CW00693164

Flat Horses

of 2005

Flat Horses

of 2005

Edited by Graham Dench
and Nick Pulford

Associate editor
Tracey Scarlett

Cover photographs: Motivator forges clear in the Derby, by AFP Photo/ John D McHugh.
Hurricane Run at Longchamp by Racing Post.

Other photographs: Racingfotos.com, Getty, APRH, Caroline Norris, Japan Racing Association, NTRA, Reuters, Stefano Grasso, Healy Racing, AFP, Associated Press, PA, Gerry Cranham, Empics, Edward Whitaker, Martin Lynch, Patrick McCann, Hong Kong Jockey Club, Scoop/Dyga, Frank Sorge, John Beasley, Dan Abraham.

Programming and data by Brett Campbell, Terry Day and Kevin Smith.

Special thanks for their invaluable assistance to Mark Bowers, James Crispe, John Kettle, Victor Jones and Andy Smith.

Published in 2006 by Highdown,
an imprint of Raceform Ltd,
Compton, Newbury, Berkshire RG20 6NL.
Raceform Ltd is a wholly-owned subsidiary of Trinity Mirror plc.

A catalogue record for this book is available from the British Library.

ISBN 1-905156-19-7

Designed by Robin Gibson.
Printed in Great Britain by William Clowes Ltd, Beccles, Suffolk.

Flat Horses

of 2005

Contents

Foreword

by Michael Bell

THE 2005 season proved to be the most memorable of my training career. We were fortunate enough to be the recipient in the autumn of 2003 of a yearling by the new sire sensation Montjeu, to be called Motivator. He was to take us on an extraordinary rollercoaster of emotion as a three-year-old, which reached its peak on the first Saturday in June and its low exactly a year to the day after his first Group 1 win in the Racing Post Trophy, when he sustained a career-ending injury in his final bit of work prior to the Breeders' Cup. Breaking bad news to owners is probably the hardest and worst part of a trainer's job, but ringing Harry Herbert to tell him what had happened was desperate.

But we can still look back on what a scintillating performance Motivator put up in the Derby and appreciate what a refreshing result it was for racing to have the sacred winner's enclosure at Epsom packed full to bursting by members of the Royal Ascot Racing Club.

Motivator was our one live bullet to achieve victory in an English Classic, and the fact that he lasted all year from the Dante through to the Arc was an achievement in itself when you consider the rate of attrition at the highest level.

It must be long odds against the winners of the 1,000 Guineas, the 2,000 Guineas, the Oaks and the Derby not winning another race that season, but I don't think that should detract from any of the winning performances. As any trainer will tell you, just try winning one of them.

In my opinion there were some outstanding three-year-old colts around, with Hurricane Run, Dubawi, Shamardal, Oratorio, David Junior and Motivator all to the fore. The fillies were probably not a vintage crop but Virginia Waters and Eswarah were very good on their respective big days. As usual the big battalions fought out most of the major races, while the jockeys' titles both provided very refreshing outcomes. Jamie Spencer being crowned champion jockey would have been a surprise choice at the beginning of the year given his unhappy time in Ireland. However, he came back a happy and determined man and ran out a clear winner, having ridden with great dash all year.

Naturally, we were all thrilled that Hayley Turner, our stable apprentice, managed to finish joint champion with Saleem Golam for the apprentices' title. It was a huge achievement on her behalf and it was just reward for all her hard work. She is a very talented rider and I will be doing all I can to ensure that she maintains the momentum.

I will never forget 2005, and to have headed the trainers' table for three weeks between the Derby and Royal Ascot was a thrill probably never to be repeated. We will not give up trying, though, and when the new crop of yearlings arrive we will always keep our fingers crossed that a new Motivator has walked in. Here's hoping!

Introduction

by Graham Dench

FLAT HORSES OF 2005 has a more international outlook than either of its predecessors, reflecting the increasingly global nature of the sport, and in particular the continuing emergence of Japan and Hong Kong as major forces on the world stage.

There is still space for every Group 1 winner in Britain, France and Ireland, as well as others from Germany, Italy and Dubai, but a later publication date has allowed us to cover the entire calendar year for the first time, and thus to include Ouija Board's superb win at the prestigious international meeting at Sha Tin in December, as well as Alkaased's thrilling Japan Cup success and the Arima Kinen, the Christmas Day target of the brilliant Japanese Triple Crown winner Deep Impact and the Juddmonte runner-up Zenno Rob Roy.

In an effort to embrace all of the top horses featured in the World Thoroughbred Racehorse Rankings, which for the first time in 2005 were published at regular intervals throughout the year, we have also extended our coverage of the top performers in America. Besides the winners of their Triple Crown races and Ghostzapper, who ran only once but still has claims to being regarded the best horse to race anywhere in the world in 2005, we have included the likes of Borrego, Flower Alley, Pleasant Home and Stevie Wonderboy. And no book of this nature would be complete without the wonderful Makybe Diva, whose third Melbourne Cup win justified inevitable comparisons with the great Phar Lap.

The writing line-up is as impressive as ever. James Willoughby's work is to the fore once again, and he has employed his sharp intellect and specialist knowledge to great effect, not only on Horse of the Year Hurricane Run, but also on some of the issues surrounding racing in America. The *Racing Post*'s editorial director Brough Scott and the paper's leading columnists David Ashforth, Paul Haigh and Howard Wright also feature, alongside writers as talented as Lee Mottershead, Tom O'Ryan, Richard Austen and Steve Dennis.

Besides the top 100, which is the section most readers will turn to first, we have highlighted the juveniles we expect to make their mark in the big races of 2006 in our 'Young Pretenders' section. This includes all of the highest-rated juveniles who did not make the top 100, plus others who figure prominently in the ante-post lists for the Classics or else particularly caught the eye of our race-readers.

Flat Horses also offers an international classification to rival the official version, based on the Racing Post Ratings compiled by Paul Curtis, Simon Turner and Sam Walker and taking into account the best races in Europe, North America, Australia, Hong Kong, Japan and the UAE.

Finally, the book contains an A to Z directory of every horse who raced in Britain in 2005, complete with definitive Racing Post Rating.

In short, it's the ultimate guide.

The top 100 horses

of 2005

Figure in bold by each horse's name is its definitive Racing Post Rating

Pedigree assessments by Tony Morris (TM) and Janet Hickman (JH)

Ace (Ire)

4yo bay colt **124**

Danehill (USA) - Tea House (Sassafras (Fr))

Owner Mrs J Magnier, M Tabor, Mrs H McCalmont

Trainer A P O'Brien

Breeder Norelands Bloodstock

Career: **12** starts | won **3** | second **2** | third **3** | **£502,967** win and place

By Alan Sweetman

THERE was no shame in the fact that a horse of Ace's ability could not manage in 2005 to supplement the three wins that he gained the previous year. The reason lies in the ambitious and courageous manner in which he was campaigned.

In eight races, starting off in the Prix Ganay in April, and culminating in a tremendous effort to take second place behind Shirocco in the Breeders' Cup Turf, the Danehill colt never stepped away from the highest level of competition and consistently proved himself superior to all but a handful of his contemporaries.

All this was in marked contrast to the way in which Aidan O'Brien marshalled his three-year-old season in 2004, when Ace made his belated racecourse debut in a humble Navan maiden and worked his way up in stages to the Queen Elizabeth II Stakes – a first taste of the Group 1 fare that was to become his staple. In a strong renewal, Ace emerged with credit in fifth behind Rakti. It was a performance that seemed to augur well for his second season.

The decision to send Ace to Longchamp for the Ganay set the tone for a high-flying campaign in 2005. Although it required the disqualification of Pride from second to effect his promotion to third place behind the previous season's Arc hero Bago, it was a promising beginning. The next port of call was the Tattersalls Gold Cup at The Curragh in May, with Bago again in the field for a contest with a rare depth of quality for such an early stage of the Irish season, bringing together the two outstanding Irish-trained three-year-old colts of 2004, Grey Swallow and Azamour. It resulted in another third placing for Ace, and a narrowing of the gap with Bago, who had to settle for second as Grey Swallow took the honours, with Azamour back in fourth after a luckless passage.

Ace again clashed with Azamour in the Prince of Wales's Stakes at York. This was generally viewed as a match between Azamour and Ouija

Ace failed to win in a busy season but was placed in five races at the top level, providing a good form benchmark

Board, but the filly failed to run her race after losing a shoe, and it was left to the two Irish raiders to fight it out after the remarkably versatile Australian performer Elvstroem had dropped away. It took a while for Azamour to assert, and Ace consolidated his growing reputation with a clear second-best, five lengths in front of Elvstroem.

O'Brien now stepped Ace up to a mile and a half for the first time in the King George at Newbury. Sent off a 13-2 chance in a field of 12, he was well in the hunt until running out of steam from over a furlong out, ending up fifth as Azamour triumphed in stylish fashion. It looked as if Ace did not see out the trip, but that did not dissuade Kieren Fallon from giving him an aggressive ride from the front when he was dropped back in trip to contest the Juddmonte International at York. It was a tactic that backfired, setting up a duel between the Italian-trained Electrocutionist and Japanese raider Zenno Rob Roy. However, his length fourth confirmed that he was tantalisingly close to netting a Group 1.

There was to be no lowering in class, and his next race was in the Irish Champion Stakes, this time as the stable's second-string. Partnered by Seamus Heffernan, he produced another honest display to take fourth place behind his stable's three-year-old standard-bearer Oratorio.

Ace's odyssey now took him to America to contest the Joe Hirsch Turf Classic Invitational over a mile and a half at Belmont Park. His stamina

2005 Race record

2nd John Deere Breeders' Cup Turf (Grade 1) (Belmont Park, October 29) 3yo+ 1m4f Yielding **124** 13 ran. *9th early, headway on inside to go 4th 3f out, went 2nd 2f out, soon hard ridden, kept on but no impression (K Fallon), beaten $1\frac{3}{4}$l by Shirocco*

3rd Joe Hirsch Turf Classic Invitational (Grade 1) (Turf) (Belmont Park, October 1) 3yo+ 1m4f Firm **118** 7 ran. *Pressed leader, every chance on inside 2f out, kept on under pressure (P Valenzuela), beaten 1l by Shakespeare*

4th Baileys Irish Champion Stakes (Group 1) (Leopardstown, September 10) 3yo+ 1m2f Good to yielding **123** (TS 105) 10 ran. *Held up in rear, progress approaching straight, 4th over 1f out, kept on under pressure (J A Heffernan), beaten $1\frac{3}{4}$l by Oratorio*

4th Juddmonte International Stakes (Group 1) (York, August 16) 3yo+ 1m$2\frac{1}{2}$f Good **123** (TS 122) 7 ran. *Led after 1f, quickened over 4f out, headed over 1f out, no extra inside final furlong (K Fallon), beaten 1l by Electrocutionist*

5th King George VI And Queen Elizabeth Diamond Stakes (Group 1) (Newbury, July 23) 3yo+ 1m4f Good to firm **113** (TS 101) 12 ran. *Chased leaders, effort on outer over 3f out, every chance 2f out, weakened over 1f out (K Fallon), beaten 9l by Azamour*

2nd Prince of Wales's Stakes (Group 1) (York, June 15) 4yo+ 1m$2\frac{1}{2}$f Good to firm **123** (TS 117) 8 ran. *Tracked leaders, effort and went 2nd over 3f out, edged left and led over 1f out, soon headed, ran on (K Fallon), beaten $1\frac{1}{2}$l by Azamour*

3rd Tattersalls Gold Cup (Group 1) (Curragh, May 22) 4yo+ 1m$2\frac{1}{2}$f Good to yielding **123** (TS 70) 6 ran. *Tracked leader in 2nd, led 2f out, headed $1\frac{1}{2}$f out, 3rd and kept on inside final furlong (K Fallon), beaten $1\frac{3}{4}$l by Grey Swallow*

3rd Prix Ganay (Group 1) (Longchamp, April 24) 4yo+ 1m$2\frac{1}{2}$f Very soft **118** (TS 51) 9 ran. *Prominent, went 2nd over 4f out, disputing 2nd and pushed along straight, ran on under pressure to line, finished 4th, placed 3rd (K Fallon), beaten $1\frac{3}{4}$l by Bago*

2004

5th Queen Elizabeth II Stakes (Sponsored By NetJets) (Group 1) (Ascot, September 25) 3yo+ 1m Good to firm **109** (TS 100) 11 ran ● **1st** Desmond Stakes (Group 3) (Leopardstown, August 15) 3yo+ 1m Good to firm **118** (TS 83) 5 ran ● **1st** Luas To Leopardstown Race (Leopardstown, July 24) 3yo 1m Good to firm **112** (TS 105) 4 ran ● **1st** Nobber Maiden (Navan, June 11) 3yo 1m Good **83** 14 ran

held up well and the margins were narrow, but once again his fate was a minor share of the money.

Four weeks later the two horses who had beaten him, Shakespeare and English Channel, were again in opposition in the Breeders' Cup Turf at the same venue. Ace, visored for the first time, turned the tables in convincing fashion as the European horses dominated the race. Fallon afterwards claimed that if he had not been locked in for a stride or two before the final turn, he might have given Shirocco a run for his money, but in reality Azamour was the unluckier in third. Still, with another familiar rival Bago in fourth, this was indisputably Ace's finest hour.

Tough and consistent, and a top-class performer over ten furlongs and a mile and a half, he deserves to win a Group 1. The Tattersalls Gold Cup at The Curragh could provide him with an early opportunity to rectify the omission as a five-year-old.

Ace

bay colt, 23-4-2001

Danehill b 1986	Danzig	Northern Dancer	Nearctic **Natalma**
		Pas de Nom	Admirals Voyage Petitioner
	Razyana	His Majesty	Ribot Flower Bowl
		Spring Adieu	Buckpasser **Natalma**
Tea House b 1980	Sassafras	Sheshoon	Precipitation Noorani
		Ruta	Ratification Dame d'Atour
	House Tie	Be Friendly	Skymaster Lady Sliptic
		Mesopotamia	Zarathustra Agars Plough

Bred by Norelands Bloodstock in Ireland. E300,000 Goffs Orby yearling.

Sire Danehill

Won 4 of 9 races, inc. Haydock Park Sprint Cup-Gr1. Died May 2003. Stood at Coolmore Stud, latterly at Ir200,000gns. Sire of Gr1 winners: Danish (QE II Challenge Cup), Kissing Cousin (Coronation), Danehill Dancer (Phoenix, National), Tsukuba Symphony (NHK Mile Cup), Desert King (National, Irish 2,000, Irish Derby), Fairy King Prawn (Yasuda Kinen), Tiger Hill (GP von Baden [twice], Bayerisches Zuchtrennen), Indian Danehill (Prix Ganay), Wannabe Grand (Cheveley Park), Aquarelliste (Prix de Diane, Prix Vermeille, Prix Ganay), Banks Hill (Coronation, Breeders' Cup F & M Turf, Prix Jacques le Marois), Mozart (July Cup, Nunthorpe), Regal Rose (Cheveley Park), Dress To Thrill (Matriarch), Fine Motion (Shuka Sho, QE II Commemorative Cup), Landseer (Poule d'Essai des Poulains), Rock Of Gibraltar (Grand Criterium, Dewhurst, 2,000 Guineas, Irish 2,000, St James's Palace, Sussex, Prix du Moulin), Westerner (Prix du Cadran [twice], Prix Royal-Oak [twice], Gold Cup), Clodovil (Poule d'Essai des Poulains), Intercontinental (Matriarch, Breeders' Cup F & M Turf), Light Jig (Yellow Ribbon), Spartacus (Phoenix, Gran Criterium), Grey Lilas (Prix du Moulin), North Light (Derby), Luas Line (Garden City H.), Oratorio (Prix Jean-Luc Lagardere, Eclipse, Irish Champion), George Washington (Phoenix, National), Horatio Nelson (Prix Jean-Luc Lagardere), Rumplestiltskin (Moyglare Stud, Prix Marcel Boussac).

Dam Tea House

Won 4 of 13 starts at 2 (6f) and 3 (8f) in Europe and North America, including 8f Listed event in Ireland at 3. Dam of: Mr Sunday Sport (1985 c by Henbit; winner), Sybillin (1986 g by Henbit; Flat/hurdle/chase winner), Come To Tea (1988 f by Be My Guest; winner), Sure Haven (1989 g by Sure Blade; winner), Butter Knife (1990 f by Sure Blade; unraced, grand-dam of Gr3 winner Contemporary), Danish (1991 f by Danehill; Queen Elizabeth II Challenge Cup-Gr1), Tea Service (1992 f by Roi Danzig; Listed-placed winner), Teio License (1994 c by Fool's Holme; winner), Teishebaini (1995 c by Hamas; Listed winner), Hawkeye (1998 c by Danehill; Gr3 winner), Devered (1999 c by Desert King; unraced), Ace (2001 c by Danehill; Gr3 winner). Died without further produce.

Pedigree assessment

The combination of Danehill with this family has been very fruitful. Danish, Hawkeye and Ace have resulted from the Danehill-Tea House union, while Twine's son Restructure is by the same sire and additional talented family members are by other sons of Danzig. Hawkeye recorded several Group 1 places but failed to win beyond Group 3 level, just like Ace at the time of writing. The aim for Ace now is to emulate his sister, Danish, who was a Grade 1 winner at Keeneland, rather than his brother. *JH*

Afleet Alex (USA)

3yo bay colt **126**

Northern Afleet (USA) - Maggy Hawk (USA) (Hawkster (USA))

Owner Cash Is King Stable

Trainer T F Ritchey

Breeder John Martin Silverland

Career: **12** starts	won **8**	second **2**	third 1	**£1,556,273** win and place

By James Willoughby

WHEN the names in his pedigree have become archaic, the particulars of his racing record obsolete and his connections passed away, people will still talk about Afleet Alex. He will forever be the horse who got up from his knees.

It might have been notable in any minor race, a what-happened-next moment to go with countless others from this chaotic sport. It was a lot more significant than that, however, because it occurred at the top of the straight in the Preakness Stakes.

Afleet Alex was starting to accelerate at the time. He had just been unleashed by his jockey Jeremy Rose after moving up from the rear like a certain winner. The only horse in front was Scrappy T, an outsider running the race of his life.

At the apex of the turn, Ramon Dominguez pulled his whip on the leader. There is nothing remarkable in that, except for the rider brandished it in his left hand and administered it with such force on Scrappy T's left flank that even a horse made of marble would have recoiled.

Scrappy T was surprised in mid-stride. He flinched immediately with the force of his rider's savagery, veering to his right uncontrollably. And his weight received the impulsion provided by centrifugal force.

The only thing that could arrest his momentum was Afleet Alex. He struck the onrushing rival squarely in the shoulder, causing him to clip heels and his knees to buckle, so that his head plummeted towards the dirt. Instinctively and brilliantly, Rose yanked at his head like a rodeo rider astride a malicious mustang, and the impossible happened: Afleet Alex came up from the floor like Jake LaMotta in Raging Bull.

When it was clear that Rose had kept his seat, the onlooker sensed immediately what was about to occur. It was a scene out of some Rocky film in which our hero shakes off double vision, sets his jaw and comes back from oblivion: Afleet Alex just had to go on to victory – and he did.

Jeremy Rose celebrates after Afleet Alex's Preakness win at Pimlico, where the colt got off his knees to triumph

Biology provides a very plausible explanation for seemingly incredible recoveries which are far from unprecedented in horseracing. Miracle comebacks take place a few times a season in jumps racing, though only every few years on the Flat. Most famous in US racing is Alysheba's stumble at the two-furlong pole in the 1987 Kentucky Derby, from which he got back up to beat Bet Twice. But it was nothing compared to the misadventure that befell Afleet Alex.

The resulting shock is a catalyst for the release of adrenalin in the horse, just as it would be if a predator's teeth and claws were felt around the flanks. But who cares if Afleet Alex's brush with disaster was not all it appeared? The viewer cannot help but to develop a visceral urge for the unfortunate animal to recover and to invest in the full extent of the event's apparent impossibility once it has transpired.

Afleet Alex didn't just win. Having regained his balance, he ducked back inside Scrappy T with incredible deftness and composure and began to absolutely pour it on, overwhelming his errant rival as soon as the furlong pole, then surging away to finish five lengths ahead of him. He sprinted across the line like a wild horse, to extend the theme outlined above.

2005 Race record

1st Belmont Stakes (Grade 1) (Belmont Park, June 11) 3yo 1m4f Fast **126** 11 ran. *Taken across behind field and joint 9th on first turn, smooth headway over 2f out, quickened to lead straight, driven clear, ran on well (J Rose), beat Andromeda's Hero by 7l*

1st Preakness Stakes (Grade 1) (Pimlico, May 21) 3yo 1m1½f Fast **122** 14 ran. *Raced in 10th, good headway on inside 3f out, close 2nd when clipped heels and almost fell entering straight, recovered to lead over 1f out, ran on well (J Rose), beat Scrappy T by 4¾l*

3rd Kentucky Derby (Grade 1) (Churchill Downs, May 7) 3yo 1m2f Fast **119** 20 ran. *Mid-division, progress between horses over 3f out, ridden and every chance over 1f out, ran on at same pace (J Rose), beaten 1l by Giacomo*

1st Arkansas Derby (Grade 2) (Oaklawn Park, April 16) 3yo 1m1f Fast **117** 10 ran. *5th early, headway 4-wide to lead over 2f out, quickened clear, impressive (J Rose), beat Flower Alley by 8l*

6th Rebel Stakes (Grade 3) (Oaklawn Park, March 19) 3yo 1m½f Fast 6 ran. *3rd early, went 2nd after 3f, weakened quickly 1½f out (J R Velazquez), beaten 12½l by Greater Good*

1st Mountain Valley Stakes (Oaklawn Park, March 5) 3yo 6f Fast 6 ran. *5th early, 3rd halfway, led just over 1f out, ran on well (J Rose), beat Razor by 2¾l*

2004

2nd Bessemer Trust Breeders' Cup Juvenile (Grade 1) (Dirt) (Lone Star Park, October 30) 2yo 1m½f Fast **119** 8 ran ● **2nd** Champagne Stakes (Grade 1) (Belmont Park, October 9) 2yo 1m½f Fast **119** 8 ran ● **1st** Hopeful Stakes (Grade 1) (Saratoga, August 21) 2yo 7f Sloppy **111** 7 ran ● **1st** Sanford Stakes (Grade 2) (Saratoga, July 29) 2yo 6f Fast **120** 11 ran ● **1st** Allowance Race (Delaware Park, July 12) 2yo 5½f Sloppy 5 ran ● **1st** Maiden Special Weight (Delaware Park, June 26) 2yo 5½f Fast 6 ran

Once the incident had been replayed on national television a few thousand times, it finally came to the attention of the many that, if the explanation for this amazing event lay in the winner's unnatural powers, it was consistent to excuse him his Kentucky Derby defeat. Afleet Alex had been beaten a half-length and the same by Giacomo and Closing Argument after appearing to hold every chance.

In the immediate aftermath of Churchill Downs, the consensus was nothing like so clear. Had his journeyman jockey Rose delivered him off a hot pace too soon? Had the punishing workout regimen set out by his trainer Tim Ritchey diminished his energy resources? Having seen Afleet Alex at Pimlico, most were inclined to go one way or the other.

The most plausible explanation is that Rose mistimed a move which took him up to the leaders shortly after turning for home. The straight at Churchill Downs is one of the longest in the US, and jockeys who excel there – most notably the recently retired Pat Day – are renowned for their patience.

Afleet Alex secures a second Classic success as he wins the Belmont by seven lengths, but he did not run again

Nobody was looking to criticise Rose or Ritchey after the Belmont Stakes. Sent off the 11-10 favourite to defeat ten rivals, including Giacomo, who was fully ten lengths behind him in the Preakness, he delivered a commanding performance.

Fears that a mile and a half may prove his undoing looked to be little justified, but Rose hid him well off the pace to make sure and picked his way through the field steadily and efficiently. He split Giacomo and Southern Africa while full of running as they turned into the straight and sprinted away to beat late-charging Andromeda's Hero by seven lengths.

In the course of running a mile and a half in a fast time, Afleet Alex posted a final quarter-mile split of 24.4 seconds – the fastest in the race since Arts And Letters in 1969. That wasn't his only standout statistic, either.

Afleet Alex is the only horse in the last 40 years to win from six furlongs to a mile and a half in the same season, gaining the former accreditation in a Listed race at Oaklawn Park in March. And he has won at six different distances, often by wide margins, including a record eight-length victory in the Grade 2 Arkansas Derby at Oaklawn in April. The only blot on his record came when he was diagnosed with a lung infection after running poorly in the Rebel Stakes, again at Oaklawn, between the two victories just mentioned.

Like Smarty Jones the year before him, there can be no doubt that Afleet Alex had the ability to win the Triple Crown. He had the toughness and the stamina to go with his talent, and it was only the strong pace that caught him out in the Kentucky Derby.

So the search for a successor to Affirmed will stretch into its 28th year. Perhaps this time span gives the quest an added cachet, but there is a serious danger that the demands of three Classics in little more than a month is more than the modern thoroughbred can bear.

Once again, the series exacted a wicked toll on its competitors. Of the original 20 who lined up for the Kentucky Derby, no fewer than 12 were either knocked out for the campaign there and then, or later sustained season- or career-ending injuries. The fallen included five of the first six home.

Since 1995, there have been eight horses who competed in all three legs of the Triple Crown and were successful in two. Afleet Alex, Smarty Jones and Charismatic never raced again; Silver Charm and Real Quiet were knocked out for the campaign; Point Given raced just twice more and War Emblem just three more times; even the tough gelding Funny Cide stood only two more outings before returning to action as a four-year-old.

It is lamentable that the values which the Triple Crown seeks to showcase are anachronistic, but now could be the time for an overhaul of its scheduling. Top-class horses are hardly ever asked to run in three punishing races within the same period during the rest of their career.

It is an entirely separate argument that dictates that the British Triple Crown should not be tampered with, for there is no demonstrable harm caused by horses being forced through the series in pursuit of kudos. Unless the three legs of the US Triple Crown are spaced more kindly, it will continue to destroy the careers of talented horses who could otherwise bolster competition at the highest levels of the sport.

Afleet Alex's medical book received its red entry after the Belmont. In late July, he returned sore after routine exercise and was diagnosed with a fractured left ankle. A screw was inserted but the injury still had not healed by November and the decision was made to retire him the following month.

Afleet Alex will stand for $40,000 at Gainesway Farm in Kentucky – a relatively modest covering fee considering his level of ability. This can be accounted for by his unfashionable pedigree. He is by Northern Afleet,whose other best runners are G P Fleet, Unforgettable Max and Saint Afleet, all removed from the highest class. His legacy is far less likely to be measured through his progeny than it is for that incomparable moment at Pimlico.

Afleet Alex

bay colt, 9-5-2002

Northern Afleet b 1993	Afleet	Mr Prospector	Raise A Native Gold Digger
		Polite Lady	Venetian Jester Friendly Ways
	Nuryette	Nureyev	Northern Dancer Special
		Stellarette	Tentam Square Angel
Maggy Hawk b 1994	Hawkster	Silver Hawk	Roberto Gris Vitesse
		Strait Lane	Chieftain Level Sands
	Qualique	Hawaii	Utrillo Ethane
		Dorothy Gaylord	Sensitivo Gaylord's Touch

Bred by John Martin Silvertand in Florida. $75,000 Fasig-Tipton Midlantic May 2-year-old.

Sire Northern Afleet

Won 5 of 21 races, inc. San Fernando S.-Gr2, San Carlos H.-Gr2, San Diego H.-Gr3. Also Gr3-placed at 2, Gr1-placed at 3 and 4. Medium-sized (16.0hh), well-made individual. Smart at 2 and 3, best at 4 between 7 and 9 furlongs on dirt. Also stakes-placed on turf. Half-brother to Gr1 winner Tap To Music (by Pleasant Tap) and to stakes winner Boss Soss. Dam unraced half-sister to Gr1 winner Cuddles. Grand-dam Gr3 winner. Same immediate family as Fantastic Light, Swain, Seaside Attraction, Hiaam, etc. Stands at Taylor Made Farm, Nicholasville, Kentucky, at a 2006 fee of $20,000. Sire of 4 crops of racing age, inc. notable winners: G P Fleet (Gr3), Saint Afleet (Gr2), Afleet Alex (Hopeful S-Gr1, Preakness S.-Gr1, Belmont S.-Gr1).

Dam Maggy Hawk

Raced only at 2 years, won 1 of 4 starts. Half-sister to useful winners Cue The Groom (by Blushing Groom; dam of Italian Gr3 winner Vale Mantovani) and Santa Rosa Island (by Valiant Nature). Dam 2-y-o Grade 1 winner, sister to smart Gr3 4th-placed Honolulu Honey, half-sister to Listed winner Peaks Mill (by Stalwart). Grand-dam unraced half-sister to Island Charm (by Hawaii; Gr3 winner, Gr1-placed) and to another winner by Hawaii. Family of Quill (champion; dam of One For All, Caucasus, Last Feather, grand-dam of Run The Gantlet) and Count Amber. Dam of: Jolie Hawk (1999 f by Mister Jolie; unraced), Unforgettable Max (2000 c by Northern Afleet; stakes winner, Gr2-placed), Afleet Alex (2002 c by Northern Afleet; Classic winner). She has a yearling filly named John's Diamond, by Tour d'Or, and a filly foal by Quiet American.

Pedigree assessment

There was not much doubt about the identity of America's best three-year-old after the Preakness Stakes, and none at all after the Belmont. The shame was that Afleet Alex, having registered excellent performances to win those Classics, was unable to reappear, but only Flower Alley really made much progress afterwards in the sophomore division, so Afleet Alex's status as number one was never under threat. Like several other US Classic victors in recent years, he was cheaply bred, by a horse who fell some way short of the top class, and his dam, who fetched only $5,000 as a yearling, came from one of the less successful offshoots of a high-class family. He will stand for $40,000 at Gainesway Farm in Kentucky – a relatively modest fee for a horse of his ability. *TM*

Alcazar (Ire)

10yo bay gelding **117**

Alzao (USA) - Sahara Breeze (Ela-Mana-Mou)

Owner J Repard, F Melrose, O Pawle, M Stokes, R Black

Trainer H Morrison

Breeder J Repard

Career: **28** starts	won **12**	second **3**	third **3**	**£419,989** win and place

By Howard Wright

WHERE to start with Alcazar? Should it be with his breeding? While nowadays Alcazar does not begin to find his stride until the 14-furlong pole, his sire Alzao fell short of early promise and managed only one Pattern win over a mile and a half, by a nose in an Italian Group 3, while his dam Sahara Breeze, a miler maiden and half-sister to the Fillies' Mile winner Ivanka, was best known for her French Group 1 juvenile winner Lady Of Chad.

Should we start with Alcazar's medical history? Twice absent for long spells in the sick bay – hence his low-mileage record for a ten-year-old of 28 races – he had three years out between his last start for John Dunlop as a three-year-old and his winning handicap reappearance for Hughie Morrison, and another 18 months off the track immediately after that.

Alcazar had been prepared for a hat-trick attempt in Nottingham's Further Flight Stakes on his reappearance in 2005, until the entry became muddled on its electronic route to Weatherbys. Instead he was forced into an inadequate 12 furlongs in Newbury's John Porter Stakes, where he ran with credit, but about a stone below his best, to finish sixth to Day Flight.

However, Alcazar's best was not far away, in the Sagaro Stakes to be exact, in which two years previously he was in turn first past the post, disqualified and reinstated on appeal to the Jockey Club disciplinary panel.

There was no such controversy this time, and with the race moved from the building site that was Ascot in 2005 to Lingfield, Alcazar showed that he can handle most types of course by drawing away with Franklins Gardens on the turn for home and getting on top near the finish. The rest were beaten at least five lengths, and Alcazar matched his best-ever Racing Post Rating of 117.

The two principals met again in the Emirates Airline Yorkshire Cup, a more strongly contested race but with a less strong pace to beyond

Alcazar (left), at the grand old age of ten, scores his first Group 1 win in the Prix du Cadran at Longchamp

midway than at Lingfield, and over a shorter trip. Alcazar lacked the foot to make a serious challenge and finished fourth behind Franklins Gardens, who made all the running.

Alcazar's next race, the Group 2 Bonusprint.com Henry II Stakes at Sandown, produced a similarly pedestrian pace but he was ridden with more enterprise and was driven into the lead just inside the final furlong, only to be run out of the five-figure prizes in the last 75 yards by Fight Your Corner and Lochbuie.

This was the fourth time Alcazar had finished in the first three in a Group 1 or 2 race without winning, but he finally made the breakthrough in the Pattern's second strata on his next run, in the Darley Prix Kergorlay at Deauville. Having tracked the pace-setters from the off, Alcazar took up the running from Ostankino well over a furlong out and, despite hanging right under pressure, he ran on under strong driving to win by two lengths from the six years younger favourite Reefscape, who took second place close home.

The generally steadier pace of the Prix du Cadran, rather than the extra five furlongs, appeared to catch him out next time. Reefscape turned the tables, both in running style, by being with the leaders from the start until leading over a furlong out, and result, by staying on to win by two lengths, while Alcazar stayed on from the two-furlong mark to dead-heat for second with Ostankino, another four-year-old.

However, with a better gallop and on slightly softer ground, revenge on both rivals was not long delayed. Three weeks to be exact, and back

2005 Race record

1st Prix Royal Oak (Group 1) (Longchamp, October 23) 3yo+ 1m7½f Soft **117** (TS 114) 11 ran. *Towards rear, 8th halfway, pushed along to challenge 1½f out, led over 1f out, ran on well to line (M Fenton), beat Reefscape by nk*

2nd Dead-heat Prix du Cadran Casino Les Princes Barriere de Cannes (Group 1) (Longchamp, October 2) 4yo+ 2m4f Good to soft **117** (TS 8) 10 ran. *Raced in 7th, effort over 2f out, stayed on down outside under strong pressure to share 2nd on line (M Fenton), beaten 2l by Reefscape*

1st Darley Prix Kergorlay (Group 2) (Deauville, August 21) 3yo+ 1m7f Soft **117** (TS 91) 11 ran. *Always close up, disputed 3rd halfway, 2nd straight, led well over 1f out, hung right under pressure inside final furlong (M Fenton), beat Reefscape by 2l*

3rd bonusprint.com Henry II Stakes (Group 2) (Sandown, May 30) 4yo+ 2m½ Good **110** (TS 92) 16 ran. *Settled midfield, progress well over 2f out, driven to lead just inside final furlong, headed last 75yds (M Fenton), beaten 1¾l by Fight Your Corner*

4th Emirates Airline Yorkshire Cup (Group 2) (York, May 13) 4yo+ 1m6f Good to soft **110** (TS 80) 9 ran. *Slowly into stride, soon chasing leaders, ridden over 3f out, kept on same pace final 2f (M Fenton), beaten 4¾l by Franklins Gardens*

1st Hesmonds Stud Sagaro Stakes (Group 3) (Lingfield, April 27) 4yo+ 2m Soft **117** (TS 64) 9 ran. *Held up in midfield, headway 6f out, chased winner over 4f out, driven to lead near finish (M Fenton), beat Franklins Gardens by nk*

6th Dubai Tennis Championships Stakes (Registered As The John Porter Stakes) (Group 3) (Newbury, April 16) 4yo+ 1m4f Soft **104** (TS 69) 13 ran. *Chased clear leader, left in lead inside final 5f, headed over 4f out, weakened (M Fenton), beaten 8¼l by Day Flight*

Other wins

2004 **1st** totesport Willie Park Stakes (Listed) (Musselburgh, November 3) 3yo+ 2m Good to soft **112** (TS 58) 6 ran ● **1st** HBLB "Further Flight" Stakes (Listed) (Nottingham, March 31) 4yo+ 1m6f Good **106** (TS 45) 6 ran **2003** **1st** Bovis Homes Sagaro Stakes (Group 3) (Ascot, April 30) 4yo+ 2m Good **110** (TS 57) 7 ran ● **1st** 'Further Flight' Stakes (Listed) (Nottingham, April 1) 4yo+ 1m6f Good **111** (TS 49) 11 ran **2001** ● **1st** Abu Dhabi Rated Stakes (Handicap) (Newmarket, September 22) 3yo+ (0-100) 1m6f Good **106** (TS 93) 9 ran **1998** **1st** CIU Serlby Stakes (Listed) (Doncaster, November 7) 3yo+ 1m4f Soft **117** (TS 104) 6 ran ● **1st** Newton Fund Managers Conditions Stakes (Haydock, October 14) 3yo+ 1m4f Soft **104** (TS 95) 6 ran ● **1st** Stanley Casinos Rated Stakes (Handicap) (Haydock, September 5) 3yo+ (0-105 handicap) 1m4f Good **111** (TS 76) 9 ran

at Longchamp for the Prix Royal-Oak. Taking advantage of the absence of Westerner, behind whom he had been placed in the previous two runnings, Alcazar hit Group 1-winning form for the first time.

He was held up until past halfway, and after moving into third place on the home turn, he galloped into the lead over a furlong out and had enough in reserve to repel Reefscape, who had been restrained even farther behind, by a neck.

Alcazar became only the second ten-year-old to win a Group 1 race in Europe –- after Yavana's Pace – as well as the oldest-ever winner of the Royal-Oak.

Now that's where the 2005 story of Alcazar starts – at the end, and at the top.

Alcazar

bay gelding, 11-5-1995

Alzao b 1980	Lyphard	Northern Dancer	Nearctic Natalma
		Goofed	Court Martial Barra
	Lady Rebecca	Sir Ivor	Sir Gaylord Attica
		Pocahontas	Roman How
Sahara Breeze b 1986	Ela-Mana-Mou	Pitcairn	Petingo Border Bounty
		Rose Bertin	High Hat Wide Awake
	Diamond Land	Sparkler	Hard Tack Diamond Spur
		Canaan	Santa Claus Rustic Bridge

Bred by J Repard in Ireland

Sire Alzao

Won 4 of 12 races, inc. Premio Ellington-Gr3. Also 2nd in La Coupe de Maisons-Laffitte and respectable 8th of 19 in Champion S. (only Gr1 start) at 3. Strong, compact sort, effective on any going, scored sole Pattern win in only race at 12f. Retired from stud duty. Last stood at Coolmore at a fee of €7,500. Sire of 18 crops of racing age, inc. notable winners: Alcando (Beverly Hills H.-Gr1), Mirror Black (Gr2), Pass The Peace (Cheveley Park S.-Gr1), Noble Patriarch (Gr3), Capricciosa (Moyglare Stud S.-Gr1, Cheveley Park S.-Gr1), Second Set (Sussex S.-Gr1), Bobzao (Gr2), Stubass (Gr2), Alpride (Beverly Hills H.-Gr1, Yellow Ribbon Invitational S.-Gr1), Prince Firebird (Gr3), Relatively Special (Gr3), Sheridan (Gr3), Unblest (Gr2), Wind In Her Hair (Aral Pokal-Gr1), Last Second (Gr2), Matiya (Irish 1,000 Guineas-Gr1), Solar Crystal (Gr3), Waky Nao (Premio Vittorio di Capua-Gr1), Token Gesture (Gr3), Alborada (Champion S.-Gr1 twice), Alcazar (Prix Royal Oak-Gr1), Epistolaire (Gr2), Shahtoush (Oaks S.-Gr1), Winona (Irish Oaks-Gr1), Eurolink Raindance (Gr3), Lady Upstage (Gr2), Timi (Oaks d'Italia-Gr1), Balthazar (Gr3), Albanova (Deutschland Preis-Gr1, Aral Pokal-Gr1, Preis von Europa-Gr1), Contemporary (Gr3), Special Kaldoun (Gr2), Bailador (Gr3), Luvah Girl (Gr2), Angara (Beverly D S.-Gr1), Maraahel (Gr3).

Dam Sahara Breeze

Placed 2nd and 3rd in 2 starts at 2 years, placed 3rd once from 2 starts at 3. Leggy, somewhat nervous individual with a round action. Modest maiden, appeared to act on fast and soft ground, and to stay 10f. Dam of: Eurodouble (1992 g by Double Schwartz; unplaced), Sheeny Raisin (1993 f by Double Schwartz; placed), Rapier (1994 c by Sharpo; winner), Alcazar (1995 g by Alzao; Gr1 winner), Lady Of Chad (1997 f by Last Tycoon; Gr1 winner), Pelagia (1998 f by Lycius; placed 4th once, dam of Gr2-placed Upper Hand), Aqaba (1999 f by Lake Coniston; placed), Danzig River (2001 g by Green Desert; winner). Had dead foal by Double Schwartz in 1991, not covered 1995 and 2002, barren to Alzao in 2000, to Sadler's Wells in 2002, and to Rock Of Gibraltar in 2004.

Pedigree assessment

Alcazar may be long in the tooth, but he has had only 28 races. His tally of 12 victories and six minor placings provide testimony to honest, consistent endeavour, all the more remarkable for the fact that he has had a history of physical ailments. He came from the tenth crop of Alzao, which included three other Group 1 winners – Alborada (Champion Stakes, twice), Shahtoush (Oaks) and Winona (Irish Oaks) – who all attained that standard way back in 1998. *TM*

Alexander Goldrun (Ire)

4yo bay filly **122**

Gold Away (Ire) - Renashaan (Fr) (Darshaan)

Owner Mrs N O'Callaghan

Trainer J S Bolger

Breeder Dermot Cantillon

Career: **24** starts | won **9** | second **5** | third **4** | **£1,551,364** win and place

By Richard Austen

ALEXANDER GOLDRUN ran in the first Irish two-year-old race of her year and she's still running. She remains in training as a five-year-old and if she ever stopped over in one place for long she would probably have quite a following. As one of the best older fillies or mares on the Flat in Ireland for many a year, however, she has to be campaigned on the international stage.

Since winning the Guineas Trial at Leopardstown in May 2004, Alexander Goldrun has run in only Group 1 events and that has taken her to France and Britain three times, Hong Kong twice and to Dubai and Singapore once each. From 14 Group 1 races, only four have been on home soil.

She's also had four Group 1 victories. The Prix de l'Opera was described in Flat Horses of 2004, but she wasn't finished that year and found easily her greatest booty, about £734,000, on the other side of the world that December when holding on very gamely and by a hair's breadth in the Hong Kong Cup.

On her own patch there is no filly to touch Alexander Goldrun, a point already evident to backers weighing up the Audi Pretty Polly Stakes at The Curragh in June 2005 and confirmed when Alexander Goldrun came from the back to score readily, with four-year-olds filling the first five places.

The tactics were familiar by now, often due to slow starts but also seemingly a matter of preference for Kevin Manning, who has ridden Alexander Goldrun throughout her career. "When he sits out the back like that it can wreck your nerves," observed Lee Smith, the filly's groom, later on. "It's just as well he knows her well and they get on good."

Red Bloom and Hazarista, second and fifth in the Pretty Polly, were the only older horses to take her on when the Alexander Goldrun

Alexander Goldrun makes a rare appearance on home soil, winning the Group 1 Pretty Polly Stakes at The Curragh

roadshow went to Glorious Goodwood for the Nassau Stakes. Eight three-year-olds who tried to strike a blow for youth at Goodwood included the Newmarket 1,000 winner Virginia Waters, Irish 1,000 runner-up Penkenna Princess, Oaks runner-up Something Exciting and Musidora winner Secret History.

The 13-8 favourite, Alexander Goldrun got a bump on the way, but still gave a comfortable reprise of her Pretty Polly performance in quickening to the front and holding off Cassydora and Red Bloom.

These were Group 1 events, but in most of her other races in 2005 Alexander Goldrun was sent in search of more notable scalps. In most instances they showed that she does have limitations. In one instance it provided the best opposition she has ever faced and the opportunity to register a career-best.

First, though, the limitations. Alexander Goldrun has been kept almost entirely to races at around a mile and a quarter since her second in the Irish Guineas and, over shorter distances, both the Dubai Duty Free at Nad Al Sheba in March and the Falmouth at Newmarket in July helped to show why. She has a fine turn of foot, but she is vulnerable to high-class milers – she was not going to outsprint Soviet Song in a steadily run race.

Perhaps soft ground does not see her at her peak either, because although she has won on heavy and her third in the Singapore Airlines International Cup at Kranji in May was a creditable result, it did not threaten her best form.

2005 Race record

8th Cathay Pacific Hong Kong Cup (Group 1) (Sha Tin, December 11) 3yo+ 1m2f Good to firm **116** 10 ran. *Held up, switched to inside 2f out, close 6th when not clear run 1 1/2f out, no chance after (K J Manning), beaten 4l by Vengeance Of Rain*

8th Emirates Airline Champion Stakes (Group 1) (Newmarket, October 15) 3yo+ 1m2f Good to soft **113** (TS 99) 15 ran. *Held up, headway over 1f out, no extra inside final furlong (K J Manning), beaten 5 3/4l by David Junior*

3rd Prix de l'Opera Casino Barriere d'Enghien (Group 1) (Longchamp, October 2) 3yo+ 1m2f Good to soft **109** (TS 82) 9 ran. *Held up, 8th straight, pushed along on outside 1 1/2f out, nearest at finish (K J Manning), beaten 1 1/4l by Kinnaird*

3rd Baileys Irish Champion Stakes (Group 1) (Leopardstown, September 10) 3yo+ 1m2f Good to yielding **122** (TS 104) 10 ran. *Slowly into stride, held up, not clear run under 4f out, switched to outer, stayed on well (K J Manning), beaten 3/4l by Oratorio*

1st Vodafone Nassau Stakes (Group 1) (Goodwood, July 30) 3yo+ 1m2f Good to soft **114** (TS 113) 11 ran. *Held up, steady progress from 3f out, slight bump 2f out, ridden to lead over 1f out, in command final furlong (K J Manning), beat Cassydora by 1 1/4l*

2nd UAE Equestrian And Racing Federation Falmouth Stakes (Group 1) (Newmarket (July), July 5) 3yo+ 1m Good **117** (TS 85) 7 ran. *Always prominent, ridden and every chance inside final furlong, unable to quicken (K J Manning), beaten 2 1/2l by Soviet Song*

1st Audi Pretty Polly Stakes (Group 1) (Curragh, June 25) 3yo+ 1m2f Good to firm **117** (TS 87) 10 ran. *Slowly into stride, held up in rear, switched to outer 2f out, challenged 1f out, soon led, stayed on well (K J Manning), beat Red Bloom by 1 1/2l*

3rd Singapore Airlines International Cup (Group 1) (Kranji, May 15) 3yo+ 1m2f Soft **108** 15 ran. *Midfield, headway to go 6th straight, switched inside over 1f out, every chance 1f out until weakened 120yds out (K J Manning), beaten 3 1/2l by Mummify*

6th Dubai Duty Free Sponsored By Dubai Duty Free (Turf) (Group 1) (Nad Al Sheba, March 26) 4yo+ 1m1f Good to firm **107** 14 ran. *In touch towards rear, ridden 2f out, ran on final 1f, not reach leaders (K J Manning), beaten 4 1/4l by Elvstroem*

Other notable wins

2004 **1st** Cathay Pacific Hong Kong Cup (Group 1) (Sha Tin, December 12) 3yo+ 1m2f Good to firm **118** 14 ran ● **1st** Prix de l'Opera Casino Barriere d'Enghien (Group 1) (Longchamp, October 3) 3yo+ 1m2f Good **118** (TS 87) 10 ran

In her last three starts as a four-year-old, Alexander Goldrun was below form and without such obvious excuses in the book, though for lesser mortals a trip to Hong Kong in December would provide a ready one. The Prix de l'Opera and Champion Stakes also saw her under-perform.

It does not take the gloss off her record. Those runs are heavily outweighed by her achievements and it can be claimed that the pick of those also came in defeat, when taking on colts in the Irish Champion Stakes at Leopardstown. In form terms, it was the best so far from Alexander Goldrun, who found her way blocked on the turn but finished best of all. Her margin of defeat to Oratorio and Motivator was half a length and a head.

Alexander Goldrun

bay filly, 9-2-2001

Gold Away ch 1995	Goldneyev	Nureyev	**Northern Dancer** Special
		Gold River	Riverman Glaneuse
	Blushing Away	Blushing Groom	Red God Runaway Bride
		Sweet Revenge	Raja Baba Away
Renashaan b 1989	Darshaan	Shirley Heights	Mill Reef Hardiemma
		Delsy	Abdos Kelty
	Gerbera	Lyphard	**Northern Dancer** Goofed
		Greenway	Targowice Gracious

Bred by Dermot Cantillon in Ireland. Ir40,000gns Goffs November foal.

Sire Gold Away

Won 5 of 16 races, inc. Prix Thomas Bryon-Gr3, Prix de Guiche-Gr3, Prix Edmond Blanc-Gr3, Prix du Muguet-Gr2. Also 2nd 4 times and 3rd once in Gr1. Never out of the frame. Medium-sized (15.3hh), well-made sort. High-class performer with a sharp turn of foot, effective on any going. Stayed 9f, but also smart at 6.5f and very best form at 8f in final start. Stands at Haras du Quesnay, Deauville, France, at a 2006 fee of €5,000. Sire of 3 crops of racing age, inc. notable winners: Alexander Goldrun (Prix de l'Opera-Gr1, Hong Kong Cup-Gr1, Pretty Polly S.-Gr1, Nassau S.-Gr1), Clifden (Gr3).

Dam Renashaan

Won 2 of 8 races, inc. Listed at Longchamp. Also Gr3-placed at 3. Smart performer with a useful turn of foot, effective on any ground. Probably did not quite get 10f. Best performance came after long lay-off. Dam of: Highshaan (1994 f by Pistolet Bleu; winner), Renazig (1995 g by Polish Precedent; winner), Renaleon (1996 g by Generous; winner), Kalliopino (1998 f by Machiavellian; unraced), Medecis (1999 c by Machiavellian; Gr3 winner), Alexander Goldrun (2001 f by Gold Away; multiple Gr1 winner), Rio (2002 c by Namid; unraced). She has a yearling colt by Machiavellian and a colt foal by Pivotal. Covered by Sadler's Wells in 2005.

Pedigree assessment

Alexander Goldrun doubled her tally of Group 1 scores in 2005 with successes in the Pretty Polly Stakes on The Curragh and the Nassau Stakes at Goodwood, but her lifetime best performance surely came when she finished third behind Oratorio and Motivator in the Irish Champion. In the light of that run, her subsequent displays were a shade disappointing, but she has been a splendid servant to her connections, a game, hardy and thoroughly admirable racemare. She is much the best product of her sire (who remains available at a bargain fee), and her dam, who was sold for 640,000gns at the 2004 Newmarket December Sales, was mated in 2005 to exploit the much-publicised 'nick' between Sadler's Wells and Darshaan. *TM*

Alkaased (USA)

5yo bay horse **125**

Kingmambo (USA) - Chesa Plana (Niniski (USA))

Owner M R Charlton

Trainer L M Cumani

Breeder Clovelly Farms

Career: **16** starts	won **6**	second **7**	third **0**	**£1,672,129** win and place

By Nicholas Godfrey

WHEN Monte Carlo-based businessman Mike Charlton shelled out 42,000gns to buy Alkaased at the end of his three-year-old season, the son of Kingmambo could boast just a lowly Ripon maiden-race success from six starts.

Admittedly, the colt had shown a degree of promise, and the figure was rather less than the $325,000 that Hamdan Al Maktoum had paid for him as a yearling. But he came with a distinct risk attached, a history of minor ailments that screamed out caveat emptor. "We were told he had never scoped clean and would never be given a clean bill of health by the vet," Charlton confided, speaking just over two years after taking the plunge in October 2003 at the Tattersalls Horses In Training Sales. "I bought him knowing the risk," he added. "In fact, if someone had gone to 50,000, they'd have got him." Which would have been a shame for Charlton, under the circumstances. Barely half an hour before he spoke, the owner had watched Alkaased complete a magnificent rags-to-riches story with a thrilling success under Frankie Dettori in the Japan Cup, the horse establishing a track record time – unofficially a world record for 2,400 metres on turf – in one of the most prestigious races on the planet. While lucrative enough in itself, the nail-biting victory also provided the ticket to a place at stud in the host nation after the Maktoums bought him back in a deal that was reportedly of the multi-million-pound variety.

That unforgettable victory in Tokyo, achieved by a nostril hair from a talent-laden field, was the culmination of an ascent through the ranks that was nothing short of remarkable and meant he retired with two Group 1 victories to his name. Not bad for a horse bought as a prospective handicapper before Charlton sent him to Luca Cumani, who duly demonstrated his peerless prowess when it comes to managing improvement in older horses.

Having been trained by Sir Michael Stoute for his first two seasons,

Photograph courtesy of Japan Racing Association

Alkaased (near side) completes his rise to the top level with a narrow victory over Heart's Cry in the Japan Cup

Alkaased's form in 2004 following his move was highly progressive. He routed his rivals in a cracking renewal of Haydock's Old Newton Cup off a mark of 94 before scoring in Listed company at Glorious Goodwood and then confirming that he might well be more than just a very decent middle-distance handicapper with a determined effort in Kempton's September Stakes.

Not for the first time, Alkaased clearly appreciated the fast ground that day as he went down by just a half-length to dual Group 1 winner Mamool, chasing the winner hard through the final furlong. The performance augured well. Here was a tough nut to crack, a resolute galloper seemingly guaranteed to produce a relentless effort in the last couple of furlongs of his races.

Any doubts over whether Alkaased could handle yet another step up in class were erased straight away at the start of his fourth season in training with a decisive victory over Gamut in the Group 2 Jockey Club Stakes at Newmarket in May. Although the contest was not as strong as it could have been, the winner looked very much still on the upgrade in scoring much more easily than the length-and-a-half verdict implied.

The inevitable move into the highest grade came a month later in the Coronation Cup, where Alkaased yet again acquitted himself well in finishing runner-up to Yeats, aboard whom a masterful Kieren Fallon pinched the race. Alkaased did exceptionally well to get as close as he did, having been held up in last place by Jimmy Fortune and given far too much to do. "I think my horse and jockey were a bit outfoxed," said Cumani.

2005 Race record

1st Japan Cup (Group 1) (Tokyo, November 27) 3yo+ 1m4f Firm **125** 18 ran. *Missed break, raced in 12th, headway 5f out, 5th straight, ridden under 2f out, led 1f out, driven out, just held on (L Dettori), beat Heart's Cry by nose*

5th Emirates Airline Champion Stakes (Group 1) (Newmarket, October 15) 3yo+ 1m2f Good to soft **119** (TS 105) 15 ran. *Held up, headway over 1f out, stayed on same pace inside final furlong (G Mosse), beaten 4¼l by David Junior*

2nd Prix Foy Gray d'Albion Barriere (Group 2) (Longchamp, September 11) 4yo+ 1m4f Good to soft **122** (TS 115) 6 ran. *Held up in rear, 5th 5f out, 4th straight, went 2nd 1½f out, soon ridden, beaten inside final furlong (K Fallon), beaten 2½l by Pride*

1st Grand Prix de Saint-Cloud (Group 1) (Saint-Cloud, June 26) 4yo+ 1m4f Good to soft **125** (TS 124) 11 ran. *Held up, headway on inside to go 3rd 5f out, went 2nd entering straight, led 1½f out, soon 2 lengths clear, driven out (L Dettori), beat Policy Maker by 2l*

2nd Vodafone Coronation Cup (Group 1) (Epsom, June 3) 4yo+ 1m4f Good **118** (TS 105) 7 ran. *Held up in last, some progress and 5th straight, chased winner 2f out, kept on but hopeless pursuit after (J Fortune), beaten 2½l by Yeats*

1st UltimatePoker.com Jockey Club Stakes (Group 2) (Newmarket, May 1) 4yo+ 1m4f Good to firm **121** (TS 63) 5 ran. *Started slowly, held up, headway to lead over 2f out, edged right over 1f out, ridden clear, eased near finish (J Fortune), beat Gamut by 1½l*

2004

2nd Pentax UK September Stakes (Group 3) (Kempton, September 4) 3yo+ 1m4f Good to firm **118** (TS 81) 4 ran ● **1st** Glorious Stakes (Listed) (Goodwood, July 30) 4yo+ 1m4f Good to firm **114** (TS 112) 9 ran ● **1st** bet365 Old Newton Cup (Heritage Handicap) (Haydock, July 3) 3yo+ (0-110 handicap) 1m4f Good **111** (TS 104) 15 ran ● **2nd** Fifty Years of Twinning Classified Stakes (Newmarket, June 5) 3yo+ (0-90) 1m4f Good to firm **102** (TS 38) 9 ran

Other runs

2003 **2nd** Tote Placepot Rated Stakes (Handicap) (Leicester, October 13) 3yo (0-90 handicap) 1m4f Good to firm **100** (TS 76) 8 ran ● **2nd** NGK Spark Plugs Handicap (Newmarket, October 4) 3yo (0-95 handicap) 1m6f Good to firm **102** (TS 83) 8 ran ● **1st** Family Day Maiden Stakes (Ripon, August 25) 3yo+ 1m4½f Good to firm **86** 4 ran ● **2nd** Great Yarmouth Glass Maiden Stakes (Yarmouth, July 3) 3yo+ 1m3½f Good **87** (TS 80) 7 ran 2002 ● **4th** Federation of Bloodstock Agents Maiden Stakes (Div II) (Newmarket, October 18) 2yo 1m Good **83** (TS 66) 16 ran ● **4th** McKeever St. Lawrence Conditions Stakes (Doncaster, September 11) 2yo 7f Good **86** (TS 61) 6 ran

While the Epsom run suggested the rapidly improving Alkaased had the potential to win a Group 1 event, his next outing in the Grand Prix de Saint-Cloud was no easy option. Run on ground almost certainly a bit faster than the official good to soft, the French contest attracted a top-class field, headed by the previous year's Arc winner, Bago, and Yeats.

In the event, though, they all had to give best to Alkaased. Never a flashy sort, he crowned his amazing rise to the summit with a trademark display. With new rider Dettori hugging the rail throughout behind a generous pace, Alkaased moved upsides Bago's pacemaker Imago Mundi halfway up the straight before settling the issue, driven out to score by a couple of lengths from Policy Maker.

Though this was an impressive performance, there were a couple of question marks over the form, namely Bago and Yeats, neither of whom turned up with their A-game. The disappointing Bago was niggled and scrubbed along some way from home, while Yeats found zero when asked for an effort. They did little to enhance their reputations, and in doing so they probably ensured that Alkaased was not quite accorded the credit he deserved for the win, although such an accusation could not be levelled at those responsible for calculating his Racing Post Rating. At 125, it would be the highest of his career, a mark matched only in the Japan Cup.

Alkaased now featured among the leading fancies for the King George, but Cumani took the bold decision to miss the midsummer highlight and put him away for an ambitious autumn campaign focusing on four major international targets: the Arc, the Breeders' Cup Turf, the Japan Cup and the Hong Kong Vase. For a time, it looked as if the masterplan was set to blow up in the trainer's face. Although Alkaased was a beaten favourite in his Arc trial, the Prix Foy, where he could not peg back Pride, this was considered a minor blip on his first outing for 77 days, Cumani claiming the horse needed the race after watching him tire in the final furlong. "He had too many spaghettis while he was on holiday and was a little bit overweight," he said.

However, Alkaased was forced to miss the Arc itself when a small cut became infected, and he could finish only fifth to outsider David Junior on an attempted retrieval mission in the Champion Stakes. While this was no disgrace at a trip too sharp for him in a race considered no more than an afterthought, further disappointment was to follow when an unsatisfactory blood count meant he had to forgo the Breeders' Cup. At least these setbacks ensured he arrived a fresh horse in Tokyo for a race in which conditions were designed to suit him, rock-hard ground and a guaranteed fast pace being tailor-made. For good measure, Dettori was back on board, Alkaased having been ridden by others since his Saint-Cloud victory. Nonetheless, this was a tall order. The 18-strong field assembled in late November for what is arguably the most international race on the calendar looked one of the strongest in its history, with an Arc winner in Bago (again) plus two horses with victories at the Breeders' Cup in Ouija Board and US-trained Better Talk Now.

Furthermore, the quality of Japanese-trained horses has done nothing but improve in recent years, with the result that the Japan Cup has become a much stiffer task for the visitors. Before 2005, domestically trained horses had won six of the previous seven renewals, and even in the absence of superstar three-year-old Deep Impact, who avoided the race in favour of the Arima Kinen on Christmas Day, the home defence looked formidable, headed as it was by 2004 winner Zenno Rob Roy. An equine pin-up at home, the five-year-old was sent off a short-priced favourite to become the first horse to win back-to-back runnings of the Japan Cup.

Such a stellar field produced one of the races of the season. Alkaased was sent off fourth favourite, shortest of the visitors at the surprisingly miserly price of 9.6-1, indicative of his rider's popularity even in Japan. He missed a beat at the traps, which enabled Dettori to angle him across to the rail and soon he was travelling comfortably, settled in mid-division and making steady headway down the back straight behind a scorching pace set by 2003 winner Tap Dance City.

Although for a while it looked as if the leader might have stolen the race, he folded two furlongs out, when Kieren Fallon kicked the gallant Ouija Board in pursuit and Zenno Rob Roy arrived on the scene in menacing fashion on the outside. As Ouija Board's effort petered out, Alkaased grabbed the favourite a furlong out under the strongest of driving from Dettori. But he was immediately attacked by domestic hope Heart's Cry, who sneaked up Alkaased's inner with a desperate late lunge, drifting across Ouija Board in the process. With a crowd of 95,635 going mad in the stands, Alkaased and Heart's Cry crossed the line seemingly in unison. Given the hosts' reputation for promptness in declaring results, it was an agonising few minutes before Alkaased's number appeared on the screens to confirm that he had become the first British-trained winner of the event since Pilsudski in 1997 – by a nose. Even then, there was a stewards' inquiry before it was confirmed that Dettori had landed his third success following Singspiel (1996) and Falbrav (2002). The rider appeared more emotional than usual after winning such a richly endowed contest for his mentor Cumani, to whom he was apprenticed at the very start of a fantastic riding career.

Cumani, for his part, was unstinting in his praise for Dettori. "He is probably the best rider we've seen in the world for a very, very long time," he said. Alkaased, the horse who inspired this love-in, hadn't done so badly himself. In winning, he shaved a tenth off the previous track best, his time of 2min 22.1sec bettering a mark set by Horlicks in 1989, confirming his status as one of the most progressive racehorses of recent seasons; talented, consistent and admirably resilient.

As for Charlton, who had just seven horses in training at the time of the Japan Cup – Alkaased the only one with Cumani – the owner soon abandoned plans to run the winner in Hong Kong once Sheikh Mohammed weighed in with an offer for the horse's services as a stallion at Hokkai Stud, the Japanese arm of his Darley operation.

Charlton couldn't help but admit how lucky he had been over his allegedly risky purchase. "While I thought he might improve as a four-year-old, this is a million-to-one shot," he said. "When I bought him, I thought he might be the type of older horse Luca does so well with – I hoped we might try to win a nice handicap at Royal Ascot."

The formidably gritty Alkaased never did quite manage that. Not that his owner was complaining.

Alkaased *bay horse, 19-2-2000*

Parents	Grandparents	Great-grandparents	Great-great-grandparents
Kingmambo b 1990	Mr Prospector	Raise A Native	Native Dancer Raise You
		Gold Digger	Nashua Sequence
	Miesque	Nureyev	**Northern Dancer** Special
		Pasadoble	Prove Out Santa Quilla
Chesa Plana b 1989	Niniski	Nijinsky	**Northern Dancer** Flaming Page
		Virginia Hills	Tom Rolfe Ridin' Easy
	Top Of The League	High Top	Derring-Do Camenae
		Home and Away	Home Guard Garden of Eden

Bred by Clovelly Farms in Kentucky. $325,000 Keeneland September yearling; 42,000gns Tattersalls Autumn 4-y-o.

Sire Kingmambo

Won 5 of 13 races, inc. Poule d'Essai des Poulains-Gr1, St James's Palace S.-Gr1, Prix du Moulin-Gr1). Among the best milers of his generation. Sire of: American Boss (Gr2), El Condor Pasa (NHK Mile Cup-Gr1, Japan Cup-Gr1, Grand Prix de Saint-Cloud-Gr1), Mambo Twist (Gr3), Parade Ground (Gr2), Admire Mambo (Gr2), Lemon Drop Kid (Futurity S.-Gr1, Belmont S.-Gr1, Travers S.-Gr1, Whitney S.-Gr1, Woodward H.-Gr1), Monarch's Maze (Gr2), Bluemamba (Poule d'Essai des Pouliches-Gr1), King Cugat (Gr2), Kingsalsa (Gr3), King's Best (2,000 Guineas-Gr1), Parade Leader (Gr2), Penny's Gold (Gr3), King Fidelia (Gr3), Malhub (Golden Jubilee S.-Gr1), Okawango (Grand Criterium-Gr1), Voodoo Dancer (Garden City H.-Gr1), Dubai Destination (Queen Anne S.-Gr1), Walzerkonigin (Gr2), Alkaased (Grand Prix de Saint-Cloud-Gr1, Japan Cup-Gr1), Governor Brown (Gr3), Russian Rhythm (1,000 Guineas-Gr1, Coronation S.-Gr1, Nassau S.-Gr1, Lockinge S.-Gr1), Illustrious Miss (Gr3), Mambo Slew (Gr3), Notable Guest (Gr3), Rule Of Law (St Leger S.-Gr1), Tarfah-Gr3), Divine Proportions (Prix Morny-Gr1, Prix Marcel Boussac-Gr1, Poule d'Essai des Pouliches-Gr1, Prix de Diane-Gr1, Prix d'Astarte-Gr1), Virginia Waters (1,000 Guineas-Gr1).

Dam Chesa Plana

Won 3 of 27 races, inc. 1 Listed. Also placed 7 times in Pattern races, twice in Gr1. Smart performer, effective at a variety of distances, placed in German Classics at 1m and 1m6f. Dam of: Burgundian Red (1997 c by Red Ransom; winner), Vielle Senlis (1998 f by Cryptoclearance; winner), Stickwithsterling (1999 c by Silver Hawk; placed), Alkaased (2000 c by Kingmambo; dual Gr1 winner), unnamed (2001 f by Distant View; died as a foal), Lady Circe (2002 f by Spinning World; winner) Glory Pass (2003 c by Tiznow; unraced to date). She has a yearling filly by Woodman, and a colt foal by Lucius. Covered by E Dubai in 2005.

Pedigree assessment

The summer break that Alkaased was allowed after his victory in the Grand Prix de Saint-Cloud served him admirably. When he got his proper distance and underfoot conditions, in the Japan Cup, he was a monster, lowering the world record for 2,400m to an amazing 2:22.1. The ever-acquisitive Sheikh Mohammed made an offer that could not be refused, and Alkaased remained in Japan for stud duties at Darley's Hokkaido branch. Kingmambo's stock have done well in Japan. *TM*

Amadeus Wolf

2yo bay colt **120**

Mozart (Ire) - Rachelle (Ire) (Mark Of Esteem (Ire))

Owner J Duddy & B McDonald

Trainer K A Ryan

Breeder Ascagnano S P A

Career: **5** starts | won **3** | second **1** | third **1** | **£190,645** win and place

By Tom O'Ryan

IT SPEAKS volumes for Kevin Ryan's rapid climb through the training ranks that, in the space of seven years, he has gone from fledgling recruit, with only a handful of modest horses, to become a prolific producer of winners, a leading light in the North of England, and one of the country's most prosperous practitioners.

Ryan's considerable talents were showcased to a much wider audience in 2005, largely thanks to the notable exploits of Amadeus Wolf and Palace Episode, who were both juvenile winners at the highest level.

Success in the Scottish Equitable Gimcrack Stakes heralded Amadeus Wolf as a rising star. Anyone who, for whatever reason, had any doubt about the true merit of that performance, was presented with further proof of this likeable colt's burgeoning ability in the Shadwell Stud Middle Park Stakes, in which he supplied Ryan with his first Group 1 triumph with his first runner in that superior grade.

Amadeus Wolf, who had changed hands as a yearling for €87,000, failed to reach his reserve when re-offered at the Newmarket Breeze-Up Sales as a two-year-old. How many would-be buyers, one wonders, have since had cause for regret at allowing him to walk away unsold from that auction?

He can hardly have hidden his light under a bushel, as the first time he ran, at Ayr the following month, he was sent off a well-supported 5-4 favourite and won handsomely in maiden company on rain-softened ground.

That the Coventry Stakes, at Royal Ascot at York, was chosen as his next assignment confirmed that Amadeus Wolf was already regarded as an above-average performer by those who knew him best. He performed admirably there, coming out comfortably best of those drawn in double figures and finishing third to Red Clubs, with Pacific Pride dividing the pair at the line.

Amadeus Wolf and Red Clubs were to become regular rivals. But, before they crossed swords again, Amadeus Wolf was switched to five furlongs

Amadeus Wolf lands the Group 1 Middle Park Stakes for trainer Kevin Ryan, who enjoyed a memorable season

at Chester, where, after slightly spoiling his chance by drifting to his right rounding the home turn, he suffered an odds-on defeat at the hands of Mullaad, who sneaked through on the rails to nail him late.

There was no disgrace in that defeat, given that Mullaad went on to finish third in the Richmond Stakes at Goodwood, before renewing rivalry again with Amadeus Wolf in the Gimcrack.

The return to six furlongs in York's historic contest plainly suited Amadeus Wolf, who produced a gritty display to turn the Coventry tables on Red Clubs, who, this time, had to play second fiddle, one and a half lengths behind the winner, though he was conceding a 5lb Royal Ascot penalty. Assertive, a Listed winner, was comfortably held in third, while Mullaad stumbled at the start and finished among the backmarkers, as did Pacific Pride, the Coventry Stakes runner-up.

Ryan targeted the Middle Park as his next objective for Amadeus Wolf, and it provided a real acid test for the Yorkshire-based colt after a six-week break. In opposition among the six-strong field were Ivan Denisovich, winner of the July Stakes and runner-up in the Prix Morny, the Richmond Stakes winner Always Hopeful, the progressive Group 3 winner Prince Of Light, and old rival Red Clubs, this time meeting Amadeus Wolf on level terms.

Ryan had hoped that the ground at Newmarket would remain good,

2005 **Race record**

1st Shadwell Stud Middle Park Stakes (Group 1) (Newmarket, September 30) 2yo 6f Good to soft **120** (TS 119) 6 ran. *Tracked leader, ridden to lead over 1f out, ran on under pressure (N Callan), beat Red Clubs by 1¼l*

1st Scottish Equitable Gimcrack Stakes (Group 2) (York, August 17) 2yo 6f Good **111** (TS 109) 13 ran. *Tracked leaders, effort 2f out, stayed on to lead last 75yds (N Callan), beat Red Clubs by 1½l*

2nd Littlewoods Bet Direct Conditions Stakes (Chester, July 8) 2yo 5f Good to firm **93** (TS 62) 8 ran. *With leader, led and edged right over 1f out, headed inside final furlong, ran on (N Callan), beaten nk by Mullaad*

3rd Coventry Stakes (Group 2) (York, June 14) 2yo 6f Good to firm **99** (TS 96) 14 ran. *Tracked leaders on stands' side, kept on same pace final furlong (N Callan), beaten 3l by Red Clubs*

1st DM Hall EBF Ayr Maiden Stakes (Ayr, May 26) 2yo 6f Soft **85** (TS 62) 6 ran. *Dwelt, soon led, pushed along 2f out, kept on strongly (N Callan), beat Glasshoughton by 2½l*

as it had been at York, believing his contender to be most effective under such conditions. Aidan O'Brien had similar sentiments about Ivan Denisovich, who had reportedly been unsuited by soft ground when a two-length second to Silca's Sister in the Prix Morny. Overnight rain, though, eased the going, which was officially changed to good to soft.

Not that it hindered Amadeus Wolf, who was sent off the 4-1 joint-second favourite and hammered home his growing prowess in no uncertain style. After tracking the leader Always Hopeful, he went to the front more than a furlong out and ran on strongly to beat his old foe Red Clubs by one and a quarter lengths, to provide his regular rider Neil Callan, a former journeyman jockey who has risen firmly to the fore in the last couple of years, with his first Group 1 victory. Always Hopeful was a further two lengths back in third, a length ahead of the 2-1 favourite Ivan Denisovich.

Ryan promptly drew stumps for the season with Amadeus Wolf, whose victory earned him a much-improved Racing Post Rating of 120 – a figure that puts him just behind dual Group 1 winner George Washington (121), on a par with Horatio Nelson, and just ahead of Sir Percy (119), who won the Dewhurst.

Whether or not Amadeus Wolf can last out a mile in top company next season is the proverbial 64,000-dollar question. But he will, in any case, understandably be trained with the 2,000 Guineas firmly in mind, by a man who just three weeks after the Middle Park crowned a memorable campaign by winning a second Group 1 juvenile event with Palace Episode in the Racing Post Trophy at Doncaster.

Should Amadeus Wolf line up at Newmarket for the Guineas, he will be his trainer's first Classic runner. That would be yet another milestone for Ryan in a career which, like this admirably classy and talented colt, has not been lacking in pace or high achievement.

Amadeus Wolf *bay colt, 28-1-2003*

Mozart b 1998	Danehill	Danzig	Northern Dancer
			Pas de Nom
		Razyana	His Majesty
			Spring Adieu
	Victoria Cross	Spectacular Bid	Bold Bidder
			Spectacular
		Glowing Tribute	Graustark
			Admiring
Rachelle b 1998	Mark Of Esteem	Darshaan	Shirley Heights
			Delsy
		Homage	Ajdal
			Home Love
	Rose Violet	Alleged	Hoist The Flag
			Princess Pout
		Shawnee Creek	Mr Prospector
			Back Ack

Bred by Ascagnano SPA in Ireland. €87,000 Milan yearling, 50,000gns (retained) Tattersalls breeze-up 2yo

Sire Mozart

High-class 2yo, won 2 (both 7f, including Tattersalls Houghton Sales Stakes) of 3 starts, also 4th Dewhurst S. At 3, developed into top-class sprinter, won 3 (Jersey S-Gr3, July Cup-Gr1, Nunthorpe S-Gr1) of 7 starts, also 2nd Irish 2,000 Guineas. Half-brother to Grade 2 winner England Expects out of unraced half-sister to Kentucky Derby winner Sea Hero, Grade 1 winner Hero's Honor and several other high-class US performers.Stood only season at Coolmore, died 2002. Only foals 2003, sire of: Amadeus Wolf (Middle Park S-Gr1), Dandy Man (Listed), Johannes (Gr1-placed), Modeeroch (Listed).

Dam Rachelle

Won 1 (8f at 3) of 7 starts at 2 and 3 in Italy, unplaced in remainder. By top-class miler and fair sire who is capable of getting top-level winners, out of 1993 Oaks d'Italia runner-up Rose Violet, herself a half-sister to Grade 3 winner and decent US sire Storm Creek. Dam of: Amadeus Wolf (2003 c by Mozart; Middle Park S-Gr1), 2004 f by Zamindar, 2005 c by Rock Of Gibraltar.

Pedigree assessment

The two questions here are (a) will Amadeus Wolf stay a mile, and (b) is he likely to 'train on'? He is from Mozart's only crop, so there is no evidence to guide us here. Although Mozart was a sprinter, he could have been expected to last a mile on pedigree, and he will get some talented milers. Amadeus Wolf's family is not one of sprinters – his grand-dam put in her best performance over 12 furlongs – and there is a decent chance the Middle Park Stakes winner can step up another couple of furlongs. As for 'training on', Amadeus Wolf's pedigree gives no strong pointers either way, though it is possible the colt has less scope for improvement than some of his contemporaries. *JH*

Artie Schiller (USA)

4yo bay colt **124**

El Prado (Ire) - Hidden Light (USA) (Majestic Light (USA))

Owner Timber Bay Farm and Mrs Thomas J Walsh

Trainer J Jerkens

Breeder Haras Du Mezeray

Career: **19** starts | won **10** | second **4** | third **2** | **£1,070,555** win and place

By James Willoughby

LEGENDARY US trainer Allen Jerkens is still trying to win a Breeders' Cup race after more than two decades. It took his son Jimmy just one horse.

Artie Schiller had a successful campaign as a three-year-old in 2004 and started favourite for the Breeders' Cup Mile at Lone Star. Connections were in two minds as to whether he was ready for the big time, but decided to take their chance. Every door slammed in his face, however, and the season ended with a degree of frustration.

The heavy defeat provoked discussions as to whether to concentrate on a repeat bid for the Mile at Belmont or aim Artie Schiller for the Turf. A son of the Sadler's Wells stallion El Prado, he certainly had the pedigree for running over middle distances. It was decided early in 2005 to defer a step up in distance until later in the campaign.

The sun was to shine more than once on his connections for this decision. On a beautiful day in April at Keeneland, Artie Schiller returned to action with a devastating display in the Grade 2 Maker's Mark Mile. Always travelling well under Edgar Prado, the four-year-old scooted clear after straightening for home to beat Gulch Approval by two and a quarter lengths.

The Grade 2 Dixie Handicap on the Preakness day card at Pimlico the following month was to be the watershed. "This race will be the deciding point in mapping out his campaign," Jerkens jnr said.

The Dixie was over nine furlongs, a distance that Artie Schiller had won over four times. His handler's uncertainty over longer distances had emanated from a defeat by the top-class Kitten's Joy on his only try at a mile and a quarter, but the impression that Artie Schiller did not get home had to be tempered by his simply being defeated by a better horse.

Yet again the result was inconclusive. In a steadily run race, Artie Schiller failed by a nose to concede 6lb to the much inferior Cool Conductor.

The Grade 1 Manhattan Handicap at Belmont in June finally proved

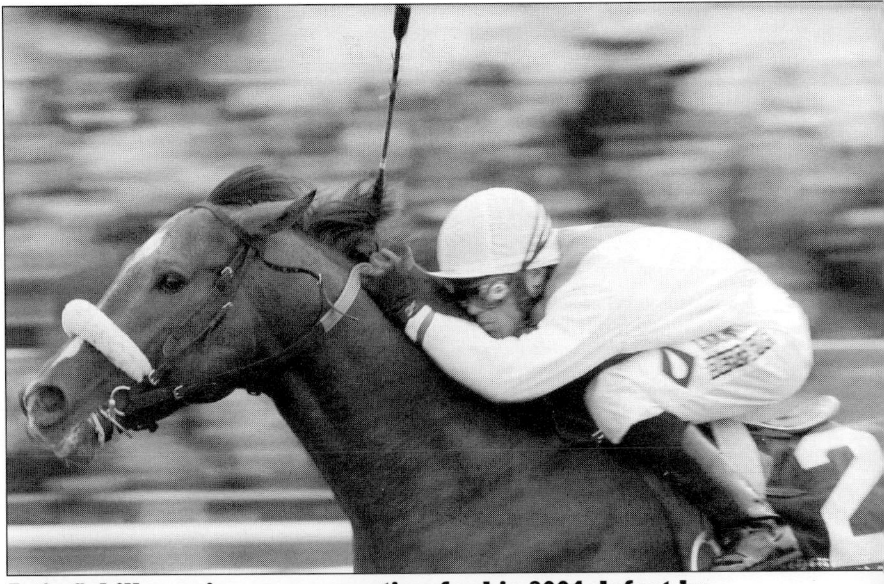

Artie Schiller gains compensation for his 2004 defeat by landing the Breeders' Cup Mile at Belmont Park

that a mile and a quarter was too far. The colt ran a creditable race to finish a close-up third to Good Reward, but it really appeared as though the trip caught him out. "He wasn't there the last half-furlong," said his trainer. "He is probably best at up to nine furlongs."

Dead aim was now set on the Breeders' Cup Mile. There were four and a half months to go, and a careful campaign would have to be set in order to get Artie Schiller to Belmont in peak condition. He had already had three races and suffered two defeats, so a break was in order.

Having learned at the foot of a master during a 20-year tenure as his father's assistant, Jerkens jnr, 54, delivered Artie Schiller ready to run the race of his life on Breeders' Cup day. He used a pair of Grade 2 handicaps in New York to put an edge on the colt, victory in the Bernard Baruch at Saratoga being followed by honourable defeat in the Kelso at Belmont.

So often it takes defeat to reveal the true requirements of high-class horses. Though conceding 8lb to the ill-starred former Sir Michael Stoute and Amanda Perrett-trained six-year-old Funfair was no disgrace, Artie Schiller was more inconvenienced by tactics than weight. He raced far too close to the pace for a horse with a finishing kick, and some were inclined to lay the blame at the door of his jockey Richard Migliore.

Artie Schiller had been Migliore's ride as a three-year-old, but now there was some conjecture as to whether he should be replaced. It turned out to be a moot point, for the veteran New York rider was ruled out by

2005 Race record

1st Netjets Breeders' Cup Mile (Grade 1) (Turf) (Belmont Park, October 29) 3yo+ 1m Yielding **124** 12 ran. *Always close up, 4th straight, ran on to lead inside final furlong, driven out (G K Gomez), beat Leroidesanimaux by 3/4l*

2nd Kelso Breeders' Cup Handicap (Grade 2) (Belmont Park, October 2) 3yo+ 1m Firm **120** 10 ran. *Pressed leader throughout, every chance under strong pressure final furlong, unable to quicken close home (R Migliore), beaten hd by Funfair*

1st Bernard Baruch Handicap (Grade 2) (Saratoga, August 1) 3yo+ 1m1f Good **122** 5 ran. *Always close up, went 2nd before halfway, led inside final furlong, ran on well (R Migliore), beat Silver Tree by 1/2l*

3rd Manhattan Handicap (Grade 1) (Belmont Park, June 11) 3yo+ 1m2f Firm **120** 11 ran. *Led over 2f, restrained and moved to outside, went 2nd well over 1f out, every chance final furlong, no extra close home (E Prado), beaten 1/2l by Good Reward*

2nd Dixie Stakes (Grade 2) (Turf) (Pimlico, May 21) 3yo+ 1m1f Good **120** 5 ran. *Pressed leader off slow pace, not much room on inside but every chance from over 1f out, stumbled slightly final stages, just held (E Prado), beaten shd by Cool Conductor*

1st Maker's Mark Mile Stakes (Grade 2) (Keeneland, April 15) 4yo+ 1m Firm **117** 10 ran. *In touch, close 5th halfway, headway 4-wide to press leader entering straight, led well over 1f out, driven clear final furlong (E Prado), beat Gulch Approval by 2 1/4l*

Other wins

2004 **1st** Jamaica Handicap (Grade 2) (Belmont Park, September 26) 3yo 1m1f Firm **121** 6 ran ● **1st** National Museum of Racing Hall of Fame Stakes (Handicap) (Grade 2) (Saratoga, August 9) 3yo 1m1f Firm **116** 8 ran ● **1st** Hill Prince Stakes (Grade 3) (Belmont Park, June 6) 3yo 1m1f Firm 6 ran ● **1st** Woodlawn Stakes (Pimlico, May 15) 3yo 1m1/2f Firm 13 ran ● **1st** Allowance race (Aqueduct, May 1) 3yo+ 1m Good 7 ran **2003** **1st** Allowance race (Belmont Park, September 17) 2yo 1m Firm 11 ran ● **1st** Maiden Special Weight (Belmont Park, July 16) 2yo 6f Firm 12 ran

injury sustained in a paddock accident a week before the Breeders' Cup. The big-race seat went to rising star Garrett Gomez, who made the best possible start to Breeders' Cup day when steering Stevie Wonderboy to victory in the Juvenile.

Racing analysts in the US label horses the beneficiary of a 'perfect trip' when they receive the ideal run through the race. That was most certainly the case with Artie Schiller in the Mile, but not with his most dangerous opponent, Leroidesanimaux.

While the latter was caught wide and had to accelerate while losing ground, Artie Schiller drafted behind rivals, skimmed the rails into the straight and had only to be angled around one rival to prevail by three-quarters of a length from the odds-on favourite, who must be regarded as unlucky. He wasn't the only one, either, for the ex-French filly Gorella and her former compatriot Whipper were hampered while filling out third and fourth placings.

Nevertheless, it was a victory not just for Artie Schiller but for persistence and planning. And those are qualities the Jerkens family know plenty about.

Artie Schiller

bay colt, 23-4-2001

El Prado gr 1989	Sadler's Wells	Northern Dancer	Nearctic
			Natalma
		Fairy Bridge	Bold Reason
			Special
	Lady Capulet	Sir Ivor	Sir Gaylord
			Attica
		Cap And Bells	Tom Fool
			Ghazni
Hidden Light b 1983	Majestic Light	Majestic Prince	Raise A Native
			Gay Hostess
		Irradiate	Ribot
			High Voltage
	Tallahto	Nantallah	Nasrullah
			Shimmer
		Legato	Dark Star
			Vulcania

Bred by Haras du Mezeray in Kentucky. $67,000 Keeneland September yearling.

Sire El Prado

Won 4 of 9 races, inc. Railway S.-Gr3, National S.-Gr1, Beresford S.-Gr2. Strong, well-made, 16.0hh. Named joint-best 2-y-o in Ireland in International Classifications, best form at 1m on soft ground. Stands at Adena Springs Kentucky, at a 2006 fee of $125,000. Sire of 10 crops of racing age, inc. notable winners: Chindi (Gr3), El Cielo (Gr3), Nite Dreamer (Gr3), Shires Ende (Gr3), Sweet And Ready (Gr2), Air Rocket (Gr3), Swinging On Ice (Gr2), Mr Livingston (Gr3), Medaglia d'Oro (Travers S.-Gr1, Whitney H.-Gr1, Donn H.-Gr1), Senor Swinger (Gr2), Shaconage (Gr3), Spanish Sun (Gr2), Artie Schiller (Breeders' Cup Mile-Gr1), Borrego (Pacific Classic-Gr1, Jockey Club Gold Cup-Gr1), Kitten's Joy (Secretariat S.-Gr1, Joe Hirsch Turf Classic S.-Gr1), Timo (Gr3), Asi Siempre (Gr3).

Dam Hidden Light

Won 6 of 12 races, inc. Santa Anita Oaks-Gr1, Hollywood Oaks-Gr1, Del Mar Oaks-Gr2. High-class performer on dirt and turf, effective sprinting and up to 9f. Ranked joint 4th-best of her sex at 3. Dam of: Liginsky (1989 c by Nijinsky; winner), Hidden Dark (1990 f by Ferdinand; placed), Step In Toe (1991 f by Ferdinand; winner), Hidden Dance (1993 f by Nureyev; unraced), Shaheen (1994 c by Danzig; winner), Citrus Sun (1995 g by Danzig; unplaced), Mr Kris (1997 c by Kris S; winner), Avalon Bay (1998 f by Broad Brush; winner), Speed To Burn (1999 f by Red Ransom; winner, Gr2-placed), Orellana (2000 f by With Approval; winner), Artie Schiller (2001 c by El Prado; Gr1 winner), Our Table Mountain (2003 f by Fusaichi Pegasus; unraced to date in South Africa). She has a yearling colt in France by With Approval, and a filly foal in Kentucky by Elusive Quality. Barren in 1992, 1996 and 2002. Not covered in 2005.

Pedigree assessment

Sadler's Wells has become notorious for his inability to get a runner capable of winning a Graded race on dirt, but his son El Prado has proved surprisingly effective in the American environment, delivering products who are at home on both the main track and the turf course. Champion sire there in 2003 and runner-up in 2004, El Prado began his stud career at a fee of $7,500 and once stood for only $5,000, but since the emergence of Medaglia d'Oro (a dirt specialist), he has become ever more popular and will cover at $125,000 in 2006. No wonder, with grass performers Kitten's Joy and Artie Schiller and dirt star Borrego all featuring in his 2001 crop. Artie Schiller's dam was adept on both surfaces, but had produced nothing of note until she gave birth to him at the age of 18. *TM*

Ashado (USA)

4yo brown filly **123**

Saint Ballado (Can) - Goulash (USA) (Mari's Book (USA))

Owner Starlight Stables & P Saylor & J Martin

Trainer T Pletcher

Breeder Aaron U Jones & Marie D Jones

Career: **21** starts | won **12** | second **4** | third **3** | **£2,189,732** win and place

By David Ashforth

AT THE Keeneland Sales, the land of dreams, a lot can happen in a short time. On a September Monday in 2002, sandwiched between lots fetching \$300,000 and \$260,000, lot 226, a yearling filly by Saint Ballado out of Goulash, was bought by Starlight Stables for \$170,000. She was named Ashado, partly Goulash, partly Ballado.

Jack and Laurie Wolf, and their partners Paul Saylor and Johns Martin, hoped she would be a star. Barry Berkelhammer, their agent, was confident that she would be. When Ashado was sent to another rising star, trainer Todd Pletcher, Berkelhammer told him, "I hope you like her, because this is the best that it gets." It got much better.

Back at Keeneland, three years later, on a November Monday, Ashado entered the ring again, as lot 189. Jack Wolf and Pletcher had a small bet on how much Ashado would fetch. Wolf thought between \$7 million and \$8 million, but Pletcher was right on the button. In his catalogue, Pletcher had written \$9m.

This time it was Sheikh Mohammed who bought Ashado, for the highest auction price ever paid for a mare. Ashado was sent to Darley's nearby Jonabell Farm, the home of the stallions Cherokee Run, Holy Bull and Street Cry. \$9 million was an awful lot of money, but Ashado was an awful lot of horse.

By the time the turn of 2005 made Ashado a four-year-old, exceptional success had raised exceptional expectations. Ashado had been good from the start, winning the Grade 1 Spinaway Stakes at Saratoga before finishing runner-up to the outstanding Halfbridled in the 2003 Breeders' Cup Juvenile Fillies at Santa Anita.

As a three-year-old, in 2004, Ashado achieved the unique distinction of winning both the Kentucky Oaks and Breeders' Cup Distaff in the same year. It earned her the Eclipse Award as the top filly of her generation.

Ashado wins the Grade 1 Beldame Stakes, her final victory before being bought for $9 million by Sheikh Mohammed

The award was richly deserved, for Ashado worked for her success, winning at an exalted level in Louisiana and Kentucky, New York, Pennsylvania and Texas – the scene, at Lone Star Park, of her Breeders' Cup triumph, Pletcher's first.

In her first two seasons, Ashado never finished out of the first three. Punters had enormous faith in her. In 15 races as a three and four-year-old, Pletcher's champion started favourite 14 times but, as a four-year-old, justifying the odds became tougher, and Ashado's performances less consistent.

Odds-on when out of the frame in a Grade 1 handicap at Oaklawn Park, Ashado was again beaten when odds-on in a Grade 3 handicap at Pimlico before bouncing back with convincing wins in Grade 1 handicaps at Belmont and Saratoga. Then there was the worst performance of her career, the only bad one, in the Grade 1 Personal Ensign Stakes at Saratoga.

It was out of character, for Ashado was tough, reliable, consistent and willing. She didn't run bad races and, afterwards, it was discovered that she had bruised her foot.

Just over a month later, at Belmont, Ashado bounced back to win the Grade 1 Beldame Stakes, hanging on from Happy Ticket after going clear. Pletcher thought she could do better. The Breeders' Cup was next.

There were records at stake. Azeri, herself the winner of the Distaff in 2002, boasted lifetime earnings of $4,079,820; Ashado was closing in, with $3,711,440. The Distaff was her last race. If she finished in the first two, the record for America's highest-earning filly or mare would

2005 Race record

3rd Emirates Airlines Breeders' Cup Distaff (Grade 1) (Belmont Park, October 29) 3yo+ 1m1f Fast **115** 13 ran. *Prominent, 2nd straight, led briefly 2f out, ridden and no extra final furlong (J R Velazquez), beaten 9½l by Pleasant Home*

1st Beldame Stakes (Grade 1) (Dirt) (Belmont Park, October 1) 3yo+ 1m2f Fast **121** 7 ran. *Pressed leader, led 3f out, 2 lengths clear over 1f out, driven out (J R Velazquez), beat Happy Ticket by ½l*

4th Dead-heat Personal Ensign Stakes (Grade 1) (Saratoga, August 26) 3yo+ 1m2f Fast **105** 7 ran. *Raced in 2nd behind clear leader until weakening well over 1f out (J R Velazquez), beaten 15l by Shadow Cast*

1st Go For Wand Handicap (Grade 1) (Saratoga, July 31) 3yo+ 1m1f Fast **123** 5 ran. *Pressed leader until went on over 2f out, clear over 1f out, ridden out (J R Velazquez), beat Bending Strings by 9 ½l*

1st Ogden Phipps Handicap (Grade 1) (Dirt) (Belmont Park, June 18) 3yo+ 1m½ Fast **119** 5 ran. *Soon led, narrow advantage until ridden clear 2f out, ridden out (J R Velazquez), beat Society Selection by 3l*

2nd Pimlico Breeders' Cup Distaff Handicap (Grade 3) (Pimlico, May 20) 3yo+ 1m½ Sloppy **114** 4 ran. *Led, 2½ lengths clear approaching final furlong, headed and no extra well inside final furlong (J R Velazquez), beaten ¾l by Silmaril*

5th Apple Blossom Handicap (Grade 1) (Oaklawn Park, April 9) 4yo+ 1m½ Fast **113** 7 ran. *Raced in 2nd, pressed leader over 3f out, remained prominent until weakened quickly last 100yds (J R Velazquez), beaten 2l by Dream Of Summer*

Other wins

2004 **1st** Breeders' Cup Distaff (Grade 1) (Dirt) (Lone Star Park, October 30) 3yo+ 1m1f Fast **117** 11 ran ● **1st** Cotillion Handicap (Grade 2) (Philadelphia Park, October 2) 3yo 1m½ Fast **115** 6 ran ● **1st** Coaching Club American Oaks (Grade 1) (Dirt) (Belmont Park, July 24) 3yo 1m2f Fast **115** 6 ran ● **1st** Kentucky Oaks (Grade 1) (Dirt) (Churchill Downs, April 30) 3yo 1m1f Muddy **115** 11 ran ● **1st** Fair Grounds Oaks (Grade 2) (Fair Grounds, March 6) 3yo 1m½ Fast **113** 6 ran **2003** **1st** Demoiselle Stakes (Grade 2) (Aqueduct, November 29) 3yo+ 1m1f Fast 7 ran ● **1st** Spinaway Stakes (Grade 1) (Saratoga, August 29) 2yo 7f Fast **99** 6 ran ● **1st** Schuylerville Stakes (Grade 2) (Saratoga, July 23) 2yo 6f Sloppy **95** 7 ran ● **1st** Maiden (Belmont Park, June 18) 2yo 5½f Sloppy 5 ran

be hers. If she won, Ashado would also be the only horse since Bayakoa, in 1990, to successfully defend her Distaff title. It was a big day, the closing ceremony on a splendid, diligent career.

So it was an anti-climax when Ashado finished third, more so because the race became an unexpected procession. There was little in Pleasant Home's past performances to suggest victory, and nothing to suggest dominance, yet on the stretch to the wire, there was no shouting worth the effort unless Pleasant Home was your horse. It was an astonishing nine and a quarter lengths back to Society Selection, with Ashado a neck away.

The final public fanfare was not at the racetrack but in the sales ring. It will be interesting to see if Ashado's sons and daughters inherit her fine qualities.

Ashado *brown filly, 4-2-2001*

Saint Ballado br 1989	Halo	Hail To Reason	Turn-to Nothirdchance
		Cosmah	Cosmic Bomb Almahmoud
	Ballade	Herbager	Vandale Flagette
		Miss Swapsco	Cohoes Soaring
Goulash b 1993	Mari's Book	Northern Dancer	Nearctic Natalma
		Mari Her	Maribeau Hem And Haw
	Wise Bride	Blushing Groom	Red God Runaway Bride
		Wising Up	Smarten Hardly

Bred by Aaron & Marie Jones in US. $170,000 Keeneland September yearling

Sire Saint Ballado

Won 4 of 9 races, inc. Sheridan S.-Gr3, Arlington Classic-Gr2. Earned $302,820. Strong, lengthy, 16.2hh. Smart performer at around a mile on his day. Brother to champion racemare Glorious Song (dam of Rahy and Singspiel) and to champion 2-y-o Devil's Bag. Died in 2002. Stood last at Taylor Made Farm, Nicholasville, Kentucky, at a fee of $125,000. Sire of 10 crops of racing age, inc. notable winners: Captain Bodgit (Florida Derby-Gr1), Fantasy Angel (Gr3), Sister Act (Hempstead H.-Gr1), Sweetsouthernsaint (Gr3), Straight Man (Gr2), Yankee Victor (Metropolitan H.-Gr1), Flame Thrower (Gr2), Lindsay Jean (Gr3), Popular (Gr3), Saint Marden (Gr3), Freedom's Daughter (Gr2), Ocean Terrace (Gr3), Saint Liam (Donn H.-Gr1, Stephen Foster H.-Gr1, Woodward S.-Gr1, Breeders' Cup Classic-Gr1), Saintly Look (Gr3), Savedbythelight (Gr2), Ashado (Spinaway S.-Gr1, Kentucky Oaks-Gr1, Coaching Club American Oaks-Gr1, Breeders' Cup Distaff-Gr1, Ogden Phipps H.-Gr1, Go For Wand H.-Gr1, Beldame S.-Gr1), Lord of the Game (Gr2), St Averil (Gr2).

Dam Goulash

Unraced at 2, won 6 of 12 starts at 3 and 4 at around 8f, inc minor stakes, also 2nd Linda Vista H-Gr3. By stakes-placed son of Northern Dancer who is also broodmare sire of Gr1 winners Behrens and Congaree. Dam unplaced half-sister to Gr3 winner Wised Up and useful French 10f horse Smart Wise. Grand-dam very smart US dirt 2yo/3yo over around 7-8f. Dam of: Ballado's Halo (1999 f by Saint Ballado; stakes-placed winner), Saint Stephen (2000 c by Saint Ballado; Gr2-placed winner), Ashado (2001 f by Saint Ballado; Gr1 winner), Storm Creek Rising (2002 c by Storm Creek; stakes-placed winner), Sunriver (2003 c by Saint Ballado; placed), 2004 c by Storm Creek.

Pedigree assessment

Few fillies as accomplished as Ashado are offered at public auction, and none has made the $9 million she cost Sheikh Mohammed at Keeneland last November. It is almost futile to speculate whether she will be worth that sum; her owner wants mares of her calibre in his US broodmare collection, and Ashado's acquisition is priceless to him. It is her performances that make her valuable. Although she is well bred and is by a sire favoured by Sheikh Mohammed and his team, her pedigree falls short of spectacular and Saint Ballado is yet to make a major impact as a broodmare sire. Storm Cat has been mooted as a mate for her in 2006, and the product of such a union is obvious material to excel over 8-9f on dirt. *JH*

Attraction

4yo bay filly **113**

Efisio - Flirtation (Pursuit Of Love)

Owner Duke Of Roxburghe

Trainer M Johnston

Breeder Floors Farming

Career: **15** starts | won **10** | second **2** | third **0** | **£899,597** win and place

By David Carr

ATTRACTION was by almost any reckoning an outstanding racehorse. Her story was certainly a remarkable one – the filly with the conformation so unattractive that she was not considered worth taking to the sales ring and rejected by two trainers who were convinced she would never make it to the track. She confounded the doubts by proving herself a top two-year-old and then recovered from serious injury to complete a unique 1,000 Guineas/Irish 1,000 Guineas double.

The scriptwriter always kept a dramatic twist for her final scene, whether it be the come-from-behind victory in the Cherry Hinton Stakes on what turned out to be her final start as a juvenile, or the emotional victory in the Sun Chariot Stakes at three after three successive defeats. And the last act of all had a happy ending too, in Ireland this time as she signed off with a fifth Group 1 victory in the Matron Stakes at Leopardstown in September.

Adopting her trademark position in front, she made all under Kevin Darley and showed all of her customary zest to hold off Chic and the latest 1,000 Guineas winner Virginia Waters. After that there was talk of another tilt at the Sun Chariot or the Breeders' Cup but it all came to nought as she picked up a minor injury and was retired to stud.

The Matron victory was another example of 'bouncebackability' from a filly whose knack of overcoming adversity contributed much to her popularity. The previous month she had managed only fourth place when dropped to Group 3 company for the first time since she was a two-year-old in the Hungerford Stakes at Newbury, headed approaching the final furlong on the softening ground and beaten over six lengths behind Sleeping Indian.

That understandably caused some to question whether she retained her ability, for she had also come unstuck in a bold bid to land the

Attraction scores the fifth Group 1 win of her career with a smooth success in the Matron Stakes at Leopardstown

Champions Mile in Hong Kong – part of the Asian Mile Challenge – on her reappearance in May.

The Lockinge is the more usual starting point for top milers at four, but defying convention has paid off many times in the past for Attraction's trainer Mark Johnston, who was quick to point out that second place at Sha Tin was worth very nearly as much as first at Newbury, and that the ground is much less likely to come up unsuitably soft in the Far East than in Berkshire in mid-May.

As it was, the weather may actually have played a part in her downfall at Sha Tin, as the race was run in stiflingly hot and humid conditions and Attraction was scarcely at the races after missing the break. She threatened briefly to get into it after halfway, but faded in the straight to finish 11th behind Bullish Luck, who quietened Silent Witness's legion of supporters by beating the champion sprinter by a short head.

Attraction's fame preceded her to Hong Kong, where she was labelled 'Freak' by the *South China Morning Post* ahead of her clash with 'Monster' Silent Witness, and she unquestionably had the following more associated with a top jumper than a leading Flat horse – as witnessed by the outpourings that followed her retirement.

But racing is not The X-Factor or Strictly Come Dancing and merit is not measured by a popularity poll. Nor is it judged solely by the prestige of victories earned. There is the objective analysis of form to consider as well. On that reckoning – and that one alone – Attraction was not quite the outstanding filly her supporters might have you believe.

2005 Race record

1st Coolmore Fusaichi Pegasus Matron Stakes (Group 1) (Leopardstown, September 10) 3yo+ 1m Good to yielding **113** (TS 82) 9 ran. *Made all, clear early straight, ridden and swished tail briefly over 1f out, kept on well (K Darley), beat Chic by 3/4l*

4th stanjamesuk.com Hungerford Stakes (Group 3) (Newbury, August 13) 3yo+ 7f Good **105** (TS 99) 9 ran. *Led, ridden over 2f out, headed over 1f out, beaten when bumped inside final furlong (K Darley), beaten 6 1/4l by Sleeping Indian*

11th Champions Mile (Group 1) (Sha Tin, May 14) 3yo+ 1m Good to firm **88** 13 ran. *Started slowly, niggled along to dispute 7th on inside, ridden over 3f out, 5th straight, weakened 1 1/2f out (K Darley), beaten 15l by Bullish Luck*

2004

1st Kingdom of Bahrain Sun Chariot Stakes (Group 1) (Newmarket, October 2) 3yo+ 1m Good **123** (TS 117) 5 ran ● **2nd** Coolmore Fusaichi Pegasus Matron Stakes (Group 1) (Leopardstown, September 11) 3yo+ 1m Good to firm **123** (TS 104) 6 ran ● **10th** Prix Fresnay-le-Buffard-Jacques Le Marois (Group 1) (Deauville, August 15) 3yo+ 1m Soft **75** (TS 45) 10 ran ● **2nd** UAE Equestrian And Racing Federation Falmouth Stakes (Group 1) (Newmarket (July), July 6) 3yo+ 1m Good to firm **116** (TS 103) 7 ran ● **1st** Coronation Stakes (Group 1) (Ascot, June 18) 3yo 1m Firm **121** (TS 121) 11 ran ● **1st** Boylesports Irish 1,000 Guineas (Group 1) (Curragh, May 23) 3yo 1m Good to firm **118** (TS 93) 15 ran ● **1st** UltimateBet.com 1,000 Guineas Stakes (Group 1) (Newmarket, May 2) 3yo 1m Good **115** (TS 105) 16 ran

Other runs

2003 **1st** Chippenham Lodge Stud Cherry Hinton Stakes (Group 2) (Newmarket (July), July 8) 2yo 6f Good **117** (TS 110) 8 ran ● **1st** Queen Mary Stakes (Group 3) (Ascot, June 18) 2yo 5f Good to firm **116** (TS 111) 14 ran ● **1st** Hilary Needler Trophy (Listed) (Beverley, June 4) 2yo 5f Good to firm **104** (TS 95) 9 ran ● **1st** EBF Carlton Miniott Novice Fillies' Stakes (Thirsk, May 17) 2yo 5f Good **91** (TS 89) 6 ran ● **1st** Harby Novice Median Auction Stakes (Nottingham, April 29) 2yo 5f Good **86** (TS 65) 9 ran

She failed to show her very best in her final season – it was not only disgruntled favourite backers who thought she might well have been beaten in the Matron had Christophe Soumillon not come so wide into the straight on Chic. But even in her Classic season she did not hit the heights sometimes claimed for her. Hers was not a vintage generation of fillies and it did not take a performance too far out of the ordinary by Group 1 standards to see off her contemporaries in either Guineas or in the Coronation Stakes.

And when taking on her elders she only just got the better of Chic in the Sun Chariot and found Soviet Song too good in the Falmouth Stakes. She did not make the top 40 in the World Thoroughbred Racehorse Rankings for 2004 – and failed to make the world's top 50 in the last published list of 2005.

But there was much more to Attraction than her bare form and she will be remembered long after most on those lists have been forgotten. As her owner-breeder, the Duke of Roxburghe, said on the filly's retirement: "She gave me the most exciting thrill I'm ever going to have in racing and probably anything else in my life."

Attraction

bay filly, 19-2-2001

Efisio b 1982	Formidable	Forli	Aristophanes Trevisa
		Native Partner	Raise A Native Dinner Partner
	Eldoret	High Top	Derring-Do Camenae
		Bamburi	Ragusa Kilifi
Flirtation b 1994	Pursuit Of Love	Groom Dancer	Blushing Groom Featherhill
		Dance Quest	Green Dancer Polyponder
	Eastern Shore	Sun Prince	Princely Gift Costa Sola
		Land Ho	Primera Lucasland

Bred by Floors Farming in England.

Sire Efisio

Won 8 of 26 races, inc. Horris Hill S.-Gr3, Challenge S.-Gr3, Premio Emilio Turati-Gr1, Premio Chiusura-Gr2. Also 3rd in Prix Jacques le Marois at 4. Smallish (15.3hh), lengthy, strong-quartered type. Best at 7-8f. Round-actioned, but effective on any ground. Inclined to get worked up in preliminaries, but always raced genuinely. The only Gr1 winner by his sire (high-class sprinting 2-y-o who did not quite fulfil expectations. Half-brother to Mountain Bear (G1 winner in US) and to 3 other winners, and to dam of Timboroa (G1 winner in Italy & US). Dam won 2 races, half-sister to 2 other winners. Family of Princely Gift. Sire of 14 crops of racing age, inc: Casteddu (Gr3), Pips Pride (Phoenix S.-Gr1), Young Ern (Gr3), Hever Golf Rose (Prix de l'Abbaye de Longchamp-Gr1), Tomba (Prix de la Foret-Gr1), Uruk (Gr3), Heads Will Roll (Gr3), Frizzante (July Cup-Gr1), Guys And Dolls (Gr3), Pearly Shells (Prix Vermeille-Gr1), Le Vie dei Colori (Premio Vittorio di Capua-Gr1), Attraction (1,000 Guineas-Gr1, Irish 1,000 Guineas-Gr1, Coronation S.-Gr1, Sun Chariot S.-Gr1, Matron S.-Gr1), Enforcer (Gr3).

Dam Flirtation

Ran only once, 5th in 7f maiden at Haydock as a 3-y-o. Tall, leggy type in training. Showed some promise on debut, though clearly backward and green. Failed to reappear. Quite well-bred. Half-sister to several winners, inc. Gr2-placed, Listed-winning stayer Carmita (by Caerleon). By a high-class 6-7f performer out of a placed half-sister to Listed winners Easy Landing and Lifting, and to the dam of Gr1 winner Lord Of Men and Gr1-placed Her Ladyship. Noted family of top-class miler Sonic Lady, descending from July Cup winner Lucasland. Dam of: Aunty Mary (1999 f by Common Grounds; winner), Attraction (2001 f by Efisio; multiple Gr1 winner), Infantryman (2002 c by Inchinor; unraced). She has a colt foal by Oasis Dream, and was covered by Cape Cross.

Pedigree assessment

We did not see the best of Attraction in 2005, but that great public favourite was able to add a fifth Group 1 victory to her record at Leopardstown before her enforced retirement from training. Perhaps the Matron Stakes provided the luckiest of her triumphs, as Chic was given an awful lot to do and almost made up the ground, but there were other good runners in arrears, and Attraction, heroine of the 2004 Newmarket and Curragh 1,000 Guineas, proved herself clearly superior to the latest winners of those Classics, Virginia Waters and Saoire. Many will hope that she proves just as successful in her new role as a broodmare in the Duke of Roxburghe's Floors Stud. *TM*

Avonbridge

5yo bay horse **119**

Averti (Ire) - Alessia (Caerleon (USA))

Owner D J Deer

Trainer R Charlton

Breeder D J and Mrs Deer

Career: **22** starts | won **7** | second **4** | third **4** | **£334,587** win and place

By Lee Mottershead

GOD, it is said, loves a trier. If that is the case, the Almighty must be ever so fond of Avonbridge. Perhaps that's why this supremely consistent sprinter finally tasted Group 1 glory on his very last racecourse appearance.

With or without divine assistance, Avonbridge did indeed claim much-deserved top-flight honours when he captured what was a remarkable race for the British invaders on the Prix de l'Arc de Triomphe undercard. Eleven of the first 12 horses home in the Prix de l'Abbaye, France's premier sprint, were trained in Britain. Three of the first five home, including the winner, were trained by Roger Charlton. If that doesn't merit a God Save the Queen and three cheers for 'Rog', nothing does.

However, while Britain has become accustomed to whipping *les locals* in the Abbaye, Avonbridge had never become accustomed to winning Group 1 races, in no small part because he had never won one. That's not to say he had not tried.

To employ an increasingly fashionable phrase, Avonbridge danced at every dance, or at least almost every dance. From his Group-race debut at Deauville in August 2003 onwards, the entire raced 15 times, and each time he raced, he raced in Group company. A half-brother to Charlton's 2003 Abbaye hero Patavellian, he went into the 2005 season as the winner of the Prix du Gros-Chene in 2004, the same year in which he also finished fourth in the Nunthorpe and fifth in both the Abbaye and Golden Jubilee Stakes.

At the start of 2004 he was beaten a short head in the Palace House Stakes by subsequent July Cup winner Frizzante. In 2005, as in 2004, he began his year in the Newmarket Group 3 dash, and this time he won it. Under regular rider Steve Drowne, he led starting into the Dip and kept going in characteristically game fashion to deny Ashdown Express by half a length. Charlton hailed it the "best performance" ever put up

Avonbridge (right) gains his reward for years of honest endeavour with a Group 1 win in the Prix de l'Abbaye

by the son of Averti. There would, though, be better to come.

But not back at Chantilly. Avonbridge was unable to repeat his previous year's win in the Gros-Chene, even if third place was hardly a disgrace. As a result of that defeat, Avonbridge was sent off at 40-1 for the July Cup, and he came close to springing one of the shocks of the season. Avonbridge grabbed the lead at halfway and came close to holding that lead all the way to the line.

Unfortunately for Avonbridge, his connections and his backers, six furlongs had always been a tad further than the five-year-old's stamina could take. Just as unfortunately, Avonbridge had to cope with the stiff Newmarket hill at the end of the demanding race. And very unfortunately for Avonbridge's regular rider Steve Drowne, the only horse to come past him up that final hill was Pastoral Pursuits, a horse he had partnered in eight of his previous nine races.

"You're telling me," said Drowne, when asked if it was additionally galling to have been denied by Pastoral Pursuits, while Charlton called his somewhat luckless runner-up 'Mr Consistent'. That consistency seemed to disappear next time out in the Nunthorpe, in which Avonbridge could manage only seventh, but that result was explained away by a subsequent dirty scope. The horse showed himself to be back on track when third in the Diadem Stakes and then, another seven days into the calendar, came the Abbaye.

It took Avonbridge about one minute to win the race and then about another 15 minutes to keep it. Slowly away as ever, Drowne's ally scythed through the field to stake his claim, only to veer a little when stablemate

2005 Race record

1st Prix de L'Abbaye de Longchamp Majestic Barriere (Group 1) (Longchamp, October 2) 2yo+ 5f Good to soft **119** (TS 99) 17 ran. *Towards rear after 2f, headway final 2f to lead last strides (S Drowne), beat Striking Ambition by sht-nk*

3rd totepool Diadem Stakes (Group 2) (Newmarket, September 25) 3yo+ 6f Good **114** (TS 113) 13 ran. *Soon led, ridden and headed inside final furlong, stayed on (S Drowne), beaten 3/4l by Baron's Pit*

7th VC Bet Nunthorpe Stakes (Group 1) (York, August 18) 2yo+ 5f Good to firm **111** (TS 96) 16 ran. *With leaders, kept on same pace inside final furlong (S Drowne), beaten 2 1/4l by La Cucaracha*

2nd Darley July Cup (Group 1) (Newmarket (July), July 7) 3yo+ 6f Good to soft **118** (TS 106) 19 ran. *Raced far side, chased leaders until led halfway, ridden and headed well inside final furlong (S Drowne), beaten 1 1/2l by Pastoral Pursuits*

3rd Prix du Gros-Chene (Group 2) (Chantilly, June 5) 3yo+ 5f Good **112** (TS 77) 11 ran. *Middivision, disputing 5th and pushed along halfway, ran on final furlong, took 3rd close home (S Drowne), beaten 1 1/2l by The Trader*

1st VCbet Palace House Stakes (Group 3) (Newmarket, April 30) 3yo+ 5f Good to firm **119** (TS 99) 9 ran. *Always prominent, ridden to lead 1f out, ran on (S Drowne), beat Ashdown Express by 1/2l*

2004

5th Prix de l'Abbaye de Longchamp Majestic Barriere (Group 1) (Longchamp, October 3) 2yo+ 5f Good **109** (TS 106) 15 ran ● **4th** Victor Chandler Nunthorpe Stakes (Group 1) (York, August 19) 2yo+ 5f Soft **113** (TS 103) 12 ran ● **4th** King George Stakes (Group 3) (Goodwood, July 29) 3yo+ 5f Good to firm **116** (TS 107) 13 ran ● **5th** Golden Jubilee Stakes (Group 1) (Ascot, June 19) 3yo+ 6f Firm **111** (TS 111) 14 ran ● **1st** Prix du Gros-Chene (Group 2) (Chantilly, June 6) 3yo+ 5f Good to soft **116** (TS 100) 8 ran ● **2nd** Victor Chandler Palace House Stakes (Group 3) (Newmarket, May 1) 3yo+ 5f Good **114** (TS 77) 13 ran

Other wins

2003 **1st** Axminster Carpets Cathedral Stakes (Listed) (Salisbury, June 15) 3yo+ 6f Good to firm **119** (TS 71) 6 ran **2002** ● **1st** Newton Fund Managers Rockingham Stakes (Listed) (York, October 12) 2yo 6f Good to firm **110** (TS 78) 7 ran ● **1st** Seven Points Nursery Stakes (Handicap) (Goodwood, September 13) 2yo (0-85 handicap) 6f Good **98** (TS 92) 15 ran ● **1st** Sponsor A Race Median Auction Maiden Stakes (Div I) (Lingfield, August 29) 2yo 6f Good to firm **89** (TS 86) 15 ran

Striking Ambition ducked out 50 yards from home. The chain reaction caused Eisteddfod to receive a bump and persuaded the Longchamp stewards to have one of the inquiries they so enjoy. They enjoyed this one so much that it took them an age to resolve it.

"They're talking about throwing the first two out," said a gobsmacked Charlton, who for good measure also had the second, Striking Ambition, as well as the fifth, Patavellian. Agony. But then, with the words "le resultat est maintenu", came the ecstasy. Avonbridge had kept the race.

That was Avonbridge's last race. He now goes to Whitsbury Manor Stud to replace his deceased sire. He goes there as a Group 1 winner. It would have been an injustice had he not.

Avonbridge

bay horse, 18-3-2000

Parents	Grandparents	Great-grandparents	Great-great-grandparents
Averti br 1991	Warning	Known Fact	In Reality Tamerett
		Slightly Dangerous	Roberto Where You Lead
	Imperial Jade	Lochnager	Dumbarnie Miss Barbara
		Songs Jest	Song Lady Jester
Alessia b 1992	Caerleon	Nijinsky	Northern Dancer Flaming Page
		Foreseer	Round Table Regal Gleam
	Kiss	Habitat	Sir Gaylord Little Hut
		Miss Petard	Petingo Miss Upward

Bred by D J and Mrs Deer in Britain

Sire Averti

Won 5 of 41 starts from 2 to 8. Useful 2yo, won 2 (6f) of 3 starts. Unplaced in 3 3yo starts (6-7f), thereafter smart and tough sprinter, best form over 5f, gained main victory in G3 King George S but G1-placed in Nunthorpe S and Prix de l'Abbaye. Returned to racecourse as an 8yo after first year at stud. Bred for speed, by pacey miler noted for speedy offspring out of smart 2yo/sprinter from fast family. Stood initially at Fawley Stud, later switched to Whitsbury Manor Stud, died December 2004. First foals 2000, quickly established himself as useful source of smart 2yos and sprinters, sire of: Avertina (Listed), Avonbridge (Prix de l'Abbaye-Gr1), Wunders Dream (Gr2).

Dam Alessia

Won 1 (7f at 2) of 10 start from 2 to 4. Sister to smart 12-14f filly Casey and half-sister to very useful stayer Crack out of useful sprinter Kiss. Next dam is Ribblesdale Stakes winner Miss Petard, from family of Derby winner Oath. Dam of: Patavellian (1998 g by Machiavellian; Prix de l'Abbaye-Gr1), Alashaan (1999 f by Darshaan; placed), Avonbridge (2000 c by Averti; Prix de l'Abbaye-Gr1), Avessia (2001 f by Averti; placed 4th), 2002 died as a foal, 2004 f by Averti. Mare died 2004.

Pedigree assessment

Alessia at first glance might look an unlikely source of two Prix de l'Abbaye winners, given that her sister stayed very well and her grand-dam won the Ribblesdale Stakes, but her pedigree can be read another way. Her sire Caerleon was responsible for several good sprinters, her dam Kiss was third in the 1981 Portland Handicap, her maternal grandsire is speed influence Habitat, and the sire of her grand-dam is speedy juvenile Petingo, later a top-class miler. Avonbridge effectively is taking the place of his sire at Whitsbury Manor Stud in 2006. Averti quickly established himself as a useful sire of fast juveniles and sprinters, and breeders will be looking for the same from Avonbridge. *JH*

Azamour (Ire)

4yo bay colt **129**

Night Shift (USA) - Asmara (USA) (Lear Fan (USA))

Owner H H Aga Khan

Trainer John M Oxx

Breeder H H Aga Khan

Career: **12** starts | won **6** | second **1** | third **3** | **£1,499,557** win and place

By Richard Austen

THE DERBY winner tries for Group 1 success at a mile and a quarter and the Sussex Stakes winner goes sprinting. They try and in 2005 they fail. Versatility in a top-flight racehorse is easier said than done, so ring the bells for a horse who won top-ranking Group 1 events at three years or above over a mile, over a mile and a quarter and over a mile and a half – Azamour, now retired to the Aga Khan's Gilltown Stud in Ireland.

Daylami, moving up in trip, and Falbrav and Rakti, moving down, have all done the treble in recent years and in the process established themselves among the most exciting racehorses of recent years. Likewise Azamour.

Gilltown was already birthplace and stallion residence not only to Daylami, but also to Kalanisi, who won the Queen Anne, Champion Stakes and Breeders' Cup Turf in one campaign as a four-year-old, although he did it three years before the Queen Anne was raised from Group 2.

One big help in establishing a colt's versatility is to give it a chance and keep it in training. At the end of his three-year-old season, Azamour would have been a dual Group 1 winner and worth his place at stud, but what he was truly capable of as a racehorse would still to a significant extent have been informed guesswork.

"His three-year-old career was not a true reflection of his ability and we thought there was more improvement to come," said the Aga Khan.

If the Aga Khan had come to a different, safety-first conclusion and retired him, Azamour could hardly have been said to have established his reputation for reliability after just seven races (even his eventual 12 was hardly being over-raced) and the composed stride and dynamic finish that became his hallmarks would not have found their most spectacular setting, a top race at a mile and a half.

The top older horses, all condition, power and presence, are one of the sport's most compelling sights – not surprisingly, seeing as the Flat

Azamour scores an impressive victory in the King George at Newbury, proving his class from a mile to 12 furlongs

thoroughbred seldom reaches its physical peak until it is four years old, at least – and Azamour was a superb-looking individual even as a three-year-old, catching the eye when the ultra-discerning John Oxx sent him over to Newmarket for the Guineas as a 25-1 shot. He went on to win the St James's Palace and the Irish Champion that season and was a short-priced favourite when back in Britain for two more top events in 2005.

The only occasion he did not start favourite as a four-year-old was on his reappearance in a star-studded Tattersalls Gold Cup at The Curragh, a race that caused jockey Mick Kinane plenty of exasperation when Azamour came a hampered fourth.

Kinane's view that he should have beaten Grey Swallow, Bago and Ace did not go unchallenged, but he would have his chance for revenge. Ace, in fact, was present every time Azamour set foot on a racecourse at four, a fine yardstick for when the result did or did not do Azamour justice.

Next up was the Prince of Wales's Stakes at Royal Ascot at York, where Ouija Board shared star billing but had a troubled preparation and an even more troubled race, leaving Azamour to play the lead role.

Australian challenger Elvstroem had nearly stolen the Prix d'Ispahan from the front and tried to perfect the trick here, sticking far side in the straight as nearly all the rest came up the centre. Ace was set alight at

2005 Race record

3rd John Deere Breeders' Cup Turf (Grade 1) (Belmont Park, October 29) 3yo+ 1m4f Yielding **126** 13 ran. *Held up, shuffled back to 11th 2½f out, headway and 6th straight, switched right over 1f out, stayed on strongly (M J Kinane), beaten 2l by Shirocco*

5th Baileys Irish Champion Stakes (Group 1) (Leopardstown, September 10) 3yo+ 1m2f Good to yielding **122** (TS 104) 10 ran. *Settled towards rear, ridden early straight, 3rd on inner 1f out, no extra close home (C Soumillon), beaten 2¼l by Oratorio*

1st King George VI And Queen Elizabeth Diamond Stakes (Group 1) (Newbury, July 23) 3yo+ 1m4f Good to firm **129** (TS 115) 12 ran. *Held up, smooth headway from over 3f out, led well over 1f out, stayed on strongly (M J Kinane), beat Norse Dancer by 1¼l*

1st Prince of Wales's Stakes (Group 1) (York, June 15) 4yo+ 1m2½f Good to firm **126** (TS 120) 8 ran. *Held up, headway over 3f out, led 1f out, ran on well (M J Kinane), beat Ace by 1½l*

4th Tattersalls Gold Cup (Group 1) (Curragh, May 22) 4yo+ 1m2½f Good to yielding **124** (TS 69) 6 ran. *Held up in touch, last into straight, 5th 1½f out, 4th when not clear run 1f out, kept on same pace (M J Kinane), beaten 2l by Grey Swallow*

Other runs

2004 **3rd** Emirates Airline Champion Stakes (Group 1) (Newmarket, October 16) 3yo+ 1m2f Soft **122** (TS 87) 11 ran ● **1st** Baileys Irish Champion Stakes (Group 1) (Leopardstown, September 11) 3yo+ 1m2f Good to firm **126** (TS 126) 8 ran ● **1st** St James's Palace Stakes (Group 1) (Ascot, June 15) 3yo 1m Good to firm **120** (TS 123) 11 ran ● **2nd** Boylesports Irish 2,000 Guineas (Group 1) (Curragh, May 22) 3yo 1m Good to firm **118** (TS 83) 8 ran ● **3rd** UltimateBet.com 2,000 Guineas Stakes (Group 1) (Newmarket, May 1) 3yo 1m Good **120** (TS 111) 14 ran **2003** **1st** Juddmonte Beresford Stakes (Group 2) (Curragh, October 12) 2yo 1m Good to yielding **109** (TS 66) 6 ran ● **1st** Pizza Stop EBF Maiden (Curragh, September 14) 2yo 7f Good to firm **97** (TS 59) 9 ran

the head of the latter group, with Azamour three lengths behind him and closing. With a steady challenge over three furlongs, Azamour always looked like winning and, with Elvstroem already done for, he got to Ace 150 yards out and went on to score by one and a half lengths going away.

"I've always believed he'd stay and he wants at least ten furlongs now. I wouldn't have any reservations about 12," said Kinane.

"If we had serious doubts we wouldn't even try him over it," said Oxx, as Azamour finished preparations for the following month's King George VI and Queen Elizabeth Diamond Stakes. At Newbury instead of Ascot and on fast ground instead of what could easily be a soft surface for the Arc, connections were giving Azamour's stamina every chance to last out.

Others in the race unsurprisingly seemed intent on testing it as much as was possible. Pace-setting Gamut and Mubtaker consequently went too quickly mid-race and were found out over three furlongs from home, which brought Doyen, Ace, Bago, Grey Swallow and Eswarah into the firing line and saw a brief bunching of the field as Azamour and Norse Dancer began their moves from the back. If Azamour stayed, he would win, that much was crystal clear as he made up his ground apparently

Azamour scores the second Royal Ascot win of his career, this time at York, by landing the Prince of Wales's Stakes

travelling so well within himself, while all the others looked to have been asked for their maximum.

Azamour had Ace to aim at again on the outside, but not for long, and Doyen was swiftly despatched as well to leave Bago as the only target ahead. Even the Arc winner had no answer when Azamour swept past just before the furlong pole. Norse Dancer joined in the battle for second (and won it by a whisker) as the three of them drew well clear, but there was no more than a brief skirmish for first. Azamour maintained his lead at just over a length.

"I knew they'd gone a hell of a pace and that they'd pay the price," Kinane reported. "I had every confidence in the horse and didn't want to mess him about early on. I wasn't going to compete until late on."

If there were regrets about the King George, they were that the clash of generations featured only one three-year-old, the Oaks winner Eswarah, and that plenty of the older brigade were clearly not on their game.

In the Irish Champion seven weeks later, conversely, Motivator and Oratorio were present and correct but Azamour gave the first disappointing show of his career, Kinane already disappointed as he was missing the ride with a broken wrist.

It looked promising for Azamour rounding the turn as he made headway in the middle of a bunched field, but Christophe Soumillon later reported that the 6-4 favourite then lost his footing. His effort was short-lived, and not only did he fail to reel in Oratorio and Motivator, he was passed by Alexander Goldrun and Ace.

"I couldn't believe it when he didn't produce his usual burst of speed because he's so reliable, and it was the first time he's run below par," reflected Oxx.

A pulled back muscle was diagnosed, on his off-hind quarters. A hoof abscess confirmed his absence from the Arc, and the Breeders' Cup Turf would now be his final race.

Ten years earlier, soft ground at Belmont tipped the balance firmly in favour of Ridgewood Pearl, Oxx's last Breeders' Cup runner. He did not want the same for Azamour, however, even though the colt was stronger and thought better able to deal with a soft surface than in 2004.

"I am never optimistic and I am even less optimistic now," said Oxx after receiving one damp going report. In similar vein Kinane observed: "We went to the wrong place this year. We needed California."

In the event, though, the going did not seem to be the deciding factor and Kinane, who had been forced in the run-up to talk about Rock Of Gibraltar's fast-finishing defeat in the 2002 Mile, was left to reflect on a very similar scenario in the 2005 Turf.

A chance can go in the bat of an eyelid round those tight American tracks and how Kinane must have wished for the wide-open spaces and long straight of a York or Newbury. Azamour's jockey tucked him in on the inside from his low draw, finding himself well back at halfway, then probably checked as he lost ground rather than made it at a crucial stage early on the turn.

If this sounds more about the jockey than the horse, that is because in the midst of all the mayhem, Azamour ran his usual race, travelling well and finishing well. Unfortunately, before he could do the last bit, he lost further momentum as he angled out in the straight, and although he made up over three lengths to master Bago late on, it brought him only third. He got to Ace's quarters as well but Shirocco, who had got first run on them all, was not threatened. Azamour finished full of running but was still two lengths down at the finish. In other circumstances he might well have won.

"I have never been so close to a horse in my career," Kinane reflected. "He's boisterous, exuberant and can be a real handful at times. He's a character of a horse but a very honest and genuine one. I've ridden him in every important piece of work he's had, except when I was off injured."

Oxx's parting words on his stable star, who had surgery for colic in late November, were: "He was such a phenomenal horse and he won over all sorts of distances. I know he got beaten plenty of times, but horses who come from behind like he did are going to run into trouble sometimes."

Azamour

bay colt, 8-3-2001

Night Shift b 1980	Northern Dancer	Nearctic	Nearco Lady Angela
		Natalma	Native Dancer Almahmoud
	Ciboulette	Chop Chop	Flares Sceptical
		Windy Answer	Windfields Reply
Asmara b 1993	Lear Fan	Roberto	Hail To Reason Bramalea
		Wac	Lt Stevens Belthazar
	Anaza	Darshaan	Shirley Heights Delsy
		Azaarika	Ribero Arcana

Bred by H H Aga Khan's Studs in Ireland.

Sire Night Shift

Won 1 (6f maiden) of 7 starts. Small (15.2 hh), quite well-made individual. A poor racehorse, evidently not very sound or injury-prone in training. Brother to Fanfreluche (champion filly in Canada, winner of Gr1-calibre events in USA, dam of major US winners L'Enjoleur and D'Accord, and of Canadian champions La Voyageuse and Medaille d'Or). Also brother to passable sire Barachois and half-brother to the dam of Russian Bond (Gr2). Stands at Coolmore Stud, Ireland, fee (2004) €20,000 (Oct 1). Sire of 16 crops of racing age, inc Gr1 winners: In The Groove (Irish 1,000 Guineas, York International S., Champion S., Coronation Cup), Nicolotte (Premio Vittorio di Capua), Listening (Hollywood Oaks, Milady H.), Lochangel (Nunthorpe S.), Daryaba (Prix de Diane, Prix Vermeille), Night Style (Gran Criterium), Azamour (St James's Palace S., Irish Champion S., Prince of Wales's S., King George VI & Queen Elizabeth S.).

Dam Asmara

Won 2 of 10 races, inc. Trigo S.-Listed). Also 2nd 3 times (2 Listed), 3rd once (Listed), 4th once (Gr3). Leggy sort. Smart performer, successful on fast and soft ground. Showed progressive form at 3, stayed 10.5f well, but poorest effort only attempt at 12f. Half-sister to Prix Ganay winner Astarabad (by Alleged) and to 6 other winners. By a leading miler and successful sire out of a Listed winner who is grand-dam of Gr3-placed Listed winner Anzari (by Nicolotte). Dam of: Arameen (1998 f by Halling; winner), Ahsanabad (1999 c by Muhtarram; Gr3-placed winner), Arawan (2000 c by Entrepreneur; winner), Azamour (2001 c by Night Shift; multiple Gr1 winner), Arafan (2002 c by Barathea; placed), Ardalan (2003 c by Sinndar; unplaced). She has a yearling colt by Selkirk.

Pedigree assessment

In his juvenile days Azamour gave a strong hint that he would stay rather better than the vast majority of Night Shift's stock, who have tended to be sprinters and milers. In 2004 he confirmed that impression by adding an Irish Champion Stakes victory to his score in the St James's Palace, and we made the point here a year ago that he should not be ruled out if he were to line up for a top 12-furlong event in 2005. The King George VI & Queen Elizabeth Stakes established beyond doubt that he was an accomplished performer at that distance – and the best-ever son of his sire, who was 20 years old when he was conceived. A thoroughly sound, genuine racehorse with an excellent turn of foot, he should find enthusiastic support in his new role as a stallion at his owner's Gilltown Stud. *TM*

Bago (Fr)

4yo bay colt **126**

Nashwan (USA) - Moonlight's Box (USA) (Nureyev (USA))

Owner Niarchos Family

Trainer J E Pease

Breeder Niarchos Family

Career: **16** starts | won **8** | second **1** | third **5** | **£1,551,515** win and place

By Paul Haigh

ANY ARC winner who stays in training for another year is a celebrity by definition. Sadly, the 2004 Longchamp hero Bago never quite lived up to his billing in 2005.

A season spent entirely in Group 1 company started well with victory in the ten-furlong Prix Ganay. Very well in fact, because although this soft-ground performance was not reckoned impressive at the time, the subsequent form of the disqualified second, Pride, Reefscape and the down-the-field Ace suggests it may have been a lot better than it then looked.

Following this evidence that he'd at least trained on, the Niarchos four-year-old was made short-priced favourite for the Tattersalls Gold Cup, again over ten furlongs, at The Curragh; but here, not for the first time – because there'd already been doubts about his effectiveness, perhaps even about his resolution, when asked to race anywhere but at his beloved Longchamp – he delivered the first of a series of puzzling performances that were never quite bad, but never quite befitting a champion either.

In the absence of his pacemaker, who was injured in transit, Bago travelled well before hitting what we later learned was a characteristic 'flat spot' just before the home turn, and although he later improved quickly to give himself every chance of cutting down the leader Grey Swallow, his fans were disappointed to see him fail to do so. Still, Ace was third and Azamour only fourth, so there was nothing much wrong with the run.

A month later Bago reappeared in the Grand Prix de Saint-Cloud, a race that was expected to suit him better as its 12 furlongs was more likely to bring his proven stamina into play. But once again he hit the flat spot as the field quickened; once again he ran on late but with no obvious relish, and although in retrospect there was no particular shame in going down to the eventual Japan Cup winner Alkaased and Policy Maker, there was no great credit in it either.

It was after Saint-Cloud that Jonathan Pease called in the vets in the

Bago (far side) lands the Prix Ganay on his reappearance, but the 2004 Arc winner was unable to win again

belief that, while he was acting very satisfactorily at home, something was niggling Bago and preventing him from producing his best in the heat of competition. A back problem was diagnosed, and, it was hoped, corrected in time for the King George VI and Queen Elizabeth Stakes, run at Newbury while Ascot was being rebuilt. Yet again came the flat spot, yet again the respectable rather than the brilliant run. He was mown down by Azamour, then at the peak of his form and superbly ridden by Mick Kinane, who may just have got the better of Thierry Gillet on this occasion. More worryingly, Bago failed to get past long-standing Group 1 maiden Norse Dancer.

Pease then gave Bago a full three-month break from the racecourse as he prepared for another crack at the Arc, and was rewarded by what was probably his star's best performance of the season as, once again back on his favourite course, Bago came charging through from well back to catch all but the brilliant Hurricane Run and Westerner, with Shirocco behind him in fourth. Maybe the back was better. Maybe we were about to see the real Bago at last. No, we discovered in the Breeders' Cup at Belmont, we weren't – because in the Turf, in spite of being given every chance by Gillet, he failed to confirm the form with either the winner Shirocco, or the second Ace, and was once again overtaken by Azamour, who finished strongly late.

Bago's last outing of the season, and of his career, came in the Japan Cup at Fuchu. Once again he pleased his trainer beforehand. Once again he failed in the race, finishing only eighth behind Alkaased. This time, however, he did have some very plausible and obvious excuses. First the

2005 Race record

8th Japan Cup (Group 1) (Tokyo, November 27) 3yo+ 1m4f Firm **118** 18 ran. *Raced in 11th, 12th straight, ridden 2f out, stayed on same pace (T Gillet), beaten 4¾l by Alkaased*

4th John Deere Breeders' Cup Turf (Grade 1) (Belmont Park, October 29) 3yo+ 1m4f Yielding **123** 13 ran. *Midfield, 4th straight on inside, went 3rd over 1f out, one pace final furlong (T Gillet), beaten 2¾l by Shirocco*

3rd Prix de l'Arc de Triomphe Lucien Barriere (Group 1) (Longchamp, October 2) 3yo+ 1m4f Good to soft **126** (TS 127) 15 ran. *Held up towards rear, 14th straight, headway from well over 1f out, ran on to take 3rd close home (T Gillet), beaten 3½l by Hurricane Run*

3rd King George VI And Queen Elizabeth Diamond Stakes (Group 1) (Newbury, July 23) 3yo+ 1m4f Good to firm **125** (TS 113) 12 ran. *Held up in touch, headway to lead 2f out, soon ridden and headed, kept on but no extra inside final furlong, lost 2nd close home (T Gillet), beaten 1¼l by Azamour*

3rd Grand Prix de Saint-Cloud (Group 1) (Saint-Cloud, June 26) 4yo+ 1m4f Good to soft **116** (TS 116) 11 ran. *Held up towards rear, 8th and slightly hampered straight, switched right 2f out, ridden to take 3rd close home (T Gillet), beaten 4l by Alkaased*

2nd Tattersalls Gold Cup (Group 1) (Curragh, May 22) 4yo+ 1m2½f Good to yielding **125** (TS 72) 6 ran. *Settled 3rd, 4th and pushed along before straight, improved into 3rd under 2f out, 2nd and edged right 1f out, kept on (T Gillet), beaten ¾l by Grey Swallow*

1st Prix Ganay (Group 1) (Longchamp, April 24) 4yo+ 1m2½f Very soft **121** (TS 54) 9 ran. *Raced in 2nd after 3f, disputing 5th straight, shaken up and 4 lengths off leader 2f out, driven to lead final furlong, ran on gamely, pushed out (T Gillet), beat Pride by sht-nk*

Other runs

2004 **1st** Prix de l'Arc de Triomphe Lucien Barriere (Group 1) (Longchamp, October 3) 3yo+ 1m4f Good **129** (TS 130) 19 ran ● **3rd** Prix Niel Casino Barriere d'Enghien (Group 2) (Longchamp, September 12) 3yo 1m4f Soft **117** (TS 116) 8 ran ● **3rd** Juddmonte International Stakes (Group 1) (York, August 17) 3yo+ 1m2½f Good **123** (TS 96) 9 ran ● **1st** Juddmonte Grand Prix de Paris (Group 1) (Longchamp, June 27) 3yo 1m2f Good to soft **113** (TS 71) 4 ran ● **1st** Prix Jean Prat (Group 1) (Chantilly, June 6) 3yo 1m1f Good to soft **118** (TS 102) 8 ran **2003** **1st** Criterium International (Group 1) (Saint-Cloud, November 1) 2yo 1m Very soft **118** (TS 110) 7 ran ● **1st** Prix des Chenes (Group 3) (Longchamp, September 20) 2yo 1m Good **113** (TS 77) 7 ran ● **1st** Prix des Aigles (Longchamp, September 2) 2yo 1m Soft **98** 7 ran ● **1st** Prix de Bourguebus (Unraced Colts & Geldings) (Round Course) (Deauville, August 5) 2yo 1m Good to soft **94** 11 ran

race was run on lightning-fast ground. Second he was struck into in the straight. Third he lost a shoe in the process of that collision. So once again – and just as well for his purchasers from Japan, where he is to stand at stud – there was no shame, just mild disappointment.

Bago retired with the excellent record of eight victories, five of them at Group 1 level; the only race in which he was ever out of the frame was his last. There has to be at least a suspicion, however, that his problems, such as they were, were never so much physical as psychological.

Bago

bay colt, 3-2-2001

Parents	Grandparents	Great-grandparents	Great-great-grandparents
Nashwan ch 1986	Blushing Groom	Red God	Nasrullah
			Spring Run
		Runaway Bride	Wild Risk
			Aimee
	Height Of Fashion	Bustino	Busted
			Ship Yard
		Highclere	Queen's Hussar
			Highlight
Moonlight's Box b 1996	Nureyev	Northern Dancer	Nearctic
			Natalma
		Special	Forli
			Thong
	Coup de Genie	Mr Prospector	Raise A Native
			Gold Digger
		Coup de Folie	Halo
			Raise The Standard

Bred by Niarchos Family in France

Sire Nashwan

Won 6 of 7 races, inc. 2,000 Guineas-Gr1, Derby-Gr1, Eclipse Stakes-Gr1, King George VI & Queen Elizabeth Stakes-Gr1. Big, rangy individual and a superb mover. A tip-top performer from 8-12f, much the most impressive of his generation. Died in July 2002. Sire of: Wandesta (Santa Ana H.-Gr1, Santa Barbara H.-Gr1, Matriarch S.-Gr1), Aqaarid (Fillies' Mile-Gr1), Didina (Gr2), Myself (Gr3), Silent Warrior (Gr3), Swain (Coronation Cup-Gr1, King George VI & Queen Elizabeth S.-Gr1 [twice]), Bint Salsabil (Gr3), Bint Shadayid (Gr3), One So Wonderful (York International S.-Gr1), Elhayq (Gr2), Haami (Gr3), Rabah (Gr3), Special Nash (Gr2), Mistle Song (Gr3), Nadia (Prix Saint-Alary-Gr1), Najah (Gr2), With Reason (Gr3), Miss Nashwan (Gr3), Bago (Criterium International-Gr1, Prix Jean Prat-Gr1, Grand Prix de Paris-Gr1, Prix de l'Arc de Triomphe-Gr1, Prix Ganay-Gr1).

Dam Moonlight's Box

Unraced, but half-sister to Gr1 winner Denebola and Gr3 winners Snake Mountain and Loving Kindness, her dam's only other racing-age produce. Dam of Bago (2001 c by Nashwan; 4-time Gr1 winner), Million Wishes (2002 f by Darshaan; winner), Wulimaster (2003 c by Hernando; unraced to date). She has a yearling filly by Selkirk.

Pedigree assessment

Our confidence that Bago would add to his tally of Group 1 wins in 2005 was promptly justified by a game performance in the Prix Ganay, but that was to be his last victory. He was in the frame in five subsequent efforts, all at the top level, and as he actually ran to a higher mark in three of those races than he had at Longchamp, he could hardly be accused of falling too far from grace. What he didn't do was improve on his second-season form, which had seemed a reasonable expectation in view of what Swain – his sire's only previous top-class colt – had achieved as an older horse. Because of Nashwan's rather disappointing record, it would probably have been difficult for Bago to attract appropriate support at stud in Europe, so it was no surprise to learn that he would start as a stallion in Japan. Unfortunately, from that angle, he gave a dull display in the Japan Cup, his final start. *TM*

Bandari (Ire)

6yo bay horse **123**

Alhaarth (Ire) - Miss Audimar (USA) (Mr Leader (USA))

Owner Hamdan Al Maktoum

Trainer M Johnston

Breeder Rathasker Stud

Career: **29** starts | won **11** | second **2** | third **4** | **£531,843** win and place

By John Hopkins

"THIS is a race I have a love affair with, but I also have a love affair with this horse," said trainer Mark Johnston. Bandari endured a mixed time in 2005, and the Group 1 success his trainer covets for him looks as far away as ever, but there can be no doubt that his resilient Hardwicke Stakes success at Royal Ascot at York provided Johnston with an emotional highlight amid another hugely successful campaign for the trainer.

A 10-1 chance in a field of six for the Group 2 Hardwicke over a mile and a half, Bandari, or rather jockey Willie Supple, went against the grain for the York meeting, sticking to the far rail off the home turn. The manoeuvre may have been a decisive one, as Bandari, who led four furlongs out and with the rail to help, battled all the way up the straight, giving his rider added satisfaction in fighting off owner Hamdan Al Maktoum's first string Maraahel by half a length. It was Johnston's fourth success in the Hardwicke in seven years and one in which he took evident pleasure – he would later describe the winner, very much the type of stable stalwart he loves to train, as "a fantastic horse".

It may be churlish, but it should be noted that everything fell into place for Bandari in the Hardwicke. Maraahel would later post superior efforts at a mile and a quarter; third-home Gamut would undoubtedly have preferred much softer ground than the official firm; Powerscourt in fourth was out of form at that stage and the fifth, Doyen, was a shadow of the horse who so dominated the race a year earlier. Those gripes aside, this was still a performance to match Bandari's best. Racing Post Ratings awarded Bandari a mark of 123 for the race, equalling his previous highs in landing the 2002 Gordon Stakes and the 2004 Princess of Wales's Stakes, in which he took the scalp of Sulamani.

Johnston's delight was tempered by a note of frustration that Bandari was capable of beating Group 1 performers, but seemingly not in Group

Bandari (right), given an astute ride by Willie Supple, wins the Group 2 Hardwicke Stakes from Maraahel

1 races. A winner of 11 races over five seasons, and six times in Group company, he had been beaten seven times in the top grade.

In a bid to remedy that situation, Bandari was sent to Germany after a two-month absence for the Group 1 Rheinland-Pokal over a mile and a half at Cologne. This was no penalty kick: the race featured Deutsches Derby winner Nicaron, the 6-4 favourite, and the globetrotting Simonas was also preferred to Bandari in the market. But conditions on the day proved more problematic to the British raider. Having challenged the front-running Czech-trained Darsalam from some way out, Bandari eventually tired in the very soft ground inside the final furlong and did well to hang on to second, five lengths behind Darsalam, a stronger stayer whose triumphs included the previous year's Deutsches St Leger. Richard Hills, Bandari's jockey, said: "He ran a great race in the circumstances. But he's a much better horse on top of the ground." To add to the sense of frustration at an opportunity missed, Darsalam had been trained for his first two career starts by Johnston.

"I suppose he has been a bit erratic," admitted Johnston at one stage, and that well sums up the rest of Bandari's campaign. He had three starts before the Hardwicke, taking time to find his form. His reappearance effort, when ninth of 13 to Day Flight in the John Porter Stakes at Newbury, was indifferent at best, although his length-and-a-half third of five to Alkaased in the Group 2 Jockey Club Stakes at Newmarket in May reads much better. His next run, when fifth to Yeats in the Coronation Cup,

2005 Race record

4th 32Red.com September Stakes (Group 3) (Newmarket (July), September 3) 3yo+ 1m4f Good to firm **100** (TS 71) 6 ran. *Chased leaders, ridden and every chance 2f out, soon weakened (W Supple), beaten 18l by Imperial Stride*

2nd Rheinland-Pokal der Sparkasse KolnBonn (Group 1) (Cologne, August 14) 3yo+ 1m4f Very soft **116** 7 ran. *Went 2nd after 2f, with leader in back straight, hard ridden well over 1f out, kept on same pace (R Hills), beaten 5l by Darsalam*

1st Hardwicke Stakes (Group 2) (York, June 18) 4yo+ 1m4f Firm **123** (TS 103) 6 ran. *Tracked leader, stayed far side entering straight and led 4f out, held on gamely (W Supple), beat Maraahel by ½l*

5th Vodafone Coronation Cup (Group 1) (Epsom, June 3) 4yo+ 1m4f Good **111** (TS 98) 7 ran. *Tracked winner, challenged briefly over 4f out, outpaced over 3f out, lost 2nd and beaten over 2f out (R Hills), beaten 6¾l by Yeats*

3rd UltimatePoker.com Jockey Club Stakes (Group 2) (Newmarket, May 1) 4yo+ 1m4f Good to firm **119** (TS 63) 5 ran. *Tracked leader, ridden and every chance over 2f out, stayed on same pace final furlong (R Hills), beaten 1½l by Alkaased*

9th Dubai Tennis Championships Stakes (Registered As The John Porter Stakes) (Group 3) (Newbury, April 16) 4yo+ 1m4f Soft **94** (TS 56) 13 ran. *Held up in rear, headway 6f out, soon pushed along, weakened from 3f out (R Hills), beaten 19l by Day Flight*

Other wins

2004 **1st** Princess of Wales's cantorodds.com Stakes (Group 2) (Newmarket (July), July 7) 3yo+ 1m4f Good to firm **123** (TS 69) 8 ran ● **1st** betfair.com Brigadier Gerard Stakes (Group 3) (Sandown, June 1) 4yo+ 1m2f Good to soft **122** (TS 77) 9 ran ● **1st** Breitling Watches & Waltons of Chester Huxley Stakes (for the Tradesman's Cup) (Listed) (Chester, May 6) 4yo+ 1m2½f Good to soft **114** (TS 90) 10 ran ● **1st** Ruinart Champagne Conditions Stakes (Newmarket, May 1) 4yo+ 1m2f Good **109** (TS 62) 10 ran **2002** **1st** Great Voltigeur Stakes (Group 2) (York, August 20) 3yo 1m4f Good **118** (TS 105) 6 ran ● **1st** Peugeot Gordon Stakes (Group 3) (Goodwood, July 30) 3yo 1m4f Good to firm **123** (TS 100) 4 ran ● **1st** attheraces Sky Channel 418 Derby Trial Stakes (Group 3) (Lingfield, May 11) 3yo 1m3½f Good **118** (TS 88) 6 ran **2001** ● **1st** Tote Bookmakers Silver Tankard Stakes (Listed) (Pontefract, October 22) 2yo 1m Soft **113** (TS 85) 12 ran ● **1st** Carrick Architects EBF Novice Stakes (Ayr, September 22) 2yo 1m Good to firm **91** (TS 65) 5 ran ● **1st** EBF Journal Maiden Stakes (Beverley, August 15) 2yo 7½f Good **90** (TS 46) 11 ran

suggested that a domestic Group 1 success may continue to be beyond his reach.

Post-Germany, Bandari ran in the Group 3 September Stakes at Newmarket, but again turned in a stinker, with no apparent excuse, finishing 18 lengths behind the progressive Imperial Stride in fourth. Perhaps the hard race in Germany had taken its toll, as he wasn't seen again.

Doubtless the quest for Group 1 success will occupy Johnston's thoughts when he considers Bandari's campaign in 2006. Having sent out Yavana's Pace to win the Cologne race at the age of ten, it would not be beyond the trainer to conjure a similar feat from Bandari, but such a victory remains unlikely in the domestic arena and he increasingly looks a horse for whom everything has to drop right.

Bandari

bay horse, 29-4-1999

Alhaarth b 1993	Unfuwain	Northern Dancer	Nearctic Natalma
		Height Of Fashion	Bustino Highclere
	Irish Valley	Irish River	Riverman Irish Star
		Green Valley	Val de Loir Sly Pola
Miss Audimar b 1981	Mr Leader	Hail To Reason	Turn-to Nothirdchance
		Jolie Deja	Djeddah Bellesoeur
	Quick Selection	Viceregal	Northern Dancer Victoria Regina
		Lachine	Grey Sovereign Loved One

Bred by Rathasker Stud in Ireland. Ir£40,000 Goffs Orby yearling

Sire Alhaarth

Won 8 of 17 races. At 2, won 5 (inc. Vintage S-Gr3, Solario S-Gr3, Champagne S-Gr2, Dewhurst S-Gr1) of 5. At 3, won 1 (Prix du Rond-Point-Gr2) of 7, also 3rd Sussex S-Gr1. At 4, won 2 (Curragh International-Gr2, Prix Dollar-Gr2) of 5, also 3rd Irish Champion S-Gr1. By top-class, very well-bred 12f performer with strong stud record. Half-brother to Gr3 winner Green Pola out of unplaced half-sister to top-class 2yo Green Dancer. Stands at Derrinstown Stud, 2006 fee €30,000. First foals 1999, sire of: Bandari (Gr2), Dominica (Gr2), Misterah (Gr3), Maharib (Gr3), Phoenix Reach (Canadian International-Gr1, Hong Kong Vase-Gr1, Dubai Sheema Classic-Gr1), Hoh Buzzard (Gr2), Haafhd (2,000 Guineas-Gr1, Champion S-Gr1).

Dam Miss Audimar

Won 4 of 20 starts at 2 and 3 in US, including 2 stakes events at 3, also 3rd Boiling Springs H-Gr3. By high-class US performer and fair sire, out of US stakes winner from family of Group 1 winners Park Express, Shinko Forest, Waky Nao. Half-sister to US stakes winner Charge My Account (by Majestic Prince). Dam of: Belle Of Kentucky (1986 f by Key To Content; winner), Express Account (1987 f by Carr de Naskra; winner), Noora Park (1988 f by Ahonoora, winner), Rosy Sunset (1989 f by Red Sunset; unplaced, dam of Grade 3 winner Evening Promise), Orry Main (1991 c by Don't Forget Me; winner), Diaghilef (1992 c by Royal Academy; winner), Gaily Eagle (1993 c by Mujtahid; stakes winner in Japan), Kilcora (1995 f by Mujadil; winner), Admire Missile (1996 c by Mujtahid; placed), Keltech Night (1997 f by Night Shift; unraced), Gold Standard (1998 c by Goldmark; winner), Bandari (1999 c by Alhaarth; Gr2 winner), Given A Choice (2002 c by Trans Island; winner), 2003 f by Fruits Of Love.

Pedigree assessment

Bandari's credentials are well established. He is tough, in common with both his sire and dam, and at the age of seven in 2006 he should still show smart form. After all, Alcazar and Millenary were older than that when excelling in 2005. Further ahead, Bandari looks a natural for a jumps-oriented stud. *JH*

Borrego (USA)

4yo chestnut colt **127**

El Prado (Ire) - Sweet As Honey (USA) (Strike The Gold (USA))

Owner Kelly, Ralls, Foster, Scott, Greely

Trainer C B Greely

Breeder J Kelly, C Beau Greely & B & Dr S Bradley

Career: **20** starts | won **5** | second **6** | third **2** | **£1,092,494** win and place

By James Willoughby

STAMINA is an important quality to preserve in the thoroughbred for more reasons than just tradition. Those horses who exhibit the combination of endurance, toughness and resilience are also those who tend to be sound.

The desire to breed for speed has consistently worked against this ideal, nowhere more demonstrably than in the US. As average running times have improved – reflecting the breed's athletic improvement – so the leading horses have become more fragile.

The annual average starts per runner has been on a downward curve for over 25 years. In 1975, US racehorses averaged 10.23 runs per year. By 2000, it was 7.11 – a decline of more than 30 per cent. While fashion and medication have played their part, the increasing number of top horses who fall by the wayside each year reflects a trend in stallion selection that values precocity and commercial appeal over soundness and durability.

In order for stamina to maintain its value, there must be races in which it can be put to good effect. With the exception of the Belmont Stakes, however, all important races once run at a mile and a half or more on dirt have been reduced in distance.

The Grade 1 Jockey Club Gold Cup at Belmont in October provides a fine example. Established in 1919, it was run over two miles between 1921 and 1975, making it second in distance only to the two-and-a-quarter-mile Display Handicap among important US races during this period.

In 1976, the race was cut back to a mile and a half, with a further reduction to its current distance of a mile and a quarter instituted for the 1990 running. It is no coincidence that as the test it provides has become more commonplace, so the race's prestige has been reduced.

The 87th running of the Jockey Club Gold Cup in 2005 could not compare with that of 1978, when Exceller defeated the previous season's Triple Crown winner Seattle Slew by a nose, but it did produce one of the most

Borrego scores a comfortable win in the Jockey Club Gold Cup, having got the strong pace that suits him so well

impressive winners in Borrego. The four-year-old was able to coast the final furlong on the way to defeating Suave by four and a half lengths. The runner-up, it should be noted, was beaten with considerably less ease by Saint Liam in the subsequent Breeders' Cup Classic.

That the latest Jockey Club Gold Cup reduced most of the field to running the final quarter-mile as slow as in the race's heyday was a factor of the pace. They went much too fast down the back straight into a headwind that had taken its toll before the turn for home had been made. Borrego relished the test of stamina, not least because he was able to observe the leaders wilting from a position well in rear.

As jockey Garrett Gomez put Borrego into gear before reaching the sweeping home bend, the Travers hero Flower Alley and Hollywood Gold Cup winner Lava Man were backing out of a savage duel. What a difference a strong gallop makes, for the latter had thrashed Borrego when gifted an easy lead at the Los Angeles track. This time, the habitual strong finisher ran past him as if he were standing still – which he very nearly was.

Though wildly impressive, this had to be a flattering account of Borrego's powers. The opposite impression was provided by the steadily run Breeders' Cup Classic four weeks later, when he lost ground at the start on the leaders without them expending much effort, was forced to accelerate while his rivals were themselves quickening, then tired in the straight to finish a remote tenth.

If we are looking for a more honest assessment of Borrego, it is necessary

2005 Race record

10th Breeders' Cup Classic - Powered by Dodge (Grade 1) (Dirt) (Belmont Park, October 29) 3yo+ 1m2f Fast **108** 13 ran. *Held up, 11th and driven straight, never a factor (G K Gomez), beaten 10½l by Saint Liam*

1st Jockey Club Gold Cup (Grade 1) (Dirt) (Belmont Park, October 1) 3yo+ 1m2f Fast **127** 8 ran. *Detached in last to 3f out, rapid headway around outside to lead 2f out, 7 lengths clear over 1f out, easily (G K Gomez), beat Suave by 4½l*

1st Pacific Classic (Grade 1) (Del Mar, August 21) 3yo+ 1m2f Fast **119** 11 ran. *Held up in 9th, stayed on down outside final 2f to lead well inside final furlong (G K Gomez), beat Perfect Drift by ½l*

2nd Hollywood Gold Cup (Grade 1) (Dirt) (Hollywood Park, July 9) 3yo+ 1m2f Fast **105** 9 ran. *Held up in rear, headway on outside to go 5th under 2f out, switched inside over 1f out, stayed on to take 2nd final 100yds (G K Gomez), beaten 8¾l by Lava Man*

4th Californian Stakes (Grade 2) (Hollywood Park, June 18) 3yo+ 1m1f Fast **95** 7 ran. *Raced in 5th, 4-wide and ridden entering straight, one pace (G K Gomez), beaten 7l by Lava Man*

3rd Mervyn Leroy Handicap (Grade 2) (Hollywood Park, May 14) 3yo+ 1m½ Fast **110** 7 ran. *Raced in 3rd, headway down outside from over 1f out, ran on (G K Gomez), beaten ½l by Ace Blue*

3rd Santa Anita Handicap (Grade 1) (Dirt) (Santa Anita, March 5) 4yo+ 1m2f Fast **112** 11 ran. *Raced in 6th, 7th 2f out, stayed on final 1½f to take 3rd close home (G K Gomez), beaten 2¾l by Rock Hard Ten*

1st Allowance Optional Claiming (Santa Anita, February 11) 4yo+ 1m½ Sloppy 5 ran. *Held up in 5th, headway on inside to lead 100yds out, ran on well (T Baze), beat Forty Suertudo by 2l*

Other wins

2003 **1st** Allowance Optional Claiming Race (Santa Anita, December 27) 2yo 1m½ Fast 8 ran ● **1st** Maiden Special Weight (Santa Anita, October 26) 2yo 1m Firm 10 ran

to revert to the Pacific Classic at Del Mar in August. Here, he underlined that stamina is his long suit when requiring all but the last few steps of the mile and a quarter to overhaul perennial place-getter Perfect Drift, Lava Man and Dubai World Cup third Choctaw Nation in a blanket finish. Nobody could describe Borrego as impressive on this occasion, but he was certainly gritty and determined.

As a three-year-old, Borrego was regarded as one of the best horses not to win a major race, placings in three Grade 2s suggesting he had the ability to blossom into a stakes winner when strengthening. After a winter break, this potential was further underlined when he ran third to Rock Hard Ten in the Santa Anita Handicap in March, before it was realised in the Pacific Classic. The switch to waiting tactics proved to be a key.

Fortunately for those who enjoy watching a throwback, this outstanding prospect for champion older horse will be around for another year. Whereas Saint Liam, Rock Hard Ten, Roses In May and Ghostzapper have departed the scene, Borrego stays. And stays. And stays.

Borrego

chestnut colt, 17-5-2001

El Prado gr 1989	Sadler's Wells	Northern Dancer	Nearctic Natalma
		Fairy Bridge	Bold Reasom Special
	Lady Capulet	Sir Ivor	Sir Gaylord Attica
		Cap And Bells	Tom Fool Ghazni
Sweet As Honey b 1995	Strike The Gold	Alydar	**Raise A Native** Sweet Tooth
		Majestic Gold	Hatchet Man Majestic Secret
	Cup Of Honey	Raise A Cup	**Raise A Native** Spring Sunshine
		Honey Deb	Herbager Smart Deb

Bred by Jon Kelly, Beau Greely, Sam Bradley, Brad Scott in US. Not Sold $20,000 Keeneland September yearling

Sire El Prado

Won 4 of 9 races, inc. Railway S.-Gr3, National S.-Gr1, Beresford S.-Gr2. Strong, well-made, 16.0hh. Named joint-best 2-y-o in Ireland in International Classifications, best form at 1m on soft ground. Stands at Adena Springs Kentucky, at a 2006 fee of $125,000. Sire of 10 crops of racing age, inc. notable winners: Chindi (Gr3), El Cielo (Gr3), Nite Dreamer (Gr3), Shires Ende (Gr3), Sweet And Ready (Gr2), Air Rocket (Gr3), Swinging On Ice (Gr2), Mr Livingston (Gr3), Medaglia d'Oro (Travers S.-Gr1, Whitney H.-Gr1, Donn H.-Gr1), Senor Swinger (Gr2), Shaconage (Gr3), Spanish Sun (Gr2), Artie Schiller (Breeders' Cup Mile-Gr1), Borrego (Pacific Classic-Gr1, Jockey Club Gold Cup-Gr1), Kitten's Joy (Secretariat S.-Gr1, Joe Hirsch Turf Classic S.-Gr1), Timo (Gr3), Asi Siempre (Gr3).

Dam Sweet As Honey

Unplaced at 2 in US, only season to race. By Kentucky Derby winner but modest sire. Dam Cup Of Honey minor US stakes winner and Gr3 placed, also dam of La Brea S-Gr1, Milady H-Gr1 winner I Ain't Bluffing (f by Pine Bluff) and champion Canadian 2yo Truth Of It All (Proud Truth), plus British Listed-placed 6f 2yo winner Cup Of Tricks (Clever Trick). Dam of: Lizzy's Bluff (1999 f by Pine Bluff; unraced), Diamond Rocket (2000 c by Touch Gold; winner), Borrego (2001 c by El Prado; Gr1 winner), In Great Taste (2002 c by Dixie Union; unplaced), 2004 c by Festival Of Light, 2005 f by Aptitude. In foal to El Prado, sold $850,000 2005 Keeneland November Sale.

Pedigree assessment

An obvious candidate to lead the way among older North American horses in 2006. Looking further ahead, Borrego has the right credentials to make a popular stallion. His sire, whose reputation has risen inexorably, had a superb 2005 and that will heighten interest in his sons. *JH*

Bullish Luck (USA)

6yo bay gelding **122**

Royal Academy (USA) - Wild Vintage (USA) (Alysheba (USA))

Owner Wong Wing Keung

Trainer A S Cruz

Breeder Max Morris & Isabel Morris

Career: **37** starts | won **9** | second **6** | third **4** | **£1,895,817** win and place

By Nick Pulford

AL MOUGHAZEL had eight starts for Pip Payne in Britain and was then sold to race in Hong Kong, where new owner Wong Wing Keung decided to give him a head start by re-naming him Bullish Luck. It was an apposite choice, for here is a horse that needs more than a slice of luck every time he goes to the racetrack. That largely explains why he has managed only seven wins from 29 starts in Hong Kong despite possessing the ability to win an international Group 1 over a mile and finish a desperately close second in another at ten furlongs.

He is a frustrating horse and often it has been too much for his owner, who has swapped jockeys more often than Henry VIII changed wives. Sometimes the changes have been enforced, but still Bullish Luck has had 10 different partners – including some of the world's elite, like Gerald Mosse, Christophe Soumillon and Felix Coetzee, stable jockey to Bullish Luck's trainer Tony Cruz.

Soumillon, Coetzee and Australia's Brett Prebble took it in turns through the revolving door for Bullish Luck's first three runs of 2005, all in local Group 1 and Group 2 events. Soumillon and Prebble both won classy mile events with last-to-first runs down the outside – the runner-up each time was Ain't Here, at a distance of a length and three-quarters.

In between, Coetzee was on board for a ten-furlong race. Bullish Luck, without the strong pace he needs, found trouble early in the straight and his late run was only good enough for fifth place. Coetzee, who had failed by a short head to catch Alexander Goldrun in the Hong Kong Cup the previous December, was out the door again.

Bullish Luck re-entered the international arena for his fourth start of the year. Prebble was on board for the Group 1 QEII Cup over ten furlongs, but he appeared to get too far out of his ground and, despite the usual late flourish, sixth place was the best Bullish Luck could manage behind Vengeance Of Rain.

Bullish Luck (right) swoops late in the Champions Mile to end the unbeaten record of his stablemate Silent Witness

Gerald Mosse was the new man in the saddle for Bullish Luck's next crack at international competition, the Group 1 Champions Mile. All eyes, though, were on unbeaten stablemate Silent Witness, who was sent off at 1-5. Only two rivals were under 20-1 – Bullish Luck at a shade over 8-1 and Mark Johnston's Attraction at 10-1.

The Cruz horses made it a race to remember. Silent Witness set a fast pace under Coetzee, which proved too much for slow-starting Attraction but was perfect for Bullish Luck. Mosse was able to slip through on the inside on the turn, and this proved the difference between victory and defeat. Bullish Luck collared Silent Witness in the dying strides to score by a short head, with the consistent Ain't Here two lengths back in third.

Cruz sent both stable stars to the Group 1 Yasuda Kinen in Tokyo, where the fates weren't so kind to Bullish Luck. Silent Witness was relegated to third in a bobbing finish, with Bullish Luck a length and a quarter behind in fourth. Mosse was stopped in his run on the turn, with Cruz saying that "he could have won with the perfect run of the race".

Mosse retained the ride when Bullish Luck returned in the autumn for the new Hong Kong season, when a handicap defeat and a close second in the trial for the Hong Kong Mile did not matter much. The big target was the Mile itself at the December international meeting, where Bullish Luck started 3-1 favourite, with Rakti 7-2 and Yasuda Kinen winner Asakusa Den'En 4-1. Bullish Luck was out of luck again, though. Mosse

2005 Race record

4th Cathay Pacific Hong Kong Mile (Group 1) (Sha Tin, December 11) 3yo+ 1m Good to firm **118** 13 ran. *Dwelt, 10th straight, headway well over 1f out, 8th 1f out, ran on, nearest at finish (G Mosse), beaten 2¼l by Hat Trick*

2nd Cathay Pacific International Mile Trial (Group 2) (Sha Tin, November 20) 3yo+ 1m Good to firm **121** 14 ran. *Slowly away, challenged wide on turn, ran on strongly to lead well inside final furlong, caught on line (G Mosse), beaten nk by Dave's Best*

6th Sha Tin Trophy Handicap (Group 3) (Sha Tin, October 16) 3yo+ 1m Good to firm **121** 14 ran. *Positioned last, held up when attempting to improve on turn and in early straight, ran on well inside final furlong (G Mosse), beaten 3l by Best Gift*

4th Yasuda Kinen (Grade 1) (Tokyo, June 5) 3yo+ 1m Firm **119** 18 ran. *In rear to straight, strong run final 2f, nearest at finish (G Mosse), beaten 1¾l by Asakusa Den'En*

1st Champions Mile (Group 1) (Sha Tin, May 14) 3yo+ 1m Good to firm **122** 13 ran. *Held up in rear, slipped through on inside on turn to be 6th entering straight, ran on strongly under pressure to lead last strides (G Mosse), beat Silent Witness by shd*

6th Audemars Piguet QE II Cup (Group 1) (Sha Tin, April 24) 3yo+ 1m2f Good to firm **118** 13 ran. *Last to over 1½f out, stayed on strongly down outside final furlong, nearest finish (B Prebble), beaten 3¾l by Vengeance Of Rain*

1st Chairman's Trophy (Group 2) (Sha Tin, March 19) 3yo+ 1m Good to firm **120** 11 ran. *Dropped in rear early, picked up well to lead 150yds out, ran on strongly (B Prebble), beat Ain't Here by 1¾l*

5th Hong Kong Gold Cup (Group 1) (Sha Tin, February 20) 3yo+ 1m2f Good **114** 14 ran. *In rear,good late progress, never nearer (F Coetzee), beaten 3½l by Perfect Partner*

1st Stewards' Cup (Group 1) (Sha Tin, January 16) 3yo+ 1m Good to firm **122** 12 ran. *Settled 7l off lead in last, quickened up very well to lead 1f out, drew clear, impressive (C Soumillon), beat Ain't Here by 1¾l*

Other notable runs

2004 **2nd** Cathay Pacific Hong Kong Cup (Group 1) (Sha Tin, December 12) 3yo+ 1m2f Good to firm **122** 14 ran ● **1st** Hong Kong Gold Cup (Group 1) (Sha Tin, February 22) 3yo+ 1m2f Good to firm **118** 13 ran ● **1st** High Island Handicap (Sha Tin, February 1) 1m Good to firm 13 ran ● **1st** Chang Yiang Handicap (Sha Tin, January 1) 1m Good to firm 14 ran **2003** **1st** Pearce Memorial Challenge Cup (Handicap) (Sha Tin, April 13) 7f Good 14 ran **2001** ● **1st** HBG Properties Conditions Stakes (Ayr, September 21) 2yo 7f Good **98** 6 ran ● **1st** NGK Spark Plugs Maiden Stakes (Newmarket (July), June 22) 2yo 6f Good to firm **82** (TS 49) 11 ran

was unable to find the same charmed run on the inside that he had in the Champions Mile, and by the time he got to the outside it was too late. Bullish Luck finished best of all but was beaten two and a quarter lengths into fourth behind Hat Trick, the other Japanese raider.

It seems odds-on that 2006 will start with a change of jockey for Bullish Luck. There is a select but small pool in Hong Kong, so it could be Coetzee's turn again. Bullish Luck is clearly a top-class miler and, if things had turned out better in 2005, he could have won three international Group 1s. His next attempt might come in the Dubai Duty Free in March. Fingers crossed.

Bullish Luck

bay gelding, 3-4-1999

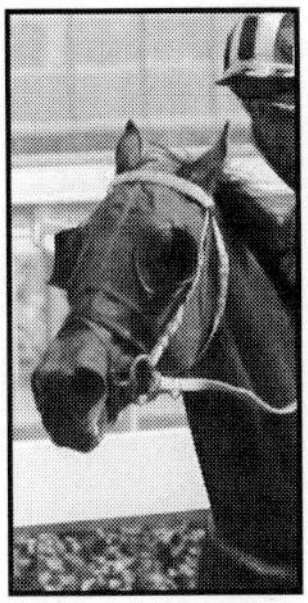

Parents	Grandparents	Great-grandparents	Great-great-grandparents
Royal Academy b 1987	Nijinsky	Northern Dancer	Nearctic Natalma
		Flaming Page	Bull Page Flaring Top
	Crimson Saint	Crimson Satan	Spy Song Papila
		Bolero Rose	Bolero First Rose
Wild Vintage br 1990	Alysheba	Alydar	Raise A Native Sweet Tooth
		Bel Sheba	Lt Stevens Belthazar
	Vintage	Foolish Pleasure	What A Pleasure Fool-Me-Not
		Prix	Vaguely Noble Margarethen

Bred by Max & Isobel Morris in US. 50,000gns Tattersalls October yearling. Raced in Britain as Al Moughazel.

Sire Royal Academy

Won 4 of 7 starts. At 2, won 1 (6f) of 2 starts. At 3, won 3 (Tetrarch S-Gr3, July Cup-Gr1, Breeders' Cup Mile-Gr1) of 5 starts, also 2nd Irish 2,000 Guineas-Gr1, Haydock Sprint Cup-Gr1. By Triple Crown winner and outstanding sire, though with patchy record as sire of sires, out of US stakes winner. Half-brother to Gr2 winner Pancho Villa, stakes winner Alydariel (dam of Gr2 winner Jeune Homme), Gr2 winner Terlingua (dam of Storm Cat). Stands at Ashford in US, 2006 fee $15,000. First foals 1992, sire of Gr1 winners (northern hemisphere foals): Oscar Schindler (Irish St Leger x 2), Ali-Royal (Sussex S), Carmine Lake (Prix de l'Abbaye), Sleepytime (1,000 Guineas), Zalaiyka (Poule d'Essai des Pouliches), Lavery (Phoenix S), Val Royal (Breeders' Cup Mile), Bullish Luck (HK Gold Cup, Stewards' Cup, Champions Mile).

Dam Wild Vintage

Winner over 10f at 3 in France, placed several times. Half-sister to Juvenia (by Trempolino; Prix Marcel Boussac-Gr1), In Extremis (by Sharpen Up; Gr3 winner), Milesime (dam of Gr2 winner Millemix). Family of Galileo, Generous, Horatio Nelson, Imagine, Triptych. Dam of: Vino Veritas (1996 f by Chief's Crown; unplaced), Green Wilderness (1997 f by Green Dancer; placed), Wild Liffey (1998 f by Irish River; unraced), Bullish Luck (1999 g by Royal Academy; HK Gold Cup-Gr1, Stewards' Cup-HKGr1, Champions Mile-HKGr1), Only Vintage (2000 g by Diesis; bumper/hurdle winner), Vintage Gold (2001 c by Lear Fan; non-winner), Wild Academy (2003 f by Royal Academy; unraced), 2004 f by Alhaarth.

Pedigree assessment

The horse we formerly knew as Al Moughazel has become Royal Academy's most prolific northern hemisphere-bred top-level winner. He is one of over 100 stakes winners worldwide for the Ashford shuttler. You will find sprinters, milers, middle-distance horses and stayers in Royal Academy's record, depending on the dam's contribution, and Wild Vintage brought a touch of stamina to Bullish Luck. As a gelding, he will race on in 2006, but as a seven-year-old he will do well to repeat his recent feats. *JH*

Cape Of Good Hope

7yo chestnut gelding **121**

Inchinor - Cape Merino (Clantime)

Owner Guy and Alexander Carstairs

Trainer D Oughton

Breeder Mrs D Ellis

Career: **43** starts | won **7** | second **7** | third **9** | **£1,585,641** win and place

By Nick Pulford

DAVID OUGHTON, Cape Of Good Hope's trainer, made a prediction in Flat Horses of 2004: "He'll win a big one, there's no doubt about that."

It was a bold claim, considering the gelding was rising seven and had just completed a winless campaign, albeit one that saw him make the frame four times in international Group 1 company, in Hong Kong, Britain and Japan, and on three more occasions in domestic Group 1s in his native Hong Kong.

Cape Of Good Hope had been given plenty of chances at the top level and had come up short every time. Oughton's prediction nevertheless proved correct. And not just once, but twice.

Group 1 wins came Cape Of Good Hope's way in Britain and Australia during 2005, a fitting reward for this tough globetrotter who has raced between nine and 11 times in each of his four years under Oughton's care, and finished in the first four on 28 occasions.

Australia was Cape Of Good Hope's first port of call in 2005. Five furlongs has always been too sharp for him and, predictably, that trip found him out in the Group 1 Lightning Stakes at Flemington. It didn't help that he was opposed by the two of the best Australian sprinters, Fastnet Rock and Alinghi, who were separated by a neck in a thrilling finish. Cape Of Good Hope, game as ever, was a length back in third.

A fortnight later, Cape Of Good Hope was out again in the Australia Stakes at Moonee Valley, where the trip was six furlongs and the Lightning principals were missing. The big question mark this time was whether he would handle the tricky track, and the omens weren't good when he was drawn seven of ten, but he sped home by a length and three-quarters from Super Elegant, a dual Group 1 winner the previous year.

Cape Of Good Hope had his Group 1 win at last, but there was no resting on his laurels. After two more defeats at home by Silent Witness

Cape Of Good Hope (right) gains his Royal meeting win at the fourth attempt, mastering Galeota in the Golden Jubilee

(taking the score to 10-0 in Silent Witness's favour), Cape Of Good Hope returned to England for another crack at Royal Ascot, where he had finished second in the King's Stand and third in the Golden Jubilee in 2004. Royal Ascot's transfer to York was not in his favour, however, as Oughton believes he is really a seven-furlong horse and needs a stiff test at sprint trips. It was the now familiar story in the King's Stand, in which Cape Of Good Hope ran gamely into fourth but found speedier types too good over five furlongs. A low draw didn't help as he raced virtually alone on the far side through the final two furlongs.

He didn't have any more luck in the Golden Jubilee draw, starting from stall two, but two factors played in his favour: the six-furlong trip and the blistering pace set by Galeota. Mick Kinane joined the main field this time and he was the only one able to catch Galeota, taking the lead at the furlong pole and holding his rival's renewed challenge by a head. The time was two-tenths of a second inside the course record.

Cape Of Good Hope was given a well-earned break before his next overseas assignment, the Grade 1 Sprinters Stakes at Nakayama in early October, but he was joined on the flight from Hong Kong by Silent Witness and finished a well-beaten 11th behind his old rival.

Then it was back to Australia for a double bid in the Group 1 Salinger Stakes and the Group 2 Age Classic, both over six furlongs at Flemington. Cape Of Good Hope was third in both, each time behind emerging sprint filly Glamour Puss.

As usual, he arrived back in Hong Kong in good shape and was aimed at the Group 1 Hong Kong Sprint, starting favourite in the absence of Silent Witness. He beat all the overseas raiders but still finished only

2005 Race record

5th Cathay Pacific Hong Kong Sprint (Group 1) (Sha Tin, December 11) 3yo+ 5f Good to firm **106** 12 ran. *Always prominent on far side, ridden 1½f out, no extra final furlong (M J Kinane), beaten 3¾l by Natural Blitz*

3rd The Age Classic (Group 2) (Flemington, November 5) 3yo+ 6f Good 9 ran. *Always in touch on stands' side, ran on final furlong, nearest at finish (G Childs), beaten 2½l by Glamour Puss*

3rd Seppelt Salinger Stakes (Group 1) (Flemington, October 29) 3yo+ 6f Good **118** 15 ran. *Always in touch on stands' side, ran on well final furlong (B Prebble), beaten 1½l by Glamour Puss*

11th Sprinters Stakes (Grade 1) (Nakayama, October 2) 3yo+ 6f Firm **107** 16 ran. *Raced in midfield throughout (B Prebble), beaten 5¼l by Silent Witness*

1st Golden Jubilee Stakes (British Leg of The Global Sprint Challenge) (Group 1) (York, June 18) 3yo+ 6f Firm **120** (TS 119) 15 ran. *In touch, went right and headway over 2f out, ridden to lead narrowly 1f out, ran on (M J Kinane), beat Galeota by hd*

4th King's Stand Stakes (Group 2) (York, June 14) 3yo+ 5f Good to firm **117** (TS 85) 16 ran. *Raced wide, always prominent, ridden well over 1f out, driven and one pace inside final furlong (M J Kinane), beaten 2¼l by Chineur*

3rd Chairman's Sprint Prize (Group 1) (Sha Tin, April 3) 3yo+ 6f Good to firm **113** 14 ran. *Settled behind midfield, quickened 2f out and made up good ground in straight (B Prebble), beaten 3¾l by Silent Witness*

5th Centenary Sprint Cup (Group 1) (Sha Tin, February 27) 3yo+ 5f Good to yielding **96** 11 ran. *Rear, headway 2f out, no extra (G Schofield), beaten 8l by Silent Witness*

1st Timbercorp Australia Stakes (Group 1) (Moonee Valley, February 19) 3yo+ 6f Good **121** 9 ran. *Raced in 2nd until led over 1f out, ran on well (B Prebble), beat Super Elegant by 1¾l*

3rd TEAC Lightning Stakes (Group 1) (Flemington, February 5) 3yo+ 5f Good to soft **118** 12 ran. *Settled towards rear, headway over 2f out, ran on well, nearest finish (M J Kinane), beaten 1¼l by Fastnet Rock*

Other notable runs

2004 **2nd** Cathay Pacific Hong Kong Sprint (Group 1) (Sha Tin, December 12) 3yo+ 5f Good to firm **121** 14 ran ● **3rd** Sprinters Stakes (Grade 1) (Nakayama, October 3) 3yo+ 6f Heavy **109** 16 ran ● **4th** Darley July Cup (Group 1) (Newmarket (July), July 8) 3yo+ 6f Good to soft **114** (TS 97) 20 ran ● **3rd** Golden Jubilee Stakes (Group 1) (Ascot, June 19) 3yo+ 6f Firm **115** (TS 117) 14 ran ● **2nd** King's Stand Stakes (Group 2) (Ascot, June 15) 3yo+ 5f Good to firm **114** (TS 102) 19 ran **2003** **3rd** Hong Kong Sprint (Group 1) (Sha Tin, December 14) 3yo+ 5f Good to firm **121** 14 ran

fifth behind Natural Blitz in a race that emphasised the strength in depth of Hong Kong sprinting.

It is hard to believe that Cape Of Good Hope improved at the age of seven, but Oughton believes the 2004 trip to Britain may have been the making of him. He enjoyed a blissful summer at Amanda Perrett's Pulborough stables, interspersed with a spot of racing.

Getting away from it all clearly agrees with Cape Of Good Hope, and he is sure to have his passport stamped a few more times during 2006.

Cape Of Good Hope *chestnut gelding, 21-1-1998*

Inchinor ch 1990	Ahonoora	Lorenzaccio	Klairon Phoenissa
		Helen Nichols	Martial Quaker Girl
	Inchmurrin	Lomond	Northern Dancer My Charmer
		On Show	Welsh Pageant African Dancer
Cape Merino ch 1991	Clantime	Music Boy	Jukebox Veronique
		Penny Pincher	Constable Midnight Dollar
	Laena	Roman Warrior	Porto Bello Colliers
		Poshteen	Royal Smoke Camlet

Bred by Mrs D Ellis in Britain. 25,000gns Doncaster St Leger yearling

Sire Inchinor

Won 5 of 10 starts, inc. Greenham S.-Gr3, Criterion S.-Gr3, Hungerford S.-Gr3. Also 2nd in Dewhurst S., 3rd in Sussex S. Small ($15.1\frac{1}{2}$ hh), well-made, attractive sort, and a grand mover. Very game, consistent performer, effective in most conditions (not raced on extremes). Speedy, owned a sharp turn of foot, stayed a mile well. Died in 2003. Stood at Woodland Stud, Newmarket, last fee £10,000. Sire of 9 crops of racing age, inc. notable winners: Golden Silca (Gr2), Palanca (Gr3), Summoner (Queen Elizabeth II S.-Gr1), Umistim (Gr3), Bannister (Gr2), Cape Of Good Hope (Australia S.-Gr1, Golden Jubilee S.-Gr1), Orientor (Gr3), Felicity (Gr3), Latice (Prix de Diane-Gr1), Secret Melody (Gr3), Satchem (Gr3), In Clover (Gr3), Silca's Sister (Prix Morny-Gr1).

Dam Cape Merino

Won 4 of 9 starts from 2 to 5. At 2, won 2 (5-6f, inc. Redcar Tote Two-Year-Old Trophy) from 4 starts. At 3, won 1 (5f Bovis Hcap) of 4 starts. Unraced at 4, won sole start (5f) at 5. By smart and very tough sprinter who tended to get tough progeny, out of placed 2yo. Dam of: Cape Of Good Hope (1998 c by Inchinor; Australia S-AusGr1, Golden Jubilee S-Gr1), Cape St Vincent (2000 c by Paris House; winner), Cape Columbine (2002 f by Diktat; Gr3-placed winner), Gabriella (2003 f by Cape Cross; unraced), 2004 c by Inchinor.

Pedigree assessment

Cape Of Good Hope has long established himself as by far the most prominent runner from this family in modern times, and he has now put Group 1 wins on the catalogue page. Meanwhile, his half-sister Cape Columbine came close in 2005 to adding a Group 1 place, having finished fifth in the 1,000 Guineas and fourth in the Coronation Stakes. No wonder the 2004 brother to Cape Of Good Hope made 400,000gns at Part 1 of the Tattersalls October Yearling Sale. That alone is a superb return on the 6,200gns Cape Merino cost as a nine-year-old mare in 2000. *JH*

Caradak (Ire)

4yo bay colt **118**

Desert Style (Ire) - Caraiyma (Ire) (Shahrastani (USA))

Owner H H Aga Khan

Trainer John M Oxx

Breeder H H Aga Khan's Studs

Career: **10** starts | won **5** | second **1** | third **1** | **£189,799** win and place

By Graham Dench

IT WILL be interesting to see how Godolphin intend to campaign Caradak, who was by no means one of their higher-profile back-end purchases but was certainly among the more interesting of them.

Although he will be five in 2006, Caradak is still relatively lightly raced, and he has the advantage of having so far won nothing better than a Group 3, which will help him from a penalty standpoint until he moves back into Group 1 company. However, his former trainer John Oxx seemed uncertain of his ideal trip, and prime opportunities will be less abundant if, as is eminently possible, he is better at seven furlongs than he is at a mile, and better on fast ground than on soft.

Caradak certainly stays a mile – three of his five wins have come at the trip – but it appears to stretch his stamina and his very best performances have both been over seven furlongs, when beating Arakan in the Emirates Airline Minstrel Stakes at The Curragh and when caught close home by Court Masterpiece in the Prix de la Foret Casino Barriere at Longchamp on Arc weekend.

The Foret was Caradak's first run in a Group 1, an earlier intended appearance in the Prix du Moulin having been abandoned when Oxx concluded that he had found a mile a shade too far when only scrambling home in the Desmond Stakes at Leopardstown. A 4-5 chance to complete a hat-trick that day, Caradak looked set to win well when he went to the front well over a furlong from home, but he failed to get away from his rivals and held on by just a short head from 20-1 shot Mustameet.

It was an unimpressive performance and Oxx concluded: "This wasn't as good as Caradak's last run and he didn't run up to his rating. I also think he didn't get the trip in a fast-run race. It was just his courage that got him home. I had planned to run him in the Prix du Moulin in three weeks' time, but now I might give him a break and freshen him up for the Foret and hope that the ground will be all right by then."

Caradak (right) gamely holds off Mustameet in the Group 3 Desmond Stakes to complete a midsummer hat-trick

By "all right", Oxx meant not too soft. In that respect he was unlucky. The going on Arc weekend was officially soft and, although the race times suggested it was not too bad, it was probably softer than Caradak would have preferred.

Oxx could have few complaints about the standard of opposition that Caradak encountered at Longchamp, however, for in truth it was a Group 1 in name only, with the race's 2004 winner Somnus the sole runner in a field of eight demonstrably in that class, and even he had been running below form all season.

Regular rider Mick Kinane adopted his usual prominent position on Caradak, who was second into the straight and once again took it up around a furlong and a half from the finish. However, this time Caradak could not quite hold on, the four-year-old succumbing to a perfectly timed challenge by Gerald Mosse on fellow Group 1 virgin Court Masterpiece.

Kinane told Oxx that Caradak had been very brave again, but had been unable to accelerate as he normally does because of the ground. All five of Caradak's wins had been gained in mid-summer on ground officially described as good to firm, and soft ground was said to have been a factor in his defeat in the Challenge Stakes at Newmarket 12 months previously, when he did best of a small group that raced near the stands rail but was only sixth overall.

2005 Race record

2nd Prix de la Foret Casino Barriere de Biarritz (Group 1) (Longchamp, October 1) 3yo+ 7f Soft **116** (TS 99) 8 ran. *Prominent, 2nd straight, shaken up 2f out, led 1½f out, ran on until headed on line (M J Kinane), beaten hd by Court Masterpiece*

1st Desmond Stakes (Group 3) (Leopardstown, August 14) 3yo+ 1m Good to firm **114** (TS 88) 8 ran. *Settled moderate 3rd, improved into 2nd approaching straight, led over 1f out, kept on well, all out (M J Kinane), beat Mustameet by shd*

1st Emirates Airline Minstrel Stakes (Group 3) (Curragh, July 17) 4yo+ 7f Good to firm **118** (TS 116) 6 ran. *Always prominent, 2nd and challenged under 3f out, led 2f out, ridden clear over 1f out, easily (M J Kinane), beat Arakan by 3½l*

1st Budweiser Celebration Stakes (Listed) (Curragh, June 26) 3yo+ 1m Good to firm **116** (TS 115) 9 ran. *Always prominent, 2nd early straight, led 1½f out, stayed on well final furlong (F M Berry), beat Kings Point by 2l*

9th Glencairn Stakes (Listed) (Leopardstown, June 1) 4yo+ 1m Good to firm **93** (TS 59) 9 ran. *Tracked leaders in 4th, lost place early straight, no extra over 1f out (M J Kinane), beaten 10½l by Lord Admiral*

2004

6th Victor Chandler Challenge Stakes (Group 2) (Newmarket, October 16) 3yo+ 7f Soft **104** (TS 89) 12 ran ● **3rd** Ben Dunne Memorial Solonaway Stakes (Listed) (Curragh, September 19) 3yo+ 1m Good **112** (TS 84) 10 ran ● **1st** King Charlemagne Platinum Stakes (Listed) (Cork, August 2) 3yo+ 1m Good to firm **110** 4 ran ● **1st** McDonogh Style Concepts Maiden (Galway, July 27) 3yo 7f Good to firm **99** 9 ran ● **4th** Business Is Better With Vodafone (C & G) Maiden (Leopardstown, July 14) 3yo+ 1m Good to yielding **59** (TS 52) 9 ran

Caradak's 2005 campaign had begun inauspiciously when he trailed home last of nine in a Listed race at Leopardstown in June, but he had quickly put that reverse behind him with a good win in similar company at The Curragh on Irish Derby day and a first Group 3 success in the Minstrel Stakes on the same course. He was at his most impressive in the latter race, when he was sent to the front two furlongs out and soon had the race in safe keeping, coming home an easy three-and-a-half-length winner from British challenger Arakan.

There was talk after the Foret of Caradak returning to Newmarket for a second crack at the Challenge Stakes, but Oxx decided that it would be unfair to submit him to another overseas journey so soon and said he would wait for Hong Kong, where he would have faced a rematch with Court Masterpiece.

However, there was no trip to Hong Kong, not this time anyway. It emerged at the end of November that Godolphin had bought him from the Aga Khan, along with Irish Oaks heroine Shawanda, Queen Anne winner Valixir and the improving Group 2 filly Oiseau Rare.

Caradak is likely to be in action in Dubai before returning to Europe, when we can expect to see him contesting some of the better races at seven furlongs and possibly a mile when the ground is on top. Unless Godolphin read his form differently.

Caradak

bay colt, 23-2-2001

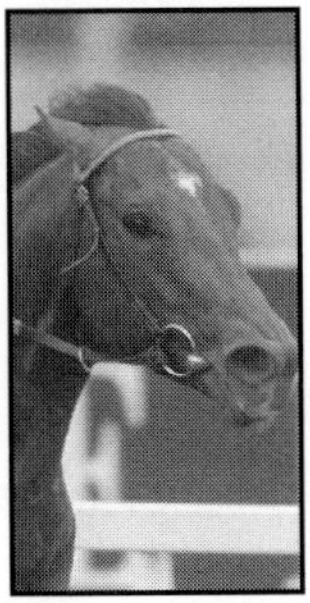

Desert Style b 1992	Green Desert	Danzig	**Northern Dancer** Pas de Nom
		Foreign Courier	Sir Ivor Courtly Dee
	Organza	High Top	Derring-do Camenae
		CantonSilk	Runnymede Clouded Lamp
Caraiyma b 1992	Shahrastani	Nijinsky	**Northern Dancer** Flaming Page
		Shademah	Thatch Shamim
	Caraniya	Darshaan	Shirley Heights Delsy
		Callianire	Sir Gaylord Passionata

Bred by Aga Khan in Ireland

Sire Desert Style

High-class 6-7f 2yo, won 2 (6f) of 5 starts, also 3rd Phoenix S-Gr1, National S-Gr1. At 3, high-class 6-7f performer, won 3 (Tetrarch S-Gr3, Ballycorus S-Gr3, Phoenix Sprint S-Gr3) of 6 starts, also 2nd Hong Kong International Bowl-Gr2. Only once out of first 3 in 11 starts. By top-class sprinter-miler and good sire who is influence for speed. Dam quite useful 10f 3yo winner, half-sister to 7f Gr1 winner Brocade (dam of Gr1 winners Barathea, Gossamer, and Gr winners Free At Last, Zabar). First foals 1997. Stands at Morristown Lattin Stud in Ireland, 2006 fee €10,000. Sire of (northern hemisphere): Bachir (Poule d'Essai des Poulains-Gr1, Irish 2,000 Guineas-Gr1), Jessica's Dream (Gr3), Next Desert (Deutsches Derby-Gr1), Caradak (Gr3), Captain Hurricane (Gr2), Cool Creek (Gr2).

Dam Caraiyma

Unraced at 2, won 1 (9f) of 5 starts at 3, also placed over 8-9f. By dual Derby winner but largely disappointing sire. Sister to smart 2yo/10-12f performer Cajarian, half-sister to high-class 2005 10f Hong Kong performer Floral Dynamite (by Danehill) out of an 8f 2yo/12f 3yo winner. Dam of: Caraiyni (1997 c by Be My Chief; unplaced, Caraman (1998 c by Grand Lodge; hurdle winner), Carallia (1999 c by Common Grounds; winner), Caradak (2001 c by Desert Style; Gr3 winner), Canndar (2002 c by Celtic Swing; unraced), Carakiysa (2003 f by Docksider; unraced), 2004 c by Medicean.

Pedigree assessment

Caradak is a member of the significant batch of purchases made by Sheikh Mohammed in the autumn of 2005. Relatively lightly raced and progressive to date, he is from a family whose members tend to improve with age. So far, 7-8f has been his distance, and that concurs with his pedigree. *JH*

Carlotamix (Fr)

2yo grey colt **117**

Linamix (Fr) - Carlitta (USA) (Olympio (USA))

Owner H H Aga Khan

Trainer A Fabre

Breeder Snc Lagardere Elevage

Career: **3** starts | won **3** | **£138,901** win and place

By Robert Carter

DEAUVILLE has made great efforts in the past quarter-century to expand its appeal into as much of a year-round affair as possible, both as a place to live or to visit and as a racing town.

The training centre, which now has a permanent population of between 280 and 300 horses and is home to the likes of Yves de Nicolay, Eric Danel and Stephane Wattel, has been one example.

Racing has also expanded, beginning with an October meeting to coincide with the sales. They then tried a May one in 1996, importing Group races from Chantilly, Longchamp and Saint-Cloud to increase interest. However, when Evry closed at the end of that year, the early meeting was switched to July, inheriting the feature races from that course.

All this extra use, some of it in answer to the demand from the trainers based in the town, took its toll on the racing surface. A new turf course was therefore built inside the main circuit. But several wet summers still increased the problem and the bewildering spectacle of fields racing wide, or even round the extreme outside of the final turn, became familiar. At some stage, the ground would improve and an enterprising rider would try the inside again. If his horse ran well, then everyone else would return to the normal route. The new course, which was in use from 1998 to 2002, took some of the pressure off the main one but not enough. So it vanished under the present dirt track, which was first tried in the summer of 2003 and used fully in December of that year.

The main course still has its problems though. It was in such a state after the opening weekend of the 2005 summer meeting that the authorities made a last-minute switch for the Tuesday. Runners for the eight races were declared under the assumption that they would all be run on the turf but five of them were moved to the dirt.

Nine were declared for the first such contest, the Prix d'Etreham, but four were scratched. That left Lanfranc, third in both his races, to lead

Carlotamix (near side) completes an unbeaten campaign with victory in the Group 1 Criterium International

from the odds-on Happy Owners, who had finished second in both of his. The two debutants, Zanazeem and Carlotamix, followed them. Lanfranc fought off the favourite in the straight but had no answer when Carlotamix quickened past with a furlong to run. Carlotamix, who started third favourite, bounded clear and went on to register a claim as the best French juvenile. His four victims ran 13 times afterwards without winning any of them until the fourth, Zanazeem, was successful back on the dirt in a maiden at Deauville on December 14.

It is not too surprising that Carlotamix handled the dirt so well. His dam is American and won on dirt while her sire won four Derbys, the Arkansas, Minnesota, American (at Arlington) and Hollywood, all but the last of which were on dirt. It is not likely that we shall see Carlotamix on that surface again, though, unless it is in the Breeders' Cup Classic.

Carlotamix reappeared in the Prix des Chenes at Longchamp, a race that attracted only four runners for the third time in the last ten years. You might think that it doesn't deserve to survive but its previous three winners were Dalakhani, Bago and Helios Quercus, all of whom took the path that Carlotamix was to follow and went on to win the Criterium International.

2005 Race record

1st Criterium International (Group 1) (Saint-Cloud, October 30) 2yo 1m Soft **117** (TS 74) 6 ran. *Held up in 5th to straight, brought to stands' side, confidently ridden, led inside final furlong, pushed out (C Soumillon), beat Stormy River by 3l*

1st Prix des Chenes (Group 3) (Longchamp, September 17) 2yo 1m Good to soft **106** (TS 62) 4 ran. *Raced in 2nd, pushed along to lead 1½f out, ran on steadily to line, pushed out (T Jarnet), beat Linda's Lad by ½l*

1st Prix d'Etreham (All-Weather) (Deauville, August 2) 2yo 7½f Standard **77** 5 ran. *Raced in 4th, headway 1½f out to lead inside final furlong, soon clear, easily (C Soumillon), beat Lanfranc by 3l*

Two of the runners in the Chenes were trained by Andre Fabre but neither was in there to help the other. Fortunately for Carlotamix and Linda's Lad, the Mick Channon-trained Zato set a good pace. Christophe Soumillon was replacing the injured Mick Kinane on the Aga's Shalapour in the Irish St Leger, so the lucky chance ride on Carlotamix went to Thierry Jarnet, who did not receive any rides from Fabre for several years after mistaking the winning post on Daring Miss in the 1999 Prix de Royallieu, a crime he committed again in the same race with the Francois Rohaut-trained Whortleberry in 2003.

Jarnet tracked Zato until going on over one furlong from home and then pushed the colt out to hold the efforts of Linda's Lad by half a length. Zato finished three lengths back. Jarnet also won the day's other Group 3 event, the Prix du Prince d'Orange, on Corre Caminos. This gelded son of Montjeu, trained by Mikel Delzangles, beat Ruwi by one and a half lengths and, although he later finished behind that rival in the Prix Dollar, he should continue to improve in 2006.

Carlotamix started favourite for the first time in the Criterium International at Saint-Cloud, another course where soft ground plays tricks with tactics. Bribon set a good pace to the Irish raider Poseidon Adventure while Soumillon held up Carlotamix fifth of the six runners. As they approached the straight, he edged out and then made for the stands side. Porto Santo, a colt who had won two early races but was running for the first time since May, followed him across and they reached the hedge one and a half furlongs from home.

Meanwhile, the Swedish-owned Stormy River had been last of the four on the far side but moved up to take over there with one furlong to run. It was difficult to tell how the two sides compared but Carlotamix probably already had the advantage and he quickly established his superiority in the final furlong, winning by three lengths. Porto Santo stuck to him as far as the distance and only failed to beat Stormy River by a neck.

Soumillon announced afterwards that Carlotamix was the best French juvenile, but he has only competed in small fields and still has plenty of progress to make if he is to be compared with the likes of Dalakhani or Bago.

Carlotamix

grey colt, 22-3-2003

Linamix gr 1987	Mendez	Bellypha	Lyphard Belga
		Miss Carina	Caro Miss Pia
	Lunadix	Breton	Relko La Melba
		Lutine	Alcide Mona
Carlitta b 1996	Olympio	Naskra	Nasram Iskra
		Carols Christmas	Whitesburg Light Verse
	Creamery	Secretariat	Bold Ruler Somethingroyal
		Cream 'n Crimson	Vaguely Noble Crimson Lass

Bred by SNC Lagardere Elevage in France.

Sire Linamix

Won 4 of 10 starts, inc. Prix La Rochette-Gr3, Prix de Fontainebleau-Gr3, Poule d'Essai des Poulains-Gr1. Also 2nd in Grand Criterium, Prix Jacques le Marois, Prix du Moulin de Longchamp and Champion Stakes (all Gr1). Big, angular, round-actioned, free-running sort; not the best of forelegs. Stands at Haras du Val Henry at a fee of €50,000. Sire of 12 crops of racing age, inc. notable winners Diamond Mix (Gr2), Housamix (Gr2), Miss Satamixa (Prix Jacques le Marois-Gr1), Walk On Mix (Gr2), Manninamix (Gr3), Clodora (Gr2), Fragrant Mix (Grand Prix de Saint-Cloud-Gr1), Oa Baldixe (Gr3), Diamonixa (Gr3), Pinmix (Gr3), Sagamix (Prix de l'Arc de Triomphe-Gr1), Amilynx (Prix Royal-Oak-Gr1, twice), Artistique (Gr3), Sage et Jolie (Gr2), Slickly (Grand Prix de Paris-Gr1, Prix du Moulin de Longchamp-Gr1, Premio Vittorio di Capua-Gr1, twice), Goldamix (Criterium de Saint-Cloud-Gr1), Miraculous (Gr3), Diamilina (Gr2), Fair Mix (Prix Ganay-Gr1), Vahorimix (Poule d'Essai des Poulains-Gr1, Prix Jacques le Marois-Gr1), Bernimixa (Gr2), Martaline (Gr2), Diasilixa (Gr3), Visorama (Gr3), Walkamia (Gr3), Cherry Mix (Gran Premio del Jockey Club-Gr1), Fracassant (Gr2), Linda Regina (Gr3), Lord du Sud (Gr2), Millemix (Gr2), Reefscape (Prix du Cadran-Gr1), Carlotamix (Criterium International-Gr1), Manbala (Gr3). Champion sire in France 1998 and 2004.

Dam Carlitta

Won 3 of 18 races, inc. 1 Listed. Quite useful performer, winner on dirt, but best form at a mile on turf, successful in Remington Park Oaks. Dam of: Carlix (2002 c by Linamix; winner), Carlotamix (2003 c by Linamix; Gr1 winner). She has a yearling filly, Carlaxna, by Linamix.

Pedigree assessment

The late Jean-Luc Lagardere was a regular buyer of fillies and mares in America, though never at the top level of the market. His purchases tended to have some respectable form and to come from families which lacked fashionability, and the policy paid off famously, because when they were mated with Lagardere's own stallion Linamix, top runners were frequently produced. The strategy was not one that the Aga Khan would ever have employed in his breeding operation, but he recognised the success attained from it and by acquiring the entire Lagardere bloodstock holdings – some 200 head – in the spring of 2005 he placed faith in it. He soon reaped rewards, notably through Vadawina and Valixir, but by the end of the year Carlotamix promised to prove the most significant individual among the horses in training. He will stay ten furlongs, possibly even a mile and a half. *TM*

Cesario (Jpn)

3yo brown filly **116**

Special Week (Jpn) - Kirov Premiere (Sadler's Wells (USA))

Owner Carrot Farm

Trainer Katsuhiko Sumii

Breeder Northern Farm

Career: **6** starts | won **5** | second **1** | **£1,395,734** win and place

By James Willoughby

A STATE-FUNDED racing industry unified towards the common good; the world's highest prize-money structure; a breeding industry committed to developing middle-distance horses. It sounds like Utopia, but it is actually Japan.

No wonder that Japanese thoroughbreds have made such an international impact within the last 10 years. It was only in 1995 that Fujiyama Kenzen became the first horse to win a Pattern race outside their domestic scene in the Group 2 Hong Kong International Cup at Sha Tin.

Japanese success has spread to most corners of the racing globe since. In 1998, Seeking The Pearl broke new ground in Europe when successful in the Group 1 Prix Maurice de Gheest at Deauville. Like Fujiyama Kenzen, the filly was trained by the enterprising Hideyuki Mori.

Agnes World planted the Japanese flag in Britain when defying a poor draw to win the Group 1 July Cup in 2000, while Dubai was added to the list the following year via Stay Gold's narrow defeat of home favourite Fantastic Light in the Dubai Sheema Classic, which was then classified as only a Group 2.

When Cesario became the first Japanese-trained winner of a Grade 1 race in the US in the 2005 American Oaks at Hollywood Park in July, her triumph recalled the country's less than illustrious racing past. To be specific, a 40-year period of fruitless toil to land a major race abroad.

Cesario's victory – by four lengths over the useful yardstick Melhor Ainda – was not the first by a Japanese runner in any US race. In 1958, Hakuchikara broke the ice when winning a valuable handicap at Santa Anita. His victory tempted eight further raids from back home for the Washington DC International at Laurel Park between 1962 and 1976, but none was successful.

Sporadic attempts in the intervening period mostly ended in hapless

Cesario lands the Grade 1 American Oaks, becoming Japan's first major winner in the US in almost 50 years

defeat. Ski Captain, for instance, was only 14th in the 1995 Kentucky Derby, while Taiki Blizzard was unplaced in the 1996 and 1997 Breeders' Cup Classic.

Undaunted by these discouraging examples, Katsuhiko Sumii took it upon himself to put the record straight. In 2004, he ventured to California as the guest of Neil Drysdale, observing the working practices of the English-born trainer that have seen him ensconced in the US Racing Hall of Fame.

"Neil, of course, takes care of his horses very well," Sumii commented at the time. "But I think a key factor in his training is caring for the mental attitude of his horses. He wants them to enjoy their work."

Easier said than done. During 2005, a faction of 25 trainers, including Richard Mandella, expressed welfare concerns for horses associated with the sun-baked track surfaces of southern California. A raft of injuries to thoroughbreds trained by Eoin Harty on the West Coast had led to his patron Sheikh Mohammed moving his entire string elsewhere.

Given the demands of this challenge, Sumii had to wait until the right horse came along, but he needed no further prompting when Cesario underlined her class and toughness to win the Grade 1 Yushun Himba (Japanese Oaks) at Tokyo in May. While she prevailed by only a neck, it was clear she was worth a deal more in coming from an unpromising position two furlongs out.

The diminutive Cesario arrived on the backstretch at Hollywood Park in superb condition. She did not please all observers with a puzzling workout

2005 Race record

1st American Oaks (Grade 1) (Hollywood Park, July 3) 3yo 1m2f Firm **116** 12 ran. *Raced in 3rd, led approaching 2f out, ran on strongly (Y Fukunaga), beat Melhor Ainda by 4l*

1st Yushun Himba (Japanese Oaks) (Grade 1) (Tokyo, May 22) 3yo 1m4f Firm **114** 18 ran. *Raced in 16th, 12th 2f out, strong run to lead close home (Y Fukunaga), beat Air Messiah by nk*

2nd Oka Sho (Group 1) (Japanese 1,000 Guineas) (Hanshin, April 10) 3yo 1m Firm **114** 18 ran. *Raced in 6th, 10th 2f out, finished fast (M Yoshida), beaten hd by Rhein Kraft*

1st Jiji Press Hai Flower Cup (Grade 3) (Nakayama, March 19) 3yo 1m1f Firm 14 ran. *Close up in 2nd or 3rd, 2nd straight, led over 1f out, ran on well (Y Fukunaga), beat Slew Rate by 2½l*

1st Kanchiku Sho (Nakayama, January 9) 3yo 1m2f Firm 16 ran. *Raced in 3rd, led inside final furlong, ridden out (Y Fukunaga), beat Admire Fuji by nk*

2004

1st Maiden (Unraced) (Hanshin, December 25) 2yo 1m Firm 16 ran

three days before the race, however. Timed in a moderate 52 seconds for four furlongs, she had broken slowly and barely risen above a canter until the final 110 yards of the exercise, though her connections expressed themselves well pleased.

A source of further uncertainty among punters was the identity of Cesario's jockey. Films of her keynote success back home encouraged the perception that Yuinichi Fukunaga, 28, had somewhat eccentric methods, despite standing third in his domestic rankings and collecting four Group 1 races in 2005.

Perhaps Fukunaga was aware that Cesario had won despite him last time out, for he kept the filly much closer to the pace in the early stages of the Hollywood Oaks. Furthermore, he managed to save ground around the tight first turn despite being drawn furthest outside in a field of 12.

Having tracked runaway leader Isla Cozzene through brisk fractions during the first third of the race, Cesario could be seen going very well at the head of the chasing pack. By the end of the back straight, she took over, doing so with little apparent effort while one or two behind began to feel the pace.

Cesario had a decent cushion over hot favourite Melhor Ainda on the crown of the bend, the latter having stumbled at the start. What's more, the Japanese filly was still going through the gears, and her desire to clear away from the field was still unquenched. She opened out in the straight with terrific zest, powering away throughout a final furlong that must have made those connected with her burst with pride. In the process, Cesario earned a special place in her country's racing history.

She was named after the heroine in Twelfth Night who posed as a man called Cesario in order to rise above the expectations of her sex. Perhaps this Hollywood story was a case of life imitating art.

Cesario

brown filly, 31-3-2002

Special Week br 1995	Sunday Silence	Halo	Hail To Reason Cosmah
		Wishing Well	Understanding Mountain Flower
	Campaign Girl	Maruzensky	Nijinsky Shill
		Lady Shiraoki	Saint Crespin Miss Ashiyagawa
Kirov Premiere b 1990	Sadler's Wells	Northern Dancer	Nearctic Natalma
		Fairy Bridge	Bold Reason Special
	Querida	Habitat	Sir Gaylord Little Hut
		Principia	Le Fabuleux Pia

Bred by Northern Farm in Japan

Sire Special Week

Won 10 of 17 starts in Japan from 2 to 4 at up to 2m. At 3, won Japanese Derby, 2nd Japanese St Leger, 3rd Japan Cup, Japanese 2,000 Guineas. At 4, won Japan Cup-Gr1, Tenno Sho (Spring)-Gr1, Tenno Sho (Autumn)-Gr1. By 1989 North American Horse of the Year and outstanding Japanese-based stallion. Dam, from modest family, by a champion Japanese 2yo. Stands at Shadai Stallion Station. First foals 2001, sire of: Cesario (American Oaks-Gr1, Japanese Oaks-Gr1), Inti Raimi (Gr2), Smooth Baritone (Gr3).

Dam Kirov Premiere

Won 5 of 13 starts in 3 seasons. At 2, won 9f maiden from 3 starts in Ireland. At 3 in Ireland, won 3 handicaps (10-12f) from 5 starts. Switched to US, won 1 (Rutgers Breeders' Cup H-Gr3) of 5 starts, also, 2nd Athenia H-Gr3. Sister to smart 10-12f colt Theatre Critic, half-sister to Be Discreet (dam of smart miler Gothenberg, grand-dam of smart 2005 2yo Amadeus Mozart). By outstanding sire and broodmare sire, out of winning half-sister to outstanding 6-8f colt Chief Singer. Third dam is Oaks winner Pia. Sold $280,000 1994 Keeneland November Sale. Sent to Japan, dam of: Proton (1996 c by Sunday Silence; winner), Millennium Dancer (1997 c by Sunday Silence; winner), Farukh (1999 c by Sunday Silence; non-winner), Kirov Opera (2000 c by Pentire; non-winner), Dark Potential (2001 c by Dance In The Dark; placed), Cesario (2002 f by Special Week; Gr1 winner), Silk Pleiades (2003 f by Admire Vega; non-winner), 2004 f in Australia by Fusaichi Pegasus, 2005 f in Australia by French Deputy.

Pedigree assessment

Sunday Silence's sons are now taking over from the great sire, who died in 2002. Special Week, also sire of the 2005 Japanese Derby runner-up Inti Raimi, is one of the many making a big impact in his native country – and now abroad. Cesario is from a strong European family and has obvious broodmare potential. *JH*

Cherry Mix (Fr)

4yo grey colt **118**

Linamix (Fr) - Cherry Moon (USA) (Quiet American (USA))

Owner Godolphin

Trainer Saeed Bin Suroor

Breeder S N C Lagardere Elevage

Career: **15** starts | won **4** | second **4** | third **2** | **£495,864** win and place

By Graham Dench

IF THE Godolphin team were hoping for another Sulamani when they bought the Prix de l'Arc de Triomphe second Cherry Mix privately from the Lagardere family at the end of 2004 they must have viewed his first four races in their colours with increasing horror. Thank heavens for the relatively easy pickings that are available at Group 1 level in Italy at the back-end.

The Prix du Jockey-Club winner Sulamani proved a superb standard bearer after he was purchased from the Niarchos family following his second to Godolphin's Marienbard in the 2002 Arc, landing Dubai's Sheema Classic on his first appearance under their tutelage and going on to win another four major internationals before his retirement.

Cherry Mix had not enjoyed success on Sulamani's level when Godolphin bought him – prior to his Group 2 success at Deauville he had gained both of his previous wins at provincial tracks – and his shock second in the Arc, in which he looked the winner when bursting clear in the last two furlongs and was only cut down late by Bago, does not look such strong form with hindsight as it did at the time. However, he had scope for improvement, and looked the type with which Godolphin can excel.

Cherry Mix could be excused his indifferent fourth to Chiquitin at Nad Al Sheba on his debut for Godolphin, as it was no secret he needed the race, and it was run over an inadequate ten furlongs on dirt. The Sheema Classic was a different matter, however, for even though the likes of Powerscourt and Phoenix Reach featured among some pretty smart opponents, he stood out on his effort in the Arc. It was back to the drawing board after he beat only his stablemate Fight Your Corner in a field of 11, with no obvious excuse.

A host of attractive opportunities went by without Cherry Mix in the summer, and more than five months had passed before he was seen in public again in the Grosser Preis von Baden. A hot favourite in a field

Photograph courtesy of Stefano Grasso

Cherry Mix (centre) scores a Group 1 win in the Gran Premio del Jockey Club, but overall he had a disappointing season

which included the Gold Cup winner Westerner, who was racing over his shortest distance in more than a year, Cherry Mix looked to have a perfect opportunity to put himself back in the picture for another crack at the Arc, but he had to make his own running. Headed with two furlongs to go, he finished only fifth behind Warrsan.

It was hardly an auspicious return to action, and one wonders if he would still have been allowed his chance in the Arc if Godolphin had another realistic candidate. However, Doyen's campaign had gone from bad to worse and they had no alternative. Incredibly, Cherry Mix went to Longchamp as Godolphin's sole representative the entire weekend.

In the build-up to the race Frankie Dettori warned punters not to overlook the colt's chance, reasoning that he is a horse who is possibly unsuited by heat and sun and that he seemed a much happier horse than he had been earlier in the year, but yet again Cherry Mix disappointed, looking a shadow of the horse that had excelled 12 months previously. He trailed home a poor 12th of 15, beating just the three rank outsiders.

There must have been a temptation for Godolphin to cut their losses and call it a day, but they were no doubt conscious of the difference a Group 1 win would make to his future as a stallion and well aware of the opportunities on offer in Italy in the autumn.

Fifty years on from the great Ribot's win in the race, the Gran Premio del Jockey Club at the San Siro is not the race it was, and if ever Cherry Mix was to win a Group 1 this was surely it.

2005 — Race record

9th Cathay Pacific Hong Kong Vase (Group 1) (Sha Tin, December 11) 3yo+ 1m4f Good to firm **115** 12 ran. *Tracked leader after 2½f, 2nd straight, hard ridden and every chance 1f out, soon beaten (L Dettori), beaten 5l by Ouija Board*

1st Gran Premio del Jockey Club (Group 1) (San Siro, October 16) 3yo+ 1m4f Soft **118** 8 ran. *Pressed leader, led over 8f out, 2 lengths clear when shaken up over 1f out, comfortably (L Dettori), beat Salutino by 2l*

12th Prix de l'Arc de Triomphe Lucien Barriere (Group 1) (Longchamp, October 2) 3yo+ 1m4f Good to soft **98** (TS 100) 15 ran. *Prominent, 2nd straight, weakened well over 1f out, eased (L Dettori), beaten 21l by Hurricane Run*

5th Grosser Volkswagen Preis von Baden (Group 1) (Baden-Baden, September 4) 3yo+ 1m4f Good **117** 9 ran. *Raced wide early, led after 1½f to 2f out, ridden over 1f out, one pace and lost 3rd close home (L Dettori), beaten 3l by Warrsan*

10th Dubai Sheema Classic Sponsored By Dubai Water Front (Turf) (Group 1) (Nad Al Sheba, March 26) 4yo+ 1m4f Good to firm **105** 11 ran. *Mid-division, ridden straight, weakened final 2f (L Dettori), beaten 10l by Phoenix Reach*

4th Sh Maktoum bin Rashid Al Maktoum Challenge RIII (Group 2) (Dirt) (Nad Al Sheba, March 5) 4yo+ 1m2f Fast **104** 10 ran. *Mid-division, 6th and ridden straight, stayed on final 1f, not reach leaders (L Dettori), beaten 6¼l by Chiquitin*

Other runs

2004 **2nd** Prix de l'Arc de Triomphe Lucien Barriere (Group 1) (Longchamp, October 3) 3yo+ 1m4f Good **128** (TS 129) 19 ran ● **1st** Grand Prix de Deauville Lucien Barriere (Group 2) (Deauville, August 29) 3yo+ 1m4½f Heavy **120** (TS 33) 7 ran ● **1st** Prix Frederic de Lagrange (Listed) (Vichy, July 24) 3yo 1m4f Holding **109** 9 ran ● **2nd** Prix Auriban (Saint-Cloud, July 4) 3yo 1m2½f Good to soft **105** (TS 41) 7 ran ● **3rd** Prix Hocquart (Group 2) (Longchamp, May 13) 3yo 1m4f Very soft **105** (TS 88) 6 ran ● **2nd** Prix Noailles (Group 2) (3yo Colts & Fillies) (Longchamp, April 11) 3yo 1m3f Good to soft **107** (TS 98) 9 ran ● **3rd** Prix Maurice Caillault (Listed) (Saint-Cloud, March 18) 3yo 1m2½f Good to soft **93** (TS 45) 8 ran **2003** **2nd** Prix de la Sorbonne (Longchamp, October 12) 2yo 1m½ Very soft 10 ran ● **1st** Prix des Carpes (Apprentices) (Maiden Colts & Geldings) (Fontainbleau, September 28) 2yo 1m Soft 12 ran

Facing seven undistinguished rivals, he was sent to the front with more than a mile to go and was never seriously troubled, winning comfortably by two lengths from the German three-year-old Salutino. Cherry Mix was evidently much more relaxed than he had been at Longchamp, and Dettori was confident throughout. He was Godolphin's 999th winner, and surely one of their most welcome of 2005, for it had been an indifferent year for the team as a whole, and not just Cherry Mix.

Shirocco went on to Breeders' Cup success the season after taking the 2004 Gran Premio del Jockey Club, but he had beaten a genuine Group 1 performer in Electrocutionist, and he was only three at the time. It is difficult to be as optimistic about Cherry Mix, who ended his season on another low. He finished only ninth behind Ouija Board when his sights were raised again for the Hong Kong Vase, and so he has it all to prove again now.

Cherry Mix

grey colt, 15-2-2001

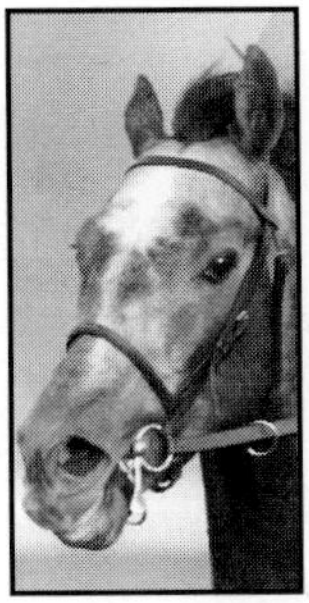

Linamix gr 1987	Mendez	Bellypha	Lyphard Belga
		Miss Carina	Caro Miss Pia
	Lunadix	Breton	Relko La Melba
		Lutine	Alcide Mona
Cherry Moon b 1995	Quiet American	Fappiano	Mr Prospector Killaloe
		Demure	Dr Fager Quiet Charm
	Datsdawayitis	Known Fact	In Reality Tamerett
		Baton Twirler	Reverse Dixie B

Bred by SNC Lagardere Elevage in France

Sire Linamix

Won 4 of 10 starts, inc. Prix La Rochette-Gr3, Prix de Fontainebleau-Gr3, Poule d'Essai des Poulains-Gr1. Also 2nd in Grand Criterium, Prix Jacques le Marois, Prix du Moulin de Longchamp and Champion Stakes (all Gr1). Big, angular, round-actioned, free-running sort; not the best of forelegs. Stands at Haras du Val Henry at a fee of E50,000. Sire of 12 crops of racing age, inc. notable winners Diamond Mix (Gr2), Housamix (Gr2), Miss Satamixa (Prix Jacques le Marois-Gr1), Walk On Mix (Gr2), Manninamix (Gr3), Clodora (Gr2), Fragrant Mix (Grand Prix de Saint-Cloud-Gr1), Oa Baldixe (Gr3), Diamonixa (Gr3), Pinmix (Gr3), Sagamix (Prix de l'Arc de Triomphe-Gr1), Amilynx (Prix Royal-Oak-Gr1, twice), Artistique (Gr3), Sage et Jolie (Gr2), Slickly (Grand Prix de Paris-Gr1, Prix du Moulin de Longchamp-Gr1, Premio Vittorio di Capua-Gr1, twice), Goldamix (Criterium de Saint-Cloud-Gr1), Miraculous (Gr3), Diamilina (Gr2), Fair Mix (Prix Ganay-Gr1), Vahorimix (Poule d'Essai des Poulains-Gr1, Prix Jacques le Marois-Gr1), Bernimixa (Gr2), Martaline (Gr2), Diasilixa (Gr3), Visorama (Gr3), Walkamia (Gr3), Cherry Mix (Gran Premio del Jockey Club-Gr1), Fracassant (Gr2), Linda Regina (Gr3), Lord du Sud (Gr2), Millemix (Gr2), Reefscape (Prix du Cadran-Gr1), Carlotamix (Criterium International-Gr1), Manbala (Gr3). Champion sire in France 1998 and 2004.

Dam Cherry Moon

Won 4 of 21 starts in North America from 2 to 4, including minor stakes at 3. Most wins at up to 8f. By top-class 9-10f dirt performer who has had just sporadic success as a sire. Half-sister to 2yo stakes winner Dawaytogold (f Candi's Gold) out of minor winner, from workmanlike family. Dam of: Cherry Mix (2001 c by Linamix; Gran Premio del Jockey Club-Gr1), Moon Mix (2003 c by Linamix; unraced).

Pedigree assessment

Cherry Mix has joined Linamix's long list of Group 1 winners, at the end of a largely disappointing season for the Godolphin colt. In common with the sire's 2005 Criterium International winner Carlotamix, Cherry Mix is out of a useful US racemare from an unspectacular family. It is a formula that worked well for Cherry Mix's breeder, Jean-Luc Lagardere. More Group 1s surely will be the target for 2006, and if Cherry Mix enhances his reputation he should find a good slot at stud in Europe, particularly as his sire is now elderly. *JH*

Collier Hill

7yo chestnut gelding **117**

Dr Devious (Ire) - Polar Queen (Polish Precedent (USA))

Owner R H Hall & Ashley Young

Trainer G A Swinbank

Breeder George Strawbridge

Career: **31** starts | won **10** | second **6** | third **4** | **£471,342** win and place

By Tom O'Ryan

GREAT game, this, for creating fairytales. Who, for instance, could possibly have predicted that a horse bought out of the bargain basement at Ascot Sales as an unraced three-year-old, and who posted his first win in a modest bumper at Catterick, would end up becoming a celebrated Classic hero?

Step forward Collier Hill, whose rise from rags to riches has been nothing short of extraordinary, and whose heady achievements have no doubt fuelled the dreams of anyone willing to take a chance on a cheap purchase, by providing spectacular proof that – just occasionally – you might stumble on a horse with hidden star quality.

That Collier Hill fits that bill is without question. His bumper win apart, he ran a further four times under National Hunt rules, winning a novices' hurdle at Kelso in December 2003, but coming up short in three further efforts that season, which included two odds-on defeats.

On the Flat, however, his career has continued to follow an upward curve throughout. His first Flat win, in May 2002, was achieved in a low-grade handicap at Ayr, where he earned himself a Racing Post Rating of 73. Contrast that with the figure of 117 he received for gloriously winning the Irish Field St Leger at The Curragh in September 2005.

Collier Hill started 2005 as a horse on the upgrade. His two wins from seven starts the previous year had comprised a Listed handicap at Hamilton in May and a Group 3 contest at Taby in September. With that, connections, led by trainer Alan Swinbank, decided to see what Dubai had to offer and, come February, Collier Hill made an immediate impact at Nad Al Sheba. Despite having invariably shown a preference for a dig in the ground previously, the seven-year-old coped admirably with the good-to-firm surface and belied his 20-1 odds by notching a handicap victory by one and a quarter lengths.

The following month, Collier Hill, raised 6lb for his earlier success,

Collier Hill (centre) completes his remarkable rise to Group 1 level with a gutsy win in the Irish St Leger

and racing off a handicap mark of 112, was beaten two lengths into fourth place in another handicap at Nad Al Sheba.

His third and final start in Dubai was in no less a contest than the Group 1 Sheema Classic at the end of March, in which Collier Hill started at 40-1. The Yorkshire challenger, however, ran a blinder. Once again tackling 12 furlongs, he was beaten just over two lengths into third by the winner Phoenix Reach, only a short head behind Razkalla, who had won Collier Hill's previous race.

Having been granted the month of April to get over his winter exertions, Collier Hill turned out in Cologne on May 1 and, sent off the 13-10 favourite, adopted unusual tactics for him in making every yard of the running and staying on strongly to win the Group 2 Gerling-Preis on soft ground.

His next outing was not until late July when he was on his travels again; this time to Dusseldorf for the Group 1 Deutschlandpreis. It was a tough test against a high-class home-team, but Collier Hill, by now as reliable as they come, ran a fine race in defeat to be beaten just under two lengths into second by Gonbarda, a nose ahead of favourite Simonas.

The Irish St Leger was his swansong for the campaign, and what a memorable outcome he delivered. All eyes were on Vinnie Roe, the local hero, who was bidding to win this all-aged Classic for an outstanding fifth time. Also in opposition were the Coronation Cup winner Yeats and the Irish Derby third Shalapour.

Collier Hill, a 10-1 chance, clearly faced a tall order, but he typically remained undaunted and, relishing the step up to a mile and three-quarters, showed great battling qualities to land the prize by half a length from

2005 Race record

1st Irish Field St Leger (Group 1) (Curragh, September 17) 3yo+ 1m6f Good **117** (TS 81) 9 ran. *Settled 5th, progress early straight, 2nd and challenged inside final furlong, stayed on well to lead close home (Dean McKeown), beat The Whistling Teal by 1/2l*

2nd Deutschlandpreis - Preis der Freunde und Forderer (Group 1) (Dusseldorf, July 24) 3yo+ 1m4f Good **117** 9 ran. *Disputed 3rd, hard ridden to lead narrowly 1 1/2f out, headed just over 1f out, just held on for 2nd (Dean McKeown), beaten 1 3/4l by Gonbarda*

1st Gerling-Preis (Group 2) (Cologne, May 1) 4yo+ 1m4f Soft **114** 7 ran. *Made all, strongly pressed 2f out, soon ridden, hard driven to assert final 100yds (Dean McKeown), beat Simonas by 3/4l*

3rd Dubai Sheema Classic Sponsored By Dubai Water Front (Turf) (Group 1) (Nad Al Sheba, March 26) 4yo+ 1m4f Good to firm **116** 11 ran. *In touch, 4th and ridden straight, stayed on well near finish (Dean McKeown), beaten 2l by Phoenix Reach*

4th Crown Promenade Hotel Trophy (Handicap) (Turf) (Nad Al Sheba, March 10) 4yo+ (100-112 handicap) 1m4f Good to firm **115** 10 ran. *Mid-division, ridden straight, progress 2f out, stayed on same pace (Dean McKeown), beaten 2l by Razkalla*

1st Elnadim Sponsored by Derrinstown Stud (Handicap) (Turf) (Nad Al Sheba, February 25) 4yo+ (90-110 handicap) 1m4f Good to firm **115** 12 ran. *Mid-division, ridden 5f out, ran on to lead 1f out, driven out (Dean McKeown), beat Corriolanus by 1 1/4l*

Other wins

2004 **1st** Stockholm Cup International (Group 3) (Taby, September 12) 3yo+ 1m4f Good to firm **110** 10 ran ● **1st** Saffie Joseph & Sons Braveheart Rated Stakes (Handicap) (Listed) (Hamilton, May 14) 4yo+ (0-110 handicap) 1m4f Good to soft **107** (TS 95) 12 ran **2003** **1st** bet365 Old Newton Cup (Handicap) (Haydock, July 5) 3yo+ (0-110 handicap) 1m4f Good **100** (TS 85) 19 ran ● **1st** Tote betXpress Handicap (Hamilton, May 4) 4yo+ (0-85 handicap) 1m5f Good to soft **94** (TS 81) 15 ran **2002** 1st McEwan's 70/- Ale Stayers Handicap (Ayr, September 21) 3yo+ (0-95 handicap) 1m5f Good **86** (TS 4) 12 ran ● **1st** St Modwen Properties Plc Apprentice Classified Stakes (Newcastle, June 5) 3yo+ (0-60) 1m4 1/2f Soft **61** 7 ran ● **1st** 'Petronella' Classified Stakes (Ayr, May 31) 3yo+ (0-60) 1m5f Good to soft **73** 9 ran

outsider The Whistling Teal, with the gallant Vinnie Roe the same margin away in third and Yeats in fourth.

It was a magical victory, not only for Collier Hill, but for trainer Swinbank, enjoying by far his biggest success, and Dean McKeown, the horse's regular jockey, who had never ever ridden in a Classic in Britain and who was thanking his lucky stars at having registered such a notable success in the twilight of his career.

The Collier Hill faiytale was forced to endure a nightmare scenario in October. Following a reported rift between his connections, the horse was sent to Tattersalls Autumn Sales in Newmarket to dissolve the ownership partnership.

Fittingly, after being knocked down for 97,000gns, he returned to Swinbank, the trainer who had originally bought him for just 5,500gns, and who has since placed him to win prize-money in excess of £470,000. "Like winning the Irish St Leger all over again," was Swinbank's understandable reaction at retaining his celebrated Classic hero.

Collier Hill *chestnut gelding, 26-3-1998*

Dr Devious ch 1989	Ahonoora	Lorenzaccio	Klairon Phoenissa
		Helen Nichols	Martial Quaker Girl
	Rose Of Jericho	Alleged	Hoist The Flag Princess Pout
		Rose Red	**Northern Dancer** Cambrienne
Polar Queen b 1992	Polish Precedent	Danzig	**Northern Dancer** Pas de Nom
		Past Example	Buckpasser Bold Example
	Rain Date	Rainbow Quest	Blushing Groom I Will Follow
		Roussalka	Habitat Oh So Fair

Bred by George Strawbridge in Britain. 3,000gns Ascot 3yo, 97,000gns Tattersalls Autumn 7yo

Sire Dr Devious

At 2, from 6 starts, won 4 over 6-7f (inc. Superlative S-L, Vintage S-Gr3, Dewhurst S-Gr1). At 3, from 9 starts, won 2 (Derby-Gr1, Irish Champion S-Gr1), also 2nd Irish Derby-Gr1. Sire high-class sprinter and very successful stallion who also was responsible for Indian Ridge. Dam also foaled Group winners Archway, Royal Court. To stud in Japan in 1993, switched to Ireland for 1997 season, exported to Italy before 2002 season. Stands at Allevamenti della Berardenga, 2005 fee €9,000. Sire of: Collier Hill (Irish St Leger-Gr1), Devious Indian (Gr3), Doc Holiday (Gr3), Duca d'Atri (Gr2), Devious Boy (Gr2), Where We Left Off (Gr3), Kinnaird (Prix de l'Opera-Gr1), Day Walker (Gr3).

Dam Polar Queen

Unraced at 2, won first (7f maiden) of 2 starts at 3.By outstanding miler who overall had fairly moderate stallion career but was capable of siring outstanding performers. Dam unraced daughter of high-class 2yo and 8-10f filly Roussalka, who is also ancestress of 1,000 Guineas winner Ameerat. Family of Oh So Sharp.Sold 3,500gns 2001 Tattersalls December Sales. Dam of: Collier Hill (1998 g by Dr Devious; Irish St Leger-Gr1), Sicamous (1999 c by Selkirk; winner in Slovakia), 2002 c by Benny The Dip, 2004 c by Sure Blade, 2005 c by Cyrano de Bergerac. In foal to Slip Anchor.

Pedigree assessment

Collier Hill and fellow Group 1 winner Kinnaird made it a notable 2005 for Dr Devious, now in Italy. Collier Hill's immediate family cannot be blamed for its paucity of good performers, for the gelding's grand-dam had two foals registered, and his dam has just three offspring of racing age. It is also not known for stayers. The gelded Collier Hill, might struggle to land another Group 1 but, with another season of astute placing, should be able to add to his black type.*JH*

Court Masterpiece

5yo bay horse **117**

Polish Precedent (USA) - Easy Option (Ire) (Prince Sabo)

Owner Maktoum Al Maktoum

Trainer E A L Dunlop

Breeder Gainsborough Stud Management

Career: **25** starts | won **6** | second **5** | third **5** | **£428,301** win and place

By Steve Dennis

WHEN Court Masterpiece finished fourth behind Iffraaj in the Victoria Cup at Lingfield on his seasonal debut in May, his connections would surely have been thrilled. In lugging 9st 10lb to an honourable defeat, he recorded his second-highest Racing Post Rating, and a big handicap looked certain to come his way, possibly even a Listed race. But a Group 1? I'll have some of what you're drinking.

The Listed race came his way two runs later at Goodwood in early June when, relishing the easy conditions, he drew off in the final furlong to beat Elliots World by nine lengths. Kieren Fallon got off and said: "I don't understand it – he's never run like that before. It was so easy. If only they were all as easy as that."

The transformation was abrupt. The sharp mile and good to soft ground proved ideal for Court Masterpiece, who had won another Listed race over course and distance almost two years earlier. He had also finished fourth to Chic in the Group 2 Celebration Mile over the same track and trip. Success can be simplified – find out what works and stick to it.

Ed Dunlop set out to maximise the potential of his newest Pattern plaything and stepped him up to Group 3 company, first at Newmarket and then at Lingfield. Each time he came off second best, and at this stage he remained nothing more than a crossover horse, one too high in the ratings for handicaps but yet to truly establish himself at Group level. There was only one thing for it. Back to Goodwood.

The Group 2 Betfair Cup, registered as the Lennox Stakes, is a johnny-come-lately of a Pattern race and its first-place prize-money of £72,500 is out of all proportion to its prestige. That prize-money lured 14 hopefuls to the Sussex Downs, including Dubai World Cup fourth Jack Sullivan. He had yet to win on turf and was sent away a 33-1 shot, but was stopped from causing a shock only by the determined late challenge of Court Masterpiece, who wrested the lead from him inside the final furlong and

Court Masterpiece (right) gets up in the dying strides to land the Group 1 Prix de la Foret at Longchamp

held on to it by a short head in the face of a renewed challenge.

If the form was dubious, Court Masterpiece's fighting spirit was not. He demonstrated it twice more in defeat, both times under his Group 2 penalty, when a game third in the Celebration Mile, won for a second year by Chic, and when third in the Park Stakes behind Iffraaj, another former handicapper making hay while the sun shone on a less than vintage bunch of seven-furlong/mile horses. Was Court Masterpiece now a better horse than 12 months earlier? Only by a pound or two, despite his black type. He had run to a near-identical level in the Celebration Mile and Park Stakes as he had in 2004, and his Lennox Stakes win could be construed as being no more than due reward for his tenacity and his trainer's opportunism in finding such a valuable soft option.

That was as nothing, however, compared to Dunlop's next trick. The Prix de la Foret at Longchamp's Arc meeting is a race of declining prestige, but it does hold Group 1 status and, run over seven furlongs on what is always likely to be softish ground, it looked a good spot for Court Masterpiece to try his luck at the highest level for the first time.

If the race was of its usual calibre, Dunlop must have reasoned, Court Masterpiece might even be placed. His hunch was rewarded with an appalling event for Group 1 standard. The Foret drew a field that wouldn't have looked out of place in a Listed contest and, as we've seen, a Listed race over seven furlongs on soft ground represents pennies from heaven for Court Masterpiece, who flashed home fast and late under Gerald Mosse to pip Caradak by a head in a blanket finish. His Racing Post Rating was identical to the one he had recorded when seeing off Elliots World at Goodwood, but this time Group 1 honours came with

2005 Race record

5th Cathay Pacific Hong Kong Mile (Group 1) (Sha Tin, December 11) 3yo+ 1m Good to firm **117** 13 ran. *Held up towards rear, 9th straight on inside, stayed on up rails but never reached challenging position (K Fallon), beaten 2½l by Hat Trick*

1st Prix de la Foret Casino Barriere de Biarritz (Group 1) (Longchamp, October 1) 3yo+ 7f Soft **117** (TS 100) 8 ran. *Held up, disputing 6th straight, good headway over 1½f out in centre, ridden and ran on well to lead on line (G Mosse), beat Caradak by hd*

3rd GNER Park Stakes (Group 2) (Doncaster, September 8) 3yo+ 7f Good to firm **117** (TS 58) 11 ran. *Stumbled start and behind, headway well over 1f out, soon ridden and kept on well final furlong, nearest finish (R L Moore), beaten 3l by Iffraaj*

3rd totesport Celebration Mile (Group 2) (Goodwood, August 28) 3yo+ 1m Good **113** (TS 78) 8 ran. *Held up in touch, tracked leaders over 2f out, not much room soon after, went 3rd final furlong but easily outpaced (P Robinson), beaten 5l by Chic*

1st Betfair Cup (Registered As The Lennox Stakes) (Group 2) (Goodwood, July 26) 3yo+ 7f Good to soft **117** (TS 95) 14 ran. *Tracked leaders, effort 2f out, ridden to lead inside final furlong, just held on (P Robinson), beat Jack Sullivan by shd*

2nd Ladbrokes Silver Trophy Stakes (Group 3) (Lingfield (AW), July 9) 4yo+ 1m Standard **115** (TS 108) 12 ran. *Held up in midfield, headway over 1f out, ran on to press winner final 75yds, just held (T E Durcan), beaten nk by Autumn Glory*

2nd Haven And British Holidays Criterion Stakes (Group 3) (Newmarket (July), June 25) 3yo+ 7f Good **115** (TS 84) 8 ran. *Held up, headway and not clear run over 1f out, ridden and every chance inside final furlong, ran on (L Dettori), beaten shd by Vortex*

1st UBS Laing & Cruickshank On The House Stakes (Listed) (Goodwood, June 3) 3yo+ 1m Good to soft **117** (TS 72) 6 ran. *Held up, smooth headway over 2f out, led over 1f out, soon clear, very easily (K Fallon), beat Elliots World by 9l*

2nd Abbey Park Conditions Stakes (Leicester, May 23) 3yo+ 7f Soft **106** (TS 68) 5 ran. *Held up, switched right and headway over 2f out, ridden to lead and edged leftinside final furlong, headed post (J P Murtagh), beaten hd by Azarole*

4th totesport Victoria Cup (Heritage Handicap) (Lingfield, May 7) 4yo+ 7f Good **116** (TS 109) 18 ran. *Dwelt, held up in centre group, going easily over 2f out, brought to near side, driven and stayed on same pace final furlong (K Fallon), beaten 3l by Iffraaj*

Other wins

2004 **1st** totesport International Stakes (Heritage Handicap) (Ascot, July 24) 3yo+ 7f Good to firm **117** (TS 107) 21 ran 2003 **1st** Vodafone Thoroughbred Stakes (Listed) (Goodwood, August 2) 3yo 1m Good **106** (TS 97) 12 ran ● **1st** Convivial Maiden Stakes (York, August 21) 2yo 6f Good **88** (TS 80) 6 ran

it, along with the increased potential for a stud career.

Dunlop now had nothing to lose, and an invitation to run in the Hong Kong Mile was swiftly snapped up. On fast ground that wouldn't have been helpful, he kept on to be nearest at the finish behind the Japanese-trained Hat Trick. Kieren Fallon confessed that the final half-furlong had found him out, but Court Masterpiece appeared to run to form again.

If he stays in training at the age of six, he is unlikely to find any further improvement, and opportunities will be limited by his Group 1 penalty. However, he has already exceeded all reasonable expectations.

Court Masterpiece

bay horse, 12-5-2000

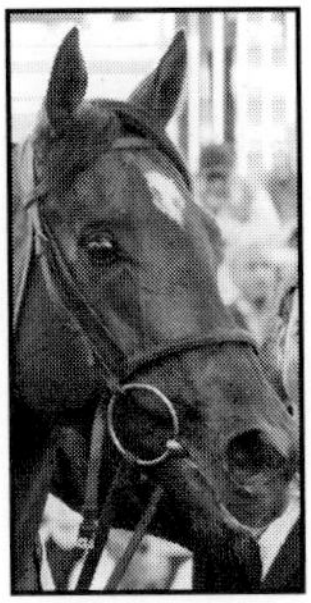

Polish Precedent b 1986	Danzig	Northern Dancer	Nearctic Natalma
		Pas de Nom	Admiral's Voyage Petitioner
	Past Example	Buckpasser	Tom Fool Busanda
		Bold Example	Bold Lad (USA) Lady Be Good
Easy Option ch 1992	Prince Sabo	Young Generation	Balidar Brig O'Doon
		Jubilee Song	Song Sylvanecte
	Brazen Faced	Bold And Free	Bold Lad (IRE) Free And Easy
		Maurine	Worden Muscida

Bred by Gainsborough Stud Management in Britain

Sire Polish Precedent

Won 7 of 9 races, inc. Prix du Palais Royal-Gr3, Prix de la Jonchere-Gr3, Prix Messidor-Gr3, Prix Jacques le Marois, Prix du Moulin de Longchamp-Gr1. Big, lengthy sort, top-class miler, inferior only to Zilzal at 3. Sire of: Red Route (Gr2), Pilsudski (Grosser Preis von Baden-Gr1, Breeders' Cup Turf-Gr1, Eclipse S.-Gr1, Irish Champion S.-Gr1, Champion S.-Gr1, Japan Cup-Gr1), Pure Grain (Irish Oaks-Gr1, Yorkshire Oaks-Gr1), Riyadian (Gr2), Predappio (Gr2), Social Harmony (Gr3), Noushkey (Gr3), Polish Summer (Gr2), Sobieski (Gr2), First Charter (Gr3), Rakti (Derby Italiano-Gr1, Premio Presidente della Repubblica-Gr1, Champion S.-Gr1, Prince of Wales's S-Gr1, Queen Elizabeth II S.-Gr1, Lockinge S.-Gr1), Court Masterpiece (Prix de la Foret-Gr1).

Dam Easy Option

At 2, won 2 (inc. St Hugh's S-L) of 3 starts. At 3, won 1 (5f) of 3 starts. At 4, placed 3 times from 5 starts inc. 2nd Prix du Gros-Chene-Gr3, also 4th Prix de l'Abbaye-Gr1. Best at 5f, lightly raced. By high-class 2yo who has done best at stud with juveniles. Half-sister to useful sprint 2yo Wanton (dam of Gr2 winner Rumpipumpy and Irish 1,000 Guineas winner Classic Park, grand-dam of Derby 2nd Walk In The Park).Dam of: Pride In Me (1998 f by Indian Ridge; winner), Maybe Forever (1999 f by Zafonic; Gr3 winner), Court Masterpiece (2000 c by Polish Precedent; Prix de la Foret-Gr1), Generous Option (2002 f by Cadeaux Genereux; winner), Easy Air (2003 c by Zafonic; unraced), 2004 f by Zamindar, 2005 c by Zamindar. Due to Cape Cross.

Pedigree assessment

Has progressed with age, in common with many of his sire's best offspring. This is basically a fast family that, with appropriate mating, can produce performers who last further, and Polish Precedent has injected a little stamina here. Court Masterpiece's pedigree is not flashy, but his late sire was renowned for the odd outstanding performer in a mixed stud career and the dam's family is strengthening with a number of recent talented performers. That, allied to the horse's own tough racing record, suggests that Court Masterpiece deserves a fair chance at stud in time. *JH*

David Junior (USA)

3yo chestnut colt **126**

Pleasant Tap (USA) - Paradise River (USA) (Irish River (Fr))

Owner Roldvale Limited

Trainer B J Meehan

Breeder A I Appleton

Career: **9** starts | won **5** | second **1** | third **1** | **£335,179** win and place

By Richard Austen

THERE is something of the boy who cried wolf about the Champion Stakes victory of David Junior. While Brian Meehan has won the last two Cheveley Parks, David Junior was the first of his three-year-olds or older horses to win a Group 1 in Britain but by no means the first to try.

For much of the season David Junior seemed a fairly typical Meehan charge, highly regarded but found wanting when let loose in the top brigade. But he kept coming back for more, and when he was given his third crack at a Group 1 prize in the Emirates Airline-sponsored Champion, he ran out the clear-cut winner.

David Junior is the most highly rated winner Meehan has sent out, well clear of the likes of Tomba, Indian Prince, Kaieteur, Tumbleweed Ridge and Bad As I Wannabe. There's the chance of better to come for this progressive colt.

He should be a superb standard bearer in 2006, Meehan's first season at Manton, which has been vacated by John Gosden, although there's always a cloud lurking over a horse as good as he is, one touched upon by Jamie Spencer in his post Champion Stakes observations.

"He'll be one hell of a horse next year," said Spencer, "and provided Godolphin don't nick him, he could make my season."

There is scope for disappointment on the latter score, however, with owner David Sullivan, the top-shelf publisher and Birmingham City owner, hitting an ominous note with his post-race comment that "there's more money in football" – shortly before being presented with the trophy by one Sheikh Mohammed.

"If Birmingham were playing today I would not have been here," continued Sullivan, who named the colt after one of his sons. "This is my 30th season owning horses and I have broken even for the last five. That is a miracle. I used to have 60 broodmares but there is even less money in that."

David Junior, ridden by champion jockey Jamie Spencer, springs a surprise in the Group 1 Champion Stakes

If he wants to balance the books for the 2006 season, for which he had four or so horses lined up "for old time's sake", Sullivan knows who to call. And he is clearly none too sentimental, for he had already sold the useful Jack Sullivan, whom he named after his other son.

Meehan characteristically picked up on David Junior's potential very early and, after two maiden races as a juvenile, he reappeared in the 2,000 Guineas. The average price of the trainer's domestic Group 1 runners since the turn of the century is 38-1, and 100-1 seemed a fair reflection of David Junior's chance.

Eleventh place did not suggest too dramatic a reappraisal was needed, but that was 11th of 19 and David Junior was beaten only about five lengths, keeping on well after trouble in running had put him towards the back just as the race began in earnest.

Listed races at Newmarket and Sandown, contrastingly, served up tepid opposition on the day and David Junior pulverised a total of nine rivals with runaway mile-and-a-quarter wins that revived hopes he could be high class at a mile. His seventh in the Sussex Stakes when returned to Group 1 company, at 11-1, seemed to dispel that notion, and second of five when 4-6 for the Rose of Lancaster Stakes at Haydock showed there were flaws back at the longer trip as well. The latter race had been a messy one, however, and his defeat of Hazyview in the Select Stakes at Goodwood in September, where he justified favouritism this time, also suggested he had more to give granted a stronger pace.

2005 Race record

1st Emirates Airline Champion Stakes (Group 1) (Newmarket, October 15) 3yo+ 1m2f Good to soft **126** (TS 113) 15 ran. *Held up, headway over 2f out, led over 1f out, driven out (J P Spencer), beat Pride by ¾l*

1st Select Racing UK On Sky 432 Stakes (Group 3) (Goodwood, September 11) 3yo+ 1m2f Good to firm **117** (TS 46) 8 ran. *Tracked leading pair, effort over 2f out, ridden to lead just over 1f out, edged right and driven out (J P Spencer), beat Hazyview by 1½l*

2nd Petros Rose of Lancaster Stakes (Group 3) (Haydock, August 6) 3yo+ 1m2½f Good to firm **112** (TS 53) 5 ran. *Held up in touch, ridden to take 2nd 1f out, no impression on winner (R Hills), beaten 3l by Notable Guest*

7th Cantor Spreadfair Sussex Stakes (Group 1) (Goodwood, July 27) 3yo+ 1m Soft **114** (TS 99) 12 ran. *Tracked leaders, ridden and effort over 2f out, hanging right after, weakened inside final furlong (R Hills), beaten 5½l by Proclamation*

1st Fink Gala Stakes (Listed) (Sandown, July 1) 3yo+ 1m2f Good **119** (TS 97) 6 ran. *Slowly into stride, held up in last pair, progress just over 2f out, led over 1f out, soon ridden clear, eased near finish, impressive (R Hills), beat Forward Move by 5l*

1st Shadwell Estate Fairway Stakes (Listed) (Newmarket, May 21) 3yo 1m2f Good **113** (TS 62) 5 ran. *Held up, headway over 4f out, led over 2f out, ridden clear approaching final furlong (R Hills), beat Hallhoo by 8l*

11th UltimatePoker.com 2,000 Guineas Stakes (Group 1) (Newmarket, April 30) 3yo 1m Good to firm **106** (TS 81) 19 ran. *Held up, ran on inside final furlong, never nearer (R Hills), beaten 5¼l by Footstepsinthesand*

2004

1st Allied Irish Bank (GB) Maiden Stakes (Ascot, September 24) 2yo 7f Good to firm **83** 5 ran

● **3rd** Brough Castle Maiden Stakes (Thirsk, September 14) 2yo 7f Good **82** (TS 77) 12 ran

The likely stronger pace was a less prominent feature of the Champion Stakes than the vastly stronger field. Alexander Goldrun, Alkaased, Oratorio and Rakti already had 14 Group 1 victories between them, while Chic, Pinson, Pride and Touch Of Land had chalked up Group 2 wins. Layman and Echo Of Light were Godolphin's chosen representatives, with Rob Roy and Maraahel joining Chic from Sir Michael Stoute's stable.

Holding David Junior up in third last, Jamie Spencer was able to ride a confident race and they crept closer on the outside from three and a half furlongs out. When the Godolphin pacemaker gave way, David Junior found himself disputing the lead with Maraahel approaching the final furlong and was swiftly in charge. He held Pride by three-quarters of a length, with Maraahel third and the favourite Oratorio, who did not get the best of runs, fourth.

The Haydock Sprint Cup and Champion Stakes were the crowning glories in Spencer's championship-winning season, one year after an Irish championship, and the perfect response following his exit from Ballydoyle. Spencer was champion-elect by Champions Day but Robert Winston had been three in front and odds-on when suffering a broken jaw in a fall in August.

David Junior

chestnut colt, 18-4-2002

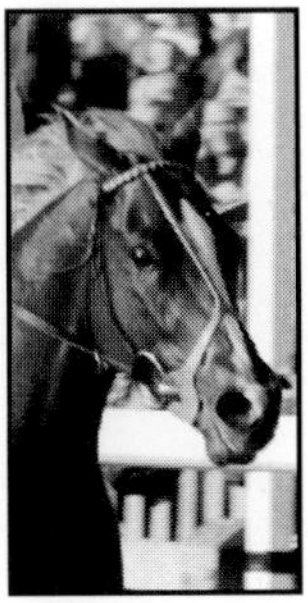

Pleasant Tap b 1987	Pleasant Colony	His Majesty	Ribot Flower Bowl
		Sun Colony	Sunrise Flight Colonia
	Never Knock	Stage Door Johnny	Prince John Peroxide Blonde
		Never Hula	**Never Bend** Hula Hula
Paradise River b 1994	Irish River	Riverman	**Never Bend** River Lady
		Irish Star	Klairon Botany Bay
	North Of Eden	Northfields	Northern Dancer Little Hut
		Tree Of Knowledge	Sassafras Sensibility

Bred by Arthur I. Appleton in Florida. Unsold $55,000 Keeneland November foal; $175,000 Fasig-Tipton Florida 2-y-o.

Sire Pleasant Tap

Won 9 of 32 races, inc. Malibu S.-Gr2, Commonwealth BC H.-Gr3, Churchill Downs H-Gr3, Suburban H.-Gr1, Jockey Club Gold Cup S.-Gr1. Also 2nd in 4 Gr1 races, inc. Breeders' Cup Sprint at 4, and Breeders' Cup Classic at 5, 3rd in Kentucky Derby. Big (16.2), quite well-made individual. Tough, sound, consistent high-class performer in all four seasons' racing, champion at five. Stands at Lane's End Farm, Versailles, Kentucky, at a fee of $10,000 (live foal). Sire of 10 crops of racing age, inc. notable winners: Lager (Gr3), Pleasant Breeze (Gr2), Tap To Music (Gazelle H.-Gr1), Sapphire N' Silk (Gr2), Tap Dance City (Japan Cup-Gr1), I Believe In You (Hollywood Starlet S.-Gr1), Palmeiro (Gr3), Tap Dance (Gr2), Tap The Admiral (Gr2), PT's Grey Eagle (Ancient Title H.-Gr1), Tap Day (Gr2), David Junior (Champion S.-Gr1).

Dam Paradise River

Ran only as a 4-y-o, placed 3rd twice (both on turf) from 7 starts. Sister to multiple Gr1 winner Paradise Creek, half-sister to Gr1 winners Wild Event (c by Wild Again) and Forbidden Apple (c by Pleasant Colony). Dam of: Blood Simple (2000 c by Kingmambo; unplaced), Boatswain (2001 c by Swain; winner), David Junior (2002 c by Pleasant Tap; Gr1 winner), Kid Carousel (2003 c by Lemon Drop Kid; unraced to date). She has a yearling colt by Theatrical ($200,000 to John McCormack Bloodstock at Keeneland September 2005).

Pedigree assessment

Pleasant Tap was a top-class runner, and an extremely versatile one in the context of American racing; at four he was runner-up in the Breeders' Cup Sprint, and 12 months later second in the Breeders' Cup Classic. He also had a Grade 2 second on turf to his credit as a two-year-old, and at five he was named the best older horse in the nation. That highly commendable record did not make him a favourite with breeders, probably because his sire had become recognised principally for stock who were not precocious and who had stamina in excess of speed. Perhaps European buyers ought to have cottoned on to his potential before. David Junior is surely his best product to date, and his Champion Stakes form clearly made him one of the best of his generation. He will surely enjoy another productive campaign in 2006. *TM*

Deep Impact (Jpn)

3yo bay colt **125**

Sunday Silence (USA) - Wind In Her Hair (Ire) (Alzao (USA))

Owner Kaneko Makoto Holdings Co Ltd

Trainer Y Ikee

Breeder Northern Farm

Career: **8** starts | won **7** | second **1** | **£3,472,988** win and place

By Nicholas Godfrey

DURING 2005, the spacecraft Deep Impact was busy exploring the galaxy, sending back information from which NASA researchers hoped to shed further light on the origins of the solar system.

You didn't need to go quite as far to locate the most spectacular Classic performer of 2005, though he, too, was called Deep Impact. A son of bloodstock legend Sunday Silence, the colt raced exclusively in Japan, but the three extraordinary performances with which he became that nation's sixth Triple Crown winner were quite simply out of this world. When he suffered his first defeat on Christmas Day, the Japanese certainly treated it as if a stellar being had suddenly crashed down to earth.

Until the unwelcome reality check provided by that half-length reverse to Japan Cup runner-up Heart's Cry in the prestigious Arima Kinen, there seemed no limit to the claims made on behalf of Deep Impact by his supporters. Here was the best horse in the history of Japanese racing, they dared to suggest, one who might even be the best racehorse on the planet.

In October, with a stunning display in the Kikuka Sho (Japanese St Leger), Deep Impact became only the second unbeaten horse to secure Japan's Triple Crown, following Symboli Rudolf in 1984, and the first of any kind since Narita Brian ten years later.

He had already attained iconic status in Japan, where he became a national hero attracting huge crowds to the racecourse. Such is his popularity that he has been made odds-on favourite for every one of his eight starts – including on the day he was beaten, when he was sent off a 1-3 chance despite being the only three-year-old racing against 15 older horses, including the exalted Zenno Rob Roy.

Even that ludicrously short price represented a value option compared to the dividend on offer on his previous outing in the Kikuka Sho. That

Photograph courtesy of Japan Racing Association

First leg of a stunning Triple Crown for Deep Impact, who wins the Japanese 2,000 Guineas in unbelievable style

day, with a multitude of fans close to hysteria clapping and cheering his every move, Deep Impact achieved a new first. Having never been sent off at a bigger price than 1-3 and winning at 1-10 on no fewer than four occasions, Deep Impact's supporters were rewarded with no profit whatsoever. Such was the level of money wagered on him that successful punters simply got their money back, a 100 yen bet yielding exactly that, 100 yen, breaking all natural rules of gambling in that while you couldn't win, theoretically you could lose.

By that stage, the deceptively unimposing colt was on the verge of achieving the seemingly impossible in terms of Japanese racing: becoming more famous than his celebrated sire, who died prematurely of laminitis at the age of 16 in 2002. Deep Impact arrived in the penultimate crop of Sunday Silence, who imbued him with his trademark attributes of agility and pace, qualities that are usually seen to best effect on faster ground. He also possesses a remarkable change of pace, often employed to dramatic effect at the end of his races, when sectional times suggested Deep Impact really did accelerate rather than simply slowing down less quickly than his rivals, as is generally the case.

Visually, he could be absolutely breathtaking, as evinced by his unforgettable victory in the Satsuki Sho, Japan's version of the 2,000 Guineas at Nakayama in April. Having won three races beforehand in more than promising fashion, the Yasuo Ikee-trained colt was already

2005 Race record

2nd Arima Kinen (The Grand Prix) (Group 1) (Nakayama, December 25) 3yo+ 1m4½f Firm **125** 16 ran. *(Y Take), beaten ½l by Heart's Cry*

1st Kikuka Sho (Japanese St Leger) (Grade 1) (Kyoto, October 23) 3yo 1m7f Firm **115** 16 ran. *Broke well, always in touch and pulling for first 5f, racing in 7th to straight, good headway to go 2nd over 1f out, driven to lead 80yds out, ran on well (Y Take), beat Admire Japan by 2l*

1st Kobe Shimbun Hai St Leger Trial (Grade 2) (Hanshin, September 25) 3yo 1m2f Firm 13 ran. *Held up towards rear, headway on final turn, 5th straight, led inside final furlong, comfortably (Y Take), beat Six Sense by 2½l*

1st Tokyo Yushun (Japanese Derby) (Grade 1) (Tokyo, May 29) 3yo 1m4f Firm **125** 18 ran. *Towards rear early, 10th straight, rapid headway 2f out, led over 1f out, ridden clear and ran on well (Y Take), beat Inti Raimi by 5l*

1st Satsuki Sho (Grade 1) (Nakayama, April 17) 3yo 1m2f Firm **119** 18 ran. *Stumbled start and lost 5 lengths, on outside and in rear until headway 4f out, 9th straight, strong run to lead inside final furlong, driven out (Y Take), beat Six Sense by 2½l*

1st Hochi Hai Yayoi Sho Stakes (Grade 2) (Nakayama, March 6) 3yo 1m2f Firm 10 ran. *Held up in 7th, headway and 3rd straight, led 1f out, ridden out with hands and heels (Y Take), beat Admire Japan by nk*

1st Wakagoma Stakes (Kyoto, January 22) 3yo 1m2f Firm 7 ran. *Held up, last at halfway, 6th straight, quickened to lead 1f out, soon clear, easily (Y Take), beat Keiai Hennessy by 5l*

2004

1st Two Year Old Newcomer (Hanshin, December 19) 2yo 1m2f Firm 9 ran

being touted as a potential superstar. In this respect, it was appropriate that he was ridden in all his races by Yutaka Take, the poster boy of Japanese racing.

What Deep Impact did to a maximum field of 18 featuring all Japan's leading three-year-old colts had to be seen to be believed. He completely overwhelmed his rivals despite stumbling on leaving the stalls, nearly losing his rider and ceding the field a five-length start. Passing the packed stands first time around after a couple of furlongs, Deep Impact was 17th of 18, before he set about circling the entire field, Take bringing him six or seven wide around the home turn. Although a handful were still in front of him a furlong and a half out, he swamped them in a matter of strides after just a couple of gentle taps to win easily from 123-1 shot Six Sense, runner-up to Ouija Board in Hong Kong at the end of the year.

This was an astounding, electrifying performance – and it was by no means a one-off, for Deep Impact's comfortable victory six weeks later in the Tokyo Yushun, the Japanese Derby, was not far removed in its brilliance. A superlative Deep Impact equalled the track record with another awe-inspiring display against 17 rivals. Slow from the gate again, he was taken wide by Take, who nudged him on after turning for home. The race was over in an instant; a nonchalant victor strolled away from second

Photograph courtesy of Japan Racing Association

Deep Impact strolls home a five-length winner of the Japanese Derby, equalling the course record in the process

favourite Inti Raimi to win by five lengths. Six Sense was two and a half lengths behind in third. Deep Impact's connections were now set on his completing the Triple Crown; after a summer break, all roads led to the Kikuka Sho at Kyoto in October. Having duly taken a Grade 2 trial at Hanshin with his signature late burst, Deep Impact was the subject of enormous attention in the run-up to the Classic and prompted scarcely credible levels of interest on the day itself.

Special programmes were broadcast on TV, newspapers ran special pullouts and columns to highlight the significance of the attempted feat, while huge numbers of reporters and photographers shadowed his every move. The attendance figure of 136,701 was a record, but it did few favours to a highly excited Deep Impact, who became unsettled by the noise. Though the field contained many of the same horses he had beaten previously, earning a slice of racing history was far from straightforward.

For once Deep Impact managed a good break but he sped into the first turn, seemingly persuaded by the roars of the crowd that it was time to go about his business. Pulling with open mouth and head high, he was close to out of control as he passed the stands before finally being settled in mid-division in a field that had become quite strung out. Rounding the home turn, Admire Japan was kicked clear in a bid to steal the race; Deep Impact moved into second, still around ten lengths behind the runaway leader. A thrilling burst of speed later, he collared the leader about 80 metres from the line and won going away by two lengths. "I gave him the go sign and he flew," said Take, who was partnering his 50th Group or Grade 1 winner. "He's the best horse in the world today."

A subsequent decision to avoid the Japan Cup was a little disappointing, though his chosen target, the 2,500-metre Arima Kinen Grand Prix, is reputed to be the most popular race in the country. The end-of-season highlight is a natural target for Japan's best horses – and in no way was the 50th renewal a soft option for Deep Impact, featuring as it did such horses as Heart's Cry, Zenno Rob Roy and Lincoln, second, third and fourth behind Alkaased in the Japan Cup.

The race garnered huge interest in Japan, where a sell-out crowd of 162,000 travelled to Nakayama in expectation of another Deep Impact cakewalk. Only Zenno Rob Roy, himself considered a superstar in his home nation, was sent off in single figures behind the odds-on favourite, before producing a tame display on his final outing before retirement.

Though he failed to produce his usual explosive brilliance, Deep Impact never really had the run of the race. As usual, Take settled him at the rear on his first outing against older horses. Although the eventual winner Heart's Cry is also famed as a come-from-behind performer, his rider Christophe Lemaire adopted a much more prominent position than usual on the four-year-old, a tactic that looked a masterstroke when a tepid pace ensued.

Having started to improve midway through the race, Deep Impact was forced to challenge seven or eight horses wide turning for home. When Heart's Cry hit the front just over a furlong out, Deep Impact was only a length down, out wider on the track. For the first time in his life, though, there was no jet propulsion, more of a grinding effort that saw him closest at the line, still a half-length behind.

Sent off just over 16-1 fourth choice in the market, an outstanding victor was greeted not with the cheers he deserved, but virtual silence as the crowd mourned their fallen hero. Take accepted a degree of culpability. "The horse was good enough to win and I feel responsible," he said. "It just goes to show that I have a lot more to prove because I couldn't get the job done. But today he didn't fly like he did in the past races, he just ran."

Perhaps, though, it wasn't quite time to don the sackcloth and ashes. Developing an emotional attachment to a racehorse is one of the joys of the sport, but while it could hardly be anything other than disappointing that Deep Impact failed to sprint past Heart's Cry, a sober reading of the bare form still marks him out as one of the best horses in the world, deserving of a rating in the mid-120s on a line through the winner's Japan Cup form, not too far adrift of Hurricane Run and with similarly abundant potential as he matures.

Even brilliant racehorses get beaten sometimes, and the good news is that Deep Impact is scheduled to stay in training in 2006 with the Arc as his ultimate target. Then we might find out how good he really is. Though no longer unbeaten, he is pretty special.

Deep Impact

bay colt, 25-3-2002

Sunday Silence br 1986	Halo	Hail To Reason	Turn-to Nothirdchance
		Cosmah	Cosmic Bomb Almahmoud
	Wishing Well	Understanding	Promised Land Pretty Ways
		Mountain Flower	Montparnasse Edelweiss
Wind In Her Hair b 1991	Alzao	Lyphard	Northern Dancer Goofed
		Lady Rebecca	Sir Ivor Pocahontas
	Burghclere	Busted	Crepello Sans le Sou
		Highclere	Queens Hussar Highlight

Bred by Northern Farm in Japan. 70,000,000 yen JRHA Select Foal Sale in Japan

Sire Sunday Silence

Won 9 (6-10f) of 14 races. At 2, won 1 of 3 starts. At 3, won 7 (inc. San Felipe H-Gr2, Santa Anita Derby-Gr1, Kentucky Derby-Gr1, Preakness S-Gr1, Super Derby-Gr1, Breeders' Cup Classic-Gr1) of 9 starts, also 2nd Belmont S-Gr1. At 4, won 1 (Californian S-Gr1) of 2 starts. By smart turf performer and very good US sire, out of a US stakes winner. Retired to Shadai Stallion Station in Japan, died August 2002. First foals 1992, sire of Gr1 winners (northern hemisphere foals): Dance Partner, Fuji Kiseki, Genuine, Marvelous Sunday, Tayasu Tsuyoshi, Bubble Gum Fellow, Dance In The Dark, Ishino Sunday, Silence Suzuka, Stay Gold, Special Week, Admire Vega, Stinger, To The Victory, Agnes Flight, Air Shakur, Cheers Grace, Believe, Manhattan Cafe, Mejiro Bailey, Admire Max, Durandal, Gold Allure, Admire Groove, Heavenly Romance, Neo Universe, Peace Of World, Still In Love, Zenno Rob Roy, Dance In The Mood, Daiwa El Cielo, Daiwa Major, Hat Trick, Heart's Cry, Suzuka Mambo, Air Messiah, Deep Impact. Also sire of European Group winners Sunday Picnic (Gr3), Silent Honor (Gr3), Layman (Gr3), Sundrop (Gr3)

Dam Wind In Her Hair

At 2, placed over 7f from 2 starts. At 3, won 2 (both 10f Listed) of 6 starts, also 2nd Oaks. At 4, won 1 (Aral Pokal-Gr1) of 5 starts, also 3rd Yorkshire Oaks-Gr1. Half-sister to Gr3 winner Capo di Monte. Dam useful middle-distance filly, very closely related to top-class 12f filly Height Of Fashion (dam of Nayef, Nashwan, Unfuwain) out of Prix de Diane winner Highclere. Dam of: Glint In Her Eye (1996 f by Arazi; unplaced), Veil Of Avalon (1997 f by Thunder Gulch; Gr3 winner), Lady Blond (1998 f by Seeking The Gold; winner), Stars In Her Eyes (1999 c by Woodman; placed), Like The Wind (2000 f by Danehill; unraced), Black Tide (2001 c by Sunday Silence; Japanese Gr2 winner), Deep Impact (2002 c by Sunday Silence; Japanese Triple Crown winner), On Fire (2003 c by Sunday Silence; placed).

Pedigree assessment

The appositely named Deep Impact is due to be seen in action outside Japan in 2006, though his influence has already been felt outside his native country. At Keeneland in November, his half-sister Glint In Her Eye (in foal to Empire Maker) was sold for $1,050,000, a sum that had much to do with her half-brother (and a little to do with her second foal, 2005 Listed-placed juvenile Jeremy). Deep Impact, by an outstanding and much-missed sire out of a mare from an excellent middle-distance family, is certain to draw great support when he does retire to stud. *JH*

Divine Proportions (USA)

3yo bay filly **123**

Kingmambo (USA) - Myth To Reality (Fr) (Sadler's Wells (USA))

Owner Niarchos Family

Trainer P Bary

Breeder Flaxman Holdings Limited

Career: **10** starts | won **9** | second **0** | third **0** | **£907,630** win and place

By Lee Mottershead

THE French are a wonderful people, blessed with comfortable trains, the world's most uplifting national anthem and crusty bread to die for. They do, however, have their own singular traits and bijou peculiarities. They are, for example, more than a little partial to a good riot; they have an unquenchable thirst for industrial action; they positively gorge themselves on the smelliest cheeses and, between five and seven each evening, or so they would have us believe, they almost all indulge in the country's favourite pastime, extra-marital nookie. And, on top of all that, they – and here we focus on the French racing community – do love to come out with a tasty superlative.

Perhaps because the French, by and large, are not weighed down by old-fashioned English reserve, they are prone to eulogise left, right and centre. Sometimes the horses are just so special that those who own, train or ride them can appear to be on the verge of spontaneously combusting when asked about the latest dazzling display. For proof positive, one need look no further than Divine Proportions.

There had been plenty said about Divine Proportions during a sparkling two-year-old campaign. After her second career success at Chantilly, trainer Pascal Bary described her as "lovely and progressive", while in the aftermath of her next victory at Maisons-Laffitte, he called her a "true professional". Her Prix Morny triumph led to Bary hailing her "truly a top-class performer" and he topped that with a "fantastic" after the Prix Marcel Boussac. There was more to come at three.

At various stages in 2005, either Bary, rider Christophe Lemaire or Niarchos family spokesman Alan Cooper used the following superlatives to describe Divine Proportions: "extraordinary", "breathtaking", "formidable" (possibly in French or English, take your pick), "a phenomenon", "a dream", "a champion", "super", "something special", "in a different class", "absolutely magnificent" and "really quite good"

Christophe Lemaire is able to take things easy in the closing stages as Divine Proportions wins the Pouliches

(sorry, made the last one up). According to Lemaire, she may well have had "four lungs", but he was adamant that she possessed "a monstrous amount of gas". All that and a pretty white face too.

However, while we have no need to challenge Lemaire on the gas front, there was one thing said about Divine Proportions that can be cast aside without any sense of uncertainty. Taking the employment of superlatives to the level of the ridiculous, Bary claimed that his leading lady was "the best" since Sea-Bird. Thankfully, he later suggested that he had done so with tongue firmly in cheek. That's just as well, for even Divine Proportions' most devoted fans would laugh at such a comparison. They would, though, tell you there was no better three-year-old filly in her generation. And they would be right.

But just how good was she? We had hoped to get an early chance of finding out in the 1,000 Guineas. Not surprisingly, the home-bred daughter of Kingmambo went into winter quarters as favourite for the premier mile fillies' Classic. A precedent had been set two years earlier when Bary and the Niarchos family had been responsible for the Guineas favourite, Six Perfections, a filly who possessed a similar juvenile profile to Divine Proportions. However, another precedent had been set by Six Perfections' Newmarket excursion. For she suffered a nightmare passage, seemingly being taken across most of the heath en route to finishing second behind Russian Rhythm. As such, it was not the greatest shock

2005 Race record

4th Prix du Haras de Fresnay-le-Buffard-Jacques le Marois (Group 1) (Deauville, August 14) 3yo+ 1m Good to soft **114** (TS 107) 6 ran. *Held up in 4th, headway over 1½f out, ridden over 1f out, soon beaten (C P Lemaire), beaten 4¾l by Dubawi*

1st Prix d'Astarte (Group 1) (Straight Course) (Deauville, July 31) 3yo 1m Good to soft **121** (TS 117) 10 ran. *Held up in 9th, headway when momentarily short of room towards outside 1½f out, led 1f out, ran on strongly (C P Lemaire), beat Shapira by 2l*

1st Prix de Diane Hermes (Group 1) (Chantilly, June 12) 3yo 1m2½f Good **120** (TS 114) 10 ran. *Always close up, 3rd straight, left in lead 2½f out, ridden 1½f out, clear 1f out, ran on well (C P Lemaire), beat Argentina by 3l*

1st Gainsborough Poule d'Essai des Pouliches (Group 1) (Grande Piste) (Longchamp, May 15) 3yo 1m Soft **123** (TS 121) 8 ran. *Soon pressing leader, settled disputing 2nd after 1½f, 2nd straight, led 2f out, quickened clear from 1 ½f out, easily (C P Lemaire), beat Toupie by 5l*

1st Prix de la Grotte (Group 3) (Longchamp, April 24) 3yo 1m Very soft **117** (TS 78) 9 ran. *In touch, 4th towards outside straight, shaken up 1½f out, quickened to challenge over 1f out, led 150yds out, ran on well (C P Lemaire), beat Ysoldina by 2l*

2004

1st Prix Marcel Boussac Royal Barriere Deauville (Group 1) (Longchamp, October 3) 2yo 1m Good **114** (TS 111) 10 ran ● **1st** Prix Morny Casinos Barriere (Group 1) (Deauville, August 22) 2yo 6f Very soft **117** (TS 117) 9 ran ● **1st** Prix Robert Papin (Group 2) (Maisons-Laffitte, July 25) 2yo 5½f Good **103** (TS 76) 8 ran ● **1st** Prix du Bois (Group 3) (Chantilly, June 28) 2yo 5f Good **111** (TS 100) 7 ran ● **1st** Prix Chateau Bouscat (Unraced) (Maisons-Laffitte, May 26) 2yo 5f Good to soft **80** 9 ran

to discover that Divine Proportions would stay at home to tackle the French 1,000 Guineas.

If the memory of what happened to Six Perfections was at the root of the decision, it was not mentioned. Instead, it was said that Divine Proportions had been slow to come to hand, and so would benefit from running in the domestic Classic, held two weeks later than the British original. Even so, she was deemed sufficiently ready to make her seasonal reappearance seven days before the 1,000 Guineas would be run. The Group 3 Prix de la Grotte was selected as her first port of call.

The Grotte, run over the same Longchamp mile as the Marcel Boussac and Poule d'Essai des Pouliches, was not expected to place excessive demands on Divine Proportions, and it did not. However, it confirmed she had lost none of her ability. Understandably a shade keen on her return, she still reserved more than enough energy for the business end of the race, leading 150 yards out before running out a two-length winner from Ysoldina. The unbeaten record had been maintained, and there was now no doubt whatsoever who would start favourite for the Pouliches.

Not only did Divine Proportions start favourite for the French Guineas, she started the sort of red-hot favourite that is almost unheard of in a major European Classic. On British industry prices, she was 2-7, while on the French pari-mutuel she was considerably shorter. So frightening

Divine Proportions lands her second Classic in the Diane, her task having been made easier by Vadawina's injury

was the filly's reputation that only seven horses – none of whom were shorter than 10-1 – took her on.

It is impossible to overstate how easily Divine Proportions won. She treated her opponents with nothing less than disdain, unleashing a bravura performance, the ease of which one could scarcely believe. Never off the bridle, even after being sent to the front early in the straight, she sauntered home, oozing class. "She has made herself into a star," said Cooper, while Lemaire noted that "Divine Proportions has never been put under pressure in any of her seven races". You couldn't really argue with either of them.

The Prix de Diane seemed certain to represent a harder test. For a start, Divine Proportions was facing by some way her stiffest stamina test after connections decided not to send her to Britain for the Coronation Stakes. Just as relevant, she was arguably about to face her sternest ever challenger in Vadawina, the runaway winner of the Group 1 Prix Saint-Alary. This would not be easy.

It was easy. Yes, her task was facilitated by Vadawina incurring what would be a career-ending injury, but this was still a beautifully sweet tour de force. In front early in the straight, she never looked in the remotest danger of being beaten thereafter. Like Peintre Celebre in the 1997 Prix de l'Arc de Triomphe, she visibly quickened twice inside the final three furlongs, once to go clear, then once more to go further clear. It was a breathtaking exhibition of consummate brilliance. The winning time was the fastest for the race in 20 years.

Even more pertinently, Divine Proportions had done what the greatest filly ever to carry the Niarchos colours had not. Miesque had been beaten in the Diane. Divine Proportions won it. A link with history had been made, and it was a link that showed Divine Proportions in a most favourable light.

It was after the Diane that Bary made his famous Sea-Bird reference. Ironically, though, Divine Proportions never quite seemed the same filly again, at least not in the heat of competitive action. The first sign that all might not be well came in the Prix d'Astarte. For, although the filly would land her fifth Group 1 triumph in the Deauville event, she did so without ever really catching fire. To be fair to her, she was at one point short of room, but even when she went to win her race, it was more workmanlike than brilliant.

But Bary had not lost the faith, and nor had punters. After a workout five days before the Prix Jacques le Marois, a race sponsored by the Niarchos family, Divine Proportions was described as being in "impeccable condition" by her trainer. She would need to be, for her rivals included runaway Queen Anne Stakes winner Valixir, Irish 2,000 Guineas victor Dubawi and the previous weekend's Prix Maurice de Gheest first Whipper. She was sent off 5-6 favourite to beat them all, but she beat none of them. The early stages went as one would have wanted them to go, and she appeared dangerous when looming large just inside the quarter-mile pole, but then there was nothing. The dazzling acceleration, the change of pace, the victory were all missing. For the first time in her life, she had been defeated, her fourth place not what had been expected.

And that was that. Two weeks later plans to send her to the Breeders' Cup Mile were abandoned when she was retired, the announcement coming alongside a revelation that she had suffered a tendon injury in the Marois. Bary was dejected but relieved at the same time. "The news is very hard to take," he said, "but it does give us an explanation for her disappointing run at Deauville."

Three months after her retirement, Divine Proportions was declared champion three-year-old filly at the season-end Cartier Awards. She deserved the accolade. At the time, though, she had an official international rating of only 122, a mark 2lb below triple Melbourne Cup heroine Makybe Diva. On Racing Post Ratings, her best effort, in the Pouliches, only merited a figure of 123. As a mark of comparison, Dubawi posted an RPR of 128 in the Marois, while Shawanda was deemed to have matched Divine Proportions' personal best when netting the Irish Oaks. One season earlier, Ouija Board had run to an RPR of 124 when landing the Epsom Oaks. Perspective is a calming influence.

Divine Proportions never raced outside France, never won anything but a fillies' race and, on the one occasion she met the boys, she sank. On form figures she was no wonder woman, and certainly not in the same league as Miesque, even if she did win the Diane and Miesque did not. But so what? Visually she was stunning – a filly with "a monstrous amount of gas" and an inordinate amount of ability.

Divine Proportions *bay filly, 13-3-2002*

Parents	Grandparents	Great-grandparents	Great-great-grandparents
Kingmambo b 1990	Mr Prospector	Raise A Native	Native Dancer
			Raise You
		Gold Digger	Nashua
			Sequence
	Miesque	Nureyev	**Northern Dancer**
			Special
		Pasadoble	Prove Out
			Santa Quilla
Myth To Reality b 1986	Sadler's Wells	**Northern Dancer**	Nearctic
			Natalma
		Fairy Bridge	Bold Reason
			Special
	Millieme	Mill Reef	Never Bend
			Milan Mill
		Hardiemma	Hardicanute
			Grand Cross

Bred by Flaxman Holdings Ltd in Kentucky

Sire Kingmambo

Won 5 of 13 races, inc. Poule d'Essai des Poulains-Gr1, St James's Palace S.-Gr1, Prix du Moulin-Gr1). Among the best milers of his generation. Sire of: American Boss (Gr2), El Condor Pasa (NHK Mile Cup-Gr1, Japan Cup-Gr1, Grand Prix de Saint-Cloud-Gr1), Mambo Twist (Gr3), Parade Ground (Gr2), Admire Mambo (Gr2), Lemon Drop Kid (Futurity S.-Gr1, Belmont S.-Gr1, Travers S.-Gr1, Whitney S.-Gr1, Woodward H.-Gr1), Monarch's Maze (Gr2), Bluemamba (Poule d'Essai des Pouliches-Gr1), King Cugat (Gr2), Kingsalsa (Gr3), King's Best (2,000 Guineas-Gr1), Parade Leader (Gr2), Penny's Gold (Gr3), King Fidelia (Gr3), Malhub (Golden Jubilee S.-Gr1), Okawango (Grand Criterium-Gr1), Voodoo Dancer (Garden City H.-Gr1), Dubai Destination (Queen Anne S.-Gr1), Walzerkonigin (Gr2), Alkaased (Grand Prix de Saint-Cloud-Gr1, Japan Cup-Gr1), Governor Brown (Gr3), Russian Rhythm (1,000 Guineas-Gr1, Coronation S.-Gr1, Nassau S.-Gr1, Lockinge S.-Gr1), Illustrious Miss (Gr3), Mambo Slew (Gr3), Notable Guest (Gr3), Rule Of Law (St Leger S.-Gr1), Tarfah-Gr3), Divine Proportions (Prix Morny-Gr1, Prix Marcel Boussac-Gr1, Poule d'Essai des Pouliches-Gr1, Prix de Diane-Gr1, Prix d'Astarte-Gr1), Virginia Waters (1,000 Guineas-Gr1).

Dam Myth To Reality

Won 4 of 14 races, inc. 3 Listed. Good, consistent, mostly provincial performer, well suited by 12f, runner-up in Gr3 Prix Minerve. By the outstanding sire of the age out of a placed full-sister to Derby winner Shirley Heights. Dam of: Sonofogy (1992 g by Ogygian; winner), Magic Spin (1993 f by Lord Avie; winner), Assos (1994 g by Alleged; Listed winner), Mambo Jambo (1995 f by Kingmambo; winner, dam of Gr1-placed Ocean Silk), Fireinthewind (1996 c by Alleged; winner), Indigo Myth (1997 g by Kingmambo; Listed-placed winner), Meteorite Sun (1998 g by Miesque's Son; winner), Whipper (2001 c by Miesque's Son; triple Gr1 winner), Divine Proportions (2002 f by Kingmambo; five-time Gr1 winner), Anse Victorin (2003 f by Mt Livermore; unraced to date). She has a yearling colt by Lemon Drop Kid.

Pedigree assessment

Divine Proportions' invincibility was never soundly based. Her dominance of France's distaff milers didn't make her great, and in the Diane Vadawina was going just as well when she suffered her injury. She clearly did not run to her form when finally beaten in the Marois, but her best had never matched up to the best displayed by Dubawi. Still, her sharp turn of foot had always served her admirably among the fillies, and she will be a valuable broodmare for the Niarchos interests. *TM*

Donna Blini

2yo chestnut filly **110**

Bertolini (USA) - Cal Norma's Lady (Ire) (Lyphard's Special (USA))

Owner Mrs T S M Cunningham

Trainer B J Meehan

Breeder James Thom and Sons

Career: **4** starts | won **3** | second **1** | **£154,981** win and place

By Graham Dench

THE YEAR 2006 will mark the start of an exciting new chapter in the life of Brian Meehan, who moves from Newlands Stables in Upper Lambourn to the Sangster family's superb Manton training complex near Marlborough.

Meehan has big shoes to fill, for Barry Hills, Peter Chapple-Hyam and most recently John Gosden sent out a steady stream of top-class winners from the estate over the last 20 years, among them Classic winners like Sir Harry Lewis, Rodrigo de Triano, Dr Devious, Turtle Island, Spectrum, Lahan and Zenda. However, Meehan's own career has been on a upward curve ever since he set out on his own in 1993 after six years assisting his mentor Richard Hannon, and he is unlikely to let the side down.

He is expected to start with at least 130 horses in his care, and two of them are already Group 1 winners, Donna Blini and David Junior having helped him towards his most successful season yet with wins in the Sky Bet Cheveley Park Stakes and the Emirates Airline Champion Stakes respectively, shortly before the announcement of the move.

Gosden enjoyed Classic glory in his first season at Manton in 2000 through Lahan, who won the 1,000 Guineas despite a preparation repeatedly hampered by the weather, with 12 inches of rain falling on the estate in March alone, and four work days reportedly being lost through snow. Meehan, who is still awaiting his first taste of success at that level, will be taking Lahan's victory as a good omen, for the Guineas will be his first big target with Donna Blini.

However, while Donna Blini went into winter quarters with stronger juvenile form than Lahan, she looks less certain to appreciate the longer trip and she will have a worrying trend to buck. For the last Cheveley Park winner to win the Guineas was Sayyedati in 1993, and she of course was a rare talent.

Donna Blini stretches out to crown her first season with victory in the Group 1 Cheveley Park Stakes at Newmarket

Arguably of even greater concern is the fact that none of the intervening 12 winners has gone on to win a major prize of any description at three, the latest to disappoint having been Donna Blini's own stablemate Magical Romance, whose season went from bad to worse after she finished only in mid-division in the French 1,000 Guineas and the Oaks. Indeed, while the 1998 Cheveley Park winner Wannabe Grand went agonisingly close in the Guineas, it is placed fillies such as Harayir and Russian Rhythm who have the better record in recent times.

Donna Blini did not cause quite such a shock as Magical Romance had in the Cheveley Park, but she was only fifth favourite in a market dominated by Flashy Wings and Nidhaal, having been off the track since July. Her jockey Mick Kinane was also returning from a long absence, for the filly was his first ride since he fractured his right wrist in two places in August.

Donna Blini was understandably a shade keen after her layoff, but if Kinane was at all rusty it did not show, as he was as cool as ever. He kept Donna Blini much handier than favourite Flashy Wings behind the pace set by rank outsider Dizzy Dreamer, and he pinched a handy advantage when asking the filly to quicken to the front with more than a furlong to go.

However, Donna Blini had only just enough left to hold the challenges of Wake Up Maggie and Flashy Wings by a neck and the same, and although Kinane is optimistic that she will stay further, it was a performance that tended to confirm that speed is her most potent weapon. Indeed

2005 **Race record**

1st Sky Bet Cheveley Park Stakes (Group 1) (Newmarket, September 29) 2yo 6f Good **110** (TS 95) 10 ran. *Tracked leader, raced keenly, led over 1f out, driven out (M J Kinane), beat Wake Up Maggie by nk*

1st Chippenham Lodge Stud Cherry Hinton Stakes (Group 2) (Newmarket (July), July 5) 2yo 6f Good **100** (TS 93) 8 ran. *Made virtually all, driven out (M J Kinane), beat Salut d'Amour by nk*

2nd Hilary Needler Trophy (Listed) (Beverley, June 1) 2yo 5f Good **94** (TS 70) 12 ran. *Chased leaders far side, headway well over 1f out, soon ridden, chased winner inside final furlong, kept on (J Fortune), beaten 1l by Clare Hills*

1st toteexacta EBF Maiden Fillies' Stakes (Newmarket, May 7) 2yo 5f Good **73** (TS 49) 9 ran. *Went left start, chased leader, led over 1f out, ran on well, eased near finish (L Dettori), beat Aliceinwonderland by 1¼l*

many will be fancying the strong-finishing Flashy Wings to turn the tables if they meet again in the Guineas.

Kinane said afterwards: "I was delighted to get a lead and I was going the pace I wanted to be going. I was always happy with her. She was a shade fresh, but I knew when we quickened we were going to take some pegging back. She's scopey enough to get further. She's pacy and relaxes to give herself every opportunity."

Donna Blini had begun her career on the same course, when a good winner of a maiden that did not turn out particularly well, and she had gone on to Beverley for the Listed Hilary Needler Stakes with plenty going for her, not least the plum draw. She met her only defeat there, going down by a length to Clare Hills in a race that failed to conform to the typical Beverley sprint blueprint – although she eventually crossed over, the winner was one of several to race up the nearside – but nevertheless showing improved form.

Meehan opted to miss Royal Ascot at York, where his filly would have had the option of either the Queen Mary Stakes or the Albany, and that decision paid off when Donna Blini was next seen back at Newmarket in the Chippenham Lodge Stud-sponsored Cherry Hinton Stakes. With Kinane on board for the first time, she made the most of her draw, quickly grabbing the rail from stall two and making just about all before holding on gamely from the Queen Mary second Salut d'Amour and the Albany fourth Spinning Queen in another finish of necks.

The seven-furlong Rockfel Stakes was nominated afterwards as a possible autumn target for Donna Blini, but Meehan evidently had a change of heart, for when she did eventually reappear in the Cheveley Park Stakes he explained her absence by saying: "She hasn't run since the Cherry Hinton as there wasn't an awful lot for her and we did not want to go beyond six furlongs."

Not exactly the ringing endorsement of her stamina that ante-post punters might have been hoping for.

Donna Blini

chestnut filly, 27-3-2003

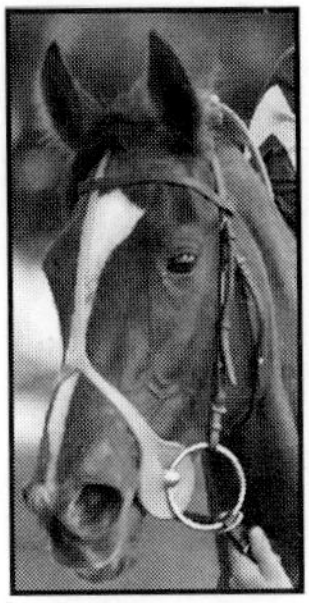

Bertolini b 1996	Danzig	**Northern Dancer**	Nearctic Natalma
		Pas de Nom	Admirals Voyage Petitioner
	Aquilegia	Alydar	Raise A Native Sweet Tooth
		Courtly Dee	Never Bend Tulle
Cal Norma's Lady b 1988	Lyphard's Special	Lyphard	**Northern Dancer** Goofed
		My Bupers	Bupers Princess Revoked
	June Darling	Junius	Raja Baba Solid Thought
		Beau Darling	Darling Boy Fair Astronomer

Bred by James Thom and sons in Britain. 20,000gns Doncaster St Leger yearling

Sire Bertolini

Won 2 of 23 starts from 2 to 5. At 2, won 1 (July S-Gr3) of 7 starts over 6-7f, also 2nd Prix Robert Papin-Gr2, Middle Park S-Gr1. At 3, won 1 (European Free Hcap-Listed) of 7 starts, also 2nd Haydock Sprint Cup-Gr1, 3rd Jersey S-Gr3, July Cup-Gr1, Prix Maurice de Gheest-Gr1. At 4, from 6 starts, 2nd Dubai Golden Shaheen-Listed, Nunthorpe S-Gr1, 3rd King's Stand S-Gr2. At 5, from 3 starts, 3rd Golden Shaheen-Gr3. Superbly bred, by outstanding sprint sire out of Gr2 turf winner. Aquilegia full-sister to 1983 North American champion 2yo filly Althea (grand-dam of Gr1 winners Arch, Balletto) and Gr2 winner Aishah, and half-sister to several other stakes winners and to Foreign Courier (dam of Green Desert). First (British-conceived) foals 2003. Stood at Overbury Stud until 2005, standing in 2006 at Kildangan Stud, fee €15,000. Sire of: Bow Bridge (Listed), Donna Blini (Cheveley Park S-Gr1), Tabaret (Listed).

Dam Cal Norma's Lady

Won 3 of 17 starts. At 2, won 3 (6-7f) of 6 starts. At 3, 2nd once over 7f from 4 starts. At 4, unraced. At 5, 3rd once over 9f from 7 starts. Modest, ran off 94 at 2 but later rated in the 40s. Sire high-class 2yo/8-12f performer who made little mark at stud. Dam unraced grand-daughter of high-class 2yo/8-10f filly Fair Astronomer, also ancestress of Gr1 winners Anka Germania, Deputy Commander, Lord Grillo, Malhub, Mourjane. Dam of: Under Pressure (1994 f by Keen; winner), Magical (1995 c by Magic Ring; Gr3 winner), Sabre Lady (1997 f by Sabrehill; winner), Dundonald (1999 g by Magic Ring; winner), Jordans Elect (2000 g by Fleetwood; winner), Bijou Dan (2001 g by Bijou d'Inde; winner), Donna Blini (2003 f by Bertolini; Cheveley Park S-Gr1), 2005 f by Averti.

Pedigree assessment

This pedigree, if read without knowledge of the holder, suggests a fairly precocious individual who might just last 1m but probably will be better at shorter and has a good chance of being a sprinter. Donna Blini, from a hitherto low-key branch of a good family, has 'outrun' her pedigree in class terms, but it could well be a good indicator in stamina terms. Physically, she looks likely to be more than a one-season wonder, but it would be no surprise to see her contesting sprints in her 3yo season. *JH*

Dubawi (Ire)

3yo bay colt **128**

Dubai Millennium - Zomaradah (Deploy)

Owner Godolphin

Trainer Saeed Bin Suroor

Breeder Darley

Career: **8** starts | won **5** | second **1** | third **1** | **£699,341** win and place

By Richard Austen

THERE is a centuries-old bond between man and horse that underpins the sport but often gets obscured. The romance is not always so evident in the era of banded racing at one end of the scale, and in the domination of a handful of bloodstock empires at the other.

On October 19, 2005, Godolphin registered their 1,000th win worldwide. Their 2005 season, however, was largely about one horse and a reminder that its owner's involvement in the sport is not merely that of a rich man seeking entertainment from his hobby, or a repeated test of just what money can buy. Success in horseracing has been a long-running advert for Dubai, but with Sheikh Mohammed and the Godolphin racehorse Dubawi there was something very personal.

What can make one horse special to a man who has been associated with thousands of them? It's simple – Dubawi is a son of Dubai Millennium, Sheikh Mohammed's paragon among racehorses. The Sheikh was present throughout the operation on Dubai Millennium's fractured leg that saved him for stud, and there again as his best among the thousands fought in vain against a rare disease only the next year. He was there too for the autopsy.

Dubai Millennium had just 54 living foals and Sheikh Mohammed set about recruiting as many under the Maktoum banner as was possible and desirable. That meant all but four. Seven-figure cheques were reputedly flying hither and thither, so spare a thought for Palides Investments, who had a foal share with Darley in their colt, but bought out Darley's share at auction, for $1.6 million, and have yet to see him run.

Others who kept their Dubai Millenniums were Khalid Abdullah, with the useful Quickfire, the Britton House Stud, whose Carisolo won a maiden in the USA in December, and Lordship Stud, whose Blessing was unraced in France.

Dubawi (right) puts up his best performance of the year with victory over Whipper in the Prix Jacques le Marois

Three years on from the sire's death, as his progeny got ready for the track, Sheikh Mohammed desperately wanted to recognise the father in his sons, for others to recognise him, and for one of those sons to prove good enough to stand in Dubai Millennium's box at Dalham Hall.

Four years on and there turned out to be only one viable candidate. Ten had won for them before Godolphin packed their bags for winter quarters in Dubai, but the unbeaten Dubawi, the first to make the racecourse, would be the only significant Classic contender.

Dubawi had the look of his sire, albeit in a much more compact version. Winning the National Stakes in style had taken him to the fore in betting for the Guineas and Derby, and his chance for the former received a huge boost when Shamardal, Godolphin's recent draft and the top-rated two-year-old in Europe, was prepared instead for the Kentucky Derby. That plan crashed and burned in the UAE Derby but Shamardal was not rerouted to the Rowley Mile.

Breezing home many lengths in front in his trial at Nad Al Sheba showed, contrastingly, that Dubawi's wellbeing was in no doubt and when he lined up at Newmarket on April 30 he was 11-8 favourite against 18 rivals.

Sheikh Mohammed's willing it to happen was not enough and Dubawi's Guineas challenge ended not in victory, but in fifth place to Footstepsinthesand, representing archrivals Coolmore and one of Coolmore's own first-season sires, Giant's Causeway.

"In 18 years of my career I don't think I've been so nervous," said Frankie Dettori, Sheikh Mohammed's jockey, afterwards. "It's a shame

2005 Race record

2nd Queen Elizabeth II Stakes sponsored by Barclays plc (Group 1) (Newmarket, September 24) 3yo+ 1m Good **121** (TS 96) 6 ran. *Raced centre, held up, switched left and headway to join stands' side group 2f out, soon ridden and every chance, unable to quicken near finish (L Dettori), beaten 3/4l by Starcraft*

1st Prix du Haras de Fresnay-le-Buffard-Jacques le Marois (Group 1) (Deauville, August 14) 3yo+ 1m Good to soft **128** (TS 121) 6 ran. *Raced in 3rd, led over 1 1/2f out, pushed out, ran on well (K McEvoy), beat Whipper by 1 1/2l*

3rd Vodafone Derby Stakes (Group 1) (Epsom, June 4) 3yo 1m4f Good **116** (TS 112) 13 ran. *Took keen hold, tracked leaders, progress and 4th straight, ridden to chase winner well over 1f out, no impression, lost 2nd last 150yds (L Dettori), beaten 8l by Motivator*

1st Boylesports Irish 2,000 Guineas (Group 1) (Curragh, May 21) 3yo 1m Good **126** (TS 57) 8 ran. *Settled in 4th, smooth headway to lead 2f out, soon quickened clear and edged right, eased close home, impressive (L Dettori), beat Oratorio by 2l*

5th UltimatePoker.com 2,000 Guineas Stakes (Group 1) (Newmarket, April 30) 3yo 1m Good to firm **111** (TS 90) 19 ran. *Tracked leaders, ridden and hung left over 1f out, stayed on same pace (L Dettori), beaten 3l by Footstepsinthesand*

2004

1st Dunnes Stores National Stakes (Group 1) (Curragh, September 19) 2yo 7f Yielding **122** (TS 119) 7 ran ● **1st** Weatherbys Superlative Stakes (Group 3) (Newmarket (July), July 8) 2yo 7f Good to soft **104** (TS 85) 12 ran ● **1st** Green & Black's Organic Chocolate EBF Maiden Stakes (Goodwood, June 4) 2yo 6f Good to firm **99** (TS 79) 5 ran

that all the dreams we had for six months have been broken."

What motivates Sheikh Mohammed? The same as most of us judged by translations of his poetry (Jilted, The Night, etc) published in collections such as Poems From The Soiree on sheikhmohammed.com, but his verse also broaches a single-minded pursuit of success in sport that racing will recognise instantly. In Challenge, he writes:

"From my love of hardships I am elated when more difficult
I am accustomed to hardships, eager to confront them
I exhausted the unyielding land without tiring
I exhausted birds in the sky and my accusers"

Defeat in the Guineas, then, might not be the end of his aspirations for Dubawi. Three weeks later Dubawi tried his first step to redemption in the Irish Guineas.

He'd hung badly to his left on the firm going at Newmarket and he shot off to his right once sent about his business at The Curragh, but on easy ground on the second occasion Dubawi was able to make impressive forward motion with it.

Rebel Rebel was too far adrift on that side of the track to be impeded, while the likes of Oratorio and Democratic Deficit on the other side were not faring much better. Those three had all been among the principals at Newmarket, but Dettori never had to raise his whip as Dubawi dismissed them comfortably.

Dubawi, beaten favourite in the 2,000 Guineas, bounces back to land the Irish equivalent at The Curragh

With the task now to enhance his reputation rather than salvage it, it was a case of bigger the better for Dubawi's remaining assignments. The Derby was a good place to start.

Rivals had emerged from interesting sources. Footstepsinthesand's absence at The Curragh presaged his retirement but Shamardal was back as a French Classic winner, while the forces were massing among the offspring of another Coolmore sire, Montjeu, Dubai Millennium's great rival for plaudits in the summer of 2000. A great rival, but one he never met in action, Dubai Millennium's injury having been sustained one day after Sheikh Mohammed's proposal that they meet in a $6 million match.

At Epsom, Dubawi was taken on by three of Montjeu's sons in Motivator, Walk In The Park and Kings Quay. Dubai Millennium had met his only defeat in the Derby, and Dettori had still not won it, but early in the straight in the 2005 running he must have held hopes on strong-travelling third favourite Dubawi, only to have them extinguished as Motivator went further and further ahead.

Close home, Dubawi lost second as well, to Walk In The Park, and others were closing fast. Dubawi did not get the trip and was not at all disgraced in the circumstances, but that day he would not have beaten Motivator at a mile and a quarter.

Dubawi returned to a mile. Missing the St James's Palace, when rain failed to arrive, left Shamardal to make championship claims but he then had to be retired and that meant Godolphin's season as a force in the top races now depended almost entirely on Dubawi.

Their time may come later, as it did with their sire, but among the other offspring of Dubai Millennium, the likes of Centaurus, Echo Of

Light and Belenus flickered briefly as three-year-olds.

Dubawi was the only one to keep the flame alive and this he did most brightly in the Jacques Le Marois. There were just four serious runners but it was the most eagerly anticipated mile race of the season, boasting Valixir, who had emerged among the very best older horses, Whipper, a Group 1 winner in each of his three seasons, and spiciest of all Divine Proportions, the five-time Group 1-winning filly.

Just inside the final two furlongs, Dubawi took over from his pacemaker. He asked a stiff question and the first reply, dismayingly for the faithful who had backed her down to 5-6 favouritism, was a tame one from Divine Proportions; next, Valixir buckled and hung away his chance; Whipper, the previous year's winner, emerged from Dubawi's slipstream but Dubawi was going on much too strongly for him and won by a length and a half.

It might not have been the enthralling clash envisaged by the racing public, but Dubawi's performance was up with the best of his age at the distance in 2005.

"This is a dream," said Sheikh Mohammed from the winner's enclosure. "To be here with a son of Dubai Millennium, the best horse I ever saw."

One absentee from the celebrations was Dettori, injured and replaced by the excellent Kerrin McEvoy, and though Dettori was on board again when Dubawi ran in the following month's Queen Elizabeth II at Newmarket, this time the celebrations were absent.

In their place, Dettori was plunged into soul-searching depths and the rest of the Godolphin camp left dismayed. Defeat in itself was not the issue. It was the manner of defeat, with the jockey failing to stick to their pre-race plan when he ignored his own pacemaker and instead followed Rakti away from the stands side. Dubawi joined the main action eventually but was seen off by three-quarters of a length by Starcraft.

"It was a complete cock-up," observed Simon Crisford, Godolphin's racing manager. "I've said my sorries and it's in the past now," said Dettori the next day.

Alas, Dubawi the racehorse was a thing of the past as well. The Breeders' Cup Mile had been next on the agenda but an injured hind ligament saw all engagements struck off.

Sheikh Mohammed has his successor to Dubai Millennium at Dalham Hall. "He looks like Dubai Millennium and he has his heart, so he is very close to my heart," he said.

The Crown Prince of Dubai sees his involvement as a rebirth in the heritage of the Darley Arabian and Godolphin Arabian. Dubawi was not a rebirth of Dubai Millennium but, from that small and solitary crop, an individual as classy as Dubawi was at Deauville, and a Classic winner to boot, is surely the most the Sheikh could have planned for.

The Darley advert for Dubawi's stud services reads: "The world revolves around the son".

Dubawi

bay colt, 7-2-2002

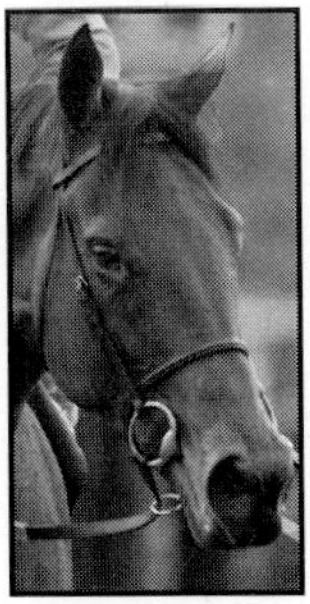

Dubai Millennium b 1996	Seeking The Gold	Mr Prospector	Raise A Native Gold Digger
		Con Game	Buckpasser Broadway
	Colorado Dancer	Shareef Dancer	Northern Dancer Sweet Alliance
		Fall Aspen	Pretense Change Water
Zomaradah b 1995	Deploy	Shirley Heights	Mill Reef Hardiemma
		Slightly Dangerous	Roberto Where You Lead
	Jawaher	Dancing Brave	Lyphard Navajo Princess
		High Tern	High Line Sunbittern

Bred by Darley in England.

Sire Dubai Millennium

Won 9 of 10 races, inc. Prix Eugene Adam-Gr3, Prix Jacques le Marois-Gr1, Queen Elizabeth II S.-Gr1, Dubai World Cup-Gr1, Prince of Wales's S.-Gr1. Big (16.2hh), strong, handsome individual, not the best of movers in his slower paces, but a powerful galloper, effective on any turf surface and on dirt. Very well-bred, by a dual Grade 1 winner, out of a Gr2 winner whose own dam was the outstanding broodmare of modern times. Deceased. Stood one season at Dalham Hall Stud, Newmarket, at a fee of £100,000. Sire of one crop of racing age, inc. notable winner: Dubawi (National S.-Gr1, Irish 2,000 Guineas-Gr1, Prix Jacques le Marois-Gr1).

Dam Zomaradah

Won 6 of 12 races, inc. Oaks d'Italia-Gr1, E.P. Taylor S.-Can Gr1, Royal Whip S.-Gr2, Premio Lydia Tesio-Gr2. Also 3rd in Breeders' Cup Filly and Mare Turf S. High-class, round-actioned, consistent performer, acted on any going. Well suited by 11f, should have stayed further, but disappointed in only race at 12f. Very well-bred. The best daughter of her sire, out of a non-winning half-sister to Derby winner High-Rise. Dam of: Dubawi (2002 c by Dubai Millennium; triple Gr1 winner), Princess Nada (2003 f by Barathea; placed twice to date). She has a colt foal by Alhaarth. Barren to Sadler's Wells in 2001, and to both Singspiel and Halling in 2004.

Pedigree assessment

The interim report on Dubai Millennium's first and only crop, which included a Group 1 winner, was favourable. But Dubawi was again the only one who truly excelled as a three-year-old. In 2004 we formed the impression that he might display some of the staying qualities of his dam, but as it turned out, he emulated his sire by failing to get home in the Derby, and he earned his credits as an undoubtedly gifted miler, one of the best of his generation in Europe. He has now retired to stud, commanding a fee of £25,000 at Dalham Hall, where he will no doubt be able to count on strong support from members of the Maktoum family. *TM*

Electrocutionist (USA)

4yo bay colt **125**

Red Ransom (USA) - Elbaaha (Arazi (USA))

Owner Earle I Mack

Trainer V Valiani

Breeder Compagnia Generale Srl

Career: **8** starts | won **6** | second **1** | third **1** | **£712,588** win and place

By Paul Haigh

RIBOT was the first, of course, but more recently both Falbrav and, to a slightly lesser extent, Rakti have taught us that Italian champions are not to be underestimated. The latest in the line is 2004 Derby Italiano winner Electrocutionist, who began campaigning internationally in 2005 with advance notices that at least matched those of the latter pair. One respected Italian journalist even went so far as to say in July that: "Although Falbrav improved afterwards, Electrocutionist is a better horse now than Falbrav was when he came to Luca Cumani."

A lot was obviously expected, but it was only partially delivered. Electrocutionist's season nevertheless impressed Godolphin enough for a transfer to be negotiated in the autumn.

It began on May 22 with an effortless six-length victory in a Group 2 at the Capannelle. The starting price of 1-25 told us all we needed to know both about the quality of the opposition and the esteem in which Electrocutionist was held. Four weeks later he went to San Siro for his first Group 1 of the year, the 12-furlong Gran Premio di Milano, and, at odds of 2-9 in a small field, put away his only serious rival – the useful French middle-distance performer Vol de Nuit.

Trainer Valfredo Valiani then began to prepare him for the King George at Newbury in July, but a slight setback meant he missed the race and his revised target became the Juddmonte International at York on August 16. He was stabled with Cumani, although Valiani continued to supervise his training, and soon returned impressively to form.

There were problems all year with the going at York and it may have been that Electrocutionist didn't find the consistency of the Knavesmire perfectly to his liking in the Juddmonte. After looking for a while early in the straight to have been briefly outpaced, he was wound up by Mick Kinane in his most irresistible form and gradually began to wear them down, then came with a rush down the outside in the last half-furlong

Electrocutionist (left) pips Zenno Rob Roy in a thrilling finish to the International, which truly lived up to its name

to cut down the Japanese champion Zenno Rob Roy and win by a neck. Maraahel was just a head further back in third, and the subsequent Breeders' Cup Turf runner-up Ace was only half a length behind him in fourth. Norse Dancer too had every chance going into the final furlong, but he faded into fifth.

At the time much of the credit went to Kinane who, it was generally felt, had simply outridden Yutaka Take on the runner-up, but those closest to Electrocutionist were just as impressed by the horse even though he had achieved no more than what looked like a scrambling victory in a bunch finish. Valiani immediately declared the Arc as his prime target, and his jockey, the hero of the hour, was positively effusive. "He can be better than this at a mile and a half with a quicker surface," said Kinane. "I would have beaten them more easily over further. He's definitely an Arc horse."

Largely because there is usually plenty of cut in the ground at Longchamp in October it was decided, however, to follow a different course with him and send him to North America, the plan being to target the $2 million Canadian International at Woodbine, and then if all went well in Toronto to go on to the Breeders' Cup Turf at Belmont.

The weather went against Electrocutionist in a big way, though. First Paris dodged most of the expected rain, then it poured so relentlessly on Long Island that Belmont had to put up with record rainfall by the middle of October, and then, in the last few days before the Canadian

2005 Race record

3rd Pattison Canadian International (Grade 1) (Woodbine, October 23) 3yo+ 1m4f Yielding **114** 10 ran. *Settled in 8th, taken to outside and headway 2f out, ridden under 1½f out, one pace when struck by rival's whip over 1f out, finished 4th, beaten 6l by Relaxed Gesture, placed 3rd (M J Kinane)*

1st Juddmonte International Stakes (Group 1) (York, August 16) 3yo+ 1m2½f Good **125** (TS 125) 7 ran. *Held up in last, headway over 2f out, ran on to lead near finish (M J Kinane), beat Zenno Rob Roy by nk*

1st Gran Premio di Milano (Group 1) (San Siro, June 19) 3yo+ 1m4f Good to firm **117** 5 ran. *Made all, pushed along over 3f out, ridden 2f out, driven out, ran on well (E Botti), beat Vol De Nuit by ¾l*

1st Premio Carlo d'Alessio (Group 2) (Capannelle, May 22) 4yo+ 1m4f Good to firm **118** 5 ran. *Made all, went clear from over 2f out, easily (E Botti), beat Fielding by 6l*

2004

2nd Gran Premio del Jockey Club (Group 1) (San Siro, October 17) 3yo+ 1m4f Soft **125** 9 ran ● **1st** Premio Giuseppe Fassati (San Siro, September 19) 3yo 1m3f Good to soft 6 ran ● **1st** Gran Premio d'Italia (Listed) (San Siro, June 27) 3yo 1m2f Good 12 ran ● **1st** Premio Angelo Gardenghi (Unraced) (San Siro, April 7) 3yo 1m1f Good 15 ran

International, Toronto too was hit by steady downpours.

The official going at Woodbine on October 23 was yielding, but that was probably a generous description of ground that only the eventual winner, Relaxed Gesture, really handled. Electrocutionist, the hot favourite, was never travelling, failed completely to produce his usual finishing burst and was beaten a total of just under six lengths by the two Americans, Relaxed Gesture and Meteor Storm, and Grey Swallow – although, after a stewards' inquiry over slight interference that probably would not even have been called in Britain, Electrocutionist was rather fortunately promoted to third.

This defeat, one of only two blemishes on his eight-race career record, can almost certainly be excused on account of the ground. It was a disappointing way for him to end his season, though, and gave encouragement to those who suspected he might just have been overrated. It is his only other defeat, however, on which it may be more sensible to judge him. That came in the 2004 Gran Premio del Jockey Club when, again on ground much softer than he prefers, he went down by only a head to Shirocco. The Breeders' Cup Turf winner may have improved a little for the transfer to Andre Fabre, but he was a very good colt when trained by Andreas Schutz too, and for Electrocutionist to have finished so close to him on ground that would certainly have favoured Shirocco was in retrospect a major achievement.

With his distinct going preference Electrocutionist looks a perfect type for either Japan or Hong Kong, or both, but wherever he gets the fast ground he needs to show his very best he should be a formidable opponent to anything in 2006 – perhaps even to Hurricane Run.

Electrocutionist

bay colt, 24-2-2002

Parents	Grandparents	Great-grandparents	Great-great-grandparents
Red Ransom b 1987	Roberto	Hail To Reason	Turn-to Nothirdchance
		Bramalea	Nashua Rarelea
	Arabia	Damascus	Sword Dancer Kerala
		Christmas Wind	Nearctic Bally Free
Elbaaha ch 1994	Arazi	Blushing Groom	Red God Runaway Bride
		Danseur Fabuleux	Northern Dancer Fabuleux Jane
	Gesedeh	Ela-Mana-Mou	Pitcairn Rose Bertin
		Le Melody	Levmoss Arctic Melody

Bred by Compagnia Generale SRL in Kentucky.

Sire Red Ransom

Won 2 of 3 starts. Strong, 16.1hh, well-made sort. Speedy and precocious, but seemed likely to stay beyond a mile and establish himself in top-flight company until injury cut him short. From the family of Classic winners Juliette Marny, Julio Mariner and Scintillate, plus Be Careful, Showdown, Matatina, etc. Stands at Dalham Hall Stud, Newmarket, at a 2006 fee of £25,000. Sire of 12 crops of racing age, inc. notable winners: Bail Out Becky (Del Mar Oaks-Gr1), Petrouchka (Gr3), Sri Pekan (Gr2), Upper Noosh (Gr3), Trail City (Gr2), Wandering Star (Gr2), Intikhab (Gr2), Rojo Dinero (Gr3), Comic Strip (Gr3), Stay Sound (Gr3), Crystal Symphony (Gr3), Perfect Sting (Garden City H.-Gr1, Queen Elizabeth II Challenge Cup S.-Gr1, Breeders' Cup Filly & Mare Turf-Gr1), Pico Teneriffe (Gr3), China Visit (Gr2), Ekraar (Gran Premio del Jockey Club-Gr1), Shining Hour (Gr3), Slew The Red (Gr3), New Economy (Gr2), Mr Mellon (Gr2), Van Rouge (Gr3), Cassis (Gr3), Casual Look (Oaks S.-Gr1), Fairly Ransom (Gr2), Ransom o' War (Gr2), Electrocutionist (Gran Premio di Milano-Gr1, York International S.-Gr1), Western Ransom (Gr3), Red Clubs (Gr2).

Dam Elbaaha

Won 1 of 11 races. Also placed 2nd 4 times, 3rd twice, 4th 3 times. Useful, honest and consistent performer, indifferent to ground conditions. Lacked a change of pace, but stayed 14f well and promised to stay further. From the family of Ardross, Scorpion, etc. Dam of: Hatalan (1999 f by Mark Of Esteem; placed), Retooff (2000 f by Cadeaux Genereux; unraced), Electrocutionist (2001 c by Red Ransom; dual Gr1 winner), Myloveportofino (2002 f by Distant View; unplaced), Grigorieva (2003 f by Woodman; unraced to date). She has a yearling filly by Intikhab, her colt foal by Namid died, and she was covered by Montjeu in 2005.

Pedigree assessment

The performances in Britain of such as Falbrav and Rakti, who both started their racing careers in Italy, have ensured a new-found respect for form in that country, and Electrocutionist advertised it again with a fine victory in York's International, battling on gamely at the end of a stirring race in which the first four finished within a length. His subsequent disappointing effort at Woodbine was a rare lapse, and he will surely enjoy other days in the limelight. He is an accomplished performer from 10-12 furlongs and the best son of his sire to have raced in Europe to date. Remarkably, he was one of six tail-female descendants of 1965 Musidora Stakes heroine Arctic Melody to win in Pattern company in 2005. *TM*

Elvstroem (Aus)

5yo bay horse **121**

Danehill (USA) - Circles Of Gold (Aus) (Marscay (Aus))

Owner Elvstroem Syndicate

Trainer T Vasil

Breeder F B J Tagg

Career: **32** starts | won **10** | second **4** | third **5** | **£2,281,766** win and place

By James Willoughby

THE tenth Dubai World Cup night at Nad Al Sheba brought together some high-class thoroughbreds from disparate nations. The feature races were won by trainers representing USA, Great Britain, South Africa, the UAE and, for the first time, Australia.

The last-named country was the origin of Dubai Duty Free winner Elvstroem, who annexed the Group 1 contest under a superb ride from Nash Rawiller. The Victoria-based jockey dictated a steady pace, which he quickened off the home turn to beat the American-trained Whilly by two and three-quarter lengths.

According to Racing Post Ratings, this represented improvement over his domestic form, but would it stand up? Tactics had surely played a big part. If the Dubai Duty Free form was reliable, Elvstroem would surely reproduce it. Australian horses have carved out something of a reputation for their toughness and consistency. These are qualities which are increasingly precious, with so many top runners from the US and Europe falling by the wayside.

After Dubai, Elvstroem headed east to Sha Tin, where he received a sound thrashing in the Queen Elizabeth II Cup. The Hong Kong Derby winner Vengeance Of Rain fought out the finish with South African Greys Inn as Elvstroem faded into ninth.

This performance was lengths below what Elvstroem appeared to show in Dubai, but it turned out to represent form not far short of the level he achieved on his other starts in 2005. In effect, it provided the first piece of supporting evidence that his victory in the desert was flattering.

Elvstroem arrived in England to contest the Group 1 Juddmonte Lockinge Stakes, for which he had to be supplemented for £16,000. He was stationed at Newmarket with Geoff Wragg, but had little time to settle into his new surroundings with only a 20-day intermission before he would race at Newbury.

Elvstroem quickens clear to win the Dubai Duty Free, but he was unable to score again when tried in Europe

The ground came up fast at Newbury and, despite the familiarity he should have had with the terrain, Elvstroem was beaten for pace, all ends up, by Rakti. He finished fourth, passed inside the final two furlongs by Mac Love and Hurricane Alan, and beaten more than six lengths as the winner lowered the track record.

Elvstroem was back in the role of a flat-track bully when he made the front right from the stalls in the Prix d'Ispahan. The usual moderate opening stages at Longchamp allowed him to get there without undue energy loss, but Rawiller was intent on kicking on running down the false straight, an infamous bear-trap at Longchamp.

The sectional times confirmed that this was a precarious manoeuvre as Elvstroem recorded a split of near 22 seconds too far from home to sustain. Nonetheless, it took a good one to beat him in Valixir, and the five-year-old held on gamely to finish in front of Cacique and Touch Of Land as the winner swaggered two lengths clear.

Even when able to resume his favoured tactics – he had also made all to beat Makybe Diva in the 2004 Caulfield Cup – Elvstroem had failed to recapture his Dubai form. It now seemed that only a similarly freakish race would enable him to do so, which was going to leave him short of the necessary standard for Group 1 racing in Europe.

Sure enough, he confirmed this impression when found out in the closing furlongs of the Prince of Wales's Stakes at York in June. His connections said the ground was too loose for him, but it was the same for all. He finished more than six lengths behind as Azamour and Ace drew clear.

2005 Race record

4th Grand Prix de Saint-Cloud (Group 1) (Saint-Cloud, June 26) 4yo+ 1m4f Good to soft **115** (TS 115) 11 ran. *Held up in rear, headway 5f out, 4th straight, went 3rd approaching final furlong, lost 3rd close home (Nash Rawiller), beaten 4¼l by Alkaased*

3rd Prince of Wales's Stakes (Group 1) (York, June 15) 4yo+ 1m2½f Good to firm **114** (TS 107) 8 ran. *Took keen hold in front, stayed far side, headed over 1f out, kept on same pace (Nash Rawiller), beaten 6½l by Azamour*

2nd Prix d'Ispahan (Group 1) (Longchamp, May 22) 4yo+ 1m1f Good **115** (TS 108) 8 ran. *Led, pushed along 2f out, headed just inside final furlong, kept on (Nash Rawiller), beaten 2l by Valixir*

4th Juddmonte Lockinge Stakes (Group 1) (Newbury, May 14) 4yo+ 1m Firm **113** (TS 84) 8 ran. *Led 1f, stayed tracking winner until ridden and one pace from inside final 2f (Nash Rawiller), beaten 6¼l by Rakti*

9th Audemars Piguet QE II Cup (Group 1) (Sha Tin, April 24) 3yo+ 1m2f Good to firm **113** 13 ran. *Raced in 6th on outside, effort and unable to quicken 2f out (Nash Rawiller), beaten 6¼l by Vengeance Of Rain*

1st Dubai Duty Free Sponsored By Dubai Duty Free (Turf) (Group 1) (Nad Al Sheba, March 26) 4yo+ 1m1f Good to firm **121** 14 ran. *Made all, set slow pace, ridden 1½f out, quickened clear final 1f, pushed out (Nash Rawiller), beat Whilly by 2¾l*

4th Australian Cup (Group 1) (Flemington, March 12) 3yo+ 1m2f Good **119** 7 ran. *Broke well, cover 3 lengths off lead 2nd, 6 length 3rd midway, stayed on (Nash Rawiller), beaten 4½l by Makybe Diva*

1st St George Stakes (Group 2) (Caulfield, February 26) 3yo+ 1m1f Good **119** 4 ran. *Broke well and driven along to settle in 2nd, took lead soon after straightening, kicked well clear and held on final stages (Nash Rawiller), beat Makybe Diva by shd*

1st C F Orr Stakes (Group 1) (Caulfield, February 12) 3yo+ 7f Good to soft **119** 15 ran. *Broke well, three wide without cover in 4th, 2 lengths off lead, similar position turning for home, all out, just held on (Nash Rawiller), beat Savabeel by hd*

Other wins

2004 **1st** Carlton Draught Caulfield Cup (Group 1) (Handicap) (Caulfield, October 16) 3yo+ 1m4f Soft **119** 18 ran ● **1st** Turnbull Stakes (Group 2) (Flemington, October 2) 4yo+ 1m2f Good 16 ran ● **1st** Emirates Airline Underwood Stakes (Group 1) (Caulfield, September 19) 3yo+ 1m1f Good to soft **119** 16 ran ● **1st** Autumn Classic (Group 2) (Caulfield, February 28) 3yo 1m1f Good 9 ran **2003** **1st** AAMI Victoria Derby (Group 1) (Flemington, November 1) 3yo 1m4½f Slow **112** 14 ran ● **1st** Guineas Prelude (Group 3) (Caulfield, September 21) 3yo 7f Good 11 ran ● **1st** Handicap (Swan Hill, June 7) 2yo 6½f Good to soft 10 ran

Later the same month, trainer Tony Vasil elected to try a change of tactics with Elvstroem. No doubt he was influenced by the combination of a mile and a half and the forecast of easier ground in the Grand Prix de Saint-Cloud. It made little difference, as a never-dangerous Elvstroem was beaten more than four lengths by the subsequent Japan Cup winner Alkaased.

Elvstroem made a decent contribution towards the first half of the European season, though he was exposed as being below the level requisite for Group 1 success. He ran consistently well, however, and provided another clue to how Antipodean form stacks up with the rest of the world.

Elvstroem

bay horse, 14-11-2000

Parents	Grandparents	Great-grandparents	Great-great-grandparents
Danehill b 1986	Danzig	Northern Dancer	Nearctic Natalma
		Pas de Nom	Admirals Voyage Petitioner
	Razyana	His Majesty	Ribot Flower Bowl
		Spring Adieu	Buckpasser Natalma
Circles Of Gold ch 1991	Marscay	Biscay	Star Kingdom Magic Symbol
		Heart Of Market	To Market Accroche Coeur
	Olympic Aim	Zamazaan	Exbury Toyama
		Gold Vink	Gold Sovereign Goudvink

Bred by Frank Tagg, Frank Meduri and Garry Moffitt in Australia. Aus$330,000 (spun) William Inglis Easter yearling

Sire Danehill

Won 4 of 9 races, inc. Haydock Park Sprint Cup-Gr1. Died May 2003. Stood at Coolmore Stud, latterly at a fee of Ir200,000gns. Sire of Gr1 winners: Danish (QE II Challenge Cup), Kissing Cousin (Coronation), Danehill Dancer (Phoenix, National), Tsukuba Symphony (NHK Mile Cup), Desert King (National, Irish 2,000, Irish Derby), Fairy King Prawn (Yasuda Kinen), Tiger Hill (GP von Baden [twice], Bayerisches Zuchtrennen), Indian Danehill (Prix Ganay), Wannabe Grand (Cheveley Park), Aquarelliste (Prix de Diane, Prix Vermeille, Prix Ganay), Banks Hill (Coronation, Breeders' Cup F & M Turf, Prix Jacques le Marois), Mozart (July Cup, Nunthorpe), Regal Rose (Cheveley Park), Dress To Thrill (Matriarch), Fine Motion (Shuka Sho, QE II Commemorative Cup), Landseer (Poule d'Essai des Poulains), Rock Of Gibraltar (Grand Criterium, Dewhurst, 2,000 Guineas, Irish 2,000, St James's Palace, Sussex, Prix du Moulin), Westerner (Prix du Cadran [twice], Prix Royal-Oak [twice], Gold Cup), Clodovil (Poule d'Essai des Poulains), Intercontinental (Matriarch, Breeders' Cup F & M Turf), Light Jig (Yellow Ribbon), Spartacus (Phoenix, Gran Criterium), Grey Lilas (Prix du Moulin), North Light (Derby), Luas Line (Garden City H.), Oratorio (Prix Jean-Luc Lagardere, Eclipse, Irish Champion), George Washington (Phoenix, National), Horatio Nelson (Prix Jean-Luc Lagardere), Rumplestiltskin (Moyglare Stud, Prix Marcel Boussac).

Dam Circles Of Gold

Won 6 of 43 starts over 6-12f inc Australian Oaks-AusGr1. Also 2nd Caulfield Cup-AusGr1. Sire Marscay top-class 2yo, former champion sire and multiple champion broodmare sire in Australia. Dam of: Gold Rush (1998 c by Octagonal; non-winner), Lady Circles (1999 f by Ascot Knight; placed), Elvstroem (2000 c by Danehill; Dubai Duty Free-Gr1, Caulfield Cup-AusGr1, Victoria Derby-AusGr1, C F Orr S-AusGr1, Underwood S-AusGr1), Hveger (2001 f by Danehill; AusGr1-placed winner), Gold Centre (2002 c by Danehill; winner), 2003 c by Fusaichi Pegasus.

Pedigree assessment

The Australian obsession with Danehill, together with the nation's enthusiasm for international success, found its perfect object in Elvstroem. He stood his first season in 2005 at Blue Gum Farm in Victoria, Australia, where his fee was Aus$38,500. That is a substantial one for a new stallion in Australia, but Elvstroem appears to have the attributes to make an impact as a stallion. *JH*

Eswarah

3yo bay filly **116**

Unfuwain (USA) - Midway Lady (USA) (Alleged (USA))

Owner Hamdan Al Maktoum

Trainer M A Jarvis

Breeder Shadwell Estate Company Limited

Career: **5** starts | won **3** | second **0** | third **0** | **£258,394** win and place

By Steve Dennis

LIKE mother, like daughter. Nineteen years after Midway Lady provided trainer Ben Hanbury with his second British Classic by winning the Oaks (she had also provided his first, in the 1,000 Guineas), her 10th foal emulated her by becoming trainer Michael Jarvis's second British Classic winner following his 1,000 Guineas win with Ameerat in 2001.

That's where the grip on the imagination slackens. Oaks winners have recently become makeweights in the racing year; no Oaks winner since Time Charter in 1982 has subsequently been able to win an all-aged European Group 1 contest open to both colts and fillies. Eswarah ran just five times in a four-month career and her last two runs were disappointing ones. You may have forgotten her already.

Unraced as a two-year-old when in training with Hanbury, the daughter of Unfuwain was transferred to Jarvis upon Hanbury's retirement and made her debut for him in a ten-furlong Newbury maiden in the middle of April. She had evidently shown enough at home to be sent away favourite, took up the running at the furlong pole and saw off her 15 rivals by a comfortable two and a half lengths. "She was obviously difficult last year, but she's got some talent. I wouldn't rule her out of the Oaks," said Angus Gold, racing manager to owner Hamdan Al-Maktoum.

She returned to Newbury and duly won her Oaks trial, coming home an eased-down two-length winner of the Listed Swettenham Stud Fillies' Trial Stakes from Favourita, although the weakness of the field can be illustrated by her odds of 1-2. The Oaks was now inevitable – her stamina could virtually be taken for granted, she had done nothing wrong on the racecourse, and in a year without an outstanding candidate she made plenty of appeal.

She had 11 rivals at Epsom, headed by Ballydoyle's 1,000 Guineas winner Virginia Waters, who had finished only eighth in the Irish 1,000.

Eswarah lands the Oaks at Epsom, only seven weeks after making her racecourse debut, but she did not win again

The pair were joint-favourites at 11-4, with the John Dunlop-trained Cassydora, easy winner of the Lingfield Oaks Trial, next in the market. It was not a strong Oaks; form from the better juvenile races the previous season was practically non-existent, although Cheveley Park Stakes winner Magical Romance took her chance, a 50-1 'hope' on her first attempt beyond a mile.

Eswarah's stamina was in no doubt, so while Magical Romance made the running, Richard Hills had his filly poised in the perfect Epsom position – two or three off the leaders – ready to pounce when the leader inevitably ran out of puff. Magical Romance did well to take them past the three-furlong pole, but Hills soon asserted on Eswarah and very quickly had all beaten bar Something Exciting, trained by David Elsworth and ridden by Richard Quinn. Something Exciting looked a real danger inside the last two furlongs, but Eswarah had as yet untapped reserves and stayed on strongly to win by a length and a half, with the Jim Bolger-trained Pictavia flying late on for third, three lengths back.

It was a visually impressive performance, as Eswarah showed class and commitment to repel the runner-up's challenge. We had an unbeaten Oaks winner, of whom her trainer said: "This filly is exceptional. She's a credit to Ben [Hanbury], who has been very helpful to me. He always said she was good. I asked him 'Listed good?' and he said, 'Better than that'."

However, if the style had been good, the substance was provoking unease, and Racing Post handicapper Paul Curtis called her "an average Oaks

2005 **Race record**

4th Aston Upthorpe Yorkshire Oaks (Group 1) (York, August 17) 3yo+ 1m4f Good **110** (TS 96) 11 ran. *Held up, headway over 4f out, hung left and led over 1f out, headed just inside final furlong, faded (R Hills), beaten 3½l by Punctilious*

8th King George VI And Queen Elizabeth Diamond Stakes (Group 1) (Newbury, July 23) 3yo+ 1m4f Good to firm **95** (TS 83) 12 ran. *Mid-division, took closer order and travelling well over 3f out, ridden over 2f out, weakened over 1f out (R Hills), beaten 18l by Azamour*

1st Vodafone Oaks (Group 1) (Epsom, June 3) 3yo 1m4f Good **116** (TS 105) 12 ran. *Settled midfield, 5th and going easily straight, progress to lead over 2f out, driven and pressed well over 1f out, stayed on strongly (R Hills), beat Something Exciting by 1½l*

1st Swettenham Stud Fillies' Trial Stakes (Listed) (Newbury, May 13) 3yo 1m2f Good to firm **97** (TS 14) 6 ran. *Held up in rear but in touch, steady headway from 3f out to lead inside final 2f, quickened clear final furlong, very easily (R Hills), beat Favourita by 2l*

1st Robert Sangster Memorial Maiden Fillies' Stakes (Newbury, April 15) 3yo 1m2f Good to soft **92** (TS 61) 16 ran. *Tracked leaders, quickened over 2f out to lead 1f out, shaken up and ran on strongly inside final furlong (R Hills), beat Alumni by 2½l*

winner" in allotting her a Racing Post Rating of 118, a figure that was 6lb below that of the previous year's winner, Ouija Board.

Even that figure needed marking down before the end of the year, for Something Exciting did nothing for the form when only fourth in the Ribblesdale Stakes at Royal Ascot at York, and further evidence that the Epsom form was only of limited usefulness came when the French filly Shawanda knocked spots off an Irish Oaks field that included Pictavia and Ribblesdale winner Thakafaat.

Eswarah was in her box. Connections were not tempted by the Irish Oaks or the Nassau Stakes and preferred instead to throw her to the lions in the King George VI and Queen Elizabeth Diamond Stakes at Newbury. The aforementioned Time Charter had been the last Oaks winner to land the King George, and she won it as a four-year-old. Pawneese had been the last three-year-old to do the double in the same year, in 1976, and Eswarah was now being asked to succeed where the likes of Oh So Sharp and Sun Princess had failed.

Her connections are to be congratulated for their sporting behaviour as Eswarah was the only three-year-old in the field, but she was out of her depth and ran like it. She went 'pop' with more than two furlongs to run and beat only four home, trailing in about 18 lengths behind Azamour. Gold said: "Richard said he got there nicely, but she emptied out more quickly than expected."

The needle was still hovering over empty when Eswarah found her elders her betters in the Yorkshire Oaks at the Ebor meeting, leading briefly before fading into fourth behind Punctilious. That was that. Just over a week later she had been retired with a knee injury.

Eswarah

bay filly, 21-2-2002

Parents	Grandparents	Great-grandparents	Great-great-grandparents
Unfuwain b 1985	Northern Dancer	Nearctic	Nearco Lady Angela
		Natalma	Native Dancer Almahmoud
	Height Of Fashion	Bustino	Busted Ship Yard
		Highclere	Queen's Hussar Highlight
Midway Lady b 1983	Alleged	Hoist The Flag	Tom Rolfe Wavy Navy
		Princess Pout	Prince John Determined Lady
	Smooth Bore	His Majesty	Ribot Flower Bowl
		French Leave	Damascus Marche Lorraine

Bred by Shadwell Estate Co. in England.

Sire Unfuwain

Won 6 of 10 starts, inc. Chester Vase-Gr3, Princess of Wales's S.-Gr2, John Porter S.-Gr3, Jockey Club S.-Gr2. Also 2nd in King George VI & Queen Elizabeth S., 4th in Prix de l'Arc de Triomphe. Strong, rangy, 16.1hh, good-bodied sort. Genuine and consistent, stayed 12f well. By the world's leading sire, and half-brother to Nashwan. Dam a Gr2 winner. Deceased. Stood at Nunnery Stud, last advertised fee £30,000. Sire of 12 crops of racing age, inc. notable winners: Bolas (Irish Oaks-Gr1), Alpha City (Gr3), Mamlakah (Gr3), Alhaarth (Dewhurst S.-Gr1), Gulland (Gr3), Dano-Mast (Gr2), Zahrat Dubai (Nassau S.-Gr1), Lahan (1,000 Guineas-Gr1), Petrushka (Irish Oaks-Gr1, Yorkshire Oaks-Gr1, Prix de l'Opera-Gr1), Amiwain (Gr2), Lailani (Irish Oaks-Gr1, Nassau S.-Gr1, Flower Bowl Invitational H.-Gr1), Ranin (Gr3), Fruhlingssturm (Gr2), Medici (Gr3), Eswarah (Oaks S.-Gr1), Perfect Hedge (Gr3), Ruwi (Gr2), Thakafaat (Gr2), Vadawina (Prix Saint-Alary-Gr1).

Dam Midway Lady

Won 5 of 6 starts, inc. May Hill S.-Gr3, Prix Marcel Boussac-Gr1, 1,000 Guineas-Gr1, Oaks S.-Gr1. Top-class performer at 2 and 3, stayed 12f well, would have got further. Big, rangy, good-topped sort, susceptible to leg problems. Bought for Shadwell $3.3 million out of training, 1986 Keeneland November Sales, to stud at 4 years, and dam of: Umnitayee (1988 f by Green Desert; Gr1-placed winner), Sharayif (1989 f by Green Desert; unraced), Alasad (1990 g by Kris; winner), Tharqaam (1991 c by Nashwan; unraced), Fatehalkhair (1992 g by Kris; winner), Abuijood (1995 g by Marju; winner), Haafiz (1996 c by Green Desert; stakes-placed winner), Iktinas (1999 c by Unfuwain; placed, died at 3), Itnab (2000 f by Green Desert; Gr3 winner), Eswarah (2002 f by Unfuwain; Classic winner), Shumookh (2003 c by Mujahid; unraced to date). She has a filly foal by Cape Cross and has returned to him. Not covered in 1992, slipped to Nashwan in 1994, barren to Indian Ridge in 1997 and 1998, to Green Desert in 2001, and to Elnaadim in 2004.

Pedigree assessment

Like Footstepsinthesand and Motivator, Eswarah preserved an unbeaten record while registering her Classic success, and, as with the colts, that was the last win of her career. She looked good when she became the first daughter of an Oaks winner to emulate her dam since Mirska – out of 1899 heroine Musa – in 1912, but hers was no vintage Classic, and her limitations were thoroughly exposed later on. It seems likely that she was only the second-best filly in the late Unfuwain's 2002 crop, behind French-trained Vadawina, another who went into early retirement. *TM*

Flower Alley (USA)

3yo chestnut colt **126**

Distorted Humor (USA) - Princess Olivia (USA) (Lycius (USA))

Owner Laura & Eugene Melnyk

Trainer T Pletcher

Breeder George Brunacini & Bona Terra Farms

Career: **10** starts | won **4** | second **3** | third **1** | **£1,269,706** win and place

By Nicholas Godfrey

FLOWER ALLEY, among the best of a thin US Classic crop in 2005, was guided towards his greatest triumph with the pinpoint accuracy of a tracer bullet by the nation's champion trainer, Todd Pletcher. In terms of international recognition, an admirably stubborn effort in finishing runner-up to Saint Liam in the Breeders' Cup Classic in October ensured Flower Alley's name appeared on the global radar. However, it was his victory two months previously in Saratoga's Travers Stakes, historic centrepiece of America's most storied meeting, which provided the major highlight of his season, a rich reward for the precision planning of his trainer, who targeted the $1 million contest known as the 'Midsummer Derby' rather than being tempted by other lucrative targets for a slowish learner.

Pletcher had to acquire such patience. Time is never in abundant supply for a US-trained three-year-old in the spring of a Classic campaign, and so it proved for Flower Alley.

Such is its towering status in US racing that the Kentucky Derby has a habit of forcing trainers' hands; Flower Alley's Churchill Downs campaign was fatally compromised by his lack of experience and maturity. He did not race until December of his two-year-old season. After three more races – two victories and a sound beating at the hands of Afleet Alex – Flower Alley was sent off at over 40-1 for the Kentucky Derby where his trainer, in a bid to overcome the colt's greenness and a perceived lack of focus, took the calculated risk of equipping him with blinkers. But while Flower Alley always raced in them afterwards, they appeared to offer only limited assistance at Churchill Downs as he finished ninth behind Giacomo. Still, the performance was not entirely without merit as he missed a beat at the gate before being hustled up on the inside to chase a stern pace. "If there is such a thing as running a good ninth, Flower Alley's performance in the Kentucky Derby qualifies," wrote

Flower Alley lands the Grade 1 Travers Stakes at Saratoga, the highlight of a fine campaign as a three-year-old

Dave Litfin in the *Daily Racing Form*.

Pletcher agreed, but he chose to forgo the remaining two legs of the Triple Crown, instead playing the long game and freshening up Flower Alley for a summer campaign focusing on the Travers.

The colt returned two months later in Grade 2 company at Belmont, where he was beaten just a half-length by the top-class Roman Ruler in a race that did not really go his way as he was forced to press the pace on the outside before just losing out. Yes, Flower Alley was a beaten favourite, but the Pletcher masterplan was gradually coming together, as a decisive victory next time out in the Grade 2 Jim Dandy Stakes made plain. That performance was all the more impressive as the lack of pace had forced jockey John Velazquez to send his mount into a front-running duel. Not that it ever looked like stopping him, and his trainer suggested better was to come. "Mentally, he's still getting there," said Pletcher. "I still don't think he's run his best race yet."

Primed to the second, Flower Alley must have managed something close to that when beating a strong field in the Grade 1 Travers. Flower Alley and Bellamy Road had the ten-furlong event largely to themselves. The front-running Bellamy Road fought gallantly to withstand two separate attacks from his rival, who tracked him in second throughout. Flower Alley applied pressure six furlongs out and again, tellingly, around the home turn. Flower Alley took command after entering the stretch to win going away by two and a half lengths, with a one-paced Roman Ruler

2005 Race record

2nd Breeders' Cup Classic - Powered by Dodge (Grade 1) (Dirt) (Belmont Park, October 29) 3yo+ 1m2f Fast **126** 13 ran. *Raced in 3rd, pushed along 2f out, disputed lead 1½f out, kept on gamely under pressure (J R Velazquez), beaten 1l by Saint Liam*

4th Jockey Club Gold Cup (Grade 1) (Dirt) (Belmont Park, October 1) 3yo+ 1m2f Fast **100** 8 ran. *Disputed lead until headed over 2f out, weakened (J R Velazquez), beaten 15½l by Borrego*

1st Travers Stakes (Grade 1) (Saratoga, August 27) 3yo 1m2f Fast **126** 7 ran. *Raced in 2nd, led 1½f out, driven out (J R Velazquez), beat Bellamy Road by 2½l*

1st Jim Dandy Stakes (Grade 2) (Saratoga, July 30) 3yo 1m1f Fast **115** 5 ran. *Raced in 2nd until led over 5f out, drew clear final 1½f, (J R Velazquez), beat Reverberate by 5¼l*

2nd Dwyer Stakes (Grade 2) (Belmont Park, July 4) 3yo 1m½ Fast **115** 6 ran. *Held up on outside of tightly packed field in 4th or 5th, pressed leader from over 1f out, stayed on gamely but always held (J R Velazquez), beaten ½l by Roman Ruler*

9th Kentucky Derby (Grade 1) (Churchill Downs, May 7) 3yo 1m2f Fast **107** 20 ran. *Close up until outpaced approaching straight (J Chavez), beaten 7½l by Giacomo*

2nd Arkansas Derby (Grade 2) (Oaklawn Park, April 16) 3yo 1m1f Fast **102** 10 ran. *Raced in 3rd, went 2nd over 2f out, outpaced by winner and edged right but held on for 2nd (J Chavez), beaten 8l by Afleet Alex*

1st Lane's End Stakes (Grade 2) (Turfway Park, March 26) 3yo 1m1f Muddy **101** 9 ran. *2nd early, 3rd halfway, 4th when hampered entering straight, stayed on strongly final furlong to lead close home (J Chavez), beat Wild Desert by ½l*

1st Maiden Special Weight (Gulfstream Park, February 19) 3yo Fast 12 ran. *Led narrowly 2f, 4th halfway, headway to press leader 2f out, soon looked held, rallied under pressure to lead close home (J Chavez), beat Wall Street by ¾l*

2004

3rd Maiden Special Weight (Calder, December 18) 2yo 6f Fast 8 ran

nearly three more lengths back in third. "He's an awesome horse," said the victorious Velazquez.

Maybe so, but his next outing was chalk to the Travers cheese. Back at Belmont, Flower Alley was strongly fancied to beat the older generation in the Jockey Club Gold Cup but the race was a disaster. Pletcher's tactic of employing a 'rabbit' to ensure a good pace backfired in spectacular fashion as a headstrong Flower Alley battled his own pacemaker, pulling hard before coming a distant fourth behind the commanding Borrego.

With the benefit of hindsight, that most exact of sciences, this was a race to ignore, but Flower Alley had few supporters ahead of the Breeders' Cup Classic where, according to Racing Post Ratings, he went on to equal his Travers form in defeat. Flower Alley ceded only grudgingly to Saint Liam, eventually beaten just a length after a performance that fully redeemed his reputation. With the exception of the brilliant Afleet Alex, there were few better than him in the US among 2005's Classic generation. Flower Alley stays in training in 2006, and he is likely to thrive – if it can be assumed he now knows what he is doing after those growing pains.

Flower Alley

chestnut colt, 7-5-2002

Distorted Humor ch 1993	Forty Niner	**Mr Prospector**	**Raise A Native** **Gold Digger**
		File	Tom Rolfe Continue
	Danzig's Beauty	Danzig	**Northern Dancer** Pas de Nom
		Sweetest Chant	Mr Leader Gay Sonnet
Princess Olivia ch 1995	Lycius	**Mr Prospector**	**Raise A Native** **Gold Digger**
		Lypatia	Lyphard Hypatia
	Dance Image	Sadler's Wells	**Northern Dancer** Fairy Bridge
		Diamond Spring	Vaguely Noble Dumfries

Bred by George Brunacini & Bona Terra Farms in Kentucky. $50,000 Keeneland November foal; $165,000 Keeneland September yearling.

Sire Distorted Humor

Won 8 of 23 starts, inc. Salvator Mile-Gr3, Commonwealth Breeders' Cup S.-Gr2, Churchill Downs H-Gr2, Ack Ack H.-Gr3. Also 6 times placed at Graded level, inc. 3rd in Cigar Mile. Showed high-class form up to 9f in each of three seasons, best from 7-8f at 5 years. Always Lasix user from midway in 3-y-o campaign. Neat, well-made sort, 15.3hh. Stands at WinStar Farm, Versailles, Kentucky, at a 2006 fee of $150,000. Sire of 4 northern hemisphere crops of racing age, inc. Awesome Humor (Spinaway S.-Gr1), Funny Cide (Kentucky Derby-Gr1, Preakness S.-Gr1, Jockey Club Gold Cup-Gr1), Go Rockin' Robin (Gr2), Humorous Lady (Gr2), Sensibly Chic (Gr2), Commentator (Whitney H.-Gr1), Fourty Niners Son (Clement L. Hirsch Turf Championship H.-Gr1), Flower Alley (Travers S.-Gr1), Original Spin (Gr3). Also sire of Australian Gr1 winner Rinky Dink.

Dam Princess Olivia

Won 3 of 24 races. Useful sprinter on dirt at 2, modest form later, unplaced in all 7 starts on turf. Quite well-bred. By a Middle Park S. winner and Classic-placed miler. Half-sister to Internet Commander, a major stakes winner in Jamaica, from the family of Lyphard. Dam of: He's Souper (2001 c by Alphabet Soup; winner), Flower Alley (2002 c by Distorted Humor; Gr1 winner), Ludington (2003 c by Black Minnaloushe; unraced to date). She has a yearling filly by Victory Gallop.

Pedigree assessment

Distorted Humor stood at only $12,500 when his first star, Kentucky Derby and Preakness hero Funny Cide, was conceived, but he soon became busily employed at a fee of $60,000, covering 156 mares in his 2003 book, 145 in 2004, and 115 in 2005. Next season his fee will be $150,000, reflecting another fine season in which he was represented by three individual Grade 1 winners. Flower Alley was the best of them, as his Travers victory and Breeders' Cup second clearly demonstrated. After Afleet Alex, he was the best three-year-old around in the States, and as he remains lightly raced, with scope for improvement, he should prove a legitimate candidate for top honours in 2006. He gets ten furlongs really well. *TM*

Footstepsinthesand

3yo bay colt **118**

Giant's Causeway (USA) - Glatisant (Rainbow Quest (USA))

Owner Michael Tabor

Trainer A P O'Brien

Breeder Hascombe and Valiant Studs

Career: **3** starts | won **3** | **£226,450** win and place

By Alan Sweetman

HOW GOOD could he have been? That is the inevitable question to be posed about Footstepsinthesand, retired with a foot injury as the unbeaten winner of three races. On the day that Kieren Fallon rode him to victory in the 2,000 Guineas at Newmarket it was easy enough to pick holes in his form. For all his supremacy, it was hard to overlook the fact that he was chased home by a pair of 100-1 shots, Rebel Rebel and Kandidate, and that three other runners priced at 66-1 or above finished within five lengths of him. If further evidence was needed of the suspect nature of the form, it was apparent that Dubawi, the one horse in the race who had been widely billed as a potential star of the season, had failed to deliver.

And yet the manner of his triumph was so thoroughly authoritative, the issue settled with a surge of acceleration towards the outside of the field over a furlong out, that it is possible to believe that he might have been very good indeed. Ultimately, perhaps, Fallon's very presence in the saddle provides the most telling evidence of the colt's nascent ability.

Fallon had returned to the land of his birth, where his raw natural talent had first been harnessed under Kevin Prendergast's tutelage, to take over from Jamie Spencer as Ballydoyle stable jockey. In a sense, it was an easy decision for the Coolmore power brokers. A multiple British champion, who had served two of the greatest trainers of the modern era with distinction, Fallon was the outstanding candidate in terms of riding ability and international experience. However, there has been enough in his past to give even his most fervent admirer the occasional shudder of anxiety, and some observers privately wondered whether a skeleton in the cupboard would eventually rattle its way into the public eye.

Fallon secured not only the prime job in Irish racing, but also an implicit vote of confidence in his professional integrity. People who make decisions at this level do not act on the spur of the moment, or without giving due

Footstepsinthesand takes the 2,000 Guineas in good style, but his unbeaten three-race career was soon at an end

consideration to implications beyond the short term. It would be incomprehensible if the appointment had been made without rigorous scrutiny being applied to any issue that might ultimately reflect doubt on its wisdom.

By all accounts, Fallon settled into his new role with a relish that impressed everyone at Ballydoyle. He threw himself into the routine of work-riding with enthusiasm, wasted no time in getting to know the horses, and quickly developed a rapport with Aidan O'Brien that was based on mutual respect. The change of scene seemed to make a difference to the jockey on a personal level. Within weeks of the start of the season, he already seemed more relaxed on an Irish racecourse than he had ever looked in Britain.

However, these were early days, and still anxious times for the Ballydoyle camp after the difficulties of 2004, even though the seeds of optimism had been planted by a late autumnal rally spearheaded by a group of talented juveniles. The new stable jockey faced his first serious test, not on the racecourse, but on the gallops, in trying to assess the relative merits of potential Classic prospects, including the Middle Park winner Ad Valorem, the Prix Jean-Luc Lagardere winner Oratorio, and Footstepsinthesand, a dark bay colt by Giant's Causeway who had blazed onto the scene with two victories in the space of eight days in October.

When bookmakers had initially priced up the Tifrums Maiden at Naas, they put in as favourite Olympic, an unraced Danzig colt from Ballydoyle. With the O'Brien two-year-olds at last in good form, and Spencer in the saddle, it seemed a reasonable assumption. But those

2005 Race record

1st UltimatePoker.com 2,000 Guineas Stakes (Group 1) (Newmarket, April 30) 3yo 1m Good to firm **118** (TS 99) 19 ran. *Tracked leaders, pulled hard, ridden to lead and edged left over 1f out, ran on (K Fallon), beat Rebel Rebel by 1¼l*

2004

1st Kilavullan Stakes (Group 3) (Leopardstown, October 25) 2yo 7f Soft **112** (TS 114) 6 ran ●
1st Tifrums EBF (C & G) Maiden (Naas, October 17) 2yo 6f Yielding to soft **97** (TS 94) 20 ran

who had been watching the gallops at Ballydoyle, and others privy to the right information, were keenly aware that the Giant's Causeway colt invariably ridden in his work by apprentice Colm O'Donoghue was a different kettle of fish. O'Brien allowed O'Donoghue to keep the ride at Naas, and a few early birds availed of a little 20-1 at morning prices. On track the gamble steamrolled from an opening 10-1 to 3-1 favouritism as Olympic drifted from 2-1 to 7-2, and Footstepsinthesand scampered home by four and a half lengths.

O'Brien's immediate reaction was that Footstepsinthesand would not run again as a two-year-old, but he changed his mind in time for a tilt at the Killavullan Stakes over seven furlongs at Leopardstown just eight days later, with Spencer on board this time. Here the standard was set by Gaff, a colt who had started his career at Keeneland in the spring before joining Dermot Weld, for whom he won a Listed race at Fairyhouse on his Irish debut. Gaff proved no match for Footstepsinthesand, who quickened to the front off the final turn in the decisive move of the race. Spencer was enthusiastic, and O'Brien, confident that the colt would be suited by better ground, faced into the winter in the knowledge that he had another string to his bow for the 2,000 Guineas.

According to Coolmore Stud's lavish brochure for 2006, Fallon identified Footstepsinthesand as the best racehorse in Ballydoyle in his very first week in the yard. The response may be "well he would say that, wouldn't he?" and we have a right to be cynical about the lexicon of stallion advertising, but the facts seem to bear out such a claim. Fallon did not agonise for long in choosing his Guineas mount in preference to the fundamentally idle Oratorio, and the personal significance of the decision, though doubtless taken in conjunction with O'Brien and the Coolmore team, should not be underestimated.

The Guineas was the first real test of his new alliance, Newmarket the perfect stage on which to show the British racing public that his career had taken on another incarnation. On the day, Footstepsinthesand looked a class apart in quickening away from his rivals. A top-class miler with enough in his pedigree to suggest that he might have stayed the Derby trip, his retirement was the cause of general regret, and a particular loss to O'Brien and Fallon, even though they would find compensation in the later achievements of the Guineas fourth Oratorio.

Footstepsinthesand

bay colt, 15-2-2002

Parents	Grandparents	Great-grandparents	Great-great-grandparents
Giant's Causeway ch 1997	Storm Cat	Storm Bird	Northern Dancer South Ocean
		Terlingua	Secretariat Crimson Saint
	Mariah's Storm	Rahy	**Blushing Groom** Glorious Song
		Immense	Roberto Imsodear
Glatisant b 1991	Rainbow Quest	**Blushing Groom**	Red God Runaway Bride
		I Will Follow	Herbager Where You Lead
	Dancing Rocks	Green Dancer	Nijinsky Green Valley
		Croda Rossa	Grey Sovereign Crenelle

Bred by Hascombe & Valiant Studs in England; 170,000gns Tattersalls October (Part 1) yearling.

Sire Giant's Causeway

Won 9 of 13 starts, inc. Curragh Futurity S.-Gr3, Prix de la Salamandre-Gr1, Gladness S.-Gr3, St James's Palace S.-Gr1, Eclipse S.-Gr1, Sussex S.-Gr1, York International S.-Gr1, Irish Champion S.-Gr1. Also 2nd in 2,000 Guineas, Irish 2,000 Guineas, Queen Elizabeth II S. and Breeders' Cup Classic. A striking individual, and a tough, top-class performer from 8-10.5f. By a champion North American sire out of a winner of 6 Graded races. Stands at Ashford Stud, Kentucky, at a (2006) fee of $300,000. Sire of 2 crops of racing age, inc: Aragorn (Gr2), Footstepsinthesand (2,000 Guineas-Gr1), Maids Causeway (Coronation S.-Gr1), My Typhoon (Gr2), Naissance Royale (Gr2), Shamardal (Dewhurst S.-Gr1, Poule d'Essai des Poulains-Gr1, Prix du Jockey Club-Gr1, St James's Palace S.-Gr1), Diamond Omi (Gr2), First Samurai (Hopeful S-Gr1, Champagne S.-Gr1), Frost Giant (Gr3).

Dam Glatisant

Won 2 of 9 races, inc. Prestige S.-Gr3. Also placed 2nd in Listed mile at Newmarket at 3. Attractive sort, smart performer at 2 before injury to a hind leg. Showed high-class form only once at 3, acquired blinkers. Seemed to stay 10f. Never tested on soft ground. By a top-notch runner, sire and broodmare sire. Dam won Nassau S., 3rd in Coronation S., 4th in Yorkshire Oaks. Dam of: Frappe (1996 c by Inchinor; winner), Margot (1998 f by Sadler's Wells; unplaced), Theme Song (1999 g by Singspiel; winner), Marie Laurencin (2000 f by Peintre Celebre; placed), Footstepsinthesand (2002 c by Giant's Causeway; Gr1 winner). She has a yearling filly by Dansili and was covered by Pivotal in 2004. Slipped to Caerleon in 1997, and to Selkirk in 2002 and 2003.

Pedigree assessment

What are we to make of Footstepsinthesand? He looked good when he won the 2,000 Guineas, preserving an unbeaten record, but he failed to reappear to defend a reputation that might have flattered him. He was covering mares in the southern hemisphere when the older generations might have been testing his mettle. This was not what we might have expected from a son of the so-called 'Iron Horse' of 2000, but it turned out that Footstepsinthesand was not the only Giant's Causeway product who had his fragility exposed in 2005; Shamardal's career also ended early, Maids Causeway spent months on the sidelines, and the sire's best juvenile filly in the States, Diamond Omi, was still more unfortunate, succumbing to pneumonia. Perhaps Footstepsinthesand was a good Classic winner; unfortunately, there is nothing in his record that enables him to be rated as such. *TM*

George Washington (Ire)

2yo bay colt **121**

Danehill (USA) - Bordighera (USA) (Alysheba (USA))

Owner Mrs John Magnier, M Tabor & D Smith

Trainer A P O'Brien

Breeder Lael Stables

Career: **5** starts | won **4** | second **0** | third **1** | **£317,349** win and place

By James Willoughby

TALENT streaked with temperament. It is a familiar paradox with racehorses. Perhaps the best ones know they are good and desire to express their individuality. After all, we expect them to stand out on the track, so why should they melt into the crowd off it?

When George Washington won the Group 2 Anheuser-Busch Railway Stakes on Irish Derby day at The Curragh, he was intent on asserting himself in both these regards. On the track, he needed only shaking up to beat Amigoni and three others by upwards of three-quarters of a length. Off it, he showed the capricious streak of a Hollywood star.

George Washington stood in the winner's enclosure and surveyed the scene around him with interest. He clearly enjoyed the limelight of the number-one spot, for he refused to co-operate when the time came to lead him away. It took handfuls of grass and the company of a stablemate to subjugate his wilfulness.

There was really no need for George Washington to draw attention to himself in this way; he had done more than enough on the track. The only blot on his performance was a tendency to race freely through the early stages, though a slow gallop had certainly not helped him to keep his exuberance in check.

George Washington had also raced freely when breaking his maiden. It took him two starts to do it, first time out running a race full of promise when only third to League Champion at Newmarket in May. The experience had not been lost on him, however, for he made short work of six rivals at The Curragh three weeks later.

With three starts under his belt after his Railway success, it was time for George Washington to get a shot at the big time. It always helps a horse move up in class if its jockey has faith, and it is hard to get a more glowing recommendation than this: "This horse is class and the best two-year-old around," Fallon said after the Railway Stakes.

George Washington lands the Phoenix by eight lengths, one of the most visually impressive wins of the year

O'Brien admitted that he did not initially have the Independent Waterford Wedgwood Phoenix Stakes specifically in mind. As with most of Ireland's juvenile Pattern races, the Ballydoyle trainer has an outstanding record in this Group 1, having won it every year between 1998 and 2003, his run broken only when the David Wachman-trained Damson defeated Oratorio.

Interestingly, George Washington differed from those six winners in using the Railway Stakes as his prep. Johannesburg (2001), Spartacus (2002) and One Cool Cat (2003) had run in the Group 3 Anglesey Stakes, which comes two weeks later and is thus only four weeks prior to the Phoenix.

Of O'Brien's six previous Railway Stakes winners – King Of Kings, Bernstein, Honours List, Rock Of Gibraltar, Hold That Tiger and Antonius Pius – only Hold That Tiger went on to run in the Phoenix, finishing last of nine behind his lesser-fancied stable companion Spartacus.

Significantly, O'Brien had allowed the other five time off for development, stepping them up in trip for a major race in the autumn. Did he initially consider George Washington to be of this type?

Certainly, George Washington is no sprinter on pedigree. Though sharing

2005 **Race record**

1st Laing O'Rourke National Stakes (Group 1) (Curragh, September 18) 2yo 7f Good **113** (TS 113) 7 ran. *Held up, stumbled shortly after start, 3rd and headway 2f out, led over 1f out, edged left, kept on well (K Fallon), beat Golden Arrow by 2l*

1st Independent Waterford Wedgwood Phoenix Stakes (Group 1) (Entire Colts & Filllies) (Curragh, August 7) 2yo 6f Good **121** (TS 115) 7 ran. *Bumped shortly after start, held up in 6th, smooth headway to lead 1½f out, soon quickened clear, impressive (K Fallon), beat Amadeus Mozart by 8l*

1st Anheuser-Busch Adventure Parks Railway Stakes (Group 2) (Curragh, June 26) 2yo 6f Good to firm **105** (TS 68) 5 ran. *Pulled hard early, settled 3rd, ridden to lead over 1f out, edged left, stayed on well (K Fallon), beat Amigoni by ¾l*

1st Boylesports 1800 221 321 EBF Maiden (Curragh, May 22) 2yo 6f Yielding **89** (TS 65) 7 ran. *Restrained early, held up in touch, 5th 2f out, quickened to lead under 1f out, soon clear, easily (K Fallon), beat Global Wings by 2l*

3rd Wyck Hall Stud Maiden Stakes (Newmarket, May 1) 2yo 5f Good to firm **86** (TS 77) 10 ran. *Slowly into stride, headway over 1f out, ran on well (K Fallon), beaten 1½l by League Champion*

his sire Danehill with Spartacus, he is not nearly so speedily bred as Ballydoyle's other five Phoenix winners. His dam Bordighera, by the Kentucky Derby winner Alysheba, won over 13 furlongs and was herself the daughter of Blue Tip. The latter won the Group 3 Prix Penelope over a mile and a quarter and was placed in the EP Taylor Stakes and Prix de l'Opera during the early 1970s.

Bordighera's most notable offspring prior to George Washington is the Irish Champion Stakes winner Grandera. We will refer to him again later, for reasons that those who remember the Grand Lodge colt will be able to anticipate. Suffice to say for now that Grandera was best at around a mile and a quarter.

Whether his preparation was a little ad hoc or not, George Washington arrived on Phoenix Stakes day at the beginning of August in screaming physical condition. Perhaps he had shown so much speed at home as to tip the hand of his trainer to attempt a race that is often the preserve of sprinting types.

What followed was particularly interesting when you take on board that George Washington was by no means hard-trained to a peak. "He has never worked more than four furlongs at home," said O'Brien.

George Washington produced the two-year-old performance of the season, crushing six rivals by a very wide margin in a sensational time. And how easily he did it, cruising behind the leaders for the first two-thirds of the six-furlong contest, having caught a bump and lost his balance leaving the stalls.

It was clear that he was charging for the lead when switched left to find a clear run up the rail two furlongs out, and he nearly jumped out of Fallon's hands to find the front soon after, running on very strongly

A second Group 1 victory for George Washington in the National, confirming his status as Guineas favourite

without ever feeling the whip. The winning margin was eight lengths over his stable companion Amadeus Mozart, with two and a half lengths back to the Coventry Stakes winner Red Clubs. In truth, it was impossible to quantify George Washington's superiority.

It behoves us to treat such commanding performances from two-year-olds with suspicion, following not the odd striking precedent. Senior Irish handicapper Garry O'Gorman was one who warned that the Phoenix Stakes could have dubious substance.

"Although the time of the race was exceptional and the winner put up an impressive performance, there was a soft underbelly in the fact that the form horses disappointed. I don't want to get carried away," O'Gorman said.

Fair enough, but you cannot cheat the clock. Allowing for weight-for-age, George Washington's time was 25lb better than that of Osterhase in a Group 3 race for older horses later on the card. Race-to-race time comparisons are dangerous, but the point is made for illustrative purposes here in full knowledge of the additional context provided by the other races on the card.

Osterhase ran to a Racing Post Rating of 115 in a competitive sprint. Just how lowly can you assess his time? If George Washington was flattered by weak competition and recorded a time performance a stone below his supposed merit, for example, Osterhase comes out in the realms of a 0-70 handicapper. Sprint races have to be seriously slowly run to fall to such levels, and it is just not logical to believe that George

Washington's far superior time does not confirm his merit lies in the 120s.

While George Washington had the platform of a strong pace to run at in the Phoenix, his subsequent win in the Group 1 Laing O'Rourke National Stakes did not afford him a similar opportunity. Again, he had the services of a pacemaker, but the field rather ignored Amigoni and became stretched out more as a result of a troublesome start, in which George Washington himself caught the worst of it and ended up towards the tail of the field.

From this moderate position, he needed the hurry-up from Fallon earlier than was good for him. The jockey could not be blamed for this, for an uncertain tactical situation was unfolding in front of him. Above all else, Fallon's job was to ensure that the colt was not left with too much to do.

George Washington never looked like being beaten, but having to rush through a quickening field while short of cover had its effect – he did not display anything like the surge of the Phoenix Stakes. Still, a two-length win in Group 1 company can hardly be regarded as disappointing, for all that his six rivals, headed by Golden Arrow and Heatseeker, remain uncertain blue-chip performers.

No winner of the Phoenix Stakes has won a Classic since Turtle Island in 1993, and only one of the previous six winners won a race as a three-year-old. The trends pertaining to the National Stakes are altogether different, however, with a roster of previous champions including subsequent Group 1 winners Dubawi, Refuse To Bend, Hawk Wing, Sinndar, King Of Kings and Desert King.

Plenty regard George Washington as a prohibitive price at odds of around 3-1 for the 2,000 Guineas. It is easy to hide behind the price when condemning his Classic prospects, however. While some of O'Brien's red-hot juveniles burned themselves out by the following spring, there are reasons to believe that George Washington may be one to deliver at Newmarket.

But what of the 'Grandera factor' alluded to above? While George Washington has hardly needed to be touched by the whip, he did receive one reminder in the closing stages of the National Stakes, from which he recoiled slightly and flashed his tail. Moreover, he was also inclined to edge left when asked to stretch. All this can be attributed to inexperience, but could it be more than that?

Grandera showed his own distinct waywardness while progressing into a high-class horse for James Fanshawe, then Saeed Bin Suroor in 2001 and 2002. Towards the end of his career, what had been merely quirks became more serious, culminating in a thoroughly irresolute display on his final racecourse outing in the 2003 King George at Ascot.

It would be speculation to suggest that George Washington's prospects will be severely limited by dishonesty, but distinct signs of a highly spirited nature are already transparent. It would be ironic were he to emerge as the type of character ill suited to his name. For now, he gets the benefit of the doubt.

George Washington *bay colt, 1-3-2003*

Danehill b 1986	Danzig	Northern Dancer	Nearctic **Natalma**
		Pas de Nom	Admiral's Voyage Petitioner
	Razyana	His Majesty	Ribot Flower Bowl
		Spring Adieu	Buckpasser **Natalma**
Bordighera ch 1992	Alysheba	Alydar	Raise a Native Sweet Tooth
		Bel Sheba	Lt Stevens Belthazar
	Blue Tip	Tip Moss	Luthier Top Twig
		As Blue	Blue Tom As Well

Bred by Lael Stables in Ireland. 1,150,000gns Tattersalls October 1 yearling.

Sire Danehill

Won 4 of 9 races, inc. Cork and Orrery Stakes-Gr3, Haydock Park Sprint Cup-Gr1. Also 3rd in 2,000 Guineas. Died May 2003. Stood at Coolmore Stud, latterly at a fee of Ir200,000gns. Sire of Gr1 winners: Danish (Queen Elizabeth II Challenge Cup), Kissing Cousin (Coronation), Danehill Dancer (Phoenix, National), Tsukuba Symphony (NHK Mile Cup), Desert King (National, Irish 2,000 Guineas, Irish Derby), Fairy King Prawn (Yasuda Kinen), Tiger Hill (Grosser Preis von Baden [twice], Bayerisches Zuchtrennen), Indian Danehill (Prix Ganay), Wannabe Grand (Cheveley Park), Aquarelliste (Prix de Diane, Prix Vermeille, Prix Ganay), Banks Hill (Coronation, Breeders' Cup Filly & Mare Turf, Prix Jacques le Marois), Mozart (July Cup, Nunthorpe), Regal Rose (Cheveley Park), Dress To Thrill (Matriarch), Fine Motion (Shuka Sho, Queen Elizabeth II Commemorative Cup), Landseer (Poule d'Essai des Poulains), Rock Of Gibraltar (Grand Criterium, Dewhurst, 2,000 Guineas, Irish 2,000 Guineas, St James's Palace, Sussex, Prix du Moulin), Westerner (Prix du Cadran [twice], Prix Royal-Oak [twice], Gold Cup), Clodovil (Poule d'Essai des Poulains), Intercontinental (Matriarch, Breeders' Cup Filly & Mare Turf), Light Jig (Yellow Ribbon), Spartacus (Phoenix, Gran Criterium), Grey Lilas (Prix du Moulin), North Light (Derby), Luas Line (Garden City H.), Oratorio (Prix Jean-Luc Lagardere, Eclipse, Irish Champion), George Washington (Phoenix, National), Horatio Nelson (Prix Jean-Luc Lagardere), Rumplestiltskin (Moyglare Stud, Prix Marcel Boussac).

Dam Bordighera

Ran only at 3 years, won 1 of 5 races, also Listed-placed at Chantilly. Dam of: Fifty Five (1997 f by Lake Coniston; winner in France), Grandera (1998 c by Grand Lodge; dual Gr1 winner), Tropezina (1999 f by Entrepreneur; unraced), Roman Love (2001 f by Perugino; placed 4th in only start), Ampelio (2002 c by Grand Lodge; 800,000gns yearling, unplaced in 2 starts), George Washington (2003 c by Danehill; dual Gr1 winner). Her yearling is a colt by Grand Lodge, her foal is a colt by Pivotal, and she was covered by Montjeu in 2005. Not covered in 1999.

Pedigree assessment

The hyping of horses trained at Ballydoyle reached a new level with the reported comment by Aidan O'Brien that George Washington was "by far the best two-year-old" that he had ever trained. The colt certainly has some smart form, notably in the Phoenix Stakes, but he was rather less convincing in the National Stakes. Even so, he is entitled to train on and make an impact at the top level, certainly at a mile, probably up to ten furlongs. *TM*

Ghostzapper (USA)

5yo bay horse **135**

Awesome Again (Can) - Baby Zip (USA) (Relaunch (USA))

Owner Stronach Stables

Trainer R J Frankel

Breeder Adena Springs

Career: **11** starts | won **9** | second **0** | third **1** | **£1,937,148** win and place

By James Willoughby

INJURY turned out to be the spectre that Ghostzapper could not overcome. Ghostzapper's 2004 Breeders' Cup Classic win invited some kind of historical perspective. Were we watching one of the all-time greats or simply a horse taking apart relatively weak opponents?

Even without reference to the time of 1min 59.02sec – a race record – it seemed unlikely that the latter possibility were true. The horses in closest proximity to him at the end of that Lone Star Park romp – Roses In May and Pleasantly Perfect – had already established themselves as top-class runners and were beaten by three lengths and another four.

Rather than take on the demands of a trip to the Dubai World Cup, Ghostzapper spent the following winter at the plush Palm Meadows training centre in Florida built by his owner Frank Stronach. In March, he turned in his first piece of serious work over six furlongs under his regular rider Javier Castellano. His trainer Bobby Frankel earmarked the Grade 2 Oaklawn Park Handicap the following month for his seasonal debut.

An unexpected hurdle presented itself, however, in the shape of an outbreak of the bacterial disease strangles at Palm Meadows, forcing Frankel to ship Ghostzapper and 13 stable companions to Churchill Downs. While the five-year-old thankfully did not contract the potentially fatal condition, instead he came down with a sinus infection that forced him to miss his intended reappearance.

After sufficient time was allowed for Ghostzapper to recover – a hole was drilled in the side of his head in order for his sinuses to drain – Frankel considered his star ready to resume competition at the end of May in the historic Metropolitan Handicap at Belmont Park, the track over which he was undefeated in four races and had repelled Saint Liam in the previous season's Woodward Stakes.

Only five horses opposed Ghostzapper in the 'Met Mile', but all were Graded stakes winners. There was market support for the impressive

Ghostzapper scores an easy victory in the Met Mile on his seasonal debut, but the 'world champ' never ran again

Carter Handicap winner Forest Danger, but the Horse of the Year still went off at a shade better than 1-2.

Ghostzapper toyed with them throughout. After a brisk opening half-mile, he was cruising just behind the leaders Love Of Money and Forest Danger. It took less than a furlong for Ghostzapper to wrap up the contest. He surged to a length lead by the three-furlong pole, with his rider doing little, and cruised into the straight with his opponents already beginning to look exhausted.

Had Castellano asked Ghostzapper for more effort, he could easily have broken the track record, but the jockey was mindful that this was only a step on the way to a defence of his title in the Breeders' Cup Classic. The great horse sauntered over the line more than six lengths ahead of outsider Silver Wagon, with Sir Shackleton third. Both placed horses went on to underline the merit of the form.

The time of 1min 33.29sec was the fastest in the Met Mile for 10 years, but a second short of the record. Nonetheless, it was a tremendous performance visually in a race that was also won by the likes of Holy Bull, Gulch, Forego, Buckpasser, Kelso and Native Dancer.

"All the years I have been watching Spectacular Bid, Affirmed and Secretariat, I wondered if I would ever get one like that," Frankel said afterwards. "This might be the horse."

Though it is difficult to compare horses from different generations, it is nevertheless a fascinating exercise. For Ghostzapper, the context provided

2005 Race record

1st Metropolitan Handicap Stakes (Grade 1) (Belmont Park, May 30) 3yo+ 1m Fast **135** 6 ran. *Close up in 3rd, led over 2f out, soon clear, pushed out, easily (J Castellano), beat Silver Wagon by 6¼l*

Other runs

2004 **1st** Breeders' Cup Classic - Powered by Dodge (Grade 1) (Dirt) (Lone Star Park, October 30) 3yo+ 1m2f Fast **135** 13 ran ● **1st** Woodward Stakes (Grade 1) (Dirt) (Belmont Park, September 11) 3yo+ 1m1f Fast **129** 7 ran ● **1st** Philip H Iselin Breeders' Cup Handicap (Grade 3) (Monmouth Park, August 21) 3yo+ 1m1f Sloppy 6 ran ● **1st** Tom Fool Handicap (Grade 2) (Belmont Park, July 4) 3yo+ 7f Fast **122** 4 ran 2003 **1st** Vosburgh Stakes (Grade 1) (Belmont Park, September 27) 3yo+ 6½f Fast **125** 10 ran ● **3rd** Kings Bishop Stakes (Grade 1) (Dirt) (Saratoga, August 23) 3yo 7f Fast **119** 13 ran ● **1st** Allowance race (Saratoga, July 26) 3yo+ 7f Fast 6 ran ● **1st** Allowance race (Belmont Park, June 20) 3yo+ 6f Muddy 6 ran 2002 ● **4th** Allowance race (Santa Anita, December 26) 2yo 6f Fast 8 ran ● **1st** Maiden Special Weight (Hollywood Park, November 16) 2yo 6½f Fast 10 ran

by American stars of the past is most exacting.

If the measure of greatness is races won, Ghostzapper would have to match the 39 victories of Kelso, not to mention Forego's 34 or Citation's 32; if it is track records broken, he would need to augment his record by eight to reach the mark of nine established by Swaps and by three to equal Man O'War and Secretariat; if it is Grade 1 wins then Affirmed had 14 and Spectacular Bid 13 compared to his three.

Once again, however, the racing fan was left with more questions than answers. On June 12, it was announced that Ghostzapper was retired with a fracture of the sesamoid bone on his near-fore limb. He was retired to his owner's stud Adena Springs in Kentucky to stand for $200,000. Incidentally, he will be covering alongside 2004 Epsom Derby winner North Light, who is valued at a quarter of this sum.

Poring over the elongated careers of the greats who offered Ghostzapper far stiffer comparison in an academic sense than his contemporaries did on the track, it really does seem as though they belonged to a different species. If only horses were campaigned as aggressively as in the past; if only they could stand up to the rigours of competition so robustly.

Will US racing ever see horses again to match those listed above? The depressing fact is that thoroughbreds are neither so tough since selective breeding compromised their soundness, nor so free to pursue lengthy careers since their reputations became so carefully protected.

The fact is that great horses of the past were persevered with after their injuries had healed, not sent to stud as soon as an excuse presented itself. It is true that Secretariat became too valuable to remain in training back in 1973, and there were other examples before him of champion racehorses whose stud value evidently exceeded the joy for their connections of watching them run, but nothing compared to the scale of the modern day.

Ghostzapper

bay horse, 6-4-2000

Awesome Again b 1994	Deputy Minister	Vice Regent	Northern Dancer Victoria Regina
		Mint Copy	Bunty's Flight Shakney
	Primal Force	Blushing Groom	Red God Runaway Bride
		Prime Prospect	Mr Prospector Square Generation
Baby Zip b 1991	Relaunch	In Reality	Intentionally My Dear Girl
		Foggy Note	The Axe Silver Song
	Thirty Zip	Tri Jet	Jester Haze
		Sailaway	Hawaii Quick Wit

Bred by Adena Springs in Kentucky.

Sire Awesome Again

Won 9 of 12 races, inc. Jim Dandy S.-Gr2, Stephen Foster H.-Gr2, Whitney H,-Gr1, Saratoga Cup H.-Gr2, Hawthorne Gold Cup H.-Gr3, Breeders' Cup Classic S.-Gr1. Medium-sized (16.0hh), well-made sort. Well-bred. Half-brother to champion 2-y-o Macho Uno (by Holy Bull). By a champion 2-y-o and champion sire. Dam won 4 races (6-7f), half-sister to dam of Miss Ra He Ha (Gr3). Grand-dam smart stakes winner at 5 years, from family of 1987 champion older mare North Sider. Stands at Adena Springs Kentucky, 2005 fee $125,000. Sire of 3 racing crops, inc: Awesome Time (Gr3), Ghostzapper (Vosburgh S.-Gr1, Woodward S.-Gr1, Breeders' Cup Classic S.-Gr1, Metropolitan Handicap-Gr1), Hotstufanthensome (Gr3), Snorter (Gr3), Toccet (Champagne S.-Gr1, Hollywood Futurity-Gr1), Round Pond (Acorn S.-Gr1), Spun Sugar (Gr2), Wilko (Breeders' Cup Juvenile S.-Gr1).

Dam Baby Zip

Won 4 of 16 races, inc. one minor stakes race. Just a useful sprinter. Unplaced only 2 efforts on grass. Sister to one and half-sister to nine other winners, inc. Win River Win (by Virginia Rapids, champion imported horse in Turkey). Dam tough, smart performer on dirt and grass, Gr1-placed, stakes winner (5 Listed) in each of 4 racing seasons. Half-sister to hardy sprinter Cutter Sam and to dam of Kentucky Derby winner Lil E. Tee. Dam of: Catch The Ghost (1996 f by Silver Ghost; winner), Getaway Girl (1997 f by Silver Deputy; winner), City Zip (1998 c by Carson City; Gr1 winner), Zip To The Wire (1999 f by Birdonthewire; placed), Ghostzapper (2000 c by Awesome Again; multiple Gr1 winner), Aristocrat (2002 c by Awesome Again; placed 4th on debut), Casperina (2003 f by Golden Missile; unraced to date). She has a yearling colt by Mr Greeley, and a colt foal by Sligo Bay, and was covered by El Prado in 2005.

Pedigree assessment

In 2004 we concluded our observations on Ghostzapper with a welcome for the news that he would remain in training, along with the prediction: "So long as he remains sound, another flawless season seems a certainty." It turned out to be all too true. Ghostzapper was flawless, but his season amounted to only one start, when he gave another breathtaking display in the Metropolitan Handicap. He was being aimed at the Suburban Handicap when examination of his near-fore disclosed a hairline fracture of the sesamoid, and his career was over. He was the best son of his sire, certainly the best American-trained horse since Cigar, and perhaps the best since Spectacular Bid. *TM*

Giacomo (USA)

3yo grey colt **121**

Holy Bull (USA) - Set Them Free (USA) (Stop The Music (USA))

Owner Mr & Mrs J S Moss

Trainer J Shirreffs

Breeder Mr & Mrs J S Moss

Career: **10** starts | won **2** | second **2** | third **3** | **£1,028,495** win and place

By James Willoughby

THE Kentucky Derby is an extraordinary race won by extraordinary horses. It is run like the July Cup with another half-mile tacked on the end.

There is about the race a beautiful brutality. Few horses are ever the same again. For some, it is their rite of passage from raw talent to rounded racehorse; for others, it is their ruination.

Every contender is trained to the minute, brought to a peak through a series of prep races used to give them the necessary toughness to come through the test. It is hard for us to understand this in Europe because we have no race that requires a similar grounding.

Brilliant horses can and do rise above the humbling fractions of the Derby. Fusaichi Pegasus came into the race as a strutting peacock of a colt in 2000 but produced a blue-collar effort to prevail; further back Silver Charm, Sunday Silence, Alysheba, Ferdinand, Spectacular Bid, Affirmed, Seattle Slew and Secretariat carried top-class credentials into the race and came out the other side. And there are many other examples stretching back into the mists of time.

For every one of these celebrated champions is another type of winner: Charismatic, Grindstone, Go For Gin, Sea Hero, Lil E Tee or Strike The Gold, not necessarily the best of their generation but capable of lifting their game through a combination of rare stamina or rare guts in this unusual environment.

Giacomo can safely be added to this list. The 50-1 chance became the second-longest priced winner of the great race in 131 runnings, owing his success in a large part to the fierce pace.

His starting price was a fair reflection of his form. The grey colt had yet to win outside maiden company and had been beaten fair and square in two of California's key Derby trials. Only his jockey Mike Smith seemed to derive encouragement from the latter, a two-length fourth behind

Giacomo (left) scores an upset win in the Kentucky Derby after coming from way off a very strong pace

Buzzards Bay in a below-par running of the Santa Anita Derby.

If Giacomo had failed to set the pulse racing with his tactical speed, at least he had kept galloping at Santa Anita. And that was to prove a key attribute.

Giacomo's fellow outsider Spanish Chestnut set the pace at Churchill Downs, acting as 'rabbit' for the much-fancied Blue Grass Stakes winner Bandini, who also carried the livery of Michael Tabor. To his credit, the leader lasted until exiting the back straight, where Giacomo was still languishing well in rear.

Turning for home, it looked as if the race was going to take shape as expected. The hot favourite Bellamy Road shaded the lead with Afleet Alex running on behind him. But in a matter of strides, the whole race was turned on its head.

Dirt horses stretched beyond breaking point can stop very quickly. A horse who looks to be going well will often have nothing left for the drawn-out closing furlongs and will suddenly lose its action. When this affliction overcomes several contenders concurrently, the resulting chaotic scenario is often referred to in the US as a 'pace meltdown'.

With all around him in turmoil, Smith began to thread Giacomo from the rear with the composure of a man walking down the street as buildings collapsed around his ears. At the furlong pole, it looked as though everything was running on the spot, with one exception: Giacomo was still passing rivals and lurched to the front down the middle of the track in the final 50 yards. Closing Argument, who did best of the front runners, and Afleet Alex, whose jockey Jeremy Rose had made a mistimed move, filled out the places, a half-length and the same behind.

It would be harsh to describe a Classic victory as a fluke, but this was the best opportunity if you were so inclined. For those of a more generous

2005 **Race record**

7th Belmont Stakes (Grade 1) (Belmont Park, June 11) 3yo 1m4f Fast **99** 11 ran. *Tracked leaders in 5th, went up on outside and led or disputed from 3f out, headed entering straight, soon weakened (M E Smith), beaten 18l by Afleet Alex*

3rd Preakness Stakes (Grade 1) (Pimlico, May 21) 3yo 1m1½f Fast **102** 14 ran. *Raced in 11th, pushed along over 4f out, 6th straight, went 3rd inside final furlong, kept on but never threatened first two (M E Smith), beaten 9¾l by Afleet Alex*

1st Kentucky Derby (Grade 1) (Churchill Downs, May 7) 3yo 1m2f Fast **121** 20 ran. *In rear, headway to go 9th straight, stayed on strongly down outside to lead final strides, driven out (M E Smith), beat Closing Argument by ½l*

4th Santa Anita Derby (Grade 1) (Dirt) (Santa Anita, April 9) 3yo 1m1f Fast **117** 11 ran. *Raced in 3rd, went 2nd over 1½f out, outpaced by winner and just held on for 2nd (M E Smith), beaten 2l by Buzzards Bay*

2nd San Felipe Stakes (Grade 2) (Santa Anita, March 19) 3yo 1m½ Fast **108** 8 ran. *Raced in 8th on inside, switched outside and headway well over 3f out, went 4th 1½f out, kept on (M E Smith), beaten 6½l by Consolidator*

3rd Sham Stakes (Santa Anita, February 5) 3yo 1m1f Fast 9 ran. *6th early, headway on outside to go 3rd after 4f, 3-wide into straight, kept on same pace under pressure final 1½f (M E Smith), beaten 1¼l by Going Wild*

2004

2nd Hollywood Futurity (Grade 1) (Hollywood Park, December 18) 2yo 1m½ Fast **119** 7 ran ● **3rd** Allowance Race (Hollywood Park, November 14) 2yo 1m½ Fast 5 ran ● **1st** Maiden Special Weight (Santa Anita, October 22) 2yo 1m½ Fast 7 ran ● **5th** Maiden Special Weight (Hollywood Park, July 15) 2yo 5½f Fast 9 ran

disposition, let us say that Giacomo had taken the invitation offered to him by the run of the race. And to do it required incredible resolution.

Not that Smith nor trainer John Shirreffs gave a damn how it was regarded. Instead, they set about preparing Giacomo for the second leg of the Triple Crown, the Preakness Stakes at Pimlico, two weeks after the first Saturday in May.

The Preakness was a different type of race – the first half-mile was a second slower – and it produced a different result, Afleet Alex wildly impressive as he overcame being brought to his knees at the top of the straight to record a four-and-three-quarter-length win over Scrappy T, who had not run in the Derby. Giacomo ran exactly as he had done at Churchill Downs, except this time the leaders did not stop and his late surge was enough only for third, five lengths behind the runner-up.

Worse was to follow in the Belmont Stakes. A bedraggled Giacomo barely picked up his hooves, finishing seventh as Afleet Alex once again put on a show. This time, it looked as though Giacomo was wrong.

Sure enough, bone chips were discovered in Giacomo's near-fore ankle and right knee which required surgery and ruled him out for the remainder of the season. He returned to training in September and the prognosis is excellent for his continued racing career.

Giacomo's mission is not just to regain his form but to get a little respect.

Giacomo

grey colt, 16-2-2002

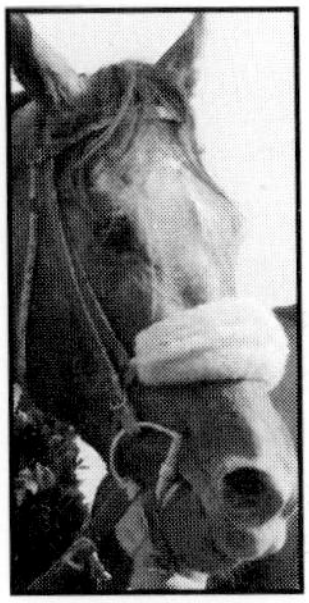

Holy Bull gr 1991	Great Above	Minnesota Mac	Rough'N Tumble Cow Girl
		Ta Wee	Intentionally Aspidistra
	Sharon Brown	Al Hattab	The Axe Abyssinia
		Agathea's Dawn	Grey Dawn Agathea
Set Them Free b 1990	Stop The Music	Hail to Reason	Turn-to Nothirdchance
		Bebopper	Tom Fool Bebop
	Valseuse	Tyrant	Bold Ruler Anadem
		Barbarossa	Cambremont Barbara

Bred by Jerry and Ann Moss in Kentucky.

Sire Holy Bull

Won 13 of 16 races, inc. Futurity S.-Gr1, Hutcheson S.-Gr2, Florida Derby-Gr1, Blue Grass S.-Gr2, Metropolitan H.-Gr1, Dwyer Stakes (8.5)-Gr2, Haskell Invitational H.-Gr1, Travers S.-Gr1, Woodward S.-Gr1. Horse of the Year at 3. Big (16.2hh), strong, well-made sort. Clearly the best of his crop, top-class from 8-10f. Retired after injury to near-fore in second start at four. By a good sprinter who was out of Dr Fager's half-sister, a champion sprint filly. Dam won 3 races, by high-class winner and successful sire. From a family noted for winner production, occasionally of high quality. Stands at Darley's Jonabell Stud, Lexington, Kentucky at a 2006 fee of $15,000. Sire of 8 crops of racing age, inc. notable winners: Confessional (Frizette S.-Gr1), Crash Course (Gr3), Holywood Picture (Gr3), Turnofthecentury (Gr3), Macho Uno (Breeders' Cup Juvenile S.-Gr1), Pohave (Triple Bend Invitational H.-Gr1), Thunder Blitz (Gr3), Giacomo (Kentucky Derby-Gr1).

Dam Set Them Free

Won 5 of 12 races, inc. 3 Listed. Lightly raced sprinter with smart form, successful on dirt and turf. Half-sister to French Gr3-placed Listed winner Vachti (f by Crystal Palace; dam of Gr3-placed Secret Saver). Dam unraced half-sister to Listed winner River Rose (by Riverman; dam of high-class performers Baiser Vole [Gr1], Tenue de Soiree, Squill, Neverneyev, Rio Verde). Grand-dam unraced half-sister to top-class sprinter-milers Barbaresque (by Ocarina) and Barbare (by Sicambre). Third dam half-sister to Eclipse S. winner Mystery, out of exceptional racemare Mistress Ford. Dam of: Scoville (1997 c by Sheikh Albadou; unraced), Valedon (1998 c by Valiant Nature; unraced), Styler (1999 f by Holy Bull; winner), Sea Jewel (2000 f by Sea Hero; Gr2-placed winner), Giacomo (2002 c by Holy Bull; Classic winner), Falcon Scott (2003 c by Swain; unraced to date). She has a yearling colt and a colt foal, both by Pleasant Tap.

Pedigree assessment

Giacomo was a surprise winner of the Kentucky Derby, having won nothing other than a maiden previously, so it was rather less surprising that he failed to follow up in the other Triple Crown events. But what was really disappointing was that in neither the Preakness nor the Belmont did his form seem to match up to the best of his juvenile performances, when runner-up in the Hollywood Futurity. If he is not destined to remain one of those who achieve only their 15 minutes of fame, he needs to come back stronger and more competitive in 2006. His sire, of course, came back after Kentucky Derby failure to establish himself as a true champion. *TM*

Goodricke

3yo bay colt **122**

Bahamian Bounty - Star (Most Welcome)

Owner Sheikh Mohammed

Trainer D R Loder

Breeder Red House Stud

Career: **11** starts | won **5** | second **4** | third **0** | **£236,383** win and place

By Richard Austen

JAMIE SPENCER will surely enjoy many more Group 1 successes, and so too will Sheikh Mohammed, but Goodricke's William Hill Sprint Cup was the last Group 1 for David Loder, as a trainer anyway. Loder decided for the second time to retire, and switch to being a bloodstock agent. Once the young man in a hurry, among the country's top trainers within five years of taking out a licence, Loder retired at the age of 41.

A spectacular success with his two-year-olds, in particular, Loder lost plenty of them to Godolphin, including Goodricke's sire Bahamian Bounty, even before he was selected to take charge of Sheikh Mohammed's juveniles on their way to Saeed Bin Suroor. So there was an irony in Loder's final success at the top level – and his first since 1998 – coming not with a juvenile but with a three-year-old Sheikh Mohammed left with him.

An earlier highlight in Loder's career was overseeing the start and name change for one of the equine greats. "From 60 yearlings in the yard my pin landed on the right one," is how he described picking out the youngster that would be Dubai Millennium.

It was when Loder moved to France with Godolphin in 1999 that things went wrong. A key factor for the trainer was ill health after a virus. "With my temperament, what with getting stewed up, the virus kept coming back all the time," he has revealed. On Sprint Cup day, he was at Newmarket, explaining: "I'm not mentally strong enough to handle the excitement of a day like this. It was no reflection of the horse's chance."

At the off, that chance was rated at 14-1 by the bookmakers. A month earlier he would have been among the longshots, but a half-length second in the Prix Maurice de Gheest put him in a different light, making Whipper go all the way to the line and drawing well clear of the rest.

Prior to that, Goodricke had run largely in handicaps in 2005, emerging on the line to dead-heat in one at Salisbury in May and the following

Jamie Spencer punches the air in delight as Goodricke lands the Group 1 Sprint Cup at Haydock for David Loder

month adding a conditions stakes at Newbury. And after Goodricke had weaved a way through the pack and passed all except New Seeker in the Totesport International at Newbury in July, Loder had reflected that "This was my Derby." Group 1 success seemed a long way off.

One of the hallmarks of Spencer's riding is a synergy with his mount, both seemingly filled with easy confidence. Goodricke is not one of those typical mounts. Visored and tongue tied all season, he looked more the type that needed confidence forced on him, along with a sense of urgency, and Loder's comments when Goodricke got off the mark in April as a two-year-old were not so wide of the mark well over a year later. "He was very lazy in the stalls and very lazy in the race and he is going to have to learn to jump better," he said that day.

Olivier Peslier was reading from a similar script when, after the Maurice de Gheest, he reported that, "I was pushing him from the start and then suddenly he accelerated for 100 yards at the furlong marker."

Although a bit of give in the ground was thought to suit him well, the concern at Haydock, on good going and with half a furlong less to travel, was that Goodricke would never have a scent of victory.

Most were in contention approaching the furlong marker, but it was Goodricke who got to front-running Patavellian and Etlaala first, and under repeated encouragement from the whip he was always going to keep ahead of other strong finishers in La Cucaracha, Ashdown Express, Somnus and Fayr Jag, enabling Spencer to pass the post stood up in his irons and punching the air.

Among the few that never threatened were Proclamation (11th) and

2005 Race record

1st William Hill Sprint Cup (Group 1) (Haydock, September 3) 3yo+ 6f Good **122** (TS 103) 17 ran. *Hampered start, soon switched right, held up, headway 2f out, ridden over 1f out, led inside final furlong, ran on (J P Spencer), beat La Cucaracha by 1l*

2nd Prix Maurice de Gheest (Group 1) (Deauville, August 7) 3yo+ 6½f Good **122** (TS 76) 13 ran. *Towards rear and pushed to stay in touch after 2f, ridden and good headway from 1½f out, 2nd 1f out, every chance 100yds out, not pass winner (O Peslier), beaten ½l by Whipper*

2nd totesport International Stakes (Heritage Handicap) (Newbury, July 23) 3yo+ 7f Good to firm **110** (TS 82) 24 ran. *Mid-division on stands' side, ridden and good headway over 1f out, stayed on strongly to go 2nd close home (J P Spencer), beaten ½l by New Seeker*

1st Coolmore Choisir Conditions Stakes (Newbury, June 30) 3yo 6f Good **111** (TS 88) 8 ran. *Held up in rear but in touch, steady headway over 1f out to lead just inside final furlong, soon clear, easily (J P Spencer), beat Visionist by 4l*

2nd Vodafone Surrey Stakes (Listed) (Epsom, June 3) 3yo 7f Good **102** (TS 82) 9 ran. *Dwelt, outpaced, 8th straight, good progress on outer 2f out, hung badly left 1f out, stayed on to take 2nd last stride (J P Spencer), beaten 1l by Galeota*

7th williamhillpoker.com Stakes (0-110 handicap) (Registered As The Merrion Stakes) (Listed) (York, May 11) 3yo 7f Soft **65** (TS 51) 10 ran. *Badly hampered and saddle slipped start, behind until headway over 2f out, soon ridden and beaten (J P Spencer), beaten 17½l by Wise Dennis*

1st Dead-heat betfair.com Handicap (Salisbury, May 1) 3yo (0-100) 6f Good to soft **108** (TS 91) 11 ran. *Dwelt, behind, headway 2f out, soon ridden, went 2nd and edged right just inside final furlong, ran on well to dead heat final stride (Martin Dwyer), dead-heated with Resplendent Glory*

2004

9th Coventry Stakes (Group 2) (Ascot, June 15) 2yo 6f Good to firm **86** (TS 71) 13 ran ● **1st** EBF Novice Stakes (Nottingham, May 14) 2yo 6f Good to soft **91** (TS 67) 7 ran ● **1st** "Original" Median Auction Maiden Stakes (Leicester, April 24) 2yo 5f Good to soft **86** (TS 45) 5 ran ● **2nd** French Brothers Median Auction Maiden Stakes (Windsor, April 5) 2yo 5f Good to soft **70** (TS 59) 8 ran

Gift Horse (last) and they headed the betting, newcomers to a Group 1 sprint comprised chiefly of the usual suspects. Proclamation was owned by Princess Haya of Jordan, Sheikh Mohammed's wife, who described this domestic as "great fun. There's been a lot of teasing in the house."

Spencer's reaction was more heated. "This is not about horses or about me," he said. "David has been one of my best friends for a long time, and it is upsetting and sad that his career is ending. I was just delighted that I could do this today for him."

When Spencer left the stable jockey job at Ballydoyle, Loder's support was instrumental in putting him back among the winners in Britain and on course for his first jockeys' title. Goodricke's success was reward for the jockey's steadfastness as well, as but for riding for Loder at the Royal meeting, Spencer might have been the regular big-race partner of Proclamation.

Goodricke

bay colt, 12-3-2002

Bahamian Bounty ch 1994	Cadeaux Genereux	Young Generation	Balidar Brig O'Doon
		Smarten Up	Sharpen Up L'Anguissola
	Clarentia	Ballad Rock	Bold Lad True Rocket
		Laharden	Mount Hagen Sinella
Star b 1995	Most Welcome	Be My Guest	Northern Dancer What A Treat
		Topsy	Habitat Furioso
	Marista	Mansingh	Jaipur Tutasi
		Evendo	Derring-Do Christmas Eve

Bred by Red House Stud in England. 110,000gns Tattersalls October (Part 1) yearling.

Sire Bahamian Bounty

Won 3 of 7 races, inc. Prix Morny-Gr1, Middle Park S.-Gr1. Also 4th in Dewhurst S. and July Cup. Medium-sized (16.0hh), well-made individual, and a fluent mover. High-class sprinter, best at 6f. Failed to stay 1m in Poule d'Essai des Poulains. Well-bred. By a top-class miler and successful sire. Half-brother to 2 other winners. Dam won 5 races from 2-5 years, Gr3-placed at 2. Grand-dam unraced half-sister to 2 winners and to dam of Gr3 winner Hawkins. Third dam won and placed twice from only 3 starts, half-sister to Stilvi (Gr3 winner, dam of Gr1 winners Tachypous, Tromos and Tyrnavos, Gr2 winner Tolmi, and Listed winner Taxiarchos). Stands at the National Stud, Newmarket, at a 2006 fee of £10,000. Sire of 5 crops of racing age, inc. notable winners: Naahy (Gr3), Pastoral Pursuits (July Cup-Gr1), Goodricke (Haydock Sprint Cup-Gr1).

Dam Star

Ran only at 2 years, won 1 of 3 races. Showed quite useful form in brief career, winning debut (median auction race at Nottingham) by 6 lengths. Half-sister to Superstrike (by Superlative; dual Gr3 winner in US) and Four-Legged Friend (by Aragon; Listed 2-y-o winner at Newmarket). Dam of: Petrean (1999 f by Petong; unplaced), Asbo (2000 f by Abou Zouz; placed; sold 47,000gns, in foal to Bahamian Bounty, at Tattersalls July 2005), Pastoral Pursuits (2001 c by Bahamian Bounty; Gr1 winner), Goodricke (2002 c by Bahamian Bounty; Gr1 winner), Starstone (2003 f by Diktat; unraced to date). She produced a colt foal by Nayef in 2005, and died, in foal to Dubai Destination, in July. Barren to Diktat in 2004.

Pedigree assessment

Having shown much-improved form when dividing Whipper and Patavellian in the Prix Maurice de Gheest, Goodricke confirmed his Group 1 calibre with a performance of at least equal distinction in the Haydock Park Sprint Cup. It was a shame that we did not see him again, but he promises to prove a significant recruit to the ranks of Godolphin in 2006. He tends to be a slow starter, which may sometimes count against him, but he is no less effective at seven furlongs than he is at six, so there will be plenty of options for him. He is a full-brother to Pastoral Pursuits, who improved from three to four, and there seems to be no reason why Goodricke should fail to do the same. *TM*

Grey Swallow (Ire)

4yo grey colt **126**

Daylami (Ire) - Style Of Life (USA) (The Minstrel (Can))

Owner Murry Rose Bloodstock

Trainer D K Weld

Breeder Mrs C L Weld

Career: **12** starts | won **5** | second **0** | third **1** | **£810,043** win and place

By James Willoughby

HIS are summers of lofty heights and autumns of spiralling decline. He is shimmering in full flight but pale in submission. Grey Swallow is a perplexing creature. He has won first time out in each of his three campaigns, but has twice finished the season in disappointment.

In 2005, his reappearance hinted at a glorious year, but it proved to be a false impression. Form students will point out that his defeat of Bago, Ace and an unfortunate Azamour in the Group 1 Tattersalls Gold Cup at The Curragh in May does not make for a solid guide. After all, the placed horses are not the most difficult to beat in the world, reaching the frame nine times between them subsequently without winning a race.

Nevertheless, there is no denying the style in which it was achieved. Grey Swallow travelled smoothly towards the inside, picked up well to lead a furlong and a half out and ran on well to win by three-quarters of a length. It was close for the minor placings.

Grey Swallow received an astute tactical ride from Pat Smullen. He was the first to make his effort and was able to build momentum while others were getting in each other's way. Azamour, in particular, looked as if he would have made a race of it had he not been bottled up when the winner first moved out to challenge.

The fragility of this form provides no explanation for Grey Swallow's disappointing showing in the King George at Newbury, however. He never looked at one with himself when trailing home a well-beaten seventh of 12, the winner Azamour getting a clear run this time.

Trainer Dermot Weld was inclined to blame the fast going, having previously stated that the colt is a heavy-shouldered type. While he clearly acts well with some cut, it was good to firm when he won the Irish Derby in such grand style in 2004, however. It could be argued that the uphill finish at The Curragh lessened the concussion on that occasion, but excuses based on ground conditions often mask an underlying problem. To be

Grey Swallow (left) beats a star-studded field on his 2005 debut in the Tattersalls Gold Cup, but he did not win again

fair, he did not move with complete freedom.

Weld afforded Grey Swallow seven weeks off to recover from his Newbury debacle, and he looked in good shape when reappearing in the Baileys Irish Champion Stakes at Leopardstown in September. Worse was to follow, however.

Grey Swallow just didn't have it. He was sufficiently well positioned to take part in the closing stages of the race with no tactical disadvantage, but did not pick up as Oratorio and Motivator fought it out.

This was puzzling. Though Grey Swallow could be forgiven his King George flop – any horse can have an off-day – it now seemed as though there were serious issues surrounding the colt.

While moving up the ranks, Grey Swallow had made corresponding progress physically – a trait of many by his sire Daylami who are often still unfurnished as three-year-olds. His reappearance was just about the best effort of his life and suggested he could make a strong challenge for some of Europe's best races. So it had to be regarded as a serious fall from grace that he was making so little impact at a time when he was reaching full strength.

Weld still elected to take up Grey Swallow's engagement in the Pattison Canadian International at Woodbine, worth more than £170,000 to the

2005 Race record

4th Pattison Canadian International (Grade 1) (Woodbine, October 23) 3yo+ 1m4f Yielding **114** 10 ran. *Held up, headway on outside to go 2nd over 2f out, lost 2nd 1½f out, one pace when rider's whip struck rival over 1f out, finished 3rd, beaten 4¾l by Relaxed Gesture, disqualified, placed 4th (P J Smullen)*

6th Baileys Irish Champion Stakes (Group 1) (Leopardstown, September 10) 3yo+ 1m2f Good to yielding **113** (TS 96) 10 ran. *Tracked leaders in 5th, 4th and effort 3f out, 3rd early straight, soon no extra (P J Smullen), beaten 6¾l by Oratorio*

7th King George VI And Queen Elizabeth Diamond Stakes (Group 1) (Newbury, July 23) 3yo+ 1m4f Good to firm **108** (TS 96) 12 ran. *Held up in mid-division, took closer order 4f out, ridden over 2f out, weakened 1f out (P J Smullen), beaten 12l by Azamour*

1st Tattersalls Gold Cup (Group 1) (Curragh, May 22) 4yo+ 1m2½f Good to yielding **126** (TS 73) 6 ran. *Settled 4th, 3rd 4f out, improved into 2nd 2f out, led 1½f out, kept on well final furlong (P J Smullen), beat Bago by ¾l*

Other runs

2004 **18th** Prix de l'Arc de Triomphe Lucien Barriere (Group 1) (Longchamp, October 3) 3yo+ 1m4f Good **98** (TS 90) 19 ran ● **4th** Baileys Irish Champion Stakes (Group 1) (Leopardstown, September 11) 3yo+ 1m2f Good to firm **123** (TS 123) 8 ran ● **1st** Budweiser Irish Derby (Group 1) (Curragh, June 27) 3yo 1m4f Good to firm **126** (TS 125) 10 ran ● **3rd** Boylesports Irish 2,000 Guineas (Group 1) (Curragh, May 22) 3yo 1m Good to firm **116** (TS 81) 8 ran ● **4th** UltimateBet.com 2,000 Guineas Stakes (Group 1) (Newmarket, May 1) 3yo 1m Good **118** (TS 108) 14 ran ● **1st** Leopardstown 2,000 Guineas Trial Stakes (Listed) (Leopardstown, April 18) 3yo 1m Soft **110** (TS 69) 5 ran **2003** **1st** Killavullan Stakes (Group 3) (Leopardstown, October 27) 2yo 7f Good **117** (TS 100) 4 ran ● **1st** G.P.T. Access Equipment EBF Maiden (Galway, July 28) 2yo 7f Soft **105** 9 ran

winner. He looked to be about to lay down a serious challenge swinging for home. In now depressingly familiar style, however, his run rather flattened out.

Grey Swallow was third past the post, beaten nearly five lengths by former stable companion Relaxed Gesture, but was demoted to fourth after Smullen was adjudged to have struck Mick Kinane, the jockey on fourth-home Electrocutionist, over the head. The placings were reversed.

Though Grey Swallow's performance was not a total disgrace, we know he is so much better than that. Smullen was not despondent, however. "The horse ran a very brave race," he said.

Stallion duties in 2006 were an option for Grey Swallow but it must be admitted he is not the most fashionably bred. Although Grey Swallow was a smart-two-year-old, his sire Daylami's tendency to produce slow-developing stock is likely to diminish his commercial appeal in the middle bracket of stallions in which he will have to operate.

Connections ultimately opted to keep him in training and at the end of the year Weld nominated an ambitious tilt at the Dubai World Cup as the five-year-old's likely first target of 2006. He has never raced on dirt, but he has come to hand early in each of his three seasons so far and could be a major contender.

Grey Swallow *grey colt, 19-2-2001*

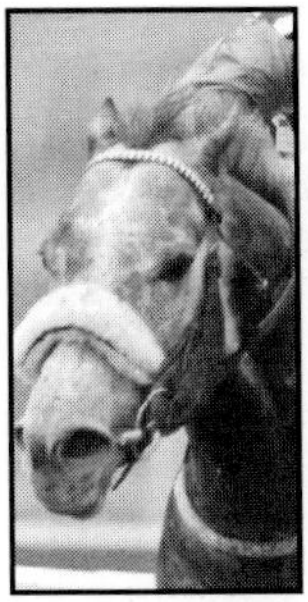

Daylami gr 1994	Doyoun	Mill Reef	Never Bend
			Milan Mill
		Dumka	Kashmir
			Faizebad
	Daltawa	Miswaki	Mr Prospector
			Hopespringseternal
		Damana	Crystal Palace
			Denia
Style Of Life b 1985	The Minstrel	Northern Dancer	Nearctic
			Natalma
		Fleur	Victoria Park
			Flaming Page
	Bubinka	Nashua	Nasrullah
			Segula
		Stolen Date	Sadair
			Stolen Hour

Bred by Mrs C.L. Weld in Ireland. 150,000gns Newmarket Houghton yearling.

Sire Daylami

Won 11 of 21 races, inc. Prix de Fontainebleau-Gr3, Poule d'Essai des Poulains-Gr1, Tattersalls Gold Cup-Gr2, Eclipse S.-Gr1, Man o'War S.-Gr1, Coronation Cup-Gr1, King George VI & Queen Elizabeth S.-Gr1, Irish Champion S.-Gr1, Breeders' Cup Turf-Gr1). High-class performer in all 4 seasons, noted for toughness, honesty, consistency and a rare zest for racing. Effective on any surface, and endowed with superior powers of acceleration. Well-made individual, just over 16.0hh, and very well-bred. Half-brother to Dalakhani (4 Gr1 wins) and Daymarti (Gr1-placed Listed winner). Sire won 2,000 Guineas, 3rd in Derby, also sire of Kalanisi; dam Listed winner, also Gr3-placed. Stands at Gilltown Stud, Ireland, at a 2004 fee of €20,000. Sire of 3 crops of racing age, inc. notable winner: Grey Swallow (Irish Derby-Gr1, Tattersalls Gold Cup-Gr1).

Dam Style Of Life

Won 2 of 10 races. Useful, consistent performer up to a mile, indifferent to ground conditions. Wore blinkers in both wins (Phoenix Park and Naas), but always raced gamely enough. Sister to Seasonal Pickup (won 4 Listed, Gr3-placed), half-sister to 2 other winners. By a dual Derby winner and successful sire out of a Gr3 winner who was sister to Listed winner Stoshka and half-sister to Gr2-placed Taufan (useful sire). Dam of: Style For Life (1990 f by Law Society; Listed-placed winner; dam of Gr1 winner in Italy), The Breadman (1991 g by Thatching; unplaced), Stylish Ways (1992 g by Thatching; Gr3-placed winner), Yudrik (1994 g by Lahib; winner), Central Lobby (1995 c by Kenmare; Gr3-placed winner), Rustic (1996 f by Grand Lodge; Gr3-placed winner), unnamed (1997 c by Caerleon; unraced), Irish Style (1999 f by Mujadil; winner), Grey Swallow (2001 c by Daylami; triple Gr1 winner), Moonlight Dance (2002 f by Sinndar; Gr3 winner). She has a filly foal by Daylami, and was covered in 2005 by Refuse To Bend.

Pedigree assessment

After an in-and-out campaign at three, Grey Swallow seemed to have got his career back on track when he came out best of a distinguished field for the Tattersalls Gold Cup. But the rest of his season turned out to be disappointing, and his two Group 1 wins on The Curragh stand out way above his other performances in his three seasons in training. He remains the only Pattern winner to date in the record of Daylami, but he is no longer the only one produced by his dam, as Moonlight Dance, who showed little in 2004, made striking progress in her second season. When three months' pregnant by High Chaparral, she won the Gr3 International Stakes, and at the December Sales she was sold to Japan for 800,000gns. *TM*

Heart's Cry (Jpn)

4yo bay colt **125**

Sunday Silence (USA) - Irish Dance (Jpn) (Tony Bin)

Owner Shadai Race Horse Co Ltd

Trainer K Hashiguchi

Breeder Shadai Farm

Career: **16** starts | won **4** | second **4** | third **2** | **£2,847,851** win and place

By Nicholas Godfrey

THANKS in no small part to a masterly change of tactics from his rider Christophe Lemaire, the top-class Japanese four-year-old Heart's Cry was able to produce an end-of-season performance that suggested he was among the very best racehorses in the world.

On Christmas Day, the Japan Cup runner-up stunned a crowd of 162,000 at Nakayama racecourse by winning the prestigious Arima Kinen, a lucrative 2,500-metre event reputed to attract more betting turnover than any other race in the world. Fervent Japanese racing enthusiasts had descended in their droves hoping to see another brilliant performance from the superstar colt Deep Impact, the spectacular Triple Crown winner hitherto unbeaten in seven starts. And they were disappointed.

The hot favourite, brought from the rear in customary fashion, was unable to reel in the year-older Heart's Cry, himself known as a come-from-behind performer but this time ridden much more prominently before gatecrashing the party to record his first success in more than 18 months. Reports that the victory was greeted by silence might be a little wide of the mark. If you listened carefully, it was probably just about possible to hear the sound of a pin dropping.

Like Deep Impact, Heart's Cry is a son of the exalted Sunday Silence, whose dominion over the Japanese bloodstock scene continued in 2005, despite his premature death three years earlier. Bred by the Yoshida family's Shadai operation, Heart's Cry also races in their ownership, and he showed immense promise from the outset in scoring three times in his first five starts, culminating in victory in a Group 2 Derby trial.

Yet despite a tremendous effort to finish second to King Kamehameha in the Classic itself, where a signature late burst failed by a length and a half, the colt developed into the most frustrating of performers.

Highly tried thereafter, he simply could not win, though he became well known for a powerful late charge of the type exemplified in his

Photograph courtesy of Japan Racing Association

Heart's Cry stuns the Nakayama crowd by ending the brilliant Deep Impact's unbeaten run in the Arima Kinen

performance in the 2005 Japan Cup. Heart's Cry was second favourite for the Japan Cup, possibly because the guaranteed fast pace and long straight at Tokyo racecourse seemed likely to play to his strengths. They did. But for a nod of the head, he would have won after weaving through horses and charging up Alkaased's inside in the final furlong.

On paper, the Arima Kinen a month later seemed unlikely to suit quite as much, the shorter straight at Nakayama not ideal for such a confirmed hold-up horse. Heart's Cry was sent off fourth best at just over 16-1 in a strong 16-runner field featuring, alongside the iconic Deep Impact, all Japan's leading older horses, among them the 2004 winner Zenno Rob Roy and Lincoln, close-up third and fourth in the Japan Cup.

An unexpectedly slow pace might also have worked against Heart's Cry, but in the event it compromised the favourite instead. As Yutaka Take positioned Deep Impact well to the rear, Lemaire took the bold move to settle his mount just off the leaders.

Deep Impact started to make a move at halfway before challenging six or seven horses wide at the final turn, as he had in many of his previous races. In front of him this time, however, was another horse with excellent acceleration in the shape of Heart's Cry, who took it up just over a furlong out. Although Deep Impact cut into his rival's lead, he could not get upsides,

2005 Race record

1st Arima Kinen (The Grand Prix) (Group 1) (Nakayama, December 25) 3yo+ 1m4½f Firm **125** 16 ran. *Always close up, led over 1f out, driven out, ran on well (C P Lemaire), beat Deep Impact by ½l*

2nd Japan Cup (Group 1) (Tokyo, November 27) 3yo+ 1m4f Firm **125** 18 ran. *Held up in 16th, 14th straight towards inside, 8th 1f out, ran on strongly while edging left final furlong, just failed (C P Lemaire), beaten shd by Alkaased*

6th Tenno Sho (Autumn) (Grade 1) (Tokyo, October 30) 3yo+ 1m2f Firm **118** 18 ran. *Held up, disputing 10th entering straight, stayed on final 2f (C P Lemaire), beaten 2¼l by Heavenly Romance*

2nd Takarazuka Kinen (Grade 1) (Hanshin, June 26) 3yo+ 1m3f Firm **122** 15 ran. *Held up in rear, 12th straight, ran on strongly final 1½f, finished well (N Yokoyama), beaten nk by Sweep Tosho*

5th Tenno Sho (Spring) (Group 1) (Kyoto, May 1) 4yo+ 2m Firm **114** 18 ran. *Held up towards rear, 16th straight, ran on strongly from over 1f out, nearest finish (N Yokoyama), beaten 4l by Suzuka Mambo*

2nd Sankei Osaka Hai (Group 2) (Hanshin, April 3) 4yo+ 1m2f Firm 9 ran. *Dropped out in last 4 lengths behind field, disputing 8th straight, strong run to take 2nd well inside final furlong, not reach winner (N Yokoyama), beaten 1¼l by Sunrise Pegasus*

2004

9th Arima Kinen (Grade 1) (Nakayama, December 26) 3yo+ 1m4½f Firm **114** 15 ran ● **10th** Deadheat Japan Cup (Grade 1) (Tokyo, November 28) 3yo+ 1m4f Firm **112** 16 ran ● **7th** Kikuka Sho (Japanese St Leger) (Grade 1) (Kyoto, October 24) 3yo 1m7f Firm **118** 18 ran ● **3rd** Kobe Shimbun Hai (Group 2) (Hanshin, September 26) 3yo+ 1m2f Firm 8 ran ● **2nd** Tokyo Yushun (Japanese Derby) (Group 1) (Tokyo, May 30) 3yo 1m4f Firm **123** 18 ran ● **1st** Kyoto Shimbun Hai (Group 2) (Kyoto, May 8) 3yo 1m3f Firm 11 ran ● **14th** Satsuki Sho (Japanese 2,000 Guineas) (Grade 1) (Nakayama, April 18) 3yo 1m2f Firm **101** 18 ran ● **1st** Wakaba Stakes (Hanshin, March 20) 3yo 1m2f Firm 14 ran ● **3rd** Kisaragi Sho (NHK Sho) (Group 3) (Kyoto, February 15) 3yo 1m1f Firm 14 ran ● **1st** Three-year-old Newcomer Race (Kyoto, January 5) 3yo 1m2f Firm 10 ran

eventually going down to his first defeat by half a length.

While a shocked crowd tried to suspend its disbelief, Lemaire pumped his fist after crossing the line. Speaking of the crucial tactical switch, he said: "I watched the video of the Japan Cup and made some mental notes from it – I reflected long and hard. He had run so well, I decided I would change, and in my mind the front-runners definitely have an edge here."

Heart's Cry achieved a Racing Post Rating of 125 for his victory, the equal of his Japan Cup mark, thereby confirming that he had produced another display right from the top drawer under divergent circumstances. Deep Impact will not be short of supporters should the pair ever meet again, an intriguing prospect that looks more than likely given that both horses are set to stay in training. In 2005, though, Heart's Cry just had the edge.

Given such talent, it is tempting to consider that the fates had to let things drop right for Heart's Cry one day. It just needed someone to give them a little shove in the right direction.

Heart's Cry

bay colt, 15-4-2001

Sunday Silence br 1986	Halo	Hail To Reason	Turn-to Nothirdchance
		Cosmah	Cosmic Bomb Almahmoud
	Wishing Well	Understanding	Promised Land Pretty Ways
		Mountain Flower	Montparnasse Edelweiss
Irish Dance b 1990	Tony Bin	Kampala	Kalamoun State Pension
		Severn Bridge	Hornbeam Priddy Fair
	Buper Dance	Lyphard	Northern Dancer Goofed
		My Bupers	Bupers Princess Revoked

Bred by Shadai Farm in Japan.

Sire Sunday Silence

Won 9 (6-10f) of 14 races. At 2, won 1 of 3 starts. At 3, won 7 (inc. San Felipe H-Gr2, Santa Anita Derby-Gr1, Kentucky Derby-Gr1, Preakness S-Gr1, Super Derby-Gr1, Breeders' Cup Classic-Gr1) of 9 starts, also 2nd Belmont S-Gr1. At 4, won 1 (Californian S-Gr1) of 2 starts. By smart turf performer and very good US sire, out of a US stakes winner. Retired to Shadai Stallion Station in Japan, died August 2002. First foals 1992, sire of Gr1 winners (northern hemisphere foals): Dance Partner, Fuji Kiseki, Genuine, Marvelous Sunday, Tayasu Tsuyoshi, Bubble Gum Fellow, Dance In The Dark, Ishino Sunday, Silence Suzuka, Stay Gold, Special Week, Admire Vega, Stinger, To The Victory, Agnes Flight, Air Shakur, Cheers Grace, Believe, Manhattan Cafe, Mejiro Bailey, Admire Max, Durandal, Gold Allure, Admire Groove, Heavenly Romance, Neo Universe, Peace Of World, Still In Love, Zenno Rob Roy, Dance In The Mood, Daiwa El Cielo, Daiwa Major, Hat Trick, Heart's Cry, Suzuka Mambo, Air Messiah, Deep Impact. Also sire of European Group winners Sunday Picnic (Gr3), Silent Honor (Gr3), Layman (Gr3), Sundrop (Gr3).

Dam Irish Dance

Unraced at 2, raced 20 times from 3 to 5 in Japan, won 9 races at 4 and 5, notably Niigata Daishoten-Gr3 and Niigata Kinen-Gr3, both over 10f, also 2nd All Comers S-Gr2. By Arc winner and excellent middle-distance Japanese sire. Dam unraced sister to Group 3 winner Lyphard's Special, half-sister to champion North American sprinter My Juliet and Listed-placed My Potters (dam of Irish Oaks winner Winona). Grand-dam My Bupers also dam of $10.2m yearling Snaafi Dancer (unraced). Dam of: Agnes Shiranui (1998 c by Sunday Silence; winner), Emerald Isle (1999 f by Sunday Silence; winner), Heart's Cry (2001 c by Sunday Silence; Gr1 winner), 2003 c by El Condor Pasa.

Pedigree assessment

The combination of Sunday Silence as sire and Tony Bin as broodmare sire has been very successful; two notable recent examples are Heart's Cry and fellow top-level winner Admire Groove. Although Heart's Cry is from the family of champion North American sprinter My Juliet, most members stay further. Heart's Cry's dam Irish Dance was best over 10f, and his grand-dam's brother Lyphard's Special was a 12f Group winner. Heart's Cry is an obvious contender for the top Japanese 12f+ prizes in 2006, and the identity of his sire guarantees him initial popularity at stud. *JH*

Horatio Nelson (Ire)

2yo bay colt **120**

Danehill (USA) - Imagine (Ire) (Sadler's Wells (USA))

Owner Mrs John Magnier & Mrs David Nagle

Trainer A P O'Brien

Breeder Beaverstone & Tower Bloodstock

Career: **5** starts | won **4** | second **1** | **£284,235** win and place

By Alan Sweetman

IN THE year that marked the 200th anniversary of the Battle of Trafalgar it was fitting that one of the best juveniles of the season should bear the name of Britain's greatest naval hero. It was, however, a touch ironic that the name was secured by an Irish-based owner, since Horatio Nelson is best remembered in Ireland for his Pillar, Dublin's most distinctive monumental landmark until blown up by Republicans in 1966 as a symbolic gesture against the country's colonial past.

In common with many of Aidan O'Brien's juveniles during the 2005 season, Horatio Nelson, a son of Danehill and dual Classic winner Imagine, looked some way short of being fully primed for his first outing, in a maiden over seven furlongs at The Curragh on the Friday evening before the Irish Derby. In front on settling down, he maintained his effort in promising fashion despite drifting to the left under pressure, causing some slight inconvenience to the one-length runner-up Heliostatic, though not enough for there to have been any real prospect of the placings being altered in the ensuing stewards' inquiry. It was a fine start, and Heliostatic, considered an excellent long-term prospect by his trainer Jim Bolger, was not long in endorsing the form with a comfortable maiden win.

Next on the agenda for Horatio Nelson was the Weatherbys Superlative Stakes at Newmarket, a contest that had been won the year before by the subsequent National Stakes and Irish 2,000 Guineas winner Dubawi, whose victims had included the Breeders' Cup Juvenile winner Wilko. It again looked a decent contest on paper, but the Irish raider proved far too good. After setting a steady early pace Kieren Fallon raised the tempo from around two furlongs down, and when the colt responded to a couple of cracks of the whip it was only a matter of how far he would win. In the end, the margin was two and a half lengths to Leo, later the winner of a sub-standard edition of the Royal Lodge, with solid yardstick Yasoodd close behind in third.

Kieren Fallon and Horatio Nelson after their triumph at Longchamp, but there were no smiles after the Dewhurst

As O'Brien's grip on the juvenile scene developed inexorably, there were few takers when it was announced that Horatio Nelson would run in the Group 2 Futurity Stakes at The Curragh. Silent Times, the sole British visitor in a field of five, made the running at a good pace, but it was plain sailing for the Ballydoyle colt, who stretched clear to score by two and a half lengths from the rank outsider Galantas, with Silent Times third. Given his provenance and his pedigree, it was hardly surprising that he was now being seen as a leading candidate for the 2006 Derby.

Horatio Nelson was declared for the National Stakes merely as a precautionary measure in the event of any last-minute hitch with George Washington, and instead was routed towards the Prix Jean-Luc Lagardere, a race regarded fondly by O'Brien, who had won it for the fifth time with Oratorio in 2004. Under a well-crafted educational ride by Fallon, he had little difficulty in maintaining his unbeaten record at the main expense of the Solario Stakes winner Opera Cape. Although the race has not proved a reliable guide to Ballydoyle's Derby aspirations in the past, the roll of honour has included Rock Of Gibraltar and Oratorio, both of whom went on to contest the Dewhurst shortly afterwards.

2005 Race record

2nd Darley Dewhurst Stakes (Group 1) (Newmarket, October 15) 2yo 7f Good to soft **120** (TS 119) 8 ran. *Held up, ridden and not clear run over 1f out, ran on well inside final furlong (K Fallon), beaten nk by Sir Percy*

1st Prix Jean-Luc Lagardere (Grand Criterium) (Group 1) (Longchamp, October 2) 2yo 7f Good to soft **118** (TS 101) 6 ran. *Disputed lead until led after 3f, narrowly headed 1½f out, soon regained lead, ridden approaching final furlong, ran on well (K Fallon), beat Opera Cape by 1½l*

1st Galileo European Breeders' Fund Futurity Stakes (Group 2) (Curragh, August 20) 2yo 7f Good **113** (TS 105) 5 ran. *Close up in 2nd, improved to lead over 1½f out, ridden clear final furlong, easily (K Fallon), beat Galantas by 2½l*

1st Weatherbys Superlative Stakes (Group 3) (Newmarket (July), July 7) 2yo 7f Good to soft **106** (TS 103) 11 ran. *Made all, ridden over 1f out, ran on well (K Fallon), beat Leo by 2½l*

1st Blue Square Casino EBF Maiden (Curragh, June 24) 2yo 7f Good to firm **85** (TS 52) 12 ran. *Soon led, strongly pressed 2f out, driven out and ran on well final furlong, drifted left, comfortably (K Fallon), beat Heliostatic by 1l*

A year earlier Oratorio had been a 15-2 chance when a creditable second in the Newmarket event that is so often the defining race of the juvenile season in Britain, but when Horatio Nelson and Opera Cape renewed rivalry just 13 days after their Longchamp meeting, the Irish colt was sent off the 8-11 favourite to preserve his unbeaten record. Still, with the opposition headed by another unbeaten runner in Sir Percy, and Coventry Stakes winner Red Clubs also in the field, the race looked well up to standard.

After the outsider Humungous had made the running, the crucial moment came as Horatio Nelson was squeezed for room between Red Clubs and Palace Episode over a furlong out. Sir Percy took the initiative, and though Horatio Nelson ran on well when switched it never looked as if he would rescue the situation, with Sir Percy holding him by a neck despite idling slightly in front. Opera Cape reproduced his Longchamp effort to take third, with Red Clubs a further three and a half lengths behind him in fourth.

After a lean season for the British two-year-olds, a genuine Classic contender had emerged in the cheaply bought Sir Percy, but much of the bookmaker reaction and media attention predictably remained focused on Ballydoyle. With the Phoenix and National Stakes winner George Washington apparently set to lead the stable's challenge for the 2,000 Guineas, Horatio Nelson held his place in the vanguard of the Derby picture. He is somewhat in the mould of Generous, a half-brother to his dam, and the trip looks tailor-made for him. If we are ever to see another monument raised in Ireland to Horatio Nelson, it will surely be to the equine version, a hero not of Trafalgar, but perhaps of Epsom and The Curragh.

Horatio Nelson

bay colt, 30-4-2003

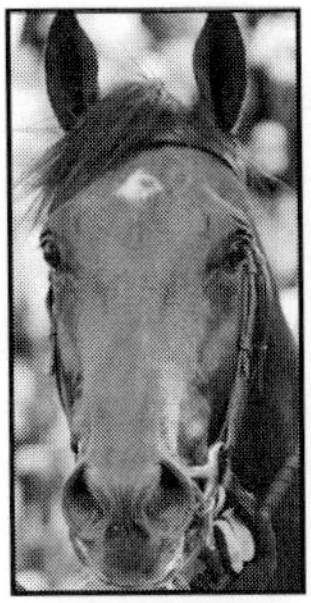

Danehill b 1986	Danzig	**Northern Dancer**	**Nearctic** **Natalma**
		Pas de Nom	Admiral's Voyage Petitioner
	Razyana	His Majesty	Ribot Flower Bowl
		Spring Adieu	Buckpasser **Natalma**
Imagine b 1998	Sadler's Wells	**Northern Dancer**	**Nearctic** **Natalma**
		Fairy Bridge	Bold Reason Special
	Doff The Derby	Master Derby	Dust Commander Madam Jerry
		Margarethen	Tulyar Russ-Marie

Bred by Beaverstone & Tower Bloodstock in Ireland.

Sire Danehill

Won 4 of 9 races, inc. Haydock Park Sprint Cup-Gr1. Died May 2003. Stood at Coolmore Stud, latterly at Ir200,000gns. Sire of Gr1 winners: Danish (QE II Challenge Cup), Kissing Cousin (Coronation), Danehill Dancer (Phoenix, National), Tsukuba Symphony (NHK Mile Cup), Desert King (National, Irish 2,000, Irish Derby), Fairy King Prawn (Yasuda Kinen), Tiger Hill (GP von Baden [twice], Bayerisches Zuchtrennen), Indian Danehill (Prix Ganay), Wannabe Grand (Cheveley Park), Aquarelliste (Prix de Diane, Prix Vermeille, Prix Ganay), Banks Hill (Coronation, Breeders' Cup F & M Turf, Jacques le Marois), Mozart (July Cup, Nunthorpe), Regal Rose (Cheveley Park), Dress To Thrill (Matriarch), Fine Motion (Shuka Sho, QE II Commemorative Cup), Landseer (Poule d'Essai des Poulains), Rock Of Gibraltar (Grand Criterium, Dewhurst, 2,000 Guineas, Irish 2,000, St James's Palace, Sussex, Prix du Moulin), Westerner (Prix du Cadran [twice], Prix Royal-Oak [twice], Gold Cup), Clodovil (Poule d'Essai des Poulains), Intercontinental (Matriarch, Breeders' Cup F & M Turf), Light Jig (Yellow Ribbon), Spartacus (Phoenix, Gran Criterium), Grey Lilas (Prix du Moulin), North Light (Derby), Luas Line (Garden City H.), Oratorio (Prix Jean-Luc Lagardere, Eclipse, Irish Champion), George Washington (Phoenix, National), Horatio Nelson (Prix Jean-Luc Lagardere), Rumplestiltskin (Moyglare Stud, Prix Marcel Boussac).

Dam Imagine

Won 4 of 10 races, inc. Park S.-Gr3, Irish 1,000 Guineas-Gr1, Oaks S.-Gr1. Strongly built, close-coupled individual, with admirable temperament, effective on both fast and soft ground. Half-sister to multiple Gr1 winner Generous (by Caerleon) and Gr3 winner Wedding Bouquet (by Kings Lake). Family of Trillion, Triptych, etc. Dam of: Horatio Nelson (2003 c by Danehill; Gr1 winner). Her yearling is a colt by Rock Of Gibraltar and she has a filly foal by the same horse.

Pedigree assessment

Notwithstanding the contradictory hype from Ballydoyle that favours George Washington, stablemate Horatio Nelson arguably has the better form in the book. What he achieved at Longchamp pretty well matched the other Danehill colt's mark in the National Stakes, and he exceeded it in the Dewhurst. It seems reasonable to assume that Horatio Nelson will be aimed at the Derby, and there can be little doubt that he will have the stamina for the job. When Danehill's mates provide staying qualities, distance is rarely a problem for his stock. We may also count on Horatio Nelson's having the requisite class, as son of an Oaks winner, and 'nephew' of an outstanding dual Derby hero. An uncomplicated colt with an admirable attitude, Horatio Nelson belongs on any Derby shortlist. *TM*

Hurricane Run (Ire)

3yo bay colt **133**

Montjeu (Ire) - Hold On (Ger) (Surumu (Ger))

Owner M Tabor

Trainer A Fabre

Breeder Gestut Ammerland

Career: **7** starts | won **6** | second **1** | **£1,624,650** win and place

By James Willoughby

AS LA MARSEILLAISE drifted on the breeze to announce another French-trained winner of the Prix de l'Arc de Triomphe, the focus of pomp and pageantry at Longchamp rested on Le Tricolore. Its broad bands of blue, white and red signify the republic's ideological foundation of liberty, equality and fraternity, but they could also represent the united forces behind the winner, Hurricane Run.

The first colour symbolises the blue-chip investment made by the team at Coolmore when Hurricane Run was acquired in mid-season; white is for Kieren Fallon's blemish-free performance in the saddle; red is the Napoleonic hue of the little general, Andre Fabre, who trained the colt to perfection.

Three colours and three stories. Each one a separative narrative but combining to shape the career of the outstanding racehorse in Europe during 2005.

Blue. The identity of Hurricane Run's sire Montjeu may have been the catalyst behind his change of ownership. When the 1999 Arc winner began to emerge as a potent progenitor, his son took on added value following his second to Shamardal in the Prix du Jockey-Club in June.

Hurricane Run arrived at the post at Chantilly as hot favourite. He was coming off a five-length victory in the Group 2 Prix Hocquart at Longchamp the previous month. A good gallop had really suited him on that occasion, and he had powered away after following the pace to beat Silver Cross, Orion Star and Ruwi – all with black type already next to their names – in spectacular style.

That was Hurricane Run's coming-out party. Though always held in high regard, he had barely been tested in two previous outings, at Longchamp. He made one start as a juvenile, winning a late-season newcomers' event, then reappeared in April and landed a minor event over the Hocquart distance of 11 furlongs.

Hurricane Run stamps himself Europe's Horse of the Year with a clear-cut triumph in the Prix de l'Arc de Triomphe

The only doubt over Hurricane Run after his first three starts was his attitude under pressure. In common with others by his sire, he owned a rather spirited nature that inclined him towards some degree of individuality. This had manifested itself in the latter stages of the Hocquart as a tendency to come off a true line.

Notwithstanding his inexperience, it is likely that he would have maintained his unbeaten record in the Jockey-Club had his rider Christophe Soumillon kept him closer to the pace. He was undone by both a steady early gallop and a brilliant tactical ride by Frankie Dettori on the winner.

Hard though Hurricane Run charged, he could reach only Shamardal's throat latch as the pair winged past the line, again spoiling the momentum of his finishing effort by edging both ways. This meandering provides some degree of absolution for Soumillon, but the impression was that the best horse finished second.

Part of the deal struck by his German owner Gestut Ammerland on sale of the colt to Magnier and his associates was that he should race in the stud's colours in the Irish Derby. He would remain in training with Fabre, but Fallon would take over from Soumillon in the irons.

White. It is not without irony that the colour is applied to Fallon, for his life out of the saddle has hardly been blemish-free. Nevertheless, the back of a horse is an oasis of calm when compared with the maelstrom in which he has been caught up on some occasions.

2005 Race record

1st Prix de l'Arc de Triomphe Lucien Barriere (Group 1) (Longchamp, October 2) 3yo+ 1m4f Good to soft **133** (TS 133) 15 ran. *Held up to straight, squeezed through on inside 2½f out, led inside final furlong (K Fallon), beat Westerner by 2l*

1st Prix Niel Casino Barriere (Group 2) (Longchamp, September 11) 3yo 1m4f Good to soft **123** (TS 114) 5 ran. *Raced in 2nd, pressing leader 3f out, led entering straight, pushed along 1½f out, driven clear final furlong (K Fallon), beat Runaway by 3l*

1st Budweiser Irish Derby (Group 1) (Curragh, June 26) 3yo 1m4f Good to firm **126** (TS 103) 9 ran. *Held up, last 3f out, smooth headway on outer early straight, ridden to lead inside final furlong, edged right, kept on well (K Fallon), beat Scorpion by ½l*

2nd Prix du Jockey Club (Group 1) (Chantilly, June 5) 3yo 1m2½f Good **116** (TS 109) 17 ran. *Held up in touch, disputing 7th on outside straight, pushed along over 2f out, finished strongly final 150yds (C Soumillon), beaten nk by Shamardal*

1st Prix Hocquart (Group 2) (Longchamp, May 9) 3yo 1m3f Good **117** (TS 106) 6 ran. *In touch, disputing 3rd halfway, effort in centre 1½f out, ran on to lead approaching final furlong, quickened clear, pushed out (C Soumillon), beat Silver Cross by 5l*

1st Prix de Ferrieres (Longchamp, April 15) 3yo 1m3f Heavy **83** (TS 61) 7 ran. *Made all, quickened clear when pressed a[pproaching final furlong, hung badly left final furlong, very easily (C Soumillon), beat Warning Sign by 3l*

2004

1st Prix de Belleville (Unraced Colts & Geldings) (Longchamp, October 21) 2yo 1m1f Holding (TS 79) 9 ran

As a jockey, Fallon has chiselled away at his shortcomings like an archaeologist uncovering hidden treasure with a toothpick. His tool is the intuitive process of linking cause and effect in the most common tactical situations in which a rider finds himself. Repeat the process of self-correction in a few thousand races, and the ability to sit in the most favourable spots and pick the right running lanes to find the gaps begins to look instinctive.

When Fallon climbed aboard Hurricane Run for the first time at The Curragh in June, his racing brain told him to keep it simple. He believed himself on a horse with an advantage in talent over his eight rivals that did not require the bolster of a great tactical ride. So he took the safe route down the outside.

This strategy got the job done, but few come wide on the round course at The Curragh without some degree of additional toil. And Hurricane Run was still inexperienced, so much so that he seemed to go a little in snatches as the pace lifted and fell.

Nevertheless, Hurricane Run reeled in Scorpion inside the final furlong and went on to win by half a length with something in hand. It was just the type of Fallon ride that really fills a horse with confidence for its later assignments.

Red. Andre Fabre is an expressed admirer of the Emperor Napoleon. Comparisons between their professional exploits are trite, but the necessity for forward planning is a theme of both the military strategist and the racehorse trainer.

Hurricane Run (right) gains compensation for his French Derby defeat by landing the Irish equivalent in great style

It was no stroke of genius that Fabre worked back from the Arc when planning Hurricane Run's autumn campaign, neither did it require an inspirational decision to select the Prix Niel as his prep race. The point is that anything done well is made to look simple.

When the colt returned for the Niel in September he had to be at the right level to derive benefit from the race without it taking something out of him. Fabre's calculations were on the mark, though a three-length defeat of his Listed-winning stablemate Runaway did not impress everyone, particularly as the runner-up was tenderly handled. Hurricane Run was entitled to be rusty, but it was still of some concern that he lugged into the rail inside the final furlong. Despite this, the trainer described it as a "perfect prep".

Three weeks later, Fallon and Hurricane Run came together at the top of their form for the Arc. The former was already enjoying one of the best days of his career, having gained a brace of Group 1 victories atop Rumplestiltskin in the Prix Marcel Boussac and Horatio Nelson in the Prix Jean-Luc Lagardere. At the same time, the colt was in screaming condition for the most important race of his career.

Before the field had gone a quarter of a mile, Hurricane Run looked in trouble. He seemed to need encouragement to stay with the pack, though his jockey later said he remained unconcerned and was only "hunting along". It was not the gait of a potential winner, however.

Hurricane Run's indolence – it proved to be nothing more – took the tactical impetus out of Fallon's hands. He was playing catch-up and found himself still languishing in rear as they came down the false straight. With just two horses behind him and no escape route to the outside, the Irishman had his right boot against the rail and his back against the wall.

The advantage for his rider was that Hurricane Run was now taking him forward through the field. When a gap appeared, he would have the momentum to take it, and, slipping past outsider Samando just before straightening up, Fallon saw a path open along the inside.

With room to run, Hurricane Run began to charge up towards the lead. Up front, Motivator had taken it up and was going for home, but the Derby winner seemed to falter approaching the final furlong. This was the break Fallon needed, for, when the leader hung left in a state of weariness, Hurricane Run needed no further bidding, pouring it on to overpower Westerner half a furlong out and beating the fine stayer by two lengths. Bago was a length and a half further behind in third.

When the video is reviewed, it seems as though Hurricane Run did less hard running during the Arc than any horse to have scored in modern times. He needed to engage overdrive for little over a furlong to prevail, partly a factor of his superior ability and partly down to the benefit of saving ground and getting cover on the inside, which rather sucked him into contention.

Though some regarded the latest Arc as less than a vintage renewal, the form did not work out too badly. Admittedly, the placed horses disappointed somewhat afterwards, but fourth-placed Shirocco won the Breeders' Cup Turf at Belmont – a race from which Hurricane Run had to be scratched after coughing – and seventh-placed Pride was runner-up in the Champion Stakes at Newmarket and the Hong Kong Cup.

Hurricane Run will be back in 2006 to augment his record. His sire went on to land the King George at Ascot in great style, but was not at his best when only fourth to Sinndar in his defence of the Arc.

This precedent poses an interesting question: does a King George bid deny Hurricane Run the mid-season pause that refreshes? Will he be campaigned aggressively during the opening months or saved for the international races during the autumn?

Moreover, will his quirks become more significant? It is easy to gloss over his alarming lack of fluency during the early stages of the Arc, but it may prove that he will become increasingly idle. These are all questions that will be answered if he is to break through to the superhorse category.

The significance of what is gone is far clearer. Just as the French flag is unrecognisable without one of its constituent colours, so Hurricane Run would not have been the same horse without one of the influential trinity.

Without his new owners, Fallon would not have got the ride; without Fallon, the colt might not have received a brilliant ride; without Fabre, Fallon might not have had the horse to do it.

Hurricane Run

bay colt, 13-4-2002

Montjeu b 1996	Sadler's Wells	Northern Dancer	Nearctic Natalma
		Fairy Bridge	Bold Reason Special
	Floripedes	Top Ville	High Top Sega Ville
		Toute Cy	Tennyson Adele Toumignon
Hold On ch 1991	Surumu	Literat	Birkhahn Lis
		Surama	Reliance Suncourt
	Hone	Sharpen Up	Atan Rocchetta
		Lucy	Sheshoon Laverock

Bred by Gestut Ammerland in Ireland.

Sire Montjeu

Won 11 of 16 races, inc. Prix Greffulhe-Gr2, Prix du Jockey-Club-Gr1, Irish Derby-Gr1, Prix Niel-Gr2, Prix de l'Arc de Triomphe-Gr1, Tattersalls Gold Cup-Gr1, Grand Prix de Saint-Cloud-Gr1, King George VI & Queen Elizabeth S.-Gr1, Prix Foy-Gr2. Also 2nd in Prix Lupin at 3, and in Champion S. at 4. Tallish, well-made, but not strikingly handsome individual. Not a good mover in his slower paces, seemed unsuited by firm ground, but acted on any other, and possessed a tremendous turn of foot. One of the best 12f horses of recent times. Well-bred. The best son of his outstanding sire. Out of a lightly-raced high-class stayer (won Prix de Lutece-Gr3, 2nd in Prix Royal-Oak-Gr1), who was among the best daughters of her sire. Family of multiple Pattern-winning stayer Dadarissime, Gr3 winner Le Mamamouchi and Dear Doctor (Arlington Million). Stands at Coolmore Stud at a (2006) fee of €125,000. Sire of 2 racing crops, inc: Corre Caminos (Gr3), Hurricane Run (Irish Derby-Gr1, Prix de l'Arc de Triomphe-Gr1), Montare (Gr2), Motivator (Racing Post Trophy-Gr1, Derby S.-Gr1), Scorpion (Grand Prix de Paris-Gr1, St Leger-Gr1).

Dam Hold On

Won 2 of 8 races. Also Listed-placed, runner-up in Dortmunder Stutenpreis. Useful performer. Stayed 11f well, not raced beyond. Half-sister to smart middle-distance colts Hondo Mondo (by Caerleon; Gr2 winner, twice Gr1-placed) and Hondero (by Damister; Gr3 winner). By a top-class winner and multiple champion sire out of a four-time Listed winner in Belgium who produced two winners of the Derby Belge. Dam of: Hibiscus (1996 c by Law Society; Gr3 winner, Gr1-placed), Hotline (1997 c by Java Gold; winner), Hold The Gold (1998 f by Java Gold; unraced), Farazdaq (2000 g by Linamix; Listed-placed winner), Hold Off (2001 f by Bering; unraced) Hurricane Run (2002 c by Montjeu; Irish Derby, Prix de l'Arc de Triomphe), unnamed (2003 f by Peintre Celebre; unraced to date). She has a yearling colt by Boreal, and was covered by Montjeu in 2005.

Pedigree assessment

There might have been some doubt about the identity of the best three-year-old in Europe before the Arc; after it there was no doubt about the identity of the best of any age group. Hurricane Run's performance at Longchamp was sensational, and it was heartening to learn that he would return to action in 2006. There are sound reasons for believing that he will prove even more formidable at four, and if all goes well with him he will start at short odds to emulate Ribot and Alleged as a dual Arc hero. The tough German influences in his pedigree will stand him in good stead. *TM*

Iffraaj

4yo bay colt **121**

Zafonic (USA) - Pastorale (Nureyev (USA))

Owner Sheikh Ahmed Al Maktoum

Trainer M A Jarvis

Breeder Darley

Career: **9** starts | won **5** | second **0** | third **1** | **£156,124** win and place

By David Carr

RACING'S answer to the 'transfer window' is Godolphin's recruitment drive in the closing weeks of the campaign, which has seen numerous good horses snapped up in recent years. While Imperial Stride, Palace Episode and Proclamation played the Wayne Rooney role in the latest transfer season, as headline-grabbing youngsters with the world seemingly at their feet, Iffraaj may be the Frank Lampard – a less-heralded acquisition who turns out to be an invaluable, top-notch performer.

The lack of prominence given to the four-year-old's name in reports on the team announced to be heading out to Dubai probably owed something to his having finished down the field on his final appearance in Sheikh Ahmed Al Maktoum's colours in the Prix de la Foret at Longchamp in October. But the soft ground was all against him that day and he had shown himself a Group 1 winner in the making on a more suitable surface at Doncaster the previous month.

The seven-furlong Park Stakes, won by future July Cup winner Pastoral Pursuits in its first running with Group 2 status in 2004, attracted another quality field. Iffraaj proved up to the task, but he had to battle, fighting back splendidly to short-head the Hungerford winner Sleeping Indian on the line after losing the lead to him at the furlong pole. The runner-up is a high-class colt, well enough thought of by trainer John Gosden to be pitched into the Queen Elizabeth II Stakes next time out, and the pair drew fully three lengths clear of third-placed Court Masterpiece, who went on to win the Foret.

Iffraaj's route to the top may also have disguised his merit as he worked his way up through handicaps. He had a BHB rating of only 86 at the start of the year, but that was because he had had a leg problem after a promising reappearance as a three-year-old and missed the rest of 2004. Michael Jarvis knew he was "too nice a horse to give up on" after just

Iffraaj (far side) fights back in dogged fashion to overcome Sleeping Indian in the Group 2 Park Stakes at Doncaster

three career races and had nursed him back to health by the spring, seeing his faith rewarded when the colt made a successful reappearance at Kempton over six furlongs and then followed up, over an extra furlong, in the Victoria Cup at Lingfield.

An entry in the Group 1 Golden Jubilee Stakes at Royal Ascot at York showed the regard in which he was held even then, but the Wokingham Handicap was his chosen target at the Royal meeting. This traditional sprint lost a little of its usually fierce competitiveness for its temporary change of venue, with a reduced safety limit and several unable to handle the very quick ground – the effects of racing on which were subsequently blamed by Jarvis for Iffraaj's disappointing effort in the July Cup at Newmarket the following month.

However, the manner of his success was still striking, as the only fright he gave supporters was when he was reluctant to go in the stalls. He travelled well before hitting the front two furlongs out and held on by a comfortable two lengths from Beckermet to land the ante-post gamble of the week, costing the bookmakers a reported £1m.

Notwithstanding the speed he showed that day, it bears repeating that Iffraaj showed his best form over seven furlongs at Doncaster and ran

2005 Race record

7th Prix de la Foret Casino Barriere de Biarritz (Group 1) (Longchamp, October 1) 3yo+ 7f Soft **108** (TS 94) 8 ran. *In touch, 3rd straight, ridden to chase leaders over 1½f out, crossed by Mirabilis over 1f out but looked held at time (P Robinson), beaten 3½l by Court Masterpiece*

1st GNER Park Stakes (Group 2) (Doncaster, September 8) 3yo+ 7f Good to firm **121** (TS 62) 11 ran. *Close up, led well over 1f out, soon ridden and headed 1f out, driven and rallied inside final furlong to lead on line (P Robinson), beat Sleeping Indian by shd*

14th Darley July Cup (Group 1) (Newmarket (July), July 7) 3yo+ 6f Good to soft **92** (TS 79) 19 ran. *Raced far side, chased leaders, ridden over 1f out, soon weakened (P Robinson), beaten 10½l by Pastoral Pursuits*

1st Wokingham Stakes (Heritage Handicap) (York, June 18) 3yo+ (0-110 handicap) 6f Firm **119** (TS 118) 17 ran. *Raced far side, led 2f out, stayed on well inside final furlong, readily (P Robinson), beat Beckermet by 2l*

1st totesport Victoria Cup (Heritage Handicap) (Lingfield, May 7) 4yo+ 7f Good **112** (TS 100) 18 ran. *Raced centre, with leaders, led over 2f out, ridden and in command 1f out, stayed on well (P Robinson), beat Moayed by 2l*

1st JSC PR Straight From Horse's Mouth Handicap (Kempton, March 28) 4yo+ (0-100 handicap) 6f Good **106** (TS 98) 9 ran. *Tracked leaders, shaken up and quickened over 1f out, led final half furlong, comfortably (P Robinson), beat High Reach by 1l*

Other runs

2004 **4th** bet365 Call 08000 322365 Handicap (Newmarket, April 15) 3yo (0-95 handicap) 7f Good **94** (TS 66) 20 ran 2003 **1st** "Barry Lynn's 60th Birthday" Maiden Stakes (Warwick, September 20) 2yo 7f Good to firm **86** (TS 74) 8 ran ● **3rd** Pacemaker EBF Maiden Stakes (Sandown, August 29) 2yo 7f Soft **80** (TS 58) 14 ran

that day as though he will get further. Jarvis had been looking forward to trying him at a mile – over which trip the four-year-old's half-sister Jathaabeh gained her biggest success in a Newmarket handicap in 2000 – and it will be interesting to see how Godolphin campaign him as a five-year-old.

Handicaps are firmly out for him now and a Group 2 winner's penalty will not make him easy to place, but there will be more opportunities if he stays a mile – and the way he progressed throughout 2005 makes it dangerous to write off the prospect of further improvement from a colt who has run only nine times in three seasons.

If he does land that Group 1 success, it will only twist the knife further for Peter Goulandris. His Post And Rail had Iffraaj back in third place when winning a maiden as the pair made their debuts at Sandown in August 2003 – with future Derby winner North Light second and Group 1-placed Maraahel fourth. But while the placed horses have gone on to glory his colt has been sidelined by injury and was finally retired in April, a clear case of 'what might have been'.

Iffraaj *bay colt, 22-2-2001*

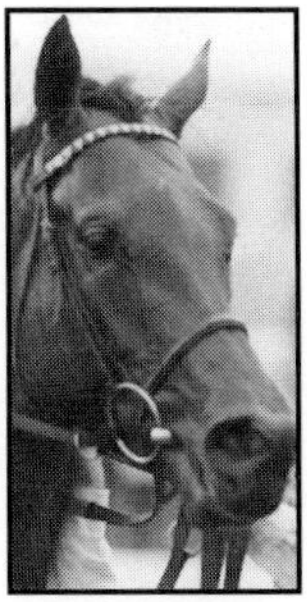

Zafonic br 1990	Gone West	Mr Prospector	Raise A Native Gold Digger
		Secrettame	Secretariat Tamerett
	Zaizafon	The Minstrel	**Northern Dancer** Fleur
		Mofida	Right Tack Wold Lass
Pastorale ch 1988	Nureyev	**Northern Dancer**	Nearctic Natalma
		Special	Forli Thong
	Park Appeal	Ahonoora	Lorenzaccio Helen Nichols
		Balidaress	Balidar Innocence

Bred by Darley in Britain

Sire Zafonic

Won 5 of 7 races at 2 and 3. At 2, won all 4 starts inc. Prix Morny-Gr1, Prix de la Salamandre-Gr1, Dewhurst S-Gr1. At 3, won 1 (2,000 Guineas-Gr1) of 3 starts. Bled when well beaten in Sussex S on final start. Stood at Banstead Manor Stud, died September 2002. First foals 1995, sire of: Xaar (Prix de la Salamandre-Gr1, Dewhurst S-Gr1), Alrassaam (Gr2), Kareymah (Gr3), Shenck (Gr2), Pacino (Gr2), Clearing (Gr3), Count Dubois (Gran Criterium-Gr1), Ozone Layer (Gr3), Dupont (Gr2), Ibn Al Haitham (Gr3), Maybe Forever (Gr3), Zee Zee Top (Prix de l'Opera-Gr1), Zipping (Gr2), Aynthia (Gr3), Trade Fair (Gr3), Zafeen (St James's Palace S-Gr1), Iffraaj (Gr2), Flashy Wings (Gr2), Guest Connections (Gr3).

Dam Pastorale

Unraced at 2, won 2 (7-8f) of 3 starts at 3, 9th Irish 1,000 Guineas on final start. By top-class miler and outstanding sire of variety of performers, out of top-class 2yo. Very closely related to Arvola (dam of Gr1 winner Diktat), half-sister to Gr1 winner Cape Cross (by Green Desert). Second dam Balidaress also dam of Gr1 winners Alydaress (Irish Oaks) and Desirable (Cheveley Park S), ancestress of Gr1 winners Russian Rhythm, Shadayid. Dam of: Krosno (1994 c by Kris; winner), In Arcadia (1995 c by Slip Anchor; winner), Kareymah (1996 f by Zafonic; Gr3 winner), Jathaabeh (1997 f by Nashwan; winner), Benkram (1999 c by Zafonic; winner), Akrmina (2000 f by Zafonic; winner), Iffraaj (2001 c by Zafonic; Gr2 winner), My Dubai (2002 f by Dubai Millennium; placed), 2004 c by Bering 2005 c by Dubai Destination.

Pedigree assessment

Another high-level runner from a superb family. With speed on both sides of his pedigree, Iffraaj was bred to excel at distances less than a mile. In 2005 he stepped up on his earlier form, thus following a similar path to his close relatives Cape Cross and Diktat. That pair also performed with distinction at five, so anticipate more in 2006 from Iffraaj. He is, however, a lightly raced son of a stallion who has sired his share of delicate performers. *JH*

Imperial Stride

4yo bay colt **128**

Indian Ridge - Place De L'Opera (Sadler's Wells (USA))

Owner Saeed Suhail

Trainer Sir Michael Stoute

Breeder Cliveden Stud Ltd

Career: **11** starts | won **6** | second **0** | third **0** | **£145,102** win and place

By Tom O'Ryan

SOMETIMES it takes patience. Sometimes it takes skill. Sometimes it takes a combination of the two. Step forward Sir Michael Stoute, who put his masterly training talents to good use to enable Imperial Stride, after a 'missing' season, to finally fulfil his sizeable juvenile potential in 2005.

To appreciate the job done on this beautifully bred colt during the latest campaign, one has to be aware of the big picture. As a two-year-old Imperial Stride had promised to be the real deal. An easy winner at Yarmouth on his debut in May, he found no difficulty making it two out of two at Doncaster in July. A setback denied him any opportunity for further experience before he reappeared in the autumn in no less a race than the Group 1 Dewhurst Stakes. Looking a little raw, he underlined his talent by finishing sixth, beaten little more than two lengths by surprise winner Milk It Mick.

His first season having promised so much, Imperial Stride's three-year-old campaign unsurprisingly started off on a traditional 2,000 Guineas route in the Craven Stakes. The outsider of the five runners, he raced keenly off a modest early pace and dropped away in the closing stages to finish a well-held fourth behind Haafhd, the subsequent Guineas winner. Then, in what proved another severely interrupted season, no more was seen of him until October when he ran twice more at Newmarket, finishing a hardly mind-blowing seventh of 16 in an all-aged Group 3 race, racing keenly again on his first encounter with soft ground, and then ninth of 11 in Listed company.

The jury, as they say, was out on Imperial Stride at the beginning of his latest campaign. He had promised plenty but, thus far, had failed to deliver. The fact that he had been retained for a further season at Freemason Lodge, however, was a plus point and the first evidence of the reasons why was uncovered at Royal Ascot at York in June.

Imperial Stride wins the September Stakes to complete a four-timer, prompting Godolphin to snap him up for 2006

Having finished unplaced in a seven-furlong handicap at the same course the previous month, Imperial Stride started unfancied at 25-1 in the Wolferton Handicap, over ten furlongs, but gained a handsome triumph, scoring by one and three-quarter lengths from Mullins Bay, who went on to prove himself considerably better than a handicapper as the season unfolded. He was on his way again.

It was back to Newmarket at the end of June for Imperial Stride's next start, which saw him line up alongside only three others in an uncompetitive Listed race over 12 furlongs. Imperial Stride won again, unchallenged, by 17 lengths. He could hardly have done more than win by that wide margin, pulling the proverbial bus, and it was hardly surprising to see Stoute target the Group 2 Scottish Derby at Ayr midway through the following month as Imperial Stride's next assignment.

In another four-runner contest, the principal focus was on only two of the runners; Imperial Stride, who was sent off the 1-2 favourite, and Powerscourt, who had, up until then, failed to discover his best form of the previous year. Richard Hills, regular rider of Imperial Stride, adopted no-nonsense tactics on his mount and made every yard of the running over the ten furlongs. Needing only to shake up the colt inside the final quarter-mile, he gained a comfortable length-and-a-quarter success over Powerscourt, who was to go on and win the Arlington Million, a race he had lost in the stewards' room the previous season.

The impression gained from his cosy victory at Ayr was that Imperial Stride, with his confidence clearly sky-high, could climb even further up the ladder. And so it proved.

He turned out next at Newmarket for the Group 3 September Stakes, transferred from Kempton, and duly made it four wins on the bounce

2005 Race record

1st 32Red.com September Stakes (Group 3) (Newmarket (July), September 3) 3yo+ 1m4f Good to firm **128** (TS 99) 6 ran. *Held up, headway to lead 2f out, soon hung right, ridden inside final furlong, edged left, ran on (R Hills), beat Mamool by 1¼l*

1st Daily Record Scottish Derby (Group 2) (Ayr, July 18) 3yo+ 1m2f Good **123** (TS 107) 4 ran. *Made all, shaken up 2f out, comfortably (R Hills), beat Powerscourt by 1¼l*

1st Ballygallon Stud Fred Archer Stakes (Listed) (Newmarket (July), June 25) 4yo+ 1m4f Good **123** (TS 76) 4 ran. *Tracked clear leader until led stands' side over 7f out, overall leader 3f out, clear over 1f out, eased final furlong (R Hills), beat Albinus by 17l*

1st Wolferton Handicap (Listed) (York, June 17) 4yo+ (0-110 handicap) 1m2½f Good to firm **117** (TS 101) 20 ran. *Tracked leaders, led over 2f out, ran on (R Hills), beat Mullins Bay by 1¾l*

10th Bank of Scotland Corporate Banking Hambleton Handicap (Listed) (York, May 12) 4yo+ (0-110 handicap) 7f Soft **91** (TS 75) 12 ran. *Always in rear (M J Kinane), beaten 9l by Quito*

Other runs

2004 **9th** Best Bet John 0800 587 7086 Ben Marshall Stakes (Listed) (Newmarket, October 30) 3yo+ 1m Good to soft **97** (TS 89) 11 ran ● **7th** Rolls-Royce Motor Cars London Darley Stakes (Group 3) (Newmarket, October 16) 3yo+ 1m1f Soft **102** (TS 81) 16 ran ● **4th** bet365 Craven Stakes (Group 3) (Newmarket, April 15) 3yo 1m Good **101** (TS 63) 5 ran **2003** **6th** Darley Dewhurst Stakes (Group 1) (Newmarket, October 18) 2yo 7f Good to firm **113** (TS 102) 12 ran ● **1st** skybet.com Conditions Stakes (Doncaster, July 10) 2yo 7f Good to firm **101** (TS 77) 4 ran ● **1st** EBF Novice Stakes (Yarmouth, May 28) 2yo 6f Good to firm **78** (TS 56) 6 ran

when giving the classy Mamool 5lb and a one-and-a-quarter-length beating, with the remainder of the six-strong field, which included a below-form Bandari, beaten more than 14 lengths.

His Racing Post Rating having risen from 91 to 128 through the season, Imperial Stride had earned another crack at Group 1 company in either the Champion Stakes or the Prix de l'Arc de Triomphe before his already memorable campaign came to an end. Joe Mercer, racing manager to owner Saeed Suhail, was also reported as saying that the Breeders' Cup Turf at Belmont Park could be up for serious consideration.

As it turned out, Imperial Stride was not seen out again. Indeed, the only subsequent headlines he made came when it was reported that he had changed ownership and stables, having been snapped up by Sheikh Mohammed to join Godolphin.

It was a great pity that a horse of such burgeoning prowess did not get the opportunity to tackle Group 1 company for the first time since his juvenile days, but it must have been hugely satisfying to connections that his early potential was largely fulfilled.

The burning question now is, just how much more is there to come from him for his new connections as a five-year-old? If he enjoys another uninterrupted campaign there will be no shortage of opportunity for him. He looks the sort Godolphin could send almost anywhere.

Imperial Stride *bay colt, 11-3-2001*

Indian Ridge ch 1985	Ahonoora	Lorenzaccio	Klairon Phoenissa
		Helen Nichols	Martial Quaker Girl
	Hillbrow	Swing Easy	Delta Judge Free Flowing
		Golden City	Skymaster West Shaw
Place de l'Opera b 1993	Sadler's Wells	Northern Dancer	Nearctic Natalma
		Fairy Bridge	Bold Reason Special
	Madame Dubois	Legend Of France	Lyphard Lupe
		Shadywood	Habitat Milly Moss

Bred by Cliveden Stud in Britain. 375,000gns Tattersalls October yearling

Sire Indian Ridge

Won 5 of 11 starts from 2 to 4. At 2, won 2 of 4 starts. At 3, won Jersey S-Gr3 from 4 starts. At 4, won Duke of York S-Gr3 and King's Stand S-Gr2 from 3 starts. By top-class sprinter and excellent sire who got top-class horses across the distance spectrum. Stands at Irish National Stud, 2006 fee €75,000. First foals 1991, sire of: Fumo di Londra (Gr3), Island Magic (Gr3), Ridgewood Ben (Gr3), Blomberg (Gr3), Definite Article (National S-Gr1), Ridgewood Pearl (Irish 1,000 Guineas-Gr1, Coronation S-Gr1, Prix du Moulin-Gr1, Breeders' Cup Mile-Gr1), Tumbleweed Ridge (Gr3), Compton Place (July Cup-Gr1), Handsome Ridge (Gr2), Indian Rocket (Gr2), Bardonecchia (Gr3), Cassandra Go (Gr2), Namid (Prix de l'Abbaye-Gr1), St Clair Ridge (Gr3), Indian Mary (Gr3), Nicobar (Gr2), Domedriver (Breeders' Cup Mile-Gr1), High Pitched (Gr3), Indian Creek (Gr2), Monturani (Gr2), Munir (Gr3), Nayyir (Gr2), Sights On Gold (Gr3), Campsie Fells (Gr3), Indian Haven (Irish 2,000 Guineas-Gr1), Imperial Stride (Gr2), Relaxed Gesture (Canadian International-Gr1), Sleeping Indian (Gr3), Snow Ridge (Gr2), Tahreeb (Gr3), Noelani (Gr3).

Dam Place de l'Opera

Unraced at 2, won 2 (12f) of 5 starts at 3, also 3rd 12f Listed race. Half-sister to Count Dubois (Gran Criterium-Gr1) and Indian Haven (by Indian Ridge; Irish 2,000 Guineas-Gr1) out of high-class 12f+ filly Madame Dubois. Family of high-class 2yo Daggers Drawn. Dam of: High Pitched (1998 by Indian Ridge; Gr3 winner), Zero Tolerance (2000 g by Nashwan; winner), Imperial Stride (2001 c by Indian Ridge; Gr2 winner), Noble Concorde (2002 c by Daylami; unplaced), Hala Bek (2003 c by Halling; unraced), 2004 c by King's Best.

Pedigree assessment

This is a stout family whose members can show speed when sired by fast stallions. Indian Ridge goes particularly well with the family, but though he introduced speed in the case of Indian Haven, he sired two of his rare middle-distance horses in the brothers High Pitched and Imperial Stride. Neither were precocious, and there has to be a fair chance that Imperial Stride will make further progress as a five-year-old. *JH*

Intercontinental

5yo bay mare **120**

Danehill (USA) - Hasili (Ire) (Kahyasi)

Owner Juddmonte Farms

Trainer R J Frankel

Breeder Juddmonte Farms

Career: **22** starts | won **13** | second **3** | third **4** | **£1,107,311** win and place

By Robert Carter

WOODY STEPHENS was once asked what chance there is of training a horse to stay further than its natural distance. His reply was that the best hope was the first time over the new trip because the horse did not know what was being asked of it. Stephens trained five consecutive winners of the Belmont Stakes, starting with Conquistador Cielo in 1982. That colt set a track record at Belmont Park, when winning the Grade 1 Metropolitan Mile by seven and a quarter lengths. Six days later he won the Belmont over another half-mile by 14 lengths.

The form book suggested that it was impossible. Likewise Intercontinental winning the ten-furlong Breeders' Cup Filly and Mare Turf. Intercontinental had left Europe with a useful record of four wins from nine outings, but she was thought to be better at seven furlongs than one mile. She had won seven Graded stakes in California, Kentucky and New York but they were all at either one mile or over an extra half-furlong. Intercontinental had been beaten on both occasions that she tried nine furlongs. Furthermore, she finished a well-beaten fifth in the Grade 1 Diana Handicap at Saratoga in July 2004, a day on which the going was officially yielding. Similar conditions prevailed on Breeders' Cup day.

It was her run in the 1,000 Guineas that first shaped popular opinion of Intercontinental as a non-stayer. She arrived at Newmarket with a record of three wins and a third in the Grand Criterium. Christophe Soumillon sent her to the front over one furlong out but she was caught by Russian Rhythm in the final furlong and then also by the unlucky Six Perfections and beaten almost three lengths.

What is apparent with hindsight is that she had finished third in what was one of the best runnings of the Classic for many years. Six of the first eight finishers went on to Group 1 or Grade 1 success and another was a Group 2 winner. But Intercontinental was beaten in three of her

Intercontinental lands the Breeders' Cup Filly & Mare Turf, emulating her sister Banks Hill, the 2001 winner

next four races, ending with a close fourth behind Etoile Montante in the Prix de la Foret, and the non-staying label stuck.

She joined Bobby Frankel and won her first three races, including the Jenny Wiley Stakes at Keeneland and the Just A Game Handicap at Belmont. She then failed in the Diana and was second in a sprint before ending 2004 with victory over Etoile Montante in the Grade 1 Matriarch Stakes at Hollywood Park. Intercontinental started favourite for all but those last two races in 2004 and for all her six races leading up to the Breeders' Cup in 2005. She returned in the Jenny Wiley but fought for her head in the early stages and Jerry Bailey allowed her to go on starting down the back straight. She had been held up in all her races at four and was again in her next three outings of 2005, only one of which she won.

The last of those three was the John C Mabee Handicap, the second time that Intercontinental had attempted nine furlongs. She was ridden by Alex Solis and, for once, started odds against. As usual, she pulled, but Solis was able to settle her in fourth on the rail. Unfortunately, that is where she remained and she was beaten by Amorama and Island Fashion. Solis tried to extricate her in the straight but Pat Valenzuela, riding the runner-up, would not allow it.

Bailey was back for her next two races and reverted to front-running tactics. Intercontinental turned the tables on Amorama in the Palomar Handicap and then controlled the pace throughout to beat Wend in the WinStar Galaxy. It was the seventh time that Bailey had won on her.

However, he took the mount on Ouija Board in the Filly and Mare

2005 Race record

1st Emirates Airline Breeders' Cup Filly & Mare Turf (Grade 1) (Turf) (Belmont Park, October 29) 3yo+ 1m2f Yielding **120** 14 ran. *Made all, quickened 2 lengths clear under 1½f out, ridden out (R Bejarano), beat Ouija Board by 1¼l*

1st WinStar Galaxy Stakes (Grade 2) (Keeneland, October 9) 3yo+ 1m Firm **117** 9 ran. *Made all, driven out (J D Bailey), beat Wend by ¾l*

1st Palomar Breeders' Cup Handicap (Grade 2) (Turf) (Del Mar, September 3) 3yo+ 1m½ Firm **118** 5 ran. *Pulled hard early, made most (J D Bailey), beat Amorama by 1¼l*

3rd John C Mabee Handicap (Grade 1) (Del Mar, July 23) 3yo+ 1m1f Firm **116** 8 ran. *Restrained early, soon pulled her way up to track leaders, not clear run over 1f out, stayed on to take 3rd close home (A Solis), beaten 1½l by Amorama*

1st Royal Heroine Invitational Stakes (Grade 3) (Turf) (Hollywood Park, July 3) 3yo+ 1m Firm 5 ran. *Pulled hard in rear early, headway on outside to go 2nd over 2f out, led 1½f out, ran on well (J D Bailey), beat Ticker Tape by 1¼l*

2nd Just A Game Breeders' Cup Stakes (Grade 2 Handicap) (Belmont Park, June 11) 3yo+ 1m Firm **117** 9 ran. *Outpaced early but soon in touch in rear, headway to go 2nd 1½f out, kept on but no impression on winner (J D Bailey), beaten 2½l by Sand Springs*

1st Jenny Wiley Stakes (Grade 3) (Keeneland, April 17) 4yo+ 1m½ Firm **116** 7 ran. *Pulled very hard early, close up until led after 3f, made rest, 2 lengths clear approaching final furlong, ridden out (J D Bailey), beat Delta Princess by 1l*

Other wins

2004 1st Matriarch Stakes (Grade 1) (Hollywood Park, November 28) 3yo+ 1m Firm **118** 9 ran ● **1st** Just A Game Breeders' Cup Handicap (Grade 2) (Belmont Park, June 5) 3yo+ 1m Firm 8 ran ● **1st** Jenny Wiley Stakes (Grade 3) (Keeneland, April 18) 4yo+ 1m½ Firm 8 ran ● **1st** Allowance Race (Santa Anita, March 28) 4yo+ 1m Firm 5 ran **2003 1st** Prix Amandine (Listed) (Straight Course) (Deauville, July 11) 3yo 7f Good to soft **105** (TS 87) 12 ran ● **1st** Prix Birdaine (Maisons-Laffitte, April 18) 3yo 6f Good **104** 7 ran **2002 1st** Prix des Melezes (Longchamp, September 12) 2yo 7f Good 7 ran ● **1st** Prix de la Potiniere (Deauville, August 18) 2yo 6½f Good to soft 6 ran

Turf and Frankel turned to Rafael Bejarano. Bejarano, 23, began riding in December 1999 and became champion apprentice in Peru. He moved to the United States in 2002 and now divides his time between Kentucky and New York, claiming his 1,000th American success in mid-October.

The Filly and Mare Turf started in front of the stands. Intercontinental, who was drawn four from the outside, broke well and took it up soon after passing the post for the first time. She had pulled her way into a two-length lead starting down the back straight but Bejarano was able to restrain her. She stretched clear on the final turn and had two and a half lengths to spare over Ouija Board entering the straight. Ouija Board halved the lead but Bejarano only had to push his mount out.

Hasili, also the dam of Banks Hill, had thus produced her second winner of the race in five runnings. Primal Force, dam of Awesome Again (1998 Classic) and Macho Uno (2000 Juvenile), is the only other mare to have produced two Breeders' Cup winners. Intercontinental will now try her luck in the breeding arena.

Intercontinental

bay mare, 19-3-2000

Danehill b 1986	Danzig	Northern Dancer	Nearctic Natalma
		Pas de Nom	Admiral's Voyage Petitioner
	Razyana	His Majesty	Ribot Flower Bowl
		Spring Adieu	Buckpasser Natalma
Hasili b 1991	Kahyasi	Ile de Bourbon	Nijinsky Roseliere
		Kadissya	Blushing Groom Kalkeen
	Kerali	High Line	High Hat Time Call
		Sookera	Roberto Irule

Bred by Juddmonte Farms in England.

Sire Danehill

Won 4 of 9 races, inc. Haydock Park Sprint Cup-Gr1. Died May 2003. Stood at Coolmore Stud, latterly at a fee of Ir200,000gns. Sire of Gr1 winners: Danish (QE II Challenge Cup), Kissing Cousin (Coronation), Danehill Dancer (Phoenix, National), Tsukuba Symphony (NHK Mile Cup), Desert King (National, Irish 2,000, Irish Derby), Fairy King Prawn (Yasuda Kinen), Tiger Hill (GP von Baden [twice], Bayerisches Zuchtrennen), Indian Danehill (Prix Ganay), Wannabe Grand (Cheveley Park), Aquarelliste (Prix de Diane, Prix Vermeille, Prix Ganay), Banks Hill (Coronation, Breeders' Cup F & M Turf, Prix Jacques le Marois), Mozart (July Cup, Nunthorpe), Regal Rose (Cheveley Park), Dress To Thrill (Matriarch), Fine Motion (Shuka Sho, QE II Commemorative Cup), Landseer (Poule d'Essai des Poulains), Rock Of Gibraltar (Grand Criterium, Dewhurst, 2,000 Guineas, Irish 2,000, St James's Palace, Sussex, Prix du Moulin), Westerner (Prix du Cadran [twice], Prix Royal-Oak [twice], Gold Cup), Clodovil (Poule d'Essai des Poulains), Intercontinental (Matriarch, Breeders' Cup F & M Turf), Light Jig (Yellow Ribbon), Spartacus (Phoenix, Gran Criterium), Grey Lilas (Prix du Moulin), North Light (Derby), Luas Line (Garden City H.), Oratorio (Jean-Luc Lagardere, Eclipse, Irish Champion), George Washington (Phoenix, National), Horatio Nelson (Prix Jean-Luc Lagardere), Rumplestiltskin (Moyglare Stud, Prix Marcel Boussac).

Dam Hasili

Won 4 of 17 races, inc. 1 Listed at Nantes. Also 2nd 3 times, 3rd once, 4th 4 times. Light-framed, not particularly robust, but strong-quartered type, about 15.3hh. Smart performer in French provinces at 2, and held her form well, though not quite as competitive, in Paris at 3. Dam of: Dansili (1996 c by Danehill; Gr2 winner), Banks Hill (1998 f by Danehill; Gr1 winner), Heat Haze (1999 f by Green Desert; Gr1 winner), Intercontinental (2000 f by Danehill; Gr1 winner), Cacique (2001 c by Danehill; Gr2 winner), Champs Elysees (2003 c by Danehill; unraced to date). She was barren to Zafonic in 1997, and to Danehill in 2002, slipped in 2004 after coverings by Danehill and Rock Of Gibraltar. Her foal is a colt by Sadler's Wells.

Pedigree assessment

Hasili may not have been much of a racemare, but she became the six-million-dollar broodmare when her daughter Intercontinental captured the Breeders' Cup Filly & Mare Turf, leading home the first three in the 2004 renewal. Under a canny ride she was able to emulate her sister, Banks Hill, winner of that race four years earlier. Also sister to Dansili and Cacique, and three-parts sister to Heat Haze, Intercontintental went into retirement as her dam's highest earner, having banked over $2 million. *TM*

Kane Hekili (Jpn)

3yo chestnut colt **117**

Fuji Kiseki (Jpn) - Life Out There (USA) (Deputy Minister (Can))

Owner Kaneko Makoto Holdings Co Ltd

Trainer Katsuhiko Sumii

Breeder Northern Farm

Career: **11** starts | won **7** | second **1** | third **0** | **£1,653,602** win and place

By Nicholas Godfrey

NO WINNER in the short history of the Japan Cup Dirt has gone on to achieve further fame on the international stage after victory in the richly endowed event that takes place 24 hours before its vastly more revered turf equivalent at Tokyo racecourse in November.

However, that situation could be about to change following the thrilling triumph of Japan's outstanding dirt performer Kane Hekili in a blanket finish to the sixth running of the £1.15 million Grade 1 event in 2005.

Japanese-trained horses are an ever-increasing force on the international scene, and in the immediate aftermath of the three-year-old's narrow success Katsuhiko Sumii, who in 2005 landed major prizes in America with Cesario and in Hong Kong with Hat Trick, was avidly eyeing rich prizes around the world in 2006.

The Dubai World Cup and top-level races in the USA offer obvious potential targets for a colt who has been beaten just once on dirt. But the trainer also hinted at the intriguing possibility of a crack at the turf in Europe, where he feels a more forgiving surface might suit Kane Hekili, whose name is derived from Polynesian mythology and means 'spirit of thunder'.

The colt's form on the prevalent firm turf at home left a lot to be desired before the switch to dirt racing at the outset of his three-year-old campaign proved the making of him. Winless in a pair of starts on the grass the previous season, the chestnut son of Fuji Kiseki, a son of the now departed bloodstock legend Sunday Silence, proved an instant hit on his first two dirt starts in February 2005, scoring by a total of 20 lengths. A return to the grass for a Group 3 event in March showed little improvement, though it did at least mark the beginning of superstar jockey Yutaka Take's association with the colt.

That was it as far as the turf was concerned for Kane Hekili, who immediately recaptured his winning form with a nine-length victory on

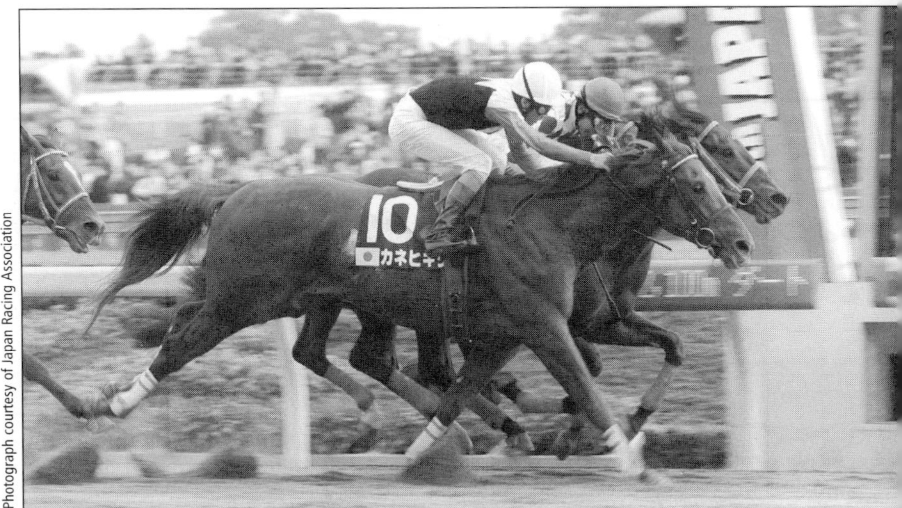

Photograph courtesy of Japan Racing Association

Kane Hekili (near side) wins a dramatic tussle in the Japan Cup Dirt, proving his first-class credentials on the surface

the dirt at Kyoto. Next he graduated to Grade 3 over a mile at Tokyo racecourse in June before a pair of victories in two of the nation's most prestigious dirt events, the Japan Dirt Derby and the Derby Grand Prix, both Grade 1 events over a mile and a quarter.

The unbeaten record on dirt bit the dust in a one-mile Grade 3 event at Tokyo in October. Racing over a trip a little short of his best, Kane Hekili slipped on the turf surface of the chute used at the start, which left him with an enormous amount of ground to make up. After a tremendous turn of speed in the straight, he got to within two lengths of the winner Sunrise Bacchus, a talented colt in receipt of 7lb whom he had defeated on his previous outing.

Sunrise Bacchus was among 15 rivals a month later in the sixth running of the Japan Cup Dirt, where punters clearly expected Kane Hekili to resume winning ways. With around £55 million in the pool, he was sent off 11-10 favourite from a field that also included the previous year's winner Time Paradox and a trio of overseas visitors in the US dirt specialists Lava Man and Tap Day, plus the Andrew Reid-trained Eccentric, all-weather horse of the season in Britain for 2005. However, the Lingfield Winter Derby winner's audacious bid for one of the world's top dirt prizes was akin to Accrington Stanley winning a few minor matches and then thinking they can take on Chelsea at Stamford Bridge. The non-leaguer was routed, coming home a distant last under Darryll Holland, well adrift of the 15th-placed horse. Mind you, the Americans did not fare much better. Far in front of them, the race developed into an absolute classic as Kane Hekili just got the nod after a bitter three-way struggle up the

2005 Race record

1st Japan Cup Dirt (Grade 1) (Tokyo, November 26) 3yo+ 1m2½f Fast **117** 16 ran. *Raced in 8th or 9th, headway on outside over 2f out, disputed lead approaching final furlong until led post (Y Take), beat Seeking The Dia by nose*

2nd Tokyo Chunichi Sports Hai Musashino Stakes (Grade 3) (Tokyo, October 29) 3yo+ 1m Standard 16 ran. *Slipped after start and dropped to rear, stayed on strongly on wide outside from 2f out, not reach winner (Y Take), beaten 1¾l by Sunrise Bacchus*

1st Derby Grand Prix (Grade 1) (Morioka, September 19) 3yo 1m2f Standard 12 ran. *3rd early, 4th straight, led 2f out, ran on strongly (Y Take), beat Sunrise Bacchus by 2½l*

1st Japan Dirt Derby (Grade 1) (Ohi, July 13) 3yo 1m2f Standard 14 ran. *Raced in 5th, 4th halfway, led well over 2f out, ran on strongly (Y Take), beat Maple Eight by 5l*

1st Unicorn Stakes (Grade 3) (Tokyo, June 4) 3yo 1m Standard 16 ran. *Raced in 3rd, 2nd straight, led inside final furlong, ran on strongly (Y Take), beat Agnes Jedi by 1¾l*

1st Tango Stakes (Kyoto, April 30) 3yo 1m1f Standard 14 ran. *Raced in 6th, 2nd straight, led under 2f out, soon clear, easily (Y Take), beat Eishin Newton by 9l*

7th Mainichi Hai (Grade 3) (Hanshin, March 26) 3yo 1m2f Firm 14 ran. *Raced in 2nd, weakened over 1f out (Y Take), beaten 5½l by Rosenkreuz*

1st Allowance (Nakayama, February 26) 3yo 1m1f Muddy 10 ran. *Raced in 2nd until led over 3f out, soon clear, very easily (O Peslier), beat Shuzan Eagle by 12l*

1st Maiden (Kyoto, February 13) 3yo 1m1f Standard 16 ran. *Led over 2f out, easily (Kenichi Ikezoe), beat San Season by 8l*

2004

11th Maiden (Kokura, August 21) 2yo 1m1f Firm 13 ran ● **4th** Maiden (Unraced) (Niigata, July 31) 2yo 7f Firm 14 ran

straight to the backdrop of a roaring, excitable crowd of more than 56,000. Having been brought smoothly from midfield to hit the front two furlongs out, Kane Hekili was soon under pressure as longshot Star King Man challenged on the rails, and then a second outsider, Seeking The Dia, who ran in Britain and France in 2004, pushed up in between the pair.

The three hit the wire virtually in a line after what was described as a "neck-and-neck-neck [sic] rally" by local journalists, the bob of heads just going to Kane Hekili by a nostril hair. He stopped the clock at 2min 8sec dead, a new track record.

Afterwards, Sumii was soon looking ahead to 2006. "I will have to discuss with the owner any possibility of overseas challenges," said the trainer. "I think perhaps he could adapt well to the softer turf in Europe, but if he was to run in dirt races in the USA or Dubai, I would have to build him up in a different manner with emphasis on strength in order to deal with the faster track."

Kane Hekili, the second three-year-old winner of the race after Kurofune in 2001, carries the same colours as brilliant Japanese Triple Crown winner Deep Impact. Take commented: "He has proved himself to be the dirt champion in his three-year-old season, and, as we already have a champion three-year-old on turf, I hope he will continue his career as King of Dirt."

Kane Hekili

chestnut colt, 26-2-2002

Fuji Kiseki br 1992	Sunday Silence	Halo	Hail To Reason Cosmah
		Wishing Well	Understanding Mountain Flower
	Millracer	Le Fabuleux	Wild Risk Anguar
		Marston's Mill	In Reality Millicent
Life Out There ch 1992	Deputy Minister	Vice Regent	Northern Dancer Victoria Regina
		Mint Copy	Bunty's Flight Shakney
	Silver Valley	Mr Prospector	Raise A Native Gold Digger
		Seven Valleys	Road At Sea Proud Pied

Bred by Northern Farm in Japan. 20,000,000 yen 2002 JRHA Select Foal Sale

Sire Fuji Kiseki

Champion 2yo in Japan, won all 3 starts over 6-8f, inc. Asahi Hai Sansai S-Gr1. Won sole start (Gr2) over 10f at 3. Sire top-class US 10f dirt performer and outstanding Japanese sire of 8f+ performers (Fuji Kiseki his first Gr1 winner). Dam useful dual winner in US from family of Mill Reef, also dam of Japanese Gr3 winner Shinin' Racer (by Northern Taste). Stands at Shadai Stallion Station. First foals 1996, sire of: Air Pierre (Gr3), Tosho Andre (Gr3), Daitaku Riva (Gr2), Grand Pas de Deux (Gr3), Mitsuwa Top Lady (Gr3), Tenshino Kiseki (Gr3), Kitasan Hibotan (Gr3), Osumi Cosmo (Gr3), Our Fuji (Gr3), Rock Of Cashel (AusGr3), Wana (Gr3), Meisho Oscar (Gr2), Tamamo Hot Play (Gr2), Kane Hekili (Japan Dirt Derby-Gr1, Derby Grand Prix-Gr1, Japan Cup Dirt-Gr1), Grace Tiara (Gr3).

Dam Life Out There

Unraced. By outstanding dirt sire out of dual 4yo stakes winner in US. Full-sister to unbeaten dual 2yo winner and good sire Silver Deputy, very closely related to minor US stakes winner Buzzys Gold (by Touch Gold). Sent to Japan early 1999. Dam of: Shape Up (1997 f by Kingmambo; winner), Splintered Life (1998 f by Woodman; unraced), Ninety Proof (1999 c by Wild Again; winner in Japan), Out Of The Whim (2000 f by Sunday Silence; non-winner), Kane Hekili (2002 c by Fuji Kiseki; Gr1 winner), 2004 c by Admire Vega.

Pedigree assessment

Although bred in Japan, Kane Hekili effectively has an American dirt pedigree, so it is no surprise that he is dirt-oriented. The fact that he stays 10f (which is his maximum trip on pedigree) means that he has obvious international possibilities in 2006. *JH*

Kinnaird (Ire)

4yo chestnut filly **111**

Dr Devious (Ire) - Ribot's Guest (Ire) (Be My Guest (USA))

Owner Mrs R J Jacobs

Trainer P C Haslam

Breeder Victor Stud

Career: **16** starts | won **6** | second **3** | third **2** | **£240,639** win and place

By Tom O'Ryan

EVERY trainer in the land dreams that the very next horse to come into their yard will be the one they've been waiting for all their life. For Patrick Haslam, Kinnaird was that horse.

Having first taken out a training licence in 1972, aged just 23 and after two years assisting the late, great George Todd, Haslam gradually proved himself to be a very able dual-purpose practitioner, courtesy of such horses as Royal Hunt Cup winner Hawkley, Group-winning juvenile Godstone and dual Bunbury Cup winner Mummy's Treasure.

In 1988, however, Haslam dramatically quit the sport and walked away. In the early years of marriage, and with a young son, he felt an urgent need to spend more time with his family. "I was consumed by racing and had been for so long, that I just felt life had flashed by and I was stuck in a rut. I thought I'd be able to do something else, and I didn't want life to go by without at least trying something else," is how he recalls his feelings at the time.

The lure of racing, however, proved too strong. After two years, Haslam was back. Not in Newmarket, where he'd previously been based, but at Middleham, giving his usual 100 per cent commitment to the profession – and way of life – to which he was clearly addicted.

That Haslam is a man for all seasons is illustrated by the fact that in 2004, and after three winners from three runners at Cheltenham, he was able to claim the rare feat of having figured on the scoreboard at all of Britain's 59 racecourses.

It is doubtful if even the shrewd Haslam instantly felt that Kinnaird was heaven-sent when she arrived at his historic Manor House yard after changing hands for just 8,000gns at Doncaster's Breeze-Up Sales as a juvenile in the spring of 2003. Five months on, however, and she'd won five of her six races, including the Group 2 May Hill Stakes at Doncaster.

Her second season saw her fail to win in five starts, but she was beaten

Kinnaird wins the Group 1 Prix de l'Opera, providing Pat Haslam with the highlight of his training career

only four lengths into fourth place by Attraction in the Irish 1,000 Guineas. Furthermore, she finished second in a Group 2 race at The Curragh and in Group 3 races at Deauville and Chepstow.

And so it was that she started 2005 with solid Pattern-race credentials. The first of her five races saw her tackle the Group 2 Ridgewood Pearl Stakes at The Curragh in late May. Luck wasn't with her. Sent off the 11-8 joint-favourite in a five-strong field, she was denied a clear run through the final two furlongs and had to settle for third prize behind Airwave, the other joint-favourite, and Miss Trish.

Compensation was sought in the Windsor Forest Stakes, another Group 2 affair, at the Royal Ascot at York meeting some three weeks later, but she trailed home seventh of the eight runners after being eased by jockey Kevin Darley, who reported that his mount has slipped coming out of the stalls and had hung right throughout.

Kinnaird did not reappear until mid-September when she returned to The Curragh for the Group 2 Blandford Stakes. A 12-1 chance in an 11-strong field, she ran a fine race to finish third to Red Bloom, the favourite, beaten two and a half lengths.

It was, by now, more than two years since Kinnaird had won a race and, into the autumn, the clock was clearly ticking on her career. Arc day at Longchamp was her next stop for the Group 1 Prix de l'Opera, which attracted a strong field, led by the odds-on Alexander Goldrun, winner of the race the previous year. Kinnaird was a largely unconsidered 33-1 shot; only two horses in the nine-strong field started at longer odds.

2005 Race record

5th Premio Lydia Tesio (Group 1) (Capannelle, October 23) 3yo+ 1m2f Heavy **96** 9 ran. *Raced in 2nd, pushed along to chase leader 3f out, driven and every chance 2f out, no extra final furlong (K Darley), beaten 9l by Dubai Surprise*

1st Prix de l'Opera Casino Barriere d'Enghien (Group 1) (Longchamp, October 2) 3yo+ 1m2f Good to soft **111** (TS 84) 9 ran. *Raced in 2nd, led narrowly entering straight, ridden to take lead 1f out, ran on gamely, ridden out (K Darley), beat Mona Lisa by 1/2l*

3rd Irish National Stud Blandford Stakes (Group 2) (Curragh, September 18) 3yo+ 1m2f Good to firm **110** (TS 67) 11 ran. *Tracked leaders, ridden early straight, 5th 1 1/2f out, kept on under pressure final furlong (D Holland), beaten 2 1/2l by Red Bloom*

7th Windsor Forest Stakes (Group 2) (York, June 15) 4yo+ 1m Good to firm **75** (TS 67) 8 ran. *Slipped start, soon chasing leaders, driven along over 4f out, hung right and lost place over 2f out, eased (K Darley), beaten 18l by Peeress*

3rd Ridgewood Pearl Stakes (Group 2) (Curragh, May 21) 4yo+ 1m Good **99** (TS 41) 5 ran. *Tracked leaders on far rail, 3rd halfway, not clear run from 2f out, last 1f out, ridden and kept on (M J Kinane), beaten 1 3/4l by Airwave*

Other wins

2003 **1st** Betdaq May Hill Stakes (Group 2) (Doncaster, September 11) 2yo 1m Good **104** (TS 107) 10 ran ● **1st** NSPCC Shergar Cup Juvenile (Auction Race) (Ascot, August 9) 2yo 7f Good to firm **96** (TS 89) 10 ran ● **1st** Lewis Geipel Challenge Cup Conditions Stakes (Thirsk, July 25) 2yo 7f Soft **87** (TS 95) 6 ran ● **1st** Scottish Daily Mail Novice Auction Stakes (Qualifier for the Hamilton Park 2YO Series Final) (Hamilton, June 26) 2yo 6f Firm **80** (TS 36) 6 ran ● **1st** Ben Raceday Maiden Auction Fillies' Stakes (Qualifier for Hamilton Park 2-Y-O Series Final) (Hamilton, June 12) 2yo 6f Good to soft **70** 14 ran

On her favoured good-to-soft ground, and with Darley back on board, she found – for once – everything falling right for her in what proved to be a tactical affair, run at a steady pace. Never out of the first two, she duelled throughout with the Aidan O'Brien-trained Mona Lisa, a 25-1 shot, and the pair of them fought out a thrilling finish, with Kinnaird taking the spoils by half a length. In a finish that clearly favoured fillies who had been ridden prominently, Alexander Goldrun did best of those trying to come from off the pace and stayed on to finish third, three-parts of a length behind Mona Lisa.

It was a wonderful result for Kinnaird, a reward for her consistency at the top level since the start of her three-year-old days. As for Haslam, it provided an even greater reward – the first-ever Group 1 triumph of his long career – ironically on a day when he was at Kelso, saddling two jumps winners.

Kinnaird had her final race before being retired to the paddocks in Italy towards the end of October and failed to shine when finishing unplaced in the Group 1 Premio Lydia Tesio. It didn't much matter in the whole scheme of things.

The cheaply bought filly had proved an outstanding bargain. "Tough, genuine, consistent, bombproof – and the best I've trained," was her trainer's grateful summing-up.

Kinnaird

chestnut filly, 27-2-2001

Dr Devious ch 1989	Ahonoora	Lorenzaccio	Klairon
			Phoenissa
		Helen Nichols	Martial
			Quaker Girl
	Rose Of Jericho	Alleged	Hoist The Flag
			Princess Pout
		Rose Red	**Northern Dancer**
			Cambrienne
Ribot's Guest ch 1994	Be My Guest	**Northern Dancer**	Nearctic
			Natalma
		What A Treat	Tudor Minstrel
			Rare Treat
	Raysiya	Cure The Blues	Stop The Music
			Quick Cure
		Rilasa	St Paddy
			Sarila

Bred by Victor Stud in Ireland. €10,000 Goffs October yearling, 8,000gns Doncaster Breeze-Up 2yo

Sire Dr Devious

At 2, from 6 starts, won 4 over 6-7f (inc. Superlative S-L, Vintage S-Gr3, Dewhurst S-Gr1). At 3, from 9 starts, won 2 (Derby-Gr1, Irish Champion S-Gr1), also 2nd Irish Derby-Gr1. Sire high-class sprinter and very successful stallion who also was responsible for Indian Ridge. Dam also foaled Group winners Archway, Royal Court. To stud in Japan in 1993, switched to Ireland for 1997 season, exported to Italy before 2002 season. Stands at Allevamenti della Berardenga, 2005 fee €9,000. Sire of: Collier Hill (Irish St Leger-Gr1), Devious Indian (Gr3), Doc Holiday (Gr3), Duca d'Atri (Gr2), Devious Boy (Gr2), Where We Left Off (Gr3), Kinnaird (Prix de l'Opera-Gr1), Day Walker (Gr3).

Dam Ribot's Guest

In Italy, unraced at 2, unplaced in 2 starts at 3. Sire high-class 2yo and miler who was very good sire of variety of performers, mainly in 8-12f bracket. Dam triple 10-12f winner at 3, also dam of quite useful middle-distance fillies Raysiza, Razana. Decent middle-distance family. Dam of: Silvertine (2000 f by Alzao; placed), Kinnaird (2001 f by Dr Devious; Prix de l'Opera-Gr1), Invisible Quest (2002 f by Intikhab; non-winner), Chief Guest (2003 c by Namid; unraced), 2005 c by Dubai Destination.

Pedigree assessment

Derby winner Dr Devious was a top-class two-year-old, but progressive middle-distance performers rather than smart juveniles are his forte. Kinnaird has been his juvenile standout, but on pedigree we might have expected her to improve her record with greater maturity and a step up in trip, and she did that at Longchamp in October. She is from a good European middle-distance family and will be given every chance to enhance its record at stud by her owner, a member of a notable European breeding dynasty. *JH*

La Cucaracha

4yo bay filly **116**

Piccolo - Peggy Spencer (Formidable (USA))

Owner Guy Reed

Trainer B W Hills

Breeder Guy Reed

Career: **12** starts | won **6** | second **3** | third **1** | **£298,177** win and place

By Rodney Masters

IN THE art of bridge building, neither Isambard Kingdom Brunel, Costain, John Laing, nor any other construction colossus, would be capable of getting the job done with greater haste or elegance than La Cucaracha. In the space of 26 days, she successfully spanned a handicap and a Group 1. When underfoot conditions were favourable, La Cucaracha was to prove a formidable opponent for the best of sprinters during 2005.

Her achievement in seizing a 0-105 at York, then returning to the same venue to overwhelm rivals who included past and future Group 1 winners in the Nunthorpe, was testimony to canny placement by Barry Hills, who never forfeited conviction in his filly's ability despite her frustrating stress fracture injuries, which had reared during her juvenile days and then again the following season.

Initially, we must focus on her finest hour at York, which provided the moment in a lifetime for owner-breeder Guy Reed, a Yorkshireman who had seen talents such as Warpath, Dakota and Shotgun carry his colours over almost 40 years, but was celebrating his first strike in a Group 1. As the back slapping of congratulations came from every direction, the owner reminisced, with a question. "I made my first purchase in 1968. How long ago is that?" he asked.

Michael Hills had arrived at York flush with belief in the four-year-old. Back in Lambourn the previous weekend, his mount had produced her best-ever work session on the Faringdon Road gallop. Plan A, formulated between the jockey and his father, was to sit off the pace and arrive on the scene much later than on the previous month's visit to York, where she had seized control entering the final furlong and stayed on to win by three-parts of a length.

However, the script was one thing, reality was another. What does a jockey do when a gap opens sooner than he planned to make his dart

La Cucaracha (near side) lands the Group 1 Nunthorpe at York, just 26 days after a handicap win at the same track

for home? Hills decided not to squander the opportunity, arrowed for the breach with the quickening filly, and soon found himself in front. Now came the toughest part, fending off challengers.

Typically, it was that old warhorse The Tatling who came at La Cucaracha the hardest. He was closing her down. La Cucaracha clearly thought she had done enough and, as was feared, she was idling in front. Would she hold on? She did, but by only a head.

Prior to 2005, the daughter of Piccolo had visited the racecourse on just five occasions. Her juvenile season promised plenty, but was terminated before the summer. By then she'd won both her races, at Leicester – by five lengths from an odds-on shot – and Newbury, showing on both occasions the ability to quicken which was to become her trademark.

There's a well-proven theory in Lambourn that when a Hills-trained juvenile wins first time out, it's more than likely to win at Group-race level at some stage of its career. This filly had looked the likely favourite for the Queen Mary, but by mid-May the injury problem intervened and she failed to see the track again that year.

In 2004, she was limited to just three races, all at Listed level, but failed to win, and once more her season was shut down before the end of May. Under the circumstances, it was a tribute to Reed and Hills that they didn't cut and run and despatch her to the paddocks.

She was back in 2005 with a proper campaign to justify her trainer's faith. It launched with a win at one of his favourite meetings, the Doncaster Lincoln fixture, where she overcame ground that was a shade slower than ideal in the Listed Cammidge Trophy.

2005 Race record

2nd William Hill Sprint Cup (Group 1) (Haydock, September 3) 3yo+ 6f Good **116** (TS 98) 17 ran. *Midfield, headway over 2f out, edged left over 1f out, went 2nd inside final furlong, stayed on (M Hills), beaten 1l by Goodricke*

1st VC Bet Nunthorpe Stakes (Group 1) (York, August 18) 2yo+ 5f Good to firm **116** (TS 101) 16 ran. *Held up in midfield, headway 2f out, quickened to lead just inside final furlong, held on towards finish (M Hills), beat The Tatling by hd*

1st Skybet Dash (Heritage Handicap) (York, July 23) 3yo+ (0-105 handicap) 6f Good to firm **116** (TS 100) 15 ran. *Held up in midfield, smooth headway 2f out, led entering final furlong, kept on (M Hills), beat Connect by 3/4l*

2nd Cuisine De France Summer Stakes (Group 3) (York, July 8) 3yo+ 6f Good to soft **104** (TS 104) 11 ran. *Tracked leaders, led well over 1f out, headed just inside final furlong, no extra (M Hills), beaten 3l by Lucky Spin*

1st Ballyogan Stakes (Group 3) (Leopardstown, June 1) 3yo+ 6f Good to firm **108** (TS 77) 8 ran. *Tracked leaders in 5th, progress on outer early straight, ridden to lead over 1f out, kept on well (M Hills), beat Alexander Icequeen by 1/2l*

9th Duke of York Hearthstead Homes Stakes (Group 2) (York, May 11) 3yo+ 6f Soft **96** (TS 70) 11 ran. *Held up, headway on outer to chase leaders 2f out, soon ridden and weakened well over 1f out (M Hills), beaten 5l by The Kiddykid*

1st Stanleybet Cammidge Trophy (Listed) (Doncaster, April 2) 3yo+ 6f Good **103** (TS 81) 11 ran. *Held up in touch on outer, good headway over 2f out, ridden to lead 1f out, kept on strongly (M Hills), beat The Kiddykid by 1/2l*

Other runs

2004 **3rd** Telectronics System Leisure Stakes (Listed) (Windsor, May 24) 3yo+ 6f Good to firm **96** (TS 75) 9 ran ● **6th** Cantor Sport Carnarvon Stakes (Listed) (Newbury, May 14) 3yo 6f Good **91** (TS 59) 11 ran ● **2nd** EBF Lansdown Fillies' Stakes (Listed) (Bath, April 27) 3yo+ 5f Good **103** (TS 82) 14 ran 2003 **1st** Sanctuary Group Fillies' Conditions Stakes (Newbury, May 16) 2yo 5f Good to firm **96** (TS 85) 5 ran ● **1st** Brooklands Racing First For Horse Sponsorship Median Auction Maiden Stakes (Leicester, April 26) 2yo 5f Good to firm **87** (TS 72) 14 ran

The Doncaster form was turned inside out when she failed to handle York's soft surface in the Group 2 Duke of York, but Hills found the perfect opening in Ireland when, well backed, she bounced off the drying ground at Leopardstown with a commanding display in the Group 3 Ballyogan Stakes.

Post Nunthorpe, she may well have added another Group 1 at Haydock but for a high draw. As it was, she found herself isolated down the stands side and Goodricke got first run. She was beaten a length, and that performance must rank as one of her best.

All along, Hills had hankered after a challenge on the Hong Kong Sprint. In fact, he had mentioned Sha Tin as far back as the spring, reckoning everything there would be in her favour. Unfortunately, injury intervened once more and she missed the engagement.

The cheering news is that La Cucaracha will remain in training. She may yet make it to Hong Kong one day.

La Cucaracha

bay filly, 26-3-2001

Piccolo b 1991	Warning	Known Fact	In Reality Tamerett
		Slightly Dangerous	Roberto Where You Lead
	Woodwind	Whistling Wind	Whistler Good As Gold
		Garden Green	Pinturischio Focal
Peggy Spencer ch 1992	Formidable	Forli	Aristophanes Trevisa
		Native Partner	Raise A Native Dinner Partner
	Careful Dancer	Gorytus	Nijinsky Glad Rags
		Be Noble	Vaguely Noble Be Careful

Bred by Guy Reed in Britain

Sire Piccolo

Won 4 of 21 starts. At 2, won 1 (6f maiden) of 6 starts, also 3rd Tattersalls Houghton Sales S. At 3, won 2 (Chipchase S-Listed, Nunthorpe S-Gr1 on disqualification) of 11 starts, also 2nd Mehl-Mulhens-Rennen-Gr2, Phoenix Sprint S-Gr3, Haydock Sprint Cup-Gr1. At 5, won 1 (King's Stand S-Gr2) of 4 starts, also 2nd July Cup-Gr1, 3rd Benazet Rennen-Gr3. Initially tried at 3 over 8f, far better over 5-6f. Sire top-class miler who generally has been an influence for speed at stud. Dam 6f 2yo winner, half-sister to smart sprinter Le Johnstan. First foals 1997, sire of (northern hemisphere): Pan Jammer (Gr3), La Cucaracha (Nunthorpe S-Gr1), Pickle (Gr3), Ajigolo (Gr2).

Dam Peggy Spencer

Won 3 of 16 starts. At 2, unplaced sole start. At 3, won 2 (6-7f) of 9 starts. At 4, won 1 (7f) of 6 starts. All wins on all-weather, highest winning mark 66. By top-class 2yo and fair speed sire, out of unplaced half-sister to smart 10-12f filly Darine. Third dam is high-class 2yo Be Careful. Dam of: Sammy Samba (1998 g by Be My Chief; bumper/hurdle winner), unnamed (1999 c by Slip Anchor), Takes Two To Tango (2000 f by Groom Dancer; winner), La Cucaracha (2001 f by Piccolo; Nunthorpe S-Gr1), unnamed (2002 f by Pursuit Of Love), 2004 f by Pursuit Of Love, 2005 c by Piccolo.

Pedigree assessment

Guy Reed's homebred owes much to Lavington Stud in Sussex, home to Piccolo and to the late Formidable. Both stallions are regarded as transmitters of speed, and that has enabled La Cucaracha – whose female family is not known for sprinters – to possess such pace. With just one strain of both Northern Dancer and Native Dancer in the fifth generation, and several other common factors missing from her pedigree, La Cucaracha will have almost all mating options open to her when she eventually retires to the paddocks. *JH*

Leroidesanimaux (Brz)

5yo chestnut horse **127**

Candy Stripes (USA) - Dissemble (Ahonoora)

Owner T.N.T. Stud

Trainer R J Frankel

Breeder Haras Baga Do Sul

Career: **13** starts | won **9** | second **2** | third **0** | **£876,787** win and place

By Nicholas Godfrey

BUT for a compromising draw and potentially even more compromising footwear, we might well be lauding the muscular American-trained Leroidesanimaux as a Breeders' Cup Mile winner with a near-flawless record. We might even be identifying the Brazilian-bred, whose name means 'King of the Animals', as the best turf miler in the world in 2005, despite the claims of several others in Europe.

But we can't, because circumstances conspired to defeat Leroidesanimaux at Belmont on the day it mattered most, when a valiant performance was not enough to hold the top-class Artie Schiller, who outran him in the stretch to beat him by three-quarters of a length. Such are the margins on which exalted reputations are brought into question, and usually diminished.

Leroidesanimaux had not done too much wrong previously. Transferred to Bobby Frankel's yard by his owners, Goncalo Torrealba's TNT Stud, after a promising two-year-old season in Brazil in 2003, his American record thereafter was impeccable.

Few trainers have enjoyed as much success with imports as Frankel, who made his name largely with ex-European horses sent to him by Khalid Abdullah's Juddmonte operation.

After finishing fourth on his US debut in January 2004, Leroidesanimaux went unbeaten in five further starts that year, culminating in Grade 1 victory in the one-mile Citation Handicap at Hollywood Park in November. Though his previous victories had all been achieved in lesser company, the Brazilian emigrant had already done much to demonstrate both class and versatility, recording a set of excellent speed figures while racing in front, stalking the pace, or producing a turn of foot from behind. Despite having to race as a four-year-old, he set a track record (also at Hollywood Park) in May when still five months short of his actual fourth birthday.

The Brazilian-bred Leroidesanimaux established himself as the top US miler, despite defeat at the Breeders' Cup

Nevertheless, he was hardly a household name by the time of his seasonal debut in 2005 in March in the Grade 1 Frank E Kilroe Mile, a handicap at Santa Anita. "He is quite possibly the best turf horse in the nation, and virtually no one even knows how to pronounce his name," said the *Daily Racing Form* before Leroidesanimaux showed competitive instinct to match his tactical speed in surviving a race-long pace duel.

A six-month break followed after an unspecified minor setback during which time Leroidesanimaux was shipped to Frankel's East Coast stable. He returned with yet another victory at Saratoga in a Grade 2 handicap where he conceded weight to rivals who made the mistake of granting him an easy lead. He was not fully extended to post another track record, albeit one on extremely fast ground.

If that display was hugely competent, Leroidesanimaux was nothing short of spectacular next time out on much softer ground in the Atto Mile at Woodbine in Canada. While his rivals represented a substandard Grade 1 field, they were overwhelmed by the odds-on favourite, who took control on the inside after two furlongs of the mile contest before going on to win by nearly eight lengths from the outsider Mobil. Though it was easy to pick holes in the form, the manner of the victory was hugely impressive.

On the back of such a display, Leroidesanimaux would probably have been fancied to beat even the top Europeans in the Breeders' Cup Mile, for which he was supplemented at a cost of $135,000. Without the likes of Shamardal, Dubawi, Starcraft, Divine Proportions and Rakti in

2005 Race record

2nd Netjets Breeders' Cup Mile (Grade 1) (Turf) (Belmont Park, October 29) 3yo+ 1m Yielding **123** 12 ran. *Pressed leaders on outside, went 2nd well over 2f out, led over 1f out to inside final furlong, ran on same pace (J R Velazquez), beaten 3/4l by Artie Schiller*

1st Atto Mile (Grade 1) (Woodbine, September 18) 3yo+ 1m Yielding **127** 9 ran. *Led over 5f out, quickened clear well over 1f out (J R Velazquez), beat Mobil by 7 3/4l*

1st Fourstardave Handicap (Grade 2) (Turf) (Saratoga, August 27) 3yo+ 1m 1/2 Firm **124** 6 ran. *Made all, driven out (J R Velazquez), beat Silver Tree by 1 1/4l*

1st Frank E Kilroe Mile Handicap (Grade 1) (Turf) (Santa Anita, March 5) 4yo+ 1m Good **122** 9 ran. *Led or disputed until ridden clear over 1f out, driven out (J K Court), beat Buckland Manor by 1l*

Other wins

2004 **1st** Citation Handicap (Grade 1) (Hollywood Park, November 27) 3yo+ 1m 1/2 Firm **121** 10 ran ● **1st** Morvich Stakes (Handicap) (Grade 3) (Santa Anita, October 30) 3yo+ 6 1/2f Firm **120** 6 ran ● **1st** Inglewood Handicap (Grade 3) (Hollywood Park, May 1) 3yo+ 1m 1/2 Firm 9 ran ● **1st** Allowance Optional Claiming (Santa Anita, March 20) 4yo+ 1m Firm 6 ran ● **1st** Allowance Race (Santa Anita, January 31) 4yo+ 1m Firm 11 ran **2003** **1st** Maiden (Gavea, May 31) 2yo 6 1/2f Good 10 ran

opposition, he was sent off a strong 7-4 favourite, and would have been even shorter were it not for his unappetising draw, 11 of 12 on a turf track where double-figure gate positions have enjoyed scant success in recent seasons, albeit from a limited sample of runners.

More worryingly, it emerged on the morning of the race that Leroidesanimaux would run in two aluminium bar shoes, which offer less traction than conventional racing plates, after he was found to be slightly sore. Although the Belmont turf track features a one-turn mile with a long straight run from the gate rather than an immediate bend, from his wide draw Leroidesanimaux was unable to dominate in his customary fashion. Instead, he pressed the pace behind Sand Springs and Ad Valorem.

Jockey John Velazquez claimed that his mount pulled too hard, in contrast to eventual winner Artie Schiller, one of a handful of legitimate rivals on paper, who benefited from a ground-saving trip in behind. Leroidesanimaux finally got to the lead two out, but while he fought back once headed, he simply could not hold Artie Schiller and he only just managed to withstand the closing pack to retain second by a nose. "He's a better horse than that," said Frankel. "Running in two aluminium plates, that had to hurt him." Given his hitherto unblemished record, defeat could be regarded only as a disappointment, one that could not help but raise questions about the true worth of his earlier victories, despite the visual impression and the persuasive evidence of the clock. Had he simply been beating up the generally inferior opposition that prevails in North American turf races?

We will never receive a satisfactory answer. Soon after the Breeders' Cup it was announced that Leroidesanimaux was to be retired to stud.

Leroidesanimaux *chestnut horse, 27-9-2000*

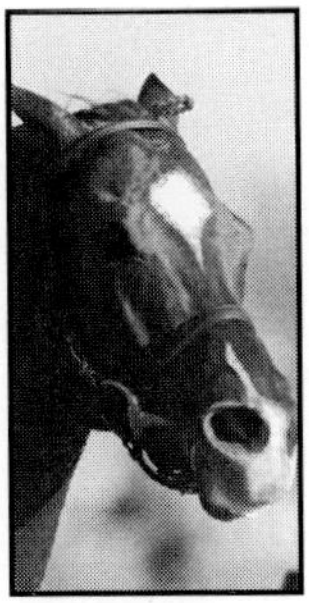

Candy Stripes ch 1982	Blushing Groom	Red God	Nasrullah
			Spring Run
		Runaway Bride	Wild Risk
			Aimee
	Bubble Company	Lyphard	Northern Dancer
			Goofed
		Prodice	Prominer
			Euridice
Dissemble ch 1989	Ahonoora	Lorenzaccio	Klairon
			Phoenissa
		Helen Nichols	Martial
			Quaker Girl
	Kerali	High Line	High Hat
			Time Call
		Sookera	Roberto
			Irule

Bred by Haras Bage do Sul in Brazil.

Sire Candy Stripes

Won 2 of 6 races. Also 2nd (promoted from 3rd) in Poule d'Essai des Poulains. Quite attractive, 15.3hh. Smart performer, dogged by leg problems. Unraced after May at 3, and after June at 4. By a top-class miler and champion sire out of a minor winner who was sister to Grade 1-winning mare Sangue. Half-brother to Bubble Gum Fellow (champion 2-y-o in Japan) and Intimiste (Gr1 winner in France). Stands at Haras Carampangue in Argentina. Sire of 16 racing crops and 55 stakes winners inc. Gr1 winners Seaborg, Different, Emigrant, Fanon, Body Glove, Victory Stripes, Leroidesanimaux, Equipado and Invasor.

Dam Dissemble

Unraced. Sold 3,000gns as filly out of training, Tattersalls 1992 December Sales. By a high-class sprinter and successful sire. Half-sister to Hasili (dam of Gr2 winner Dansili, Gr1 winners Banks Hill, Heat Haze and Intercontinental, and to Gr2 winner Cacique) and to Skiable (dam of disqualified Gr1 'winner' Three Valleys). Dam a winner, half-sister to Gr1-winning sprinter So Factual. Grand-dam won Cheveley Park Stakes. Dam of: Disport (1994 c by Blue Stag; Gr3 winner in Brazil), Direct Dial (1995 c by Pour Henri; winner), Blond Temptation (1996 f by Pour Henri; unplaced), Uapybo (1998 c by Blush Rambler; Gr1 winner in Brazil; 3rd in Derby Paulista), Zaragoza Girl (1999 f by Trempolino; winner), Leroidesanimaux (2000 c by Candy Stripes; multiple Gr1 winner). Her yearling filly by War Chant died, but she has a Giant's Causeway colt foal, and was covered in 2005 by Storm Cat.

Pedigree assessment

In 2005 there was never any doubt that Brazilian-bred Leroidesanimaux was the best grass-course miler in North America – until his defeat by Artie Schiller at the Breeders' Cup. The five-year-old had won eight in a row before he came to Belmont Park as a hot favourite, and while it seemed a pity that he could not confirm his title credentials on the big day, his Atto Mile form at Woodbine still looked better than anything Artie Schiller ever accomplished. Leroidesanimaux is a well-bred individual, although his dam was sold cheaply as an unraced three-year-old. At that time her half-sister Hasili had yet to establish herself as one of the world's outstanding broodmares. Dissemble's 2005 mating with Storm Cat provided a sure indication of the lofty status she has now attained. *TM*

Linda's Lad

2yo bay colt **110**

Sadler's Wells (USA) - Colza (USA) (Alleged (USA))

Owner S Mulryan

Trainer A Fabre

Breeder Niarchos Family

Career: **6** starts | won **3** | second **3** | third **0** | **£166,652** win and place

By Robert Carter

ANDRE FABRE gained his tenth Group 1 success of the year, and Christophe Soumillon his 12th, when Linda's Lad won the Criterium de Saint-Cloud. But it is more significant for French racing that the winner of the final Group 1 event of the season is owned by Sean Mulryan. The Irishman has rapidly expanded his team of jumpers in France and was the leading owner, on first place earnings, in 2005 but his enthusiasm for the Flat has been less evident.

Mulryan and his wife sold their house and their cars to fund their first residential development, at Ballymore Eustace in Co Kildare. That was in 1982 and they called their company Ballymore Properties. It now has head offices in Dublin and London. Mulryan has concentrated on developments in capital cities, including Bratislava, Prague and Budapest.

Like any true Irishman, he bought jumpers when he turned his attention to racing. Dovaly, winner of the Galway Plate in 2000, and Forget The Past, successful in a Grade 1 novice chase at the Leopardstown Christmas meeting in 2004, have been among his best at home. But he chose an entirely new path when he began investing in French jumpers, trying to win the big races in that country rather than paying inflated prices for horses with form and importing them to Britain or Ireland.

Mulryan, 51, has had expert assistance from his trainer, Arnaud Chaille-Chaille, and his racing manager, the bloodstock agent Herve Barjot, who runs the Irish part of his own Pegasus Farms enterprise from Kilmoney Stud in Co Kildare. Mulryan was not in the leading 100 owners over jumps in France in 2003 but he was fourth in 2004. Magalen Bryant headed the list thanks to the efforts of 92 different horses. Mulryan was represented by seven. They started 27 times, for 18 wins and six places.

Such success encouraged further expansion in 2005 and 25 horses had contributed 33 wins and 32 places from 74 starts by the beginning of December. Bonbon Rose, Cyrlight, Kiko, Mid Dancer, Polivalente, Sunspot

Linda's Lad wins the Group 1 Criterium de Saint-Cloud, confirming his status as France's top staying juvenile

and Zaiyad were all Graded race winners. Mulryan has made little impact in Britain, although Ballymore Properties has sponsored races on Hennessy day at Newbury since 2002 and Ambobo carried his colours to victory in a Grade 2 novice hurdle at Cheltenham in January 2005.

Ballymore Eustace is still an important part of Mulryan's life. He now lives at the Ardenode Stud there, an establishment that produced the likes of Ragusa and the Irish 2,000 Guineas winner, Ballymore. The Mullions, who owned Ardenode at the time, also had considerable success in France so Mulryan is following the tradition of the farm. He had ten wins on the Flat in 2004 and 11 wins from 15 starters by the beginning of December. He has also invested in broodmares, including Ebaraya, a daughter of Sadler's Wells who cost €925,000 at Goffs November Sales in 2002. Barjot paid 475,000gns for a yearling filly by Sadler's Wells out of Infamy at Newmarket in October 2005. So Ardenode should once again be producing big winners on the Flat before too long.

French racing was full of staying-bred two-year-olds not so many years ago. Now horses like Linda's Lad are something of a rarity. Few French trainers would feel the need to start a son of Sadler's Wells in early July. But Fabre has a stable bursting with talent. The experience of his two seconds helped Linda's Lad when he was faced with his first serious test at Deauville in August. No-one was sure where the best ground was and two jockeys stuck to the rails while the rest raced out in the middle.

Championship Point, the Mick Channon-trained favourite, led the main group into the straight with Linda's Lad tracking him and racing in fifth

2005 Race record

1st Criterium de Saint-Cloud (Group 1) (Saint-Cloud, November 12) 2yo 1m2f Heavy **110** (TS 70) 5 ran. *Raced in 2nd, led over 1½f out, soon driven, headed 100yds out, rallied to lead again close home, driven out (C Soumillon), beat Fauvelia by 1l*

1st Prix de Conde (Group 3) (Longchamp, October 16) 2yo 1m1f Good **105** (TS 63) 6 ran. *Made all, ridden approaching final furlong, just held on (C Soumillon), beat Best Name by shd*

2nd Prix des Chenes (Group 3) (Longchamp, September 17) 2yo 1m Good to soft **105** (TS 60) 4 ran. *Raced in 3rd, pushed along 2f out, ridden and went 2nd over 1f out, kept on but not reach winner (O Peslier), beaten ½l by Carlotamix*

1st Criterium du Fonds European de l'Elevage (Listed) (Deauville, August 20) 2yo 1m Very soft **102** (TS 71) 10 ran. *Raced in 5th, headway to lead narrowly approaching final furlong, stayed on, just held on (C Soumillon), beat Championship Point by hd*

2nd Prix du Putois (Compiegne, July 29) 2yo 7f Good to soft 12 ran. *Raced in 3rd, went 2nd approaching final furlong, kept on but never threatened winner (C Soumillon), beaten 1½l by Kakofonic*

2nd Prix Cocktail FM (Unraced Colts & Geldings) (Straight) (Deauville, July 7) 2yo 7f Good **76** (TS 62) 16 ran. *Always prominent, went 2nd approaching final furlong, stayed on but no chance with winner (C Soumillon), beaten 2½l by El Capitano*

overall. He led more than a furlong out and went at least half a length up. But Championship Point rallied gamely and Linda's Lad had to be ridden right out. Daaly Babet, who had led on the rails most of the way, kept on for third.

Olivier Peslier rode Linda's Lad in the Prix des Chenes, the only time Soumillon missed the mount. Had he been there, rather than in Ireland, he would have been claimed for the winner in any case. Linda's Lad started favourite but could never catch his stablemate. That must have persuaded Soumillon to adopt front-running tactics when they were reunited in the Prix de Conde. Linda's Lad was untidy on the top bend, edging out to his left while his head was turned to the right, but he seemed in control until inside the final furlong. Then Best Name, a son of King's Best who was making his debut, produced a strong run. Linda's Lad was already under driving when the threat emerged but he kept on just well enough. Fauvelia finished one and a half lengths back in third but made more of a race of it in the Criterium de Saint-Cloud. She hit the front inside the final furlong and Soumillon had to work his hardest before Linda's Lad could regain the advantage.

Linda's Lad was the best stayer in a weak division but it remains to be seen how far his stamina and durability can carry him. However, he has already earned €234,980, a handsome return on the €140,000 he cost as a yearling at Deauville. His chances of adding to that success in races like the Prix Noailles, Hocquart and Greffulhe, none of which attracted more than eight runners last year, must be good. But he had better watch out for the likes of Best Name.

Linda's Lad

bay colt, 23-02-2003

Sadler's Wells b 1981	Northern Dancer	Nearctic	Nearco Lady Angela
		Natalma	Native Dancer Almahmoud
	Fairy Bridge	Bold Reason	Hail To Reason Lalun
		Special	Forli Thong
Colza b 1991	Alleged	Hoist The Flag	Tom Rolfe Wavy Navy
		Princess Pout	Prince John Determined Lady
	Dockage	Riverman	Never Bend River Lady
		Golden Alibi	Empery Charming Alibi

Bred by Niarchos family in Britain

Sire Sadler's Wells

Won 6 of 11 races, inc. Beresford S.-Gr3, Irish Derby Trial-Gr2, Irish 2,000 Guineas-Gr1, Eclipse S.-Gr1, Phoenix Champion S.-Gr1. Also 2nd in Prix du Jockey-Club-Gr1, King George VI & Queen Elizabeth S.-Gr1. Impeccably bred top-class performer from 8-12f, handsome, tough and consistent. Sire of Gr1 winners: Braashee, French Glory, In The Wings (3), Old Vic (2), Prince Of Dance, Scenic, Salsabil (5), Opera House (3), Runyon, Saddlers' Hall, El Prado, Johann Quatz, Masad, Barathea (2), Fatherland, Fort Wood, Intrepidity (3), Carnegie (2), King's Theatre (2), Northern Spur (2), Moonshell, Muncie, Poliglote, Chief Contender, Dance Design, Darazari, Luna Wells, Cloudings, Ebadiyla (2), Entrepreneur, In Command, Kayf Tara (4), Dream Well (2), Greek Dance, King Of Kings (2), Leggera, Commander Collins, Daliapour, Montjeu (6), Saffron Walden, Aristotle, Beat Hollow (4), Subtle Power, Galileo (3), Imagine (2), Milan, Perfect Soul, Sequoyah, Sligo Bay, Ballingarry, Black Sam Bellamy (2), Gossamer (2), High Chaparral (6), Islington (4), Quarter Moon, Sholokov, Alberto Giacometti, Brian Boru (2), Doyen, Powerscourt (2), Refuse To Bend (4), Yesterday, Quiff, Yeats, Playful Act, Linda's Lad.

Dam Colza

Won sole start at 2, over 8f. Unplaced sole start at 3 (12f Listed). By dual Arc winner and very good stamina-oriented sire. Half-sister to smart 2yo/miler Wharf (Storm Bird), to 8f 3yo Listed winner Mooring (Zafonic) and to dam of high-class 10f colt Chelsea Manor (Grand Lodge). Dam Listed winner, out of unraced half-sister to outstanding 12f performer and broodmare Dahlia. Dam of: Cooper Island (1996 c by Generous; placed on Flat, hurdles winner), Ulterior Motives (1997 c by Selkirk; Gr3-placed winner), Lilyfoot (1998 f by Sanglamore; winner), Volantis (1999 c by Bluebird; winner), Cheeky Madam (2000 f by Night Shift; placed), Latinia (2001 f by Barathea; placed), Linda's Lad (2003 c by Sadler's Wells; Gr1 winner), 2004 f by Hernando. In foal to Ocean Of Wisdom.

Pedigree assessment

Linda's Lad, already a Group 1 winner over 10f, is certain to stay 12f. Family members can excel over shorter when sired by more speed-oriented stallions, but the combination of Sadler's Wells as sire and Alleged as broodmare sire should ensure Linda's Lad stays well. That sire combination is also responsible for St Leger winner Brian Boru. *JH*

Maids Causeway (Ire)

3yo chestnut filly **115**

Giant's Causeway (USA) - Vallee Des Reves (USA) (Kingmambo (USA))

Owner Martin S Schwartz

Trainer B W Hills

Breeder The Vallee Des Reves Syndicate

Career: **11** starts | won **4** | second **4** | third **1** | **£350,996** win and place

By Mark Blackman

"She was her father's daughter." It would be a fitting epitaph for the racing career of Maids Causeway. Just as her sire, the 'Iron Horse' Giant's Causeway, appeared almost to sense the winning line, and to thrust at it with a determination that suggested he knew its significance, so Maids Causeway's two finest hours on the track were gained with a palpable will to win under maximum pressure. No wonder regular jockey Michael Hills was moved to describe her as "one of the bravest fillies I have ever ridden".

The first signs that she had acquired the determination of her sire came in a busy two-year-old season. Never out of the first three in seven starts – four in Pattern company – she had closed out that campaign with a short-head defeat of Penkenna Princess in the Group 2 Rockfel Stakes at Newmarket, rallying in the most courageous fashion to snatch victory in the last few inches. It was a deserved second Group win, but with potential stars of the calibre of Divine Proportions and Playful Act heading up the 1,000 Guineas market, Maids Causeway wintered at between 20-1 and 33-1 for the first fillies' Classic. The general feeling was that, tough though she was, she was exposed as not up to that level.

When the race took place she was favourite – and she hadn't even set foot on the racecourse for a trial. Instead, behind in her work, she had been given a racecourse gallop, and while Divine Proportions stayed in France and Playful Act struggled to come to herself, punters latched on to the tough Barry Hills filly as the highest-rated runner in what looked a substandard renewal. Another factor in her appeal to punters was probably the 2,000 Guineas success 24 hours earlier of Footstepsinthesand – also from the first crop of Giant's Causeway.

Awash with sweat in the parade ring, as her trainer warned she could be, Maids Causeway nonetheless went down to post calmly. Prominent from the moment the gates opened, she ran her customary solid race

Maids Causeway at York's Royal meeting, where she won the Group 1 Coronation Stakes in game fashion

and hit the front under the Hills roust with a quarter-mile to go, but she had no response to the withering last-to-first thrust of the Kieren Fallon-ridden Virginia Waters.

From the furlong pole she was fighting only to hold on to second. She did so, two and a half lengths adrift of the enigmatic Ballydoyle filly and half a length in front of the Masaka Stakes winner Vista Bella. As Virginia Waters did nothing comparable before or after, Maids Causeway could be counted unlucky to have run into her on her red-letter day.

Three weeks later, Maids Causeway sought revenge on Virginia Waters in the Irish 1,000 Guineas at The Curragh, but in a strange race, in which the first ten home were covered by less than three lengths, she could finish only a staying-on fifth, with Virginia Waters back in eighth. The first two home were Saoire and Penkenna Princess, who had finished some way adrift of her at Newmarket. A high draw had proved essential, with the first three occupying the three highest stalls and Maids Causeway was arguably unlucky again – she had been drawn in six, and was first home of those with single-figure berths.

The traditional meeting of Guineas principals in the Coronation Stakes was her next assignment, albeit decamped to York. Many of those she

2005 Race record

7th Kingdom of Bahrain Sun Chariot Stakes (Group 1) (Newmarket, October 1) 3yo+ 1m Good to soft **66** (TS 29) 10 ran. *Led centre group, headed over 3f out, weakened over 2f out, eased over 1f out (M Hills), beaten 24l by Peeress*

1st Coronation Stakes (Group 1) (York, June 17) 3yo 1m Good to firm **115** (TS 98) 10 ran. *With leaders, led over 4f out, faltered and headed well inside final furlong, shaken up to lead post (M Hills), beat Karen's Caper by shd*

5th Boylesports Irish 1,000 Guineas (Group 1) (Curragh, May 22) 3yo 1m Good to yielding **105** (TS 84) 18 ran. *Tracked leaders on stands' side, 9th over 3f out, kept on under pressure from 1½f out (M Hills), beaten 1½l by Saoire*

2nd UltimatePoker.com 1,000 Guineas Stakes (Group 1) (Newmarket, May 1) 3yo 1m Good to firm **109** (TS 99) 20 ran. *Chased leaders, led 2f out, ridden over 1f out, headed and unable to quicken inside final furlong (M Hills), beaten 2½l by Virginia Waters*

2004

1st Owen Brown Rockfel Stakes (Group 2) (Newmarket, October 16) 2yo 7f Soft **106** (TS 96) 8 ran ● **2nd** Meon Valley Stud Fillies' Mile (Group 1) (Ascot, September 25) 2yo 1m Good to firm **111** (TS 105) 9 ran ● **3rd** betfair.com May Hill Stakes (Group 2) (Doncaster, September 9) 2yo 1m Good **111** (TS 105) 8 ran ● **1st** Swynford Paddocks Hotel Sweet Solera Stakes (Group 3) (Newmarket (July), August 7) 2yo 7f Good to firm **99** (TS 71) 11 ran ● **2nd** Star Stakes (Listed) (Sandown, July 22) 2yo 7f Good to firm **100** (TS 93) 9 ran ● **1st** EBF Maiden Fillies' Stakes (Kempton, June 23) 2yo 7f Good **83** (TS 22) 8 ran ● **2nd** Wedgewood Estates Maiden Auction Fillies' Stakes (Newbury, June 9) 2yo 6f Good to firm **81** (TS 76) 19 ran

had clashed swords with at Newmarket and The Curragh – notably Virginia Waters – lined up again, but it was Maids Causeway who was to enjoy her day in the sun.

Always in the front rank, she took a clear lead with half a mile to run and soon had several rivals at full stretch. The exception, coming smoothly from off the pace, was Karen's Caper, the Nell Gwyn winner and 1,000 Guineas fourth.

As Karen's Caper challenged at the furlong marker, Maids Causeway appeared to falter, and surrendered her lead. She had lost a shoe and pricked a foot. It should have spelt the end of her chance, but she dug deep, responded to her rider's drive and, incredibly, got back up in the dying strides to break her Group 1 duck. Once again, there were shades of Giant's Causeway.

On pulling her up, a concerned Hills quickly dismounted. As well as hurting a foot, it transpired that Maids Causeway had pulled muscles in her hip. She was to be out of action for four months, and when she did return to the track it was to result in the worst performance of her career – a remote seventh to Peeress in the Sun Chariot Stakes.

American-based owner Martin Schwartz put her up for auction at the Tattersalls December Sales, where she would have been the star attraction, but Sheikh Mohammed stepped in and bought her privately. He will not regret it if she makes the start at stud her father did.

Maids Causeway *chestnut filly, 11-3-2002*

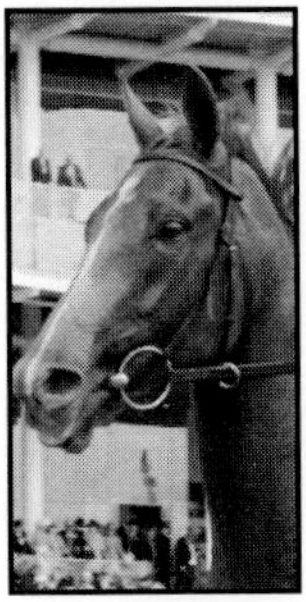

Giant's Causeway ch 1997	Storm Cat	Storm Bird	**Northern Dancer** South Ocean
		Terlingua	Secretariat Crimson Saint
	Mariah's Storm	Rahy	Blushing Groom Glorious Song
		Immense	Roberto Imsodear
Vallee des Reves b 1996	Kingmambo	Mr Prospector	Raise A Native Gold Digger
		Miesque	**Nureyev** Pasadoble
	Venise	**Nureyev**	**Northern Dancer** Special
		Virunga	Sodium Vale

Bred by Vallee des Reves Syndicate in Ireland; 25,000gns Tattersalls December yearling (retained).

Sire Giant's Causeway

Won 9 of 13 starts, inc. Curragh Futurity S.-Gr3, Prix de la Salamandre-Gr1, Gladness S.-Gr3, St James's Palace S.-Gr1, Eclipse S.-Gr1, Sussex S.-Gr1, York International S.-Gr1, Irish Champion S.-Gr1. Also 2nd in 2,000 Guineas, Irish 2,000 Guineas, Queen Elizabeth II S. and Breeders' Cup Classic. A striking individual, and a tough, top-class performer from 8-10.5f. Big, strong, consistent, effective on fast and soft turf and on dirt. By a champion North American sire out of a winner of 6 Graded races. Stands at Ashford Stud, Kentucky, at a (2006) fee of $300,000. Sire of 2 crops of racing age, inc: Aragorn (Gr2), Footstepsinthesand (2,000 Guineas-Gr1), Maids Causeway (Coronation S.-Gr1), My Typhoon (Gr2), Naissance Royale (Gr2), Shamardal (Dewhurst S.-Gr1, Poule d'Essai des Poulains-Gr1, Prix du Jockey Club-Gr1, St James's Palace S.-Gr1), Diamond Omi (Gr2), First Samurai (Hopeful S-Gr1, Champagne S.-Gr1), Frost Giant (Gr3).

Dam Vallee des Reves

Unraced. Sold 320,000gns, carrying to Danehill, 1999 Tattersalls December Sales. By a Classic-winning miler and internationally successful sire. Half-sister to Verveine (Gr2 winner, dam of Victory Cry, Volga, Vallee Enchantee), Vanishing Prairie (winner, dam of Vespone, La Sylphide) and Vetheuil (Gr2 winner). Dam unraced half-sister to Vin de France (Gr1), Vacarme (Gr2) and Vosges (Gr1-placed winner, dam of Gr1 winner Victoire Bleue, grand-dam of Gr2 winner Vertical Speed). Dam of: unnamed (2000 f by Danehill; unraced), Dream Valley (2001 f by Sadler's Wells; unplaced), Maids Causeway (2002 f by Giant's Causeway; Gr1 winner), unnamed (2003 c by Galileo; unraced to date). She has a yearling colt by Montjeu and a filly foal by Statue Of Liberty.

Pedigree assessment

The season's three-year-old distaff milers turned out to be rather less distinguished than we imagined in the spring. Maids Causeway, already considered among the best of her generation after a busy season at two, gave a good account of herself in the 1,000 Guineas, did not quite match that form in the Irish equivalent, and when she exceeded it, in her ultra-game Coronation Stakes victory, it was at the cost of an injury that left her on the sidelines for months. Who knows? But for that mishap she might have progressed. Instead, she came back as a shadow of her former self, and the overall impression of her record is that she was fortunate to gain a Group 1 success in a far-from-vintage year. *TM*

Makybe Diva

7yo bay mare **124**

Desert King (Ire) - Tugela (USA) (Riverman (USA))

Owner Emily Krstina Pty Ltd Syndicate

Trainer Lee Freedman

Breeder Emily Krstina Pty Ltd

Career: **36** starts | won **15** | second **4** | third **3** | **£5,795,063** win and place

By Paul Haigh

WHEN 2005 began, the seven-year-old mare, Makybe Diva had already established herself as one of the giants of Australian racing. By the time it ended she was being talked of, seriously and by serious people, as a latter-day counterpart of Phar Lap, Australian racing's all-time greatest and one of the country's enduring icons.

What she'd done already was win two Melbourne Cups, something no other female and only a tiny handful of males had ever achieved, and win them in succession as well as prove herself over a variety of distances as a major contender for the unofficial title 'best horse in Australia'.

If she'd been retired on January 1, 2005, which according to the calculations of Britain, the country in which she was foaled, would have been her sixth birthday, she'd still have had her place in history, and would still have been talked about for years to come in a country in which racing really matters to the average member of the sporting public in a way that seems strange even to devotees in other major racing nations.

What she did in 2005 was just plain ridiculous – the sort of thing that gets scoffed at when readers are invited to believe it in bad novels. And what made the whole country besotted with her by the time she had finished – her career as well as her season unless her fan club can somehow persuade her adoring owner, Tony Santic, to rethink his decision to retire her at the height of her powers - was the manner in which she accomplished it. The style and the joie de vivre that became her defining characteristics – her sheer pleasure in racing – were wondrous to behold.

Makybe Diva's 2005 didn't start in particularly spectacular fashion. 'First up', as the Aussies put it, she was given what looked like a pipe opener even by the standards of a racing fraternity that thinks nothing of asking two-mile specialists to go sprinting in the Group 1 CF Orr Stakes over seven furlongs in February. In retrospect, though, there was a hint of things to come in her fast-finishing seventh of 15, behind middle-distance

Makybe Diva cements her place among the icons of Australian racing with her third Melbourne Cup triumph

star Elvstroem. Eight days later she was beaten again by Elvstroem, then at the peak of the form that enabled him to win the Dubai Duty Free the following month, this time by only a head in the four-runner St George Stakes over nine furlongs.

It was the third outing of her campaign that announced she was in the process of improving her already special status as a champion of extraordinary versatility. In winning the A$1 million Group 1 Australian Cup over ten furlongs at Flemington, another weight-for-age race, she came with her trademark mid-straight surge to turn the tables decisively on Elvstroem, who could finish only fourth, yet had the former Caulfield Cup winner Mummify, who went on to beat Phoenix Reach and Alexander Goldrun in the Singapore International Airlines Cup two months later.

'The Diva' then took her songsheets to Sydney for Australia's second-richest weight-for-age race, the A$2 million BMW at Rosehill; and the ease with which she overwhelmed New South Wales champion Grande Armee suggested she had no real rivals left on home soil.

The decision to send her to Japan was in the circumstances perfectly understandable, not just because of the colossal prize-money available, but because at that time of year anyway, there were no fields left for her to conquer in Australia. Besides, her idolisers reasoned, if she could turn in performances like those at ten furlongs, who could the Japanese put up to beat her in the two-mile Spring Tenno Sho?

Her failures in Japan, both in a prep race and in the Tenno Sho itself,

2005 **Race record**

1st Emirates Melbourne Cup (Group 1) (Handicap) (Flemington, November 1) 3yo+ 2m Good to soft **124** 24 ran. *Held up on inside, 15th 5f out, switched off rail and headway over 3f out, 8th straight six-wide, led over 1f out, ran on strongly (G Boss), beat On A Jeune by 1¼l*

1st Carlton Draught Cox Plate (Group 1) (Moonee Valley, October 22) 3yo+ 1m2f Slow **116** 14 ran. *Settled in midfield, 9 lengths behind leaders, brought wide and smooth headway nearing turn, kept on well for strong win (G Boss), beat Lotteria by 1¼l*

1st Turnbull Stakes (Group 2) (Flemington, October 1) 1m2f Good 16 ran. *Settled in rear 9 lengths behind the leaders, came to the extreme outside on the turn and quickly made ground, won in cosy fashion (Steven King), beat Lad Of The Manor by ¾l*

2nd Dato Tan Chin Nam Stakes (Group 2) (Moonee Valley, September 10) 1m Good to soft 12 ran. *Settled in rear 12 lengths behind leaders, travelled wide and widest of all on the turn, stayed on strongly, just failed (G Boss), beaten shd by Lad Of The Manor*

1st Memsie Stakes (Group 2) (Caulfield, August 27) 7f Good 7 ran. *Broke well before settling down in rear 8 lengths behind leaders, still 7 or 8 lengths off turning in, finished strongly, impressive (Steven King), beat Barely A Moment by ½l*

7th Tenno Sho (Spring) (Group 1) (Kyoto, May 1) 4yo+ 2m Firm **107** 18 ran. *Raced in 12th, 10th straight, headway on outside to reach 5th 1f out, no extra (G Boss), beaten 4½l by Suzuka Mambo*

7th April Stakes (Nakayama, April 10) 4yo+ 1m2f Firm 12 ran. *Raced in 10th, never a factor (G Boss), beaten 5l by Suzuno March*

1st BMW Classic (Group 1) (Rosehill, March 19) 3yo+ 1m4f Soft **119** 11 ran. *Moderately away and given time to settle in midfield 7 lengths behind leaders, still 10 lengths behind turning in, finished strongly (G Boss), beat Grand Armee by 2l*

1st Australian Cup (Group 1) (Flemington, March 12) 3yo+ 1m2f Good **121** 7 ran. *Broke well, settled in rear 12 lengths behind leaders until good headway turning for home, pulled clear, easily (G Boss), beat Winning Belle by 1l*

2nd St George Stakes (Group 2) (Caulfield, February 26) 3yo+ 1m1f Good **114** 4 ran. *Broke well, settled in rear 3 lengths behind leaders until good headway when straightening up (G Boss), beaten shd by Elvstroem*

7th C F Orr Stakes (Group 1) (Caulfield, February 12) 3yo+ 7f Good to soft **109** 15 ran. *Settled in midfield, 10 lengths behind leaders, under pressure and still well back turning in, ran on strongly close home (Steven King), beaten 1¾l by Elvstroem*

Other wins

2004 **1st** Emirates Melbourne Cup (Group 1) (Handicap) (Flemington, November 2) 3yo+ 2m Good to soft **123** 24 ran ● **1st** Schweppes Sydney Cup (Group 1) (Handicap) (Randwick, April 17) 3yo+ 2m Good **115** 10 ran **2003** 1st Tooheys New Melbourne Cup (Group 1) (Handicap) (Flemington, November 4) 3yo+ 2m Good **114** 23 ran **2002** ● **1st** Queen Elizabeth Stakes (Grade 2 Handicap) (Flemington, November 9) 1m4½f Good 13 ran ● **1st** Grade 4 Handicap (Werribee, October 30) 1m2f Good 12 ran ● **1st** Fillies & Mares (Flemington, October 7) 1m2f Good 12 ran ● **1st** (Ballaratt, September 17) 1m2f Good 12 ran ● **1st** (Sale, September 3) 1m½f Good 10 ran ● **1st** Maiden (Wangaratta, August 13) 1m Good 14 ran

have been explained in various ways. Some thought they showed she was not quite herself when she was over there. Some that the firm ground was all against one who had shown she liked a bit of give. Some said she just did not travel, which seemed strange considering interstate travel in Australia never bothered her. Some wondered whether all the racing had not finally taken its toll.

There were those who preferred the more obvious explanation: that she may well have been a very big fish back home, but Japan, in racing terms at least, was just a bigger pond. Whatever the reason for her no more than respectable effort in seventh it should be noted that four lengths in front of her in third place in the Japanese two-mile championship event was Eye Popper, who she was to meet again during her triumphant finale.

Naturally she was given a good break by trainer Lee Freedman after that unsuccessful foray following such a busy (southern hemisphere) autumn. She returned in startling fashion in late August with a comfortable two-length victory in the Memsie Stakes, another Group 1 over seven furlongs – a distance at which, by most of the accepted rules of the game even in Australia, she really had no business winning. Although she failed to follow up in the Group 1 Dato Tan Chin Nam Stakes over the slightly longer trip of a mile, around the tight Moonee Valley track, her narrow defeat by Lad Of The Manor was put down by her fans to overconfidence on the part of her regular jockey, Glen Boss.

Sure enough, three weeks later, this time with Boss unavailable, she was reunited with her Memsie Stakes partner Steven King for the Group 2 Turnbull Stakes at Caulfield over ten furlongs in which she had no difficulty turning round the form with Lad Of The Manor. So impressive were these three performances that she was an obvious favourite for the race her connections had already declared to be her main target for the year, the Australasian equivalent of the Arc or the King George, the Cox Plate over the same ten-furlong trip at Moonee Valley in late October.

Doubts about her ability to take the championship race may have derived from the dissimilarity of the course to Flemington, scene of her greatest triumphs, and to the sheer improbability of what she was being asked to achieve. But there was absolutely no mistaking her enthusiasm for the job as she skipped down to the start like a ballerina, pricking her ears constantly at the capacity crowd and at everything that caught her attention as she waited to be loaded.

Even from the wide gate she dominated her field throughout, and although she had to challenge ten wide on the turn into the short straight, she was so obviously going better than anything else that her fans, many of whom, including her owner, sported weird-looking eye masks in the distinctive red, white and blue Santic colours, had already started to celebrate before she hit the front. At the line, idling a bit as was her habit once she had spent what seemed to her to be long enough in front, she had a length and a quarter to spare over Lotteria.

Freedman had always insisted the Cox Plate was the race he wanted for her CV, and that an attempt at the unprecedented third Melbourne Cup would be entirely dependent on her post-Cox condition, as well as on the prevailing track conditions. If this was a ploy to guarantee that enough water was poured on by the Flemington authorities to encourage the top-weight's appearance it certainly worked. Freedman was satisfied. Makybe Diva turned out, and in what seemed in a way almost an action replay of her Cox plate victory the great mare had her field well beaten even before she took the lead two furlongs out.

Boss's ecstasies after another length-and-a-quarter confirmation of her supremacy were themselves something to behold, but so too were the mare's; and it is surely not to be guilty of anthropomorphism to suggest she enjoyed the race and its aftermath almost as much as her connections – perhaps even more so than an emotional Santic himself, who immediately invoked the "nothing left to prove" rule in announcing her retirement to the paddocks.

All that was left was to work out exactly where Makybe Diva stood in terms of global class. Her detractors, of whom there are still a few, most of them outside Australia, would point to the fact that the Melbourne Cup is "just a handicap" – although by doing so they betray their ignorance of the true nature of 'The Race That Stops A Nation' as it is a compacted handicap, quite unlike the Cesarewitch, with which it has been rather absurdly compared, and one that is invariably contested by the best horses in Australasia who have even the remotest hope of getting the trip. Detractors also point to her failures in Japan on her only attempts outside Australia, as well as the defeats of her one-time rival, Elvstroem, when he came to Europe as indications that she was no more than a local heroine found wanting by the highest international standards.

Well, Elvstroem may have been past his best by the time he raced on this side of the world, and in any case two other formlines are relevant in questioning these assessments. First she was well below her best in Japan if an apparently reliable line through Eye Popper is anything to go by. In Kyoto she was getting 4lb from Eye Popper, whose second in the Caulfield Cup shows pretty clearly that he adapted well on his own excursion to Australia. At Flemington she gave him 9lb and beat him further than he had beaten her in the Tenno Sho.

Even more significantly, her defeats of Vinnie Roe suggest that at two miles and more she was as much superior to the redoubtable Irish stayer as was Westerner. Given her amazing versatility, is it too fanciful to suppose that if she'd been sent to Longchamp rather than to Moonee Valley and Flemington she, rather than the superb Wildenstein stayer, might have given Hurricane Run most to do in the 2005 Arc?

One more point to make about the idolised mare is that there is absolutely no doubt that, even at her relatively advanced age, she was still improving when she was retired. She was a freak in the best possible sense of the word – certainly one of the greatest ever seen on the Australian turf, and just possibly, particularly in view of the astounding variety of her triumphs, one of the best seen anywhere.

Makybe Diva

bay mare, 21-3-1999

Parents	Grandparents	Great-grandparents	Great-great-grandparents
Desert King b 1994	Danehill	Danzig	**Northern Dancer** Pas de Nom
		Razyana	His Majesty Spring Adieu
	Sabaah	Nureyev	**Northern Dancer** Special
		Dish Dash	Bustino Loose Cover
Tugela br 1995	Riverman	Never Bend	Nasrullah Lalun
		River Lady	Prince John Nile Lily
	Rambushka	Roberto	Hail To Reason Bramalea
		Katsura	**Northern Dancer** Noble Fancy

Bred by Emily Krstina (Aust) Pty Ltd in England. Unsold 1999 Tattersalls December Foal Sale.

Sire Desert King

Won 5 of 12 races, inc. National S.-Gr1, Tetrarch S.-Gr3, Irish 2,000 Guineas-Gr1, Irish Derby-Gr1. Also placed 2nd in York International S., Irish Champion S. Attractive, robust-looking individual, particularly impressive behind the saddle. Powerful galloper, with a rather round action, effective on firmish and softish ground. High-class performer from 8-12f. Bred on similar lines ot Maroof (Danzig-Dish Dash). Stands in Japan. Sire of: Makybe Diva (Melbourne Cup-Gr1, three times), Maranilla (Gr3), Mr Dinos (Prix Royal-Oak-Gr1, Gold Cup-Gr1), Place Rouge (Gr3), Rageman (Gr3), Darsalam (Aral Pokal-Gr1), Chelsea Rose (Moyglare Stud S.-Gr1), Mango Mischief (Gr3), North Queen (Gr3).

Dam Tugela

Ran twice unplaced as 2-y-o. Leggy, poor individual, showed no form. Sold 21,000gns 1997 Tattersalls December Sales; re-sold, carrying Makybe Diva, 60,000gns 1998 Tattersalls December Sales. Quite well-bred. Half-sister to minor winners in England and Japan. By a leading sire and notable broodmare sire. Dam Listed winner, half-sister to 9 other winners. To stud at 3 years and dam of: Makybe Diva (1999 f by Desert King; multiple Gr1 winner), Celtic Reign (2000 f by Woodman; unraced), Valkyrie Diva (2001 f by Jade Robbery; unraced). She has a 2-y-o colt by Redoute's Choice. Barren to End Sweep in 2002.

Pedigree assessment

The accomplishment of a unique feat does not necessarily denote greatness, and it might still be argued that such as Carbine (who conceded 53lb to his runner-up and won in record time in 1890) and Phar Lap (who triumphed easily under 9st 12lb in 1930) gave greater displays than Makybe Diva in the Melbourne Cup. But by winning it for a third time, the English-bred mare secured a place both in history and in the hearts of her adopted nation. And whose name might be cited as her equal among racemares active anywhere in the world in 2005? It was not just her Flemington handicap performance, as joint-top weight with Vinnie Roe, that advertised her merit; she also reigned supreme in Australia's top weight-for-age event, the W.S. Cox Plate. In the year when Danehill became champion sire in Britain, his grand-daughter was surely the best racemare on the planet. *TM*

Maraahel (Ire)

4yo bay colt **124**

Alzao (USA) - Nasanice (Ire) (Nashwan (USA))

Owner Hamdan Al Maktoum

Trainer Sir Michael Stoute

Breeder Shadwell Estate Company Limited

Career: **15** starts | won **3** | second **3** | third **4** | **£368,132** win and place

By Tony Smurthwaite

MARAAHEL'S consistency and application have carried him to the precipice of fame, but so far no further. Oddly, a 2005 record of one win from seven starts might suggest fun was frugally rationed.

Not so, as the smallish bay with the white face offered his people most to cherish when, in fact, beaten. A cosy winner of the Huxley Stakes at Chester in May, he was runner-up in the Group 2 Hardwicke Stakes at the Royal meeting, third in the Group 1 Emirates Airline Champion Stakes at Newmarket and third again in the Group 1 Hong Kong Cup at Sha Tin.

Yet those accomplishments were merely ballast to his mid-summer *piece de resistance*, a painfully close third in a cosmopolitan running of the Group 1 Juddmonte International Stakes, a half-length in front of Ace, for Ballydoyle and Ireland, but a head behind Japan's 2004 Horse of the Year Zenno Rob Roy, who in turn was beaten a solitary neck by Italy's new relentless galloper, Electrocutionist.

There may have been no Azamour, Motivator was missing, and Oratorio was also an absentee, but only those who show can bask in the glow and for Maraahel it was his moment for a near miss that felt like a career high point. Such was the proximity to victory that inevitably a review of the race would examine ways in which Maraahel might have, in other circumstances, won.

Once the pacesetting Ace began to tire there were five in a row fanned across the track with barely a furlong to run. Maraahel was the first to attack, but he was overwhelmed initially by Japan, and then by Italy, in those agonising final yards. He was in front a stride before the line, as trainer Sir Michael Stoute noted afterwards.

Yet so exotic was the intercontinental exacta that poor old Maraahel was largely ignored. He had run the race of his life so far, and yet his

Maraahel at Chester, on his way to his sole win of a season that also saw him make the frame in three Group 1 events

placing would simply provide munitions to those wanting to denigrate the International as relatively substandard.

Fifteen days later it looked as if the naysayers had a point. Stoute prepared Maraahel for the Group 3 Strensall Stakes, again at York although now over nine furlongs, with the biggest threat seemingly posed by Mullins Bay, up from handicaps after winning the John Smith's Cup.

No contest? Not quite. Fast ground and a strong pace appeared to diminish Maraahel, who with his high knee action edged left and was roundly beaten into third by Mullins Bay, with the modest Godolphin performer Andean taking second, a gaping four lengths clear of the Juddmonte International's top Brit.

Post-race verdicts concluded that the Strensall came too quickly after the International, and so Maraahel was given a break during which time Stoute and O'Brien continued their engrossing duel for the trainers' title.

Come Champions Day at Newmarket on October 15 Stoute threw everything at the feature event, the Champion Stakes. Chic, Rob Roy and Maraahel all appeared in a 15-runner line-up, whereas O'Brien played only Eclipse and Irish Champion winner Oratorio.

At 25-1, Maraahel's mid-summer effort was clearly overlooked, yet

2005 Race record

3rd Cathay Pacific Hong Kong Cup (Group 1) (Sha Tin, December 11) 3yo+ 1m2f Good to firm **124** 10 ran. *Held up, 8th straight, headway on outside from well over 1f out, ridden 1f out, no extra last 50yds (R Hills), beaten 1¼l by Vengeance Of Rain*

3rd Emirates Airline Champion Stakes (Group 1) (Newmarket, October 15) 3yo+ 1m2f Good to soft **123** (TS 109) 15 ran. *Held up in touch, ridden to lead over 1f out, soon headed, stayed on same pace inside final furlong (R Hills), beaten 2l by David Junior*

3rd William Hill Poker Grand Prix Strensall Stakes (Group 3) (York, August 31) 3yo+ 1m1f Good to firm **114** (TS 88) 6 ran. *Tracked leaders, headway 3f out, ridden to chase leading pair well over 1f out, one pace (R Hills), beaten 4¼l by Mullins Bay*

3rd Juddmonte International Stakes (Group 1) (York, August 16) 3yo+ 1m2½f Good **123** (TS 123) 7 ran. *Dwelt, soon tracking leaders, led over 1f out, no extra and headed near finish (R Hills), beaten ½l by Electrocutionist*

2nd Hardwicke Stakes (Group 2) (York, June 18) 4yo+ 1m4f Firm **122** (TS 102) 6 ran. *Dwelt, held up, effort and went 2nd over 1f out, soon ridden to challenge, no extra inside final furlong (R Hills), beaten ½l by Bandari*

1st Jardine Lloyd Thompson Huxley Stakes (for the Tradesman's Cup) (Group 3) (Chester, May 5) 4yo+ 1m2½f Good to soft **120** (TS 109) 10 ran. *Held up, headway over 3f out, led over 1f out, driven out (R Hills), beat Solskjaer by 1l*

5th Dubai Tennis Championships Stakes (Registered As The John Porter Stakes) (Group 3) (Newbury, April 16) 4yo+ 1m4f Soft **108** (TS 73) 13 ran. *Chased leaders, led over 4f out, headed approaching final 2f, weakened (W Supple), beaten 8l by Day Flight*

8th Dubai Sheema Classic Sponsored By Dubai Water Front (Turf) (Group 1) (Nad Al Sheba, March 26) 4yo+ 1m4f Good to firm **111** 11 ran. *In touch, 3rd and ridden straight, effort 2f out, weakened final 1f (R Hills), beaten 6l by Phoenix Reach*

Other wins

2004 **1st** ABN Amro Stakes (Registered As The Gordon Stakes) (Group 3) (Goodwood, July 27) 3yo 1m4f Good **116** (TS 95) 8 ran **2003** **1st** EBF Frier Wood Maiden Stakes (Pontefract, September 25) 2yo 1m Good to firm **77** (TS 65) 9 ran

in beating all bar David Junior and Pride he finished a place ahead of Oratorio. Stoute's representative was visored for the first time and, as at York, after travelling well he hit the front around a furlong from home only to flatten out. Another sound effort, but overshadowed by others.

More of the same was the order when Maraahel was dispatched to Hong Kong for the ten-furlong Cup, worth nearly £700,000 to the winner. Track notes recorded his evident wellbeing for his rematch with the French mare Pride and as the gates cracked open the two European challengers lay together at the back. Both travelled well and made their move in the straight, both wide, but both failed to get to the winner, Vengeance Of Rain. There was only a neck in it back to Pride, with Maraahel a length away third, fractionally closer to her than at Newmarket. It was arguably his best effort to date.

In 2006 he will resume his struggle to escape the periphery in Dubai, where either the Duty Free or the World Cup itself await. It remains to be seen if he has the pace to win in the very best company.

Maraahel

bay colt, 24-2-2001

Parents	Grandparents	Great-grandparents	Great-great-grandparents
Alzao br 1980	Lyphard	Northern Dancer	Nearctic Natalma
		Goofed	Court Martial Barra
	Lady Rebecca	Sir Ivor	Sir Gaylord Attica
		Pocahontas	Roman How
Nasanice b 1995	Nashwan	Blushing Groom	Red God Runaway Bride
		Height Of Fashion	Bustino Highclere
	Mathaayl	Shadeed	Nijinsky Continual
		Manal	Luthier Top Twig

Bred by Shadwell Estate Co in Ireland

Sire Alzao

Won 4 of 12 races, inc. Premio Ellington-Gr3. Also 2nd in La Coupe de Maisons-Laffitte and respectable 8th of 19 in Champion S. (only Gr1 start) at 3. Strong, compact sort, effective on any going, scored sole Pattern win in only race at 12f. Retired from stud duty. Last stood at Coolmore at a fee of €7,500. Sire of 18 crops of racing age, inc. notable winners: Alcando (Beverly Hills H.-Gr1), Mirror Black (Gr2), Pass The Peace (Cheveley Park S.-Gr1), Noble Patriarch (Gr3), Capricciosa (Moyglare Stud S.-Gr1, Cheveley Park S.-Gr1), Second Set (Sussex S.-Gr1), Bobzao (Gr2), Stubass (Gr2), Alpride (Beverly Hills H.-Gr1, Yellow Ribbon Invitational S.-Gr1), Prince Firebird (Gr3), Relatively Special (Gr3), Sheridan (Gr3), Unblest (Gr2), Wind In Her Hair (Aral Pokal-Gr1), Last Second (Gr2), Matiya (Irish 1,000 Guineas-Gr1), Solar Crystal (Gr3), Waky Nao (Premio Vittorio di Capua-Gr1), Token Gesture (Gr3), Alborada (Champion S.-Gr1 twice), Alcazar (Prix Royal Oak-Gr1), Epistolaire (Gr2), Shahtoush (Oaks S.-Gr1), Winona (Irish Oaks-Gr1), Eurolink Raindance (Gr3), Lady Upstage (Gr2), Timi (Oaks d'Italia-Gr1), Balthazar (Gr3), Albanova (Deutschland Preis-Gr1, Aral Pokal-Gr1, Preis von Europa-Gr1), Contemporary (Gr3), Special Kaldoun (Gr2), Bailador (Gr3), Luvah Girl (Gr2), Angara (Beverly D S.-Gr1), Maraahel (Gr3).

Dam Nasanice

Unraced at 2, won 1 (9f) of 6 starts at 3, placed twice over 10-12f, also ran with credit in Listed races over 8-10f. By Guineas and Derby winner with decent stud record overall. Very closely related to smart 12f filly Sahool (by Nashwan's half-brother Unfuwain out of Mathaayl), bred along similar lines to smart 2yo Muhbubh. Grand-dam Manal sister to high-class French 10f+ colts Tip Moss and Twig Moss. Dam of: Huja (2000 f by Alzao; Gr3-placed winner), Maraahel (2001 c by Alzao; Gr3 winner), Mostashaar (2002 c by Intikhab; winner), 2003 c by Anabaa, 2004 f by Green Desert.

Pedigree assessment

Having been tried at up to 15 furlongs – in the St Leger – Maraahel has found 10 to 12 furlongs more his forte. That is the distance bracket in which both his sire and dam showed talent. Maraahel's family close up features several smart juveniles, including Muhbubh and Asfurah, but there are several very talented middle-distance horses in it too. Expect more in 2006 from Maraahel, whose sire Alzao is adept at siring tough performers, with Alcazar the extreme example. *JH*

Millenary

8yo bay horse **121**

Rainbow Quest (USA) - Ballerina (Ire) (Dancing Brave (USA))

Owner L Neil Jones

Trainer J L Dunlop

Breeder Abergwaun Farms

Career: **35** starts | won **12** | second **6** | third **8** | **£958,431** win and place

By Howard Wright

JOHN DUNLOP had his tongue firmly in his cheek when he said of Millenary, after the 2005 Lonsdale Cup: "One day he'll make into a nice horse, once we know what his distance is!" He might have been joking, but he had a point.

Millenary, who won four of his five races as a three-year-old, was sent down the modern route for a St Leger winner after his Classic success, and ran over farther than a mile and a half in only three of his next 16 outings. He won just once in each season for three years, following the single Group 1 victory that marks the pinnacle of his career, but when he did tackle two miles for the first time, he went down by a short head to the gallant Persian Punch in that memorable Jockey Club Cup of 2003.

The desire to keep Millenary to middle distances was understandable. Looking to promote a stallion career for a son of Rainbow Quest out of a half-sister to a Princess Royal Stakes winner and the dam of Spectrum, without drawing too much attention to the so-called stigma of being a St Leger winner, connections appear to have decided that the middle-distance bracket made most appeal.

Yet for all Millenary's obvious quality, he was not able to win more than those single races a season over 12 furlongs. Then he was moved up to the staying category, where the difference in pace and quality of the opposition brought out the best in his turn of foot. Despite the earlier good intentions, as Millenary left the Dunlop yard in November 2005 to stand at stud in Co Kilkenny, he was already carrying the label of "a jumps stallion".

In ratings terms, Millenary's final two seasons, which comprised 11 races and only one over shorter than 14 furlongs, were not so consistently outstanding as the previous four, but that may be as much a consequence of staying horses in general being unable to impress the handicappers as any decline in overall ability. The fact is that in the company he was

Millenary signed off his long and consistent career with popular wins in the Lonsdale Cup and Doncaster Cup

asked to keep in that period, he won four Group 2 races and one Group 3, comprising the Yorkshire Cup, Doncaster Cup twice, Lonsdale Cup and Jockey Club Cup.

He achieved all this while acquiring blinkers to offset his increasingly noticeable quirkiness. He simply needed to be held up until the last possible moment, and had to be handled with the respect that any 'old gentleman' might expect.

Tailed-off last and hanging violently in the Yorkshire Cup, despite starting favourite, and a distant fourth of five behind Gamut in the Princess of Wales's Stakes, Millenary's opening two races of 2005 hinted that perhaps his departure for stud had been delayed too long. However, despite again hanging in the straight, he picked up when third – admittedly never dangerous and beaten over eight lengths – to Distinction and Golden Quest in the Goodwood Cup, and then came two superb displays by Richard Quinn, and Millenary.

Quinn's performance in fooling, humouring, cajoling, kidding and finally delivering Millenary with a late, late surge to turn the tables on Distinction by two and a half lengths in the Weatherbys Insurance Lonsdale Cup, without the winner hardly knowing he had been in a race, was put up among the three candidates for Racing Post readers to vote for the Flat Ride of the Season. The paper's northern racecourse reporter Tom O'Ryan described the achievement as "jockeyship at its best, poetry in motion".

Yet when Quinn repeated his trickery three weeks later in the GNER Doncaster Cup, producing Millenary with silky-smooth precision to head the progressive handicap specialist Sergeant Cecil well inside the final furlong, the jockey was moved to remark about "a carbon copy of York,

2005 Race record

3rd Jockey Club Cup (Group 3) (Newmarket, October 15) 3yo+ 2m Good to soft **114** (TS 110) 10 ran. *Held up, headway over 2f out, ridden over 1f out, ran on near finish (T Quinn), beaten 1½l by Cover Up*

1st GNER Doncaster Cup (Group 2) (Doncaster, September 8) 3yo+ 2m2f Good **115** (TS 72) 7 ran. *Held up and behind, steady headway 4f out, close up on bridle over 1f out, quickened to lead well inside final furlong (T Quinn), beat Sergeant Cecil by ¾l*

1st Weatherbys Insurance Lonsdale Cup (Group 2) (York, August 16) 3yo+ 2m Good **121** (TS 116) 8 ran. *Held up in last, steady headway over 2f out, pulled outside 1f out, quickened to lead inside final furlong, soon clear (T Quinn), beat Distinction by 2½l*

3rd Lady O Goodwood Cup (Group 2) (Goodwood, July 28) 3yo+ 2m Soft **115** (TS 107) 10 ran. *Held up behind, ridden and stayed on from 3f out, hung right from over 2f out, went 3rd just inside final furlong, never on terms with leading pair (T Quinn), beaten 8½l by Distinction*

4th Princess of Wales's Edward St George Memorial Stakes (Group 2) (Newmarket (July), July 6) 3yo+ 1m4f Good to soft **106** (TS 47) 5 ran. *Held up, some headway over 1f out, never dangerous (T Quinn), beaten 12½l by Gamut*

9th Emirates Airline Yorkshire Cup (Group 2) (York, May 13) 4yo+ 1m6f Good to soft **89** (TS 58) 9 ran. *Held up, headway on outer and hung right 4f out, weakened quickly over 1f out, eased inside final furlong (T Quinn), beaten 22l by Franklins Gardens*

Other wins

2004 **1st** Persian Punch Jockey Club Cup (Group 3) (Newmarket, October 16) 3yo+ 2m Soft **121** (TS 96) 11 ran ● **1st** Dead-heat GNER Doncaster Cup (Group 2) (Doncaster, September 9) 3yo+ 2m2f Good **120** (TS 46) 8 ran ● **1st** Emirates Airline Yorkshire Cup (Group 2) (York, May 13) 4yo+ 1m6f Good to soft **121** (TS 74) 10 ran 2003 **1st** Princess of Wales's UAE Equestrian And Racing Federation Stakes (Group 2) (Newmarket (July), July 8) 3yo+ 1m4f Good **121** (TS 103) 6 ran 2002 **1st** Princess of Wales's UAE Equestrian And Racing Federation Stakes (Group 2) (Newmarket (July), July 9) 3yo+ 1m4f Good to soft **118** (TS 108) 7 ran 2001 **1st** Sagitta Jockey Club Stakes (Group 2) (Newmarket, May 4) 4yo+ 1m4f Good **121** (TS 91) 7 ran 2000 ● **1st** Rothmans Royals St Leger Stakes (Group 1) (Doncaster, September 9) 3yo 1m6½f Good to firm **119** (TS 91) 11 ran ● **1st** Peugeot Gordon Stakes (Group 3) (Goodwood, August 1) 3yo 1m4f Good to firm **118** (TS 100) 10 ran ● **1st** Victor Chandler Chester Vase (Group 3) (Chester, May 9) 3yo 1m4½f Good **104** (TS 102) 8 ran ● **1st** Peter Smith Memorial Maiden Stakes (Newbury, April 14) 3yo 1m3f Soft **85** (TS 4) 6 ran

if not a tad better".

The level of form might not have been quite so high, though there was no knowing how much the winner had in hand, but the execution probably matched Quinn's description, because the Doncaster Cup distance of two and a quarter miles, over which he dead-heated in 2004, appeared to be the extreme limit of Millenary's stamina. Dunlop commented: "Last year he only just got home, so even more patience had to be exercised today. It was absolute perfection."

Beaten into third place behind Cover Up on his last start in the Jockey Club Cup, Millenary deserves to be remembered best for York and Doncaster in 2005. They were the days when everything came together in the right place.

Millenary *bay horse, 21-4-1997*

Rainbow Quest b 1981	Blushing Groom	Red God	Nasrullah Spring Run
		Runaway Bride	Wild Risk Aimee
	I Will Follow	Herbager	Vandale Flagette
		Where You Lead	Raise A Native Noblesse
Ballerina b 1991	Dancing Brave	Lyphard	Northern Dancer Goofed
		Navajo Princess	Drone Olmec
	Dancing Shadow	Dancer's Image	Native Dancer Noors Image
		Sunny Valley	Val de Loir Sunland

Bred by Abergwaun Farms.

Sire Rainbow Quest

Won 6 of 14 starts, inc. Great Voltigeur Stakes-Gr2, Coronation Cup-Gr1, Prix de l'Arc de Triomphe-Gr1. Medium-sized (16.0hh), attractive, good mover, somewhat light and leggy in training. Top-class performer in each of 3 seasons, only once out of the frame. Among the best sons of his sire (also got Nashwan, Arazi, etc). Dam a Gr3 winner at 12f, half-sister to Slightly Dangerous (Gr3 winner, 2nd in Oaks, dam of Warning, Commander In Chief, Dushyantor, Yashmak, etc). Stands at Banstead Manor Stud, Cheveley, Newmarket, at a fee of £35,000 (Oct. 1). Sire of 16 crops of racing age, inc. Gr1 winners: Knight's Baroness (Irish Oaks), Quest For Fame (Derby S., Hollywood Turf H.), Saumarez (Grand Prix de Paris, Prix de l'Arc de Triomphe), Sought Out (Prix du Cadran), Armiger (Racing Post Trophy), Bright Generation (Oaks d'Italia), Raintrap (Prix Royal Oak, Canadian International Championship S., San Juan Capistrano H.), Urgent Request (Santa Anita H.), Rainbow Dancer (Hollywood Turf H., Oak Tree Turf Championship S.), Sakura Laurel (Spring Tenno Sho, Arima Kinen), Sunshack (Critérium de Saint-Cloud, Coronation Cup, Prix Royal-Oak), Spectrum (Irish 2,000 Guineas, Champion S.), Fiji (Gamely H., Yellow Ribbon S.), Croco Rouge (Prix Lupin, Prix d'Ispahan), Nedawi (St Leger S.), Special Quest (Criterium de Saint-Cloud), Edabiya (Moyglare Stud S.), Millenary (St Leger S.).

Dam Ballerina

Won 1 of 5 races. Lengthy, quite attractive type, good mover. Seemed to stay 10f. Lightly raced. Very well-bred, by a top-class runner and good sire. Dam of: Little Giant (1996 c by Caerleon; placed at 2 in Ireland), Millenary (1997 c by Rainbow Quest; Classic winner), Head In The Clouds (1998 f by Rainbow Quest; Gr3 winner), Angel Of The Gwaun (1999 f by Sadler's Wells; unraced), Let The Lion Roar (2001 c by Sadler's Wells; Classic-placed winner), Dancingintheclouds (2002 f by Rainbow Quest; unplaced), King In Waiting (2003 c by Sadler's Wells; unraced to date). She has a yearling colt by Sadler's Wells, called Lion On The Prowl.

Pedigree assessment

This great public favourite gave racegoers memorable treats in the Lonsdale Cup and the Doncaster Cup, coming from far off the pace to win with nonchalant ease. It is sad that there is no future as a Flat stallion for such a tough and talented performer. Cursed with the stigma of "stayer", he could only go into NH production, and, as he is not a big horse, he may not be cut out for success in that role. *TM*

Motivator

3yo bay colt **129**

Montjeu (Ire) - Out West (USA) (Gone West (USA))

Owner The Royal Ascot Racing Club

Trainer M L W Bell

Breeder Deerfield Farm

Career: **7** starts	won **4**	second **2**	third **0**	**£1,192,457** win and place

By Brough Scott

AT THE start of the year the main ambition for the Motivator team was to win the Derby. On the fourth of June he did just that in the most spectacular style imaginable. That his seven-race career ended in October with a slight sense of mission unfulfilled is as much a compliment as a complaint.

For as Motivator drew further and further clear of his Epsom rivals, the medium-sized, livewire bay was already a better-known horse than any Derby winner in memory. Not just because he had, in the 239 members of the Royal Ascot Racing Club, more owners than any previous victor, but because his trainer Michael Bell had granted the public, through this writer's columns in the *Racing Post*, quite unprecedented access to the preparation of a Derby favourite. We knew his dreams. And after Epsom, the sky was quite legitimately the limit.

Motivator's three subsequent defeats temper rather than tarnish a reputation that had been built on a lot more than newspaper hyperbole, which his trainer handled with a skill to match his openness. In January, while the colt was still on his trotting break, Bell was completely clear about the challenge ahead. "I am sure he is good enough," he said, "but we have to avoid him either getting jazzed up or jarred up. He is so active that he will get himself fit, we must be sure not to overstress him or work him on anything like firm ground."

From the very first visit you could appreciate the reality of Bell's dilemma. Even at the trot, Motivator was always ready to crackle and one explosive, pirouetting turn beside the Bury Road as a giant car transporter hissed its brakes would have scarred a nervous or bad-tempered rider for life. But in Shane Fetherstonhaugh he had one of those calm, skilful partners whom trainers treasure. In the wrong hands Motivator's temperament could have become a problem. He was in the right ones.

But dealing with the mental and physical conditioning is only one half

Motivator, primed to the minute by trainer Michael Bell, comes home five lengths clear in the Vodafone Derby

of a Classic colt's campaign. The strategy of where to run, which jockey to book and what tactics to take is all-consumingly important and, with anything but a hundred per cent success rate, endlessly debatable. The path chosen by Bell and the Royal Ascot racing managers, Harry Herbert and John Warren, through to Epsom was a case study in excellence.

With former rider Kieren Fallon pledged to Ballydoyle, they booked dual Derby winner Johnny Murtagh. In conjunction with him they opted to avoid the full-blown trauma of the 2,000 Guineas for the lesser test and greater distance of the Dante Stakes and took the earlier opportunity to give Motivator's mind and body a public spin round the Epsom contours. In fact the ground on 2,000 Guineas day was so firm that Motivator would have been a scratching, while York turned out conveniently soft for the Dante.

In this seasonal debut the colt was impressive enough without being devastating. He was a bit fresh in the paddock, raced keenly behind a slow pace set by Falstaff, the Ballydoyle pacemaker, was still on the bridle behind the 2,000 Guineas third Kandidate when Murtagh loosed him

2005 Race record

5th Prix de l'Arc de Triomphe Lucien Barriere (Group 1) (Longchamp, October 2) 3yo+ 1m4f Good to soft **125** (TS 125) 15 ran. *Always in touch, 5th straight, led over 1f out to inside final furlong, one pace (J P Murtagh), beaten 4¼l by Hurricane Run*

2nd Baileys Irish Champion Stakes (Group 1) (Leopardstown, September 10) 3yo+ 1m2f Good to yielding **125** (TS 107) 10 ran. *Tracked leaders, 3rd halfway, improved to lead travelling well entering straight, headed inside final furlong, kept on well (K Darley), beaten ½l by Oratorio*

2nd Coral-Eclipse Stakes (Group 1) (Sandown, July 2) 3yo+ 1m2f Good to firm **123** (TS 102) 7 ran. *Took keen hold, led for 2f, tracked leader until led again over 2f out, ridden 2 lengths clear over 1f out, headed and no extra final 75yds (J P Murtagh), beaten ½l by Oratorio*

1st Vodafone Derby Stakes (Group 1) (Epsom, June 4) 3yo 1m4f Good **129** (TS 128) 13 ran. *Tracked leader for 2f, went 2nd again over 4f out, led over 2f out, soon quickened right away, ridden out, impressive (J P Murtagh), beat Walk In The Park by 5l*

1st totesport Dante Stakes (Group 2) (York, May 12) 3yo 1m2½f Soft **119** (TS 104) 6 ran. *Tracked leaders, smooth headway over 2f out, quickened to lead over 1f out, hung badly right inside final furlong, stayed on, comfortably (J P Murtagh), beat The Geezer by 1½l*

2004

1st Racing Post Trophy (Group 1) (Doncaster, October 23) 2yo 1m Soft **118** (TS 118) 8 ran ●
1st Learndirect Maiden Stakes (Newmarket (July), August 13) 2yo 1m Soft **92** (TS 76) 11 ran

over a furlong out, and had an easy length and a half over the improving The Geezer at the line.

But, as usual, there were doubts to be answered. The form's value was queried by Kandidate's obvious failure to stay, by a dreadful display from the Ballydoyle number one Albert Hall, and by the subsequent Jersey and Sussex Stakes hero Proclamation exhausting himself by pulling Frankie Dettori's arms half out of their sockets. Motivator also hung sharply right in the final furlong with maybe a hint of knee action, just as he had at Doncaster. How would this and his temperament play at Epsom?

The answer: "perfectly." Bell shrewdly saddled the horse in the quiet of the racecourse stables. His two strong attendants, James Cronin and Roy Thorpe, kept the colt straight in the long, drawn-out preliminaries. Johnny Murtagh settled him calmly close behind the Chester Vase winner Hattan, went to the front a full quarter-mile from home and sailed away in majesty. As he passed the line Motivator looked every inch a true champion. So do his subsequent defeats at Sandown, Leopardstown and Longchamp represent a decline, or an early overrating?

The answer here is probably "a bit of both". Certainly events and tactics and preparation never dropped together so well, and there are a number of arguments for suggesting that Motivator never peaked so perfectly again. For the Derby took a lot out of him – on the morning after, he looked a wreck, he had lost a shoe and all his fizz. And while the four-week break to the Eclipse Stakes seemed long enough, on the day both

Motivator (left) warms up for Epsom with a smooth win in the Dante Stakes at York on his reappearance

the race shape and the weather certainly conspired against the Derby winner.

The unlucky defection of Shamardal took the natural pace-setter out of the contest, leaving Motivator always running too freely at the head of affairs. And the drying ground produced a surface on which Motivator was clearly head-in-the-air uncomfortable as Oratorio ran him down by half a length in the closing stages.

Murtagh has suggested this experience slightly altered the colt's attitude for the rest of his races and certainly Dettori was privately unimpressed when he rode Motivator in a gallop before the Irish Champion Stakes; on dismounting he dismayed Fetherstonhaugh by saying "this is not the horse that won the Derby." Despite all this Motivator ran on much better at Leopardstown (with Kevin Darley deputising for the suspended Murtagh), albeit going down to Oratorio by exactly the same distance as at Sandown.

If there were excuses in Ireland (and few were needed against the likes of Azamour, Grey Swallow and Alexander Goldrun) they seemed to come from the run of the race, not the condition of the horse. Riding a mile-and-a-half winner in a ten-furlong race, Darley always wanted to play his cards early rather than late. His own pacemaker Temple Place was spent before the turn, while Hazarista (for Azamour) had gone before the straight, leaving Motivator no option but to kick for home.

Despite the early strike of his Derby victory, a horse as eager and quick to manoeuvre as Motivator seemed more natural with closing, rather than forcing, tactics. It was the way he was ridden at home and it became the hoped-for plan for what looked a vintage running of the Arc de Triomphe and for which a flood of ex-pat British money made Motivator favourite. It didn't quite work out.

It wouldn't have made much difference, but the fact remains that after turning into the straight close behind the leaders a gap appeared to the inside and Murtagh had no option to take it. The sprint was on, and over the next 300 yards Motivator outran Shawanda and Westerner to the outside of him. At the furlong pole he had the lead but he had used his juice. The others were swamping him and he faded to finish fifth, four and a quarter lengths behind Hurricane Run. "He stopped very quick," said Murtagh. "Didn't have the stamina," concluded Raceform.

They cited the softer ground at Longchamp rather than Epsom but having walked both courses on the morning of the respective races, I find that not reason enough. The Arc winning time of 2min 27.40sec confirms the surface as hardly super testing, just as the Epsom clocking of 2min 35.69sec reminds us how much more severe (and therefore more stamina testing) a course it is than Longchamp.

What was different in Paris was the quality of the opposition he was sprinting against. His effort gained a Racing Post Rating of 125, the same as at Leopardstown, 2lb better than Sandown but, significantly, still 4lb shy of his career-peak 129 in the Derby. As a colt he had held together pretty well, but the figures confirm what the eye remembers.

"Might-have-beens" are never more than speculation, but the theory, first voiced by Dettori, that Motivator might have always been saving himself a fraction after Epsom was hardly debunked by his two bits of work in preparation for the Breeders' Cup. The horse, in readiness for American competition rules, had been treated with bute and Salix and was more impressive than he had been all season. "He drew right away," said Fetherstonhaugh, "just as he used to do as a two-year-old. We came back in high hopes and it was only just before we got back to the yard that he came lame with me. You wonder if there had been something there all along."

The injury had been high up in the pelvic region and needed seven weeks' box confinement. But the horse made a complete recovery and before the end of the year was reported in lively – soon to be libidinous – form in his new home at The Royal Studs. In view of the injury, those of us who castigated the earlier decision to cash in Motivator for some £6 million are having to sneer on the other side of our faces. But what should not be in question is the ability that was being sold.

Times change and it is now 70 years since Federico Tesio said that the most important thing in racing was "a piece of wood, the winning post at Epsom." But those who use the new stallion will still be right to remember that Motivator was, as he was pledged to be, a very, very good horse on Derby Day.

Motivator

bay colt, 22-2-2002

Montjeu b 1996	Sadler's Wells	Northern Dancer	Nearctic Natalma
		Fairy Bridge	Bold Reason Special
	Floripedes	Top Ville	High Top Sega Ville
		Toute Cy	Tennyson Adele Toumignon
Out West br 1994	Gone West	Mr Prospector	Raise A Native Gold Digger
		Secrettame	Secretariat Tamerett
	Chellingoua	Sharpen Up	Atan Rocchetta
		Uncommitted	Buckpasser Lady Be Good

Bred by Deerfield Farm in England. 75,000gns Tattersalls October, Part 1, yearling.

Sire Montjeu

Won 11 of 16 races, inc. Prix Greffulhe-Gr2, Prix du Jockey-Club-Gr1, Irish Derby-Gr1, Prix Niel-Gr2, Prix de l'Arc de Triomphe-Gr1, Tattersalls Gold Cup-Gr1, Grand Prix de Saint-Cloud-Gr1, King George VI & Queen Elizabeth S.-Gr1, Prix Foy-Gr2. Also 2nd in Prix Lupin at 3, and in Champion S. at 4. Tallish, well-made, but not strikingly handsome individual. Possessed a tremendous turn of foot. One of the best 12f horses of recent times. Well-bred. The best son of his outstanding sire. Out of a lightly-raced high-class stayer (won Prix de Lutece-Gr3, 2nd in Prix Royal-Oak-Gr1), who was among the best daughters of her sire. Family of multiple Pattern-winning stayer Dadarissime, Gr3 winner Le Mamamouchi and Dear Doctor (Arlington Million). Stands at Coolmore Stud at a (2006) fee of €125,000. Sire of 2 racing crops, inc: Corre Caminos (Gr3), Hurricane Run (Irish Derby-Gr1, Prix de l'Arc de Triomphe-Gr1), Montare (Gr2), Motivator (Racing Post Trophy-Gr1, Derby S.-Gr1), Scorpion (Grand Prix de Paris-Gr1, St Leger-Gr1).

Dam Out West

Won 2 (1 Listed) of 5 races. Also 3rd once and 4th twice. Leggy individual, who showed useful form in good company until poor effort in fifth start. Quite well-bred. By one of Mr Prospector's best sons at stud. Half-sister to US Gr3-placed multiple turf winner Auggies Here (c by Hilal) and to lesser winners by Northern Baby and Miswaki. Dam placed in France and US, half-sister to US Gr1 winner and sire Wavering Monarch. Dam of: Warsaw Girl (2000 f by Polish Precedent; winner), Gabana (2001 f by Polish Precedent; placed), Motivator (2002 c by Montjeu; Classic winner), Imperial Star (2003 c by Fantastic Light; unraced to date). She has a yearling colt by Montjeu.

Pedigree assessment

"If he truly takes after his sire, he must be considered a first-rate Derby candidate," was how we summed up Motivator a year ago. As it turned out, he was a true son of Montjeu, most effective at middle distances, and with some of the same quirks, but we were probably a little too carried away by his authoritative performance at Epsom; the form did not read so well when it was tested subsequently, and after the Arc it was clear that Motivator was just the second-best son of Montjeu from his first crop. While Hurricane Run races on, Motivator is being launched on a stud career at Sandringham, with a powerful syndicate of prominent breeders to back him. The Derby could use a boost from a winner making a decided success of his term at stud. Perhaps it is a good omen that the last to have made a significant mark – Shirley Heights – also stood at Sandringham. *TM*

Nannina

2yo bay filly **114**

Medicean - Hill Hopper (Ire) (Danehill (USA))

Owner Cheveley Park Stud

Trainer J H M Gosden

Breeder Cheveley Park Stud

Career: **5** starts | won **3** | second **0** | third **1** | **£136,353** win and place

By Lee Mottershead

THERE they were, two fine fillies, stood just feet away from each other in the Goodwood winner's enclosure. One, Dame Vera Lynn, a veritable national heroine, deservedly one of Britain's most treasured ladies. The other, Nannina, just crowned winner of the Prestige Stakes and not long off adding Group 1 honours to her name. Yet, despite racing with such distinction in her first season, Nannina had to wait until the final day of 2005 to receive meaningful acclaim. She can't sing, either.

At the end of her two-year-old campaign, Nannina was not a sexy horse. She was a top-flight winner and the season's joint top-rated two-year-old filly on Racing Post Ratings, alongside Alexandrova, New Girlfriend, and Silca's Sister, and superior to the Prix Marcel Boussac winner Rumplestiltskin. She was also the representative of leading connections, but she had failed to capture the imagination of either punters or bookmakers. So it was a huge surprise that on New Year's Eve, when ante-post Classic bets are seldom at the top of backers' agendas, Nannina was the subject of a monster plunge for the 1,000 Guineas, the race that trainer John Gosden has insisted is her major target, and, in his opinion, an attainable one at that.

As a result of that plunge, Nannina was slashed by most layers, most notably to 7-1 from 16-1 by Ladbrokes. Yet even if Nannina never sets foot on a racecourse again, the supremely successful Cheveley Park Stud will have boosted its glorious broodmare band with another Group 1 winner to add to the likes of Russian Rhythm, a horse who won the Classic that Nannina will attempt to secure at Newmarket in May. And, if she manages that feat, she will become a relatively rare beast indeed – a Guineas winner to have started her racing life at Pontefract.

There may have been some prepared to take 16-1 Guineas quotes as soon as Nannina passed the Pontefract post, for seldom has the Yorkshire venue played host to such an impressive two-year-old newcomer. The

Nannina goes to post at Newmarket before her short-head success over Alexandrova in the Group 1 Fillies' Mile

Pontefract hill is among the most severe in Flat racing, but the home-bred Nannina positively ate it, overcoming a wide draw before surging home for an impressive three-length victory. So far, so good.

The next start was not so good. Gosden sent Nannina the obvious way, to the Cherry Hinton Stakes, but in a contest won by subsequent Cheveley Park Stakes winner Donna Blini, the 11-4 second favourite flattered only to deceive, eventually taking fifth after being swamped inside the final furlong. The first attempt at Group glory had failed, and so would the second, although a third-place finish to Mixed Blessing in the Princess Margaret Stakes at Newbury was more forgivable given that Nannina was stuck out away from the action for most of a race in which she also suffered an untimely bump. Gosden thought she should have been second.

The betting market expected her to be second the next time she ran, this time over seven furlongs for the first time, in Goodwood's Prestige Stakes. But this time she proved up to Group class. Trapped on the fence for much of the straight, she quickened smartly once a gap materialised and, at the post, was actually striding clear under Jimmy Fortune for a length-and-a-quarter defeat of Rising Cross, with Mixed Blessing back in third.

2005 Race record

1st Meon Valley Stud Fillies' Mile (Group 1) (Newmarket, September 24) 2yo 1m Good **114** (TS 107) 6 ran. *Chased leaders, switched right over 2f out, soon ridden, ran on under pressure to lead near finish (J Fortune), beat Alexandrova by shd*

1st Sixty Years On Prestige Stakes (Group 3) (Goodwood, August 28) 2yo 7f Good **104** (TS 68) 9 ran. *Slowly into stride, soon tracked leaders, pulled out and ridden over 1f out, driven to lead last 150yds, ran on well near finish (J Fortune), beat Rising Cross by 1¼l*

3rd Princess Margaret Stakes (Group 3) (Newbury, July 23) 2yo 6f Good to firm **101** (TS 97) 12 ran. *Raced in centre, chased leaders, ridden and effort 2f out, kept on under pressure inside final furlong (J Fortune), beaten 3l by Mixed Blessing*

5th Chippenham Lodge Stud Cherry Hinton Stakes (Group 2) (Newmarket (July), July 5) 2yo 6f Good **94** (TS 87) 8 ran. *Always prominent, chased winner over 2f out, ridden and every chance 1f out, no extra well inside final furlong (J Fortune), beaten 2l by Donna Blini*

1st EBF toteplacepot Maiden Fillies' Stakes (Pontefract, June 19) 2yo 6f Good to firm **79** (TS 62) 14 ran. *Towards rear, ridden and headway when switched right over 1f out, strong run to lead well inside final furlong, readily (J Fortune), beat Crimson by 3l*

In winning the Group 3 prize she had given her Cheveley Park sire Medicean his first Pattern success from his first crop of runners, while she had earned herself a tilt at either the Meon Valley-sponsored Fillies' Mile or the Prix Marcel Boussac.

Connections took the domestic option, not surprisingly given that the Fillies' Mile – so often an event of huge future significance – looked to have served up one of its weakest renewals. Only six youngsters lined up for the race, staged at Newmarket due to Ascot's redevelopment, and therefore over a straight mile as opposed to around a bend. None of the sextet really set the pulse racing and, as it turned out, none of them really set the pulse racing afterwards.

Nannina did nothing wrong – indeed she did just about everything right – but a game short-head triumph didn't trigger an ante-post odds feeding frenzy. That came three months later. Nevertheless, the second, Alexandrova, was representing Aidan O'Brien off the back of a ten-length maiden win, while Nasheej, three lengths further back in third, had already pocketed the May Hill Stakes. Gosden, who was netting his third Fillies' Mile in six years, reasoned that it was "good form" and confirmed that he saw Nannina "as a Guineas filly", with the Prix de Diane a more obvious longer-term target than the Oaks, for which her stamina would seem suspect on breeding.

From what we have seen so far, Nannina is no superstar. She is not flashy, explosive or obviously brilliant. That is what she is not. What she is, though, is talented, tough and a battler. Such qualities served Dame Vera well. Perhaps they will for Nannina too.

Nannina

bay filly, 9-2-2003

Medicean ch 1997	Machiavellian	Mr Prospector	Raise A Native
			Gold Digger
		Coup de Folie	Halo
			Raise The Standard
	Mystic Goddess	Storm Bird	**Northern Dancer**
			South Ocean
		Rose Goddess	Sassafras
			Cocarde
Hill Hopper b 1991	Danehill	Danzig	**Northern Dancer**
			Pas de Nom
		Razyana	His Majesty
			Spring Adieu
	Sea Harrier	Grundy	Great Nephew
			Word From Lundy
		Anchor	Major Portion
			Ripeck

Bred by Cheveley Park Stud Ltd in England.

Sire Medicean

Won 6 of 12 starts, inc. Celebration Mile S.-Gr2, Lockinge S.-Gr1, Queen Anne S.-Gr2, Eclipse S.-Gr1. Also 3rd in St James's Palace S., Sussex S., York International S. 4th in Queen Elizabeth II S. Strong, well-made, 16.1hh. Fine mover. Honest consistent performer, effective on any ground. Stands at Cheveley Park Stud, Newmarket, at a 2006 fee of £17,500. Sire of 1 crop of racing age, inc. notable winners: Abigail Pett (Gr3), Nannina (Fillies' Mile-Gr1).

Dam Hill Hopper

Won 4 of 7 races, inc. Criterion S.-Gr3. Also placed 2nd twice. Useful performer, effective on fast and soft ground. Half-sister to 4 other winners, inc. Water Boatman (Gr1 winner in Australia). From the celebrated Arches Hall Stud family of Ark Royal, Cut Above, Bireme, Buoy, etc. Dam of: Rainbow Hill (1997 g by Rainbow Quest; winner), Sea Vixen (1998 f by Machiavellian; winner), Arachine (1999 g by Indian Ridge; winner), Groom Raider (2001 c by Groom Dancer; winner), Nannina (2003 f by Medicean; Gr1 winner). Sold 67,000gns Tattersalls 2003 December Sale. She has a yearling colt by Kyllachy, a filly foal by Redback, and is due to Redback again in 2006. Barren to Groom Dancer in 2000 and to Machiavellian in 2002.

Pedigree assessment

The rise of Cheveley Park Stud as a home of prominent stallions continues. Its Pivotal will be the highest-priced horse in service – at £65,000 – in England in 2006, its Kyllachy obtained excellent results with his first auctioned yearlings in 2005, and its Medicean is off to a flyer with his first runners, Abigail Pett and Nannina having notched three Pattern victories between them. Nannina's most important win came at Group 1 level in the Fillies' Mile, when her gameness was much in evidence as she thwarted a determined rival in Alexandrova. The effort was all the more creditable, as she had gone in her coat and would have been excused a below-par run. A classy, progressive filly with a turn of foot, she may well prove Classic calibre. There is sufficient stamina in her background to suggest that the Oaks trip may not be beyond her. *TM*

Norse Dancer (Ire)

5yo bay horse **125**

Halling (USA) - River Patrol (Rousillon (USA))

Owner J C Smith

Trainer D R C Elsworth

Breeder Ralph Ergnist and Bruno Faust

Career: **30** starts | won **4** | second **3** | third **3** | **£720,660** win and place

By Steve Dennis

THE peace and quiet of a Whitsbury morning is broken by the steady thunk, thunk, thunk of David Elsworth throwing darts at a photograph of Baron de Coubertin, founder of the modern Olympics. After inspecting his handiwork and congratulating himself on his 'grouping', he hands the darts to Jeff Smith. Thunk, thunk, thunk. Classy stuff. Smith passes the darts to Norse Dancer, who shuffles into position and, sticking his tongue out with concentration, takes aim and lets fly. All three of his darts miss, one just a fraction away, and Elsworth and Smith mutter in unison: "Story of your life, mate."

De Coubertin's famous dictum that "it's not winning that's important, but taking part" doesn't wash down Whitsbury way. Norse Dancer has run in 22 Group 1 races during his four seasons on the track and never once has he won, although he has finished second three times, third three times and fourth four times.

Norse Dancer has finished in the first four in (deep breath) the 2,000 Guineas, Derby, Sussex Stakes (twice), Lockinge Stakes, Eclipse Stakes, Juddmonte International, Irish Champion Stakes, Champion Stakes and King George. It is no wonder that after his defeat in the latter in 2005, Smith said: "Sometimes you just want to sit down and cry."

In Flat Horses of 2004, Smith was quoted as saying: "We'll win the bloody lot next year." And 2005 started promisingly, with the big bay finishing strongly and relentlessly to snatch the Group 3 Earl of Sefton Stakes from Hurricane Alan in the dying strides by a neck.

Hurricane Alan gained his revenge in the Betfred Mile at Sandown next time out, but the dawdling pace didn't suit Norse Dancer and, in any case, the Betfred was 'only' a Group 2. A rich crop of Group 1 races was there to be harvested, and the first port of call was The Curragh, for the Tattersalls Gold Cup.

Unfortunately, it was a very hot contest, and Norse Dancer failed to

Norse Dancer starts his season with a Group 3 victory in the Earl of Sefton Stakes, but a Group 1 continued to elude him

give of his very best in any case, beating only the pacemaker home behind Grey Swallow. He fared no better next time out in the Prince of Wales's Stakes at Royal Ascot at York, trailing in a distant sixth behind Azamour after slipping leaving the back straight on what was widely derided as unsatisfactory ground.

So far, no good. Elsworth decided to shake the mix a little and, instead of heading to Glorious Goodwood at the end of July for the Sussex Stakes, as he had the previous two seasons, Norse Dancer was rerouted to Newbury for the King George VI and Queen Elizabeth Diamond Stakes, transferred from Ascot.

Norse Dancer, who hadn't tried a mile and a half since finishing fourth to Kris Kin in the Derby more than two years earlier, ran arguably the race of his life. John Egan kept his gallant partner to the rear for the first mile before beginning to make headway on the rail three furlongs out. He was soon under pressure, but responded valiantly to every request Egan made of him. Although Azamour had gone beyond recall, Norse Dancer collared Bago in the last 100 yards to take second prize, a length and a quarter behind the winner. It was the biggest payday of his life. In collecting £154,770, he took his win-and-place-money haul to over £700,000 – almost ten times his win-only earnings – and, as mentioned earlier, left Smith looking for a chair and a handkerchief.

That performance might have been expected to prove a springboard

2005 Race record

11th Cathay Pacific Hong Kong Vase (Group 1) (Sha Tin, December 11) 3yo+ 1m4f Good to firm **112** 12 ran. *Held up, disputed 2nd $1^1/_2$f out, hampered final furlong, no chance after (Martin Dwyer), beaten $7^1/_2$l by Ouija Board*

11th Prix de l'Arc de Triomphe Lucien Barriere (Group 1) (Longchamp, October 2) 3yo+ 1m4f Good to soft **101** (TS 102) 15 ran. *Last straight, always behind (J F Egan), beaten $19^1/_2$l by Hurricane Run*

8th Baileys Irish Champion Stakes (Group 1) (Leopardstown, September 10) 3yo+ 1m2f Good to yielding **108** 10 ran. *Held up, 6th halfway, 7th 3f out, no extra straight (J F Egan), beaten $9^1/_4$l by Oratorio*

5th Juddmonte International Stakes (Group 1) (York, August 16) 3yo+ 1m$2^1/_2$f Good **117** (TS 116) 7 ran. *Held up in touch, effort 4f out, challenged over 1f out, weakened inside final furlong (J F Egan), beaten 4l by Electrocutionist*

2nd King George VI And Queen Elizabeth Diamond Stakes (Group 1) (Newbury, July 23) 3yo+ 1m4f Good to firm **125** (TS 113) 12 ran. *Held up, headway over 3f out, stayed on inside final furlong but not trouble winner (J F Egan), beaten $1^1/_4$l by Azamour*

6th Prince of Wales's Stakes (Group 1) (York, June 15) 4yo+ 1m$2^1/_2$f Good to firm **87** (TS 79) 8 ran. *In rear soon, soon nudged along, slipped bend over 5f out, headway over 4f out, ridden and weakened 3f out (J F Egan), beaten 21l by Azamour*

5th Tattersalls Gold Cup (Group 1) (Curragh, May 22) 4yo+ 1m$2^1/_2$f Good to yielding **118** (TS 65) 6 ran. *Held up, 5th and pushed along halfway, effort on outer entering straight, 4th $1^1/_2$f out, soon no extra (J F Egan), beaten $4^1/_2$l by Grey Swallow*

5th betfred.com Mile (Group 2) (Sandown, April 23) 4yo+ 1m Good **113** (TS 83) 8 ran. *Held up in midfield, ridden on outere over 2f out, soon not quicken, one pace from over 1f out (T Quinn), beaten 2l by Hurricane Alan*

1st Weatherbys Earl of Sefton Stakes (Group 3) (Newmarket, April 13) 4yo+ 1m1f Good to firm **120** (TS 112) 10 ran. *Held up, headway over 2f out, edged right and ran on to lead near finish (J F Egan), beat Hurricane Alan by nk*

Other wins

2004 **1st** totesport Sovereign Stakes (Group 3) (Salisbury, August 12) 3yo+ 1m Good to soft **116** (TS 100) 12 ran **2002** **1st** Alfred Franks & Bartlett Sunglasses Novice Stakes (Ascot, July 13) 2yo 7f Good **101** (TS 97) 9 ran ● **1st** Herbert And Gwen Blagrave Maiden Stakes (Salisbury, June 27) 2yo 7f Firm **86** (TS 29) 9 ran

to Group 1 glory, but it was not to be. Norse Dancer was one of the five stretched across the track entering the final furlong of York's Juddmonte International but was the first to crack, eventually finishing fifth behind Electrocutionist. He then failed to register his presence in the Irish Champion Stakes, the Prix de l'Arc de Triomphe and the Hong Kong Vase, his final attempt to net that elusive victory at the highest level before the Group 1 trophy cupboard was locked up for the winter.

Norse Dancer hasn't won a Group 1, but he is a high-class horse in terms of rating and earnings, he is tough and genuine, and he brings his connections untold pleasure. Elsworth and Smith can put away the darts for now, but 2006, when Norse Dancer will resume in Dubai at the Carnival, could yet hear a relieved cry of 'Bullseye!' from the long-suffering pair.

Norse Dancer

bay horse, 3-4-2000

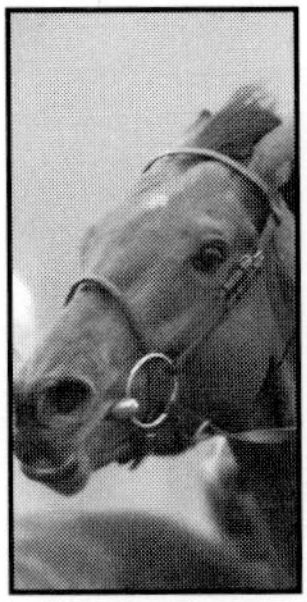

Halling ch 1991	Diesis	Sharpen Up	Atan
			Rocchetta
		Doubly Sure	Reliance
			Soft Angels
	Dance Machine	Green Dancer	Nijinsky
			Green Valley
		Never A Lady	Pontifex
			Camogie
River Patrol b 1988	Rousillon	Riverman	Never Bend
			River Lady
		Belle Dorine	Marshua's Dancer
			Palsy Walsy
	Boathouse	Habitat	Sir Gaylord
			Little Hut
		Ripeck	Ribot
			Kyak

Bred by Ralph Ergnist and Bruno Faust in Ireland. 26,000gns Tattersalls December foal

Sire Halling

Won 12 (8-10f) of 18 races from 3 to 5. Won 4 (inc. Cambridgeshire) at 3, won 4 (inc. Eclipse S-Gr1, York International-Gr1) at 4, won 4 (inc. Prix d'Ispahan-Gr1, Eclipse S-Gr1, York International-Gr1) at 5. Originally based at Dalham Hall Stud, switched before 2004 season to Emirates Stud Farm in Dubai, 2005 fee £30,000. First foals 1998, sire of: Chancellor (Gr2), Dandoun (Gr2), Giovane Imperatore (Gr2), Fisich (Gr2), Mkuzi (Gr3), Nordhal (Gr2), Vanderlin (Gr3), Franklins Gardens (Gr2), Norse Dancer (Gr3), Hattan (Gr3), Pinson (Gr2), The Geezer (Gr3).

Dam River Patrol

Won 1 of 8 starts in Britain. Placed over 7f at 2, won over 10f at 3, when also Listed placed over 10f. Later placed in US. Half-sister to St Leger third Dry Dock, to smart 7-8f colt Showboat and to dam of Gr1-winning 2yo Mail The Desert. Sold 17,000gns carrying Norse Dancer at 1999 Tattersalls December Sale. Dam of: Regal Patrol (1994 g by Red Ransom; winner), Russillo (1995 c by Belmez; winner), Rouanne (1996 f by Unfuwain; winner), Riviera Ligure (1997 f by Hernando; unraced), Norse Dancer (2000 c by Halling; Gr3 winner), River Blue (2001 f by Ashkalani; placed), Rosewater (2002 f by Winged Love; placed), Rhapsody In Blue (2003 f by Winged Love; unraced), 2005 f by Samum. In foal to Galileo.

Pedigree assessment

In Flat Horses of 2004, the conclusion stated: "One Group 3 success does no justice to Norse Dancer". The same applies 12 months on, though substitute "one" with "two". With his King George second, Norse Dancer still managed to be one of the highlights of a marvellous year for Halling, who was also responsible for Oaks runner-up Something Exciting and St Leger runner-up The Geezer – who are both stablemates of Norse Dancer – plus Group/Graded winners Franklins Gardens, Hattan, Mkuzi, Nordhal, Pinson and Vanderlin. That list will help to elevate the appeal of Halling's sons as stallions, though as yet there is no sign of such a role for Norse Dancer. Instead, his task doubtless remains to land that elusive Group 1. *JH*

North Light (Ire)

4yo bay colt **121**

Danehill (USA) - Sought Out (Ire) (Rainbow Quest (USA))

Owner Ballymacoll Stud

Trainer Sir Michael Stoute

Breeder Ballymacoll Stud Farm Ltd

Career: **7** starts | won **3** | second **3** | third **0** | **£1,097,275** win and place

By Steve Dennis

IT TAKES a brave man – some might say a foolhardy one – to call for another card at the blackjack table when already holding two picture cards. The chances of drawing up an ace to embellish an already enviable hand are long indeed; the prudent and pragmatic would stick, not twist.

It may be a strained analogy, but it gives some insight into the dilemma facing the lucky man or woman with the task of deciding the destiny of a Derby winner at the end of its three-year-old season.

Some such horses have already performed such feats that another year going round the track could hardly endow them with further value or prestige. Injury spikes the careers of others, and there are some whose success owed more to their peers' shortcomings than to their own excellence. Owners of these horses 'stick', and sweep up the chips in the shape of a lucrative stallion valuation.

It takes either a bold player or a high-roller with bottomless resources to 'twist'. Sometimes – and examples such as Royal Palace, Teenoso and High Chaparral are very good ones – a Derby winner who falls short of the highest rank can indeed reap a rich harvest at four. On other occasions – and Slip Anchor, Quest For Fame and High-Rise are equally good examples – they can't.

So, Peter Reynolds, manager of the Ballymacoll Stud – will you twist or stick?

North Light looked a good case for a career extension at the beginning of 2005. With just six runs behind him he most emphatically did not have too many miles on the clock, and there were lucid and widely accepted reasons for his three defeats. One was first time out at two, and on his final two starts, in the Irish Derby and Prix de l'Arc de Triomphe, he was hamstrung by fast ground that prevented him from realising his already proven potential. At four he would be stronger and his targets could be

North Light chases in vain in the Brigadier Gerard Stakes, which turned out to be his one and only race at four

cherry-picked so that his efforts might bear greater fruit. His entry in this book 12 months ago ended with the words: "North Light has already shown himself to be a fine Derby winner. He could yet prove to be a prodigious one."

Reynolds balanced all, and brought all to mind. He decided to 'twist'. North Light would race on at four.

Halfway through April, he was reported as on course to reappear in the ten-furlong Group 1 Tattersalls Gold Cup at The Curragh, but the focus was then shifted to the Group 3 Brigadier Gerard Stakes ten days later as he had been held up in his work and Sir Michael Stoute "didn't want to rush the horse". Other pertinent reasons were the considerably weaker opposition at Sandown compared to the Irish race, and the greater convenience of a short box trip as opposed to a flight.

Reynolds said: "We're very excited about his four-year-old campaign but he had a minor setback that put him a bit behind schedule, so he may need the run, and having to concede weight makes the challenge tough enough. We hope he runs well and that the race doesn't become too much of a tactical contest."

The last point was no doubt connected to the fact that North Light was competing over a trip slightly shorter than any he had run over as a three-year-old, and only four horses turned up at Sandown to take him

2005 Race record

2nd betfair.com Brigadier Gerard Stakes (Group 3) (Sandown, May 31) 4yo+ 1m2f Good to firm **121** (TS 80) 5 ran. *Chased leading pair, ridden 3f out, floundering 2f out, ran on to chase winner last 100yds, gaining at finish (J P Murtagh), beaten ½l by New Morning*

Other runs

2004 **5th** Prix de l'Arc de Triomphe Lucien Barriere (Group 1) (Longchamp, October 3) 3yo+ 1m4f Good **123** (TS 122) 19 ran ● **2nd** Budweiser Irish Derby (Group 1) (Curragh, June 27) 3yo 1m4f Good to firm **125** (TS 124) 10 ran ● **1st** Vodafone Derby Stakes (Group 1) (Epsom, June 5) 3yo 1m4f Good **124** (TS 123) 14 ran ● **1st** totesport Dante Stakes (Group 2) (York, May 12) 3yo 1m2½f Good to soft **120** (TS 92) 10 ran **2003** **1st** Uniq Foodservice Gold Cup EBF Maiden Stakes (Goodwood, September 24) 2yo 1m Good to firm **87** (TS 56) 5 ran ● **2nd** Pacemaker EBF Maiden Stakes (Sandown, August 29) 2yo 7f Soft **88** (TS 67) 14 ran

on, all in receipt of weight from the Derby winner. As it turned out, the race was not a particularly tactical one, as the Ballymacoll-bred filly New Morning set a decent pace and was never headed, running out a half-length winner.

North Light ran a very strange race. When Johnny Murtagh asked him for an effort at the head of the straight, North Light put his head in the air and looked for all the world like a horse who had never raced in earnest in his life. Two furlongs out it seemed as though he would finish last, and it was only after changing his legs twice and generally taking an age to compose himself that he finally buckled down and ran the final 100 yards like a Derby winner should, although that only brought him second place. Stoute said: "He was a bit rusty and he took a long time to get going, I thought he was not going to pick up at all."

Mention was made of the Hardwicke Stakes at Royal Ascot at York being his next target, but he missed that race. The following week brought the news that North Light had sustained a pelvic injury and would be retired forthwith.

The sportsman's gesture that had added so much spice to the Flat season had backfired. Like many of the stars of 2004 who had been expected to sparkle in 2005 – Doyen, Quiff, Papineau, Var, to name but four –North Light had tried and failed to match expectations. His stud career goes ahead nevertheless – he will stand his first season at Frank Stronach's Adena Springs Farm in Kentucky – but the opportunity to stamp himself into the fabric of the folklore of the Turf has gone forever.

Perhaps the last word should be left to the man who had the courage to call for another card with the odds arguably stacked against him. When the news of North Light's retirement broke, Reynolds was heard to say: "It's a bit of a disaster. Keeping a Derby winner in training at four is always risky."

North Light *bay colt, 1-3-2001*

Danehill b 1986	Danzig	Northern Dancer	Nearctic **Natalma**
		Pas de Nom	Admiral's Voyage Petitioner
	Razyana	His Majesty	Ribot Flower Bowl
		Spring Adieu	Buckpasser **Natalma**
Sought Out b 1988	Rainbow Quest	Blushing Groom	Red God Runaway Bride
		I Will Follow	Herbager Where You Lead
	Edinburgh	Charlottown	Charlottesville Meld
		Queen's Castle	Sovereign Path Country House

Bred by Ballymacoll Stud Farm Ltd in Ireland

Sire Danehill

Won 4 of 9 races, inc. Haydock Park Sprint Cup-Gr1. Died May 2003. Stood at Coolmore Stud, latterly at a fee of Ir200,000gns. Sire of Gr1 winners: Danish (QE II Challenge Cup), Kissing Cousin (Coronation), Danehill Dancer (Phoenix, National), Tsukuba Symphony (NHK Mile Cup), Desert King (National, Irish 2,000, Irish Derby), Fairy King Prawn (Yasuda Kinen), Tiger Hill (GP von Baden [twice], Bayerisches Zuchtrennen), Indian Danehill (Prix Ganay), Wannabe Grand (Cheveley Park), Aquarelliste (Prix de Diane, Prix Vermeille, Prix Ganay), Banks Hill (Coronation, Breeders' Cup F & M Turf, Prix Jacques le Marois), Mozart (July Cup, Nunthorpe), Regal Rose (Cheveley Park), Dress To Thrill (Matriarch), Fine Motion (Shuka Sho, QE II Commemorative Cup), Landseer (Poule d'Essai des Poulains), Rock Of Gibraltar (Grand Criterium, Dewhurst, 2,000 Guineas, Irish 2,000, St James's Palace, Sussex, Prix du Moulin), Westerner (Prix du Cadran [twice], Prix Royal-Oak [twice], Gold Cup), Clodovil (Poule d'Essai des Poulains), Intercontinental (Matriarch, Breeders' Cup F & M Turf), Light Jig (Yellow Ribbon), Spartacus (Phoenix, Gran Criterium), Grey Lilas (Prix du Moulin), North Light (Derby), Luas Line (Garden City H.), Oratorio (Prix Jean-Luc Lagardere, Eclipse, Irish Champion), George Washington (Phoenix, National), Horatio Nelson (Prix Jean-Luc Lagardere), Rumplestiltskin (Moyglare Stud, Marcel Boussac).

Dam Sought Out

Won 5 (14-20f) of 21 starts, inc. Prix du Cadran-Gr1, Prix Kergorlay-Gr2. By top-class 8-12f performer and very good stamina-oriented sire, out of 2yo Gr3 winner. Dam of: Treasure Chest (1995 g by Last Tycoon; winner), Hidden Bounty (1996 g by Generous; hurdle/chase winner), Cover Up (1997 g by Machiavellian; Gr3 winner), Search Me (1998 c by Suave Dancer; unraced), Researched (1999 g by Danehill; Listed winner), North Light (2001 c by Danehill; Gr1 winner), Paper Hunt (2002 c by Indian Danehill; died as a yearling), Seeking Kali (2003 f by Kalanisi; unraced), 2005 c by Danehill Dancer.

Pedigree assessment

It will be fascinating to see how North Light fares at Adena Springs in Kentucky, where his debut fee in 2006 is $50,000. In the last 20 years, Derby winners Shahrastani, Quest For Fame and Benny The Dip have retired to stud in the US, and all were exported within a few years. North Light is a mile-and-a-half European performer, from a stamina-rich European family, by a sire who has few US stallion sons. Expect a fair proportion of his progeny to return to Europe, and the remainder should include a high proportion of turf performers. *JH*

Oratorio (Ire)

3yo bay colt **126**

Danehill (USA) - Mahrah (USA) (Vaguely Noble)

Owner Mrs John Magnier & M Tabor

Trainer A P O'Brien

Breeder Barronstown Stud & Orpendale

Career: **15** starts | won **6** | second **3** | third **1** | **£1,085,278** win and place

By Richard Austen

"IT IS BETTER to have loafed and lost than never to have loafed at all," said James Thurber. Oratorio loafed and lost all right, and might have left it at that, but he was good enough also to loaf and win. Lazy was the word mentioned most in his context, but he it was who turned around a 25-length deficit with Motivator to beat him twice.

Setting the tone, Aidan O'Brien described Oratorio in April as "a lazy worker at home. All he does is eat and sleep, and he would be happy doing nothing else." Not that Oratorio would be granted his wish, far from it, and after seven races as a two-year-old, he was about to make the first of his eight starts in 2005 in the 2,000 Guineas.

Lazy at home and not that zealous on the track either, Oratorio played along eventually to make his second season even more rewarding than the first, which had brought victory in the Prix Jean-Luc Lagardere and second place in the Dewhurst. All those races at three years were Group 1, making it 11 of his 15 outings all told.

Oratorio has now been granted retirement, which must sound pretty relaxing to him, but knowing Coolmore, it's unlikely that he'll get that much in the way of repose in his new capacity either. In 2005, for instance, their One Cool Cat covered 162 mares in his first season.

Oratorio did not book his stud place on Guineas Day and was not expected to. "It wasn't an easy choice," Kieren Fallon asserted when explaining why he opted to ride Footstepsinthesand. "Oratorio is a lazy worker and Footstepsinthesand isn't. Horses who do more in their work are easier to get to the track without a prep run but Oratorio has good form."

His keeping-on fourth to his stablemate was a bit below that form but entirely satisfactory for Oratorio and it brought him on as well, judged by the Irish version three weeks later when he finished runner-up. Oratorio warmed to his task at The Curragh, too, although Fallon's later observation

Kieren Fallon is at his driving best as Oratorio wears down Motivator to land the Eclipse Stakes at Sandown

that "he nearly clipped Dubawi's heels on the line" was putting the situation in a rather rosy light.

It was hard to put any gloss on a lacklustre show in the Derby next time, except that Oratorio came home unscathed. With fancied runners (he was an 8-1 chance) that finish as far back as he did, that is usually in some doubt. Epsom can provide a ready excuse – Oratorio floundered on the descent and never adjusted to even more alien surroundings on his final start either – but connections opted to fit him with a visor when he was dragged off his chaise-longue to run again only ten days later.

He did better than at Epsom, a lot better, but when his jockey later claimed that, "If I could have had him handy in the St James's Palace I think he'd have won," that rather glossed over the fact that Oratorio had spent three-quarters of that York event skulking towards the back and grabbed third only when the race up front was all over.

Oratorio's career was threatening to subside into a series of defeats marked by varying degrees of recalcitrance but, lo and behold, it was at this juncture that all the positive thinking and faith from his connections began to pay off. The headgear was not seen again and, for whatever reason, the lentissimo version of Oratorio was not seen again either, in three remaining European starts anyway. Oratorio had seemed a most

2005 Race record

11th Breeders' Cup Classic - Powered by Dodge (Grade 1) (Dirt) (Belmont Park, October 29) 3yo+ 1m2f Fast **107** 13 ran. *Mid-division, driven 3f out, 7th and one pace straight (K Fallon), beaten 12l by Saint Liam*

4th Emirates Airline Champion Stakes (Group 1) (Newmarket, October 15) 3yo+ 1m2f Good to soft **121** (TS 107) 15 ran. *Prominent, not clear run and lost place over 1f out, switched right, ran on inside final furlong (K Fallon), beaten 3¼l by David Junior*

1st Baileys Irish Champion Stakes (Group 1) (Leopardstown, September 10) 3yo+ 1m2f Good to yielding **126** (TS 108) 10 ran. *Held up, 7th and driven along halfway, 5th and headway 3f out, 2nd early straight, led inside final furlong, kept on well under pressure (K Fallon), beat Motivator by ½l*

1st Coral-Eclipse Stakes (Group 1) (Sandown, July 2) 3yo+ 1m2f Good to firm **124** (TS 103) 7 ran. *Chased leading pair and ran in snatches, driven 2f out, chased leader over 1f out, ran on to lead final 75yds (K Fallon), beat Motivator by ½l*

3rd St James's Palace Stakes (Group 1) (York, June 14) 3yo 1m Good to firm **113** (TS 112) 8 ran. *In touch, soon pushed along, lost place 4f out, hard ridden and headway over 1f out, took 3rd near line (K Fallon), beaten 4¾l by Shamardal*

10th Vodafone Derby Stakes (Group 1) (Epsom, June 4) 3yo 1m4f Good **88** (TS 80) 13 ran. *Settled midfield, ridden over 4f out, 7th and under pressure straight, soon beaten (M J Kinane), beaten 25l by Motivator*

2nd Boylesports Irish 2,000 Guineas (Group 1) (Curragh, May 21) 3yo 1m Good **119** (TS 53) 8 ran. *Towards rear, driven along halfway, headway over 2f out, 2nd and no impression from 1½f out, kept on inside final furlong without troubling winner (K Fallon), beaten 2l by Dubawi*

4th UltimatePoker.com 2,000 Guineas Stakes (Group 1) (Newmarket, April 30) 3yo 1m Good to firm **112** (TS 91) 19 ran. *Soon driven along in rear, not clear run well over 1f out, soon hung right, ran on inside final furlong, nearest finish (J P Murtagh), beaten 2¾l by Footstepsinthesand*

2004

2nd Darley Dewhurst Stakes (Group 1) (Newmarket, October 16) 2yo 7f Soft **119** (TS 119) 9 ran ● **1st** Prix Jean-Luc Lagardere (Group 1) (Longchamp, October 3) 2yo 7f Good **118** (TS 98) 6 ran ● **1st** Galileo EBF Futurity Stakes (Group 2) (Curragh, August 21) 2yo 7f Good to firm **114** (TS 94) 5 ran ● **2nd** Independent Waterford Wedgwood Phoenix Stakes (Group 1) (Curragh, August 8) 2yo 6f Good to firm **111** (TS 86) 6 ran ● **1st** Dubai Duty Free Anglesey Stakes (Group 3) (Curragh, July 18) 2yo 6½f Good **112** (TS 97) 8 ran ● **7th** Coventry Stakes (Group 2) (Ascot, June 15) 2yo 6f Good to firm **91** (TS 77) 13 ran ● **1st** Boylesports Everyday Specials EBF Maiden (Curragh, May 23) 2yo 6f Good to firm **87** (TS 59) 7 ran

unlikely candidate on Derby Day to be Motivator's nemesis, but so it proved.

When they met again in the Coral-Eclipse at Sandown, the mile and a quarter looked to be in Oratorio's favour and shorter than ideal for Motivator, but few predicted that the changed conditions could make all the difference. The only plausible dangers to the Derby winner in the Eclipse seemed to have been removed when Shamardal was crocked after his declaration and Starcraft lost his cool in the preliminaries.

A huge crowd flocked to Sandown to acclaim a champion. But while

Oratorio confirms the Eclipse form with a second victory over Motivator, this time in the Irish Champion Stakes

Motivator duly hit the front, this time he did not stretch clear. The Derby winner had a clear advantage entering the final furlong even, but he and his jockey were showing signs of increasing unease and from thereon in it was Fallon who was getting much the better tune on 12-1 chance Oratorio, who was driven past the 2-5 shot close home.

The pace was muddling, two outsiders weren't far away at the post and Motivator must have been well below his best, or so said many. O'Brien, though, had told Fallon beforehand that Oratorio was only just coming to himself.

Oratorio had, characteristically, gone in snatches. "He's a lazy horse but he tries and he responds," reported Fallon after earning a two-day whip ban. "He's the sort of horse who will only give you half of what he's capable of."

Galvanising was what Oratorio needed, and he certainly got it when Fallon was on board. Small wonder O'Brien opted to have the colt renew his grudging partnership with the stable jockey in the Baileys Irish Champion Stakes in September, rather than sending Fallon to Doncaster to ride favourite Scorpion in the same day's St Leger.

Both Oratorio and Motivator were having their first starts since the Eclipse, Oratorio because he had been jarred up at Sandown, and while Motivator led for most of the last two furlongs again, Oratorio went by him again. The Eclipse had been a pretty accurate guide to their respective merits after all, at least over a mile and a quarter on a sound surface, but as one indication that this was not such a widespread view going into the rematch, Motivator started 3-1 second favourite and Oratorio was at 7-1.

With two pacemakers ensuring a fast pace, Oratorio soon had Fallon punching away, but as the field bunched right up rounding the turn, Oratorio answered him and came right round the outside and into a challenging position. With Motivator the target once again, Oratorio flashed his tail when hit with the whip but produced an admirable response when Fallon went for everything halfway up the straight and, if anything, having led 100 yards out, his half-length victory looked a shade comfortable.

Others were in close attendance, but this time they were names of real repute: Alexander Goldrun, Ace, Azamour (the 6-4 favourite, who was found to have tweaked a back muscle) and Grey Swallow were all well established as Group 1 performers.

"Oratorio is an amazing horse," enthused O'Brien afterwards, with words that unsurprisingly made the autumn advertising copy. "He has everything – speed, stamina and a big heart, and Kieren was brilliant on him."

With an Eclipse and Irish Champion under his belt, it was no surprise, and entirely merited, that Oratorio started favourite for the other Champion Stakes at Newmarket in October. Public confidence in him had been turned around to such a degree, in fact, that he was sent off at 9-4, with the next best in a 15-runner field on 6-1. That overstated his potential dominance, however, and he could not afford the troubled passage that eventually ensued from stall two in the big field. Fallon was left to describe this as his worst day in the year, as traffic problems sentenced both Oratorio and the Dewhurst favourite Horatio Nelson to minor honours, the former passing the post in a never-threatening fourth behind David Junior, Pride and Maraahel.

O'Brien had surprised Channel 4 viewers by giving some contradictory signals just before the race, revealing that Oratorio's build-up to the Champion had been punctuated by signs of a "little infection" on the Thursday, followed by a perfect scope on the Friday.

The luck in running ensured that Oratorio was not at his peak at Newmarket and, although he started at just 68-10 at Belmont Park two weeks later, the switch to sand for the Breeders' Cup Classic did the same job even more effectively.

Circumstances, rather than his own idiosyncrasies, had prevented Oratorio from showing his class on his last two starts, but his standing as a high-class mile-and-a-quarter horse had already been put well beyond doubt. He acted on soft ground and good to firm. Oratorio will stand at Coolmore in 2006 at a fee of €30,000, and with his masters not too shy to point out that two of his predecessors as Eclipse and Irish Champion winners were Sadler's Wells and Giant's Causeway.

Oratorio

bay colt, 29-4-2002

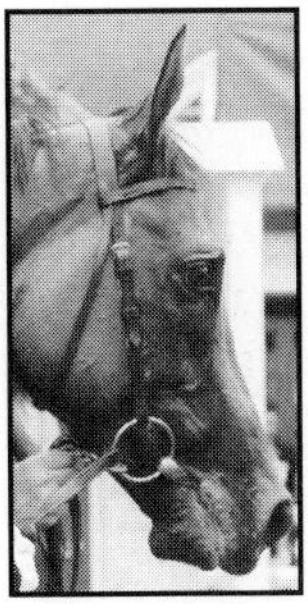

Danehill b 1986	Danzig	Northern Dancer	Nearctic **Natalma**
		Pas de Nom	Admiral's Voyage Petitioner
	Razyana	His Majesty	Ribot Flower Bowl
		Spring Adieu	Buckpasser **Natalma**
Mahrah b 1987	Vaguely Noble	Vienna	Aureole Turkish Blood
		Noble Lassie	Nearco Belle Sauvage
	Montage	Alydar	Raise A Native Sweet Tooth
		Katonka	Minnesota Mac Minnetonka

Bred by Barronstown Stud & Orpendale.

Sire Danehill

Won 4 of 9 races, inc. Haydock Park Sprint Cup-Gr1. Also 3rd in 2,000 Guineas. Died May 2003. Stood at Coolmore Stud, latterly at a fee of Ir200,000gns. Sire of Gr1 winners: Danish (QE II Challenge Cup), Kissing Cousin (Coronation), Danehill Dancer (Phoenix, National), Tsukuba Symphony (NHK Mile Cup), Desert King (National, Irish 2,000 Guineas, Irish Derby), Fairy King Prawn (Yasuda Kinen), Tiger Hill (GP von Baden [twice], Bayerisches Zuchtrennen), Indian Danehill (Prix Ganay), Wannabe Grand (Cheveley Park), Aquarelliste (Prix de Diane, Prix Vermeille, Prix Ganay), Banks Hill (Coronation, Breeders' Cup F & M Turf, Prix Jacques le Marois), Mozart (July Cup, Nunthorpe), Regal Rose (Cheveley Park), Dress To Thrill (Matriarch), Fine Motion (Shuka Sho, QE II Commemorative Cup), Landseer (Poule d'Essai des Poulains), Rock Of Gibraltar (Grand Criterium, Dewhurst, 2,000 Guineas, Irish 2,000 Guineas, St James's Palace, Sussex, Prix du Moulin), Westerner (Prix du Cadran [twice], Prix Royal-Oak [twice], Gold Cup), Clodovil (Poule d'Essai des Poulains), Intercontinental (Matriarch, Breeders' Cup F & M Turf), Light Jig (Yellow Ribbon), Spartacus (Phoenix, Gran Criterium), Grey Lilas (Prix du Moulin), North Light (Derby), Luas Line (Garden City H.), Oratorio (Prix Jean-Luc Lagardere, Eclipse, Irish Champion), George Washington (Phoenix, National), Horatio Nelson (Prix Jean-Luc Lagardere), Rumplestiltskin (Moyglare Stud, Prix Marcel Boussac).

Dam Mahrah

Won 1 of 6 races. Also 2nd twice and 3rd once. Earned £4,318. From a good US family. Dam of Kanun (1992 f by Dancing Brave; unraced), Fahim (1993 c by Green Desert; winner, Gr1-placed in US), Hawzah (1994 f by Green Desert; unraced), Khafaya (1995 f by Unfuwain; placed), Hadeb (1996 f by Unfuwain; winner), Elauyun (1997 f by Muhtarram; unraced), Mowaadah (1998 f by Alzao; Listed winner), Miss Mirage (2000 f by Alhaarth; winner), Glimmering (2001 f by Sadler's Wells; winner), Oratorio (2002 c by Danehill; triple Gr1 winner). Barren to Alhaarth in 1999, not covered in 2002, and barren to Montjeu in 2004. She has a colt foal by Danehill Dancer.

Pedigree assessment

Oratorio won only twice in a busy campaign of eight starts, but took the scalp of Derby hero Motivator on both occasions, at Sandown and Leopardstown. He retired as the clear pick of Danehill's 2002 crop and is guaranteed strong support in his first stud season at Coolmore, where his fee will be €30,000. The Danehill factor will surely stand him in good stead, but it is a remarkable fact that there has never been a successful sire out of a Vaguely Noble mare. *TM*

Ouija Board

4yo bay filly **118**

Cape Cross (Ire) - Selection Board (Welsh Pageant)

Owner Lord Derby

Trainer E A L Dunlop

Breeder Stanley Estate and Stud Co

Career: **13** starts | won **7** | second **1** | third **3** | **£1,729,767** win and place

By Nicholas Godfrey

FILLIES like Ouija Board are a rare and special breed. On their own, Ouija Board's amazing exploits in 2004 would have been enough to ensure a long-term place in our affections, whatever had gone on to happen after she was kept in training in 2005.

If Ouija Board was already the most popular horse in training on the Flat at the start of the season, even her most ardent fans must have been left pinching themselves when she fought her way back from a litany of injuries to end the campaign with a thrilling Group 1 success in Hong Kong in December. This had been the fairytale that threatened to turn into a horror story until Ouija Board managed to conjure up a happy ending. At the time of writing, there might yet be another sequel.

The owner-trainer team behind Ouija Board could never be accused of having drawn the losing ticket in the lottery of life. The 19th Earl of Derby is a man in danger of giving the aristocracy a good name, while Ed Dunlop cheerfully admits to having been born with a silver spoon. Yet given their travails with Britain's equine wonder woman for much of the 2005 season, they could have been forgiven for thinking they had exhausted their quota of good karma.

After she had won a pair of Classics and the Breeders' Cup Filly & Mare Turf in Texas, *Racing Post* readers voted Ouija Board their Horse of the Year for 2004. In 2005, her well-documented problems began in the spring when she threw a splint, the first in a many and varied list of setbacks.

Her belated seasonal debut in June at the York version of Royal Ascot came only after another minor problem, some slight bruising having emerged on the inside of her heels – and those closest to the filly must have wished they had shown even greater patience. Although Dunlop suggested publicly that the filly would improve for the outing in the Group 1 Prince of Wales's Stakes, he probably hoped for better than

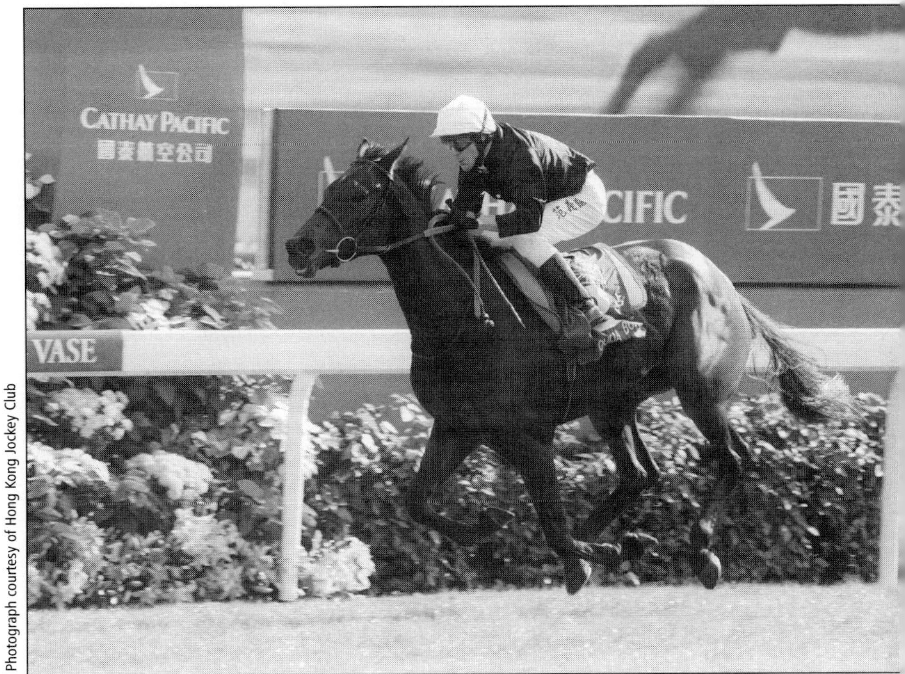

Photograph courtesy of Hong Kong Jockey Club

Ouija Board caps her impressive autumn comeback with a clear-cut success in the Group 1 Hong Kong Vase

seventh of eighth behind Azamour, beaten around 30 lengths. Only two horses had beaten Ouija Board the previous season; six now managed it in one race. But there was a huge mitigating factor in that Ouija Board lost a shoe after two furlongs, suffering a quarter crack on her off-fore in the process.

A nuclear bone scan revealed that Ouija Board had suffered a small stress fracture to her near-fore cannonbone. Lord Derby said he would not hesitate to retire the filly to his paddocks rather than risk her welfare; although Dunlop issued reassuring statements at the time that the injury was not thought to be career-threatening, he later admitted that he had been more worried than he had been prepared to let on. "I'd closed the book halfway through the season," he said in the autumn. "Mentally I'd finished the story." Fortunately, Ouija Board thrived after a spell of box-rest, so much so that an ambitious autumn campaign focusing on a return visit to the Breeders' Cup was planned.

It was far from straightforward, of course. Ouija Board's intended return in the September Stakes was shelved after a minor bout of coughing, with the result that she did not reappear until the Group 3 Princess Royal Stakes in late September, moved from Ascot to the Rowley Mile. Though she was favoured by race conditions, Ouija Board's performance did more

2005 Race record

1st Cathay Pacific Hong Kong Vase (Group 1) (Sha Tin, December 11) 3yo+ 1m4f Good to firm **119** 12 ran. *Held up towards rear, 10th straight, headway 2f out, quickened through gap to lead just inside final furlong, driven clear, ran on well (K Fallon), beat Six Sense by 2³/₄l*

5th Japan Cup (Group 1) (Tokyo, November 27) 3yo+ 1m4f Firm **118** 18 ran. *Raced in 10th, headway 5f out, 3rd straight, went 2nd over 2f out, lost 2nd just over 1f out, staying on at one pace when carried left 80yds out (K Fallon), beaten 2¹/₄l by Alkaased*

2nd Emirates Airline Breeders' Cup Filly & Mare Turf (Grade 1) (Turf) (Belmont Park, October 29) 3yo+ 1m2f Yielding **118** 14 ran. *8th early, headway to go 3rd 2f out, went 2nd over 1f out, kept on (J D Bailey), beaten 1¹/₄l by Intercontinental*

1st Princess Royal John Doyle Stakes (Group 3) (Newmarket, September 24) 3yo+ 1m4f Good **109** (TS 78) 13 ran. *Held up, headway to lead 3f out, ridden clear final furlong (L Dettori), beat Briolette by 2¹/₂l*

7th Prince of Wales's Stakes (Group 1) (York, June 15) 4yo+ 1m2¹/₂f Good to firm **67** (TS 58) 8 ran. *Held up in rear, effort over 4f out, soon beaten, 6th when eased inside final furlong (J P Spencer), beaten 30l by Azamour*

Other runs

2004 **1st** Alberto VO5 Breeders' Cup Filly & Mare Turf (Grade 1) (Lone Star Park, October 30) 3yo+ 1m3f Yielding **121** 12 ran ● **3rd** Prix de l'Arc de Triomphe Lucien Barriere (Group 1) (Longchamp, October 3) 3yo+ 1m4f Good **123** (TS 124) 19 ran ● **1st** Darley Irish Oaks (Group 1) (Curragh, July 18) 3yo 1m4f Good to firm **117** (TS 117) 7 ran ● **1st** Vodafone Oaks (Group 1) (Epsom, June 4) 3yo 1m4f Good **124** (TS 120) 7 ran ● **1st** R.L. Davison Pretty Polly Stakes (Listed) (Newmarket, May 2) 3yo 1m2f Good **111** (TS 81) 9 ran 2003 **3rd** EBF Montrose Fillies' Stakes (Listed) (Newmarket, November 1) 2yo 1m Good to soft **92** (TS 76) 12 ran ● **1st** EBF Novice Stakes (Yarmouth, October 21) 2yo 7f Good to firm **91** (TS 45) 6 ran ● **3rd** Beech House Stud EBF Maiden Stakes (Newmarket, October 3) 2yo 7f Good to firm **74** (TS 66) 23 ran

than enough to suggest she might still be capable of leaving her mark in better grade. Frankie Dettori, riding her for the first time, ensured she had a serious workout, driving her out to score by two and a half lengths from Briolette, much to the excitement – or was it relief? – of the Newmarket crowd.

Though she didn't need to be anywhere near her best to win for the first time in 11 months, Ouija Board pleased her connections to such a degree that they momentarily considered another crack at the Arc before settling on their principal target, a second trip to the Breeders' Cup Filly & Mare Turf, this time at Belmont Park in New York.

Dunlop sounded confident. "This time, it will be cooler, we'll be on a lovely European-style turf course with big, sweeping bends," he said. "She's the freshest horse in training; if she were 4-1, I'd lump on." However, the race was also a furlong shorter than in 2004, the rain got into the ground and Ouija Board was drawn wide in gate 13 of 14 against a stronger field.

Ouija Board (left) emerges from a three-month layoff to land the Group 3 Princess Royal Stakes at Newmarket

Ridden by local hero Jerry Bailey, she was sent off 2-1 favourite – and the partnership produced a truly gallant effort. A truly gallant effort in defeat, that is. From stall number one, potentially doubtful stayer Intercontinental, deserted by Bailey for Ouija Board, enjoyed an easy lead under Rafael Bejarano and conserved enough stamina to get home by just over a length from the favourite.

In effect Intercontinental stole the race. Ouija Board was much the best of the rest and clearly back in business, as she demonstrated a month later in an even more prestigious contest, the Japan Cup, where she was reunited with old sparring partner Kieren Fallon.

Back to her optimum trip of a mile and a half on very fast ground, she finished fifth behind thrilling winner Alkaased in a stellar field, having looked for a second as if she might even win the race once Fallon kicked her after the dying pacemaker on turning for home. Later, the rider was to suggest he had gone too soon, but while eventual runner-up Heart's Cry did interfere slightly with Ouija Board as he attempted to nail Alkaased, it would be stretching things to suggest she was unlucky, although she was beaten only two lengths.

The intention to stay in the Far East for the Hong Kong international meeting a couple of weeks later was immediately confirmed, connections briefly toying with a tilt at the mile-and-a-quarter Cup before plumping for the two-furlong-longer Vase.

Though the competition here was up to Group 1 standard, in reality it wasn't quite at the level of Japan, where Ouija Board had been close on a 12-1 chance. In Hong Kong, she was only 5-2 against 11 rivals including a strong team of British-based travellers comprising Norse Dancer, Warrsan and Cherry Mix. A bigger danger appeared to be Arc runner-up Westerner; the Gold Cup winner, 9-4 favourite, headed a four-strong raiding party from France.

This race, though, was all about Ouija Board, who was dubbed a "wonder filly" by course commentator David Raphael after a stunning victory. Fallon must have given the Ouija Board fan club serious concerns as he buried her at the back of the pack before nosing and weaving her way through the gaps. Still with a worrying amount to do at the top of the short straight, she unleashed a tremendous turn of foot when asked to accelerate, going clear in a handful of strides to record a convincing two-and-three-quarter-length verdict over Japanese-trained outsider Six Sense. None of the other British-trained horses made the places; Westerner was fifth.

Fallon admitted he had been somewhat further behind than he would have liked ideally. "The one thing which went wrong was that I had to take her back in the early stages, but I knew if I didn't get her settled she definitely wouldn't finish," he said. "But I've ridden some seriously good fillies like Bosra Sham and Islington, and on this evidence she must be right up there with them."

For Lord Derby and Dunlop, her first victory against the colts provided ample reward for the decision to keep her in training. Indeed, despite all the earlier anxieties, the filly's excited owner was speaking in terms of postponing Ouija Board's retirement and a proposed visit to Sadler's Wells for at least the early part of 2006 to send her to the Dubai Sheema Classic.

"A week ago I would have said there was no question of her being kept in training," said Lord Derby. "But after that emphatic victory it would be silly to rule it out as I recognise I will probably not have another horse like this again."

According to Racing Post Ratings, Ouija Board barely needed to improve on her previous two performances to win, being awarded a mark of 119. International handicappers, on hand to finalise their ratings ahead of the publication of the World Racehorse Rankings, suggested she would be rated only around 117 for the victory.

These ratings, perfectly understandable given the quality of the opposition, are not those of a superstar, just as they were not in 2004, when Ouija Board achieved her highest Racing Post Rating in the Epsom Oaks with a mark of 124.

Which just goes to show that sometimes ratings are not quite enough. How else do you explain to her legion of fans the ridiculous suggestion that racing's Queen of Hearts is anything other than a superstar?

Ouija Board

bay filly, 6-3-2001

Cape Cross b 1994	Green Desert	Danzig	Northern Dancer Pas de Nom
		Foreign Courier	Sir Ivor Courtly Dee
	Park Appeal	Ahonoora	Lorenzaccio Helen Nichols
		Balidaress	Balidar Innocence
Selection Board b 1982	Welsh Pageant	Tudor Melody	Tudor Minstrel Matelda
		Picture Light	Court Martial Queen Of Light
	Ouija	Silly Season	Tom Fool Double Deal
		Samanda	Alycidon Gradisca

Bred by Stanley Estate & Stud Co. in England.

Sire Cape Cross

Won 5 of 19 races, inc. Lockinge S.-Gr1, Queen Anne S.-Gr2, Goodwood Mile-Gr2. Also 2nd 3 times, 3rd 3 times and 4th 3 times. Big, strong, well-made type. High-class miler, notably game and consistent. Unraced beyond 9f (which he appeared to stay), effective on firm, good and good to soft ground. Well-bred. Half-brother to 4 winners, inc. Lord Of Appeal (Listed) and the dams of Kareymah (Gr3) and Diktat (Gr1). By a top-class sprinter-miler out of a champion 2-y-o filly whose siblings include Gr1 winners Desirable (dam of Shadayid, Gr1) and Alydaress and Gr1-placed Nashamaa, plus the dams of Russian Rhythm and Bin Ajwaad. Stands at Kildangan Stud, Co. Kildare, Ireland, at a (2006) fee of €50,000. Sire of 3 crops of racing age, inc: Hazyview (Gr3), Mac Love (Gr3), Mazuna (Gr3), Mokabra (Gr3), Ouija Board (Oaks S.-Gr1, Irish Oaks-Gr1, Breeders' Cup Filly & Mare Turf-Gr1).

Dam Selection Board

Ran only twice, placed 2nd in Ayr maiden at 2, unplaced at 3. Plain, leggy, evidently less than sound. Well-bred. Sister to top-class miler Teleprompter, half-sister to Chatoyant (c by Rainbow Quest; Gr3), Message Pad (c by Rousillon; Gr3-placed) and Rosia Bay (f by Blakeney; winner, dam of Gr1 winners Ibn Bey and Roseate Tern). Dam of: Officer Cadet (1987 c by Shernazar; winner), Draft Board (1989 f by Rainbow Quest; winner), Star Selection (1991 g by Rainbow Quest; Listed-placed winner), Pass Mark (1992 f by Never So Bold; placed), Cruinn A Bhord (1995 f by Inchinor; winner), Victor Ludorum (1996 f by Rainbow Quest; unraced), Spectrometer (1997 c by Rainbow Quest; winner), unnamed (1998 g by Rainbow Quest; unraced), Coalition (1999 g by Polish Precedent; winner), Ouija Board (2001 f by Cape Cross; Oaks winner), Illuminati (2002 g by Inchinor; unplaced). Died in 2002.

Pedigree assessment

Ouija Board's season did not work out as her many fans would have liked, but her performances in New York, Japan and Hong Kong indicated that she had retained her ability. She was the principal reason for the advance in her sire's fee from €20,000 to €50,000, and for his increased popularity among breeders, but she continues to stand out in his record, and his only Pattern winners to date are those who came from his first crop. Ouija Board is also by far the most important of her dam's 11 foals, the last of whom, Illuminati, seems to be only plating calibre. Let's hope she enjoys further success if she races on, and produces worthy stock when she eventually retires. *TM*

Palace Episode (USA)

2yo bay colt **114**

Machiavellian (USA) - Palace Weekend (USA) (Seattle Dancer (USA))

Owner Mrs T Marnane

Trainer K A Ryan

Breeder C W Clay and Runnymede Farm

Career: **5** starts | won **3** | second **0** | third **1** | **£160,480** win and place

By Howard Wright

THERE is more than a temptation to regard the Racing Post Trophy as a Classic trial; it seems to be an almost obligatory train of thought among some media correspondents as soon as the winner crosses the line at Doncaster each October. That temptation should be resisted.

When Phil Bull instigated "the provision of a high-class two-year-old race over a distance demanding stamina", he did so with one aim in mind. His thinking was contained in the essay on Miralgo, winner of the inaugural Timeform Gold Cup, in *Racehorses of 1961*, Bull's own publication.

As with the quotation above, the published explanation was not Bull's; he had long given up writing for the annual he founded. They belonged to the editor Arthur Shaw, a brilliant writer whose skills were subsumed by the criterion of anonymity that exists to this day.

Shaw pointed out that British racing lagged "far behind other countries" in putting on a high-value, back-end, two-year-old race – "Hence the Timeform Gold Cup, the primary purpose of which is to give a really worthwhile opportunity to high-class two-year-olds bred to stay."

No mention of trying to spot the following year's Classic winners; just the fulfilment of what Bull regarded, and Shaw articulated, as the "need for a race that would attract the best staying two-year-olds in the country."

Bull had more than one progressive idea which many people, mostly occupying Establishment seats, felt would upset the status quo far more than was good for the game. Overnight declaration of runners and starting stalls come to mind, and a valuable mile race for two-year-olds was another.

The majority of Bull's campaigns came to fruition, in time. He could actually do something about the mile race, and Bull's own company Timeform provided sponsorship for what proved to be the richest two-year-old race run outside the US, and the fifth biggest stake of the year.

Sales races, in which owners' entry fees create a prize fund out of proportion to those for Pattern races, currently eclipse the major juvenile

Palace Episode, belying his status as rank outsider, takes the Racing Post Trophy in the style of a progressive colt

Group races. However, the event that Bull created, which has been kept alive by sponsorship in the intervening years from the Observer, William Hill and, since 1989, the Racing Post, remains true to the original cause.

The owners of Palace Episode, winner of the 2005 Racing Post Trophy, were credited with a first prize of £125,280, second among Britain's non-sales juvenile races to the £145,000 that Sir Percy earned for beating Horatio Nelson, with Palace Episode fifth, in the Darley Dewhurst Stakes.

Equally important, in assessing the value of the Racing Post Trophy, Palace Episode was the best staying two-year-old of 2005.

No-one would have thought so after his debut, not even owner Con Marnane, the County Tipperary pinhooker who paid $100,000 for him as a yearling. Marnane took back Palace Episode for 44,000 guineas at the Newmarket Breeze-Up sales as a two-year-old intending to send him to a similar auction in Germany, but then decided to let him join Amadeus Wolf with Kevin Ryan.

Palace Episode was well regarded enough to start second favourite on his debut, but it was at Catterick of all places, in a late July maiden over six furlongs on firm ground. He defied an unfavourably wide draw and won quite comfortably by a length from Johannes.

The impression that Palace Episode would improve from his debut, given a stiffer test of stamina, was confirmed in the Acomb Stakes at York, for though among the outsiders, he won going away from Araafa.

He was withdrawn from Doncaster's Champagne Stakes after scoping unsatisfactorily and reappeared in the Group 2 Royal Lodge Stakes, which was moved to Newmarket. Though the mile should have suited him, the below-par pace did not, and he merely plugged on into third behind Leo.

2005 **Race record**

1st Racing Post Trophy (Group 1) (Doncaster, October 22) 2yo 1m Heavy **114** (TS 112) 7 ran. *Tracked leaders, headway 3f out, led well over 1f out, ridden approaching final furlong, flashed tail and stayed on well (N Callan), beat Winged Cupid by 1½l*

5th Darley Dewhurst Stakes (Group 1) (Newmarket, October 15) 2yo 7f Good to soft **101** (TS 99) 8 ran. *Chased leader until led well over 1f out, headed and weakened 1f out (N Callan), beaten 7¼l by Sir Percy*

3rd totesport.com Royal Lodge Stakes (Group 2) (Newmarket, September 25) 2yo 1m Good **104** (TS 103) 8 ran. *Always prominent, ridden and every chance over 1f out, stayed on same pace final furlong (N Callan), beaten 1¾l by Leo*

1st Acomb Stakes (Listed) (York, August 16) 2yo 7f Good **101** (TS 75) 8 ran. *Chased leaders, effort over 3f out, stayed on down wide outside to lead last 75yds (K Fallon), beat Araafa by 1¼l*

1st Louisburg And Sphinx Maiden Stakes (Catterick, July 20) 2yo 6f Firm **74** (TS 49) 10 ran. *Held up on outside, headway 2f out, led inside final furlong, comfortably (N Callan), beat Johannes by 1l*

Exactly the opposite seemed to be the case when Palace Episode came out three weeks later for the Dewhurst Stakes, because he and Humungous disputed a strong pace, and when the pack came at them Palace Episode faded tamely on the dead ground to finish fifth behind Sir Percy.

At Doncaster for the Racing Post Trophy, patience was back as the watchword for regular jockey Neil Callan, influenced no doubt by an official going description of heavy.

Stamina was not the issue, and at last it came into play for Palace Episode, who started the outsider of seven. He was driven to the front over a furlong out, was headed for the more favourable stands-rail pitch and kept on to beat the hitherto-unbeaten pair Winged Cupid and odds-on Septimus.

The odds and ground conditions might suggest Palace Episode's win was a fluke, but the way the race was run and the winning time say it would be folly to downrate him. The point made in 1961 by Arthur Shaw about France's Grand Criterium and the fact that it is frequently run on heavy going, remains pertinent in relation to Britain's equivalent: "[It] is nonetheless almost always won by a top-class horse, who takes no harm from it, trains on and confirms his merit as a three-year-old."

Over the years the Doncaster race has proved the point times over, from Miralgo, Noblesse and Vaguely Noble to the four winners before Palace Episode – High Chaparral, Brian Boru, American Post and Motivator.

Palace Episode, who will need at least ten furlongs as a three-year-old and should stay a mile and a half, but will probably need at least some cut in the ground to be at his best, will get his chance to show whether he "takes no harm from [the race], trains on and confirms his merit" in new colours. He missed an engagement at the Newmarket horses in training sales the week after Doncaster, and was bought by Godolphin in a private sale, reputedly for a seven-figure sum.

Palace Episode

bay colt, 2-5-2003

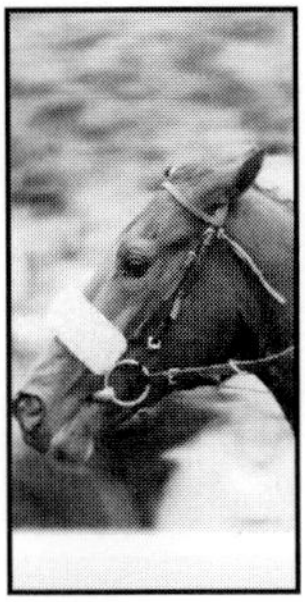

Machiavellian b 1987	Mr Prospector	Raise A Native	Native Dancer Raise You
		Gold Digger	Nashua Sequence
	Coup de Folie	Halo	Hail To Reason Cosmah
		Raise The Standard	Hoist The Flag Natalma
Palace Weekend b 1995	Seattle Dancer	Nijinsky	Northern Dancer Flaming Page
		My Charmer	Poker Fair Charmer
	Royal Run	Wavering Monarch	Majestic Light Uncommitted
		Kazadancoa	Green Dancer Khazaeen

Bred by Catesby W. Clay and Runnymede Farm in Kentucky. $100,000 Keeneland September yearling; unsold 44,000gns Tattersalls 2-y-o.

Sire Machiavellian

Won 4 of 7 races, inc. Prix Morny-Gr1, Prix de la Salamandre-Gr1. Also 2nd in 2,000 Guineas, 4th in Irish 2,000 Guineas. Medium-sized (16.0hh), quick-actioned, with a useful turn of foot. Seemingly acted on any ground, though not raced in very soft conditions. Barely lasted a mile. Died in June 2004, stood at Dalham Hall Stud, Newmarket, last fee £100,000. Sire of 12 crops of racing age, inc. Gr1 winners: Vettori (Poule d'Essai des Poulains), Invermark (Prix du Cadran), Rebecca Sharp (Coronation S.), Almutawakel (Prix Jean Prat, Dubai World Cup-UAE), Best Of The Bests (Prix d'Ispahan), Medicean (Lockinge S., Eclipse S.), Patavellian (Prix de l'Abbaye de Longchamp), Storming Home (Champion S., Charles Whittingham Memorial H., Clement L. Hirsch Memorial Championship S.), Street Cry (Dubai World Cup-UAE, Stephen Foster H.), Right Approach (Dubai Duty Free [dead-heat]-UAE Gr1), Palace Episode (Racing Post Trophy-Gr1).

Dam Palace Weekend

Unraced. Quite well-bred. By a Gr2-winning half-brother to Seattle Slew and Lomond. Half-sister to Tejano Run (c by Tejano; Gr2 winner, 2nd in Kentucky Derby) and More Royal (c by Mt Livermore; Gr2-placed in England, Gr2 winner in US). Dam of: Rich Pickins (1999 c by Smart Strike; winner), Stylish Guy (2000 c by Swain; winner), Adventure (2001 f by Unbridled's Song; winner), Towering Palace (2002 f by Unbridled's Song; winner), Palace Episode (2003 c by Machiavellian; Gr1 winner). She was barren in 2004, but has a colt foal by Distorted Humor.

Pedigree assessment

Emphatically best on the day when landing Doncaster's Group 1 contest on heavy ground, but previously successful on good and firm surfaces, Palace Episode showed progressive form throughout the season. He seems sure to train on, promising to stay middle distances at three. Of course, that is precisely what his sire, Machiavellian, failed to do, but his stock have rarely taken after him, and in aptitudinal terms they have tended to be sons of their dams. As a non-runner, Palace Weekend provides no clues in that regard, but as half-sister to a Kentucky Derby runner-up and as daughter of a half-brother to US Triple Crown hero Seattle Slew, there is stamina enough in her background. Whether her colt has sufficient quality to claim a Classic for her new connections remains to be seen. There are others who make more appeal at this stage. *TM*

Pastoral Pursuits

4yo bay colt **123**

Bahamian Bounty - Star (Most Welcome)

Owner The Pursuits & National Stud Partnership

Trainer H Morrison

Breeder Red House Stud

Career: **10** starts | won **6** | second **2** | third **0** | **£264,496** win and place

By Graham Dench

PASTORAL PURSUITS' claim to be regarded as Europe's top sprinter rests entirely on his win in the Darley July Cup at Newmarket. It is a valid claim for all that, and while his superiority is only marginal over contemporaries that are headed on Racing Post Ratings by his younger brother Goodricke, injury denied him the opportunity to extend it. For just three weeks after the July Cup came the news that Pastoral Pursuits had suffered "a minor leg injury" and was to be retired to the National Stud, who had shrewdly bought into him in the spring.

He had reportedly returned from his first piece of work since Newmarket with a bit of a heat in his near foreleg – ironically, it had been an injury to his off fore that had brought a highly progressive juvenile campaign to a premature halt two years earlier – and while trainer Hughie Morrison reckoned he could have been all right again granted a month or six weeks off, the season would have been all but over by the time he was back to full fitness.

The July Cup was a landmark first Group 1 win for Morrison, who started training in 1996 and quickly established himself as a skilled practitioner under both codes, as well as one noted for his patience with older horses, a facet of his talent that gained further significant reward when veteran Alcazar won the Prix Royal-Oak at Longchamp later in the season.

However, Pastoral Pursuits was very nearly pulled out after an overnight deluge brought 10mm of rain, for soft ground was thought to be against him and he had been withdrawn in similar circumstances at three.

Morrison, who was staying locally, was filled with gloom when he heard how much rain the track had taken and initially phoned his yard to instruct staff not to bring Pastoral Pursuits. The consequences of his change of heart were, in his own words, "immense".

Pastoral Pursuits scores a clear-cut win in the July Cup, but he never got the chance to contest another Group 1

Running over six furlongs for the first time in almost a year, having been a well-beaten seventh of ten behind Valixir after slipping badly on the home bend in the Queen Anne Stakes on his only previous start of the year, Pastoral Pursuits was a 22-1 chance in a field of 19 headed by the top 2004 sprinter Somnus and the highly progressive former handicappers Soldier's Tale and Iffraaj. On paper he did not have a great deal going for him, and he was deserted even by his regular rider Steve Drowne, whose association with fellow outsider Avonbridge went back even further.

However, the times suggested the going was much nearer good than the official good to soft, and though the now all-too-familiar splitting of the field made it a somewhat unsatisfactory affair, there was no apparent fluke about Pastoral Pursuits' success. In the hands of new partner John Egan, he was always prominent among the far-side group and went after the leader Avonbridge approaching the furlong pole. He got to the front well inside the final furlong and kept on strongly to beat Avonbridge by a length and a half.

While some of his rivals plainly failed to give their running, the runner-up went on to win the Prix de l'Abbaye, which many regard as Europe's premier sprint, and the winning margin was a wide one by championship sprint standards.

It is doubtful if the Abbaye would have been on Pastoral Pursuits' agenda had he remained in training, as he never raced at five furlongs, but he would have been an ideal type for the Haydock Sprint Cup, in which a head-to-head with Goodricke would have made for a fascinating clash. Siblings of their class that are so closely matched in terms of both ability

2005 Race record

1st Darley July Cup (Group 1) (Newmarket (July), July 7) 3yo+ 6f Good to soft **123** (TS 111) 19 ran. *Raced far side, always prominent, chased leader over 1f out, ran on under pressure to lead well inside final furlong (J F Egan), beat Avonbridge by 1½l*

7th Queen Anne Stakes (Group 1) (York, June 14) 4yo+ 1m Good to firm **90** (TS 77) 10 ran. *In rear, slipped bend over 4f out, lost place over 2f out (S Drowne), beaten 15½l by Valixir*

Other runs

2004 **5th** Prix de la Foret (Group 1) (Longchamp, October 9) 3yo+ 7f Soft **116** (TS 66) 7 ran ● **1st** GNER Park Stakes (Group 2) (Doncaster, September 9) 3yo+ 7f Good to firm **121** (TS 95) 8 ran ● **1st** Racing UK Stakes (Registered As The Hackwood Stakes) (Listed) (Newbury, July 17) 3yo+ 6f Good **110** (TS 93) 11 ran ● **2nd** IG Index 30th Anniversary Surrey Stakes (Listed) (Sandown, June 3) 3yo 7f Good **118** (TS 96) 6 ran 2003 **1st** Coral Sirenia Stakes (Group 3) (Kempton, September 6) 2yo 6f Good **107** (TS 82) 9 ran ● **1st** Ian Hutchinson Memorial Conditions Stakes (Windsor, August 10) 2yo 6f Good to firm **110** (TS 84) 5 ran ● **1st** Averti Maiden Auction Stakes (Chepstow, July 25) 2yo 6f Good **90** (TS 73) 11 ran ● **2nd** Clio Renault Sport V6 EBF Median Auction Maiden Stakes (Windsor, June 9) 2yo 6f Good to firm **72** (TS 53) 20 ran

and aptitude are few and far between, though coincidentally two of the best, the Classic-winning pair Julio Mariner and Juliette Marny, were bred by Morrison's father, James.

Unfortunately Pastoral Pursuits and Goodricke never met, for Goodricke, who beat the Nunthorpe winner La Cucaracha in the Haydock race, did not emerge as a Group 1 performer until after Pastoral Pursuits had been retired. The figures suggest there would have been precious little between them.

Pastoral Pursuits, a boisterous character who evidently had an aversion to being saddled, was in Morrison's view "not the most natural-looking sprinter, but a perfect size and a perfect athlete." He won six of his ten races, five of them over six furlongs, a distance over which he was beaten only once, when second from a moderate draw at Windsor on his racecourse debut.

He won three times at two, twice by extravagant margins, and Morrison hoped he would make a live 2,000 Guineas challenger after he landed Kempton's Sirenia Stakes in fast time. However, he did not reappear at three until June and he was not tried at a mile for another year. Though his running in the Queen Anne can hardly be accepted as conclusive, his breeding and style of running suggested that the distance would have stretched him in any case. He stayed seven furlongs well enough to win Doncaster's Park Stakes at three, but the evidence suggests he was essentially a sprinter.

He was a pretty good one too, and but for his injuries he might have been an even better one.

Pastoral Pursuits

bay colt, 3-4-2001

Parents	Grandparents	Great-grandparents	Great-great-grandparents
Bahamian Bounty ch 1994	Cadeaux Genereux	Young Generation	Balidar Brig O'Doon
		Smarten Up	Sharpen Up L'Anguissola
	Clarentia	Ballad Rock	Bold Lad True Rocket
		Laharden	Mount Hagen Sinella
Star b 1995	Most Welcome	Be My Guest	Northern Dancer What A Treat
		Topsy	Habitat Furioso
	Marista	Mansingh	Jaipur Tutasi
		Evendo	Derring-Do Christmas Eve

Bred by Red House Stud in England. 110,000gns Tattersalls October (Part 1) yearling.

Sire Bahamian Bounty

Won 3 of 7 races, inc. Prix Morny-Gr1, Middle Park S.-Gr1. Also 4th in Dewhurst S. and July Cup. Medium-sized (16.0hh), well-made individual, and a fluent mover. High-class sprinter, best at 6f. Failed to stay 1m in Poule d'Essai des Poulains. Well-bred. By a top-class miler and successful sire. Half-brother to 2 other winners. Dam won 5 races from 2-5 years, Gr3-placed at 2. Grand-dam unraced half-sister to 2 winners and to dam of Gr3 winner Hawkins. Third dam won and placed twice from only 3 starts, half-sister to Stilvi (Gr3 winner, dam of Gr1 winners Tachypous, Tromos and Tyrnavos, Gr2 winner Tolmi, and Listed winner Taxiarchos). Stands at the National Stud, Newmarket, at a 2006 fee of £10,000. Sire of 5 crops of racing age, inc. notable winners: Naahy (Gr3), Pastoral Pursuits (July Cup-Gr1), Goodricke (Haydock Sprint Cup-Gr1).

Dam Star

Ran only at 2 years, won 1 of 3 races. Showed quite useful form in brief career, winning debut (median auction race at Nottingham) by 6 lengths. Half-sister to Superstrike (by Superlative; dual Gr3 winner in US) and Four-Legged Friend (by Aragon; Listed 2-y-o winner at Newmarket). Dam of: Petrean (1999 f by Petong; unplaced), Asbo (2000 f by Abou Zouz; placed; sold 47,000gns, in foal to Bahamian Bounty, at Tattersalls July 2005), Pastoral Pursuits (2001 c by Bahamian Bounty; Gr1 winner), Goodricke (2002 c by Bahamian Bounty; Gr1 winner), Starstone (2003 f by Diktat; unraced to date). She produced a colt foal by Nayef in 2005, and died, in foal to Dubai Destination, in July. Barren to Diktat in 2004.

Pedigree assessment

This was a good year for the National Stud's stallion Bahamian Bounty, who served his second three-figure book and was represented by his first Group 1 winners. He was not always so popular, for Pastoral Pursuits came from a crop of only 25, and his full-brother Goodricke from one of 31, but their victories in two of Britain's best-contested six-furlong events will ensure big books for the foreseeable future. Pastoral Pursuits had no opportunity to confirm his newly acquired status as Britain's top sprinter, an injury ending his career shortly afterwards. In 2006 he will stand alongside his sire at a fee of £6,000. Although he peaked at four, he did have smart form, including a Group 3 victory, to his credit at two, and breeders will surely trust him to get precocious stock. *TM*

Peeress

4yo chestnut filly **117**

Pivotal - Noble One (Primo Dominie)

Owner Cheveley Park Stud

Trainer Sir Michael Stoute

Breeder Cheveley Park Stud

Career: **12** starts | won **6** | second **1** | third **3** | **£283,879** win and place

By David Carr

NEWMARKET may be the 'headquarters' of British Flat racing, but it is not necessarily an ideal place to stage a Group 1 race.

Contests designed to prove who is best can raise more questions than they answer there, as too often fields split into two or more groups and leave endless debates over, say, whether Rock Of Gibraltar really was better than Hawk Wing in the 2,000 Guineas of 2002, or Starcraft better than Dubawi in the Queen Elizabeth II Stakes in the latest season.

But those results stand up well compared with the farce of a race for the latest Sun Chariot Stakes. The one-mile contest was raised to Group 1 status in 2004, but its second running in that grade was more reminiscent of the Lincoln Handicap, so profound was the effect of the draw.

Ten runners went to post, but they split into three groups leaving the stalls and it was clear from a long way out that the trio who raced against the far rail had the upper hand on the softened ground. Peeress, Summitville and Musicanna came home clear of the rest, who might as well have waited around for the Cambridgeshire 40 minutes later for all the chance they seemed to have.

All credit, however, to Kevin Darley for a finely judged ride to take advantage of conditions on Peeress, who took command over two furlongs out and passed the post a length and a half in front. But it would be a brave punter who took the result as evidence that Peeress is a better filly than, say, her own stable companions Chic and Favourable Terms, who started at shorter odds but could not overcome the disadvantage of an unfavourable draw. And subsequent events underlined the impression that the result was questionable to say the least.

Summitville, a 50-1 shot who had won once from six outings in Listed and Group 3 company earlier in 2005, failed to reproduce her

Peeress (second left) makes the most of an advantageous draw to land the Group 1 Sun Chariot Stakes at Newmarket

apparently improved form in two outings afterwards, and Peeress herself could manage only fourth in the Group 2 Challenge Stakes back at Newmarket a fortnight later. On the other hand Chic finished a close seventh in the Champion Stakes on the same card, showing form that would have had her dead-heating for the Sun Chariot on Racing Post handicapper Paul Curtis's figures.

Peeress is undoubtedly a progressive and smart filly, whatever the exact merit of her form. Once-raced as a two-year-old, she improved with virtually every run the next season and won three times – though her biggest impact on the headlines was providing Kieren Fallon's 100th winner of the season in a handicap at Newmarket.

She immediately rewarded the decision to keep her in training in 2005 with a smooth victory in Listed company at York in May and went on to prove herself one of the best four-year-old milers of her sex around. She took the Group 2 Windsor Forest Stakes at the Royal meeting by an authoritative two lengths from Sundrop – gaining revenge on a filly who had beaten her a fortnight earlier at Epsom, a track which seemed not to suit. And there was no disgrace in finishing third on her Group 1 debut in the Falmouth Stakes at Newmarket in July, given that the first two were top fillies Soviet Song and Alexander Goldrun.

The good news is that she stays in training and, as she has not had much racing, it would be no surprise to see her progressing again. The enhanced programme of Pattern races for mares should provide her with plenty of opportunities.

She is certainly one to look forward to next season for Sir Michael Stoute,

2005 Race record

4th VC Bet Challenge Stakes (Group 2) (Newmarket, October 15) 3yo+ 7f Good to soft **106** (TS 101) 15 ran. *Prominent, chased leader 3f out, led well over 1f out, soon headed, weakened inside final furlong (M J Kinane), beaten 7l by Le Vie Dei Colori*

1st Kingdom of Bahrain Sun Chariot Stakes (Group 1) (Newmarket, October 1) 3yo+ 1m Good to soft **116** (TS 87) 10 ran. *Raced on far side, chased overall leader, led overall over 2f out, driven out (K Darley), beat Summitville by 1½l*

3rd UAE Equestrian And Racing Federation Falmouth Stakes (Group 1) (Newmarket (July), July 5) 3yo+ 1m Good **117** (TS 84) 7 ran. *Led, headed 7f out, led 6f out, ridden and headed inside final furlong, no extra (M J Kinane), beaten 2¾l by Soviet Song*

1st Windsor Forest Stakes (Group 2) (York, June 15) 4yo+ 1m Good to firm **117** (TS 110) 8 ran. *Tracked leaders, effort 2f out, ran on gamely to lead last 100yds (M J Kinane), beat Sundrop by 2l*

2nd Princess Elizabeth Stakes (Sponsored By Vodafone) (Group 3) (Epsom, June 3) 3yo+ 1m½ Good **105** (TS 28) 3 ran. *Tracked leader, effort to challenge over 2f out, soon outpaced by winner, one pace after (M J Kinane), beaten 2l by Sundrop*

1st Michael Seely Memorial Fillies' Stakes (Listed) (York, May 13) 3yo+ 7f Good to soft **103** (TS 72) 5 ran. *Tracked leaders, shaken up to lead over 1f out, ran on well, readily (M J Kinane), beat Dumnoni by 2½l*

Other runs

2004 **4th** Littlewoods Bet Direct EBF Fleur De Lys Fillies' Stakes (Listed) (Lingfield (AW), October 31) 3yo+ 1m Standard **89** (TS 66) 12 ran ● **3rd** Albert Stakes (0-100 handicap) (Goodwood, July 29) 3yo 7f Good to firm **105** (TS 82) 17 ran ● **1st** racingpost.co.uk Fillies' Rated Stakes (0-100 handicap) (Newmarket (July), July 6) 3yo 7f Good to firm **103** (TS 88) 9 ran ● **1st** Anthony Fawcett Memorial Fillies' Handicap (Thirsk, June 15) 3yo+ (0-90) 1m Firm **93** (TS 72) 8 ran ● **1st** EBF Maiden Fillies' Stakes (Bath, May 27) 3yo 1m Firm **68** (TS 26) 11 ran **2003** **3rd** EBF Balaton Lodge Maiden Fillies' Stakes (Div II) (Newmarket, November 1) 2yo 7f Good to soft **84** (TS 74) 18 ran

as he bids to defend the trainers' championship that he won for the eighth time in 2005 after a ding-dong battle with Aidan O'Brien which enlivened the closing weeks of the turf season.

The lead changed hands several times through the summer and the Irishman was odds-on to land the British crown for the third time until a luckless Champions Day. The defeats of Horatio Nelson and Oratorio that day marked the final turning point, and his failure to win the Racing Post Trophy left him with too much ground to make up.

Stoute deserves plenty of credit given that his 2004 stars North Light and Quiff made little contribution in 2005, both retired after meeting defeat on their only outing, while exciting four-year-old Imperial Stride left for Godolphin before taking up his engagement in the Champion Stakes, for which he would have been a leading fancy.

Surprisingly, Peeress was Stoute's only Group 1 winner of the season, but along with Maraahel, Distinction and Imperial Stride she was one of four to contribute £100,000 or more towards a prize-money total in excess of £2.25m.

Peeress

chestnut filly, 1-2-2001

Parents	Grandparents	Great-grandparents	Great-great-grandparents
Pivotal ch 1993	Polar Falcon	Nureyev	Northern Dancer Special
		Marie d'Argonne	Jefferson Mohair
	Fearless Revival	Cozzene	Caro Ride The Trails
		Stufida	Bustino Zerbinetta
Noble One ch 1996	Primo Dominie	Dominion	Derring-Do Picture Palace
		Swan Ann	My Swanee Anna Barry
	Noble Destiny	Dancing Brave	Lyphard Navajo Princess
		Tender Loving Care	Final Straw Silk Stocking

Bred by Cheveley Park Stud Ltd in England.

Sire Pivotal

Won 4 of 6 races, inc. King's Stand S.-Gr2, Nunthorpe S.-Gr1. Powerfully built, attractive sort, 16.3hh, who always impressed in appearance and condition. High-class sprinter on fast ground. Stands at Cheveley Park Stud, Newmarket, at a fee of £65,000 (Oct 1). Sire of 6 crops of racing age, inc. notable winners: Golden Apples (Del Mar Oaks-Gr1, Beverly D S.-Gr1, Yellow Ribbon S.-Gr1), Kyllachy (Nunthorpe S.-Gr1), Low Pivot (Gr3), Needwood Blade (Gr3), Ratio (Gr3), Silvester Lady (Preis der Diana-Gr1), Captain Rio (Gr2), Chorist (Pretty Polly S.-Gr1), Megahertz (John C. Mabee H.-Gr1), Ringmoor Down (Gr3), Stolzing (Gr3), Humouresque (Gr3), Pivotal Point (Gr2), Somnus (Haydock Sprint Cup-Gr1, Prix Maurice de Gheest-Gr1, Prix de la Foret-Gr1), Lucky Spin (Gr3), Peeress (Sun Chariot S.-Gr1), Penkenna Princess (Gr3), Saoire (Irish 1,000 Guineas-Gr1), Windsor Knot (Gr3), Leo (Gr2).

Dam Noble One

Won 2 of 5 races. Useful sprint performer who competed at Listed level. Appeared not to get 6f in testing conditions. Quite well-bred sister to one winner and half-sister to 4 others. Dam of: Peeress (2001 f by Pivotal; Gr1 winner), Carte Royale (2002 c by Loup Sauvage; winner), Eastern Empress (2003 f by Mujadil; placed). Her yearling is a colt by Kyllachy, and she has been covered by Pivotal.

Pedigree assessment

Cheveley Park Stud has bred a number of first-class advertisements for its own flagship stallion, and Peeress emulated Kyllachy and Chorist by graduating at Group 1 level in the Sun Chariot Stakes. In common with most of Pivotal's stock, she is an honest, genuine performer, and she appears to be equally at home at seven furlongs or a mile. The penalty for having won at the top level meant that she had a stiff task against the colts in the Challenge Stakes, but she turned in a creditable effort, beating many more than beat her. If the plan to race her again at five is adhered to, she will again face difficult tasks, but it is not beyond the bounds of possibility that she has further improvement in her. *TM*

Phoenix Reach (Ire)

5yo bay horse **119**

Alhaarth (Ire) - Carroll's Canyon (Ire) (Hatim (USA))

Owner Winterbeck Manor Stud

Trainer A M Balding

Breeder Miss Christine Kiernan

Career: **14** starts	won **5**	second **2**	third **1**	**£1,975,483** win and place

By Graham Dench

YOU HAVE to wonder what Phoenix Reach might have achieved if he had stayed free of injury. With earnings pushing the £2 million mark from Group 1 wins in Canada, Hong Kong and Dubai, his four seasons in training have hardly been unproductive. Yet Andrew Balding has seldom had an entirely trouble-free run with him, for besides viral infections, colic and many of the other ailments that are so common in the equine world, Phoenix Reach has required surgery under general anaesthetic on no fewer than five occasions.

The 2005 season started brilliantly for Phoenix Reach, but it was over by August after he came off the gallops with a hairline fracture to his off-fore pastern. By Phoenix Reach's standards it was not a serious setback – an unrelated injury to the same leg following his debut at two had required no fewer than four operations – and it did not require surgery. But it was enough to thwart connections' plans for a busy autumn campaign in which a trip to Australia for a crack at the Cox Plate or to Belmont for the Breeders' Cup Turf were options, as were a return to Hong Kong for the Cathay Pacific Hong Kong Vase, which he won in 2004, and another shot at the Japan Cup, in which he had finished sixth.

Although never previously seen before June, Phoenix Reach had begun his travels as early as March, little more than three months after his Sha Tin defeat of Sights On Gold. This time he went to Dubai, for the Sheema Classic. Facing ten rivals, among them the previous year's Arc runner-up Cherry Mix and disqualified Arlington Million winner Powerscourt, Phoenix Reach faced a tough task from his outside draw. However, there was no shortage of optimism in the Balding camp, for he had enjoyed an unusually smooth preparation and he had worked so well that the headgear that had been introduced for his Canadian International win at Woodbine at three was dispensed with.

The Sheema Classic showed Martin Dwyer at his best and confirmed

Phoenix Reach (noseband) strikes for home in the Sheema Classic, a race that is likely to be his first target in 2006

him a match for almost anyone on the big occasions. He needed a cool head, for having dropped Phoenix Reach in to the inside rail from stall 11 he had to sit and suffer behind what looked a far from breakneck pace and just hope that the gaps came for him. Phoenix Reach had a wall of horses in front of him when Razkalla set sail for home, but when a gap appeared he picked up impressively, hitting the front well inside the final furlong and going on for a two-length success.

Dwyer acknowledged his good fortune, but also paid tribute to his sometimes underrated mount, a “real professional” and “a star”.

From Nad Al Sheba it was back to Sha Tin for the Audemars Piguet QE II Cup. The race was over ten furlongs, a distance at which Phoenix Reach had yet to win, but that was only part of the problem. For Phoenix Reach missed vital work after being cast in his box and suffering a pinched girth, and on top of that he was hit with another unfavourably high draw, which over the shorter distance around Sha Tin was an even bigger worry than it had been in Dubai. If that was not enough, he found himself checked at a crucial stage early in the straight. It did not cost him the race, but he would have been a place or two closer than fifth behind the local star Vengeance Of Rain.

Phoenix Reach stayed in the Far East for the Singapore Airlines International Cup at Kranji, which attracted a field worthy of the name. Opposed by runners from Australia, France, Germany, Ireland, South Africa and the United States, not to mention half a dozen locals, Phoenix Reach enjoyed the strong pace and hit the front with a furlong and a

2005 Race record

10th King George VI And Queen Elizabeth Diamond Stakes (Group 1) (Newbury, July 23) 3yo+ 1m4f Good to firm **97** (TS 85) 12 ran. *Took keen hold in mid-division, lost position over 5f out, not a danger after (Martin Dwyer), beaten 19l by Azamour*

2nd Singapore Airlines International Cup (Group 1) (Kranji, May 15) 3yo+ 1m2f Soft **117** 15 ran. *Midfield, pushed along and headway over 3f out, ridden to lead narrowly 1½f out, headed and no extra last 100yds (Martin Dwyer), beaten ¾l by Mummify*

5th Audemars Piguet QE II Cup (Group 1) (Sha Tin, April 24) 3yo+ 1m2f Good to firm **119** 13 ran. *Raced in 8th, stayed on steadily final 2f (Martin Dwyer), beaten 3¼l by Vengeance Of Rain*

1st Dubai Sheema Classic Sponsored By Dubai Water Front (Turf) (Group 1) (Nad Al Sheba, March 26) 4yo+ 1m4f Good to firm **119** 11 ran. *Towards rear, ridden and progress 2f out, ran on well to lead final 165yds, driven out (Martin Dwyer), beat Razkalla by 2l*

Other runs

2004 **1st** Cathay Pacific Hong Kong Vase (Group 1) (Sha Tin, December 12) 3yo+ 1m4f Good to firm **120** 12 ran ● **6th** Japan Cup (Grade 1) (Tokyo, November 28) 3yo+ 1m4f Firm **116** 16 ran ● **10th** King George VI And Queen Elizabeth Diamond Stakes (Group 1) (Ascot, July 24) 3yo+ 1m4f Good to firm **108** (TS 76) 11 ran ● **6th** Grand Prix de Saint-Cloud (Group 1) (Saint-Cloud, July 4) 3yo+ 1m4f Good to soft **114** (TS 98) 10 ran ● **6th** Prince of Wales's Stakes (Group 1) (Ascot, June 16) 4yo+ 1m2f Good to firm **115** (TS 108) 10 ran **2003** **1st** Pattison Canadian International (Grade 1) (Woodbine, October 19) 3yo+ 1m4f Yielding **118** 10 ran ● **3rd** Seabiscuit St Leger Stakes (Group 1) (Doncaster, September 13) 3yo 1m6½f Good **117** (TS 103) 12 ran ● **1st** Peugeot Gordon Stakes (Group 3) (Goodwood, July 29) 3yo 1m4f Good **113** (TS 97) 10 ran ● **1st** Stan James 08000 383384 Maiden Stakes (Newbury, July 3) 3yo 1m4f Good **88** (TS 82) 14 ran **2002** ● **2nd** Herbert And Gwen Blagrave Maiden Stakes (Salisbury, June 27) 2yo 7f Firm **86** (TS 29) 9 ran

half to go. However, he was then challenged on both sides, and while he was too strong for Alexander Goldrun, whom he beat two and three-quarter lengths, he found the Lee Freedman-trained Mummify three-quarters of a length too good for him.

Balding and Dwyer could hardly have been more thrilled with Phoenix Reach had he won, but their excitement was tempered when the five-year-old returned home with an ulcer on the cornea of an eye which required him to undergo surgery yet again and then treatment for six weeks through a catheter. Balding somehow still managed to prepare Phoenix Reach for the King George VI and Queen Elizabeth Stakes at Newbury, but the training regime was upset once again little more than a week before the race when the horse had the stuffing knocked out of him by a bad reaction to treatment for a bout of colic. While he would have struggled against Azamour at Newbury with a trouble-free preparation, he returned with a cut to his near-fore and bruising, so his tenth of 12 was no reflection of his true ability.

It was a disappointing end to a campaign that had begun so well, but Phoenix Reach will be back in 2006 for one last season. The world, as ever, is his oyster, but first stop will be Dubai again for the Sheema Classic.

Phoenix Reach

bay horse, 5-3-2000

Alhaarth b 1993	Unfuwain	Northern Dancer	Nearctic Natalma
		Height Of Fashion	Bustino Highclere
	Irish Valley	Irish River	Riverman Irish Star
		Green Valley	Val de Loir Sly Pola
Carroll's Canyon ch 1989	Hatim	Exclusive Native	Raise A Native Exclusive
		Sunday Purchase	TV Lark Dame Fritchie
	Tuna	Silver Shark	Buisson Ardent Palsaka
		Vimelette	Vimy Sea Parrot

Bred by Christine Kiernan in Ireland. Ir£16,000 Goffs November foal, 36,000gns Doncaster St Leger yearling

Sire Alhaarth

Won 8 of 17 races. At 2, won 5 (inc. Vintage S-Gr3, Solario S-Gr3, Champagne S-Gr2, Dewhurst S-Gr1) of 5. At 3, won 1 (Prix du Rond-Point-Gr2) of 7, also 3rd Sussex S-Gr1. At 4, won 2 (Curragh International-Gr2, Prix Dollar-Gr2) of 5, also 3rd Irish Champion S-Gr1. By top-class, very well-bred 12f performer with strong stud record. Half-brother to Gr3 winner Green Pola out of unplaced half-sister to top-class 2yo Green Dancer. Stands at Derrinstown Stud, 2006 fee €30,000. First foals 1999, sire of: Bandari (Gr2), Dominica (Gr2), Misterah (Gr3), Maharib (Gr3), Phoenix Reach (Canadian International-Gr1, Hong Kong Vase-Gr1, Dubai Sheema Classic-Gr1), Hoh Buzzard (Gr2), Haafhd (2,000 Guineas-Gr1, Champion S-Gr1).

Dam Carroll's Canyon

Unraced. By well-bred Gr1 winner but disappointing sire, half-sister to Arc winner Carroll House (by Lord Gayle). Dam of: The Director (1993 g by Prince Rupert; winner), Kilbride Lass (1994 f by Lahib; unraced), unnamed (1995 c by Indian Ridge), Capriolo (1996 g by Priolo; Flat/hurdle winner), Athlumney Pearl (1997 f by Lycius; unraced), Arenas (1999 c by Revoque; winner), Phoenix Reach (2000 c by Alhaarth; Canadian International-Gr1, Hong Kong Vase-Gr1, Dubai Sheema Classic-Gr1), Royal Canyon (2001 f by Royal Applause; unplaced), Coill Cri (2002 f by Shinko Forest; unplaced), Shafrons Canyon (2003 f by Lend A Hand; unplaced), 2004 f by Indian Danehill.

Pedigree assessment

A tough and very high-class performer, in the mould of his sire Alhaarth and 'uncle' Carroll House. Fitness permitting, he should continue to collect various currencies from around the world. As a Flat stallion prospect in Britain and Ireland, he lacks the British/Irish Group 1 win and the flashy distaff family that studs like, though he is just the sort of horse that breeders want to produce and owners want to race. *JH*

Pinson (Ire)

3yo grey colt **120**

Halling (USA) - Tadorne (Fr) (Inchinor)

Owner Baron Guy de Rothschild

Trainer J-C Rouget

Breeder Baron Guy de Rothschild

Career: **6** starts | won **4** | second **1** | third **0** | **£103,547** win and place

By Robert Carter

THIS would have been a very different story if it had ended in August. Pinson was a revelation at Deauville and seemed assured of a great future. Jean-Claude Rouget, his trainer, said: "He's making enormous progress and we are taking things step by step. He's not entered in the Arc and we will go steady this year, as the plan is to keep him in training as a four-year-old."

The next step turned out to be the Emirates Airline Champion Stakes, but who can blame his connections for supplementing him for the Newmarket race? Rouget had a fast-improving young horse. Why not press on when he was in top form? Baron Guy de Rothschild, his owner-breeder, had celebrated his 96th birthday in May, though he was spry enough to go racing at Longchamp and Deauville and to be interviewed after welcoming back his winner. The Baron still keeps eight mares at his Haras de Meautry but he had cut down on his breeding and racing interests in the early 1990s.

When Pinson won the Group 3 Prix Daphnis at Longchamp in June, he was the Baron's first Pattern winner since Bleu de France was successful in the 1989 Prix Saint-Roman. The temptation to find out just how good this new star was must have been very strong. The grey may still develop into a far better four-year-old but it will be for new connections. He left Rouget's yard in Pau on November 19 and will be part of the Godolphin team when he reappears.

Pinson, incidentally, was first registered as a bay but he is in fact a dark grey with some much lighter markings, particularly the spots on his haunches. His four wins helped his trainer, whose 242 wins in 1994 remain a French record, to top the 200 mark for a sixth time. It was also Rouget's best-ever season on earnings. He would have beaten Andre Fabre in some years, but the perennial champion chose 2005 to have his own best season since 1997.

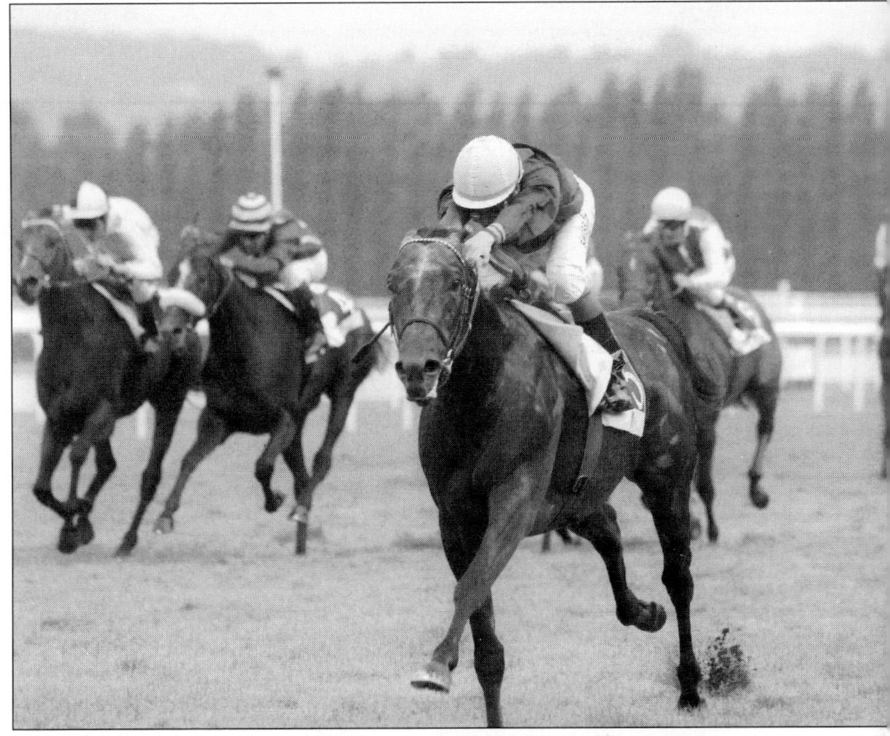

Pinson scores an easy win in the Prix Guillaume d'Ornano, stamping himself as a highly progressive three-year-old

Rouget starts off most of his horses in the south before asking them to take on the Parisians. Pinson, however, made his racecourse debut at the first meeting of the year at Longchamp towards the end of March. He stayed on from last place in the straight to take second in the final strides, a performance that ensured he would start odds-on when he next ran at Maisons-Laffitte six weeks later. He won by a neck, but with something in hand, from Blue Kite, who had added blinkers since finishing four lengths behind him on their debuts. It was the start of a sequence of four victories, during which Pinson was asked to stay a little further each time. His progress caught backers by surprise and, possibly his trainer as well, for he defeated better-fancied stable companions in both his Group-race victories.

Ioritz Mendizabal, who rode Pinson in his first three races, broke his left collarbone in a fall on a spare ride at Toulouse on June 19 and did not reappear until August 7. In his absence, Stephane Pasquier, whose progress had been as dramatic as that of Pinson, took the ride. Pasquier rode 23 winners in 2001, then 62, 74 and 100 in the next three years before finishing runner-up to Christophe Soumillon in 2005.

2005 **Race record**

10th Emirates Airline Champion Stakes (Group 1) (Newmarket, October 15) 3yo+ 1m2f Good to soft **105** (TS 90) 15 ran. *Chased leader until over 7f out, remained handy until weakened over 1f out (S Pasquier), beaten 12l by David Junior*

1st Prix Guillaume d'Ornano (Group 2) (Deauville, August 20) 3yo 1m2f Very soft **120** (TS 99) 6 ran. *Held up, 5th straight, brought to stands' rails, led distance, easily (S Pasquier), beat Ruwi by 6l*

1st Prix Daphnis (Group 3) (Longchamp, June 27) 3yo 1m1f Good **111** (TS 104) 8 ran. *Last until headway on inside from 2f out, slipped through on rail to lead inside final furlong, driven out (S Pasquier), beat Melanosporum by 1½l*

1st Prix Cambis (Longchamp, June 1) 3yo 1m½f Good **98** (TS 49) 5 ran. *Tracked leader until led approaching final furlong, ran on well, comfortably (I Mendizabal), beat Lonesome Me by ¾l*

1st Prix Vitiges (Maiden) (Right-handed) (Maisons-Laffitte, May 4) 3yo 1m Good **88** (TS 80) 10 ran. *Raced in 4th, headway 2f out, led approaching final furlong, ran on well, comfortably (I Mendizabal), beat Blue Kite by nk*

2nd Prix du Dragon (Unraced Colts & Geldings) (Longchamp, March 24) 3yo 1m Very soft **90** 9 ran. *Held up in rear, stayed on strongly final furlong to take 2nd close home, promising (I Mendizabal), beaten 3l by Anabaa Boy*

Pasquier kept Pinson last of the eight runners in the Prix Daphnis, a rare race of any significance on the 'moyenne piste' at Longchamp. They were still last early in the shorter than usual straight but Pasquier switched between Home Call and Musketier over 300 yards out. Once on the rails, he drove Pinson to hit the front with a furlong to run. Meanwhile, Olivier Peslier had been obliged to bring the Rouget-trained Melanosporum round the outside and the best he could do was to snatch second on the line.

Mendizabal was back in time for Deauville's Prix Guillaume d'Ornano but he chose Ruwi, who started at 9-10. Pasquier again rode Pinson. They raced in two files down the middle of the back straight, with Chrysander leading Kocab, Pinson and Ruwi and the other two wider out. All six continued well away from the rails on the turn but Pasquier set to work approaching the straight. They were in line abreast two furlongs from home, with Pinson nearest the stands side and Ruwi furthest out, but Pinson responded to that early pressure. He quickened up, and moved wider of his rivals, but ducked both left and right on several occasions before drawing right away in the final furlong for an impressive six-length victory.

Pasquier kept the mount at Newmarket while Mendizabal rode a winner at Marseille-Borely. Pinson started fourth favourite for the Champion and was best backed of the four French raiders, but he was found wanting in the final quarter-mile and faded into tenth place. The verdict, for now, must be that he was flattered by his Deauville win, which was gained on much softer ground. With a little luck, however, he will have the chance to disprove that opinion.

Pinson

grey colt, 4-4-2002

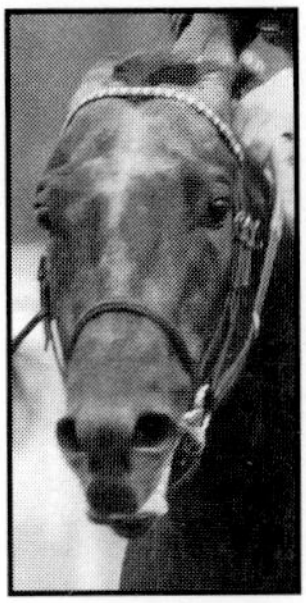

Parents	Grandparents	Great-grandparents	Great-great-grandparents
Halling ch 1991	Diesis	Sharpen Up	Atan Rocchetta
		Doubly Sure	Reliance Soft Angels
	Dance Machine	Green Dancer	Nijinsky GreenValley
		Never A Lady	Pontifex Camogie
Tadorne gr 1997	Inchinor	Ahonoora	Lorenzaccio Helen Nichols
		Inchmurrin	Lomond On Show
	Tambura	Kaldoun	Caro Katana
		Belle du Bresil	Akarad White Face

Bred by Baron Guy de Rothschild in Ireland

Sire Halling

Won 12 (8-10f) of 18 races from 3 to 5. Won 4 (inc. Cambridgeshire) at 3, won 4 (inc. Eclipse S-Gr1, York International-Gr1) at 4, won 4 (inc. Prix d'Ispahan-Gr1, Eclipse S-Gr1, York International-Gr1) at 5. Originally based at Dalham Hall Stud, switched before 2004 season to Emirates Stud Farm in Dubai, 2005 fee £30,000. First foals 1998, sire of: Chancellor (Gr2), Dandoun (Gr2), Giovane Imperatore (Gr2), Fisich (Gr2), Mkuzi (Gr3), Nordhal (Gr2), Vanderlin (Gr3), Franklins Gardens (Gr2), Norse Dancer (Gr3), Hattan (Gr3), Pinson (Gr2), The Geezer (Gr3).

Dam Tadorne

From 11 starts at 2 and 3 in France, won 3 races at up to 8f, also placed twice at 3 in 8f Listed events. By high-class 2yo/miler and good sire, half-sister to smart 2yo Ximb and very useful 2yo/miler Welcome Millenium. Dam of: Pinson (2002 c by Halling; Gr2 winner), Nageur (2003 c by Celtic Swing), Tarpon (2004 c by Vettori).

Pedigree assessment

The lightly raced Pinson is an obvious candidate to progress at 4, and his pedigree is consistent with that. Halling progressed well at 4 and 5, and he has numerous offspring who have followed that pattern. *JH*

Pleasant Home (USA)

4yo bay filly **124**

Seeking The Gold (USA) - Our Country Place (USA) (Pleasant Colony (USA))

Owner Phipps Stable

Trainer C McGaughey III

Breeder Phipps Stable

Career: **12** starts | won **5** | second **2** | third **3** | **£724,295** win and place

By James Willoughby

A NEW chapter was added to the annals of the Phipps family when Pleasant Home scored a wildly impressive victory in the Breeders' Cup Distaff. The black silks with cherry cap have been carried by some of the most famous thoroughbreds in US racing history, but Pleasant Home would hardly have merited a footnote in this story had she not turned up at Belmont Park. She was unheralded at 30-1, odds that were much inflated by the presence of the star filly Ashado, who was expected to end her racing career by successfully defending the title she had won so grittily at Lone Star Park.

If Pleasant Home was overlooked, perhaps she should not have been. Brought along in typically patient style by her Hall of Fame trainer Shug McGaughey, for whom she was a ninth Breeders' Cup winner, the progressive filly had appeared unlucky when second in Keeneland's influential Spinster Stakes, hampered as she started to run on strongly from off the pace.

"She closed a lot of ground at Keeneland, which is tough to do at that track," McGaughey said when discussing Pleasant Home's chances positively before the Breeders' Cup.

Neither was Pleasant Home exposed. She had made just 11 starts before Belmont, winning four times, including the same Grade 3 Bed o'Roses Handicap at Aqueduct in April that her full-sister Country Hideaway had landed five years earlier.

Whatever latent talent she possessed was drawn out when a strong pace transpired in the Distaff. Moreover, Belmont is unique in presenting only one turn for runners to negotiate in nine-furlong races – ideal for the long-striding Pleasant Home.

Capeside Lady won the early lead, but she had to work hard to get there – the first quarter of 23.33sec was faster than in the subsequent Classic but gained her an advantage of only a length. Despite an unabating

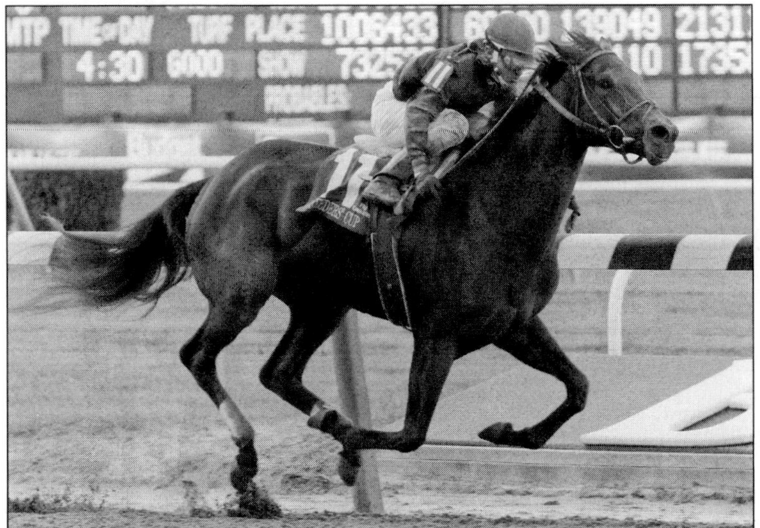

Pleasant Home upsets the odds in the Breeders' Cup Distaff, scorching to victory by more than nine lengths

tempo, the majority of the field raced close up and most of those prominent were probably doing too much.

After a half-mile, Pleasant Home had only one behind her while racing on the rail, but she began to make ground as the early pace took its effect on the leaders. Halfway around the turn, she got a dream run that carried her right to the heels of Ashado and Society Selection.

Jockey Cornelio Velasquez had only one decision to make – and it was an easy one. With Pleasant Home so full of running, he was able to hook her out and around horses entering the straight, rather than persisting with his challenge on the inside.

As soon as she straightened up, Pleasant Home's raking stride did the rest, taking her further and further clear until the line interrupted her increasing margin as it reached nine and a quarter lengths. Society Selection was second and Ashado third, the last-named filly deprived by a photo from overtaking Azeri as the all-time money-winning female.

Pleasant Home's margin of victory was the second-biggest in Cup history, fittingly eclipsed only by Inside Information, who carried very similar livery when winning the 1995 edition of the Distaff by 13 and a half lengths. Apart from these two, the Phipps colours have reached the Breeders' Cup winner's enclosure on five other occasions – all of their horses born and raised at the historic Claiborne Farm in Kentucky.

In 1989 at Gulfstream Park, the family enjoyed its most lucrative day when Dancing Spree won the Sprint and Rhythm the Juvenile, but it is the other three victories which have far greater recognition.

At Churchill Downs the previous year, Personal Ensign played her part

2005 Race record

1st Emirates Airlines Breeders' Cup Distaff (Grade 1) (Belmont Park, October 29) 3yo+ 1m1f Fast **124** 13 ran. *In touch, headway on outside over 3f out, 5th and ridden straight, led and ridden clear over 1f out, impressive (C Velasquez), beat Society Selection by 9¼l*

2nd Juddmonte Spinster Stakes (Grade 1) (Dirt) (Keeneland, October 9) 3yo+ 1m1f Fast **112** 11 ran. *Held up in rear, headway on outside over 2f out, ran on under pressure to take 2nd well inside final furlong (C Velasquez), beaten 1¾l by Pampered Princess*

2nd Ballerina Stakes (Grade 1) (Saratoga, August 28) 3yo+ 7f Muddy **109** 7 ran. *Outpaced early, raced in 6th, headway 2f out, ran on to take 2nd well inside final furlong (C Velasquez), beaten 5¼l by Happy Ticket*

3rd Allowance Optional Claiming Race (Saratoga, August 14) 4yo+ 6f Fast **96** 6 ran. *Behind to halfway, 4th straight, stayed on final furlong, nearest at finish (C Velasquez), beaten 3¼l by Smokey Glacken*

4th Pimlico Breeders' Cup Distaff Handicap (Grade 3) (Pimlico, May 20) 3yo+ 1m½ Sloppy **94** 4 ran. *Raced in 2nd, effort when bumped 1½f out, soon weakened (C Velasquez), beaten 7¼l by Silmaril*

1st Bed O'Roses Breeders' Cup Handicap (Grade 3) (Aqueduct, April 23) 3yo+ 1m Good **109** 7 ran. *Held up in 6th, headway to lead just inside final furlong, drew clear (C Velasquez), beat Traci Girl by 5¼l*

1st Allowance Race (Gulfstream Park, March 27) 4yo+ 1m Fast 7 ran. *Raced in 4th, ridden to lead inside final furlong, driven out (C Velasquez), beat Birthday Song by ¾l*

3rd Allowance Optional Claiming Race (Gulfstream Park, January 16) 4yo+ 1m1f Good 8 ran. *Always prominent, led narrowly 2½f out until headed over 1f out, stayed on (C Velasquez), beaten 1l by Valliant Dancer*

2004

3rd Allowance Race (Belmont Park, October 24) 3yo+ 1m½ Fast 5 ran ● **1st** Allowance Race (Belmont Park, September 22) 3yo+ 1m½ Fast 8 ran ● **1st** Maiden Special Weight (Belmont Park, July 5) 3yo+ 7½f Fast 6 ran ● **4th** Maiden Special Weight (Aqueduct, April 24) 3yo+ 7f Fast 9 ran

in one of the most thrilling races ever when retaining her unbeaten record in a gut-wrenching duel in the Distaff with Kentucky Derby victress Winning Colors. Personal Ensign went on to produce the 1996 Juvenile Fillies winner My Flag, who in turn threw the winner of the 2003 renewal of the latter contest, Storm Flag Flying.

Because of her size, Pleasant Home did not make the racecourse until the April of her three-year-old season in 2004. She had a couple of brief interruptions due to physical setbacks – "nothing major" according to her trainer – and did not begin to blossom until the Aqueduct victory mentioned above.

It is easy to see that Pleasant Home has all the credentials of a successful broodmare. She will retire to Claiborne and visit Ghostzapper's sire Awesome Again in 2006. Look for her as the dam of a Breeders' Cup winner from 2010 onwards. It would hardly be the biggest surprise in the world.

Pleasant Home

bay filly, 5-5-2001

Seeking The Gold b 1985	**Mr Prospector**	Raise A Native	Native Dancer Raise You
		Gold Digger	Nashua Sequence
	Con Game	Buckpasser	Tom Fool Busanda
		Broadway	Hasty Road Flitabout
Our Country Place br 1992	Pleasant Colony	His Majesty	Ribot Flower Bowl
		Sun Colony	Sunrise Flight Colonia
	Maplejinsky	Nijinsky	Northern Dancer Flaming Page
		Gold Beauty	**Mr Prospector** Stick To Beauty

Bred by Phipps Stable in US

Sire Seeking The Gold

Won 8 of his 15 starts. At 2, won sole start. At 3, won 6 (inc. Super Derby-Gr1, Peter Pan S-Gr2, Dwyer S-Gr1), also 2nd 5 times inc. Travers S-Gr1, Wood Memorial S-Gr1, Haskell Invitational H-Gr1, Breeders' Cup Classic-Gr1. At 4, won 1, also 2nd Metropolitan H-Gr1. By outstanding sire, half-brother to Gr1 winner Fast Play (by Seattle Slew) and Gr3 winner Stacked Pack (by Majestic Light). Stands at Claiborne Farm, Kentucky, 2006 fee $125,000. Sire of Gr1 winners: Heavenly Prize (Frizette S, Alabama S, Gazelle H, Beldame S, Apple Blossom H, Hempstead H, Go For Wand H, John A Morris H), Secret Savings (Doncaster H-Aus), Squire Jones (British Columbia Derby-Can), Flanders (Frizette S, Spinaway S, Breeders' Cup Juvenile Fillies), Seeking The Pearl (NHK Mile Cup, Prix Maurice de Gheest), Cape Town (Florida Derby), Meiner Love (Sprinters S-Jap), Dubai Millennium (Prix Jacques le Marois, QEII S, Dubai World Cup, Prince of Wales's S), Gold Tiara (Nanbu Jai-Jap), Lujain (Middle Park S), Oh What A Windfall (Matron S), Cash Run (Breeders' Cup Juvenile Fillies), Catch The Ring (Canadian Oaks-Can), Dream Supreme (Test S, Ballerina H), Favorite Funtime (Santa Maria H), Victory Ride (Test S), Pleasant Home (Breeders' Cup Distaff).

Dam Our Country Place

Unraced. By top-class 10-12f performer and very good sire who imparted stamina, out of dual 3yo Grade 1 winner. Half-sister to outstanding filly Sky Beauty, family of Dayjur. Dam of: Country Hideaway (1996 f by Seeking The Gold; Gr2 winner), Matlacha Pass (1997 f by Seeking The Gold; winner), Seeking A Home (1998 c by Seeking The Gold; unraced), Home Sweet Home (1999 f by Seeking The Gold; unplaced), Preaching (2000 f by Pulpit; placed), Pleasant Home (2001 f by Seeking The Gold; Breeders' Cup Distaff-Gr1), 2002-05 no foal. In foal to Seeking The Gold.

Pedigree assessment

A superbly bred distaffer who has now put in a superb performance. Pleasant Home is by a speed-oriented sire out of a mare from a fairly speedy family, and it is a reasonable bet that Pleasant Colony's stamina helped her to stay the nine furlongs of the Distaff well. The Seeking The Gold-Pleasant Colony cross also yielded Cash Run. Pleasant Home, from a long line of talented racemares, is an immensely valuable broodmare prospect for the Phipps family. *JH*

Powerscourt

5yo bay horse **124**

Sadler's Wells (USA) - Rainbow Lake (Rainbow Quest (USA))

Owner Mrs John Magnier

Trainer A P O'Brien

Breeder Juddmonte Farms

Career: **21** starts | won **5** | second **6** | third **3** | **£1,068,673** win and place

By Paul Haigh

POWERSCOURT, retired to stud following a setback while he was being prepared for the Breeders' Cup Turf, was a horse with two reputations. On our side of the Atlantic he was a bit of an enigma, a horse you couldn't quite get a handle on, a flatterer who more than occasionally deceived. On the American side he was a star, the best horse in successive Arlington Millions; the moral winner, many thought, of the 2004 Breeders' Cup Turf, who would have been the actual winner if he hadn't been unleashed too soon.

The difference between the two Powerscourts was probably nothing much more complicated than Salix (or Lasix as it used to be known), the anti-bleeding diuretic that's permitted over there but very definitely not over here; but to give him the benefit of the doubt there may have been just a bit more to it than that. It could have been that tight-turning American tracks and the even pace at which American races are run just suited him. It could also have been that he didn't quite stay 12 furlongs, which could account for the in-and-out pattern of his career; and that August, when they run the Million, just might have been his time of year. Perhaps his victory in the 2003 Great Voltigeur at the York August meeting, when he appeared to outbattle his Leger-winning stablemate Brian Boru, was a flash in the pan that gave everybody the wrong idea about his stamina – including Jamie Spencer at Lone Star Park.

Powerscourt's 2005 began with some people wondering whether his first past the post before disqualification in the 2004 Arlington Million was going to prove the highlight of his career. When he disappointed in fifth, though beaten only just over three lengths behind Phoenix Reach, in the Sheema Classic at the Dubai World Cup meeting it just seemed to confirm the suspicion that he was good, but not that good. The Sheema Classic was over 12 furlongs, however; and so too was his next run in the Hardwicke Stakes at Royal Ascot at York, when even the drop down

Powerscourt (right) lands the Arlington Million, gaining compensation for his 2004 disqualification from first place

to Group 2 failed to address what seemed to be a pattern of regression as he trailed in more than ten lengths behind the winner, Bandari.

Just over a month later he was sent for the Scottish Derby at Ayr, another Group 2, now open to older horses, where his length-and-a-quarter defeat by what may have been a very high-class horse in Imperial Stride suggested either that he was already in better form than he had been at York, or that the much-criticised ground at York had been to blame for his Hardwicke flop, or that the return to ten furlongs was more to his liking. Then came his second trip to Chicago.

Kieren Fallon was very bullish about him, insisting he was "just coming right" and "certain to run a very good race". There still looked plenty of room for doubt, though, as he faced not just the 2004 Breeders' Cup Turf winner Better Talk Now, who cut him down with ease after he had been clear halfway up the straight in Texas, but Kitten's Joy, allegedly the best turf horse in America for a long time, whose pencilled-in plans included the Arc and the Japan Cup and who as a three-year-old had actually recorded a faster time than Powerscourt in winning the Grade 1 Secretariat Stakes over the same ten furlongs little more than an hour after Powerscourt's controversial Million disqualification in 2004.

The race itself proved no contest, however, for Powerscourt travelled as well as Fallon predicted he would, pounced on the leaders entering the straight and drew away even more impressively than he had the year before to win by an extending three lengths from Kitten's Joy, with Better Talk Now no better than fourth. It would have been no surprise if the five-year-old had been retired on the spot, because that revenge victory, both on the Breeders' Cup Turf winner and on the Arlington stewards,

2005 Race record

1st Arlington Million (Grade 1) (Arlington, August 13) 3yo+ 1m2f Yielding **124** 10 ran. *Raced in 6th, took closer order from 4f out, 4th straight, driven to challenge final furlong, led 100yds out, ran on strongly (K Fallon), beat Kitten's Joy by 3l*

2nd Daily Record Scottish Derby (Group 2) (Ayr, July 18) 3yo+ 1m2f Good **118** (TS 104) 4 ran. *Chased winner, effort over 2f out, hung left over 1f out, kept on inside final furlong (K Fallon), beaten 1¼l by Imperial Stride*

4th Hardwicke Stakes (Group 2) (York, June 18) 4yo+ 1m4f Firm **106** (TS 87) 6 ran. *Held up, effort 3f out, soon ridden beaten 2f out (J P Murtagh), beaten 10½l by Bandari*

5th Dubai Sheema Classic Sponsored By Dubai Water Front (Turf) (Group 1) (Nad Al Sheba, March 26) 4yo+ 1m4f Good to firm **114** 11 ran. *Mid-division, ridden straight, stayed on near finish, never troubled leaders (K Fallon), beaten 3l by Phoenix Reach*

Other notable runs

2004 **4th** Cathay Pacific Hong Kong Cup (Group 1) (Sha Tin, December 12) 3yo+ 1m2f Good to firm **118** 14 ran ● **3rd** John Deere Breeders' Cup Turf (Grade 1) (Lone Star Park, October 30) 3yo+ 1m4f Yielding **119** 8 ran ● **3rd** Baileys Irish Champion Stakes (Group 1) (Leopardstown, September 11) 3yo+ 1m2f Good to firm **124** (TS 125) 8 ran ● **4th** Arlington Million XXII (Grade 1) (Arlington, August 14) 3yo+ 1m2f Firm **118** 13 ran ● **2nd** Grosser Dallmayr-Preis Bayerisches Zuchtrennen (Group 1) (Munich, August 1) 3yo+ 1m2f Good **115** 9 ran ● **2nd** Prince of Wales's Stakes (Group 1) (Ascot, June 16) 4yo+ 1m2f Good to firm **121** (TS 114) 10 ran ● **1st** Tattersalls Gold Cup (Group 1) (Curragh, May 23) 4yo+ 1m2½f Good to firm **122** (TS 101) 6 ran **2003** **3rd** Irish Field St Leger (Group 1) (Curragh, September 13) 3yo+ 1m6f Good to firm **121** (TS 36) 6 ran ● **1st** Daily Telegraph Great Voltigeur Stakes (Group 2) (York, August 19) 3yo 1m4f Good to firm **121** (TS 102) 9 ran ● **1st** Seapoint Race (Leopardstown, July 16) 3yo+ 1m2f Good **112** (TS 82) 5 ran **2002** ● **2nd** Racing Post Trophy (Group 1) (Doncaster, October 26) 2yo 1m Soft **111** (TS 73) 9 ran ● **1st** www.punchestown.com EBF Maiden (Punchestown, October 17) 2yo 7½f Soft **92** 17 ran

had certainly done enough to establish his right to stand in the USA.

However, Aidan O'Brien, and no doubt Fallon too, were obviously convinced that American conditions were the key to him, and that under them he could cope with the return to 12 furlongs and set his record straight in the Breeders' Cup Turf itself. Two weeks before Belmont and what should have been his final race, however, came the news that he "wasn't quite himself" and that those of us who had bought into the theory that the trip as much as anything else – even the Salix – was what really determined the level of his performances were not going to get the chance to be proved right or wrong.

He retired to Coolmore's Ashford Stud in Kentucky with a career record of only five victories from 21 outings, a pretty poor return for a horse with pretensions to championship status; but in retrospect, and in view not just of his two Millions but of his three-quarter length third to Azamour in a strong-looking 2004 Irish Champion Stakes, he was always very near the best around over ten furlongs and on his favoured fast ground. He should make a very interesting American-based representative of his illustrious sire, Sadler's Wells.

Powerscourt

bay horse, 1-4-2000

Sadler's Wells b 1981	Northern Dancer	Nearctic	Nearco Lady Angela
		Natalma	Native Dancer Almahmoud
	Fairy Bridge	Bold Reason	Hail To Reason Lalun
		Special	Forli Thong
Rainbow Lake b 1990	Rainbow Quest	Blushing Groom	Red God Runaway Bride
		I Will Follow	Herbager Where You Lead
	Rockfest	Stage Door Johnny	Prince John Peroxide Blonde
		Rock Garden	Roan Rocket Nasira

Bred by Juddmonte Farms in England.

Sire Sadler's Wells

Won 6 of 11 races, inc. Beresford S.-Gr3, Irish Derby Trial-Gr2, Irish 2,000 Guineas-Gr1, Eclipse S.-Gr1, Phoenix Champion S.-Gr1. Also 2nd in Prix du Jockey-Club-Gr1, King George VI & Queen Elizabeth S.-Gr1. Impeccably bred top-class performer from 8-12f, handsome, tough and consistent. Sire of Gr1 winners: Braashee, French Glory, In The Wings (3), Old Vic (2), Prince Of Dance, Scenic, Salsabil (5), Opera House (3), Runyon, Saddlers' Hall, El Prado, Johann Quatz, Masad, Barathea (2), Fatherland, Fort Wood, Intrepidity (3), Carnegie (2), King's Theatre (2), Northern Spur (2), Moonshell, Muncie, Poliglote, Chief Contender, Dance Design, Darazari, Luna Wells, Cloudings, Ebadiyla (2), Entrepreneur, In Command, Kayf Tara (4), Dream Well (2), Greek Dance, King Of Kings (2), Leggera, Commander Collins, Daliapour, Montjeu (6), Saffron Walden, Aristotle, Beat Hollow (4), Subtle Power, Galileo (3), Imagine (2), Milan, Perfect Soul, Sequoyah, Sligo Bay, Ballingarry, Black Sam Bellamy (2), Gossamer (2), High Chaparral (6), Islington (4), Quarter Moon, Sholokov, Alberto Giacometti, Brian Boru (2), Doyen, Powerscourt (2), Refuse To Bend (4), Yesterday, Quiff, Yeats, Playful Act, Linda's Lad.

Dam Rainbow Lake

Won 3 of 6 races, inc. Lancashire Oaks-Gr3. Lean, leggy type in training. High-class performer at best. Stayed 12f. Well-bred. Sister and half-sister to 5 other winners, inc. Vertex (c by Shirley Heights; Listed in Italy). Dam of: Brimming (1995 c by Generous; winner), Barbican (1996 c by Caerleon; unplaced), Unaware (1997 g by Unfuwain; winner), Polish Lake (1998 f by Polish Precedent; unraced), Lake Of Dreams (1999 g by Polish Precedent; unplaced), Powerscourt (2000 c by Sadler's Wells; dual Gr1 winner), Kind (2001 f by Danehill; winner), Marella (2002 f by Desert Prince; unplaced), Electric Storm (2003 c by Zafonic; unraced to date). She has a yearling colt by Sadler's Wells, was barren to him in 2005, and covered by him again.

Pedigree assessment

Clearly the best horse in the 2004 Arlington Million, but relegated from first to fourth, Powerscourt was even more emphatically the outstanding runner on parade in the 2005 renewal; indeed, he won with a career-best performance. Although he stayed a mile and a half, and contrived third place in an Irish St Leger, he proved most effective at ten furlongs, which was also his sire's optimum trip. His dam's stud record was disappointing until she visited Sadler's Wells, so it is no surprise that she has been a regular mate for the long-time champion in recent years. *TM*

Pride (Fr)

5yo chestnut mare **123**

Peintre Celebre (USA) - Specificity (USA) (Alleged (USA))

Owner N P Bloodstock

Trainer A de Royer-Dupre

Breeder N P Bloodstock

Career: **19** starts | won **5** | second **4** | third **3** | **£591,420** win and place

By Richard Austen

FROM the front end of a pantomime horse in Stockport to the highest-paid actor in the world – a spell away from Britain can see talent blossom. Pride's story was not quite of Charlie Chaplin proportions, but the mare undoubtedly moved in very different circles when she returned in 2005.

Pride's initial appearances in Britain were in 2003. Trained by Gerard Butler, she was beaten at evens on the Lingfield all-weather, won at Newbury in what the *Racing Post* described as "a shocking maiden for the course" and ended in mid-division in a Listed race at Doncaster, officially rated 80 at the time. In 2005 there was no mixing with the hoi polloi.

With Alain de Royer-Dupre in France for 2004, Pride won the Group 3 Prix Allez France at Chantilly in May and the Group 2 Prix du Conseil de Paris at Longchamp in October. She ran three times at Group 1 level, on the first occasion going down by about four lengths in the Grand Prix de Saint-Cloud and on the third by just over eight, meeting trouble in running, when 13th of 20 in the Arc.

That Pride had improved again for 2005 was immediately apparent when she ran the Arc winner to a short neck in the Ganay. The Form Book has her in sixth, but Pride was demoted after hanging right and causing interference before she lost out to Bago's late run up the rails.

A 33-1 shot when last seen in Britain, Pride was back as an 8-1 chance at Epsom in the Coronation Cup. Her sixth of seven was an anti-climax, but that first disappointment for de Royer-Dupre would also be her last.

In the Prix Jean Romanet at Deauville in August, Pride went one better than in 2004 when she came with a smooth challenge to catch front-running favourite Red Bloom. Next was the Prix Foy Gray d'Albion Barriere at Longchamp on the day of Arc trials. A year earlier, Pride ran on the same card in the Vermeille and was unlucky, coming fast but too late after getting squeezed out at a vital stage. Perusing the 2005 Foy line-up, from an

Pride beats Alkaased and Shirocco in the Prix Foy, starting a fine autumn campaign where she mixed with the best

end-of season perspective anyway, she looks most unlucky in coming up against Alkaased and Shirocco, but their career-defining victories lay in the future and on September 11 neither the Japan Cup winner nor the Breeders' Cup Turf winner was a match for her.

Pride took up the running just inside the final two furlongs. Both the favourites had a crack at her in what was the fastest of the three trials, but Shirocco and Alkaased were seen off in turn as Pride went on to score by two and a half lengths. "She is quite a difficult ride and tended to pull hard last year," said de Royer-Dupre. "She is more relaxed this year and the way she won the Prix Foy came as no surprise to me."

In the Arc three weeks later, Pride started 16-1 compared to 33-1 12 months earlier. One thing stayed the same, though, as she failed to get a clear run and ended up just a length closer to the winner.

Two opportunities remained for Pride to add a Group 1 triumph to her three at Group 2 level. The Champion Stakes at Newmarket attracted four runners from France, with Christophe Lemaire, who had ridden Pride on her last three starts, deserting her for Touch Of Land. "Maybe Christophe thinks that Touch Of Land has a better chance. Maybe Christophe is wrong," said de Royer-Dupre, and as Touch Of Land weakened out of contention approaching the final furlong, Pride was just warming up. However, her strong run in the wake of David Junior never promised to get her past him.

One reason given for the jockey's switch of allegiance was that Lemaire

2005 Race record

2nd Cathay Pacific Hong Kong Cup (Group 1) (Sha Tin, December 11) 3yo+ 1m2f Good to firm **122** 10 ran. *Held up, 9th straight, headway on outside from 2f out, took 2nd 100yds out, ran on (C Soumillon), beaten nk by Vengeance Of Rain*

2nd Emirates Airline Champion Stakes (Group 1) (Newmarket, October 15) 3yo+ 1m2f Good to soft **122** (TS 108) 15 ran. *Held up, headway over 1f out, ran on (C Soumillon), beaten 3/4l by David Junior*

7th Prix de l'Arc de Triomphe Lucien Barriere (Group 1) (Longchamp, October 2) 3yo+ 1m4f Good to soft **117** (TS 118) 15 ran. *Towards rear when not clear run approaching straight, stayed on, never a factor (C P Lemaire), beaten 7 1/4l by Hurricane Run*

1st Prix Foy Gray d'Albion Barriere (Group 2) (Longchamp, September 11) 4yo+ 1m4f Good to soft **123** (TS 116) 6 ran. *Held up, went 3rd 5f out, 3rd straight, led on rails just inside final 2f, ran on well (C P Lemaire), beat Alkaased by 2 1/2l*

1st Prix Jean Romanet (Group 2) (Deauville, August 21) 4yo+ 1m2f Soft **116** (TS 84) 12 ran. *4th straight, smooth headway from well over 1f out, led 100yds out, ran on well (C P Lemaire), beat Red Bloom by 3/4l*

6th Vodafone Coronation Cup (Group 1) (Epsom, June 3) 4yo+ 1m4f Good **105** (TS 92) 7 ran. *Held up in rear, last and in touch straight, soon outpaced, no danger after (O Peslier), beaten 8 1/2l by Yeats*

6th Prix Ganay (Group 1) (Longchamp, April 24) 4yo+ 1m2 1/2f Very soft **118** (TS 51) 9 ran. *Held up, 8th straight, progress on outside 1 1/2f out, hung right and bumped Short Pause, finished 2nd, btn sht nk by Bago, placed 6th (I Mendizabal)*

Other runs

2004 **1st** Prix du Conseil de Paris (Group 2) (Longchamp, October 17) 3yo+ 1m4f Heavy **116** (TS 114) 8 ran ● **13th** Prix de l'Arc de Triomphe Lucien Barriere (Group 1) (Longchamp, October 3) 3yo+ 1m4f Good **113** (TS 107) 19 ran ● **3rd** Prix Vermeille Fouquet's Barriere (Group 1) (Longchamp, September 12) 3-4yo 1m4f Soft **113** (TS 107) 13 ran ● **2nd** Prix Jean Romanet (Group 2) (Deauville, August 22) 4yo+ 1m2f Very soft **113** (TS 65) 13 ran ● **5th** Grand Prix de Saint-Cloud (Group 1) (Saint-Cloud, July 4) 3yo+ 1m4f Good to soft **112** (TS 96) 10 ran ● **3rd** Prix Corrida (Group 2) (Saint-Cloud, May 31) 4yo+ 1m2 1/2f Good to soft **107** (TS 71) 10 ran ● **1st** Prix Allez France (Group 3) (Chantilly, May 7) 4yo+ 1m2f Soft **107** (TS 83) 11 ran ● **4th** Prix de l'Axe Majeur (Longchamp, April 22) 4yo+ 1m2f Good to soft **100** 13 ran 2003 **7th** Auker Rhodes Blue Parrot EBF Gillies Fillies' Stakes (Listed) (Doncaster, November 7) 3yo+ 1m2 1/2f Good **93** (TS 77) 16 ran ● **1st** CiSTM Maiden Stakes (Newbury, October 25) 3yo 1m2f Good to firm **78** (TS 68) 8 ran ● **2nd** Venner Shipley Maiden Stakes (Div I) (Lingfield (AW), October 8) 3yo+ 1m Standard **66** (TS 18) 12 ran 2002 ● **3rd** Prix de Noiremare (Deauville, August 31) 2yo 7f Good to soft 14 ran

was keen to ride Touch Of Land in Hong Kong. That was another bad call, for he had to make do with a cut of fifth prize-money in the Cup, while up ahead Pride was earning Christophe Soumillon a share of almost £228,000 more. The main prize, though, eluded Pride by a neck. Trying to come from ninth of ten in the straight was too much and the local champion Vengeance Of Rain proved just too strong.

The consistent Pride is expected to be at stud in 2006. With a bit more give in the ground at Sha Tin, or a bit more luck, she would have retired with a Group 1 win.

Pride *chestnut mare, 20-4-2000*

Peintre Celebre ch 1994	Nureyev	Northern Dancer	Nearctic Natalma
		Special	Forli Thong
	Peinture Bleue	Alydar	Raise A Native Sweet Tooth
		Petroleuse	Habitat Plencia
Specificity b 1988	Alleged	Hoist The Flag	Tom Rolfe Wavy Navy
		Princess Pout	Prince John Determined Lady
	Mandera	Vaguely Noble	Vienna Noble Lassie
		Foolish One	Tom Fool Miss Disco

Bred by NP Bloodstock Ltd in France

Sire Peintre Celebre

Won 5 (8-12f) of 7 races. Won once from 2 starts at 2, won 4 (Prix Greffulhe-Gr2, Prix du Jockey-Club-Gr1, Grand Prix de Paris-Gr1, Prix de l'Arc de Triomphe-Gr1) from 5 starts at 3. Sire top-class miler and outstanding sire, with several good stallion sons. Dam 12f Grade 2 winner, out of Group 3-winning half-sister to outstanding 12f filly Pawneese. Stands at Coolmore Stud (2001 in Japan), 2006 fee €25,000. First foals 2000, sire of (northern hemisphere foals): Dai Jin (Deutsches Derby-Gr1, Aral Pokal-Gr1), Pride (Gr2), Super Celebre (Gr2), Vallee Enchantee (Hong Kong Vase-Gr1), Castledale (Santa Anita Derby-Gr1, Shoemaker Breeders' Cup Mile-Gr1), Mister Monet (Gr2), Pearl Of Love (Gran Criterium-Gr1).

Dam Specificity

Unraced at 2, won 2 of 7 starts at 3 and 4. At 3, won 1 (12f) of 2 starts. At 4, won 16f George Stubbs S-Listed, also 2nd Cesarewitch H, 3rd Prix Belle de Nuit-Listed. By dual Arc winner and heavy stamina influence, out of 12f Gr3 winner. Half-sister to St Leger winner and Derby second Touching Wood. Grand-dam Foolish One half-sister to Bold Ruler. Dam of: Specifically (1994 f by Sky Classic; winner, dam of 2005 Gr2 winner Speciosa and SW Major Rhythm), Westwego (1995 c by Gone West; winner), Bulacan (1996 c by Dynaformer; winner), Noble Calling (1997 c by Caller ID; Flat/hurdle winner), Only The Lonely (1998 f by Bering; winner), Tenderly (1999 f by Danehill; placed), Pride (2000 f by Peintre Celebre; Gr2 winner), Infinity (2001 f by Bering; unplaced), Malakas (2002 c by Bering; unplaced), Right Stuff (2003 c by Dansili; unraced), 2005 f by Polish Precedent.

Pedigree assessment

An admirable filly with a touch more pace than her pedigree suggested she might have. She was the flagbearer in 2005 for Peintre Celebre, who can be forgiven an apparently quiet year as his three-year-olds were conceived in Japan. This is an excellent family, and interestingly Pride's vastly inferior half-sister Specifically has already produced two stakes winners, notably 2005 Rockfel Stakes winner Speciosa (by Danehill Dancer). A lovely broodmare prospect. *JH*

Proclamation (Ire)

3yo grey colt **128**

King's Best (USA) - Shamarra (Fr) (Zayyani)

Owner H R H Princess Haya Of Jordan

Trainer J Noseda

Breeder Cathal M Ryan

Career: **6** starts | won **4** | second **0** | third **0** | **£238,438** win and place

By James Willoughby

THE Cantor Spreadfair Sussex Stakes at Goodwood in July produced one of the major talking points of the season. That the winner Proclamation quickened impressively is in no doubt. But was he worth more than the half-length margin over Soviet Song or was the runner-up the moral winner?

It was a debate that found no solution in a rematch, nor was there evidence in the later performances of the two horses. Proclamation was soundly beaten in the William Hill Sprint Cup at Haydock on his subsequent outing, and Soviet Song did not race again.

The strong-finishing Soviet Song was said to be unlucky because she had to wait to deliver her effort after being trapped in a pocket by Proclamation. That may be the case, but she did not accelerate with the same vigour as the winner and only the latter's tendency to idle resulted in the proximity of the two at the finish.

Proclamation initially started his run from behind Soviet Song as they came down the hill. He had been ridden extremely confidently by Mick Kinane after Ad Valorem had cut out a strong pace, with Mac Love and Tucker keeping the leader honest.

Even at this brisk tempo, Proclamation was inclined to race keenly. Approaching the two-furlong pole, Kinane began to make his move down the outside as Soviet Song waited. The chance was there for the mare to be constricted, and Kinane made no mistake. Once the tactical advantage had accrued, he put Proclamation into overdrive at the point he sensed his ensnared opponent was at her most vulnerable.

Changing his legs and responding to the impetus with no hesitation, Proclamation unleashed a tremendous burst that overwhelmed his 11 opponents. It was a turn of speed the like of which is rarely seen in a top-class mile race, akin perhaps to that produced by Mark Of Esteem in the 1996 Queen Elizabeth II Stakes.

Proclamation, under a fine ride from Mick Kinane, holds off Soviet Song to land the Group 1 Sussex Stakes

The surge took Proclamation into a clear lead at the furlong pole, but he began to hang markedly right. Only the far rail arrested his deviation, but he was concurrently pulling himself up and had to be driven out firmly towards the line.

Proclamation's tendency to idle and hang makes him a difficult horse to assess. It was also in evidence on the two starts preceding his seminal moment, a three-length defeat of the useful Tucker in a Listed race over the Sussex Stakes course and distance in late May and a superb win in the Jersey Stakes at York the following month.

The colt certainly wasn't aided by a wide draw in the seven-furlong Jersey, but he produced another good turn of speed, circling the field to defeat Camacho by two and a half lengths. He would have won by twice as far if he had been well drawn and had refrained from hanging, this time to the left.

The speed and acceleration Proclamation revealed had taken his trainer Jeremy Noseda by surprise. Though deserving of a good deal of credit for nurturing such a quirky individual, the trainer was the first to admit that his early assessments of the big, grey colt were somewhat awry.

Before Proclamation's racecourse debut in a backend Newmarket maiden in 2004, Noseda referred to him as "a backward horse who will develop into a nice handicapper next year". It wasn't gauging his potential that proved the trainer's most notable misjudgement, it was assessing his distance requirements.

With the misapprehension that he was handling a Derby contender, Noseda had started Proclamation's three-year-old campaign in the totesport

2005 Race record

11th William Hill Sprint Cup (Group 1) (Haydock, September 3) 3yo+ 6f Good **105** (TS 87) 17 ran. *Slowly into stride, held up, hung left when headway over 1f out, weakened inside final furlong (L Dettori), beaten 5½l by Goodricke*

1st Cantor Spreadfair Sussex Stakes (Group 1) (Goodwood, July 27) 3yo+ 1m Soft **128** (TS 113) 12 ran. *Dwelt, held up in last, good progress on outer 2f out, quickened impressively to lead over 1f out and soon clear, idled and hung right, held on (M J Kinane), beat Soviet Song by ½l*

1st Jersey Stakes (Group 3) (York, June 15) 3yo 7f Good to firm **121** (TS 113) 21 ran. *Steadied start, held up and behind, hampered bend over 4f out, headway on outside over 2f out, led 1f out, edged left, ran on strongly (J P Murtagh), beat Camacho by 2½l*

1st Empire Property Group Cup Stakes (Registered As The Heron Stakes) (Listed) (Goodwood, May 28) 3yo 1m Good **116** (TS 102) 9 ran. *Took keen hold, held up in rear, headway over 2f out, quickened to lead approaching final furlong, edged right and soon pushed clear, comfortably (L Dettori), beat Tucker by 3l*

6th totesport Dante Stakes (Group 2) (York, May 12) 3yo 1m2½f Soft **74** (TS 52) 6 ran. *Took keen hold, chased leading pair, effort 3f out, soon ridden and beaten 2f out (L Dettori), beaten 27l by Motivator*

2004

1st Federation of Bloodstock Agents Maiden Stakes (Newmarket, October 15) 2yo 1m Soft **90** (TS 90) 21 ran

Dante Stakes at York in May. He was soon disabused of the notion that the colt needed a trip, however, for Proclamation would do nothing but pull hard for the majority of the extended mile and a quarter and finished a distant last of six behind Motivator.

With his stamina potential more clearly defined, Noseda gave Proclamation the experience he needed over shorter distances. His wins at Goodwood and York detailed above were the perfect provision for the step up to Group 1 level, and the trainer gained the ultimate vindication for his revised strategy in the defeat of Soviet Song.

After the Sussex, it sounded very much as if Noseda was angling towards the Queen Elizabeth II Stakes for his born-again miler, but he ended up avoiding a clash with Dubawi in favour of the Sprint Cup at Haydock.

Though some took his sound defeat in midfield behind Goodricke as evidence that the trip was too short, in truth Proclamation was never travelling well. It was discovered that he had incurred some muscle damage.

The experiment with Proclamation over sprint distances is unlikely to be repeated in 2006, but there should be plenty of opportunities to explore the depth of his talent over a mile. He has been transferred to Sheikh Mohammed's Godolphin operation, having run his last two races in the colours of the Sheikh's wife, Princess Haya of Jordan.

Provided Proclamation's idiosyncrasies do not take on a darker aspect, he is an exciting prospect for all the top mile races. But as he has already shown in the closing stages, there are two ways he can go.

Proclamation

grey colt, 1-5-2002

Parents	Grandparents	Great-grandparents	Great-great-grandparents
King's Best b 1997	Kingmambo	Mr Prospector	Raise A Native Gold Digger
		Miesque	Nureyev Pasodoble
	Allegretta	Lombard	Agio Promised Lady
		Anatevka	Espresso Almyra
Shamarra gr 1993	Zayyani	Darshaan	Shirley Heights Delsy
		Zariya	Blushing Groom Zahra
	Shannfara	Zeddaan	Grey Sovereign Vareta
		Shahana	Wild Risk Princess Yasmin

Bred by Cathal M. Ryan in Ireland. 84,000gns Tattersalls October (1) yearling.

Sire King's Best

Won 3 of 6 races, inc. 2,000 Guineas S.-Gr1. Strong, handsome individual, 16.0½ hh. Tip-top miler on Guineas performance, beating Giant's Causeway, but inclined to be headstrong, and below par in Dewhurst and Craven S. Missed Derby through muscle problems, fractured off-fore cannon-bone in Irish Derby. Stamina for 12f unproven. Seemingly indifferent to ground conditions. From the family of Galileo, etc. Stands at Kildangan Stud, Monaterevin, Co. Kildare at a 2006 fee of €35,000. Sire of 2 crops of racing age, inc. notable winners: Dubai Surprise (Gr3), Oiseau Rare (Gr2), Proclamation (Sussex S.-Gr1).

Dam Shamarra

Unraced. Half-sister to Gr2-placed winner Shantaroun, from same immediate family as multiple Gr1-winning miler Sendawar, tracing to Teresina, one of the foundation mares of the Aga Khan's Studs. Dam of: Princess Claudia (1998 f by Kahyasi; placed), Denmark (1999 c by Danehill; winner), No Refuge (2000 c by Hernando; Listed winner), Sweet Home Alabama (2001 f by Desert Prince; unplaced; covered by Key of Luck this year), Proclamation (2002 c by King's Best; Gr1 winner). Mare died 2002.

Pedigree assessment

Proclamation ran like a mad thing in the Dante, giving Frankie Dettori a nightmare experience, but he came back to register a splendid hat-trick over shorter trips, and was particularly impressive in the Sussex Stakes. At Goodwood he utilised his brilliant acceleration to clear away from his opposition in a matter of strides, his performance suggesting that he might prove equally dominant in sprints. Haydock proved otherwise, but he scoped badly after that race and was not seen out again. The best son of his sire to date, and from a top Aga Khan family, Proclamation has joined Godolphin and will surely be a leading candidate for mile honours again in 2006. He is still lightly raced, and promises to improve as he matures and becomes a more settled individual. *TM*

Punctilious

4yo bay filly **116**

Danehill (USA) - Robertet (USA) (Roberto (USA))

Owner Godolphin

Trainer Saeed Bin Suroor

Breeder Bjorn E Nielsen

Career: **15** starts | won **6** | second **2** | third **2** | **£476,834** win and place

By Mark Blackman

A FEW eyebrows were raised when Frankie Dettori chose to ride Musidora Stakes winner Punctilious over 1,000 Guineas runner-up Sundrop in the 2004 Oaks, but in both the short and the long term, the Italian was proved to be absolutely spot-on. Punctilious finished third to Ouija Board in that Classic, three places ahead of her stablemate, and at the end of their four-year-old campaigns it was Punctilious again who gained that elusive Group 1 success, while Sundrop had to settle for minor Pattern laurels.

Such an outcome would have been hard to predict in July. Sundrop had run out a very impressive winner at Epsom's Derby meeting and finished second at Royal Ascot at York. Punctilious, on the other hand, had finished last of five in the Group 3 Brigadier Gerard Stakes and beaten just one home as favourite for the Group 2 Lancashire Oaks at Haydock. A Group 1 winner in waiting? At that stage, a success at any level would have been welcome.

It was probably with that in mind that the Godolphin team lowered her sights for a fillies' Listed race at Newbury in July – her first start outside Group company since gaining the second of her two juvenile successes.

By that stage, the yard was firing on more cylinders than had been the case earlier in the campaign, and that, combined with the drop in class, helped her to regain winning ways with an authoritative two-length defeat of Natalie Jane, who had finished four places ahead of her at Haydock. Punctilious had seemingly simply taken time to find her feet as a four-year-old.

Just 17 days later, Punctilious lined up as the 13-2 fourth favourite for the Group 1 Aston Upthorpe Yorkshire Oaks at York, scene of her Musidora romp, but also of a lacklustre fourth to Quiff in the 2004 Yorkshire Oaks. Ahead of her in the market were a trio of high-class three-year-olds –

Punctilious (second left), after four placings at the top level, finally lands a Group 1 win in the Yorkshire Oaks

Oaks heroine Eswarah, Lancashire Oaks winner and Irish Oaks runner-up Playful Act, and the progressive French Listed winner Shamdala. With Luca Cumani's well-regarded Dash To The Top also in the line-up, and Richard Gibson sending over the previous year's Italian Group 1 winner Lune d'Or from France, this was a race in which Punctilious would need to be back to her very best to continue her winning ways.

She was slow to break from the stalls – a trait that had begun to surface in one or two of her recent starts – but Kerrin McEvoy refused to panic and did not make his forward move until the final bend had been safely negotiated. From there, Punctilious made smooth headway to challenge with over a furlong to run, and as Eswarah hung left and Dash To The Top went right, Punctilious was able to surge into the lead inside the final furlong. From there, she was always going to land the spoils, despite edging a shade to the outside herself, and at the line she had half a length to spare over Dash To The Top, with Lune d'Or two lengths back in third and Eswarah only fourth.

It was a deserved first Group 1 success for Punctilious, earning a career-best Racing Post Rating of 116. While those who immediately followed her home failed to boost the form subsequently, sixth-placed Shamdala went from strength to strength, winning two Group races and finishing third in the Prix Royal-Oak.

It was mission accomplished for a filly kept in training at four solely in order to upgrade her black-type status. Clearly, too, Punctilious was a filly who had grown up as a racer. McEvoy, who had been standing in for the injured Dettori, commented after the Yorkshire Oaks: "Last year

2005 Race record

10th E P Taylor Stakes (Grade 1) (Woodbine, October 23) 3yo+ 1m2f Yielding **98** 12 ran. *Lost 4l start, last until headway around outside after 2f, went 3rd 6f out, remained prominent until weakened over 1f out (L Dettori), beaten 8¼l by Honey Ryder*

4th Park Hill Stakes (Group 2) (Doncaster, September 7) 3yo+ 1m6½f Good to firm **114** (TS 96) 11 ran. *Dwelt, held up in rear, effort on outside 4f out, stayed on same pace final 2f (L Dettori), beaten 3¾l by Sweet Stream*

1st Aston Upthorpe Yorkshire Oaks (Group 1) (York, August 17) 3yo+ 1m4f Good **116** (TS 101) 11 ran. *Slowly into stride, headway over 3f out, stayed on to lead inside final furlong, held on well (K McEvoy), beat Dash To The Top by ½l*

1st EBF Chalice Stakes (Listed) (Newbury, July 31) 3yo+ 1m4f Good to soft **109** (TS 109) 8 ran. *Held up in rear, steady headway on outside from 3f out, led inside final 2f, driven out (K McEvoy), beat Natalie Jane by 2l*

7th bet365 Lancashire Oaks (Group 2) (Haydock, July 2) 3yo+ 1m4f Good to firm **103** (TS 58) 8 ran. *Prominent, ridden over 2f out, no extra over 1f out (K McEvoy), beaten 2¾l by Playful Act*

5th betfair.com Brigadier Gerard Stakes (Group 3) (Sandown, May 31) 4yo+ 1m2f Good to firm **112** (TS 71) 5 ran. *Settled in last pair, ridden over 2f out, no impression until stayed on inside final furlong (L Dettori), beaten 2½l by New Morning*

Other runs

2004 **2nd** E P Taylor Stakes (Grade 1) (Woodbine, October 24) 3yo+ 1m2f Good **114** 8 ran ● **4th** Aston Upthorpe Yorkshire Oaks (Group 1) (York, August 18) 3yo+ 1m4f Soft **92** (TS 56) 8 ran ● **2nd** Darley Irish Oaks (Group 1) (Curragh, July 18) 3yo 1m4f Good to firm **114** (TS 115) 7 ran ● **1st** Ribblesdale Stakes (Group 2) (Ascot, June 17) 3yo 1m4f Good to firm **111** (TS 112) 9 ran ● **3rd** Vodafone Oaks (Group 1) (Epsom, June 4) 3yo 1m4f Good **108** (TS 99) 7 ran ● **1st** Tattersalls Musidora Stakes (Group 3) (York, May 11) 3yo 1m2½f Good to soft **108** (TS 41) 6 ran **2003** **3rd** Meon Valley Stud Fillies' Mile (Group 1) (Ascot, September 27) 2yo 1m Good to firm **110** (TS 107) 7 ran ● **1st** Butler & Co Equine Tax Planning EBF Novice Stakes (Salisbury, September 4) 2yo 1m Good to firm **94** (TS 74) 7 ran ● **1st** EBF Maiden Fillies' Stakes (Yarmouth, July 3) 2yo 7f Good **79** (TS 71) 6 ran

she didn't like much of the stick, but today under full pressure she responded very well."

Punctilious was not to win again. Reunited with Dettori, she was stepped up to an extended mile and three-quarters for the Group 2 Park Hill Stakes at Doncaster in September, but another slow start and her 5lb penalty proved her undoing. Responding gamely to pressure, she ran on all the way to the line, but was never able to get to Sweet Stream – a Group 1 winner to whom she was forced to concede 5lb – Kastoria and Songerie.

Hopes were high that she could sign off with victory in the Grade 1 EP Taylor Stakes at Woodbine in Canada in October, in which she had finished second 12 months earlier. Losing four lengths at the start was a fatal if increasingly predictable hurdle to overcome, however, and she never figured. Her closing shot was a tame tenth of 12 behind Honey Ryder.

Punctilious

bay filly, 7-5-2001

Danehill b 1986	Danzig	**Northern Dancer**	Nearctic **Natalma**
		Pas de Nom	Admiral's Voyage Petitioner
	Razyana	His Majesty	Ribot Flower Bowl
		Spring Adieu	Buckpasser **Natalma**
Robertet b 1986	Roberto	Hail To Reason	Turn-to Nothirdchance
		Bramalea	Nashua Rarelea
	Ethics	Nijinsky	**Northern Dancer** Flaming Page
		Fairness	Cavan Equal Venture

Bred by Bjorn Neilsen in England.

Sire Danehill

Won 4 of 9 races, inc. Haydock Park Sprint Cup-Gr1. Died May 2003. Stood at Coolmore Stud, latterly at a fee of Ir200,000gns. Sire of Gr1 winners: Danish (QE II Challenge Cup), Kissing Cousin (Coronation), Danehill Dancer (Phoenix, National), Tsukuba Symphony (NHK Mile Cup), Desert King (National, Irish 2,000, Irish Derby), Fairy King Prawn (Yasuda Kinen), Tiger Hill (GP von Baden [twice], Bayerisches Zuchtrennen), Indian Danehill (Prix Ganay), Wannabe Grand (Cheveley Park), Aquarelliste (Prix de Diane, Prix Vermeille, Prix Ganay), Banks Hill (Coronation, Breeders' Cup F & M Turf, Prix Jacques le Marois), Mozart (July Cup, Nunthorpe), Regal Rose (Cheveley Park), Dress To Thrill (Matriarch), Fine Motion (Shuka Sho, QE II Commemorative Cup), Landseer (Poule d'Essai des Poulains), Rock Of Gibraltar (Grand Criterium, Dewhurst, 2,000 Guineas, Irish 2,000, St James's Palace, Sussex, Prix du Moulin), Westerner (Prix du Cadran [twice], Prix Royal-Oak [twice], Gold Cup), Clodovil (Poule d'Essai des Poulains), Intercontinental (Matriarch, Breeders' Cup F & M Turf), Light Jig (Yellow Ribbon), Spartacus (Phoenix, Gran Criterium), Grey Lilas (Prix du Moulin), North Light (Derby), Luas Line (Garden City H.), Oratorio (Prix Jean-Luc Lagardere, Eclipse, Irish Champion), George Washington (Phoenix, National), Horatio Nelson (Prix Jean-Luc Lagardere), Rumplestiltskin (Moyglare Stud, Marcel Boussac).

Dam Robertet

Won 2 of 15 races, inc. Grand Prix de Deauville-Gr2. Also 3rd in Prix Royal-Oak at 3. Burly staying type, admirably consistent, best effort at 15.5f. By a Derby winner and successful sire. Dam unraced sister to Eclipse S. winner Solford, half-sister to numerous other winners. Died in 2001, having produced: Redwood Falls (1992 f by Dancing Brave; Listed winner), Requin (1993 c by Thatching; winner, died at 3 years), Ruwenzori (1994 f by Alzao; placed), Rubis Royal (1995 c by Bluebird, winner over jumps), Red Valley (1997 f by Wolfhound; unplaced), Red Star (1998 f by Lure; winner), Risk Seeker (2000 c by Elmaamul; triple Gr3 winner), Punctilious (2001 f by Danehill; Gr1 winner).

Pedigree assessment

Punctilious took a while to find her best form in 2005, but after a Listed win at Newbury she reached a new peak to collect her first Group 1 victory in the Yorkshire Oaks. The waiting tactics were perhaps overdone in the Park Hill, but her performance was highly creditable in light of her 5lb penalty. The stamina influences on the distaff side of her pedigree always suggested that she should be one of the staying Danehills, and there can be no doubt now that she stayed 14f well. In common with her dam, she was not at her best on really soft ground. *TM*

Rakti

6yo bay horse **129**

Polish Precedent (USA) - Ragera (Ire) (Rainbow Quest (USA))

Owner Gary A Tanaka

Trainer M A Jarvis

Breeder Azienda Agricola Rosati Colarieti

Career: **26** starts | won **11** | second **4** | third **1** | **£1,870,762** win and place

By David Ashforth

IT WAS all in the mind. Unfortunately, the mind it was in was Rakti's, and Rakti's mind was unpredictable, mildly disturbed and, eventually, rather tiresome.

Rakti was a talented nuisance most of his life, his outstanding ability persuading connections to tolerate his outstanding delinquency. Trainer Michael Jarvis, as calm and patient as Rakti was agitated and impatient, confessed, "There are certain places on Newmarket Heath I wouldn't dream of taking him."

Rakti worked on his own, prone to taking unscheduled flight if asked to walk across the gallops. He was a trial, and had been since he first appeared in Britain, behind, but not in, the starting stalls for the 2002 Champion Stakes.

In 2003 he redeemed himself by winning the same Group 1 race and, in 2004, as a five-year-old, he won the Group 1 Prince of Wales's Stakes at Royal Ascot and, dropped to a mile, the Group 1 Queen Elizabeth II Stakes. When Jupiter was in harmony with Mars, Rakti was very good indeed.

Sandwiched between those glowing tributes to his talent was a less glowing tribute to the inside of his head, which instructed Rakti to pull fatally hard in the Coral-Eclipse Stakes at Sandown, albeit on ground softer than ideal, and to be awkward in the Irish Champion Stakes.

So Rakti started his fifth and final season with a high reputation for ability and a low reputation for reliability. The question was always, "Good afternoon, Dr Jekyll, or is it Mr Hyde?"

Rakti had never failed to win his first race of the season – perhaps each new season was upon him before he remembered that racecourses were places for playing tricks. The latest season got off to a breathtaking start, at Newbury on May 14, in the Group 1 Juddmonte Lockinge Stakes.

Everything was in Rakti's favour, a galloping mile, on fast ground, against

Rakti sets a course record in the Lockinge at Newbury, but he could not get near the same level of form again

opponents with dubious Group 1 credentials. He humbled them, galloping powerfully away with the prize and the course record – slashed by 1.4 seconds. Race times can be fragile measures, and the merit of Rakti's achievement was compromised by the fact that, with the help of a strong following wind, every runner bar one broke the record.

The champion miler had confirmed his status but hopes that Rakti would dominate the season foundered on his fragile temperament. Sent to Royal Ascot at York for the Group 1 Queen Anne Stakes, Rakti was on edge in the parade ring before a witless spectator sent him over the edge.

According to jockey Philip Robinson, as he steered Rakti towards the track, a woman repeatedly made clicking noises with her tongue. Rakti shot off, nearly bolting to the start and, although Robinson regained control, Rakti's mental equilibrium had been lost. Still odds on, Rakti finished a creditable but well-beaten second to the improving Valixir.

Jarvis then gave Rakti a break, presenting him at Newmarket for the Queen Elizabeth II Stakes, in which he had excelled at Ascot the previous year. During preparations for the race, Rakti simmered quietly but discouragingly and, in the race, facing Dubawi and Starcraft, ploughed his own furrow towards the centre of the track. For Rakti, the day's race tactics mattered little – the ground was slower than ideal, and Rakti was not on his best form. He finished an anonymous fourth of six, unable to challenge either Starcraft or Dubawi.

Rakti's behavioural idiosyncrasies encouraged doubts about the likelihood of him recapturing his captivating best. "You have to keep kidding him the whole time," Robinson observed. "He can change in a second!" It was a challenge but, in truth, it was wearisome. Rakti had not run a

2005 Race record

11th Cathay Pacific Hong Kong Mile (Group 1) (Sha Tin, December 11) 3yo+ 1m Good to firm **114** 13 ran. *Slowly into stride, soon racing in 6th, 7th on inside straight, one pace final 1½f (P Robinson), beaten 4½l by Hat Trick*

6th Emirates Airline Champion Stakes (Group 1) (Newmarket, October 15) 3yo+ 1m2f Good to soft **119** (TS 104) 15 ran. *Held up, pulled hard, not clear run over 1f out, hampered inside final furlong, not trouble leaders (P Robinson), beaten 4¼l by David Junior*

4th Queen Elizabeth II Stakes sponsored by Barclays plc (Group 1) (Newmarket, September 24) 3yo+ 1m Good **114** (TS 86) 6 ran. *Led centre group, staying on same pace when edged left inside final furlong (P Robinson), beaten 3¾l by Starcraft*

2nd Queen Anne Stakes (Group 1) (York, June 14) 4yo+ 1m Good to firm **122** (TS 120) 10 ran. *Soon led, headed over 1f out, no extra (P Robinson), beaten 1½l by Valixir*

1st Juddmonte Lockinge Stakes (Group 1) (Newbury, May 14) 4yo+ 1m Firm **129** (TS 100) 8 ran. *Led after 1f, came readily clear inside final 2f, edged left inside final furlong, easily (P Robinson), beat Mac Love by 5l*

Other wins

2004 **1st** Queen Elizabeth II Stakes (Sponsored By NetJets) (Group 1) (Ascot, September 25) 3yo+ 1m Good to firm **128** (TS 122) 11 ran ● **1st** Prince of Wales's Stakes (Group 1) (Ascot, June 16) 4yo+ 1m2f Good to firm **128** (TS 118) 10 ran **2003** **1st** Emirates Airline Champion Stakes (Group 1) (Newmarket, October 18) 3yo+ 1m2f Good to firm **125** (TS 104) 12 ran ● **1st** Premio Presidente della Repubblica (Group 1) (Capannelle, May 11) 4yo+ 1m2f Good **114** 8 ran **2002** ● **1st** Premio Villa Borghese (Listed) (Capannelle, September 8) 3yo 1m2f Good to soft 7 ran ● **1st** Derby Italiano (Group 1) (Capannelle, May 26) 3yo 1m4f Good to firm **116** 16 ran ● **1st** Premio Botticelli (Listed) (Capannelle, May 1) 3yo 1m2½f Good 10 ran ● **1st** Premio Barba Toni (Conditions Race) (Capannelle, March 10) 3yo 1m3f Heavy 8 ran **2001** ● **1st** Premio Furigolo (Conditions Race) (Capannelle, November 25) 2yo 1m2f Soft 9 ran ● **1st** Premio Teatro Gozzoli (Maiden) (Pisa, November 2) 2yo 1m2f Good 7 ran

bad race but nor, after the Lockinge, had he succeeded in dominating his rivals.

The Breeders' Cup Mile was considered but the combination of a hefty supplementary fee, and the prospect of noisy pre-race preliminaries deterred Jarvis and owner Gary Tanaka, who had negotiated Rakti's sale with a view to him standing at Huma Park Stud in Ireland in 2006.

Instead, Rakti returned to Newmarket for the Champion Stakes. The ground was against him and punters had lost faith – he started at 12-1. Fighting for his head behind a modest pace, Rakti did not get the best of runs and, under the circumstances, ran respectably to finish sixth of 15, just over four lengths behind the unexpected winner, David Junior.

For his final appearance, connections decided to contest the Hong Kong Mile. Despite a troubled journey from Britain, Rakti started as the second favourite, but went out in a whimper. When Robinson asked for an effort in the straight, there was no response and, although Rakti ran on a little at the end, he beat only two rivals.

For all the frustrations, Rakti took to stud a record that included six Group 1 successes, and some mighty performances.

Rakti

bay horse, 10-2-1999

Polish Precedent b 1986	Danzig	Northern Dancer	Nearctic
			Natalma
		Pas de Nom	Admiral's Voyage
			Petitioner
	Past Example	Buckpasser	Tom Fool
			Busanda
		Bold Example	Bold Lad
			Lady Be Good
Ragera b 1992	Rainbow Quest	Blushing Groom	Red God
			Runaway Bride
		I Will Follow	Herbager
			Where You Lead
	Smageta	High Top	Derring-Do
			Camenae
		Christine	Crocket
			Denning Report

Bred by Azienda Agricola Rosati Colarieti in England.

Sire Polish Precedent

Won 7 of 9 races, inc. Prix du Palais Royal-Gr3, Prix de la Jonchere-Gr3, Prix Messidor-Gr3, Prix Jacques le Marois, Prix du Moulin de Longchamp-Gr1. Big, lengthy sort, top-class miler, inferior only to Zilzal at 3. Sire of: Red Route (Gr2), Pilsudski (Grosser Preis von Baden-Gr1, Breeders' Cup Turf-Gr1, Eclipse S.-Gr1, Irish Champion S.-Gr1, Champion S.-Gr1, Japan Cup-Gr1), Pure Grain (Irish Oaks-Gr1, Yorkshire Oaks-Gr1), Riyadian (Gr2), Predappio (Gr2), Social Harmony (Gr3), Noushkey (Gr3), Polish Summer (Gr2), Sobieski (Gr2), First Charter (Gr3), Rakti (Derby Italiano-Gr1, Premio Presidente della Repubblica-Gr1, Champion S.-Gr1, Prince of Wales's S-Gr1, Queen Elizabeth II S.-Gr1, Lockinge S.-Gr1), Court Masterpiece (Prix de la Foret-Gr1).

Dam Ragera

Placed twice from 3 starts at 3 in Italy, modest performer on limited evidence available. Dam of: Riksha (1997 f by Zilzal; won 12 races in Italy), Rasana (1998 f by Royal Academy; unplaced in Italy and Ireland), Rakti (1999 c by Polish Precedent; triple Gr1 winner), Radha (2000 f by Bishop Of Cashel; unraced).

Pedigree assessment

Rakti again demonstrated merit of a high order over a mile when victorious in the Lockinge Stakes – which was perhaps even a career-best performance – but he was unable to build on that early-season triumph. There were probably excuses in addition to reasons, but he has always been less than a straightforward character. Let's just remember that, like Azamour and few others in recent years, at his peak he was capable of top-class form at a mile, ten and 12 furlongs. In 2006 he will be resident at Huma Park Stud in Ireland, and if he cannot quite claim to have been the best son of his sire on the racecourse, he did match Pilsudski's score of six Group 1 victories. *TM*

Reefscape

4yo grey colt **119**

Linamix (Fr) - Coraline (Sadler's Wells (USA))

Owner K Abdullah

Trainer A Fabre

Breeder Juddmonte Farms

Career: **19** starts | won **5** | second **7** | third **2** | **£361,750** win and place

By Robert Carter

NOBODY would place Reefscape among the very best. He won only twice in nine appearances in 2005 and his overall record is five wins from 19 runs. But he is a versatile and durable racehorse with plenty of good qualities, and he deserves respect. Reefscape raced from April to December and, having started with a Group 1 second (albeit promoted from third) over ten and a half furlongs, he gained his most prestigious success at almost twice that distance in the Group 1 Prix du Cadran.

His season split into two halves. In the first, he was competing at around one and a half miles, as he had done in 2004. He won twice over the trip that year before finishing seventh to Blue Canari in the Prix du Jockey-Club. In the second half of 2005, he switched to longer distances, again as he had done the year before, when he ended the season by winning the Group 2 Prix Chaudenay.

Christophe Soumillon chose Short Pause, fit from his second in the Prix d'Harcourt three weeks earlier, when Reefscape made his reappearance in the Prix Ganay. Reefscape was always close up and stayed on in good style behind Bago and Pride. But Pride had hampered Short Pause when making her run and was put back to sixth behind him, thus handing Reefscape second prize.

It was an excellent effort, suggesting that he should prosper at one and a half miles. However, Soumillon and the others allowed Kieren Fallon to lull them to sleep in the Coronation Cup. Reefscape kept on to finish third to Yeats, three lengths behind the runner-up Alkaased, who added another two lengths to his superiority in the Grand Prix de Saint-Cloud. Reefscape could never strike a blow in either race and the first phase of his season ended when he was beaten inches by Short Pause in the Listed Prix de Reux at Deauville.

He returned to longer distances in the Group 2 Prix Kergorlay two

Reefscape draws clear in the Group 1 Prix du Cadran to cement his status as the best French stayer after Westerner

weeks later but, though staying on from the rear to beat Ostankino for second, could not catch Alcazar, to whom he was conceding 2lb. Allez Olive was fourth. They met again in the Prix Gladiateur, when Soumillon was much closer to the pace throughout. Ostankino tried to make all but Reefscape caught him halfway through the final furlong and ran on to win by three-quarters of a length, with Allez Olive third and the ever-disappointing Blue Canari fourth.

It was Soumillon's enterprise that made sure of victory in the Cadran. His mount was running against a number of horses he had met before and, like them, he was far from certain to stay the longer trip. Cut Quartz, beaten three lengths by Westerner in the race 12 months earlier, was the only proven stayer but he had not approached that form in his two races in 2005. It was anybody's guess who would see it out best.

Soumillon, who rarely makes the running, set off in front. And, since his nine rivals accepted it, he was able to dictate a slow pace until a mile out, where the ten-year-old Terrazzo pulled his way to the front. Terrazzo is another Juddmonte-bred, but he never ran for Prince Khalid while in training with Roger Charlton. However, he did win a nine-furlong handicap for Jimmy FitzGerald, at Musselburgh in May 1999, before moving to France.

A fair stayer in his day but now playing second fiddle to his stable companion, Allez Olive, Terrazzo hung on until early in the straight. Reefscape took over again inside the final quarter-mile and ran on gamely to hold the dead-heaters Alcazar and Ostankino by two lengths, with Allez Olive a creditable fourth.

The first four in the Cadran ran again in the Prix Royal-Oak. Reefscape again started favourite. Richard Hughes had him at the back early on but had closed up running down to the straight. Reefscape stayed on but

2005 Race record

6th Cathay Pacific Hong Kong Vase (Group 1) (Sha Tin, December 11) 3yo+ 1m4f Good to firm **117** 12 ran. *Raced in 3rd to straight, ridden and outpaced approaching final furlong, rallied closing stages (R Hughes), beaten 4¼l by Ouija Board*

2nd Prix Royal-Oak (Group 1) (Longchamp, October 23) 3yo+ 1m7½f Soft **117** (TS 114) 11 ran. *Held up, 10th halfway, pushed along over 3f out, ridden over 1f out and went 2nd final furlong, nearest at finish (R Hughes), beaten nk by Alcazar*

1st Prix du Cadran Casino Les Princes Barriere de Cannes (Group 1) (Longchamp, October 2) 4yo+ 2m4f Good to soft **119** (TS 10) 10 ran. *Set slow pace until headed 1m out, close 3rd straight, led over 1½f out, ran on well (C Soumillon), beat Alcazar by 2l*

1st Prix Gladiateur Royal Thalasso Barriere (Group 3) (Longchamp, September 11) 4yo+ 1m7½f Good to soft **118** (TS 29) 7 ran. *Raced in close 2nd, pressing leader 2f out, ridden to lead 100yds out, driven out (C Soumillon), beat Ostankino by ¾l*

2nd Darley Prix Kergorlay (Group 2) (Deauville, August 21) 3yo+ 1m7f Soft **117** (TS 90) 11 ran. *Mid-division, 7th straight, headway well over 1f out, stayed on under pressure to take 2nd close home (C Soumillon), beaten 2l by Alcazar*

2nd Prix de Reux (Listed) (Deauville, August 6) 3yo+ 1m4½f Good to soft **114** (TS 54) 7 ran. *Held up, ridden to chase leader over 1½f out, hard ridden to dispute lead 100yds out, hung right and headed close home (C Soumillon), beaten shd by Short Pause*

5th Grand Prix de Saint-Cloud (Group 1) (Saint-Cloud, June 26) 4yo+ 1m4f Good to soft **113** (TS 113) 11 ran. *Disputed 5th, ridden and outpaced over 3f out, effort on outside from 2f out, never able to challenge (C Soumillon), beaten 5¼l by Alkaased*

3rd Vodafone Coronation Cup (Group 1) (Epsom, June 3) 4yo+ 1m4f Good **113** (TS 100) 7 ran. *Held up in midfield, 6th straight, soon outpaced, hanging badly over 2f out, kept on to take 3rd last 75yds (C Soumillon), beaten 5½l by Yeats*

2nd Prix Ganay (Group 1) (Longchamp, April 24) 4yo+ 1m2½f Very soft **118** (TS 51) 9 ran. *In touch, pushed along and disputing 2nd straight, driven and in front rank over 1f out, stayed on to line, finished 3rd, placed 2nd (O Peslier), beaten 1½l by Bago*

Other wins

2004 **1st** Prix Chaudenay Casino Barriere de Menton (Group 2) (Longchamp, October 2) 3yo 1m7f Good **118** (TS 118) 7 ran ● **1st** Prix de l'Avre (Listed) (Longchamp, May 19) 3yo 1m4f Good **101** (TS 80) 7 ran ● **1st** Prix du Connetable (Chantilly, May 4) 3yo 1m4f Good to soft (TS 77) 5 ran

Alcazar was a neck too good. Ostankino came sixth and Allez Olive ninth.

Reefscape finally reverted to one and a half miles for the Hong Kong Vase. Neither the distance nor the firm ground was in his favour but he was able to take a good position. His rivals were too fast for him in the dash for home but he rallied to finish sixth, only a neck behind Westerner.

It was said after the Cadran that in 2006 he would be aimed at the Ascot Gold Cup. Westerner won at York thanks to courage and class, rather than stamina, and Reefscape certainly doesn't stay any better than him. Nor would he be allowed to dictate a slow pace. He seems best at around two miles, and he clearly likes Longchamp, where he has won four times and finished runner-up on his remaining three visits, albeit with the help of the stewards in the Ganay.

Reefscape

grey colt, 22-1-2001

Parents	Grandparents	Great-grandparents	Great-great-grandparents
Linamix gr 1987	Mendez	Bellypha	Lyphard, Belga
		Miss Carina	Caro, Miss Pia
	Lunadix	Breton	Relko, La Melba
		Lutine	Alcide, Mona
Coraline b 1994	Sadler's Wells	Northern Dancer	Nearctic, Natalma
		Fairy Bridge	Bold Reason, Special
	Bahamian	Mill Reef	Never Bend, Milan Mill
		Sorbus	Busted, Censorship

Bred by Juddmonte Farms in Britain

Sire Linamix

Won 4 of 10 starts, inc. Prix La Rochette-Gr3, Prix de Fontainebleau-Gr3, Poule d'Essai des Poulains-Gr1. Also 2nd in Grand Criterium, Prix Jacques le Marois, Prix du Moulin de Longchamp and Champion Stakes (all Gr1). Big, angular, round-actioned, free-running sort; not the best of forelegs. Stands at Haras du Val Henry at a fee of €50,000. Sire of 12 crops of racing age, inc. notable winners Diamond Mix (Gr2), Housamix (Gr2), Miss Satamixa (Prix Jacques le Marois-Gr1), Walk On Mix (Gr2), Manninamix (Gr3), Clodora (Gr2), Fragrant Mix (Grand Prix de Saint-Cloud-Gr1), Oa Baldixe (Gr3), Diamonixa (Gr3), Pinmix (Gr3), Sagamix (Prix de l'Arc de Triomphe-Gr1), Amilynx (Prix Royal-Oak-Gr1, twice), Artistique (Gr3), Sage et Jolie (Gr2), Slickly (Grand Prix de Paris-Gr1, Prix du Moulin de Longchamp-Gr1, Premio Vittorio di Capua-Gr1, twice), Goldamix (Criterium de Saint-Cloud-Gr1), Miraculous (Gr3), Diamilina (Gr2), Fair Mix (Prix Ganay-Gr1), Vahorimix (Poule d'Essai des Poulains-Gr1, Prix Jacques le Marois-Gr1), Bernimixa (Gr2), Martaline (Gr2), Diasilixa (Gr3), Visorama (Gr3), Walkamia (Gr3), Cherry Mix (Gran Premio del Jockey Club-Gr1), Fracassant (Gr2), Linda Regina (Gr3), Lord du Sud (Gr2), Millemix (Gr2), Reefscape (Prix du Cadran-Gr1), Carlotamix (Criterium International-Gr1), Manbala (Gr3). Champion sire in France 1998 and 2004.

Dam Coraline

Unraced at 2, won 1 (12.5f) of 5 starts at 3 in France. Sister to stakes-placed fillies New Abbey and Trellis Bay, and minor winner Spanish Wells (dam of Spanish Don). Half-sister to Irish Oaks winner Wemyss Bight (dam to Sadler's Wells of top-class 10-12f colt Beat Hollow), Gr3 winner Yaralino, Listed winner Vacamonte and unplaced Hope (dam of Gr1 winners Oasis Dream and Zenda). Dam of: Martaline (1999 c by Linamix; Gr2 winner), Clear Thinking (2000 g by Rainbow Quest; Gr2-placed winner), Reefscape (2001 c by Linamix; Prix du Cadran-Gr1), Diamond Reef (2002 f by Alzao; non-winner), Grand Coral (2003 f by Grand Lodge; unraced), 2004 c by Halling, 2005 f by King's Best.

Pedigree assessment

It is no surprise to see Reefscape excel beyond a mile and a half. Both his dam's earlier foals showed at least smart form over 12 furlongs and beyond, including Reefscape's brother Martaline. This family can produce speedy performers with help from fast stallions, but the combination of Linamix and broodmare sire Sadler's Wells ensured Reefscape fell at the other end of the scale. He has to be a leading candidate to take over the staying mantle of Westerner, and it is also worth remembering that he has high-class form over 12 furlongs. *JH*

Relaxed Gesture (Ire)

4yo chestnut colt **123**

Indian Ridge - Token Gesture (Ire) (Alzao (USA))

Owner Moyglare Stud Farm

Trainer Christophe Clement

Breeder Moyglare Stud Farm

Career: **12** starts | won **4** | second **5** | third **2** | **£732,108** win and place

By Nicholas Godfrey

IT MIGHT have been an unknown Spaniard, or possibly Woody Allen, depending on which internet site you visit. But someone definitely once said that if you want to make God laugh, you should tell Him your plans.

Dermot Weld probably has the proverb embossed on his psyche after his experiences with Relaxed Gesture, a talented racehorse who had the Irish trainer eyeing virtually every middle-distance Classic he could find in the early part of 2004.

Yet when Relaxed Gesture finally came good, not before time, with a commanding victory in the Canadian International in October 2005, he was under the tutelage of New York-based Christophe Clement. Weld could have been forgiven if he allowed himself a rueful smile. In his care, Relaxed Gesture had followed a promising juvenile campaign with a resilient effort first time out as a three-year-old to finish second to Yeats in the Derrinstown Stud Derby Trial, prompting his trainer to set about planning an ambitious programme on both sides of the Atlantic.

That's when the Almighty had His giggle at the trainer's expense. Relaxed Gesture never raced again as a three-year-old after making a habit of missing intended engagements. Plans to target the Belmont Stakes were abandoned owing to the exploits of Smarty Jones, while injury meant Relaxed Gesture was pulled out of the Italian Derby on the morning of the race and later withdrawn from the French Derby.

Even worse followed. Relaxed Gesture was being lined up for the Irish Derby when he suffered a serious pelvic injury. In the autumn, in search of softer opposition and faster ground, his owners Moyglare Stud switched their small, athletic colt to Clement's New York barn to be readied for a US campaign as a four-year-old.

Much of 2005 proved another exercise in frustration, though this time injury had nothing to do with it. After a pair of flashy allowance-race

Corey Nakatani celebrates Relaxed Gesture's victory over a high-class field in the Canadian International at Woodbine

victories in the spring, each of his next four outings came in either a Grade 1 or Grade 2 event in New York on fast ground. Usually rallying gamely after racing close to the pace, Relaxed Gesture was defeated just a half-length, a head and a pair of three-quarter-length margins which meant that, while he had never been out of the first three in nine previous races on turf, he arrived at the Canadian International still searching for his first success at Pattern level.

Clement explained his decision to take Relaxed Gesture to Woodbine on the basis that the opposition was likely to be easier than at the Breeders' Cup, but the 68th running of a $2 million event won in the past by such luminaries as Secretariat, Dahlia, Exceller and Singspiel nevertheless attracted one of its superior fields.

Encountering ground softer than good for the first time since leaving Europe and belying suggestions that he preferred it faster, Relaxed Gesture also benefited from a change of tactics and a masterly ride by the patient Corey Nakatani. With one eye perhaps on potential stamina worries for a son of Indian Ridge, the rider settled his mount towards the rear well off an urgent gallop set by King's Drama, who was pressed by Yeats, driven up to dispute the lead after missing the break. Having set a suicidal pace, the leaders faltered on leaving the far turn, enabling domestic hope Meteor Storm to pick up a clear lead.

Both Electrocutionist and Grey Swallow attempted to improve but neither

2005 Race record

1st Pattison Canadian International (Grade 1) (Woodbine, October 23) 3yo+ 1m4f Yielding **123** 10 ran. *Patiently ridden in 9th, smooth headway 7-wide on home turn, led well over 1f out, ridden clear, easily (C Nakatani), beat Meteor Storm by 4½l*

3rd Man O'War Stakes (Grade 1) (Belmont Park, September 10) 3yo+ 1m3f Firm **119** 11 ran. *Chased clear leader, led narrowly just under 2f out, held on gamely until headed and no extra inside final furlong (C Nakatani), beaten ¾l by Better Talk Now*

2nd Sword Dancer Invitational Stakes (Grade 1) (Saratoga, August 13) 3yo+ 1m4f Good **114** 8 ran. *Led narrowly until headed over 4f out, stayed on under pressure but always held final furlong (J Santos), beaten ¾l by King's Drama*

2nd Bowling Green Handicap (Grade 2) (Turf) (Belmont Park, July 16) 3yo+ 1m3f Firm **114** 7 ran. *Raced in 3rd, 4th 2f out, close 2nd approaching final furlong, stayed on gamely under pressure (B Blanc), beaten hd by Cacht Wells*

2nd Manhattan Handicap (Grade 1) (Belmont Park, June 11) 3yo+ 1m2f Firm **114** 11 ran. *Raced in 3rd on outside, dropped back to 7th 4f out, still 7th 2f out, stayed on well to take 2nd on line (B Blanc), beaten ½l by Good Reward*

1st Allowance Race (Belmont Park, May 14) 3yo+ 1m2f Firm 6 ran. *Raced in 4th, led over 1f out, ran on well (B Blanc), beat Ershaad by 1¼l*

1st Allowance Race (Keeneland, April 14) 4yo+ 1m1f Firm 11 ran. *Held up in 6th, led well over 1f out, soon clear, easily (B Blanc), beat British Blue by 7l*

Other runs

2004 **2nd** Derrinstown Stud Derby Trial Stakes (Group 2) (Leopardstown, May 9) 3yo 1m2f Good to yielding **108** (TS 74) 4 ran **2003** **8th** Bessemer Trust Breeders' Cup Juvenile (Grade 1) (Dirt) (Santa Anita, October 25) 2yo 1m½ Fast **79** 12 ran ● **2nd** Juddmonte Beresford Stakes (Group 2) (Curragh, October 12) 2yo 1m Good to yielding **108** (TS 66) 6 ran ● **1st** Irish Stallion Farms EBF Maiden (Leopardstown, August 17) 2yo 7f Good to firm **86** (TS 39) 14 ran ● **3rd** Jumeirah International EBF Maiden (Curragh, July 13) 2yo 7f Good **79** (TS 72) 8 ran

had any answer to a decisive move from Relaxed Gesture, who swept past seven wide on entering the straight before going away to score comfortably from the dogged Meteor Storm. Grey Swallow, unable to land a telling blow, plugged on at one pace for third ahead of Electrocutionist, only for the places to be reversed when the stewards found that Pat Smullen had accidentally hit the latter with his whip. Weld never did get any luck when Relaxed Gesture was in the vicinity.

Although connections of several of his main rivals could offer an excuse of some sort – King's Drama and Yeats compromising themselves up front, Electrocutionist reportedly not liking the ground, softer than the official description – the winner looked hugely impressive. *Racing Post* handicappers assessed the form at a mark of 123, only 4lb below the 127 achieved by Shirocco in the Breeders' Cup Turf, run in similar conditions only six days later thanks to an annual fixture clash we could perhaps do without.

Relaxed Gesture was sent to Florida for a winter break soon after his Canadian victory ahead of a 2006 campaign in which he seems destined to figure towards the top end of the perennially weak US turf division.

Relaxed Gesture

chestnut colt, 12-3-2001

Indian Ridge ch 1985	Ahonoora	Lorenzaccio	Klairon Phoenissa
		Helen Nichols	Martial Quaker Girl
	Hillbrow	Swing Easy	Delta Judge Free Flowing
		Golden City	Skymaster West Shaw
Token Gesture b 1994	Alzao	Lyphard	Northern Dancer Goofed
		Lady Rebecca	Sir Ivor Pocahontas
	Temporary Lull	Super Concorde	Bold Reasoning Prime Abord
		Magazine	Prince John Day Line

Bred by Moyglare Stud Farm in Ireland

Sire Indian Ridge

Won 5 of 11 starts from 2 to 4. At 2, won 2 of 4 starts. At 3, won Jersey S-Gr3 from 4 starts. At 4, won Duke of York S-Gr3 and King's Stand S-Gr2 from 3 starts. By top-class sprinter and excellent sire who got top-class horses across the distance spectrum. Stands at Irish National Stud, 2006 fee €75,000. First foals 1991, sire of: Fumo di Londra (Gr3), Island Magic (Gr3), Ridgewood Ben (Gr3), Blomberg (Gr3), Definite Article (National S-Gr1), Ridgewood Pearl (Irish 1,000 Guineas-Gr1, Coronation S-Gr1, Prix du Moulin-Gr1, Breeders' Cup Mile-Gr1), Tumbleweed Ridge (Gr3), Compton Place (July Cup-Gr1), Handsome Ridge (Gr2), Indian Rocket (Gr2), Bardonecchia (Gr3), Cassandra Go (Gr2), Namid (Prix de l'Abbaye-Gr1), St Clair Ridge (Gr3), Indian Mary (Gr3), Nicobar (Gr2), Domedriver (Breeders' Cup Mile-Gr1), High Pitched (Gr3), Indian Creek (Gr2), Monturani (Gr2), Munir (Gr3), Nayyir (Gr2), Sights On Gold (Gr3), Campsie Fells (Gr3), Indian Haven (Irish 2,000 Guineas-Gr1), Imperial Stride (Gr2), Relaxed Gesture (Canadian International-Gr1), Sleeping Indian (Gr3), Snow Ridge (Gr2), Tahreeb (Gr3), Noelani (Gr3).

Dam Token Gesture

At 2, won 2 (inc. Weld Park S-Gr3) of 3 starts over 7f. At 3, won 2 (both 10f, inc. Listed) of 6 starts. Half-sister to Gr2 winner Wait Till Monday, Listed winner Rare Holiday, smart jumper Blazing Spectacle and to dam of top-class hurdler Rhinestone Cowboy. Dam Temporary Lull unraced daughter of a CCA Oaks winner. Dam of: Turn Of Phrase (1999 g by Cadeaux Genereux; Flat/hurdle winner), Evolving Tactics (2000 c by Machiavellian; American Derby-Gr2), Relaxed Gesture (2001 c by Indian Ridge; Canadian International-Gr1), Delicate Flower (2002 f by Sadler's Wells; unraced), 2003 c by Sadler's Wells, 2004 f by Sadler's Wells.

Pedigree assessment

This strong international family tends to produce horses who stay in excess of a mile, and Relaxed Gesture is typical despite being by Indian Ridge. Family members tend to be tough and progressive, in which case Relaxed Gesture has a good chance of enhancing his record in 2006. *JH*

Rob Roy (USA)

3yo brown colt **118**

Lear Fan (USA) - Camanoe (USA) (Gone West (USA))

Owner Philip Newton

Trainer Sir Michael Stoute

Breeder Millsec Ltd

Career: **6** starts | won **2** | second **1** | third **1** | **£50,278** win and place

By John Hopkins

REMARKABLY, in what proved to be another title-winning year, Sir Michael Stoute endured a wretched time in the home Classics. Shanghai Lily, 19th of 20 in the 1,000 Guineas, and Rob Roy, last of 19 in the 2,000 Guineas, were notable disappointments. Unlike the former, Rob Roy was at least able to return to the track, giving notice in the autumn that he remains a colt of some potential.

Available at 25-1 for the Guineas after his maiden success at two, Rob Roy was around 10-1 by the time April arrived. Backers at the initial price were entitled to be on good terms with themselves, with the colt reported to be working consistently well in the spring and firmly established as Stoute's contender for a race he had won five times. Further encouragement was provided when Stoute announced that Rob Roy would return in the Craven Stakes, a race he often targets with his principal Newmarket hope, and which Shadeed and Doyoun had won for him en route to Guineas glory.

Perhaps the main worry for ante-post backers was the form of Rob Roy's Newmarket maiden over seven furlongs the previous October. For all that he was an impressive winner, the 22 horses he defeated had not covered themselves in glory in the meantime, mustering no wins and just four places between them before the Craven.

Rob Roy did not win the Craven, but his reputation and his Guineas prospects were enhanced nevertheless. In a messy race, Mick Kinane had to sit and suffer as his mount was hemmed in by Montgomery's Arch until inside the final furlong. Finishing in taking fashion, he would have won in another stride but instead had to settle for a head second to Irish raider Democratic Deficit, who came from behind but had the benefit of an unhindered run.

The race was difficult to assess formwise, particularly with the 2-1 favourite Etlaala performing dismally, but the positives stacked up. The

Rob Roy (far side) caps his autumn comeback with victory in the Joel Stakes, with the promise of better to come

now twice-raced colt would have learned plenty from the experience, and Stoute was happy: "I was very pleased. He picked up, his attitude was good, and we are hopeful." Established runners, like Iceman and Montgomery's Arch, were in behind. And the omens were favourable, as Stoute's King's Best, so brilliant when winning the Guineas, had also been beaten in unfortunate fashion in the Craven. Coral cut the Classic second favourite's odds to 11-2. The momentum continued into the Guineas, with Rob Roy reported by one enthusiastic watcher to have "strode out majestically" on the gallops a week before the race.

On the day, only Dubawi started at shorter odds in a field of 19. However, Rob Roy's backers were in for an almighty shock. They barely got any sort of run for their money, for Rob Roy was one of the first beaten, backpedalling from two furlongs out and finishing stone last, Kinane reporting that he had lost his action.

It was too bad to be true and so it proved. Rob Roy was later revealed to have injured his right shin, which needed to be blistered. "We will give him quite a bit of time," said Stoute.

When Rob Roy did return, it was in a fairly low-key manner, in a conditions event over a mile at Doncaster's St Leger meeting. It wasn't a great race and it wasn't a particularly great comeback, the 13-8 joint-favourite travelling well until the closing stages, at which point his head

2005 Race record

14th Emirates Airline Champion Stakes (Group 1) (Newmarket, October 15) 3yo+ 1m2f Good to soft **95** (TS 79) 15 ran. *Tracked leaders, raced keenly, weakened over 1f out (M J Kinane), beaten 17½l by David Junior*

1st Rolls-Royce Motor Cars London Joel Stakes (Group 3) (Newmarket, September 30) 3yo+ 1m Good to soft **118** (TS 84) 10 ran. *Always prominent, chased leader halfway, ridden to lead 1f out, ran on (M J Kinane), beat Ancient World by ¾l*

3rd Wilfreda Beehive Trophy (Conditions Stakes) (Doncaster, September 9) 3yo 1m Good to soft **98** (TS 88) 7 ran. *Tracked leading pair, carried head high, effort over 1f out, unable quicken inside final furlong (J P Spencer), beaten 2¾l by Elliots World*

19th UltimatePoker.com 2,000 Guineas Stakes (Group 1) (Newmarket, April 30) 3yo 1m Good to firm **54** (TS 14) 19 ran. *Tracked leaders, raced keenly, weakened well over 2f out, eased (M J Kinane), beaten 28l by Footstepsinthesand*

2nd bet365 Craven Stakes (Group 3) (Newmarket, April 14) 3yo 1m Good to firm **114** (TS 82) 8 ran. *Tracked leaders, raced keenly, not clear run over 1f out, ran on well inside final furlong (M J Kinane), beaten hd by Democratic Deficit*

2004

1st Beech House Stud EBF Maiden Stakes (Newmarket, October 1) 2yo 7f Good **83** (TS 96) 23 ran

came up and he found only the one pace, finishing a two-and-three-quarter-length third to the relatively exposed Elliots World. Taking a charitable view, Rob Roy may have needed the run and may have found the testing ground against him. Alternatively, with neither his maiden nor the Craven working out, maybe he just wasn't that good.

Yet confirmation that Rob Roy was indeed a talent to be reckoned with came just three weeks later. Stepped back up to Group 3 company in a strong renewal of the Joel Stakes at Newmarket, run over a mile on good to soft ground, Rob Roy was always prominent and ran on strongly inside the final furlong to beat Ancient World, a Group 1 winner in Italy the previous autumn, by three-quarters of a length. Established Group performers/top handicappers Polar Ben, Babodana and St Andrews were in behind. Stoute enthused: "That was really pleasing. He was just a little rusty for a while and then Mick got hold of him and he was going away at the end."

At the time, Stoute said he would put Rob Roy away for the season, but he was supplemented for the Group 1 Champion Stakes, in which the trainer ran three in a bid to protect his lead over Aidan O'Brien in the title race. Rob Roy was sent off a 12-1 shot in a race featuring such top-class performers as Oratorio, Alkaased and Rakti, but again he ran disappointingly on his first attempt at a mile and a quarter, weakening inside the last to finish a dismal 14th of 15 after racing keenly.

If one ignores the Champion, which had all the appearance of an afterthought, and concentrates on the Joel success, Rob Roy could yet develop into a top-class performer at a mile. After all, Stoute's prowess at improving his lightly raced older horses is legendary.

Rob Roy

brown colt, 27-3-2002

Lear Fan br 1981	Roberto	Hail To Reason	Turn-to Nothirdchance
		Bramalea	Nashua Rarelea
	Wac	Lt Stevens	Nantallah Rough Shod
		Belthazar	War Admiral Blinking Owl
Camanoe br 1996	Gone West	Mr Prospector	Raise A Native Gold Digger
		Secrettame	Secretariat Tamerett
	Prodigious	Pharly	Lyphard Comely
		Vichy	Restless Native Boda

Bred by Millsec Ltd in US. $300,000 Keeneland September yearling

Sire Lear Fan

Won 5 of 8 starts at 2 and 3. At 2, won all 3 starts over 7-8f, inc. Champagne S-Gr2. At 3, won Craven S-Gr3, Prix Jacques le Marois-Gr1, also 2nd Prix du Moulin, 3rd 2,000 Guineas. Unplaced Breeders' Cup Mile final start. Stood at Gainesway Farm, retired autumn 2004. First foals 1986, sire of (northern hemisphere runners): Le Famo (Gr3), Run Don't Fly (Gr2), Sikeston (Gran Criterium-Gr1, Premio Parioli-Gr1, Premio Vittorio di Capua-Gr1x2, Premio Presidente della Repubblica-Gr1x2, Premio Roma-Gr1), Corrupt (Gr2), Dampierre (Gr3), Fanmore (Gr2), Casual Lies (Gr3), Glaieul (Criterium de Saint-Cloud-Gr1), Verveine (Gr2), Codified (Gr3), Lear White (Gr3), Windsharp (San Luis Rey S-Gr1, Beverly Hills H-Gr1), Labeeb (Hollywood Derby-Gr1), Loup Solitaire (Grand Criterium-Gr1), Fantastic Fellow (Gr3), Ryafan (Prix Marcel Boussac-Gr1, Yellow Ribbon S-Gr1, Matriarch S-Gr1, QE II Challenge Cup-Gr1), Tiraaz (Prix Royal-Oak-Gr1), Lear Spear (Gr2), Sarafan (Eddie Read H-Gr1), Chopinina (Gr3), Dublino (Del Mar Oaks-Gr1), Far Lane (Gr3), Finery (Gr3), Rob Roy (Gr3).

Dam Camanoe

Unraced at 2, unplaced in 2 3yo starts over 8f. By US Gr 1 winner and very good sire who is mainly influence for speed, out of French 8-10f winner. Half-sister to Grade 1 winner Super Staff (Secretariat) and high-class 10-12f performer Public Purse. Dam of: Rob Roy (2002 c by Lear Fan; Gr3 winner), 2004 c by Yankee Victor.

Pedigree assessment

Rob Roy's pedigree is that of a progressive miler. Lear Fan, as the accompanying list suggests, has been a prolific source of tough, talented, older horses. Camanoe, too, is from a good but not precocious family. On this basis, soundness permitting, Rob Roy should have a good season in 2006. *JH*

Roses In May (USA)

5yo brown horse **128**

Devil His Due (USA) - Tell A Secret (USA) (Speak John)

Owner Kenneth L & Sarah K Ramsey

Trainer Dale Romans

Breeder Margaux Farm Llc

Career: **13** starts | won **8** | second **4** | third **0** | **£2,932,147** win and place

By James Willoughby

THE Dubai World Cup fell to an American-trained horse for the fifth time in its ten runnings when Roses In May put up a commanding display at Nad Al Sheba in March. That he never raced again would seem to add further weight to the theory that victory in the world's richest race is a double-edged sword.

"Don't go to Dubai," screamed a headline in the *Daily Racing Form* in 2004. The article was a plea to the connections of the top-class dirt horse Medaglia d'Oro as they considered a trip to the desert. "If he goes to Dubai, there is a very strong chance he will not be even close to the same horse when he returns," wrote the respected journalist Mike Watchmaker.

The same theory could be applied to Roses In May 12 months later. A relatively late-developing colt, he had capped a lucrative four-year-old season with a fine second to Ghostzapper in the Breeders' Cup Classic at Lone Star Park. He returned to action early in 2005 by occupying the same place in the Grade 1 Donn Handicap at Gulfstream behind the subsequent winner of the Classic, Saint Liam.

In truth, the connections of Roses In May were hardly on the horns of a dilemma in shipping their horse to Dubai. The five-year-old's owner Ken Ramsey is an astute judge of the form book and was well aware that the absence of Ghostzapper and any credible challenger from the home team would present Roses In May with a clear opportunity. And even if the travelling left its mark, there was ample compensation from the huge prize-money on offer.

Roses In May duly reached the post at Nad Al Sheba as a short-priced favourite with British bookmakers. His 11 opponents had nothing in their past performances to worry him, for even the highest-rated among them, fellow US raider Congrats, could not boast of a Grade 1 win and was at least 7lb inferior according to most ratings.

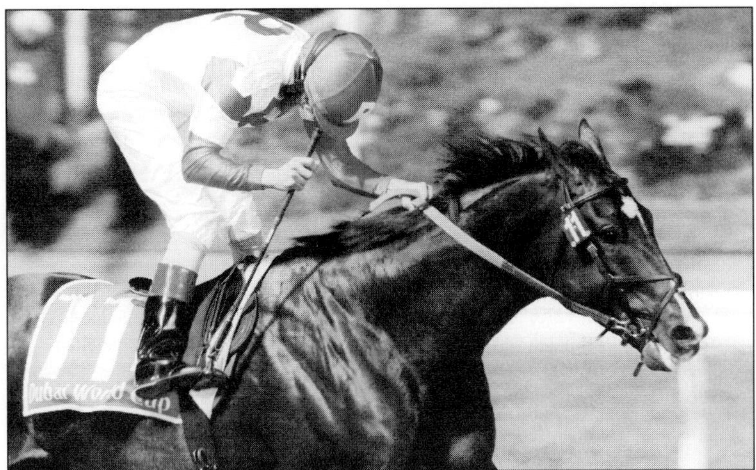

Roses In May wins the Dubai World Cup as a hot favourite should, but he soon joined America's long wounded list

In a well-run race, the South African challenger Yard-Arm took command from the outset. Behind him could soon be seen Roses In May, and the latter took over the lead when the pace appeared to slacken approaching halfway.

To those unfamiliar with the way dirt horses operate, the fact that Roses In May appeared to require encouragement from his jockey John Velazquez as he barrelled towards the end of the back straight might have been construed as a negative. A completely different dynamic is at work than on turf, however, owing to the comparatively upside-down nature of competition which features a fast first half of the race and a slow finish.

Dirt horses must be asked to run earlier because the surface just does not facilitate acceleration, and in familiar style Roses In May began to grind his opponents into submission. First the Gerard Butler-trained Jack Sullivan had a crack at him, then the late-charging US runner Choctaw Nation, but he turned both challengers away with authority and strode through the final half-furlong unopposed. The strong finish of Dynever reduced the winning margin to three lengths.

It was a performance that compared very favourably with the majority of those that had gone before it in the World Cup, both in terms of style and performance and merit. Naturally, it could not compare in either facet with the imperious Dubai Millennium, whose demolition job in 2000 was backed up by the race's record time of 1min 59.50sec.

For the record, Roses In May clocked 2min 2.17sec on a track that was playing slower than on some occasions in World Cup history. Among US-trained winners, this is faster than Cigar and Silver Charm, but slower than Captain Steve and Pleasantly Perfect.

More to the point, Roses In May promised better to come. "He was

2005 Race record

1st Dubai World Cup Sponsored By Emirates Airline (Dirt) (Group 1) (Nad Al Sheba, March 26) 4yo+ 1m2f Fast **128** 12 ran. *Tracked leaders, led halfway, ridden straight, quickened clear over 2f out, driven out (J R Velazquez), beat Dynever by 3l*

2nd Donn Handicap (Grade 1) (Gulfstream Park, February 5) 3yo+ 1m1f Fast **123** 6 ran. *Led or disputed until headed over 2f out, outpaced by winner but kept on to hold 2nd (J R Velazquez), beaten 3¾l by Saint Liam*

Other runs

2004 **2nd** Breeders' Cup Classic (Grade 1) (Dirt) (Lone Star Park, October 30) 3yo+ 1m2f Fast **130** 13 ran ● **1st** Kentucky Cup Classic Handicap (Grade 2) (Turfway Park, September 18) 3yo+ 1m1f Fast **127** 6 ran ● **1st** Whitney Handicap (Grade 1) (Saratoga, August 7) 3yo+ 1m1f Fast **121** 9 ran ● **1st** Prairie Meadows Cornhusker Breeders' Cup Handicap (Grade 3) (Prairie Meadows, July 3) 3yo+ 1m2f Fast 6 ran ● **1st** Optional Claimer (Churchill Downs, May 21) 3yo+ 1m½f Fast 5 ran ● **1st** Allowance Race (Keeneland, April 17) 4yo+ 1m½f Fast 8 ran 2003 **6th** Jerome Handicap (Grade 2) (Belmont Park, September 13) 3yo 1m Fast **92** 9 ran ● **1st** Allowance Race (Saratoga, August 17) 3yo+ 1m1f Fast 6 ran ● **2nd** Allowance Race (Churchill Downs, June 22) 3yo+ 1m½f Fast 8 ran ● **1st** Maiden Special Weight (Churchill Downs, May 25) 3yo+ 1m½f Sloppy 8 ran ● **2nd** Maiden Special Weight (Churchill Downs, May 3) 3yo+ 7f Fast 7 ran

better today than before the Classic," said his trainer Dale Romans after the race. "We are going to take him back to Kentucky and give him a little break."

Such was the impact of Roses In May's victory back home that one or two even began to question whether he could step out from Ghostzapper's shadow when the pair renewed rivalry. Sadly this point was academic, for injuries forced the retirement of Ghostzapper in June and Roses In May in August.

Roses In May's torn tendon, which came to light after a workout in which he had pleased all about him, was particularly disappointing given that it rendered the older horse division even weaker in the US.

Though Roses In May's abbreviated career will be used by those intent on bolstering their case against American horses running in the Dubai World Cup, this would be unfair. In common with Medaglia d'Oro, who also succumbed to injury after finishing an excellent second to Pleasantly Perfect at Nad Al Sheba, he had endured plenty of hard races before the World Cup and was on his final tour of duty.

In truth, the outcry against the World Cup from some within the US racing establishment has a protectionist ring. It could easily be argued that the real agenda is to maintain the standing of domestic events, such as the Santa Anita Handicap.

There is an inescapable irony in the 'Big Cap' being afflicted by the magnet of bigger prize-money elsewhere. The catalyst for its own showcase status in the late 1930s was a $100,000 purse which lured famous horses of the day to California from the longer-established races on the opposite coast. What goes around comes around, so they say.

Roses In May *brown horse, 9-2-2000*

Devil His Due br 1989	Devil's Bag	Halo	Hail To Reason Cosmah
		Ballade	Herbager Miss Swapsco
	Plenty O'Toole	Raise A Cup	Raise A Native Spring Sunshine
		Li'l Puss	Noble Jay Li'l Sis
Tell A Secret b/br 1977	Speak John	Prince John	Princequillo Not Afraid
		Nuit de Folies	Tornado Folle Nuit
	Secret Retreat	Clandestine	Double Jay Conniver
		Retirement	Royal Gem Marie J.

Bred by Margaux Farm in Kentucky. $19,000 Keeneland September yearling, $115,000 Ocala April 2-y-o.

Sire Devil His Due

Won 11 of 41 races, inc. Gotham S. [dead-heat]-Gr2, Wood Memorial S.-Gr1, Gulfstream Park H.-Gr1, Excelsior H.-Gr2, Suburban H.-Gr1 [twice], Pimlico Special H-Gr1, Broward H.-Gr3, Brooklyn H.-Gr2, Suburban H.-Gr1. Also 2nd in 9 other Gr1 races. Tough, honest performer, who stayed 10f well, and who ran without medication in 40 of 41 races. Well-made, 16.1hh. The best son of his sire (champion 2-y-o, won 8 of 9 races), out of a tough Gr1-placed racemare, from a good, but not exceptional, family. Stands at Margaux Farm, Midway, Kentucky, at a 2006 fee of $15,000 (live foal). Sire of 7 crops of racing age, inc. notable winners: Buckle Down Ben (Gr3), She's A Devil Due (Gr2), Spite The Devil (Gr3), Roses In May (Whitney H.-Gr1, Dubai World Cup-Gr1).

Dam Tell A Secret

Won 9 of 49 races. Also placed 26 times, inc. Gr3-placed at 4 and 5 years. Hardy campaigner, most effective at 7-8f. From a family noted more for its toughness than its class. The best of 5 winners from her dam (bred 1 other stakes-placed performer). Dam of: Secret Threat (1985 f by Mr Leader; placed, dam of Gr3 winner Gleefully), Playful Secret (1998 f by Play Fellow; unraced), Lismore Lass (1989 f by Vigors; stakes winner), Oscar Max (1990 g by Temperence Hill; stakes-placed winner), Foxhart (1991 g by Irish Tower; winner), Forbes Castle (1993 c by Air Forbes Won; winner), Hidden Message (1995 c by Cryptoclearance; winner), Pizza N Beer (1997 c by Farma Way; winner), I Already Know (1999 f by Captain Bodgit; unraced), Roses In May (2000 c by Devil His Due; dual Gr1 winner). Barren in 1987 and 1996, dead foal in 1994. Died in 2000.

Pedigree assessment

The product of parents who proved their toughness and durability over long periods, Roses In May showed that he was near the top of his class as a four-year-old, winning five in a row before taking second place to Ghostzapper in the Breeders' Cup Classic. He was the natural favourite for the Dubai World Cup and won it, apparently without being extended, but as was the case with a number of other visitors to Nad Al Sheba in the past, the trip took its toll, and instead of going on to challenge for Horse of the Year honours at home, he stayed on the sidelines. The form he showed in 2004 and in Dubai would have made him a serious rival to Saint Liam at the Breeders' Cup, though that horse did beat him comfortably, albeit with a 2lb advantage, in the Donn Handicap. *TM*

Rumplestiltskin (Ire)

2yo bay filly **112**

Danehill (USA) - Monevassia (USA) (Mr Prospector (USA))

Owner Mrs J Magnier/M Tabor/Niarchos Family

Trainer A P O'Brien

Breeder Quay Bloodstock & Niarchos Family

Career: **6** starts | won **5** | second **0** | third **1** | **£350,807** win and place

By Alan Sweetman

THE Rumplestiltskin of the Brothers Grimm is described at one stage as "a ridiculous little man hopping on one leg", making it curiously inappropriate that one of the most stylish juveniles of 2005 bears his name. That she is a filly makes it more than a little bizarre. Ballydoyle has embellished the sport with some wonderfully evocative names over the years, so we should excuse this aberration, and if she turns out to be a Classic winner in 2006 it will hardly matter.

The turn of foot that was to characterise Rumplestiltskin's best performances was evident when she made her initial appearance as the odds-on favourite for a maiden over six furlongs at Naas in May. At the furlong pole it looked as if the front-running Always A Star might maintain her advantage, but Rumplestiltskin delivered a late burst of speed under Seamus Heffernan to win by half a length. It was a performance that ensured that she again started favourite when returning to Naas for the Swordlestown Stud Sprint Stakes in the first week of June. Twelve months earlier this six-furlong contest had been won by Damson as a prelude to her victory in the Queen Mary, and Rumplestiltskin's opponents included Waterways, a filly already nominated as a possible contender for the Royal meeting after her win in the Marble Hill Stakes at The Curragh.

The Marble Hill form had been franked by runner-up BA Foxtrot's six-length win in the Woodcote Stakes at Epsom, and Waterways held an edge in terms of experience. However, a 5lb penalty for her Listed success took its toll, and after attempting to make all she was a sitting duck as Rumplestiltskin quickened to take control from a furlong down, despite drifting to the left, indicating that she still had a bit to learn. On ground that was officially slower, her winning time was marginally better than Damson's, though visually her performance was perhaps less striking.

Nonetheless, her reputation was sufficient to make her 5-4 favourite for the Albany Stakes at the Royal meeting at York. This newly promoted

Rumplestiltskin scores her second Group 1 victory under a cool ride from Kieren Fallon in the Prix Marcel Boussac

Group 3 event over six furlongs attracted a field of 14, including La Chunga, whose defeat on her debut over five furlongs at Sandown had put paid to an intended bid for the Queen Mary. La Chunga went to the front two furlongs down, and took control of the race as Rumplestiltskin failed this time to find another gear and again showed a tendency to hang to the left. The winner's long-priced stablemate Vague came with a late run to take second, with Rumplestiltskin relegated to third, though an encouraging five lengths clear of the second favourite Spinning Queen in fourth. Aidan O'Brien said on a number of occasions afterwards that his filly was not at her best on the day, without offering any specific excuse.

In August she was given the chance to atone in the Group 2 Robert Griffin Debutante Stakes at The Curragh. By this stage the Albany form was beginning to look insecure. La Chunga had finished only fourth when favourite for the Princess Margaret, Vague had been a beaten favourite in a Listed race at Sandown, and while Spinning Queen had performed with credit to take third place in the Cherry Hinton she was a beaten favourite for the Sweet Solera at Newmarket on the eve of Rumplestiltskin's Curragh race.

Vague travelled from Britain to renew rivalry, but the market suggested that the unbeaten Modeeroch, winner of the Listed Tyros Stakes at Leopardstown on her second start, was the principal danger. Given an attacking ride, Modeeroch established a clear advantage under two furlongs down, but when Kieren Fallon asked Rumplestiltskin for her effort she acclerated inside the last half-furlong and won going away by two lengths. Vague was fourth.

The prospect of a showdown in the Moyglare between Rumplestiltskin and the Lowther winner Flashy Wings was briefly offered, but the clash

2005 **Race record**

1st Prix Marcel Boussac - Criterium des Pouliches (Group 1) (Longchamp, October 2) 2yo 1m Good to soft **112** (TS 110) 15 ran. *Moved sharply right in 1st furlong, 6th straight, not clear run well over 1f out, switched left and headway 1½f out, driven to lead well inside final furlong (K Fallon), beat Quiet Royal by 1l*

1st Moyglare Stud Stakes (Group 1) (Curragh, September 4) 2yo 7f Good **107** (TS 82) 9 ran. *Slowly into stride and held up in rear, headway on outer 2f out, led 1f out, kept on well (K Fallon), beat Ugo Fire by nk*

1st Robert H. Griffin Debutante Stakes (Group 2) (Curragh, August 7) 2yo 7f Good **106** (TS 74) 7 ran. *Tracked leaders in 4th, headway into 2nd 1f out, led over 100yds from finish, soon clear, easily (K Fallon), beat Modeeroch by 2l*

3rd Albany Stakes (Group 3) (York, June 17) 2yo 6f Good to firm **93** (TS 84) 14 ran. *Chased leaders towards far side, hung left and kept on same pace final 2f (K Fallon), beaten 4½l by La Chunga*

1st Swordlestown Stud Sprint Stakes (Listed) (Naas, June 6) 2yo 6f Good **103** (TS 97) 8 ran. *Tracked leaders, 5th halfway, 3rd 2f out, quickened to challenge when edged left 1f out, soon led, stayed on well (K Fallon), beat Waterways by 1½l*

1st Windscreen Centre Naas Fillies Maiden (Naas, May 14) 2yo 6f Good **88** (TS 75) 13 ran. *Tracked leaders, 3rd after halfway, 2nd and ran on strongly inside final furlong to lead close home (J A Heffernan), beat Always A Star by ½l*

did not materialise. Instead, with a low key-challenge from Britain for the Group 1 event, the 2-7 offered about Rumplestiltskin seemed a fair reflection of the overall standard.

It looked a straightforward task, but after missing the break Rumplestiltskin made heavy weather of it. Produced on the outside, she laboured to gain the upper hand and failed to quicken away, getting home by just a neck from Ugo Fire, a filly having her eighth start and only once successful, in an auction maiden in the early part of the season. Ardbrae Lady, the 100-1 outsider of the nine-strong field, was third. Objectively, the race's credibility as a genuine Group 1 test was called into question by the fact that Ugo Fire and Ardbrae Lady had almost precisely duplicated their running in a Listed race at The Curragh.

Fallon's claim that the filly had been almost knocked over shortly after the start was not borne out by video evidence, and the general feeling was that Rumplestiltskin now had something to prove. She did so in style in the Prix Marcel Boussac at Longchamp. Brought to the inside by Fallon in the early stages, she travelled supremely well in the straight and, after a few anxious moments, accelerated from a furlong and a half down when the gaps opened. On a day that showcased many facets of Fallon's talents, this ride typified his patience and coolness under pressure. It was a reassuring performance on which to sign off, and the form stood up when runner-up Quiet Royal won the Prix Miesque, a Group 3 event at Maisons-Laffitte. On the eve of the Boussac, Ugo Fire's victory in the CL Weld Park Stakes had advanced the suspect Moyglare form, and Rumplestiltskin went into the winter as a prime contender for the 1,000 Guineas.

Rumplestiltskin

bay filly, 17-2-2003

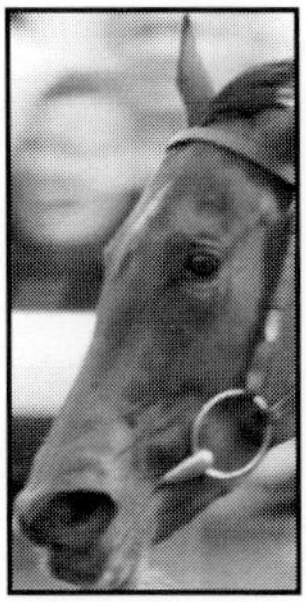

Danehill b 1986	Danzig	**Northern Dancer**	Nearctic **Natalma**
		Pas de Nom	Admiral's Voyage Petitioner
	Razyana	His Majesty	Ribot Flower Bowl
		Spring Adieu	Buckpasser **Natalma**
Monevassia b 1994	Mr Prospector	Raise A Native	Native Dancer Raise You
		Gold Digger	Nashua Sequence
	Miesque	Nureyev	**Northern Dancer** Special
		Pasadoble	Prove Out Santa Quilla

Bred by Quay Bloodstock and Samac Ltd in Ireland. 550,000gns Tattersalls Houghton yearling

Sire Danehill

Won 4 of 9 races, inc. Haydock Park Sprint Cup-Gr1. Died May 2003. Stood at Coolmore Stud, latterly at Ir200,000gns. Sire of Gr1 winners: Danish (QE II Challenge Cup), Kissing Cousin (Coronation), Danehill Dancer (Phoenix, National), Tsukuba Symphony (NHK Mile Cup), Desert King (National, Irish 2,000, Irish Derby), Fairy King Prawn (Yasuda Kinen), Tiger Hill (GP von Baden [twice], Bayerisches Zuchtrennen), Indian Danehill (Prix Ganay), Wannabe Grand (Cheveley Park), Aquarelliste (Prix de Diane, Prix Vermeille, Prix Ganay), Banks Hill (Coronation, Breeders' Cup F & M Turf, Prix Jacques le Marois), Mozart (July Cup, Nunthorpe), Regal Rose (Cheveley Park), Dress To Thrill (Matriarch), Fine Motion (Shuka Sho, QE II Commemorative Cup), Landseer (Poule d'Essai des Poulains), Rock Of Gibraltar (Grand Criterium, Dewhurst, 2,000 Guineas, Irish 2,000, St James's Palace, Sussex, Prix du Moulin), Westerner (Prix du Cadran [twice], Prix Royal-Oak [twice], Gold Cup), Clodovil (Poule d'Essai des Poulains), Intercontinental (Matriarch, Breeders' Cup F & M Turf), Light Jig (Yellow Ribbon), Spartacus (Phoenix, Gran Criterium), Grey Lilas (Prix du Moulin), North Light (Derby), Luas Line (Garden City H.), Oratorio (Prix Jean-Luc Lagardere, Eclipse, Irish Champion), George Washington (Phoenix, National), Horatio Nelson (Prix Jean-Luc Lagardere), Rumplestiltskin (Moyglare Stud, Prix Marcel Boussac).

Dam Monevassia

Ran only twice, viz. 2nd of 5 at Deauville at 2 years, 4th of 6 at Saint-Cloud at 3 years. Seemingly a modest performer on the scant available evidence. Immaculately bred sister to Classic-winning miler and high-ranking sire Kingmambo and to Miesque's Son (Gr3 winner, sire of Whipper). Out of an exceptional racemare. Dam of: Trevi Fountain (2000 g by Sadler's Wells; unplaced), Moonawara (2001 f by Sadler's Wells; unraced), Woman Secret (2002 f by Sadler's Wells; unraced), Rumplestiltskin (2003 f by Danehill; dual Gr1 winner). She has a yearling colt by Danehill ($170,000 to Mark Johnston at Keeneland) and a colt foal by Storm Cat.

Pedigree assessment

A short-priced favourite for all her six races, Rumplestiltskin justified the confidence placed in her five times. What is more, hers was a progressive campaign, and she wound up with an undeniably authoritative display in the Prix Marcel Boussac. But was she just a two-year-old? It is possible that her busy first season was all about striking while the iron was hot, because she did seem to lack some physical scope. Still, if she makes it to post on the Rowley Mile, there will be no better-bred filly in the line-up. *TM*

Saint Liam (USA)

5yo bay horse **129**

Saint Ballado (Can) - Quiet Dance (USA) (Quiet American (USA))

Owner Mr & Mrs W K Warren

Trainer R Dutrow Jr

Breeder Edward P Evans

Career: **20** starts | won **9** | second **6** | third **1** | **£2,334,285** win and place

By Nicholas Godfrey

BY THE time Saint Liam ended his racing career with a convincing victory in the Breeders' Cup Classic, the admirable five-year-old had thoroughly earned the right to be called America's leading older horse. During a season of solid achievement in dirt racing's fiercest arenas, it was hardly his fault if he suffered by comparison to his immediate predecessor, for the brilliant Ghostzapper cast the most imposing of shadows.

Despite being retired after only one start in 2005, Ghostzapper's weight-conceding romp in the Metropolitan Handicap in May could easily be regarded as the best performance of the season in ratings terms. Still, it was merely a single outing, and Ghostzapper's subsequent retirement through injury created a huge opportunity for another horse to step up to the plate. By season's end, it was Saint Liam, trained in New York by the controversial Richard Dutrow jr, who had hit the winning home run with a decisive success in the Classic at Belmont Park that confirmed his status as Ghostzapper's rightful successor.

Coincidentally, it was against Ghostzapper in September 2004 that Saint Liam had produced his breakthrough performance in giving his esteemed rival a fright in Belmont's Woodward Stakes, sustaining only a narrow defeat after racing stride for stride with the best horse in the world for most of the nine-furlong trip.

While his progression to the very top after such an auspicious performance could have been forecast, it did not come without the odd bump in the road. Saint Liam has a history of foot problems, plus a disturbing tendency to lug out in his races, and an otherwise excellent 2005 record was besmirched by one major blemish in the shape of a horrid performance in the storied Santa Anita Handicap in March.

Then there was his outspoken trainer Dutrow, the subject of much gossip and innuendo with regard to performance-enhancing drugs, a spectre that haunts American racing. In June and July, Dutrow served a 60-day

Saint Liam (left) charges to victory in the Breeders' Cup Classic, a glorious end to an outstanding final season

suspension in New York for a medication violation dating back two years that resulted in his stable star's being officially transferred for a spell into the care of Bobby Frankel. When Saint Liam arrived in his barn, Frankel had just said goodbye to his own standard bearer. That was Ghostzapper, of course.

Saint Liam, a Kentucky-bred son of Saint Ballado bought for just $130,000 at Fasig-Tipton's Saratoga sale, was originally trained by Tony Reinstedler, for whom he won two of eight starts before joining Dutrow in the autumn of his three-year-old campaign. He showed great promise in his first four starts for his new handler, including a pair of placed efforts in Grade 2 company, before a setback with quarter cracks on his feet meant a five-month spell on the sidelines.

When Saint Liam returned, it was to tangle with Ghostzapper in the Woodward, after which Dutrow, in a bid to cure the horse's unfortunate predilection for drifting out, equipped him with the blinkers that were to become his trademark. Never again would he race without the shocking pink blinds that matched his silks, and his 2004 season concluded with a game victory in the Grade 2 Clark Handicap at Churchill Downs that augured well. Saint Liam's first outing of 2005, in Gulfstream Park's Donn

2005 Race record

1st Breeders' Cup Classic - Powered by Dodge (Grade 1) (Dirt) (Belmont Park, October 29) 3yo+ 1m2f Fast **127** 13 ran. *Raced in 4th, driven to challenge 1½f out, led over 1f out, ran on well, driven out (J D Bailey), beat Flower Alley by 1l*

1st Woodward Stakes (Grade 1) (Belmont Park, September 10) 3yo+ 1m1f Fast **125** 5 ran. *Raced in 4th, smooth headway on outside over 3f out, led over 2f out, pushed out, easily (J D Bailey), beat Sir Shackleton by 2l*

2nd Whitney Handicap (Grade 1) (Saratoga, August 6) 3yo+ 1m1f Fast **129** 8 ran. *Chased clear leader, effort over 2f out, 1½ lengths down approaching final furlong, stayed on under strong driving final furlong, never nearer (E Prado), beaten nk by Commentator*

1st Stephen Foster Handicap (Grade 1) (Dirt) (Churchill Downs, June 18) 3yo+ 1m1f Fast **122** 8 ran. *Always close up, led over 2f out, ran on well (E Prado), beat Eurosilver by 2¾l*

6th Santa Anita Handicap (Grade 1) (Dirt) (Santa Anita, March 5) 4yo+ 1m2f Fast **116** 11 ran. *Raced in 3rd on outside, effort over 2f out, one pace (E Prado), beaten 4¼l by Rock Hard Ten*

1st Donn Handicap (Grade 1) (Gulfstream Park, February 5) 3yo+ 1m1f Fast **129** 6 ran. *Disputed lead after 2f until led over 2f out, drew clear while drifting right final 2f (E Prado), beat Roses In May by 3¾l*

Other runs

2004 **1st** Clark Handicap (Grade 2) (Churchill Downs, November 26) 3yo+ 1m1f Fast **115** 9 ran ● **2nd** Woodward Stakes (Grade 1) (Dirt) (Belmont Park, September 11) 3yo+ 1m1f Fast **129** 7 ran ● **3rd** Oaklawn Handicap (Grade 2) (Oaklawn Park, April 3) 4yo+ 1m1f Fast 6 ran ● **2nd** New Orleans Handicap (Grade 2) (Fair Grounds, February 29) 4yo+ 1m1f Fast 8 ran ● **1st** Allowance Optional Claiming Race (Gulfstream Park, January 18) 4yo+ 1m½f Fast 8 ran **2003** **1st** Allowance Race (Aqueduct, December 12) 3yo+ 1m½f Fast 9 ran ● **6th** Allowance race (Saratoga, August 24) 3yo+ 1m1f Fast 9 ran ● **9th** National Musuem Of Racing Hall of Fame Stakes (Grade 2 Handicap) (Saratoga, August 4) 3yo 1m1f Yielding 11 ran ● **2nd** Iowa Derby (Prairie Meadows, July 5) 3yo 1m½f Fast 6 ran ● **1st** Allowance Race (Churchill Downs, June 8) 3yo+ 1m½f Fast 6 ran ● **2nd** Allowance (Churchill Downs, May 25) 3yo 1m½f Sloppy 6 ran ● **7th** Arkansas Derby (Grade 2) (Dirt) (Oaklawn Park, April 12) 3yo 1m1f Fast 12 ran ● **1st** Maiden Special Weight (Gulfstream Park, March 28) 3yo 1m½f Fast 9 ran ● **2nd** Maiden Special Weight (Gulfstream Park, February 22) 3yo 7f Fast 11 ran

Handicap, fully confirmed the impression that here was a major player at the top level.

He and Classic runner-up Roses In May produced a contest similar in style to the previous year's battle with Ghostzapper – with one crucial difference: this time Saint Liam won the battle. After racing four wide through the first turn, Saint Liam squared off with Roses In May, both running hard through fast fractions until the former powered away to score in emphatic style by nearly four lengths from a top-class rival who won the Dubai World Cup on his next start.

Saint Liam was receiving weight in the nine-furlong event but, make no mistake, this was an outstanding performance. Racing Post Ratings awarded Saint Liam a mark of 129, the joint-highest of his career, while respected commentator Mike Watchmaker, writing in the *Daily Racing Form*, described the winner as a "powerhouse", despite his having drifted out worryingly yet again in the stretch.

Instead of being sent across the world to Dubai, Saint Liam was sent across the continent for the $1 million Santa Anita Handicap, assigned top weight against a classy field of West Coast horses on his first attempt at ten furlongs. In retrospect, connections could have been forgiven for thinking that perhaps they should have risked the Dubai trip instead. Made 11-10 favourite despite being drawn on the outside in a field of 11, Saint Liam faded badly to finish sixth behind a dominant Rock Hard Ten.

Perhaps being shipped into a vastly different climate for a race not won by such a visitor for nearly 20 years played a part; perhaps his feet had troubled him. Either way, after such a mediocre run Saint Liam would not be tried again at the trip until the Classic.

Fortunately, the 'Big Cap' proved only a temporary blip, as a back-to-form Saint Liam recorded a comfortable Grade 1 victory over seasoned, if unspectacular, performers next time out in the Stephen Foster Handicap at Churchill Downs in June, when Frankel's name appeared on the racecard owing to Dutrow's ban.

Dutrow was out of the sin bin by the time Saint Liam reappeared at Saratoga in the nine-furlong Whitney Handicap, the first of a two-part epic full of the intriguing tactical nuances that can make American racing utterly compelling at times, in spite of its homogeneity.

Co-star in the Whitney was the Nick Zito-trained four-year-old Commentator – blisteringly fast but untried beyond seven furlongs - and Saint Liam proved vulnerable giving plenty of weight to such a rising star, aboard whom Gary Stevens produced the most astute of rides to steal what amounted to a two-horse race.

It was a case of different track, same names just over a month later at Belmont when Saint Liam, with Jerry Bailey replacing usual rider Edgar Prado, returned to the Woodward – and another clash with Commentator, this time at level weights.

In an attempt to soften up his representative's main rival, Dutrow employed a pair of 'rabbits', pacemakers designed to prevent Commentator from having things his own way. Though it was considered unsporting in some quarters, the ploy could not have worked better. Commentator, who resented the company up front, could not escape the attentions of the Dutrow team until the far turn. Saint Liam, meanwhile, enjoyed an untroubled passage in fourth; he soon joined Commentator and went past without any fuss as his rival folded dramatically. With Bailey still holding him tight, Saint Liam scored an effortless victory; a stuttering Commentator finished third, more than 14 lengths back.

Seven weeks later at Belmont Park, Saint Liam was sent off a worthy 9-4 favourite for the Breeders' Cup Classic, a race that was worth $4.68

million but lacked the field to match such an immense prize. As was the case for much of the day as a whole, the 13-strong field was denuded of stars, with the likes of Ghostzapper, Roses In May, the brilliant three-year-old Afleet Alex and Kentucky Derby winner Giacomo either retired or injured.

Indeed, apart from Saint Liam and impressive Jockey Club Gold Cup winner Borrego, there were few others who looked to hold a serious chance, albeit in a race that has produced its share of surprises over the years. The list of absentees, already lengthy, was added to the day before the race when Rock Hard Ten, expected to be the main market rival to Saint Liam, was a late withdrawal with a hoof injury.

Most of those who did show up failed to thrive. Three visitors from Europe, headed by Australia's Queen Elizabeth II Stakes winner Starcraft, trained in England by Luca Cumani and supplemented for $800,000, failed to land a significant blow, while Borrego finished tenth after what his rider described as a "clunker". Though some were worried about the trip and others the draw, Saint Liam did not clunk, despite losing ground by stepping out to the right when breaking awkwardly from his box inside Starcraft, who was widest of all. Bailey bided his time before moving Saint Liam up to a solid stalking position down the back stretch alongside Travers Stakes winner Flower Alley, a few lengths off Sun King and Suave in front. Flower Alley and Saint Liam, the latter out wide as usual, moved closer in tandem rounding the turn.

Flower Alley hit the front at the top of the stretch as the front-runners gave in, but Saint Liam immediately offered an intimidating presence on his outside, and he took command about a furlong out with a relentless gallop. Though his tenacious rival refused to buckle under, Saint Liam scored by a length, a winning margin that doesn't quite do justice to his superiority.

The bare form could not be rated alongside his best, but it meant an enormous amount to both jockey and trainer. Winning rider Bailey hinted, not for the first time, that he was on the verge of retirement, while the Breeders' Cup gave Dutrow powerful ammunition against his most trenchant critics. On the very day that security at the racecourse barns at Belmont was among the tightest ever seen in a bid to prevent any potential illegitimacies, the 46-year-old trainer sent out not one but two winners, Saint Liam's Classic success being preceded by Silver Train's victory in a thrilling renewal of the Sprint.

Saint Liam, officially retired soon after the race, takes up stallion duties in 2006 at a fee of $50,000, having proved conclusively that he was the number one American-trained horse still active at the end of 2005 – waywardness, dodgy feet, allegedly suspicious trainer and all.

While late-season ratings issued by the international handicappers left him 6lb behind world rankings leader Hurricane Run, it was still a fine achievement by a fine racehorse. Even if he wasn't Ghostzapper.

Saint Liam

bay horse, 13-4-2000

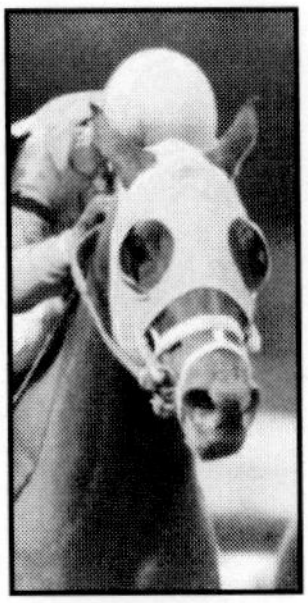

Saint Ballado br 1989	Halo	Hail To Reason	Turn-to Nothirdchance
		Cosmah	Cosmic Bomb Almahmoud
	Ballade	Herbager	Vandale Flagette
		Miss Swapsco	Cohoes Soaring
Quiet Dance gr 1993	Quiet American	Fappiano	Mr Prospector Killaloe
		Demure	Dr Fager Quiet Charm
	Misty Dancer	Lyphard	Northern Dancer Goofed
		Flight Dancer	Misty Flight Courbette

Bred by Edward P. Evans in Kentucky. $130,000 Saratoga yearling.

Sire Saint Ballado

Won 4 of 9 races, inc. Sheridan S.-Gr3, Arlington Classic-Gr2. Earned $302,820. Strong, lengthy, 16.2hh. Smart performer at around a mile on his day. Brother to champion racemare Glorious Song (dam of Rahy and Singspiel) and to champion 2-y-o Devil's Bag. Died in 2002. Stood last at Taylor Made Farm, Nicholasville, Kentucky, at a fee of $125,000. Sire of 10 crops of racing age, inc. notable winners: Captain Bodgit (Florida Derby-Gr1), Fantasy Angel (Gr3), Sister Act (Hempstead H.-Gr1), Sweetsouthernsaint (Gr3), Straight Man (Gr2), Yankee Victor (Metropolitan H.-Gr1), Flame Thrower (Gr2), Lindsay Jean (Gr3), Popular (Gr3), Saint Marden (Gr3), Freedom's Daughter (Gr2), Ocean Terrace (Gr3), Saint Liam (Donn H.-Gr1, Stephen Foster H.-Gr1, Woodward S.-Gr1, Breeders' Cup Classic-Gr1), Saintly Look (Gr3), Savedbythelight (Gr2), Ashado (Spinaway S.-Gr1, Kentucky Oaks-Gr1, Coaching Club American Oaks-Gr1, Breeders' Cup Distaff-Gr1, Ogden Phipps H.-Gr1, Go For Wand H.-Gr1), Lord Of The Game (Gr2), St Averil (Gr2).

Dam Quiet Dance

Won 6 of 23 races. Placed 2nd in Demoiselle S.-Gr1 at 2, won minor stakes race at 4. Failed fully to realise juvenile promise, but proved useful at around a mile on dirt. Half-sister to multiple US Gr3 winner Misty Gallore (by Halo) and to multiple English/Irish Gr1 winner Minstrella (by The Minstrel). Dam of: Quiet Broad (1999 f by Broad Brush; winner), Saint Liam (2000 c by Saint Ballado; multiple Gr1 winner), Congressionalhonor (2001 c by Forestry; Gr3 winner), Dance Quiet (2002 c by Saint Ballado; unplaced), Beatem Buster (2003 f by Honour And Glory; unraced to date). Barren in 2004, she has a filly foal by Tiznow, and was covered in 2005 by A.P. Indy.

Pedigree assessment

Because the likes of Ghostzapper, Roses In May, Rock Hard Ten and Afleet Alex were all absentees, the 2005 Breeders' Cup Classic could hardly be called a vintage renewal, but Saint Liam gave a convincing display to notch his fourth Grade 1 triumph of the campaign and thereby stake a serious claim for Horse of the Year honours. He has now retired to Lane's End Farm, ranking as the best son of his sire, who exceeded expectations at stud by proving no less successful than his brother Devil's Bag, a significantly more accomplished athlete. Saint Liam's prospects as a stallion will depend on the perceptions of breeders, who may look askance at his lack of precocity and sprinting ability. *TM*

Saoire

3yo chestnut filly **109**

Pivotal - Polish Descent (Ire) (Danehill (USA))

Owner Joseph Joyce

Trainer Ms F M Crowley

Breeder Mrs M L Parry

Career: **9** starts | won **2** | second **2** | third **1** | **£210,598** win and place

By Alan Sweetman

FRANCES CROWLEY entered the pages of Irish racing history in 2005 when saddling Saoire to win the Boylesports Irish 1,000 Guineas, the first time that an Irish Classic had been won by a female licence-holder. Back in the 1940s Mrs Toby Wellesley prepared Grand Weather to win the Irish 2,000 Guineas and Morning Wings to capture the Irish 1,000 Guineas, but in those less emancipated days her triumphs were officially credited to her head man, Eddie McGrath.

The world has moved on since then, but lest anyone make the mistake that attitudes have changed completely it is worth reflecting that Crowley is often described in the media in terms of her relationship to various males. She is indeed Joe Crowley's daughter, Pat Smullen's wife, and Aidan O'Brien's sister-in-law, but it is important to recognise that she has made her own distinctive mark on the Irish racing scene. In 1994 she became the first woman to win the Irish amateur championship, and the following year she retained the title with a very respectable tally of 31 wins. Since taking out a trainers' licence she has landed valuable prizes over jumps with the likes of Moscow Express, Sackville and Nil Desperandum.

Saoire had already advertised Crowley's skills during a fine juvenile campaign which held out the prospect that she would be even more effective when stepping up to a mile. A short-head defeat of Mona Lisa at Leopardstown had been followed by placings over seven furlongs at The Curragh in both the Group 1 Moyglare Stud Stakes, in which she justified a supplementary entry with her third behind Chelsea Rose, and the Group 3 CL Weld Park Stakes, when she handled soft ground efficiently in second behind Jazz Princess. A length and a half behind her in third in the Park Stakes was Virginia Waters, a Ballydoyle-trained filly who had already shown considerable promise.

Crowley had reckoned from the outset that she would get the best of

History in the making as the Frances Crowley-trained Saoire (right) defeats Penkenna Princess in the Irish 1,000 Guineas

Saoire as a three-year-old, and did not shirk from throwing her in at the deep end to make her seasonal debut in the 1,000 Guineas at Newmarket. Her rivals included Virginia Waters, who had already got her year off to a winning start in a Guineas trial at Leopardstown, and Pictavia, the filly who had kept her out of second place in the Moyglare. Without the benefit of an outing it looked a demanding assignment, and Saoire's task was compromised early on when she got involved in a scrimmage with Penkenna Princess. Nor did she get the clearest of passages as she began her challenge, and her eventual sixth of 20 was a creditable effort as Virginia Waters took the glory in commanding fashion.

Just three weeks later, Saoire renewed rivalry with Virginia Waters and the Newmarket runner-up Maids Causeway at The Curragh. This time everything fell into place. They finished pretty much in a heap, and were spread across the track, but Mick Kinane had Saoire well positioned throughout in a race that plainly favoured the highest-drawn runners, and after getting to the front early in the final furlong she stuck to her guns to resist Penkenna Princess by a short head. The only slight regret for Crowley was that it was not shared with her husband, who had been committed to riding the 33-1 fourth Utterly Heaven for his retaining stable. Unfortunately the rest of the season was to prove an

2005 Race record

5th Coolmore Fusaichi Pegasus Matron Stakes (Group 1) (Leopardstown, September 10) 3yo+ 1m Good to yielding **109** (TS 77) 9 ran. *Settled in 2nd, ridden 3f out, 3rd and outpaced early straight, kept on final furlong (D P McDonogh), beaten 1¾l by Attraction*

6th Darley Irish Oaks (Group 1) (Curragh, July 17) 3yo 1m4f Good to firm **103** (TS 103) 13 ran. *Mid-division, 7th halfway, 5th approaching straight, kept on same pace (P J Smullen), beaten 10l by Shawanda*

8th Audi Pretty Polly Stakes (Group 1) (Curragh, June 25) 3yo+ 1m2f Good to firm **109** 10 ran. *Settled 5th, ridden early straight, close 5th when hampered and checked under 1f out, no extra (F M Berry), beaten 3¾l by Alexander Goldrun*

1st Boylesports Irish 1,000 Guineas (Group 1) (Curragh, May 22) 3yo 1m Good to yielding **108** (TS 87) 18 ran. *Always prominent, challenged 1½f out, led under 1f out, soon strongly pressed, all out (M J Kinane), beat Penkenna Princess by shd*

6th UltimatePoker.com 1,000 Guineas Stakes (Group 1) (Newmarket, May 1) 3yo 1m Good to firm **104** (TS 95) 20 ran. *Held up, headway halfway, ridden over 2f out, stayed on same pace final furlong (J P Spencer), beaten 4½l by Virginia Waters*

2004

2nd C L Weld Park Stakes (Group 3) (Curragh, October 2) 2yo 7f Yielding to soft **102** (TS 100) 9 ran ● **3rd** Moyglare Stud Stakes (Group 1) (Curragh, September 5) 2yo 7f Good to firm **105** (TS 99) 12 ran ● **1st** Irish Stallion Farms EBF Fillies Maiden (Leopardstown, August 15) 2yo 7f Good to firm **81** (TS 32) 18 ran ● **2nd** Irish Stallion Farms EBF Fillies Maiden (Limerick, July 22) 2yo 7f Good **79** 13 ran

anti-climax for the filly whose Guineas triumph averted an overseas monopoly of the Irish Classics in 2005.

Stepped up to ten furlongs in the Audi Pretty Polly Stakes at The Curragh in June, she was thoroughly outgunned, along with other members of the Classic generation, as Alexander Goldrun led home a clean sweep of the first five placings for the four-year-old contingent. She ended up eighth of the ten runners, though there was some consolation in the fact that she was still close up in fifth when hampered early in the final furlong. The following month she contested the Darley Irish Oaks, and fortune again deserted her, with Smullen reporting that she had lost a shoe at the top of the hill, preventing her from striding out properly.

It was back to one mile for her final start in the Coolmore Fusaichi Pegasus Matron Stakes at Leopardstown in September. Equipped with blinkers for the first time, she tracked Attraction through the first half of the race but was outpaced off the home turn before keeping on to take fifth place, second-best of the three-year-olds and only a short head and a neck behind her old rival Virginia Waters.

At the Moyglare Dinner in December, the senior steward of the Turf Club made a special presentation to Crowley to mark Saoire's Classic triumph. No such courtesies were afforded to Mrs Wellesley all those years ago, but perhaps, in some small part, the gesture can be interpreted as a memorial to her pioneering achievement.

Saoire

chestnut filly, 29-4-2002

Pivotal ch 1993	Polar Falcon	Nureyev	**Northern Dancer** Special
		Marie d'Argonne	Jefferson Mohair
	Fearless Revival	Cozzene	Caro Ride The Trails
		Stufida	Bustino Zerbinetta
Polish Descent b 1993	Danehill	Danzig	**Northern Dancer** Pas de Nom
		Razyana	His Majesty Spring Adieu
	Nolnocan	Colum	Santa Claus Mitigation
		Cotoneaster	Never Say Die What Joy

Bred by Mrs Louise Parry in Wales. 4,000gns Newmarket December foal, €65,000 Tattersalls Ireland September yearling.

Sire Pivotal

Won 4 of 6 races, inc. King's Stand S.-Gr2, Nunthorpe S.-Gr1. Powerfully built, attractive sort, 16.3hh. High-class sprinter on fast ground. Stands at Cheveley Park Stud, Newmarket, at a fee of £65,000 (Oct 1). Sire of 6 crops of racing age, inc. notable winners: Golden Apples (Del Mar Oaks-Gr1, Beverly D S.-Gr1, Yellow Ribbon S.-Gr1), Kyllachy (Nunthorpe S.-Gr1), Low Pivot (Gr3), Needwood Blade (Gr3), Ratio (Gr3), Silvester Lady (Preis der Diana-Gr1), Captain Rio (Gr2), Chorist (Pretty Polly S.-Gr1), Megahertz (John C. Mabee H.-Gr1), Ringmoor Down (Gr3), Stolzing (Gr3), Humouresque (Gr3), Pivotal Point (Gr2), Somnus (Haydock Sprint Cup-Gr1, Prix Maurice de Gheest-Gr1, Prix de la Foret-Gr1), Lucky Spin (Gr3), Peeress (Sun Chariot S.-Gr1), Penkenna Princess (Gr3), Saoire (Irish 1,000 Guineas-Gr1), Windsor Knot (Gr3), Leo (Gr2).

Dam Polish Descent

Unraced. Quite respectably bred. By a top-class sprinter and highly successful sire. Half-sister to 4 winners, inc. Gr3-placed Wistful Tune (by Ballad Rock) and Listed-placed Wild Outcast (by Wolverlife). Dam half-sister to 8 other winners, inc. Lady Eileen (Listed; by Taufan). Dam of: Naomi de Bergerac (1997 f by Cyrano de Bergerac; winner), unnamed (1998 c by Alhijaz; died as a foal), Foronlymo (1999 g by Forzando; winner), Whittle Warrior (2000 g by Averti; winner), Newtown Chief (2001 g by So Factual; unplaced), Saoire (2002 f by Pivotal; Classic winner). She has a colt foal by Auction House, and has been tested in foal to Kyllachy. Not covered in 2002, had early abortion after coverings by Mister Baileys and Primo Valentino in 2003.

Pedigree assessment

Pivotal's star remained in the ascendant in 2005, and Saoire's contribution typified much of the success enjoyed to date by the Cheveley Park stallion. The Irish Guineas heroine came as the product of a cheap mare from a less than aristocratic background, and though it might be deemed unfortunate that her breeder, Louise Parry, parted with her for such a small sum, rewards came later. The filly's half-sister fetched 65,000gns and her dam realised 180,000gns, both at the December Sales. Shortly afterwards Mrs Parry learned that she was to receive the TBA's award as small breeder of the year – a fitting accolade for the producer of the first Classic winner born and raised in Wales. Although Saoire did not win again after her big triumph, she actually ran to a higher mark twice. *TM*

Scorpion (Ire)

3yo bay colt **123**

Montjeu (Ire) - Ardmelody (Law Society (USA))

Owner Mrs John Magnier & M Tabor

Trainer A P O'Brien

Breeder Grangemore Stud

Career: **7** starts	won **3**	second **2**	third **0**	**£659,897** win and place

By Lee Mottershead

AS ALL MEN know, some colours work for us, some colours work against us. No new man needs Trinny or Susannah to tell him that, while one hombre might look fabulous wearing dark green, another sporting the same shade can resemble an excessively boiled vegetable. Indeed, some colours work just perfectly. And that was surely on the minds of all who gazed on Frankie Dettori in the Doncaster paddock after his St Leger success on Scorpion. There can be no doubt. The deep dark blue of the Magnier silks suited his tanned skin a treat.

Yet, sadly, the two will complement each other no more. Hostilities erupted in the autumn between Flat racing's two superpowers. For so long the towering forces both on the track and in the breeding shed, the Coolmore and Maktoum camps found themselves at loggerheads, divided by a large slice of animosity and frost. Like JR Ewing and Cliff Barnes, or Ken Barlow and Mike Baldwin before them, Sheikh Mohammed and John Magnier were in the middle of their own Cold War. And Scorpion sat close to the heart of that conflict.

It had been a major surprise when Dettori announced he was going to team up with Scorpion in the first place. The Godolphin stable jockey, so closely associated with Sheikh Mohammed, had never previously ridden a winner for Scorpion's trainer Aidan O'Brien, while the occasions when he had taken mounts for him had been few and far between. So when Dettori declared in the run-up to the Leger that he would act as Kieren Fallon's deputy on Scorpion, he had effectively broken a major news story. Two months later, with the St Leger triumph firmly locked away, Dettori would break an even bigger one.

By the Tuesday in mid-November when Dettori appeared as Simon Mayo's guest on BBC Radio Five Live, the man he calls "the boss", Sheikh Mohammed, was in the middle of a major fallout with Magnier, the man half of Ireland calls "the boss". The dispute had kicked off a

Scorpion (right) wins the St Leger, but the main talking point was Frankie Dettori's presence in the saddle

few weeks earlier at the time of the major European yearling sales when the Maktoum family made clear it would not be buying progeny sired by Coolmore stallions. The shock announcement sent a shiver through the breeding industry, and triggered inevitable speculation as to what had prompted the move. No official answer ever came, but confirmation of the depth of enmity felt from Dubai towards an area of Tipperary arrived in Mayo's afternoon programme.

Mayo asked Dettori about winning the Leger for Coolmore. Dettori, who at the time of the race itself, answered a similar question with the words, "it's weird", this time went much further.

"In hindsight it perhaps wasn't the best thing to do," he said. "It's like Michael Schumacher one day driving for Ferrari and then driving another car. I didn't do anything wrong, as it was an important race and I thought the horse could win, so I rode it and did my job. But it left a bit of a sour taste with everybody, so perhaps I shouldn't have done it. They are our main rivals, and you can't be black one day and then white another day. I made a winning mistake, but it doesn't reflect well on my team when they see me ride for the main opposition." Partnering Scorpion had been, admitted Dettori, "a mistake". Would he ride for O'Brien again. "No", he would not.

But he did ride Scorpion that day at Doncaster, and, with no little irony, the horse's triumph was in no small part down to Dettori's brilliance. The Italian's place on the colt's back had first come about because Fallon had opted to take what would be the winning ride on Oratorio in the same day's Irish Champion Stakes. Dettori himself had been supposed

2005 Race record

10th Prix de l'Arc de Triomphe Lucien Barriere (Group 1) (Longchamp, October 2) 3yo+ 1m4f Good to soft **110** (TS 111) 15 ran. *Prominent, 4th straight, ridden 2f out, soon weakened and eased (coupled with Hurricane Run) (M J Kinane), beaten 13½l by Hurricane Run*

1st Ladbrokes St Leger Stakes (Group 1) (Doncaster, September 10) 3yo 1m6½f Heavy **120** (TS 72) 6 ran. *Made all, quickened over 4f out, shaken up over 3f out, 3 lengths clear when jinked left and brushed rail just inside final furlong, held on towards finish (L Dettori), beat The Geezer by 1l*

1st Juddmonte Grand Prix de Paris (Group 1) (Longchamp, July 14) 3yo 1m4f Good **123** (TS 118) 9 ran. *Close up, 2nd halfway, joined leader 3f out, led straight, driven 2f out, joined 1½f out, ridden clear, ran on strongly final stages, readily (K Fallon), beat Desideratum by 2½l*

2nd Budweiser Irish Derby (Group 1) (Curragh, June 26) 3yo 1m4f Good to firm **122** (TS 102) 9 ran. *Always prominent, 2nd from before halfway, challenged travelling well entering straight, led under 2f out, headed inside final furlong, kept on well under pressure (C O'Donoghue), beaten ½l by Hurricane Run*

16th Prix du Jockey Club (Group 1) (Chantilly, June 5) 3yo 1m2½f Good **97** (TS 92) 17 ran. *Held up in 16th, shaken up over 2f out, no impression (K Fallon), beaten 10l by Shamardal*

2nd Airlie Stud Gallinule Stakes (Group 3) (Curragh, May 22) 3yo 1m2f Good to yielding **108** (TS 38) 6 ran. *Settled 5th, driven along approaching straight, 4th 2f out, switched left over 1f out, ran on well close home, just failed (K Fallon), beaten shd by Im Spartacus*

1st Carrickmines Maiden (Leopardstown, May 8) 3yo+ 1m2f Soft to heavy **101** (TS 96) 10 ran. *Chased leaders, niggled along in 6th approaching straight, ridden on outer in moderate 5th 2f out, went 2nd 1f out, stayed on strongly final furlong to lead inside final 100yds, snugly at the finish (K Fallon), beat Magnolia Lane by ½l*

to be at Leopardstown to act as Johnny Murtagh's supersub aboard Derby hero Motivator. However, with dry conditions in Ireland threatening to rule out Motivator, Dettori opted to jump ship, desert Motivator and offer his services to the Scorpion team. Dettori's offer was gratefully accepted.

His enthusiasm for Scorpion's claims was understandable, for Scorpion's claims were strong indeed, strong enough for the son of Montjeu to be sent off a red-hot 10-11 favourite. That price reflected a career that had included no two-year-old racing, but one that had marked him down as among the best of his generation in the build-up to the world's oldest Classic.

Competitive life for Scorpion began at Leopardstown in early May. A €260,000 purchase, he went to the Dublin track with a tall reputation, and, despite beating Magnolia Lane by only half a length, he did enough to suggest that the reputation could be justified. As green as you like, he took an age to wear down his rival but one always sensed that he was going to get there and, under a beautifully educational Fallon ride, get there he did.

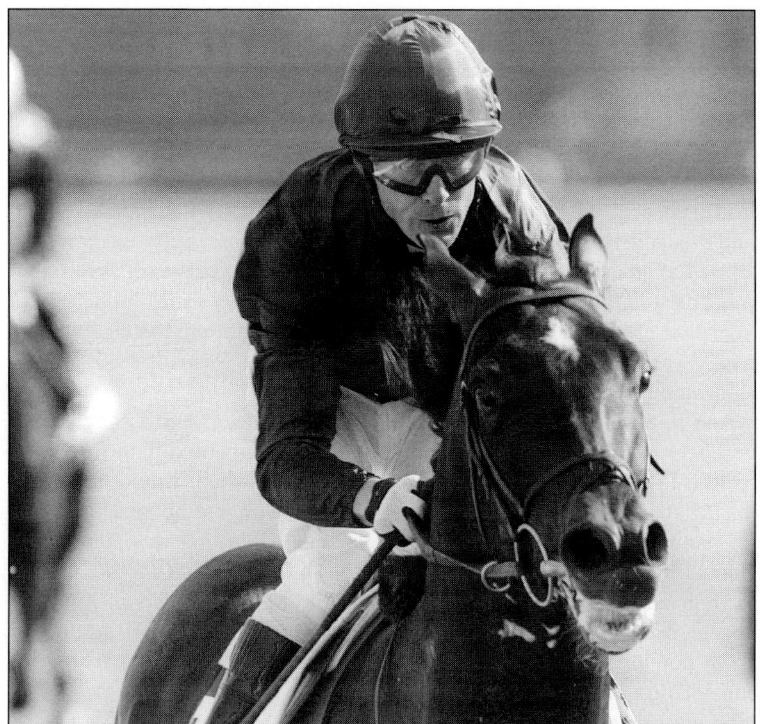

Scorpion, with Kieren Fallon in the saddle, follows up his Irish Derby second with victory in the Grand Prix de Paris

Described after Leopardstown by O'Brien as "one of our top horses", Scorpion was out again only 14 days later, this time at The Curragh, where he took his place in the Group 3 Gallinule Stakes, and this time got beat, albeit only by a short head, his lack of experience proving his undoing. Another defeat followed, but this time a far more comprehensive one, when he trailed in 16th of 17, ten lengths behind Godolphin's Shamardal, in the Prix du Jockey-Club. Fallon blamed the "lack of pace", but to the impartial observer Scorpion just looked a bit slow.

Given the way he had flopped at Chantilly, it was understandable that Scorpion should be sent off at 25-1 for the Irish Derby, a race in which he did not even start as Ballydoyle first string. Nor did Fallon ride for Ballydoyle, the pilot instead preferring to side with Coolmore's high-profile acquisition Hurricane Run, the Andre Fabre-trained horse who had come so close to catching Shamardal in the Jockey-Club. Fallon's decision proved spot on, but it still proved to be a massive day for Scorpion, who made Fallon and Hurricane Run work harder than seemed at one stage likely. Hurricane Run won, but Scorpion was beaten only half a length into second. A reputation had been restored.

Then it was back to France, but this time with an altogether more positive result. The Grand Prix de Paris, a prize most recently staged over a mile and a quarter in June, was for the first time being run over a mile and a half in July. The revamped race proved to be a perfect vehicle for Scorpion to parade his talents. Despite misbehaving in the preliminaries, in the process incurring a €10,000 fine for O'Brien, Scorpion was magnificent in the race. Always prominent in an event contested on quick ground and at a generous pace by French Group 1 standards, Scorpion was sent on by Fallon at the top of the Longchamp straight. Game, set and match was immediately his. Giving plenty every time Fallon's stick hit his rump, Scorpion careered away, bounding two and a half lengths clear of the well-regarded Desideratum. The victorious rider was suitably pleased, remarking that "the horse was just perfect today".

And so it was that Scorpion started favourite for the St Leger. There had been some racecourse rumour that O'Brien wanted to aim straight for the Prix de l'Arc de Triomphe but, while Scorpion would indeed go for the Arc, he would go for the Leger first. Fallon was not at Doncaster, and neither was O'Brien nor Magnier, but while this was clearly not Coolmore's biggest priority on the day, Scorpion still added another Classic to their cupboard. For Dettori, it would be a tenth British Classic, but not, as it turned out, one he will look back on with the most fondness.

On horribly heavy ground that did not play to Scorpion's strengths, the odds-on favourite was nursed around Town Moor by his new jockey. The pace dictated by Dettori was no better than steady, only increased to any great degree when the turn for home had been completed. Up the straight, Scorpion's five opponents were dismissed one by one, all that is except The Geezer, whose late challenge looked ever more dangerous when the pacesetter veered dramatically into the rail after Dettori gave him a hefty smack just inside the final furlong. Class will out, however, and Scorpion was soon back on track and never really in danger of losing. He got the money by a length. Everybody associated with the winner, for a while at least, was happy.

Scorpion went for the Arc, but, like all St Leger winners who go for the Arc, he was beaten, finishing tenth of 15 under Mick Kinane, as Fallon again deserted him to win the European championship on Hurricane Run. And it was as Magnier celebrated Hurricane Run's election as Horse of the Year at the Cartier awards, one day after Dettori's Five Live interview, that the big man gave his thoughts on the hot topic. He wanted, he said, to thank O'Brien and all who made Coolmore's great year possible, "least of all Frankie Dettori". And there was more. "Frankie," said Magnier, "we still love you and we forgive you, because you know not what you do."

Scorpion races on as a four-year-old. If Fallon ever deserts him again, it's a pretty safe bet that one leading jockey will not be ringing or be rung for the ride.

Scorpion

bay colt, 5-2-2002

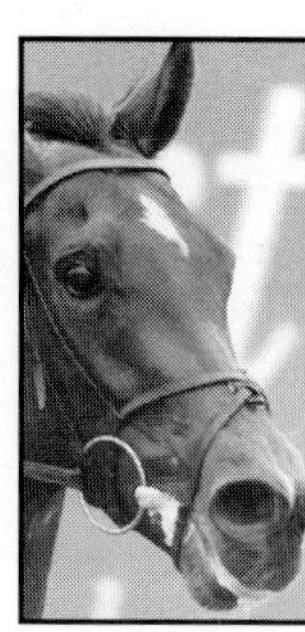

Montjeu b 1996	Sadler's Wells	Northern Dancer	Nearctic Natalma
		Fairy Bridge	Bold Reason Special
	Floripedes	Top Ville	High Top Sega Ville
		Toute Cy	Tennyson Adele Toumignon
Ardmelody b 1987	Law Society	Alleged	Hoist The Flag Princess Pout
		Bold Bikini	Boldnesian Ran-Tan
	Thistlewood	Kalamoun	Zeddaan Khairunissa
		Le Melody	Levmoss Arctic Melody

Bred by Grangemore Stud in Ireland. €260,000 Goffs Orby yearling.

Sire Montjeu

Won 11 of 16 races, inc. Prix Greffulhe-Gr2, Prix du Jockey-Club-Gr1, Irish Derby-Gr1, Prix Niel-Gr2, Prix de l'Arc de Triomphe-Gr1, Tattersalls Gold Cup-Gr1, Grand Prix de Saint-Cloud-Gr1, King George VI & Queen Elizabeth S.-Gr1, Prix Foy-Gr2. Also 2nd in Prix Lupin at 3, and in Champion S. at 4. Tallish, well-made, but not strikingly handsome individual. One of the best 12f horses of recent times. Well-bred. The best son of his outstanding sire. Out of a lightly raced high-class stayer (won Prix de Lutece-Gr3, 2nd in Prix Royal Oak-Gr1). Family of multiple Pattern-winning stayer Dadarissime, Gr3 winner Le Mamamouchi and Dear Doctor (Arlington Million). Stands at Coolmore Stud at a (2006) fee of €125,000. Sire of 2 racing crops, inc: Corre Caminos (Gr3), Hurricane Run (Irish Derby-Gr1, Prix de l'Arc de Triomphe-Gr1), Montare (Gr2), Motivator (Racing Post Trophy-Gr1, Derby S.-Gr1), Scorpion (Grand Prix de Paris-Gr1, St Leger-Gr1).

Dam Ardmelody

Unraced. Half-sister to 8 winners (1 Listed). By an Irish Derby winner, out of an unraced sister to Karol (Listed winner, Gr2-placed), and half-sister to 8 other winners, inc. champion stayer Ardross (13 Pattern races) and Gesedeh (Gr3 winner). Grand-dam won twice, half-sister to Arctique Royal (Irish 1,000 Guineas). Next dam won Musidora Stakes and is ancestress of 6 individual Pattern winners in 2005. Dam of: Memories (1991 f by Don't Forget Me; Gr2 winner), Victor Tycoon (1992 c by Last Tycoon; winner), Danish Rhapsody (1993 g by Danehill; Listed winner, Gr3-placed), Garuda (1994 c by Danehill; Listed winner, Gr1-placed), Like My Style (1995 f by Alzao; unraced), Social Scene (1996 f by Grand Lodge; winner), Darkling (1997 f by Grand Lodge; placed), unnamed (2000 f by Peintre Celebre; died as a foal), Scorpion (2002, by Montjeu; dual Gr1 winner). She has a yearling filly by Galileo. Not covered in 1997, 2004 and 2005, barren to Spectrum in 1999, and to Peintre Celebre in 2001.

Pedigree assessment

Scorpion probably ran his best race in defeat as runner-up to Hurricane Run in the Irish Derby. His victories in the Grand Prix de Paris and St Leger were gained against relatively weak competition. As he flopped badly in the Prix du Jockey-Club and the Arc, it may be that he has two ways of running, but his pedigree always marked him out to be a true stayer who would need at least a mile and a half. It is hard to see him as a dominant performer at four, but there will surely be opportunities for him in Group 1 staying tests. *TM*

Sergeant Cecil

6yo chestnut gelding **116**

King's Signet (USA) - Jadidh (Touching Wood (USA))

Owner Terry Cooper

Trainer B R Millman

Breeder D E Hazzard

Career: **35** starts | won **6** | second **12** | third **5** | **£429,855** win and place

By Steve Dennis

WHAT'S he doing in here? This book is for Group 1 winners – Classic heroes, sprint kings, magical milers. Look, old chap, it's just not done to let the rank and file in. Dam was a hurdler, I hear. Not our type at all. Handicapper, you know.

He may be a little too blue-collar for the blue-bloods, but Sergeant Cecil's exploits in 2005 entitled him to look anyone in the eye. No horse has ever done what Sergeant Cecil did – win the three great staying handicaps, Northumberland Plate, Ebor and Cesarewitch – in the same season. It was a feat that saw him voted a runaway winner in the poll for ROA/Racing Post Horse of the Year.

The ranks of staying handicappers are generally characterised by plenty of guts and precious little glory – rarely mentioned in dispatches and often dismissed as betting-shop fodder. That was Sergeant Cecil when the season started, yet by its end he was front-page news.

His transformation coincided with his association with Alan Munro, who enjoyed a remarkable return to race-riding in 2005. Munro won the 1991 Derby and King George aboard Generous before carving out a career in Hong Kong, but he began a sabbatical in 2000 during which time he practised martial arts and reached the level of black belt in karate.

On his return to Britain he struck up an instant rapport with trainer Rod Millman, with winners flowing from day one. Munro rode 60 winners in the year – 19 for Millman – but his three aboard Sergeant Cecil far outshone his other victories.

The first leg of the unique hat-trick came in the two-mile John Smith's Northumberland Plate at Newcastle, his fourth outing of the season. Munro gave him a confident ride, sticking to the rail throughout and relying on his mount's ability to find a turn of foot when all around him were keeping on at one pace. The gaps opened up and the £104,000 prize was his by a length and a half from Tungsten Strike. Millman said: "As they say,

Alan Munro urges the gallant Sergeant Cecil into the lead in the Cesarewitch, creating a slice of Turf history

this was the plan, so I don't know where he'll go next."

If everything after that was a bonus, Sergeant Cecil was ready to cash in. A narrow defeat at Glorious Goodwood was a stepping-stone to the Totesport Ebor at York where, off a 4lb higher mark, he was given what the *Racing Post* analyst called "a balls-of-steel ride" by Munro. Held up off the pace, his stealthy progress through the field was rewarded with running room when required and he hit the front in the last half-furlong, eventually beating Carte Diamond by a length.

With his stable star in such irrepressible form, Millman went gunning for Group-race prestige in the Doncaster Cup, and it took a horse of the calibre of Millenary, under a brilliant ride from Richard Quinn, to deny him. Sergeant Cecil had come so far in such a short space of time, but his defining moment would require him to go just a little bit further. Two and a quarter miles, to be precise, in the Totesport Cesarewitch at Newmarket on Champions Day.

Sergeant Cecil was 5lb well-in for the great autumn marathon, the handicapper being unable to reassess him following his Doncaster run, and despite racing off an official rating of 104, comfortably his highest ever, he was sent away the 10-1 third-favourite in a field of 34.

It was a rough race, although in his customary fashion Munro kept Sergeant Cecil hidden away from the firing line until beginning an irrepressible, implacable challenge with two furlongs to run. It looked as though King Revo had gone beyond recall, but Munro and Sergeant Cecil had no intention of playing second fiddle and they hit the front on the hill, pulling out enough to win by three-quarters of a length. The crowd greeted them like prodigals, and rightly so. When you think you've

2005 Race record

1st totesport Cesarewitch (Heritage Handicap) (Newmarket, October 15) 3yo+ 2m2f Good to soft **116** (TS 108) 34 ran. *Held up, headway 2f out, stayed on to lead near finish (A Munro), beat King Revo by 3/4l*

2nd GNER Doncaster Cup (Group 2) (Doncaster, September 8) 3yo+ 2m2f Good **111** (TS 68) 7 ran. *Held up in rear, headway 4f out, effort 2f out, ridden to lead 1f out, headed and not quicken well inside final furlong (A Munro), beaten 3/4l by Millenary*

1st totesport Ebor (Heritage Handicap) (York, August 17) 3yo+ 1m6f Good **109** (TS 89) 20 ran. *Took keen hold, held up and behind, headway 3f out, squeezed through and stayed on well to lead inside final furlong (A Munro), beat Carte Diamond by 1l*

3rd Tatler Summer Season Stakes (Handicap) (Goodwood, July 26) 3yo+ (0-105 handicap) 1m6f Good to soft **106** (TS 98) 13 ran. *Held up in rear, progress on outer over 3f out, stayed on but always held final furlong (A Munro), beaten 1 1/4l by Golden Quest*

1st John Smith's Northumberland Plate (Heritage Handicap) (Newcastle, June 25) 3yo+ 2m Good **101** (TS 56) 20 ran. *Held up on inside, smooth headway over 2f out, weaved through to lead inside final furlong, kept on strongly (A Munro), beat Tungsten Strike by 1 1/2l*

3rd Vodafone Handicap (Epsom, June 4) 4yo+ (0-100 handicap) 1m4f Good **101** (TS 100) 20 ran. *Settled in midfield, progress on outer 3f out, pressed winner well over 1f out, soon outpaced, lost 2nd near finish (A Munro), beaten 2 1/2l by Crow Wood*

2nd paddypower.com Stakes (Handicap) (Newbury, May 14) 4yo+ (0-100 handicap) 1m4f Firm **100** (TS 48) 10 ran. *In rear, headway on rails over 3f out, not much room over 2f out, switched right and headway over 1f out, took 2nd inside final furlong but no chance with winner (A Munro), beaten 3l by Flamboyant Lad*

12th bet@bluesq.com Great Metropolitan Stakes (Handicap) (Epsom, April 20) 4yo+ (0-95 handicap) 1m4f Good to soft **66** (TS 40) 13 ran. *Behind, effort on inside 3f out, soon weakened (A Munro), beaten 27l by Tender Falcon*

Other wins

2004 **1st** Sony Wega Handicap (Ascot, July 9) 3yo+ (0-90 handicap) 1m4f Good **95** (TS 83) 11 ran 2003 **1st** Hampton Court Handicap (Sandown, July 4) 3yo+ (0-90 handicap) 1m6f Good **93** 10 ran ● **1st** Betting Brain Has Evolved Handicap (Sandown, May 27) 3yo+ (0-85 handicap) 1m6f Good to firm **87** 10 ran

seen it all before, it is most welcome to discover that isn't the case.

Millman took the applause and spread the praise, saying: "It was wonderful just to have been able to have a crack and unbelievable to have achieved it. The credit has to go to a good horse, good staff and a good jockey. Alan Munro has been amazing and rides this horse so well. We shall have to start thinking about the Cup races for him next season."

With Westerner ensconced at Coolmore, there is room at the top of the staying division. Sergeant Cecil has rather run himself out of handicaps, so the Cup route may become a necessity. His detractors may have damned him hitherto with the badge of 'handicapper'. but he wore that badge like a medal and won himself a lasting place in Turf history. The story may not be over; 2006 may bring him a Group 1 garnish and another place in these pages. Sergeant Cecil, we salute you.

Sergeant Cecil *chestnut gelding, 2-5-1999*

King's Signet ch 1989	Nureyev	Northern Dancer	Nearctic Natalma
		Special	Forli Thong
	Sigy	Habitat	Sir Gaylord Little Hut
		Satu	Primera Creation
Jadidh b 1988	Touching Wood	Roberto	Hail To Reason Bramalea
		Mandera	Vaguely Noble Foolish One
	Petrol	Troy	Petingo La Milo
		Rambling Rose	Silly Season Honeysuckle Rose

Bred by Don Hazzard in Britain

Sire King's Signet

Unraced at 2, won 2 (both 6f) of 6 starts at 3, won 3 (inc. Stewards' Cup, Listed Scarbrough S) of 6 starts at 4. Progressed into very useful sprinter, though well beaten only 2 starts in Pattern company. By top-class miler and outstanding sire of variety of performers, mainly milers and sprinters. Half-brother to Gr3 winners Radjhasi and Sicyos out of outstanding sprinter. First foals 1995, exported after 2000 covering season to Saudi Arabia. Very modest record overall from very limited chances, sire of: Bali Royal (Listed winner), Sergeant Cecil (Gr2 placed).

Dam Jadidh

Unraced at 2, placed over 14f only Flat start at 3. Placed over 2m1f in 8 subsequent Flat starts. Won 6 (2m1f to 2m6f) of 57 starts over hurdles from 3 to 9. By St Leger winner with poor stud record. Half-sister to Listed winner Refuse To Lose. Dam half-sister to useful 2yo Rahik (grand-dam of Gr3-winning 2yo Kings Point) out of smart sprinter Rambling Rose. Dam of: Sergeant Cecil (1999 g by King's Signet; Gr2-placed winner), Jayer Gilles (2000 g by Busy Flight; placed), 2003 c by Kayf Tara.

Pedigree assessment

Sergeant Cecil has outrun his pedigree in terms of both stamina and class. Although his dam was a hurdler by a St Leger winner, she is from a fairly pacy family, and speed underpins King's Signet's performance and pedigree. It is tempting to attribute Sergeant Cecil's stamina to maternal grandsire Touching Wood, but in the end the gelding is one of those Flat horses best judged without reference to his pedigree. *JH*

Shamardal (USA)

3yo bay colt **127**

Giant's Causeway (USA) - Helsinki (Machiavellian (USA))

Owner Godolphin

Trainer Saeed Bin Suroor

Breeder Brilliant Stable

Career: **7** starts	won **6**	second **0**	third **0**	**£1,099,290** win and place

By Lee Mottershead

RICHIE BENAUD, the legendary cricket commentator, said goodbye in the summer of 2005, and so did Shamardal. Like Benaud, Shamardal went out at the top, exiting stage left at the very height of his powers. Like Benaud, Shamardal bade farewell while following the tried and trusted formula of "always leave them wanting more". And, like Benaud, Shamardal swapped the British winter for the Australian summer. The similarities are uncanny.

Shamardal was a racehorse with a very special story, a story that contained many an unanswered question. What would have happened if he had been able to run in the Eclipse? Didn't he get lonely always being out in front? And were we supposed to emphasise the 'ar' or the 'dal'? So many questions, so few answers.

Then there's the irony, never more evident than in the Dubai desert on Nad Al Sheba racecourse. It was here that Shamardal made his first public appearance of a three-year-old campaign that had been long anticipated. We had wanted so much to see Shamardal at three because Shamardal had been so very good at two. He had been champion juvenile, the best of his generation, the unbeaten 'go to whoa' winner of three starts, most significantly the title-deciding Dewhurst Stakes. He had gone into the winter as ante-post favourite for the 2,000 Guineas, and, without any doubt, the horse to beat at Newmarket. Unfortunately for those who had backed Shamardal for the Guineas, Shamardal would never get to Newmarket.

He did not go because of Godolphin. Eight days after his Dewhurst tour de force, Shamardal had been transferred from Mark Johnston to Saeed Bin Suroor. Instead of wintering on the North Yorkshire moors of Middleham, he would winter in the sunny climes of the United Arab Emirates. And instead of going for Classic glory in the Guineas, he would run in the UAE Derby with one eye focused firmly on the Kentucky

Shamardal (near side) after his narrow victory in the French Guineas under a fine ride from Frankie Dettori

equivalent, that Run for the Roses that has always eluded Godolphin's grasp.

The decision to direct Shamardal towards Churchill Downs via Nad Al Sheba was greeted with surprise but, more than that, it was greeted with relish by the conspiracy theorists. It was said in the build-up to the UAE Derby that Shamardal was being sacrificed so that stablemate Dubawi – a son of Sheikh Mohammed's beloved Dubai Millennium – would face an easier task in the Guineas. The accusation was dismissed by Godolphin, who reasoned that the Kentucky Derby was a huge race, but even if talk of Shamardal being a sacrificial lamb was scurrilous and untrue, the decision to race Shamardal on dirt in the desert was one that backfired spectacularly.

And herein lies the irony. For it was in Sheikh Mohammed's own back garden – albeit one covered mostly with sand, along with a little grass – and on the racecourse and the race night that he established to focus the sporting world's attention on Dubai, that Shamardal suffered the only defeat of his otherwise flawless career. More than that, this was a defeat of monumental proportions.

To quote Godolphin racing manager Simon Crisford, it all went "pear-shaped". Shamardal went off like the proverbial clappers. Racing on dirt for the first – and, as things turned out, last – time, he began at a rare rate of knots, his enthusiasm for the early exchanges increased by the

2005 Race record

1st St James's Palace Stakes (Group 1) (York, June 14) 3yo 1m Good to firm **127** (TS 126) 8 ran. *Made all, quickened 3f out, clear 2f out, readily (K McEvoy), beat Ad Valorem by 3l*

1st Prix du Jockey Club (Group 1) (Chantilly, June 5) 3yo 1m2½f Good **117** (TS 110) 17 ran. *Made all, ridden and quickened clear 1½f out, held on well (L Dettori), beat Hurricane Run by nk*

1st Gainsborough Poule d'Essai des Poulains (Group 1) (Grande Piste) (Longchamp, May 15) 3yo 1m Soft **117** (TS 112) 15 ran. *Made all, driven out, just held on (L Dettori), beat Indesatchel by hd*

9th UAE Derby Sponsored By Saeed & Mohammed Al Naboodah (Dirt) (Group 2) (Nad Al Sheba, March 26) 3yo 1m1f Fast **69** 12 ran. *Led, disputed lead halfway, ridden straight, headed 2½f out, weakened quickly, eased final 1½f (L Dettori), beaten 46l by Blues And Royals*

2004

1st Darley Dewhurst Stakes (Group 1) (Newmarket, October 16) 2yo 7f Soft **125** (TS 127) 9 ran ● **1st** Veuve Clicquot Vintage Stakes (Group 2) (Goodwood, July 28) 2yo 7f Good **114** (TS 99) 10 ran ● **1st** EBF Maiden Stakes (Ayr, July 12) 2yo 6f Good **95** (TS 97) 7 ran

attention of eyeballing rivals. Then, as the field swung for home, he stopped as if shot, gone in a stride, a spent force. A weary, dejected sight, he carried Frankie Dettori past the post 46 lengths behind Godolphin second-string Blues And Royals.

The script had not gone according to plan. "If he'd kept up that pace, he'd be a motorbike, not a racehorse," said Dettori.

Yet on that Nad Al Sheba night, even Shamardal's future as a racehorse seemed open to doubt. His reputation – which just minutes earlier had been towering – was now in tatters.

Soon news emerged that Shamardal was slightly shinsore and would not be asked to contest the Kentucky Derby. His future once again lay in Europe – and his future would turn out to be extremely bright indeed.

He returned to action 15 days after Dubawi had finished fifth in the Guineas. There was, however, still a Guineas for him to race in, albeit at Longchamp rather than at Newmarket. The Poule d'Essai des Poulains did not look a great race on paper and, despite his ignominious effort at Nad Al Sheba, Shamardal was sent off 4-1 favourite in Britain and at little more than 3-1 on Longchamp's pari-mutuel.

Crisford admitted that it was a case of having to "start all over again" for the former two-year-old champion, who went to Paris seeking to give Godolphin a boost after a spring that had not gone according to plan. Shamardal did exactly what his connections needed him to do.

But here comes further irony. For although Shamardal returned to winning ways in the Poulains, his was a triumph that was largely credited to the efforts of Dettori. Godolphin's No.1 excels at Longchamp, and nobody came close to riding it better in the French Guineas. After Shamardal

Frankie Dettori drives Shamardal to complete the second leg of a French Classic double in the Prix du Jockey-Club

bounced out of the stalls with ears pricked, the boy in blue opted to let him exploit his inside draw and bowl along in front. Yet this was no ordinary piece of front-running riding. This was a masterclass in waiting in front.

Dettori judged the pace to a nicety. Making the most of both Longchamp's turning mile and the easy lead, he utilised Shamardal's energy reserves to perfection. As the line drew closer, the colt's stride shortened and his rivals closed, but where it mattered he was still in front, albeit only narrowly, by a head from Indesatchel.

Remarkably, just three weeks later, Dettori and Shamardal were allowed to stage a repeat at Chantilly when the son of Giant's Causeway returned to France to bid for back-to-back Classics in the Prix du Jockey-Club.

Once more, it was as if the Gods were smiling on Shamardal. For a start, the Jockey-Club was being run over its new, reduced distance of ten and a half furlongs. That suited Shamardal. What suited him even more was the way the race panned out.

At Chantilly, as at Longchamp, Dettori was allowed free rein in front. He set exactly the pace he wanted, and that pace was slow. The first three horses passing the chateau were three of the first five to finish. It was a race in which sitting close to the head of affairs reaped dividends and none sat closer to the pace than Shamardal.

Having rushed his mount to the front before slowing the tempo after three furlongs, the Godolphin number one injected real speed into the contest only 300 metres from home. The Jockey-Club had turned into a sprint up half the Chantilly straight and nothing behind Shamardal was better positioned for that sprint than Shamardal himself.

But despite being a dual Classic hero, Shamardal was once more semi-snubbed in victory. Many pundits argued that this was the race that Hurricane Run had lost, not the race that Shamardal had won. It was, they insisted, all down to Dettori.

Poor old Shamardal. Despite suddenly not being able to lose, he could not win.

Thank goodness, then, for the St James's Palace Stakes. For at Royal Ascot at York, Dettori could not receive the plaudits, for Dettori was not there. He was absent through suspension. Dubawi was absent because of the ground. Despite his sterling performances, Shamardal, it seemed, was still playing second fiddle to his exalted Godolphin companion. Both horses were entered at the final declaration stage, with Dubawi considered much the likeliest runner thanks to the forecast rain.

But the rain did not come, and neither did Dubawi. And in staying away, Dubawi left the path clear for Shamardal to achieve his finest hour and post one of the year's greatest performances.

Ridden by Kerrin McEvoy, the horse was quite brilliant. Again sent straight to the front, he once more made all, but this time there was no doubting his huge supremacy. Always moving superbly, he came clear with effortless ease when the question was popped. Entering the final furlong, his advantage had stretched to about six lengths, and despite being eased down close home he was still three lengths too strong for Ad Valorem and nearly five lengths too strong for an admittedly below-par Oratorio. It was a visually stunning performance.

The excitement generated by Shamardal's display was heightened in the winner's enclosure when Sheikh Mohammed declared that Shamardal would take on Motivator at Sandown. It was the sort of great-for-racing decision that has typified Godolphin's approach to the sport. We awaited the clash with relish but were not allowed to taste it.

Shamardal had run his last race. On the eve of the Eclipse, he was retired after being diagnosed with an osteochondral fracture fragment in his right-fore fetlock, an injury that was deemed to have occurred on the gallops two mornings earlier. The Shamardal story – at least the racecourse element – was over. He would become a dual-hemisphere shuttle stallion.

Still there were so many questions left unanswered. In particular there was Sandown. Certainly it was possible to argue that Shamardal would have won the Eclipse. But no matter. For while it remains possible to knock what Shamardal did at Longchamp and Chantilly, he still did it. He ended his racing life unbeaten on turf, the winner of six of his seven starts, a champion two-year-old, a dual Classic winner and the first horse ever to complete the Prix du Jockey-Club-St James's Palace Stakes double.

Shamardal was hailed by Bin Suroor as "one of the best horses Godolphin has had". And he was.

Shamardal *bay colt, 27-3-2002*

Parents	Grandparents	Great-grandparents	Great-great-grandparents
Giant's Causeway ch 1997	Storm Cat	Storm Bird	Northern Dancer South Ocean
		Terlingua	Secretariat Crimson Saint
	Mariah's Storm	Rahy	Blushing Groom Glorious Song
		Immense	Roberto Imsodear
Helsinki b 1993	Machiavellian	Mr Prospector	Raise A Native Gold Digger
		Coup de Folie	Halo Raise The Standard
	Helen Street	Troy	Petingo La Milo
		Waterway	Riverman Boulevard

Bred by Brilliant Stable in USA. Unsold $485,000 as Keeneland November foal; 50,000gns Tattersalls Houghton yearling.

Sire Giant's Causeway

Won 9 of 13 starts, inc. Curragh Futurity S.-Gr3, Prix de la Salamandre-Gr1, Gladness S.-Gr3, St James's Palace S.-Gr1, Eclipse S.-Gr1, Sussex S.-Gr1, York International S.-Gr1, Irish Champion S.-Gr1. Also 2nd in 2,000 Guineas, Irish 2,000 Guineas, Queen Elizabeth II S. and Breeders' Cup Classic. A striking individual, and a tough, top-class performer from 8-10.5f. Big, strong, consistent, effective on fast and soft turf and on dirt. By a champion North American sire out of a winner of 6 Graded races. Stands at Ashford Stud, Kentucky, at a (2006) fee of $300,000. Sire of 2 crops of racing age, inc: Aragorn (Gr2), Footstepsinthesand (2,000 Guineas-Gr1), Maids Causeway (Coronation S.-Gr1), My Typhoon (Gr2), Naissance Royale (Gr2), Shamardal (Dewhurst S.-Gr1, Poule d'Essai des Poulains-Gr1, Prix du Jockey Club-Gr1, St James's Palace S.-Gr1), Diamond Omi (Gr2), First Samurai (Hopeful S-Gr1, Champagne S.-Gr1), Frost Giant (Gr3).

Dam Helsinki

Ran only at 3 years, won 1 (10f newcomers' race at Deauville) out of 3 starts. Placed 3rd in Listed, 6th in Gr3. Late May foal who was slow to come to hand, seemingly frail. Appeared to stay 12f. Sister to Street Cry (earned $5 million, Gr1 winner in Dubai and US), half-sister to Listed winner Historian (f by Pennekamp), Listed-placed winner Sovetsky (c by Soviet Star) and to 3 lesser winners, inc. Grecian Slipper (dam of 2 Gr3 winners). By the leading European-based son of Mr Prospector out of a winner of the Irish Oaks. From a notable Ballymacoll Stud family. Dam of: Lushs Lad (1998 c by Wolfhound; winner), Helsinka (2000 f by Pennekamp; placed), Shamardal (2002 c by Giant's Causeway; quadruple Gr1 winner), Emirates World (2003 c by Maria's Mon; unraced to date). She has a yearling filly by Unbridled's Song, and a colt foal by Cherokee Run.

Pedigree assessment

But for the misconceived plan to turn him into a dirt horse, the record would show that Shamardal retired undefeated. Unfortunately, the record also shows that he retired early without having been tested by older horses – and early enough to be covering mares in the southern hemisphere at the time we might have been learning just how good he was. Three more Group 1 victories certainly added to his reputation, but he certainly would not have beaten Hurricane Run in the Prix du Jockey-Club at the race's traditional distance. Shamardal will be at Kildangan at a fee of €40,000 in 2006. *TM*

Shawanda (Ire)

3yo bay filly **123**

Sinndar (Ire) - Shamawna (Ire) (Darshaan)

Owner H H Aga Khan

Trainer A de Royer-Dupre

Breeder H H The Aga Khan's Studs

Career: **7** starts | won **5** | second **1** | third **0** | **£313,182** win and place

By Lee Mottershead

SOME things that used to happen do not anymore. Things that once were, no longer are. The Tories used to be the natural party of government. They no longer are. The United Kingdom used to win the Eurovision Song Contest. She no longer does. Tomatoes used to taste like tomatoes. Now, by and large, they don't taste of anything. There are countless examples. Take fillies winning the Arc. That doesn't happen anymore either.

Go back a few decades and it used to. Return to the late 1970s and early 1980s, and it actually happened quite a lot. Five consecutive Arcs from 1979 were won by fillies, the quintet including the mighty All Along in 1983. Since then, only Urban Sea has been good enough to triumph in the rotten renewal of 1993. All that being the case, perhaps we should not have been surprised that Shawanda was unable to buck the trend in 2005.

It is testament to the impression that Shawanda had made in the run-up to the Prix de l'Arc de Triomphe that so much was expected of her on the big day. It is because she had looked so dazzling in Group 1 company prior to the Arc that she was sent off at just 3-1 on the British industry betting. And dazzling is exactly what she had looked. Nay, more than that, she had looked awesome.

She was, of course, born to do the job. Owned and bred by the Aga Khan, Shawanda is a daughter of the Aga's dual Derby and Arc-winning stallion Sinndar. Her dam, Shamawna, once finished second in the Prix du Royaumont, a 12-furlong fillies' Group 3 run on French Derby weekend at Chantilly.

It was in the same race that Shawanda first made a big impression herself. She went into the contest with three runs to her name, none of which had come as a juvenile. She finished second on her April debut at Maisons-Laffitte before posting easy wins at Chantilly and Longchamp.

Shawanda quickens right away from Playful Act and company for a highly impressive win in the Irish Oaks

Returning to Chantilly for the Royaumont, the Alain de Royer-Dupre-trained filly did the job in fine style, making virtually all under Christophe Soumillon to beat Royal Highness – a subsequent Group 2 winner – by two and a half lengths. It was a display that earned her a crack at Classic glory.

A fee of €40,000 was paid to put Shawanda into the Darley Irish Oaks, a heat that contained the Epsom Oaks third as well as the winners of the Irish 1,000 Guineas, Ribblesdale Stakes and Lancashire Oaks. On reflection, those facts are deceptive, because the form of the Irish Oaks did not, in truth, amount to much, with few of the beaten horses achieving anything of note over the following months.

Nothing, however, should be taken away from Shawanda, for the manner of her victory was spectacular. Performing on the fastest ground she had encountered, she annihilated the opposition. Sauntering into the lead at the quarter-mile pole, the noseband-wearing lady careered away under no meaningful pressure, bounding five lengths clear at the line. She was, in the words of her smitten jockey Soumillon, "my easiest Group 1 winner", and value for double the margin.

It was just as easy in the Prix Vermeille. Having been rated at the time the equal of compatriot Divine Proportions (RPR 123) by Racing Post

2005 **Race record**

6th Prix de l'Arc de Triomphe Lucien Barriere (Group 1) (Longchamp, October 2) 3yo+ 1m4f Good to soft **120** (TS 120) 15 ran. *Always in touch, slipped through on inside to lead approaching straight, headed over 1f out, one pace (coupled with Windya) (C Soumillon), beaten 6l by Hurricane Run*

1st Prix Vermeille Lucien Barriere (Group 1) (Longchamp, September 11) 3-4yo 1m4f Good to soft **121** (TS 93) 6 ran. *Led after 3f, quickened over 1½f out, comfortably (C Soumillon), beat Royal Highness by ¾l*

1st Darley Irish Oaks (Group 1) (Curragh, July 17) 3yo 1m4f Good to firm **123** (TS 119) 13 ran. *Tracked leaders, 5th approaching straight, smooth headway to lead 2f out, soon quickened clear, impressive (C Soumillon), beat Playful Act by 5l*

1st Prix de Royaumont (Group 3) (Chantilly, June 4) 3yo 1m4f Good **114** (TS 85) 5 ran. *Made all, ridden clear over 1f out, easily (C Soumillon), beat Royal Highness by 2½l*

1st Prix de la Seine (Listed) (Longchamp, May 15) 3yo 1m3f Soft **105** (TS 91) 6 ran. *Led over 1m out, quickened 2f out, ran on well (C Soumillon), beat Asi Siempre by 1½l*

1st Prix de la Fosse Aux Biches (Maiden) (Chantilly, April 29) 3yo 1m2f Very soft **101** (TS 63) 15 ran. *Raced in 3rd, left in lead 5f out (leader fell and brought down the 2nd), went clear over 1f out, ran on (C Soumillon), beat Bastet by 2½l*

2nd Prix Dushka (Unraced Fillies) (Maisons-Laffitte, April 1) 3yo 1m2½f Heavy **84** (TS 71) 14 ran. *Led to approaching final furlong, kept on steadily (C Soumillon), beaten 1l by L'Enjoleuse*

handicapper Paul Curtis, Shawanda had enjoyed a summer holiday in Deauville. She made her return in the race annually billed by the French as the 'Prix de Diane d'automne', and treated us to the same brilliance we had enjoyed at The Curragh. Her lustre frightened off all but five rivals, but those five need not have turned up if winning had been their aim, for Shawanda was way too wonderful. She won without coming off the bridle. It was a devastating exhibition of class on four legs. The Arc beckoned.

She did not run badly in the big one, but she could manage only sixth. Aided by her pacemaker, Windya, who appeared to do the perfect job, she had the race run to suit, and, as heads were turned for home, it was her head that moved to the front. But in front it could not stay, and Shawanda faded into a disappointing finishing position, even if she was beaten less than six lengths by Hurricane Run.

An excuse, and a valid one, was soon forthcoming. Shawanda had sustained a hairline fracture to her off-hind leg. Georges Rimaud, the Aga Khan's spokesman, noted that the injury "does explain why she didn't quite live up to our expectations". The filly's treatment involved two months of box rest and coincided with her purchase by Godolphin, for whom she will no doubt try again to win the Arc.

She probably won't win it. But then again, the UK probably won't win the Eurovision Song Contest.

Shawanda

bay filly, 3-3-2002

Sinndar b 1997	Grand Lodge	Chief's Crown	Danzig Six Crowns
		La Papagena	Habitat Magic Flute
	Sinntara	Lashkari	**Mill Reef** Larannda
		Sidama	Top Ville Stoyana
Shamawna b 1989	Darshaan	Shirley Heights	**Mill Reef** Hardiemma
		Delsy	Abdos Kelty
	Shamsana	Nijinsky	Northern Dancer Flaming Page
		Shanizadeh	Baldric Safiah

Bred by H H Aga Khan's Studs in Ireland.

Sire Sinndar

Won 7 of 8 races, inc. National S.-Gr1, Irish Derby Trial S.-Gr3, Derby S.-Gr1, Irish Derby-Gr1, Prix Niel-Gr2, Prix de l'Arc de Triomphe-Gr1. Strong, lengthy, 16.0 1/2 hh. Not striking in appearance, but improved physically through his second season. Effective on soft ground, ideally suited by a fast-run 12f. The best son of his sire and from family of outstanding runners Apollonia, Acamas, Akarad, Akiyda and Darshaan. Stands in 2006 at Haras de Bonneval at a fee of €20,000. Sire of 2 crops of racing age, inc. notable winners: Moonlight Dance (Gr2), Shawanda (Irish Oaks-Gr1).

Dam Shamawna

Ran only at 3 years, won 2 of 5 races. Also 3rd in Prix de Royaumont and 4th in Prix Cleopatre. Showed quite smart form, raced only on fastish ground, and not after August. By an outstanding runner, successful sire and exceptional broodmare sire. Traces to the grand-dam of Blushing Groom. Dam of: Shawalan (1994 c by Shernazar; placed), Shamawan (1995 c by Kris; winner), Shawana (1996 f by Turtle Island; unraced), Shawara (1998 f by Barathea; winner), Shambar (1999 c by Linamix; placed), Shamsada (2000 f by Kahyasi; placed), Shawanda (2002 f by Sinndar; dual Gr1 winner). Her foal is a filly by Kalanisi, and she was covered by Galileo in 2005. Barren to Subotica in 1997, to Grand Lodge in 2001, to Peintre Celebre in 2003 and to King's Best in 2004.

Pedigree assessment

Shawanda did nothing wrong until the Arc, turning in an eye-catching display of brilliance at The Curragh, and coasting home at Longchamp for her Group 1 triumphs. It may be that she did nothing wrong in the Arc either, as, although her trademark change of gear failed to function and she wound up only sixth, she returned lame on her off-hind. Surprisingly allowed to transfer to Godolphin at the end of the year, Shawanda should show to advantage in top-level competition again in 2006 if she returns sound and in good heart. She has still had little racing and is entitled to improve on what she has shown to date. Her sire, sadly neglected in Ireland (where he attracted only 27 mares in 2005), has switched to France in search of keener patronage. *TM*

Shirocco (Ger)

4yo bay colt **127**

Monsun (Ger) - So Sedulous (USA) (The Minstrel (Can))

Owner Baron Georg Von Ullmann

Trainer A Fabre

Breeder Baron Georg Von Ullmann

Career: **9** starts	won **4**	second **1**	third **3**	**£1,144,753** win and place

By David Ashforth

FEW TRAINERS exude as strong a sense of being in command as Andre Fabre, France's champion trainer for the 19th consecutive year in 2005. Methodical, organised and rigorous in his thinking, Fabre's manner is forensic, legalistic, with a rational man's distaste for imprecision and ignorance. Economical in his statements, for all Fabre's years of success, there remains an air of mystery about him.

That sense of mystery, and mastery, extends across the Atlantic, to the Breeders' Cup, where Fabre's success with Shirocco in the Turf at Belmont in October made him the most successful European trainer since the event began, with four winners – albeit from 38 runners. One of those wins alone, that of the unconsidered Arcangues at odds of over 133-1 in the 1993 Classic at Santa Anita, gave Fabre a special place in Breeders' Cup history.

Fabre does things his own way, which extends to a consistent, and laudable, rejection of the use of Salix, so commonly resorted to by other European trainers when racing in North America. At Belmont, as usual, all five of Aidan O'Brien's representatives raced on Salix as, among others, did Ed Dunlop's Ouija Board in the Filly & Mare Turf, John Oxx's Azamour in the Turf and Luca Cumani's Starcraft in the Classic.

When in Rome, it is often advisable to do as the Romans do, but should that principle apply when European horsemen visit North American racetracks? European trainers use Salix – prohibited across Europe – not because their horses have significant bleeding problems, the ostensible justification for using Salix, but for fear of being at a competitive disadvantage. Salix, a strong diuretic, can result in improved performance but does not always do so.

The fact that the use of Salix is permissible on racedays does not make it desirable and it is incongruous to see trainers who support the European ban on Salix happily resorting to it in the USA. Even from a purely

Christophe Soumillon celebrates as Shirocco builds on his Arc fourth with victory in the Breeders' Cup Turf

pragmatic perspective, how certain is it that European-trained horses, often racing on Salix for the first time, after a demanding transatlantic journey, will perform better with Salix than without it?

As Charlie Brooks so succinctly put it in the *Daily Telegraph*: "Why would you fly a horse to America, which presumably dehydrates it, rehydrate it by your chosen method, then dehydrate it again giving it Salix and expect it to run well?"

Neither Shirocco nor Valixir, Fabre's runner in the Mile, raced on Salix. It certainly didn't stop Shirocco.

He was a late-season star. The Turf was only Shirocco's third appearance of the year, and his third for Fabre. Bred in Germany by Baron Georg von Ullmann, the son of Monsun was initially sent to Andreas Schutz's yard at Cologne. "He was quite slow to come to hand as a two-year-old," said Schutz, "and was simply not forward enough to run that year."

As a three-year-old, with Andreas Suborics as his regular partner, Shirocco made rapid strides. On his fourth appearance, he comfortably defeated a large field to win the Group 1 Deutsches Derby at Hamburg on testing ground, racing prominently throughout. Schutz had a high opinion of him. "We haven't seen the best of Shirocco yet," he said, promptly naming the Prix de l'Arc de Triomphe as his autumn target.

2005 Race record

1st John Deere Breeders' Cup Turf (Grade 1) (Belmont Park, October 29) 3yo+ 1m4f Yielding **127** 13 ran. *Raced in 2nd behind clear leader, led over 2½f out, ridden over 1f out, driven out (C Soumillon), beat Ace by 1¾l*

4th Prix de l'Arc de Triomphe Lucien Barriere (Group 1) (Longchamp, October 2) 3yo+ 1m4f Good to soft **125** (TS 126) 15 ran. *Always in touch, 6th straight, stayed on final 2f, took 4th on line (S Pasquier), beaten 4¼l by Hurricane Run*

3rd Prix Foy Gray d'Albion Barriere (Group 2) (Longchamp, September 11) 4yo+ 1m4f Good to soft **121** (TS 112) 6 ran. *Disputed 3rd, 4th 5f out, went 2nd approaching straight, ridden and disputing 2nd 1½f out, one pace final furlong (C Soumillon), beaten 4½l by Pride*

2004

1st Gran Premio del Jockey Club (Group 1) (San Siro, October 17) 3yo+ 1m4f Soft **125** 9 ran ● **3rd** Grosser Volkswagen Preis Von Baden (Group 1) (Baden- Baden, September 5) 3yo+ 1m4f Soft **122** 11 ran ● **1st** BMW Deutsches Derby (Group 1) (Hamburg, July 4) 3yo 1m4f Heavy **122** 18 ran ● **3rd** Oppenheim-Union-Rennen (Group 2) (Cologne, June 13) 3yo 1m3f Soft **111** 8 ran ● **1st** RWE Aqua Derby-Trial (Listed) (Mulheim, May 15) 3yo 1m3f Good 9 ran ● **2nd** Preis Dolce Vita des Eiscafe' Venezia Im Schwanenmarkt (Maiden) (Krefeld, March 27) 2yo 1m3f Soft 4 ran

After a two-month break, Shirocco reappeared in the Group 1 Grosser Preis von Baden. Said to be only 90 per cent fit, with the officially soft going at Baden-Baden regarded as insufficiently yielding for Shirocco's taste, he put up a sterling performance to finish third, only a length behind the winner, Warrsan.

Ground conditions were clearly important to Shirocco and, when the soft ground traditionally associated with the Arc failed to materialise, his connections withdrew him. Instead, he finished his three-year-old season in Italy, narrowly defeating the highly regarded local champion Electrocutionist in the Group 1 Gran Premio del Jockey Club at San Siro. In 2005 Electrocutionist would win the Group 1 Juddmonte International at York.

It was almost a year before Shirocco appeared again, an absence blamed on a string of niggling injuries. In August 2005, still in Baron von Ullmann's ownership, he was moved to Fabre's yard.

The Baron's patronage of Fabre was interesting because Von Ullmann, who is chairman of Cologne racecourse, has strong roots in Germany's racing industry. His previous stars, including Monsun, Tiger Hill and Sumitas, were all trained in Germany. A prominent European banker, Von Ullmann and his mother own the Gestut Schlenderhan, one of that country's oldest and most influential studs.

When Shirocco joined Fabre, he was already close to racing fitness for, a month later, he finally reappeared, ridden by Christophe Soumillon in one of Longchamp's Arc trials, the Prix Foy. He finished a very acceptable third.

His run in the Arc, on rain-softened ground, was hugely encouraging,

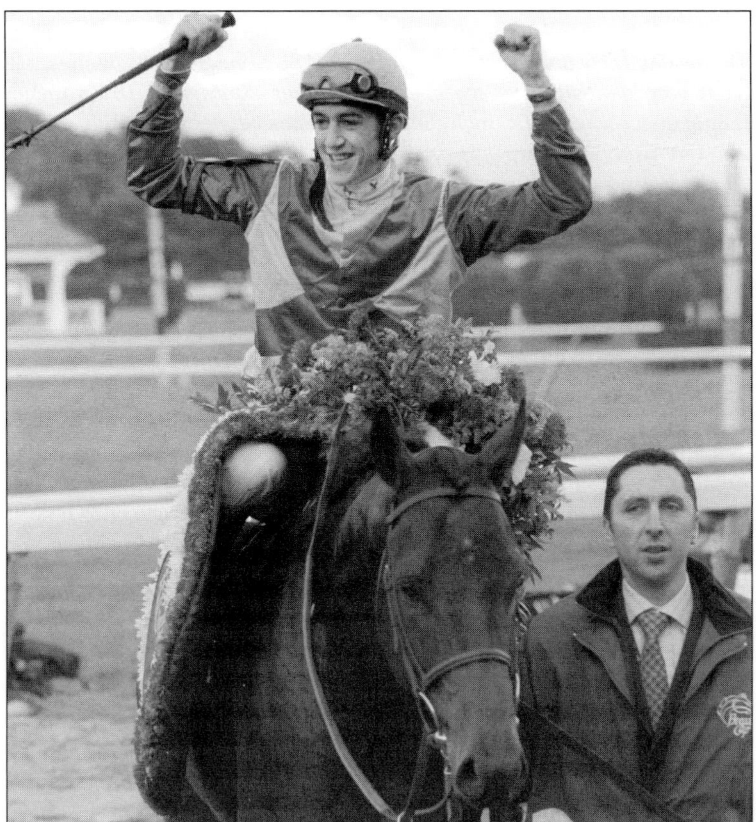

Shirocco and Christophe Soumillon return to the Belmont winner's circle after leading Europe's 1-2-3-4 in the Turf

bearing more the appearance of a dress rehearsal than of the day of days. Very much the second string to stablemate and Irish Derby winner Hurricane Run, who was ridden by Kieren Fallon, Shirocco started at 25-1 but, with a more positive ride, might have improved on his fourth place.

With Soumillon riding the Aga Khan's impressive Irish Oaks and Prix Vermeille winner Shawanda for Alain de Royer-Dupre, Stephane Pasquier partnered Shirocco. He gave his mount a lot to do and Shirocco responded stoutly in the straight to reach the heels of Bago, if not of Hurricane Run, the winner, and Westerner.

Given that it was only his second race after an 11-month absence, it was a striking effort but Shirocco's options were clearly limited by his need for soft ground. It was fortunate for his connections that the Breeders' Cup was at Belmont in 2005, and that New York was experiencing exceptional rainfall.

Records for monthly rainfall in the city's Central Park extend back to 1869. The record was set in September 1882, when 16.85 inches fell. That record was almost matched in October 2005, with 16.73 inches falling on Central Park, including 3.48 inches between October 22 and 26. The Breeders' Cup was run on October 29. In parts of Long Island, where Belmont is situated, rainfall in October exceeded 21 inches.

The turf track at Belmont is not of the rapidly draining, sand-based variety seen at some American racetracks. The dry spell that set in during the second half of Breeders' Cup week was not enough to nullify the earlier deluge and it was significant that John Oxx, Azamour's trainer, expressed serious apprehension at the likely conditions. Three days before the big day, Oxx dismissed suggestions that a few dry days could turn conditions around.

In anticipation of soft going, a gamble developed on Shirocco, who was more likely than most runners to put up an improved performance. Available at 16-1 a fortnight before Breeders' Cup day, and 10-1 a week before, Shirocco's 'industry' SP in Britain was 5-1, at which odds he was joint-third favourite with Shakespeare, behind Azamour and Bago. On Belmont's pari-mutuel, Shirocco paid 8.8-1.

There was never any doubt that Shirocco would be ridden much closer to the pace than in the Arc. His strength was stamina on soft ground and Soumillon quickly established a position behind the 'rabbit' Shake The Bank, a pacemaker for Better Talk Now, the previous year's Turf winner.

It was an uncomplicated race. Having taken the lead before the home straight, Soumillon steadily turned the screw. Shirocco maintained a resolute momentum and, although his European rivals – Ace, Azamour and Bago – all strove bravely to throw down a challenge, none caused serious nervousness among Shirocco's supporters. He won by a length and three-quarters and a neck from Ace and the strong-finishing Azamour, and in doing so became the first German-bred to triumph in a Breeders' Cup race.

Europe's four Turf representatives occupied the first four places, almost six lengths ahead of the rest of the field. Belmont's soft turf course certainly favoured the Europeans, on a day when they had little else to celebrate.

"I was always confident," said Fabre, "because he ran such a fantastic race in the Arc and could have done a bit better. He acts on any ground but is a strong galloper and today's conditions favoured him. He is a typical representative of German breeding – a staying horse with a big heart."

Shirocco will stay in training as a five-year-old and be aimed at major races in Europe and America. His programme is certain to be strongly influenced by prevailing ground conditions, for to show his best, he clearly needs it soft. That requirement makes another appearance in the Arc more likely than a defence of his Breeders' Cup crown, for Churchill Downs, the 2006 venue, would not suit Shirocco as well as Belmont.

Shirocco

bay colt, 10-4-2001

Monsun b 1990	Konigsstuhl	Dschingis Khan	Tamerlane Donna Diana
		Konigskronung	Tiepoletto Kronung
	Mosella	Surumu	Literat Surama
		Monasia	Authi Monacensia
So Sedulous b 1991	The Minstrel	Northern Dancer	Nearctic Natalma
		Fleur	Victoria Park Flaming Page
	Sedulous	Tap On Wood	Sallust Cat O'Mountaine
		Pendulina	Prince Tenderfoot Rosemarin

Bred by Baron Georg von Ullmann in Germany.

Sire Monsun

Won 12 of 23 starts, inc. Grosser Preis der Steigenberger Hotels-Gr3, Grosser Hertie Preis-Gr2, Aral Pokal-Gr1, Preis von Europa-Gr1 [twice], Gerling Preis-Gr2 [twice], Preis von Europa-Gr1, Grosser Hansa Preis-Gr2. Strong, 16.1hh, attractive individual. High-class middle-distance performer, effective on top of the ground, but especially proficient on rain-affected surface. Very genuine and consistent. Stands at Gestut Schlenderhan at a 2006 fee of €60,000 (Oct 1). Sire of 7 crops of racing age, inc. notable winners: Network (Gr2), Samum (Deutsches Derby-Gr1, Grosser Preis von Baden-Gr1), Speedmaster (Gr2), Subiaco (Gr2), Noroit (Gr2), Simoun (Gr2), Guadalupe (Oaks d'Italia-Gr1), Salve Regina (Preis der Diana-Gr1), Aubonne (Gr3), Royal Fantasy (Gr2), Amarette (Preis der Diana (Gr1), Assiun (Gr3), Give Me Five (Gr3), Shirocco (Deutsches Derby-Gr1, Gran Premio del Jockey Club-Gr1, Breeders' Cup Turf-Gr1), Vallera (Gr3), Anna Monda (Premio Vitorio di Capua-Gr1), Arcadio (Gr3), Manduro (Gr3), Royal Highness (Gr2), Sorrent (Gr3).

Dam So Sedulous

Won 2 of 11 races. Placed 4th in mile Listed race at Deauville. Rather small, a tail-flasher, but game and consistent. Showed quite useful form, seemed to act on any ground. Same family as Noble Dancer (multiple Gr1 winner in US), Cavan (Belmont Stakes) and Indiana (St Leger). Dam of: Satchmo (1996 c by Surumu; Listed winner), Subiaco (1997 c by Monsun; Gr2 winner, Derby 2nd), Shoah (1999 f by Acatenango; winner), Storm Trooper (2000 c by Monsun; winner, Derby 3rd), Shirocco (2001 c by Monsun; Derby winner), September Storm (2002 c by Monsun; winner). She was not covered in 1997, and was barren to Monsun in 2003. Her yearling is a Monsun filly, already named So Squally.

Pedigree assessment

A Group 1 winner at three in his native Germany and in Italy, Shirocco enhanced his reputation with two sterling efforts in even more competitive company after his transfer to Andre Fabre. His Arc performance, in fourth place to Hurricane Run, marked him down as a legitimate contender for the Breeders' Cup Turf, and there he reversed Longchamp form with Bago to win with a career-best display. He now ranks as the top runner for his outstanding sire, whose first three products out of So Sedulous finished second, third and first in the Deutsches Derby. Shirocco will be in action again in 2006, and he can be depended upon to make his presence felt over a mile and a half in the very best of company. *TM*

Silca's Sister

2yo chestnut filly **114**

Inchinor - Silca-Cisa (Hallgate)

Owner Aldridge Racing Limited

Trainer M R Channon

Breeder E Aldridge

Career: **3** starts | won **2** | second **0** | third **0** | **£147,427** win and place

By Steve Dennis

WHAT must Sheikh Mohammed's birthday be like? A crowd of friends and family, plenty to eat and drink, an inviting pile of presents with his name on them. He opens his presents, has a quick look, then puts them away in a cupboard for six months.

That may sound ridiculous, but it is, in essence, the tactic used by the Sheikh when he goes cherry-picking for future stars to wear the Godolphin blue. His purchases are immediately retired for the season, no matter what objectives had been planned by their former trainers and no matter what the state of development of a particular horse. The 2005 season saw Imperial Stride, Plea Bargain, Proclamation, Royal Proposal and the US-trained juvenile Discreet Cat enter the Godolphin fold well before the end of the season, along with the Prix Morny winner Silca's Sister, who had had just three runs in the space of six weeks while in the care of Mick Channon. None of the six was seen out again.

Simon Crisford, Godolphin's racing manager, said: "Silca's Sister was bought as a long-term prospect and therefore will not race again this year. At this stage the plan is not to run again prior to the 1,000 Guineas. The plan will be not only to race her next season, but the season after that as well."

Silca's Sister has already outstripped her sister, the hardy miler Golden Silca, in that she has a Group 1 win under her belt, something her full-sibling failed to manage in 44 starts, although she was runner-up in the 1999 Irish 1,000 Guineas. If she has been endowed with the same toughness as was her sister, she should prove a formidable weapon for Godolphin in the top races.

The daughter of Inchinor made her debut in a maiden at the Newmarket July meeting and was expected to win first time out. Reports of her prowess on the gallops saw her sent off a 9-4 favourite to beat 11 rivals but she showed little sparkle in finishing a disappointing fifth behind Nidhaal,

Silca's Sister defeats the colts in the Prix Morny before being added to Godolphin's extensive shopping list

who would go on to be runner-up in the Princess Margaret Stakes and fifth in the Cheveley Park Stakes.

The good to soft ground was put forward as a reason for Silca's Sister's lacklustre showing, so when she encountered a faster surface at Newbury in another six-furlong maiden a fortnight later, she was expected to redeem herself. She did.

After she had justified favouritism with a three-length defeat of Dazed (who ended the season a maiden after six starts), a clearly relieved Channon said: "Newmarket was very disappointing. She had looked such a talented filly at home, but she ran no race. She has put that right today and is clearly a decent filly – Listed or Group class. We won't be ducking and diving and she will be pitched into a better race next time."

The manner of her victory – she was eased down in the closing stages after showing an eye-catching turn of foot to settle affairs approaching the furlong marker – allied to her morning exertions did indeed merit Channon raising his sights with the filly. With stablemate Flashy Wings earmarked for the Lowther Stakes, Channon set Silca's Sister the stiffer test of the Group 1 Darley Prix Morny at Deauville, in which she would take on colts for the first time.

The market leaders for the Morny were the Ballydoyle representative

2005 Race record

1st Darley Prix Morny (Group 1) (Deauville, August 21) 2yo 6f Soft **114** (TS 91) 7 ran. *Always close up, led distance, driven out (T E Durcan), beat Ivan Denisovich by 2l*

1st London Clubs Maiden Fillies' Stakes (Newbury, July 22) 2yo 6f Good to firm **95** (TS 86) 9 ran. *Tracked leaders, led well over 1f out, soon quickened clear, eased near finish (T E Durcan), beat Dazed by 3l*

5th Heathavon Stud EBF Maiden Fillies' Stakes (Newmarket (July), July 7) 2yo 6f Good to soft **72** (TS 65) 12 ran. *Ridden along, chased leaders, one pace when carried left over 1f out, well beaten after (T E Durcan), beaten 8¾l by Nidhaal*

Ivan Denisovich, winner of the July Stakes at Newmarket, and impressive Prix Robert Papin winner New Girlfriend, trained by Robert Collet.

The abrupt step up into the highest class was a big hurdle for Silca's Sister to overcome, as was the testing Deauville turf, but she took over from Ivan Denisovich more than a furlong from home and strode away under Ted Durcan to win by two lengths, with Always Hopeful, previously winner of the Richmond Stakes, a nose away third. Kieren Fallon, rider of the runner-up, was moved to say: "It's the worst ground I've ever ridden on anywhere in the world." So much for the excuses offered after Silca's Sister's debut defeat!

Durcan, on the other hand, said: "I was scared about the ground before the race. She made huge progress between her first and second races, and has done the same thing again. I just gave her one slap and she picked up."

It was a performance of high promise, proving her ability to handle both soft and fast ground at the top level against colts and fillies. It was a performance that whetted the appetite, and Channon was hungry to take on all-comers, saying: "All the top races have now become options and they include the Cheveley Park, the Fillies' Mile and the Prix Marcel Boussac – and I'm not worried about the mile."

Sadly, the big Group 1s of the autumn went by without Silca's Sister, as three weeks later Sheikh Mohammed came calling and whisked her away, two months before the end of the season. Godolphin were not represented in either the Cheveley Park, the Fillies' Mile or the Marcel Boussac, notwithstanding the fact that in Silca's Sister they owned a filly who would quite feasibly have started favourite for any one of those races. Their plan of inaction seemed a waste of resources.

In 2006 (Godolphin willing) Silca's Sister is likely to be seen to best effect at a mile; she is most unlikely to stay further. She entered the winter as second favourite for the 1,000 Guineas at a general 8-1, behind Marcel Boussac winner Rumplestiltskin and a place ahead of her former stablemate Flashy Wings; the last filly to take the Morny was Divine Proportions, and she won two Classics. Silca's Sister may well have the ability to meet her halfway.

Silca's Sister

chestnut filly, 26-2-2003

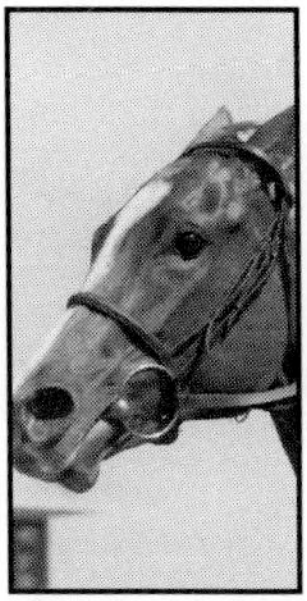

Inchinor ch 1990	Ahonoora	Lorenzaccio	Klairon Phoenissa
		Helen Nichols	Martial Quaker Girl
	Inchmurrin	Lomond	Northern Dancer My Charmer
		On Show	Welsh Pageant African Dancer
Silca-Cisa ch 1989	Hallgate	Vaigly Great	**Great Nephew** Dervaig
		Beloved Mistress	Rarity Fizzy
	Princess Silca Key	Grundy	**Great Nephew** Word From Lundy
		Recline	Wollow Balista

Bred by Eddie Aldridge in England.

Sire Inchinor

Won 5 of 10 starts, inc. Greenham S.-Gr3, Criterion S.-Gr3, Hungerford S.-Gr3. Also 2nd in Dewhurst S., 3rd in Sussex S. Small (15.11/2 hh), well-made, attractive sort, and a grand mover. Very game, consistent performer, effective in most conditions (not raced on extremes). Speedy, owned a sharp turn of foot, stayed a mile well. Died in 2003. Stood at Woodland Stud, Newmarket, last fee £10,000. Sire of 9 crops of racing age, inc. notable winners: Golden Silca (Gr2), Palanca (Gr3), Summoner (Queen Elizabeth II S.-Gr1), Umistim (Gr3), Bannister (Gr2), Cape Of Good Hope (Golden Jubilee S.-Gr1), Orientor (Gr3), Felicity (Gr3), Latice (Prix de Diane-Gr1), Secret Melody (Gr3), Satchem (Gr3), In Clover (Gr3), Silca's Sister (Prix Morny-Gr1).

Dam Silca-Cisa

Won 2 of 15 races. Also placed 7 times, inc. Listed at 4. Lightly built individual, not the best of movers, but with a quick action. Useful sprinter on fast ground, less effective on soft. Stayed 6f, untested beyond. From an excellent family. Dam of: Muso Corto (1995 c by Reprimand; winner), Golden Silca (1996 f by Inchinor; Classic-placed Gr2 winner), King Silca (1997 g by Emarati; winner), Silca Legend (1998 c by Efisio; Listed-placed winner), For Evva Silca (1999 f by Piccolo; placed), Green Manalishi (2001 g by Green Desert; winner), Silca's Sister (2003 f by Inchinor; Gr1 winner). She has a yearling filly by Pivotal. Barren to Polar Falcon in 2000, and to Inchinor in 2002, not covered in 2004. Covered by Cape Cross in 2005.

Pedigree assessment

When Inchinor died, following colic surgery, in 2003, he had had only one Group 1 winner as a sire – Summoner in the 2001 Queen Elizabeth II Stakes. The tally now stands at four, after Latice's score in the 2004 Prix de Diane, and the triumphs this season of Cape Of Good Hope (Golden Jubilee Stakes) and Silca's Sister (Prix Morny). Deauville's testing ground may have been a factor in the Morny result, but the sister to tough and talented Golden Silca accomplished her task in exemplary style – and on only her third appearance. Unfortunately, we obtained no further evidence of the filly's merit in the months that followed, but she seemed to be a filly who was entitled to progress and get a mile as a three-year-old. *TM*

Silent Witness (Aus)

6yo bay gelding **128**

El Moxie (USA) - Jade Tiara (Aus) (Bureaucracy (NZ))

Owner Arthur Antonio da Silva & Betty da Silva

Trainer A S Cruz

Breeder I K Smith

Career: **20** starts | won **18** | second **1** | third **1** | **£3,470,972** win and place

By Paul Haigh

SILENT WITNESS began 2005 as probably the most famous racehorse in the world. For sheer number of fans and certainly for sheer weight of adulation no horse anywhere even came close. The son of the previously obscure, then Tasmanian-based American stallion El Moxie (by Conquistador Cielo) out of the not otherwise notable mare Jade Tiara, he had transcended his breeding in such outrageous fashion that he had achieved championship status without ever tasting defeat. Winner of all his first 13 races, including the world's richest five-furlong event, the Hong Kong Sprint, in successive years, he was a true phenomenon – the kind of 'freak' that stirs every racing imagination.

The form book said he was not only the best horse ever to race in Hong Kong, where he was a national hero to compare with any film or pop star, but the best turf sprinter anywhere on earth. His idolaters, who included his ebullient owner Arthur Antonio ('Archie') da Silva, seemed to believe he was not only unbeaten but invincible (although to be fair to Archie, he did concede prophetic awareness of the truth that "if you run them often enough, all horses get beaten"). The Hong Kong Jockey Club gave him his own website. A magnificent memorial tome was already in preparation to commemorate the feats of the horse whose Chinese title translates as 'Master of the Elite'. And still the rumour continued to circulate that all that had gone before was just prologue, and that not until 'the great one' stepped up in trip would we see just how exceptionally good he was.

When you're that far up there really is nowhere much to go but down; and down – to some extent anyway – was where Silent Witness went in 2005. Not for a little while, however – and not before Silent Witness fever had reached boiling point in Hong Kong, or before he'd topped the remarkable feat of 16 consecutive wins achieved by the great Ribot, as well as by American champions Citation and Cigar.

Photograph courtesy of Hong Kong Jockey Club

Felix Coetzee salutes the fans as Silent Witness scores his 16th straight win with another dominant performance

In his first race of 2005, the Group 1 Bauhinia Sprint Trophy at Sha Tin, he started at 1-20, the minimum odds permitted by the Hong Kong tote, and won in a blistering 55.3 seconds that, on ground officially described as good, bettered both of his Hong Kong Sprint winning times by more than a second. He was followed home at his now more or less standard winning distance of a length and three-quarters by stablemate Country Music, with Planet Ruler third.

A month later, again starting at 1-20, he again beat Country Music and another inmate of the hugely powerful Tony Cruz stable, Multidandy, by two lengths and four and a half in the Group 1 Centenary Sprint Cup. That brought his winning run to 15. Planet Ruler finished fourth.

He equalled the 16-victory mark with which Archie had become a little fixated in another Group 1, the Chairman's Sprint Prize over six furlongs on April 3. Again he started at 1-20. The 2004 Hong Kong Derby second Tiber was beaten a length and three-quarters, with Cape Of Good Hope third. Again, Planet Ruler was one of his victims in fourth. Even more significantly, as it later turned out, Natural Blitz finished sixth.

The scene was set for the day on which he was to achieve the 17th straight win that now obsessed every racegoer and quite a few non-racing persons in Hong Kong. The HKJC offered free Silent Witness souvenir hats at Sha Tin station. When only 10,000 hats arrived, disappointed fans staged a mini-riot that saw 23 people taken to hospital. The stands

2005 Race record

1st Sprinters Stakes (Grade 1) (Nakayama, October 2) 3yo+ 6f Firm **123** 16 ran. *Tracked leaders, disputing 3rd straight, ridden to lead inside final furlong, ran on well (F Coetzee), beat Durandal by 1¼l*

3rd Yasuda Kinen (Grade 1) (Tokyo, June 5) 3yo+ 1m Firm **121** 18 ran. *Tracked leader, led 2f out until caught 50yds out, lost 2nd last stride (F Coetzee), beaten ½l by Asakusa Den'En*

2nd Champions Mile (Group 1) (Sha Tin, May 14) 3yo+ 1m Good to firm **122** 13 ran. *Led until headed last strides (F Coetzee), beaten shd by Bullish Luck*

1st The Queen's Silver Jubilee Cup (Group 2) (Sha Tin, April 24) 3yo+ 7f Good to firm **117** 11 ran. *Prominent early dictating pace, 1l advantage into straight, asked for effort 2f out, cruised home unchallenged (F Coetzee), beat Town Of Fionn by 1¾l*

1st Chairman's Sprint Prize (Group 1) (Sha Tin, April 3) 3yo+ 6f Good to firm **128** 14 ran. *Settled 3-4l off leaders, steadily made up ground rounding home turn, wore down leader 1½ furlongs out (F Coetzee), beat Tiber by 1¾l*

1st Centenary Sprint Cup (Group 1) (Sha Tin, February 27) 3yo+ 5f Good to yielding **125** 11 ran. *Disputed lead, quickened when challenged 1f out, won easily (F Coetzee), beat Country Music by 2l*

1st Bauhinia Sprint Trophy (Group 1) (Sha Tin, January 23) 3yo+ 5f Good **123** 7 ran. *Broke well and led early, lost lead 4f out, regained 1½f out, responded well when challenged final furlong, drew clear (F Coetzee), beat Country Music by 1¾l*

Other runs

2004 **1st** Cathay Pacific Hong Kong Sprint (Group 1) (Sha Tin, December 12) 3yo+ 5f Good to firm **127** 14 ran ● **1st** Cathay Pacific International Sprint Trial (Group 2) (Sha Tin, November 21) 3yo+ 5f Good to firm **127** 10 ran ● **1st** Chairman's Sprint Prize (Group 1) (Sha Tin, April 25) 3yo+ 6f Good to firm **125** 13 ran ● **1st** Centenary Sprint Cup (Group 1) (Sha Tin, March 13) 3yo+ 5f Good to firm **127** 10 ran ● **1st** Bauhinia Sprint Trophy (First Leg of the Champion Sprint Series) (Group 1) (Sha Tin, February 1) 3yo+ 5f Good to firm **128** 7 ran **2003** **1st** Hong Kong Sprint (Group 1) (Sha Tin, December 14) 3yo+ 5f Good to firm **127** 14 ran ● **1st** International Sprint Trial (Group 2) (Sha Tin, November 22) 3yo+ 5f Good to firm **130** 9 ran ● **1st** Sha Tin Sprint Trophy (Group 3 Handicap) (Sha Tin, October 11) 5f Good **121** 14 ran ● **1st** Sha Tin Vase (Group 2 Handicap) (Sha Tin, June 7) 3yo+ 5f Good to yielding **124** 7 ran ● **1st** Sound Print Handicap (Sha Tin, March 23) 3yo 6f Good 14 ran ● **1st** Gay Eighties Handicap (Sha Tin, February 23) 3yo 5f Good to firm 14 ran ● **1st** Mastermind Handicap (Sha Tin, January 19) 3yo 6f Good to firm 14 ran **2002** ● **1st** Hennessy Handicap (Sha Tin, December 26) 3yo 5f Good 14 ran

by the winning post were packed with young racegoers whose faces had been painted in the black and green da Silva colours. When the great horse came out on to the course the noise was worthy of a Cup final.

The race was the Group 2 Queen's Silver Jubilee Cup over seven furlongs, and yet again Silent Witness's odds were 1-20. Yet again he didn't let anyone down, stealing a lead of a couple of lengths within half a furlong after his usual brilliant start, and holding it comfortably all the way to the line. There were one or two who were unconvinced by the performance; who felt there might not have been all that much left as Felix Coetzee rode him out hands and heels in the seventh furlong; who didn't think

Photograph courtesy of Japan Racing Association

Silent Witness, after two defeats over a mile, returns to six furlongs to win the Grade 1 Sprinters Stakes in Japan

he looked as though he'd really relish an eighth.

But never mind all that. The crowd went wild. So did the connections, as well as the thousands back in the city clustered round specially erected TV screens. For Hong Kongers there was now no doubt: Silent Witness bestrode the world.

Now at last came the long-awaited step up from sprint distances. His 18th race, the Group 1 Champions Mile, attracted the Mark Johnston-trained filly Attraction, as well as every one of the best milers in Hong Kong; yet despite the fact that it was the toughest test of his career, at least since his first Hong Kong Sprint, and against a completely different set of horses, he started at odds of 1-5 on the Hong Kong tote – testament once more to the adulation he enjoyed.

Again he led. Again Coetzee kicked off the home turn and seemed to have opened a winning lead. Gradually, inexorably, however, in the last furlong, another stablemate, Bullish Luck, who'd failed by only a short head to catch Alexander Goldrun in the Hong Kong Cup five months earlier, began to wear him down. Even with 50 yards to go the hero still had half a length in hand, but as they hit the line his stride just shortened. Bullish Luck ended the unbeaten record by a short head.

Undismayed, Cruz and da Silva stuck to their previous intention, and went to Japan for their champion's first outing outside Hong Kong in the Group 1 Yasuda Kinen, which had been won in 2000 by the Hong Kong hero he'd superseded, Fairy King Prawn. Bullish Luck was going too, but even his trainer seemed to believe Silent Witness would reverse the Champions Mile form.

In the Yasuda Kinen Silent Witness ran another wonderful race over a distance we know now, but did not know then, was just too far for him. Racing three wide into the straight after never really having settled, he took it up with just over a furlong to go and looked likely to win until weakening in the last few strides and going down by a neck and a head to Asakusa Den'En and the subsequent Grade 1 Takarazuka Kinen winner (from Zenno Rob Roy among others) Sweep Tosho.

It was now that connections were forced to realise the truth: that the great sprinter was just that. Perhaps one of the greatest of all time, but a sprinter nevertheless. Appropriately enough, after a short break, it was the six-furlong Grade 1 Sprinters Stakes at Nakayama that was chosen for his return and, as all his fans fervently hoped, his rehabilitation. Sure enough, in Japan's major sprint, he made short work of the Japanese champion Durandal and Admire Max, with his old rival Cape Of Good Hope a long way down the field. The winning distance was only a length and a quarter, but he had the race safe a long way out. The time of 1min 7.3sec showed just what it takes to beat the Japanese sprinters on their home ground.

The champ, it seemed, was back. A third consecutive Hong Kong Sprint appeared a formality, and after that Archie had promised to do more than just consider the possibility of a triumphal tour of Europe in 2006. Royal Ascot, the July Cup and the Prix de l'Abbaye all seemed at his mercy in view of the form he'd already shown against horses who fought over them in 2004 and 2005.

Early in November, though, the word went out that he was not quite himself, having picked up a virus in Japan that he was unable to shake. Unwisely perhaps, he was kept in training in the hope that he might recover in time for the international meeting on December 11. But he wasn't well enough to run in the Sprint Trial on November 20, won decisively by Planet Ruler – and then came two bits of news that shocked every one of his legion of fans. For the first time ever Silent Witness had been beaten by a workmate in an exercise gallop, and then a week later he could finish only fifth of eight in a barrier trial. The bid to bring him back in time for the Sprint had foundered altogether.

A long period of rest and recuperation was required, and so the Grand Tour of Europe looks unlikely to take place. He's still the world's highest-rated turf sprinter, still unbeaten at sprint distances, still the idol not just of Hong Kong but of many internationalists around the world. At the time of writing, however, there seems no evidence of a return to his previous irresistible vigour, and there has to be a doubt whether at the age of seven there ever quite will be.

In a final irony for 2005, the Hong Kong Sprint on December 11 went to Natural Blitz from Planet Ruler. The winning time of 57.6sec was nearly a second slower than Silent Witness had put up on identical ground a year earlier.

Silent Witness

bay gelding, 1-10-1999

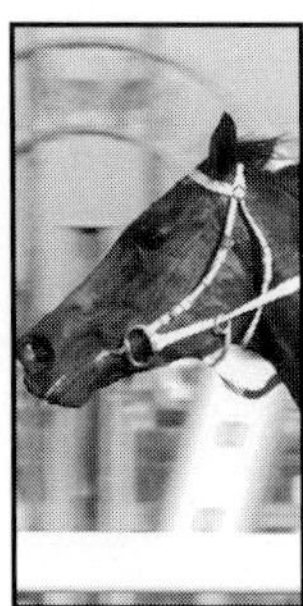

El Moxie b 1986	Conquistador Cielo	Mr Prospector	Raise A Native Gold Digger
		K D Princess	Bold Commander Tammy's Turn
	Raise The Standard	Hoist The Flag	Tom Rolfe Wavy Navy
		Natalma	Native Dancer Almahmoud
Jade Tiara b 1993	Bureaucracy	Lord Ballina	Bletchingly Sunset Girl
		Tulla Doll	Oncidium Doll
	Jade Amanda	Grosvenor	Sir Tristram My Tricia
		Comptroller	Smuggler Shifnals Pride

Bred by I Smith in Australia.

Sire El Moxie

Raced in US, won 6 of 19 starts from 2 to 4 at 6.5f to 8.5f. Modest, raced mostly at minor US tracks including in claiming company. By Belmont winner and fair sire, out of half-sister to Northern Dancer. Dam Raise The Standard also dam of Coup de Folie, ancestress of Gr1 winners Bluemamba, Coup de Genie, Denebola, Exit To Nowhere, Machiavellian, Orpen, Way Of Light. Stands at Emirates Park Stud, Australia. First foals 1992, sire of: Alfa (Caulfield Guineas-AusGr1), El Mirada (AJC All-Aged S-AusGr1), Silent Witness (Hong Kong Sprint-Gr1x2, Sprinters S-JapGr1, HK Bauhinia Sprint Trophy-Gr1x2, HK Chairman's Sprint Prize-Gr1x2, HK Centenary Sprint Cup-Gr1x2), Always Flying (HKGr3), Winestock (Sires' Produce S-AusGr1).

Dam Jade Tiara

Won 4 (5-6f) of 12 starts, including once at 2. By high-class 2yo and middle-distance performer but modest sire, out of minor 6.5f winner. Dam of: Silent Witness (1999 g by El Moxie; Gr1 winner), Crown Rubiton (2000 g by Rubiton; placed), Very Fit (2001 g by Woodman; winner in Hong Kong), 2002 c by Commands; 2003 f by Encosta de Lago.

Pedigree assessment

Silent Witness has outrun his pedigree in class terms, but his ability has an obvious possible source. His sire El Moxie might have been a modest runner, but he is from a superb family that has yielded three particularly notable stallions in recent generations – Danehill, Halo and Northern Dancer. High-flying relatives are a bit further back in Jade Tiara's pedigree, but she showed speed, and that is the forte of her son. *JH*

Sir Percy

2yo bay colt **119**

Mark Of Esteem (Ire) - Percy's Lass (Blakeney)

Owner A E Pakenham

Trainer M P Tregoning

Breeder The Old Suffolk Stud

Career: **4** starts | won **4** | **£201,632** win and place

By Rodney Masters

HOW IRONIC. Since Marcus Tregoning trains for four of the Maktoum brothers, betting was the seven-star Burj Al Arab hotel to a humble wadi that when Sheikh Hamdan's Kingwood House stable produced an unbeaten Group 1-winning juvenile with 2,000 Guineas and Derby potential it would be owned by one of the quartet.

But the endearing story of Sir Percy was to germinate from the other end of racing's spectrum. In doing so, it offered bona fide hope to the sport's nickel-and-dime players in pursuit of the Classic pot.

Tregoning, typically, was far too modest to admit it, but those close to the trainer will confirm he's blessed with an encyclopedic brain when it comes to equine breeding matters, and, as a consequence, he was unable to resist tossing in a speculative bid of 16,000 guineas when the thoroughly likeable colt, by Mark Of Esteem and out of a mare unbeaten as a juvenile, circled the yearling sales auction ring.

Three months later, in pressing need of a larger car to transport his expanded family, he reluctantly parted with the imposing colt, whom he sold to Anthony and Victoria Pakenham with the proviso that the jaunty youngster remained in the yard. So Tregoning got his new set of wheels, and the colt, who was to prove his best-ever two-year-old, stayed under his tutelage.

Prep work on Farncombe Down consistently proved well above average, and the Lambourn Valley drums were beating a confident message for Sir Percy prior to his debut, over six furlongs at Goodwood in late May, when he was duly backed from 10-1 to 8-1. Despite a stumble exiting the stalls, and displaying the anticipated signs of inexperience, he closed down the leaders with an impressively lengthening stride inside the final two furlongs to win with something to spare. The trainer was adamant that he viewed the colt as more

Sir Percy gets the better of Horatio Nelson in the Dewhurst at Newmarket, completing an unbeaten juvenile campaign

of a middle-distance three-year-old.

After Sir Percy again demonstrated that long raking stride to win at Salisbury, Tregoning delivered the outstanding racing prophecy of 2005. "Sir Percy will go for the Veuve Clicquot Vintage Stakes," he said, "and after he's won that, he'll win the Dewhurst." At the time it was pooh-poohed by many as tongue in cheek, but Tregoning doesn't normally play that particular joker, and, accordingly, there would have been good reason to conclude that he believed the colt was blessed with the required talent.

With the ground soft at Goodwood, the trainer walked the course to plot the best route, and Martin Dwyer followed his instructions to the letter, coming up the centre to grab Cool Creek and Black Charmer close home. At the time, it hardly looked a vintage renewal of the Vintage, but over the coming weeks this Group 2 was to gain more of a gloss. The runner-up went on to win the Mill Reef at Newbury, while Aussie Rules, well held in fourth, was successful in the Somerville Tattersall at Newmarket. Such evidence was most encouraging, and it's worth remembering that several previous winners of the Goodwood race went on to success in the Classics, including Shamardal, Don't Forget Me, Dr Devious and Mister Baileys.

Two of that quartet, Dr Devious and Sharmardal, also won the Dewhurst, and Sir Percy joined them on the roll of honour in the most prestigious of juvenile races – a success that came as no surprise to anyone who had witnessed his final two pieces of work. Jockey Dwyer, the best of judges, went into the race brimming over with confidence.

The main opposition came in the shape of the first two home in

2005 **Race record**

1st Darley Dewhurst Stakes (Group 1) (Newmarket, October 15) 2yo 7f Good to soft **119** (TS 120) 8 ran. *Held up, switched right and headway over 1f out, ridden to lead well inside final furlong, just held on (Martin Dwyer), beat Horatio Nelson by nk*

1st Veuve Clicquot Vintage Stakes (Group 2) (Goodwood, July 27) 2yo 7f Soft **112** (TS 108) 7 ran. *Chased leader, ridden to challenge over 1f out, hung left entering final furlong, straightened and ran on well to lead near finish (Martin Dwyer), beat Cool Creek by nk*

1st New Wiltshire Stand Champagne Auction Stakes (Conditions Race) (Salisbury, June 23) 2yo 6f Good to firm **91** (TS 76) 8 ran. *Tracked leaders, slightly hampered well over 1f out, driven to lead just inside final furlong, stayed on strongly (Martin Dwyer), beat Dont Dili Dali by 1¼l*

1st Royal Sussex Regiment Maiden Auction Stakes (Goodwood, May 28) 2yo 6f Good **82** (TS 82) 11 ran. *Went right start, stumbled and behind, headway and switched right 2f out, switched left 1f out, rapid headway to lead final 50yds, comfortably (Martin Dwyer), beat Right Again by 1¾l*

Longchamp's Grand Criterium earlier in the month, Horatio Nelson, who was 8-11 favourite to maintain his unbeaten record, and Opera Cape. Once again, Sir Percy demonstrated that the most potent weapon in his arsenal was the ability to quicken his stride in an instant. True, he got first run on the favourite and there was a lot of fuss in the debriefing that the latter had been unlucky in running before going down to a neck defeat. But repeated replays of the final two furlongs suggest Sir Percy won on merit, for even after Horatio Nelson was clear of the trouble, Sir Percy actually extended his advantage. At no stage did he look likely to get caught, even though he was idling in front.

So now, is it the 2,000 Guineas or the Derby, or both? Tregoning is an expert judge when it comes to assessing a trip, and he's of the belief that a mile and a quarter will be the optimum distance, though he is encouraged that the dam is by Blakeney and so there's every chance of him getting the Derby trip.

There is, of course, another question. Will the owners see off the cherry pickers from Godolphin? It was rumoured in Lambourn, though never confirmed, that they'd come visiting even before the Dewhurst.

At the time of writing, the Pakenhams, to their credit, seem determined to see him carry their colours next year. Anthony Pakenham said: "We bought him to race and to sell him now would be awful. You could buy five horses for four times what he cost and they might never see a racecourse. It would be a shame not to have a go at the Classics."

All that is required in early spring is a prediction from Tregoning. Ideally, somewhere between the Cheltenham Festival and the Craven meeting, he'll declare: "Sir Percy will go for the 2,000 Guineas, and after he has won that, he'll win the Derby."

Come on, Marcus.

Sir Percy

bay colt, 27-1-2003

Mark Of Esteem b 1993	Darshaan	Shirley Heights	Mill Reef Hardiemma
		Delsy	Abdos Kelty
	Homage	Ajdal	Northern Dancer Native Partner
		Home Love	Vaguely Noble Homespun
Percy's Lass b 1984	Blakeney	Hethersett	Hugh Lupus Bride Elect
		Windmill Girl	Hornbeam Chorus Beauty
	Laughing Girl	Sassafras	Sheshoon Ruta
		Violetta	Pinza Urshalim

Bred by The Old Suffolk Stud in England. 20,000gns Tattersalls December foal, 16,000gns Tattersalls October 2 yearling

Sire Mark Of Esteem

Won 4 of 7 races, inc. 2,000 Guineas S.-Gr1, Goodwood Mile-Gr2, Queen Elizabeth II S.-Gr1. Small (15.3hh), rather lightly-built, but quite attractive, and a smooth-actioned, athletic mover. Untested beyond a mile or on soft ground. Stands at Dalham Hall Stud, Newmarket, at a fee of £7,000. Sire of 6 crops of racing age, inc. notable winners: Ameerat (1,000 Guineas-Gr1), Spring Oak (Gr3), Millennium Dragon (Gr3), Redback (Gr3), High Accolade (Gr2), Uraib (Gr2), African Dream (Gr3), Needlecraft (Gr3), Sir Percy (Dewhurst S.-Gr1).

Dam Percy's Lass

Won 5 of 13 races, inc. September S.-Gr3. Also Gr2-placed and 5th in King George VI & Queen Elizabeth S. at 4. Attractive individual and a good walker. High-class performer who became temperamental and unreliable at 4. Stayed 12f well. Died in 2003, having produced: Blue Lion (1990 g by Lomond; winner, Gr3-placed), Morpeth (1991 c by Sadler's Wells; unplaced), Lion Tower (1992 c by Soviet Star; placed), unnamed (1995 c by Shirley Heights; unraced), Lionne (1996 f by Darshaan; unraced, dam of winners), Norvin (1997 g by Nashwan; unraced), unnamed (1998 f by Barathea; unraced), Love Token (1999 f by Mark Of Esteem; winner), Lady Karr (2001 f by Mark Of Esteem; winner), Sir Percy (2003 c by Mark Of Esteem; Gr1 winner). Slipped to Polish Precedent in 1993, to Shirley Heights in 1994, and to Mark Of Esteem in 2002, barren to Mark Of Esteem in 2000.

Pedigree assessment

Arguments raged after the Dewhurst as to which of the first two home was actually the better colt; Sir Percy undeniably had the clearer passage, and there was not much between him and Horatio Nelson at the finish. Each has a sire who would not have had a prayer of staying the Derby distance, but has proved capable of getting accomplished 12-furlong performers, and in Sir Percy's case, in addition to his paternal half-brother High Accolade, we may cite his dam, Percy's Lass, as a factor for class and stamina. Sir Percy has done nothing wrong to date, is a likeable colt, and could progress to be a Derby candidate. But he is a bit of a character, and his dam exhibited plenty of the cussedness often associated with the family. It is to be hoped that he will not deteriorate temperamentally. *TM*

Soviet Song (Ire)

5yo bay mare **124**

Marju (Ire) - Kalinka (Ire) (Soviet Star (USA))

Owner Elite Racing Club

Trainer J R Fanshawe

Breeder Elite Racing Club

Career: **18** starts | won **8** | second **4** | third **2** | **£967,113** win and place

By Richard Austen

THERE was no real cause for disappointment in Soviet Song's latest season, the fourth from this marvellous mare, so let's say instead that there could have been still more cause for celebration.

Racecourse executives were denied a fortune in entrance fees when Soviet Song's owners were called upon to support their darling only three times in 2005, but those members of the Elite Racing Club were not short-changed. They celebrated a fifth Group 1 success after the hat-trick in 2004 and the Fillies' Mile that marked Soviet Song's emergence in the top flight way back in 2002.

First the bad news, and there was plenty of it, though none of the tragic variety or even that serious, except when taken in aggregate.

A fetlock injury the previous season necessitated two months' box rest over the winter, and when she was in good form on the gallops just before the Lockinge Stakes, she scoped badly and everything had to be put on hold again.

A bad cough in the week after the Sussex Stakes ruled out assignments in late summer, while a bruised off-fore foot in mid-September meant no Matron Stakes, Sun Chariot or Breeders' Cup.

However, small windows of opportunity remained. On June 15, Soviet Song was there for the Windsor Forest Stakes and on July 5 and 27 she attempted to repeat her 2004 victories in the Falmouth Stakes and the Sussex.

She was easily the best horse in the Windsor Forest and gave no more than 5lb to any of her rivals, but it was well documented that her preparation had not been trouble free and she was allowed to go off second favourite before coming in third, James Fanshawe confirming that he had run her in that race rather than the Queen Anne "so that she would have less of a hard race and it would put her right."

Soviet Song scores a repeat win in the Falmouth Stakes at Newmarket, her only success in a troubled season

Faith in his view was evident when Soviet Song started 7-4 favourite for her second Falmouth, much preferred to top Irish filly Alexander Goldrun, to the Windsor Forest one-two Peeress and Sundrop, and to three of the season's more worthy Guineas contenders.

The big concern for Fanshawe, reportedly, was that Attraction was not present to set a good pace, which is some measure of his confidence as the Mark Johnston-trained filly was the only one in their division who could seriously be fancied to beat Soviet Song.

Soviet Song did just that twice in 2004, including in this race, and none of her 2005 Falmouth opponents could offer the same sort of test, even with the favourite held up off a slow pace. "You don't change things for a big race, you have to ride them the way they like to be ridden," said Johnny Murtagh.

Peeress had a three-length advantage over her one and a half furlongs out, but Soviet Song comfortably turned that around once switched to the centre. A slowly run mile was probably even more of an obstacle to Alexander Goldrun, whose big wins were at around a mile and a quarter and, as the betting suggested, came second.

"Before she ran at York she was just getting by her lead horse on the gallops, but on Wednesday she flew by him," said the winning trainer.

Punters reckoned that the latter scenario was also the most likely outcome when Soviet Song took on the colts at Goodwood for the Sussex Stakes, but although that surge accounted for 10 of her rivals, it could not get her past Proclamation.

In 2004, Soviet Song got first run on Nayyir, but in 2005 it was the

2005 Race record

2nd Cantor Spreadfair Sussex Stakes (Group 1) (Goodwood, July 27) 3yo+ 1m Soft **123** (TS 111) 12 ran. *Held up in rear, effort when not clear run 2f out, plenty to do after, progress to chase winner last 150yds, ran on strongly, post came too soon (J P Murtagh), beaten 1/2l by Proclamation*

1st UAE Equestrian And Racing Federation Falmouth Stakes (Group 1) (Newmarket (July), July 5) 3yo+ 1m Good **124** (TS 91) 7 ran. *Held up, headway over 1f out, ridden to lead inside final furlong, ran on (J P Murtagh), beat Alexander Goldrun by 2 1/2l*

3rd Windsor Forest Stakes (Group 2) (York, June 15) 4yo+ 1m Good to firm **113** (TS 106) 8 ran. *Tracked leaders, effort over 3f out, kept on same pace approaching final furlong (J P Murtagh), beaten 3 3/4l by Peeress*

Other runs

2004 **6th** Queen Elizabeth II Stakes (Sponsored By NetJets) (Group 1) (Ascot, September 25) 3yo+ 1m Good to firm **103** (TS 93) 11 ran ● **1st** Coolmore Fusaichi Pegasus Matron Stakes (Group 1) (Leopardstown, September 11) 3yo+ 1m Good to firm **124** (TS 106) 6 ran ● **1st** Cantor Odds Sussex Stakes (Group 1) (Goodwood, July 28) 3yo+ 1m Good **122** (TS 118) 11 ran ● **1st** UAE Equestrian And Racing Federation Falmouth Stakes (Group 1) (Newmarket (July), July 6) 3yo+ 1m Good to firm **122** (TS 111) 7 ran ● **2nd** Queen Anne Stakes (Group 1) (Ascot, June 15) 4yo+ 1m Good to firm **119** (TS 108) 16 ran ● **1st** Ridgewood Pearl Stakes (Group 2) (Curragh, May 22) 4yo+ 1m Good to firm **118** (TS 81) 5 ran ● **3rd** Betfred.com Mile (Group 2) (Sandown, April 24) 4yo+ 1m Good to soft **111** (TS 104) 10 ran ● **2nd** Surrey Herald Snowdrop Fillies' Stakes (Listed) (Kempton, April 10) 4yo+ 1m Good to soft **106** (TS 69) 8 ran 2003 **5th** Queen Elizabeth II Stakes (Sponsored By NetJets) (Group 1) (Ascot, September 27) 3yo+ 1m Good to firm **111** (TS 97) 8 ran ● **4th** Netjets Prix du Moulin de Longchamp (Group 1) (Longchamp, September 7) 3yo+ 1m Good to soft **114** (TS 85) 14 ran ● **2nd** Coronation Stakes (Group 1) (Ascot, June 20) 3yo 1m Good to firm **118** (TS 115) 9 ran ● **4th** Sagitta 1,000 Guineas Stakes (Group 1) (Newmarket, May 4) 3yo 1m Good to firm **108** (TS 96) 19 ran 2002 ● **1st** Meon Valley Stud Fillies' Mile (Group 1) (Ascot, September 28) 2yo 1m Good to firm **112** (TS 100) 10 ran ● **1st** Milcars Sweet Solera Stakes (Listed) (Newmarket (July), August 10) 2yo 7f Soft **111** (TS 74) 8 ran ● **1st** EBF Median Auction Maiden Fillies' Stakes (Kempton, July 17) 2yo 6f Good to firm **83** (TS 74) 15 ran

mare's turn to get a taste of her own medicine as Mick Kinane on the second favourite seized the initiative and did not relinquish it, the pair having the finish to themselves.

There was only half a length between them, but while 20,000 Elite Club owners may disagree, it's no certainty by any means that the order would have been reversed had the two of them been let loose at the same time.

What's beyond dispute is that the other top mile races were much the poorer without her. Soviet Song's has been a great and now long-running success story, so if the owners had called it quits on the track with her, a horse they bred, there could have been few quibbles. However, she will be back for more in 2006.

"She knows she is out of the ordinary," said Fanshawe. "She has that air of superiority that commands her a lot of respect. She is the best horse I have ever trained and she knows it."

Soviet Song

bay mare, 18-2-2000

Marju b 1988	Last Tycoon	Try My Best	**Northern Dancer** Sex Appeal
		Mill Princess	Mill Reef Irish Lass
	Flame Of Tara	Artaius	Round Table Stylish Pattern
		Welsh Flame	Welsh Pageant Electric Flash
Kalinka b 1994	Soviet Star	Nureyev	**Northern Dancer** Special
		Veruschka	Venture Marie d'Anjou
	Tralthee	Tromos	Busted Stilvi
		Swalthee	Sword Dancer Amalthee

Bred by Elite Racing Club.

Sire Marju

Won 3 of 7 races, inc. Craven Stakes-Gr3, St James's Palace Stakes-Gr1. Also 2nd in the Derby (to Generous). Had an abbreviated first season owing to a slight setback, in-and-out at 3 because of a persistent stifle problem, and eventually lost his action completely. Good-bodied, lengthy, short-legged, showing quality. Among the best sons of his sire (also got Ezzoud, Bigstone, Taipan and Mahogany). Half-brother to 10 other winners, inc. Salsabil, Danse Royale, Song Of Tara and Flame Of Athens. Out of a top-class 8-12f runner, from an extremely successful family. Stands at Derrinstown Stud, Co. Kildare, (2006) fee €25,000 (Oct. 1). Sire of 11 crops of racing age, inc. notable winners: My Emma (Prix Vermeille-Gr1), Sil Sila (Prix de Diane-Gr1, Yorkshire Oaks-Gr1), Della Scala (Gr3), Mahboob (Gr3), Oriental Fashion (Gr2), Miletrian (Gr2), Naheef (Gr3), Marbye (Prix d'Astarte-Gr1), Soviet Song (Fillies' Mile (Gr1), Falmouth S.-Gr1 x2, Sussex S.-Gr1, Matron S.-Gr1), Stormont (Gr2), Brunel (Gr2), Red Feather (Gr2), Bobs Pride (Gr3).

Dam Kalinka

Won 1 of 10 races. Also 2nd once, 3rd once, 4th 4 times, and placed 4th and 6th (poor form) in 2 outings over hurdles. Big, leggy sort. Fairly useful, showed quite consistent form at 3. Quite well-bred. Half-sister to 12f winner Dancing Tralthee (by Dancing Brave). By a high-class miler and successful sire, out of smart racemare (won Rockfel and Lupe S, both Listed) who was sister to 6 lesser winners, inc. dam of US Gr3 winners Club Champ and Ask Anita. Dam of: Baralinka (1999 f by Barathea; winner), Soviet Song (2000 f by Marju; multiple Gr1 winner), Penzance (2001 c by Pennekamp; Flat winner and Gr1 hurdles winner), Kazatzka (2002 f by Groom Dancer; placed). Her yearling is a filly by Marju, she has a filly foal by Red Ransom, and was covered by Marju in 2005.

Pedigree assessment

Soviet Song had an abbreviated season, but both at Newmarket, where she won one of the best-contested fillies' races of the year, and at Goodwood, where she was arguably unlucky as Proclamation's runner-up, she proved that she was every bit as good as she had been in 2004. One of those horses who has effectively 're-written' her pedigree, Soviet Song has far exceeded expectations in a thoroughly meritorious career. She is the best daughter of her sire, whose fillies have generally proved superior to his colts, and she is unquestionably the best runner to have emerged in recent generations from a family whose prominent performers have been few and far between. Let's hope the decision to race on is suitably rewarded. *TM*

Starcraft (NZ)

5yo chestnut horse **127**

Soviet Star (USA) - Flying Floozie (NZ) (Pompeii Court (USA))

Owner The Australian Syndicate

Trainer L M Cumani

Breeder G J Chittick

Career: **22** starts	won **11**	second **3**	third **4**	**£1,289,010** win and place

By Brough Scott

THERE are many ways of judging a trainer, but the one they themselves know, and sometimes fear, the most is how they handle horses from other people. The better the horse, the further away the original territory, the bigger the challenge. So step forward Luca Cumani.

In 2003 he took on the Italian champion Falbrav and made him into a superstar with five Group 1 wins and that photo-finish third in the Breeders' Cup. In 2005 he took on the Australian giant Starcraft and won the Prix du Moulin and the Queen Elizabeth II Stakes. When that was finished he took the former Sir Michael Stoute reject Alkaased to win the Japan Cup. To hit the jackpot with one, or even two, transferred horses might be considered good fortune, but with three in three years, that's little short of genius.

In every sense Starcraft, who arrived in the first week of February, was the biggest challenge of them all. To start with, there was the size of him. At 16.3 hands and no less than 570 kilos he was 33 kilos heavier than Falbrav – and we thought him a monster. But much more important than the shape, was the extent, the distance and the time zone of his victories. Cumani knew this huge horse was talented, but how would he gauge his fitness, what would be his best trip, and when would he acclimatise?

Starcraft's nine successes (eight in Australia and one in New Zealand) had included three at Group 1 level from seven furlongs to a mile and a half, from soft ground to firm. With a fast-finishing third in the prestigious Cox Plate as his Australian swansong he had to be good. But arriving in Britain in deepest winter direct from the heat of his own high summer, he didn't even know what year it was.

Foaled in New Zealand in October 2000, he was a four-year-old in the southern hemisphere. Up in Newmarket he was a five-year-old and a very chilly one at that. When he finally made it out on to Warren Hill

Starcraft, having set a steady pace, puts in a storming finish to score his first European victory in the Moulin

he had more blankets and head coverings than an Arctic explorer. "I felt rather sorry for him," remembered Cumani. "The one place we could not cover was his stomach and his baffled system grew a woolly coat there. We obviously would have to take our time."

It wasn't until April that the big horse began to flourish and by the end of May the word was well and truly out. "Starcraft," wrote the *Racing Post*'s Newmarket correspondent Tony Elves, "looked appropriately named as he cruised up to his workmates with Dettori's arms fully stretched." The horse was well, but what was his trip? His first entry was in the one-mile Queen Anne Stakes at Royal Ascot at York. But the Cox Plate had been over ten furlongs, he had won the Australian Derby over a soft 12 furlongs, and owner Paul Makin had said that he should aim for the July Cup over six.

He ran a cracker in the Queen Anne to be a two-length third to Valixir, just half a length behind the odds-on Rakti. It was the first sight for most of us. What we saw was this huge chestnut thing with such an enormous stride that his limbs seemed to be moving slower than the others when he was actually overtaking. We were sure he would need further. When he turned up in the Eclipse 18 days later, the scene seemed set. Only for Starcraft, quite literally, to blow it.

Everyone who deals with thoroughbreds will have had at least one experience when something switches in a horse's head and cool goes to

2005 Race record

7th Breeders' Cup Classic - Powered by Dodge (Grade 1) (Dirt) (Belmont Park, October 29) 3yo+ 1m2f Fast **113** 13 ran. *In touch in mid-division, pushed along 2½f out and some headway, 8th straight, unable to quicken (P Valenzuela), beaten 7½l by Saint Liam*

1st Queen Elizabeth II Stakes sponsored by Barclays plc (Group 1) (Newmarket, September 24) 3yo+ 1m Good **122** (TS 98) 6 ran. *Raced stands' side, tracked leaders, led that group and overall leader over 2f out, soon ridden, stayed on gamely (C P Lemaire), beat Dubawi by ¾l*

1st Netjets Prix du Moulin de Longchamp (Group 1) (Longchamp, September 4) 3yo+ 1m Good **127** (TS 104) 9 ran. *Made all, ridden 1f out, ran on strongly (C P Lemaire), beat Gorella by 2½l*

6th Coral-Eclipse Stakes (Group 1) (Sandown, July 2) 3yo+ 1m2f Good to firm **103** (TS 81) 7 ran. *Slowly into stride, took keen hold, soon chased leaders, ridden over 2f out, weakened rapidly well over 1f out (P Robinson), beaten 11l by Oratorio*

3rd Queen Anne Stakes (Group 1) (York, June 14) 4yo+ 1m Good to firm **121** (TS 119) 10 ran. *Led early, held up, headway over 3f out, stayed on well final furlong (D Holland), beaten 2l by Valixir*

Other runs

2004 **3rd** Carlton Draught Cox Plate (Group 1) (Moonee Valley, October 23) 3yo+ 1m2f Good **119** 13 ran ● **3rd** Yalumba Stakes (Group 1) (Caulfield, October 9) 3yo+ 1m2f Good **116** 9 ran ● **2nd** Kelt Capital Stakes (Group 1) (Hastings, October 2) 3yo+ 1m2f Good to soft **109** 11 ran ● **1st** Hawke's Bay Stoney Bridge Stakes (Group 2) (Hastings, September 18) 1m Firm 12 ran ● **1st** Mudgway Partsworld Stakes (Group 1) (Hastings, August 28) 3yo+ 7f Firm **113** 16 ran ● **1st** San Miguel AJC Australian Derby (Group 1) (Randwick, April 10) 3yo 1m4f Soft **113** 13 ran ● **1st** STC Tulloch Stakes (Group 2) (Rosehill, April 3) 1m2f Good 14 ran ● **1st** San Miguel Chipping Norton Stakes (Group 1) (Warwick Farm, March 6) 3yo+ 1m Soft **117** 9 ran ● **2nd** Cadbury Guineas (Group 1) (Flemington, February 14) 3yo 1m Good **117** 10 ran ● **1st** VRC Debonair Stakes (Group 3) (Flemington, January 31) 3yo 7f Good to soft 12 ran 2003 **1st** QTC Peintre Celebre Handicap (Eagle Farm, December 13) 1m Good 14 ran ● **1st** QTC Leopardstown Handicap (Eagle Farm, December 3) 1m Good 12 ran ● **1st** BTC Network Ten Maiden Handicap (Doomben, November 19) 1m Good 11 ran ● **4th** QTC Mercedes-Benz Maiden Handicap (Eagle Farm, November 4) 7f Good 10 ran ● **11th** Tattersall's 2-y-o Stakes (Listed) (Eagle Farm, June 21) 7f Good 14 ran ● **2nd** Ipswich TC Qtis 2-y-o Maiden Handicap (Ipswich, June 11) 6½f Good to soft 11 ran ● **3rd** QTC River 94.9 Tile Wizards Handicap (Eagle Farm, February 15) 6f Good 10 ran

chaos. Not many have it in the paddock at Sandown. Suddenly Starcraft was a dangerous lunatic, plunging about and at one stage almost leaping out into the crowd. Philip Robinson had been booked for the ride. He was used to the combustible Rakti but he hadn't banked on anything like this.

Not surprisingly the race proved a fiasco. Starcraft pulled hard behind a slow pace before dropping away disappointingly in the straight to finish 11 lengths off the winner Oratorio. Cumani was back to the drawing board. Enquiries to Australia brought the not entirely helpful "didn't we tell you he had done it before" response, veterinary examination suggested

Starcraft lands a second Group 1 triumph in the Queen Elizabeth II Stakes, leaving Dubawi trailing in his wake

an injury high up in the pelvis, and the trainer publicly fed the press with the cryptic "psychological training."

In reality this involved boxing Starcraft down to Newmarket's July course every Friday for "paddock schooling" during the evening meetings which have become such sell-out events in mid-summer. The first time Starcraft nearly went over backwards in a repeat of his Sandown antics, but he was good as gold on future occasions, no doubt aware that any behaviour of his own was unlikely to match what humans got up to when the racing gave way to the pop music which was the real attraction. Either way, Starcraft got psychologically and physically on track and was a massive model of deportment before his next race, the nine-runner Prix du Moulin over the Longchamp mile.

In the race he was a revelation. With no one keen to make the running jockey Christophe Lemaire dictated a steady pace over the first three furlongs before flying home in 1min 36.10sec, the second-fastest time clocked for the race. The sectionals were revealing; Starcraft's opening three furlongs were in a sedentary 39.1 seconds, the last five, with the likes of Valixir, Whipper and Gorella all coming at him, were knocked off in an astonishing 57 seconds flat. Starcraft was fast.

It was no great surprise to the Cumani team but somehow the enormity of the Aussie's talent had not been fully rumbled by the British public. When Starcraft came out for the Queen Elizabeth II Stakes, transferred from Ascot to Newmarket, he was only third choice in the betting and his subsequent victory was submerged under discussions of how much Frankie Dettori had, or had not, erred on the Godolphin hope Dubawi.

Over the years Sheikh Mohammed's men have been admirably generous and circumspect in defeat. Just for once they lost it and used a full-scale blaming of the jockey to explain away their little horse's defeat. Dettori himself contributed, saying that "the best horse lost" and claiming that his tracking of Rakti in the centre of the course, rather than (as per the Godolphin plan) his own pacemaker Blatant on the rail, and his forced return to tackle Starcraft, lost him 20 yards. It was all nonsense.

According to the Turftrax GPS tracking system, over the whole straight Newmarket mile Dubawi had actually run slightly less far than the winner. What's more, Dettori still had plenty of horse underneath him when he came over to do battle with an already driven Starcraft. Dubawi was a brilliant little runner but never quite the reincarnation of his ill-fated sire Dubai Millennium that he was hailed as. At Newmarket – look at the video – the Aussie giant was just too strong for him.

Cumani first talked of a Dubawi rematch in the Breeders' Cup and of proving Starcraft "The World's Best Miler." But then he and Makin opted for an even bolder plan, to stump up the $800,000 late entry fee to put their champion in the Breeders' Cup Classic on the Belmont dirt. Makin had made some of his millions gambling in Hong Kong and lived on the maxim that "life isn't a dress rehearsal". But this was something else and it took Cumani's perspective to make sense of the punt.

"My American trainer friends all tell me that you can never be sure whether a horse will adapt to the surface first time," he said. "They may work well on it but you can't be sure what will happen until the real pressure is applied. We can't be sure with this horse. But he is big, mature and bold. He has a chance."

This turned out to be a perfect horoscope-style prediction. Starcraft did indeed work brilliantly on the dirt and for a few brief moments running to the final turn looked to have Belmont and the world at his mercy. But when he hit the straight, he seemed to hit a wall. His huge stride lost both its rhythm and its bite and suddenly he was just another floundering sand-caked loser in the dirt.

It was his last race. In 2006 he will be doing the stallion shuttle in what will presumably be a reinforced plane between Suffolk's Cheveley Park and Arrowfield Stud in Australia. He was a terrific performer and reflected great credit on his connections. But even in that last race he kept a bit of mystery to himself. Perhaps it was not the surface but because, racing at the choke-out American rhythm, he just did not stay. Maybe, even after 22 races, no one, not even Cumani, was yet certain of his optimum trip.

Starcraft

chestnut horse, 21-10-2000

Soviet Star b 1984	Nureyev	Northern Dancer	Nearctic Natalma
		Special	Forli Thong
	Veruschka	Venture	Relic Rose O' Lynn
		Marie d'Anjou	Vandale Marigold
Flying Floozie ch 1993	Pompeii Court	Tell	Round Table Nas-Mahal
		Port Damascus	Damascus Paris Pike
	Lucky Heiress	Battle-Waggon	Never Say Die Carrozza
		Entrancing Bell	Bellborough Entrancing

Bred by G J Chittick in New Zealand. NZ$80,000 New Zealand Bloodstock Premier Sale yearling.

Sire Soviet Star

Won 8 of 14 starts, inc. Prix de Fontainebleau-Gr3, Poule d'Essai des Poulains-Gr1, Sussex Stakes-Gr1, Prix de la Foret-Gr1, Sandown Mile-Gr2, July Cup-Gr1, Prix du Moulin de Longchamp-Gr1. Also 2nd in Prix Jean Prat, St James's Palace Stakes & Prix du Moulin de Longchamp at 3, and in Queen Anne Stakes at 4. Medium-sized (16.0 hands), lengthy, quite good-looking. Top-class performer from 6-8 furlongs, barely stayed 9f. Highly strung, inclined to be impetuous, but raced gamely and consistently. Stands at Ballylinch Stud, Co. Kilkenny, Ireland, at a 2006 fee of €12,000. Sire of 9 European-conceived crops of racing age, inc. notable winners Bon Point (Gr2), Soviet Line (Lockinge Stakes-Gr1, twice), Freedom Cry (Gr2), Volochine (Gr2), Wessam Prince (Gr3), Advancing Star (Gr3), Ashkalani (Poule d'Essai des Poulains-Gr1, Prix du Moulin de Longchamp-Gr1), Sensation (Gr2), Clerio (Gr3), Starborough (Prix Jean Prat-Gr1, St James's Palace Stakes-Gr1), Limpid (Grand Prix de Paris-Gr1), Democratic Deficit (Gr2). Also sire, from 1 NZ-conceived crop, of Russian Pearl (Bayer Classic-Gr1), Starcraft (Chipping Norton S.-Gr1, Australian Derby-Gr1, Mudgway S.-Gr1, Prix du Moulin de Longchamp-Gr1, Queen Elizabeth II S.-Gr1) and Stardane (Gr3).

Dam Flying Floozie

Ran only at 3 years, placed 3rd once from 4 starts. Earned NZ$400. Well bred. Sister to Happy Heiress (Gr2 winner in South Africa, dam of Gr3 and Listed winners there). Dam of: Forum Floozie (1998 f by Danasinga; won 5 races in Australia), Wise Choice (1999 g by Danasinga; won 5 races in Hong Kong), Starcraft (2000 c by Soviet Star; multiple Gr1 winner), Pin Up (2001 f by Pins; won 2 of 3 starts to date in Australia). She has a yearling filly and a filly foal, both by Danasinga. Barren to Danasinga in 2002, covered by Pins in 2004 and sent to Australia in March 2005.

Pedigree assessment

Starcraft turned in a first-rate performance to make all in the the Prix du Moulin, and while his subsequent victory over Dubawi in the Queen Elizabeth II Stakes was rather more controversial, he impressed again with an admirable attitude. From the only crop conceived in New Zealand by Soviet Star, who had spells in England and Japan before he found a permanent home in Ireland, Starcraft comes from a long-established successful family in the southern hemisphere. He will spend his first stud season at Cheveley Park in 2006, and it remains to be seen what kind of support he receives from British breeders; he certainly advertised his racing qualities well enough during his period with Luca Cumani. *TM*

Stevie Wonderboy (USA)

2yo chestnut colt **119**

Stephen Got Even (USA) - Heat Lightning (USA) (Summer Squall (USA))

Owner The Merv Griffin Ranch Co

Trainer Doug O'Neill

Breeder J Gunther, T Holmes & W Zent

Career: **5** starts | won **3** | second **1** | third **1** | **£511,531** win and place

By James Willoughby

JOCKEYS provided the most compelling narrative to the 22nd Breeders' Cup at Belmont Park. Edgar Prado rode his first winner at the annual meeting in 42 tries, on Folklore in the opening Juvenile Fillies, then promptly gained his second on Silver Train in the Sprint two races later. And Jerry Bailey landed his fifth Classic on Saint Liam before confirming he was thinking long and hard about retirement.

The most poignant story was that of rising star Garrett Gomez. The Arizona-born rider might be described as an overnight success 17 years in the making, because his talent was obvious to many when he first appeared at tiny Santa Fe Downs in 1988.

Gomez had taken the reins on eight Breeders' Cup mounts before partnering the highly promising colt Stevie Wonderboy in the latest renewal of the Juvenile. His best finishes had come in 1999, when he was second in the Classic on Budroyale and third in the Turf on Buck's Boy.

Those high-profile mounts saw him rise to prominence within two years, but Gomez was to prove his own worst enemy when drug addiction soon arrested the momentum of his career. For that and other personal problems, he was out of the saddle for 21 months before returning to action in September 2004.

Gomez found love – that of his second wife Pam – to get him back on the straight and narrow, and he found Stevie Wonderboy to get him in the winner's enclosure at the Breeders' Cup for the first time at the age of 33.

A big, rangy colt by the middle-distance dirt horse Stephen Got Even, Stevie Wonderboy came into the Juvenile with the reputation but not the record. True, he had won the Del Mar Futurity with an eye-catching wide sweep, but ranged against him at Belmont were two colts in First Samurai and Henny Hughes that had established formidable form credentials. Moreover, they had done it over course and distance, whereas Stevie Wonderboy had to ship in from his home base in California.

Stevie Wonderboy scores a stylish win in the Breeders' Cup Juvenile, and looks a first-rate Kentucky Derby prospect

Any fears that Stevie Wonderboy would not acclimatise were assuaged by a sensational gallop on the Monday before the race. Despite his rider hardly letting out a reef, the two-year-old notched a time which was the fastest of 137 horses to work that morning, including some useful older runners. Still, workouts are one thing and races are another.

While his passage through the race was relatively untroubled compared to his rider's journey through life, Stevie Wonderboy caught a bump after half a mile of the Juvenile that left him in a most unpromising position. Here, Gomez displayed that characteristic common to all great riders, no matter what the individual demands of their racing environment throughout the world: a cool head.

Races at Belmont over the mile and half a furlong trip on dirt take place around just one turn. This has the effect of rendering them a stern test of stamina, for a fearsome gallop can build up down the long back straight. The pace meant that the leaders would come back to Stevie Wonderboy, and that there was still time for the colt to overcome the interference.

Gomez angled his mount in and out of traffic with great prescience. And just before the field straightened up, Stevie Wonderboy could be seen as a menacing presence behind the more strained forms of Henny Hughes and First Samurai. The latter, in particular, looked used up by the stern pace, perhaps recoiling from the stress of a Grade 1 double in the Hopeful Stakes at Saratoga and the Champagne at Belmont.

2005 Race record

1st Bessemer Trust Breeders' Cup Juvenile (Grade 1) (Belmont Park, October 29) 2yo 1m½f Fast **119** 14 ran. *Held up in touch, good headway from halfway and 3rd straight, driven 2f out, finished well from 1f out to lead close home, driven out (G K Gomez), beat Henny Hughes by 1¼l*

1st Del Mar Futurity (Grade 2) (Del Mar, September 7) 2yo 7f Fast **110** 11 ran. *Held up in rear, headway on outside on final turn, 6th straight, led distance, ridden out (G K Gomez), beat The Pharaoh by 5l*

1st Maiden Special Weight (Del Mar, August 6) 2yo 6½f Fast **107** 9 ran. *Pressed leaders, led 2f out, soon clear, ridden out (G K Gomez), beat Long Rider by 4l*

3rd Hollywood Juvenile Chapionship Stakes (Grade 3) (Hollywood Park, July 16) 2yo 6f Fast **100** 5 ran. *Dwelt start, raced in 4th, came wide and 3rd straight, ran on steadily (G K Gomez), beaten 1¼l by What A Song*

2nd Maiden Special Weight (Hollywood Park, June 18) 2yo 5½f Fast 7 ran. *Towards rear, hampered 4f out, went 3rd 2f out, stayed on steadily to take 2nd close home (G K Gomez), beaten 3¼l by What A Song*

Henny Hughes, by contrast, was not stopping and looked for a moment approaching the furlong pole as if he could not be caught. Down the outside, however, Gomez began to get a tremendous response from Stevie Wonderboy and his mount wore down his persistent foe half a furlong out, winning by more than a length and in the manner of a strong stayer. First Samurai was two lengths further back, with a five-length gap behind him to Brother Derek, subsequent winner of the Hollywood Futurity.

Named after the recording star for whom the colt's veteran owner Merv Griffin once served as agent, Stevie Wonderboy had put his own name up in lights. And here indeed is a superstar, for the winning time of 1min 41.64sec was superb when conditions were taken into account.

Each successive winner of the Juvenile before Stevie Wonderboy has added to the increasingly tiresome diatribe that none has landed the Kentucky Derby. It is ridiculous to conclude that this collective failure amounts to a jinx. In Stevie Wonderboy, the Juvenile has one of its best chances to divest itself of a stigma that led to some talented youngsters skipping the race in 2004. He is lightly raced, physically robust in appearance and has the pedigree to stay a mile and a quarter with ease.

Of course, there are plenty of pitfalls to avoid before Stevie Wonderboy can wear the blanket of roses, and his trainer Doug O'Neill is comparatively inexperienced with Classic prospects, having worked his way up by improving claiming horses in California.

Nevertheless, the more often you watch the Juvenile on tape, the more starry Stevie Wonderboy's outlook becomes. He would have won more easily had his run started from closer to the pace and passed the line travelling much faster than the runner-up, who is a decent horse in his own right and will make a top-class sprinter.

Provided he comes through his prep races without accident, Stevie Wonderboy is a terrific prospect for the Triple Crown.

Stevie Wonderboy

chestnut colt, 27-3-03

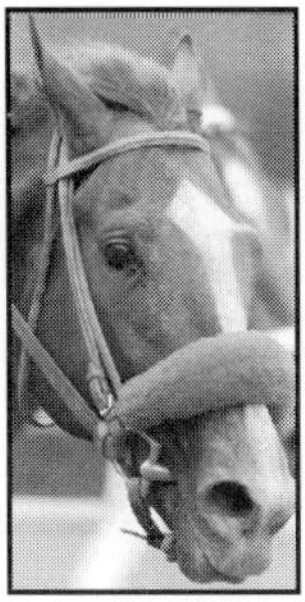

Stephen Got Even b 1996	A P Indy	Seattle Slew	Bold Reasoning My Charmer
		Weekend Surprise	Secretariat Lassie Dear
	Immerse	Cox's Ridge	Best Turn Our Martha
		Baroness Direct	Blushing Groom Avum
Heat Lightning br 1993	Summer Squall	Storm Bird	Northern Dancer South Ocean
		Weekend Surprise	Secretariat Lassie Dear
	Mystical Mood	Roberto	Hail To Reason Bramalea
		Mystery Mood	Night Invader Moaning Low

Bred by John Gunther, Tony Holmes, Walter Zent in US. $100,000 Fasig-Tipton Florida Calder Selected 2yo

Sire Stephen Got Even

Placed only start at 2. Developed into top-class 8f+ colt at 3 and 4, won 5 of 10 starts, notably 9f Gallery Furniture.com S-Gr2 at 3 and 9f Donn H-Gr1 at 4. By top-class 9f+ performer and outstanding sire of dirt performers, mostly over 8f+. Stands alongside his sire at Lane's End Farm, Kentucky, 2006 fee $25,000. First foals 2002, sire of: Don't Get Mad (Gr2), For All We Know (Gr2), Stevie Wonderboy (Breeders' Cup Juvenile-Gr1)

Dam Heat Lightning

Placed at 2, 3 and 4 on dirt in US. By Preakness Stakes winner and very good dirt sire, chief winners Charismatic and Storm Song. Dam high-class US 2yo, Gr3 winner, 2nd Frizette S-Gr1, 3rd Matron S-Gr1, also dam of high-class 8-10f colt Fair Judgment (Alleged) and grand-dam of several minor US stakes winners. Grand-dam Mystery Mood Gr1 placed, dam of smart German miler Maximilian and grand-dam of Australian Gr1 winner Istidaad. Dam of: Game Called (1998 c by Miswaki; winner), Our Imperial Bay (1999 c by Smart Strike; winner), Summer Scene (2000 f by Belong To Me; winner), Summer Flash (2001 f by Belong To Me; winner), Ogden Dunes (2002 c by Swain; winner), Stevie Wonderboy (2003 c by Stephen Got Even; Gr1 winner), 2004 f by Mr Greeley. In foal to Birdstone, sold $1,100,000 2005 Keeneland November Sale.

Pedigree assessment

Stevie Wonderboy's performances at 2 suggest he should stay further than a mile at 3, and that concurs with his pedigree. Stephen Got Even stayed well in US terms, and there is some stamina in Heat Lightning's background. There is also plenty of encouragement that the Breeders' Cup Juvenile winner can enhance his record at 3. Certainly in pedigree terms, the Kentucky Derby is within Stevie Wonderboy's compass. *JH*

The Geezer

3yo chestnut colt **119**

Halling (USA) - Polygueza (Fr) (Be My Guest (USA))

Owner J C Smith

Trainer D R C Elsworth

Breeder Wickfield Farm Partnership

Career: **12** starts | won **4** | second **4** | third **1** | **£241,653** win and place

By Richard Austen

GOING into the latest season, David Elsworth could claim to have trained a British Classic winner, but not for its Classic victory. Island Sands was unbeaten in two juvenile starts for Elsworth in 1999 but caught the eye of Godolphin in the process.

Bidding to put his own name in the record books, Elsworth was represented in all five Classics in 2005. In the two Guineas, his runners failed to rise to the occasion, Tucker (33-1) finishing tenth in the 2,000, while Cape Columbine (10-1) and Simply Sunshine (25-1) were fifth and 15th respectively in the 1,000.

Within three weeks the dream was revived in the Epsom trials as The Geezer kept on stoutly to run Motivator to one and a half lengths in the Dante Stakes and Something Exciting won the Lupe. "Each year we have a dream, a Derby horse, a Classic horse," said the trainer, but when Something Exciting (7-1) beat all except Eswarah in the Oaks, all hopes rested with The Geezer.

Although there can be some dramatic changes with relatively young and inexperienced horses, and The Geezer had already improved about two and a half stone in 2005, there was no striking reason why he should turn the tables on Motivator judged solely on the Dante.

The trainer must have been bitterly disappointed nevertheless, for whereas Something Exciting's bid was alive still entering the final furlong, 10-1 shot The Geezer at the same stage had no chance whatsoever of beating Motivator and he lost out to six of the others as well after attempting to come from last place.

When The Geezer stepped out in the King Edward VII Stakes at York 13 days later, Elsworth predicted that he would run well, while adding "let's face it, he couldn't run worse than he did at Epsom."

A five-runner line-up suggested The Geezer would be messed around less than in the Derby, but the final furlong showed how three horses

The Geezer scores his most important win in the Group 3 ABN Amro Stakes, but he came up short at a higher level

can make things most uncomfortable for each other and The Geezer was the proverbial meat in the sandwich. Maintaining his effort at the time, he might have been second but probably no better.

"He takes a long time to do anything," was Elsworth's realistic comment, a trait that did not rule him out of St Leger considerations, of course, particularly when The Geezer embarked on his pre-Doncaster campaign with two victories. The second of those, in the ABN Amro Stakes (the Gordon Stakes) with plenty of give in the ground at Goodwood, came impressively by five lengths.

Ending up second in the Great Voltigeur back at York in August, after he'd struck for home looking the winner three furlongs out, queered the pitch somewhat for some observers, as did his pedigree, but there was never any question of The Geezer missing the final Classic.

Facing only five rivals made him a very serious contender, for all that one of those was Scorpion at 10-11, and heavy going could have opened it up for The Geezer as well. In the event he got every yard and was staying on best of all, but he did not take Classic glory. Boxed in halfway up the straight, the 7-2 second favourite was out in time to chase Scorpion through the final furlong, but while reducing the deficit all the way to the post, he went down by a length.

"I wouldn't swap my horse for the winner," said a philosophical Elsworth afterwards. In November, however, after a below-form fourth in a Longchamp Group 2, came news that owner Jeff Smith had swapped him, for an unspecified sum, and The Geezer had joined Godolphin.

2005 Race record

4th Prix Chaudenay Casino Barriere de Menton (Group 2) (Longchamp, October 1) 3yo 1m7f Soft **110** (TS 109) 7 ran. *In touch, headway to go 2nd over 4f out, driven to chase leader 2f out, no extra inside final furlong (J F Egan), beaten 3l by Shamdala*

2nd Ladbrokes St Leger Stakes (Group 1) (Doncaster, September 10) 3yo 1m6½f Heavy **119** (TS 71) 6 ran. *Held up in touch, not clear run on inside over 3f out, switched right over 2f out, went 2nd 1f out, stayed on, not quite reach winner (T Quinn), beaten 1l by Scorpion*

2nd Daily Telegraph Great Voltigeur Stakes (Group 2) (York, August 16) 3yo 1m4f Good **117** (TS 90) 6 ran. *Held up, went prominent 8f out, shaken up to lead over 3f out, 3 lengths clear over 1f out, ridden inside final furlong, headed near finish (T Quinn), beaten ½l by Hard Top*

1st ABN Amro Stakes (Registered As The Gordon Stakes) (Group 3) (Goodwood, July 26) 3yo 1m4f Good to soft **119** (TS 88) 5 ran. *Dwelt, soon close up, tracked leader 4f out, shaken up to lead 2f out, readily drew clear over 1f out (T Quinn), beat Unfurled by 5l*

1st H20 July Trophy (Listed) (Haydock, July 2) 3yo 1m4f Good to firm **108** (TS 69) 5 ran. *Held up in rear, headway over 4f out, led over 1f out, tail flashed when ridden and soon edged left inside final furlong, driven out (T Quinn), beat Eraser by 1l*

3rd King Edward VII Stakes (Group 2) (York, June 17) 3yo 1m4f Good to firm **110** (TS 89) 5 ran. *Close up, ridden to challenge 1f out, every chance when hampered well inside final furlong, not recover (T Quinn), beaten 1½l by Plea Bargain*

8th Vodafone Derby Stakes (Group 1) (Epsom, June 4) 3yo 1m4f Good **104** (TS 97) 13 ran. *Soon last and not going well, still last straight, effort and not clear run on inner over 2f out, plugged on from over 1f out, no chance (T Quinn), beaten 15½l by Motivator*

2nd totesport Dante Stakes (Group 2) (York, May 12) 3yo 1m2½f Soft **116** (TS 101) 6 ran. *Tracked leaders, pushed along well over 1f out, ridden to chase winner inside final furlong, switched left and kept on (T Quinn), beaten 1½l by Motivator*

1st Dubai Duty Free Golf World Cup Conditions Stakes (Newbury, April 15) 3yo 1m2f Good to soft **103** (TS 15) 6 ran. *Tracked leaders, led over 2f out, pushed clear final furlong, easily (T Quinn), beat Thunderwing by 5l*

1st JSC Congratulates Anna Lisa And SJ Maiden Stakes (Kempton, March 28) 3yo 1m3f Good **89** (TS 60) 11 ran. *Held up in rear, steady headway from 4f out, shaken up and quickened from 2f out, led final half furlong, comfortably (T Quinn), beat Bravemore by 1¼l*

2004

2nd betdirect.co.uk Maiden Stakes (Div II) (Lingfield (A.W), November 27) 2yo 1m2f Standard **81** (TS 41) 10 ran ● **4th** Testers Of Edenbridge All New Discovery 3 Maiden Stakes (Div II) (Lingfield (AW), October 31) 2yo 1m Standard **66** (TS 64) 12 ran

It will be interesting to see how they campaign The Geezer, who was looking more and more the strong-galloping staying type in 2005 and one particularly well suited by good ground or softer.

A strapping sort who could improve further, he came up just short in Group 1 and Group 2 company as a three-year-old, but in four runs at a lower level in the latest season he won them all.

The Geezer

chestnut colt, 4-3-2002

Parents	Grandparents	Great-grandparents	Great-great-grandparents
Halling ch 1991	Diesis	Sharpen Up	Atan Rocchetta
		Doubly Sure	Reliance Soft Angels
	Dance Machine	Green Dancer	Nijinsky GreenValley
		Never A Lady	Pontifex Camogie
Polygueza ch 1993	Be My Guest	Northern Dancer	Nearctic Natalma
		What A Treat	Tudor Minstrel Rare Treat
	Polifontaine	Bold Lad (USA)	Bold Ruler Misty Morn
		Mortefontaine	Polic Brabantia

Bred by Wickfield Farm Partnership in Britain. 21,000gns Tattersalls December foal

Sire Halling

Won 12 (8-10f) of 18 races from 3 to 5. Won 4 (inc. Cambridgeshire) at 3, won 4 (inc. Eclipse S-Gr1, York International-Gr1) at 4, won 4 (inc. Prix d'Ispahan-Gr1, Eclipse S-Gr1, York International-Gr1) at 5. Originally based at Dalham Hall Stud, switched before 2004 season to Emirates Stud Farm in Dubai, 2005 fee £30,000. First foals 1998, sire of: Chancellor (Gr2), Dandoun (Gr2), Giovane Imperatore (Gr2), Fisich (Gr2), Mkuzi (Gr3), Nordhal (Gr2), Vanderlin (Gr3), Franklins Gardens (Gr2), Norse Dancer (Gr3), Hattan (Gr3), Pinson (Gr2), The Geezer (Gr3).

Dam Polygueza

At 2, ran 4, placed once over 7f. At 3, ran 12, won 7f maiden, unplaced remaining starts. By high-class 2yo/miler and very good sire of variety of performers. Very closely related to dam of useful miler John Ferneley and high-class hurdler Intersky Falcon. Dam Polifontaine half-sister to Irish 1,000 Guineas winner Katies. Dam of: Big Sinisa (1998 c by Barathea; Listed-placed winner), 1999 c by Revoque, Jouvert (2000 c by Grand Lodge; unplaced), Doctored (2001 c by Dr Devious; winner), The Geezer (2002 c by Halling; Gr3 winner), Flight Captain (2003 c by In The Wings; winner).

Pedigree assessment

This is a family whose talented members in recent generations have tended to excel at around a mile. The Geezer has smart form over 12 furlongs and beyond, but on pedigree a mile and a quarter is more his trip. Halling's record for siring progressive performers suggests The Geezer could show improved form in 2006. *JH*

Turtle Bowl (Ire)

3yo bay colt **117**

Dyhim Diamond (Ire) - Clara Bow (Fr) (Top Ville)

Owner B Van Dalfsen

Trainer F Rohaut

Breeder A D Crichton

Career: **10** starts | won **5** | second **1** | third **1** | **£228,022** win and place

By Robert Carter

OF ALL the changes made to the Pattern-race calendar in France, the shortening of the Prix Jean Prat to one mile was the most pointless. Nine furlongs is a useful intermediate distance. The only important race at that trip is the Prix d'Ispahan. There is nothing above Group 3 otherwise. The new Jean Prat emerges as a consolation for Guineas losers and, on the evidence of its first year, no competition for the St James's Palace Stakes.

Its one strong point could be that it is the last Group 1 mile restricted to three-year-olds. If the calendar was not so thickly sown with good races matching them with older horses, between July and October, it would make some sense to move it to the autumn. As things stand, it will need to attract a stronger field than in 2005 or its Group 1 status will be challenged.

Most owners and trainers have been happy with the changes, although there was some criticism of the dropping of the Prix Lupin. Several trainers said that it would have been the ideal preparatory race for their Prix du Jockey-Club hopes. Others pointed out that, while the Lupin had been axed, the Prix Saint-Alary had both survived and retained its Group 1 status. For some reason, it has always proved difficult to win both the Saint-Alary and the Diane. That was never the case with the Lupin and it should have been downgraded from Group 1 years ago.

The Jean Prat no longer operated as an intermediate race – one which Bago had made good use of on his reappearance in 2004 – but the first Prix du Jockey-Club to be run at 2,100 metres fulfilled that function perfectly. Shamardal dropped back to one mile for the St James's Palace Stakes and should have stepped up again for the Coral-Eclipse. Hurricane Run went on to win the Irish Derby and the third, Rocamadour, contested the Jean Prat.

The character of the new races will change in time. For the moment,

Turtle Bowl wins the Group 1 Prix Jean Prat and, while he did not race again at three, he is expected back in 2006

though, they were pretty much the same. There had been either 14 or 15 runners in the Jockey-Club in four of the five previous years. This time there were 17.

Everybody called it the French Derby. No-one seemed worried by the shorter trip. The Grand Prix de Paris had only once attracted a field larger than eight since 1996. This time there were nine runners but no-one mistook it for a Derby, even though it is now run over the Classic distance. The Jean Prat attracted a field of eight just as it had in each of the three previous years.

Francois Rohaut was the first provincial trainer to produce a Group 1 winner. He saddled Balbonella, who carried the colours of his parents until being sold to Maktoum Al Maktoum a few days before the race, to win the Prix Robert Papin (since demoted to Group 2) in 1986. Rohaut, who is based at Pau, has trained other good horses like Pearly Shells and Torrestrella, but he had to wait 19 years for his first Group 1-winning colt.

Turtle Bowl ran four times as a two-year-old without leaving the south-west. He made his debut with a third at Bordeaux, then added a late-season win and a second on soft ground at Toulouse, one of Rohaut's favourite courses. He started his second season with another win there on March 2.

Turtle Bowl turned his fitness to advantage in the Listed Prix Montenica but his limitations were exposed by his defeats in the Prix de Fontainebleau and the Poule d'Essai. However, although he had won the Montenica on sticky ground, his trainer believed that the soft going

2005 Race record

1st Prix Jean Prat (Group 1) (Chantilly, July 3) 3yo 1m Good **117** (TS 103) 8 ran. *Held up, 7th and pushed along straight, driven 1½f out and headway, quickened and challenged final furlong, led 100yds out, pushed out (O Peslier), beat Starpix by 1l*

1st Prix de la Jonchere (Group 3) (Chantilly, June 12) 3yo 1m Good **114** (TS 95) 7 ran. *Always close up, 3rd straight, joined leader over 2f out, led well over 1f out, ran on well (O Peslier), beat Mathematician by 3l*

8th Gainsborough Poule d'Essai des Poulains (Group 1) (Grande Piste) (Longchamp, May 15) 3yo 1m Soft **104** (TS 92) 15 ran. *9th straight, one pace final 2f (D Boeuf), beaten 6½l by Shamardal*

4th Prix de Fontainebleau (Group 3) (Longchamp, April 24) 3yo 1m Very soft **98** (TS 23) 7 ran. *Held up, 5th and pushed along straight, never able to challenge (O Peslier), beaten 3½l by Laverock*

1st Prix Montenica (Listed) (Maisons-Laffitte, March 15) 3yo 7f Heavy **94** 8 ran. *Raced in 5th, slightly outpaced 2f out, headway on inside to lead well inside final furlong, ran on well (O Peslier), beat Mathematician by 1l*

1st Prix Provincial (Toulouse, March 2) 3yo 7f Good to firm 7 ran. *Always prominent, led 150yds out, quickened clear, easily (F X Bertras), beat Michelucci by 2½l*

2004

2nd Prix Sud Radio (Toulouse, December 4) 2yo 1m Very soft 9 ran ● **1st** Prix de Minimes (Toulouse, November 15) 2yo 1m Very soft 11 ran ● **5th** Prix de Saon (Straight Course) (Deauville, October 19) 2yo 7½f Soft **75** 6 ran ● **3rd** Prix du Four a Chaux (Unraced Colts & Geldings) (Bordeau Le Bouscat, September 20) 2yo 1m Good to soft 10 ran

at Longchamp was against him each time. Rohaut also claimed that Turtle Bowl was a sufferer in the crowding that took place when a big field was competing for position after the first furlong. Gharir was definitely a victim and he stayed on for third. Turtle Bowl raced in ninth, just behind Gharir, improved to sixth over one furlong from home, then declined to eighth.

Good going seems to have done the trick when he won the Group 3 Prix de la Jonchere, which had been moved to Chantilly to act as a prep for the Jean Prat. Turtle Bowl was always close up behind the front-running favourite, Early March, and moved into second on the outside early in the straight. Starpix, another south-west raider, made his challenge on the inside. The three were in line approaching the final furlong when Starpix hit the rails and almost came down. His chance was gone and Turtle Bowl was left in command.

Starpix took him on again in the Jean Prat and they were the last two as far as the straight while Rocamadour made the running. Turtle Bowl moved up on the outside of the odds-on Ad Valorem but hung in and hampered the Irish colt before hitting the front 100 yards out. He ran on to beat Starpix, who had been tracking him and kept absolutely straight while pinching second from Rocamadour. There was talk of an autumn campaign in the United States but Rohaut decided to keep Turtle Bowl for 2006.

Turtle Bowl

bay colt, 9-4-2002

Dyhim Diamond ch 1994	Night Shift	Northern Dancer	Nearctic Natalma
		Ciboulette	Chop Chop Windy Answer
	Happy Landing	Homing	Habitat Heavenly Thought
		Laughing Goddess	Green God Gay Baby
Clara Bow b 1990	Top Ville	High Top	Derring-Do Camenae
		Sega Ville	Charlottesville La Sega
	Kamiya	Kalamoun	Zeddaan Khairunissa
		Shahinaaz	Venture Cherry

Bred by Andrew Crichton in Ireland.

Sire Dyhim Diamond

Won 5 of 26 races, inc. Prix de Seine-et-Oise-Gr3, Benazet Rennen-Gr3. Also placed 10 times, and 4th in Prix Maurice de Gheest-Gr1. Medium-sized (16.0½hh), strong, good-quartered individual. Smart sprinter in Pattern company from 2-5 years, best at 4, modest form at 6 in US. Brother to Creaking Board (Gr1 in US, dam of Gr3 winner in US) and Dakhla Oasis (Gr2 in Germany). Stands at Haras de la Tuilerie, France at a fee of €2,000. Sire of 2 crops of racing age, inc. notable winner: Turtle Bowl (Prix Jean Prat-Gr1).

Dam Clara Bow

Unplaced in all 7 starts, 2 at 2 years, 5 at 3 years. Showed no form in varied company, including a seller, from 7-10f. Half-sister to Listed winner Houwayda (by Carwhite) and a winner in Morocco by Sarhoob. Dam won 2, placed 2 from only 5 starts, half-sister to Gr3 winners Karamita (dam of Gr1 winner Kartajana) and Karadar, and to the dam of Gr1 winner Khariyda. From a notable Aga Khan family. Dam of: Olden Waal (1994 f by Nashamaa; winner), Olden Maas (1995 f by Sanglamore; winner), Olde Vechte (1997 f by Tenby; unraced), Whitton Court (1998 c by Cardoun; Listed-placed winner), Turtle Bow (1999 f by Turtle Island; Gr2 winner, Gr1-placed), Lady Zorreghuietta (2000 f by Anabaa; unraced), Super Bowl (2001 c by Green Tune; unraced), Turtle Bowl (2002 c by Dyhim Diamond; Gr1 winner). She has a yearling colt by Rock Of Gibraltar, and a colt foal by High Chaparral, and was covered by Galileo in 2005.

Pedigree assessment

A modest Group 3-calibre sprinter allowed few chances at stud would normally seem an unlikely sort to get a Group 1-winning miler. A mare who finished unplaced in all her seven races, including a seller, would seem a doubtful proposition to produce one. But the union of Dyhim Diamond and Clara Bow turned up trumps, and when Turtle Bowl won the Prix Jean Prat it really was not a total surprise. Clara Bow had already produced a filly of some distinction in Turtle Bow, a Group 2 scorer also placed in Group 1. And her second notable runner already had a Group 3 win under his belt before he quickened up nicely to dispose of Starpix in the Jean Prat. He did not reappear, but is expected to be in training once again in 2006. *TM*

Vadawina (Ire)

3yo bay filly **116**

Unfuwain (USA) - Vadaza (Fr) (Zafonic (USA))

Owner H H Aga Khan

Trainer A Fabre

Breeder M Lagardere

Career: **4** starts | won **3** | second **0** | third **0** | **£151,036** win and place

By Robert Carter

MAY 22 was the day that the Aga Khan knew that he had found a bargain when he bought the bloodstock of the late Jean-Luc Lagardere. Vadawina won him the Prix Saint-Alary and half an hour later her close relative Valixir completed a Group 1 double in the Prix d'Ispahan for what Paris-Turf once called L'Aga...dere.

Unfortunately Vadawina only ran once more. She fractured her near hind pastern when finishing fourth in the Prix de Diane Hermes, and was thus prevented from testing the questionable stamina of Divine Proportions.

Vadawina made her debut in the Prix Astronomie, over one and a half miles at Saint-Cloud, before working her way down to the ten furlongs of the Saint-Alary. Andre Fabre also ran Vagamixa in the Astronomie and, since she had won her only race, at Lyon-Villeurbanne one month earlier, she was assumed to be the better half of the coupling. Interestingly Vagamixa is the 14th foal produced by Vadsa, whose first was Vadlava, the third dam of Vadawina. Vadlava was also the granddam of Valima, who had become the first of the Lagardere horses to win for the Aga when she took the Listed Prix Imprudence at Maisons-Laffitte on April 5.

Christophe Soumillon, who could have ridden either filly, was at Newmarket where he finished third in the Earl of Sefton Stakes on Valixir. Mathieu Sautjeau, who had ridden Vagamixa on her debut, kept the mount. David Michaux, who was able to claim, got the call on Vadawina. He settled her in a share of fifth place as far as the straight, while Medaille led from Pyrana and Vagamixa. Pyrana then took over but Vadawina came bounding down the outside to catch her a furlong from home. Vadawina, who was receiving 12lb, swept clear to win by four lengths with Vagamixa only sixth. Michaux was winning his 33rd race and added another later in the afternoon.

Vadawina wins the Prix Saint-Alary in great style, but injury on her next start, in the Diane, ended her brief career

Pyrana had run third to Argentina in a Listed event over ten and a half furlongs at Saint-Cloud on March 19, and defeat in the Astronomie did not stop her connections from trying again at level weights in the Prix Cleopatre 18 days later. Vadawina, ridden by Soumillon this time, was drawn on the rail and broke best. But she was soon joined by Chavela, who took over with a mile to run. Then Pyrana closed up on her outside and Vadawina began to pull, only settling when she moved out from behind the leader.

Vadawina led again straightening for home. She was quickly in command, despite edging to her right from two furlongs out, and won with her ears pricked. Soumillon had kept her going, and in a fairly straight line, with flicks of the whip and she was not troubled by the late effort of Montare. Pyrana finished four and a quarter lengths back in fifth.

Vadawina's racing reputation will rest on her impressive performance in the Saint-Alary. Michaux contributed a good pace on her stable companion Scartara while the favourite relaxed in seventh as far as the straight. No-one rides Longchamp better than Soumillon. He could have chosen to come up the outside, the way that she had been ridden in both her races at Saint-Cloud. But he did not take the chance of seeing whether she would hang right again. So he switched to the rails early in the straight and was quickly close behind the leaders.

2005 **Race record**

4th Prix de Diane Hermes (Group 1) (Chantilly, June 12) 3yo 1m2½f Good **107** (TS 106) 10 ran. *Held up, headway on inside and 5th straight, soon 2nd, every chance well over 1f out, soon ridden and one pace (C Soumillon), beaten 4¼l by Divine Proportions*

1st Prix Saint-Alary (Group 1) (Longchamp, May 22) 3yo 1m2f Good **116** (TS 110) 8 ran. *Held up in 7th, headway on inside over 2f out, switched off rail to lead just under 1½f out, quickened clear, impressive (C Soumillon), beat Argentina by 4l*

1st Prix Cleomene (Prix Cleopatre) (Group 3) (Saint-Cloud, May 1) 3yo 1m2½f Good to soft **105** (TS 74) 8 ran. *Led 3f, 2nd straight, led again over 2f out, ridden out (C Soumillon), beat Montare by 1½l*

1st Prix Astronomie (Saint-Cloud, April 13) 3yo 1m4f Very soft **90** (TS 29) 8 ran. *Raced in 5th or 6th on outside, smooth headway to lead final furlong, impressive (D Michaux), beat Pyrana by 4l*

There were moments when he might have been in trouble. Instead it was Olivier Peslier on Argentina who found himself caught when Scartara began to weaken and had to manoeuvre to the outside. Meanwhile Vadawina had quickened almost onto the heels of the leader, Naissance Royale, switched between that one and the previously unbeaten Perfect Hedge with one and a half furlongs to run and was soon in an unassailable lead. Argentina stayed on but Soumillon was taking it easy in the final 80 yards. Vadawina scored by four lengths in the fastest time for the race since Behera won it for the Aga in 1989.

Behera is one of only three Saint-Alary winners to miss the Diane in the last 30 years. Sickness kept her out until the autumn, when she ran second in the Arc. Five of her 13 immediate predecessors completed the double. Another five were second and two finished third, often behind fillies they had beaten at Longchamp. However, Zainta, victorious for the Aga in 1998, is the only one to complete the Saint-Alary and Diane double in the past 15 years.

Divine Proportions and Vadawina were both provided with leaders in the Diane, for which the Niarchos pair were favourites on the Pari-Mutuel at 4-5, with the Aga's coupling at 13-10. Alharmina was quickly away and set a good pace for Vadawina, who pulled early before settling near the back. She had only Paita, who was several lengths adrift, behind her approaching the straight but the rest of the field followed the pacemakers in coming a little wide.

Vadawina kept to the rails and went from nowhere to challenging in a matter of strides. She was almost level with two furlongs to run but was soon in trouble. She found nothing under pressure, then lost her action in the final furlong and was passed by Argentina and Paita. She finished one and a quarter lengths behind Argentina and about one and a half in front of Perfect Hedge, who had been five and a half lengths behind her at Longchamp. Her injury must have happened just as she was about to make a race of it and her career was over in the space of 61 days.

Vadawina *bay filly, 7-2-2002*

Parents	Grandparents	Great-grandparents	Great-great-grandparents
Unfuwain b 1985	Northern Dancer	Nearctic	Nearco Lady Angela
		Natalma	Native Dancer Almahmoud
	Height Of Fashion	Bustino	Busted Ship Yard
		Highclere	Queen's Hussar Highlight
Vadaza b 1997	Zafonic	Gone West	Mr Prospector Secrettame
		Zaizafon	The Minstrel Mofida
	Vadlamixa	Linamix	Mendez Lunadix
		Vadlava	Bikala Vadsa

Bred by SNC Lagardere Elevage in Ireland.

Sire Unfuwain

Won 6 of 10 starts, inc. Chester Vase-Gr3, Princess of Wales's S.-Gr2, John Porter S.-Gr3, Jockey Club S.-Gr2. Also 2nd in King George VI & Queen Elizabeth S., 4th in Prix de l'Arc de Triomphe. Strong, rangy, 16.1hh, good-bodied sort, fine walker and a relentless galloper with a roundish action. Genuine and consistent, stayed 12f well and would have got extended distances. By the world's leading sire, and half-brother to Nashwan. Dam a Gr2 winner, herself a daughter of multiple Gr1-winning parents. Deceased. Stood at Nunnery Stud, last advertised fee £30,000. Sire of 12 crops of racing age, inc. notable winners: Bolas (Irish Oaks-Gr1), Alpha City (Gr3), Mamlakah (Gr3), Alhaarth (Dewhurst S.-Gr1), Gulland (Gr3), Dano-Mast (Gr2), Zahrat Dubai (Nassau S.-Gr1), Lahan (1,000 Guineas-Gr1), Petrushka (Irish Oaks-Gr1, Yorkshire Oaks-Gr1, Prix de l'Opera-Gr1), Amiwain (Gr2), Lailani (Irish Oaks-Gr1, Nassau S.-Gr1, Flower Bowl Invitational H.-Gr1), Ranin (Gr3), Fruhlingssturm (Gr2), Medici (Gr3), Eswarah (Oaks S.-Gr1), Perfect Hedge (Gr3), Ruwi (Gr2), Thakafaat (Gr2), Vadawina (Prix Saint-Alary-Gr1).

Dam Vadaza

Won 1 of 7 starts. Also placed 2nd twice (1 Listed) and 3rd twice (1 Listed). Useful performer on Paris courses. Stayed 10f well. Not so good after four-month layoff in summer at 3. Well-bred. By a champion two-year-old and Classic-winning miler with a creditable stud record. Half-sister to Valixir (by Trempolino; Gr1 winner). Dam a Listed winner, half-sister to Vadlawys (by Always Fair; Gr2 winner) and Val Royal (by Royal Academy; Gr1 winner). To stud at 4 years. Dam of Vadawina (2002 f by Unfuwain; Gr1 winner), Vadazing (2003 f by Spinning World; unraced to date). Her yearling is a filly by Trempolino, and she has a filly foal by Sagacity. Covered by Peintre Celebre in 2005.

Pedigree assessment

Within a couple of months of his purchase of the late Jean-Luc Lagardere's bloodstock holdings, the Aga Khan obtained a notable dividend in the form of a Longchamp Group 1 double, courtesy of Vadawina (Prix Saint-Alary) and Valixir (Prix d'Ispahan). The colt subsequently notched a second win at that level, and, with better luck, the filly might have emulated him; she was going every bit as well as Divine Proportions in the Prix de Diane when she faltered, and she was later found to have suffered a fracture of her near-hind pastern. The loss to the Aga's racing interests may yet be offset by her contribution to his stud. Vadawina comes from a family which Lagardere had developed with great success, and it seems safe to predict that she will thrive in her new environment. *TM*

Valixir (Ire)

4yo bay colt **126**

Trempolino (USA) - Vadlamixa (Fr) (Linamix (Fr))

Owner H H Aga Khan

Trainer A Fabre

Breeder Snc Lagardere Elevage

Career: **16** starts	won **8**	second **1**	third **4**	**£570,654** win and place

By Richard Austen

AT THE end of 2004 Valixir had most of what it took to be a winner in top-class company, but something was missing. Stamina and maturity were the chief candidates. One you can readily do something about, and the erstwhile Arc candidate was an improved horse at four dropped back markedly in distance. The other can be more problematic, a matter chiefly of waiting and hoping, and although Valixir is now a dual Group 1 winner, something is undoubtedly missing still.

Valixir has had time to shed the immaturity pinpointed by connections during his three-year-old campaign, and it seems fair enough to replace the word "immature" with those of "often uncooperative". Flat Horses of 2004 observed that "If he ever wises up, Valixir will be some horse." Some horse he was indeed in 2005, a match for the very best that could be mustered at around a mile, but the latest season was perhaps less about him wising up, as us wising up to him.

The process began immediately with an instructive performance in the nine-furlong Earl of Sefton Stakes at Newmarket in April when he came there to win, but didn't. It was not the first time Valixir had looked less than hearty, and whether he would kick the habit or suffer a relapse was the big question to be answered every time he ran afterwards. There were two major positive aspects to this "effort" as well, namely that giving away weight put this up with the best of his previous form, and that the shorter distance was absolutely no problem, giving him every chance of being as good at a mile.

Nine furlongs would do, however, when a good opportunity for Group 1 success presented itself in the Prix d'Ispahan at Longchamp. There were seven rivals but only one – Elvstroem – set a challenge. The front-runner turned into a good target when he began to flag and Valixir built up his momentum in pursuit; Valixir went by for a two-length verdict.

Rakti promised to be much tougher to pass at York in the Queen Anne,

Valixir is kept up to his work in the Queen Anne Stakes to record a second successive Group 1 victory

judged on his runaway Lockinge victory anyway, but there's even more of a need to hold your breath when Rakti's running than there is with Valixir. Rakti's on-the-edge demeanour going to post was a warning signal, though he still went off at 5-6 compared to Valixir's 4-1.

Entering the straight, the favourite was in front by a length and a half, Akimbo had first strike at him and was gone again, and now it was the turn of Valixir and Christophe Soumillon. Valixir's ability got him there comfortably enough and it was up to his temperament to take him past. Earlier evidence suggested Valixir was in front soon enough, but he went two lengths clear by the furlong pole, and although Rakti stuck on well and Starcraft emerged from the pack, he had made the decisive move. He did not change his mind and passed the line still a length and a half to the good. Soumillon's outstretched whip did one orbit before he lobbed it backhand into the packed enclosure.

Just how well earned his celebrations were, we may never know, because horses as good as this do not often have disparaging observations made about them by their connections, but Soumillon taking over from Eric Legrix had also been one of the ingredients of the d'Ispahan victory. The role of Andre Fabre, Valixir's master trainer, was doubtless integral too and six weeks later, in what seemed a miraculous turnaround bearing in mind what happened in the Earl of Sefton, they were celebrating again as Valixir then made it three wins in a row. Although the Prix Messidor did not look a demanding assignment on paper, a small field presented pitfalls and he demonstrated a new trick by making all.

There were no more Group 3s after that, but in taking on the best at

2005 Race record

10th Netjets Breeders' Cup Mile (Grade 1) (Turf) (Belmont Park, October 29) 3yo+ 1m Yielding **93** 12 ran. *10th straight, always in rear (C Soumillon), beaten 15½l by Artie Schiller*

5th Netjets Prix du Moulin de Longchamp (Group 1) (Longchamp, September 4) 3yo+ 1m Good **115** (TS 84) 9 ran. *Always close up, 4th straight, switched left 2f out, ridden 1½f out, one pace (C Soumillon), beaten 6¼l by Starcraft*

3rd Prix du Haras de Fresnay-le-Buffard-Jacques le Marois (Group 1) (Deauville, August 14) 3yo+ 1m Good to soft **122** (TS 117) 6 ran. *Last to over 2f out, switched left over 1½f out, stayed on while hanging left under strong driving from over 1f out (C Soumillon), beaten 2¼l by Dubawi*

1st Prix Messidor (Group 3) (Straight Course) (Maisons-Laffitte, July 24) 3yo+ 1m Good **125** (TS 110) 6 ran. *Made all, clear over 1f out, comfortably (C Soumillon), beat Special Kaldoun by 1l*

1st Queen Anne Stakes (Group 1) (York, June 14) 4yo+ 1m Good to firm **126** (TS 125) 10 ran. *Tracked leaders, led over 1f out, ran on strongly (C Soumillon), beat Rakti by 1½l*

1st Prix d'Ispahan (Group 1) (Longchamp, May 22) 4yo+ 1m1f Good **121** (TS 112) 8 ran. *In touch, progress and 4th straight, pushed along and headway from 2f out, challenged approaching final furlong, led just inside final furlong, ran on well (C Soumillon), beat Elvstroem by 2l*

3rd Weatherbys Earl of Sefton Stakes (Group 3) (Newmarket, April 13) 4yo+ 1m1f Good to firm **119** (TS 111) 10 ran. *Tracked leaders, challenged and hung right over 1f out, not running on when not much room towards finish (E Legrix), beaten 1½l by Norse Dancer*

Other runs

2004 **10th** Prix de l'Arc de Triomphe Lucien Barriere (Group 1) (Longchamp, October 3) 3yo+ 1m4f Good **117** (TS 112) 19 ran ● **1st** Prix Niel Casino Barriere d'Enghien (Group 2) (Longchamp, September 12) 3yo 1m4f Soft **118** (TS 119) 8 ran ● **1st** Prix Eugene Adam (Group 2) (Maisons-Laffitte, July 14) 3yo 1m2f Soft **117** 6 ran ● **3rd** Prix du Jockey Club (Group 1) (Chantilly, June 6) 3yo 1m4f Good to soft **117** (TS 110) 15 ran ● **3rd** Prix Lupin (Group 1) (3yo Colts & Fillies) (Longchamp, May 16) 3yo 1m2½f Good to firm **112** (TS 95) 5 ran ● **1st** Prix Matchem (Listed) (Straight Course) (Maisons-Laffitte, April 20) 3yo 1m1f Holding **97** (TS 77) 5 ran **2003** **2nd** Prix des Chenes (Group 3) (Longchamp, September 20) 2yo 1m Good **105** (TS 72) 7 ran ● **1st** Prix Irish River (Deauville, August 12) 2yo 6f Good to soft **98** 6 ran ● **1st** Prix Hunyade (Unraced Colts & Geldings) (Maisons-Laffitte, July 15) 2yo 6f Good 10 ran

a mile in three subsequent starts, Valixir buckled and there was not nearly enough that Soumillon could do about it.

Bad ground was blamed for his Jacques Le Marois defeat, but he ended up racing on the worst of it because he hung so badly left. A hard race that day was mentioned when he was only fifth to Starcraft in the Moulin, and after the Breeders' Cup Mile, Soumillon said he could not go on the bridle on the yielding ground as Valixir was always out the back.

Something was still missing, but perhaps new owners Godolphin will find it.

Valixir

bay colt, 31-3-2001

Trempolino ch 1984	Sharpen Up	Atan	Native Dancer Mixed Marriage
		Rocchetta	Rockefella Chambiges
	Trephine	Viceregal	Northern Dancer Victoria Regina
		Quiriquina	Molvedo La Chaussee
Vadlamixa gr 1992	Linamix	Mendez	Bellypha Miss Carina
		Lunadix	Breton Lutine
	Vadlava	Bikala	Kalamoun Irish Bird
		Vadsa	Halo Rainbow's Edge

Bred by SNC Lagardere Elevage in Ireland

Sire Trempolino

Won 4 of his 11 starts at 2 and 3. at 2, won 1 (8f) of 3 starts, also 3rd Criterium de Maisons-Laffitte-Gr2. At 3, won 3 (inc. Prix Niel-Gr2, Prix de l'Arc de Triomphe-Gr1) of 8 starts, also 2nd Prix Lupin-Gr1, Prix du Jockey-Club-Gr1, Breeders' Cup Turf-Gr1, 3rd Grand Prix de Paris-Gr1, Prix Guillaume d'Ornano-Gr2. By high-class 2yo and very good sire who also produced good stallions Diesis, Kris, Selkirk and Sharpo, out of Group-placed half-sister to top-class 10-12f performer Trepan. Originally stood in Kentucky, switched to France after 1999 covering season. Stands at Haras du Mezeray, 2006 fee €8,000. First foals 1989, sire of (northern hemisphere): Summer Ensign (Gr3), Trampoli (Gr2), Cox Orange (Gr3), Dernier Empereur (Champion S-Gr1), Hidden Trick (Gr2), Kindergarten (Gr3), Talloires (Gr2), Triarius (Gr3), Germany (Bayerisches Zuchtrennen-Gr1, Grosser Preis von Baden-Gr1), For Valour (Gr3), Neuilly (Gr3), Saugerties (Gr3), Arkadian Hero (Gr2), Snow Polina (Beverly D S-Gr1), Juvenia (Prix Marcel Boussac-Gr1), Valixir (Prix d'Ispahan-Gr1, Queen Anne S-Gr1).

Dam Vadlamixa

Won 2 of her 11 starts at 2 and 3 in France. At 2, won 8f maiden, placed 4 times. At 3, won 8f Listed event. By top-class miler and excellent sire, mainly of 8-12f performers. Half-sister to Breeders' Cup Mile winner Val Royal (by Royal Academy) and 12f Gr2 winner Vadlawys (by Always Fair). Family of Poulains winner Vahorimix (by Linamix). Dam of: Vadaza (1997 f by Zafonic, Listed-placed winner, dam of 2005 Gr1 winner Vadawina), Vadlaviria (1998 f by Bering; winner), Vallahilla (1999 f by Danehill; placed), Vadagreen (2000 c by Green Desert; unraced), Valixir (2001 c by Trempolino; Prix d'Ispahan-Gr1, Queen Anne S-Gr1), Vadasin (2002 c by Sinndar; placed), Celebre Vadala (2003 f by Peintre Celebre; unraced).

Pedigree assessment

The Aga Khan's purchase of the late Jean-Luc Lagardere's bloodstock has received a rapid and substantial reward, largely owing to Vadlamixa. She is dam of Valixir and grand-dam of Vadawina, both Group 1 winners in 2005 for the Aga Khan. Hopefully Valixir, in time, will have better fortune at stud than his close relative Vahorimix, who was infertile. In the meantime, the Godolphin acquisition is an obvious candidate for the top European events over eight or ten furlongs. *JH*

Vengeance Of Rain (NZ)

4yo bay gelding **127**

Zabeel (NZ) - Danelagh (Aus) (Danehill (USA))

Owner Exors of the late Chow Nam & Raymond Gianco

Trainer D Ferraris

Breeder K Biggs Enterprise Pty Ltd Et Al

Career: **16** starts | won **8** | second **1** | third **3** | **£2,345,916** win and place

By Nick Pulford

EVEN AS the 2005 Hong Kong international races were being run, the local police were battening down the hatches in preparation for expected violent protests at the World Trade Organisation talks, which commenced in the city two days later.

At the turn of the millennium, anti-globalisation protesters would have found some resonance within Hong Kong's racing community. Enterprising European and Australian trainers saw Hong Kong's big races as easy pickings, and some local owners and trainers complained about the vast sums of prize-money that were disappearing abroad.

Things are different now. Hong Kong won three of the four December international races in 2002, two in 2003, one in 2004 and two again in 2005. In addition, Hong Kong horses kept both of their other international Group 1 prizes at home in 2005, and won three overseas Group 1s.

It was into this new era of Hong Kong success that David Ferraris stepped in the summer of 2003. By the end of his first campaign, the four-times South African champion trainer's stable housed a horse to take on the world. The horse was Vengeance Of Rain, a New Zealand-bred who had raced in Australia as a two-year-old under the name of Subscribe. He had been regarded highly enough to start 6-4 favourite in Group 1 company at Flemington, finishing fifth behind a horse (Winestock) that he had beaten in his previous race. It took him a little while to find his feet in Hong Kong, but 2005 was his year. He cut a swathe through all levels of competition, stepping up in class and distance to end the year as the winner of the World Racing Championships. The series may not carry much weight any longer, but Vengeance Of Rain's success serves as confirmation that Hong Kong horses cannot be taken lightly nowadays.

Vengeance Of Rain was winless in four Hong Kong starts as he turned into 2005, and he was coming off a four-month break necessitated by a stress fracture to a scapula. After two impressive handicap wins off low

Photograph courtesy of Hong Kong Jockey Club

Vengeance Of Rain (left) holds off Pride in the Hong Kong Cup, his second Group 1 win in international company

weights, Ferraris set course for the Hong Kong Derby – the race, as with Derbys around the world, that is the most treasured by owners. Hong Kong's version is held in March, for four-year-olds, over ten furlongs, but it is still a Derby.

The Derby was Vengeance Of Rain's first level-weights race in Hong Kong, but his progress was obvious and he started a warm favourite. Unleashing his now trademark kick, he won by two and three-quarter lengths from Russian Pearl. There was a sad postscript when, three days later, while on a business trip to China, Vengeance Of Rain's owner Chow Nam died.

The next logical step up for Vengeance Of Rain was the Queen Elizabeth II Cup over the same course and distance six weeks later. It attracted Phoenix Reach, fresh from his Sheema Classic win in Dubai, and highly rated runners from Australia and South Africa, but Vengeance Of Rain defied the competition to score by three-quarters of a length from South Africa's Greys Inn. Russian Pearl finished third, beaten exactly the same distance as he had been in the Derby, with Phoenix Reach fifth.

Clearly the best 'staying' horse in Hong Kong, Vengeance Of Rain ended his season with victory in the historic Champions & Chater Cup – one of only four races in Hong Kong run at a mile and a half. He lasted home by half a length from Best Gift, who was later to frank the form by finishing third behind Ouija Board in the Hong Kong Vase.

Vengeance Of Rain – "a big, burly horse who needs a lot of work", according to Ferraris – took time to come right in the 2005/06 Hong Kong season, but a confident Ferraris told anybody who would listen that the

2005 Race record

1st Cathay Pacific Hong Kong Cup (Group 1) (Sha Tin, December 11) 3yo+ 1m2f Good to firm **127** 10 ran. *Raced in 5th to straight, headway from well over 1f out to lead 150yds out, ran on well (A Delpech), beat Pride by nk*

1st Cathay Pacific International Cup Trial (Group 2) (Sha Tin, November 13) 3yo+ 1m2f Good to firm **120** 8 ran. *Settled in mid-division, ran on under pressure final 2f to lead on line (A Delpech), beat Green Treasure by shd*

5th Sha Tin Trophy Handicap (Group 3) (Sha Tin, October 16) 3yo+ 1m Good to firm **121** 14 ran. *Drawn wide (11 of 14), settled 3rd last, headway on rails from well over 1f out, nearest at finish (A Delpech), beaten 3l by Best Gift*

8th National Day Cup Premier Handicap (Sha Tin, October 2) 7f Good 14 ran. *Held up 4th last, stayed on final 2f, nearest at finish (A Delpech), beaten 4½l by Fokine*

1st Hong Kong Champions & Chater Cup (Group 1) (Sha Tin, May 29) 3yo+ 1m4f Good **118** 9 ran. *Raced in 7th, headway and 5th straight, ran on to lead 100yds out, driven out (A Delpech), beat Best Gift by ½l*

1st Audemars Piguet QE II Cup (Group 1) (Sha Tin, April 24) 3yo+ 1m2f Good to firm **124** 13 ran. *Raced in 5th on inside, switched out entering straight, led 1f out, driven out (A Delpech), beat Greys Inn by ¾l*

1st Mercedes-Benz Hong Kong Derby (Group 1) (Sha Tin, March 13) 4yo 1m2f Good to yielding **121** 14 ran. *Always close up, racing in 6th, headway 3f out, 3rd straight, led 1½f out, ran on well (A Delpech), beat Russian Pearl by 2¾l*

1st Centenary Vase Handicap (Group 3) (Sha Tin, January 30) 4yo+ 1m2f Good **111** 14 ran. *Held up, led well inside final furlong (A Delpech), beat Floral Dynamite by 1¼l*

1st Fairy King Prawn Handicap (Sha Tin, January 16) 1m Good to firm 13 ran. *Mid-division, headway well over 1f out, led 1f out, readily (A Delpech), beat Grand Zulu by 1¾l*

Other runs

2004 **3rd** Guangzhou Handicap (Sha Tin, September 11) 1m Good to firm 13 ran ● **2nd** Hong Kong ROA Trophy (Handicap) (Sha Tin, June 20) 1m Good to firm 13 ran ● **3rd** Sheung Shui Handicap (Sha Tin, May 26) 7f Good 14 ran ● **10th** Li Cup (Handicap) (Sha Tin, May 1) 6f Good to firm 14 ran 2003 **5th** VRC Sires' Produce Stakes (Group 1) (Flemington, March 10) 2yo 7f Good **107** 14 ran ● **1st** Veuve Clicquot Stakes (Caulfield, March 1) 2yo 6f Good 16 ran ● **3rd** Stakes Race (Flemington, February 15) 2yo 5½f Good 13 ran

gelding would win the Hong Kong Cup. Ferraris was right.

While Alexander Goldrun, the previous year's winner, was trapped on the rail, Vengeance Of Rain kicked hard down the outside and was always going well enough to hold the late challenge of Pride by a neck, with Maraahel third. Russian Pearl was fourth, the usual two and three-quarter lengths behind. A Racing Post Rating of 127 marked out Vengeance Of Rain's win as the best ten-furlong performance of the year on turf.

Ferraris has made no secret of his desire to test his stable star outside Hong Kong, but the late Chow Nam's son, Raymond, is less keen, mindful of the problems that beset Silent Witness after his win in Japan.

All being well, Vengeance Of Rain will be ready and waiting in Hong Kong, however, when the international raiders return in April for the QEII Cup. And they know he will be no pushover.

Vengeance Of Rain

bay gelding, 21-9-2000

Zabeel b 1986	Sir Tristram	Sir Ivor	Sir Gaylord Attica
		Isolt	Round Table All My Eye
	Lady Giselle	Nureyev	**Northern Dancer** Special
		Valderna	Val de Loir Derna
Danelagh b 1995	Danehill	Danzig	**Northern Dancer** Pas de Nom
		Razyana	His Majesty Spring Adieu
	Palatious	Semipalatinsk	Nodouble School Board
		Delicious Blue	Rascolnik All In Vain

Bred by K Biggs Enterprises & Partners in New Zealand. NZ$300,000 New Zealand Bloodstock Premier yearling. Known as Subscribe when he raced in Australia

Sire Zabeel

At 2, won 1 (7f) of 3 starts. At 3, won 5 over 6-10f (inc. Australian Guineas-Gr1, Moonee Valley S-Gr2, Alister Clark S-Gr2). At 4, won 1 (Craiglee S-Gr2), also 3rd Underwood S-Gr1. In total, won 7 of 19 starts. By useful French 10-12f performer and outstanding NZ sire, out of unraced twin Lady Gizelle. Brother to Charming Life (dam of Gr winners Kingfisher Mill, Wellbeing), half-brother to Gr1 winner Baryshnikov (Kenmare). Grand-dam Valderna half-sister to Gr1 winners Detroit (Arc) and Durtal (Cheveley Park S). Stands at Cambridge Stud, New Zealand, 2005 fee NZ$95,000. Sire of Gr1 winners: Cronus, Jezabeel (x2, inc. Melbourne Cup), Octagonal (x10, inc. Cox Plate), Bezeal Bay, Might And Power (x7, inc. Caulfield Cup, Melbourne Cup, Cox Plate), Mouawad (x3), Champagne (x2), Greene Street, Our Unicorn, Zacheline (x2), Zonda, Able Master, Dignity Dancer (x2), Inaflury, Sky Heights (x3, inc. Caulfield Cup), Dress Circle, Grand Echezeaux, Hades, Hill Of Grace, Don Eduardo, Bazelle, Lad Of The Manor, Shower Of Roses, St Reims (x2), Zagalia, Grey's Inn (x3 in S Africa), Reset (x2), Unearthly, Vengeance Of Rain (x4, in HK), Vouvray, Dizelle, Savabeel (x2, inc. Cox Plate), Railings (x2, inc. Caulfield Cup).

Dam Danelagh

Won 4 of her 18 starts, all stakes, notably 6f Blue Diamond S-Aus Gr1 at 2, also 2nd VATC 1,000 Guineas-Gr1. By top-class 6-8f performer and outstanding shuttle sire, out of dual Gr2 winner who won over 6-16f. Sister to useful 7-8f filly Villa Bled, half-sister to useful sprinter Well Done (Last Tycoon), dam sister to several at-least-useful performers, notably high-class 6f+ filly Memphis Blues. Dam of: Vengeance Of Rain (2000 c by Zabeel; HK Derby-Gr1, QE II Cup-Gr1, Champions & Chater Cup-Gr1, HK Cup-Gr1), Dizelle (2001 f by Zabeel; AJC Australian Oaks-Gr1), Hachiman (2002 c by Fusaichi Pegasus; unplaced), 2003 foal died, 2004 f by Elusive Quality, 2005 foal died. Mare sent to US December 2005.

Pedigree assessment

Has established himself as a world-class 8-10f performer. Accompanying him is his full-sister Dizelle, winner of the Australian Oaks and a Group 2 mile event in 2005. This touch of stamina comes from their NZ-based sire and their grand-dam, a stakes winner over two miles. The dam - now part of Darley's collection - was also talented but far more speedy. The gelded Vengeance of Rain is an obvious contender in 2006 for the top races he collected so prolifically in 2005. *JH*

Vinnie Roe (Ire)

7yo brown horse **119**

Definite Article - Kayu (Tap On Wood)

Owner Seamus Sheridan

Trainer D K Weld

Breeder Mrs Virginia Moeran

Career: **29** starts | won **13** | second **4** | third **5** | **£1,263,315** win and place

By Alan Sweetman

TO BE strictly pedantic the Irish St Leger ceased to be a Classic in the generally accepted sense once it was opened to older horses in 1983. However, in an era in which it has become almost a contradiction in terms to refer to a high-class three-year-old stayer, the change has been so obviously beneficial as to satisfy all but the most rigidly conservative.

For a while in the 1980s the three-year-olds still held sway, but Ibn Bey's victory in 1990 began a sequence of dominance by older horses. A pattern of dual winners developed. Vintage Crop became the first horse to win it twice in a row, Oscar Schindler followed suit, and so too did Kayf Tara. Thus, in 2001, recent history was all against the Irish Derby seventh Vinnie Roe when Dermot Weld committed him to the race in preference to a tilt at the St Leger at Doncaster. The opposition included the previous year's Doncaster winner Millenary, as well as the remarkable Persian Punch and a subsequent Arc winner in Marienbard, but Vinnie Roe had found his vocation. A two-length victory over Millenary was a prelude to an enduring love affair with the race.

Vinnie Roe started the 2005 season with Weld focused on preparing him for an attempt to win the Irish St Leger for the fifth year in a row. He began in May in the Saval Beg Stakes over a mile-and-six at Leopardstown, a Listed race that had provided him with a winning start to the season in 2002, as well as an odds-on defeat behind an enterprisingly-ridden winner in 2004. After taking the lead from his pacemaker Mutakarrim over a furlong and a half out, he won comfortably. It was a performance that suggested little apparent diminution of his formidable powers, and Weld now turned his attention to a second attempt on the Gold Cup in which he had lost out by only a neck to Royal Rebel in 2002. The switch to York produced a strong version of this traditional Ascot showpiece, and the seven-year-old gave a characteristically honest

Vinnie Roe starts his season on a winning note in the Saval Beg Stakes, but a fifth Irish St Leger triumph eluded him

performance to take third behind the outstanding French stayer Westerner, who would later finish second to Hurricane Run in the Arc.

For the fourth successive year, Weld elected to use the Ballyroan Stakes at Leopardstown in mid-August as the stepping-stone to the Irish St Leger. Having won the Listed mile-and-a half contest in 2002, as well as on his belated seasonal debut the following year, and lost out by only a neck to Foreign Affairs in 2004, he was opposed this time by two talented members of the Classic generation, the former Moyglare winner Chelsea Rose and the Irish Derby third Shalapour. It was hardly discouraging that he was relegated to third over a trip short of his best, and on ground that was a bit quick for him, but doubts set in during the build-up to his major target, with Weld reporting that he had missed a few days' work.

As already noted, the Irish St Leger has been essentially the preserve of older horses since 1990, but the 2005 edition took the trend to a new level, with the first three places occupied by horses with a combined age of 23. When Vinnie Roe went to the front two furlongs down after travelling well into the straight, it looked as if he was going to maintain his grip on the race, but the old fire was absent and fellow seven-year-old Collier Hill proved too strong, with the nine-year-old The Whistling Teal also

2005 Race record

8th Emirates Melbourne Cup (Group 1) (Handicap) (Flemington, November 1) 3yo+ 2m Good to soft **119** 24 ran. *Raced wide in 15th or 16th, 14th straight, soon ridden, kept on at same pace (P J Smullen), beaten 5¹/₄l by Makybe Diva*

3rd Irish Field St Leger (Group 1) (Curragh, September 17) 3yo+ 1m6f Good **116** (TS 79) 9 ran. *Tracked leaders in 3rd, led 2f out, strongly pressed well inside final furlong, headed and no extra close home (P J Smullen), beaten 1l by Collier Hill*

3rd Ballyroan Stakes (Listed) (Leopardstown, August 14) 3yo+ 1m4f Good to firm **115** (TS 91) 6 ran. *Settled 3rd, improved to lead approaching straight, strongly pressed 2f out, headed over 1f out, no extra inside final furlong (P J Smullen), beaten 2¹/₄l by Chelsea Rose*

3rd Gold Cup (Group 1) (York, June 16) 4yo+ 2m4f Good to firm **116** 17 ran. *Tracked leaders, kept on same pace final 2f (P J Smullen), beaten 5¹/₄l by Westerner*

1st Saval Beg Stakes (Listed) (Leopardstown, May 25) 3yo+ 1m6f Good to firm **114** (TS 79) 12 ran. *Tracked leaders in 4th, 3rd approaching straight, led over 1¹/₂f out, kept on well, comfortably (P J Smullen), beat Mutakarrim by 1¹/₂l*

Other notable runs

2004 **2nd** Emirates Melbourne Cup (Group 1) (Handicap) (Flemington, November 2) 3yo+ 2m Good to soft **126** 24 ran ● **1st** Irish Field St Leger (Group 1) (Curragh, September 18) 3yo+ 1m6f Good **123** (TS 86) 13 ran **2003** **4th** Prix Royal-Oak (Group 1) (Longchamp, October 26) 3yo+ 1m7¹/₂f Holding **115** (TS 66) 14 ran ● **5th** Prix de l'Arc de Triomphe Lucien Barriere (Group 1) (Longchamp, October 5) 3yo+ 1m4f Holding **120** (TS 107) 13 ran ● **1st** Irish Field St Leger (Group 1) (Curragh, September 13) 3yo+ 1m6f Good to firm **122** (TS 38) 6 ran ● **1st** Ballyroan Stakes (Listed) (Leopardstown, August 17) 3yo+ 1m4f Good to firm **107** (TS 59) 6 ran **2002** **4th** Tooheys New Melbourne Cup (Handicap) (Group 1) (Flemington, November 5) 3yo+ 2m Good **125** 23 ran ● **1st** Jefferson Smurfit Memorial Irish St Leger (Group 1) (Curragh, September 14) 3yo+ 1m6f Good to firm **121** (TS 102) 8 ran ● **1st** Ballyroan Stakes (Listed) (Leopardstown, August 18) 3yo+ 1m4f Good **118** (TS 98) 8 ran ● **2nd** Gold Cup (Group 1) (Ascot, June 20) 4yo+ 2m4f Good to firm **116** (TS 21) 15 ran ● **1st** Saval Beg Stakes (Listed) (Leopardstown, May 30) 3yo+ 1m6f Soft **116** 7 ran **2001** ● **1st** Prix Royal-Oak (Group 1) (Longchamp, October 28) 3yo+ 1m7¹/₂f Heavy **116** (TS 91) 13 ran ● **1st** Jefferson Smurfit Memorial Irish St Leger (Group 1) (Curragh, September 15) 3yo+ 1m6f Good to firm **124** (TS 97) 8 ran ● **1st** Ballycullen Stakes (Listed) (Curragh, August 25) 3yo+ 1m6f Good **113** (TS 43) 8 ran ● **1st** www.ppg.ie Challenge Stakes (Listed) (Leopardstown, July 21) 3yo+ 1m6f Good **107** 6 ran **2000** ● **1st** EBF Eyrefield Stakes (Listed) (Leopardstown, November 12) 2yo 1m1f Soft **106** 19 ran ● **1st** Goffs Median Auction Maiden (Leopardstown, June 28) 2yo 7f Good to firm **86** 9 ran

overtaking him in the closing stages.

Despite this disappointment, Weld stuck to his plan of giving the old warrior a final shot at the Melbourne Cup, in which he had finished fourth behind stablemate Media Puzzle in 2002, and a gallant second to Makybe Diva in 2004. Drawn widest of all, he never threatened to spoil the local fairytale, but kept on to finish a respectable eighth as Makybe Diva sealed her reputation. He was retired after a career distinguished by extraordinary determination, consistency and durability.

Vinnie Roe

brown horse, 6-4-1998

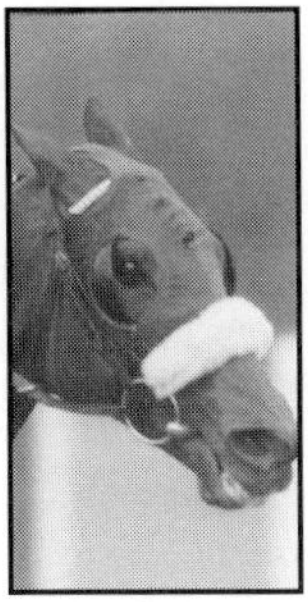

Definite Article b 1992	Indian Ridge	Ahonoora	**Lorenzaccio** Helen Nichols
		Hillbrow	Swing Easy Golden City
	Summer Fashion	Moorestyle	Manacle Guiding Star
		My Candy	**Lorenzaccio** Candy Gift
Kayu ch 1985	Tap On Wood	Sallust	Pall Mall Bandarilla
		Cat O'Mountaine	Ragusa Marie Elizabeth
	Ladytown	English Prince	Petingo English Miss
		Supreme Lady	Grey Sovereign Ulupis Sister

Bred by Virginia Moeran in Ireland. Ir48,000gns Goffs November foal, Ir£50,000 Goffs Orby yearling

Sire Definite Article

Won 5 of 11 starts, won both starts at 2 including National S-Gr1. Won 1 (Silver S-Listed) of 4 starts at 3, also 2nd Irish Derby-Gr1. Won 2 (Mooresbridge S-Listed, Tattersalls Gold Cup-Gr2) of 5 starts at 4. Effective 10-12f, stayed better than pedigree indicates. By top-class sprinter and excellent sire. Half-brother to Salford Express (Dante S-Gr2), and Salford City (Greenham S-Gr3). Stands at Morristown Lattin Stud in Ireland, 2005 fee €8,000. First foals 1998, sire of: Vinnie Roe (Irish St Leger-Gr1 (x4), Prix Royal-Oak-Gr1), Grammarian (Gr2), Supreme Rabbit (HKGr2), Lochbuie (Gr2).

Dam Kayu

Unraced. By top-class miler who is also broodmare sire of Ridgewood Pearl (by Indian Ridge), out of half-sister to Irish St Leger winner M-Lolshan, from family of Arc fourth Acropolis, Fairy Queen, Right Wing and Tashawak. Dam of: Rich Victim (1992 c by Lapierre; HK stakes winner), Vincitore (1993 c by Petorius; winner), Acquaiura (1994 f by Astronef; winner), Khartoum (1996 c by Common Grounds; winner), Divine Prospect (1997 f by Namaqualand; winner), Vinnie Roe (1998 c by Definite Article; Irish St Leger-Gr1 x 4, Prix Royal-Oak-Gr1). Mare died 2003.

Pedigree assessment

Vinnie Roe's long and distinguished career on the racecourse has ended, but an even busier one awaits him at Coolmore, where he joins the jumps division. His toughness, durability, class and pedigree – which offers speed and provides an outcross for most mares, Flat and National Hunt will ensure he covers a large book. *JH*

Virginia Waters (USA)

3yo bay filly **115**

Kingmambo (USA) - Legend Maker (Ire) (Sadler's Wells (USA))

Owner Mrs John Magnier & M Tabor

Trainer A P O'Brien

Breeder Barnett Enterprises

Career: **12** starts | won **3** | second **1** | third **2** | **£311,745** win and place

By Richard Austen

THE CASE of the Missing Guineas Winner could almost as easily be about Virginia Waters as Footstepsinthesand. And that's despite Virginia Waters running six times after her Classic triumph, whereas her stablemate was never seen again. Virginia Waters only once got in the places after the 1,000 Guineas and mostly looked a living ghost in comparison to the filly who had scorched up the Rowley Mile on May 1.

What made Virginia Waters' post-Guineas season so disappointing was that her Guineas win looked so good. Coming from last to first in a 20-runner field tends to make a big impression, and doing it with so little exertion from the usually vigorous Kieren Fallon seemed to confirm that she would rank highly even among Guineas winners.

While Satin Kiss, Karen's Caper, Maids Causeway and Cape Columbine crossed swords up front, scanning towards the stands side and further back through the field revealed Fallon making assured progress on Virginia Waters. Although she hung right, there were only one or two taps of the whip before she had the race in the bag early in the final furlong. She was a serene two and a half lengths clear as the battle raging for second was won by Maids Causeway, ahead of Vista Bella and Karen's Caper.

"Kieren weighed up the race and told us how he was going to ride her," said O'Brien. "Everything went exactly to his plan."

Four days earlier, however, the jockey might well have been plotting victory on board the same owner's long-time Guineas favourite Damson. That David Wachman-trained filly made it to Newmarket, but only as far as the gallops, and was withdrawn after a bad scope immediately after her final workout.

Although Fallon had not committed himself to Damson, Virginia Waters turned up comparatively unheralded and with a second-best feel to her among her owner's options, let alone the whole field, and her jockey's

Virginia Waters wins the 1,000 Guineas in great style, but she could not match that form in six subsequent runs

post-race observation was that "she is obviously a better filly than I thought she was."

Virginia Waters had already left her trainer pleasantly surprised when overcoming the ring-rustiness exhibited by much of his team and winning her trial at Leopardstown by three lengths. The ground that day was soft, misleading some into thinking that the fast ground at Newmarket would be against her, and the form, although a clear step up on what she had done as a two-year-old, was nothing special. None of her Guineas rivals boasted anything markedly better, though, and favouritism had eventually gone to the previous October's narrow Rockfel Stakes winner Maids Causeway, who was making her reappearance.

Virginia Waters' performances after the Guineas initially demanded explanation, with a return to much softer ground and her coming into season the following day both offered for her managing only eighth when 11-10 for the Irish Guineas, and lack of stamina the obvious culprit when her promising effort got as far only as the two-furlong marker and she finished fourth in the Oaks.

When next seen out, however, back at a mile and on fast ground in the Coronation Stakes, Fallon switched to Damson as Virginia Waters came sixth to Maids Causeway. Sixth again was the result in the Nassau when Virginia Waters tried a mile and a quarter.

Going down by three-quarters of a length and half a length to the 2004

2005 Race record

10th Kingdom of Bahrain Sun Chariot Stakes (Group 1) (Newmarket, October 1) 3yo+ 1m Good to soft 10 ran. *Raced in centre group, in rear, effort over 3f out, no impression, weakened over 2f out (K Fallon), beaten 47l by Peeress*

3rd Coolmore Fusaichi Pegasus Matron Stakes (Group 1) (Leopardstown, September 10) 3yo+ 1m Good to yielding **110** (TS 78) 9 ran. *Tracked leaders on inner, 4th halfway, 3rd 3f out, moderate 2nd and ridden straight, kept on under pressure from over 1f out (K Fallon), beaten 1¼l by Attraction*

6th Vodafone Nassau Stakes (Group 1) (Goodwood, July 30) 3yo+ 1m2f Good to soft **108** (TS 107) 11 ran. *Held up towards rear, not much room 3f out, ridden and effort over 2f out, chased leading trio 1f out, no impression, weakened near finish (K Fallon), beaten 3½l by Alexander Goldrun*

6th Coronation Stakes (Group 1) (York, June 17) 3yo 1m Good to firm **103** (TS 86) 10 ran. *In touch, effort on wide outside 3f out, soon edged right, kept on same pace final 2f (J P Murtagh), beaten 5l by Maids Causeway*

4th Vodafone Oaks (Group 1) (Epsom, June 3) 3yo 1m4f Good **106** (TS 96) 12 ran. *Held up in last pair, 8th and progress straight, switched right to chase leading pair well over 1f out, no impression, weakened final furlong (K Fallon), beaten 5½l by Eswarah*

8th Boylesports Irish 1,000 Guineas (Group 1) (Curragh, May 22) 3yo 1m Good to yielding **102** 18 ran. *Held up, 10th after halfway, ridden 2f out, kept on same pace from over 1f out (K Fallon), beaten 2¾l by Saoire*

1st UltimatePoker.com 1,000 Guineas Stakes (Group 1) (Newmarket, May 1) 3yo 1m Good to firm **115** (TS 105) 20 ran. *Held up, headway over 2f out, hung right and led inside final furlong, ran on well (K Fallon), beat Maids Causeway by 2½l*

1st Dimitrova 1,000 Guineas Trial Stakes (Group 3) (Leopardstown, April 10) 3yo 7f Yielding to soft **105** (TS 58) 6 ran. *Tracked leaders in 4th, progress early straight, led under 1f out, stayed on well (K Fallon), beat Sweet Treat by 3l*

2004

2nd Flame Of Tara EBF Stakes (Listed) (Curragh, October 10) 2yo 6f Yielding to soft **92** (TS 58) 10 ran ● **3rd** C L Weld Park Stakes (Group 3) (Curragh, October 2) 2yo 7f Yielding to soft **98** (TS 95) 9 ran ● **1st** Loder EBF Fillies Race (Curragh, September 18) 2yo 7f Yielding **89** (TS 72) 10 ran ● **8th** Go And Go Round Tower Stakes (Group 3) (Curragh, September 5) 2yo 6f Good to firm **84** 11 ran

Guineas heroine Attraction and dual Celebration Mile winner Chic in the Matron Stakes at Leopardstown made better reading, without living up to her former image. However, at the same venue as, and exactly five months after, her greatest triumph, tailing off in the Sun Chariot was an unequivocably sorry way to end the career of a Classic winner.

Does her Guineas triumph need a reappraisal? Not in a major way. Some other connections will wish their charges had gone hammer and tongs a little less soon in that race, but enough of the principals were principals throughout to make it seem most unlikely that Virginia Waters' was purely some kind of tactical triumph.

O'Brien's verdict, once she was retired, is that he "never managed to get her back to the pitch that she was on Guineas day," and that seems a fair assessment.

Virginia Waters

bay filly, 15-2-2002

Kingmambo b 1990	Mr Prospector	Raise A Native	Native Dancer Raise You
		Gold Digger	Nashua Sequence
	Miesque	Nureyev	**Northern Dancer** **Special**
		Pasadoble	Prove Out Santa Quilla
Legend Maker b 1994	Sadler's Wells	**Northern Dancer**	Nearctic Natalma
		Fairy Bridge	Bold Reason **Special**
	High Spirited	Shirley Heights	Mill Reef Hardiemma
		Sunbittern	Sea Hawk Pantoufle

Bred by Barnett Enterprises in Kentucky.

Sire Kingmambo

Won 5 of 13 races, inc. Poule d'Essai des Poulains-Gr1, St James's Palace S.-Gr1, Prix du Moulin-Gr1). Among the best milers of his generation. Sire of: American Boss (Gr2), El Condor Pasa (NHK Mile Cup-Gr1, Japan Cup-Gr1, Grand Prix de Saint-Cloud-Gr1), Mambo Twist (Gr3), Parade Ground (Gr2), Admire Mambo (Gr2), Lemon Drop Kid (Futurity S.-Gr1, Belmont S.-Gr1, Travers S.-Gr1, Whitney S.-Gr1, Woodward H.-Gr1), Monarch's Maze (Gr2), Bluemamba (Poule d'Essai des Pouliches-Gr1), King Cugat (Gr2), Kingsalsa (Gr3), King's Best (2,000 Guineas-Gr1), Parade Leader (Gr2), Penny's Gold (Gr3), King Fidelia (Gr3), Malhub (Golden Jubilee S.-Gr1), Okawango (Grand Criterium-Gr1), Voodoo Dancer (Garden City H.-Gr1), Dubai Destination (Queen Anne S.-Gr1), Walzerkonigin (Gr2), Alkaased (Grand Prix de Saint-Cloud-Gr1, Japan Cup-Gr1), Governor Brown (Gr3), Russian Rhythm (1,000 Guineas-Gr1, Coronation S.-Gr1, Nassau S.-Gr1, Lockinge S.-Gr1), Illustrious Miss (Gr3), Mambo Slew (Gr3), Notable Guest (Gr3), Rule Of Law (St Leger S.-Gr1), Tarfah-Gr3), Divine Proportions (Prix Morny-Gr1, Prix Marcel Boussac-Gr1, Poule d'Essai des Pouliches-Gr1, Prix de Diane-Gr1, Prix d'Astarte-Gr1), Virginia Waters (1,000 Guineas-Gr1).

Dam Legend Maker

Won 2 of 7 races. Also placed 3rd in Gr2. Smart middle-distance/staying performer. Well suited by 12f, probably stayed 13.5f. Half-sister to Gr2 winner Amfortas (by Caerleon) and Listed-placed Dollar Bird (by Kris). By the leading European sire of his era out of a full sister to High Hawk (Gr1 winner; dam of multiple Gr1 winner In the Wings, Gr2 winner Hunting Hawk, and Gr3 winner Hawker's News). Same family as High-Rise (Derby) and Zomaradah (Oaks d'Italia; dam of Dubawi). Outstanding family, notable for middle-distance performers. Dam of: Qurrah (1999 f by Zafonic; placed), Chevalier (2000 c by Danehill; winner, Gr1-placed), Canterbury Lace (2001 f by Danehill; unraced), Virginia Waters (2002 f by Kingmambo; Gr1 winner), Eiwa Virginia (2003 c by Kingmambo; unraced to date). She has a yearling colt by Danehill, and a colt foal by Kingmambo.

Pedigree assessment

Virginia Waters seduced us into believing that she was a top-class filly with a smooth victory in the 1,000 Guineas. Nothing that she did afterwards confirmed that impression, and ultimately we had to conclude that she had beaten a poor group in her Classic: the three-year-old distaff milers of 2005 were simply not up to scratch. She was not entirely discredited as fourth of 12 in the Oaks, but she patently did not see out the trip and was wisely not asked to go that distance again. *TM*

Walk In The Park (Ire)

3yo bay colt **121**

Montjeu (Ire) - Classic Park (Robellino (USA))

Owner Michael Tabor

Trainer J E Hammond

Breeder Lodge Park Stud

Career: **8** starts | won **1** | second **3** | third **3** | **£329,715** win and place

By Richard Austen

WALK IN THE PARK'S performance in the Derby was such that Alan Munro, his jockey, could have been excused a similar reaction to that of John Matthias in 1981. Matthias it was who had to put his head down so far out and from so far off the pace on Glint Of Gold in his Derby, that he reported afterwards: "In the straight I just kept pushing and when I came between them I thought I'd won – Shergar had gone so far clear I didn't see him."

Munro did not have quite so far to scan up the track, but while Motivator was making his summit bid, Walk In The Park had not yet got beyond the foothills. When a big gap appeared on the inside rounding Tattenham Corner, Walk In The Park was able to take advantage, but there were seven horses in front of him, he was about ten lengths off the lead and he was already being firmly ridden.

Kings Quay, Almighty and Unfurled were readily taken care of, but Walk In The Park was still at a severe disadvantage with the four others as he angled out to make his final push. He passed Gypsy King at the furlong marker, Hattan a few strides later and Dubawi with a hundred yards to go. Motivator, though, was totally out of reach.

Munro's task on the 11-1 shot was always going to be hard because the colt was not adaptable tactically. Walk In The Park was already an infamous hard-puller and he runs like a hard-pulling stayer, an uncommon combination, in a successful racehorse certainly. It was widely expected that the strong Derby pace would prompt a career-best performance, but maximising his potential still required his being held up to help him settle.

Settled might not be the right word, but Walk In The Park was under control as Munro held him up among the backmarkers from his high draw, one from the outside in a field of 13. Straining at the bit, Walk In The Park hampered The Geezer in his desire to move forward, but could

Walk In The Park at Epsom on Derby Day, when he finished well for second place but too late to catch Motivator

still get only two behind him as he embarked on that descent to Tattenham Corner.

For those intent on it, finding cover in the Derby is usually fairly easy, and so is forfeiting a suitable challenging position in the process. But the most important thing was to stop Walk In The Park pulling. Without that, he would not have been able to make his run up the straight.

Evidence that nurturing him for such an effort was not so easy came on his starts either side of Epsom. In the Lingfield Derby Trial, with Walk In The Park already talked of as trainer John Hammond's first Derby runner, he started 6-4 favourite but a slow pace meant that Kieren Fallon's effort to settle him did not succeed and he was still fighting for his head entering the straight. He kept on to get within a neck of victory, but he was always being held in the run to the post. Losing out to Kong in a sprint was nothing for a horse of his calibre to brag about.

Hammond's wife Georgina reflected that "you reckon on getting the sun in Barbados and the speed in England, but we didn't get it."

Walk In The Park's race after Epsom was the Irish Derby, for which he was 100-30 second favourite to Hurricane Run. "My horse had no

2005 **Race record**

8th Budweiser Irish Derby (Group 1) (Curragh, June 26) 3yo 1m4f Good to firm **92** 9 ran. *Raced keenly on outer, 4th halfway, weakened entering straight (A Munro), beaten 19½l by Hurricane Run*

2nd Vodafone Derby Stakes (Group 1) (Epsom, June 4) 3yo 1m4f Good **121** (TS 118) 13 ran. *Settled in last trio, progress on inner and 9th straight, soon ridden, taken to outer 2f out, driven and ran on to take 2nd last 150yds (A Munro), beaten 5l by Motivator*

2nd Letheby & Christopher Derby Trial Stakes (Group 3) (Lingfield, May 7) 3yo 1m3½f Good **108** (TS 48) 6 ran. *Took keen hold, held up in last pair, hampered 10f out, progress over 2f out, challenged entering final furlong, not quicken and always held (K Fallon), beaten nk by Kong*

2004

3rd Criterium International (Group 1) (Saint-Cloud, October 31) 2yo 1m Very soft **112** (TS 99) 8 ran ● **1st** Prix Adaris (Saint-Cloud, October 22) 2yo 1m Very soft **98** 6 ran ● **2nd** Prix Hauban (Saint-Cloud, October 7) 2yo 1m Good **90** (TS 42) 10 ran ● **3rd** Prix du Canouvert (Chantilly, September 13) 2yo 7f Good **80** (TS 68) 15 ran ● **3rd** Prix de Marolles (Unraced Colts & Geldings) (Straight Course) (Deauville, July 10) 2yo 7f Soft 7 ran

cover. There wasn't much pace and he just ran too freely," said Munro after his mount was the last to finish. A respiratory tract infection gave additional explanation for the scale of defeat and the colt also returned jarred up. Missing from the big autumn prizes, Walk In The Park does, however, stay in training.

As a two-year-old Walk In The Park had taken four runs to get off the mark, at short odds in a conditions race at Saint-Cloud in October, and he had finished only third behind Helios Quercus when stepped up to Group 1 company for the Criterium International on the same course on his final start. But he clearly wasn't doing himself any justice, for he reportedly would get to the start white with sweat, and then take a fierce hold when the race got underway.

Though apparently calmer in 2005, Walk In The Park will surely still be one of the most characterful horses when he returns to action. "He's just an aggressive horse," said Munro. "He's highly strung, always has been, always will be," said Hammond, who reckons that travel helps his charge and who also took him to Epsom ten days before the Derby for some experience of the place.

Even if he is as quiet as a church mouse, Walk In The Park will nevertheless be a striking sight – there cannot be many taller Flat horses. Hammond, of course, trained his sire Montjeu, who incredibly is also the father of Motivator and Hurricane Run in his first crop. Let's hope that Walk In The Park gets plenty of opportunities to improve his standing. In comparing him to Montjeu, Hammond gave a good general summary of Walk In The Park's current status when he said "he looks like him, acts like him and runs quite like him."

Walk In The Park

bay colt, 20-1-2002

Montjeu b 1996	Sadler's Wells	Northern Dancer	Nearctic Natalma
		Fairy Bridge	Bold Reason Special
	Floripedes	Top Ville	High Top Sega Ville
		Toute Cy	Tennyson Adele Toumignon
Classic Park b 1994	Robellino	Roberto	Hail To Reason Bramalea
		Isobelline	Pronto Isobella
	Wanton	Kris	Sharpen Up Doubly Sure
		Brazen Faced	Bold And Free Maurine

Bred by Lodge Park Stud in Ireland. €130,000 Goffs Orby yearling, 270,000gns Tattersalls Breeze-up 2yo

Sire Montjeu

Won 11 of 16 races, inc. Prix Greffulhe-Gr2, Prix du Jockey-Club-Gr1, Irish Derby-Gr1, Prix Niel-Gr2, Prix de l'Arc de Triomphe-Gr1, Tattersalls Gold Cup-Gr1, Grand Prix de Saint-Cloud-Gr1, King George VI & Queen Elizabeth S.-Gr1, Prix Foy-Gr2. Also 2nd in Prix Lupin at 3, and in Champion S. at 4. Tallish, well-made, but not strikingly handsome individual. Not a good mover in his slower paces, seemed unsuited by firm ground, but acted on any other, and possessed a tremendous turn of foot. One of the best 12f horses of recent times. Well-bred. The best son of his outstanding sire. Out of a lightly-raced high-class stayer (won Prix de Lutece-Gr3, 2nd in Prix Royal Oak-Gr1), who was among the best daughters of her sire. Family of multiple Pattern-winning stayer Dadarissime, Gr3 winner Le Mamamouchi and Dear Doctor (Arlington Million). Stands at Coolmore Stud at a (2006) fee of €125,000. Sire of 2 racing crops, inc: Corre Caminos (Gr3), Hurricane Run (Irish Derby-Gr1, Prix de l'Arc de Triomphe-Gr1), Montare (Gr2), Motivator (Racing Post Trophy-Gr1, Derby S.-Gr1), Scorpion (Grand Prix de Paris-Gr1, St Leger-Gr1).

Dam Classic Park

Won 3 of 14 starts at 2 and 3. At 2, won 1 (5f maiden) of 8 starts, Listed placed 3 times over 5-6f. At 3, won 2 (7-8f, notably Irish 1,000 Guineas-Gr1) of 6 starts, unplaced in remainder. Half-sister to useful 2yos Birthday Suit (Daylami), Magongo (Be My Chief) and Wilde Rufo (Sharrood), plus Grade 2 winner Rumpipumpy (Shirley Heights). Sire high-class 2yo and decent stallion, dam useful sprint 2yo, half-sister to smart 2yo/sprinter Easy Option (dam of Gr1 winner Court Masterpiece). Dam of: Cool Storm (1999 f by Rainbow Quest; unplaced), Park Crystal (2000 f by Danehill; unraced), Mufradat (2001 f by Desert Prince; winner), Walk In The Park (2002 c by Montjeu; Classic-placed winner), Secret World (2003 c by Spinning World; unraced).

Pedigree assessment

Only stout stallions can sire middle-distance performers from this tough, speedy family. Shirley Heights's daughter Rumpipumpy is a good example, and Walk In The Park is another. More typical of the family's pace is Court Masterpiece, by a top-class miler. Montjeu is an obvious candidate to do well with his older progeny, and Walk In The Park is an obvious candidate to convert a Group 1 place to a Group 1 win. *JH*

Warrsan (Ire)

7yo bay horse **122**

Caerleon (USA) - Lucayan Princess (High Line)

Owner Saeed Manana

Trainer C E Brittain

Breeder Saeed Manana

Career: **43** starts | won **9** | second **9** | third **4** | **£1,654,749** win and place

By Steve Dennis

YOU never know where you are with Warrsan. It could be Tokyo, Paris, Epsom, Hong Kong or the Black Forest. You know what you'll get, though – an honest, hard-working performance against the best horses in the world, with the strong possibility of a big bag of foreign banknotes to take through customs on the way home. Robert Louis Stevenson said to travel hopefully is a better thing than to arrive, and Warrsan seems to have spent his whole life travelling hopefully. In the last three seasons, he has not raced in Britain after the end of July.

His favourite destination seems to be Baden-Baden, as he gained his sole success of 2005 at the German spa track when he repeated his victory of 12 months earlier in the Group 1 Grosser Preis von Baden in September. German Group 1 races are sometimes – and sometimes rightly – seen as a soft touch, but the Grosser Preis never falls into that category and this renewal was no exception, with Gold Cup winner Westerner, Arc runner-up Cherry Mix and the first and second in the Deutsches Derby, Nicaron and Night Tango, all in opposition.

Warrsan went to Baden-Baden in better form than he had done the previous year, following a barnstorming fourth in the King George VI and Queen Elizabeth Diamond Stakes at Newbury, where he seemed to relish the change in venue and improved markedly on his efforts at its traditional Ascot home in the previous two years. Kerrin McEvoy was in no doubt about his wellbeing and, on the good ground the old warhorse relishes, gave him a fine forcing ride, keeping him in the first three throughout and driving him home through the final quarter-mile to beat the local filly Gonbarda by a length and a quarter, with future Arc runner-up Westerner only third.

Warrsan's first target of the season had been a third Coronation Cup, something no horse had achieved, and his tune-up behind Alkaased in the Jockey Club Stakes at Newmarket led punters to make him second

Warrsan scores his second successive win in the Grosser Preis von Baden, in another season of globetrotting

favourite at Epsom behind his Newmarket conqueror. However, the hat-trick proved beyond him. Unsuited by the pedestrian pace set by all-the-way winner Yeats, he was left floundering when the pace quickened and a one-paced fourth was the best he could muster.

He looked lethargic at Royal Ascot at York two weeks later when fifth behind Azamour in the Prince of Wales's Stakes, but his Newbury effort illustrated that the flame still burned brightly within him and the Grosser Preis proved it.

The final quarter of the year brings with it a richer harvest in the shape of international competition of the highest order and, as in 2004, Warrsan had his tickets booked. The softish ground at Longchamp was not in his favour but he ran a solid race in the Arc to be eighth behind Hurricane Run, a place better than 12 months earlier. Eight weeks later he was in Tokyo for the Japan Cup and again ran an almost identical race to the previous year, trailing in a never-dangerous 13th behind Alkaased, who had also taken his measure half a year and half a world away at Newmarket in May.

Warrsan is a tough cookie, but the searching demands of a season in Group 1 company and the strength-sapping effect of long-distance travel seemed too much even for him. Perhaps he was a little world-weary, for the outcome of his final outing, in the Hong Kong Vase at Sha Tin, again mirrored his 2004 performance. He was never seen with a chance and

2005 Race record

12th Cathay Pacific Hong Kong Vase (Group 1) (Sha Tin, December 11) 3yo+ 1m4f Good to firm **101** 12 ran. *Prominent early, 5th over 3f out, weakened well over 2f out, last straight (J P Spencer), beaten 14½l by Ouija Board*

13th Japan Cup (Group 1) (Tokyo, November 27) 3yo+ 1m4f Firm **113** 18 ran. *Raced in 9th, 13th straight, never a factor (J P Spencer), beaten 8¼l by Alkaased*

8th Prix de l'Arc de Triomphe Lucien Barriere (Group 1) (Longchamp, October 2) 3yo+ 1m4f Good to soft **118** (TS 119) 15 ran. *Prominent, 8th straight, ridden 2f out, soon one pace (K McEvoy), beaten 9l by Hurricane Run*

1st Grosser Volkswagen Preis von Baden (Group 1) (Baden-Baden, September 4) 3yo+ 1m4f Good **122** 9 ran. *Led 1½f, always close up, 3rd and stayed towards inside straight, led 2f out, driven out (K McEvoy), beat Gonbarda by 1¼l*

4th King George VI And Queen Elizabeth Diamond Stakes (Group 1) (Newbury, July 23) 3yo+ 1m4f Good to firm **117** (TS 105) 12 ran. *Held up towards rear, headway and not clear run briefly over 3f out, stayed on to go 4th inside final furlong, never troubled leaders (S Sanders), beaten 6¼l by Azamour*

5th Prince of Wales's Stakes (Group 1) (York, June 15) 4yo+ 1m2½f Good to firm **97** (TS 89) 8 ran. *Chased leaders, pushed along and lost place over 4f out, kept on final 2f to take moderate 5th (D Holland), beaten 15½l by Azamour*

4th Vodafone Coronation Cup (Group 1) (Epsom, June 3) 4yo+ 1m4f Good **112** (TS 98) 7 ran. *Chased leaders, 3rd and ridden straight, chased winner over 2f out to 2f out, one pace after (D Holland), beaten 6¼l by Yeats*

4th UltimatePoker.com Jockey Club Stakes (Group 2) (Newmarket, May 1) 4yo+ 1m4f Good to firm **113** (TS 58) 5 ran. *Held up in touch, ridden and every chance over 2f out, weakened over 1f out (D Holland), beaten 6½l by Alkaased*

Other wins

2004 **1st** Grosser Volkswagen Preis Von Baden (Group 1) (Baden- Baden, September 5) 3yo+ 1m4f Soft **126** 11 ran ● **1st** Vodafone Coronation Cup (Group 1) (Epsom, June 4) 4yo+ 1m4f Good **124** (TS 100) 11 ran **2003** **1st** Vodafone Coronation Cup (Group 1) (Epsom, June 6) 4yo+ 1m4f Good **121** (TS 99) 9 ran ● **1st** Sagitta Jockey Club Stakes (Group 2) (Newmarket, May 2) 4yo+ 1m4f Good to soft **120** (TS 81) 6 ran ● **1st** Dubai Irish Village Stakes (Registered As The John Porter Stakes) (Group 3) (Newbury, April 12) 4yo+ 1m4f Good to firm **116** (TS 88) 9 ran **2002** **1st** Qualitair Holdings Conditions Stakes (Newmarket (July), July 19) 3yo+ 1m4f Good to firm **109** (TS 76) 4 ran ● **1st** Bonusprint Rated Stakes Showcase Handicap (Goodwood, May 23) 4yo+ (0-100 handicap) 1m6f Good **104** (TS 85) 11 ran **2001** **1st** Jim Macdonald-Buchanan Handicap (Sandown, July 26) 3yo (0-85 handicap) 1m6f Good to firm **85** (TS 68) 10 ran

finished last behind Ouija Board. Even the most warm-hearted analysis could conclude that the dust of past campaigns was finally weighing heavy on his legs.

He saw out 2005 with more than £1.6m in earnings, just shy of his older half-brother Luso, who had an equally extensively stamped passport and boasted consecutive wins in the Hong Kong Vase for Clive Brittain in the days when it was a Group 2. Brittain, in the twilight of his career, may yet unearth another with their toughness and ability, but when Warrsan finally ends his days on the road he will be a hard act to follow.

Warrsan

bay horse, 28-2-1998

Caerleon b 1980	Nijinsky	Northern Dancer	Nearctic Natalma
		Flaming Page	Bull Page Flaring Top
	Foreseer	Round Table	Princequillo Knight's Daughter
		Regal Gleam	Hail To Reason Miz Carol
Lucayan Princess b 1983	High Line	High Hat	Hyperion Madonna
		Time Call	Chanteur Aleria
	Gay France	Sir Gaylord	Turn-to Somethingroyal
		Sweet and Lovely	Tanerko Lilya

Bred by Saeed Manana in Ireland.

Sire Caerleon

Won 4 of 8 races, inc. Anglesey S.-Gr3, Prix du Jockey-Club-Gr1, Benson & Hedges Gold Cup-Gr1. Also 2nd in Irish Derby. Good-looking, compact, top-class middle-distance performer. Died in February 1998. Sire of Gr 1 winners: Caerwent (National S.), Welsh Guide (Gran Premio d'Italia, Premio Roma), Kostroma (Yellow Ribbon S., Santa Barbara Handicap, Beverly D S.), Atoll (Oaks d'Italia), Caerlina (Prix de Diane), Generous (Dewhurst S., Derby S., Irish Derby, King George VI & Queen Elizabeth S.), In A Tiff (Derby Italiano), Only Royale (Yorkshire Oaks x 2), Biwa Heidi (Hanshin Sansai Himba S.) Tenby (Grand Criterium), Moonax (St Leger S., Prix Royal-Oak), Auriette (Gamely Handicap), Fusaichi Concorde (Tokyo Yuushun), Grape Tree Road (Grand Prix de Paris), Lady Carla (Oaks S.), Shake The Yoke (Coronation S.), Cape Verdi (1,000 Guineas S.), Mukhalif (Derby Italiano), Sunspangled (Fillies' Mile), Marienbard (Deutschlandpreis, Grosser Preis von Baden, Prix de l'Arc de Triomphe), Preseli (Moyglare Stud Stakes), Warrsan (Coronation Cup x 2, Grosser Preis von Baden x 2).

Dam Lucayan Princess

Won 2 of 4 races. inc. Sweet Solera S.-Listed. Leggy, light-framed, attractive sort, effective on any ground, stayed 12f well. Same family as Kris Kin. Dam of: Celia Brady (1988 f by Last Tycoon; winner), Lucca (1989 f by Sure Blade; unplaced), Needle Gun (1990 c by Sure Blade; Gr2 winner, Gr1-placed), Luana (1991 f by Shaadi; winner, Listed-placed), Luso (1992 c by Salse; multiple Gr1 winner), Lunda (1993 f by Soviet Star; unplaced) Cloud Castle (1995 f by In The Wings; Gr3 winner), Maskunah (1997 f by Sadler's Wells; unraced) Warrsan (1998 c by Caerleon; quadruple Gr1 winner), Mreef (1999 c by Sadler's Wells; unraced), Mantesera (2000 f by In The Wings; unraced).

Pedigree assessment

Those who thought that Warrsan was a back-number after his failure to complete a treble in the Coronation Cup were made to think again. He had not yet finished at the top level, going on to score a fine victory over Gonbarda and Westerner in the Grosser Preis von Baden, a race he had also won in 2004. The doughty old warrior was not at his best in the Arc, and never reached contention in the Japan Cup, but overall he has enjoyed a wonderful career, and must rank as the best of three half-brothers who have earned fortunes as well as plaudits for honest endeavour over long periods. *TM*

Westerner

6yo bay horse **129**

Danehill (USA) - Walensee (Troy)

Owner Ecurie Wildenstein

Trainer E Lellouche

Breeder Dayton Investments Ltd

Career: **28** starts | won **11** | second **9** | third **2** | **£1,072,584** win and place

By Paul Haigh

WESTERNER began the year already rated by many the outstanding stayer of recent times, certainly the best so far in the 21st century, and maybe the best since Ardross. He ended it with that reputation intact, and far from humiliated too in his bid to translate his supremacy to 12 furlongs.

For his first outing since running out a comfortable winner from Bekhara and Alcazar in his second Prix Royal-Oak the previous October he was offered what looked an undemanding test in the Group 3 Prix de Barbeville over half a furlong shy of two miles at Longchamp. Although starting at a relatively generous 3-5 – a price perhaps explained by the suspicion that he might be lacking a bit of fitness on very soft ground – he came home for Olivier Peslier a length and a half in front of Allez Olive, with Gloirez and Le Carre behind.

Three weeks later he moved up to Group 2 level in the Prix Vicomtesse Vigier over the same course and distance, although the apparent step up in class was slightly illusory as he had more or less the same group of horses to beat. The fact that he did so much more easily than in the Prix de Barbeville, this time extending his winning margin over Allez Olive to five lengths, may have been confirmation that he was just in need of the race in April. It may also have been an indication that, although, as he'd already proved, he had the ability to act on any sort of ground, the good going he encountered in the Vicomtesse Vigier suited him best of all.

The two races set him up in any case for what was to be his major early season target: the Gold Cup at Royal Ascot at York – the race in which his defeat the previous year by Godolphin's Papineau had inspired his owner Alec Wildenstein's ill-advised remark about dope-testing machines having broken down. This time the ground was officially good to firm. Although doubts had already begun to be voiced about the actual quality

Westerner (right), under a well-judged ride by Olivier Peslier, wins the Gold Cup by a neck from Distinction

of the Knavesmire going, it seemed to make little difference to the French champion. Nursed along just behind the leaders by Peslier in what looked like a deliberate decision not to ask too many questions of his stamina over two and a half miles, the son of Danehill picked up Distinction without fuss, and then held that horse's renewed challenge much more comfortably than the neck winning margin suggests. The bare form of the Gold Cup form may seem to have been devalued by the runner-up's subsequent failures, but Distinction, who had breathing problems later in the year, was a pretty good horse at that stage of the season. The ultra-reliable Vinnie Roe, more than five lengths back in third, provided an accurate measure of the class of Westerner's performance.

With his credentials as a stayer established beyond argument – he had now won the Prix du Cadran and the Prix Royal-Oak twice each as well as put his Gold Cup record straight – his trainer, Elie Lellouche, now began the ambitious project of converting him back into a middle-distance horse. More than two months later Westerner reappeared in the Group 1 Grosser Volkswagen Preis von Baden at Baden-Baden, with doubts about his versatility seemingly confirmed by Peslier's decision to partner instead the more recognised 12-furlong performer Prospect Park

2005 Race record

5th Cathay Pacific Hong Kong Vase (Group 1) (Sha Tin, December 11) 3yo+ 1m4f Good to firm **117** 12 ran. *Mid-division, close 8th on outside straight, ridden approaching final furlong, stayed on under pressure but never able to challenge (O Peslier), beaten 4l by Ouija Board*

2nd Prix de l'Arc de Triomphe Lucien Barriere (Group 1) (Longchamp, October 2) 3yo+ 1m4f Good to soft **129** (TS 130) 15 ran. *Tracked leaders, 3rd straight, hard ridden and every chance 1f out, ran on same pace (O Peslier), beaten 2l by Hurricane Run*

3rd Grosser Volkswagen Preis von Baden (Group 1) (Baden-Baden, September 4) 3yo+ 1m4f Good **118** 9 ran. *Mid-division, 5th straight, kept on to take 3rd close home (S Pasquier), beaten 2½l by Warrsan*

1st Gold Cup (Group 1) (York, June 16) 4yo+ 2m4f Good to firm **124** 17 ran. *Tracked leaders going well, steadied over 4f out and over 2f out, shaken up and headway to lead 1f out, pushed out towards finish (O Peslier), beat Distinction by nk*

1st Prix Vicomtesse Vigier (Group 2) (Longchamp, May 22) 4yo+ 1m7½f Good **116** (TS 106) 8 ran. *Always in touch and going well, 4th halfway, smooth headway to lead 2f out, soon quickened clear, easily (O Peslier), beat Allez Olive by 5l*

1st Prix de Barbeville (Group 3) (Longchamp, April 30) 4yo+ 1m7½f Very soft **119** (TS 79) 9 ran. *Held up towards rear, last from over 4f out to straight, steady progress on outside to lead inside final furlong, ran on well (O Peslier), beat Allez Olive by 1½l*

Other notable runs

2004 **1st** Prix Royal-Oak (Group 1) (Longchamp, October 24) 3yo+ 1m7½f Heavy **119** (TS 85) 8 ran ● **1st** Prix du Cadran Casino Les Princes Barriere de Cannes (Group 1) (Longchamp, October 3) 4yo+ 2m4f Good **117** (TS 75) 8 ran ● **1st** Prix Gladiateur Royal Thalasso Barriere (Group 3) (Longchamp, September 12) 4yo+ 1m7½f Soft **121** (TS 38) 8 ran ● **2nd** Gold Cup (Group 1) (Ascot, June 17) 4yo+ 2m4f Good to firm **119** (TS 100) 13 ran ● **2nd** Prix Vicomtesse Vigier (Group 2) (Longchamp, May 23) 4yo+ 1m7½f Good **113** 6 ran ● **1st** Prix de Barbeville (Group 3) (Longchamp, April 22) 4yo+ 1m7½f Good to soft **120** 6 ran **2003** **1st** Prix Royal-Oak (Group 1) (Longchamp, October 26) 3yo+ 1m7½f Holding **120** (TS 71) 14 ran ● **1st** Prix du Cadran - Casinos Barriere (Group 1) (Longchamp, October 5) 4yo+ 2m4f Holding **122** 10 ran ● **2nd** Prix Gladiateur Royal Thalasso Barriere (Group 3) (Longchamp, September 14) 4yo+ 1m7½f Good to soft **113** (TS 19) 9 ran ● **2nd** Prix Kergorlay (Group 2) (Deauville, August 24) 3yo+ 1m7f Good to soft **112** (TS 95) 9 ran ● **2nd** Prix Maurice de Nieuil (Group 2) (Maisons-Laffitte, July 19) 4yo+ 1m6f Good to soft **110** (TS 98) 7 ran ● **1st** Prix de la Porte de Madrid (Listed) (Longchamp, May 8) 4yo+ 1m4f Soft **100** (TS 43) 8 ran **2002** **1st** Prix du Coeur Volant (Maisons-Laffitte, May 7) 3yo 1m Soft 8 ran

for Carlos Laffon-Parias.

Stephane Pasquier inherited the ride and, while Pasquier did nothing even Westerner's hyper-critical owner could positively identify as wrong, his relative unfamiliarity with his mount might have contributed partly to the fact that Westerner seemed rather caught by surprise when asked for his finishing effort after only ten and a half furlongs. He ran on strongly in the end but, even so, his defeat, albeit by only a length and three-quarters and the same by course specialist Warrsan and the excellent German filly Gonbarda, must have left his connections feeling

Westerner and Olivier Peslier warm up for the Gold Cup with an easy win in the Group 2 Prix Vicomtesse Vigier

slightly disappointed, if not wondering whether the attempted re-direction of his career had been a mistake.

Wildenstein is not the type of man to admit error after just one piece of questionable evidence, though, and few were surprised to hear that in spite of this defeat – or, conversely, because of its apparent promise – the Arc, over the same trip, was still on Westerner's agenda. In the run-up to the race several respected judges, including the *Racing Post*'s Tom Segal, put him up as a serious possible for the 12-furlong championship, and the fact that he started at one-third of the odds of his Baden-Baden conqueror made it clear that at his own favourite course punters were pretty sure Westerner could at least turn the tables on Warrsan.

A cloudburst that just about coincided with the start ensured that the 2005 Arc was run at what may have been a steadier pace than usual, although the actual race time was standard for the conditions. Perhaps surprisingly in the circumstances, though, the great stayer was not outpaced in the straight, and possibly hit the front for a stride or two half a furlong out before the irresistible surge of Hurricane Run proved too much for him by two lengths. He was followed home, however, by, in finishing order, the previous year's Arc winner, Bago; the subsequent Breeders' Cup Turf winner, Shirocco; the Derby winner, Motivator; the brilliant Irish Oaks and Prix Vermeille winner, Shawanda, and the subsequent Champion Stakes and Hong Kong Cup second, Pride. Peslier deserved great praise for his immaculate ride, but the real point was that Westerner had entirely vindicated his owner's and trainer's judgement by running what was probably the race of his life. The international handicappers thought so too, raising him to a rating of 126 that at the time put him behind only Hurricane Run and the retired American champion Ghostzapper in the list of the world's leading horses.

That performance could only have boosted his value at stud, but even so there was some surprise at the news later that month that Wildenstein had received what must have been too tempting an offer for even him to refuse. Rather than race on in 2006, Westerner will stand, primarily as a jumping stallion, at Coolmore in 2006. He was, however, to have one more run before retirement – in what looked like a bid to confirm his middle-distance class beyond doubt: the Hong Kong Vase at Sha Tin on December 11. In retrospect, that race, eight months after he'd begun his season as a stayer, may have been a classic case of one demand too many, although few thought so beforehand, since Westerner was sent off favourite to beat his only obvious rival if he could repeat his Arc form, the superb filly Ouija Board, now fully restored to her best after a season interrupted by injury.

Just before they turned into the straight it did seem that Westerner was going as well as any, and course commentator David Raphael (probably the best in the world) in fact gave his name that little shift in tone that said he felt sure he was going to play a part in the finish. When Peslier asked Westerner for acceleration this time, though, there wasn't enough there, and he could only run on steadily at his own pace into fifth, while Ouija Board streaked clear of the Japanese Six Sense, the local horse Best Gift, and the French filly Shamdala. The time for the race of just over 2min 28sec on firm going – almost identical to that of the Arc, run on ground with much more give – perhaps went some way towards explaining Westerner's failure to match the middle-distance specialists for pace.

In a way it was a pity that his honourable career should have finished on this relatively low note, but there was certainly no shame in the defeat. He retires with a record of 11 victories (five of them Group 1), nine seconds and two thirds from 28 starts that says plenty about his honesty and consistency. As a son of the great Danehill out of the Prix Vermeille winner Walensee, he's almost too well bred for a jumping sire, and one shudders a bit to think of the sort of hurdlers he's likely to sire.

If there was one great regret about his career, though, it was this: just after his Gold Cup there was talk about a possible tilt at the Melbourne Cup. There he would have met Makybe Diva. An admittedly debatable form line through Vinnie Roe suggests there might not have been that much between them. Now that would have been a race worth seeing.

Westerner *bay horse, 17-5-1999*

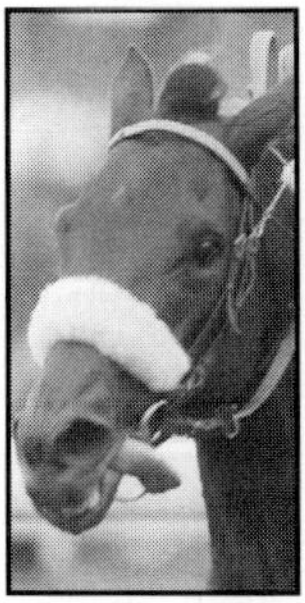

Danehill b 1986	Danzig	Northern Dancer	Nearctic **Natalma**
		Pas de Nom	Admiral's Voyage Petitioner
	Razyana	His Majesty	Ribot Flower Bowl
		Spring Adieu	Buckpasser **Natalma**
Walensee b 1982	Troy	Petingo	Petition Alcazar
		La Milo	Hornbeam Pin Prick
	Warsaw	Bon Mot	Worden Djebel Idra
		War Path	Blue Prince Alyxia

Bred by Dayton Investments Ltd in England.

Sire Danehill

Won 4 of 9 races, inc. Haydock Park Sprint Cup-Gr1. Died May 2003. Stood at Coolmore Stud, latterly at a fee of Ir200,000gns. Sire of Gr1 winners: Danish (QE II Challenge Cup), Kissing Cousin (Coronation), Danehill Dancer (Phoenix, National), Tsukuba Symphony (NHK Mile Cup), Desert King (National, Irish 2,000, Irish Derby), Fairy King Prawn (Yasuda Kinen), Tiger Hill (GP von Baden [twice], Bayerisches Zuchtrennen), Indian Danehill (Prix Ganay), Wannabe Grand (Cheveley Park), Aquarelliste (Prix de Diane, Prix Vermeille, Prix Ganay), Banks Hill (Coronation, Breeders' Cup F & M Turf, Prix Jacques le Marois), Mozart (July Cup, Nunthorpe), Regal Rose (Cheveley Park), Dress To Thrill (Matriarch), Fine Motion (Shuka Sho, QE II Commemorative Cup), Landseer (Poule d'Essai des Poulains), Rock Of Gibraltar (Grand Criterium, Dewhurst, 2,000 Guineas, Irish 2,000, St James's Palace, Sussex, Prix du Moulin), Westerner (Prix du Cadran [twice], Prix Royal-Oak [twice], Gold Cup), Clodovil (Poule d'Essai des Poulains), Intercontinental (Matriarch, Breeders' Cup F & M Turf), Light Jig (Yellow Ribbon), Spartacus (Phoenix, Gran Criterium), Grey Lilas (Prix du Moulin), North Light (Derby), Luas Line (Garden City H.), Oratorio (Prix Jean-Luc Lagardere, Eclipse, Irish Champion), George Washington (Phoenix, National), Horatio Nelson (Prix Jean-Luc Lagardere), Rumplestiltskin (Moyglare Stud, Prix Marcel Boussac).

Dam Walensee

Won 3 of 9 races, inc. Prix Vermeille-Gr1. Progressed rapidly to rank among the best of her age and sex in Europe at 3, woefully disappointing in varied company at 4. Stayed 12f well. Dam of: Waldensian (1988 c by Shareef Dancer; winner), War Arrow (1990 g by Top Ville; winner over jumps), Wild Ride (1991 c by Niniski; placed), Wild Life (1993 f by Nashwan; unraced); World Cup (1994 g by Epervier Bleu; unraced), Wagram (1995 f by Nashwan; unraced), War Game (1996 f by Caerleon; Gr2 winner), Watteau (1998 g by Loup Solitaire; winner), Westerner (1999 c by Danehill; 5-time Gr1 winner), Wildest Hope (2001 c by Wolfhound; placed). Died in 2001.

Pedigree assessment

The best long-distance performer in Europe over the last few years, Westerner earned his long-coveted Gold Cup triumph in 2005 and ultimately proved that he was not just a one-dimensional athlete. He put up a tremendous performance in the Arc, the best of his distinguished career. In 2006 he will join the NH division of the Coolmore stallion empire. It is to be hoped that he will not be entirely neglected by breeders for the Flat, as the attributes of toughness, honesty and class that served him so well are sorely needed in a species that is becoming progressively less sound. *TM*

Whipper (USA)

4yo bay colt **124**

Miesque's Son (USA) - Myth To Reality (Fr) (Sadler's Wells (USA))

Owner R C Strauss

Trainer Robert Collet

Breeder Flaxman Holdings Ltd

Career: **19** starts | won **6** | second **2** | third **2** | **£732,962** win and place

By Steve Dennis

PERHAPS it was the sea air. Perhaps a fresh breeze blowing through his mane, the cries of the seagulls in his ears and the tang of salt in his nostrils improved him 10lb. He would be a certainty at Laytown, had he not earned himself a berth at stud through his unique achievements. Whipper *was* Deauville, and 2006 will not be the same on the Normandy coast.

Like many a prodigal son, he wasn't wanted at first. The first time he went to Deauville he passed through the ring as a yearling without attracting a bid. Those who kept their hands in their pockets lived to regret it.

As a two-year-old he returned to win the Group 1 Prix Morny over six furlongs on soft ground. The following year he landed the Group 1 Prix Jacques le Marois over a mile, again on soft ground, and was beaten only a neck by Somnus in the Group 1 Prix Maurice de Gheest over the incongruous trip of six and a half furlongs.

These are the only three races at the highest level staged at Deauville – and, with the Maurice de Gheest only recently elevated to Group 1 status, no horse had won them all. Yet.

Whipper began his third and final year on the track in the Prix du Muguet at Saint-Cloud in May. Despite his Marois victory he was never a natural miler, much more a seven-furlong horse stretching out, and his late thrust brought him only third place behind Martillo.

It was a similar story in the Prix du Chemin de Fer du Nord at Chantilly the following month, when the good ground was another factor stacked against him, and he was only fourth behind Cacique.

These contests, however, were simply *amuse-gueules*, hors d'oeuvres, gulped down to the sound of the engraver sharpening his steel to chisel a new entry in the record books. Trainer Robert Collet had said, after Whipper's defeat in the Prix du Muguet: "The main target is a second attempt to win the Prix Jacques le Marois. He has been specially

Whipper (near side) completes the set of Deauville Group 1s with victory over Goodricke in the Prix Maurice de Gheest

left in training with that race in view."

Fortunately for the engraver, Deauville and Whipper himself, he was first set the task of going one better in the Maurice de Gheest. Whipper had 12 rivals and was made a strong favourite to see them off despite the presence in the field of Somnus, his nemesis of 12 months earlier. Racing off the pace as usual under Christophe Soumillon, Whipper moved through menacingly to challenge a furlong and a half out and was in front at the furlong pole. He had to roll up his sleeves to see off the persistent threat of Goodricke by half a length, but no wonder – Goodricke went on to win the William Hill Sprint Cup at Haydock.

The clean sweep was swept. The hometown favourite had come good when the occasion demanded and left the experienced Collet, trainer of many top horses including champion sprinter and Breeders' Cup Mile winner Last Tycoon and Japan Cup winner Le Glorieux, purring. He said: "Whipper is out of the ordinary and you're lucky if you have just one horse like him in your stable in your career."

A week later, Whipper made what would be his last visit to Deauville's straight mile for the Marois, although this time he was not expected to sign off in glory as Irish 2,000 Guineas winner Dubawi, Queen Anne Stakes winner Valixir and unbeaten dual Classic winner Divine Proportions barred his way. It was something of a family affair, Divine Proportions being practically his sister (same dam, sires are brothers), and Whipper took the measure of his year-younger sibling in some style. Unfortunately, he had to give best by a length and a half to Dubawi, who got first run on him and always held the upper hand – indeed, Whipper

2005 Race record

4th Netjets Breeders' Cup Mile (Grade 1) (Turf) (Belmont Park, October 29) 3yo+ 1m Yielding **122** 12 ran. *Midfield, 6th straight, switched outside inside final furlong, ran on well final 100yds, nearest finish (J P Murtagh), beaten 1l by Artie Schiller*

4th Netjets Prix du Moulin de Longchamp (Group 1) (Longchamp, September 4) 3yo+ 1m Good **121** (TS 93) 9 ran. *Always close up, switched out and chased winner from well over 1f out, lost 2nd close home (I Mendizabal), beaten 3¼l by Starcraft*

2nd Prix du Haras de Fresnay-le-Buffard-Jacques le Marois (Group 1) (Deauville, August 14) 3yo+ 1m Good to soft **124** (TS 119) 6 ran. *Raced in 5th, headway to go 2nd 1½f out, stayed on under pressure but always held (O Peslier), beaten 1½l by Dubawi*

1st Prix Maurice de Gheest (Group 1) (Deauville, August 7) 3yo+ 6½f Good **123** (TS 77) 13 ran. *Mid-division, disputed 6th halfway, headway 2f out, led 1f out, ran on under pressure to hold runner-up, driven out (C Soumillon), beat Goodricke by ½l*

4th Prix du Chemin de Fer du Nord (Group 3) (Chantilly, June 12) 4yo+ 1m Good **111** (TS 54) 6 ran. *Held up, 5th straight on inside, not much room 2f out, headway over 1f out, ridden and unable to quicken final furlong (S Maillot), beaten 3l by Cacique*

3rd Prix du Muguet (Group 2) (Saint-Cloud, May 1) 4yo+ 1m Good to soft **118** (TS 105) 9 ran. *Held up in rear, 8th straight, headway from 2f out, finished well (S Maillot), beaten 1½l by Martillo*

Other wins

2004 **1st** Prix Fresnay-le-Buffard-Jacques Le Marois (Group 1) (Deauville, August 15) 3yo+ 1m Soft **124** (TS 103) 10 ran ● **1st** Prix Djebel (Listed) (Straight) (Maisons-Laffitte, April 6) 3yo 7f Holding **115** (TS 107) 6 ran **2003** **1st** Criterium de Maisons-Laffitte (Group 2) (Maisons-Laffitte, October 31) 2yo 6f Holding **116** (TS 95) 10 ran ● **1st** Prix Morny Casinos Barriere (Group 1) (Deauville, August 31) 2yo 6f Soft **117** (TS 101) 8 ran ● **1st** Prix de Longchamp (Chateaubriant, August 18) 2yo 5½f Soft 7 ran

looked to be going up and down on the spot in the last 100 yards over a trip that stretched his elastic to transparency. In his subsequent outings, Whipper did his utmost to demonstrate that he was more than a one-trick pony. He was fourth to Starcraft in the Prix du Moulin, perhaps feeling the effects of two quick races and again running on empty at the end of the mile, and then filled the same position in the Breeders' Cup Mile at most un-Deauville-like Belmont Park, remarkably doing all his best work in the closing stages behind Artie Schiller. That race turned out to be his swansong, for a mooted trip to Hong Kong was dismissed.

Ultimately, Whipper fell between the two stools of the sprint division and the milers, and his connections will be eternally grateful that an unremarkable stretch of grass in a French seaside resort caught his fall and elevated him to great heights. Without Deauville, Whipper would have been no more than a name in the form book.

Without Whipper, Deauville will be shorn of its most enduring – and record-breaking – equine attraction. When the racing carnival swings into Deauville in the summer, when the smart yachts fill up the harbour and the helicopters scatter the seagulls, Whipper won't be there. He'll be missed.

Whipper

bay colt, 13-3-2001

Miesque's Son b 1992	Mr Prospector	Raise A Native	Native Dancer Raise You
		Gold Digger	Nashua Sequence
	Miesque	Nureyev	**Northern Dancer** **Special**
		Pasadoble	Prove Out Santa Quilla
Myth To Reality b 1986	Sadler's Wells	**Northern Dancer**	Nearctic Natalma
		Fairy Bridge	Bold Reason **Special**
	Millieme	Mill Reef	Never Bend Milan Mill
		Hardiemma	Hardicanute Grand Cross

Bred by Flaxman Holdings Ltd in Kentucky. $4,000 Keeneland November foal; Euros 30,000 Deauville yearling (private sale).

Sire Miesque's Son

Won 1 (Prix de Ris-Orangis-Gr3) of 9 races. Also 2nd in Prix Maurice de Gheest and Prix de la Foret. Quite well-made, close-coupled individual. Had training problems at 2 and 3, smart 6-7f performer at 4, best with some give in the ground. Impeccably bred. Brother to Classic winner and successful sire Kingmambo, half-brother to dual Classic winner East Of The Moon (f by Private Account), Gr3 winner Mingun (c by A.P. Indy), and to Gr3-placed winner Moon Is Up (f by Woodman). Out of an outstanding racemare, one of the best milers of her sex in recent times. Stands at Haras des Chartreux, France, 2006 fee €7,500. Sire of 6 crops of racing age, inc: Miesque's Approval (Gr3), Whipper (Prix Morny-Gr1, Prix Jacques le Marois-Gr1, Prix Maurice de Gheest-Gr1).

Dam Myth To Reality

Won 4 of 14 races, inc. 3 Listed. Good, consistent, mostly provincial performer, well suited by 12f, respectable 5th in Gr2 Prix de Royallieu, runner-up in Gr3 Prix Minerve. Effective on any ground. Did not progress at four. Very well bred. By the outstanding sire of the age out of a placed full-sister to Derby winner Shirley Heights. Dam of: Sonofogy (1992 g by Ogygian; winner), Magic Spin (1993 f by Lord Avie; winner), Assos (1994 g by Alleged; Listed winner), Mambo Jambo (1995 f by Kingmambo; winner, dam of Gr1-placed Ocean Silk), Fireinthewind (1996 c by Alleged; winner), Indigo Myth (1997 g by Kingmambo; Listed-placed winner), Meteorite Sun (1998 g by Miesque's Son; winner), Whipper (2001 c by Miesque's Son; triple Gr1 winner), Divine Proportions (2002 f by Kingmambo; five-time Gr1 winner), Anse Victorin (2003 f by Mt Livermore; unraced to date). She has a yearling colt by Lemon Drop Kid.

Pedigree assessment

If Whipper was supposed to be the poor relation of Divine Proportions, it never showed. The pair have the same dam, and their sires are brothers, Kingmambo being far superior to Miesque's Son as both racehorse and sire, but while the filly kept hitting the headlines with her long unbeaten streak, she never ran to a better figure than the colt at his peak. And when they finally met, a below-par Divine Proportions finished more than three lengths behind her brother in the Prix Jacques le Marois. A high-class sprinter-miler who looked unlucky in traffic at the Breeders' Cup, Whipper has now retired to Ballylinch Stud at a fee of €12,000. He should be able to count on strong support from Irish breeders. *TM*

Yeats (Ire)

4yo bay colt **122**

Sadler's Wells (USA) - Lyndonville (Ire) (Top Ville)

Owner Mrs John Magnier

Trainer A P O'Brien

Breeder Barrowsdale Stud & Orpendale

Career: **8** starts	won **4**	second **1**	third **0**	**£267,004** win and place

By Steve Dennis

ONE OF Aidan O'Brien's main requirements at Ballydoyle is to unearth and polish to a shine new stallions to keep Coolmore in clover and – to the benefit of both racegoers and the bloodstock industry – there is greater lustre these days in horses who have shown the capability to race beyond their three-year-old season.

O'Brien's newly adopted policy of keeping a handful of older horses in training was instantly rewarded by the second Breeders' Cup Turf success of Derby winner High Chaparral in 2003. Others to have embellished their standing thanks to another season in which to strengthen and mature include Arlington Million winner Powerscourt and now Yeats, who turned what might have been a career of unfulfilled talent into one that can now boast success at the highest level.

Yeats, frequently described by O'Brien as an "uncomplicated horse", still had plenty to prove at the beginning of 2005. Unbeaten in three starts, including the Derrinstown Stud Derby Trial, he was a hot favourite for the 2004 Derby until being withdrawn three days before the race owing to "muscle stiffness between his hip and backbone". The uncomplicated horse evidently had his intricacies.

He returned to action 51 weeks after his Derrinstown win, in the Group 3 Mooresbridge Stakes, and would have disappointed no-one save the odds-on backers in finishing runner-up to Cairdeas, beaten six lengths in wearying conditions. The winner had a run under his belt and Yeats patently looked in need of one – we could expect a different horse next time out. Next time O'Brien would do with him exactly what he had wanted to do with him the previous year – send him to Epsom to run in a Group 1 over a mile and a half.

This time, though, he had to make do with the Coronation Cup, and few on the Downs that summer afternoon would have begrudged O'Brien a wistful wonder about what might have been.

Kieren Fallon, making the most of an easy lead, keeps Yeats (right) up to his work to win the Coronation Cup

His uncomplicated horse ran a very uncomplicated race, setting a steady pace under Kieren Fallon, quickening clear from his six rivals three furlongs out and maintaining his gallop to the line. Yeats had run the race of his life in beating Alkaased by two and a half lengths, and it was hardly his fault that his rivals had contributed to their own downfall by allowing him an easy lead.

It was a visually very impressive display, and Fallon said on his return: "He's everything you want in a horse." O'Brien was slightly more loquacious, saying: "As I was watching that my mind went back to last year when Yeats was favourite for the Derby. I might have over-trained him for the Derby, which could have brought on his problems, and we learned a lot from that. Every run will bring him on this year."

Connections of Alkaased had no qualms about taking on Yeats again and the pair renewed rivalry in the Grand Prix de Saint-Cloud, joined by Arc winner Bago in a high-quality contest for which Yeats was made second favourite. Yeats followed a decent pace set by Bago's pacemaker and was third on the home turn, but when asked for a decisive effort he flattened out in two strides and eventually trailed in ninth behind Alkaased.

Was the Coronation Cup a fluke? What was more probable was that Yeats is a more delicate horse than his physique indicates, and the demands of another run in top company so soon after his Epsom exertions proved his undoing.

2005 Race record

6th Pattison Canadian International (Grade 1) (Woodbine, October 23) 3yo+ 1m4f Yielding **105** 10 ran. *Missed break, soon recovered to press leader, pushed along to lead under 4f out, headed over 3f out, 5th straight, soon ridden and one pace (K Fallon), beaten 12l by Relaxed Gesture*

4th Irish Field St Leger (Group 1) (Curragh, September 17) 3yo+ 1m6f Good **115** (TS 79) 9 ran. *Held up in touch, 5th and headway when checked briefly over 2f out, 4th and stayed on well inside final furlong (K Fallon), beaten 1½l by Collier Hill*

9th Grand Prix de Saint-Cloud (Group 1) (Saint-Cloud, June 26) 4yo+ 1m4f Good to soft **83** (TS 83) 11 ran. *Soon racing in 3rd, went 2nd over 5f out to well over 2f out, 3rd straight, soon weakened (J Fortune), beaten 20l by Alkaased*

1st Vodafone Coronation Cup (Group 1) (Epsom, June 3) 4yo+ 1m4f Good **122** (TS 109) 7 ran. *Made all, set steady pace until kicked clear 3f out, driven 2f out, stayed on well, unchallenged (K Fallon), beat Alkaased by 2½l*

2nd High Chaparral EBF Mooresbridge Stakes (Group 3) (Curragh, May 2) 4yo+ 1m2f Heavy **111** (TS 109) 4 ran. *Chased leaders in 3rd, pushed along before straight, 2nd 2f out, no impression from over 1f out, eased close home (K Fallon), beaten 6l by Cairdeas*

Other runs

2004 **1st** Derrinstown Stud Derby Trial Stakes (Group 2) (Leopardstown, May 9) 3yo 1m2f Good to yielding **111** (TS 77) 4 ran ● **1st** P.W.McGrath Memorial Ballysax Stakes (Group 3) (Leopardstown, April 18) 3yo 1m2f Soft **117** (TS 56) 3 ran **2003** **1st** Korean Racing Association EBF Maiden (Curragh, September 21) 2yo 1m Good to firm **94** (TS 66) 15 ran

O'Brien took Yeats back to Ballydoyle and pondered his next move. He now had a son of Sadler's Wells with a Group 1 victory to his name, two things that generally lead to a stud career. However, the next task for Yeats was to try to win a race that tends to have a negative impact on potential stallions: a St Leger.

He went to The Curragh after a break of two and a half months in a bid to bring Vinnie Roe's domination of the Irish St Leger to an end, and the pair were made joint-favourites. Yeats seemed to see out the longer trip but never looked in a position to win, taking fourth in a blanket finish behind Collier Hill, half a length adrift of Vinnie Roe.

It was not a performance to suggest that further glories lay just around the corner, and that conclusion was borne out in Yeats's final outing of the year, in the Canadian International at Woodbine. He joined a decent European raiding party that included his compatriot Grey Swallow and Juddmonte winner Electrocutionist, but the tourists were turned over in one of those neat little coincidences that racing occasionally delights us with.

The race went to the Christophe Clement-trained Relaxed Gesture, who had last been seen in action in Europe when chasing home Yeats in the Derrinstown Stud Derby Trial. It was as good an indication as any that we may have seen the best of Yeats; at least we had the chance to.

Yeats

bay colt, 23-4-2001

Sadler's Wells b 1981	Northern Dancer	Nearctic	Nearco Lady Angela
		Natalma	Native Dancer Almahmoud
	Fairy Bridge	Bold Reason	Hail To Reason Lalun
		Special	Forli Thong
Lyndonville b 1988	Top Ville	High Top	Derring-Do Camenae
		Sega Ville	Charlottesville La Sega
	Diamond Land	Sparkler	Hard Tack Diamond Spur
		Canaan	Santa Claus Rustic Bridge

Bred by Barronstown Stud & Orpendale in Ireland.

Sire Sadler's Wells

Won 6 of 11 races, inc. Beresford S.-Gr3, Irish Derby Trial-Gr2, Irish 2,000 Guineas-Gr1, Eclipse S.-Gr1, Phoenix Champion S.-Gr1. Also 2nd in Prix du Jockey-Club-Gr1, King George VI & Queen Elizabeth S.-Gr1. Impeccably bred top-class performer from 8-12f, handsome, tough and consistent. Sire of Gr1 winners: Braashee, French Glory, In The Wings (3), Old Vic (2), Prince Of Dance, Scenic, Salsabil (5), Opera House (3), Runyon, Saddlers' Hall, El Prado, Johann Quatz, Masad, Barathea (2), Fatherland, Fort Wood, Intrepidity (3), Carnegie (2), King's Theatre (2), Northern Spur (2), Moonshell, Muncie, Poliglote, Chief Contender, Dance Design, Darazari, Luna Wells, Cloudings, Ebadiyla (2), Entrepreneur, In Command, Kayf Tara (4), Dream Well (2), Greek Dance, King Of Kings (2), Leggera, Commander Collins, Daliapour, Montjeu (6), Saffron Walden, Aristotle, Beat Hollow (4), Subtle Power, Galileo (3), Imagine (2), Milan, Perfect Soul, Sequoyah, Sligo Bay, Ballingarry, Black Sam Bellamy (2), Gossamer (2), High Chaparral (6), Islington (4), Quarter Moon, Sholokov, Alberto Giacometti, Brian Boru (2), Doyen, Powerscourt (2), Refuse To Bend (4), Yesterday, Quiff, Yeats, Playful Act, Linda's Lad.

Dam Lyndonville

Won 1 of 3 starts. Showed progressive form in brief career, stayed 14f well. Dam of: Tsukuba Symphony (1993 c by Danehill; Gr3 winner in Japan), Anchored In Love (1994 f by Alzao; unplaced), Lady Fairy (1996 f by Fairy King; unplaced), Lion Of Judah (1997 c by Caerleon; unplaced), Chalice Wells (1998 f by Sadler's Wells; unraced), Solskjaer (2000 c by Danehill; Gr2 winner), Yeats (2001 c by Sadler's Wells; Gr1 winner), Magnolia Lane (2002 f by Sadler's Wells; placed).

Pedigree assessment

Yeats was the unbeaten Derby favourite when muscle problems interrupted his career in May 2004, and it was almost a year before he could return to action. His victory in the Coronation Cup looked good, but perhaps only because Alkaased was given too much to do, and his subsequent form suggests that he was probably never Derby calibre. He had been entered in the Gold Cup, and that might have proved a realistic target, as he seems to be a natural stayer, lacking in the speed department. Though bred on the same cross as Montjeu, with the same sire and broodmare sire, he has none of the acceleration we came to associate with that dual Derby hero, and if he finds a berth at stud it is likely to be in the company of NH mares. *TM*

Zenno Rob Roy (Jpn)

5yo bay horse **124**

Sunday Silence (USA) - Roamin Rachel (USA) (Mining (USA))

Owner Mrs Kumiko Oosako

Trainer Kazuo Fujisawa

Breeder Shiraoi Farm

Career: **20** starts | won **7** | second **6** | third **4** | **£5,791,477** win and place

By Paul Haigh

ZENNO ROB ROY ended 2004 with his fame at its height. His triumph in the world's biggest betting race, the Arima Kinen at the end of December, meant he had swept Japan's three major autumn Group 1s, and his election as Japanese Horse of the Year was a formality. If anyone had predicted then that the son of Sunday Silence would somehow manage to go through 2005 without a victory, they'd have been laughed at.

That's what's happened, though, and while it is true that he never ran a bad race, it was very disappointing for a horse who had appeared to have the world at his feet. Perhaps those three stellar performances came when he was at a freakish peak. Although he achieved similar ratings on occasions in 2005, he simply wasn't able to force his head in front where it mattered.

Unraced at two, he won three out of four before finishing second in the 2003 Japanese Derby. He then won again at Grade 2 level before being sent off second favourite for the 15-furlong Kikuka Sho, the Japanese St Leger, in which he never got a run and finished only fourth. Third place in the Arima Kinen rounded off a three-year-old season that left him near the top, though not quite the leader of his generation.

At four he ran second three times from four starts before hitting the purple patch that elevated him to superstar status. An ambitious plan for 2005 was laid out by trainer Kazuo Fujisawa that included raids abroad before another attempt on Japan's autumn Triple Crown.

Phase one went wrong, however, when, under Kent Desormeaux – Olivier Peslier had been his previous partner – he could finish only third behind Sweep Tosho and Heart's Cry in the Takarazuka Kinen at Hanshin. Undeterred, connections stuck to the original itinerary and took him to York for phase two, the Juddmonte International in August. He lodged with Geoff Wragg at Newmarket.

Japan's 2004 Horse of the Year Zenno Rob Roy in action at York in the Juddmonte International Stakes

Virtually throughout the ten and a half furlongs of the Juddmonte he looked the likely winner, and it was only in the last strides that the Italian champion, Electrocutionist, got up to beat him. The general opinion was that Yutaka Take had simply been outmuscled in the finish by the power of Mick Kinane, but a pattern of being run down after having looked the winner had begun to emerge.

The pattern was maintained on his return to Japan where, this time under another new jockey, Norohiro Yokoyama, his attempt to retain the Autumn Tenno Sho on October 30 was foiled by Heavenly Romance, although he did turn the Hanshin tables on both Sweep Tosho in fifth and Heart's Cry in sixth. The pace had been muddling, but Zenno Rob Roy had looked to have it in safe keeping until the mare, who had been under strong pressure for some way, came to beat him by a head.

In spite of these defeats he was made favourite at only a shade of odds-against for the Japan Cup on November 27. Once again, reunited with Kent Desormeaux, he came with his now standard mid-straight run and just headed the eventual winner, Alkaased, a furlong out; but once again, instead of drawing away as he had a year earlier, he folded when Alkaased fought back. He finished third, beaten nearly two lengths by Alkaased and Heart's Cry. Those who had formed the view after York that what he needed was stronger handling were confounded by the fact that only Frankie Dettori on the winner could be reckoned to have matched Desormeaux for vigour.

Some allowance for his failure to get home has to be made for the fact

2005 Race record

8th Arima Kinen (The Grand Prix) (Group 1) (Nakayama, December 25) 3yo+ 1m4½f Firm **117** 16 ran. *(K Desormeaux), beaten 5¼l by Heart's Cry*

3rd Japan Cup (Group 1) (Tokyo, November 27) 3yo+ 1m4f Firm **122** 18 ran. *Raced in 13th, 10th straight, strong run down outside to dispute lead briefly just over 1f out, soon headed, stayed on same pace (K Desormeaux), beaten 1¾l by Alkaased*

2nd Tenno Sho (Autumn) (Grade 1) (Tokyo, October 30) 3yo+ 1m2f Firm **122** 18 ran. *Settled in midfield, 9th straight, good headway well over 1f out, every chance final furlong, ran on (N Yokoyama), beaten hd by Heavenly Romance*

2nd Juddmonte International Stakes (Group 1) (York, August 16) 3yo+ 1m2½f Good **124** (TS 124) 7 ran. *Held up in touch, headway over 2f out, switched right over 1f out, stayed on well, no extra near finish (Y Take), beaten nk by Electrocutionist*

3rd Takarazuka Kinen (Grade 1) (Hanshin, June 26) 3yo+ 1m3f Firm **120** 15 ran. *Raced in 6th, headway on inside to go 3rd over 3f out, 4th straight, switched left over 1f out, went 2nd 100yds out, lost 2nd close home (K Desormeaux), beaten 1½l by Sweep Tosho*

2004

1st Arima Kinen (Grade 1) (Nakayama, December 26) 3yo+ 1m4½f Firm **122** 15 ran ● **1st** Japan Cup (Grade 1) (Tokyo, November 28) 3yo+ 1m4f Firm **124** 16 ran ● **1st** Tenno Sho (Grade 1) (Tokyo, October 31) 3yo+ 1m2f Good **124** 17 ran ● **2nd** Kyoto Daishoten (Grade 2) (Kyoto, October 10) 3yo+ 1m4f Firm 10 ran ● **4th** Takarazuka Kinen (Grade 1) (Hanshin, June 27) 3yo+ 1m3f Firm **116** 15 ran ● **2nd** Tenno Sho (Spring) (Grade 1) (Kyoto, May 2) 4yo+ 2m Firm **116** 18 ran ● **2nd** Nikkei Sho (Grade 2) (Nakayama, March 27) 4yo+ 1m4½f Firm 14 ran

Other runs

2003 **3rd** Arima Kinen (Grade 1) (Nakayama, December 28) 3yo+ 1m4½f Firm **115** 12 ran ● **4th** Kikuka Sho (Japanese St Leger) (Grade 1) (Kyoto, October 26) 3yo 1m7f Firm **116** 18 ran ● **1st** Japanese St Leger Trial (Grade 2) (Hanshin, September 28) 3yo 1m2f Firm 13 ran ● **2nd** Tokyo Yushun (Japanese Derby) (Grade 1) (Tokyo, June 1) 3yo 1m4f Firm **120** 18 ran ● **1st** Japanese Derby Trial (Grade 2) (Tokyo, May 3) 3yo 1m4f Firm 15 ran ● **1st** Yamabuki Sho (Nakayama, April 12) 3yo 1m3f Firm 10 ran ● **3rd** Sumire Stakes (Hanshin, March 2) 3yo 1m3f Good 10 ran ● **1st** Maiden (Unraced) (Nakayama, February 9) 3yo 1m Good 15 ran

that at 2min 22.1sec this was unofficially the fastest 2,400 metres ever run; but it did seem he was beaten by two better, and perhaps more determined, horses.

By the time Zenno Rob Roy turned out on Christmas Day for the Arima Kinen his status as the great hero of Japanese racing had already been lost to the three-year-old Triple Crown winner Deep Impact. But once again, in his final race before retirement to stud, the fire that had enabled him to break the Nakayama course record a year earlier was missing as he was beaten more than five lengths into eighth behind old rival Heart's Cry, Deep Impact and Lincoln.

Perhaps it was the third horse home who provided the best evidence of what looked like gradual deterioration. For the now fallen idol had finished just in front of Lincoln in the Japan Cup.

Zenno Rob Roy

brown horse, 27-3-2000

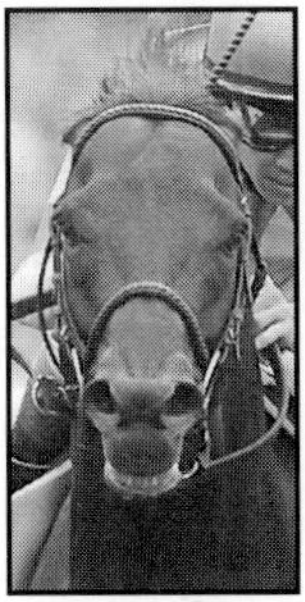

Sunday Silence br 1986	Halo	Hail To Reason	Turn-to Nothirdchance
		Cosmah	Cosmic Bomb Almahmoud
	Wishing Well	Understanding	Promised Land Pretty Ways
		Mountain Flower	Montparnasse Edelweiss
Roamin Rachel b 1990	Mining	Mr Prospector	Raise A Native Gold Digger
		I Pass	Buckpasser Impish
	One Smart Lady	Clever Trick	Icecapade Kankatee Miss
		Pia's Lady	Pia Star Plucky Roman

Bred by Shiraoi Farm in Japan. 90,000,000 yen JRHA Select Foal Sale

Sire Sunday Silence

Won 9 (6-10f) of 14 races. At 2, won 1 of 3 starts. At 3, won 7 (inc. San Felipe H-Gr2, Santa Anita Derby-Gr1, Kentucky Derby-Gr1, Preakness S-Gr1, Super Derby-Gr1, Breeders' Cup Classic-Gr1) of 9 starts, also 2nd Belmont S-Gr1. At 4, won 1 (Californian S-Gr1) of 2 starts. By smart turf performer and very good US sire, out of a US stakes winner. Retired to Shadai Stallion Station in Japan, died August 2002. First foals 1992, sire of Gr1 winners (northern hemisphere foals): Dance Partner, Fuji Kiseki, Genuine, Marvelous Sunday, Tayasu Tsuyoshi, Bubble Gum Fellow, Dance In The Dark, Ishino Sunday, Silence Suzuka, Stay Gold, Special Week, Admire Vega, Stinger, To The Victory, Agnes Flight, Air Shakur, Cheers Grace, Believe, Manhattan Cafe, Mejiro Bailey, Admire Max, Durandal, Gold Allure, Admire Groove, Heavenly Romance, Neo Universe, Peace Of World, Still In Love, Zenno Rob Roy, Dance In The Mood, Daiwa El Cielo, Daiwa Major, Hat Trick, Heart's Cry, Suzuka Mambo, Air Messiah, Deep Impact. Also sire of European Group winners Sunday Picnic (Gr3), Silent Honor (Gr3), Layman (Gr3), Sundrop (Gr3).

Dam Roamin Rachel

Won sole 2yo start, top-class dirt filly at 3 and 4 in US. From 15 starts, she won 9 races, 7 of them stakes, notably Beaumont S-Gr2 at 3 and Ballerina H-Gr1, Brown & Williamson H-Gr3 at 4. Best at up to 8f. Sister to minor US stakes winner Hello Rachel and minor winner Choice Claim (dam of Gr3 winner Another), half-sister to unraced Tangled (dam of Gr1 winner Cats Cradle). Sire Mining fast Gr1-winning son of Mr Prospector. Dam of: Indy Bold (1996 f by A P Indy; unraced), Darling My Darling (1997 f by Deputy Minister; stakes winner, Gr1-placed), Qawaqeb (1998 c by A P Indy; winner), Stray Cat (1999 f by Storm Cat; unplaced), Zenno Rob Roy (2000 c by Sunday Silence; Japan Cup-Gr1), Grande Gloria (2001 c by Sunday Silence; non-winner). Mare died 2001.

Pedigree assessment

Another in the long line of top-class middle-distance performers by Sunday Silence, and one sure to draw heavy interest at stud. He is from a speed-oriented US family, and on pedigree it is slightly surprising he has classy (Japanese) form over two miles. The ten furlongs of the Juddmonte International is more in keeping with his background. *JH*

The young pretenders

of 2005

Figure in bold by each horse's name is its definitive Racing Post Rating

Comments by Richard Austen (RA) and Graham Dench (GD)

Pedigree assessments by Janet Hickman

Ajigolo 110

ch c Piccolo - Ajig Dancer (Niniski (USA)) January 17
Owner Timberhill Racing Partnership **Trainer** M R Channon **Breeder** Timber Hill Racing Partnership
10 starts: won **3**, second **1**, third **1** **£61,296** win & place prize-money

AJIGOLO is likely to be hard to place at three, but he deserves plenty of credit for the level he reached at two. So too does trainer Mick Channon.

The product of a mating between two horses who both did well for Channon, Ajigolo's season started at Goodwood in April, when he was joint favourite but got too worked up to do himself any sort of justice. It ended at the meeting transferred from Ascot to Salisbury in October, when he was sent off a ridiculously generous 25-1 and failed by only a head to concede a 7lb penalty to Hunter Street in the Group 3 Cornwallis Stakes. He ran ten times in all.

The penalty had been incurred at Baden-Baden the previous month, when he landed the odds in the six-runner Group 2 Maurice Lacroix Trophy. That was his third win of the season, following a smart success at Salisbury less than a fortnight after his inauspicious debut, and a novice

Race record

2nd skybet.com Cornwallis Stakes (Group 3) (Salisbury, October 8) 2yo 5f Good **110** (TS 102) 12 ran.
6th Dubai Duty Free Mill Reef Stakes (Group 2) (Newbury, September 17) 2yo 6f Good to firm **105** (TS 99) 13 ran.
1st Maurice Lacroix-Trophy (Group 2) (Baden-Baden, September 2) 2yo 6f Good **107** 6 ran.
3rd Costcutter Roses Stakes (Listed) (York, August 17) 2yo 5f Good **97** (TS 74) 10 ran.
1st SimblyBiz 1000 Member Firms Celebration Novice Stakes (Doncaster, July 14) 2yo 6f Good to firm **91** (TS 70) 6 ran.
4th Norfolk Stakes (Group 3) (York, June 16) 2yo 5f Good to firm **90** (TS 84) 12 ran.
5th Kerry Spring Water Rochestown Stakes (Listed) (Cork, June 12) 2yo 6f Good **80** 6 ran.
10th bonusprint.com National Stakes (Listed) (Sandown, May 30) 2yo 5f Good **52** (TS 46) 11 ran.
1st George Smith Horseboxes Maiden Stakes (Salisbury, May 12) 2yo 5f Good to firm **88** (TS 88) 9 ran.
7th EBF Patrick Hogan "Betfair" Lifetime In Racing Maiden Stakes (Goodwood, April 30) 2yo 5f Good 7 ran.

Pedigree assessment

Sire Piccolo (Warning) Quite useful 5f 2yo winner, then tough and high-class sprinter over next two seasons, won Nunthorpe S-Gr1 (awarded race) and King's Stand S-Gr2. Speedily bred, by top-class miler who generally was influence for speed, out of dual 6f 2yo winner from fast family. First foals 1997, prolific sire of 2yo and sprint winners, sires occasional very talented performer (notably La Cucaracha). **Dam Ajig Dancer** Won 4 of 26 races from 2 to 4. Minor winner over 5f at 2, later won 3 races over 7f and showed form over 5-6f. Tough, fairly modest. By top-class stayer out of unraced sister to smart sprinter Puissance from fast family. Her 2 earlier foals feature quite useful dual 2004 5f 2yo winner Indiannie Star (by Fraam). **Conclusion** His forte already is speed, and he will continue to sprint. Both sire and dam were tough and durable performers who did well at 4, so Ajigolo should continue to run well, even if he misses the highest class.

Ajigolo gets off the mark at Salisbury in May

win at Doncaster in July. His limitations were exposed when he stepped up in grade in races like the Norfolk Stakes and the Mill Reef, and as he looks a sprinter pure and simple, and a precocious one at that, he may struggle to pay his way again. *GD*

Alexander Alliance (Ire) 112

b f Danetime (Ire) - Geht Schnell (Fairy King (USA)) April 18
Owner Noel O'Callaghan **Trainer** T Stack **Breeder** Roger & Henry O'Callaghan
2 starts: won **1**, second **1**, **£37,336** win & place prize-money

ALEXANDER ALLIANCE probably caught a tartar when fancied for a winning debut in a huge field of maidens at The Curragh in September, for fellow newcomer Art Museum, who beat her a length, went on to put up a smart performance in a Listed race over the same course and distance a fortnight later and was due to represent Aidan O'Brien in the Middle Park Stakes until withdrawn with a vet's certificate.

Any ordinary maiden race ought to have been there for the taking, but connections stepped Alexander Alliance straight up to Listed company for the Flame Of Tara Stakes, also at The Curragh, the following month.

She was more than up to the task too, for she travelled well and quickened in the style of a classy filly to score by three and a half lengths from the Group-placed Karaminskaya, with the rest well beaten off. In doing so she recorded a Racing Post Rating that would theoretically have made her the winner of the Cheveley Park Stakes and would have put her very much in the reckoning for either the Prix Marcel Boussac or the Fillies' Mile.

The 1,000 Guineas is understandably Alexander Alliance's target, and a preliminary outing is said to be ground dependent. Having so far avoided the sort of race from which the leading ante-post fancies usually emerge she could represent a bit of value. *GD*

Race record

1st Flame Of Tara EBF Stakes (Listed) (Curragh, October 9) 2yo 6f Good to yielding **112** (TS 69) 8 ran.
2nd Bloodstock Underwriting EBF Maiden (Curragh, September 4) 2yo 6f Good **80** (TS 43) 26 ran.

Pedigree assessment

Sire Danetime (Danehill) Fair 6f winner at 2, progressed into high-class 6f performer at 3 and 4, won Stewards' Cup, placed Haydock Sprint Cup-Gr1 and July Cup-Gr1. By top-class sprinter-miler and outstanding sire out of 7f 3yo winner. Good source of 2yos and sprinters, some very useful. **Dam Geht Schnell** Placed at 2 over 5f, unplaced at 3 over 5-7f. By very good sire out of half-sister to high-class sprinter Anita's Prince. Her 8 earlier foals feature 2yo Listed winners Inzar's Best (by Inzar) and Ruby Rocket (Indian Rocket) plus Listed-placed 7f 2yo/3yo winner Cool Panic (Brave Act). **Conclusion** Bred to the same cross as two of Danetime's best runners, Baltic Kid (out of mare by Fairy King) and The Kiddykid (out of mare by Fairy King's brother Sadler's Wells). Expect Alexander Alliance to be a tough sprinter, for her pedigree suggests distinct stamina limitations.

Alexandrova (Ire) 114

b f Sadler's Wells (USA) - Shouk (Shirley Heights) April 23
Owner Mrs John Magnier, M Tabor & D Smith **Trainer** A P O'Brien **Breeder** Quay Bloodstock
4 starts: won **1**, second **1**, third **1** **£47,010** win & place prize-money

WITH Sadler's Wells for her sire and her dam Shouk a Shirley Heights winner from a middle-distance family Luca Cumani has done really well with, Alexandrova has the breeding of a filly who was always likely to make a much better three-year-old than a two-year-old. Yet she still ended the season the joint-top two-year-old filly on Racing Post Ratings, sharing that position with Nannina, who beat her a short head in the Fillies' Mile at Newmarket, New Girlfriend and Silca's Sister.

Her pedigree is plainly much stouter than Nannina's, and she is also surely going to be much better suited by a mile and a half than her stable-mates Rumplestiltskin and Race For The Stars, or for that matter Donna Blini, Flashy Wings, New Girlfriend or Silca's Sister. Indeed she looks a worthy winter favourite for the Oaks, despite having won only one of her four juvenile starts, for the Newmarket form already puts her within touching distance of the level typically required at Epsom and she has much less to prove than most of the others being touted.

Alexandrova had no obvious excuse when beaten by Nannina at Newmarket – indeed one could argue that she got first run on her rival when going to the front, looking the likelier winner, at around the furlong marker – but there was a lot to like about her performance, and with the pair pulling three lengths clear the form looks rock solid. The time before, when first stepped up to a mile, Alexandrova had been a runaway ten-length winner at Tralee, form that was franked when runner-up Nautical Star went on to run another O'Brien Oaks possible, Chenchikova, considerably closer at Tipperary next time. Earlier defeats were over an inadequate seven furlongs, her debut at The Curragh coming in Listed company and her Goodwood third in a maiden which turned out to be well above average, with the first two places occupied by the Marcel Boussac third Deveron and the Listed winner Innocent Air. She looks a major contender for the top fillies' races at around a mile and a half. *GD*

Race record

2nd Meon Valley Stud Fillies' Mile (Group 1) (Newmarket, September 24) 2yo 1m Good **114** (TS 106) 6 ran.

1st Irish Stallion Farms EBF Fillies Maiden (Tralee, August 22) 2yo 1m Good **99** 8 ran.

3rd EBF New Ham Maiden Fillies' Stakes (Goodwood, July 28) 2yo 7f Soft **81** (TS 79) 11 ran.

6th Blue Square Stakes (Registered as Balanchine Stakes) (Listed) (Curragh, June 24) 2yo 7f Good to firm **83** 11 ran.

Pedigree assessment

Sire Sadler's Wells (Northern Dancer) Smart 7-8f winner at 2, improved into top-class 8-12f colt at 3, won Irish 2,000 Guineas-Gr1, Eclipse S-Gr1, Irish Champion S-Gr1. Outstanding sire, particularly of 3yo+ over 8-12f, also has good record with autumn 2yos. **Dam Shouk** At 2, placed once over 7f in 2 starts. At 3, won over 11f only completed start. At 4, showed fair form over 10-12f in 4 starts. Very closely related to smart 10f+ filly Puce (by Darshaan; dam to Sadler's Wells of useful 12f colt Pukka, and dam to Barathea of smart 12f filly Pongee) and half-sister to smart stayer Golden Quest (Rainbow Quest). Her 3 earlier foals feature Cheveley Park Stakes winner Magical Romance and 7f 2yo winner Saree (both by Barathea, a son of Sadler's Wells), plus 10f 3yo winner Grand Wizard (Grand Lodge). **Conclusion** Very well bred, from a family that has done well of late. Will need at least 10f, will stay 12f, and bred to make good progress from 2 to 3.

Always Hopeful 112

b c Mind Games - Expectation (Ire) (Night Shift (USA)) February 20

Owner J C Fretwell **Trainer** E J O'Neill **Breeder** Lostford Manor Stud

6 starts: won **2**, second **1**, third **2** **£95,739** win & place prize-money

THE progeny of Mind Games are usually only modest or fair performers, but Eoghan O'Neill and John Fretwell's shopping spree at the 2004 yearling sales unearthed the best yet when they took home Always Hopeful. A clear-cut winner of the Richmond Stakes and third in both the Prix Morny and Middle Park, Always Hopeful heads off the likes of Dazzling Bay and Romantic Myth among his sire's stock on Racing Post Ratings.

Always Hopeful is far more typical of one by Mind Games in being a sprinter, though his best efforts were over six furlongs rather than five. He ran over the minimum when winning a maiden event at Nottingham second time up and when fifth, giving weight to virtually all the rest, in the Weatherbys Super Sprint on his third outing. There was also more give in the ground when Always Hopeful was in the front rank throughout to take the Sterling Insurance Richmond at Goodwood and when he made the running in those two Group 1 assignments afterwards.

Losing out to Silca's Sister and Ivan Denisovich at Deauville and to Amadeus Wolf and Red Clubs at Newmarket represented Always Hopeful's best efforts on the figures, but placing a sprinter of this quality can be an awful lot easier at two than three, and when he was sold at auction in October for 270,000 guineas, it was no surprise to hear that Always Hopeful was heading for Hong Kong. His yearling price had been 32,000 guineas. *RA*

Race record

3rd Shadwell Stud Middle Park Stakes (Group 1) (Newmarket, September 30) 2yo 6f Good to soft **110** (TS 106) 6 ran.

3rd Darley Prix Morny (Group 1) (Deauville, August 21) 2yo 6f Soft **112** (TS 86) 7 ran.

1st Sterling Insurance Richmond Stakes (Group 2) (Goodwood, July 29) 2yo 6f Good to soft **108** (TS 103) 6 ran.

5th Weatherbys Super Sprint (Newbury, July 16) 2yo 5f Good to firm **88** (TS 66) 25 ran.

1st EBF Median Auction Maiden Stakes (Nottingham, June 15) 2yo 5f Good **87** (TS 86) 10 ran.

2nd turftours.com "Come To The Irish Derby" Maiden Stakes (Newmarket, May 29) 2yo 5f Good to firm **81** (TS 74) 12 ran.

Pedigree assessment

Sire Mind Games (Puissance) Smart triple 5f 2yo winner, later won 4 5f races at 3 and 4, notably Palace House S-Gr3 and Temple S-Gr2 (twice). Once-raced at 5 after first year at stud. First foals 1998, influence for speed, does best with sprint 2yos (notably Romantic Myth). **Dam Expectation** Unplaced in 5 2yo outings over 5-6f, unplaced sole start at 3. By very good sire who is basically influence for speed, out of daughter of Irish 1,000 Guineas winner Front Row, from family of smart miler Long Row and Irish Oaks winner Possessive Dancer. Her 3 earlier foals include Always Hopeful's very close relative Polly Plunkett (by Puissance), a dual 1m 3yo winner, and dual 6f 2yo winner Enford Princess (by Pivotal). **Conclusion** Many of Mind Games's most talented progeny have their best season at 2, and Expectation is from a family whose members tend to do well as juveniles. Always Hopeful has already done admirably, but on pedigree he might struggle to enhance his record.

Amadeus Wolf 120

See entry in the top 100 horses, page 36

Always Hopeful comes home clear in the Richmond Stakes

Arabian Prince (USA) 104

b c Fusaichi Pegasus (USA) - Add (USA) (Spectacular Bid (USA)) May 13
Owner Mrs John Magnier & M Tabor **Trainer** A P O'Brien **Breeder** Eagle Holdings
4 starts: won **1**, second **1**, third **1** **£22,420** win & place prize-money

ARABIAN PRINCE began his two-year-old career at shorter odds than his stablemate Septimus for the same maiden and ended it crossing swords with him again in the Racing Post Trophy, but at 14-1 compared to Septimus' 5-6. He lost to Septimus on both occasions and his form also falls well short of that shown by several of his other stablemates, but Arabian Prince has a turn of foot and is likely to be a more potent force in Group events as a three-year-old when the ground is a lot less testing than it was at Doncaster.

After a half-length second to Septimus on that debut at Leopardstown in September, having himself hit the front inside the final furlong, Arabian Prince made up a lot of ground to score by a neck at 8-13 in a similar event at The Curragh eight days later, also over seven furlongs.

His next start confirmed that there was plenty of ability there, and again perhaps significantly more than the bare result suggested, when Arabian Prince came third in a Group 3 over one mile on good ground at Salisbury. It was a rather frantic, bunched finish to the Autumn Stakes, and Arabian Prince had to be extricated from a pocket to launch his bid, taken wide to the outside. Once there, he passed half a dozen rivals to lead and look the likely winner a furlong out, only to be run out of it by Blitzkrieg and the Aidan O'Brien-trained favourite Dylan Thomas in the last 75 yards. Given the way Arabian Prince went that day, there did not look much chance that a slog in the mud on Town Moor would be his cup of tea. *RA*

Race record

5th Racing Post Trophy (Group 1) (Doncaster, October 22) 2yo 1m Heavy **104** (TS 95) 7 ran.
3rd skybet.com Autumn Stakes (Group 3) (Salisbury, October 8) 2yo 1m Good **99** (TS 99) 12 ran.
1st Tinnakill House EBF Maiden (Curragh, September 18) 2yo 7f Good **86** (TS 72) 18 ran.
2nd Irish Stallion Farms EBF Maiden (Leopardstown, September 10) 2yo 7f Good to yielding **87** (TS 80) 13 ran.

Pedigree assessment

Sire Fusaichi Pegasus (Mr Prospector) Placed only start at 2, top-class 8-10f dirt performer at 3, won Kentucky Derby-Gr1. By outstanding sire out of stakes-placed sister to Preakness Stakes winner Pine Bluff. First foals 2002, has compiled strong record, mainly in US. Has sired smart US 2yos Roman Ruler, Superfly, but progeny appear to progress well from 2 to 3, sire of US Grade 1 winners Roman Ruler and Bandini, plus Belmont 2nd Andromeda's Hero. Quieter in Europe, though sire of Witten and Gr2-placed Scandinavia. **Dam Add** Won 4 races at 3 and 4 in US, also placed in minor stakes. By outstanding dirt performer but largely disappointing sire. From superb family, half-sister to Group 1 winner Jade Robbery and high-class US performers Chequer and Numerous (all by Mr Prospector) out of a smart very close relative of Nureyev. Her 9 earlier foals feature 4 winners, notably minor US stakes winner Inflate, plus the unraced dam of smart 8f+ US dirt performer Desert Hero. **Conclusion** Bred along very similar lines to Chequer, Jade Robbery and Numerous, all of whom were best at around a mile. Arabian Prince will be, too. His pedigree suggests he will train on, but it also suggests he will like dirt.

Art Museum (USA) 109

b c Storm Cat (USA) - Totemic (USA) (Vanlandingham (USA)) April 1
Owner Mrs John Magnier & M Tabor **Trainer** A P O'Brien **Breeder** Strategy Bloodstock
2 starts: won **2, £34,627** win & place prize-money

ART MUSEUM was denied the opportunity to prove himself at top level when he was withdrawn from the Middle Park Stakes on the morning of the race, having failed to recover in time from the bruised foot he suffered a couple of days previously. On paper he was Aidan O'Brien's second string behind the eventual fourth Ivan Denisovich, but he would not be one to underestimate, for he had looked a colt of real potential when winning his only two races – the same two races, incidentally, Ad Valorem had picked up prior to winning the 2004 Middle Park.

We did not see Art Museum in public until September, but his reputation preceded him to the track for his debut in a six-furlong maiden at The Curragh. He started at odds-on in a field of 26 and came home a comfortable length winner from another fancied newcomer in Alexander Alliance, who went on to record a smart win in a Listed race. It was a Listed race next for Art Museum too, back at The Curragh a fortnight later, and he took the step up in class readily in his stride, leading 100 yards or so from the finish and running on strongly to beat Leitra comfortably by two lengths. It looked a strong Listed race, despite a small

Race record

1st Laing O'Rourke Blenheim Stakes (Listed) (Curragh, September 18) 2yo 6f Good **109** (TS 63) 6 ran.
1st Bloodstock Underwriting EBF Maiden (Curragh, September 4) 2yo 6f Good **88** (TS 51) 26 ran.

Pedigree assessment

Sire Storm Cat (Storm Bird) Top-class US dirt 2yo, very lightly raced at 3. By top-class European 2yo from strong, speedy family of Royal Academy. Excellent sire, particularly of dirt performers, good record with European 2yos (Denebola, Hold That Tiger, One Cool Cat) and older 7-10f performers (Aljabr, Black Minnaloushe, Giant's Causeway, Nebraska Tornado, Sophisticat). **Dam Totemic** Won 5 of 15 starts at 2 and 3 in US, notably Honeybee S-Gr3 and a Listed event at 3. Effective on dirt at around 1m. By top-class turf/dirt performer who stayed well, from fair US family. Her 7 earlier foals include Art Museum's full-sister Cherokee, a 6f 2yo Gr3 winner on her debut but disappointing subsequently over 6-8f, plus high-class 8-9f performer Lil's Lad (by Pine Bluff). **Conclusion** Another who might prove best on dirt in time. Cherokee eventually was tried in a sprint, but Art Museum is likely to be effective over 1m.

field, and well-beaten fourth Rhythm'n Roots, the only horse to emerge from it and run again, franked the form with a Listed win and two cracking efforts when giving lumps of weight in decent nurseries.

Art Museum's sister Cherokee was seen only twice in 2005, as a pacemaker in the French 1,000 Guineas and then dropped back to six furlongs. Hopefully a better fate awaits Art Museum, although he too will have a stamina issue to address if connections are set on a Classic campaign. *GD*

Atlantic Waves (Ire) 96

b c Sadler's Wells (USA) - Highest Accolade (Shirley Heights) May 2
Owner Jaber Abdullah **Trainer** M Johnston **Breeder** Premier Bloodstock
2 starts: won **1**, second **0** third **0** **£6,239** win & place prize-money

THIS colt was much talked about after his successful debut and, although beaten on his only other start, it's well worth remembering the name for 2006. Atlantic Waves is a May foal by Sadler's Wells out of a Shirley Heights mare from a famous family. On paper, his two-year-old career should pale into insignificance beside what he achieves over middle distances as a three-year-old.

Taking to the field first in a seven-furlong maiden at Leicester on August 7, Atlantic Waves was the ninth runner and first winner among his exalted sire's 2005 juveniles. The 11-2 fourth favourite, he was always in the front rank and scored by five lengths. Runner-up Bold And Free won next time for Godolphin and third-placed Speciosa went on to take the Rockfel Stakes.

Atlantic Waves' second assignment was a Group 3 at Salisbury two months later, following a slight setback. The Racing Post Trophy was in the back of connections' minds, "if he puts up a good performance", and

Race record

5th skybet.com Autumn Stakes (Group 3) (Salisbury, October 8) 2yo 1m Good **96** (TS 96) 12 ran.

1st EBF John Virgo Maiden Stakes (Div II) (Leicester, August 7) 2yo 7f Good **89** (TS 90) 11 ran.

Pedigree assessment

Sire Sadler's Wells (Northern Dancer) Smart 7-8f winner at 2, improved into top-class 8-12f colt at 3, won Irish 2,000 Guineas-Gr1, Eclipse S-Gr1, Irish Champion S-Gr1. Outstanding sire, particularly of 3yo+ over 8-12f, also has good record with autumn 2yos. **Dam Highest Accolade** Made debut in September of 3yo season, won 1 (10f) of 3 starts. By Derby winner and very good sire with excellent broodmare sire record, out of half-sister to top-class 12f filly Awaasif (dam of Snow Bride, grand-dam of Lammtarra). Her 3 earlier foals, all by Sadler's Wells, include 10f 3yo winner Urowells. **Conclusion** Horses from this excellent family only occasionally excel at two; most do far better at 3. Certainly none of Highest Accolade's three earlier foals showed much at 2. On that basis, expect much better at 3 from Atlantic Waves, who will stay 10f and should stay 12f.

he started second favourite in a 12-runner line-up. The final furlong, however, saw him fade out of contention and into fifth behind 20-1 winner Blitzkrieg. He beat Bold And Free by less far than at Leicester.

The Racing Post Trophy was reportedly still on the agenda the following week but he did not take his place. Atlantic Waves has got something to prove, but it's far too soon to be writing him off. "He always stood out from the pack at home," said Johnston after Leicester, "but I've tried to ignore it because you knew this was going to be one for next season rather than this." *RA*

Aussie Rules (USA) 109

gr c Danehill (USA) - Last Second (Ire) (Alzao (USA)) February 6

Owner Mrs J Magnier, M Tabor, F Salman **Trainer** A P O'Brien **Breeder** Belgrave Bloodstock Ltd

4 starts: won **2**, second **1**, third **0** **£58,370** win & place prize-money

THE Somerville Tattersall winner Aussie Rules needs to improve significantly at three to make his mark at Group 1 level in Britain or Ireland, but he is from a family that gets better and better and it would be dangerous to dismiss the notion. Many of the most distinguished

Aussie Rules (far side) short-heads Killybegs in the Somerville Tattersall Stakes at Newmarket

members of the family have been trained by Sir Mark Prescott, among them the dam Last Second and Alborada. Prescott also had the younger half-sister Intrigued, who looked an Oaks filly at two but unfortunately failed to see the track in 2005.

It was a shame that injury intervened when Aussie Rules was set to be given his first chance at Group 1 level in the Gran Criterium at San

Race record

1st Somerville Tattersall Stakes (Group 3) (Newmarket, September 29) 2yo 7f Good **109** (TS 90) 9 ran.
2nd Go And Go Round Tower Stakes (Group 3) (Curragh, September 4) 2yo 6f Good **109** (TS 39) 6 ran.
4th Veuve Clicquot Vintage Stakes (Group 2) (Goodwood, July 27) 2yo 7f Soft **107** (TS 101) 7 ran.
1st Netjets Maiden (Curragh, June 25) 2yo 6f Good **89** (TS 85) 9 ran.

Pedigree assessment

Sire Danehill (Danzig) Useful 6f 2yo winner, improved at 3 into top-class sprinter, won Haydock Sprint Cup-Gr1 but also smart over 1m. Excellent sire, has done well with 2yos (inc Aussie Rules, George Washington, Golden Arrow, Horatio Nelson, Ivan Denisovich, Rumplestiltskin in 2005) and older progeny, mainly at up to 1m but capable of getting top-class 10f+ performers from stoutly bred dams. Best progeny include Aquarelliste, Banks Hill, Cacique, Desert King, Intercontinental, Landseer, Mozart, North Light, Oratorio, Rock Of Gibraltar, Westerner. **Dam Last Second** Won both starts at 2 over 6-7f, inc. Gr3 event. Won Nassau S-Gr2 and Sun Chariot S-Gr2 at 3, both over 10f, also 2nd Coronation S-Gr1 over 1m. Disappointing in 2 4yo starts. By useful 1m+ performer and good sire, particularly of fillies. Half-sister to smart fillies Alleluia, Alouette (dam of Gr1 winners Albanova, Alborada) and Arrikala, plus unplaced Jude (dam of Gr1 winners Quarter Moon, Yesterday). Her 3 earlier foals feature very useful 7f 2yo/10f 3yo winner Approach and very useful 9f 2yo winner Intrigued (both by Darshaan). **Conclusion** Superbly bred, and certainly a top-class prospect on pedigree. Family members tend to be better at 3+. Aussie Rules should be effective over 1m and has decent chance of staying 10f.

Siro, for the step up to a mile looked sure to suit him and a reproduction of his narrow Newmarket defeat of Killybegs, or even his earlier Group 3 second to Abigail Pett at The Curragh, would have given him a major chance – provided he handled the prevailing soft ground. There was a question mark in that area, for Aidan O'Brien had reported that Aussie Rules had not enjoyed the loose ground when only fourth to Sir Percy in the Vintage Stakes at Goodwood, in which he started favourite on the back of a good win at The Curragh on his debut. *GD*

Balthazaar's Gift (Ire) 112

b c Xaar - Thats Your Opinion (Last Tycoon) March 23
Owner Ryder Racing Ltd **Trainer** K A Ryan **Breeder** Pat Beirne
6 starts: won **3**, second **1**, third **0** **£99,654** win & place prize-money

KEVIN RYAN lost a Group 1 winner when Godolphin swooped for Racing Post Trophy winner Palace Episode at the end of the season, but he had recently gained a classy juvenile himself when Balthazaar's Gift was switched to him from Nick Littmoden's stable.

Littmoden had alluded to Balthazaar's Gift's potential when he was an easy winner of a Windsor maiden, and sixth place in the Gimcrack

Race record

1st Criterium de Maisons-Laffitte (Group 2) (Maisons-Laffitte, November 1) 2yo 6f Good to soft **112** (TS 93) 10 ran.

1st Newton Investment Management Rockingham Stakes (Listed) (York, October 8) 2yo 6f Good to soft **106** (TS 102) 8 ran.

12th Dubai Duty Free Mill Reef Stakes (Group 2) (Newbury, September 17) 2yo 6f Good to firm **88** (TS 79) 13 ran.

6th Scottish Equitable Gimcrack Stakes (Group 2) (York, August 17) 2yo 6f Good **96** (TS 89) 13 ran.

1st Attachmate WRQ Maiden Stakes (Windsor, July 25) 2yo 5f Good to soft **82** (TS 42) 7 ran.

2nd St.James Security Maiden Auction Stakes (Carlisle, July 15) 2yo 5f Good to firm **61** (TS 57) 6 ran.

Pedigree assessment

Sire Xaar (Zafonic) Outstanding 2yo over 6-7f, won Dewhurst S-Gr1, Prix de la Salamandre-Gr1. Showed high-class form over 8-10f at 3 and 4, gained only win in Craven S-Gr3 but Gr1 placed in Irish Champion and Eclipse S. By outstanding 2yo/miler who has done particularly well with 2yos, out of smart 2yo/sprinter from outstanding family. First foals 2002, good record with 2yos, particularly over 6-7f, sire of Balthazaar's Gift, Mystical Land, Sir Xaar, Tony James, Wake Up Maggie. **Dam Thats Your Opinion** Unraced at 2, placed over 12f on 3yo debut, unplaced in 7 subsequent starts at 3 and 4 over 8-16f. By top-class sprinter-miler and fair sire, out of dual 7-9f 2yo Listed winner. Her 2 previous foals include one unplaced on the Flat and over hurdles. **Conclusion** The two main questions with Balthazaar's Gift are a) how far will he stay, and b) will he progress at 3? His pedigree gives him a good chance of staying 1m, but also raises a slight question mark about his potential to progress. His grand-dam disappointed badly at 3, and Xaar's northern hemisphere stakes performers have tended to excel at 2, much like those of Zafonic.

behind the Ryan-trained Amadeus Wolf was a step in the right direction. But the colt beat only one home in the Mill Reef Stakes at Newbury the following month and was moved shortly afterwards.

Dropped in class a shade for a Listed race at York on his debut for his new stable, Balthazaar's Gift beat the Norfolk Stakes winner Masta Plasta in style by two and a half lengths, admittedly in receipt of 7lb. Then a month later he was stepped back up to Group 2 company for the Criterium de Maisons-Laffitte and crowned a memorable season for Ryan by providing him with his first winner in France, coming late to beat the Prix du Bois winner Gwenseb a neck. With the Cornwallis fourth Curtail a further two and a half lengths back in third and further solid yardsticks left further behind it was a cracking effort from Balthazaar's Gift, who clearly had no problem with the testing conditions and put up one of the best two-year-old performances of the year over a sprint distance.

Although the dam stayed middle distances, Ryan sees speed as Balthazaar's Gift's main asset. He reckons he will make an even better three-year-old, and indeed he might. But he may need to, for the better sprinting juveniles can be notoriously hard to place in their second season. *GD*

Best Alibi (Ire) 106

b c King's Best (USA) - Chauncy Lane (Ire) (Sadler's Wells (USA)) February 25
Owner Maktoum Al Maktoum **Trainer** Sir Michael Stoute **Breeder** Robert Scarborough
4 starts: won **1**, second **0**, third **1** **£16,941** win & place prize-money

"WE thought if he was going to go for a Group race, it might as well be a Group 1," said Joe Mercer, racing manager to Maktoum Al Maktoum, explaining why a £17,500 supplementary fee was paid to enter Best Alibi for the Racing Post Trophy rather than the Horris Hill. "We would prefer good ground though . . . we don't want a quagmire."

The press suggested Best Alibi's participation also had something to do with the £216,000 up for grabs in the Racing Post Trophy and the proximity to Sir Michael Stoute in the trainers' championship of Aidan O'Brien, who was mob-handed in the race as usual. In the event, Best Alibi got his quagmire instead of good ground and he took just £10,800 of the prize-money as he stuck on from the back into fourth of seven, but O'Brien's team managed only third, fifth and sixth, and Stoute's title was assured.

Best Alibi was not an obvious Group 1 candidate for Stoute, never having ventured out of maiden company hitherto and with three runs needed to get off the mark. He looked to be learning all the time, though, and overcame some trouble in running when he did go in at Leicester in October. The step up to one mile at Doncaster would suit him too. In going down by four lengths in the Group 1, Best Alibi showed he is worth a place in middle-distance Group events in 2006. *RA*

Race record

4th Racing Post Trophy (Group 1) (Doncaster, October 22) 2yo 1m Heavy **106** (TS 99) 7 ran.

1st EBF ladbrokes.com Reference Point Maiden Stakes (Div II) (Leicester, October 11) 2yo 7f Good to firm **83** (TS 84) 13 ran.

3rd EBF Maiden Stakes (Yarmouth, September 14) 2yo 7f Good to firm **83** (TS 76) 15 ran.

7th betfredcasino.com EBF Maiden Stakes (Sandown, August 19) 2yo 7f Soft **61** (TS 35) 8 ran.

Pedigree assessment

Sire King's Best (Kingmambo) Smart dual 7f 2yo winner, won 2,000 Guineas in 2 completed 3yo outings. By top-class 2yo/miler and excellent sire. Half-brother to several good performers, notably Arc winner Urban Sea (dam of Galileo), from very strong middle-distance family. First foals 2002, emerging as good sire, has fair record with 2yos (inc. Gr winner Dubai Surprise), but better record with 3yos (inc Gr1 winners Dubai Surprise, Proclamation, and Gr2 winner Oiseau Rare). Progeny often stay 10f or further, with help from dam. **Dam Chauncy Lane** Unraced at 2, won 2 (10-11f) of 7 starts at 3 and 4. By outstanding sire, sister to useful 10f+ colt Astor Place, very closely related to Irish 2,000 Guineas winner Fourstars Allstar and smart 5-8f US gelding Fourstardave (both by Compliance, by Northern Dancer). Her 3 previous foals (one conceived in New Zealand) include French jumps winner Clemax (by Linamix) and 6f 3yo winner Oakbridge (by Indian Ridge). **Conclusion** Has the pedigree to do better at 3, when he will stay at least 1m and probably 10f, though 12f looks just beyond him on paper.

Black Charmer (Ire) 111

b c Black Minnaloushe (USA) - Abla (Robellino (USA)) January 16
Owner A D Spence **Trainer** M Johnston **Breeder** Annalee Bloodstock and Rockhart Trading Ltd
5 starts: won **1**, second **1**, third **3** **£30,555** win & place prize-money

BLACK CHARMER may have won only once from five starts but there was improvement every time and he was close up behind the best of his contemporaries when he packed up for the season after Glorious Goodwood.

All those runs came in just under eight weeks, beating Charles Darwin in the second of his six-furlong maidens at Doncaster, then vaulting straight into Group company. Another of Aidan O'Brien's celebrity name club, Ivan Denisovich, came by him for a clear-cut triumph in the July Stakes at Newmarket but there was little in it when Black Charmer tried the same front-running tactics against Amigoni in the Anglesey Stakes at The Curragh and against a collection of useful or better colts in the seven-furlong Vintage Stakes at Goodwood. The Vintage winner, only a

Black Charmer - a Group-race winner in waiting

neck and short head in front of Black Charmer, was subsequent Dewhurst hero Sir Percy.

Black Charmer is probably bred to get a mile and there is not much to lose in giving him a shot at it, but he looked more of a speed sort in the summer as a juvenile. He also had the look of a sprinter physically. He was bought at the breeze-up sales for 40,000 guineas. *RA*

Race record

3rd Veuve Clicquot Vintage Stakes (Group 2) (Goodwood, July 27) 2yo 7f Soft **111** (TS 106) 7 ran.

2nd Dubai Duty Free Anglesey Stakes (Group 3) (Curragh, July 17) 2yo 6½f Good to firm **107** (TS 91) 5 ran.

3rd TNT July Stakes (Group 2) (Newmarket (July), July 6) 2yo 6f Good to soft **103** (TS 75) 11 ran.

1st Spinal Injuries Association Charity Raceday EBF Median Auction Maiden Stakes (Doncaster, June 12) 2yo 6f Good to firm **77** (TS 77) 13 ran.

3rd Derek Guy Lifetime In Racing Maiden Auction Stakes (Doncaster, June 4) 2yo 6f Good to firm **76** (TS 77) 16 ran.

Pedigree assessment

Sire Black Minnaloushe (Storm Cat) Won both 2yo starts over 6f, one of them Listed. At 3, won 2 (Irish 2,000 Guineas-Gr1, St James's Palace S-Gr1) of 9 starts, also 3rd Sussex S-Gr1. Unplaced all starts over 10f. By top-class 2yo/dirt performer and extremely fashionable sire of both turf and dirt performers. Half-brother to top-class 2yo/miler Pennekamp out of a high-class 2yo. First foals 2003, decent start with first 2yos, sire of US Gr3 winner Stream Cat as well as Black Charmer. **Dam Abla** Unplaced over 1m at 2 on only start. By high-class 2yo and decent sire of variety of performers, out of useful 12f filly Sans Blague, next dam 1,000 Guineas third Joking Apart. Half-sister to useful 2yo Nettle (Kris). Her only previous foal is minor US stakes winner Chenia (by Sahm). **Conclusion** Has raced so far over 6-7f, but 1m should be within his compass. Black Minnaloushe is untested yet with his 3yos, but he made good progress from 2 to 3 and should get fair proportion of milers, with some sprinters.

Blitzkrieg (Ire) 101

b g Barathea (Ire) - Eman's Joy (Lion Cavern (USA)) March 8
Owner R J Baines **Trainer** V Smith **Breeder** Rathbarry Stud
5 starts: won **2**, second **1**, third **0** **£30,801** win & place prize-money

IN JUST his second season training, former dual-code jockey Vince Smith had his first Group winner. Blitzkrieg was sent off at 20-1 against the representatives of Ballydoyle and Godolphin, among others, in the skybet.com Autumn Stakes at Salisbury, transferred from Ascot. In a 12-runner field, Blitzkrieg was drawn two, jockey Seb Sanders held him up towards the rear, guided him swiftly to the far rail and waited for a gap. Three furlongs out, he had ground to make up on six or seven rivals and two of those were directly ahead of him. All manner of challenges were being laid down as first Well Armed provided space and leader Silver Blue rolled left soon afterwards. The gap and the time to take advantage were both small but, in the words of Sanders, Blitzkrieg "was brave, put his head down and showed a nice turn of foot". The Aidan O'Brien-trained favourite Dylan Thomas was coming back at him at the finish but Blitzkrieg had a neck to spare.

The Autumn Stakes was the final leg in a story of constant improvement from Blitzkrieg, who had been gelded one day after his one previous win at 16-1 in a maiden at Epsom in July. Jamie Spencer ensured his fate after that last-gasp short-head victory, dismounting to tell Smith that the very coltish Blitzkrieg was doing only half of what he was capable of. Blitzkrieg is a rangy individual but if he makes any further improvement it will be in different hands following his sale to Hong Kong. *RA*

Race record

1st skybet.com Autumn Stakes (Group 3) (Salisbury, October 8) 2yo 1m Good **101** (TS 101) 12 ran.

2nd Romans Novice Stakes (Sandown, September 14) 2yo 7f Good to soft **95** (TS 82) 7 ran.

5th Queen's Own Yorkshire Dragoons Ladies Day Stakes (Nursery) (Doncaster, September 8) 2yo 1m Good to firm **81** (TS 52) 13 ran.

1st Hogg Robinson EBF Maiden Stakes (Epsom, July 28) 2yo 7f Good **76** (TS 76) 6 ran.

16th Strutt & Parker EBF Maiden Stakes (Newmarket (July), July 5) 2yo 7f Good **57** (TS 52) 20 ran.

Pedigree assessment

Sire Barathea (Sadler's Wells) Useful 7f winner at 2, progressed into top-class miler, won Irish 2,000 Guineas and Breeders' Cup Mile. Also showed smart form over 6f and 12f. Good record as a sire, including with 2yos (Barathea Guest, Charming Prince, Magical Romance, Opera Cape, Tobougg) and older performers mainly over 1m+ (Enrique, Pongee), also gets occasional good sprinter (Tante Rose). **Dam Eman's Joy** Unraced at 2, won 6f maiden from 7 starts at 3, also placed over 6-8f. By top-class 2yo who was later smart over 7-8f and had just sporadic success as a sire, out of very useful sprint 2yo. Half-sister to smart miler Eton Lad. Her only previous foal is Raven, unplaced at 2 and 3 over 6-8f. **Conclusion** Has already won a Gr3 event over 1m, and that should be the limit of his stamina. Pedigree suggests he should continue to show smart form at 3.

Blue Mirage (Ire) 94

b c King's Best (USA) - Catch The Blues (Ire) (Bluebird (USA)) February 22
Owner Godolphin **Trainer** Saeed Bin Suroor **Breeder** Mrs Helen Keaveney
2 starts: won **1**, second **0**, third **0** **£3,560** win & place prize-money

FEW Flat races were won by a wider margin in 2005 than the Doncaster maiden won by Blue Mirage, who made every yard and came home a very easy 14-length winner. One has to treat the form with caution, as Blue Mirage had been beaten almost as far when only fourth at Warwick on his debut, and there is a strong suspicion he handled the soft ground better than most. What's more, he was one of only four in the field to race up the far side. However, Queen's Composer, who followed him home, went on to run a series of solid races, and the Aidan O'Brien favourite James Joyce, who led the pack home on the stands' side and was third overall, further franked the form when winning a similar race next time. Blue Mirage was given quotes of 25-1 in places for the 2,000 Guineas, and he may well be one of the best prospects among those Godolphin raced themselves. The likelihood, however, is that they will have stronger Guineas candidates among their acquisitions from other stables. *GD*

Race record

1st Gibson Booth EBF October Maiden Stakes (Div II) (Doncaster, October 21) 2yo 7f Soft **94** (TS 94) 14 ran.

4th Dodie Receives Her Government Inheritance Maiden Stakes (Div I) (Warwick, September 17) 2yo 7f Good **61** (TS 45) 10 ran.

Pedigree assessment

Sire King's Best (Kingmambo) Smart dual 7f 2yo winner, won 2,000 Guineas in 2 completed 3yo outings. By top-class 2yo/miler and excellent sire. Half-brother to several good performers, notably Arc winner Urban Sea (dam of Galileo), from very strong middle-distance family. First foals 2002, emerging as good sire, has fair record with 2yos (inc. Gr winner Dubai Surprise), but better record with 3yos (inc Gr1 winners Dubai Surprise, Proclamation, and Gr2 winner Oiseau Rare). Progeny often stay 10f or further, with help from dam. **Dam Catch The Blues** Placed over 6f in 2 2yo outings, thereafter won 3 (5-7f) of 20 starts from 3 to 5. Progressive, showed best form at 4 and 5, won Ballyogan S-Gr3, placed in several Pattern sprints, notably Cork & Orrery S-Gr3 twice, Haydock Sprint Cup-Gr1. By top-class sprinter, grand-dam half-sister to Prix du Jockey-Club winner Caracolero and Betty's Secret (dam of Istabraq, Secreto). Her 3 earlier foals feature 7f 3yo winner Beacon Wood (by Woodman). **Conclusion** Has already won over 7f, but far from certain to last 1m and may prove best over 6-7f. Every encouragement on pedigree that he can progress from 2 to 3.

Carlotamix 117

See entry in the top 100 horses, page 86

Championship Point (Ire) 107

b c Lomitas - Flying Squaw (Be My Chief (USA)) February 3
Owner John Livock Bloodstock Limited **Trainer** M R Channon **Breeder** Mount Coote Stud
3 starts: won **2**, second **1**, **£45,948** win & place prize-money

CHAMPIONSHIP POINT was not seen in Britain after his win in the Chesham Stakes at York, and as that form was nothing special by the standards we are accustomed to at the Royal meeting he could easily have slipped under the radar. However, his season was not over, and closer inspection of his subsequent defeat at Deauville in August reveals he was a top-flight two-year-old after all.

A hot favourite for a 10-runner Listed race run over a mile on testing ground, his head defeat at the hands of the then unheralded Linda's Lad after a good battle must have come as a disappointment to his connections. However, what nobody could have known at the time was that the winner was Group 1 class. Linda's Lad was beaten only narrowly by a subsequent Group 1 winner, Carlotamix, in a Group 3 at Longchamp the following month, and after winning at that level on the same course he was a Group 1 winner himself at Saint-Cloud in mid-November. What's more, several of the other beaten horses at Deauville also franked the form, so Championship Point's Racing Post Rating of 107 is unlikely to be far wide of thc mark.

Championship Point had made a winning debut back in May at Newbury, a course at which Mick Channon introduces many of his best juveniles, and he had gone on to beat Global Genius and ten others in the Chesham, a race that caters principally for future middle-distance performers, since it is open exclusively to juveniles by sires who won over

Race record

2nd Criterium du Fonds Europeen de l'Elevage (Listed) (Deauville, August 20) 2yo 1m Very soft **107** (TS 76) 10 ran.

1st Chesham Stakes (Listed) (York, June 14) 2yo 7f Good to firm **89** (TS 87) 12 ran.

1st Paddy Power Supports Brooke Hospital For Animals Maiden Stakes (Div I) (Newbury, May 14) 2yo 6f Firm **83** (TS 71) 10 ran.

Pedigree assessment

Sire Lomitas (Niniski) Won both 2yo starts, thereafter top-class German 12f performer, also placed in US turf Graded races over 8-11f. By top-class stayer and good sire, out of smart German 2yo/3yo at up to 10f. Very good sire, particularly of 3yo+ over 10f+. Progeny tend to progress well with age. **Dam Flying Squaw** Smart 2yo, won 3 of 6 races, notably Moet & Chandon Rennen-Gr2, also 4th Phoenix S-Gr1. Unplaced sole run at 3. By top-class 2yo out of 6f 2yo winner, next dam very smart 6-8f filly Fluke. Her 4 earlier foals include 1m 3yo winner Flying Carpet (by Barathea). **Conclusion** Has good chance of proving effective over 10f. Dam had little chance to prove herself at 3, but family members generally do well after their 2yo season and Championship Point should continue to show smart form.

Smart prospect Championship Point wins the Chesham

ten furlongs or more. The Chesham has a chequered history, but the previous two runnings yielded Group or Grade 1 winners in Milk It Mick, Pearl Of Love and Wilko. If there was another one in the 2005 field the chances are it was Championship Point, although he may have to go abroad again. He has already shown he acts on any going. *GD*

Chenchikova (Ire) 84

b f Sadler's Wells (USA) - Kasora (Ire) (Darshaan) January 16
Owner Mrs John Magnier **Trainer** A P O'Brien **Breeder** Tower Bloodstock
1 start: won **1**, **£8,331** win & place prize-money

ANTE-POST layers are notoriously prone to over-reaction when a well-bred juvenile from a leading stable makes a winning debut, and Chenchikova is a case in point. Although she faced 15 rivals in a maiden race at Tipperary on her debut the truth of the matter is that they were a pretty ordinary bunch, and while she won nicely, by two lengths from Nautical Design, it would be impossible to rate the form anything special. Yet in at least one quarter she was immediately promoted to favouritism for the Oaks. Aidan O'Brien said afterwards that she might not run again, and that was the case, yet Chenchikova went into winter quarters still disputing favouritism in most lists with two stablemates who have shown form more than 20lb superior and are already proven at Group 1 level. While Rumplestiltskin looks unlikely to be aimed at the Oaks, it is hard to justify having Chenchikova at the same sort of odds as Alexandrova, who was beaten just a short head in the Fillies' Mile and had earlier given Nautical Design a ten-length thrashing.

Chenchikova may yet win the Oaks, for she has any amount of untapped potential and could hardly be in better hands or better bred for the job. But it requires a leap of faith to be backing her to do so before she has proven herself in better company than she met at Tipperary. *GD*

Race record

1st Irish Stallion Farms EBF Maiden (Tipperary, September 15) 2yo 7½f Yielding **84** 16 ran.

Pedigree assessment

Sire Sadler's Wells (Northern Dancer) Smart 7-8f winner at 2, improved into top-class 8-12f colt at 3, won Irish 2,000 Guineas-Gr1, Eclipse S-Gr1, Irish Champion S-Gr1. Outstanding sire, particularly of 3yo+ over 8-12f, also has good record with autumn 2yos. **Dam Kasora** Unraced. By top-class 12f performer, very good sire and outstanding broodmare sire, out of high-class 8-12f filly Kozana. Her 5 earlier foals feature Derby/dual Breeders' Cup Turf winner High Chaparral and 2005 10f 3yo winner Helena Molony (both by Sadler's Wells), plus fair 7-8f 2yo Treasure The Lady (Indian Ridge). **Conclusion** Bred to do far better at 3 than 2, and to appreciate 12f. An obvious candidate to develop into an Oaks filly.

City Of Troy 100

ch c Grand Lodge (USA) - Arazena (USA) (Woodman (USA)) January 24
Owner M Tabor, Mrs J Magnier & D Smith **Trainer** Sir Michael Stoute
Breeder Darpat S L
3 starts: won **2**, second **0**, third **0** **£17,351** win & place prize-money

CITY OF TROY probably owes his prominence in ante-post lists for the 2,000 Guineas and the Derby to the outstanding record of trainer Sir Michael Stoute in those races, for in truth his form leaves him a fair way short of the level required to win a Classic. However, that's not to say he is not a promising individual, and he was significantly shorter until meeting his first defeat when a hot favourite for the Royal Lodge Stakes at Newmarket.

He had made a big impression on his debut in a well-contested conditions race at Newbury, weaving his way through from the back after a slow start and quickening up takingly without having at all a hard race. He got his head in front on the line and beat the subsequent big sales-race winner Murfreesboro and League Champion, his performance looking all the better when one considers every one of his seven opponents was a previous winner. Then at the St Leger meeting at Doncaster he accounted for another strongish field, getting up late once again to beat previous Sandown maiden winner Art Deco by half a length after the runner-up had got first run on him.

It may pay to forgive City Of Troy his admittedly disappointing fourth to Leo in the Royal Lodge, as the tactical nature of the race did not lend itself to the come-from-behind style that had looked so good on his previous two starts. The trials will establish whether or not he is a genuine Classic contender, but he still might be. If he does not quite make the grade he still ought to have a Group race or two in him. He has the looks and pedigree to make a better three-year-old, and he has the temperament too. And he could not be in better hands. *GD*

Race record

4th totesport.com Royal Lodge Stakes (Group 2) (Newmarket, September 25) 2yo 1m Good **100** (TS 99) 8 ran.

1st Pack It In Stakes (Conditions Race) (Doncaster, September 7) 2yo 7f Good to firm **97** (TS 84) 7 ran.

1st Racing UK Conditions Stakes (Newbury, July 16) 2yo 7f Good to firm **92** (TS 71) 8 ran.

Pedigree assessment

Sire Grand Lodge (Chief's Crown) Top-class 2yo, won Dewhurst S-Gr1, later top-class 8-10f colt, won St James's Palace S-Gr1. Very good sire, has good record with 2yos (Chateau Istana, Queen's Logic, Raise A Grand) but better one with 3yos over 1m+ (Grandera, Indian Lodge, Sinndar). **Dam Arazena** Won 1 (11f at 3) of 11 starts at 2 and 3 in France, placed 4 times. By high-class 2yo who has patchy stud career but can sire genuinely top-class performers, out of daughter of 1,000 Guineas and Oaks winner Mysterious. Half-sister to dam of Grade 2 winner Quest (c by Seeking The Gold). This is her first foal. **Conclusion** On pedigree, he looks likely to be effective at a mile, with possibilities of staying slightly further. There are some talented 2yos in the pedigree, but he should be at least as effective at 3 as at 2.

Close To You (Ire) 112

b c Shinko Forest (Ire) - Maritana (USA) (Rahy (USA)) March 27

Owner Miss J A Leighs **Trainer** T G Mills **Breeder** Kevin B Lynch

7 starts: won **4**, second **0**, third **0** **£57,311** win & place prize-money

CLOSE TO YOU did not always speak up for himself, but his excited stable have made a game bid to make up the deficit. Four wins from seven starts hints strongly enough that he was well above the average, and with the last of those victories he proved himself a smart performer.

Close To You's last four outings were all on soft or good to soft ground, which connections are now adamant is against him. His first three successes, making impressive progress in mid-summer, were a maiden at Folkestone (well backed second time out), a novice stakes on the Lingfield all-weather and an auction stakes at Newbury.

The going turned soft for the last-named and Close To You coped easily the best in a strong field for that class, beating Silent Times by five lengths, but that was not the case at all in two of his three ventures in Group events afterwards. He was sixth of seven when favourite in the Solario at Sandown and seventh of eight when 20-1 in the Dewhurst. In between those reverses, however, came victory, or a share of victory, in the intercasino.com Champagne Stakes at Doncaster, where front-running Silent Times this time kept on a lot better but Close to You joined him through the final two furlongs and battled his way to parity on the line.

There was no equivocating in the response from Richard Ryan, assistant to trainer Terry Mills. "He absolutely hated the ground with a passion – we were going to pull him out but he had a good draw. He is an absolute monster when he gets fast ground and he'll be a 2,000 Guineas horse next year. He won't run on soft again. He's flying at home and beating older horses, so we knew we had something special." *RA*

Race record

7th Darley Dewhurst Stakes (Group 1) (Newmarket, October 15) 2yo 7f Good to soft **83** (TS 79) 8 ran.

1st Dead-heat intercasino.com Champagne Stakes (Group 2) (Doncaster, September 9) 2yo 7f Good to soft **112** (TS 77) 7 ran.

6th Iveco Daily Solario Stakes (Group 3) (Sandown, August 20) 2yo 7f Soft **96** (TS 81) 7 ran.

1st Happy Valley Auction Stakes (Conditions Race) (Newbury, July 24) 2yo 7f Soft **105** (TS 93) 10 ran.

1st Ladbrokes Freephone 0800 524524 Novice Stakes (Lingfield (AW), July 9) 2yo 7f Standard **73** (TS 73) 7 ran.

1st Barry Dennis Betting Shop Median Auction Maiden Stakes (Folkestone, June 24) 2yo 7f Good to firm **74** (TS 45) 11 ran.

8th carpetright.co.uk EBF Median Auction Maiden Stakes (Windsor, June 6) 2yo 6f Good to firm **64** (TS 44) 16 ran.

Pedigree assessment

Sire Shinko Forest (Green Desert) High-class sprinter in Japan, won 9 of 29 starts from 3 to 6. By top-class 6-8f and speed influence, out of high-class 10f filly Park Express. Half-brother to high-class 8-10f filly Dazzling Park (Warning). First (Irish-conceived) foals 2001, decent record with 2yos and sprinters. **Dam Maritana** Unraced. By smart 2yo/miler and very good sire, out of very useful 10f+ filly Mariella, next dam Oaks winner Monade. Her 2 earlier foals include triple 6f 2yo winner Clocking Off (Night Shift). **Conclusion** Pedigree is a combination of speed and stamina. He should stay a mile but probably no further.

Confidential Lady 108

b f Singspiel (Ire) - Confidante (USA) (Dayjur (USA)) April 4

Owner Cheveley Park Stud **Trainer** Sir Mark Prescott **Breeder** Cheveley Park Stud Ltd

7 starts: won **4**, second **1**, third **1** **£58,693** win & place prize-money

IT'S a shame that Confidential Lady failed to give her running when second favourite for the Prix Marcel Boussac at Longchamp in October. She might not have coped with Rumplestiltskin in any case, but she had

Confidential Lady makes all in Sandown's Star Stakes

beaten the runner-up Quiet Royal when an all-the-way winner of the Group 3 Prix du Calvados at Deauville on her previous start, and the time before that she had beaten the Boussac third Deveron when just touched off by Nasheej after racing alone for much of the way in the Sweet Solera Stakes at Newmarket.

In all probability she was simply over the top in the Boussac. Although she held a prominent position from the start, it was clear to connections

Race record

10th Prix Marcel Boussac - Criterium des Pouliches (Group 1) (Longchamp, October 2) 2yo 1m Good to soft **93** (TS 86) 15 ran.

1st Prix du Calvados (Group 3) (Deauville, August 20) 2yo 7f Very soft **108** (TS 105) 11 ran.

2nd Swynford Paddocks Hotel Sweet Solera Stakes (Group 3) (Newmarket (July), August 6) 2yo 7f Good **108** (TS 91) 8 ran.

1st BT Challenge Star Stakes (Listed) (Sandown, July 21) 2yo 7f Good to firm **102** (TS 84) 11 ran.

1st Award Winning Coachman Caravans Novice Stakes (Beverley, July 2) 2yo 7½f Good **87** (TS 85)6 ran.

1st EBF Zetland Median Auction Maiden Stakes (Catterick, June 29) 2yo 7f Firm **73** (TS 62) 8 ran.

3rd BT Local Business Champagne Maiden Stakes (Hamilton, June 8) 2yo 6f Good **66** (TS 52) 9 ran.

Pedigree assessment

Sire Singspiel (In The Wings) Useful 7f 2yo winner, later tough, progressive and top-class 10-12f performer, gained 5 Gr1 wins inc. Japan Cup, Dubai World Cup, Juddmonte International. By top-class 12f colt and very good sire out of top-class racemare, half-brother to Rahy. Very good sire, tends to get progressive individuals who excel over 1m+. **Dam Confidante** Placed over 7f sole 2yo start, won twice over 7f at 3, Listed placed over 1m. By outstanding sprinter out of useful half-sister to Affirmed. Half-sister to very useful 7f 2yo White Crown (by Secreto). Her 3 earlier foals include 7f 3yo winners Crown Counsel and Registrar (both by Machiavellian). **Conclusion** Has done well for a Singspiel 2yo and has the pedigree to make further progress. Certain to stay 1m, should be effective over 10f but major question mark over 12f for her.

a long way out that she was not going well, and she trailed home tenth of 15. She was entitled to have gone off the boil, for it was her seventh race in a campaign that had begun with defeat over an inadequate six furlongs at Hamilton in June and had gone on to embrace front-running wins over seven furlongs at Catterick, Beverley and Sandown.

Confidential Lady is entitled to a crack at the 1,000 Guineas, but her owners, Cheveley Park Stud, have another major contender in Fillies' Mile winner Nannina. They are also very conscious of the fact that Sir Mark Prescott seldom hits stride until June or July, in which case the Coronation Stakes may be a more realistic target. In all probability she will stay a bit further than a mile. *GD*

Cool Creek (Ire) 111

b c Desert Style (Ire) - Shining Creek (Can) (Bering) April 5
Owner Michael Pescod & Justin Dowley **Trainer** R Hannon **Breeder** Miss S Von Schilcher
10 starts: won **3**, second **2**, third **1** **£118,393** win & place prize-money

COOL CREEK stayed in the States after his ill-starred last of 12 in the Breeders' Cup Juvenile, but some sterling efforts in Britain and Ireland previously entitle him to inclusion here. In truth, although he started at

Race record

12th Lane's End Breeders' Futurity (Grade 1) (Keeneland, October 8) 2yo 1m½f Fast 12 ran.
1st Dubai Duty Free Mill Reef Stakes (Group 2) (Newbury, September 17) 2yo 6f Good to firm **111** (TS 109) 13 ran.
4th intercasino.com Champagne Stakes (Group 2) (Doncaster, September 9) 2yo 7f Good to soft **108** (TS 72) 7 ran.
2nd Tattersalls Ireland Sale Stakes (Curragh, August 20) 2yo 6f Good **105** (TS 82) 26 ran.
2nd Veuve Clicquot Vintage Stakes (Group 2) (Goodwood, July 27) 2yo 7f Soft **111** (TS 107) 7 ran.
4th TNT July Stakes (Group 2) (Newmarket (July), July 6) 2yo 6f Good to soft **102** (TS 74) 11 ran.
1st Spindrifter Conditions Stakes (Pontefract, June 27) 2yo 6f Good to firm **86** (TS 56) 5 ran.
9th Coventry Stakes (Group 2) (York, June 14) 2yo 6f Good to firm **82** (TS 73) 14 ran.
1st Federation of Bloodstock Agents Conditions Stakes (Newmarket, April 12) 2yo 5f Good to firm **78** (TS 74) 4 ran.
3rd EBF Maiden Stakes (Kempton, April 2) 2yo 5f Good to soft **76** (TS 34) 5 ran.

Pedigree assessment

Sire Desert Style (Green Desert) High class over 6-7f at both 2 and 3, won 5 of 11 starts, Gr1 placed in Phoenix and National S at 2, won 3 Gr3 races at 3. By top-class sprinter-miler and speed influence, dam half-sister to dam of top-class milers Barathea and Gossamer. Decent sire, has good record with 2yos and older horses, mainly at up to 1m, notable performers Bachir, Cape Town, Caradak, Jessica's Dream, Next Desert. **Dam Shining Creek** Winner at 2 and 3 in Italy over 1m. By top-class 12f performer and very good sire, out of useful 2yo, next dam high-class 2yo/miler Photo Flash. Shining Creek half-sister to dam of 2005 10f French stakes winners Archange d'Or and Russian Hill. Her 3 earlier foals have achieved little. **Conclusion** Should stay 1m but no further.

industry odds of only 15-2 at Belmont it was unrealistic to expect him to shine there. The distance of a mile represented unknown territory – even seven furlongs appeared to stretch him and his biggest win came back at six furlongs on his final start in Britain – and while his stable are not averse to running decent horses on the all-weather tracks, particularly at Lingfield, they had never seen fit to try Cool Creek in public on an artificial surface before.

Despite minor wins at Newmarket and Pontefract, it was not until Newmarket's July Stakes that Cool Creek established himself as a genuine Group-class juvenile with his strong-finishing fourth to Ivan Denisovich. Although beaten only narrowly by Sir Percy in the Vintage Stakes at Goodwood, the form was not that strong and seven furlongs arguably looked far enough for him. Back at six furlongs he looked better again, failing narrowly against the subsequent Cheveley Park runner-up Wake Up Maggie when a hot favourite to provide the stable with yet another valuable sales prize at The Curragh, and wearing down solid yardstick Sir Xaar near the finish of a Dubai Duty Free Mill Reef Stakes at Newbury that attracted an unusually big field but looked devoid of Classic contenders. *GD*

Cross Channel (USA) 98

ch f Giant's Causeway (USA) - Sterling Pound (USA) (Seeking The Gold (USA))
March 18
Owner Cliveden Stud **Trainer** E A L Dunlop **Breeder** Cliveden Stud Ltd
3 starts: won **1**, second **0**, third **1** **£9,923** win & place prize-money

IT WAS apparent early in his career that Ed Dunlop had a way with fillies, and his success with Ouija Board merely underlined the point. Nobody is suggesting that Cross Channel is another Ouija Board, but she's a promising filly – one of several Dunlop can look forward to in 2006.

Cross Channel was quietly fancied for the Fillies' Mile at Newmarket in September, but while her fifth of six behind Nannina, left behind in the final furlong, technically represented improved form, it was clear that more was expected of her. Dunlop is seldom one to over-hype his horses, but he had nominated the Fillies' Mile as a likely target immediately after her impressive Newmarket maiden win almost two months earlier, when she had confirmed the promise of her debut in a similar race that had worked out particularly well by settling nicely in front and storming home two and a half lengths clear of Shortest Day, with the rest six lengths and upwards further back.

With Nidhaal and Eilean Ban having shown form of a similar level at two it is hard to know quite where Cross Channel will fit into the stable's Classic plans, but there will be no shortage of options. A beautifully bred filly from a good American family, she is almost certainly capable of better. *GD*

Race record

5th Meon Valley Stud Fillies' Mile (Group 1) (Newmarket, September 24) 2yo 1m Good **98** (TS 83) 6 ran.

1st Blue Square 0800 587 0200 EBF Maiden Fillies' Stakes (Newmarket (July), July 30) 2yo 7f Good to firm **88** (TS 88) 15 ran.

3rd Brackett Green Maiden Stakes (Newmarket (July), July 15) 2yo 7f Good to firm **87** (TS 83) 18 ran.

Pedigree assessment

Sire Giant's Causeway (Storm Cat) Top-class 2yo, won all 3 races over 6-7f inc. Prix de la Salamandre-Gr1, then tough and top-class 8-10f 3yo, won 5 more Gr1 events. By outstanding US sire out of high-class US 8-9f filly. First foals 2002, quickly established as a leading sire in both Europe and US on turf and dirt. Capable of siring top-class 2yos (Shamardal, and First Samurai in US in 2005), even better record with 3yos, mainly at 8-10f (Footstepsinthesand, Maids Causeway, Mona Lisa, Shamardal). **Dam Sterling Pound** Unplaced sole 2yo start, thereafter won 5 of 16 starts at 3 and 4, notably Gr3 dirt event. By top-class 6f+ dirt performer and excellent sire out of minor stakes winner, family of Ajdal and Arazi. Her 4 earlier foals feature smart 10f winner Sabre d'Argent (by Kris S) and high-class 7f+ dirt performer Exchange Rate (Danzig). **Conclusion** Has pedigree to make good progress from 2 to 3, when she should be suited by 1m. Just an outside chance she will stay 10f.

Deveron (USA) 105

b/br f Cozzene (USA) - Cruisie (USA) (Assert) February 8

Owner Saif Ali **Trainer** C E Brittain **Breeder** Dr Kramer & Cozzene Syndicate

5 starts: won **1**, second **1**, third **2** **£41,358** win & place prize-money

DEVERON was switched to join Saeed Bin Suroor at the end of 2005 and will carry the royal blue Godolphin colours at three. Her record suggests she has limitations, for she was beaten three times in Group company

Race record

3rd Prix Marcel Boussac - Criterium des Pouliches (Group 1) (Longchamp, October 2) 2yo 1m Good to soft **105** (TS 102) 15 ran.

6th Sixty Years On Prestige Stakes (Group 3) (Goodwood, August 28) 2yo 7f Good **93** (TS 56) 9 ran.

3rd Swynford Paddocks Hotel Sweet Solera Stakes (Group 3) (Newmarket (July), August 6) 2yo 7f Good **102** (TS 85) 8 ran.

1st EBF New Ham Maiden Fillies' Stakes (Goodwood, July 28) 2yo 7f Soft **87** (TS 86) 11 ran.

2nd Brackett Green Maiden Stakes (Newmarket (July), July 15) 2yo 7f Good to firm **87** (TS 84) 18 ran.

Pedigree assessment

Sire Cozzene (Caro) Unraced at 2, top-class 8-9f turf performer in US, won Breeders' Cup Mile. Very good sire, mainly of turf performers, capable of siring smart 2yos but better record with 3yos+, mainly over 8-12f. Progeny include Alphabet Soup, Environment Friend, Running Stag, Tikkanen. **Dam Cruisie** Unplaced at 2, won 3 races at 3 on turf and dirt in US. By top-class 12f performer, half-sister to 2 Graded winners out of half-sister to smart 1m+ trio Arkadina, Blood Royal, Gregorian. Her 7 previous foals include 4 winners, among them a minor US 2yo stakes winner by Capote. **Conclusion** Fair amount of stamina in this pedigree. Deveron has good chance of staying 10f and may last 12f. Bred to progress well from 2 to 3.

Deveron wins a hot maiden at Glorious Goodwood

after her second-time-out win in a seven-furlong maiden at Glorious Goodwood. However, the Goodwood maiden could scarcely have worked out better – she had the subsequent Washington Singer winner Innocent Air in second and the Fillies' Mile runner-up Alexandrova in third – and her subsequent third behind Rumplestiltskin in the Prix Marcel Boussac at Longchamp confirmed Clive Brittain's high opinion of her. The winner was clearly better class on the day, but Deveron was beaten only two and a half lengths and had some useful rivals behind her.

It is hard to know where Deveron will fit in Godolphin's pecking order, but there may still be better to come from her. She will stay at least a mile and a quarter. *GD*

Dickensian (Ire) 99

br c Xaar - Cappella (Ire) (College Chapel) March 6
Owner Godolphin **Trainer** Saeed Bin Suroor **Breeder** Mrs Ellen Lyons
4 starts: won **2**, second **1**, third **0** **£11,032** win & place prize-money

THE stallion Xaar enjoyed big-race successes with 2005 two-year-olds Balthazaar's Gift, Sir Xaar and Wake Up Maggie, and Dickensian was made joint-favourite to give him another in the Horris Hill Stakes at Newbury in October. It did not happen. The Godolphin colt never managed better than mid-division, ending up only fractionally worse than his main market rivals Stepping Up and Yasoodd but giving no cause for cheer.

Perhaps the good to soft ground at Newbury was too much for him. Either way, Dickensian looked highly promising before that, winning two of his three starts and improving each time. The wins came in a six-furlong maiden at Chepstow in June and a seven-furlong novice stakes at Leicester in September, in the latter facing only four rivals and starting 11-10 but leaving a big impression with the way he breezed home in front of the Newmarket maiden winner Tell.

Even if Dickensian gets a mile, he may not be one for the Guineas judged on the conclusion of Simon Crisford, Godolphin's racing manager, that "there were no obvious Classic contenders from this season's two-year-old crop" when he announced new purchases in November. *RA*

Race record

8th Stan James Horris Hill Stakes (Group 3) (Newbury, October 22) 2yo 7f Good to soft **95** (TS 59) 13 ran.

1st EBF Kegworth Novice Stakes (Leicester, September 19) 2yo 7f Good to firm **99** (TS 90) 5 ran.

2nd EBF Rollits Solicitors And Peter Stockill Limited Novice Stakes (Beverley, July 18) 2yo 7½f Good **93** (TS 90) 6 ran.

1st Saltwell Signs Maiden Stakes (Chepstow, June 29) 2yo 6f Good **85** (TS 60) 15 ran.

Pedigree assessment

Sire Xaar (Zafonic) Outstanding 2yo over 6-7f, won Dewhurst S-Gr1, Prix de la Salamandre-Gr1. Showed high-class form over 8-10f at 3 and 4, gained only win in Craven S-Gr3 but Gr1 placed in Irish Champion and Eclipse Stakes. By outstanding 2yo/miler who has done particularly well with 2yos, out of smart 2yo/sprinter from outstanding family. First foals 2002, good record with 2yos, particularly over 6-7f, sire of Balthazaar's Gift, Mystical Land, Sir Xaar, Tony James, Wake Up Maggie. **Dam Cappella** Won 2 (5f) of 8 2yo starts, placed once over 6f from 9 3yo starts. By high-class sprinter and speed influence, from speedy family. Her 2 earlier foals comprise 6f 2yo/3yo winner Azuree (by Almutawakel) and 10f winner Red Birr (Bahhare). **Conclusion** Lots of speed and precocity in this pedigree. Has already won over 7f, but on pedigree he is more likely to be a sprinter than a miler.

Donna Blini 110

See entry in the top 100 horses, page 122

Dylan Thomas (Ire) 101

b c Danehill (USA) - Lagrion (USA) (Diesis) April 23

Owner Mrs John Magnier & M Tabor **Trainer** A P O'Brien

Breeder Tower Bloodstock

4 starts: won **2**, second **1**, third **0** **£101,984** win & place prize-money

DYLAN THOMAS is the sort of strapping son of Danehill that should develop into a fine three-year-old, and he didn't do badly at two either. Making his debut, at the end of June, over an extended seven furlongs immediately marked him down as a different type to his half-sister Queen's Logic, a top-class sprinting two-year-old in 2001, but he showed a degree of precocity in justifying favouritism in that maiden at Tipperary and followed up with a valuable prize at Leopardstown in September.

The latter was landed after some uncomfortable moments, as Dylan Thomas went left and then badly right, but the form justified his inclusion in Group races thereafter. Both were at a mile and although he was a beaten favourite in the Autumn Stakes at Salisbury, his rallying effort after taking a keen hold got him to within a neck of winner Blitzkrieg. Dylan Thomas was far less competitive when 5-1 third favourite on heavy going in the Racing Post Trophy at Doncaster two weeks later, but O'Brien had warned that better ground would suit him.

Dylan Thomas shapes as if he will get beyond a mile. There are mixed signals for stamina from the pedigree, with plenty who stayed middle distances to be put against the far more illustrious achievements of Queen's Logic and the dam's brother Pure Genius, who was runner-up in a Middle Park. The dam herself was a fair middle-distance maiden who did half of her racing in headgear. *RA*

Race record

6th Racing Post Trophy (Group 1) (Doncaster, October 22) 2yo 1m Heavy **101** (TS 90) 7 ran.

2nd skybet.com Autumn Stakes (Group 3) (Salisbury, October 8) 2yo 1m Good **100** (TS 100) 12 ran.

1st Irish Breeders Foal Levy Stakes (Leopardstown, September 10) 2yo 7f Good to yielding **101** (TS 97) 12 ran.

1st Irish Stallion Farms EBF Maiden (Tipperary, June 30) 2yo 7½f Firm **87** 10 ran.

Pedigree assessment

Sire Danehill (Danzig) Useful 6f 2yo winner, improved at 3 into top-class sprinter, won Haydock Sprint Cup-Gr1 but also smart over 1m. Excellent sire, has done well with 2yos (inc Aussie Rules, George Washington, Golden Arrow, Horatio Nelson, Ivan Denisovich, Rumplestiltskin in 2005) and older progeny, mainly at up to 1m but capable of getting top-class 10f+ performers from stoutly bred dams. Best progeny include Aquarelliste, Banks Hill, Cacique, Desert King, Intercontinental, Landseer, Mozart, North Light, Oratorio, Rock Of Gibraltar, Westerner. **Dam Lagrion** Unraced at 2, placed over 10-13f at 3 and 4, very modest, often blinkered. By top-class 2yo and very good sire, particularly of fillies. Half-sister to smart 2yo Pure Genius. Her 7 earlier foals feature top-class 6f 2yo Queen's Logic (by Grand Lodge); most of the rest were modest. **Conclusion** Likely to be effective over 1m. On pedigree, he is not the most obvious candidate to make substantial progress from 2 to 3, though it is worth remembering injury prevented Queen's Logic from proving herself fully at 3.

Final Verse 106

b c Mark Of Esteem (Ire) - Tamassos (Dance In Time (Can)) February 22

Owner Athos Christodoulou **Trainer** Sir Michael Stoute **Breeder** A Christodoulou

4 starts: won **1**, second **2**, third **0** **£19,942** win & place prize-money

FINAL VERSE had questions to answer when he trailed in last of four in a Newmarket conditions stakes just three weeks after his promising debut success at Doncaster, when he was his stable's first juvenile winner of the season. However, by the end of the season he had redeemed himself to such an extent that we have little hesitation in recommending him as a colt to keep on the right side of in 2006.

His second to Prince Of Light under a big weight in a strongly contested nursery at York's Ebor meeting represents high-class form of its type, and he went on to run even better when upped to Group 3 company in the Horris Hill Stakes at Newbury at the back-end, finding only the Ballydoyle-based raider Hurricane Cat too good in a field of 13, despite starting slowly and looking green still under pressure. Final Verse got pretty warm both at York and Newbury, but it did not appear to have an adverse effect on his performance. On the contrary, he ran his two best races.

What makes Final Verse a particularly attractive proposition as a three-year-old is his pedigree, for his dam Tamassos, a 12-furlong winning half-sister to the so-called 'stun gun' victim Ile de Chypre, has produced a host of winners in a long and distinguished career at stud, among them the good middle-distance performers Carry The Flag and Posidonas. The family nearly all improve with age and two-year-old wins are usually a bonus. *GD*

Race record

2nd Stan James Horris Hill Stakes (Group 3) (Newbury, October 22) 2yo 7f Good to soft **106** (TS 71) 13 ran.

2nd Irwin Mitchell Solicitors Stakes (Nursery) (York, August 16) 2yo 6f Good **99** (TS 97) 17 ran.

4th Lexus Conditions Stakes (Newmarket (July), July 29) 2yo 7f Good **82** (TS 81) 4 ran.

1st St Johns Ambulance Maiden Stakes (Doncaster, July 7) 2yo 6f Good **79** (TS 82) 16 ran.

Pedigree assessment

Sire Mark Of Esteem (Darshaan) Won 7f maiden at 2, top-class miler at 3, won 2,000 Guineas-Gr1, Celebration Mile-Gr2, Queen Elizabeth II S-Gr1. By top-class 12f colt and very good sire, out of unraced half-sister to Gr1 winner Local Talent and Gr2 winner Local Suitor. Decent stallion, sires occasional talented 2yo (notably Sir Percy in 2005) but much better record with 3yos+, mainly over 8-12f (notably Ameerat, High Accolade). **Dam Tamassos** Winner over 10f at 3. Very closely related to top-class 10f performer Ile de Chypre (by Ile de Bourbon). Her 13 previous foals feature top-class 12f performer Posidonas and one-time useful 12f colt Maniatis (both by Slip Anchor), plus smart 10-12f horse Carry The Flag (Tenby) and useful 12f colt Zalongo **Conclusion** Bred along very similar lines to Posidonas, from a family whose members tend to progress well with age and stay at least 10f. Final Verse should do likewise.

Fire And Rain (Fr) 95

b c Galileo (Ire) - Quatre Saisons (Fr) (Homme De Loi (Ire)) April 21
Owner Michael Tabor **Trainer** A P O'Brien **Breeder** Whitewood Stables
1 start: won **1**, **£6,981** win & place prize-money

NEWMARKET maidens vary considerably in quality – even those run at the big autumn meetings – but we are confident that the mile race won by Fire And Rain on Cheveley Park day was a strong one. Third

Fire And Rain makes a winning debut at Newmarket

favourite for a race in which his stable's subsequent Group 1 winners Black Sam Bellamy and Powerscourt were both beaten, Fire And Rain looked as if he was going to have to play second fiddle to market leader Mashaahed when the unlucky Newbury sixth was seemingly going much the better two out, but the further they went the stronger he looked. Having hit the front inside the final furlong Fire And Rain was firmly in charge at the finish. The winning margin was a length, and there were another five back to subsequent Houghton Stakes runner-up Red Rocks.

Kieren Fallon spoke glowingly at Newmarket of both Fire And Rain and the stable's earlier winner Aussie Rules, and both look set to go on to much better things. Fire And Rain does not look the sort who is going to do anything very quickly, and he is sure to appreciate stepping up to middle distances. *GD*

Race record

1st Macmillan Cancer Relief Coffee Morning Maiden Stakes (Newmarket, September 29) 2yo 1m Good **95** (TS 87) 16 ran.

Pedigree assessment

Sire Galileo (Sadler's Wells) Impressive winner of only 2yo start, outstanding 12f 3yo, won Derby, Irish Derby, King George, also 2nd Irish Champion S over 10f. Superb pedigree, by outstanding sire out of Arc heroine. First foals 2003, has sired 7f Listed winner Innocent Air, should do far better with 3yos, mainly over 10f+. **Dam Quatre Saisons** Unraced, by French 10f Gr1 winner. Half-sister to dam of 2yo Gr1 winner Beckett (Fairy King) out of half-sister to Gr1 winners Entrepreneur (Sadler's Wells) and Exclusive (Polar Falcon, dam of Chic) plus Oaks 2nd Dance A Dream (Sadler's Wells). Her 2 earlier foals include French sprint winner Festivite. **Conclusion** Bred along similar lines to Dance A Dream and Entrepreneur. Has good chance of lasting 12f and the pedigree to make good progress from 2 to 3.

Flashy Wings 111

ch f Zafonic (USA) - Lovealoch (Ire) (Lomond (USA)) March 13
Owner Jaber Abdullah **Trainer** M R Channon **Breeder** Redmyre Bloodstock and S Hillen
6 starts: won **4**, second **1**, third **1** **£180,159** win & place prize-money

FLASHY WINGS spent almost the entire season at, or near, the head of betting for the 1,000 Guineas. "There's been a lot of hype about her," said Mick Channon, her trainer, after a successful maiden debut at Newmarket in April, and there would be a lot more. It was not long before she added substantial achievement.

Channon was unable to contain his enthusiasm for Flashy Wings as she followed up in a conditions stakes at Newbury and the Queen Mary at York, a three-length dismissal of fellow co-favourite Salut D'Amour and two other Listed winners in the latter confirming that he had made no mistake in his impressions.

There were worries about her wellbeing before the Queen Mary, but worries in the betting market rather than for her trainer, Channon pointing out how some stiffness the day after a piece of work can get blown out of all proportion. Those who laid Flashy Wings were swiftly confounded.

Channon's 1998 and 2001 two-year-old fillies Bint Allayl and Queen's Logic were by now being mentioned every time that Flashy Wings was, and the latest star followed the same route as her predecessors after the Royal meeting by going to York for the Jaguar Cars Lowther Stakes, in which she had to carry a penalty. La Chunga, another impressive scorer

Race record

3rd Sky Bet Cheveley Park Stakes (Group 1) (Newmarket, September 29) 2yo 6f Good **108** (TS 94) 10 ran.
2nd Watership Down Stud Sales Race (Newbury, September 17) 2yo 6½f Good to firm **103** 23 ran.
1st Jaguar Cars Lowther Stakes (Group 2) (York, August 18) 2yo 6f Good to firm **111** (TS 110) 6 ran.
1st Queen Mary Stakes (Group 2) (York, June 15) 2yo 5f Good to firm **110** (TS 110) 17 ran.
1st Sanctuary Group Fillies' Conditions Stakes (Newbury, May 13) 2yo 5f Good to firm **100** (TS 69) 3 ran.
1st Letheby & Christopher Supports Stable Lads Canteen Maiden Fillies' Stakes (Newmarket, April 13) 2yo 5f Good to firm **79** (TS 81) 13 ran.

Pedigree assessment

Sire Zafonic (Gone West) Outstanding 2yo, won all 4 races over 6-7f inc. Prix Morny-Gr1, Prix de la Salamandre-Gr1, Dewhurst S-Gr1. Won 2,000 Guineas in short 3yo campaign. Decent sire, particularly of 2yos (Count Dubois, Flashy Wings, Xaar, Zipping) and 6-9f performers (Dupont, Iffraaj, Pacino, Zafeen, Zee Zee Top). **Dam Lovealoch** Won over 7f at 2, later a useful 8-10f filly. By 2,000 Guineas winner who had just sporadic success as a sire, out of fairly useful 11f+ filly. Her 6 earlier foals include 3 3yo Flat winners in France/Italy. **Conclusion** Talented 2yos by her sire often fail to sustain their form, but the dam was progressive and most of her foals have not been precocious. Balancing this, Flashy Wings is bred to show smart form over around 1m at 3 but other fillies may have more scope for improvement.

at the Royal meeting, and Aidan O'Brien's maiden winner Beauty Bright were the only serious rivals in the betting and the race, with Flashy Wings disputing the lead three furlongs out and looking authoritative, although the winning margin was only a length.

Channon was by now speculating that dropping her in for a later challenge would suit, and was thoroughly convinced after Flashy Wings met her first defeat, at odds of 4-9 in a field of 23 no less, when chasing the bumper pot in the Watership Down Stud Sales Race at Newbury in September. Flashy Wings ran because she had her ground and lost because she was idling in front in the centre of the course and left Expensive to mug her on the stand rail.

That race was some way below Flashy Wings' best form, but the Cheveley Park 12 days later was much more like it and she left the best impression as well, very strong at the finish after finally getting that waiting ride, though ending up only third was something of a dampener. Beaten, but not by far – two necks – Flashy Wings ended the season at 12-1 for the 1,000 Guineas, having been as short as 7-1 after the Lowther.

Flashy Wings was turned over on her only start beyond six furlongs (six and a half) but it will be surprising if she does not get a mile at three, judged both on pedigree and performance. Her trainer repeatedly made the point that, being a daughter of Zafonic, she would not be risked on soft ground. Flashy Wings looks a realistic Guineas contender, though as connections and commentators were all quick to point out, the sad experience of Bint Allayl and Queen's Logic shows that getting to the track on Guineas day cannot be taken for granted. *RA*

Frost Giant (USA) 108

ch c Giant's Causeway (USA) - Takesmybreathaway (USA) (Gone West (USA))
February 22
Owner Michael Tabor **Trainer** A P O'Brien **Breeder** J M J Stables Corporation
2 starts: won **1**, second **0**, third **1** **£32,827** win & place prize-money

COINCIDENCE or calculation marks Frost Giant out among the host of promising two-year-olds sent out by Aidan O'Brien in 2005. He won the Group 3 Killavullan Stakes at Leopardstown at the end of October and so, 12 months earlier, did another son of Giant's Causeway, the subsequent 2,000 Guineas winner Footstepsinthesand.

Both colts made their debuts less than two weeks earlier, though Frost Giant did not win his, taking third in a Doncaster maiden. That was on soft ground and the Killavullan was on heavy, with Frost Giant establishing the upper hand in the war of attrition from one and a half furlongs out, the other four runners strung out behind.

One of the differences between Frost Giant and Footstepsinthesand was a lack of market support for the younger colt, who started third favourite in both his races.

Frost Giant must stay a mile judged on his hard-working win in the mud over seven furlongs, but a mile and a quarter might be the limit judged on pedigree. *RA*

Race record

1st Killavullan Stakes (Group 3) (Leopardstown, October 31) 2yo 7f Heavy **108** (TS 92) 5 ran.

3rd Gibson Booth EBF October Maiden Stakes (Div I) (Doncaster, October 21) 2yo 7f Soft **69** (TS 60) 14 ran.

Pedigree assessment

Sire Giant's Causeway (Storm Cat) Top-class 2yo, won all 3 races over 6-7f inc. Prix de la Salamandre-Gr1, then tough and top-class 8-10f 3yo, won 5 more Gr1 events. By outstanding US sire out of high-class US 8-9f filly. First foals 2002, quickly established as a leading sire in both Europe and US on turf and dirt. Capable of siring top-class 2yos (Shamardal, and First Samurai in US in 2005), even better record with 3yos, mainly at 8-10f (Footstepsinthesand, Maids Causeway, Mona Lisa, Shamardal). **Dam Takesmybreathaway** Unplaced in both 2yo starts over 6f. By top-class dirt runner and highly rated sire. Very closely related to very smart 7-8f performer Mutakddim (Seeking The Gold) out of half-sister to Breeders' Cup Juvenile winner Rhythm (Mr Prospector). This is her first foal. **Conclusion** From an excellent US family with fair amount of speed. Although the dam is bred along very similar lines to Rhythm, family members tend to do best at 3+ and Frost Giant should do likewise. He has a good chance of lasting 1m but is unlikely to get much further.

George Washington 121

See entry in the top 100 horses, page 152

Gin Jockey (Fr) 98

b c Soviet Star (USA) - Singing Lark (Fr) (Pampabird) April 23
Owner Bob Lalemant **Trainer** R Hannon **Breeder** P Chedeville
2 starts: won **2**, **£28,656** win & place prize-money

GIN JOCKEY still has a bit to prove, but he has done everything asked of him so far and at this stage looks the best Classic prospect among Richard Hannon's colts. On his racecourse debut he won a maiden at Newmarket's July Meeting that has a very strong tradition, making the most of the near-side rail and just holding on from the subsequent Royal Lodge second Kilworth after leading throughout. The following month he was sent to Deauville for a race catering for French-breds in which he was one of six previous winners, and he won again, albeit only narrowly from the filly Stadore, the pair finishing clear.

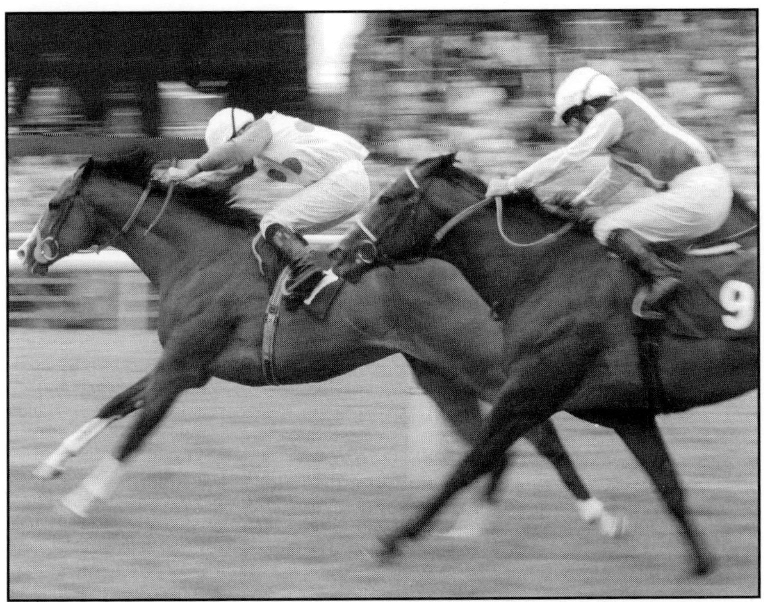

Gin Jockey makes all on Newmarket's July course

The Deauville race, in which Gin Jockey again helped force it throughout, worked out well, with the runner-up going on to win a Listed race and fourth-placed Fauvelia finishing second in a Group 1, but the winner

Race record

1st Prix des Yearlings (French-Bred) (Deauville, August 10) 2yo 7f Good **98** (TS 86) 7 ran.

1st Strutt & Parker EBF Maiden Stakes (Newmarket (July), July 5) 2yo 7f Good **83** (TS 79) 20 ran.

Pedigree assessment

Sire Soviet Star (Nureyev) Smart 2yo winner, later tough and top-class 6-8f performer. Decent sire, can get smart 2yos but most of his talented progeny best at 7-10f (Ashkalani, Democratic Deficit, Sensation, Soviet Line, Starborough, Starcraft, Volochine among them). Gets occasional good sprinter and 12f+ horse. **Dam Singing Lark** Unplaced in France. By smart French 8-10f performer, full-sister to Arc winner Subotica. Her 2 earlier foals include French placed 2yo Singing Princess (Roi Gironde). **Conclusion** His distance looks to be around 8-9f. The sire tends to get progressive progeny, while the dam's family is not precocious, so expect this one to make a bigger impact at 3.

himself was not seen out again, pulled back muscles persuading connections to put him away for the winter and give him plenty of time.

The Craven Stakes looks a likely starting point for Gin Jockey in 2006, and if he improves enough to win there Hannon will have a live candidate for the 2,000 Guineas, which he has already won three times. The French equivalent is an obvious alternative, and he ought to stay a bit further too, as his dam was a sister to the Arc winner Subotica. *GD*

Godfrey Street 107

ch c Compton Place - Tahara (Ire) (Caerleon (USA)) April 21
Owner J A Leek and Partners **Trainer** R Hannon **Breeder** Miss S N Ralphs
11 starts: won **3**, second **2**, third **1** **£67,913** win & place prize-money

GODFREY STREET'S first season saw him repay his purchase price ten times over. Having been bought for 6,000 guineas as a yearling, he won £67,913 in prize money and another 78,000 guineas was turned down when, after 11 starts, he made his final appearance of the year in the Newmarket sale ring.

Confirming that confounding expectations was what he was all about in 2005, consider this observation from Richard Hannon junior after Godfrey Street gained the first of two wins on the Lingfield Polytrack, on his second outing. "He's got a lot of speed," said Hannon, "and wants very quick ground." The first part of that statement rang as true in September as it had in May, but easily his biggest success and best form came when Godfrey Street coped the best of nine runners in the Polypipe Flying Childers Stakes on heavy ground at Doncaster. It was Godfrey Street's second run of the meeting, three days after his close fifth in the St Leger

Race record

7th skybet.com Cornwallis Stakes (Group 3) (Salisbury, October 8) 2yo 5f Good **101** (TS 92) 12 ran.

1st Polypipe Flying Childers Stakes (Group 2) (Doncaster, September 10) 2yo 5f Heavy **107** (TS 103) 9 ran.

5th £300,000 St Leger Yearling Stakes (Doncaster, September 7) 2yo 6f Good to firm **91** (TS 84) 22 ran.

2nd Costcutter Roses Stakes (Listed) (York, August 17) 2yo 5f Good **103** (TS 79) 10 ran.

1st Celebrate Your Wedding At Lingfield Racecourse Novice Stakes (Lingfield (AW), August 5) 2yo 5f Standard **94** (TS 63) 7 ran.

3rd Vodafone Racegoers Club Nursery (Handicap) (Goodwood, July 30) 2yo 6f Good to soft **83** (TS 85) 13 ran.

6th Betfair Molecomb Stakes (Group 3) (Goodwood, July 26) 2yo 5f Good to soft **92** (TS 92) 15 ran.

24th Weatherbys Super Sprint (Newbury, July 16) 2yo 5f Good to firm **36** (TS 13) 25 ran.

2nd Warwick International Novice Stakes (Chester, June 25) 2yo 5f Good **83** (TS 73) 7 ran.

1st Lingfield Leisure Club Median Auction Maiden Stakes (Div I) (Lingfield (AW), May 24) 2yo 5f Standard **81** (TS 80) 10 ran.

4th EBF Maiden Stakes (Kempton, March 26) 2yo 5f Good to soft **61** (TS 63) 10 ran.

Pedigree assessment

Sire Compton Place (Indian Ridge) Smart sprint 2yo, won July Cup-Gr1 at 3. By top-class sprinter and excellent sire out of fair 2yo, half-brother to Grade 3 winner Mantles Star (Beveled). Decent record with 2yos and sprinters, among them Boogie Street, Hunter Street, If Paradise, Pacific Pride, Pleasure Place, Shifting Place. **Dam Tahara** Unraced at 2, unplaced in 2 starts at 3. By top-class 10-12f colt and very good sire of variety of performers, out of high-class 2yo/miler Tarwiya. Family of smart sprint 2yo Blue Dakota (Namid). Her 4 earlier foals include 2 3yo winners in Europe. **Conclusion** Undoubtedly a sprinter. Bred to be reasonably precocious, but there is sufficient encouragement on both sides of his pedigree that he can continue to show smart form at 3.

Yearling Stakes, the second time he'd been below his best over six furlongs from as many attempts.

Godfrey Street's nearest victim, at three-quarters of a length, at Doncaster was Hunter Street, who met him on three other occasions. Results in the Molecomb Stakes and the Cornwallis Stakes saw them finish the other way round but confirmed that the pair were closely matched, in the latter race with Godfrey Street carrying a 7lb penalty and getting a poor run. Their fourth encounter was at Tattersalls where Hunter Street also failed to meet his reserve, although he was sold privately afterwards to continue his career in the United States.

The urge to cash in with horses of this type is understandable, as mentioned in last year's Flat Horses, when considering the record of recent Flying Childers winners. Sprinters of this grade are notoriously difficult to place in their second seasons in Britain. Connections of Chateau Istana, the 2004 winner, didn't even try, but gained a spectacular reward in November when winning a HK$1m (£75,000) handicap at Sha Tin. The horse was rather less fortunate in doing so under the new name Chateau King Prawn. *RA*

Golden Arrow (Ire) 108

b c Danehill (USA) - Cheal Rose (Ire) (Dr Devious (Ire)) February 13
Owner Dr R Lambe **Trainer** D K Weld **Breeder** Mrs Monica Hackett
4 starts: won **1**, second **1**, third **1** **£73,925** win & place prize-money

FEW two-year-olds run to the level that Golden Arrow appeared to achieve first time out at Cork in June. The only newcomer in a field of six for a six-furlong Listed race that attracted five previous winners, he came from off the pace to lead before the furlong pole and then scoot three lengths clear of previous Gowran Park winner Duff, with subsequent Group winners Ugo Fire and Ajigolo further back. As trainer Dermot Weld said, "he knew his job."

While Golden Arrow failed to go on and win a Group race himself, and in the course of three subsequent outings improved by only a few pounds on Racing Post Ratings, he was highly tried, twice coming up against George Washington. Weld reportedly retains the highest hopes for him.

Beaten little more than two lengths into fourth in the Railway Stakes at The Curragh later in June, for which he was supplemented, Golden Arrow got marginally closer when stepped up to Group 1 company and upped to seven furlongs for the National Stakes on the same course in September, a race in which his trainer has a fine record. He was flattered a little to run the slow-starting winner to two lengths, but he stayed on best of the others to take second inside the final furlong and delighted Weld, who hailed the winner as "an exceptional horse" and had no hesitation in nominating the 2,000 Guineas as his own colt's target. *GD*

Race record

2nd Laing O'Rourke National Stakes (Group 1) (Curragh, September 18) 2yo 7f Good **108** (TS 107) 7 ran.

3rd Go And Go Round Tower Stakes (Group 3) (Curragh, September 4) 2yo 6f Good **104** (TS 34) 6 ran.

4th Anheuser-Busch Adventure Parks Railway Stakes (Group 2) (Curragh, June 26) 2yo 6f Good to firm **98** (TS 61) 5 ran.

1st Kerry Spring Water Rochestown Stakes (Listed) (Cork, June 12) 2yo 6f Good **104** 6 ran.

Pedigree assessment

Sire Danehill (Danzig) Useful 6f 2yo winner, improved at 3 into top-class sprinter, won Haydock Sprint Cup-Gr1 but also smart over 1m. Excellent sire, has done well with 2yos (inc Aussie Rules, George Washington, Golden Arrow, Horatio Nelson, Ivan Denisovich, Rumplestiltskin in 2005) and older progeny, mainly at up to 1m but capable of getting top-class 10f+ performers from stoutly bred dams. Best progeny include Aquarelliste, Banks Hill, Cacique, Desert King, Intercontinental, Landseer, Mozart, North Light, Oratorio, Rock Of Gibraltar, Westerner. **Dam Cheal Rose** Placed twice over 7f from 6 starts at 2, placed twice over 7-8f from 10 starts at 4. Tough, showed fair amount of ability despite failing to win. By top-class 2yo and Derby winner, half-sister to smart sprint 2yo Buffalo Berry (Sri Pekan) out of very close relative of top-class sprinter Nabeel Dancer. This is her first foal. **Conclusion** Already proven at 7f, but not certain to stay much further.

Gwenseb (Fr) 107

ch f Green Tune (USA) - La Popesse (USA) (St Jovite (USA)) April 16
Owner Wertheimer Et Frere **Trainer** C Laffon-Parias **Breeder** Mme M-T & G Geffrelot
7 starts: won **3**, second **2**, third **1** **£93,050** win & place prize-money

THE dam La Popesse was a middle-distance winner, ploughing through the mud over an extended mile and a half for her final win, and her first two French runners were a middle-distance/jumps winner and a Green Tune colt who made his debut over a mile and a quarter before winning once over nine furlongs. A second visit to the 1994 French Guineas winner Green Tune, however, produced one of the season's top two-year-old sprinters in France in the three-time winner Gwenseb.

Making her debut in mid-May, Gwenseb had four races in just over six weeks and won three of them, namely a newcomers race at Longchamp, a Listed race at Longchamp and the Prix du Bois at Chantilly. She had impressed sufficiently to start 8-11 in the last-named Group 3.

Six furlongs at Maisons-Laffitte, however, proved a less happy hunting ground and Gwenseb's customary attempts to come from off the pace resulted in only minor rewards in both the Robert Papin (as 6-4 favourite) and the Eclipse. By the Criterium de Maisons-Laffitte in November,

Golden Arrow makes a stylish winning debut at Cork

Gwenseb's star had fallen far enough for her to start the longest priced of three runners sent out by Carlos Laffon-Parias. There was a marked upturn in fortunes as she beat her stablemates, but she failed by a neck to reel in British challenger Balthazaar's Gift. Soon pushed along in rear, Gwenseb was finally running as her pedigree suggested, as if ready for a step up in trip. *RA*

Race record

2nd Criterium de Maisons-Laffitte (Group 2) (Maisons-Laffitte, November 1) 2yo 6f Good to soft **107** (TS 89) 10 ran.

6th Prix Eclipse (Group 3) (Maisons-Laffitte, September 30) 2yo 6f Good **99** (TS 97) 9 ran.

3rd Prix Robert Papin (Group 2) (Maisons-Laffitte, July 24) 2yo 5½f Good **100** (TS 43) 9 ran.

1st Prix du Bois (Group 3) (Chantilly, July 3) 2yo 5f Good **103** (TS 95) 7 ran.

1st Prix La Fleche (Listed) (Longchamp, June 16) 2yo 5f Good **102** (TS 94) 6 ran.

2nd Prix du Mont de Po (Chantilly, May 27) 2yo 5f Good **87** (TS 60) 6 ran.

1st Prix Port-Royal (Unraced) (Longchamp, May 19) 2yo 5f Good to soft **85** (TS 77) 9 ran.

Pedigree assessment

Sire Green Tune (Green Dancer) Useful 6f 2yo winner, top-class miler at 3 and 4, won Poule d'Essai des Poulains, Prix d'Ispahan. By top-class 2yo and very good middle-distance sire, half-brother to top-class 2yo/sprinter Pas de Reponse and smart 2yo Didyme, family of Storm Bird. Good sire, decent record with 2yos in second half of season, better record with 3yos, mainly over 8-10f.
Dam La Popesse Won 3 (10f at 2, 11-13f at 3) of 22 starts in 3 seasons. By top-class 12f performer but modest sire, out of half-sister to 2yo Group 1 winner Will Dancer (by Green Dancer), from good French family of mainly 1m+ performers. Her 2 previous foals are 9f 3yo winner Les Annees Pop (Green Tune) and triple 10-12f 3yo winner Pop Art (Bering), now a useful French jumper.
Conclusion Bred to stay 1m, but not certain to stay that far as she has shown more speed than her background indicates.

Heatseeker (Ire) 107

ch c Giant's Causeway (USA) - Rusty Back (USA) (Defensive Play (USA))
January 22
Owner Rick Barnes **Trainer** David Wachman **Breeder** Richard F Barnes
3 starts: won **2**, second **0**, third **1** **£40,286** win & place prize-money

THE expected good publicity from Damson failed to materialise in her second season but trainer David Wachman had some fine standard-bearers nevertheless in 2005 thanks to the likes of Fracas, Indesatchel and Luas Line. And 15 two-year-old wins give plenty of hope for the future.

Heatseeker supplied two of those successes, in a six-furlong maiden at Naas in July and an £11,542 race over an extended seven at Tipperary in August, but it was his final start and first defeat that demonstrated most clearly that he should be a horse to reckon with in good races in 2006. The National Stakes was dominated in the betting by George Washington, who started 2-11, with Heatseeker the second choice at 9-1. Heatseeker never looked like winning, caught flat-footed well over two furlongs out and appearing green, but he stuck to his guns to finish third of seven to the hotpot, beaten two and a half lengths, and that suggested he can develop into a smart sort next year.

Race record

3rd Laing O'Rourke National Stakes (Group 1) (Entire Colts & Fillies) (Curragh, September 18) 2yo 7f Good **107** (TS 105) 7 ran.

1st Irish Stallion Farms EBF Race (Tipperary, August 4) 2yo 7½f Good to yielding **88** 8 ran.

1st Yeomanstown And Morristown Lattin Studs EBF Maiden (Naas, July 20) 2yo 6f Good to firm **86** (TS 85) 8 ran.

Pedigree assessment

Sire Giant's Causeway (Storm Cat) Top-class 2yo, won all 3 races over 6-7f inc. Prix de la Salamandre-Gr1, then tough and top-class 8-10f 3yo, won 5 more Gr1 events. By outstanding US sire out of high-class US 8-9f filly. First foals 2002, quickly established as a leading sire in both Europe and US on turf and dirt. Capable of siring top-class 2yos (Shamardal, and First Samurai in US in 2005), even better record with 3yos, mainly at 8-10f (Footstepsinthesand, Maids Causeway, Mona Lisa, Shamardal). **Dam Rusty Back** Unraced. By smart 10f turf colt, later top-class 10f dirt performer. Half-sister to Grade 1 winner Spanish Fern out of sister to Al Bahathri. This is her first foal. **Conclusion** Should make good progress from 2 to 3, when he will be effective over 1m and is likely to last 10f.

Wachman sounded pleased, stating: "I'm happy with that. He is still a big, raw horse and he was doing his best work towards the finish. He should be a nice middle-distance horse next year, but he needs good ground." *RA*

Heliostatic (Ire) 86

ch c Galileo (Ire) - Affianced (Ire) (Erin's Isle) February 6
Owner Mrs J S Bolger **Trainer** J S Bolger **Breeder** J S Bolger
2 starts: won **1**, second **1** **£11,943** win & place prize-money

HELIOSTATIC was not seen again after winning his maiden at The Curragh in July, but there is little cause for concern. For Jim Bolger holds him in such high regard that he said at the time he was tempted to put him away there and then, with a view to bringing him back in the Derrinstown Stud Derby Trial.

It would be impossible to rate Heliostatic's maiden win as anything special, for one has to go right down to seventh-placed Border Cat in order to find a subsequent winner, and his success came in a Listowel nursery. But Heliostatic won comfortably, having been up there throughout and in front with more than two furlongs to go, and in doing so more than confirmed the promise he had shown when chasing home the

Race record

1st Jumeirah EBF Maiden (Curragh, July 17) 2yo 7f Good to firm **86** (TS 60) 9 ran.
2nd Blue Square Casino EBF Maiden (Curragh, June 24) 2yo 7f Good to firm **83** (TS 49) 12 ran.

Pedigree assessment

Sire Galileo (Sadler's Wells) Impressive winner of only 2yo start, outstanding 12f 3yo, won Derby, Irish Derby, King George, also 2nd Irish Champion S over 10f. Superb pedigree, by outstanding sire out of Arc heroine. First foals 2003, has sired 7f Listed winner Innocent Air, should do far better with 3yos, mainly over 10f+. **Dam Affianced** Useful 2yo, won twice over 7f at 2 inc. Listed event. At 3, won 10f handicap, also stakes placed over 10-14f. Tough. By top-class turf 10f+ performer out of fair filly. Half-sister to several talented runners inc. high-class 2yo/10-12f colt Sholokhov (Sadler's Wells). This is her first foal. **Conclusion** There are several useful 2yos in this family, but talented members tend to train on well. Heliostatic should do likewise, especially as his sire is likely to get progressive performers. He probably will need at least 10f and should stay 12f.

subsequent triple Group winner and Dewhurst second Horatio Nelson in a similar race over the same course and distance the previous month, when both colts were making their debuts.

Heliostatic's pedigree suggests he could improve out of recognition when stepped up to middle distances. He is from the first crop of the 2001 Derby and Irish Derby winner Galileo – he had the distinction of being Galileo's first runner in Ireland – and his dam Affianced was a middle-distance filly who was placed in a Group 3. Bolger trained Affianced, and he also trained her sire Erin's Isle, who was a redoubtable middle-distance stayer and among the horses who helped the trainer make a name for himself. Heliostatic has scope for plenty of physical improvement, so underestimate him at your peril. *GD*

Horatio Nelson 120

See entry in the top 100 horses, page 178

Hurricane Cat (USA) 108

b c Storm Cat (USA) - Sky Beauty (USA) (Blushing Groom (Fr)) March 28
Owner Mrs John Magnier & M Tabor **Trainer** A P O'Brien **Breeder** Pacelco S A
3 starts: won **2**, second **0**, third **0** **£30,551** win & place prize-money

IT IS almost anybody's guess where Hurricane Cat fits within the Ballydoyle pecking order, but he is clearly a decent prospect and he will deserve respect wherever he turns up at three. He followed the example of George Washington and Ivan Denisovich in getting beaten first time out, but the experience he acquired when seventh of 23 at Newmarket in September clearly was not lost on him. He could scarcely have been more impressive at Cork a fortnight later, where he treated 17 rivals with contempt and came home eight lengths clear, and his success there earned him a crack at something better.

Hurricane Cat had to work much harder in order to cope with the step up to Group 3 class for the Stan James Horris Hill Stakes at Newbury – jockey Colm O'Donoghue picked up a four-day whip ban after getting him home by three-quarters of a length from Final Verse – but it was a competitive affair and it represented another much-improved performance. There should be more improvement to come, especially as his rider felt he was in front soon enough and that the good to soft ground was not ideal. It will be interesting to see how Aidan O'Brien places him. *GD*

Race record

1st Stan James Horris Hill Stakes (Group 3) (Newbury, October 22) 2yo 7f Good to soft **108** (TS 73) 13 ran.
1st Blackwater Maiden (Cork, October 15) 2yo 7f Yielding to soft **95** 18 ran.
7th Hungry Horse EBF Maiden Stakes (Newmarket, September 30) 2yo 7f Good to soft **72** (TS 70) 23 ran.

Pedigree assessment

Sire Storm Cat (Storm Bird) Top-class US dirt 2yo, very lightly raced at 3. By top-class European 2yo from strong, speedy family of Royal Academy. Excellent sire, particularly of dirt performers, good record with European 2yos (Denebola, Hold That Tiger, One Cool Cat) and older 7-10f performers (Aljabr, Black Minnaloushe, Giant's Causeway, Nebraska Tornado, Sophisticat). **Dam Sky Beauty** Outstanding dirt racemare. Won 15 of 21 starts from 2 to 5, inc. 9 Gr1 events from 2 to 4, champion North American older mare. By top-class turf miler and outstanding sire, out of dual Grade 1 winner Maplejinsky. Half-sister to dam of Breeders' Cup Distaff winner Pleasant Home. Her 5 earlier foals include 5f 2yo winner Desert Tigress and a winner at around 1m on dirt in US (both by Storm Cat) plus a sprint winner by Danzig. **Conclusion** Superbly bred. Every encouragement on pedigree that he should progress well from 2 to 3, when a mile should be his trip. The problem is, will dirt turn out to be his surface?

Hurricane Cat wins the Horris Hill, but it's hard work

Innocent Air 101

ch f Galileo (Ire) - Minskip (USA) (The Minstrel (Can)) February 14
Owner K Abdullah **Trainer** J H M Gosden **Breeder** Juddmonte Farms Ltd
3 starts: won **1**, second **1**, third **0** **£17,288** win & place prize-money

INNOCENT AIR failed to win her first two starts but the second of those performances persuaded John Gosden to stop the pussy-footing in maidens and raise her to Listed level. The move paid off with a victory in the Stan James Stakes (the Washington Singer) at Newbury in August that saw her enter ante-post lists for the Oaks. At season's close, bookmakers had her at 25-1 for Epsom.

Taking on mostly colts, Innocent Air started at 10-1 at Newbury in a market dominated by Godolphin's maiden winner Emirates Skyline. The chief danger, however, turned out to be another filly, Galileo's Star, and front-running Innocent Air was not too hard pressed to hold her at bay by a couple of lengths. Thc winner was not seen again, Gosden having hinted strongly that that would be the case when he described her as having "a mile and a half written all over her."

The first three in that Listed event (a one-two for Galileo, incidentally) had only one start between them afterwards, but the next three all registered positive results. As Gosden suspected, the form of Innocent Air's second start, in a Goodwood maiden, made good reading later on, with the winner Deveron taking third at both Group 3 and Group 1 level, and third-placed Alexandrova going down by a short-head in the Fillies' Mile. *RA*

Race record

1st Stan James Stakes (Registered As The Washington Singer Stakes) (Listed) (Newbury, August 12) 2yo 7f Good to firm **101** (TS 78) 9 ran.

2nd EBF New Ham Maiden Fillies' Stakes (Goodwood, July 28) 2yo 7f Soft **86** (TS 84) 11 ran.

4th betdirectcasino.com EBF Maiden Stakes (Lingfield, July 16) 2yo 7f Good to firm **61** (TS 54) 14 ran.

Pedigree assessment

Sire Galileo (Sadler's Wells) Impressive winner of only 2yo start, outstanding 12f 3yo, won Derby, Irish Derby, King George, also 2nd Irish Champion S over 10f. Superb pedigree, by outstanding sire out of Arc heroine. First foals 2003, Innocent Air his only stakes winner at 2, should do far better with 3yos, mainly over 10f+. **Dam Minskip** From 6 starts, won 5f maiden at 2, 4th twice over 7-8f at 3. By Derby winner and very good sire of variety of performers. Sister to smart 8-12f gelding Savinio, very closely related to smart 2yo Ballet de France (by Northern Dancer, dam of Muhtarram), half-sister to very smart 12f performer St Hilarion (Sir Ivor). Her 9 earlier foals feature smart 10f colt Skipping (Rainbow Quest), very useful 10f+ filly Minority (Generous), and several other 1m+ winners at 3+. **Conclusion** With a sire likely to do well with his middle-distance 3yos and a dam whose progeny have done best at 3+, Innocent Air has the background to step up considerably on her 2yo form. Will stay 10f and likely – though not certain – to stay 12f.

Ivan Denisovich (Ire) 112

b c Danehill (USA) - Hollywood Wildcat (USA) (Kris S (USA)) March 9

Owner Mrs John Magnier, M Tabor, I Cowan **Trainer** A P O'Brien **Breeder** Irving Cowan

6 starts: won **2**, second **2**, third **0** **£116,754** win & place prize-money

DEFEATS of increasing severity in three Group 1 events showed that Ivan Denisovich has a good way to go before he's a serious Classic contender, but the ground was blamed for all three.

After the Prix Morny on soft ground at Deauville, where Ivan Denisovich was beaten two lengths by Silca's Sister into second but showed his best form, Kieren Fallon stated bluntly that "he really shouldn't have run. You can't ride a horse of this quality on such a poor surface." Going into the following month's Middle Park at Newmarket, the jockey reported that he'd be "disappointed if he didn't win, provided it doesn't rain", but rain it did and on good to soft Ivan Denisovich, failing to show much fluency, could only keep on for fourth.

Ballydoyle regularly gambles these days that one of their juveniles will adapt to racing on dirt at the Breeders' Cup and the punt in 2005 was on Ivan Denisovich.

Johannesburg won for the stable in 2001, and Wilko in 2004 showed again that the Europeans are not without hope, but most of those who have crossed the Atlantic to run in the Juvenile have looked hopeless and that includes Ivan Denisovich in the latest running. His dam was a celebrated Breeders' Cup winner and she had already produced a Breeders' Cup winner. But O'Brien summed it up for Ivan Denisovich when he said: "It was a struggle. It just didn't work."

Ivan Denisovich's first three starts, contrastingly, brought improvement each time and victories by four and a half lengths in a maiden at Leopardstown and two lengths in a good renewal of the TNT July Stakes at Newmarket. With the ground in the latter race probably faster than the official good to soft, Ivan Denisovich quickened well to come from off the pace and score with authority.

His only run beyond six furlongs was at the Breeders' Cup, but he may get a mile judged on pedigree. His Danzig close relation War Chant gained his Breeders' Cup success in the 2000 Mile and their dam Hollywood Wildcat took the nine-furlong Distaff. *RA*

Race record

12th Bessemer Trust Breeders' Cup Juvenile (Grade 1) (Belmont Park, October 29) 2yo 1m½f Fast **35** 14 ran.

4th Shadwell Stud Middle Park Stakes (Group 1) (Newmarket, September 30) 2yo 6f Good to soft **107** (TS 102) 6 ran.

2nd Darley Prix Morny (Group 1) (Deauville, August 21) 2yo 6f Soft **112** (TS 87) 7 ran.

1st TNT July Stakes (Group 2) (Newmarket (July), July 6) 2yo 6f Good to soft **109** (TS 81) 11 ran.

1st Irish Stallion Farms EBF Maiden (Leopardstown, June 1) 2yo 6f Good to firm **94** (TS 86) 12 ran.

2nd Paddy Power Supports Brooke Hospital For Animals Maiden Stakes (Div II) (Newbury, May 14) 2yo 6f Firm **87** (TS 88) 10 ran.

Pedigree assessment

Sire Danehill (Danzig) Useful 6f 2yo winner, improved at 3 into top-class sprinter, won Haydock Sprint Cup-Gr1 but also smart over 1m. Excellent sire, has done well with 2yos (inc Aussie Rules, George Washington, Golden Arrow, Horatio Nelson, Ivan Denisovich, Rumplestiltskin in 2005) and older progeny, mainly at up to 1m but capable of getting top-class 10f+ performers from stoutly bred dams. Best progeny include Aquarelliste, Banks Hill, Cacique, Desert King, Intercontinental, Landseer, Mozart, North Light, Oratorio, Rock Of Gibraltar, Westerner. **Dam Hollywood Wildcat** Top-class 8-9f dirt filly at 3 and 4, gained Gr1 wins in Hollywood Oaks, Breeders' Cup Distaff, Gamely H. By excellent sire of both turf and dirt performers, most of whom stay 1m+, from relatively modest family. Her 6 earlier foals feature Breeders' Cup Mile winner War Chant (Danzig) and minor dirt stakes winners Double Cat (Storm Cat) and Ministers Wild Cat (Deputy Minister), both effective 6-8f. **Conclusion** Superbly bred, but not a straightforward Guineas candidate as he may not quite stay 1m. The dam is transmitting a fair amount of speed, and it may well be that Ivan Denisovich proves best over 6-7f.

Killybegs (Ire) 109

b c Orpen (USA) - Belsay (Belmez (USA)) March 27

Owner John C Grant & D M James **Trainer** B W Hills **Breeder** E O'Leary

4 starts: won **2**, second **1**, third **1** **£32,052** win & place prize-money

GOING for win number six in the race, Barry Hills's representative in the latest Champagne Stakes at Doncaster was Killybegs. The Orpen colt was putting an unbeaten record on the line, having upset a Godolphin odds-on shot in a Newmarket maiden in July and then shown how it should be done when taking a median auction novice event at Redcar the following month by six lengths at 5-6.

In a seven-runner Champagne field, Killybegs was supported into favouritism but failed to emulate Sexton Blake, Sure Blade, Auction House, Distant Music and Etlaala on the roll of honour. He was only a length and three-quarters behind dead-heaters Silent Times and Close To You, after chasing the pace and hanging left, and was himself involved in a desperately tight finish in the Somerville Tattersall Stakes at Newmarket three weeks later, but that too went against him after he'd made the running and then been joined in battle by Aussie Rules.

Killybegs has improved every time in terms of form and should stay a mile, but he entered winter quarters a 50-1 chance for the Guineas. *RA*

Race record

2nd Somerville Tattersall Stakes (Group 3) (Newmarket, September 29) 2yo 7f Good **109** (TS 90) 9 ran.

3rd intercasino.com Champagne Stakes (Group 2) (Doncaster, September 9) 2yo 7f Good to soft **107** (TS 72) 7 ran.

1st Redcar Racecourse Wedding Receptions Novice Median Auction Stakes (Redcar, August 20) 2yo 7f Good **103** (TS 74) 8 ran.

1st Limbrick Architects Maiden Stakes (Newmarket (July), July 16) 2yo 6f Good to firm **76** (TS 82) 9 ran.

Pedigree assessment

Sire Orpen (Lure) Top-class 2yo, won both starts (6f) inc. Prix Morny-Gr1. At 3, 3rd Irish 2,000 Guineas-Gr1 from 4 starts. By sub-fertile dual Breeders' Cup Mile winner, half-brother to dam of Pouliches winner Bluemamba (Kingmambo), dam very closely related to immensely influential broodmare Coup de Folie. First foals 2001, fair sire, decent record with 2yos at up to 7f and 3yo+ over 6-10f. **Dam Belsay** Unraced at 2, unplaced at 3 in 2 starts over 7-10f. By top-class 12f performer and just fair sire in short stallion career. Very closely related to high class 7 8f filly Crystal Gazing. Her 4 earlier foals include 6f 2yo/8f 3yo winner Tsaroxy (Xaar) and 6f 2yo winner Lady's Mantle (Sri Pekan), both fair. **Conclusion** A mile should be his trip.

La Chunga (USA) 106

br f More Than Ready (USA) - Gypsy Monarch (USA) (Wavering Monarch (USA)) February 6

Owner Sir Robert Ogden **Trainer** J Noseda **Breeder** Brilliant Stables Inc Et Al

4 starts: won **1**, second **1**, third **1** **£57,338** win & place prize-money

FLASHY WINGS versus La Chunga in the Lowther Stakes at York in August was the first big clash among the latest crop of fillies. Flashy Wings had set out her stall with a three-length victory over La Chunga's stablemate Salut d'Amour in the Queen Mary there in June, a victory followed two days later by La Chunga's three-and-a-half-length win in the Albany Stakes.

La Chunga's arrival at the Royal meeting had been comparatively unheralded and she started at 10-1, with only a third place in a Sandown

La Chunga wins the Albany Stakes in great style

maiden to her name. After she'd shown a clean pair of heels to her 13 rivals, though, trainer Jeremy Noseda (also responsible for 50-1 runner-up Vague) revealed that La Chunga had been five lengths better than

Race record

2nd Jaguar Cars Lowther Stakes (Group 2) (York, August 18) 2yo 6f Good to firm **106** (TS 104) 6 ran.
4th Princess Margaret Stakes (Group 3) (Newbury, July 23) 2yo 6f Good to firm **105** (TS 101) 12 ran.
1st Albany Stakes (Group 3) (York, June 17) 2yo 6f Good to firm **106** (TS 102) 14 ran.
3rd bonusprint.com EBF Maiden Fillies' Stakes (Sandown, May 30) 2yo 5f Good **78** (TS 76) 11 ran.

Pedigree assessment

Sire More Than Ready (Southern Halo) High-class US dirt 2yo, later high-class 6-8f performer, also 4th Kentucky Derby. By high-class 8-10f dirt runner and very good sire, particularly in South America, out of half-sister to Grade 1 winner Bail Out Becky. First foals 2002, fair record with 2yos and older horses, mainly over 6-8f, few runners in Europe. **Dam Gypsy Monarch** Won 2 (turf and dirt, over 8f+) of 24 starts in US in 3 seasons. By top-class 8-10f performer and fair sire, half-sister to smart US dirt sprinter Mint (Runaway Groom) and useful miler Minge Cove (Sandpit). Her only previous foal is a sprint winner in the US. **Conclusion** She has a fair chance of lasting 8f, but might prove best at slightly shorter. Has already done well on turf, but she has the pedigree to appreciate dirt.

Salut d'Amour at home, which had therefore led to some surprise when La Chunga met with debut defeat on the same day that Salut d'Amour won the National Stakes.

Flashy Wings did not run between her two York assignments but La Chunga did, going down by three and a half lengths to Mixed Blessing in the Princess Margaret at Newbury. At 11-10, that looked disappointing for La Chunga, but the winner raced on an apparently firmer strip of ground and the vanquished favourite, conceding 5lb, was reportedly distressed afterwards.

In the Lowther, it was La Chunga who received 2lb from Flashy Wings, but it was not enough. While La Chunga had every chance, battling it out with the Mick Channon-trained filly and Aidan O'Brien's Beauty Bright over the last two furlongs, she looked to be beaten rather more comfortably into second than the eventual margin of a length suggests.

"We are very good but Flashy Wings is very, very special," Noseda reflected. "We will go for the Cheveley Park and have another whirl but if she is in that sort of form she will probably be too good for us." Flashy Wings was beaten in the Cheveley Park but not by La Chunga, who was an intended runner the week before but did not take her place.

La Chunga was bought earlier in the year for Sir Robert Ogden, the one-time champion National Hunt owner. At $270,000, she fell nearly five million dollars short of the top-priced lot at her 2005 Calder Selected 2-Y-Os In Training Sale in March. *RA*

Leo **108**

ch c Pivotal - Miss Penton (Primo Dominie) March 7

Owner H R H Princess Haya Of Jordan **Trainer** J H M Gosden **Breeder** Hascombe and Valiant Studs

7 starts: won **2**, second **2**, third **0** **£65,611** win & place prize-money

LEO was transferred to Godolphin at the end of his two-year-old campaign, despite failing to cut much ice in the Breeders' Cup Juvenile at Belmont Park on his final start.

His disappointing ninth there is easy to forgive – the race was run on an unfamiliar dirt surface and came at the end of a busy season – and the switch from John Gosden's care to that of Saeed Bin Suroor was entirely understandable given that the Pivotal colt had been running in the colours of Sheikh Mohammed's wife, Princess Haya of Jordan, whose classy three-year-old Proclamation had already made a similar move from Jeremy Noseda's stable. What made the transfer all the more predictable is that Leo's Royal Lodge Stakes defeat of Kilworth at Newmarket, where the Godolphin challenger True Cause could do no better than fifth, ensured that he would end the season rated a street in front of any of Godolphin's own juveniles, even if it was a substandard running of the race.

The Royal Lodge was devalued by the absence of a Ballydoyle challenger, and also by a steady pace, which flattered both Leo and Kilworth, who had both been up there throughout. While Leo appeared to enjoy the track better than Goodwood and reversed recent running with True Cause, who had beaten him a neck in a Listed race there, the form is suspect, and the subsequent Racing Post Trophy winner Palace Episode is among those who clearly did not give their running. Leo had been beaten comprehensively by Horatio Nelson in the Group 3 Superlative Stakes at Newmarket's July meeting, and his only previous win had come in a maiden at Doncaster in May, albeit one with a strong tradition.

It remains to be seen where Leo fits into Godolphin's plans, but his pedigree suggests stamina limitations and he is more exposed than most, so he is not one to get too excited about. *GD*

Race record

9th Bessemer Trust Breeders' Cup Juvenile (Grade 1) (Belmont Park, October 29) 2yo 1m½f Fast **81** 14 ran.

1st totesport.com Royal Lodge Stakes (Group 2) (Newmarket, September 25) 2yo 1m Good **108** (TS 108) 8 ran.

2nd Stardom Stakes (Listed) (Goodwood, September 10) 2yo 1m Good to firm **99** (TS 99) 8 ran.

6th Criterium du Fonds Europeen de l'Elevage (Listed) (Deauville, August 20) 2yo 1m Very soft **95** (TS 62) 10 ran.

2nd Weatherbys Superlative Stakes (Group 3) (Newmarket (July), July 7) 2yo 7f Good to soft **100** (TS 96) 11 ran.

1st EBF Zetland Maiden Stakes (Doncaster, May 28) 2yo 6f Good to firm **85** (TS 83) 11 ran.

4th totesport 0800 221 221 EBF Maiden Stakes (York, May 12) 2yo 6f Soft **62** (TS 56) 11 ran.

Pedigree assessment

Sire Pivotal (Polar Falcon) Won 2 races over 5-6f at 2, high-class sprinter at 3, won King's Stand S-Gr2 and Nunthorpe S-Gr1. By top-class sprinter-miler. Excellent sire, strong record with 2yos and also with 3yo+ over variety of trips. Particularly strong record with fillies (including in last 2 seasons Chorist, Megahertz, Peeress, Penkenna Princess, Saoire), who tend to stay better than colts (Pivotal Point, Somnus). **Dam Miss Penton** Unraced at 2, placed over 6-7f from 6 starts at 3. By top-class 2yo who is influence for speed and precocity, out of 1,000 Guineas winner. Her 2 earlier foals include useful Italian 2yo/miler Balkenhol (Polar Falcon). **Conclusion** Very closely related to Balkenhol, who stays a mile. Leo does too, but that should be his limit as there is plenty of speed in his background.

Linda's Lad 110

See entry in the top 100 horses, page 216

Mostaqeleh (USA) 88

ch f Rahy (USA) - Istiqlal (USA) (Diesis) April 23

Owner Hamdan Al Maktoum **Trainer** J L Dunlop **Breeder** Shadwell Farm Llc

3 starts: won **2**, second **0**, third **1** **£17,729** win & place prize-money

ON THE bare ratings, Mostaqeleh has a long way to go before she is worth a crack at the established Group-race performers, but the style of what she did as a two-year-old demands that she gets her chance. John

Dunlop knows the family well and sent out her half-brother Muqbil to win the 2003 Greenham before he took 12th in the Guineas on his way to showing smart form over a mile and a quarter.

Shaping satisfactorily behind Silca's Sister when both fillies made their debuts in July, Mostaqeleh returned to Newbury for her two starts afterwards and won them both. There was nothing too flash about the way she justified favouritism in a six-furlong fillies' maiden in August, but placed horses Erytheis and Short Dance both won twice afterwards and Mostaqeleh won as a 1-2 shot should when she turned out next in a fillies' conditions stakes over seven furlongs at the same course.

I'm In Love, the 25-1 second in Mostaqeleh's last race, scored next time and is being targeted at the Guineas by George Margarson. Mostaqeleh is 25-1 or 33-1 in most lists for that Classic but ante-post backers were denied an opportunity to judge her in useful company when she passed up a couple of Group-race engagements in the autumn on account of soft going. *RA*

Race record

1st Dubai Duty Free Full of Surprises EBF Fillies' Conditions Stakes (Newbury, September 16) 2yo 7f Good to firm **88** (TS 74) 7 ran.

1st stanjamesuk.com EBF Maiden Fillies' Stakes (Div II) (Newbury, August 12) 2yo 6f Good to firm **83** (TS 81) 15 ran.

3rd London Clubs Maiden Fillies' Stakes (Newbury, July 22) 2yo 6f Good to firm **76** (TS 73) 9 ran.

Pedigree assessment

Sire Rahy (Blushing Groom) High-class 6f 2yo, 2nd Middle Park S-Gr1. Useful miler in Britain at 3, later smart on dirt at around 1m in US. By top-class miler and excellent sire, half-brother to Singspiel from outstanding family. Very good sire, does get high-class 2yos (Noverre) but most progeny best as 3yo+ over 1m+ (Fantastic Light, Serena's Song). **Dam Istiqlal** Unraced. By top-class 2yo and very good sire, particularly of fillies. Half-sister to top-class miler Bahri (by Riverman) and high-class 2yo/10f colt Bahhare (Woodman). Her 4 earlier foals feature smart 8-10f colt Muqbil (Swain), plus 1m 3yo winner Hureya (Woodman). **Conclusion** Will stay a mile, and has outside chance of lasting 10f.

Nakheel 109

b c Sadler's Wells (USA) - Matiya (Ire) (Alzao (USA)) March 12

Owner Hamdan Al Maktoum **Trainer** M Johnston **Breeder** Shadwell Estate Company Limited

2 starts: won **2**, **£23,940** win & place prize-money

"NEXT year, we'll be aiming for the top," says Mark Johnston of Nakheel. And what's more, Johnston will still have the horse in his stable. Shamardal went to Godolphin in 2004 followed by Winged Cupid in 2005, but the situation for Johnston looks a lot rosier this time round, with horses of striking promise in Nakheel and Atlantic Waves and an established Group-race performer in Black Charmer.

Mostaqeleh ends her first season in style at Newbury

Not seen out until mid-September, Nakheel was favourite to make a winning debut in a Hamilton maiden. He ran green and, although successful, he did not ultimately win in quite the style that might be expected of an 8-13 shot.

Johnston had every confidence in him, though, and when contesting the Listed totesport.com Silver Tankard at Pontefract one month later Nakheel could hardly have justified that good opinion in better style. Bandari won the Tankard for Johnston four years before by nine lengths. Nakheel was only four in front in 2005, but the style of it could hardly have been more promising and this son of Sadler's Wells and an Irish Guineas winner is very much one to follow in 2006. *RA*

Race record

1st totesport.com Silver Tankard Stakes (Listed) (Pontefract, October 17) 2yo 1m Good to soft **109** (TS 110) 7 ran.

1st Hamilton Park Autumn Finale Maiden Stakes (Hamilton, September 18) 2yo 1m½f Good to firm **79** (TS 78) 9 ran.

Pedigree assessment

Sire Sadler's Wells (Northern Dancer) Smart 7-8f winner at 2, improved into top-class 8-12f colt at 3, won Irish 2,000 Guineas-Gr1, Eclipse S-Gr1, Irish Champion S-Gr1. Outstanding sire, particularly of 3yo+ over 8-12f, also has good record with autumn 2yos. **Dam Matiya** High-class 2yo, won over 7f, 3rd Fillies' Mile. At 3, won Irish 1,000 Guineas-Gr1, 2nd 1,000 Guineas-Gr1, 3rd Prix de Diane-Gr1. By very good sire, particularly of fillies, out of smart miler. Her 3 earlier foals include 7f 2yo winner Aljazeera (Swain). **Conclusion** Likely to be best at further than a mile at 3. His distance looks like 10f, and he has an outside chance of lasting 12f.

Nannina 114

See entry in the top 100 horses, page 244

Nasheej (USA) 108

b f Swain (Ire) - El Nafis (USA) (Kingmambo (USA)) March 15
Owner Malih L Al Basti **Trainer** R Hannon **Breeder** D Henderson
5 starts: won **3**, second **0**, third **2** **£92,661** win & place prize-money

NASHEEJ is going to have her work cut out at the highest level in 2006 if her three-length third behind Nannina and Alexandrova in the Fillies' Mile at Newmarket is an accurate reflection of her ability. There's a chance, however, that we did not see the best of her that day. The front-running tactics that were employed for the first time might not have suited her ideally, and she had no answer when the two principals challenged. The situation was accepted, otherwise she would not have been beaten quite so far.

She started favourite that day, having improved from race to race and won three of her four previous starts, including a Group 3 and a Group 2. A gambled-on winner of a maiden at Newbury first time out, she was then pitched straight into Listed company at Sandown but did not enjoy the run of the race and was beaten into third behind Confidential Lady, doing good work at the finish and showing much-improved form in defeat nevertheless. She had a point to prove when she took on Confidential

Race record

3rd Meon Valley Stud Fillies' Mile (Group 1) (Newmarket, September 24) 2yo 1m Good **107** (TS 97) 6 ran.

1st Murphy's Fastflow May Hill Stakes (Group 2) (Doncaster, September 8) 2yo 1m Good to firm **108** (TS 99) 8 ran.

1st Swynford Paddocks Hotel Sweet Solera Stakes (Group 3) (Newmarket (July), August 6) 2yo 7f Good **105** (TS 88) 8 ran.

3rd BI Challenge Star Stakes (Listed) (Sandown, July 21) 2yo 7f Good to firm **99** (TS 79) 11 ran.

1st Mountgrange Stud Maiden Fillies' Stakes (Newbury, June 30) 2yo 7f Good **80** (TS 64) 17 ran.

Pedigree assessment

Sire Swain (Nashwan) Unraced at 2, top-class 10f+ performer from 3 to 6. Progressive, tough, won Irish Champion S and two editions of King George, also showed top-class form over 10f on dirt (placed Dubai World Cup, Breeders' Cup Classic). First foals 2000, capable of siring useful 2yos but most progeny better at 3, mostly over 9-12f. **Dam El Nafis** Won over 1m at 2, unplaced at 3 over 7-10f. By top-class 2yo/miler out of sister to Seattle Dancer and half-sister to Lomond and Seattle Slew. Her only previous foal was placed over 8-9f at 2 and 3. **Conclusion** The most prominent 2yo by her sire, but her pedigree suggests she should make further progress at 3. Her trip looks to be 10f, and she is not certain to last 12f.

Lady again in the Sweet Solera Stakes at Newmarket, and while she emerged the narrow winner, it was a case of 'honours even', for Confidential Lady, who raced wide of the others for much of the way, was conceding a 3lb penalty.

Confidential Lady was a late withdrawal from Doncaster's May Hill Stakes with a vet's certificate, but Nasheej still had no easy task, for this time it was she that had to concede a 3lb penalty. With hot favourite Pure Illusion failing to live up to expectations she came home a good winner from High Heeled Sneakers and Speciosa, who both went to post outsiders yet subsequently confirmed there was no fluke at all about their performances. Richard Hughes, substituting for the injured Pat Dobbs, was taken with Nasheej and said: "She's a great ride, she just does enough and she was never running away. She hangs in there and when you really go for her she picks up. She's very talented."

Just how talented still remains to be seen, but if a mile proves on the sharp side for her at three, there must be a fair chance she will get a mile and a half. *GD*

New Girlfriend (Ire) 114

b f Diesis - New Story (USA) (Dynaformer (USA)) April 21
Owner R C Strauss **Trainer** Robert Collet **Breeder** Kilfrush Stud
3 starts: won **2**, second **0**, third **0** **£72,277** win & place prize-money

FORGIVE New Girlfriend her disappointing effort in the Prix Morny and there are grounds for regarding her as Europe's most exciting two-year-old filly of 2005. And she can be forgiven that run.

On a day when there were widespread misgivings about the state of the rain-softened, and possibly over-used, ground, she looked ill at ease throughout, just as her trainer Robert Collet feared she might be. She had gone to the meeting with a major chance of beating Ivan Denisovich and the other colts but raced too keenly through the early stages and was beaten with more than a furlong to go. Christophe Soumillon accepted the situation and she came home fifth behind the other filly in the line-up, Silca's Sister, beaten almost eight lengths. Soumillon reported that she "had no action and was never balanced."

It was obvious that Collet thought a lot of New Girlfriend when he launched her career in the five-furlong Prix Yacowlef, a Listed race for juveniles that have never run, on the same course the previous month. The filly did not let him down and just 17 days later she was pitched straight into Group 2 company for the Prix Robert Papin at Maisons-Laffitte, a race with a rich tradition. Second favourite in a market dominated by the Prix du Bois winner Gwenseb, she was simply in a different class to her eight rivals. Having settled well in a handy position, New Girlfriend went smoothly to the front with more than a furlong to go and came home an easy three-length winner from her stablemate Queensalsa, with Soumillon looking around for non-existent dangers. It was a most impressive sight and has been rated high-class form, as good as any recorded by a two-year-old filly all year.

While New Girlfriend clearly has plenty of speed, her pedigree suggests there should not be too much doubt about her getting a mile at three. After all, Diesis tends to impart a fair measure of stamina, and the dam New Story finished second in the Marcel Boussac before winning over ten furlongs at three. Collet is in no doubt at all that she is a Classic filly, but he is in no hurry to choose between the 1,000 Guineas and the Poule d'Essai des Pouliches. The Pouliches usually offers much the easier pickings, but Collet is not a trainer to duck a challenge, so it will be no surprise at all if she turns up at Newmarket in May. If she does, she must not be underestimated. *GD*

Race record

5th Darley Prix Morny (Group 1) (Deauville, August 21) 2yo 6f Soft **93** (TS 60) 7 ran.
1st Prix Robert Papin (Group 2) (Maisons-Laffitte, July 24) 2yo 5½f Good **114** (TS 55) 9 ran.
1st Prix Yacowlef (Listed) (Unraced) (Deauville, July 7) 2yo 5f Good **101** (TS 95) 8 ran.

Pedigree assessment

Sire Diesis (Sharpen Up) Top-class 6-7f 2yo, won Middle Park S-Gr1, Dewhurst S-Gr1. Showed just useful form over 7-8f in 2 3yo starts. Brother to Kris. Excellent sire, particularly of fillies. Does get high-class 2yos but better record with 3yo+ over 7f+, talented fillies often stay 10f+. **Dam New Story** High-class 2yo, won 5f maiden and 2nd 1m Prix Marcel Boussac-Gr1. Showed smart form at 3 over 8-10f. By excellent sire of 1m+ dirt and turf performers, out of unraced daughter of US 2yo stakes winner. Her only previous foal is fair French miler New Largue (Distant View). **Conclusion** Should prove effective over 1m and has fair chance on pedigree of lasting 10f, although it is worth bearing in mind she showed lots of speed at 2.

Nidhaal (Ire) 104

ch f Observatory (USA) - Jeed (Ire) (Mujtahid (USA)) March 7
Owner Hamdan Al Maktoum **Trainer** E A L Dunlop **Breeder** Shadwell Estate Company Limited
4 starts: won **2**, second **1**, third **0** **£40,774** win & place prize-money

NIDHAAL could manage only fifth of ten in the Cheveley Park, for which she started 3-1 second favourite. She looked to have every chance in the race but reportedly returned lame. She had won two of her previous three races and she was unfortunate not to have won all three. Her defeat came in the Group 3 Princess Margaret at Newbury second time out when she beat Nannina and La Chunga, both of them major race winners in 2005, into third and fourth. It made for very strange reading at the

Nidhaal and Richard Hills on their way to post at Newbury

end of the season that this trio lost out to Mixed Blessing, on whom Kieren Fallon had steered a lonely but victorious course by the stands rail. Mixed Blessing was sent off at 28-1 in the Cheveley Park.

Nidhaal's successes were impressive ones, in a maiden at Newmarket earlier in July and a Listed race at Salisbury in September. There were 12 runners for the latter race but Nidhaal started 5-4, with only two others in single figures, and favourite backers were never worried. There is stamina in her excellent family but Nidhaal's dam showed stamina limitations in her brief career, so did her first foal, and Nidhaal is unlikely to be suited by a mile judged on her style of racing so far. *RA*

Race record

5th Sky Bet Cheveley Park Stakes (Group 1) (Newmarket, September 29) 2yo 6f Good **101** (TS 87) 10 ran.

1st EBF/Irish Thoroughbred Marketing Dick Poole Fillies' Stakes (Listed) (Salisbury, September 1) 2yo 6f Good to firm **99** (TS 89) 12 ran.

2nd Princess Margaret Stakes (Group 3) (Newbury, July 23) 2yo 6f Good to firm **104** (TS 100) 12 ran.

1st Heathavon Stud EBF Maiden Fillies' Stakes (Newmarket (July), July 7) 2yo 6f Good to soft **98** (TS 100) 12 ran.

Pedigree assessment

Sire Observatory (Distant View) Useful 6f 2yo. Progressed into top-class miler at 3, won 2 7f Gr3 events and 1m Queen Elizabeth II S-Gr1. Lightly raced at 4, won 9f Prix d'Ispahan-Gr1. By top-class miler out of useful 6f 2yo. Half-brother to high-class 8-12f filly High Praise (Quest For Fame). First foals 2003, decent start, sire of Violette (Firth of Clyde S-Gr3). **Dam Jeed** Won sole start at 2 over 6f, unplaced both 3yo starts over 6-7f. By high-class 2yo but modest sire, out of half-sister to top-class 12f colts Assert and Bikala. Her only previous foal is Mostanad (Alhaarth), placed over 5f at 3. **Conclusion** Has a good chance of lasting a mile, but there is a fair amount of speed in this pedigree and Nidhaal may end up best at around 7f.

Opera Cape 114

b c Barathea (Ire) - Optaria (Song) March 31
Owner J C Smith **Trainer** S Kirk **Breeder** Littleton Stud
6 starts: won **2**, second **2**, third **2** **£120,804** win & place prize-money

OPERA CAPE is easily the best horse trained by Sylvester Kirk, so good that he will be racing for Godolphin instead in his second season. It took Opera Cape three runs to get off the mark, while the stable was going through a very quiet time, but he took that Goodwood maiden in clear-cut fashion (from a Godolphin horse) and Group races were on the agenda for him in three starts afterwards, two of them Group 1.

Leaping up the rankings with a tenacious and clear-cut victory in the Group 3 Iveco Daily Solario Stakes at Sandown, Opera Cape then took on the best around in the Jean-Luc Lagardere at Longchamp and the Dewhurst at Newmarket. He mounted a game but unavailing challenge to Horatio Nelson in the former, coming off second best, and stuck on well again when drawing clear of the fourth horse in the Dewhurst, having no answer however to the late surges of Sir Percy and Horatio Nelson again.

"He's a bloody good prospect and franked the form from Paris," said Kirk after the Dewhurst. "He's a proper Guineas contender." He would surely have been forgiven another expletive when news came through soon afterwards that Opera Cape would henceforth be a contender for the boys in blue. *RA*

Race record

3rd Darley Dewhurst Stakes (Group 1) (Newmarket, October 15) 2yo 7f Good to soft **114** (TS 114) 8 ran.

2nd Prix Jean-Luc Lagardere (Grand Criterium) (Group 1) (Longchamp, October 2) 2yo 7f Good to soft **114** (TS 96) 6 ran.

1st Iveco Daily Solario Stakes (Group 3) (Sandown, August 20) 2yo 7f Soft **110** (TS 97) 7 ran.

1st Vodafone EBF Maiden Stakes (Goodwood, July 30) 2yo 7f Good to soft **86** (TS 84) 12 ran.

2nd George Smith Horseboxes EBF Maiden Stakes (Salisbury, July 9) 2yo 7f Firm **86** (TS 72) 16 ran.

3rd Herbert And Gwen Blagrave EBF Maiden Stakes (Salisbury, June 23) 2yo 7f Good to firm **77** (TS 32) 11 ran.

Pedigree assessment

Sire Barathea (Sadler's Wells) Useful 7f winner at 2, progressed into top-class miler, won Irish 2,000 Guineas and Breeders' Cup Mile. Also showed smart form over 6f and 12f. Good record as a sire, including with 2yos (Barathea Guest, Charming Prince, Magical Romance, Tobougg) and older performers mainly over 1m+ (Enrique, Pongee), also gets occasional good sprinter (Tante Rose). **Dam Optaria** Won over 5f at 2, placed over 5-6f at 3. Sire influential speed stallion, dam unplaced, grand-dam 5f 2yo winner. Her 7 earlier foals feature Opera Cape's full-sister Opera Glass, a fair 1m 3yo winner, plus smart stayer Grey Shot (Sharrood), useful sprinter Night Shot (Night Shift) and fair 7-9f filly Highland Shot (Selkirk). **Conclusion** Optaria, despite her speedy background, produces horses who do far better at 3+ than at 2. Opera Cape is by a sire with a good 2yo record, but there is encouragement in his pedigree that he can do at least as well at 3 at around 1m.

Palace Episode 114

See entry in the top 100 horses, page 268

Porto Santo (Fr) 110

b c Kingsalsa (USA) Exciting Times (Fr) (Jeune Homme (USA)) February 10
Owner Aleyrion Bloodstock Ltd **Trainer** P Demercastel **Breeder** Earl Elevage De La Source
3 starts: won **2**, second **0**, thrid **1** **£37,642** win & place prize-money

PORTO SANTO'S half-sister Gorella developed into a classy performer in 2005, with four Group 1 placings after her Group 2 win in the Prix de Sandringham, including in the Prix du Moulin and the Breeders' Cup Mile. Judged on two-year-old form, Porto Santo can do just as well at three, for in a campaign restricted to just three starts he has already shown form every bit as good as that shown by Gorella at a similar stage.

Porto Santo contributed twice to the good spring enjoyed by first-season sire Kingsalsa, winning a five-furlong newcomers race impressively at Chantilly in April and following up with another decisive win over an extra half-furlong at Maisons-Laffitte the following month. He looked set to take high rank among France's two-year-olds, but the obvious summer targets went by without him and the season was virtually over when he was next seen on the track at Saint-Cloud at the end of October. Stepped up to a mile on soft ground in the Group 1 Criterium International after two sprinting wins, it would have been asking a lot of him to beat Carlotamix, but he chased the favourite home up the nearside in a race

Race record

3rd Criterium International (Group 1) (Saint-Cloud, October 30) 2yo 1m Soft **110** (TS 65) 6 ran.
1st Prix Dagor (Maisons-Laffitte, May 31) 2yo 5½f Good **98** (TS 17) 8 ran.
1st Prix du Premier Pas (Unraced) (Chantilly, April 25) 2yo 5f Heavy **88** (TS 40) 11 ran.

Pedigree assessment

Sire Kingsalsa (Kingmambo) High-class 7-8f 2yo, later high-class and tough miler in France. By top-class 2yo/miler and excellent sire, mainly of 8-12f performers. Half-brother to top-class 10f colt Al Nasr (Lyphard). First foals 2003, decent start, also sire of Listed winner Salsalava and multiple Group-placed Queensalsa. **Dam Exciting Times** Placed over 6f at 2 in France. By high-class 8-10f performer and modest sire, dam grand-daughter of top-class 10-12f filly Crepellana. Her one previous foal is top-class miler Gorella (by Grape Tree Road). **Conclusion** This arm of a once-prominent family is reviving rapidly thanks to the progeny of Exciting Times. Gorella, useful at 2, stepped up considerably at 3 and it is possible Porto Santo will do the same. He also will be a miler.

in which the small field split into two groups racing wide apart, and he only just failed to snatch second. All things considered, it was a very good effort, and one he can build on at three. *GD*

Poseidon Adventure (Ire) 105

b c Sadler's Wells (USA) - Fanny Cerrito (USA) (Gulch (USA)) January 16
Owner Mrs John Magnier & M Tabor **Trainer** A P O'Brien **Breeder** Tower Bloodstock
3 starts: won **1**, second **1**, third **0** **£17,154** win & place prize-money

AIDAN O'BRIEN has a wealth of horses like this every year, two-year-olds by Sadler's Wells who should come into their own in a second season and for whom he must, justifiably, hold Group-race ambitions. Poseidon Adventure was not seen out until mid-September and was a beaten favourite over seven furlongs first time out. He was a tougher proposition over the straight mile at Newbury over five weeks later, grittily asserting at even money in another big field of maidens, and that resulted in a crack at the Criterium International at Saint-Cloud nine days later.

Second favourite Poseidon Adventure was beaten about six lengths into fourth of six, after the favourite and three-length winner Carlotamix and third-placed Porto Santo came to the stands side in the straight. "He

Race record

4th Criterium International (Group 1) (Saint-Cloud, October 30) 2yo 1m Soft **105** (TS 58) 6 ran.

1st EBF Greene King IPA Maiden Stakes (Div I) (Newbury, October 21) 2yo 1m Good to soft **84** (TS 56) 17 ran.

2nd Irish Stallion Farms EBF (C & G) Maiden (Tipperary, September 15) 2yo 7½f Yielding **83** 16 ran.

Pedigree assessment

Sire Sadler's Wells (Northern Dancer) Smart 7-8f winner at 2, improved into top-class 8-12f colt at 3, won Irish 2,000 Guineas-Gr1, Eclipse S-Gr1, Irish Champion S-Gr1. Outstanding sire, particularly of 3yo+ over 8-12f, also has good record with autumn 2yos. **Dam Fanny Cerrito** Unraced. By top-class 6-10f dirt performer out of top-class 9-12f turf racemare Sabin. Her 2 earlier foals, both by Sadler's Wells, are 1m 2yo winner Kisses For Me, later Listed placed over 9-12f, and 12-14f placed 3yo Saphila. **Conclusion** Likely to need further than 1m, and likely – though not certain – to stay 12f. Every chance on pedigree he can step up on his 2yo form.

had a hard race at Newbury last time out and this outing may have come a little quick," said jockey Kieren Fallon. No excuses were really needed, though, as Poseidon Adventure was making a huge step up to Group 1 level.

Two previous visits by his dam to Sadler's Wells resulted in a fair maiden who stayed a mile and three-quarters, and the useful Kisses For Me, who was placed in Listed races and acted as pacemaker in the 2004

A maiden win earns Poseidon Adventure a step up in class

Oaks. A prominent showing in the spring trials will be needed, but there must be hopes that Poseidon Adventure can make a Classic line-up on his own merits. *RA*

Prince Of Light (Ire) 102

ch c Fantastic Light (USA) - Miss Queen (USA) (Miswaki (USA)) May 4
Owner Claire Riordan and Kieran Coughlan **Trainer** M Johnston
Breeder High Bramley Grange Stud Ltd
5 starts: won **3**, second **0**, third **1** **£51,300** win & place prize-money

MARK JOHNSTON lacked a Shamardal in his two-year-old team of 2005, but if there was a shortage of brilliance at the very top end, there was strength in depth to make up for it. Prince Of Light proved something of a slow burner and he was not initially campaigned like a future Group 1 contender, but by the end of September he found himself representing his stable in Newmarket's Middle Park Stakes. What's more, only the Ballydoyle colt Ivan Denisovich started at shorter odds for the race.

Prince Of Light disappointed in fifth place behind Amadeus Wolf, but the easy ground may have been a factor, even though he had overcome similar conditions when winning his maiden at Goodwood in July. He looked very good on ground that the times suggested was riding faster than it was officially described when beating Final Verse in a hot nursery at York's Ebor meeting, when he travelled strongly all the way and overcame a big weight, and he had coped with the step up to Group 3 company in a 32.Red.com Sirenia Stakes transferred from Kempton to Newmarket and run on fast ground, beating the filly Ann Summers Gold by three-quarters of a length despite hanging left.

Prince Of Light clearly has more natural speed than one might expect of a son of Fantastic Light and might not be easy to place at three, but he ought to stay further than six furlongs. *GD*

Race record

5th Shadwell Stud Middle Park Stakes (Group 1) (Newmarket, September 30) 2yo 6f Good to soft **97** (TS 88) 6 ran.

1st 32Red.com Sirenia Stakes (Group 3) (Newmarket (July), September 3) 2yo 6f Good to firm **102** (TS 80) 9 ran.

1st Irwin Mitchell Solicitors Stakes (Nursery) (York, August 16) 2yo 6f Good **102** (TS 102) 17 ran.

1st Turf Club EBF Maiden Stakes (Goodwood, July 26) 2yo 6f Good to soft **83** (TS 73) 8 ran.

3rd SimblyBiz 1000 Member Firms Celebration Novice Stakes (Doncaster, July 14) 2yo 6f Good to firm **73** (TS 55) 6 ran.

Pedigree assessment

Sire Fantastic Light (Rahy) Useful dual 7-8f 2yo winner, later progressive, tough and top-class 10-12f performer, won 6 Gr1 events inc. Hong Kong Cup, Tattersalls Gold Cup, Prince of Wales's S, Breeders' Cup Turf. By high-class 2yo/miler and very good sire, brother to high-class 10f filly Hi Dubai, from excellent 1m+ family. First foals 2003, sire of stakes winners Jalisco Light (in Japan), Prince Of Light (Gr3), Under The Rainbow (Listed). **Dam Miss Queen** Placed at 2, dirt sprint winner at 3 in US. By top-class 2yo and very good sire of variety of performers, half-sister to smart 2yo Tajannub out of a tough and useful US turf filly. Her 3 earlier foals include 5f Gr2 2yo winner Chateau Istana (by Grand Lodge) and useful 7f 2yo/1m 3yo winner Mandobi (Mark Of Esteem). **Conclusion** Another talented 2yo from this family, but he has the pedigree to be effective too at 3, when his ideal trip on pedigree looks to be 8-9f.

Quiet Royal (USA) 108

b f Royal Academy (USA) - Wakigoer (USA) (Miswaki (USA)) February 10
Owner Wertheimer Et Frere **Trainer** Mme C Head-Maarek
Breeder Wertheimer Et Frere
5 starts: won **2**, second **2**, third **0** **£93,588** win & place prize-money

QUIET ROYAL was not quite the best French-trained two-year-old filly of 2005, but she was not far off it. Her length second to Rumplestiltskin in the Prix Marcel Boussac at Longchamp on Arc day was a terrific effort, collared only in the last 50 yards or so after bursting to the front on the outside of the pack looking the likely winner, and she ran to a similar level when landing the odds in the Group 3 Prix Miesque at Maisons-Laffitte in the last week of the turf season. She and Mednaya had a steadily run race more or less to themselves most of the way there, and having taken it up well over a furlong from home Quiet Royal was totally dominant, winning in style by two lengths, with another five back to the Rockfel second Violette.

A Compiegne winner in the summer, having made her debut behind another classy filly in New Girlfriend, Quiet Royal may be aimed for the 1,000 Guineas. However, she got first run on Rumplestiltskin in the Boussac, so there are no obvious grounds for her turning the tables, and she might be better off in the Pouliches, which is normally the softer option. *GD*

Race record

1st Prix Miesque (Group 3) (Straight) (Maisons-Laffitte, November 1) 2yo 7f Good to soft **108** (TS 84) 7 ran.

2nd Prix Marcel Boussac - Criterium des Pouliches (Group 1) (Longchamp, October 2) 2yo 1m Good to soft **108** (TS 107) 15 ran.

2nd Prix du Calvados (Group 3) (Deauville, August 20) 2yo 7f Very soft **105** (TS 100) 12 ran.

1st Prix de la Belette (Compiegne, July 29) 2yo 7f Good to soft **98** 8 ran.

4th Prix Yacowlef (Listed) (Unraced) (Deauville, July 7) 2yo 5f Good **94** (TS 87) 8 ran.

Pedigree assessment

Sire Royal Academy (Nijinsky) Useful 6f 2yo winner, top-class 6-8f 3yo, won July Cup and Breeders' Cup Mile. By Triple Crown winner and excellent sire out of fast racemare Crimson Saint, half-brother to dam of Storm Cat. Good sire, strong record with 2yos, mainly over 5-7f, older progeny have excelled over wide variety of trips but mainly at up to 10f. **Dam Wakigoer** Winner at 3 in France at around 1m, later placed on dirt in US. In total, won 1 of 10 starts from 2 to 4. By top-class French 2yo, very good sire and excellent broodmare sire. Very closely related to top-class 8-10f dirt/turf performer Dare And Go (Alydar). Her 2 earlier foals, both by Royal Academy, feature smart 7-9f filly Acago. **Conclusion** Already Group 1-placed over 1m, and should be effective over that trip at 3. She may stay slightly further, although the 10.5f of the Diane may prove just beyond her on pedigree.

Race For The Stars (USA) 101

b f Fusaichi Pegasus (USA) - La Lorgnette (Can) (Val De L'Orne (Fr)) May 7
Owner Mrs John Magnier **Trainer** A P O'Brien **Breeder** Strategy Bloodstock
4 starts: won **2**, second **1**, third **0** **£35,232** win & place prize-money

RACE FOR THE STARS does not feature that prominently in the ratings lists after her first season, not even among two-year-olds from her own stable, but she figured at 14-1 or 16-1 in winter lists for the 1,000 Guineas. That stable is Ballydoyle and among the many positive remarks Aidan O'Brien has made about his 2005 flock of juveniles, those on Race For The Stars sounded particularly noteworthy.

"She's a lovely filly and Kieren has always liked her," said O'Brien after the Oh So Sharp Stakes at Newmarket in October. "He was very worried about the ground and said she really wants it fast . . . Hopefully she'll come back for the Guineas. That is why we came here. Alexandrova will hopefully get the Oaks trip but this filly is different."

Starting favourite in the Oh So Sharp two weeks after comfortably seeing off some fairly useful rivals in a fillies' race at The Curragh that Virginia Waters had won 12 months previously, Race For The Stars left it late to launch her challenge. She had to, following interference at the start and some patient route-finding in a 12-runner field, but she did the job well once in the clear and cut down the very promising Sir Michael Stoute-trained second favourite, Scottish Stage, close home.

The strong signs were there that Race For The Stars was held in high regard when, despite defeat on her debut, O'Brien made her next start in the Moyglare Stud Stakes. "We were surprised she got beaten first time out and she didn't get things together in the Moyglare," he said later. Further sorties at Group 1 level are on the cards if the trainer's words are anything to go by. It will be fascinating to see in how many respects she can resemble her half-brother, the mercurial and sometimes magisterial Hawk Wing. *RA*

Race record

1st Finnforest Oh So Sharp Stakes (Listed) (Newmarket, October 1) 2yo 7f Good to soft **101** (TS 93) 12 ran.

1st Loder EBF Fillies Race (Curragh, September 17) 2yo 7f Good **99** (TS 69) 5 ran.

9th Moyglare Stud Stakes (Group 1) (Curragh, September 4) 2yo 7f Good **85** 9 ran.

2nd Grangecon Stud EBF Fillies Maiden (Curragh, August 7) 2yo 6f Good **83** (TS 73) 18 ran.

Pedigree assessment

Sire Fusaichi Pegasus (Mr Prospector) Placed only start at 2, top-class 8-10f dirt performer at 3, won Kentucky Derby-Gr1. By outstanding sire out of stakes-placed sister to Preakness Stakes winner Pine Bluff. First foals 2002, has compiled strong record, mainly in US. Has sired smart US 2yos Roman Ruler, Superfly, but progeny appear to progress well from 2 to 3, sire of US Grade 1 winners Roman Ruler, Bandini, plus Belmont 2nd Andromeda's Hero. Quieter in Europe, though sire of useful 2yos Scandinavia and Witten. **Dam La Lorgnette** Useful 2yo and champion 3yo filly in Canada, effective 8-10f. By Prix du Jockey-Club winner, grand-dam champion 2yo/3yo filly in Argentina. Her 10 earlier foals feature top-class 8-10f colt Hawk Wing (Woodman) and 2yo Canadian stakes winner Alexandrina (Conquistador Cielo; dam of 12f Gr1 turf winner Thornfield). **Conclusion** The dam previously has produced Hawk Wing and Alexandrina to sons of Mr Prospector, and Race For The Stars is another bred to that formula. Family members, though sometimes smart at 2, generally do better at 3+. Expect more from Race For The Stars at 3, when she should be effective over 8-10f but will struggle to last 12f.

Rampallion 87

b c Daylami (Ire) - Minute Waltz (Sadler's Wells (USA)) February 17
Owner Duke Of Devonshire **Trainer** J H M Gosden **Breeder** Side Hill Stud
1 start: won **1**, **£7,176** win & place prize-money

WE WERE allowed only one glimpse of Rampallion at two, but we are confident he is a really smart prospect. Favourite to beat 21 similarly inexperienced rivals in a mile maiden at Newmarket in October in which trainer John Gosden has an outstanding recent record, he was

Hawk Wing's promising half-sister Race For The Stars

held up in touch but lost his position through scrimmaging after halfway. To his credit, he picked up again impressively, collaring the leaders on the uphill finish and winning a shade comfortably by three-quarters of a length from Sandglass. The bare form is nothing special, but he shaped like a colt who will go on to better things, as did several of his beaten rivals.

Rampallion is from a family Gosden knows well, and although the mare May Ball, the most talented of the dam's progeny he has had so far, ultimately proved best at sprint distances, half-brothers such as Daunt and Taunt stayed much better. Gosden reckons he will be suited by further at three, and few would argue, but whether he gets a mile and a half remains to be seen. *GD*

Race record

1st 340th Anniversary Of Horse Racing In America EBF Maiden Stakes (Newmarket, October 14) 2yo 1m Good to soft **87** (TS 83) 22 ran.

Pedigree assessment

Sire Daylami (Doyoun) Very smart 1m winner at 2, top-class miler at 3 (won Poulains), later top-class and very tough 10-12f performer, won Eclipse S, King George and Breeders' Cup Turf. First foals 2001, decent stud record, best known for Irish Derby/Tattersalls Gold Cup winner Grey Swallow, can sire useful 2yos over 7f+ but most progeny make good progress from 2 to 3 and stay at least 10f. **Dam Minute Waltz** Unraced. By outstanding sire and excellent broodmare sire, sister to useful 1m 2yo Marcham and half-sister to two useful milers, out of a useful miler from strong family. Her 9 earlier foals feature very high-class 6-7f filly May Ball (Cadeaux Genereux) and several 3yo+ winners over 1m and further. **Conclusion** Rampallion, by a sire whose progeny tend to progress well, is the only one of his dam's offspring to win at 2. That suggests he can do well at 3. He should stay 10f and might just last 12f.

Red Clubs (Ire) 116

br c Red Ransom (USA) - Two Clubs (First Trump) January 17
Owner R J Arculli **Trainer** B W Hills **Breeder** J Fike
9 starts: won **3**, second **2**, third **1** **£148,229** win & place prize-money

WE SAW few smarter two-year-olds in 2005 than Red Clubs, who beat a strong field in the Coventry Stakes at York and went on to finish in the frame in some of the season's top juvenile races. However, there must be a doubt about his maintaining such a lofty position in the pecking order at three.

Barry Hills's previous Coventry winners Sure Blade and Royal Applause both went on to even better things at three, but Red Clubs looks less likely to do so. Unlike the subsequent St James's Palace and Queen Elizabeth II winner Sure Blade, Red Clubs had a tough schedule at two and he does not have the pedigree of a colt who will improve for the step up to a mile at three. And unlike the Cork & Orrery and Haydock Sprint winner Royal Applause, who went through the season unbeaten, Red Clubs was beaten no fewer than six times. He was beaten in the Gimcrack and the Middle Park, both of which Royal Applause won, and also in the Phoenix Stakes and the Dewhurst.

The burning question at the end of Royal Applause's juvenile campaign was: Will he stay a mile? Red Clubs has already hinted at the answer

Race record

4th Darley Dewhurst Stakes (Group 1) (Newmarket, October 15) 2yo 7f Good to soft **106** (TS 104) 8 ran.

2nd Shadwell Stud Middle Park Stakes (Group 1) (Newmarket, September 30) 2yo 6f Good to soft **116** (TS 114) 6 ran.

2nd Scottish Equitable Gimcrack Stakes (Group 2) (York, August 17) 2yo 6f Good **112** (TS 108) 13 ran.

3rd Independent Waterford Wedgwood Phoenix Stakes (Group 1) (Entire Colts & Filllies) (Curragh, August 7) 2yo 6f Good **90** (TS 80) 7 ran.

7th TNT July Stakes (Group 2) (Newmarket (July), July 6) 2yo 6f Good to soft **102** (TS 74) 11 ran.

1st Coventry Stakes (Group 2) (York, June 14) 2yo 6f Good to firm **108** (TS 108) 14 ran.

1st British Legion Punters Novice Stakes (Newmarket, May 25) 2yo 6f Good to firm **101** (TS 91) 8 ran.

1st EBF Patrick Hogan "Betfair" Lifetime In Racing Maiden Stakes (Goodwood, April 30) 2yo 5f Good **79** (TS 83) 7 ran.

6th Creature Comforts EBF Maiden Stakes (Newmarket, April 14) 2yo 5f Good to firm **48** (TS 50) 8 ran.

Pedigree assessment

Sire Red Ransom (Roberto) Impressive winner of both 2yo starts in sprints, placed at 3 on only other start. Very good sire, had strong European record before switch to stand in Britain, has sired high-class 2yos (Shining Hour, Sri Pekan, Titian Time), milers (China Visit, Intikhab) and 10f+ performers (Casual Look, Ekraar, Electrocutionist, Ransom o'War). **Dam Two Clubs** Useful 6f performer, won 5 of 12 starts inc. Listed events at 2 and 3. By top-class 2yo and influence for speed, out of sprinting sister to top-class sprinter Petong. Half-sister to smart sprint 2yo Gipsy Fiddler (Bairn). She has one earlier foal who has yet to make a mark. **Conclusion** Red Clubs, from a fast family, will continue to do best in sprints. He is quite precociously bred and is not certain to step up on his juvenile form.

to that one, for when stepped up to seven furlongs for the Dewhurst Stakes he weakened to finish around five lengths in fourth behind Sir Percy. There may have been other factors – he had, after all had a tough time – but he shaped for all the world like a non-stayer. His doubtful stamina had been an issue ever since he attracted 2,000 Guineas quotes following his Coventry Stakes defeat of Pacific Pride at York, for speed looked his most potent weapon that day and the dam's side of his pedigree is dominated by sprinters.

Whatever his future – and there is nothing to lose by trying a mile in the 2,000 Guineas, as Royal Applause did – Red Clubs deserves real credit for his achievements at two. For the Coventry, his third successive win after an inauspicious start, worked out well, with Amadeus Wolf in third and Sir Xaar fourth, and he put up particularly good efforts in second against Amadeus Wolf in both the Gimcrack Stakes, in which he emerged the best horse in the race under his penalty, and the Middle Park. Indeed, at six furlongs he was a match for all but the very best. *GD*

Royal Proposal 98

b f King's Best (USA) - Mrs Ting (USA) (Lyphard (USA)) April 8
Owner Ms Nicola Mahoney **Trainer** L M Cumani **Breeder** Eric Puerari and Michel Henochsberg
2 starts: won **1**, second **1**, **£7,191** win & place prize-money

FIRST time out as a two-year-old is not usually the occasion to latch on to a horse trained by Luca Cumani. He's had 87 such juveniles in the last five seasons and only four have won. The bells started ringing, therefore, when Royal Proposal was backed down to 5-2 favouritism for her debut in a maiden at Nottingham in August and quickened up well to justify all the confidence.

The 11 fillies behind her that day all ended the turf season apparently exposed as fair at best, but Cumani was already talking of the Fillies' Mile as a possible engagement for Royal Proposal, once he had given her another run for education. His 2004 runner in that Nottingham race, who came second, was his Fillies' Mile contender Dash To The Top.

Royal Proposal did not make it to that Group 1 but that does not mean her second start was a disaster. She was beaten at 5-6 in a Newmarket conditions stakes, but by only a short head. Royal Proposal looked sure to win when going on with a quarter-mile left to run, but Eilean Ban pipped her on the post after the pair had drawn clear.

The performance did not put off Godolphin anyway, as they bought Royal Proposal within another fortnight and put her away for the winter.

At the time of writing, she stood at 25-1 and 33-1 for the Guineas and Oaks. A 115,000-guinea yearling, she is not at all certain to get the Oaks trip on pedigree, although her sire King's Best has had good middle-distance winners. *RA*

Race record

2nd EBF Fillies' Conditions Stakes (Newmarket (July), September 2) 2yo 7f Good to firm **98** (TS 93) 6 ran.
1st BBAG Yearling Sale EBF Maiden Fillies' Stakes (Nottingham, August 17) 2yo 1m Good **81** (TS 57) 12 ran.

Pedigree assessment

Sire King's Best (Kingmambo) Smart dual 7f 2yo winner, won 2,000 Guineas in 2 completed 3yo outings. By top-class 2yo/miler and excellent sire. Half-brother to several good performers, notably Arc winner Urban Sea (dam of Galileo), from very strong middle-distance family. First foals 2002, emerging as good sire, has fair record with 2yos (inc. Gr winner Dubai Surprise), but better record with 3yos (inc Gr1 winners Dubai Surprise, Proclamation, and Gr2 winner Oiseau Rare). Progeny often stay 10f or further, with help from dam. **Dam Mrs Ting** Unplaced in 3 starts at 2 and 3 over 8-10f. By top-class miler and outstanding sire, sister to top-class 8-10f performer Al Nasr and half-sister to high-class miler Kingsalsa (Kingmambo). Her 6 earlier foals feature smart miler Tripat (Persian Bold). **Conclusion** Some family members are useful at 2, most are better at 3. The same goes for King's Best as a sire, so expect more from Royal Proposal at 3 over a mile.

Rumplestiltskin 112

See entry in the top 100 horses, page 328

Scottish Stage (Ire) 100

ch f Selkirk (USA) - Drama Class (Ire) (Caerleon (USA)) February 25
Owner Ballymacoll Stud **Trainer** Sir Michael Stoute **Breeder** Ballymacoll Stud Farm Ltd
2 starts: won **1**, second **1**, **£9,486** win & place prize-money

IT'S a measure of the regard in which Lingfield's Polytrack surface is held these days that Sir Michael Stoute should choose to launch one of his brightest hopes on it.

Scottish Stage had been touted as one of Stoute's better prospects before she made her debut in a maiden in which only two of her rivals had any racecourse experience, and a smart change of gear in the home straight enabled her to overcome a very slow start and distinct signs of greenness with a last-strides defeat of Mary Delaney. While there was no mistaking her promise, it took a leap of faith to fancy her for the Listed Oh So Sharp Stakes at Newmarket just eight days later, yet Scottish Stage was sent

A winning debut for Scottish Stage on Lingfield's Polytrack

off second favourite in a field of 12. Slowly away again, she recovered to travel comfortably towards the rear before making good headway to look the likely winner after hitting the front inside the last two furlongs. It was only near the finish that Hawk Wing's half-sister Race For The Stars took her measure, and the pair were nicely clear of a field that included the subsequent Radley Stakes winner Short Dance in fourth. Interestingly, Jamie Spencer felt she had got to the front a bit soon.

Scottish Stage is from the middle-distance family of Oaks and St Leger winner Sun Princess, but she has clearly inherited some speed from her sire Selkirk. It looks a winning combination. *GD*

Race record

2nd Finnforest Oh So Sharp Stakes (Listed) (Newmarket, October 1) 2yo 7f Good to soft **100** (TS 92) 12 ran.

1st Gigabyte Technology Maiden Stakes (Lingfield (AW), September 23) 2yo 7f Standard **70** (TS 67) 13 ran.

Pedigree assessment

Sire Selkirk (Sharpen Up) Very useful 1m 2yo winner, later top-class 7-8f colt, won Queen Elizabeth II S-Gr1 and 3 Gr2 events. By sire of Diesis, Kris, Sharpo and Trempolino out of high-class miler and excellent broodmare. Very good sire, decent source of 2yos (Red Bloom, Sulk) but better record with 3yos, mainly over 1m+ (Altieri, Favourable Terms, Field Of Hope, Prince Kirk, Wince), sires occasional talented sprinter (Etlaala, The Trader). **Dam Drama Class** Unraced at 2, quite useful 10f winner at 3. By top-class 10-12f colt and very good sire, mainly of middle-distance performers. Dam 12f winner, sister to top-class 2yo Prince Of Dance and useful stayer Ballet Prince out of Oaks winner Sun Princess. Her only previous foal, Highland Diva (Selkirk), was unplaced in 2 outings at 2 and 3 over 7-10f. **Conclusion** This is a stout family, and as a result Scottish Stage should last 10f, though 12f may be just beyond her. Bred to make good progress from 2 to 3.

Septimus (Ire) 108

b c Sadler's Wells (USA) - Caladira (Ire) (Darshaan) April 4
Owner D Smith, Mrs J Magnier & M Tabor **Trainer** A P O'Brien **Breeder** Barronstown Stud & Orpendale
3 starts: won **2**, second **0**, third **1** **£92,926** win & place prize-money

AIDAN O'BRIEN had three runners in the Racing Post Trophy, with most of his hopes apparently pinned on Septimus at odds of 5-6. The Sadler's Wells colt arrived unbeaten in two starts over the previous six weeks, the first of them a maiden at Leopardstown that brought back memories of Footstepsinthesand's eyecatching debut in 2004 as the stable jockey was on board another runner, in this case Arabian Prince, that drifted in the betting, while Septimus was backed from 20-1 to 10-1 and with Wayne Lordan on top he caught his stablemate in the final furlong.

O'Brien extolled the virtues of both colts and Septimus was put next into a six-runner field for the Group 2 Juddmonte Beresford Stakes at The Curragh. None of the six had won more than a maiden. Septimus was the 4-6 favourite and justified the support, though not without a few moments of concern as he had to knuckle down to haul in Rekaab.

The going was good for the Beresford, but heavy at Doncaster for the Racing Post Trophy, and in the latter Septimus never looked likely to come out on top. Fallon can often be seen pushing along before the other principals but it was quickly obvious that this was a case of real concern. Palace Episode was travelling with vastly more fluency and Septimus could not get to front-running Winged Cupid either.

"He's a good-moving Sadler's Wells and it's very bad ground," was how O'Brien saw the Racing Post performance. It would be no surprise whatsoever if Septimus still turns out to be a Derby contender. *RA*

Race record

3rd Racing Post Trophy (Group 1) (Doncaster, October 22) 2yo 1m Heavy **108** (TS 102) 7 ran.
1st Juddmonte Beresford Stakes (Group 2) (Curragh, October 9) 2yo 1m Good **107** (TS 107) 6 ran.
1st Irish Stallion Farms EBF Maiden (Leopardstown, September 10) 2yo 7f Good to yielding **89** (TS 81) 13 ran.

Pedigree assessment

Sire Sadler's Wells (Northern Dancer) Smart 7-8f winner at 2, improved into top-class 8-12f colt at 3, won Irish 2,000 Guineas-Gr1, Eclipse S-Gr1, Irish Champion S-Gr1. Outstanding sire, particularly of 3yo+ over 8-12f, also has good record with autumn 2yos. **Dam Caladira** Unraced at 2, 10f winner on debut at 3, unplaced only subsequent outing. By outstanding broodmare sire who links very well with Sadler's Wells. Half-sister to several fair winners, out of half-sister to Lord Gayle. Her 6 earlier foals include a 7f 3yo winner in Italy by Charnwood Forest. **Conclusion** Bred to a sire-broodmare sire combination responsible for several top-class 10-12f performers, including High Chaparral, Islington and Yesterday in recent seasons. Will stay at least 10f, and has a good chance of proving effective at 12f. Bred to step up on 2yo form at 3.

Short Skirt 94

br f Diktat - Much Too Risky (Bustino) March 16
Owner J M Greetham **Trainer** Sir Michael Stoute **Breeder** J M Greetham
2 starts: won **1**, second **0**, third **0** **£4,459** win & place prize-money

ODDS of 16-1 for a well-bred Sir Michael Stoute-trained newcomer in a Newmarket maiden in August were made to look ridiculous when Short Skirt won by six lengths. Minutes later she was quoted at only 33-1 for the Oaks. There is no denying she did the job in fine style, but from an end-of-season perspective the substance of what Short Skirt achieved that day is open to serious question, given the exceedingly low-level subsequent performances of most behind her.

Short Skirt had one more opportunity to show her own worth when she was stepped straight up to Group company for the Rockfel nearly two months later. She was made 11-4 favourite too but faded into mid-division from her wide draw. That obviously leaves Short Skirt with plenty to prove as a Group-race performer but the family record suggests there should be improvement and she looks the sort to make up into an imposing sort physically. *RA*

Race record

7th Owen Brown Rockfel Stakes (Group 2) (Newmarket, October 15) 2yo 7f Good to soft **94** (TS 90) 14 ran.

1st David Thom Memorial EBF Maiden Fillies' Stakes (Div I) (Newmarket (July), August 26) 2yo 7f Good to soft **91** (TS 91) 12 ran.

Pedigree assessment

Sire Diktat (Warning) Unplaced sole start at 2, later top-class 6-8f performer, won Prix Maurice de Gheest-Gr1, Haydock Sprint Cup-Gr1, also won 2 7f Gr3 races and Gr1 placed over 1m. By top-class miler, from excellent family of 2yos and milers. First foals 2002, quite promising sire, has produced smart 2yos (inc Gr3 winner Diktatorial and Listed winners Dixie Belle, Rajeem) and 3yos at up to around a mile (inc. 1,000 Guineas third Vista Bella). **Dam Much Too Risky** Won both 2yo starts over 7-8f, placed over 1m from 2 starts at 3. By top-class 12f+ performer and stamina influence, out of 2yo winner. Half-sister to Gr1 winners Arctic Owl (14f) and Marooned (2m in Australia). Her 13 earlier foals include very useful sprint 2yo Seductress (by Known Fact), high-class 10-14f filly Whitewater Affair (Machiavellian), high-class 10-12f colt Little Rock (Warning), and quite useful 10f or 11f 3yo winners L'Affaire Monique and Rich Affair (both by Machiavellian). **Conclusion** Bred along very similar lines to Seductress and Little Rock. Seductress is the odd one out in this family; other members do far better at 3+ than at 2 and generally stay at least 10f. Short Skirt is likely to appreciate around 10f but might struggle to last further.

Silca's Sister 114

See entry in the top 100 horses, page 368

Silent Times (Ire) 112

b c Danehill Dancer (Ire) - Recoleta (USA) (Wild Again (USA)) March 17
Owner J C Fretwell **Trainer** E J O'Neill **Breeder** Gerrardstown House Stud
5 starts: won **2**, second **2**, third **1** **£59,801** win & place prize-money

SILENT TIMES would have been an appropriate enough name for a Eoghan O'Neill-trained runner in 2004, but 2005 was a spectacularly different story for the young trainer. After an ultimately torrid time trying to get established at Newmarket, 2004 saw him send out the winners of three races, but O'Neill and his new landlord and backer John Fretwell were laying down the groundwork for 2005. It was a partnership born in the *Racing Post* classifieds.

With a string made up mostly of two-year-olds, all of them reportedly for sale, O'Neill won more than 30 races and more than £320,000 in 2005, including Group races with Always Hopeful and Silent Times.

Silent Times showed easily his best form on the last of five starts, in the intercasino.com Champagne Stakes at Doncaster. After winning at York on his second maiden start, front-running Silent Times had been beaten five lengths by Close To You, one of his Champagne rivals, in an auction event on soft ground at Newbury. Close To You found Silent Times much tougher to pass at Doncaster – impossible to pass, in fact, as the two of them dominated some better-fancied rivals. Any number of times it looked as if Silent Times would concede a decisive advantage to Close To You, but he kept coming back and they were inseparable at the line.

"He's got to run that way," said O'Neill. "He's a strong horse with a

Race record

1st Dead-heat intercasino.com Champagne Stakes (Group 2) (Doncaster, September 9) 2yo 7f Good to soft **112** (TS 77) 7 ran.

3rd Galileo European Breeders' Fund Futurity Stakes (Group 2) (Curragh, August 20) 2yo 7f Good **100** (TS 92) 5 ran.

2nd Happy Valley Auction Stakes (Conditions Race) (Newbury, July 24) 2yo 7f Soft **91** (TS 77) 10 ran.

1st Fit As A Butchers Dog Challenge Maiden Stakes (York, July 8) 2yo 7f Good to soft **88** (TS 85) 13 ran.

2nd Freephone Stanleybet EBF Maiden Stakes (Ayr, June 18) 2yo 7f Good to soft **88** (TS 56) 8 ran.

Pedigree assessment

Sire Danehill Dancer (Danehill) Top-class 6-7f 2yo, won Phoenix S-Gr1 and National S-Gr1. Smart form over 6-8f at 3, won Greenham S-Gr1, 3rd Prix Maurice de Gheest-Gr1. By top-class sprinter-miler and excellent sire, mainly of 2yos and horses at up to 10f, out of grand-daughter of top-class sprinter Lianga. Decent sire, has good record with 2yos (inc. SWs Misu Bond, Nordtanzerin, Salut d'Amour, Silent Times, Speciosa, Strut in 2005) and progeny at up to 1m, best runners Choisir, Indesatchel, Monsieur Bond, Where Or When. **Dam Recoleta** Placed at 2, won on dirt at 3 in US. By Breeders' Cup Classic winner and very good dirt sire. Sister to top-class 8-10f dirt colt Offlee Wild from strong middle-distance dirt/turf family. Her 3 previous foals include two 9f+ winners by Diesis. **Conclusion** Silent Times comes from a stout family in US terms, and family members tend to progress well from 2 to 3. He will have no problem with 1m but his sire should ensure 10f is too far for him.

Silent Times (far side) and Close To You can't be separated

lovely big stride and there's no point in holding him up. You have to let him use himself, enjoy himself. He trains on his own at home."

A Breeders' Cup bid was abandoned because Silent Times had to be supplemented. Unraced so far on firmer than good, he made all his starts over seven furlongs but looks sure to get a mile. Though no match for Horatio Nelson at The Curragh, he is a strapping sort with the scope to improve further. Having sold 24 of the 30 juveniles he started 2005 with, O'Neill hopes to have about 50 in residence in 2006. *RA*

Sir Percy 119

See entry in the top 100 horses, page 378

Sir Xaar (Ire) 110

b/br c Xaar - Cradle Brief (Ire) (Brief Truce (USA)) March 24

Owner Pinnacle Xaar Partnership **Trainer** B Smart **Breeder** Mick Quinn and Peter Jones

9 starts: won **3**, second **2**, third **0** **£55,685** win & place prize-money

SIR XAAR appeared to achieve a Racing Post Rating of 110 when running Cool Creek to a head in the Mill Reef Stakes at Newbury, and if that figure is a genuine reflection of his ability at the end of a busy first season it places him high up the juvenile classification. However, with third-placed Nantyglo having earlier been beaten in two nurseries off marks in the 80s the form is by no means rock solid, and Sir Xaar's two best previous figures fell some way short on 103.

He was a very useful two-year-old, but one with limitations. A winner at Doncaster and Pontefract on his first two starts, he was put firmly in his place three times in Group company before the Mill Reef, including in the Coventry Stakes and the Gimcrack at York, and he was also beaten in a nursery at Redcar, albeit giving 22lb to subsequent Listed winner Wovoka. His only significant success came in a Listed race at Ripon, when he beat a promising sort in Johannes.

He may struggle to improve again at three, but he has already done his connections proud. After all, he cost them only 9,000 guineas. *GD*

Race record

2nd Dubai Duty Free Mill Reef Stakes (Group 2) (Newbury, September 17) 2yo 6f Good to firm **110** (TS 108) 13 ran.

1st Ripon Champion Two Yrs Old Trophy, 2005 (Listed) (Ripon, August 29) 2yo 6f Good to firm **103** (TS 86) 9 ran.

5th Scottish Equitable Gimcrack Stakes (Group 2) (York, August 17) 2yo 6f Good **97** (TS 90) 13 ran.

2nd Cleveland Nursery (Redcar, August 7) 2yo 6f Good to firm **103** (TS 80) 8 ran.

5th Happy Valley Auction Stakes (Conditions Race) (Newbury, July 24) 2yo 7f Soft **79** (TS 63) 10 ran.

6th Weatherbys Superlative Stakes (Group 3) (Newmarket (July), July 7) 2yo 7f Good to soft **88** (TS 83) 11 ran.

4th Coventry Stakes (Group 2) (York, June 14) 2yo 6f Good to firm **98** (TS 95) 14 ran.

1st Griffvale Ltd Supporting Chancy Conditions Stakes (Pontefract, May 27) 2yo 6f Good to firm **87** (TS 91) 4 ran.

1st Book Your Wedding Here Auction Stakes (Doncaster, May 19) 2yo 6f Good to firm **78** (TS 68) 18 ran.

Pedigree assessment

Sire Xaar (Zafonic) Outstanding 2yo over 6-7f, won Dewhurst S-Gr1, Prix de la Salamandre-Gr1. Showed high-class form over 8-10f at 3 and 4, gained only win in Craven S-Gr3 but Gr1 placed in Irish Champion and Eclipse S. By outstanding 2yo/miler who has done particularly well with 2yos, out of smart 2yo/sprinter from outstanding family. First foals 2002, good record with 2yos, particularly over 6-7f, sire of Balthazaar's Gift, Mystical Land, Sir Xaar, Tony James, Wake Up Maggie. **Dam Cradle Brief** Unraced. By top-class 8-10f colt but modest sire, half-sister to useful sprinter Tiger Royal (Royal Academy) out of half-sister to dam of top-class 12-14f colt Oscar Schindler (Royal Academy). Her 2 earlier foals include quite useful 8-12f filly Fuerta Ventura (Desert Sun). **Conclusion** Sir Xaar has already shown he is one of the speedier members of the family, and 1m looks to be his limit in stamina terms.

Speciosa (Ire) 108

b f Danehill Dancer (Ire) - Specifically (USA) (Sky Classic (Can)) April 28

Owner Michael H Sly, Dr T Davies Mrs Pam Sly **Trainer** Mrs P Sly

Breeder K and Mrs Cullen

6 starts: won **2**, second **1**, third **2** **£57,255** win & place prize-money

THIS, given her trainer's description, sounds like a frightening creature from the Fens. "She's got a severe temperament," said Pam Sly. "We've got her on a magnesium-based product, which they apparently give to mental patients." Her owners were offered £200,000 for her, though, and that was before easily her biggest triumph.

Speciosa required four runs in maidens before she won one, but only two in Group events. The maiden form was only fair, her last-gasp victory over an extended seven furlongs at Beverley in August failing to improve things on that score, but 50-1 and 20-1 in those two Group races afterwards both badly underestimated her.

The first attempt brought a close third in the May Hill at Doncaster. That came with front-running tactics (tried once before) and so did Speciosa's win in the Owen Brown Rockfel Stakes on the bookies'

Race record

1st Owen Brown Rockfel Stakes (Group 2) (Newmarket, October 15) 2yo 7f Good to soft **108** (TS 107) 14 ran.

3rd Murphy's Fastflow May Hill Stakes (Group 2) (Doncaster, September 8) 2yo 1m Good to firm **102** (TS 92) 8 ran.

1st EBF BP Acetyls Saltend Maiden Fillies' Stakes (Beverley, August 20) 2yo 7½f Good **74** (TS 66) 8 ran.

3rd EBF John Virgo Maiden Stakes (Div II) (Leicester, August 7) 2yo 7f Good **69** (TS 69) 11 ran.

8th EBF Maiden Fillies' Stakes (Nottingham, July 9) 2yo 6f Good to firm **51** (TS 45) 14 ran.

2nd EBF Go Racing In Yorkshire Maiden Stakes (Ripon, June 9) 2yo 6f Good to firm **70** (TS 64) 9 ran.

Pedigree assessment

Sire Danehill Dancer (Danehill) Top-class 6-7f 2yo, won Phoenix S-Gr1 and National S-Gr1. Smart form over 6-8f at 3, won Greenham S-Gr1, 3rd Prix Maurice de Gheest-Gr1. By top-class sprinter-miler and excellent sire, mainly of 2yos and horses at up to 10f, out of grand-daughter of top-class sprinter Lianga. Decent sire, has good record with 2yos (inc. SWs Misu Bond, Nordtanzerin, Salut d'Amour, Silent Times, Speciosa, Strut in 2005) and progeny at up to 1m, best runners Choisir, Indesatchel, Monsieur Bond, Where Or When. **Dam Specifically** Winner at 2 in US. By top-class 10-12f US turf performer out of useful stayer Specificity. Half-sister to top-class 10-12f filly Pride (by Peintre Celebre), family of Touching Wood. Her 5 earlier foals include 10f 2yo/3yo winner Thundermill (by Thunder Gulch), smart US 8-10f turf horse Major Rhythm (Rhythm), and modest 5-6f 4yo winner Shadow Jumper (Dayjur). **Conclusion** Speed on the sire's side, stamina on the dam's. Speciosa should have no problem with 1m, but her sire might prevent her from staying much further.

benefit of a Champions Day at Newmarket the following month, when she avoided various shenanigans in the pack and kept on just too strongly for the only serious pursuer, Violette.

Victory had gone to a trainer based near Peterborough with only nine Flat horses, one who has had ten Flat winners aggregate in the last five seasons and a best jumps total of 12 back in 1998/99. Meanwhile, as was swiftly pointed out in the press afterwards, Sheikh Mohammed's Rockfel runner finished last. "They told me you can't train horses here as there are no hills to gallop them up," said Sly. "But we've proved them wrong."

Sly said she had not given the Guineas a thought. Bookmakers have not given Speciosa much of a thought for the Classic either, with 50-1 still available at the end of the season. At 30,000 guineas from the Doncaster Breeze-Up Sales, Speciosa is already well bought and she will be suited by the step back up from seven furlongs. *RA*

Star Cluster 88

b f Observatory (USA) - Didicoy (USA) (Danzig (USA)) March 15
Owner K Abdullah **Trainer** H R A Cecil **Breeder** Juddmonte Farms Ltd
1 start: won **1**, **£4,270** win & place prize-money

IT WILL be a sad day when Henry Cecil no longer has a two-year-old worthy of inclusion in this list, but Star Cluster's presence here is not a matter of mere tokenism. Her Racing Post Rating may leave her a lot to find if she is to trouble the best of her age in 2006, but she won what turned out a decent maiden in good style on her only appearance, and she is undoubtedly promising.

A market drifter for an 18-runner fillies' race at Newmarket in July, despite having shown plenty of promise at home, she was settled in mid-field in the far-side group which allowed Cross Channel plenty of rope. Cross Channel was still clear two furlongs out, and it is very much to Star Cluster's credit that she picked up well enough to lead near the finish and win by a neck and the same from Deveron, who was clear herself on the stands side, and Cross Channel in a time only half a second outside the two-year-old course record. The form worked out well – the placed horses both won decent maidens on their next outings and ended the season contesting Group 1 races – but Star Cluster herself had problems and missed an intended engagement in the Radley Stakes.

Star Cluster is from an excellent Juddmonte family. Her dam Didicoy is a half-sister to the brilliant Xaar and was a smart sprint winner herself

Race record

1st Brackett Green Maiden Fillies' Stakes (Newmarket (July), July 15) 2yo 7f Good to firm **88** (TS 85) 18 ran.

Pedigree assessment

Sire Observatory (Distant View) Useful 6f 2yo. Progressed into top-class miler at 3, won 2 7f Gr3 events and 1m Queen Elizabeth II S-Gr1. Lightly raced at 4, won 9f Prix d'Ispahan-Gr1. By top-class miler out of useful 6f 2yo. Half-brother to high-class 8-12f filly High Praise (Quest For Fame). First foals 2003, decent start, sire of Nidhaal (Listed winner) and Violette (Firth of Clyde S-Gr3). **Dam Didicoy** Useful 6f performer at 2 and 3, won 3 of 6 starts, placed in Gr3 and Listed company. By outstanding speed-oriented stallion, out of useful sprinter Monroe. Half-sister to top-class 2yo/8-10f colt Xaar and several other talented runners. Her 10 earlier foals include Grade 2-winning 7-9f filly Didina and modest 7-8f winner Fen Gypsy (both by Nashwan), plus 10f winners Didifon, Espionage (Listed winner) and Explode (Listed placed), all by Zafonic. **Conclusion** Very strong family with fair amount of pace. Star Cluster should stay 1m but not much further.

Speciosa becomes a first Group winner for Pam Sly

in the Abdullah colours towards the end of Jeremy Tree's distinguished career as a trainer. She has plenty to recommend her, and it will be interesting to see how she figures in one of the Guineas trials. *GD*

Stormy River (Fr) 111

gr c Verglas (Ire) - Miss Bio (Fr) (River Mist (USA)) April 7
Owner Ecurie Mister Ess A S **Trainer** N Clement **Breeder** J & Mlle Marie-Laure Collet
3 starts: won **1**, second **2**, **£60,148** win & place prize-money

THIS French-trained colt was not a high-profile performer during his first season, but he might just have been but for the opportunism of Christophe Soumillon. The ride in question came in the Criterium International at Saint-Cloud at the end of October when the partnership of Soumillon and Carlotamix started even-money favourite in a six-runner field and Stormy River was 7-1. Entering the straight, these two looked the ones to concentrate on but Soumillon let the four ahead of him continue up the far rail while he steered for the opposite side of the track. Stormy River was one of the four and won that race pretty comfortably, from Poseidon Adventure, but only while Carlotamix was three lengths in front overall.

It cannot be said that staying where he did cost Stormy River the race. It's a matter of conjecture and that conclusion would be taking it much too far, but he is probably a smart performer, at the least, and that makes him well worth a place in further high-class events. His trainer, Nicolas Clement, decided he was worth a supplementary entry for the Saint-Cloud Group 1 after Stormy River had won his previous start, a maiden at Clairefontaine, by eight lengths. *RA*

Race record

2nd Criterium International (Group 1) (Saint-Cloud, October 30) 2yo 1m Soft **111** (TS 66) 6 ran.

1st Prix des Equiday's (Prix de Saint-Mars d'Egrenne) (Maiden) (Clairefontaine, October 15) 2yo 7f Soft **104** 12 ran.

2nd Prix Diatome (Left-Handed) (Maisons-Laffitte, September 21) 2yo 1m Good **81** (TS 62) 6 ran.

Pedigree assessment

Sire Verglas (Highest Honor) High-class 6f 2yo, won Coventry S-Gr3, 3rd Phoenix S-Gr1. At 3, 2nd Irish 2,000 Guineas. By leading French sire, mainly of progeny around 6-9f. Half-brother to high-class sprinter Cassandra Go (by Indian Ridge). First foals 2001, sire of Grade 2 winner Blackdoun and Listed winners Joursanvault and Ozone Bere. **Dam Miss Bio** Unraced. By smart miler mainly known as a French jumps sire. Half-sister to smart French/US 2yo/3yo Fantastic Filly (Myrakalu). Her only previous foal is 3yo French winner Norman Bio (by Chef de Clan) **Conclusion** Bred to appreciate around 1m, might find 10f just too far.

Strike Up The Band 106

b c Cyrano De Bergerac - Green Supreme (Primo Dominie) February 13

Owner The Oak Apple Syndicate **Trainer** D Nicholls **Breeder** Miss A J Rawding and P M Crane

6 starts: won **3**, second **3**, **£75,558** win & place prize-money

WHEN Strike Up The Band lined up for his debut at Pontefract in late April, his trainer David Nicholls had a record of one win from 27 two-year-olds first time out over the previous four and a bit seasons. That became two from 28 in impressive fashion as this half-brother to one of the stable's stars, Fire Up The Band, justified favouritism by seven lengths.

Nicholls tells it how it is and did not hold back in his post-race description of Strike Up The Band. "I haven't had many good two-year-olds," he said, "but this is the best." Everything seen afterwards confirmed his good opinion and suggested that Strike Up The Band could eventually take high rank among Nicholls' older horses as well.

Defeat in the Lily Agnes at Chester looked unlucky, decided by a short head after Strike Up The Band had gone around the houses, but he took a Listed race at Goodwood next time and was a slow-starting second in the Norfolk Stakes and the Windsor Castle Stakes in the space of three days at the Royal Ascot meeting at York.

He was a beaten favourite in those two Royal races but this was by no means a case of the bubble bursting. In form terms, Strike Up The Band was getting better and better and he showed more again when returned to Goodwood for the Betfair Molecomb Stakes. There looked to be plenty of interesting contenders in a 15-runner field – the Norfolk winner Masta Plasta was there for a start – and Strike Up The Band had to pass nearly all of them after being settled well off the pace from his widest draw. But he arrived at the head of affairs before the furlong marker and had three-quarters of a length in hand at the line.

The Nunthorpe, Gimcrack and Redcar Two-Year-Old Trophy were all mentioned as possible targets but Strike Up The Band was not seen again. It is not yet clear whether he will stay six furlongs but all ground seemed to come alike to him as a two-year-old. *RA*

Race record

1st Betfair Molecomb Stakes (Group 3) (Goodwood, July 26) 2yo 5f Good to soft **106** (TS 107) 15 ran.

2nd Windsor Castle Stakes (Listed) (York, June 18) 2yo 5f Firm **103** (TS 98) 8 ran.

2nd Norfolk Stakes (Group 3) (York, June 16) 2yo 5f Good to firm **98** (TS 93) 12 ran.

1st Baker Tilly Trophy Stakes (Registered As The Aubigny Stakes) (Listed) (Goodwood, May 18) 2yo 5f Good to firm **96** (TS 100) 8 ran.

2nd Joseph Heler Lily Agnes Conditions Stakes (Chester, May 4) 2yo 5f Good to soft **97** (TS 97) 10 ran.

1st EBF betfred.com Maiden Stakes (Pontefract, April 27) 2yo 5f Good **92** (TS 82) 9 ran.

Pedigree assessment

Sire Cyrano de Bergerac (Bold Lad Ire) Smart 2yo and 3yo at 5-6f. By good speed-oriented sire, grand-dam high-class 2yo/miler. Fair sire, has good record with 2yos, talented older performers generally best at up to 1m (Millkom a notable exception). **Dam Green Supreme** Unraced. By top-class 2yo and speed influence, out of a useful sprint 2yo. Half-sister to dam of Grade 2 winner Hail The Chief (Be My Chief). Her 6 earlier foals include high-class sprinters Sampower Star (by Cyrano de Bergerac) and Fire Up The Band (Prince Sabo). **Conclusion** The dam has already produced two talented sprinters, and Strike Up The Band is her third. Both Strike Up The Band's brother and half-brother progressed well with age, so Strike Up The Band has a good chance of enhancing his record at 3.

True Cause (USA) 100

ch c Storm Cat (USA) - Dearly (Rahy (USA)) March 4

Owner Godolphin **Trainer** Saeed Bin Suroor **Breeder** Darley

4 starts: won **2**, second **1**, third **0** **£23,979** win & place prize-money

HERE'S a sobering thought. True Cause, who barely registered on the consciousness of many racing enthusiasts, was Godolphin's highest-rated juvenile of 2005 judged on Racing Post Ratings. He was the only one to reach three figures, and even then it was only by the skin of his teeth.

Only those most closely involved will know how many two-year-olds were on Godolphin's books in 2005, but there was speculation that the figure exceeded 200. What we can say is that they raced 73 of them in

Britain, of which there were 32 individual winners of 37 races, not one of them at Group level.

While it is with three-year-olds and older horses that Sheikh Mohammed's operation has tended to enjoy its most significant wins over the years, they enjoyed Group 1 juvenile success with Dubawi in 2004, when there was no shortage of candidates for the 'young pretenders' section of Flat Horses. Indeed at the end of 2004 it was more a case of 'which ones dare we leave out?' than 'what on earth can we include?'. How could an organisation that has so many of the world's most choicely bred thoroughbreds at its command perform so abysmally?

Clearly there was a change of policy, and in fairness we may yet see the benefits when they are three-year-olds in 2006. Let's hope so, for on form one would be hard pressed to nominate a single likely Group-race winner from the 73 we have seen so far. No wonder Godolphin were busier than ever transferring horses already belonging to members of the Maktoum family and their associates to Saeed Bin Suroor, and buying many more privately. Things will not look so bleak with colts like Palace Episode, Winged Cupid, Opera Cape and Leo to call upon, plus fillies like Silca's Sister, Royal Proposal and Deveron.

As for True Cause, he was unlucky to run into an opponent of Opera Cape's calibre on his debut at Goodwood and on his next two starts he won a novice event at Nottingham and a Listed race at Goodwood. But he hung both times, and although at Goodwood his effort was purposely delayed, he took time to hit top gear and got up only in the last strides. Had True Cause's campaign ended at Goodwood we would probably have been predicting that he would at least take the step up to minor Group races in his stride in 2006, but now we are not so sure. For he was given his chance in the Royal Lodge Stakes, run at Newmarket, and rather blotted his copy-book by finishing only fifth behind Leo, the colt he had beaten at Goodwood. Although True Cause ran close to his Goodwood

Race record

5th totesport.com Royal Lodge Stakes (Group 2) (Newmarket, September 25) 2yo 8f Good **99** (TS 98) 8 ran.

1st Stardom Stakes (Listed) (Goodwood, September 10) 2yo 8f Good to firm **100** (TS 100) 8 ran.

1st EBF Colwick Park Novice Stakes (Nottingham, August 15) 2yo 8f Good **84** (TS 85) 4 ran.

2nd Vodafone EBF Maiden Stakes (Goodwood, July 30) 2yo 7f Good to soft **85** (TS 79) 12 ran.

Pedigree assessment

Sire Storm Cat (Storm Bird) Top-class US dirt 2yo, very lightly raced at 3. By top-class European 2yo from strong, speedy family of Royal Academy. Excellent sire, particularly of dirt performers, good record with European 2yos (Denebola, Hold That Tiger, One Cool Cat) and older 7-10f performers (Aljabr, Black Minnaloushe, Giant's Causeway, Nebraska Tornado, Sophisticat). **Dam Dearly** Won 1 (7f maiden) of 2 2yo starts, won 2 (9f Listed and 10f Gr3) of 5 3yo starts. By high-class 2yo/miler and excellent sire, out of 11f Grade 3 turf winner. Half-sister to top-class US 2yo dirt filly Balletto (Timber Country) from outstanding family of Bertolini and Green Desert. **Conclusion** Reproduces the sire-maternal grandsire combination of Giant's Causeway. Will be effective over 1m, just a slim chance of staying 10f.

Ugo Fire signs off with a Group 3 win at The Curragh

figure, Leo showed improved form in something of a tactical race and was four lengths too good for him. True Cause's own improvement seemed to have flattened out. *GD*

Ugo Fire (Ire) 106

b f Bluebird (USA) - Quiet Mouse (USA) (Quiet American (USA)) January 27
Owner Norman Ormiston **Trainer** Kevin Prendergast **Breeder** Sweetman Bloodstock
9 starts: won **2**, second **1**, third **2** **£123,628** win & place prize-money

RUMPLESTILTSKIN may not have been at her very best when Ugo Fire ran her to a neck in the Moyglare Stud Stakes, but even if the winner is taken out of calculations it was still a pretty smart performance by the Kevin Prendergast-trained filly, who had Ardbrae Lady two and a half lengths further back in third in a field of nine.

The Moyglare was Ugo Fire's eighth race in a season that began just two days after Kicking King won the Cheltenham Gold Cup. Her only win prior to the Moyglare had been gained in a maiden auction at Leopardstown, on her third start, when she bolted up by seven lengths, to the relief of her trainer, who could hardly believe she had been beaten at Navan the time before. The Moyglare was not her last appearance, however, and she went on to give the form some much-needed credibility by beating the subsequent Rockfel third Abigail Pett in efficient fashion in the Group 3 CL Weld Park Stakes at The Curragh.

The Irish 1,000 Guineas will be Ugo Fire's main target in 2006, and the Athasi Stakes was nominated as the likely scene of her reappearance. She will be vulnerable to less exposed rivals, but should give an honest account of herself. *GD*

Race record

1st C.L.Weld Park Stakes (Group 3) (Curragh, October 1) 2yo 7f Yielding **106** (TS 79) 8 ran.

2nd Moyglare Stud Stakes (Group 1) (Curragh, September 4) 2yo 7f Good **106** (TS 81) 9 ran.

3rd Tattersalls Ireland Sale Stakes (Curragh, August 20) 2yo 6f Good **93** (TS 69) 26 ran.

4th Independent Waterford Wedgwood Phoenix Stakes (Group 1) (Entire Colts & Filllies) (Curragh, August 7) 2yo 6f Good **84** (TS 74) 7 ran.

3rd Blue Square Stakes (Registered as Balanchine Stakes) (Listed) (Curragh, June 24) 2yo 7f Good to firm **94** (TS 66) 11 ran.

4th Kerry Spring Water Rochestown Stakes (Listed) (Cork, June 12) 2yo 6f Good **88** 6 ran.

1st Irish Stallion Farms EBF Auction Maiden (Leopardstown, May 8) 2yo 6f Soft to heavy **89** (TS 82) 11 ran.

4th Tattersalls (Ireland) Auction Maiden (Navan, April 16) 2yo 5f Soft to heavy **67** 6 ran.

7th Tally Ho Stud EBF Maiden (Curragh, March 20) 2yo 5f Soft **57** 12 ran.

Pedigree assessment

Sire Bluebird (Storm Bird) Useful 2yo, progressed into top-class sprinter at 3, won King's Stand S-Gr1, Ballyogan S-Gr3, 3rd July Cup-Gr1. By top-class 2yo who is also sire of Mujadil and Storm Cat. Bred along similar lines to Indian Skimmer. Decent sire, good record with 2yos but better one with 3yo+, mostly at up to 1m, best progeny Delilah, Dolphin Street, Fly To The Stars, Lake Coniston. **Dam Quiet Mouse** Unraced. By top-class US 8-10f dirt performer, out of fair 8-10f 3yo Fife. Half-sister to quite useful 2yo Witch Of Fife (dam of smart 2yo Ho Choi), from family of Prix Vermeille winner Pearly Shells. This is her first foal. **Conclusion** The stamina on the dam's side should ensure Ugo Fire stays 1m, but she may not last 10f.

Violette 110

b f Observatory (USA) - Odette (Pursuit Of Love) March 31

Owner C G Rowles Nicholson **Trainer** Sir Mark Prescott **Breeder** Limestone Stud

10 starts: won **4**, second **4**, third **1** **£125,864** win & place prize-money

SIR MARK PRESCOTT'S two-year-olds are better known for having three runs than ten. And for finishing far less prominently than Violette, the industrious filly who bucked the trends from Heath House in 2005.

Juveniles, particularly first time out, have been just about the only area in which to tread carefully with a stable renowned for its excellent strike-rate, so Violette going in at 4-6 on her debut on June 5 was eyecatching to say the least. Sir Mark also appeared to abandon the rules of a lifetime by running a horse out of its depth when Violette took the field in a Group

3 on her third start and was well held, but she quickly showed that the decision had not been so misguided.

A four-runner race at Hamilton in August did not demand much more as Violette took her tally to two wins from five outings, but she looked a different horse in good races thereafter. First, a valuable fillies' nursery

Race record

3rd Prix Miesque (Group 3) (Straight) (Maisons-Laffitte, November 1) 2yo 7f Good to soft **94** (TS 68) 7 ran.

2nd Owen Brown Rockfel Stakes (Group 2) (Newmarket, October 15) 2yo 7f Good to soft **110** (TS 109) 14 ran.

2nd totepool Two-Year-Old Trophy (Listed) (Redcar, October 1) 2yo 6f Good to firm **96** (TS 96) 24 ran.

1st TSG Firth of Clyde Stakes (Group 3) (Ayr, September 17) 2yo 6f Good **107** (TS 105) 12 ran.

1st EBF Carrie Red Fillies' Nursery (Handicap) (Doncaster, September 7) 2yo 6½f Good to firm **96** (TS 83) 17 ran.

1st Nessco Telecoms Novice Stakes (Hamilton, August 10) 2yo 6f Good to firm **80** (TS 44) 4 ran.

2nd EBF Novice Fillies' Stakes (Haydock, August 6) 2yo 6f Good to firm **85** (TS 77) 5 ran.

7th Princess Margaret Stakes (Group 3) (Newbury, July 23) 2yo 6f Good to firm **85** (TS 81) 12 ran.

2nd Western Daily Press Race Club/EBF Novice Stakes (Bath, June 11) 2yo 5f Firm **81** (TS 58) 3 ran.

1st Draycott Ward Median Auction Maiden Fillies' Stakes (Bath, June 5) 2yo 5½f Good **71** (TS 56) 11 ran.

Pedigree assessment

Sire Observatory (Distant View) Useful 6f 2yo. Progressed into top-class miler at 3, won 2 7f Gr3 events and 1m Queen Elizabeth II S-Gr1. Lightly raced at 4, won 9f Prix d'Ispahan-Gr1. By top-class miler out of useful 6f 2yo. Half-brother to high-class 8-12f filly High Praise (Quest For Fame). First foals 2003, decent start, also sire of Listed winner Nidhaal. **Dam Odette** Placed over 5-6f all 4 starts at 2, won twice over 5-6f at 3. By top-class sprinter and fair sire, out of smart 5f 2yo On Tiptoes. Her 3 earlier foals include 5f 3yo winner On Point (by Kris) and very useful 6f 2yo/7f 3yo winner Silca's Gift (Cadeaux Genereux). **Conclusion** This is a speedy family, and there has to be a major doubt Violette will stay 1m. So far she has shown smart form over 6-7f, and on pedigree that should be her trip at 3, too.

at Doncaster in September fell to her late burst and some cool route-finding from her jockey, and ten days later she was again going on much too strongly for the rest in the final furlong of a Group 3 at Ayr.

A huge pot narrowly escaped her grasp in the Redcar sales race, as 6-4 favourite Violette beat her stands-side group clearly enough but hung away from them and lost out on the other side to Misu Bond, who was drawn one. Evaluating that race nearly always demands a dose of aspirin but Violette gave an unequivocal demonstration of her class when taking second again when stepped back up to seven furlongs for the Rockfel at Newmarket, looking rather unlucky too as she got checked in her run before losing out to Speciosa by a neck. She may have been over the top when taken to Maisons-Laffitte for her final outing.

Violette is from a speedy family but the Rockfel performance gives hope that she will stay a mile. Whether she has the scope to improve again in her second season, however, must be open to question. *RA*

Wake Up Maggie (Ire) 109

b f Xaar - Kalagold (Ire) (Magical Strike (USA)) March 21
Owner J G Lambton **Trainer** C F Wall **Breeder** Rathmoyle Exports Ltd
4 starts: won **2**, second **2**, **£149,479** win & place prize-money

"THERE was no disgrace to be second. Posterity may say that this was not a vintage running of this race but, for the moment, they are the best around and the form was strong." Chris Wall's calm reflection on the Cheveley Park Stakes was, on the face of it, remarkably calm seeing as his Wake Up Maggie had just been denied the £104,806 first prize in that Group 1 by a neck, but by that stage the filly had already put more than that in the bank. The decision to retain her for 20,000 guineas at the breeze-up sales was an exceedingly wise one.

The lion's share, to put it mildly, of those earnings came via the Tattersalls Ireland Sale Stakes at The Curragh in August, when Wake Up Maggie overturned a deficit with the far-side group to win by two lengths from the subsequent Mill Reef winner Cool Creek. Wake Up Maggie had been unlucky not to beat another useful Richard Hannon horse, Godfrey Street, on the Lingfield all-weather earlier that month following her highly promising debut success at Sandown.

Not much more luck in running would have been required for Wake Up Maggie to emerge first in the Cheveley Park, in which Donna Blini got first run and just held on, but Flashy Wings was close up as well and finishing even faster. That run confirmed that Wake Up Maggie should stay beyond six furlongs, and she is bred to get a mile. She had an interrupted preparation for the Cheveley Park, having been on a course of antibiotics shortly after her Curragh win. *RA*

Race record

2nd Sky Bet Cheveley Park Stakes (Group 1) (Newmarket, September 29) 2yo 6f Good **109** (TS 94) 10 ran.

1st Tattersalls Ireland Sale Stakes (Curragh, August 20) 2yo 6f Good **103** (TS 80) 26 ran.

2nd Celebrate Your Wedding At Lingfield Racecourse Novice Stakes (Lingfield (AW), August 5) 2yo 5f Standard **90** (TS 59) 7 ran.

1st RBL 60th Anniversary End of WWII Maiden Auction Stakes (Sandown, July 21) 2yo 5f Good to firm **81** (TS 79) 15 ran.

Pedigree assessment

Sire Xaar (Zafonic) Outstanding 2yo over 6-7f, won Dewhurst S-Gr1, Prix de la Salamandre-Gr1. Showed high-class form over 8-10f at 3 and 4, gained only win in Craven S-Gr3 but Gr1 placed in Irish Champion and Eclipse S. By outstanding 2yo/miler who has done particularly well with 2yos, out of smart 2yo/sprinter from outstanding family. First foals 2002, good record with 2yos, particularly over 6-7f, sire of Balthazaar's Gift, Mystical Land, Sir Xaar, Tony James. **Dam Kalagold** Won over 1m at 2, unplaced at 3 over 7-12f. By smart 7-8f performer but modest sire, out of unraced half-sister to useful 12f colt Gorgeous Strike. Her 2 earlier foals have made no impact. **Conclusion** This is an otherwise modest family in recent generations. Wake Up Maggie has shown speed, but on pedigree she has every chance of lasting 1m.

Wake Up Maggie beats Cool Creek at The Curragh

Winged Cupid (Ire) 111

b c In The Wings - Sweet Emotion (Ire) (Bering) April 18
Owner Joy and Valentine Feerick **Trainer** M Johnston **Breeder** Longfield Stud
3 starts: won **2**, second **1**, **£64,166** win & place prize-money

WINGED CUPID is the latest of Mark Johnston's juveniles to get the call-up from Godolphin. He's not nearly so obvious a candidate for Classic glory as Shamardal was 12 months earlier, but very few could be and Winged Cupid met his only defeat as a two-year-old when runner-up at Group 1 level in a bog, so it's easy to see why Godolphin have decided that the best is yet to come.

Winged Cupid did not have the Derby entry as a two-year-old, something the Godolphin purse will surely deal with before long, but his then owners were looking forward to top middle-distance races after he won his first two starts, in August and September, on fast ground over a mile.

A maiden when second favourite at Sandown kicked things off, and Winged Cupid headed the betting for the Haynes, Hanson and Clark Conditions Stakes at Newbury. The past winners that ensure this race gets such high billing are heroes of mostly former decades, but in winning his renewal with indisputable authority, always in the front rank and setting a new juvenile course record, Winged Cupid gave every indication that he could give it further lustre.

The Racing Post Trophy was set as his next target and, although having to overcome a foot abscess to take part, Winged Cupid started second favourite to the Ballydoyle hotpot Septimus. Winged Cupid dealt with him comfortably enough but a bold front-running effort failed to hold off the 20-1 shot Palace Episode.

A highly profitable investment at 9,000 guineas as a foal – he was also unsold at 24,000 guineas as a yearling – Winged Cupid is by a notable stamina influence in In The Wings but the dam's family means he is not 100 per cent sure to get a mile and a half. "He's a very weak horse," said Johnston after the Racing Post Trophy, "and there is a huge amount of room for improvement." *RA*

Race record

2nd Racing Post Trophy (Group 1) (Doncaster, October 22) 2yo 1m Heavy **111** (TS 107) 7 ran.

1st Haynes, Hanson And Clark Conditions Stakes (Newbury, September 16) 2yo 1m Good to firm **103** (TS 96) 11 ran.

1st Mildmay Vets EBF Maiden Stakes (Sandown, August 11) 2yo 1m Good to firm **78** (TS 75) 9 ran.

Pedigree assessment

Sire In The Wings (Sadler's Wells) Won both 2yo starts (6-7f), inc. Listed event, 10f Gr3 winner from just 2 3yo starts, top-class 4yo over 12f, won Coronation Cup, Grand Prix de Saint-Cloud, Breeders' Cup Turf. By outstanding middle-distance sire, out of high-class 12f filly. Very good sire, occasionally gets smart 2yos but far better record with progeny aged 3+. Capable of siring smart milers, but most progeny best over 10f+. **Dam Sweet Emotion** Unraced at 2, quite useful 1m winner at 3. By top-class 12f performer and good sire, out of unraced half-sister to high-class 6-8f colts Great Commotion and Lead On Time. Her 2 earlier foals have run but have made little mark. **Conclusion** Bred to make good progress from 2 to 3. Will stay 10f, but 12f is not guaranteed as there is a fair amount of speed on dam's side.

With Interest 82

b c Selkirk (USA) - With Fascination (USA) (Dayjur (USA)) March 17
Owner George Strawbridge **Trainer** A M Balding **Breeder** George Strawbridge
1 start: won **1**, **£4,966** win & place prize-money

WITH INTEREST is one of those once-raced maiden winners who dealt with the opposition put in front of him in such style that he might be capable of the step up required to figure in useful company as a three-year-old. It is a big step up, without doubt, as the form at Newbury that afternoon in October was unexceptional, but 10-1 shot With Interest was value for more than his two-length winning margin and, if his stable's record is anything to go by, he should be all the better for a run under his belt. The Horris Hill was mentioned as a further option for this scopey individual, but he did not race again.

There is conflicting evidence in the pedigree as to whether he will stay beyond a mile. One brother was running over middle distances in France in 2005, but With Interest is probably a racehorse of an entirely different calibre. *RA*

Race record

1st Newvoicemedia Maiden Stakes (Div I) (Newbury, October 7) 2yo 7f Good to firm **82** (TS 66) 19 ran.

Pedigree assessment

Sire Selkirk (Sharpen Up) Very useful 1m 2yo winner, later top-class 7-8f colt, won Queen Elizabeth II S-Gr1 and 3 Gr2 events. By sire of Diesis, Kris, Sharpo and Trempolino out of high-class miler and excellent broodmare. Very good sire, decent source of 2yos (Red Bloom, Sulk) but better record with 3yos, mainly over 1m+ (Altieri, Favourable Terms, Field Of Hope, Prince Kirk, Wince), sires occasional talented sprinter (Etlaala, The Trader). **Dam With Fascination** High-class 6-7f 2yo in France, won Prix de Cabourg-Gr3, 2nd Prix Morny-Gr1, Prix de la Salamandre-Gr1. Unplaced both 3yo starts over 7f. By outstanding sprinter who is influence for speed, out of top-class US filly Fran's Valentine (over 1m+ from 2 to 5). Half-sister to top-class 10-12f US turf horse With Anticipation (Relaunch). Her 4 earlier foals include 1m 2yo and 10f 3yo winners (both by Nashwan) and a Selkirk colt placed over 10-12f in France. **Conclusion** Bred to be best at around a mile, and on pedigree he should make good progress from 2 to 3.

Racing Post Classification

The Racing Post Classification lists the Racing Post Ratings for the world's leading racehorses. The classification takes into account performances in Group 1 and Grade 1 races worldwide, Group racing as a whole throughout Europe and all racing in Britain and Ireland. They provide a fascinating insight into the relative merits of the best horses who represented each of the major racing nations in 2005. Racing Post Ratings are compiled by our team of independent handicappers who rely primarily on collateral form as the basis of the figures. The ratings incorporate weight-for-age allowances to facilitate direct comparison of the merit of horses of different ages. The 'distance(s)' column in the table indicates the distance, or distances, at which the horse achieved the rating

Note that the classification for dirt horses includes three-year-olds and upwards

European two-year-olds

Rating	Name & sex	Trainer	Country	Distance(s)
121	**George Washington (Ire) C**	A P O'Brien	Ireland	6f
120	**Amadeus Wolf C**	K A Ryan	UK	6f
	Horatio Nelson (Ire) C	A P O'Brien	Ireland	7f
119	**Sir Percy C**	M P Tregoning	UK	7f
117	**Carlotamix (Fr) C**	A Fabre	France	8f
116	**Red Clubs (Ire) C**	B W Hills	UK	6f
114	**Alexandrova (Ire) F**	A P O'Brien	Ireland	8f
	Nannina F	J H M Gosden	UK	8f
	New Girlfriend (Ire) F	Robert Collet	France	6f
	Opera Cape C	S Kirk	UK	7f
	Palace Episode (USA) C	K A Ryan	UK	8f
	Silca's Sister F	M R Channon	UK	6f
112	**Alexander Alliance (Ire) F**	T Stack	Ireland	6f
	Always Hopeful C	E J O'Neill	UK	6f
	Balthazaar's Gift (Ire) C	K A Ryan	UK	6f
	Close To You (Ire) C	T G Mills	UK	7f
	Ivan Denisovich (Ire) C	A P O'Brien	Ireland	6f
	Rumplestiltskin (Ire) F	A P O'Brien	Ireland	8f
	Silent Times (Ire) C	E J O'Neill	UK	7f
111	**Black Charmer (Ire) C**	M Johnston	UK	7f
	Cool Creek (Ire) C	R Hannon	UK	6f, 7f
	Flashy Wings F	M R Channon	UK	6f
	Stormy River (Fr) C	N Clement	France	8f
	Winged Cupid (Ire) C	M Johnston	UK	8f
110	**Ajigolo C**	M R Channon	UK	5f
	Donna Blini F	B J Meehan	UK	6f
	Lateral C	P Schiergen	Germany	8f
	Linda's Lad C	A Fabre	France	10f
	Porto Santo (Fr) C	P Demercastel	France	8f
	Sir Xaar (Ire) C	B Smart	UK	6f
	Violette F	Sir Mark Prescott	UK	7f

Three-year-olds

Rating	Name & sex	Trainer	Country	Distance(s)
133	**Hurricane Run (Ire) C**	A Fabre	France	12f
129	**Motivator C**	M L W Bell	UK	12f
128	**Dubawi (Ire) C**	Saeed Bin Suroor	UK	8f
	Proclamation (Ire) C	J Noseda	UK	8f
127	**Shamardal (USA) C**	Saeed Bin Suroor	UK	8f
126	**David Junior (USA) C**	B J Meehan	UK	10f
	Oratorio (Ire) C	A P O'Brien	Ireland	10f
125	**Deep Impact (Jpn) C**	Y Ikee	Japan	12f
123	**Dance Hero (Aus) G**	Mrs Gai Waterhouse	Australia	7f
	Divine Proportions (USA) F	P Bary	France	8f
	Scorpion (Ire) C	A P O'Brien	Ireland	12f
	Shawanda (Ire) F	A De Royer-Dupre	France	12f
122	**Goodricke C**	D R Loder	UK	6f, 7f
121	**English Channel (USA) C**	T Pletcher	USA	12f
	Layman (USA) C	Saeed Bin Suroor	UK	8f
	Walk In The Park (Ire) C	J E Hammond	France	12f
120	**Pinson (Ire) C**	J-C Rouget	France	10f
	Plastered (Aus) G	L Smith	Australia	12f
	Ruwi C	J-C Rouget	France	10f
119	**Ad Valorem (USA) C**	A P O'Brien	Ireland	8f
	Anna Monda (Ger) F	P Rau	Germany	8f
	Gorella (Fr) F	P L Biancone	USA	8f
	Gun Salute (USA) C	W Mott	USA	10f
	Linngari (Ire) C	Sir Michael Stoute	UK	8f
	Outback Prince (Aus) C	A Cummings	Australia	12f
	Six Sense (Jpn) C	H Nagahama	Japan	12f
	Tails Of Triomphe (Aus) G	T O'Sullivan	Australia	13f
	The Geezer C	D R C Elsworth	UK	12f, 15f
	Willow O Wisp (USA) G	V Cerin	USA	10f
118	**Barely A Moment (Aus) C**	T McEvoy	Australia	6f
	Big Planet (Jpn) C	K Minai	Japan	8f
	Footstepsinthesand C	A P O'Brien	Ireland	8f
	Hard Top (Ire) C	Sir Michael Stoute	UK	12f
	Lords A Leaping (Nz) C	R Smerdon	Australia	12f

Three-year-olds continued

Rating	Name & sex	Trainer	Country	Distance(s)
	Rob Roy (USA) C	Sir Michael Stoute	UK	8f
	Stormhill (Aus) C	T Martin	Australia	12f
117	Admire Japan (Jpn) C	H Matsuda	Japan	12f
	Eremein (Aus) G	A Denham	Australia	12f
	Galeota (Ire) C	R Hannon	UK	6f
	Indesatchel (Ire) C	David Wachman	Ireland	8f
	Irish Darling (Aus) F	T Vasil	Australia	10f
	Shinzig (Aus) C	C Waller	NZ	7f
	Stella Grande (Aus) G	Lee Freedman	Australia	12f
	Stormy Cafe (Jpn) C	F Kojima	Japan	10f
	Turtle Bowl (Ire) C	F Rohaut	France	8f
	Vitesse Dane (Aus) F	Kris Lees	Australia	12f
116	Air Messiah (Jpn) F	Y Ito	Japan	10f
	Alayan (Ire) C	John M Oxx	Ireland	10f
	Avalon G	A P O'Brien	Ireland	12f
	Cesario (Jpn) F	Katsuhiko Sumii	Japan	10f
	Douro Valley (Aus) G	P Moody	NZ	13f
	Eswarah F	M A Jarvis	UK	12f
	Gharir (Ire) C	J E Hammond	France	8f
	Inti Raimi (Jpn) C	S Sasaki	Japan	12f
	Melhor Ainda (USA) F	R J Frankel	USA	10f
	Munsef C	J L Dunlop	UK	12f
	Nicaron (Ger) C	H Steinmetz	Germany	12f
	Not A Single Doubt (Aus) C	T Vasil	Australia	7f
	Nota Bene C	D R C Elsworth	UK	6f
	Pentathlon (Nz) G	J Wheeler	NZ	12f
	Runaway C	A Fabre	France	12f
	Salutino (Ger) C	A Schutz	Germany	12f
	Shalapour (Ire) C	John M Oxx	Ireland	12f
	Unfurled (Ire) C	J L Dunlop	UK	14f
	Vadawina (Ire) F	A Fabre	France	10f
115	Camacho C	H R A Cecil	UK	6f
	Chelsea Rose (Ire) F	C Collins	Ireland	9f, 12f
	Cupid's Glory G	Sir Mark Prescott	UK	8f

Rating	Name & sex	Trainer	Country	Distance(s)
	Darci Brahma (Nz) C	M Walker	NZ	8f
	Dash To The Top F	L M Cumani	UK	12f
	Desideratum C	A Fabre	France	12f
	God's Own (Aus) C	J B Cummings	Australia	8f
	Helios Quercus (Fr) C	C Diard	France	8f
	Iceman C	J H M Gosden	UK	8f
	Jambalaya (USA) G	Catherine Day Phillips	Canada	10f
	Karen's Caper (USA) F	J H M Gosden	UK	8f, 9f
	Kylikwong (Aus) F	Mick Price	Australia	10f
	Lions Gate (Aus) C	T McEvoy	Australia	13f
	Maids Causeway (Ire) F	B W Hills	UK	8f
	Manduro (Ger) C	P Schiergen	Germany	10f
	Miss Sally (Ire) F	M Halford	Ireland	6f
	Oiseau Rare (Fr) F	A Fabre	France	13f
	Paratroopers (Aus) C	J Hawkes	Australia	8f
	Rebel Rebel (Ire) C	R J Frankel	USA	8f
	Rhein Kraft (Jpn) F	T Setoguchi	Japan	8f, 10f
	Rocamadour C	M R Channon	UK	8f
	Royal Highness (Ger) F	P Bary	France	12f
	Saxon (Aus) C	G Ryan	Australia	12f
	Starpix (Fr) C	J-C Rouget	France	8f
	Sweet Talker (USA) F	Helen Pitts	USA	9f
	Virginia Waters (USA) F	A P O'Brien	Ireland	8f

Four-year-olds-plus

Rating	Name & sex	Trainer	Country	Distance(s)
129	**Azamour (Ire) C**	John M Oxx	Ireland	12f
	Rakti H	M A Jarvis	UK	8f
	Westerner H	E Lellouche	France	12f
128	**Imperial Stride C**	Sir Michael Stoute	UK	12f
	Silent Witness (Aus) G	A S Cruz	HK	5f
127	**Leroidesanimaux (Brz) H**	R J Frankel	USA	8f
	Shirocco (Ger) C	A Fabre	France	12f
	Starcraft (Nz) H	L M Cumani	UK	8f

Four-year-olds plus continued

Rating	Name & sex	Trainer	Country	Distance(s)
	Vengeance Of Rain (Nz) G	D Ferraris	HK	10f
126	Bago (Fr) C	J E Pease	France	12f
	Grey Swallow (Ire) C	D K Weld	Ireland	11f
	Valixir (Ire) C	A Fabre	France	8f
125	Alkaased (USA) H	L M Cumani	UK	12f
	Electrocutionist (USA) C	V Valiani	Italy	10f
	Heart's Cry (Jpn) C	K Hashiguchi	Japan	12f
	Norse Dancer (Ire) H	D R C Elsworth	UK	12f
124	Ace (Ire) C	A P O'Brien	Ireland	12f
	Artie Schiller (USA) C	J Jerkens	USA	8f
	Grand Armee (Aus) G	Mrs Gai Waterhouse	Australia	10f
	Makybe Diva M	Lee Freedman	Australia	16f
	Maraahel (Ire) C	Sir Michael Stoute	UK	10f
	Powerscourt H	A P O'Brien	Ireland	10f
	Soviet Song (Ire) M	J R Fanshawe	UK	8f
	Whipper (USA) C	Robert Collet	France	8f
	Zenno Rob Roy (Jpn) H	Kazuo Fujisawa	Japan	10f
123	Asakusa Den'En H	Michifumi Kono	Japan	8f
	Bandari (Ire) H	M Johnston	UK	12f
	Greys Inn (USA) H	M F De Kock	South Africa	10f, 12f
	Hat Trick (Jpn) C	Katsuhiko Sumii	Japan	8f
	Kitten's Joy (USA) C	Dale Romans	USA	8f
	Le Vie Dei Colori H	L M Cumani	UK	7f
	Pastoral Pursuits C	H Morrison	UK	6f
	Pride (Fr) M	A De Royer-Dupre	France	12f
	Relaxed Gesture (Ire) C	Christophe Clement	USA	12f
122	Alexander Goldrun (Ire) F	J S Bolger	Ireland	10f
	Bullish Luck (USA) G	A S Cruz	HK	8f
	Daiwa Major (Jpn) C	H Uehara	Japan	8f
	Gamut (Ire) H	Sir Michael Stoute	UK	12f
	Lincoln (Jpn) H	H Otonashi	Japan	12f
	Majors Cast (Ire) C	J Noseda	UK	8f
	Russian Pearl (Nz) G	A S Cruz	HK	10f

Rating	Name & sex	Trainer	Country	Distance(s)
	Tycoon C	M Al Kurdi	United Arab Emirates	12f
	Warrsan (Ire) H	C E Brittain	UK	12f
	Yeats (Ire) C	A P O'Brien	Ireland	12f
121	**Autumn Glory (Ire) H**	G Wragg	UK	8f
	Cacique (Ire) C	A Fabre	France	8f
	Cape Of Good Hope G	D Oughton	HK	6f
	Chineur (Fr) C	M Delzangles	France	5f
	Darsalam (Ire) C	A Shavuyev	Czech Republic	12f
	Distinction (Ire) G	Sir Michael Stoute	UK	20f
	Elvstroem (Aus) H	T Vasil	Australia	9f
	Epalo (Ger) H	A Schutz	Germany	10f
	Iffraaj C	M A Jarvis	UK	7f
	Mamool (Ire) H	Saeed Bin Suroor	UK	12f
	Millenary H	J L Dunlop	UK	16f
	Natural Blitz (Aus) G	D Cruz	HK	5f
	Nayyir G	G A Butler	UK	8f
	North Light (Ire) C	Sir Michael Stoute	UK	10f
	Singletary (USA) H	D Chatlos Jr	USA	8f
	Sleeping Indian C	J H M Gosden	UK	7f
	Super Kid (Nz) H	J Moore	HK	7f
	Tiber (Ire) H	J Moore	HK	8f
	Touch Of Land (Fr) H	H-A Pantall	France	10f
120	**Alinghi (Aus) F**	R J Frankel	USA	6f
	Better Talk Now (USA) G	H G Motion	USA	11f
	Cosmo Bulk (Jpn) H	K Tabe	Japan	12f
	Court's In Session (Aus) G	G Walter	Australia	8f
	Delzao (Aus) C	R Smerdon	Australia	10f
	Golden Quest G	M Johnston	UK	16f
	Green Treasure (Aus) G	D Cruz	HK	10f
	Intercontinental M	R J Frankel	USA	10f
	King's Drama (Ire) G	R J Frankel	USA	11f
	Perfect Partner (Aus) G	A S Cruz	HK	10f
	Policy Maker (Ire) H	E Lellouche	France	12f
	Railings (Aus) G	J Hawkes	Australia	12f
	Right Approach H	M F De Kock	South Africa	9f
	Spark Of Life (Aus) G	A Denham	Australia	6f
	Sunrise Pegasus (Jpn) H	S Ishizaka	Japan	12f

Four-year-olds-plus continued

Rating	Name & sex	Trainer	Country	Distance(s)
	Sweet Return H	R McAnally	USA	9f, 10f
	The Duke (Aus) G	C Fownes	HK	8f
119	**Avonbridge H**	R Charlton	UK	5f
	Balance Of Game (Jpn) H	Y Munakata	Japan	8f
	Best Gift (Nz) G	J Moore	HK	12f
	Castledale (Ire) C	Jeff Mullins	USA	8f
	Chic M	Sir Michael Stoute	UK	8f
	Coin Toss (Jpn) H	Kazuo Fujisawa	Japan	12f
	Dave's Best G	C H Yip	HK	8f
	Day Flight C	J H M Gosden	UK	12f
	Durandal (Jpn) H	M Sakaguchi	Japan	6f
	Fields Of Omagh (Aus) G	D Hayes	Australia	10f
	Fourty Niners Son (USA) C	N Drysdale	USA	10f
	Lachlan River (Nz) G	John Morrisey	Australia	10f, 12f
	Lad Of The Manor (Nz) G	R Hoysted	Australia	10f
	Leprechaun Kid (USA) G	M Mitchell	USA	10f
	Limehouse (USA) C	T Pletcher	USA	8f
	Mubtaker (USA) H	M P Tregoning	UK	12f, 13f
	Mullins Bay C	A P O'Brien	Ireland	9f
	Ouija Board F	E A L Dunlop	UK	12f
	Phoenix Reach (Ire) H	A M Balding	UK	10f, 12f
	Quito (Ire) R	D W Chapman	UK	6f
	Reefscape C	A Fabre	France	20f
	Saturn (Ire) G	C Fownes	HK	10f
	Shakespeare (USA) C	W Mott	USA	12f
	Simonas (Ire) H	A Wohler	Germany	12f
	Sweep Tosho (Jpn) F	A Tsurudome	Japan	11f
	Vinnie Roe (Ire) H	D K Weld	Ireland	16f
	Winning Belle (Nz) M	Mrs Gai Waterhouse	Australia	10f
	Wolf Whistle (SAF) G	M F De Kock	South Africa	9f
	Yard-Arm (SAF) G	M L W Bell	UK	8f
118	**Admire Max (Jpn) H**	M Hashida	Japan	6f, 8f
	Ain't Here (Aus) G	D Hall	HK	8f
	Altieri H	V Caruso	Italy	10f
	Andean C	Saeed Bin Suroor	UK	9f

Rating	Name & sex	Trainer	Country	Distance(s)
	Babodana H	M H Tompkins	UK	8f
	Buckland Manor (USA) H	J Paco Gonzalez	USA	8f
	Caradak (Ire) C	John M Oxx	Ireland	7f
	Cherry Mix (Fr) C	Saeed Bin Suroor	UK	12f
	Company (Jpn) C	H Otonashi	Japan	8f
	Country Music (Aus) G	A S Cruz	HK	5f
	Desert War (Aus) G	Mrs Gai Waterhouse	Australia	8f
	Designed For Luck (USA) G	V Cerin	USA	8f
	Film Maker (USA) M	H G Motion	USA	12f
	Gift Horse G	D Nicholls	UK	6f
	Heavenly Romance (Jpn) M	S Yamamoto	Japan	10f
	Host (Chi) H	T Pletcher	USA	8f
	Key Of Destiny (SAF) G	M F De Kock	South Africa	9f
	King Of Happiness (USA) H	N Drysdale	USA	8f
	Martillo (Ger) H	R Suerland	Germany	8f
	Mummify (Aus) G	Lee Freedman	Australia	10f, 12f
	New Seeker G	C G Cox	UK	7f
	Osumi Haruka (Jpn) M	M Ando	Japan	11f
	Razkalla (USA) G	Saeed Bin Suroor	UK	12f
	Red Fort (Ire) G	N Drysdale	USA	10f
	Regal Roller (Aus) G	C McDonald	Australia	7f
	Savabeel (Aus) C	G Rogerson	Australia	7f
	Soldier Hollow H	P Schiergen	Germany	10f
	Solskjaer (Ire) H	A P O'Brien	Ireland	10f
	Striking Ambition H	R Charlton	UK	5f
	Suzuka Mambo (Jpn) C	M Hashida	Japan	12f, 16f
	The Tatling (Ire) G	J M Bradley	UK	5f
117	**A Bit O'Gold (Can) G**	Catherine Day Phillips	Canada	10f, 11f
	Al Nitak (SAF) G	S Seemar	United Arab Emirates	7f
	Alcazar (Ire) G	H Morrison	UK	15f, 16f, 20f
	America Alive (USA) C	N J Howard	USA	9f
	Angara F	P L Biancone	USA	10f
	Arakan (USA) H	Sir Michael Stoute	UK	7f
	Barolo G	W R Swinburn	UK	12f
	Benbaun (Ire) G	M J Wallace	UK	5f
	Blatant G	Saeed Bin Suroor	UK	8f

Four-year-olds-plus continued

Rating	Name & sex	Trainer	Country	Distance(s)
	Casual Pass (Aus) G	M Ellerton	Australia	9f
	Collier Hill G	G A Swinbank	UK	12f, 14f
	County Tyrone (Aus) G	Kris Lees	Australia	16f
	Court Masterpiece H	E A L Dunlop	UK	7f, 8f
	Dance In The Mood (Jpn) F	Kazuo Fujisawa	Japan	10f
	Dizelle (Aus) F	J Hawkes	Australia	12f
	Fastnet Rock (Aus) C	Paul Perry	Australia	6f
	Floral Dynamite (Aus) H	A S Cruz	HK	10f
	Franklins Gardens H	M H Tompkins	UK	14f, 16f
	Geordieland (Fr) C	J-M Beguigne	France	12f
	Hazyview C	N A Callaghan	UK	8f, 10f
	Hurricane Alan (Ire) H	R Hannon	UK	8f
	Jack Sullivan (USA) G	G A Butler	UK	7f, 8f
	Laura's Lucky Boy (USA) C	Richard E Mandella	USA	10f
	Lilando (Aus) G	A Noblet	NZ	5f
	Lochbuie (Ire) C	G Wragg	UK	13f
	Majestic Missile (Ire) C	W J Haggas	UK	5f
	Marend (Fr) G	D Sepulchre	France	13f
	Maruka Kiseki (Jpn) C	T Setoguchi	Japan	6f
	Megahertz M	R J Frankel	USA	10f
	Notable Guest (USA) C	Sir Michael Stoute	UK	11f
	Orientor H	J S Goldie	UK	5f
	Ostankino (Fr) C	E Lellouche	France	15f, 16f, 20f
	Our Smoking Joe (Aus) G	Lee Freedman	Australia	10f
	Peeress F	Sir Michael Stoute	UK	8f
	Percussionist (Ire) G	J Howard Johnson	UK	14f
	Planet Ruler (Aus) G	A Lee	HK	5f, 7f
	Riskaverse (USA) M	Patrick J Kelly	USA	10f
	Soldier's Tale (USA) C	J Noseda	UK	6f
	Telegnosis (Jpn) H	H Sugiura	Japan	8f
	The Trader (Ire) G	M Blanshard	UK	5f
	Three Valleys (USA) C	R J Frankel	USA	8f
	Toulouse Lautrec (Aus) G	J Hawkes	Australia	10f
	Voix Du Nord (Fr) C	D Smaga	France	11f

Rating	Name & sex	Trainer	Country	Distance(s)
	Wonder Again (USA) M	James J Toner	USA	10f
116	**Allez Olive (Ire) G**	Mme C Jung	France	20f
	Ancient World (USA) G	Saeed Bin Suroor	UK	8f
	Ashdown Express (Ire) G	C F Wall	UK	6f
	Baltic King H	H Morrison	UK	6f
	Baron's Pit H	Mrs A J Perrett	UK	6f
	Brunel (Ire) C	W J Haggas	UK	8f
	Byron C	Saeed Bin Suroor	UK	7f
	Carte Diamond (USA) C	B Ellison	UK	14f
	Corridor Creeper (Fr) G	J M Bradley	UK	5f
	Distinctly Secret (Nz) G	M Walker	NZ	10f
	Eisteddfod G	P F I Cole	UK	6f
	G P Fleet (USA) G	Steve Flint	USA	9f
	Good Reward (USA) C	C McGaughey III	USA	10f
	Hookipa Wave (Jpn) C	Y Ninomiya	Japan	10f
	Kinetics (Jpn) H	M Shinkawa	Japan	8f
	La Cucaracha F	B W Hills	UK	5f, 6f
	Mac Love G	J Akehurst	UK	8f
	Mahtoum (Aus) G	Kim Moore	Australia	12f
	Meteor Storm H	W Dollase	USA	8f, 9f, 12f
	Multidandy (Aus) G	A S Cruz	HK	5f
	Palette Natural (Nz) G	J Size	HK	8f
	Polar Ben G	J R Fanshawe	UK	8f
	Prospect Park C	C Laffon-Parias	France	10f, 12f
	Punctilious F	Saeed Bin Suroor	UK	12f
	Sand Springs (USA) M	W Mott	USA	8f, 9f, 10f
	Scintillation (Aus) G	C S Shum	HK	8f
	Sergeant Cecil G	B R Millman	UK	18f
	Shakis (Ire) H	Doug Watson	United Arab Emirates	9f
	Short Pause H	A Fabre	France	11f
	Silver Tree (USA) H	W Mott	USA	9f
	Stream Of Gold (Ire) C	Sir Michael Stoute	UK	8f
	Super Elegant (Aus) G	T Vasil	Australia	6f
	Tap Dance City (USA) H	S Sasaki	Japan	10f, 12f
	The Whistling Teal G	G Wragg	UK	14f
	Tosho Knight (Jpn) C	K Yasuda	Japan	16f

Four-year-olds-plus continued

Rating	Name & sex	Trainer	Country	Distance(s)
	Valentino (Fr) G	A De Royer-Dupre	France	8f
	Vol De Nuit C	L Brogi	Italy	10f, 12f
	We All Love Aleyna (USA) G	J W Sadler	USA	8f
	Weightless G	Mrs A J Perrett	UK	10f
	Wend (USA) F	W Mott	USA	8f
	With Reason (USA) G	Saeed Bin Suroor	UK	8f
115	Adreamisborn (USA) G	J Hollendorfer	USA	8f
	Alost (Fr) G	A Spanu	France	10f, 12f
	Balmont (USA) C	J Noseda	UK	6f
	Bowman's Crossing (Ire) G	D Oughton	HK	8f
	Cairdeas (Ire) C	D K Weld	Ireland	10f
	Cajun Beat (USA) G	R J Frankel	USA	8f
	Celtic Mill G	D W Barker	UK	6f
	Cinque Cento (Aus) F	Tony Wildman	Australia	12f
	Cut Quartz (Fr) H	R Gibson	France	20f
	Dubai Success H	B W Hills	UK	12f
	Fayr Jag (Ire) G	T D Easterby	UK	6f
	Flip Flop (Fr) F	B Cecil	USA	10f
	Forestier (Fr) H	E Danel	France	20f
	Fracassant (Ire) C	R Gibson	France	12f, 13f
	Frank Sonata C	M G Quinlan	UK	12f
	Glamour Puss (Nz) F	Danny O'Brien	Australia	6f
	Grand Emporium (SAF) G	Saeed Bin Suroor	UK	9f
	High Intelligent (Aus) G	J Size	HK	7f, 8f
	Hollow Bullet (Aus) F	J McArdle	Australia	10f
	Hugs Dancer (Fr) G	D Hayes	Australia	8f, 16f
	Jubilation H	F Reuterskiold	Sweden	9f
	Kamsky (Aus) G	J B Cummings	Australia	13f
	Le Carre (USA) G	A De Royer-Dupre	France	16f
	Lord Du Sud (Fr) C	J-C Rouget	France	12f
	Lucky Strike G	A Trybuhl	Germany	6f, 7f
	Malinas (Ger) C	P Schiergen	Germany	12f
	Mustanfar (USA) C	K McLaughlin	USA	9f

Rating	Name & sex	Trainer	Country	Distance(s)
	Omikron (Ire) C	J Barton	United Arab Emirates	12f
	Osterhase (Ire) G	J E Mulhern	Ireland	5f, 6
	Papineau H	Saeed Bin Suroor	UK	14f
	Patezza (Aus) G	G Walter	Australia	7f, 8f
	Prince Arch (USA) C	K McPeek	USA	11f, 12f
	Prince Kirk (Fr) H	E Borromeo	Italy	10f
	Red Bloom F	Sir Michael Stoute	UK	10f
	Red Oog (Aus) G	J Pride	Australia	7f
	Revved Up (USA) G	Christophe Clement	USA	10f
	Sambuca (SAF) G	A T Millard	HK	10f
	Seihali (Ire) H	D Selvaratnam	United Arab Emirates	8f
	Sidewinder (Jpn) H	S Kitahashi	Japan	8f
	Soaring Free (Can) G	M Frostad	Canada	6f
	Somnus G	T D Easterby	UK	6f
	Special Kaldoun (Ire) H	D Smaga	France	8f
	St Andrews (Ire) H	M A Jarvis	UK	10f
	St Basil (Nz) G	B Laming	Australia	7f
	Suggestive G	W J Haggas	UK	7f
	T. H. Approval (USA) C	E Inda	USA	12f
	Takeover Target (Aus) G	J Janiak	Australia	7f
	Vortex G	Miss Gay Kelleway	UK	7f
	Whilly (Ire) C	Doug O'Neill	USA	9f
	Win Radius (Jpn) H	Kazuo Fujisawa	Japan	8f

Dirt

Rating	Name & sex	Trainer	Country	Distance(s)
135	**Ghostzapper (USA) H**	R J Frankel	USA	8f
129	**Saint Liam (USA) H**	R Dutrow Jr	USA	9f
128	**Roses In May (USA) H**	Dale Romans	USA	10f
127	**Borrego (USA) C**	C B Greely	USA	10f
126	**Afleet Alex (USA) C**	T F Ritchey	USA	12f
	Flower Alley (USA) C	T Pletcher	USA	10f
125	**Bellamy Road (USA) C**	N Zito	USA	9f
124	**Lava Man (USA) G**	D O'Neill	USA	10f

Dirt continued

Rating	Name & sex	Trainer	Country	Distance(s)
	Pleasant Home (USA) F	C McGaughey III	USA	9f
123	**Ashado (USA) F**	T Pletcher	USA	9f
	Commentator (USA) G	N Zito	USA	9f
	Perfect Drift (USA) G	Murray W Johnson	USA	10f
	Rock Hard Ten (USA) C	Richard E Mandella	USA	9f
	Sir Shackleton (USA) C	N Zito	USA	9f
122	**Dynever (USA) H**	Christophe Clement	USA	10f
	Forest Danger (USA) C	T Pletcher	USA	7f
	I'm The Tiger (USA) G	R J Frankel	USA	6f
	Super Frolic (USA) H	V Cerin	USA	10f
	Sweet Symphony (USA) F	W Mott	USA	10f
121	**Bandini (USA) C**	T Pletcher	USA	9f
	Buzzards Bay (USA) C	Ronald W Ellis	USA	9f
	Declan's Moon (USA) F	Ronald W Ellis	USA	9f
	Giacomo (USA) C	J Shirreffs	USA	10f
	Sis City (USA) F	R Dutrow Jr	USA	9f
	Suave (USA) C	P McGee	USA	10f
120	**Choctaw Nation (USA) G**	Jeff Mullins	USA	10f
	Closing Argument (USA) C	K McLaughlin	USA	10f
	Consolidator (USA) C	D Wayne Lukas	USA	9f
	General John B (USA) G	Roger Stein	USA	9f
	Happy Ticket (USA) F	A Leggio Jr	USA	10f
	Leave Me Alone (USA) F	J Eric Kruljac	USA	7f
	Purge (USA) C	T Pletcher	USA	8f
	Silver Train (USA) C	R Dutrow Jr	USA	6f
	Summerly (USA) F	S Asmussen	USA	9f
	Taste Of Paradise (USA) H	G Mandella	USA	6f
	Wilko (USA) C	Craig Dollase	USA	9f

The directory

The directory lists every horse who ran in Britain in 2005, plus top overseas performers. Each entry includes the horse's full form figures, with distance and going (in raised figures) for each run, wins-places-runs statistics for 2005 and total prize-money for 2005. Each horse is given a definitive Racing Post Rating, and an all-weather rating (a) where appropriate

A Bid In Time (Ire) *D Shaw* 36 a6
4 b f Danetime (Ire) - Bidni (Ire)
11^{6sd} 12^{5sd} 12^{6g} 7^{5g} 9^{5gf} 11^{6s} 15^{5gf}
0-0-7

A Bit Of Fun *J T Stimpson* a46
4 ch g Unfuwain (USA) - Horseshoe Reef
4^{11sd} **0-0-1**

A Little Bit Yarie *K R Burke* 61
4 b g Paris House - Slipperose
14^{5hy} 6^{5s} **0-0-2**

A Little Tipsy *D Haydn Jones* a18
3 b g Tipsy Creek (USA) - My Hearts Desire
14^{10sd} 12^{9sd} 17^{8g} **0-0-3**

A Monk Swimming (Ire) *Miss J S Davis* a2
4 br g Among Men (USA) - Sea Magic (Ire)
12^{12sd} **0-0-1**

A One (Ire) *H J Manners* 67 a37
6 b g Alzao (USA) - Anita's Contessa (Ire)
9^{9sd} 5^{10gs} 12^{6gf} 3^{10f} 5^{8gf} 10^{7gf} 3^{10gf} 7^{10gf}
13^{8gf} **0-1-9 £882**

A Qui Le Tour *M R Hoad* 18
3 b g Pyramus (USA) - Dolphin Beech (Ire)
12^{10sd} 7^{8g} **0-0-2**

A Teen *P Howling* 35 a53
7 ch h Presidium - Very Good
11^{6sd} 4^{6sd} 6^{5sd} 6^{6sd} 10^{5sd} 9^{7sd} 8^{7sd} 6^{6s} 10^{6sd}
5^{6sd} 8^{6g} 7^{6gs} 7^{5sd} 3^{5sd} **0-1-14 £208**

A Thousand Smiles (Ire) *M A Jarvis* 68 a58
3 b f Sadler's Wells (USA) - Bluffing (Ire)
4^{10gs} 2^{14g} 3^{12s} 3^{10sd} **0-3-4 £2,651**

A Woman In Love *Miss B Sanders* a54
6 gr m Muhtarram (USA) - Ma Lumiere (Fr)
11^{6sd} **0-0-1**

Aahgowangowan (Ire) *M Dods* 71
6 b m Tagula (Ire) - Cabcharge Princess (Ire)
5^{6gs} 10^{5g} 1^{6gf} 8^{5g} 4^{6gs} 6^{5gf} 2^{6gf} 12^{6gf} 2^{6g}
7^{5gs} 9^{6g} 12^{5g} **1-2-12 £8,730**

Aamaaq *J L Dunlop* 84
2 b c Danehill (USA) - Alabaq (USA)
3^{7g} 4^{7gf} 2^{8g} 2^{8g} **0-3-4 £4,762**

Aastral Magic *R Hannon* 82 a67
3 b f Magic Ring (Ire) - Robanna
12^{8gs} 5^{7g} 7^{6g} 8^{7f} 1^{7gf} 8^{7g} 6^{7g} 22^{7gf} 9^{7g}
11^{7sd} **1-0-10 £7,077**

Abbajabba *C W Fairhurst* 54
9 b g Barrys Gamble - Bo' Babbity
16^{8g} 12^{7s} 14^{6g} **0-0-3**

Abbey Cat (Ire) *G A Swinbank* 65
2 b f Indian Danehill (Ire) - Catfoot Lane
6^{5gf} 3^{5s} 2^{6gs} 2^{5gf} 1^{5g} 2^{7gf} 4^{6f} 3^{7g} **1-4-8**
£10,041

Abbey Hill *W S Kittow* 24 a29
8 b m Then Again - Galley Bay
10^{12sd} 9^{10hy} 11^{12g} **0-0-3**

Abbeygate *T Keddy* a59
4 b g Unfuwain (USA) - Ayunli
1^{8sd} 2^{9sd} 1^{7sd} 4^{8sd} 1^{8sd} 5^{8sd} 5^{8sd} **3-1-7**
£9,276

Abbielou *B J Meehan* 73 a57
2 ch f Bertolini (USA) - Rockstine (Ire)
3^{5gf} 3^{5gs} 4^{5gf} 7^{5gf} 1^{5gf} 25^{5gf} 8^{5gs} 8^{5sd}
1-2-8 £5,725

Abbondanza (Ire) *J Howard Johnson* 67
2 b c Cape Cross (Ire) - Ninth Wonder (USA)
3^{8gf} 6^{8s} **0-1-2 £560**

Abelard (Ire) *R A Fahey* 56 a40
4 b g Fasliyev (USA) - Half-Hitch (USA)
11^{5sd} 7^{6sd} 10^{7sd} 9^{7g} 4^{5gf} 4^{5s} 7^{5gf} 3^{6gf} 11^{6gf}
4^{5gf} 6^{6g} 17^{6gf} **0-3-12 £738**

Aberdeen Park *Mrs H Sweeting* 63 a52
3 gr f Environment Friend - Michelee
7^{7g} 8^{7gf} 5^{8gf} 5^{7gf} 7^{8gs} 5^{7s} 5^{7gf} 6^{10g} 17^{10g}
5^{8sf} 6^{8sd} **0-0-11**

Aberdovey *M L W Bell* 81 a31
3 b f Mister Baileys - Annapurna (Ire)
9^{9g} 5^{7g} 1^{8gf} 8^{8g} 2^{8g} 4^{8gf} 6^{9gs} 11^{8sd}
1-0-8 £9,261

Abeurbe Condita (Ire) *E S McMahon* 21
2 ch c Titus Livius (Fr) - Avantage Service (Ire)
7^{8g} **0-0-1**

Abhisheka (Ire) *Saeed Bin Suroor* 66
2 b f Sadler's Wells (USA) - Snow Bride (USA)
6^{7g} 6^{8s} **0-0-2**

Abide (Fr) *R Hannon* 77
3 ch f Pivotal - Ariadne (Ger)
2^{8g} 2^{8g} 3^{7g} 3^{8gf} 1^{7gf} 5^{7f} 7^{8gf} 11^{8g} 11^{8f}
9^{8g} **1-4-10 £9,850**

Abientot (Ire) *B J Meehan* 85 a73
3 b g Danetime (Ire) - Clandolly (Ire)
2^{7sd} 1^{7sd} 1^{5gf} 8^{6gf} 6^{6gf} 5^{5gf} 3^{5gf} 1^{5gs} 6^{5g}
3-2-9 £22,628

Abigail Pett *J S Bolger* 107
2 ch f Medicean - Kalindi
7^{7g} 1^{7gf} 1^{6gf} 1^{6g} 2^{7y} 3^{7gs} 2^{7hy} **3-3-7**
£99,582

Able Baker Charlie (Ire) *J R Fanshawe* 99
6 b g Sri Pekan (USA) - Lavezzola (Ire)
12^{9g} 3^{8gf} 6^{8gf} 1^{10gs} 11^{10g} **1-1-5**
£14,065

Able Charlie (Ger) *Mrs Tracey Barfoot-Saunt* 75
3 ch g Lomitas - Alula (Ger)
5^{7gf} 7^{8gf} 7^{8g} 7^{7g} 2^{8g} 11^{7g} 15^{8gf} 1^{7g} 9^{7gf}
1-1-9 £4,086

Able Mind *A C Whillans* 64 a47
5 b g Mind Games - Chlo-Jo
5^{8gs} 1^{8gf} 3^{10gf} 3^{8gf} 5^{11gs} 5^{10s} 10^{12s} 6^{9sd}
1-1-8 £4,384

Aboustar *M Brittain* a53
5 b g Abou Zouz (USA) - Three Star Rated (Ire)
5^{5sd} 1^{6sd} 6^{6sd} 8^{6sd} 2^{6sd} 11^{6sd} **1-1-6**
£1,910

Above Board *R F Marvin* a30
10 b g Night Shift (USA) - Bundled Up (USA)
13^{6sd} 7^{6sd} 11^{6sd} 11^{6sd} 10^{6sd} 7^{6sd} 7^{6sd}
0-0-7

Aboyne (Ire) *M G Quinlan* 65 a66
2 b c Mull Of Kintyre (USA) - Never End
1^{5s} 3^{5g} 5^{6gf} 6^{6gf} 5^{7g} 3^{7sd} 3^{7sd} 23^{6g} 7^{8g} 2^{7gf}
20^{8hy} 6^{8sd} 7^{9sd} **1-3-13 £5,649**

Absent Friends *J Balding* 66 a82
8 b g Rock City - Green Supreme
8^{5sd} 5^{5sd} 2^{6sd} 7^{5sd} 8^{5sd} 9^{5s} 2^{5f} 1^{5gf} 7^{5g} 15^{5gs}
9^{5g} 14^{6sd} **1-2-12 £4,664**

Absinther *M R Bosley* 46
8 b g Presidium - Heavenly Queen
12^{10gf} 5^{12gf} 8^{12gf} 4^{11gs} PU^{10f} **0-0-5**

Absolutely Perhaps (Ire) *D Morris* 55 a55
3 b f Daylami (Ire) - Dream Lover
6^{9sd} 5^{12gf} 9^{12gf} **0-0-3**

Absolutelythebest (Ire) *J G M O'Shea* 81
4 b g Anabaa (USA) - Recherchee

4^{14gs} 10^{16g} 2^{14gf} 5^{13gf} 6^{12g} 6^{17f} **0-1-6 £2,734**

Abstract Art (USA) *N A Callaghan* 72 a72
2 ch c Distorted Humor (USA) - Code From Heaven (USA)
2^{7g} 4^{7gf} 7^{8g} 2^{8sd} **0-2-4 £2,683**

Abstract Folly (Ire) *J D Bethell* 62 a64
3 b g Rossini (USA) - Cochiti
5^{7gs} 8^{8s} 6^{10g} 3^{10gf} 6^{10gf} 7^{12gf} 4^{8g} 5^{10g} 2^{10gf} 1^{8gf} 16^{10gf} 12^{9gf} 2^{9sd} 6^{8sf} **1-4-14 £5,835**

Acca Larentia (Ire) *Mrs H O Graham* 35
4 gr f Titus Livius (Fr) - Daisy Grey
9^{8sd} 14^{7g} 4^{12s} 16^{12gf} 7^{8g} 5^{8gf} **0-0-6**

Acceleration (Ire) *R Allan* 67 a60
5 b g Groom Dancer (USA) - Overdrive
8^{16sd} 6^{14gs} 7^{18gs} 6^{16gf} **0-0-4**

Accendere *R M Beckett* a64
4 b g Machiavellian (USA) - Littlewick (Ire)
9^{7sd} 2^{7sd} 1^{8sd} 7^{8sd} **1-1-4 £3,391**

Accent (Ire) *Sir Mark Prescott* 32 a45
2 b g Beckett (Ire) - Umlaut
7^{6sd} 7^{5sd} 9^{6gf} **0-0-3**

Accepting *J Mackie* 49
8 b g Mtoto - D'Azy
8^{16gf} 9^{17g} **0-0-2**

Acciacatura (USA) *G Wragg* 64
4 gr f Stravinsky (USA) - Lady In Waiting (USA)
5^{6g} 10^{8s} **0-0-2 £256**

Accomplish *W J Haggas* 62 a57
3 b f Desert Story (Ire) - Last Ambition (Ire)
3^{8gs} 1^{8sd} 14^{10gf} 8^{10gf} 3^{10gf} 7^{8gf} 4^{8gf} 1^{10gf} 13^{9sd} **2-2-9 £6,929**

Accumulate *R A Fahey* 13
2 b g Second Empire (Ire) - Bee-Bee-Gee (Ire)
12^{5gf} 15^{6g} **0-0-2**

Ace (Ire) *A P O'Brien* 124
4 b c Danehill (USA) - Tea House
3^{11vs} 3^{11gy} 2^{10gf} 5^{12gf} 4^{10g} 4^{10gy} 3^{12f} 2^{12y} **0-3-8 £446,888**

Ace Baby *Mrs L Stubbs* 64
2 b g First Trump - Mise En Scene
4^{5s} 1^{5s} 2^{5s} 6^{5gs} 3^{6g} 9^{5g} **1-2-6 £5,852**

Ace Club *J Hetherton* 24 a59
4 ch g Indian Rocket - Presently
6^{6sd} 2^{6sd} 11^{6sd} 9^{7sd} 7^{7sd} 13^{6gs} 20^{5gf} 17^{7gf} 10^{5g} 13^{8g} 10^{5sd} 10^{5sd} 7^{6sd} 2^{7sd} 1^{6sd} 8^{7ss} 3^{6sd} 8^{7sd} **1-3-18 £2,931**

Ace Coming *D B Feek* a6
4 b g First Trump - Tarry
11^{10sd} **0-0-1**

Ace Of Hearts *C F Wall* 109
6 b g Magic Ring (Ire) - Lonely Heart
16^{7gf} 6^{9g} 8^{8gf} 3^{8g} 1^{9gf} 1^{8gf} 7^{8gf} 1^{8gf} 10^{9g} 5^{9s} **3-1-10 £90,085**

Ace-Ma-Vahra *S R Bowring* a45
7 b m Savahra Sound - Asmarina
7^{8sd} **0-0-1**

Acheekyone (Ire) *B J Meehan* 80 a75
2 b c Indian Ridge - Tafrah (Ire)
2^{6gf} 3^{7gf} 2^{7gf} 1^{7sd} **1-3-4 £8,878**

Achill Bay (Ire) *Saeed Bin Suroor* 88
2 b c Peintre Celebre (USA) - Albacora (Ire)
2^{7g} 1^{8gs} **1-1-2 £10,591**

Acknowledgement *I A Wood* 87 a70
3 b c Josr Algarhoud (Ire) - On Request (Ire)
7^{8sd} 3^{10sd} 4^{10sd} 4^{10gs} 5^{10s} 11^{10gf} **0-1-6 £1,824**

Acomb *N Wilson* 89 a80
5 b g Shaamit (Ire) - Aurora Bay (Ire)
6^{7sd} 3^{9sd} 1^{9sd} 7^{9sd} 5^{8gf} 17^{8gf} 6^{8g} 1^{7g} 1^{7gs} 1^{7gf} 13^{7gs} 13^{8g} 3^{7g} 7^{7ft} 11^{7sd} **4-2-15 £27,431**

Acorazado (Ire) *C P Morlock* 43 a69
6 b g Petorius - Jaldi (Ire)
6^{6sd} 5^{9sd} 4^{9sd} 2^{9sd} 4^{8sd} 9^{8gs} 12^{10gf} 10^{7sd} 12^{9sd} 9^{6sd} **0-1-10 £1,296**

Acrobatic (USA) *R Charlton* 75
2 ch c Storm Boot (USA) - Alvernia (USA)
6^{8g} 4^{8g} 2^{8gs} **0-1-3 £1,349**

Acropolis (Ire) *A P O'Brien* 112
4 b c Sadler's Wells (USA) - Dedicated Lady (Ire)
2^{10s} 3^{13gs} 4^{10gy} 5^{12g} **0-2-4 £17,342**

Act Friendly (Ire) *Saeed Bin Suroor* 80
2 b f Sadler's Wells (USA) - Ozone Friendly (USA)
7^{8gs} 2^{8s} **0-1-2 £1,416**

Active Account (USA) *J R Holt* 55 a58
8 b/br g Unaccounted For (USA) - Ameritop (USA)
8^{12gf} 7^{10s} 9^{12gf} 8^{11gs} 15^{11g} 9^{14sd} 1^{8ss} 11^{14sd} **1-0-8 £2,415**

Active Asset (Ire) *M R Channon* 83
3 ch g Sinndar (Ire) - Sacristy
5^{8g} 12^{10gf} 12^{8gf} 6^{10gf} 1^{10g} 6^{11gf} 5^{10gf} 3^{10gf} 3^{10gf} 4^{11gs} 6^{10gs} 2^{10gf} 4^{9g} 6^{10s} 3^{10g} 5^{10g} 6^{10s} **1-4-17 £18,595**

Active Audience (Ire) *A Berry* 63
2 b f Fasliyev (USA) - Luisa Demon (Ire)
3^{5s} 5^{5gs} 7^{5g} 7^{6gf} 5^{6g} 3^{5g} 9^{5g} 12^{6hy} **0-2-8 £1,047**

Activist *D Carroll* a65
7 ch g Diesis - Shicklah (USA)
12^{15s} 2^{14sd} 4^{14sd} 7^{17sd} **0-1-4 £876**

Activity (Ire) *M J Gingell* 67
6 gr g Pennekamp (USA) - Actoris (USA)
7^{7g} **0-0-1**

Activo (Fr) *S Dow* a93
4 b g Trempolino (USA) - Acerbis (Ger)
16^{8g} 3^{10g} 4^{8g} 10^{8s} 6^{7s} 1^{11g} 1^{9g} 2^{10sd} 5^{8sd} **2-1-9 £12,420**

Actuality *M P Tregoning* 71 a83
3 b g So Factual (USA) - Cottage Maid
8^{8g} 5^{9g} 3^{7g} 5^{10g} 12^{8gf} 1^{7sd} 2^{8sd} **1-1-7 £4,556**

Acuzio *W M Brisbourne* 60 a59
4 b g Mon Tresor - Veni Vici (Ire)
2^{9sd} 4^{8gs} 6^{8g} 9^{10gf} 3^{8s} 2^{11g} 2^{10f} 8^{10f} 2^{10gf} 4^{10gf} 5^{9gf} 6^{10gf} **0-6-12 £4,578**

Ad Valorem (USA) *A P O'Brien* 119
3 b c Danzig (USA) - Classy Women (USA)
2^{8gf} 5^{8g} 3^{8s} 6^{8f} 9^{8y} **0-2-5 £90,613**

Adage *L M Cumani* 70
2 b f Vettori (Ire) - Aymara
10^{7gf} 9^{8g} 3^{8gf} **0-0-3 £692**

Adalar (Ire) *P W D'Arcy* 44 a45
5 br g Grand Lodge (USA) - Adalya (Ire)
10^{9sd} 9^{9sd} 5^{9sd} 4^{8g} 3^{10f} 12^{10f} 10^{8gf} 5^{8gf} 5^{10g} 7^{9sd} **0-1-10 £527**

Adantino *B R Millman* 73 a74
6 b g Glory Of Dancer - Sweet Whisper
2^{6sd} 4^{5sd} 14^{7sd} 5^{7sd} 2^{6sd} 6^{6gf} 10^{6sd} 2^{6f} 1^{6sd} 7^{6gf} 7^{6sd} 12^{6sd} 2^{6sd} 2^{6gf} 2^{6gf} 1^{6gs} 6^{6f} 3^{6sd} 5^{6g} 9^{6g} **2-7-20 £16,653**

Adeje Park (Ire) *P W Chapple-Hyam* 91
2 ch f Night Shift (USA) - Iyandas (Ity)
5^{5gf} 1^{5g} 4^{6g} 14^{6gf} **1-0-4 £7,166**

Adelfia (Ire) *Sir Michael Stoute* a58
2 ch f Sinndar (Ire) - Adaiyka (Ire)
4^{7sd} **0-0-1 £238**

Adelphi Theatre (USA) *R Rowe* 67 a55
8 b g Sadler's Wells (USA) - Truly Bound (USA)
8^{14gs} 10^{14g} 16^{20s} 11^{16g} 9^{16sd} **0-0-5**

Adjami (Ire) *A King* 52
4 b g Entrepreneur - Adjriyna
12^{11gs} **0-0-1**

Adjawar (Ire) *J J Quinn* 49
7 b g Ashkalani (Ire) - Adjriyna
13^{10g} **0-0-1**

Administrator *C A Cyzer* 54 a24
3 ch g Unfuwain (USA) - Squaw Talk (USA)
12^{10g} 6^{10s} 11^{14s} 4^{12f} 7^{13gf} 8^{12sd} **0-0-6**
£315

Admiral (Ire) *R C Guest* 80
4 b c Alhaarth (Ire) - Coast Is Clear (Ire)
5^{16gf} 9^{10g} **0-0-2**

Admiral Compton *J R Boyle* 72 a84
4 ch g Compton Place - Sunfleet
4^{8sd} 8^{8sd} 14^{8gf} 10^{10gf} 4^{8gf} 6^{8gf} 9^{9g} 16^{8gf}
4^{8sd} 10^{10sd} 3^{10sd} **0-1-11 £1,929**

Admiral's Cruise (USA) *B J Meehan* 100
3 b c A.P. Indy (USA) - Ladies Cruise (USA)
4^{10gf} 1^{9gs} 2^{10g} 2^{10gf} 1^{10s} 1^{9gs} 2^{10gs}
2-3-7 £25,867

Adobe *W M Brisbourne* 63 a53
10 b g Green Desert (USA) - Shamshir
3^{8g} 7^{9sd} 7^{8g} 4^{7sd} 2^{8f} 3^{9sd} 6^{8g} 6^{8gf} 4^{8gf} 9^{8gf}
3^{8gf} 12^{9sd} 3^{9sd} 3^{9sd} 1^{9sd} 5^{9sd} 7^{9ss}
1-6-17 £5,103

Adoniel (Ire) *P W Chapple-Hyam* 54
2 b c Fasliyev (USA) - Serene Princess (USA)
9^{6g} **0-0-1**

Adorata (Ger) *J Jay* 61 a48
4 b f Tannenkonig (Ire) - Adora (Ger)
4^{7s} 8^{8s} 11^{10gf} 12^{10gf} 10^{7sd} 10^{8sd} **0-0-6**
£267

Adoration *M Johnston* 91
3 b g Royal Applause - Unconditional Love (Ire)
1^{6s} 5^{7g} 1^{7g} 10^{8gf} 12^{8gf} 5^{8g} 2^{9gs} 14^{8g} 3^{9g}
2^{8gs} 10^{8gf} 1^{9gs} 7^{9gs} **3-3-13 £28,935**

Advanced *R Charlton* 98
2 b c Night Shift (USA) - Wonderful World (Ger)
1^{6gf} 2^{7g} 9^{6g} 1^{6g} 7^{6gs} **2-0-5 £15,832**

Aegean Dancer *B Smart* 71 a59
3 b g Piccolo - Aegean Flame
2^{6gf} 2^{6gf} 2^{6f} 1^{6sd} **1-3-4 £6,944**

Aeronaut *J M Bradley* 18 a27
2 b g Averti (Ire) - Roufontaine
7^{5gf} 16^{7gf} 12^{5sf} **0-0-3**

Aeroplane *P W Chapple-Hyam* 72
2 b c Danehill Dancer (Ire) - Anita At Dawn (Ire)
2^{6gs} **0-1-1 £1,684**

Afadan (Ire) *J R Jenkins* a74
7 br g Royal Academy (USA) - Afasara (Ire)
10^{12sd} 10^{12sd} **0-0-2**

Afleet Alex (USA) *T F Ritchey* a126
3 b c Northern Afleet (USA) - Maggy Hawk (USA)
1^{6ft} 6^{9ft} 1^{9ft} 3^{10ft} 1^{10ft} 1^{12ft} **4-1-6**
£1,175,938

Afrad (Fr) *N J Henderson* 96
4 gr g Linamix (Fr) - Afragha (Ire)
7^{14gf} 1^{12gs} 1^{21s} 28^{18gs} **2-0-4 £33,823**

African Blues *M R Hoad*
2 ch g College Chapel - Pearl Dawn (Ire)
PU^{5s} 6^{5g} 13^{8g} **0-0-3**

African Breeze *R M Whitaker* 70
3 b f Atraf - Luanshya
14^{6hy} 5^{6gf} 7^{7f} 5^{7gs} 4^{6g} 6^{6gf} 1^{6g} 2^{7gf} 12^{8gf}
5^{6gf} 16^{6g} 7^{7gf} **1-1-12 £6,985**

African Concerto (Ire) *S Kirk* 65 a67
2 b c Mozart (Ire) - Out Of Africa (Ire)
9^{6gf} 6^{6gf} 4^{5f} 12^{6s} 3^{6sd} **0-1-5 £981**

African Dream *P W Chapple-Hyam* 94 a104
4 b g Mark Of Esteem (Ire) - Fleet Hill (Ire)
8^{10sd} 8^{9gf} **0-0-2**

African Gift *J G Given* 68 a59
3 b f Cadeaux Genereux - African Light
14^{8g} 7^{8s} 3^{5sd} 1^{6g} 1^{6g} 3^{5s} 8^{6sd} 7^{6hy}
2-2-8 £8,434

African Sahara (USA) *Miss D Mountain* 87 a79
6 br h El Gran Senor (USA) - Able Money (USA)
10^{9gf} 7^{8g} 12^{10gs} 4^{8gf} 16^{8g} 5^{8gf} 4^{8g} 3^{8gf} 3^{8gf}
7^{8g} 8^{8g} 2^{8gf} 3^{8gf} 5^{9sd} 10^{8g} 9^{8gs} 13^{8gf} 6^{8sd}
1^{8s} 1^{9sd} 9^{8sd} 2^{10sd} 8^{11sd} 7^{9sd} **2-4-24**
£15,835

African Star *J M Bradley* 48
4 b g Mtoto - Pass The Rose (Ire)
12^{8gf} 5^{8f} 12^{6sd} 17^{6g} 9^{10f} **0-0-5**

African Storm (Ire) *S Kirk* 48
3 b g Fasliyev (USA) - Out Of Africa (Ire)
7^{5g} 10^{7gf} **0-0-2**

African Sunrise (USA) *Saeed Bin Suroor* 47
2 b/br f Tale Of The Cat (USA) - Nature's Magic (USA)
15^{7g} **0-0-1**

Africanus (Ire) *Saeed Bin Suroor* 74 a74
3 b c Dubai Millennium - Asfurah (USA)
3^{7gf} 2^{9sd} **0-1-2 £1,896**

After Lent (Ire) *P A Blockley* 52 a34
4 b g Desert Style (Ire) - Yashville
10^{9sd} 6^{10f} 9^{10f} 1^{10gf} 9^{12sd} 11^{10gs} **1-0-6**
£1,512

After The Rainbow *E A L Dunlop* 76
2 b c Montjeu (Ire) - Rainbow Goddess
7^{7g} 6^{7g} **0-0-2**

After The Show *Rae Guest* a78
4 b g Royal Applause - Tango Teaser
1^{5sd} 2^{5sd} 4^{5sf} 1^{5sd} **2-1-4 £7,878**

After You *B W Hills* a76
2 b f Pursuit Of Love - Los Alamos
1^{7sd} **1-0-1 £4,303**

Afton *J Balding*
3 ch f Bien Bien (USA) - Madam Zando
15^{6s} 7^{7sd} **0-0-2**

Against All Odds *W G M Turner*
3 br g Vettori (Ire) - Only In Dreams
10^{10g} **0-0-1**

Agamard *M P Tregoning* 60
2 b c Red Ransom (USA) - Zobaida (Ire)
11^{7gf} **0-0-1**

Age Of Kings (USA) *J H M Gosden* 75
3 b g Kingmambo (USA) - Everhope (USA)
2^{7s} 3^{10g} 3^{8g} **0-2-3 £2,871**

Agent Kensington *N I M Rossiter* 23 a53
3 b f Mujahid (USA) - Monawara (Ire)

10^{7sd} 15^{8g} 14^{6g} 13^{6s} **0-0-4**

Aggi Mac *N Bycroft* 43 a46
4 b f Defacto (USA) - Giffoine
9^{11gf} 6^{10gf} 7^{11gf} 10^{9gf} 6^{12gf} 10^{11gf} 9^{11gs} 6^{16gf} 5^{16sd} 7^{12g} 3^{11sd} 5^{11ss} 2^{11sd} **0-2-13 £631**

Aggravation *D R C Elsworth* 68 a78
3 b g Sure Blade (USA) - Confection
3^{7sd} 8^{7sd} 3^{6sd} 9^{7sd} 6^{6sd} 9^{8gf} 15^{7gs} 7^{8gf} 7^{10f} 1^{8sd} 7^{8sd} 2^{8gf} 6^{8g} 3^{8g} 2^{8gs} 7^{8f} 7^{6s} 3^{6sd} 7^{6sd} **1-5-19 £8,394**

Agilete *J R Boyle* 78 a68
3 b g Piccolo - Ingerence (Fr)
5^{7g} 2^{7gf} 5^{7gf} 3^{7gf} 3^{6gf} 3^{6gf} 4^{7gf} 9^{7gf} 5^{8sd} 8^{6sd} **0-4-10 £5,707**

Aguila Loco (Ire) *Stef Liddiard* a56
6 ch g Eagle Eyed (USA) - Go Likecrazy
3^{6sd} 5^{7sd} 7^{6sd} 1^{6sd} 11^{7sd} 5^{7sd} 12^{6sd} 9^{6sd} 12^{6sd} 6^{6sd} **1-1-10 £3,125**

Ahaz *J F Coupland* 25 a47
3 b g Zaha (Can) - Classic Faster (Ire)
8^{6sd} 4^{6sd} 13^{7gs} 9^{9sd} 3^{8sd} 11^{8g} 13^{7gf} 9^{5f} 14^{6g} 14^{6f} 12^{7gs} 5^{7sd} 12^{7sf} 5^{7sd} 10^{9sd} **0-1-15 £618**

Ahdaaf (USA) *J L Dunlop* 85
3 b/br f Bahri (USA) - Ashraakat (USA)
8^{7f} 3^{8gs} 3^{7gf} 1^{7g} 2^{8gf} 14^{8gs} 9^{8g} **1-3-7 £10,808**

Ahmedy (Ire) *M R Channon* 80
2 b g Polish Precedent (USA) - Nawaji (USA)
2^{7g} 1^{7gf} 6^{8g} **1-1-3 £5,109**

Aiguille (USA) *R Hannon* 74
3 b c Royal Academy (USA) - Premier Peak (USA)
3^{7g} 11^{7gf} 6^{7g} 3^{7gf} 4^{8gf} 1^{8f} 10^{10gf} 11^{10gs} 7^{7gf} **1-2-9 £6,407**

Aimee Vibert *W R Swinburn* 68
3 b f Zilzal (USA) - Rose Vibert
7^{8g} 5^{8g} 3^{8gf} 8^{10g} **0-1-4 £390**

Aintnecessarilyso *J M Bradley* 61 a55
7 ch g So Factual (USA) - Ovideo
12^{6sd} 10^{7sd} 8^{7sd} 3^{6sd} 1^{6gf} 10^{6s} 12^{6g} 2^{6f} 7^{6sd} 3^{6f} 3^{6sd} 4^{6g} 4^{6f} 13^{6gf} 7^{6gs} 14^{6f} 7^{6gs} 8^{6sd} 1^{6g} UR^{6g} 11^{5sd} 5^{6sf} 11^{5sd} 2^{7sd} 5^{6ss} **2-5-25 £7,448**

Air Biscuit (Ire) *C F Wall* 45 a61
2 b f Galileo (Ire) - Surprise Visitor (Ire)
11^{6gs} 5^{7sd} 9^{7sd} **0-0-3**

Air Commodore (USA) *H R A Cecil* 68
3 ch c Diesis - La Sky (Ire)
6^{10gf} **0-0-1**

Air Mail *N Wilson* a62
8 b g Night Shift (USA) - Wizardry
1^{8sd} 9^{7sd} **1-0-2 £2,569**

Air Of Esteem *Ian Emmerson* 33 a54
9 b g Forzando - Shadow Bird
6^{8sd} 1^{8sd} 8^{9sd} 11^{8sd} 3^{8sd} 1^{8sd} 10^{9gf} **2-1-7 £3,144**

Air Of Supremacy (Ire) *Mrs K Walton* 54 a52
4 gr g Royal Applause - Lap Of Luxury
6^{9sd} 8^{8gf} 12^{10gf} **0-0-3**

Airbuss (Ire) *M R Channon* a66
2 b c Mozart (Ire) - Kardelle
5^{8sd} **0-0-1**

Airedale Lad (Ire) *R M Whitaker* 49 a48
4 b g Charnwood Forest (Ire) - Tamarsiya (USA)
2^{8gs} 4^{8gf} 10^{10gf} 5^{8gf} 10^{8gf} 8^{8g} 6^{10s} 3^{10g} 3^{8g} 5^{10g} 6^{11gs} 4^{8sd} 6^{8s} 5^{8sd} 11^{11ss} **0-3-15 £1,816**

Airgusta (Ire) *C P Morlock* a58
4 b g Danehill Dancer (Ire) - Ministerial Model (Ire)
2^{16sd} 5^{16sd} 1^{17sd} 7^{14sd} 2^{17sd} 12^{13sd} 10^{8sd} 3^{17sd} 7^{16sd} 8^{14sd} 5^{14ss} **1-3-11 £3,141**

Airwave *A P O'Brien* 105
5 b m Air Express (Ire) - Kangra Valley
3^{7hy} 1^{8g} 6^{8gf} **1-1-3 £62,659**

Ajigolo *M R Channon* 110
2 ch c Piccolo - Ajig Dancer
7^{5g} 1^{5gf} 10^{5g} 5^{6g} 4^{5gf} 1^{6gf} 3^{5g} 1^{6g} 6^{6gf} 2^{5g} **3-2-10 £61,296**

Akarem *K R Burke* 108
4 b c Kingmambo (USA) - Spirit Of Tara (Ire)
1^{9hy} 9^{8g} 3^{9g} 3^{14gf} 4^{12gf} 7^{10gy} 11^{12g} 2^{12hy} **1-2-8 £29,352**

Akash (Ire) *M Johnston* 71 a55
5 b g Dr Devious (Ire) - Akilara (Ire)
13^{10sd} 13^{10gs} 9^{10s} 10^{11gs} **0-0-4**

Akathea *Christian Wroe* 30
4 b f Barathea (Ire) - Dubai Lady
8^{8gf} 8^{10gs} 11^{10gs} **0-0-3**

Akhdaar (Ire) *Miss D A McHale* 13 a5
3 b g City Honours (USA) - Huldine
8^{11gs} 15^{12s} 13^{12sd} 12^{16s} 11^{18gf} 12^{15gf} 8^{14hy} 11^{11sd} **0-0-8**

Akimbo (USA) *H R A Cecil* 110 a89
4 b c Kingmambo (USA) - All At Sea (USA)
2^{7gs} 1^{7f} 5^{8gf} 10^{8sd} **1-1-4 £12,717**

Akona Matata (USA) *C E Brittain* 72
3 b c Seeking The Gold (USA) - Oh What A Dance (USA)
7^{10gf} 6^{10gf} 3^{7gf} **0-0-3 £525**

Al Alba (USA) *R Hannon* 71
3 b f Distant View (USA) - Noblissima (Ire)
7^{7sd} 7^{8g} 2^{7hy} 2^{9g} 8^{9hy} 8^{11vs} 8^{8g} 2^{8s} 7^{8gs} 1^{8s} 8^{8hd} **1-2-11 £12,341**

Al Awwam *W M Brisbourne* a55
6 b g Machiavellian (USA) - Just A Mirage
3^{7sd} 1^{6sd} 2^{5sd} 10^{6sd} **1-2-4 £2,123**

Al Dhahab (USA) *C E Brittain* 55
2 b f Seeking The Gold (USA) - South Of Saturn (USA)
4^{7gf} 13^{8s} **0-0-2 £438**

Al Eile (Ire) *John Queally* 103
5 b g Alzao (USA) - Kilcsem Eile (Ire)
4^{14gf} 3^{22f} **0-1-2 £4,949**

Al Hazim (Ire) *L M Cumani* 67
2 b c Danehill (USA) - Dathiyna (Ire)
12^{7g} 6^{7gs} 5^{8g} 7^{7gs} **0-0-4**

Al Maradi *C E Brittain* 67
2 b c Xaar - Diamond Park (Ire)
7^{8gf} 9^{8gf} 3^{8g} 13^{10g} 13^{8g} **0-1-5 £700**

Al Rayanah *G Prodromou* a53
2 b f Almushtarak (Ire) - Desert Bloom (Fr)
6^{5sd} 2^{7sd} 5^{7sd} **0-1-3 £1,019**

Al Shamara *I W McInnes* 57 a47
2 b f Alhaarth (Ire) - Shamriyna (Ire)
5^{5gs} 3^{6gs} 4^{7gf} 7^{7f} 3^{7sd} 7^{7gf} 5^{7gf} 8^{7gf} 9^{8gf} **0-2-9 £1,084**

Alabama Twist *W J Haggas* 74
3 b g Magic Ring (Ire) - Glass
4^{6s} 5^{6g} 3^{5gs} 5^{7gf} 1^{6f} 4^{7gf} 5^{6g} 4^{7g} 6^{8s} **1-1-9 £4,989**

Alafdal (USA) *R Allan*
5 b g Gone West (USA) - Aqaarid (USA)
PU^{10sd} **0-0-1**

Alafzar (Ire) *P D Evans* 47 a61
7 b g Green Desert (USA) - Alasana (Ire)
3^{8sd} 8^{9sd} 7^{7g} **0-1-3 £374**

Alagon (Ire) *Ian Williams*
5 b g Alzao (USA) - Forest Lair
15^{20s} **0-0-1**

Alam (USA) *P Monteith* 57
6 b g Silver Hawk (USA) - Ghashtah (USA)
9^{13g} 11^{15s} **0-0-2**

Alambic *Sir Mark Prescott* 36 a36
2 gr f Cozzene (USA) - Alexandrine (Ire)
11^{7sd} 10^{7gf} 13^{7gf} **0-0-3**

Alamiyan (Ire) *Sir Michael Stoute* 95
3 b c King's Best (USA) - Alasana (Ire)
1^{8g} 9^{8g} 1^{10gf} 6^{10s} 6^{10s} **2-0-5 £16,148**

Alani (Ire) *Jedd O'Keeffe* 49
3 b f Benny The Dip (USA) - Toi Toi (Ire)
10^{12g} 12^{12g} 11^{10g} 11^{12g} 11^{10gf} 11^{9gf} 1^{16gf}
5^{16gf} 7^{16gf} 10^{16gf} **1-0-10 £2,912**

Alarm Call *T D Easterby* 34
2 b f Mind Games - Warning Bell
14^{6gf} 8^{7g} 7^{7gf} **0-0-3**

Alasao *S C Burrough* 30
2 b g Inchinor - Daisy May
14^{7f} **0-0-1**

Alasoun (Ire) *Sir Michael Stoute* 63
2 b c Kalanisi (Ire) - Alasana (Ire)
6^{8s} **0-0-1**

Alastair Smellie *S L Keightley* a38
9 ch g Sabrehill (USA) - Reel Foyle (USA)
8^{6sd} 9^{7sd} 8^{6sd} 8^{6sd} **0-0-4**

Albadi *C E Brittain* 2 a32
4 b g Green Desert (USA) - Lyrist
19^{6gf} 16^{7gf} 6^{7sd} 11^{8sd} **0-0-4**

Albahja *M A Jarvis* 102
3 b f Sinndar (Ire) - Eshq Albahr (USA)
3^{10gs} 3^{11gs} 1^{12gf} 2^{10gf} 2^{12gf} 9^{15gf} **1-4-6**
£23,809

Albashoosh *D Nicholls* 58 a31
7 b g Cadeaux Genereux - Annona (USA)
9^{6s} 9^{6g} 6^{7gf} 9^{6f} 8^{7sd} 13^{6sd} **0-0-6**

Albert Hall *A P O'Brien* 96
3 b c Danehill (USA) - Al Theraab (USA)
5^{10s} 5^{8g} **0-0-2 £10,149**

Albertine *John Berry*
5 b m Bahhare (USA) - Rosa Royale
9^{7sd} **0-0-1**

Albinus *A M Balding* 104
4 gr g Selkirk (USA) - Alouette
5^{11g} 2^{12g} 2^{12g} 8^{12g} **0-1-4 £10,437**

Alcazar (Ire) *H Morrison* 117
10 b g Alzao (USA) - Sahara Breeze
6^{12s} 1^{16s} 4^{14gs} 3^{16g} 1^{15s} 2^{20gs} 1^{16s} **3-2-7**
£206,610

Alcestes Selection *J Pearce* 50
2 b f Selkirk (USA) - Attitre (Fr)
12^{8g} 5^{7hy} **0-0-2**

Alcharinga (Ire) *T J Etherington* a61
3 b g Ashkalani (Ire) - Bird In Blue (Ire)
4^{6sd} 8^{7sd} 5^{6sd} **0-0-3 £260**

Alchemist Master *R M Whitaker* 78 a82
6 b g Machiavellian (USA) - Gussy Marlowe
8^{8f} 15^{7gf} 8^{7gf} 2^{7f} 1^{7gf} 3^{7gf} 9^{8gf} 6^{7g} F^{7gf}
12^{7g} 1^{7gf} 2^{7sd} 7^{7sd} **2-2-13 £15,023**

Alcott (Fr) *J Jay* 43 a54
3 ch g Medaaly - Louisa May (Ire)
11^{8sd} 6^{8sd} 7^{9sd} 12^{10g} 12^{10g} 8^{12g} 3^{11sd} 4^{8sd}
4^{11ss} 9^{9ss} **0-1-10 £207**

Aldabra *Sir Michael Stoute* 51
3 b c Green Desert (USA) - Krisalya
8^{8gs} 7^{7g} **0-0-2**

Aldbury Grey (Ire) *W R Swinburn* 59
2 gr f Alhaarth (Ire) - Alphilda
2^{6gf} 6^{6g} 10^{6g} **0-1-3 £1,344**

Alderney Race (USA) *R Charlton* 109
4 ch c Seeking The Gold (USA) - Oyster Catcher (Ire)
4^{6g} 4^{6gf} 6^{6f} 5^{6gf} **0-1-4 £4,676**

Aldora *J Ryan* 108 a55
6 b m Magic Ring (Ire) - Sharp Top
7^{8gs} 1^{8g} 3^{7gs} 8^{10s} 11^{10hy} 10^{9sd} **1-0-6**
£20,400

Aleron (Ire) *J J Quinn* 75
7 b g Sadler's Wells (USA) - High Hawk
3^{11gs} 6^{12gs} **0-1-2 £1,072**

Aleshanee *J R Best* 21
3 b f Bold Edge - Nesyred (Ire)
13^{6gf} 14^{5hd} 12^{5f} **0-0-3**

Alessandria *E A L Dunlop* 77
2 b f Sunday Silence (USA) - Tereshkova (USA)
1^{8g} **1-0-1 £4,628**

Alessano *G L Moore* 81 a77
3 ch g Hernando (Fr) - Alessandra
4^{10sd} 6^{10sd} 5^{10sd} 4^{12gs} 3^{12gf} 2^{11gs} 3^{12gf} 1^{11g}
5^{10s} **1-4-9 £10,129**

Aletta *W J Haggas* 53
2 b f Dansili - Bombalarina (Ire)
3^{5g} **0-1-1 £523**

Alexander Alliance (Ire) *T Stack* 112
2 b f Danetime (Ire) - Geht Schnell
2^{6g} 1^{6gy} **1-1-2 £37,336**

Alexander Capetown (Ire) *D Nicholls* 65
3 b f Fasliyev (USA) - Hawas
3^{5g} 2^{7gs} 17^{8gf} 7^{7gs} 8^{6gf} **0-2-5 £2,859**

Alexander Goldrun (Ire) *J S Bolger* 122
4 b f Gold Away (Ire) - Renashaan (Fr)
6^{9gf} 3^{10s} 1^{10gf} 2^{8g} 1^{10gs} 3^{10gy} 3^{10gs} 8^{10gs} 8^{10gf}
2-4-9 £466,449

Alexander Sapphire (Ire) *N B King* a56
4 gr f Pennekamp (USA) - Beautiful France (Ire)
6^{12sd} 2^{11sd} 1^{12sd} 12^{14sd} 10^{12sd} 12^{14sd}
1-1-6 £3,371

Alexandrova (Ire) *A P O'Brien* 114
2 b f Sadler's Wells (USA) - Shouk
6^{7gf} 3^{7s} 1^{8g} 2^{8g} **1-2-4 £47,010**

Alexia Rose (Ire) *A Berry* 74 a66
3 b f Mujadil (USA) - Meursault (Ire)
9^{6s} 5^{6gs} 8^{6gf} 8^{6gf} 7^{6gf} 3^{6gf} 5^{5gf} 11^{6gf} 10^{5g}
10^{5s} 5^{6sd} 6^{5sd} **0-1-12 £1,543**

Aleyah *C F Wall* 43
3 ch f Bachir (Ire) - Silver Peak (Fr)
12^{8g} 4^{7gf} 7^{8gf} 6^{7gf} **0-0-4**

Alf Tupper *M H Tompkins* 63
2 b g Atraf - Silvery
10^{7gs} 10^{8g} 13^{8gs} **0-0-3**

Alfaasil *D M Fogarty* 22
3 b c Darshaan - Bright Halo (Ire)
8^{10gf} **0-0-1**

Alfie Lee (Ire) *D A Nolan* 65
8 ch g Case Law - Nordic Living (Ire)
12^{5g} 6^{5gf} 8^{5s} 11^{5gf} 8^{5gf} 12^{5g} 5^{5g} 11^{5gf} 9^{5gf}

11^{6g} **0-0-10**

Alfie Noakes *Mrs A J Perrett* 95
3 b g Groom Dancer (USA) - Crimson Rosella
1^{10gf} 9^{13gf} 7^{15gs} 9^{12g} **1-0-4 £6,877**

Alfie Tupper (Ire) *S Kirk* 76
2 ch g Soviet Star (USA) - Walnut Lady
1^{7gf} **1-0-1 £3,250**

Alfonso *B W Hills* 91
4 ch g Efisio - Winnebago
3^{8gs} 9^{7gf} 9^{10gs} 9^{8s} 15^{8gs} 16^{8gs} **0-1-6 £1,710**

Alfred The Great (Ire) *P C Haslam* 78
3 b g King's Best (USA) - Aigue
4^{8g} 3^{10gs} 1^{12s} **1-1-3 £5,052**

Alfridini *D R C Elsworth* 73 a76
4 ch g Selkirk (USA) - Vivre En Paix
10^{10sd} 6^{10sd} 7^{10gf} 4^{8gf} 16^{10g} 14^{8gf} **0-1-6 £334**

Alghaazy (Ire) *M D Hammond* 51
4 b g Mark Of Esteem (Ire) - Kentmere (Fr)
8^{12gf} 5^{12g} 9^{14f} 2^{17f} 3^{15g} 11^{13gf} 2^{16gf} **0-3-7 £2,263**

Algharb *W J Haggas* 89
3 b/br g Mujahid (USA) - Actress
4^{7g} 2^{7gf} 1^{6gf} 5^{6g} 1^{6gf} 3^{6gf} 4^{6gf} 6^{6g} **2-2-8 £14,076**

Alhaadh (USA) *J H M Gosden* 26
3 b f Diesis - Wishah (USA)
11^{8g} **0-0-1**

Alhaajes (USA) *B W Hills* 16
2 b c Bahri (USA) - Mamlakah (Ire)
11^{7s} **0-0-1**

Alhaitham (USA) *J L Dunlop* 84
2 b c Storm Cat (USA) - Bint Salsabil (USA)
6^{7g} 2^{7gf} 2^{7gs} **0-2-3 £4,542**

Alhamazing (Ire) *F Turner* 33
2 b c Alhaarth (Ire) - Bee Off (Ire)
1^{7gf} 7^{7gf} 10^{8gf} **1-0-3 £7,092**

Ali Bruce *G L Moore* 79 a85
5 b g Cadeaux Genereux - Actualite
2^{8sd} 4^{8sd} 6^{6sd} 8^{8sd} 1^{6sd} 6^{7g} 2^{8gf} 12^{7g} 3^{7sd} 2^{7g} 2^{6gf} 1^{7sd} 3^{7g} 4^{7sd} 11^{7g} **2-6-15 £16,980**

Ali D *G Woodward* 68 a6
7 b g Alhijaz - Doppio
13^{8sd} 9^{8g} 1^{8gf} 1^{8gf} 5^{8gf} 2^{8gf} 5^{8s} 5^{10g} 6^{10gf} 11^{8gs} 3^{9gf} **2-2-11 £9,531**

Ali Deo *S J Mahon* 63 a51
4 ch g Ali-Royal (Ire) - Lady In Colour (Ire)
3^{11f} 7^{12gf} 4^{12sd} 9^{10g} **0-1-4 £838**

Ali The Minx *S Kirk* 19
3 b f King's Theatre (Ire) - Sarah's Dream (Ire)
11^{9sd} 8^{8gf} 14^{7g} **0-0-3**

Ali Zandra *Julian Poulton* 5 a23
4 b f Prince Sabo - Priceless Fantasy
11^{7sd} 8^{11sd} 13^{12gf} 9^{7g} **0-0-4**

Alice Amelia *C R Egerton* a45
2 b f Alhaarth (Ire) - Wondrous Maid (Ger)
9^{6sd} **0-0-1**

Aliceinwonderland *David Wachman* 81
2 b f Danehill (USA) - Grail (USA)
2^{5g} 3^{7gf} 3^{7gf} **0-3-3 £3,835**

Alinda (Ire) *W R Swinburn* 35
4 b f Revoque (Ire) - Gratclo
12^{8gs} **0-0-1**

Alisdanza *G A Swinbank* 57
3 b f Namaqualand (USA) - Enchanting Eve
8^{7g} 12^{6g} 6^{10gf} 5^{9gf} 13^{8gf} **0-0-5**

Alistair John *Mrs G S Rees* a35
2 b g Komaite (USA) - Young Rosein
10^{6sd} 9^{9sd} 12^{9sd} **0-0-3**

Alkaadhem *M P Tregoning* 114
5 b h Green Desert (USA) - Balalaika
1^{9gf} 4^{9gf} 6^{9gf} 7^{12g} 3^{10g} **1-0-5 £148,468**

Alkaased (USA) *L M Cumani* 125
5 b h Kingmambo (USA) - Chesa Plana
1^{12gf} 2^{12g} 1^{12gs} 2^{12gs} 5^{10gs} 1^{12f} **3-2-6 £1,589,270**

Alkhabar (USA) *J L Dunlop* 29
2 b c Kingmambo (USA) - Ashraakat (USA)
12^{7gs} **0-0-1**

All A Dream *Mrs L Williamson* a77
3 br f Desert Story (Ire) - Alioli
3^{10sd} 2^{9sd} 6^{7sd} 7^{10g} 10^{11gf} 3^{8sd} 4^{9sd} 7^{8sd} **0-2-8 £6,502**

All Being Well *Miss B Sanders* 50 a35
3 ch g Bien Bien (USA) - Princess Moodyshoe
14^{7sd} 10^{10s} 12^{8sd} 18^{12gf} **0-0-4**

All Bleevable *Mrs S Lamyman* 48 a53
8 b g Presidium - Eve's Treasure
4^{14sd} 1^{14sd} 6^{14sd} 5^{18gs} 7^{16g} 7^{22s} 9^{14sd} 4^{16sd} 2^{14ss} 5^{14sd} **1-1-10 £1,348**

All For Laura *D R Loder* 103
3 ch f Cadeaux Genereux - Lighthouse
2^{6g} 2^{6gf} 4^{6g} 5^{6s} 7^{5gf} 5^{6s} **0-2-6 £9,339**

All Ivory *R Charlton* 101
3 ch c Halling (USA) - Ivorine (USA)
5^{7g} 2^{7g} 1^{7g} 5^{7gf} 1^{7gf} 4^{7gf} 2^{8gf} 2^{8s} 1^{7g} **3-3-9 £34,963**

All On My Own (USA) *I W McInnes* a27
10 ch g Unbridled (USA) - Someforall (USA)
5^{7sd} 6^{8sd} 7^{11sd} 11^{11sd} **0-0-4**

All Quiet *R Hannon* 83 a78
4 b f Piccolo - War Shanty
1^{7sd} 3^{7sd} 4^{7gf} 5^{7gf} 1^{8gf} 4^{7gf} 1^{8g} 5^{7gf} 3^{8g} **3-1-9 £19,802**

All Star (Ger) *N J Henderson* 82
5 b g Lomitas - Alte Garde (Fr)
2^{13gf} 2^{14g} 2^{14gs} 5^{16g} **0-3-4 £4,595**

All That And More (Ire) *B W Hills* 92
3 ch c Unfuwain (USA) - Ideal Lady (Ire)
1^{8g} 1^{9g} 1^{10gf} 9^{10s} **3-0-4 £18,743**

All The Good (Ire) *G A Butler* 60 a80
2 ch c Diesis - Zarara (USA)
5^{8gs} 1^{10sd} **1-0-2 £5,129**

All Too Beautiful (Ire) *A P O'Brien* 111
4 b f Sadler's Wells (USA) - Urban Sea (USA)
1^{10s} **1-0-1 £29,000**

Allegretto (Fr) *S Kirk* 45 a43
3 b c Anabaa (USA) - Aimores (Ire)
12^{6gf} 7^{8s} 12^{9sd} 6^{7sd} 10^{7gf} **0-0-5**

Allegretto (Ire) *Sir Michael Stoute* 63
2 ch f Galileo (Ire) - Alleluia
5^{8s} **0-0-1**

Allez Mousson *A Bailey*
7 b g Hernando (Fr) - Rynechra
10^{12sd} **0-0-1**

Allied Cause *L M Cumani* 60
3 ch f Giant's Causeway (USA) - Alligram (USA)

8^{8gf} 6^{8gf} 13^{8f} **0-0-3 £163**

Allied Victory (USA) *E J Alston*
5 b h Red Ransom (USA) - Coral Dance (Fr)
PU^{10g} **0-0-1**

Allizam *E S McMahon* 18
3 b g Tragic Role (USA) - Mazilla
10^{10g} 13^{8g} 11^{10gs} 12^{10gf} **0-0-4**

Allouette *J M P Eustace* 45 a12
2 b f Largesse - Alo Ez
11^{8g} 7^{10hy} 10^{9sd} **0-0-3**

Allstar Princess *E J Alston* 10 a29
3 b f Environment Friend - Turf Moor (Ire)
8^{8s} 9^{9sd} 13^{9sd} 10^{6s} 16^{6gf} 12^{6sd} **0-0-6**

Allstars Rocket *K G Wingrove*
12 b g Puissance - Sally Delight
10^{14sd} **0-0-1**

Allsussedup *E J O'Neill* 50 a54
2 b g Bertolini (USA) - Beau Duchess (Fr)
3^{5sd} 14^{5g} 5^{5g} 6^{5sd} 7^{7sd} **0-1-5 £524**

Almanshood (USA) *P L Gilligan* 75 a72
3 b/br c Bahri (USA) - Lahan
5^{11gs} 2^{10gf} 6^{12g} 5^{11g} 6^{10gf} 3^{10gf} 8^{8sd} 1^{9sd} 10^{8sd}
1-2-9 £5,465

Almansoor (Ire) *B W Hills* 67
3 b c Sadler's Wells (USA) - Groom Order
11^{8gf} 3^{10gs} 9^{12s} **0-0-3 £1,102**

Almansoora (USA) *Saeed Bin Suroor* 73
3 b f Bahri (USA) - Bashayer (USA)
11^{7f} **0-0-1**

Almara *Miss K B Boutflower* 46
5 b m Wolfhound (USA) - Alacrity
2^{7f} 10^{6g} 11^{8gf} 5^{5f} 9^{5f} 13^{6f} **0-1-6**
£740

Almaty Express *J R Weymes* 62 a64
3 b g Almaty (Ire) - Express Girl
8^{5s} 5^{5gf} 6^{6gf} 6^{6g} 7^{5gf} 2^{5g} 4^{5g} 1^{5sd} 6^{6gf} 8^{5g}
9^{5g} 8^{5sd} 10^{5sd} 8^{6sd} 1^{5sd} 2^{5sd} **2-2-16**
£8,199

Almavara (USA) *J Noseda* 72 a73
3 b/br c Fusaichi Pegasus (USA) - Name Of Love (Ire)
6^{8sd} 1^{9sd} 10^{10gf} 9^{16g} 3^{12g} **1-0-5 £4,659**

Almendrados (Ire) *J Noseda* 95
3 b f Desert Prince (Ire) - Sevi's Choice (USA)
9^{7gf} 3^{10gf} **0-0-2 £3,080**

Almighty (USA) *A P O'Brien* 104
3 b c Sadler's Wells (USA) - Saganeca (USA)
4^{10ys} 2^{12gs} 12^{12g} 9^{16gf} **0-1-4 £15,839**

Almisq (USA) *J Ryan* 42 a41
4 ch f Diesis - Inscrutable Dancer (USA)
11^{8g} 14^{6g} 6^{10sd} 12^{14sd} **0-0-4**

Almizan (Ire) *G L Moore* 78
5 b g Darshaan - Bint Albaadiya (USA)
9^{18g} 6^{13s} 3^{16gf} 20^{18g} 10^{14gf} 5^{12g} **0-1-6**
£2,069

Almost Innocent (Ire) *J H M Gosden* 78
3 b f Danehill (USA) - Puzzled Look (USA)
5^{7gs} 4^{8gf} 1^{8g} 6^{7gf} **1-0-4 £4,060**

Almost Perfect (Ire) *Ian Williams* 45
3 ch f Priolo (USA) - Talbiya (Ire)
14^{8g} 17^{6g} 12^{6s} 15^{6s} 19^{6gf} **0-0-5**

Almost Spinning (Ire) *M R Channon* 84
2 ch f Spinning World (USA) - Almost A Lady (Ire)
3^{6gs} 4^{6gf} 2^{7gs} 1^{8gf} 5^{8gf} 7^{7gf} 14^{7gs} **1-2-7**
£17,352

Almost Welcome *S Dow* a47
4 b g First Trump - Choral Sundown
5^{12sd} 6^{16sd} **0-0-2**

Almowj *C E Brittain* 62 a62
2 b c Fasliyev (USA) - Tiriana
5^{6gf} 3^{6g} 10^{7sd} 5^{7sd} **0-1-4 £866**

Almuraad (Ire) *Sir Michael Stoute* 104
4 b c Machiavellian (USA) - Wellspring (Ire)
3^{10g} 5^{10gs} **0-0-2 £2,224**

Almutasader *J A B Old* 16
5 b h Sadler's Wells (USA) - Dreamawhile
16^{16g} **0-0-1**

Along Came Molly *B J Meehan* a48
3 ch f Dr Fong (USA) - Torrid Tango (USA)
9^{9sd} **0-0-1**

Along The Nile *Mrs J R Ramsden* 85
3 b g Desert Prince (Ire) - Golden Fortune
7^{10s} 4^{12g} 2^{11gs} 6^{10f} 5^{10s} 3^{8g} 1^{8gf} 1^{8gf} 7^{8gf}
1^{8g} **3-2-10 £22,502**

Alpaga Le Jomage (Ire) *M J Polglase* 83 a69
3 b g Orpen (USA) - Miss Bagatelle
8^{6sd} 4^{5sd} 19^{6hy} 3^{5s} 7^{6gs} 4^{5s} 9^{6gs} 8^{5g} 6^{5gf}
4^{5gf} 6^{5gf} 4^{5gf} 9^{6gf} 17^{6gs} 17^{5gs} 12^{5sd} 12^{6sd}
2^{6sd} 8^{5sd} 10^{5sd} **0-2-20 £6,529**

Alpha Echo (USA) *M F Harris* a34
6 b/br h Spinning World (USA) - Add (USA)
12^{6sd} 11^{9sd} **0-0-2**

Alpha Zeta *D Nicholls* 4
4 b g Primo Dominie - Preening
10^{11gf} 9^{7g} **0-0-2**

Alphecca (USA) *K G Reveley* 22
4 b g Kingmambo (USA) - Limbo (USA)
6^{11g} **0-0-1**

Alphonsina *Mrs L Williamson*
3 b f Josr Algarhoud (Ire) - Club Elite
12^{6sd} **0-0-1**

Alphun (Ire) *K J Burke* 60 a58
3 b g Orpen (USA) - Fakhira (Ire)
6^{6sd} 5^{8g} 7^{7gf} 5^{6gf} 10^{8f} **0-0-5**

Alpine Gold (Ire) *J L Dunlop* 86
3 b f Montjeu (Ire) - Ski For Gold
5^{10gf} 6^{12gs} 9^{12g} 9^{12g} 6^{16g} 5^{16gs} **0-0-6**
£325

Alpine Hideaway (Ire) *J S Wainwright* 53
12 b g Tirol - Arbour (USA)
5^{8gf} 6^{8gf} 9^{7g} 8^{8g} 13^{8gs} **0-0-5**

Alpine Maiden *T P Tate* 33
2 br f Diktat - Alpine Time (Ire)
14^{7s} 7^{8gs} 6^{7g} **0-0-3**

Alpine Reel (Ire) *W R Swinburn* 87
4 b g Danehill Dancer (Ire) - Alpine Flair (Ire)
1^{7g} 1^{8gf} **2-0-2 £9,646**

Alpine Special (Ire) *S Wilson* 79 a75
4 gr g Orpen (USA) - Halomix
3^{12sd} 5^{14sd} 2^{12gs} 2^{12gf} 9^{12sh} **0-3-5**
£2,642

Alqaayid *P W Hiatt* 56 a57
4 b g Machiavellian (USA) - One So Wonderful
9^{7sd} 8^{8sd} 8^{8sd} 5^{7sd} 5^{7sd} 7^{10s} 5^{8gs} 5^{10f} 12^{10g}
3^{11g} 14^{10gs} **0-0-11 £1,241**

Alrafid (Ire) *G L Moore* 45
6 ch g Halling (USA) - Ginger Tree (USA)
10^{10g} **0-0-1**

Alrafidain (Ire) *M Johnston* 90
3 b g Monsun (Ger) - Demeter (USA)
1^{12gs} 6^{10gf} **1-0-2 £4,754**

Alright My Son (Ire) *R Hannon* 81
3 b c Pennekamp (USA) - Pink Stone (Fr)
5^{8gs} 16^{8gf} 7^{9gf} 8^{10gf} 7^{8g} 5^{9gf} 8^{7g} 6^{7g} 9^{10g} 6^{8gs} **0-0-10 £442**

Alsadaa (USA) *J H M Gosden* 79
2 b c Kingmambo (USA) - Aljawza (USA)
3^{7gf} **0-1-1 £858**

Alsharq (Ire) *M P Tregoning* 70 a27
3 b f Machiavellian (USA) - Balaabel (USA)
10^{7sd} 13^{8g} 1^{7gf} 5^{7gf} 6^{10gf} **1-0-5 £3,474**

Alta Petens *Mrs J Chapple-Hyam* 92 a83
3 b f Mujadil (USA) - Be Exciting (Ire)
3^{6g} 4^{6g} 6^{6s} 7^{6sd} 10^{7sd} **0-0-5 £2,991**

Altenburg (Fr) *Mrs N Smith* 53
3 b c Sadler's Wells (USA) - Anna Of Saxony
4^{12gf} **0-0-1 £262**

Altesse *G Wragg* 64
3 br f Highest Honor (Fr) - All Is Fair
3^{7g} 7^{6gf} **0-1-2 £518**

Altieri *V Caruso* 118
7 ch h Selkirk (USA) - Minya (USA)
1^{10f} 1^{10hy} 1^{10gf} 3^{10gf} 6^{8g} 3^{8s} 9^{10hy} **3-1-7 £273,858**

Altilhar (USA) *G L Moore* 74 a74
2 b c Dynaformer (USA) - Al Desima
7^{7gf} 15^{7gs} 3^{7sd} 1^{7sd} **1-1-4 £5,171**

Altitude Dancer (Ire) *A Crook* a13
5 b g Sadler's Wells (USA) - Height Of Passion
9^{14sd} **0-0-1**

Alugat (Ire) *Mrs A Duffield* 74 a59
2 b g Tagula (Ire) - Notley Park
13^{6sd} 1^{5gf} 4^{5gs} 6^{5gs} 7^{5g} 8^{6s} 6^{5sd} **1-0-7 £5,344**

Alumni *B W Hills* 103
3 ch f Selkirk (USA) - Ajuga (USA)
2^{10gs} 1^{11gs} 6^{10s} 9^{12g} 7^{10s} **1-1-5 £31,205**

Alvarinho Lady *D Haydn Jones* 57
3 b f Royal Applause - Jugendliebe (Ire)
12^{6g} 14^{6gf} 16^{6gf} **0-0-3**

Alvarita *Sir Mark Prescott* 105 a96
3 gr f Selkirk (USA) - Alborada
1^{8f} 12^{8g} 4^{8sd} 1^{11vs} **2-0-4 £23,763**

Alwariah *C E Brittain* 55 a51
2 b f Xaar - Signs And Wonders
6^{6gs} 13^{6g} 7^{7gs} 5^{6sd} **0-0-4**

Always Baileys (Ire) *M Johnston* 81
2 ch g Mister Baileys - Dubiously (USA)
11^{5g} 5^{5gf} 1^{6f} 5^{7gf} 11^{6gf} 1^{7gs} 4^{7s} 2^{8g} 5^{8g} 12^{8g} **2-1-10 £20,368**

Always Believe (USA) *Mrs P Ford* a28
9 b g Carr De Naskra (USA) - Wonder Mar (USA)
11^{9sd} 9^{9sd} 11^{12sd} **0-0-3**

Always Emirates (USA) *Saeed Bin Suroor* 84
2 b c Danzig (USA) - Country Belle (USA)
4^{6g} 2^{7gf} **0-1-2 £3,108**

Always Esteemed (Ire) *K A Ryan* 90 a104
5 b g Mark Of Esteem (Ire) - Always Far (USA)
10^{10sd} 3^{9sd} 9^{8g} 17^{8gs} 10^{9g} 17^{10g} 9^{12gs} **0-1-7 £5,500**

Always Flying (USA) *N Wilson* 31 a57
4 ch g Fly So Free (USA) - Dubiously (USA)
5^{12sd} 6^{9sd} 6^{12s} 7^{9sd} 11^{12sd} **0-0-5**

Always Hopeful *E J O'Neill* 112
2 b c Mind Games - Expectation (Ire)
2^{5gf} 1^{5g} 5^{5gf} 1^{6gs} 3^{6s} 3^{6gs} **2-1-6 £95,739**

Always Mine *N A Callaghan* 40 a63
3 ch f Daylami (Ire) - Mamoura (Ire)
7^{12sd} 6^{13sd} 5^{12gs} 5^{10sd} **0-0-4**

Always Turn Left (Ire) *H S Howe* 49
2 b f King's Theatre (Ire) - Light-Flight (Ire)
7^{6gf} 9^{7s} 7^{7g} **0-0-3**

Always Waining (Ire) *P L Clinton* 37
4 b g Unfuwain (USA) - Glenarff (USA)
16^{12gs} **0-0-1**

Alwaysforsale (Ire) *J S Moore* a50
2 b g City On A Hill (USA) - Prague Spring
6^{8sd} **0-0-1**

Alzarma *P D Evans* 49 a54
3 b g Alzao (USA) - Skimra
3^{5sd} 5^{6gf} 3^{6hy} 2^{6sd} 11^{6sd} 2^{7gf} 3^{7f} 9^{5sd} 12^{7ss} **0-5-9 £2,471**

Am Brose (USA) *L M Cumani* 101
6 ch h Nureyev (USA) - Madame Premier (USA)
10^{6gf} 8^{6gf} 8^{8gf} 8^{8g} 2^{6s} 8^{6g} 12^{5gf} 23^{6gs} 19^{6g} **0-1-9 £2,976**

Amadeus Mozart (Ire) *A P O'Brien* 97
2 b c Mozart (Ire) - Lindesberg
7^{6hy} 3^{7gf} 3^{6gs} 2^{6g} **0-3-4 £43,097**

Amadeus Rock (USA) *J H M Gosden* 57
2 b/br g Forest Wildcat (USA) - Downtown Blues (USA)
7^{7g} 5^{8s} **0-0-2**

Amadeus Wolf *K A Ryan* 120
2 b c Mozart (Ire) - Rachelle (Ire)
1^{6s} 3^{6gf} 2^{5gf} 1^{6g} 1^{6gs} **3-2-5 £190,645**

Amanda's Lad (Ire) *M C Chapman* 58 a61
5 b g Danetime (Ire) - Art Duo
2^{5sd} 9^{5sd} 3^{6sd} 1^{6sd} 6^{6sd} 6^{6sd} 11^{7sd} 9^{5gf} 5^{5gf} 2^{5f} 10^{5gf} 6^{5gf} 10^{5gf} 1^{5g} 4^{5gf} 4^{5gf} 5^{5sd} 9^{6sd} 3^{5sd} 4^{5ss} 1^{6sd} 6^{7sd} 4^{6sd} **3-6-23 £8,802**

Amanderica (Ire) *M C Chapman*
3 b f Indian Lodge (Ire) - Striking Gold (USA)
6^{8sd} **0-0-1**

Amaya Silva *S Dow* a34
3 b f Silver Patriarch (Ire) - Queen Of Tides (Ire)
13^{10sd} **0-0-1**

Amazin *N P Littmoden* 85 a63
3 b c Primo Dominie - Aegean Blue
7^{6gs} 10^{6gf} 14^{7g} 4^{6g} 8^{8gs} 2^{7gf} 8^{7gf} 2^{8gf} 1^{7gs} 10^{7sd} 13^{5gs} **1-2-11 £8,327**

Amazing Grace Mary *S R Bowring* 6 a26
3 b f Dancing Spree (USA) - Frisky Miss (Ire)
10^{5sd} 8^{5sd} 13^{5s} 14^{6sd} 11^{7sd} 11^{6ss} 10^{6ss} **0-0-7**

Amber Glory *K A Ryan* 74 a69
2 b f Foxhound (USA) - Compton Amber
3^{5g} 1^{5sd} 2^{5s} 3^{5g} 1^{5s} 11^{5gf} 5^{5g} 14^{5gf} 12^{5gf} 11^{6gs} 7^{5g} 2^{5hy} 3^{5sd} 4^{5sd} 2^{6sd} **2-5-15 £17,908**

Amber Nectar Two *A G Newcombe* 40 a43
5 b g Bluegrass Prince (Ire) - Another Batchworth
15^{5hy} 16^{7sh} 28^{6y} 22^{5y} 8^{6g} 12^{5g} 6^{5g} 6^{6y} 5^{5sd} 11^{6sd} 2^{6sd} 5^{5sd} **0-1-12 £422**

Amber Spirit *Peter Grayson* a33
2 ch f Zaha (Can) - Classic Faster (Ire)
7^{7ft} 11^{9sd} 8^{10sd} **0-0-3**

Amberlina (Ire) *Patrick Morris* 52 a47
3 b f Monashee Mountain (USA) - Try My Rosie

10^{7sd} 8^{7sd} 10^{12gf} 11^{9f} 13^{8gf} 9^{10sd} 2^{10gf} 6^{9sd} 5^{12sd} 9^{12sd} **0-1-10 £913**

Ambersong *A W Carroll* a43
7 ch g Hernando (Fr) - Stygian (USA)
6^{9sd} **0-0-1**

Ameeq (USA) *G L Moore* 74
3 b/br c Silver Hawk (USA) - Haniya (Ire)
4^{11g} 4^{12gf} 2^{10g} 2^{10g} 4^{10gs} **0-2-5 £3,203**

Amelia (Ire) *J Balding* 64 a48
7 b m General Monash (USA) - Rose Tint (Ire)
16^{6g} 6^{5sd} 2^{5g} 15^{6gf} 10^{6sd} 10^{6s} 9^{5sd} 7^{5gf} 5^{6gf} 10^{6gf} 9^{6g} 7^{5gf} 8^{5sd} **0-1-13 £965**

Ameliore (Ire) *G C Bravery*
2 b f Dansili - Common Consent (Ire)
10^{5gf} **0-0-1**

American Cousin *D Nicholls* 56
10 b g Distant Relative - Zelda (USA)
10^{6gf} 2^{5gf} 1^{5gf} 7^{5g} 13^{6gs} 6^{5gf} 6^{5gf} **1-1-7 £2,418**

American Embassy (USA) *V Smith* a17
5 b h Quiet American (USA) - Foreign Courier (USA)
12^{8sd} **0-0-1**

Amerigo Vespucci *J Noseda* 74 a70
3 b g Zafonic (USA) - Amellnaa (Ire)
3^{10sd} 5^{8gf} 1^{10f} **1-1-3 £4,015**

Ames Souer (Ire) *D Carroll* 41 a32
2 b f Fayruz - Taispeain (Ire)
7^{6s} 11^{5sf} 12^{6sd} **0-0-3**

Amethyst Rock *P L Gilligan*
7 b g Rock Hopper - Kind Lady
15^{8g} **0-0-1**

Amica *G L Moore* 85
3 b f Averti (Ire) - Friend For Life
3^{6g} 7^{6gf} 11^{7gf} 4^{7f} 4^{8gf} 1^{8g} 10^{8g} 1^{9g} 9^{8gs} 6^{8gf} **2-1-10 £13,294**

Amigoni (Ire) *A P O'Brien* 108
2 b c Danehill (USA) - Elite Guest (Ire)
5^{5f} 1^{7g} 8^{6gf} 2^{6gf} 1^{6gf} 4^{6gs} 5^{7gs} 6^{7g} **2-1-8 £68,214**

Amigra (Ire) *Miss J S Davis* a41
3 b f Grand Lodge (USA) - Beaming
9^{8sd} 7^{7sd} 5^{9sd} 10^{8sd} 12^{5gf} **0-0-5**

Amir Zaman *J R Jenkins* 15 a77
7 ch g Salse (USA) - Colorvista
2^{12sd} 8^{9sd} 3^{12sd} 7^{12sd} 5^{15s} 13^{12gs} 12^{16sf} 9^{14sd} **0-2-8 £2,794**

Amira *B W Hills* 68
3 b f Efisio - Princess Athena
5^{5gf} 2^{5gf} 5^{7gs} 6^{6gs} 1^{5gf} 3^{6g} 7^{5gf} **1-1-7 £5,825**

Ammirare *C W Thornton* 46
3 b f Diktat - Mathaayl (USA)
5^{5s} 12^{7s} 11^{7gf} 11^{7gs} 11^{9gf} **0-0-5**

Amnesty *G L Moore* 65
6 ch g Salse (USA) - Amaranthus
3^{10s} 4^{10s} 2^{10hy} **0-2-3 £1,817**

Amoli (Ire) *K A Ryan* 61
3 b f Sadler's Wells (USA) - Eilanden (Ire)
8^{12g} 8^{13f} 7^{12ss} **0-0-3**

Among Dreams *A G Newcombe* a2
4 ch f Among Men (USA) - Russell Creek
13^{7sd} 8^{8sd} **0-0-2**

Among Thieves (Ire) *M D I Usher* a20
5 b m Among Men (USA) - Abbessingh
6^{7sd} **0-0-1**

Amorada *H Morrison* 44
2 b f Pursuit Of Love - Duena
8^{6gs} 8^{7gf} 13^{7gf} **0-0-3**

Amorist (Ire) *Sir Mark Prescott* 58 a71
3 b g Anabaa (USA) - Moivouloirtoi (USA)
7^{8sd} 6^{8sd} 8^{6sd} 3^{10sd} 15^{13s} 2^{8gs} 5^{8hy} 3^{7sd} 1^{8sd} 1^{8sd} 4^{8sd} 5^{8sd} **2-3-12 £7,645**

Ample Note *W R Swinburn* 38
3 b g Piccolo - Abundance
10^{7gf} **0-0-1**

Amusement *D G Bridgwater* a49
9 ch g Mystiko (USA) - Jolies Eaux
9^{14sd} 5^{12sd} 3^{12sd} 7^{12sd} 2^{9sd} 4^{8sd} **0-2-6 £794**

Amwaal (USA) *J L Dunlop* 72
2 b c Seeking The Gold (USA) - Wasnah (USA)
6^{7gs} 2^{7gf} 4^{8gs} **0-1-3 £2,832**

Amwell Brave *J R Jenkins* 56 a69
4 b g Pyramus (USA) - Passage Creeping (Ire)
2^{12sd} 6^{13sd} 14^{12sd} 4^{11g} 5^{12g} 8^{14gs} 4^{12g} 5^{12sd} 10^{12sd} 3^{12sd} 1^{12sd} 2^{12sd} 5^{14sd} **1-4-13 £5,198**

Amy Louise (Ire) *T D Barron* 71
2 ch f Swain (Ire) - Mur Taasha (USA)
3^{6gf} 2^{6g} 4^{6g} **0-2-3 £2,703**

Amygdala *Saeed Bin Suroor* 59 a68
2 b f Royal Applause - Touch And Love (Ire)
10^{7gf} 3^{6sd} 5^{7s} **0-1-3 £672**

Anaamil (Ire) *M A Jarvis* 82
3 b f Darshaan - Noushkey
1^{11s} 8^{12gf} **1-0-2 £3,610**

Anak Pekan *M A Jarvis* 111
5 ch g In The Wings - Trefoil (Fr)
1^{19gs} 6^{16g} 6^{16gf} **1-0-3 £70,020**

Analyze (Fr) *Andrew Reid* a84
7 b g Anabaa (USA) - Bramosia
4^{8sd} 2^{8sd} 10^{8sd} **0-1-3 £1,267**

Anaphora (Ire) *Kevin Prendergast* 43
3 b f Goofalik (USA) - Annaberta (Ger)
10^{11g} 9^{10y} 6^{12s} **0-0-3**

Anatolian Star (USA) *J A R Toller* 62
3 ch g Rahy (USA) - Rosebrook (USA)
13^{7gf} 11^{7gs} 3^{7g} **0-0-3 £519**

Anchor Date *Stef Liddiard* 80 a80
3 b c Zafonic (USA) - Fame At Last (USA)
2^{6gf} 6^{7gf} 2^{7gf} 4^{7gf} 2^{7gs} 2^{7gf} 1^{6gf} 7^{7gf} 3^{7sd} 6^{8sd} **1-5-10 £11,004**

Ancient World (USA) *Saeed Bin Suroor* 116
5 b/br g Spinning World (USA) - Headline
3^{9gf} 2^{8gs} **0-1-2 £12,697**

And Again (USA) *J R Fanshawe* 59
2 b f In The Wings - Garah
4^{7g} **0-0-1 £238**

And I *M P Tregoning* 63 a67
2 b f Inchinor - Fur Will Fly
6^{6gf} 2^{7sd} 19^{7gf} **0-1-3 £1,396**

Andaluza (Ire) *P D Cundell* 55 a80
4 b f Mujadil (USA) - Hierarchy
1^{7sd} 16^{7g} 18^{7gf} 12^{7g} 11^{7sd} **1-0-5 £3,370**

Andean *Saeed Bin Suroor* 118
4 b c Singspiel (Ire) - Anna Matrushka
1^{10g} 2^{9gf} 3^{10gf} **1-2-3 £24,940**

Andorran (Ger) *Mrs J R Ramsden* 54
2 b c Lando (Ger) - Adora (Ger)

5^{6f} 7^{5g} 11^{6gs} 11^{7hy} 4^{7g} **0-0-5 £557**

Andre Chenier (Ire) *P Monteith* 70
4 b g Perugino (USA) - Almada (Ger)
3^{12s} **0-1-1 £543**

Andronikos *P F I Cole* 111
3 ch c Dr Fong (USA) - Arctic Air
5^{7gs} 1^{6s} 2^{6gf} 5^{6g} 5^{6g} 2^{6gs} 13^{7gs} **1-2-7 £37,648**

Anduril *I W McInnes* 84 a80
4 ch g Kris - Attribute
3^{9sd} 1^{9sd} 4^{9sd} 2^{9sd} 3^{9sd} 6^{10g} 2^{8s} 4^{8s} 2^{8s} 1^{8g} 10^{8g} 4^{8g} 9^{8gf} 4^{8gf} 2^{9sd} 5^{8gf} 9^{8g} 2^{10g} 4^{8g} 4^{10s} 13^{9gs} **2-8-21 £19,629**

Andy Mal *R A Fahey* 38
3 b f Mark Of Esteem (Ire) - Sunflower Seed
6^{10gf} 10^{8gf} 7^{7f} 15^{9gf} 4^{11gf} **0-0-5 £280**

Anemometer *Saeed Bin Suroor* 64
2 b f Sunday Silence (USA) - Anna Palariva (Ire)
12^{8g} 2^{8gs} **0-1-2 £1,027**

Anemone *B J Meehan* 51 a57
2 gr f Arkadian Hero (USA) - Noble Haven
10^{6gf} 5^{6gf} 3^{6g} 3^{6sd} 6^{6sd} 5^{7sd} 6^{6sd} **0-1-7 £1,399**

Anemos (Ire) *B G Powell* 51
10 ch g Be My Guest (USA) - Frendly Persuasion
12^{8sd} 7^{8gf} 5^{10f} 16^{12gf} 8^{8hd} **0-0-5**

Anfield Dream *J R Jenkins* 77 a77
3 b c Lujain (USA) - Fifth Emerald
2^{6sd} 1^{6sd} 3^{7sd} 1^{5sd} 2^{5sd} 1^{6gs} 8^{6gs} 11^{5gf} 6^{5g} 7^{6sd} 14^{7gf} 4^{6sd} 2^{5sd} **3-4-13 £21,184**

Angaric (Ire) *B Smart* 68
2 ch g Pivotal - Grannys Reluctance (Ire)
3^{5gf} 6^{5g} 5^{5g} 7^{6f} 7^{6g} 23^{6gf} **0-1-6 £627**

Angel Rays *G A Butler* 63
3 ch f Unfuwain (USA) - Success Story
4^{6g} 7^{7gf} 4^{6g} **0-0-3 £553**

Angel River *J Ryan* 54 a56
3 ch f Bold Edge - Riviere Rouge
9^{6sd} 1^{7sd} 3^{7sd} 10^{7sd} 4^{6gf} 7^{6sd} 5^{7gf} 3^{6gf} 15^{7g} 7^{7f} 16^{7gf} 7^{6f} 2^{6gf} 4^{8sd} 4^{7sd} 17^{7g} 6^{6sd} 7^{7sd} 5^{7sd} 4^{6sd} 10^{6sd} **1-3-21 £4,227**

Angel Sprints *L G Cottrell* 94
3 b f Piccolo - Runs In The Family
10^{6gs} 7^{6g} 7^{7gf} 3^{6gf} 6^{6gf} 1^{6g} 3^{6g} 1^{5gs} 5^{6g} **2-1-9 £14,716**

Angel Voices (Ire) *K R Burke* 81
2 b f Tagula (Ire) - Lithe Spirit (Ire)
3^{7g} 3^{7gy} 7^{6g} **0-2-3 £25,357**

Angelina Bankes *R A Harris* 52 a56
2 b f Observatory (USA) - Cloche Call
4^{5sd} 3^{5gs} 8^{5sd} 7^{6g} 4^{7g} 1^{7sd} 5^{9sd} 7^{9sd} 10^{7sd} 8^{7sd} **1-1-10 £4,380**

Angelo's Pride *J A Osborne* a63
4 ch g Young Ern - Considerable Charm
11^{8sd} 5^{9sd} 3^{9sd} 1^{10sd} 1^{11sd} **2-1-5 £5,921**

Angelofthenorth *J D Bethell* 79
3 b f Tomba - Dark Kristal (Ire)
1^{5gs} 1^{5gs} 7^{6s} 16^{5gf} 9^{5g} 4^{5g} 5^{5gf} 7^{5gf} 5^{5gf} 8^{6gf} 12^{5s} 3^{5s} 3^{5s} **2-2-13 £9,166**

Angie And Liz (Ire) *P D Evans* 34 a56
2 b f Spectrum (Ire) - Mary Magdalene
7^{5g} 5^{5sd} 5^{6sd} 2^{6sd} 12^{6gs} 11^{7sd} 1^{6sd} 2^{5sd} **1-2-8 £4,356**

Angus Newz *M Quinn* 86 a37
2 ch f Compton Place - Hickleton Lady (Ire)
9^{5gf} 8^{5sd} 5^{5g} 1^{6gf} 3^{6gf} 1^{5gs} 3^{6gf} 1^{6gf} 3^{6gf} 4^{6gs} 3^{6s} **3-4-11 £16,306**

Anissati *C E Brittain* 37 a53
3 ch f Machiavellian (USA) - Inchacooley (Ire)
6^{11g} 6^{7f} 9^{7gf} 6^{7gs} 4^{9sf} 1^{7sd} 10^{11g} 3^{6sd} 5^{8sd} **1-1-9 £2,449**

Ann Summers Gold (USA) *B J Meehan* 97
2 b f Yankee Victor (USA) - Inoma Slew (USA)
3^{5gs} 2^{6gf} **0-2-2 £9,660**

Anna Monda (Ger) *P Rau* 119
3 ch f Monsun (Ger) - Anna Of Kiev
1^{6s} 1^{8s} 7^{8g} 7^{7gs} 1^{8g} 1^{8s} **4-0-6 £216,738**

Anna Pallida *W R Swinburn* 83
4 b f Sadler's Wells (USA) - Masskana (Ire)
12^{8g} 4^{10gf} 6^{10gf} 3^{12gf} 7^{12gs} **0-0-5 £1,607**

Anna Pavlova *R A Fahey* 90
2 b f Danehill Dancer (Ire) - Wheeler's Wonder (Ire)
4^{6gf} 1^{6gf} 4^{6gf} 1^{8gf} 1^{8gf} **3-0-5 £35,868**

Anna Walhaan (Ire) *Ian Williams* 23
6 b g Green Desert (USA) - Queens Music (USA)
7^{8gf} 11^{10gf} **0-0-2**

Annabelle Ja (Fr) *D R C Elsworth* 81 a88
2 b f Singspiel (Ire) - Alamea (Ire)
6^{6gs} 2^{8gf} 2^{8g} 3^{8sd} 1^{7sd} **1-3-5 £8,039**

Annakita *W J Musson* 39 a56
5 b m Unfuwain (USA) - Cuban Reef
1^{14sd} 10^{16g} **1-0-2 £2,895**

Annals *R C Guest* 63
3 b f Lujain (USA) - Anna Of Brunswick
14^{7f} **0-0-1**

Annambo *D Morris* 81 a81
5 ch g In The Wings - Anna Matrushka
12^{12s} 8^{12gf} 6^{14gf} 2^{12gf} 16^{12gs} 1^{15gf} 12^{16g} 2^{17sd} 9^{12sd} 12^{12sd} **1-2-10 £9,859**

Anne Of Cleves *D R Loder* 41
3 b f Diktat - Anna Matrushka
5^{8gf} **0-0-1**

Annibale Caro *Sir Mark Prescott* 88
3 b g Mtoto - Isabella Gonzaga
3^{12gf} 1^{12gf} 1^{11gf} 5^{12gf} **2-0-4 £11,258**

Annies Valentine *J Gallagher* 29 a9
2 b f My Best Valentine - Shashi (Ire)
9^{5g} 14^{6gf} 11^{7sd} **0-0-3**

Annitas Dream (Ire) *T Hogan* 35 a32
4 b f Desert Prince (Ire) - Divine Pursuit
15^{8ft} 17^{8gf} 23^{8hy} 8^{7sd} **0-0-4**

Anniversary Guest (Ire) *Lucinda Featherstone* 46 a46
6 b/br m Desert King (Ire) - Polynesian Goddess (Ire)
6^{16gf} 1^{15gf} 11^{16g} 4^{17sf} **1-0-4 £1,526**

Annus Iucundus (Ire) *E J O'Neill* a66
4 b f Desert King (Ire) - Mezzanine
12^{10sd} 2^{13sd} 2^{13sd} 1^{13sd} 1^{17sd} 9^{16sd} 6^{16sd} **2-2-7 £5,645**

Another Bottle (Ire) *T P Tate* 105
4 b g Cape Cross (Ire) - Aster Aweke (Ire)
1^{10gf} 8^{10gf} 2^{8gf} 14^{10g} 1^{8gf} 10^{8s} 20^{9s} **2-1-7 £39,644**

Another Choice (Ire) *N P Littmoden* 89 a90
4 ch g Be My Guest (USA) - Gipsy Rose Lee (Ire)
4^{10sd} 13^{10gs} 2^{11s} 12^{12gs} 17^{12gs} **0-1-5 £3,243**

Another Con (Ire) *P Howling* 37 a56

4 b f Lake Coniston (Ire) - Sweet Unison (USA)
5 11sd 5 14sd 12 12sd 8 13sd 9 14sd 2 10sd 7 10sd 1 9sd 1 12sd 13 10g 5 12sd 7 12gf 10 12sd 11 17sd 9 9sf 10 9sd **2-1-16 £3,405**

Another Faux Pas (Ire) *R Hannon* 77 a68
4 b f Slip Anchor - Pirie (USA)
8 10sd 6 8gf 3 9g 2 8f 2 8gf 2 8gf 19 8gs 1 10g **1-4-8 £7,643**

Another Genepi (USA) *J W Hills* 77 a70
2 br f Stravinsky (USA) - Dawn Aurora (USA)
7 7gf 2 7sd **0-1-2 £1,216**

Another Glimpse *Miss B Sanders* a55
7 b g Rudimentary (USA) - Running Glimpse (Ire)
6 6sd **0-0-1**

Another Misk *M E Sowersby* 32 a53
3 ch g Storm Boot (USA) - Pure Misk
5 9sd 5 12sd 12 6sd 9 8gf 4 9sd 6 7f **0-0-6**

Another Mistress *R M Flower*
3 b f Slip Anchor - Mellow Miss
15 10gs 14 12sd **0-0-2**

Another Plan (Ire) *M G Quinlan*
3 b g Entrepreneur - Tammany Hall (Ire)
13 9sd **0-0-1**

Anousa (Ire) *P Howling* 85
4 b c Intikhab (USA) - Annaletta
8 12gf 6 12g 12 12gf **0-0-3 £307**

Ans Bach *Saeed Bin Suroor* 88
2 b c Green Desert (USA) - Bezzaaf
1 6g 9 6gf 4 6g **1-0-3 £5,604**

Ansells Joy *B Smart* 32 a60
2 b f Primo Valentino (Ire) - Eastern Ember
6 5gf 16 6gf 3 9sd 11 8sd **0-1-4 £368**

Ansells Legacy (Ire) *A Berry* 53
3 b g Charnwood Forest (Ire) - Hanzala (Fr)
5 8gs 9 8gf 2 8g 6 8gf 4 8g 10 8gf 7 9gf **0-1-7 £1,343**

Anthemion (Ire) *Mrs J C McGregor* 65
8 ch g Night Shift (USA) - New Sensitive
5 7gf 14 9gs 10 8gs 15 8g 7 9f 14 8s 8 8gf 2 8gf 1 9gf 1 8g 7 9gf 6 9gf 4 9gf 9 7gf 12 8gf 11 8g 8 8gf 13 9g **2-1-18 £10,281**

Antica (Ire) *M H Tompkins* 80
2 ch f Raise A Grand (Ire) - Travel Tricks (Ire)
6 6gf 2 6g 3 6s 1 6g **1-2-4 £4,278**

Anticipating *G L Moore* 65
5 b g Polish Precedent (USA) - D'Azy
5 10g 7 10g **0-0-2**

Antigone's Fire *P D Niven* a32
6 b m Lycius (USA) - Buzzbomb
13 12sd **0-0-1**

Antigoni (Ire) *A M Balding* 61 a70
2 ch f Grand Lodge (USA) - Butter Knife (Ire)
4 6gf 6 6gf 4 6sd **0-0-3 £904**

Antley Court (Ire) *R Hollinshead* a52
3 ch g Tagula (Ire) - Changed Around (Ire)
15 10s 6 9sd 3 11sd **0-1-3 £496**

Antoinette (USA) *Sir Michael Stoute* 65
3 b f Silver Hawk (USA) - Excellentadventure (USA)
8 9gs 9 10gf 8 12g **0-0-3**

Antonius Pius (USA) *A P O'Brien* 108
4 b c Danzig (USA) - Catchascatchcan
8 8f 15 6f **0-0-2**

Antony Ebeneezer *C R Dore* a39
6 ch h Hurricane Sky (Aus) - Captivating (Ire)
8 12sd 6 14sd 5 12sd **0-0-3**

Antrim (Ire) *R A Fahey* a14
3 b g Giant's Causeway (USA) - Kylemore (Ire)
5 12sd **0-0-1**

Anuvasteel *N A Callaghan* 83 a83
4 gr g Vettori (Ire) - Mrs Gray
12 10sd 5 10sd 3 10sd 1 9sd 3 9sd 11 8sd 4 9gs 2 10gf 1 10gf 3 8gf 8 10gf 8 12gf 12 10gf **2-3-13 £13,430**

Any Offer (Ire) *B J Meehan* 10 a2
2 b g Desert Prince (Ire) - Gold Mist
8 6gf 9 7sd 12 7gf **0-0-3**

Anyone Can Whistle *G G Margarson* 57
2 ch g Zilzal (USA) - Dame Jude
14 6gf 8 6gf 7 7gf 2 6gf 3 8gf 2 6gs 12 6gf 10 7gf 12 8g 10 8sd **0-3-10 £2,636**

Aoninch *Mrs P N Dutfield* 70
5 ch m Inchinor - Willowbank
6 13f 2 10gf 3 12gf 3 10gf 2 12f 4 10g 1 12gf 9 13gf 9 14g **1-5-9 £11,127**

Apache Indian (USA) *P W Chapple-Hyam* 24
2 b c Black Minnaloushe (USA) - Dove Shoot (USA)
11 7g **0-0-1**

Apache Nation (Ire) *M Dods* 61
2 b g Fruits Of Love (USA) - Rachel Green (Ire)
7 7gf 3 7gf 10 7gf **0-1-3 £664**

Apache Point (Ire) *N Tinkler* 67 a50
8 ch g Indian Ridge - Ausherra (USA)
6 9sd 3 8sd 10 9sd 7 8sd 1 9g 1 10gs 4 9gf 3 10gf 10 11g 7 9gf 7 9gf 2 10g 12 9g 9 9gf **2-2-14 £9,989**

Aperitif *D Nicholls* 67
4 ch g Pivotal - Art Deco Lady
9 7s 17 10gf UR 7gf 8 7gs 12 7gf 16 7g **0-0-6**

Apetite *N Bycroft* 28
3 ch g Timeless Times (USA) - Petite Elite
15 6g **0-0-1**

Apex *N Tinkler* 92 a91
4 ch g Efisio - Royal Loft
2 6gs 8 8s 6 7gf 5 6sd 14 6g 16 6g 5 6s 11 7sd 10 7gf 17 7s **0-1-10 £2,476**

Aphrodelta *P D Cundell* a51
3 b f Delta Dancer - Mouton (Ire)
6 6sd 12 7sd 10 6s 10 8sd **0-0-4**

Appalachian Trail (Ire) *I Semple* 103 a103
4 b g Indian Ridge - Karinski (USA)
5 9sd 10 8g 6 8g 3 8gs 2 7gf 15 7gf 6 7gs 6 7gf 1 7gf 2 9sd 2 7sd **1-4-11 £30,043**

Appetina *J Parkes* a30
4 b f Perugino (USA) - Tina Heights
9 11sd 14 8sd **0-0-2**

Apple Annie *M E Sowersby* 34
2 b f Benny The Dip (USA) - Aneen Alkamanja
8 5gs 13 6gf 10 7gf **0-0-3**

Apple Of My Eye *J R Jenkins* 24
3 b f Fraam - Fresh Fruit Daily
9 7gs PU 6gf **0-0-2**

Apple Wood *Denis P Quinn* 52 a43
5 b g Woodborough (USA) - Appelania
8 8hy 3 7hy 20 8hy 2 8g 2 7sd 14 7y **0-3-6 £1,855**

Apply Dapply *H Morrison* 64
2 b f Pursuit Of Love - Daring Destiny
7 6g **0-0-1**

Appointed Time *D Haydn Jones* 1
3 b f Nomination - Tymeera
12 8gf 14 8g 12 10gf **0-0-3**

Appolonious *E A Wheeler* 55 a53
4 b g Case Law - Supreme Thought
8^{7sd} 7^{7sd} 3^{7sd} 3^{7sd} 5^{7gf} 3^{6sd} 4^{8f} **0-4-7 £845**

Appreciated *W J Haggas* a56
2 b f Most Welcome - Align
7^{7sd} 4^{7sd} 7^{8sd} **0-0-3**

Apres Ski (Ire) *J W Hills* 38
2 b c Orpen (USA) - Miss Kinabalu
11^{7g} **0-0-1**

April Shannon *J E Long*
3 b f Tipsy Creek (USA) - Westering
16^{10g} **0-0-1**

Apron (Ire) *J Ryan*
4 b f Grand Lodge (USA) - Sultana
11^{10g} 11^{12sd} 11^{9sd} **0-0-3**

Apsara *G M Moore* 70
4 br f Groom Dancer (USA) - Ayodhya (Ire)
11^{11s} 6^{12f} 12^{10g} 3^{10gf} 5^{10gf} 4^{10g} 10^{12gf} 8^{14g} 8^{12g} **0-2-9 £884**

Apt To Run (USA) *E A L Dunlop* 72 a61
2 b c Aptitude (USA) - Tufa
6^{8g} 7^{8gf} 5^{7sd} **0-0-3**

Aquilonia *R Charlton* 66
3 b f Giant's Causeway (USA) - Leonila (Ire)
14^{10gs} 4^{10gf} 5^{10gf} 15^{12gf} 8^{11s} **0-0-5 £353**

Araafa (Ire) *J Noseda* 105
2 b c Mull Of Kintyre (USA) - Resurgence
1^{7g} 2^{7g} 6^{7g} 3^{7gs} **1-2-4 £15,667**

Arabian Dancer *M R Channon* 83
3 b f Dansili - Hymne (Fr)
8^{6gf} 2^{6gf} 5^{6g} 2^{6gf} 10^{7g} 2^{6gf} 8^{6gs} **0-3-7 £6,291**

Arabian Moon (Ire) *R Brotherton* 61 a53
9 ch g Barathea (Ire) - Excellent Alibi (USA)
5^{16sd} 6^{16sd} 19^{18g} 14^{12g} 1^{12g} 1^{14gf} 5^{12gf} 12^{11g} 7^{10gs} 7^{12sd} 8^{12sd} **2-0-11 £6,113**

Arabian Prince (USA) *A P O'Brien* 104
2 b c Fusaichi Pegasus (USA) - Add (USA)
2^{7gy} 1^{7g} 3^{8g} 5^{8hy} **1-2-4 £22,420**

Arabian Sea (Ire) *C E Brittain* 76
2 b c Sadler's Wells (USA) - Teggiano (Ire)
9^{5gf} 6^{7gf} 3^{7g} 12^{8g} **0-0-4 £1,438**

Arabian Spell (Ire) *R Gibson* 92
3 ch f Desert Prince (Ire) - Truly Bewitched (USA)
5^{8hy} 7^{8vs} 2^{8gs} 1^{8gf} 7^{8s} **1-1-5 £5,866**

Arabie *Ian Williams* 82 a70
7 b g Polish Precedent (USA) - Always Friendly
7^{7sd} 5^{7sd} 2^{10sd} 5^{9sd} 1^{10g} 4^{10g} 3^{10gf} 10^{10gf} 3^{10gf} 3^{10g} 2^{10gf} 10^{9gs} 8^{9gf} 12^{10gf} **1-4-14 £9,549**

Araglin *Miss S J Wilton* 11 a50
6 b g Sadler's Wells (USA) - River Cara (USA)
11^{12sd} 7^{15gf} **0-0-2**

Aragon's Boy *N Wilson* 51
5 ch g Aragon - Fancier Bit
6^{8g} 15^{7g} **0-0-2**

Aragorn (Ire) *N Drysdale* 102
3 ch c Giant's Causeway (USA) - Onaga (USA)
1^{7g} 3^{7gs} 8^{7gf} 5^{7gf} 1^{9f} **2-0-5 £56,298**

Arakan (USA) *Sir Michael Stoute* 117
5 br h Nureyev (USA) - Far Across
2^{8s} 5^{8f} 5^{7g} 8^{6gs} 2^{7gf} 5^{7gs} 1^{7gf} 4^{7gf} 1^{7g} 3^{7gs} **2-3-10 £92,380**

Aramat *R A Farrant* 26
3 b f Cigar - Winze Kible
10^{7g} 14^{7gs} **0-0-2**

Aravalli (Ire) *D J Daly* 60 a69
2 b f Desert Style (Ire) - Hayward
8^{6gf} 6^{7gf} 5^{7gf} 1^{7sf} **1-0-4 £3,737**

Arawan (Ire) *M W Easterby*
5 b g Entrepreneur - Asmara (USA)
12^{9sd} **0-0-1**

Arbella *W R Swinburn* 64
3 ch f Primo Dominie - Kristal Bridge
5^{8g} 2^{12f} **0-1-2 £1,042**

Arbors Little Girl *B R Millman* a43
3 b f Paris House - Arbor Ealis (Ire)
6^{8sd} **0-0-1**

Arc El Ciel (Arg) *Stef Liddiard* a87
7 b g Fitzcarraldo (Arg) - Ardoise (USA)
6^{6sd} 3^{7sd} 6^{6sd} 7^{7sd} 9^{7sd} **0-1-5 £2,069**

Arcangela *J G Given* 53
2 b f Galileo (Ire) - Crafty Buzz (USA)
8^{8gf} 7^{8s} **0-0-2**

Arch Folly *J G Portman* 63
3 b g Silver Patriarch (Ire) - Folly Fox
11^{11gs} 5^{12g} 7^{13g} 3^{14g} 10^{14gf} 3^{16g} 8^{17gs} **0-2-7 £1,203**

Archduke Ferdinand (Fr) *A King*
7 ch g Dernier Empereur (USA) - Lady Norcliffe (USA)
13^{14gf} **0-0-1**

Archenko *A Berry* a13
5 b g Weldnaas (USA) - Silverdale Rose
14^{11sd} 12^{9sd} **0-0-2**

Archerfield (Ire) *R Johnson* 43 a8
4 ch f Docksider (USA) - Willow River (Can)
7^{8sd} 7^{8gf} 18^{8gf} 4^{10g} 10^{14gf} **0-0-5**

Archerfield Links (USA) *N A Callaghan* 83
2 b/br c Brahms (USA) - Georgian Bay (USA)
4^{7gs} 1^{8g} 1^{8g} 5^{8s} **2-0-4 £9,678**

Archie Babe (Ire) *J J Quinn* 58
9 ch g Archway (Ire) - Frensham Manor
8^{12gs} 9^{12g} 5^{12s} 8^{22s} 13^{16gs} **0-0-5**

Archie Glenn *M S Saunders* a19
3 b c Lake Coniston (Ire) - La Ballerine
5^{7sd} **0-0-1**

Archie Wright *R Hannon* 56
3 ch g Lake Coniston (Ire) - Roisin Clover
14^{7gf} 4^{7f} 2^{8gf} 5^{8gf} 8^{8f} 3^{7f} 5^{8gf} 4^{10hd} **0-3-8 £1,795**

Archimboldo (USA) *T Wall* 80
2 ch g Woodman (USA) - Awesome Strike (USA)
12^{6g} 7^{7gf} 3^{6g} 1^{8f} 7^{8f} 5^{8gf} **1-0-6 £5,908**

Archirondel *M D Hammond* 68
7 b g Bin Ajwaad (Ire) - Penang Rose (NZ)
1^{10g} 3^{11g} 8^{10gf} 5^{9g} 7^{10gf} 3^{12gs} 5^{9gf} 6^{10g} 5^{10g} 6^{10g} 12^{14gf} **1-2-11 £5,028**

Archivist (Ire) *M Blanshard* 43
2 b c Kalanisi (Ire) - Mill Rainbow (Fr)
10^{7gf} 10^{8s} **0-0-2**

Archon Star (Ire) *C G Cox* 79
2 b c Ashkalani (Ire) - Scandalous
8^{6gf} 2^{6f} 3^{7gf} 1^{7s} 13^{7hy} 10^{8g} 3^{7gs} **1-3-7 £5,688**

Arctic Burst (USA) *D Shaw* 36 a50
5 b/br g Royal Academy (USA) - Polar Bird
4^{5sd} 1^{6sd} 6^{5sd} 5^{6sd} 7^{5gf} 10^{5gs} 6^{5gf} 12^{5sd}

1-0-8 £1,470

Arctic Cove *M D Hammond* 66 a69
4 b g Vettori (Ire) - Sundae Girl (USA)
6^{10gf} 4^{10gf} 6^{11s} 4^{12g} 1^{13f} 10^{14g} 3^{14ft}
1-1-7 £5,134

Arctic Desert *A M Balding* 82 a77
5 b g Desert Prince (Ire) - Thamud (Ire)
7^{7g} 10^{7gs} 7^{7g} 5^{6gf} 12^{6gf} 16^{7gs} 2^{7gf} 2^{7gf} 10^{7g} 6^{7gf} 10^{8sd} 7^{9sd} 4^{8sd} 10^{6sd} **0-2-14 £4,521**

Arctic Queen *P A Blockley* a19
4 br f Linamix (Fr) - Thamud (Ire)
10^{8sd} 9^{6sd} **0-0-2**

Arculinge *M Blanshard* 56 a52
2 b f Paris House - Calamanco
5^{6sd} 9^{6gs} 9^{6g} **0-0-3**

Ardasnails (Ire) *K G Wingrove* a24
3 b g Spectrum (Ire) - Fey Lady (Ire)
10^{9sd} 10^{10s} 16^{14g} **0-0-3**

Ardent Prince *Mrs H Dalton* 2 a57
2 b g Polar Prince (Ire) - Anthem Flight (USA)
16^{8s} 3^{7sd} **0-1-2 £477**

Ardglass (Ire) *Mrs P Townsley* 61 a57
3 b g Danehill Dancer (Ire) - Leggagh Lady (Ire)
3^{8hy} 7^{8sd} 7^{10s} 5^{10g} 10^{12sd} **0-1-5 £503**

Ardkeel Boy (Ire) *B Palling*
2 ch g Simply Great (Fr) - Wot-A-Noise (Ire)
13^{8sd} 12^{9sd} 9^{6sd} **0-0-3**

Ardkeel Lass (Ire) *P D Evans* 14 a52
4 ch f Fumo Di Londra (Ire) - Wot-A-Noise (Ire)
8^{6sd} 6^{6sd} 10^{5sd} 9^{6sd} 2^{6sd} 10^{5g} 13^{5hd} 2^{6sd} 4^{5sd} 10^{5sd} 1^{5ss} 8^{5sd} 5^{6sd} 1^{6sd} 4^{5ss}
2-2-15 £4,103

Ardwelshin (Fr) *C J Down* 10
7 b g Ajdayt (USA) - Reem Dubai (Ire)
13^{8g} 11^{8g} **0-0-2**

Areyoutalkingtome *C A Cyzer* 101
2 b c Singspiel (Ire) - Shot At Love (Ire)
7^{7gs} 2^{8gf} 6^{8g} **0-1-3 £2,923**

Arfinnit (Ire) *Mrs A L M King* 56 a44
4 b g College Chapel - Tidal Reach (USA)
12^{5gs} 8^{6sd} 11^{7gs} 14^{6g} 14^{7gf} 8^{6f} 4^{6f} 11^{6f} 9^{6gf} 1^{6f} 8^{5g} 2^{6g} **1-1-12 £2,041**

Argamia (Ger) *P J McBride* a6
9 br m Orfano (Ger) - Arkona (Ger)
8^{16sd} **0-0-1**

Argent *Miss L A Perratt* 50 a18
4 b g Barathea (Ire) - Red Tiara (USA)
12^{9sd} 1^{8gs} 10^{8gf} 8^{9gf} **1-0-4 £3,484**

Argentum *Lady Herries* 69
4 b g Sillery (USA) - Frustration
4^{14g} 6^{12gf} 1^{16gf} 1^{16gf} 3^{16gf} **2-2-5 £10,927**

Argonaut *Ian Williams* a27
5 b g Rainbow Quest (USA) - Chief Bee
13^{9sd} **0-0-1**

Ariadaeus (USA) *M J Wallace*
3 b f Thunder Gulch (USA) - Rills (USA)
11^{12sd} **0-0-1**

Arian's Lad *B Palling* 66
4 b g Prince Sabo - Arian Da
5^{7g} 2^{7gf} 5^{7g} 14^{6g} 5^{6gs} **0-1-5 £1,087**

Aricovair (Ire) *Mrs A J Bowlby* a19
5 ch g Desert Prince (Ire) - Linoise (Fr)
11^{16sd} **0-0-1**

Ariesanne (Ire) *A C Whillans* a33
4 ch f Primo Dominie - Living Legend (Ity)
9^{9hy} 12^{8ss} 7^{6sd} **0-0-3**

Arinos (Ger) *B J Curley* 59 a56
5 ch g Platini (Ger) - Arionette
12^{12sd} 8^{15gs} 5^{14gs} 13^{14g} 4^{11sd} **0-0-5 £253**

Ariodante *J M P Eustace* 53
3 b g Groom Dancer (USA) - Maestrale
11^{8gs} 15^{8gf} **0-0-2**

Arisea (Ire) *R C Guest* 39
2 b f Cape Cross (Ire) - Castelfranca (Ire)
8^{5g} 8^{7gf} 6^{7gf} **0-0-3**

Aristi (Ire) *M Quinn* 66 a60
4 b f Dr Fong (USA) - Edessa (Ire)
0^{11g} 0^{10g} 0^{10vs} 1^{13vs} 11^{11gf} 12^{12gf} 6^{12sd} 3^{13gs} 3^{17sd} 1^{17sd} 6^{14g} 1^{18gs} 6^{16g} **3-2-13 £13,916**

Aristofilia *P F I Cole* 74
2 b f Bahhare (USA) - Noble Story
2^{5gf} 4^{7gf} 3^{7g} **0-2-3 £2,668**

Ark Admiral *J Pearce* a48
6 b g Inchinor - Kelimutu
14^{10sd} 4^{14sd} 10^{12sd} 4^{12sd} **0-0-4**

Arkadia Honey *J L Spearing* 56
2 ch f Tomba - Arkadia Park (Ire)
7^{6g} 5^{6gs} 3^{5gs} **0-1-3 £676**

Arkadian Blues *Mrs L Stubbs* 35 a20
2 ch g Arkadian Hero (USA) - Nashville Blues (Ire)
4^{5s} 5^{5sd} **0-0-2 £260**

Arkholme *P Winkworth* 74
4 b g Robellino (USA) - Free Spirit (Ire)
13^{8g} 11^{8g} 9^{8gf} 7^{9gf} 10^{7gf} 13^{8gs} **0-0-6**

Arm Candy (Ire) *J A R Toller* 88
2 br f Nashwan (USA) - Bedara
6^{7gf} 1^{7gs} 10^{7gs} **1-0-3 £7,163**

Armagnac *M A Buckley* 85
7 b g Young Ern - Arianna Aldini
9^{5gs} 3^{6g} 11^{7gf} 7^{7gf} 6^{6gf} 8^{6g} 9^{6g} 4^{7gf} 10^{7gf} 15^{6g} 9^{7g} 3^{7g} **0-2-12 £2,369**

Armatore (USA) *E R Oertel* 36 a64
5 b g Gone West (USA) - Awesome Account (USA)
4^{10sd} 2^{9sd} 10^{10sd} 8^{9sd} 11^{9sd} 12^{8gf} 8^{10g}
0-1-7 £1,352

Armatrading (Ire) *J S Moore* 20 a48
3 ch f Rossini (USA) - Queenfisher
10^{7sd} 5^{8sd} 6^{10sd} 4^{9sd} 7^{10sd} 10^{9sd} 5^{10sd} 3^{8sd} 5^{12s} **0-1-9 £209**

Armenian Heritage *M G Quinlan* 83
2 b f Bluebird (USA) - Blueberry Walk
3^{8hy} 5^{8gf} 7^{8g} **0-1-3 £1,702**

Armentieres *Mrs E Slack* a41
4 b f Robellino (USA) - Perfect Poppy
8^{17sd} **0-0-1**

Arminius (Ire) *R Hannon* 86
2 b c Shinko Forest (Ire) - Tribal Rite
7^{5gf} 1^{7g} **1-0-2 £4,784**

Arms Acrossthesea *J Balding* 51 a38
6 b g Namaqualand (USA) - Zolica
10^{11sd} 12^{9sd} 9^{9sd} 7^{11gf} 19^{10gf} 10^{10gs} 12^{8g} 9^{9gf} 3^{8gf} 4^{8gf} 5^{8gf} 11^{8gs} 7^{8sd} **0-1-13 £548**

Army Of Angels (Ire) *Saeed Bin Suroor* 105
3 ch c King's Best (USA) - Angelic Sounds (Ire)
2^{7gf} 8^{8gf} **0-1-2 £3,314**

Arnbi Dancer *Mrs N S Sharpe* a36
6 b g Presidium - Travel Myth
10^{8sd} 12^{9sd} **0-0-2**

Arnie De Burgh *D J Daly* 66 a60
3 br c Amfortas (Ire) - Align
13^{8s} 4^{6gf} 6^{6gf} 2^{7gf} 13^{7gf} 10^{6sd} 12^{6sd}
0-2-7 £1,484

Arnprior (USA) *M Johnston* 60
3 ch f Royal Academy (USA) - Cool Ashlee (USA)
5^{7g} 2^{6g} 8^{7f} 3^{7gs} 7^{7gf} 4^{7f} 1^{8gf} 10^{8g} 7^{7g} 7^{7gf}
9^{10g} 5^{10gf} 13^{10s} **1-2-13 £4,983**

Arogant Prince *A W Carroll* a51
8 ch g Aragon - Versaillesprincess
2^{6sd} 9^{6sd} 6^{7sd} 11^{7sd} 5^{7sd} 9^{9sd} 12^{9sd} 11^{7sd}
10^{5sd} **0-1-9 £425**

Arous (Fr) *J L Dunlop* 68
3 br f Desert King (Ire) - Moneefa
6^{7g} 3^{8gs} 2^{7gf} 3^{9gf} 4^{7gf} **0-2-5 £2,195**

Arpa (Ire) *R Hannon* 64
2 br f Mozart (Ire) - National Portrait (Ire)
5^{6f} **0-0-1**

Arpetcheeo (USA) *D Carroll* a51
3 b/br c Deputy Minister (Can) - Lizanne (USA)
8^{9sd} 8^{9sd} 7^{9sd} **0-0-3**

Arran Scout (Ire) *T G McCourt* 73 a72
4 b g Piccolo - Evie Hone (Ire)
1^{9sd} 8^{9sd} 6^{9sd} 1^{8sd} 16^{8g} 2^{9f} 3^{8gf} 4^{8gf} 10^{8gf}
10^{8gf} 16^{10hy} 11^{7hy} **2-2-12 £9,277**

Arrivato *A M Balding* 61 a39
3 b f Efisio - Beloved Visitor (USA)
3^{7s} 5^{6s} 10^{8gf} 9^{8gf} 9^{8sd} **0-0-5 £581**

Arry Dash *M J Wallace* 89 a74
5 b g Fraam - Miletrian Cares (Ire)
6^{9sd} 8^{8sd} 8^{10sd} 4^{10sd} 3^{10gs} 8^{12sd} 5^{11g} 4^{10g} 2^{8gf}
6^{8gf} 7^{8gf} 2^{8gf} 6^{8f} 1^{8gs} 11^{9gs} 3^{8g} 9^{8gs}
1-5-17 £8,385

Arsad (Ire) *C E Brittain* 50
2 b f Cape Cross (Ire) - Astuti (Ire)
9^{8g} 10^{8g} **0-0-2**

Art Class *G L Moore* 64 a2
3 b f Mtoto - Arpello
11^{8sd} 4^{14s} 6^{8g} 13^{16g} 7^{13f} **0-0-5 £240**

Art Critic (USA) *P W Chapple-Hyam* 40
2 b/br f Fusaichi Pegasus (USA) - Performing Arts
12^{6s} **0-0-1**

Art Deco (Ire) *C R Egerton* 94
2 ch c Peintre Celebre (USA) - Sometime (Ire)
1^{7s} 2^{7gf} **1-1-2 £7,331**

Art Elegant *G A Swinbank* 66 a66
3 b g Desert Prince (Ire) - Elegant (Ire)
17^{7g} 14^{8s} 8^{7f} 4^{7sd} 8^{8g} 2^{6gf} 6^{6g} 2^{9s} 5^{8g} 2^{8s}
4^{6sf} **0-3-11 £3,903**

Art Eyes (USA) *D R C Elsworth* 113
3 ch f Halling (USA) - Careyes (Ire)
8^{8g} 3^{9gs} 6^{10gf} 3^{12gf} 1^{12g} 4^{12gf} 2^{12s} 4^{14g} 5^{15gf}
4^{12g} 1^{14g} 6^{16gs} **2-3-12 £54,735**

Art Historian (Ire) *P F I Cole* 64
2 b g Barathea (Ire) - Radhwa (Fr)
5^{5s} 9^{6g} 6^{7gf} 11^{8g} 11^{6gf} **0-0-5**

Art Investor *Unknown* 77
2 b g Sinndar (Ire) - Maid For Romance
4^{7gf} 5^{8gf} 3^{9gf} **0-1-3 £1,217**

Art Market (Can) *P F I Cole* 98
2 ch c Giant's Causeway (USA) - Fantasy Lake (USA)
3^{6gf} 1^{6gf} 3^{6gf} 10^{6gf} **1-2-4 £10,319**

Art Modern (Ire) *Mrs A J Perrett* 82 a75
3 ch g Giant's Causeway (USA) - Sinead (USA)
1^{8sd} 6^{10g} 5^{8gf} 2^{10gs} 14^{9g} 6^{10g} **1-1-6**
£6,332

Art Museum (USA) *A P O'Brien* 109
2 b c Storm Cat (USA) - Totemic (USA)
1^{6g} 1^{6g} **2-0-2 £34,627**

Art Royal (USA) *Mrs A J Perrett* 69
3 b c Royal Academy (USA) - Chelsea Green (USA)
6^{7gf} 2^{8g} **0-1-2 £1,281**

Art Work *J H M Gosden* 81 a84
3 b f Zafonic (USA) - Bayswater
9^{7gs} 1^{8g} 5^{8sd} 8^{8gf} **1-0-4 £5,018**

Artful Whisper (USA) *M A Buckley* 61 a30
3 b/br f Machiavellian (USA) - Speak Softly To Me (USA)
8^{8gf} 5^{8gf} 7^{9gs} 3^{11gf} 7^{10gf} 12^{9sd} **0-0-6**
£372

Arthurs Dream (Ire) *J G M O'Shea* 68
3 b c Desert Prince (Ire) - Blueprint (USA)
6^{10g} 2^{10gs} 9^{10f} 6^{12gf} 6^{10gf} 2^{11s} 9^{12gf} 3^{12hd}
8^{12gs} **0-2-9 £2,723**

Arthurs Legacy *J A R Toller*
3 b g Josr Algarhoud (Ire) - Loch Clair (Ire)
11^{12sd} **0-0-1**

Artic Bliss *P W Hiatt* 46 a17
3 ch f Fraam - Eskimo Nel (Ire)
14^{8gs} 11^{7sd} 9^{8g} 20^{6g} 7^{8gf} **0-0-5**

Artie *T D Easterby* 91
6 b g Whittingham (Ire) - Calamanco
11^{5g} 9^{5s} 11^{6g} 9^{6f} 7^{6gf} 7^{5gf} 10^{5g} 2^{6g} 7^{6gf}
5^{6g} 2^{6g} 1^{5g} 10^{6gs} 5^{6g} 14^{6g} **1-2-15**
£15,315

Artie Schiller (USA) *J Jerkens* 124
4 b c El Prado (Ire) - Hidden Light (USA)
1^{8f} 2^{9g} 3^{10f} 1^{9g} 2^{8f} 1^{8y} **3-3-6**
£754,166

Artie's Lad (Ire) *D Nicholls* 67 a39
4 ch g Danehill Dancer (Ire) - Bold Avril (Ire)
6^{6sd} 2^{6g} 13^{5gf} 6^{5gs} 12^{6sd} **0-1-5 £1,036**

Artistic Belle (Ire) *J M Bradley* 65
4 b f Orpen (USA) - Rite Of Spring
8^{6f} 6^{6g} 4^{6gf} 5^{5g} 7^{6g} 15^{6s} 9^{6gf} **0-1-7**
£436

Artistic Lady *M A Jarvis* 50
2 br f Jade Robbery (USA) - Noble Lily (USA)
8^{6gs} **0-0-1**

Artistic Style *B Ellison* 101
5 b g Anabaa (USA) - Fine Detail (Ire)
3^{7s} 5^{10gs} 6^{10gs} 6^{12g} 19^{10gf} 9^{8gf} 20^{10g} 4^{9g}
1^{10s} 7^{10gs} 15^{12hy} **1-1-11 £13,062**

Artists Touch (Ire) *N P Littmoden*
2 b g Alhaarth (Ire) - Alla Marcia (Ire)
11^{9sd} **0-0-1**

Arturius (Ire) *Sir Michael Stoute* 91
3 b c Anabaa (USA) - Steeple
5^{10gf} 1^{9gs} **1-0-2 £3,454**

Artushof (USA) *J Noseda* a72
3 b c Danzig (USA) - Maidee (USA)
3^{8sd} 3^{9sd} 4^{9sd} **0-2-3 £1,616**

Artzola (Ire) *C A Horgan* a49
5 b m Alzao (USA) - Polistatic
8^{10sd} 11^{10sd} 1^{9sf} 6^{9sd} **1-0-4 £1,477**

As Handsome Does *N Tinkler* 61 a45
3 ch g Handsome Ridge - Fast To Light
15^{8s} 13^{6s} 3^{6f} 7^{6f} 12^{8gf} 5^{6gf} 14^{6g} 10^{6sf}

12^{7sd} 8^{6ss} **0-1-10 £398**

Asaateel (Ire) *G L Moore* 74
3 br c Unfuwain (USA) - Alabaq (USA)
5^{10s} 1^{10s} 5^{12gf} 3^{12g} 11^{12g} 9^{11g} **1-1-6 £5,988**

Asaawir *M R Channon* 98
2 b f Royal Applause - Triple Joy
14^{6gf} 1^{6gf} 2^{6g} 1^{6gf} 6^{6gf} 4^{7gf} 10^{7gs} 3^{7gs} **2-2-8 £26,081**

Asawer (Ire) *Sir Michael Stoute* 105
3 b f Darshaan - Sassy Bird (USA)
1^{10gf} 3^{12gf} 2^{12gf} 8^{14s} 4^{12gf} 1^{10gf} 3^{12g} 3^{10s} 13^{10hy} **2-4-9 £52,970**

Asbo *Dr J D Scargill* 54
5 b m Abou Zouz (USA) - Star
8^{8gf} 6^{6gf} 4^{6gf} **0-1-3**

Asbury Park *E S McMahon* 70 a53
2 b c Primo Valentino (Ire) - Ocean Grove (Ire)
3^{8gs} 6^{8gs} 9^{9sd} **0-1-3 £483**

Ascari *A L Forbes* a34
9 br g Presidium - Ping Pong
7^{12sd} 8^{12sd} **0-0-2**

Ash Bold (Ire) *B Ellison* a13
8 ch g Persian Bold - Pasadena Lady
10^{7sd} 12^{9sd} **0-0-2**

Ash The Cash (Ire) *K F Clutterbuck*
3 b g High Roller (Ire) - Angela's Pet (Ire)
7^{6sd} **0-0-1**

Ashaawes (USA) *Saeed Bin Suroor* 96
2 b c Kingmambo (USA) - Crown Of Crimson (USA)
1^{7g} 4^{7g} **1-0-2 £6,317**

Ashado (USA) *T Pletcher* a123
4 b/br f Saint Ballado (Can) - Goulash (USA)
5^{9ft} 2^{9sy} 1^{9ft} 1^{9ft} 4^{10ft} 1^{10ft} 3^{9ft} **3-1-7 £552,613**

Asharon *C E Brittain* 84 a88
3 b c Efisio - Arriving
1^{7sd} 1^{10sd} 3^{9sd} 17^{9g} 5^{10gs} 3^{9gf} 10^{10g} 13^{10gf} 4^{10gf} **2-1-9 £21,078**

Ashburnham (Ire) *N I M Rossiter* 45 a62
2 b f Intikhab (USA) - Blu Tamantara (USA)
12^{7gf} 5^{7gs} 13^{8gf} 3^{7sd} PU^{7f} 12^{6sd} **0-1-6 £700**

Ashdown Express (Ire) *C F Wall* 116
6 ch g Ashkalani (Ire) - Indian Express
2^{6gf} 2^{5gf} 6^{6gf} 6^{5gf} 6^{6gs} 2^{6gf} 7^{7gs} 4^{6g} 3^{6g} 1^{6gf} 7^{6g} **1-4-11 £68,420**

Ashdown Princess (Ire) *C F Wall* 23
3 b f King's Theatre (Ire) - Indian Express
12^{10gf} **0-0-1**

Ashes (Ire) *K R Burke* 76 a67
3 b f General Monash (USA) - Wakayi
UR^{5sd} 2^{6sd} 3^{5sd} 2^{5gs} 1^{5g} 10^{5gs} 5^{5gs} 3^{5s} 1^{5s} 3^{5sd} 7^{5gf} 1^{5g} 8^{5gf} 13^{5s} 6^{5sf} 5^{6sd} 11^{5sd} **3-5-17 £14,051**

Ashes Regained *B W Hills* 82
2 b c Galileo (Ire) - Hasty Words (Ire)
4^{7gs} **0-0-1 £551**

Ashkal Way (Ire) *B Ellison* 106
3 ch g Ashkalani (Ire) - Golden Way (Ire)
2^{8g} 1^{8gf} 3^{8gs} 2^{10s} 1^{10g} 7^{10gf} 15^{9s} **2-3-7 £60,438**

Ashmolian (Ire) *R Charlton* 48
2 b g Grand Lodge (USA) - Animatrice (USA)
10^{8gf} 15^{8gs} **0-0-2**

Ashstanza *Mrs L Richards* 46
4 gr g Ashkalani (Ire) - Poetry In Motion (Ire)
8^{10g} 17^{10gf} 9^{9g} 11^{10f} 8^{12f} 20^{8gf} **0-0-6**

Ashwell Rose *R T Phillips* a36
3 b f Anabaa (USA) - Finicia (USA)
8^{10sd} **0-0-1**

Asian Heights *G Wragg* 41
7 b h Hernando (Fr) - Miss Rinjani
13^{12s} 10^{12gs} **0-0-2**

Ask For Rain *B W Hills* 48
3 gr f Green Desert (USA) - Requesting
7^{8gf} 6^{7g} **0-0-2**

Ask The Clerk (Ire) *Mrs P Sly* 79
4 b g Turtle Island (Ire) - Some Fun
6^{7gs} 9^{6s} 4^{7g} 13^{7gf} 5^{6g} 2^{7g} 4^{8gf} 4^{7g} 13^{7gs} **0-2-9 £2,255**

Askwith (Ire) *J D Bethell* 59
3 b g Marju (Ire) - Hayward
9^{12g} 7^{10s} 8^{10gf} 2^{11gf} 6^{10g} 5^{10gf} 1^{10g} 10^{10gf} 7^{10s} **1-1-9 £3,753**

Asmaradana *P F I Cole* 47
2 b c Groom Dancer (USA) - Nsx
9^{5gf} 7^{5gs} 8^{7gf} **0-0-3**

Aspen Falls (Ire) *Sir Mark Prescott* 77
2 ch f Elnadim (USA) - Esquiline (USA)
2^{6f} 4^{6s} 5^{5gf} 2^{7f} 1^{7g} 11^{8g} **1-2-6 £9,362**

Assertive *R Hannon* 103
2 ch c Bold Edge - Tart And A Half
2^{5g} 4^{5gf} 1^{6gf} 1^{6g} 6^{6g} 3^{6g} **2-2-6 £34,408**

Asset (Ire) *R Hannon* 98
2 b c Marju (Ire) - Snow Peak
4^{6gs} 1^{6gf} 3^{7s} **1-0-3 £8,783**

Assir *J H M Gosden* 58
3 gr f Daylami (Ire) - Etaaq (Ire)
10^{10gf} 8^{12gf} **0-0-2**

Assumption (Ire) *S C Williams* 40 a47
2 b f Beckett (Ire) - Native Force (Ire)
9^{7gs} 4^{7sd} **0-0-2**

Asteem *M E Sowersby* 44 a2
3 b g Mark Of Esteem (Ire) - Amidst
9^{9sd} 9^{6gs} 8^{7gf} 10^{8f} 6^{7g} **0-0-5**

Aston Lad *M D Hammond* 34
4 b g Bijou D'Inde - Fishki
8^{15s} **0-0-1**

Astorygoeswithit *Julian Poulton* 63 a65
2 b g Foxhound (USA) - La Belle Mystere
8^{6sd} 2^{7g} 3^{7sd} 13^{8s} 9^{6g} 1^{7sd} 11^{7sd} 11^{8sd} 8^{7sd} **1-2-9 £3,181**

Astrobella *M H Tompkins* 74
2 ch f Medicean - Optimistic
4^{6gs} 1^{7s} **1-0-2 £3,468**

Astrocharm (Ire) *M H Tompkins* 108
6 b m Charnwood Forest (Ire) - Charm The Stars
3^{12g} 3^{12gf} 4^{16g} 7^{14g} 3^{14s} 5^{16g} 5^{14g} 8^{16g} **0-3-8 £25,855**

Astronomical (Ire) *Miss S J Wilton* 87
3 b c Mister Baileys - Charm The Stars
5^{8g} 1^{8gf} 4^{8gf} 13^{10gs} 12^{10gs} 6^{10g} 8^{8g} **1-0-7 £8,575**

Astronova *M H Tompkins* 53
2 ch f Bahamian Bounty - Astrolove (Ire)
12^{6g} 10^{6g} 8^{6s} **0-0-3**

Aswan (Ire) *S R Bowring* 18 a72

7 ch g Ashkalani (Ire) - Ghariba
6^{9sd} 5^{9sd} 10^{9sd} 1^{7sd} 2^{6sd} 20^{8g} 16^{8g} 6^{8sd} 1^{9sf} 7^{8sd} **2-1-10 £6,480**

At The Bar *Miss A Stokell* 51 a42
2 ch c Compton Place - Miss Tress (Ire)
10^{5gs} 7^{5sd} 2^{5sd} 6^{5sd} 6^{6gf} 4^{5gf} 6^{6gf} 8^{5g} 11^{5sd} 9^{5sd} 8^{7gf} 14^{5gf} 12^{7gf} 6^{5gf} 6^{6gf} 8^{6g} 7^{8g} 14^{7gf} **0-1-18 £1,017**

At The Money *J M P Eustace* 56
2 b g Robellino (USA) - Coh Sho No
8^{6s} 9^{7gf} 5^{7g} 3^{8hy} **0-1-4 £702**

Atacama Star *B G Powell* 74
3 ch g Desert King (Ire) - Aunty (Fr)
8^{8g} 10^{9g} 6^{8f} 7^{7gs} 14^{7gf} 1^{10f} 3^{12f} 8^{10g} **1-0-8 £5,303**

Atali (USA) *Mrs A J Perrett*
2 b f Cherokee Run (USA) - Zaghruta (USA)
18^{7g} **0-0-1**

Athena's Dream *C F Wall* 65
2 b f Robellino (USA) - Greek Dream (USA)
13^{6gf} 5^{6g} **0-0-2**

Athens (Ire) *T Keddy* 47 a63
3 b c Saddlers' Hall (Ire) - Athene (Ire)
5^{7sd} 5^{6s} 1^{7sd} 3^{12sd} 4^{12sd} **1-1-5 £3,789**

Atlantic Ace *B Smart* a67
8 b g First Trump - Risalah
4^{9sd} 4^{9sd} **0-0-2 £317**

Atlantic Breeze *B J McMath* 34
4 br f Deploy - Atlantic Air
12^{10g} 8^{10g} 13^{16g} **0-0-3**

Atlantic City *Mrs L Richards* 54 a68
4 ch g First Trump - Pleasuring
1^{12sd} 7^{12sd} 6^{10sd} 10^{12sd} 6^{12g} **1-0-5 £3,328**

Atlantic Quest (USA) *R A Harris* a89
6 b g Woodman (USA) - Pleasant Pat (USA)
1^{7sd} 1^{7sd} **2-0-2 £9,615**

Atlantic Viking (Ire) *Unknown* 85
10 b g Danehill (USA) - Hi Bettina
15^{6s} 16^{5g} 10^{5g} 12^{5g} **0-0-4**

Atlantic Waves (Ire) *M Johnston* 96
2 b c Sadler's Wells (USA) - Highest Accolade
1^{7g} 5^{8g} **1-0-2 £6,239**

Atriffic Story *Miss Gay Kelleway* 62 a53
3 ch g Atraf - Composition
5^{8sd} 7^{7sd} 9^{8gf} 4^{10f} 3^{12f} 1^{12gf} 3^{14g} **1-2-7 £4,244**

Attacca *J R Weymes* 59 a39
4 b g Piccolo - Jubilee Place (Ire)
6^{7s} 3^{6gf} 8^{7gf} 9^{7f} 5^{6gs} 3^{7gf} 7^{8gf} 16^{7gf} 6^{7gf} 1^{7f} 9^{7sf} **1-1-11 £4,099**

Attack Minded *L R James*
4 ch g Timeless Times (USA) - French Ginger
12^{12gf} **0-0-1**

Atticus Trophies (Ire) *K McAuliffe* 70 a55
2 b g Mujadil (USA) - Nezool Almatar (Ire)
12^{5gf} 3^{6g} 10^{7sd} 20^{7s} 8^{7sd} **0-1-5 £648**

Attila The Hun *F Watson* 47
6 b g Piccolo - Katya (Ire)
14^{5g} 7^{6gf} 10^{5gf} 6^{6gf} **0-0-4**

Attishoe *Miss B Sanders* a52
3 b f Atraf - Royal Shoe
8^{8sd} 7^{10sd} 10^{12sd} **0-0-3**

Attitude Annie *S Dow* 27 a54
2 b f Josr Algarhoud (Ire) - Eclectic
15^{6gf} 4^{7sd} **0-0-2 £276**

Attorney *N E Berry* 74 a71
7 ch g Wolfhound (USA) - Princess Sadie
1^{6sd} 1^{5sd} 1^{6sd} 1^{6sd} 5^{6sd} 11^{5sd} 7^{6sd} 3^{7s} 1^{6sd} 1^{6s} 10^{6g} 2^{5gs} 6^{6gf} 1^{6g} 1^{5gf} 6^{6g} 2^{6gs} 11^{5g} 2^{6sd} 1^{5gf} 8^{6g} 7^{5sd} 9^{6sd} 8^{6sd} 8^{6sd} **9-4-25 £27,123**

Attraction *M Johnston* 113
4 b f Efisio - Flirtation
11^{8gf} 4^{7g} 1^{8gy} **1-0-3 £117,748**

Attune *B J Meehan* 97 a99
4 br f Singspiel (Ire) - Arriving
6^{7g} 8^{8gf} 5^{7g} 3^{7g} 2^{7g} 9^{8gs} 3^{8sd} **0-3-7 £15,200**

Au Revoir *C W Thornton* 44
3 ch f Efisio - Blow Me A Kiss
8^{6gs} 6^{7gs} 10^{6g} PU^{8gs} **0-0-4**

Aubaine (USA) *J H M Gosden* 78
2 b/br f Fusaichi Pegasus (USA) - Valencay (Ire)
10^{6gf} 1^{7gf} 4^{7gf} **1-0-3 £11,605**

Auburn Lodge (Ire) *J J Lambe* 55
4 ch f Grand Lodge (USA) - Hadawah (USA)
2^{8g} 2^{12gf} 2^{11s} 2^{9g} 6^{10y} 9^{8g} 13^{13f} 9^{12g} 12^{12f} **0-4-9 £4,110**

Auction Room (USA) *B W Hills* 78
2 b f Chester House (USA) - Didina
7^{7g} 2^{7g} 1^{8g} 4^{8g} 4^{7gs} **1-1-5 £6,309**

Audience *J Akehurst* 103
5 b g Zilzal (USA) - Only Yours
5^{8g} 14^{7gf} 8^{8gs} 11^{7s} 3^{8g} 1^{8gf} 12^{8gf} 10^{8gs} 16^{8gf} 11^{9g} 9^{8g} 7^{8gs} 8^{10g} 4^{8s} **1-1-14 £16,436**

Auditorium *Mrs A J Perrett* 100
4 b g Royal Applause - Degree
3^{7gs} 5^{8gf} 10^{10g} **0-0-3 £1,578**

Auentraum (Ger) *K McAuliffe* 49 a54
5 br g Big Shuffle (USA) - Auenglocke (Ger)
12^{6sd} 7^{5gf} 10^{6gs} 4^{6sd} 6^{6sf} 4^{5sd} 4^{7sd} 4^{8sd} 10^{6sd} **0-0-9**

Augustine *P W Hiatt* a62
4 b/br g Machiavellian (USA) - Crown Of Light
8^{8sd} 8^{9sd} 4^{9sd} 9^{10sd} 1^{8sd} 1^{10sd} 3^{8sd} 2^{8sd} **2-2-8 £6,901**

Augustus Livius (Ire) *W Storey* 13
2 b g Titus Livius (Fr) - Regal Fanfare (Ire)
8^{5gf} 16^{8gf} 13^{7s} 4^{7s} **0-0-4**

Aunt Julia *R Hannon* 105
3 b f In The Wings - Original
5^{10gs} 3^{10gs} 3^{10gf} 1^{10gf} 3^{12gs} 7^{12g} **1-2-6 £12,459**

Aurora Jane (Fr) *B W Hills* 58
2 ch f Distant View (USA) - Alto Jane
5^{6s} 12^{7gf} **0-0-2**

Aussie Rules (USA) *A P O'Brien* 109
2 gr c Danehill (USA) - Last Second (Ire)
1^{6g} 4^{7s} 2^{6g} 1^{7g} **2-1-4 £58,370**

Australie (Ire) *J R Fanshawe* 108
4 b f Sadler's Wells (USA) - Asnieres (USA)
4^{10s} 7^{11s} 3^{12gs} 5^{11vs} **0-1-4 £11,059**

Austrian (UAE) *M Johnston* 86
2 ch c Jade Robbery (USA) - Anne D'Autriche (Ire)
3^{6gf} 1^{8s} **1-1-2 £6,467**

Authenticate *E S McMahon* 67 a66
3 b f Dansili - Exact Replica
13^{7f} 7^{10gf} 3^{7gf} 1^{7gf} 6^{8g} 4^{7gf} 7^{9sd} **1-2-7**

£3,900

Authority (Ire) *Lady Herries* 79
5 b g Bluebird (USA) - Persian Tapestry
1^{10gs} 2^{10gf} **1-1-2 £4,634**

Automation *C W Thornton*
2 b f Tamure (Ire) - Anatomic
13^{6gf} **0-0-1**

Autumn Daze *M Wigham* a21
3 b f Danzig Connection (USA) - Autumn Stone (Ire)
10^{10sd} 11^{5sd} 9^{6sd} **0-0-3**

Autumn Dream *Miss J E Foster* 18
3 b f Primo Dominie - Red Cascade (Ire)
12^{7gf} **0-0-1**

Autumn Fantasy (USA) *M R Hoad*
6 b g Lear Fan (USA) - Autumn Glory (USA)
13^{17sd} **0-0-1**

Autumn Glory (Ire) *G Wragg* 121 a119
5 b h Charnwood Forest (Ire) - Archipova (Ire)
1^{8g} 2^{8gs} 3^{10g} 1^{8sd} 13^{7gs} 5^{8g} **2-1-6**
£76,077

Autumn Wealth (Ire) *Mrs A J Perrett* 107
4 ch f Cadeaux Genereux - Prickwillow (USA)
1^{12g} 4^{12gs} 8^{15gf} 5^{12g} 7^{13s} 2^{14hy} **1-1-6**
£30,600

Auvergne *S J Mahon* 79
3 b c Green Desert (USA) - Aquaba (USA)
3^{7s} 1^{7gs} 4^{7gs} 6^{7gf} 9^{7gf} 2^{8g} 3^{7g} 14^{7gf} 3^{8g}
13^{8sh} **1-4-10 £7,006**

Auwitesweetheart *B R Millman* 88
3 b f Josr Algarhoud (Ire) - Miss Kirsty (USA)
2^{6s} 3^{5gs} 1^{5g} 4^{6g} 2^{5gf} 2^{6gf} 2^{6gf} 5^{5gs} 7^{5g} 5^{5gs}
8^{6g} **1-5-11 £12,510**

Avalon *Jonjo O'Neill* 116
3 b g Kingmambo (USA) - Lady Carla
1^{10gf} 3^{12g} 4^{14g} **1-0-3 £22,865**

Avanti *Dr J R J Naylor* 50 a54
9 gr g Reprimand - Dolly Bevan
11^{12sd} 8^{17sd} 4^{10s} 1^{12sd} 6^{12gf} **1-0-5**
£2,968

Avanti Avanti (USA) *R Hannon* a77
3 b c Royal Academy (USA) - Norelands (USA)
2^{8sd} 1^{8sd} **1-1-2 £4,750**

Aveiro (Ire) *G C H Chung* 32 a60
9 b g Darshaan - Avila
6^{12sd} 3^{12sd} 6^{14sd} 6^{12g} 6^{12sd} **0-1-5 £367**

Avenches (Ger) *M J McGrath* a21
5 ch m Dashing Blade - Altja (Ger)
3^{10sd} 8^{12sd} **0-0-2 £305**

Avenlea *G L Moore* a50
4 b g Averti (Ire) - Cloudslea (USA)
7^{7sd} 6^{5sd} **0-0-2**

Aventura (Ire) *S R Bowring* 54 a74
5 b g Sri Pekan (USA) - La Belle Katherine (USA)
1^{9sd} 5^{9sd} 3^{8sd} 8^{7g} 13^{10g} **1-1-5 £3,988**

Averami *A M Balding* a43
4 b/br f Averti (Ire) - Friend For Life
7^{7sd} **0-0-1**

Averlline *B De Haan* a45
4 b f Averti (Ire) - Spring Sunrise
8^{8sd} 10^{8sd} **0-0-2**

Aversham *Jonjo O'Neill* 86
5 b h Averti (Ire) - Vavona
25^{6gf} BD^{6g} 9^{7gf} 6^{6gf} 7^{6gf} 4^{6g} 13^{7gf}
0-0-7 £699

Avertible *M W Easterby* 28
2 b g Averti (Ire) - Better Still (Ire)
11^{5gf} 14^{5s} 11^{5gf} 14^{6gf} 8^{8gf} **0-0-5**

Avesa *D A Nolan*
5 br m Averti (Ire) - Andalish
10^{11g} 9^{8gs} **0-0-2**

Avesomeofthat (Ire) *Mrs P N Dutfield* 58
4 b g Lahib (USA) - Lacinia
8^{10gf} 6^{12gf} 7^{14gf} 7^{18gf} **0-0-4**

Aviation *G M Moore* 71
3 b g Averti (Ire) - Roufontaine
11^{6gf} 5^{6g} 7^{6gf} 2^{7f} 4^{8gf} 4^{9gf} 5^{8gf} 1^{8g}
1-1-8 £4,988

Avicia *C A Horgan* a68
3 ch f Vettori (Ire) - Amarice
3^{12sd} 5^{12sd} 3^{13sd} 9^{14sd} 7^{12sd} **0-2-5**
£1,205

Aviemore *J R Cornwall* 76
3 b g Selkirk (USA) - Film Script
11^{10gf} 4^{10gs} 10^{11gs} 7^{12gf} 6^{10gs} 8^{10g} **0-0-6**
£384

Avit (Ire) *P L Gilligan* 48 a49
5 ch m General Monash (USA) - Breakfast Boogie
1^{6g} 3^{6gs} 2^{6sd} 2^{6f} 7^{7f} 4^{5sd} 10^{7sd} 9^{6f} 6^{5f} 6^{5sd}
7^{5ss} 5^{6sd} **1-3-12 £2,563**

Avizandum (Ire) *T J Etherington* a54
3 b g Daggers Drawn (USA) - Miss Dilletante
6^{7sd} 5^{7sd} 5^{6sd} 9^{5sd} 10^{6gf} 4^{5sd} 9^{6sd} 4^{6sd} 8^{7sd}
0-0-9

Avoca Dancer (Ire) *M Johnston* 65
2 ch f Compton Place - Kashra (Ire)
5^{6g} 3^{6gf} 6^{6g} 7^{7gf} 8^{7s} **0-1-5 £1,200**

Avonbridge *R Charlton* 119
5 b h Averti (Ire) - Alessia
1^{5gf} 3^{5g} 2^{6gs} 7^{5gf} 3^{6g} 1^{5gs} **2-3-6**
£182,786

Avontuur (Fr) *D W Chapman* 50 a41
3 ch g Kabool - Ipoh (Fr)
14^{10g} 7^{11s} 5^{7f} 7^{8gf} 5^{9sd} 2^{7gs} 9^{9gf} 7^{9gf} 10^{10gf}
0-1-9 £1,108

Awaaser (USA) *J A Osborne* 39 a54
3 ch f Diesis - Forest Storm (USA)
5^{7g} 13^{6g} 2^{9sd} 1^{9sf} **1-1-4 £1,859**

Awake *Miss D A McHale* 68 a85
8 ch g First Trump - Pluvial
2^{6sd} 4^{5sd} 7^{6sd} 4^{6sd} 10^{6sd} 5^{5sd} 4^{5sd} 9^{6sd} 5^{5sd}
12^{5gs} 10^{5g} 15^{5gf} 7^{6gf} 7^{6g} 13^{7g} 13^{6g} 13^{5ft}
14^{6sd} **0-1-18 £1,054**

Awaken *Miss Tracy Waggott* 54
4 b f Zafonic (USA) - Dawna
3^{8g} 4^{11gf} 3^{8gf} 3^{10gs} 1^{10g} 10^{11g} **1-3-6**
£4,221

Awarding *Dr J R J Naylor* 53 a52
5 ch g Mark Of Esteem (Ire) - Monaiya
5^{5gf} 7^{6sd} 7^{7gf} 13^{9sd} 15^{8gf} 2^{7gf} 7^{8g} 17^{7gf}
17^{5gf} 10^{6g} 10^{7sf} 8^{8sd} 3^{7sd} 2^{7sd} **0-3-14**
£1,908

Awash (USA) *H R A Cecil* 76
3 ch c Coronado's Quest (USA) - All At Sea (USA)
4^{10gf} 1^{13gf} **1-0-2 £4,001**

Awatuki (Ire) *A P Jarvis* 76
2 b c Distant Music (USA) - Itkan (Ire)
5^{6gs} 2^{7s} **0-1-2 £675**

Awwal Marra (USA) *E W Tuer* 45
5 ch m King Of Kings (Ire) - Secretariat Lass (USA)
5^{12gf} 7^{12g} 13^{14f} 8^{12f} 13^{16gf} 10^{10gs} **0-0-6**

Axis Shield (Ire) *J G Portman* 16 a47

2 b f Shinko Forest (Ire) - La Doyenne (Ire)
13^{6gf} 4^{7sd} 2^{7sd} 7^{6sd} 4^{6sf} 11^{7ss} 4^{6sd}
0-1-7 £758

Ayala Cove (USA) *P C Haslam* 37
2 ch f Mt. Livermore (USA) - Kitra (USA)
9^{6gf} 8^{6gf} 13^{6gf} **0-0-3**

Ayam Jantan *M Johnston* 58
2 ch g Cadeaux Genereux - Madame Est Sortie (Fr)
11^{6gf} 7^{7gf} 4^{7g} **0-0-3 £477**

Ayam Zaman (Ire) *M A Jarvis* 86
3 b f Montjeu (Ire) - Kardashina (Fr)
3^{11g} F^{11gf} **0-0-2 £5,500**

Aylmer Road (Ire) *P F I Cole* 79
3 b c Groom Dancer (USA) - Pekan's Pride
6^{8gs} 3^{10gf} 3^{10gf} 1^{12f} 7^{12g} 6^{12gf} 4^{14gf} 16^{12g} 3^{12gs} 5^{16g} **1-3-10 £7,284**

Aysgarth Flyer (Ire) *I Semple* 52 a62
2 b g Soviet Star (USA) - Why Worry Now (Ire)
7^{7sd} 5^{7f} 6^{7g} 6^{6gf} 2^{8gf} 5^{8g} 5^{9sd} 1^{6sd} 4^{6sd}
1-1-9 £2,615

Azahara *K G Reveley* 61
3 b f Vettori (Ire) - Branston Express
15^{12g} 7^{8g} 11^{10g} 10^{8g} 6^{8s} 5^{10g} 6^{12gf} 6^{11gf} 3^{10g} 6^{10g} 9^{8s} **0-1-11 £388**

Azamour (Ire) *John M Oxx* 129
4 b c Night Shift (USA) - Asmara (USA)
4^{11gy} 1^{10gf} 1^{12gf} 5^{10gy} 3^{12y} **2-1-5**
£760,449

Azarole (Ire) *J S Moore* 114 a108
4 b g Alzao (USA) - Cashew
1^{7gs} 7^{7gs} 1^{7s} 3^{8gf} 10^{7gs} 9^{6gs} 2^{8sd} **2-2-7**
£26,486

Azeezah *R M H Cowell* 54 a45
3 ch f Hernando (Fr) - Brave Vanessa (USA)
10^{9sd} 8^{9sd} 10^{7g} 4^{6g} 7^{6sd} 8^{7sd} 4^{6f} 10^{6gf} 12^{9sd}
0-0-9 £270

Azime (Ire) *C E Brittain* 63
2 b c Cape Cross (Ire) - Adjisa (Ire)
6^{8s} 5^{8gf} 8^{9gf} **0-0-3**

Azizam *P W Chapple-Hyam* 81 a29
3 ch f Singspiel (Ire) - Perdicula (Ire)
7^{10gf} 2^{10gf} 1^{10gf} 9^{10gs} 13^{11gf} 14^{12sd} **1-1-6**
£5,096

Azreme *P Howling* 75 a53
5 ch h Unfuwain (USA) - Mariette
9^{7gs} 8^{7sd} 19^{8g} 11^{7g} 3^{8gs} 7^{7gs} 9^{7gs} 7^{8gs} 5^{7g} 5^{8s} 11^{7hy} 11^{10sd} 8^{9sd} **0-1-13 £1,053**

Azuree (Ire) *D W Chapman* 59 a51
3 b f Almutawakel - Cappella (Ire)
7^{6sd} 3^{6sd} 12^{7sd} 4^{5sd} 6^{6sd} 9^{5sd} 13^{5sd} 6^{5sd} 13^{6gf} 6^{6sd} 5^{5sd} 4^{5sd} 4^{5gf} 12^{6gf} 1^{6gf} 11^{7f} 6^{5sd} 17^{6gf} 3^{6s} 4^{6gf} 1^{6gf} 3^{6gf} 13^{7sd} **2-4-23 £7,500**

Azygous *J Akehurst* 87 a81
2 ch g Foxhound (USA) - Flag
1^{5sd} 1^{5sd} 13^{5gf} 3^{5gf} 3^{5gf} 4^{6gf} 7^{5gf} 4^{5g} 2^{5g} 2^{5g} 8^{6sd} **2-4-11 £17,386**

Ba Clubman (Ire) *B D Leavy* a53
5 b g Royal Abjar (USA) - Ah Ya Zein
7^{7sd} 2^{6sd} 5^{6sd} 1^{7sd} 5^{7sd} 7^{7sd} 4^{6sd} 3^{9sd} 8^{7sd} 12^{7sd} 16^{10g} 10^{9sd} **1-2-12 £2,278**

Ba Foxtrot *M R Channon* 105
2 b c Foxhound (USA) - Aunt Susan
1^{5gs} 1^{5hy} 2^{5gy} 1^{6g} 13^{6gf} 4^{6gf} 18^{6gf} 10^{6gs}
3-1-8 £46,199

Baan (USA) *M Johnston* 102
2 ch c Diesis - Madaen (USA)
1^{7g} 2^{8g} 2^{8s} 1^{9gs} **2-0-4 £18,673**

Baba Ghanoush *W Jarvis* 51 a71
3 ch f Zaha (Can) - Vrennan
8^{7g} 4^{7sd} 1^{7sd} **1-0-3 £3,580**

Babatac (Ire) *G Prodromou*
3 b g Diktat - Babsy Babe
8^{8gf} **0-0-1**

Babe Maccool (Ire) *B W Hills* 88
3 ch g Giant's Causeway (USA) - Kotama (USA)
1^{8gf} 3^{8gf} 1^{8g} 1^{10gf} 10^{10s} 6^{10gf} 13^{10gf}
3-1-7 £22,338

Babeth (Ire) *A M Balding* 63 a61
2 b f Indian Lodge (Ire) - Almond Flower (Ire)
8^{6gf} 4^{6s} 2^{6sd} 1^{5sd} **1-1-4 £4,629**

Babodana *M H Tompkins* 118 a109
5 ch h Bahamian Bounty - Daanat Nawal
7^{8hy} 3^{8g} 3^{8s} 8^{8gf} 4^{8sd} 5^{8gs} 3^{7gf} 4^{8g} 4^{8gs} 11^{7gs} 5^{8s} **0-3-11 £32,630**

Baboosh (Ire) *M Wigham* a58
4 b f Marju (Ire) - Slipper
10^{8sd} **0-0-1**

Baby Barry *R A Fahey* 56 a60
8 b g Komaite (USA) - Malcesine (Ire)
3^{7sd} 3^{8gs} 7^{9sd} 2^{9sd} 2^{8gf} 3^{8sd} 3^{9sd} 8^{9sd} 4^{8gf} 7^{10g} 2^{8s} 7^{9sd} **0-7-12 £5,339**

Bacharach (Ire) *R F Fisher* 69
2 b g Indian Lodge (Ire) - Katherine Gorge (USA)
6^{6g} 5^{7gs} 3^{7gf} **0-1-3 £589**

Bachelor Affair *W Jarvis* 61 a47
3 b g Bachir (Ire) - Profit Alert (Ire)
2^{7f} 3^{8g} 6^{7gf} 6^{7gf} 9^{10gf} 11^{9sd} 8^{6g} **0-2-7**
£2,005

Back At De Front (Ire) *R A Harris* a20
4 b f Cape Cross (Ire) - Bold Fashion (Fr)
13^{5sd} **0-0-1**

Back In Spirit *E S McMahon* a46
5 ch g Primo Dominie - Pusey Street Girl
12^{7sd} 3^{6sd} 10^{6sd} 10^{6sd} **0-1-4 £416**

Back To Reality *B Palling* 29
3 ch g Magic Ring (Ire) - Arian Da
11^{8gs} 9^{12g} 7^{14g} 16^{8g} **0-0-4**

Backgammon *K G Reveley* 85
4 b g Sadler's Wells (USA) - Game Plan
11^{12gs} 1^{13gs} 9^{14s} 4^{12f} 6^{12g} 15^{12gf} 6^{13gs}
1-0-7 £7,598

Backlash *A W Carroll* 27 a48
4 b f Fraam - Mezza Luna
5^{12sd} 6^{8sd} 2^{9sd} 2^{9sd} 10^{7g} 10^{9sd} 10^{7gf} 9^{10f}
0-2-8 £701

Backstreet Lad *Evan Williams* 56 a47
3 b g Fraam - Forest Fantasy
4^{10gs} 2^{10g} 6^{12sd} 7^{12g} 3^{10f} **0-2-5 £1,465**

Baddam *J L Dunlop* 92
3 b c Mujahid (USA) - Aude La Belle (Fr)
3^{11gs} 1^{14g} 2^{14gf} 1^{14gf} 1^{15gs} 15^{18gs} **3-2-6**
£21,995

Badou *L Montague Hall* a43
5 b g Averti (Ire) - Bint Albadou (Ire)
6^{8sd} 7^{7sd} 5^{5sd} **0-0-3**

Baffle *T Hogan* a27
4 b f Selkirk (USA) - Elude
9^{8sd} 11^{10sd} 11^{7f} 15^{14y} **0-0-4**

Bago (Fr) *J E Pease* 126
4 b c Nashwan (USA) - Moonlight's Box (USA)
1^{11vs} 2^{11gy} 3^{12gs} 3^{12gf} 3^{12gs} 4^{12y} 8^{12f}

1-4-7 £438,151

Bahama Belle *Mrs L C Jewell* a38
4 b f Bahamian Bounty - Barque Bleue (USA)
10^{7sd} **0-0-1**

Bahama Reef (Ire) *B Gubby* 35 a56
4 b g Sri Pekan (USA) - Caribbean Dancer
5^{8sd} 8^{8sd} 11^{8gf} 9^{8sd} 10^{8gf} 12^{8sd} 9^{8sd}
0-0-7

Bahamian Ballet *E S McMahon* 75 a69
3 ch g Bahamian Bounty - Plie
3^{6g} 1^{6g} 8^{6sd} **1-1-3 £4,423**

Bahamian Bay *M Brittain* a48
3 b f Bahamian Bounty - Moly
1^{5sd} 13^{5sd} 4^{5sd} 4^{6sd} **1-0-4 £1,463**

Bahamian Belle *P S McEntee*
5 b m Bahamian Bounty - Marjorie's Memory (Ire)
6^{13sd} **0-0-1**

Bahamian Breeze *D M Simcock* a59
4 b g Piccolo - Norgabie
7^{5sf} **0-0-1**

Bahamian Duke *K R Burke* 50
2 ch g Bahamian Bounty - Madame Sisu
6^{5gf} 5^{5g} 10^{6gf} **0-0-3**

Bahamian Pirate (USA) *D Nicholls* 110
10 ch g Housebuster (USA) - Shining Through (USA)
6^{6g} 5^{5gf} 7^{6gs} 11^{5s} 8^{5gf} 6^{6g} 4^{5g} 11^{6g}
0-0-8 £3,162

Bahamian Spring (Ire) *D Shaw* a56
3 b g Danehill Dancer (Ire) - Siana Springs (Ire)
2^{7sd} 11^{8sd} 10^{7sd} 3^{9sd} 17^{6hy} 13^{8sd} **0-2-6**
£1,271

Bahar Shumaal (Ire) *C E Brittain* 106
3 b c Dubai Millennium - High Spirited
2^{8f} 1^{10gf} 5^{12gf} 10^{8gs} 12^{9gs} **1-1-5**
£28,199

Bahara *M R Channon* 77
3 b f Barathea (Ire) - Brigadiers Bird (Ire)
2^{5gs} 4^{6g} 3^{6f} 8^{7g} 6^{7g} 5^{6gf} 14^{6hy} **0-1-7**
£4,224

Bahhmirage (Ire) *C N Kellett* a46
2 ch f Bahhare (USA) - Border Mirage
9^{8sd} 11^{7sd} **0-0-2**

Bahia Breeze *Rae Guest* 106
3 b f Mister Baileys - Ring Of Love
7^{7gf} 8^{8gf} 4^{8g} 4^{8g} **0-0-4 £8,085**

Bahiano (Ire) *C E Brittain* 103 a103
4 ch g Barathea (Ire) - Trystero
4^{8gf} 5^{8ft} 7^{8gf} 5^{7sd} 4^{7sd} 8^{8gs} 6^{7g} 3^{7gf} 2^{6g}
4^{7gf} 8^{8sd} 3^{7g} 8^{7gf} 9^{6g} 9^{7gf} 7^{9sd} 3^{8sd}
0-5-17 £24,928

Bahrall *A P Jarvis* 37 a25
2 b g Bahri (USA) - Navajo Love Song (Ire)
11^{8gf} 12^{8sd} **0-0-2**

Baie Des Flamands (USA) *Miss S J Wilton* 83
3 b c Kingmambo (USA) - Isle De France (USA)
7^{8gf} 6^{8g} 9^{10g} 2^{10gf} 1^{10g} 13^{10s} 6^{10gf} 2^{10g} 8^{10g}
1-2-9 £7,508

Bailaora (Ire) *B W Duke* 46
4 b/br g Shinko Forest (Ire) - Tart (Fr)
5^{8hy} 12^{12gf} **0-0-2**

Bailey Gate *R Hannon* 92
3 b f Mister Baileys - Floppie (Fr)
10^{6gf} 4^{6gf} 1^{6gf} 5^{6gf} 10^{6g} 14^{6g} 9^{6gf} 7^{6g}
1-0-8 £7,870

Baileys Applause *C A Dwyer* 50 a59
3 b f Royal Applause - Thicket
2^{5sd} 4^{5sd} 1^{5sd} 6^{5gf} 4^{5sd} 5^{6f} 6^{5gs} 9^{5sd} 3^{5sd}
10^{6gs} **1-2-10 £4,146**

Baileys Encore *M Johnston* 84
2 b g Mister Baileys - Exclusive Life (USA)
6^{7gs} 3^{7g} 7^{6g} 8^{7g} 3^{8s} 5^{8hy} **0-2-6 £1,864**

Baileys Honour *A G Newcombe* 46 a64
3 b f Mark Of Esteem (Ire) - Kanz (USA)
1^{9sd} 3^{9sd} 6^{12sd} 8^{9sd} 14^{8g} 10^{9sd} 14^{8gf} 7^{14g}
1-1-8 £3,404

Baileys Polka *J G Given* 68 a50
2 b f Polish Precedent (USA) - Mistitled (USA)
2^{7s} 5^{9sd} **0-1-2 £1,248**

Bailieborough (Ire) *Robert Gray* 89
6 b g Charnwood Forest (Ire) - Sherannda (USA)
5^{7g} 2^{7gf} 2^{9gs} 6^{8g} 6^{8gf} 3^{8gf} 7^{8gs} 7^{8g} 1^{9f} 4^{9gf}
1^{8g} 4^{7f} 1^{8gf} 1^{7gf} 1^{8gs} 12^{8gs} 12^{9gs} 11^{7s}
5-2-18 £26,597

Baizically (Ire) *J A Osborne* 66
2 ch c Galileo (Ire) - Baize
7^{7gf} **0-0-1**

Bajan Parkes *H Candy* 91
2 b/br g Zafonic (USA) - My Melody Parkes
1^{6f} **1-0-1 £3,620**

Baker Of Oz *D Burchell* 58 a21
4 b g Pursuit Of Love - Moorish Idol
2^{10s} 5^{10gf} 4^{8s} 13^{9sd} 7^{8g} 13^{9sd} **0-1-6**
£1,010

Bakke *B I Case* 29 a56
3 b g Danehill (USA) - Valagalore
4^{6sd} 14^{7g} 12^{7gf} 13^{10sd} **0-0-4 £267**

Baklawa *B J Meehan* 68 a63
2 br f Zafonic (USA) - Baked Alaska
7^{6gf} 5^{7gs} 4^{7sd} 5^{7sd} **0-0-4 £350**

Balakiref *M Dods* 83 a81
6 b g Royal Applause - Pluck
6^{6s} 5^{7s} 7^{6g} 5^{6gf} 5^{6g} 15^{6g} 2^{6s} 12^{6g} 1^{6gs} 4^{6s}
2^{6hy} 3^{7s} 7^{6sf} 4^{6sd} 8^{7sd} **1-4-15 £13,234**

Balalaika Tune (Ire) *B R Foster* a34
6 b m Lure (USA) - Bohemienne (USA)
8^{9sd} 11^{9sd} **0-0-2**

Balance Of Power *R Charlton* 86
3 b g Sadler's Wells (USA) - Cattermole (USA)
2^{12gf} 1^{12g} 10^{14gf} **1-1-3 £6,283**

Balasari (Ire) *Miss Kariana Key* a7
5 b g Sri Pekan (USA) - Balaniya (USA)
12^{11sd} **0-0-1**

Balavista (USA) *R Charlton* 97 a76
4 br c Distant View (USA) - Balabina (USA)
2^{7g} 16^{8gs} 1^{8g} 8^{8sd} 2^{8g} 11^{8g} **1-2-6**
£17,025

Baldassare *J Noseda* 86
3 ch c Grand Lodge (USA) - Royal York
6^{10gf} 2^{12s} **0-1-2 £1,033**

Balearic Star (Ire) *B R Millman* 77 a63
4 b g Night Shift (USA) - La Menorquina (USA)
11^{8g} 3^{8gf} 12^{10g} 5^{8gf} 5^{8gf} 12^{8g} 11^{8gf} 7^{7f}
11^{10sd} 3^{8sd} 3^{8sd} 8^{8sd} **0-3-12 £1,559**

Balerno *R Ingram* 67 a65
6 b g Machiavellian (USA) - Balabina (USA)
10^{7sd} 10^{7sd} 1^{7sd} 2^{8sd} 8^{7sd} 6^{8sd} 3^{7sd} 2^{7gf} 1^{8sd}
10^{10sd} 15^{8gf} 8^{9g} 3^{8gs} 12^{8gf} 4^{7s} 1^{7g} 11^{7f}
1^{7sd} 9^{8f} 5^{7g} 7^{8gs} **4-4-21 £15,783**

Balfour House *R A Harris*
2 b g Wizard King - Tymeera

7^{5sd} **0-0-1**

Balgarth (USA) *K J Burke* 41 a66
3 b g Zamindar (USA) - Vaguely Regal (Ire)
3^{6sd} 8^{8sd} 7^{6g} 16^{6gf} 11^{6s} 13^{6g} **0-1-6 £536**

Bali Royal *T Stack* 108
7 b m King's Signet (USA) - Baligay
12^{5gf} 1^{5g} 10^{5s} 9^{6g} **1-0-4 £42,553**

Ballan *G L Moore* 69
2 b g Mujahid (USA) - Imperial Jade
10^{6gs} 3^{5g} 3^{6gf} 9^{5g} **0-2-4 £953**

Balik Pearls *N A Callaghan* 71 a75
2 b f Xaar - Miss Mercy (Ire)
3^{6g} 2^{7f} 10^{7gf} 7^{6gs} 1^{6sd} 3^{6sd} **1-1-6 £6,513**

Balkan Knight *D R C Elsworth* 109
5 b h Selkirk (USA) - Crown Of Light
2^{12gs} 1^{14gs} 2^{12g} 6^{16g} 2^{14gs} 4^{14g} 1^{14g} **2-4-7 £88,338**

Ball Boy *G Haine* 75 a76
3 b g Xaar - Tanz (Ire)
1^{12sd} 4^{12g} 7^{11gs} **1-0-3 £3,997**

Ball Games *James Moffatt* a18
7 b g Mind Games - Deb's Ball
13^{10g} 8^{12sd} **0-0-2**

Ballare (Ire) *P J Makin* a50
6 b g Barathea (Ire) - Raindancing (Ire)
12^{8sd} 5^{7sd} 11^{7sd} 7^{10g} 4^{8gf} 6^{7g} 2^{9gf} 2^{9gf} 11^{7sd} **0-0-9 £1,187**

Ballast (Ire) *L M Cumani* 110
4 ch c Desert Prince (Ire) - Suedoise
10^{8gs} 1^{8gs} 2^{8gf} 15^{7gs} 15^{8gf} **1-1-5 £35,608**

Ballet Ballon (USA) *M A Jarvis* 79 a77
3 b f Rahy (USA) - Bella Ballerina
5^{8g} 3^{8gf} 3^{8gf} 1^{10gf} 8^{10gf} 4^{10gf} 4^{12sd} 10^{12sf} **1-3-8 £5,669**

Ballet Be (Ire) *H S Howe*
2 b f Beckett (Ire) - Coppelia (Ire)
16^{6gf} 5^{5s} **0-0-2**

Ballet Slippers (Ire) *John Joseph Murphy* 52
2 b f Mozart (Ire) - American Queen (Fr)
8^{5s} 8^{6g} 11^{6g} 9^{6s} 8^{6hy} **0-0-5**

Balletomaine (Ire) *B W Hills* 67 a56
3 b f Sadler's Wells (USA) - Ivy (USA)
11^{10g} 8^{10gf} 3^{12sd} 1^{12f} 10^{14gf} 6^{16s} 3^{14gf} 14^{12sd} **1-2-8 £3,837**

Balletto *K R Burke*
3 b f Robellino (USA) - Denial
PU^{8s} **0-0-1**

Balloura (USA) *W J Haggas* 57
2 b f Swain (Ire) - Mowaadah (Ire)
4^{7g} 4^{7g} **0-0-2 £380**

Bally Hall (Ire) *M J Gingell* 63
5 b g Saddlers' Hall (Ire) - Sally Rose
16^{10gf} 15^{11gf} 4^{10gf} 9^{10gf} 10^{11gf} **0-0-5 £267**

Ballybeg (Ire) *R Hannon* 64 a59
2 b g Mujadil (USA) - Sabaniya (Fr)
7^{6gf} 6^{6g} 6^{7gf} 14^{7g} 3^{7sd} **0-1-5 £555**

Ballybunion (Ire) *N E Berry* 71 a63
6 ch g Entrepreneur - Clarentia
7^{6sd} 3^{6sd} 2^{6sd} 3^{7sd} 9^{5sd} 17^{6gs} 5^{7g} 9^{6gf} 5^{6g} 1^{5gf} 4^{5g} 2^{6gf} 2^{5gf} 4^{6gf} 3^{5f} 10^{6f} 1^{5gf} 1^{5g} 7^{6g} 5^{6sd} 7^{5sd} **3-5-21 £12,648**

Ballycroy Girl (Ire) *A Bailey* 65 a60
3 ch f Pennekamp (USA) - Hulm (Ire)
6^{9sd} 11^{7g} 7^{7g} 8^{7s} 9^{7g} 4^{7sd} 11^{7g} 1^{7gf} 6^{7gf} 10^{7g} **1-0-10 £3,598**

Ballygally Bay *S J Mahon* 75
3 b g Erhaab (USA) - Indigo Dawn
4^{10g} 3^{12gf} 3^{11g} 6^{12gf} **0-1-4 £1,051**

Ballygriffin Kid *Miss Gay Kelleway* 49 a68
5 gr g Komaite (USA) - Ballygriffin Belle
3^{7sd} 3^{7sd} 4^{9sd} 1^{8sd} 3^{7sd} 2^{8sd} 2^{10sd} 4^{9sd} 3^{8sd} 3^{12sd} 5^{10sd} 6^{10gf} **1-7-12 £7,391**

Ballyhooligan (Ire) *Jamie Poulton* 12 a48
2 b c Imperial Ballet (Ire) - Cancan Madame (USA)
8^{6gf} 6^{5sd} 11^{7sd} **0-0-3**

Ballyhurry (USA) *J S Goldie* 76 a66
8 b g Rubiano (USA) - Balakhna (Fr)
5^{9sd} 5^{9sd} 7^{7gs} 1^{7g} 4^{8g} 2^{7gf} 1^{8g} 9^{7gs} 5^{7f} 7^{8gf} 5^{7gf} 4^{7g} 5^{7gf} 3^{7gf} 5^{8gf} 1^{9gf} 5^{8gf} **3-2-17 £14,889**

Ballyrush (Ire) *Miss D A McHale* a50
5 ch g Titus Livius (Fr) - Mandoline (Ire)
5^{8sd} 11^{7sd} 12^{8sd} 10^{8sd} 10^{8sd} 1^{8sd} 10^{8sd} 4^{8ss} 7^{7sd} 5^{8ss} **1-0-10 £1,433**

Balmacara *B G Powell* 40 a8
6 b m Lake Coniston (Ire) - Diabaig
8^{8gf} 4^{10f} 5^{10f} 11^{12sd} 4^{12gf} 11^{10g} 8^{10f} **0-0-7 £258**

Balmont (USA) *J Noseda* 115
4 b c Stravinsky (USA) - Aldebaran Light (USA)
8^{6gf} 3^{5gf} 3^{6f} 5^{6gs} 2^{6g} 15^{5gf} **0-3-6 £55,736**

Balthasar *K G Wingrove* 20 a35
3 b g Lujain (USA) - Anatase
8^{5sd} 16^{7g} 12^{9sf} 7^{6sd} 12^{5ss} **0-0-5**

Balthazaar's Gift (Ire) *K A Ryan* 112
2 b c Xaar - Thats Your Opinion
2^{5gf} 1^{5gs} 6^{6g} 12^{6gf} 1^{6gs} 1^{6gs} **3-1-6 £99,654**

Baltic Boy *W Jarvis* a44
3 ch g Bachir (Ire) - Sparkling Isle
9^{10sd} 11^{10sd} 12^{10sd} **0-0-3**

Baltic Dip (Ire) *R Hannon* 87 a61
3 b f Benny The Dip (USA) - Drei (USA)
5^{8gs} 5^{8sd} 4^{8g} 6^{7gf} **0-0-4 £2,521**

Baltic King *H Morrison* 116
5 b h Danetime (Ire) - Lindfield Belle (Ire)
4^{5gs} 2^{6gf} 1^{6gf} 13^{5gf} 6^{6gf} 2^{5g} 9^{6gf} 5^{5gf} 4^{6g} 2^{6gs} **1-3-10 £51,541**

Baltic Princess (Fr) *M Johnston* 25
2 ch f Peintre Celebre (USA) - Snow House (Ire)
8^{8gf} **0-0-1**

Baltic Rhapsody *M A Jarvis* 57 a59
2 b f Polish Precedent (USA) - Rensaler (USA)
7^{6g} 6^{6g} 7^{6sd} 4^{7sd} 7^{8sd} **0-0-5 £228**

Balwearie (Ire) *Miss L A Perratt* 62
4 b g Sesaro (USA) - Eight Mile Rock
11^{7g} 9^{9gf} 4^{8s} 9^{7gf} 2^{8g} 1^{10g} 2^{12gf} 3^{12gf} 4^{10gf} 1^{12g} 1^{13s} 7^{12s} **3-3-12 £13,628**

Balyan (Ire) *J Howard Johnson* 94
4 b g Bahhare (USA) - Balaniya (USA)
8^{19gs} 20^{16g} 14^{11gf} **0-0-3**

Bamboo Banks (Ire) *J L Dunlop*
2 b g Indian Lodge (Ire) - Emma's Star (Ity)
12^{7gf} **0-0-1**

Bamzooki *D J Daly* 66 a61

3 b f Zilzal (USA) - Cavernista
6^{7sd} 8^{8gf} 3^{8f} 5^{10gf} 3^{9g} 8^{8gs} 10^{7sd} 8^{10sd}
0-1-8 £1,163

Bananchi (Ire) *John A Quinn*
3 b/br f Key Of Luck (USA) - Borneo
9^{7sd} 18^{6g} **0-0-2**

Banba (Ire) *K R Burke* 86
3 b f Docksider (USA) - See Gold (Fr)
4^{10s} 1^{10gf} 1^{8g} PU^{10gs} 4^{8gf} 6^{10g} 8^{10gf} 14^{8g}
2-0-8 £14,340

Band *E S McMahon* 54 a68
5 b g Band On The Run - Little Tich
4^{7s} 5^{8gs} 12^{10gf} 10^{8g} 4^{8gf} 1^{8sd} 12^{8gf} 1^{9sd}
5^{9sd} 8^{9sd} 4^{8sd} 5^{8sd} **2-1-12 £6,545**

Band Of Gold *J J Sheehan* 51 a50
3 ch f Spectrum (Ire) - Intellectuelle
12^{8gs} 9^{8sd} 9^{8g} **0-0-3**

Bandama (Ire) *Mrs A J Perrett* 74
2 b c Green Desert (USA) - Orinoco (Ire)
16^{7gs} 3^{7gf} **0-1-2 £812**

Bandari (Ire) *M Johnston* 123
6 b h Alhaarth (Ire) - Miss Audimar (USA)
9^{12s} 3^{12gf} 5^{12g} 1^{12f} 2^{12vs} 4^{12gf} **1-1-6**
£124,673

Bandos *I Semple* 70
5 ch g Cayman Kai (Ire) - Lekuti
9^{7f} 12^{7g} 10^{7gs} 6^{10g} 6^{8gf} 8^{7gf} 11^{6gf} 3^{8g} 11^{7g}
10^{8gf} **0-1-10 £519**

Banjo Bay (Ire) *D Nicholls* 71
7 b g Common Grounds - Thirlmere
6^{7gf} 8^{6s} 2^{7g} 1^{6g} 2^{7g} 7^{7gf} 7^{6g} 7^{6g} 12^{5g}
1-2-9 £4,697

Banjo Patterson *G A Huffer* 96
3 b c Green Desert (USA) - Rumpipumpy
1^{6g} 1^{6gf} 1^{7gf} 12^{6g} **3-0-4 £17,565**

Bank On Benny *P W D'Arcy* 59 a62
3 b g Benny The Dip (USA) - Green Danube (USA)
10^{10sd} 10^{10sd} 8^{10gf} 19^{12gf} 7^{17gs} 4^{16sf} 2^{17sd}
3^{16sd} **0-2-8 £1,693**

Bank On Him *G L Moore* a67
10 b g Elmaamul (USA) - Feather Flower
1^{10sd} **1-0-1 £3,010**

Banknote *A M Balding* 94
3 b c Zafonic (USA) - Brand
1^{8g} 5^{8g} 8^{10g} 1^{8gf} 1^{8g} **3-0-5 £21,895**

Banningham Blaze *A W Carroll* 43 a29
5 b m Averti (Ire) - Ma Pavlova (USA)
13^{12gf} 12^{14sd} 7^{12sd} **0-0-3**

Bansha Bandit (Ire) *A B Haynes* 41 a25
3 b g Imperial Ballet (Ire) - Lagta
7^{8gf} 11^{12gf} 4^{12gf} 10^{16g} 13^{12sd} **0-0-5**
£265

Bantikhi (Ire) *C Boutin* 75 a51
2 b c Intikhab (USA) - Limited Option (Ire)
7^{7sd} 6^{6sd} 8^{5g} 1^{7g} 5^{9g} 7^{8vs} **1-0-6**
£4,707

Banzine (Ire) *M Johnston* 47
3 b c Barathea (Ire) - Banque Privee (USA)
11^{10g} 5^{8gf} 6^{8g} **0-0-3**

Barabella (Ire) *Miss Z C Davison* 22 a30
4 gr f Barathea (Ire) - Thatchabella (Ire)
10^{10sd} 12^{12sd} 10^{8sd} 6^{7s} **0-0-4**

Barabinka (Ire) *P F I Cole* 59
3 b g Barathea (Ire) - Starlight Smile (USA)
10^{10gf} UR^{11g} UR^{10g} UR^{10gs} **0-0-4**

Barachois Gaudy *R Hollinshead*
3 br f Nomination - Barachois Princess (USA)
12^{7sd} **0-0-1**

Baranook (Ire) *B J Llewellyn* a18
4 b g Barathea (Ire) - Gull Nook
7^{12sd} **0-0-1**

Barataria *G Wragg* 68
3 ch c Barathea (Ire) - Aethra (USA)
8^{8g} 3^{8hy} 7^{10g} **0-1-3 £535**

Barathea Blue *M C Pipe* 72 a69
4 ch g Barathea (Ire) - Empty Purse
10^{10gf} 9^{10g} 13^{12gs} 4^{14gs} 15^{16g} 6^{14ft} 5^{14sd}
0-0-7 £286

Barathea Dreams (Ire) *J S Moore* 87 a67
4 b g Barathea (Ire) - Deyaajeer (USA)
11^{7sd} 1^{8g} 7^{8g} 10^{8g} 7^{8g} 9^{7gf} 1^{8gs} 9^{8g} 8^{8g}
2-0-9 £25,935

Barb (Ire) *J L Dunlop* 17
2 b f Docksider (USA) - Classical Flair (USA)
13^{6gs} 9^{6gf} **0-0-2**

Barbary Coast (Fr) *W R Muir* 71
3 b c Anabaa (USA) - Viking's Cove (USA)
5^{8gf} 11^{8gf} 7^{8gf} 6^{8gf} 6^{6gf} 8^{7g} **0-0-6**

Barbirolli *W M Brisbourne* 72 a74
3 b g Machiavellian (USA) - Blushing Barada (USA)
4^{9gs} 6^{12gf} 3^{10gf} 6^{11s} 5^{10g} 5^{8gf} 5^{8gs} 1^{10g} 3^{9sd}
4^{10gf} 7^{10s} 9^{8g} 13^{10gf} 5^{9ft} 6^{10sd} **1-2-15**
£8,272

Barcardero (USA) *M Johnston* 85
3 b c Danzig (USA) - Very Confidential (USA)
1^{9gf} 3^{8gs} 1^{12gf} **2-0-3 £12,547**

Barella (Ire) *B G Powell* 61 a42
6 b g Barathea (Ire) - Daniella Drive (USA)
6^{7hy} 3^{11s} 3^{9y} 15^{12f} 3^{10gf} 16^{12gf} 3^{12gf} 12^{12g}
6^{10s} 10^{14sd} **0-4-10 £2,271**

Bargain Hunt (Ire) *W Storey* 46
4 b g Foxhound (USA) - Atisayin (USA)
17^{10gs} 12^{12gf} 3^{8gf} 9^{10g} **0-1-4 £523**

Barking Mad (USA) *C R Dore* 87 a84
7 b/br g Dayjur (USA) - Avian Assembly (USA)
1^{9sd} 3^{9sd} 2^{11gs} 1^{12gf} 7^{12gs} 2^{12s} 6^{12gf} 2^{11g} 1^{12gf}
3^{12gf} 2^{10g} 12^{12gf} 2^{12gf} 2^{12g} 10^{10hy} 10^{9sd} 6^{12sd}
3-8-17 £19,766

Barnamaj (USA) *E A L Dunlop* 43
2 b/br g Seeking The Gold (USA) - Ranin
13^{7gs} 10^{9gf} **0-0-2**

Barnbrook Empire (Ire) *B J Llewellyn* 58 a57
3 b f Second Empire (Ire) - Home Comforts
16^{8gf} 16^{6gs} 8^{5gf} 2^{7g} 4^{8gf} 2^{8gf} 9^{8gf} 3^{10sd} 6^{10g}
3^{12gf} 6^{12gf} 3^{12gf} 10^{13sd} **0-3-13 £2,933**

Barndeh (Ire) *M A Jarvis* 61
2 b g Marju (Ire) - Sweetest Thing (Ire)
10^{7gs} 8^{8g} 19^{8s} **0-0-3**

Barney Gold *A G Newcombe* a11
2 br c Superior Premium - Cyber Babe (Ire)
12^{7sd} 11^{7sd} **0-0-2**

Barney McAll (Ire) *R T Phillips* 84
5 b g Grand Lodge (USA) - Persian Song
9^{10gf} 12^{13gf} **0-0-2**

Barodine *H R A Cecil* 78
2 ch c Barathea (Ire) - Granted (Fr)
4^{7gs} 2^{8gf} **0-1-2 £2,179**

Barolo *W R Swinburn* 117
6 b g Danehill (USA) - Lydia Maria
3^{12g} 10^{20gf} **0-1-2 £1,788**

Baron De Hoyland *J R Norton* 17
2 b g First Trump - Efficacy
10^{6gf} 12^{7s} 16^{7gf} **0-0-3**

Baron Rhodes *J S Wainwright* 86
4 b f Presidium - Superstream
8^{5s} 3^{5g} 9^{5gf} 6^{6gf} 1^{6gf} 6^{6gf} 7^{5gf} 5^{5gf} 2^{5g} 7^{5gf} 7^{6gs} 6^{6s} 6^{6gs} 7^{7gf} 12^{7g} 20^{7s} **1-2-16 £11,280**

Baron's Pit *Mrs A J Perrett* 116
5 b h Night Shift (USA) - Incendio
3^{6gf} 7^{6g} 5^{6gf} 1^{6g} 10^{7gs} **1-1-5 £50,230**

Barons Spy (Ire) *R J Price* 64 a60
4 b g Danzero (Aus) - Princess Accord (USA)
12^{8g} 7^{8gf} 8^{8gf} 11^{7gf} 2^{7g} 11^{9sd} 1^{9sd} 10^{10sd} **1-1-8 £4,045**

Barranco (Ire) *G L Moore*
4 b g Sadler's Wells (USA) - Belize Tropical (Ire)
PU^{13sd} **0-0-1**

Barrissimo (Ire) *W J Musson* 38 a56
5 b g Night Shift (USA) - Belle De Cadix (Ire)
11^{8sd} 12^{8sd} 22^{8g} 4^{8sd} 14^{8gs} 6^{9sd} 10^{12sd} 6^{9sd} 8^{8gs} **0-0-9**

Barrow (Swi) *Ferdy Murphy*
8 br g Caerleon (USA) - Bestow
PU^{22s} **0-0-1**

Barton Sands (Ire) *Andrew Reid* 77 a77
8 b g Tenby - Hetty Green
8^{10sd} 2^{10sd} 5^{10sd} 1^{10sd} 2^{10sd} 13^{10sd} 1^{10sd} 4^{10sd} 3^{12sd} 3^{12sd} 1^{10sd} 14^{11g} 3^{10gf} 1^{8gf} 2^{8gf} 4^{8gf} 18^{8gf} 11^{8gf} 14^{12sd} 4^{10sd} 2^{10sd} **4-6-21 £18,751**

Bartra Rock (Ire) *G A Swinbank* 70 a56
6 br g Persian Bold - Cool Gales
11^{10gf} 3^{12f} 2^{13s} 4^{13gf} 13^{16sd} 3^{14gf} 3^{14gf} 1^{14gf} 4^{12g} 5^{14gf} 13^{14s} **1-2-11 £6,779**

Barzak (Ire) *S R Bowring* 41 a70
5 b g Barathea (Ire) - Zakuska
1^{7sd} 2^{9sd} 5^{8sd} 1^{9sd} 5^{9sd} 5^{9sd} 11^{8g} 10^{8gf} 10^{9sd} 7^{7sf} 4^{7sd} 9^{8sd} **2-1-12 £8,117**

Basiliko (USA) *P W Chapple-Hyam* 73 a53
2 ch g Fusaichi Pegasus (USA) - Shootforthestars (USA)
11^{7gf} 5^{8g} 4^{8s} 9^{10sd} **0-0-4 £258**

Basinet *J J Quinn* 49
7 b g Alzao (USA) - Valiancy
10^{10g} **0-0-1**

Baskerville *P W Chapple-Hyam* 78
2 b c Foxhound (USA) - Miss Up N Go
4^{8g} 2^{7s} **0-1-2 £2,087**

Basque *M Johnston* 54
2 b f King's Best (USA) - Proud Titania (Ire)
5^{6g} 6^{8g} 6^{7s} **0-0-3**

Basserah (Ire) *B W Hills* 78
3 b f Unfuwain (USA) - Blueberry Walk
6^{10gf} 2^{7g} 1^{8g} 2^{8gf} 10^{8gf} **1-2-5 £11,214**

Batchworth Beau *E A Wheeler* a35
4 ch g Bluegrass Prince (Ire) - Batchworth Belle
11^{8sd} **0-0-1**

Bathwick Alice *B R Millman* 73 a60
2 b f Mark Of Esteem (Ire) - Ciel De Feu (USA)
3^{5sd} 6^{6gs} 5^{6g} 9^{6sd} 7^{7gs} 1^{6sd} 2^{5gs} 4^{6gf} 1^{6gf} 6^{5gf} 4^{6gs} **2-1-11 £10,888**

Bathwick Bruce (Ire) *B R Millman* a27
7 b g College Chapel - Naivity (Ire)
9^{11sd} 9^{12sd} **0-0-2**

Bathwick Emma (Ire) *P D Evans* 76 a39
2 ch f Raise A Grand (Ire) - Lindas Delight
11^{5s} 7^{5sd} 2^{6s} 4^{6g} 12^{6gf} 2^{6gf} 5^{7g} 3^{6g} 2^{6f} 5^{7g} 6^{6g} 7^{6g} 1^{6s} **1-4-13 £7,574**

Bathwick Intyre (Ire) *B R Millman* 56 a54
2 b g Mull Of Kintyre (USA) - Miss Siham (Ire)
3^{5sd} 7^{5g} 5^{5gf} 5^{5g} 21^{5gf} 7^{6g} 15^{7gf} 7^{5f} **0-0-8 £415**

Bathwick Prince *B R Millman* 63
2 b g Superior Premium - Gay Ming
3^{5s} 7^{5gs} 2^{5g} 5^{5gf} 5^{6gf} 20^{5gf} 8^{5g} 10^{6g} 2^{5g} 3^{6gs} 15^{7g} 8^{6s} **0-4-12 £4,726**

Bathwick Rox (Ire) *B R Millman* 59 a61
2 b g Carrowkeel (Ire) - Byproxy (Ire)
9^{5hy} 7^{5f} 5^{7gf} 10^{7gf} 16^{7g} 4^{8g} 2^{8sd} 4^{7sd} 3^{9sd} **0-2-9 £1,448**

Batik (Ire) *L M Cumani* 86
4 gr f Peintre Celebre (USA) - Dali's Grey
1^{12s} 1^{12gf} 5^{12gs} 13^{14gs} 7^{14hy} 5^{12hy} **2-0-6 £13,847**

Batool (USA) *D Nicholls*
6 b m Bahri (USA) - Mrs Paddy (USA)
14^{7sd} **0-0-1**

Battalion (Ire) *Sir Michael Stoute* 64
2 b c Grand Lodge (USA) - The Faraway Tree
4^{8hy} **0-0-1 £246**

Battledress (Ire) *K J Condon* 67 a75
3 b g In The Wings - Chaturanga
2^{12sd} 2^{12gs} 1^{12f} 14^{12gf} 12^{11gf} **1-2-5 £5,524**

Battling Mac (Ire) *L A Dace* 86 a67
7 ch g Ashkalani (Ire) - Questing Star
13^{8s} LFT^{12g} 5^{8gf} 6^{9gy} 2^{8g} 16^{8g} 5^{9gf} LFT^{8sd} 12^{8sd} 9^{10sd} **0-1-10 £1,655**

Baudolino *R J Price*
8 br g Bin Ajwaad (Ire) - Stos (Ire)
11^{10g} **0-0-1**

Bauer (Ire) *L M Cumani* 49
2 gr c Halling (USA) - Dali's Grey
15^{7gf} 13^{7gf} **0-0-2**

Bauhinia *J A R Toller* 54 a56
3 b f Spectrum (Ire) - Juvenilia (Ire)
7^{6gf} 8^{6g} 3^{8f} 6^{9sd} 2^{9sd} **0-1-5 £1,272**

Bavarica *Miss J Feilden* 61 a63
3 b f Dansili - Blue Gentian (USA)
9^{6gf} 6^{7sd} 5^{8g} 3^{8sf} 10^{8sd} 11^{10sd} **0-1-6 £374**

Bay Diamond *R Hannon* 38 a26
2 b c Lujain (USA) - La Nureyeva (USA)
7^{5gs} 9^{5sd} 8^{6g} 6^{5f} 12^{8f} **0-0-5**

Bay Hawk *B G Powell* 57 a71
3 b c Alhaarth (Ire) - Fleeting Vision (Ire)
10^{12g} 4^{12sd} 8^{12g} **0-0-3 £304**

Bay Story (USA) *M Johnston* 107
3 b c Kris S (USA) - Sweeping Story (USA)
2^{12gf} 1^{12s} 2^{12gf} 6^{12gs} 1^{12gf} 5^{12s} 10^{12g} 3^{14g} 6^{15gs} 8^{12g} **2-3-10 £30,837**

Bayadere (Ger) *K F Clutterbuck* a27
5 br m Lavirco (Ger) - Brangane (Ire)
12^{9sd} **0-0-1**

Bayard (USA) *J R Fanshawe* 60
3 gr g Lord Avie (USA) - Mersey
9^{12gs} **0-0-1**

Bayeux (USA) *Saeed Bin Suroor* 95
4 b g Red Ransom (USA) - Elizabeth Bay (USA)
5^{8g} 6^{8gf} 10^{8gf} 7^{10g} 6^{10gf} 12^{15gs} **0-0-6**

£1,718

Bayeux De Moi (Ire) *Mrs A J Perrett* 97
3 b c Barathea (Ire) - Rivana
2^{10gf} 4^{12s} 5^{10s} 3^{12gf} 4^{10s} **0-2-5 £9,599**

Bayhope *M J Wallace* 28
2 b c Muhtarram (USA) - Sunday Night (Ger)
18^{6gf} 7^{5g} 3^{7gf} 7^{8gf} **0-0-4 £360**

Baylaw Star *K A Ryan* 92 a76
4 b g Case Law - Caisson
5^{6sd} 6^{8sd} 7^{8sd} 1^{7s} 1^{9sd} 10^{8g} 10^{7gf} 4^{8gs} 1^{7gf} 4^{8g} 3^{7g} 1^{8g} 1^{7g} 13^{8g} 16^{8gs} **5-1-15 £23,679**

Baymist *M W Easterby* 60
3 b f Mind Games - Milliscent
17^{6s} 6^{6gs} 5^{6gs} 17^{6gf} 18^{5gf} 14^{5s} 9^{5s} **0-0-7**

Bayreuth *J G Given* 58 a58
3 ch f Halling (USA) - South Shore
7^{8g} 7^{12sd} 4^{10g} 12^{10gs} **0-0-4 £264**

Baysgarth Park *J R Weymes* 32 a34
2 ch f Rambling Bear - Bayrami
8^{5gs} 3^{5sd} 7^{5g} 10^{6gf} 9^{5f} 7^{6gf} 10^{5gf} 7^{5gf} 9^{5g} 10^{7f} **0-0-10 £360**

Baytown Flyer *Mrs L Richards* 45 a50
5 ch m Whittingham (Ire) - The Fernhill Flyer (Ire)
5^{5sd} 9^{6sd} 3^{7sd} 8^{6sd} 4^{6sd} 7^{6sd} 10^{6sd} 5^{6gs} 3^{6sd} 1^{6sd} 9^{7sd} 4^{6g} 7^{6gf} 8^{6gf} 7^{6f} 10^{6gf} **1-2-16 £2,022**

Baytown Lulu *H S Howe* 49 a50
2 b f Timeless Times (USA) - Judys Girl (Ire)
4^{5gs} 2^{5sd} 5^{5g} 3^{5s} 1^{5s} 5^{6gf} 6^{5f} 2^{5sd} 4^{5g} 4^{6gf} 5^{5gf} 4^{6f} 5^{6f} 2^{6f} 3^{5gf} 6^{5sd} 6^{7f} 9^{6sd} **1-3-18 £6,926**

Baytown Shamrock (Ire) *G H Jones*
4 b f First Trump - Siana Springs (Ire)
15^{5gf} **0-0-1**

Baytown Valentina *P S McEntee* 56
2 b f Lugana Beach - Baytown Rhapsody
6^{5s} 8^{5gf} 7^{6gs} 4^{6g} 7^{6gf} 7^{5gf} 8^{6gf} 1^{5f} 13^{7gs} 6^{5g} 13^{6gf} **1-0-11 £3,341**

Bazelle *D Shaw* 82 a80
3 ch f Ashkalani (Ire) - Dona Royale (Ire)
3^{8g} 2^{10gf} 5^{12gf} 2^{10gf} 5^{10gf} 1^{9sd} 4^{9sd} 5^{12sd} **1-3-8 £7,938**

Be Bop *N Tinkler*
3 ch g Groom Dancer (USA) - Norpella
8^{12sd} **0-0-1**

Be Bop Aloha *John Berry* 49
3 b f Most Welcome - Just Julia
15^{7gf} 5^{10gf} 7^{10gf} 8^{10f} **0-0-4**

Be Like A Lion *B Palling* 55 a27
2 b f Hunting Lion (Ire) - Princess Kelly
2^{5gf} 14^{6g} 8^{5gs} 8^{6sd} **0-0-4 £724**

Be Lucky Lady (Ger) *N B King* 28 a55
3 b f Law Society (USA) - Ballata (Ger)
9^{10sd} 7^{7gf} 8^{10sd} 10^{11g} 9^{9sf} **0-0-5**

Be My Charm *M Blanshard* 66 a55
2 b f Polish Precedent (USA) - Demerger (USA)
2^{5gf} 4^{5gf} 3^{5gs} 5^{5g} 5^{5g} 3^{6gf} 9^{6sd} **0-2-7 £2,882**

Be My Queen (Ire) *A P O'Brien* 98
2 b f Sadler's Wells (USA) - Multimara (USA)
6^{7y} 8^{8s} **0-0-2**

Be Wise Girl *A W Carroll* 79 a60
4 ch f Fleetwood (Ire) - Zabelina (USA)
2^{9sd} 7^{12sd} 4^{10sd} 5^{9sd} 1^{12sd} 4^{12hy} 8^{12g} 2^{10gf} 9^{12g} **1-3-9 £5,294**

Beacon Rambler *F Watson*
3 ch g Cayman Kai (Ire) - Bunty's Friend
14^{7gf} 13^{6gf} **0-0-2**

Beady (Ire) *B Smart* a51
6 b g Eagle Eyed (USA) - Tales Of Wisdom
8^{11sd} 9^{14sd} 2^{17sd} 8^{16sd} **0-1-4 £730**

Beamish Prince *G M Moore* 54
6 ch g Bijou D'Inde - Unconditional Love (Ire)
9^{10g} 13^{12g} **0-0-2**

Beamsley Beacon *M Dods* 49 a55
4 ch g Wolfhound (USA) - Petindia
3^{6sd} 2^{6sd} 2^{5sd} 2^{6sd} 2^{5sd} 3^{6sd} 1^{5sd} 3^{5sd} 10^{6sd} 6^{5gf} 3^{5sd} 5^{5ss} 2^{6sd} 3^{6ss} **1-10-14 £4,600**

Beat The Heat (Ire) *Jedd O'Keeffe* 56
7 b g Salse (USA) - Summer Trysting (USA)
8^{11s} **0-0-1**

Beau Artiste *N Wilson* 58
5 ch g Peintre Celebre (USA) - Belle Esprit
8^{10gf} 10^{10g} **0-0-2**

Beau Jazz *W De Best-Turner* 30 a28
4 br g Merdon Melody - Ichor
12^{9sd} 7^{6g} 17^{7gf} **0-0-3**

Beau Marche *B G Powell* 38 a65
3 b g My Best Valentine - Beau Dada (Ire)
6^{6sd} 4^{7sd} 7^{6sd} 7^{6sd} 3^{6sd} 10^{6sd} 11^{5f} 17^{7gs} 10^{6sd} 12^{7gf} 7^{8gf} 13^{7g} 7^{8gf} 5^{8hd} **0-1-14 £796**

Beau Nash (USA) *P W Chapple-Hyam* 85
2 b c Barathea (Ire) - Style N' Elegance (USA)
6^{6gf} 3^{7s} 1^{7gf} 10^{7gs} **1-1-4 £6,333**

Beauchamp Quest *G F Bridgwater* a24
6 b g Pharly (Fr) - Beauchamp Kate
6^{12sd} 10^{12sd} 9^{12sd} **0-0-3**

Beauchamp Spark *D G Bridgwater*
4 ch g Pharly (Fr) - Beauchamp Buzz
12^{12sd} **0-0-1**

Beauchamp Star *P D Evans* a56
4 ch f Pharly (Fr) - Beauchamp Cactus
5^{10sd} 2^{9sd} 12^{9sd} 7^{9sd} **0-1-4 £754**

Beauchamp Tiger *G A Butler* 62 a73
3 b g Pharly (Fr) - Beauchamp Jade
9^{10gs} 2^{13sd} 9^{10gs} 10^{7sd} **0-1-4 £1,193**

Beauchamp Trump *G A Butler* 71 a69
3 b g Pharly (Fr) - Beauchamp Kate
4^{9gf} 2^{18gf} 8^{16g} 4^{13f} 1^{16g} 9^{16g} 7^{12sd} BD^{17sd} 8^{12sd} **1-1-9 £5,172**

Beauchamp Turbo *G A Butler* 55 a58
3 ch g Pharly (Fr) - Compton Astoria (USA)
8^{10g} 9^{8gf} 2^{10sd} 11^{10g} 9^{11f} 6^{10f} 15^{16g} **0-1-7 £859**

Beauchamp Twist *M R Hoad* 57
3 b f Pharly (Fr) - Beauchamp Cactus
5^{11gs} 2^{12g} 4^{13g} 4^{11gs} 3^{10gf} 7^{12f} 2^{12g} 6^{12f} 2^{11gs} 4^{15gf} **0-3-10 £4,046**

Beauchamp Unique *G A Butler* 53 a63
2 b f Compton Admiral - Beauchamp Jade
10^{7s} 14^{8gs} 1^{7sd} **1-0-3 £1,423**

Beauchamp United *G A Butler* 72 a17
2 b g Compton Admiral - Beauchamp Kate
4^{7gf} 12^{8s} 4^{7s} 11^{9sd} **0-0-4 £740**

Beauchamp Utopia *G A Butler* 70
2 ch f Compton Admiral - Compton Astoria (USA)

2^{6gf} **0-1-1 £2,010**

Beaufort *D K Ivory* 70
3 b g Yaheeb (USA) - Royal Blaze
10^{10g} 4^{10gs} 7^{10gs} **0-0-3 £296**

Beaumont Girl (Ire) *Miss M E Rowland* 53
3 ch f Trans Island - Persian Danser (Ire)
14^{8gf} 7^{11gf} 2^{10g} 1^{14g} 7^{12g} 6^{10s} 9^{14ss}
1-1-7 £3,695

Beauteous (Ire) *M J Polglase*
6 ch g Tagula (Ire) - Beauty Appeal (USA)
9^{8sd} **0-0-1**

Beautiful Mover (USA) *J W Hills* 60
3 ch f Spinning World (USA) - Dancer's Glamour (USA)
12^{7f} 6^{7gf} 2^{8f} 10^{9gf} 9^{7g} 9^{6gf} 6^{10s} **0-1-7**
£1,260

Beautiful Noise *M G Quinlan* 60 a26
4 b f Piccolo - Mrs Moonlight
9^{10gf} 15^{8gf} 11^{6gf} 12^{6f} 10^{7gy} 4^{5y} 8^{5g} 14^{8y}
9^{9ss} **0-0-9 £290**

Beautiful South *N Wilson* 48
2 b f Forzando - Fly South
11^{5g} 9^{5s} 7^{5g} 6^{5gf} 2^{5f} 4^{5gf} 2^{5gf} 12^{5gs} 10^{6g}
18^{6s} 10^{6g} **0-2-11 £2,519**

Beauty Bright (Ire) *A P O'Brien* 100
2 b f Danehill (USA) - Dietrich (USA)
3^{6gf} 1^{5f} 3^{6gf} 6^{6g} 8^{7gs} **1-1-5 £26,423**

Beauty Of Dreams *M R Channon* 62 a63
4 b f Russian Revival (USA) - Giggleswick Girl
4^{7sd} 4^{7sd} 6^{8sd} 10^{9sd} 2^{9gf} 5^{9f} 6^{8s} 1^{8f} 8^{8gf}
3^{8f} 5^{8g} 3^{9gf} 3^{8gs} 4^{9g} 5^{9gf} 2^{8gf} 13^{8g}
1-4-17 £7,852

Beauty Talk *C A Cyzer* 62
3 b f Mark Of Esteem (Ire) - Daralaka (Ire)
8^{10gf} 15^{12sd} 5^{8f} **0-0-3**

Beautyandthebeast *John M Oxx* 103
3 ch f Machiavellian (USA) - Nicola Bella (Ire)
1^{9s} 10^{10sh} 1^{7g} 1^{8gf} 4^{7f} 6^{9gy} 8^{10gf} **3-0-7**
£47,500

Beaver Diva *W M Brisbourne* a35
4 b f Bishop Of Cashel - Beaver Skin Hunter
4^{7sd} 2^{5sd} 13^{6sd} **0-1-3 £425**

Beaver Lodge (Ire) *B P J Baugh* 16 a36
8 gr g Grand Lodge (USA) - Thistlewood
10^{12sd} 8^{12sd} 10^{16gf} **0-0-3**

Beaver Patrol (Ire) *R F Johnson Houghton* 98
3 ch g Tagula (Ire) - Erne Project (Ire)
4^{8gs} 8^{8gs} 5^{7s} 5^{8g} 9^{7g} 7^{8gf} 8^{10gs} 5^{10g} 6^{7g} 4^{6gf}
1^{6gf} 6^{6s} 3^{6s} **1-2-13 £13,453**

Bebe Factual (Ger) *J D Frost* a35
4 b c So Factual (USA) - Bebe Kamira (Ger)
8^{12sd} **0-0-1**

Beckermet (Ire) *R F Fisher* 112
3 b g Second Empire (Ire) - Razida (Ire)
4^{6s} 4^{5gs} 3^{5g} 12^{5g} 2^{6gf} 2^{6f} 8^{6g} 4^{6gf} 1^{6gf} 11^{6gf}
15^{6g} 3^{6gf} 11^{5gf} **1-4-13 £54,175**

Beckett Hall (Ire) *R Hannon* 73
2 ch c Beckett (Ire) - Date Mate (USA)
5^{6gf} 5^{6gs} 3^{7g} **0-1-3 £766**

Becktara (Ire) *K A Ryan* 62 a25
2 b g Beckett (Ire) - Northern Tara (Ire)
9^{5g} 11^{5gs} 6^{5gf} 4^{5g} 7^{6g} 9^{6gf} 9^{5sd} **0-0-7**
£414

Becky Moss (USA) *Miss E C Lavelle* 66 a68
2 b/br f Red Ransom (USA) - British Columbia
8^{6gf} 4^{5gf} 2^{5sd} 5^{5gs} 3^{5gf} RR^{7gs} **0-2-6**
£2,246

Becky's Dancer *W M Brisbourne*
2 ch f Rock City - Hill Farm Dancer
9^{8s} 11^{7sd} 13^{9sd} **0-0-3**

Bedouin Blue (Ire) *P C Haslam* 70 a37
2 b g Desert Style (Ire) - Society Fair (Fr)
5^{7g} 2^{7gf} 8^{9sd} **0-1-3 £993**

Bedtime Blues *J A Glover* a48
3 b f Cyrano De Bergerac - Boomerang Blade
4^{6sd} 6^{7sd} 12^{6sd} **0-0-3 £260**

Bee Minor *Ms Deborah J Evans* 57
4 b f Barathea (Ire) - Bee Off (Ire)
10^{6gf} **0-0-1**

Bee Seventeen (USA) *P F I Cole* 71
2 b f Chester House (USA) - Stormy Squab (USA)
2^{6gf} 7^{6gf} 2^{7gf} 8^{6gf} 6^{7g} **0-2-5 £2,517**

Bee Stinger *I A Wood* 66 a59
3 b g Almaty (Ire) - Nest Egg
5^{6gf} 3^{6gf} 10^{6gf} 5^{6g} 10^{6sd} 3^{6gf} 10^{6gf}
0-1-7 £1,210

Beeches Theatre (Ire) *R Brotherton* 14 a27
3 b f King's Theatre (Ire) - Sandpiper
11^{6sd} 4^{6sd} 7^{6sd} 10^{6sd} 12^{5sd} 6^{5s} 11^{6hy} 7^{5sd}
0-0-8

Beejay *P F I Cole* 67 a59
4 b f Piccolo - Letluce
9^{5sd} 8^{6g} 5^{6f} 8^{6g} **0-0-4**

Befitting *J A Osborne* 41 a35
3 b g Inchinor - Ellebanna
11^{8gf} 8^{12sd} **0-0-2**

Before The Dawn *A G Newcombe* 18 a32
3 b f Lugana Beach - Chayanee's Arena (Ire)
7^{6sd} 16^{7gf} 13^{7f} **0-0-3**

Before Time *Mrs A M Thorpe* 41
3 ch g Giant's Causeway (USA) - Original Spin (Ire)
14^{10gf} **0-0-1**

Before You Go (Ire) *T G Mills* 41 a77
2 b c Sadler's Wells (USA) - Here On Earth (USA)
15^{7g} 1^{8sd} **1-0-2 £4,792**

Befriend (USA) *W M Brisbourne* 45 a54
5 ch m Allied Forces (USA) - Approcheer (USA)
6^{9sd} 4^{6sd} 11^{9sd} 4^{8g} 9^{8s} 2^{7sd} 8^{8g} 11^{7gs} 9^{8gf}
7^{6gf} 13^{8gf} **0-1-11 £685**

Being There *P F I Cole* a46
2 b g Bien Bien (USA) - Segsbury Belle
7^{9sd} **0-0-1**

Bekoning (Ire) *M Quinn* 46 a47
2 b c Beckett (Ire) - Echoing
6^{8gs} 10^{6hy} 7^{7sd} **0-0-3 £234**

Bel Cantor *W J H Ratcliffe* 75 a70
2 b c Largesse - Palmstead Belle (Ire)
2^{5g} 4^{5gs} 3^{5gf} 3^{5s} 4^{5f} 9^{6gf} 2^{5f} 3^{6sd} 11^{5sd}
8^{5sf} 4^{5sd} 3^{8sd} **0-6-12 £5,945**

Belenus (Ire) *Saeed Bin Suroor* 110
3 ch c Dubai Millennium - Ajhiba (Ire)
3^{11gf} 2^{10gf} 2^{10gf} **0-2-3 £18,810**

Belgian Quarter *Mrs L Stubbs* 39 a57
2 b g Bertolini (USA) - Gold Luck (USA)
10^{7gf} 4^{8sd} 5^{8gs} **0-0-3**

Belisco (USA) *C A Dwyer* a54
4 b g Royal Academy (USA) - A Mean Fit (USA)
3^{9sd} 7^{9sd} 11^{10sd} 13^{10sd} 9^{8sd} **0-1-5 £373**

Bella Bertolini *M A Jarvis* 65 a56
2 b f Bertolini (USA) - Fly Like The Wind
13^{5gf} 2^{5gf} 7^{5gf} 8^{6sd} **0-1-4 £1,272**

Bella Boy Zee (Ire) *A W Carroll* 23 a17
4 b f Anita's Prince - Waikiki (Ger)
13^{5gf} 14^{6s} 10^{5sd} **0-0-3**

Bella Estella (Ger) *Ian Williams* a8
4 gr f Sternkoenig (Ire) - Bankula (Ger)
12^{9sd} **0-0-1**

Bella Fiorella (Ire) *R C Guest* 49
2 b f Shinko Forest (Ire) - Phylella
9^{5s} 6^{5g} 8^{6s} 12^{6gf} 7^{6gf} 15^{5g} **0-0-6**

Bella Miranda *H Morrison* 66 a47
3 ch f Sinndar (Ire) - Bella Lambada
6^{10sd} 4^{8sd} 14^{10sd} 7^{12sd} 1^{12f} 4^{12gs} 9^{17sd}
1-0-7 £3,615

Bella Pavlina *R A Harris* 55 a61
7 ch m Sure Blade (USA) - Pab's Choice
7^{11sd} 6^{12sd} 4^{12sd} 4^{12sd} 4^{12sd} 1^{9sd} 6^{9sd} 8^{10sd}
4^{12sd} 3^{12gf} 1^{10s} 13^{10sd} **2-1-12 £4,641**

Bella Plunkett (Ire) *W M Brisbourne* 34 a26
3 ch f Daggers Drawn (USA) - Amazona (Ire)
8^{7sd} 8^{8gf} **0-0-2**

Bella Tutrice (Ire) *M J Attwater* 10 a64
4 b f Woodborough (USA) - Institutrice (Ire)
8^{6sd} 4^{6sd} 8^{6sd} 1^{5sd} 1^{5sd} 15^{5gs} 9^{5sd} **2-0-7**
£2,922

Bellabelini (Ire) *S Kirk* a60
2 b f Bertolini (USA) - Bethania
7^{6sf} 2^{6sd} **0-1-2 £850**

Bellalini *Peter Grayson* 36
2 b f Bertolini (USA) - Primum Tempus
6^{7gf} 10^{7gf} **0-0-2**

Bellalou *Mrs S A Watt* 45 a56
3 b f Vettori (Ire) - Spinning Mouse
3^{9sd} 6^{9sd} 6^{9sd} 10^{12f} 1^{12sd} 9^{14f} 5^{10gf} 3^{12gf}
9^{11sd} **1-2-9 £3,810**

Bellanora *R F Johnson Houghton* 66 a43
2 b f Inchinor - Barberello (Ire)
2^{6gs} 4^{6g} 11^{7sd} **0-1-3 £1,303**

Belle Chanson *J R Boyle* 48 a49
3 b f Kingsinger (Ire) - Tallulah Belle
15^{7gs} 17^{8gf} 7^{8sd} 9^{10sd} 10^{10sd} 10^{10gf} 2^{10sd}
3^{10f} 7^{10g} **0-2-9 £643**

Belle Encore *A P Jarvis* 61 a49
3 b f Prince Sabo - Frisson
12^{7sd} 8^{8gs} 2^{7gf} 5^{6g} 10^{6gf} 5^{7g} 9^{6gf} 8^{5gf} 8^{6sd}
0-1-9 £1,625

Belle Largesse *W De Best-Turner* 43
3 b f Largesse - Palmstead Belle (Ire)
10^{7s} 12^{6gf} 9^{6gf} 9^{8gf} 7^{8g} **0-0-5**

Belle Rouge *C A Horgan* 68
7 b m Celtic Swing - Gunner's Belle
11^{16gs} **0-0-1**

Bellini Star *P D Evans* 61 a49
2 b g Fraam - Rewardia (Ire)
8^{7gf} 11^{7g} 5^{7gf} 6^{8gf} 5^{8hy} 7^{7sd} **0-0-6**

Bells Beach (Ire) *P Howling* a19
7 b m General Monash (USA) - Clifton Beach
13^{6sd} **0-0-1**

Bellsbank (Ire) *A Bailey* 74
2 b f Beckett (Ire) - Fag End (Ire)
6^{6gs} 2^{7gf} 4^{6g} 3^{6gs} 4^{7gf} 2^{6gs} 1^{7hy} **1-3-7**
£7,535

Belly Dancer (Ire) *P F I Cole* 84
3 gr f Danehill Dancer (Ire) - Persian Mistress (Ire)
2^{7g} 2^{7gf} 1^{7gs} 5^{7g} 4^{6g} **1-2-5 £11,451**

Belpasso (Ire) *B Smart* 72
2 ch c Danehill Dancer (Ire) - Beltisaal (Fr)
4^{6gf} **0-0-1 £368**

Belrose (Ire) *Mrs C A Dunnett*
3 b f Robellino (USA) - Blue Bay (Ger)
11^{7sd} **0-0-1**

Beltane *W De Best-Turner* 15 a29
7 b g Magic Ring (Ire) - Sally's Trust (Ire)
13^{8sd} 7^{8sd} 13^{10gf} 11^{10gf} 19^{12g} **0-0-5**

Belton *Ronald Thompson* 33 a11
3 b g Lujain (USA) - Efficacious (Ire)
10^{11sd} 14^{7gs} 12^{8gs} 15^{10g} **0-0-4**

Ben Bacchus (Ire) *P A Blockley* 51 a51
3 b g Bahhare (USA) - Bodfaridistinction (Ire)
10^{10g} 5^{12sd} 12^{16g} 11^{10gs} 10^{11gs} 3^{12gf} 9^{14sf}
0-1-7 £545

Ben Casey *B Smart* 43 a62
3 b g Whittingham (Ire) - Hot Ice (Ire)
5^{6sd} 5^{5sd} 5^{5g} 2^{5sd} 1^{5gf} 7^{6sd} 18^{6g} 3^{6sd} 3^{5sd}
2^{6ss} **0-4-10 £1,664**

Ben Hur *W M Brisbourne* 58 a61
6 b g Zafonic (USA) - Gayane
7^{9sd} 5^{12gs} 1^{10f} 4^{8gf} 3^{8f} 6^{10g} 2^{10sd} 6^{10f} 8^{10g}
3^{9gf} 6^{9g} 12^{10gs} **1-3-12 £4,457**

Ben Kenobi *Mrs P Ford* 50 a43
7 ch g Accondy (Ire) - Nour El Sahar (USA)
7^{7sd} 9^{7sd} 14^{10gs} 6^{11gf} 1^{10gf} 6^{9sd} 14^{11g}
1-0-7 £2,688

Ben Lomand *B W Duke* 21 a42
5 ch g Inchinor - Benjarong
11^{7sd} 10^{8sd} 14^{6gs} **0-0-3**

Ben's Revenge *M Wellings* 18 a41
5 b g Emperor Jones (USA) - Bumble Boogie (Ire)
2^{12sd} 6^{12sd} 9^{9sd} 6^{12sd} 12^{12sd} 12^{13sd} 12^{12s}
0-1-7 £418

Benbaun (Ire) *M J Wallace* 117
4 b g Stravinsky (USA) - Escape To Victory
2^{5g} 15^{5gf} 1^{5gf} 5^{5gf} 1^{5g} 2^{6gy} 10^{5gs} 6^{5gf}
2-2-8 £128,479

Benbrook *J L Dunlop* 56
2 b c Royal Applause - Muffled (USA)
9^{6gf} 6^{6gf} 5^{7g} 7^{7s} **0-0-4**

Benbyas *D Carroll*
8 b g Rambo Dancer (Can) - Light The Way
10^{12sd} **0-0-1**

Bendarshaan *R Hannon* 90
5 b g Darshaan - Calypso Run
2^{12gf} 4^{12gs} 10^{12gf} 5^{12f} 3^{12g} 7^{12g} 16^{20gf} 5^{14gf}
2^{16gf} 6^{15gf} 9^{12g} 1^{16gf} 5^{17f} 7^{14s} **1-2-14**
£13,113

Benedict *John Berry* 102
3 b g Benny The Dip (USA) - Abbey Strand (USA)
3^{7g} 1^{8g} 3^{8g} 2^{8gs} 1^{8gs} 1^{8gf} 2^{8g} 4^{10gs}
3-4-8 £31,104

Benedict Bay *J A Geake* 58
3 b c In The Wings - Persia (Ire)
3^{10s} 8^{11g} 12^{14gf} 5^{16s} **0-1-4 £690**

Beneking *D Burchell* 36 a53
5 b/br g Wizard King - Gagajulu
9^{8f} 10^{9sd} 1^{7sd} 2^{8sd} 2^{7sd} **1-2-5 £2,506**

Benjamin (Ire) *Jane Southcombe* 8
7 b g Night Shift (USA) - Best Academy (USA)
10^{10f} **0-0-1**

Benjum *B I Case* a55
2 ch g Benny The Dip (USA) - Boojum
12^{8gf} 10^{9sd} **0-0-2**

Bennanabaa *S C Burrough* 30 a39
6 b g Anabaa (USA) - Arc Empress Jane (Ire)
13^{8hd} 12^{5g} 11^{6sd} 3^{6sd} 13^{7sd} **0-1-5 £211**

Benny The Bus *Mrs G S Rees* 71 a74
3 b g Komaite (USA) - Amy Leigh (Ire)
2^{5sd} 10^{6gf} 2^{6sd} 3^{6sd} 8^{7g} 3^{7sd} 2^{7sd} 7^{6sd} 4^{7gf}
18^{7g} 8^{7sd} **0-5-11 £5,072**

Bens Georgie (Ire) *D K Ivory* 70 a65
3 ch f Opening Verse (USA) - Peperonata (Ire)
9^{7sd} 3^{6sd} 3^{6sd} 5^{7sd} 2^{6gs} 3^{6gf} 2^{6g} 14^{6g} 1^{6sd}
5^{6sd} **1-5-10 £6,996**

Bentley Brook (Ire) *P A Blockley* 80 a70
3 ch c Singspiel (Ire) - Gay Bentley (USA)
2^{8gs} 2^{8gs} 1^{8g} 3^{8gf} 10^{8gf} 5^{10g} 3^{8gf} 9^{10g} 10^{11sd}
1-3-9 £9,096

Bentley's Bush (Ire) *R Hannon* 78
3 ch f Barathea (Ire) - Veiled Threat (Ire)
13^{7s} 6^{8s} 9^{7gf} 11^{9gs} **0-0-4 £420**

Bentong (Ire) *P F I Cole* a72
2 b c Anabaa (USA) - Miss Party Line (USA)
1^{7sd} **1-0-1 £3,698**

Berham Maldu (Ire) *I A Wood* a12
3 b f Fraam - Corniche Quest (Ire)
6^{7sd} 11^{7sd} **0-0-2**

Berkeley Heights *Jennie Candlish*
5 b m Hector Protector (USA) - Dancing Heights (Ire)
6^{17sd} 8^{14sd} **0-0-2**

Berkhamsted (Ire) *J A Osborne* 84
3 b c Desert Sun - Accounting
5^{10gs} **0-0-1 £328**

Bermuda Beauty (Ire) *J M Bradley* 55 a49
2 b f Elnadim (USA) - Believing
6^{5g} 3^{5g} 2^{5g} 2^{7gf} 9^{6f} 3^{5sd} 4^{5gf} 1^{5f} 4^{6gs} 5^{5gf}
1^{6gf} 5^{6g} 8^{6gf} 4^{5f} 6^{6sd} **2-4-15 £8,101**

Bernie's Beau (Ire) *R Hollinshead* 65
2 br f Namid - Otter's Field (Ire)
6^{5gf} 2^{5g} 3^{5g} 12^{6g} 2^{5g} 14^{5gf} **0-3-6**
£3,020

Berry Racer (Ire) *Mrs S D Williams* a18
4 ch f Titus Livius (Fr) - Opening Day
14^{7sd} 10^{7sd} **0-0-2**

Berti Bertolini *T G Mills* 58 a59
2 b g Bertolini (USA) - Cosmic Countess (Ire)
8^{7sd} 10^{6g} 9^{6s} **0-0-3**

Bertie Arms *J M Jefferson*
5 gr m Cloudings (Ire) - Pugilistic
9^{10gf} **0-0-1**

Bertie Bear *G G Margarson* 20
2 b c Bertolini (USA) - Philarmonique (Fr)
23^{7gs} 9^{6g} 12^{9sf} **0-0-3**

Bertie Southstreet *J R Best* 80
2 b/br g Bertolini (USA) - Salvezza (Ire)
3^{5s} 4^{5gf} 4^{5g} 4^{6gf} 1^{5f} **1-1-5 £7,265**

Berties Brother *D G Bridgwater* 5 a47
2 ch g Forzando - Sweets (Ire)
11^{7gf} 6^{9sd} 9^{9sd} **0-0-3**

Berties Connection *Julian Poulton* 48 a56
6 b g Danzig Connection (USA) - Bertie's Girl
6^{8sd} 13^{7g} 10^{14gf} **0-0-3**

Bertocelli *K F Clutterbuck* 9 a38
4 ch g Vettori (Ire) - Dame Jude
10^{7sd} 10^{11g} **0-0-2**

Bertrose *J L Dunlop* 70
3 ch g Machiavellian (USA) - Tularosa
7^{10gs} 12^{12gf} **0-0-2**

Bessemer (Jpn) *D Carroll* 74 a80
4 b g Carnegie (Ire) - Chalna (Ire)
11^{8gf} 11^{10s} 11^{8g} 1^{10gf} 2^{9f} 1^{9gf} 1^{8gf} 4^{10gf}
7^{9gf} 4^{7sd} 2^{8gf} 3^{7g} 13^{7g} 11^{8g} 3^{8sd} 1^{6sd} 3^{6sd}
8^{6sd} **4-5-18 £16,903**

Best About *D R Loder*
3 ch f King's Best (USA) - Up And About
12^{9sd} **0-0-1**

Best Alibi (Ire) *Sir Michael Stoute* 106
2 b c King's Best (USA) - Chauncy Lane (Ire)
7^{7s} 3^{7gf} 1^{7gf} 4^{8hy} **1-1-4 £16,941**

Best Be Going (Ire) *W R Swinburn* 87
5 b g Danehill (USA) - Bye Bold Aileen (Ire)
2^{10gf} 15^{10gf} 3^{10gf} 2^{10gf} **0-3-4 £5,929**

Best Before (Ire) *Ms V S Lucas* 80 a67
5 b g Mujadil (USA) - Miss Margate (Ire)
2^{8sd} 15^{8g} 15^{8g} 1^{10f} 2^{10gf} 4^{8gf} 8^{10g} 1^{9g} 10^{7gf}
2-2-9 £6,566

Best Desert (Ire) *J R Best* 53
4 b g Desert Style (Ire) - La Alla Wa Asa (Ire)
16^{10hy} 13^{10gf} 3^{7gf} 15^{7f} 9^{12gf} 8^{7g} **0-1-6**
£219

Best Double *G A Butler* 69 a71
2 ch f Compton Place - Bestemor
9^{6gs} 2^{6s} 2^{6sd} 9^{7gf} 6^{7gs} 2^{7g} 3^{7s} 2^{5sd} 3^{5sf}
0-6-9 £7,689

Best Flight *N Wilson* 55 a56
5 gr g Sheikh Albadou - Bustling Nelly
8^{12sd} 7^{10g} 9^{10g} **0-0-3**

Best Game *D W Thompson* 64 a58
3 b g Mister Baileys - Bestemor
4^{8sd} 9^{9sd} 2^{9sd} 1^{8gf} 6^{8g} 3^{10gf} 6^{8gf} 7^{9gf} 1^{7gf}
5^{7gs} 13^{8gf} 10^{7gf} **2-2-12 £7,239**

Best Guess (USA) *P W Chapple-Hyam* 70
2 b/br f Stormin Fever (USA) - Probing (USA)
2^{6g} 1^{6g} 8^{7g} **1-1-3 £5,315**

Best Lady (Ire) *B W Hills* 66
2 b f King's Best (USA) - Sassenach (Ire)
11^{7g} 6^{7s} 3^{8g} **0-1-3 £712**

Best Lead *Ian Emmerson* 57 a63
6 b g Distant Relative - Bestemor
4^{5sd} 3^{5gs} 13^{5gf} 1^{5gf} 8^{5gf} **1-1-5 £3,642**

Best Of Friends *P T Midgley* 30
2 ch f Silver Wizard (USA) - Feiticeira (USA)
4^{5g} 5^{5s} **0-0-2 £258**

Best Of The Blues *J G M O'Shea* 58 a58
5 b g Whittingham (Ire) - Gold And Blue (Ire)
5^{9sd} 7^{9sd} 5^{8g} 7^{7gf} 11^{9sd} 10^{10gf} 14^{10g}
0-0-7

Best Offer *M G Quinlan* 26
2 b f Danehill Dancer (Ire) - Mary Hinge
12^{5s} 9^{5g} 9^{5g} 11^{5gf} **0-0-4**

Best Port (Ire) *J Parkes* 68 a53
9 b g Be My Guest (USA) - Portree
6^{12sd} 8^{16gf} 3^{14gf} 1^{16f} 6^{16gf} **1-1-5**
£4,008

Best Prospect (Ire) *M Dods* 89
3 b g Orpen (USA) - Bright Prospect (USA)
3^{10g} 1^{10g} 2^{10gf} 2^{10gf} 3^{10s} 4^{10g} 3^{9g} 5^{8g}
1-4-8 £24,426

Best Side (Ire) *Kevin Prendergast* 100
3 b f King's Best (USA) - Mood Swings (Ire)
5^{9s} 1^{8gy} 7^{7g} 2^{8gf} 5^{9gf} 3^{12gf} 7^{12gf} 6^{12gf}
1-2-8 £22,705

Best Way (Ire) *Sir Michael Stoute* 55

2 ch c King's Best (USA) - Green Jannat (USA)
8^{7gf} **0-0-1**

Bestam *Mrs A V Roberts* 62
6 b g Selkirk (USA) - Showery
13^{12gf} 10^{10s} **0-0-2**

Bestbyfar (Ire) *J G Given* 52 a21
3 b g King's Best (USA) - Pippas Song
8^{8hy} 12^{7sd} 6^{8gf} 10^{7f} 10^{10sd} 19^{10gs} 13^{10g} **0-0-7**

Bethanys Boy (Ire) *B Ellison* 61 a78
4 ch g Docksider (USA) - Daymoon (USA)
6^{7gf} 6^{7g} 2^{9sd} 5^{8g} 5^{10g} 4^{9sd} 1^{12sd} 4^{12gs} 1^{12sd} 2^{14ft} 1^{12sf} 5^{12sd} 3^{12sd} **3-4-13 £13,067**

Bettys Pride *M Dods* 62
6 b m Lion Cavern (USA) - Final Verdict (Ire)
3^{5g} 4^{5gf} 12^{5gf} 4^{5gf} 14^{5gf} 9^{5gf} 8^{5g} 3^{5g} 4^{5gf} 6^{5g} 13^{5gf} **0-3-11 £1,832**

Between Friends *A Berry* 50 a40
3 b f Slip Anchor - Charisse Dancer
4^{12gs} 6^{12gs} 7^{8gs} 7^{12gf} 11^{13sd} 8^{9sf} 12^{11g} **0-0-7 £365**

Beveller *W M Brisbourne* 47 a57
6 ch g Beveled (USA) - Klairover
13^{6sd} 5^{6sd} 2^{7sd} 4^{7sd} 3^{7sd} 11^{6sd} 8^{6sd} 4^{7gf} 4^{6f} 4^{7sd} 9^{8gf} **0-3-11 £1,787**

Beverley Beau *Mrs L Stubbs* 61 a51
3 b g Inchinor - Oriel Girl
5^{6sd} 3^{5sd} 7^{5gs} 6^{6sd} 6^{5s} 2^{5f} 5^{5f} 7^{5sd} 4^{5gf} 7^{5gf} 3^{5gf} 9^{5gf} 9^{5gf} 4^{6g} 10^{5g} 5^{5sd} 2^{6sd} 7^{5sd} 4^{6sd} **0-5-19 £2,697**

Beverley Hills (Ire) *J Howard Johnson* 27
2 gr f Mozart (Ire) - Attachment (USA)
7^{6gf} 10^{5gf} 9^{6gf} **0-0-3**

Beverley Polo (Ire) *M W Easterby* 53
2 br c Prince Sabo - Justfortherecord
1^{5gs} 7^{5g} 8^{5gf} **1-0-3 £2,597**

Bevier *T Wall* a4
11 b g Nashwan (USA) - Bevel (USA)
12^{12sd} **0-0-1**

Beyonce *D E Cantillon* 49 a25
3 b f Halling (USA) - Day Fairy (Ire)
4^{8g} 6^{9g} 10^{8sd} **0-0-3 £263**

Beyond The Clouds (Ire) *J S Wainwright* 72
9 b g Midhish - Tongabezi (Ire)
5^{5gf} 4^{5f} 10^{5g} 7^{5gf} **0-0-4 £522**

Beyond The Pole (USA) *B R Johnson* a48
7 b g Ghazi (USA) - North Of Sunset (USA)
9^{13sd} 4^{12sd} 7^{12sd} **0-0-3**

Bibury Lodge *M R Channon* 52 a55
2 gr g Indian Lodge (Ire) - Pearl Bright (Fr)
7^{8gf} 13^{7f} 3^{7sd} **0-1-3 £391**

Bid For Fame (USA) *J Pearce* 69 a71
8 b/br g Quest For Fame - Shroud (USA)
13^{14g} 1^{14sd} 2^{12sd} 3^{12sd} 3^{12sd} 4^{11gs} 3^{14sd} 8^{12sd} 6^{14sd} 5^{16sd} **1-4-10 £5,365**

Bienheureux *Miss Gay Kelleway* 66 a73
4 b g Bien Bien (USA) - Rochea
3^{13sd} 4^{12sd} 2^{13sd} 2^{12sd} 8^{12sd} 5^{17sd} 3^{12gf} 17^{14gf} 5^{15gf} 4^{12g} 5^{12g} 3^{12sd} 2^{12sd} 4^{14sd} 3^{12sd} 3^{12sd} 10^{14sd} **0-8-17 £5,928**

Bienvenue *M P Tregoning* a67
4 ch f Bien Bien (USA) - Mossy Rose
8^{12sf} **0-0-1**

Big Bad Bob (Ire) *J L Dunlop* 114
5 br h Bob Back (USA) - Fantasy Girl (Ire)
9^{9gf} 2^{10gf} 9^{10gf} 5^{10g} 2^{10g} 8^{10gf} **0-2-6 £6,995**

Big Band Music (USA) *D R Loder* 85 a92
3 br c Dixieland Band (USA) - Bashfulcharmer (USA)
1^{8sd} 2^{7sd} 8^{8g} 5^{7gf} **1-1-4 £8,675**

Big Bertha *M D Hammond* a81
7 ch m Dancing Spree (USA) - Bertrade
1^{12sd} 2^{16sd} 7^{16sd} 7^{17sd} **1-1-4 £4,375**

Big Bradford *W R Muir* 76 a73
4 b g Tamure (Ire) - Heather Honey
10^{7gs} 12^{6gs} 8^{6gf} 6^{7gf} 3^{6gf} 3^{7gf} 3^{7gf} 2^{7g} 20^{7gf} 4^{6g} 8^{8sd} 5^{7sd} 8^{7sd} 8^{7sd} **0-3-14 £3,813**

Big Moment *Mrs A J Perrett* 101
7 ch g Be My Guest (USA) - Petralona (USA)
9^{19gs} 3^{12g} 4^{16gf} 9^{14gs} 9^{14g} 13^{12gs} **0-1-6 £4,920**

Big Mystery (Ire) *S C Williams* 20 a49
4 b f Grand Lodge (USA) - Mysterious Plans (Ire)
1^{7sd} 9^{8sd} 18^{8gf} 3^{9sf} 10^{9sd} 7^{9sd} **1-1-6 £1,507**

Big Smoke (Ire) *J C Tuck* a19
5 gr g Perugino (USA) - Lightning Bug
9^{12sd} **0-0-1**

Bigalo's Banjo *J J Quinn* a57
2 b/br g Fraam - Polly Particular
4^{9sd} 6^{6sd} 9^{9sd} **0-0-3**

Bigalos Bandit *J J Quinn* 101
3 ch c Compton Place - Move Darling
2^{5gf} 2^{5gf} 16^{5s} 10^{5g} 7^{5g} **0-2-5 £10,315**

Bijli (Ire) *J Akehurst* 9
2 gr c Key Of Luck (USA) - More Magnanimous
4^{5gf} **0-0-1 £410**

Bijou Dan *I Semple* 60 a71
4 ch g Bijou D'Inde - Cal Norma's Lady (Ire)
3^{9sd} 3^{7sd} 6^{9sd} 2^{7sd} 4^{7gs} 5^{8g} 3^{7gf} 11^{8s} 3^{9s} 5^{10gs} 5^{11gf} 8^{8gf} 11^{8gf} 1^{9sd} 2^{9sd} **1-6-15 £7,844**

Bilkie (Ire) *John Berry* 51
3 ch g Polish Precedent (USA) - Lesgor (USA)
9^{6g} 8^{7gf} 12^{9sd} **0-0-3**

Bill Bennett (Fr) *J Jay* 63 a56
4 b g Bishop Of Cashel - Concert
11^{16sd} 7^{16sd} 13^{12sd} 4^{12sd} 10^{18gs} 6^{17sd} 12^{14g} 2^{14sd} 7^{12sd} 2^{16sd} 8^{14ss} 2^{12ss} **0-3-12 £1,271**

Billanroy (Ire) *M H Tompkins* 56
2 ch c Inchinor - Charm The Stars
9^{7gf} 13^{7s} **0-0-2**

Billet (Ire) *Anthony Mullins* 63 a56
3 b f Danehill (USA) - Tathkara (USA)
8^{7sd} 17^{6s} 9^{9gf} 4^{7g} 9^{7g} 11^{5gf} 6^{7gf} 7^{10gf} 8^{12gf} 6^{6g} **0-1-10 £363**

Billich *E J O'Neill* 70 a76
2 ch c Observatory (USA) - Pomponette (USA)
5^{6g} 10^{6gs} 6^{7g} 2^{8sd} **0-1-4 £1,123**

Billie Bunter (Ire) *Eamon Tyrrell* a50
4 b c Perugino (USA) - Last Finale (USA)
6^{9sd} **0-0-1**

Billy Allen (Ire) *F Chappet* a102
4 b c Night Shift (USA) - Daintree (Ire)
1^{12sd} 1^{10sd} 1^{10sd} 11^{10sd} 1^{9g} 4^{10ft} **4-0-6 £95,759**

Billy Bling (Ire) *R Hannon* a67
2 b g Enrique - Shewillifshewants (Ire)
12^{7sd} 3^{6sd} **0-1-2 £520**

Billy Flynn (Ire) *Miss D Mountain* a45
4 b g General Monash (USA) - Word Of Honor (Fr)
7^{13sd} 5^{12sd} 9^{12sd} 12^{12g} **0-0-4**

Billy One Punch *P W Chapple-Hyam* 65
3 b c Mark Of Esteem (Ire) - Polytess (Ire)
5^{8gs} 3^{7gs} 2^{6gf} 5^{7gf} **0-2-4 £1,938**

Billy's Brother *M A Buckley*
3 ch g Wolfhound (USA) - Chili Lass
11^{7sd} 13^{9ss} **0-0-2**

Bin Rahy (Ire) *M R Channon* 60 a68
2 ch c Rahy (USA) - Belle Genius (USA)
11^{6gs} 7^{8hy} 3^{7sd} **0-1-3 £558**

Binaa (Ire) *S C Williams* a55
4 b f Marju (Ire) - Hadeb
4^{8sd} 4^{9sd} 7^{6sd} 12^{7sd} **0-0-4 £527**

Binanti *P R Chamings* 93 a92
5 b g Bin Ajwaad (Ire) - Princess Rosananti (Ire)
3^{8sd} 12^{7sd} 4^{8g} 5^{7gf} 11^{8gf} 7^{7gf} 6^{8sd} 9^{6gf} 7^{7sd}
4^{7g} 5^{7g} 2^{7sd} 3^{8sd} 3^{7sd} **0-4-14 £8,599**

Bincrafty *J S Moore* 56 a41
2 b g Benny The Dip (USA) - Spanish Craft (Ire)
5^{5sd} 4^{5sd} 12^{7sd} 5^{8g} 11^{7sd} 7^{8sd} **0-0-6**

Bingo One (Ire) *M Dods* 61
2 b f Mujahid (USA) - Barque Bleue (USA)
2^{5s} 1^{6gs} **1-1-2 £5,060**

Binnion Bay (Ire) *J J Bridger* 50 a56
4 b g Fasliyev (USA) - Literary
5^{8sd} 6^{6sd} 3^{7sd} 5^{8sd} 3^{7sd} 7^{7sd} 2^{7sd} 6^{7sd} 8^{7gf}
7^{5gs} 14^{6gf} 11^{6g} 8^{6gf} 3^{7gf} 16^{10g} 11^{8sd} 8^{5sd}
0-4-17 £1,716

Bint Al Hammour (Ire) *M R Channon* 50
2 b f Grand Lodge (USA) - Forest Lair
15^{7gf} 11^{7s} 10^{6gs} 6^{8gf} **0-0-4**

Bint Il Sultan (Ire) *W M Brisbourne* 51 a36
3 b f Xaar - Knight's Place (Ire)
11^{7sd} 11^{7sd} 4^{8gf} 4^{10g} 10^{9gf} 4^{9gf} 8^{9gf} 6^{10f}
8^{8gf} 10^{8s} 8^{11g} **0-2-11 £835**

Bint Royal (Ire) *Miss V Haigh* 65 a48
7 ch m Royal Abjar (USA) - Living Legend (USA)
7^{7sd} 10^{6sd} 6^{6sd} 3^{5gf} 12^{7s} 8^{6sd} 9^{6gs} 8^{6gf} 4^{6gf}
7^{6gf} 6^{6gf} **0-1-11 £1,177**

Binty *J L Spearing* 56
3 b f Prince Sabo - Mistral's Dancer
6^{5f} 8^{6gf} 1^{6gf} 13^{6gf} 4^{6gs} **1-0-5 £3,373**

Bird Away *R M Beckett* 58
3 b f Bien Bien (USA) - Grace Browning
2^{10s} 4^{12s} 7^{12s} 8^{14g} 8^{12gf} **0-1-5 £2,022**

Bird Over *R M Beckett* 89 a86
3 b f Bold Edge - High Bird (Ire)
1^{7sd} 1^{6sd} 1^{6s} 6^{6s} 1^{6gf} 8^{7g} 2^{6gf} 7^{6g} 5^{6gs} 8^{7sd}
4-1-10 £20,064

Birdwatch *K G Reveley* 22
7 b g Minshaanshu Amad (USA) - Eider
12^{12gs} 11^{14gf} 11^{12gf} 9^{17f} **0-0-4**

Biriyani (Ire) *W R Swinburn* 60 a40
3 b f Danehill (USA) - Breyani
4^{6gs} 4^{8sd} 9^{10gs} **0-0-3 £702**

Birkside *W R Swinburn* 50 a60
2 ch g Spinning World (USA) - Bright Hope (Ire)
10^{7gf} 5^{7sd} **0-0-2**

Birth Of The Blues *J C Fox* a6
9 ch g Efisio - Great Steps
12^{10sd} **0-0-1**

Birthday Star (Ire) *W J Musson* 59 a67
3 b g Desert King (Ire) - White Paper (Ire)
8^{7sd} 4^{7sd} 3^{8sd} 10^{8s} 10^{8gs} 6^{10gf} 4^{12gf} 2^{12gf}
18^{12gf} **0-2-9 £2,179**

Bish Bash Bosh (Ire) *W M Brisbourne*
4 b f Bien Bien (USA) - Eurolink Virago
10^{9sd} **0-0-1**

Bishops Court *Mrs J R Ramsden* 99
11 ch g Clantime - Indigo
7^{5g} 1^{5gs} 13^{5gs} 5^{5g} 17^{5g} 5^{5gf} 4^{5gf} 7^{5s}
1-0-8 £9,244

Bishops Finger *Jamie Poulton* 52 a68
5 b g Bishop Of Cashel - Bit Of A Tart
4^{10sd} 2^{10sd} 10^{10sd} 1^{10sd} 10^{10sd} 12^{12sd} 10^{9g}
8^{10sd} 1^{10sd} 10^{10gf} 3^{11gs} 6^{10sd} **2-2-12**
£7,381

Bitter Chill *P W Chapple-Hyam* 79 a57
2 b c Agnes World (USA) - Azula
3^{7gs} 11^{8s} 6^{7sd} 10^{8sd} **0-1-4 £938**

Bjorling *M J Gingell* a1
4 ch g Opening Verse (USA) - Pola Star (Ire)
6^{8sd} **0-0-1**

Black As Soot (Ire) *E F Vaughan* 68
2 br g Key Of Luck (USA) - Meigiu (Ire)
5^{7g} 8^{7gs} 5^{7gf} 4^{7gs} 7^{7gf} **0-1-5 £146**

Black Beauty *M G Quinlan* 36
2 br c Diktat - Euridice (Ire)
12^{8g} **0-0-1**

Black Charmer (Ire) *M Johnston* 111
2 b c Black Minnaloushe (USA) - Abla
3^{6gf} 1^{6gf} 3^{6gs} 2^{6gf} 3^{7s} **1-3-5 £30,555**

Black Draft *Jean-Rene Auvray* 42 a34
3 b/br g Josr Algarhoud (Ire) - Tilia
10^{7sd} 16^{6gf} 9^{8g} 6^{12sd} 6^{12sd} **0-0-5**

Black Falcon (Ire) *Ian Williams* 79 a87
5 ch g In The Wings - Muwasim (USA)
7^{12sd} 7^{12sd} 11^{11gs} 13^{10s} 11^{10g} 8^{11g} 7^{10g} 4^{10g}
2^{11gf} 15^{11gs} 5^{10g} **0-1-11 £2,652**

Black Jade *M A Jarvis* 52
2 b c Averti (Ire) - Rivermead (USA)
8^{5gf} 13^{6gf} **0-0-2**

Black Oval *M J Polglase* 55 a39
4 b f Royal Applause - Corniche Quest (Ire)
9^{5sd} 7^{7sd} 6^{6sd} 9^{7sd} 11^{6gs} 8^{5s} 5^{5gf} 4^{5gf} 9^{5gf}
4^{6gf} 3^{6gf} 2^{6gf} 9^{7gs} 10^{7g} 17^{6f} 10^{6gf} 12^{6gf}
17^{6gf} 7^{6sd} 6^{9sd} 9^{5sd} 6^{7sd} 9^{6sd} **0-2-23**
£2,483

Black Sabbeth *Miss A Stokell* 42 a9
4 br g Desert Story (Ire) - Black Orchid (Ire)
11^{6sd} 13^{6sd} 7^{6sd} 4^{5gf} 14^{5g} **0-0-5**

Black Sea Pearl *P W D'Arcy* a61
2 b/br f Diktat - Made Of Pearl (USA)
10^{7sd} 6^{9sd} 4^{6sd} **0-0-3 £259**

Black Swan (Ire) *G A Ham*
5 b g Nashwan (USA) - Sea Spray (Ire)
11^{17sd} **0-0-1**

Black Velvet *M P Tregoning* 94 a59
3 br g Inchinor - Three Owls (Ire)
8^{7gf} 9^{7gf} 16^{8gf} 7^{7gf} 10^{8sd} 15^{7s} **0-0-6**

Black Wadi *T Keddy* 48
3 br f Desert King (Ire) - Tamelia (USA)
9^{8g} **0-0-1**

Blackbury *J W Unett* a39
3 b f Overbury (Ire) - Fenian Court (Ire)
6^{12sd} 9^{9sd} **0-0-2**

Blackheath (Ire) *D Nicholls* 78
9 ch g Common Grounds - Queen Caroline (USA)

20^{5g} 12^{5s} 17^{5gf} 11^{5gf} 5^{6f} 6^{6gf} 7^{6g} 14^{6gf} 6^{5gf} 3^{6gf} 1^{6gf} 3^{6gf} 5^{6gf} **1-1-13 £4,745**

Blackmail (USA) *Miss B Sanders* 72 a72
7 b g Twining (USA) - Black Penny (USA)
5^{13sd} 2^{10sd} 5^{10sd} 3^{10sd} 7^{10sd} 9^{13sd} 3^{10sd} 8^{12sd} 1^{8sd} 3^{8f} 2^{10gf} 1^{12gf} 4^{12g} 2^{12f} 1^{12f} 2^{12gf} 2^{12gf} 5^{14gf} 7^{10g} 1^{12g} 8^{12g} 3^{12gs} 6^{12gs} 5^{10sd} **4-10-24 £24,273**

Blacknyello Bonnet (USA) *D W P Arbuthnot* 4
3 b f Seeking The Gold (USA) - Salt It (USA)
18^{10g} 14^{12sd} **0-0-2**

Blackpool *A Senior*
2 br f Averti (Ire) - Prima Venture
16^{5gs} **0-0-1**

Blackthorn *M Appleby* 50
6 ch g Deploy - Balliasta (USA)
10^{10g} 12^{12gf} 5^{16f} 4^{14gf} 12^{12sd} **0-0-5**

Blacktoft (USA) *E A L Dunlop* 34
2 b/br c Theatrical - Black Truffle (USA)
14^{8g} **0-0-1**

Blade Runner (Ire) *D Haydn Jones*
3 ch f Daggers Drawn (USA) - Leitrim Lodge (Ire)
6^{6sd} **0-0-1**

Blade's Edge *A Bailey* a33
4 b g Daggers Drawn (USA) - Hayhurst
6^{7sd} 8^{9sd} **0-0-2**

Blades Boy *K A Ryan* 69 a52
3 ch g Paris House - Banningham Blade
8^{6sd} 6^{5s} 1^{5gs} 2^{5g} 4^{6gf} 15^{5g} 3^{5gf} 6^{5gf} 9^{5gf} 6^{6sd} 11^{5gf} 9^{5gf} 17^{5gf} **1-3-13 £5,044**

Blades Girl *K A Ryan* 87
2 ch f Bertolini (USA) - Banningham Blade
1^{5gf} 4^{6gf} 12^{6g} 2^{6g} **1-1-4 £55,812**

Blaeberry *Miss E C Lavelle* 67 a67
4 b f Kirkwall - Top Berry
2^{8sd} 8^{8gf} 3^{10gf} 13^{10sd} 6^{8gf} **0-2-5 £1,656**

Blaenavon *D W P Arbuthnot* 17 a48
3 b f Cadeaux Genereux - One Of The Family
7^{10gf} 5^{10sd} 8^{12sd} **0-0-3**

Blaise Hollow (USA) *R Charlton* 96
3 b g Woodman (USA) - Castellina (USA)
4^{9g} 1^{10gf} 3^{10g} 10^{10gs} **1-2-4 £12,580**

Blaise Wood (USA) *A L Forbes* 19
4 b g Woodman (USA) - Castellina (USA)
7^{12g} **0-0-1**

Blake Hall Lad (Ire) *P S McEntee* 40 a55
4 b g Cape Cross (Ire) - Queen Of Art (Ire)
4^{9sd} 8^{7sd} 20^{10g} 12^{8g} 12^{12sd} 12^{9sd} 12^{8sd} 8^{12sd} 16^{8g} 8^{8hy} 10^{8sd} **0-0-11 £258**

Blakeshall Boy *A J Chamberlain* 8 a37
7 b g Piccolo - Giggleswick Girl
13^{6f} 8^{7sd} **0-0-2**

Blakeshall Hope *A J Chamberlain* 41 a57
3 ch g Piccolo - Elite Hope (USA)
3^{9sd} 6^{12sd} 10^{9sd} 3^{9sd} 8^{9sd} 7^{9sd} 7^{8gf} **0-2-7 £796**

Blakeshall Quest *R Brotherton* 46 a62
5 b m Piccolo - Corniche Quest (Ire)
10^{6sd} 4^{6sd} 8^{7sd} 6^{6sd} 11^{7sd} 3^{6sd} 1^{6sd} 3^{7sd} 9^{7sd} 5^{6gf} 12^{6s} 11^{6gf} 9^{6s} 12^{6sd} 9^{6sd} **1-2-15 £2,164**

Blandford Flyer *W R Swinburn* 46 a64
2 b c Soviet Star (USA) - Vento Del Oreno (Fr)
11^{7gf} 9^{7gf} 5^{7sd} 6^{7sd} **0-0-4**

Blatant *Saeed Bin Suroor* 117
6 ch g Machiavellian (USA) - Negligent
4^{8gf} 3^{8g} 4^{8s} **0-0-3 £24,800**

Blau Grau (Ger) *N E Berry*
8 gr g Neshad (USA) - Belle Orfana (Ger)
18^{10gf} 7^{12sd} **0-0-2**

Blaze Of Colour *P F I Cole* 93 a93
4 ch f Rainbow Quest (USA) - Hawait Al Barr
2^{12sd} 2^{12sd} 2^{12sd} 3^{12gf} **0-3-4 £15,266**

Blazing Bailey *S C Williams* 70 a46
3 b g Mister Baileys - Wannaplantatree
13^{7sd} 10^{10gf} 1^{14gf} 2^{14gf} 5^{14gf} 5^{14gf} 9^{14gf} **1-1-7 £4,817**

Blazing Heights *J S Goldie* 74
2 b g Compton Place - Harrken Heights (Ire)
6^{6gf} 1^{6g} 6^{6g} 2^{5g} **1-1-4 £8,460**

Blazing The Trail (Ire) *C J Mann* 65
5 ch g Indian Ridge - Divine Pursuit
4^{11s} 8^{11gf} **0-0-2 £274**

Blazing View (USA) *N Tinkler* 40
3 b f Bahri (USA) - Dixie Eyes Blazing (USA)
9^{8s} 6^{6gs} 7^{6f} 11^{7f} 13^{6gf} **0-0-5**

Blendon Belle (Fr) *A G Newcombe* 16 a45
3 b f Lugana Beach - Palace Green (Ire)
10^{6sd} 10^{8gf} 13^{7gf} 9^{5sd} 2^{5sd} 9^{5ss} 10^{5sd} **0-1-7 £412**

Blendon Boy (Ire) *A G Newcombe* 57 a31
3 b g Brave Act - Negria (Ire)
8^{8gs} 10^{9sd} 7^{8gf} 15^{10g} 17^{12gs} 12^{9sd} **0-0-6**

Blessed Place *D J S Ffrench Davis* 67 a59
5 ch g Compton Place - Cathedra
5^{6sd} 7^{6sd} 3^{5sd} 2^{6sd} 2^{5g} 2^{6sd} 1^{6sd} 7^{5sd} 1^{6g} 5^{5gf} 2^{6gf} 8^{5g} 4^{6gf} 4^{5gf} 2^{5hd} 1^{6gs} 9^{5g} 2^{6sd} 1^{5sd} **4-7-19 £15,877**

Bling *W Jarvis* 95
2 ch g Mark Of Esteem (Ire) - Show Off
10^{5gf} 2^{5f} 1^{6gs} 6^{6gf} 16^{6g} **1-1-5 £4,661**

Bling Bling (Ire) *Mrs A J Perrett* 69
3 b f Indian Ridge - Sweeping
5^{7g} 4^{8gs} 4^{10g} 4^{10gf} **0-0-4 £859**

Blinis (Ire) *P R Rodford* 50 a57
3 ch g Danehill Dancer (Ire) - Richly Deserved (Ire)
12^{8gs} 4^{9sd} 3^{10gs} 4^{9sd} **0-0-4 £625**

Blissphilly *R A Fahey* a21
3 b f Primo Dominie - Majalis
10^{7sd} 6^{6sd} 9^{8sd} **0-0-3**

Blitzkrieg (Ire) *V Smith* 101
2 b g Barathea (Ire) - Eman's Joy
16^{7g} 1^{7g} 5^{8gf} 2^{7gs} 1^{8g} **2-1-5 £30,801**

Blonde Streak (USA) *T D Barron* 86
5 ch m Dumaani (USA) - Katiba (USA)
2^{8s} 8^{8g} 8^{8gf} 16^{8g} 4^{8gf} 14^{10gs} 7^{8g} 8^{8gs} 1^{8g} **1-1-9 £9,987**

Blood Money *N A Callaghan* 52
3 b g Dracula (Aus) - Guinea
11^{8gf} 13^{10g} 7^{11gf} 13^{14gf} 7^{10gf} 12^{8g} **0-0-6**

Bloodstocktv *D R C Elsworth* 66
2 b g Lujain (USA) - Bella Helena
2^{5gs} 7^{5gf} 5^{6gf} 1^{5g} 8^{6gf} 10^{5hy} **1-1-6 £3,675**

Blu Manruna *J Akehurst* 65 a65
2 ch c Zaha (Can) - Vrennan
7^{6gf} 3^{7gf} 7^{6gs} 7^{7s} 3^{6gs} 6^{6g} 8^{6sd} 10^{7g} 5^{7sd} 5^{7sd} 4^{7sd} **0-2-11 £1,525**

Blue A Fuse (Ire) *M Brittain* 41

5 b m Bluebird (USA) - Gleaming Heather (USA)
$8^{9gs}\ 8^{12gf}$ **0-0-2**

Blue Army (Ire) *A B Haynes* 36
2 ch g Titus Livius (Fr) - Trojan Tale (USA)
$5^{5gs}\ 18^{5s}\ 6^{6g}$ **0-0-3**

Blue Aura (Ire) *R Charlton* 77
2 b c Elnadim (USA) - Absent Beauty (Ire)
$8^{6g}\ 1^{6g}$ **1-0-2 £4,264**

Blue Azure (USA) *G A Butler* 59 a21
3 b/br f American Chance (USA) - Kibitzing (USA)
$3^{5gf}\ 6^{8gs}\ 7^{8sd}$ **0-1-3 £522**

Blue Bajan (Ire) *Andrew Turnell* 77 a84
3 b g Montjeu (Ire) - Gentle Thoughts
$7^{9sd}\ 5^{12gs}\ 6^{10g}\ 6^{8g}\ 2^{10gf}\ 1^{12gf}\ 3^{11gf}\ 6^{12gs}\ 16^{10gs}$
$1^{12gf}\ 1^{12sd}$ **3-2-11 £15,092**

Blue Beacon *K A Ryan* 39 a58
2 b f Fantastic Light (USA) - Blue Duster (USA)
$14^{8g}\ 5^{9sd}$ **0-0-2**

Blue Dakota (Ire) *J Noseda* 25
3 b c Namid - Touraya
12^{5s} **0-0-1**

Blue Danielle (Ire) *A D Brown*
2 ch f Blue Ocean (USA) - Imco Lucent (Ity)
11^{8ss} **0-0-1**

Blue Empire (Ire) *C R Dore* 72 a73
4 b g Second Empire (Ire) - Paleria (USA)
$5^{9sd}\ 4^{9sd}\ 10^{9sd}\ 3^{7sd}\ 6^{7sd}\ 1^{9sd}\ 9^{8gf}\ 1^{7sd}\ 2^{8g}$
$5^{9sd}\ 2^{7gf}\ 6^{7g}\ 1^{8gf}\ 7^{7g}\ 6^{8gf}\ 10^{7sd}\ 8^{7sd}\ 8^{10sd}$
$14^{8gf}\ 11^{8sf}\ 8^{9sd}\ 3^{8sd}\ 3^{8sd}$ **3-5-23**
£13,616

Blue Ette (Ire) *G A Swinbank* 31
5 b g Blues Traveller (Ire) - Princess Roxanne
$8^{8g}\ 11^{11gf}$ **0-0-2**

Blue Eyed Girl (Ire) *N P Littmoden*
2 b f Whittingham (Ire) - Highland Blue
11^{8gf} **0-0-1**

Blue Grouse (USA) *Saeed Bin Suroor* 78 a77
2 gr/ro f Maria's Mon (USA) - Enrich (USA)
$2^{7g}\ 1^{7sd}$ **1-1-2 £5,080**

Blue Hawk (Ire) *R Dickin* a21
8 ch g Prince Of Birds (USA) - Classic Queen (Ire)
8^{14sd} **0-0-1**

Blue Hedges *H J Collingridge* 62 a57
3 b c Polish Precedent (USA) - Palagene
$16^{10s}\ 8^{8gf}\ 17^{8f}\ 5^{10gf}\ 5^{11gf}\ 7^{14gf}\ 7^{12sd}$
0-0-7

Blue Hills *P W Hiatt* 58 a65
4 br g Vettori (Ire) - Slow Jazz (USA)
$3^{12sd}\ 3^{14sd}\ 11^{16sd}\ 3^{12sd}\ 3^{13sd}\ 2^{12sd}\ 5^{12sd}\ 3^{12sd}$
$11^{15gs}\ 1^{12sd}\ 13^{13gs}\ 6^{12f}\ 6^{12g}\ 6^{13gf}\ 7^{12f}\ 10^{13gs}$
$9^{14ft}\ 9^{12sd}\ 1^{14ss}$ **2-5-19 £8,375**

Blue Java *H Morrison* 76 a63
4 ch g Bluegrass Prince (Ire) - Java Bay
$1^{7gf}\ 3^{8gf}\ 1^{7g}\ 4^{7g}\ 11^{7gf}\ 4^{7g}\ 8^{7g}\ 9^{8sd}\ 10^{8sd}$
2-1-9 £12,198

Blue Jeans *R Hannon* 67
2 b f Royal Applause - Holly Blue
$5^{5g}\ 5^{5g}\ 2^{5gf}\ 12^{5g}\ 2^{6g}\ 4^{6gf}\ 7^{6gf}\ 12^{7gs}$
0-2-8 £3,698

Blue Knight (Ire) *D Nicholls* 72 a62
6 ch g Bluebird (USA) - Fer De Lance (Ire)
$3^{5sd}\ 8^{6sd}\ 2^{6gf}\ 6^{7sd}\ 8^{6gs}\ 5^{6gf}\ 10^{6f}\ 2^{6gf}\ 11^{7g}$
$5^{5f}\ 12^{6gf}\ 1^{5gf}\ 3^{5gf}\ 5^{5gs}$ **1-4-14 £5,681**

Blue Line *M Madgwick* 66
3 gr f Bluegrass Prince (Ire) - Out Line
$7^{6gf}\ 3^{6gf}\ 9^{6g}\ 5^{7gf}\ 3^{7gf}\ 6^{7g}\ 8^{7gf}\ 9^{7g}$
0-2-8 £1,522

Blue Lullaby (Ire) *D R C Elsworth* 81 a54
3 b f Fasliyev (USA) - Whispering (Ire)
$10^{7sd}\ 5^{7g}\ 3^{7gf}\ 5^{7gf}\ 6^{6gf}\ 1^{7g}\ 2^{8f}\ 8^{7g}$
1-1-8 £7,830

Blue Maeve *A D Brown* 70 a58
5 b g Blue Ocean (USA) - Louisville Belle (Ire)
$7^{5f}\ 3^{5gf}\ 11^{5gf}\ 13^{5f}\ 9^{5gf}\ 10^{5gf}\ 2^{5gf}\ 7^{5g}\ 2^{5g}$
$11^{6g}\ 13^{5gf}\ 8^{5g}\ 10^{5sd}\ 5^{5sd}\ 5^{6sd}\ 2^{6sd}$
0-4-16 £3,814

Blue Mariner *J Jay* 58 a63
5 b g Marju (Ire) - Mazarine Blue
$5^{10sd}\ 11^{10sd}\ 7^{10sd}\ 6^{7sd}\ 9^{6g}\ 4^{8g}\ 7^{8gf}\ 9^{7sd}$
0-0-8

Blue Minx (Ire) *J S Moore* 55 a55
2 b f Darnay - Sea Idol (Ire)
$10^{5sd}\ 3^{5gs}\ 1^{5sd}\ 1^{5g}\ 6^{5s}\ 5^{5g}\ 8^{5g}\ 4^{6f}\ 4^{5g}\ 2^{5g}$
$3^{5gf}\ 7^{5g}\ 7^{5sd}\ 11^{6gf}\ 8^{5gs}\ 5^{5sd}\ 11^{5sd}\ 8^{5sd}$
2-2-18 £7,587

Blue Mirage (Ire) *Saeed Bin Suroor* 94
2 b c King's Best (USA) - Catch The Blues (Ire)
$4^{7g}\ 1^{7s}$ **1-0-2 £3,560**

Blue Monday *R Charlton* 113
4 b g Darshaan - Lunda (Ire)
$3^{10gs}\ 1^{10gf}\ 4^{12f}\ 2^{10gf}\ 1^{9s}$ **2-3-5**
£134,696

Blue Moon Hitman (Ire) *R Brotherton* 59 a60
4 ch g Blue Ocean (USA) - Miss Kookaburra (Ire)
$3^{5sd}\ 12^{6sd}\ 5^{5sd}\ 3^{5sd}\ 3^{5sd}\ 10^{6sd}\ 1^{5sd}\ 2^{5sd}\ 2^{5sd}$
$3^{5sd}\ 2^{5g}\ 6^{5gf}\ 5^{5f}\ 10^{5sd}\ 3^{5sd}$ **1-8-15**
£6,571

Blue Opal *Miss S E Hall* 55 a57
3 b f Bold Edge - Second Affair (Ire)
$4^{7g}\ 19^{7gf}\ 8^{7gs}\ 1^{11sd}\ 4^{12sd}$ **1-0-5 £3,889**

Blue Otis (Ire) *Mrs H Sweeting*
3 ch f Docksider (USA) - Minstrel's Gift
13^{8sd} **0-0-1**

Blue Patrick *K A Ryan* 73 a82
5 gr g Wizard King - Great Intent
$3^{11sd}\ 2^{8sd}\ 1^{9sd}\ 13^{9gs}\ 1^{10gf}\ 5^{9gf}\ 6^{10gf}\ 9^{11gf}$
$16^{10gf}\ 5^{7sd}\ 3^{8gf}\ 7^{9g}\ 11^{8gf}\ 5^{10gf}\ 1^{9sd}\ 2^{8sd}$
3-4-16 £13,365

Blue Power (Ire) *K R Burke* 49 a58
4 b g Zieten (USA) - La Miserable (USA)
$2^{5sd}\ 8^{5sd}\ 6^{5sd}\ 3^{5sd}\ 3^{5sd}\ 15^{5gs}\ 10^{6g}\ 7^{5s}\ 9^{5sd}$
0-3-9 £1,486

Blue Quiver (Ire) *C A Horgan* 48 a62
5 b g Bluebird (USA) - Paradise Forum
$6^{8sd}\ 3^{8g}\ 5^{9sd}\ 9^{10s}\ 2^{9sd}\ 10^{10sd}\ 3^{9sd}\ 1^{9sd}\ 9^{10sd}$
1-3-9 £3,978

Blue Spinnaker (Ire) *M W Easterby* 111
6 b g Bluebird (USA) - Suedoise
$11^{8g}\ 2^{7s}\ 9^{10gf}\ 12^{10gf}\ 11^{10g}\ 13^{8gf}\ 6^{9g}\ 3^{10s}$
$17^{9s}\ 14^{8g}$ **0-1-10 £11,000**

Blue Splendour (Ire) *W G M Turner*
2 b f Bahhare (USA) - Swirl
$13^{6g}\ 5^{7gf}$ **0-0-2**

Blue Streak (Ire) *Mrs H Sweeting* 25 a40
8 ch g Bluebird (USA) - Fleet Amour (USA)
$6^{9sd}\ 11^{9sd}\ 9^{10gf}\ 11^{12gf}\ 17^{11g}\ 9^{10g}\ 5^{11sd}\ 10^{11ss}$
0-0-8

Blue Tomato *J M Bradley* 79 a91
4 b g Orpen (USA) - Ocean Grove (Ire)
$6^{6sd}\ 4^{6sd}\ 6^{5sd}\ 2^{6g}\ 11^{6g}\ 9^{6f}\ 12^{5gf}\ 3^{8gf}\ 3^{8g}$
$8^{7gf}\ 3^{7gf}\ 3^{6gf}\ 9^{6gs}\ 11^{6f}\ 11^{6f}$ **0-4-15**

£7,457

Blue Torpedo (USA) *Mrs A J Perrett* 94
3 ch g Rahy (USA) - Societe Royale
6^{10gs} 3^{10s} 1^{10g} 6^{12gf} 7^{10s} 2^{10g} 3^{10g} 1^{11gf} 5^{12g} 4^{12gs} **2-3-10 £19,303**

Blue Train (Ire) *Sir Michael Stoute* 83 a87
3 b g Sadler's Wells (USA) - Igreja (Arg)
1^{9sd} 6^{10gs} 8^{10gf} **1-0-3 £3,989**

Blue Trojan (Ire) *S Kirk* 89 a90
5 b g Inzar (USA) - Roman Heights (Ire)
3^{8sd} 10^{7g} 11^{9gf} 9^{8g} 8^{9sd} 7^{8sd} 4^{9sf} 8^{9sd} **0-1-8 £1,475**

Blue Viking (Ire) *J R Weymes*
4 b g Danetime (Ire) - Jenny Spinner (Ire)
13^{14gf} **0-0-1**

Blue Water *M Mullineaux* a18
5 b m Shaamit (Ire) - November Song
12^{14sd} **0-0-1**

Blue Wing *R Flint* a29
4 b g Bluebird (USA) - Warbler
10^{7sd} **0-0-1**

Blueberry Rhyme *P T Midgley* 58 a55
6 b g Alhijaz - Irenic
6^{5sd} 9^{5gs} 17^{6s} 11^{5sd} 4^{6gs} 11^{6g} 16^{6g} 6^{6g} **0-0-8**

Blueberry Tart (Ire) *J M P Eustace* 76 a69
3 b f Bluebird (USA) - Tart (Fr)
4^{8g} 4^{8gs} 3^{9gf} 7^{10gf} 7^{10g} 9^{8gf} 15^{6g} 2^{8sd} 2^{9sd} 5^{8sd} **0-4-10 £3,332**

Bluebok *J M Bradley* 85
4 ch g Indian Ridge - Blue Sirocco
4^{6g} 9^{6gf} 2^{5gf} 4^{5gf} 1^{6f} 1^{5gf} 3^{6gf} 2^{5gf} 10^{5g} 2^{5s} 6^{5gs} 11^{5g} 9^{5gf} **2-4-13 £18,022**

Bluefield (Ire) *Mrs K Walton* a4
4 b g Second Empire (Ire) - Imco Reverie (Ire)
17^{8s} 11^{11sd} **0-0-2**

Bluegrass Boy *J A Geake* 62
5 b g Bluegrass Prince (Ire) - Honey Mill
7^{10g} 11^{10gf} 7^{10gf} 8^{13gf} 12^{10g} **0-0-5**

Blues In The Night (Ire) *P J Makin* 68
2 ch g Bluebird (USA) - Always True (USA)
10^{7g} 6^{7gf} **0-0-2**

Blues Princess *R A Fahey* a7
5 b m Bluebird (USA) - Queen Shirley (Ire)
12^{5sd} 9^{6sd} **0-0-2**

Bluetoria *Miss Victoria Roberts*
4 b f Vettori (Ire) - Blue Birds Fly
16^{13s} **0-0-1**

Bluff *W J Haggas* 76
3 b g Bluebird (USA) - Show Off
1^{7gf} 10^{7gf} 7^{6g} 7^{7gf} 2^{7gf} 7^{7g} 9^{8g} 6^{7gf} **1-1-8 £4,707**

Blunham *M C Chapman* 28 a7
5 b g Danzig Connection (USA) - Relatively Sharp
12^{6sd} 7^{8sd} 5^{6s} 9^{6gf} 16^{10gf} **0-0-5**

Blushing Hilary (Ire) *B Smart* 72 a64
2 ch f City On A Hill (USA) - Trinida
6^{6f} 4^{7g} 3^{7gf} 4^{7gs} 5^{7gf} 9^{7g} 4^{9sd} 2^{8g} 8^{8g} 9^{8gs} **0-2-10 £3,726**

Blushing Russian (Ire) *J M Bradley* 48 a54
3 b g Fasliyev (USA) - Ange Rouge
11^{9sd} 7^{8gf} 8^{8gf} 9^{10g} 8^{6g} 2^{7sd} 10^{7sd} 2^{7sd} 1^{7sd} 7^{8sd} 3^{7ss} **1-3-11 £2,501**

Blythe Knight (Ire) *E A L Dunlop* 107 a110
5 ch h Selkirk (USA) - Blushing Barada (USA)
2^{10sd} 2^{10g} 6^{8g} 4^{10hy} 3^{10gf} 4^{9g} 12^{10g} 8^{8gf} 4^{10gf} 7^{11gf} 3^{10gs} 7^{9s} 8^{8gs} **0-2-13 £39,367**

Blythe Spirit *C R Dore* 72 a81
6 b g Bahamian Bounty - Lithe Spirit (Ire)
4^{5sd} 8^{6sd} 6^{5sd} 5^{5sd} 13^{5gs} 10^{6s} 8^{5gs} 10^{5gs} 11^{6sd} 9^{5g} 9^{6g} 5^{5g} 9^{5gs} 6^{6sd} 11^{7sd} 6^{6sd} 2^{6sd} **0-1-17 £1,264**

Bo McGinty (Ire) *R A Fahey* 93
4 ch g Fayruz - Georges Park Lady (Ire)
9^{5gs} 6^{5g} 11^{5gs} 14^{6s} 8^{7gf} 4^{7g} 8^{5g} 16^{6g} 3^{6gf} 5^{6gf} 8^{6gf} 2^{6g} 9^{6g} 1^{6gf} 18^{6g} 8^{6s} 9^{5g} **1-2-17 £16,197**

Boanerges (Ire) *J M Bradley* 59 a51
8 br g Caerleon (USA) - Sea Siren
8^{5g} 5^{5g} 11^{5f} 1^{6sd} 2^{5g} 6^{5sd} 2^{6gs} 12^{6sd} 2^{6sd} 1^{6sd} **2-3-10 £4,509**

Bob Baileys *P R Chamings* 34 a50
3 b g Mister Baileys - Bob's Princess
6^{8sd} 14^{10gf} 7^{8sf} 12^{10sd} **0-0-4**

Bob's Flyer *J G M O'Shea* a35
3 br f Lujain (USA) - Gymcrak Flyer
8^{5sd} **0-0-1**

Bob's Your Uncle *J G Portman* 55 a54
2 br g Zilzal (USA) - Bob's Princess
5^{7gf} 12^{7gf} 4^{7gf} 6^{8f} 9^{10g} 4^{7sd} 10^{9sd} **0-0-7 £250**

Bobby Charles *Dr J D Scargill* 86 a69
4 ch g Polish Precedent (USA) - Dina Line (USA)
1^{10sd} 6^{10sd} 2^{10sd} 1^{10s} 1^{12s} 2^{10s} 1^{10hy} **4-2-7 £20,941**

Bobby Kennard *J A Osborne* 60 a63
6 b g Bobinski - Midnight Break
10^{10sd} 5^{12sd} 14^{14gf} 1^{11gs} 13^{17g} 5^{12sd} **1-0-6 £2,625**

Bobering *B P J Baugh* a46
5 b g Bob's Return (Ire) - Ring The Rafters
11^{8sd} 10^{9sd} 5^{9sd} 2^{9sd} 14^{10sd} 5^{9sf} 3^{9sd} 6^{12sf} 4^{8sd} 3^{9sd} **0-3-10 £849**

Bobski (Ire) *G A Huffer* 86 a79
3 b g Victory Note (USA) - Vivid Impression
1^{6sd} 1^{7sd} 1^{7gf} 12^{7gf} 5^{7g} 6^{8gf} 12^{7sd} **3-0-7 £14,623**

Bobsleigh *H S Howe* 74 a61
6 b g Robellino (USA) - Do Run Run
5^{16sd} 7^{15gs} 2^{16s} 6^{15s} 14^{20s} 15^{18g} 8^{14g} 5^{16gf} 7^{21s} 1^{14gf} 9^{14gs} 5^{16gf} **1-1-12 £5,393**

Bodden Bay *D Carroll* 63 a63
3 b g Cayman Kai (Ire) - Badger Bay (Ire)
2^{6sd} 1^{6sd} 5^{7sd} 1^{6gf} 2^{6sd} 5^{6sd} 12^{6gf} 19^{6gf} 13^{7sd} 7^{6sd} 4^{7sd} **2-2-11 £6,797**

Bodfari Dream *M Mullineaux* a35
4 ch f Environment Friend - Al Reet (Ire)
9^{9sd} 11^{9sd} **0-0-2**

Bodfari Signet *Mrs S C Bradburne* 25
9 ch g King's Signet (USA) - Darakah
11^{12gf} **0-0-1**

Bodhi Tree (USA) *J H M Gosden* 68
3 b f Southern Halo (USA) - Dharma (USA)
6^{8g} 5^{10gs} **0-0-2**

Bogaz (Ire) *Mrs H Sweeting* 72 a67
3 b g Rossini (USA) - Fastnet
12^{7sd} 2^{7sd} 5^{7sd} 6^{8gf} 3^{8gf} 13^{8g} 3^{8gf} 13^{8g} 8^{8gf} 1^{7gs} 3^{8gf} 15^{8g} 15^{7hy} 13^{7sd} **1-4-14 £6,360**

Boing Boing (Ire) *Miss S J Wilton* 32
5 b g King's Theatre (Ire) - Limerick Princess (Ire)

14^{8gs} **0-0-1**

Boisdale (Ire) *S L Keightley* 58 a59
7 b g Common Grounds - Alstomeria
$7^{5sd}\ 13^{6sd}\ 12^{5sd}\ 2^{7sd}\ 2^{6sd}\ 6^{6sd}\ 2^{6s}\ 1^{6sd}$
1-3-8 £5,327

Bojangles (Ire) *R Brotherton* 65 a55
6 b g Danehill (USA) - Itching (Ire)
$4^{12sd}\ 6^{12sd}\ 3^{12sd}\ 5^{11sd}\ 3^{12sd}\ 4^{12sd}\ 4^{11gs}\ 1^{10hy}$
$2^{10s}\ 6^{11g}\ 16^{14gf}\ 2^{12gs}\ 12^{12gs}\ 10^{12g}\ 12^{10gf}$
$6^{8sd}\ 9^{14sd}\ 5^{8ss}$ **1-5-18 £6,463**

Bolckow *K A Ryan* 60
2 b g Marju (Ire) - Stamatina
6^{7gf} **0-0-1**

Bold Act (Ire) *H Candy* 76
3 b g Brave Act - Banco Solo
$2^{8g}\ 3^{8g}$ **0-2-2 £1,719**

Bold And Free (USA) *Saeed Bin Suroor* 89
2 ch c Giant's Causeway (USA) - Sweeping Story (USA)
$2^{7g}\ 1^{7gf}\ 7^{8g}$ **1-1-3 £7,475**

Bold Argument (Ire) *Mrs P N Dutfield* 57
2 ch c Shinko Forest (Ire) - Ivory Bride
$12^{7gf}\ 8^{6g}$ **0-0-2**

Bold Arrow *B J Llewellyn*
3 b/br g Bold Fort - Jubilee Belle
$13^{9sd}\ 7^{12gs}\ 12^{9sd}$ **0-0-3**

Bold Blade *M J Polglase* a39
4 b g Sure Blade (USA) - Golden Ciel (USA)
$5^{11sd}\ 7^{12sd}\ 9^{12sd}\ 9^{12sd}\ 6^{16sd}$ **0-0-5**

Bold Brownie *J E Long* a26
3 b f Almaty (Ire) - Polly So Bold
$13^{7gf}\ 9^{8sd}$ **0-0-2**

Bold Bunny *S C Williams* 57
4 b f Piccolo - Bold And Beautiful
$4^{7g}\ 15^{6g}\ 11^{5g}\ 14^{6gf}\ 11^{6gf}\ 9^{6gf}\ 19^{6gf}$
0-0-7 £277

Bold Cheverak *M R Channon* 71 a67
3 b g Bold Edge - Curlew Calling (Ire)
$4^{5sd}\ 4^{6sd}\ 6^{5sd}\ 3^{6sd}\ 2^{6s}\ 8^{6sd}\ 7^{5s}\ 9^{6sd}\ 15^{6gf}$
$3^{5gf}\ 1^{6gf}\ 10^{6f}\ 13^{6gf}\ 4^{6gf}\ 9^{6g}\ 9^{6gf}\ 8^{5gs}$
1-3-17 £11,660

Bold Cross (Ire) *E G Bevan* 70
2 b g Cape Cross (Ire) - Machikane Akaiito (Ire)
$7^{5s}\ 10^{6s}\ 6^{6g}\ 4^{7gf}\ 2^{7gf}\ 2^{10g}\ 2^{8g}\ 4^{8s}$
0-5-8 £4,279

Bold Crusader *Saeed Bin Suroor* 79
2 b c Cape Cross (Ire) - Tee Cee
$3^{6gf}\ 1^{7s}$ **1-1-2 £6,367**

Bold Desire *M L W Bell* 56
3 b f Cadeaux Genereux - Polish Romance (USA)
$8^{6g}\ 3^{6g}$ **0-1-2 £592**

Bold Diktator *W R Muir* 75 a55
3 b g Diktat - Madam Bold
$5^{8gs}\ 8^{8gf}\ 5^{10sd}\ 3^{8gf}\ 3^{8gf}\ 11^{9gf}\ 4^{8gf}\ 1^{8f}\ 1^{7gf}$
$7^{8gf}\ 5^{8f}\ 4^{7gf}\ 2^{8f}\ 9^{8gs}$ **2-4-14 £11,945**

Bold Eagle (Ire) *Sir Michael Stoute* 88
3 ch c Rainbow Quest (USA) - Britannia (Ger)
$4^{10g}\ 2^{10gf}\ 5^{12gf}\ 1^{10g}\ 6^{12g}$ **1-1-5 £6,364**

Bold Eppie *P W D'Arcy* 28
3 b f Cyrano De Bergerac - So Ambitious
$9^{8g}\ 13^{8g}\ 10^{10g}\ 12^{14sd}$ **0-0-4**

Bold Havana *T T Clement*
3 b f Bold Edge - Isle Of Sodor
$13^{6sd}\ 17^{6s}$ **0-0-2**

Bold Haze *Miss S E Hall* 75
3 ch g Bold Edge - Melody Park
$1^{6s}\ 9^{6gs}\ 2^{6s}\ 12^{7gf}\ 2^{6g}\ 3^{6gf}\ 4^{6gf}\ 9^{6g}\ 12^{6hy}$
1-3-9 £9,775

Bold Love *J D Bethell* 47
2 ch f Bold Edge - Noor El Houdah (Ire)
$8^{5g}\ 7^{6gf}\ 6^{5gf}$ **0-0-3**

Bold Maggie *J A Pickering* 48 a45
3 ch f Bold Edge - Vera's First (Ire)
$6^{5sd}\ 9^{5sd}\ 8^{5sd}\ 6^{6s}\ 7^{6sd}\ 2^{5gf}\ 5^{5gf}\ 13^{6sf}\ 14^{8ss}$
8^{5sd} **0-1-10 £1,058**

Bold Marc (Ire) *K R Burke* 90 a71
3 b g Bold Fact (USA) - Zara's Birthday (Ire)
$2^{5s}\ 2^{5gs}\ 4^{5gf}\ 10^{6gf}\ 7^{6gs}\ 2^{6gf}\ 2^{5gf}\ 7^{6gf}\ 5^{5gf}$
$4^{5g}\ 12^{6sd}$ **0-4-11 £16,402**

Bold Minstrel (Ire) *M Quinn* 84
3 br g Bold Fact (USA) - Ponda Rosa (Ire)
$10^{5gs}\ 13^{5gf}\ 1^{5f}$ **1-0-3 £6,973**

Bold Phoenix (Ire) *B J Curley* 49 a46
4 b g Dr Fong (USA) - Subya
$12^{9sd}\ 12^{10sd}\ 6^{10sd}\ 10^{8sd}\ 2^{7s}\ 10^{7sd}\ 2^{8g}\ 1^{7sd}$
12^{9sf} **1-2-9 £2,349**

Bold Pioneer (USA) *C P Morlock* a44
2 b c Pioneering (USA) - Uber Alyce (USA)
12^{8sd} **0-0-1**

Bold Pursuit (Ire) *S B Clark* 45
3 br g Bold Fact (USA) - Lyphard Belle
$4^{6g}\ 6^{7gf}\ 2^{7gf}\ 8^{7gs}$ **0-1-4 £1,113**

Bold Tiger (Ire) *Mrs L Stubbs* 66 a48
2 b g Bold Fact (USA) - Heart Of The Ocean (Ire)
$3^{5g}\ 5^{5gf}\ 8^{5g}\ 6^{5g}\ 13^{7gf}\ 8^{5sd}\ 6^{6sf}$ **0-1-7**
£572

Bold Trump *Mrs N S Sharpe* 40 a43
4 b g First Trump - Blue Nile (Ire)
$8^{10gf}\ 9^{12g}\ 7^{13gs}\ 4^{9sd}\ 12^{17sf}\ 3^{9sd}$ **0-1-6**
£445

Bold Wolf *Derek Kane* 55 a37
4 b g Wolfhound (USA) - Rambold
$9^{5sd}\ 13^{7s}\ 14^{8gf}\ 9^{5g}\ 6^{6gf}\ 8^{7gf}\ 14^{7s}$ **0-0-7**

Bolden *T D Easterby* 30
2 ch g Bold Edge - Enaam
$9^{5gf}\ 10^{6gf}\ 11^{5gf}\ 17^{6gf}$ **0-0-4**

Boldini (USA) *Stef Liddiard* a40
4 ch g Atticus (USA) - Bold Bold (Ire)
$9^{12sd}\ 8^{10sd}$ **0-0-2**

Bolero Again (Ire) *J R Fanshawe* 72 a66
3 b f Sadler's Wells (USA) - Gravieres (Fr)
$2^{10sd}\ 4^{10gf}\ 4^{9gs}\ 1^{10gs}\ 9^{11gs}\ 11^{10s}$ **1-1-6**
£5,756

Boleyn Castle (USA) *P S McEntee* 11 a31
8 ch g River Special (USA) - Dance Skirt (Can)
$11^{5gf}\ 11^{6sd}$ **0-0-2**

Bollin Billy *R Brotherton* 56 a65
3 b g Mind Games - Bollin Ann
$9^{6g}\ 5^{6s}\ 6^{7g}\ 2^{5s}\ 8^{5f}\ 5^{5gf}\ 3^{6gf}\ 4^{5gf}\ 9^{7gf}\ 4^{6ft}$
$1^{6sd}\ 6^{7sd}$ **1-2-12 £4,364**

Bollin David *T D Easterby* 31
2 b c Golden Snake (USA) - Bollin Ann
$8^{5g}\ 9^{7g}\ 9^{6gf}\ 8^{5gf}$ **0-0-4**

Bollin Derek *T D Easterby* 38
2 gr c Silver Patriarch (Ire) - Bollin Magdalene
$13^{7s}\ 9^{8gs}\ 14^{9g}$ **0-0-3**

Bollin Dolly *T D Easterby* 24
2 ch f Bien Bien (USA) - Bollin Roberta
8^{7gf} **0-0-1**

Bollin Edward *K A Ryan* 67
6 b g Timeless Times (USA) - Bollin Harriet

9^{7g} 4^{7s} 10^{6s} 3^{7g} 11^{7f} 13^{8s} 1^{7gf} 6^{7gf} 5^{7g}
4^{7g} 6^{7gf} 5^{7g} 5^{8s} **1-2-13 £5,925**

Bollin Michael *T D Easterby* 68
3 b c Celtic Swing - Bollin Zola
4^{9s} **0-0-1 £266**

Bollin Ruth *T D Easterby* 45
3 gr f Silver Patriarch (Ire) - Bollin Roberta
7^{10f} 8^{8s} **0-0-2**

Bollin Thomas *R Allan* 80
7 b g Alhijaz - Bollin Magdalene
8^{18g} 9^{12gf} 2^{12gs} 2^{12s} 8^{14g} 1^{13gs} 10^{16gs} 4^{16g}
7^{16g} 1^{12g} 9^{12g} 5^{13g} 4^{16g} **2-2-13**
£16,658

Bollywood (Ire) *M A Jarvis* 58 a22
2 ch g Indian Rocket - La Fille De Cirque
12^{6gf} 7^{5gs} 6^{5ss} **0-0-3**

Bolodenka (Ire) *W J Musson* 86
3 b g Soviet Star (USA) - My-Lorraine (Ire)
1^{8g} 7^{8gs} 5^{8gf} 1^{8g} 6^{8gs} 6^{9gs} **2-0-6**
£11,216

Bolshoi Ballet *R A Fahey* a49
7 b g Dancing Spree (USA) - Broom Isle
5^{12sd} **0-0-1**

Bolton Hall (Ire) *R A Fahey* 80
3 b g Imperial Ballet (Ire) - Muneera (USA)
9^{7g} 5^{7s} 3^{7g} 1^{7gf} 4^{7s} 5^{8gf} 2^{8gf} 6^{8g} 4^{9gf} 12^{10g}
4^{8gf} 2^{9gf} 3^{8g} 9^{8g} **1-4-14 £14,997**

Bomber Command (USA) *J W Hills* 35 a78
2 b c Stravinsky (USA) - Parish Manor (USA)
21^{7gs} 3^{7sd} 2^{8sd} 1^{7sd} **1-2-4 £5,270**

Bon Bon *B W Hills* 79
3 b f Efisio - Polo
7^{8gs} 1^{7g} 4^{8g} 5^{8gf} 1^{8gs} 7^{10g} 5^{11gs} **2-0-7**
£11,675

Bon Bouche *R Charlton* 2 a55
3 ch f Cadeaux Genereux - Canis Star
9^{7sd} 12^{7sd} 17^{8gf} **0-0-3**

Bon Nuit (Ire) *G Wragg* 107
3 b f Night Shift (USA) - Pray (Ire)
8^{7gf} 9^{8s} 2^{7gf} 3^{8gf} 1^{8gf} 5^{8gf} 2^{10gf} 7^{10gf}
1-3-8 £36,449

Bon Viveur *R Hannon* 63
2 b g Mozart (Ire) - Fantazia
11^{6g} 10^{7gf} 14^{7gs} **0-0-3**

Bonanza (Ire) *A P O'Brien* 77
3 b c Danehill (USA) - Mosquera (Ger)
3^{8gf} 4^{8gf} 3^{8gf} 1^{6f} 4^{6gf} **1-2-5 £8,665**

Bond Angel Eyes *B Smart* 62
2 b f Dr Fong (USA) - Speedybird (Ire)
2^{6f} 3^{6s} 4^{7gf} **0-2-3 £1,810**

Bond Babe *B Smart* 55
3 b f Forzando - Lindfield Belle (Ire)
11^{5gf} PU^{5gf} **0-0-2**

Bond Becks (Ire) *B Smart* 67 a44
5 ch g Tagula (Ire) - At Amal (Ire)
19^{5g} 18^{5gf} 8^{6f} 7^{7f} 18^{6g} 11^{5gf} 8^{5f} 13^{6gf}
9^{5g} 9^{6sd} **0-0-10**

Bond Boy *B Smart* 93
8 b g Piccolo - Arabellajill
11^{6s} 8^{5s} 8^{6g} 1^{5g} 3^{6gf} 4^{5gf} 6^{5g} 6^{6gf} 6^{6gf} 8^{5g}
1^{5s} 12^{6g} 6^{6gf} 10^{5gs} 11^{5g} **2-1-15**
£48,733

Bond Cat (Ire) *B Smart* a24
3 ch f Raise A Grand (Ire) - Merrily
10^{7sd} 14^{8gf} **0-0-2**

Bond City (Ire) *B Smart* 104 a97
3 b g Trans Island - Where's Charlotte
3^{5gs} 7^{5gf} 6^{6g} 14^{5g} 4^{5gf} 1^{5gf} 8^{5sd} 4^{6gf} 12^{5s}
5^{5g} 6^{5g} 3^{5g} 10^{5g} 21^{6gf} **1-2-14**
£21,064

Bond Cruz *B Smart* 46 a52
2 b c King's Best (USA) - Arabis
10^{7s} 6^{8s} 5^{8sd} **0-0-3**

Bond Diamond *P T Midgley* 69 a10
8 gr g Prince Sabo - Alsiba
5^{8g} 8^{8gf} 9^{8g} 4^{7g} 17^{8gf} 13^{7sd} **0-0-6**
£390

Bond Domingo *B Smart* a40
6 b g Mind Games - Antonia's Folly
3^{5sd} **0-1-1 £208**

Bond Finesse (Ire) *B Smart* 58
3 b f Danehill Dancer (Ire) - Funny Cut (Ire)
9^{6s} 1^{7gf} 9^{7gf} 13^{7gf} 2^{7gf} 6^{8gf} 10^{7g} **1-1-7**
£3,651

Bond Kop End (Ire) *B Smart* 67
2 ch g Danehill Dancer (Ire) - Slayjay (Ire)
10^{6gf} 3^{6gf} **0-1-2 £639**

Bond Millennium *B Smart* 56 a59
7 ch g Piccolo - Farmer's Pet
9^{9sd} 9^{9sd} 6^{9sd} 8^{9sd} 8^{10g} 10^{10g} 11^{10gf} 4^{9sd}
4^{9sd} 4^{8sd} 8^{9gf} 2^{9sd} **0-1-12 £426**

Bond Moonlight *B Smart* a34
4 ch g Danehill Dancer (Ire) - Interregnum
7^{11sd} 7^{12sd} 10^{8sd} **0-0-3**

Bond Playboy *B Smart* 19
5 b g Piccolo - Highest Ever (Fr)
18^{6g} **0-0-1**

Bond Puccini *B Smart* 53
3 b g Piccolo - Baileys By Name
9^{6s} 4^{5gs} 11^{6f} 9^{5gf} 11^{6g} 7^{6gf} 13^{6f} **0-0-7**
£261

Bonfire *M Johnston* 59
3 b c Machiavellian (USA) - Forest Express (Aus)
5^{7gs} **0-0-1**

Bongoali *Mrs C A Dunnett* 45 a51
3 b f Fraam - Stride Home
5^{9sd} 13^{10gf} 7^{14gf} 8^{12sd} 7^{11g} 6^{11sd} 1^{11sd} 4^{12sd}
1-0-8 £1,452

Bonjour Bond (Ire) *J G M O'Shea* 43
4 ro g Portrait Gallery (Ire) - Musical Essence
5^{16gf} 9^{16gf} 8^{18gf} **0-0-3**

Bonnabee (Ire) *C F Wall* 65 a66
3 b f Benny The Dip (USA) - Samhat Mtoto
3^{10sd} 6^{10sd} 1^{12g} 9^{12g} 5^{11g} 8^{12sd} 5^{12gs}
1-1-7 £4,028

Bonne De Fleur *B Smart* 87 a85
4 b f Whittingham (Ire) - L'Estable Fleurie (Ire)
9^{6sd} 1^{5sd} 16^{6s} 4^{5g} 2^{5gf} 9^{6gf} 6^{5gf} 2^{5gf} 6^{6g}
6^{5gf} 15^{6gf} 7^{5sd} **1-2-12 £11,123**

Bonnie Prince Blue *B W Hills* 87
2 ch c Tipsy Creek (USA) - Heart So Blue
1^{6gs} 1^{6g} 4^{6gf} **2-0-3 £20,123**

Bonny Grey *D Burchell*
7 gr m Seymour Hicks (Fr) - Sky Wave
8^{12sd} **0-0-1**

Bontadini *D Morris* 13 a34
6 b g Emarati (USA) - Kintail
9^{10sd} 9^{9sd} 7^{8sd} 8^{8g} 14^{8f} 10^{7sd} 9^{8sd} **0-0-7**

Bonus (Ire) *G A Butler* 97 a103
5 b g Cadeaux Genereux - Khamseh

$3^{6g}\ 12^{6g}\ 6^{6sd}\ 14^{6gf}\ 4^{6gf}\ 1^{6g}\ 1^{6sd}$ **2-2-7**
£19,224

Boo *K R Burke* 85 a99
3 b g Namaqualand (USA) - Violet (Ire)
$3^{7gs}\ 6^{8gs}\ 1^{9sd}\ 4^{8gf}\ 1^{8gf}\ 1^{9gf}\ 3^{10f}\ 2^{8g}\ 3^{8g}$
$9^{10g}\ 1^{9sd}\ 1^{9sd}$ **5-3-12 £35,814**

Boogie Magic *T T Clement* a44
5 b m Wizard King - Dalby Dancer
$7^{9sd}\ 11^{8sd}\ 6^{8sd}\ 4^{9sd}\ 9^{8sd}$ **0-0-5**

Boogie Street *R Hannon* 114
4 b c Compton Place - Tart And A Half
$1^{5g}\ 5^{6gf}\ 2^{5gf}\ 7^{5gf}\ 9^{6gf}\ 4^{5gf}\ 4^{5g}\ 6^{6gf}\ 3^{5gf}$
1^{5g} **2-2-10 £86,196**

Book Matched *B Smart* 42 a76
4 b g Efisio - Princess Latifa
$1^{8sd}\ 7^{8sd}\ 7^{8sd}\ 11^{8g}\ 12^{8gf}\ 11^{8gf}$ **1-0-6**
£3,376

Book Of Music (Ire) *Sir Michael Stoute* 78
2 b c Sadler's Wells (USA) - Novelette
1^{7s} **1-0-1 £3,789**

Boot 'n Toot *C A Cyzer* 84 a91
4 b f Mtoto - Raspberry Sauce
$2^{7sd}\ 1^{10sd}\ 4^{10g}\ 4^{12s}\ 9^{12g}\ 7^{8g}\ 7^{8sd}\ 1^{12g}\ 9^{12gf}$
$12^{10gf}\ 12^{10sd}\ 3^{8sd}\ 4^{10sd}\ 11^{10sd}$ **2-2-14**
£31,530

Boppys Dream *R A Fahey* 48 a37
3 ch f Clan Of Roses - Laurel Queen (Ire)
$7^{9sd}\ 4^{8g}\ 12^{8gf}\ 3^{8gf}\ 10^{8gs}\ 8^{8gf}\ 8^{9sd}\ 6^{7sd}$
0-1-8 £429

Boppys Pride *R A Fahey* a36
2 ch c Clan Of Roses - Joara (Fr)
$8^{7sd}\ 12^{7sd}\ 9^{6sd}$ **0-0-3**

Boppys Princess *R A Fahey* 79
4 b f Wizard King - Laurel Queen (Ire)
$15^{10g}\ 3^{10g}\ 1^{10s}\ 1^{10gf}\ 5^{10g}\ 9^{12gf}$ **2-1-6**
£11,343

Boquilobo *M Johnston* 75
2 b c Rainbow Quest (USA) - Moonlight Paradise (USA)
$7^{8gf}\ 7^{8gs}\ 3^{9g}$ **0-0-3 £838**

Boracay Dream (Ire) *Patrick Michael Verling* 68 a71
3 ch c Grand Lodge (USA) - Mild Intrigue (USA)
$7^{8sd}\ 3^{9sd}\ 1^{10sd}\ 4^{10sd}\ 11^{10s}\ 7^{11gf}$ **1-1-6**
£4,420

Border Alliance *D W P Arbuthnot* 50
5 ch g Selkirk (USA) - Regal Peace
$13^{8gf}\ 7^{7gs}$ **0-0-2**

Border Artist *B G Powell* 61 a61
6 ch g Selkirk (USA) - Aunt Tate
$6^{6gs}\ 2^{7gf}\ 5^{6gf}\ 5^{7g}\ 5^{7sd}$ **0-0-5 £525**

Border Castle *Miss Venetia Williams* 94
4 b g Grand Lodge (USA) - Tempting Prospect
$3^{12g}\ 7^{10gs}$ **0-1-2 £2,294**

Border Edge *J J Bridger* 78 a63
7 b g Beveled (USA) - Seymour Ann
$7^{6sd}\ 12^{10sd}\ 11^{7sd}\ 12^{7sd}\ 6^{7g}\ 14^{7gf}\ 1^{7gf}\ 15^{8g}$
$10^{8gf}\ 4^{8gf}\ 6^{7gf}\ 17^{7gf}\ 6^{10gs}\ 6^{9g}\ 2^{8gs}\ 5^{8g}\ 1^{7g}$
$1^{7s}\ 10^{8g}\ 10^{8gf}\ 8^{8f}\ 15^{7g}\ 16^{10g}\ 4^{10s}\ 14^{12sd}$
8^{10sd} **3-2-26 £15,188**

Border Hope *J S Haldane*
3 br f Ramsey Hope - Border Starlette (Ire)
$9^{9g}\ 20^{7gf}$ **0-0-2**

Border Music *A M Balding* 87 a108
4 b g Selkirk (USA) - Mara River
$4^{8sd}\ 9^{8g}\ 6^{8gf}\ 3^{7g}\ 6^{7gf}\ 4^{8g}\ 9^{8gs}\ 1^{7sd}\ 3^{6gf}\ 9^{6g}$
$4^{7g}\ 1^{7sd}\ 1^{6sd}$ **3-4-13 £32,010**

Border Tale *James Moffatt* 76 a39
5 b g Selkirk (USA) - Likely Story (Ire)
$11^{14g}\ 3^{10g}\ 4^{14gf}\ 12^{10s}\ 11^{9sd}$ **0-1-5**
£1,584

Borderlescott *R Bastiman* 104
3 b g Compton Place - Jeewan
$5^{6gf}\ 1^{6gf}\ 5^{6gf}\ 1^{6gf}\ 1^{6gf}\ 2^{6gf}\ 3^{6g}\ 1^{6s}$
4-2-8 £48,170

Borehan *M A Jarvis* 86
2 b c Agnes World (USA) - Crime Ofthecentury
$4^{6g}\ 10^{6g}$ **0-0-2 £5,384**

Boris The Spider *M D Hammond* 51 a64
4 b g Makbul - Try Vickers (USA)
$5^{14sd}\ 2^{12sd}\ 11^{12g}\ 5^{13s}\ 8^{13s}\ 7^{15s}\ 7^{14sd}$
0-1-7 £722

Born For Dancing (Ire) *B W Hills* 71 a58
3 b f Fasliyev (USA) - Fancy Boots (Ire)
$5^{5s}\ 7^{5g}\ 3^{5f}\ 7^{5gs}\ 5^{5gs}\ 1^{5g}\ 3^{6gf}\ 4^{6gf}\ 3^{5gf}\ 12^{6g}$
$6^{6g}\ 10^{5sd}\ 7^{6sd}$ **1-3-13 £6,041**

Born For Diamonds (Ire) *R E Barr* 46
3 b f Night Shift (USA) - Kirri (Ire)
$6^{6g}\ 9^{6f}\ 13^{5f}\ 12^{5gf}$ **0-0-4**

Born Ready *T D Easterby* 46
2 b c King's Best (USA) - Exactly Red (Chi)
$12^{7gs}\ 6^{7g}\ 11^{6gf}$ **0-0-3**

Born Slippy (Ire) *M G Quinlan* 46 a70
2 b c Desert Prince (Ire) - Swan's Loop
$3^{7sd}\ 8^{7gf}\ 2^{7sd}$ **0-2-3 £1,600**

Born To Be Bold *R Hannon* 79
3 ch c Bold Edge - Birthday Venture
$12^{6gs}\ 2^{6gs}\ 1^{6g}\ 4^{6gf}\ 13^{7g}\ 4^{6g}$ **1-2-6**
£5,184

Born Wild (Ger) *Sir Michael Stoute* a68
2 b f Sadler's Wells (USA) - Borgia (Ger)
3^{9sd} **0-1-1 £624**

Borodinsky *R E Barr* 59
4 b g Magic Ring (Ire) - Valldemosa
$7^{7g}\ 11^{6f}\ 3^{6f}\ 5^{8g}\ 1^{7gf}\ 3^{7gf}\ 6^{6gf}\ 2^{6gf}$
1-3-8 £5,010

Borouj (Ire) *J H M Gosden* 81
3 ch c Unfuwain (USA) - Amanah (USA)
$8^{8f}\ 2^{8gf}\ 3^{8g}\ 2^{9gs}\ 6^{10g}\ 1^{9s}$ **1-3-6**
£6,956

Borrego (USA) *C B Greely* a127
4 ch c El Prado (Ire) - Sweet As Honey (USA)
$1^{9sy}\ 3^{10ft}\ 3^{9ft}\ 4^{9ft}\ 2^{10ft}\ 1^{10ft}\ 1^{10ft}\ 10^{10ft}$
3-2-8 £800,312

Borsch (Ire) *Miss L A Perratt* 22
3 b g Soviet Star (USA) - Cheese Soup (USA)
$11^{7gs}\ 15^{9g}\ 9^{7f}$ **0-0-3**

Borthwick Girl (Ire) *B J Meehan* 105 a91
3 b f Cape Cross (Ire) - Shannon Dore (Ire)
$3^{8gs}\ 3^{8sd}\ 7^{8s}\ 2^{8gf}\ 10^{8gs}\ 3^{8s}$ **0-3-6**
£21,160

Boschette *J D Bethell* 44
3 b f Dansili - Secret Dance
$10^{8g}\ 6^{6f}\ 5^{6g}\ UR^{7gf}$ **0-0-4**

Bosky News *W G M Turner* a6
2 b g Woodborough (USA) - Express Edition
$14^{6gf}\ 10^{7sd}$ **0-0-2**

Bosphorus *D G Bridgwater* 21 a28
6 b g Polish Precedent (USA) - Ancara
$12^{9sd}\ 12^{12gf}$ **0-0-2**

Boss Mak (Ire) *V Smith* a57
2 ch g Shinko Forest (Ire) - Lucky Achievement (USA)
5^{7sd} **0-0-1**

Botteen *M P Tregoning* 85
2 br c Singspiel (Ire) - Abyaan (Ire)
3^{8gf} 1^{8g} **1-1-2 £5,227**

Bottomless Wallet *F Watson* 54
4 ch f Titus Livius (Fr) - Furry Dance (USA)
3^{10s} 7^{9s} 8^{11gf} 9^{10g} 4^{10gf} 4^{8gf} **0-1-6 £804**

Bouboulina *E A L Dunlop* a83
2 b f Grand Lodge (USA) - Ideal Lady (Ire)
1^{7sd} **1-0-1 £4,524**

Boucheen *Ms Deborah J Evans* a39
2 b g Foxhound (USA) - Anytime Baby
9^{8ss} 5^{7sd} **0-0-2**

Boule D'Or (Ire) *J Akehurst* 112 a110
4 b c Croco Rouge (Ire) - Saffron Crocus
1^{10g} 1^{10gf} 2^{10gf} 9^{10g} 7^{10gf} UR^{10gs} 8^{8gf} 3^{10g} 5^{10gf} 3^{10g} 3^{10gs} 6^{11s} 2^{10sd} **2-4-13 £111,575**

Boumsong (Ire) *R C Guest* 44
2 b c Fasliyev (USA) - Festive Season (USA)
17^{5g} 6^{5gf} 4^{5s} 7^{6gf} 13^{6f} **0-0-5**

Boundless Prospect (USA) *Miss Gay Kelleway* 89 a80
6 b g Boundary (USA) - Cape (USA)
5^{8sd} 5^{7sd} 6^{8sd} 1^{17g} 1^{8gf} 3^{8g} 3^{8gf} 2^{8gs} 2^{10g} 6^{8gf} 1^{8gf} 4^{8g} 3^{8gs} 2^{8sd} 7^{8sd} 8^{12sd} **2-6-16 £27,225**

Bountiful *M Blanshard* 44
3 gr f Pivotal - Kinsaile
5^{6gs} 10^{5s} 9^{6gs} 15^{6gf} 13^{8gf} **0-0-5**

Bouquet *J R Fanshawe* 70
3 b f Cadeaux Genereux - Bayadere (USA)
7^{7gf} 4^{8g} 6^{8gf} 15^{10gf} 2^{8gf} 4^{10g} **0-1-6 £1,840**

Bourgainville *A M Balding* 83 a94
7 b g Pivotal - Petonica (Ire)
10^{12sd} 4^{10sd} 5^{10sd} 18^{10gs} 5^{8gf} 8^{10g} 3^{10gf} 1^{9gf} 8^{12f} 5^{9g} **1-1-10 £9,911**

Bournonville *J Ryan* a48
2 b g Machiavellian (USA) - Amellnaa (Ire)
11^{7sd} 11^{10sd} 12^{7sd} **0-0-3**

Bouzouki (USA) *W R Swinburn* 61 a69
2 b/br c Distant Music (USA) - Pamina (Ire)
7^{7gf} 3^{7sd} 4^{9sd} **0-1-3 £976**

Bow Bridge *M W Easterby* 95
2 br f Bertolini (USA) - Bow Peep (Ire)
2^{5g} 1^{5s} 1^{5gs} 1^{5gs} 3^{5gf} 15^{5gs} 7^{5g} 21^{6gf} **3-2-8 £35,179**

Bow Wave *H Candy* 82 a64
3 b g Danzero (Aus) - Moxby
4^{6gf} 11^{7gf} 10^{7ft} **0-0-3 £523**

Bowl Of Cherries *I A Wood* 43 a42
2 b c Vettori (Ire) - Desert Nomad
17^{6gf} 6^{7sd} 15^{7gs} 10^{8g} 7^{8g} 15^{6gs} **0-0-6**

Bowland Boy *A Berry* 55
2 b g Diktat - Antonia's Folly
15^{5g} 3^{5gf} 5^{5g} 8^{6f} 6^{6g} 6^{6gf} 8^{5gf} 9^{5gs} 5^{6gf} 12^{6s} 18^{6s} **0-1-11 £515**

Bowlander *Miss K M George* 31 a16
2 ch g Zaha (Can) - Lambeth Belle (USA)
4^{5gf} 17^{7gf} 9^{5sd} **0-0-3 £466**

Bowled Out (Ger) *P J McBride* 72 a74
3 b f Dansili - Braissim
8^{10gf} 3^{10gf} 14^{8gf} 5^{10gs} 2^{12sd} 8^{12gf} 1^{11g} 3^{12sd} 5^{12sd} **1-3-9 £7,361**

Bowling Along *M E Sowersby* 13
4 b f The West (USA) - Bystrouska
13^{6g} **0-0-1**

Bowness *J G Given* 82 a65
3 b f Efisio - Dominio (Ire)
6^{6g} 1^{6sd} 1^{5g} 3^{5gs} 2^{5gf} 11^{6g} 2^{5gs} 16^{8g} **2-3-8 £10,985**

Bowstring (Ire) *J H M Gosden* 96
4 b f Sadler's Wells (USA) - Cantanta
5^{10gf} 6^{14s} **0-0-2 £2,000**

Box Builder *H Morrison* 70 a69
8 ch g Fraam - Ena Olley
4^{14sd} 4^{16sd} 2^{18gs} 5^{22s} **0-1-4 £1,779**

Boxhall (Ire) *W R Swinburn* 79
3 b g Grand Lodge (USA) - March Hare
6^{8g} 11^{10gf} 1^{12gf} 6^{14gf} 6^{14g} **1-0-5 £4,732**

Boxhound *N Tinkler* 42
2 b g Foxhound (USA) - Manderina
12^{6gf} 8^{6gs} 8^{6f} **0-0-3**

Boy Dancer (Ire) *D W Barker* 44
2 ch c Danehill Dancer (Ire) - Mary Gabry (Ire)
7^{5gf} 14^{8s} 8^{7s} **0-0-3**

Brabazon (Ire) *R Charlton* 64
2 b c In The Wings - Azure Lake (USA)
7^{8gf} 7^{8gs} 9^{7s} **0-0-3**

Brabinger (Ire) *B G Powell* a38
2 b g Xaar - Particular Friend
13^{7sd} 10^{7sd} 11^{8sd} **0-0-3**

Brace Of Doves *T D Barron* 74 a66
3 b g Bahamian Bounty - Overcome
3^{6sd} 2^{7gs} 3^{8s} 1^{8s} 1^{8g} 6^{8gf} 5^{8g} 11^{8g} 6^{7f} 1^{8gf} 6^{7gf} 13^{8gf} 10^{7gf} **3-3-13 £17,411**

Bracklinn *J R Fanshawe* 70 a62
3 b f Deploy - Blane Water (USA)
1^{9sd} 5^{8gf} 3^{8gf} 1^{10f} 6^{9ft} **2-1-5 £9,678**

Brads House (Ire) *J G M O'Shea* 92
3 b c Rossini (USA) - Gold Stamp
4^{10gs} 1^{11gs} 5^{11f} 3^{12g} 1^{12g} 6^{11gs} 4^{12g} 4^{14gs} 3^{15s} **2-3-9 £16,881**

Brady Boys (USA) *J G M O'Shea* a12
8 b g Cozzene (USA) - Elvia (USA)
11^{14sd} **0-0-1**

Bragadino *Lindsay Woods* 63 a40
6 b h Zilzal (USA) - Graecia Magna (USA)
12^{9sd} 8^{9sd} 16^{8s} 2^{8hy} **0-1-4 £1,256**

Brahminy Kite (USA) *M Johnston* 110
3 b g Silver Hawk (USA) - Cope's Light (USA)
2^{12gf} 4^{12gf} 3^{12gs} 5^{12g} 2^{12gs} 8^{16gs} **0-1-6 £74,942**

Bramantino (Ire) *T A K Cuthbert* 76
5 b g Perugino (USA) - Headrest
7^{11g} 1^{12gs} 2^{12gf} 3^{12f} 8^{12g} 14^{12g} 10^{12g} **1-1-7 £5,532**

Bramcote Lorne *J A Glover* 48
2 b g Josr Algarhoud (Ire) - Dreamtime Quest
10^{7s} 6^{6s} **0-0-2**

Brancacci (Ire) *R Charlton* 49 a21
2 b g Vettori (Ire) - Robsart (Ire)
6^{7g} 10^{6sd} 6^{8gs} **0-0-3**

Brandexe (Ire) *B W Hills* 52 a68
3 b f Xaar - Tintara (Ire)
3^{9sd} 8^{9sd} 5^{12f} 16^{16g} **0-1-4 £635**

Brandywell Boy (Ire) *D J S Ffrench Davis* 84 a89
2 b c Danetime (Ire) - Alexander Eliott (Ire)
4^{5gf} 2^{5gf} 4^{5gf} 3^{5gf} 1^{5g} 13^{6g} 2^{6sd} 2^{6sd}

1-4-8 £26,656

Branston Bertie *Mrs J R Ramsden* 61
2 b g Bertolini (USA) - Kauri (USA)
8^{6s} 8^{6gf} 9^{5g} 3^{6f} 12^{6g} 9^{7g} **0-1-6 £569**

Branston Lily *D Brace* 30
3 ch f Cadeaux Genereux - Indefinite Article (Ire)
15^{6g} 7^{5g} 12^{6gs} 15^{7gf} 10^{6sd} **0-0-5**

Branston Penny *P D Evans* 45 a41
3 ch f Pennekamp (USA) - Branston Jewel (Ire)
10^{7sd} 6^{9sd} 3^{8gf} 4^{10f} 10^{10f} 10^{9sd} 5^{10g} 4^{8sd} 7^{12gf} **0-1-9 £388**

Branston Tiger *Ian Emmerson* a78
6 b g Mark Of Esteem (Ire) - Tuxford Hideaway
5^{6sd} 5^{6sd} **0-0-2**

Brantwood (Ire) *A Senior* 6
5 b g Lake Coniston (Ire) - Angelic Sounds (Ire)
16^{5gf} **0-0-1**

Brave Bear *T D Easterby* 69 a23
3 br f Bold Edge - Sarah Bear
5^{6gs} 7^{5s} 11^{9sd} 1^{5s} 11^{5gf} 2^{5gs} 8^{6g} 7^{6s} 4^{6gf} 1^{5gf} 2^{6g} 1^{5g} **3-3-12 £13,573**

Brave Burt (Ire) *D Nicholls* a48
8 ch g Pips Pride - Friendly Song
4^{5sd} 12^{5sd} 5^{5sd} 3^{7sd} 1^{6sd} **1-0-5 £4,255**

Brave Chief *S R Bowring* 22 a63
4 ch g Komaite (USA) - Victoria Sioux
6^{7sd} 3^{6sd} 1^{7sd} 3^{7sd} 15^{5gf} 15^{5g} 2^{7sf} 1^{6sd} 1^{7sd} 2^{8sd} 7^{7sd} 2^{6sd} 6^{7sd} 2^{5sd} **3-6-14 £7,846**

Brave Dane (Ire) *L A Dace* 54 a38
7 b g Danehill (USA) - Nuriva (USA)
17^{7g} 11^{8gf} 9^{11f} 17^{8gf} 8^{8f} 5^{10s} 10^{8f} 12^{12sd} **0-0-8**

Brave Effect (Ire) *Mrs Dianne Sayer* 52
9 br g Bravefoot - Crupney Lass
4^{14gf} 5^{8gf} 7^{10gs} **0-0-3 £267**

Brave Fight *A King* 73 a66
2 b c Kalanisi (Ire) - Baalbek
3^{7g} 2^{8gf} 6^{8sd} **0-2-3 £2,252**

Brave Tike (Ire) *Mrs L Stubbs*
2 b g Brave Act - Karminiya (Ire)
11^{7gf} **0-0-1**

Bravely Does It (USA) *W M Brisbourne* 31
5 gr g Holy Bull (USA) - Vigors Destiny (USA)
12^{12gs} 12^{12g} 9^{12f} 10^{10gf} 13^{9sd} **0-0-5**

Bravemore (USA) *B J Meehan* 90 a91
3 b c Diesis - Private Indy (USA)
2^{11g} 1^{12sd} 8^{12gs} 4^{10g} 3^{10gf} 4^{10gf} 5^{10gf} **1-2-7 £7,203**

Bravo Maestro (USA) *D W P Arbuthnot* 79 a89
4 b g Stravinsky (USA) - Amaranthus (USA)
9^{7sd} 14^{7g} 9^{7gf} 5^{8sd} 9^{8g} 10^{10sd} **0-0-6 £438**

Bravura *G L Moore* a70
7 ch g Never So Bold - Sylvan Song
8^{10sd} 10^{10sd} 4^{10sd} 6^{12sd} **0-0-4 £259**

Brazilian Style *P Winkworth* 66
2 br f Exit To Nowhere (USA) - Cosmic Star
2^{5g} 3^{5gf} 2^{5gs} **0-2-3 £3,658**

Brazilian Terrace *M L W Bell* 64
5 ch m Zilzal (USA) - Elaine's Honor (USA)
6^{8s} **0-0-1**

Breaking Shadow (Ire) *K R Burke* 82
3 br g Danehill Dancer (Ire) - Crimbourne
19^{7g} 3^{7s} 11^{7g} 3^{7s} 2^{7g} 7^{8gs} 10^{6g} 1^{7gf} 10^{7g} 5^{7gf} 4^{8g} 11^{9gs} 14^{7s} **1-2-13 £16,183**

Breamore *Mrs A J Perrett* 64 a73
3 b c Dansili - Maze Garden (USA)
9^{9gs} 3^{12f} 3^{12sd} **0-1-3 £1,050**

Breathing Fire *W J Musson* 83
3 b g Pivotal - Pearl Venture
7^{7gf} 2^{8gs} 6^{10gf} 5^{10s} 2^{12g} 1^{10g} 9^{10hy} **1-2-7 £8,997**

Breathing Space (USA) *D J S Ffrench Davis* 42 a61
4 b/br f Expelled (USA) - Summer Retreat (USA)
13^{12sd} 14^{11gs} 13^{8g} **0-0-3**

Brecon *D R C Elsworth* 85
3 ch f Unfuwain (USA) - Welsh Valley (USA)
5^{10gf} 7^{10gf} **0-0-2 £700**

Brecon Beacon *P F I Cole* 107 a96
3 b c Spectrum (Ire) - Ffestiniog (Ire)
2^{8sd} 2^{8gs} 7^{8gf} 2^{8gf} 8^{8gs} 5^{8gf} 3^{9f} **0-3-7 £32,035**

Breeder's Folly *T J Fitzgerald* 41
3 b f Mujahid (USA) - Wynona (Ire)
7^{8g} 5^{7gf} **0-0-2**

Breezer *J A Geake* 38
5 b g Forzando - Lady Lacey
4^{12gs} **0-0-1**

Breezit (USA) *Henry De Bromhead* 51 a25
4 b f Stravinsky (USA) - Sharka
9^{6sd} 12^{6sd} 6^{8gf} 6^{7sd} **0-0-4**

Brenda Meova *B J Meehan* 94 a70
2 b f Dr Fong (USA) - Iberian Dancer (Can)
3^{5g} 3^{5sd} 4^{6gf} 1^{6sd} 5^{6g} 7^{7gf} 4^{6g} 6^{6gf} 3^{5gf} 7^{5hy} **1-3-10 £10,907**

Brendan's Surprise *K J Burke* 52 a61
3 b g Faustus (USA) - Primrose Way
7^{7sd} 7^{8sd} 11^{10sd} 15^{12g} 14^{12gs} 9^{8f} 8^{10sd} 8^{8gf} 4^{7f} 10^{7gf} 12^{8gf} 5^{10gf} 8^{13sd} 2^{6f} 2^{7g} 2^{7sd} 4^{8sd} 5^{8gs} 8^{7sd} 4^{8sd} **0-3-20 £1,324**

Brennie (Ire) *V Smith* 47 a49
4 ch f Grand Lodge (USA) - Brentsville (USA)
11^{10g} 7^{12sd} 8^{12sd} 2^{11gf} 2^{16gf} 8^{16sd} 4^{12g} 3^{12f} 3^{16gf} 2^{12sf} 2^{17sd} 7^{12sd} **0-7-12 £3,961**

Bretton *B A Pearce* a55
4 b g Polar Prince (Ire) - Understudy
4^{12sd} 1^{12sd} 4^{13sd} 8^{10sd} 1^{12sd} 9^{12sd} 8^{14sd} **2-0-7 £3,972**

Briannie (Ire) *P Butler* 49 a55
3 b f Xaar - Annieirwin (Ire)
6^{10sd} 9^{10gf} 11^{10gf} 6^{10sd} 5^{12gf} 8^{8f} 11^{16sd} **0-0-7**

Briannsta (Ire) *M R Channon* 94 a81
3 b g Bluebird (USA) - Nacote (Ire)
2^{6gs} 9^{6hy} 1^{6gs} 3^{6s} 1^{6g} 7^{6gs} 7^{6gf} 8^{6gs} 9^{6g} 4^{6gs} 8^{6gf} 2^{6gf} 17^{6g} 4^{6gf} 10^{6g} 9^{6s} 8^{6sd} **2-3-17 £29,806**

Briar Ghyll *I A Wood* a22
3 ch f Zaha (Can) - Charlotte Penny
11^{8sd} **0-0-1**

Bridal Path *Sir Mark Prescott* 76 a60
2 gr/b f Groom Dancer (USA) - Doctor's Glory (USA)
6^{5gs} 3^{6sd} 10^{7gf} 3^{5gf} 1^{5gf} 1^{5gf} 2^{6g} 5^{6f} **2-3-8 £12,571**

Bridegroom *Lady Herries* 54
3 b g Groom Dancer (USA) - La Piaf (Fr)
16^{12gs} 10^{8gf} 8^{8g} **0-0-3**

Bridewell (USA) *F Watson*
6 b g Woodman (USA) - La Alleged (USA)
6^{12gf} PU^{11gf} 15^{12s} **0-0-3**

Bridge Loan *J Noseda* 100 a90
3 ch g Giant's Causeway (USA) - Credit-A-Plenty
2^{8sd} 1^{10sd} 1^{10sd} 8^{10gs} 1^{10gf} 7^{12g} 8^{12gf} 6^{12g}
3-1-8 £22,282

Bridge Pal *P Monteith* 39
5 ch m First Trump - White Domino
8^{8gs} **0-0-1**

Bridge T'The Stars *R F Johnson Houghton* 53 a15
3 b f Josr Algarhoud (Ire) - Petra's Star
8^{6gs} 14^{8gf} 16^{7gs} 11^{8gs} 8^{8sd} 11^{11gs} **0-0-6**

Bridgewater Boys *K A Ryan* 79 a64
4 b g Atraf - Dunloe (Ire)
11^{9sd} 11^{7sd} 2^{7s} 9^{6s} 6^{8f} 8^{7g} 9^{7g} 3^{7g} 6^{8gs}
13^{8gf} 2^{8s} 8^{7hy} 6^{8sd} 2^{8sd} 3^{8sd} **0-5-15**
£4,923

Brief Goodbye *John Berry* 84
5 b g Slip Anchor - Queen Of Silk (Ire)
10^{8gf} 6^{8gf} 1^{10g} 3^{10gf} 6^{10g} 5^{12gf} 3^{10gf} 9^{12gs}
1-1-8 £6,856

Briery Blaze *Mrs K Walton* 64
2 b f Dansili - Sabonis (USA)
6^{6s} 4^{6gf} 6^{6gf} 21^{7gf} **0-0-4 £326**

Briery Lane (Ire) *Mrs K Walton* 57 a40
4 ch g Tagula (Ire) - Branston Berry (Ire)
17^{6g} 6^{6g} 3^{6gf} 9^{6f} 12^{6g} 8^{6gf} 4^{5gf} 3^{5gf} 14^{5gf}
4^{6gf} 6^{5sd} **0-2-11 £1,656**

Brigadore *J G Given* 80 a55
6 b g Magic Ring (Ire) - Music Mistress (Ire)
6^{5sd} 5^{5hy} 5^{5gs} 5^{5gf} 10^{5g} 1^{5gf} 2^{6f} 6^{5gf} 3^{5gf}
4^{5g} 1^{5gf} 5^{5g} 2^{6gf} 7^{5gs} 10^{6g} 1^{6g} 6^{6s} 11^{5s}
3-3-18 £16,327

Brigadore (USA) *W R Muir*
2 gr/ro c Sandpit (Brz) - Mersey
15^{8g} **0-0-1**

Bright *Miss J Feilden* 48 a21
2 ch g Mister Baileys - Razzle Dazzle (Ire)
12^{8sd} 8^{7g} 12^{6g} **0-0-3**

Bright Fire (Ire) *M Hill* 51
4 b f Daggers Drawn (USA) - Jarmar Moon
6^{10gf} 13^{10g} **0-0-2**

Bright Sparky (Ger) *M W Easterby* 49
2 ch g Dashing Blade - Braissim
3^{6s} 6^{6gf} 8^{6gf} 13^{8g} **0-1-4 £535**

Bright Sun (Ire) *N Tinkler* 75
4 b c Desert Sun - Kealbra Lady
6^{10s} 9^{11g} 5^{10gf} 3^{9f} 2^{12g} 6^{10g} 2^{11gf} 1^{9gf} 5^{12gf}
6^{11gf} 4^{8g} 6^{8gf} 2^{10g} 9^{10gf} 3^{10gf} **1-5-15**
£10,018

Briland (Ire) *M Halford* 90
2 b f Namid - Inourhearts (Ire)
2^{5f} 1^{6y} 5^{5gf} 5^{5gs} **1-1-4 £14,007**

Brindisi *B W Hills* 101 a101
4 b f Dr Fong (USA) - Genoa
7^{6gf} 5^{8gf} 6^{9gf} 5^{7gf} 10^{8g} 4^{8f} 6^{9g} 4^{8g} 12^{9s}
2^{8sd} 4^{9sd} **0-2-11 £15,701**

Briolette (Ire) *A P O'Brien* 105
3 b f Sadler's Wells (USA) - Cocotte
2^{10y} 2^{12g} 2^{11g} 5^{9g} 1^{12gy} 2^{12g} 6^{12g} 1^{10hy}
2-4-8 £84,327

Brios Boy *K R Burke* a23
5 ch g My Best Valentine - Rose Elegance
8^{7sd} 11^{9sd} 9^{6sd} **0-0-3**

Broadway Calling *A M Balding* a50
2 ch g Dr Fong (USA) - Manhattan Sunset (USA)
9^{8sd} **0-0-1**

Broadwood Zara *B Mactaggart* 7
2 b f Compton Admiral - Thorntoun Dancer
6^{5gf} 6^{8gf} 8^{8s} **0-0-3**

Brochrua (Ire) *J D Frost* 23
5 b m Hernando (Fr) - Severine (USA)
6^{12gs} **0-0-1**

Brockhole (Ire) *E J Alston* 54 a77
3 gr g Daylami (Ire) - Free Spirit (Ire)
2^{9sd} 6^{9gf} 7^{11g} 17^{7gf} 7^{9sd} **0-1-5 £1,290**

Broke Road (Ire) *Mrs H Dalton* 44
9 b g Deploy - Shamaka
3^{12f} 10^{12gf} **0-0-2 £427**

Broken Spur (Fr) *B W Hills* 75 a75
2 b c Bahri (USA) - Aerleon Jane
13^{6gs} 2^{6gf} 2^{7gf} 4^{7g} 5^{7g} 1^{7sd} 2^{7sd} **1-3-7**
£8,842

Bronwen (Ire) *J Noseda* 90
3 b f King's Best (USA) - Tegwen (USA)
2^{9gf} 1^{9g} 3^{11gs} 3^{14f} 1^{12g} 2^{12g} 1^{15s} 18^{18gs}
3-3-8 £20,090

Bronx Bomber *Dr J D Scargill* 46 a48
7 ch g Prince Sabo - Super Yankee (Ire)
4^{6sd} 6^{6hy} **0-0-2**

Bronze Dancer (Ire) *G A Swinbank* 70
3 b g Entrepreneur - Scrimshaw
2^{10s} 7^{10gf} 4^{10gf} 3^{12gf} 5^{12g} 13^{16gf} 7^{14s}
0-1-7 £3,282

Bronze Star *J R Fanshawe* 55
2 b f Mark Of Esteem (Ire) - White House
5^{6hy} **0-0-1**

Bronzed *J H M Gosden* 70
2 b g Bertolini (USA) - Jewel (Ire)
5^{6gs} 12^{6gs} 3^{6gf} 6^{6gf} **0-1-4 £648**

Brooklyn's Gold (USA) *Ian Williams* 63
10 b g Seeking The Gold (USA) - Brooklyn's Dance (Fr)
10^{10g} **0-0-1**

Brother Cadfael *John A Harris* a57
4 ch g So Factual (USA) - High Habit
1^{14sd} 2^{14sd} 4^{12sd} 5^{14sd} 3^{16sd} 2^{14sd} 7^{17sd} 4^{14sd}
8^{14sd} 6^{16gs} 8^{12ss} **1-3-11 £3,106**

Brother Edward (Ire) *Mrs John Harrington* 69 a51
3 b c Desert Story (Ire) - Alchiea
7^{9sd} 7^{8sd} 6^{12sd} 6^{13f} 4^{12ys} 6^{12gf} 13^{13gy}
0-0-7 £319

Brough Supreme *H Morrison* 42 a63
4 b g Sayaarr (USA) - Loriner's Lady
11^{16sd} 9^{11s} **0-0-2**

Broughton Buzzer *A G Newcombe* 58 a52
4 b f Rudimentary (USA) - Broughtons Lure (Ire)
8^{10sd} 9^{9sd} 1^{8sd} 4^{9sd} 1^{10gs} 3^{8g} 9^{10gf} 13^{9sd} 6^{8sd}
11^{8sd} **2-1-10 £4,410**

Broughton Knows *Mrs C J Ikin* 28 a70
8 b g Most Welcome - Broughtons Pet (Ire)
2^{14sd} 1^{16sd} 9^{12sd} 1^{12sd} 9^{12sd} 3^{14sd} 10^{17sd} 12^{16g}
2-2-8 £6,803

Broughton Treasure *W J Musson* 39
2 b f Bahamian Bounty - Quite Happy (Ire)
8^{5s} 8^{5gf} 3^{5g} **0-1-3 £419**

Brown Dragon *D Haydn Jones* a59
4 ch g Primo Dominie - Cole Slaw
5^{6sd} 3^{6sd} 5^{7sd} 6^{6sd} 7^{6sd} **0-1-5 £207**

Brown Fox (Fr) *C J Down* 52 a52
4 b f Polar Falcon (USA) - Garmeria (Fr)
13^{7sd} 8^{7sd} 8^{7sd} 15^{7g} **0-0-4**

Brunel (Ire) *W J Haggas* 116

4 b c Marju (Ire) - Castlerahan (Ire)
2^{8g} 2^{9g} 1^{7g} 4^{7gf} 3^{8g} 1^{8gf} **2-3-6**
£141,836

Brunelleschi *P L Gilligan* 78 a76
2 ch c Bertolini (USA) - Petrovna (Ire)
4^{6sd} 1^{5gf} 4^{5gs} 2^{5gs} 5^{5s} 9^{6sd} 3^{5sd} **1-1-7**
£7,266

Bruno Le Truffle *P F I Cole* 68 a50
3 b g Dansili - Crime Ofthecentury
5^{6sd} 2^{5s} 7^{6gs} **0-1-3 £1,732**

Brunston Castle *A W Carroll* 32 a27
5 b g Hector Protector (USA) - Villella
16^{10gf} 10^{12gf} 11^{17sd} 13^{16sd} **0-0-4**

Brut *D W Barker* 70 a60
3 b g Mind Games - Champenoise
3^{6sd} 6^{5sd} 6^{5sd} 2^{5g} 2^{6gf} 3^{5s} 3^{5g} 7^{6f} 9^{5g} 4^{7g}
5^{6g} 1^{6g} 5^{6gf} 9^{5gf} 3^{5g} 8^{6g} 2^{6gf} 2^{5g} 2^{5s}
1-8-19 £12,174

Buachaill Dona (Ire) *D Nicholls* 82
2 b c Namid - Serious Contender (Ire)
2^{6gf} **0-1-1 £1,400**

Bubbling Fun *T Wall* 68 a72
4 b f Marju (Ire) - Blushing Barada (USA)
7^{12sd} 3^{12sd} 10^{12sd} 1^{12sd} 4^{12sd} 8^{12sd} 6^{12gf} 10^{12g}
15^{12gs} 11^{10g} 11^{10gf} **1-1-11 £4,281**

Buchanan Street (Ire) *R Ford* a36
4 b g Barathea (Ire) - Please Believe Me
5^{17sd} 14^{12sd} 12^{12sd} 12^{14gf} **0-0-4**

Bucharest *R Charlton* 84
2 b c Barathea (Ire) - Zorleni
1^{6gf} 5^{7g} **1-0-2 £4,459**

Buck Whaley (Ire) *Jonjo O'Neill* 23 a48
5 ch g Fleetwood (Ire) - Kayzarana (Ire)
10^{10g} 13^{10g} 1^{11sd} **1-0-3 £1,426**

Buckle And Hyde *Mrs A L M King* 52
2 ch f Foxhound (USA) - Step On Degas
11^{6g} 16^{6g} 5^{6g} **0-0-3**

Bucks *Ian Williams* 83 a79
8 b g Slip Anchor - Alligram (USA)
3^{14gf} 3^{12g} 5^{12g} 6^{12g} 3^{12gs} 4^{13sd} 6^{12sd}
0-2-7 £5,955

Bucks Fantasy (Ire) *A Berry* 20
2 ch f Rossini (USA) - Fureur De Vivre (Ire)
11^{5gf} 5^{5f} 8^{5g} 10^{5gf} 12^{7g} 13^{7gf} **0-0-6**

Buddy Brown *J Howard Johnson* 65
3 b c Lujain (USA) - Rose Bay
9^{8g} **0-0-1**

Bulawayo *Andrew Reid* a41
8 b g Prince Sabo - Ra Ra Girl
13^{10sd} 6^{6sd} 11^{10sd} 6^{7sd} 6^{8sd} 6^{9sd} **0-0-6**

Bulberry Hill *R W Price* 43 a49
4 b g Makbul - Hurtleberry (Ire)
6^{9sd} 9^{9sd} 1^{12sd} 5^{14f} 5^{11gf} 7^{12sd} 2^{12sd} 3^{12sf}
10^{12sd} 1^{12sd} **2-2-10 £3,548**

Bull Market (Ire) *J A Osborne* a76
2 b c Danehill (USA) - Paper Moon (Ire)
2^{8sd} 2^{10sd} 1^{8sd} **1-2-3 £6,979**

Bullish Luck (USA) *A S Cruz* 122
6 b g Royal Academy (USA) - Wild Vintage (USA)
1^{8gf} 5^{10g} 1^{8gf} 6^{10gf} 1^{8gf} 4^{8f} 6^{8gf} 2^{8gf} 4^{8gf}
3-1-9 £926,391

Bullseye *P W D'Arcy* 47 a55
3 b g Polish Precedent (USA) - Native Flair
5^{6sd} 2^{5sd} 3^{6sd} 16^{8gf} 7^{8gf} 16^{8gf} **0-1-6**
£1,561

Bulwark (Ire) *Mrs A J Perrett* 97
3 b c Montjeu (Ire) - Bulaxie
3^{10s} 2^{10gf} 1^{13g} 2^{12gf} 1^{14f} 3^{14gf} 3^{14gf} 1^{15gf}
2^{16g} 1^{16g} **4-6-10 £29,535**

Bumptious *M H Tompkins* 74
4 b c Mister Baileys - Gleam Of Light (Ire)
20^{12gs} **0-0-1**

Bundaberg *P W Hiatt* 62 a69
5 b g Komaite (USA) - Lizzy Cantle
8^{11sd} 7^{9sd} 6^{10sd} 1^{8sd} 6^{11sd} 4^{9sd} 12^{10sd} 13^{8gs}
6^{10f} 7^{8s} 8^{8gf} 2^{9gf} 2^{8f} 3^{8f} 3^{10s} 13^{11gf} 5^{9gf}
2^{8gf} 3^{10g} 10^{11sd} **1-5-20 £8,144**

Bunditten (Ire) *C F Wall* 74
3 gr f Soviet Star (USA) - Felicita (Ire)
5^{5gf} 12^{6gs} **0-0-2**

Bundy *M Dods* 66
9 b g Ezzoud (Ire) - Sanctuary Cove
1^{6gs} 2^{6gs} 3^{6gs} 8^{6gf} 9^{6gf} 3^{6s} **1-3-6**
£5,823

Bunkhouse *Mrs N Macauley* 37 a42
5 ch g Wolfhound (USA) - Maid Welcome
11^{5sd} 7^{5sd} 9^{6sd} 4^{6sd} 6^{5sd} 5^{6sd} 4^{5sd} 3^{5sd} 8^{6gs}
11^{5s} 5^{6gf} 12^{6gf} 11^{9sf} **0-1-13 £470**

Bunood (Ire) *J L Dunlop* 91
2 b f Sadler's Wells (USA) - Azdihaar (USA)
1^{8g} 2^{8s} **1-1-2 £10,071**

Buon Amici *W J Musson* 41
4 b f Pivotal - Supreme Rose
8^{8s} 8^{7g} 8^{8g} **0-0-3**

Bureaucrat *J H M Gosden* 98 a91
3 b g Machiavellian (USA) - Lajna
4^{8hy} 1^{10gf} 1^{10g} 9^{12gf} 8^{10sd} **2-0-5 £7,953**

Burford Lass (Ire) *D K Ivory* 64 a10
2 b f Quws - Dancing Willma (Ire)
10^{5sd} 8^{6g} 3^{5gf} 3^{5gf} 3^{6gf} 5^{5f} **0-2-6**
£1,747

Burgundy *P Mitchell* 80 a81
8 b g Lycius (USA) - Decant
4^{10sd} 1^{10sd} 13^{10sd} 3^{10sd} 3^{10sd} 6^{10sd} 4^{10gf} 3^{9gf}
2^{10gf} 5^{10g} 5^{10g} 1^{10g} 1^{10s} 3^{10g} 4^{10g} 5^{10s} 2^{12sd}
4^{10sd} 5^{8sd} 6^{10sd} **3-6-20 £22,818**

Burhaan (Ire) *J H M Gosden* 68 a72
3 b c Green Desert (USA) - Arjuzah (Ire)
3^{6gf} 13^{6g} 7^{5gf} 6^{5gf} 6^{6s} 8^{6g} 2^{7sd} 1^{9sd} 5^{9sd}
1-2-9 £4,696

Burkees Graw (Ire) *Mrs S Lamyman* 43
4 ch g Fayruz - Dancing Willma (Ire)
6^{7g} 13^{7g} 10^{6gs} 17^{5gf} 10^{6g} 5^{5f} 11^{5gf}
0-0-7

Burley Flame *J G Given* 83 a93
4 b g Marju (Ire) - Tarsa
7^{8gf} 8^{7gs} 4^{7g} 9^{6gf} 4^{6gf} 2^{7g} 5^{8g} 2^{7gf} 8^{8g} 3^{7g}
10^{7gf} 2^{7ft} 9^{7s} **0-5-13 £7,961**

Burnbank (Ire) *W Jarvis* 59 a66
2 ch c Danehill Dancer (Ire) - Roseau
6^{7sd} 8^{8gf} **0-0-2**

Burning Incense (Ire) *R Charlton* 70
2 b c Namid - Night Scent (Ire)
11^{6gs} 5^{6g} **0-0-2**

Burning Moon *K A Morgan* 18
4 b g Bering - Triple Green
11^{10g} 16^{11gs} **0-0-2**

Burnley Al (Ire) *R A Fahey* 66 a36
3 ch g Desert King (Ire) - Bold Meadows
9^{6s} 9^{8g} 4^{8g} 9^{8gf} 2^{7gf} 3^{7gf} 6^{10g} 2^{8gf} 1^{7gf} 4^{8gf}
2^{8gf} 13^{8gf} 11^{8sd} 9^{8sd} **1-4-14 £8,988**

Burton Ash *J G Given* 73
3 b/br f Diktat - Incendio
2^{8g} 4^{8gf} 13^{8g} 5^{8g} 2^{8gf} 3^{10gf} 2^{8gf} 6^{8gs} 5^{8gf} 6^{8gf} 7^{8g} 6^{8gf} 3^{8s} **0-6-13 £4,730**

Busaco *J L Dunlop* 72
3 b c Mister Baileys - War Shanty
6^{8s} 9^{8gs} 5^{11g} 2^{12f} 6^{13gf} 1^{12g} 2^{11gf} 9^{14gf} 7^{12s} 3^{12gf} 9^{12gf} **1-3-11 £7,310**

Buscador (USA) *W M Brisbourne* a71
6 ch g Crafty Prospector (USA) - Fairway Flag (USA)
12^{9sd} 6^{9sd} 1^{9sd} 2^{9sd} 2^{9sd} 1^{9sd} 6^{9sd} 2^{9sd} 6^{9sd} 8^{9sd} **2-3-10 £7,986**

Bust (Ire) *T D Easterby* 17
3 b g Fraam - Purse
10^{7s} 12^{9gf} 10^{12g} **0-0-3**

Buster Hyvonen (Ire) *J R Fanshawe* 74 a71
3 b g Dansili - Serotina (Ire)
2^{8sd} 1^{8sd} 11^{10gs} 4^{8gf} **1-1-4 £4,120**

Busy Shark (Ire) *M R Channon* 64
2 gr g Shinko Forest (Ire) - Felicita (Ire)
6^{6f} 10^{8g} 4^{8gf} **0-0-3 £246**

Buthaina (Ire) *Mrs L Williamson* 42
5 b m Bahhare (USA) - Haddeyah (USA)
5^{10gf} 6^{8gf} 4^{9f} 5^{8gf} 4^{8f} 12^{8g} 12^{7sd} **0-0-7 £624**

Butterfly Bud (Ire) *N Tinkler* 64
2 b g Lend A Hand - Rathbawn Realm
4^{5g} 6^{5gs} 9^{6g} 2^{6gs} 15^{6gs} 4^{7gf} **0-1-6 £2,003**

Buy On The Red *W R Muir* 90
4 b g Komaite (USA) - Red Rosein
19^{6gf} 10^{6g} 9^{6g} 5^{7gf} 6^{7gf} 7^{7gf} 12^{7g} 6^{7gf} 11^{6g} **0-0-9**

Buz Kiri (USA) *A W Carroll* 38 a45
7 b g Gulch (USA) - Whitecorners (USA)
12^{11sd} 7^{9sd} 4^{13sd} 6^{17sd} 7^{12sd} 4^{12g} 4^{14g} 8^{12g} 9^{12g} 7^{14gf} 9^{12gf} **0-0-11**

Buzz Buzz *C E Brittain* a49
4 b f Mtoto - Abuzz
8^{8sd} 9^{8sd} 5^{7sd} **0-0-3**

Buzz Maite *P Butler* 19
3 b g Komaite (USA) - Scotland Bay
11^{8gf} 9^{8gf} **0-0-2**

Buzzin'Boyzee (Ire) *P D Evans* 58 a60
2 ch f Monashee Mountain (USA) - Las Bela
4^{5g} 6^{6gs} 7^{6sd} 9^{6gf} 6^{5g} 5^{5f} 1^{5sd} 9^{5g} 12^{7sd} 2^{6sd} **1-1-10 £3,756**

By Storm *John Berry* a39
2 b f Largesse - Polar Storm (Ire)
12^{7sd} 5^{5sd} 10^{5sd} **0-0-3**

Bygone Days *W J Haggas* 109
4 ch g Desert King (Ire) - May Light
10^{5s} 1^{6g} 8^{6gf} 6^{6g} 1^{6gs} **2-0-5 £26,382**

Byo (Ire) *P Howling* 67 a77
7 gr g Paris House - Navan Royal (Ire)
9^{5sd} 3^{5sd} 3^{5sd} 6^{5sd} 1^{5sd} 5^{5s} 8^{5sd} 7^{5g} 7^{5gf} 3^{5sd} 5^{5g} 4^{5gf} 5^{5gf} 8^{5g} 6^{6gs} 4^{5f} 4^{5g} 13^{5gf} 12^{5sd} 4^{5sd} 6^{5ss} 11^{6sd} 13^{5sd} **1-3-23 £5,804**

Byron *Saeed Bin Suroor* 116
4 b c Green Desert (USA) - Gay Gallanta (USA)
2^{7g} 6^{6f} **0-1-2 £14,658**

Byron Bay *I Semple* 81 a83
3 b c My Best Valentine - Candarela
7^{8gs} 1^{9gs} 8^{10gf} 2^{8gs} 5^{8gf} 12^{7g} 2^{10s} 4^{10s} 2^{8hy} 1^{8sd} **2-3-10 £18,464**

C'Est La Vie *Miss J E Foster* 51
3 ch f Bering - Action De Grace (USA)
8^{7g} 7^{8g} 8^{10gs} 3^{12f} 11^{10gf} **0-0-5 £521**

Caamora (Ire) *J Noseda* 68
2 b f Cape Cross (Ire) - Tarafiya (USA)
4^{8gf} **0-0-1 £557**

Caan *D K Ivory* 62 a45
2 br g Averti (Ire) - Bellifontaine (Fr)
5^{5gs} 4^{5gf} 6^{6f} 10^{6sd} 5^{7g} 12^{6gf} **0-0-6 £390**

Cabopino Lad (USA) *Miss Tracy Waggott* a21
3 b g Comic Strip (USA) - Roxanne (USA)
12^{12sd} 12^{12s} 14^{11ss} **0-0-3**

Cabourg (Ire) *C R Egerton* 79 a38
2 b c Danehill (USA) - Loire Valley (Ire)
8^{6sd} 3^{6gf} 2^{7gf} 4^{8gf} **0-2-4 £2,412**

Cactus King *J H M Gosden* 55 a84
2 b c Green Desert (USA) - Apache Star
13^{6gs} 3^{8sd} 1^{8sd} **1-1-3 £4,595**

Cadeaux Rouge (Ire) *D W Thompson* 39
4 ch f Croco Rouge (Ire) - Gift Of Glory (Fr)
14^{8s} 6^{12gs} 2^{14f} 5^{12gf} 12^{14f} 11^{16f} 4^{16gf} **0-1-7 £822**

Cadogen Square *Mrs Marjorie Fife* 52 a43
3 ch f Takhlid (USA) - Mount Park (Ire)
11^{6sd} 8^{5sd} 7^{6g} 2^{7gf} 2^{6sd} 14^{8gf} 2^{7gf} 8^{7f} 1^{7gf} 4^{6gf} 9^{7gs} 7^{8gf} 1^{7g} 10^{7sd} 11^{7sd} **2-3-15 £7,865**

Caerphilly Gal *P L Gilligan* 57 a56
5 b m Averti (Ire) - Noble Lustre (USA)
5^{8g} 4^{8s} 15^{8f} 11^{7g} 4^{8g} 9^{8gf} 1^{8f} 2^{7sd} 4^{6sd} 3^{8hy} 2^{8ss} 1^{7ss} 3^{7sd} 3^{7sd} 6^{7ss} **2-6-15 £5,144**

Caesar Beware (Ire) *H Candy* 101
3 b g Daggers Drawn (USA) - Red Shareef
4^{6gs} 3^{7g} **0-0-2 £3,820**

Calabaza *W Jarvis* 71
3 ch c Zaha (Can) - Mo Stopher
8^{6g} 3^{6g} 3^{6gs} 7^{6g} 10^{6g} 5^{7g} 1^{6g} 10^{6g} **1-1-8 £7,727**

Calamari (Ire) *Mrs A Duffield* 59
3 ch f Desert King (Ire) - Mrs Fisher (Ire)
4^{10gf} 5^{10gf} 4^{8s} **0-0-3 £677**

Calamintha *M C Pipe* 83
5 b m Mtoto - Calendula
1^{14gs} 8^{14gf} 22^{18gs} **1-0-3 £2,783**

Calara Hills *W M Brisbourne* 36 a30
4 ch f Bluegrass Prince (Ire) - Atlantic Line
4^{12sd} 6^{12s} 5^{16sd} 6^{10g} 6^{12gf} **0-0-5**

Calatagan (Ire) *J M Jefferson* 69 a74
6 ch g Danzig Connection (USA) - Calachuchi
4^{12sd} 16^{12g} 2^{12gf} 2^{12gf} **0-2-4 £3,588**

Calcar (Ire) *Mrs S Lamyman* a18
5 b g Flying Spur (Aus) - Poscimur (Ire)
10^{14sd} **0-0-1**

Calculaite *M Todhunter* 69 a69
4 b g Komaite (USA) - Miss Calculate
3^{9sd} 1^{9sd} 1^{8gf} 4^{8gf} 7^{8gf} 4^{10s} 5^{8gf} 1^{10g} 11^{8gf} 7^{10gs} **3-2-10 £12,434**

Calcutta *B W Hills* 100
9 b h Indian Ridge - Echoing
4^{8g} 14^{9g} 8^{8g} 21^{8gf} 10^{8gf} 5^{8gf} 5^{10gs} 2^{8gf} 3^{8gf} 5^{8g} **0-2-10 £13,036**

Caledonian (Ire) *D R C Elsworth* 44 a98
4 b g Soviet Star (USA) - Supercal

7^{10sd} 3^{10sd} 5^{10sd} 16^{10s} **0-1-4 £3,466**

Calfraz *M D Hammond* 50
3 b/br g Tamure (Ire) - Pas De Chat
11^{9gf} 8^{10gf} 6^{12f} **0-0-3**

Caliban (Ire) *Ian Williams* 28 a42
7 ch g Rainbows For Life (Can) - Amour Toujours (Ire)
10^{17sd} 11^{12gf} **0-0-2**

California Bay (Ire) *C P Donoghue* a13
5 b g Key Of Luck (USA) - Sally Gone (Ire)
12^{9sd} **0-0-1**

California Laws *T D Barron* 69 a61
3 b g Pivotal - Noor El Houdah (Ire)
5^{5gf} 5^{5g} 4^{5gs} 6^{5g} 15^{5gf} 3^{6sd} **0-1-6 £872**

Call Me George *M Johnston* 37
2 ch c Rainbow Quest (USA) - Coretta (Ire)
11^{8g} **0-0-1**

Call Me Max *E A L Dunlop* 87 a73
3 b g Vettori (Ire) - Always Vigilant (USA)
2^{9s} 2^{9sd} 5^{8gf} 1^{7gf} 1^{7gf} 4^{7g} 8^{8g} **2-3-7**
£12,630

Call Me Punch *C N Kellett* 69
4 ch g Bettergeton - Tradjazz
3^{7gs} **0-1-1 £676**

Call Me Waki (USA) *A M Balding* 74
2 ch f Miswaki (USA) - S S Capote (USA)
7^{6s} 3^{6gf} 2^{6gf} **0-1-3 £3,019**

Call My Number (Ire) *M R Channon* 79
2 b c Grand Lodge (USA) - Screen Idol (Ire)
3^{6gs} 1^{7gf} 5^{8g} **1-1-3 £5,111**

Callanish *M L W Bell* 12
2 ch f Inchinor - Lalindi (Ire)
11^{7s} 13^{8hy} **0-0-2**

Caloosa *C A Dwyer* 58
2 b c Fraam - Dominelle
5^{6gf} 11^{5gs} 4^{6gf} 12^{7g} 4^{7gf} 1^{7gf} 3^{7g} 8^{6f}
1-1-8 £4,287

Caluki *L Camici* 103 a96
8 b h Kris - Chevisaunce
1^{8s} 5^{10sd} 2^{8s} 13^{10sd} **1-0-4 £5,606**

Calusa Lady (Ire) *J A Geake* 45
5 ch m Titus Livius (Fr) - Solas Abu (Ire)
4^{7gs} 9^{6gs} 7^{6gf} 6^{6s} 12^{6gs} **0-1-5**

Calvera *B J Meehan* 56 a56
2 b g Xaar - Shona (USA)
7^{6gs} 10^{6gs} 7^{6gf} 6^{7sd} 10^{7s} 7^{6sd} 10^{6gf} 12^{7gf}
0-0-8

Caly Dancer (Ire) *D R C Elsworth* 81
3 ch g Entrepreneur - Mountain Dancer (Ire)
9^{9gf} 6^{8g} 9^{8f} 18^{8gs} 12^{7gf} **0-0-5 £228**

Calypso King *J W Hills* 88 a77
2 gr g Agnes World (USA) - T G's Girl
8^{6gf} 6^{5gs} 1^{5sd} 1^{5gf} 6^{6gf} 13^{6gf} **2-0-6**
£19,770

Camacho *H R A Cecil* 115
3 b c Danehill (USA) - Arabesque
1^{6g} 2^{7gf} 10^{6gs} 7^{6gs} **1-1-4 £30,540**

Camberwell *T G Mills* 30 a58
4 b g Royal Applause - Into Orbit
14^{7g} 10^{7sd} **0-0-2**

Cambo (Fr) *Miss Sheena West* 49 a67
4 b/br g Mansonnien (Fr) - Royal Lie (Fr)
1^{17sd} 2^{16sd} 6^{16sd} 7^{14gs} 12^{14sd} **1-1-5**
£3,997

Came Back (Ire) *J A Osborne* a35
2 ch c Bertolini (USA) - Distant Decree (USA)
7^{6sd} **0-0-1**

Camerino (USA) *Andre Hermans* a49
7 ch h Gone West (USA) - Chinese Empress (USA)
0^{12sd} 5^{16sd} 0^{13hy} 0^{11hy} **0-0-4**

Cameron Orchid (Ire) *M A Jarvis* 63 a71
3 b f Sri Pekan (USA) - London Pride (USA)
7^{8gf} 3^{10sd} 4^{12sd} 8^{12gs} 7^{12g} **0-1-5 £803**

Camille Pissarro (USA) *D J Wintle* 70 a62
5 b g Red Ransom (USA) - Serenity
10^{8sd} 16^{8gs} 1^{7sd} 1^{6g} 14^{8g} **2-0-5**
£3,199

Camp Commander (Ire) *C R Dore* 40
6 gr h Pennekamp (USA) - Khalatara (Ire)
6^{7gs} **0-0-1**

Campanile *J R Fanshawe* 70
2 ch f Zilzal (USA) - High Barn
4^{7s} **0-0-1 £441**

Campbells Lad *A Berry* 45 a44
4 b g Mind Games - T O O Mamma'S (Ire)
10^{8sd} 6^{9sd} 11^{9gf} 4^{11g} 16^{10gs} 4^{8gf} 12^{8gf} 4^{8gf}
13^{9g} 12^{11gs} 12^{7sd} **0-2-11 £274**

Campbeltown (Ire) *E J O'Neill* 103 a82
2 b c Mull Of Kintyre (USA) - Jallaissine (Ire)
7^{5gf} 2^{5sd} 2^{6gf} 7^{7gf} 1^{6sd} 2^{6sd} 2^{6sd} 6^{6gf} 1^{6gs}
3^{6gf} 2^{5g} 2^{6g} **2-7-12 £31,320**

Campeon (Ire) *J M Bradley* 69 a58
3 b g Monashee Mountain (USA) - Arcticlead (USA)
5^{6s} 6^{5g} 1^{5s} 13^{6gs} 2^{5f} 4^{5gf} 9^{5g} 8^{5gf} 5^{5g} 8^{6gf}
2^{6gf} 6^{5gf} 1^{5s} 14^{6gf} 5^{5gf} 10^{6g} 8^{5s} 2^{5gs} 1^{5s}
8^{5sf} 12^{6sd} **3-3-21 £17,233**

Camrose *J L Dunlop* 105
4 ch c Zafonic (USA) - Tularosa
8^{12gf} 6^{12gf} 4^{12g} 8^{12gf} 4^{14gs} 1^{12g} 8^{15gs} 2^{12g}
3^{12s} **1-3-9 £33,875**

Canacham *D L Williams*
6 ch m Beveled (USA) - Austral Jane
12^{10sd} 14^{7sd} **0-0-2**

Canadian Danehill (Ire) *R M H Cowell* 67 a68
3 b c Indian Danehill (Ire) - San Jovita (Can)
3^{7sd} 2^{6sd} 6^{6sd} 1^{5sd} 5^{5sd} 4^{5s} 3^{5s} 3^{7s} 1^{5f} 2^{5gf}
1^{6gf} 10^{5gf} 11^{7gf} 4^{5g} 11^{6g} 9^{7gf} 5^{6gf} 10^{5gf}
3-5-18 £17,396

Canadian Storm *A G Juckes* 25
4 gr g With Approval (Can) - Sheer Gold (USA)
8^{12gf} **0-0-1**

Canary Dancer *Miss Z C Davison* 45 a44
3 b f Groom Dancer (USA) - Bird Of Time (Ire)
8^{6sd} 6^{6sd} 2^{6sd} 5^{6f} 12^{6f} 5^{6gs} 10^{5f} 3^{6g} 5^{6f}
9^{5gf} 6^{6gf} 8^{6g} 8^{6sd} 5^{8sd} 9^{7g} 6^{8sd} 3^{6sd} 5^{7sd}
3^{8sd} 9^{6sd} 4^{8sd} 11^{6sd} **0-4-22 £1,303**

Canary Girl *P D Evans* 35 a19
2 br f Primo Valentino (Ire) - Cumbrian Concerto
12^{6gf} 8^{6gf} 11^{8g} 9^{6sd} **0-0-4**

Canary Island (Ire) *D R C Elsworth* 70
3 b g Polar Falcon (USA) - Yellow Trumpet
7^{5gs} 4^{6gf} **0-0-2**

Candleriggs (Ire) *D Nicholls* 47 a54
9 ch g Indian Ridge - Ridge Pool (Ire)
11^{7sd} 5^{6sd} 10^{6gs} 8^{7g} 4^{7g} **0-0-5**

Candy Anchor (Fr) *R E Peacock* a44
6 b m Slip Anchor - Kandavu
5^{9sd} **0-0-1**

Canina *Ms Deborah J Evans* 65 a65
2 b f Foxhound (USA) - Fizzy Fiona
5^{5g} 6^{5gf} 9^{6g} 2^{6s} 3^{6hy} 3^{5sd} 2^{5sd} 2^{5sf} 7^{6sd} 8^{5sd}

2^{6sd} **0-6-11 £4,593**

Cannygo (Ire) *R M Flower* a2
2 b g Brave Act - Cannylass (Ire)
11^{8sd} **0-0-1**

Cantabilly (Ire) *M R Channon* 70
2 b c Distant Music (USA) - Cantaloupe
5^{8g} 6^{7f} 12^{8g} **0-0-3**

Cantabria *Sir Michael Stoute* 99
2 br f Dansili - Valencia
2^{6gs} 1^{6gs} 7^{6gf} 2^{7gs} 2^{7gs} **1-3-5 £20,927**

Cantarna (Ire) *J Mackie* 75 a73
4 ch f Ashkalani (Ire) - Lancea (Ire)
3^{8s} 4^{8s} 4^{7s} 6^{7gf} 3^{7g} 4^{8gf} 5^{8g} 3^{8s} 2^{9sd} 6^{8sd} **0-4-10 £4,287**

Cantemerle (Ire) *W M Brisbourne* 35
5 b m Bluebird (USA) - Legally Delicious
7^{12s} 5^{12s} 4^{14f} **0-0-3**

Cantrip *Miss B Sanders* 63 a58
5 b m Celtic Swing - Circe
1^{13f} 5^{12gf} 2^{13gf} 6^{16g} 2^{12g} 8^{16gf} 1^{12gs} 7^{12sd} **2-2-8 £8,933**

Canvas (Ire) *H Candy* 45
2 b f Dansili - Sampan
10^{8g} **0-0-1**

Canyouwin *J H M Gosden* 24
2 b f Inchinor - Tharwa (Ire)
22^{7s} **0-0-1**

Caona (USA) *J Noseda* a70
3 b f Miswaki (USA) - Hawzah
2^{7sd} 10^{9sd} 11^{8sd} **0-1-3 £1,040**

Capable Guest (Ire) *M R Channon* 103
3 b g Cape Cross (Ire) - Alexander Confranc (Ire)
2^{8gs} 14^{8gf} 7^{8s} 6^{8g} 18^{7gf} 10^{8gf} 7^{7s} 2^{7g} 12^{7gf} 13^{8gf} 13^{8gf} 7^{8g} 10^{8g} **0-2-13 £16,447**

Cape Columbine *D R C Elsworth* 106
3 b/br f Diktat - Cape Merino
2^{7gf} 5^{8gf} 4^{8gf} 6^{8g} **0-1-4 £34,622**

Cape Courier (Ire) *I W McInnes* 45
2 b c Cape Cross (Ire) - Russian Countess (USA)
9^{6gf} 10^{5g} 12^{6g} 9^{7s} **0-0-4**

Cape Diamond (Ire) *W R Swinburn* 71
2 b c Cape Cross (Ire) - Jemalina (USA)
3^{6gs} 5^{6gf} 5^{6g} **0-1-3 £842**

Cape Enterprise (USA) *J W Hills* 71 a69
3 b c Cape Canaveral (USA) - Principessa (USA)
5^{10sd} 10^{10gs} 3^{11g} 5^{11gf} 5^{10gf} 11^{10gs} **0-1-6 £591**

Cape Fear *B J Meehan* 108 a96
4 b c Cape Cross (Ire) - Only In Dreams
3^{7sd} 2^{7gs} 0^{7g} 5^{8gs} 5^{7gf} 9^{8gs} **0-1-6 £9,518**

Cape Gigi (Ire) *B J Meehan* a38
2 b f Cape Cross (Ire) - L'Accolade (Ire)
8^{6sd} 8^{7sd} **0-0-2**

Cape Gold (Ire) *R A Fahey* 74
2 b g Cape Cross (Ire) - Filigree
2^{6g} 4^{6gf} 9^{6g} 19^{6gs} **0-1-4 £2,674**

Cape Greko *A M Balding* 96
3 ro g Loup Sauvage (USA) - Oneforthreditch (USA)
5^{8g} 3^{9gf} 5^{12gs} **0-0-3 £3,653**

Cape Latina *J R Best* 39
2 b f Cape Cross (Ire) - Latina (Ire)
13^{5gs} 6^{5f} 10^{6gf} **0-0-3**

Cape Of Good Hope *D Oughton* 121
7 ch g Inchinor - Cape Merino
3^{5gs} 1^{6g} 5^{5gy} 3^{6gf} 4^{5gf} 1^{6f} 1^{16f} 3^{6g} 3^{6g} 5^{5gf} **2-3-10 £381,162**

Cape Of Luck (Ire) *P Mitchell* 83 a86
2 b c Cape Cross (Ire) - Fledgling
1^{5gf} 2^{5gf} 5^{5g} 2^{6gf} 1^{6sd} 9^{7gs} 7^{7sd} **2-2-7 £12,893**

Cape Presto (Ire) *R Hannon* 88
2 b c Cape Cross (Ire) - Samhat Mtoto
7^{6gs} 1^{7gf} 6^{7gs} 4^{6gf} 9^{7gs} 1^{8f} 4^{8g} **2-0-7 £9,839**

Cape Royal *J M Bradley* 103 a82
5 b g Prince Sabo - Indigo
4^{5gs} 1^{5g} 3^{5gs} 14^{5gs} 5^{5s} 8^{5gs} 10^{5g} 13^{5g} 11^{5g} 10^{5sd} 10^{5gf} 11^{5s} 8^{5s} 1^{5s} 2^{5g} 6^{5g} 5^{6gf} 2^{5gf} 2^{5gs} 2^{5g} 4^{5s} 9^{5hy} **2-5-22 £52,208**

Cape Secret (Ire) *R M Beckett* 53 a56
2 b g Cape Cross (Ire) - Baylands Sunshine (Ire)
9^{8g} 9^{8gs} 4^{7sd} **0-0-3 £238**

Cape St Vincent *H Morrison* 83 a83
5 gr g Paris House - Cape Merino
6^{7sd} 9^{8sd} 2^{7sd} 4^{6s} 4^{6g} 5^{7g} 1^{6gf} 4^{6f} **1-2-8 £10,370**

Cape Sydney (Ire) *D W Barker* 44
2 b f Cape Cross (Ire) - Lady At War
6^{6g} 7^{7g} 11^{7gf} 11^{6g} **0-0-4**

Cape Unknown (USA) *G A Butler* 69 a64
3 b/br g Cape Canaveral (USA) - Danyross (Ire)
5^{7sd} 2^{6f} 2^{5g} 4^{6gf} 2^{5gf} DSQ^{6g} 6^{6sd} 11^{5f} 7^{5gf} **0-3-9 £3,707**

Cape Venus (Ire) *R Curtis* 52 a32
3 b f Cape Cross (Ire) - Lady Helen (Ire)
11^{8g} 9^{8g} 4^{7g} 12^{8ss} **0-0-4 £303**

Cape Win (Ire) *W J Haggas* 67 a69
2 b c Cape Cross (Ire) - Monarchy (Ire)
6^{7g} 7^{7s} 2^{7sd} 5^{7sf} 7^{8sd} **0-1-5 £1,400**

Capistrano *B W Hills* 45 a69
2 b c Efisio - Washita
11^{6gf} 8^{6s} 3^{6sd} **0-1-3 £564**

Capital Lass *M J Wallace* 53 a5
2 b/br f Forzando - Fair Test
1^{5gf} 9^{6g} 7^{5gs} 7^{5gf} 12^{6sd} **1-0-5 £1,498**

Capitalise (Ire) *V Smith* 46
2 b g City On A Hill (USA) - Prime Interest (Ire)
11^{7g} 11^{7gf} 12^{8s} **0-0-3**

Capitana (Ger) *N J Henderson* 85
4 ch f Lando (Ger) - Capitolina (Fr)
5^{10gf} 9^{10gf} 4^{10g} **0-0-3 £536**

Capitol Kid (Ire) *Mrs L Stubbs* 52 a64
2 b g Distant Music (USA) - Danalia (Ire)
5^{6g} 1^{6sd} 10^{6gf} 7^{7sd} 15^{6g} **1-0-5 £3,399**

Capped For Victory (USA) *W S Cunningham* 42
4 b g Red Ransom (USA) - Nazoo (Ire)
9^{7g} 13^{7gf} **0-0-2**

Capricho (Ire) *J Akehurst* 101
8 gr g Lake Coniston (Ire) - Star Spectacle
4^{6g} 10^{6gf} 15^{7g} 16^{6g} 15^{7gs} 20^{7gs} 10^{6s} 17^{7s} **0-0-8 £1,043**

Capricorn Cate *M D Hammond* 5 a2
3 b f Josr Algarhoud (Ire) - Billsha
5^{9sd} 12^{5sd} 17^{6g} 6^{6s} **0-0-4**

Capricorn Run (USA) *Saeed Bin Suroor* 84
2 b/br c Elusive Quality (USA) - Cercida (USA)
6^{7gf} 1^{7gf} 9^{7g} **1-0-3 £5,577**

Captain Bolsh *J Pearce* 65 a57
2 b g Tagula (Ire) - Bolshoi Star

6^{5g} 3^{6sd} 5^{6gf} 5^{7g} 8^{7g} 5^{6f} 5^{6gf} **0-1-7 £661**

Captain Clipper *J R Fanshawe* 82
5 b g Royal Applause - Collide
5^{10g} 8^{12gs} **0-0-2 £260**

Captain Cloudy *Miss Sheena West* 54 a50
5 b g Whittingham (Ire) - Money Supply
10^{10sd} 2^{10sd} 3^{7sd} 11^{10sd} 3^{8gf} 6^{7f} 1^{10gf} 4^{11gf} **1-3-8 £4,485**

Captain Darling (Ire) *R W Price* 44 a67
5 b g Pennekamp (USA) - Gale Warning (Ire)
1^{7sd} 8^{7sd} 10^{7sd} 4^{6sd} 7^{6s} 5^{7sd} 6^{6sd} 10^{6f} 3^{6sd} 10^{6gf} 7^{7sd} 10^{7sd} 2^{8ss} 3^{9sd} 1^{7ss} 4^{8sd} 1^{7sd} **3-3-17 £8,093**

Captain Do Ins (UAE) *J J Bridger* 3
3 b g Timber Country (USA) - Sandova (Ire)
18^{10g} 12^{8gs} 17^{10gs} **0-0-3**

Captain General *J A R Toller* 67
3 br c In The Wings - Sea Quest (Ire)
8^{12gf} 6^{12g} 5^{10s} **0-0-3**

Captain Hurricane *P W Chapple-Hyam* 66
3 b c Desert Style (Ire) - Ravine
9^{7gs} 14^{6f} **0-0-2**

Captain Johnno (Ire) *D R Loder* 82 a82
3 b g Tagula (Ire) - Thornby Park
8^{7sd} 2^{6sd} 4^{5sd} 4^{6g} 3^{6gf} PU^{6g} **0-1-6 £4,166**

Captain Margaret *J Pearce* 66 a69
3 b f Royal Applause - Go For Red (Ire)
7^{10s} 2^{10gf} 11^{10gf} 4^{11gf} 10^{10g} 5^{10f} 1^{12sd} 1^{12sd} **2-1-8 £7,133**

Captain Miller *N J Henderson* 74
9 b g Batshoof - Miller's Gait
6^{14g} 5^{16gs} 7^{22f} **0-0-3**

Captain Saif *N Wilson* 19
5 b g Compton Place - Bahawir Pour (USA)
17^{8g} 13^{7gf} 5^{12gf} **0-0-3**

Captain Smoothy *M J Gingell* 49
5 b g Charmer - The Lady Captain
10^{10gf} 6^{11gf} 5^{12gf} 7^{16g} 9^{16gf} **0-0-5**

Captain Torrance (Ire) *P W Chapple-Hyam* 52
2 b c Titus Livius (Fr) - Gay's Flutter
6^{6g} **0-0-1**

Captain Xaar (Fr) *J R Fanshawe* 43
2 b c Xaar - Rabea (USA)
19^{7s} **0-0-1**

Captivate *M J Polglase* 51 a56
2 ch f Hernando (Fr) - Catch (USA)
6^{6gf} 4^{7gf} 10^{7g} 10^{7gf} 1^{8gf} 11^{8f} 19^{8hy} 2^{8sd} 7^{8ss} **1-1-9 £3,881**

Caradak (Ire) *John M Oxx* 118
4 b c Desert Style (Ire) - Caraiyma (Ire)
9^{8gf} 1^{8gf} 1^{7gf} 1^{8gf} 2^{7s} **3-1-5 £147,745**

Caragh Mia (Ire) *G A Butler* 79 a79
3 b f Desert Prince (Ire) - Decant
1^{8gf} 10^{8gf} 2^{9sd} 12^{10gs} 3^{8gf} 12^{8gf} 4^{8sd} 5^{8sd} 4^{8sd} **1-2-9 £7,626**

Caraman (Ire) *J J Quinn* a65
7 ch h Grand Lodge (USA) - Caraiyma (Ire)
3^{12sd} **0-1-1 £520**

Carcinetto (Ire) *B Palling* 42 a55
3 b f Danetime (Ire) - Dolphin Stamp (Ire)
12^{8sd} 10^{8gs} 9^{7gf} 9^{5g} 1^{6sd} 6^{6sd} 11^{5sd} **1-0-7 £1,487**

Cardigan Kid (USA) *H Morrison* 15
2 b c Honour And Glory (USA) - Lovely Keri (USA)
12^{9gf} 15^{10g} **0-0-2**

Cardinal Venture (Ire) *K A Ryan* 100 a99
7 b g Bishop Of Cashel - Phoenix Venture (Ire)
4^{7sd} 4^{9sd} 1^{7sd} 14^{8g} 8^{8gs} 3^{7gf} 6^{7gf} 18^{8g} 14^{6gf} 11^{8gf} 5^{7g} 1^{7s} 9^{9sd} **2-1-13 £25,843**

Carefree Girl *E A Wheeler* 16 a40
2 b f Josr Algarhoud (Ire) - Double Fault (Ire)
14^{5gs} 6^{7sd} **0-0-2**

Cargo *Peter Grayson* 13 a59
6 b g Emarati (USA) - Portvasco
3^{6sd} 3^{5sd} 3^{5sd} 4^{5sd} 1^{6sd} 2^{5sd} 4^{6sd} 7^{5sd} 13^{6sd} 10^{5sd} 12^{5sd} 14^{6gf} 10^{5sd} **1-4-13 £5,414**

Caribbean Coral *J J Quinn* 95
6 ch g Brief Truce (USA) - Caribbean Star
10^{5g} 9^{5gs} 11^{5g} 7^{6f} 10^{5g} 22^{6gs} 17^{5gf} 12^{5gf} **0-0-8**

Caribbean Dancer (USA) *M Johnston* 74
3 b f Theatrical - Enticed (USA)
8^{10g} 7^{12g} 14^{12gf} 4^{12gf} 14^{14g} 13^{16g} 3^{11gf} 1^{10g} 1^{10gs} 3^{10gs} **2-2-10 £11,391**

Caribbean Nights (Ire) *T D Easterby* 37 a60
2 b g Night Shift (USA) - Caribbean Knockout (Ire)
15^{7gf} 4^{7sd} 7^{7s} 4^{7sd} 7^{7sf} **0-0-5 £463**

Caribbean Pearl (USA) *C E Brittain* 77
3 b f Silver Hawk (USA) - Ras Shaikh (USA)
4^{10s} 1^{10gf} 1^{12s} **2-0-3 £13,369**

Carisolo *Sir Michael Stoute* 63
3 b f Dubai Millennium - Solo De Lune (Ire)
5^{10gf} 3^{10gf} **0-0-2 £960**

Cark *J Balding* 46 a52
7 b g Farfelu - Precious Girl
6^{5sd} 3^{5sd} 13^{5gf} 4^{5g} 13^{5gf} 3^{5gf} 10^{5gf} 5^{5gf} 10^{5gf} 2^{5sd} 1^{5sd} 8^{5sd} 9^{5sd} 5^{5ss} 2^{5sd} **1-4-15 £3,013**

Carloman *R M Beckett* 48 a62
2 ch g King Charlemagne (USA) - Jarrayan
10^{6g} 6^{7gf} 3^{7sd} **0-1-3 £210**

Carlotamix (Fr) *A Fabre* 117 a77
2 gr c Linamix (Fr) - Carlitta (USA)
1^{8sd} 1^{8gs} 1^{8s} **3-0-3 £138,901**

Carlton Scroop (Fr) *J Jay* 36
2 ch c Priolo (USA) - Elms Schooldays
14^{7sd} 10^{8gs} 9^{8hy} **0-0-3**

Carlys Quest *Ferdy Murphy* 87
11 ch g Primo Dominie - Tuppy (USA)
2^{18g} **0-1-1 £2,908**

Carmania (Ire) *R P Elliott* a45
3 b g Desert Sun - Scatter Brain
10^{9sd} 7^{7sd} 2^{6sd} 4^{6sd} **0-1-4 £416**

Carmarthen Belle *Miss L C Siddall* 22 a18
5 b m Merdon Melody - Woodland Steps
8^{6sd} 12^{7s} 11^{7gf} 7^{9g} 9^{5gs} 8^{7g} 14^{6sd} **0-0-7**

Carmenero (Ger) *W R Muir* 80 a77
2 b g Barathea (Ire) - Claire Fraser (USA)
4^{5g} 10^{5s} 2^{6gf} 4^{6g} 4^{6gf} 13^{6gs} 5^{5g} 1^{5f} 2^{6gf} 4^{6f} 5^{6sd} **1-2-11 £6,928**

Carmina Banana *Jane Southcombe* a19
7 b m Emarati (USA) - Pettycur Bay (Fr)
11^{9sd} 9^{7gf} 11^{7sd} **0-0-3**

Carmona *M G Quinlan* a34
2 b f Rainbow Quest (USA) - El Opera (Ire)
9^{9sd} **0-0-1**

Carn Lady (Ire) *J R Fanshawe* 47 a53
2 b f Woodman (USA) - Cois Cuain (Ire)

7^{6sd} 6^{6gs} 7^{6gf} **0-0-3**

Carnivore *T D Barron* 62 a54
3 ch g Zafonic (USA) - Ermine (Ire)
7^{5g} 7^{5gs} 2^{6gf} 5^{6sd} **0-1-4 £853**

Carnt Spell *J T Stimpson* 31 a35
4 b g Wizard King - Forever Shineing
5^{12sd} 5^{12sd} 9^{12gf} **0-0-3**

Caroline's Rose *A P Jones*
7 br m Fraam - Just Rosie
11^{7gf} **0-0-1**

Caroubier (Ire) *J Gallagher* a67
5 ch g Woodborough (USA) - Patsy Grimes
5^{11sd} 12^{12sd} 5^{9sd} 8^{9sd} 11^{9sd} **0-0-5**

Carpet Ride *E A L Dunlop* 68 a62
3 ch c Unfuwain (USA) - Fragrant Oasis (USA)
8^{8gf} 5^{9sd} 7^{8g} 1^{10f} 6^{11g} 15^{10gf} 6^{9gf} 16^{8gf}
1-0-8 £5,125

Carpeting *D Morris* a53
2 b g Alhaarth (Ire) - Wigging
10^{8sd} **0-0-1**

Carr Hall (Ire) *T D Easterby* 61
2 b g Rossini (USA) - Pidgeon Bay (Ire)
5^{6g} 9^{7gf} 2^{7s} 9^{8g} 8^{7hy} 3^{8g} 12^{8gs} **0-2-7**
£1,278

Carraig (Ire) *Evan Williams* 44
3 b f Orpen (USA) - Rose Of Mooncoin (Ire)
11^{7gf} 11^{8g} 11^{8gf} 5^{7gf} 3^{8gf} 9^{8g} **0-1-6**
£376

Carrietau *J G Given* 65 a40
2 b g Key Of Luck (USA) - Carreamia
5^{6gf} 7^{7g} 13^{6g} 7^{7sd} 8^{8sd} **0-0-5**

Carry On Doc *J W Hills* 72
4 b g Dr Devious (Ire) - Florentynna Bay
11^{7g} 8^{8gf} 6^{9gf} 4^{8g} **0-0-4 £441**

Carte Diamond (USA) *B Ellison* 116
4 ch c Theatrical - Liteup My Life (USA)
2^{14g} 9^{12g} **0-1-2 £40,000**

Carte Sauvage (USA) *M F Harris* 104
4 gr/ro g Kris S (USA) - See You (USA)
2^{12gf} 3^{12gf} 8^{12gf} 5^{12gf} 8^{12g} 16^{14g} **0-2-6**
£17,838

Cartography (Ire) *Saeed Bin Suroor* 73
4 b c Zafonic (USA) - Sans Escale (USA)
6^{6gs} 4^{6g} **0-0-2 £1,273**

Cartoonist (Ire) *A King* 55
2 ch g Fruits Of Love (USA) - Verusa (Ire)
8^{8gs} 10^{8gs} 7^{8hy} **0-0-3**

Carvoeiro *C F Wall* 51 a59
3 ch f Compton Place - Shoshone
6^{10sd} 5^{12gs} 4^{12sd} 13^{9sd} **0-0-4 £268**

Casablanca Minx (Ire) *Mrs H Sweeting* 61 a60
2 br f Desert Story (Ire) - Conspire (Ire)
4^{5sd} 4^{5sd} 6^{5gf} 3^{6gf} 6^{5g} 1^{5gf} 1^{6f} 7^{6sd} 3^{6gf}
8^{6sd} 4^{6sd} 15^{7gf} 5^{6gf} 1^{7sd} 3^{7sf} 10^{8sd} 9^{7sd}
3-3-17 £11,872

Casalese *M D Hammond* 48 a13
3 ch g Wolfhound (USA) - Little Redwing
9^{9g} 8^{14gf} 10^{12gf} 7^{10g} 10^{9gf} 7^{12gf} 8^{11sd} 10^{11sd}
0-0-8

Casas (Ire) *J R Norton* a22
8 b g Tenby - Clodagh
7^{14sd} **0-0-1**

Casemate *P J Makin* 80 a77
3 b g Efisio - Flying Carpet
10^{8sd} 11^{8sd} 8^{8sd} 1^{8sd} 4^{8gs} 1^{7gs} 2^{8g} 1^{7sd} 4^{8sd}
3^{7sd} 6^{7sd} 1^{7gf} 5^{8sd} **4-3-13 £17,723**

Cash Flow *D W Barker* 25
2 b f Mtoto - Little Change
8^{7g} **0-0-1**

Cash On (Ire) *M P Tregoning* 74 a75
3 ch g Spectrum (Ire) - Lady Lucre (Ire)
6^{10sd} 6^{12gf} 4^{12gf} 1^{12sd} 11^{12sd} 8^{11g} **1-1-6**
£3,273

Cashbar *J R Fanshawe* 63
4 b f Bishop Of Cashel - Barford Sovereign
9^{8gf} 16^{8gf} **0-0-2**

Cashel Dancer *S A Brookshaw* a29
6 b m Bishop Of Cashel - Dancing Debut
7^{9sd} 11^{12sd} **0-0-2**

Cashel Mead *J L Spearing* 69 a70
5 b m Bishop Of Cashel - Island Mead
1^{5sd} 10^{5sd} 3^{6sd} 4^{5gs} 5^{5sd} 12^{6sd} 6^{6gs} 3^{5sd} 6^{5sd}
1-2-9 £4,245

Cashema (Ire) *D R MacLeod* 36 a32
4 b f Cape Cross (Ire) - Miss Shema (USA)
9^{9sd} 7^{12gs} 10^{16gf} 8^{8gf} 9^{12gf} **0-0-5**

Cashier *J H M Gosden* 98
3 gr c Alhaarth (Ire) - Cashew
2^{7gf} 1^{8g} 2^{9gf} 1^{8g} **2-2-4 £22,533**

Cashneem (Ire) *W M Brisbourne* 55
7 b g Case Law - Haanem
6^{8gs} 7^{7gs} 13^{8s} 10^{7f} 11^{7gf} 7^{7g} 10^{8gf}
0-0-7

Casino (Ire) *D P Kelly* 64
3 b g Desert Sun - Go Indigo (Ire)
4^{6s} 18^{6s} 15^{7gf} 13^{7s} **0-0-4 £259**

Casonova (Ire) *T D Easterby* 51
2 b g Trans Island - Sherna Girl (Ire)
15^{6g} 15^{7s} 4^{6gf} **0-0-3 £500**

Caspian Rose *W G M Turner* 31 a30
2 b f Paris House - Caspian Morn
8^{5sd} 11^{5gf} **0-0-2**

Cassanos (Ire) *D G Bridgwater* a49
4 b g Ali-Royal (Ire) - I'm Your Girl
9^{13sd} 12^{16sd} 6^{10sd} **0-0-3**

Cassydora *Christophe Clement* 112
3 b f Darshaan - Claxon
1^{11g} 7^{12g} 2^{10gs} 3^{10s} 11^{10y} **1-2-5**
£80,979

Castanza *M Wellings* 69 a50
3 b f Bachir (Ire) - Sylhall
7^{7sd} 5^{6sd} 1^{7s} 8^{8s} 5^{8sd} 6^{9sf} 10^{7sd} 11^{12sd}
1-0-8 £3,659

Castellano *M G Quinlan* 78
2 b c Mujahid (USA) - Megdale (Ire)
1^{6g} 4^{7g} 6^{7gf} 6^{7g} 27^{6g} 11^{8s} **1-0-6**
£3,945

Castelletto *R Hannon* 101 a30
3 b f Komaite (USA) - Malcesine (Ire)
9^{7ft} 9^{5gf} 9^{6gs} 4^{5s} 6^{5g} 9^{5g} 11^{5gs} **0-0-7**
£2,634

Casterossa *H Morrison* 63 a61
3 ch f Rossini (USA) - First Musical
9^{6gf} 6^{7gf} 11^{6sd} 3^{6gf} 8^{6g} 2^{6gf} 1^{6gs} 5^{6sd}
1-2-8 £3,909

Castle Frome (Ire) *A E Price* 44
6 b g Spectrum (Ire) - Vendimia
3^{10g} **0-1-1 £210**

Castle River (USA) *O O'Neill* 39
6 b g Irish River (Fr) - Castellina (USA)

8^{12gf} 12^{10gf} **0-0-2**

Castle Valentine *A J Lidderdale* 61 a28
3 b c Erhaab (USA) - Bassmaat (USA)
5^{8g} 13^{10sd} 13^{12gs} **0-0-3**

Castleshane (Ire) *S Gollings* 80
8 b g Kris - Ahbab (Ire)
11^{10gf} **0-0-1**

Casual Glance *A M Balding* 88 a66
3 b f Sinndar (Ire) - Spurned (USA)
5^{8g} 7^{11g} 9^{14g} 9^{12sd} 1^{12gs} 4^{14hy} **1-0-6 £6,156**

Cat's Whiskers *M W Easterby* 65
6 b g Catrail (USA) - Haut Volee
7^{8gs} 13^{8s} 10^{8gf} 12^{10gf} 4^{7gf} 16^{8gf} **0-0-6 £275**

Catabound (USA) *R Charlton* 15 a52
2 b/br g Black Minnaloushe (USA) - Castellina (USA)
13^{8gs} 6^{7sd} **0-0-2**

Catbang (Ire) *N A Callaghan* 48 a64
2 b c Zafonic (USA) - Silky Dawn (Ire)
10^{6gf} 19^{7gs} 7^{7sd} 3^{6sd} 3^{6sd} **0-2-5 £1,314**

Catch A Star *N A Callaghan* 32
3 ch f Giant's Causeway (USA) - Amy Hunter (USA)
11^{10g} **0-0-1**

Catch The Cat (Ire) *P T Midgley* 81 a45
6 b g Catrail (USA) - Tongabezi (Ire)
8^{5hy} 3^{5gs} 1^{5gf} 7^{5g} 13^{5g} 7^{5sd} 14^{5s} **1-1-7 £4,664**

Catch The Fox *J J Bridger* a23
5 b g Fraam - Versaillesprincess
8^{7sd} **0-0-1**

Catch The Wind *I A Wood* 87
4 b f Bahamian Bounty - Tinkerbird
5^{5gf} 9^{6gf} 5^{5gf} 6^{6f} 3^{5f} 13^{5g} 10^{5g} 5^{5g} **0-1-8 £1,340**

Catchthebatch *E A Wheeler* a6
9 b g Beveled (USA) - Batchworth Dancer
13^{5sd} **0-0-1**

Cate Washington *Mrs L Williamson* 48
2 b f Superior Premium - Willisa
9^{6gs} 13^{7g} 10^{7s} **0-0-3**

Categorical *Mrs J R Ramsden* 82 a78
2 b g Diktat - Zibet
9^{6gf} 4^{5gf} 1^{5sd} 3^{7hy} **1-1-4 £5,225**

Caterham Common *D W Chapman* a25
6 b g Common Grounds - Pennine Pink (Ire)
10^{6sd} 6^{8sd} **0-0-2**

Catherines Cafe (Ire) *Mrs P N Dutfield* 71
2 b f Mull Of Kintyre (USA) - Wisecrack (Ire)
6^{6g} 1^{6gf} 9^{7gf} 3^{7gs} 10^{7gf} 10^{7gs} 15^{7gs} **1-1-7 £5,224**

Catheriniski (Ire) *P A Blockley* 47 a16
3 b f Danetime (Ire) - Choralli
9^{6f} 9^{7g} 7^{10f} 11^{6sd} 7^{7sd} **0-0-5**

Cativo Cavallino *Julian Poulton* 68 a71
2 ch g Bertolini (USA) - Sea Isle
6^{5gs} 5^{6hy} 3^{5sd} 2^{5sd} **0-2-4 £1,456**

Catskill *E F Vaughan* 72
3 ch g Inchinor - Manhattan Sunset (USA)
6^{9g} 5^{8gs} 6^{8g} 2^{10g} 6^{11g} **0-1-5 £1,378**

Catspraddle (USA) *R Hannon* 70
2 ch f High Yield (USA) - Beaux Dorothy (USA)
1^{5gs} 11^{6g} 12^{6gs} **1-0-3 £5,590**

Caughnawaga (Fr) *D R C Elsworth* 46
7 b g Indian Ridge - Wakria (Ire)
17^{8g} **0-0-1**

Causeway Girl (Ire) *D M Simcock* 39
3 br f Giant's Causeway (USA) - Darbela (Ire)
11^{10g} 6^{11f} 5^{12f} 10^{10g} **0-0-4**

Caustic Wit (Ire) *M S Saunders* 80 a76
7 b g Cadeaux Genereux - Baldemosa (Fr)
11^{5gs} 11^{5f} 7^{6f} 8^{6gf} 16^{6gf} 4^{6gf} 4^{6sd} 2^{6gs} 7^{5g} 8^{6gs} 4^{6f} 14^{6sd} **0-1-12 £2,371**

Cautiously (USA) *M Blanshard* 63 a74
4 b f Distant View (USA) - Curiously
9^{9sd} 12^{8sd} 7^{7sd} 4^{8s} 13^{8g} 8^{8g} 6^{8sd} 7^{10gf} 13^{12sd} 5^{10sd} 9^{9sf} **0-0-11 £509**

Cava Bien *B J Llewellyn* 70 a52
3 b g Bien Bien (USA) - Bebe De Cham
6^{12g} 8^{12g} 2^{14g} 8^{14f} 11^{14g} 15^{16g} 11^{12gf} 17^{10g} 13^{10g} 5^{9sd} **0-1-10 £1,072**

Cavallini (USA) *G L Moore* 90
3 b/br g Bianconi (USA) - Taylor Park (USA)
9^{8gf} 7^{10gf} 1^{10gf} 9^{11gs} 3^{12gf} 14^{10gf} **1-1-6 £6,648**

Cavan Gael (Fr) *P Howling* 75 a55
3 b c Dansili - Time Will Show (Fr)
12^{7g} 3^{8g} 14^{8g} 7^{8gf} 13^{7gf} 6^{8gf} 9^{9ft} 12^{10sd} PU^{8sf} **0-1-9 £783**

Cavaradossi *C F Wall* 52 a46
3 gr g Lake Coniston (Ire) - Floria Tosca
9^{7g} 11^{10sd} 8^{8gf} 3^{8g} 7^{8gf} 7^{8gs} 6^{8g} **0-1-7 £385**

Caveral *R Hannon* 91
4 ch f Ashkalani (Ire) - Melting Gold (USA)
6^{8g} 13^{6gs} 18^{6g} 2^{8gf} 3^{8gf} 10^{7gs} 4^{7g} 9^{8g} **0-2-8 £7,371**

Cavewarrior *J Noseda* 52 a82
2 b g Arkadian Hero (USA) - Lyna
17^{7g} 2^{7sd} 1^{6sd} 22^{6gf} 3^{6sd} **1-2-5 £5,854**

Cayenne (Ger) *D M Simcock* 53 a39
3 ch f Efisio - Carola Rouge
8^{6gf} 3^{6s} 8^{8g} 3^{8gf} 7^{7gf} 9^{9sd} 9^{7sd} **0-2-7 £1,149**

Cayman Breeze *J M Bradley* 66 a57
5 b g Danzig (USA) - Lady Thynn (Fr)
4^{7gf} 2^{7gf} 3^{6gf} 1^{7f} 8^{7gf} 1^{6f} 5^{8gf} 9^{6gs} 1^{7f} 7^{7s} 6^{6g} 4^{7sf} 6^{7sd} 3^{6sd} 6^{7sd} 1^{7sf} 2^{6sd} 6^{7sd} 3^{6sd} 3^{7sd} **4-6-20 £12,675**

Cayman Calypso (Ire) *Mrs P Sly* a57
4 ro g Danehill Dancer (Ire) - Warthill Whispers
5^{7sd} 3^{9sd} 8^{9sd} 5^{12sd} 1^{14sd} 8^{17sd} 14^{14sd} 4^{12sd} 6^{11sd} 1^{16sd} **2-1-10 £4,684**

Cayman Colony (Ire) *R Hannon* 58 a66
3 b g Namid - Imperialist (Ire)
10^{7sd} 2^{7sd} 6^{7sd} 6^{6sd} 12^{8gf} 11^{7gs} 4^{7gf} 12^{8gf} 17^{7g} 11^{7gs} 7^{7g} 11^{6sd} **0-1-12 £1,604**

Cayman King *R Craggs* 58 a56
3 b g Cayman Kai (Ire) - Distinctly Laura (Ire)
2^{5f} 6^{6gf} 8^{5sd} 16^{6gf} 11^{5ss} 2^{6sd} 10^{7ss} **0-2-7 £1,249**

Cayman Mischief *James Moffatt* 45 a13
5 b m Cayman Kai (Ire) - Tribal Mischief
9^{7sd} 6^{5s} 9^{5f} 5^{6s} 13^{5g} 12^{5gf} 8^{5gf} 10^{6g} **0-0-8**

Caymans Gift *A C Whillans* 59
5 ch g Cayman Kai (Ire) - Gymcrak Cyrano (Ire)
15^{9gs} 6^{12gs} 8^{14gs} 2^{13gs} 5^{12g} 6^{12gf} 4^{13s} **0-2-7 £857**

Cayuse *B J McMath*

3 b f Double Trigger (Ire) - Suile Mor
11^{10gf} **0-0-1**

Cd Europe (Ire) *J J Quinn* 91 a67
7 ch g Royal Academy (USA) - Woodland Orchid (Ire)
$3^{5g}\ 15^{5g}\ 10^{6gs}\ 7^{6s}\ 7^{7sd}$ **0-1-5 £2,315**

Cd Flyer (Ire) *B Ellison* 83
8 ch g Grand Lodge (USA) - Pretext
$5^{7s}\ 5^{6gs}\ 6^{7g}\ 4^{7gf}\ 13^{7g}\ 10^{6g}\ 6^{7g}\ 16^{6gf}\ 3^{6gs}\ 11^{6s}$ **0-1-10 £1,633**

Cecchetti (Ire) *Mrs H Sweeting* 40 a51
2 b f Imperial Ballet (Ire) - Quiver Tree
$5^{8s}\ 11^{7g}\ 5^{7sd}\ 13^{8sd}$ **0-0-4**

Cedar Chief *B A Pearce*
8 b g Saddlers' Hall (Ire) - Dame Ashfield
7^{12gf} **0-0-1**

Ceiriog Valley *B W Hills* 82
3 b f In The Wings - Bodfari Quarry
$12^{10g}\ 9^{12gs}\ 4^{10gs}\ 1^{12gs}\ 11^{12gs}\ 14^{14s}\ 2^{12s}$
1-1-7 £12,554

Celadon (Ire) *N P Littmoden* a20
4 b g Fasliyev (USA) - Dancing Drop
$8^{5sd}\ 16^{6gs}$ **0-0-2**

Celebration Song (Ire) *W R Swinburn* 82
2 b g Royal Applause - Googoosh (Ire)
$9^{6gf}\ 4^{6gf}\ 1^{6gf}\ 9^{6g}\ 1^{7s}$ **2-0-5 £14,509**

Celeritas (Ire) *J Gallagher* 73 a67
2 b g Titus Livius (Fr) - Shahroza (USA)
$12^{5g}\ 2^{5gf}\ 11^{6g}\ 4^{5g}\ 2^{5g}\ 5^{6sd}\ 15^{5g}\ 14^{6s}$
0-2-8 £3,224

Celestial Princess *M R Channon* 77
2 b f Observatory (USA) - Affair Of State (Ire)
$16^{6gf}\ 2^{7gf}\ 2^{7g}\ 1^{7gf}\ 10^{7gf}\ 6^{8gf}\ 23^{7gf}$
1-2-7 £6,873

Cello *R Hannon* 73
4 gr c Pivotal - Raffelina (USA)
$13^{8gf}\ 12^{10gf}\ 14^{10gs}\ 15^{8gs}\ 4^{8gs}\ 10^{10g}\ 16^{10g}$
0-0-7 £806

Celtic Blaze (Ire) *B S Rothwell* 49 a49
6 b m Charente River (Ire) - Firdaunt
$4^{22s}\ 11^{16gs}\ 12^{17gf}\ 5^{16g}\ 4^{17sd}\ 12^{14sd}$ **0-0-6 £417**

Celtic Carisma *K G Reveley* 61
3 b f Celtic Swing - Kathryn's Pet
$10^{8s}\ 8^{8s}\ 1^{12gf}\ 9^{10gf}\ 11^{12gf}\ 1^{14g}\ 1^{16gf}\ 4^{16gf}$
3-0-8 £7,593

Celtic Empire (Ire) *Jedd O'Keeffe* 41
2 b c Second Empire (Ire) - Celtic Guest (Ire)
10^{8gs} **0-0-1**

Celtic Mill *D W Barker* 115 a107
7 b g Celtic Swing - Madam Millie
$4^{5gf}\ 3^{6gf}\ 1^{5gf}\ 14^{5gf}\ F^{5gf}\ 3^{5gf}\ 8^{5gf}\ 3^{6sd}\ 1^{5sf}$
2-3-9 £76,383

Celtic Prelude (Ire) *M Johnston* 7
3 b f Celtic Swing - Presumed (USA)
12^{9g} **0-0-1**

Celtic Promise (Ire) *Mrs A J Perrett* 61
3 b f Celtic Swing - Tainted Halo (USA)
$9^{12gs}\ 4^{14g}\ 8^{14s}\ 12^{18gf}\ 14^{16g}\ 10^{14g}$ **0-0-6 £268**

Celtic Shadow (Ire) *M A Jarvis* 48
3 b g Celtic Swing - Shabby Chic (USA)
$7^{10gs}\ 7^{10gf}\ 9^{10gf}\ 14^{12gf}$ **0-0-4**

Celtic Spa (Ire) *Mrs P N Dutfield* 77
3 gr f Celtic Swing - Allegorica (Ire)
$4^{6gs}\ 16^{8g}\ 6^{7f}\ 9^{7gs}\ 3^{7gf}\ 2^{8gf}\ 2^{8f}\ 1^{8gf}\ 9^{8gf}\ 4^{8gs}\ 5^{8gs}\ 7^{10g}$ **1-3-12 £8,761**

Celtic Star (Ire) *Mrs L Williamson* 44
7 b g Celtic Swing - Recherchee
$10^{12gf}\ 8^{13gf}$ **0-0-2**

Celtic Thunder *T J Etherington* 71 a75
4 b g Mind Games - Lake Mistassiu
$9^{5gs}\ 8^{5gf}\ 3^{5f}\ 12^{6g}\ 10^{5gf}\ 3^{6sd}\ 6^{6gf}\ 13^{5g}\ 13^{6gf}$
0-2-9 £1,577

Celticello (Ire) *M A Jarvis* 93
3 b/br g Celtic Swing - Viola Royale (Ire)
$6^{8gs}\ 4^{7g}\ 1^{8s}\ 1^{8g}\ 6^{8g}$ **2-0-5 £10,008**

Celtique *M Wigham* 77 a75
3 b f Celtic Swing - Heart's Harmony
$8^{10g}\ 5^{8gs}\ 5^{10gf}\ 2^{10sd}\ 2^{10g}\ 5^{8gf}\ 3^{10f}\ 2^{12gs}\ 1^{9sd}\ 4^{9sd}$ **1-3-10 £7,594**

Cemgraft *O Brennan* 43
4 b f In The Wings - Soviet Maid (Ire)
$12^{12gf}\ 6^{7f}\ 11^{7gf}\ 8^{10gs}$ **0-0-4**

Centaurus *Saeed Bin Suroor* 113
3 gr c Daylami (Ire) - Dandanna (Ire)
$5^{8gs}\ 1^{12s}\ 3^{14g}\ 2^{14g}$ **1-1-4 £20,515**

Ceol Na Sraide (Ire) *B S Rothwell* 30
6 b m King's Theatre (Ire) - My Lady's Key (USA)
10^{10s} **0-0-1**

Cerebus *M J Polglase* 73 a76
3 b f Wolfhound (USA) - Bring On The Choir
$2^{6sd}\ 2^{7sd}\ 1^{6sd}\ 1^{5sd}\ 6^{7sd}\ 3^{6sd}\ 2^{5sd}\ 6^{5gs}\ 2^{5s}$
$2^{6sd}\ 7^{6s}\ 7^{5gs}\ 11^{6g}\ 2^{6gs}\ 3^{5g}\ 12^{6gs}\ 3^{6sd}\ 5^{5s}$
$4^{6ss}\ 2^{7sd}$ **2-10-20 £17,334**

Ceredig *N A Callaghan* 66
2 b g Lujain (USA) - Anneli Rose
$4^{5gs}\ 8^{5g}\ 5^{5gs}$ **0-0-3 £327**

Certain Circles (USA) *A M Balding* 72 a72
2 b c King Cugat (USA) - Daily Special (USA)
$1^{6f}\ 8^{7g}\ 10^{6gf}\ 5^{7sd}\ 4^{7sd}$ **1-0-5 £3,286**

Certain Justice (USA) *Stef Liddiard* 76 a82
7 gr g Lit De Justice (USA) - Pure Misk
$1^{7sd}\ 9^{9sd}\ 3^{8gf}\ 2^{7g}\ 5^{7gf}\ 1^{6sd}\ 4^{6gs}\ 8^{7gf}\ 6^{8g}$
$9^{7s}\ 2^{7sd}$ **2-2-11 £11,051**

Cerulean Rose *A W Carroll* 76
6 ch m Bluegrass Prince (Ire) - Elegant Rose
$11^{5gf}\ 2^{6g}\ 3^{5gf}\ 2^{6g}\ 2^{6f}\ 7^{5gf}\ 3^{5gf}\ 2^{5gf}\ 5^{5s}$
$5^{5f}\ 4^{6g}\ 10^{6f}\ 3^{6g}\ 6^{6g}\ 3^{6g}$ **0-8-15 £9,684**

Cesar Manrique (Ire) *B W Hills* 82
3 ch g Vettori (Ire) - Norbella
$6^{6gf}\ 8^{6gs}\ 12^{5gf}\ 5^{6gf}\ 6^{6gf}\ 5^{6gf}\ 6^{6g}\ 8^{6gf}$
C-0-8

Cesare *J R Fanshawe* 102 a106
4 b g Machiavellian (USA) - Tromond
$1^{7s}\ 1^{8s}\ 1^{8sd}\ 3^{8gs}$ **3-1-4 £43,067**

Cesario (Jpn) *Katsuhiko Sumii* 116
3 b f Special Week (Jpn) - Kirov Premiere
$1^{10f}\ 1^{9f}\ 2^{8f}\ 1^{12f}\ 1^{10f}$ **4-1-5 £1,359,247**

Cetshwayo *J M P Eustace* 25 a60
3 ch g Pursuit Of Love - Induna
$7^{7sd}\ 11^{10s}$ **0-0-2**

Cezzaro (Ire) *T A K Cuthbert* 43
7 ch g Ashkalani (Ire) - Sept Roses (USA)
$10^{12gf}\ 12^{13s}\ 4^{12gf}\ 6^{12gf}\ 10^{12f}$ **0-0-5**

Chaco (Ire) *Saeed Bin Suroor* 42
2 b c Cape Cross (Ire) - Carotene (Can)
17^{8gs} **0-0-1**

Chadlington (Ire) *E J O'Neill* 81

2 b c Robellino (USA) - Tweed Mill
9^{7gf} 2^{7gs} **0-1-2 £1,496**

Chadwell Lad *R M H Cowell*
4 b g Vettori (Ire) - Elle Reef
9^{12sd} 6^{12sd} **0-0-2**

Chairman Bobby *W S Cunningham* 47 a27
7 ch g Clantime - Formidable Liz
12^{6sd} 12^{6gf} 7^{6gf} **0-0-3**

Chairman Rick (Ire) *D Nicholls* 60 a38
3 b g Danehill Dancer (Ire) - Come Together
5^{7g} 12^{5g} 4^{9gf} 6^{7f} 10^{6f} 15^{6g} 17^{6g} **0-0-7 £392**

Chaka Zulu *A C Whillans* 65
8 b g Muhtarram (USA) - African Dance (USA)
13^{12sd} 3^{14gf} 2^{12gf} 1^{15g} 2^{14g} 1^{12gf} 2^{14gf} 3^{16gf} 2^{16gf} **2-6-9 £12,717**

Chalentina *H R A Cecil* 73
2 b f Primo Valentino (Ire) - Chantilly Myth
4^{6gf} 7^{8g} 3^{7gs} **0-1-3 £888**

Chalet *M J Wallace* 56
3 b f Singspiel (Ire) - Douce Maison (Ire)
5^{9g} 2^{12f} **0-1-2 £1,045**

Chalice Welcome *J A Supple* 36
2 b g Most Welcome - Blue Peru (Ire)
9^{6gf} 8^{8g} 11^{6g} 10^{8gf} **0-0-4**

Chalison (Ire) *R Hannon* 73 a55
3 b c Anabaa (USA) - Raincloud
2^{7s} 6^{8g} 3^{7sd} **0-2-3 £1,687**

Chalmaty *D W Thompson*
3 b f Almaty (Ire) - Chalice
16^{7gf} 15^{5gf} 12^{7g} **0-0-3**

Chambray (Ire) *A M Balding* 53
4 b f Barathea (Ire) - Spurned (USA)
6^{12s} 7^{16g} 13^{12hy} **0-0-3**

Chaminade (USA) *Sir Michael Stoute* 50
2 b f Danzig (USA) - Flute (USA)
6^{6gf} **0-0-1**

Champagne Brandy (Ire) *P D Evans* 18
3 ch f Spectrum (Ire) - Petite Liqueurelle (Ire)
7^{10g} 14^{10g} **0-0-2**

Champagne Cracker *I Semple* 72
4 ch f Up And At 'Em - Kiveton Komet
9^{5g} 5^{5gf} 3^{5gf} 2^{5gf} 1^{5g} 3^{5gf} 10^{5gf} 10^{5g} **1-3-8 £9,109**

Champagne Lujain *M W Easterby*
3 b g Lujain (USA) - Brief Glimpse (Ire)
12^{9gf} **0-0-1**

Champagne Moment *J A Glover* 44
2 ch f Perryston View - Ashleen
5^{6gs} 2^{6gf} 13^{6gf} 4^{6gf} 6^{5g} 9^{7gf} **0-1-6 £796**

Champagne Rossini (Ire) *M C Chapman* 53 a48
3 b g Rossini (USA) - Alpencrocus (Ire)
9^{8sd} 7^{10g} 3^{8sd} 7^{7gs} 2^{8gf} F^{8gf} 6^{10g} 6^{10gf} 13^{7gs} 8^{7sd} **0-1-10 £1,571**

Champagne Shadow (Ire) *G L Moore* a76
4 b c Kahyasi - Moet (Ire)
RR^{16g} 1^{12sd} **1-0-2 £3,474**

Champain Sands (Ire) *E J Alston* 60 a54
6 b g Green Desert (USA) - Grecian Bride (Ire)
1^{9sd} 5^{9sd} 3^{8gs} 6^{9gf} 2^{8s} 4^{9s} 7^{8gf} 2^{9gf} 11^{10g} 9^{9gf} 4^{8gf} 5^{9g} **1-4-12 £4,186**

Champara (Ire) *E J O'Neill* 71
2 b c Monashee Mountain (USA) - Zoya (Ire)
1^{6f} **1-0-1 £4,014**

Champion Lion (Ire) *J R Boyle* 66 a57
6 b g Sadler's Wells (USA) - Honey Bun
5^{10g} 15^{10s} 5^{10g} 5^{10g} 9^{10gs} 2^{12sd} 5^{12sd} 8^{12sd} **0-1-8 £751**

Champions Gallery *D R C Elsworth* 94
2 b c Dansili - Pure
9^{7gf} 1^{7f} 6^{8g} **1-0-3 £4,604**

Championship Point (Ire) *M R Channon* 107
2 b c Lomitas - Flying Squaw
1^{6f} 1^{7gf} 2^{8vs} **2-1-3 £45,948**

Champoluc (Ire) *W R Swinburn* a58
4 ch f Indian Ridge - Just Ice
2^{7sd} 9^{7sd} **0-1-2 £1,063**

Chance For Romance *W R Muir* 73
4 ch f Entrepreneur - My First Romance
5^{6g} 8^{6gf} **0-0-2**

Chancellor (Ire) *Andrew Reid* 106
7 ch h Halling (USA) - Isticanna (USA)
6^{10g} 6^{10gs} 5^{12g} 3^{10g} 14^{12gf} 18^{10gs} 5^{10g} 8^{10g} 5^{12hy} 15^{10gs} 9^{10s} **0-1-11 £13,435**

Changiz *J A Geake* 54
2 b g Foxhound (USA) - Persia (Ire)
12^{6gs} 11^{8g} 7^{8g} 14^{8gs} **0-0-4**

Channel Crossing *A Bailey* 55
3 b g Deploy - Wave Dancer
4^{12gf} 10^{10gs} 7^{12s} **0-0-3 £259**

Chantaco (USA) *A M Balding* 89 a80
3 b c Bahri (USA) - Dominant Dancer
1^{7sd} 3^{7sd} 3^{8gs} 4^{10s} 3^{11g} 1^{10s} **2-1-6 £15,244**

Chantelle's Dream *Ms J S Doyle* 46 a49
3 ch f Compton Place - Polar Peak
15^{5gf} 2^{5f} 14^{6sd} 16^{5g} 2^{5sd} 4^{5sd} **0-2-6 £850**

Chanteuse Noire (USA) *J Noseda* 71
2 b f War Chant (USA) - Galeta (Arg)
9^{7gf} 5^{7gf} 3^{6gf} **0-1-3 £661**

Chantilly Beauty (Fr) *R Pritchard-Gordon* 105 a79
3 b f Josr Algarhoud (Ire) - Lysabelle (Fr)
5^{7ft} 8^{8ft} 4^{11s} 2^{8gf} 4^{8gf} 1^{7gs} 7^{8s} 7^{10hy} **1-1-8 £71,768**

Chantry Falls (Ire) *G C H Chung* a57
5 b g Mukaddamah (USA) - Woodie Dancer (USA)
2^{9sd} 3^{10sd} 1^{9sd} 10^{9sd} 8^{9sd} 7^{11sd} **1-2-6 £2,070**

Chapter (Ire) *R Hannon* 75
3 ch g Sinndar (Ire) - Web Of Intrigue
11^{9g} 9^{8gf} 1^{8gf} 3^{8gf} UR^{8f} 5^{9g} UR^{10g} 14^{8g} **1-1-8 £4,215**

Chara *J R Jenkins* 43
4 ch f Deploy - Subtle One (Ire)
8^{12s} 7^{12gf} 9^{13f} PU^{12gf} **0-0-4**

Charade (Ire) *M A Jarvis* a59
3 b f Danehill (USA) - Actoris (USA)
4^{9sd} 4^{12sd} **0-0-2 £575**

Charanne *J M Bradley*
2 b f Diktat - Mystique
15^{5gs} **0-0-1**

Charismatic Cat (USA) *A P O'Brien* 93
3 b c Storm Cat (USA) - The Franchise (USA)
5^{7s} 3^{7f} 12^{7g} 3^{9g} 1^{8gf} 1^{8f} 2^{7gf} 2^{8gf} 2^{8gf} **2-4-9 £20,219**

Charissa *P F I Cole*
2 b f Fasliyev (USA) - Nefeli
8^{5gs} **0-0-1**

Charles Darwin (Ire) *M Blanshard* 89
2 ch c Tagula (Ire) - Seymour (Ire)
7^{5g} 6^{5gf} 2^{6gf} 2^{5gs} 6^{5gf} 1^{5gf} 10^{5gf} 1^{6g} 3^{6g} 2^{6hy} 4^{6gs} 5^{6gs} **2-4-12 £13,685**

Charles Parnell (Ire) *M Dods* 70
2 b c Elnadim (USA) - Titania
3^{6g} 3^{6g} 5^{6gs} **0-2-3 £1,102**

Charles Street Lad (Ire) *M A Jarvis* 57
2 b c Mull Of Kintyre (USA) - Tropicana (Ire)
15^{6gf} 5^{6gs} 8^{7s} 8^{6g} **0-0-4**

Charleston *R Rowe* a47
4 ch g Pursuit Of Love - Discomatic (USA)
6^{13sd} **0-0-1**

Charleston Lover (Ger) *S Dow* 65
4 ch c Dashing Blade - Carella (Ger)
1^{10sd} 2^{10sd} 5^{8sd} 5^{10gf} 3^{10gf} 9^{12gf} 3^{10gf} 2^{8gf} 7^{8gs} **1-3-9 £4,901**

Charley's Aunt (Ire) *N P Littmoden* a57
2 ch f King Charlemagne (USA) - Dane's Lady (Ire)
7^{5sd} 7^{5sf} **0-0-2**

Charlie Bear *Miss Z C Davison* 67 a59
4 ch c Bahamian Bounty - Abi
9^{8g} 9^{7g} 6^{8gf} 11^{7g} 5^{7sd} **0-0-5**

Charlie Cool *W J Haggas* 94
2 ch c Rainbow Quest (USA) - Tigwa
2^{7g} 1^{7gf} 7^{8g} **1-1-3 £9,423**

Charlie Delta *D Carroll* 78 a75
2 b g Pennekamp (USA) - Papita (Ire)
6^{5f} 7^{6f} 1^{6f} 4^{6gf} 4^{5gf} 5^{6gf} 7^{5g} 1^{6g} 3^{6gs} 8^{6g} 4^{6s} 5^{6sd} 8^{7sf} 7^{7sd} 3^{5sd} 7^{7sd} **2-2-16 £12,760**

Charlie George *P Monteith* 47
4 ch g Idris (Ire) - Faithful Beauty (Ire)
4^{9gf} 16^{8s} 5^{11s} 10^{12f} 10^{11gf} 6^{12g} **0-0-6**

Charlie Hather *N Tinkler* 47
2 ch g Sugarfoot - Scoffera
8^{5f} 6^{7gf} 2^{6gf} 5^{6gf} 11^{7gf} 14^{7gf} **0-1-6 £900**

Charlie Kennet *Mrs H Sweeting* 76 a63
7 b g Pyramus (USA) - Evaporate
3^{10sd} 5^{12sd} 2^{12sd} 1^{12sd} 4^{12sd} 5^{12sd} 5^{11sd} 7^{12sd} 1^{10sd} 1^{10g} 1^{10gs} 14^{12g} 1^{10s} 6^{11gs} 13^{10g} 3^{10s} 7^{9sd} **5-3-17 £25,699**

Charlie Tango (Ire) *D W Thompson* 63
4 b g Desert Prince (Ire) - Precedence (Ire)
1^{9f} 3^{9gs} 9^{8gf} 8^{8gf} 6^{9gf} 3^{8gf} 6^{8gf} 4^{8gs} 2^{10g} 4^{9gf} **1-5-10 £5,123**

Charlie Tokyo (Ire) *R Hannon* 79
2 b c Trans Island - Ellistown Lady (Ire)
1^{6gf} 4^{6gf} 2^{7gs} 3^{7g} 6^{8gf} 9^{8g} 2^{8g} **1-3-7 £10,484**

Charlieslastchance *Ms J S Doyle*
3 b f Sure Blade (USA) - Sea Mist (Ire)
13^{10gf} 12^{12sd} **0-0-2**

Charllen *E S McMahon* 54 a53
2 ch f Band On The Run - Breezy Day
7^{5g} 9^{6sd} 3^{7gf} 9^{8g} 3^{7sd} 10^{7sd} **0-2-6 £717**

Charlotte Vale *M D Hammond* 78
4 ch f Pivotal - Drying Grass Moon
3^{13gs} 11^{14s} 2^{12g} 1^{12gf} 7^{14gf} 7^{12gf} 3^{12g} 6^{14s} 4^{14s} **1-4-9 £8,664**

Charlton *T G Mills* 93 a73
2 b g Inchinor - Sabina
4^{6s} 1^{6sd} 8^{7gf} 1^{6g} 6^{6g} 5^{6g} 5^{6gs} **2-0-7 £18,482**

Charlwood (Ire) *P Mitchell* 37 a37
2 b f Barathea (Ire) - King Of All (Ire)
13^{6gf} 11^{7gf} 8^{6sd} **0-0-3**

Charmatic (Ire) *Andrew Turnell* 73
4 br f Charnwood Forest (Ire) - Instamatic
8^{10gs} 1^{11g} 2^{13gs} 6^{14gf} 5^{12s} 10^{10gf} 1^{8gf} 1^{10g} 3^{8gf} 7^{10gs} 4^{11gf} 10^{10g} 12^{10gf} 10^{10gf} **3-1-14 £17,212**

Charming Ballet (Ire) *N P Littmoden* 70 a72
2 b g Imperial Ballet (Ire) - Some Merit
8^{5g} 4^{5gs} 3^{6gf} 8^{6gs} 2^{6sd} 1^{5sf} 6^{5sd} **1-1-7 £5,283**

Charming Princess *P T Midgley* a3
2 b f Primo Valentino (Ire) - Via Dolorosa
6^{5sd} **0-0-1**

Charming Rogue *S Kirk* 56 a56
3 gr g Robellino (USA) - Silver Charm
13^{10gs} 6^{12gf} 9^{12sd} 5^{12gf} **0-0-4**

Charnock Bates One (Ire) *J J Quinn* 62 a56
4 b f Desert Sun - Fleetwood Fancy
10^{10s} 8^{10s} 9^{10gf} 5^{10gf} 6^{10g} 13^{10s} 12^{10g} 7^{12g} 14^{9gf} 12^{10s} 3^{9sd} 5^{10sd} **0-1-12 £380**

Charnwood Street (Ire) *D Shaw*
6 b g Charnwood Forest (Ire) - La Vigie
10^{17sd} 12^{17sd} **0-0-2**

Chase The Ace *T D Easterby* 73
2 b g Foxhound (USA) - Quiz Show
9^{5gf} 3^{5gs} 2^{5gf} 7^{6gf} 4^{6gf} 4^{7g} 10^{7gf} 6^{6g} 2^{5g} 2^{6g} **0-4-10 £5,708**

Chase The Fox *Julian Poulton*
2 ch f Foxhound (USA) - La Belle Dominique
5^{5gf} **0-0-1**

Chase The Lady (USA) *D J S Ffrench Davis* 10
2 ch f Atticus (USA) - Nunatak (USA)
15^{6gs} 10^{7g} PU^{9sd} **0-0-3**

Chasing A Dream *B W Hills* a69
2 b f Pursuit Of Love - Preening
3^{7sd} **0-1-1 £639**

Chasing The Dream (Ire) *P R Webber* 67 a56
4 b f Desert Sun - Dream Of Jenny
3^{7g} 8^{8sd} 8^{7gf} 6^{5gf} 15^{6gf} 10^{8f} 8^{6gf} **0-1-7 £554**

Chaski (USA) *Saeed Bin Suroor* 73 a61
2 gr/ro f Gone West (USA) - Zelanda (Ire)
6^{6gf} 2^{6gf} 5^{6sd} 2^{5s} 1^{5gf} 9^{6gf} **1-1-6 £7,012**

Chaste *V Smith* 51
5 gr m Groom Dancer (USA) - Brilliant Timing (USA)
2^{7sd} 11^{7gs} 13^{8g} 6^{6gf} 8^{7gf} **0-0-5 £973**

Chateau Nicol *B G Powell* 96 a94
6 b g Distant Relative - Glensara
3^{6sd} 4^{7gs} 3^{6s} 2^{8gs} 9^{6g} 13^{7gf} 7^{8g} 13^{7gf} 3^{6g} 19^{7gf} 12^{6gs} 10^{7sd} 8^{7s} 12^{7sd} 1^{6sf} 5^{7sd} 7^{6sd} **1-4-17 £16,053**

Chater Knight (Ire) *W R Muir* a63
4 b g Night Shift (USA) - Neat Dish (Can)
1^{11sd} **1-0-1 £2,839**

Chatila (USA) *J H M Gosden* 95
2 b f Red Ransom (USA) - Silvester Lady
1^{6gf} 3^{7gf} 8^{8gs} **1-0-3 £6,670**

Chatshow (USA) *A W Carroll* 81 a72
4 br g Distant View (USA) - Galanty Show
3^{6sd} 1^{5sd} 5^{5sd} 2^{5sd} 7^{5gs} 5^{5sd} 4^{6sd} 1^{5sd} 1^{5gf} 4^{5sd} 4^{5g} 4^{6gf} 5^{5f} 3^{5gf} 8^{6g} 5^{6gf} 1^{6g} 2^{6gf} 9^{6gf} 5^{6gf} 3^{5gs} 8^{5g} 9^{6gs} 16^{6g} **4-5-24 £21,225**

Cheap N Chic *B J Meehan* 81 a79
2 ch f Primo Valentino (Ire) - Amber Mill
6^{6g} 2^{6gf} 3^{6gf} 4^{6gf} 1^{6f} 6^{7gf} 7^{6gf} 7^{6sd}
1-2-8 £13,056

Cheeky Chi (Ire) *P S McEntee* 19 a40
4 gr f Desert Style (Ire) - Grey Patience (Ire)
10^{6sd} 7^{5sd} 9^{6s} 12^{6g} 4^{6sd} 7^{8ss} **0-0-6**

Cheeney Basin (Ire) *M C Chapman* a29
7 ch g King's Signet (USA) - Gratclo
11^{6sd} 11^{6sd} **0-0-2**

Cheerleader *M A Jarvis* 89
3 ch f Singspiel (Ire) - India Atlanta
3^{10f} 2^{10gf} 2^{10gf} 1^{9gf} 9^{10s} 18^{8gf} 8^{10g}
1-3-7 £6,902

Cheese 'n Biscuits *M Wigham* 69 a86
5 b m Spectrum (Ire) - Bint Shihama (USA)
1^{7sd} 1^{7sd} 1^{7sd} 3^{7sd} 11^{6g} 9^{7hy} 6^{7sd} 12^{7sd}
3-1-8 £14,890

Chehalis Mist (Ire) *M J Wallace* a69
3 b c Orpen (USA) - Classic Heights
4^{8sd} 4^{9sd} **0-0-2 £646**

Chelsea Chelsea *P F I Cole* 63
2 ch c Medicean - Shoshone
10^{7gf} 8^{8g} **0-0-2**

Chelsey Jayne (Ire) *M R Channon* 53
2 b f Galileo (Ire) - Lady Lahar
7^{7gf} 6^{8gf} 8^{8gs} 4^{10hy} **0-0-4 £253**

Chenchikova (Ire) *A P O'Brien* 84
2 b f Sadler's Wells (USA) - Kasora (Ire)
1^{7y} **1-0-1 £8,331**

Cheney Hill *H Candy* 50
2 b g Compton Place - Catriona
7^{6gs} **0-0-1**

Cherish *Rae Guest* 56 a42
2 br f Nashwan (USA) - Chere Amie (USA)
5^{6g} 7^{6g} 9^{7sd} **0-0-3**

Cherished Number *I Semple* 72 a76
6 b g King's Signet (USA) - Pretty Average
1^{9sd} 1^{9sd} 2^{9sd} 8^{9sd} 10^{8g} 9^{9gf} 1^{8gf} 7^{9gf} 3^{9gf}
9^{9gf} 7^{8gf} 9^{9sd} 8^{9sd} **3-2-13 £12,060**

Cherokee Nation *P W D'Arcy* a83
4 br g Emperor Jones (USA) - Me Cherokee
6^{7sd} 5^{8sd} 5^{6sd} 7^{6sd} 12^{8sd} 12^{7gf} 11^{6gs} 14^{6sd}
12^{10sd} **0-0-9 £162**

Cherokee Vision *P W D'Arcy* 52 a55
2 b g Primo Valentino (Ire) - Me Cherokee
10^{5gf} 9^{6sd} 4^{7sd} 6^{7gf} **0-0-4 £278**

Cherry Mix (Fr) *Saeed Bin Suroor* 118 a104
4 b c Linamix (Fr) - Cherry Moon (USA)
4^{10ft} 10^{12gf} 5^{12g} 12^{12gs} 1^{12s} 9^{12gf} **1-0-6**
£130,904

Chess Board *Sir Mark Prescott* 56 a36
2 b c Vettori (Ire) - Cruinn A Bhord
8^{6s} 11^{6sd} 7^{7s} **0-0-3**

Chessee (Ire) *B J Meehan* 50 a33
2 b f Green Desert (USA) - Le Montrachet
11^{6gf} 7^{6gf} 10^{6sd} 11^{7f} **0-0-4**

Chestall *R Hollinshead* 7 a46
4 b g Polar Prince (Ire) - Maradata (Ire)
5^{11sd} 6^{17g} 9^{17sd} 8^{17sd} **0-0-4**

Cheveley Flyer *J Pearce* 61
2 ch c Forzando - Cavern Breeze
11^{7gs} 5^{7s} 7^{7g} 4^{8gf} 5^{8hy} **0-0-5 £399**

Cheviot Heights *Mrs A J Perrett* 69
2 b f Intikhab (USA) - Cheviot Hills (USA)
3^{7gf} 2^{7gs} **0-2-2 £1,854**

Chia (Ire) *D Haydn Jones* 68 a68
2 ch f Ashkalani (Ire) - Motley
6^{6gf} 6^{6gf} 7^{5g} 2^{6f} 9^{8g} 9^{8s} 6^{7sd} 3^{8sd} **0-2-8**
£2,102

Chic *Sir Michael Stoute* 119 a102
5 ch m Machiavellian (USA) - Exclusive
6^{8sd} 12^{8s} 1^{8g} 2^{8gy} 5^{8gs} 7^{10gs} **1-1-6**
£97,437

Chicago Nights (Ire) *Ronald Thompson*
3 ch f Night Shift (USA) - Enclave (USA)
13^{6sd} **0-0-1**

Chicherova (Ire) *T D Barron* 50
2 b f Soviet Star (USA) - Ruby Rose
7^{6gf} 6^{5gf} 9^{7g} **0-0-3**

Chickado (Ire) *D Haydn Jones* 19 a62
4 b f Mujadil (USA) - Arcevia (Ire)
2^{6sd} 4^{6sd} 6^{6sd} 6^{6sd} 15^{6gs} 8^{6sd} 9^{6sd} 2^{6sd} 7^{7sd}
1^{7sd} 8^{8sd} **1-2-11 £4,654**

Chicken Soup *D Carroll* 69 a70
3 br g Dansili - Radiancy (Ire)
15^{8g} 3^{10f} 15^{10gf} 3^{10f} 5^{8gf} 3^{8g} 3^{7sd} 1^{8sd}
1-3-8 £5,436

Chicks Babe *B Palling* a37
3 br f Chickawicka (Ire) - Ballasilla
8^{9sd} 13^{10sd} 10^{9sd} 12^{8f} **0-0-4**

Chief Argent (Ire) *J Howard Johnson* 51
2 b c Robellino (USA) - Running Tycoon (Ire)
7^{6s} 6^{7s} **0-0-2**

Chief Commander (Fr) *Mrs J Chapple-Hyam* a76
2 b/br c Commands (Aus) - Neeran (USA)
2^{7sd} 2^{7sd} **0-2-2 £2,346**

Chief Dipper *P J McBride* 6 a74
3 b g Benny The Dip (USA) - Cuban Reef
1^{9sd} 1^{8sd} 17^{10g} 5^{8sd} 3^{10sd} 8^{9sd} 11^{12sd} 5^{9sd}
7^{7sd} **2-1-9 £7,324**

Chief Exec *C A Cyzer* 71 a85
3 br g Zafonic (USA) - Shot At Love (Ire)
4^{7sd} 13^{7g} 7^{7gf} 5^{6gf} 4^{6sd} 8^{8gs} 5^{7sd} 4^{7sd} 4^{7sd}
8^{8sd} **0-0-10 £2,636**

Chief Scout *B J Meehan* 87 a74
3 br g Tomba - Princess Zara
10^{8gs} 4^{8gs} 7^{8gf} 9^{6gf} 2^{7gf} 11^{7sd} 14^{7gs} 4^{7s}
0-2-8 £3,916

Chigorin *Miss S J Wilton* 67 a20
4 b g Pivotal - Belle Vue
7^{10gs} 2^{10s} 3^{10gs} 16^{12gf} 14^{10sd} 6^{10s} 1^{11gs} 10^{12gs}
1-2-8 £5,260

Chilali (Ire) *A Berry* 26 a46
3 b f Monashee Mountain (USA) - Pam Story
6^{5sd} 5^{5sd} 10^{5sd} 9^{5sd} 7^{5f} 16^{5f} 7^{5gf} 16^{5gf}
0-0-8

Chillin Out *W Jarvis* a46
3 ch c Bahamian Bounty - Steppin Out
4^{6sd} 12^{6sd} 8^{6sd} **0-0-3 £267**

Chillipetals *D Shaw* 37 a28
2 br f Averti (Ire) - Island Mead
10^{6g} 13^{6gf} 10^{8sd} **0-0-3**

Chilly Cracker *R Hollinshead* 68 a66
3 ch f Largesse - Polar Storm (Ire)
14^{5gs} 2^{6hy} 7^{5gf} 7^{5g} 11^{5sd} 2^{6g} 9^{6gf} 9^{7gf} 6^{6gs}
2^{5gs} 10^{5gf} 4^{5sd} 3^{7sd} 11^{5sd} 2^{6sd} 8^{6ss} 12^{6sd}
9^{7sd} **0-5-18 £5,567**

Chiloe Wigeon (Ire) *M J Grassick* 60
2 ch f Docksider (USA) - Shore Lark (USA)

9^{7g} 5^{7s} **0-0-2**

Chilsdown *E J O'Neill* 69
2 b c Mozart (Ire) - Goodwood Blizzard
7^{5g} 4^{8g} 4^{8g} 15^{7gs} **0-0-4 £764**

Chiltai (Ire) *Mervyn Torrens* 36 a29
4 b g Taipan (Ire) - Chilling
15^{5sh} 8^{7g} 7^{5g} 4^{8g} 9^{7gf} 3^{5g} 9^{5gy} 8^{5f} 8^{5sh} 5^{5ss} **0-1-10 £714**

Chimali (Ire) *J R Boyle* a77
4 b g Foxhound (USA) - Mari-Ela (Ire)
8^{6sd} 8^{6sd} 8^{6sd} **0-0-3**

Chin Dancer *B R Millman*
3 ch f Inchinor - Red Hot Dancer (USA)
8^{12gf} 12^{16g} **0-0-2**

China Pearl *R Hannon* 74
2 ch g Benny The Dip (USA) - Seek The Pearl
14^{7gf} 15^{8s} 6^{8g} 2^{8gs} 9^{9gf} **0-1-5 £1,266**

Chinalea (Ire) *C G Cox* 81
3 b g Danetime (Ire) - Raise-A-Secret (Ire)
3^{5s} 4^{5gf} 2^{6gf} 2^{6g} 5^{6gf} 1^{5s} 13^{6g} 8^{5gs} 3^{5g} 8^{6g} **1-5-10 £11,087**

Chineur (Fr) *M Delzangles* 121
4 b c Fasliyev (USA) - Wardara
1^{6g} 1^{6hy} 1^{5s} 1^{5gf} 9^{5gf} 4^{5gs} 5^{6gs} 8^{5gf} **4-0-8 £148,777**

Chingola *R M Whitaker* 34 a24
3 b f Atraf - Sulaka
11^{6g} 10^{7sd} 7^{6ss} **0-0-3**

Chippewa River *M Dods* 23
2 b g Pursuit Of Love - Sharp Top
10^{6g} 17^{6gs} **0-0-2**

Chiqitita (Ire) *Miss M E Rowland* 14
4 b f Saddlers' Hall (Ire) - Funny Cut (Ire)
10^{12gf} **0-0-1**

Chisel *M Wigham* 33
4 ch g Hector Protector (USA) - Not Before Time (Ire)
11^{12sd} 13^{10sd} 9^{8s} 8^{5f} 12^{7g} **0-0-5**

Chiselled (Ire) *K R Burke* 65
3 b g Rossini (USA) - Con Dancer
5^{5g} 5^{5gf} 8^{5g} **0-0-3**

Chisom *M W Easterby* 58 a24
2 b g Averti (Ire) - Cinder Hills
3^{5gs} 8^{6g} 7^{5sd} **0-1-3 £640**

Chocolate Boy (Ire) *G L Moore* 66 a66
6 b g Dolphin Street (Fr) - Kawther
10^{12sd} 2^{12sd} 8^{13sd} 1^{12sd} 7^{12s} 2^{12gf} 3^{12f} 4^{12gf} 11^{12g} 7^{12sd} 6^{16sd} **1-3-11 £4,957**

Chocolate Caramel (USA) *Mrs A J Perrett* 90
3 b g Storm Creek (USA) - Sandhill (Brz)
5^{10gs} 1^{10s} 4^{12gf} 2^{12gs} 5^{12g} 2^{14s} 6^{16gs} **1-2-7 £12,456**

Choir Practice *J H M Gosden* 74
2 b f Benny The Dip (USA) - Choirgirl
3^{6gs} 4^{7gs} 6^{7gf} **0-1-3 £1,761**

Chookie Heiton (Ire) *I Semple* 112
7 br g Fumo Di Londra (Ire) - Royal Wolff
24^{6gf} 14^{6f} 2^{5g} 10^{6gf} 3^{6g} 1^{5g} 7^{6gf} 12^{6g} 10^{7gf} **1-2-9 £28,787**

Chookie Windsor *I Semple* 56 a56
2 b g Lake Coniston (Ire) - Lady Of Windsor (Ire)
8^{6g} F^{6gs} 3^{6gf} 5^{8gf} 4^{7g} 10^{8s} 4^{9sd} **0-0-7 £1,272**

Choosy (Ire) *R Hannon* 94
2 b f Kalanisi (Ire) - Hawksbill Special (Ire)
10^{7gf} 2^{6gs} 1^{6s} 4^{7gs} **1-1-4 £8,962**

Choreographic (Ire) *R A Fahey* 54 a7
3 b g Komaite (USA) - Lambast
13^{7s} 3^{5gs} 13^{6gs} 8^{7gf} 5^{8gf} 7^{9gf} BD^{8g} 13^{10gf} 14^{6gf} 14^{5gf} 11^{7sd} 10^{8sd} **0-0-12 £522**

Choreography *M L W Bell* 50
2 ch c Medicean - Stark Ballet (USA)
6^{7gf} **0-0-1**

Choristar *W R Muir* 61 a64
4 ch g Inchinor - Star Tulip
2^{6sd} 4^{7sd} 4^{7sd} 8^{6sd} 7^{7gf} 5^{7gf} 5^{7gf} 3^{10f} **0-2-8 £2,109**

Chorus *B R Millman* a63
8 b m Bandmaster (USA) - Name That Tune
3^{7sd} 2^{7sd} 5^{5sd} 4^{6sd} 11^{7sd} 6^{7sd} 6^{8sd} 9^{7sd} 11^{9sd} 5^{7sd} 10^{6sd} 14^{7gf} **0-2-12 £1,213**

Chorus Beauty *N I M Rossiter*
4 b f Royal Applause - Happy Lady (Fr)
13^{9sd} **0-0-1**

Choysia *D W Barker* 88
2 b f Pivotal - Bonica
1^{5gf} 17^{5gf} 5^{6g} 1^{5gf} 2^{5gs} 8^{6g} **2-1-6 £13,826**

Chris Corsa *M L W Bell* 80
2 b g Mark Of Esteem (Ire) - Risque Lady
4^{6gf} 6^{7gf} 1^{7s} 7^{7gs} 13^{8g} 12^{7gs} **1-0-6 £2,649**

Chrissam Express (Ire) *Karen McLintock* 55
3 b g Fayruz - Miss Nutwood (Ire)
4^{5g} 7^{6gf} **0-0-2**

Christa Bee *E J O'Neill* 80 a65
2 b f Groom Dancer (USA) - Beleza (Ire)
1^{5sd} 1^{5g} 4^{6gf} 4^{6gf} 5^{6g} **2-0-5 £6,894**

Christian Bendix *P Howling* 37 a49
3 ch g Presidium - Very Good
10^{6g} 13^{6g} 7^{7sd} 7^{6sd} 3^{6sd} 9^{6sd} 3^{6sd} 5^{6ss} 2^{6sd} **0-3-9 £1,404**

Christmas Player (USA) *J H M Gosden* 46 a61
2 b/br f Theatrical - Christmas Gift (USA)
13^{7gf} 5^{10sd} **0-0-2**

Christom *Mrs Tracey Barfoot-Saunt* 27
3 b g Groom Dancer (USA) - Throw Away Line (USA)
16^{12g} 14^{10gf} 13^{12sd} 7^{8g} 16^{10g} **0-0-5**

Chromboy (Ger) *N B King* 27 a40
5 ch g Kornado - Chroma (Ger)
6^{10gs} 5^{13sd} 11^{14g} 12^{12sd} **0-0-4**

Chronomatic *M H Tompkins* 79
2 gr g Mister Baileys - Sky Red
2^{6gs} 2^{6g} 5^{6gf} 4^{6gs} 25^{6g} 3^{6gs} **0-3-6 £5,035**

Chrysander *M R Channon* 109
3 b c Cadeaux Genereux - Jumairah Sun (Ire)
1^{8gs} 3^{8gs} 2^{8gf} 4^{8g} 4^{10g} 6^{10vs} 3^{7hy} 1^{8hy} **2-1-8 £31,026**

Chunky Bell *P T Midgley* 42
2 b c Easycall - Lady Susan
9^{5g} 6^{6gf} 5^{6gs} 10^{6gf} **0-0-4 £316**

Ci Ci La Femme *Lindsay Woods* 29
3 b f Atraf - Shalati (Fr)
10^{5hy} 16^{7g} 9^{6sd} **0-0-3**

Cicatrice *D R Gandolfo* 49 a47
4 ch g Wolfhound (USA) - Capricious Lady (Ire)
7^{10sd} 1^{8sd} 12^{10sd} 9^{8gf} 7^{7sd} **1-0-5 £1,533**

Ciccone *W Jarvis* 63
2 ch f Singspiel (Ire) - Untold Riches (USA)

7^{6gf} 9^{7g} **0-0-2**

Ciel Bleu *John E Kiely* 39
3 ch f Septieme Ciel (USA) - Valthea (Fr)
18^{10g} 13^{12y} **0-0-2**

Cilla's Smile *M A Buckley* 39 a49
3 b f Lake Coniston (Ire) - Tinkerbird
12^{6g} 4^{6sd} 8^{5s} 7^{6gf} 16^{6gf} 10^{6sd} **0-0-6**

Cils *Eamon Tyrrell* 59 a54
4 b f Zilzal (USA) - My Valentina
2^{7sd} 13^{6s} 7^{9s} 8^{7gf} 5^{8g} **0-1-5 £1,038**

Cimyla (Ire) *C F Wall* 103 a112
4 b g Lomitas - Coyaima (Ger)
2^{8gs} 7^{8g} 4^{8s} 24^{9s} 1^{9sd} 1^{10sd} **2-1-6 £28,212**

Cinder Maid *J G Portman* a37
3 b f Piccolo - Bella Helena
11^{7sd} 12^{10sd} **0-0-2**

Cindertrack *J A Osborne* 67 a64
2 b g Singspiel (Ire) - Beading
6^{7g} 4^{8g} 6^{8sd} **0-0-3 £321**

Cinematic (Ire) *M H Tompkins* 73
2 b c Bahhare (USA) - Eastern Star (Ire)
10^{6g} 3^{6g} 1^{6g} 13^{6g} **1-1-4 £4,731**

Circassian (Ire) *J Howard Johnson* 106
4 b g Groom Dancer (USA) - Daraliya (Ire)
5^{21s} 1^{16g} 1^{14g} **2-0-3 £19,586**

Circle Of Wolves *H J Manners*
7 ch g Wolfhound (USA) - Misty Halo
15^{12s} **0-0-1**

Circuit Dancer (Ire) *A Berry* 93
5 b g Mujadil (USA) - Trysinger (Ire)
3^{6s} 5^{6gf} 12^{6g} 11^{5g} 12^{6g} 7^{6gf} 9^{6gf} 6^{6gf} 17^{6g} 4^{7gf} 24^{6g} 10^{7g} **0-0-12 £2,102**

Circumspect (Ire) *P C Haslam* 51 a50
3 b g Spectrum (Ire) - Newala
10^{7g} 7^{10gf} 11^{9sd} **0-0-3**

Cirrious *B Palling* 64
4 gr f Cloudings (Ire) - Westfield Mist
7^{10g} 7^{12hy} 1^{12g} 3^{10gf} 5^{12gf} **1-1-5 £4,105**

Citelle (Ire) *Mrs P N Dutfield* 59
2 ch f City On A Hill (USA) - La Rochelle (Ire)
12^{6gf} 1^{7gf} 7^{7g} 5^{10g} 10^{8gs} **1-0-5 £3,250**

Cithogue (Ire) *J R Fanshawe* a50
2 ch f Machiavellian (USA) - Another Dancer (Fr)
10^{8sd} **0-0-1**

City Chancer (Ire) *Sir Mark Prescott* 65 a41
2 b g Kalanisi (Ire) - Rachrush (Ire)
7^{6gf} 9^{6sd} **0-0-2**

City For Conquest (Ire) *K R Burke* 80
2 b f City On A Hill (USA) - Northern Life (Ire)
6^{5g} 7^{5hy} 1^{5f} 3^{5f} 1^{5gf} 4^{5gf} 8^{5gf} 2^{5g} 4^{5g} 4^{5g} **2-1-10 £12,117**

City General (Ire) *J S Moore* 52 a54
4 ch g General Monash (USA) - Astra (Ire)
5^{7sd} 5^{8sd} 1^{7sd} 9^{8sd} 3^{8s} 11^{7gf} 7^{6gf} 5^{8gf} 10^{7gf} 6^{8f} 1^{7f} 15^{7gf} **2-0-12 £4,836**

City Of Troy *Sir Michael Stoute* 100
2 ch c Grand Lodge (USA) - Arazena (USA)
1^{7gf} 1^{7gf} 4^{8g} **2-0-3 £17,351**

City Palace *Evan Williams* 56
4 ch g Grand Lodge (USA) - Ajuga (USA)
10^{10gf} **0-0-1**

Clafoutis (USA) *Sir Michael Stoute* a64
2 ch f Unbridled's Song (USA) - Sous Entendu (USA)
4^{6sd} **0-0-1 £287**

Clambake (Ire) *M P Tregoning* 64
3 ch f Grand Lodge (USA) - Sometime (Ire)
5^{8g} 5^{10gf} 8^{8g} **0-0-3**

Clann A Cougar *P A Blockley*
5 ch g Bahamian Bounty - Move Darling
10^{8sd} **0-0-1**

Clap *J A Osborne* 29
3 b f Royal Applause - Devastating
14^{7g} **0-0-1**

Clara Bow (Ire) *B W Hills* 82 a69
3 b f Sadler's Wells (USA) - Brigid (USA)
2^{8g} 4^{8gf} 1^{7gf} 2^{7gs} 5^{7g} 7^{8gs} 4^{7s} 8^{7sd} **1-2-8 £9,228**

Claradotnet *Mrs L Williamson* 11 a41
5 b m Sri Pekan (USA) - Lypharitissima (Fr)
14^{16g} 3^{12sd} 6^{14sd} 9^{14ss} **0-1-4 £367**

Clare Galway *B G Powell* a52
4 b f Compton Place - Oublier L'Ennui (Fr)
6^{10sd} 8^{10sd} **0-0-2**

Clare Hills (Ire) *K R Burke* 98
2 b f Orpen (USA) - Morale
1^{5s} 1^{5g} 4^{5gf} 5^{6g} 6^{6g} **2-0-5 £22,171**

Claret And Amber *R A Fahey* 86 a89
3 b g Forzando - Artistic Licence
10^{8g} 8^{8g} 12^{8s} 9^{7sd} 2^{9sd} 3^{7sd} **0-2-6 £2,570**

Clash Of The Ash (USA) *J S Bolger* 95
3 b g King Of Kings (Ire) - Ceirseach (Ire)
4^{7s} 3^{10ys} 4^{10gf} 15^{12gy} **0-1-4 £6,665**

Classic Calvados (Fr) *P D Niven* 21
6 b/br g Thatching - Mountain Stage (Ire)
12^{10gf} **0-0-1**

Classic Croco (Ger) *Mrs Jeremy Young* a89
4 gr g Croco Rouge (Ire) - Classic Light (Ire)
9^{12sd} 7^{12sd} **0-0-2**

Classic Encounter (Ire) *D M Simcock* 99
2 b c Lujain (USA) - Licence To Thrill
3^{5gf} 1^{5gf} 3^{5gf} 9^{5g} **1-1-4 £12,962**

Classic Event (Ire) *T D Easterby* 64
4 ch g Croco Rouge (Ire) - Delta Town (USA)
5^{16g} 8^{12s} 2^{16gf} 7^{16g} 4^{16gf} **0-1-5 £1,341**

Classic Expression *E S McMahon* 28
4 ch f Classic Cliche (Ire) - Breezy Day
11^{8sd} 6^{10gs} 10^{11g} **0-0-3**

Classic Guest *M R Channon* a47
3 b f Xaar - My Lass
7^{7sd} 11^{7sd} **0-0-2**

Classic Lease *J Mackie*
4 b g Cyrano De Bergerac - Vado Via
10^{12g} UR^{8g} **0-0-2**

Classic Punch (Ire) *D R C Elsworth* 79
2 b c Mozart (Ire) - Rum Cay (USA)
8^{7g} 3^{8gs} **0-1-2 £828**

Classic Role *L Wells* a72
6 b g Tragic Role (USA) - Clare Island
7^{12sd} **0-0-1**

Classic Style (Ire) *T D Easterby* 53 a32
3 b f Desert Style (Ire) - Classic Ring (Ire)
7^{7s} 3^{8sd} 10^{8g} 9^{7gf} **0-0-4 £412**

Claureen Prince (Ire) *R M H Cowell* a49
6 ch g Prince Of Birds (USA) - Arkadina's Million
8^{8sd} 5^{8sd} 9^{7sd} **0-0-3**

Clear Impression (Ire) *P W Chapple-Hyam* 85
3 b f Danehill (USA) - Shining Hour (USA)
1^{6gs} 7^{7gs} **1-0-2 £6,743**

Clear Thinking *Miss Venetia Williams* 107
5 b g Rainbow Quest (USA) - Coraline
5^{16s} 10^{16gs} **0-0-2 £1,250**

Clear Veneer (USA) *M Johnston* 56
2 ch f Diesis - Forest Treasure (Ire)
10^{6gf} 6^{5gf} 6^{6gf} 5^{6gf} 9^{8gf} **0-0-5**

Clear Vision *Mrs A J Perrett* a60
2 b f Observatory (USA) - Claxon
7^{8sd} **0-0-1**

Clearing Sky (Ire) *J R Boyle* 63 a63
4 gr f Exploit (USA) - Litchfield Hills (USA)
8^{6sd} 13^{7sd} 2^{6sd} 10^{6sd} 3^{6gf} 10^{6s} 1^{5hd} 2^{6sd} 8^{6g} 8^{5sd} **1-3-10 £4,761**

Cleaver *Lady Herries* 72
4 ch g Kris - Much Too Risky
15^{9g} 1^{10s} **1-0-2 £3,462**

Cleveland *R Hollinshead* 63
3 b g Pennekamp (USA) - Clerio
7^{10s} 17^{8gs} 6^{6g} 13^{6g} 8^{6gf} 8^{6g} **0-0-6**

Cleveland Way *D Carroll* 28 a48
5 b g Forzando - Fallal (Ire)
12^{7sd} 9^{6sd} 1^{7sd} 12^{7sd} 5^{6sd} 9^{6sd} 3^{6sd} 7^{7sd} 6^{7sd} 10^{6sd} 1^{6sd} 9^{6sd} 8^{6sd} 7^{6sd} 12^{7sd} 6^{6g} 11^{6sd} 8^{7ss} 8^{8sd} **2-1-19 £3,156**

Cliffie (Ire) *A D Brown* 27
3 ch g Timeless Times (USA) - Suppression
8^{8f} 7^{12f} 7^{12g} **0-0-3**

Climate (Ire) *K A Ryan* 65
6 ch g Catrail (USA) - Burishki
6^{8gf} **0-0-1**

Climate Change (USA) *J H M Gosden* 96
3 ch c Langfuhr (Can) - Summer Mist (USA)
1^{10gf} 1^{9g} 2^{9g} 7^{12g} **2-1-4 £16,746**

Clinet (Ire) *J W Hills* 101 a83
3 b f Docksider (USA) - Oiche Mhaith
1^{9sd} 6^{8sd} 5^{8gf} 2^{8g} 1^{7g} 3^{7gf} 8^{7gs} 3^{8f} 2^{7gf} 3^{8g} 3^{7g} **2-6-11 £37,951**

Clipper Hoy *Mrs H Sweeting* a79
3 ch c Bahamian Bounty - Indian Flag (Ire)
13^{5sd} 7^{5sd} 2^{5sd} 1^{5sd} **1-1-4 £3,524**

Clipperdown (Ire) *W R Swinburn* 91 a93
4 b g Green Desert (USA) - Maroussie (Fr)
1^{8gf} 4^{8g} 1^{10gf} 6^{10gf} 7^{10g} 2^{10gf} 1^{10sd} 9^{10g} **3-1-8 £29,406**

Cloann (Ire) *E A Wheeler* 67 a55
3 b f Danetime (Ire) - Rustic Lawn
9^{6sd} 2^{5sd} 8^{5g} 4^{5f} 3^{5gf} 4^{6gf} 6^{6gf} 1^{6f} 13^{6gf} 8^{5g} 2^{6f} 10^{5f} 6^{6gf} 8^{5gf} 4^{5sd} 7^{5sd} **1-2-16 £6,245**

Cloonavery (Ire) *B Llewellyn* 63
3 b g Xaar - Hero's Pride (Fr)
6^{10gf} 5^{12f} **0-0-2**

Close To You (Ire) *T G Mills* 112 a73
2 b c Shinko Forest (Ire) - Maritana (USA)
8^{6gf} 1^{7gf} 1^{7sd} 1^{7s} 6^{7s} 1^{7gs} 7^{7gs} **4-0-7 £57,311**

Cloud Atlas (Ire) *S Kirk* 52 a76
2 b g Monashee Mountain (USA) - Blue Sioux
6^{7g} 2^{6sd} 2^{6sd} **0-2-3 £2,333**

Cloud Catcher (Ire) *M Appleby* 3 a4
4 br f Charnwood Forest (Ire) - Notley Park
4^{8sd} 13^{17sd} 9^{12sd} 10^{7g} **0-0-4**

Cloud Dancer *K A Ryan* 76 a92
6 b m Bishop Of Cashel - Summer Pageant
7^{8sd} 2^{9sd} 9^{6sd} 5^{7sd} 12^{7sd} 5^{6gf} 5^{6gf} 14^{7gf} **0-1-8 £2,084**

Clove (USA) *J A Osborne* 76 a61
3 b f Distant View (USA) - Nidd (USA)
5^{5gf} 3^{5g} 12^{6gf} 5^{6gf} 9^{5g} 9^{5sd} 6^{6ss} **0-1-7 £1,568**

Club Captain (USA) *G A Butler* 48
2 b g Red Ransom (USA) - Really Fancy (USA)
9^{6gs} **0-0-1**

Clueless *N G Richards* 95
3 b g Royal Applause - Pure
4^{10gf} 2^{12s} 2^{12g} 1^{12gf} 5^{12gf} 1^{10gf} 2^{10s} **2-3-7 £24,508**

Cnoc Na Gaoithe (USA) *E A L Dunlop* 75 a72
2 ch g Rahy (USA) - Momentous (USA)
14^{6s} 1^{6sd} 4^{7g} 10^{7sd} 12^{8sd} **1-0-5 £4,293**

Coalite (Ire) *B Palling* 71
2 b g Second Empire (Ire) - Municipal Girl (Ire)
10^{6gf} 10^{6gf} 3^{5g} 11^{6g} **0-1-4 £536**

Coalpark (Ire) *M Johnston* 77
2 b f Titus Livius (Fr) - Honey Storm (Ire)
1^{7gf} 8^{7gs} **1-0-2 £4,446**

Coat Of Honour (USA) *J Howard Johnson* 57
5 gr g Mark Of Esteem (Ire) - Ballymac Girl
14^{12f} **0-0-1**

Coburn (Fr) *B J Meehan* 92 a77
2 b c Pivotal - Source De Reve (Fr)
5^{5g} 2^{6sd} 3^{6gs} 2^{7sd} 5^{7gf} 2^{6g} 4^{6gf} **0-4-7 £22,295**

Coccinelle (Ire) *K A Morgan* 25
7 b m Great Marquess - Nuit D'Ete (USA)
9^{16gf} **0-0-1**

Cockatoo (USA) *J H M Gosden* 51
2 b c Dynaformer (USA) - Enticed (USA)
11^{7g} **0-0-1**

Cockney Tai (Ire) *Patrick Morris* 54 a34
5 b m Taipan (Ire) - Cockney Ground (Ire)
11^{12g} 2^{12g} 11^{13gf} 7^{12g} 9^{11g} 6^{12f} 6^{12g} 4^{10gf} 1^{10gf} 8^{9sf} **1-1-10 £5,066**

Coco Reef *M Mullineaux* a32
4 b f Kingsinger (Ire) - Highland Blue
8^{6sd} 11^{7sd} 12^{5sd} **0-0-3**

Coconut Beach *C Roche* 98
4 b c Sadler's Wells (USA) - Eversince (USA)
5^{16s} 5^{19gs} 3^{20gf} 19^{16g} **0-1-4 £8,500**

Coconut Moon *E J Alston* 46 a70
3 b f Bahamian Bounty - Lunar Ridge
10^{6gf} 8^{6g} 1^{5sd} 3^{5sd} **1-1-4 £3,852**

Coconut Squeak *Stef Liddiard* 103 a66
3 b f Bahamian Bounty - Creeking
3^{7sd} 2^{7sd} 4^{7gs} 10^{6gf} 2^{6gf} 1^{6gf} 4^{7gf} 2^{6gs} 2^{6g} 3^{6gf} 2^{6gf} 2^{6g} 3^{6gf} 4^{7g} 1^{6s} 10^{6gs} 5^{6s} **2-9-17 £37,924**

Coda Agency *D W P Arbuthnot* 55
2 b g Agnes World (USA) - The Frog Lady (Ire)
8^{7g} 7^{8g} 6^{8gf} **0-0-3**

Code (Ire) *Miss Z C Davison*
4 b g Danehill (USA) - Hidden Meaning (USA)
13^{12g} **0-0-1**

Code Orange *J H M Gosden* 72 a50
3 b f Green Desert (USA) - Warning Belle
11^{7sd} 2^{6g} 1^{6gf} 7^{6gs} **1-1-4 £5,269**

Coeur Courageux (Fr) *D Flood* 103 a88
3 b c Xaar - Linoise (Fr)
2^{7sd} 1^{7sd} 13^{8s} 3^{8g} 7^{7g} 9^{8gs} **1-2-6**

£9,600

Coeur D'Alene *Dr J R J Naylor* 43 a51
4 gr g Hernando (Fr) - Chambre Separee (USA)
9^{14s} 11^{12sd} 8^{13sd} **0-0-3**

Coffin Dodger *C N Allen* 34 a16
2 ch f Dracula (Aus) - Karakul (Ire)
8^{5gf} 7^{5sd} 6^{6g} 4^{7gf} 6^{6f} **0-0-5**

Coffs Harbour (USA) *E A L Dunlop* 59
2 b c Swain (Ire) - Tethkar
8^{7gf} 3^{8s} 12^{6sd} 14^{7gs} **0-1-4 £552**

Cois Na Tine Eile *P W Hiatt* 53 a33
3 br f Cois Na Tine (Ire) - Water Pixie (Ire)
9^{10g} 1^{11gs} 4^{12f} 3^{12f} 2^{12gf} 5^{12g} 2^{16g} 11^{12sf}
1-2-8 £4,721

Cold Climate *Bob Jones* 55 a60
10 ch g Pursuit Of Love - Sharpthorne (USA)
11^{6gs} 15^{6gs} 3^{6g} 6^{7sd} **0-1-4 £247**

Cold Cure *B Palling* 41 a14
2 b c Averti (Ire) - Forest Song
6^{5gs} 7^{5f} 10^{7sd} 9^{6sd} **0-0-4**

Cold Play *C J Mann* a53
3 ch g Inchinor - Ice House
9^{8sd} 12^{10sd} 6^{9sd} 9^{12sd} **0-0-4**

Cold Turkey *G L Moore* 98 a98
5 b/br g Polar Falcon (USA) - South Rock
1^{12sd} 3^{12sd} 1^{12sd} 2^{12sd} 4^{13sd} 1^{16gs} 12^{19gs} 2^{16sd}
10^{16g} 8^{16sd} 3^{16sd} 1^{12sd} **4-3-12 £56,596**

Cole (Ire) *J Howard Johnson* 50
2 b g Distant Music (USA) - Dark Albatross (USA)
4^{6gf} 10^{5gs} 7^{5g} **0-0-3**

Colemanstown *B Ellison* 48 a68
5 b g Charnwood Forest (Ire) - Arme Fatale (Ire)
3^{8sd} 6^{9sd} 1^{8sd} 3^{8sd} 6^{7gs} 11^{6g} 3^{9sd} 5^{7sd} 14^{7g}
10^{9sd} **1-3-10 £4,197**

Coleorton Dancer *K A Ryan* 108
3 ch g Danehill Dancer (Ire) - Tayovullin (Ire)
1^{6s} 5^{8gs} 2^{6gs} 4^{5gf} 18^{6g} 5^{6gs} 14^{6g} 20^{6g}
1-1-8 £22,749

Coleorton Dane *K A Ryan* 79 a54
3 gr g Danehill Dancer (Ire) - Cloudy Nine
15^{7g} 2^{7s} 4^{8gf} 11^{8gf} 14^{7gf} 8^{6gs} 16^{8gf} 12^{7sd}
4^{7sd} **0-1-9 £3,501**

Coleorton Foxe (Ire) *K A Ryan* 40
2 ch f Foxhound (USA) - Tayovullin (Ire)
10^{5gf} 8^{5gf} **0-0-2**

Colinca's Lad (Ire) *G C H Chung* 94 a67
3 b g Lahib (USA) - Real Flame
4^{10s} 5^{10s} 8^{12hy} 12^{12sd} 6^{9sd} **0-0-5 £980**

Colinette *H Candy* 46
2 b f Groom Dancer (USA) - Collide
11^{8gs} **0-0-1**

Colisay *Mrs A J Perrett* 109 a103
6 b g Entrepreneur - La Sorrela (Ire)
7^{8gs} 2^{10gf} 5^{10g} 17^{10gf} 5^{10g} 5^{9gf} 9^{9s} 2^{8gs} 4^{10s}
9^{10sd} **0-2-10 £12,891**

Collateral Damage (Ire) *T D Easterby* 79 a62
2 b c Orpen (USA) - Jay Gee (Ire)
3^{5sd} 4^{6gf} 2^{7s} 3^{7g} 1^{7s} 5^{7s} **1-3-6 £7,411**

Collect *M H Tompkins* 68
3 b f Vettori (Ire) - Ring Fence
8^{8g} 6^{8gs} 2^{8gf} 8^{7gf} 4^{10gs} 8^{10gs} **0-1-6**
£1,813

College Queen *S Gollings* 60
7 b m Lugana Beach - Eccentric Dancer
7^{5gf} 4^{5g} 11^{5g} 7^{6g} 13^{6g} 12^{5gf} **0-0-6**

£306

College Rebel *J F Coupland* a34
4 b f Defacto (USA) - Eccentric Dancer
4^{9sd} 6^{12sd} 6^{8sd} 9^{12ss} 9^{8sd} 6^{9sd} **0-0-6**

College Time (Ire) *P A Blockley* a13
4 b g Danetime (Ire) - Respectful (Ire)
10^{6sd} **0-0-1**

Colleton River (Ire) *W J Haggas* 71 a73
4 gr g Croco Rouge (Ire) - Midnight Angel
1^{12sd} 10^{12g} 2^{16g} 3^{16gf} 7^{18g} 16^{16gf} **1-2-6**
£4,931

Collette's Choice *R A Fahey* 43 a41
2 b f Royal Applause - Brilliance
11^{7gs} 6^{5sd} 8^{6g} 9^{8g} **0-0-4**

Collier Hill *G A Swinbank* 117
7 ch g Dr Devious (Ire) - Polar Queen
1^{12gf} 4^{12gf} 3^{12gf} 1^{12s} 2^{12g} 1^{14g} **3-2-6**
£324,243

Colloquial *H Candy* 96
4 b g Classic Cliche (Ire) - Celia Brady
2^{10gf} 2^{10gf} 5^{13gf} 10^{16g} 1^{14g} 1^{16gs} **2-2-6**
£13,411

Colloseum *T J Etherington* 51 a55
4 b g Piccolo - Trig Point
7^{7sd} 3^{7sd} 9^{7sd} 6^{9gf} 5^{9sd} 3^{6gf} 11^{6sd} 15^{6f} 2^{7gf}
1^{7sd} 12^{7sf} **1-3-11 £3,078**

Colmar Supreme *R Hannon* 72 a70
2 b f Woodborough (USA) - Child Star (Fr)
9^{5gs} 5^{7gf} 3^{6f} 6^{6gf} 2^{7g} 10^{7g} 7^{8g} 1^{7gs} 3^{7sd}
3^{7sd} **1-3-10 £6,569**

Colonel Bilko (Ire) *Miss S J Wilton* 62 a62
3 b g General Monash (USA) - Mari-Ela (Ire)
4^{6sd} 8^{6sd} 7^{7gs} 5^{6gf} 9^{7gf} 3^{6sd} 4^{6sd} 2^{7gf} 6^{7gf}
6^{8f} 2^{7gs} 10^{7sd} 5^{10g} 10^{9sd} 9^{8sd} 7^{7sd}
0-3-16 £4,586

Colonel Cotton (Ire) *D Nicholls* 93
6 b g Royal Applause - Cutpurse Moll
5^{5g} 11^{6f} 13^{5gf} 18^{6gs} 15^{6g} 8^{5g} 26^{6g}
0-0-7 £1,875

Colonial Girl (Ire) *T D Easterby* 60
3 b f Desert Style (Ire) - Telemania (Ire)
11^{5s} 4^{6gs} 6^{5g} 2^{6f} 4^{6gs} 3^{6f} 6^{6g} 4^{7gf} 8^{6g}
0-2-9 £2,060

Colophony (USA) *K A Morgan* a69
5 ch g Distant View (USA) - Private Line (USA)
9^{13sd} 5^{12sd} **0-0-2**

Colorus (Ire) *R A Fahey* 95 a77
2 b c Night Shift (USA) - Duck Over
1^{5sd} 4^{5g} 3^{5gf} 8^{5hy} 20^{6gf} **1-1-5 £6,695**

Colorwise (Ire) *P C Haslam* 14
2 b f Spectrum (Ire) - Night Owl
8^{5g} **0-0-1**

Colour Blind (Ire) *M L W Bell* a24
3 b g Spectrum (Ire) - Sarooh's Love (USA)
9^{9sd} 11^{12sd} **0-0-2**

Colour Code (Ire) *N P Littmoden* 21 a56
4 b g Spectrum (Ire) - Viendra Nur (USA)
6^{10sd} 6^{9sd} 13^{10sd} 15^{8gs} 13^{8gf} 8^{10gs} **0-0-6**

Colourful Era *D G Bridgwater* 67 a67
11 ch g Indian Ridge - Clare Celeste
3^{7sd} 5^{7sd} 7^{7sd} 14^{10sd} 1^{6sd} 2^{6gs} 14^{5gs} 13^{6gf}
11^{6sd} **1-2-9 £5,065**

Colourpoint (USA) *C E Brittain* 76
2 b/br f Forest Wildcat (USA) - Farrfesheena (USA)
9^{5g} 10^{6gf} 2^{5g} 2^{5f} 5^{6gf} 16^{7gf} 14^{5g} 7^{5hy} PU^{6sd}

0-2-9 £6,741

Coltchester (Ire) *Peter Grayson* a56
2 b c Tagula (Ire) - Eveam (Ire)
12^{6sd} 5^{6sd} **0-0-2**

Colton *J M P Eustace* 64
2 b g Zilzal (USA) - Picot
7^{6gf} 9^{7gf} **0-0-2**

Colway Ritz *W Storey* 54
11 b g Rudimentary (USA) - Million Heiress
10^{14g} 8^{12s} 10^{11g} 5^{11gf} 3^{12s} 5^{12f} 8^{12gf} 4^{16gf} 5^{12gf} **0-1-9 £420**

Comcatchini *J R Best*
3 ch g Compton Place - Baileys Firecat
15^{7gf} **0-0-1**

Come Away With Me (Ire) *M A Buckley* 72
5 b m Machiavellian (USA) - Vert Val (USA)
5^{5g} 1^{5gf} 4^{6gf} 3^{5gf} 6^{5gf} 8^{5gf} **1-1-6 £4,396**

Come On *J Hetherton* 51 a1
6 b g Aragon - All On
12^{5sd} 9^{6s} 13^{7g} 8^{5gf} 5^{5s} 2^{8gf} 6^{8gf} **0-1-7 £832**

Come On Jonny (Ire) *R M Beckett* 106
3 b g Desert King (Ire) - Idle Fancy
1^{10g} 3^{10gs} 2^{12gs} 1^{12g} 4^{12gs} 2^{10s} 9^{12gs} 1^{12hy} **3-3-8 £66,305**

Come Out Fighting *P A Blockley* 91
2 b c Bertolini (USA) - Ulysses Daughter (Ire)
3^{5g} 1^{5gf} 1^{5g} 6^{6hy} **2-1-4 £16,582**

Come To Daddy (Ire) *F Jordan* 29
3 ch g Fayruz - Forgren (Ire)
PU^{11gf} 17^{10g} 15^{10g} **0-0-3**

Come What Augustus *R M Stronge* 52
3 b g Mujahid (USA) - Sky Red
8^{10s} 6^{10gf} 16^{10g} **0-0-3**

Come What July (Ire) *Mrs N Macauley* 65 a88
4 b g Indian Rocket - Persian Sally (Ire)
6^{12sd} 1^{14sd} 1^{12sd} 3^{11sd} 3^{12sd} 8^{12sd} 2^{12sd} 7^{12sd} 15^{12g} 6^{11g} 10^{10gf} 1^{12gf} 1^{14sd} 8^{12gf} 10^{14gf} 6^{12g} 14^{10gf} 9^{12gf} BD^{17sd} 10^{12sd} 5^{11sd} 5^{16sd} 5^{12sd} **4-3-23 £15,420**

Comeintothespace (Ire) *A Bailey* 74 a74
3 b g Tagula (Ire) - Playa Del Sol (Ire)
1^{9sd} 1^{9sd} 2^{10sd} 14^{10g} 4^{10sd} 6^{8g} 2^{8gf} 8^{10f} 8^{8g} 9^{10gf} 7^{8g} 4^{8gf} 4^{7gf} 2^{8gf} 11^{8gf} 4^{8gf} 7^{8gs} 9^{8g} 12^{9ft} 12^{10sd} **2-4-20 £13,350**

Comic Strip *Sir Mark Prescott* 106
3 b g Marju (Ire) - Comic (Ire)
4^{10s} **0-0-1 £5,000**

Comic Tales *M Mullineaux* 36 a43
4 b g Mind Games - Glorious Aragon
4^{6sd} 3^{6sd} 13^{9sd} 4^{6sd} 6^{5sd} 10^{5s} 3^{6sd} 5^{6g} 2^{5sd} **0-3-9 £857**

Comical Errors (USA) *P C Haslam* 54 a49
3 b g Distorted Humor (USA) - Fallibility (USA)
7^{10sd} 7^{10g} 10^{10g} 11^{12f} 10^{12sd} **0-0-5**

Command Respect *E F Vaughan*
2 b f Commands (Aus) - The Blade (Ger)
11^{6sd} **0-0-1**

Commander Wish *Lucinda Featherstone* 69 a48
2 ch c Arkadian Hero (USA) - Flighty Dancer
7^{6g} 3^{6g} 12^{6gf} 12^{6g} 17^{7s} 7^{7sd} **0-1-6 £920**

Commando Scott (Ire) *I W McInnes* 92 a81
4 b g Danetime (Ire) - Faye
13^{6g} 10^{7s} 3^{6s} 8^{6g} 12^{7gs} 10^{6gs} 6^{7ft} 3^{7gs} 6^{7s} 13^{7s} **0-2-10 £3,626**

Commendable Coup (USA) *T D Barron* a58
3 b/br g Commendable (USA) - Bird Dance (USA)
4^{8sd} 6^{7sd} **0-0-2 £262**

Commentary *W J Haggas* 85
2 b f Medicean - Eloquent
4^{6g} 1^{7gf} 2^{7g} 2^{7gs} **1-2-4 £8,237**

Commitment Lecture *M Dods* 69
5 b m Komaite (USA) - Hurtleberry (Ire)
2^{9gs} 2^{9g} 7^{9s} 8^{9gs} 4^{8gf} 3^{8g} 1^{8gs} 5^{8gf} 9^{8g} 10^{8gf} 2^{8gf} 8^{7hy} **1-4-12 £7,918**

Common World (USA) *T Hogan* 108
6 ch h Spinning World (USA) - Spenderella (Fr)
15^{8s} 1^{9s} 3^{8g} 2^{8gs} 5^{8hy} 2^{10y} 12^{8g} 5^{8gf} 14^{8gf} 1^{10y} 12^{8gf} 1^{8gy} 7^{10g} 6^{10gy} 5^{8gf} 2^{7sh} 1^{9s} 7^{8s} 9^{7sh} **4-4-19 £114,319**

Communication *Joseph Quinn* 75
3 b c Machiavellian (USA) - Kundalini (USA)
11^{8gs} 8^{9s} 4^{10f} 7^{10gs} 4^{10g} 3^{12gf} 6^{12gy} 11^{12y} **0-1-8 £2,133**

Compass Point (USA) *Patrick Morris* 39 a43
8 b g Northern Flagship (USA) - Eastern Emblem (USA)
4^{12sd} 9^{9sd} 7^{10sd} 3^{12sd} 6^{10ys} 6^{12g} 9^{12gf} **0-1-7 £206**

Competitor *J Akehurst* 40 a63
4 b c Danzero (Aus) - Ceanothus (Ire)
7^{10sd} 14^{10gf} 10^{12sd} 11^{12sd} 11^{12sd} 1^{10sd} **1-0-6 £2,518**

Compromiznotension (Ire) *M A Jarvis* 78
2 br g Key Of Luck (USA) - Music Khan
3^{6s} **0-1-1 £639**

Compton Arrow (Ire) *A W Carroll* a23
9 b g Petardia - Impressive Lady
12^{5sd} 8^{6sd} **0-0-2**

Compton Banker (Ire) *P D Evans* 57 a61
8 br g Distinctly North (USA) - Mary Hinge
8^{6sd} 9^{7sd} 8^{7sd} 3^{8sd} 9^{9sd} 2^{8s} 7^{8t} 10^{8f} 10^{8gf} 6^{8g} 12^{7gf} 10^{8f} **0-2-12 £1,441**

Compton Bay *M Brittain* 27 a43
5 b g Compton Place - Silver Sun
4^{6sd} 5^{7sd} 9^{8sd} 4^{7sd} 11^{8gf} 10^{7sd} **0-0-6**

Compton Bolter (Ire) *G A Butler* 114 a115
8 b g Red Sunset - Milk And Honey
2^{10sd} 2^{9sd} 3^{12sd} 4^{10sd} 4^{10sd} 2^{12g} 8^{12s} 1^{12g} 5^{13f} 4^{12g} 4^{12g} 1^{11gf} 3^{12g} 3^{10sd} 2^{12sd} **2-6-15 £78,700**

Compton Classic *J S Goldie* 55
3 b c Compton Place - Ayr Classic
8^{5gs} 4^{5gs} 2^{5gs} 7^{5s} 10^{6f} 7^{5g} 15^{6gf} 4^{5g} 5^{5gf} 13^{6s} 16^{5gf} 13^{6gf} 11^{5g} 6^{5s} 14^{5s} **0-2-15 £1,317**

Compton Court *A M Balding* 73
3 b g Compton Place - Loriner's Lass
6^{6gs} 5^{7gf} 6^{8gf} 3^{10g} 2^{8g} **0-2-5 £2,803**

Compton Dragon (USA) *R Johnson* 69 a80
6 ch g Woodman (USA) - Vilikaia (USA)
8^{9sd} 8^{9sd} 12^{9sd} 7^{10sd} 12^{8gs} 12^{10gf} 5^{8g} 4^{9gs} 3^{10g} 9^{10gf} 1^{10g} 4^{10s} 8^{10g} 6^{9gf} 12^{10gf} **1-2-15 £4,734**

Compton Drake *G A Butler* 87 a86
6 b g Mark Of Esteem (Ire) - Reprocolor
4^{10sd} 1^{11gs} 7^{10gf} 11^{10gf} 13^{12g} 6^{12gf} 8^{10gf} 9^{10gf} 11^{8g} **1-0-9 £7,499**

Compton Earl *J J Lambe* 27
5 ch h Efisio - Bay Bay

12^{5g} 16^{9f} 12^{7f} **0-0-3**

Compton Eclaire (Ire) *B Ellison* 61 a54
5 ch m Lycius (USA) - Baylands Sunshine (Ire)
9^{10g} 7^{16gf} 3^{12g} 3^{12sd} 6^{12g} 4^{12gf} 4^{12gf} 1^{16gf} 2^{14gf} **1-3-9 £5,530**

Compton Eclipse *J J Lambe* 73
5 ch h Singspiel (Ire) - Fatah Flare (USA)
23^{7hy} 11^{7g} 3^{8f} 17^{7gf} 1^{8gf} 4^{8f} 9^{10gy} 15^{9g} **1-1-8 £4,763**

Compton Express *Jamie Poulton* a44
2 gr f Compton Place - Jilly Woo
7^{7sd} **0-0-1**

Compton Flyer *J M Bradley* 53
2 ch c Compton Admiral - Elegantissima
7^{6gf} 12^{6gf} 5^{6gf} 12^{7g} 12^{6gs} **0-0-5**

Compton Lad *D A Nolan* 50 a50
2 b g Compton Place - Kintara
5^{5s} 4^{5sd} 11^{5sd} 3^{5sd} 3^{5s} 6^{5gs} 3^{5gf} 8^{5gf} 4^{5gf} 7^{5gf} 9^{5g} 6^{5g} 6^{6gf} 7^{5gf} **0-2-14 £1,866**

Compton Micky *J Balding* 61 a50
4 ch g Compton Place - Nunthorpe
7^{7sd} 3^{6gf} 5^{6sd} 12^{7g} 9^{6gf} 15^{8g} 8^{6sd} 5^{6gf} **0-1-8 £377**

Compton Plume *M W Easterby* 76
5 ch g Compton Place - Brockton Flame
9^{6g} 9^{5f} 2^{6f} 1^{6gf} 6^{5g} 2^{6gf} 5^{6gf} 3^{5g} 10^{5g} 11^{7g} **1-3-10 £6,585**

Compton Quay *Miss K M George* 59
3 ch g Compton Place - Roonah Quay (Ire)
11^{8gf} 9^{10gf} 9^{10gf} **0-0-3**

Compton Spark *J S Goldie* 47 a38
3 ch g Compton Place - Rhinefield Beauty (Ire)
11^{9sd} 7^{7gs} 6^{5sd} 4^{7gf} 6^{6s} 2^{6f} 7^{5f} 6^{7f} 7^{6g} 12^{6gf} **0-1-10 £797**

Compton's Eleven *M R Channon* 104 a103
4 gr g Compton Place - Princess Tara
1^{6gf} 8^{6gf} 8^{8gf} 2^{7gf} 8^{6g} 3^{5gs} 13^{6gf} 9^{6gs} 2^{7gf} 8^{7gf} 5^{7g} 12^{7gs} 2^{7s} 5^{7gf} 5^{7g} 6^{7gf} 2^{7gs} 2^{7gs} 6^{7sd} **1-6-19 £71,660**

Comtake Dot Com (Ire) *M R Bosley* 26
4 b f Tagula (Ire) - Be Prepared (Ire)
9^{7gf} 10^{5gs} 15^{5hd} **0-0-3**

Concert Time *C R Dore* a37
3 ch f Timeless Times (USA) - Thalya
9^{5sd} 7^{6sd} 6^{7sd} **0-0-3**

Conchonita *B Palling*
5 b m Bishop Of Cashel - Cactus Road (Fr)
10^{12sd} **0-0-1**

Conciliate *R M H Cowell* 59 a56
2 b c Mujahid (USA) - Admonish
9^{5gs} 6^{5g} 1^{5sd} 4^{6gf} 6^{6gf} 2^{5f} 4^{5g} 4^{5g} 14^{6gf} 3^{5g} 11^{5gf} 7^{5sd} **1-2-12 £5,456**

Confetti *W J Haggas* 38 a47
3 ch f Groom Dancer (USA) - Fabulous
8^{9sd} 7^{8g} **0-0-2**

Confide (Ire) *G A Swinbank* 59
3 ch g Namid - Confidential
5^{7gf} 5^{7gf} 8^{7g} 2^{9gf} **0-1-4 £1,078**

Confidential Lady *Sir Mark Prescott* 108
2 b f Singspiel (Ire) - Confidante (USA)
3^{6g} 1^{7f} 1^{7g} 1^{7gf} 2^{7g} 1^{7vs} 10^{8gs} **4-2-7 £58,693**

Confucius Miracle (Ire) *J R Boyle* 78 a62
2 ch c Docksider (USA) - Bay Bay
5^{5sd} 4^{6sd} 1^{6gs} **1-0-3 £4,472**

Confuzed *A P Jones* 34 a55
5 b g Pivotal - Times Of Times (Ire)
1^{10sd} 8^{12sd} 4^{10sd} 15^{10s} 12^{10gf} 10^{8sd} **1-0-6 £1,473**

Congressional (Ire) *M A Jarvis* 76 a54
2 b f Grand Lodge (USA) - Gilah (Ire)
5^{7sd} 2^{7gf} 1^{8gf} 8^{8g} **1-1-4 £6,916**

Conjecture *R Bastiman* 81 a65
3 b c Danzig (USA) - Golden Opinion (USA)
5^{6sd} 1^{5sd} 8^{6sd} 1^{5g} 2^{5gf} 3^{5gf} 4^{5gf} **2-2-7 £11,822**

Conjuror *A M Balding* 84
4 b g Efisio - Princess Athena
15^{5gs} 5^{5s} 8^{6g} 3^{6gf} 5^{6gf} 2^{6gf} 7^{7gf} 3^{6s} 2^{7gf} 3^{7g} 1^{7g} **1-5-11 £9,843**

Conkering (USA) *J R Fanshawe* 83 a58
2 ch c Horse Chestnut (SAF) - Nunbridled (USA)
9^{7sd} 2^{7gs} 3^{8g} **0-2-3 £2,257**

Connect *M H Tompkins* 105
8 b g Petong - Natchez Trace
5^{6g} 2^{6gf} 10^{6g} 7^{5g} 1^{5gf} 2^{6gf} 21^{6gs} 8^{6g} 4^{6gf} 10^{6gf} 11^{6g} 5^{6s} 7^{5s} **1-2-13 £25,171**

Connotation *P W Chapple-Hyam* a78
3 b f Mujahid (USA) - Seven Wonders (USA)
5^{8sd} 4^{9sd} 5^{7sd} 1^{9sd} **1-0-4 £3,889**

Connotation (USA) *Saeed Bin Suroor* 66 a70
3 b/br f Menifee (USA) - Refer (USA)
2^{8ft} 4^{10gf} **0-1-2 £3,028**

Conscript (Ire) *A L T Moore* 83
3 b c Mujadil (USA) - Battle Queen
7^{10g} 7^{11gs} 2^{11gf} 1^{10gf} 6^{10gf} 6^{12gs} **1-0-6 £4,655**

Consensus (Ire) *M Brittain* 57 a65
6 b m Common Grounds - Kilbride Lass (Ire)
7^{5sd} 11^{6g} 6^{5g} 13^{6gf} **0-0-4**

Consent *Mrs J R Ramsden* 50
2 ch f Groom Dancer (USA) - Preference
9^{7g} 9^{7gf} 7^{7g} **0-0-3**

Conservation (Fr) *P W Chapple-Hyam* 57
2 b c Green Desert (USA) - Lightly Dancing (Fr)
4^{6s} **0-0-1 £319**

Consider This *W M Brisbourne* 58
3 b f Josr Algarhoud (Ire) - River Of Fortune (Ire)
9^{8gs} 11^{7g} 13^{8gf} 7^{8gf} **0-0-4**

Considerthelilies (Ire) *Miss L A Perratt* 49
2 b f Mull Of Kintyre (USA) - Gilding The Lily (Ire)
11^{6g} 6^{5gf} 9^{7s} **0-0-3**

Considine (USA) *P Howling* 68 a73
4 b g Romanov (Ire) - Libeccio (NZ)
4^{12sd} 5^{16sd} 8^{17sd} 9^{13s} 11^{14g} 4^{14f} 5^{12gf} 2^{16f} 3^{16gf} 6^{16g} 1^{17g} 5^{16gf} 4^{14gf} 6^{14g} 1^{16gf} 7^{17g} 4^{14gf} 7^{16s} 2^{16gf} 10^{16sd} 24^{18gs} **2-1-21 £11,225**

Consonant (Ire) *D G Bridgwater* 89 a97
8 ch g Barathea (Ire) - Dina Lina (Fr)
2^{10sd} 13^{9sd} 8^{12g} 6^{10gf} 4^{10s} 5^{8gf} 6^{8gs} 9^{10gf} 11^{10sd} 6^{7s} 8^{8sd} 2^{9sd} 1^{9sd} 8^{12sd} **1-2-14 £11,240**

Constable Burton *Mrs A Duffield* 62 a64
4 b g Foxhound (USA) - Actress
4^{8sd} 11^{7sd} 6^{7sd} 3^{7gf} 1^{10gf} 7^{8gf} 7^{9gf} **1-1-7 £3,915**

Constant Cheers (Ire) *W R Swinburn* 61
2 b g Royal Applause - Juno Marlowe (Ire)
7^{7gs} 8^{7gs} 14^{7gf} **0-0-3**

Constructor *C A Cyzer* 59 a69
4 b g So Factual (USA) - Love And Kisses
2^{7sd} 5^{7sd} 6^{6g} 11^{6sd} 13^{7g} 4^{8sd} 3^{7g} 11^{10gf} 3^{7sd} 5^{9sd} 5^{6sd} 3^{10sd} **0-4-12 £2,445**

Consular *M A Jarvis* 99
3 br c Singspiel (Ire) - Language Of Love
5^{10g} 2^{12gf} 1^{12g} 3^{12gf} 12^{10gs} 6^{12gf} **1-2-6 £10,251**

Contact Dancer (Ire) *C F Swan* 96
6 b g Sadler's Wells (USA) - Rain Queen
3^{19gs} 3^{16g} 10^{20gf} 18^{16g} **0-2-4 £15,578**

Contented (Ire) *Mrs L C Jewell* 65 a66
3 b c Orpen (USA) - Joyfullness (USA)
4^{8sd} 4^{8sd} 5^{9sd} 15^{10g} 11^{7g} 10^{10gf} 8^{7sd} 4^{7sd} **0-0-8 £544**

Continent *D Nicholls* 101
8 ch g Lake Coniston (Ire) - Krisia
11^{6g} 6^{5s} 8^{6s} 15^{6g} 17^{6f} 3^{6gf} 22^{6g} 13^{6s} **0-1-8 £5,500**

Continental Flyer (Ire) *M Dods* 39
3 b f Piccolo - Sunshine Coast
8^{6gf} RR^{6gf} **0-0-2**

Conviction *Mrs A L M King* 14 a51
4 b g Machiavellian (USA) - Beldarian (Ire)
8^{10sd} 12^{9sd} 16^{10s} 13^{11gf} **0-0-4**

Convince (USA) *M A Buckley* 81
4 ch g Mt. Livermore (USA) - Conical
6^{5gs} 1^{5g} 4^{6g} 5^{5gf} 13^{5gs} 6^{6gf} 5^{5g} 14^{5g} **1-0-8 £3,866**

Cookie Cutter (Ire) *K R Burke* 70 a57
3 b f Fasliyev (USA) - Cut The Red Tape (Ire)
9^{6y} 3^{5g} 10^{5gf} 2^{6gf} 2^{6g} 8^{6gf} 2^{5y} 3^{5sd} 6^{5sd} **0-5-9 £4,554**

Cool As A Moose *N Tinkler*
3 b g Groom Dancer (USA) - Purbeck (Ire)
8^{9g} **0-0-1**

Cool Bathwick (Ire) *G H Yardley*
6 b g Entrepreneur - Tarafa
18^{12gf} 13^{14ft} **0-0-2**

Cool Creek (Ire) *R Hannon* 111
2 b c Desert Style (Ire) - Shining Creek (Can)
3^{5gs} 1^{5gf} 9^{6gf} 1^{6gf} 4^{6gs} 2^{7s} 2^{6g} 4^{7gs} 1^{6gf} 12^{9ft} **3-2-10 £118,393**

Cool Customer (USA) *E A L Dunlop* 72
2 b c Gone West (USA) - Radu Cool (USA)
4^{8gs} 11^{8gs} **0-0-2 £316**

Cool Ebony *M Dods* 73
2 br c Erhaab (USA) - Monawara (Ire)
10^{7g} 8^{7gf} 5^{9g} **0-0-3**

Cool Hunter *W R Swinburn* 86
4 ch g Polar Falcon (USA) - Seabound
11^{8g} 8^{8g} 3^{8gf} 4^{8g} 1^{10gs} 4^{10gs} 11^{10g} **1-1-7 £5,351**

Cool Isle *K A Ryan* 53 a54
2 b f Polar Prince (Ire) - Fisher Island (Ire)
8^{5gf} 5^{5s} 8^{6f} 10^{6gf} 2^{7g} 2^{7sd} 4^{9sd} 3^{7ss} **0-3-8 £2,219**

Cool Panic (Ire) *M L W Bell* 98
3 b c Brave Act - Geht Schnell
1^{7g} 6^{7gf} 2^{7s} 11^{6gs} 20^{6g} **1-1-5 £13,678**

Cool Sands (Ire) *D Shaw* 65 a68
3 b g Trans Island - Shalerina (USA)
6^{6sd} 4^{5sd} 1^{6sd} 2^{7sd} 11^{6s} 4^{7s} 3^{8g} 5^{8gf} 10^{7gf} 7^{7sd} 14^{7g} 13^{6hy} 1^{6sd} 2^{5ss} 4^{7sd} 3^{7sd} 8^{7sd} **2-5-17 £8,960**

Cool Sting (Ire) *A M Balding* 72
2 b g Bluebird (USA) - Honey Bee
2^{6gf} 5^{6gf} 6^{7gf} 8^{6gs} **0-1-4 £1,414**

Cool Temper *P F I Cole* 63
9 b g Magic Ring (Ire) - Ovideo
14^{10gf} 5^{8gf} 19^{8g} BD^{8g} **0-0-4**

Coola Tagula (Ire) *C W Thornton* 25 a23
3 b g Tagula (Ire) - Second Craft (Ire)
10^{6s} 18^{6g} 7^{9g} 7^{6sd} 15^{8gf} **0-0-5**

Coolbythepool *M J Gingell* 27
5 b g Bijou D'Inde - Alchi (USA)
11^{11g} 13^{7g} 17^{12g} **0-0-3**

Cooleycall Star (Ire) *A G Juckes* a50
4 b g Foxhound (USA) - Ozwood (Ire)
5^{6sd} 3^{6sd} 3^{6sd} 2^{6sd} 2^{7sd} 2^{6sd} 2^{8sd} 9^{9sd} 5^{6sd} **0-6-9 £2,132**

Coolfore Jade (Ire) *R A Harris* a53
5 ch m Mukaddamah (USA) - Cashel Princess (Ire)
3^{8sd} 5^{12sd} 9^{8sd} 6^{9sd} 8^{8sd} 1^{9sd} 2^{12sd} 2^{9sd} 1^{12sd} 12^{9sd} 3^{12sd} **2-4-11 £4,677**

Coombe Centenary *S Dow* 47 a54
3 b f Robellino (USA) - Shining Dancer
5^{10sd} 12^{10sd} 2^{10sd} 5^{10sd} 9^{10gs} 8^{10gf} 15^{10g} **0-1-7 £1,256**

Copeland *M C Pipe* 82
10 b g Generous (Ire) - Whitehaven
13^{19gs} **0-0-1**

Copper Bay (Ire) *A King* 73 a69
3 b g Revoque (Ire) - Bahia Laura (Fr)
11^{10gf} 9^{12g} 3^{10gs} 3^{12sd} 6^{14g} 2^{10s} **0-3-6 £2,248**

Coppermalt (USA) *R Curtis* a50
7 b g Affirmed (USA) - Poppy Carew (Ire)
8^{17sd} 5^{14sd} 4^{16sd} 8^{14ss} **0-0-4**

Coppice (Ire) *L M Cumani* 89
4 ch g Rainbow Quest (USA) - Woodwin (Ire)
7^{10ys} 2^{8y} 1^{8f} 1^{8gf} 4^{8g} **2-1-5 £11,089**

Coppington Flyer (Ire) *B W Duke* a50
5 ch m Eagle Eyed (USA) - Miss Flite (Ire)
5^{9sd} 3^{9sd} 13^{10sd} 4^{10sd} 9^{8sd} 5^{10sd} 7^{9sd} 11^{9sd} **0-1-8 £412**

Coquet Island *G M Moore* 67
2 ch g Alhaarth (Ire) - Abir
2^{5g} 3^{5gf} 5^{5g} 6^{5f} 14^{5gf} **0-2-5 £2,402**

Coqueteria (USA) *G Wragg* 96
4 b f Cozzene (USA) - Miss Waikiki (USA)
8^{7gs} 5^{7g} 6^{8gf} 8^{8g} 2^{10gf} **0-1-5 £8,375**

Coquin D'Alezan (Ire) *W Jarvis* a69
4 ch g Cadeaux Genereux - Nwaahil (Ire)
7^{9sd} 3^{7sd} 7^{6sd} **0-1-3 £543**

Cora Pearl (Ire) *M J Polglase* 39
2 b f Montjeu (Ire) - Castara Beach (Ire)
14^{8gf} 5^{7g} 11^{8g} **0-0-3**

Coranglais *J M Bradley* 68 a61
5 ch g Piccolo - Antonia's Folly
9^{6sd} 4^{6sd} 7^{6s} 1^{6gf} 5^{5gf} 6^{7sd} 1^{6gf} 3^{5g} 3^{6gf} 5^{6gf} 7^{6gf} 3^{6g} 4^{6g} 11^{6g} **2-4-14 £11,004**

Corcoran (USA) *Mrs A J Perrett* 95
3 b f Lear Fan (USA) - Corsini
3^{10gf} 4^{10gf} 5^{12g} **0-0-3 £6,917**

Cordage (Ire) *Karen McLintock* 67 a56
3 ch g Dr Fong (USA) - Flagship
3^{10gs} 3^{12sd} 11^{11gf} 9^{10g} 6^{8g} 4^{10g} **1-0-6 £4,376**

Cordial (Ire) *J J Quinn* 92 a90

5 gr g Charnwood Forest (Ire) - Moon Festival
3^{9sd} 1^{10sd} 5^{12sd} 1^{12sd} 10^{12sd} 5^{14gs} 17^{18gs} 8^{15s}
2-1-8 £15,268

Cordier *D R Loder* 47 a69
3 b g Desert Style (Ire) - Slipper
1^{10sd} 7^{10sd} 10^{10g} **1-0-3 £4,173**

Corker *D B Feek* 64 a51
3 ch g Grand Lodge (USA) - Immortelle
9^{9sd} 1^{12gf} 7^{10g} 4^{12s} 7^{15gf} **1-0-5 £4,118**

Corky (Ire) *I W McInnes* 86 a73
4 b g Intikhab (USA) - Khamseh
9^{7g} 1^{7gs} 8^{7g} 8^{8g} 6^{8gs} 12^{8g} 10^{9sd} 1^{8hy} 9^{8sd}
4^{7sd} 3^{9sd} **2-1-11 £10,483**

Cormorant Wharf (Ire) *G L Moore* a76
5 b g Alzao (USA) - Mercy Bien (Ire)
2^{10sd} 1^{9sd} 2^{10sd} **1-2-3 £5,477**

Corniche Dancer *M R Channon* 40
3 b f Marju (Ire) - Sellette (Ire)
10^{6gf} 13^{6g} **0-0-2**

Cornish Gold *D W Thompson* 34 a41
4 b f Slip Anchor - Sans Diablo (Ire)
4^{10sd} 6^{12sd} 4^{10sd} 9^{9sd} 10^{14sd} 15^{8s} 9^{9gf} 15^{8gf}
0-0-8

Cornus *M J Polglase* 103 a102
3 ch g Inchinor - Demerger (USA)
6^{7gf} 6^{6s} 3^{6gf} 10^{5gs} 5^{6g} 4^{5sd} 5^{6gs} 3^{6g} 5^{5gf}
3^{5gs} 1^{5g} 12^{5sf} 5^{6sf} 3^{5sd} 8^{7sd} 3^{6sd} **1-4-16**
£18,145

Coronado Forest (USA) *M R Hoad* a51
6 b g Spinning World (USA) - Desert Jewel (USA)
8^{8sd} 8^{10sd} 13^{10sd} 6^{12sd} 8^{12sd} 3^{8sd} 1^{7sd} 1^{8sd}
9^{7sf} 12^{10sd} 8^{7sd} 8^{8sd} 10^{8sd} **2-1-13**
£3,155

Coronado's Gold (USA) *V Smith* 55
4 ch g Coronado's Quest (USA) - Debit My Account (USA)
10^{8g} 14^{10gf} 5^{12gf} 14^{8g} **0-0-4**

Coronation Flight *G A Swinbank* 17
2 b f Missed Flight - Hand On Heart (Ire)
12^{7s} **0-0-1**

Coronation Queen *S Kirk* 36
2 b f Pivotal - Coffee Ice
11^{8gs} **0-0-1**

Coronilla (Ire) *E J O'Neill* 25 a21
2 b f Mozart (Ire) - Fragrant
11^{5sd} 9^{6g} **0-0-2**

Correct Time (Ire) *N P Littmoden* 54 a36
2 b c Danetime (Ire) - Solo Symphony (Ire)
8^{5gf} 4^{5gf} 8^{5sd} **0-0-3 £262**

Corrib (Ire) *B Palling* 78 a75
2 b f Lahib (USA) - Montana Miss (Ire)
1^{5g} 1^{6gf} 5^{6g} 11^{7gf} 5^{6sd} 8^{7g} **2-0-6**
£6,625

Corrib Drift (USA) *Jamie Poulton* 19
5 ch g Sandpit (Brz) - Bygones (USA)
9^{12gs} **0-0-1**

Corrib Eclipse *Ian Williams* 102 a105
6 b g Double Eclipse (Ire) - Last Night's Fun (Ire)
7^{16s} 11^{20gf} 5^{16sd} 2^{18gs} **0-1-4 £4,673**

Corridor Creeper (Fr) *J M Bradley* 116
8 ch g Polish Precedent (USA) - Sonia Rose (USA)
1^{5g} 1^{5g} 4^{5g} 3^{5g} 5^{6g} 4^{5gf} 1^{5s} 4^{5gs} 4^{5g} 13^{5gf}
5^{5g} 2^{5g} 3^{5s} **3-3-13 £93,660**

Corriolanus (Ger) *P Mitchell* 114 a105
5 b h Zamindar (USA) - Caesarea (Ger)
2^{10g} 1^{12gf} 2^{12gf} 5^{10sd} 6^{12g} 3^{11g} 20^{10gf}
1-2-7 £93,857

Cortesia (Ire) *P W Chapple-Hyam* 52
2 ch f Courteous - Cecina
9^{7s} **0-0-1**

Corton Denham *G P Enright* 35
4 ch g Wolfhound (USA) - Wigit
12^{10g} 15^{8gf} 10^{5gf} 7^{8gf} **0-0-4**

Corum (Ire) *J H M Gosden* 50
2 b c Galileo (Ire) - Vallee Des Reves (USA)
10^{7s} **0-0-1**

Cosmic Destiny (Ire) *E F Vaughan* 65 a59
3 b f Soviet Star (USA) - Cruelle (USA)
2^{5sd} 4^{6sd} 16^{5gs} 6^{5gf} 3^{5gf} 3^{5g} 14^{5gf} 6^{6g} 3^{5gs}
7^{5f} 3^{5s} 1^{5gf} 15^{5gf} **1-5-13 £6,886**

Cost Analysis (Ire) *M A Jarvis* 66 a58
3 ch g Grand Lodge (USA) - Flower Girl
14^{8s} 12^{8g} 3^{7gf} 6^{8g} 8^{7gf} 5^{7sd} 5^{5sd} 4^{9sd}
0-1-8 £641

Costa Del Sol (Ire) *Miss Victoria Roberts* 20
4 ch g General Monash (USA) - L'Harmonie (USA)
12^{7gf} **0-0-1**

Costa Packet (Ire) *A M Balding* 37
2 ch f Hussonet (USA) - Costa Balena (Chi)
12^{6gf} **0-0-1**

Cote D'Argent *M Johnston* 86
2 b c Lujain (USA) - In The Groove
3^{7gf} 5^{7gf} 3^{7gf} 1^{7s} **1-2-4 £5,565**

Cottam Grange *M W Easterby* 47
5 b g River Falls - Karminski
3^{12gf} 3^{16g} 5^{13gf} 4^{10g} **0-2-4 £1,328**

Cottingham (Ire) *M C Chapman* 52
4 b g Perugino (USA) - Stately Princess
14^{7gf} 8^{11gf} 11^{12g} 5^{10g} **0-0-4**

Cotton Easter *Mrs A J Bowlby* 55 a49
4 b f Robellino (USA) - Pluck
11^{8gs} 5^{10hy} 5^{13sd} **0-0-3**

Cotton Eyed Joe (Ire) *G A Swinbank* 27 a44
4 b g Indian Rocket - Cwm Deri (Ire)
11^{12f} 12^{15g} 9^{16gf} 7^{11ss} 2^{11sd} **0-1-5 £419**

Councellor (Fr) *Stef Liddiard* 81 a81
3 b c Gilded Time (USA) - Sudden Storm Bird (USA)
11^{7g} 4^{6g} 3^{8gf} 3^{8gf} 2^{6g} 2^{7gf} 1^{7g} 4^{6g} 1^{7g} 18^{7gf}
3^{9gs} 2^{7sd} **2-5-12 £16,324**

Council Member (USA) *Saeed Bin Suroor* 112
3 b c Seattle Slew (USA) - Zoe Montana (USA)
1^{7gs} 7^{7gf} 5^{8gs} 5^{8gs} 1^{7gf} 12^{7gs} **2-0-6**
£33,355

Counsel's Opinion (Ire) *C F Wall* 111 a111
8 ch g Rudimentary (USA) - Fairy Fortune
1^{10sd} 12^{10sd} 1^{12g} 3^{10gs} 3^{10gs} 5^{10gf} 6^{12gs} 2^{12g}
4^{11gf} 14^{9s} **2-3-10 £47,102**

Count Boris *J A Geake* 68
4 b g Groom Dancer (USA) - Bu Hagab (Ire)
1^{11gs} 4^{10s} 11^{12gf} 5^{12gf} 7^{12gf} 11^{12g} 8^{12s}
1-0-7 £3,057

Count Cougar (USA) *S P Griffiths* 62 a73
5 b g Sir Cat (USA) - Gold Script (USA)
4^{6sd} 5^{6sd} 4^{6sd} 4^{5sd} 1^{6sd} 3^{5gf} 1^{6sd} 1^{6sd} 4^{6sd}
3^{5gf} 14^{5gf} 15^{5gf} 10^{6sd} 5^{7sd} 12^{7sd} **3-2-15**
£7,793

Count Kristo *C G Cox* 75
3 br g Dr Fong (USA) - Aryadne
3^{11gf} 4^{10gf} 9^{8f} **0-1-3 £1,658**

Count The Trees *W G M Turner* 20 a40
2 ch f Woodborough (USA) - Numerate

7^{6gf} 10^{6sd} 11^{7sd} 10^{7sd} 5^{10sd} 7^{9sd} **0-0-6**

Count Trevisio (Ire) *Saeed Bin Suroor* 77
2 b c Danehill (USA) - Stylish
1^{7g} 8^{8s} **1-0-2 £3,315**

Countback (Fr) *A W Carroll* a60
6 b g Anabaa (USA) - Count Me Out (Fr)
10^{12sd} 5^{12sd} 7^{12sd} 4^{17sd} 4^{17sd} 3^{17sd} 4^{14sd}
0-1-7 £430

Countdown *Miss J A Camacho* 63 a86
3 ch g Pivotal - Quiz Time
16^{5gs} 17^{7hy} 3^{6sf} 3^{6sd} **0-2-4 £1,694**

Countess Carmine *P C Haslam* 67
2 b f Royal Applause - Red Ryding Hood
12^{5g} 14^{5gf} 8^{5g} 11^{5g} **0-0-4**

Countess Foley *D Burchell* 29 a51
3 b f Wizard King - Princess Foley (Ire)
7^{7sd} 5^{6sd} 7^{9sd} 8^{7sd} 9^{10gs} 18^{8g} 14^{7g} **0-0-7**

Counting Blessings *M L W Bell* 52
3 b f Compton Place - Banco Suivi (Ire)
11^{10gs} 9^{10gs} 13^{10s} 3^{8gf} 4^{8gf} 5^{7f} **0-2-6**
£710

Counting House (Ire) *R Charlton* 73
2 ch c King's Best (USA) - Inforapenny
7^{7gf} **0-0-1**

Country Affair (USA) *John A Quinn* 67 a70
2 ch c Vettori (Ire) - Nany's Affair (USA)
11^{8g} 3^{9sd} **0-1-2 £552**

Country Pursuit (USA) *C E Brittain* 97 a83
3 ch c Theatrical - Jade Flush (USA)
10^{8s} 4^{8g} 3^{10gf} 6^{10g} 3^{12s} 3^{10gs} 1^{12sd} 2^{12gf} 6^{14g}
1-3-9 £8,696

Country Reel (USA) *Saeed Bin Suroor* 96
5 b/br h Danzig (USA) - Country Belle (USA)
8^{6gf} 16^{6f} **0-0-2**

Countrywide Belle *K A Ryan* 73 a58
2 b f Josr Algarhoud (Ire) - Dancing Bluebell (Ire)
4^{5sd} 1^{5sd} 2^{5g} 5^{5gf} 5^{5gs} 2^{6gf} 12^{6gs} 16^{8g} 17^{6gf}
14^{7g} 13^{6s} 1^{8sd} 2^{9sd} 10^{8sd} 3^{9sd} 4^{9sd}
2-4-16 £9,683

Countrywide Dancer (Ire) *K W Hogg* 40
5 b m Danehill Dancer (Ire) - Meadow Grass (Ire)
10^{8gf} 8^{5f} 5^{7g} 12^{6f} 13^{5gf} 10^{8gf} **0-0-6**

Countrywide Girl (Ire) *A Berry* 32 a52
6 ch m Catrail (USA) - Polish Saga
2^{7sd} 1^{7sd} 9^{7g} 4^{7sd} **1-1-4 £1,899**

Countrywide Luck *N P Littmoden* 80 a77
4 b g Inchinor - Thelma
6^{14gs} 14^{12gf} 17^{12gs} 7^{12gf} 6^{12gs} 2^{12g} 8^{12gs} 6^{11gf}
8^{12g} 11^{12gs} 2^{12sd} 3^{12sd} 4^{12sd} **0-3-13**
£5,358

Countrywide Sun *A C Whillans*
3 b g Benny The Dip (USA) - Sundae Girl (USA)
10^{10gf} **0-0-1**

County Clare *Eoin Doyle* 50
3 ch f Barathea (Ire) - Input
7^{6sd} 5^{7gf} 15^{6gf} **0-0-3**

Coup D'Etat *J L Dunlop* 95
3 b c Diktat - Megdale (Ire)
1^{7g} 8^{8gs} 1^{7gf} 2^{8gs} 11^{7s} 4^{8gf} 14^{8gs} **2-1-7**
£21,214

Courageous Dove *A Bailey* 26
4 gr g Overbury (Ire) - Mazzelmo
10^{12gf} 9^{12gf} 8^{10gs} 10^{9sd} **0-0-4**

Courageous Duke (USA) *J Noseda* 105
6 b g Spinning World (USA) - Araadh (USA)
4^{10gf} 6^{10gf} 2^{10gf} 1^{11gf} 13^{10g} **1-1-5**
£54,333

Courageously *P F I Cole* 66 a48
3 b g Aljabr (USA) - Eishin Eleuthera (Ire)
8^{7g} 11^{7sd} 5^{10gf} 1^{8g} 3^{8gf} 3^{8g} 6^{10gf} 3^{8gf} 10^{8gf}
6^{8gf} 5^{8gf} 8^{10s} 6^{8gf} **1-3-13 £4,896**

Courant D'Air (Ire) *Lucinda Featherstone* a37
4 b g Indian Rocket - Red River Rose (Ire)
7^{12sf} **0-0-1**

Cours De La Reine (Ire) *Mrs J Chapple-Hyam* 95
3 b f Fasliyev (USA) - Society Queen (Ire)
4^{10g} 10^{10hy} **0-0-2 £3,333**

Court Alliance *R J Price* 43 a32
6 ch g Alhijaz - Fairfields Cone
5^{12s} 2^{11gs} 8^{13sd} 9^{14g} 9^{12gf} **0-1-5 £379**

Court Emperor *R J Price* 39
5 b g Mtoto - Fairfields Cone
10^{12hy} 9^{12gf} 6^{12g} 9^{12sd} 10^{14sd} **0-0-5**

Court Masterpiece *E A L Dunlop* 117 a115
5 b h Polish Precedent (USA) - Easy Option (Ire)
4^{7g} 2^{7s} 1^{8gs} 2^{7g} 2^{8sd} 1^{7gs} 3^{8g} 3^{7gf} 1^{7s} 5^{8gf}
3-6-10 £250,231

Court Of Appeal *B Ellison* 93 a86
8 ch g Bering - Hiawatha's Song (USA)
5^{12gf} 1^{12sd} 3^{12gs} 4^{12gs} 11^{14g} 15^{12f} 2^{12sd} 1^{12gf}
1^{12gf} 3^{14gf} 7^{12g} **3-2-11 £11,292**

Court Of Justice (USA) *K A Morgan* 37
9 b g Alleged (USA) - Captive Island
8^{12s} **0-0-1**

Court One *R J Price* 46
7 b g Shareef Dancer (USA) - Fairfields Cone
12^{16gf} 2^{14g} 9^{17g} **0-1-3 £432**

Court Ruler *R J Price*
3 b g Kayf Tara - Fairfields Cone
7^{10s} 13^{17gs} **0-0-2**

Cousteau *P W Chapple-Hyam* 77
2 ch c Spinning World (USA) - Wavy Up (Ire)
2^{7gf} 2^{7s} **0-2-2 £2,790**

Coustou (Ire) *R M Stronge* 68
5 b g In Command (Ire) - Carranza (Ire)
1^{12s} 15^{13s} 13^{12gs} **1-0-3 £2,965**

Coventina (Ire) *J L Dunlop* 97
4 gr f Daylami (Ire) - Lady Of The Lake
2^{16gs} 3^{14s} **0-1-2 £7,627**

Cover Drive (USA) *R Simpson* 70 a78
2 br c Giant's Causeway (USA) - Woodland Orchid (Ire)
7^{5gf} 5^{8g} 4^{8gf} 1^{7ft} **1-0-4 £3,296**

Cover Up (Ire) *Sir Michael Stoute* 112
8 b g Machiavellian (USA) - Sought Out (Ire)
9^{16g} 2^{22f} 3^{16gf} 4^{16g} 7^{18g} 1^{16gs} **1-1-6**
£46,030

Cozinneta (USA) *P W Chapple-Hyam* 65
2 gr/ro f Cozzene (USA) - Inny River (USA)
6^{8gf} 12^{8s} **0-0-2**

Crabadabadoo *M R Channon* 23
2 b f Tagula (Ire) - Kastaway
15^{6g} **0-0-1**

Crackleando *A R Dicken*
4 ch g Forzando - Crackling
PU^{15s} **0-0-1**

Crafty Fancy (Ire) *D J S Ffrench Davis* 36 a77
4 ch f Intikhab (USA) - Idle Fancy
10^{8sd} 17^{7gs} **0-0-2**

Cragganmore Creek *D Morris* a53
2 b g Tipsy Creek (USA) - Polish Abbey

1^{9sd} **1-0-1 £1,405**

Craic Sa Ceili (Ire) *M S Saunders* 63 a63
5 b m Danehill Dancer (Ire) - Fay's Song (Ire)
9^{9sd} 5^{7sd} 6^{7sd} 3^{7sd} 2^{7sd} 7^{9sd} 5^{9sd} 7^{8sd} 7^{6s} 3^{8gs} 2^{7g} 10^{7sd} 10^{9sd} 10^{8sd} **0-4-14 £2,742**

Crail *C F Wall* 72 a85
5 b g Vettori (Ire) - Tendency
6^{10sd} 1^{9sd} 10^{8gf} 8^{8g} 13^{10s} 2^{9sf} 3^{9sd} **1-2-7 £5,982**

Crathorne (Ire) *M Todhunter* 68
5 b g Alzao (USA) - Shirley Blue (Ire)
3^{16g} 2^{12s} 4^{12gs} 1^{12f} 3^{15gf} 5^{14gf} **1-3-6 £6,317**

Crazy Bear (Ire) *K A Ryan* 53 a53
2 ch f King Charlemagne (USA) - Specifiedrisk (Ire)
10^{6g} 11^{7gf} 2^{8sd} **0-1-3 £836**

Crazy Flirt (Ire) *A E Jones* 17
3 b f King's Best (USA) - Itab (USA)
12^{7gf} 15^{10gs} **0-0-2**

Cream Of Esteem *M Todhunter* 47
3 b g Mark Of Esteem (Ire) - Chantilly (Fr)
6^{7g} 9^{7s} 8^{8g} 7^{8gf} 4^{10g} 9^{9gf} 2^{12g} 5^{11gf} **0-1-8 £1,075**

Creambiscuit *N P Littmoden* 56
2 ch c Cadeaux Genereux - Star Ridge (USA)
7^{5gf} 8^{5gs} 3^{5g} **0-1-3 £670**

Creative Mind (Ire) *E J O'Neill* 80
2 b f Danehill Dancer (Ire) - Inventive
2^{7gf} 1^{7gf} 2^{7hy} 2^{7g} **1-3-4 £9,046**

Credential *John A Harris* 76
3 b c Dansili - Sabria (USA)
5^{8gs} 4^{8g} 7^{8g} 3^{8s} **0-1-4 £898**

Credit (Ire) *J Howard Johnson* 84
4 b g Intikhab (USA) - Tycooness (Ire)
8^{8gf} 19^{10g} **0-0-2**

Cree *W R Muir* 74 a62
3 b g Indian Ridge - Nightitude
5^{6sd} 5^{5g} 2^{5s} 3^{6gf} 4^{6f} 7^{6gf} 3^{6gf} 2^{6g} 3^{6gf} 1^{6g} 4^{6gf} 7^{7g} 7^{6sd} 12^{6g} **1-5-14 £11,930**

Creek Dancer *Rae Guest* 56 a53
3 b f Josr Algarhoud (Ire) - Dance Land (Ire)
10^{8g} 6^{8g} 10^{11g} 4^{7gs} 6^{9sd} 4^{8gf} 6^{10gs} 9^{8g} 2^{8gf} 2^{10gf} 4^{8s} 5^{10hd} 13^{8gf} 2^{10g} **0-3-14 £2,966**

Creme Brulee *C R Egerton* a61
2 b f College Chapel - Balinsky (Ire)
6^{6sf} **0-0-1**

Creme De La Creme (Ire) *D R Loder* a38
3 b f Montjeu (Ire) - Pride Of Place (Ire)
11^{9sd} **0-0-1**

Creskeld (Ire) *B Smart* 69 a93
6 b g Sri Pekan (USA) - Pizzazz
1^{8sd} 11^{9sd} 11^{8g} 12^{8s} 12^{8g} 3^{8g} **1-1-6 £14,149**

Cresta Gold *A Bailey* 70 a70
2 b f Halling (USA) - Fleet Hill (Ire)
5^{6gf} 5^{7gf} 4^{8g} 10^{8g} 4^{7sf} **0-0-5 £655**

Crested *Saeed Bin Suroor* 82
2 ch c Fantastic Light (USA) - Dunnes River (USA)
11^{7gf} 1^{8g} 16^{8s} **1-0-3 £4,186**

Crestfallen (Ire) *E J O'Neill* 48
2 b f Fasliyev (USA) - Cresalin
7^{5gf} 5^{5g} 17^{6s} **0-0-3**

Cretan Gift *N P Littmoden* a64
14 ch g Cadeaux Genereux - Caro's Niece (USA)
9^{6sd} **0-0-1**

Crete (Ire) *W J Haggas* 84
3 b g Montjeu (Ire) - Paesanella
3^{8s} 3^{9g} 1^{12gf} 3^{12gf} 2^{12gf} 6^{14gf} **1-2-6 £10,415**

Crewes Miss Isle *A G Newcombe* a44
4 b f Makbul - Riviere Rouge
10^{7sd} 8^{5sd} 12^{6sd} **0-0-3**

Crime Scene (Ire) *M Johnston* 75
2 b c Royal Applause - Crime (USA)
1^{6g} **1-0-1 £6,864**

Criminal Act (USA) *B W Hills* 83
2 b c Bahri (USA) - Captive Island
3^{6gs} 2^{7gs} 1^{8gf} 12^{8g} **1-2-4 £10,383**

Crimson (Ire) *M R Channon* 67
2 b f Fasliyev (USA) - Fey Lady (Ire)
5^{6g} 2^{6gf} 6^{6gf} 6^{6g} 10^{6g} 6^{6gf} 20^{7gf} 12^{5gf} **0-1-8 £1,524**

Crimson Bow (Ger) *J G Given* 40 a39
3 ch f Night Shift (USA) - Carma (Ire)
10^{8g} 8^{10s} 5^{12sd} 15^{12g} **0-0-4**

Crimson Flame (Ire) *M R Channon* 77
2 b g Celtic Swing - Wish List (Ire)
5^{7f} 4^{7g} 4^{7g} 3^{8gf} 4^{8gf} 6^{8gf} 4^{8g} 3^{8gf} 4^{9g} **0-2-9 £5,270**

Crimson Sun (USA) *Saeed Bin Suroor* 105
3 b c Danzig (USA) - Crimplene (Ire)
3^{7gf} 5^{7gf} **0-1-2 £3,780**

Cripsey Brook *K G Reveley* 85
7 ch g Lycius (USA) - Duwon (Ire)
7^{10gs} 3^{11g} 2^{10f} 2^{10g} 6^{12gf} 3^{10g} 4^{12gf} DSQ^{11gs} 1^{10gf} 11^{10gf} **1-3-10 £13,285**

Crisp Note (Ire) *R Bastiman* 55
3 b f Victory Note (USA) - Shirley Venture
4^{9gf} 10^{8g} 11^{10gf} 8^{12g} 9^{12sd} 5^{11hy} **0-0-6 £774**

Cristoforo (Ire) *B J Curley* 102
8 b g Perugino (USA) - Red Barons Lady (Ire)
1^{14g} 2^{15gs} 4^{12g} **1-1-3 £17,188**

Critic (Ire) *M L W Bell* 83
2 b g Fasliyev (USA) - Scruple (Ire)
8^{6gf} 2^{6gf} 3^{7g} 4^{8s} **0-1-4 £2,713**

Critical Stage (Ire) *J D Frost* 58
6 b g King's Theatre (Ire) - Zandaka (Fr)
7^{12gf} **0-0-1**

Crociera (Ire) *M H Tompkins* a55
4 b g Croco Rouge (Ire) - Ombry Girl (Ire)
6^{10sd} **0-0-1**

Crocodile Bay (Ire) *J A Osborne* 92 a51
2 b c Spectrum (Ire) - Shenkara (Ire)
5^{5sd} 1^{5g} 1^{5g} 2^{5gf} 8^{6g} 3^{7gf} 7^{6gf} 6^{7s} 3^{8gf} 3^{6g} **2-4-10 £20,021**

Crocodile Kiss (Ire) *J A Osborne* a52
3 b f Rossini (USA) - Pipe Opener
4^{9sd} 7^{7sd} **0-0-2**

Crocodile Star (USA) *J A Osborne* 50
2 b/br g Woodman (USA) - Rhumba Rage (USA)
12^{6gf} 8^{7gf} 8^{7s} **0-0-3**

Croft (Ire) *J W Hills* 70 a53
2 b g Mull Of Kintyre (USA) - Home Comforts
7^{5sd} 6^{5gf} 6^{7g} 6^{7gf} 7^{7gf} 3^{8gf} 8^{8sd} **0-1-7 £417**

Cromarty Bay *J J Bridger* a38
4 b f Victory Note (USA) - Cromarty

9^{10sd} 4^{12sd} RR^{8sd} **0-0-3 £267**

Cronkyvoddy *M J Wallace* 57
4 b g Groom Dancer (USA) - Miss Pout
5^{10gf} 7^{10gf} 16^{8f} **0-0-3**

Croon *L M Cumani* a76
3 b c Sinndar (Ire) - Shy Minstrel (USA)
5^{10sd} **0-0-1**

Crooner (Ire) *W R Muir* 82 a54
2 b c Titus Livius (Fr) - John's Ballad (Ire)
13^{6gf} 8^{6sd} 1^{6gs} 3^{6g} 12^{5gf} 9^{6gs} 11^{6gs}
1-0-7 £5,174

Crosby Hall *L M Cumani* 80
2 b c Compton Place - Alzianah
7^{5f} 1^{5g} 2^{6gf} 5^{6gf} **1-1-4 £9,980**

Crosby Jubilee (Ire) *J R Weymes*
4 b g Shinko Forest (Ire) - Quicksand (Ire)
12^{12gs} 7^{8sd} **0-0-2**

Crosby Vision *J R Weymes* 74
2 b c Agnes World (USA) - Aegean Blue
4^{6g} 4^{7s} 1^{7g} **1-0-3 £5,544**

Crosby Waltzer *John A Harris*
5 b m Terimon - Mary Macblain
9^{8sd} **0-0-1**

Cross Ash (Ire) *R Hollinshead* a33
5 ch g Ashkalani (Ire) - Priorite (Ire)
9^{9sd} **0-0-1**

Cross Channel (USA) *E A L Dunlop* 98
2 ch f Giant's Causeway (USA) - Sterling Pound (USA)
3^{7gf} 1^{7gf} 5^{8g} **1-1-3 £9,923**

Cross My Mind *T Keddy* 88 a83
3 b g Cape Cross (Ire) - Dynamic Dream (USA)
5^{7gf} 14^{8gf} 2^{6sd} 2^{7gf} 1^{7gf} 2^{7g} **1-3-6**
£11,423

Cross My Shadow (Ire) *M F Harris* 55 a43
3 b g Cape Cross (Ire) - Shadowglow
7^{8sd} 4^{8g} 2^{8f} 3^{7f} 7^{7f} 8^{8gf} 7^{7gf} 17^{7g} 8^{7s} 4^{7gf}
4^{10gf} 9^{8gs} 5^{9sd} 6^{8sd} **0-2-14 £1,551**

Cross The Line (Ire) *A P Jarvis* 75 a79
3 b g Cape Cross (Ire) - Baalbek
8^{9gs} 7^{7gf} 1^{8gf} 2^{8g} 2^{8sd} **1-2-5 £8,324**

Cross Time (USA) *M R Channon* 86
3 b c Cape Cross (Ire) - Reine Maid (USA)
2^{8s} 3^{9gf} 5^{10gs} 1^{8gf} 14^{8gf} 2^{8gf} 9^{8gf} 5^{10g} 7^{8gf}
4^{10g} 2^{12g} 3^{12gf} 6^{11g} **1-4-13 £15,006**

Crosspeace (Ire) *M Johnston* 114
3 b c Cape Cross (Ire) - Announcing Peace
2^{6gf} 8^{8gs} 1^{7gf} 12^{7gf} 2^{8gs} 3^{9g} 2^{10g} 3^{10gf} 4^{9s}
1^{12hy} **2-6-10 £104,492**

Crow Wood *J J Quinn* 106
6 b g Halling (USA) - Play With Me (Ire)
12^{10gs} 6^{10gs} 5^{10s} 3^{10gf} 1^{12g} 2^{12f} 2^{10g} 10^{14g}
11^{14g} **1-3-9 £70,343**

Crowberry *P S McEntee* 49 a48
4 b g Orpen (USA) - Cloudberry
3^{5sd} 8^{5g} 6^{6gf} 6^{5sd} 11^{6sd} 12^{6sd} 16^{6g}
0-1-7 £414

Crown Agent (Ire) *M E Sowersby* 47
5 b g Mukaddamah (USA) - Supreme Crown (USA)
7^{10gf} 13^{10g} **0-0-2**

Crown Of Medina *W R Swinburn* 47 a69
3 ch g Fraam - Medina De Rioseco
8^{7sd} 1^{6sd} 11^{6gf} 6^{6g} 12^{7sd} 4^{6sd} 8^{6sd} 12^{6gf}
3^{6sd} **1-1-9 £4,332**

Crownfield *K G Reveley* 64
6 b g Blushing Flame (USA) - Chief Island
14^{12s} 5^{12gf} 4^{14gf} 5^{16gf} 8^{15gf} 3^{17g} 5^{12gf} 4^{14gf}
0-0-8 £797

Cruise Director *W J Musson* 94 a90
5 b g Zilzal (USA) - Briggsmaid
4^{12sd} 2^{12sd} 5^{12sd} 4^{12sd} 8^{10s} 2^{12gs} 1^{12s} 16^{14gs}
1-2-8 £17,565

Crusader's Gold (Fr) *T D Easterby* 63
2 b c Lujain (USA) - Rain And Shine (Fr)
16^{6gf} 14^{6gf} 3^{7gf} 3^{7gf} 3^{7gf} 5^{8gf} 6^{7g} **0-2-7**
£1,694

Crush On You *R Hollinshead* 44 a39
2 b f Golden Snake (USA) - Mourir D'Aimer (USA)
5^{7f} 8^{7gf} 3^{7g} 10^{7gf} 4^{6sd} 6^{9sd} 11^{9sd} 5^{9sd}
0-1-8 £628

Crusoe (Ire) *A Sadik* a61
8 b g Turtle Island (Ire) - Self Reliance
5^{8sd} 1^{7sd} 3^{7sd} 1^{6sd} 3^{8sd} 4^{7sd} 7^{7sd} 6^{7sd} 7^{9sd}
4^{9sd} 12^{6sd} 12^{8sd} 4^{7sd} 2^{8sd} 8^{9sd} 13^{9sd} 14^{8sd}
10^{8sd} **2-3-18 £5,855**

Crusty Miss *M Sheppard*
6 b m Chaddleworth (Ire) - Miss Crusty
12^{9sd} 12^{6sd} **0-0-2**

Crux *C W Thornton* 55 a40
3 b g Pivotal - Penny Dip
8^{5s} 6^{6g} 13^{6g} 7^{6g} 11^{7gf} 11^{8ss} 7^{8sd} 5^{9ss}
0-0-8

Cruzspiel *J R Fanshawe* 111
5 br g Singspiel (Ire) - Allespagne (USA)
8^{16s} 4^{12g} 10^{16g} 1^{22f} 7^{16gf} 8^{16g} **1-0-6**
£21,326

Cryfield *N Tinkler* 60 a45
8 b g Efisio - Ciboure
13^{7s} 11^{7sd} 6^{8s} 2^{8gf} 5^{7gf} 8^{8g} 3^{8gf} 3^{8gf} 6^{8gf}
9^{8gf} 3^{8g} 4^{10g} 10^{8s} 7^{9ss} **0-5-14 £3,002**

Crystal (Ire) *B J Meehan* 44 a89
4 b f Danehill (USA) - Solar Crystal (Ire)
4^{12sd} 8^{16gf} **0-0-2 £522**

Crystal Air (Ire) *Miss J Feilden* 73
2 b f Distant Music (USA) - Columbian Sand (Ire)
5^{5gf} 1^{6gs} 5^{7gs} 9^{7gs} **1-0-4 £4,340**

Crystal Bay (Ire) *A Berry* 7
2 b f Carrowkeel (Ire) - Cajo (Ire)
15^{5s} 11^{5gf} 11^{6gf} 8^{5gf} 11^{5gf} 10^{7gf} 10^{6gf}
0-0-7

Crystal Mystic (Ire) *B Palling* 63
3 b g Anita's Prince - Out On Her Own
13^{8gs} 2^{6gs} 1^{6gf} 2^{6g} 7^{7gf} 3^{7g} **1-3-6**
£5,785

Cuccinello (Ire) *A Berry* 6
2 b f Makbul - Costa Verde
9^{6g} 10^{5gs} 12^{7gf} **0-0-3**

Cuddly Toy (Ire) *W J Haggas* 27 a60
2 b f King Charlemagne (USA) - Smart Pet
9^{5g} 14^{6gs} 1^{7ft} **1-0-3 £2,639**

Cuesta Canyon (Ire) *M J Polglase* 38
2 b g Indian Ridge - Perfect Plum (Ire)
13^{6sd} 7^{7f} 11^{7gf} 6^{6gf} 13^{7ss} **0-0-5**

Cuevas Bay *R Hannon* 34
3 b f Robellino (USA) - Down The Valley
6^{8s} **0-0-1**

Culture Queen *M P Tregoning* 81
2 b f King's Best (USA) - Cultured Pearl (Ire)
6^{6s} 8^{6gf} 2^{5gf} 1^{6g} **1-1-4 £5,787**

Cultured *Mrs A J Bowlby* 58 a40
4 b f Danzero (Aus) - Seek The Pearl

5^{8g} 11^{10sd} **0-0-2**

Cumberland Road *P C Haslam* 59 a61
2 ch g Efisio - Thatcher's Era (Ire)
12^{6gf} 4^{6sd} 5^{7gf} 12^{7ss} **0-0-4 £237**

Cumbrae (Ire) *Mrs H Sweeting* 24 a54
2 b g Mull Of Kintyre (USA) - Maura's Pet (Ire)
8^{5gs} 5^{5gs} 1^{7sd} **1-0-3 £2,590**

Cumbrian Knight (Ire) *J M Jefferson* 64 a66
7 b g Presenting - Crashrun
8^{12gf} 4^{11gf} 13^{10gf} 4^{12gf} 7^{14gf} 5^{12g} 1^{14sd} 10^{14sd} **1-0-8 £3,329**

Cumbrian Princess *M Blanshard* a54
8 gr m Mtoto - Cumbrian Melody
10^{10sd} 1^{9sd} 8^{9sd} **1-0-3 £2,879**

Cunegonde *G L Moore* 31
2 ch f Observatory (USA) - Brave Princess
21^{7s} **0-0-1**

Cunning Pursuit *N J Henderson* 37
4 b g Pursuit Of Love - Mistitled (USA)
9^{12gf} **0-0-1**

Cup Of Love (USA) *Rae Guest* 63 a62
3 ch f Behrens (USA) - Cup Of Kindness (USA)
12^{8g} 11^{10gf} 1^{10f} 2^{12gf} 1^{10gf} 3^{10f} 6^{12sd} 7^{8sd} **2-2-8 £5,829**

Cupid's Glory *Sir Mark Prescott* 115
3 b g Pursuit Of Love - Doctor's Glory (USA)
7^{8gs} 1^{8gf} 2^{8gs} 2^{7g} **1-2-4 £25,776**

Curbridge Bell *M R Channon*
2 ch f Fraam - Stride Home
13^{9sd} **0-0-1**

Curragh Dancer (Fr) *Saeed Bin Suroor* 49
2 ch c Grand Lodge (USA) - Native Twine
10^{7gs} 13^{7g} **0-0-2**

Currency *J M Bradley* 88 a83
8 b g Sri Pekan (USA) - On Tiptoes
3^{7sd} 8^{5sd} 10^{6sd} 12^{6sd} 13^{6gf} 7^{6f} 4^{6gf} 5^{6f} 1^{6gf} 1^{6g} 12^{6gf} 7^{6g} 15^{6gf} 1^{6gf} 3^{6g} 6^{6gf} 10^{6gf} 14^{6g} 13^{6gf} 13^{6gs} **3-3-20 £23,685**

Cursum Perficio *W R Muir* 73
3 b g Tagula (Ire) - Simply Sooty
9^{7g} 6^{8gs} 4^{8g} 6^{7gs} 4^{7gf} 1^{8gf} **1-0-6 £4,882**

Curtail (Ire) *I Semple* 104
2 b c Namid - Nipitinthebud (USA)
11^{5g} 4^{5s} 2^{6gf} 2^{5g} 4^{6g} 1^{6g} 5^{6g} 8^{6g} 1^{5g} 4^{5g} 3^{6gs} **2-3-11 £42,179**

Curtain Bluff *M R Channon* 85 a85
3 b g Dansili - Gayane
3^{8g} 5^{7g} 2^{8g} 1^{7f} 4^{7g} 9^{8gs} 2^{8g} 3^{8sd} 8^{7gf} 14^{8gf} 3^{8gs} 7^{8s} 10^{8g} **1-5-13 £11,642**

Cusoon *G L Moore* 82 a74
3 b g Dansili - Charming Life
12^{7g} 8^{7gf} 1^{8gf} 6^{7gf} 10^{8gs} 11^{8g} 5^{7g} 13^{8g} 2^{10sd} 4^{10sd} **1-1-10 £5,029**

Cusp *Mrs A M Thorpe* 11
5 b m Pivotal - Bambolona
11^{16g} **0-0-1**

Cut And Dried *D M Simcock* 54 a61
4 ch g Daggers Drawn (USA) - Apple Sauce
7^{5sd} 5^{5sd} 8^{5sd} 7^{6gf} 12^{7sd} **0-0-5**

Cut Glass *C E Brittain* 59
2 ch f Fantastic Light (USA) - Shady Point (Ire)
12^{7gf} 8^{7gf} **0-0-2**

Cut Ridge (Ire) *J S Wainwright* 55
6 b m Indian Ridge - Cutting Ground (Ire)
10^{7gf} 3^{7g} 6^{8gs} 5^{6gf} 10^{7f} 6^{7g} 16^{7s} **0-1-7 £535**

Cutlass Gaudy *R Hollinshead* 46
3 br c Nomination - Cutlass Princess (USA)
14^{6g} 13^{6gs} 10^{6gf} 10^{6g} 6^{8g} 6^{6f} 14^{6g} 15^{6gf} **0-0-8**

Cyber Santa *J Hetherton* 51
7 b g Celtic Swing - Qualitair Ridge
12^{16gs} 3^{12gf} 1^{12g} 12^{11gf} **1-1-4 £2,892**

Cyclical *G A Butler* 94
3 b c Pivotal - Entwine
6^{6gs} 17^{6s} **0-0-2**

Cyclonic *J R Fanshawe* 64
3 br c Pivotal - Rainy Day Song
11^{6s} 8^{7gf} 7^{7gf} 2^{6f} 4^{6g} **0-1-5 £1,370**

Cyfrwys (Ire) *B Palling* 69 a52
4 b f Foxhound (USA) - Divine Elegance (Ire)
5^{7f} 3^{6g} 4^{6g} 1^{6g} 12^{7g} 2^{6gf} 4^{6g} 5^{7g} 12^{6gf} 7^{6g} 2^{6g} 9^{6sd} **1-3-12 £8,243**

Czarina Waltz *Miss Gay Kelleway* a55
6 b m Emperor Jones (USA) - Ballerina Bay
10^{8sd} PU^{9sd} **0-0-2**

Daanet Al Dunya (USA) *Saeed Bin Suroor* 40
2 ch f Rahy (USA) - Jood (USA)
6^{7gf} **0-0-1**

Daaweitza *B Ellison* 65 a65
2 ch c Daawe (USA) - Chichen Itza
6^{6gf} 7^{7gf} 9^{7gs} 6^{7hy} 2^{6gs} 16^{6g} 10^{7s} 4^{6sd} 7^{6sd} 4^{8sd} **0-1-10 £2,808**

Dabbers Ridge (Ire) *B W Hills* 90
3 b c Indian Ridge - Much Commended
2^{7g} 2^{7g} 1^{7s} 3^{7g} 2^{7g} 4^{8g} 4^{7gf} 2^{7s} **1-6-8 £18,608**

Dado Mush *T T Clement* 31 a36
2 b c Almushtarak (Ire) - Princess Of Spain
9^{6s} 10^{6sd} **0-0-2**

Daedal *M L W Bell* 58
2 b f Dr Fong (USA) - Datura
5^{7g} 3^{7f} 7^{7gf} 10^{7g} 9^{7g} **0-1-5 £634**

Dafa *B J Curley* 21 a49
9 b g Deploy - Linpac North Moor
1^{12sd} 11^{11gs} PU^{10s} **1-0-3 £1,494**

Dafore *R Hannon* 81 a67
4 b c Dr Fong (USA) - Aquaglow
9^{8sd} 3^{10s} 7^{11s} 4^{10gf} 7^{10g} 12^{8gf} 5^{8gs} 7^{10g} 6^{10gs} 6^{8g} 9^{10s} **0-1-11 £1,617**

Daggernought (USA) *J W Hills* 102 a63
2 b c Diesis - Quittance (USA)
5^{6gs} 2^{6f} 3^{7g} 9^{7sd} 4^{8f} 1^{7gs} 5^{7gs} **1-2-7 £6,941**

Dagola (Ire) *C A Dwyer* 56 a66
4 b g Daggers Drawn (USA) - Diabola (USA)
11^{9sd} 7^{9sd} DSQ^{12sd} 4^{12sd} 4^{10sd} 8^{9sd} 7^{10gf} 11^{10gf} 3^{10sd} 12^{10sd} 8^{10sd} **0-1-11 £637**

Dahaaleez (USA) *M P Tregoning* 79
2 b c Red Ransom (USA) - Raajiya (USA)
11^{6gf} 5^{7g} 5^{7g} 1^{7g} **1-0-4 £5,239**

Dahliyev (Ire) *W R Swinburn* 67
3 b g Fasliyev (USA) - Thaidah (Can)
10^{7g} 8^{8gf} 5^{10gf} 10^{10g} 11^{10gf} 11^{10hd} 14^{10gs} **0-0-7**

Dahman *Saeed Bin Suroor* 85
3 b g Darshaan - Nuriva (USA)
1^{8gf} 2^{10gf} 3^{11gs} 6^{12gs} **1-2-4 £9,734**

Dahteer (Ire) *M R Channon* 91

3 b g Bachir (Ire) - Reematna
3^{6gs} 3^{6gf} 5^{7g} 14^{6gf} 8^{6g} 10^{6g} **0-2-6**
£5,333

Daintree Affair (Ire) *Mrs H Sweeting* a31
5 b g Charnwood Forest (Ire) - Madam Loving
9^{5sd} **0-0-1**

Daisy Bucket *D M Simcock* a42
3 b f Lujain (USA) - Masrora (USA)
6^{7sd} **0-0-1**

Daisy Pooter (Ire) *T D Barron* 43 a53
3 b f Charnwood Forest (Ire) - Idrak
5^{6sd} 4^{6sd} 8^{5sd} 8^{5g} 7^{6gs} 8^{6g} **0-0-6**

Daisys Girl *S C Williams* 50 a47
3 b f Inchinor - Andbell
14^{10sd} 4^{7sd} 8^{9sd} 9^{7gs} 3^{7f} 14^{8gf} 11^{7gf} 3^{7gf}
4^{10f} 10^{8s} 9^{10gf} 3^{7f} 12^{7g} 12^{8g} **0-3-14**
£1,474

Dakota Blackhills *J G Given* 59 a17
4 b g Singspiel (Ire) - Lady Blackfoot
5^{9gf} 7^{8gf} 6^{10g} 15^{10gf} 16^{8gs} 10^{7sf} **0-0-6**

Dakota Rain (Ire) *M A Jarvis* 86
3 br g Indian Ridge - Mill Rainbow (Fr)
5^{8g} 2^{8g} 2^{8g} 1^{8g} 6^{8g} **1-2-5 £8,846**

Daldini *Mrs S J Smith* 76
3 b g Josr Algarhoud (Ire) - Arianna Aldini
6^{7gf} 9^{8gf} 12^{9g} 12^{12g} 7^{11g} **0-0-5**

Dalida *Miss M E Rowland* 41 a28
4 ch f Pursuit Of Love - Debutante Days
10^{8sd} 6^{8sd} 7^{8gf} DSQ^{10g} **0-0-4**

Dalkeys Lass *Mrs L B Normile* 17
4 gr f Wolfhound (USA) - Dalkey Sound
5^{11g} 6^{12gf} **0-0-2**

Dalmarnock (Ire) *P D Niven*
4 ch g Grand Lodge (USA) - Lochbelle
16^{10g} 18^{8gf} **0-0-2**

Dalpe *A J Lidderdale* a53
4 ch g Siphon (Brz) - Double Stake (USA)
2^{8sd} **0-1-1 £1,208**

Dalriath *M C Chapman* 18
6 b m Fraam - Alsiba
10^{12f} 11^{10gf} **0-0-2**

Dama'A (Ire) *J H M Gosden* 77
2 b f Green Desert (USA) - Lady Miletrian (Ire)
2^{6gf} **0-1-1 £1,700**

Damburger Xpress *D M Simcock* 66
3 b g Josr Algarhoud (Ire) - Upping The Tempo
5^{8gf} 12^{7gf} 5^{8g} 2^{9gf} 5^{10s} **0-1-5 £863**

Dame De Noche *J G Given* 94
5 b m Lion Cavern (USA) - Goodnight Kiss
4^{5s} 8^{6gf} 3^{5gf} 2^{5gf} 5^{5g} 9^{5gs} 9^{5g} 9^{5s} 12^{6g} 10^{6gf}
0-2-10 £6,184

Damelza (Ire) *T D Easterby* 82
2 b f Orpen (USA) - Damezao
3^{6gf} 1^{7gf} 7^{6gs} 1^{8g} 15^{7gs} 8^{7hy} **2-1-6**
£11,466

Damson (Ire) *David Wachman* 102
3 b f Entrepreneur - Tadkiyra (Ire)
9^{8gy} 7^{8gf} 9^{6g} **0-0-3 £851**

Dan Buoy (Fr) *A King* 64
2 b c Slip Anchor - Bramosia
6^{8gs} **0-0-1**

Dan Dare (USA) *Sir Michael Stoute* 76
2 b c Dynaformer (USA) - Etheldreda (USA)
2^{8g} 4^{8gf} **0-1-2 £2,057**

Dan Di Canio (Ire) *A G Newcombe* 45 a62
4 b g Bahri (USA) - Khudud
2^{8sd} 2^{9sd} 2^{8sd} 10^{9sd} 18^{7gs} 8^{8sd} 7^{7g} 9^{8f} 10^{6sd}
0-3-9 £2,996

Dan's Heir *P C Haslam* 63 a64
3 b g Dansili - Million Heiress
2^{9sd} 4^{12g} 1^{12sd} 2^{12g} **1-3-4 £5,230**

Danaatt (USA) *K R Burke* 41 a24
3 b f Gulch (USA) - Agama (USA)
4^{7f} 4^{6gs} 7^{7gf} 6^{6gf} 14^{7g} 8^{8sd} 6^{6ss} 6^{8sd}
0-0-8

Danakim *J R Weymes* 48 a50
8 b g Emarati (USA) - Kangra Valley
8^{5sd} 1^{5sd} 2^{6sd} 12^{5sd} 7^{5sd} 3^{5sd} 8^{5sd} 11^{6sd} 12^{6g}
4^{6f} 2^{5f} 7^{5g} 8^{5gf} 11^{5g} 5^{6gf} 4^{6f} 11^{6sd} 12^{6g}
14^{6sd} 11^{5sd} **1-4-20 £3,130**

Danamour (Ire) *M P Tregoning* a75
2 b g Dansili - Love And Affection (USA)
7^{8sd} 1^{9sd} **1-0-2 £3,727**

Danawi (Ire) *R Hannon* 87 a66
2 ch c Elnadim (USA) - Just Rainbow (Fr)
10^{7gf} 2^{6g} 2^{6s} 2^{6s} 5^{6sd} **0-3-5 £3,965**

Dance A Daydream *J R Fanshawe* a36
2 b f Daylami (Ire) - Dance A Dream
9^{9sd} **0-0-1**

Dance Hall Diva *M D I Usher* 27
3 b f Zaha (Can) - Eastwell Star
15^{8g} 12^{10g} **0-0-2**

Dance In Style *J Mackie* 48 a68
4 b f Desert Style (Ire) - Loves To Dance (Fr)
8^{9sd} 8^{9sd} 13^{10gs} 10^{10gf} 4^{9sd} 2^{8sd} 1^{9sd}
1-1-7 £3,487

Dance Light (Ire) *T T Clement* 49
6 b m Lycius (USA) - Embracing
6^{14gf} 5^{16gf} 9^{17g} **0-0-3**

Dance Night (Ire) *Miss L A Perratt* 84
3 b c Danehill Dancer (Ire) - Tiger Wings (Ire)
9^{5g} 6^{5g} 25^{6g} **0-0-3**

Dance On The Top *J R Boyle* 77 a93
7 ch g Caerleon (USA) - Fern
4^{8sd} 8^{10sd} 6^{8sd} 3^{7sd} 2^{8gf} 3^{8gf} 4^{8gf} 1^{8gf} 6^{8g}
6^{8g} 9^{8gf} 7^{8g} **1-3-12 £7,353**

Dance Partner *J H M Gosden* 91 a89
3 b f Danzero (Aus) - Dancing Debut
7^{9gs} 2^{12sd} 1^{10sd} 1^{10gs} 1^{10gf} 2^{11gs} 1^{12g} 3^{10sd}
4-2-8 £36,245

Dance Party (Ire) *M W Easterby* a49
5 b m Charnwood Forest (Ire) - Society Ball
7^{9sd} **0-0-1**

Dance Sauvage *B W Hills* 41
2 ch g Groom Dancer (USA) - Peace Dance
10^{6gf} 8^{7gs} 12^{7g} **0-0-3**

Dance School *D R Loder* 70
2 b f Zafonic (USA) - Dust Dancer
4^{7gf} 5^{7gf} **0-0-2 £407**

Dance Sequel *Sir Michael Stoute* 55
2 ch f Selkirk (USA) - Dance Sequence (USA)
10^{6gf} 10^{7g} 12^{8g} **0-0-3**

Dance To My Tune *M W Easterby* 81
4 b f Halling (USA) - Stolen Melody
2^{12g} 5^{10gs} 4^{10s} 2^{12gs} 3^{12s} 1^{12g} 14^{12gf} 5^{10gs}
7^{10gs} 3^{12g} 10^{12gs} 4^{14s} 2^{12gs} **1-6-13**
£13,515

Dance To The Blues (Ire) *B De Haan* 71 a71
4 br f Danehill Dancer (Ire) - Blue Sioux
2^{6sd} 9^{6sd} 4^{5sd} 3^{5gf} 5^{6hy} 3^{5gf} 5^{6g} 1^{5f} 2^{5gf}

2^{5gf} 1^{6g} 2^{6sd} **2-5-12 £12,783**

Dance Troupe *J Jay* 79 a57
3 b f Rainbow Quest (USA) - Dansara
3^{13s} 5^{12g} 2^{12g} 2^{12vs} 2^{11s} 2^{13vs} 2^{11sd} 9^{14sd}
0-3-8 £13,192

Dance World *Miss J Feilden* 82
5 b g Spectrum (Ire) - Dansara
6^{16gs} 10^{12gf} 10^{11g} 11^{12gs} **0-0-4 £310**

Danceinthevalley (Ire) *G A Swinbank* 76 a55
3 b g Imperial Ballet (Ire) - Dancing Willma (Ire)
4^{9sd} 7^{10sd} 2^{10gf} 2^{10g} 4^{9f} 1^{8s} 10^{8g} 1^{8g} 5^{8g}
6^{10g} **2-2-10 £10,379**

Dancer's Serenade (Ire) *T P Tate* 95
3 b g Almutawakel - Dance Serenade (Ire)
2^{10g} 1^{10s} 7^{12g} 1^{10g} 5^{10gf} 4^{10s} 6^{10g} 8^{10g}
2-1-8 £17,300

Dancers Of Kerry (Ire) *E J O'Neill* 40 a33
2 br f Imperial Ballet (Ire) - Knockanure (USA)
10^{8sd} 6^{8gf} 10^{7gf} **0-0-3**

Dances With Angels (Ire) *J W Unett* a49
5 b m Mukaddamah (USA) - Lady Of Leisure (USA)
4^{14sd} 1^{12sd} 3^{14sd} 3^{11sd} 2^{14sd} 5^{12sd} 8^{17sd} 3^{12sd}
1-4-8 £2,520

Dancing Bay *N J Henderson* 109
8 b g Suave Dancer (USA) - Kabayil
4^{22f} 5^{16s} 4^{16gs} 4^{16s} **0-0-4 £8,361**

Dancing Beauty (Ire) *T T Clement* a29
3 b f Charnwood Forest (Ire) - Viennese Dancer
13^{8g} 10^{7sd} 14^{10sd} **0-0-3**

Dancing Dane (Ire) *T D Easterby* 37
2 ch g Danehill Dancer (Ire) - Tifosi (Ire)
15^{6gf} 10^{7gf} 8^{6gf} 4^{7g} 12^{8g} **0-0-5 £238**

Dancing Deano (Ire) *R M Whitaker* 63
3 b g Second Empire (Ire) - Ultimate Beat (USA)
8^{6gf} 1^{6gs} 3^{7gf} 2^{6gf} 5^{7f} 11^{5gs} 2^{6g} 3^{6g} 5^{6gf}
4^{7g} 9^{7g} **1-4-11 £6,897**

Dancing Edge *N Tinkler* 52
2 ch g Bold Edge - Rockin' Rosie
8^{5g} 9^{5g} 2^{5s} 5^{5g} 15^{5gf} 5^{6gf} 1^{6gf} 5^{6gf} 7^{7g} 10^{8gf}
1-1-10 £4,192

Dancing Flame *E J Alston* 56
2 b f Groom Dancer (USA) - Catch The Flame (USA)
2^{5s} 6^{5gs} 6^{6f} 6^{6gf} 5^{7gf} 4^{7gf} 7^{8gs} **0-1-7**
£1,257

Dancing Guest (Ire) *G G Margarson* 69
2 ch f Danehill Dancer (Ire) - Saibhreas (Ire)
10^{6gf} 9^{6g} 1^{7s} **1-0-3 £3,149**

Dancing Lyra *R A Fahey* 85 a83
4 b g Alzao (USA) - Badaayer (USA)
16^{10gs} 6^{10gf} 13^{12gf} 3^{12gf} 4^{12gf} 7^{15gf} 6^{12g} 4^{13gf}
7^{12g} 8^{11gf} 8^{14g} 3^{12sd} **0-2-12 £3,720**

Dancing Melody *J A Geake* 58
2 b f Dr Fong (USA) - Spring Mood (Fr)
9^{6gf} 12^{6gf} 4^{6gs} 8^{7g} 17^{7g} **0-0-5 £248**

Dancing Moonlight (Ire) *Mrs N Macauley* a26
3 b f Danehill Dancer (Ire) - Silver Moon
10^{8sd} 5^{6sd} 6^{7sd} 13^{6sd} 10^{11sd} 12^{7ss} **0-0-6**

Dancing Mystery *E A Wheeler* 87 a108
11 b g Beveled (USA) - Batchworth Dancer
1^{5sd} 6^{5ft} 3^{5ft} 1^{5sd} 5^{5g} 7^{5gs} 4^{5f} 13^{5gf} 7^{5gf}
7^{5sd} 10^{5s} 6^{5g} 5^{5gs} 3^{5g} 4^{5g} 6^{6g} 9^{6sd} 8^{5sf} 8^{5sd}
2-2-19 £38,905

Dancing On *G A Butler*
2 ch f Pivotal - Dance On
F^{6gf} **0-0-1**

Dancing Pearl *C J Price* a40
7 ch m Dancing Spree (USA) - Elegant Rose
4^{14sd} **0-0-1**

Dancing Rose (Ire) *C G Cox* 87
3 b f Danehill Dancer (Ire) - Shinkoh Rose (Fr)
1^{7gf} 3^{7g} 5^{7gf} 12^{7g} **1-1-4 £8,431**

Dancing Shirl *C W Fairhurst* 18 a36
3 b f Dancing Spree (USA) - Shirl
7^{10gs} 10^{12g} 12^{8gf} 8^{8sd} 10^{12s} 8^{12sf} **0-0-6**

Dancing Storm *W S Kittow* 60 a54
2 b f Trans Island - Stormswell
4^{6gs} 6^{6g} 6^{6g} 9^{7sd} **0-0-4**

Dancing Tilly *R A Fahey* a38
7 b m Dancing Spree (USA) - L'Ancressaan
10^{14sd} 7^{12sd} **0-0-2**

Dancingintheclouds (Ire) *J L Dunlop* 66
3 b f Rainbow Quest (USA) - Ballerina (Ire)
9^{10gs} 7^{10gf} 5^{12gf} **0-0-3**

Dancinginthedark (Ire) *B R Millman* 59 a52
3 b f Fasliyev (USA) - Moviegoer
6^{7sd} 3^{7g} 6^{8s} 4^{7g} 5^{6g} 5^{7g} 8^{10gs} **0-1-7**
£794

Dandoun *C A Dwyer* 73 a97
7 b h Halling (USA) - Moneefa
4^{9sd} 11^{7sd} 12^{9sd} 6^{8s} 13^{8gf} **0-0-5**
£1,476

Dandygrey Russett (Ire) *B D Leavy* 65 a72
4 gr f Singspiel (Ire) - Christian Church (Ire)
5^{10sd} 4^{10sd} 5^{12sd} 5^{10s} 2^{10g} 5^{9g} 7^{12sd} **0-1-7**
£1,358

Dane Rhapsody (Ire) *B Palling* 48 a40
4 b f Danetime (Ire) - Hil Rhapsody
5^{7gf} 9^{6s} 6^{8gf} 9^{7sd} 6^{7f} 7^{6f} 5^{7g} 3^{6f} 7^{6g} 4^{5hd}
6^{6sd} 6^{7sf} 8^{6sd} **0-1-13 £385**

Dane's Castle (Ire) *B J Meehan* a59
3 b g Danetime (Ire) - Faypool (Ire)
7^{6sd} **0-0-1**

Dane's Rock (Ire) *M S Saunders* 52 a53
3 b g Indian Danehill (Ire) - Cutting Ground (Ire)
6^{7sd} 4^{8sd} 1^{8sd} 11^{9sd} 2^{9sd} 3^{8sd} 5^{7s} 5^{7gf} 12^{8gf}
6^{8f} 13^{7f} 1^{8f} 6^{7sf} 6^{9sd} 5^{9sd} **2-1-15**
£6,732

Danebank (Ire) *J Mackie* 60
5 b g Danehill (USA) - Snow Bank (Ire)
2^{14gf} 7^{14gf} **0-1-2 £1,139**

Danehill Angel *M J Polglase* 10 a25
3 ch f Danehill Dancer (Ire) - Ace Girl
11^{8sd} 10^{7sd} 9^{8sd} 12^{8hd} 10^{7g} 12^{7sd} **0-0-6**

Danehill Dazzler (Ire) *A P Jarvis* 83 a76
3 b f Danehill Dancer (Ire) - Finnegans Dilemma (Ire)
1^{8g} 4^{8gs} 4^{7gf} 6^{8gf} 10^{10g} 23^{7gf} 1^{7g} 5^{8g} 9^{7sd}
2-0-9 £13,797

Danehill Folly (Ire) *J M Bradley*
2 b g Danehill Dancer (Ire) - Theorique (Ire)
9^{6gf} 11^{5gs} 10^{6f} 14^{5gs} **0-0-4**

Danehill Stroller (Ire) *R M Beckett* 77
5 b g Danetime (Ire) - Tuft Hill
3^{6gf} 9^{6gf} 14^{6gf} 3^{6gf} 5^{6f} **0-2-5 £1,618**

Danehill Willy (Ire) *N A Callaghan* 95
3 b g Danehill Dancer (Ire) - Lowtown
4^{10gf} 6^{12gf} 11^{10gf} 2^{10gf} 1^{10gs} 1^{10gf} 2^{10gf} 13^{10gf}
10^{10s} **2-2-9 £46,130**

Danelor (Ire) *R A Fahey* 91 a84
7 b g Danehill (USA) - Formulate
10^{8sd} 5^{9sd} 4^{9sd} 1^{11sd} 5^{10sd} 6^{10gs} 1^{10gs} 8^{10gs}

14^{10g} 3^{10g} 5^{10gf} 12^{9gs} 3^{10s} 5^{9sf} 2^{11sd} 2^{11sd} **2-2-16 £21,392**

Danescourt (Ire) *J M Bradley* 52 a43
3 b g Danetime (Ire) - Faye
9^{6hy} 5^{5gf} 10^{6sd} 8^{6sd} 7^{6g} 8^{7f} 9^{6g} 9^{6gs} 12^{6gf} 14^{7gf} 13^{6f} 10^{5g} 9^{5g} **0-0-13**

Danethorpe Lady (Ire) *D Shaw* 35 a34
3 b f Brave Act - Annie's Travels (Ire)
10^{5sd} 11^{5g} 10^{5sd} 8^{6sd} 6^{6s} 12^{7gf} 12^{6gf} 11^{6sd} **0-0-8**

Danetime Lady (Ire) *Niall Moran* 76 a29
5 b m Danetime (Ire) - Hawattef (Ire)
7^{7sd} 8^{9sd} 14^{11sd} 6^{7f} 4^{6gf} 2^{6gf} 8^{6g} 12^{6g} 12^{6gf} 7^{5g} **0-1-10 £2,178**

Danetime Lord (Ire) *A Berry* 49
2 b c Danetime (Ire) - Seven Sisters (USA)
6^{5gf} 9^{5g} 10^{6g} **0-0-3**

Danettie *W M Brisbourne* 56 a59
4 b f Danzero (Aus) - Petite Heritiere
4^{9sd} 6^{7sd} 12^{8gf} 3^{9sd} 6^{9sd} 4^{10sd} 2^{9gf} 6^{8sd} 1^{8sd} 1^{8sd} 2^{9ss} **2-3-11 £4,781**

Daneway *H R A Cecil* a58
2 ch f Danehill Dancer (Ire) - Scylla
8^{8sd} **0-0-1**

Danger Bird (Ire) *R Hollinshead* 19 a52
5 ch m Eagle Eyed (USA) - Danger Ahead
3^{9sd} 9^{12sd} 7^{9sd} 10^{9sd} 6^{9sd} 4^{9sd} 7^{9sf} 8^{10g} 6^{9sd} 11^{12sf} 2^{9sd} 10^{9sd} **0-2-12 £867**

Danger Zone *Mrs A J Perrett* 73 a74
3 b g Danzero (Aus) - Red Tulle (USA)
17^{8gs} 9^{8gf} 4^{7gf} 3^{7gf} 1^{7g} 2^{7sd} 2^{7gf} 5^{7gf} 5^{7g} 11^{8sd} 2^{10sd} **1-5-11 £8,150**

Dangermouse *A G Newcombe* 49 a46
2 b f Afternoon Deelites (USA) - Ghost Dance (Ire)
5^{5s} 4^{6gf} 7^{5f} 4^{7gf} 5^{6gf} 10^{7g} 7^{7gs} 6^{7sd} **0-0-8**

Dangerous Dave *Jamie Poulton* a25
6 b g Superpower - Lovely Lilly
8^{7sd} 10^{10sd} **0-0-2**

Daniel O'Donnell *C E Brittain* 47 a71
3 b c Komaite (USA) - Light Slippers (Ire)
2^{6sd} 5^{7sd} 6^{6gf} 15^{8gs} 11^{8sd} **0-1-5 £1,245**

Daniel Thomas (Ire) *Mrs A J Perrett* 86
3 b c Dansili - Last Look
3^{8gs} **0-1-1 £1,947**

Daniella *Rae Guest* 71
3 b f Dansili - Break Point
15^{8g} 6^{8g} 3^{7gf} 8^{6gf} 2^{7f} 4^{6gf} 1^{6gf} 5^{6g} 6^{6g} **1-2-9 £5,838**

Danielle Taylor *N Tinkler*
3 b f Fraam - Mayor
12^{8g} 15^{6s} PU^{6gf} **0-0-3**

Danielle's Lad *B Palling* 72 a70
9 b g Emarati (USA) - Cactus Road (Fr)
10^{8hy} 15^{7gf} 5^{9sd} 1^{8gf} 10^{8g} 10^{8g} 9^{8sd} 5^{9sd} **1-0-8 £4,317**

Danifah (Ire) *P D Evans* 77
4 b f Perugino (USA) - Afifah
1^{6gs} 13^{7gf} 5^{8gf} 8^{8g} 10^{8gf} 7^{8g} 13^{7gf} **1-0-7 £3,912**

Danish Blues (Ire) *R M Flower*
2 b g Danetime (Ire) - Sing A Song (Ire)
11^{6sd} 11^{8gs} 10^{8sd} **0-0-3**

Danish Express (Ire) *P Winkworth* 77 a72
2 b c Danetime (Ire) - Jungle Story (Ire)
2^{5s} 1^{6gf} 7^{6g} 4^{5gf} 14^{6gs} 6^{6sd} 3^{5g} **1-2-7 £7,014**

Danish Monarch *David Pinder* 50 a23
4 b g Great Dane (Ire) - Moly
9^{6sd} 12^{8g} 9^{8gf} 7^{7gf} 11^{8gf} 6^{8gf} 10^{7g} 14^{10g} 2^{10g} 4^{10f} 7^{11g} **0-1-11 £430**

Danjet (Ire) *P D Evans* 87 a80
2 bl f Danehill Dancer (Ire) - Jet Lock (USA)
2^{5sd} 1^{5gs} 2^{5g} 2^{5sd} 5^{5gs} 6^{5g} 10^{5gf} 1^{5g} 17^{5gf} 9^{5gs} 9^{5gf} 6^{6g} 9^{6gf} 8^{5g} **2-3-14 £29,521**

Danny The Dip *J J Bridger* 60 a44
2 b g Prince Sabo - Ann's Pearl (Ire)
7^{5gf} 5^{5s} 6^{5sd} 1^{5g} 7^{5gs} 11^{5gf} 6^{5gf} 7^{6gs} **1-0-8 £3,376**

Dansa Queen *W R Swinburn* a69
2 gr f Dansili - Pericardia
12^{7sd} 1^{7sd} **1-0-2 £4,524**

Danse Du Flambe *D J S Ffrench Davis* 50 a53
2 ch f Zaha (Can) - Amber Rose (Ire)
10^{6g} 10^{6g} 10^{7sd} 9^{7g} 1^{8gf} 10^{8hy} 8^{9sd} 7^{7sd} **1-0-8 £2,996**

Danse Spectre (Ire) *E J O'Neill* a61
3 b f Spectrum (Ire) - Danse Royale (Ire)
13^{10s} 1^{10sd} **1-0-2 £4,070**

Dansili Dancer *C G Cox* 96
3 b g Dansili - Magic Slipper
2^{8g} 1^{8g} 5^{8gs} 5^{10s} 2^{10g} **1-2-5 £11,987**

Danski *P J Makin* 70
2 b c Dansili - Manila Selection (USA)
5^{7s} **0-0-1**

Dante's Devine (Ire) *A Bailey* a34
4 b g Ashkalani (Ire) - Basilea (Fr)
10^{8sd} 11^{10sd} **0-0-2**

Dante's Diamond (Ire) *G A Swinbank* 73
3 b g Orpen (USA) - Flower From Heaven
12^{8s} 7^{8gf} 5^{7gf} 9^{7g} 2^{7gf} 2^{7gf} 6^{7gf} 2^{8gf} 9^{8gf} 7^{8gf} 14^{7g} **0-3-11 £3,881**

Danum *R Hollinshead* 43 a48
5 b g Perpendicular - Maid Of Essex
5^{8sd} 3^{9sd} 8^{12sd} 5^{9sd} 10^{9sd} 9^{8sd} 4^{9sd} 3^{12s} 18^{10gf} 4^{12sd} **0-2-10 £399**

Danzar *M Brittain* 63
3 b g Danzero (Aus) - Tarf (USA)
6^{6gf} 6^{6gf} **0-0-2**

Danzare *Mrs A J Hamilton-Fairley* 59 a63
3 b f Dansili - Shot Of Redemption
8^{8gf} 11^{8g} 3^{8gs} 11^{10g} 1^{10g} 2^{9sd} 13^{10sd} **1-2-7 £4,774**

Danzatrice *C W Thornton* 42
3 b f Tamure (Ire) - Miss Petronella
8^{8g} 10^{10gf} **0-0-2**

Danze Romance *S Woodman*
4 b f Danzero (Aus) - By Arrangement (Ire)
15^{12gs} 14^{10gf} 12^{10gf} **0-0-3**

Danzig River (Ire) *D Nicholls* 92
4 b g Green Desert (USA) - Sahara Breeze
13^{5g} 4^{5gs} 6^{5s} 13^{6s} 11^{6g} 8^{5g} 8^{6g} 5^{7g} 3^{6gs} 3^{6s} 18^{6g} **0-2-11 £5,637**

Danzili Bay *P W Chapple-Hyam* 95
3 b c Dansili - Lady Bankes (Ire)
2^{6gs} 1^{6gf} 4^{6g} 1^{6gf} 4^{6gf} **2-1-5 £21,265**

Danzolin *W R Muir* 60 a61
4 b f Danzero (Aus) - Howlin' (USA)
6^{7sd} 4^{9sd} 7^{10s} 9^{9f} 12^{9sd} 10^{8gf} 2^{8f} **0-1-7 £1,034**

Dara Girl (Ire) *L Montague Hall* a39
3 br f Key Of Luck (USA) - Tavildara (Ire)
9^{8sd} 9^{10sd} **0-0-2**

Dara Mac *L P Grassick* 58 a57
6 b g Presidium - Nishara
6^{8s} 9^{7s} 8^{7g} 17^{8g} 6^{8gf} 4^{8gf} 2^{7g} 2^{8g} 5^{7g} 6^{8gf} 8^{9sd} 2^{9sd} 6^{9sd} **0-3-13 £3,109**

Dara Mate Mac *N Bycroft* 7
4 b g Komaite (USA) - Nishara
11^{6gf} **0-0-1**

Darasim (Ire) *Jonjo O'Neill* 88
7 b g Kahyasi - Dararita (Ire)
6^{14s} 9^{16s} 14^{16g} 13^{20gf} 4^{12s} **0-0-5 £1,341**

Darghan (Ire) *W J Musson* 66
5 b g Air Express (Ire) - Darsannda (Ire)
15^{8gf} 12^{8f} 10^{8gf} 8^{8gf} 2^{10gf} 6^{10g} 5^{12g} 2^{12f} 6^{14g} **0-2-9 £1,678**

Daring Affair *K R Burke* 77 a74
4 b f Bien Bien (USA) - Daring Destiny
2^{11gs} 13^{9sd} 1^{10s} 8^{10hy} 3^{12sd} 3^{11sd} 2^{9sd} **1-4-7 £9,390**

Daring Gamble *I W McInnes*
8 b m Barrys Gamble - Rachel Sharp
13^{7sd} 13^{6sd} **0-0-2**

Daring Games *B Ellison* 29 a25
4 b f Mind Games - Daira
13^{8g} 5^{8sd} 7^{12gs} 8^{6gs} **0-0-4**

Daring Ransom (USA) *J Noseda* 103
3 b g Red Ransom (USA) - Young And Daring (USA)
3^{9gf} 2^{10gf} 2^{12g} 4^{16gf} 5^{14g} **0-3-5 £18,907**

Dark Champion *R E Barr* 67
5 b g Abou Zouz (USA) - Hazy Kay (Ire)
3^{6g} 2^{7gf} 5^{7f} 10^{6f} 14^{6g} 2^{6g} 11^{6s} 15^{6gf} 6^{6g} 3^{6g} 2^{6g} 2^{6gf} 8^{5s} **0-6-13 £6,057**

Dark Chapel *M Dods* 48
2 b g College Chapel - Possibility
7^{8gf} **0-0-1**

Dark Charm (Fr) *R A Fahey* 85
6 b g Anabaa (USA) - Wardara
9^{7gs} 6^{8gf} 1^{8g} 4^{8gf} 6^{8gf} 13^{8g} 17^{8gf} 7^{8gf} 1^{9gf} 9^{8gf} **2-0-10 £11,998**

Dark Cheetah (USA) *A P O'Brien* 107
3 b c Storm Cat (USA) - Layounne (USA)
6^{8vs} 15^{8s} 6^{7g} 4^{6gf} 11^{5g} 14^{6g} 2^{6g} **0-2-7 £9,659**

Dark Day Blues (Ire) *M D Hammond* 37 a50
4 ch g Night Shift (USA) - Tavildara (Ire)
8^{9sd} 11^{8sd} 7^{9sd} 5^{8gf} 8^{8gf} 15^{10g} 11^{10g} 14^{12g} **0-0-8**

Dark Empress (Ire) *R M Beckett* 78
4 br f Second Empire (Ire) - Good Reference (Ire)
16^{8g} 16^{8gf} 9^{8gf} **0-0-3**

Dark Islander (Ire) *J W Hills* 92 a81
2 br c Singspiel (Ire) - Lamanka Lass (USA)
5^{6sd} 1^{7gf} 4^{7sd} 3^{7gs} **1-0-4 £4,939**

Dark Missile *A M Balding* 79
2 b f Night Shift (USA) - Exorcet (Fr)
14^{7f} 1^{6g} **1-0-2 £5,629**

Dark Moon *A M Balding* 50
2 b f Observatory (USA) - Lady Donatella
10^{5gf} 9^{6gf} 8^{7g} **0-0-3**

Dark Night (Ire) *D W Barker* a37
2 b g Night Shift (USA) - Shamaness (USA)
11^{7sd} 8^{7sd} 10^{9sd} **0-0-3**

Dark Parade (Arg) *G L Moore* a61
4 b c Parade Marshal (USA) - Charming Dart (Arg)
1^{16sd} 1^{14sd} 2^{17sd} 3^{16sd} **2-2-4 £5,655**

Dark Planet *C E Brittain* 60
2 ch c Singspiel (Ire) - Warning Shadows (Ire)
8^{7gf} 9^{7gs} 8^{9g} 4^{8g} **0-0-4 £433**

Dark Raider (Ire) *A P Jones* a26
4 br/gr f Definite Article - Lady Shikari
10^{9sd} **0-0-1**

Dark Shadows *W Storey* 32
10 b g Machiavellian (USA) - Instant Desire (USA)
5^{16gf} **0-0-1**

Dark Society *A W Carroll* a63
7 b g Imp Society (USA) - No Candles Tonight
1^{10sd} **1-0-1 £2,935**

Darko Karim *R J Hodges* 70 a53
3 b g Groom Dancer (USA) - Russian Rose (Ire)
12^{9g} 2^{10s} 5^{10gs} 13^{7g} 8^{12gf} 2^{11sd} 10^{14sd} **0-2-7 £1,796**

Darla (Ire) *J W Payne* 58 a58
4 b f Night Shift (USA) - Darbela (Ire)
11^{6g} 6^{6g} 13^{6gf} 7^{6sd} 10^{6gf} **0-0-5**

Darling Deanie (Ire) *D R C Elsworth* 75
3 ch f Sinndar (Ire) - Blushing Melody (Ire)
11^{8gf} 10^{10g} 6^{10g} 1^{12gs} 3^{12gf} 6^{14gf} 9^{14s} **1-1-7 £4,910**

Darn Good *A King* 70
4 ch g Bien Bien (USA) - Thimbalina
10^{15gs} 9^{20s} 9^{16gs} 4^{18g} 6^{18g} 5^{14gf} 8^{16gf} 2^{16gf} 7^{14gf} 6^{17g} 14^{16g} 8^{17f} **0-1-12 £2,358**

Darsalam (Ire) *A Shavuyev* 121
4 ch c Desert King (Ire) - Moonsilk
1^{12g} 1^{16s} 9^{20gf} 1^{12vs} **3-0-4 £90,636**

Darsharp *Miss Gay Kelleway* 46 a46
3 b f Josr Algarhoud (Ire) - Dizzydaisy
7^{7g} 5^{8f} 5^{8sd} 8^{8g} **0-0-4**

Dart Along (USA) *R Hannon* 81
3 b c Bahri (USA) - Promptly (Ire)
3^{6gs} 1^{6gf} 5^{7gf} 4^{6gf} 4^{6gf} 14^{7gf} 12^{8g} 15^{7g} **1-1-8 £7,468**

Darting (USA) *G A Butler* 78
4 b f Sahm (USA) - Mur Taasha (USA)
3^{8s} **0-0-1 £1,018**

Darusso *J S Moore* 68
2 ch g Daylami (Ire) - Rifada
8^{7g} 8^{7gf} 3^{7s} 4^{8gf} 3^{8f} 6^{10f} 7^{8g} **0-2-7 £1,080**

Dasar *M Brittain* a52
5 ch m Catrail (USA) - Rising Of The Moon (Ire)
4^{7sd} 7^{6sd} 6^{7sd} 3^{7sd} 5^{6sd} 4^{8sd} **0-1-6 £211**

Dash Of Lime *J Akehurst* 64 a42
3 b f Bold Edge - Green Supreme
7^{6g} 1^{6s} 6^{6g} 12^{7g} **1-0-4 £4,381**

Dash To The Front *J R Fanshawe* 75
2 b f Diktat - Millennium Dash
2^{7gf} **0-1-1 £782**

Dash To The Top *L M Cumani* 115
3 b f Montjeu (Ire) - Millennium Dash
1^{10gf} 5^{12gf} 2^{12g} 4^{12gs} RR^{13s} **1-1-5 £89,048**

Dasheena *M J Polglase* 63
2 b f Magic Ring (Ire) - Sweet And Lucky
9^{5s} 13^{6gf} 7^{5gf} 1^{6f} 8^{7gf} 7^{6gf} **1-0-6 £3,698**

Dashfa Baileys *C A Dwyer* 46 a39
2 ch g Mark Of Esteem (Ire) - Dahshah
8^6gs 9^6gf 9^7sd 11^9sd **0-0-4**

Dashing Dane *D W Chapman*
5 b h Danehill (USA) - Baldemara (Fr)
12^9sd **0-0-1**

Dashing Home (Ire) *Noel Meade* 104
6 b g Lahib (USA) - Dashing Rose
9^10gf 2^14gf 14^12gy 3^13f 6^12g **0-0-5**
£7,528

Daughters World *J R Best* 52
2 b f Agnes World (USA) - Priluki
9^5gf 11^5g 6^5gf **0-0-3**

Daunted (Ire) *P A Blockley* a48
9 b g Priolo (USA) - Dauntess
4^16sd 7^12sd **0-0-2 £259**

Dave (Ire) *J R Best* 41
4 b g Danzero (Aus) - Paradise News
12^5hd 11^8ss **0-0-2**

Davenport (Ire) *B R Millman* 86 a87
3 b g Bold Fact (USA) - Semence D'Or (Fr)
4^7sd 4^9sd 1^8s 1^8gs 9^8gf 9^8gf 4^9g 3^8g 7^10g 1^8s
4^8sd 11^9sf **3-1-12 £12,818**

David Junior (USA) *B J Meehan* 126
3 ch c Pleasant Tap (USA) - Paradise River (USA)
11^8gf 1^10g 1^10g 7^8s 2^11gf 1^10gf 1^10gs
4-1-7 £327,036

David's Symphony (Ire) *A W Carroll* 20 a52
3 ch g Almutawakel - Habemus (Fr)
1^6sd 12^8g 12^9sd 8^6sd 9^6sd 12^7sd 8^9sd
1-0-7 £1,466

Davidia (Ire) *S Kirk* 64
2 b g Barathea (Ire) - Green Life
7^6gf 10^7gf **0-0-2**

Davids Mark *J R Jenkins* 48 a53
5 b g Polar Prince (Ire) - Star Of Flanders
10^6sd 6^5sd 11^5gf 8^6sd 6^6sd **0-0-5**

Davy Crockett *M Dods* 71
3 b g Polar Prince (Ire) - Sing With The Band
4^8g 4^8gf 9^8g 14^7gf 6^10gf 5^7gf 8^8gf 10^6g 11^7gs
0-0-9 £662

Davy's Luck *J M Bradley* 52
5 ch m Zahran (Ire) - Cursneh Decone
6^8g **0-0-1**

Dawaleeb (Ire) *M P Tregoning* 65
2 b f Alhaarth (Ire) - Summerhill
7^6gf 6^7g 3^6gf **0-1-3 £780**

Dawn Assault (Ire) *P F I Cole* 54
2 b c Night Shift (USA) - Thermopylae
18^7g 9^7gf 6^7g 5^8f **0-0-4**

Dawn At Sea *J R Fanshawe* 68
3 b f Slip Anchor - Finger Of Light
7^10gf 2^12gf 3^10gf 4^12g 12^16g 3^11g **0-1-6**
£2,311

Dawn Quest (USA) *Saeed Bin Suroor* 79
2 b c Dynaformer (USA) - Sun And Shade
2^7s 1^8gf 3^10g **1-1-3 £8,423**

Dawn Surprise (USA) *Saeed Bin Suroor* 89
4 b f Theatrical - Lignify (Arg)
9^8g 8^7s **0-0-2**

Dawn's Last Shot (Ire) *J L Dunlop* 58
3 b g Son Of Sharp Shot (Ire) - Dawn Star
9^10g 10^10gs **0-0-2**

Day Care *Mrs A J Perrett* 52
4 gr c Daylami (Ire) - Ancara
5^10s **0-0-1**

Day Flight *J H M Gosden* 119
4 b c Sadler's Wells (USA) - Bonash
1^10g 1^12s 1^13gs 2^12gs 1^12gs 2^12hy **4-2-6**
£143,814

Day One *R J Price* 43 a63
4 ch c Daylami (Ire) - Myself
4^12sd 9^10sd 9^12sd 10^10g 17^12hy 10^12g 9^13gf 13^17sd
0-0-8 £266

Day To Remember *E F Vaughan* 93
4 gr g Daylami (Ire) - Miss Universe (Ire)
12^10gs 9^10g 2^10s 5^12g 15^14g **0-1-5**
£4,146

Daybreak Dancer (Ire) *G A Huffer* 86 a57
3 b/br g Fasliyev (USA) - Darkling (Ire)
7^5sd 8^6sd 4^6sd 3^8sd 6^7gs 8^5gf 1^6gf 1^7gf 6^5gf
15^6gf **2-0-10 £8,332**

Daybreaking (Ire) *R F Johnson Houghton* 32
3 br c Daylami (Ire) - Mawhiba (USA)
11^8gs **0-0-1**

Daydream Dancer *C G Cox* 60
4 gr f Daylami (Ire) - Dancing Wolf (Ire)
2^12g 3^11gf 6^12g 11^14gf 3^12f 2^12g 6^12g 10^10g
0-3-8 £2,770

Daygar *M G Quinlan* 28 a54
3 b c Spectrum (Ire) - Milly Ha Ha
9^8sd 13^10sd 7^7s 7^10g **0-0-4**

Daylami Star *J H M Gosden* 80 a73
2 gr c Daylami (Ire) - Ascot Cyclone (USA)
6^7f 4^8sd 4^8g 4^8g 2^9gf 1^10g **1-1-6**
£9,553

Dayoff (Ire) *P D Evans* 63 a28
4 gr f Daylami (Ire) - Dabtara (Ire)
15^10s 18^10gf 13^11g 9^12gf 2^10gf 8^8g 6^9sd
0-1-7 £1,141

Dayrose *Sir Michael Stoute* 52
2 ch f Daylami (Ire) - Blush Rambler (Ire)
10^7s **0-0-1**

Dazed (Ire) *J H M Gosden* 80
2 b f Danehill (USA) - Puzzled Look (USA)
8^6g 5^7gf 5^7g 2^6gf 8^7gf 7^7g **0-1-6**
£1,720

Dazzler Mac *N Bycroft* 54
4 b g Komaite (USA) - Stilvella
6^7gs 9^6gf 7^7g **0-0-3**

Dazzling Bay *T D Easterby* 94
5 b g Mind Games - Adorable Cherub (USA)
22^6gf 8^5g 6^5g 7^6gf 9^5g 15^6gf **0-0-6**
£900

Dazzling Blaze (Ire) *Mrs A J Perrett* 37
2 b c Spectrum (Ire) - Tomanivi
14^6gf 13^7gf 12^7g **0-0-3**

Dazzling Daisy *M Wigham* a28
8 b m Shareef Dancer (USA) - Mariette
12^7sd 9^10sd 11^9sd 10^8sd 9^7f **0-0-5**

De La Rue (USA) *M G Quinlan* a58
2 b c Louis Quatorze (USA) - Primevere (USA)
4^9sf **0-0-1**

Dean's Yard *Sir Michael Stoute* 78 a74
2 b g Machiavellian (USA) - Abbey Strand (USA)
3^7gf 7^7gs 2^7sd **0-2-3 £1,819**

Debbie *B D Leavy* a44
6 b m Deploy - Elita
1^12sd **1-0-1 £1,515**

Debs Broughton *W J Musson* 44 a41

3 b f Prince Sabo - Coy Debutante (Ire)
17^{8s} 14^{8g} 9^{8gs} 10^{8gs} 14^{10gs} 8^{8sd} 3^{8sd}
0-1-7 £217

Decent (Ire) *W J H Ratcliffe* 50 a42
2 b f Desert Sun - Guyum
5^{6f} 10^{6gf} 6^{7sd} 11^{7sd} **0-0-4**

Decisive *P Bowen* 58 a71
6 b g Alhaarth (Ire) - Alys
9^{16sd} 16^{18g} 6^{15gf} **0-0-3**

Decree Nisi *Mrs A Duffield* 58
2 ch g Compton Place - Palisandra (USA)
6^{7s} 5^{8gf} **0-0-2**

Dee Day (Ire) *M L W Bell* 80
2 gr c Daylami (Ire) - Woodwin (Ire)
4^{8gf} 3^{8g} 1^{9g} **1-1-3 £5,098**

Deeday Bay (Ire) *C F Wall* 65 a73
3 b f Brave Act - Skerries Bell
8^{7gf} 12^{6gf} 8^{8gs} 2^{7sd} 14^{7hy} **0-1-5**
£1,074

Deedayboots *G M Moore* 37
2 b g Allied Forces (USA) - Dusty Shoes
9^{7gf} 7^{6gf} 14^{7g} **0-0-3**

Deekazz (Ire) *F Watson*
6 b m Definite Article - Lyric Junction (Ire)
11^{12sd} **0-0-1**

Deep Impact (Jpn) *Y Ikee* 125
3 b c Sunday Silence (USA) - Wind In Her Hair (Ire)
1^{10f} 1^{10f} 1^{10f} 1^{12f} 1^{10f} 1^{15f} 2^{12f} **6-1-7**
£3,436,501

Deep Purple *A M Balding* 73
4 b g Halling (USA) - Seal Indigo (Ire)
10^{12gs} **0-0-1**

Deep Sleep *M H Tompkins* 67 a24
2 b c Tipsy Creek (USA) - Tiempo
7^{7g} 5^{6s} 10^{6sd} **0-0-3**

Deeper In Debt *J Akehurst* 72 a80
7 ch g Piccolo - Harold's Girl (Fr)
13^{8gf} 10^{8gs} 1^{8gf} 1^{8gf} 3^{8g} 6^{8gf} 10^{8sd} 2^{7sd}
1^{9sd} **3-2-9 £11,736**

Deepwater Bay (USA) *A M Balding* 79
2 b c Chester House (USA) - Gem Treck (USA)
4^{7gf} 2^{8gf} **0-1-2 £1,413**

Defi (Ire) *I Semple* 89 a68
3 b c Rainbow Quest (USA) - Danse Classique (Ire)
2^{8gf} 10^{9gf} 6^{8gf} 5^{10gf} 5^{8g} 3^{8gf} 6^{9gf} 11^{12g} 3^{9gf}
12^{8g} 9^{9sd} **0-2-11 £6,311**

Defining *J R Fanshawe* 114
6 b g Definite Article - Gooseberry Pie
3^{14gs} 5^{16g} 4^{14gf} 1^{12gf} 14^{14g} 2^{12gs} **1-2-6**
£33,119

Definite Guest (Ire) *R A Fahey* 73
7 gr g Definite Article - Nicea (Ire)
11^{8s} 11^{8g} **0-0-2**

Definitely Royal (Ire) *R M H Cowell* 33 a18
3 b f Desert Prince (Ire) - Specifically (USA)
8^{8sd} 9^{8gf} **0-0-2**

Degas Art (Ire) *D R C Elsworth* 83
2 b g Danehill Dancer (Ire) - Answer
9^{7gf} 2^{7s} **0-1-2 £1,166**

Degree Of Honor (Fr) *J G Given* 48 a37
3 ch f Highest Honor (Fr) - Sheba Dancer (Fr)
12^{8gf} 2^{12gf} 6^{12gf} 6^{9gf} UR^{11gf} 8^{12gf} 2^{10g} 7^{11g}
3^{11sd} 4^{11sd} **0-3-10 £1,780**

Deira (USA) *C E Brittain* 66
2 b f Green Desert (USA) - New Sayyedati (USA)
7^{6gs} 3^{7gf} 9^{6gf} 4^{7gs} **0-2-4 £1,103**

Deirdre's Dilemma (Ire) *G C Bravery* 30
3 b f Primo Dominie - Sartigila
12^{6g} 9^{8g} **0-0-2**

Dejeeje (Ire) *D W Chapman* 13 a37
4 ch g Grand Lodge (USA) - Christan (Ire)
12^{9sd} 3^{8sd} 6^{9sd} 11^{8gf} 4^{12sd} 15^{14g} 11^{9sd}
0-1-7 £208

Del Mar Sunset *W J Haggas* 84 a88
6 b g Unfuwain (USA) - City Of Angels
9^{10sd} 6^{8sd} 2^{10s} 10^{8s} 4^{7gf} 4^{7gf} 6^{8gf} 3^{8g} 1^{8gf}
1^{10gf} 4^{9g} 2^{10g} 2^{10gf} 2^{10gf} 5^{9sd} 6^{9sd}
2-6-16 £17,514

Delcienne *G G Margarson* 47
4 b f Golden Heights - Delciana (Ire)
9^{10g} 8^{8f} 10^{10gf} 10^{8f} 5^{9gf} 11^{8g} 12^{8hd} 17^{8gf}
5^{10g} 6^{8g} 5^{10gs} 7^{14hy} **0-0-12**

Delightful Gift *D W Barker* 33 a38
5 b m Cadeaux Genereux - Delightful Chime (Ire)
3^{7sd} 4^{8sd} 3^{7sd} 8^{7gf} 6^{8gf} 9^{9gf} **0-2-6 £421**

Delightfully *Jean-Rene Auvray* a51
4 b f Definite Article - Kingpin Delight
3^{10sd} 6^{12sd} 6^{13sd} 3^{12sd} 7^{12sd} **0-2-5 £851**

Della Salute *A M Balding* 82
3 gr f Dansili - Marie Dora (Fr)
6^{7s} 10^{7f} 3^{7gf} 1^{8f} 5^{7f} 2^{8gf} 3^{10f} 5^{9s} 1^{8f} 4^{9g}
5^{8g} **2-3-11 £12,656**

Dellagio (Ire) *Rae Guest* 37 a63
4 b c Fasliyev (USA) - Lady Ounavarra (Ire)
6^{7sd} 8^{6sd} 10^{5gf} 10^{6sd} 14^{6gf} 15^{6f} 10^{5gf} 17^{6g}
1^{5sd} 3^{5sd} 1^{5sd} 2^{5sd} 2^{5sd} **2-3-13 £4,348**

Delorain (Ire) *J A R Toller* 23
2 b c Kalanisi (Ire) - Lady Nasrana (Fr)
11^{7s} **0-0-1**

Delphie Queen (Ire) *Unknown* 100
4 ch f Desert Sun - Serious Delight
6^{6g} 6^{7hy} 11^{7g} 5^{6g} 8^{7gf} 5^{7g} 14^{8g} **0-0-7**
£2,000

Delta Shamrock *K A Ryan*
3 b c Montjoy (USA) - Miss Paradiso (Ire)
12^{7sd} 12^{6sd} **0-0-2**

Dematraf (Ire) *Ms Deborah J Evans* 64 a64
3 gr f Atraf - Demolition Jo
1^{6f} 13^{5gf} 9^{6g} 3^{6sd} 13^{5gf} 13^{6ss} 11^{7sd}
1-1-7 £3,680

Demi Tasse *J M P Eustace* 55
3 b f Largesse - Not A Word
6^{9g} 4^{10gf} 5^{12gf} 7^{12gf} **0-0-4 £271**

Democratic Deficit (Ire) *J S Bolger* 113
3 b c Soviet Star (USA) - Grandiose Idea (Ire)
1^{8gf} 6^{8gf} 3^{8g} 1^{7gf} 3^{8gf} 13^{6g} 6^{8gf} 4^{9gf} 5^{9gs}
2-1-9 £101,292

Demolition Molly *R F Marvin* 38
4 b f Rudimentary (USA) - Persian Fortune
17^{5gf} 10^{5g} 18^{5gf} 9^{5gf} 19^{5gf} 14^{6sd} 17^{5gf}
0-0-7

Demon Docker (Ire) *P W Chapple-Hyam* a72
2 ch c Docksider (USA) - Green Moon (Fr)
1^{9sd} **1-0-1 £3,737**

Den Perry *A Berry* a34
3 ch c Tipsy Creek (USA) - Beverley Monkey (Ire)
12^{7sd} 7^{7sd} 4^{7sd} **0-0-3**

Denise Best (Ire) *Miss K M George* a38
7 ch m Goldmark (USA) - Titchwell Lass
5^{14sd} **0-0-1**

Dennick *P C Haslam* 53 a55
3 b g Nicolotte - Branston Dancer
6^{7sd} 4^{7sd} 6^{7gf} 13^{7gf} 10^{9sd} **0-0-5**

Denounce *H R A Cecil* 62
4 b c Selkirk (USA) - Didicoy (USA)
7^{8g} **0-0-1**

Denver (Ire) *B J Meehan* 41 a92
4 b c Danehill (USA) - Born Beautiful (USA)
5^{10sd} 14^{8gs} 19^{8g} **0-0-3 £640**

Depressed *Andrew Reid* 79 a69
3 ch f Most Welcome - Sure Care
1^{6sd} 3^{6sd} 4^{6g} 1^{6gf} 6^{6g} 3^{6gf} 2^{6gf} 4^{6gf} 7^{6sd}
2-3-9 £12,876

Deputy Consort (USA) *J H M Gosden* 61
2 b c Stravinsky (USA) - Possible Consort (USA)
13^{6gf} 6^{6gf} 7^{7g} 8^{7gs} **0-0-4**

Derwent (USA) *R H Buckler* 61
6 b/br g Distant View (USA) - Nothing Sweeter (USA)
5^{12f} **0-0-1**

Desert Arc (Ire) *W M Brisbourne* 65
7 b g Spectrum (Ire) - Bint Albadou (Ire)
5^{6g} 16^{6g} 13^{6gf} 4^{7gf} 12^{6gf} 13^{6gf} 6^{6g} 3^{6gf}
14^{6g} **0-1-9 £435**

Desert Battle (Ire) *Ian Williams* 28
4 ch g Desert Sun - Papal
11^{10hy} 11^{8g} 6^{10s} **0-0-3**

Desert Bounty *G M Moore* 51
2 b f Bahamian Bounty - Aldevonie
8^{5gf} 6^{5gf} **0-0-2**

Desert Buzz (Ire) *J Hetherton* 48 a23
3 b g Desert Story (Ire) - Sugar
16^{10gs} 3^{10gf} 8^{10gf} 5^{8gf} 7^{8f} 10^{7f} 8^{6gf} 10^{7gf}
11^{9sd} 12^{10g} **0-0-10 £519**

Desert Chief *Saeed Bin Suroor* 95
3 b c Green Desert (USA) - Oriental Fashion (Ire)
1^{7g} 1^{8gf} **2-0-2 £10,894**

Desert Classic *E A L Dunlop* 62 a62
3 b f Green Desert (USA) - High Standard
4^{9sd} 4^{12g} 10^{12g} **0-0-3 £539**

Desert Coral (Ire) *P A Blockley* 34
4 ch f Desert Story (Ire) - Sleeping Beauty
12^{10gf} 3^{12f} 9^{13gf} **0-0-3 £522**

Desert Cristal (Ire) *J R Boyle* 87 a87
4 ch f Desert King (Ire) - Damiana (Ire)
8^{8g} 6^{8g} 11^{10s} 1^{10g} 6^{11gs} 7^{10g} 6^{10s} 7^{10sd}
1-0-8 £10,069

Desert D'Argent (Ire) *M Johnston* 82
2 ch f Desert Story (Ire) - Petite-D-Argent
1^{6g} 1^{7hy} **2-0-2 £18,310**

Desert Daisy (Ire) *Mrs L Stubbs* a48
4 gr f Desert Prince (Ire) - Pomponette (USA)
1^{7sd} 14^{7sd} 9^{7sd} **1-0-3 £1,501**

Desert Demon (Ire) *B W Hills* 62
3 b g Unfuwain (USA) - Baldemosa (Fr)
9^{7s} 9^{6g} **0-0-2**

Desert Destiny *Saeed Bin Suroor* 108
5 b g Desert Prince (Ire) - High Savannah
8^{9g} 9^{10gf} 1^{8gf} 9^{7gs} 13^{7g} 7^{9g} 6^{9s} **1-0-7**
£61,194

Desert Dreamer (Ire) *P R Chamings* 89 a90
4 b g Green Desert (USA) - Follow That Dream
2^{7sd} 15^{7gs} 5^{8sd} 4^{6g} 6^{7gf} 3^{6gf} 4^{6gf} 8^{7gf} 9^{6sd}
7^{8gf} 1^{6s} 4^{5s} 9^{7sd} 18^{6g} 1^{7sd} 3^{6g} 2^{7s}
2-3-17 £20,896

Desert Dust *R M H Cowell* a57
2 b c Vettori (Ire) - Dust
6^{6sd} 7^{6sd} 8^{6sd} **0-0-3**

Desert Express (Ire) *G A Swinbank* 26
3 b g Shinko Forest (Ire) - Perfect Guest
13^{6s} 12^{7g} 8^{7gs} **0-0-3**

Desert Fantasy (Ire) *M Meade* 109
6 b g Desert King (Ire) - Petite Fantasy
17^{8g} 3^{7g} 11^{6gf} 15^{8gf} **0-1-4 £3,080**

Desert Flair *R Hannon* 72
2 b f Desert Style (Ire) - Celtic Cross
8^{6g} 4^{7g} 3^{6gf} 2^{7gf} **0-2-4 £2,661**

Desert Flora (Ire) *E A L Dunlop* a66
2 gr f Green Desert (USA) - Requesting
1^{6sd} **1-0-1 £5,005**

Desert Fury *R Bastiman* 41 a48
8 b g Warning - Number One Spot
5^{8sd} 4^{9sd} 9^{9sd} 5^{8sd} 1^{9sd} 11^{8gf} 3^{10g} 1^{8sd} 4^{9sd}
2-1-9 £2,954

Desert Glory (Ire) *D R Loder* 41
3 gr f Desert Prince (Ire) - True Love
13^{8g} **0-0-1**

Desert Google *C F Wall* 65 a34
3 b f Green Desert (USA) - Khambani (Ire)
17^{8g} 7^{8g} 4^{8g} 3^{7gf} 12^{8gf} 3^{9gf} 12^{8gf} 6^{8sd} 4^{10gf}
0-2-9 £1,504

Desert Hawk *W M Brisbourne* 61 a44
4 b g Cape Cross (Ire) - Milling (Ire)
14^{8g} 5^{8gf} 3^{10gf} 5^{12g} 10^{10gf} 3^{8gf} 6^{8gf} 11^{8gf}
7^{14ss} **0-2-9 £1,079**

Desert Hunter (Ire) *M D Hammond* 52 a22
2 b g Desert Story (Ire) - She-Wolff (Ire)
10^{5gs} 6^{6g} 6^{5sd} 14^{6s} **0-0-4**

Desert Image (Ire) *C Tinkler* 54 a71
4 b g Desert King (Ire) - Identical (Ire)
10^{10sd} 11^{8gf} 2^{12sd} 6^{14sd} **0-1-4 £1,088**

Desert Imp *B W Hills* 90 a84
3 b f Green Desert (USA) - Devil's Imp (Ire)
1^{7f} 7^{7g} 9^{7g} 6^{8gs} 2^{7g} 7^{7gf} 10^{8sd} **1-1-7**
£10,128

Desert Island Disc *Dr J R J Naylor* 74 a52
8 b m Turtle Island (Ire) - Distant Music
9^{10s} 4^{12gf} 7^{12gf} 6^{12g} 6^{12gf} 6^{12gf} 8^{12f} 3^{12gf}
7^{12f} 6^{10gf} 10^{12g} 2^{11gf} 2^{12g} 1^{16gf} 4^{16g} 3^{16g}
4^{12gf} 7^{12gs} 3^{16s} 7^{13sd} **1-6-20 £11,574**

Desert Leader (Ire) *W M Brisbourne* 65 a85
4 b g Green Desert (USA) - Za Aamah (USA)
8^{8g} 4^{7gs} 8^{8f} 6^{7g} 2^{9sd} 10^{8gf} 3^{9sd} 1^{9sd} 1^{9sd}
2^{9sd} 6^{9sd} **2-3-11 £10,710**

Desert Light (Ire) *D Shaw* 53 a56
4 b g Desert Sun - Nacote (Ire)
9^{5sd} 8^{5gf} 4^{5gf} 14^{5gf} 2^{5sd} 4^{5sd} 2^{5sd} 6^{5sd} 5^{5sd}
8^{5sd} 6^{6sd} **0-2-11 £1,118**

Desert Lightning (Ire) *J Noseda* 74 a68
3 ch g Desert Prince (Ire) - Saibhreas (Ire)
1^{7sd} 3^{8gs} 17^{9g} **1-0-3 £4,395**

Desert Lord *A Berry* 98 a70
5 b g Green Desert (USA) - Red Carnival (USA)
9^{8gf} 10^{6ft} 15^{5ft} 8^{8gf} 9^{8gf} 11^{7gf} 6^{7gf} 9^{6gf}
7^{6gf} 5^{6gf} 5^{6gf} 1^{5gf} 7^{6gf} 6^{5gf} 22^{6gs} 25^{6g} 6^{5gs}
16^{6s} 11^{5g} **1-0-19 £9,578**

Desert Lover (Ire) *R J Price* 53 a54
3 b g Desert Prince (Ire) - Crystal Flute
5^{7gs} 11^{6g} 10^{7gf} 18^{6gf} 5^{7sf} 11^{7sd} 5^{6sd} 2^{6sd}
1^{7ss} 9^{6sd} 3^{7ss} 6^{9ss} **1-2-12 £2,093**

Desert Moonbeam (Ire) *R J Hodges* 39
3 b f Desert Prince (Ire) - Pip's Dream

6^{6gs} 9^{7gf} 15^{10gf} PU^{12sd} **0-0-4**

Desert Move (Ire) *M R Channon* 97
3 b f Desert King (Ire) - Campestral (USA)
6^{10gs} 4^{10gf} 7^{12gf} 3^{15gs} 3^{12gf} **0-1-5**
£8,702

Desert Omen (Ire) *M Johnston* 60 a65
3 b g Desert Style (Ire) - Gratclo
3^{7sd} 5^{7g} 4^{9sd} 6^{8gf} 16^{8gf} 12^{9sd} 5^{7f} 3^{8f} 11^{7g}
0-1-9 £1,050

Desert Opal *D W Chapman* 75 a72
5 ch g Cadeaux Genereux - Nullarbor
11^{9sd} 10^{7sd} 11^{7sd} 4^{7s} 10^{9sd} 15^{6g} 13^{6sd} 6^{7gs}
5^{8gf} 10^{6g} 1^{6sd} 1^{6sd} 22^{7s} 10^{6sd} 6^{6sd}
2-0-15 £7,040

Desert Quest (Ire) *P F Nicholls* 98
5 b g Rainbow Quest (USA) - Jumilla (USA)
3^{10gf} 4^{10gf} **0-2-2 £3,467**

Desert Realm (Ire) *M Johnston* 97
2 b c Desert Prince (Ire) - Fawaayid (USA)
10^{6s} 2^{5s} 3^{5g} 1^{6gf} 6^{6gs} 10^{5g} 7^{6gf} **1-2-7**
£7,224

Desert Reign *A P Jarvis* 77
4 ch g Desert King (Ire) - Moondance
6^{11g} 3^{10gf} 4^{10g} 8^{9gs} **0-2-4 £1,342**

Desert Sea (Ire) *C Tinkler* 62 a54
2 b c Desert Sun - Sea Of Time (USA)
11^{7sd} 11^{7gf} 7^{8s} **0-0-3**

Desert Secrets (Ire) *J G Portman* 69 a42
3 b f Almutawakel - Shaping Up (USA)
10^{10gf} 5^{10gf} 2^{12g} 7^{10sd} **0-1-4 £1,060**

Desert Star *Sir Michael Stoute* 52
5 b g Green Desert (USA) - Phantom Gold
16^{8gs} **0-0-1**

Desert Storm (Den) *Rae Guest* 70
3 br g Desert Prince (Ire) - Boss Lady (Ire)
8^{10g} 2^{10s} 2^{11g} 2^{12g} 2^{12s} **0-4-5 £4,646**

Desert Stream (Ire) *M Johnston* 63
4 ch g Desert Sun - Prime Site (Ire)
2^{11gf} 6^{12gs} 10^{12gf} 7^{14gf} **0-1-4 £744**

Deserted Island (Ire) *N Wilson* 19
2 b f Desert Style (Ire) - Osprey Point (Ire)
8^{6gf} 9^{6gf} **0-0-2**

Deserted Prince (Ire) *M J Wallace* 65 a54
2 b c Desert Prince (Ire) - Pool Party (USA)
8^{6gf} 7^{6g} 2^{7gf} 8^{7gf} 8^{8f} 10^{8g} 1^{8g} 8^{7sd}
1-1-8 £4,462

Desertina (Ire) *R M Whitaker* 39 a54
3 b f Spectrum (Ire) - Kayanga
6^{6s} 9^{6g} 13^{8s} 2^{6gs} 5^{6gf} 5^{7sd} 1^{6sd} 1^{6sd} 2^{6sd}
11^{6sf} 7^{6sd} **2-2-11 £4,183**

Deserving *W J Haggas* 68 a60
2 b f Grand Lodge (USA) - Superstar Leo (Ire)
2^{5g} 2^{5gf} 7^{5gf} 11^{6hy} 5^{5sf} 9^{6sd} 11^{6sd} **0-2-7**
£3,016

Desiree (Ire) *John Berry* 48
4 b f Desert Story (Ire) - Elba (Ire)
12^{10s} 2^{12gf} 11^{14sd} **0-1-3 £460**

Desperate Dan *J A Osborne* 96 a91
4 b g Danzero (Aus) - Alzianah
6^{5g} 4^{6gf} 3^{6gf} 13^{6g} 12^{6gf} 2^{6gs} 12^{5g} 4^{5sf} 6^{6sd}
0-3-9 £7,852

Desperation (Ire) *K R Burke* 71 a78
3 b g Desert Style (Ire) - Mauras Pride (Ire)
1^{10sd} 1^{10sd} 4^{12sd} 10^{10sd} 17^{12gs} 7^{10g} 4^{12g} 6^{11gf}
3^{10gf} 5^{10s} 2^{10sd} 2^{11g} 8^{11gs} 2^{11sd} **2-4-14**
£15,272

Detonate *Mrs C A Dunnett* 61 a53
3 b g Mind Games - Bron Hilda (Ire)
15^{5s} 10^{5f} 7^{5sd} 11^{5gf} 8^{7gf} 5^{5gs} 6^{5sd} 8^{5g} 10^{5gf}
6^{5gf} 11^{5gs} 11^{5sd} **0-0-12**

Detonateur (Fr) *Ian Williams* 46
7 b g Pistolet Bleu (Ire) - Soviet Princess (Ire)
8^{13gs} **0-0-1**

Detroit City (USA) *P J Hobbs* 91 a77
3 gr/ro c Kingmambo (USA) - Seattle Victory (USA)
9^{10sd} 1^{12sd} 1^{12sd} 1^{12sd} 5^{15gs} 6^{14gf} 1^{14g} 2^{15gs}
4-0-8 £19,945

Deutschland (USA) *M A Jarvis* 69
2 b g Red Ransom (USA) - Rhine Valley (USA)
4^{6g} 5^{7gf} 4^{7s} **0-0-3 £664**

Developer (Ire) *T G Mills* 69 a52
2 b g Danehill Dancer (Ire) - Via Camp
11^{6gf} 8^{6sd} 4^{5g} 7^{5gs} 8^{5gs} **0-0-5 £324**

Deveron (USA) *C E Brittain* 105
2 b/br f Cozzene (USA) - Cruisie (USA)
2^{7gf} 1^{7s} 3^{7g} 6^{7g} 3^{8gs} **1-3-5 £41,358**

Devil's Bite *M C Chapman*
4 ch g Dracula (Aus) - Niggle
7^{10hy} **0-0-1**

Devils Delight (Ire) *C W Thornton* 32
3 b f Desert King (Ire) - Devil's Crown (USA)
14^{9gf} 5^{14gf} 6^{14g} **0-0-3**

Devils River (Ire) *N A Twiston-Davies* 64
3 b g Anabaa (USA) - Riviere Du Diable (USA)
7^{10gs} **0-0-1**

Devine Command *R Ingram* 58 a67
4 b g In Command (Ire) - Adriya
1^{8sd} 3^{8sd} 7^{7sd} 6^{7gf} 8^{8gf} 7^{8gf} 17^{10gf} 3^{11gf} 9^{12gs}
6^{10sd} 5^{11g} **1-2-11 £4,376**

Devine Dancer *H Candy* a47
2 ch f Woodborough (USA) - Princess Londis
8^{6sd} 7^{7sd} **0-0-2**

Devious Ayers (Ire) *J M Bradley* 45 a26
4 br g Dr Devious (Ire) - Yulara (Ire)
12^{7sd} 14^{8gf} 1^{7f} 14^{10gf} 14^{10gf} 18^{7g} 5^{8g} 7^{8f}
9^{8hd} 8^{6sd} 5^{8g} **1-0-11 £2,562**

Devise (Ire) *M S Saunders*
6 b g Hamas (Ire) - Soreze (Ire)
15^{6g} **0-0-1**

Devon Flame *Mrs Jeremy Young* 83
6 b g Whittingham (Ire) - Uaeflame (Ire)
16^{6g} 1^{6gf} 1^{6gf} 3^{6gf} 8^{6gf} 4^{5gs} 3^{5s} 13^{6g}
2-2-8 £14,748

Devon Ruby *Mrs A Duffield* 42 a52
2 ch f Zilzal (USA) - Last Result
7^{7gf} 13^{7gf} 8^{8gs} 4^{7sd} 11^{10g} 7^{7sd} 7^{8sd} 4^{7ss}
0-0-8

Dexileos (Ire) *David Pinder* 38 a53
6 b g Danehill (USA) - Theano (Ire)
1^{6sd} 5^{7sd} 13^{7sd} 10^{6sd} 6^{8s} 11^{7gf} 10^{8sd}
1-0-7 £1,487

Dextrous *P T Midgley* a40
8 gr g Machiavellian (USA) - Heavenly Cause (USA)
10^{8sd} 4^{12ss} **0-0-2**

Deyaree (Ire) *M R Channon* 56
2 ch c Grand Lodge (USA) - Legende D'Or (Fr)
10^{7g} 12^{7gf} **0-0-2**

Dhaular Dhar (Ire) *B W Hills* 83
3 b c Indian Ridge - Pescara (Ire)
11^{9gf} 8^{7g} 8^{8gf} 9^{8gs} 6^{7gf} 4^{9gf} 5^{9g} 2^{9g} 9^{8gf}

5^{9gs} 1^{8g} **1-1-11 £9,562**

Dhehdaah *Mrs P Sly* 65
4 b g Alhaarth (Ire) - Carina Clare
1^{11s} 4^{12s} 9^{13gs} 5^{12gf} 5^{12g} 10^{12gs} **1-0-6 £3,751**

Dhekraa (Ire) *M A Jarvis* 91
2 b f Fasliyev (USA) - White Heat
1^{6g} 5^{6gf} 7^{6g} 1^{6gf} 3^{5g} 11^{6gf} **2-1-6 £11,816**

Diablerette *M Johnston* 76
2 b f Green Desert (USA) - Scandalette
5^{6gf} 1^{6gf} **1-0-2 £4,768**

Dial Square *P Howling* 38 a52
4 b g Bluegrass Prince (Ire) - Honey Mill
11^{10sd} 1^{10sd} 6^{10sd} 4^{10sd} 2^{8sd} 5^{7sd} 10^{10sd} 3^{8sd} 7^{10sd} 7^{8sd} 4^{8g} 6^{10sd} 10^{8f} 6^{10sd} 13^{10sd} 15^{8g} 11^{7f} 17^{8g} 7^{7sd} **1-2-19 £2,502**

Diamond Circle *B W Hills* 89
3 br f Halling (USA) - Canadian Mill (USA)
1^{10gf} 7^{10gf} 7^{12gf} 2^{15gf} 1^{14s} 6^{16s} **2-1-6 £12,953**

Diamond Dan (Ire) *P D Evans* 3 a47
3 b g Foxhound (USA) - Kawther
16^{6gf} 9^{6sd} 8^{7sd} 6^{8sd} **0-0-4**

Diamond Darren (Ire) *Miss Victoria Roberts* a12
6 ch g Dolphin Street (Fr) - Deerussa (Ire)
10^{14sd} **0-0-1**

Diamond De Triano (USA) *P W Chapple-Hyam* 62
2 b/br f Forest Wildcat (USA) - Hot Princess
7^{6gs} 10^{6s} 2^{6hy} **0-1-3 £1,329**

Diamond Diggins (Ger) *W Figge* 76
3 ch c Kendor (Fr) - Diana Dancer (Fr)
3^{8g} 2^{9g} 2^{10g} 2^{10s} 3^{9s} 6^{8gf} 3^{12s} **0-0-7 £7,735**

Diamond Green (Fr) *R J Frankel* 113
4 br c Green Desert (USA) - Diamonaka (Fr)
2^{10g} 7^{10gf} 2^{8y} **0-2-3 £17,638**

Diamond Heritage *J A Glover* a24
3 ch g Compton Place - Eccolina
8^{5sd} 6^{6sd} **0-0-2**

Diamond Hombre (USA) *J W Hills* 59
3 gr c Two Punch (USA) - Flowing (USA)
9^{8g} 7^{7gf} 10^{6g} 8^{6gf} 6^{8f} 8^{7gf} **0-0-6**

Diamond Josh *P D Evans* 46 a59
3 ch g Primo Dominie - Exit
3^{5sd} 6^{6s} 15^{7gf} 1^{6sd} **1-1-4 £2,118**

Diamond Joshua (Ire) *N B King* 31
7 b g Mujadil (USA) - Elminya (Ire)
8^{14g} **0-0-1**

Diamond Katie (Ire) *Rae Guest* 74
3 b f Night Shift (USA) - Fayrooz (USA)
4^{6g} 2^{6gf} 3^{6g} 1^{5gf} 4^{5gf} 5^{5gf} 6^{5s} 4^{6gf} **1-2-8 £6,515**

Diamond Max (Ire) *John Berry* 81 a75
7 b g Nicolotte - Kawther
10^{7sd} 6^{6sd} 4^{7sd} 4^{8sd} 5^{8sd} 4^{8s} **0-0-6 £1,468**

Diamond Ring *Jennie Candlish* 43 a27
6 b m Magic Ring (Ire) - Reticent Bride (Ire)
7^{5sd} 9^{6gf} 3^{6f} 4^{5f} 10^{8g} **0-1-5 £370**

Diamond Shannon (Ire) *D Carroll* 39 a47
4 b f Petorius - Balgren (Ire)
8^{7sd} 12^{8gs} 13^{9sd} 9^{8sf} **0-0-4**

Diamond Vein *S P Griffiths* 20
6 b g Green Dancer (USA) - Blushing Sunrise (USA)
11^{12gs} **0-0-1**

Diamond World *C A Horgan* 33 a42
2 b f Agnes World (USA) - In A Twinkling (Ire)
11^{6gf} 11^{7sd} **0-0-2**

Diamonds And Dust *M H Tompkins* 96 a91
3 b g Mister Baileys - Dusty Shoes
4^{8sd} 9^{8gs} 1^{8gs} 6^{10gf} 14^{8gf} 6^{8gf} 12^{9gs} **1-0-7 £14,901**

Diane's Choice *J Akehurst* 71
2 ch f Komaite (USA) - Ramajana (USA)
6^{5gs} 3^{6g} 3^{5gs} 9^{5hy} **0-2-4 £777**

Diatonic *D Carroll* 28 a47
3 b g Deploy - Vic Melody (Fr)
8^{12sd} 11^{9sd} 11^{10g} 9^{12sd} 9^{12sd} 3^{9sd} 12^{11sd} 9^{9sd} **0-1-8 £212**

Dickensian (Ire) *Saeed Bin Suroor* 99
2 br c Xaar - Cappella (Ire)
1^{6g} 2^{7g} 1^{7gf} 8^{7gs} **2-1-4 £11,032**

Dickie Deadeye *J A Geake* 75 a23
8 b g Distant Relative - Accuracy
4^{12g} 1^{13s} 15^{14s} 9^{12g} 10^{12gs} 12^{12gs} 16^{12sd} **1-1-7 £8,712**

Dickie's Dream (Ire) *P J McBride* 66
2 b c Xaar - Swallowtailed Kite (USA)
9^{8g} 9^{8s} **0-0-2**

Dictatrix *J M P Eustace* 68
2 gr f Diktat - Apennina (USA)
1^{6hy} **1-0-1 £4,469**

Diction (Ire) *K R Burke* a69
3 br f Diktat - Waft (USA)
3^{7sd} 13^{7sd} 10^{7sd} 13^{8sd} **0-1-4 £834**

Didn't We (Ire) *T G Mills* 74 a71
2 b c Mujadil (USA) - Non Dimenticar Me (Ire)
2^{6g} 4^{6sd} **0-1-2 £1,617**

Didnt Tell My Wife *Julian Poulton* 63 a55
6 ch g Aragon - Bee Dee Dancer
10^{9sd} 5^{8s} 5^{8g} 6^{8gs} 10^{8gf} 10^{7g} 7^{10g} 4^{8hy} 6^{8ss} 7^{8sd} **0-1-10**

Didoe *P W Hiatt* 55 a32
6 br m Son Pardo - My Diamond Ring
11^{9sd} 11^{9sd} 11^{9sd} 4^{10gf} 4^{10f} 3^{10gf} 7^{10gf} 2^{8gf} 2^{8g} 3^{8f} 10^{8g} 14^{11gf} 5^{8g} 9^{8f} **0-4-14 £4,170**

Diego Cao (Ire) *G L Moore* 95
4 b g Cape Cross (Ire) - Lady Moranbon (USA)
3^{10g} PU^{12hy} **0-1-2 £2,105**

Diequest (USA) *Mrs P Ford* a34
4 ch g Diesis - Nuance (Ire)
11^{9sd} 7^{14sd} 9^{11sd} **0-0-3**

Dig Deep (Ire) *W J Haggas* 81 a79
3 b g Entrepreneur - Diamond Quest
4^{6sd} 1^{7sd} 1^{7gf} 4^{7sd} 7^{8s} **2-0-5 £10,355**

Digger Girl (USA) *N A Callaghan* a43
2 b/br f Black Minnaloushe (USA) - Careyes (Ire)
11^{9sd} **0-0-1**

Digital *M R Channon* 83
8 ch g Safawan - Heavenly Goddess
7^{7gs} 4^{7s} 9^{7g} 8^{8g} 9^{7gf} 14^{7gs} 4^{7gf} 2^{7gf} 5^{7g} 6^{7gf} 1^{7gf} 16^{7gf} 2^{7g} 1^{6gf} 2^{6gf} 7^{7g} 5^{7gf} 9^{7gf} 11^{7g} 6^{7g} **2-3-20 £13,623**

Diktalex (Ire) *W G M Turner* 58 a55
2 b f Diktat - Kingdom Royale (Ire)
9^{5gs} 10^{7sd} 11^{6s} 3^{6sf} 2^{6sd} 5^{6sd} 3^{6sd} **0-3-7 £1,647**

Diktatit *R C Guest* 49

3 b f Diktat - Mystique Smile
4^{5g} 5^{5s} 12^{5f} 16^{5g} 13^{5gf} **0-0-5 £312**

Diktatorial *A M Balding* 95
3 br c Diktat - Reason To Dance
15^{8gf} 9^{8g} 8^{7g} 4^{7hy} **0-0-4 £673**

Diktatorship (Ire) *J H M Gosden* 69
2 b g Diktat - Polka Dancer
5^{6gf} 7^{7gf} 7^{7gf} 4^{8gf} 4^{7gs} **0-0-5 £518**

Dilala (Ire) *B W Hills* 66
3 b f Barathea (Ire) - Deyaajeer (USA)
5^{7gs} 6^{7gf} 3^{11gf} 4^{12gf} 2^{10gs} 2^{12gf} 4^{10gf}
0-3-7 £3,530

Dillons Dilemma (Ire) *E Sheehy* 88
3 ch c Monashee Mountain (USA) - God Speed Her
1^{12hy} 2^{12gf} 10^{16gf} **1-0-3 £8,860**

Dilsaa *K A Ryan*
8 ch g Night Shift (USA) - Llia
13^{11sd} **0-0-1**

Dimashq *Ronald Thompson* 47
3 b f Mtoto - Agwaas (Ire)
13^{7g} 7^{9gf} 6^{11gf} 2^{12gf} 9^{16g} 8^{14g} 3^{14g} 4^{16gf} 1^{13g}
10^{12sd} 7^{12ss} **1-2-11 £2,785**

Dimelight *D R C Elsworth* 63 a69
2 b f Fantastic Light (USA) - Dime Bag
8^{7gf} 3^{10sd} **0-1-2 £762**

Dimple Chad *W Storey* 75
6 b g Sadler's Wells (USA) - Fern
10^{14gs} 6^{12gs} 9^{12g} **0-0-3**

Dine 'N' Dash *A G Newcombe* 32 a33
4 ch g Komaite (USA) - Instinction
4^{6sd} 9^{6gs} 10^{7f} **0-0-3**

Dingaan (Ire) *A M Balding* 81
2 b c Tagula (Ire) - Boughtbyphone
9^{5g} 3^{6f} 3^{6gf} **0-2-3 £1,671**

Dinner Date *T Keddy* 56 a60
3 ch c Groom Dancer (USA) - Misleading Lady
10^{9sd} 5^{9sd} 6^{10s} 14^{8gs} 5^{8gf} 18^{10gf} 9^{11gf} 1^{10gf}
12^{13gf} 6^{10sd} 6^{12sd} **1-0-11 £2,912**

Direct Debit (Ire) *M L W Bell* 70
2 b c Dansili - Dimple
5^{7gf} **0-0-1**

Disco Diva *P Howling* a46
4 ch f Spectrum (Ire) - Compact Disc (Ire)
8^{8sd} 7^{7sd} 9^{7sd} 6^{7sd} 11^{8sd} **0-0-5**

Disco Lights *D J Daly* 70 a60
2 b f Spectrum (Ire) - Discomatic (USA)
3^{8g} 2^{8gs} 3^{9sd} 6^{8sd} **0-3-4 £2,545**

Discomania *J A Glover* 68 a65
3 b g Pursuit Of Love - Discomatic (USA)
5^{9sd} 7^{12sd} 9^{9sd} 6^{10s} 3^{14g} 2^{14gf} 8^{14gf} 10^{14g}
10^{12gf} 7^{14gf} **0-2-10 £1,620**

Discotheque (USA) *B J Meehan* 72 a65
2 ch f Not For Love (USA) - Disco Darlin' (USA)
6^{5gf} 4^{6gf} 4^{6gf} 5^{6sd} 6^{6sd} **0-0-5 £715**

Discuss (USA) *Sir Michael Stoute* 103 a95
3 b f Danzig (USA) - Private Line (USA)
1^{8g} 8^{8gf} 4^{10gf} 2^{8f} 8^{8g} 5^{8sd} **1-1-6**
£17,027

Disguise *J J Quinn* 78
3 b g Pursuit Of Love - Nullarbor
2^{5f} 1^{6gf} 6^{6g} 18^{5g} 16^{6s} **1-1-5 £4,547**

Dishdasha (Ire) *C R Dore* 38 a54
3 b g Desert Prince (Ire) - Counterplot (Ire)
6^{6sd} 8^{6sd} 6^{7sd} 2^{6sd} 3^{6sd} 9^{6sd} 1^{6sd} 7^{6sd} 6^{6f}
11^{6sd} 7^{6gf} 9^{7gs} 11^{8gf} **1-2-13 £2,216**

Disobey *C A Murphy* 72 a47
3 b f Machiavellian (USA) - Polisonne
15^{10gs} 6^{9gf} 9^{8g} 2^{10g} 6^{12sd} 1^{8gy} **1-1-6**
£9,506

Dispol Charm (Ire) *D W Chapman*
3 br f Charnwood Forest (Ire) - Phoenix Venture (Ire)
11^{5sd} 6^{8sd} **0-0-2**

Dispol Foxtrot *Miss V Scott* 79 a61
7 ch m Alhijaz - Foxtrot Pie
1^{8s} 3^{8gs} 8^{8s} 12^{8g} 5^{8gs} 8^{12gf} 3^{9gf} 6^{8gs} 8^{8gs}
11^{11gs} 1^{9g} 2^{10gf} 9^{10s} 6^{10hy} 1^{8sd} 1^{8sd}
4-3-16 £20,518

Dispol Holly *P T Midgley*
2 b f Woodborough (USA) - Tinker Osmaston
12^{5g} **0-0-1**

Dispol In Mind *A Berry* 38 a36
3 b f Mind Games - Sans Diablo (Ire)
12^{6sd} 9^{5g} 12^{6g} 14^{5gf} 15^{5g} **0-0-5**

Dispol Isle (Ire) *T D Barron* 65
3 gr f Trans Island - Pictina
2^{7gs} 3^{7gf} 11^{7gf} 5^{6f} 8^{7gf} 5^{7gf} 6^{6gf} 2^{8gf} 9^{8gf}
10^{8s} 7^{7hy} **0-3-11 £2,728**

Dispol Katie *T D Barron* 91
4 ch f Komaite (USA) - Twilight Time
7^{5s} 3^{5s} 8^{5g} 15^{5gf} 8^{5gf} 1^{7f} 10^{6gf} 2^{7f} 4^{7f}
1^{7gs} 5^{7gf} 6^{8g} 4^{7gf} 5^{8gf} **2-2-14 £15,814**

Dispol Lady *P T Midgley* 44
2 b f Foxhound (USA) - River Of Fortune (Ire)
13^{5gf} 7^{5gf} 7^{5gf} **0-0-3**

Dispol Peto *Ian Emmerson* a61
5 gr g Petong - Plie
4^{7sd} 1^{7sd} 4^{7sd} 2^{7sd} 5^{7sd} 9^{7sd} **1-1-6**
£3,689

Dispol Samurai *T D Barron* 44
2 gr g Shinko Forest (Ire) - Natural Pearl
14^{6g} 16^{6g} 5^{7gf} 8^{5g} **0-0-4**

Dispol Shabama *P T Midgley* 50
2 gr f Bahamian Bounty - Bogus Mix (Ire)
5^{5s} 10^{5s} 1^{7f} 7^{7g} 4^{6gf} 5^{7gf} 14^{7g} 9^{7gf}
1-0-8 £3,486

Dispol Valentine *P T Midgley* 49
2 b f Whittingham (Ire) - Bint Baddi (Fr)
6^{5hy} 7^{5g} 10^{6gf} 2^{7gf} 16^{7gf} 9^{6g} 9^{5ss} **0-1-7**
£858

Dispol Veleta *T D Barron* 83 a52
4 b f Makbul - Foxtrot Pie
10^{8sd} 4^{8s} 4^{8s} 1^{8gs} 1^{8gs} 6^{8g} 7^{8s} 5^{8g} 12^{8g}
5^{10gs} 4^{10gs} 7^{8gf} 9^{9g} 17^{8g} 10^{10gs} **2-1-15**
£14,230

Dispol Verity *W M Brisbourne* 44
5 b m Averti (Ire) - Fawley Mist
10^{8gf} 6^{8gf} 8^{7g} 10^{7sd} 8^{7g} 9^{7f} 14^{7g} 1^{7g} 10^{7hy}
1-0-9 £1,505

Distant Country (USA) *R A Harris* 71 a81
6 b g Distant View (USA) - Memsahb (USA)
2^{7sd} 1^{8sd} 3^{8g} 8^{8gf} 6^{8gf} 6^{8gf} 2^{9gf} 5^{10sd} 12^{7gf}
5^{8gf} 11^{8gf} 5^{8gf} 6^{8gf} 8^{8gf} 7^{9sf} 10^{7sd} 4^{7sd} 3^{7sd}
1-4-18 £8,930

Distant Cousin *M A Buckley* 51 a64
8 b g Distant Relative - Tinaca (USA)
5^{12sd} 5^{14sd} 2^{12sd} 1^{12sd} 8^{14gf} 2^{12sd} 9^{12sd}
1-2-7 £4,079

Distant Drums (Ire) *B W Hills* 38
2 ch f Distant Music (USA) - No Hard Feelings (Ire)
18^{7s} **0-0-1**

Distant Mind (Ire) *Mrs C A Dunnett* 51

2 b f Distant Music (USA) - Mind Song
11^{5gf} 9^{6gf} 11^{6gf} 15^{6g} **0-0-4**

Distant Prospect (Ire) *A M Balding* 94
8 b g Namaqualand (USA) - Ukraine's Affair (USA)
10^{18g} 11^{19gs} 4^{18gs} 10^{18gs} **0-0-4 £778**

Distant Shores (Ire) *J L Spearing* 43
2 b f Averti (Ire) - Adeptation (USA)
10^{5g} 7^{5g} 12^{6g} 6^{6gs} **0-0-4**

Distant Times *T D Easterby* 81
4 b c Orpen (USA) - Simply Times (USA)
12^{6s} 15^{6g} 1^{6g} 8^{5gf} 10^{6gf} 11^{8g} **1-0-6 £3,850**

Distant Vision (Ire) *Mark Campion* 36
2 br f Distant Music (USA) - Najeyba
6^{7gf} 6^{7g} **0-0-2**

Distinction (Ire) *Sir Michael Stoute* 121
6 b g Danehill (USA) - Ivy Leaf (Ire)
6^{13gs} 2^{20gf} 1^{16s} 2^{16g} 6^{18g} 19^{16gs} **1-2-6 £137,625**

Distinctive Look (Ire) *J H M Gosden* 77
2 b f Danehill (USA) - Magnificient Style (USA)
3^{7gs} 4^{8g} 9^{8s} **0-1-3 £1,063**

Distinctive Mind *T D Easterby* 37
3 b g Mind Games - Primum Tempus
11^{6f} **0-0-1**

Distinctive Voice *Saeed Bin Suroor* 76
2 ch g Mark Of Esteem (Ire) - Potri Pe (Arg)
3^{8gs} 3^{8gs} **0-2-2 £1,416**

Distinctly Game *K A Ryan* 103
3 b c Mind Games - Distinctly Blu (Ire)
4^{6g} 6^{5g} 9^{5gf} 11^{5gf} 8^{5gf} 25^{6gs} 19^{6g} **0-0-7 £1,400**

Distinctly Jim (Ire) *B Smart* 59
2 ch g City On A Hill (USA) - Bucaramanga (Ire)
2^{6f} 10^{7gf} 10^{7gf} **0-1-3 £1,084**

Ditto's Dream *Julian Poulton* a21
3 ch f Case Law - Precious Air (Ire)
5^{7sd} **0-0-1**

Ditton Dancer *J J Quinn* 63
2 ch f Danehill Dancer (Ire) - Dubai Lady
7^{5g} 1^{7gf} 8^{6g} 14^{8hy} **1-0-4 £4,319**

Dium Mac *N Bycroft* 64
4 b g Presidium - Efipetite
4^{6gf} 4^{6gf} 5^{7gf} 11^{6g} 5^{9gf} 6^{7gf} 2^{8gf} 1^{9gf} 10^{10s} **1-2-9 £4,668**

Divani (Ire) *J Pearce*
3 b f Shinko Forest (Ire) - Supreme Crown (USA)
13^{6gf} 9^{5g} **0-0-2**

Divine Gift *M A Jarvis* 100
4 b g Groom Dancer (USA) - Child's Play (USA)
8^{8g} 14^{8gs} 2^{10gs} 2^{10gf} 3^{10f} 7^{8gf} **0-3-6 £16,751**

Divine Proportions (USA) *P Bary* 123
3 b f Kingmambo (USA) - Myth To Reality (Fr)
1^{8vs} 1^{8s} 1^{11g} 1^{8gs} 4^{8gs} **4-0-5 £632,242**

Divine Spirit *M Dods* 86 a80
4 b g Foxhound (USA) - Vocation (Ire)
16^{5g} 13^{6g} 11^{5gf} 11^{5f} 7^{6gf} 5^{6g} 10^{6gf} 2^{6g} 2^{6gf} 3^{5gf} 8^{5gf} 6^{6gf} 3^{5g} 4^{5gf} 4^{5g} 10^{5g} 5^{6s} 3^{6sd} 7^{5s} 4^{5sd} **0-4-20 £8,721**

Divine White *Mrs A J Perrett* 56 a62
2 ch f College Chapel - Snowy Mantle
9^{6gs} 14^{6gf} 2^{6sd} 6^{7s} 4^{7sd} **0-1-5 £951**

Divinely Decadent (Ire) *P W Chapple-Hyam* 98
3 br f Turtle Island (Ire) - Divine Prospect (Ire)
5^{7gf} 8^{7g} 8^{10gf} 9^{10g} 12^{7g} **0-0-5 £1,250**

Divisive *M Blanshard* 37 a52
2 b f Alhaarth (Ire) - Hakkaniyah
17^{7g} 6^{7sd} 3^{9sd} **0-1-3 £426**

Dixie Belle *M G Quinlan* 93
2 b f Diktat - Inspiring (Ire)
1^{6gf} 4^{6g} 1^{6g} 5^{6gf} 4^{6g} **2-0-5 £20,587**

Dixie Edwards (Ire) *M Quinn*
4 ch c Titus Livius (Fr) - Fairy Oak (Ire)
7^{6gs} **0-0-1**

Dixieanna *B W Hills* 77 a65
3 ch f Night Shift (USA) - Dixielake (Ire)
2^{6gs} 4^{5s} 1^{6gf} 3^{6g} 6^{6gf} 4^{6gf} 4^{5gs} 8^{5g} 3^{6s} 7^{5sd} **1-3-10 £8,966**

Dizzy Dreamer (Ire) *P W Chapple-Hyam* 95
2 b f Spinning World (USA) - Divine Prospect (Ire)
1^{6gf} 8^{7gf} 10^{7vs} 8^{6g} **1-0-4 £4,280**

Dizzy Future *B J Llewellyn* 57 a63
3 b g Fraam - Kara Sea (USA)
7^{9sd} 8^{8sd} 2^{12sd} 15^{12gf} 5^{14gf} 4^{16gf} 2^{13sd} 12^{12sd} **0-2-8 £1,760**

Dizzy In The Head *I Semple* 79 a67
6 b g Mind Games - Giddy
PU^{6sd} 14^{5g} 14^{6s} 10^{5f} 2^{5s} 1^{5gf} 2^{6f} 7^{6g} 9^{5g} 7^{6s} 4^{6gf} 28^{6g} 6^{5gf} 6^{5sd} 1^{5s} 12^{5sf} 10^{6sd} 11^{5sd} **2-2-18 £11,446**

Dizzy Lizzy *Nick Williams* 46
3 gr f Sendawar (Ire) - Black Velvet (Fr)
6^{10gf} 13^{9sd} **0-0-2**

Dmitri *J D Frost* 31 a50
5 b g Emperor Jones (USA) - Shining Cloud
9^{10gs} 13^{7gf} 6^{6sd} 10^{8hd} **0-0-4**

Dock Tower (Ire) *M E Sowersby* 54 a28
3 b g Docksider (USA) - Thakhayr
10^{10gf} 11^{11g} 12^{12sd} 3^{12gf} **0-1-4 £516**

Docklands Dude (Ire) *M Meade*
3 ch g Namid - Cheeky Weeky
13^{6sd} **0-0-1**

Doctor Bailey *M R Channon* 42
3 b g Mister Baileys - Frustration
5^{12g} **0-0-1**

Doctor Dash *D R C Elsworth* 97
2 ch g Dr Fong (USA) - Dashiba
2^{6gf} 3^{6gf} 1^{8gs} 8^{8g} 9^{8g} **1-2-5 £16,552**

Doctor Dennis (Ire) *J Pearce* 52 a58
8 b g Last Tycoon - Noble Lustre (USA)
3^{7sd} 4^{7sd} 6^{7sd} 2^{7sd} 2^{6sd} 9^{7sd} 3^{6sd} 6^{6sd} 9^{7s} 8^{7g} 4^{6gf} 2^{7f} 1^{7g} 1^{6sd} 3^{7sd} 5^{7sd} 2^{7sd} 3^{7sd} **2-8-18 £6,115**

Doctor Of Laws *M J Wallace* 80 a87
2 b c Dr Fong (USA) - Mavourneen (USA)
1^{8sd} 3^{7sd} 3^{8g} **1-1-3 £5,957**

Doctor Scott *M Johnston* 88
2 b c Medicean - Milly Of The Vally
1^{8gf} 4^{8gs} 5^{8gs} 4^{10s} **1-0-4 £6,816**

Doctor's Cave *K O Cunningham-Brown* 75 a71
3 b g Night Shift (USA) - Periquitum
5^{7sd} 7^{5sd} 13^{6gs} 6^{8g} 5^{6gf} 10^{6g} 9^{6gf} 6^{7f} 9^{6sd} 20^{7gf} 12^{6g} 8^{6sd} 9^{6sd} **0-0-13 £507**

Doctored *D C O'Brien* 79
4 ch g Dr Devious (Ire) - Polygueza (Fr)
7^{12gf} 12^{12gf} 2^{10gf} 4^{11g} 2^{11gf} 4^{10gf} 7^{10g} 14^{12f} 9^{10g} 3^{11gs} 13^{12gf} **0-3-11 £3,628**

Dodgem (USA) *Saeed Bin Suroor* 31
2 b/br c Forestry (USA) - Concentric (USA)

7^{7s} **0-0-1**

Dogbiscuit (Ire) *A Berry*
2 b c Beckett (Ire) - Hever Golf Lady
11^{6g} 17^{6g} 11^{7sd} **0-0-3**

Doitforreel (Ire) *R M Beckett* 78 a68
3 b f Princely Heir (Ire) - Chehana
3^{6gf} 15^{6g} 11^{5gf} 1^{7gf} 7^{7f} 8^{7gf} 2^{7gf} 10^{6g} 8^{7g} 10^{7sd} **1-2-10 £6,171**

Doitnow (Ire) *R A Fahey* 88 a84
4 b g Princely Heir (Ire) - Tony's Gift
7^{6sd} 2^{6g} 11^{6gs} 7^{7gf} 12^{6gf} 9^{6gf} 8^{7gf} 8^{6g} 21^{7gf} 13^{7g} **0-1-10 £2,228**

Dolce Maria (Ire) *Michael Cunningham* 53 a50
2 b/br f Trans Island - The State Of Her (Ire)
8^{6gf} 13^{7gf} 12^{6f} 10^{6g} 10^{7sd} 3^{6sd} 9^{6sd} **0-1-7 £366**

Dolce Piccata *B J Meehan* 69 a61
4 ch f Piccolo - Highland Rhapsody (Ire)
8^{5sd} 6^{5gf} 2^{5f} 8^{5f} 4^{6gf} 6^{5g} **0-1-6 £1,632**

Dollivius (Ire) *Ms Deborah J Evans* 50 a58
4 b f Titus Livius (Fr) - Dollar Magic
12^{5sd} 10^{5sd} 13^{5sd} 10^{5sd} 9^{5g} 12^{5gf} 4^{5sd} 11^{5f} 7^{5sd} 6^{7g} 9^{7gf} 13^{7g} **0-0-12**

Dolls House *M H Tompkins* 27
3 b f Dancing Spree (USA) - Kip's Sister
6^{6gs} 14^{7gf} 11^{7s} 12^{12sd} **0-0-4**

Dolly *R J Hodges* 44
3 b f Thowra (Fr) - Sweet Symphony (Ire)
8^{6gs} 15^{8g} 8^{7gf} 10^{6g} 5^{6gf} 13^{5f} **0-0-6**

Dolly Brown *T D Easterby* 51
2 ch f Bertolini (USA) - Birichino
6^{6gf} 6^{6hy} 10^{6s} **0-0-3**

Dolly Wotnot (Ire) *N P Littmoden* a29
4 b f Desert King (Ire) - Riding School (Ire)
8^{10sd} **0-0-1**

Dolzago *G L Moore* a45
5 b g Pursuit Of Love - Doctor's Glory (USA)
13^{12sd} 10^{13sd} **0-0-2**

Domenico (Ire) *J R Jenkins* 66 a21
7 b g Sadler's Wells (USA) - Russian Ballet (USA)
9^{14sd} 1^{14g} 7^{16g} 33^{18gs} **1-0-4 £4,208**

Dominello *R A Fahey* 22
2 b c Primo Valentino (Ire) - Forever Nellie
9^{5gf} 13^{5g} **0-0-2**

Dominer (Ire) *J M Bradley* 56 a34
3 b g Desert Prince (Ire) - Smart (Ire)
6^{7s} 1^{7gf} 6^{8gf} 12^{7gs} 8^{7gs} 11^{7g} 6^{7gf} 4^{7f} 8^{7sd} 13^{8g} 6^{7ss} **1-0-11 £1,512**

Domirati *J D Bethell* 73
5 b g Emarati (USA) - Julia Domna
7^{5gf} 12^{6gf} 5^{5gf} 6^{6g} 12^{5gs} 3^{5gf} 8^{5g} **0-1-7 £657**

Don Argento *Mrs A J Bowlby*
4 gr g Sri Pekan (USA) - Grey Galava
F^{11gs} **0-0-1**

Don Jose (USA) *J H M Gosden* 76
2 b/br c Dynaformer (USA) - Panthera (USA)
5^{8gf} 9^{8gs} **0-0-2**

Don Pasquale *J T Stimpson* 73 a76
3 br g Zafonic (USA) - Bedazzling (Ire)
3^{9sd} 4^{9sd} 2^{9sd} 3^{9sd} 4^{8s} 15^{8g} 10^{10s} 12^{12sd} **0-3-8 £2,864**

Don Pele (Ire) *S Kirk* 96
3 b c Monashee Mountain (USA) - Big Fandango
5^{6gf} 4^{6gf} 14^{6g} 7^{6gf} 14^{7s} 6^{6gs} 15^{6g} **0-0-7 £2,750**

Don Peter (Ire) *R M Beckett* 52 a66
2 b g Princely Heir (Ire) - Easy Going
7^{5g} 2^{5sd} 4^{5g} 7^{5g} 7^{5gf} 4^{5f} 6^{5g} **0-1-7 £1,154**

Don Tenorio (Ire) *S Kirk* 44 a54
2 ch c Fruits Of Love (USA) - Moonlight Partner (Ire)
13^{5s} 11^{6s} 7^{7g} 8^{8sd} **0-0-4**

Don'Tcallmeginger (Ire) *M H Tompkins* 64
2 ch c Fruits Of Love (USA) - Scotia Rose
8^{7g} 5^{7s} 5^{9g} **0-0-3**

Don't Sioux Me (Ire) *C R Dore* 34
7 b g Sadler's Wells (USA) - Commanche Belle
6^{10gf} 7^{10g} **0-0-2**

Don't Tell Daddy *Ronald Thompson* 32
2 ch g Atraf - Star Dancer
7^{5g} 13^{6gs} 15^{6g} 11^{8gs} **0-0-4**

Don't Tell Mum (Ire) *R Hannon* 98
3 b f Dansili - Zinnia
5^{7gs} 1^{6g} 10^{6g} **1-0-3 £7,945**

Don't Tell Sue *B W Hills* 70 a70
2 ch c Bold Edge - Opopmil (Ire)
1^{5gs} 10^{5gs} 11^{7gs} 5^{6gs} 3^{5g} 5^{5g} 3^{5hy} 2^{5sd} **1-3-8 £8,518**

Dona Vitoria *S Kirk* 61 a35
2 b f Diktat - Salanka (Ire)
16^{6gf} 4^{6gf} 13^{7sd} **0-0-3 £452**

Donastrela (Ire) *A M Balding* 72 a72
4 b f Tagula (Ire) - David's Star
5^{14gs} 3^{13f} 2^{12g} 5^{13gf} 3^{12gf} 5^{10gf} 11^{12f} 3^{14sd} **0-4-8 £3,652**

Donegal Shore (Ire) *Jennie Candlish* 40 a61
6 b h Mujadil (USA) - Distant Shore (Ire)
7^{8sd} 1^{7sd} 2^{6sd} 5^{7sd} 4^{8sd} 2^{9sd} 6^{8g} 11^{9sd} 10^{9sd} 9^{8g} 7^{8sd} 6^{6sd} 5^{7ss} **1-2-13 £3,054**

Donna Blini *B J Meehan* 110
2 ch f Bertolini (USA) - Cal Norma's Lady (Ire)
1^{5g} 2^{5g} 1^{6g} 1^{6g} **3-1-4 £154,981**

Donna Giovanna *J A Osborne* 68 a70
2 b f Mozart (Ire) - Chelsea (USA)
4^{5g} 3^{6gf} 4^{7gf} 10^{7g} 6^{7sd} **0-1-5 £1,480**

Donna's Double *Karen McLintock* 58
10 ch g Weldnaas (USA) - Shadha
3^{11gf} 2^{12g} 2^{10gs} 6^{12gf} 5^{10g} 3^{12gf} 1^{10s} 3^{10g} 2^{10gf} 3^{10gs} 11^{13s} 6^{12gf} 3^{10s} 10^{14s} **1-8-14 £7,997**

Dont Call Me Babe *J R Best*
3 b g Easycall - Ok Babe
12^{10sd} 10^{8sd} **0-0-2**

Dont Call Me Derek *J J Quinn* 95
4 b g Sri Pekan (USA) - Cultural Role
8^{12hy} 1^{17s} **1 0 2 £13,264**

Dont Dili Dali *J S Moore* 91
2 b f Dansili - Miss Meltemi (Ire)
5^{6g} 2^{6gf} 2^{6gf} 2^{7gf} 2^{7gs} 1^{7g} 1^{8s} 7^{7g} 3^{7gf} 9^{6g} **2-5-10 £50,841**

Donya One *L M Cumani* 62
3 b f Cadeaux Genereux - Fadhah
5^{6gs} 9^{6gf} 3^{6gf} 6^{8gf} 13^{7gf} 11^{6gf} 3^{7gf} 15^{7g} **0-1-8 £1,198**

Donyana *M A Jarvis* 79 a78
3 b f Mark Of Esteem (Ire) - Albarsha
5^{8gf} 11^{8s} 6^{10sd} **0-0-3 £180**

Doohulla (USA) *G A Butler* 92 a72

4 ch f Stravinsky (USA) - Viva Zapata (USA)
6^{5s} 7^{6gf} 4^{6gf} 7^{7g} 1^{6gf} 9^{6gf} 4^{5gf} 10^{7sd}
1-0-8 £10,904

Dora's Green *M Blanshard* 48
2 b f Rambling Bear - Compradore
12^{5gf} 2^{5gf} 10^{5g} **0-1-3 £1,051**

Dorchester *W J Musson* 74
8 b g Primo Dominie - Penthouse Lady
10^{7s} 12^{6g} 9^{6g} 2^{6g} 11^{6g} 14^{6g} **0-1-6**
£1,110

Doric (USA) *B Ellison* 94
4 ch g Distant View (USA) - Doree (USA)
21^{7gf} 7^{7s} 3^{6g} 7^{8gf} 2^{6gf} 12^{7g} **0-2-6**
£6,283

Doringo *J L Spearing* 55
4 b g Prince Sabo - Mistral's Dancer
8^{7s} 12^{8gs} 2^{8gf} 4^{8f} 10^{10g} 5^{8g} 1^{8f} 5^{8f} 4^{10s}
12^{10gf} **1-1-10 £4,198**

Doris Souter (Ire) *D J Wintle* 64 a68
5 b/br m Desert Story (Ire) - Hope And Glory (USA)
11^{10sd} 13^{10sd} 7^{10gf} **0-0-3**

Dorn Dancer (Ire) *D W Barker* 66
3 b f Danehill Dancer (Ire) - Appledorn
18^{7g} 5^{5s} 11^{6gs} 8^{6s} 7^{7g} 5^{6gf} 5^{6g} 4^{5gs} 13^{6g}
10^{6s} 13^{6g} 7^{6g} **0-0-12 £648**

Dorn Hill *D G Bridgwater* 54 a47
3 b f Lujain (USA) - Benedicite
4^{6gf} 3^{7gf} 2^{6gf} 8^{5g} 7^{7sf} 17^{6g} 1^{6sd} 12^{6ss}
1-2-8 £3,160

Double Carpet (Ire) *G Woodward* 58
2 b c Lahib (USA) - Cupid Miss
13^{6g} 5^{6gf} 9^{6g} **0-0-3**

Double Dawn *B De Haan* 61
3 b f Double Trigger (Ire) - Spring Sunrise
4^{7gf} 7^{8gf} 7^{8f} **0-0-3 £330**

Double Deputy (Ire) *Saeed Bin Suroor* 91
4 b c Sadler's Wells (USA) - Janaat
3^{12g} 8^{10g} 1^{14g} 5^{15s} **1-1-4 £11,671**

Double Emblem (Ire) *B R Foster*
8 ch m Weld - Sultry
12^{12sd} **0-0-1**

Double Kudos (Fr) *Jamie Poulton* 81 a78
3 gr c Highest Honor (Fr) - Black Tulip (Fr)
3^{12sd} 2^{10sd} 4^{10g} 3^{10gf} 9^{10g} 8^{14gf} 5^{12sd}
0-3-7 £3,002

Double M *Mrs L Richards* 57 a77
8 ch g First Trump - Girton Degree
5^{5sd} 1^{6sd} 1^{7sd} 12^{6sd} 16^{6gf} 11^{6g} 13^{6g} 7^{5gf}
9^{6sd} 7^{6gf} 7^{6f} 9^{5gf} 11^{5gf} 11^{6gs} 7^{7sd} 9^{7sd}
2-0-16 £6,923

Double Margin (USA) *Jamie Poulton*
3 b g Boundary (USA) - Maniches Slew (USA)
12^{12sd} 10^{10gf} **0-0-2**

Double Oh Seven (Ire) *J W Unett* 62 a5
2 ch c Alhaarth (Ire) - Liberi Versi (Ire)
12^{6g} 4^{7g} 17^{7gs} 9^{7g} 9^{7sd} **0-0-5 £255**

Double Ransom *Mrs L Stubbs* 59 a64
6 b g Bahamian Bounty - Secrets Of Honour
7^{10sd} 7^{8sd} 9^{8s} 7^{9gs} 6^{8s} 6^{8s} 2^{9s} 7^{12gs} 4^{8s} 10^{10s}
9^{10sd} **0-2-11 £1,546**

Double Royal (Ire) *Mrs T J Hill* a53
6 b g Ali-Royal (Ire) - Royal Wolff
3^{12sd} 1^{12sd} 6^{14sd} 7^{14sd} 12^{17sd} **1-1-5**
£3,464

Double Spectre (Ire) *Jean-Rene Auvray* 69
3 b g Spectrum (Ire) - Phantom Ring
4^{9g} 5^{10gf} 3^{8f} 2^{10g} 7^{10g} **0-1-5 £1,818**

Double Turn *Mrs S J Smith* 46
5 ch g Double Trigger (Ire) - Its My Turn
17^{14g} 9^{16g} 10^{17g} 7^{16f} **0-0-4**

Double Valentine *R Ingram* 40 a60
2 ch f Primo Valentino (Ire) - Charlottevalentina (Ire)
8^{6f} 10^{5gs} 7^{6sd} 10^{5sd} 12^{6sd} **0-0-5**

Double Vodka (Ire) *C Grant* 83
4 b/br g Russian Revival (USA) - Silius
2^{8s} 4^{8f} 1^{10s} 5^{10gf} 10^{8g} 17^{10gs} 7^{10g} 3^{10s}
1-2-8 £11,267

Doughty *D J Wintle* 38 a49
3 b g Bold Edge - Marquante (Ire)
6^{5sd} 4^{5s} 2^{5sd} 7^{5sd} 6^{7sd} 8^{6ss} 7^{9sd} 9^{7sd} 4^{6ss}
7^{9ss} **0-1-10 £414**

Dove Cottage (Ire) *W S Kittow* 66
3 b g Great Commotion (USA) - Pooka
7^{8s} 12^{7gs} 15^{8g} 10^{8gf} 1^{10g} 3^{10s} 8^{10s}
1-1-7 £5,403

Dovedale *H S Howe* 64 a54
5 b m Groom Dancer (USA) - Peetsie (Ire)
6^{12hy} 4^{12gf} 5^{12gf} 1^{13sd} 6^{11gf} **1-0-5**
£1,746

Dovedon Hero *P J McBride* 84 a86
5 ch g Millkom - Hot Topic (Ire)
3^{12sd} 6^{12sd} 4^{12sd} 6^{12sd} 9^{12sd} 6^{12sd} 1^{16gf} 6^{12gf}
12^{14gf} 9^{15gf} 3^{16gf} 7^{12sf} 5^{14sd} 9^{12sd} 3^{12sd}
1-2-15 £17,697

Dover Street *E F Vaughan* 66
3 ch g Zafonic (USA) - Seeker
8^{12gf} 9^{10gf} 6^{8g} 4^{10f} **0-0-4 £258**

Dower House *Andrew Turnell* 76 a92
10 ch g Groom Dancer (USA) - Rose Noble (USA)
1^{9sd} 5^{9sd} 1^{12sd} 4^{10sd} 1^{12sd} 5^{10gs} 6^{10s} 9^{10g} 4^{12sd}
1^{10sd} **4-0-10 £27,285**

Downland (Ire) *N Tinkler* 71
9 b g Common Grounds - Boldabsa
5^{7gf} 13^{7s} 4^{7g} 6^{7gf} 14^{8g} 3^{8gf} 1^{7f} 2^{7g} 2^{7gs}
9^{7g} 7^{7gf} 16^{6g} 17^{7gf} **1-3-13 £7,715**

Downland (USA) *J L Dunlop* 60
3 gr f El Prado (Ire) - Quelle Affaire (USA)
7^{7gf} 3^{7gf} 8^{8s} 9^{8f} 11^{7g} **0-1-5 £812**

Doyen (Ire) *Saeed Bin Suroor* 113
5 b h Sadler's Wells (USA) - Moon Cactus
5^{12f} 6^{12gf} 6^{10g} **0-0-3 £20,952**

Dr Fox (Ire) *M Wigham* a42
4 b g Foxhound (USA) - Eleonora D'Arborea
5^{9sd} 8^{9sd} **0-0-2**

Dr Pertseff *P F I Cole* 53
2 ch c Dr Fong (USA) - Superspring
13^{5g} 11^{6gs} 6^{5g} **0-0-3**

Dr Saddler *D Mullarkey* a30
9 b g Saddlers' Hall (Ire) - Dama De Noche
10^{10sd} **0-0-1**

Dr Sharp (Ire) *T P Tate* 93
5 ch g Dr Devious (Ire) - Stoned Imaculate (Ire)
1^{18g} 10^{19gs} 2^{16g} 9^{20gf} 13^{14g} 6^{14gs} 2^{20s}
1-2-7 £17,164

Dr Synn *J Akehurst* 74
4 br g Danzero (Aus) - Our Shirley
5^{8gs} 3^{7gf} 1^{7g} 13^{7gf} 7^{7g} 6^{7hy} **1-0-6**
£4,085

Dr Thong *P F I Cole* 86 a84
4 ch c Dr Fong (USA) - Always On My Mind
11^{7f} 3^{8g} 6^{8gf} 12^{7gf} 5^{8gs} 16^{7gf} 1^{8sd} 5^{8sd} 6^{9sd}

1-0-9 £5,066

Dr Zalo *P J Makin* 78 a62
3 ch g Dr Fong (USA) - Azola (Ire)
2^{6gf} 4^{5gf} 3^{6sd} 8^{6gf} 5^{6f} 10^{8f} 13^{6gf} **0-2-7 £2,736**

Dragon Dancer *G Wragg* 63
2 b c Sadler's Wells (USA) - Alakananda
7^{7gf} **0-0-1**

Dragon Flyer (Ire) *M Quinn* 88 a93
6 b m Tagula (Ire) - Noble Rocket
5^{5sd} 6^{5sd} 12^{5g} 4^{5s} 6^{5g} 6^{5g} 8^{5g} 15^{5g} 7^{6g} 4^{5gf} 7^{5g} 7^{5g} **0-0-12 £2,159**

Dragon Slayer (Ire) *M J Attwater* 76 a76
3 ch g Night Shift (USA) - Arandora Star (USA)
4^{6sd} 3^{6sd} 2^{7sd} 1^{6sd} 9^{8g} 3^{6gf} 1^{9g} 1^{8gf} 8^{9g} 10^{8gs} 2^{9sd} 2^{9sd} **3-5-12 £16,280**

Dramatic Review (Ire) *P C Haslam* 52 a35
3 b g Indian Lodge (Ire) - Dramatic Shift (Ire)
8^{9sd} 2^{9g} 3^{8gf} 4^{10gf} 2^{9hy} **0-4-5 £2,295**

Dramaticus *B Palling* 50
3 b g Indian Ridge - Corinium (Ire)
8^{6s} 10^{6s} 9^{7s} **0-0-3**

Drawback (Ire) *J A Osborne* a54
2 b g Daggers Drawn (USA) - Sacred Heart (Ire)
5^{7sd} **0-0-1**

Drawn Out (Ire) *P C Haslam* 52
2 ch g Daggers Drawn (USA) - Fastnet
15^{5g} 6^{6g} 13^{6gf} 3^{7g} 7^{7gf} 3^{7gf} 11^{7g} **0-2-7 £965**

Dreadnought *J R Fanshawe* 18 a69
3 b g Slip Anchor - Fleet Amour (USA)
6^{11gs} 5^{12sd} 6^{12sd} **0-0-3**

Dream Alive *M Blanshard* 53
4 b g Unfuwain (USA) - Petite Sonnerie
15^{8s} 10^{10gf} 18^{12gf} 6^{8gf} 10^{10gf} 8^{14gf} **0-0-6**

Dream Along *Mrs A J Perrett*
3 b g Sinndar (Ire) - Dream Quest
UR^{10sd} **0-0-1**

Dream Champion *M R Channon* a71
2 b c Fraam - Forest Fantasy
2^{9sd} **0-1-1 £1,106**

Dream Easy *P L Gilligan* a56
4 b g Pyramus (USA) - Hush Baby (Ire)
3^{12sd} 6^{12sd} **0-1-2 £475**

Dream Factor (Ire) *J O'Reilly* 61 a57
2 br f Bold Fact (USA) - Bobby's Dream
6^{5sd} 1^{5sd} 8^{5gs} 5^{5gf} 7^{7gs} 7^{6gf} 4^{6gf} 3^{6g} 2^{5gf} 5^{5g} 12^{5sd} 7^{7sd} **1-1-12 £4,428**

Dream Fantasy (Ire) *Sir Mark Prescott* 98 a95
2 b g Barathea (Ire) - Night Mirage (USA)
1^{6g} 1^{7gf} 1^{9sd} 2^{9gs} 2^{8gs} 7^{8hy} **3-2-6 £22,028**

Dream Forest (Ire) *Mrs P N Dutfield* 59
2 b c Raise A Grand (Ire) - Theresa Green (Ire)
7^{5gf} **0-0-1**

Dream Magic *M J Ryan* a74
7 b g Magic Ring (Ire) - Pip's Dream
3^{9sd} 1^{13sd} 3^{12sd} 4^{12sd} F^{12sd} **1-2-5 £4,534**

Dream Merchant (Ire) *P J Hobbs* 71
5 b h Deputy Minister (Can) - User Friendly
2^{12gf} 4^{14g} 5^{14gf} 6^{14gf} 2^{16gf} 4^{16gf} **0-2-6 £3,334**

Dream Mountain *M Johnston* 64 a57
2 b c Mozart (Ire) - Statua (Ire)
3^{6gf} 2^{6gf} 1^{7gf} 15^{8s} 8^{8sd} 5^{7sd} **1-2-6 £4,589**

Dream Of Dubai (Ire) *P Mitchell* a43
4 b f Vettori (Ire) - Immortelle
7^{7sd} 7^{8sd} 7^{10sd} 5^{8sd} **0-0-4**

Dream Of Paradise (USA) *Mrs L Williamson* 51 a48
2 ch f Atticus (USA) - Scrumptious (USA)
3^{7f} 7^{6gf} 5^{5gf} 5^{8g} 6^{9sd} 10^{7s} 4^{7sd} **0-0-7 £760**

Dream Rose (Ire) *M R Channon* 76
2 b f Anabaa (USA) - Hiddnah (USA)
2^{5gs} 5^{5gs} 2^{6gf} 9^{7gf} 2^{7gs} 3^{8g} 4^{8gf} **0-4-7 £6,588**

Dream Theme *B W Hills* 75
2 b c Distant Music (USA) - Xaymara (USA)
8^{6g} 3^{7gf} **0-1-2 £391**

Dream To Dress (USA) *D K Weld* 109
3 ch f Theatrical - Journey Of Hope (USA)
3^{8ys} 1^{10y} 8^{12g} 7^{10gf} 7^{9g} 2^{12g} 6^{12g} **1-2-7 £11,508**

Dream Tonic *M R Channon* 81
3 b c Zafonic (USA) - Dream On Deya (Ire)
11^{10gf} 7^{7g} 12^{9gf} 8^{7g} 2^{7gf} 12^{8gf} 8^{6gf} 9^{8g} 6^{7gf} 1^{8gf} 1^{8gf} 1^{8gf} 10^{9g} 6^{8g} 16^{8g} 15^{7hy} **3-1-16 £17,358**

Dreamer's Lass *J M Bradley* 26
3 b f Pyramus (USA) - Qualitair Dream
14^{5gf} **0-0-1**

Dreams Forgotten (Ire) *P R Hedger* 43 a1
5 b m Victory Note (USA) - Sevens Are Wild
14^{10sd} 5^{7s} 15^{6gs} **0-0-3**

Dreams Of Zena *D Burchell* 8
6 b m Dreams End - Billan Tara
8^{7f} **0-0-1**

Dress Pearl *J G Given*
4 b f Atraf - Dress Design (Ire)
13^{7sd} **0-0-1**

Drink To Me Only *J R Weymes* 47 a51
2 b g Pursuit Of Love - Champenoise
9^{5gs} 3^{5gf} 7^{5gf} 12^{6gs} 9^{5gf} 13^{7g} 13^{6gs} 5^{5sd} **0-0-8 £514**

Drive Me Wild (Ire) *R Charlton* 53 a31
3 b c Indian Ridge - Wild Bluebell (Ire)
10^{8g} 7^{8g} 6^{8gf} 7^{10sd} 12^{12gf} **0-0-5**

Drizzle *M J Gingell*
4 ch g Hector Protector (USA) - Rainy Sky
14^{7sd} **0-0-1**

Droopys Joel *S C Williams* a45
3 b g Primo Dominie - Zaima (Ire)
7^{6sd} 13^{8sd} 9^{6sd} **0-0-3**

Drum Dance (Ire) *N Tinkler* 65
3 b g Namid - Socialite (Ire)
1^{6s} 10^{6gs} 11^{6gf} 4^{6f} 5^{6gf} 6^{7gf} 9^{6gf} 5^{6g} 14^{6g} 19^{7gf} **1-0-10 £4,128**

Drumacole Artist (Ire) *W A Murphy* 8
4 b g Foxhound (USA) - Ever So Artful
14^{5s} 10^{6sd} **0-0-2**

Drumming Party (USA) *A M Balding* 60
3 b/br g War Chant (USA) - Santaria (USA)
7^{8gs} 8^{7gs} 5^{7g} **0-0-3**

Drumroll (Ire) *Miss J Feilden* a59
3 b g Diktat - Mystic Tempo (USA)
8^{8sd} 10^{9sd} 3^{9sd} 6^{9sd} **0-1-4 £501**

Drury Lane (Ire) *D W Chapman* 56

5 b/br g Royal Applause - Ghost Tree (Ire)
11^{6gf} 1^{6g} 10^{6gf} 13^{7f} 4^{6gf} 8^{6g} 12^{7sd} 13^{7sd}
1-1-8 £3,626

Dry Ice (Ire) *H Candy* 83
3 b g Desert Sun - Snowspin
2^{8gf} 5^{8f} **0-1-2 £2,188**

Dubai Ace (USA) *Miss Sheena West* a45
4 b g Lear Fan (USA) - Arsaan (USA)
12^{10sd} **0-0-1**

Dubai Around (Ire) *M D Hammond* 53
2 ch g Zinaad - Triple Transe (USA)
6^{6g} 6^{8s} 8^{6gs} **0-0-3**

Dubai Dreams *S R Bowring* a62
5 b g Marju (Ire) - Arndilly
10^{11sd} 2^{9sd} 1^{8sd} 1^{11sd} 13^{10sd} 13^{9sd} 6^{7sd} 5^{7sd}
10^{8sd} **2-1-9 £3,418**

Dubai Lightning (USA) *J G M O'Shea*
5 br g Seeking The Gold (USA) - Heraklia (USA)
12^{7sd} **0-0-1**

Dubai Melody (USA) *J H M Gosden* 62
2 ch f Woodman (USA) - Dabaweyaa
6^{8g} **0-0-1**

Dubai On *M P Tregoning* 88 a72
2 b f Daylami (Ire) - Cambara
1^{7sd} 1^{10g} **2-0-2 £11,173**

Dubai Success *B W Hills* 115
5 b h Sadler's Wells (USA) - Crystal Spray
3^{12s} 3^{16s} 8^{13f} 3^{12gs} 2^{12gs} 17^{14g} 1^{12hy} 5^{16g}
7^{12gs} **1-3-9 £41,920**

Dubai Surprise (Ire) *Saeed Bin Suroor* 113
3 b f King's Best (USA) - Toujours Irish (USA)
1^{8gf} 1^{10hy} **2-0-2 £106,202**

Dubai Typhoon (USA) *C E Brittain* 92
2 ch c Thunder Gulch (USA) - Dubian
3^{7g} 5^{7gf} 1^{8g} 8^{6gf} **1-1-4 £4,850**

Dubai Venture *Sir Michael Stoute* 99
3 ch c Rainbow Quest (USA) - Bombazine (Ire)
1^{10gf} 2^{10gf} 8^{12gf} 2^{10gf} 2^{12gf} 7^{12gf} **1-3-6**
£13,403

Dubawi (Ire) *Saeed Bin Suroor* 128
3 b c Dubai Millennium - Zomaradah
5^{8gf} 1^{8g} 3^{12g} 1^{8gs} 2^{8g} **2-2-5 £546,379**

Dublin Dice (Ire) *B W Hills* 27
2 b g Orpen (USA) - Cullinan Diamond (Ire)
7^{6gf} **0-0-1**

Dubonai (Ire) *G M Moore* a54
5 ch g Peintre Celebre (USA) - Web Of Intrigue
4^{9sd} **0-0-1**

Duc's Dream *D Morris* 38 a56
7 b g Bay Tern (USA) - Kala's Image
3^{12sd} 4^{12sd} 7^{11sd} 5^{11s} 1^{12sd} 8^{11f} **1-1-6**
£1,875

Ducal Diva *J R Weymes* 27 a19
3 b f Bahamian Bounty - Lucky Thing
7^{5sd} 6^{5s} **0-0-2**

Duck Row (USA) *J A R Toller* 94
10 ch g Diesis - Sunny Moment (USA)
10^{9s} 9^{8gs} 6^{8s} **0-0-3 £450**

Duckett (Ire) *Julian Poulton* a36
5 b g Charnwood Forest (Ire) - Lovat Spring (USA)
13^{6sd} 7^{5sd} 13^{5sd} **0-0-3**

Dudley Docker (Ire) *D Carroll* 69 a71
3 b g Victory Note (USA) - Nordic Abu (Ire)
PU^{11gs} 11^{8gf} 5^{8f} 2^{7gf} 1^{8gf} 7^{8gf} 5^{8g} 13^{8s} 4^{8sd}
11^{8sd} 5^{8sd} **1-1-11 £4,916**

Due Respect (Ire) *D T Hughes* 98
5 b h Danehill (USA) - Stylish
2^{8s} 15^{8gs} 13^{8g} 16^{8gf} 6^{8hy} 14^{8sh} **0-1-6**
£11,514

Duel In The Sands *D Shaw* 57 a50
2 ch g Allied Forces (USA) - Kildine (Ire)
11^{6g} 12^{7s} 5^{8gf} 12^{7hy} 2^{9sd} **0-1-5 £415**

Duelling *J H M Gosden* 80
2 ch f Diesis - Enemy Action (USA)
7^{5gf} 1^{6gf} 7^{6g} 4^{6gf} 9^{6gs} **1-0-5 £5,545**

Duelling Banjos *J Akehurst* 81 a72
6 ch g Most Welcome - Khadino
4^{12sd} 1^{12sd} 1^{10s} 1^{10s} 4^{11g} 9^{12gf} 14^{10gs} 10^{12gs}
15^{10g} 6^{10hy} 9^{12sd} 4^{10sd} **3-0-12 £11,421**

Duka *W R Muir* a45
2 b g Diktat - Shalverton (Ire)
11^{8sd} **0-0-1**

Duke Of Venice (USA) *Saeed Bin Suroor* 100
4 b g Theatrical - Rihan (USA)
16^{16g} 6^{12gs} **0-0-2 £420**

Dulce Sueno *I Semple* 46
2 b f Lahib (USA) - Graceland Lady (Ire)
5^{5g} 5^{6gf} 9^{7s} **0-0-3**

Dumaran (Ire) *P A Blockley* 96 a93
7 b g Be My Chief (USA) - Pine Needle
8^{10sd} 4^{10gs} 9^{10gs} 14^{8g} 4^{10gs} 5^{10s} 10^{8g} UR^{10g}
0-1-8 £2,500

Dumnoni *Julian Poulton* 96 a95
4 b f Titus Livius (Fr) - Lamees (USA)
2^{8gs} 2^{7gs} 4^{8gf} 5^{8s} 7^{7g} 6^{8sd} **0-2-6**
£15,060

Dunaskin (Ire) *Karen McLintock* 107
5 b g Bahhare (USA) - Mirwara (Ire)
3^{10gs} 15^{12gf} 12^{11gf} 6^{10s} **0-1-4 £5,717**

Duncanbil (Ire) *J J Bridger* a35
4 b f Turtle Island (Ire) - Saintly Guest
11^{10sd} 10^{6sd} 4^{6sd} 8^{10sd} **0-0-4**

Dundonald *M Appleby* 51 a51
6 ch g Magic Ring (Ire) - Cal Norma's Lady (Ire)
5^{9sd} 2^{9sd} 8^{7sd} 1^{7sd} 11^{9sd} 5^{7sd} 6^{9sd} 4^{9sd} 7^{10gf}
5^{7gf} 7^{8f} 9^{9sd} **1-1-12 £1,923**

Dundry *G L Moore* 86
4 b g Bin Ajwaad (Ire) - China's Pearl
5^{11gs} 11^{10s} 2^{14gs} 1^{14s} 8^{14gf} 7^{15gs} 2^{14g} 11^{14gs}
6^{15s} **1-2-9 £16,508**

Dune Melody (Ire) *J S Moore* 82
2 b f Distant Music (USA) - Desert Gift
2^{5gs} 3^{5g} 4^{5gf} 3^{6f} 1^{6s} 13^{6gf} 10^{6gf} 4^{6g} 3^{6gf}
9^{7gs} **1-3-10 £22,505**

Dune Raider (USA) *K A Ryan* 83
4 b g Kingmambo (USA) - Glowing Honor (USA)
9^{10gs} 17^{13s} 7^{16g} 7^{10gs} 5^{12g} 2^{11gf} 2^{12gf} 3^{17g}
3^{16gf} 6^{20s} **0-2-10 £5,853**

Dunelight (Ire) *C G Cox* 84
2 ch c Desert Sun - Badee'A (Ire)
2^{7gf} 3^{7g} 1^{8g} **1-2-3 £6,748**

Dunmaglass (USA) *P F I Cole* 47
3 ch g Cat Thief (USA) - Indian Fashion (USA)
5^{12gf} **0-0-1**

Dunmore Derry (Ire) *B J Meehan* a59
3 b c Montjeu (Ire) - Louju (USA)
6^{10sd} 8^{10sd} **0-0-2**

Dunn Deal (Ire) *W M Brisbourne* 74
5 b g Revoque (Ire) - Buddy And Soda (Ire)
11^{5gs} 3^{5hy} 2^{6s} 6^{6s} 2^{5gs} 3^{6g} 12^{5gf} 3^{5g} 3^{5s}

5^{5gf} 2^{6g} 5^{5gf} 3^{6g} 1^{6g} 1^{6g} 8^{6g} 19^{6g} 12^{6gf} 14^{6gs} **2-8-19 £24,405**

Dunnett Again (Ire) *Mrs C A Dunnett* 50 a41
4 b c Petardia - Pat Said No (Ire)
4^{7gf} 7^{7gs} 14^{8g} 14^{8gf} 14^{7gf} 7^{7g} 9^{8hy} 5^{7sd} 5^{6sd} 2^{7sd} **0-1-10 £705**

Duroob *K R Burke* 81
3 b g Bahhare (USA) - Amaniy (USA)
2^{10g} 10^{10gs} 8^{12gs} 5^{12gf} 3^{12g} 5^{14g} 4^{15gf} 4^{17g} 8^{13g} 5^{16gf} 10^{17gs} **0-1-11 £4,363**

Dusty City (Ire) *W G M Turner* 76 a79
2 ch g City On A Hill (USA) - Christan (Ire)
4^{5g} 1^{5g} 3^{5sd} 3^{5gs} 5^{6gf} 2^{5gf} **1-3-6 £9,228**

Dusty Dane (Ire) *W G M Turner* 61 a60
3 b g Indian Danehill (Ire) - Teer On Eer (Ire)
5^{10sd} 4^{9sd} 6^{11gs} 6^{12g} **0-0-4 £258**

Dusty Dazzler (Ire) *W G M Turner* a92
5 ch m Titus Livius (Fr) - Satinette
9^{5sd} 11^{5sd} **0-0-2**

Dusty Devil *W G M Turner* 36 a55
2 ch g Fumo Di Londra (Ire) - Lady Sabina
3^{5sd} 8^{5sd} 4^{5gf} 5^{5sd} 5^{6f} 8^{7sd} **0-0-6 £670**

Dutch Key Card (Ire) *C Smith* 52 a73
4 b g Key Of Luck (USA) - Fanny Blankers (Ire)
3^{5sd} 1^{5sd} 7^{6sd} 14^{5gs} 8^{6sd} 16^{5gf} 8^{5gf} 14^{5gf} 9^{5g} 5^{6gs} 4^{5ss} **1-1-11 £3,769**

Duty (Ire) *Sir Michael Stoute* a42
2 b c Rainbow Quest (USA) - Wendylina (Ire)
8^{9sd} **0-0-1**

Duxford *D K Ivory* a59
4 ch g Young Ern - Marsara
3^{7sd} **0-1-1 £498**

Dvinsky (USA) *A W Carroll* 76 a73
4 b g Stravinsky (USA) - Festive Season (USA)
8^{8sd} 2^{7sd} 9^{9sd} 4^{7sd} 2^{6sd} 5^{6sd} 2^{7sd} 3^{6g} 1^{7gs} 7^{7gf} 4^{6gf} 2^{7f} 4^{7gf} 3^{8gf} 8^{6gf} 7^{7g} 7^{7gf} 2^{7gf} 4^{6gs} 5^{8g} 3^{8gf} 6^{7sd} 2^{7s} 8^{7gf} 12^{8g} 6^{7g} **1-10-26 £14,037**

Dyanita *B W Hills* 68 a73
2 b f Singspiel (Ire) - Dance Clear (Ire)
6^{7gf} 6^{7g} 2^{7sd} **0-1-3 £1,212**

Dylan (Ire) *N Tinkler* 53 a22
2 b g Mull Of Kintyre (USA) - Rose Of Shuaib (Ire)
5^{7g} 11^{6gf} 10^{6gf} 8^{6gf} 13^{6gf} 6^{7sd} **0-0-6**

Dylan Thomas (Ire) *A P O'Brien* 101
2 b c Danehill (USA) - Lagrion (USA)
1^{7f} 1^{7gy} 2^{8g} 6^{8hy} **2-1-4 £101,984**

Dynacam (USA) *Sir Michael Stoute* 79 a54
2 b f Dynaformer (USA) - Najecam (USA)
5^{7sd} 12^{7sd} 1^{10hy} **1-0-3 £3,406**

Dynamic Rhythm (USA) *J Noseda* 74
2 b c Kingmambo (USA) - Palme D'Or (Ire)
7^{7gs} 2^{8s} **0-1-2 £1,490**

Dynamite Blond *Miss D Mountain* 48 a3
2 b f Xaar - Hannalou (Fr)
12^{5sd} 8^{6gf} 6^{6gf} 7^{6gf} UR^{6gf} 17^{7gf} **0-0-6**

Dynamite Deano *D K Ivory* 53 a48
2 b g Dracula (Aus) - Katy Ivory (Ire)
7^{6sd} 8^{7g} 10^{7sd} **0-0-3**

Dysonic (USA) *D Burchell* 43 a48
3 b g Aljabr (USA) - Atyab (USA)
9^{10gf} 16^{12s} 8^{10g} 7^{7g} 5^{5sd} 15^{6f} 6^{9sd} **0-0-7**

Dzhani *S C Williams* 10
2 b c Singspiel (Ire) - Heuston Station (Ire)
15^{8s} **0-0-1**

E Bride (USA) *T T Clement* 50 a6
3 gr/ro f Runaway Groom (Can) - Fast Selection (USA)
9^{8s} 9^{10g} 14^{10g} 5^{10g} 7^{12gf} 12^{8sd} 13^{11sd} 13^{10sd} **0-0-8**

E Minor (Ire) *T Wall* a38
6 b m Blushing Flame (USA) - Watch The Clock
4^{17sd} 11^{12sd} **0-0-2**

Eabha (Ire) *G A Swinbank* 47
4 b/br f Danzero (Aus) - Decant
5^{9f} **0-0-1**

Eager Angel (Ire) *R F Marvin* a17
7 b m Up And At 'Em - Seanee Squaw
10^{6sd} 10^{7sd} 11^{6sd} **0-0-3**

Earl Kraul (Ire) *G L Moore* 71 a59
2 b g Imperial Ballet (Ire) - Bu Hagab (Ire)
11^{6g} 5^{7f} 9^{7sd} 3^{7gs} 8^{7sd} **0-1-5 £576**

Earl Of Spectrum (Ger) *J L Spearing* 47 a29
4 b g Spectrum (Ire) - Evry (Ger)
8^{7sd} 6^{10g} 7^{12gs} **0-0-3**

Earlsfield Raider *G L Moore* 50
5 ch g Double Trigger (Ire) - Harlequin Walk (Ire)
3^{22s} 11^{18g} **0-1-2 £834**

Early Evening *H Candy* 50
2 b f Daylami (Ire) - Regent Court (Ire)
7^{6gf} **0-0-1**

Earth Master (Ire) *S Kirk* 79 a20
2 gr g Grand Lodge (USA) - Beautiful France (Ire)
7^{7ys} 1^{7g} 13^{8gf} 12^{7hy} 11^{8sd} **1-0-5 £9,234**

Earthling *D W Chapman* 20 a56
4 b g Rainbow Quest (USA) - Cruising Height
6^{9sd} 14^{8g} 6^{7gf} 13^{9sd} **0-0-4**

Easibet Dot Net *I Semple* 77 a55
5 gr g Atraf - Silvery
2^{12gf} 10^{10g} 1^{11gf} 5^{10gf} 4^{11gf} 7^{12sd} 9^{12gs} **1-1-7 £5,442**

East Cape *N Tinkler* 40 a48
8 b g Bering - Reine De Danse (USA)
3^{13gs} 3^{14sd} 7^{14sd} 7^{16gf} 10^{10g} 10^{13s} 5^{12sd} 4^{12ss} 6^{11sd} 9^{12sd} **0-2-10 £810**

East Riding *Miss A Stokell* 34 a29
5 b m Gothenberg (Ire) - Bettynouche
9^{11sd} 9^{11sd} 6^{8s} 13^{9g} **0-0-4**

Eastborough (Ire) *B G Powell* 81 a78
6 b g Woodborough (USA) - Easter Girl
4^{10sd} 3^{12sd} 1^{12sd} 6^{12sd} 7^{10sd} 4^{17sd} 3^{15gs} 1^{13gs} 7^{14g} 5^{14gs} 8^{14sd} 2^{13gf} 13^{11g} 1^{11gf} 3^{16gf} 3^{10gf} 12^{12f} 8^{9sd} 10^{10sd} 7^{12sd} **3-5-20 £19,900**

Easter Egg (USA) *J H M Gosden* 62
3 b f Danzig (USA) - Sugar Hill Chick (USA)
7^{8g} 10^{7gs} 8^{7gf} **0-0-3**

Easter Ogil (Ire) *Jane Southcombe* 44 a84
10 ch g Pips Pride - Piney Pass
3^{8sd} 1^{10sd} 9^{10sd} 8^{13sd} 2^{9gs} 13^{10hy} 10^{11gf} 9^{10sd} 11^{12sd} **1-1-9 £3,408**

Eastern Empress *W R Swinburn* 68
2 b f Mujadil (USA) - Noble One
11^{6gf} 8^{6g} 3^{6g} **0-1-3 £656**

Eastern Hope (Ire) *Mrs L Stubbs* 49 a58
6 b g Danehill Dancer (Ire) - Hope And Glory (USA)
8[9sd] 2[7g] 12[8g] **0-1-3 £790**

Eastern Mandarin *Karen McLintock* 41
3 b g Tipsy Creek (USA) - Hotel Street (USA)
9[7gs] 14[7s] 8[8gf] 10[7gf] 3[7f] 18[7g] 13[6gf] 10[7gf]
0-1-8 £425

Eastern Tribute (USA) *A C Whillans*
9 b g Affirmed (USA) - Mia Duchessa (USA)
10[9s] **0-0-1**

Eastfields Lad *S R Bowring* 27 a14
3 b g Overbury (Ire) - Honey Day
9[6sd] 6[7gf] 13[8g] 9[11sd] 7[8sd] **0-0-5**

Eastwell Magic *J G Given*
3 b f Polish Precedent (USA) - Kinchenjunga
14[10s] **0-0-1**

Easy Air *E A L Dunlop* a75
2 ch c Zafonic (USA) - Easy Option (Ire)
1[6sd] **1-0-1 £3,860**

Easy Feeling (Ire) *R Hannon* 77 a59
3 b f Night Shift (USA) - Talena
14[7gf] 4[7gf] 8[6g] 5[7gf] 7[7gf] 4[7gf] 3[7gf] 2[9g] 9[7g]
13[7gf] 9[7sd] 10[7sd] 6[6sd] **0-2-13 £2,998**

Easy Laughter (Ire) *A King* 69 a73
4 b c Danehill (USA) - All To Easy
12[7g] 9[7g] 10[8g] 10[10g] 6[8g] 2[7gs] 10[8sd] 6[7sd] 1[9sd]
3[9sd] 4[12sd] **1-3-11 £5,263**

Easy Mover (Ire) *Rae Guest* 74
3 ch f Bluebird (USA) - Top Brex (Fr)
14[9g] 5[8g] 3[8f] 2[10g] 3[10g] 3[8g] 9[9g] **0-3-7**
£3,974

Eathie *R F Marvin*
3 ch g Bluegrass Prince (Ire) - Persian Fortune
13[6g] **0-0-1**

Ebert *P J Makin* 54 a69
2 b g Polish Precedent (USA) - Fanfare
7[7g] 3[7sd] 2[8sd] **0-2-3 £1,617**

Ebinzayd (Ire) *L Lungo* 55
9 b g Tenby - Sharakawa (Ire)
8[17gf] **0-0-1**

Ebony Lady *R M Whitaker* 46
2 br f Vettori (Ire) - Keen Melody (USA)
8[7g] 15[9g] 12[7gf] 11[8s] **0-0-4**

Ebony Lord *A M Balding* 54
2 b c Fraam - Dorissio (Ire)
9[7g] 6[7gf] 4[7gs] PU[7sd] **0-0-4**

Ebonywood (USA) *P C Haslam* 76
2 b f Montbrook (USA) - Brazen Blaze (USA)
3[6g] 3[6gf] 6[7gf] 2[6g] 8[6gy] **0-2-5 £3,927**

Eboracum (Ire) *T D Easterby* 69
4 b f Alzao (USA) - Fire Of London
13[8g] 4[9gf] **0-0-2 £514**

Eborarry (Ire) *T D Easterby* 56
3 b g Desert Sun - Aztec Princess
17[10f] 1[8gf] 5[10g] 13[8gf] 7[8gf] 14[10g] **1-0-6**
£3,406

Ebraam (USA) *E A L Dunlop* 52
2 b c Red Ransom (USA) - Futuh (USA)
13[7g] **0-0-1**

Ebtikaar (Ire) *J L Dunlop* 98
3 b c Darshaan - Jawlaat (USA)
3[10gf] 2[10g] 1[12gf] 7[16gf] 8[11gs] 2[12gf] 3[12gs] 1[12s]
11[12hy] **2-4-9 £22,829**

Eccentric *Andrew Reid* 111 a113
4 ch g Most Welcome - Sure Care
1[10sd] 1[8sd] 2[10sd] 1[10sd] 1[10sd] 5[9g] 1[10g] 9[8sd] 6[10gs]
2[11gf] 1[10g] 8[10gf] 8[9gs] 16[11ft] **6-2-14**
£199,192

Eccentricity (USA) *H R A Cecil* 75
3 ch f Kingmambo (USA) - Shiva (Jpn)
2[8g] **0-1-1 £1,544**

Eccollo (Ire) *Saeed Bin Suroor* 46
3 b c Spectrum (Ire) - Taking Liberties (Ire)
8[10s] **0-0-1**

Echelon *Sir Michael Stoute* 102
3 b f Danehill (USA) - Exclusive
3[7gs] 9[8gf] 3[6g] 2[8gf] 1[8gf] 4[8s] 1[7g] **2-3-7**
£50,940

Echo Of Light *Saeed Bin Suroor* 113
3 b c Dubai Millennium - Spirit Of Tara (Ire)
2[8g] RO[10gs] 1[11gf] 1[10gs] 15[10gs] **2-1-5**
£16,460

Eclipse Park *M J McGrath* a72
2 ch c Rainbow Quest (USA) - Gino's Spirits
6[7sd] 5[8sd] **0-0-2**

Ecomium (Ire) *J Noseda* 111 a104
4 b c Sadler's Wells (USA) - Encens
6[10sd] 4[10gs] 7[8gs] 2[10s] **0-1-4 £8,660**

Economic (Ire) *Saeed Bin Suroor* 76
2 b c Danehill Dancer (Ire) - Warusha (Ger)
4[7s] 1[8hy] **1-0-2 £2,397**

Edaara (Ire) *W J Haggas* 82
2 ch f Pivotal - Green Bonnet (Ire)
3[7gf] 2[8gs] **0-2-2 £4,213**

Edas *L M Cumani* 86
3 b c Celtic Swing - Eden (Ire)
4[10s] 6[10g] 1[10gf] 4[10f] 11[12g] 10[9g] 11[10s]
1-0-7 £4,200

Eddies Jewel *I W McInnes* 50 a35
5 b g Presidium - Superstream
8[9sd] 9[7g] 4[7s] 1[8gf] 7[8g] 7[7gs] 7[8g] 2[8g] 12[9sd] 3[7g]
10[7sd] **1-2-11 £2,191**

Eden Rock (Ire) *Sir Michael Stoute* 104
4 b g Danehill (USA) - Marlene-D
1[8gf] 12[8gf] 8[8gf] 4[8gf] 13[9gf] **1-1-5**
£9,483

Eden Star (Ire) *D K Ivory* 46 a50
3 b f Soviet Star (USA) - Gold Prospector (Ire)
4[5sd] 4[6sd] 3[6sd] 7[7sd] 7[6sd] 1[6sd] 14[6gs] 8[7gf] 3[6gf]
3[6f] 11[6f] 11[8f] UR[6gf] 7[6sd] 11[7g] 12[7sd]
1-3-16 £2,812

Edge Fund *Miss Gay Kelleway* 71 a6
3 b g Bold Edge - Truly Madly Deeply
6[6gs] 12[6g] 14[6gf] 11[6g] 5[6gf] 8[8gf] 2[8gf] 1[8g] 4[8g]
12[8g] 5[7f] 8[8f] 11[7gs] 14[8sd] **1-1-14**
£5,189

Edge Of Blue *R Hannon* 62
3 b g Bold Edge - Blue Goddess (Ire)
3[5g] 15[6gf] 9[6gf] 7[7gf] 5[5gf] 11[7gf] 17[6gf]
0-1-7 £578

Edge Of Italy *C G Cox* 39
3 ch f Bold Edge - Brera (Ire)
13[5gf] 13[7gf] 13[6gs] **0-0-3**

Edged In Gold *P J Makin* 49 a61
3 ch f Bold Edge - Piccante
8[5sd] 5[5sd] 6[5g] 1[5sd] 18[5g] 16[5gf] 11[5sd]
1-0-7 £2,957

Edgehill (Ire) *R Ford* 62 a68
4 b g Ali-Royal (Ire) - Elfin Queen (Ire)
5[10sd] 6[10sd] 11[8gf] 6[10gf] 12[10gf] 1[12gf] 4[12gs] 4[14g]
5[10gf] 1[12sd] **2-1-10 £6,961**

Edict *C J Down* 51 a49
3 br f Diktat - Pericardia
7^{8g} 8^{8gf} 12^{8f} 4^{12sd} 13^{9sf} 13^{12sd} 6^{12sd}
0-0-7

Edin Burgher (Fr) *T T Clement* a61
4 br g Hamas (Ire) - Jaljuli
4^{7sd} 7^{8sd} 1^{6sd} 1^{6sd} **2-0-4 £3,665**

Edward (Ire) *A P Jarvis* 56
3 b g Namid - Daltak
7^{6g} 11^{6g} **0-0-2**

Eeshee *S L Keightley* 46 a53
2 b f Distant Music (USA) - Madame Curie
15^{6gs} 6^{6g} 2^{5sd} **0-1-3 £1,196**

Effective *A P Jarvis* 85 a71
5 ch g Bahamian Bounty - Efficacy
10^{7sd} 5^{7sd} 3^{7s} 5^{7g} 3^{7gf} 1^{6g} 1^{5gf} 1^{6f} 4^{6sd}
1^{6s} 7^{6g} 6^{5g} **4-2-12 £18,773**

Efiacto *N Bycroft*
2 ch g Defacto (USA) - Efipetite
8^{5s} **0-0-1**

Efidium *N Bycroft* 77
7 b g Presidium - Efipetite
11^{6s} 8^{8g} 9^{8gf} 3^{7f} 10^{8gf} 2^{7f} 4^{7f} 4^{7gf} 6^{8gf}
7^{7g} 3^{8gf} 5^{7gf} 11^{7gf} 1^{8g} 10^{7g} 8^{6g} 7^{8gf} 8^{7gf}
1-3-18 £7,448

Efimac *N Bycroft* 53 a37
5 b m Presidium - Efipetite
9^{7g} 6^{7gf} 12^{7gf} 9^{8g} 4^{7gf} 4^{7g} 7^{11gf} 4^{8g} 9^{8gf}
15^{8gf} 4^{7g} 9^{8sd} 10^{8sd} 9^{6sd} **0-1-14 £810**

Efistorm *J Balding* a74
4 b g Efisio - Abundance
13^{6sd} 10^{5sd} 3^{5sd} **0-1-3 £1,004**

Eforetta (Ger) *D J Wintle* 41 a54
3 ch f Dr Fong (USA) - Erminora (Ger)
13^{6sd} 1^{7sd} 2^{9sd} 9^{8gf} 11^{8gs} 11^{6sd} 9^{8sd}
1-1-7 £2,352

Efrhina (Ire) *Stef Liddiard* 70 a70
5 ch m Woodman (USA) - Eshq Albahr (USA)
1^{12sd} 1^{11sd} 2^{12sd} 6^{12sd} 8^{12sd} 5^{12sd} 8^{11g} 3^{11sd}
1^{14sd} 2^{12f} 5^{13f} 14^{10g} 4^{12gf} 7^{12g} 10^{14gf} 4^{12g}
8^{14ft} 6^{12sd} 1^{11sd} 7^{12sd} 6^{12sd} **4-2-21**
£14,503

Egeria (Ire) *J R Fanshawe* 64
3 gr f Daylami (Ire) - Spring
7^{12g} 4^{12gf} 5^{12gf} 7^{12gf} 4^{14gf} **0-0-5 £634**

Ego Trip *M W Easterby* 68
4 b g Deploy - Boulevard Rouge (USA)
5^{12s} 5^{12gf} 8^{13s} 1^{12g} 7^{12gs} 6^{12gs} 2^{14s} 5^{12s} 3^{14s}
1-2-9 £6,433

Egyptian Lord *Peter Grayson* 50 a68
2 ch g Bold Edge - Calypso Lady (Ire)
11^{5g} 9^{5gf} 8^{6sd} 3^{5gf} 14^{6gf} 3^{7sd} 5^{6sd} 6^{6sd} 1^{5sd}
2^{5sd} **1-2-10 £6,377**

Eidsfoss (Ire) *T T Clement* 38 a40
3 b g Danehill Dancer (Ire) - Alca Egeria (Ity)
9^{9sd} 13^{10gs} 7^{8f} 5^{7gf} 12^{6sd} 11^{9sd} **0-0-6**

Eight Ellington (Ire) *R M Stronge* 16 a48
4 b g Ali-Royal (Ire) - Where's Charlotte
4^{7sd} 1^{9sd} 12^{8sd} 9^{10sd} 12^{10s} 7^{8f} **1-0-6**
£1,298

Eight Trumps *A Dickman*
5 ch g First Trump - Misty Silks
7^{12sd} **0-0-1**

Eijaaz (Ire) *Mrs L Stubbs* 63 a69
4 b g Green Desert (USA) - Kismah
12^{8sd} 1^{10sd} 3^{10sd} 10^{10sd} 4^{10sd} 4^{10s} 6^{10s} 8^{10gf}
3^{10gf} 1^{10g} 3^{10g} 4^{10gf} 7^{11gf} 4^{10gf} 10^{10gf}
2-3-15 £8,413

Eilean Ban (USA) *E A L Dunlop* 99
2 ch f Silver Hawk (USA) - Isla Del Rey (USA)
2^{7g} 1^{7gf} 6^{8gs} **1-1-3 £8,744**

Eisteddfod *P F I Cole* 116
4 ch g Cadeaux Genereux - Ffestiniog (Ire)
3^{6g} 4^{7gf} 5^{6gs} 1^{6g} 1^{6g} 2^{6g} 1^{6gs} 7^{5gs} **3-3-8**
£81,434

Ekaterina *W Storey* 14
3 b f Merdon Melody - Hsian
7^{9gs} 10^{7gs} **0-0-2**

Ektishaaf *C F Wall* 72 a59
3 b f Mujahid (USA) - Tahnee
4^{7f} 8^{8gf} 7^{9sd} 13^{7g} 18^{8gf} **0-0-5 £292**

El Alamein (Ire) *Sir Mark Prescott* 48 a20
2 ch g Nashwan (USA) - El Rabab (USA)
7^{6s} 9^{6hy} 10^{7sd} **0-0-3**

El Barco (Ire) *K A Ryan* 26
2 b g Carrowkeel (Ire) - Life On The Street
7^{5s} 6^{5g} 9^{6gf} **0-0-3**

El Capitan (Fr) *N A Callaghan* 73 a73
2 b c Danehill Dancer (Ire) - Fille Dansante (Ire)
4^{6gf} 2^{6sd} 3^{7sd} 17^{6g} 9^{6g} 3^{8g} 9^{8g} **0-3-7**
£2,656

El Chaparral (Ire) *W J Haggas* 74 a81
5 b g Bigstone (Ire) - Low Line
4^{9sd} 9^{10sd} 7^{12sd} 6^{13sd} 1^{9sd} 6^{9sd} 8^{8g} 6^{10gf} 12^{10gf}
3^{12gf} 3^{12gf} 1^{12sd} 6^{10gf} 3^{10gf} UR^{11gs} 9^{10s} 2^{12sd}
6^{10s} 9^{12sd} 6^{12sd} 2^{9sd} **2-5-21 £9,918**

El Coto *E S McMahon* 101
5 b g Forzando - Thatcherella
16^{8g} 4^{8gs} 6^{8gs} 6^{7s} 4^{7s} 1^{7gf} **1-1-6**
£16,112

El Dee (Ire) *D Carroll* 46
2 br g Brave Act - Go Flightline (Ire)
8^{7gf} 9^{7gf} 11^{8gf} 11^{8s} **0-0-4**

El Faro (Fr) *M R Channon* 60
2 b c Fantastic Light (USA) - Pagoda (Fr)
8^{8s} **0-0-1**

El Giza (USA) *Miss J R Tooth* a44
7 ch g Cozzene (USA) - Gazayil (USA)
12^{9sd} 3^{9sd} 7^{9sd} 7^{12sd} 13^{10s} 11^{9sd} **0-1-6**
£213

El Magnifico *P D Cundell* a28
4 b g Forzando - Princess Poquito
9^{9sd} 13^{14sd} **0-0-2**

El Palmar *J Pearce* 66 a64
4 b g Case Law - Aybeegirl
2^{7sd} 4^{8sd} 8^{7sd} 5^{7s} 17^{7g} 1^{8sd} 6^{9sd} **1-1-7**
£3,539

El Potro *E S McMahon* a67
3 b c Forzando - Gaelic Air
4^{6sd} 3^{6sd} 6^{6ft} 4^{5sd} 1^{5sd} 1^{5sd} **2-0-6**
£6,904

El Rey Del Mambo (USA) *G A Butler* 88
3 b g Kingmambo (USA) - Scarab Bracelet (USA)
3^{6gf} 1^{6gf} 4^{7gf} 5^{7gf} 4^{7gs} 8^{8gf} 15^{6gf} **1-1-7**
£7,984

El Rey Royale *M D Hammond* 60
3 b g Royal Applause - Spanish Serenade
9^{8gf} 9^{10s} 5^{10gf} 11^{8gf} 2^{10g} 3^{10gf} 18^{10g} 14^{14g}
0-2-8 £2,177

El Tiger (Ger) *B J Curley*
4 b g Tiger Hill (Ire) - Elea (Ger)

11^{12gs} 10^{12s} 13^{8s} **0-0-3**

Ela Figura *M Appleby* 15 a46
5 ch m The West (USA) - Chili Bouchier (USA)
9^{5sd} 3^{5sd} 6^{5sd} 14^{6gf} **0-1-4 £210**

Ela Paparouna *H Candy* 81 a82
4 b f Vettori (Ire) - Pretty Poppy
1^{7gf} 4^{8g} 2^{7sd} 7^{7g} 14^{7g} **1-1-5 £6,227**

Ela Re *Mrs S J Smith* a16
6 ch g Sabrehill (USA) - Lucia Tarditi (Fr)
13^{16sd} **0-0-1**

Elaala (USA) *M Todhunter* 59 a46
3 ch f Aljabr (USA) - Nufuth (USA)
6^{10g} 6^{12s} 10^{12g} 7^{10sd} 5^{12sd} 4^{14g} **0-1-6 £231**

Eldon Outlaw *B Storey* 46
2 b g Hunting Lion (Ire) - La Noisette
7^{6gs} 12^{7gf} 12^{5g} **0-0-3**

Eldori *M S Saunders*
2 b f Vettori (Ire) - Elderberry
13^{7sd} **0-0-1**

Election Seeker (Ire) *G L Moore* 73
3 b g Intikhab (USA) - Scottish Eyes (USA)
1^{8gf} **1-0-1 £3,588**

Electric Warrior (Ire) *K R Burke* 49
2 b g Bold Fact (USA) - Dungeon Princess (Ire)
9^{6gf} **0-0-1**

Electrocutionist (USA) *V Valiani* 125
4 b c Red Ransom (USA) - Elbaaha
1^{12gf} 1^{12gf} 1^{10g} 3^{12y} **3-1-4 £552,817**

Elegant Times (Ire) *T D Easterby* 71
2 b f Dansili - Simply Times (USA)
4^{6g} 3^{7gf} 8^{7gf} **0-1-3 £1,149**

Element Of Truth (USA) *L M Cumani* 88
3 ch f Atticus (USA) - My Shafy
1^{8g} 5^{10gf} 3^{7gf} 12^{8g} **1-1-4 £9,007**

Elgin Marbles *R Hannon* 76
3 b g Lujain (USA) - Bold Gem
14^{6g} 10^{6gs} 4^{6gf} 12^{7gf} **0-0-4 £530**

Elidore *B Palling* 74
5 b m Danetime (Ire) - Beveled Edge
5^{10s} 5^{10s} 3^{8g} 6^{8gf} 3^{8g} 1^{8gf} 1^{8gf} 8^{8gf} 12^{8g} 7^{8gf} 13^{8gs} **2-2-11 £7,900**

Eliminator *I W McInnes* 69
2 ch c Observatory (USA) - Effie
13^{6gs} 2^{6gf} 4^{6gf} 6^{7gs} **0-1-4 £1,387**

Elise *Sir Michael Stoute* 78
2 b f Fantastic Light (USA) - Napoleon's Sister (Ire)
6^{7gf} 9^{8gf} 1^{8gs} **1-0-3 £4,947**

Elisha (Ire) *D M Simcock* 70 a46
3 ch f Raise A Grand (Ire) - Social Butterfly (USA)
6^{6gf} 2^{6f} 9^{6g} 13^{6g} 7^{6gf} 6^{6gf} 5^{5g} 12^{6sd} 17^{6gf} **0-1-9 £1,030**

Elite Land *N Bycroft* 47
2 b c Namaqualand (USA) - Petite Elite
16^{5g} 5^{5g} 10^{7gf} 11^{6gf} 11^{7g} 8^{8g} 10^{10g} 7^{8gf} **0-0-8**

Elizabethan Age (Fr) *W J Haggas* 70 a67
3 b f King's Best (USA) - Dolydille (Ire)
5^{8s} 4^{8g} 3^{10gf} 2^{8g} 2^{8g} 1^{7sd} **1-2-6 £6,668**

Elkhorn *A M Balding* 76
3 b g Indian Ridge - Rimba (USA)
10^{7g} 5^{7gf} 4^{7gs} 12^{7g} 7^{6g} **0-0-5 £442**

Ellamyte *G F Bridgwater* 10 a37
5 b m Elmaamul (USA) - Deanta In Eirinn
8^{5sd} 10^{8sd} 9^{6sd} 10^{5sd} 5^{5sd} 14^{5s} 6^{6sd} 17^{6g} **0-0-8**

Ellcon (Ire) *A Bailey* 68
2 b f Royal Applause - Carranita (Ire)
7^{5gs} 4^{5s} 13^{5gf} 3^{5f} 7^{5gf} **0-1-5 £914**

Elle Nino *G Wragg* 39 a72
3 b f Inchinor - Robellino Miss (USA)
14^{8g} 5^{10sd} 7^{8sd} 13^{8gs} **0-0-4**

Ellen Mooney *Mrs G S Rees* a58
6 ch m Efisio - Budby
6^{9sd} 5^{9sd} **0-0-2**

Ellens Academy (Ire) *E J Alston* 94
10 b g Royal Academy (USA) - Lady Ellen
11^{6g} 5^{6gf} 2^{5gf} 3^{6g} 11^{6gf} 2^{6g} 5^{5g} 15^{6g} 7^{6g} 9^{6gf} 22^{6g} **0-3-11 £12,507**

Ellens Princess (Ire) *R Hannon* 59 a60
3 b f Desert Prince (Ire) - Lady Ellen
3^{7sd} 16^{6gs} 3^{6gs} 6^{7gf} 9^{7g} 1^{7g} **1-2-6 £4,504**

Elleray (Ire) *J G Given* a38
3 b f Docksider (USA) - Saint Ann (USA)
12^{10sd} **0-0-1**

Ellerslie Jack (Ire) *T P Tate* 53 a18
3 b g Danetime (Ire) - White Jasmin
10^{5gs} 8^{6gf} 9^{8g} 11^{7sd} **0-0-4**

Ellerslie Tom *P Bowen* 69
3 br g Octagonal (NZ) - Tetravella (Ire)
1^{12gf} **1-0-1 £3,406**

Ellesappelle *K R Burke* 67
2 b f Benny The Dip (USA) - Zizi (Ire)
3^{6g} 2^{6s} 9^{8g} 3^{7gf} 11^{7g} **0-3-5 £2,932**

Elli Lewtia *J Jay* 33
2 ch f Tomba - Troia (Ire)
5^{5gf} 16^{8g} 23^{7s} **0-0-3**

Ellina *J Pearce* 68 a79
4 b f Robellino (USA) - Native Flair
3^{12s} 2^{12s} 5^{12sd} 8^{12f} 7^{13f} 9^{12g} 13^{12gf} 1^{14sd} 1^{17sd} 5^{12g} 4^{16g} 1^{14ft} 4^{17sd} **3-2-13 £10,860**

Elliot's Choice (Ire) *R A Harris* 48 a61
4 b g Foxhound (USA) - Indian City
11^{7sd} 1^{5sd} 12^{5gf} 8^{5gf} 4^{5sd} 7^{5g} 8^{6g} 16^{5g} **1-0-8 £3,721**

Elliots World (Ire) *M Johnston* 111
3 b c King's Best (USA) - Morning Welcome (Ire)
2^{10gs} 18^{8gf} 9^{8g} 2^{8gs} 3^{10gf} 3^{10gs} 4^{8gs} 2^{8gf} 1^{8gs} **1-6-9 £47,294**

Ellis Cave *M J Polglase* 38 a38
3 gr g Diktat - Cole Slaw
11^{6sd} 6^{5sd} 12^{6sd} 8^{8sd} 4^{5s} 6^{5s} 4^{6sd} 5^{6sd} 7^{6s} 12^{7f} 7^{11gs} **0-0-11**

Ello Lucky (Ire) *J M Bradley* 33 a20
3 b f Key Of Luck (USA) - Ellopassoff
11^{8sd} 10^{7sd} 18^{8g} 9^{7s} 10^{7gf} **0-0-5**

Ellway Heights *W M Brisbourne* 56
8 b g Shirley Heights - Amina
6^{12gf} 5^{12gf} 2^{16gf} 1^{16gf} **1-1-4 £4,165**

Ellway Prospect *M G Rimell* 39 a44
5 ch m Pivotal - Littlemisstrouble (USA)
6^{16sd} 6^{17sd} 9^{15gs} 10^{17sd} **0-0-4**

Elms Schoolboy *J M P Eustace* 47 a50
3 ch g Komaite (USA) - Elms Schoolgirl
13^{8gf} 9^{8sd} 5^{8gf} 5^{12gf} 5^{10f} 4^{11g} 1^{8sd} 15^{8g} 8^{8sd} 8^{8ss} **1-0-10 £1,494**

Elopement (Ire) *D J Daly* 58 a40

3 ch f Machiavellian (USA) - Melanzane
8^{8sd} 4^{8gs} 4^{8f} **0-0-3 £683**

Eloquent Knight (USA) *W R Muir* 70 a72
3 gr c Aljabr (USA) - Matinee Mimic (USA)
6^{7g} 1^{8gs} 2^{8gf} 4^{10gs} 6^{10gf} 5^{11sd} 6^{10sd} **1-1-7 £6,578**

Elraawy (USA) *E A L Dunlop* 82
3 b/br g Red Ransom (USA) - Fatina
6^{10gf} 6^{10gf} 2^{10g} 6^{12gf} 2^{10g} 1^{12gs} 13^{11gf} **1-1-7 £9,374**

Elrafa Mujahid *E R Oertel* 73 a81
3 b f Mujahid (USA) - Fancier Bit
4^{7sd} 10^{8g} 1^{7gs} 5^{7f} 12^{8gf} 7^{7s} 12^{8sd} 1^{8sd} 10^{8sd} **2-0-9 £8,064**

Elsie Hart (Ire) *T D Easterby* 74
3 b f Revoque (Ire) - Family At War (USA)
17^{6hy} 5^{7gs} 14^{6g} 19^{7hy} 12^{8s} **0-0-5**

Elsinora *A G Juckes*
4 b f Great Dane (Ire) - Deanta In Eirinn
15^{8gf} **0-0-1**

Elusive Double (Ire) *D K Weld* 96
3 ch c Grand Lodge (USA) - Lady Luck (Ire)
3^{7hy} 21^{8gf} 13^{8gf} 10^{8g} 4^{8y} **0-0-5 £6,292**

Elusive Dream *Sir Mark Prescott* 98
4 b g Rainbow Quest (USA) - Dance A Dream
4^{14g} 5^{18gs} 3^{17s} **0-1-3 £8,972**

Elusive Warrior (USA) *Mrs A J Perrett* 75 a59
2 b g Elusive Quality (USA) - Love To Fight (Can)
4^{6f} 3^{6gf} 3^{6gf} 12^{7g} 5^{7sd} **0-2-5 £1,740**

Elvina *A G Newcombe* 62 a61
4 b f Mark Of Esteem (Ire) - Pharaoh's Joy
3^{5sd} 12^{6sd} 12^{5gf} 3^{5gf} 6^{5gf} 10^{6gf} 2^{5sd} 1^{5gf} 3^{5gf} 6^{5hd} 11^{6g} 3^{5ss} **1-5-12 £7,004**

Elvina Hills (Ire) *W G M Turner* 60
3 ch f Bluebird (USA) - Women In Love (Ire)
4^{7gf} 7^{8f} **0-0-2 £267**

Elvstroem (Aus) *T Vasil* 121
5 b h Danehill (USA) - Circles Of Gold (Aus)
1^{7gs} 1^{9g} 4^{10g} 1^{9gf} 9^{10gf} 4^{8f} 2^{9g} 3^{10gf} 4^{12gs} **3-2-9 £869,697**

Elzees *Miss J S Davis* a49
4 b g Magic Ring (Ire) - White Flash
7^{10sd} **0-0-1**

Emaradia *A W Carroll* a46
4 ch f Emarati (USA) - Rewardia (Ire)
6^{7sd} 4^{5sd} 5^{6sd} 7^{6sd} 3^{5sd} **0-1-5 £207**

Emarati's Image *B Forsey* 9 a37
7 b g Emarati (USA) - Choir's Image
11^{6sd} 5^{5sd} 4^{5sd} 15^{5s} **0-0-4**

Embark *J R Fanshawe* 7
3 b f Soviet Star (USA) - Shore Line
17^{7g} **0-0-1**

Embassy Lord *J O'Reilly* 50 a51
4 b g Mind Games - Keen Melody (USA)
10^{5sd} 13^{5sd} 12^{6gf} 11^{7gf} **0-0-4**

Embraceable (Ire) *J S Moore* 51 a18
2 b f Mull Of Kintyre (USA) - Embracing
7^{5g} 15^{6gf} 11^{7g} 10^{9sd} **0-0-4**

Emerald Bay (Ire) *M Johnston* 91
3 b c King's Best (USA) - Belle Etoile (Fr)
2^{8s} 1^{8g} 1^{8gf} 4^{8gf} 3^{8gf} 3^{10gf} 5^{9gf} **2-2-7 £18,201**

Emerald Dancer *H Morrison* 46 a56
3 b f Groom Dancer (USA) - Green Bonnet (Ire)
6^{8gf} 4^{8sd} 2^{12sd} 3^{12sf} 8^{10sd} 6^{10sd} **0-2-6 £641**

Emerald Destiny (Ire) *D Carroll* 41
3 b g Key Of Luck (USA) - Green Belt (Fr)
10^{12sd} 8^{8gf} 8^{11gf} 7^{11gf} 10^{12gf} **0-0-5**

Emerald Lodge *J Noseda* 88
3 b c Grand Lodge (USA) - Emerald Peace (Ire)
11^{5s} 9^{6gs} 8^{5gf} 1^{6g} 5^{6gf} **1-0-5 £7,300**

Emerald Storm (USA) *M Johnston* 80
3 ch f Diesis - Green Lady (Ire)
1^{10gf} **1-0-1 £5,512**

Emeraude Du Cap *J O'Reilly* 17
3 b f Tipsy Creek (USA) - High Typha
12^{5g} 13^{7gs} **0-0-2**

Emile Zola *Miss Venetia Williams* 78
3 b c Singspiel (Ire) - Ellie Ardensky
11^{10gs} 5^{12gf} 3^{12gf} 2^{12gf} 3^{12g} 7^{14gf} **0-2-6 £3,862**

Emilion *W J Haggas* 53
2 ch f Fantastic Light (USA) - Riberac
5^{6g} **0-0-1**

Emily (Fr) *C E Brittain* 62
2 b f Dansili - Palomelle (Fr)
2^{5gf} 2^{6g} 6^{6g} 6^{6f} **0-2-4 £2,522**

Emily's Pet (Ire) *B W Duke* a41
2 ch g Raise A Grand (Ire) - Zaola (Ire)
12^{7gf} 8^{7sd} **0-0-2**

Emily's Place (Ire) *M H Tompkins* 67
2 b f Mujadil (USA) - Dulcinea
6^{6gf} 7^{6g} 3^{6g} **0-1-3 £650**

Emily's Will (Ire) *M J Wallace* 52 a42
2 ch f Night Shift (USA) - Flush Rush
6^{5sd} 3^{5s} 8^{5gs} 3^{6f} 6^{5gf} 3^{6gf} 8^{8gf} **0-1-7 £1,777**

Eminence Gift *K R Burke* 58 a53
3 b f Cadeaux Genereux - Germane
6^{9sd} 5^{8s} 3^{7gf} 1^{10g} 1^{10g} 7^{12sd} 2^{11gs} 3^{10s} **2-3-8 £7,545**

Emirates Gold (Ire) *Saeed Bin Suroor* 95
2 b c Royal Applause - Yara (Ire)
1^{6gs} 10^{6gf} 2^{7g} 2^{8gs} **1-2-4 £11,022**

Emirates Sevens (USA) *Saeed Bin Suroor* 67 a74
2 b c Fusaichi Pegasus (USA) - Lite Light (USA)
3^{7f} 4^{8sd} **0-0-2 £1,075**

Emirates Skyline (USA) *Saeed Bin Suroor* 97
2 b c Sunday Silence (USA) - The Caretaker
1^{7gs} 4^{7gf} 1^{7gs} **2-0-3 £13,644**

Emirates To Dubai (USA) *Saeed Bin Suroor* 63
2 ch c Storm Cat (USA) - Morn Of Song (USA)
6^{7gf} **0-0-1**

Emma Lilley (USA) *J G M O'Shea* 49 a53
3 ch f Theatrical - Changed Tune (USA)
7^{10sd} 8^{12sd} 4^{12sd} 3^{10s} 5^{12f} 13^{10gf} 9^{11g} 7^{12sd} 10^{12sd} **0-1-9 £507**

Emotive *I A Wood* 47 a31
2 b c Pursuit Of Love - Ruby Julie
13^{7gs} 8^{6gs} 5^{7f} 7^{7sd} **0-0-4**

Empangeni *J L Dunlop* 79
3 b g Mtoto - Shibui
12^{12g} 9^{11g} 1^{13gf} 7^{14gf} 1^{16gf} 1^{16g} 3^{16gf} 2^{18gs} **3-2-8 £12,748**

Emperor Cat (Ire) *P A Blockley* 24 a51
4 b g Desert Story (Ire) - Catfoot Lane
3^{8sd} 2^{7sd} 8^{9sd} 5^{8sd} 3^{7sd} 5^{7sd} 4^{6sd} 8^{7sd} 12^{8g} **0-2-9 £1,037**

Emperor's Well *M W Easterby* 68
6 ch g First Trump - Catherines Well
10^{8s} 16^{8g} 3^{10gf} 12^{11gf} 10^{9gf} 8^{8gf} 1^{8gf} 4^{8gf} 5^{8gf} 2^{8gs} 15^{8gf} 9^{8gf} **1-2-12 £6,116**

Emphasis *Mrs A J Perrett* 55 a67
2 ch f Pivotal - Matoaka (USA)
7^{6gs} 5^{7g} 4^{7sd} **0-0-3 £348**

Empire City (USA) *Sir Mark Prescott* 57 a41
3 b g Carson City (USA) - Teeming Shore (USA)
7^{6gf} 4^{6s} 10^{5g} 10^{8sd} **0-0-4 £337**

Empire Dancer (Ire) *C N Allen* 36
2 b c Second Empire (Ire) - Dance To The Beat
12^{7s} **0-0-1**

Empire Of The Sun *P J Makin* a40
4 b f Second Empire (Ire) - Splicing
11^{8sd} 11^{7sd} 5^{8sd} **0-0-3**

Empress Jain *M A Jarvis* 75
2 br f Lujain (USA) - Akhira
1^{5g} 9^{5g} 5^{5g} 6^{6gf} 4^{6g} 1^{5gf} **2-0-6 £10,086**

Empress Josephine *J R Jenkins* a51
5 b m Emperor Jones (USA) - Valmaranda (USA)
8^{6sd} 11^{6sd} 5^{6sd} 3^{5sd} 8^{5sd} 10^{5sd} 2^{5ss} 4^{5sd} **0-2-8 £787**

Empty Gesture *J R Best* 48 a59
3 b g Cadeaux Genereux - Broken Spectre
9^{7sd} 9^{7gf} 12^{6gf} 18^{7g} **0-0-4**

Enborne Again (Ire) *R A Fahey* a19
3 ch g Fayruz - Sharp Ellie (Ire)
6^{8sd} 13^{8sd} 13^{11ss} **0-0-3**

Encanto (Ire) *J S Moore* 58
3 ch f Bahhare (USA) - Born To Glamour
9^{6g} 11^{6gf} 8^{6gf} 8^{6gf} LFT^{8gf} 14^{8gf} **0-0-6**

Enchanting Times (Ire) *D G Bridgwater* 59 a50
2 b f Danetime (Ire) - Enchanted Isle
3^{5s} 5^{5gs} 3^{5sd} 10^{6sd} 3^{5gf} 2^{5f} 5^{6sd} 5^{5g} 4^{8gf} 2^{7f} 2^{6g} 9^{7sd} **0-7-12 £3,056**

Enchantment *J M Bradley* 84
4 b f Compton Place - Tharwa (Ire)
10^{5g} 7^{5g} 10^{5s} **0-0-3**

Encora Bay *P R Chamings* 62
4 b f Primo Dominie - Brave Revival
2^{6gf} **0-1-1 £1,118**

Encounter *A D Brown* 36 a38
9 br g Primo Dominie - Dancing Spirit (Ire)
6^{7sd} 10^{9sd} 10^{8g} 6^{11g} 7^{8gf} **0-0-5**

Encrypt (Ire) *K A Morgan* 45 a23
3 ch f Entrepreneur - Just An Illusion (Ire)
5^{10s} 11^{10gf} 11^{10g} 12^{10sd} 4^{13g} 4^{14hy} **0-0-6**

Endless Chimes *Mrs H Sweeting* 19
2 br f Timeless Times (USA) - Belltina
7^{6g} 7^{6f} 4^{7f} **0-0-3**

Endless Night *H Morrison* 62 a65
2 ch c Dracula (Aus) - La Notte
3^{6s} 5^{5sd} 4^{6sd} **0-1-3 £614**

Endless Peace (Ire) *J W Unett* a55
4 ch f Russian Revival (USA) - Magical Peace (Ire)
7^{7sd} 2^{9sd} 5^{9sd} 3^{9sd} 8^{9sd} 12^{6sd} 2^{9sd} 10^{9sd} 9^{7sd} 8^{8sd} 8^{9sd} **0-3-11 £1,811**

Endless Summer *A W Carroll* 93 a70
8 b g Zafonic (USA) - Well Away (Ire)
11^{5s} 4^{6g} 11^{6gf} 9^{6g} 8^{5g} 17^{6s} 12^{6sf} 7^{6sd} 7^{6sd} **0-1-9 £900**

Endure (Ire) *Saeed Bin Suroor* 40
3 b f Green Desert (USA) - Sister Golden Hair (Ire)
7^{7g} 7^{7gf} **0-0-2**

Enemies Of Jazz (USA) *M W Easterby* 12 a45
3 gr g Pioneering (USA) - Just About Enough (USA)
8^{6sd} 8^{5sd} 10^{5sd} 10^{8gf} **0-0-4**

Enforcer *W R Muir* 112
3 b c Efisio - Tarneem (USA)
4^{7g} 2^{8gs} 3^{8gs} 1^{9gf} 3^{8g} 1^{10g} 13^{8gf} 9^{10gs} 1^{10s} 3^{10g} 6^{10gf} 2^{10gf} 1^{9gs} **4-6-13 £189,544**

Enford Princess *R Hannon* 86
4 b f Pivotal - Expectation (Ire)
7^{7gf} 2^{8g} 4^{7g} 2^{7gf} 2^{8gs} 6^{8g} 7^{7s} 2^{8gs} 5^{7g} 3^{7s} **0-5-10 £11,113**

English Archer *J R Weymes* 57
2 b g Rock City - Fire Sprite
4^{7gf} 6^{8gf} **0-0-2 £302**

English City (Ire) *B Smart* 60 a39
2 ch c City On A Hill (USA) - Toledana (Ire)
13^{5s} 7^{6gf} 4^{7gf} 8^{7sd} 15^{7gf} **0-0-5 £338**

English Rocket (Ire) *D J S Ffrench Davis* 63 a51
4 b g Indian Rocket - Golden Charm (Ire)
14^{8sd} 12^{10sd} 6^{7s} 10^{8gf} 2^{8gs} 9^{8g} 7^{8s} **0-1-7 £1,057**

English Victory *T G Mills* 71 a74
3 ch c Grand Lodge (USA) - Amandine (Ire)
12^{10g} 7^{9gs} 3^{10gs} 4^{12sd} 4^{12gf} **0-1-5 £1,128**

Enjoy The Buzz *J M Bradley* 62 a53
6 b h Prince Of Birds (USA) - Abaklea (Ire)
4^{6s} 2^{5gf} 15^{5gf} 2^{6g} 1^{6gf} 1^{5gf} 4^{5f} 8^{6s} 4^{6sd} 2^{5gf} 6^{6g} 4^{5g} 13^{6g} 3^{5gs} 13^{6gf} 10^{6gf} 4^{6sd} **2-4-17 £8,997**

Enjoy The Moment *J A Osborne* 71
2 b g Generous (Ire) - Denial
9^{8gs} 6^{9gf} **0-0-2**

Enna (Pol) *T M Jones*
6 ch m Don Corleone - Elba (Pol)
10^{10sd} **0-0-1**

Ennobling *E F Vaughan* a58
2 b f Mark Of Esteem (Ire) - Noble Dane (Ire)
5^{7sd} 7^{8sd} **0-0-2**

Enrichetta (Ire) *W R Swinburn* 71
2 ch f Primo Dominie - My Lewicia (Ire)
13^{7gf} 3^{6g} 1^{6gf} **1-1-3 £5,067**

Entailment *Miss Gay Kelleway* 75 a63
3 b g Kris - Entail (USA)
11^{6g} 15^{5gf} 5^{7gf} 2^{8gf} 5^{8gf} 10^{9sd} 10^{8s} 12^{8sd} 7^{14sd} 11^{12sd} **0-1-10 £1,304**

Entertain *Ms Deborah J Evans* 54 a57
3 b f Royal Applause - Darshay (Fr)
7^{10sd} 8^{8sd} 10^{8sd} 10^{10sd} 2^{12sd} 5^{12sd} 7^{12sd} 6^{10s} 13^{10gf} 8^{7g} 2^{7gf} 1^{6sd} 2^{7f} 8^{9sd} 10^{8gf} 12^{6gf} 8^{6sd} 12^{7gf} 14^{7sf} **1-3-19 £4,668**

Entertaining *H Candy* 70
3 b f Halling (USA) - Quaver (USA)
5^{7gf} 4^{7gf} 6^{6gf} 7^{6g} 2^{7g} **0-1-5 £1,430**

Enthusius *M L W Bell* 41
2 b c Generous (Ire) - Edouna (Fr)
11^{8gf} 13^{8s} **0-0-2**

Entranced *Miss J A Camacho* 46 a69
2 b f Saddlers' Hall (Ire) - Vent D'Aout (Ire)
11^{7s} 1^{9sd} **1-0-2 £4,197**

Envision *R Hannon* 87
2 b g Pivotal - Entwine
4^{5gf} 1^{6g} 7^{6gf} 4^{8gs} **1-0-4 £14,973**

Epaminondas (USA) *A J Chamberlain*

4 ch g Miswaki (USA) - Nora Nova (USA)
PU^{12sd} **0-0-1**

Epices *Sir Mark Prescott* 36
3 b g Mtoto - French Spice
6^{12gf} 16^{14s} 13^{9ft} **0-0-3**

Epicurean *J G Given* 69
3 ch f Pursuit Of Love - Arminda
1^{7gf} 3^{8gf} 12^{10gf} 8^{8g} 9^{12gf} **1-1-5 £3,600**

Epineuse *J R Best* 31
2 b f Gorse - Four-Legged Friend
12^{5gs} 14^{6gs} 8^{6gf} **0-0-3**

Epitomise *R M Beckett* 60 a61
3 b f Mind Games - Yanomami (USA)
8^{7sd} 1^{7sd} 4^{7sd} 6^{7sd} 2^{7sd} 8^{7sd} 5^{7sd} 2^{7gf} 1^{6gf}
7^{6g} **2-2-10 £8,415**

Eqdaam (USA) *M Al Muhairi* 81 a48
3 b c Diesis - Awaamir
6^{8hy} 13^{9g} 5^{10g} 3^{8gf} 3^{8gf} 5^{8gf} 11^{7ft} 6^{8ft}
0-2-8 £2,374

Equilibria (USA) *G L Moore* 55 a43
3 b g Gulch (USA) - Julie La Rousse (Ire)
9^{6sd} 17^{7gf} 4^{6f} 3^{7sd} 5^{8sd} 2^{12gs} **0-2-6**
£972

Eraser *E Borromeo* 106
3 gr c Linamix (Fr) - Kamakha (Ire)
1^{9g} 4^{9g} 13^{11g} 2^{12gf} 4^{12gs} 7^{12s} **1-1-6**
£26,301

Erhgent Sea *T M Jones* 11
2 gr g Erhaab (USA) - Gentle Gypsy
10^{7s} 9^{7g} **0-0-2**

Ermine Grey *A W Carroll* 74 a84
4 gr g Wolfhound (USA) - Impulsive Decision (Ire)
6^{9sd} 2^{9sd} 11^{8sd} 4^{8g} 12^{9gs} 10^{8gf} 4^{10gs} 3^{10gs}
0-3-8 £5,038

Ermine Sea *J H M Gosden* 64
2 b c Rainbow Quest (USA) - Bint Pasha (USA)
12^{8gs} **0-0-1**

Ernmoor *J R Best* 41
3 b g Young Ern - Linpac North Moor
9^{7g} 11^{7sd} **0-0-2**

Errachidia (Ire) *M J Wallace* a20
5 b m King Of Kings (Ire) - Sunset Reigns (Ire)
12^{5sd} **0-0-1**

Erracht *Mrs H Sweeting* a10
7 gr m Emarati (USA) - Port Na Blath
13^{5sd} **0-0-1**

Erupt *R E Barr* 14
12 b g Beveled (USA) - Sparklingsovereign
10^{8g} **0-0-1**

Erytheis (USA) *Sir Michael Stoute* 89
2 b f Theatrical - Enthused (USA)
2^{6gf} 2^{6g} 1^{6gf} 1^{6gs} 5^{6s} **2-2-5 £16,528**

Escalade *Barry Potts* 34 a42
8 b g Green Desert (USA) - Sans Escale (USA)
6^{9sd} 3^{12sd} 4^{12sd} 5^{11sd} 9^{9sd} 6^{11s} 4^{12sd}
0-1-7 £213

Escape Clause (USA) *Sir Michael Stoute* 76
2 b c Red Ransom (USA) - Promptly (Ire)
3^{7s} **0-1-1 £583**

Escape Plan (Ire) *E J O'Neill* 98
2 b c Key Of Luck (USA) - Magic Garter
1^{6s} 2^{6g} 1^{6g} 10^{6g} 9^{6gf} 4^{6gs} 8^{6hy} **2-1-7**
£15,295

Escayola (Ire) *W J Haggas* 92 a79
5 b g Revoque (Ire) - First Fling (Ire)
10^{16g} 5^{16g} 11^{12gs} 8^{18gs} 5^{16sd} **0-0-5 £461**

Escobar (Pol) *Mrs P Townsley* a55
4 b g Royal Court (Ire) - Escola (Pol)
6^{10sd} 6^{10sd} 2^{7sd} 2^{8sd} 9^{9sd} **0-2-5 £1,379**

Escoffier *Mrs A J Perrett* 35 a64
3 b g Entrepreneur - Gooseberry Pie
14^{10gs} 9^{12sd} 3^{10sd} **0-1-3 £619**

Eskdale (Ire) *R F Fisher* 2
3 b g Perugino (USA) - Gilding The Lily (Ire)
11^{10sd} 10^{9sd} 15^{8s} **0-0-3**

Eskimo Nell *T D Easterby* 52
2 b f Polar Prince (Ire) - We'Re Joken
6^{5s} 3^{5gs} 7^{6f} 3^{5g} **0-2-4 £1,409**

Eskimo's Nest *D Shaw* 49 a54
3 b f Polar Falcon (USA) - White House
8^{7gs} 8^{7gf} 7^{9sd} 3^{8gf} 7^{9sd} 8^{7sf} 10^{7sd} 7^{8sd} 9^{12sd}
0-1-9 £435

Esoterica (Ire) *T D Barron* 59
2 b g Bluebird (USA) - Mysterious Plans (Ire)
3^{5g} **0-1-1 £526**

Espada (Ire) *J J Bridger* 18 a34
9 b g Mukaddamah (USA) - Folk Song (Can)
12^{7s} 12^{8sd} **0-0-2**

Esperance (Ire) *J Akehurst* 42 a54
5 ch g Bluebird (USA) - Dioscorea (Ire)
3^{10sd} 4^{10sd} 4^{10sd} 2^{9sd} 4^{8sd} 2^{10sd} 1^{10sd} 5^{12gf}
12^{10s} 10^{13sd} 11^{12gf} 7^{10sd} 4^{12sd} 2^{10sd} 7^{10sd}
12^{10gf} 7^{10g} **1-4-17 £3,441**

Espere D'Or *M Wellings* a24
8 b g Golden Heights - Drummer's Dream (Ire)
9^{8sd} 8^{7sd} 11^{7sd} 8^{9sd} 12^{9sd} **0-0-5**

Esprit De Corps *Sir Mark Prescott* a61
3 b c Hernando (Fr) - Entente Cordiale (USA)
6^{10sd} **0-0-1**

Esquillon *S Parr* 49
3 b f High Estate - Our Aisling
10^{10g} 5^{10f} 10^{10gf} 11^{14gf} 7^{16g} 2^{16gf} 9^{14g} 4^{14g}
0-1-8 £832

Esquire *Saeed Bin Suroor* 70
3 b c Dubai Millennium - Esperada (Arg)
10^{8gf} 8^{8g} **0-0-2**

Essex Star (Ire) *Miss J Feilden* 61 a48
4 b f Revoque (Ire) - Touch Of White
9^{9sd} 5^{7s} 1^{7g} 2^{6g} 3^{6gs} 9^{7s} 9^{8sd} 12^{8hy} 6^{8sd}
5^{7sf} **1-2-10 £2,876**

Establishment *C A Cyzer* 76 a67
8 b g Muhtarram (USA) - Uncharted Waters
4^{16sd} 4^{16sd} 6^{16g} 10^{22s} 7^{14sd} 1^{16gs} 6^{16gs} 11^{21s}
4^{16g} 3^{16gf} 26^{18gs} 4^{16s} **1-0-12 £9,853**

Estancia *H Morrison* 49
3 b f Grand Lodge (USA) - Donostia
5^{10s} 10^{10g} 11^{10gs} 6^{12f} 12^{14g} **0-0-5**

Estepona *J Howard Johnson* 87
4 ch g Polar Falcon (USA) - Kingdom Ruby (Ire)
4^{10g} 1^{10gf} 2^{10gf} 2^{10g} 2^{11gf} 1^{12g} 3^{12hy}
2-5-7 £22,254

Esterelle (USA) *H J Manners*
10 ch m Trempolino (USA) - Duck Flighting (USA)
PU^{18gf} **0-0-1**

Esthlos (Fr) *J Jay* a61
2 ch c Limnos (Jpn) - Cozzie
4^{7sd} 3^{7sd} **0-1-2 £466**

Estiqraar (Ire) *J L Dunlop* 75
2 b c Alhaarth (Ire) - Hureya (USA)
3^{7s} 2^{8gf} **0-2-2 £1,974**

Estoille *Mrs S Lamyman* 57
4 b f Paris House - Nampara Bay
18^{5hy} 14^{6gs} 3^{6gf} 8^{6gf} 15^{5gf} 5^{5gf} **0-1-6**
£873

Estrelle (Ger) *H R A Cecil* 79
3 ch f Sternkoenig (Ire) - Enrica
2^{9g} 2^{11g} 2^{12gf} 4^{12g} 3^{12gs} 5^{12s} **0-4-6**
£5,264

Eswarah *M A Jarvis* 116
3 b f Unfuwain (USA) - Midway Lady (USA)
1^{10gs} 1^{10gf} 1^{12g} 8^{12gf} 4^{12g} **3-0-5**
£258,394

Etaar *E A L Dunlop* 75
3 b c Zafonic (USA) - Hawayah (Ire)
7^{7gf} 1^{8s} 4^{8gf} **1-0-3 £4,010**

Etching (USA) *W Storey* 64 a26
5 b m Groom Dancer (USA) - Eternity
7^{12gf} 11^{16gf} 4^{14g} 10^{17sd} 1^{13gf} 4^{12gf} 13^{12gs}
14^{14gf} 5^{12g} 2^{12gf} 18^{12gs} 10^{12sd} **1-1-12**
£4,794

Etendard Indien (Fr) *N J Henderson*
4 b g Selkirk (USA) - Danseuse Indienne (Ire)
9^{16gs} **0-0-1**

Eternal Bloom *M Brittain*
7 b m Reprimand - Forever Roses
13^{5sd} **0-0-1**

Eternal Sunshine (Ire) *R P Elliott*
3 b f Rossini (USA) - Sweet As A Nut (Ire)
7^{6sd} **0-0-1**

Eternally *R M H Cowell* 6 a23
3 ch c Timeless Times (USA) - Nice Spice (Ire)
7^{6sd} 11^{5sd} 8^{5sd} 5^{5s} 8^{6sd} 13^{6sd} 10^{5sd}
0-0-7

Etesaal (USA) *Saeed Bin Suroor* 114
5 b/br h Danzig (USA) - Electric Society (Ire)
4^{10gf} 4^{10gf} 3^{10gf} 1^{10gf} 11^{10gf} 10^{12gf} 1^{10g} 1^{10gf}
3-2-8 £53,402

Etijahaat (Ire) *C W Fairhurst* 89 a7
3 b g King's Best (USA) - Dance Ahead
4^{7g} 6^{10gf} 3^{6gf} 17^{8gf} 10^{10g} 11^{7sd} **0-1-6**
£1,195

Etlaala *B W Hills* 113
3 ch c Selkirk (USA) - Portelet
8^{8gf} 7^{5gf} 7^{6f} 3^{6gs} 6^{6g} 10^{6g} 8^{7gs} **0-1-7**
£31,070

Etoile Russe (Ire) *P C Haslam* 63
3 b g Soviet Star (USA) - To The Skies (USA)
10^{10sd} 10^{8g} 10^{8gf} 5^{7g} 3^{8g} **0-1-5 £649**

Eton (Ger) *D Nicholls* 61
9 ch g Suave Dancer (USA) - Ermione
18^{12g} 14^{10g} 4^{12s} 11^{11gf} 9^{12gf} 6^{10gf} 1^{10gf} 5^{12gf}
4^{12f} 3^{10s} 17^{10gs} **1-1-11 £3,856**

Ettrick Water *L M Cumani* 104
6 ch g Selkirk (USA) - Sadly Sober (Ire)
6^{8g} 23^{7gf} 5^{7g} 7^{8gf} 6^{8g} 14^{8gs} **0-0-6**
£1,400

Euippe *J G Given* a38
4 b f Air Express (Ire) - Myth
9^{16sd} 12^{16sd} **0-0-2**

Euphoria *B J Meehan* 55
3 b f Unfuwain (USA) - Maria Isabella (Fr)
10^{9gs} 7^{8gs} **0-0-2**

Eurana *S C Williams* 47
2 ch f Mark Of Esteem (Ire) - Intervene
14^{6gf} 11^{6g} **0-0-2**

Euro Route (Ire) *G J Smith* 58 a27
4 b g Desert Style (Ire) - Fresh Look (Ire)
14^{8g} 11^{9y} 20^{8gf} 9^{8gs} 12^{7g} 4^{16sd} **0-0-6**

European (Arg) *R M Beckett* 91
5 br g Nugget Point - Enfeitada (Arg)
15^{7gf} 12^{8g} 16^{7gf} 12^{8g} 15^{7gf} **0-0-5**

European Dream (Ire) *R C Guest* 68
2 br c Kalanisi (Ire) - Tereed Elhawa
12^{7gf} 8^{7g} 1^{7s} 5^{8gf} 4^{7hy} **1-0-5 £2,955**

Europrime Games *M E Sowersby* 36
7 b g Mind Games - Flower Princess
7^{10gs} 6^{10gs} **0-0-2**

Eva Jean *H Morrison*
4 b f Singspiel (Ire) - Go For Red (Ire)
13^{10g} 15^{10s} **0-0-2**

Eva Soneva So Fast (Ire) *J L Dunlop* 85
3 ch g In The Wings - Azyaa
3^{10gf} 10^{11gf} **0-1-2 £1,486**

Evaluator (Ire) *T G Mills* 107
4 b g Ela-Mana-Mou - Summerhill
6^{8g} 11^{8g} 2^{10g} 1^{10gf} 1^{10gs} 12^{10gf} 2^{9s}
2-2-7 £68,171

Evanesce *M R Channon* 56 a56
3 b f Lujain (USA) - Search Party
7^{7sd} 6^{7sd} 12^{7sd} 11^{6gf} 2^{6gf} 6^{6g} 3^{7gf} 6^{6gf} 5^{7f}
5^{6gf} 6^{6gf} 6^{6gf} **0-2-12 £1,923**

Even Hotter *D W P Arbuthnot* a49
4 b f Desert Style (Ire) - Level Pegging (Ire)
6^{7sd} 10^{7sd} 6^{8sd} 14^{8gf} 12^{7sd} **0-0-5**

Ever Cheerful *G C H Chung* 54 a73
4 b g Atraf - Big Story
1^{7sd} 8^{7sd} 6^{7sd} 7^{5g} 11^{6gf} 7^{6sd} 3^{7sd} 8^{7sd} 5^{7sd}
5^{7sd} 1^{7sd} 2^{5sd} 4^{6sd} **2-2-13 £7,176**

Ever Special (Ire) *P C Haslam* 41
2 b g Fruits Of Love (USA) - El Corazon (Ire)
11^{6g} 10^{7gf} 12^{9g} **0-0-3**

Everest (Ire) *B Ellison* 88
8 ch g Indian Ridge - Reine D'Beaute
18^{8g} 13^{8gf} 9^{8gs} 7^{8f} 12^{8g} 6^{8gf} 6^{8g} 4^{8s} 6^{8g}
1^{8s} 1^{8gf} 10^{9g} 7^{8g} 9^{8gs} 2^{8hy} **2-1-15**
£11,760

Eversden (USA) *C G Cox* 76
2 b c Red Ransom (USA) - Who Did It And Run (USA)
2^{5gf} 1^{5g} 10^{6g} **1-1-3 £5,505**

Every Bodys Angel *P J Makin* a28
2 b f Josr Algarhoud (Ire) - Piccante
10^{7sd} **0-0-1**

Evidential *Sir Michael Stoute*
2 b f Sadler's Wells (USA) - Prove
16^{8s} **0-0-1**

Evolution Ex (USA) *J H M Gosden* 86
3 b/br g Bahri (USA) - Zoe's Gold (USA)
2^{10g} 2^{11s} 1^{10gf} 4^{10g} 3^{10gf} 7^{10gf} 6^{8gf} **1-2-7**
£11,605

Ewar Finch (Fr) *K O Cunningham-Brown* 51 a43
3 b f Kayf Tara - Ewar Empress (Ire)
7^{12s} 3^{12s} 7^{10gf} 8^{12g} 7^{12sd} 10^{12sd} 9^{11g} 6^{14hy}
10^{12sf} 10^{14sf} 11^{10sd} **0-0-11 £565**

Excellent *Sir Michael Stoute* 62
2 ch f Grand Lodge (USA) - Exclusive
10^{7g} **0-0-1**

Exclusive Air (USA) *H H G Owen* a10
6 ch g Affirmed (USA) - Lac Dessert (USA)
6^{8sd} 7^{12sd} **0-0-2**

Excusez Moi (USA) *C E Brittain* 106 a78

3 b c Fusaichi Pegasus (USA) - Jiving
9^{7ft} 3^{7ft} 1^{7g} 7^{7gs} 6^{10gs} 3^{7g} 8^{6gf} 13^{6g} 9^{7gf}
2^{6gs} 4^{6g} **1-4-11 £19,875**

Exexel *P F I Cole* a62
2 br f Dansili - Only In Dreams
4^{5sd} 2^{5sd} 5^{5sd} 13^{6sd} **0-1-4 £1,307**

Exhibit One (USA) *Sir Michael Stoute* 75
3 b f Silver Hawk (USA) - Tsar's Pride
4^{10gf} 4^{12gf} 2^{11gf} 1^{12gf} **1-1-4 £5,118**

Exit Smiling *G C H Chung* 68 a65
3 ch g Dr Fong (USA) - Away To Me
4^{9sd} 4^{7sd} 2^{6sd} 3^{6s} 6^{7sd} 6^{6g} 14^{6gs} 11^{5sd} 12^{7sd}
0-2-9 £1,268

Exmoor *R Charlton* 88
3 b g Cape Cross (Ire) - Royal Jade
1^{6gs} 2^{6g} 2^{6g} 7^{6gf} 14^{6g} **1-2-5 £6,983**

Exmoor Dancer (Ire) *H S Howe* a30
2 b f Mujahid (USA) - Amy G (Ire)
9^{5f} 11^{6sd} **0-0-2**

Exotic Venture *R M Beckett* a55
2 b f Piccolo - Bay Risk
6^{8sd} **0-0-1**

Expected Bonus (USA) *Jamie Poulton* a38
6 b/br g Kris S (USA) - Nidd (USA)
7^{8sd} **0-0-1**

Expensive *C F Wall* 100
2 b f Royal Applause - Vayavaig
5^{6gf} 2^{6gf} 4^{6gf} 2^{6gf} 1^{6gf} 1^{7gf} 13^{7gs} **2-2-7**
£151,969

Expensive Problem *R M Beckett* 67 a72
2 b c Medicean - Dance Steppe
13^{6gf} 4^{6gf} 5^{7gf} 2^{7sd} 5^{7g} 11^{7gs} **0-1-6**
£1,683

Explosive Fox (Ire) *C P Morlock* 65 a66
4 gr g Foxhound (USA) - Grise Mine (Fr)
7^{16sd} 8^{11s} 10^{12gf} 1^{12sd} 3^{14f} 9^{14gf} 10^{14sd}
1-1-7 £3,204

Exponential (Ire) *S C Williams* a62
3 b g Namid - Exponent (USA)
20^{7hy} 13^{6sf} 11^{7sd} **0-0-3**

Expression Echo (Ire) *A G Newcombe* 60
3 b f Bahhare (USA) - Bint Alreeys
12^{8g} 4^{10g} 4^{10gf} 10^{12gs} 9^{11sd} **0-0-5 £327**

Expulsion (USA) *A Senior*
4 b f Expelled (USA) - Solar Beam (USA)
8^{7g} 12^{6sd} **0-0-2**

Extemporise (Ire) *T T Clement* 51 a48
5 ch g Indian Ridge - No Rehearsal (Fr)
4^{7s} 6^{6s} 16^{7gf} 3^{6g} 5^{8sd} 7^{6hy} 9^{9sd} **0-1-7**
£217

Extra Cover (Ire) *Ronald Thompson* 59 a53
4 b g Danehill Dancer (Ire) - Ballycurrane (Ire)
7^{6sd} 4^{8sd} 1^{12sd} 3^{11sd} 11^{12gf} 7^{16sd} 6^{12sd} 6^{9sd}
3^{8gf} 6^{12gf} 6^{6gf} 6^{9sd} 1^{8gs} 3^{10g} 2^{12g} 11^{12gf} 11^{12sd}
2-4-17 £8,793

Extra Mark *J R Best* 65 a63
3 b g Mark Of Esteem (Ire) - No Comebacks
9^{8gf} 5^{5gs} 6^{6gf} 6^{6sd} 6^{6sd} **0-0-5**

Extreme Beauty (USA) *C E Brittain* 89 a49
3 ch f Rahy (USA) - Mediation (Ire)
11^{8ft} 8^{9ft} 11^{7gs} 13^{7g} 1^{7gf} 10^{8f} 10^{10g} 7^{7g}
14^{7g} **1-0-9 £8,839**

Extreme Measures *Saeed Bin Suroor* 86
2 b c Montjeu (Ire) - Fade
1^{7gf} 5^{7gf} **1-0-2 £6,397**

Extremely Rare (Ire) *M S Saunders* 81 a65
4 b f Mark Of Esteem (Ire) - Colourflash (Ire)
4^{6hy} 5^{6sd} 8^{6s} 10^{6sd} 2^{6gs} 1^{6gs} 4^{6gs} 1^{5gf} 2^{6gf}
7^{5gf} 3^{5g} 12^{5g} 1^{6g} 11^{6sd} **3-3-14**
£17,785

Eyes Dont Lie (Ire) *D A Nolan* 22
7 b g Namaqualand (USA) - Avidal Park
9^{12gs} 9^{13gs} 14^{9gf} 7^{16gf} **0-0-4**

Ezz Elkheil *J R Jenkins* 61 a75
6 b g Bering - Numidie (Fr)
14^{10sd} 2^{12sd} 5^{12sd} 2^{12sd} 5^{12sd} 7^{12gf} 5^{12sd} 2^{12sd}
7^{12sd} **0-3-9 £2,806**

Fabrian *R J Price* 79 a36
7 b g Danehill (USA) - Dockage (Can)
4^{7sd} 3^{8g} 1^{7g} 7^{8gf} 1^{10g} 5^{10gf} 1^{8g} 3^{8gf} 3^{8gf}
2^{10gf} 5^{9gs} 1^{8gs} 4^{10g} 6^{8g} 7^{7gf} 2^{7g} 2^{8gf}
4-6-17 £24,195

Fabuloso *V Smith* 38
4 b f Dr Fong (USA) - Shafir (Ire)
6^{11g} 6^{8g} **0-0-2**

Fabulous Bird *R Hannon* 47
2 b f Robellino (USA) - Cockatrice
14^{6gs} 12^{7g} **0-0-2**

Fabulous Emperor (Ire) *Jamie Poulton* 56 a70
3 b c Imperial Ballet (Ire) - Al Cairo (Fr)
2^{10sd} 9^{10gf} 8^{12gs} 13^{10sd} **0-1-4 £1,288**

Face The Limelight (Ire) *Jedd O'Keeffe* 46
6 b g Quest For Fame - Miss Boniface
8^{9g} 6^{11gf} **0-0-2**

Factor Twenty (Ire) *C A Murphy* 62 a27
3 b f Revoque (Ire) - Swirl
4^{7sd} 17^{12gf} 9^{8g} **0-0-3**

Factual Lad *B R Millman* 77
7 b g So Factual (USA) - Surprise Surprise
1^{10gf} 3^{10s} 4^{10gf} 7^{10g} 8^{10g} **1-0-5 £5,113**

Fadansil *J Wade* 40
2 b c Dansili - Fatah Flare (USA)
7^{5gf} 6^{7g} 12^{7gf} **0-0-3**

Faint Heart (Ire) *David Wachman* 96
3 b f Sadler's Wells (USA) - Never So Fair
3^{8s} 2^{10sh} 4^{11gs} **0-2-3 £17,500**

Fair Along (Ger) *P J Hobbs* a68
3 b g Alkalde (Ger) - Fairy Tango (Fr)
7^{10sd} 1^{11sd} 8^{9sd} 4^{12sd} 3^{9sd} **1-1-5 £4,054**

Fair Compton *R Hannon* 64 a63
4 b f Compton Place - Fair Eleanor
5^{6sd} 9^{7sd} 5^{6g} 1^{6f} 15^{6gf} 12^{6g} 5^{6f} 7^{6sd} 12^{5gs}
9^{6gf} **1-0-10 £3,056**

Fair Options *A P Jones* 41 a38
4 gr g Marju (Ire) - Silver Singing (USA)
8^{7sd} 13^{6sd} 10^{8f} 16^{6f} 7^{8g} 7^{8g} **0-0-6**

Fair Rosamond (Ire) *R Simpson* 75 a77
2 ch f Alhaarth (Ire) - Virgin Stanza (USA)
3^{6g} 4^{5f} 2^{6gf} 5^{7sd} 3^{7sd} 14^{7gf} 2^{7ft} **0-4-7**
£4,250

Fair Shake (Ire) *Karen McLintock* 81
5 b g Sheikh Albadou - Shamrock Fair (Ire)
14^{7gf} 1^{7s} 7^{6s} 10^{7gs} 2^{8g} 2^{8g} 6^{8gs} 3^{8g} 8^{8g}
13^{8gs} 9^{7s} 19^{7s} **1-3-12 £9,571**

Fair Spin *M D Hammond* 62
5 ch g Pivotal - Frankie Fair (Ire)
3^{12s} 7^{10g} 16^{12gs} 16^{14g} 7^{9hy} **0-1-5 £677**

Fairgame Man *J S Wainwright* 54 a34
7 ch g Clantime - Thalya
5^{6sd} 7^{6sd} 11^{6sd} 13^{5gf} 5^{5gf} 7^{5gf} 9^{5g} 5^{6g} 3^{6gs}

8^{5g} 1^{6gf} 10^{6gf} 6^{6gs} 9^{5gf} 12^{6g} **1-1-15 £3,228**

Fairland (Ire) *S Dow* a41
6 b g Blues Traveller (Ire) - Massive Powder
7^{13sd} 11^{13sd} 8^{12sd} **0-0-3**

Fairlie *K G Reveley* 67
4 b f Halling (USA) - Fairy Flax (Ire)
6^{11g} 7^{12g} 4^{10gf} 2^{8gf} 1^{8gf} 12^{8gf} 8^{8gf} 9^{8g} 1^{10gf} 10^{10g} 5^{10gf} 13^{10gs} **2-1-12 £9,885**

Fairmile *W R Swinburn* 91
3 b g Spectrum (Ire) - Juno Marlowe (Ire)
1^{10s} 1^{12g} 9^{12hy} **2-0-3 £13,066**

Fairmorning (Ire) *C N Kellett* 32 a44
6 b g Ridgewood Ben - The Bratpack (Ire)
5^{14sd} 7^{14sd} 4^{17sd} 6^{14sd} 12^{12gf} 9^{16gf} **0-0-6**

Fairy Dance (Ire) *G Wragg* 10
3 b f Zafonic (USA) - Oh So Well (Ire)
15^{7gf} **0-0-1**

Fairy Monarch (Ire) *P T Midgley* 56 a4
6 b g Ali-Royal (Ire) - Cookawara (Ire)
8^{11sd} 3^{10gf} 2^{8g} 4^{7gf} 3^{8gf} 6^{12f} 1^{8gf} 3^{10gf} 3^{8gf} 12^{9gf} 5^{9gf} 11^{8gf} **1-5-12 £6,421**

Fairy Tail (Ire) *J A Osborne* 45 a34
3 b c Princely Heir (Ire) - Batilde (Ire)
8^{6g} 8^{7sd} 10^{9sd} 9^{8gf} **0-0-4**

Fairytale Of York (Ire) *D Carroll* a30
2 b f Imperial Ballet (Ire) - Pekanski (Ire)
12^{9sd} 10^{9sf} 11^{9sd} **0-0-3**

Faith And Reason (USA) *Saeed Bin Suroor* 84
2 b c Sunday Silence (USA) - Sheer Reason (USA)
9^{7gf} 1^{7gf} 1^{8g} **2-0-3 £12,980**

Faith Healer (Ire) *John Berry* 39 a31
4 br f Key Of Luck (USA) - Cindy's Star (Ire)
13^{10sd} 11^{8gs} 8^{8g} **0-0-3**

Faithfull Girl (Ire) *Miss Z C Davison*
3 b f Second Empire (Ire) - Cairde Nua (Ire)
9^{8f} **0-0-1**

Faithisflying *D W Chapman* 36 a47
3 ch g Wolfhound (USA) - Niggle
4^{6sd} UR^{6sd} 4^{7sd} 8^{6sd} 4^{6sd} 3^{6sd} 11^{5sd} 14^{6gf} 6^{7gf} 6^{5gf} 7^{6g} 7^{5g} 11^{6gf} 9^{6sd} 9^{5sd} 2^{6sd} 5^{6sd} 13^{6sd} 3^{6ss} 4^{8sd} 2^{7sd} **0-4-21 £1,256**

Fajr (Ire) *N B King* 59 a61
3 b c Green Desert (USA) - Ta Rib (USA)
13^{10gf} 6^{7g} 3^{8g} 3^{7sd} **0-2-4 £1,043**

Falcon Dive (USA) *R Hannon* 41 a71
2 ch c Diesis - Yanaseeni (USA)
9^{6gs} 7^{7sd} 9^{7sd} **0-0-3**

Falcon Goer (USA) *Miss B Sanders* 33 a20
3 b f Zamindar (USA) - Elizabeth Eliza (USA)
7^{6sd} 13^{6g} 16^{8gs} 10^{6sd} 11^{6s} 14^{10sd} **0-0-6**

Faleh (USA) *W J Haggas* 80
3 ch f Silver Hawk (USA) - Marasem
5^{8g} 1^{7gs} 3^{7g} **1-1-3 £5,542**

Falkirk *M Johnston* 38
2 ch c Selkirk (USA) - Fig Tree Drive (USA)
10^{8g} **0-0-1**

Fall In Line *Sir Mark Prescott* a37
5 gr g Linamix (Fr) - Shortfall
16^{12sd} **0-0-1**

Fallal Parc *M F Harris* 30 a47
2 ch g Tachyon Park - Fallal (Ire)
6^{5sd} 16^{6gf} 8^{5gf} 6^{5sd} **0-0-4**

Falmer For All (Ire) *J Ryan* 16 a25
7 b g Warcraft (USA) - Sunset Walk
10^{8g} 9^{7sd} 8^{9sd} **0-0-3**

Falstaff (Ire) *A P O'Brien* 109
3 b c Montjeu (Ire) - Dance Of Love (Ire)
1^{7hy} 5^{10vs} 3^{10s} 17^{11g} **1-0-4 £27,844**

Famcred *L M Cumani* 82
2 b f Inchinor - Sumingasefa
2^{6g} 1^{7gf} 1^{7g} **2-1-3 £13,776**

Fame *P J Hobbs* 53
5 ch g Northern Amethyst - First Sapphire
7^{10g} **0-0-1**

Familiar Affair *T D Barron* a57
4 b g Intikhab (USA) - Familiar (USA)
8^{9sd} 8^{8sd} **0-0-2**

Familiar Territory *Saeed Bin Suroor* 95
2 br c Cape Cross (Ire) - Forever Fine (USA)
1^{8g} 3^{9gs} 2^{8s} **1-1-3 £9,779**

Family 'n Friends *C A Cyzer* 35 a13
3 b f Unfuwain (USA) - Springs Welcome
13^{9sd} 11^{9gs} 13^{12gf} 7^{12f} F^{16s} **0-0-5**

Fancy Day *B W Hills* 60 a71
2 b f Zafonic (USA) - Hiwaayati
3^{5gf} 1^{7sd} **1-0-2 £4,758**

Fancy You (Ire) *A W Carroll* 46
2 b f Mull Of Kintyre (USA) - Sunset Park (Ire)
4^{5s} 6^{5gs} 8^{6gf} 24^{6gf} **0-0-4 £314**

Fangorn Forest (Ire) *K A Ryan* 84 a62
2 b f Shinko Forest (Ire) - Edge Of Darkness
1^{5gf} 3^{5g} 11^{6gf} 10^{6g} 4^{7gs} 16^{7s} 2^{7sd} 6^{9sd} **1-2-8 £10,447**

Fann (USA) *C E Brittain* 69
2 b f Diesis - Forest Storm (USA)
6^{7f} 7^{7g} 7^{7gf} 3^{8g} 5^{7gs} **0-1-5 £1,832**

Fantaisiste *P F I Cole* 89 a86
3 b f Nashwan (USA) - Fantastic Belle (Ire)
2^{6gf} 4^{6gf} 3^{7gf} 11^{7g} 2^{7gf} 2^{7sd} 2^{7gf} 7^{7sd} 7^{8sd} **0-5-9 £9,825**

Fantastic Champion (Ire) *J R Cornwall* 67
6 b g Entrepreneur - Reine Mathilde (USA)
9^{14g} **0-0-1**

Fantastic Luck (Ire) *J L Dunlop* 34
3 b g Josr Algarhoud (Ire) - Fantastic Fantasy (Ire)
14^{10gs} 10^{14f} **0-0-2**

Fantastic Night (Den) *Rae Guest* 43
3 ch f Night Shift (USA) - Gaelic's Fantasy (Ire)
10^{8g} **0-0-1**

Fantastisch (Ire) *H R A Cecil* 74
2 b f Fantastic Light (USA) - Alexandra S (Ire)
4^{8g} 11^{8s} **0-0-2 £301**

Fantasy Believer *J J Quinn* 100
7 b g Sure Blade (USA) - Delicious
15^{6g} 17^{7gf} 30^{6gf} 11^{6gs} 5^{7gf} 16^{7gf} 5^{6g} 1^{6gf} 3^{6gf} 2^{6gf} 6^{6gf} 3^{6gs} 13^{6gf} 5^{6g} UR^{5g} 11^{6s} 19^{5hy} **1-3-17 £33,947**

Fantasy Crusader *R M H Cowell* 61 a55
6 ch g Beveled (USA) - Cranfield Charger
19^{10gf} 11^{8f} 6^{10sd} 2^{10f} 13^{8f} 11^{8gf} 10^{10s} 5^{8gs} 9^{10gf} 16^{10g} 13^{8gf} 10^{9gf} 8^{10sd} 12^{8f} 6^{7sd} 1^{9sd} 10^{9sd} 3^{10sd} 5^{8sd} 12^{10sd} **1-2-20 £2,728**

Fantasy Defender (Ire) *J J Quinn* 57 a55
3 b g Fayruz - Mrs Lucky
11^{9sd} 7^{8gf} 1^{7f} 2^{7g} 11^{8gf} 13^{7s} 9^{7gf} 10^{7gf} 9^{8gf} 12^{9sd} 13^{8sd} 2^{9sd} 6^{8sd} 7^{8sd} **1-2-14 £4,170**

Fantasy Explorer *J J Quinn* 51
2 b g Compton Place - Zinzi

7^{5g} 7^{5gf} 5^{6gf} **0-0-3**

Fantasy Feeling *P T Midgley*
3 b g Easycall - Priceless Fantasy
11^{7g} **0-0-1**

Fantorini (USA) *J H M Gosden* 89
3 b g Theatrical - Beyrouth (USA)
4^{10g} 4^{12gf} 5^{10gs} 1^{10g} 14^{10s} 1^{10g} **2-0-6**
£13,605

Faqaraat (USA) *M Johnston* 74
2 b/br f War Chant (USA) - Fatwa (Ire)
4^{7gf} **0-0-1 £451**

Far Note (USA) *S R Bowring* 58 a69
7 ch g Distant View (USA) - Descant (USA)
5^{5sd} 12^{7sd} 12^{5sd} 9^{6gf} 10^{6sd} 13^{6g} 13^{7g} 3^{6gf}
3^{6sd} 11^{6gf} 14^{6s} 1^{6sd} 3^{7sd} 7^{7sd} **1-3-14**
£3,942

Far Pavilions *G A Swinbank* 104 a70
6 b g Halling (USA) - Flambera (Fr)
10^{9sd} 1^{14g} 1^{14gf} 1^{14g} 3^{16g} **3-1-5**
£46,220

Farasha *M A Jarvis* 60
2 b f Indian Ridge - Felona
9^{6gf} 5^{6gf} 6^{6f} 8^{7g} 7^{6gf} **0-0-5**

Faraway Echo *James Moffatt* 43
4 gr f Second Empire (Ire) - Salalah
10^{16g} 7^{11sd} **0-0-2**

Fardi (Ire) *A Berry* 69
3 b g Green Desert (USA) - Shuruk
8^{6g} 5^{6gf} 7^{7gf} 7^{6gf} 11^{7g} **0-0-5**

Farewell Gift *R Hannon* 80
4 b g Cadeaux Genereux - Daring Ditty
13^{6gs} 14^{7gf} 3^{7gf} 7^{7gf} 2^{9g} 10^{7gf} 14^{6s} 16^{7s}
0-2-8 £2,691

Farnborough (USA) *R J Price* 59 a62
4 b g Lear Fan (USA) - Gretel
5^{9sd} 6^{14sd} 2^{9sd} 3^{10sd} 1^{9sd} 2^{9sd} 1^{9sd} 2^{12sd} 3^{9sd}
8^{11gf} 3^{12gs} 3^{12gs} 5^{11g} 10^{12sd} **2-7-14**
£8,078

Farne Island *L M Cumani* 59 a62
2 ch c Arkadian Hero (USA) - Holy Island
7^{6gs} 5^{6s} 3^{7sd} **0-1-3 £210**

Farne Isle *G A Harker* 65
6 ch m Midnight Legend - Biloela
8^{11gf} 2^{12gf} **0-1-2 £1,265**

Farriers Charm *D J Coakley* 69 a61
4 b f In Command (Ire) - Carn Maire
4^{9gf} 3^{8gf} 10^{7gf} 8^{8g} 8^{9sd} **0-1-5 £967**

Farringdon *M P Tregoning* 48
2 b c Sadler's Wells (USA) - Rebecca Sharp
12^{7g} **0-0-1**

Farthing (Ire) *Miss A Stokell* 55 a52
3 b f Mujadil (USA) - Neat Shilling (Ire)
4^{6sd} 2^{7sd} 5^{6sd} 3^{7sd} 4^{7sd} 2^{7sd} 4^{6g} 5^{7s} 13^{6s}
4^{6sd} 5^{6g} 9^{8g} 5^{5f} 12^{6f} 18^{7gf} 11^{8g} 7^{7gf} 12^{7sd}
0-3-18 £1,734

Fashion Chic *Stef Liddiard* 30 a39
2 b f Averti (Ire) - Fashion Bride (Ire)
8^{5sd} 6^{5sd} 4^{5gs} 8^{5sd} 9^{8sd} 8^{6sd} **0-0-6 £264**

Fashion House (USA) *Saeed Bin Suroor* 70 a59
3 b f Quiet American (USA) - Polish Style (USA)
6^{7ft} 6^{8gf} 4^{8gf} 10^{7sd} 14^{10gf} **0-0-5 £283**

Fashionable *B W Hills* 101
3 ch f Nashwan (USA) - Fine Detail (Ire)
1^{8gf} 1^{10gf} 9^{12gf} 7^{10gf} **2-0-4 £20,630**

Fast Bowler *J M P Eustace* 75
2 b g Intikhab (USA) - Alegria
1^{6gf} **1-0-1 £4,173**

Fast Heart *B J Meehan* 104 a103
4 b g Fasliyev (USA) - Heart Of India (Ire)
2^{5sd} 7^{5gs} 6^{5gs} 6^{5gf} 2^{5g} 9^{5g} 8^{5g} 6^{5gf} 5^{5sd} 14^{5s}
10^{5gf} 12^{6gf} 9^{5gf} 18^{6s} 15^{5hy} **0-2-15**
£13,982

Fast Lightning (Ire) *W J Haggas* 55
2 b g Barathea (Ire) - Poleaxe
10^{6g} **0-0-1**

Fasylitator (Ire) *D K Ivory* 70 a87
3 b c Fasliyev (USA) - Obsessed
4^{7sd} 1^{9sd} 6^{7sd} 5^{7gs} 10^{8sd} 1^{9sd} 7^{8gf} 9^{10g} 2^{8gf}
1^{10sd} 3^{10sd} 1^{8sd} **4-2-12 £15,166**

Fateful Attraction *I A Wood* 51 a60
2 b f Mujahid (USA) - Heavens Above (Fr)
12^{5s} 15^{6gf} 12^{7gf} 7^{7gs} 6^{7sd} 11^{8g} 1^{7sd} 5^{7sd}
1-0-8 £1,522

Fatherghent (Ire) *Niall Moran* 51 a10
3 b g Bold Fact (USA) - Dance In The Wings
7^{10g} 5^{8f} 2^{10gf} 13^{10gf} 13^{10sd} **0-1-5**
£1,256

Favour *Mrs J R Ramsden* 67
5 b m Gothenberg (Ire) - Prejudice
6^{6gf} 4^{6gf} 7^{6gs} 13^{8gf} 10^{7g} UR^{6gf} **0-0-6**

Favourable *A W Carroll*
4 b f Mark Of Esteem (Ire) - Top Society
11^{10gf} **0-0-1**

Favourable Terms *Sir Michael Stoute* 109
5 b m Selkirk (USA) - Fatefully (USA)
1^{7g} 8^{8gs} 5^{10y} **1-0-3 £33,963**

Favouring (Ire) *R A Fahey* a59
3 ch g Fayruz - Peace Dividend (Ire)
7^{5sd} 10^{7g} 4^{6sd} 3^{6sd} 8^{6sd} **0-1-5 £532**

Favourita *C E Brittain* 102
3 b f Diktat - Forthwith
3^{7gf} 12^{8gf} 2^{10gf} 3^{10gf} 6^{8gf} 8^{12g} 4^{10gf} 15^{8g}
0-3-8 £16,660

Fayr Firenze (Ire) *M F Harris* 49 a48
4 b g Fayruz - Shillay
9^{8sd} 7^{6sd} 9^{6sd} 1^{7sd} 10^{7sd} 3^{6sd} 3^{7gf} 17^{7gf} 6^{6f}
5^{8f} **1-2-10 £2,079**

Fayr Jag (Ire) *T D Easterby* 115
6 b g Fayruz - Lominda (Ire)
11^{6s} 12^{5gf} 8^{5gf} 11^{6g} 4^{6gf} 3^{6g} 12^{6g} 6^{5gf} 5^{6g}
2^{6g} 2^{6g} 7^{7gf} **0-3-12 £34,399**

Fayr Sky (Ire) *J J Quinn* 68
2 b f Fayruz - Dutosky
6^{5gf} 4^{5gf} 1^{5gf} 4^{6g} 6^{7gf} **1-1-5 £3,721**

Fayrz Please (Ire) *M C Chapman* 44 a37
4 ch g Fayruz - Castlelue (Ire)
12^{6s} 14^{6sd} UR^{11gf} 10^{12gf} 14^{10s} 13^{8g} 13^{6gf}
9^{7gf} 8^{7g} 7^{6sd} 4^{6sd} **0-0-11 £245**

Fear To Tread (USA) *J L Dunlop* 71
2 ch f Peintre Celebre (USA) - Pleine Lune (Ire)
7^{7s} 6^{8g} 5^{7gf} 7^{7gs} **0-0-4**

Fearless Spirit (USA) *J H M Gosden* 80
3 ch f Spinning World (USA) - Hot Princess
6^{10gf} 5^{10g} 1^{12gf} 10^{12gf} 8^{10gf} **1-0-5**
£2,562

Fearnofoe (Ire) *B Palling* 6
2 b g Desert Style (Ire) - College Lane (Fr)
13^{8g} 9^{8gf} **0-0-2**

Feast Of Romance *C R Dore* 57 a69
8 b g Pursuit Of Love - June Fayre

2^{7sd} 1^{7sd} 3^{6sd} 1^{6sd} 1^{7sd} 4^{6sd} 2^{6s} 4^{6sd} 7^{6gs}
10^{7sd} 8^{6gf} 12^{5gf} 17^{5gf} 12^{6g} 12^{8gs} 3^{8sd} 5^{6sd}
12^{8sd} 13^{8ss} 11^{7sd} **3-4-20 £10,219**

Feathergrass (Ire) *S Kirk* 65 a36
3 b f Fasliyev (USA) - Jamaican Punch (Ire)
6^{7gs} 5^{8gs} 6^{8gf} 13^{8gf} 11^{7sd} **0-0-5**

Feed The Meter (Ire) *M J Ryan* 82
5 b m Desert King (Ire) - Watch The Clock
1^{12g} 4^{12gf} 1^{12gf} 1^{12gf} 1^{12gf} 3^{12gf} 3^{12gf} 2^{12gf}
4-3-8 £18,996

Feel The Need *G A Swinbank*
3 ch g Chocolat De Meguro (USA) - Mary Miller
16^{9gf} 10^{12ss} **0-0-2**

Feel The Pride (Ire) *Jonjo O'Neill*
7 b m Persian Bold - Nordic Pride
12^{14g} **0-0-1**

Feelin Irie (Ire) *N Tinkler* 65
2 b c Key Of Luck (USA) - Charlotte's Dancer
10^{5g} 8^{5gs} 7^{6g} 9^{5gf} 9^{6g} 4^{7gf} 1^{8gf} 17^{8g}
1-0-8 £3,705

Fei Mah *J R Jenkins* 3
3 b f Vettori (Ire) - Bluewain Lady
10^{5sd} 12^{6g} **0-0-2**

Felicitous *Saeed Bin Suroor* 76
2 b f King's Best (USA) - Embassy
3^{6gf} 2^{6gf} **0-2-2 £2,594**

Felin Gruvy (Ire) *R F Johnson Houghton* 71
2 b f Tagula (Ire) - Felin Special
10^{6gs} 2^{6gs} 5^{6g} **0-1-3 £1,776**

Fellbeck Fred *C W Thornton*
3 gr c Paris House - Wyse Folly
8^{8sd} **0-0-1**

Fellow Ship *P Butler* a46
5 b g Elmaamul (USA) - Genoa
9^{8sd} 9^{8sd} 7^{16sd} 5^{13sd} 5^{12sd} 12^{12s} **0-0-6**

Feminist (Ire) *J M Bradley* 36 a54
3 b f Alhaarth (Ire) - Miss Willow Bend (USA)
8^{6sd} 4^{5sd} 8^{6sd} 3^{5sd} 2^{6sd} 7^{5sd} 7^{6sd} 11^{5sd} 15^{5gs}
6^{5g} 1^{5sd} 1^{5sd} 12^{5f} 17^{5g} 8^{5sd} 12^{6sd} 10^{5sd}
2-2-17 £5,309

Fen Game (Ire) *J H M Gosden* 72
3 b g Montjeu (Ire) - Hatton Gardens
11^{8gs} 7^{10f} 5^{12f} 1^{12gf} **1-0-4 £4,334**

Fen Guest *Rae Guest* 58
2 b f Woodborough (USA) - Crackling
4^{5f} **0-0-1 £262**

Fen Gypsy *P D Evans* 52
7 b g Nashwan (USA) - Didicoy (USA)
10^{8gs} 7^{8f} 16^{8g} 8^{8gf} 15^{7gf} **0-0-5**

Fen Shui (UAE) *Saeed Bin Suroor* 96
3 b f Timber Country (USA) - Crystal Gazing (USA)
10^{8gf} 12^{12g} **0-0-2**

Fenners (USA) *M Johnston* 79
2 ch c Pleasant Tap (USA) - Legal Opinion (Ire)
3^{6gf} 6^{7f} 1^{8gf} **1-1-3 £3,567**

Fenwicks Pride (Ire) *A Berry* 48 a41
7 b g Imperial Frontier (USA) - Stunt Girl (Ire)
12^{7sd} 7^{5sd} 2^{6g} 7^{7g} 17^{7g} 12^{6gf} 3^{6g} 2^{7sd} 3^{6sd}
8^{6sd} **0-4-10 £1,269**

Fern House (Ire) *A Berry* 11
3 b g Xaar - Certain Impression (USA)
RO^{7g} 11^{6g} 8^{8gf} **0-0-3**

Fern Valley *M J Attwater*
3 ch g Young Ern - Croft Sally
12^{6sd} 13^{7sd} 10^{7sd} 13^{7sd} **0-0-4**

Ferrando *Mrs J R Ramsden* 50
3 b g Hernando (Fr) - Oh So Misty
10^{7g} PU^{8g} **0-0-2**

Ferrara Flame (Ire) *R Brotherton* 59 a59
3 b f Titus Livius (Fr) - Isolette
2^{9sd} 4^{11sd} 5^{12sd} 9^{7gs} 9^{10s} 3^{8g} 4^{12sd} 1^{7g} 12^{8gf}
1-2-9 £4,250

Ferrero *W McKeown* 51
2 br c Distant Music (USA) - Charitable (Ire)
9^{5gf} 6^{5g} 5^{5gs} **0-0-3**

Ferroli *J Balding*
2 b g Efisio - Ordained
13^{5gf} **0-0-1**

Festive Chimes (Ire) *N B King* a22
4 b f Efisio - Delightful Chime (Ire)
11^{9sd} 13^{8sd} 9^{6sd} **0-0-3**

Feu D'Artifice (USA) *R Hannon* 76 a69
2 b c Stravinsky (USA) - Alashir (USA)
3^{7sd} 4^{7g} 2^{8hd} **0-2-3 £1,759**

Ffizzamo Go *Mrs A J Hamilton-Fairley*
4 b g Forzando - Lady Lacey
13^{17sd} **0-0-1**

Fibou (USA) *Saeed Bin Suroor* 42
2 ch f Seeking The Gold (USA) - Lilium
12^{6gf} **0-0-1**

Fictional *E S McMahon* 102
4 b c Fraam - Manon Lescaut
3^{5gf} 9^{5s} 3^{5g} 3^{5gs} 1^{5gf} 14^{5gf} 1^{6g} 27^{6g}
2-2-8 £31,407

Fiddlers Creek (Ire) *R Allan* 66 a84
6 b g Danehill (USA) - Mythical Creek (USA)
1^{9sd} 9^{12sd} 9^{12sd} 6^{10sd} 11^{10g} 8^{9gs} 2^{8gs} 14^{8g}
UR^{12sd} **1-1-9 £7,892**

Fiddlers Wood *V Smith* 92
2 b g Spectrum (Ire) - Tanasie
14^{8g} 4^{8gs} 2^{10s} 8^{10hy} **0-1-4 £5,426**

Fiddles Music *D Burchell* 38
4 b f Fraam - Fiddles Delight
6^{10hy} **0-0-1**

Fidra (Ire) *H Morrison* a63
3 gr f Vettori (Ire) - Doon Point
3^{8sd} 5^{8sd} **0-1-2 £536**

Fiefdom (Ire) *M Johnston* 96
3 br c Singspiel (Ire) - Chiquita Linda (Ire)
4^{10gs} 4^{8g} **0-1-2 £6,110**

Field Spark *J G Given* 62 a61
5 b g Sillery (USA) - On The Top
2^{12sd} 3^{12gf} 3^{12g} 4^{12f} 9^{12f} 4^{14sd} 6^{17sd} 6^{12sf}
8^{12g} **0-3-9 £2,320**

Fiennes (USA) *R C Guest* 32
7 b/br g Dayjur (USA) - Artic Strech (USA)
11^{5g} 18^{5gf} 9^{5f} 15^{7g} **0-0-4**

Fiery Angel (Ire) *A G Newcombe* a6
4 ch f Machiavellian (USA) - Flaming June (USA)
8^{5sd} **0-0-1**

Fiesty Madam *Miss I E Craig* 28
4 ch f Bien Bien (USA) - Riverine
6^{10gs} 9^{10gf} 5^{10g} 9^{8gs} **0-0-4**

Fife And Drum (USA) *Miss J Feilden* 41 a21
8 b/br g Rahy (USA) - Fife (Ire)
13^{9sd} 15^{12sd} 11^{10sd} 8^{10gf} 9^{10g} 8^{12gf} 2^{8gf} 19^{8gf}
0-1-8 £1,191

Fifth Column (USA) *D W Thompson*
4 b g Allied Forces (USA) - Miff (USA)
13^{12gs} 17^{7f} 15^{8gf} **0-0-3**

Figaro Flyer (Ire) *P Howling* 88 a72
2 b g Mozart (Ire) - Ellway Star (Ire)
3^{5gf} 2^{5gf} 1^{6f} 3^{6sd} 4^{6gf} 1^{6gf} 1^{5gf} 2^{5gs} 6^{5g} 3^{5gs} 6^{5g} 1^{6sd} **4-4-12 £28,221**

Figaro's Quest (Ire) *P F I Cole* 66
3 b g Singspiel (Ire) - Seren Quest
2^{12g} 13^{12g} 8^{13g} 9^{12f} 9^{14g} 3^{16s} 4^{12gf} 7^{16g} 2^{12f} 2^{12f} 4^{12gs} **0-4-11 £3,349**

Figgy's Brew *C G Cox* 16
3 ch f Ashkalani (Ire) - Marabela (Ire)
11^{8gf} 11^{8sd} **0-0-2**

Fight The Feeling *J W Unett* a48
7 ch g Beveled (USA) - Alvecote Lady
2^{17sd} 4^{17sd} **0-1-2 £421**

Fight Your Corner *Saeed Bin Suroor* 113
6 b h Muhtarram (USA) - Dame Ashfield
1^{12gf} 2^{12gf} 11^{12gf} 1^{16g} 7^{20gf} **2-1-5 £107,668**

Fighter Command *Evan Williams* 42 a61
4 ch g Docksider (USA) - Rose Alto
6^{9sd} 8^{10gf} 6^{12sd} 6^{12sd} **0-0-4**

Figjam *J R Best* 86 a76
2 b g Groom Dancer (USA) - Sheila's Secret (Ire)
14^{5gs} 2^{5sd} 1^{5g} 1^{5g} 1^{5gf} 13^{5gs} 6^{6g} 2^{6gs} 8^{5g} **2-2-9 £12,796**

Figurative (Ire) *G A Swinbank* 36
3 b g Machiavellian (USA) - Marble Maiden
9^{8hy} 10^{7gs} 12^{8g} **0-0-3**

Filey Buoy *R M Whitaker* 45 a56
3 b g Factual (USA) - Tugra (Fr)
11^{10gf} 6^{10gf} 5^{8gf} 6^{8gf} 3^{10g} 5^{12g} 6^{8gf} 9^{10g} 12^{10g} 2^{7sd} 3^{7sd} 2^{8sd} 1^{7sd} 8^{8sd} **1-4-14 £3,238**

Fillameena *P T Midgley* 54 a54
5 b m Robellino (USA) - Lotus Moon
13^{10gf} 6^{8sd} 13^{10gf} 3^{12g} 4^{13gs} 2^{14sd} 6^{17sd} 4^{16sd} 2^{12sf} 9^{13sd} **0-3-10 £1,653**

Filliemou (Ire) *A W Carroll* 35
4 gr f Goldmark (USA) - St Louis Lady
12^{8gf} 11^{7g} 7^{10s} 12^{8gf} 7^{8hd} **0-0-5**

Final Bid (Ire) *M G Quinlan* 60 a67
2 b c Mujadil (USA) - Dusky Virgin
6^{6gf} 6^{7gs} 7^{7gf} 9^{7sd} 2^{7sf} **0-1-5 £1,114**

Final Overture (Ire) *J S Wainwright* 10
3 b f Rossini (USA) - Two Magpies
4^{9gf} **0-0-1 £261**

Final Promise *J A Geake* 74
3 b c Lujain (USA) - Unerring
9^{6gf} 3^{7gs} 5^{8gf} 12^{8g} 1^{8gs} 11^{9g} 11^{8s} 16^{8s} **1-1-8 £4,571**

Final Tune (Ire) *D Nicholls* 63
2 ch g Grand Lodge (USA) - Jackie's Opera (Fr)
8^{7gs} 4^{6gs} 5^{6gf} **0-0-3 £431**

Final Verse *Sir Michael Stoute* 106
2 b c Mark Of Esteem (Ire) - Tamassos
1^{6g} 4^{7g} 2^{6g} 2^{7gs} **1-2-4 £19,942**

Finalmente *N A Callaghan* 86
3 b g Kahyasi - Sudden Spirit (Fr)
11^{10gf} 6^{11g} 7^{12gf} 11^{10gf} 1^{14gf} **1-0-5 £4,237**

Financial Future *C Roberts* 65
5 b g Barathea (Ire) - In Perpetuity
9^{12s} 6^{10s} 5^{12gs} 4^{12gf} 2^{12s} **0-1-5 £1,236**

Find It Out (USA) *T D Barron* 56
2 b g Luhuk (USA) - Ursula (Ven)
5^{8gs} 4^{8gf} **0-0-2 £280**

Fine Cuisine (Ire) *R Bastiman*
3 b f Entrepreneur - Hillside Rose (Ire)
12^{11sd} 8^{11hy} **0-0-2**

Fine Lady *M Johnston* 7
3 ch f Selkirk (USA) - Rua D'Oro (USA)
12^{10s} 15^{8s} 6^{8gf} **0-0-3**

Fine Palette *B J Llewellyn* 64
5 ch g Peintre Celebre (USA) - Filly Mignonne (Ire)
11^{11g} 5^{12gf} 6^{10gf} 10^{10gs} **0-0-4**

Fine Silver (Ire) *P F I Cole* 107
4 gr c Intikhab (USA) - Petula
1^{8gs} 12^{8g} 7^{7s} 11^{9g} 13^{10gf} 8^{8gf} 11^{12sd} **1-0-7 £29,000**

Fine Thanks *D Haydn Jones*
4 b f Danzig Connection (USA) - Dim Ots
9^{6sd} 18^{7gf} **0-0-2**

Finished Article (Ire) *P A Blockley* 77 a41
8 b g Indian Ridge - Summer Fashion
13^{7gs} 9^{10gs} 7^{8gf} 11^{9sd} 18^{10g} **0-0-5**

Finland (UAE) *Mrs A Duffield* 66
3 b g Timber Country (USA) - Najm Al Bahar (Fr)
9^{10g} 5^{9gs} 4^{12f} 5^{11g} 4^{12gf} 6^{12gs} 12^{14g} **0-0-7 £543**

Finnegans Rainbow *M C Chapman* 57 a58
3 ch g Spectrum (Ire) - Fairy Story (Ire)
7^{8sd} 11^{9sd} 7^{12gs} 9^{12gf} 4^{11g} 7^{12sd} 5^{14gf} 2^{12g} 6^{12s} 8^{12s} 2^{11sd} 4^{8ss} 3^{11ss} 6^{11sd} 4^{11sd} **0-3-15 £1,682**

Finsbury *C F Wall* 68 a69
2 br/gr g Observatory (USA) - Carmela Owen
4^{6g} 4^{6sd} 4^{7sd} **0-0-3 £746**

Fiore Di Bosco (Ire) *T D Barron* 59
4 b f Charnwood Forest (Ire) - Carabine (USA)
8^{6g} 7^{6gf} 12^{7gf} 4^{6g} 11^{7gf} 10^{6g} **0-0-6 £277**

Fir Tree *S R Bowring* 38 a43
5 b g Mistertopogigo (Ire) - Marina's Song
10^{7g} 14^{6sf} 12^{5sd} 2^{5sd} 2^{9sd} **0-2-5 £841**

Fire And Rain (Fr) *A P O'Brien* 95
2 b c Galileo (Ire) - Quatre Saisons (Fr)
1^{8g} **1-0-1 £6,981**

Fire At Will *A W Carroll* 59 a59
3 b c Lugana Beach - Kahyasi Moll (Ire)
1^{7sd} 7^{7sd} 7^{9sd} 7^{9sd} 5^{7gs} 2^{7sd} **1-1-6 £4,829**

Fire Two *M R Channon* 80
2 b c Cape Cross (Ire) - Reematna
3^{7gs} 2^{8g} 2^{9g} 2^{8gf} 9^{8s} **0-4-5 £4,862**

Fire Up The Band *D Nicholls* 114
6 b g Prince Sabo - Green Supreme
1^{5gs} 8^{5s} 5^{7gs} 1^{5g} 10^{6f} 4^{5gf} 3^{5gf} 1^{5s} 13^{5gf} 8^{5gf} 3^{5gs} **3-2-11 £109,372**

Firebird *I I Candy* 43 a44
4 b f Soviet Star (USA) - Al Corniche (Ire)
9^{6g} 7^{6gf} 10^{8gf} 11^{6gf} 6^{6g} 9^{6sd} **0-0-6**

Firebird Rising (USA) *R Brotherton* 35 a40
4 b f Stravinsky (USA) - Capable (USA)
4^{7sd} 7^{8sd} 7^{8sd} 6^{8sd} 4^{10sd} 6^{10s} 8^{7gf} 8^{7g} 6^{12gf} 6^{7sd} 7^{8ss} 7^{8sd} **0-0-12**

Firenze *J R Fanshawe* 96
4 ch f Efisio - Juliet Bravo
3^{6g} 1^{6gf} 1^{6gf} 6^{6g} 3^{6g} 11^{6s} **2-2-6 £16,739**

Firesong *S Kirk* 83
3 b g Dansili - Leaping Flame (USA)

5^{9gs} 2^{10g} 1^{9f} 11^{11gf} 7^{8g} **1-1-5 £3,640**

Firework *E A Wheeler* 63
7 b g Primo Dominie - Prancing
7^{6f} 13^{6f} 17^{6gf} 6^{5gf} 10^{6g} 1^{6gf} 14^{6f} 9^{6f}
1-0-8 £2,723

Firmount (Ire) *B S Rothwell* 48 a23
3 b/br g Lujain (USA) - Monkey Business
13^{8gf} 12^{5sd} 9^{5gf} 14^{5gf} 15^{5s} 10^{6sd} **0-0-6**

First Among Equals *Miss J R Tooth* 56 a27
2 b f Primo Valentino (Ire) - Margarets First
5^{5f} 8^{5gf} 3^{6gf} 3^{6gf} 1^{5gf} 7^{6gf} 5^{5gf} 10^{5gf} 9^{5sd}
11^{6sd} **1-2-10 £5,252**

First Approval *B W Hills* 74
2 b f Royal Applause - Gaijin
10^{6gf} 2^{6f} 8^{6g} **0-1-3 £1,505**

First Ballot (Ire) *D R C Elsworth* 106
9 br g Perugino (USA) - Election Special
3^{12g} 7^{16g} 12^{14gs} **0-0-3 £2,257**

First Byte *Miss D A McHale* 53 a43
2 b f Primo Valentino (Ire) - Shark Games
3^{5g} 10^{5gs} 6^{6gf} 3^{6f} 1^{6gf} 3^{6gf} 5^{7f} 5^{7g} 6^{6gf}
3^{7gf} 7^{5sd} 12^{9sd} 9^{7sd} **1-1-13 £4,257**

First Candlelight *A M Balding* 37
4 b f First Trump - No Candles Tonight
12^{6gf} **0-0-1**

First Dawn *D K Ivory* 46 a35
4 ch f Dr Fong (USA) - Delight Of Dawn
14^{8gf} 13^{6g} 11^{6gf} 11^{7f} 9^{6sd} 10^{5g} 5^{6f} 12^{6f}
4^{7gs} 6^{6g} **0-0-10 £301**

First Dynasty (USA) *Miss S J Wilton* 69 a61
5 b/br g Danzig (USA) - Willow Runner (USA)
8^{12sd} 4^{10s} 5^{10g} 3^{13gs} 11^{12gf} **0-1-5 £914**

First Eclipse (Ire) *G Woodward*
4 b f Fayruz - Naked Poser (Ire)
14^{6sd} **0-0-1**

First Empire (Ire) *M J Wallace* 73
2 b c Desert Prince (Ire) - Second Prayer (Ire)
10^{6gf} 6^{7gf} 4^{6gs} 1^{7gf} 3^{7gf} 12^{7gf} 12^{8gf}
1-1-7 £6,649

First Fought (Ire) *D McCain* 66
3 b g Germany (USA) - Royal Flame (Ire)
4^{10gs} 2^{8gf} 7^{9s} 6^{8gf} **0-1-4 £2,821**

First Generation *T Hogan* 51
3 b g Primo Dominie - My Cadeaux
15^{7g} 10^{7gf} 4^{6gf} 11^{8f} 7^{7g} **0-0-5 £328**

First Look (Fr) *P Monteith* 54
5 b g Acatenango (Ger) - First Class (Ger)
6^{11gs} **0-0-1**

First Maite *S R Bowring* 46 a52
12 b g Komaite (USA) - Marina Plata
6^{7g} 10^{8g} 10^{5gf} UR^{7gf} 3^{7sd} 7^{9sd} 2^{6g} 7^{6sd} 3^{7sd}
5^{8sd} **0-3-10 £1,195**

First Of May *Miss Z C Davison* 46 a48
4 b f Halling (USA) - Finger Of Light
7^{12sd} 4^{10sd} 6^{10sd} 4^{9sd} 11^{10sd} 7^{9sd} 13^{9sd} 0^{8s}
16^{11g} 6^{9gf} 11^{8gf} 5^{8g} 5^{8sd} 11^{10sd} 8^{8sd}
0-0-15

First Rhapsody (Ire) *T J Etherington* 66 a46
3 b f Rossini (USA) - Tinos Island (Ire)
11^{8sd} 8^{9sd} 3^{6s} 2^{7gs} 1^{6g} 3^{6gf} 15^{6s} 4^{6g}
1-2-8 £6,959

First Row (Ire) *D T Hughes* 103 a73
3 b c Daylami (Ire) - Ballet Society (Fr)
2^{10sd} 1^{12s} 3^{12gs} 5^{12gf} 4^{12gs} 5^{14gf} 6^{12hy}
1-2-7 £20,851

First Show *J Noseda* 79 a54
3 b c Cape Cross (Ire) - Rose Show
10^{10sd} 7^{8sd} 4^{10gf} 4^{12g} 5^{12gf} 5^{10g} 4^{8gf} 1^{8g} 2^{8s}
1-2-9 £6,002

First Slip *Mrs A J Perrett* a71
2 b c Slip Anchor - Nanouche
2^{8sd} 3^{8sd} **0-2-2 £1,570**

Fisberry *M S Saunders* 85 a59
3 gr c Efisio - Elderberry
5^{7sd} 10^{7sd} 1^{6g} 1^{6gf} 12^{6g} **2-0-5**
£10,452

Fisby *K J Burke* 78 a78
4 ch g Efisio - Trilby
13^{10sd} 4^{9sd} 1^{10sd} 2^{9sd} 1^{10sd} 5^{10sd} 12^{10g} 16^{8gf}
4^{10gf} 3^{9sd} 1^{11gf} 2^{12gs} 5^{12gs} **3-3-13**
£14,260

Fisher Bridge (Ire) *W R Swinburn* a62
2 ch c Singspiel (Ire) - Kristal Bridge
4^{9sd} **0-0-1 £276**

Fisher's Dream *J R Norton* a22
4 b g Groom Dancer (USA) - Cremets
11^{6sd} 10^{7sd} **0-0-2**

Fishlake Flyer (Ire) *D Carroll* 55
4 b f Desert Style (Ire) - Millitrix
9^{5gf} 11^{5gs} 12^{5gf} **0-0-3**

Fisola (Ire) *C G Cox* 76
2 b f Fasliyev (USA) - Afisiak
1^{5gf} 2^{5gf} 20^{6gf} 11^{5g} **1-1-4 £6,095**

Fit To Fly (Ire) *R C Guest* 49 a41
4 b g Lahib (USA) - Maid Of Mourne
5^{7s} 6^{8gf} 9^{14sd} 7^{6gf} 7^{6gf} 5^{8sd} **0-0-6**

Fitasabuckstoat (Ire) *A Berry* 35
2 b g Fayruz - Bardia
6^{5s} 8^{5s} 8^{5gs} 7^{6gf} 6^{6f} 11^{5g} **0-0-6**

Fitting Guest (Ire) *G C Bravery* 71 a6
4 ch g Grand Lodge (USA) - Sarah-Clare
20^{8g} 16^{6g} 3^{7gf} 11^{8gf} 8^{8g} 19^{10gf} 10^{8g} 12^{8sd}
14^{10gf} **0-1-9 £527**

Fitzsimons (Ire) *A M Hales* 47 a37
2 b g Carrowkeel (Ire) - Our Pet
8^{6g} 8^{6g} 5^{7gf} 8^{7gf} 13^{7g} 6^{7gf} 11^{7gf} 7^{10sd}
0-0-8

Fitzwarren *A D Brown* 56 a51
4 b g Presidium - Coney Hills
11^{5gf} 11^{5gf} 7^{6gf} 5^{6f} 12^{6f} 5^{7gf} 13^{6gf} 13^{8gf}
13^{6g} 3^{7sd} 6^{6sd} 6^{6sd} **0-1-12 £211**

Five Fields (USA) *J H M Gosden* 85
3 b/br f Chester House (USA) - Diese (USA)
8^{8gs} 3^{8f} 1^{10f} 8^{10s} **1-1-4 £4,403**

Five Years On (Ire) *R M Beckett* 42
4 b g Desert Sun - Snowspin
14^{7gs} 15^{10gf} 14^{7g} 17^{8gf} **0-0-4**

Fiveoclock Express (Ire) *N Wilson* 69 a74
5 gr g Woodborough (USA) - Brooks Masquerade
9^{12sd} 1^{9sd} 2^{9sd} 5^{10sd} 9^{8sd} 7^{8gs} 8^{8sd} 8^{7gs} 5^{10sd}
1^{10f} 1^{10f} 1^{12f} 7^{10gf} 4^{10gf} 3^{10g} 7^{10g}
4-2-16 £13,826

Fizz *Mrs N Macauley* 36
3 ch f Bold Edge - Join The Clan
6^{5gf} F^{6gf} 6^{7gf} **0-0-3**

Fizzlephut (Ire) *Miss J R Tooth* 87 a75
3 b g Indian Rocket - Cladantom (Ire)
7^{7sd} 10^{6g} 3^{5s} 1^{5f} 1^{5g} 4^{5gs} 14^{6g} 11^{5g} 6^{6gs}
5^{5sd} **2-1-10 £11,241**

Fizzy Lady *R A Harris* a38

4 b f Efisio - The Frog Lady (Ire)
13^{11sd} 12^{9sd} 9^{9sd} **0-0-3**

Fizzy Lizzy *H E Haynes* 38 a48
5 b m Cool Jazz - Formidable Liz
11^{7sd} 4^{6sd} 7^{6g} 11^{6f} 6^{6sd} 9^{7sd} **0-0-6**

Flag Lieutenant *Sir Michael Stoute* 76 a75
3 b g Machiavellian (USA) - Fairy Godmother
5^{10sd} 2^{11gs} 8^{12gf} 8^{12sd} **0-1-4 £1,036**

Flag Of Truce *Saeed Bin Suroor* 81
3 b c Dubai Millennium - Flagbird (USA)
3^{8g} **0-1-1 £746**

Flag Point (Ire) *J L Dunlop* 62
3 b c Indian Danehill (Ire) - Bianca Cappello (Ire)
6^{10gf} 11^{12gf} 3^{12f} 14^{12g} **0-1-4 £704**

Flamand (USA) *L M Cumani* 61 a48
3 ch f Miswaki (USA) - Sister Sorrow (USA)
8^{10g} 6^{8f} 5^{8sd} **0-0-3**

Flamboyant Lad *B W Hills* 103
4 ch c Nashwan (USA) - Cheeky Charm (USA)
4^{12gf} 1^{12f} 10^{12f} 11^{12gf} 4^{11gf} **1-1-5**
£17,945

Flame Queen *Mrs C A Dunnett* 43
4 b f The West (USA) - Red Cloud (Ire)
13^{6gf} 7^{8g} 8^{6g} 10^{7gf} 11^{7gf} **0-0-5**

Flaming Cat (Ire) *C Grant* 49
2 b/br c Orpen (USA) - Brave Cat (Ire)
13^{5s} 9^{6gf} 5^{5f} **0-0-3**

Flaming Eyes (Ger) *W R Swinburn* a68
4 b f Imperial Ballet (Ire) - Fantastic Flame (Ire)
3^{12sd} **0-1-1 £512**

Flaming Shot (Ire) *Jennie Candlish* 51 a14
3 b c Son Of Sharp Shot (Ire) - Brockton Flame
8^{9gf} 8^{6g} 8^{9sd} **0-0-3**

Flaming Weapon *G L Moore* 52 a41
3 b g Unfuwain (USA) - Flame Valley (USA)
13^{7sd} 4^{10gs} 8^{11g} 10^{12sd} 5^{10g} **0-0-5 £273**

Flamjica (USA) *J A R Toller* 66 a58
4 ch f Real Quiet (USA) - Fiamma (Ire)
16^{8g} 10^{8g} 6^{12sd} 9^{10g} 9^{9sd} **0-0-5**

Flapdoodle *A W Carroll* 23 a14
7 b m Superpower - My Concordia
13^{5sd} 9^{5g} 7^{5sd} **0-0-3**

Flaran *J A R Toller* 69 a52
5 b g Emarati (USA) - Fragrance
1^{5gf} 8^{5g} 4^{5g} 7^{5g} 9^{6f} 4^{5gf} 10^{6sd} **1-1-7**
£4,313

Flash And Dazzle (Ire) *J H M Gosden* 64 a58
2 b f Bertolini (USA) - Corn Futures
10^{6gs} 4^{6gf} 6^{7sd} 9^{7sf} **0-0-4 £390**

Flash Ram *T D Easterby* 78
4 b g Mind Games - Just A Gem
7^{7s} 8^{7gs} 7^{8g} 1^{8g} 1^{8gs} 7^{8gf} 3^{8g} **2-0-7**
£8,844

Flashing Floozie *J M P Eustace* 51
2 ch f Muhtarram (USA) - High Habit
9^{6gs} **0-0-1**

Flashy Wings *M R Channon* 111
2 ch f Zafonic (USA) - Lovealoch (Ire)
1^{5gf} 1^{5gf} 1^{5gf} 1^{6gf} 2^{7gf} 3^{6g} **4-2-6**
£180,159

Flaunt N Flirt *M Blanshard* 49
3 b/br f Erhaab (USA) - Lets Fall In Love (USA)
12^{8gf} 7^{8gs} 9^{8gf} 11^{12sd} **0-0-4**

Flaxby *J D Bethell* 66
3 b g Mister Baileys - Harryana
2^{7g} 8^{8g} 11^{7g} 4^{7s} 7^{7gf} 8^{6g} 4^{6g} 7^{6g} 9^{7gf}
0-1-9 £1,659

Fleece *H R A Cecil* 64
3 b f Daylami (Ire) - Gold Dodger (USA)
2^{12gs} 3^{10g} **0-1-2 £2,267**

Fleet Anchor *J M Bradley* 52 a49
4 b g Fleetwood (Ire) - Upping The Tempo
9^{7gs} 10^{8gf} 4^{8gf} 6^{8f} 12^{9sd} 5^{8f} 17^{10f} 2^{8gs} 5^{7gf}
UR^{8gf} 11^{8f} 10^{8g} 3^{8sd} 4^{8sd} 8^{9sf} 6^{8ss}
0-2-16 £1,289

Fleetfoot Mac *B Storey* 24
4 b g Fleetwood (Ire) - Desert Flower
14^{10g} **0-0-1**

Fleeting Memory *Sir Michael Stoute* 75
2 b f Danehill (USA) - Flight Of Fancy
6^{8g} **0-0-1**

Fleetwood Bay *V R A Dartnall* 70
5 b g Fleetwood (Ire) - Caviar And Candy
3^{10gf} 10^{10gs} **0-1-2 £566**

Fletcher *H Morrison* 18
11 b g Salse (USA) - Ballet Classique (USA)
12^{14g} 17^{12gf} **0-0-2**

Fleurance *J A R Toller* 22 a9
3 br f High Estate - Fragrance
10^{6gf} 11^{7gs} 11^{8sd} **0-0-3**

Flick N Flack *D W Thompson* 22
2 b g Namaqualand (USA) - Riyoom (USA)
8^{7gf} **0-0-1**

Flight Captain *M G Quinlan* 79
2 ch c In The Wings - Polygueza (Fr)
8^{7gf} 4^{7g} 1^{7g} **1-0-3 £4,634**

Flight Of Esteem *W R Swinburn* 88 a87
5 b g Mark Of Esteem (Ire) - Miss Up N Go
10^{10g} 10^{10gf} 3^{12g} 5^{12gs} 3^{12sd} **0-2-5**
£2,512

Flighty Fellow (Ire) *T D Easterby* 92
5 ch g Flying Spur (Aus) - Al Theraab (USA)
4^{8gs} 6^{7gf} 5^{8gf} 15^{7gf} 8^{8gf} 6^{8gf} **0-0-6**
£1,899

Flint River *H Morrison* 86 a86
7 b g Red Ransom (USA) - She's All Class (USA)
7^{8sd} 3^{7sd} 12^{9sd} 1^{7gs} 12^{8g} 3^{7gf} 4^{7gf} 3^{7gf} 10^{8gf}
11^{7gf} 5^{6g} 9^{6gf} 5^{7gf} 14^{7s} 6^{6sd} **1-3-15**
£12,731

Flipando (Ire) *T D Barron* 98
4 b g Sri Pekan (USA) - Magic Touch
2^{8g} 13^{8gs} 4^{7g} 5^{8gf} 5^{8gf} 6^{8gf} 10^{7g} 2^{8gf} 3^{8g}
0-3-9 £16,995

Flitcroft (Ire) *J Mackie*
3 b f Bahhare (USA) - Lear's Crown (USA)
9^{8g} PU^{14g} **0-0-2**

Flite Of Araby *R J Price* a54
8 b g Green Desert (USA) - Allegedly Blue (USA)
3^{7sd} 10^{8sd} 3^{9sd} 3^{8sd} 4^{9sd} 7^{9sd} 2^{12sd} 2^{9sd} 10^{9sd}
0-5-9 £2,091

Floating Banker *P Winkworth* 61
2 b c Zieten (USA) - Form At Last
5^{7g} 4^{7gf} 5^{6gf} 11^{5gs} **0-0-4 £293**

Floodlight Fantasy *E S McMahon* 63
2 b c Fantastic Light (USA) - Glamadour (Ire)
12^{7gf} 5^{7g} 11^{7gf} **0-0-3**

Floosie (Ire) *N P Littmoden* 28 a36
3 b f Night Shift (USA) - German Lady
4^{7sd} 8^{7sd} 7^{7sd} 8^{10sd} 8^{9sd} 8^{10g} 7^{10gs} 6^{11sd} 5^{9sd}
12^{10g} **0-0-10 £265**

Flor Y Nata (USA) *Sir Mark Prescott* 82 a88
2 b f Fusaichi Pegasus (USA) - Rose Of Zollern (Ire)
3^{6sd} 1^{7sd} 3^{7sd} 1^{7sd} 3^{7gs} 6^{7sd} **2-2-6 £10,059**

Floragalore *O Sherwood* 46
4 b f Dr Fong (USA) - Valagalore
5^{12s} **0-0-1**

Floral Bazaar *G M Moore* 48
2 b f Bahamian Bounty - Aonach Mor
4^{5f} 2^{6gf} 10^{6gf} 5^{7gf} 13^{7g} 11^{7gf} 5^{7g} 10^{8g} **0-1-8 £1,272**

Floral Print (USA) *M Johnston* 63
3 b f Rahy (USA) - Royal Fandango (USA)
5^{7g} 4^{8s} 3^{9gs} 10^{8g} 8^{11gf} **0-0-5 £809**

Florida Heart *A M Balding* a80
4 ch f First Trump - Miami Dancer (USA)
9^{8sd} 4^{8sd} **0-0-2 £532**

Florida Legend (Ire) *Miss J Feilden* 37
2 ch f Beckett (Ire) - Sunlit Ride
8^{7gs} **0-0-1**

Florino *A W Carroll* 37
3 b f Polish Precedent (USA) - Flourish
11^{10g} 7^{8g} **0-0-2**

Flossytoo *J Balding* 43
3 b f Royal Applause - Nite-Owl Dancer
14^{5g} 8^{5g} 16^{6g} **0-0-3**

Flotta *B G Powell* 88 a88
6 ch g Elmaamul (USA) - Heavenly Goddess
2^{12sd} 10^{14gf} 1^{12gf} 7^{12gf} 3^{14g} 4^{11gf} **1-2-6 £10,786**

Flower Alley (USA) *T Pletcher* a126
3 ch c Distorted Humor (USA) - Princess Olivia (USA)
1^{0ft} 1^{9my} 2^{9ft} 9^{10ft} 2^{9ft} 1^{9ft} 1^{10ft} 4^{10ft} 2^{10ft} **4-3-9 £1,268,332**

Flower Haven *M J Gingell* 53 a53
3 b f Dr Fong (USA) - Daisy May
4^{12gf} 6^{12sd} 3^{12g} 9^{12g} **0-1-4 £786**

Flower Market *R Hannon* 70
2 ch f Cadeaux Genereux - Marl
3^{6gf} 1^{6g} 10^{6gf} **1-1-3 £5,562**

Flower Seeker *Ms Deborah J Evans* a17
3 b f Lujain (USA) - Kingpin Delight
8^{7sd} 12^{6sd} **0-0-2**

Fluorescent *L M Cumani* 68
2 b f Fantastic Light (USA) - Frangy
8^{7g} 2^{7hy} **0-1-2 £1,332**

Flur Na H Alba *J J Quinn* 76
6 b g Atraf - Tyrian Belle
11^{6gf} 8^{7g} 12^{7gf} 3^{5gf} 4^{6gf} 12^{5g} 1^{5g} 4^{6gf} 6^{7gf} 16^{5g} **1-1-10 £6,188**

Flushing Meadows (USA) *Saeed Bin Suroor* 83
4 b c Grand Slam (USA) - Sheepish Grin (USA)
8^{7gf} 8^{7gf} 12^{7ft} **0-0-3**

Fly Back *M Dods* 32
6 ch g Fraam - The Fernhill Flyer (Ire)
13^{7g} 9^{8gf} **0-0-2**

Fly By Jove (Ire) *A M Balding* 11
2 b c Fasliyev (USA) - Flyleaf (Fr)
6^{5s} **0-0-1**

Fly Me To The Moon (Ger) *C E Brittain* 62
2 b f Galileo (Ire) - Four Roses (Ire)
4^{7f} **0-0-1 £313**

Fly More *J M Bradley* 58 a53
8 ch g Lycius (USA) - Double River (USA)
11^{6sd} 9^{5sd} 13^{5sd} 10^{5gs} 12^{5sd} 14^{5gf} 8^{5gf} 6^{5gf} 8^{5f} 1^{6s} 6^{5f} 3^{5gf} 5^{5gf} 13^{6gf} 9^{6g} 18^{6g} 7^{5g} 5^{5g} **1-1-18 £3,244**

Fly To Dubai (Ire) *R McGlinchey* 81 a76
3 b g Fly To The Stars - Morna's Fan (Fr)
2^{8sd} 1^{9sd} 1^{10gf} 2^{8gf} 1^{8gf} 3^{9sd} 1^{8gf} 10^{7gf} 3^{8gf} 7^{8gf} 7^{9y} 8^{10g} 11^{10g} **4-3-13 £23,710**

Flying Adored *J L Dunlop* 79
4 b f Polar Falcon (USA) - Shining High
7^{10s} 6^{10g} 15^{8g} **0-0-3**

Flying Bantam (Ire) *R A Fahey* 89 a84
4 b g Fayruz - Natural Pearl
1^{6s} 5^{6s} 8^{6gf} 7^{7f} 4^{7gf} 13^{6gf} 5^{6g} 6^{6s} 5^{7gf} 3^{7gf} 5^{7ft} 5^{6gs} 5^{7s} **1-1-13 £11,970**

Flying Clarets (Ire) *R A Fahey* 69
2 b f Titus Livius (Fr) - Sheryl Lynn
5^{6gf} 4^{6gf} 3^{6g} 13^{6g} 11^{6g} 3^{7gf} 5^{8g} 2^{7gf} **0-3-8 £3,164**

Flying Dancer *R A Harris* 57 a55
3 b f Danzero (Aus) - Alzianah
6^{6sd} 6^{6sd} 12^{5gs} 4^{5g} 14^{6gs} 5^{6f} 6^{7gf} 6^{6gf} 2^{5g} 5^{7sf} 10^{7sd} 6^{5ss} **0-1-12 £1,045**

Flying Doctor *G M Moore* 50
2 b g Mark Of Esteem (Ire) - Vice Vixen (Can)
7^{6g} 8^{6gf} 5^{7gf} 6^{8gf} **0-0-4**

Flying Edge (Ire) *E J Alston* 71 a59
5 b g Flying Spur (Aus) - Day Is Dawning (Ire)
1^{6sd} 3^{6gf} 3^{6gf} 1^{6gs} 12^{6gf} 3^{6f} 2^{7gf} 14^{6gf} 1^{6g} **3-4-9 £11,178**

Flying Heart *M R Channon* 62 a50
3 ch f Bahamian Bounty - Flying Wind
5^{6sd} 8^{6gf} 4^{5gf} 1^{5s} 6^{5s} 10^{5g} 4^{5gf} 9^{5gs} 8^{5gf} 6^{5s} 2^{5gf} 5^{5g} 16^{5s} UR^{5gs} **1-1-14 £4,369**

Flying Key (Ire) *J D Bethell* 65 a49
2 b f Key Of Luck (USA) - Belle Bijou
5^{6sd} 1^{6gf} 3^{6gf} 3^{7g} 1^{7gf} 4^{7gf} 9^{7g} 8^{7gf} **2-1-8 £13,607**

Flying Lyric (Ire) *A King* 60
7 b g Definite Article - Lyric Junction (Ire)
10^{12gf} 7^{11gs} **0-0-2**

Flying Pass *D J S Ffrench Davis* a55
3 b g Alzao (USA) - Complimentary Pass
10^{8sd} **0-0-1**

Flying Penne *M R Channon* 52 a36
2 b f Pennekamp (USA) - Flying Wind
9^{5gf} 8^{7g} 3^{5f} 6^{5s} 13^{7gs} 8^{9sd} **0-0-6 £410**

Flying Rani (Ire) *Declan Gillespie* 52 a56
2 b f Mujadil (USA) - New Tycoon (Ire)
7^{7ys} 2^{7sd} **0-1-2 £1,100**

Flying Ridge (Ire) *A M Balding* 44 a25
3 ch f Indian Ridge - Jarrayan
13^{6gf} 11^{6sd} 5^{5g} **0-0-3**

Flying Spirit (Ire) *G L Moore* 78
6 b g Flying Spur (Aus) - All Laughter
11^{13s} 6^{11gf} 8^{10gf} 5^{12g} 8^{12g} 2^{12g} 5^{12g} **0-1-7 £4,750**

Flying Spud *A J Chamberlain* a42
4 ch g Fraam - Lorcanjo
17^{8gs} 12^{12sd} 8^{14sd} 9^{9sd} 13^{9sd} **0-0-5**

Flying Tackle *I W McInnes* 57 a48
7 ch g First Trump - Frighten The Life
5^{6sd} 6^{5sd} 4^{5sd} 6^{6s} 8^{5gs} 5^{5gf} 7^{5f} 2^{5gf} 4^{5g} 1^{5gf} 4^{5gf} 11^{5gf} **1-3-12 £4,715**

Flying With Eagles *M D I Usher* 17
4 ch g Most Welcome - Super Sol
10^{16gf} 10^{12sd} **0-0-2**

Flylowflylong (Ire) *I Semple* 69 a77
2 b f Danetime (Ire) - Jellybeen (Ire)
2^{5gs} 4^{6g} 4^{6s} 1^{6gs} 10^{6gf} 5^{6gf} 4^{8gf} 3^{6s} 8^{6hy} 1^{7sd} **2-2-10 £11,779**

Focus Group (USA) *H R A Cecil* 94
4 b g Kris S (USA) - Interim
1^{8gs} **1-0-1 £11,303**

Foley Millennium (Ire) *M Quinn* 98 a88
7 ch g Tagula (Ire) - Inshirah (USA)
1^{5sd} 1^{5sd} 6^{6sd} 2^{5gs} 7^{5g} 19^{5gf} 4^{5gf} 3^{5gs} 1^{6gf} 3^{5s} 1^{5gf} 1^{5g} 1^{5gf} 14^{5gf} **6-3-14 £45,671**

Foley Prince *Stef Liddiard* 58
4 b g Makbul - Princess Foley (Ire)
12^{8g} 8^{8gf} 12^{8gf} 16^{8gf} **0-0-4**

Folga *J G Given* 90
3 b f Atraf - Desert Dawn
5^{5gf} 2^{6gf} 1^{5gf} 5^{6g} 2^{5gf} 2^{5gf} 2^{5g} 2^{6gf} 6^{5gs} 1^{5g} 9^{6g} 11^{5gf} 8^{6s} **2-5-13 £31,605**

Folio (Ire) *W J Musson* 83 a87
5 b g Perugino (USA) - Bayleaf
6^{8sd} 6^{8sd} 6^{7sd} 7^{7sd} 15^{7gf} 4^{7gf} 19^{8gf} 3^{8g} 10^{8s} 2^{8gf} 2^{10g} 11^{10g} **0-3-12 £5,756**

Follingworth (Ire) *A D Brown* 41
2 ch f Midhish - Pennine Way (Ire)
10^{8g} 8^{7gf} 10^{7s} 12^{8hy} **0-0-4**

Follow Me In (Ire) *K R Burke* 47
2 b f Elnadim (USA) - Arjan (Ire)
6^{5g} 3^{5g} 9^{5sd} **0-0-3 £519**

Follow My Lead *B W Hills* 68 a41
3 b f Night Shift (USA) - Launch Time (USA)
8^{6sd} 4^{8g} 5^{8gf} 1^{8g} 3^{8g} 3^{8g} 5^{8s} **1-3-7 £4,584**

Follow My Trail (Ire) *B Smart* 56
2 br g Indian Danehill (Ire) - Lady Stalker
7^{7gf} 11^{7gf} 5^{8gf} **0-0-3**

Follow The Colours (Ire) *J W Hills* 60 a65
2 b c Rainbow Quest (USA) - Gardenia (Ire)
8^{7gf} 6^{7sd} 5^{8sd} **0-0-3**

Follow The Game *W R Swinburn* 38 a57
3 b g Mind Games - Play The Game
5^{7sd} 11^{7gf} 12^{8sf} **0-0-3**

Following Flow (USA) *R Hollinshead* 80 a83
3 b/br g King Of Kings (Ire) - Sign Here (USA)
8^{8sd} 2^{9sd} 9^{8hy} 12^{8gf} 2^{8gf} 7^{8gf} 10^{9sd} 5^{9sd} 10^{7sd} **0-2-9 £4,278**

Folly Mount *M W Easterby* a35
3 b g Anabaa (USA) - Height Of Folly
6^{7sd} 7^{6sd} 9^{6sd} 9^{11sd} **0-0-4**

Fong's Thong (USA) *B J Meehan* 74
4 ch c Dr Fong (USA) - Bacinella (USA)
10^{8g} **0-0-1**

Fonic Rock (Ire) *M L W Bell* 54
2 b f Zafonic (USA) - Blue Crystal (Ire)
14^{6gs} 7^{7gf} 10^{7gf} **0-0-3**

Font *J R Fanshawe* 78
2 b c Sadler's Wells (USA) - River Saint (USA)
5^{8gs} **0-0-1**

Fontaine House *T T Clement* 56 a18
3 b f Pyramus (USA) - Primavera
9^{7s} 9^{1g} 6^{8g} 6^{6g} 6^{7g} 12^{6sd} 13^{7ss} **0-0-7**

Fonthill Road (Ire) *R A Fahey* 109
5 ch g Royal Abjar (USA) - Hannah Huxtable (Ire)
1^{5g} 2^{5gs} 2^{6gs} 7^{5g} 5^{6gf} 2^{6gs} 7^{5g} 2^{6g} **1-4-8 £69,285**

Food For Thought *K R Burke* 58 a56
2 b f Mind Games - Ladycake (Ire)
7^{5gf} 4^{5gf} 4^{6gf} 2^{7sd} 3^{8sd} **0-2-5 £1,497**

Foodbroker Founder *D R C Elsworth* 86
5 ch g Groom Dancer (USA) - Nemea (USA)
17^{10g} 6^{12gf} 12^{10gs} 3^{10g} **0-1-4 £1,105**

Foolish Groom *R Hollinshead* 70
4 ch g Groom Dancer (USA) - Scared
16^{10g} 3^{8gs} 2^{8g} 5^{7g} 5^{8gf} 2^{8gs} 1^{8gf} 4^{8s} 9^{8gf} 14^{8gs} **1-4-10 £6,861**

Fools Entire *Miss J Feilden* 36 a52
4 ch g Fraam - Poly Blue (Ire)
10^{7gf} 15^{7gf} 2^{9sd} 5^{9sd} 12^{9sd} 8^{11sd} **0-1-6 £846**

Football Crazy (Ire) *P Bowen* 84
6 b g Mujadil (USA) - Schonbein (Ire)
2^{14gf} **0-1-1 £2,139**

Footstepsinthesand *A P O'Brien* 118
3 b c Giant's Causeway (USA) - Glatisant
1^{8gf} **1-0-1 £185,600**

For Life (Ire) *A P Jarvis* 69
3 b g Bachir (Ire) - Zest (USA)
3^{6g} 4^{6g} 12^{6s} 11^{8g} 6^{6g} **0-1-5 £838**

For Once *Saeed Bin Suroor* 49
2 b c Green Desert (USA) - Belle Argentine (Fr)
6^{6gf} 11^{7s} **0-0-2**

For Scarlett (USA) *J Noseda* 71
3 br f Red Ransom (USA) - Lady Dixie (USA)
6^{7s} 4^{5gf} 2^{6gf} 15^{6gf} **0-1-4 £1,844**

Forces Sweetheart *M L W Bell* 68
2 b f Allied Forces (USA) - Talighta (USA)
5^{5gs} 2^{5g} 2^{5g} 1^{5gf} 6^{5g} 9^{6gf} 13^{6gf} 13^{6g} 14^{5hy} **1-2-9 £5,590**

Fordhill (Ire) *E A L Dunlop* 40
2 b f Danehill (USA) - Ultra Finesse (USA)
14^{7g} **0-0-1**

Forehand (Ire) *E F Vaughan* 55
3 b f Lend A Hand - Set Trail (Ire)
10^{10gf} 2^{10g} 1^{10g} 11^{9gf} 13^{12gs} **1-1-5 £4,251**

Foreign Affairs *Sir Mark Prescott* 109
7 ch h Hernando (Fr) - Entente Cordiale (USA)
2^{12s} 2^{14gf} 1^{12gs} 2^{12g} **1-2-4 £39,552**

Foreign Edition (Ire) *J H M Gosden* 91
3 b g Anabaa (USA) - Palacegate Episode (Ire)
1^{6g} 7^{7gf} 4^{6gs} **1-0-3 £8,001**

Foreign Envoy (Ire) *B W Hills* 45 a48
2 ch g Grand Lodge (USA) - Soviet Artic (Fr)
9^{7gf} 7^{7sd} **0-0-2**

Foreplay (Ire) *E A L Dunlop* 69 a68
2 b f Lujain (USA) - Watch Me (Ire)
3^{6g} 4^{6g} 1^{6sd} **1-1-3 £4,470**

Forest Air (Ire) *B R Johnson* a30
5 br m Charnwood Forest (Ire) - Auriga
12^{10sd} 7^{10sd} 9^{10sd} **0-0-3**

Forest Dane *Mrs N Smith* 52 a59
5 b g Danetime (Ire) - Forest Maid
6^{7sd} 3^{7sd} 8^{7sd} 5^{7sd} 8^{6s} 9^{7gf} 5^{6f} 9^{7f} 5^{5g} 6^{7g} 6^{6gf} 5^{5g} 15^{8gf} 1^{5g} **1-1-14 £1,891**

Forest Knight (Ire) *T F Lacy* 14 a56
4 b c Charnwood Forest (Ire) - Kristabelle (Ire)
5^{6sd} 6^{5sd} 8^{5sd} 13^{7sd} 8^{9sd} 12^{7g} 6^{7sd} 12^{6sd} **0-0-8**

Forest Lodge (Ire) *D R C Elsworth* 44
2 ch f Indian Lodge (Ire) - Folkboat

8^{8g} 13^{8gs} **0-0-2**

Forest Magic (Ire) *A P Jarvis* 80
5 b g Charnwood Forest (Ire) - Adultress (Ire)
18^{12g} 9^{15gs} **0-0-2**

Forest Of Love *B W Hills* 73 a72
3 br f Charnwood Forest (Ire) - Touch And Love (Ire)
4^{7gs} 3^{8g} 3^{10g} 2^{9sd} 5^{8sd} 5^{7g} 1^{7sd} **1-3-7**
£5,753

Forest Rail (Ire) *L Corcoran* a26
5 b m Catrail (USA) - Forest Heights
12^{6sd} 6^{7sd} 11^{11sd} **0-0-3**

Forest Viking (Ire) *J S Wainwright* 59
3 b g Orpen (USA) - Berhala (Ire)
2^{10gs} 2^{10f} 2^{10gf} 6^{12g} 14^{9gf} **0-3-5**
£3,011

Forever Fantasy (Ire) *J L Dunlop* 54
4 b g Daylami (Ire) - Gay Fantasy
3^{12gf} **0-1-1 £435**

Forever Free (Ger) *P Mitchell* 96
5 ch g Platini (Ger) - Forever Nice (Ger)
8^{8g} 3^{8gf} 9^{8gf} 22^{8g} **0-1-4 £5,729**

Forever My Lord *D K Ivory* 46 a15
7 b g Be My Chief (USA) - In Love Again (Ire)
5^{10f} 7^{12gf} 6^{16gf} 1^{12gf} 9^{12gf} 7^{10f} 3^{12g} 7^{14sd}
11^{12gs} **1-1-9 £3,190**

Forever Phoenix *R M H Cowell* 103 a104
5 b m Shareef Dancer (USA) - With Care
4^{5sd} 10^{6gf} 11^{5ft} 1^{6gf} 8^{7gf} 6^{6s} 2^{6gf} 11^{5g} 4^{6g}
4^{6g} 3^{5sd} 4^{5g} 6^{5s} 7^{6g} 3^{5gf} **1-3-15**
£54,412

Forever Rocky *F Jordan* 40
2 b c Kayf Tara - Song For Jess (Ire)
14^{6gf} 11^{6gs} 10^{6gf} 12^{8gf} **0-0-4**

Forfeiter (USA) *G M Lyons* 66 a82
3 ch g Petionville (USA) - Picabo (USA)
1^{7sd} 7^{9sd} 9^{7g} 8^{7gs} 10^{7gf} 9^{7gf} 5^{7gf} 3^{8gf} 3^{8sh}
1-1-9 £7,341

Forgery (Ire) *G A Butler* 97
3 ch g Dr Devious (Ire) - Memory Green (USA)
2^{10gs} 6^{11f} **0-1-2 £3,929**

Form And Beauty (Ire) *C Roberts* 58
3 b c Orpen (USA) - Formezza (Ire)
3^{8s} 12^{8sd} 7^{11gf} **0-0-3 £533**

Formal Approval (USA) *M Johnston* 63
3 b f Kingmambo (USA) - Eloquent Minister (USA)
3^{9gs} 3^{7gf} 3^{7g} 5^{12gf} 9^{12s} 3^{12s} **0-4-6**
£3,116

Formal Decree (Ger) *Mrs J R Ramsden* 74
2 b c Diktat - Formida (Fr)
9^{6g} 2^{5gf} 6^{5gf} 6^{8gf} 11^{8gf} 3^{8gs} **0-2-6**
£2,930

Formidable Will (Fr) *M W Easterby* 52 a70
3 b g Efisio - Shewillifshewants (Ire)
13^{8gs} 15^{7gf} 13^{11gf} 2^{8gf} 8^{8f} 1^{8sd} 1^{8sd} 13^{8sd}
12^{8sd} **2-1-9 £5,408**

Forpetesake *Miss V Scott* 37 a46
3 ch g Primo Dominie - Showcase
10^{9sd} 12^{7sd} 8^{11gf} 6^{11gs} 9^{12gf} 12^{11sd} **0-0-6**

Forrest Gump *C J Teague* 38 a57
5 ch g Zilzal (USA) - Mish Mish
6^{11sd} 2^{9sd} 11^{9sd} 10^{9sd} 10^{9sd} 12^{8gf} 6^{12gf} 6^{12f}
0-1-8 £475

Forroger (Can) *V Smith* 73
2 b/br c Black Minnaloushe (USA) - Count On Romance (Can)
5^{7s} 4^{8hy} **0-0-2 £282**

Fort Augustus (USA) *E A L Dunlop* 15
3 b c Quiet American (USA) - Fife (Ire)
14^{10s} **0-0-1**

Fort Dignity (USA) *Sir Michael Stoute* 113
4 b c Seeking The Gold (USA) - Kitza (Ire)
4^{9gf} 1^{8gf} 7^{9g} **1-0-3 £20,700**

Forthright *G L Moore* 75 a77
4 b g Cadeaux Genereux - Forthwith
9^{10sd} 7^{10sd} 5^{11g} **0-0-3**

Fortiszamo *A W Carroll* 39 a57
3 b g Forzando - Flamingo Times
4^{8sd} 10^{6gf} 11^{8g} 16^{8g} 10^{9sd} 13^{9sd} **0-0-6**
£315

Fortress *W J Haggas* 63 a62
2 b f Generous (Ire) - Imperial Bailiwick (Ire)
4^{6sd} 6^{7sd} 4^{6g} 4^{5gf} 5^{5gs} 4^{6sd} **0-0-6**
£1,154

Fortunate Isle (USA) *B W Hills* 80
3 ch c Swain (Ire) - Isla Del Rey (USA)
1^{8f} **1-0-1 £6,214**

Fortune Island (Ire) *M C Pipe* 96
6 b g Turtle Island (Ire) - Blue Kestrel (Ire)
5^{16gs} 15^{16g} 1^{16gs} 3^{16gf} 4^{21s} 21^{18gs} 2^{16s}
1-1-7 £16,394

Fortune Point (Ire) *A W Carroll* 60 a67
7 ch g Cadeaux Genereux - Mountains Of Mist (Ire)
2^{7sd} 14^{10sd} 3^{9sd} 19^{10g} 10^{8g} 7^{10gf} 7^{10sd}
0-2-7 £1,561

Fortune's Fair *J A Glover* 48
3 b g Forzando - River's Rising (Fr)
14^{8s} 8^{7gf} 5^{7gf} 10^{8gf} **0-0-4**

Fortunes Favourite *J E Long* 47 a49
5 ch m Barathea (Ire) - Golden Fortune
5^{12sd} 3^{9sd} 1^{9sd} 11^{12sd} 16^{12gs} 3^{10s} 10^{9sd} 12^{10g}
2^{9sf} 11^{9ss} **1-3-10 £2,518**

Forty Forte *Miss S J Wilton* 4 a21
9 b g Pursuit Of Love - Cominna
11^{9sd} 8^{9sd} 12^{9sd} 13^{8g} **0-0-4**

Forward Move (Ire) *R Hannon* 111
3 ch c Dr Fong (USA) - Kissing Gate (USA)
6^{8gf} 4^{10gs} 7^{10gf} 2^{10g} 1^{8gs} 7^{8g} 8^{8gs} **1-1-7**
£30,460

Forzenuff *J R Boyle* 32 a51
4 b g Mujadil (USA) - Sada
2^{5sd} 4^{6sd} 10^{6sd} 10^{7gs} 5^{6sd} 12^{7gf} 8^{6gf} 7^{6sd}
4^{5ss} **0-1-9 £472**

Forznar Ridge *C Roberts*
5 b g Forzando - Narbonne
13^{6sd} **0-0-1**

Fosroc (USA) *J S Moore* 56
3 ch g Royal Anthem (USA) - Stellar Blush (USA)
5^{10f} 5^{12g} 5^{10g} 15^{14g} 8^{14gf} 7^{10f} **0-0-6**

Fossgate *J D Bethell* 66 a8
4 ch g Halling (USA) - Peryllys
11^{8s} 4^{9s} 1^{10gf} 13^{10sd} **1-0-4 £4,666**

Four Amigos (USA) *D Nicholls* 80 a56
4 b g Southern Halo (USA) - Larentia
2^{5s} 5^{5s} 16^{5g} 4^{5gs} 10^{5g} 10^{6s} 11^{5sd} 9^{6sd}
0-1-8 £2,600

Four Kings *R Allan* 42 a42
4 b c Forzando - High Cut
9^{5g} 13^{7g} 8^{6gf} 14^{8gf} 10^{8gf} 3^{5sd} 13^{9sd}
0-1-7 £210

Four Pleasure *H R A Cecil* 62
3 ch f King's Best (USA) - Please

5^{10gf} 6^{10g} 5^{7g} **0-0-3**

Foursquare Flyer (Ire) *J Mackie* 76
3 ch g Tagula (Ire) - Isla (Ire)
8^{8g} 2^{10gf} 3^{10gf} 4^{10gf} 5^{10g} **0-2-5 £2,684**

Fourswainby (Ire) *B Ellison*
4 b g Foxhound (USA) - Arena
9^{12ss} **0-0-1**

Fourth Dimension (Ire) *N Wilson* 58
6 b g Entrepreneur - Isle Of Spice (USA)
6^{12gs} 13^{21s} **0-0-2**

Fox *C E Brittain* 96 a82
3 b c Diktat - Badawi (USA)
7^{6gs} 6^{8gf} 2^{7gf} 11^{7gf} 8^{7gf} 13^{7sd} **0-1-6 £2,052**

Fox Covert (Ire) *D W Barker* 55 a52
4 b g Foxhound (USA) - Serious Contender (Ire)
16^{6gs} 12^{6gf} 4^{5gs} 10^{5gf} 18^{6gf} 12^{5gf} 13^{5gf} 1^{6gf} 7^{6g} 19^{6g} 7^{6gf} 5^{5gf} 12^{6sd} 2^{5sd} **1-2-14 £3,423**

Fox Flight (Ire) *D W Barker*
2 b g Brave Act - Danz Danz
17^{6gf} 13^{6g} **0-0-2**

Fox Mask (USA) *J G M O'Shea* 35
3 b f Lion Cavern (USA) - Curiously
13^{8g} 16^{11gs} **0-0-2**

Foxhaven *P R Chamings* 105
3 ch c Unfuwain (USA) - Dancing Mirage (Ire)
4^{7s} 10^{8g} 4^{10gf} 2^{10g} 5^{10gs} 1^{12s} **1-1-6 £57,564**

Foxies Future (Ire) *J R Weymes* a56
4 b f General Monash (USA) - Indescent Blue
6^{7sd} 4^{7sd} 2^{6sd} 9^{6sd} 11^{6sd} 5^{6sd} 3^{6sd} 1^{6sd} **1-2-8 £2,493**

Foxilla (Ire) *D R C Elsworth* 44
4 ch f Foxhound (USA) - Lilissa (Ire)
12^{10gf} **0-0-1**

Foxtrotromeoyankee *L A Dace* a48
5 b g Tragic Role (USA) - Hope Chest
7^{10sd} 13^{10sd} **0-0-2**

Foxy Gwynne *A M Balding* 79
3 b f Entrepreneur - Nahlin
4^{8gf} 2^{8gs} 3^{10g} 3^{10g} 9^{9g} **0-3-5 £3,083**

Foxysox *C F Wall* 81
2 ch f Foxhound (USA) - Triple Tricks (Ire)
7^{6gf} 3^{6g} 5^{6gf} 3^{6g} 5^{6gs} **0-2-5 £25,623**

Fraamex *M R Channon* a61
2 ch g Fraam - Scenic Air
4^{8sd} **0-0-1**

Frabrofen *James Moffatt* a5
4 b f Mind Games - Oh My Oh My
13^{6sd} **0-0-1**

Fracas (Ire) *David Wachman* 114
3 b c In The Wings - Klarifi
1^{10ys} 1^{10gs} 1^{10sh} 4^{12g} 7^{12gf} **3-0-5 £159,382**

Fragile Witness *J R Norton*
3 b g Fraam - Heavenly Abstone
9^{7f} **0-0-1**

Framily Love *P W Chapple-Hyam*
3 gr g Fraam - Asian Love
11^{8sd} **0-0-1**

Francescas Boy (Ire) *P D Niven* 41
2 b g Titus Livius (Fr) - Mica Male (Ity)
15^{7g} 10^{6gs} 5^{7g} **0-0-3**

Francis Cadell *D R Loder* a100
3 b c Cadeaux Genereux - Ruby Affair (Ire)
2^{6sd} 2^{7sd} **0-2-2 £18,568**

Francis Flute *B Mactaggart* 59
7 b g Polar Falcon (USA) - Darshay (Fr)
2^{7g} 6^{7g} 11^{8g} **0-1-3 £864**

Frank Crow *I Semple* 76
2 b c Josr Algarhoud (Ire) - Belle De Nuit (Ire)
3^{6g} 2^{6g} 1^{7g} 13^{8s} **1-2-4 £7,910**

Frank Sonata *M G Quinlan* 115
4 b c Opening Verse (USA) - Megdale (Ire)
2^{14s} 2^{12s} 7^{14gs} 3^{12g} 6^{11gf} 4^{12gs} 5^{12gs} 3^{16hy} **0-4-8 £28,640**

Frank's Quest (Ire) *A B Haynes* 10 a62
5 b g Mujadil (USA) - Questuary (Ire)
11^{9sd} 10^{8sd} 11^{8sd} 10^{8sd} 1^{8sd} 7^{7sd} 14^{8gs} 2^{9sd} 12^{7sd} 11^{9sd} **1-1-10 £2,306**

Franklins Gardens *M H Tompkins* 117
5 b h Halling (USA) - Woodbeck
2^{16s} 1^{14gs} 6^{20gf} 8^{14g} 24^{16gs} **1-1-5 £96,000**

Franksalot (Ire) *Miss B Sanders* 73 a77
5 ch g Desert Story (Ire) - Rosie's Guest (Ire)
8^{6sd} 2^{6sd} 4^{7gf} 6^{7gf} 9^{6gf} 8^{6g} 2^{7gf} 5^{9g} 3^{7g} 4^{7g} 6^{7f} 1^{6sd} **1-3-12 £7,992**

Franky'N'Jonny *I A Wood* 57 a53
2 b f Groom Dancer (USA) - Bron Hilda (Ire)
9^{5gf} 6^{6gf} 3^{6g} 6^{6sd} 4^{7gs} 6^{7sd} 5^{6g} 5^{7g} 6^{6f} 3^{8g} **0-2-10 £1,292**

Fransiscan *P C Haslam* 44 a33
3 ch g Fraam - Ordained
7^{9sd} 3^{8sd} 9^{14gf} 3^{12gf} 5^{16g} **0-2-5 £778**

Frantastik Lady (Ire) *A Kinsella*
2 b f Key Of Luck (USA) - Kenderah (Fr)
12^{9sd} **0-0-1**

Frascati *A Berry* 89 a84
5 b m Emarati (USA) - Fizzy Fiona
4^{5s} 7^{5s} 14^{5s} 6^{5g} 8^{5gf} 5^{5g} 4^{5gf} 3^{5gf} 4^{5f} 2^{5gf} 2^{5gf} 3^{5gf} 8^{5gs} 2^{5gf} 5^{5g} 6^{5sf} 5^{5sd} **0-4-17 £14,710**

Fraternity *J A Pickering* 66 a68
8 b g Grand Lodge (USA) - Catawba
1^{9sd} 1^{8sd} 1^{9sd} 1^{6sd} 2^{8sd} 1^{9sd} 8^{7sd} 8^{9sd} 12^{8gf} 1^{8s} 6^{10gf} 17^{7g} 10^{8s} **6-1-13 £13,739**

Fratt'n Park (Ire) *J J Bridger* 66
2 b f Tagula (Ire) - Bouffant
9^{6gf} 9^{6g} 4^{5gf} 4^{5g} 6^{6gf} 4^{6s} 5^{6g} 7^{6gs} 5^{6gf} 2^{5gs} 7^{6g} 6^{6s} **0-1-12 £3,953**

Freak Occurence (Ire) *Miss E C Lavelle* 79
4 b g Stravinsky (USA) - Date Mate (USA)
6^{8hy} 3^{8gf} 1^{10g} 3^{10gf} 9^{10gf} 8^{10g} 4^{8gs} 8^{10hy} **1-2-8 £5,435**

Freddie Freccles *J G Given* a39
4 ch g Komaite (USA) - Leprechaun Lady
7^{12sd} 9^{12sd} 13^{9sd} **0-0-3**

Frederick James *H E Haynes* 7
11 b g Efisio - Rare Roberta (USA)
14^{7gf} **0-0-1**

Fredricksburg (Ire) *J H M Gosden* 74
2 gr g Fantastic Light (USA) - Rahaam (USA)
10^{7gf} 4^{7g} 8^{8g} 12^{8f} 4^{10f} **0-0-5 £670**

Free Angel (USA) *M Wigham* 56 a64
3 b f Mystery Storm (USA) - No Makeup (USA)
4^{7gf} 4^{7sd} 5^{6gf} 1^{7sd} **1-0-4 £1,846**

Free Lift *R Charlton* 84 a78
3 ch f Cadeaux Genereux - Step Aloft

4^{7f} 9^{7gf} 7^{7g} 1^{6g} 5^{6sd} **1-0-5 £7,307**

Free Option (Ire) *W J Musson* a60
10 ch g Indian Ridge - Saneena
6^{8sd} 4^{8sd} **0-0-2**

Free Silver (Ire) *Miss K B Boutflower* 36
2 b f Lujain (USA) - Joonayh
10^{6gf} **0-0-1**

Free Style (Ger) *Mrs H Sweeting* 41 a57
5 ch m Most Welcome - Furiella
5^{12sd} 10^{12sd} 3^{13sd} 5^{13sd} 6^{12sd} 6^{13sd} 4^{12sd} 1^{13sd} 3^{14f} 1^{12sd} 11^{12g} 13^{16sd} 5^{12sd} 4^{12sd} 6^{12sd} 9^{16sd} **2-1-16 £5,710**

Free To Air *A M Balding* 75
2 b c Generous (Ire) - Petonica (Ire)
4^{8gf} 5^{9gf} 7^{10g} **0-0-3 £406**

Free Wheelin (Ire) *J Akehurst* 57 a43
5 b g Polar Falcon (USA) - Farhana
14^{6s} 6^{6s} 5^{5gs} 2^{6g} 5^{6gf} 5^{6s} 4^{6gs} 9^{6g} 8^{5sd} 6^{6sd} 11^{7ss} 12^{7sd} **0-2-12 £1,138**

Freefall (Ire) *C A Dwyer* a58
4 ch f Peintre Celebre (USA) - Irish Company (USA)
9^{9sd} 2^{12sd} 5^{12sd} 7^{12sd} **0-1-4 £1,042**

Freeloader (Ire) *J W Hills* 91 a83
5 b g Revoque (Ire) - Indian Sand
1^{8gf} 2^{8gf} 15^{8g} 3^{8gf} 3^{8gs} 6^{9gf} 9^{10sd} 5^{8g} **1-2-8 £16,218**

Freeze The Flame (Ger) *C R Egerton* a56
2 b g In The Wings - Fantastic Flame (Ire)
8^{7sd} 8^{6sd} **0-0-2**

Fregate Island (Ire) *W J Haggas* 68 a84
2 gr g Daylami (Ire) - Briery (Ire)
15^{8s} 8^{6g} 1^{7sd} 3^{8sd} 1^{8sd} **2-1-5 £8,914**

French Gold *N Wilson* 43
3 b f Bien Bien (USA) - Shalad'Or
8^{10f} 16^{8gf} 6^{12gf} 2^{11gs} 6^{12g} **0-1-5 £751**

French Kisses *Ronald Thompson* 34 a32
3 b f Paris House - Clashfern
5^{8sd} 11^{9sd} 4^{7sd} 6^{8gf} 11^{8gf} 11^{10g} **0-0-6**

French Mannequin (Ire) *P A Blockley* 61 a60
6 b/br m Key Of Luck (USA) - Paris Model (Ire)
5^{13sd} 1^{12sd} 5^{16sd} 1^{17sd} 5^{12s} 6^{16g} 2^{13f} 14^{18g} 6^{13gf} 1^{12sd} 2^{12gf} 1^{16gf} 5^{14gf} 4^{14gf} **4-2-14 £13,653**

French Opera *J A Osborne* a60
2 b g Bering - On Fair Stage (Ire)
9^{8sd} 7^{9sd} 6^{9sf} **0-0-3**

French Risk (Ire) *Evan Williams* 40
5 b g Entrepreneur - Troyes
11^{11gf} 9^{12gf} 10^{15g} **0-0-3**

French School *D R Loder* 28
3 b f Desert Prince (Ire) - Bint Shihama (USA)
11^{8g} 13^{7gf} **0-0-2**

French Sovereign (USA) *M G Quinlan* a57
2 b/br c Louis Quatorze (USA) - Conectis (Ire)
13^{7sd} **0-0-1**

Frenchgate *M E Sowersby* 36
4 br g Paris House - Let's Hang On (Ire)
16^{8g} 5^{6f} 10^{8g} **0-0-3**

Frenchmans Lodge *L A Dace* 50 a51
5 b g Piccolo - St Helena
12^{6sd} 12^{5sd} 2^{5sd} 10^{6sd} F^{5sd} 5^{5sd} 4^{5sd} 6^{5sd} 3^{5g} 11^{5gf} 2^{6gf} 10^{6f} 7^{5f} 11^{5sd} 8^{6f} 10^{7f} 1^{6g} 11^{7sd} 5^{6g} 13^{6sd} **1-3-20 £4,027**

Freshwinds *S L Keightley* a40
3 ch g Bahamian Bounty - La Noisette
9^{7sd} 3^{6sd} **0-1-2 £492**

Friar Tuck *Miss L A Perratt* 49
10 ch g Inchinor - Jay Gee Ell
8^{6gs} 10^{6gs} 11^{6gs} 6^{5gf} **0-0-4**

Frida *P D Cundell*
3 b f Lujain (USA) - Ishona
11^{8sd} **0-0-1**

Friedhelmo (Ger) *S B Clark* 59 a53
9 ch g Dashing Blade - Fox For Gold
4^{12gs} 3^{12gf} 8^{14f} 3^{12sd} 13^{12f} 1^{14g} 5^{16gf} 10^{14gf} 6^{12sd} 13^{17sf} 13^{15s} **1-1-11 £3,856**

Friends Hope *P A Blockley* 68 a59
4 ch f Docksider (USA) - Stygian (USA)
5^{7sd} 1^{9sd} 4^{7sd} 6^{10s} 2^{10gf} 2^{11gf} 18^{12f} 10^{8gf} 12^{8sd} 7^{10sd} **1-2-10 £5,095**

Frimley's Matterry *R E Barr* 55
5 b g Bluegrass Prince (Ire) - Lonely Street
6^{6gs} 5^{6gf} 7^{7f} 4^{6g} 11^{6gf} 15^{7g} 8^{6g} 8^{6gf} 10^{8gf} 8^{6gf} 6^{6gf} **0-0-11**

Frith (Ire) *Mrs L B Normile* 75
3 b g Benny The Dip (USA) - Melodist (USA)
5^{10gf} **0-0-1**

Frogmill Prince *M W Easterby* 47 a49
2 b g Pursuit Of Love - Exotic Forest
7^{5g} 7^{6sd} 11^{6gf} 9^{6sd} **0-0-4**

Frogs' Gift (Ire) *G M Moore* 42
3 gr f Danehill Dancer (Ire) - Warthill Whispers
8^{7f} 5^{6gf} 9^{7g} **0-0-3**

From The North (Ire) *J R Weymes* 40
4 ch f Foxhound (USA) - Best Swinger (Ire)
8^{5gf} 11^{8sd} 9^{7g} **0-0-3**

Fromsong (Ire) *D K Ivory* 97 a103
7 b g Fayruz - Lindas Delight
7^{5gs} 13^{6gs} 3^{5g} 10^{5gf} 1^{5gf} 2^{5gf} 10^{5g} 10^{6gf} 4^{5s} 4^{5gf} 7^{5s} 13^{5g} 8^{5gf} 1^{6sd} 1^{5sd} 7^{6sd} 2^{6sd} **3-4-17 £29,178**

Front Rank (Ire) *K C Bailey* 63
5 b h Sadler's Wells (USA) - Alignment (Ire)
3^{12s} 8^{14g} **0-1-2 £423**

Front Stage (Ire) *Sir Michael Stoute* 101 a80
3 b/br c Grand Lodge (USA) - Dreams
1^{8sd} 1^{10g} 2^{10g} 13^{12g} 7^{12gf} **2-1-5 £19,594**

Frontier *B J Llewellyn* 82
8 b g Indian Ridge - Adatiya (Ire)
7^{11g} 4^{10s} 5^{10gf} 1^{10gf} 17^{12f} 4^{10gs} **1-0-6 £7,607**

Frontlinefinancier *N I M Rossiter* 60 a59
5 b g Bluegrass Prince (Ire) - Bunny Gee
1^{14sd} 2^{14sd} 2^{13sd} 1^{17g} 1^{16g} 14^{21s} 3^{17sd} **3-3-7 £9,306**

Frootie Tooty (Ire) *J R Weymes* 29 a26
2 ch f Fruits Of Love (USA) - Tana Mana (Ire)
10^{7g} 11^{7sd} 12^{6gf} **0-0-3**

Frost Giant (USA) *A P O'Brien* 108
2 ch c Giant's Causeway (USA) - Takesmybreathaway (USA)
3^{7s} 1^{7hy} **1-1-2 £32,827**

Fruhlingssturm *M A Jarvis* 111
5 b h Unfuwain (USA) - Fruhlingserwachen (USA)
5^{10gs} 13^{10g} 16^{10gs} 3^{10g} 1^{10g} 7^{10gs} **1-1-6 £24,525**

Fruit Of Glory *J R Jenkins* 104
6 b m Glory Of Dancer - Fresh Fruit Daily
1^{6gf} 4^{5g} 3^{6g} 2^{5g} 12^{6gs} 1^{6g} 11^{5g} 10^{5gf} 7^{6g} **2-3-9 £50,726**

Fruit Salad *M Johnston* 68
2 b f Fruits Of Love (USA) - Jerre Jo Glanville (USA)
$3^{6gf} 2^{7gf} 2^{7g} 6^{8g} 1^{7gf}$ **1-3-5 £6,940**

Fu Manchu *Jonjo O'Neill* 99
3 b g Desert Style (Ire) - Robsart (Ire)
$3^{10gs} 3^{10gf}$ **0-0-2 £4,525**

Fuel Cell (Ire) *M E Sowersby* 69 a72
4 b c Desert Style (Ire) - Tappen Zee
$9^{10sd} 3^{10sd} 6^{10g} 4^{8sd} 5^{10g} 10^{10gf} 6^{8gf} 10^{12gs} 1^{10sd} 11^{10sd} 11^{9g} 5^{8gs}$ **1-1-12 £4,270**

Fuerta Ventura (Ire) *K J Condon* 101
3 b/br f Desert Sun - Cradle Brief (Ire)
$1^{8hy} 1^{9sh} 1^{9s} 5^{10s} 9^{11s} 4^{12gf} 4^{14gf} 4^{12g} 2^{12gs}$ **3-1-9 £42,889**

Full As A Rocket (Ire) *D Nicholls* 52
4 b g Foxhound (USA) - Taysala (Ire)
$6^{12gs} 5^{12gs} 8^{8g} 4^{12gf}$ **0-0-4 £320**

Full Of Zest *Mrs A J Perrett* 64 a64
3 ch f Pivotal - Tangerine
$3^{8gf} 4^{9sd} 3^{10g} 4^{9sd}$ **0-1-4 £1,764**

Full Spate *J M Bradley* 76 a38
10 ch g Unfuwain (USA) - Double River (USA)
$9^{7sd} 10^{6s} 9^{6g} 2^{6g} 6^{6gs} 4^{6gf} 6^{6g} 1^{6gf} 3^{6g} 7^{6g} 5^{6gs} 8^{6gs} 1^{6gf} 2^{6f} 5^{6g} 6^{6gs} 4^{6g}$ **2-3-17 £9,248**

Fullandby (Ire) *T J Etherington* 94 a77
3 b g Monashee Mountain (USA) - Ivory Turner
$9^{8g} 2^{9sd} 3^{8gs} 1^{7sd} 2^{7gs} 2^{6g} 1^{6gf} 8^{6gf} 2^{5g} 1^{6s}$ **3-5-10 £26,760**

Fulvio (USA) *P Howling* 54 a61
5 b g Sword Dance - One Tuff Gal (USA)
$2^{8sd} 7^{7sd} 6^{7sd} 1^{8sd} 1^{7sd} 9^{7sd} 1^{7sd} 13^{8g} 6^{7sd} 4^{7f} 4^{7gf} 7^{8f} 8^{8f} 5^{7sd} 2^{7sf} 2^{7sf} 3^{8ss} 5^{7sd} 6^{7ss}$ **3-4-19 £6,091**

Fun Time *M R Channon* a61
2 br f Fraam - Kissing Time
$1^{7sd} 8^{8sd}$ **1-0-2 £1,426**

Fun To Ride *M W Easterby* 79
4 ch f Desert Prince (Ire) - Zafaaf
$8^{6gs} 15^{5g} 6^{5gf} 23^{6gs} 3^{6gs} 14^{5gs}$ **0-1-6 £1,047**

Funfair Wane *D Nicholls* 93
6 b g Unfuwain (USA) - Ivory Bride
$9^{6g} 2^{5gf} 18^{6gs} 18^{6gf} 26^{6g}$ **0-1-5 £4,576**

Furs N Gems *T D Easterby* 36 a47
2 ch f Foxhound (USA) - Just A Gem
$4^{5sd} 8^{5gf} 3^{6sd} 6^{7sd} 9^{7gf} 5^{6gf} 17^{6s} 14^{6gs}$ **0-1-8 £523**

Further Outlook (USA) *D Carroll* 87
11 gr g Zilzal (USA) - Future Bright (USA)
$5^{5gs} 10^{5gs} 6^{5g} 2^{6gf} 4^{5gf} 7^{6gf} 13^{5g} 7^{5gs} 2^{5gs} 10^{5g} 2^{6g} 6^{6g} 1^{5gs}$ **1-3-13 £8,765**

Fusili (Ire) *N P Littmoden* 74 a69
2 ch f Silvano (Ger) - Flunder
$2^{5s} 6^{5gf} 4^{6gs} 2^{8gs} 4^{7gs} 19^{6g} 3^{8g} 11^{8gs} 1^{9sd} 4^{8sd}$ **1-3-10 £6,838**

Fusilier *Sir Michael Stoute* 26
2 ch c Medicean - Fearless Revival
11^{7gs} **0-0-1**

Fusillade (Ire) *A J Lockwood*
5 ch g Grand Lodge (USA) - Lili Cup (Fr)
16^{12f} **0-0-1**

Fuss *P J Hobbs* 45 a47
4 b f Unfuwain (USA) - First Sapphire
$16^{10gs} 8^{14gf} 3^{14g} 4^{17f} 1^{16gs} 3^{16gf} 8^{16g} 3^{16sd}$ **1-3-8 £4,394**

Futoo (Ire) *G M Moore* 73 a50
4 b g Foxhound (USA) - Nicola Wynn
$10^{12gs} 6^{9gs} 13^{10g} 1^{9s} 5^{8g} 10^{9gs} 3^{10gs} 8^{10g} 6^{10gf} 12^{10gs} 11^{10hy} 6^{11sd}$ **1-0-12 £4,566**

Futun *L M Cumani* 73
2 b c In The Wings - Svanzega (USA)
3^{7g} **0-1-1 £763**

Future Deal *C A Horgan* 69 a69
4 b f First Trump - Katyushka (Ire)
$4^{8sd} 2^{7gf} 5^{10g} 5^{7sd} 8^{10gf} 5^{9sd}$ **0-1-6 £1,401**

Fyodor (Ire) *W J Haggas* 80 a97
4 b g Fasliyev (USA) - Royale Figurine (Ire)
$2^{5g} 1^{5gf} 1^{6sd} 2^{5sd} 1^{5sd}$ **3-2-5 £23,912**

Fyvie *E A L Dunlop* a69
2 ch f Grand Lodge (USA) - Island Of Silver (USA)
2^{8sd} **0-1-1 £1,163**

Gabana (Ire) *C F Wall* a65
4 br f Polish Precedent (USA) - Out West (USA)
$8^{8sd} 9^{9sd} 6^{9sd}$ **0-0-3**

Gabla (NZ) *R C Guest* a32
9 b g Prince Of Praise (NZ) - Dynataine (NZ)
12^{12sd} **0-0-1**

Gabor *D W Thompson* 51 a41
6 b g Danzig Connection (USA) - Kiomi
$3^{16gf} 2^{16gf} 7^{12sd}$ **0-2-3 £1,396**

Gaelic Colleen *J Gallagher* 13 a4
2 b f Bertolini (USA) - Peruvian Jade
$8^{5g} 9^{6gf} 10^{6gf} 8^{7sd}$ **0-0-4**

Gaelic Games (UAE) *M Johnston* 56 a59
2 b c Jade Robbery (USA) - Colleen (Ire)
$9^{10g} 9^{8gf} 6^{9sd}$ **0-0-3**

Gaelic Princess *A G Newcombe* 88 a81
5 b m Cois Na Tine (Ire) - Berenice (Ity)
$3^{8sd} 3^{8sd} 8^{9sd} 7^{10sd} 7^{9sd} 1^{8f} 1^{7gf} 12^{8gf} 9^{8g} 1^{7gf} 4^{7s} 6^{7gf} 14^{8gf} 5^{9sd} 5^{9sd} 6^{8sd}$ **3-2-16 £19,585**

Gaelic Roulette (Ire) *J Jay* 50 a55
5 b m Turtle Island (Ire) - Money Spinner (USA)
$10^{14gs} 7^{14gs} 7^{12gf} 6^{12f} 4^{17sd}$ **0-0-5**

Gala Casino King (Ire) *M Dods* 59
2 ch c Elnadim (USA) - Fashion Scout (Ire)
$8^{6gf} 13^{7g}$ **0-0-2**

Gala Evening *Sir Michael Stoute* 76
3 b c Daylami (Ire) - Balleta (USA)
$4^{10gs} 7^{10g} 2^{11gf}$ **0-1-3 £2,593**

Gala Jackpot (USA) *A M Balding* 45 a22
2 b/br g Crafty Prospector (USA) - True At Heart (USA)
$5^{5f} 9^{6sd} 9^{6gf}$ **0-0-3**

Gala Sunday (USA) *M W Easterby* 55 a49
5 b g Lear Fan (USA) - Sunday Bazaar (USA)
$7^{10gs} 3^{12f} 11^{13gf} 2^{10s} 16^{10gs} 5^{9sf} 11^{9sd}$ **0-2-7 £1,203**

Galactic Star *Sir Michael Stoute* 59
2 ch c Galileo (Ire) - Balisada
5^{7s} **0-0-1**

Galandora *Dr J R J Naylor* 44
5 b m Bijou D'Inde - Jelabna
$9^{16g} 4^{16gs} 6^{16gf} 14^{17g} 9^{16gs} 6^{16gf} 11^{16g} 7^{15gf}$ **0-0-8**

Galaxy Bound (Ire) *E A L Dunlop* 63
2 b g Mark Of Esteem (Ire) - Diner De Lune (Ire)
$12^{7gf} 7^{7gf} 5^{7g} 7^{8gf} 10^{7gs}$ **0-0-5**

Galaxy Dancer (Ire) *N B King* a37

3 b g Starborough - Missy Dancer
7^{7sd} 12^{8sd} **0-0-2**

Galaxy King (Ire) *M Johnston*
2 b c Kalanisi (Ire) - Local Lass
18^{8s} 10^{9sd} **0-0-2**

Galeota (Ire) *R Hannon* 117
3 b c Mujadil (USA) - Refined (Ire)
3^{7gs} 1^{7g} 2^{6f} 18^{6gs} 13^{6g} **1-2-5 £81,860**

Galey River (USA) *G L Moore* a45
6 ch g Irish River (Fr) - Carefree Kate (USA)
4^{16sd} **0-0-1**

Galient (Ire) *M A Jarvis* 60
2 b c Galileo (Ire) - Endorsement
7^{8gs} **0-0-1**

Galileo's Star (Ire) *B W Hills* 96
2 ch f Galileo (Ire) - Anazara (USA)
5^{7gf} 1^{7gs} 2^{7gf} 6^{8s} **1-1-4 £10,501**

Gallant Boy (Ire) *P D Evans* 68
6 ch g Grand Lodge (USA) - Damerela (Ire)
1^{12gf} 1^{13gf} 3^{12gf} 15^{12f} 7^{12g} 12^{12g} **2-1-6 £9,512**

Gallantian (Ire) *Alan Fleming* 75
3 gr g Turtle Island (Ire) - Galletina (Ire)
4^{10gf} 22^{10gf} 3^{12ys} 6^{14g} **0-1-4 £1,050**

Gallantry *Sir Michael Stoute* 88
3 b c Green Desert (USA) - Gay Gallanta (USA)
10^{8gs} 1^{7gf} 12^{7gf} 4^{7gf} **1-0-4 £4,356**

Gallas (Ire) *P A Blockley* 54 a51
4 b g Charnwood Forest (Ire) - Nellie's Away (Ire)
5^{12sd} 2^{8g} 2^{8gf} 17^{8gf} 3^{7gf} 8^{8f} 7^{10sd} 6^{8hy} 6^{9sf} 7^{14sd} 4^{11sd} **0-3-11 £2,470**

Gallego *R J Price* 64 a55
3 br c Danzero (Aus) - Shafir (Ire)
11^{9sd} 10^{9sd} 4^{12sd} 8^{9sd} 2^{9sd} 1^{8sd} 1^{10g} 1^{9sd} 12^{10gf} 6^{8gf} 2^{8gf} 2^{8gs} 2^{8gf} 10^{8gf} 8^{10g} 10^{5sd} **3-4-16 £10,077**

Gallery Breeze *P A Blockley* 78 a70
6 b m Zamindar (USA) - Wantage Park
1^{9sd} 9^{9sd} 2^{9sd} 7^{9sd} 2^{9sd} 2^{8g} 1^{9s} 3^{9gf} 5^{8gf} 1^{10gs} 6^{12gf} 14^{10g} **3-3-12 £19,310**

Gallery Girl (Ire) *T D Easterby* 98
2 ch f Namid - September Tide (Ire)
7^{5s} 3^{6gf} 1^{6g} 2^{7gf} 2^{6g} 3^{6gf} 8^{7gs} 2^{6s} **1-5-8 £48,999**

Galley Law *R Craggs* 58 a60
5 ch g Most Welcome - Miss Blitz
3^{9sd} 6^{12sd} 3^{9sd} 1^{8sd} 2^{8s} 9^{8sd} 13^{10g} 5^{12sd} 9^{12sd} **1-3-9 £2,253**

Galloping Foxley (Ire) *R M Flower*
3 ch g Indian Rocket - Croeso Adref
13^{7gf} 12^{8sd} **0-0-2**

Gamble In Gold (Ire) *R Hannon* 90
2 b f Monashee Mountain (USA) - Starisa (Ire)
1^{5gs} 2^{5gs} 6^{5g} 6^{5gf} **1-1-4 £10,900**

Gamble Of The Day (USA) *Sir Michael Stoute* 53
3 ch c Cozzene (USA) - Sue Warner (USA)
7^{8f} 7^{9g} **0-0-2**

Gambling Spirit *H Candy* 37 a68
3 ch f Mister Baileys - Royal Roulette
1^{13sd} 12^{10hy} **1-0-2 £3,877**

Game Flora *M E Sowersby* 49
4 b f Mind Games - Breakfast Creek
11^{8g} 4^{6g} 15^{8g} 9^{8gf} 14^{7g} 8^{6gf} 11^{6f} **0-0-7**

Game Guru *M J Attwater* 58 a59
6 b g First Trump - Scarlett Holly
10^{8sd} 8^{11sd} 4^{9sd} 3^{8sd} 2^{12sd} 2^{11sd} 1^{12sd} 3^{11gs} 7^{12g} 5^{10gs} 4^{8gs} 16^{10gf} 9^{12sd} 13^{8sd} 14^{12sd} **1-3-15 £5,397**

Game Lad *T D Easterby* 99
3 b g Mind Games - Catch Me
7^{7gf} 2^{6g} 3^{7gf} 3^{7gf} 11^{7g} 4^{10g} 3^{8g} 1^{7g} 1^{7s} 6^{7s} **2-3-10 £19,225**

Gameset'N'Match *Miss M P Bryant* 52
4 b g Hector Protector (USA) - Tanasie
12^{6gf} 8^{7gf} 6^{8f} 16^{8gf} 4^{8g} 8^{10g} **0-0-6**

Gamesters Lady *W M Brisbourne* 82 a77
2 br f Almushtarak (Ire) - Tycoon Tina
7^{5s} 9^{5sd} 1^{6g} 2^{7gf} 5^{7g} 2^{7g} 1^{7sd} 2^{7gf} 7^{8g} 5^{7s} 12^{7gs} **2-3-11 £14,064**

Gamut (Ire) *Sir Michael Stoute* 122
6 b h Spectrum (Ire) - Greektown
2^{12gf} 3^{12f} 1^{12gs} 9^{12gf} 5^{13g} 5^{14g} **1-1-6 £94,330**

Gandalf *J R Fanshawe* 80 a83
3 b g Sadler's Wells (USA) - Enchant
11^{10sd} 1^{12sd} 9^{10gf} 6^{12gs} **1-0-4 £3,649**

Gandiloo Gully *J D Bethell* a42
4 ch f Master Willie - Happydrome
12^{10gs} 4^{7sd} 9^{8sd} 9^{7sd} **0-0-4**

Gandor (Ire) *J H M Gosden* 62
2 b c Cape Cross (Ire) - Daftiyna (Ire)
8^{7gf} **0-0-1**

Ganymede *J G M O'Shea* 79
4 gr g Daylami (Ire) - Germane
2^{12gf} 4^{13gf} 6^{15gf} 8^{14gf} **0-1-4 £2,427**

Gardasee (Ger) *T P Tate* 55
3 gr g Dashing Blade - Gladstone Street (Ire)
6^{12g} 11^{16g} **0-0-2**

Garden Society (Ire) *T T Clement* 93 a94
8 ch g Caerleon (USA) - Eurobird
10^{12sd} 1^{16sd} 2^{17sd} 1^{13gf} 8^{13gf} 1^{16g} 14^{14gs} 4^{20s} 1^{16sd} BD^{17sd} 7^{12sd} **4-1-11 £38,194**

Garhoud *Miss K M George* 50
3 b g Grand Lodge (USA) - Puce
11^{12g} 1^{12s} **1-0-2 £3,357**

Garibaldi (Ger) *D R C Elsworth* 75 a71
3 ch c Acatenango (Ger) - Guanhumara
5^{8sd} 2^{8sd} 4^{10gf} 9^{10gs} 8^{10g} 1^{12sd} **1-1-6 £5,207**

Garlogs *A Bailey* 54 a54
2 b g Hunting Lion (Ire) - Fading
2^{5gs} 1^{5g} 7^{5gf} 6^{5gf} 8^{6g} 6^{7ss} 3^{5sd} 2^{5sd} 6^{6sd} **1-3-9 £6,617**

Garnett (Ire) *D E Cantillon* 62 a78
4 b g Desert Story (Ire) - In Behind (Ire)
3^{12sd} 1^{13sd} 1^{16sd} 1^{16sd} 4^{12gs} **3-1-5 £10,541**

Garnock Venture (Ire) *A Berry* 37 a51
4 b g Mujadil (USA) - Stay Sharpe (USA)
8^{6sd} 8^{7sd} 4^{7sd} 3^{7sd} 10^{9sd} 7^{7sd} 3^{7sd} 6^{7gs} 5^{7gf} 10^{7sd} 6^{6sd} 10^{7ss} 9^{8sd} **0-2-13 £752**

Garple Burn *J Akehurst* 53 a59
3 b g Zaha (Can) - Skedaddle
12^{8sd} 4^{10sd} 8^{10sd} 15^{10s} 14^{12g} 7^{10g} 3^{12sd} **0-1-7 £692**

Garrigon *P A Blockley* 61 a62
4 b g Hector Protector (USA) - Queen Of The Keys
2^{11sd} 2^{12sd} 6^{10sd} 11^{12sd} 2^{13sd} 5^{13sd} 8^{12f} 7^{9gf} 8^{12sd} **0-3-9 £2,605**

Garstang *Peter Grayson* 51
2 ch g Atraf - Approved Quality (Ire)

9^{5sd} 8^{5gf} 2^{5s} 3^{5gf} 4^{5s} 1^{5gf} 4^{5gf} 4^{5gf} 8^{6gf}
1-2-9 £4,598

Garw Valley *M Wigham* a28
6 b m Mtoto - Morgannwg (Ire)
12^{9sd} **0-0-1**

Gary's Lady *M Mullineaux*
4 b f Bahamian Bounty - St Lucia (Ire)
12^{7gf} 14^{8gf} **0-0-2**

Gasping (USA) *M R Channon* 13 a66
3 b f Rahy (USA) - Millstream (USA)
5^{7sd} 4^{7sd} 3^{7sd} 2^{6sd} 15^{7gf} **0-2-5 £2,127**

Gateland *W R Swinburn* 60 a61
2 b/br c Dansili - Encorenous (USA)
7^{7sd} 5^{8gf} **0-0-2**

Gates Of Eden (USA) *M L W Bell* 66
2 b f Kingmambo (USA) - Amethyst (Ire)
3^{7f} 5^{7gf} **0-0-2 £627**

Gattuso *Ms Deborah J Evans* 54 a67
2 b g Zilzal (USA) - Daanat Nawal
5^{6sd} 4^{7gf} 6^{5g} 14^{6gf} 5^{5gf} 7^{6sd} 7^{5hy} 2^{7sd} 10^{7sf}
10^{6sd} 4^{7sd} **0-1-11 £1,702**

Gaudalpin (Ire) *E R Oertel* 43 a60
3 b f Danetime (Ire) - Lila Pedigo (Ire)
9^{6sd} 9^{6g} 5^{5gs} 3^{6sd} 2^{6sd} 1^{7sd} 5^{7sd} 9^{6sd} 9^{7sf}
2^{6sd} 2^{6sd} **1-4-11 £3,423**

Gavarnie Beau (Ire) *M Blanshard* 62 a67
2 b g Imperial Ballet (Ire) - Mysticism
6^{5gf} 6^{6sd} 2^{5gf} 3^{5sd} 6^{5sf} 5^{6sd} **0-2-6**
£1,830

Gavioli (Ire) *J M Bradley* 60 a31
3 b g Namid - Pamina (Ire)
19^{6s} 17^{6gs} 13^{6gf} 4^{5g} 1^{6gf} 10^{5f} 6^{6gf} 3^{6g} 10^{6g}
11^{5ft} **1-1-10 £3,828**

Gavroche (Ire) *J R Boyle* 99 a98
4 b c Docksider (USA) - Regal Revolution
5^{13sd} 11^{12gs} 6^{10gf} 2^{10gf} 2^{10gf} 4^{10gf} 1^{10gf} 3^{10g}
1^{10g} 1^{10g} 11^{10gs} 4^{9sd} **3-2-12 £30,324**

Gawain (USA) *M P Tregoning* 70
3 ch g Horse Chestnut (SAF) - Maid Of Camelot
2^{13gf} 7^{12g} **0-1-2 £1,108**

Gay Romance *B W Hills* a67
4 ch f Singspiel (Ire) - Gaijin
5^{8sd} 8^{7sd} 2^{9sd} **0-1-3 £1,042**

Gebora (Fr) *B R Foster* a48
6 ch g Villez (USA) - Sitapanoki (Fr)
6^{9sd} 9^{12sd} 10^{9sd} 10^{12sd} **0-0-4**

Gee Dee Nen *M H Tompkins* 78
2 b c Mister Baileys - Special Beat
5^{7gs} 5^{8g} 1^{8s} 6^{8s} **1-0-4 £7,962**

Gee Four (Ire) *E S McMahon* 52 a44
2 br c Bold Fact (USA) - Hay Knot
6^{5s} 5^{5g} 14^{5s} 1^{5gf} 10^{7sd} 8^{6g} 4^{5gf} 8^{6sd} 18^{7gf}
1-0-9 £2,811

Geller *R T Phillips* 11
4 b g Mind Games - Time To Tango
13^{10gs} 11^{16s} **0-0-2**

Gem Bien (USA) *D W Chapman* 60 a61
7 b g Bien Bien (USA) - Eastern Gem (USA)
9^{8sd} 14^{11sd} 12^{7sd} 3^{8sd} 1^{7sd} 2^{9sd} 2^{9sd} 1^{8sd}
6^{7sd} 7^{9sd} 5^{7sd} 4^{7sd} 4^{8gf} 1^{9sd} 7^{7g} 1^{9sd} 7^{9gf}
2^{8gf} 7^{8gf} 15^{8s} 9^{9sd} 1^{9sd} **5-4-22**
£13,069

Gemini Joy *J Balding*
5 ch m Milieu - Monibell
8^{8sd} **0-0-1**

Gemini Lady *Mrs J C McGregor* 44
5 b m Emperor Fountain - Raunchy Rita
7^{8gs} 7^{9gf} 8^{13gs} **0-0-3**

Gems Bond *J S Moore* 47
5 b g Magic Ring (Ire) - Jucinda
6^{8f} 14^{8g} 4^{8f} 10^{8g} **0-0-4**

Gems Of Araby *H R A Cecil* 74
3 b f Zafonic (USA) - Clepsydra
8^{10gs} 2^{10g} 6^{9gs} 3^{10gf} **0-1-4 £2,184**

Genari *P F I Cole* 93
2 b c Generous (Ire) - Sari
2^{6f} 1^{6gf} 5^{7gf} 3^{7g} 1^{8g} 8^{8g} **2-2-6**
£20,572

Genau (Ire) *Mrs L Stubbs* 71 a70
2 ch g Grand Lodge (USA) - Intizaa (USA)
5^{6g} 3^{7hy} 3^{9sd} **0-1-3 £1,191**

General Factotum (Ire) *G A Swinbank* 43
3 br f General Monash (USA) - Cool Gales
9^{8g} 4^{10gs} 8^{8g} **0-0-3 £294**

General Feeling (Ire) *S Kirk* 84 a83
4 b g General Monash (USA) - Kamadara (Ire)
1^{6g} 5^{6gs} 14^{8g} 9^{6gf} 7^{8gf} 9^{7gf} 9^{7gf} 5^{6g} 8^{6s}
4^{7sd} 10^{7sd} 1^{6sd} 5^{7sd} 1^{7sd} 12^{6sd} 2^{6sd}
3-1-16 £11,094

General Flumpa *C F Wall* 64 a65
4 b g Vettori (Ire) - Macca Luna (Ire)
8^{12sd} 7^{13gs} 6^{14f} 7^{15gf} 1^{13gs} 9^{12gs} **1-0-6**
£2,977

General Haigh *J R Best* 51 a47
3 b g Mujahid (USA) - Stygian (USA)
12^{6sd} 17^{8gf} 6^{6gs} 8^{6gf} 9^{6sd} 15^{7gf} 17^{8g} 6^{10gf}
13^{8f} **0-0-9**

General Jist *Evan Williams* 33 a40
3 ch g Opening Verse (USA) - Pharling
8^{9sd} 12^{7gs} 12^{10sd} 11^{10sd} 13^{11sd} **0-0-5**

General Max (Ire) *A Crook* 40
3 b g General Monash (USA) - Sawaki
3^{12s} 8^{12gs} 12^{8gf} 10^{10g} 6^{10s} 12^{8g} **0-0-6**
£819

General Nuisance (Ire) *A J Chamberlain* a12
3 ch g General Monash (USA) - Baywood
13^{7sd} **0-0-1**

General Oliver (Ire) *K G Wingrove*
5 b g General Monash (USA) - Sea Idol (Ire)
9^{7sd} **0-0-1**

Generator *Dr J D Scargill* a72
3 ch c Cadeaux Genereux - Billie Blue
4^{7sd} 2^{6sf} **0-1-2 £1,262**

Generosia *A M Balding* 54
2 b f Generous (Ire) - Come On Rosi
9^{8g} 16^{7s} **0-0-2**

Generous Lad (Ire) *Miss J S Davis* 62
2 b g Generous (Ire) - Tudor Loom
12^{8s} 1^{8gf} 10^{8f} 10^{10g} **1-0-4 £3,125**

Generous Measure *J M P Eustace* 57
3 b g Largesse - Stormy Heights
8^{8gs} 12^{10f} 13^{10sd} 14^{14g} **0-0-4**

Generous Option *M Johnston* 89
3 ch f Cadeaux Genereux - Easy Option (Ire)
2^{6s} 1^{7g} 5^{6s} 6^{8g} 11^{7gs} 7^{7g} 5^{7g} **1-1-7**
£15,362

Genghis (Ire) *P Bowen* 70
6 br g Persian Bold - Cindy's Baby
7^{16gf} **0-0-1**

Gennie Bond *R Hannon* 73

3 b f Pivotal - Miriam
2^{6gs} 5^{6gf} 5^{8gs} 13^{8gf} 4^{6g} 11^{6g} **0-1-6**
£2,341

Genoa Star *T J Pitt* 40 a27
2 b f Woodborough (USA) - Naval Dispatch
8^{5s} 11^{5gs} 11^{6gf} 6^{6gf} 8^{7f} 4^{6gf} 15^{6gf} 7^{6sd}
0-0-8

Genre *R Hannon* 101
2 b c Orpen (USA) - Blue Indigo (Fr)
5^{7gf} 3^{7f} 5^{7g} 2^{8g} 9^{8gf} 1^{8g} 1^{8s} 3^{10s} **2-2-8**
£19,450

Gentian *Sir Mark Prescott* 39 a43
2 ch f Generous (Ire) - French Spice
10^{7sd} 4^{7g} 13^{8gs} **0-0-3 £346**

Gentle Peace (Ire) *J W Unett* 62 a67
4 b f Orpen (USA) - Habaza (Ire)
7^{7hy} 12^{7sh} 2^{9g} 11^{8gf} 6^{7ys} 5^{8g} 6^{9f} 2^{12g} 2^{13g}
8^{12g} 3^{12gy} 9^{12g} 4^{10gf} 1^{12sd} 9^{14sd} 5^{9sd}
1-5-16 £6,459

Gentle Response *B R Johnson* 13 a43
5 b m Puissance - Sweet Whisper
5^{7sd} 4^{6sd} 7^{6sd} 8^{7sd} 4^{5sd} 13^{5f} **0-0-6**

Gentle Warning *M Appleby* a12
5 b m Parthian Springs - Manx Princess
12^{9sd} 13^{14sd} **0-0-2**

Genuine Surprise (Ire) *A P Jarvis* 48
3 br f Definite Article - Morning Surprise
6^{7gs} 10^{7gs} 14^{9g} 5^{10g} **0-0-4**

Geojimali *J S Goldie* 33
3 ch g Compton Place - Harrken Heights (Ire)
13^{8gf} 9^{7gf} **0-0-2**

Geometric *R Hannon* a61
3 b g Octagonal (NZ) - Liska's Dance (USA)
5^{8sd} 9^{9sd} 9^{10sd} 16^{8g} **0-0-4**

Geordie Dancer (Ire) *A Berry* 66
3 b g Dansili - Awtaar (USA)
11^{6s} 5^{7f} 9^{7f} 7^{7g} 2^{6gf} 5^{6gf} 2^{6gf} 15^{5gf} 1^{6gf}
8^{5g} 18^{7gf} **1-2-11 £4,618**

George Romney (USA) *Mrs L J Mongan* 38 a61
6 b g Distant View (USA) - Polish Socialite (USA)
11^{12sd} 2^{7sd} 3^{6sd} 12^{6s} 4^{6sd} 9^{7gf} 13^{6gs}
0-2-7 £794

George Stubbs (USA) *B Ellison* 64
7 b/br g Affirmed (USA) - Mia Duchessa (USA)
6^{11gf} 8^{16g} 2^{13gf} 4^{12g} 4^{16gf} **0-1-5 £1,574**

George The Best (Ire) *M D Hammond* 72 a49
4 b g Imperial Ballet (Ire) - En Retard (Ire)
11^{6s} 1^{6gs} 10^{6sd} 14^{5g} 4^{6s} 7^{6gs} 11^{6sd} 10^{5s}
7^{6sd} **1-0-9 £4,051**

George The Second *Mrs H Sweeting* 55 a53
2 b c Josr Algarhoud (Ire) - Pink Champagne
5^{7gf} 10^{7g} 10^{7g} 5^{7sd} 10^{7sd} 10^{8sd} **0-0-6**

George Washington (Ire) *A P O'Brien* 121
2 b c Danehill (USA) - Bordighera (USA)
3^{5gf} 1^{6y} 1^{6gf} 1^{6g} 1^{7g} **4-1-5 £317,349**

George's Flyer (Ire) *R A Fahey* 65 a63
2 b c Daggers Drawn (USA) - Winged Victory (Ire)
4^{5hy} 6^{6s} 7^{7f} 3^{7gf} 12^{8g} 8^{8gs} 7^{8sd} 1^{7sd} 7^{8sd}
1^{9sd} **2-1-10 £7,345**

Georgia Jed (Ire) *A Berry* 24
2 b g Even Top (Ire) - Klipspinger
9^{5g} 5^{6gf} 8^{5gf} 4^{8s} **0-0-4 £987**

Georgie's Lass (Ire) *C Roberts* 45
6 gr m Flemensfirth (USA) - Rongai (Ire)
5^{12gs} 9^{16gf} **0-0-2**

Geri Roulette *S C Burrough*
7 b m Perpendicular - Clashfern
11^{12sd} **0-0-1**

Germanicus *R Charlton* 68
3 b g Desert King (Ire) - Simacota (Ger)
7^{10gf} 2^{12g} 1^{12gf} 10^{12gf} **1-1-4 £4,866**

Geronimo *Miss Gay Kelleway* a42
8 b g Efisio - Apache Squaw
6^{7sd} 11^{10sd} **0-0-2**

Get To The Point *Miss J Feilden* 49 a52
4 ch g Daggers Drawn (USA) - Penny Mint
7^{8sd} 8^{6s} 5^{7sd} 11^{7sd} 6^{9sd} 7^{7gf} 1^{8g} 16^{8gf} 8^{7f}
3^{8g} 12^{8sd} 13^{9ss} **1-1-12 £2,915**

Getbuzzin *M J Wallace* 67 a64
2 ch g Bold Edge - Berenice (Ity)
2^{5gs} 3^{5sd} 3^{6gf} 10^{6gf} **0-1-4 £2,849**

Gettysburg (Ire) *J Howard Johnson* 52
2 b g Imperial Ballet (Ire) - Two Magpies
6^{7gf} 10^{6gf} 13^{9g} **0-0-3**

Ghaill Force *P Butler* 52 a57
3 b g Piccolo - Coir 'A' Ghaill
4^{7sd} 4^{7s} 6^{7s} 14^{10sd} 8^{8gf} 12^{7g} 5^{7gf} 4^{8g} 6^{8gf}
11^{10gf} **0-0-10 £290**

Ghajariy (USA) *G C Bravery* 3
2 b/br g Stormin Fever (USA) - Jetapat (USA)
9^{6gs} **0-0-1**

Ghasiba (Ire) *C E Brittain* 56
3 gr f Daylami (Ire) - Night Owl
7^{8s} 17^{8g} 8^{10f} 10^{9g} **0-0-4**

Ghostly Pet (Ire) *Unknown* 53
2 b/br g Spectrum (Ire) - Fabulous Pet
8^{8gf} 15^{8g} 14^{8s} **0-0-3**

Ghostzapper (USA) *R J Frankel* a135
5 b h Awesome Again (Can) - Baby Zip (USA)
1^{8ft} **1-0-1 £234,375**

Ghurra (USA) *E A L Dunlop* 91
3 b f War Chant (USA) - Futuh (USA)
7^{7gf} 2^{7gf} 6^{7g} 5^{8g} 4^{7gf} 2^{9s} 5^{10gf} **0-2-7**
£7,423

Giacomo (USA) *J Shirreffs* a121
3 gr c Holy Bull (USA) - Set Them Free (USA)
3^{9ft} 2^{9ft} 4^{9ft} 1^{10ft} 3^{10ft} 7^{12ft} **1-2-6**
£961,914

Giant Leap *G L Moore* 55
3 ch f Giant's Causeway (USA) - Home Truth
6^{8g} 10^{8g} 12^{10g} 10^{7g} 10^{10g} **0-0-5**

Giant's Rock (Ire) *B J Llewellyn* 58 a69
3 ch g Giant's Causeway (USA) - En Garde (USA)
6^{10sd} UR^{7sd} 2^{8sd} 9^{8gs} **0-1-4 £1,046**

Gibbs Camp *E A L Dunlop* a59
2 b f Marju (Ire) - Serengeti Bride (USA)
10^{7sd} 7^{6sd} 4^{7sd} **0-0-3 £274**

Gibraltar Bay (Ire) *T G Mills* 88 a87
3 b f Cape Cross (Ire) - Secrets Of Honour
1^{9sd} 1^{9sd} 5^{12sd} 1^{12gs} 2^{12gf} 3^{14gf} 8^{12gf} 2^{12sd}
3-3-8 £15,471

Gidam Gidam (Ire) *J Mackie* 66 a69
3 b g King's Best (USA) - Flamands (Ire)
4^{10sd} 11^{11sd} 4^{12gf} 5^{14f} 8^{14g} 7^{16g} 12^{16gf} 10^{14g}
0-0-8 £898

Gift Aid *P J Makin* 34 a49
2 b c Generous (Ire) - Sans Diablo (Ire)
14^{6gf} 7^{8gs} 6^{6sd} 13^{5gs} **0-0-4**

Gift Horse *D Nicholls* 118
5 ch g Cadeaux Genereux - Careful Dancer

1^{6g} 3^{6gs} 1^{6g} 1^{6gs} 17^{6g} **3-1-5 £91,023**

Gifted Flame *T D Barron* 77
6 b g Revoque (Ire) - Littleladyleah (USA)
6^{8g} 2^{7f} 1^{7gf} 5^{7gf} 3^{8g} 8^{8gf} 4^{7gf} 11^{8s}
1-2-8 £7,103

Gifted Gamble *K A Ryan* 98
3 b c Mind Games - Its Another Gift
2^{6s} 5^{6hy} 3^{7s} 5^{7g} 8^{7s} 6^{6gf} 7^{6g} **0-2-7**
£8,035

Gifted Glori *T D Barron* 50
2 ch g Vettori (Ire) - Azira
6^{6gs} 6^{6gf} 9^{7g} 6^{6gf} 13^{6hy} **0-0-5**

Gifted Lass *J Balding* 12
3 b f Bold Edge - Meeson Times
12^{5gf} **0-0-1**

Gifted Musician *J L Dunlop* 75
3 b c Sadler's Wells (USA) - Photogenic
9^{12gf} 8^{12g} 6^{10s} 1^{12s} **1-0-4 £4,210**

Gig Harbor *P R Chamings* 69 a107
6 b g Efisio - Petonica (Ire)
1^{12sd} 5^{12sd} 2^{10sd} 1^{12sd} 10^{10sd} 11^{9gf} 11^{16sd}
2-1-7 £31,381

Giganticus (USA) *B W Hills* 91
2 ch c Giant's Causeway (USA) - Shy Princess (USA)
6^{7g} 1^{6g} **1-0-2 £4,641**

Gigs Magic (USA) *J G Given* 61 a70
2 ch g Gulch (USA) - Magic Of Love
9^{6gf} 2^{6sd} 4^{6g} 9^{6sd} 17^{6g} **0-1-5 £1,851**

Giko *Jane Southcombe* 36
11 b g Arazi (USA) - Gayane
2^{12g} 10^{14gf} 12^{10gf} 7^{11gs} 8^{11gf} **0-0-5**
£525

Gildas Fortuna *P C Haslam* 42
3 b f Fort Wood (USA) - Gleaming Sky (SAF)
7^{8gf} 9^{7g} 12^{8s} **0-0-3**

Gilded Cove *R Hollinshead* a81
5 b h Polar Prince (Ire) - Cloudy Reef
7^{6sd} 7^{6sd} 5^{6sd} 1^{6sd} 4^{5sd} 1^{5sd} 4^{6sd} 2^{6sd} 10^{6sd}
3^{5sd} 1^{5sd} 2^{5sf} 2^{6sd} 9^{6sd} **3-4-14**
£14,774

Gillipops (Ire) *R Hannon* 68 a61
2 b f Xaar - Snoozeandyoulose (Ire)
3^{5gs} 4^{5sd} 2^{6gf} 1^{7gf} 11^{6gf} 4^{7gf} 11^{8g} **1-2-7**
£6,591

Gilly's General (Ire) *J W Unett* a26
5 ch g General Monash (USA) - Good Aim (Ire)
9^{7sd} 12^{7sd} **0-0-2**

Gilt Linked *B W Hills* 82
2 b f Compton Place - Copy-Cat
4^{5g} 15^{5gf} 10^{6gs} 3^{5gf} 1^{5gs} 9^{5hy} **1-0-6**
£5,388

Gimasha *W Jarvis* 102
3 b f Cadeaux Genereux - First Waltz (Fr)
10^{6g} 2^{5gf} 1^{5g} 1^{6gf} 1^{6gf} 11^{6g} 1^{6g} **4-1-7**
£33,572

Gin Jockey (Fr) *R Hannon* 98
2 b c Soviet Star (USA) - Singing Lark (Fr)
1^{7g} 1^{7g} **2-0-2 £28,656**

Ginger Cookie *B Smart* 24 a40
3 ch f Bold Edge - Pretty Pollyanna
8^{5g} 11^{6gf} 5^{7sd} 3^{7sd} 2^{7sd} 11^{8sd} 6^{7sd} **0-2-7**
£633

Ginger For Pluck *J G Given* a20
3 b f Revoque (Ire) - Naughty Pistol (USA)
10^{9sd} 13^{6sd} **0-0-2**

Ginger Ice *G G Margarson*
5 ch g Bahamian Bounty - Sharp Top
7^{8sd} **0-0-1**

Ginger Spice (Ire) *W J Haggas* 87 a15
3 ch f Cadeaux Genereux - Pop Queen
2^{7gs} 4^{7s} 1^{8s} 4^{8g} 15^{8gs} 11^{7ft} **1-1-6**
£8,724

Gingerbread *B Ellison* 2
4 ch g Pharly (Fr) - Gay Sarah
6^{8gs} **0-0-1**

Gingiefly *J L Dunlop* 63
3 b c Sinndar (Ire) - Native Ring (Fr)
7^{11g} 11^{12g} 4^{12gs} **0-0-3 £558**

Gingko *P R Webber* 29 a81
8 b g Pursuit Of Love - Arboretum (Ire)
3^{10sd} 6^{12sd} 1^{10sd} 1^{10sd} 13^{10gs} 14^{10s} 5^{10sd}
2-1-7 £10,723

Giocoso (USA) *B Palling* 88
5 b h Bahri (USA) - Wing My Chimes (USA)
1^{8g} 6^{7gf} 13^{8g} 17^{9gs} **1-0-4 £7,258**

Girandola *R F Johnson Houghton* 65 a47
2 b c Observatory (USA) - Honeyspike (Ire)
5^{6g} 10^{6sd} **0-0-2**

Girardii *R Charlton* 61
2 ch c Sinndar (Ire) - Armeria (USA)
18^{7gf} 8^{8g} **0-0-2**

Girlsweekend *Mrs L J Mongan* 68 a65
3 b f Benny The Dip (USA) - Snoozy
3^{6sd} 4^{5s} 5^{5gf} 12^{6gf} **0-1-4 £952**

Gitche Manito (Ire) *A King* 75 a71
3 b g Namid - Chasing Rainbows
2^{10g} 11^{8gf} 4^{11gf} 3^{10g} 3^{10g} 5^{12sd} 14^{11gs}
0-3-7 £3,136

Giunchiglio *W M Brisbourne* 57 a68
6 ch g Millkom - Daffodil Fields
6^{12sd} 6^{9f} 11^{12gf} 6^{13gs} 8^{12gs} 5^{12gf} 6^{11gf} 16^{10gf}
7^{12gf} 7^{12gf} 4^{12sd} 8^{12sd} 3^{11sd} 6^{12sd} 10^{10sd}
0-1-15 £209

Give It Time *J G Given* 55
2 b f Kayf Tara - Startino
7^{8s} **0-0-1**

Give Me The Night (Ire) *E A L Dunlop* 90 a84
2 b f Night Shift (USA) - There With Me (USA)
2^{5gs} 1^{5sd} 4^{5g} 16^{5gf} 2^{5g} 1^{5gf} 8^{5gf} 7^{6gf} 7^{5g}
1^{5g} **3-2-10 £17,759**

Givemethemoonlight *Stef Liddiard* a29
6 ch m Woodborough (USA) - Rockin' Rosie
10^{9sd} **0-0-1**

Given A Chance *Mrs S Lamyman* 51 a43
4 b/br g Defacto (USA) - Milly Molly Mango
10^{9sd} 13^{8sd} 5^{9sd} 6^{8sd} 1^{16gs} 14^{16gs} 5^{12g} 13^{17gf}
1-0-8 £1,599

Given A Choice (Ire) *J G Given* 88
3 b g Trans Island - Miss Audimar (USA)
4^{9g} 3^{12gf} 1^{11gf} 11^{12gf} 1^{11gf} 9^{14gf} 7^{10gf}
2-1-7 £15,224

Giverny Spring *J W Hills* 67
2 b f Lujain (USA) - Matisse
3^{7gf} 5^{7gf} 13^{7gf} **0-1-3 £752**

Giving *G Wragg* 78
2 gr f Generous (Ire) - Madiyla
8^{6gf} 1^{7gf} 8^{7gs} **1-0-3 £4,836**

Gizmondo *M L W Bell* 37
2 ch c Lomitas - India Atlanta
14^{8gf} **0-0-1**

Gjovic *B J Meehan* 80
4 br g Singspiel (Ire) - Photo Call
8^{10g} 2^{10gf} 8^{10g} 3^{10gf} 3^{8gf} 5^{8gf} 2^{10g} 3^{11gf} 4^{9gf}
0-5-9 £6,308

Glad Big (Ger) *J A Osborne* 65 a69
3 b g Big Shuffle (USA) - Glady Sum (Ger)
3^{6s} 3^{9sd} 5^{7gs} **0-1-3 £1,048**

Gladys Aylward *D A Nolan*
5 b m Polar Falcon (USA) - Versami (USA)
11^{8gf} 9^{8gf} **0-0-2**

Glamaraazi (Ire) *R A Fahey* 49
2 b f Orpen (USA) - Raazi
5^{5gf} **0-0-1**

Glaramara *A Bailey* 93 a97
4 b g Nicolotte - Digamist Girl (Ire)
2^{7sd} 6^{8sd} 1^{6sd} 4^{7sd} 6^{6g} 20^{6gf} 6^{8gs} 8^{6g} 2^{6gf}
8^{6gf} 8^{5gf} 4^{6gf} 12^{6gf} **1-2-13 £22,475**

Glasnas Giant *J Pearce* 58 a41
2 b f Giant's Causeway (USA) - Gleefully (USA)
2^{5gs} 7^{5gf} 7^{6gf} 9^{7sd} **0-1-4 £1,316**

Glasshoughton *M Dods* 73
2 b c Dansili - Roseum
4^{5g} 2^{6s} 2^{6s} 4^{6gf} 3^{5gs} 4^{6g} 11^{5g} **0-2-7**
£4,751

Glasson Lodge *A L Forbes* 42 a56
3 b f Primo Dominie - Petrikov (Ire)
2^{9sd} 3^{9sd} 1^{9sd} 4^{10sd} 4^{10g} 2^{8sd} 13^{8g} 10^{9sd} 11^{7gf}
11^{9ss} **1-3-10 £4,565**

Glastonbury (Ire) *Peter McCreery*
9 b g Common Grounds - Harmonious
5^{7f} **0-0-1**

Glebe Garden *M Wigham* 62
4 b f Soviet Star (USA) - Trounce
12^{7gf} 14^{7g} 15^{6gf} 10^{7f} 12^{8gf} **0-0-5**

Glen Ida *M L W Bell* 104
3 ch c Selkirk (USA) - Yanka (USA)
1^{9g} 5^{10gs} 3^{10g} 8^{10gf} 4^{9g} PU^{9gf} **1-0-6**
£12,724

Glen Innes (Ire) *D R Loder* a102
4 b f Selkirk (USA) - Shinko Hermes (Ire)
2^{9sd} 8^{8sd} **0-1-2 £4,514**

Glenbuck (Ire) *A Bailey* 67 a73
2 b g Mujadil (USA) - Bryna (Ire)
10^{6gf} 6^{7g} 8^{7gf} 3^{6gs} 6^{6s} 15^{8gs} 7^{6hy} 1^{7s} 7^{8hy}
2^{7sd} **1-2-10 £5,011**

Glencairn Star *J S Goldie* 74 a71
4 b g Selkirk (USA) - Bianca Nera
2^{6sd} 5^{7sd} 17^{6s} 7^{7s} 2^{6g} 3^{6gf} 10^{8gf} **0-3-7**
£3,285

Glencalvie (Ire) *J Akehurst* 77 a81
4 ch g Grand Lodge (USA) - Top Of The Form (Ire)
3^{6gs} 3^{7g} 6^{7gf} 4^{7f} 1^{8g} 10^{8gs} 3^{8sd} 3^{8sd} 1^{8sd}
2-4-9 £11,906

Glendale *D K Ivory* a60
4 ch g Opening Verse (USA) - Kayartis
4^{10sd} 2^{10sd} 5^{10sd} 3^{12sd} 1^{10sd} 1^{10sd} 3^{10sd} 11^{9sd}
2-3-8 £6,011

Glendening *D Nicholls* 54 a53
2 b g Mark Of Esteem (Ire) - Mistook (USA)
9^{5gf} 7^{6s} 7^{6gf} 2^{7sd} 12^{7g} 4^{7g} 8^{6gf} 3^{7gf} 2^{7gf}
5^{8gf} **0-3-10 £2,820**

Glenmuir (Ire) *B R Millman* 80
2 b g Josr Algarhoud (Ire) - Beryl
1^{5gs} 2^{5g} 2^{6gf} 2^{6gf} 4^{7s} 8^{7gs} 4^{7gf} 4^{6g} 17^{6g}
1-2-9 £12,317

Glenree *Eamon Tyrrell* 53 a59
4 b g Wizard King - The Prussian Queen
17^{7g} 7^{8hy} 2^{9sd} **0-1-3 £862**

Glenrowan (USA) *M P Tregoning* 53 a59
2 b f Danzig (USA) - Pricket (USA)
12^{6gf} 6^{6sd} 11^{7gf} 12^{5gf} **0-0-4**

Glenviews Oldport (USA) *Peter Grayson* 28 a56
3 ch f Old Trieste (USA) - Port Plaisance (USA)
13^{7gf} 12^{6gf} 12^{7gf} 18^{7gf} 7^{6sd} 5^{7sd} 2^{10sd} 4^{9sd}
11^{10sd} 4^{9sd} **0-1-10 £429**

Glenviews Surlami (Ire) *R C Guest* 34 a18
4 gr f Daylami (Ire) - Surmise (USA)
6^{12sd} 5^{12f} 4^{11gf} **0-0-3**

Glenviews Youngone (Ire) *Peter Grayson* a70
2 b f Namid - Baltic Beach (Ire)
3^{5sd} 1^{5sd} 4^{5sd} **1-1-3 £3,605**

Glide *J A B Old* 11
4 ch g In The Wings - Ash Glade
9^{18g} **0-0-1**

Glistening *Sir Michael Stoute* 102
3 b c Sadler's Wells (USA) - Shining Water
2^{10g} 1^{12gf} 5^{12g} 2^{14gf} 6^{14g} 5^{14g} **1-2-6**
£14,273

Glitterati *R Charlton* 53
2 b f Observatory (USA) - Stardom
12^{6gs} **0-0-1**

Global Achiever *G C H Chung* 39 a77
4 b g Key Of Luck (USA) - Inflation
6^{6sd} 5^{6sd} 1^{5sd} 11^{6sd} 7^{5sd} 9^{6g} UR^{6f} 10^{5f} 11^{6sd}
12^{6sd} 9^{5sd} 4^{6sd} 12^{7sd} **1-0-13 £3,415**

Global Banker (Ire) *G C H Chung* 20 a32
3 b g Desert Prince (Ire) - Luisa Demon (Ire)
12^{7g} 8^{5sd} 15^{6gf} **0-0-3**

Global Genius (Ire) *B W Hills* 85
2 gr c Galileo (Ire) - Vadsagreya (Fr)
3^{6gf} 2^{7gf} 2^{7gs} 1^{7gf} 7^{8gf} **1-3-5 £18,117**

Global Guardian *Mrs G S Rees* 65 a58
2 ch g Dr Fong (USA) - Penmayne
7^{6gf} 5^{6f} 8^{6gf} 5^{7gf} 7^{7gf} 3^{7g} 9^{6hy} 4^{7sd}
0-1-8 £649

Global Warning (USA) *M Johnston* 64
2 b g Red Ransom (USA) - Wild Planet (USA)
3^{5gs} 4^{6g} **0-1-2 £940**

Globalized (Ire) *Mrs P Sly* 75
3 b g Spectrum (Ire) - Smaointeach (Ire)
5^{7s} 7^{9gy} 11^{11gf} 5^{8f} 2^{10f} 10^{10gs} 10^{10g}
0-1-7 £1,712

Globe *M Meade* 42
2 b f Agnes World (USA) - Hoist (Ire)
8^{5f} 10^{6gf} 5^{5gf} **0-0-3**

Globe Trekker (USA) *James Moffatt* 18
3 gr f Aljabr (USA) - Amazonia (USA)
9^{10g} 12^{8g} **0-0-2**

Glorious Step (USA) *J H M Gosden* 65
3 b f Diesis - Bessie's Chips (USA)
8^{8gf} **0-0-1**

Glorious Westport (Ire) *E S McMahon* 46 a60
3 b c Erhaab (USA) - Generate
9^{10gs} 12^{10g} 8^{11gf} 2^{12sd} 17^{12gf} 10^{12g} **0-1-6**
£744

Glory Oatway (Ire) *D Flood* a28
3 b f Desert Prince (Ire) - Seasonal Blossom (Ire)
11^{8sd} 5^{12f} **0-0-2**

Glory Quest (USA) *Miss Gay Kelleway* a67
8 b g Quest For Fame - Sonseri

4^{16sd} 6^{12sd} **0-0-2 £265**

Gloved Hand *J G Given* 91 a91
3 b f Royal Applause - Fudge
7^{6hy} 8^{6g} 1^{6g} 5^{6gf} 7^{6g} 4^{8g} 11^{8g} 8^{8sd}
1-0-8 £9,809

Glowette (Ire) *I W McInnes* 29
3 ch f General Monash (USA) - Why Not Glow (Ire)
7^{9hy} 13^{8f} 4^{10gf} 12^{13g} 13^{10sd} 14^{7sd} **0-0-6**

Glowing Dawn (Ire) *Miss J S Davis* 57
3 b f Definite Article - Alizee (Ire)
9^{8s} 10^{8f} 7^{7g} 11^{7g} 12^{6gs} **0-0-5**

Gnillah *B W Hills* 48
2 b f Halling (USA) - Dimakya (USA)
9^{7gf} **0-0-1**

Go Amwell *J R Jenkins* a51
2 b c Kayf Tara - Daarat Alayaam (Ire)
10^{7sd} 8^{7sd} **0-0-2**

Go Figure (Ire) *B J Meehan* 72
2 ch g Desert Prince (Ire) - Interpose
8^{6gs} 3^{6gf} 4^{7g} 4^{6g} 5^{6g} 5^{7g} **0-1-6 £1,330**

Go Free *C J Down* 50 a51
4 gr g Easycall - Miss Traxdata
2^{7sd} 6^{10sd} 3^{10sd} 4^{12sd} 2^{12sd} 3^{12sd} 1^{13sd} 11^{17g}
2^{12g} 5^{12g} 7^{10g} 7^{16sd} **1-5-12 £3,647**

Go Garuda *D W P Arbuthnot* 39 a68
4 b g Air Express (Ire) - Free As A Bird
3^{8sd} 8^{9sd} 9^{8sd} 2^{8sd} 7^{10sd} 8^{8gs} 8^{10sd} **0-2-7**
£1,611

Go Go Girl *D W P Arbuthnot* 64 a46
5 ch m Pivotal - Addicted To Love
9^{6sd} 8^{6gs} 6^{6gs} 4^{6gf} 5^{6g} 10^{7g} **0-0-6 £281**

Go Green *P D Evans* 55
4 ch f Environment Friend - Sandra Mac
11^{12g} 4^{10g} 3^{10s} 1^{12gs} 8^{12g} 10^{12g} 6^{12gf} 4^{12f}
7^{16gf} **1-1-9 £2,968**

Go Like The Wind *Rae Guest* a37
3 br f Cape Cross (Ire) - Fly Like The Wind
6^{6sd} 9^{6sd} 18^{6s} **0-0-3**

Go Mo (Ire) *S Kirk* 87 a82
3 b g Night Shift (USA) - Quiche
10^{7g} 1^{6gf} 7^{6g} 1^{7gf} 6^{7gs} 10^{6gf} 6^{7g} 9^{7sd} 6^{8s}
7^{8g} 4^{6gs} 6^{6sd} **2-1-12 £16,639**

Go Padero (Ire) *M Johnston* 91
4 ch g Night Shift (USA) - Watch The Clock
15^{8gf} 3^{7gs} 15^{7g} 7^{8g} 15^{7gf} 18^{8gs} **0-1-6**
£1,587

Go Solo *G A Swinbank* 86
4 b g Primo Dominie - Taza
11^{7g} 13^{7gs} 6^{8f} 6^{9f} 1^{8gf} 2^{8gf} 1^{8gf} 1^{9gf} 3^{9gf}
3^{10gf} 4^{10g} 6^{8gf} **3-3-12 £20,073**

Go Tech *T D Easterby* 98 a97
5 b g Gothenberg (Ire) - Bollin Sophie
13^{10gs} 7^{8gf} 11^{10gf} 8^{9gf} 1^{10f} 15^{10g} 8^{10gf} 8^{11gf}
6^{10gf} 5^{10g} 1^{10g} 7^{10g} 4^{12sd} 8^{10sd} **2-0-14**
£27,880

Go Yellow *P D Evans* 72
4 b g Overbury (Ire) - Great Lyth Lass (Ire)
1^{7s} 5^{7gs} 13^{7gf} 7^{7f} 9^{7gf} 9^{8gf} 8^{7f} 7^{8gf} 6^{6g}
1-0-9 £3,478

Goblin *D E Cantillon* 61 a59
4 b g Atraf - Forest Fantasy
12^{12sd} 10^{10gs} 9^{10gf} **0-0-3**

Godfrey Street *R Hannon* 107 a94
2 ch c Compton Place - Tahara (Ire)
4^{5gs} 1^{5sd} 2^{5g} 24^{5gf} 6^{5gs} 3^{6gs} 1^{5sd} 2^{5g} 5^{6gf}
1^{5hy} 7^{5g} **3-3-11 £67,913**

Gogetter Girl *J Gallagher* 47 a48
3 b f Wolfhound (USA) - Square Mile Miss (Ire)
3^{7sd} 9^{9sd} 9^{7sd} 9^{7gf} 5^{8gs} 8^{8f} 19^{6g} 7^{7f} 16^{6gf}
5^{10sd} **0-1-10 £376**

Golano *P R Webber* 80 a83
5 gr g Linamix (Fr) - Dimakya (USA)
1^{12sd} 7^{12sd} 9^{11gs} 7^{10g} 12^{12sd} **1-0-5**
£6,032

Golband *L M Cumani* 69 a76
3 b f Cadeaux Genereux - Hatheethah (Ire)
7^{6g} 9^{5gf} 8^{5sd} 4^{6sd} 8^{5gf} 2^{6gf} 1^{6g} 14^{6g} 1^{6sd}
13^{6sd} **2-1-10 £7,964**

Gold Dragon *W Jarvis* 46
2 ch g Piccolo - Fredora
15^{6g} 8^{6gs} 14^{6g} **0-0-3**

Gold Express *W A O'Gorman* a76
2 b c Observatory (USA) - Vanishing Point (USA)
8^{7sd} **0-0-1**

Gold Fervour (Ire) *W M Brisbourne* a37
6 b g Mon Tresor - Fervent Fan (Ire)
3^{8sd} 12^{8sd} 8^{9sd} 10^{12sd} **0-1-4 £219**

Gold Guest *P D Evans* 63 a69
6 ch g Vettori (Ire) - Cassilis (Ire)
1^{9sd} 5^{9sd} 11^{10sd} 2^{9sd} 9^{9sd} 1^{12gs} 6^{10gf} 6^{11f}
7^{7sd} 7^{8gf} 1^{10f} 3^{10g} 11^{8g} 6^{10g} **3-2-14**
£9,783

Gold Gun (USA) *M A Jarvis* 100
3 b c Seeking The Gold (USA) - Possessive Dancer
1^{11gs} 3^{12g} 16^{12hy} **1-1-3 £8,101**

Gold Heritage (USA) *Saeed Bin Suroor* 71
3 b/br c Seeking The Gold (USA) - Heritage Of Gold (USA)
4^{8gf} 6^{11g} 3^{10g} **0-1-3 £772**

Gold Queen *M R Channon* 83
3 b f Grand Lodge (USA) - Silver Colours (USA)
3^{9gs} 8^{7gs} 7^{8s} 8^{8gf} **0-0-4 £1,050**

Gold Ring *J A Geake* 95
5 ch g Groom Dancer (USA) - Indubitable
4^{12s} 11^{12g} 9^{16g} **0-0-3 £788**

Gold Strike (Ire) *Miss D A McHale*
3 ch f Rainbow Quest (USA) - Turban
11^{8sd} **0-0-1**

Golda Seek (USA) *P C Haslam* 55
2 b f Seeking The Gold (USA) - Golightly (USA)
3^{5gf} 5^{5gf} 8^{5gf} 16^{5gf} **0-1-4 £739**

Goldbricker *W M Brisbourne* a48
5 b g Muhtarram (USA) - Sally Slade
10^{9sd} **0-0-1**

Golden Acer (Ire) *R Hannon* 95
2 ch c Elnadim (USA) - Shifty Lady (Ire)
3^{6f} 3^{6g} 1^{5f} 1^{5gf} 2^{5g} 2^{5gf} 9^{5g} **2-4-7**
£19,650

Golden Alchemist *M D I Usher* 76
2 ch g Woodborough (USA) - Pure Gold
6^{6gf} 12^{7g} 4^{6g} 2^{6g} 12^{7gs} 5^{7gs} **0-1-6**
£2,105

Golden Anthem (USA) *J Pearce* 88
3 ch f Lion Cavern (USA) - Bacinella (USA)
6^{8g} 12^{7gf} 7^{7gs} 8^{7g} 9^{7gf} **0-0-5**

Golden Applause (Fr) *Mrs A L M King* 77
3 b f Royal Applause - Golden Circle (USA)
2^{8gf} 2^{8gf} 1^{8s} 5^{8s} **1-2-4 £7,230**

Golden Arrow (Ire) *D K Weld* 108
2 b c Danehill (USA) - Cheal Rose (Ire)
1^{6g} 4^{6gf} 3^{6g} 2^{7g} **1-1-4 £73,925**

Golden Asha *N A Callaghan* 88
3 ch f Danehill Dancer (Ire) - Snugfit Annie
$2^{5gs}\ 2^{6gs}\ 5^{7f}\ 1^{6f}\ 2^{6g}\ 2^{5gf}\ 1^{5g}\ 1^{5g}\ 2^{5gs}\ 8^{5s}$
3-5-10 £20,629

Golden Boot *A Bailey* 72
6 ch g Unfuwain (USA) - Sports Delight
$4^{14gf}\ 3^{12gf}\ 1^{12gf}\ 3^{12gf}\ 1^{16s}\ 5^{17g}\ 10^{13g}$
2-1-7 £11,273

Golden Bounty *N Wilson* 35 a47
6 b g Bahamian Bounty - Cumbrian Melody
$9^{5sd}\ 10^{5sd}\ 13^{5hy}\ 13^{5gs}$ **0-0-4**

Golden Chalice (Ire) *Miss E C Lavelle* 86
6 ch g Selkirk (USA) - Special Oasis
7^{8gf} **0-0-1**

Golden Chance (Ire) *M W Easterby* 50
8 b g Unfuwain (USA) - Golden Digger (USA)
$6^{13gs}\ 3^{16gf}\ 5^{12gf}\ 5^{14gf}\ 8^{12f}$ **0-0-5 £416**

Golden Chica (Ire) *J R Jenkins*
2 b f Imperial Ballet (Ire) - Sunday Sport Star
$4^{5gf}\ 15^{6gf}$ **0-0-2**

Golden Dixie (USA) *R A Harris* 94 a77
6 ch g Dixieland Band (USA) - Beyrouth (USA)
$1^{6sd}\ 5^{6sd}\ 7^{6sd}\ 2^{5sd}\ 7^{6s}\ 2^{6g}\ 5^{6g}\ 9^{6gs}\ 1^{5gs}\ 1^{5gf}$
$3^{6gf}\ 6^{6gf}\ 5^{6gf}\ 4^{6gf}\ 8^{6gf}\ 2^{5g}\ 2^{5gs}\ 3^{6g}\ 5^{6gf}$
12^{6s} **3-6-20 £24,174**

Golden Dynasty *R Hannon* 65
3 ch c Erhaab (USA) - Ajeebah (Ire)
$4^{10gf}\ 11^{10gf}\ 3^{12gf}\ 11^{10g}\ 1^{10g}\ 7^{11gf}\ 7^{10hd}\ 13^{12g}$
1-1-8 £4,429

Golden Feather *R C Guest* 86
3 ch c Dr Fong (USA) - Idolize
$1^{8gs}\ 8^{8gf}\ 2^{10gf}$ **1-1-3 £7,471**

Golden Fields (Ire) *Jennie Candlish*
5 b m Definite Article - Quickstep Queen (Fr)
PU^{12ss} **0-0-1**

Golden Fitz (Arg) *R M Stronge* a40
6 ch g Fitzcarraldo (Arg) - Good Last (Arg)
$9^{17sd}\ 11^{13sd}$ **0-0-2**

Golden Fury *J L Dunlop* 89
3 ch c Cadeaux Genereux - Galaxie Dust (USA)
$1^{8gs}\ 7^{8g}\ 2^{9g}\ 4^{8gf}\ 1^{9g}\ 9^{9gs}$ **2-1-6**
£12,477

Golden Gate (Ire) *M L W Bell* 65
3 b g Giant's Causeway (USA) - Bay Queen
$7^{8s}\ 3^{10gs}\ 2^{10g}\ 1^{12f}\ 3^{12f}\ 2^{12gf}$ **1-3-6**
£6,515

Golden Grimshaw (Ire) *Andrew Lee* 85
3 b g Grand Lodge (USA) - Daftiyna (Ire)
$4^{8gs}\ 8^{8g}\ 1^{10g}\ 1^{10g}\ 14^{10g}$ **2-0-5 £16,263**

Golden Island (Ire) *J W Hills* 101
4 ch f Selkirk (USA) - Daftiyna (Ire)
$3^{8gf}\ 2^{8gs}\ 17^{8gf}\ 11^{8gf}\ 2^{8s}\ 1^{8g}\ 5^{8s}\ 10^{8s}$
1-3-8 £21,944

Golden Legacy (Ire) *R A Fahey* 98 a88
3 b f Rossini (USA) - Dissidentia (Ire)
$6^{7sd}\ 6^{7gf}\ 11^{8gf}\ 10^{6g}\ 10^{8gf}$ **0-0-5**
£1,875

Golden Measure *G A Swinbank* 58
5 b g Rainbow Quest (USA) - Dawna
$8^{10gs}\ 7^{12gs}\ 11^{8g}\ 2^{14f}\ 4^{13s}\ 3^{16gf}\ 17^{10g}\ 5^{15s}$
0-2-8 £2,443

Golden Odyssey (Ire) *K G Reveley* 42
5 ch m Barathea (Ire) - Opus One
$4^{12gs}\ 9^{14gf}$ **0-0-2 £427**

Golden Queen *M D I Usher* a36
4 b f Unfuwain (USA) - Queen Linear (USA)
6^{13sd} **0-0-1**

Golden Quest *M Johnston* 120 a106
4 ch g Rainbow Quest (USA) - Souk (Ire)
$12^{14gs}\ 1^{16g}\ 2^{20gf}\ 2^{16sd}\ 1^{14gs}\ 2^{16s}$ **2-3-6**
£72,532

Golden Remedy *A R Dicken* 27
4 b f Dr Fong (USA) - Golden Daring (Ire)
$8^{9s}\ 9^{7gf}\ 5^{6gf}\ 15^{5gf}\ 11^{7gf}\ 14^{8gf}\ 11^{8sd}$
0-0-7

Golden Shadow (Ire) *J H M Gosden* 72
2 ch f Selkirk (USA) - Balnaha
$5^{8gf}\ 2^{8gs}\ 3^{8gf}\ 12^{8s}$ **0-2-4 £2,052**

Golden Spectrum (Ire) *R A Harris* 64 a58
6 ch g Spectrum (Ire) - Plessaya (USA)
$5^{6sd}\ 2^{7sd}\ 9^{9sd}\ 4^{6sd}\ 3^{7g}\ 1^{8g}\ 3^{7sd}\ 3^{7s}\ 3^{7g}\ 11^{7g}$
$5^{8s}\ 1^{8g}\ 1^{8f}\ 14^{8gf}\ 11^{8g}\ 6^{9sd}\ 4^{9sf}\ 5^{7sd}\ 2^{7sd}$
$12^{6sf}\ 2^{7sd}\ 9^{8sd}$ **3-7-22 £13,508**

Golden Sprite *B R Millman* 61
2 b f Bertolini (USA) - Shalad'Or
$13^{7f}\ 5^{7gf}\ 3^{7gf}\ 9^{8g}$ **0-1-4 £500**

Golden Square *A W Carroll* 52 a60
3 ch g Tomba - Cherish Me
$3^{9sd}\ 8^{9sd}\ 10^{8sd}\ 14^{11gs}\ 3^{8gs}\ 10^{8g}\ 2^{8f}\ 8^{10gf}$
$12^{8gf}\ 16^{8gf}\ 3^{8gs}\ 2^{9sd}\ 9^{8g}\ 2^{9sd}\ 9^{9sd}\ 11^{7gs}$
$3^{9sd}\ 2^{8sd}$ **0-8-18 £4,951**

Golden Treasure *J J Sheehan* a52
3 b f Octagonal (NZ) - Karaferya (USA)
$5^{10sd}\ 10^{12sd}\ 10^{9sd}\ 16^{10g}$ **0-0-4**

Goldeva *R Hollinshead* 103
6 gr m Makbul - Gold Belt (Ire)
$5^{6s}\ 7^{6gf}\ 11^{6gs}\ 3^{6g}\ 9^{7gf}\ 13^{6g}\ 11^{6gs}$ **0-1-7**
£8,000

Goldhill Prince *Andrew Reid* 69 a69
3 b g Prince Sabo - Lady Mabel
$4^{6sd}\ 2^{6sd}\ 7^{6sd}\ 3^{6sd}\ 1^{5sd}\ 3^{5sd}\ 10^{7sd}\ 8^{5sd}\ 7^{6sd}$
$8^{5f}\ 17^{7gs}\ 3^{6f}\ 6^{5sd}\ 4^{6f}\ 6^{6g}\ 8^{5gs}\ 6^{6f}\ 8^{5s}\ 13^{5gf}$
7^{6gf} **1-2-20 £5,603**

Goldstar Dancer (Ire) *J J Quinn* 48 a49
3 b c General Monash (USA) - Ravensdale Rose (Ire)
$3^{10ys}\ 5^{10ys}\ 5^{10sh}\ 7^{9gf}\ 4^{12sd}\ 2^{12sd}$ **0-2-6**
£918

Golo Gal *Mrs L J Mongan* 59 a66
3 b g Mark Of Esteem (Ire) - Western Sal
$9^{8gf}\ 7^{8gf}\ 3^{12sd}\ 7^{10sd}$ **0-1-4 £516**

Gone Fishing (Ire) *M A Jarvis* 72
3 ch f Cadeaux Genereux - Dabbing (USA)
$4^{6g}\ 6^{7g}\ 1^{8g}\ 17^{8gs}$ **1-0-4 £3,924**

Gone Too Far *P Monteith* 65
7 b g Reprimand - Blue Nile (Ire)
$1^{16f}\ 1^{16gf}\ 6^{14gf}\ 3^{16g}$ **2-0-4 £7,557**

Gone'N'Dunnett (Ire) *Mrs C A Dunnett* 79 a76
6 b g Petardia - Skerries Bell
$1^{6sd}\ 11^{6sd}\ 3^{6sd}\ 10^{5sd}\ 10^{6sd}\ 7^{6sd}\ 2^{5sd}\ 7^{6sd}$
$1^{5gs}\ 1^{6sd}\ 3^{6sd}\ 9^{5gf}\ 9^{5g}\ 1^{6gs}\ 14^{5gf}\ 10^{5f}\ 8^{6f}$
$6^{6g}\ 12^{6g}\ 6^{6g}\ 9^{5gs}\ 11^{6sd}\ 8^{6g}\ 9^{5sf}\ 2^{6sd}\ 2^{6sd}$
5^{5sd} **4-5-27 £22,102**

Gonfilia (Ger) *Saeed Bin Suroor* a94
5 b m Big Shuffle (USA) - Gonfalon
7^{8sd} **0-0-1**

Good Article (Ire) *A P Jones* a44
4 b g Definite Article - Good News (Ire)
$12^{11sd}\ 5^{10sd}\ 9^{8sd}$ **0-0-3**

Good Companion (Ire) *J L Dunlop* 57
2 ch c Elnadim (USA) - Broadway Rosie
$8^{6g}\ 9^{6g}\ 4^{6s}$ **0-0-3**

Good Investment *P C Haslam* 60
3 b g Silver Patriarch (Ire) - Bundled Up (USA)
13^12g 10^10f 1^10gf 15^10gf 11^10g **1-0-5 £5,025**

Good Time Bobby *Miss Kate Milligan* 9
8 b g Primitive Rising (USA) - Goodreda
13^8sd 7^7gf **0-0-2**

Good Wee Girl (Ire) *S Woodman* 50 a42
3 b f Tagula (Ire) - Auriga
6^8sd 7^7gf 7^6g 8^6gf 8^7g 9^7f 6^8f 7^10f 8^8s 7^7f 6^7g 7^7sd 13^7sd **0-0-13**

Goodbye Girl (Ire) *Mrs C A Dunnett* 54 a20
2 b f Shinko Forest (Ire) - Adieu Cherie (Ire)
10^5g 5^6f 8^6s 1^7gf 4^7f 2^6f 11^7g 12^7sd 10^6sd 11^8hy **1-1-10 £3,625**

Goodbye Mr Bond *E J Alston* 88
5 b g Elmaamul (USA) - Fifth Emerald
5^8g 4^8gf 3^8s 6^8g 2^8gf 3^8gf 2^8gf 2^10gs 8^10g 6^10g 10^10gf 3^8gf 6^8gs 2^9gs 3^8s **0-8-15 £26,670**

Goodenough Blue *J S King* 19
3 b f Bluegrass Prince (Ire) - Goodenough Girl
9^10s 9^10gf 7^12sd **0-0-3**

Goodenough Mover *Andrew Turnell* 92 a94
9 ch g Beveled (USA) - Rekindled Flame (Ire)
6^6g 11^6g 1^6f 10^6g 14^7gf 10^6g 8^6gf 2^6g 15^6gs 3^6sd 1^7sd **2-2-11 £17,065**

Goodricke *D R Loder* 122
3 b c Bahamian Bounty - Star
1^6gs 7^7s 2^7g 1^6g 2^7gf 2^7g 1^6g **3-3-7 £226,955**

Goodtime Girl (Ire) *T D Easterby* 48
2 ch f Shinko Forest (Ire) - Titchwell Lass
8^5f 4^5gs 8^5gf 11^5gf 13^6gf 10^6gf **0-0-6 £262**

Goodwood March *J L Dunlop* 42
2 b f Foxhound (USA) - Military Tune (Ire)
10^6gf **0-0-1**

Goodwood Spirit *J L Dunlop* 88
3 b c Fraam - Rechanit (Ire)
11^7gf 3^8gs 6^8gf 1^8gf 4^8f 5^8gs 4^7g 3^7g 3^8g 3^8g **1-4-10 £12,827**

Goose Chase *C J Mann* 71 a70
3 b g Inchinor - Bronzewing
1^8gs 2^8sd 6^8gf 3^8g 12^8gf **1-2-5 £4,038**

Gordonsville *A M Balding* 73
2 b c Generous (Ire) - Kimba (USA)
4^8g **0-0-1 £335**

Gordy's Joy *G A Ham* 7
5 b m Cloudings (Ire) - Beatle Song
9^18gf **0-0-1**

Gorgeous Boy (Ire) *P L Gilligan* 13 a34
3 ch g Forzando - Instil
11^6g 11^7sd 6^6ss **0-0-3**

Gortumblo *K Bishop* 72 a52
3 b g Sri Pekan (USA) - Evergreen (Ire)
5^6g 14^6g 6^6gf 8^8sd 8^10sd **0-0-5 £276**

Gossip Queen (Ire) *Paul Magnier* 44 a38
3 b f Daggers Drawn (USA) - Kifenia (Ire)
7^6sd 8^7gf 11^10gf LFT^8hy **0-0-4**

Got To Be Cash *W M Brisbourne* 47 a40
6 ch m Lake Coniston (Ire) - Rasayel (USA)
10^10hy 15^10gf 5^11g 7^10g 2^10gf 9^10g 10^10gf 4^10g 7^10g 6^9sd **0-1-10 £768**

Gouranga *H Candy* 70
2 b f Robellino (USA) - Hymne D'Amour (USA)
3^8g **0-1-1 £667**

Government (Ire) *M C Chapman* a45
4 b g Great Dane (Ire) - Hidden Agenda (Fr)
3^6sd 10^7sd 11^7sd **0-1-3 £524**

Gower Song *D R C Elsworth* 63 a69
2 b f Singspiel (Ire) - Gleaming Water
7^6gs 3^8sd **0-1-2 £434**

Gozetan Lace *D W Barker*
3 ch f Barathea (Ire) - Little Change
14^12s 11^8sd **0-0-2**

Gracechurch (Ire) *M R Channon* 79
2 b g Marju (Ire) - Saffron Crocus
2^7gf 4^7gs 6^7g 3^7gf 2^8gf 1^8hd 10^8g 8^8s **1-3-8 £9,939**

Graceful Air (Ire) *J R Weymes* 65
4 b f Danzero (Aus) - Samsung Spirit
3^9g 11^8gf 1^10gf 6^10gf 4^8gf 1^9gf **2-0-6 £12,440**

Graceful Flight *P T Midgley* 44
3 gr f Cloudings (Ire) - Fantasy Flight
7^6s 10^6f 17^5gf 11^6gf 4^6gf 11^8gf 15^6gf **0-0-7 £270**

Gracie's Gift (Ire) *A G Newcombe* 64 a46
3 b g Imperial Ballet (Ire) - Settle Petal (Ire)
1^6sd 2^5gf 9^7gf 5^6g 6^6f **1-1-5 £2,199**

Graduate Boy *M Todhunter* 12
2 b g College Chapel - Lamsonetti
11^5g **0-0-1**

Graft *Mrs P Townsley* a66
6 b g Entrepreneur - Mariakova (USA)
9^10sd **0-0-1**

Grafton (Ire) *J D Bethell* 62
2 b g Desert Style (Ire) - Gracious Gretclo
9^5g 16^6gf 6^6gs 2^6f 14^6g 17^6g **0-1-6 £1,138**

Graham Island *G Wragg* 86
4 b g Acatenango (Ger) - Gryada
12^14gs 1^14gf 5^16gf **1-0-3 £6,952**

Grain Of Truth *Sir Michael Stoute* 70
2 b f Gulch (USA) - Pure Grain
6^7g **0-0-1**

Gralmano (Ire) *K A Ryan* a6
10 b g Scenic - Llangollen (Ire)
12^12sd **0-0-1**

Gramada (Ire) *P A Blockley* 59 a64
3 b f Cape Cross (Ire) - Decatur
4^6sd 9^7gs 5^8g 10^10gf 5^12sd 4^12hd 1^12gf 8^12gf 3^9sd **1-1-9 £3,902**

Gramm *Unknown* 94
2 b c Fraam - Beacon Silver
1^7g 3^7s 18^6gf 2^8g 2^10g 1^8s **2-2-6 £19,139**

Grammaticus *K A Ryan* 20
2 b c Zaha (Can) - Autumn Stone (Ire)
7^6s 11^8sd **0-0-2**

Grampian *J G Given* 109
6 b h Selkirk (USA) - Gryada
4^12g 6^16s 10^12s 1^12g 6^12f 4^12gf 2^14g 3^14g 5^14g **1-2-9 £43,275**

Gran Clicquot *G P Enright* 46 a47
10 gr m Gran Alba (USA) - Tina's Beauty
5^10sd 10^8f 3^8gf 8^9gf 8^8gf 8^10sd **0-1-6 £595**

Gran Dana (Ire) *G Prodromou* 45 a49

5 b g Grand Lodge (USA) - Olean
12^{13sd} 6^{14sd} 8^{10sd} 10^{13sd} 5^{12sd} 10^{12sd} 1^{11gs}
4^{12gf} 10^{12gf} 3^{11g} 5^{16gs} 6^{10g} 6^{12sd} **1-1-13**
£1,758

Granary Girl *J Pearce* 57 a57
3 b f Kingsinger (Ire) - Highland Blue
6^{8sd} 5^{8sd} 9^{9sd} 6^{9sd} 2^{9sd} 9^{9sd} 5^{9sd} 6^{9sd} 1^{9sd}
13^{9sd} 1^{10g} 4^{8gf} 7^{10f} 3^{10gf} 8^{10gf} 4^{10sd} 4^{10g}
1^{10g} 1^{10sd} **4-2-19 £11,092**

Grand Central (Ire) *F Poulsen* 111
3 b c Sadler's Wells (USA) - Rebecca Sharp
2^{8ys} 3^{10sh} 9^{12g} 7^{8gf} 1^{10gf} 4^{10y} **1-0-6**
£43,474

Grand Cherokee (Ire) *B Ellison* 68 a20
2 gr c Fayruz - Divine Apsara
10^{6sd} 7^{6gs} 4^{7gf} 4^{6g} 7^{8gf} **0-0-5 £939**

Grand Course (Ire) *Rae Guest* 71
3 ch f Grand Lodge (USA) - Star Of The Course (USA)
7^{8g} 7^{8gs} 2^{7g} 1^{10gf} 7^{12g} 7^{10gs} 13^{8gf} **1-1-7**
£4,686

Grand Court (Ire) *R J Price*
2 b f Grand Lodge (USA) - Nice One Clare (Ire)
19^{7g} **0-0-1**

Grand Design *C A Cyzer* 56 a53
3 b f Danzero (Aus) - Duende
9^{8sd} 12^{9gs} 4^{7g} 11^{7sd} **0-0-4 £259**

Grand Emporium (SAF) *Saeed Bin Suroor* 115 a118
5 b g National Assembly (Can) - Whistling Dixie (SAF)
1^{8ft} 4^{9ft} 2^{8ft} 1^{8ft} 7^{8f} 3^{9g} 13^{8gf} **2-1-7**
£409,291

Grand Entrance (Ire) *C R Egerton* 72 a73
2 b c Grand Lodge (USA) - Alessia (Ger)
4^{6gf} 4^{6gs} 2^{7sd} 9^{7gs} **0-1-4 £1,837**

Grand Girl *C N Kellett* 11 a4
3 b f Mark Of Esteem (Ire) - Ayunli
12^{9sd} 12^{10hy} 10^{11sd} 11^{10g} 19^{6f} **0-0-5**

Grand Ideas *Julian Poulton* 46 a63
6 br g Grand Lodge (USA) - Afrafa (Ire)
2^{8sd} 3^{8sd} 5^{10sd} 3^{8sd} 11^{8s} 9^{7sd} 9^{8gf} 11^{7gf}
0-3-8 £2,085

Grand Jour (Ire) *K McAuliffe* 69 a73
2 b c Grand Lodge (USA) - Reveuse De Jour (Ire)
13^{6g} 4^{7sd} 4^{6hy} 8^{8sd} 7^{10sd} 1^{7sd} **1-0-6**
£5,174

Grand Ocean (Ire) *C A Dwyer* 54 a60
3 b g Grand Lodge (USA) - In Full Cry (USA)
2^{8sd} 2^{10gs} **0-1-2 £1,752**

Grand Opera (Ire) *J Howard Johnson* 74
2 b c City On A Hill (USA) - Victoria's Secret (Ire)
2^{6gs} 3^{7gs} 3^{8gf} 4^{7gf} 5^{8gf} **0-2-5 £3,375**

Grand Option *B W Duke* 55 a46
3 ch g Compton Place - Follow The Stars
8^{6gs} 11^{7gs} 7^{6gf} 13^{6gf} 7^{6gf} 6^{6gf} 8^{6sd}
0-0-7

Grand Parrot *W De Best-Turner* 4
2 b c Prince Sabo - Silkstone Lady
9^{6hy} 15^{6s} **0-0-2**

Grand Passion (Ire) *G Wragg* 111 a105
5 b g Grand Lodge (USA) - Lovers' Parlour
9^{10sd} 7^{10gs} 4^{10gf} 4^{10g} 4^{10gf} 4^{10g} **0-0-6**
£5,984

Grand Rebecca (Ire) *G A Huffer* 27
2 ch f Namid - Krayyalei (Ire)
16^{6gf} **0-0-1**

Grand Sefton *J G Portman* 42 a64
2 br g Pivotal - Nahlin
11^{7gf} 9^{8g} 3^{7sd} **0-1-3 £467**

Grand Seigneur (Ire) *D R Loder* a83
3 b c Grand Lodge (USA) - Commanche Belle
5^{8sd} 1^{10sd} **1-0-2 £4,225**

Grand Show *W R Swinburn* 70 a88
3 b g Efisio - Christine Daae
9^{6gf} 2^{6sd} 7^{5s} **0-1-3 £1,912**

Grand View *J R Weymes* 49 a58
9 ch g Grand Lodge (USA) - Hemline
3^{6sd} 2^{6gs} 1^{6sd} 4^{6g} 4^{6sd} 8^{6g} 6^{6f} 16^{6g}
1-2-8 £2,732

Grandad Bill (Ire) *T D Easterby* 67
2 ch c Intikhab (USA) - Matikanehanafubuki (Ire)
4^{5g} 5^{6gf} 1^{7g} 9^{7gs} **1-0-4 £4,170**

Grande Roche (Ire) *G A Swinbank* 73 a47
3 b g Grand Lodge (USA) - Arabian Lass (SAF)
6^{7gs} 7^{8gs} 8^{8g} 2^{10gf} 5^{10gs} 2^{10gf} 2^{9sd} **0-3-7**
£3,108

Grande Terre (Ire) *R A Fahey* 63 a51
4 b f Grand Lodge (USA) - Savage (Ire)
4^{8sd} 10^{9sd} 1^{7g} 1^{8g} 7^{8gf} 7^{8g} 8^{8g} 7^{8gf}
2-0-8 £7,586

Grandma Lily (Ire) *D Carroll* 61 a79
7 b m Bigstone (Ire) - Mrs Fisher (Ire)
6^{6sd} 6^{8sd} 1^{6sd} 8^{6sd} 10^{6gf} 3^{6s} 7^{6g} 6^{5gf} 7^{5gf}
6^{5gf} **1-1-10 £3,940**

Grandma Ryta *John Berry* 35
3 br f Cyrano De Bergerac - Tamara
7^{5s} 4^{8gf} 4^{7gf} **0-0-3**

Grandma's Girl *Robert Gray* 64 a60
3 b f Desert Style (Ire) - Sakura Queen (Ire)
4^{8gf} 6^{10gf} 6^{9gf} 4^{8gs} 4^{9sd} 2^{10g} 4^{10s} 6^{12g} 8^{11sd}
0-1-9 £1,923

Grandos (Ire) *T D Easterby* 56
3 b g Cadeaux Genereux - No Reservations (Ire)
11^{8gf} 7^{6g} **0-0-2**

Granita *M Blanshard* 37 a47
3 b/br f Machiavellian (USA) - Actualite
9^{7sd} 14^{8gs} 19^{7gf} 16^{12sd} 12^{6sd} **0-0-5**

Granston (Ire) *J D Bethell* 93
4 gr g Revoque (Ire) - Gracious Gretclo
5^{8g} 2^{8g} 2^{8f} 3^{8gf} 6^{8gf} 6^{8g} 6^{8s} 1^{8g} 1^{8gf} 3^{8gf}
9^{8s} **2-4-11 £32,198**

Grantley Adams *M R Channon* 96
2 b g Dansili - Noble Peregrine
4^{5gs} 7^{6gf} 4^{6gf} 2^{7f} 3^{6gf} 1^{6gf} 2^{6gs} 2^{6gf} 3^{6hy}
1^{6gf} 2^{6g} **2-3-11 £27,417**

Grasp *G L Moore* 64
3 b g Kayf Tara - Circe
14^{14gs} 7^{14g} 4^{16g} 4^{16g} 1^{17gs} **1-0-5**
£4,493

Grasslandik *Miss A Stokell* 12 a31
9 b g Ardkinglass - Sophisticated Baby
7^{5sd} 13^{5sd} 6^{5sd} 14^{5gf} 14^{5gf} 12^{5sd} **0-0-6**

Grateful *D R C Elsworth* 32
2 ch f Generous (Ire) - Duende
19^{7s} **0-0-1**

Gravardlax *Miss D A McHale* 53 a60
4 ch g Salse (USA) - Rubbiyati
8^{10sd} 7^{14sd} 4^{10sd} 8^{12sd} 3^{12sd} 9^{16sd} 11^{12gf} 8^{12gs}
4^{10gf} 10^{10gf} 10^{14f} 10^{10gf} 6^{12ss} **0-2-13**
£1,067

Gravinsky (USA) *Mrs A J Perrett* 71
2 b/br c Theatrical - Prospectress (USA)
5^{7gf} **0-0-1**

Graze On *J J Quinn* 80
3 b g Factual (USA) - Queens Check
11^{6g} 6^{6g} 3^{6gf} 6^{6gf} 7^{6gf} 4^{7gs} 7^{6gf} 1^{6gf} **1-1-8 £4,160**

Graze On Too (Ire) *J J Quinn* 29
2 b f Rainbow Quest (USA) - Whispering (Ire)
3^{7s} **0-1-1 £477**

Grazeon Gold Blend *J J Quinn* 89
2 ch g Paris House - Thalya
4^{5gf} 1^{5g} 1^{5gs} 5^{5hy} 16^{6g} 17^{6s} **2-0-6 £20,087**

Great As Gold (Ire) *B Ellison* a38
6 b g Goldmark (USA) - Great Land (USA)
8^{14ss} **0-0-1**

Great Aunt *A M Balding* 32 a54
3 br f Dansili - Shebasis (USA)
8^{8sd} 7^{8sd} 9^{10gf} 15^{12sd} 14^{10sd} **0-0-5**

Great Belief (Ire) *T D McCarthy* 53
3 b g Namid - Fairy Lore (Ire)
6^{5s} 9^{6g} 7^{5s} 9^{6gf} 11^{5gf} 13^{5s} **0-0-6**

Great Britain *Saeed Bin Suroor* 104
3 b c Green Desert (USA) - Park Appeal
1^{7gf} 4^{7gf} **1-0-2 £4,952**

Great Chieftain (Ire) *R A Fahey* 69
2 b g Lend A Hand - Well Wisher (USA)
7^{5gf} 4^{5s} 3^{5gf} **0-1-3 £660**

Great Composer (Ire) *Mrs A J Perrett* a51
2 b c Mozart (Ire) - Talena
9^{7sd} 7^{7sd} 9^{7sd} **0-0-3**

Great Fox (Ire) *P L Gilligan* 82
4 b c Foxhound (USA) - Good Enough (Ire)
1^{5g} 9^{6gf} 20^{5hy} **1-0-3 £5,992**

Great General (Ire) *T T Clement* 50 a27
3 ch g General Monash (USA) - Racing Brenda
12^{7sd} 7^{10sd} 8^{10gs} 11^{10gf} 8^{10s} 13^{10g} **0-0-6**

Great Orator (USA) *H Candy* 76
3 b g Bahri (USA) - Verbal Intrigue (USA)
2^{10g} 3^{10gs} **0-2-2 £2,002**

Great Plains *Mrs A J Perrett* 95
3 b c Halling (USA) - West Dakota (USA)
1^{7g} 3^{8g} 7^{10gf} 2^{10s} **1-2-4 £7,726**

Great Tidings *M Johnston* 45
2 b g Fantastic Light (USA) - On The Tide
7^{8gf} 14^{7gf} **0-0-2**

Great View (Ire) *Mrs A L M King* 67 a56
6 b g Great Commotion (USA) - Tara View (Ire)
7^{13sd} 5^{14sd} 10^{10sd} 5^{12hy} 2^{12gf} 8^{12gf} 7^{11g} 3^{12gf} 5^{12g} 2^{12g} 3^{12g} 3^{13gf} 1^{12gf} 9^{12gs} 3^{12g} **1-6-15 £8,912**

Greatcoat *J G Given*
3 ch g Erhaab (USA) - Vaula
13^{9gf} **0-0-1**

Greatest By Phar *J Akehurst* a30
4 b g Pharly (Fr) - Greatest Friend (Ire)
7^{12sd} **0-0-1**

Grecian Gold (Ire) *C G Cox* 78
3 b g Lujain (USA) - Falconera (Ire)
2^{7gf} **0-1-1 £1,426**

Grecianette (Ire) *J A R Toller* 60 a65
2 b f Night Shift (USA) - Alexandria (Ire)
3^{6sd} 4^{6gs} 3^{6sd} 8^{5hy} **0-2-4 £1,717**

Greek Renaissance (Ire) *M P Tregoning* 74
2 b c Machiavellian (USA) - Athene (Ire)
7^{8gf} **0-0-1**

Greek Secret *T D Easterby* 71
2 b g Josr Algarhoud (Ire) - Mazurkanova
7^{5gs} 2^{5f} 3^{6g} 3^{5gf} 3^{5gs} 8^{6g} 1^{6gf} 10^{7g} 9^{6s} **1-4-9 £8,182**

Green 'N' Gold *M D Hammond* 51
5 b m Cloudings (Ire) - Fishki
8^{18gs} 5^{14gf} 6^{16gf} **0-0-3**

Green Calibre *Sir Michael Stoute* 76
2 b c Green Desert (USA) - Air Of Distinction (Ire)
7^{7g} 4^{8g} 2^{8gf} 5^{8gf} **0-1-4 £1,700**

Green Falcon *Mrs S Lamyman* 54 a35
4 b g Green Desert (USA) - El Jazirah
11^{9sd} 5^{12g} 8^{10s} 6^{8g} 5^{8g} 5^{10gf} 2^{12gf} 11^{11g} **0-1-8 £1,060**

Green Ginger *C N Kellett*
9 ch g Ardkinglass - Bella Maggio
11^{14sd} **0-0-1**

Green Lemon (USA) *G A Butler* 56 a75
2 b c Lemon Drop Kid (USA) - Heavenly Calm (USA)
10^{7gf} 3^{8sd} 2^{9sd} **0-2-3 £1,830**

Green Manalishi *D W P Arbuthnot* 104 a102
4 b g Green Desert (USA) - Silca-Cisa
9^{5gf} 11^{5g} 5^{5s} 1^{5g} 1^{5gs} 4^{5s} 2^{5g} 8^{6gf} 1^{5gs} 8^{5s} 4^{6sd} 4^{6sd} **3-1-12 £42,572**

Green Noon (Fr) *R Charlton* 98
4 b f Green Tune (USA) - Terring (Fr)
3^{10g} 6^{12gs} 13^{8g} **0-0-3 £3,500**

Green Park (Ire) *R Hannon* 89
2 b g Shinko Forest (Ire) - Danccini (Ire)
2^{5g} 1^{5g} 1^{5gf} 8^{5gf} 10^{6gs} 4^{6gf} 8^{5g} **2-1-7 £17,893**

Green Pirate *R Craggs* 53 a70
3 b g Bahamian Bounty - Verdura
1^{7sd} 9^{7sd} 11^{7gf} 10^{7sd} 7^{6sd} 6^{7sd} **1-0-6 £3,454**

Green Pride *R Hannon* 89
2 b c Piccolo - Little Greenbird
6^{5g} 1^{5s} 1^{5gf} 5^{5gf} 3^{6g} 6^{6gf} 5^{6gs} **2-1-7 £12,977**

Green Room (Fr) *J L Dunlop* 57
2 b f In The Wings - Scarlet Plume
8^{7s} **0-0-1**

Greenbelt *G M Moore* a64
4 b g Desert Prince (Ire) - Emerald (USA)
8^{8sd} 2^{9sd} 9^{8sd} 2^{8sd} 1^{8sd} **1-2-5 £4,008**

Greenmeadow *S Kirk* 58 a67
3 b f Sure Blade (USA) - Pea Green
10^{8sd} 4^{8gs} 6^{6g} 1^{9sd} 11^{9ft} **1-0-5 £3,420**

Greenslades *P J Makin* 103 a97
6 ch h Perugino (USA) - Woodfield Rose
8^{7g} 2^{6g} 4^{6g} 1^{6g} 17^{6g} 2^{6g} 4^{6gs} 7^{7sd} **1-3-8 £21,234**

Greenwich Meantime *Mrs J R Ramsden* 77 a77
5 b g Royal Academy (USA) - Shirley Valentine
2^{12sd} 1^{12g} 2^{14g} 2^{12gf} 4^{17gf} 4^{16gf} 2^{14gf} 5^{14gf} 1^{14gf} 1^{16gf} **3-4-10 £18,553**

Greenwich Village *W J Knight* 63
2 b c Mtoto - D'Azy
7^{8gs} **0-0-1**

Greenwood *P G Murphy* 80 a75
7 ch g Emarati (USA) - Charnwood Queen
4^{7sd} 8^{6sd} 3^{7sd} 2^{6sd} 4^{6sd} 5^{7s} 4^{6gs} 12^{6g} 2^{7gf} 7^{7gs} 4^{7gf} 6^{7gf} 12^{8gs} 6^{7g} 6^{6sd} 6^{7g} 5^{7g} 1^{6g} 3^{6g} 10^{7sd} **1-4-20 £11,064**

Gregs Girl *M Madgwick* 5
3 b f Bluegrass Prince (Ire) - Ninotchka

14^{7gf} 14^{8f} 8^{10g} **0-0-3**

Grenadier (Ire) *Miss L C Siddall*
8 b g Sadler's Wells (USA) - Sandhurst Goddess
18^{8s} **0-0-1**

Grenane (Ire) *P D Evans* 62 a69
2 b c Princely Heir (Ire) - Another Rainbow (Ire)
6^{5gs} 6^{5sd} 1^{6f} 2^{6gf} 5^{5gf} 2^{6g} 2^{6gf} 3^{7gf} 9^{7gs} 2^{6sd} 6^{7sf} 1^{6sd} 4^{7sd} **2-4-13 £13,114**

Grey Admiral (USA) *B R Johnson* a39
4 gr g Cozzene (USA) - Remarkable Style (USA)
15^{12sd} **0-0-1**

Grey Boy (Ger) *R A Fahey* 79
4 gr g Medaaly - Grey Perri
5^{8g} 14^{10g} 1^{8gf} 1^{8g} 20^{8gs} 7^{8g} 3^{8f} 9^{7g} 14^{7s} **2-1-9 £8,488**

Grey Clouds *T D Easterby* 76
5 gr m Cloudings (Ire) - Khalsheva
8^{10g} 14^{8gf} 9^{10gf} 4^{10gf} 4^{11gf} 7^{10gf} **0-0-6 £821**

Grey Cossack *J Balding* 67
8 gr g Kasakov - Royal Rebeka
7^{6g} 12^{6g} 3^{6g} 6^{6gf} 7^{6gf} 14^{7g} 10^{6gs} **0-1-7 £873**

Grey Outlook *Miss L A Perratt* 67
2 ch f Observatory (USA) - Grey Galava
11^{7gf} 4^{8s} 2^{8s} **0-1-3 £2,087**

Grey Paint (USA) *J H M Gosden* 56 a73
2 gr/ro g El Prado (Ire) - Devil's Art (USA)
20^{8gs} 9^{8gs} 1^{9sd} **1-0-3 £3,386**

Grey Plover (Ire) *J L Dunlop* 97
3 b f Alzao (USA) - Firecrest (Ire)
5^{9gs} 4^{10gf} 7^{10gf} 2^{12f} 1^{12s} 2^{14s} 6^{16hy} **1-2-7 £6,406**

Grey Swallow (Ire) *D K Weld* 126
4 gr c Daylami (Ire) - Style Of Life (USA)
1^{11gy} 7^{12gf} 6^{10gy} 4^{12y} **1-0-4 £168,486**

Grey Time Girl *A Berry*
2 gr f Timeless Times (USA) - Royal Comedian
10^{5gf} 13^{7g} **0-0-2**

Greytown *M A Jarvis* 67
2 gr f Daylami (Ire) - Hawayah (Ire)
11^{7gs} 6^{7gf} **0-0-2**

Grezie *T D McCarthy* 58 a59
3 gr f Mark Of Esteem (Ire) - Lozzie
3^{8sd} 3^{8sd} 5^{8sd} 5^{8sd} 3^{7sd} 11^{7s} 12^{7gs} 4^{7gf} 16^{7gf} 7^{7g} 1^{7f} 5^{7gf} 11^{7gf} 9^{7sd} 10^{7sd} **1-4-15 £4,732**

Grigorovitch (Ire) *I Semple* 91
3 b c Fasliyev (USA) - Hasty Words (Ire)
5^{6gs} 4^{5s} 3^{5gf} 9^{6s} 5^{6g} 8^{5gf} 1^{5gf} 6^{5gs} 1^{5g} 3^{5g} 4^{5g} **2-4-11 £22,624**

Grimes Faith *R Hannon* 76 a80
2 b c Woodborough (USA) - Emma Grimes (Ire)
4^{5s} 1^{5sd} 4^{5sd} 1^{5f} 2^{5sd} 9^{6sd} **2-1-6 £9,097**

Gringo *B W Hills* 81
3 gr g Alzao (USA) - Glen Falls
9^{7gf} 3^{8gs} 1^{8gf} 1^{10g} 2^{10g} 9^{10gs} 6^{10hy} **2-2-7 £10,351**

Grizedale (Ire) *J Akehurst* 84
6 ch g Lake Coniston (Ire) - Zabeta
16^{7gs} 4^{7gf} 12^{7gs} 10^{7gf} 1^{8gs} 10^{7gf} 15^{7g} 2^{7g} PU^{7s} **1-1-9 £5,184**

Grooms Affection *K A Morgan*
5 b g Groom Dancer (USA) - Love And Affection (USA)
19^{12hy} **0-0-1**

Groomsman *Ms V S Lucas* 69
3 b g Groom Dancer (USA) - Trois Heures Apres
7^{10g} 8^{10gs} 17^{12gf} 1^{8gf} 8^{8gf} 2^{8f} 11^{8gf} 7^{12gf} 3^{10gf} **1-1-9 £5,305**

Grosvenor Square (Ire) *Saeed Bin Suroor* 90
3 b c Dubai Millennium - Embassy
12^{9gf} 7^{10s} 10^{8s} **0-0-3**

Ground Rules (USA) *V Smith* 70
3 b c Boundary (USA) - Gombeen (USA)
1^{8gf} **1-0-1 £2,733**

Group Captain *S Kirk* 97 a77
3 b g Dr Fong (USA) - Alusha
1^{10sd} 13^{10gf} 10^{10s} 9^{8gf} 1^{10gf} 4^{12gf} 1^{11gs} 9^{12g} 8^{10g} 9^{15gs} 8^{11gf} 1^{12hy} 5^{12hy} **4-0-13 £43,987**

Group One's Hope *A W Carroll*
9 b m Absalom - Hopeful Waters
11^{12sd} **0-0-1**

Grove Cherry (Ire) *M H Tompkins* 49
2 b f City On A Hill (USA) - Kaliningrad (Ire)
7^{7gs} 13^{6gf} **0-0-2**

Growler *D Nicholls* 69
4 ch g Foxhound (USA) - Femme Femme (USA)
14^{7g} 10^{7gf} 9^{7gs} 16^{6g} 1^{8f} 8^{7f} 9^{6s} 11^{8g} 1^{6f} **2-0-9 £6,486**

Grub Street *J Parkes*
9 b g Barathea (Ire) - Broadmara (Ire)
8^{7sd} **0-0-1**

Grumpyintmorning *M J Gingell* 52 a59
6 b g Magic Ring (Ire) - Grecian Belle
1^{7sd} 2^{7sd} 8^{8sd} 11^{7sd} 11^{7gf} 14^{8sf} 11^{8sd} **1-1-7 £2,516**

Grunzig *Mrs C A Dunnett*
3 ch g Danzig Connection (USA) - Great Exception
8^{12sd} **0-0-1**

Guadaloup *M Brittain* 65 a55
3 ch f Loup Sauvage (USA) - Rash
2^{5g} 2^{7g} 10^{7gf} 2^{7g} 5^{6g} 8^{6gf} 4^{7sd} 7^{8sd} **0-3-8 £4,682**

Guadiana (Ger) *A W Carroll* 51 a54
3 b f Dashing Blade - Gamberaia (Ire)
6^{7gf} 11^{8g} 5^{8gf} 10^{11gf} 3^{9sf} 9^{10sd} 7^{9sd} 11^{11sd} **0-1-8 £213**

Guadiaro (USA) *B W Hills* 70
3 b c El Prado (Ire) - Splendid (Ire)
2^{6gf} 9^{7gs} 8^{7gf} 8^{7g} 3^{7gf} 9^{7gf} 3^{7g} **0-3-7 £2,502**

Guanyin *J G Given* 44 a39
2 b f Zaha (Can) - Misty Moon
9^{7s} 8^{8s} 10^{9sd} 6^{10sd} **0-0-4**

Gue De Bost *M R Hoad*
3 b c Pyramus (USA) - Nordesta (Ire)
7^{6gf} **0-0-1**

Guest Connections *M R Channon* 99
2 b g Zafonic (USA) - Llyn Gwynant
5^{5gf} 1^{6g} 1^{6gf} 9^{7gs} 5^{6g} 12^{7gs} **2-0-6 £39,414**

Guideline *M W Easterby* 64
2 b g Diktat - Polisonne
5^{6g} 7^{6g} 6^{5gf} 15^{5hy} **0-0-4**

Guild's Delight (Ire) *W S Kittow*
6 b g College Chapel - Tamburello (Ire)
11^{10f} **0-0-1**

Guilded Warrior *W S Kittow* a70

2 b g Mujahid (USA) - Pearly River
6^{6sd} 1^{6sd} **1-0-2 £4,299**

Guildenstern (Ire) *H Morrison* 91 a81
3 b c Danetime (Ire) - Lyphard Abu (Ire)
1^{6s} 1^{6sd} 1^{6g} 3^{6gs} 2^{7g} 16^{6g} 9^{7g} 15^{6g} 17^{7gf} 12^{7gf} **3-2-10 £26,520**

Guilia *Rae Guest* 73
2 ch f Galileo (Ire) - Lesgor (USA)
1^{7g} **1-0-1 £4,221**

Guinea A Minute (Ire) *P D Evans* 51 a53
3 ch f Raise A Grand (Ire) - Repique (USA)
12^{7sd} 7^{7s} 9^{6g} 9^{7sd} 3^{7g} 4^{7g} 12^{9gf} 6^{8gf} 7^{7gs} **0-2-9 £383**

Gulchina (USA) *D R C Elsworth* a59
3 b f Gulch (USA) - Harda Arda (USA)
3^{7sd} 5^{8sd} 14^{8gf} **0-1-3 £652**

Gulf (Ire) *D R C Elsworth* 109
6 ch g Persian Bold - Broken Romance (Ire)
2^{13f} 3^{12g} **0-1-2 £9,240**

Gulf Of Mexico (USA) *Saeed Bin Suroor* 77
4 b c Smart Strike (Can) - Apalachee Princess (USA)
4^{5gf} **0-0-1 £1,040**

Guns Blazing *D K Ivory* 66 a36
6 b g Puissance - Queen Of Aragon
12^{5g} 9^{5gf} 13^{5gs} 11^{6g} 6^{5gs} 3^{5gs} 9^{5f} 10^{6sd} 8^{5gf} **0-0-9 £638**

Gurrun *N A Callaghan* 78 a66
3 b c Dansili - Mashmoon (USA)
3^{7sd} 1^{8sd} 4^{8sd} 5^{10sd} 2^{12sd} 13^{11gs} 4^{10gf} 1^{10f} 3^{10f} 1^{11g} 9^{12g} 1^{12f} 1^{12gf} 6^{12gf} **5-3-14 £19,716**

Gus *B W Hills* 55 a51
2 b c Dr Fong (USA) - Tender Moment (Ire)
7^{7gf} 7^{7sd} **0-0-2**

Gustavo *Miss Venetia Williams* 65
4 b g Efisio - Washita
15^{11gs} 1^{10gs} 4^{10hy} **1-1-3 £3,581**

Guto *K A Ryan* 87 a63
2 b g Foxhound (USA) - Mujadilly
3^{5sd} 1^{5gf} 2^{5g} 1^{5g} 2^{6s} **2-3-5 £23,879**

Guyana (Ire) *S Kirk* 41 a61
3 b g Lend A Hand - Romora (Fr)
7^{8sd} 9^{8g} 14^{7gf} **0-0-3**

Gwenseb (Fr) *C Laffon-Parias* 107
2 ch f Green Tune (USA) - La Popesse (USA)
1^{5gs} 2^{5g} 1^{5g} 1^{5g} 3^{6g} 6^{6g} 2^{6gs} **3-3-7 £93,050**

Gwilym (Ger) *D Haydn Jones* 76
2 b c Agnes World (USA) - Glady Rose (Ger)
10^{6gf} 7^{7g} 7^{6gs} 2^{5gf} 4^{5g} **0-1-5 £2,065**

Gwungy *W Jenks*
5 b g Mind Games - Kinlet Vision (Ire)
13^{9sd} **0-0-1**

Gwyneth *J L Dunlop* 63
3 b f Zafonic (USA) - Llyn Gwynant
5^{8f} 8^{10g} 9^{8g} **0-0-3**

Gyflym *J Balding*
3 b f Atraf - Bold Gift
11^{6gs} 11^{6s} 4^{8sd} **0-0-3**

Gymbolini *N P Littmoden* 58 a51
2 b f Bertolini (USA) - Gymcrak Flyer
5^{5g} 12^{5gf} 9^{6sd} 4^{5sd} 2^{6gf} 5^{7g} 2^{6sd} 14^{7sd} **0-2-8 £3,100**

Gypsy Fair *T D Barron* a70
3 b f Compton Place - Marjorie's Memory (Ire)
2^{6sd} 5^{6sd} 2^{5sd} 2^{5sd} 3^{6sd} **0-4-5 £3,645**

Gypsy King (Ire) *A P O'Brien* 113
3 b c Sadler's Wells (USA) - Love For Ever (Ire)
1^{10gs} 5^{12g} UR^{12gf} **1-0-3 £68,950**

Gypsy Royal (Ire) *G Woodward* 54
3 b f Desert Prince (Ire) - Menominee
4^{7gf} 8^{7g} 12^{7gf} 12^{8g} **0-0-4 £426**

Gypsy's Kiss *B P J Baugh* 37
2 b g Cyrano De Bergerac - Reina
13^{6gf} 11^{6g} **0-0-2**

H Harrison (Ire) *I W McInnes* 86 a52
5 b g Eagle Eyed (USA) - Penrose (Ire)
19^{5gs} 9^{7f} 11^{8g} 5^{8sd} 4^{8gf} 3^{7gf} 1^{7gf} 1^{7g} 3^{7f} 13^{6gf} 2^{6g} 2^{7gf} 2^{8gf} 12^{7g} 7^{8gf} 11^{7g} 9^{7g} **2-4-17 £31,969**

Haadef *J Howard Johnson* 43
4 b c Sadler's Wells (USA) - Taqreem (Ire)
7^{12g} **0-0-1**

Haatmey *M R Channon* 80
3 b g Josr Algarhoud (Ire) - Raneen Alwatar
8^{10gs} 9^{11f} **0-0-2**

Habanero *R Hannon* 93 a81
4 b c Cadeaux Genereux - Queen Of Dance (Ire)
3^{8sd} 11^{7gf} 16^{8gf} 1^{10gf} 1^{8gf} 5^{9gf} 2^{8f} 2^{8s} 2^{8gf} 1^{8gs} 2^{8g} 18^{8gs} **3-5-12 £25,329**

Habitual Dancer *Jedd O'Keeffe* 68
4 b g Groom Dancer (USA) - Pomorie (Ire)
3^{18gs} 14^{16g} 4^{15s} **0-1-3 £896**

Habshan (USA) *C F Wall* 86 a77
5 ch g Swain (Ire) - Cambara
7^{8gf} 1^{8gf} 4^{8g} 2^{8g} 5^{8g} 8^{8sd} **1-2-6 £10,102**

Hachita (USA) *H R A Cecil* 98
3 ch f Gone West (USA) - Choice Spirit (USA)
3^{8gf} 1^{7gf} 8^{8gf} 7^{8f} 9^{7g} **1-1-5 £14,528**

Hadath (Ire) *B G Powell* 46 a67
8 br g Mujtahid (USA) - Al Sylah
13^{7sd} 9^{6sd} 3^{7sd} 5^{8sd} 1^{6sd} 2^{6sd} 9^{6sd} 2^{7sd} 1^{6sd} 1^{7sd} 7^{7gs} 8^{7gs} 1^{6sd} 4^{6sd} 10^{6sd} 9^{7sd} 6^{6sd} 1^{7sd} 3^{6sd} **5-4-19 £16,937**

Haddaaf (USA) *J L Dunlop* 81
3 b g Kingmambo (USA) - Bint Salsabil (USA)
4^{8gf} 7^{10gf} 8^{8g} 5^{8g} **0-0-4 £337**

Hadrian (Ire) *M Johnston* 95
3 b c King's Best (USA) - Wanton
4^{7gf} 4^{8gf} 7^{7gf} 7^{7g} 1^{9gf} 1^{8gf} 2^{10gf} **2-2-7 £21,048**

Haenertsburg (Ire) *A L Forbes* 43 a44
3 b f Victory Note (USA) - Olivia's Pride (Ire)
7^{6sd} 7^{7sd} 6^{8sd} 10^{6g} 5^{8gs} 5^{7gf} 3^{7gf} 6^{7gf} 3^{9sd} 6^{10g} 11^{9ss} **0-2-11 £663**

Hahns Peak *Mrs A L M King* 22
2 b g Mujahid (USA) - Fille Genereux
7^{5gf} 6^{6f} **0-0-2**

Haiban *G A Butler* 74
3 b c Barathea (Ire) - Aquarela
12^{9g} 2^{10gf} 5^{12gf} 3^{12g} 15^{14gs} **0-2-5 £1,918**

Haifa (Ire) *Mrs A Duffield* 70
2 ch f Spectrum (Ire) - Mrs Fisher (Ire)
3^{7s} 1^{6hy} **1-1-2 £3,748**

Hail The Chief *R Hannon* 62 a96
8 b h Be My Chief (USA) - Jade Pet
15^{10s} 6^{10hy} 8^{9sd} 2^{8sd} 1^{9sd} 3^{8sd} 3^{9sd} **1-2-7 £10,010**

Haithem (Ire) *D Shaw* a33
8 b g Mtoto - Wukk (Ire)
11^{7sd} 6^{9sd} 11^{9sd} 8^{9sd} 12^{8sd} **0-0-5**

Haiti Dancer *I A Wood* 61
2 b f Josr Algarhoud (Ire) - Haitienne (Fr)
9^{5s} 10^{6gs} 10^{6g} 1^{7gs} 12^{7g} 12^{7g} 8^{8s} **1-0-7 £3,024**

Halcyon Express (Ire) *Mary Meek* 66
3 b g Mujadil (USA) - Hakkaniyah
5^{8gs} 7^{8gf} 8^{10gf} 8^{7g} **0-0-4**

Halcyon Lodge (Fr) *P F I Cole* 53
2 ch f Grand Lodge (USA) - Halcyon Daze
5^{5gs} 2^{5g} 10^{6g} 3^{5f} 9^{5g} 5^{6gf} 11^{6gs} **0-2-7 £1,807**

Halcyon Magic *M Wigham* 57 a50
7 b g Magic Ring (Ire) - Consistent Queen
8^{7sd} 3^{8sd} 3^{12sd} 5^{12sd} 3^{12sd} 1^{9sd} 5^{8sd} 2^{8gs} 1^{10sd} 4^{8f} 4^{8gf} 11^{12sd} 9^{10sd} 8^{12sd} 2^{9sd} **2-6-15 £5,053**

Half Pint Bill *W G M Turner* 69 a54
2 b g Green Horizon - Anywhichway
6^{5s} 3^{5hy} 15^{6gf} 9^{5gf} 5^{5sd} 1^{5f} 3^{6sd} 5^{5f} 6^{5hy} 9^{6sd} **1-2-10 £3,785**

Halfwaytoparadise *M L W Bell* 69
2 b f Observatory (USA) - Always On My Mind
2^{6gs} 3^{6gs} 2^{6gs} 2^{6s} **0-4-4 £3,764**

Halkin (USA) *J H M Gosden* 84
3 b/br c Chester House (USA) - Estala
3^{8g} 2^{8g} **0-2-2 £2,020**

Halla San *Mrs J R Ramsden* 72
3 b g Halling (USA) - St Radegund
5^{10g} 7^{12gs} 6^{12gf} 4^{12g} 5^{12g} 4^{10gf} 2^{10g} 1^{10s} 1^{11g} **2-1-9 £11,132**

Hallahoise Hydro (Ire) *B S Rothwell* 39 a13
4 ch g Lake Coniston (Ire) - Flo Bear (Ire)
14^{6g} 13^{6g} 14^{7sd} 13^{7sd} 11^{5sd} **0-0-5**

Halland *A King*
7 ch g Halling (USA) - Northshiel
9^{22s} **0-0-1**

Hallandale *P W D'Arcy* 60 a64
2 b f Bold Edge - Halland Park Girl (Ire)
8^{5gf} 6^{7gf} 9^{6g} 13^{6g} 16^{10g} 1^{7sd} **1-0-6 £3,035**

Halle Bop *Saeed Bin Suroor* 89 a82
3 b f Dubai Millennium - Napoleon's Sister (Ire)
19^{7g} 2^{7g} 11^{6g} 11^{8sd} **0-1-4 £2,296**

Hallhoo (Ire) *M R Channon* 103
3 gr c Indian Ridge - Nuit Chaud (USA)
3^{8g} 1^{10gs} 7^{12gs} 2^{10g} 3^{10g} 5^{10gf} 8^{10s} 11^{10g} **1-2-8 £28,740**

Halliard *H R A Cecil* 69
3 b f Halling (USA) - Felucca
7^{8gf} 6^{8g} 4^{10gf} 3^{11gf} **0-0-4 £857**

Hallowed Dream (Ire) *B Cecil* 104 a70
3 b f Alhaarth (Ire) - Salul
6^{10sd} 2^{10gf} 6^{10gf} 2^{11gf} 12^{10f} **0-2-5 £109,947**

Hallucinate *R A Fahey* 62
3 b g Spectrum (Ire) - Swift Spring (Fr)
16^{10g} 6^{10gs} 6^{12gs} 7^{12g} 3^{11gf} 4^{12gf} 12^{14gf} **0-1-7 £632**

Halmahera (Ire) *K A Ryan* 92
10 b g Petardia - Champagne Girl
4^{6s} 9^{6g} 8^{6f} 16^{6gf} 19^{6gs} 8^{6gs} 14^{6g} 11^{6gf} **0-0-8 £750**

Hamaasy *D Nicholls* 69 a49
4 b g Machiavellian (USA) - Sakha
10^{6sd} 7^{5sd} 1^{7gs} 15^{6g} 14^{7gf} 4^{6f} 15^{6g} 4^{7g} 12^{6gf} 6^{6gf} 15^{7gf} 16^{5gf} **1-1-12 £5,267**

Hambleden *M A Jarvis* 98
8 b g Vettori (Ire) - Dalu (Ire)
13^{12f} 2^{12gf} 9^{12gf} 7^{12g} 5^{12gf} **0-1-5 £2,926**

Hamburg Springer (Ire) *M J Polglase* 43 a44
3 b g Charnwood Forest (Ire) - Kyra Crown (Ire)
9^{6sd} 6^{8sd} 7^{8sd} 1^{6sd} 4^{7sd} 6^{6sd} 6^{8sd} 8^{10gf} 8^{10s} 15^{11gf} 11^{7gf} 11^{7gf} 5^{9gf} 15^{10g} 10^{10g} 9^{11sd} **1-0-16 £1,438**

Hammer Of The Gods (Ire) *Julian Poulton* a73
5 ch g Tagula (Ire) - Bhama (Fr)
2^{5sd} 1^{6sd} **1-1-2 £4,474**

Hana Dee *M R Channon* 43 a47
4 b f Cadeaux Genereux - Jumairah Sun (Ire)
11^{7sd} 6^{9sd} 9^{7sd} 3^{9sd} 9^{9sd} 13^{8f} 5^{15g} 3^{16gs} 7^{16gf} 3^{12g} 5^{16sd} **0-3-11 £1,218**

Hand Chime *E R Oertel* 59 a68
8 ch g Clantime - Warning Bell
5^{7sd} 5^{8gf} 6^{7gf} 1^{7sd} 5^{7sd} 2^{7sd} 4^{7sd} 4^{8sd} 14^{7sd} 8^{7sd} **1-1-10 £4,834**

Hand Of Destiny (USA) *N P Littmoden* a55
2 ch c High Yield (USA) - Special Happening (USA)
9^{6sf} 6^{7sd} 10^{6sd} **0-0-3**

Handa Island (USA) *M W Easterby* 41 a32
6 br g Pleasant Colony (USA) - Remote (USA)
11^{14gf} 7^{14gf} 15^{16g} 12^{12g} 6^{14ss} 12^{11sd} **0-0-6**

Handsome Cross (Ire) *D Nicholls* 91
4 b g Cape Cross (Ire) - Snap Crackle Pop (Ire)
11^{5gs} 4^{5gf} 3^{5g} 2^{5g} 2^{5gf} 1^{5g} 5^{5gs} 6^{5gf} 10^{5s} 12^{5gf} 12^{6g} **1-4-11 £14,634**

Handsome Lady *I Semple* 45 a6
3 ch f Handsome Ridge - Il Doria (Ire)
16^{5g} 12^{6sd} 7^{5gs} **0-0-3**

Handy Station (Ire) *J J Quinn*
4 b f Desert Style (Ire) - Art Age
12^{6sd} **0-0-1**

Haneen (USA) *J L Dunlop* 70
2 b f Bahri (USA) - Tamgeed (USA)
7^{7g} 10^{8s} **0-0-2**

Hang Loose *R Charlton* 66
2 b c Agnes World (USA) - My Cadeaux
3^{6g} **0-1-1 £656**

Hannah's Tribe (Ire) *C W Moore* 31 a22
3 b f Daggers Drawn (USA) - Cala-Holme (Ire)
9^{9sd} 9^{11sd} 9^{12g} 6^{12sd} **0-0-4**

Hanoona (Ire) *M R Channon* 96
2 ch f Zafonic (USA) - Wedoudah (Ire)
1^{6gf} 5^{7gf} 5^{7g} 8^{7g} **1-0-4 £4,711**

Hanseatic League (USA) *M Johnston* 80
3 b g Red Ransom (USA) - Rhine Valley (USA)
6^{6hy} 8^{6g} 3^{8gf} 5^{10gf} 5^{8gf} 2^{8g} **0-2-6 £3,229**

Hansomelle (Ire) *B Mactaggart* 74
3 b f Titus Livius (Fr) - Handsome Anna (Ire)
2^{8hy} 7^{8gf} 6^{7g} 10^{8g} 7^{8gf} 7^{8f} 6^{9gf} **0-1-7 £3,223**

Happy Camper (Ire) *J J Best* 36 a17
5 b g Pennekamp (USA) - Happy Dancer (USA)
13^{6sd} 9^{9sd} 10^{6gf} 9^{8f} **0-0-4**

Happy Event *B R Millman* 43

3 b g Makbul - La Belle Vie
14^{6gs} 8^{6gs} 12^{6gf} **0-0-3**

Happy Harry (Ire) *B Storey* 40
2 b g Raphane (USA) - Zalotti (Ire)
5^{5f} 12^{5gf} 6^{5gf} 5^{7f} 7^{6gf} 5^{5g} 5^{8gf} 10^{7gf}
0-0-8

Harambee (Ire) *J A Geake* a41
5 b m Robellino (USA) - Hymenee (USA)
14^{10sd} 8^{16sd} **0-0-2**

Harare *R J Price* 50 a58
4 b g Bahhare (USA) - Springs Eternal
15^{8gs} 13^{8g} 7^{11gf} 3^{9sd} 7^{8ss} 9^{9sd} 7^{12sd} 3^{9ss}
0-2-8 £592

Harbour House *J J Bridger* 46 a41
6 b g Distant Relative - Double Flutter
6^{5sd} 5^{5g} 7^{6sd} 8^{6f} 11^{7gf} 5^{7s} 8^{7g} 4^{6sd}
0-0-8

Harbour King (Fr) *N I M Rossiter*
6 b/br h Darshaan - Zinarelle (Fr)
12^{9sd} 11^{12sd} **0-0-2**

Harcourt (USA) *M Madgwick* 83
5 b h Cozzene (USA) - Ballinamallard (USA)
4^{10s} 8^{12gs} 2^{10gf} 3^{12gf} 13^{10s} 12^{10gs} **0-3-6**
£3,803

Hard Nose (Ire) *D J Wintle* 34
5 b h Entrepreneur - Cutlers Corner
8^{10g} **0-0-1**

Hard To Believe (Ire) *M G Quinlan* 26
2 b f Revoque (Ire) - Alexanders Way (Fr)
17^{6gf} 22^{7gs} **0-0-2**

Hard To Catch (Ire) *D K Ivory* 76 a73
7 b g Namaqualand (USA) - Brook's Dilemma
15^{6gs} 11^{6gf} 7^{5f} 7^{6gf} 11^{6gf} 6^{6sd} 6^{6f} 3^{6sd} 5^{5g}
2^{7sd} 2^{5gf} 16^{7g} 3^{6sd} 2^{6sd} **0-5-14 £4,671**

Hard To Explain (Ire) *E J O'Neill* 76 a73
2 br c Marju (Ire) - Kesh Kumay (Ire)
3^{8g} 2^{9g} 1^{9sd} **1-1-3 £6,017**

Hard Top (Ire) *Sir Michael Stoute* 118
3 b c Darshaan - Well Head (Ire)
1^{11gf} 1^{12g} 5^{15hy} **2-0-3 £93,170**

Hardy Norseman (Ire) *W Jarvis* 69 a65
2 b g Mull Of Kintyre (USA) - Miss Willow Bend (USA)
5^{5gf} 4^{6gf} 4^{5gf} 13^{6gs} 7^{6sd} 9^{5sd} **0-0-6**
£534

Harik *G L Moore* 35 a58
11 ch g Persian Bold - Yaqut (USA)
3^{16sd} 6^{16sd} 6^{14g} **0-0-3 £364**

Harlestone Grey *J L Dunlop* 56
7 gr g Shaamit (Ire) - Harlestone Lake
10^{12g} 9^{20s} 11^{16s} **0-0-3**

Harlestone Linn *J L Dunlop* 56
3 ch g Erhaab (USA) - Harlestone Lake
5^{12s} 11^{13g} 7^{14f} 9^{14gf} 9^{16g} 5^{16g} **0-0-6**

Haroldini (Ire) *J Balding* 49 a36
3 b g Orpen (USA) - Ciubanga (Ire)
8^{5g} 8^{7gf} 7^{7f} 6^{6f} 3^{6g} 12^{6g} 3^{5g} 7^{5sd} **0-2-8**
£814

Haroum (USA) *Mrs H Dalton*
2 ch c Diesis - Up Her Sleeve (USA)
17^{7gf} **0-0-1**

Harrington Bates *R M Whitaker* 57 a26
4 ch g Wolfhound (USA) - Fiddling
14^{5gf} 9^{6g} 11^{5gf} 10^{5gf} 16^{7g} 11^{6gf} 3^{6g} 9^{6s}
4^{6gf} 17^{6g} 9^{7sd} **0-1-11 £982**

Harrison's Flyer (Ire) *J M Bradley* 87 a83
4 b g Imperial Ballet (Ire) - Smart Pet
6^{5s} 12^{5gf} 6^{6sd} 1^{5g} 3^{5gs} 4^{5g} 12^{5g} 7^{5gs} 1^{6sd}
2^{6gf} 5^{5gf} 4^{5gs} 1^{5g} 15^{5s} 8^{5sd} 11^{6sf} 10^{6sd}
3-1-17 £21,528

Harry B *R J Price*
6 b g Midyan (USA) - Vilcabamba (USA)
9^{12sd} **0-0-1**

Harry May *C L Tizzard* 64
3 b g Lujain (USA) - Mrs May
6^{8gf} 5^{9gf} 10^{10gf} 5^{10gf} 7^{12gf} 5^{8f} 2^{10g} 3^{12g}
0-2-8 £1,196

Harry The Hoover (Ire) *M J Gingell* 12 a54
5 b g Fayruz - Mitsubishi Style
12^{7sd} 2^{7sd} 9^{6sd} 13^{7s} 6^{6sd} 9^{7sd} 10^{7sd}
0-1-7 £426

Harry Tu *E R Oertel* a38
5 b g Millkom - Risky Tu
8^{12sd} 8^{13sd} **0-0-2**

Harry Up *K A Ryan* 85 a86
4 ch g Piccolo - Faraway Lass
17^{5gf} 12^{6f} 2^{5gf} 11^{5gf} 11^{6g} 5^{5gs} 5^{6sd} 1^{6sd}
1-1-8 £4,997

Harrycat (Ire) *V Smith* 67 a68
4 b g Bahhare (USA) - Quiver Tree
4^{12sd} 4^{12gf} 7^{12gf} **0-0-3 £580**

Harrys House *J J Quinn* 68 a59
3 gr g Paris House - Rum Lass
14^{5s} 14^{6s} 12^{6gs} 10^{5f} 6^{5gs} 5^{5g} 18^{5gf} 10^{6gf}
1^{5s} 8^{5sd} 17^{5s} 11^{6sd} **1-0-12 £3,373**

Hartshead *G A Swinbank* 99
6 b g Machiavellian (USA) - Zalitzine (USA)
9^{6g} 3^{7g} 6^{6gf} 1^{8gf} 2^{7g} 3^{8gf} 9^{6g} 4^{8gf} 5^{8gf} 1^{8g}
2-4-10 £39,830

Harvest Queen (Ire) *P J Makin* a63
2 ch f Spinning World (USA) - Royal Bounty (Ire)
4^{7sd} **0-0-1 £349**

Harvest Warrior *T D Easterby* 90
3 br g Mujahid (USA) - Lammastide
7^{7gf} 11^{8gs} 18^{8gf} 8^{6g} 10^{7g} 2^{8g} 7^{8s} **0-1-7**
£1,756

Hashima (USA) *C E Brittain* 58 a59
3 b f Kingmambo (USA) - Fairy Heights (Ire)
6^{6gf} 6^{7f} 4^{8f} 11^{8g} 9^{6g} 3^{9sd} 10^{8f} 4^{9sd}
0-1-8 £692

Hasty Passion *W G M Turner* 61 a41
2 b f Diktat - Passionelle
7^{5sd} 4^{5s} 3^{5s} 11^{6gs} 12^{6g} 2^{5gs} 4^{5f} 4^{6g} 12^{6gf}
1^{5f} 11^{7gs} **1-2-11 £4,910**

Hatch A Plan (Ire) *Mrs A J Hamilton-Fairley* 73
4 b g Vettori (Ire) - Fast Chick
4^{10gf} 8^{12gf} 6^{10gf} 4^{10gf} 5^{10gf} SU^{10g} **0-0-6**
£594

Hathlen (Ire) *G L Moore* 73 a66
4 b g Singspiel (Ire) - Kameez (Ire)
3^{12sd} 2^{14g} 7^{16gs} 4^{14gf} 8^{14gf} 9^{12f} 5^{16sd} 3^{14gf}
10^{16g} **0-2-9 £2,699**

Hattan (Ire) *C E Brittain* 113
3 ch c Halling (USA) - Luana
6^{8g} 8^{10gf} 3^{10gs} 1^{12gs} 6^{12g} 5^{12gs} 2^{10g} 6^{15hy}
1-2-8 £81,950

Haunt The Zoo *John A Harris* a50
10 b m Komaite (USA) - Merryhill Maid (Ire)
3^{8sd} 6^{8sd} 3^{8sd} 6^{9sd} 3^{9sd} 8^{8sd} 1^{8sd} 2^{9sd} 4^{8sd}
8^{8sd} 2^{8sd} 12^{9sd} **1-5-12 £4,762**

Haunting Memories (Ire) *M A Jarvis* 98
3 b c Barathea (Ire) - King Of All (Ire)

8^{7s} 4^{7g} 19^{8gf} 17^{7g} **0-0-4 £1,104**

Havantadoubt (Ire) *Miss Z C Davison* a29
5 ch m Desert King (Ire) - Batiba (USA)
10^{8sd} 9^{12sd} 9^{14sd} **0-0-3**

Hawk Arrow (Ire) *H Morrison* 72
3 ch c In The Wings - Barbizou (Fr)
5^{11g} 5^{10g} 1^{12gf} 2^{12gf} 14^{12gf} **1-1-5 £4,837**

Hawkes Bay *M H Tompkins* 92
3 b c Vettori (Ire) - Nordico Princess
1^{7s} 3^{7gf} 3^{8gf} **1-2-3 £10,753**

Hawkes Run *Ian Williams* a70
7 b g Hernando (Fr) - Wise Speculation (USA)
2^{12sd} 6^{16sd} 4^{12sd} 5^{12sd} **0-1-4 £1,331**

Hawkit (USA) *P D Evans* 81 a73
4 b g Silver Hawk (USA) - Hey Ghaz (USA)
7^{10sd} 7^{7sd} 11^{9sd} 2^{7sd} 4^{9sd} 2^{10gs} 3^{11gf} 5^{9gf} 13^{12sd} 6^{9sd} 13^{12sd} **0-3-11 £2,634**

Hawks Home (USA) *Saeed Bin Suroor* 79
2 b c Distant View (USA) - Altamura (USA)
5^{8g} 1^{8gs} **1-0-2 £3,129**

Hawksmoor (Ire) *L A Dace* 69 a1
3 b c In The Wings - Moon Cactus
9^{11gs} 12^{10s} 9^{9sd} 13^{16sd} **0-0-4**

Hawridge King *W S Kittow* 72
3 b g Erhaab (USA) - Sadaka (USA)
3^{8gs} 3^{8gf} 5^{10gf} 2^{10gf} 8^{10g} 4^{10gs} 4^{11g} 3^{10gf} 2^{12g} **0-5-9 £4,850**

Hawridge Prince *L G Cottrell* 97
5 b g Polar Falcon (USA) - Zahwa
5^{10g} 9^{13f} **0-0-2 £1,250**

Hawridge Sensation *L G Cottrell* 61
3 ch g Polish Precedent (USA) - Looks Sensational (USA)
8^{8g} 6^{8g} 19^{10gf} 7^{7g} 1^{7gf} 7^{7g} 12^{7f} **1-0-7 £2,919**

Hawridge Star (Ire) *W S Kittow* 82
3 b g Alzao (USA) - Serenity
4^{10g} 9^{10gf} 10^{10gs} 2^{10gs} 14^{11gf} **0-1-5 £1,422**

Haystacks (Ire) *James Moffatt*
9 b g Contract Law (USA) - Florissa (Fr)
17^{16g} **0-0-1**

Hayyani (Ire) *K McAuliffe* 82 a82
3 ch g Almutawakel - Just Rainbow (Fr)
2^{6sd} 4^{5f} 9^{8g} 1^{7gf} 2^{7sd} 11^{10g} 4^{8sd} 12^{8sd} **1-2-8 £9,816**

Hazarista (Ire) *John M Oxx* 111
4 b f Barathea (Ire) - Hazaradjat (Ire)
5^{10gf} 9^{10gs} 9^{12g} 9^{10gy} **0-0-4 £3,546**

Hazelhurst (Ire) *J Howard Johnson* 65
2 b f Night Shift (USA) - Iktidar
6^{6gf} 5^{5gf} 2^{6gf} 5^{6s} 4^{7s} **0-1-5 £1,594**

Hazelnut *J R Fanshawe* 49
2 b f Selkirk (USA) - Cashew
6^{7s} **0-0-1**

Hazewind *P D Evans* 76
4 gr g Daylami (Ire) - Fragrant Oasis (USA)
2^{7g} 4^{8g} 7^{10gf} 3^{8gf} 1^{7g} 5^{8gf} 3^{7gf} 5^{7g} 10^{8g} 7^{8g} 4^{7g} 15^{7gf} 7^{7g} 10^{8gf} 5^{7g} **1-4-15 £9,840**

Hazeymm (Ire) *M R Channon* 102
2 b c Marju (Ire) - Shimna
2^{7gf} 5^{7g} 1^{8gf} **1-1-3 £11,083**

Hazyview *N A Callaghan* 117
4 b c Cape Cross (Ire) - Euridice (Ire)
5^{9gf} 2^{10g} 3^{9g} 1^{9g} 8^{10gf} 1^{8g} 4^{10gf} 5^{8gf} 2^{10gf} 4^{10gf} 6^{9gs} **2-3-11 £111,840**

He's A Diamond *T G Mills* 49 a63
3 ch g Vettori (Ire) - Azira
8^{8sd} 5^{7sd} 13^{8gs} 7^{7gf} **0-0-4**

He's A Rascal (Ire) *A J Lidderdale* 22 a40
7 b g Fumo Di Londra (Ire) - Lovely Ali (Ire)
6^{12sd} 9^{15gf} **0-0-2**

He's A Rocket (Ire) *K R Burke* 58 a66
4 b g Indian Rocket - Dellua (Ire)
7^{5sd} 7^{5sd} 3^{5sd} 1^{5sd} 2^{5sd} 1^{5sd} 2^{5sd} 3^{5sd} 7^{6gs} 11^{5g} 2^{5gf} 5^{5gf} 2^{5sd} 4^{5gf} 1^{5sd} 4^{5g} 9^{5gs} 12^{5gf} 5^{5gf} 6^{6gs} 1^{5sd} 1^{5ss} 6^{5sd} 5^{5sd} **5-7-24 £16,006**

He's A Star *Miss Gay Kelleway* 64 a59
3 ch g Mark Of Esteem (Ire) - Sahara Belle (USA)
1^{7gs} 9^{8g} 4^{7gf} 5^{8s} 14^{7gf} 1^{10g} 15^{10g} 10^{10gf} 2^{12gf} 6^{12gs} 2^{14ss} 3^{14sd} 6^{16sd} **2-3-13 £9,678**

Head Above Clouds (Ire) *E J Alston*
2 b c Cloudings (Ire) - Troys Guest (Ire)
14^{7sd} **0-0-1**

Head Boy *S Dow* 44 a44
4 ch g Forzando - Don't Jump (Ire)
7^{7sd} 15^{8gf} 17^{7gf} 4^{9gf} 4^{10sd} 12^{10s} 6^{10sd} 15^{10g} **0-0-8 £318**

Head To Kerry (Ire) *D J S Ffrench Davis* 52 a57
5 b g Eagle Eyed (USA) - The Poachers Lady (Ire)
4^{10sd} 4^{10f} 5^{14sd} 4^{12gf} 10^{11gf} 3^{14g} 6^{12sd} **0-2-7 £463**

Headland (USA) *D W Chapman* 53 a67
7 b/br g Distant View (USA) - Fijar Echo (USA)
4^{7sd} 1^{6sd} 11^{6sd} 4^{6sd} 8^{7sd} 9^{7sd} 3^{7g} 3^{7sd} 2^{6sd} 4^{7sd} 4^{7sd} 16^{8gf} 3^{6sd} 7^{6g} 7^{8gf} **1-4-15 £5,060**

Heads Turn (Ire) *E J Alston* 41
2 ch f Grand Lodge (USA) - Belle Origine (USA)
11^{6g} 6^{7s} 11^{6gs} **0-0-3**

Healey (Ire) *I W McInnes* a33
7 ch g Dr Devious (Ire) - Bean Siamsa
6^{9sd} **0-0-1**

Health Spa *B R Johnson* 40 a44
2 b f King's Theatre (Ire) - Thermal Spring
17^{7s} 10^{8sd} 10^{6sd} **0-0-3**

Heart Of Eternity (Ire) *J R Boyle* 23 a43
3 b f Namid - Kurfuffle
7^{6sd} 15^{6gf} **0-0-2**

Heart Springs *Dr J R J Naylor* 66 a33
5 b m Parthian Springs - Metannee
4^{14gf} 1^{18g} 2^{18g} 3^{16gs} 10^{14gs} 6^{16gf} 11^{16sd} **1-2-7 £5,860**

Heart Stopping (USA) *B W Hills* 57 a59
3 b f Chester House (USA) - Clog Dance
5^{10gs} 3^{8g} 12^{8gs} 6^{9sd} **0-1-4 £532**

Heart's Cry (Jpn) *K Hashiguchi* 125
4 b c Sunday Silence (USA) - Irish Dance (Jpn)
2^{10f} 5^{16f} 2^{11f} 6^{10f} 2^{12f} 1^{12f} **1-2-6 £1,920,257**

Heartbeat *I A Wood* 39 a46
4 b f Pursuit Of Love - Lyrical Bid (USA)
2^{10sd} 10^{9sd} 3^{10sd} 9^{12sd} 14^{10g} 12^{8gf} 10^{10sd} 5^{8g} 7^{10gf} 12^{10f} 11^{8ss} **0-2-11 £1,096**

Heartcrusher (Ire) *G A Swinbank* 66 a54
3 ch f Alhaarth (Ire) - Windini
7^{8s} 10^{8hy} 10^{8hy} 3^{9gf} 20^{8g} 1^{9sd} **1-1-6 £3,552**

Hearthstead Dancer (USA) *M Johnston* 76
2 b/br f Royal Academy (USA) - Amity (USA)
1^{7gf} 4^{7hy} **1-0-2 £4,916**

Hearthstead Wings *M Johnston* 107
3 b g In The Wings - Inishdalla (Ire)
4^{10gs} 8^{12gs} 8^{10g} 5^{16gf} 3^{12gf} 4^{14g} 6^{16s} 14^{14g} 3^{12hy} 1^{13gs} 8^{12gs} 2^{16s} **1-1-12 £29,909**

Heartsonfire (Ire) *P W D'Arcy* 48 a64
3 bl f Bold Fact (USA) - Jazirah
5^{6sd} 4^{7sd} 8^{7sd} 9^{5gs} 2^{6sd} 10^{6gf} **0-1-6 £1,022**

Heat Alert (USA) *A M Balding* 51
3 b/br f Valid Expectations (USA) - Melt My Heart (USA)
4^{7gf} 9^{8f} 11^{7f} 12^{7gf} 6^{8gs} **0-0-5 £261**

Heat Of The Night *P W Chapple-Hyam* 87 a85
3 b f Lear Fan (USA) - Hot Thong (Brz)
1^{9sd} 1^{9sd} 6^{8gs} 7^{7gf} 5^{8gf} 4^{8gf} **2-0-6 £13,538**

Heathcote *G L Moore* 85
3 b g Unfuwain (USA) - Chere Amie (USA)
3^{12gf} 6^{10g} 1^{12gs} 4^{15gs} 7^{14gf} 12^{14g} **1-0-6 £5,686**

Heather Moor (USA) *Sir Michael Stoute* a72
2 b f Diesis - High Walden (USA)
2^{7sd} **0-1-1 £1,392**

Heatherlea Laird (NZ) *A King* 49
5 ch g His Royal Highness (NZ) - Misty Gleam (NZ)
12^{14gf} 11^{14g} **0-0-2**

Heathers Furio (Ire) *R P Elliott*
3 b f Spectrum (Ire) - Almi Ad (USA)
11^{9sd} **0-0-1**

Heathwood (Ire) *J H M Gosden* 71 a77
3 b g Green Desert (USA) - Woodsia
7^{7g} 1^{7sd} 6^{8g} 6^{8g} 4^{7g} 3^{8g} 4^{8f} 3^{10gs} **1-2-8 £5,948**

Heathyards Joy *R Hollinshead* 45 a51
4 ch f Komaite (USA) - Heathyards Lady (USA)
7^{7sd} 9^{6sd} 10^{7s} 10^{7gf} 2^{10f} 2^{9sd} 7^{10g} 11^{8f} 6^{9sd} 6^{11g} 3^{9sd} 10^{12sd} 10^{9ss} **0-3-13 £1,687**

Heathyards Pride *R Hollinshead* 68 a84
5 b g Polar Prince (Ire) - Heathyards Lady (USA)
13^{11g} 6^{12g} 11^{10gf} 3^{12sd} 2^{12gf} 2^{12g} 1^{12g} 7^{13gf} 3^{12sd} 2^{12gf} 3^{12sf} 1^{14sd} 1^{12sd} **3-6-13 £22,424**

Heathyardsblessing (Ire) *R Hollinshead* 43 a43
8 b g Unblest - Noble Nadia
9^{7sd} 4^{5sd} 13^{5sd} 8^{6sd} 4^{5sd} 2^{6sd} 4^{6sd} 3^{6sd} 3^{5s} 8^{6sd} **0-3-10 £872**

Heatseeker (Ire) *David Wachman* 107
2 ch c Giant's Causeway (USA) - Rusty Back (USA)
1^{6gf} 1^{7gy} 3^{7g} **2-0-3 £40,286**

Heaven Can Wait (Ire) *J L Dunlop* 65
2 b f Mull Of Kintyre (USA) - Heavenward (USA)
5^{6gf} 4^{7g} 5^{7gf} 9^{8f} 2^{7g} 10^{7gs} 13^{7s} **0-1-7 £1,380**

Heaven Knows *W J Haggas* 73 a76
2 ch c Halling (USA) - Rambling Rose
5^{6s} 3^{6s} 1^{6sf} **1-1-3 £4,909**

Heaven Sent *Sir Michael Stoute* 72
2 ch f Pivotal - Heavenly Ray (USA)
7^{7gf} 3^{7gf} **0-1-2 £744**

Heavens Walk *P J Makin* 59 a31
4 ch c Compton Place - Ghost Dancing
12^{5gs} 5^{5gf} 11^{5sd} **0-0-3**

Hebenus *T A K Cuthbert* 40
6 b g Hamas (Ire) - Stinging Nettle
13^{7gs} 8^{6gf} 7^{6f} 15^{8gf} **0-0-4**

Heidi's Dash (Ire) *R Charlton* 68 a52
3 b f Green Desert (USA) - Child Prodigy (Ire)
10^{5sd} 2^{5gf} 5^{5g} 4^{5sd} 8^{5gf} 1^{5f} 7^{5f} 11^{5gf} **1-1-8 £6,142**

Height Of Fury (Ire) *J L Dunlop* 71
2 b c Sadler's Wells (USA) - Height Of Fantasy (Ire)
6^{7gs} 8^{7gf} 6^{7gf} **0-0-3**

Height Of Glory (Ire) *N A Callaghan* 59 a55
3 ch c Grand Lodge (USA) - Ghayah (Ire)
2^{5sd} 3^{5sd} 4^{6f} 9^{10gf} **0-1-4 £2,098**

Height Of Spirits *T D McCarthy* 57 a61
3 b g Unfuwain (USA) - Kimono (Ire)
7^{10sd} 6^{8sd} 4^{7sd} 14^{7gs} 9^{8sd} 6^{10gf} 9^{12gf} 7^{10gf} 5^{10s} 6^{12gs} **0-0-10 £401**

Heisse *Ian Williams* a80
5 b g Darshaan - Hedera (USA)
7^{12sd} 6^{12sd} **0-0-2**

Helen House *M H Tompkins* 54
3 b f Tipsy Creek (USA) - Tiempo
14^{6g} 5^{6s} 11^{7gf} **0-0-3**

Heliostatic (Ire) *J S Bolger* 86
2 ch c Galileo (Ire) - Affianced (Ire)
2^{7gf} 1^{7gf} **1-1-2 £11,943**

Hellbent *A W Carroll* 59 a57
6 b g Selkirk (USA) - Loure (USA)
5^{6sd} 10^{6sd} 10^{5sd} 6^{5sd} 11^{5sd} 1^{5sd} 3^{6sd} 2^{5sd} 7^{5sd} 4^{5g} 4^{5gf} 5^{5sd} 1^{5sd} 3^{5gf} 4^{6sd} 12^{6sd} 9^{5sd} 6^{5g} **2-3-18 £5,633**

Hello It's Me *H J Collingridge* 90 a99
4 ch g Deploy - Evening Charm (Ire)
6^{12sd} 2^{13sd} 4^{16gs} 9^{16s} 6^{12g} 6^{12g} 9^{12g} **0-1-7 £5,843**

Hello Roberto *R A Harris* 42 a52
4 b f Up And At 'Em - Hello Hobson'S (Ire)
18^{6s} 11^{6g} 13^{5gf} 7^{5g} 13^{6gf} 10^{5f} 16^{5gf} 12^{5gf} 1^{5sd} 6^{6sd} 6^{5gf} 7^{5sd} 6^{5sd} 3^{5ss} 4^{5sd} **1-1-15 £1,695**

Helm (Ire) *R Rowe* 58 a58
4 b g Alhaarth (Ire) - Pipers Pool (Ire)
7^{16sd} 5^{15s} 13^{18g} 14^{16g} **0-0-4**

Helm Bank *J L Dunlop* 110 a105
5 b h Wild Again (USA) - Imperial Bailiwick (Ire)
5^{9sd} 8^{7gf} 9^{9ft} 6^{7gf} 16^{10gf} 1^{8gf} 4^{8gf} 7^{8gs} 4^{8gf} 11^{8s} 7^{9gs} 7^{10sd} **1-1-12 £26,224**

Helvetio *D K Weld* 106
3 b c Theatrical - Personal Love (USA)
2^{10hy} 2^{10g} 1^{10gy} 3^{16gf} 6^{12gf} 8^{10gy} **1-3-6 £30,598**

Hembury Fort (Ire) *W S Kittow* 73
2 b g Mujahid (USA) - Overcome
7^{5s} 3^{6gf} 5^{6gf} PU^{6gf} **0-1-4 £707**

Henchman *W J Haggas* a66
2 b g Anabaa (USA) - Gay Heroine
17^{7gs} 4^{7sd} 7^{7sd} **0-0-3 £302**

Henry Hall (Ire) *N Tinkler* 85
9 b h Common Grounds - Sovereign Grace (Ire)
16^{5gs} 10^{5gf} 10^{5g} 2^{5gf} 3^{5gf} 3^{5g} 4^{5gs} 5^{5f} 4^{5gf} 14^{5gs} **0-3-10 £5,503**

Henry Holmes *Mrs L Richards* a51
2 b g Josr Algarhoud (Ire) - Henrietta Holmes (Ire)
8^{8sd} **0-0-1**

Henry Island (Ire) *Mrs A J Bowlby* 54
12 ch g Sharp Victor (USA) - Monterana

12^{15gs} 17^{17g} 6^{16gf} 3^{15gf} 9^{16gf} **0-1-5**
£218

Henry Tun *J Balding* 51 a63
7 b g Chaddleworth (Ire) - B Grade
3^{5sd} 1^{5sd} 4^{5sd} 6^{5sd} 5^{5sd} 4^{5sd} 2^{5sd} 2^{5gf} 7^{5gf} 12^{5gf} 12^{5ft} 8^{5ss} 2^{5sd} 12^{5sd} **1-4-14**
£5,733

Herbie Goes Green *W Storey* 15
3 gr g Environment Friend - Sallyoreally (Ire)
7^{7gf} 10^{8g} 12^{7g} **0-0-3**

Hereditary *Mrs L C Jewell* a54
3 ch c Hernando (Fr) - Eversince (USA)
10^{6sd} 7^{7sd} 7^{8sd} 9^{8sd} 3^{12sd} 9^{12gf} **0-1-6**
£382

Heres The Plan (Ire) *M G Quinlan* 34
3 b f Revoque (Ire) - Fanciful (Ire)
7^{7gs} **0-0-1**

Hermitage Court (USA) *M J McGrath* 48 a76
4 ch g Out Of Place (USA) - Russian Act (USA)
13^{12gf} 10^{12g} 5^{7sd} 13^{6sd} **0-0-4**

Hernando's Boy *K G Reveley* 70
4 b g Hernando (Fr) - Leave At Dawn
6^{12g} 2^{16gf} 3^{14f} 6^{14gf} 3^{14s} 1^{14s} **1-3-6**
£7,188

Herne Bay (Ire) *R S Brookhouse*
5 b g Hernando (Fr) - Charita (Ire)
9^{14sd} **0-0-1**

Herninski *P C Haslam* 64 a30
2 b f Hernando (Fr) - Empress Dagmar
4^{6f} 11^{7gf} 4^{7gf} 4^{8g} 13^{8gs} 12^{8sd} **0-1-6**
£914

Herodotus *K O Cunningham-Brown*
7 b g Zafonic (USA) - Thalestria (Fr)
13^{9sd} **0-0-1**

Heron's Wing *Lady Herries* a63
4 ch g Hernando (Fr) - Celtic Wing
2^{10sd} 7^{12sd} **0-1-2 £874**

Herring (Ire) *D J Coakley* 69
2 b c Orpen (USA) - Moorfield Daisy (Ire)
3^{8gs} **0-1-1 £513**

Heureux (USA) *J Howard Johnson* 81
2 b c Stravinsky (USA) - Storm West (USA)
3^{6gf} 2^{6g} 1^{6g} 17^{8s} **1-1-4 £14,686**

Heversham (Ire) *J Hetherton* 48 a20
4 b g Octagonal (NZ) - Saint Ann (USA)
14^{10g} 12^{7g} 11^{8s} 15^{8gf} 19^{8gf} 16^{8s} 11^{9sd}
0-0-7

Hewaraat (Ire) *B W Hills* 75
3 b g Fasliyev (USA) - Maraatib (Ire)
6^{6g} 3^{6gs} 2^{5g} 2^{6gf} 1^{6g} 9^{6g} 2^{6gf} **1-4-7**
£8,668

Hey Presto *R Rowe* 73 a75
5 b g Piccolo - Upping The Tempo
3^{7sd} 12^{8sd} 8^{7gf} 5^{7g} 5^{7gf} 1^{7f} 17^{7g} 9^{8sd}
1-1-8 £4,241

Heybrook Boy (USA) *Michael McElhone* 71 a73
3 ch g Woodman (USA) - Liberada (USA)
1^{9sd} 9^{10g} 7^{12g} 9^{12sd} 6^{12gf} **1-0-5 £3,373**

Hezaam (USA) *C W Fairhurst* 75 a55
4 b g Red Ransom (USA) - Ashraakat (USA)
8^{10gs} 7^{12gs} 17^{14s} 17^{12gf} 3^{12gf} 7^{12gf} 9^{12gs} 9^{12sd}
0-1-8 £901

Hi Dancer *P C Haslam* 46 a17
2 b g Medicean - Sea Music
5^{6s} 7^{6gf} 7^{5sd} 6^{8g} **0-0-4**

Hi Katriona (Ire) *D J S Ffrench Davis* 59 a65
2 b f Second Empire (Ire) - Hi Bettina
9^{5hy} 6^{6gf} 3^{6f} 4^{7f} 5^{9sd} 8^{7ft} **0-0-6**
£1,219

Hiamovi (Ire) *R M H Cowell* 33 a69
3 b g Monashee Mountain (USA) - Dunfern
1^{5sd} 2^{5sd} 1^{6sd} 2^{5sd} 2^{5sd} 5^{6sd} 7^{5sd} 4^{5s} 15^{6hy}
9^{6sd} 12^{6sd} 9^{6sd} 5^{6sd} **2-3-13 £7,259**

Hiats *C J Teague* 13
3 b g Lujain (USA) - Naulakha
14^{7g} **0-0-1**

Hiawatha (Ire) *A M Hales* 58 a59
6 b g Danehill (USA) - Hi Bettina
14^{10sd} 7^{9sd} 8^{9sd} 13^{10gf} 3^{13gf} 12^{12gs} 8^{14sd} 12^{11gf}
3^{10sd} 1^{9sd} 8^{10g} 8^{9sd} 6^{9sd} 2^{10sd} **1-3-14**
£2,604

Hiccups *D Nicholls* 81
5 b g Polar Prince (Ire) - Simmie's Special
11^{5s} 4^{6s} 4^{6g} 1^{7f} 7^{7g} 6^{6gf} 14^{6g} 5^{6gf} 20^{6g}
1-1-9 £7,928

Hidden Chance *R Hannon* 76
3 ch f Hernando (Fr) - Catch (USA)
10^{8g} 1^{7gf} 2^{10f} 7^{12f} 1^{10gf} 6^{10g} 3^{10gs} 3^{12f} 7^{10gf}
3^{12gs} **2-3-10 £10,566**

Hidden Dragon (USA) *P A Blockley* 98 a111
6 b g Danzig (USA) - Summer Home (USA)
1^{5sd} 2^{6sd} 3^{5sd} 2^{5sd} 4^{6sd} 9^{5sd} 2^{5gs} 8^{5gs} 18^{5g}
12^{7gf} 13^{6gs} 3^{6g} 17^{6gs} 5^{6g} **1-5-14**
£30,807

Hidden Hope *G Wragg* 107
4 ch f Daylami (Ire) - Nuryana
2^{12gf} **0-1-1 £19,800**

Hidden Star *F Jordan* 71 a57
3 br g Lujain (USA) - Inimitable
7^{6s} 3^{6gf} 12^{6gf} 3^{6gf} 11^{6gf} 3^{8g} 7^{8gf} 2^{8gs} 10^{8g}
12^{8s} 5^{6sf} **0-4-11 £3,977**

Hiddensee (USA) *M Johnston* 99
3 b g Cozzene (USA) - Zarani Sidi Anna (USA)
3^{10g} 2^{12s} 1^{12gs} 1^{15gs} 6^{12gf} 2^{13gf} 8^{14gf} 2^{14gs}
2-3-8 £30,408

Higgys Prince *A P Jones* 16
3 b g Prince Sabo - Themeda
14^{8g} 10^{6g} **0-0-2**

High (Ire) *W J Musson* 33 a61
3 b g Desert Story (Ire) - Sesame Heights (Ire)
7^{8sd} 8^{7sd} 4^{9sd} 8^{8sd} 15^{10gs} **0-0-5 £314**

High Accolade *M P Tregoning* 114
5 b g Mark Of Esteem (Ire) - Generous Lady
3^{13f} **0-1-1 £3,080**

High Action (USA) *Ian Williams* 108 a105
5 ch g Theatrical - Secret Imperatrice (USA)
1^{12gf} 2^{12g} 13^{16g} 1^{16sd} 11^{14g} 4^{13gf} 4^{18g} 7^{16g}
2-1-8 £54,798

High Arctic *A Bailey* 74 a61
3 b g Pivotal - Ladykirk
2^{10gs} 6^{8gf} 3^{8g} 4^{9sd} 9^{9sd} **0-2-5 £3,027**

High Authority (Ire) *Miss D Mountain* 59
3 b c Soviet Star (USA) - Moon Masquerade (Ire)
6^{10gf} 9^{10gf} **0-0-2**

High Beech (Ire) *D W P Arbuthnot*
3 b f Tagula (Ire) - Belladera (Ire)
6^{8f} 11^{7g} **0-0-2**

High Bray (Ger) *D R C Elsworth* 90
4 b g Zieten (USA) - Homing Instinct
1^{8gf} 1^{10gf} 7^{10gf} 10^{8gf} 3^{9g} 1^{7g} 1^{7g} 3^{7s}
4-2-8 £22,116

High Card *J M P Eustace* 62
3 b g So Factual (USA) - High Cut
9^{10s} 12^{8g} 7^{8g} 4^{12s} **0-0-4 £265**

High Chart *T G Mills* 58 a63
3 b f Robellino (USA) - Bright Spells
1^{7sd} 1^{8sd} 9^{7sd} 7^{8sd} 5^{7gf} 4^{8gf} 7^{6gf} 11^{7g}
2-0-8 £6,589

High Charter *J R Fanshawe* 70 a65
4 b g Polish Precedent (USA) - By Charter
1^{14g} 1^{14gs} 8^{15gf} 5^{14ft} **2-0-4 £6,291**

High Class Problem (Ire) *P F I Cole* 67
2 b c Mozart (Ire) - Sarah-Clare
10^{7gf} 5^{6gf} 5^{6gs} 5^{7g} 7^{8g} **0-0-5**

High Command *E A L Dunlop* 78 a70
2 b c Galileo (Ire) - Final Shot
2^{6sd} 9^{7gf} 2^{6gf} 1^{7gf} **1-2-4 £5,999**

High Country (Ire) *M D Hammond* 58
5 b g Danehill (USA) - Dance Date (Ire)
10^{10gs} 10^{16g} 9^{17gf} 5^{12g} 7^{12g} 8^{10g} **0-0-6**

High Curragh *K A Ryan* 85
2 b c Pursuit Of Love - Pretty Poppy
3^{5g} 1^{6g} 1^{5g} 4^{6g} 6^{6gs} 8^{6s} **2-2-6**
£15,027

High Dyke *K A Ryan* 83 a82
3 b g Mujahid (USA) - Gold Linnet
4^{9sd} 1^{8sd} 4^{9sd} 1^{9sd} 7^{9g} 6^{8gs} 1^{8gf} 13^{8gf} 9^{8gf}
5^{10g} 10^{10s} LFT^{9gs} **3-0-12 £15,865**

High Frequency (Ire) *T D Barron* 41 a56
4 ch g Grand Lodge (USA) - Freak Out (Fr)
5^{12sd} 4^{10sd} 5^{14hy} 9^{12sd} 6^{12sd} 1^{12sd} **1-0-6**
£1,687

High Heel Sneakers *P F I Cole* 104
2 b f Dansili - Sundae Girl (USA)
2^{6gs} 1^{6gf} 2^{8s} 2^{8gf} 4^{8g} **1-3-5 £42,480**

High Kick *R A Fahey* 76
4 gr g Sadler's Wells (USA) - High Tern
2^{12gs} 2^{12gf} 8^{22f} **0-2-3 £3,420**

High Lisa *J S Goldie* 44
5 ch m Bijou D'Inde - Harrken Heights (Ire)
11^{12gs} 13^{7gf} 8^{9g} 15^{7s} 19^{8s} **0-0-5**

High Meadow Girl *R Hollinshead* 63
2 b f Pursuit Of Love - Immaculate
8^{5s} 2^{6s} 6^{6gf} 9^{5g} **0-1-4 £1,070**

High Minded *K R Burke* 49
3 b g Mind Games - Pips Way (Ire)
11^{6g} 11^{7s} 8^{6gs} 15^{6s} 17^{6g} 20^{6gf} **0-0-6**

High Octave (Ire) *B G Powell* 72
2 b c Piccolo - Flight Sequence
6^{6g} 5^{6gf} 9^{7gf} 2^{6gf} **0-1-4 £1,348**

High Point (Ire) *G P Enright* 86 a87
7 b g Ela-Mana-Mou - Top Lady (Ire)
8^{12sd} 5^{18g} 5^{16sd} 7^{16g} SU^{20gf} 10^{16sd} 6^{16g} 5^{20s}
12^{18gs} 5^{16s} **0-0-10 £277**

High Policy (Ire) *R Hollinshead* a37
9 ch g Machiavellian (USA) - Road To The Top
9^{17sd} **0-0-1**

High Reach *T G Mills* 101
5 b g Royal Applause - Lady Of Limerick (Ire)
2^{6g} 1^{5s} 5^{5gs} 15^{6gf} 3^{6g} 5^{6g} 11^{7gs} 26^{6gs} 8^{6gf}
1-2-9 £15,961

High Reserve *J R Fanshawe* 92
4 b f Dr Fong (USA) - Hyabella
2^{10s} 5^{10gf} 1^{10gs} 6^{10s} 7^{10s} **1-1-5 £7,610**

High Rhythm *S C Williams* 59 a56
3 b f Piccolo - Slave To The Rythm (Ire)
2^{6gf} 6^{6gf} 3^{6g} 6^{6f} 9^{6gf} 3^{8gf} 5^{8gf} 7^{8f} 7^{8s} 3^{7sd}
6^{7sd} **0-4-11 £3,162**

High Ridge *J M Bradley* 83 a77
6 ch g Indian Ridge - Change For A Buck (USA)
3^{5gs} 5^{6gs} 1^{6f} 1^{6gf} 9^{5g} 6^{6gf} 3^{6g} 5^{6gf} 4^{6g} 8^{6gf}
3^{6gf} 3^{6gs} 4^{6g} 16^{6gf} 3^{6gf} 5^{6g} 19^{6gf} 10^{6g} 4^{6sd}
8^{6sd} **2-6-20 £18,606**

High Seasons *B R Millman* 66
2 b g Fantastic Light (USA) - El Hakma
8^{5s} 8^{6f} 2^{7gf} 5^{7gs} 11^{8f} 14^{8g} 6^{8g} **0-1-7**
£1,144

High Swainston *R Craggs* 55 a55
4 ch g The West (USA) - Reamzafonic
13^{6gf} 6^{6f} 12^{6gf} 4^{6sd} 6^{7sd} **0-0-5**

High Treason (USA) *W J Musson* 64 a66
3 ch g Diesis - Fabula Dancer (USA)
5^{10g} 2^{12sd} 5^{14g} BD^{11gf} 2^{11gf} 12^{11g} 12^{10hy}
0-2-7 £1,820

High View (USA) *F Jordan* 14
4 ch g Distant View (USA) - Disco Doll (USA)
16^{12g} 14^{8gf} 13^{10gf} 13^{10g} 15^{8hd} **0-0-5**

High Voltage *K R Burke* 93
4 ch g Wolfhound (USA) - Real Emotion (USA)
7^{6g} 14^{6g} 14^{6gf} 13^{6g} 13^{6gf} 23^{6g} 9^{5gs} 10^{6hy}
0-0-8

High Window (Ire) *G P Kelly* 44 a30
5 b g King's Theatre (Ire) - Kayradja (Ire)
7^{7sd} 7^{6gf} 13^{12s} 9^{8sd} 14^{8sd} **0-0-5**

Highband *M Madgwick*
2 b f Band On The Run - Barkston Singer
10^{5sd} **0-0-1**

Higher Love (Ire) *M L W Bell* 94
3 b f Sadler's Wells (USA) - Dollar Bird (Ire)
1^{10s} 2^{11gs} 11^{12g} 13^{12g} 10^{11g} **1-1-5**
£14,760

Higher Option (Ire) *Declan Gillespie* 44 a48
2 b f Namid - Tartan Lady (Ire)
10^{6s} 6^{6sd} **0-0-2**

Higher State *Miss J A Camacho* 82
4 b g Danehill (USA) - High And Low
9^{8s} 19^{10gs} 1^{12gs} 13^{10gs} 5^{12g} 13^{15s} **1-0-6**
£5,738

Highest Regard *P L Gilligan* 70 a84
3 b c Mark Of Esteem (Ire) - Free As A Bird
3^{7sd} 1^{8sd} 5^{7sd} 10^{8g} 1^{9sd} **2-1-5 £7,167**

Highest Return (USA) *M Johnston* 38
3 b/br g Theatrical - Hasene (Fr)
6^{12gs} 13^{10g} 12^{12g} **0-0-3**

Highindi *Sir Michael Stoute* 65
3 b f Montjeu (Ire) - Lalindi (Ire)
8^{10gf} **0-0-1**

Highland Blaze (USA) *Saeed Bin Suroor* 59
2 ch c Unbridled's Song (USA) - Green Lady (Ire)
8^{7s} **0-0-1**

Highland Cascade *J M P Eustace* 85 a60
3 ch f Tipsy Creek (USA) - Highland Hannah (Ire)
9^{5gf} 13^{6gf} 1^{6gf} 2^{6g} 8^{6sd} 3^{6gf} 12^{6gs} **1-2-7**
£10,228

Highland Diva (Ire) *Sir Michael Stoute* 48
3 ch f Selkirk (USA) - Drama Class (Ire)
10^{10gf} **0-0-1**

Highland Fair (Ire) *D W Barker* 32 a14
3 b f Orpen (USA) - Fairy Highlands (Ire)
9^{8sd} 9^{7g} 9^{10gs} **0-0-3**

Highland Games (Ire) *L M Cumani* 89

5 b g Singspiel (Ire) - Highland Gift (Ire)
$6^{12f}\ 18^{12gs}\ 2^{16gf}\ 11^{16g}\ 2^{16gf}\ 2^{16g}\ 27^{18gs}$
0-3-7 £9,206

Highland Lass *Mrs H Sweeting*
4 b f Nicolotte - Portvasco
14^{7sd} **0-0-1**

Highland Song (Ire) *R F Fisher* 60 a71
2 ch g Fayruz - Rose 'n Reason (Ire)
$1^{5g}\ 4^{5f}\ 4^{6sd}\ 6^{5gf}\ 9^{7gf}\ 6^{6gf}\ 4^{6s}\ 3^{6hy}\ 3^{6sd}\ 8^{6sd}$
1-3-10 £8,990

Highland Warrior *J S Goldie* 88
6 b g Makbul - Highland Rowena
$1^{5s}\ 7^{5gs}\ 2^{6gf}\ 9^{6s}\ 2^{5g}\ 5^{5gs}\ 20^{6gs}\ 8^{5gf}\ 4^{5g}$
$8^{6g}\ 10^{5g}\ 5^{6hy}$ **1-2-12 £24,769**

Highlander *Saeed Bin Suroor* 84
2 ch c Elusive Quality (USA) - Highland Ceilidh (Ire)
1^{8s} **1-0-1 £3,354**

Highlight Girl *A W Carroll* 18
4 ch f Forzando - Norska
$9^{10g}\ 13^{12g}\ 12^{14sd}\ 10^{12g}$ **0-0-4**

Highliner *Mrs L Williamson* 66 a60
3 b c Robellino (USA) - Bocas Rose
$6^{9g}\ 2^{12gf}\ 5^{12s}\ 8^{12s}\ 5^{8sd}\ 8^{10sd}$ **0-1-6**
£820

Hilarious (Ire) *Dr J R J Naylor* 31
5 b m Petorius - Heronwater (Ire)
9^{10g} **0-0-1**

Hilites (Ire) *J S Moore* a63
4 ch f Desert King (Ire) - Slayjay (Ire)
10^{7sd} **0-0-1**

Hill Fairy *T P Tate* 45
3 ch f Monsun (Ger) - Homing Instinct
$5^{12gf}\ 5^{9gf}\ 13^{14g}$ **0-0-3**

Hill Farm Shanty *M Wellings* 43
3 b g Slip Anchor - Hill Farm Blues
4^{12g} **0-0-1 £265**

Hill Of Almhuim (Ire) *K R Burke* 75
2 b g City On A Hill (USA) - Kitty Kildare (USA)
$1^{6gf}\ 6^{7g}\ 7^{7gf}\ 3^{6gs}\ 5^{6gs}\ 7^{7hy}$ **1-1-6**
£9,131

Hill Of Clare (Ire) *J W Payne* 53
3 gr f Daylami (Ire) - Sarah-Clare
$5^{7g}\ 8^{8gs}$ **0-0-2**

Hill Of Grace *J Noseda* 64 a70
2 ch f Desert Prince (Ire) - Tycoon's Dolce (Ire)
$4^{6gf}\ 11^{6gf}\ 1^{6sd}\ 8^{7g}\ 7^{7sd}\ 13^{8hy}$ **1-0-6**
£4,178

Hill Of Howth (Ire) *K A Ryan* 81 a46
2 b c Danehill Dancer (Ire) - Elton Grove (Ire)
$2^{6s}\ 6^{6sd}\ 9^{6gf}\ 3^{7g}\ 14^{8g}\ 8^{8g}\ 9^{8sd}$ **0-2-7**
£3,267

Hill Spirit *D R C Elsworth* 75
2 b c Polish Precedent (USA) - Homing Instinct
$5^{6gf}\ 2^{8gf}\ 3^{7f}\ 7^{8s}$ **0-2-4 £1,921**

Hillbilly Cat (USA) *T D Barron* 56
2 ch g Running Stag (USA) - Flashy Cat (USA)
$7^{5gs}\ 4^{5g}$ **0-0-2 £261**

Hillfield Flyer (Ire) *Samuel Murphy* 51 a47
5 b m Flying Spur (Aus) - Paul's Lass (Ire)
$10^{7ys}\ 12^{7hy}\ 8^{5s}\ 22^{6y}\ 4^{5y}\ 4^{5g}\ 7^{7g}\ 10^{7g}\ 10^{6g}$
6^{8sd} **0-1-10 £523**

Hills Of Gold *M W Easterby* 79
6 b g Danehill (USA) - Valley Of Gold (Fr)
$6^{7gs}\ 10^{8g}\ 2^{8gs}\ 4^{8gf}\ PU^{8g}\ 13^{7g}\ 11^{8g}$
0-1-7 £3,405

Hills Spitfire (Ire) *W R Swinburn* 82 a68
4 b/br g Kahyasi - Questina (Fr)
$3^{12gf}\ 3^{12g}\ 6^{12sd}\ 7^{14s}\ 4^{13sd}\ 7^{16gs}$ **0-2-6**
£1,712

Hillside Heather (Ire) *A Berry* 42 a40
3 ch f Tagula (Ire) - Danzig Craft (Ire)
$10^{5gs}\ 12^{6gs}\ PU^{6gf}\ 12^{6f}\ 7^{6g}\ 10^{6gf}\ 13^{5gf}\ 15^{6gf}$
$7^{6sd}\ 11^{6sd}\ 12^{7sd}\ 13^{6sd}$ **0-0-12**

Hilltime (Ire) *J J Quinn* 58
5 b g Danetime (Ire) - Ceannanas (Ire)
$4^{10gf}\ 1^{12f}\ 2^{10gf}$ **1-1-3 £4,128**

Hilltop Destiny *V Smith* 43 a61
2 b c Sure Blade (USA) - Saferjel
$11^{8g}\ 6^{7s}\ 3^{7sd}$ **0-1-3 £549**

Hilltop Fantasy *V Smith* a50
4 b f Danzig Connection (USA) - Hilltop
4^{7sd} **0-0-1 £249**

Hilltop Rhapsody *D J Daly* 64
4 b f Bin Ajwaad (Ire) - Saferjel
$11^{7g}\ 7^{8gf}\ 7^{7gf}$ **0-0-3**

Hilly Be *J R Jenkins* 43 a43
4 b f Silver Patriarch (Ire) - Lolita (Fr)
$5^{7f}\ 9^{9sd}\ 16^{12g}$ **0-0-3**

Hilversum *Miss J A Camacho* a45
3 ch f Polar Falcon (USA) - Silky Heights (Ire)
6^{9sd} **0-0-1**

Himist (Ire) *W Storey*
3 b g Lahib (USA) - Tara View (Ire)
$15^{7g}\ 10^{10g}\ 10^{8g}\ 11^{7g}$ **0-0-4**

Hinterland (Ire) *M A Jarvis* 101
3 b/br c Danzig (USA) - Electric Society (Ire)
$1^{8g}\ 1^{8gs}\ 9^{8g}$ **2-0-3 £13,937**

Hippodrome (Ire) *A P O'Brien* 103
3 b c Montjeu (Ire) - Moon Diamond
$10^{10ys}\ 1^{10g}\ 2^{10gf}\ 32^{18gs}\ 2^{12y}$ **1-2-5**
£11,386

Historic Appeal (USA) *M R Channon* 73
2 b g Diesis - Karasavina (Ire)
$6^{8g}\ 9^{8gs}\ 3^{8gs}$ **0-1-3 £783**

Historic Place (USA) *J A Geake* 81
5 b g Dynaformer (USA) - Captive Island
$13^{14s}\ 6^{16g}\ 2^{16gs}\ 6^{21s}\ 12^{16g}\ 2^{16gs}\ 7^{16s}$
0-2-7 £4,125

Hit's Only Money (Ire) *P A Blockley* 48 a66
5 br g Hamas (Ire) - Toordillon (Ire)
$12^{6gs}\ 6^{9sd}$ **0-0-2**

Hits Only Cash *J Pearce* 74 a56
3 b g Inchinor - Persian Blue
$5^{6g}\ 3^{6s}\ 6^{6g}\ 1^{7s}\ 4^{8gs}\ 7^{6g}\ 11^{6sd}$ **1-1-7**
£4,509

Hits Only Heaven (Ire) *J Pearce* 74 a87
3 ch g Bold Fact (USA) - Algonquin Park
$2^{6g}\ 1^{7g}\ 1^{8sd}\ 6^{7sd}\ 1^{8sd}$ **3-1-5 £13,635**

Hits Only Jude (Ire) *J Pearce* 76 a77
2 gr g Bold Fact (USA) - Grey Goddess
$5^{5gf}\ 5^{5hy}\ 3^{6g}\ 3^{6s}\ 6^{6g}\ 2^{6s}\ 2^{6sd}$ **0-3-7**
£5,219

Hits Only Life (USA) *J Pearce* a47
2 b g Lemon Drop Kid (USA) - Southern Day (USA)
$12^{7sd}\ 9^{7sd}$ **0-0-2**

Hogan's Heroes *G A Butler* 45
2 b g Alhaarth (Ire) - Icicle
$12^{5gf}\ 12^{6gs}$ **0-0-2**

Hogmaneigh (Ire) *S C Williams* 80 a71
2 b c Namid - Magical Peace (Ire)

1^{6gs} 4^{6sd} **1-0-2 £4,013**

Hoh Bla Daa *S Kirk* 70
2 b c Cape Cross (Ire) - Monte Calvo
14^{7g} 8^{7gf} 4^{7f} 11^{8g} **0-0-4 £363**

Hoh Bleu Dee *T Keddy* 60 a62
4 b g Desert Style (Ire) - Ermine (Ire)
13^{7sd} 8^{7sd} 8^{9sd} 6^{7sd} 4^{7sd} 6^{9sd} 5^{9sd} 11^{8g} 14^{8s} 3^{8gf} 8^{7gf} 2^{9sd} 2^{10sd} **0-3-13 £2,547**

Hoh Hedsor *S Kirk* 42
3 ch f Singspiel (Ire) - Ghassanah
9^{10s} 13^{10g} **0-0-2**

Hoh Hoh Hoh *A M Balding* 92
3 ch g Piccolo - Nesting
2^{5gf} 11^{6g} **0-1-2 £2,299**

Hoh Intrepid (Ire) *M L W Bell* 49
3 b f Namid - Bazaar Promise
16^{8g} 13^{8gs} 8^{8g} 16^{8s} **0-0-4**

Hoh My Darling *M L W Bell* 70
3 br f Dansili - Now And Forever (Ire)
8^{12g} 7^{10s} 1^{10f} 4^{10gf} 4^{10gf} 2^{10f} 3^{10f} **1-2-7 £6,855**

Hoh Wotanite *A M Balding* 61
2 ch c Stravinsky (USA) - West One
8^{6gs} 8^{5gs} **0-0-2**

Hoh's Back *Paul Johnson*
6 b g Royal Applause - Paris Joelle (Ire)
9^{8sd} **0-0-1**

Holbeck Ghyll (Ire) *A M Balding* 79
3 ch g Titus Livius (Fr) - Crimada (Ire)
12^{7sd} 6^{7gf} 4^{6gf} 2^{6f} 1^{5gf} 1^{6f} 1^{5g} **3-1-7 £18,141**

Holda (Ire) *B J Meehan* 74
2 b f Docksider (USA) - Spring Symphony (Ire)
1^{7s} **1-0-1 £4,319**

Holiday Camp (USA) *B W Hills* 96
3 b c Chester House (USA) - Arewehavingfunyet (USA)
7^{8gs} 4^{8s} 2^{8g} 1^{8gf} 4^{8gf} 1^{8s} 7^{10g} 6^{8g} **2-1-8 £14,883**

Holiday Cocktail *S C Williams* 70 a68
3 b g Mister Baileys - Bermuda Lily
2^{6gf} 3^{5gs} 11^{6gs} 7^{7hy} 4^{8s} 1^{7sd} **1-3-6 £4,894**

Hollow Jo *J R Jenkins* 54 a59
5 b g Most Welcome - Sir Hollow (USA)
15^{5gf} 14^{6gf} 15^{6g} 4^{7g} 8^{7gf} 15^{8gf} 4^{7sd} 3^{7sd} 1^{7sd} 1^{6sd} **2-1-10 £4,151**

Holly Games *M R Bosley* 22
6 b m Mind Games - Young Holly
11^{5g} 13^{6s} 8^{5f} **0-0-3**

Holly Rocket *J E Long* a13
4 b f Sayaarr (USA) - Start Again (Ire)
16^{6s} 10^{9sd} 11^{9sf} 7^{12sd} **0-0-4**

Holly Springs *Mrs C A Dunnett* 72 a59
3 b f Efisio - Anotheranniversary
2^{5gf} 3^{6gf} 3^{5gf} 4^{6gf} 4^{6g} 9^{6sd} 9^{5sd} 11^{5sd} **0-2-8 £3,744**

Holly Walk *A G Juckes* 25 a35
4 ch f Dr Fong (USA) - Holly Blue
4^{14sd} 9^{13g} **0-0-2**

Hollywood Henry (Ire) *P A Blockley* 52 a50
5 b g Bahhare (USA) - Takeshi (Ire)
8^{8sd} 14^{8f} 9^{8g} 3^{8hd} 7^{9sd} 5^{9sf} 7^{8ss} 9^{12sd} 6^{11sd} **0-1-9 £390**

Holy Blessing (Ire) *T D Easterby* 43
2 b f Almutawakel - Chancel (USA)
13^{5gf} 4^{6gf} 9^{7gf} 9^{7g} 10^{6gf} **0-0-5 £318**

Home Affairs *Sir Michael Stoute* 114
3 b c Dansili - Orford Ness
1^{8g} 3^{7gf} 4^{8g} 7^{8gf} 6^{8gs} **1-1-5 £79,199**

Homebred Star *G P Enright* a51
4 ch g Safawan - Celtic Chimes
1^{8sd} 10^{8sd} **1-0-2 £1,453**

Hometomammy *P W Hiatt* a54
3 b g Diktat - Catania (USA)
10^{9sd} **0-0-1**

Homme Dangereux *C R Egerton* 53 a53
3 b g Royal Applause - Happy Lady (Fr)
2^{7sd} 8^{7s} 7^{7gf} 4^{7f} 1^{8f} **1-1-5 £3,700**

Honey Flame *A P Jarvis* 44 a31
2 b f Fumo Di Londra (Ire) - Dulzie
6^{6gs} 16^{6gs} 6^{7ft} **0-0-3**

Honey Gold (Ire) *D R Loder* 25
3 ch f Indian Ridge - Half-Hitch (USA)
12^{7gs} **0-0-1**

Honey Ryder *N A Callaghan* 89
3 b f Compton Place - Urania
1^{6g} 7^{6gf} 5^{7gf} 8^{7g} 8^{5g} 10^{5g} **1-0-6 £9,484**

Honor Me (Ire) *J J Quinn* 3
2 b f Beckett (Ire) - Christmas Kiss
7^{7s} **0-0-1**

Honorary Citizen *D Haydn Jones* 58 a44
3 b g Montjoy (USA) - Heart So Blue
12^{10gf} 4^{8g} 5^{7sd} 16^{10g} 6^{10gf} 12^{8g} 4^{8f} 11^{9sd} 6^{8sd} 10^{12sd} **0-0-10 £620**

Honour High *Lady Herries* 52
3 gr g Cloudings (Ire) - Meant To Be
6^{10gs} 9^{12g} **0-0-2**

Hope An Glory (Ire) *N P Littmoden* 74 a61
3 ch g Nashwan (USA) - Susi Wong (Ire)
5^{7sd} 1^{10f} 2^{12f} 12^{10gf} 9^{10gf} 3^{12gf} **1-2-6 £6,573**

Hope Sound (Ire) *B Ellison* 58
5 b g Turtle Island (Ire) - Lucky Pick
7^{16s} 6^{12s} 4^{12s} 11^{12gs} 13^{12g} 5^{14gs} 5^{16gf} 3^{17f} **0-1-8 £701**

Hope's Eternal *J L Dunlop* 59
2 ro c Highest Honor (Fr) - Tennessee Moon
15^{7gf} 12^{8g} 8^{8gf} **0-0-3**

Hopeful Mission *K R Burke* a49
4 b g Bien Bien (USA) - Tiama (Ire)
6^{11sd} 3^{12sd} 7^{12sd} 11^{14sd} 8^{16sd} 8^{12sd} **0-0-6 £360**

Hopeful Purchase (Ire) *W J Haggas* 82
2 ch c Grand Lodge (USA) - Funoon (Ire)
3^{7s} **0-1-1 £583**

Hopelessly Devoted *N Tinkler* a29
3 b f Compton Place - Alpi Dora
10^{6sd} 8^{7sd} 9^{5sd} 14^{7gs} **0-0-4**

Horatio Nelson (Ire) *A P O'Brien* 120
2 b c Danehill (USA) - Imagine (Ire)
1^{7gf} 1^{7gs} 1^{7g} 1^{7gs} 2^{7gs} **4-1-5 £284,235**

Horeion Directa (Ger) *Andreas Lowe* 111
6 ch h Big Shuffle (USA) - Hosianna (Ger)
1^{8s} 5^{8s} 8^{7g} 8^{8g} 1^{7gs} F^{8sd} **2-0-6 £48,651**

Hormuz (Ire) *Paul Johnson*
9 b g Hamas (Ire) - Balqis (USA)
11^{7sd} **0-0-1**

Hornpipe *Sir Michael Stoute* 95

3 b g Danehill (USA) - Dance Sequence (USA)
5^{6gf} 1^{5g} 19^{6g} 4^{5g} 9^{5g} 7^{6g} **1-0-6**
£8,147

Hors La Loi (Fr) *Ian Williams* a71
9 ch g Exit To Nowhere (USA) - Kernia (Ire)
5^{14sd} **0-0-1**

Horsefair Dancer *T D Barron* 41
2 b f Almaty (Ire) - Minskip Miss
8^{5g} 11^{6gf} 5^{5g} 3^{6gf} 16^{6gf} **0-1-5 £450**

Hot (Ire) *R Hannon* 99 a94
2 b c Xaar - Solar Display (USA)
6^{5s} 6^{5hy} 1^{5g} 1^{5f} 7^{5gf} 4^{6gf} 1^{6sd} 3^{6gf} 9^{6gf} 7^{6gf}
3-0-10 £24,294

Hot Baby (Ire) *D R Loder* 39
2 gr f Linamix (Fr) - House In Wood (Fr)
15^{8g} **0-0-1**

Hot Lips Page (Fr) *Ian Williams* a52
4 b f Hamas (Ire) - Salt Peanuts (Ire)
13^{7sd} 10^{7sd} 12^{8sd} **0-0-3**

Hotchpotch (USA) *J R Best* 46
2 b c Dayjur (USA) - Anagram (USA)
9^{6gs} 8^{5gf} 8^{5gs} **0-0-3**

Hotel Du Cap *G Wragg* 70
2 br c Grand Lodge (USA) - Miss Riviera Golf
9^{7gs} 4^{7gs} 3^{8g} **0-1-3 £1,252**

Hotham *H Candy* 73
2 b g Komaite (USA) - Malcesine (Ire)
3^{6gs} 6^{6gs} 5^{5g} 3^{6gs} **0-2-4 £2,934**

Houdini Bay (Ire) *R P Elliott* a48
3 b f Indian Lodge (Ire) - Do The Right Thing
7^{7sd} 5^{8sd} 3^{6sd} 1^{7sd} 8^{8sd} **1-0-5 £1,654**

Hounded *M A Jarvis* 63
2 b c Foxhound (USA) - Cyclone Flyer
5^{6gf} 8^{6g} **0-0-2**

House Martin *C R Dore* 77 a59
3 b/br f Spectrum (Ire) - Guignol (Ire)
4^{8gf} 4^{10gf} 2^{10gs} 9^{10gs} 4^{9f} 18^{8g} 8^{9sd} **0-1-7**
£2,077

House Of Kaiser *M W Easterby* 53 a52
3 b g Josr Algarhoud (Ire) - Boulevard Rouge (USA)
7^{8g} 4^{7f} 9^{6gf} 11^{12g} 4^{10g} 8^{10g} 3^{9gf} 11^{8gf} 4^{12sf}
10^{8sd} **0-1-10 £1,273**

Hout Bay *R A Fahey* 61
8 ch g Komaite (USA) - Maiden Pool
8^{5f} 12^{5g} 12^{5g} 10^{6g} 11^{6g} 11^{6g} 10^{6g} 9^{5s}
0-0-8

Hov *D Shaw* a34
5 gr g Petong - Harifa
12^{9sd} 12^{7sd} 13^{8sd} **0-0-3**

How's Things *R A Harris* a4
5 b g Danzig Connection (USA) - Dim Ots
12^{7sd} 12^{9sd} **0-0-2**

Howards Call *I Semple* 42
2 b g Easycall - Bouchra (Ire)
4^{5g} 5^{6s} 6^{5g} 7^{5gf} **0-0-4 £519**

Howards Dream (Ire) *D A Nolan* 28
7 b g King's Theatre (Ire) - Keiko
12^{12gs} 10^{13gs} 15^{9gf} 4^{13s} 6^{13gf} 11^{11gf} 4^{10g}
14^{13s} 13^{12s} **0-0-9 £1,500**

Howards Prince *I Semple* 74
2 gr g Bertolini (USA) - Grey Princess (Ire)
4^{5gs} 6^{5s} 4^{5gf} 1^{5gf} 10^{5gf} 17^{6gs} 11^{5g}
1-0-7 £5,399

Howards Princess *I Semple* 77
3 gr f Lujain (USA) - Grey Princess (Ire)
3^{5gs} 10^{6g} 2^{5s} 1^{5gf} 4^{5gs} 10^{6g} 5^{6gf} 1^{6gf} 3^{5g}
12^{7gf} 2^{5s} **2-4-11 £11,936**

Howle Hill (Ire) *A King* 105 a111
5 b g Ali-Royal (Ire) - Grandeur And Grace (USA)
1^{10sd} 3^{10sd} 14^{10sd} 6^{13f} 5^{12g} 9^{16sd} 12^{14g}
1-1-7 £15,540

Hows That *K R Burke* a61
3 ch f Vettori (Ire) - Royalty (Ire)
1^{7sd} 2^{7sd} 3^{9sd} 3^{7sd} 5^{8sd} 6^{6sd} 8^{8ss} 11^{6sd} 14^{7sd}
1-2-9 £4,021

Huboob (Fr) *Eoin Doyle* 60
3 b g Almutawakel - Atnab (USA)
4^{10gf} 13^{10y} 13^{10sh} **0-0-3 £294**

Hue *B Ellison* 73 a28
4 ch g Peintre Celebre (USA) - Quandary (USA)
5^{9s} 2^{9gs} 2^{9gs} 4^{9g} 8^{12sd} **0-2-5 £2,950**

Huggin Mac (Ire) *N Bycroft*
4 b f Spectrum (Ire) - Little Love
LFT^{8g} **0-0-1**

Huggle *Julian Poulton* 65
2 b c Groom Dancer (USA) - Perle De Sagesse
8^{8gf} 5^{8gs} 5^{8hy} **0-0-3**

Hugo The Boss (Ire) *J R Boyle* 43 a49
3 ch g Trans Island - Heartland
1^{8sd} 7^{7sd} 3^{6sd} 7^{7gs} 8^{8sd} 12^{10gf} 13^{7sd} 11^{6sd}
12^{10sd} **1-1-9 £1,853**

Hugs Destiny (Ire) *M A Barnes* 63 a64
4 b g Victory Note (USA) - Embracing
6^{12sd} 11^{18gs} 10^{12sd} 7^{14g} 7^{9gf} 5^{8f} 7^{11gf} 2^{9gf}
6^{10g} 6^{12gf} 7^{10gf} **0-1-11 £1,062**

Hula Ballew *M Dods* 70
5 ch m Weldnaas (USA) - Ballon
3^{8s} 3^{8g} 2^{8g} 6^{8g} 2^{8gs} 3^{8gf} 2^{8gf} 2^{9gf} 3^{8gf} 6^{9gf}
1^{8gf} 2^{8f} 5^{8gs} 8^{8gf} 7^{8gf} **1-9-15 £12,563**

Hum (Ire) *Miss D A McHale* a48
4 ch f Cadeaux Genereux - Ensorceleuse (Fr)
5^{14sd} 11^{8sd} 4^{8sd} 7^{9sd} 9^{12sd} 16^{7g} 13^{12sd}
0-0-7 £282

Humble Gift *Mrs L J Mongan* a7
2 ch f Cadeaux Genereux - West Humble
13^{7sd} **0-0-1**

Humble Opinion *B J Meehan* 92
3 br g Singspiel (Ire) - For More (Fr)
7^{9g} 2^{8g} 2^{8gf} 1^{8gf} 2^{7gf} 3^{8gf} 10^{10gf} 7^{9gf}
1-4-8 £17,079

Humdinger (Ire) *John A Harris* 46 a14
5 b m Charnwood Forest (Ire) - High Finish
11^{14sd} 8^{12sd} 8^{12sd} 3^{12s} 5^{10gs} 10^{12gf} 8^{16gf}
0-0-7 £414

Humid Climate *R A Fahey* a53
5 ch g Desert King (Ire) - Pontoon
7^{12sd} **0-0-1**

Humility *C A Cyzer* 46 a55
4 b f Polar Falcon (USA) - Rich In Love (Ire)
8^{6s} 9^{6sd} 7^{7gf} 5^{7gf} 7^{5gf} 1^{7sd} 3^{7sf} 2^{7sd}
1-2-8 £4,053

Humourous (Ire) *Saeed Bin Suroor* 83
3 b c Darshaan - Amusing Time (Ire)
7^{12g} **0-0-1**

Humungous (Ire) *C R Egerton* 96 a96
2 ch c Giant's Causeway (USA) - Doula (USA)
6^{6g} 1^{7f} 6^{7gf} 1^{7sd} 6^{7gs} **2-0-5 £13,387**

Hunipot *M E Sowersby* 30
3 ch f Aragon - Acinom
6^{7gf} 12^{10g} 17^{6f} **0-0-3**

Hunter Street *P W Chapple-Hyam* 104
2 b c Compton Place - Sewards Folly
3^{5gf} 1^{6gf} 8^{6gs} 4^{5gs} 5^{5g} 2^{5hy} 1^{5g} **2-2-7 £46,359**

Hunting Haze *Miss S E Hall* 60
2 b g Foxhound (USA) - Second Affair (Ire)
4^{6gf} 5^{6g} 10^{6g} 6^{7gf} **0-0-4 £336**

Hunting Lodge (Ire) *H J Manners* 89 a73
4 ch g Grand Lodge (USA) - Vijaya (USA)
1^{8sd} 3^{10gs} 9^{8gf} 16^{12f} **1-0-4 £5,240**

Hunting Party (Ire) *B W Hills* 66
2 ch c Grand Lodge (USA) - Delilah (Ire)
5^{6gf} 7^{7g} **0-0-2**

Hurricane Alan (Ire) *R Hannon* 117 a108
5 b/br h Mukaddamah (USA) - Bint Al Balad (Ire)
3^{10sd} 2^{8g} 2^{9gf} 1^{8g} 3^{8f} 10^{8gf} 5^{10gf} **1-4-7 £115,390**

Hurricane Cat (USA) *A P O'Brien* 108
2 b c Storm Cat (USA) - Sky Beauty (USA)
7^{7gs} 1^{7ys} 1^{7gs} **2-0-3 £30,551**

Hurricane Coast *K McAuliffe* 79 a97
6 b g Hurricane Sky (Aus) - Tread Carefully
10^{7sd} 3^{6sd} 9^{7sd} 2^{6sd} 7^{6sd} 10^{6sd} 4^{6sd} 7^{6g} 1^{7sd} 16^{6gf} 10^{6sd} 2^{6g} 1^{7hy} 9^{6sd} 12^{7s} 8^{7sd} 13^{10sd} 11^{8sd} 2^{9sd} 3^{8sd} 7^{7sd} **2-5-21 £13,529**

Hurricane Floyd (Ire) *D Flood* 49
7 ch g Pennekamp (USA) - Mood Swings (Ire)
11^{8gf} **0-0-1**

Hurricane Run (Ire) *A Fabre* 133
3 b c Montjeu (Ire) - Hold On (Ger)
1^{11hy} 1^{11g} 2^{11g} 1^{12gf} 1^{12gs} 1^{12gs} **5-1-6 £1,618,312**

Hurry Up Helen (Ire) *Mrs L Stubbs* 60
2 b f In The Wings - Imitation
12^{8gs} 5^{9g} **0-0-2**

Husam (Ire) *P W Chapple-Hyam* a48
2 b c Marju (Ire) - Licentious
10^{7sd} **0-0-1**

Husky (Pol) *B G Powell* a27
7 b g Special Power - Hallo Bambina (Pol)
12^{10sd} 12^{10sd} **0-0-2**

Huw The News *S C Burrough* a1
6 b g Primo Dominie - Martha Stevens (USA)
12^{9sd} 8^{12sd} **0-0-2**

Huxley (Ire) *D J Wintle* 70 a39
6 b g Danehill Dancer (Ire) - Biddy Mulligan
2^{10f} 1^{8g} 12^{9sd} 10^{8g} 9^{10g} 15^{7gf} 11^{8g} 13^{10gf} 13^{8hy} 10^{6sd} **1-1-10 £3,495**

Hygieia *A D Smith*
3 b c Silver Wizard (USA) - Defy Me
10^{6sd} **0-0-1**

Hymn Of Victory (Ire) *T I Ftherington* 40 a32
3 b c Bluebird (USA) - Vaga Follia (Ire)
11^{8gf} 8^{6sd} 16^{6gf} 6^{5g} 11^{6g} 12^{5sd} **0-0-6**

Hypnosis *D W Barker* 65
2 b f Mind Games - Salacious
9^{5gf} 9^{6g} 7^{5gf} 2^{5gf} 14^{6s} **0-1-5 £1,120**

Hypnotic *M L W Bell* 82
3 ch c Lomitas - Hypnotize
7^{8gf} 11^{7g} 1^{8g} 6^{10g} 10^{8g} **1-0-5 £7,035**

I Got Rhythm *K G Reveley* 54
7 gr m Lycius (USA) - Eurythmic
1^{14g} 2^{12gf} 8^{13s} **1-1-3 £1,944**

I Had A Sister (Bel) *P S McEntee* a19
4 ch g Bid For Blue - Texas Cowgirl (Ire)
12^{10sd} 11^{9sd} **0-0-2**

I Have Dreamed (Ire) *T G Mills* 77
3 b c Montjeu (Ire) - Diamond Field (USA)
1^{10g} **1-0-1 £3,818**

I Wish *Miss J R Tooth* 62 a64
7 ch m Beveled (USA) - Ballystate
7^{7sd} 4^{8sd} 5^{7sd} 10^{8sd} 10^{8gf} 3^{6gs} 6^{6gf} 1^{6sd} 7^{6f} 6^{6gf} 4^{6s} 1^{6f} 7^{6gf} 4^{6sd} 11^{7gf} 4^{6gs} 7^{7sd} 2^{7sd} 2^{7sf} 2^{7sd} **2-4-20 £8,677**

I'Ll Do It Today *J M Jefferson* a58
4 b g Mtoto - Knayton Lass
5^{12ss} 1^{14sd} **1-0-2 £2,987**

I'Ltellthejokes (Ire) *M W Easterby* 30
2 b f Mull Of Kintyre (USA) - Persian Flower
13^{5gf} 4^{6s} 9^{5gf} **0-0-3 £267**

I'm Aimee *P D Evans* 39 a50
3 ch f Timeless Times (USA) - Marfen
5^{5sd} 3^{6sd} 3^{6sd} 8^{7sd} 2^{6sd} 6^{7sd} 6^{7sd} 4^{7g} 4^{6hy} 4^{6sd} **0-3-10 £1,522**

I'm In Love (USA) *M A Magnusson* 78 a73
2 b/br f Zafonic (USA) - Bank On Her (USA)
7^{5g} 2^{7gf} 1^{8sd} **1-1-3 £8,215**

I'm So Lucky *M Johnston* 107
3 b g Zilzal (USA) - City Of Angels
3^{12gs} 1^{11f} 6^{12g} 4^{12gf} 1^{10g} 6^{10g} 5^{10gf} **2-1-7 £40,989**

Iamback *Miss Gay Kelleway* 49 a53
5 b m Perugino (USA) - Smouldering (Ire)
6^{9sd} 3^{9sd} 10^{9sd} 4^{7sd} 4^{9sd} 4^{9sd} 2^{8g} 2^{10gs} 7^{8sd} 5^{7sd} 4^{9f} 1^{12gf} UR^{13s} 3^{12gf} 3^{16g} 5^{12f} 10^{12g} 12^{12gf} 3^{16gf} 6^{12sd} 7^{17sf} 4^{12sd} 1^{14sd} 2^{13sd} 7^{14sd} 6^{12sd} 9^{11ss} 5^{12sd} 7^{16sd} **2-7-29 £7,320**

Iannis (Ire) *J Noseda* 71
2 b c Danehill Dancer (Ire) - Suave Lady (Fr)
3^{6g} **0-1-1 £872**

Iberus (Ger) *S Gollings* 58 a61
7 b g Monsun (Ger) - Iberica (Ger)
7^{10gf} 8^{10gf} 4^{8sd} **0-0-3 £252**

Icannshift (Ire) *T M Jones* 56 a44
5 b g Night Shift (USA) - Cannikin (Ire)
9^{10sd} 8^{10sd} 6^{8sd} 10^{10sd} 2^{11gs} 4^{12s} 4^{12gf} 4^{12gf} 8^{11g} 2^{10f} 14^{10gf} 8^{10gf} 2^{10g} 3^{10g} 3^{10gf} 8^{11g} 1^{12g} 12^{12gs} 14^{10sd} **1-5-19 £4,724**

Ice And Fire *J T Stimpson* 37 a54
6 b g Cadeaux Genereux - Tanz (Ire)
7^{10g} 17^{14g} 5^{12sf} 1^{14ss} 8^{14sd} 6^{14sd} 6^{14ss} **1-0-7 £1,419**

Ice Dragon *M H Tompkins* 36 a44
4 b f Polar Falcon (USA) - Qilin (Ire)
14^{7sd} 7^{6sd} 7^{5sd} 6^{7g} 3^{9sd} 5^{10sd} 12^{14gf} 10^{10gf} **0-1-8 £452**

Ice Of Battle (USA) *Mrs A J Perrett* 56
3 b c Diesis - Dance Gaily (USA)
4^{10gf} **0-0-1 £274**

Ice Planet *D Nicholls* 98
4 b g Polar Falcon (USA) - Preference
10^{6g} 9^{7s} 3^{5gf} 1^{5gf} 2^{5g} 4^{5gf} 1^{6gf} 2^{6gf} 5^{6g} 1^{6gs} 15^{6g} **3-3-11 £46,628**

Ice Princess (Ire) *David Wachman* 87
2 b f Grand Lodge (USA) - Ghana (Ire)
1^{7gf} 7^{7g} 11^{8y} **1-0-3 £9,234**

Ice Ruby *D Shaw*
3 b f Polar Prince (Ire) - Simply Style
10^{6s} **0-0-1**

Icecap *W G M Turner* 58 a28
5 b m Polar Falcon (USA) - Warning Light

12^{7sd} 5^{7f} 12^{6gf} 4^{8f} 3^{10f} 4^{10f} **0-1-6**
£879

Iced Diamond (Ire) *W M Brisbourne* 58 a68
6 b g Petardia - Prime Site (Ire)
3^{6sd} 3^{6sd} 8^{7sd} 1^{7sd} 1^{7sd} 6^{7sd} 9^{7sd} 6^{7g} 8^{7gf} 8^{8gf} 3^{7gf} 4^{7gs} 8^{7gf} 3^{7gf} 10^{7g} 4^{7sd} **2-4-16**
£8,318

Iceman *J H M Gosden* 115
3 b c Polar Falcon (USA) - Virtuous
4^{8gf} 13^{8gf} **0-0-2** **£2,500**

Iceni Warrior *P S McEntee* 22 a43
3 b g Lake Coniston (Ire) - Swing Job
8^{6sd} 12^{6sd} 4^{5sd} 11^{5gf} 17^{6gf} 10^{10sd} **0-0-6**
£286

Icey Run *D G Bridgwater* 9 a4
5 b g Runnett - Polar Storm (Ire)
13^{17sd} 13^{10f} **0-0-2**

Idarah (USA) *W J Haggas* 73
2 gr/ro c Aljabr (USA) - Fatina
7^{8g} 4^{8gf} 1^{8s} **1-0-3** **£5,596**

Idealistic (Ire) *L M Cumani* 97
4 b f Unfuwain (USA) - L'Ideale (USA)
9^{12gf} 5^{12gf} 4^{12gf} 1^{12f} 1^{12g} 5^{12g} 9^{14hy}
2-0-7 **£29,955**

Idle Power (Ire) *J R Boyle* 96 a90
7 b g Common Grounds - Idle Fancy
8^{7gs} 1^{6g} 13^{7g} 10^{6g} 12^{7gf} 3^{7gf} 9^{7gf} 2^{7gf} 1^{6gs} 15^{6gf} 5^{6g} 8^{7gf} 10^{6gf} 4^{6s} 5^{6sd} 7^{7sd} 10^{6sf}
2-3-17 **£21,920**

If Dubai (USA) *R Hannon* 49
3 b f Stephen Got Even (USA) - Quillummo (USA)
9^{7gf} 11^{8f} **0-0-2**

If Paradise *R Hannon* 109 a82
4 b c Compton Place - Sunley Stars
7^{5sd} 2^{6g} 1^{5gs} 4^{5g} 5^{5g} 2^{5g} 6^{6gf} 6^{5gf} 8^{6gf} 7^{5s} 4^{5g} 8^{5g} 4^{5g} 5^{5s} 12^{6s} **1-2-15** **£25,615**

Iffraaj *M A Jarvis* 121
4 b c Zafonic (USA) - Pastorale
1^{6g} 1^{7g} 1^{6f} 14^{6gs} 1^{7gf} 7^{7s} **4-0-6**
£151,136

Iffy *R Lee* 78
4 b g Orpen (USA) - Hopesay
6^{10gf} 4^{10gf} 3^{10gf} 2^{10gf} 1^{10gf} 5^{11gf} 1^{10gf} 6^{10g} 7^{9g} 9^{12gs} **2-2-10** **£12,385**

Ifit (Ire) *M R Channon* a51
3 b f Inchinor - Robin
3^{9sd} 9^{8sd} 1^{10sd} **1-1-3** **£3,295**

Iftikhar (USA) *W M Brisbourne* a63
6 b g Storm Cat (USA) - Muhbubh (USA)
4^{12sd} 3^{9sd} 1^{9sd} 6^{9sd} **1-1-4** **£3,343**

Ignition *W M Brisbourne* 70
3 ch f Rock City - Fire Sprite
7^{8g} 3^{9s} 8^{10g} 1^{8gf} 6^{8gf} 2^{9gf} 5^{9gf} 1^{9g} 15^{10gf} 1^{8g} **3-2-10** **£13,473**

Il Castagno (Ire) *B Smart* 77 a42
2 ch c Night Shift (USA) - Cartesian
10^{6g} 7^{7s} 5^{6g} 7^{7g} 2^{6gf} 1^{7g} 5^{7hy} 9^{7sd}
1-1-8 **£8,257**

Il Divo *C Grant*
2 b g Tipsy Creek (USA) - Be My Hattie
8^{5s} 13^{6gf} **0-0-2**

Il Pranzo *P D Evans* 61 a77
3 b g Piccolo - St Helena
1^{6sd} 3^{6sd} 5^{9sd} 2^{7sd} 10^{6sd} 5^{6sd} 2^{5sd} 11^{7sd} 12^{6gs} 11^{6gf} 2^{6sd} 7^{6sd} 12^{6gf} 8^{6g} 8^{6sd} 8^{5gf} 11^{8gf} 9^{5s} **1-4-18** **£8,414**

Ile Michel *Lady Herries* 72
8 b g Machiavellian (USA) - Circe's Isle
4^{8gf} 3^{9gf} 2^{10gf} 6^{10g} **0-2-4** **£2,033**

Illuminati *L Corcoran* 54
3 b g Inchinor - Selection Board
5^{12s} 5^{11s} **0-0-2**

Illuminise (Ire) *E A L Dunlop* 70
2 ch f Grand Lodge (USA) - Brief Escapade (Ire)
5^{7g} **0-0-1**

Illustrious Blue *J A Osborne* 77 a74
2 b/br c Dansili - Gipsy Moth
2^{7gf} 2^{7s} 3^{8g} 2^{8gs} 2^{9sd} 4^{8g} **0-5-6**
£5,589

Illustrious Duke *M Mullineaux* 49 a49
7 b g Dancing Spree (USA) - Killick
6^{7sd} 2^{7sd} 5^{9sd} 4^{7gs} 4^{7sd} 4^{9sd} 6^{7sd} 11^{10gs} 17^{8g}
0-1-9 **£952**

Im Spartacus *D Flood* 108 a85
3 b g Namaqualand (USA) - Captivating (Ire)
8^{7ft} 8^{8ft} 3^{9ft} 5^{9ft} 4^{10gs} 2^{10gs} 1^{10gs} 1^{10gy} 5^{10g}
2-2-9 **£73,389**

Imagine That *Peter Grayson*
2 b f Bertolini (USA) - Rythm N Time
10^{5gs} 8^{5gf} **0-0-2**

Imco Sasihill (Ire) *P S McEntee* 42 a76
5 b h Danehill (USA) - Sasimoto (USA)
2^{5sd} 4^{5sd} 9^{7sd} 7^{5gs} 6^{6sd} **0-1-5** **£1,297**

Imlaak *James Moffatt* 62
3 ch c Giant's Causeway (USA) - Karen S (USA)
6^{10gf} 5^{10gf} 8^{11gf} **0-0-3**

Immaculate Red *R Bastiman* 25 a63
2 ch g Woodborough (USA) - Primula Bairn
12^{5gf} 8^{6gf} 2^{5sd} **0-1-3** **£419**

Impasse Carraire *P C Haslam* 20
3 ch f Piccolo - Magical Dancer (Ire)
8^{9gs} 17^{7gf} **0-0-2**

Impeccable Guest (Ire) *P C Haslam* 59 a49
2 b f Orpen (USA) - Perfect Guest
8^{6gs} 6^{7gf} 3^{7gf} 8^{8g} 4^{7sd} **0-1-5** **£744**

Impeller (Ire) *W R Muir* 104
6 ch g Polish Precedent (USA) - Almaaseh (Ire)
5^{8gs} 9^{10gf} 4^{8g} 7^{10g} 7^{8gf} 9^{10g} 10^{10gs} 8^{8gs} 1^{9g} 5^{11gf} 2^{9g} 2^{9gf} 5^{10gf} 6^{10gf} 8^{9s} 7^{8gs} 10^{10gs}
1-2-17 **£26,097**

Imperative (USA) *M J Gingell* 30 a42
5 ch g Woodman (USA) - Wandesta
6^{9sd} 10^{12sd} 11^{12sd} 9^{12sd} 9^{12s} 13^{14sd} **0-0-6**

Imperatrice *G A Ham*
3 b f Emperor Jones (USA) - Fine Honor (Fr)
13^{9sd} 9^{9sd} **0-0-2**

Imperial Dragon (USA) *W A O'Gorman* 28
5 b g Meadowlake (USA) - South Cove
20^{8gf} 6^{5gs} **0-0-2**

Imperial Echo (USA) *T D Barron* 88
4 b g Labeeb - Regal Baby (USA)
10^{6g} 10^{6g} 6^{6gf} 2^{6gf} 5^{6gf} 11^{6gf} 3^{6g} 8^{6g} 6^{7gf} 14^{6gf} 6^{6g} 5^{7g} 8^{7s} 5^{7s} **0-1-14** **£4,033**

Imperial Gain (USA) *W R Swinburn* 70 a63
2 ch g High Yield (USA) - Empress Jackie (USA)
5^{6g} 2^{6gs} 8^{6sd} **0-1-3** **£1,105**

Imperial Gem (Ire) *Rae Guest* 66 a47
2 b f Inchinor - Pie In The Sky
8^{5gf} 5^{5gf} 14^{5g} 6^{6gs} 8^{6sd} 13^{7sd} 6^{6sd} 4^{6sd}
0-0-8

Imperial Harry *P W Chapple-Hyam* 57

2 b c Alhaarth (Ire) - Serpentara
8^{8gs} **0-0-1**

Imperial Heights *I A Wood* 53 a7
2 b c Imperial Ballet (Ire) - Ruby Princess (Ire)
10^{6sd} 12^{7f} 8^{6f} **0-0-3**

Imperial Lucky (Ire) *M J Wallace* 59 a64
2 b f Desert Story (Ire) - Irina (Ire)
5^{5gf} 4^{5gf} 3^{6f} 2^{5g} 14^{6gf} 1^{7gf} 2^{7sd} 5^{7gf} 3^{8f} 1^{7gf} **2-4-10 £13,629**

Imperial Miss (Ire) *B W Duke* a38
3 b f Imperial Ballet (Ire) - Miss Flite (Ire)
5^{9sd} 11^{8sd} **0-0-2**

Imperial Royale (Ire) *P L Clinton* a55
4 ch g Ali-Royal (Ire) - God Speed Her
1^{12sd} 7^{12sd} 15^{12sd} 11^{9sd} **1-0-4 £1,477**

Imperial Rule (Ire) *M P Tregoning* 75
3 b g Second Empire (Ire) - Alikhlas
17^{10g} 9^{7g} 2^{6g} 5^{7gf} 2^{6g} 1^{6g} **1-2-6 £6,703**

Imperial Soldier *M J Wallace* a63
2 b c Fasliyev (USA) - Hopping Higgins (Ire)
7^{7sd} 8^{6sd} **0-0-2**

Imperial Stride *Sir Michael Stoute* 128
4 b c Indian Ridge - Place De L'Opera
10^{7s} 1^{10gf} 1^{12g} 1^{10g} 1^{12gf} **4-0-5 £126,440**

Imperial Sword *T D Barron* 72
2 b g Danehill Dancer (Ire) - Hajat
4^{6gf} 1^{6s} 6^{6gf} 5^{6gs} 3^{6g} 13^{5g} **1-1-6 £6,257**

Imperial Treasure (Fr) *J J Sheehan* 41 a52
3 b f Octagonal (NZ) - Imperial Prospect (USA)
7^{7sd} 8^{8sd} 13^{9sd} 8^{7gf} 10^{10g} 12^{10g} 4^{10sd} **0-0-7**

Imperialistic (Ire) *K R Burke* 83
4 b f Imperial Ballet (Ire) - Shefoog
6^{8gs} 3^{8s} 10^{8gs} 6^{8g} 9^{8g} 5^{8gs} 3^{7g} 4^{8hy} 3^{7s} 7^{10hy} **0-3-10 £4,833**

Imperioli *P A Blockley* 1
3 b g Fraam - Jussoli
11^{8gf} 10^{12g} 11^{12sd} **0-0-3**

Imperium *Stef Liddiard* 63 a59
4 b g Imperial Ballet (Ire) - Partenza (USA)
7^{5gf} 9^{5f} 8^{5gf} 12^{5gf} 5^{5gf} 10^{6g} 10^{5gf} 3^{6f} 6^{5gf} 2^{6g} 11^{8f} 3^{7gf} 7^{5gs} 3^{5sd} 7^{6sd} 8^{7sd} **0-4-16 £3,009**

Impostor (Ire) *J R Fanshawe* a52
2 b g In The Wings - Princess Caraboo (Ire)
7^{8sd} **0-0-1**

Improvise *C E Brittain* 88
3 b f Lend A Hand - Mellow Jazz
1^{6gs} 4^{7gf} 7^{7g} 2^{7gf} **1-1-4 £11,937**

Impulsive Madam *S Kirk* 38 a39
2 b f Diktat - Decorous (Ire)
9^{8gf} 6^{7f} 6^{7sd} **0-0-3**

Impulsivo *Simon Earle* 34 a49
5 ch g Millkom - Joytime
5^{10sd} 18^{10g} 8^{12sd} 8^{13gf} 13^{12g} **0-0-5**

Imtalkinggibberish *J R Jenkins* 64 a64
4 b g Pursuit Of Love - Royal Orchid (Ire)
2^{5sd} 1^{5sd} 2^{5sd} 10^{5sd} 5^{5gf} 11^{5gf} 13^{6gs} 9^{6g} **1-2-8 £4,997**

In A Fit *P Howling* a42
4 b f Intikhab (USA) - Millfit (USA)
12^{6sd} 9^{6sd} 7^{7sd} 8^{7sd} **0-0-4**

In A Flash (Ire) *N A Callaghan* 78
2 b c Night Shift (USA) - Belle De Cadix (Ire)
6^{6gs} 3^{7g} 2^{7g} 1^{7gs} 4^{8g} **1-1-5 £7,063**

In Deep *Mrs P N Dutfield* 62
4 b f Deploy - Bobbie Dee
6^{10g} 5^{10gf} 7^{12gf} 6^{14gs} 1^{14gs} 13^{16g} **1-0-6 £3,720**

In Dream's (Ire) *B Gubby* 53 a6
3 b g Dr Fong (USA) - No Sugar Baby (Fr)
8^{8sd} 10^{7g} 15^{8gf} 7^{6gf} 16^{10f} 6^{8gf} 4^{9gf} 15^{8gf} **0-0-8 £450**

In Dubai (USA) *M P Tregoning* 81
2 ch f Giant's Causeway (USA) - Bahr
3^{6gf} 4^{7s} 2^{8g} 1^{8s} **1-2-4 £7,589**

In Fashion *R J Hodges* 41
2 b f Bertolini (USA) - Dress Design (Ire)
11^{5g} 8^{5g} **0-0-2**

In Full Cry *M Johnston* 83
2 ch c Grand Lodge (USA) - Red Roses Story (Fr)
1^{6gf} **1-0-1 £4,550**

In Good Faith (USA) *N J Henderson* 65 a70
4 b/br f Dynaformer (USA) - Healing Hands
5^{10sd} 5^{12g} **0-0-2**

In Hope *Andrew Reid* 49 a50
2 b f Most Welcome - Frankie Fair (Ire)
12^{5gf} 4^{5sd} 4^{5g} 6^{5gf} 4^{5sd} 6^{5g} 7^{7sd} 3^{6sd} 4^{5sd} 5^{7sd} **0-1-10 £1,865**

In Reality *W J Haggas* 73
2 ch f Fantastic Light (USA) - Poppadam
7^{7gf} 4^{6gs} 2^{6gf} **0-1-3 £2,005**

In Rhubarb *I W McInnes* 45 a37
3 ch g Piccolo - Versami (USA)
7^{5sd} 4^{5g} 10^{5g} 17^{5gf} 4^{5f} 4^{5f} 11^{5gf} **0-1-7**

In Some Style (Ire) *D Haydn Jones* 44
2 ch f Grand Lodge (USA) - Lovisa (USA)
10^{7gs} 12^{6gs} 10^{7gf} **0-0-3**

In The Fan (USA) *J L Dunlop* 87
3 b g Lear Fan (USA) - Dippers (USA)
10^{7gs} 15^{8gs} **0-0-2**

In The Fashion (Ire) *J Noseda* 94
2 b f In The Wings - Tropical Lass (Ire)
4^{6g} 4^{7gf} 1^{7gf} 7^{7g} **1-0-4 £7,395**

In The Fountain (Ire) *C A Dwyer* 53 a37
2 b f Mozart (Ire) - Riviere Du Diable (USA)
8^{5g} 2^{6g} 3^{6gf} 3^{7f} 8^{7sd} 8^{7g} 8^{5sd} **0-2-7 £2,136**

In The Know *J H M Gosden* a72
3 b c Desert Prince (Ire) - Evocatrice
3^{8sd} **0-1-1 £650**

In The Lead (USA) *J L Dunlop* 82
3 b/br f Bahri (USA) - Air De Noblesse (USA)
4^{8g} 3^{10gf} 2^{12gf} 4^{12gf} 2^{11s} 5^{12gf} 4^{14g} 2^{10gs} **0-4-8 £4,838**

In The Pink (Ire) *M A Buckley* 71 a67
5 gr m Indian Ridge - Norfolk Lavender (Can)
5^{7g} 1^{8gf} 6^{7f} 10^{7g} 7^{8g} 2^{8g} 6^{10gs} 11^{8g} 6^{9sd} 11^{10sd} 5^{9sd} **1-1-11 £5,935**

In The Shadows *W S Kittow*
3 b f Lujain (USA) - Addicted To Love
13^{8s} 19^{10g} 9^{12sd} **0-0-3**

Inagh *R C Harper* 41
3 b f Tipsy Creek (USA) - Compton Amber
14^{7g} 4^{5f} 18^{6g} 13^{5gs} **0-0-4**

Inaminute (Ire) *R A Harris* 52 a57
2 ch f Spectrum (Ire) - Phantom Ring

4^{5gs} 9^{5gf} 6^{5sd} 2^{6sd} 2^{7sd} **0-2-5 £2,050**

Inbuilt Beauty (USA) *C E Brittain* 68
2 gr f Giant's Causeway (USA) - Ela Athena
11^{7g} 7^{6s} 5^{7gf} **0-0-3**

Inca Soldier (Fr) *R C Guest* 28 a63
2 br c Intikhab (USA) - Chrysalu
10^{6s} 4^{7sd} **0-0-2 £351**

Inca Wood (UAE) *R McGlinchey* 61
3 b f Timber Country (USA) - Lady Icarus
7^{12gf} 9^{12g} **0-0-2**

Incense *M S Saunders* 67 a49
3 b f Unfuwain (USA) - Blessed Honour
5^{8gf} 3^{8gs} 2^{8g} 4^{7g} 12^{7sd} 4^{10f} 7^{7g} **0-2-7 £3,600**

Inch By Inch *P J Makin* 82 a78
6 b m Inchinor - Maid Welcome
3^{5gf} 9^{6sd} 1^{6f} 1^{6sd} 12^{5g} 4^{5g} 6^{5g} 6^{6gf} 15^{6g} 6^{7sd} **2-1-10 £10,081**

Inch High *J S Goldie* 41 a50
7 ch g Inchinor - Harrken Heights (Ire)
3^{7sd} 11^{9sd} 5^{7sd} 8^{7sd} 13^{7g} 9^{6sd} 13^{6gs} 12^{7g} 2^{8gf} 10^{7g} 8^{8gf} 16^{8gf} **0-2-12 £656**

Inchcape Rock *J G M O'Shea* 56
3 ch g Inchinor - Washm (USA)
7^{8gs} 10^{8g} 7^{10gf} 10^{8gs} 3^{8g} 4^{7gs} 10^{8f} 8^{7g} 6^{10g} **0-1-9 £654**

Inchdhuaig (Ire) *P C Haslam* 56 a53
2 ch g Inchinor - Be Thankfull (Ire)
7^{6gf} 4^{5g} 5^{5gf} 6^{6hy} 5^{7sd} **0-0-5 £335**

Inchdura *N Tinkler* 46 a47
7 ch g Inchinor - Sunshine Coast
10^{7g} 16^{11g} 9^{8gf} 6^{8gf} 9^{9sd} 3^{8s} 11^{8g} 5^{8sd} 6^{8ss} 5^{8sd} 4^{8sd} 4^{8ss} **0-1-12 £465**

Inchloch *Miss Venetia Williams* 84
3 ch g Inchinor - Lake Pleasant (Ire)
3^{8gf} 3^{8gf} 1^{10gf} 3^{10g} 4^{10g} 5^{10hy} **1-4-6 £6,701**

Inchloss (Ire) *E S McMahon* 78
4 b g Imperial Ballet (Ire) - Earth Charter
15^{8gf} 13^{8g} 3^{8g} 7^{8gf} 11^{8g} 6^{8gs} 12^{8g} 11^{8gs} 10^{8g} **0-0-9 £1,052**

Inchmarlow (Ire) *T H Caldwell* 55
2 b g Cape Cross (Ire) - Glenstal Priory
11^{6g} 6^{6gf} 6^{6gf} 7^{6gs} 6^{6g} 12^{7s} **0-0-6**

Inchnadamph *T J Fitzgerald* 90
5 b g Inchinor - Pelf (USA)
3^{12g} 4^{12s} 1^{14g} 2^{15gf} 1^{14gf} 1^{16g} 12^{14gs} 3^{18gs} **3-3-8 £37,536**

Inchpast *M H Tompkins* 89 a86
4 ch c Inchinor - Victor Ludorum
3^{14gf} 5^{14gf} 1^{14gf} 1^{14gf} 6^{16sd} 2^{14gf} 3^{16gf} 7^{16g} 16^{18gs} **2-3-9 £19,122**

Incidentally (Ire) *R Hannon* 69
2 ch c Inchinor - Top Sauce
4^{6gf} **0-0-1 £545**

Incline (Ire) *R McGlinchey* 76 a35
6 b g Danehill (USA) - Shalwar Kameez (Ire)
8^{8hy} 17^{8sh} 12^{7gf} 4^{7g} 14^{5ys} 2^{7g} 10^{7s} 7^{7sd} **0-1-8 £2,178**

Incorporation *M Appleby* 45 a41
6 b g In The Wings - Danishkada
7^{14gf} 9^{12g} 9^{14sd} 12^{15gf} **0-0-4**

Incroyable *Sir Mark Prescott* 80 a81
4 gr f Linamix (Fr) - Crodelle (Ire)
1^{16sd} 8^{14gs} 5^{16gf} 4^{14gf} 2^{14g} **1-1-5 £5,720**

Incursion *D Nicholls* 84
4 b g Inchinor - Morgannwg (Ire)
9^{12gs} 3^{16gs} 6^{12g} 15^{14gs} **0-1-4 £1,079**

Indalo Grey (Ire) *Stef Liddiard* a65
9 gr g Toca Madera - Pollyfaster
2^{12sd} 3^{17sd} **0-2-2 £1,273**

Indebted *P W D'Arcy* 34 a79
3 b f Royal Applause - Briggsmaid
2^{10sd} 1^{9sd} 8^{8s} 2^{9sd} 9^{8sd} 13^{7sd} 3^{9sd} 7^{12sd} **1-3-8 £7,186**

Indecent Proposal *D R C Elsworth* 79
2 gr f Pursuit Of Love - Impulsive Decision (Ire)
UR^{5gf} 9^{6gf} 7^{5gf} 4^{6gs} 3^{6g} 5^{6gs} 2^{5gf} 2^{6f} 1^{6g} 5^{5g} 4^{5hy} **1-3-11 £9,357**

Indesatchel (Ire) *David Wachman* 117
3 b c Danehill Dancer (Ire) - Floria (Ire)
1^{7hy} 1^{7gs} 1^{7hy} 2^{8s} 8^{8gf} 9^{6gy} 8^{7sh} **3-1-7 £158,489**

India Run (Ire) *J L Dunlop* 62
2 b c Hernando (Fr) - Sirdhana
7^{7g} 3^{8gf} **0-1-2 £446**

Indian Agent (Ire) *M D I Usher* 54 a54
2 b f Indian Lodge (Ire) - Faraway Moon
4^{5g} 4^{5sd} 13^{6sf} **0-0-3 £578**

Indian Ballet *M A Jarvis* 35
2 ch f Indian Ridge - Bolshaya
15^{7s} **0-0-1**

Indian Bazaar (Ire) *R A Harris* 54 a45
9 ch g Indian Ridge - Bazaar Promise
11^{5gs} 10^{5gf} 12^{5g} 2^{6f} 2^{5gf} 7^{6f} 3^{5gf} 9^{5g} 3^{5gf} 4^{5gf} 9^{5gf} 3^{5hd} 10^{6f} 9^{5g} 7^{5g} 4^{5sd} 5^{5sd} **0-4-17 £3,718**

Indian Blaze *Andrew Reid* a53
11 ch g Indian Ridge - Odile
3^{10sd} 5^{10sd} 4^{8sd} 9^{10sd} 4^{10sd} 1^{10sd} **1-1-6 £1,677**

Indian Call *E S McMahon* 8 a9
4 ch g Classic Cliche (Ire) - Crees Sqaw
13^{5sd} 12^{8g} **0-0-2**

Indian Chase *Dr J R J Naylor* 55 a58
8 b g Terimon - Icy Gunner
9^{17sd} 5^{15gs} 4^{16gs} 11^{22s} 1^{16sd} 7^{17g} 4^{14sd} 8^{14sd} 2^{17sd} 2^{17sd} 10^{14sd} 11^{16sd} 5^{16gf} 7^{16gf} **1-2-14 £3,470**

Indian Dawn (Ire) *T H Caldwell* 50
2 b c Indian Lodge (Ire) - Degree Of Charm (Ire)
5^{5g} 7^{5gf} 5^{6f} 11^{8gs} **0-0-4**

Indian Dove (Ire) *G A Butler* a44
3 b f Indian Danehill (Ire) - African Dance (USA)
8^{10sd} 12^{10sd} **0-0-2**

Indian Edge *B Palling* 58 a53
4 ch g Indian Rocket - Beveled Edge
3^{7sd} 2^{7s} 3^{7gs} 2^{9sd} 8^{7g} **0-4-5 £1,475**

Indian Flyer (Ire) *T D Easterby* 41
3 ch g Indian Ridge - Gazar
9^{9gs} 6^{7f} 8^{7g} 10^{11gf} **0-0-4**

Indian Gem *P A Blockley* 41 a48
4 ch f Bijou D'Inde - Cayla
9^{7sd} 5^{6sd} 7^{7sd} 8^{7f} 6^{6gf} 11^{7g} 7^{6gf} 9^{6sd} **0-0-8**

Indian Kate *R Brotherton*
2 b f Komaite (USA) - Indian Nectar
11^{6f} 13^{7g} 12^{5sd} **0-0-3**

Indian Lady (Ire) *Mrs P N Dutfield* 62

2 b f Namid - Lady Eberspacher (Ire)
4^{5gs} 5^{6gs} 1^{6f} 4^{6gf} 9^{5gf} **1-0-5 £3,786**

Indian Love (Fr) *M A Jarvis* 51
2 b f Indian Danehill (Ire) - La Desirade (Fr)
11^{8g} 15^{8s} **0-0-2**

Indian Maiden (Ire) *M S Saunders* 111 a83
5 br m Indian Ridge - Jinsiyah (USA)
4^{6sd} 1^{6sd} 1^{6sd} 1^{6sd} 3^{6hy} 1^{5s} 4^{6gf} 3^{5g} 1^{6g} 10^{6g}
3^{6gs} 8^{5s} 1^{6g} 6^{6g} 2^{6g} 10^{6g} 1^{6s} 3^{5g} 9^{6s}
7-4-19 £111,862

Indian Music *A Berry* a26
8 b g Indian Ridge - Dagny Juel (USA)
8^{7sd} 9^{7sd} 13^{7sd} **0-0-3**

Indian Pearl (Ire) *R J Hodges* 54
3 b f Indian Lodge (Ire) - Thatchabella (Ire)
2^{5s} 12^{6hy} **0-1-2 £820**

Indian Pipe Dream (Ire) *J H M Gosden* 98
3 br c Indian Danehill (Ire) - Build A Dream (USA)
1^{10g} 4^{12gs} 2^{15gs} 1^{14gf} 6^{16gf} 1^{14gs} 1^{16s} 5^{17s}
4-1-8 £36,299

Indian Sky (Ire) *B R Millman* a50
3 b g Indian Lodge (Ire) - Bolero
12^{7sd} 10^{9sd} 17^{8s} 17^{7s} **0-0-4**

Indian Solitaire (Ire) *B P J Baugh* 9 a61
6 b g Bigstone (Ire) - Terrama Sioux
11^{12sd} 12^{12g} 6^{13sd} 11^{14sd} **0-0-4**

Indian Spark *J S Goldie* 71
11 ch g Indian Ridge - Annes Gift
9^{6s} 2^{6g} 4^{5g} 8^{6g} 12^{6gf} 10^{6gf} 8^{5gf} 6^{6gf} 5^{6g}
2^{6gf} 5^{6s} 4^{6gf} 3^{6gf} 6^{7g} 3^{5gf} **0-4-15**
£4,991

Indian Steppes (Fr) *Julian Poulton* 93 a89
6 b m Indian Ridge - Ukraine Venture
2^{7sd} 3^{5sd} 5^{7sd} 5^{7sd} 1^{7sd} 6^{7gf} 5^{8s} 8^{7gf}
1-2-8 £12,116

Indian Sundance (Ire) *R A Fahey* 37
2 b g Namid - Can't Afford It (Ire)
9^{6gf} 5^{5f} 14^{6gf} **0-0-3**

Indian Trail *D R C Elsworth* 102
5 ch g Indian Ridge - Take Heart
1^{6gf} 6^{6gf} 8^{6gs} **1-0-3 £29,750**

Indian Warrior *J Jay* 27 a37
9 b g Be My Chief (USA) - Wanton
7^{7g} 6^{6gs} 15^{7s} 6^{7sd} **0-0-4**

Indian Well (Ire) *S Kirk*
3 b g Indian Lodge (Ire) - Pride Of Pendle
10^{10s} **0-0-1**

Indian Wizard (Ire) *P Howling* 65 a69
2 b g Indian Ridge - Ragtime Rumble (USA)
8^{5hy} 6^{6f} 4^{6sd} 6^{6sd} 8^{7f} 6^{7gs} 6^{7g} 5^{7sd} 9^{7gf} 9^{6f}
1^{7g} 4^{9sd} **1-0-12 £3,849**

Indian's Landing (Ire) *Jennie Candlish* 50 a44
4 b g Barathea (Ire) - We've Just Begun (USA)
7^{7hy} 5^{7gf} 5^{10gf} 9^{12f} 11^{8g} 5^{9sd} 7^{12sd} 3^{9sd} 10^{9sd}
0-1-9 £211

Indiana Blues *A M Balding* 65
4 ch f Indian Ridge - Blue Siren
4^{6g} 12^{5gf} 3^{6gf} **0-1-3 £1,189**

Indiara (Ire) *E A L Dunlop* 56 a53
2 b c Indian Ridge - Siwaayib
10^{7g} 12^{7g} 7^{7sd} **0-0-3**

Indie Skies *M W Easterby* 21
3 b f Diktat - Dalu (Ire)
14^{6gf} 12^{8gf} 9^{8g} **0-0-3**

Indigene *Miss J R Gibney* 7 a26
2 b g Pivotal - River City Moon (USA)
8^{5sd} 9^{7g} **0-0-2**

Indigo Cat (USA) *A P O'Brien* 114
3 ch c Storm Cat (USA) - Bluemamba (USA)
1^{10g} 2^{11gf} 1^{10gf} **2-0-3 £35,242**

Indigo Dancer *C F Wall* 42
2 b g Groom Dancer (USA) - Violet (Ire)
16^{7gs} 12^{7gf} 11^{7gf} **0-0-3**

Indigo Nights (Ire) *Mrs A Duffield* 81
2 b f Danehill Dancer (Ire) - Bent Al Fala (Ire)
2^{5g} 3^{6gf} 1^{5gs} 1^{5g} **2-2-4 £10,512**

Indigo Sky (Ire) *B G Powell* 51 a68
4 gr c Adieu Au Roi (Ire) - Urban Sky (Fr)
10^{10sd} 7^{8sd} 13^{10sd} 9^{12gf} 6^{9g} 5^{10gf} 5^{12f} 13^{8gf}
0-0-8

Indonesia *M Johnston* 73 a69
3 ch g Lomitas - Idraak
6^{12sd} 3^{12g} **0-1-2 £538**

Inducement *R M Stronge* 43
9 ch g Sabrehill (USA) - Verchinina
10^{13s} 11^{12g} **0-0-2**

Industrial Spirit *G C H Chung* 91
3 b c Chester House (USA) - Celibataire (Fr)
2^{8gf} 1^{8gs} 4^{8gf} 9^{8g} **1-1-4 £5,541**

Industrial Star (Ire) *M D Hammond* 64
4 ch g Singspiel (Ire) - Faribole (Ire)
13^{9g} 5^{12g} **0-0-2**

Inescapable (USA) *A W Carroll* a45
4 b c Cape Town (USA) - Danyross (Ire)
14^{8gf} 8^{7sf} 11^{9sf} 9^{7sd} 2^{7sd} **0-1-5 £420**

Infatuate *J R Fanshawe* 82
3 b g Inchinor - First Fantasy
9^{7g} 4^{8g} 1^{8g} 10^{8gs} 3^{8gf} 6^{10gf} **1-0-6**
£5,741

Infidelity (Ire) *A Bailey* 35 a6
4 b f Bluebird (USA) - Madaniyya (USA)
10^{12sd} 11^{8gf} 9^{10g} 15^{9g} 11^{11g} **0-0-5**

Influence *R Hannon* 44
2 ch g Inchinor - Gentle Persuasion
11^{7gf} **0-0-1**

Ingleby Arch (USA) *T D Barron* 86
2 b c Arch (USA) - Inca Dove (USA)
4^{5g} 4^{6g} 3^{6gs} 1^{6g} 3^{7gf} 9^{6gf} 4^{8gs} **1-1-7**
£8,755

Ingleby Cross *J D Bethell* 47 a34
3 b f Cape Cross (Ire) - No Islands
8^{8g} 6^{10s} 7^{7gf} 12^{8gf} 8^{8s} 7^{8g} 4^{11sd} 7^{11sd}
0-0-8

Ingleton *G L Moore* 87
3 b c Komaite (USA) - Dash Cascade
11^{6gf} 9^{6gs} 16^{6g} 5^{5g} 10^{7s} 5^{5s} 8^{6g} 7^{5gs} 16^{7hy}
5^{5s} **0-0-10**

Ingratitude (Ire) *R M Beckett* 77
2 ch c Inchinor - Merci (Ire)
10^{6g} 4^{6g} 3^{6g} 4^{6gs} **0-1-4 £1,335**

Inherit (Ire) *R A Fahey* 56 a31
3 b g Princely Heir (Ire) - Flora Wood (Ire)
7^{7gf} 3^{6gf} 5^{6g} 12^{7sd} 8^{7sd} **0-1-5 £652**

Ink In Gold (Ire) *B G Powell* 47 a38
4 b g Intikhab (USA) - Your Village (Ire)
7^{12sd} 11^{12sd} 10^{12gf} 6^{12g} 6^{14sd} 14^{16sd}
0-0-6

Inka Dancer (Ire) *B Palling* 56 a42
3 ch f Intikhab (USA) - Grannys Reluctance (Ire)
5^{8g} 18^{6gf} 13^{7gs} 9^{7g} 1^{7gf} 9^{9sd} **1-0-6**

£3,066

Inn A Spin (Ire) *N Tinkler*
2 ch f Spinning World (USA) - Harmonic Sound (Ire)
6^{7gf} **0-0-1**

Inn For The Dancer *Mrs H Dalton* 55
3 b g Groom Dancer (USA) - Lady Joyce (Fr)
11^{10gs} 5^{10g} 7^{11g} 12^{12sd} 2^{8gf} **0-1-5 £776**

Innclassic (Ire) *Jane Southcombe* 46 a50
4 b f Stravinsky (USA) - Kyka (USA)
7^{7sd} 11^{7sd} 13^{6gf} 13^{6gf} 2^{5sd} 5^{5g} 2^{5sd} 3^{5ss} 13^{5sd} 5^{5sd} 6^{5sd} **0-3-11 £1,057**

Innocent Air *J H M Gosden* 101
2 ch f Galileo (Ire) - Minskip (USA)
4^{7gf} 2^{7s} 1^{7gf} **1-1-3 £17,288**

Innocent Rebel (USA) *A King* 60
4 ch g Swain (Ire) - Cadeaux D'Amie (USA)
7^{13gf} 6^{16gs} 9^{16gf} **0-0-3**

Innocent Splendour *E A L Dunlop* 73 a74
3 b f Mtoto - Maureena (Ire)
7^{10g} 5^{10gf} 12^{8gf} 9^{8gf} 1^{9ft} **1-0-5 £3,538**

Innpursuit *J M P Eustace* 72 a46
3 b g Inchinor - Quest For The Best
4^{8g} 10^{10gf} 11^{8sd} **0-0-3 £327**

Innstyle *J L Spearing* 7
4 b f Daggers Drawn (USA) - Tarneem (USA)
7^{6hy} 14^{6f} **0-0-2**

Inshaad (Ire) *E A L Dunlop* 17
3 b f Alhaarth (Ire) - Jedwa (Ire)
9^{10gf} **0-0-1**

Inside Story (Ire) *J Noseda* 87 a72
3 b c Rossini (USA) - Sliding
1^{7sd} 7^{7g} 4^{7gf} 3^{10s} **1-0-4 £6,134**

Insider *J A Glover* 39 a38
3 ch f Docksider (USA) - Inquirendo (USA)
9^{6gs} 7^{7sd} 10^{7g} 6^{9sd} 10^{12gf} **0-0-5**

Insignia (Ire) *W M Brisbourne* 59 a52
3 b g Royal Applause - Amathea (Fr)
5^{10g} 9^{8gf} 6^{8gs} 15^{11g} 7^{9sd} 7^{9sd} 9^{9sd} 3^{9ss} **0-1-8 £218**

Insignificance *K G Wingrove* a42
5 b g Bishop Of Cashel - Summer Pageant
6^{9sd} 11^{9sd} 5^{12sd} **0-0-3**

Insinuation (Ire) *D R Loder* 68
3 b f Danehill (USA) - Hidden Meaning (USA)
5^{10f} 5^{12gf} **0-0-2**

Inspector Blue *H J Collingridge* 11
7 ch g Royal Academy (USA) - Blue Siren
11^{7f} **0-0-1**

Inspectors Choice (Ire) *Patrick Morris* 68 a31
4 ch f Spectrum (Ire) - Morcote (Ire)
9^{8g} 11^{8s} 2^{7gf} 5^{8gf} 6^{7g} 10^{7gf} 5^{8f} 9^{8sd} **0-1-8 £1,427**

Inspired Act (Ire) *P S McEntee* a33
4 ch f Fayruz - Rainery (Ire)
6^{5sd} 10^{6sd} 6^{6sd} 11^{5sd} 7^{5sd} **0-0-5**

Instant Hit *M Woods* 65 a72
6 b g Indian Ridge - Pick Of The Pops
4^{9sd} 9^{9sd} 6^{9sd} 7^{9sd} 9^{7sd} 8^{7hy} 7^{6gy} 5^{7g} 14^{8g} **0-0-9 £266**

Instinct *M D Hammond* 37
4 b g Zafonic (USA) - Gracious Gift
12^{6gf} 14^{6g} 12^{6gf} 14^{6gf} 16^{7gf} 10^{6sd} **0-0-6**

Instructor *R A Fahey* 87 a89
4 ch g Groom Dancer (USA) - Doctor's Glory (USA)
3^{9sd} 1^{8sd} 7^{8sd} 8^{8s} 14^{8g} 8^{10gf} 4^{10gf} 9^{10g} 1^{11gf} 1^{9gf} 3^{10gf} 1^{10gf} 9^{10g} 6^{10g} 2^{10g} **4-2-15 £24,938**

Insubordinate *J S Goldie* 60
4 ch g Subordination (USA) - Manila Selection (USA)
15^{7s} 11^{6gs} 7^{6gs} 5^{6gs} 5^{8g} 10^{8s} 5^{6g} 9^{6g} **0-0-8**

Intavac Boy *C W Thornton* 61 a63
4 ch g Emperor Fountain - Altaia (Fr)
12^{8g} 9^{7gf} 4^{8gs} 8^{10s} 5^{9gf} 3^{10gf} 8^{10g} 2^{10g} 9^{12g} 1^{12gf} 2^{12sd} 4^{12sd} 13^{14sd} **1-3-13 £6,633**

Intavac Girl *C W Thornton* 27
2 b f Sinndar (Ire) - Messila Rose
14^{6gf} 5^{7g} 10^{6gs} **0-0-3**

Intend To Leave (Ire) *Saeed Bin Suroor* 76
3 b c Dubai Millennium - Sheer Audacity
2^{10gs} **0-1-1 £1,228**

Intended *A M Balding* 63 a55
3 b f Singspiel (Ire) - Introducing
3^{8f} 5^{12g} 8^{10g} 14^{10g} 6^{10gf} 6^{8ss} 7^{10sd} 12^{9sd} **0-1-8 £630**

Inter Vision (USA) *A Dickman* 96 a80
5 b g Cryptoclearance (USA) - Fateful (USA)
5^{7sd} 8^{6sd} 7^{6s} 4^{5gs} 7^{5gf} 6^{6g} 3^{5gf} 1^{6f} 1^{6g} 11^{6gf} 3^{6g} 1^{6g} 15^{6gs} **3-3-13 £26,515**

Intercontinental *R J Frankel* 120
5 b m Danehill (USA) - Hasili (Ire)
1^{9f} 2^{8f} 1^{8f} 3^{9f} 1^{9f} 1^{8f} 1^{10y} **5-2-7 £662,082**

Interim Payment (USA) *R Charlton* 86
3 b f Red Ransom (USA) - Interim
1^{10gf} 1^{10gf} 3^{10gf} 5^{11gf} 7^{12gf} **2-1-5 £12,430**

Internationalguest (Ire) *D G Bridgwater* 55 a44
6 b g Petardia - Banco Solo
11^{13gs} 15^{12gf} 6^{12sd} 6^{11gs} **0-0-4**

Intigold *A Berry* 61 a56
2 ch g Intikhab (USA) - Golden Daring (Ire)
8^{6gf} 4^{5gf} 5^{6gs} 4^{5gf} 6^{5gf} 8^{5g} 3^{5gf} 6^{5gf} 6^{6sd} 6^{7gf} 11^{6gf} 13^{6gs} 16^{7gf} **0-1-13 £1,127**

Intimate Friend (USA) *Miss Diana Weeden* 53
4 b f Expelled (USA) - Intimate (USA)
11^{6s} 13^{7gf} 9^{8f} 6^{6gf} 14^{5f} **0-0-5**

Into The Breeze (Ire) *J W Hills* 86 a42
5 b g Alzao (USA) - Catalane (USA)
12^{8sd} 11^{8gs} 1^{7gf} **1-0-3 £4,795**

Into The Dark *Saeed Bin Suroor* 114
4 ch c Rainbow Quest (USA) - Land Of Dreams
2^{11gf} 5^{12gs} 4^{9gs} 3^{10s} **0-2-4 £17,280**

Into The Shadows *K G Reveley* 87
5 ch m Safawan - Shadows Of Silver
4^{14gs} 4^{14g} 2^{14g} 1^{12gs} 11^{12gf} 3^{11gs} 5^{12g} 6^{12s} **1-2-8 £14,540**

Intoview *C A Dwyer* 22 a36
2 b f Perryston View - Leave It To Lib
7^{6gf} 4^{6f} 10^{5gf} 9^{7sd} 8^{5f} **0-0-5**

Intoxicating *R F Johnson Houghton* 107
3 b g Mujahid (USA) - Salalah
4^{6gf} 2^{7gf} 1^{6gf} 5^{6gs} 16^{7gf} 11^{6g} 6^{7g} 1^{6gf} 12^{6g} **2-1-9 £34,888**

Intrepid Jack *H Morrison* 105
3 b c Compton Place - Maria Theresa
1^{6gf} 1^{6gf} 4^{6gf} 2^{6g} 8^{6g} **2-1-5 £32,679**

Intricate Web (Ire) *E J Alston* 81 a62
9 b g Warning - In Anticipation (Ire)

12^{8s} 4^{11s} 4^{11g} 2^{10gf} 1^{10s} 4^{11g} 4^{10gs} 7^{10gf} 6^{10gs} 2^{10gf} 14^{8gs} 8^{10g} 9^{10gf} 13^{9sd} 11^{11sd} **1-2-15 £7,513**

Intriguing Glimpse *Miss B Sanders* 93
4 b/br f Piccolo - Running Glimpse (Ire)
8^{5gs} 7^{5g} 12^{6gf} 3^{5gf} 1^{5gf} 3^{5g} 6^{5gf} 3^{5s} 1^{5g} 3^{5g} 5^{5g} 4^{5g} 6^{6gs} **2-4-13 £19,266**

Invasian (Ire) *H R A Cecil* 86
4 ch g Desert Prince (Ire) - Jarrayan
10^{10gf} 8^{8gf} 30^{9s} **0-0-3**

Investment Wings (Ire) *M Johnston* 72
3 b g In The Wings - Superb Investment (Ire)
4^{11gs} 10^{12gf} 4^{12g} 3^{14gf} 2^{15gs} **0-2-5 £5,560**

Invincible Desire *J O'Reilly*
2 b c Tanodaman - Into The Box
13^{7gf} 16^{6gs} **0-0-2**

Iola *B R Millman*
2 ch f Bluebird (USA) - Interregnum
13^{5sd} **0-0-1**

Ionian Spring (Ire) *C G Cox* 91 a99
10 b g Ela-Mana-Mou - Well Head (Ire)
3^{10sd} 6^{9sd} 3^{10gs} 4^{10gs} 1^{10g} 13^{10gf} 4^{10gs} 6^{10gf} 2^{9g} 2^{10s} 7^{9sd} **1-5-11 £15,969**

Iopes (Ire) *Liam Roche* a20
2 b f City On A Hill (USA) - Jemapel (Ire)
9^{7sd} **0-0-1**

Iota (Ger) *P Schiergen* 112
3 b f Tiger Hill (Ire) - Iora (Ger)
1^{10s} 1^{11s} 1^{11s} 5^{12g} 8^{10y} **3-0-5 £146,037**

Iphigenia (Ire) *P W Hiatt* 56 a67
4 b/br f Orpen (USA) - Silver Explosive
9^{7sd} 12^{7sd} 10^{7sd} 12^{8sd} 8^{8sd} 6^{8sd} 9^{7g} 6^{7sd} 7^{7sd} 12^{7gf} 7^{7sd} 10^{7g} **0-0-12**

Ipledgeallegiance (USA) *Miss Tracy Waggott* 45
9 b g Alleged (USA) - Yafill (USA)
4^{14gf} **0-0-1**

Irelands Cross (Ire) *K A Ryan* 64
2 b c Agnes World (USA) - Zaizafonic Davis (Ire)
3^{7g} 3^{7gf} 4^{7gf} 4^{7hy} **0-2-4 £1,678**

Iridescence *Sir Mark Prescott* 57
2 br f Daylami (Ire) - Eilean Shona
8^{6gf} 5^{6gf} 10^{6gf} PU^{8g} **0-0-4**

Irish Ballad *W R Swinburn* 65
3 b g Singspiel (Ire) - Auenlust (Ger)
7^{10gf} 11^{10gf} 1^{12f} 7^{14g} 6^{13gf} 6^{16g} **1-0-6 £2,877**

Irish Hawk (Ger) *M F Harris*
3 ch g Platini (Ger) - Irishfritter (USA)
17^{8g} **0-0-1**

Irish Legend (Ire) *C Roberts* a47
5 b g Sadler's Wells (USA) - Wedding Bouquet
6^{16sd} 10^{17sd} 13^{17sd} **0-0-3**

Irish Piper *T D Easterby* 38 a40
3 b g Piccolo - Freddie's Recall
8^{7sd} 9^{6g} 9^{6s} 6^{7gf} 12^{10gf} **0-0-5**

Irish Playwright (Ire) *D G Bridgwater*
5 b g King's Theatre (Ire) - Marino Waltz
16^{10g} **0-0-1**

Irish Whispers (Ire) *B G Powell* 68
2 b c Marju (Ire) - Muneera (USA)
5^{5gf} 4^{6f} 12^{7gf} 7^{7gf} 7^{8gf} 13^{8gf} 15^{8g} **0-0-7 £418**

Iron Mountain (Ire) *Mrs L C Jewell* 45 a36
10 b g Scenic - Merlannah (Ire)
13^{10sd} 9^{10sd} 8^{12s} 10^{13sd} **0-0-4**

Iron Warrior (Ire) *G M Moore* 47 a34
5 b g Lear Fan (USA) - Robalana (USA)
6^{13s} 6^{13s} 8^{17sd} **0-0-3**

Irony (Ire) *A M Balding* 96
6 gr g Mujadil (USA) - Cidaris (Ire)
13^{7gs} 4^{7gf} 1^{7f} 2^{7gf} 17^{7g} 9^{7gf} 10^{8gf} 10^{7gf} 9^{7gf} **1-2-9 £10,896**

Iroquois Chief (USA) *C N Kellett* a35
6 b g Known Fact (USA) - Celtic Shade
13^{7sd} 10^{5sd} **0-0-2**

Is *Rae Guest* 58 a24
2 br f Diktat - Blackpool Belle
6^{7gs} 12^{7sd} **0-0-2**

Is It Me (USA) *P A Blockley* 63 a54
2 ch c Sky Classic (Can) - Thea (Ger)
4^{6f} 5^{8gf} 2^{8hd} 3^{10f} 4^{9sd} 8^{8ss} **0-0-6 £2,056**

Isa'Af (Ire) *P W Hiatt* 72 a73
6 b g Darshaan - Shauna's Honey (Ire)
2^{12sd} 6^{12sd} 7^{14g} 1^{14gs} 5^{15gf} 4^{14gf} 9^{16sd} 5^{12sd} **1-1-8 £4,882**

Isabella Bay *M Wellings* 52
5 b m Meqdaam (USA) - Orchard Bay
4^{11gf} 11^{11g} 10^{11g} **0-0-3 £265**

Isabella Rossini *A M Hales* 45 a63
3 br f Rossini (USA) - Misty Rain
2^{10sd} 11^{10g} 8^{10gf} 10^{10sd} 11^{8gf} 3^{12sd} 3^{11gs} 4^{12gf} 8^{10sd} 3^{12gf} 2^{12gf} 5^{12sd} 6^{13sd} 11^{13g} 8^{9sd} 7^{10sd} 6^{12sd} 10^{7sd} **0-4-18 £2,985**

Isharram (Ire) *A Berry* 42
2 ch f Muhtarram (USA) - Ishaam
11^{5gs} 6^{5g} 12^{6gf} 4^{7g} 8^{6gf} 4^{7f} 9^{7gf} 11^{7gf} 9^{6gf} **0-0-9 £262**

Isidore Bonheur (Ire) *G A Swinbank* 90
4 b g Mtoto - Way O'Gold (USA)
10^{8s} 9^{8gf} 5^{10f} 12^{10g} 2^{7g} 4^{7gf} 2^{8g} 3^{10gf} 1^{9g} 5^{10g} **1-3-10 £20,296**

Isis (USA) *H R A Cecil* 68
2 b f Royal Academy (USA) - Incredulous (Fr)
3^{6gf} 5^{6gf} **0-1-2 £634**

Isitloveyourafter (Ire) *G L Moore* 43
3 b f Orpen (USA) - Pericolo (Ire)
3^{10g} 11^{8f} 12^{10g} **0-1-3 £216**

Iskander *K A Ryan* 77
4 b g Danzero (Aus) - Amber Mill
8^{8s} 11^{8g} 1^{8gf} 2^{8f} 3^{8g} 2^{10gf} 3^{9gf} 7^{8gf} 4^{10g} 3^{8g} 11^{9gf} 5^{8g} 2^{8gf} **1-6-13 £10,601**

Island Babe (USA) *Saeed Bin Suroor* 51
2 b f Kingmambo (USA) - Shinko Hermes (Ire)
10^{7gf} **0-0-1**

Island Myth (Ire) *M P Tregoning* a70
2 ch g Inchinor - Jersey Lillie (Ire)
12^{7sd} 2^{9sd} 4^{9sd} **0-1-3 £1,387**

Island Odyssey *E A L Dunlop* 63 a62
2 b f Dansili - Tetravella (Ire)
9^{6sd} 4^{7gf} 2^{6sd} 4^{7gf} **0-1-4 £1,530**

Island Prince (Ire) *Mrs A Duffield* 74
2 b g Mull Of Kintyre (USA) - Green Flower (USA)
4^{5gf} 1^{5gf} 6^{6f} 4^{5g} 5^{5g} 3^{6g} 8^{5hy} **1-1-7 £4,328**

Island Rapture *J A R Toller* 71 a79
5 b m Royal Applause - Gersey
4^{9sd} 4^{8sd} 2^{8sd} 2^{10sd} 4^{8gf} 5^{8gf} 8^{8g} 7^{9gf} 2^{8sd}

2^{8sd} 11^{8sd} **0-4-11 £7,373**

Island Sound *D R C Elsworth* 99
8 b g Turtle Island (Ire) - Ballet
8^{10gs} **0-0-1**

Island Swing (Ire) *J L Spearing* 66
3 ch f Trans Island - Farmers Swing (Ire)
16^{6hy} 11^{6gf} 7^{7gs} 3^{6g} 5^{5gf} 7^{6gf} 10^{5gf} 1^{6gf} 10^{6gf} 5^{6gf} 6^{6gf} **1-1-11 £5,284**

Island Warrior (Ire) *B P J Baugh* a15
10 b g Warcraft (USA) - Only Flower
10^{14sd} **0-0-1**

Islands Farewell *D Nicholls* a50
5 b g Emarati (USA) - Chief Island
3^{11sd} 5^{17sd} 3^{12sd} **0-2-3 £421**

Isle De Maurice *D B Feek* 68 a71
3 b g Sinndar (Ire) - Circe's Isle
2^{9sd} 1^{12sd} 5^{12gs} 4^{12g} 15^{14s} 8^{16g} 13^{12sd} **1-1-7 £4,920**

Isle Dream *John A Harris* 12 a3
3 ch f Forzando - La Volta
7^{8gf} 4^{10g} 17^{6gf} 19^{8g} 9^{6ss} 12^{8sd} **0-0-6 £318**

Isleofhopeanteears (Ire) *A E Jones* a46
6 b g College Chapel - Fontaine Lodge (Ire)
5^{9sd} 14^{10hy} 3^{8gf} 5^{10sd} **0-0-4 £315**

Isphahan *A M Balding* 79
2 b c Diktat - Waltzing Star (Ire)
8^{8g} 2^{7f} 1^{7f} **1-1-3 £2,740**

Issa *J L Dunlop* 18
3 b f Pursuit Of Love - Catawba
11^{8gs} 9^{10gf} 16^{10g} **0-0-3**

Issy Blue *J A Osborne*
3 b f Inchinor - Mountain Bluebird (USA)
13^{10g} **0-0-1**

It Must Be Speech *S L Keightley* 43 a50
4 b g Advise (Fr) - Maiden Speech
8^{8sd} 6^{9sd} 9^{12sd} 7^{12sd} 6^{9sd} 5^{9sd} 10^{8s} 9^{10s} 6^{10gs} 5^{12sd} 8^{16sd} 2^{8sd} 9^{10sd} **0-1-13 £423**

It's A Dream (Fr) *D R C Elsworth* a79
2 b c Kaldounevees (Fr) - Bahia Mar (USA)
1^{8sd} **1-0-1 £3,776**

It's Basil *Mrs A J Perrett* 36 a48
2 b g Foxhound (USA) - Marabela (Ire)
11^{7g} 9^{7g} 9^{7sd} **0-0-3**

It's Firefly *Miss Sheena West* a47
3 ch g Fumo Di Londra (Ire) - Try The Duchess
10^{8sd} **0-0-1**

It's My Party *W G M Turner* 44
4 b g Danzero (Aus) - Addicted To Love
8^{14s} **0-0-1**

It's Peggy Speech *S L Keightley* a35
3 b f Bishop Of Cashel - Marsara
9^{5sd} **0-0-1**

It's The Limit (USA) *W K Goldsworthy* 98
6 b g Boundary (USA) - Beside (USA)
3^{12f} 8^{16g} 13^{16g} **0-1-3 £2,505**

It's Twilight Time *R Hannon*
2 b f Royal Applause - Mainly Sunset
12^{6gs} **0-0-1**

It's Unbelievable (USA) *B J Meehan* 69
2 b/br g Stravinsky (USA) - Churn Dat Butter (USA)
4^{8gf} **0-0-1 £600**

Italian Mist (Fr) *Julian Poulton* 33 a66
6 b g Forzando - Digamist Girl (Ire)
7^{6sd} 4^{6sd} 12^{7sd} 6^{5sd} 7^{7sd} 5^{5sd} 7^{5g} **0-0-7 £261**

Italian Romance *M L W Bell* 45
2 b c Medicean - Polish Romance (USA)
9^{7g} **0-0-1**

Italic *Mrs A J Perrett* 63
2 ch f Medicean - Ink Pot (USA)
9^{7g} 3^{8gs} **0-1-2 £761**

Itcanbedone Again (Ire) *Ian Williams* a47
6 b g Sri Pekan (USA) - Maradata (Ire)
7^{9sd} **0-0-1**

Itqaan (USA) *M P Tregoning* 81
3 b f Danzig (USA) - Sarayir (USA)
1^{8g} 8^{8g} 4^{10gf} **1-0-3 £5,422**

Its Alex (Ire) *R J Hodges* a42
4 ch g Tagula (Ire) - Shrewd Girl (USA)
8^{6sd} 10^{6sd} 12^{9sf} **0-0-3**

Ivan Denisovich (Ire) *A P O'Brien* 112 a35
2 b c Danehill (USA) - Hollywood Wildcat (USA)
2^{6f} 1^{6gf} 1^{6gs} 2^{6s} 4^{6gs} 12^{9ft} **2-2-6 £116,754**

Ivana Illyich (Ire) *J S Wainwright* 59
3 ch f Tipsy Creek (USA) - Tolstoya
14^{8gf} 13^{11g} 10^{10gf} 3^{8gs} 3^{10g} 8^{9gf} 5^{8gf} 4^{7gs} 11^{8gf} 5^{8g} 8^{10g} 12^{10g} **0-2-12 £1,447**

Ivans Ride (Ire) *S Kirk* 56 a61
2 b g Night Shift (USA) - Ride Bold (USA)
15^{5g} 7^{5g} 8^{7g} 7^{7gf} 5^{10f} 4^{9sd} 3^{9sd} **0-1-7 £692**

Ivory Key (Ire) *Patrick Morris* 42 a41
3 b/br c Key Of Luck (USA) - Belike The Wind (Ire)
10^{8ys} 12^{8hy} 14^{8gf} 7^{8sd} 7^{11sd} 5^{12sd} **0-0-6**

Ivory Lace *S Woodman* 79 a76
4 b f Atraf - Miriam
3^{6sd} 6^{6sd} 2^{7sd} 7^{8sd} 14^{5gf} 2^{5gf} 5^{5gf} 10^{6g} 7^{6f} 8^{7g} 4^{6g} 7^{6g} 2^{7sd} 5^{6sd} **0-5-14 £3,542**

Ivy Bridge (Ire) *T D Easterby* 41
2 b f Namid - Chinon (Ire)
11^{6gf} 7^{6g} 12^{6gs} 10^{5g} **0-0-4**

Iwunder (Ire) *H Candy* 73
3 b f King's Best (USA) - Sweetest Thing (Ire)
4^{8g} 3^{8s} 4^{8f} 7^{8f} **0-1-4 £1,379**

Izmail (Ire) *P D Evans* 22
6 b g Bluebird (USA) - My-Lorraine (Ire)
14^{5gf} **0-0-1**

Izzet Muzzy (Fr) *I W McInnes* 47 a59
7 ch g Piccolo - Texanne (Bel)
7^{6sd} 4^{6sd} 7^{7sd} 5^{6g} 2^{6gs} 1^{5s} 12^{5gf} 8^{7sd} **1-1-8 £2,063**

J R Stevenson (USA) *E R Oertel* 57 a64
9 ch g Lyphard (USA) - While It Lasts (USA)
7^{10sd} 9^{10sd} 3^{9sd} 6^{10g} 4^{10gs} 6^{12sd} 2^{12sd} 6^{12sd} 8^{16sf} 7^{12sd} **0-2-10 £1,560**

Jaad *M Johnston* 80
2 b c Elnadim (USA) - Off The Blocks
1^{8gf} 6^{7gs} **1-0-2 £4,498**

Jaafi (Ire) *M P Tregoning* 72
3 b c Celtic Swing - Bustinetta
5^{10gf} 1^{11gf} 2^{12g} **1-1-3 £4,480**

Jaamid *M A Buckley* 66
3 b g Desert Prince (Ire) - Strictly Cool (USA)
5^{9gs} 15^{7g} 8^{7gf} 16^{10gf} 5^{7gs} 5^{8g} 11^{8gf} 15^{10gs} **0-0-8**

Jaassey *M R Channon* 59
2 b g Josr Algarhoud (Ire) - Saaryeh
2^{5s} 5^{5hy} 12^{5s} 2^{7f} 4^{8g} **0-2-5 £2,340**

Jabraan (USA) *Saeed Bin Suroor* 60
3 b c Aljabr (USA) - Miss Zafonic (Fr)
3^{7gf} **0-1-1 £852**

Jacaranda (Ire) *Mrs A L M King* 71 a68
5 ch g Bahhare (USA) - Near Miracle
7^{10sd} 3^{12sd} 11^{12sd} 9^{10gf} 3^{10gf} 7^{10gf} 3^{10g} 9^{11gf} 3^{10gf} 9^{10g} 4^{10g} 4^{11gf} 11^{10gs} **0-3-13 £2,917**

Jack Attack *J R Weymes* 54 a37
2 b g Bertolini (USA) - Mark Of Respect
5^{7s} 5^{7gf} 6^{8gs} 9^{9sd} **0-0-4**

Jack Dawson (Ire) *John Berry* 70 a84
8 b g Persian Bold - Dream Of Jenny
5^{12sd} 2^{12sd} 5^{16g} 4^{16sd} **0-1-4 £2,813**

Jack Durrance (Ire) *G A Ham* 40
5 b g Polish Precedent (USA) - Atlantic Desire (Ire)
10^{12gf} **0-0-1**

Jack Frost Nipping (USA) *B Smart* 73
2 b c Miswaki (USA) - Sulalat
4^{7gf} **0-0-1 £294**

Jack It (Ire) *M R Channon* 19 a34
2 b f Distant Music (USA) - Oklahoma
6^{5sd} 7^{5s} 4^{5f} **0-0-3**

Jack Of Trumps (Ire) *G Wragg* 94 a84
5 b h King's Theatre (Ire) - Queen Caroline (USA)
1^{12sd} 10^{12gs} 2^{12gf} 3^{13gs} 2^{11gf} 2^{12gf} 15^{12g} 7^{12gs} 6^{10gs} **1-3-9 £16,902**

Jack Reacher *M Johnston* 65
2 b g Royal Applause - Mrs P
14^{6gf} 4^{6gf} 10^{6g} **0-0-3 £316**

Jack Rolfe *G L Moore* 58
3 b g Polish Precedent (USA) - Haboobti
8^{10gf} 5^{10gs} 5^{10g} **0-0-3**

Jack Sullivan (USA) *G A Butler* 117 a117
4 ch g Belong To Me (USA) - Provisions (USA)
3^{8ft} 1^{9ft} 1^{8ft} 4^{10ft} 7^{8sd} 2^{7gs} 2^{8gf} 8^{7gf} 12^{10ft} **2-3-9 £325,856**

Jack The Giant (Ire) *B W Hills* 77
3 b g Giant's Causeway (USA) - State Crystal (Ire)
9^{10gs} 5^{10gf} 4^{8gf} 3^{8gf} 4^{8g} 2^{8gf} 2^{9gf} 1^{9g} 4^{8g} **1-2-9 £7,200**

Jackadandy (USA) *B Storey* 66
3 b g Lear Fan (USA) - Chandra (Can)
6^{10gs} 4^{16gf} **0-0-2 £220**

Jackie Francis (Ire) *P S McEntee* 45 a30
2 b c Fasliyev (USA) - Appalachia (Ire)
5^{5gf} 12^{5gf} 6^{5gf} 7^{5sd} 6^{5gf} **0-0-5**

Jackie Kiely *P Howling* 82 a60
4 ch g Vettori (Ire) - Fudge
6^{9sd} 9^{10gs} 9^{9g} 9^{10gf} 5^{10gf} 8^{10gf} 3^{10gf} 14^{12gf} 6^{12f} 3^{10g} 4^{10f} 13^{10gf} 5^{10gf} 9^{10g} 1^{10g} 2^{10s} 1^{10g} 7^{9gf} 8^{12sd} 14^{10g} 1^{12sd} 3^{16sd} 4^{17sd} 11^{14sd} **3-5-24 £10,665**

Jackie The Kat (Ire) *Miss D Mountain* 37 a29
2 b/br c Diktat - Abundance
10^{5g} 10^{6sd} 8^{7gf} 12^{7g} 4^{8hd} 17^{8gf} **0-0-6 £312**

Jacks Delight *C N Kellett* 40 a47
5 b g Bettergeton - Impromptu Melody (Ire)
3^{6sd} 15^{8gf} 6^{7sd} 4^{6gf} 4^{6gf} 2^{6sd} 4^{7sd} 4^{5sd} 2^{6sd} 2^{7ss} 2^{8sd} **0-7-11 £1,901**

Jadalee (Ire) *M P Tregoning* 85
2 b c Desert Prince (Ire) - Lionne
7^{7g} 2^{8gf} 1^{10f} **1-0-3 £5,100**

Jadan (Ire) *E J Alston* 81
4 b g Imperial Ballet (Ire) - Sports Post Lady (Ire)
7^{5g} 6^{5gs} 5^{5f} 7^{5gs} 7^{5gf} 1^{5g} 4^{5g} 9^{5gf} 7^{5gf} 7^{5s} 7^{5g} 18^{6gs} **1-0-12 £7,720**

Jadeeron *Miss D A McHale* 25 a66
6 b g Green Desert (USA) - Rain And Shine (Fr)
7^{13sd} 2^{14sd} 9^{16sd} 7^{13sd} 10^{12sd} 7^{12sd} 5^{16sd} 15^{14g} 6^{12sd} 4^{17sd} 5^{14sd} 5^{12ss} 10^{14ss} 6^{17sd} 5^{16sd} **0-1-15 £1,076**

Jagged (Ire) *J R Jenkins* 63 a57
5 b g Sesaro (USA) - Latin Mass
9^{5sd} 11^{5sd} 9^{5sd} 12^{5gf} 4^{5gs} 14^{5gf} 8^{5gf} 8^{5gs} 4^{5gf} 3^{5s} 14^{5gf} 10^{5ft} **0-0-12 £934**

Jagger *G A Butler* 110
5 gr g Linamix (Fr) - Sweetness Herself
UR^{10sd} 5^{12gf} 7^{12gf} 3^{12gs} 6^{14g} 1^{13gf} 5^{18g} 6^{16g} **1-1-8 £26,775**

Jahia (NZ) *P T Midgley* 53 a56
6 br m Jahafil - Lana (NZ)
9^{7sd} 9^{8sd} 1^{7sd} 2^{8sd} 8^{8sd} 15^{7gs} 7^{7f} 14^{7gs} 15^{7gf} 2^{5gf} 3^{6gf} 3^{5g} 14^{6gf} 3^{5g} 13^{5gf} **1-5-15 £4,075**

Jair Ohmsford (Ire) *W J Musson* 73
6 b g Hamas (Ire) - Harry's Irish Rose (USA)
2^{12s} 3^{14s} 3^{14g} **0-3-3 £3,641**

Jaish (USA) *J L Dunlop* 87
2 b/br f Seeking The Gold (USA) - Khazayin (USA)
1^{6gf} 7^{7gf} 3^{8s} **1-1-3 £7,044**

Jakarmi *B Palling* 70 a71
4 b g Merdon Melody - Lady Ploy
9^{12sd} 10^{12sd} 3^{10s} 2^{10g} 14^{12gf} 3^{9sd} 11^{12gs} 5^{8g} 3^{10g} 2^{9sd} 5^{11sd} 9^{9sd} **0-5-12 £3,848**

Jake Black (Ire) *J J Quinn* 80 a59
5 b g Definite Article - Tirhala (Ire)
5^{9sd} 11^{12sd} 1^{10g} 6^{10gf} 6^{10g} 1^{10g} 1^{12gf} 10^{12g} **3-0-8 £18,881**

Jakeal (Ire) *R M Whitaker* 38 a40
6 b g Eagle Eyed (USA) - Karoi (Ire)
15^{6gs} 11^{7g} 9^{8s} 8^{7gf} 8^{8gf} 9^{7g} 5^{5sd} 8^{6sd} 9^{5ss} 7^{6sd} 11^{6sd} 4^{7sd} 10^{8sd} **0-0-13**

Jakeini (Ire) *E S McMahon* 52 a56
2 b c Rossini (USA) - Talita Kumi (Ire)
9^{6gs} 4^{6s} 8^{6sf} **0-0-3 £346**

Jalamid (Ire) *J H M Gosden* 107
3 b g Danehill (USA) - Vignelaure (Ire)
1^{8gs} 6^{8gs} 17^{8gf} 1^{8gf} 4^{8gf} **2-0-5 £26,054**

Jalissa *R Charlton* 83
3 b f Mister Baileys - Julia Domna
1^{6gs} 9^{6gf} 9^{7f} 3^{7s} 12^{7g} 4^{8gs} 10^{8g} **1-2-7 £7,357**

Jalldee (Fr) *Saeed Bin Suroor* 90
3 b g Green Desert (USA) - Princess Haifa (USA)
1^{9gf} 1^{10gs} 4^{12g} **2-0-3 £10,549**

Jalouhar *B P J Baugh* 35 a53
5 b g Victory Note (USA) - Orient Way (Ire)
3^{6sd} 2^{6sd} 1^{6sd} 5^{6sd} 2^{6sd} 3^{6sd} 4^{6sd} 4^{7sd} 4^{6sd} 4^{6sd} 8^{7sd} 9^{6gs} 3^{6sd} 3^{6sd} 2^{6sd} 4^{6sd} 1^{6ss} **2-7-17 £5,235**

Jalwada *D Selvaratnam* 76
3 b f Cadeaux Genereux - Wedoudah (Ire)
2^{10gf} 8^{10gf} 6^{6ft} **0-1-3 £1,520**

Jamaahir (USA) *J L Dunlop* 56
2 b c Bahri (USA) - Elrehaan
7^{7s} **0-0-1**

Jamaar *C N Kellett* 58 a54
3 ch g Nashwan (USA) - Kissogram

8[8sd] 9[10gf] 4[10gf] 6[12g] **0-0-4 £383**

Jamaaron *W G M Turner* 66 a64
3 ch c Bachir (Ire) - Kentmere (Fr)
6[9g] 9[10sd] 7[10gs] 5[11gs] 8[8gf] 2[10f] 16[10gs]
0-1-7 £738

Jamaican (UAE) *M J McGrath* 58 a59
3 ch g Timber Country (USA) - Notting Hill
6[10sd] 4[10sd] 9[12g] 12[13g] 1[12sd] 5[12f] 8[14gf] 9[12f]
10[16s] **1-0-9 £2,891**

Jamaican Flight (USA) *Mrs S Lamyman* 21 a28
12 b h Sunshine Forever (USA) - Kalamona (USA)
10[14sd] 10[17sd] 9[17sd] 14[10gf] 8[12gf] 9[16sd] 7[14ss]
6[12sd] **0-0-8**

Jamehir (Ire) *J Noseda* 73
3 gr c Machiavellian (USA) - Crodelle (Ire)
5[8gf] 7[10gs] 4[10gf] 4[14g] 8[12g] 3[12g] 3[12gf] **0-2-7**
£1,916

James Caird (Ire) *M H Tompkins* 97 a84
5 ch g Catrail (USA) - Polish Saga
5[8gf] 4[10gf] 2[8gf] 3[10gf] 4[10g] 7[10gf] 1[9gs] 7[10g] 3[9g]
6[9g] 12[8g] 6[8sd] **1-4-12 £29,654**

James Joyce (Ire) *A P O'Brien* 84
2 b c Danehill (USA) - Crumpetsfortea (Ire)
3[7s] 1[7hy] **1-1-2 £9,742**

James Street (Ire) *J R Best* 61 a66
2 b g Fruits Of Love (USA) - Humble Mission
11[6gf] 11[5gf] 5[6gf] 7[7gf] 3[6sd] 7[7gs] **0-1-6**
£770

James The Third *S C Williams* 71
2 b c Diktat - Attention Seeker (USA)
7[7gf] 3[7hy] **0-1-2 £666**

Jamestown *C Smith* a25
8 b g Merdon Melody - Thabeh
8[7sd] 10[8ss] **0-0-2**

Jamie's Princess (Ire) *I A Wood* 11 a33
2 b f Mujadil (USA) - Widows Walk
PU[7g] 11[7f] 11[8sd] 8[8sd] **0-0-4**

Jamieson Gold (Ire) *B W Hills* 88
2 b g Desert Style (Ire) - Princess Of Zurich (Ire)
2[6gs] 2[6gf] 1[6g] 6[7g] 3[8s] **1-2-5 £11,223**

Jane Jubilee (Ire) *M Johnston* 75
3 b f Mister Baileys - Elsie Bamford
5[7g] 7[8gf] 7[8gf] 8[8gf] 5[10g] **0-0-5 £782**

Jaolins *M Appleby* a12
4 b f Groom Dancer (USA) - On The Top
11[6sd] 10[7sd] **0-0-2**

Jardines Lookout (Ire) *A P Jarvis* 103
8 b g Fourstars Allstar (USA) - Foolish Flight (Ire)
6[14gs] 12[16g] 15[20gf] **0-0-3 £2,100**

Jarvo *Mark Campion* 58 a52
4 b g Pursuit Of Love - Pinkie Rose (Fr)
7[9sd] 5[7sd] 17[8gs] 4[8sd] 5[10gf] 7[12gf] 4[10gf] 2[10f]
4[12f] 3[10f] 11[8gf] 9[9sd] **0-2-12 £1,605**

Jasmine Hill *R A Fahey* 32
3 ch f Timeless Times (USA) - Coney Hills
14[6gf] 5[5g] 8[6gf] 11[6sd] **0-0-4**

Jasmine Pearl (Ire) *T M Jones* 49 a44
4 b f King Of Kings (Ire) - Tumbleweed Pearl
10[7sd] 6[6sd] 6[6g] 2[5s] 2[5sd] 7[5gf] 3[6s] 2[5f] 4[5f] 6[5sd]
4[6f] 1[6f] 8[5g] 6[6gf] 3[6f] 7[5g] 7[5sd] **1-5-17**
£5,380

Jath *Julian Poulton* 96 a92
4 b f Bishop Of Cashel - Night Trader (USA)
1[10hy] 18[10gs] 4[7gs] 6[10gf] 11[10s] 5[10hy] 12[10sd] 10[10sd]
1-0-8 £10,297

Java Dancer *T D Easterby* 4
4 b g Danehill Dancer (Ire) - Evasive Step
14[8s] **0-0-1**

Java Dawn (Ire) *T E Powell* a42
5 b m Fleetwood (Ire) - Krakatoa
10[16sd] 11[13sd] **0-0-2**

Jawleyford Court *C Smith* a31
6 b m Moshaajir (USA) - Mrs Jawleyford (USA)
5[8sd] 10[8sd] **0-0-2**

Jay Gee's Choice *B G Powell* 63 a50
5 b g Barathea (Ire) - Llia
15[8gf] 8[8g] 15[8gf] 11[8sd] 8[8gs] **0-0-5**

Jay Jay Rocket (USA) *J Howard Johnson* 36
2 b c Kissin Kris (USA) - Party's At Home (USA)
8[5gf] 8[5g] 6[5gf] **0-0-3**

Jayanjay *Miss B Sanders* 96 a84
6 b g Piccolo - Morica
9[6g] 3[6gf] 8[6sd] 11[6gs] 11[6gf] 8[5s] 6[5g] 13[6gf] 1[5g]
1[6gs] 11[6sd] 4[7sd] 10[7sd] **2-0-13 £29,196**

Jaycee Star (Ire) *D Flood* a32
4 ch f Idris (Ire) - Shantung (Ire)
10[9sd] 13[8sd] 13[7sd] 10[10s] **0-0-4**

Jayer Gilles *Dr J R J Naylor* 71 a67
5 br g Busy Flight - Jadidh
11[12sd] 10[14gs] 5[14gf] 2[18g] 5[18g] 4[16gs] 10[21s] 3[18gf]
5[16g] 5[17g] 6[17sd] **0-2-11 £2,471**

Jazrawy *Miss Gay Kelleway* 67 a64
3 b g Dansili - Dalila Di Mare (Ire)
9[8g] 11[10s] 5[10gf] 4[10g] 12[10sd] 12[8sd] 6[8sd]
0-0-7 £265

Jazz At The Sands (USA) *D Shaw* 48 a44
2 ch c Forest Wildcat (USA) - Dahlia's Krissy (USA)
5[5s] 6[5sd] 5[5g] 13[5hy] 9[5sd] 6[5sd] **0-0-6**

Jazz Scene (Ire) *M R Channon* 90
4 b g Danehill Dancer (Ire) - Dixie Jazz
12[8gf] 5[10gf] 8[8gf] 8[8gf] 8[10gs] 13[8g] 12[10s] 8[9g]
3[9gf] 4[10f] 2[10g] 4[13gf] 2[10gf] 13[10gs] 1[11gf] 7[10gf]
2[9gf] 5[9gf] **1-4-18 £18,994**

Jazzy Millennium *B R Millman* 48
8 ch g Lion Cavern (USA) - Woodcrest
8[7s] 4[6gf] 14[7f] **0-0-3**

Je Suis Belle *Miss Gay Kelleway* 67 a66
3 ch f Efisio - Blossom
5[9sd] 7[7s] 6[10gs] 6[10gf] 8[10sd] 8[10sd] 3[11sd] 8[12sd]
7[11sd] 4[10sd] **0-1-10 £506**

Jeanmaire (Ire) *H Morrison* 90
2 b f Dansili - Lovely Lyca
3[6gf] 1[6gs] 2[6gf] 3[6gf] 4[5g] 8[5g] 7[6s] **1-3-7**
£14,775

Jebel Al Tariq (Ire) *W J Musson*
3 b g Desert Style (Ire) - Song Of The Glens
7[6sd] **0-0-1**

Jebel Ali (Ire) *B Gubby* 62
2 b c Fruits Of Love (USA) - Assertive Lass (USA)
7[7s] 6[8g] 6[9g] 10[8gf] **0-0-4**

Jedburgh *J L Dunlop* 112
4 b c Selkirk (USA) - Conspiracy
1[7gf] 10[7g] 5[7gf] 1[7gf] 5[6gf] 4[7gf] 5[7g] 6[7gf]
2-0-8 £45,472

Jedeydd *J S Wainwright* 51 a47
8 b g Shareef Dancer (USA) - Bilad (USA)
7[6gs] 10[7s] 7[5gf] 8[6gf] 7[6gs] 4[6gf] 2[7g] 7[8gf] 6[7gf]
5[7s] 5[7sd] 5[6sd] **0-1-12 £1,060**

Jeepstar *S C Williams* 95
5 b g Muhtarram (USA) - Jungle Rose

3^{14g} 9^{12gs} 3^{12gs} 2^{12g} 4^{12gf} 3^{14gf} 1^{16gf} 14^{16g} 2^{14g} 7^{14gs} 5^{12hy} 9^{12hy} **1-5-12 £28,815**

Jeffslottery *D W Lewis* 46
3 b g Rock City - Thieves Welcome
10^{12gs} 3^{12s} 4^{9gs} 6^{8gs} 5^{9g} UR^{7gf} 10^{8gf} 4^{12f} **0-0-8 £1,080**

Jellytot (USA) *D Carroll* 63
2 b f Minardi (USA) - Dounine
5^{5gf} 6^{5gf} 6^{6g} 4^{5gf} 10^{5g} 9^{8g} **0-0-6**

Jember Red *B Smart* 39
2 b f Polish Precedent (USA) - Arabellajill
6^{6g} **0-0-1**

Jenise (Ire) *Mark Campion* a61
2 b f Orpen (USA) - Griqualand
5^{6sf} **0-0-1**

Jenna Stannis *W Storey* 64
3 ch f Wolfhound (USA) - Darling Splodge
2^{10f} 13^{10gf} 7^{12gf} 8^{10gf} 10^{12gs} 6^{10gf} 8^{10f} 7^{10g} **0-1-8 £1,263**

Jennverse *D K Ivory* 58 a63
3 b f Opening Verse (USA) - Jennelle
6^{5sd} 5^{5sd} 1^{6sd} 6^{6sd} 1^{7sd} 9^{7sd} 6^{6s} 5^{9sd} 13^{8gf} 2^{7gs} 9^{7gf} 9^{7sd} 10^{6g} **2-1-13 £7,239**

Jenny Soba *R M Whitaker* 59
2 b f Observatory (USA) - Majalis
4^{6gs} 8^{6g} 7^{7gf} 8^{8gf} **0-0-4 £633**

Jeremy (USA) *Sir Michael Stoute* 98
2 b c Danehill Dancer (Ire) - Glint In Her Eye (USA)
2^{6gs} 2^{7gf} 1^{6g} 2^{6hy} **1-3-4 £13,293**

Jerome *D W Thompson* 61 a29
4 b g Nicolotte - Mim
6^{8g} 8^{7g} 5^{9g} 9^{9sd} 6^{9gf} 10^{8gf} 6^{10g} 11^{7sf} 3^{7s} 4^{6g} 7^{8s} 7^{8sd} **0-1-12 £484**

Jerry Joslyn (Ire) *J Jay*
3 b f General Monash (USA) - Princess Of Dance (Ire)
10^{6sd} **0-0-1**

Jerry's Girl (Ire) *Miss L A Perratt* 57
3 ch f Danehill Dancer (Ire) - Lurgoe Lady (Ire)
6^{5g} 4^{5s} 9^{5gf} 8^{5gf} **0-0-4 £273**

Jessica Wigmo *A W Carroll* 32 a52
2 b f Bahamian Bounty - Queen Of Shannon (Ire)
15^{6g} 5^{5sd} 9^{5sd} 9^{6sd} **0-0-4**

Jessie *C W Thornton* a38
6 ch m Pivotal - Bold Gem
8^{7sd} 3^{7sd} **0-1-2 £210**

Jessinca *A P Jones*
9 b m Minshaanshu Amad (USA) - Noble Soul
13^{8sd} **0-0-1**

Jeu De Mot (Ire) *J H M Gosden* 94
2 b c Montjeu (Ire) - Nwaahil (Ire)
2^{7g} 1^{7gs} 3^{8gs} **1-1-3 £10,178**

Jeune Loup *P C Haslam* a44
3 b g Loup Sauvage (USA) - Secret Waters
7^{7sd} **0-0-1**

Jewel In The Sand (Ire) *R Hannon* 103
3 b f Bluebird (USA) - Dancing Drop
3^{5gf} **0-1-1 £3,080**

Jezawi (Ire) *M A Jarvis* 55
2 b c Danzig (USA) - Nuts In May (USA)
10^{6g} 8^{6s} **0-0-2**

Jidaar (Ire) *M Johnston* 46
2 b c Grand Lodge (USA) - Banaadir (USA)
8^{6gs} **0-0-1**

Jidiya (Ire) *S Gollings* 69 a73
6 b g Lahib (USA) - Yaqatha (Ire)
1^{9sd} 10^{10sd} 8^{10sd} 11^{12sd} 1^{14sd} 4^{10g} 11^{12g} 15^{10g} 12^{12sd} 7^{14sd} **2-1-10 £7,108**

Jihaaz (Ire) *B W Hills* 65
2 ch c Elnadim (USA) - Gazar
6^{6gf} 6^{7g} **0-0-2**

Jill Dawson (Ire) *John Berry*
2 b f Mull Of Kintyre (USA) - Dream Of Jenny
14^{6s} **0-0-1**

Jilly Why (Ire) *Ms Deborah J Evans* 78 a63
4 b f Mujadil (USA) - Ruwy
10^{6sd} 9^{5sd} 8^{5sd} 1^{6g} 4^{5g} 11^{6sd} 8^{5sd} **1-0-7 £3,965**

Jimmy Byrne (Ire) *R C Guest* 49
5 ch g Red Sunset - Persian Sally (Ire)
9^{11s} 13^{9sd} **0-0-2**

Jimmy Ryan (Ire) *T D McCarthy* 108
4 b c Orpen (USA) - Kaysama (Fr)
2^{5g} **0-1-1 £6,600**

Jimmy The Guesser *N P Littmoden* 71 a82
2 ch g Piccolo - Brush Away
11^{6gf} 3^{6sd} 6^{5g} 4^{5g} 2^{6gs} 1^{6sd} 6^{6sd} 1^{6sd} **2-2-8 £11,794**

Jimmyling (Ire) *J O'Reilly* a4
3 b g Timeless Times (USA) - Miss Walsh
11^{8sd} **0-0-1**

Jinksonthehouse *M D I Usher* 34 a31
4 b f Whittingham (Ire) - Aldwick Colonnade
11^{6sd} 11^{6sd} 17^{8gf} 15^{5g} **0-0-4**

Jive Time (USA) *K A Ryan* 57 a28
2 b g Silver Hawk (USA) - Bold Ballerina
7^{6gf} 7^{7s} 9^{7sd} **0-0-3**

Jockser (Ire) *J W Mullins* 14
4 b g Desert Story (Ire) - Pupa Fiorini (Ity)
12^{12gs} **0-0-1**

Jodonstay *D Shaw* 44 a26
5 b m Komaite (USA) - Cliburnel News (Ire)
10^{6sd} 10^{7sd} 6^{6sd} 5^{6gf} 11^{7g} 18^{6g} 13^{7sd} **0-0-7**

Joe Jo Star *P A Blockley* 49 a50
3 b g Piccolo - Zagreb Flyer
6^{10g} 4^{12f} 15^{8gf} 16^{5g} 5^{8f} 10^{10gf} 8^{10g} 6^{7sd} 4^{9sd} 1^{9sd} 10^{6sd} **1-0-11 £1,782**

Joely Green *N P Littmoden* 44 a51
8 b g Binary Star (USA) - Comedy Lady
2^{17sd} 8^{12sd} 5^{17sd} 3^{16gs} **0-1-4 £1,051**

Joey *R Hollinshead* 58 a48
3 b f Polar Prince (Ire) - Understudy
9^{9sd} 5^{8g} 6^{12sd} 4^{10g} 4^{10g} 8^{12sd} 5^{9sd} 10^{14sd} **0-1-8 £428**

Joey Perhaps *J R Best* 53 a50
4 b g Danzig Connection (USA) - Realms Of Gold (USA)
13^{7sd} 12^{12sd} 7^{13sd} 2^{8gf} 12^{11g} 1^{10f} 10^{10f} 4^{9sd} 10^{9sd} 14^{12gf} **1-1-10 £3,880**

Johannes (Ire) *D Nicholls* 102
2 b c Mozart (Ire) - Blue Sirocco
2^{6f} 1^{6g} 2^{6gf} **1-2-3 £24,834**

John Bratby (USA) *P J Makin* a50
3 b/br c Royal Academy (USA) - Side Saddle (Ire)
5^{7sd} **0-0-1**

John Charles (Ire) *D R C Elsworth* a60
3 b c Fraam - Norwegian Queen (Ire)
2^{9sd} **0-1-1 £1,003**

John Claude (Ire) *Ronald Thompson* 67 a21
2 b g Night Shift (USA) - Koukla Mou
4^{5g} 3^{5gf} 3^{5gf} 4^{5g} 5^{5gf} 1^{5g} 7^{6gs} 10^{5gf} 4^{6hy}

11^{5hy} 11^{5sd} **1-2-11 £6,056**

John Forbes *B Ellison* 74 a34
3 b g High Estate - Mavourneen (USA)
3^{9gs} 4^{8g} 1^{11gs} 4^{12gs} 7^{10g} 11^{8sd} **1-0-6 £5,713**

John Keats *J H M Gosden* 82
2 b g Bertolini (USA) - Nightingale
12^{6gf} 1^{6gf} 8^{6gs} 1^{6g} **2-0-4 £8,775**

John O'Groats (Ire) *B Mactaggart* a10
7 b g Distinctly North (USA) - Bannons Dream (Ire)
10^{6g} 7^{6ss} **0-0-2**

John Robie (USA) *J Parkes* 76 a69
3 ch g Rahy (USA) - Diamond Flower (USA)
4^{5gs} 3^{6gf} 3^{5gf} 13^{6s} 1^{7sd} **1-2-5 £6,120**

John Terry (Ire) *Mrs A J Perrett* 75
2 b c Grand Lodge (USA) - Kardashina (Fr)
1^{6s} 8^{7gs} **1-0-2 £5,772**

John The Hat *D Burchell* 33 a11
3 b g Killer Instinct - Bijou Princess
10^{6gs} 7^{9sd} 11^{12sd} **0-0-3**

Johnny Alljays (Ire) *P A Blockley* a53
4 b g Victory Note (USA) - It's Academic
1^{12sd} 1^{14sd} 3^{14sd} 3^{17sd} 3^{12sd} **2-2-5 £3,553**

Johnny Alpha (Ire) *P W Chapple-Hyam* 69
2 b c Namid - Green's Maud Earl
2^{5gs} 6^{6gs} 4^{6g} **0-1-3 £4,819**

Johnny Chi (Ire) *P W D'Arcy* a24
3 ch g Indian Lodge (Ire) - Bring Me Home (Ire)
10^{12sd} 9^{11gs} 9^{9sd} 13^{16s} **0-0-4**

Johnny Jumpup (Ire) *R M Beckett* 108
3 ch c Pivotal - Clarice Orsini
2^{7gs} 2^{8s} 5^{8g} 7^{8g} 8^{8s} **0-2-5 £40,610**

Johnny Parkes *H Candy* 84
4 b g Wolfhound (USA) - Lucky Parkes
8^{5gf} 9^{5gs} 11^{6gf} 2^{5g} 15^{5gs} **0-1-5 £1,621**

Johnny Rook (Ire) *B R Johnson* 74 a71
4 ch g Woodman (USA) - Tani (USA)
9^{12sd} 10^{10sd} 9^{12s} 9^{12sd} 3^{12sd} 1^{14sd} 2^{16gf} **1-2-7 £4,212**

Johnny The Fish *B J Meehan* 96
2 b g Most Welcome - Ewenny
8^{6f} 4^{6f} 3^{6gf} 2^{7gs} 1^{7gf} 5^{7gf} 1^{6gf} **2-2-7 £182,494**

Johnston's Diamond (Ire) *E J Alston* 96 a81
7 b g Tagula (Ire) - Toshair Flyer
4^{6sd} 3^{6sd} 4^{5sd} 3^{6g} 14^{6s} 7^{5gs} 12^{6s} 5^{7gf} 7^{7f} 12^{6gf} 3^{6sd} 1^{6gs} 7^{6g} 3^{6g} 15^{6s} 12^{6sd} **1-4-16 £17,143**

Joint Acquisition (Ire) *M R Channon* 12
2 b g Mull Of Kintyre (USA) - Vieux Carre
12^{7g} 15^{7gs} **0-0-2**

Joint Aspiration *J Noseda* 107
3 ch f Pivotal - Welcome Home
2^{8gs} 13^{8gf} 7^{8gy} 10^{12g} 9^{9gf} 8^{10gs} 8^{10s} 4^{8gs} 2^{8g} 1^{9g} **1-2-10 £36,220**

Joking John *C W Fairhurst* 35 a13
2 b g Compton Admiral - Bo' Babbity
8^{5gf} 11^{5sd} 9^{6hy} **0-0-3**

Joli Classical (Ire) *R J Hodges* 59
3 b f Classic Cliche (Ire) - Mesp (Ire)
8^{11g} 6^{10gs} 4^{10f} 8^{12gf} **0-0-4**

Jolie (Ire) *R Dickin* 70
3 b f Orpen (USA) - Arabian Dream (Ire)
10^{8gs} 3^{8g} 12^{8gf} 1^{6g} 16^{7gf} 14^{6g} **1-1-6 £4,016**

Jollys Pride *K F Clutterbuck* 11 a48
4 b g Orpen (USA) - Greek Night Out (Ire)
12^{10sd} 8^{7sd} 11^{8sd} 4^{8sd} 10^{9sd} 5^{10gs} 8^{12sd} **0-0-7**

Jomus *L Montague Hall* 50 a65
4 b g Soviet Star (USA) - Oatey
9^{12sd} 16^{12sd} 9^{10sd} 5^{10sd} 5^{8sd} 2^{10sd} 2^{8sd} 2^{7sd} 5^{7f} 4^{10s} 7^{10g} 5^{8sd} 6^{10gf} 2^{10sd} 2^{10sd} **0-5-15 £4,039**

Jonanaud *H J Manners* 68
6 b g Ballet Royal (USA) - Margaret Modes
4^{10s} 3^{15s} 6^{14gs} 10^{16gs} **0-1-4 £974**

Jonathan Josh (NZ) *N J Henderson* 77
4 b g Prized (USA) - Mac's Gold (NZ)
5^{12s} **0-0-1**

Jonny Ebeneezer *D Flood* 108 a72
6 b g Hurricane Sky (Aus) - Leap Of Faith (Ire)
3^{6gf} 2^{7gf} 4^{6gf} 3^{7gf} 4^{7gf} 10^{7sd} 10^{6g} 10^{6gy} 6^{5g} **0-3-9 £32,351**

Jonnyem *G A Swinbank* 43
4 b g Emarati (USA) - Deerlet
11^{6gs} 7^{6gf} **0-0-2**

Jonquil (Ire) *J H M Gosden* 95
3 ch c Machiavellian (USA) - Jumilla (USA)
7^{9gf} 4^{9gf} 6^{10g} **0-0-3 £2,824**

Jonquil Lad *J L Spearing* 40
4 b g Superlative - Daffodil Express (Ire)
13^{8s} 12^{9sd} 4^{11gf} 12^{13gf} **0-0-4 £282**

Jools *D K Ivory* 83 a67
7 b g Cadeaux Genereux - Madame Crecy (USA)
3^{7sd} 3^{9sd} 12^{9sd} 4^{8g} 12^{7gs} 3^{7gf} 2^{7gf} 1^{8gf} 1^{8g} 15^{8g} 5^{8f} 15^{8gf} 6^{8gs} 16^{8g} 9^{7gs} 19^{10g} **2-4-16 £15,782**

Jordan's Light (USA) *R C Guest* 62
2 gr/ro c Aljabr (USA) - Western Friend (USA)
12^{6gf} 6^{7g} 11^{7g} 8^{7gf} **0-0-4**

Jordan's Ridge (Ire) *P Monteith* 17
9 b/br g Indian Ridge - Sadie Jordan (USA)
12^{16g} 13^{14gf} **0-0-2**

Jordans Elect *I Semple* 80
5 ch g Fleetwood (Ire) - Cal Norma's Lady (Ire)
15^{8gf} 2^{9gf} 5^{9gf} 4^{8g} 3^{9gf} 8^{9gf} 4^{8gf} 2^{9g} 14^{10gf} **0-3-9 £6,431**

Jordans Spark *P Monteith* 53
4 ch g Opening Verse (USA) - Ribot's Pearl
5^{9gs} 5^{8gs} 14^{9g} 4^{8g} 4^{8gf} 8^{8gf} 11^{10s} 5^{8gf} 7^{9gf} 1^{8s} **1-0-10 £3,279**

Josear *C J Down* 52 a57
3 b g Josr Algarhoud (Ire) - Real Popcorn (Ire)
4^{9sd} 9^{8sd} 6^{8sd} 1^{8sd} 4^{9sd} 4^{10gf} 2^{12s} 3^{12sd} 4^{10gs} 2^{12sd} 2^{12sd} 7^{12sd} 4^{12gf} **1-4-13 £4,694**

Joseph Henry *M Johnston* 100
3 b g Mujadil (USA) - Iris May
3^{7gf} 10^{7s} 4^{7g} 17^{6gf} 12^{6g} 4^{7s} 9^{6gf} 20^{6g} **0-1-8 £4,630**

Josephus (Ire) *R Charlton* 97
4 ch c King Of Kings (Ire) - Khulasah (USA)
15^{8gf} 10^{7g} 14^{7gf} 9^{7g} PU^{7gf} **0-0-5**

Josh *M A Jarvis* 103
3 b g Josr Algarhoud (Ire) - Charlie Girl
5^{7gf} 3^{6hy} 4^{6gf} 3^{6g} 15^{7gf} 2^{8gf} 5^{7gf} 4^{8g} 12^{7gs} **0-2-9 £14,642**

Josh You Are *M R Channon* 43
2 b g Josr Algarhoud (Ire) - Cibenze

11^{6gf} 12^{7gf} 6^{7gs} **0-0-3**

Joshua's Gold (Ire) *D Carroll* 66 a63
4 b g Sesaro (USA) - Lady Of The Night (Ire)
14^{8s} 2^{9sd} 7^{8g} 3^{7f} 1^{7g} 3^{7g} 3^{8gf} 2^{8g} 2^{8gf} 4^{7sd} 4^{8gf} 13^{9gf} 7^{9sd} **1-6-13 £8,424**

Jostle *S C Williams* 56 a64
3 b g Josr Algarhoud (Ire) - Russell Creek
10^{8sd} 5^{9sd} 4^{8sd} 4^{8sd} 6^{8sd} 5^{8sd} 10^{8gs} 3^{8gf} 6^{7g} 9^{10f} 5^{6g} 14^{5g} 7^{6sd} **0-1-13 £1,103**

Jostling *G L Moore* 54
3 b f Josr Algarhoud (Ire) - Arpero
7^{14g} 12^{10gs} **0-0-2**

Joy And Pain *J R Boyle* 64 a77
4 b g Pursuit Of Love - Ice Chocolate (USA)
4^{7sd} 2^{7sd} 2^{6sd} 1^{6sd} 9^{6gs} 15^{6g} 6^{7f} 12^{8sd} 2^{6sd} 10^{6sd} **1-3-10 £6,728**

Joy In The Guild (Ire) *W S Kittow* 33
2 b f Mull Of Kintyre (USA) - About Face
11^{6g} 10^{6gs} 14^{6gf} 12^{6g} **0-0-4**

Joy Will Tell You *M S Saunders* 14
2 b f Piccolo - Magical Dancer (Ire)
10^{6f} 13^{7g} 8^{8gf} **0-0-3**

Joyce's Choice *J S Wainwright* 44
6 b g Mind Games - Madrina
12^{5hy} 14^{5gf} 9^{6f} 13^{6gf} 14^{5g} **0-0-5**

Joyeaux *S L Keightley* 74 a71
3 b f Mark Of Esteem (Ire) - Divine Secret
6^{6sd} 1^{5s} 7^{5gs} 1^{5s} 11^{5g} 3^{5gs} 10^{6s} 4^{6sd} 2^{5sd} **2-2-9 £9,483**

Jubilee Coin *J A Geake* 36 a8
3 ch f Fumo Di Londra (Ire) - Money Supply
6^{6hy} 12^{7gf} 12^{6sd} **0-0-3**

Jubilee Dawn *H Candy* 59 a31
3 b f Mark Of Esteem (Ire) - Eveningperformance
7^{7gf} 3^{7gf} 9^{7gf} 8^{7sd} **0-1-4 £543**

Jubilee Dream *Mrs L J Mongan* 68 a65
3 b g Bluebird (USA) - Last Dream (Ire)
11^{7gf} 4^{10gf} 4^{10g} 10^{9gs} 2^{9gf} 9^{10g} 8^{10sd} **0-1-7 £2,501**

Jubilee Prince *A E Jones* a28
5 b g Petong - Efficacious (Ire)
9^{9sd} 9^{9sd} 8^{10gf} **0-0-3**

Jubilee Street (Ire) *Mrs A Duffield* 83
6 b g Dr Devious (Ire) - My Firebird
7^{7s} 7^{7gs} 1^{7f} 1^{7gf} 2^{8g} 2^{7gf} 2^{8gf} 5^{7f} UR^{7gf} 2^{7gf} 1^{7g} 1^{8gf} 11^{7s} 13^{7s} **4-4-14 £34,784**

Jucebabe *J L Spearing* 62
2 b f Zilzal (USA) - Jucea
3^{6gs} 5^{6g} 10^{6s} **0-1-3 £619**

Judd Street *R F Johnson Houghton* 91 a93
3 b g Compton Place - Pudding Lane (Ire)
1^{5sd} 3^{6gs} 3^{5gf} 3^{5gf} 3^{6g} 1^{6sd} 2^{5g} 2^{5g} **2-5-8 £22,790**

Judda *R F Marvin*
4 b g Makbul - Pepeke
15^{7gf} **0-0-1**

Judge (USA) *B J Meehan* 93
2 b c Giant's Causeway (USA) - Autumn Leaf (USA)
2^{7gf} 1^{8g} **1-1-2 £6,054**

Judge Damuss (Ire) *A Crook* 24
3 ch c Tagula (Ire) - Acicula (Ire)
9^{7s} **0-0-1**

Judraan *M A Jarvis* 80
2 b c Alhaarth (Ire) - Sakha
6^{6gs} 4^{6g} 3^{7gf} 1^{8gf} **1-1-4 £4,408**

Jumanji (Ire) *M J Attwater* a53
2 b f Imperial Ballet (Ire) - Toshair Flyer
8^{9sd} 4^{7sd} **0-0-2 £278**

Jumbajukiba *Mrs A J Perrett* 91
2 b c Barathea (Ire) - Danseuse Du Soir (Ire)
6^{6gf} 7^{6g} 1^{6f} 2^{7hy} **1-1-4 £9,241**

Jumeirah Scarer *M R Channon* 68
4 b g Tagula (Ire) - Mountain Harvest (Fr)
4^{8f} 3^{7s} 3^{8g} 8^{10gf} 14^{9gs} 7^{8gf} **0-0-6 £1,708**

Jun Fan (USA) *B Ellison* 43 a58
3 br g Artax (USA) - Ringside Lady (NZ)
12^{6g} 4^{6s} 4^{5sd} 7^{6sd} 7^{5sd} **0-0-5 £529**

Junebug Symphony (Ire) *V Smith* 58 a38
3 b f Indian Lodge (Ire) - Ladies View (Ire)
5^{6s} 12^{5hy} 9^{7s} 10^{6g} 4^{8gf} 2^{8g} 11^{8gf} 15^{7gy} 7^{5g} 7^{7f} 12^{8sd} 10^{7ss} **0-1-12 £1,332**

Jungle Drums (Ire) *J L Dunlop* 51
3 b c Nashwan (USA) - Conspiracy
9^{8gs} 9^{9gs} 8^{10gf} **0-0-3**

Jungle Lion *J R Norton* a57
7 ch g Lion Cavern (USA) - Star Ridge (USA)
6^{14sd} 2^{12sd} 5^{14sd} 1^{12sd} 11^{12sd} **1-1-5 £1,871**

Juniper Banks *Miss A Stokell* 48 a46
4 ch g Night Shift (USA) - Beryl
7^{5sd} 6^{6sd} 13^{6sd} 9^{5sd} 9^{5sd} 5^{6sd} 11^{5s} 10^{5gf} 12^{7f} 1^{6gs} 10^{7g} 16^{6g} **1-0-12 £2,917**

Juniper Girl (Ire) *M L W Bell* 67
2 b f Revoque (Ire) - Shajara (Fr)
4^{8gs} 1^{7g} **1-0-2 £4,739**

Junkanoo *K G Reveley* 62
9 ch g Generous (Ire) - Lupescu
1^{16s} **1-0-1 £5,538**

Jupiters Princess *J R Best* 25 a14
7 b m Jupiter Island - Capricious Lass
11^{8f} 10^{10sd} **0-0-2**

Juror (USA) *Sir Michael Stoute* 83
2 gr c Royal Academy (USA) - Paper Princess (USA)
2^{7g} **0-1-1 £1,584**

Just A Fluke (Ire) *M R Bosley* 66
4 b g Darshaan - Star Profile (Ire)
7^{10s} 3^{10gf} 10^{12gf} 13^{10g} 8^{10gf} 15^{10gf} **0-1-6 £788**

Just A Glimmer *L G Cottrell* a70
5 b m Bishop Of Cashel - Rockin' Rosie
11^{7sd} **0-0-1**

Just A Try (USA) *R Hannon* 74 a71
3 ch c Lure (USA) - Boubasis (USA)
7^{7sd} 3^{8sd} 5^{7gs} 6^{9g} 1^{8gf} 6^{10s} 5^{8gf} **1-1-7 £4,097**

Just Beware *Miss Z C Davison* 39 a58
3 b f Makbul - Bewails (Ire)
7^{8sd} 7^{9sd} 3^{10sd} 7^{10sd} 9^{10gf} 9^{9sd} 13^{12sd} 12^{10sd} 8^{10sd} 11^{12sd} **0-1-10 £792**

Just Bond (Ire) *B Smart* 61 a57
3 b g Namid - Give Warning (Ire)
11^{8hy} 7^{8g} 6^{7g} 3^{7f} 3^{7g} 2^{7gf} 7^{7gf} 4^{7gf} 5^{9sd} 3^{8gf} **0-5-10 £2,711**

Just Bonnie *J M Bradley* 39
3 b c Lujain (USA) - Fairy Flight (Ire)
11^{6gf} 10^{7gf} 6^{6g} 15^{7gs} **0-0-4**

Just Cliff *W R Muir* a44
3 b c Handsome Ridge - Justfortherecord

9^{6sd} 5^{7sd} 6^{9sd} 9^{7sd} **0-0-4**

Just Colin (Ire) *A B Haynes* 10 a7
3 b g Shinko Forest (Ire) - Peaches And Cream (Fr)
8^{7sd} 11^{10sd} 10^{8g} **0-0-3**

Just Dashing *J E Long* a14
6 b g Arrasas (USA) - Smitten
11^{10sd} 8^{7sd} **0-0-2**

Just Down The Road (Ire) *D Haydn Jones* 69
2 b f Night Shift (USA) - Avigail (USA)
4^{5s} 4^{5f} 3^{7gf} 14^{7g} 20^{6g} **0-1-5 £1,052**

Just Fly *Dr J R J Naylor* 77 a85
5 b g Efisio - Chrysalis
7^{7sd} 2^{7gf} 12^{8gf} 8^{7g} 7^{8gf} 13^{7g} 4^{7g} 4^{8sd} 4^{10sd}
0-2-9 £3,124

Just Freya *R Dickin*
4 b f Chaddleworth (Ire) - Country Kizzie
17^{10g} 13^{10gs} 11^{9sd} **0-0-3**

Just Intersky (USA) *P W Chapple-Hyam* 73
2 gr c Distant View (USA) - Hexane (Fr)
1^{6g} **1-0-1 £3,458**

Just James *D Nicholls* 107
6 b g Spectrum (Ire) - Fairy Flight (Ire)
8^{7g} 10^{7gs} 18^{7gf} 24^{6g} **0-0-4**

Just Magical *Mrs C A Dunnett* 28
8 b m Emperor Jones (USA) - Magnetic Point (USA)
8^{8f} 9^{10gf} 10^{16gs} 14^{10g} **0-0-4**

Just Observing *E A L Dunlop* 75 a73
2 ch g Observatory (USA) - Just Speculation (Ire)
6^{6gf} 2^{7sd} 3^{7g} 2^{7gf} 3^{8gs} **0-4-5 £3,831**

Just Tallulah *N P Littmoden* 18
2 b f Tomba - Tallulah Belle
4^{5s} **0-0-1 £367**

Just The Job Too (Ire) *L Corcoran*
8 b/br g Prince Of Birds (USA) - Bold Encounter (Ire)
12^{16sd} **0-0-1**

Just Waz (USA) *R M Whitaker* 65 a46
3 ch g Woodman (USA) - Just Tops (USA)
5^{12g} 6^{12gf} 3^{12g} 3^{10g} 5^{12gs} 6^{12s} 5^{14s} 7^{16sf}
0-1-8 £1,877

Just Wiz *J Jay* a48
9 b g Efisio - Jade Pet
7^{9sd} 4^{9sd} 6^{11gs} 9^{8ss} 3^{11sd} **0-1-5 £210**

Justalord *A Crook* 59 a89
7 b g King's Signet (USA) - Just Lady
6^{5sd} 10^{5sd} 8^{5sd} 2^{5sd} 8^{5gs} 10^{5g} 11^{5sd}
0-1-7 £2,056

Justaquestion *H Morrison* 81 a74
3 b f Pursuit Of Love - Queenbird
8^{7sd} 8^{8gs} 9^{7gf} 6^{7s} 11^{7g} 11^{8gs} 4^{8g} **0-0-7**
£467

Justcallmehandsome *D J S Ffrench Davis* 42 a32
3 ch g Handsome Ridge - Pearl Dawn (Ire)
7^{8hy} 12^{7sd} **0-0-2**

Juste Pour L'Amour *V Smith* 81
5 ch g Pharly (Fr) - Fontaine Lady
9^{9g} 12^{8gf} 6^{7gs} 3^{7g} 2^{8g} 4^{9gf} 5^{7g} 7^{10g} 9^{7gf}
6^{8g} 13^{8gf} **0-2-11 £3,473**

Justenjoy Yourself *R W Price* 49 a48
3 b f Tipsy Creek (USA) - Habibi
6^{7sd} 3^{6sd} 1^{6sd} 6^{6sd} 8^{5sd} 4^{7s} 7^{6sd} 5^{6sd} 5^{6sd}
9^{7s} 2^{5f} 12^{6g} 9^{5sd} 10^{6gf} 11^{6gf} 10^{6gf}
1-2-16 £2,434

Justice Jones *Mrs P Ford* 20 a3
4 b g Emperor Jones (USA) - Rally For Justice
18^{8g} 12^{10g} 8^{11sd} 8^{11sd} **0-0-4**

Juwwi *J M Bradley* 48 a49
11 ch g Mujtahid (USA) - Nouvelle Star (Aus)
3^{5sd} 11^{5sd} 10^{5sd} 11^{5sd} 5^{5sd} 7^{5sd} 9^{6sd} 2^{5sd}
3^{6sd} 7^{6sd} 3^{6g} 3^{6gf} 12^{5s} 8^{6ss} **0-5-14**
£1,587

Juxta Pose *H Morrison* 49 a44
2 b c Josr Algarhoud (Ire) - Shi Shi
9^{8g} 12^{8gf} 6^{8sd} **0-0-3**

Kabeer *P S McEntee* 73 a94
7 ch g Unfuwain (USA) - Ta Rib (USA)
2^{10sd} 2^{10sd} 1^{8sd} 7^{10sd} 1^{8sd} 7^{8sd} 12^{8gf} 5^{8gf}
6^{7gf} **2-2-9 £12,243**

Kabis Amigos *D Nicholls* 76
3 ch c Nashwan (USA) - River Saint (USA)
5^{10gf} 12^{12g} 4^{10g} 12^{8s} 1^{8gf} 11^{8g} **1-0-6**
£3,701

Kahira (Ire) *M L W Bell* 50
3 ch f King's Best (USA) - Sine Labe (USA)
10^{8g} **0-0-1**

Kahlua Bear *Miss K B Boutflower* 40 a64
3 b g Mister Baileys - Crystal Magic
5^{9sd} 12^{6s} 11^{8gf} 15^{8gf} 6^{7g} **0-0-5**

Kahlua Kiss *W R Muir* 73
2 b f Mister Baileys - Ring Queen (USA)
9^{7gf} 1^{7gf} 12^{8g} **1-0-3 £3,620**

Kahramana *D R Loder* 33
3 b f Hernando (Fr) - Come On Rosi
7^{7f} 11^{7gf} **0-0-2**

Kajul *C A Horgan* 12 a25
4 b f Emperor Jones (USA) - Andbell
9^{5f} 12^{7gf} 6^{6sd} 8^{9sd} **0-0-4**

Kal *Jean-Rene Auvray* 22 a36
2 b f Kalanisi (Ire) - Towaahi (Ire)
10^{6f} 10^{7sd} 7^{10f} **0-0-3**

Kalaam *G P Enright* a3
3 b g Silver Patriarch (Ire) - Phil's Folly
6^{12sd} **0-0-1**

Kaladin *G L Moore* 58
2 b g Kalanisi (Ire) - Minstrel's Gift
12^{8g} 19^{8gs} 6^{7gs} **0-0-3**

Kalahari Dream (Ire) *W R Swinburn* 63
3 b f Desert Story (Ire) - Hope And Glory (USA)
10^{8gf} 10^{8gf} 6^{10gf} 7^{10f} **0-0-4**

Kalamkar (Ire) *Sir Michael Stoute* 102
3 gr c Daylami (Ire) - Kalamba (Ire)
5^{10gf} 4^{12gs} **0-0-2 £3,250**

Kalani Star (Ire) *I W McInnes* 62 a65
5 b g Ashkalani (Ire) - Bellissi (Ire)
5^{8sd} 6^{7sd} 4^{9sd} 5^{9sd} 3^{9sd} 6^{10sd} 5^{7s} 6^{8g} 11^{8s}
2^{7gf} 2^{7f} 3^{7gf} 8^{7g} 3^{8f} 2^{7gf} 2^{7gf} 3^{7s} 3^{7f} 7^{8g}
3^{8gf} 9^{7s} 15^{9gf} **0-10-22 £6,417**

Kalankari (Ire) *A M Balding* 77
2 b/br c Kalanisi (Ire) - Stately Princess
10^{7f} 4^{7g} 5^{7s} 2^{8f} 2^{8f} 2^{8g} **0-3-6 £4,495**

Kalantera (Ire) *A M Balding* 35
2 b g Kalanisi (Ire) - Tintera (Ire)
13^{8g} 12^{8gs} **0-0-2**

Kalatime (Ire) *A M Balding* 59
2 b/br f Kalanisi (Ire) - Dream Time
11^{7f} 5^{8g} **0-0-2**

Kalishka (Ire) *R Allan* 59
4 b g Fasliyev (USA) - Andromaque (USA)
3^{9gs} 12^{12g} 12^{8s} 9^{13s} 5^{11gf} 15^{10gs} **0-1-6**
£558

Kaliyoun (Ire) *A Crook* 41

4 b g Grand Lodge (USA) - Kaliana (Ire)
13^{18gs} 10^{12s} 14^{10gf} 9^{14f} 6^{14f} 10^{11g} 7^{10gf} 7^{12gf} 6^{14gf} 7^{10g} 14^{12sd} **0-0-11**

Kallista's Pride *J R Best* 73 a64
5 b m Puissance - Clan Scotia
3^{6sd} 9^{6sd} 3^{6sd} 12^{6s} 1^{6f} 8^{5gf} 1^{6gf} 10^{5sd} 3^{6gf} LFT^{5gf} 1^{6g} 1^{6gf} 1^{5g} 2^{6f} 2^{6g} 2^{6sd} 9^{6sd} 2^{7sd} **5-7-18 £22,291**

Kalmini (USA) *Miss Sheena West* 73
3 b/br f Rahy (USA) - Kilma (USA)
3^{10g} 8^{10s} 8^{10gf} 9^{10g} **0-1-4 £1,448**

Kaluana Court *R J Price* 62
9 b m Batshoof - Fairfields Cone
5^{18g} 2^{14gs} 4^{15gf} 2^{17g} 2^{15gf} 12^{21s} 2^{14gf} 8^{16g} 11^{16g} 10^{18gs} **0-4-10 £4,889**

Kalush *Ronald Thompson* 36 a27
4 b g Makbul - The Lady Vanishes
12^{12sd} 10^{9sd} 7^{8gf} 14^{12gf} **0-0-4**

Kamakiri (Ire) *R Hannon* 103
3 b c Trans Island - Alpine Flair (Ire)
1^{7gf} 10^{8s} 13^{7gf} 3^{8g} 12^{7gs} **1-0-5 £19,320**

Kamanda Laugh *B W Hills* 103
4 ch g Most Welcome - Kamada (USA)
9^{8g} 3^{8gs} 12^{7gf} 1^{8g} 7^{7gs} 11^{8gs} 6^{8s} 1^{8g} **2-1-8 £28,038**

Kamari Gold *M Mullineaux* 39
2 b c Cloudings (Ire) - Manse Key Gold
13^{7s} 5^{7hy} 10^{6hy} **0-0-3**

Kamenka *R A Fahey* 38
4 ch f Wolfhound (USA) - Aliuska (Ire)
8^{7s} 12^{7gf} **0-0-2**

Kames Park (Ire) *I Semple* 88
3 b g Desert Sun - Persian Sally (Ire)
2^{8gs} 2^{10gs} 11^{12g} 3^{8g} 7^{8g} **0-2-5 £10,708**

Kanad *E A L Dunlop* 83
3 b g Bold Edge - Multi-Sofft
8^{7g} 5^{8gf} 3^{10s} 2^{10g} 4^{11gf} 8^{10g} **0-2-6 £3,905**

Kandidate *C E Brittain* 113 a106
3 b c Kabool - Valleyrose (Ire)
1^{9sd} 4^{8ft} 9^{9ft} 4^{9ft} 3^{8gf} 3^{8gf} 4^{10s} 5^{8gf} 9^{8s} 5^{8gf} 8^{8g} 14^{7gs} 5^{10sd} **1-2-13 £78,724**

Kane Hekili (Jpn) *Katsuhiko Sumii* a117
3 ch c Fuji Kiseki (Jpn) - Life Out There (USA)
1^{9sd} 1^{9my} 7^{10f} 1^{9sd} 1^{8sd} 1^{10sd} 1^{10sd} 2^{8sd} 1^{11ft} **7-0-9 £1,647,868**

Kangarilla Road *J R Boyle* 73 a75
6 b g Magic Ring (Ire) - Kangra Valley
1^{5sd} 6^{5gf} 3^{5f} 6^{5gf} 3^{6f} 4^{5gf} 8^{5f} 12^{6gf} 3^{5g} 19^{5gf} **1-3-10 £5,831**

Kangaruz (Ire) *A M Balding* 54
2 b c Fayruz - Super Zoe
2^{6f} 2^{5f} 8^{5g} 6^{5f} 11^{5gs} **0-2-5 £1,892**

Kanpai (Ire) *J G M O'Shea* 55
3 br g Trans Island - David's Star
2^{12gf} 7^{12gs} 12^{16g} 5^{17gs} **0-1-4 £732**

Kanz Wood (USA) *A W Carroll* a39
9 ch g Woodman (USA) - Kanz (USA)
7^{7sd} 7^{7sd} 7^{7sd} 9^{9sd} 10^{9sd} **0-0-5**

Kapaje *J Gallagher* 28
3 b f Lake Coniston (Ire) - Reina
8^{7gf} 12^{8gf} **0-0-2**

Kapellmeister (Ire) *C R Egerton* 70 a71
2 b c Mozart (Ire) - March Hare
4^{7sd} 2^{6gf} **0-1-2 £1,755**

Karaoke (Ire) *S Kirk* 75 a80
5 b g Mujadil (USA) - Kayoko (Ire)
7^{9sd} 4^{12sd} 2^{10sd} 17^{11gs} 2^{10sd} 13^{11g} 2^{10g} 5^{10gf} 7^{10gf} 10^{10g} 9^{10gf} 7^{10g} 11^{10gf} 8^{10gf} 9^{10gf} 15^{10gf} 7^{10sd} 2^{12sd} 2^{10sd} 2^{10sd} **0-6-20 £8,082**

Karashino (Ire) *R A Fahey* 73 a7
3 ch f Shinko Forest (Ire) - Karisal (Ire)
1^{6s} 4^{6s} 13^{6gf} 10^{6gf} 8^{5s} 12^{6ss} 10^{7sd} **1-1-7 £4,090**

Karathaena (Ire) *M E Sowersby* 52
5 b m Barathea (Ire) - Dabtara (Ire)
5^{10gs} 6^{10gs} **0-0-2**

Kareeb (Fr) *W J Musson* 77 a79
8 b g Green Desert (USA) - Braari (USA)
2^{7sd} 1^{7sd} 3^{8sd} 18^{8g} 14^{7g} 3^{7gf} 1^{7g} 3^{7gf} 14^{7gf} 9^{7sd} 3^{7gf} 4^{8gf} 12^{7g} 7^{7sd} **2-6-14 £12,327**

Karen's Caper (USA) *J H M Gosden* 115
3 b f War Chant (USA) - Miss Caerleona (Fr)
1^{7gf} 4^{8gf} 2^{8gf} 4^{8g} 6^{8gy} 2^{9f} 9^{10y} **1-2-7 £161,272**

Karlani (Ire) *Sir Michael Stoute* 70
2 b/br g Fantastic Light (USA) - Karliyka (Ire)
8^{8g} 9^{8g} 3^{8hy} **0-1-3 £491**

Karliyna (Ire) *Sir Michael Stoute* 89
3 br f Rainbow Quest (USA) - Karliyka (Ire)
7^{10gs} 1^{10f} 2^{10gf} 8^{12gs} 7^{10g} **1-1-5 £10,359**

Karlu (Ger) *J L Dunlop* 88
3 ch g Big Shuffle (USA) - Krim (Ger)
2^{8gs} 3^{10s} 2^{12g} 1^{12gs} 10^{14s} **1-3-5 £11,965**

Karminskey Park *T J Etherington* 71 a67
6 b m Sabrehill (USA) - Housefull
4^{5sd} 2^{6sd} 2^{6sd} 1^{6g} 8^{6sd} 6^{6gs} 3^{6s} 6^{5gf} **1-3-8 £6,417**

Karrnak *Miss J Feilden* 79 a44
3 b c Hernando (Fr) - Maiden Aunt (Ire)
9^{10gf} 14^{10gs} 5^{10f} 10^{16g} 6^{10sd} **0-0-5**

Karshaan (Fr) *P Winkworth* 66
2 b g Kahyasi - Mon Petitnamour (Ire)
8^{7gf} 7^{7gf} 5^{8gs} **0-0-3**

Kartikeya (USA) *J R Fanshawe* a35
2 b/br f War Chant (USA) - Egoli (USA)
10^{6sf} **0-0-1**

Kasarami (Ire) *J S Goldie* 45
2 b g Bluebird (USA) - Masakira (Ire)
5^{6gf} 8^{7g} 5^{6gf} **0-0-3**

Kashtanka (Ire) *J Balding* a32
3 ch g Ashkalani (Ire) - Spark (Ire)
14^{6gf} 12^{7sd} 9^{6ss} 9^{5sd} **0-0-4**

Kassiopcia (Ire) *M R Channon* 66
2 b f Galileo (Ire) - Brush Strokes
4^{8s} **0-0-1 £354**

Kasthari (Ire) *J Howard Johnson* 109
6 gr g Vettori (Ire) - Karliyka (Ire)
7^{16g} 3^{18g} **0-0-2 £11,000**

Kastoria (Ire) *John M Oxx* 114
4 ch f Selkirk (USA) - Kassana (Ire)
2^{13gf} 1^{12g} 2^{12gf} 1^{12gf} 2^{15gf} 2^{13s} **2-4-6 £79,093**

Katana *I A Wood* 39 a30
3 b f Spectrum (Ire) - Karlaska
15^{14g} 7^{10g} UR^{10g} 9^{10sd} 12^{8f} 8^{8sd} 3^{11hy} 6^{11sd}

0-1-8 £367

Katchit (Ire) *M R Channon* 72 a47
2 b g Kalanisi (Ire) - Miracle
4^{7gs} 3^{7gf} 2^{8gs} 5^{8ss} **0-2-4 £2,580**

Katejackiera (Ire) *R A Fahey* 27 a35
2 b f Rossini (USA) - The Merry Widow (Ire)
12^{5g} 11^{6sd} 8^{7gf} **0-0-3**

Katheer *M P Tregoning* 73
3 b g Anabaa (USA) - Elhida (Ire)
11^{8gf} 1^{6gs} 4^{6gf} **1-0-3 £3,633**

Kathology (Ire) *D R C Elsworth* 55 a83
8 b g College Chapel - Wicken Wonder (Ire)
1^{5sd} 7^{5sd} 5^{5sd} 14^{5gs} **1-0-4 £3,370**

Kathryn Janeway (Ire) *W R Muir* 65
3 b f In The Wings - Freak Out (Fr)
2^{8g} 4^{10g} 6^{10gf} 4^{10g} 13^{12g} **0-1-5 £1,694**

Kathys Job *A D Smith* a4
3 b f Silver Wizard (USA) - Kathy Fair (Ire)
8^{7sd} **0-0-1**

Katie Boo (Ire) *A Berry* 77
3 br f Namid - Misty Peak (Ire)
6^{5s} 5^{6g} 10^{6gf} 8^{6s} 8^{6g} **0-0-5**

Katie Killane *M Wellings* 20 a40
3 ch f Komaite (USA) - Efficacy
5^{6sd} 6^{6sd} 3^{6sd} 5^{5sd} 12^{5g} 13^{6sd} **0-1-6 £206**

Katie Lawson (Ire) *D Haydn Jones* a42
2 b f Xaar - Idle Chat (USA)
9^{7sd} 12^{7sd} 8^{8sd} **0-0-3**

Katies House *J J Quinn* 24
2 gr f Paris House - Rum Lass
11^{6gs} 9^{7s} **0-0-2**

Katies Tuitor *B W Duke* 64 a72
2 b g Kayf Tara - Penny Gold (Ire)
5^{8gs} 1^{8sd} **1-0-2 £3,387**

Katiypour (Ire) *Miss B Sanders* 92 a96
8 ch g Be My Guest (USA) - Katiyfa
1^{7sd} 2^{7sd} 1^{6sd} 1^{6sd} 4^{7sd} 8^{7g} 5^{7g} 2^{7gf} 1^{7gf} 6^{9g} 3^{7gf} 4^{7gf} 10^{6gf} 3^{7g} 6^{6sd} **4-4-15 £41,217**

Katrina Ballerina (Ire) *P C Haslam*
2 b f Imperial Ballet (Ire) - Sheznice (Ire)
10^{5sd} **0-0-1**

Katsumoto (Ire) *N P Littmoden* 29 a60
2 ch g Muhtarram (USA) - Self Assured (Ire)
22^{8gs} 9^{8sd} 7^{9sd} **0-0-3**

Katy Jem *D M Simcock* 62
3 b f Night Shift (USA) - Top Jem
8^{8g} **0-0-1**

Katy O'Hara *Miss S E Hall* a23
6 b m Komaite (USA) - Amy Leigh (Ire)
6^{7sd} **0-0-1**

Kavachi (Ire) *E A L Dunlop* 59 a67
2 b c Cadeaux Genereux - Answered Prayer
5^{8sd} 7^{9g} **0-0-2**

Kaveri (USA) *C E Brittain* 82 a82
2 b/br f War Chant (USA) - Valid Bonnet (USA)
9^{5gf} 4^{6gf} 1^{7g} 10^{8s} 3^{7sd} **1-1-5 £6,494**

Kavi (Ire) *Simon Earle* 56 a76
5 ch g Perugino (USA) - Premier Leap (Ire)
1^{12sd} 2^{13sd} 1^{12sd} 9^{12sd} 2^{12sd} 6^{14gs} 5^{13gf} **2-2-7 £8,906**

Kawacatoose (Ire) *G C Bravery* 31 a34
3 b g Imperial Ballet (Ire) - Cree's Figurine
11^{6sd} 10^{6sd} 9^{8g} **0-0-3**

Kawn *M P Tregoning* 38
3 b f Cadeaux Genereux - Khubza
6^{7g} **0-0-1**

Kay Two (Ire) *Ms F M Crowley* 105
3 ch c Monashee Mountain (USA) - Tricky
4^{5g} 6^{5gf} 5^{5gf} 6^{5g} 3^{6g} 5^{6gy} 12^{7sh} 4^{6gy} 5^{5ys} **0-1-9 £7,317**

Kayf Aramis *J L Spearing* 52
3 b g Kayf Tara - Ara
13^{10gf} 5^{13gf} 3^{16g} 4^{16s} 4^{16g} 8^{17g} 6^{18gs} **0-2-7 £500**

Kaylianni *M R Channon* 86
2 b f Kalanisi (Ire) - Vivianna
8^{8g} 6^{7gs} **0-0-2 £352**

Kaymich Perfecto *R M Whitaker* 80 a59
5 b g Sheikh Albadou - Manhattan Diamond
6^{8s} 4^{8gs} 2^{8gf} 3^{7f} 1^{9f} 3^{8gf} 7^{10g} 6^{8gf} 3^{9gf} 5^{9gf} 1^{8gf} 2^{8gf} 5^{8g} 2^{8g} 5^{8gf} 10^{8g} 13^{10s} 10^{10sd} **2-7-18 £12,164**

Kayrati *J Wade* 49
2 b f Cayman Kai (Ire) - Emmajoun
6^{5gf} 7^{6gf} 11^{5gf} 4^{6gf} 9^{5gf} 10^{5gf} **0-0-6**

Kazatzka *J R Fanshawe* 46 a58
3 ch f Groom Dancer (USA) - Kalinka (Ire)
3^{9sd} 8^{10sd} 7^{9gf} **0-1-3 £529**

Keel (Ire) *J A Osborne* 68
2 b g Carrowkeel (Ire) - First Degree
6^{7gf} 2^{6g} 6^{6g} **0-1-3 £1,263**

Keelings Donabate *K R Burke* a43
2 b g Desert Style (Ire) - Sideloader Special
5^{7sd} **0-0-1**

Keeneland Swan (USA) *Hideyuki Mori* 114
6 ch h Distant View (USA) - To Act (USA)
9^{6f} 15^{6f} 1^{6f} 2^{6f} 10^{7g} 10^{6f} 12^{6gs} 5^{6f} **1-1-8 £457,968**

Keenstar *Jedd O'Keeffe*
2 ch f Keen - Sweet Solitaire
7^{8sd} **0-0-1**

Keep Attacking (Ire) *A M Balding* 57
2 b f Hernando (Fr) - Mara River
6^{7gs} 7^{7gf} 10^{7g} 10^{8g} 8^{7gs} **0-0-5**

Keep Bacckinhit (Ire) *G L Moore* 51 a51
3 b f Raise A Grand (Ire) - Taispeain (Ire)
9^{7gs} 7^{6g} 6^{7g} 16^{6gf} 13^{7sd} **0-0-5**

Keep Me Warm *P A Blockley* a73
3 ch g Atraf - Little Greenbird
3^{7sd} 1^{7sd} **1-1-2 £3,361**

Keep On Movin' (Ire) *N A Callaghan* 70 a60
4 b f Danehill Dancer (Ire) - Tormented (USA)
5^{12sd} 4^{12s} 8^{12sd} 10^{10sd} **0-0-4 £262**

Keepasharplookout (Ire) *C W Moore* 27 a46
3 b g Rossini (USA) - Zoyce
6^{6sd} 10^{7sd} 6^{7s} **0-0-3**

Keeper's Lodge (Ire) *E S McMahon* 73 a66
4 ch f Grand Lodge (USA) - Gembira (USA)
7^{8gf} 5^{10gf} 8^{10gs} 9^{9sd} 4^{10gs} 2^{11g} 2^{10g} 9^{8gs} 8^{11gs} 8^{10gf} **0-2-10 £2,686**

Keepers Knight (Ire) *Karen McLintock* 59 a59
4 b c Sri Pekan (USA) - Keepers Dawn (Ire)
10^{12sd} 5^{12sd} 2^{12sd} 4^{12gf} 2^{16gf} 7^{14gf} 4^{16gf} **0-2-7 £2,125**

Kelly Nicole (Ire) *C Von Der Recke* 81 a64
3 b f Rainbow Quest (USA) - Banquise (Ire)
9^{7sd} 2^{7sd} 8^{9sd} 4^{8s} 5^{11gs} 1^{10g} 1^{9s} 1^{8g} 8^{8gs} 12^{10gf} 10^{9g} 13^{12s} **3-1-12 £13,926**

Keltic Rainbow (Ire) *D Haydn Jones* 48 a48
4 b f Spectrum (Ire) - Secrets Of Honour
1^{12sd} 3^{12sd} 8^{11sd} 3^{12sd} 8^{14sd} 12^{12sd} 4^{12sd} 3^{12gs} 4^{12g} 5^{12sd} 10^{12g} 2^{14sd} 6^{12sd} 11^{14ss} **1-3-14 £2,817**

Kelucia (Ire) *J S Goldie* 88
4 ch f Grand Lodge (USA) - Karachi (Spa)
6^{8gf} 12^{7g} 7^{7gf} 5^{8s} 1^{8g} **1-0-5 £7,934**

Kempsey *J J Bridger* 67 a66
3 ch g Wolfhound (USA) - Mockingbird
3^{5sd} 4^{6sd} 8^{6sd} 2^{6sd} 4^{5sd} 10^{6sd} 5^{6g} 10^{6sd} 1^{5gs} 4^{5g} 8^{5s} 12^{5gs} 4^{6s} 5^{6sd} 7^{5sd} **1-2-15 £7,099**

Kenmore *B W Hills* 99
3 b c Compton Place - Watheeqah (USA)
1^{6g} 4^{7s} 6^{7g} 14^{7g} 1^{7gs} **2-0-5 £17,268**

Kennington *Mrs C A Dunnett* 68 a77
5 ch g Compton Place - Mim
11^{6sd} 9^{5sd} 1^{6sd} 1^{6s} 7^{5hy} 10^{5sd} 7^{6g} 3^{6g} 11^{6g} 4^{5gs} 4^{5gf} 2^{6sd} 1^{6g} 4^{6g} 6^{5gs} 6^{6sd} 3^{6sd} 1^{5sd} **4-3-18 £14,563**

Kenny The Truth (Ire) *B D Leavy* a31
6 b g Robellino (USA) - Just Blink (Ire)
7^{8sd} 4^{8sd} 9^{7sd} 14^{8sd} **0-0-4**

Kensington (Ire) *P D Evans* 67 a69
4 b g Cape Cross (Ire) - March Star (Ire)
14^{6s} 13^{6s} 13^{6g} 4^{5f} 12^{6f} 1^{6f} 3^{6f} 3^{7g} 6^{7s} 1^{5g} 1^{7sd} 2^{6sd} 3^{7sd} **3-4-13 £12,455**

Kentavr's Dream *P Howling* 28 a24
2 b f Robellino (USA) - Very Good
15^{6gf} 9^{6sd} **0-0-2**

Kentucky Blue (Ire) *T D Easterby* 71
5 b g Revoque (Ire) - Delta Town (USA)
9^{12gf} 9^{12g} **0-0-2**

Kentucky Bullet (USA) *A G Newcombe* 28 a54
9 b g Housebuster (USA) - Exactly So
4^{11sd} 2^{12sd} 2^{11sd} 9^{12sd} 3^{11sd} 8^{10gf} 1^{12sd} 11^{10g} 2^{12sd} 1^{11sd} 6^{12sd} 1^{11ss} **3-4-12 £7,559**

Kentucky Express *T D Easterby* 59
4 b c Air Express (Ire) - Hotel California (Ire)
5^{6g} 7^{6s} 9^{5f} 11^{6g} **0-0-4**

Kenwyn *Simon Earle* 68 a38
3 b g Efisio - Vilany
4^{7gf} 11^{7sd} 5^{8gf} 14^{8gf} 8^{8gs} **0-0-5 £356**

Keon (Ire) *R Hollinshead* 62 a66
3 b c Rossini (USA) - Lonely Brook (USA)
3^{7sd} 6^{7g} 11^{8g} 11^{8gf} 12^{9sd} 17^{8g} 5^{9gf} 8^{9sd} 7^{6sf} 8^{8sd} **0-1-10 £531**

Kept Faith (Ire) *Saeed Bin Suroor* 73
2 ch c Storm Cat (USA) - Good Mood (USA)
2^{6gf} 8^{6gs} **0-1-2 £1,284**

Ker Lani (Fr) *R Pritchard-Gordon* 77
2 b f Ashkalani (Ire) - Hier Deja (Fr)
3^{5gs} 3^{5g} 6^{5f} **0-2-3 £4,430**

Kerashan (Ire) *Sir Michael Stoute* 105 a101
3 b g Sinndar (Ire) - Kerataka (Ire)
1^{9g} 2^{10g} 2^{10gs} 13^{12s} 3^{10sd} 1^{12g} 4^{12s} **2-3-7 £48,699**

Keresforth *Mrs L C Jewell* 24 a64
3 b g Mind Games - Bullion
11^{6sd} 1^{5sd} 8^{5sd} 7^{5sd} 5^{6sd} 4^{5sd} 10^{7sd} 15^{5gf} 10^{6g} 9^{6gf} 11^{6sd} **1-0-11 £3,359**

Kernel Dowery (Ire) *W R Swinburn* 56 a60
5 b g Sri Pekan (USA) - Lady Dowery (USA)
2^{12sd} 3^{10f} 4^{12g} 3^{13gf} 2^{13gf} 8^{12g} 4^{10g} 4^{11gf} **0-5-8 £3,011**

Kerriemuir Lass (Ire) *M A Jarvis* 61
2 b f Celtic Swing - Shabby Chic (USA)
8^{8g} **0-0-1**

Kerry'Skick *P R Hedger* 68
3 b c Diktat - Urchin (Ire)
4^{8gs} 8^{8g} 4^{8gs} **0-0-3 £694**

Kerry's Blade (Ire) *P C Haslam* 56
3 ch g Daggers Drawn (USA) - Treasure (Ire)
13^{10f} 9^{10gf} 13^{10gs} **0-0-3**

Keshya *N P Littmoden* 75 a72
4 b f Mtoto - Liberatrice (Fr)
3^{9sd} 4^{10s} 2^{8s} 1^{9sd} 7^{9sd} 2^{8g} 12^{8g} 7^{10s} 3^{8hy} RR^{10sd} **1-4-10 £7,230**

Kettong (Ire) *M D Hammond*
5 b m Among Men (USA) - Kettenblume
12^{7sd} **0-0-1**

Kevins View (Ire) *A W Carroll* 28
9 ch g Brief Truce (USA) - Day Dress
13^{12s} 5^{17f} 10^{14gf} **0-0-3**

Kew Green (USA) *P R Webber* 109 a110
7 b/br g Brocco (USA) - Jump With Joy (USA)
2^{10sd} 3^{9sd} 1^{10sd} 1^{10gs} 1^{9g} 15^{10g} 29^{9s} 1^{10sd} **4-2-8 £96,326**

Kew The Music *M R Channon* 69 a74
5 b g Botanic (USA) - Harmonia
1^{7sd} 3^{7sd} 4^{8sd} 4^{7sd} 7^{9sd} 3^{7gf} 3^{8gf} 2^{8g} 4^{8hy} 5^{7gf} 10^{7gf} 6^{7s} 3^{7g} 4^{7f} 2^{7g} 4^{7gf} 8^{7gs} 4^{7hy} 4^{6sd} 6^{6sd} **1-7-20 £10,500**

Key Factor *M W Easterby* a19
4 b f Defacto (USA) - Onemoretime
10^{9sd} **0-0-1**

Key In *I W McInnes* 51
4 ch f Unfuwain (USA) - Fleet Key
6^{12s} 6^{16gs} 7^{16f} 14^{14f} **0-0-4**

Key Of Gold (Ire) *A G Juckes* a44
4 b g Key Of Luck (USA) - Damaslin
9^{9sd} 5^{9sd} 13^{6sd} **0-0-3**

Key Of Magic (Ire) *J Hetherton* 6 a10
2 b g Key Of Luck (USA) - Desirous Of Peace
12^{7sd} 5^{5gf} 11^{6sd} **0-0-3**

Key Of Solomon (Ire) *H Morrison* 58 a56
3 ch g Machiavellian (USA) - Minerva (Ire)
4^{9gs} 10^{8sd} 8^{10g} **0-0-3 £525**

Key Partners (Ire) *P A Blockley* 66
4 b g Key Of Luck (USA) - Teacher Preacher (Ire)
10^{8gs} 13^{7g} 9^{8g} 7^{10gf} 13^{8g} **0-0-5**

Key Time (Ire) *Sir Mark Prescott* 66 a48
3 b g Darshaan - Kasota (Ire)
9^{8sd} 8^{7sd} 8^{7sd} 11^{7sd} 4^{11gf} 2^{12s} 1^{16g} **1-1-7 £5,744**

Keyaki (Ire) *C F Wall* 83
4 b f Shinko Forest (Ire) - Woodie Dancer (USA)
4^{6g} 1^{7g} 4^{7gf} 9^{8g} 6^{8g} 11^{7g} 7^{7g} **1-0-7 £8,346**

Keyalzao (Ire) *A Crook* 38
3 b f Alzao (USA) - Key Partner
6^{8sd} 6^{12s} 6^{7f} 5^{7gf} 9^{7g} **0-0-5**

Keylime (Ire) *J Noseda* 52
3 b f Green Desert (USA) - Comme D'Habitude (USA)
7^{7gf} 3^{8gf} 11^{6g} **0-1-3 £550**

Keys Of Cyprus *D Nicholls* 69
3 ch g Deploy - Krisia
1^{6gf} 12^{6g} **1-0-2 £3,513**

Kez *V Smith* 65
9 b g Polar Falcon (USA) - Briggsmaid

10[15gf] 5[12f] 10[12g] 8[12gf] **0-0-4**

Khabfair *Mrs A J Perrett* 103
4 b c Intikhab (USA) - Ruby Affair (Ire)
8[7gf] 9[7gf] 22[7gf] 6[6gf] 13[5s] 4[6gf] 7[6g] 4[7gf] 5[6s] **0-0-9 £3,408**

Khalidia (USA) *M A Magnusson* a68
4 b g Boundary (USA) - Maniches Slew (USA)
11[7sd] **0-0-1**

Khanjar (USA) *K R Burke* 79 a79
5 ch g Kris S (USA) - Alyssum (USA)
11[10sd] 7[8g] 2[8gf] 8[11gf] 5[8gf] 6[8gf] 4[9gf] 3[9sd] 2[9sd] 3[9sd] 3[12sd] 1[12sd] **1-5-12 £10,574**

Kharaline (Ire) *K R Burke* 27
3 b f Spectrum (Ire) - Kharaliya (Fr)
10[9s] 12[7gs] **0-0-2**

Kharish (Ire) *J Noseda* 99
3 b g Desert Prince (Ire) - Moy Water (Ire)
2[11f] 8[12gf] 3[10gf] 3[10g] 6[10g] **0-2-5 £12,191**

Khe Sanh *R A Harris* 65 a77
3 b f Mtoto - Hoh Chi Min
1[8sd] 3[8sd] 12[8g] 8[8g] 5[8gf] 7[8g] 6[8sd] F[7sd] **1-1-8 £4,631**

Khorkina (Ire) *J G Given* 17
2 b f Soviet Star (USA) - Philgwyn
13[6gf] 9[6gf] 18[8s] **0-0-3**

Khyber Kim *H Candy* 106
3 b g Mujahid (USA) - Jungle Rose
1[11g] 2[10gs] 1[10gs] **2-1-3 £19,623**

Khyber Knight (Ire) *Jane Southcombe* 42
2 b f Night Shift (USA) - Peshawar
5[5gs] 10[5g] 17[7gf] **0-0-3**

Kiama *H Morrison* 70 a66
3 b f Dansili - Catriona
8[8g] 3[10g] 2[11g] 5[12sd] 2[12sd] 2[12g] 2[16g] 11[14g] **0-5-8 £4,838**

Kibosh (Ire) *P D Evans* 39
2 b f Elnadim (USA) - Dazzling Fire (Ire)
14[5g] 5[6gf] 7[6f] 7[5gf] **0-0-4**

Kick And Prance *J A Geake* 60
2 ch c Groom Dancer (USA) - Unerring
7[7g] 14[7gf] 6[8gs] **0-0-3**

Kid'Z'Play (Ire) *J S Goldie* 64
9 b g Rudimentary (USA) - Saka Saka
7[14gs] 5[13gs] 6[12s] 11[12s] **0-0-4**

Kiev (Ire) *D G Bridgwater* 49 a42
5 b g Bahhare (USA) - Badrah (USA)
2[12s] 6[14gf] 3[12gf] 8[12gf] 12[16gs] 7[17sd] 10[18gf] 5[13sd] 9[17sf] **0-1-9 £786**

Kilbarri *M Johnston* 68
2 b c Zafonic (USA) - Gentle Dame
5[6s] 3[6gs] 4[7gf] 5[7gf] 1[8g] **1-1-5 £4,720**

Kildonan Castle *Mrs G S Rees* 56 a35
2 b c Forzando - Katie Komaite
13[6g] 5[5g] 11[6sd] 8[6g] 13[6gf] 8[7g] **0-0-6**

Kill Cat (Ire) *A Peraino* 105 a91
4 b/br c Catrail (USA) - Feather River (USA)
10[7ft] 2[7ft] 3[8ft] 8[7sd] 6[7gs] 2[8hy] **0-3-6 £36,981**

Killala (Ire) *R N Bevis* 39 a18
5 b g Among Men (USA) - Hat And Gloves
13[8gf] 8[8gf] 9[8g] 9[10gf] 10[9sd] 7[9sd] **0-0-6**

Killarney Beauty *W Jarvis* 77
2 b f Komaite (USA) - Royal Girl
2[5gf] 1[6g] 4[5gf] 4[6s] **1-1-4 £8,071**

Killasser Pride *G L Moore* 30 a26
3 b g Halling (USA) - Mavura
5[8gf] 10[12sd] **0-0-2**

Killena Boy (Ire) *W Jarvis* 87
3 b g Imperial Ballet (Ire) - Habaza (Ire)
1[10s] 1[8g] 5[8g] 3[8gf] 6[8gs] 7[7gf] 2[8gf] 4[9gs] **2-2-8 £13,683**

Killer Katy *K R Burke* 55
2 ch f Primo Valentino (Ire) - Lake Mistassiu
2[5g] **0-1-1 £1,254**

Killing Me Softly *J Gallagher* a30
4 b g Kingsinger (Ire) - Slims Lady
10[9sd] **0-0-1**

Killoch Place (Ire) *W Storey*
4 b g Compton Place - Hibernica (Ire)
11[8sd] **0-0-1**

Killybegs (Ire) *B W Hills* 109
2 b c Orpen (USA) - Belsay
1[6gf] 1[7g] 3[7gs] 2[7g] **2-1-4 £32,052**

Kilmeena Star *J C Fox* a46
7 b g So Factual (USA) - Kilmeena Glen
12[6sd] 5[6sd] 10[6sd] 9[6sd] 11[7sd] 6[5sd] 10[6sd] **0-0-7**

Kilmovee *N Tinkler* a53
3 gr f Inchinor - Christmas Rose
5[6sd] 6[6sd] 9[6sd] 8[6sd] 4[7sd] 6[9sd] **0-0-6**

Kilt (Fr) *Mrs L Williamson* a46
7 ch g Luchiroverte (Ire) - Unite Ii (Fr)
8[9sd] PU[7gs] **0-0-2**

Kilworth (Ire) *N A Callaghan* 105
2 gr c Kalanisi (Ire) - Perugia (Ire)
2[7g] 2[7g] 5[7s] 1[8g] 2[8g] 7[8hy] **1-3-6 £26,225**

Kimberley Hall *John A Harris* 15
3 ch f Bachir (Ire) - Sedna (Fr)
13[8g] 13[7gs] 5[8gf] 9[6sd] 13[7sd] 13[8sd] **0-0-6**

Kincaid *M F Harris* 36
2 ch g Dr Fong (USA) - Peacock Alley (Ire)
10[6f] 8[7g] 9[7s] **0-0-3**

Kind (Ire) *R Charlton* 108
4 b f Danehill (USA) - Rainbow Lake
3[5s] 1[6gf] 3[6gf] 5[6gs] 5[6g] **1-2-5 £25,168**

Kind Emperor *P L Gilligan* 73
8 br g Emperor Jones (USA) - Kind Lady
1[11f] 1[10g] 13[10gf] 9[11g] **2-0-4 £7,579**

Kindlelight Debut *N P Littmoden* 76 a75
5 b m Groom Dancer (USA) - Dancing Debut
10[8sd] 10[6sd] 8[8sd] 1[8f] 5[8f] 2[8gf] 3[7f] 1[7sd] 1[7sd] 5[8g] 2[8g] 5[8g] 8[7sd] 6[7g] 5[8gf] 5[8g] 3[8gf] 4[8g] 8[8gs] 3[9sd] 7[7sd] 6[8sd] 4[9sd] **3-5-23 £14,474**

Kindling *M Johnston* 100
3 br f Dr Fong (USA) - Isle Of Flame
7[10gf] 6[10g] 4[12gf] 2[12gs] 6[12gf] 5[12g] 4[12gs] 1[12gs] 1[12gs] 3[13s] 1[16s] **3-2-11 £34,603**

Kindness *David Pinder* 61
5 ch m Indian Ridge - Kissing Gate (USA)
4[8g] 1[8gf] 5[8f] 10[8gf] 2[9g] 7[8f] 13[8gf] **1-1-7 £4,667**

Kineta (USA) *J L Dunlop* 67
2 b f Miswaki (USA) - Kibitzing (USA)
8[6gf] 3[6gs] **0-1-2 £888**

Kinetic Power (Ire) *D R C Elsworth* a44
2 gr c Alhaarth (Ire) - Nichodoula
8[9sd] **0-0-1**

Kinfayre Boy *K W Hogg* 51

3 b g Grey Eagle - Amber Gambler (Ity)
7^{12s} 3^{12f} 9^{12f} 14^{16g} PU^{12gf} **0-0-5 £528**

King After *J R Best* 67 a65
3 b g Bahamian Bounty - Child Star (Fr)
3^{10sd} 9^{10sd} 12^{11sd} 3^{10sd} 6^{8sd} 9^{7gf} 14^{6gs} 7^{7gf} 1^{8gf} 3^{10gf} **1-3-10 £4,888**

King Alfie *A B Haynes* 69 a65
2 gr g Foxhound (USA) - Its All Relative
3^{6gf} 4^{6gf} 7^{6gs} 2^{6gf} 4^{6gf} 2^{6g} 1^{7g} 6^{8gf} 1^{7gf} 6^{7sd} PU^{7sd} **2-3-11 £9,361**

King At Last *K Bell* a56
6 b g Zamindar (USA) - Louis' Queen (Ire)
7^{8sd} 11^{8sd} 3^{9sd} 8^{9sd} 9^{9sd} **0-1-5 £544**

King Cugat Kid (USA) *P W Chapple-Hyam* 4
2 b/br c King Cugat (USA) - Let's Dance (USA)
17^{8gs} **0-0-1**

King Darshaan *N I M Rossiter* 39 a58
5 b g Darshaan - Urchin (Ire)
9^{12gf} 1^{10sd} 4^{10sd} **1-0-3 £2,618**

King Egbert (Fr) *A W Carroll* 54
4 b g Fasliyev (USA) - Exocet (USA)
6^{6g} 9^{5gf} 7^{6gf} 8^{6gf} 13^{5gf} 16^{5g} **0-0-6**

King Eider *B Ellison* 81 a83
6 b/br g Mtoto - Hen Harrier
4^{12sd} 3^{14gs} 7^{14gf} 15^{20gf} **0-0-4 £1,563**

King Eric *C Smith* 29 a55
3 b c Green Desert (USA) - Boojum
6^{7sd} 7^{6sd} 12^{9sd} 3^{5sd} 9^{5g} 18^{7gf} 9^{6gs} 14^{5sd} 13^{7sf} 13^{8sd} **0-1-10 £523**

King Faz (Ire) *Mrs H Dalton* 62
2 b c Fasliyev (USA) - White Satin (Ire)
8^{5gf} 4^{6gf} 13^{6g} **0-0-3 £499**

King Flyer (Ire) *Miss J Feilden* 60 a69
9 b g Ezzoud (Ire) - Al Guswa
1^{16sd} 13^{16sd} 2^{14gf} 11^{14gf} 9^{16gf} 13^{16g} **1-1-6 £4,227**

King Forever *D E Cantillon* 78 a56
3 b g King's Best (USA) - Elude
4^{7g} 4^{8gs} 6^{10g} 8^{9g} 8^{6g} 5^{9sd} 11^{10sd} **0-0-7 £949**

King Gabriel (Ire) *D J S Ffrench Davis* 61
3 b g Desert King (Ire) - Broken Spirit (Ire)
4^{7gs} 12^{10gf} 9^{12gf} 10^{12g} **0-0-4 £283**

King Harson *J D Bethell* 93
6 b g Greensmith - Safari Park
6^{7s} 1^{7gs} 15^{7f} 7^{7gf} 19^{7gf} 15^{7gs} 7^{7gf} 4^{7g} 8^{7g} 10^{7s} 16^{7s} **1-0-11 £10,170**

King Henrik (USA) *A Crook* 20
3 b g King Of Kings (Ire) - Ma Biche (USA)
16^{12g} 12^{7gs} 9^{7gf} 10^{5f} 15^{5gf} **0-0-5**

King Jock (USA) *E Charpy* 108 a65
4 b/br g Ghazi (USA) - Glen Kate
8^{6gf} 13^{5ft} 1^{8gf} 3^{8gf} 4^{7hy} 5^{5sh} 2^{7gf} 15^{6gf} 6^{7gf} 6^{8g} 12^{7gy} 6^{7sh} 2^{8g} 7^{7g} **1-3-14 £59,713**

King Johannes (Ire) *J Noseda* 59
2 b c Cape Cross (Ire) - Lady Moranbon (USA)
8^{6g} **0-0-1**

King Magnus (Ire) *R Charlton* 58
2 b c Mull Of Kintyre (USA) - Sandystones
12^{6gs} 5^{6f} **0-0-2**

King Malachi (Ire) *N A Callaghan* 79
2 b c King Charlemagne (USA) - Sparky's Song
3^{5g} 2^{5gf} 1^{6gf} 2^{6g} 9^{7gs} 5^{6gf} 3^{6g} **1-3-7 £13,176**

King Marju (Ire) *K R Burke* 106 a52
3 b c Marju (Ire) - Katoushka (Ire)
3^{7gf} 10^{7gf} 6^{6g} 5^{7s} 2^{7gf} 3^{7g} 9^{7g} 9^{6s} 11^{7sd} **0-2-9 £10,286**

King Marrakech (Ire) *B P J Baugh* 38 a38
3 b g King's Best (USA) - Tenue D'Amour (Fr)
13^{7sd} 11^{9sd} 14^{7gs} 9^{6s} 13^{6f} 8^{7gs} 14^{10sd} 11^{8g} 10^{7sd} 5^{5sd} 1^{5sd} **1-0-11 £1,409**

King Nicholas (USA) *J Parkes* 41 a73
6 b g Nicholas (USA) - Lifetime Honour (USA)
3^{9sd} 7^{8sd} 2^{9sd} 4^{9sd} 5^{9sd} 6^{7gs} 9^{8hy} 12^{8sd} 11^{9sd} **0-2-9 £1,834**

King Of Argos *E A L Dunlop* 75
2 b c Sadler's Wells (USA) - Wannabe Grand (Ire)
4^{7g} **0-0-1 £371**

King Of Blues (Ire) *M A Magnusson* 74
3 ch g Bluebird (USA) - Highly Respected (Ire)
12^{8gf} 4^{8gf} 15^{8g} **0-0-3 £555**

King Of Chav's (Ire) *A Bailey* 46 a56
2 ch g Beckett (Ire) - La Paola (Ire)
8^{7gf} 10^{8gs} 9^{9sd} **0-0-3**

King Of Diamonds *J R Best* 73 a80
4 b g Mtoto - Capricious Lass
5^{8sd} 11^{12sd} 5^{10g} 13^{8g} 11^{10gf} **0-0-5**

King Of Franks (Ire) *N A Callaghan* 54
2 b c King Charlemagne (USA) - Devil's Crown (USA)
11^{6g} 10^{7gf} 6^{5g} 8^{8g} **0-0-4**

King Of Knight (Ire) *G Prodromou* 56 a73
4 gr g Orpen (USA) - Peace Melody (Ire)
1^{10sd} 5^{10sd} 4^{12sd} 2^{10sd} 9^{12gf} 14^{10gf} 15^{12sd} 6^{12sd} 8^{9sd} 5^{12sd} 8^{8sd} **1-2-11 £4,788**

King Of Love *M Johnston* 81
3 b c King's Best (USA) - Fadaki Hawaki (USA)
3^{8gs} 12^{7g} 2^{7gf} 7^{7s} 6^{7f} 5^{7gf} 6^{9g} 7^{6gf} 14^{7gf} **0-2-9 £3,014**

King Of Meze (Ire) *J S Wainwright* 61
4 b g Croco Rouge (Ire) - Cossack Princess (Ire)
3^{8gf} 2^{7g} 8^{6hy} **0-2-3 £999**

King Of Music (USA) *G Prodromou* 58 a70
4 ch g Jade Hunter (USA) - Hail Roberta (USA)
4^{10sd} 7^{10sd} 2^{9sd} 11^{8sd} 7^{11f} 4^{10g} 8^{10hy} 4^{12sd} 7^{11sd} 7^{12sd} **0-1-10 £1,828**

King Of Sting *K A Ryan* 68
3 ch c Compton Place - Dance Of The Swans (Ire)
2^{7gs} 7^{7g} 12^{7g} 11^{6sd} **0-1-4 £1,352**

King Of The Moors (USA) *T D Barron* 71
2 b g King Of Kings (Ire) - Araza (USA)
5^{7g} 5^{7g} **0-0-2**

King Of The Sun (USA) *Saeed Bin Suroor* 66
3 b c Kingmambo (USA) - Solar Bound (USA)
5^{10g} **0-0-1**

King Orchisios (Ire) *K A Ryan* 81
2 ch c Tagula (Ire) - Wildflower
1^{5g} **1-0-1 £4,186**

King Priam (Ire) *M J Polglase* a38
10 b g Priolo (USA) - Barinia
6^{14sd} 7^{12sd} 10^{12sd} 6^{17sd} **0-0-4**

King Revo (Ire) *P C Haslam* 95
5 b g Revoque (Ire) - Tycoon Aly (Ire)
7^{19gs} 8^{20gf} 10^{14gs} 2^{18gs} **0-1-4 £28,600**

King Zafeen (Ire) *M W Easterby* 57
3 b c Lend A Hand - Groom Dancing
12^{12g} 6^{11s} 7^{11gs} 15^{10f} 11^{8g} 2^{9gf} 3^{11gf} 13^{10gf} **0-2-8 £1,420**

King's Caprice *J A Geake* 95 a94
4 ch g Pursuit Of Love - Palace Street (USA)

12^{6g} 3^{7gf} 9^{7g} 16^{6gf} 10^{6gf} 11^{6g} 3^{6gf} 2^{7gf} 8^{7gs} 12^{7gs} 4^{7sd} 2^{7sd} 8^{8sd} **0-4-13**
£11,299

King's Charter (USA) *S Dow* 44 a43
2 b c Red Ransom (USA) - Extry (USA)
14^{5gf} 11^{7sd} 13^{7s} **0-0-3**

King's Envoy (USA) *Mrs J C McGregor* 41
6 b g Royal Academy (USA) - Island Of Silver (USA)
17^{9gs} 6^{16gf} 9^{15g} **0-0-3**

King's Fable (USA) *M Johnston* 52 a49
2 b c Lear Fan (USA) - Fairy Fable (Ire)
6^{7hy} 5^{10hy} 11^{10sd} **0-0-3**

King's Fantasy (USA) *D J Daly* 73 a59
2 ch c King Of Kings (Ire) - Fantasy
6^{7sd} 2^{7gf} 2^{7g} 4^{7gf} 2^{7g} **0-3-5 £3,392**

King's Gait *T D Easterby* 102
3 b g Mujahid (USA) - Miller's Gait
12^{6gf} 1^{6gs} 13^{6g} 17^{6g} 4^{5gs} 1^{5g} 2^{5hy} **2-2-7**
£34,843

King's Head (Ire) *M A Jarvis* 86
2 b c King's Best (USA) - Ustka
4^{7g} 3^{7g} 1^{8g} 6^{8gs} **1-1-4 £7,664**

King's Kama *Sir Michael Stoute* 82 a78
3 b g Giant's Causeway (USA) - Maid For The Hills
1^{9sd} 8^{10gf} 8^{8gf} **1-0-3 £3,458**

King's Majesty (Ire) *Sir Michael Stoute* 93
3 b c King's Best (USA) - Tiavanita (USA)
1^{7g} 2^{8g} **1-1-2 £14,502**

King's Minstrel (Ire) *R Rowe* a50
4 b g Cape Cross (Ire) - Muwasim (USA)
7^{10sd} 13^{10sd} 5^{10sd} 5^{10sd} 5^{10sd} 7^{12sd} **0-0-6**

King's Mountain (USA) *R M Stronge* a4
5 b g King Of Kings (Ire) - Statistic (USA)
12^{17sd} **0-0-1**

King's Ransom *A M Balding* 70 a63
2 b c Daylami (Ire) - Luana
11^{7g} 9^{8sd} **0-0-2**

King's Revenge *T D Easterby* 77 a73
2 br g Wizard King - Retaliator
6^{5g} 2^{6g} 2^{5s} 19^{6gf} 3^{7s} 7^{8sd} **0-3-6**
£2,559

King's Thought *S Gollings* 99 a94
6 b h King's Theatre (Ire) - Lora's Guest
8^{9sd} 5^{10gs} 15^{8g} 3^{10hy} 1^{10gs} 5^{10gs} 16^{12g} 6^{10g}
19^{10g} 6^{10g} **1-0-10 £20,990**

Kingdom Of Dreams (Ire) *Sir Michael Stoute* 87
3 b c Sadler's Wells (USA) - Regal Portrait (Ire)
3^{10s} 1^{9g} 1^{10gs} 4^{12gf} 7^{11gf} 3^{10g} 3^{10g} **2-3-7**
£15,998

Kingkohler (Ire) *K A Morgan* 81
6 b g King's Theatre (Ire) - Legit (Ire)
4^{12gf} 7^{12g} **0-1-2 £479**

Kings Cavalier (USA) *S Dow* 76 a62
2 b g Stormin Fever (USA) - Port Of Silver (USA)
3^{5gf} 6^{6g} 3^{6gf} 5^{6g} 7^{6sd} **0-1-5 £1,438**

Kings College Boy *R A Fahey* 79
5 b g College Chapel - The Kings Daughter
16^{6s} 3^{5g} 4^{5g} 6^{6s} 3^{5g} 4^{5gf} 1^{5gf} 5^{6g} 4^{5g} 2^{5g}
5^{6gf} 5^{6g} 4^{5g} 2^{5s} 3^{5g} 6^{5g} 17^{6hy} 14^{5s}
1-5-18 £13,252

Kings Heir (Ire) *M Johnston* 73
2 b c Princely Heir (Ire) - Unimpeachable (Ire)
7^{5gf} 2^{5gf} 3^{5g} 3^{6gf} 6^{6gs} 1^{7g} **1-3-6**
£5,771

Kings Point (Ire) *R A Fahey* 109
4 b c Fasliyev (USA) - Rahika Rose
11^{7gf} 3^{7s} 17^{8gf} 2^{8gf} 13^{10g} 14^{8gs} 5^{7gf} 1^{8gf}
6^{7g} **1-2-9 £43,539**

Kings Quay *R Hannon* 107
3 b c Montjeu (Ire) - Glen Rosie (Ire)
5^{8gs} 2^{9gf} 6^{10gs} 6^{11g} 11^{12g} 7^{9g} 3^{10gf} 7^{10s} 3^{10g}
4^{10g} 8^{10gf} 5^{10g} **0-2-12 £14,358**

Kings Rock *P A Blockley* a49
4 ch g Kris - Both Sides Now (USA)
7^{10sd} **0-0-1**

Kings Topic (USA) *A B Haynes* a67
5 ch g Kingmambo (USA) - Topicount (USA)
2^{9sd} 1^{9sd} **1-1-2 £3,400**

Kingscape (Ire) *J R Fanshawe* 65 a68
2 br g King Charlemagne (USA) - Cape Clear
9^{6gf} 2^{7sd} 5^{7gf} **0-1-3 £963**

Kingscross *M Blanshard* 89
7 ch g King's Signet (USA) - Calamanco
3^{6s} 8^{6s} 4^{6g} 5^{6gf} 5^{6gf} 11^{6g} 1^{6gf} 6^{6g} 4^{6g} 2^{6gf}
7^{6gf} 11^{6gs} 4^{6g} 7^{6s} **1-3-14 £14,715**

Kingsdon (Ire) *T J Fitzgerald* 46 a52
8 b g Brief Truce (USA) - Richly Deserved (Ire)
3^{12sd} 12^{10sd} 13^{12s} 12^{10gf} 9^{11g} 3^{10sd} 10^{10g}
9^{12sd} 18^{10g} 11^{13sd} **0-2-10 £944**

Kingsgate Prince (Ire) *J R Best* 73 a67
2 b c Desert Sun - Princess Mood (Ger)
6^{5gf} 4^{6sd} 4^{5gf} **0-0-3 £620**

Kingsholm *A M Balding* 83
3 ch g Selkirk (USA) - Putuna
12^{8gf} 2^{8g} 6^{9g} 1^{10g} **1-1-4 £9,279**

Kingsmaite *S R Bowring* 66 a92
4 b g Komaite (USA) - Antonias Melody
1^{6sd} 5^{6sd} 7^{7gf} 12^{6g} 15^{7g} 19^{6g} 6^{6sd} 3^{6sd} 4^{7sd}
1-1-9 £8,184

Kingston Harbour (Ire) *V Smith* 71 a71
4 b g Danehill (USA) - Kallavesi (USA)
1^{11sd} 3^{12sd} 3^{12sd} 4^{10gs} 6^{12sd} 6^{12gf} 12^{12gf}
1-2-7 £4,722

Kingston Rose (Ger) *P J McBride* 19 a25
4 b f Robellino (USA) - Kingston Avenue (USA)
9^{12sd} 7^{12g} **0-0-2**

Kiniska *B Palling* a40
4 b f Merdon Melody - Young Whip
6^{12sd} 3^{11sd} 8^{12sd} 8^{9sd} 10^{12sd} **0-1-5 £213**

Kinky *A Berry* 56 a56
3 b g Kingsinger (Ire) - Lucky Dip
11^{6sd} 4^{6sd} 6^{6sd} 1^{7s} 6^{8g} 13^{8g} 10^{8gf} 8^{7g} 12^{7gf}
10^{7gs} 11^{8s} 14^{8sd} **1-0-12 £3,309**

Kinnaird (Ire) *P C Haslam* 111
4 ch f Dr Devious (Ire) - Ribot's Guest (Ire)
3^{8g} 7^{8gf} 3^{10gf} 1^{10gs} 5^{10hy} **1-1-5**
£117,269

Kinrande (Ire) *P J Makin* 92
3 b g Sri Pekan (USA) - Pipers Pool (Ire)
1^{11gf} 1^{12g} 8^{12gf} 2^{12gf} **2-1-4 £13,899**

Kinsman (Ire) *T D McCarthy* 46 a62
8 b g Distant Relative - Besito
2^{7sd} 12^{7sd} 12^{7sd} 8^{7sd} 4^{7sd} 11^{10f} 13^{10gf} 7^{10sd}
9^{10sd} 6^{10sd} 1^{8sd} 8^{10sd} **1-1-12 £2,287**

Kinsya *M H Tompkins* 73
2 ch g Mister Baileys - Kimono (Ire)
7^{7gs} 6^{7g} 4^{8gf} 1^{8gs} 5^{8g} **1-0-5 £5,895**

Kintbury Cross *P D Cundell* 83
3 b g Kylian (USA) - Cebwob
3^{8gs} 14^{10gs} 2^{9g} 7^{10gf} 3^{12gf} 2^{9gs} 14^{11gf}

0-4-7 £4,192

Kintore *B Smart* a14
4 ch g Inchinor - Souadah (USA)
12^{8sd} 9^{11sd} **0-0-2**

Kipsigis (Ire) *Lady Herries* 59
4 b g Octagonal (NZ) - Kisumu
11^{10g} 9^{13gf} 5^{14gs} 12^{17g} **0-0-4**

Kirin *D E Cantillon* 69 a68
3 b c Selkirk (USA) - Amaryllis (Ire)
6^{8g} 6^{8gs} 3^{7g} 17^{8s} 10^{12sd} 5^{9sd} **0-1-6 £488**

Kirkby's Treasure *A Berry* 83
7 gr g Mind Games - Gem Of Gold
1^{7gs} 14^{8gf} 8^{7f} 4^{7g} 12^{8gf} 3^{7f} 8^{7gf} 3^{7gf} 9^{8g} 3^{6gs} 3^{7gf} 3^{7gf} 4^{6gf} 4^{7gf} 7^{7g} 7^{7s} **1-4-16 £14,394**

Kirkbys Belle (Ire) *A Berry* 27 a21
2 b f Namid - Saltwood
8^{5gs} 6^{5gf} 9^{5sd} **0-0-3**

Kirkham Abbey *J J Quinn* 57
5 b g Selkirk (USA) - Totham
16^{10gf} 9^{12g} **0-0-2**

Kirkhammerton (Ire) *M J Polglase* 37 a59
3 ch g Grand Lodge (USA) - Nawara
6^{8sd} 11^{8sd} 6^{11sd} 4^{10sd} 2^{8sd} 9^{12sd} 2^{12sd} 1^{12sd} 7^{12gf} 9^{16g} 12^{14g} 11^{12gf} 8^{12sd} **1-2-13 £4,947**

Kirkstall Lane *J H M Gosden*
2 b g Selkirk (USA) - L'Animee
11^{8hy} **0-0-1**

Kirov King (Ire) *B G Powell* 42 a56
5 b g Desert King (Ire) - Nymphs Echo (Ire)
9^{10sd} 5^{13sd} 15^{12gf} 11^{10s} **0-0-4**

Kirstys Lad *M Mullineaux* 44 a35
3 b c Lake Coniston (Ire) - Killick
7^{7g} 10^{8g} 4^{8hy} 10^{7sd} 11^{9sd} **0-0-5 £333**

Kiss The Rain *R Brotherton* 56 a56
5 b m Forzando - Devils Dirge
3^{5sd} 6^{6sd} 7^{5sd} 1^{5sd} 8^{6sd} 3^{5sd} 11^{6gf} 10^{5sd} 3^{5g} 14^{5gf} 11^{5g} 4^{5f} 3^{5sd} 12^{5g} 5^{5hd} 13^{6g} 5^{5sd} 5^{5sd} **1-4-18 £4,626**

Kissi Kissi *D Shaw*
2 b f Paris House - Miss Whittingham (Ire)
9^{5sd} 7^{5g} **0-0-2**

Kissimee *N P Littmoden* a18
2 br f Whittingham (Ire) - Shalyah (Ire)
9^{6f} 11^{7sd} **0-0-2**

Kissing A Fool *W G M Turner* 34
3 b g Tipsy Creek (USA) - Amathus Glory
10^{7gf} 13^{5g} **0-0-2**

Kissing Lights (Ire) *M L W Bell* 98
3 b f Machiavellian (USA) - Nasaieb (Ire)
8^{6gf} 8^{7gf} 7^{5g} 8^{6gs} 3^{6gf} **0-1-5 £2,252**

Kiswahili *Sir Mark Prescott* 96
3 ch f Selkirk (USA) - Kiliniski
3^{11gs} 1^{12y} 3^{16s} 4^{13vs} **1-1-4 £15,795**

Kitchen Sink (Ire) *P J Makin* 59 a59
3 ch g Bold Fact (USA) - Voodoo Rocket
8^{6g} 11^{7gf} 8^{6sd} 2^{6sd} 12^{6s} 2^{6g} 5^{6g} 6^{6g} 3^{6ft} 11^{7sd} 8^{6sd} 3^{5sd} **0-4-12 £2,484**

Kitmaah *M P Tregoning*
2 b f Alhaarth (Ire) - Kronengold (USA)
15^{6gf} **0-0-1**

Kitty *Miss J S Davis* 56 a22
3 b f Kayf Tara - Dancing Bluebell (Ire)
4^{10s} 8^{10gf} 7^{12g} 8^{12f} 14^{10sd} 14^{17gs} **0-0-6 £268**

Knead The Dough *P S McEntee* 41 a54
4 b g Wolfhound (USA) - Ridgewood Ruby (Ire)
4^{5sd} 7^{5sd} 11^{6sd} 9^{5sd} 15^{6f} 12^{6sd} 5^{5gf} 11^{5f} 11^{5sd} **0-0-9 £262**

Knickerless (Ire) *N P Littmoden* 53 a36
2 b f Fayruz - June Lady
9^{5gf} 10^{6g} 11^{7sd} **0-0-3**

Knickyknackienoo *T T Clement* 57 a57
4 b g Bin Ajwaad (Ire) - Ring Fence
8^{9sd} 8^{8sd} 12^{7s} 1^{8g} 3^{7s} 4^{7sd} 11^{8gf} 5^{8gf} 10^{7g} **1-1-9 £3,685**

Knife Artist (Ire) *P C Haslam* 9
2 b c Daggers Drawn (USA) - Akatib (Ire)
14^{6g} 10^{5g} **0-0-2**

Knight General Mac *N Bycroft*
6 b g Presidium - Agnes Jane
11^{7gf} **0-0-1**

Knight Of Hearts (Ire) *P A Blockley* a37
4 gr g Idris (Ire) - Heart To Heart (Ire)
14^{8sd} 11^{9sd} **0-0-2**

Knight Valliant *J Howard Johnson* 60
2 bl g Dansili - Aristocratique
3^{7g} **0-1-1 £560**

Knightsbridge Hill (Ire) *A King* 67
3 b c Raise A Grand (Ire) - Desert Gem
11^{7gs} 9^{10gf} 6^{11gf} **0-0-3**

Knock Bridge (Ire) *P D Evans* 77 a60
3 b f Rossini (USA) - Touraneena
8^{7sd} 2^{8s} 2^{8s} 12^{8g} 2^{8gf} 8^{9sd} 12^{10s} 4^{8g} 5^{8s} **0-3-9 £4,532**

Knockdoo (Ire) *J S Goldie* 21
12 ch g Be My Native (USA) - Ashken
12^{14sd} 6^{16gf} **0-0-2**

Knocktopher Abbey *A G Newcombe* 53
8 ch g Pursuit Of Love - Kukri
8^{8gs} 4^{8g} 7^{8gf} 12^{10g} **0-1-4 £268**

Knot In Wood (Ire) *R A Fahey* 80 a27
3 b g Shinko Forest (Ire) - Notley Park
8^{6sd} 16^{6s} 5^{6gs} 1^{6s} 4^{7gf} 4^{6gf} 1^{6gf} 1^{6gf} 10^{6gf} 2^{6gf} 8^{6gf} **3-2-11 £17,313**

Knotty Ash Girl (Ire) *D J Wintle*
6 ch m Ashkalani (Ire) - Camisha (Ire)
9^{11sd} **0-0-1**

Known Maneuver (USA) *M C Chapman* 5
7 b g Known Fact (USA) - Northernmaneuver (USA)
14^{12gs} 8^{8s} 14^{12f} **0-0-3**

Kodiac *J L Dunlop* 106
4 b c Danehill (USA) - Rafha
11^{8g} 5^{7gf} 1^{6gf} 12^{6gf} 1^{6gf} 4^{6g} 8^{6gf} **2-0-7 £18,671**

Kofi *Miss K M George* 52 a36
3 br g Emperor Fountain - La Vie En Primrose
5^{7sd} 7^{8gs} 17^{8g} **0-0-3**

Kokila *W J Haggas* a55
2 b f Indian Danehill (Ire) - Poetry In Motion (Ire)
3^{7sd} **0-1-1 £603**

Kolhapur (Ire) *J L Dunlop* 56
2 ch c Barathea (Ire) - Koniya (Ire)
7^{7gf} 16^{7g} 7^{8g} **0-0-3**

Kolibre *Mrs C A Dunnett*
2 br c Mtoto - Eternal Flame
13^{7sd} **0-0-1**

Kolyma (Ire) *J L Dunlop* 59

3 ch f Grand Lodge (USA) - Koniya (Ire)
7^{9gf} 8^{9g} 7^{10s} **0-0-3**

Komati River *M J Attwater*
6 b g Wesaam (USA) - Christening (Ire)
13^{16gs} **0-0-1**

Komena *J W Payne* 35
7 b m Komaite (USA) - Mena
6^{7g} 6^{8f} **0-0-2**

Komreyev Star *M Mullineaux* 56 a49
3 b g Komaite (USA) - L'Ancressaan
2^{7sd} 2^{9sd} 3^{8g} 1^{8gf} 7^{10g} 7^{10gf} 6^{9gf} 3^{9gf} 8^{10sd} 9^{10gf} 10^{9sd} 3^{9sd} 3^{8s} 1^{9hy} **2-6-14 £7,410**

Kong (Ire) *J L Dunlop* 112
3 b c Sadler's Wells (USA) - Hill Of Snow
2^{11gs} 1^{11g} 13^{12g} 4^{12g} 4^{15hy} 4^{12g} **1-1-6 £67,898**

Kooks (Ire) *Miss Kariana Key* 30
2 b g Titus Livius (Fr) - Lea Valley Dancer
7^{5g} 10^{6g} 10^{7gf} 7^{7g} 13^{6gf} 9^{7f} 10^{8ss} **0-0-7**

Kool Ovation *A Dickman* 77
3 b g Royal Applause - Carrie Kool
15^{7gs} 5^{5g} 4^{5gf} 1^{6gf} **1-0-4 £7,475**

Korikancha (Ire) *J Noseda* 68 a60
2 b f Fasliyev (USA) - Amravati (Ire)
4^{7gf} 9^{7g} 12^{7gf} 3^{8hy} 2^{7sd} **0-2-5 £2,050**

Korolieva (Ire) *K A Ryan* 69
2 b f Xaar - Dark Hyacinth (Ire)
4^{5gf} 3^{6g} 7^{6gf} 1^{6gf} 9^{6gs} 11^{6g} **1-1-6 £6,581**

Kostar *C G Cox* 95 a100
4 ch g Komaite (USA) - Black And Amber
3^{6gs} 10^{6gs} 8^{6gf} 1^{6gf} 4^{5gf} 1^{6gf} 15^{6gf} 2^{6sd} **2-2-8 £20,452**

Krasivi's Boy (USA) *G L Moore* 60
3 b/br c Swain (Ire) - Krasivi (USA)
5^{10s} 3^{12g} 11^{12gs} 4^{14s} 8^{14gf} 3^{14gs} 10^{16g} **0-1-7 £1,475**

Kris Spring *D R Loder* 24
3 b f Kris S (USA) - Crown Of Spring (USA)
12^{7gf} **0-0-1**

Krischera (USA) *B J Meehan* 61 a67
2 br c Kris S (USA) - Torchera (USA)
12^{7gf} 5^{6gs} 16^{8g} 3^{7sd} **0-1-4 £468**

Kristal's Queen (Ire) *J L Dunlop* 40
2 b f Sendawar (Ire) - Kristal's Paradise (Ire)
9^{7gf} 7^{7g} 9^{8s} **0-0-3**

Kristalchen *J G Given* 45
3 b f Singspiel (Ire) - Crystal Flite (Ire)
7^{11s} 14^{10f} 7^{10gf} 13^{10g} **0-0-4**

Kristensen *Karen McLintock* 83 a85
6 ch g Kris S (USA) - Papaha (Fr)
5^{12sd} 3^{18g} 3^{12gs} 6^{16g} 2^{14gf} 17^{20gf} 16^{12gf} 3^{16g} 4^{16g} **0-3-9 £6,228**

Kristiansand *P Monteith* 46
5 b g Halling (USA) - Zonda
6^{10s} 12^{10g} 6^{9gf} **0-0-3**

Kristikhab (Ire) *A Berry* 38
3 ch g Intikhab (USA) - Alajyal (Ire)
6^{5gs} 5^{7f} 5^{8f} 13^{9gf} 10^{8gf} 6^{7gf} **0-0-6**

Kristinor (Fr) *G L Moore* 67 a63
3 ch g Inchinor - Kristina
7^{7s} 5^{7f} 6^{6sd} 5^{7f} 6^{8g} 6^{6gf} 8^{7gf} 3^{8sd} 8^{9sd} 6^{8f} 7^{10sd} 4^{10sd} **0-1-12 £536**

Krugerrand (USA) *W J Musson* 94
6 ch g Gulch (USA) - Nasers Pride (USA)
7^{8g} 8^{8g} 2^{8gf} 7^{8g} 2^{9gf} 16^{8g} 18^{10g} 8^{9gf} 7^{8gs} 1^{9gs} **1-2-10 £17,774**

Krullind (Ire) *D Nicholls* 54
3 b g Rossini (USA) - Jemima Yorke
7^{6gf} 20^{7gf} 6^{6gf} **0-0-3**

Krumpet *G G Margarson* 46
3 b f Mujahid (USA) - Dame Jude
8^{6g} 12^{7g} 9^{8gf} 6^{10gf} **0-0-4**

Kryena *R F Johnson Houghton* 71 a69
3 gr f Kris - Tereyna
2^{8s} 3^{8g} 4^{10s} 3^{8g} 5^{9sd} 3^{9sd} **0-4-6 £3,937**

Kryssa *G L Moore* 80 a63
4 ch f Kris - Alessandra
5^{8gf} 4^{8g} 2^{10g} 3^{10gf} 6^{10sd} 3^{9s} 4^{10gf} 5^{10gs} 5^{10gf} 3^{8gs} **0-4-10 £6,535**

Kudbeme *N Bycroft* 74
3 b f Forzando - Umbrian Gold (Ire)
3^{7s} 5^{8s} 6^{7gs} 1^{7g} 5^{8gs} 2^{8s} 9^{8gf} 13^{8gs} **1-1-8 £9,420**

Kuka *R Hollinshead* a43
4 b g Polar Prince (Ire) - Crissem (Ire)
7^{12sd} 6^{11sd} 10^{14ss} **0-0-3**

Kumakawa *D K Ivory* 27 a55
7 ch g Dancing Spree (USA) - Maria Cappuccini
5^{7sd} 4^{8sd} 2^{8sd} 9^{9sd} 1^{7sd} 9^{7sd} 6^{8sd} 2^{7sd} 5^{8sd} 7^{7sd} 11^{6g} 11^{7sd} 7^{6g} 12^{8f} 18^{10f} 12^{8f} 13^{8gf} 9^{8hd} 13^{5sd} 12^{7f} 3^{8sd} 5^{8sd} 7^{8sd} 4^{8sd} 3^{8ss} 1^{8sd} 7^{7sd} 9^{8sd} 4^{7ss} 4^{8sd} **2-4-30 £4,163**

Kumala Ocean (Ire) *P A Blockley* 20 a35
3 ch f Blue Ocean (USA) - Kumala (Ire)
9^{9s} 6^{7sd} **0-0-2**

Kung Hei *Mrs L Stubbs* 56 a68
2 b g Primo Valentino (Ire) - Cast A Spell
3^{5sd} 5^{5g} 2^{5sd} 4^{5gf} **0-2-4 £3,375**

Kuster *L M Cumani* 76
9 b g Indian Ridge - Ustka
12^{10gf} 2^{12gf} **0-1-2 £1,078**

Kut (Ire) *J Noseda* 60
2 b c Royal Applause - Amber Tide (Ire)
7^{6g} **0-0-1**

Kwai Baby (USA) *J J Bridger* 6
4 gr f Charnwood Forest (Ire) - Roses In The Snow (Ire)
9^{11gf} 7^{12f} **0-0-2**

Kyber *R F Fisher* 34 a54
4 ch g First Trump - Mahbob Dancer (Fr)
2^{17sd} 7^{16sd} 6^{17sd} 10^{17f} 8^{15g} 11^{14s} **0-1-6 £826**

Kydd Gloves (USA) *Saeed Bin Suroor* 95
3 b f Dubai Millennium - Parade Queen (USA)
1^{8g} 1^{10g} 4^{12g} **2-0-3 £19,786**

Kyle Of Lochalsh *J S Goldie* 56 a38
5 gr g Vettori (Ire) - Shaieef (Ire)
6^{12sd} 2^{12gf} 1^{12gf} 4^{11gf} 4^{13gf} 2^{11gf} 1^{12gf} UR^{12gf} 3^{12f} 6^{12g} 12^{14g} **2-3-11 £8,894**

Kyles Prince (Ire) *P J Makin* 69 a80
3 b g In The Wings - Comprehension (USA)
5^{10gs} 2^{10sd} 1^{12sd} **1-1-3 £4,711**

Kylkenny *H Morrison* 79 a86
10 b g Kylian (USA) - Fashion Flow
2^{12sd} 1^{12sd} 3^{12sd} 2^{12sd} 3^{12gs} 6^{12gf} 1^{10s} 1^{10g} 2^{10gf} 3^{10gf} 10^{10gf} 3^{10gf} 1^{10g} 6^{10g} 13^{12f} 1^{11gs} 4^{11sd} 1^{11sd} 1^{12sd} **7-7-19 £31,767**

Kyo Bid *M Brittain*
5 b g Endoli (USA) - Hebe (Ire)
8^{12g} **0-0-1**

Kyoto Summit *L M Cumani* 83
2 ch c Lomitas - Alligram (USA)
6^{7gf} 2^{8g} 4^{8s} **0-1-3 £1,738**

L'Escapade (Ire) *D R Loder* 57
3 ch g Grand Lodge (USA) - Brief Escapade (Ire)
6^{7gf} **0-0-1**

L'Italiana (Ire) *M Dods* 40
2 b f Rossini (USA) - Paganina (Fr)
10^{6gf} 9^{7g} 9^{6gf} 4^{7gf} 11^{8g} **0-0-5 £260**

La Bella Grande (Ire) *R Charlton* 84
3 ch f Giant's Causeway (USA) - La Belle Otero (USA)
3^{7gf} 3^{8g} 1^{8g} 4^{10g} 1^{8gf} 1^{10gs} **3-2-6 £16,948**

La Bella Rosa (Ire) *J S Wainwright*
3 b f Revoque (Ire) - Tempesta Rossa (Ire)
13^{10g} 9^{12gf} **0-0-2**

La Bomba Veloce *Mrs L Williamson* 42 a25
2 b f Tomba - Charleigh Keary
15^{5gs} 7^{6s} 10^{7s} 12^{6sd} 9^{9sd} **0-0-5**

La Calera (Ger) *Lucinda Featherstone* a31
4 ch f Big Shuffle (USA) - La Luce
8^{12sd} **0-0-1**

La Chunga (USA) *J Noseda* 106
2 br f More Than Ready (USA) - Gypsy Monarch (USA)
3^{5g} 1^{6gf} 4^{6gf} 2^{6gf} **1-2-4 £57,338**

La Concha (Ire) *M J McGrath*
4 b g Kahyasi - Trojan Crown (Ire)
12^{17sd} **0-0-1**

La Cucaracha *B W Hills* 116
4 b f Piccolo - Peggy Spencer
1^{6g} 9^{6s} 1^{6gf} 2^{6gs} 1^{6gf} 1^{5gf} 2^{6g} **4-2-7 £275,729**

La Cygne Blanche (Ire) *Mrs N Macauley* a44
3 gr f Saddlers' Hall (Ire) - Ivory's Promise
9^{9sd} 5^{7sd} 9^{6sd} 10^{6sd} 10^{6sd} **0-0-5**

La Fanciulla *R Hannon* 71
2 b f Robellino (USA) - Molly Brown
5^{5gf} 7^{6gf} 2^{5g} 2^{5g} 15^{7gf} 3^{7gs} 6^{8s} **0-3-7 £6,373**

La Fonteyne *T J Fitzgerald* a27
4 b f Imperial Ballet (Ire) - Baliana
13^{9sd} 11^{9sd} 9^{11sd} **0-0-3**

La Gessa *John Berry* 63
3 gr f Largesse - En Grisaille
10^{8g} 1^{10gf} **1-0-2 £3,017**

La Gitana *A Sadik* 36 a45
5 b m Singspiel (Ire) - Iberian Dancer (Can)
9^{8sd} 7^{8sd} 7^{12sd} 4^{12sd} 1^{13sd} 3^{12sd} 10^{14sd} 11^{14sd} 6^{17sd} 11^{13sd} 9^{12sd} 8^{12gf} **1-1-12 £1,498**

La Mago *Mrs A M Naughton* 7
5 b m Wizard King - Dancing Dancer
13^{8s} 9^{10f} PU^{12gf} 9^{11g} 13^{17f} **0-0-5**

La Mottie *R M Beckett* 87
2 ch f King's Best (USA) - Bareilly (USA)
4^{6g} 1^{6gf} 2^{6gf} 12^{7gs} **1-1-4 £7,727**

La Muette (Ire) *M Appleby* 55 a6
5 b m Charnwood Forest (Ire) - Elton Grove (Ire)
8^{10s} 8^{10s} 9^{10s} 8^{8s} 14^{12sd} **0-0-5**

La Musique *P J McBride* 39 a48
3 b c Merdon Melody - Daleside Ladybird
5^{9sd} 10^{6gf} **0-0-2**

La Persiana *W Jarvis* 111
4 gr f Daylami (Ire) - La Papagena
3^{9gf} 2^{10s} 2^{10s} 2^{10gf} 1^{10gf} 1^{10g} 5^{10gf} 4^{10s} **2-4-8 £79,392**

La Professoressa (Ire) *Mrs P N Dutfield* 16 a23
4 b f Cadeaux Genereux - Fellwah (Ire)
9^{9sd} 14^{8hy} **0-0-2**

La Puce *Miss Gay Kelleway* a59
4 b f Danzero (Aus) - Verbena (Ire)
11^{12sd} 9^{9sd} 9^{9sd} 8^{8sd} **0-0-4**

La Via Ferrata (Ire) *P F I Cole* 47 a53
2 ch c Mark Of Esteem (Ire) - Verify (Ire)
7^{5g} 8^{6gf} 9^{7gf} 7^{8f} 5^{8sd} **0-0-5**

La Vie Est Belle *D Nicholls* 76
4 b f Makbul - La Belle Vie
7^{7g} 2^{5gf} 2^{5hy} 4^{6s} 9^{7g} 2^{5g} 11^{5f} 7^{6g} 12^{6g} 7^{5g} 2^{5g} 11^{5g} **0-5-12 £6,230**

La Viola *K R Burke* 60 a62
3 b f Fraam - Arasong
6^{7sd} 11^{10gf} 6^{10g} 1^{8gf} 8^{8gf} 1^{9sd} 3^{8sd} 5^{10g} 1^{9sd} 8^{9sf} 9^{7sd} **3-1-11 £8,716**

Laawaris (USA) *J A Osborne* 42 a51
4 b g Souvenir Copy (USA) - Seattle Kat (USA)
11^{12sd} 11^{12s} 6^{12sd} 9^{12sd} 6^{12gf} **0-0-5**

Labelled With Love *J R Boyle* 62 a59
5 ch g Zilzal (USA) - Dream Baby
2^{6sd} 2^{6sd} 10^{7sd} 7^{7gf} 13^{6gf} 2^{6s} 1^{6gs} 10^{6sd} 15^{6hy} 14^{6sd} **1-3-10 £5,320**

Labetera *John Joseph Murphy* 47 a24
3 b f Lujain (USA) - All Our Hope (USA)
6^{6gf} 8^{5gf} 8^{6sd} **0-0-3**

Labrett *Miss Gay Kelleway* a51
8 b g Tragic Role (USA) - Play The Game
8^{7sd} **0-0-1**

Laconia (Ire) *J S Moore* 23 a16
4 b f Orpen (USA) - Mislead (Ire)
7^{5sd} 17^{5gf} 13^{5gf} **0-0-3**

Laconicos (Ire) *W B Stone* 73 a69
3 ch g Foxhound (USA) - Thermopylae
5^{8sd} 6^{10sd} 9^{10gf} 2^{9g} 2^{8f} 6^{9sd} 9^{9sd} 4^{10sd} **0-2-8 £2,744**

Ladeena (Ire) *J L Dunlop* 71
3 b/br f Dubai Millennium - Aqaarid (USA)
4^{7gf} 9^{8g} 4^{8gf} 10^{8gf} 3^{8gs} 6^{8s} 4^{7gf} 1^{7g} 8^{7gf} **1-0-9 £5,034**

Ladies Knight *D Shaw* 34 a60
5 b g Among Men (USA) - Lady Silk
4^{5sd} 2^{5sd} 11^{6sd} 10^{6s} **0-1-4 £828**

Ladood *W J Haggas*
3 b f Unfuwain (USA) - Alshakr
10^{10gf} **0-0-1**

Ladruca *J A Glover* 12
3 b/br f Dracula (Aus) - Promissory
16^{11gf} 16^{10gf} **0-0-2**

Lady Agnes *G Wragg* 50
2 b f Singspiel (Ire) - St Radegund
11^{6s} **0-0-1**

Lady Algarhoud (Fr) *D K Ivory* 56 a70
3 b f Josr Algarhoud (Ire) - Lady Of Limerick (Ire)
1^{5sd} 3^{5sd} 1^{5sd} 8^{6s} 4^{6gs} 1^{6sd} 1^{6sd} 8^{7s} 10^{6sd} 8^{7sd} 3^{6ss} 4^{6sd} 8^{6sd} **4-3-13 £14,377**

Lady At Leisure (Ire) *M J Ryan* 14 a45
5 ch m Dolphin Street (Fr) - In A Hurry (Fr)
2^{8sd} 5^{8sd} 9^{8sd} 5^{8sd} 12^{12sd} 13^{10gf} 10^{11gf} **0-1-7 £427**

Lady Blade (Ire) *P D Evans* a45

4 b f Daggers Drawn (USA) - Singhana (Ire)
12^{10sd} 4^{9sd} 4^{10sd} 6^{9sd} 11^{10sd} 8^{10gs} 16^{8g}
0-0-7

Lady Cantankerous (Ger) *T P Tate* 25
2 b f Xaar - Lanelly (Ger)
14^{7g} 15^{7s} **0-0-2**

Lady Cree (Ire) *W R Muir* 76
2 b f Medicean - Nightitude
1^{6g} 7^{7s} 4^{6gf} 7^{7gf} 11^{7g} **1-0-5 £3,994**

Lady Diktat *P F I Cole* 79 a71
3 b f Diktat - Scared
9^{8g} 4^{8g} 2^{9gs} 4^{10gf} 5^{10gf} 2^{10gs} 3^{12gf} 4^{12sd}
0-2-8 £4,192

Lady Disdain *G M Moore* 67
2 b f Foxhound (USA) - Much Ado
3^{6gs} 3^{6g} 3^{7gf} 6^{8gs} **0-3-4 £1,782**

Lady Edge (Ire) *A W Carroll* 60
3 ch f Bold Edge - Lady Sheriff
5^{7gf} 3^{6g} 10^{7gf} 18^{6g} **0-1-4 £472**

Lady Ellendune *Andrew Turnell* 39 a43
4 b f Piccolo - Eileen's Lady
3^{8gf} 7^{10f} 10^{10f} 20^{10g} 5^{7sd} 10^{7sf} **0-1-6**
£427

Lady Erica *K R Burke*
3 b f Komaite (USA) - Zamarra
12^{5sd} **0-0-1**

Lady Eversham *W G M Turner*
2 b f Averti (Ire) - Galacia (Ire)
9^{5sd} **0-0-1**

Lady Evi *D K Ivory* a34
2 ch f Lord Of Men - Clued Up
9^{7sd} 10^{8sd} **0-0-2**

Lady Fas (Ire) *A W Carroll* 42 a38
2 b f Fasliyev (USA) - Lady Sheriff
11^{5gf} 7^{6gf} 7^{5g} 8^{5sd} 10^{6sd} **0-0-5**

Lady Filly *W G M Turner* 86
3 ch f Atraf - Just Lady
8^{5s} 7^{5gs} 5^{5gf} 2^{5f} 8^{5gf} 10^{5gf} 11^{5gs} 7^{6f}
0-1-8 £2,145

Lady Franpalm (Ire) *R A Harris* a31
5 b m Danehill Dancer (Ire) - Be Nimble
6^{6sd} 6^{6sd} 11^{5sd} **0-0-3**

Lady Georgina *J R Fanshawe* 79
4 gr f Linamix (Fr) - Georgia Venture
5^{8g} 6^{7g} 8^{7gf} 2^{9gf} 5^{9g} 17^{8g} **0-1-6**
£1,764

Lady Gregory (Ire) *John M Oxx* 73 a69
3 b f In The Wings - Athlumney Lady
2^{10gf} 2^{12sd} **0-2-2 £2,288**

Lady Hen *Miss J Feilden* 68 a65
3 b f Efisio - Royale Rose (Fr)
3^{7sd} 2^{9sd} 5^{9sd} 5^{9sd} 1^{9gf} 7^{9g} **1-2-6**
£5,156

Lady Hopeful (Ire) *Peter Grayson* 54 a54
3 b f Lend A Hand - Treble Term
5^{5gs} 6^{5sd} 5^{5gf} 3^{5sd} 6^{6sd} 9^{6g} 9^{6gf} 11^{7sd} 4^{6sd}
4^{5sd} 5^{6sd} 1^{5sd} 1^{5sd} 4^{5sd} **2-1-14 £3,287**

Lady Indiana (Ire) *J S Wainwright*
3 b f King's Theatre (Ire) - Najeyba
11^{12g} **0-0-1**

Lady Josh *W G M Turner* a42
2 b f Josr Algarhoud (Ire) - Dee-Lady
11^{7sd} 7^{6sf} 7^{6sd} 10^{7sd} **0-0-4**

Lady Karr *M Johnston* 70
4 b f Mark Of Esteem (Ire) - Percy's Lass
3^{12g} 4^{16f} 11^{12gf} 3^{12gf} 2^{12g} 8^{12gs} 3^{14g}
0-4-7 £4,182

Lady Le Saie *J R Best* 20
2 ch f Barathea (Ire) - Calypso Run
16^{6g} **0-0-1**

Lady Liesel *J L Spearing* a16
5 b m Bin Ajwaad (Ire) - Griddle Cake (Ire)
12^{9sd} **0-0-1**

Lady Livius (Ire) *R Hannon* 87
2 b f Titus Livius (Fr) - Refined (Ire)
9^{6gf} 8^{6gs} 1^{5gf} 11^{5gs} 7^{5gf} **1-0-5**
£78,300

Lady Lochinver (Ire) *M D Hammond* 51 a42
2 ch f Raise A Grand (Ire) - Opening Day
8^{8s} 2^{7s} 5^{7sd} **0-1-3 £952**

Lady Londra *D K Ivory* a65
3 b f Fumo Di Londra (Ire) - Lady Phyl
8^{6sd} 10^{7sd} 1^{6sd} 11^{7sd} 8^{6sd} 11^{6sd} 10^{7sd}
1-0-7 £3,398

Lady Lucinda *John A Harris* 33
4 b f Muhtarram (USA) - Lady Phyl
16^{7s} 12^{12gf} 6^{10gf} 10^{10gf} **0-0-4**

Lady Luisa (Ire) *Miss A Stokell*
3 b f Lujain (USA) - Lady Of Dreams (Ire)
8^{8gs} 10^{8gf} 14^{5gf} **0-0-3**

Lady Lynch (Ire) *Michael Cunningham* 51 a32
2 b f Orpen (USA) - Holly's Gold (Ire)
5^{6gf} 12^{7gf} 13^{6g} 7^{6g} 10^{8sd} **0-0-5**

Lady McNair *P D Cundell* a59
5 b m Sheikh Albadou - Bonita Bee
11^{8sd} **0-0-1**

Lady Misha *Jedd O'Keeffe* 67 a60
3 b f Mister Baileys - Hakone (Ire)
7^{10g} 5^{11s} 5^{10g} 7^{14g} 4^{12g} 6^{12gf} 14^{14s} 13^{12s}
4^{14sd} **0-0-9 £316**

Lady Mo *G G Margarson* 54 a5
4 b f Young Ern - Just Run (Ire)
14^{6g} 8^{7f} 12^{8gf} 8^{7gf} 6^{7gs} 7^{7g} 9^{8sd} 7^{6g} 14^{7gf}
0-0-9

Lady Oriande *A M Balding* a43
4 b f Makbul - Lady Roxanne
8^{6sd} 10^{6sd} **0-0-2**

Lady Palma Nova *M W Easterby* 52 a52
2 b f Danehill Dancer (Ire) - Sangra (USA)
3^{5hy} 9^{6gf} 8^{5g} 4^{6sd} 2^{7sd} **0-2-5 £2,150**

Lady Peaches *D Mullarkey* a38
4 ch f Bien Bien (USA) - Upper Club (Ire)
9^{12sd} 12^{6sd} **0-0-2**

Lady Pekan *P Howling* 56 a59
6 b m Sri Pekan (USA) - Cloudberry
2^{5sd} 2^{5sd} 6^{5sd} 8^{5sd} 1^{5sd} 8^{5sd} 2^{5sd} 10^{5sd} 14^{5g}
8^{5f} 2^{5gf} 1^{5sd} 8^{6sd} 7^{5ss} 7^{5sd} **2-4-15**
£7,551

Lady Pilot *Dr J R J Naylor* 55 a72
3 b f Dansili - Mighty Flyer (Ire)
4^{7sd} 2^{8sd} 2^{6sd} 10^{8gf} 7^{8f} 7^{8f} 7^{7g} 13^{6gf} 6^{7gf}
9^{6sd} 3^{8gs} 7^{9sd} 2^{10sd} **0-4-13 £3,953**

Lady Predominant *Robert Gray* 21 a6
4 b f Primo Dominie - Enlisted (Ire)
13^{7g} 6^{8gf} 10^{10s} 11^{14gf} 8^{12gf} 13^{12g} **0-0-6**

Lady Protector *J Balding* 40 a43
6 b m Sri Pekan (USA) - Scared
7^{5sd} 10^{5g} 9^{5g} **0-0-3**

Lady Romanov (Ire) *M H Tompkins* 54 a68
2 br f Xaar - Mixremember (Fr)

6^{6g} 10^{6s} 1^{7sd} **1-0-3 £3,042**

Lady Stratagem *E W Tuer* 9 a42
6 gr m Mark Of Esteem (Ire) - Grey Angel
2^{12sd} 6^{11sd} 14^{12s} 6^{12sd} PU^{12sd} **0-1-5**
£413

Lady Suesanne (Ire) *M J Attwater* 51 a57
3 b f Cape Cross (Ire) - Lady At War
12^{7sd} 3^{6sd} 9^{7sd} 13^{7s} 10^{6gf} 2^{6sd} 3^{5sd} 2^{6gf}
4^{8gf} 1^{7gs} 6^{8g} 8^{7sd} 7^{7gf} 3^{7sd} 11^{9sd} 2^{7sd}
1-5-16 £6,560

Lady Sunrize *P D Evans*
6 ch m Whittingham (Ire) - Scenic Air
14^{12ss} 11^{12sd} **0-0-2**

Lady Superior *R A Fahey* 56
2 b f Superior Premium - Chaloupe
2^{5gf} 7^{5g} 5^{5gf} 10^{5gf} **0-1-4 £1,704**

Lady Synthia *B Palling* 63 a56
2 b f Mull Of Kintyre (USA) - Yo-Cando (Ire)
6^{6g} 6^{6g} 3^{5sd} 12^{6sd} **0-1-4 £468**

Lady Taverner *J E Long* 57 a63
4 b f Marju (Ire) - Prompting
8^{8sd} 11^{10sd} 4^{9sd} 7^{9sd} 4^{9sd} 2^{10sd} 3^{10sd} 11^{10gf}
1^{10s} 3^{11g} 5^{12sd} 1^{12sd} 3^{10sd} 3^{14sd} **2-5-14**
£7,632

Lady Vee (Ire) *P D Niven* 49 a56
3 b f Rossini (USA) - Dama De Noche
1^{6sd} 8^{6f} 14^{6gf} 5^{6gf} 12^{6g} 8^{5sd} 6^{7sd} **1-0-7**
£2,669

Lady Xanthia *Mrs C A Dunnett* a8
4 ch f Bien Bien (USA) - Carmosa (USA)
7^{8sd} **0-0-1**

Lady Zanzara (USA) *J W Hills* 67 a62
2 ch f Lion Cavern (USA) - Pace (USA)
5^{5gf} 3^{5g} 2^{5f} 3^{5sd} 3^{5f} 3^{5f} 14^{5gf} **0-4-7**
£2,681

Lafi (Ire) *D Nicholls* 113
6 ch g Indian Ridge - Petal Girl
6^{5g} 26^{6gf} 2^{5gf} 2^{5s} 8^{6gs} 2^{6g} **0-3-6**
£32,875

Lago D'Orta (Ire) *D Nicholls* 81
5 ch g Bahhare (USA) - Maelalong (Ire)
13^{8gs} 9^{9g} 20^{7gf} 15^{8gf} **0-0-4**

Lago Di Como *R Ford* 41
8 b g Piccolo - Farmer's Pet
8^{10s} 12^{16s} 13^{12g} **0-0-3**

Lahob *P Howling* a41
5 ch g First Trump - Mystical Song
11^{12sd} 5^{9sd} 8^{9sd} **0-0-3**

Laith (Ire) *B W Hills* 81
2 b g Royal Applause - Dania (Ger)
4^{5gf} 5^{6f} 4^{6gs} 1^{5gf} 7^{5gf} **1-0-5 £4,455**

Lake Andre (Ire) *K A Ryan* 96 a97
4 b g Lake Coniston (Ire) - Shadow Casting
1^{7s} 1^{7hy} 11^{8gy} 15^{7g} 5^{5sf} 10^{6sd} **2-0-6**
£18,893

Lake Bonneville (USA) *Robert Gray* a8
2 b f Diesis - Muneefa (USA)
8^{6sd} **0-0-1**

Lake Carezza (USA) *J Noseda* 14
3 b g Stravinsky (USA) - May Wedding (USA)
11^{5gs} **0-0-1**

Lake Chini (Ire) *M A Jarvis* 58 a77
3 b g Raise A Grand (Ire) - Where's The Money
7^{6g} 1^{6ft} 10^{6sd} 1^{6sd} 13^{5sd} **2-0-5 £6,020**

Lake Diva *J G Given* a67
4 ch f Docksider (USA) - Cutpurse Moll
1^{11sd} 8^{12sd} 10^{9sd} 8^{9sd} 6^{8sd} **1-0-5**
£2,182

Lake Eyre (Ire) *J Balding* a46
6 b m Bluebird (USA) - Pooh Wee
10^{6sd} 3^{5sd} 4^{6sd} 10^{5sd} **0-1-4 £221**

Lake Garda *N Tinkler* 80
4 b g Komaite (USA) - Malcesine (Ire)
14^{6g} 7^{6s} 10^{8gs} 12^{6gs} 11^{6g} 16^{6gs} 15^{6s}
0-0-7

Lake Hero *K A Ryan* 73
2 b f Arkadian Hero (USA) - Inya Lake
7^{5gs} 1^{5gf} 6^{5gs} 8^{5gf} 1^{5gf} 19^{5gf} 3^{6gf} 7^{6gf} 8^{6gf}
11^{6gf} 3^{5gf} **2-1-11 £10,475**

Lake Poet (Ire) *C E Brittain* 92 a69
2 ch c Galileo (Ire) - Lyric
3^{6gf} 5^{7g} 6^{7gs} 3^{7sd} 5^{7s} **0-2-5 £3,043**

Lake Suprima (Ire) *R M Whitaker* 46 a31
2 b f Primo Valentino (Ire) - Sulaka
8^{5g} 11^{6sf} 3^{5sd} **0-1-3 £369**

Lake Verdi (Ire) *Jennie Candlish* a36
6 ch g Lake Coniston (Ire) - Shore Lark (USA)
8^{9sd} 9^{7sd} 8^{5sd} **0-0-3**

Lake Wakatipu *M Mullineaux* 54 a52
3 b f Lake Coniston (Ire) - Lady Broker
14^{7s} 5^{7sd} 4^{7hy} 3^{8sd} 9^{7sd} 11^{9sd} 4^{9sd} 10^{9ss}
0-1-8 £692

Lakesdale (Ire) *Miss D Mountain* 28 a54
3 b f Desert Style (Ire) - Option (Ire)
4^{8sd} 9^{9sd} 2^{10sd} 5^{9sd} 5^{9sd} 3^{10sd} 9^{7s} 6^{10sd} 4^{8sd}
6^{9g} 7^{10gs} 8^{10g} 13^{7g} 11^{10sd} **0-1-14**
£1,236

Lakeside Guy (Ire) *M Appleby* 55 a59
4 b g Revoque (Ire) - Glen Of Imaal (Ire)
12^{7sd} 4^{7sd} 10^{6sd} 1^{7sd} 3^{6sd} 10^{7sd} 5^{6sd} 7^{7sd}
7^{7sd} 5^{7sd} 3^{6g} 6^{7sd} 10^{7sd} 6^{7sd} 8^{7sd} 15^{6g} 11^{6ss}
1-2-17 £1,925

Lakota Brave *Stef Liddiard* a81
11 ch g Anshan - Pushkinia (Fr)
3^{8sd} 5^{9sd} 1^{7sd} 1^{8sd} 2^{8sd} 9^{8sd} **2-2-6**
£6,829

Lambency (Ire) *J G Given* 36 a51
2 b f Daylami (Ire) - Triomphale (USA)
9^{7s} 8^{6s} 8^{5sd} **0-0-3**

Lambriggan Lad *Miss Victoria Roberts*
3 b g Mazurek - Alfs Classic (Fr)
14^{11sd} **0-0-1**

Lamh Eile (Ire) *T D Barron* 93
3 b f Lend A Hand - Mothers Footprints (Ire)
3^{7gs} 3^{8g} 14^{7g} 7^{10gf} 9^{8g} 9^{8gf} **0-1-6**
£3,031

Lamington (Ire) *N P Littmoden* a31
2 ch g Grand Lodge (USA) - Maid Of Killeen (Ire)
12^{6sd} 9^{6g} 11^{8sd} **0-0-3**

Lamitta *M R Channon* 35
2 b f Diktat - Altaweelah (Ire)
12^{7gf} **0-0-1**

Lamon Bay (Ire) *D Carroll* a19
4 b f Perugino (USA) - Blue Jazz (Ire)
9^{7sd} 15^{8s} 11^{6sd} **0-0-3**

Lampos (USA) *Miss J A Camacho* a50
5 b/br g Southern Halo (USA) - Gone Private (USA)
4^{16sd} 5^{14sd} 2^{14sd} 5^{16sd} 7^{17sd} 7^{14sd} 11^{17sd}
0-1-7 £423

Land 'n Stars *Jamie Poulton* 104 a91
5 b g Mtoto - Uncharted Waters

1^{13sd} 6^{19gs} 3^{16sd} 6^{16g} 2^{15gs} 2^{14gf} 1^{16g} 6^{18gs}
2-3-8 £40,757

Land Of Light *Saeed Bin Suroor* 37
2 ch c Fantastic Light (USA) - Russian Snows (Ire)
10^{8g} **0-0-1**

Land Of Nod (Ire) *G Brown* a5
4 b f Barathea (Ire) - Rafif (USA)
13^{13sd} **0-0-1**

Land Sun's Legacy (Ire) *J S Wainwright*
4 b g Red Sunset - Almost A Lady (Ire)
19^{12gf} 12^{11gs} **0-0-2**

Landescent (Ire) *Miss K M George* 51 a47
5 b g Grand Lodge (USA) - Traumerei (Ger)
5^{11gs} 10^{12sd} 5^{10sd} 1^{11g} **1-0-4 £1,533**

Landucci *J W Hills* 89 a69
4 b g Averti (Ire) - Divina Luna
4^{6sd} 7^{6g} 1^{7gf} 3^{7f} 1^{7gf} 1^{7f} 3^{7gf} 1^{8f} 3^{9g} 4^{8gf}
6^{8gf} 9^{7gf} **4-1-12 £26,701**

Lane Marshal *M E Sowersby* 42
3 gr g Danzig Connection (USA) - Evening Falls
8^{10g} 14^{12g} 12^{6sd} 8^{7g} **0-0-4**

Langdale *E J Alston* 54 a64
3 ch g Dr Fong (USA) - Ciboure
7^{7sd} 9^{8sd} 7^{8g} 7^{9ft} 4^{7g} **0-0-5**

Langford *M H Tompkins* 104 a98
5 ch g Compton Place - Sharpening
11^{9g} 7^{8gf} 2^{8gf} 1^{8gf} 2^{9gf} 1^{8gf} 2^{8sd} 2^{8gf} 6^{8gf}
2^{8gf} 27^{9s} **2-5-11 £32,011**

Langston Boy *M L W Bell* 62 a76
3 b g Namid - Blinding Mission (Ire)
2^{8sd} 1^{7sd} 6^{7gs} 10^{7gf} 7^{7sd} 13^{7sd} **1-1-6**
£5,544

Lankawi *Jedd O'Keeffe* 53 a54
3 ch g Unfuwain (USA) - Zarma (Fr)
8^{9sd} 9^{8gs} 9^{7gf} 11^{12gf} 9^{13s} **0-0-5**

Lantau Peak *T D Easterby* 53 a34
2 b c Observatory (USA) - Shifty Mouse
13^{6gf} 6^{6gf} 10^{7sd} 7^{7gf} 12^{7g} 13^{7g} 7^{7gf} 17^{7gf}
0-0-8

Laphonic (USA) *T J Etherington* 49
2 b g Labeeb - Speechless (USA)
5^{7gf} 6^{9g} 2^{7s} **0-1-3 £955**

Lapwing (Ire) *Christian Wroe* 93 a36
7 b g Tagula (Ire) - Wasaif (Ire)
3^{6gf} 7^{7gf} 6^{6g} 27^{6gs} 13^{6gf} 18^{6g} 7^{8g} 11^{7ft}
0-1-8 £6,479

Laqataat (Ire) *J L Dunlop* 73
2 b f Alhaarth (Ire) - Jawlaat (USA)
9^{7gf} 2^{7gf} 4^{7s} **0-1-3 £1,610**

Lara Falana *Miss B Sanders* a67
7 b m Tagula (Ire) - Victoria Mill
7^{7sd} 2^{8sd} 8^{10sd} **0-1-3 £1,055**

Larad (Ire) *J S Moore* 60 a64
4 br g Desert Sun - Glenstal Priory
8^{9sd} 3^{9sd} 14^{10sd} 4^{12sd} 2^{12sd} 3^{17sd} 2^{13sd} 5^{9sd}
4^{12s} 4^{10gf} 11^{12sd} 7^{10g} 15^{10gf} 14^{12sd} 10^{10sd}
9^{10sd} 4^{12sd} **0-5-17 £3,163**

Lardy Lad *B Ellison* 51
2 b c Groom Dancer (USA) - Finlandaise (Fr)
6^{7g} 8^{6g} 13^{7gf} 6^{8g} **0-0-4**

Largs *J Balding* 53 a51
5 ch m Sheikh Albadou - Madam Zando
9^{7sd} 3^{6sd} 1^{6sd} 6^{6sd} 8^{6sd} 6^{6sd} 7^{6sd} 3^{5gf} 9^{5gf}
13^{5gf} 2^{5gf} 7^{5gf} 13^{5g} 1^{5g} 11^{6g} 8^{6sf} 1^{5ss} 2^{5sd}
1^{5ss} **4-4-19 £7,318**

Lark In The Park (Ire) *Mrs G S Rees* 49
5 ch m Grand Lodge (USA) - Jarrayan
5^{8gf} 12^{12f} 6^{11gf} 10^{9gf} 11^{8f} 10^{7gf} **0-0-6**

Larking About (USA) *W J Musson* 55
5 ch m Silver Hawk (USA) - Milly Ha Ha
5^{17g} 12^{17f} 9^{13gf} **0-0-3**

Larkwing (Ire) *G Wragg* 102
4 b c Ela-Mana-Mou - The Dawn Trader (USA)
3^{12gf} 4^{19gs} 9^{14g} 5^{14gs} 3^{16g} 3^{15gs} 2^{16g}
0-5-7 £17,617

Larky's Lob *J O'Reilly* 55 a67
6 b g Lugana Beach - Eucharis
8^{5sd} 9^{5sd} 3^{6gf} 7^{5gf} 5^{5gf} 4^{6gf} 9^{7gf} 6^{6g} 10^{5g}
4^{5ft} 8^{7sd} **0-2-11 £445**

Lasanga *R W Price* 48 a41
6 ch g Zamindar (USA) - Shall We Run
10^{8sd} 7^{8gs} 14^{8gf} **0-0-3**

Lasso *R Charlton* 62
3 ch f Indian Ridge - Rosse
6^{6gs} 1^{7gf} 4^{7gf} **1-0-3 £4,115**

Last Chapter (Ire) *John Berry* 32
3 b g Desert Story (Ire) - Dutosky
11^{7g} **0-0-1**

Last Offer (Ire) *M G Quinlan* 39
2 b/br f Raise A Grand (Ire) - Where's The Money
10^{7gs} **0-0-1**

Last Pioneer (Ire) *T P Tate* 66
3 b g New Frontier (Ire) - Toordillon (Ire)
6^{8s} 2^{11s} 3^{11gs} 8^{12gf} **0-1-4 £1,689**

Lasting Image *S C Williams* 28
3 br f Zilzal (USA) - Minsden's Image
9^{8gf} 16^{10g} 10^{14g} **0-0-3**

Lasting Love *C R Dore* 49 a55
2 ch f Primo Valentino (Ire) - Miss Beverley
5^{5gs} 5^{5g} 4^{6sd} 2^{6sd} 2^{6sd} 10^{6sd} **0-2-6**
£1,451

Late Arrival *M D Hammond* 52 a21
8 b g Emperor Jones (USA) - Try Vickers (USA)
6^{12sd} 1^{14f} 1^{16gf} 6^{16gf} 3^{14gf} 7^{16gf} 16^{16g}
2-1-7 £5,844

Late Night Love *K R Burke* a33
2 b f Bluebird (USA) - Syringa
11^{6sf} 10^{8sd} 11^{9sd} **0-0-3**

Lateen Sails *Saeed Bin Suroor* 110
5 ch g Elmaamul (USA) - Felucca
2^{8gs} 4^{8g} 3^{8gf} 4^{10g} 7^{12g} **0-2-5 £13,587**

Lateforbingo (Ire) *Michael Cunningham* 34 a14
4 b f Indian Rocket - Grand Princess (Ire)
13^{10f} 10^{10gf} 6^{9gf} 17^{5sh} 14^{8ss} 12^{6sd}
0-0-6

Lateral Thinker (Ire) *P D Evans* 41 a56
3 b f Desert Sun - Miss Margate (Ire)
7^{7sd} 10^{9sd} 9^{8g} 10^{7g} 4^{6s} 8^{7gf} 5^{7gf} 7^{6g} 8^{8sd}
0-0-9

Latif (USA) *Ms Deborah J Evans* 73 a47
4 b c Red Ransom (USA) - Awaamir
10^{9sd} 3^{8sd} 11^{6g} 2^{8gf} 4^{10g} 4^{8gf} 6^{7g} 3^{11gf} 2^{11gf}
5^{12gf} 7^{11g} 5^{11gs} 11^{10s} 7^{8gs} 6^{10gf} 3^{7sd}
0-4-16 £4,901

Latin Express (Ire) *W R Muir* 36 a50
3 b g Marju (Ire) - Sea Port
7^{8f} 9^{7gs} 18^{6gf} 4^{7sd} 4^{7sd} 10^{8sd} 11^{7sd}
0-0-7 £488

Latin Queen (Ire) *J D Frost* 40
5 b/br m Desert Prince (Ire) - Atlantic Dream (USA)

15^{8gs} 8^{12g} **0-0-2**

Latin Review (Ire) *A P Jarvis*
4 ch f Titus Livius (Fr) - Law Review (Ire)
13^{7sd} 13^{6sd} **0-0-2**

Latona *Saeed Bin Suroor* 60
2 b f Fantastic Light (USA) - Grecian Slipper
7^{7gf} **0-0-1**

Laugh 'n Cry *C A Cyzer* 75 a75
4 b f In The Wings - The Kings Daughter
7^{12s} 2^{10sd} 5^{8gf} 3^{8sd} 6^{9gf} **0-2-5 £2,125**

Laurel Dawn *C N Kellett* 43 a48
7 gr g Paris House - Madrina
7^{6sd} 7^{7sd} 7^{6sd} 5^{5sd} 7^{5sd} 3^{6sd} 6^{6sd} 14^{6gs} 2^{6sd} 9^{7sd} 3^{5sd} 6^{5sd} 8^{6g} 13^{5gf} 9^{6s} 10^{6sd} 12^{5sd} **0-3-17 £1,037**

Lauren Louise *T T Clement* 54 a54
3 b f Tagula (Ire) - Movie Star (Ire)
5^{6sd} 9^{7sd} 7^{7sd} 3^{7sd} 9^{8gf} 3^{6gf} 6^{7g} 5^{7gf} 9^{7gf} 8^{6sd} **0-2-10 £704**

Lauro *Miss J A Camacho* 75
5 b m Mukaddamah (USA) - Lapu-Lapu
4^{10g} 6^{8gs} 6^{11gf} 5^{9s} 13^{8gf} 15^{8gs} **0-0-6 £531**

Laurollie *Dr J R J Naylor* 54 a54
3 b f Makbul - Madonna Da Rossi
4^{9sd} 7^{9sd} 5^{8sd} 3^{9sd} 3^{10sd} 4^{9sd} 10^{8gf} 1^{10g} 5^{10g} 3^{11f} 1^{12sd} 2^{10g} 2^{12f} 12^{12g} 8^{12sd} **2-4-15 £7,735**

Lava Flow (Ire) *M L W Bell* 55
2 ch c Danehill Dancer (Ire) - Tumble
8^{5g} 6^{5gs} **0-0-2**

Lavenham (Ire) *R Hannon* 73
2 b f Kalanisi (Ire) - Antigonel (Ire)
13^{7g} 11^{7gf} 4^{6gf} 3^{6g} 12^{7gf} **0-1-5 £1,170**

Lavish Times *A Berry* a32
4 ch c Timeless Times (USA) - Lavernock Lady
10^{7sd} 7^{5sd} **0-0-2**

Law Breaker (Ire) *Miss J Feilden* 84 a80
7 ch g Case Law - Revelette
12^{6s} 6^{6s} 3^{6g} 4^{6gs} 2^{7g} 2^{7g} 10^{7gf} 9^{7gf} 6^{5gs} 4^{7sd} 11^{8gs} 2^{9sd} 8^{8sd} **0-4-13 £7,543**

Law Maker *A Bailey* 68 a78
5 b g Case Law - Bo' Babbity
1^{5sd} 2^{5sd} 1^{6sd} 2^{5f} 5^{5f} 1^{5f} 2^{5gf} 1^{6sd} 12^{6gf} 6^{6gf} 1^{6sd} 5^{5gs} 7^{5gf} 4^{6sd} 5^{5sd} 1^{5sf} **6-3-16 £18,840**

Lawaaheb (Ire) *B R Johnson* a62
4 b g Alhaarth (Ire) - Ajayib (USA)
6^{10sd} 5^{12sd} 3^{10sd} 1^{10sd} 7^{8sd} 8^{12sd} 9^{12sd} 6^{9sd} 6^{7sd} 6^{10sd} **1-1-10 £3,355**

Lay A Whisper *C G Cox* 67 a36
3 br f Night Shift (USA) - Waffle On
4^{8g} 5^{8gf} 3^{8gf} 9^{10gs} 4^{8g} 8^{7f} 7^{6g} 7^{7sd} **0-1-8 £1,609**

Layazaal (Ire) *J L Dunlop* 88
2 b c Mujadil (USA) - Law Review (Ire)
1^{6gf} 14^{6gf} 3^{7g} 4^{7gf} **1-1-4 £6,239**

Layed Back Rocky *M Mullineaux* 59 a56
3 ch c Lake Coniston (Ire) - Madam Taylor
8^{5gs} 12^{10gf} 3^{8s} 10^{8gf} 16^{8g} 6^{8s} 2^{8ss} 11^{8sd} 4^{9sd} 8^{7ss} **0-2-10 £1,525**

Laylati (Ire) *M A Jarvis* 62
2 b f Green Desert (USA) - Saeedah
4^{5gf} 3^{5gf} 3^{6gs} 4^{7gf} **0-1-4 £2,075**

Layman (USA) *Saeed Bin Suroor* 121
3 ch c Sunday Silence (USA) - Laiyl (Ire)
1^{8gf} 6^{8g} 9^{10gs} **1-0-3 £36,300**

Lazzaz *P W Hiatt* 59 a64
7 b g Muhtarram (USA) - Astern (USA)
2^{12sd} 3^{14sd} 10^{13sd} 1^{12sd} 9^{14gs} 3^{12sd} 3^{12hy} 8^{14sd} 9^{12gf} 5^{14sd} 4^{12sd} 3^{13s} 11^{12gf} **1-4-13 £5,368**

Lazzoom (Ire) *Mrs L Stubbs* 51
2 b g Zilzal (USA) - Bring On The Choir
9^{5gf} 1^{6gf} 8^{6gf} 5^{6gf} 7^{7g} 12^{7gf} **1-0-6 £2,786**

Le Chatelier (Fr) *A W Carroll* 60
6 b g Kadalko (Fr) - Tulipp D'Avril (Fr)
6^{12gf} **0-0-1**

Le Chiffre (Ire) *N G Richards* 80 a79
3 br g Celtic Swing - Implicit View
1^{8g} 3^{7sd} **1-1-2 £6,137**

Le Colombier (Ire) *J W Hills* 82
2 ch c Alhaarth (Ire) - Wide Range (Ire)
4^{7g} 3^{8g} **0-1-2 £986**

Le Corvee (Ire) *A King* 96 a94
3 b c Rossini (USA) - Elupa (Ire)
5^{8gs} 4^{11f} 8^{12g} 5^{10sd} 12^{10g} **0-0-5 £3,015**

Le Petit Diable (Ire) *J S Goldie*
3 b f Trans Island - Mevlana (Ire)
14^{8g} 13^{11g} 15^{7gf} **0-0-3**

Le Soleil (Ger) *B J Curley* a61
4 b g Monsun (Ger) - La Blue (Ger)
11^{10sd} 8^{10sd} 6^{12sd} 6^{17sd} 18^{16g} 12^{16g} 1^{12sf} **1-0-7 £1,515**

Le Tiss (Ire) *M R Channon* 90
4 b g Croco Rouge (Ire) - Manarah
5^{12gf} 7^{12f} 4^{14gs} 8^{14g} 5^{13gf} 7^{12gs} 5^{16gf} 4^{14g} 13^{14s} **0-0-9 £1,350**

Le Vie Dei Colori *L M Cumani* 123
5 b h Efisio - Mystic Tempo (USA)
1^{7gs} 6^{8f} 6^{7g} 6^{8s} 5^{8g} 1^{7gs} **2-0-6 £80,785**

League Champion (USA) *G A Butler* 107
2 b c Rahy (USA) - Meiosis (USA)
1^{5gf} 7^{6gf} 3^{7gf} 5^{7s} 1^{6gf} 4^{8gf} **2-1-6 £18,900**

League Of Nations (Ire) *P F I Cole* 73 a72
3 b c Indian Danehill (Ire) - Athens Belle (Ire)
3^{10sd} 5^{12gs} 8^{10sd} 14^{12g} 6^{14gf} 12^{12g} 1^{12f} **1-1-7 £4,382**

Leah's Pride *P Howling* a51
4 b f Atraf - First Play
12^{7sd} 7^{6sd} 9^{5sd} 6^{6sd} 2^{6sd} 9^{6sf} 8^{5sd} 3^{5sd} 1^{5sd} 7^{5sd} **1-2-10 £2,050**

Leamington Lad (Ire) *M F Harris* 48 a10
2 gr c Beckett (Ire) - Nicea (Ire)
4^{6f} 8^{7g} 12^{5sd} **0-0-3 £260**

Leaping Brave (Ire) *B R Millman* 70 a56
4 b g Indian Rocket - Island Heather (Ire)
12^{9sd} 2^{10s} 9^{10s} 3^{8gs} 10^{7g} 7^{7gf} 10^{8g} 2^{8g} **0-3-8 £2,385**

Leda *B J Meehan* 60
2 ch f Bertolini (USA) - Western Horizon (USA)
10^{6gf} 13^{7gf} **0-0-2**

Leeson Street (Ire) *M G Quinlan* a44
2 b f Xaar - Falconera (Ire)
8^{10sd} **0-0-1**

Lefonic *G C H Chung* a44
3 ch c Zafonic (USA) - La Adrada

9^{10sd} **0-0-1**

Left Hand Drive *B W Duke* 41 a47
2 b g Erhaab (USA) - Eyelet (Ire)
9^{8gs} 12^{7sd} 11^{8g} **0-0-3**

Left Nostril (Ire) *P S McEntee* 55 a42
2 b f Beckett (Ire) - Baywood
10^{5gf} 11^{5gf} 6^{5g} 4^{5sd} 8^{5gf} 6^{6f} 8^{5g} 9^{5gf} 12^{7g} 4^{5gf} 4^{6sd} 8^{6sd} 5^{7sd} **0-0-13**

Leg Spinner (Ire) *A J Martin* 92
4 b g Intikhab (USA) - Road Harbour (USA)
7^{16gf} 1^{20gf} **1-0-2 £29,000**

Legacy (Jpn) *P D Evans* 55 a44
5 b g Carnegie (Ire) - Idraak
12^{6s} 12^{6g} 13^{7gf} 15^{8g} 9^{8g} 13^{10g} 13^{9sd} 14^{10sd} **0-0-8**

Legal Belle *J L Spearing* 47
3 ch f Superpower - Legal Sound
7^{6g} 10^{7gf} 12^{6gs} 16^{6hy} **0-0-4**

Legal Call *M Appleby* 56 a26
2 b g Easycall - Legal Sound
6^{5gf} 3^{5gf} 4^{5g} 14^{6g} 7^{5sd} **0-1-5 £1,614**

Legal Dram *M Dods* a56
4 ch g Case Law - Moonshine Malt
8^{6sf} 8^{7sd} 5^{9sd} **0-0-3**

Legal Lover (Ire) *R Hollinshead* 57 a57
3 b c Woodborough (USA) - Victoria's Secret (Ire)
7^{6g} 5^{6gf} 7^{6g} 12^{8gs} 15^{8g} 7^{8gf} 8^{9sd} 11^{7gf} 7^{7sd} 1^{8sd} 1^{8ss} 6^{7sd} 4^{9sd} 5^{8sd} **2-0-14 £2,846**

Legal Set (Ire) *Miss A Stokell* 68 a74
9 gr g Second Set (Ire) - Tiffany's Case (Ire)
4^{6sd} 1^{6sd} 5^{5sd} 5^{5sd} 3^{6sd} 4^{5sd} 6^{6sd} 7^{6sd} 11^{6sd} 6^{6s} 1^{6s} 3^{6sd} 4^{6gs} 10^{6gf} 7^{6g} 7^{5gf} 13^{6gf} 5^{6f} 9^{6gf} 8^{6gs} 6^{5f} 8^{5gf} 5^{5g} 5^{6gs} 9^{5gf} 5^{5sd} 12^{6gf} 9^{6sd} 5^{6g} 14^{5sd} 4^{5sd} 4^{5sd} 9^{5sd} 2^{5sd} **2-2-34 £8,611**

Legally Fast (USA) *S C Burrough* 66
3 b c Deputy Minister (Can) - Earthly Angel (USA)
3^{12s} 3^{12f} 1^{14gf} 3^{14g} 5^{17g} 14^{16gf} 1^{12gf} **2-2-7 £7,982**

Legend Of Dance *J L Spearing* a33
3 b f Dansili - Hard Task
15^{10hy} 2^{9sd} 8^{12sd} **0-1-3 £434**

Leighton Buzzard *P W Chapple-Hyam* 57
3 b g Cyrano De Bergerac - Winsome Wooster
7^{8gf} 5^{7gf} **0-0-2**

Leitrim House *B J Meehan* 105
4 ch c Cadeaux Genereux - Lonely Heart
1^{6gf} 17^{6gs} 9^{7g} 10^{7gf} 7^{7gf} **1-0-5 £18,560**

Lekka Ding (Ire) *C F Wall* 19
3 b/br f Raise A Grand (Ire) - Non Dimenticar Me (Ire)
12^{10g} 20^{10gf} **0-0-2**

Lemon Drop Lad (USA) *Sir Michael Stoute* 72
2 ch c Lemon Drop Kid (USA) - April Starlight (USA)
8^{7gf} **0-0-1**

Lennel *A Bailey* 58 a76
7 b g Presidium - Ladykirk
7^{12sd} 2^{12sd} 1^{13sd} 3^{12sd} 5^{12sd} 6^{12sd} 6^{12sd} 14^{12sd} 7^{11gf} 6^{14g} PU^{12gf} 4^{13gs} 2^{12f} 12^{16g} 2^{15g} **1-4-15 £7,159**

Lennoxtown (Ire) *M A Jarvis* 27
2 ch c Selkirk (USA) - Pump (USA)
8^{7s} **0-0-1**

Lenoir (Ger) *V Smith* 73 a66
2 b c Lujain (USA) - Luna De Miel
11^{7g} 6^{7g} 4^{7g} 29^{6g} 4^{7g} 5^{9sd} 6^{7sd} 1^{8sd} 3^{7sd} **1-1-9 £3,201**

Lenwade *G G Margarson* 52
4 gr f Environment Friend - Branitska
14^{10gf} 10^{10f} 4^{11g} 11^{16gs} 2^{12gf} 4^{10gf} 3^{10g} 2^{12gf} 7^{12g} 1^{10f} 2^{10g} 5^{11g} 3^{12gs} **1-5-13 £4,088**

Leo *J H M Gosden* 108 a81
2 ch c Pivotal - Miss Penton
4^{6s} 1^{6gf} 2^{7gs} 6^{8vs} 2^{8gf} 1^{8g} 9^{9ft} **2-2-7 £65,611**

Leo McGarry (Ire) *S C Williams* 42
2 ch g Fantastic Light (USA) - Lilissa (Ire)
9^{6gs} 10^{6g} 9^{6gf} **0-0-3**

Leo's Lucky Star (USA) *R S Brookhouse* 99
3 b g Forestry (USA) - Leo's Lucky Lady (USA)
6^{8gs} 2^{8g} 11^{6gs} 12^{8gs} 14^{10g} 12^{8gf} 16^{7g} **0-1-7 £3,300**

Leo's Luckyman (USA) *R S Brookhouse* 107
6 b/br g Woodman (USA) - Leo's Lucky Lady (USA)
18^{10g} 1^{10s} **1-0-2 £17,400**

Leoballero *D J Daly* a81
5 ch g Lion Cavern (USA) - Ball Gown
8^{7sd} 10^{8sd} 10^{8sd} **0-0-3**

Leopoldine *H Morrison* 69
2 br f Desert Prince (Ire) - Beaming
4^{7gf} 8^{7g} 2^{6g} **0-1-3 £1,645**

Leporello (Ire) *W R Swinburn* 105
5 b h Danehill (USA) - Why So Silent
5^{10g} 7^{10gf} 2^{10g} **0-1-3 £3,711**

Leprechaun's Maite *P A Blockley* 10
3 b g Komaite (USA) - Leprechaun Lady
10^{8hy} **0-0-1**

Lerida *Miss Lucinda V Russell*
3 ch g Groom Dancer (USA) - Catalonia (Ire)
9^{10s} **0-0-1**

Leroidesanimaux (Brz) *R J Frankel* 127
5 ch h Candy Stripes (USA) - Dissemble
1^{8g} 1^{9f} 1^{8y} 2^{8y} **3-1-4 £628,058**

Les Arcs (USA) *T J Pitt* 98 a102
5 br g Arch (USA) - La Sarto (USA)
3^{7sd} 2^{8sd} 2^{7sd} 2^{7gs} 8^{8g} 1^{7g} 1^{7gf} 5^{6gf} 2^{7g} 11^{7g} 4^{6s} 8^{7sd} 1^{6sd} **3-6-13 £41,491**

Les Soeurs (Ire) *M L W Bell* 32
2 b f Indian Lodge (Ire) - Manazil (Ire)
11^{6g} 10^{7g} 14^{7gf} 13^{8gf} **0-0-4**

Leslingtaylor (Ire) *J J Quinn* 71
3 b g Orpen (USA) - Rite Of Spring
11^{6hy} 10^{6gs} 7^{6s} 10^{8g} 8^{8g} 8^{8g} 5^{11g} 1^{10gs} 5^{10g} 1^{12gf} 5^{14s} 9^{15s} **2-0-12 £7,239**

Lester Leaps In (USA) *R Hannon* 58
2 b/br c Red Ransom (USA) - Rose Aurora (USA)
9^{6gf} 7^{8gf} 11^{7g} **0-0-3**

Let It Be *K G Reveley* 72 a60
4 ch f Entrepreneur - Noble Dane (Ire)
7^{14gf} 4^{12g} 1^{14f} 3^{12gf} 1^{14gf} 4^{12gf} 8^{14gf} 7^{14g} 2^{14gf} 3^{14gf} 8^{17sd} **2-2-11 £12,315**

Let Me Try Again (Ire) *T G Mills* 96
5 b g Sadler's Wells (USA) - Dathiyna (Ire)
5^{12g} 13^{16g} **0-0-2 £513**

Let Slip *W Jarvis* 68
3 b f Second Empire (Ire) - Loose Talk
7^{8g} 2^{7g} 5^{8g} 2^{10gf} 3^{8gf} 4^{8g} 1^{10s} **1-3-7 £6,814**

Letham Spiel *M Johnston* 61
3 b c Singspiel (Ire) - Valley Of Hope (USA)

2^{10g} 8^{12gs} 3^{11g} **0-2-3 £1,587**

Lets Get It On (Ire) *J J Quinn* 69 a66
4 b f Perugino (USA) - Lets Clic Together (Ire)
9^{5g} 5^{6g} 2^{6gf} 5^{6sd} 11^{6gf} 9^{5gf} 8^{6gs} 4^{6sd} 9^{7sd} **0-1-9 £1,358**

Lets Roll *C W Thornton* 98
4 b g Tamure (Ire) - Miss Petronella
9^{12gf} 3^{12s} 4^{12gf} 1^{13gs} 9^{12gs} 3^{15gf} 5^{15gs} 1^{13g} 14^{18gs} 6^{12hy} **2-2-10 £21,621**

Levallois (Ire) *P Winkworth* 30
9 b g Trempolino (USA) - Broken Wave
12^{20s} **0-0-1**

Levantine (Ire) *John Berry* 37 a44
8 b g Sadler's Wells (USA) - Spain Lane (USA)
4^{9sd} 4^{8sd} 6^{8sd} 9^{7gf} 9^{10gf} **0-0-5**

Level Par (Ire) *J A Supple* a50
5 ch g Cadeaux Genereux - Howaida (Ire)
3^{9ss} **0-1-1 £211**

Levelled *D W Chapman* 46 a49
11 b g Beveled (USA) - Baino Charm (USA)
11^{5sd} 10^{5sd} 2^{5sd} 12^{5sd} 11^{6sd} 3^{5sd} 7^{5sd} 1^{5sd} 7^{5s} 9^{5gf} 7^{5gf} 4^{5gf} 11^{5gf} 8^{5sd} 12^{5sd} 11^{5ss} 11^{5sd} 11^{5sd} **1-3-18 £2,066**

Levera *A King* 82
2 b c Groom Dancer (USA) - Prancing
4^{6gf} 2^{6gf} 1^{6gs} **1-1-3 £7,186**

Lewis Island (Ire) *G L Moore* 65 a68
6 b g Turtle Island (Ire) - Phyllode
9^{12gs} 11^{12gs} 12^{12gf} 12^{12sd} **0-0-4**

Lewis Lloyd (Ire) *I A Wood* 45 a57
2 b c Indian Lodge (Ire) - Sandy Fitzgerald (Ire)
14^{8g} 7^{7sd} 15^{7gf} 11^{9sd} **0-0-4**

Lexicon *Miss S E Forster*
5 ch m Weldnaas (USA) - Swift Move
13^{9gf} 9^{12g} **0-0-2**

Leyaaly *Miss Z C Davison*
6 ch m Night Shift (USA) - Lower The Tone (Ire)
11^{11sd} 11^{8sd} **0-0-2**

Li Shih Chen *A P Jarvis* 63
2 ch c Dr Fong (USA) - Mad Annie (USA)
9^{6gf} 4^{6gf} **0-0-2 £371**

Liability (Ire) *Miss S E Hall* 46 a6
3 b f Bluebird (USA) - Madaniyya (USA)
5^{7g} 9^{7gf} 9^{7sd} **0-0-3**

Liakoura (Ger) *Mrs A J Perrett* 95
3 b g Royal Academy (USA) - Lady Member (Fr)
8^{8g} 2^{10gs} 13^{10g} 6^{8gs} 12^{8gs} **0-1-5 £4,725**

Liameliss *M A Allen* 49 a20
3 ch f Dr Fong (USA) - Ivory Palm (USA)
13^{10f} 6^{10gf} 3^{12gf} 11^{12sd} 15^{11gf} 7^{12f} **0-1-6 £435**

Liberate *Unknown* 44 a40
2 ch g Lomitas - Eversince (USA)
10^{7s} 8^{7hy} 9^{7sd} **0-0-3**

Liberation Square *J S Goldie* 41
2 ch g Compton Place - Class Wan
9^{5gs} 6^{6s} 7^{5g} 15^{6s} **0-0-4**

Liberty Run (Ire) *Mrs A J Hamilton-Fairley* 63
3 ch g Grand Lodge (USA) - Bathe In Light (USA)
8^{10gf} 10^{8gf} 7^{12gf} 10^{10gf} 1^{10gs} 5^{12s} **1-0-6 £2,948**

Liberty Seeker (Fr) *I Semple* 71
6 ch g Machiavellian (USA) - Samara (Ire)
2^{12gs} 4^{14g} 1^{10gf} 7^{10gf} 5^{11gf} **1-1-5 £5,613**

Libgatt (Ire) *M P Tregoning* 62
2 b f Mark Of Esteem (Ire) - Baaderah (Ire)
4^{5gf} 13^{7gf} 5^{6g} **0-0-3 £355**

Libre *Andrew Reid* 83 a80
5 b g Bahamian Bounty - Premier Blues (Fr)
4^{9sd} 10^{9sd} 2^{10s} 2^{10g} 3^{10g} 3^{8gf} 2^{8g} 2^{8gf} 5^{10g} 6^{8gf} 5^{8g} 12^{9sd} 1^{10sd} **1-6-13 £12,915**

Life Is Rosie (Ire) *D K Ivory* a39
3 ch f Rossini (USA) - Rachcara (Ire)
9^{6sd} 12^{10sd} 10^{7sd} 6^{6sd} **0-0-4**

Life Peer *M P Tregoning* 56
2 b g Mark Of Esteem (Ire) - Sadaka (USA)
14^{6gf} 9^{7gf} 13^{7g} **0-0-3**

Life's A Whirl *R Charlton* 77
3 b f Machiavellian (USA) - Spinning Top
5^{8gs} 2^{8f} 6^{8g} **0-1-3 £1,722**

Liferaft *K A Morgan* 47 a16
4 b f Kahyasi - Pontoon
11^{12sd} 9^{16gf} 5^{16s} 10^{13gs} 10^{16gf} 14^{13sd} **0-0-6**

Lifted Way *P R Chamings* 81 a8
6 b g In The Wings - Stack Rock
2^{8g} 17^{9g} 6^{8gf} 6^{8gf} 7^{8g} 9^{9gf} 14^{7sd} 12^{7g} **0-1-8 £2,115**

Liger *E A L Dunlop* 12
2 b c Fraam - Periquitum
13^{7gf} **0-0-1**

Light Meter (Ire) *J L Dunlop* 57
2 ch c Cadeaux Genereux - Zoom Lens (Ire)
6^{6gf} 12^{7f} 8^{8g} 12^{8g} **0-0-4**

Light Mozart *C E Brittain* 51 a54
2 b f Mozart (Ire) - Footlight Fantasy (USA)
9^{6gs} 6^{7sd} 4^{7sd} **0-0-3 £259**

Light Of Day (Ire) *Miss Diana Weeden* a26
2 b f Mutamam - Top Of The Morning
20^{7s} 11^{9sd} **0-0-2**

Light Of Dubai (USA) *Saeed Bin Suroor* a33
3 b f Gone West (USA) - A. P. Assay (USA)
6^{7sd} **0-0-1**

Light Of Morn *Rae Guest* 105
4 gr f Daylami (Ire) - My Emma
5^{12gf} 3^{13gf} 6^{15gf} 6^{14hy} **0-1-4 £5,920**

Light Scent (USA) *J Akehurst* 32
6 ch g Silver Hawk (USA) - Music Lane (USA)
11^{10gf} **0-0-1**

Light The Dawn (Ire) *W M Brisbourne* a32
5 ch m Indian Ridge - Flaming June (USA)
9^{6sd} 11^{6sd} 9^{7sd} 5^{6sd} 9^{5sd} **0-0-5**

Lighted Way *A M Balding* 50
3 b f Kris - Natchez Trace
13^{5gs} 9^{5s} 18^{7gf} 9^{6g} 5^{5f} 7^{5g} 8^{5hd} **0-0-7**

Lightening Fire (Ire) *B J Llewellyn* 50 a1
3 b g Woodborough (USA) - Glowlamp (Ire)
9^{10g} 3^{7gf} 12^{10gf} 17^{8gf} 3^{7gf} 3^{7g} 10^{7sd} **0-2-7 £1,383**

Lighthorne Lad *J R Jenkins* 48
3 ch g Hornbeam - Give Me A Day
3^{10g} 12^{8g} 6^{11g} 12^{8sd} **0-1-4 £364**

Lightning Affair (USA) *M Johnston* 82
2 gr c Thunder Gulch (USA) - Lady Affirmed (USA)
2^{7gf} 2^{7g} 1^{7gf} **1-2-3 £7,027**

Lightning Flash *J R Fanshawe* a86
3 br c Docksider (USA) - Threatening
1^{7sd} **1-0-1 £4,316**

Lightning Prospect *P C Haslam*
3 ch f Zaha (Can) - Lightning Blaze
12^{6sd} 7^{10gf} 8^{7gf} **0-0-3**

Lights Out (Den) *Ms C Erichsen* a98
5 b g Kateb (Ire) - Skee The Feen
3^{8sd} 7^{9g} 8^{8s} 9^{8g} 9^{9sd} 2^{8sd} 9^{10g} 1^{9sd} 1^{8sd} 8^{8sy} 11^{10sd} 9^{10sd} **2-0-12 £6,337**

Ligne D'Eau *P D Evans* 60 a63
4 ch g Cadeaux Genereux - Miss Waterline
3^{6sd} 10^{7sd} 3^{6sd} 5^{6gf} 13^{7sd} 12^{6gs} 6^{6s} 5^{6sd} 6^{7gf} 1^{7g} 9^{8gf} 9^{7gf} 7^{6sd} 11^{7sd} **1-2-14 £3,944**

Lihusn Al Haz (USA) *C E Brittain* 18
2 b/br f King Cugat (USA) - Chaste (USA)
16^{7g} **0-0-1**

Lii Najma *C E Brittain* 58
2 b f Medicean - Opari (Ire)
6^{7g} 10^{6g} **0-0-2**

Lilac *R J Price* a25
6 ch m Alhijaz - Fairfield's Breeze
7^{14sd} 8^{17sd} **0-0-2**

Lilac Mist *H R A Cecil* 78
3 b f Spectrum (Ire) - L'Ideale (USA)
2^{10gs} 2^{10g} 4^{12g} 3^{10gf} 2^{11g} 2^{10gf} 3^{10s} 7^{10gs} **0-5-8 £5,914**

Lilian *Miss Z C Davison* a30
5 b m First Trump - Lillibella
5^{10sd} 14^{13sd} **0-0-2**

Lillas Forest *P C Haslam*
3 b g Forestry (USA) - Lines Of Beauty (USA)
7^{8gs} **0-0-1**

Lillebror (Ger) *B J Curley* 60
7 b g Top Waltz (Fr) - Lady Soliciti (Ger)
2^{11s} 7^{12gf} **0-1-2 £1,050**

Lilli Marlane *N A Callaghan* a71
5 b m Sri Pekan (USA) - Fiveofive (Ire)
6^{10sd} **0-0-1**

Lillianna (Ire) *P W Hiatt* 44 a47
4 ch f Barathea (Ire) - Machikane Akaiito (Ire)
12^{9sd} 6^{7sd} 10^{8sd} 12^{7sd} 6^{9sd} 4^{9sd} 1^{10sd} 5^{9sd} 5^{10g} 7^{10sd} 7^{10f} 4^{10sd} **1-0-12 £1,449**

Lillie Le Quesne *A M Balding* 38 a57
2 b f Desert Prince (Ire) - Bathe In Light (USA)
14^{7gf} 8^{8gs} 8^{7sd} **0-0-3**

Lilly Gee (Ire) *R P Elliott* a51
4 b f Ashkalani (Ire) - Welsh Mist
10^{6sd} 6^{6sd} 8^{9sd} **0-0-3**

Lillyella (Ire) *M J Wallace* a46
2 ch f Raise A Grand (Ire) - Somers Heath (Ire)
8^{7sd} **0-0-1**

Lily Of The Guild (Ire) *W S Kittow* a48
6 ch m Lycius (USA) - Secreto Bold
4^{7sd} 7^{9sd} 9^{9sd} **0-0-3**

Lily On A Hill *B Smart* a5
2 b f City On A Hill (USA) - Gulfstream Park
12^{6sf} **0-0-1**

Limit (Ire) *M R Channon* 65 a50
3 b f Barathea (Ire) - Orlena (USA)
4^{8s} 6^{7g} 9^{7sd} 11^{8gf} 9^{7f} 17^{6g} 8^{6f} **0-1-7 £288**

Limited Magician *C Smith* 32 a25
4 b f Wizard King - Pretty Scarce
11^{6sd} 8^{5sd} 4^{6gs} 9^{5g} 6^{5sd} 12^{6ss} 5^{5sd} **0-0-7**

Limonia (Ger) *D K Ivory* 60 a57
3 b f Perugino (USA) - Limoges (Ger)
1^{6sd} 4^{6gf} 5^{5sd} 15^{6g} 3^{7sf} 4^{6sd} 7^{6sd} **1-1-7 £3,977**

Linas Selection *M Johnston* 76
2 ch c Selkirk (USA) - Lines Of Beauty (USA)
7^{6g} 4^{6s} 1^{9g} **1-0-3 £5,285**

Lincoln Dancer (Ire) *R A Fahey* 82
8 b g Turtle Island (Ire) - Double Grange (Ire)
5^{5g} 8^{5g} **0-0-2**

Lincolneurocruiser *Mrs N Macauley* 82 a67
3 b g Spectrum (Ire) - Rush Hour (Ire)
6^{8gf} 4^{7gf} 7^{8gs} 11^{6gf} 14^{8gf} 12^{5g} 3^{6g} 3^{7gf} 9^{6s} 5^{7hy} **0-2-10 £1,874**

Linda Green *M R Channon* 71 a59
4 b f Victory Note (USA) - Edge Of Darkness
5^{5sd} 8^{6sd} 3^{6sd} 7^{5gf} 6^{5gf} 2^{6hy} 7^{6gf} 1^{6g} 1^{5g} 3^{6gs} 6^{6f} 2^{6s} 5^{6gf} 4^{5gf} 1^{6gs} 3^{6gf} 3^{6g} 6^{7gf} 5^{6g} 4^{6g} 13^{6g} 5^{6g} 5^{6g} 3^{7hy} 6^{7hy} **3-8-25 £21,824**

Linda's Colin (Ire) *P W D'Arcy* 62 a67
3 b g Xaar - Capable Kate (Ire)
7^{7sd} 14^{9g} 8^{8gs} **0-0-3**

Linda's Lad *A Fabre* 110
2 b c Sadler's Wells (USA) - Colza (USA)
2^{7g} 2^{7gs} 1^{8vs} 2^{8gs} 1^{9g} 1^{10hy} **3-1-6 £166,652**

Lindbergh *R Hannon* 94 a75
3 b g Bold Edge - Halland Park Girl (Ire)
8^{7gf} 1^{5gf} 4^{5gf} 3^{5gs} 5^{6s} 12^{6sd} 10^{6sd} **1-1-7 £8,395**

Linden Lime *Jamie Poulton* 65 a65
3 ch f Double Trigger (Ire) - Linden Grace (USA)
3^{8sd} 5^{12gs} 3^{10sd} 9^{10gf} 6^{10sd} 8^{9sd} **0-2-6 £975**

Linden's Lady *J R Weymes* 59
5 b m Compton Place - Jubilee Place (Ire)
8^{7g} 6^{7f} 10^{7gf} 2^{7gf} 3^{6f} 13^{6gf} 3^{7g} 3^{8gf} 1^{8gf} 1^{7gf} 3^{8gf} 10^{7gf} 7^{8gf} 7^{7g} **2-4-14 £9,554**

Lindenburgh Way (Ire) *B J Meehan* 78
2 b c Red Ransom (USA) - Strange Destiny
4^{6gs} **0-0-1 £486**

Lindus Atenor *K R Burke* 74 a75
2 b f Fraam - Nightingale Song
5^{5gs} 2^{5gf} 1^{6sd} 3^{7gf} 1^{6sd} 4^{6gf} 3^{5gf} **2-2-7 £10,391**

Linens Flame *B G Powell* 83
6 ch g Blushing Flame (USA) - Atlantic Air
1^{14gs} 9^{14gs} 9^{14gf} 6^{14gf} 12^{15s} 10^{16s} **1-0-6 £3,536**

Linnet (Ger) *Ian Williams* 79
3 b f Dr Fong (USA) - Lauderdale (Ger)
1^{8g} 3^{10gf} 1^{10gf} 6^{10g} 5^{12gf} 6^{13gf} 3^{12g} 4^{11g} **2-2-8 £9,511**

Linngari (Ire) *Sir Michael Stoute* 119
3 ch c Indian Ridge - Lidakiya (Ire)
4^{11g} 4^{10g} 1^{9gf} 1^{8g} **2-0-4 £33,684**

Linning Wine (Ire) *P A Blockley* a97
9 b g Scenic - Zallaka (Ire)
3^{10sd} 5^{12sd} 4^{10sd} 3^{9sd} 2^{9sd} 2^{9sd} **0-4-6 £6,042**

Linton Dancer (Ire) *J R Weymes* 54
2 b f Mujadil (USA) - Daisy Grey
11^{6g} 7^{5gf} 7^{6g} 3^{7gf} 3^{8g} **0-2-5 £1,494**

Linzis Lad *K A Ryan*
3 ch g Magic Ring (Ire) - Come On Katie
11^{9sd} **0-0-1**

Lion Hunter (USA) *Miss E C Lavelle* a78

6 b g Quest For Fame - Prodigious (Fr)
9^{10sd} **0-0-1**

Lion's Domane *K W Hogg*
8 b g Lion Cavern (USA) - Vilany
14^{7sd} **0-0-1**

Lionaire (Ire) *P D Evans* 22
2 ch c Royal Academy (USA) - Higher Circle (USA)
9^{5gs} **0-0-1**

Lipizza (Ire) *N A Callaghan* 75 a72
2 b f Spinning World (USA) - Lipica (Ire)
12^{7gs} 8^{7sd} 2^{6g} 2^{6sd} 4^{7g} 1^{5hy} **1-3-6 £7,008**

Liquid Lover (Ire) *W M Brisbourne* 25 a49
3 b g Night Shift (USA) - New Tycoon (Ire)
13^{7f} 17^{8gf} 10^{12sf} 4^{11sd} 12^{11ss} 5^{9sd} 2^{12sd} 3^{12sd} **0-2-8 £632**

Lirage *M Mullineaux* 51
3 b f Wizard King - Diamond Rouge
10^{7gs} 8^{6gf} 11^{6gf} 12^{6g} 14^{8g} **0-0-5**

Lisfannon *B W Hills* 65 a48
2 ch f Bahamian Bounty - Amazed
4^{5gs} 7^{6sd} **0-0-2 £281**

Liss Ard (Ire) *John Joseph Murphy* 100
4 b c In The Wings - Beguine (USA)
2^{14hy} 9^{12gy} 6^{14gf} 3^{12gy} 9^{14g} 2^{10g} 16^{12g} 4^{12hy} **0-3-8 £13,866**

Listen To Reason (Ire) *J G Given* 56 a63
4 b g Mukaddamah (USA) - Tenalist (Ire)
6^{12sd} 6^{9sd} 5^{9sd} 5^{7g} 2^{8gf} 5^{8gf} 3^{7g} 7^{8gf} 15^{7gf} 2^{12sd} 10^{12sd} 11^{12sd} **0-3-12 £2,084**

Literatim *L M Cumani* 87
5 b g Polish Precedent (USA) - Annie Albright (USA)
5^{8gf} 7^{8gf} 15^{8gs} **0-0-3**

Little Almira *J Balding*
5 ch m Factual (USA) - Twice In Bundoran (Ire)
13^{7gf} 14^{7gs} 11^{5g} **0-0-3**

Little Biscuit (Ire) *K R Burke* 34 a48
3 ro f Indian Lodge (Ire) - Arjan (Ire)
6^{5sd} 5^{5sd} 7^{5sd} 5^{5sd} 5^{5s} **0-0-5**

Little Bob *J D Bethell* 74
4 ch g Zilzal (USA) - Hunters Of Brora (Ire)
10^{10g} 12^{11gf} 16^{9gs} 2^{10gs} 5^{10gs} 3^{10s} 12^{10s} 2^{10g} 5^{10gs} 1^{9hy} 4^{10hy} **1-3-11 £10,190**

Little Brave *C Roberts* a26
10 b g Kahyasi - Littlemisstrouble (USA)
9^{17sd} 9^{17sd} **0-0-2**

Little Britain (USA) *J Howard Johnson* 50
2 b g Stravinsky (USA) - I Don't Know (USA)
9^{6gf} 12^{6gf} **0-0-2**

Little Dunney *M W Easterby*
2 b c Timeless Times (USA) - Penny Hasset
13^{5gf} 14^{6gf} **0-0-2**

Little Edward *B G Powell* 82 a36
7 gr g King's Signet (USA) - Cedar Lady
9^{5gf} 6^{5f} 12^{6sd} 13^{6gf} 15^{5s} **0-0-5**

Little Elver *N Wilson* 48
2 gr f Inchinor - Zaragossa
14^{5g} 7^{5gf} 7^{5g} 5^{5gf} 11^{6g} 14^{6gf} 4^{5g} **0-0-7 £259**

Little Englander *M Hill*
5 b g Piccolo - Anna Karietta
15^{8gs} **0-0-1**

Little Erhaab *G L Moore* 32 a25
2 ch f Erhaab (USA) - Altara (Ire)
20^{7s} 13^{10sd} 11^{10sd} **0-0-3**

Little Eye (Ire) *J R Best* 81
4 b g Groom Dancer (USA) - Beaming
17^{10g} 5^{10gf} 6^{10gf} 2^{10g} 5^{10gs} 1^{11gf} 2^{12g} 5^{10gf} 1^{10g} **2-2-9 £9,549**

Little Eyecatcher (Ire) *T D Easterby* 49
2 b c Beckett (Ire) - Black Jack Girl (Ire)
6^{7gf} 5^{7f} **0-0-2**

Little Flute *T Keddy* 11
4 b g Piccolo - Nordic Victory (USA)
14^{5gf} **0-0-1**

Little Gannet *T D McCarthy* 37 a46
4 ro f Bien Bien (USA) - Lady Kalliste
10^{14s} 10^{13sd} 7^{13sd} **0-0-3**

Little Goldmine (Ire) *A B Haynes*
3 ch f Raise A Grand (Ire) - State Treasure (USA)
13^{7sd} 12^{8sd} **0-0-2**

Little Good Bay *J H M Gosden* 104 a103
5 b h Danehill (USA) - Brave Kris (Ire)
2^{10sd} 3^{8gf} 4^{8gf} 13^{8ft} 4^{8gs} 7^{8g} 2^{7gf} 7^{8gf} 13^{8gf} 6^{8gf} 5^{8gf} 4^{9gf} 2^{10g} 5^{10gs} **0-6-14 £26,553**

Little Indy *R Brotherton*
3 ch g Forzando - Indian Nectar
12^{7g} 13^{7sd} **0-0-2**

Little Jimbob *R A Fahey* 90
4 b g Desert Story (Ire) - Artistic Licence
4^{7gs} 1^{8gf} 14^{8g} 2^{8gf} 7^{9g} 4^{10gf} 2^{8g} 3^{8gf} 3^{8g} 8^{8gf} 14^{8gf} 5^{9g} 15^{8gf} **1-4-13 £15,513**

Little Miss Daisy *A B Haynes* 68 a43
2 br f Zilzal (USA) - Jimgareen (Ire)
4^{5gs} 5^{6sd} 6^{6gf} 8^{7gf} 5^{8gf} 2^{7g} 2^{7gs} 14^{8g} **0-2-8 £2,491**

Little Miss Gracie *A B Haynes* 103 a83
3 gr f Efisio - Circled (USA)
4^{8gs} 8^{9gf} 6^{8gf} 1^{8gs} 9^{8gs} 2^{8g} 2^{8gf} 10^{8sd} **1-2-8 £18,121**

Little Richard (Ire) *M Wellings* 29 a55
6 b g Alhaarth (Ire) - Intricacy
9^{16sd} 2^{13sd} 4^{14sd} 3^{14sd} 2^{12sd} 1^{12sd} 3^{17sd} 1^{12sd} 7^{12sd} 7^{17sd} 10^{14g} 2^{12sd} 3^{14sd} 2^{14ss} **2-7-14 £5,285**

Little Ridge (Ire) *H Morrison* 66 a85
4 b g Charnwood Forest (Ire) - Princess Natalie
1^{5sd} 3^{5sd} 10^{5gs} 12^{5s} 18^{5gs} 4^{5sd} 12^{5sd} 9^{5sd} **1-1-8 £8,134**

Little Rort (Ire) *S T Lewis*
6 b g Ali-Royal (Ire) - Florinda (Can)
12^{14sd} **0-0-1**

Little Sparkler *T D Easterby* 45 a40
2 b f Stravinsky (USA) - Idma
8^{5gf} 7^{6gf} 9^{5g} 4^{5sd} 11^{6hy} **0-0-5**

Little Task *J S Wainwright* 36
7 b g Environment Friend - Lucky Thing
7^{12gf} 13^{12gf} 7^{13gf} 8^{16gf} **0-0-4**

Little Tobias (Ire) *J S Wainwright* 25
6 ch g Millkom - Barbara Frietchie (Ire)
17^{16g} 12^{14gf} 11^{16gf} **0-0-3**

Little Trinket *M J Polglase*
2 b f Magic Ring (Ire) - Leen
11^{5sd} 10^{6sd} **0-0-2**

Little Trump *M W Easterby* 63 a51
2 ch f First Trump - Mahbob Dancer (Fr)
3^{5sd} 2^{5sd} 9^{5g} 1^{6gf} 7^{5f} **1-2-5 £3,869**

Little Venice (Ire) *C F Wall* 89
5 b m Fumo Di Londra (Ire) - Petrine (Ire)

3^{7gs} 3^{8g} 5^{8g} 8^{8g} 1^{7s} 8^{8gf} 11^{8gs} **1-1-7 £11,570**

Little Warning *R M Beckett* 34 a38
3 b f Piccolo - Iltimas (USA)
9^{6sd} 14^{6gf} 11^{6gf} **0-0-3**

Little Whitesox *J Hetherton* 39 a16
2 ch f Arkadian Hero (USA) - Due West
4^{5gf} 11^{6s} 11^{6gf} 11^{5sd} 10^{6sd} **0-0-5**

Littledodayno (Ire) *J Noseda* 78
2 b f Mujadil (USA) - Perfect Welcome
2^{5gf} 1^{6f} 2^{5g} **1-2-3 £8,617**

Littleton Telchar (USA) *J Ryan* 73 a60
5 ch g Atticus (USA) - Miss Waikiki (USA)
14^{10gs} 8^{10gf} 8^{9f} 12^{10gf} 14^{8gf} 1^{8f} 1^{8g} 3^{8gf} 4^{8gf} 7^{8gf} 3^{7gf} 8^{8g} 7^{8sd} **2-3-13 £11,507**

Littleton Zephir (USA) *Mrs P Townsley* 64 a71
6 b m Sandpit (Brz) - Miss Gorgeous (Ire)
6^{8sd} 1^{8sd} 4^{8sd} 1^{8sd} 5^{8gs} 7^{8gf} 6^{9sd} **2-0-7 £7,101**

Littletown Boy (USA) *P C Haslam*
3 gr c Stravinsky (USA) - Lady Aloma (Can)
12^{5gs} **0-0-1**

Litzinsky *J G M O'Shea* 21
7 b g Muhtarram (USA) - Boulevard Girl
15^{12g} **0-0-1**

Live And Dangerous *D Carroll* 52 a40
4 b f Mark Of Esteem (Ire) - Mazaya (Ire)
5^{6g} 5^{8sd} **0-0-2**

Live Fast (USA) *Saeed Bin Suroor* 82
2 ch c Machiavellian (USA) - Scratch Pad (USA)
2^{6gf} 2^{6gf} 2^{6gf} 11^{6g} 3^{6f} **0-4-5 £4,799**

Live Wire Lucy (USA) *Andrew Lee* 42
4 b f King Of The Heap (USA) - Approach The Bench (USA)
0^{10sd} 11^{12g} 10^{10gf} 11^{11g} 10^{13f} 12^{17g} 12^{10f} **0-0-7**

Liverti *D Carroll* 22
2 b f Averti (Ire) - Light Of Aragon
13^{6gf} 11^{7gf} **0-0-2**

Living For Gold (USA) *M Johnston* 68
3 b/br c Seeking The Gold (USA) - La Sila (USA)
5^{8g} **0-0-1**

Livvies Lady (Ire) *D K Ivory*
3 b f Opening Verse (USA) - Indian Wardance (Ity)
12^{7sd} **0-0-1**

Lizarazu (Ger) *R A Harris* 80 a78
6 b g Second Set (Ire) - Lilly (Ger)
6^{8f} 2^{8f} 1^{7gf} 1^{8gf} 3^{9g} 5^{7f} 2^{8gf} 5^{7g} 1^{8gf} 7^{8gs} 6^{9sd} 5^{8sd} 7^{8sd} **3-3-13 £13,863**

Lizzie Rocket *J O'Reilly* 52 a49
5 gr m Paris House - Jane's Affair
9^{6g} 7^{7g} 10^{7gf} 5^{6gf} 14^{7gf} 13^{6gf} 9^{7sd} 3^{7sd} 7^{7sd} 4^{6sd} 5^{8ss} 3^{7ss} 2^{5sd} 1^{5ss} **1-3-14 £1,761**

Llamadas *Andrew Reid* 66 a75
3 b g Josr Algarhoud (Ire) - Primulette
1^{7sd} 2^{7sd} 2^{7sd} 2^{7sd} 1^{9sd} 1^{7sd} 5^{9g} 10^{7sd} 9^{8sd} 1^{8sd} **4-3-10 £18,684**

Loaded Gun *W Storey* 54 a57
5 ch g Highest Honor (Fr) - Woodwardia (USA)
7^{9sd} 4^{9sd} 3^{9sd} 1^{9sd} 5^{9sd} 2^{9sd} 10^{9sd} 8^{9sd} 11^{9sd} 4^{10s} 8^{9gf} 14^{10g} **1-2-12 £2,396**

Loaderfun (Ire) *H Candy* 95
3 br g Danehill Dancer (Ire) - Sideloader Special
6^{6g} 9^{5gf} 14^{6gf} 6^{5s} **0-0-4 £682**

Lobengula (Ire) *I W McInnes* 65 a17
3 b g Spectrum (Ire) - Playwaki (USA)
7^{6gf} 1^{9gs} 15^{10gf} 14^{8sd} **1-0-4 £5,652**

Local Fancy *J M P Eustace* 75
2 b f Bahamian Bounty - Local Abbey (Ire)
4^{5gs} 1^{5s} 8^{6gf} 8^{6gf} **1-0-4 £3,785**

Local Poet *I Semple* 73 a81
4 b g Robellino (USA) - Laugharne
14^{6gf} 14^{5gf} 5^{7gf} 5^{6g} 10^{6gf} 6^{6gf} 5^{6sd} 8^{6gs} 6^{6hy} 1^{7sd} **1-0-10 £3,867**

Local Spirit (USA) *Saeed Bin Suroor* a56
2 ch f Lion Cavern (USA) - Crimson Conquest (USA)
5^{6sd} **0-0-1**

Loch Awe *J G Given* 57
2 b f Inchinor - Lochbelle
7^{6g} 6^{7s} 9^{8hy} **0-0-3**

Loch Quest (Ire) *Mrs A J Perrett* 81
3 ch g Giant's Causeway (USA) - Taibhseach (USA)
4^{12gs} 1^{12gf} 3^{11gf} 6^{10gf} 4^{12gf} 7^{12g} 10^{12gs} **1-0-7 £8,871**

Loch Verdi *A M Balding* 72
2 b f Green Desert (USA) - Lochsong
17^{6gf} 2^{5gs} **0-1-2 £1,127**

Lochbuie (Ire) *G Wragg* 117
4 b c Definite Article - Uncertain Affair (Ire)
3^{12g} 4^{13gs} 2^{16g} 12^{16g} 4^{16s} 1^{13g} 7^{15s} 5^{16gs} **1-1-8 £84,266**

Lochranza (Ire) *G Wragg* 72
3 b c Fasliyev (USA) - Mysistra (Fr)
9^{8gs} 6^{8gs} 4^{8gf} 14^{8gf} 18^{8gf} **0-0-5 £538**

Lockstock (Ire) *M S Saunders* 77 a72
7 b g Inchinor - Risalah
4^{9sd} 2^{7sd} 3^{7sd} 3^{9sd} 4^{8sd} 1^{8hy} 4^{7g} 4^{9sd} 17^{7g} 5^{8gs} 3^{9sd} **1-5-11 £8,109**

Lockstone Lad (USA) *Miss J S Davis*
2 gr c Mazel Trick (USA) - Humble (USA)
10^{5hy} **0-0-1**

Locombe Hill (Ire) *N Wilson* 78 a62
9 b g Barathea (Ire) - Roberts Pride
3^{7g} 3^{7gf} 10^{7s} 7^{7gs} 2^{7s} 2^{7sd} 1^{7sd} 4^{7sd} 15^{7g} 16^{8gf} 9^{7g} 8^{7g} 8^{7sd} 10^{8sf} 10^{7sd} **1-4-15 £7,398**

Lodger (Fr) *R J Hodges* 77
5 ch g Grand Lodge (USA) - Light River (USA)
15^{10gf} 11^{12gf} **0-0-2**

Lodgician (Ire) *J J Quinn* 58
3 b c Grand Lodge (USA) - Dundel (Ire)
10^{6gs} 16^{8g} 2^{10gf} 5^{11gf} 5^{12gf} 4^{10gf} 2^{12gf} 8^{16gf} **0-2-8 £2,659**

Logger Rhythm (USA) *R Dickin* 44
5 b g Woodman (USA) - Formidable Dancer (USA)
15^{17g} 8^{12gs} 14^{17f} **0-0-3**

Logistical *Ferdy Murphy* 50 a53
5 b g Grand Lodge (USA) - Magic Milly
1^{8sd} 5^{7sd} 10^{7gf} 7^{7sd} 2^{7gf} 9^{8gf} 11^{7g} 7^{7gf} 10^{8f} 8^{7sd} **1-1-10 £2,763**

Logsdail *G L Moore* 87 a81
5 b g Polish Precedent (USA) - Logic
9^{5gf} 14^{6g} 7^{8gf} 1^{7g} 2^{8f} 3^{7gf} 6^{9sd} 3^{8sd} **1-3-8 £8,671**

Loitokitok *P D Cundell* 31
3 b g Piccolo - Bonita Bee
11^{11g} 9^{12gf} **0-0-2**

Lojo *Miss Sheena West* 58 a58
3 ch f Pivotal - Myhat
7^{7s} 7^{8g} 4^{9sd} 6^{7gs} 8^{10gf} 6^{10g} 8^{10sd} 13^{10s} 9^{10gf} 15^{16g} **0-0-10 £422**

Lola Sapola (Ire) *N A Callaghan* 81
3 b f Benny The Dip (USA) - Cutpurse Moll
18^{8g} 6^{10g} 4^{12f} 1^{12f} 3^{12f} 9^{12g} 4^{14gf} **1-0-7 £6,951**

Lolla's Spirit (Ire) *M L W Bell* 54 a22
2 b f Montjeu (Ire) - Glenarff (USA)
8^{8g} 7^{7s} 14^{7sd} **0-0-3**

London Express (Ire) *M Johnston* 86
2 b c King Charlemagne (USA) - Robin
2^{7g} 1^{8g} 2^{8s} 2^{7s} **1-3-4 £9,277**

Londoner (USA) *S Dow* 49 a65
7 ch g Sky Classic (Can) - Love And Affection (USA)
9^{7sd} 9^{10sd} 7^{9sd} 8^{8sd} 10^{8sd} 4^{8gf} 9^{10g} 3^{7sd} 6^{9sd} 7^{9sd} 13^{10sd} **0-2-11 £724**

Lonely Ahead (USA) *C E Brittain* 97
2 b f Rahy (USA) - Sayyedati
1^{6gf} 6^{7gf} 4^{6gf} 5^{7g} 10^{6s} **1-0-5 £13,949**

Long Weekend (Ire) *D Shaw* 53 a61
7 b g Flying Spur (Aus) - Friday Night (USA)
2^{7sd} 6^{8sd} 2^{7sd} 6^{7sd} 5^{7sd} 8^{7sd} 14^{7g} 4^{6gf} 4^{6g} 10^{6sd} 5^{6gf} 9^{6gf} 7^{6gf} 7^{6g} 13^{6sd} **0-3-15 £1,973**

Longford Leader (Ire) *Edgar Byrne* 33
4 b c Indian Rocket - Bajan Girl (Ire)
9^{7f} 12^{8g} 5^{5g} 8^{5gy} 10^{7sd} 13^{7sd} **0-0-6**

Longing For Cindy (USA) *W M Brisbourne* 56 a56
3 ch f Belong To Me (USA) - I C Cindy (USA)
5^{8g} 6^{10f} 10^{12gf} 5^{9sd} 12^{10sd} 7^{10g} 5^{10gf} 12^{12sd} **0-0-8**

Longmeadows Boy (Ire) *A Berry* 32
5 b g Victory Note (USA) - Karoi (Ire)
11^{11gf} 9^{9gf} 9^{8gf} 10^{12gf} 13^{16gf} **0-0-5**

Longstone Lass *Miss Tracy Waggott* 28
5 b m Wizard King - Kamaress
9^{12sd} 7^{12gf} **0-0-2**

Look Again *Mrs A J Perrett* 99
4 ch g Zilzal (USA) - Last Look
4^{10gf} 2^{10gf} 2^{10g} 3^{12gf} 4^{10g} 17^{10gf} 9^{12s} **0-4-7 £10,522**

Look At The Stars (Ire) *R Hollinshead* 57 a47
3 b g Bachir (Ire) - Pizzazz
14^{7g} 10^{7gf} 7^{8gf} 7^{8gf} 12^{8gf} 4^{9sd} **0-0-6**

Look Here's Carol (Ire) *E S McMahon* 98
5 ch m Safawan - Where's Carol
3^{6g} 8^{7gf} 10^{7gs} 1^{6s} 9^{6gf} 6^{6g} 14^{7gf} 4^{6gs} 6^{7g} 11^{7gf} 13^{6gs} **1-1-11 £15,320**

Look Here's May *E S McMahon* a28
3 b f Revoque (Ire) - Where's Carol
10^{6sd} 13^{6sd} 10^{7sd} **0-0-3**

Look Of Eagles *P F I Cole* 66 a74
3 b f Fraam - Dreamtime Quest
10^{7sd} 1^{6f} 5^{6g} 4^{6gf} 10^{6gf} 5^{6g} 2^{7gf} 8^{7g} 2^{6ss} 1^{7sd} 3^{7sd} 5^{7sd} **2-3-12 £8,936**

Looker *R M Beckett* 75
2 b f Barathea (Ire) - Last Look
1^{8gs} 4^{8s} **1-0-2 £4,650**

Looking Great (USA) *R F Johnson Houghton* 39 a36
3 b g Gulch (USA) - Shoofha (Ire)
7^{10g} 9^{14g} 9^{12sd} 8^{10f} **0-0-4**

Looking North *Peter Grayson* 59 a50
2 gr f Paris House - Emma Amour
7^{5g} 2^{5sd} 2^{5s} 4^{5gs} 3^{5g} 9^{5sd} **0-3-6 £3,170**

Lookouthereicome *T T Clement* 37 a35
4 b f Rudimentary (USA) - Sylvatica
10^{10sd} 5^{8gf} 9^{8gf} 3^{14g} 9^{14s} **0-1-5 £527**

Looks Could Kill (USA) *E J Alston* 92 a91
3 b/br g Red Ransom (USA) - Mingling Glances (USA)
5^{7gf} 5^{7gf} 3^{8gs} 6^{8g} 6^{10g} 12^{7s} 4^{6gf} 2^{5gs} 3^{5s} 3^{7sd} 8^{9gs} 2^{6sf} 3^{6sd} 4^{7sd} **0-6-14 £13,942**

Looks The Business (Ire) *W G M Turner* 66 a69
4 b g Marju (Ire) - Business Centre (Ire)
2^{10f} 4^{11s} 3^{10f} 5^{10g} 1^{12sd} 3^{12f} 2^{12f} 5^{10sd} **1-4-8 £5,902**

Loop The Loup *K G Reveley* 68
9 b g Petit Loup (USA) - Mithi Al Gamar (USA)
12^{12gs} 2^{16gf} 3^{12gf} 3^{12gf} 1^{16gf} 1^{14gf} 8^{16gf} 5^{14g} **2-2-8 £7,205**

Lopinot (Ire) *B J Meehan* 66
2 br g Pursuit Of Love - La Suquet
11^{7gf} 3^{7gf} 24^{6g} **0-0-3 £732**

Lord Adonis (Ire) *M J Attwater* 26
2 b g Galileo (Ire) - Flaming June (USA)
11^{8hy} **0-0-1**

Lord Baskerville *W Storey* 48
4 br g Wolfhound (USA) - My Dear Watson
12^{7g} 15^{6g} 4^{7gs} 5^{6g} 3^{6g} 4^{8gf} 3^{5s} 9^{7gs} 7^{9gf} 7^{7gf} 11^{8gf} **0-2-11 £656**

Lord Chamberlain *J M Bradley* 62 a70
12 b g Be My Chief (USA) - Metaphysique (Fr)
10^{9sd} 1^{9sd} 1^{7sd} 2^{7sd} 11^{9sd} 6^{8gf} 10^{8gs} 10^{7gs} 3^{8f} 2^{8gf} 5^{8g} 4^{7sd} 6^{7g} 3^{7g} 7^{8g} 4^{8g} 10^{8gf} 1^{7s} 10^{7gf} 1^{8gf} 10^{7g} 4^{9sd} 7^{7sd} 4^{9sd} **4-4-24 £15,615**

Lord Conyers (Ire) *G Woodward* 57
6 b m Inzar (USA) - Primelta
1^{7g} 7^{7s} 13^{8gf} 9^{7gf} 14^{8gf} 13^{7gf} 10^{8g} 10^{8gs} **1-0-8 £2,765**

Lord Jack Flash *W G M Turner* 81
2 gr g Woodborough (USA) - Flair Lady
1^{5g} 2^{5gf} 4^{5gs} 2^{5f} 7^{5g} **1-1-5 £7,373**

Lord John *J Wade* 34
3 b g Piccolo - Mahbob Dancer (Fr)
10^{5g} 10^{6f} **0-0-2**

Lord Lahar *M A Buckley* a57
6 b g Fraam - Brigadiers Bird (Ire)
8^{12sd} 3^{9sd} 6^{9sd} 6^{9sd} 11^{9sd} 11^{7sd} 9^{10sd} 10^{8sd} 7^{9sd} **0-1-9 £417**

Lord Laing (USA) *H J Collingridge* a64
2 b/br g Chester House (USA) - Johanna Keene (USA)
8^{8sd} 5^{8sd} **0-0-2**

Lord Lamb *K G Reveley* 39
13 gr g Dunbeath (USA) - Caroline Lamb
8^{12gf} **0-0-1**

Lord Links (Ire) *D J Daly* 91 a70
4 ch g Daggers Drawn (USA) - Lady From Limerick (Ire)
2^{7gs} 2^{8g} 5^{8g} 3^{8g} 4^{8gf} 11^{8gs} 4^{9gs} 4^{8gf} 5^{8gs} 10^{8g} 6^{8sd} **0-4-11 £8,951**

Lord Mayfair (USA) *Miss A Stokell* 54
3 b g Silic (Fr) - Spring Wedding (USA)
13^{8g} 17^{7gf} 18^{6g} 11^{6g} 8^{11gf} 8^{8g} 5^{11gf} 6^{12gf} 6^{12gf} 6^{16s} PU^{11sd} **0-0-11 £405**

Lord Mayor *R M H Cowell* 105 a104
4 b g Machiavellian (USA) - Misleading Lady
7^{9gf} 4^{10gf} 7^{10gf} 3^{10gs} 8^{10sd} **0-1-5 £3,229**

Lord Melbourne (Ire) *A G Juckes* a51
6 b g Lycius (USA) - Adana (Ire)
9^{7sd} 6^{9sd} 12^{6sd} 4^{8sd} 7^{9sd} **0-0-5**

Lord Nellsson *Andrew Turnell* 64 a31

9 b g Arctic Lord - Miss Petronella
2^{16g} 4^{14gf} 1^{18gf} 10^{16sd} 2^{17f} 11^{18gs} **1-2-6 £5,382**

Lord Of Adventure (Ire) *Mrs L C Jewell* 64 a64
3 b g Inzar (USA) - Highly Fashionable (Ire)
4^{7sd} 8^{10sd} 7^{8gs} 11^{10s} 8^{10g} 15^{12g} 12^{12s} 11^{8hy} **0-0-8 £264**

Lord Of Dreams (Ire) *D W P Arbuthnot* 71 a74
3 ch c Barathea (Ire) - The Multiyorker (Ire)
4^{10f} 7^{8sd} 7^{8g} 11^{8s} 2^{9sd} 12^{8sd} 3^{9sd} **0-2-7 £1,782**

Lord Of The East *I W McInnes* 95 a72
6 b g Emarati (USA) - Fairy Free
10^{5s} 6^{6g} 2^{6g} 5^{6gf} 2^{7f} 1^{6gf} 1^{7sd} 3^{6sd} 6^{6gf} 1^{7g} 1^{7g} 6^{7g} 3^{7gf} 4^{7gf} 1^{7g} 1^{7g} 8^{6gf} 4^{7gs} 8^{7gs} **6-5-19 £39,828**

Lord Of The Fens *C N Kellett*
5 b g Danzig Connection (USA) - Zizi (Ire)
13^{8sd} **0-0-1**

Lord Of The Sea (Ire) *Jamie Poulton* a54
4 b g Perugino (USA) - Sea Mistress
7^{8sd} **0-0-1**

Lord Wishingwell (Ire) *J S Wainwright* a19
4 b g Lake Coniston (Ire) - Spirito Libro (USA)
10^{6sd} 10^{8sd} **0-0-2**

Lorna Dune *J G M O'Shea* 35 a33
3 b f Desert Story (Ire) - Autumn Affair
9^{9sd} 5^{11g} **0-0-2**

Los Cabos (Ire) *J H M Gosden* 75
2 b c Mozart (Ire) - Limelighting (USA)
4^{8gf} 4^{8g} 1^{8gs} **1-0-3 £4,107**

Los Organos (Ire) *P W Chapple-Hyam* 69
3 br f Turtle Island (Ire) - Spicebird (Ire)
3^{10gf} 2^{9gf} 1^{9gf} **1-2-3 £5,029**

Lost Soldier Three (Ire) *L M Cumani* 112
4 b g Barathea (Ire) - Donya
6^{16g} 1^{14g} 8^{16s} 6^{16g} 3^{15gs} 10^{16g} **1-1-6 £27,925**

Lottie *G Woodward* 43 a43
4 b f Robellino (USA) - Montserrat
14^{8sd} 4^{7sd} 10^{7sd} 7^{6g} 8^{11gf} 2^{7gf} 7^{7gf} **0-1-7 £458**

Lottie Dundass *D J Daly* 32
3 ch f Polar Falcon (USA) - Sand Grouse (USA)
8^{10g} **0-0-1**

Lotus Land (UAE) *M Johnston* 56
3 b c Timber Country (USA) - Noble Lily (USA)
12^{10gs} 6^{12g} 9^{10gf} **0-0-3**

Loua *C E Brittain* 76 a77
2 b c Lujain (USA) - Rose Bay
3^{6gf} 5^{6sd} 3^{6gf} 5^{7g} 3^{6g} 2^{6gf} 6^{6gf} 2^{6sd} **0-4-8 £4,244**

Lough Arrow (Ire) *P S Felgate* 8 a5
2 b g Carrowkeel (Ire) - State Of Dream (Ire)
10^{5g} 11^{6s} 12^{5sd} **0-0-3**

Loughlorien (Ire) *R E Barr* 58
6 b g Lake Coniston (Ire) - Fey Lady (Ire)
6^{5g} 9^{5gf} 4^{5s} 3^{5gf} 9^{6gf} 7^{6gf} 14^{6g} 13^{5gf} 5^{5gf} 7^{5gf} 3^{5gf} 7^{5gf} 8^{5gf} **0-2-13 £1,337**

Louie Louie (Ire) *N A Callaghan* 88 a82
2 b c King Charlemagne (USA) - Rose Of Mooncoin (Ire)
5^{6gs} 1^{5f} 4^{5sd} 4^{6sd} 5^{5g} 3^{8gf} 12^{6gf} 12^{7hy} **1-1-8 £6,353**

Louise D'Arzens *H R A Cecil* 70
3 br f Anabaa (USA) - Maidment
3^{10g} 2^{12hd} **0-1-2 £1,626**

Louisiade (Ire) *K A Ryan* 73 a73
4 b g Tagula (Ire) - Titchwell Lass
5^{6sd} 2^{7sd} 1^{7sd} 1^{7sd} 7^{7g} 1^{6gf} 3^{6sd} 4^{6gf} 4^{6gf} 14^{7gs} 10^{6g} 10^{7gf} 12^{7gf} 6^{6g} **3-2-14 £12,317**

Louisville Prince *A P Jones* 38 a24
4 ch g Bluegrass Prince (Ire) - Noble Soul
11^{10sd} 8^{6f} 9^{6g} 5^{6sd} 7^{7sd} 12^{11sd} **0-0-6**

Loup Sifflet (Ire) *R A Fahey* 52
3 b g Loup Sauvage (USA) - Bee-Bee-Gee (Ire)
7^{7s} 5^{6gs} 5^{8gf} 5^{8s} **0-0-4**

Louphole *P J Makin* 80 a79
3 ch g Loup Sauvage (USA) - Goodwood Lass (Ire)
11^{6gf} 11^{6sd} 9^{5gf} 11^{6gf} 5^{10gf} 9^{9g} 6^{7sd} 5^{7sd} 5^{7sd} 7^{8sd} 7^{6sd} 4^{6sd} **0-0-12 £395**

Loutasha *R F Marvin*
4 gr f Atraf - Petinata
12^{6sd} 11^{6sd} 10^{7sd} 16^{7gf} 14^{10g} **0-0-5**

Louve Heureuse (Ire) *J R Boyle* 61 a56
4 ch f Peintre Celebre (USA) - Louve Sereine (Fr)
9^{9sd} 5^{9sd} 9^{12hy} 10^{12g} 8^{11gf} 2^{10g} 3^{10g} 3^{8f} 7^{8f} 4^{10gf} 6^{10gs} 2^{8hy} 7^{9sf} 5^{10sd} 1^{8sd} 12^{8sd} **1-4-16 £3,830**

Louve Royale (Ire) *P R Webber* 90
4 ch f Peintre Celebre (USA) - Louve (USA)
7^{12g} 6^{10gf} **0-0-2 £450**

Love Affair (Ire) *R Hannon* 76 a49
3 b f Tagula (Ire) - Changing Partners
15^{7f} 1^{8gs} 2^{8g} 18^{7g} 2^{8gf} 9^{9s} 9^{8g} 6^{8gf} 8^{8gf} 11^{8sd} 12^{9sd} **1-2-11 £11,676**

Love Always *S Dow* 78
3 b f Piccolo - Lady Isabell
8^{9gs} 2^{10gf} 1^{12gf} 6^{12f} 5^{12gs} 8^{12g} **1-1-6 £6,120**

Love And Laughter (Ire) *T D Easterby* 60
3 b f Theatrical - Hoh Dear (Ire)
6^{12g} 8^{11gf} 7^{8gs} **0-0-3**

Love Angel (USA) *J J Bridger* 81
3 b/br g Woodman (USA) - Omnia (USA)
4^{7gs} 2^{8hy} 4^{8gs} 8^{10s} 2^{10g} 6^{10g} 2^{7gf} 6^{8gf} 10^{8gf} 1^{10gf} 1^{10hd} 4^{11g} 2^{11gs} 5^{10s} **2-4-14 £14,876**

Love Attack (Ire) *N B King* 37 a46
3 b f Sri Pekan (USA) - Bradwell (Ire)
3^{9sd} 4^{11sd} 6^{10g} 9^{9sd} 10^{12g} 8^{13g} 1^{10sd} **1-1-7 £1,698**

Love Beauty (USA) *M F Harris* 80
3 b/br g Seeking The Gold (USA) - Heavenly Rhythm (USA)
3^{9gs} 7^{12gf} 8^{12g} 7^{12gf} 3^{14gf} **0-0-5 £1,066**

Love From Russia *Mrs H O Graham* a41
3 b g Xaar - Heart
10^{6sd} 7^{6sd} 4^{5sd} 9^{6sd} 5^{5sd} 8^{7gf} **0-0-6**

Love In Seattle (Ire) *M Johnston* 64
5 b g Seattle Slew (USA) - Tamise (USA)
1^{8gf} 6^{8gf} **1-0-2 £4,082**

Love Me Tender *H R A Cecil* 76
3 br f Green Desert (USA) - Easy To Love (USA)
2^{7g} 8^{7gf} 2^{7gf} 4^{6f} **0-2-4 £2,571**

Love Palace (Ire) *M Johnston* 95
3 b c King's Best (USA) - Vijaya (USA)
3^{10gs} 11^{8gf} 16^{8gs} 10^{7gf} 1^{7gf} **1-0-5 £9,187**

Love Thirty *M R Channon* 92
3 b f Mister Baileys - Polished Up

4^{7gs} 18^{8gf} 3^{7gf} 10^{8gf} 4^{8gf} 13^{7g} **0-1-6 £5,633**

Love Triangle (Ire) *N B King* 13 a59
4 ch g Titus Livius (Fr) - Kirsova
11^{11sd} 10^{12sd} 8^{9sd} 11^{8sd} 12^{9sd} 8^{9sd} 13^{10gf} **0-0-7**

Love You Always (USA) *Miss J Feilden* 65 a24
5 ch g Woodman (USA) - Encorenous (USA)
9^{12sd} 10^{10gf} 4^{7gf} 7^{8gf} 6^{10gf} 1^{10gf} 3^{10gf} **1-1-7 £3,430**

Love's Design (Ire) *Miss J Feilden* 42
8 b/br g Pursuit Of Love - Cephista
9^{8gf} **0-0-1**

Lovelorn *M W Easterby* 42 a24
3 b g Mind Games - Love Letters
9^{5sd} 6^{5g} 12^{5sd} **0-0-3**

Lovely Dubai (Ire) *R Bouresly* 18 a77
2 b c Desert Prince (Ire) - Filia Ardross
11^{6gf} 10^{6g} 1^{6ft} **1-0-3 £2,765**

Lovely Hidenka (USA) *C E Brittain* 40 a45
2 b f Fusaichi Pegasus (USA) - Eliza (USA)
8^{7sd} 8^{7sd} 7^{7hy} **0-0-3**

Lover Boy (Ire) *M L W Bell* 59
2 ch c Alhaarth (Ire) - L'Amour (USA)
10^{7gf} **0-0-1**

Loves Travelling (Ire) *N Wilson* 77
5 b g Blues Traveller (Ire) - Fast Love (Ire)
14^{12s} 10^{14g} 10^{12gf} 4^{12g} 4^{12gf} 7^{12g} 10^{12gs} 15^{12g} **0-0-8 £901**

Lovingly *Sir Michael Stoute* 47
2 b f Grand Lodge (USA) - Easy To Love (USA)
6^{7g} **0-0-1**

Low Cloud *J J Quinn* 73
5 b g Danehill (USA) - Raincloud
7^{9f} 5^{10gf} 4^{8gf} 6^{8gf} 13^{10gf} **0-0-5 £314**

Low Fold Flyer *M Blanshard* 38 a16
3 ch g Fraam - Maniere D'Amour (Fr)
7^{11gf} 6^{12gf} 13^{13sd} 11^{14sd} **0-0-4**

Lowestoft Playboy *J Jay* 66 a61
3 ch g Pivotal - Red Typhoon
8^{6sd} 5^{5f} 11^{6gf} 5^{6gf} 5^{6gf} 6^{8gf} 13^{7hy} 12^{7sd} 6^{8sd} **0-0-9**

Lowicz *M Appleby* 37 a40
3 b f Polish Precedent (USA) - Eldina
6^{9sd} 8^{6s} 9^{7sd} 11^{8sd} 3^{7gf} 3^{9sd} 7^{10f} 11^{8gs} 5^{8f} 6^{8f} 13^{9sd} **0-2-11 £433**

Lowlander *D K Weld* 83
6 b g Fuji Kiseki (Jpn) - Lake Valley (USA)
3^{16gf} 19^{20gf} 13^{16gf} **0-1-3 £755**

Loyal Royal (Ire) *D R C Elsworth* 88
2 b c King Charlemagne (USA) - Supportive (Ire)
2^{6gf} 2^{6gs} 3^{6g} 12^{5g} 2^{6gs} **0-3-5 £6,948**

Loyal Tycoon (Ire) *D K Ivory* 91 a69
7 br g Royal Abjar (USA) - Rosy Lydgate
7^{6g} 5^{6gf} 12^{5g} 2^{6gf} 7^{6gf} 13^{6g} 5^{6gf} 3^{6g} 7^{6gf} 11^{7gf} 8^{7gf} 10^{6gs} 8^{6sd} **0-2-13 £3,872**

Loyalist (USA) *J G Given* a50
3 b g Valid Expectations (USA) - Chris's Commitment (USA)
7^{9sd} 12^{9sd} **0-0-2**

Loyalty Lodge (Ire) *J D Bethell*
3 ch g Grand Lodge (USA) - Gaily Grecian (Ire)
13^{10gf} **0-0-1**

Lualua *J F O'Shea* 51 a60
4 ch g Presidium - Tawny
7^{5sd} 10^{5hy} 12^{5sd} 8^{5g} 14^{6gf} **0-0-5**

Luas Line (Ire) *David Wachman* 112
3 b f Danehill (USA) - Streetcar (Ire)
3^{8gy} 5^{7gf} 4^{10f} 1^{8g} 1^{9gy} 1^{9f} 6^{9f} 11^{10y} **3-1-8 £202,908**

Luberon *M Johnston* 92
2 b c Fantastic Light (USA) - Luxurious (USA)
2^{7gf} 1^{7f} 2^{7s} 4^{7g} 1^{8g} 9^{8g} **2-2-6 £12,268**

Lucayan Dancer *D Nicholls* 84
5 b g Zieten (USA) - Tittle Tattle (Ire)
2^{10g} 11^{10g} 7^{10gf} 1^{10gf} 3^{12gf} 8^{10g} 1^{10gf} 8^{10gf} 3^{10gf} 2^{10g} 3^{9gs} 10^{12f} **2-5-12 £17,428**

Lucayan Legend (Ire) *R Hannon* 90
4 b c Docksider (USA) - Capo Di Monte
19^{10gs} 12^{8g} 9^{8g} 11^{10gf} 1^{8g} 5^{8g} 7^{8g} 14^{10gf} 10^{10g} **1-0-9 £4,853**

Lucayos *Mrs H Sweeting* 66 a64
2 ch c Bahamian Bounty - Indian Flag (Ire)
UR^{5sd} 16^{5g} 3^{5s} 2^{5g} 8^{6gf} 1^{5gf} 2^{5hy} 4^{5sd} 6^{6sd} 11^{6sd} 2^{5sd} 5^{5sd} **1-3-12 £10,056**

Luce (Ire) *H Morrison* a50
4 b f Sadler's Wells (USA) - Onaga (USA)
5^{12sd} **0-0-1**

Lucefer (Ire) *G C H Chung* 51 a47
7 b g Lycius (USA) - Maharani (USA)
4^{9sd} 12^{8gf} 4^{8gf} 5^{8gf} 6^{10f} 2^{12g} 13^{13sd} 3^{10gs} 4^{12sf} **0-3-9 £849**

Luchi *M Scudamore* a32
4 ch f Mark Of Esteem (Ire) - Penmayne
11^{7sd} 7^{7sd} **0-0-2**

Lucid Dreams (Ire) *M Wigham* 71 a67
6 b g Sri Pekan (USA) - Scenaria (Ire)
1^{8sd} 5^{8sd} 1^{8gf} 1^{7gf} 3^{7g} 7^{8gf} 14^{8gf} 8^{8gf} **3-1-8 £9,959**

Lucidity Light (Ire) *J D Bethell* 62
2 ch f Dr Fong (USA) - Moonlight (Ire)
4^{6g} 9^{6gf} 3^{7s} 6^{7s} **0-1-4 £787**

Lucidus *W J Haggas* 34
3 b g Danzero (Aus) - Lady In Colour (Ire)
8^{10g} **0-0-1**

Luciferous (USA) *Jane Southcombe* 55 a16
3 ch f Devil's Bag (USA) - Vital Laser (USA)
14^{7sd} 9^{7gf} 10^{8gf} 6^{8gf} 13^{8gf} 3^{8f} 8^{8f} **0-1-7 £709**

Lucius Verrus (USA) *D Shaw* a61
5 b g Danzig (USA) - Magic Of Life (USA)
6^{5sd} 5^{6sd} 2^{6sd} 2^{6sd} 3^{7sd} 6^{7sd} 1^{7sf} 10^{7sd} 1^{6sd} **2-3-9 £5,661**

Lucksin (Ire) *N Tinkler* 78 a60
2 b g Key Of Luck (USA) - Swallowcliffe
3^{5g} 6^{5gf} 7^{6gf} 3^{5gf} 3^{5g} 7^{5gf} 2^{5gf} 2^{5g} 5^{6sd} **0-3-9 £4,543**

Lucky April *Mrs P N Dutfield* 62 a30
2 b f Whittingham (Ire) - Lucky Dip
12^{5gs} 4^{5gf} 4^{5gf} 3^{5gf} 4^{5g} 5^{6gf} 3^{5gs} 5^{6gf} 6^{5gs} 5^{6gf} 5^{5sd} **0-1-11 £2,396**

Lucky Arthur (Ire) *Mrs L Williamson* 33 a39
4 ch f Grand Lodge (USA) - Soltura (Ire)
8^{9sd} 8^{10s} 6^{11gf} **0-0-3**

Lucky Bamblue (Ire) *P C Haslam* 35
2 b g Key Of Luck (USA) - Bamboo (Ire)
14^{7gf} 15^{8gf} 11^{7gf} **0-0-3**

Lucky Celts (Ire) *D Haydn Jones* 27 a38
2 b f Key Of Luck (USA) - Rainbow Melody (Ire)
3^{6f} 11^{6gf} 7^{5f} 7^{5g} 5^{6sd} 7^{6sd} 13^{9sd} **0-0-7 £528**

Lucky Desert (Ire) *M Quinn* 72
2 b g Desert Style (Ire) - Gertie Laurie
15^{6gf} 5^{6g} 7^{6g} **0-0-3**

Lucky Emerald (Ire) *B Palling* 50 a43
3 b f Lend A Hand - Anita's Love (Ire)
9^{7gs} 8^{6hy} 11^{6g} 9^{6g} 13^{7gf} 7^{7sf} 10^{6sd}
0-0-7

Lucky Judge *G A Swinbank* 61
8 b g Saddlers' Hall (Ire) - Lady Lydia
8^{12gs} 7^{14gs} 9^{16g} 9^{16gf} **0-0-4**

Lucky Largo (Ire) *D A Nolan*
5 b/br g Key Of Luck (USA) - Lingering Melody (Ire)
10^{8gf} 5^{10g} 5^{10s} 8^{12g} 12^{12s} **0-0-5 £750**

Lucky Leo *Ian Williams* 77 a43
5 b g Muhtarram (USA) - Wrong Bride
7^{12sd} 2^{10gs} 1^{12gf} 10^{12gf} 6^{12gf} 9^{12gf} **1-1-6**
£5,382

Lucky Lil *R M Whitaker* a25
3 ch f Cadeaux Genereux - Amalia (Ire)
13^{7sd} 12^{6sf} **0-0-2**

Lucky Lisa *R Charlton* 54
2 b f Pivotal - Topper (Ire)
11^{6g} 8^{6g} 12^{6g} **0-0-3**

Lucky Lucky (Ire) *R P Elliott* a28
3 ch f Lil's Boy (USA) - Join The Party
9^{5sd} 10^{5sd} **0-0-2**

Lucky Piscean *C W Fairhurst*
4 b g River Falls - Celestine
16^{14f} **0-0-1**

Lucky Red Pepper *M Quinn* 84
3 b g Barathea (Ire) - Mutige
10^{8gf} 2^{7gf} 4^{8g} 3^{8gf} **0-2-4 £3,803**

Lucky Spin *R Hannon* 113
4 b f Pivotal - Periscope
1^{7g} 8^{8gf} 1^{6gs} 3^{7gs} 4^{7g} 8^{6g} 6^{6g} 3^{6s} **2-2-8**
£77,429

Lucky Token (Ire) *E A L Dunlop* a59
2 gr f Key Of Luck (USA) - Shawanni
4^{7sd} **0-0-1 £348**

Lucky Uno *C Smith*
9 b g Rock City - Free Skip
11^{5sd} **0-0-1**

Lucky Valentine *G L Moore* a34
5 b m My Best Valentine - Vera's First (Ire)
8^{6sd} **0-0-1**

Luckylover *M G Quinlan* 64
2 b c Key Of Luck (USA) - Hang Fire
2^{8hy} 4^{8gs} **0-1-2 £3,439**

Lucys Lady *K R Burke* 55 a50
2 b f Primo Valentino (Ire) - Sandblaster
8^{5sd} 6^{5s} 1^{5g} 3^{5gf} 3^{6gf} 6^{6f} 4^{6sd} 1^{5gf} 7^{6sd} 8^{6sf}
2-2-10 £6,781

Lucysykes (USA) *B J Meehan* 42
2 br f Tiger Ridge (USA) - Salute The Girl (USA)
11^{7gs} 9^{8gf} **0-0-2**

Ludovico *K A Ryan* 74
2 b c Zilzal (USA) - Devastating
5^{6gf} 2^{6g} 2^{6gf} **0-2-3 £3,307**

Lugana Point *J Balding* 26 a27
3 b c Lugana Beach - Raisa Point
13^{6g} 9^{5sd} **0-0-2**

Luis Melendez (USA) *P F I Cole* 71
3 ch c Horse Chestnut (SAF) - Egoli (USA)
8^{10gf} 7^{12gs} 7^{12gs} 12^{11gf} 15^{14s} **0-0-5**

Lujain Rose *N M Babbage* 53 a47
3 b f Lujain (USA) - Rose Chime (Ire)
11^{8g} 8^{8g} 7^{10sd} 9^{10g} 12^{8gs} 4^{8gf} 7^{10gf}
0-0-7 £271

Luke After Me (Ire) *Miss Tracy Waggott* 55 a36
5 b g Victory Note (USA) - Summit Talk
9^{6gs} 4^{7g} 9^{8gf} 2^{7g} 7^{7s} 3^{6gf} 4^{7sd} **0-2-7**
£1,569

Luke Sharp *M W Easterby* 42
4 gr g Muhtarram (USA) - Heaven-Liegh-Grey
14^{8gf} 8^{10gf} 14^{11gs} **0-0-3**

Luloah *P S McEntee* 55 a58
2 b f Mujahid (USA) - Bangles
4^{5gf} 3^{5sd} 8^{5sd} 2^{5ss} 1^{5sd} **1-2-5 £3,393**

Luna Landing *Jedd O'Keeffe* 73 a44
2 ch c Allied Forces (USA) - Macca Luna (Ire)
8^{6gf} 2^{7gf} 1^{7g} 3^{7g} 11^{8gf} 8^{8g} 7^{7sd} **1-1-7**
£5,541

Lunar Express (USA) *W J Haggas* 62 a87
2 b f Giant's Causeway (USA) - June Moon (Ire)
4^{6gf} 2^{7sd} 1^{7sd} **1-1-3 £5,172**

Lunar Goddess *D R Loder* 34
2 b f Royal Applause - Moon Goddess
10^{7f} **0-0-1**

Lunar Promise (Ire) *A P Jarvis* 67 a75
3 b g Mujadil (USA) - Lunadine (Fr)
4^{8g} 5^{9sd} 1^{10gf} 2^{10sd} **1-1-4 £5,236**

Lunar River (Fr) *E A L Dunlop* 60 a34
2 b f Muhtathir - Moon Gorge
12^{7sd} 5^{8gs} 5^{7s} **0-0-3**

Lunar Sky (USA) *C E Brittain* 54 a71
3 b f Lemon Drop Kid (USA) - Celestial Bliss (USA)
8^{10sd} 7^{10sd} 1^{12sd} 7^{14g} 2^{12sd} **1-1-5**
£5,176

Lune D'Or (Fr) *R Gibson* 112
4 b f Green Tune (USA) - Luth D'Or (Fr)
3^{10gs} 3^{12g} 5^{12gs} 6^{10f} **0-2-4 £39,039**

Luscinia *N A Callaghan* 16
2 b f Bluebird (USA) - Welsh Dawn
17^{7g} 10^{7gf} 9^{6gf} 16^{8gf} **0-0-4**

Luvvie One (Ire) *P A Blockley*
2 ch f Elnadim (USA) - Crystal City
8^{5sd} **0-0-1**

Luxi River (USA) *Michael McElhone* 66 a58
5 b g Diesis - Mariella (USA)
2^{13gf} 2^{14gf} 6^{12sh} 5^{14sd} **0-2-4 £2,055**

Lyford Lass *W G Harrison* 49
4 b f Bahamian Bounty - Ladykirk
7^{10s} 11^{9gf} 9^{9f} 5^{9s} 3^{9s} **0-1-5 £598**

Lygeton Lad *Miss Gay Kelleway* 70 a105
7 b g Shaamit (Ire) - Smartie Lee
7^{9sd} 4^{10sd} 6^{8ft} 13^{9ft} 10^{9sd} 2^{7sd} 5^{7sd} 8^{7g} 6^{8gf}
2^{8gf} 9^{8g} 11^{8sd} 8^{8gf} 3^{7sd} 7^{9sd} **0-3-15**
£10,015

Lyndalee (Ire) *T D Easterby* 70
2 b f Fasliyev (USA) - Itsibitsi (Ire)
2^{5s} 2^{6g} 11^{5g} 1^{5g} 5^{5g} 6^{5gf} 11^{5gf} 16^{6gs}
1-2-8 £6,443

Lynford Lady *P W D'Arcy* a45
2 b f Zaha (Can) - Little Miss Rocker
8^{8sd} 5^{9sd} 14^{10sd} **0-0-3**

Lyric Dances (Fr) *J Jay* 44 a42
3 ch f Sendawar (Ire) - Romanche (Fr)
6^{6sd} 7^{6sd} 5^{11sd} 6^{12f} 3^{10f} 8^{12gf} 11^{10sd} 10^{12sd}
4^{12sd} 4^{12sd} **0-1-10 £418**

Lyrical Blues (Ire) *B R Millman* 76 a75

2 ch g Namid - Latest (Ire)
2^{5s} 1^{5gs} 3^{5gf} 7^{5gf} 14^{6gs} 12^{7s} 4^{6sd} 5^{7sf}
1-1-8 £5,733

Lyrical Sound (Ire) *B W Hills* 75
2 ch f Distant Music (USA) - Unscathed
6^{6gf} 1^{6g} 10^{6g} 6^{6g} **1-0-4 £6,559**

Lyrical Way *P R Chamings* 67
6 b g Vettori (Ire) - Fortunate
1^{10gf} 4^{10gf} 13^{10g} **1-0-3 £3,324**

Lysander's Quest (Ire) *R Ingram* 54 a53
7 br g King's Theatre (Ire) - Haramayda (Fr)
5^{12sd} 1^{17sd} 6^{12sd} 6^{12gf} 4^{13sd} 4^{17g} 2^{12gf} 7^{16g}
1^{16sd} 2^{15gf} 7^{17f} 10^{13sd} 8^{12sd} 4^{17sd} 2^{16sd}
2-4-15 £6,134

Lysandra (Ire) *Sir Michael Stoute* 87
3 b f Danehill (USA) - Oriane
1^{8g} 3^{10gf} 1^{10g} 3^{10gf} 9^{10gs} 7^{11gs} **2-1-6**
£12,935

Lytham (Ire) *J J Quinn* 70
4 b g Spectrum (Ire) - Nousaiyra (Ire)
5^{8s} 4^{8g} 4^{9gf} **0-1-3 £586**

Ma'Am (USA) *I A Wood* 83 a74
3 ch f Royal Anthem (USA) - Hide The Bride (USA)
2^{8gs} 5^{10gf} 5^{10gf} 7^{12gf} 7^{12g} 3^{10gs} 5^{10sd} 4^{12ss}
0-2-8 £4,247

Maarees *G P Enright*
4 b f Groom Dancer (USA) - Shemaleyah
PU^{14s} **0-0-1**

Maayafushi *M D Hammond* 50
2 ch f Fraam - Pastelle
5^{5g} 9^{7gf} 10^{7g} **0-0-3**

Mabadi (USA) *B W Hills*
2 b f Sahm (USA) - Barakat
13^{7s} **0-0-1**

Mabella (Ire) *B Llewellyn* 46
3 b f Brave Act - Wee Merkin (Ire)
11^{7gs} 8^{8gs} 7^{6gs} 8^{8gf} 12^{6g} 11^{7gf} 6^{8gf}
0-0-7

Mac Cois Na Tine *K A Ryan* 53 a42
3 b g Cois Na Tine (Ire) - Berenice (Ity)
8^{9sd} 11^{8s} 8^{7s} 13^{8g} 17^{6f} **0-0-5**

Mac Han (Ire) *Eamon Tyrrell* 63
6 ch g Pennekamp (USA) - Ryazana (Ire)
9^{14sd} 16^{10s} 13^{11gf} 7^{9gf} 9^{12g} 5^{12gf} 7^{10s}
0-0-7

Mac Love *J Akehurst* 116 a111
4 b g Cape Cross (Ire) - My Lass
4^{8s} 2^{8f} 5^{9g} 4^{8gf} 5^{8sd} 11^{8s} 9^{8gf} 5^{7gf} 6^{7gf}
0-1-9 £72,219

Mac The Knife (Ire) *M Appleby* 31 a42
4 b g Daggers Drawn (USA) - Icefern
14^{6gf} 18^{7f} 14^{6s} 7^{6gs} 15^{6g} 14^{5g} 3^{5sd} 8^{5sd}
0-1-8 £210

Mac's Elan *A B Coogan* 58
5 b g Darshaan - Elabella
9^{11s} 7^{14gs} 6^{10gs} 2^{8gs} 6^{8gs} 9^{8g} 1^{12s} 11^{10gf}
1-1-8 £3,696

Mac's Talisman (Ire) *V Smith* a57
5 ch h Hector Protector (USA) - Inherent Magic (Ire)
10^{9sd} 11^{7sd} 11^{8sd} **0-0-3**

Macabre *Saeed Bin Suroor* 82
3 b g Machiavellian (USA) - Lady In Waiting
2^{8gf} 5^{8g} **0-1-2 £1,278**

Macademy Royal (USA) *H Morrison* a71
2 b c Royal Academy (USA) - Garden Folly (USA)
3^{5sd} **0-1-1 £510**

Macanillo (Ger) *J Balding* 40 a23
7 gr g Acatenango (Ger) - Midday Girl (Ger)
11^{8g} 7^{8gf} 17^{8gf} 13^{9sf} 9^{7sd} **0-0-5**

Macaroni Gold (Ire) *D J Daly* 73 a78
5 b g Rock Hopper - Strike It Rich (Fr)
2^{16sd} 4^{16sd} 3^{17sd} 2^{16sd} 5^{20s} 10^{17gf} 4^{13gf} 10^{15gf}
4^{16g} 6^{16g} 5^{16s} 9^{16sf} **0-3-12 £4,291**

Macaulay (Ire) *R Charlton* 89
3 ch c Zafonic (USA) - Wigging
1^{7gf} 7^{8gf} 6^{8g} 10^{8gs} **1-0-4 £4,634**

Macca (Ire) *W Jarvis*
2 b c Mull Of Kintyre (USA) - Total Aloof
16^{6gs} **0-0-1**

Macedon *J S Moore* 57
2 b g Dansili - Hypnotize
4^{6gf} **0-0-1 £274**

Machhapuchhare *W M Brisbourne* a57
2 ch g Most Welcome - Spring Flyer (Ire)
12^{7sd} 8^{9sd} 8^{9sd} **0-0-3**

Machinate (USA) *W M Brisbourne* 65 a59
3 b/br g Machiavellian (USA) - Dancing Sea (USA)
10^{9sd} 1^{7g} 17^{8s} 4^{9sd} 6^{8sf} 5^{9sd} **1-0-6**
£3,484

Machinist (Ire) *D Nicholls* 97
5 br g Machiavellian (USA) - Athene (Ire)
4^{6gf} 1^{6gf} 7^{6g} 11^{6gf} 9^{6g} 5^{6gf} 9^{7g} 1^{6g} 2^{6s}
2-1-9 £30,952

Maclean *G L Moore* 56 a59
4 b g Machiavellian (USA) - Celtic Cross
7^{10gs} 15^{12sd} **0-0-2**

Macorville (USA) *G M Moore* 76
2 b g Diesis - Desert Jewel (USA)
3^{8g} 7^{9g} 2^{8gf} **0-1-3 £1,899**

Macs All Heart (Ire) *A B Coogan* 45 a43
2 ch f Alhaarth (Ire) - Top Of The Form (Ire)
13^{5gf} 10^{7s} 12^{7gs} 3^{5f} 5^{6gs} 8^{6sd} 6^{8sd} 6^{8sd} 7^{5sd}
0-1-9 £367

Macs Ransom (USA) *N A Callaghan* 57 a42
2 b f Red Ransom (USA) - Gaye's Express (USA)
8^{7g} 14^{7gf} 4^{7gf} 8^{6g} 8^{8sd} **0-0-5 £274**

Macvel (Ire) *M Blanshard* 86
2 b f Mull Of Kintyre (USA) - Velvet Appeal (Ire)
17^{6gf} 2^{6g} 2^{6gf} 1^{5gf} 1^{6gf} 3^{5s} 4^{7gf} 6^{6g}
2-3-8 £13,237

Mad *Andrew Reid* 40 a60
4 br f Pursuit Of Love - Emily-Mou (Ire)
3^{8sd} 5^{10sd} 4^{10sd} 5^{8sd} 2^{8sd} 4^{7sd} 3^{7sd} 7^{8sd} 5^{7sd}
8^{8gf} 1^{8gf} 3^{10sd} 3^{12sd} 7^{12sd} 3^{10sd} 8^{10sd} 1^{8sd}
8^{7sd} **1-6-18 £3,919**

Mad Carew (USA) *J R Boyle* 83 a86
6 ch g Rahy (USA) - Poppy Carew (Ire)
3^{10sd} 3^{12sd} 6^{12sd} 1^{12sd} 3^{12sd} 1^{10gf} 3^{10g} 1^{12gf}
1^{12gf} 5^{10gf} 9^{10gs} 4^{12g} 14^{12sd} 3^{13sd} 4^{12sf} 3^{11sd}
8^{10sd} 2^{12sd} **4-7-18 £21,226**

Mad Marty Wildcard *R Brotherton* 39 a35
3 b g Komaite (USA) - Done And Dusted (Ire)
8^{6sd} 11^{6sd} 2^{5sd} 15^{6gf} 8^{6f} 10^{6ft} 6^{5ss} 9^{5sd}
0-1-8 £430

Mad Maurice *B J Curley* 57 a53
4 ch g Grand Lodge (USA) - Amarella (Fr)
1^{10g} 5^{9sd} **1-0-2 £1,487**

Mad Professor (Ire) *P W Chapple-Hyam* 64 a49
2 b c Mull Of Kintyre (USA) - Fancy Theory (USA)
10^{6g} 5^{7gf} 10^{8gf} 6^{6gs} 6^{7g} 4^{6sd} 7^{6sd} **0-0-7**

Madaares (USA) *M Johnston* 68
2 ch c Rahy (USA) - Tajannub (USA)
6^{6g} **0-0-1**

Madam Cantyre *Mrs L Stubbs* 52 a40
2 b f Mull Of Kintyre (USA) - Canlubang
7^{5sd} 3^{6gf} 4^{5sd} 10^{5sd} **0-1-4 £424**

Madam Caversfield *P D Evans* 71
3 b f Pursuit Of Love - Madam Alison
14^{8g} 2^{7gf} 3^{8gf} 7^{8gf} 4^{8s} 3^{8g} 5^{8f} 1^{8hd} 6^{7gf} 9^{8f} 1^{10g} 2^{10s} **2-4-12 £9,604**

Madam Mac (Ire) *B J Meehan* 39
2 b f Royal Applause - Wild Woman
9^{6gf} 8^{6s} **0-0-2**

Madam Moschata *D W Barker* 55
2 b f Muhtarram (USA) - Casaque Rose (USA)
9^{6g} 4^{5gf} 7^{6f} **0-0-3 £416**

Madam Patti *B Palling* 59
2 b f Monashee Mountain (USA) - Thabeh
8^{5gf} 4^{6gs} 8^{6gf} 11^{6g} 7^{6f} 12^{5gs} **0-0-6 £326**

Madame Constanze (Ire) *Miss Gay Kelleway* 59
2 b f Mozart (Ire) - Darbela (Ire)
15^{7g} 4^{8s} **0-0-2 £372**

Madame Fatale (Ire) *Jedd O'Keeffe* 44
3 br f Daggers Drawn (USA) - Taajreh (Ire)
12^{7g} 15^{10g} 9^{10g} 6^{8f} 11^{7g} 7^{7gf} 8^{10s} **0-0-7**

Madame Guillotine *P T Midgley* 39 a36
3 b f Sure Blade (USA) - Delicious
8^{6f} 7^{6sd} 15^{6gf} 7^{7ss} 8^{9sd} 9^{8sd} **0-0-6**

Madame Medusa (Ire) *J A R Toller* 70
2 b f Mozart (Ire) - Belize Tropical (Ire)
8^{8gs} 10^{8s} **0-0-2**

Maddie's A Jem *J R Jenkins* 77 a62
5 b m Emperor Jones (USA) - Royal Orchid (Ire)
10^{6sd} 9^{6sd} 7^{6gf} 2^{6gf} 12^{6gf} 4^{6gf} **0-1-6 £2,816**

Maddox (Pol) *Mrs P Townsley* 44 a49
3 b g Upper Heights (Ger) - Muddy's Girl (Swe)
6^{6sd} 12^{7s} 7^{7gf} 6^{5g} 11^{6g} 10^{5sd} **0-0-6**

Mademoiselle *B W Hills* 58 a23
3 b f Efisio - Shall We Dance
7^{8s} 10^{8g} 14^{8g} 2^{8s} 1^{8gs} 7^{8hy} 10^{8sf} **1-1-7 £4,247**

Madge *W Storey* 40 a62
3 br f Marju (Ire) - Aymara
8^{10sd} 13^{12g} 14^{10g} 5^{8gf} 15^{8g} 15^{10gf} 11^{8gf} 10^{7f} 8^{9gf} **0-0-9**

Madhahir (Ire) *M J Gingell* a44
5 b g Barathea (Ire) - Gharam (USA)
8^{12sd} 11^{12sd} 9^{14sd} 3^{17sd} 11^{14sd} **0-0-5 £210**

Madhavi *R Hannon* 76 a53
3 gr f Diktat - Grey Galava
2^{6g} 4^{7g} 8^{7gf} 3^{8gf} 3^{8gf} 7^{6gs} 3^{7g} 3^{7g} 8^{8s} 9^{10sd} **0-4-10 £6,607**

Madiba *R T Phillips* 62 a78
6 b g Emperor Jones (USA) - Priluki
8^{12sd} 2^{14sd} 9^{16sd} 3^{16g} 9^{15gf} 7^{16gf} 14^{16sd} 10^{16g} 3^{16g} 5^{16g} 2^{16s} 12^{16g} 7^{16sd} **0-4-13 £4,179**

Madison Avenue (Ger) *T M Jones* 46 a44
8 b g Mondrian (Ger) - Madly Noble (Ger)
13^{16sd} 6^{16sd} 5^{16g} **0-0-3**

Madra Rua (Ire) *Miss L A Perratt* a20
4 b g Foxhound (USA) - Fun Fashion (Ire)
8^{7sd} 12^{8sd} **0-0-2**

Madrasee *Jane Southcombe* 55 a70
7 b m Beveled (USA) - Pendona
1^{5sd} 2^{5sd} 8^{6sd} 9^{5f} 1^{5f} 8^{6gf} 12^{6f} 12^{5f} 6^{5gf} 3^{5ft} 4^{5sd} 4^{6sd} 10^{6sd} **2-2-13 £7,818**

Madroos *J L Dunlop* 72
2 ch c Medicean - Soolaimon (Ire)
10^{7gf} 7^{7f} 3^{8s} **0-1-3 £516**

Mae Cigan (Fr) *M Blanshard* 55 a47
2 gr g Medaaly - Concert
3^{5s} 4^{5sd} 10^{6g} 7^{7sd} 8^{7gs} **0-0-5 £415**

Mafaheem *M Johnston* 91
3 b c Mujahid (USA) - Legend Of Aragon
2^{6hy} 3^{5gs} 2^{6g} 3^{7g} 6^{6gs} **0-3-5 £10,852**

Magadar (USA) *C E Brittain* 78 a62
2 b/br f Lujain (USA) - Slow Jazz (USA)
7^{6gf} 2^{6sd} 3^{6s} 14^{6gf} 2^{6gf} 2^{6g} 1^{6gf} **1-4-7 £10,531**

Magari *W M Brisbourne* 54 a53
4 b f Royal Applause - Thatcher's Era (Ire)
11^{8gf} 8^{9sd} 1^{10g} 4^{9sd} 10^{10gs} 8^{8sd} 2^{9sf} 8^{9sd} 10^{10sd} **1-1-9 £3,231**

Magdelaine *A M Hales* a24
3 b f Sinndar (Ire) - Crystal Drop
8^{11sd} **0-0-1**

Magenta Rising (Ire) *W M Brisbourne* 6 a5
5 ch m College Chapel - Fashion Queen
11^{7sd} 13^{12f} 12^{9sd} **0-0-3**

Maggie Minx (Ire) *M J Wallace* 62 a47
2 b/br f Xaar - Foolish Fun
8^{6sd} 1^{5gs} 11^{5g} 3^{5hy} 6^{5hy} 11^{6sd} **1-1-6 £5,221**

Maggie Tulliver (Ire) *W R Swinburn* 81 a77
3 b f Spectrum (Ire) - Eliza Acton
6^{10gf} 3^{12sd} 2^{14gf} 1^{14g} 6^{15gf} 6^{16g} **1-2-6 £8,701**

Maggies Farm (USA) *M Johnston* 85
2 ch f Forest Wildcat (USA) - Moss (USA)
1^{6gf} 5^{6gf} 11^{5gs} 2^{7g} 2^{8gf} **1-2-5 £8,910**

Maghazi (Ire) *M P Tregoning* 82 a71
3 b c Fasliyev (USA) - Dalayil (Ire)
4^{7sd} 2^{8sd} 2^{7gf} 1^{7gf} 2^{7gf} **1-2-5 £11,254**

Magic Amigo *J R Jenkins* 78
4 ch g Zilzal (USA) - Emaline (Fr)
4^{11gs} 15^{11g} 1^{10hy} **1-1-3 £4,442**

Magic Amour *P A Blockley* 64 a56
7 ch g Sanglamore (USA) - Rakli
16^{8gs} 14^{7gs} 1^{7gf} 1^{7gf} 5^{8g} 5^{7gf} 8^{7g} 3^{7gf} 4^{7sf} 4^{6sd} 3^{7sd} 1^{6sf} 4^{6sd} 4^{6sd} 3^{6sd} **3-3-15 £7,883**

Magic Bracelet *D J Daly* 32
3 b f Inchinor - Sharanella
9^{10g} **0-0-1**

Magic Charm *K G Wingrove* a34
7 b m Magic Ring (Ire) - Loch Clair (Ire)
9^{9sd} 6^{12sd} 11^{14sd} **0-0-3**

Magic Flo *G C Bravery* 68
3 ch f Magic Ring (Ire) - Moore Stylish
2^{8gf} 1^{8gf} 9^{8gf} 6^{8gf} 10^{8gf} 2^{8g} **1-2-6 £6,595**

Magic Glade *R Brotherton* 93 a93
6 b g Magic Ring (Ire) - Ash Glade
3^{5sd} 2^{5sd} 3^{5sd} 8^{5sd} 12^{6gf} 2^{5s} 4^{5g} 8^{5gf} 4^{5s} 13^{5gf} 11^{5sf} 11^{5sd} 7^{6sd} **0-5-13 £19,332**

Magic Instinct *M P Tregoning* 89

3 b g Entrepreneur - Passe Passe (USA)
3^{10g} 1^{10f} 7^{10g} 1^{12gf} 9^{12s} 7^{14gf} **2-1-6 £15,536**

Magic Merlin *W R Swinburn* 78 a71
4 b g Magic Ring (Ire) - St James's Antigua (Ire)
5^{8gf} 6^{7g} 9^{8sd} 9^{8sd} **0-0-4 £339**

Magic Peak (Ire) *Sir Michael Stoute* a65
2 b f Danehill (USA) - Magic Cove (USA)
2^{7sd} **0-1-1 £1,392**

Magic Red *J Ryan* a52
5 ch g Magic Ring (Ire) - Jacquelina (USA)
7^{16sd} 7^{14sd} 5^{12sd} 16^{16gs} 9^{16sd} 3^{14ss} **0-1-6 £212**

Magic Sting *M L W Bell* 87
4 ch g Magic Ring (Ire) - Ground Game
7^{11gs} 1^{11g} 1^{10s} 14^{10gf} 5^{10g} 2^{12g} 15^{10gs} 1^{10gs} 6^{10g} 2^{9gf} **3-2-10 £19,129**

Magic Verse *I W McInnes* 43
4 ch f Opening Verse (USA) - Festival Sister
15^{7s} 10^{10s} 5^{9gf} 11^{10gf} 7^{12f} 13^{10g} **0-0-6**

Magic Warrior *J C Fox* 54 a61
5 b g Magic Ring (Ire) - Clarista (USA)
6^{7gs} 9^{8gf} 6^{10sd} 1^{8g} 1^{9sd} 1^{10sd} 9^{9sd} 4^{10sd} 12^{12sd} **3-0-9 £4,494**

Magical Mimi *K G Wingrove* a55
4 b f Magic Ring (Ire) - Naval Dispatch
13^{9sd} 7^{7sd} 6^{7sd} 10^{7sd} 13^{11gs} 10^{7sd} **0-0-6**

Magical Music *J Pearce* 51 a60
2 b f Fraam - Magical Flute
14^{5gf} 7^{5g} 4^{6g} 2^{7gf} 8^{8hy} 1^{8sd} **1-1-6 £4,113**

Magical Romance (Ire) *B J Meehan* 98
3 b f Barathea (Ire) - Shouk
6^{8s} 6^{12g} 11^{10gs} 6^{7g} **0-0-4 £6,174**

Magical Wit (Ire) *Gerard Keane* 42 a59
5 ch m Bahhare (USA) - Saleemah (USA)
4^{8sd} 1^{9sd} 1^{9sd} 5^{9sd} 3^{9sd} 9^{9sd} 3^{10sd} 9^{10gf} 7^{10f} 13^{10gf} **2-2-10 £5,335**

Magical World *J M Bradley* 27 a8
2 b f Agnes World (USA) - Otaru (Ire)
8^{5gs} 5^{5sd} 7^{5gf} 14^{6g} **0-0-4**

Magico *A B Haynes* a19
4 ch g Magic Ring (Ire) - Silken Dalliance
10^{7sd} **0-0-1**

Magidene *J R Best* 49 a66
2 b g Magic Ring (Ire) - Everdene
6^{5s} 4^{5s} 9^{5sd} 1^{5sd} **1-0-4 £3,746**

Magnesium (USA) *B G Powell* 77
5 ch g Kris S (USA) - Proflare (USA)
8^{12gs} **0-0-1**

Magnolia Blossom *R A Fahey* 58 a48
2 b f Superior Premium - Cautious Joe
1^{5gf} 3^{5gf} 5^{5gf} 5^{6gf} 1^{6gf} 17^{6g} 5^{6sd} 6^{6sd} 6^{6sd} **2-0-9 £5,170**

Maguire (Ger) *M F Harris* 59 a48
4 gr g Medaaly - Mayada (USA)
12^{7f} 14^{7gf} 8^{6f} 9^{7f} 9^{7sd} 15^{10g} **0-0-6**

Mahmjra *M R Channon* 71
3 b c Josr Algarhoud (Ire) - Jamrat Samya (Ire)
9^{11gs} 3^{10gf} 1^{10g} 2^{13g} 2^{12gf} 2^{11g} 2^{14f} 4^{12g} **1-5-8 £9,404**

Mahrajaan (USA) *J H M Gosden* 71
2 b/br c Machiavellian (USA) - Karen S (USA)
4^{8gs} **0-0-1 £391**

Maid In England *J Jay* 38 a46
2 b f Mujadil (USA) - Lalique (Ire)
9^{8sd} 12^{8g} 10^{8g} **0-0-3**

Maid The Cut *A D Smith* 43 a43
4 ch f Silver Wizard (USA) - Third Dam
PU^{9sd} 7^{9sd} 5^{12f} **0-0-3**

Maidford (Ire) *M Meade* 36
2 ch f Singspiel (Ire) - Milde (USA)
11^{5gf} **0-0-1**

Maids Causeway (Ire) *B W Hills* 115
3 ch f Giant's Causeway (USA) - Vallee Des Reves (USA)
2^{8gf} 5^{8gy} 1^{8gf} 7^{8gs} **1-1-4 £221,770**

Maidstone Midas (Ire) *B R Foster*
4 b c Nashwan (USA) - Be Mine
12^{7gf} **0-0-1**

Maigue Violet (Ire) *J G Burns* 65
3 b f Night Shift (USA) - Dame's Violet (Ire)
2^{6sh} 1^{5sh} 17^{5g} 13^{5ys} **1-1-4 £10,604**

Maison Dieu *J Howard Johnson* 54
2 b/br g King Charlemagne (USA) - Shining Desert (Ire)
9^{6g} 8^{6gf} **0-0-2**

Maitre Levy (Ger) *D A Nolan* 26
7 b g Monsun (Ger) - Meerdunung (Eg)
11^{12g} **0-0-1**

Majehar *A G Newcombe* 62 a47
3 b g Marju (Ire) - Joonayh
10^{5sh} 13^{7gf} 8^{5gs} 10^{6g} 10^{8gs} 9^{5sd} 8^{8ss} 4^{9ss} **0-0-8**

Majestic Desert *M R Channon* 110
4 b f Fraam - Calcutta Queen
8^{8gf} 3^{9gf} 3^{8g} 4^{8gf} 1^{7gs} 3^{8gf} 9^{8gy} **1-2-7 £51,080**

Majestic Missile (Ire) *W J Haggas* 117
4 b c Royal Applause - Tshusick
4^{5s} 3^{5gf} 2^{5gf} 3^{5gf} 1^{5gf} 2^{5gf} 9^{5gs} **1-4-7 £70,972**

Majestic Monarch (USA) *Saeed Bin Suroor* a53
3 b c A.P. Indy (USA) - Aishah (USA)
9^{12sd} **0-0-1**

Majestic Star *M J Ryan* 52 a51
4 br f Fraam - Fun While It Lasts
7^{8sd} 7^{8sd} 12^{8f} 3^{8f} 2^{8gf} 7^{10gf} **0-2-6 £1,584**

Majestic Times (Ire) *Liam McAteer* 106
5 b g Bluebird (USA) - Simply Times (USA)
1^{6hy} 7^{6sh} 9^{7hy} 2^{6gf} 2^{5g} 4^{7gf} 5^{6g} 3^{6g} 2^{6gy} 1^{5ys} **2-5-10 £81,864**

Majestic Vision *W R Swinburn* 61 a61
4 ch g Desert King (Ire) - Triste Oeil (USA)
9^{16s} 10^{14g} 8^{12gf} 4^{12sd} 3^{12f} 8^{12g} 4^{12f} 5^{12g} 14^{12g} **0-1-9 £1,093**

Majestical (Ire) *J M Bradley* 66 a69
3 b g Fayruz - Haraabah (USA)
1^{5sd} 4^{5sd} 1^{5sd} 4^{5gs} 7^{5g} 3^{5f} 6^{5g} 5^{5sd} 2^{6gf} 8^{6g} 10^{6sd} 6^{6gf} 4^{5gf} 8^{6gf} 7^{6gf} 2^{5sd} **2-3-16 £10,515**

Majestik Mitch *C N Kellett*
2 b g Little Jim - Deal In Facts
11^{5gf} 13^{7g} 11^{6sd} 12^{5gf} **0-0-4**

Majhool *I W McInnes* 14 a45
6 b g Mark Of Esteem (Ire) - Be Peace (USA)
10^{6sd} 7^{7sd} 15^{5gf} **0-0-3**

Majik *D J S Ffrench Davis* 62 a82
6 ch g Pivotal - Revoke (USA)
1^{6sd} 1^{6sd} 2^{5sd} 3^{7s} 5^{6sd} 8^{6g} 18^{6gf} 16^{6g} 4^{6sd} 11^{5gs} 2^{6hy} 9^{7sd} **2-3-12 £13,599**

Major Broughton *W J Musson* 53 a61
2 br c Groom Dancer (USA) - Rainy Day Song
$9^{6gf} 2^{7sd} 7^{6gs} 4^{7sd} 6^{7s} 9^{8gf}$ **0-1-6**
£1,430

Major Faux Pas (Ire) *J A Osborne* 83 a87
3 b g Barathea (Ire) - Edwina (Ire)
$3^{8sd} 10^{9sd} 4^{10g} 8^{10gs} 15^{9g} 2^{10gf} 5^{8g} 8^{10s}$
0-2-8 £2,877

Major Magpie (Ire) *M Dods* 74
3 b g Rossini (USA) - Picnic Basket
$3^{7g} 3^{7g} 6^{7gf} 2^{8gf} 9^{8gf} 5^{8g} 6^{10gf} 5^{8gf}$
0-3-8 £2,636

Major Speculation (Ire) *J M Bradley* 53 a48
5 b g Spectrum (Ire) - Pacific Grove
$10^{8f} 9^{8g} 6^{8gf} 5^{10f} 5^{8sd} 6^{8sd}$ **0-0-6**

Majorca *J Howard Johnson* 64
4 b g Green Desert (USA) - Majmu (USA)
$18^{8gs} 17^{8gs} 10^{7gf} 12^{8gf} 8^{8gf} 11^{7gf} 14^{6g}$
0-0-7

Majority Vote (USA) *Saeed Bin Suroor* 67
2 b c Danzig (USA) - Shouldnt Say Never (USA)
4^{8hy} **0-0-1 £245**

Majors Cast (Ire) *J Noseda* 122
4 b c Victory Note (USA) - Ziffany
$6^{6gf} 1^{8g} 1^{8gf} 1^{8gf} 7^{9gf} 3^{7gs} 2^{7g} 2^{8g} 3^{8g} 5^{8y}$
3-4-10 £236,433

Makabul *B R Millman* 86
2 b c Makbul - Victoria Sioux
1^{5gs} **1-0-1 £5,434**

Makai *M Johnston* 70 a63
2 ch g Cayman Kai (Ire) - Young Sue
$18^{6g} 2^{6gf} 8^{6g} 4^{6s} 3^{6hy} 4^{8ss} 2^{7sd} 5^{8sd}$
0-3-8 £2,502

Makarim (Ire) *M R Bosley* a52
9 ch g Generous (Ire) - Emmaline (USA)
$3^{13sd} 5^{14sd} 2^{16sd} 8^{13sd} 3^{16sd} 8^{16sd}$ **0-3-6**
£1,405

Makderah (Ire) *M P Tregoning* 74
2 b f Danehill (USA) - Wijdan (USA)
3^{7g} **0-1-1 £812**

Make It Happen Now *S L Keightley* 47 a30
3 b/br f Octagonal (NZ) - Whittle Woods Girl
$12^{5sd} 8^{6sd} 10^{5sd} 7^{7sd} 11^{5gs} 1^{7s} 7^{8gf} 13^{5sd}$
$13^{6s} 6^{6ss}$ **1-0-10 £1,540**

Make It Snappy *M Wigham* 62 a47
3 b f Mujadil (USA) - Snap Crackle Pop (Ire)
$10^{7gs} 6^{7gf} 11^{8gf} 4^{8sd} 9^{7sd}$ **0-0-5 £278**

Make My Dream *J Gallagher* 59 a58
2 b c My Best Valentine - Sandkatoon (Ire)
$13^{5g} 8^{5g} 5^{5gf} 4^{6g} 4^{6g} 12^{5hy} 7^{6sd}$ **0-0-7**
£349

Make My Hay *J Gallagher* a48
6 b g Bluegrass Prince (Ire) - Shashi (Ire)
$1^{14sd} 5^{16sd} 3^{14ss} 12^{17sd}$ **1-1-4 £1,501**

Make Us Flush *A Berry* 60 a19
3 b f Mind Games - Pearls
$7^{5s} 10^{6s} 7^{6gf} 2^{6f} 16^{6g} 5^{6gf} 10^{5gf} 10^{5gf} 9^{6gf}$
$12^{5s} 8^{5sd} 14^{6sd}$ **0-1-12 £880**

Makfly *R Hollinshead* 77
2 b g Makbul - Flying Flip
$4^{6g} 1^{6s}$ **1-0-2 £5,099**

Making Magic *P W Hiatt* 41
5 b m Wizard King - Snowline
$11^{8g} 8^{10gf} 6^{12gf} 10^{10g} 9^{9g} 10^{8gf} 11^{10g} 10^{11sd}$
0-0-8

Making Moves *Ms Deborah J Evans* a54
2 b f Afternoon Deelites (USA) - Simona (Chi)
$7^{9sf} 4^{7sd}$ **0-0-2 £274**

Making Music *T D Easterby* 68
2 b f Makbul - Crofters Ceilidh
$8^{5gf} 2^{6gf} 9^{6s} 4^{5g} 2^{5gf} 2^{5gf} 8^{5gs} 1^{5f} 7^{6g}$
1-3-9 £8,847

Maktavish *I Semple* 81 a65
6 b g Makbul - La Belle Vie
$12^{5g} 16^{5gs} 1^{5s} 8^{5sd} 12^{5sd}$ **1-0-5**
£5,886

Maktu *M S Saunders* 34
3 ch g Bien Bien (USA) - Shalateeno
$7^{10gs} 14^{11g} 7^{12f}$ **0-0-3**

Maktub (Ity) *M A Jarvis*
6 b h Love The Groom (USA) - Carmen The Best (Ire)
7^{12g} **0-0-1**

Makybe Diva *Lee Freedman* 124
7 b m Desert King (Ire) - Tugela (USA)
$7^{7gs} 2^{9g} 1^{10g} 1^{12s} 7^{10f} 7^{16f} 1^{7g} 2^{8gs} 1^{10g}$
$1^{10sw} 1^{16gs}$ **6-0-11 £2,999,989**

Malahem (Ire) *J H M Gosden* 88
3 b g Mark Of Esteem (Ire) - Majmu (USA)
$4^{8gf} 3^{9gs} 1^{8gf} 3^{9g} 1^{8g} 18^{7gf}$ **2-2-6**
£11,508

Malahide Express (Ire) *E J Alston* 58 a42
5 gr g Compton Place - Gracious Gretclo
$9^{5gs} 5^{5gs} 5^{5gf} 3^{5gf} 9^{5gf} 12^{5sd} 10^{5ss} 12^{5sd}$
0-1-8 £422

Malaika *R Hollinshead* 59
3 b f Polar Prince (Ire) - Gold Belt (Ire)
$5^{6gf} 15^{5gs} 11^{6gf}$ **0-0-3**

Malakiya (Ire) *G A Butler* 52 a57
2 b c Sadler's Wells (USA) - State Crystal (Ire)
$8^{8g} 5^{7sd}$ **0-0-2**

Malapropism *M R Channon* 94 a98
5 ch g Compton Place - Mrs Malaprop
$13^{6gf} 4^{5ft} 7^{6gf} 2^{5ft} 7^{5gs} 17^{5g} 12^{5gs} 4^{5gs}$
$3^{5g} 15^{5g} 14^{5g} 5^{5gf} 4^{5gf} 17^{5s} 19^{6gs} 5^{5s} 3^{5gf}$
$13^{5g} 12^{5g} 5^{5gs} 9^{5s} 5^{5g} 2^{5g} 3^{5g} 5^{5hy}$
0-6-25 £31,918

Malarkey *Stef Liddiard* 83
8 b g Mukaddamah (USA) - Malwiya (USA)
$1^{16g} 5^{16g} 6^{14gf} 7^{15gf} 7^{16gs} 4^{16gf} 6^{16g} 6^{16gf}$
$4^{16g} 10^{17f} 7^{14g}$ **1-0-11 £8,943**

Malcheek (Ire) *T D Easterby* 85
3 br c Lend A Hand - Russland (Ger)
$1^{7gf} 1^{7gf} 3^{7gf} 4^{6gs} 3^{7gf} 12^{8g}$ **2-1-6**
£15,179

Maldonian *Julian Poulton* 39
3 b f Mujahid (USA) - Bellateena
$9^{7sd} 7^{10g}$ **0-0-2**

Maldoun (Ire) *R J Hodges* a12
6 b g Kaldoun (Fr) - Marzipan (Ire)
11^{12sd} **0-0-1**

Malech (Ire) *M L W Bell* 61
2 b g Bahhare (USA) - Choral Sundown
$5^{6gf} 5^{7gf} 3^{7g} 8^{8g} 15^{7g}$ **0-1-5 £484**

Malelane (Ire) *Mrs J R Ramsden* 31
2 b f Prince Sabo - Indigo
$11^{5gf} 9^{5g}$ **0-0-2**

Malibu (Ire) *S Dow* 56 a76
4 b g Second Empire (Ire) - Tootle
$8^{10sd} 8^{12sd} 3^{12sd} 8^{10sd} 1^{12sd} 9^{10gf}$ **1-1-6**
£3,922

Malinche *R Pritchard-Gordon* 91
2 ch f Hernando (Fr) - Love Letters
9^5hy 6^6s 1^6g 7^6s 3^6gs 7^7g 5^7g **1-0-7**
£14,043

Malinsa Blue (Ire) *J A Glover* 87
3 b f Desert Style (Ire) - Talina's Law (Ire)
12^7g 2^8gf 5^8gf 4^8g 3^8g 5^8gf 6^8gf 10^10g 2^7g
6^7gf 19^9gs 13^7hy **0-3-12 £6,333**

Maltese Falcon *P F I Cole* 111
5 b g Mark Of Esteem (Ire) - Crime Ofthecentury
1^5gf 9^5s 12^5gf 2^5g 2^5g 4^5gf 5^5g **1-2-7**
£23,613

Maluti *Rae Guest* 53
4 ch g Piccolo - Persian Blue
16^5gf 13^6gs 3^5gf 4^5gf 12^6gs 5^5gf 16^5gf 5^6gs
6^5gf 1^6gf 14^5g 15^6g **1-1-12 £1,745**

Malvern Light *W J Haggas* 96 a84
4 b f Zieten (USA) - Michelle Hicks
10^7g 6^6gf 21^7gf 11^7g 4^8sd 10^8gf 3^7gf 11^7gf
9^7g **0-1-9 £4,179**

Mambazo *S C Williams* 50 a61
3 b g Dansili - Kalindi
8^6s 14^8g 10^5f 7^7gf 5^6gf 10^7g 12^6g 2^5sd 3^6gf
12^6sd 13^6g 4^5sd 1^6sd 2^6ss 1^5sd **2-3-15**
£5,976

Mambo Princess (USA) *J H M Gosden* 78
3 b f Kingmambo (USA) - Tuzla (Fr)
4^7g 1^10gf 1^12y **2-0-3 £21,312**

Mambo Sun *P A Blockley* 60 a68
2 b g Superior Premium - The Manx Touch (Ire)
6^6gs 4^6gs 4^7f 13^5gf 9^7sd 6^8ss 2^8sd 3^8sd 1^7sd
1-2-9 £6,452

Mambo's Melody *P W Chapple-Hyam* 39
3 b f Kingmambo (USA) - Key Academy
8^10gf 7^10gf **0-0-2**

Mamcazma *D Morris* 83
7 gr g Terimon - Merryhill Maid (Ire)
9^12gf 4^14gf PU^16sd **0-0-3 £530**

Mamichor *J R Boyle* 65 a54
2 br c Mamalik (USA) - Ichor
10^7sd 8^7gf 9^6gs **0-0-3**

Mamool (Ire) *Saeed Bin Suroor* 121
6 b h In The Wings - Genovefa (USA)
1^12gs 4^13g 2^12gf **1-1-3 £32,900**

Mamore Gap (Ire) *M E Sowersby* 64
7 b g General Monash (USA) - Ravensdale Rose (Ire)
7^8g 1^8g 10^10gf 12^7gf **1-0-4 £2,895**

Man Crazy (Ire) *C A Dwyer* 10 a53
4 b f Foxhound (USA) - Schonbein (Ire)
5^6sd 1^6sd 4^6sd 6^7sd 3^6sd 11^6sd 8^6s **1-1-7**
£1,844

Man The Gate *P D Cundell* a53
6 b g Elmaamul (USA) - Girl At The Gate
4^12sd 5^9sd UR^12sd **0-0-3**

Mana D'Argent (Ire) *M Johnston* 88 a66
8 b g Ela-Mana-Mou - Petite-D-Argent
11^17sd 3^14gs 7^18g 6^14g 17^19gs **0-1-5**
£1,038

Manbala (Fr) *J L Dunlop* 100
2 gr f Linamix (Fr) - Do The Mambo (USA)
1^7gs 4^8g 1^8hy **2-0-3 £57,025**

Manda Island (USA) *J H M Gosden* 79
3 br f Dynaformer (USA) - Alcando
1^8gs 8^10g 6^12gf 7^10gs **1-0-4 £3,493**

Mandarin Dancer (Ire) *Miss L A Perratt* 38
2 gr f King Charlemagne (USA) - Shamneez (Ire)
8^7g 9^8gf **0-0-2**

Mandarin Grand (Ire) *Miss L A Perratt* 34
2 b f Raise A Grand (Ire) - Playa Del Sol (Ire)
7^5gf 7^6gf 6^7gf 7^7hy **0-0-4**

Mandarin Rocket (Ire) *Miss L A Perratt* 45
2 ch c Titus Livius (Fr) - Two Thousand (Ire)
4^6gf 7^5g **0-0-2 £366**

Mandarin Spirit (Ire) *G C H Chung* 79 a81
5 b g Primo Dominie - Lithe Spirit (Ire)
6^9sd 4^6sd 1^6sd 1^7sd 3^6sd 4^6sd 3^7gs 1^6s 6^6gf
2^6f 5^5gs 7^6gf 5^6gf 7^6s 6^6gf **3-3-15**
£15,454

Mandatum *L M Cumani* 87
4 b g Mtoto - Reamur
8^13s 5^14gf 1^12gf 2^15gf 8^13gf 3^14gf 8^16g
1-2-7 £6,519

Mandinka *J F Coupland* 30 a76
5 b g Distinctly North (USA) - Primo Panache
1^11sd 2^11sd 9^11gs **1-1-3 £2,533**

Maneki Neko (Ire) *E W Tuer* 72
3 b g Rudimentary (USA) - Ardbess
11^9g 5^7gs 6^7g 1^8f 4^8f 16^8gf 6^9g 11^12f SU^11gs
2-0-9 £6,791

Mango Groove (Ire) *B J Meehan* 65
3 b f Unfuwain (USA) - Solar Crystal (Ire)
11^10gs 7^10g 7^10gf 5^10f 13^10gf **0-0-5**

Mango Mischief (Ire) *J L Dunlop* 106
4 ch f Desert King (Ire) - Eurolink Mischief
6^9gf 1^10gf 5^10s 7^12g 4^10hy **1-0-5**
£34,297

Mangrove Cay (Ire) *J Hetherton* 50
3 b g Danetime (Ire) - Art Duo
6^8gf 5^8g 14^7gf **0-0-3**

Manhattan Jack *G A Swinbank* 62
4 ch g Forzando - Manhattan Diamond
7^10gs 7^10g 3^11s 9^16g 5^14g **0-0-5 £555**

Maniatis *N P Littmoden* a76
8 b g Slip Anchor - Tamassos
2^12sd 1^12sd 2^12sd 3^14sd 1^12sd 5^12sd **2-2-6**
£7,161

Manic *Andrew Reid* 65 a67
3 br f Polar Falcon (USA) - Gentle Irony
10^6sd 2^7sd 3^7sd 6^8sd 7^7sd 3^7sd 4^7sd 4^7sd 1^7sd
8^7sd 3^6g 2^6gf 2^7gf 4^6g 3^6sd 4^6gs 3^6g 6^7gf 7^6gf
12^6g 4^7sd 8^6sd **1-7-22 £11,237**

Mannello *B Palling* 49
2 b f Mamalik (USA) - Isle Of Sodor
9^6g 9^7gs 15^6gs **0-0-3**

Mannikko (Ire) *G Wragg* 63
2 gr c Green Desert (USA) - Cassandra Go (Ire)
8^6gf 6^6s 4^6hy **0-0-3 £331**

Manoubi *M Todhunter* 50
6 b g Doyoun - Manuetti (Ire)
12^14g 6^13gs **0-0-2**

Manouche *K A Ryan* 73 a50
2 b g Highest Honor (Fr) - Green Charter
10^6gf 3^7gf 3^8gf 3^8gs 11^7g 6^7gs 11^8sd 9^7sd
0-3-8 £2,336

Mansiya *C E Brittain* 63 a47
3 ch f Vettori (Ire) - Bay Shade (USA)
3^9g 2^7sd 13^11sd **0-2-3 £1,386**

Manston (Ire) *B J Meehan* 105
2 ch c Indian Ridge - Bye Bold Aileen (Ire)
10^7g 10^7gf 1^7gs 8^7g 1^6g 1^6hy 6^6gs **3-0-7**

£28,676

Mantle *J R Fanshawe* 57
3 b f Loup Sauvage (USA) - Kyle Rhea
4^{10g} **0-0-1 £347**

Manyana (Ire) *Saeed Bin Suroor* 98
4 b g Alzao (USA) - Sometime (Ire)
11^{10gf} 10^{12gf} 10^{12gf} 4^{14gf} **0-0-4 £792**

Maple Branch (USA) *R A Harris* 10
3 b f Stravinsky (USA) - Galanty Show
12^{6sd} 8^{7s} 17^{7s} 10^{6f} **0-0-4**

Maraagel (USA) *Saeed Bin Suroor* 61
2 b c Danzig (USA) - Hasnaael Reef (USA)
4^{6gf} **0-0-1 £321**

Maraahel (Ire) *Sir Michael Stoute* 124
4 b c Alzao (USA) - Nasanice (Ire)
8^{12gf} 5^{12s} 1^{10gs} 2^{12f} 3^{10g} 3^{9gf} 3^{10gs} 3^{10gf}
1-3-8 £294,395

Maraakeb (Fr) *J H M Gosden* 94
4 gr c Linamix (Fr) - Raheefa (USA)
4^{10gs} 1^{10s} 7^{10gs} 5^{10gf} 7^{12gf} 4^{12gf} 9^{11gf} 8^{10s}
11^{10gf} **1-0-9 £8,742**

Marabar *D W Chapman* 47 a54
7 b m Sri Pekan (USA) - Erbaya (Ire)
8^{7sd} 4^{6sd} 3^{7sd} 5^{7sd} 6^{6gs} 4^{7sd} 5^{8g} 7^{7s} 10^{7sd}
10^{7g} 11^{6g} 15^{7g} 7^{8sd} 12^{6sd} **0-1-14 £216**

Marachi Band (USA) *E A L Dunlop* a57
2 b f Dixieland Band (USA) - Khamsin (USA)
10^{8sd} 6^{9sd} 7^{7sd} **0-0-3**

Marajuana *J Ryan* 77 a52
3 b f Robellino (USA) - Mara River
17^{7g} 3^{7gf} 16^{7g} 14^{6s} 11^{7sd} 11^{9sd} **0-0-6**
£1,676

Maraval *M Wellings* 58 a42
2 b g Mark Of Esteem (Ire) - Mayaro Bay
11^{8g} 13^{7gf} 7^{7sd} **0-0-3**

Maravedi (Ire) *W M Brisbourne* a44
5 ch m Hector Protector (USA) - Manuetti (Ire)
6^{9sd} 8^{8sd} 6^{9sd} 6^{12sd} 9^{17sd} 9^{14sd} **0-0-6**

Marble Arch *H Morrison* 48
9 b g Rock Hopper - Mayfair Minx
13^{13s} 13^{10s} **0-0-2**

Marc Of Brilliance (USA) *M Johnston* 75
2 ch g Sunday Silence (USA) - Rahcak (Ire)
11^{7g} 3^{8g} 6^{9g} 2^{10f} 3^{10hy} **0-3-5 £2,208**

March Heir (USA) *C E Brittain* 58
3 b c Deputy Minister (Can) - Advancing Star (USA)
6^{10gf} 4^{11g} **0-0-2 £267**

Marchetta *W R Swinburn* 75 a78
3 b f Mujadil (USA) - My Lewicia (Ire)
8^{8gf} 1^{9gf} 11^{10g} 1^{10sd} 9^{10g} **2-0-5 £7,547**

Marching Song *R Hannon* 102
3 b g Royal Applause - Marl
3^{7gf} 2^{6gf} 5^{6g} 7^{7gf} 16^{7gs} **0-2-5 £6,145**

Marcus Andronicus (USA) *A P O'Brien* 99
2 b c Danehill (USA) - Fiji
1^{6s} 5^{6gf} 2^{7g} 4^{6hy} **1-1-4 £18,894**

Marcus Eile (Ire) *Robert Gray* 53 a55
4 b g Daggers Drawn (USA) - Sherannda (USA)
11^{9sd} 12^{9sd} 10^{7g} 8^{7gf} 6^{10sd} 3^{10gf} 2^{12gf} 4^{16gf}
3^{16gf} 2^{11gf} 9^{16gf} 11^{10g} **0-4-12 £2,595**

Marella *R Charlton* 41
3 b f Desert Prince (Ire) - Rainbow Lake
9^{8g} **0-0-1**

Maren (USA) *D Nicholls* 78
4 b g Gulch (USA) - Fatina
12^{8gf} 7^{7gs} 10^{8gf} 15^{10gf} 3^{8g} 7^{7gf} 8^{8gf} 10^{7gf}
6^{9gf} **0-1-9 £646**

Marengo *M J Polglase* 44 a36
11 b g Never So Bold - Born To Dance
4^{7sd} 10^{5sd} 8^{7sd} 9^{5sd} 10^{6sd} 4^{7sd} 7^{8sd} 11^{8sd}
4^{9sd} 10^{9sd} 11^{9sd} 8^{7g} 9^{10gs} 10^{9g} 15^{8s} 13^{9sd}
9^{10s} 8^{10g} 6^{7sd} 10^{8gf} 6^{6sd} 11^{8sd} 11^{7sd}
0-0-23

Margalita (Ire) *P Mitchell* a32
5 b m Sesaro (USA) - Mamma Luigi (Ire)
6^{7sd} **0-0-1**

Margaret's Dream (Ire) *D Carroll* 49 a49
4 b f Muhtarram (USA) - Acidanthera
19^{8hy} 6^{5s} 10^{5f} 9^{9g} 14^{7hy} 4^{7y} 6^{6gf} 7^{8gf} 12^{8g}
2^{7f} 3^{8g} 4^{5sh} 6^{7sd} 4^{8sd} **0-3-14 £1,831**

Margarets Choice *K A Ryan* 19 a11
2 ch f Foxhound (USA) - Its Another Gift
16^{5gf} 15^{6gf} 12^{6gf} 8^{5sd} **0-0-4**

Margarets Wish *T Wall* 25
5 gr m Cloudings (Ire) - Gentle Gain
9^{10f} 7^{11gf} **0-0-2**

Margery Daw (Ire) *P S McEntee* 52 a57
5 b m Sri Pekan (USA) - Suyayeb (USA)
4^{9sd} 1^{10sd} 3^{10sd} 3^{10sd} 7^{10sd} 8^{12sd} 7^{13sd} 2^{10sd}
8^{10sd} 10^{10sd} 3^{10g} 10^{8g} 7^{13gs} 3^{10gf} 7^{12gf} 6^{10f}
8^{10sd} 4^{12sd} 12^{10sd} 2^{12sd} 10^{17sd} 9^{10sd} 3^{10gf} 8^{10gf}
12^{12sd} **1-7-25 £5,030**

Margold (Ire) *R Hollinshead* a34
5 ch m Goldmark (USA) - Arcevia (Ire)
6^{17sd} 6^{14sd} 9^{12sd} **0-0-3**

Marhaba Million (Ire) *E McNamara* 67
3 gr g Linamix (Fr) - Modelliste
5^{10g} 7^{11gs} 6^{10f} 5^{12g} 11^{14gs} 3^{12s} 4^{12gf} 5^{13f}
8^{14gf} 3^{17gs} **0-2-10 £1,825**

Maria Bonita (Ire) *C N Kellett* 37 a51
4 b f Octagonal (NZ) - Nightitude
8^{11sd} 1^{10sd} 9^{9sd} 8^{10sd} 7^{14sd} 6^{10g} **1-0-6**
£1,459

Maria Delfina (Ire) *J H M Gosden* 72
3 ch f Giant's Causeway (USA) - Photographie (USA)
6^{10gf} 6^{10gf} 4^{13gf} 2^{13f} **0-1-4 £1,620**

Maria Maria (Ire) *Mrs N Macauley*
4 ch f Among Men (USA) - Yiayia's Girl
13^{12sd} 13^{12sd} **0-0-2**

Maria Vetsera *Sir Mark Prescott* 80
4 ch f Selkirk (USA) - Scandalette
2^{8g} 2^{10gs} **0-2-2 £3,310**

Marian's Gift *M W Easterby*
3 ch f Bold Edge - Thimbalina
16^{7g} 13^{7gs} **0-0-2**

Marianis *M S Saunders* 33 a41
3 b f Lujain (USA) - Without Warning (Ire)
7^{8sd} 10^{10gf} 5^{10gf} 12^{7sd} **0-0-4**

Marias Dream (Ire) *Eamon Tyrrell* 85
3 b/br f Desert Sun - Clifton Lass (Ire)
6^{9f} 2^{8f} 2^{9gf} 3^{8g} 1^{8gf} 2^{8gf} 15^{10gf} **1-4-7**
£11,327

Marias Magic *M Johnston* 98
4 b f Mtoto - Majoune (Fr)
2^{12gs} 2^{13gs} 9^{10g} 1^{12f} 8^{12gf} 6^{12gf} 2^{13gf} 1^{14gf}
6^{12gf} 8^{12g} 1^{14gf} 3^{15g} 6^{12gs} 6^{12hy} **3-4-14**
£28,589

Marie (Ire) *B W Hills* 67
2 gr f Observatory (USA) - Marie De Bayeux (Fr)
5^{6gf} 5^{6gf} 4^{6gs} 11^{7gs} **0-0-4 £243**

Marina Ellen (USA) *N A Callaghan* 41

2 ch f Giant's Causeway (USA) - Carsonality (USA)
$15^{7gf}\ 10^{8gf}\ 9^{7gf}$ **0-0-3**

Marinaite *S R Bowring* 77 a77
4 b f Komaite (USA) - Marina's Song
$10^{7sd}\ 8^{6sd}\ 3^{5sd}\ 1^{8sd}\ 9^{10g}\ 2^{6g}\ 12^{9sd}\ 11^{6ss}\ 9^{5sd}$ **1-2-9 £4,969**

Marinero *Lady Herries* 49 a42
2 ch g Pine Bluff (USA) - Viva Maria
$10^{9g}\ 11^{7sd}\ 7^{7sd}$ **0-0-3**

Mario Jack *M E Sowersby* 32 a12
2 ch c Atraf - Forbidden Monkey
$7^{7g}\ 15^{7gf}\ 10^{7sd}$ **0-0-3**

Maritime Blues *J G Given* 57
5 b g Fleetwood (Ire) - Dixie D'Oats
$12^{11g}\ 11^{20s}\ 5^{14gs}\ 7^{14f}$ **0-0-4**

Mark Your Card *T D Easterby*
3 ch f Mark Of Esteem (Ire) - Charolles
7^{12sd} **0-0-1**

Marker *J A Geake* 81
5 ch g Pivotal - Palace Street (USA)
$4^{5gs}\ 10^{6s}\ 10^{6g}\ 15^{6gf}\ 16^{6g}$ **0-0-5 £535**

Markestino *T D Easterby* 32
2 b g Mark Of Esteem (Ire) - Mademoiselle Chloe
$17^{8s}\ 9^{7g}\ 5^{7s}$ **0-0-3**

Market Girl *C F Wall* 55
2 b f Mark Of Esteem (Ire) - It Girl
$5^{6gs}\ 13^{6gs}$ **0-0-2**

Market Trend *M Johnston* 84
3 b f Selkirk (USA) - Equity Princess
$1^{9gs}\ 20^{8gf}\ 11^{10gf}\ 3^{12gs}\ 9^{12gf}\ 6^{12g}$ **1-0-6 £8,541**

Markington *J D Bethell* a59
2 b g Medicean - Nemesia
$4^{9sd}\ 7^{9sd}$ **0-0-2 £277**

Marko Jadeo (Ire) *S Dow* 83 a86
7 b g Eagle Eyed (USA) - Fleeting Quest
$7^{8sd}\ 8^{7sd}\ 6^{7sd}\ 1^{6sd}\ 5^{7sd}\ 8^{7g}\ 4^{7gf}\ 3^{7gf}\ 6^{6gf}\ 5^{7sd}\ 11^{7gf}\ 4^{7sd}\ 11^{7s}\ 2^{7sd}\ 7^{8sd}$ **1-2-15 £8,991**

Markovitch *P W Chapple-Hyam* 71
2 b c Mark Of Esteem (Ire) - Perdicula (Ire)
$6^{7gf}\ 4^{8g}$ **0-0-2 £537**

Markusha *Jamie Poulton* 46
7 b g Alhijaz - Shafir (Ire)
$7^{7f}\ 18^{8gf}$ **0-0-2**

Marlenes Girl (Ire) *A Berry* 45
3 ro f Foxhound (USA) - Premier Place (USA)
$13^{6g}\ 13^{6g}\ 5^{6f}\ 13^{8gf}\ 6^{7gf}$ **0-0-5**

Marmooq *M Johnston* 58
2 ch c Cadeaux Genereux - Portelet
$3^{6gf}\ 5^{7s}$ **0-1-2 £648**

Marnie *J Akehurst* a49
8 ch m First Trump - Miss Aboyne
$12^{10sd}\ 8^{8sd}\ 6^{8sd}$ **0-0-3**

Maromito (Ire) *R Bastiman* 60
8 b g Up And At 'Em - Amtico
$14^{5f}\ 13^{5gf}\ 4^{5f}$ **0-0-3 £272**

Maron *F Jordan* a23
8 b g Puissance - Will Be Bold
$10^{5sd}\ 10^{6sd}$ **0-0-2**

Maroussies Wings (Ire) *P C Haslam* 82
2 b f In The Wings - Maroussie (Fr)
$11^{7gf}\ 2^{7gf}\ 1^{8s}\ 5^{8s}$ **1-1-4 £7,477**

Marriage Value (Ire) *J A Osborne* 78
2 b f Marju (Ire) - Braari (USA)
$1^{6gs}\ 9^{6gf}$ **1-0-2 £4,852**

Marron Flore *A J Lidderdale*
2 ch f Compton Place - Flore Fair
12^{7sd} **0-0-1**

Marronnier (Ire) *T D Easterby* 68
2 ch c Vettori (Ire) - Reservation (Ire)
$8^{7gs}\ 5^{7g}\ 4^{7g}\ 6^{8gs}$ **0-0-4 £499**

Marsad (Ire) *J Akehurst* 72 a62
11 ch g Fayruz - Broad Haven (Ire)
$7^{6g}\ 14^{6s}\ 8^{6gs}\ 13^{6g}\ 15^{6g}\ 10^{6gf}\ 10^{8gf}\ 12^{6g}\ 7^{6gf}\ 11^{6gs}\ 8^{6gf}\ 10^{6gs}\ 4^{6sd}\ 7^{7sd}$ **0-0-14 £226**

Marsh Orchid *C C Bealby* a62
4 b g Lahib (USA) - Majalis
$3^{9sd}\ 6^{12sd}\ 7^{12sd}\ 18^{10gf}\ 11^{12sd}$ **0-1-5 £524**

Marshallspark (Ire) *R A Fahey* 74 a63
6 b g Fayruz - Lindas Delight
$9^{6sd}\ 11^{7sd}\ 3^{7sd}\ 3^{7sd}\ 14^{6g}\ 13^{6gf}\ 15^{6gf}\ 13^{6g}\ 1^{6gf}\ 3^{6gf}\ 6^{6sd}\ 12^{6g}\ 11^{7gf}\ 10^{7sd}$ **1-3-14 £5,174**

Marshman (Ire) *M H Tompkins* 97 a93
6 ch g College Chapel - Gold Fly (Ire)
$4^{6s}\ 11^{7g}\ 1^{7g}\ 14^{7gs}\ 8^{7g}\ 9^{7g}\ 7^{7g}\ 4^{7g}\ 6^{7gs}\ 9^{7gs}\ 3^{7sd}\ 6^{7sd}\ 7^{8sd}$ **1-2-13 £17,692**

Martharum *J J Quinn* 50 a23
2 ch f Muhtarram (USA) - Needwood Truffle (Ire)
$6^{5s}\ 2^{5g}\ 5^{5gf}\ 4^{5g}\ 4^{5g}\ 6^{5gf}\ 9^{5sd}$ **0-1-7 £1,278**

Martian Glow (Ire) *M A Jarvis* 63 a65
2 b/br f Fasliyev (USA) - Wild Missy (USA)
$2^{5gf}\ 3^{6gf}\ 3^{6sd}\ 9^{5gf}\ 8^{7sd}\ 12^{6gf}$ **0-3-6 £2,998**

Martian Mystery *R A Harris*
2 ch f Bluegrass Prince (Ire) - Martian Melody
$8^{5sd}\ 16^{7gf}$ **0-0-2**

Martillo (Ger) *R Suerland* 118 a98
5 b h Anabaa (USA) - Maltage (USA)
$10^{8ft}\ 1^{8gs}\ 6^{8gf}\ 1^{8g}\ 6^{8g}\ 2^{8s}\ 9^{8hy}$ **2-1-7 £141,806**

Martin House (Ire) *D W Thompson*
6 b g Mujadil (USA) - Dolcezza (Fr)
8^{12gf} **0-0-1**

Marvin Gardens *P S McEntee* 35 a21
2 b g Largesse - En Grisaille
$12^{6hy}\ 7^{5ss}$ **0-0-2**

Mary Carleton *R M H Cowell* 44 a49
4 ch f Halling (USA) - Anne Bonny
$1^{8sd}\ 5^{8sd}\ 4^{10sd}\ 4^{13sd}\ 4^{12sd}\ 6^{12gf}\ 13^{12gf}\ 10^{14f}\ 11^{11gf}$ **1-0-9 £1,466**

Mary Delaney (USA) *M J Wallace* a66
2 b f Hennessy (USA) - Crafty Emerald (USA)
2^{7sd} **0-1-1 £1,328**

Mary Gray *M Johnston* 69
3 gr f Mujahid (USA) - Ancestry
$5^{10f}\ 3^{12gf}\ 1^{14gf}\ 7^{14gf}\ 10^{16g}\ 1^{14gf}\ 9^{16gf}\ 4^{14g}\ 13^{14gf}\ 14^{14s}$ **2-1-10 £7,770**

Mary's Baby *Mrs A M Thorpe* 52
5 b m Magic Ring (Ire) - Everdene
$12^{7g}\ 9^{8gs}\ 8^{8f}\ 7^{8g}\ 13^{9sd}\ 14^{12g}$ **0-0-6**

Marybelle *S C Burrough* 17
3 b f Double Trigger (Ire) - Bellara
$12^{14gf}\ 11^{12g}$ **0-0-2**

Marysienka *J Balding* a30
4 b f Primo Dominie - Polish Romance (USA)

10^{6sd} 10^{6sd} 11^{6sd} 13^{5sd} **0-0-4**

Masafi (Ire) *J Howard Johnson* 104
4 b g Desert King (Ire) - Mrs Fisher (Ire)
7^{10gs} 2^{12g} 2^{13gf} 1^{13f} **1-2-4 £17,448**

Mashaahed *B W Hills* 93
2 b c In The Wings - Patacake Patacake (USA)
6^{7gf} 2^{8g} **0-1-2 £2,148**

Mashaair (Ire) *B W Hills* 73
2 ch c King's Best (USA) - Al Bahathri (USA)
4^{7gf} **0-0-1 £406**

Mashona *J L Dunlop* 29
3 b f Danzero (Aus) - Madurai
14^{6gf} **0-0-1**

Masked (Ire) *J W Hills* 84
4 b g Soviet Star (USA) - Moon Masquerade (Ire)
2^{16gf} **0-1-1 £4,139**

Masquerader (USA) *Saeed Bin Suroor* 73 a102
3 ch c Unbridled (USA) - Guise (USA)
8^{10gf} 2^{8gf} 5^{8gf} 1^{12sd} 2^{12sd} 2^{9sd} **1-3-6 £9,105**

Massey *C R Dore* 27 a81
9 br g Machiavellian (USA) - Massaraat (USA)
3^{6sd} 2^{7sd} 12^{7sd} 6^{6sd} 6^{6sd} 7^{5sd} 12^{5sd} 2^{6sd} 5^{6sd} 5^{6sd} 8^{6g} 8^{7sd} 9^{7sd} 5^{6sd} **0-3-14 £2,001**

Massif Centrale *D R C Elsworth* 103
4 ch g Selkirk (USA) - Madame Dubois
5^{12gf} 8^{14gs} 7^{12g} 12^{12g} **0-0-4 £2,250**

Masta Plasta (Ire) *J Howard Johnson* 105
2 b c Mujadil (USA) - Silver Arrow (USA)
2^{6g} 1^{5g} 1^{5gf} 8^{5gs} 10^{6gf} 2^{6gs} **2-2-6 £54,085**

Master At Arms *L M Cumani* 73
2 ch c Grand Lodge (USA) - L'Ideale (USA)
9^{7gf} 5^{7g} 4^{8g} **0-0-3 £295**

Master Bear (Ire) *R A Fahey* 52
3 b g Bluebird (USA) - Kunuz
14^{6g} 15^{6gf} 8^{5gf} 9^{6gf} 9^{7g} 8^{6g} 9^{6g} **0-0-7**

Master Ben (Ire) *S R Bowring* 41 a49
2 b g Carrowkeel (Ire) - Java Jive
9^{7s} 6^{7gf} 19^{6g} 8^{9sd} 5^{9sd} **0-0-5**

Master Cobbler (Ire) *J Akehurst* 81
3 b g Alhaarth (Ire) - Lady Joshua (Ire)
8^{9g} 10^{10gf} 4^{12gf} 4^{12gf} 3^{12gf} 4^{12g} 8^{10gf} 2^{14gf} 3^{15gf} 7^{14g} 2^{14g} 4^{17gs} 8^{16s} **0-5-13 £6,248**

Master Joseph *M R Channon* 66
3 b g Komaite (USA) - Petit Peu (Ire)
9^{10s} 7^{10gf} 4^{10g} 1^{8g} 7^{8s} 10^{8g} 6^{8gf} 4^{8gs} 6^{8gf} 8^{8gf} 4^{7gf} 5^{8gf} 9^{8s} 3^{7gf} **1-2-14 £5,549**

Master Mahogany *R J Hodges* 83
4 b g Bandmaster (USA) - Impropriety
2^{8hy} 1^{8f} 2^{10g} 3^{8g} 6^{8gf} 2^{8g} 2^{8g} 4^{8gf} 4^{8g} **1-5-9 £15,987**

Master Malarkey *Mrs C A Dunnett* a18
2 b g Tipsy Creek (USA) - Girl Next Door
13^{7sd} 12^{9sd} **0-0-2**

Master Mark *P D Evans* 49
2 b g Mark Of Esteem (Ire) - Sur Le Fil (Ire)
14^{6g} 11^{6g} 17^{7gf} 8^{7g} **0-0-4**

Master Nimbus *J J Quinn* 46
5 b g Cloudings (Ire) - Miss Charlie
10^{10gs} 2^{10g} **0-1-2 £1,062**

Master Of The Race *Sir Michael Stoute* 87
3 ch c Selkirk (USA) - Dust Dancer
2^{8gs} 2^{8g} 2^{11gf} **0-2-3 £3,664**

Master Pegasus *C F Wall* 67 a68
2 b g Lujain (USA) - Seeking Utopia
8^{6gs} 2^{7sd} **0-1-2 £952**

Master Rattle *Jane Southcombe* a36
6 b g Sabrehill (USA) - Miss Primula
10^{6sd} 1^{7g} 2^{5gs} 11^{6sd} 18^{7gs} **1-0-5 £2,215**

Master Robbie *M R Channon* 93 a99
6 b g Piccolo - Victoria's Secret (Ire)
16^{7ft} 5^{8ft} 1^{7sd} 10^{7gf} 16^{6gf} 6^{6gf} 10^{7f} 7^{7g} 10^{7g} 13^{7gf} 1^{7gf} 4^{7gf} 19^{7gf} 8^{7gf} 9^{7gf} 8^{7g} 18^{7g} 17^{7g} 7^{7gf} 10^{7g} 11^{6s} **2-0-21 £24,378**

Master Theo (USA) *Lucinda Featherstone* 78 a93
4 b g Southern Halo (USA) - Lilian Bayliss (Ire)
2^{9sd} 1^{9sd} 6^{9sd} 10^{10gs} 6^{8gf} 9^{9gs} 3^{9sd} 3^{9sd} **1-3-8 £11,613**

Master Wells (Ire) *P J Hobbs* 81
4 b g Sadler's Wells (USA) - Eljazzi
6^{18g} 4^{16g} 4^{16s} 4^{18gf} 2^{16g} 6^{14gs} 3^{16s} 6^{17g} 23^{18gs} **0-2-9 £4,277**

Master'n Commander *C A Cyzer* 69 a75
3 ch g Zafonic (USA) - Magical Retreat (USA)
11^{10gf} 12^{10gf} 5^{10g} 3^{12sd} **0-1-4 £536**

Masterman Ready *W R Swinburn* 81 a79
4 b g Unfuwain (USA) - Maria Isabella (Fr)
5^{14gs} 2^{15s} 11^{14gf} 1^{15gf} 7^{16gs} 2^{16sd} 5^{16gf} 1^{16gf} 3^{16gf} 3^{16g} **2-4-10 £15,458**

Mataa (USA) *M W Easterby* 36 a48
4 b g Stravinsky (USA) - Elusive (USA)
11^{6sd} 6^{6sd} 4^{5sd} 7^{6sd} 11^{6sd} 7^{10s} 17^{10gf} **0-0-7 £262**

Mataram (USA) *W Jarvis* 59
2 b g Matty G (USA) - Kalinka (USA)
9^{7gs} 9^{7s} 6^{6gs} **0-0-3**

Match Ball (USA) *Saeed Bin Suroor* 67
3 b/br f Grand Slam (USA) - Glitters (USA)
2^{6g} **0-1-1 £1,000**

Material Witness (Ire) *W R Muir* 106 a89
8 b g Barathea (Ire) - Dial Dream
6^{7gs} 16^{7g} 3^{7s} 9^{7gf} 18^{7gf} 17^{7gs} 3^{7s} 24^{6gs} 9^{7gf} 2^{7sd} 15^{7g} 10^{7sd} **0-2-12 £5,943**

Materialize (USA) *P J McBride* a69
2 b f Chester House (USA) - A La Mode (USA)
3^{8sd} **0-1-1 £434**

Matjar (Ire) *M A Jarvis* 60
2 ch c Grand Lodge (USA) - Tajawuz
6^{7s} **0-0-1**

Matloob *Saeed Bin Suroor* 98
4 b c Halling (USA) - Belle Argentine (Fr)
6^{12g} 6^{9gf} **0-0-2 £651**

Matsunosuke *A B Coogan* 78
3 b g Magic Ring (Ire) - Lon Isa
1^{6g} 9^{6g} 5^{6s} 9^{6g} 3^{5g} 8^{5gs} 11^{5gf} 7^{6g} 1^{5gf} 11^{5g} 3^{6gf} **2-2-11 £8,497**

Matterofact (Ire) *Mrs P N Dutfield* 77
2 b f Bold Fact (USA) - Willow Dale (Ire)
6^{5gs} 9^{6gs} 4^{6gf} 3^{5gf} 2^{5gf} 16^{6g} 1^{5f} 2^{6gf} 2^{5gf} **1-4-9 £8,511**

Matthew My Son (Ire) *F P Murtagh*
5 ch g Lake Coniston (Ire) - Mary Hinge
4^{10s} **0-0-1 £316**

Matty Tun *J Balding* 89
6 b g Lugana Beach - B Grade
11^{5g} 18^{5g} 12^{5s} 7^{5gf} 6^{5s} 1^{5gs} 5^{5g} 11^{5gs} 15^{5gs} 10^{5hy} **1-0-10 £7,028**

Matuza (Ire) *W R Muir* a77
2 ch c Cadeaux Genereux - Aoife (Ire)
1^{6sd} 1^{5sd} **2-0-2 £8,180**

Maunby Raver *P C Haslam* a47
4 ch g Pivotal - Colleen Liath
6^{7sd} 8^{7sd} **0-0-2**

Maunby Reveller *P C Haslam* 47 a29
3 b g Benny The Dip (USA) - Aunt Tate
8^{6sd} 11^{7g} 9^{10g} 12^{14gf} 2^{16g} 6^{16s} 5^{16gf}
0-1-7 £1,000

Maundy Money *M Johnston* 54
2 b c King's Best (USA) - Royal Gift
6^{6gf} 7^{6g} **0-0-2**

Maunsell's Road (Ire) *L Lungo* 54
6 b g Desert Style (Ire) - Zara's Birthday (Ire)
7^{13gs} 8^{16gf} **0-0-2**

Maureen's Lough (Ire) *Ronald Thompson*
3 b f Bachir (Ire) - Tadjnama (USA)
7^{7sd} 14^{6sd} **0-0-2**

Mauro (Ire) *A M Hales* 46 a30
3 b f Danehill Dancer (Ire) - Stop The Traffic (Ire)
12^{6sd} 16^{7gf} 8^{8gs} 13^{6gf} **0-0-4**

Mawdsley *A Senior*
8 b m Piccolo - Legendary Dancer
8^{10g} **0-0-1**

Maxamillion (Ire) *S Kirk* 71 a51
3 b g Mujadil (USA) - Manazil (Ire)
8^{10gf} 14^{12gf} 10^{8g} 10^{10sd} 6^{12gs} 3^{10hy} 2^{10hy}
0-2-7 £2,222

Maxilla (Ire) *Miss J S Davis* a26
5 b/br m Lahib (USA) - Lacinia
10^{12sd} **0-0-1**

Maximix *B W Hills*
2 gr g Linamix (Fr) - Time Will Show (Fr)
19^{7gf} **0-0-1**

Maxjack *W De Best-Turner*
2 b c Double Trigger (Ire) - Sweet Egyptian (Fr)
16^{9g} **0-0-1**

Maxolini *J J Quinn* 21
2 ch g Bertolini (USA) - Evening Falls
16^{6gf} 10^{5gf} **0-0-2**

May Morning (Ire) *B W Hills* 73
3 b f Danehill (USA) - Golden Digger (USA)
2^{8g} 4^{7g} 1^{7gf} **1-1-3 £5,955**

May's Kazan *P T Midgley*
2 b g Dracula (Aus) - Grain Storm (Ire)
11^{5gf} 6^{7g} **0-0-2**

Mayadeen (Ire) *J G M O'Shea* 85
3 b g King's Best (USA) - Inaaq
10^{9g} 2^{10gf} 11^{12gf} **0-1-3 £2,176**

Mayden Dawn *D K Ivory* a62
2 ch f Silver Wizard (USA) - Delight Of Dawn
11^{7sd} 6^{8sd} **0-0-2**

Mayfair Tambourine *W G M Turner* 30
2 ch f Tomba - Mayfair Ballerina
12^{7sd} 2^{7f} 6^{7f} 6^{6gs} **0-0-4 £717**

Maynooth Prince (Ire) *I W McInnes* 55 a44
3 b g Spectrum (Ire) - Muffle
7^{6f} 6^{12gs} 2^{8gf} 9^{8gf} 14^{8s} 6^{10sd} **0-1-6**
£852

Mayor Of Seaham (Ire) *N Wilson*
2 ch g Titus Livius (Fr) - Torrmana (Ire)
8^{7g} **0-0-1**

Maysboyo *B P J Baugh* a3
7 b g Makbul - Maysimp (Ire)
12^{12sd} 10^{12sd} **0-0-2**

Maysoor *M Johnston* 16
2 ch c Selkirk (USA) - Just Dreams
9^{10hy} **0-0-1**

Maystock *B G Powell* 73 a83
5 ch m Magic Ring (Ire) - Stockline
13^{12sd} 12^{13s} 8^{13f} 4^{12g} 6^{12f} 1^{12g} 2^{12gf} 3^{16gf}
4^{12g} 3^{14g} 8^{16gs} 1^{13sd} **2-3-12 £11,977**

Mazeej (USA) *M P Tregoning* 73
2 b f Lemon Drop Kid (USA) - Testy Trestle (USA)
3^{7g} 2^{7s} **0-2-2 £2,143**

Mazindar (USA) *P T Midgley* 43 a61
3 b/br g Zamindar (USA) - Fantastic Bloom (Ven)
4^{7sd} 2^{8sd} 12^{8sd} 9^{6sd} 10^{9sd} 13^{9gf} 13^{7g} 8^{6sd}
0-1-8 £1,314

Mazuna (Ire) *C E Brittain* 108
4 b f Cape Cross (Ire) - Keswa
6^{12gf} 6^{12gf} 8^{12gf} 11^{12s} 4^{13f} 11^{16g} 18^{10gf} 9^{13g}
7^{15gf} **0-0-9 £1,400**

Mcbain (USA) *P J Hobbs* 82
6 br g Lear Fan (USA) - River City Moon (USA)
8^{10gf} 7^{14gf} **0-0-2**

Mccormack (Ire) *M D Hammond* 59
3 b g Desert Story (Ire) - La Loba (Ire)
9^{8s} 7^{10f} 6^{12gf} **0-0-3**

Mccracken (Ire) *R Ford* a51
9 b g Scenic - Sakanda (Ire)
11^{17sd} **0-0-1**

Mceldowney *M Johnston* 78
3 b g Zafonic (USA) - Ayodhya (Ire)
10^{7g} 7^{7s} UR^{8g} 9^{8gf} 4^{8g} 7^{10gf} 1^{8gf} 6^{8g} 9^{8g}
1^{12gf} 1^{11gf} 1^{12s} 6^{12gf} 10^{12g} 7^{12g} **4-0-15**
£16,995

Mcqueen (Ire) *Mrs H Dalton* 66
5 ch g Barathea (Ire) - Bibliotheque (USA)
16^{11gs} 17^{10gs} 14^{10g} 6^{10s} 9^{12gs} **0-0-5**

Me *P W Chapple-Hyam* 70
2 b f Green Desert (USA) - Myself
5^{6gf} 9^{6g} **0-0-2**

Meadow End Boy *Bob Jones* a35
4 b g Great Dane (Ire) - Bettynouche
9^{6sd} 15^{7g} **0-0-2**

Meadow Mischief (Fr) *E A L Dunlop* 68
2 ch c Halling (USA) - Moonlight Saunter (USA)
14^{7g} 4^{8gf} **0-0-2 £435**

Meaningful *M Johnston* 67
2 b c King's Best (USA) - Kind Regards (Ire)
6^{6gf} 4^{7gf} 4^{6gf} 8^{8f} 5^{8g} **0-0-5 £660**

Meantime (USA) *J H M Gosden* 74
2 b c Point Given (USA) - Interim
8^{7g} 3^{8s} 3^{8gf} **0-0-3 £1,807**

Measured Response *J G M O'Shea* 70 a61
3 ch g Inchinor - Seal Indigo (Ire)
2^{10s} 4^{10sd} 3^{10s} 3^{8gs} **0-3-4 £2,756**

Mecca's Mate *D W Barker* 105 a67
4 gr f Paris House - Clancassie
2^{5sd} 1^{5gf} 2^{5g} 1^{6g} 7^{6gf} 3^{6gf} 1^{5gs} 4^{6g} 1^{5gs} 1^{5g}
5^{5s} 14^{6gs} 3^{5g} 6^{5gf} 12^{6s} 2^{5s} **5-5-16**
£59,189

Meddle *J Jay* 58
2 b f Diktat - Ingerence (Fr)
8^{6gs} 11^{6gf} **0-0-2**

Media Hora (Chi) *F Castro* 86 a99
5 ch h Somersham (USA) - Membrana (Chi)
7^{5sd} 10^{6g} 11^{6g} **0-0-3**

Meditation *I A Wood* 65
3 ch f Inchinor - Trojan Desert
13^{7gs} 1^{6gf} 7^{5gf} 7^{6gf} 12^{6gf} 12^{6gf} 7^{7gf} 4^{7gf} 9^{8s} 2^{7gf} 8^{7gf} **1-1-11 £5,178**

Medjugorje Message (Ire) *R A Fahey* 40 a56
3 b f Rainbow Quest (USA) - Karakia (Ire)
16^{8s} 6^{12hy} 12^{12gf} 9^{12g} 5^{12g} 2^{11sd} 5^{12sd} 1^{14sd} 2^{11sd} 5^{14ss} **1-2-10 £2,329**

Medora Leigh (USA) *J A R Toller* 64 a57
3 ch f Swain (Ire) - Gaily Tiara (USA)
16^{10g} 4^{11gf} 4^{12sd} **0-0-3 £536**

Meelup (Ire) *Jane Southcombe* 70 a70
5 ch g Night Shift (USA) - Centella (Ire)
11^{10sd} 11^{10sd} 7^{8sd} 1^{8sd} 4^{8sd} 1^{9gs} 1^{8gs} 2^{8g} 13^{8gs} 3^{8f} 3^{8sd} 4^{8gf} 1^{8gf} 6^{8gf} 3^{8s} 6^{9gs} 11^{8g} **4-3-17 £17,228**

Megabond *C A Dwyer* a49
4 b g Danehill Dancer (Ire) - Apple Peeler (Ire)
7^{9sd} 6^{9sd} 9^{8sd} **0-0-3**

Megalala (Ire) *J J Bridger* 23
4 b g Petardia - Avionne
10^{9g} **0-0-1**

Megan's Magic *M E Sowersby* 48
5 b m Blue Ocean (USA) - Hot Sunday Sport
7^{10gf} RR^{10gf} **0-0-2**

Meggido (Ire) *M P Tregoning* 78
3 b c Green Desert (USA) - No Win No Deal
4^{7g} 9^{10gf} 3^{8gf} 3^{10f} 4^{10gf} 6^{8gf} **0-1-6 £2,253**

Mehmaas *R E Barr* 53
9 b g Distant Relative - Guest List
15^{7g} 14^{8g} 12^{7g} 13^{9gf} 6^{8g} 3^{8gf} 2^{7g} 5^{8gf} 13^{8gf} 13^{8gf} 7^{8gf} 7^{6g} 8^{6sd} 13^{8s} 14^{8sd} **0-2-15 £1,284**

Meijin (Ire) *P G Murphy* 48 a40
5 b/br g Desert King (Ire) - Fortitude (Ire)
10^{7sd} 10^{7sd} 7^{10sd} 13^{11sd} 11^{10g} 12^{7f} 5^{7f} 3^{7sd} 11^{6f} 10^{6sd} 8^{7sd} **0-1-11 £210**

Meikle Barfil *R Charlton* 79 a69
3 b g Compton Place - Oare Sparrow
10^{6gf} 5^{6gf} 2^{6sd} 3^{5gs} 4^{5g} 5^{6ft} 11^{5sd} **0-3-7 £2,382**

Meikle Beoch *Mrs H Sweeting*
3 b f Magic Ring (Ire) - Portvasco
9^{6sd} 12^{8g} 15^{12sd} 8^{11sd} **0-0-4**

Mejhar (Ire) *E J Creighton* 74
5 b h Desert Prince (Ire) - Factice (USA)
5^{8sd} 6^{11sd} 2^{11sd} 4^{9sd} 1^{9sd} 2^{12sd} 2^{12sd} 8^{10f} **1-0-8 £20,017**

Mekyaas *M A Jarvis* 66
2 ch f Pivotal - Land Ahead (USA)
12^{7gf} 2^{7gf} 5^{7gf} 11^{7g} **0-1-4 £1,630**

Mel's Moment (USA) *Mrs A J Perrett* 61
3 b g Storm Creek (USA) - One Moment In Time (USA)
7^{9gs} 7^{8g} 12^{7gs} 6^{8f} **0-0-4**

Melaaya (USA) *M Johnston* 91
2 b f Aljabr (USA) - Saint Emilia (Per)
1^{6g} 6^{7gs} **1-0-2 £4,359**

Melaina *M S Saunders* 40 a29
4 b f Whittingham (Ire) - Oh I Say
14^{6gs} 12^{6g} 10^{7s} 13^{5g} 13^{5sd} 14^{6gs} 10^{6sf} 9^{6ss} **0-0-8**

Melalchrist *J J Quinn* 87
3 b g Almaty (Ire) - Lawless Bridget
10^{6hy} 15^{6gf} 2^{6gs} 4^{5g} 12^{6g} 1^{6gf} 12^{6gf} 9^{5gs} 9^{5g} **1-1-9 £16,551**

Melandre *M Brittain* 74
3 b f Lujain (USA) - Talighta (USA)
3^{5gf} 5^{5f} 6^{5gf} 11^{5g} **0-1-4 £838**

Melee *S L Keightley* 43
3 ch f Cadeaux Genereux - Nashmeel (USA)
4^{8f} **0-0-1 £313**

Melford Red (Ire) *R F Marvin* a32
5 b g Sri Pekan (USA) - Sunflower (Ire)
8^{8sd} 11^{9sd} 10^{17sd} 13^{14gf} 14^{16gf} **0-0-5**

Melodian *M Brittain* 53
10 b h Grey Desire - Mere Melody
7^{12gs} 9^{12s} 11^{12sd} **0-0-3**

Melodic Score (USA) *Saeed Bin Suroor* 77
2 b c Kingmambo (USA) - Ring Of Music
11^{7gs} 3^{7gf} 3^{8gf} **0-2-3 £1,304**

Melody King *P D Evans*
4 b g Merdon Melody - Retaliator
13^{6sd} **0-0-1**

Melody Maker *W R Swinburn* a60
2 br f Diktat - First Musical
5^{6sd} 6^{6sd} **0-0-2**

Melody Que (Ire) *J Howard Johnson* 56
3 b f Sadler's Wells (USA) - Bex (USA)
6^{8gs} 8^{12gf} 11^{12g} **0-0-3 £233**

Melograno (Ire) *Mark Campion* a51
5 ch g Hector Protector (USA) - Just A Treat (Ire)
2^{9sd} 6^{14sd} 8^{12sd} 2^{11ss} 4^{9ss} **0-2-5 £852**

Melpomene *M Johnston*
2 ch f Peintre Celebre (USA) - Lady Joyce (Fr)
11^{7s} **0-0-1**

Melrose Avenue (USA) *M Johnston* 109
3 b c Kris S (USA) - Sham Street (USA)
1^{12s} 3^{11g} 1^{16gf} 6^{12g} **2-0-4 £49,364**

Melvino *T D Barron* 72 a69
3 b g Josr Algarhoud (Ire) - Safe Secret
5^{7sd} 3^{8sd} 7^{8sd} 1^{7sd} 9^{7g} 3^{8g} 7^{9sd} 3^{8gs} 7^{8gf} 7^{10g} 14^{9gf} 4^{10gf} 9^{10gf} 5^{10gs} 1^{10f} 3^{12gf} 1^{12g} **3-5-17 £13,603**

Membership (USA) *C E Brittain* 107
5 ch h Belong To Me (USA) - Shamisen
2^{8gf} 4^{8gf} 3^{9gf} 10^{8gf} 6^{8g} 3^{7gf} **0-3-6 £27,054**

Memory Motel (Den) *Kjell Ivar Brekstad* 66
8 ch m Always Fair (USA) - Golden Line (Den)
1^{7g} 2^{9g} 15^{6g} **1-0-3 £2,468**

Memphis Belle *S Kirk* 44
2 gr f Linamix (Fr) - Clipper
10^{8gs} **0-0-1**

Memphis Man *E J O'Neill* 86
2 b c Bertolini (USA) - Something Blue
1^{5g} 6^{5gf} 8^{5g} 2^{6g} 16^{6gf} 7^{6g} **1-1-6 £5,279**

Menai Straights *P S Payne* 38 a42
4 ch g Alhaarth (Ire) - Kind Of Light
11^{7sd} 13^{6g} 11^{8gs} 7^{9sd} 7^{8gf} **0-0-5**

Menna *R Hollinshead* 9
3 b f Mark Of Esteem (Ire) - Pounelta
12^{6f} 12^{10hd} **0-0-2**

Meohmy *M R Channon* 43
2 b f Marju (Ire) - Meshhed (USA)
9^{6gf} **0-0-1**

Mephistos Kick *Jean-Rene Auvray* a52
4 b g Kingmambo (USA) - Mempari (Ire)
5^{7sd} 10^{9sd} 13^{7gs} 14^{7sd} **0-0-4**

Merayaat (Ire) *M P Tregoning* 80

3 b f Darshaan - Maddelina (Ire)
$16^{10gs} 5^{10s} 1^{14s} 2^{14gf} 6^{16gf}$ **1-1-5**
£4,433

Mercari *A R Dicken* 56 a31
3 ch f Bahamian Bounty - Aonach Mor
$5^{8sd} 7^{8s} 2^{9gs} 1^{8gs} 10^{9s} 6^{9s} 9^{8gf} 3^{9gf} 10^{8gf}$
9^{8s} **1-2-10 £4,672**

Merchant Bankes *W G M Turner* 68 a72
2 b c Observatory (USA) - Lady Bankes (Ire)
$5^{5g} 8^{5g} 2^{7f} 5^{7sd} 3^{9sd} 9^{8sd} 4^{7sd}$ **0-2-7**
£2,280

Merchymynydd (Ire) *B Palling* 25 a41
2 ch f Monashee Mountain (USA) - Santuzza (Ire)
$8^{5s} 10^{7sd} 8^{5f} 10^{5sd}$ **0-0-4**

Mercurialist *P W Chapple-Hyam* 55 a26
2 b c Foxhound (USA) - Yanomami (USA)
$10^{7gf} 8^{6gs} 8^{6gf} 9^{6sd}$ **0-0-4**

Merdiff *W M Brisbourne* a77
6 b g Machiavellian (USA) - Balwa (USA)
$1^{6sd} 4^{7sd} 8^{7sd} 7^{7sd} 7^{5sd} 5^{7sd} 2^{7sd} 5^{7sd} 5^{6sd}$
$7^{6sd} 13^{6sd} 6^{7sd}$ **1-1-12 £4,724**

Merger (USA) *D K Weld* 106
3 gr c Mr Greeley (USA) - Toledo Queen (Ire)
$2^{7hy} 2^{10gs} 6^{10gy} 2^{10gf} 3^{8gf} 6^{10g} 8^{10y}$ **0-4-7**
£31,000

Merlin's Dancer *D Nicholls* 99
5 b g Magic Ring (Ire) - La Piaf (Fr)
$1^{6g} 5^{6s} 5^{5s} 4^{6gs} 16^{6gf} 23^{6g}$ **1-1-6**
£19,217

Merlins Pride *W M Brisbourne* a37
4 b f Wizard King - Longden Pride
6^{8sd} **0-0-1**

Merlins Profit *G A Swinbank* 65 a44
5 b g Wizard King - Quick Profit
$6^{9sd} 12^{9sd} 3^{10g} 14^{12gf} 3^{9f} 1^{8gf} 3^{7gf} 4^{8gf} 1^{8gf}$
6^{8f} **2-3-10 £8,559**

Merrymadcap (Ire) *M Blanshard* 64 a68
3 b g Lujain (USA) - Carina Clare
$3^{9sd} 11^{10s} 2^{9sd} 9^{10g} 9^{10sd} 17^{7gf} 3^{9sd} 4^{9g} 2^{8gf}$
$11^{9sd} 1^{8f}$ **1-4-11 £5,875**

Merrymaker *W M Brisbourne* 78 a80
5 b g Machiavellian (USA) - Wild Pavane
$8^{13gs} 2^{12s} 5^{12gf} 4^{13gs} 3^{12gf} 4^{12gf} 5^{14gf} 2^{12g}$
$7^{12g} 2^{12gf} 5^{12g} 7^{12g} 1^{12g} 5^{12gs} 8^{12sd}$
1-3-15 £14,275

Merryvale Man *Miss Kariana Key* 48 a33
8 b g Rudimentary (USA) - Salu
$6^{18gs} 13^{16g} 11^{17sd} 14^{16g}$ **0-0-4**

Mersey Mirage *R C Guest* a26
8 b g King's Signet (USA) - Kirriemuir
$10^{9sd} 11^{5sd} 8^{6sd} 11^{7g} 7^{7sd} 16^{6f}$ **0-0-6**

Mersey Sound (Ire) *D R C Elsworth* 70 a43
7 b g Ela-Mana-Mou - Coral Sound (Ire)
$11^{14gs} 15^{14g} 10^{14sd} 11^{12gf} 16^{17g} 1^{15gf} 3^{12f}$
$2^{16gf} 1^{14gf} 4^{14gf} 2^{14gs} 5^{16gf} 1^{17f}$ **3-3 13**
£14,640

Merveilles *J H M Gosden* 90
2 b g Vettori (Ire) - Finlaggan
$1^{8gs} 4^{8gf}$ **1-0-2 £4,152**

Mescalera (Ger) *B G Powell* a42
4 b f Alkalde (Ger) - Miskinissa (Ger)
$3^{9sd} 3^{7s} 2^{7g} 9^{7s} 5^{7g} 3^{7g} 3^{7g} 2^{7s} 5^{7ss} 3^{6sd}$
12^{6sd} **0-1-11 £2,701**

Meshaheer (USA) *M P Tregoning* 107
6 b h Nureyev (USA) - Race The Wild Wind (USA)
$5^{7gs} 3^{7s} 3^{8gs}$ **0-0-3 £7,130**

Mesmeric (Ire) *B G Powell* 83
7 b g Sadler's Wells (USA) - Mesmerize
$7^{14gs} 6^{14s} 6^{20gf} 9^{16gs} 10^{16gf}$ **0-0-5 £750**

Methodical *B G Powell* 48 a55
3 b f Lujain (USA) - Simple Logic
$9^{6s} 11^{6sd} 6^{6sd} 8^{6gs} 10^{7gf}$ **0-0-5**

Methusaleh (Ire) *T D Easterby* 74
2 b g Mutamam - Madamaa (Ire)
$2^{7g} 4^{7s} 4^{7gf} 10^{8gf} 4^{9g} 5^{10g}$ **0-1-6**
£2,331

Metolica *C Smith* a39
3 b f Diktat - South Sea Bubble (Ire)
$4^{8sd} 4^{7sd} 5^{8sd} 5^{7sd} 6^{12s}$ **0-0-5**

Metropolitan Man *D M Simcock* 105
2 ch c Dr Fong (USA) - Preceder
$3^{6gs} 1^{6gf} 5^{7g}$ **1-0-3 £10,037**

Mexican (USA) *M D Hammond* a53
6 b g Pine Bluff (USA) - Cuando Quiere (USA)
$2^{8sd} 5^{8sd} 3^{8sd} 9^{8sd} 8^{8sd}$ **0-2-5 £628**

Mexican Pete *A W Carroll* 84 a74
5 b g Atraf - Eskimo Nel (Ire)
$5^{12gf} 4^{12g} 7^{12gf} 2^{12gf} 4^{12gf} 6^{12g} 6^{12f} 6^{10sd}$
0-1-8 £3,241

Mezuzah *M W Easterby* 81
5 b g Barathea (Ire) - Mezzogiorno
$2^{8s} 4^{9gs} 10^{8s} 1^{9s} 7^{8g} 11^{10gf} 3^{10g} 5^{10gf} 4^{9gs}$
1-3-9 £7,188

Mi Odds *Mrs N Macauley* a96
9 b g Sure Blade (USA) - Vado Via
$6^{8sd} 6^{9sd} 7^{7sd} 6^{9sd} 5^{12sd} 3^{9sd} 4^{9sd} 2^{12sd} 6^{12sd}$
$10^{12sd} 15^{10gf} 12^{14ft} 11^{12sd} 2^{11sd} 2^{12sd} 1^{11sd}$
$9^{9sd} 5^{11sd}$ **1-4-18 £7,840**

Miacarla *Mark Campion*
2 b f Forzando - Zarzi (Ire)
13^{6gs} **0-0-1**

Michabo (Ire) *D R C Elsworth* 89
4 b g Robellino (USA) - Mole Creek
$2^{14gs} 1^{14gf}$ **1-1-2 £9,025**

Michaels Dream (Ire) *N Wilson* 34 a49
6 b g Spectrum (Ire) - Stormswept (USA)
$9^{13gs} 7^{15g} 3^{11sd} 1^{14sd} 12^{14sd}$ **1-1-5**
£1,657

Michaels Pride (Ire) *M Johnston* 78 a43
3 b f Distant View (USA) - Ruacana Falls (USA)
$4^{6sd} 7^{8sd} 6^{7s} 1^{7s} 4^{8gf} 2^{10gs} 1^{10gf} 3^{10gf} 2^{9s}$
$1^{10gf} 1^{10g} 2^{11gf} 1^{10f} 15^{11gs} 9^{11gf} 4^{12gs} 3^{9hy}$
5-4-17 £24,033

Mickehaha *I A Wood* 71 a66
3 b c Lake Coniston (Ire) - Minnehaha
$9^{8sd} 4^{8gs} 13^{8g} 13^{8gf} 1^{10sd} 6^{10gf} 1^{10gf} 5^{10g}$
$3^{10g} 3^{10gs}$ **2-3-10 £8,123**

Mickey Pearce (Ire) *J G M O'Shea* 35
3 b g Rossini (USA) - Lucky Coin
$5^{12gf} 12^{16gf}$ **0-0-2**

Mickledo *A Bailey* 7 a44
3 b g Perryston View - Ever So Lonely
$11^{7sd} 10^{7sd} 5^{6sd} 9^{8sd} 11^{6sd} 4^{6sd} 2^{6sd} 13^{6sd}$
$12^{5sd} 6^{6sd} 11^{5f}$ **0-1-11 £410**

Mickledor (Fr) *Anthony Mullins* 50
5 ch m Lake Coniston (Ire) - Shamasiya (Fr)
$12^{7f} 8^{6g} 4^{6gs} 5^{7gf} 7^{6s}$ **0-0-5**

Mickley (Ire) *P R Hedger* a61
8 b g Ezzoud (Ire) - Dawsha (Ire)
$7^{12sd} 8^{16sd}$ **0-0-2**

Mickmacmagoole (Ire) *Seamus G O'Donnell* 43 a55

3 b g Sadler's Wells (USA) - Musk Lime (USA)
12^{7hy} 10^{7s} 15^{9gy} 6^{11g} 1^{12sf} 8^{11ss} 1^{11sd} **2-0-7 £2,839**

Mid Valley *J R Jenkins* 43 a33
2 ch c Zilzal (USA) - Isabella D'Este (Ire)
9^{5gs} 10^{5g} 10^{7sd} **0-0-3**

Midas Way *P R Chamings* 106
5 ch g Halling (USA) - Arietta's Way (Ire)
3^{12gs} 2^{12g} 14^{12g} 2^{16gf} 5^{12gs} 6^{14g} 12^{15gs} **0-3-7 £14,224**

Midcap (Ire) *B W Hills* 68 a68
3 b f Entrepreneur - Tis Juliet (USA)
7^{7sd} 4^{7sd} 2^{7s} 2^{7gf} 1^{7gf} 10^{7g} **1-2-6 £6,252**

Middle Earth (USA) *N Zito* a96
3 ch c Dixieland Band (USA) - Lite Twilight (USA)
2^{7sd} 2^{7sd} 5^{9ft} 3^{7ft} 5^{9ft} **0-2-5 £17,438**

Middle Eastern *P A Blockley* 53 a73
3 b g Mujahid (USA) - Swissmatic
6^{6gf} 14^{6gf} 6^{6gf} 3^{6g} 2^{6sd} 7^{6gf} 11^{6g} 8^{8gs} 1^{6sf} 4^{6sd} 1^{7sd} 10^{6sd} **2-2-12 £8,040**

Middleham Park (Ire) *J W Mullins* a41
5 b g Revoque (Ire) - Snap Crackle Pop (Ire)
3^{12sd} **0-1-1 £208**

Middlemarch (Ire) *J S Goldie* 94
5 ch g Grand Lodge (USA) - Blanche Dubois
12^{7s} 9^{7gf} 15^{8gf} 7^{8gf} 5^{8g} 13^{11gf} 9^{10g} 12^{9g} 7^{9g} 5^{10s} 7^{10s} **0-0-11 £362**

Middlemiss (Ire) *J W Mullins* 4
5 b m Midhish - Teresa Deevey
12^{12g} **0-0-1**

Middleton Grey *A G Newcombe* 85 a91
7 gr g Ashkalani (Ire) - Petula
7^{6sd} 5^{7sd} 4^{7g} 8^{7gs} 2^{6gf} 1^{6gs} 8^{6sd} **1-2-7 £13,525**

Middleton Minx *R M Beckett* 59 a38
2 b f Foxhound (USA) - Franica (Ire)
8^{5g} 4^{5g} 9^{5gf} 11^{6sd} 6^{7sd} 8^{6sd} **0-0-6**

Midge's Girl (Ire) *Mrs A Duffield* 44
2 b f Indian Lodge (Ire) - Blue Sky Lady (Ire)
7^{5gf} 7^{6gf} 12^{6g} **0-0-3**

Midmaar (Ire) *M Wigham* a54
4 b g Cape Cross (Ire) - Khazinat El Dar (USA)
2^{7sd} 1^{6sd} 9^{6sd} **1-1-3 £1,886**

Midnight Arrow *A Berry* a29
7 b m Robellino (USA) - Princess Oberon (Ire)
10^{13sd} 8^{12sd} 9^{14sd} **0-0-3**

Midnight Creek *A Sadik* 44 a57
7 br g Tragic Role (USA) - Greek Night Out (Ire)
6^{16gf} 10^{16g} 2^{16sd} 11^{14ss} **0-1-4 £421**

Midnight In Moscow (Ire) *P C Haslam* 20 a50
3 b g Soviet Star (USA) - Solar Display (USA)
7^{8sd} 9^{10gf} 11^{7gf} 11^{7gf} **0-0-4**

Midnight Lace *J R Boyle* 66 a71
3 ch f Tomba - Royal Passion
3^{8gf} 1^{7gf} 4^{8gs} 4^{7gf} 6^{7g} 1^{7sd} 10^{10sd} 1^{9sd} 9^{8sd} 6^{11sd} **3-1-10 £12,103**

Midnight Pearl (USA) *J Howard Johnson* 57
2 b/br f Woodman (USA) - Elegant Ridge (Ire)
5^{6gf} 7^{5f} 2^{5gf} 9^{6g} **0-1-4 £1,060**

Midnight Traveller *G C H Chung* 74 a54
2 b c Daylami (Ire) - Swift Dispersal
8^{7sd} 2^{8hy} 9^{9vs} **0-1-3 £1,130**

Midnight Tycoon *B Smart* 24 a78
3 b g Marju (Ire) - Midnight Allure
9^{5sd} 10^{5gf} **0-0-2**

Midris (Ire) *D J Daly* 93
2 ch f Namid - Dolara (Ire)
5^{7g} 3^{8g} 1^{6g} 1^{6s} **2-1-4 £20,655**

Midshipman *A W Carroll* 65 a73
7 b h Executive Man - Midler
3^{9sd} 1^{9sd} 16^{11gs} 5^{8gs} 1^{8s} 14^{10gf} 6^{9sd} 6^{9sd} **2-1-8 £10,837**

Mighty Beau (USA) *Jeff Mullins* 108
6 b g Rainbow Prospect (USA) - Mighty Lode (USA)
2^{7f} 2^{6f} 1^{7f} 2^{6f} 1^{5f} 5^{5gf} 11^{6f} **2-0-7 £87,644**

Mighty Dancer (Ire) *S Kirk* 48 a60
2 b c Danehill Dancer (Ire) - K S Sunshine (USA)
14^{7gf} 7^{8hd} 12^{8gs} 2^{7sd} 4^{8sd} 4^{8sd} **0-1-6 £1,468**

Mighty Duel *J R Norton* 30
2 b g Daggers Drawn (USA) - Runs In The Family
15^{6gf} 12^{6g} 12^{6gs} 9^{5gf} 16^{7g} **0-0-5**

Mighty Kitchener (USA) *P Howling* a61
2 br g Mighty (USA) - Libeccio (NZ)
2^{8sd} 7^{9sd} **0-1-2 £421**

Mighty Moon *Lady Herries* 69
2 gr g Daylami (Ire) - Moon Magic
4^{6g} 13^{7g} 10^{7gf} 11^{8g} **0-0-4 £273**

Mighty Mover (Ire) *B Palling* a30
3 ch c Bahhare (USA) - Ericeira (Ire)
10^{8sd} **0-0-1**

Mighty Observer (Ire) *M H Tompkins* 43
2 b g Observatory (USA) - Staff Approved
7^{7gs} 10^{6gf} 15^{6s} **0-0-3**

Mighty Pip (Ire) *M R Bosley* 43
9 b g Pips Pride - Hard To Stop
6^{10gf} 5^{10f} 7^{10f} 9^{10f} 4^{12gf} 10^{10g} 11^{10f} **0-1-7**

Mighty Splash *R Charlton* 48
2 b f Cape Cross (Ire) - Serotina (Ire)
10^{8gs} 12^{7gf} 8^{8gs} **0-0-3**

Migration *Mrs S Lamyman* 39
9 b g Rainbow Quest (USA) - Armeria (USA)
3^{11gs} 13^{14g} 8^{12gf} 12^{16gf} **0-0-4 £189**

Mikao (Ire) *M H Tompkins* 87
4 b g Tagula (Ire) - Oumaladia (Ire)
3^{10gs} 2^{10s} 1^{12gf} 4^{11gf} 2^{12g} 4^{15gs} 1^{16g} **2-3-7 £26,014**

Mikes Mate *C J Teague* 7
4 b g Komaite (USA) - Pitcairn Princess
9^{8sd} 12^{6g} **0-0-2**

Milady's Pride *Mrs C A Dunnett* 80 a74
4 ch f Machiavellian (USA) - Ideal Lady (Ire)
11^{10sd} 2^{9sd} 1^{9sd} 5^{8gs} 1^{8s} 1^{8g} 13^{9g} **3-1-7 £18,874**

Military Cross *W J Haggas* 91
2 b g Cape Cross (Ire) - Tipsy
2^{6gf} 2^{7gf} 1^{7g} 1^{7g} 13^{7gs} **2-2-5 £10,493**

Milk And Sultana *G A Ham* 57 a48
5 b m Millkom - Premier Princess
4^{10g} 8^{10gf} 3^{10g} 4^{12gf} 6^{12gf} 6^{11gf} 18^{10gs} 5^{10g} 7^{9sd} **0-1-9 £1,205**

Milk It Mick *J A Osborne* 81
4 b c Millkom - Lunar Music
6^{7gf} 5^{7hy} **0-0-2 £652**

Milky Bar Kid (Ire) *C F Wall* 52
2 ch c Night Shift (USA) - Baileys Cream
13^{6g} 10^{6gs} 12^{6g} **0-0-3**

Mill By The Stream *P T Midgley* 54 a59
3 b g Lujain (USA) - Lonesome
1^{7sd} 8^{8sd} 4^{8sd} 2^{8sd} 10^{7gs} 3^{7sd} 13^{7s} 14^{7gf} 11^{9sd} 2^{7gf} 1^{6gf} 16^{6gf} 7^{7gs} 7^{6gf} **2-3-14 £7,829**

Mill End Chateau *D K Ivory*
3 ch g Paris House - Mill End Quest
10^{8g} **0-0-1**

Millagros (Ire) *I Semple* 76
5 b m Pennekamp (USA) - Grey Galava
7^{14g} 5^{12gs} 5^{8gs} 4^{9s} 1^{11gf} 8^{12g} 4^{12gs} 3^{12g} 3^{13g} 4^{11gs} 2^{12s} **1-3-11 £10,043**

Millbrook Star (Ire) *M C Chapman* 27 a19
2 b g Orpen (USA) - Lady Bodmin (Ire)
8^{6g} 11^{7gf} 12^{7gf} 14^{6g} 15^{7gf} 9^{8gf} 8^{7sd} 9^{7s} 8^{7sd} **0-0-9**

Millenary *J L Dunlop* 121
8 b h Rainbow Quest (USA) - Ballerina (Ire)
9^{14gs} 4^{12gs} 3^{16s} 1^{16g} 1^{18g} 3^{16gs} **2-2-6 £151,500**

Millenio (Ger) *Miss Gay Kelleway* a70
5 ch g Big Shuffle (USA) - Molto In Forma (Ger)
12^{7sd} 7^{9sd} 6^{7sd} 10^{10sd} 6^{8sd} **0-0-5**

Millennium Force *M R Channon* 109
7 b g Bin Ajwaad (Ire) - Jumairah Sun (Ire)
1^{8g} 9^{7gf} 2^{7gf} 8^{8gf} 3^{7gs} 2^{6s} 3^{8s} 5^{7s} 17^{7gf} 5^{7gs} 21^{7gf} 16^{7g} **1-2-12 £57,348**

Millennium Hall *Miss Lucinda V Russell* 69
6 b g Saddlers' Hall (Ire) - Millazure (USA)
4^{12gs} 3^{12gs} 5^{12gf} 1^{13s} 3^{12g} 2^{13gs} 9^{12gf} 5^{13gf} **1-3-8 £7,437**

Millfield (Ire) *J Howard Johnson* 81
2 br c Elnadim (USA) - Eschasse (USA)
10^{5s} 1^{5f} 3^{5g} 1^{7f} 3^{6gf} 12^{6g} **2-1-6 £10,060**

Milli Wizz *W M Brisbourne*
5 b m Wizard King - State Of Love
8^{8gf} 7^{12gf} **0-0-2**

Millinsky (USA) *Rae Guest* 81
4 ch f Stravinsky (USA) - Millyant
8^{5g} 2^{5gf} 9^{5g} 1^{5gf} 1^{5gf} 1^{5g} 11^{5g} 7^{5gs} 3^{5g} 1^{5g} 2^{5gf} 9^{5s} **4-3-12 £18,288**

Million All Day (Ire) *W R Muir* 51 a53
2 gr f Daylami (Ire) - Madame Nureyev (USA)
18^{6gf} 9^{7gf} 7^{8g} 6^{8sd} **0-0-4**

Million Percent *K R Burke* 78 a81
6 b g Ashkalani (Ire) - Royal Jade
9^{6sd} 2^{6sd} 6^{5s} 14^{6gs} 7^{6g} 5^{6gf} 8^{6gf} 17^{6gf} 3^{6sd} 4^{6g} 4^{5g} 4^{6sd} 5^{6sd} 5^{6sd} **0-2-14 £4,248**

Millkom Elegance *G A Ham* a45
6 b m Millkom - Premier Princess
11^{14sd} 7^{12sd} 1^{14sd} 10^{12sd} 10^{12sd} 10^{10sd} **1-0-6 £1,491**

Millquista D'Or *G A Ham* 53
3 b f Millkom - Gild The Lily
5^{10gs} 9^{13g} 12^{10g} 7^{10g} 15^{14gf} 6^{12g} **0-0-6**

Millsy *J L Spearing* 63
3 b f Pursuit Of Love - Jucea
6^{6gf} 2^{6s} 4^{6g} 16^{6g} **0-1-4 £1,864**

Millville *M A Jarvis* 101 a99
5 ch g Millkom - Miss Topville (Fr)
5^{12gs} 5^{12g} 2^{14gf} 2^{12gf} 1^{12g} 13^{14g} 8^{14g} 3^{13gs} 3^{12sd} **1-3-9 £22,023**

Milly Waters *W M Brisbourne* 78
4 b f Danzero (Aus) - Chilly Waters
24^{7gf} 5^{7s} 12^{8gf} 7^{6s} **0-0-4**

Milton's Keen *P S McEntee* 57 a38
2 gr g Largesse - Not A Word
7^{6hy} 9^{7sd} **0-0-2**

Miltons Choice *J M Bradley* 56
2 b c Diktat - Starosta
4^{5gs} 3^{5gf} 7^{5gf} 6^{6g} 4^{6g} 5^{6g} **0-0-6 £1,474**

Mimi Mouse *T D Easterby* 95
3 br f Diktat - Shifty Mouse
12^{5s} 1^{5gf} 10^{5gf} 3^{5gf} 9^{5g} 20^{6gf} 4^{5gf} 9^{6g} 5^{5g} **1-1-9 £16,400**

Mimic *Rae Guest* 67
5 b m Royal Applause - Stripanoora
8^{6s} 6^{5gs} 10^{6g} 4^{6g} 15^{6g} 2^{6g} 8^{6gf} 12^{6gf} 5^{6g} 3^{6g} **0-3-10 £2,066**

Mimiteh (USA) *R M Beckett* 67 a36
2 ch f Maria's Mon (USA) - Green Minstrel (Fr)
7^{6gf} 2^{6g} 1^{5gf} 8^{6sd} **1-1-4 £4,665**

Min Asl Wafi (Ire) *M R Channon* 73
3 b f Octagonal (NZ) - Shy Lady (Fr)
3^{7gs} **0-1-1 £888**

Mina *Rae Guest* 65
3 ch f Selkirk (USA) - Midnight Shift (Ire)
9^{6g} 6^{6gf} 2^{6gs} 2^{6gf} 5^{6g} 2^{6g} 2^{6g} **0-4-7 £5,150**

Mina A Salem *C E Brittain* 73 a85
3 b c Singspiel (Ire) - Amber Fizz (USA)
5^{10gf} 3^{11gf} 6^{12f} 8^{8gf} 4^{10g} 2^{9ft} 1^{8sd} 2^{8sd} **1-3-8 £7,876**

Mind Alert *D Shaw* 31 a62
4 b g Mind Games - Bombay Sapphire
11^{6sd} 14^{7g} 14^{5gf} 16^{6g} 6^{7sd} 11^{6sd} 15^{7gf} 5^{7sf} 4^{7sd} 11^{7sd} 4^{6sd} 1^{6ss} 7^{5ss} 3^{6sd} 4^{5sd} 1^{6sd} **2-1-16 £3,087**

Mind How You Go (Fr) *J R Best* 70
7 b g Hernando (Fr) - Cos I Do (Ire)
6^{10g} 2^{12f} 3^{13gf} **0-1-3 £1,611**

Mind That Fox *T Wall*
3 b g Mind Games - Foxie Lady
PU^{5gf} **0-0-1**

Mindful *M J Polglase* a18
3 b c Mind Games - Blushing Victoria
8^{9sd} 7^{8sd} **0-0-2**

Mine (Ire) *J D Bethell* 113
7 b h Primo Dominie - Ellebanna
5^{8gf} 3^{8gf} 7^{8g} 2^{8s} 5^{7s} 11^{8gf} 1^{7gs} 10^{7gf} 10^{8gf} 12^{8s} 9^{7gf} **1-2-11 £58,988**

Mine Behind *J R Best* 95
5 b g Sheikh Albadou - Arapi (Ire)
14^{6g} 11^{6g} 15^{5g} 10^{6gf} 1^{7gf} 1^{6g} 6^{6gs} 15^{8gf} **2-0-8 £17,086**

Mine The Balance (Ire) *J R Best* 42 a15
2 b g Desert Style (Ire) - Dia (Ire)
5^{5s} 5^{5s} 8^{5sd} 8^{5g} **0-0-4**

Mineko *G Wragg* 77
3 b f Nashwan (USA) - Musetta (Ire)
12^{7gf} 2^{12gf} 2^{12g} 2^{14gf} 1^{10s} 9^{10hy} **1-3-6 £7,680**

Mineral Star (Ire) *M H Tompkins* 92
3 b g Monashee Mountain (USA) - Summit Talk
1^{8s} 5^{8hy} 1^{7gs} 9^{7gf} 1^{7g} 14^{7g} 8^{8gs} 13^{8g} **3-0-8 £22,842**

Ming Vase *P T Midgley* 60 a59
3 b g Vettori (Ire) - Minstrel's Dance (Can)
6^{8gs} 7^{7f} 13^{8g} 5^{8gf} 7^{7gf} 7^{9sd} 7^{8s} 2^{8sd} 7^{7sd} 12^{8sd} **0-1-10 £877**

Mini Blue (Ire) *J A Glover*
2 b f Distant Music (USA) - Sylviani
9^{5gs} 8^{5sd} **0-0-2**

Minibule (Fr) *N Wilson* a47
5 ch m Funambule (USA) - Mipour (Fr)
8^{16sd} **0-0-1**

Minimum Bid *Miss B Sanders* 75 a79
4 b f First Trump - La Noisette
1^{6sd} 2^{7sd} 11^{7sd} 1^{6sd} 4^{7sd} 3^{6sd} 5^{7sd} 8^{7f} 5^{6sd} 3^{7sd} 1^{6gf} 10^{6gf} 9^{7sd} **3-3-13 £13,181**

Minirina *C Smith* a20
5 b m Mistertopogigo (Ire) - Fabulous Rina (Fr)
7^{6sd} 7^{5sd} **0-0-2**

Minivet *R Allan*
10 b g Midyan (USA) - Bronzewing
8^{16gf} 11^{16g} 8^{17g} **0-0-3**

Mink Mitten *D J Daly* 64 a59
3 b f Polish Precedent (USA) - Trefoil (Fr)
4^{7sd} 6^{8g} 6^{10f} 3^{10gf} 3^{10g} 3^{11gf} 4^{12g} 2^{10gf} 10^{10hd} 12^{8sf} **0-2-10 £3,179**

Minnesinger *R M Beckett* 84
3 b f Fraam - Rose Alto
1^{10gs} 4^{10gf} 9^{12gs} 6^{12g} 4^{10g} 5^{10g} 8^{10g} **1-0-7 £6,908**

Minority Report *L M Cumani* 91
5 b g Rainbow Quest (USA) - Queen Sceptre (Ire)
2^{8gf} 1^{8gf} 2^{8gf} 2^{8g} 1^{7gf} **2-3-5 £17,555**

Mint *D W Barker* 74
2 b f Bahamian Bounty - Tick Tack
10^{5g} 4^{6f} 1^{5gf} 4^{5gf} 8^{5g} 12^{5g} **1-0-6 £4,714**

Minthare (Ire) *C Grant* 50
2 br c Bahhare (USA) - Mintaka (Ire)
13^{6g} 7^{7g} 12^{8gs} 5^{7gf} 12^{8s} **0-0-5**

Mintlaw *I Semple* 81
3 b f Mujahid (USA) - Rynavey
3^{8gs} 5^{10gf} 8^{10s} 7^{10s} **0-1-4 £1,711**

Mio Caro (Fr) *Noel T Chance* 35
5 ch g Bering - Composition (USA)
9^{10gf} **0-0-1**

Miracle Baby *J A Geake* 38
3 b f Atraf - Musica
6^{6g} 4^{6g} 8^{7gf} 10^{5g} **0-0-4 £237**

Miracle Girl (Ire) *M R Channon* 26
2 b f Carrowkeel (Ire) - Sandpiper
17^{7g} 10^{7g} 7^{7f} 13^{7g} 14^{8gf} **0-0-5**

Mirage Prince (Ire) *Ian Williams* 48
3 ch g Desert Prince (Ire) - Belle Bijou
10^{8g} 16^{8gf} 10^{11gf} **0-0-3**

Mirasol Princess *D K Ivory* 73 a60
4 ch f Ali-Royal (Ire) - Yanomami (USA)
14^{6gf} 13^{5gf} 5^{5gf} 4^{5gf} 5^{6g} 5^{6g} 6^{5gf} 6^{5gf} 11^{6gs} 6^{5gf} 13^{6g} 13^{5gs} 7^{5sd} 10^{9sf} 2^{6sd} 9^{6sd} 9^{6sd} 8^{5sd} **0-1-18 £1,169**

Mirjan (Ire) *L Lungo* 96
9 b g Tenby - Mirana (Ire)
7^{12s} 8^{16g} 12^{14g} 7^{18gs} **0-0-4**

Mirth *R Hannon* 71
2 b f Alhaarth (Ire) - Justine Au Jardin (USA)
14^{8g} 4^{7g} **0-0-2 £407**

Mis Chicaf (Ire) *J S Wainwright* 72
4 b f Prince Sabo - Champagne Season (USA)
6^{5gf} 13^{6g} 13^{6gf} 9^{5g} 7^{5gf} 10^{5g} 13^{5g} **0-0-7 £312**

Misaro (Ger) *R A Harris* 54 a75
4 b g Acambaro (Ger) - Misniniski
13^{6sd} 11^{6gs} 3^{6sd} 2^{7s} 1^{5ft} 2^{6sd} **1-3-6 £5,312**

Misbehaviour *J J Best* 39
6 b g Tragic Role (USA) - Exotic Forest
3^{12g} **0-1-1 £210**

Mischief *Mrs H Sweeting* 45 a44
9 ch g Generous (Ire) - Knight's Baroness
13^{10f} 6^{12f} 6^{12f} 3^{14sd} PU^{14sd} **0-1-5 £211**

Mischief Night *M Dods* 52
3 ch g Lake Coniston (Ire) - On Till Morning (Ire)
3^{12gs} 10^{12gf} 7^{10g} 13^{14gf} **0-1-4 £854**

Mishka *Julian Poulton* a58
7 b g Mistertopogigo (Ire) - Walsham Witch
6^{5sd} **0-0-1**

Miskina *W M Brisbourne* 55 a64
4 b f Mark Of Esteem (Ire) - Najmat Alshemaal (Ire)
10^{6g} 3^{7sd} 1^{7sd} 10^{6gf} 6^{7gf} 12^{6sd} 5^{7gf} 16^{7g} 1^{7sf} 6^{7sd} 3^{7sd} **2-2-11 £7,274**

Misphire *T D Easterby* 85
2 b f Mister Baileys - Bombay Sapphire
10^{6gf} 4^{5g} 3^{5gf} 7^{6g} 2^{5g} 4^{6g} 4^{6g} 1^{6gs} **1-3-8 £21,894**

Miss A Bargain (Ire) *K R Burke* a43
2 ch f Bahamian Bounty - Miss Clarinet
5^{6sd} 12^{9sd} **0-0-2**

Miss Adelaide (Ire) *B W Hills* a74
4 b f Alzao (USA) - Sweet Adelaide (USA)
2^{6sd} 2^{6sd} 12^{5sd} **0-2-3 £2,088**

Miss Amadeus (Ire) *B R Millman* 60
2 b f Mozart (Ire) - Markova's Dance
10^{6gf} 9^{7gf} 6^{6f} 15^{7gs} **0-0-4**

Miss Amour *H J Collingridge* 48 a57
3 b f Pivotal - Georgia Stephens (USA)
10^{8sd} 6^{10sd} 8^{10s} 3^{10sd} 14^{10gf} 5^{8gf} 11^{8s} 13^{8hd} 4^{8sd} 9^{10sd} **0-1-10 £429**

Miss Bear (Ire) *B Smart* 38 a53
3 b f Orpen (USA) - The Poachers Lady (Ire)
4^{8sd} 2^{12sd} 1^{11sd} 8^{12gf} 13^{12sd} 12^{12sd} **1-1-6 £2,524**

Miss Brush *J R Fanshawe* 59 a73
2 b f Foxhound (USA) - Tattinger
2^{5sd} 1^{5sd} 10^{5g} 3^{5gs} **1-1-4 £4,561**

Miss Ceylon *S P Griffiths* a3
5 b m Brief Truce (USA) - Five Islands
10^{7sd} 14^{5sd} 10^{5sd} 14^{6g} **0-0-4**

Miss Champagne (Ire) *M Quinn* 48 a43
2 b f Tagula (Ire) - Champagne Lady (Ire)
8^{6hy} 11^{7sd} 5^{8sd} **0-0-3**

Miss Chancelot *S P Griffiths*
4 b f Forzando - Suedoro
10^{5sd} 12^{5sd} 15^{5gf} **0-0-3**

Miss Chantilly *W R Swinburn*
4 ch f Kris - Jezyah (USA)
8^{7f} **0-0-1**

Miss Cotswold Lady *A W Carroll* 43 a3
3 b f Averti (Ire) - Celtic Bay (USA)
13^{6gf} 4^{8gs} 11^{7g} 9^{10f} 13^{11g} 12^{7sd} **0-0-6 £268**

Miss Cue *Miss D Mountain* a26
3 b f Polish Precedent (USA) - Sharp Girl (Fr)
12^{8sd} 11^{10sd} 8^{12sd} 11^{16s} 13^{15gf} **0-0-5**

Miss Cuisina *P D Evans* 24
3 b f Vettori (Ire) - Rewardia (Ire)
7^{10g} 6^{10gs} 8^{10g} **0-0-3**

Miss Dagger (Ire) *J R Best* 31 a53
2 b f Daggers Drawn (USA) - Royal Rumpus
$9^{5gf}\ 5^{5sd}\ 10^{5gs}$ **0-0-3**

Miss Defying *R Curtis*
3 b f Shambo - Dugy
9^{12gs} **0-0-1**

Miss Dinamite *Mrs C J Ikin*
3 b f Polar Prince (Ire) - Over The Moon
7^{12gf} **0-0-1**

Miss Dixie *Miss J A Camacho* 67 a54
2 b f Bertolini (USA) - Dixie Favor (USA)
$3^{6g}\ 10^{6gs}\ 2^{5g}\ 5^{6sd}\ 10^{5sf}$ **0-2-5 £1,950**

Miss Eloise *T D Easterby* a59
4 b f Efisio - Zaima (Ire)
$4^{11sd}\ 8^{12sd}$ **0-0-2 £256**

Miss Fiddlesticks (Ire) *J J Bridger* a20
5 b m First Trump - Tweedling (USA)
$10^{10sd}\ 12^{10sd}$ **0-0-2**

Miss Fleurie *R Craggs* a40
5 b m Alzao (USA) - Miss Sancerre
$8^{14sd}\ 5^{12sd}\ 5^{14sd}\ 4^{12sd}$ **0-0-4**

Miss Gandy *W G M Turner* 45
2 b f Vettori (Ire) - Indian Lament
$6^{5gf}\ 1^{7f}\ 8^{6gf}\ 7^{7gf}$ **1-0-4 £2,511**

Miss Glory Be *E R Oertel* 55 a59
7 b m Glory Of Dancer - Miss Blondie (USA)
$10^{9sd}\ 6^{7sd}\ 6^{9sd}\ 6^{8sd}\ 11^{10sd}\ 6^{7s}\ 3^{9sd}\ 2^{11gf}\ 8^{11g}\ 1^{10f}\ 3^{10sd}\ 6^{10s}\ 5^{10g}\ 5^{11gf}\ 4^{9sd}\ 12^{8f}\ 10^{10g}\ 8^{6sd}\ 3^{8sd}\ 7^{8sd}$ **1-4-20 £4,959**

Miss Hepburn (USA) *W R Swinburn* 59 a58
2 ch f Gone West (USA) - Circle Of Gold (Ire)
$8^{7gf}\ 16^{7g}\ 6^{7sd}$ **0-0-3**

Miss Hermione *Mrs C A Dunnett* 54
3 ch f Bahamian Bounty - Try Vickers (USA)
$10^{6gf}\ 18^{6gf}\ 7^{6g}\ 13^{7sd}$ **0-0-4**

Miss Highjinks (USA) *E J O'Neill* 32 a72
2 ch f Stravinsky (USA) - Ready For Action (USA)
$12^{7hy}\ 3^{7sd}$ **0-1-2 £552**

Miss Inch *G Wragg* 63 a48
3 b f Inchinor - Twitcher's Delight
$8^{7gs}\ 4^{9sd}$ **0-0-2 £254**

Miss Iverley *P Monteith* 36
3 b f Shambo - Blanche The Almond
6^{9gs} **0-0-1**

Miss Judgement (Ire) *W R Muir* 52
4 b f Revoque (Ire) - Mugello
$16^{6gf}\ 7^{6f}\ 10^{7gf}\ 5^{6f}\ 6^{6g}\ 11^{6gf}\ 4^{6gf}\ 11^{6gf}\ 6^{6f}$ **0-0-9**

Miss Katmandu (Ire) *G Wragg*
3 ch f Rainbow Quest (USA) - Miss Rinjani
7^{10gf} **0-0-1**

Miss Koen (Ire) *D L Williams* a48
6 b m Barathea (Ire) - Fanny Blankers (Ire)
$13^{14sd}\ 8^{10sd}\ 4^{10sd}\ 6^{7sd}\ 8^{13sd}\ 8^{8sd}$ **0-0-6**

Miss L'Augeval *N Tinkler* 55
3 b f Zilzal (USA) - Miss Sancerre
$11^{8gs}\ 8^{8gf}\ 8^{10gf}\ 11^{8gf}\ 17^{8gf}\ 10^{8gf}\ 13^{8s}$ **0-0-7**

Miss Lacey (Ire) *J A Osborne* 45
2 b f Diktat - Launch Time (USA)
$9^{6f}\ 14^{5gs}\ 8^{5g}$ **0-0-3**

Miss Lemon (Ire) *A Berry*
2 b f Tagula (Ire) - Sesame Heights (Ire)
13^{6gs} **0-0-1**

Miss Lopez (Ire) *K R Burke* a65
2 br f Key Of Luck (USA) - Legit (Ire)
5^{6sd} **0-0-1**

Miss Lovat *A Bailey* 65 a62
2 b f Wizard King - Cantina
$9^{5gs}\ 4^{5gf}\ 3^{5gf}\ 7^{5gs}\ 3^{5gf}\ 2^{5gf}\ 6^{5gf}\ 3^{6g}\ 9^{5gf}\ 1^{5sd}\ 14^{5gf}\ 17^{5gf}\ 10^{5sd}\ 8^{6sd}\ 12^{6sd}$ **1-3-15 £7,266**

Miss Madame (Ire) *Rae Guest* 69
4 b f Cape Cross (Ire) - Cosmic Countess (Ire)
$5^{8gf}\ 6^{7gf}\ 9^{8gf}$ **0-0-3**

Miss Malone (Ire) *M J Polglase* 64 a61
3 b f Daggers Drawn (USA) - Queen Molly
$3^{7sd}\ 9^{6sd}\ 4^{7sd}\ 15^{6gs}\ 2^{6f}\ 11^{6gf}\ 8^{5gf}\ 6^{7gf}\ 12^{6g}\ 12^{6gf}$ **0-2-10 £1,668**

Miss Maxi (Ire) *B Palling* 51
2 b f Bold Fact (USA) - Beautyofthepeace (Ire)
$3^{5s}\ 6^{5gs}\ 9^{6s}\ 8^{6g}\ 10^{6g}\ 17^{8g}$ **0-1-6 £542**

Miss Meggy *Miss J A Camacho* 90 a80
3 b f Pivotal - Selkirk Rose (Ire)
$10^{6gf}\ 8^{6g}\ 13^{8gf}\ 6^{7g}\ 12^{7g}\ 5^{7gf}\ 7^{6gs}\ 5^{7sd}\ 11^{7g}$ **0-0-9**

Miss Merenda *J F Panvert* a5
4 b f Sir Harry Lewis (USA) - Cool Merenda (Ire)
7^{16sd} **0-0-1**

Miss Monica (Ire) *P W Hiatt* a53
4 ch f Grand Lodge (USA) - Bea's Ruby (Ire)
$3^{9sd}\ 11^{10sd}\ 7^{9sd}\ 14^{10sd}\ 7^{11sd}\ 4^{9ss}$ **0-1-6 £543**

Miss Monza *B R Millman* 49 a45
4 b f Hazaaf (USA) - Monstrosa
$10^{7gf}\ 10^{9sd}\ 13^{7gf}\ 5^{7g}\ 5^{6gf}\ 6^{7g}\ 7^{8sd}$ **0-0-7**

Miss Mujahid Times *A D Brown* 44 a40
2 b f Mujahid (USA) - Stealthy Times
$4^{5f}\ 7^{5g}\ 6^{6g}\ 6^{5gf}\ 10^{6f}\ 7^{6g}\ 3^{6sd}\ 10^{7ss}\ 10^{6sd}\ 5^{5ss}$ **0-1-10 £474**

Miss Ocean Monarch *Miss Tracy Waggott* 13
5 ch m Blue Ocean (USA) - Faraway Grey
13^{13s} **0-0-1**

Miss Particular (Ire) *B W Hills* 84
3 b f Sadler's Wells (USA) - Viz (USA)
$2^{8gs}\ 1^{10s}\ 2^{10g}\ 1^{12s}\ 11^{15gf}$ **2-2-5 £14,234**

Miss Patricia *J G Portman* 82 a62
3 b f Mister Baileys - Zoena
$2^{7sd}\ 2^{8g}\ 2^{7f}\ 2^{8gs}\ 2^{8f}\ 7^{7gf}\ 6^{8gf}\ 7^{7g}\ 13^{8gs}$ **0-5-9 £7,607**

Miss Pebbles (Ire) *R Dickin* 78 a67
5 ch m Lake Coniston (Ire) - Sea Of Stone (USA)
$13^{8g}\ 4^{10sd}\ 3^{10gs}\ 1^{9g}\ 2^{9g}\ 4^{8g}\ 7^{10gs}\ 13^{8g}\ 4^{10gs}$ **1-3-9 £9,807**

Miss Polaris *W R Swinburn* 89 a88
4 b f Polar Falcon (USA) - Sarabah (Ire)
$2^{8sd}\ 3^{10sd}\ 2^{8s}\ 1^{8sd}\ 2^{10gf}\ 10^{9gs}$ **1-4-6 £14,348**

Miss Porcia *S L Keightley* 64 a50
4 ch f Inchinor - Krista
$9^{10sd}\ 8^{7sd}\ 13^{9sd}\ 10^{9sd}\ 15^{6gf}\ 4^{7g}\ 6^{6f}\ 5^{7gf}\ 10^{6sd}\ 7^{6s}$ **0-0-10 £268**

Miss Provvidence (Ire) *W R Swinburn* 95 a96
3 b f Grand Lodge (USA) - My Southern Love (Ity)
$3^{10gf}\ 1^{10gs}\ 1^{10gf}\ 8^{12g}\ 1^{12sd}$ **3-1-5 £23,238**

Miss Rani (Ire) *B J McMath* 52
3 b f Xaar - Bea's Ruby (Ire)
$10^{6gf}\ 7^{8gf}\ 7^{8g}\ 9^{10gf}$ **0-0-4**

Miss Redactive *M D I Usher* 62
2 b f Whittingham (Ire) - Gold And Blue (Ire)
11^{6gf} 4^{6gf} **0-0-2 £374**

Miss Ria (Arg) *G L Moore* 28
4 ch f Numerous (USA) - Gloriadora (Arg)
8^{5g} 15^{7s} **0-0-2**

Miss Rosie *T D Easterby* 52
3 b f Xaar - Disallowed (Ire)
11^{8s} 6^{8g} 8^{8gf} 11^{7f} 5^{8s} **0-0-5**

Miss Shivvy (Ire) *C F Swan* 31 a37
3 b f Montjeu (Ire) - Castellane (Fr)
9^{9sd} 7^{11sd} 14^{10y} **0-0-3**

Miss Shontaine *B G Powell* a36
3 b f Fumo Di Londra (Ire) - Stockline
8^{10gf} 9^{7sd} 11^{10sd} 4^{9sd} **0-0-4**

Miss Sure Bond (Ire) *B Smart* 60 a25
2 ch f Danehill Dancer (Ire) - Desert Rose
7^{6gf} 2^{6g} 12^{6gs} 4^{6gf} 5^{6hy} 10^{7sf} **0-1-6**
£1,548

Miss Thailand *G Wragg* 81
2 b f Grand Lodge (USA) - Miss Amanpuri
3^{6gf} **0-1-1 £876**

Miss The Boat *J L Dunlop* 77
3 b f Mtoto - Missed Again
2^{10s} 3^{10gf} 1^{12g} 5^{14gs} 8^{15gf} 2^{10gs} **1-3-6**
£4,848

Miss Tiddlypush *L R James*
4 gr f Defacto (USA) - Misty Rocket
9^{10gf} 10^{12sd} **0-0-2**

Miss Tolerance (USA) *P W D'Arcy* a51
3 ch f Mt. Livermore (USA) - Acquiesce
8^{7sd} 9^{8sd} **0-0-2**

Miss Trial *M A Jarvis* 71
3 b f Zafonic (USA) - Perfect Alibi
4^{8gf} 11^{7g} **0-0-2 £346**

Miss Truant *M L W Bell* 41
3 b f Zaha (Can) - Miss Runaway
9^{6g} 7^{7s} **0-0-2**

Miss Wedge *M R Channon* 69
2 b f Fraam - Tough Nell (Ire)
3^{6f} 4^{7gf} 5^{6gf} 2^{8g} 10^{8g} **0-2-5 £2,516**

Miss Wizz *W Storey* 46
5 b m Wizard King - Fyas
12^{6gs} 11^{6g} 3^{8gf} 12^{10gs} 6^{9gf} 2^{8gf} 2^{7gf} 7^{8gf}
14^{8gf} **0-3-9 £2,362**

Missatacama (Ire) *D J Daly* 83 a83
3 b f Desert Style (Ire) - Delta Town (USA)
3^{9sd} 1^{8g} 4^{8gf} 7^{8g} 2^{10s} 2^{10sd} 7^{9sd} 4^{8sd}
1-3-8 £16,724

Missdevina (Ire) *M G Quinlan* 63
2 b f Namid - Vintage Escape (Ire)
4^{6g} 13^{7gf} **0-0-2 £274**

Missed A Beat *M Blanshard* 78 a77
3 b f Mister Baileys - Lonely Heart
4^{6gf} 3^{7gs} 8^{7gf} 2^{7f} 12^{8gf} 4^{7gf} 6^{8gf} 5^{9g} 10^{8gs}
10^{7g} 4^{8sd} 8^{8sd} **0-2-12 £6,059**

Missed Turn *J M P Eustace* 31 a54
3 b f Mind Games - Miss Beverley
2^{8sd} 8^{8sd} 1^{8sd} 3^{8sd} 14^{8gf} 13^{8gs} 13^{7sd}
1-2-7 £3,837

Missie Baileys *Mrs L J Mongan* 23 a59
3 ch f Mister Baileys - Jilly Woo
7^{8sd} 10^{10sd} 8^{10sd} 1^{10sd} 8^{8sd} 4^{10sd} 12^{10gf} 3^{12sd}
2^{10sd} 2^{10sd} 2^{10sd} 7^{10sd} 2^{14sf} **1-5-13**
£6,449

Missin Margot *P D Evans* 49
3 b f Fraam - Abstone Queen
8^{6gf} 6^{6f} 7^{7gf} 13^{8sd} **0-0-4**

Mission Affirmed (USA) *T P Tate* 67 a79
4 ch g Stravinsky (USA) - Affirmed Legacy (USA)
2^{8sd} 7^{9sd} 1^{7sd} 5^{9gf} 6^{7g} **1-1-5 £5,166**

Missoula (Ire) *M H Tompkins* 78
2 b f Kalanisi (Ire) - Medway (Ire)
10^{7s} 1^{8gf} 3^{8gf} **1-1-3 £8,598**

Missouri (USA) *Sir Michael Stoute* 34
2 b c Gulch (USA) - Coco (USA)
13^{7gf} **0-0-1**

Missperon (Ire) *K A Ryan* 77
3 b f Orpen (USA) - Secret Hideaway (USA)
16^{7g} 4^{6hy} 9^{6s} 9^{6g} 8^{6g} 8^{6gf} 14^{5g} 10^{6g} 3^{5g}
13^{5gf} 7^{5s} **0-2-11 £1,294**

Missturner (Ire) *W Jarvis*
3 b f Danehill Dancer (Ire) - It's Academic
9^{7sd} **0-0-1**

Missus Links (USA) *C McCready* a70
4 b f Lure (USA) - Cozisaidso (USA)
7^{7sd} 2^{6sd} 4^{7sd} 1^{8gf} 3^{9g} **1-1-5 £2,216**

Missy Cinofaz *A M Balding* a66
3 ch f Zafonic (USA) - Dancing Wolf (Ire)
3^{6sd} **0-1-1 £646**

Mistatake (Ire) *K A Ryan* 65 a60
2 b g Fasliyev (USA) - Copious (Ire)
5^{7g} 6^{7gf} 6^{9sd} 3^{6gf} 4^{6sd} 6^{7sd} 3^{6sd} 3^{7sd}
0-3-8 £1,470

Mister Arjay (USA) *B Ellison* 71
5 b g Mister Baileys - Crystal Stepper (USA)
16^{10gf} 13^{8g} 4^{8g} 5^{10gf} 1^{10g} 3^{10g} 9^{11gf} 7^{10g}
6^{12gf} **1-1-9 £4,698**

Mister Aziz (Ire) *J R Jenkins* 53 a47
3 b g Mister Baileys - Aziz Presenting (Ire)
6^{5sd} 3^{5s} 5^{7gs} 7^{7gf} 9^{7f} 11^{7g} 10^{7g} 3^{6sd} 11^{8sd}
10^{7sd} **0-1-10 £768**

Mister Becks (Ire) *M C Chapman* a18
2 b g Beckett (Ire) - Cappuchino (Ire)
8^{7f} 15^{6g} 8^{5sd} 13^{7sd} 10^{7sd} **0-0-5**

Mister Benedictine *W R Muir* 81 a83
2 b g Mister Baileys - Cultural Role
5^{5gf} 2^{6f} 2^{6g} 2^{7gf} 5^{6g} 1^{7g} 1^{7gf} 5^{7sd} 12^{8g}
2-3-9 £11,581

Mister Benji *B P J Baugh* 13 a61
6 b g Catrail (USA) - Katy-Q (Ire)
1^{7sd} 2^{8sd} 6^{8sd} 8^{7sd} 17^{7gs} 7^{7sd} **1-1-6**
£3,988

Mister Buzz *M D Hammond* 46
3 b g Mind Games - Compact Disc (Ire)
17^{7s} 4^{8gs} 4^{9g} 17^{8gf} 9^{8f} 8^{8s} **0-0-6 £262**

Mister Chalk *T Keddy* a40
4 gr c Silver Patriarch (Ire) - B B Glen
6^{9sd} 5^{11sd} UR^{14sd} 3^{12sd} 12^{14sd} **0-1-5**
£205

Mister Clinton (Ire) *D K Ivory* 58 a49
8 ch g Lion Cavern (USA) - Thewaari (USA)
12^{7gf} 9^{7gf} 9^{8gf} 7^{7f} 7^{8f} 14^{10f} 8^{8g} 4^{7f} 6^{7gf}
17^{10g} 4^{8hd} 6^{8gf} 2^{8f} 6^{10g} 3^{9sd} 8^{7sd} 1^{9sd}
1-2-17 £2,493

Mister Completely (Ire) *J R Best* 42 a51
4 b g Princely Heir (Ire) - Blue Goose
10^{10sd} 4^{10g} 4^{11sd} 2^{10sd} 4^{12sd} 4^{10sd} 1^{10sd}
1-1-7 £1,875

Mister Elegant *J L Spearing* 64 a54

3 b c Fraam - Risky Valentine
3^{7gs} 10^{7gs} 14^{7gf} 9^{9g} 7^{10g} 3^{7g} 5^{7gf} 3^{7sf} 3^{7sd} **0-4-9 £1,759**

Mister Fizzbomb (Ire) *J S Wainwright* 36
2 b g Lend A Hand - Crocus (Ire)
13^{6gf} 12^{7gf} 13^{6s} **0-0-3**

Mister Genepi *W R Muir* 108
3 b c Mister Baileys - Ring Queen (USA)
5^{8gf} 7^{8gf} 3^{10gy} 14^{11g} 2^{9gf} 4^{8gs} **0-0-6 £11,570**

Mister Graham *K F Clutterbuck*
10 b g Rock Hopper - Celestial Air
12^{14sd} **0-0-1**

Mister Incredible *C A Dwyer* 64 a48
2 b c Wizard King - Judiam
8^{5gf} 4^{5gf} 9^{6sd} 7^{5g} 5^{5sd} 4^{5hy} 3^{6sd} 4^{5ss} **0-2-8 £910**

Mister Mal (Ire) *B Ellison* 67 a58
9 b g Scenic - Fashion Parade
3^{5hy} 1^{6s} 4^{6gs} 6^{6sd} 15^{6g} 11^{7g} 10^{7sd} 10^{6sd} **1-1-8 £4,275**

Mister Maq *M Dods* 61
2 b g Namaqualand (USA) - Nordico Princess
9^{7g} 11^{7s} 2^{8gf} 7^{8gf} **0-1-4 £746**

Mister Marmaduke *D A Nolan* 62 a77
4 b g Marju (Ire) - Lalique (Ire)
2^{5sd} 3^{5sd} 10^{5gs} 9^{5sd} 3^{5gf} 5^{5g} 6^{5gs} 10^{5gf} 11^{6gf} 15^{6g} 10^{5g} **0-3-11 £2,292**

Mister Minty (Ire) *D Carroll* 34
3 b c Fasliyev (USA) - Sorb Apple (Ire)
11^{12gf} 12^{12s} **0-0-2**

Mister Muja (Ire) *W R Swinburn* 59 a58
4 gr g Mujadil (USA) - Remiss (Ire)
12^{7sd} 13^{7gs} 6^{7gf} 13^{8gf} 16^{6gf} **0-0-5**

Mister Putt (USA) *Mrs N Smith* 55
7 b/br g Mister Baileys - Theresita (Ger)
7^{11gs} 8^{15s} **0-0-2**

Mister Quicksand (USA) *C N Allen* 26 a47
6 ch h Sandpit (Brz) - Get Friendly Quick (USA)
10^{10sd} 9^{17sd} 16^{8gf} 9^{12sf} 4^{11sd} 9^{10g} 10^{14sd} **0-0-7**

Mister Regent *W M Brisbourne* 14 a36
4 b g Mind Games - River Of Fortune (Ire)
8^{6sd} 9^{8sd} 12^{13gf} 13^{10gf} 11^{10gf} **0-0-5**

Mister Right (Ire) *D J S Ffrench Davis* 80
4 ch g Barathea (Ire) - Broken Spirit (Ire)
3^{8g} 2^{8gf} 1^{10gf} 4^{10gf} 1^{10gf} 3^{12gf} 7^{12g} 2^{12g} **2-5-8 £10,940**

Mister Solo (Ire) *N Tinkler*
2 b g Indian Lodge (Ire) - Carhue Gold (Ire)
14^{7s} **0-0-1**

Mister Sweets *D Carroll* 82 a67
6 ch g Nashwan (USA) - Keyboogie (USA)
2^{7sd} 5^{6sd} 2^{7gf} 6^{10s} 11^{6g} 6^{6g} 4^{7gf} **0-3-7 £2,208**

Mister Troubridge *J A Geake* 52
3 ch g Mister Baileys - So True
5^{8gs} 5^{8g} 5^{10g} **0-0-3**

Misterbianco (Ire) *B J Meehan* a52
2 br c Danehill Dancer (Ire) - Price Of Passion
8^{7sd} **0-0-1**

Misters Sister *C A Dwyer* 23
3 b f Robellino (USA) - Baileys On Line
12^{10g} 13^{12gf} **0-0-2**

Mistral Sky *Stef Liddiard* 75 a86
6 b g Hurricane Sky (Aus) - Dusk In Daytona
4^{7sd} 11^{7sd} 4^{6sd} 4^{6sd} 1^{7sd} 5^{7gs} 7^{6gs} 8^{6g} 13^{6gs} 4^{7gf} 2^{6g} 6^{6gf} 6^{6gf} 10^{7sd} 8^{6gf} 8^{6sd} **1-1-16 £15,658**

Mistress Twister *T D Barron* 78
4 b f Pivotal - Foreign Mistress
4^{8gs} 5^{8gf} 8^{8gf} 3^{10g} 5^{10g} 6^{11gf} 2^{10gf} 3^{10gs} 9^{10gf} 3^{10gf} 6^{10gf} 10^{12s} **0-3-12 £6,867**

Misty Dancer *Miss Venetia Williams* 87
6 gr g Vettori (Ire) - Light Fantastic
4^{10gf} 1^{12gf} 4^{12gf} **1-0-3 £7,718**

Misty Man (USA) *Miss J Feilden* 3 a46
7 ch g El Gran Senor (USA) - Miasma (USA)
5^{12sd} 6^{12sd} 13^{11sd} 13^{12gf} 8^{12sd} **0-0-5**

Misty Princess *D Shaw* 38 a53
3 gr f Paris House - Miss Whittingham (Ire)
5^{5sd} 7^{5s} 4^{5sd} 2^{5sd} 4^{5s} 7^{5f} 6^{5f} 10^{5sd} 4^{5gf} 12^{5gs} 10^{5ss} 7^{5sd} 10^{5sd} **0-1-13 £1,309**

Misu Bond (Ire) *B Smart* 100
2 b c Danehill Dancer (Ire) - Hawala (Ire)
4^{6g} 1^{6hy} 11^{6gf} 1^{6gf} **2-0-4 £118,059**

Mitanni (USA) *Mrs A J Perrett* 73
2 b c Lear Fan (USA) - Maria Dolores (USA)
4^{6gf} 2^{6gf} **0-1-2 £1,448**

Mitchelland *James Moffatt* 62 a44
3 b f Namaqualand (USA) - Precious Girl
4^{6s} 2^{6gs} 6^{7s} 10^{7gs} 7^{6f} 10^{6g} 10^{6ss} 14^{7sd} **0-1-8 £1,616**

Mith Hill *E A L Dunlop* 86 a79
4 b c Daylami (Ire) - Delirious Moment (Ire)
7^{12sd} 1^{12gs} 4^{12g} 14^{20gf} 6^{14g} 4^{16gs} **1-0-6 £8,067**

Mitsina *R Charlton* 42
2 ch f Fantastic Light (USA) - Rosse
8^{8gs} **0-0-1**

Mixed Blessing *A P Jarvis* 104
2 b/br f Lujain (USA) - Marjorie's Memory (Ire)
4^{6gf} 2^{6gf} 1^{6g} 3^{6g} 1^{6gf} 3^{7g} 9^{6g} 9^{6g} **2-2-8 £41,583**

Mixing *W Jarvis* 72
3 gr c Linamix (Fr) - Tuning
12^{8gf} 3^{7s} 3^{8s} 9^{14g} 5^{12gs} 1^{10gs} 13^{11gs} 9^{12gs} 16^{10s} **1-2-9 £4,629**

Mizz Tee (Ire) *T D Easterby* 86 a92
3 b f Orpen (USA) - D D's Jakette (USA)
5^{6s} 4^{8gf} 4^{7g} 15^{7g} 5^{6gf} 5^{6gf} 4^{8g} 12^{7s} 1^{10sd} 3^{9sf} 2^{9sd} **1-2-11 £16,241**

Mo Chroi *C G Cox* 24 a30
2 ch f Observatory (USA) - Away To Me
14^{6gf} 11^{8s} 9^{8sd} **0-0-3**

Moayed *N P Littmoden* 100 a104
6 b g Selkirk (USA) - Song Of Years (Ire)
1^{9sd} 2^{6sd} 5^{9sd} 2^{7sd} 7^{10sd} 12^{7gf} 8^{6gf} 2^{7g} 7^{7gf} 13^{6f} 13^{7gs} 20^{7gf} 9^{6gs} 14^{7g} 2^{7g} 16^{7gs} 21^{7gs} 10^{10sd} 5^{6sd} 3^{7sd} 5^{9sd} **1-5-21 £43,206**

Mobane Flyer *R A Fahey* 72
5 b g Groom Dancer (USA) - Enchant
3^{10g} 3^{8s} 4^{8f} 2^{9s} 2^{9gs} 9^{9gf} 3^{9gf} 12^{8gf} 7^{9g} **0-4-9 £5,240**

Mobo-Baco *R J Hodges* a64
8 ch g Bandmaster (USA) - Darakah
2^{9sd} 3^{12sd} 3^{9sd} 7^{9sd} 9^{7sd} 9^{9sd} **0-3-6 £1,628**

Mobsir *E A L Dunlop* 80
2 b c Mozart (Ire) - Pretty Sharp
2^{6g} **0-1-1 £1,224**

Mocca (Ire) *D J Coakley* 96
4 b f Sri Pekan (USA) - Ewan (Ire)
2^{12gf} 4^{12g} 6^{12g} 4^{10gf} 9^{12gf} 6^{10g} 6^{12gf} **0-1-7 £9,069**

Mocha Java *P F I Cole* 69 a67
2 b c Bertolini (USA) - Coffee Cream
4^{7gf} 3^{6gf} 8^{8gf} 13^{7g} 3^{8sd} 8^{7sd} **0-2-6 £1,258**

Modaffaa *P R Webber* a70
5 b g Darshaan - Irish Valley (USA)
10^{12sd} **0-0-1**

Modeeroch (Ire) *J S Bolger* 103
2 gr f Mozart (Ire) - Majinskaya (Fr)
1^{6f} 1^{7g} 2^{7g} 4^{6g} **2-1-4 £58,030**

Mogaamer (USA) *M P Tregoning* 98 a98
3 b g Dixieland Band (USA) - Dolly Talbo (USA)
2^{7sd} 1^{7sd} 4^{7sd} 5^{9gf} 6^{8g} 7^{7gf} **1-1-6 £9,704**

Mohafazaat (Ire) *M P Tregoning* 69 a65
3 b f Sadler's Wells (USA) - Wijdan (USA)
4^{10gs} 1^{10sd} **1-0-2 £4,435**

Mohawk Star (Ire) *Miss Venetia Williams* 48
4 ch g Indian Ridge - Searching Star
18^{10s} **0-0-1**

Mohtarres (USA) *M A Jarvis* 46
2 b c Kingmambo (USA) - Adored Slew (USA)
18^{7gs} **0-0-1**

Moi Aussi (USA) *Sir Mark Prescott* 65 a81
2 ch f Mt. Livermore (USA) - Acquiesce
4^{6sd} 3^{7gs} 8^{6sd} 9^{7sd} 4^{6sd} 8^{8g} 4^{8hy} 2^{7sd} 1^{8sd} 5^{8sd} 1^{8sd} **2-3-11 £13,487**

Mokaraba *J L Dunlop* 86
3 ch f Unfuwain (USA) - Muhaba (USA)
1^{12gs} 4^{12g} 5^{14g} 15^{16g} **1-0-4 £6,619**

Moktabes (USA) *Saeed Bin Suroor* 72 a88
3 ch c Machiavellian (USA) - Cinnamon Sugar (Ire)
12^{8s} 2^{7gf} 8^{7g} 1^{8sd} 1^{8sd} **2-1-5 £8,450**

Molcon (Ire) *E J O'Neill* 84
4 b g Danetime (Ire) - Wicken Wonder (Ire)
5^{6gf} 13^{6gf} 18^{7s} **0-0-3**

Moldavia (Ger) *N B King* 41 a58
4 b f Lagunas - Moricana (Ger)
1^{11sd} 5^{12sd} 10^{12sd} 12^{12gf} 8^{10gf} 8^{15gf} **1-0-6 £2,891**

Molem *Lady Herries* 72 a70
3 br g Green Desert (USA) - Injaad
11^{7gs} 4^{8g} 6^{10gf} 2^{8gf} 5^{10sd} **0-2-5 £1,659**

Molinia *Stef Liddiard* 67 a72
4 b f Nicolotte - Themeda
2^{7sd} 4^{7sd} 5^{7sd} 1^{9sd} 2^{8sd} 7^{8sd} 6^{7g} 11^{7s} 6^{7gf} 6^{9sd} 10^{8g} **1-2-11 £5,683**

Molly Dancer *M Meade* 49 a61
3 b f Emarati (USA) - Perfect Partner
5^{7sd} 8^{7sd} 4^{8sd} 1^{6s} 10^{7gs} 15^{6g} 15^{8hy} 10^{6sd} **1-0-8 £3,210**

Molly Marie (Ire) *T D Easterby* 74
3 b f Fasliyev (USA) - Snoozeandyoulose (Ire)
3^{6gf} 2^{5gf} 1^{6f} 5^{6gf} 8^{6gf} 9^{6gf} 7^{6gf} **1-2-7 £7,070**

Molly's Secret *Miss S J Wilton* a57
7 b m Minshaanshu Amad (USA) - Secret Miss
2^{12sd} 7^{14sd} 7^{12sd} 2^{14sd} 4^{12sd} 11^{12sd} 5^{12sd} **0-2-7 £1,262**

Mollyputtheketelon (USA) *M J Wallace* 76 a68
4 b f Rainbow Quest (USA) - Nemea (USA)
5^{10g} 7^{12s} 3^{8gf} 4^{8g} 16^{8g} 7^{9g} 6^{9sd} 12^{12sd} 5^{9sd} 2^{9sd} 11^{9sd} **0-2-11 £1,587**

Mollzam (Ire) *D Selvaratnam* a74
3 b c Danehill (USA) - Matilda Bay (Ire)
1^{6sd} 4^{9sd} 8^{8ft} **1-0-3 £4,399**

Molotov *I W McInnes* 59
5 b g Efisio - Mindomica
DSQ^{5gs} 14^{5gf} 16^{5gf} 4^{5gf} 14^{5gf} 9^{5gf} 13^{5gf} 3^{5f} 4^{5g} 13^{5sd} **0-2-10 £493**

Moment Of Clarity *R C Guest* 54 a59
3 b g Lujain (USA) - Kicka
8^{10sd} 14^{12sd} 3^{10g} 6^{13f} **0-1-4 £371**

Momtic (Ire) *W Jarvis* 112
4 ch c Shinko Forest (Ire) - Uffizi (Ire)
15^{10gs} 1^{8g} 5^{9g} 2^{8g} 1^{9g} 2^{8gf} 1^{8gf} 21^{9s} **3-2-8 £87,329**

Mon Petite Amour *D W P Arbuthnot* 33 a42
2 b f Efisio - Food Of Love
8^{5sd} 12^{5gf} **0-0-2**

Mon Plaisir *C F Wall* 62 a62
3 br f Singspiel (Ire) - Mademoiselle Chloe
6^{8g} 2^{8gf} 10^{8gf} 7^{9gf} 5^{9sd} **0-1-5 £1,217**

Mon Secret (Ire) *B Smart* 43 a60
7 b g General Monash (USA) - Ron's Secret
2^{7sd} 10^{7g} 11^{7f} 12^{8gf} 8^{8sd} **0-1-5 £834**

Mona Lisa *A P O'Brien* 111
3 ch f Giant's Causeway (USA) - Colorsnap
4^{10s} 11^{8gy} 9^{12g} 3^{8gf} 6^{10gf} 3^{12gf} 1^{12gf} 7^{10y} 7^{10gy} 2^{10gs} 10^{10y} **1-3-11 £130,539**

Monash Girl (Ire) *B R Johnson* 15
4 b f General Monash (USA) - Maricica
9^{5f} 9^{7f} **0-0-2**

Monash Lad (Ire) *M H Tompkins* 75
3 ch g General Monash (USA) - Story Time (Ire)
6^{6s} 5^{7s} 3^{7g} 8^{9g} 8^{8g} 3^{10gf} 4^{10gs} 2^{10s} **0-3-8 £3,381**

Monashee Brave (Ire) *J J Quinn* 60
2 b g Monashee Mountain (USA) - Miss Butterfield
3^{5g} **0-1-1 £688**

Monashee Express (Ire) *S C Williams* 53 a57
3 ch g Monashee Mountain (USA) - Curie Express (Ire)
7^{6gf} 4^{7sd} 4^{9sd} 11^{10g} 4^{7gf} **0-0-5**

Monashee Gold (Ire) *E J O'Neill* a73
2 b c Monashee Mountain (USA) - Onsomespecialnight (Can)
1^{9sd} **1-0-1 £2,497**

Monashee Grey (Ire) *R A Fahey* 33
2 b g Monashee Mountain (USA) - Ex-Imager
12^{6gf} 16^{6g} 11^{7g} **0-0-3**

Monashee Prince (Ire) *J R Best* 73 a73
3 ch g Monashee Mountain (USA) - Lodema (Ire)
2^{5sd} 5^{6sd} 10^{7gs} 1^{7gf} 5^{6gf} 6^{7gf} 14^{7gf} 5^{7g} 10^{7g} 10^{6sd} 10^{6sd} 3^{6sd} **1-2-12 £5,522**

Monda *Miss J A Camacho* 54 a52
3 b f Danzig Connection (USA) - Fairey Firefly
10^{7g} 1^{7g} 8^{8s} 12^{9sd} 4^{7sf} **1-0-5 £3,159**

Monets Masterpiece (USA) *Mrs A J Perrett* 77
2 b c Quiet American (USA) - Math (USA)
5^{8g} 4^{8gf} **0-0-2 £444**

Money Hills *Mrs C A Dunnett* 38 a26
3 b g Vettori (Ire) - Starfida
13^{10gf} 8^{8f} 7^{10g} 4^{11g} 9^{10sd} 13^{8g} **0-0-6**

Money Market (Ire) *R Hannon* 71
3 b g Machiavellian (USA) - Trying For Gold (USA)
8^{9gs} 2^{10gs} 6^{10s} 6^{10g} 10^{10g} **0-1-5 £1,075**

Money Mate (Ire) *C J Teague* 76

2 ch g Titus Livius (Fr) - Xania
6^{5s} 4^{5s} 6^{5f} 1^{6y} 6^{7gf} 7^{7g} **1-0-6 £5,585**

Monica Geller *M Dods* a41
7 b m Komaite (USA) - Rion River (Ire)
4^{9sd} **0-0-1**

Monkey Madge *B Smart* 55 a52
3 br f Cape Cross (Ire) - Runelia
4^{6gs} 5^{6sd} 5^{6g} 16^{6s} 8^{5ft} 6^{6sd} 4^{7ss} **0-0-7 £371**

Monkstown Road *E S McMahon* 73 a57
3 b c Makbul - Carolside
3^{6g} 7^{6s} 7^{6g} 9^{6gf} 8^{7gs} 10^{6gf} 6^{6g} 5^{6gf} 2^{7g} 1^{7gf} 7^{9sd} **1-2-11 £4,710**

Monolith *L Lungo* 82
7 b g Bigstone (Ire) - Ancara
5^{12f} **0-0-1**

Monroe Gold *Jennie Candlish* 8 a39
5 ch g Pivotal - Golden Daring (Ire)
15^{7gf} 13^{12gf} 6^{9sf} 7^{7sd} 8^{14sd} **0-0-5**

Monsal Dale (Ire) *Mrs L C Jewell* a29
6 ch g Desert King (Ire) - Zanella (Ire)
7^{12sd} **0-0-1**

Mont Etoile (Ire) *W J Haggas* 77 a64
2 b f Montjeu (Ire) - Troyes
4^{7gf} 6^{7gs} 5^{7sd} **0-0-3 £328**

Mont Saint Michel (Ire) *G Wragg* 81 a75
3 b c Montjeu (Ire) - Band Of Angels (Ire)
4^{10sd} 3^{12gs} 4^{12s} 4^{10gf} 1^{11gf} 13^{11gs} 8^{12gf} 9^{10gf} **1-1-8 £6,419**

Montage (Ire) *J Akehurst* 44
3 b g Montjeu (Ire) - Ocean View (USA)
11^{10g} 16^{10gs} **0-0-2**

Montana *J L Spearing* 68 a30
5 b g Puissance - Mistral's Dancer
9^{6gf} 3^{6g} 3^{5gf} 10^{6f} 2^{5g} 2^{5gf} 2^{6g} 3^{6g} 3^{6g} 3^{6hy} 9^{5sd} **0-6-11 £5,727**

Montara (Ire) *Barry Potts* 59
6 b g Perugino (USA) - Tatra
1^{9gf} 9^{8s} 9^{8gf} 9^{10gs} 1^{11gf} 4^{12g} 2^{10g} 2^{8g} 11^{11g} **2-2-9 £6,868**

Montcalm (Ire) *J G Given* 63 a52
3 b f Montjeu (Ire) - Autumn Fall (USA)
3^{8g} 6^{11gf} 13^{8g} 10^{9sd} 9^{14g} 8^{9hy} 11^{9sd} **0-1-7 £772**

Montchara (Ire) *G Wragg* 42
2 b c Montjeu (Ire) - Mochara
8^{6gf} **0-0-1**

Monte Carrio *C Drew*
2 ch c Observatory (USA) - Kundalini (USA)
9^{7sd} **0-0-1**

Monte Cristo (Fr) *Mrs L C Taylor* 41 a74
7 ch g Bigstone (Ire) - El Quahirah (Fr)
12^{16gs} 2^{12sd} 1^{16sd} 1^{17sd} 3^{16sf} **2-2-5 £10,059**

Monte Major (Ger) *Unknown* 34
2 ch g Trempolino (USA) - Monbijou (Ger)
12^{6g} 10^{6gf} 8^{8gf} **0-0-3**

Monte Major (Ire) *D Shaw* 41 a53
4 b g Docksider (USA) - Danalia (Ire)
12^{6sd} 13^{6sd} 8^{5sd} 8^{5sd} 10^{5gs} 7^{5gs} **0-0-6**

Monte Mayor Boy *D Haydn Jones* 66 a71
3 b g First Trump - Risalah
13^{8g} 8^{8gf} 6^{8g} 13^{8gf} 12^{10gs} UR^{9sd} 1^{8sf} 4^{8sd} **1-0-8 £2,963**

Monte Mayor Junior *D Haydn Jones* 5 a58
2 b g Mull Of Kintyre (USA) - Monte Mayor Golf (Ire)
18^{7gf} 5^{6sd} 6^{7sd} 7^{6sd} 9^{8sd} 9^{8sd} **0-0-6**

Monte Mayor Lass *D Haydn Jones*
2 gr f Baryshnikov (Aus) - Wing Partner (Ire)
10^{5g} **0-0-1**

Montecito *R Hannon* 80
3 b f Montjeu (Ire) - Dancing Fire (USA)
14^{6gs} 9^{9gf} 5^{12gf} 1^{12gf} 5^{12s} 2^{10s} 8^{11gs} 2^{12gs} 4^{12s} **1-2-9 £13,182**

Montecristo *Rae Guest* 55
12 br g Warning - Sutosky
9^{11g} **0-0-1**

Monteleone (Ire) *R Hannon* a33
3 b f Montjeu (Ire) - Rainbow Goddess
9^{10sd} 9^{9sd} **0-0-2**

Montfleur *H Candy* 66
3 b f Sadler's Wells (USA) - Mackie (USA)
10^{10gs} 6^{10gf} **0-0-2**

Montgomery's Arch (USA) *P W Chapple-Hyam* 106
3 b/br c Arch (USA) - Inny River (USA)
7^{8gf} 12^{8s} 11^{7gs} 6^{6gs} **0-0-4**

Montillia (Ire) *C F Wall* 56
3 b f Monashee Mountain (USA) - Steel Tap (Ire)
4^{5g} 1^{5gf} **1-0-2 £3,703**

Montini Royale (Ire) *M J Attwater* 52 a52
2 b f Rossini (USA) - Belmont Princess (Ire)
4^{5g} 5^{5sd} 5^{6f} 1^{7sd} 3^{6gs} 9^{7sd} 9^{7sd} 5^{6sd} 4^{6sd} 10^{6sd} **1-0-10 £3,393**

Montjeu Abu (Ire) *A Berry* 16
2 b f Montjeu (Ire) - Circus Maid (Ire)
8^{6gf} 7^{8gf} **0-0-2**

Montjeu Baby (Ire) *S Kirk* 66 a63
3 b f Montjeu (Ire) - Catch The Lights
11^{9sd} 6^{10gs} 12^{11g} 5^{8gf} 7^{10g} 11^{8gf} 14^{10g} 2^{10f} 1^{8s} 3^{10hd} 2^{10gf} 1^{9sd} 2^{8gs} **2-4-13 £9,335**

Montjeu Man *E A L Dunlop* 78
2 b c Montjeu (Ire) - Camp Fire (Ire)
12^{7g} 2^{7g} **0-1-2 £1,612**

Montlobre (Ire) *J G Given*
3 b f Petardia - Fall Of The Hammer (Ire)
12^{10gf} 14^{11g} 13^{13g} **0-0-3**

Montosari *P Mitchell* 15 a69
6 ch g Persian Bold - Sartigila
3^{16sd} 5^{16sd} 1^{12sd} 15^{12hy} 14^{14gf} 11^{15gf} 13^{12sd} 2^{16sd} 4^{16sd} **1-2-9 £4,884**

Montrachet Belle *R Johnson* 46
3 ch f Kadeed (Ire) - Swiss Hat
11^{8s} 13^{10g} 6^{9gs} 14^{8gf} 3^{9gf} 6^{9g} **0-0-6 £522**

Montreux (UAE) *J H M Gosden* 76 a80
2 b f Jade Robbery (USA) - Aldburgh
9^{7sd} 1^{8gs} 14^{7gs} 4^{8sd} **1-0-4 £5,429**

Montzando *B R Millman* 79
2 b g Forzando - Clashfern
3^{5gs} 2^{5gf} 1^{5gf} 4^{5g} 23^{5gf} 7^{6gs} 7^{6g} 18^{6gs} 11^{5gf} **1-2-9 £7,561**

Moody Tunes *K R Burke* 67 a45
2 b g Merdon Melody - Lady-Love
5^{6g} 4^{6gs} 6^{5g} 13^{7gf} 7^{6g} 6^{7sd} 4^{6hy} **0-0-7 £649**

Moohimm (Ire) *M P Tregoning* 34
2 b c Sadler's Wells (USA) - Lurina (Ire)
20^{7g} **0-0-1**

Moon Bird *C A Cyzer* 59 a68
3 b f Primo Dominie - Time For Tea (Ire)

4^{6sd} 1^{6sd} 8^{6gf} 2^{7sd} 5^{6sd} 6^{7sd} **1-1-6 £6,184**

Moon Emperor *J R Jenkins* 70 a77
8 b g Emperor Jones (USA) - Sir Hollow (USA)
5^{16sd} 2^{16sd} 5^{16gs} 3^{16g} 8^{14g} 2^{15gf} 6^{14g} 7^{16gf} 6^{16sd} 7^{16gf} 8^{16sd} **0-3-11 £2,704**

Moon Forest (Ire) *P W Chapple-Hyam* 71
3 br g Woodborough (USA) - Ma Bella Luna
5^{7g} 12^{8gs} 8^{8f} 14^{7g} **0-0-4**

Moon Mischief (Ire) *N P Littmoden* a59
3 b f Desert Sun - Moonlight Path (Ire)
5^{6sd} 5^{7sd} 8^{7sd} 1^{8sd} **1-0-4 £2,569**

Moon On A Spoon *J R Fanshawe* 65
2 b f Dansili - Tinashaan (Ire)
5^{7g} 6^{7s} **0-0-2**

Moon Ray (Ire) *M A Jarvis* 64
2 br c Xaar - Midnight Angel
6^{6g} **0-0-1**

Moon Royale *Mrs N Macauley* a8
7 ch m Royal Abjar (USA) - Ragged Moon
10^{7sd} 10^{9sd} **0-0-2**

Moon Shot *A G Juckes* a75
9 gr g Pistolet Bleu (Ire) - La Luna (USA)
2^{12sd} 8^{12sd} 9^{12sd} 5^{9sd} 4^{12sd} 2^{12sd} **0-2-6 £1,579**

Moon Spinner *Andrew Reid* a53
8 b m Elmaamul (USA) - Lunabelle
5^{10sd} 5^{10sd} 6^{12sd} 2^{13sd} 6^{12sd} 12^{13sd} 3^{16sd} 4^{14sd} **0-2-8 £1,471**

Moondancer (Ger) *B G Powell* a52
6 br g General Assembly (USA) - Miskinissa (Ger)
7^{9sd} 3^{9sd} 1^{9sd} 7^{9sd} 10^{8s} 13^{7sd} 13^{12sd} 2^{8sd} 2^{10sd} 12^{10sd} **1-2-10 £2,448**

Moonfleet (Ire) *M F Harris* 58 a36
3 b f Entrepreneur - Lunasa (Ire)
12^{9sd} 4^{10s} 10^{13g} 2^{9f} 6^{10gf} 9^{12sd} 2^{10gf} 1^{10g} 7^{13gf} 5^{10f} 6^{10f} **1-2-11 £6,544**

Moonhawk *J Howard Johnson* 76
2 b c Montjeu (Ire) - Enclave (USA)
8^{9g} 2^{8gs} 12^{7s} **0-1-3 £1,560**

Moonlight (Ger) *B G Powell* 39
2 b f Kornado - Miskinissa (Ger)
13^{6gf} 15^{8g} **0-0-2**

Moonlight Fantasy (Ire) *N Tinkler* 55
2 b g Night Shift (USA) - County Girl (Ire)
9^{8gf} 9^{8g} 9^{7gf} **0-0-3**

Moonlight Man *R Hannon* 104
4 ch c Night Shift (USA) - Fleeting Rainbow
3^{6g} 7^{7g} 9^{6gf} 7^{7gf} 13^{6g} 3^{8gf} 1^{7gf} 2^{8gf} 14^{7gf} 4^{8gf} **1-2-10 £35,390**

Moonlight Music (Ire) *E J O'Neill* 76
2 ch f Rossini (USA) - Jarmar Moon
2^{7gs} 18^{7gf} **0-1-2 £1,372**

Moonlight Song (Ire) *John A Harris* 10
8 b m Mujadil (USA) - Model Show (Ire)
16^{6g} 14^{7gf} **0-0-2**

Moonmaiden *M R Channon* 67
3 ch f Selkirk (USA) - Top Table
2^{7g} 7^{8s} 6^{7gf} 7^{8g} 19^{7gf} 1^{6g} 5^{6gf} 4^{7s} 5^{6gf} 3^{7gf} 11^{6gf} **1-2-11 £6,663**

Moonshine Beach *P W Hiatt* 86 a60
7 b g Lugana Beach - Monongelia
9^{16g} 6^{16gs} 4^{18g} 2^{18gf} 1^{16gs} 3^{15gf} 8^{21s} 6^{16g} 4^{16gf} 2^{16gf} 7^{16g} 11^{16gs} 6^{16sd} **1-2-13 £8,816**

Moonshine Bill *P W Hiatt* 55 a56
6 ch g Master Willie - Monongelia
7^{10sd} 4^{12sd} 8^{10gf} 4^{10gf} 1^{12gf} 5^{11gf} 9^{12g} 19^{10g} 8^{12sd} 10^{17sf} **1-1-10 £3,759**

Moonside *J A Geake* 36 a26
3 gr f Docksider (USA) - Moon Magic
9^{8sd} 12^{10gs} 5^{11f} 13^{14g} 12^{12f} **0-0-5**

Moonstreaker *R M Whitaker* 65
2 b g Foxhound (USA) - Ling Lane
10^{7s} 9^{7gf} 5^{7g} 3^{7gf} **0-1-4 £496**

Moonstruck *J M P Eustace* 58 a64
3 ch g Fraam - Easter Moon (Fr)
12^{9sd} 4^{7sd} 7^{7g} 11^{10sd} 12^{10sd} **0-0-5**

Moorhouse Lad *G Woodward* 77
2 b c Bertolini (USA) - Record Time
3^{6gf} 2^{5g} 9^{5g} 17^{6gf} **0-1-4 £2,774**

Moors Myth *B W Hills* 71
4 b g Anabaa (USA) - West Devon (USA)
13^{8gf} 5^{8gf} 8^{7gf} 2^{8gf} 7^{7f} 6^{7gf} **0-1-6 £1,064**

Moorside Princess *R A Fahey*
2 ch f Komaite (USA) - Moorside Girl
8^{5g} **0-0-1**

Moraadi *D W Chapman* 5
2 b f Lujain (USA) - Saleyma
14^{7gf} 15^{6gf} 11^{7sd} **0-0-3**

Morag *I A Wood* 49 a40
4 b f Aragon - Minnehaha
5^{7gs} 6^{7gf} 17^{8gf} 7^{10sd} 10^{8g} 5^{7gf} 9^{7gf} 14^{8gf} 8^{7sd} 16^{7g} 5^{6ss} **0-0-11**

Mordor (Fr) *Noel Meade* 100
3 b c Sadler's Wells (USA) - Moon Driver (USA)
1^{8gf} 5^{10gs} 6^{10gf} **1-0-3 £6,625**

More Time (Ire) *M G Quinlan* 79
2 b c Night Shift (USA) - In Your Dreams (Ire)
5^{5s} 1^{5g} 4^{5gf} 2^{6gf} 2^{6gf} 6^{6gf} 21^{6gf} 7^{6g} 5^{6gs} **1-2-9 £6,196**

Morgan Lewis (Ire) *J A Geake* 74
4 b g Orpen (USA) - Party Piece
6^{6gs} 5^{6gs} 6^{6g} 3^{6gf} 5^{7g} 14^{6g} 2^{7hy} **0-1-7 £1,865**

Morghim (Ire) *J L Dunlop* 84
2 b c Machiavellian (USA) - Saleela (USA)
1^{7gs} **1-0-1 £4,862**

Moritat (Ire) *P D Evans* 48
5 b g Night Shift (USA) - Aunty Eileen
14^{6g} 8^{6gs} 16^{6g} 4^{6gf} 11^{6s} 9^{5gf} 10^{6g} **0-0-7 £265**

Mormeatmic *M W Easterby* 61
2 b g Orpen (USA) - Mimining
3^{5g} 3^{6g} 8^{5gs} 9^{7hy} 12^{7g} 12^{6g} **0-2-6 £1,332**

Mornin Reserves *W G Harrison* 66
6 b g Atraf - Pusey Street Girl
7^{5s} 8^{5gs} **0-0-2**

Morse (Ire) *J A Osborne* 90
4 b g Shinko Forest (Ire) - Auriga
2^{6s} 4^{6gs} 1^{6g} 6^{6g} 6^{6s} 5^{7gs} 17^{6g} 5^{8g} 5^{8g} 10^{8gs} 8^{7g} 2^{6s} 6^{7s} **1-2-13 £8,469**

Mortarboard *E J O'Neill* 78
2 gr c Daylami (Ire) - Miss University (USA)
2^{8s} 6^{8s} **0-1-2 £2,450**

Morzine *R Charlton* 83
2 ch f Miswaki (USA) - Skiable (Ire)
1^{6gf} 12^{6gf} 3^{6gf} 3^{6gf} **1-2-4 £7,104**

Moscow Blue *Robert Gray* 5

4 ch g Soviet Star (USA) - Aquamarine
11^{8gs} **0-0-1**

Moscow Mary *A G Newcombe* 22
4 b f Imperial Ballet (Ire) - Baileys Firecat
10^{6g} **0-0-1**

Moss Vale (Ire) *B W Hills* 113
4 b c Shinko Forest (Ire) - Wolf Cleugh (Ire)
7^{5gf} 2^{6gy} 3^{5gf} 11^{6gs} 3^{5s} 12^{5gf} 5^{6g} 1^{6gf} 9^{5gf} 5^{6g} 3^{6gs} **1-4-11 £53,085**

Mossmann Gorge *M Wellings* 73 a65
3 b g Lujain (USA) - North Pine
9^{6sd} 8^{7sd} 7^{10gf} 2^{7gs} 1^{8g} 7^{8gf} 9^{8gf} 6^{8g} 12^{8gs} 13^{10g} 11^{7sd} 6^{12sd} **1-1-12 £5,031**

Most Definitely (Ire) *T D Easterby* 96
5 b g Definite Article - Unbidden Melody (USA)
1^{14g} 3^{16g} 7^{14g} 1^{15gf} 7^{12gs} 1^{12gf} 8^{12g} 5^{13gf} 7^{14g} 4^{15gs} 3^{12gf} **3-1-11 £29,786**

Most Famous *A D Smith* 36
2 ch f Rock City - Riverain
16^{5g} 8^{5s} 6^{5g} 12^{6g} **0-0-4**

Most-Saucy *I A Wood* 55 a44
9 br m Most Welcome - So Saucy
10^{12sd} 18^{17g} 7^{15gf} 7^{12gf} 11^{16g} 8^{16gf} **0-0-6**

Mostakbel (USA) *M D I Usher* a45
6 b/br g Saint Ballado (Can) - Shamlegh (USA)
8^{12sd} 9^{12sd} 12^{13sd} **0-0-3**

Mostanad *J M Bradley* 65
3 b g Alhaarth (Ire) - Jeed (Ire)
5^{6g} 2^{5s} 9^{6gf} 7^{6f} 6^{6gf} 9^{6f} 7^{6gf} 8^{6gf} 18^{5gf} 9^{6gs} **0-1-10 £1,296**

Mostaqeleh (USA) *J L Dunlop* 88
2 ch f Rahy (USA) - Istiqlal (USA)
3^{6gf} 1^{6gf} 1^{7gf} **2-1-3 £17,729**

Mostarsil (USA) *G L Moore* 65 a62
7 ch g Kingmambo (USA) - Naazeq
6^{10g} 11^{12gs} 7^{12gs} 10^{16gs} 1^{12sd} **1-0-5 £1,450**

Mostashaar (Fr) *Sir Michael Stoute* 111
3 b c Intikhab (USA) - Nasanice (Ire)
1^{7s} 2^{8gs} 1^{8gf} **2-1-3 £38,707**

Motarassed *J L Dunlop* 60
3 b c Green Desert (USA) - Sayedati Eljamilah (USA)
9^{8gf} 12^{8g} 9^{7gf} **0-0-3**

Mothecombe Dream (Ire) *C A Dwyer* a66
3 b c Foxhound (USA) - Another Shadow (Ire)
3^{6sd} 5^{7sd} 5^{6sd} 5^{7sd} 2^{7sd} 7^{7sd} **0-2-6 £1,245**

Motivator *M L W Bell* 129
3 b c Montjeu (Ire) - Out West (USA)
1^{10s} 1^{12g} 2^{10gf} 2^{10gy} 5^{12gs} **2-2-5 £1,067,653**

Motive (Fr) *J Howard Johnson* 100
4 ch g Machiavellian (USA) - Mistle Song
6^{12gf} 9^{10gs} 3^{10g} **0-1-3 £4,910**

Motu (Ire) *I W McInnes* 59 a65
4 b g Desert Style (Ire) - Pink Cashmere (Ire)
7^{7sd} 2^{8sd} 4^{7sd} 4^{8f} 2^{7gf} 6^{8f} 8^{8f} 6^{7g} 5^{8gf} 8^{8gf} 13^{7gf} 3^{8g} 4^{8gf} 1^{7gf} 8^{8g} 7^{8gf} 13^{7s} **1-4-17 £4,137**

Mouchoir *P J Makin* 74
2 b g Bahamian Bounty - Mouchez Le Nez (Ire)
5^{5f} 6^{6g} 2^{5gf} 1^{5gs} 8^{6gs} 6^{5g} 6^{6gs} **1-1-7 £5,535**

Mount Arafat *M Salaman* 16 a18
3 b/br g Erhaab (USA) - Cache
7^{12sd} 8^{10f} 7^{16gf} **0-0-3**

Mount Benger *Mrs A J Hamilton-Fairley* 46
5 ch g Selkirk (USA) - Vice Vixen (Can)
14^{14gs} 15^{10g} **0-0-2**

Mount Cottage *J G Given* a5
4 b f Cape Cross (Ire) - Brecon Beacons (Ire)
9^{12sd} **0-0-1**

Mount Ephram (Ire) *R F Fisher* a7
3 b g Entrepreneur - Happy Dancer (USA)
14^{11sd} 14^{10sd} **0-0-2**

Mount Hillaby (Ire) *M W Easterby* 76 a77
5 b m Mujadil (USA) - Tetradonna (Ire)
10^{9sd} 2^{9sd} 2^{9sd} 9^{7s} 1^{7gf} 7^{8gs} 4^{7g} 10^{7gf} 7^{8g} 3^{8gf} 2^{8gf} 2^{8gf} 5^{7g} **1-4-13 £10,817**

Mount Royale (Ire) *N Tinkler* 49 a63
7 ch g Wolfhound (USA) - Mahabba (USA)
10^{7sd} 6^{7sd} 5^{7sd} 4^{7sd} 4^{7sd} 3^{7sd} 10^{7f} 8^{7sd} 10^{7gs} 12^{7s} 6^{7sd} 7^{7sd} 4^{7sd} 2^{7ss} 2^{7ss} **0-3-15 £1,275**

Mount Usher *G A Swinbank* 62
3 br g Polar Falcon (USA) - Division Bell
3^{10g} 5^{9gs} 5^{7g} 8^{9gf} 7^{11gs} **0-1-5 £422**

Mount Vettore *K G Reveley* 69
4 br g Vettori (Ire) - Honeyspike (Ire)
6^{8gf} 5^{10s} 4^{7f} 3^{8gf} 8^{10g} 13^{10g} 8^{9gf} 12^{8g} 4^{8gf} 8^{9gf} 16^{9gf} **0-1-11 £1,401**

Mountain High (Ire) *Sir Michael Stoute* 106
3 b c Danehill (USA) - Hellenic
3^{8gf} 1^{10gs} 4^{12gf} 10^{9gs} **1-1-4 £14,341**

Move On (Ire) *B Ellison* 47
2 b f Night Shift (USA) - Beaufort Lady (Ire)
12^{5gf} 8^{5gf} 8^{7g} **0-0-3**

Move Over Darling (Ire) *M Johnston* 72
2 b f Singspiel (Ire) - Darling Harbour (USA)
8^{7gf} 2^{8s} **0-1-2 £1,032**

Movie King (Ire) *S R Bowring* 47 a64
6 ch g Catrail (USA) - Marilyn (Ire)
13^{10gf} 10^{10g} 11^{12sf} 3^{14sf} 4^{12sd} 11^{14sd} **0-1-6 £428**

Moyne Pleasure (Ire) *R Johnson*
7 b g Exit To Nowhere (USA) - Ilanga (Ire)
11^{11sd} **0-0-1**

Moyoko (Ire) *M Blanshard* 51
2 b f Mozart (Ire) - Kayoko (Ire)
19^{6gf} 10^{6gf} 7^{6gf} 7^{7g} 10^{7gs} **0-0-5**

Mozakhraf (USA) *K A Ryan* 67
3 b c Miswaki (USA) - Anakid (USA)
6^{6y} 4^{7f} 5^{7gf} 3^{8g} 3^{7g} **0-2-5 £1,521**

Mpenzi *J L Dunlop* 81
3 b f Groom Dancer (USA) - Muschana
8^{10gs} 13^{10gf} 3^{11gf} 2^{12f} 1^{12g} 1^{13gf} 3^{12g} 3^{12gs} 18^{13vs} **2-4-9 £11,451**

Mr Aitch (Ire) *J A Osborne* 75 a78
3 b g Soviet Star (USA) - Welsh Mist
6^{8sd} 6^{8gf} 7^{10gf} 8^{9gf} 1^{8f} **1-0-5 £3,951**

Mr Belvedere *A J Lidderdale* 41 a50
4 b g Royal Applause - Alarming Motown
3^{12sd} 4^{12sd} 5^{12g} 7^{12gf} 5^{9sd} 13^{10gs} 3^{8sd} **0-3-7 £421**

Mr Bilbo Baggins *J S Moore* a19
2 ch g Magic Ring (Ire) - I'Ll Try
12^{7sd} **0-0-1**

Mr Bountiful (Ire) *C J Teague* 36 a52
7 b g Mukaddamah (USA) - Nawadder
4^{7sd} 7^{7sd} 8^{9sd} 4^{7sd} 7^{7sd} 13^{7gf} 10^{6gf} 16^{7g}

0-0-8

Mr Cellophane *J R Jenkins* 62
2 ch g Pursuit Of Love - Fresh Fruit Daily
3^{6gs} 10^{6gf} 6^{5g} 6^{6s} **0-0-4 £634**

Mr Cheers *Miss J A Camacho* 55 a22
2 b g Bertolini (USA) - Plie
4^{5s} 5^{5gs} 10^{5gs} 13^{6sd} **0-0-4 £326**

Mr Dinglawi (Ire) *D B Feek* a47
4 b g Danehill Dancer (Ire) - Princess Leona (Ire)
4^{13sd} 11^{16sd} **0-0-2**

Mr Dinos (Ire) *P F I Cole* 104
6 b h Desert King (Ire) - Spear Dance
8^{20gf} 5^{16gf} **0-0-2 £700**

Mr Dip *L A Dace* 20 a45
5 b g Reprimand - Scottish Lady
7^{9sd} 3^{13sd} 1^{14sd} 5^{14sd} 4^{12sd} 4^{12sd} 11^{10s} 11^{10g}
9^{16sd} 3^{12sd} **1-2-10 £1,870**

Mr Ed (Ire) *P Bowen* 86
7 ch g In The Wings - Center Moriches (Ire)
7^{20gf} **0-0-1**

Mr Excel (Ire) *J A Osborne* 59 a67
2 b g Orpen (USA) - Collected (Ire)
8^{7gf} 9^{8s} 3^{7sd} 1^{9sd} **1-1-4 £2,148**

Mr Floodlight (Ire) *R Hannon* 76 a76
2 b g Bertolini (USA) - French River
11^{7f} 8^{7gs} 8^{7g} 6^{8g} 3^{8sd} 2^{7sd} **0-2-6**
£1,679

Mr Garston *M P Tregoning* 74
2 b g Mull Of Kintyre (USA) - Ninfa Of Cisterna
1^{5g} **1-0-1 £3,376**

Mr Hullabalou (Ire) *R Ingram* a33
4 b g Princely Heir (Ire) - Lomalou (Ire)
10^{6sd} 8^{7sd} **0-0-2**

Mr Jack Daniells (Ire) *Anthony Mullins* 95 a79
4 b g Mujadil (USA) - Neat Shilling (Ire)
5^{10sd} 6^{7ys} 6^{10hy} 1^{10g} 1^{9g} 1^{10gf} 10^{12gf} 10^{10g}
9^{10g} 9^{10g} **3-0-10 £28,127**

Mr Kalandi (Ire) *P W D'Arcy* 61 a65
3 gr c Grand Lodge (USA) - Singhana (Ire)
2^{9sd} 9^{10sd} 4^{9sd} 2^{8gs} 7^{8g} 6^{11g} 4^{12sd} 4^{12sd} 8^{10gf}
0-3-9 £1,855

Mr Kayos *W M Brisbourne* a27
3 b g Kayf Tara - Highland Heights (Ire)
9^{7sd} **0-0-1**

Mr Lambros *A M Balding* 88 a94
4 ch g Pivotal - Magical Veil
1^{7sd} 7^{7sd} 3^{6gf} 6^{6g} 9^{6gf} 4^{6gf} 13^{6g} 13^{7g}
1-1-8 £12,739

Mr Lear (USA) *J J Quinn* 61
6 b g Lear Fan (USA) - Majestic Mae (USA)
9^{12gs} **0-0-1**

Mr Majestic *R M Whitaker* 66
3 b g Vettori (Ire) - Alacrity
7^{8gf} 3^{10gf} 4^{9gf} 8^{10g} 2^{12gf} 4^{12gf} 7^{12s} 9^{12s}
0-2-8 £2,075

Mr Malarkey (Ire) *Mrs C A Dunnett* 91
5 b g Pivotal - Girl Next Door
12^{6g} 1^{6gf} 11^{6s} 4^{6f} 8^{6gf} 7^{6g} 2^{5gf} 3^{6gf} 7^{6gf}
4^{5g} 7^{6gf} 3^{5gf} 3^{5g} 6^{5gf} **1-3-14 £17,271**

Mr Marucci (USA) *B Ellison* 35
3 b g Miner's Mark (USA) - Appealing Style (USA)
6^{10g} **0-0-1**

Mr Maxim *R M Whitaker* 60
3 ch g Lake Coniston (Ire) - White Hare
4^{10g} 4^{11gf} 5^{12gs} 7^{11gf} 8^{10gf} 3^{12gf} 3^{14gf} 7^{13s}
0-1-8 £1,256

Mr Mayfair (Ire) *J A Osborne* a59
3 ch g Entrepreneur - French Gift
5^{7sd} 9^{6sd} **0-0-2**

Mr Midasman (Ire) *R Hollinshead* 72
4 b g Entrepreneur - Sifaara (Ire)
10^{11gs} 2^{10g} 2^{11gf} 4^{10gf} 10^{10g} 8^{10gs} 1^{11g} 5^{11gf}
1-2-8 £6,501

Mr Mischief *P C Haslam* 79 a96
5 b g Millkom - Snow Huntress
3^{12sd} 2^{14gf} 2^{14g} 2^{17gf} **0-3-4 £5,963**

Mr Motormouth *H E Haynes*
2 b c Manhal - Viola
13^{7sd} **0-0-1**

Mr Rein (Ire) *J A Osborne* a66
3 b g Indian Danehill (Ire) - Lady's Vision (Ire)
5^{9sd} 2^{9sd} 7^{12sd} 6^{10sd} **0-1-4 £1,038**

Mr Rigsby *P Howling* a66
2 gr g Forzando - Rain Splash
1^{7sd} 1^{6sd} 12^{7sd} 11^{6sd} **2-0-4 £5,337**

Mr Rooney (Ire) *M Johnston* 87
2 b c Mujadil (USA) - Desert Bride (USA)
6^{5g} 1^{5g} 3^{5gs} 9^{5g} 3^{5gf} 3^{6gf} 3^{6gf} 4^{6g} **1-1-8**
£9,401

Mr Sandicliffe *B W Hills* 95
2 b c Mujahid (USA) - Crinkle (Ire)
2^{5gf} 2^{5g} 2^{5g} 2^{6g} 2^{6gf} 4^{6g} **0-5-6**
£75,259

Mr Spliffy (Ire) *M C Chapman* a53
6 b g Fayruz - Johns Conquerer (Ire)
12^{5sd} 8^{5sd} 6^{5sd} 1^{5sd} 9^{6sd} 9^{5sd} 10^{5sd} 3^{5sd} 12^{5sd}
10^{5sd} 8^{5ss} 6^{5sd} 6^{5sd} **1-1-13 £1,661**

Mr Strowger *J C Fox* a45
4 b c Dancing Spree (USA) - Matoaka
11^{9sd} 10^{10sd} 7^{10sd} 8^{12sd} **0-0-4**

Mr Tambourine Man (Ire) *B J Llewellyn* 75 a85
4 b g Rainbow Quest (USA) - Girl From Ipanema
5^{12sd} 11^{10gf} 7^{10gf} 9^{12f} 8^{12gf} 12^{12gs} **0-0-6**

Mr Topspot (Ire) *D Morris* 10
2 b c Mister Baileys - Jugendliebe (Ire)
15^{6gs} **0-0-1**

Mr Tuplin *M J Attwater* a46
5 ch g Peintre Celebre (USA) - Fearless Revival
11^{8sd} 12^{6sd} 5^{5sd} 10^{6sd} 4^{6sd} 7^{7sd} 7^{7sd} 13^{9sd}
0-0-8

Mr Twins (Arg) *M A Barnes* a47
4 ch g Numerous (USA) - Twins Parade (Arg)
13^{10sd} 8^{10sd} **0-0-2**

Mr Uppity *Julian Poulton* a42
6 b g Shareef Dancer (USA) - Queenfisher
10^{8sd} 11^{7sd} 4^{6ss} 6^{9sd} **0-0-4**

Mr Vegas (Ire) *P W Chapple-Hyam* 108
3 b c Montjeu (Ire) - Germignaga (Ity)
10^{11hy} 3^{12gf} 2^{11gs} 1^{12s} 2^{16gf} 1^{15gs} 11^{15s}
2-2-7 £36,827

Mr Velocity (Ire) *E F Vaughan* 80
5 b g Tagula (Ire) - Miss Rusty (Ire)
13^{11gs} 5^{10s} 8^{8g} 4^{8g} **0-0-4 £526**

Mr Whizz *A P Jones* 54 a38
8 ch g Manhal - Panienka (Pol)
5^{8sd} 4^{11sd} 11^{2g} 2^{10f} 9^{10gf} 5^{12gf} 4^{12f} 2^{14gf} 6^{12gf}
8^{15gf} **1-2-10 £2,941**

Mr Wolf *D W Barker* 101
4 b g Wolfhound (USA) - Madam Millie
11^{5s} 18^{5gs} 6^{5g} 13^{5f} 12^{6g} 5^{5gf} 1^{6gf} 1^{6gf} 1^{6gf}

3^{6g} 1^{5g} 9^{6gs} 11^{5g} 17^{6gf} 2^{5g} 8^{5g} 3^{5g}
4-3-17 £29,968

Mr Wong (Ire) *M Sheppard* a57
9 br g Be My Native (USA) - Adare Boreen
6^{9sd} 10^{12sd} **0-0-2**

Mrs Chippy (Ire) *M H Tompkins* 1
3 ch f Docksider (USA) - Pile (USA)
11^{7g} **0-0-1**

Mrs Diniver (Ire) *Liam Roche* a33
2 b f Bahhare (USA) - Outstanding Order (Ire)
7^{7sd} **0-0-1**

Mrs Moh (Ire) *T D Easterby* 84
4 b f Orpen (USA) - My Gray (Fr)
6^{8gs} 18^{8gs} 17^{8g} 3^{8g} 8^{7g} 5^{7f} 7^{7gs} 3^{8gf} 7^{7g}
1^{7g} **1-2-10 £5,815**

Mrs Philip *P J Hobbs* 43
6 b m Puissance - Lightning Legacy (USA)
11^{14gf} 8^{13f} **0-0-2**

Mrs Snaffles (Ire) *Francis Ennis* 89
2 b f Indian Danehill (Ire) - Lake Nyasa (Ire)
8^{6f} 3^{6gf} 2^{7gf} 1^{6g} 4^{6gf} **1-2-5 £14,637**

Mrs Spence *M W Easterby* 54
4 b f Mind Games - Maid O'Cannie
4^{5gf} 11^{6s} 7^{5gf} 16^{5gf} **0-0-4 £322**

Ms Freebee *M Mullineaux* 16 a11
6 ch m Gunner B - Luckifosome
11^{9sd} 12^{12gf} 13^{12gf} 8^{12s} **0-0-4**

Ms Polly Garter *J M Bradley* a17
3 br f Petong - Utopia
16^{5s} 11^{5sd} **0-0-2**

Ms Rainbow Runner *P Butler* 60 a59
2 b f Josr Algarhoud (Ire) - Silk Law (Ire)
4^{6gf} 6^{6sd} 5^{6gf} 4^{6gf} 4^{5s} 8^{6g} 12^{6gf} 5^{7sd} 4^{8sd}
1^{10sd} 7^{8sd} **1-0-11 £2,461**

Ms Three *R Ford* a34
3 b f Josr Algarhoud (Ire) - Swing Along
11^{7sd} 10^{6sd} 10^{5sd} 10^{5sd} **0-0-4**

Mt Desert *J H M Gosden* 81
3 b g Rainbow Quest (USA) - Chief Bee
7^{8g} 1^{11s} 5^{12gs} 2^{13g} 11^{16g} **1-1-5 £5,992**

Muara *D W Barker* 61
3 ch f Wolfhound (USA) - Darussalam
15^{6g} 4^{6f} 4^{6gf} 1^{5f} 10^{5g} **1-0-5 £3,031**

Mubtaker (USA) *M P Tregoning* 119
8 ch h Silver Hawk (USA) - Gazayil (USA)
3^{10gf} 1^{12gf} 2^{13g} 1^{14g} 1^{12gs} 1^{12g} 9^{12gs} 4^{12gs}
3-1-8 £86,400

Mucho Loco (Ire) *J G Portman* a56
2 ch c Tagula (Ire) - Mousseux (Ire)
11^{6sd} 11^{9sd} 3^{7sd} **0-1-3 £493**

Muckle *S C Williams* 51
2 gr f Muhtarram (USA) - Crackle
9^{6gf} 12^{6g} **0-0-2**

Muddy (Ire) *N A Callaghan* 57 a27
3 ch g Monashee Mountain (USA) - Schonbein (Ire)
15^{6gs} 12^{7gf} 3^{10f} 4^{10f} 11^{12sd} 5^{9gf} 11^{10sd} 8^{7g}
11^{9sd} **0-1-9 £369**

Mufreh (USA) *A G Newcombe* a89
7 br g Dayjur (USA) - Mathkurh (USA)
4^{8sd} 9^{7sd} 3^{8sd} 4^{8sd} **0-1-4 £2,593**

Mugeba *Miss Gay Kelleway* 68 a57
4 b f Primo Dominie - Ella Lamees
3^{7sd} 9^{6sd} 2^{6s} 3^{6g} 2^{6gs} 2^{6gf} 3^{7gf} 4^{6g} 10^{6gf}
3^{7gs} 1^{7g} 5^{7gf} 4^{7gf} 8^{6g} 14^{8gs} 10^{7hy} 1^{6hy}
2-8-17 £13,334

Mujazaf *Miss Sheena West* 63
3 b g Grand Lodge (USA) - Decision Maid (USA)
6^{11g} 9^{11gs} 5^{14g} 7^{12gf} 16^{14g} 10^{16g} **0-0-6**

Mujeak (Ire) *J J Quinn* 64
2 b g Mujadil (USA) - Break For Peace (Ire)
5^{5g} **0-0-1**

Mujelle *D K Ivory* 65 a65
2 b g Mujahid (USA) - Jennelle
9^{5sd} 4^{6sd} 7^{7gf} 4^{6sd} 3^{6sd} 10^{7sd} 4^{6g} 3^{6sd} 11^{7sd}
1^{7sd} **1-2-10 £3,322**

Mujimac (Ire) *P A Blockley* 47 a54
3 b g Mujadil (USA) - Cross Dall (Ire)
5^{10sd} 6^{8sd} 11^{10sd} 8^{10gf} 11^{10g} 3^{10sd} 8^{12sd} 9^{12sd}
2^{10sd} **0-2-9 £640**

Mujkari (Ire) *J M Bradley* a26
9 ch g Mujtahid (USA) - Hot Curry (USA)
10^{9sd} **0-0-1**

Mujood *R F Johnson Houghton* 81
2 b g Mujahid (USA) - Waqood (USA)
5^{5gf} 5^{6gf} 3^{6g} 1^{6gf} 3^{7f} 12^{7gs} 2^{6gf} 5^{6g} 12^{6g}
1-3-9 £9,050

Mukafeh (USA) *E Charpy* 111 a101
4 b c Danzig (USA) - Bint Salsabil (USA)
3^{8gs} 3^{8gf} 6^{8gf} 14^{8gf} 1^{9ft} 4^{8ft} **1-1-6**
£15,218

Muktasb (USA) *D Shaw* 47 a63
4 b g Bahri (USA) - Maghaarb
5^{5sd} 2^{5sd} 8^{5gf} 14^{5g} 7^{5sd} 4^{5sd} **0-1-6**
£1,107

Mulaazem *M P Tregoning* 62
2 b c King's Best (USA) - Harayir (USA)
9^{7gf} **0-0-1**

Mulan Princess (Ire) *S C Burrough* a45
5 b m Mukaddamah (USA) - Notley Park
7^{12sd} 8^{9sd} 9^{9sd} 6^{9sd} 12^{9sd} 5^{12sd} **0-0-6**

Mulaqat *M P Tregoning* 94 a80
2 b c Singspiel (Ire) - Atamana (Ire)
8^{6gs} 4^{7f} 2^{8sd} 1^{7gf} 1^{8g} 1^{7gf} **3-1-6**
£17,854

Mulberry Lad (Ire) *P W Hiatt* 55 a56
3 b g Entrepreneur - Taisho (Ire)
6^{5gf} 6^{6gf} 12^{5gf} 6^{6f} 5^{6sd} 8^{7gf} 13^{9sd} 4^{8f} 2^{8sd}
1^{6ss} 4^{7sd} 8^{7sd} 6^{6sd} 9^{6sd} 10^{5sd} **1-1-15**
£2,093

Mulberry Wine *M Blanshard* 36
3 b f Benny The Dip (USA) - Top Berry
11^{8g} **0-0-1**

Mull Of Dubai *J S Moore* 64 a49
2 b g Mull Of Kintyre (USA) - Enlisted (Ire)
2^{6gf} 2^{6gf} 7^{6gf} 11^{6gs} 11^{7sd} 6^{7g} 13^{6g} 10^{6gs}
0-2-8 £2,400

Mullaad (Ire) *T D Easterby* 100
2 b c Mull Of Kintyre (USA) - Suaad (Ire)
2^{5gf} 1^{5g} 1^{5gf} 3^{6gs} 11^{6g} **2-1-5 £21,923**

Mullady Penelope *Mrs A Duffield* 52
2 b f Mull Of Kintyre (USA) - Gracious Imp (USA)
3^{6g} 6^{5g} **0-1-2 £642**

Mullagh (Ire) *M H Tompkins* 7
2 ch f Fantastic Light (USA) - True Joy (Ire)
7^{7gs} **0-0-1**

Mulligan's Gold (Ire) *T D Easterby* 62
2 b c Fasliyev (USA) - Magic Lady (Ire)
6^{5g} 6^{6g} 4^{6gs} **0-0-3 £276**

Mullins Bay *A P O'Brien* 119
4 b c Machiavellian (USA) - Bella Colora

8^{8s} 3^{8g} 2^{10gf} 1^{10g} 1^{9gf} 6^{8g} 2^{9gs} **2-3-7 £153,526**

Mullzima (Ire) *P D Evans* 50 a43
2 b f Mull Of Kintyre (USA) - Habaza (Ire)
6^{5g} 9^{6g} 6^{6gf} 11^{7gf} 5^{7sd} 7^{7g} 10^{7gf} 11^{8g} 8^{8gf} 9^{8sd} 12^{10sd} **0-0-11**

Multahab *Miss Gay Kelleway* 57 a51
6 b/br g Zafonic (USA) - Alumisiyah (USA)
11^{5sd} 1^{5f} 2^{6f} 10^{5g} 8^{5gf} 2^{5g} 5^{6sd} 5^{5g} 5^{5sd} 3^{6sf} 7^{6sd} 4^{6ss} **1-3-12 £4,494**

Multakka (Ire) *M P Tregoning* 83
2 b c Alhaarth (Ire) - Elfaslah (Ire)
5^{7gs} 3^{7gs} 3^{8gs} **0-2-3 £1,615**

Multiple (Ire) *J A Osborne* 77
2 b f Mull Of Kintyre (USA) - Sail Away (Ger)
2^{5gs} 4^{5gf} 2^{5g} 1^{5gf} 7^{5g} 1^{5gf} 4^{5g} 3^{5g} **2-3-8 £11,314**

Mumbling (Ire) *B G Powell* 71
7 ch g Dr Devious (Ire) - Valley Lights (Ire)
3^{13s} 4^{14g} 3^{13gf} 1^{16gf} 2^{17g} 3^{17f} **1-4-6 £12,945**

Munaa (Ire) *K R Burke* 66 a61
2 b f Alhaarth (Ire) - Beseeching (Ire)
10^{6gf} 7^{7gf} 5^{7gf} 2^{8gf} 2^{8g} 3^{8s} 2^{9sd} **0-4-7 £4,283**

Munaahej (Ire) *Mrs N Macauley*
4 b c Soviet Star (USA) - Azyaa
11^{8sd} **0-0-1**

Munaawashat (Ire) *K R Burke* 84 a68
4 b f Marju (Ire) - Simaat (USA)
13^{8gs} 9^{8gs} 1^{8g} 8^{8gs} 10^{8gf} 8^{8g} 4^{8gs} 9^{7sd} 9^{8sd} **1-0-9 £8,587**

Munaawesh (USA) *Mrs Marjorie Fife* 49 a21
4 b g Bahri (USA) - Istikbal (USA)
7^{7sd} 13^{9sd} 9^{7sd} 9^{16gs} 4^{14gf} 13^{10gs} 13^{12gf} 6^{13gf} **0-0-8**

Munaddam (USA) *Saeed Bin Suroor* 88
3 ch c Aljabr (USA) - Etizaaz (USA)
19^{7gs} **0-0-1**

Mungo Jerry (Ger) *J G Given* 79 a57
4 b g Tannenkonig (Ire) - Mostly Sure (Ire)
1^{12s} 5^{11s} 20^{14s} 9^{12g} 12^{12gs} 16^{14s} 10^{16sf} 6^{12sd} 1^{12sd} **2-0-9 £6,909**

Munnings (Ire) *P F I Cole* 85
2 b c Selkirk (USA) - Silly Goose (Ire)
5^{7gs} 4^{7gf} 2^{7g} 2^{8s} **0-2-4 £2,875**

Munsef *J L Dunlop* 116
3 b c Zafonic (USA) - Mazaya (Ire)
2^{8g} 1^{9gf} 1^{12gf} 1^{12gs} 3^{12gs} **3-2-5 £57,576**

Muntami (Ire) *John A Harris* 73
4 gr g Daylami (Ire) - Bashashah (Ire)
23^{8s} 13^{9g} 12^{10g} 15^{10g} 9^{8s} 2^{10hy} **0-1-6 £1,046**

Muqarrar (Ire) *T J Fitzgerald* a59
6 ch g Alhaarth (Ire) - Narjis (USA)
7^{10sd} 1^{12sd} 8^{12sd} 7^{12sd} 13^{14sd} 8^{12ss} 7^{12sd} **1-0-7 £1,438**

Muqtadi (Ire) *M Appleby* a49
7 b g Marju (Ire) - Kadwah (USA)
2^{6sd} 8^{9sd} 2^{8sd} **0-2-3 £895**

Muraabet *J L Dunlop* 73
3 b c Dubai Millennium - Mahasin (USA)
5^{8s} **0-0-1**

Muraqeb *Mrs Barbara Waring* a14
5 ch g Grand Lodge (USA) - Oh So Well (Ire)
9^{12sd} **0-0-1**

Murfreesboro *J H M Gosden* 95
2 b c Bahamian Bounty - Merry Rous
7^{6f} 1^{6gf} 2^{7gf} 1^{6g} **2-1-4 £131,905**

Murhef *M A Jarvis* 34
3 b g Royal Applause - Petit Point (Ire)
7^{8gf} **0-0-1**

Murielle *I Semple* 63
2 b f Diktat - Pearl Venture
4^{6g} **0-0-1 £287**

Murrieta *Miss J R Gibney* 48 a52
3 ch f Docksider (USA) - Lafleur (Ire)
7^{6s} 5^{8sd} 12^{7g} 6^{10sd} 8^{12sd} **0-0-5**

Murrumbidgee (Ire) *J W Hills* a60
2 gr c Bluebird (USA) - Blanche Neige (USA)
9^{7sd} 8^{7sd} 9^{7sd} 12^{7sd} **0-0-4**

Murtakez *R A Harris*
5 b g Alhaarth (Ire) - Raaqiyya (USA)
17^{10gs} **0-0-1**

Murts Magic (Ire) *M J McGrath*
2 ch c Rossini (USA) - Clover Tina (Ire)
14^{7gf} **0-0-1**

Murzim *J Gallagher*
6 b g Salse (USA) - Guilty Secret (Ire)
14^{12hy} 13^{13sd} **0-0-2**

Musardiere *T Hogan* 66
3 b f Montjeu (Ire) - Majestic Image
10^{10s} 4^{10s} 12^{10g} 8^{10gf} 4^{8gy} 5^{10s} 5^{8y} 2^{10y} **0-1-8 £2,219**

Museeb (USA) *J L Dunlop* 108
3 b c Danzig (USA) - Elle Seule (USA)
1^{7g} 2^{7gf} 2^{7gs} 4^{7gf} 3^{8gs} 9^{7gf} 6^{6g} **1-3-7 £22,557**

Musette (Ire) *C G Cox* 46
2 b f Mujadil (USA) - Repique (USA)
6^{5g} 11^{6g} 9^{6gf} 6^{8hd} **0-0-4**

Mushajer *M P Tregoning* 76 a74
3 gr g Linamix (Fr) - Luxurious (USA)
1^{8sd} 9^{8gs} 6^{10gf} **1-0-3 £5,200**

Music By Mozart *P W Chapple-Hyam* a70
2 b c Mozart (Ire) - Dayville (USA)
3^{6sd} **0-1-1 £575**

Music Note (Ire) *M R Channon* 80
2 b c Indian Ridge - Samara Middle East (Fr)
10^{6g} 2^{8gf} 2^{8g} 1^{8g} **1-2-4 £6,921**

Music Teacher *N A Callaghan* 63 a56
3 ch f Piccolo - Duena
3^{5gf} 8^{6g} 3^{5gf} 12^{6gf} 9^{7sd} 11^{6gf} 7^{6sd} 9^{7sd} 7^{6sd} **0-2-9 £1,177**

Musical City *B Smart* 44 a44
2 ch f City On A Hill (USA) - Royal Musical
11^{6gf} 8^{6f} 14^{6gf} 13^{7gf} 3^{6sd} **0-1-5 £215**

Musical Day *B J Meehan* 43
3 ch f Singspiel (Ire) - Dayville (USA)
10^{8gs} 10^{10g} **0-0-2**

Musical Echo *Julian Poulton* 67
2 b f Distant Music (USA) - Distant Music
5^{7gf} 4^{7gf} **0-0-2 £278**

Musical Fair *J A Glover* 80
5 b m Piccolo - Guarded Expression
6^{5g} 4^{5gf} 3^{5gf} 3^{6gf} 10^{5gf} 6^{5gf} 9^{6gf} 18^{5gs} 6^{5g} BD^{5g} 12^{5gf} **0-3-11 £2,815**

Musical Gift *P A Blockley* 46 a65
5 ch g Cadeaux Genereux - Kazoo
2^{5sd} 6^{7sd} 2^{7sd} 4^{9sd} 7^{9sd} 5^{7gs} 9^{10g} 9^{9sd} 7^{8sd}

3^{9sd} 3^{9sd} 5^{7sd} **0-4-12 £2,758**

Musical Guest (Ire) *M R Channon* 85 a68
2 b g Mozart (Ire) - Hoh Dear (Ire)
7^{6gf} 6^{6gf} 2^{6f} 6^{6gf} 6^{7gf} 4^{6g} 1^{6g} 4^{7sd} 3^{6gf} 3^{7gs} 1^{6gf} 2^{7g} 5^{6g} 3^{6gs} 11^{7gs} 18^{7s} **2-3-16 £12,714**

Musical High (Ire) *R Hannon* 77
2 b f Mozart (Ire) - Blew Her Top (USA)
4^{5g} 1^{6gf} 6^{6g} 11^{6gf} **1-0-4 £6,355**

Musical Romance (Ire) *B J Meehan* 63 a63
2 b f Mozart (Ire) - Dear Girl (Ire)
3^{5g} 14^{6gs} 3^{5gs} 7^{5gf} 2^{5sd} 9^{7sf} **0-2-6 £2,516**

Musical Shares *J A Geake* 24
4 ch g Piccolo - Ring Of Love
13^{8g} 11^{10gs} **0-0-2**

Musicanna *J R Fanshawe* 108
4 b f Cape Cross (Ire) - Upend
1^{8g} 1^{8s} 1^{8s} 3^{8gs} **3-1-4 £57,323**

Musicmaestroplease (Ire) *S Parr* a51
2 b c Rossini (USA) - Who Told Vicky (Ire)
12^{6sd} 6^{6sd} **0-0-2**

Musiotal *P A Blockley* 59 a57
4 ch g Pivotal - Bemuse
3^{6gs} 3^{6gs} 8^{8s} 2^{6g} 8^{6s} 8^{6gf} 4^{7g} 13^{6g} 6^{6s} 2^{6gf} 9^{6gf} 2^{6sf} 3^{7sd} 5^{7ss} **0-6-14 £3,733**

Mussorgsky (USA) *Sir Michael Stoute* 3 a39
2 b c Stravinsky (USA) - Mimbet (USA)
13^{7s} 6^{7sd} **0-0-2**

Must Be Magic *H J Collingridge* 10 a57
8 b g Magic Ring (Ire) - Sequin Lady
3^{9sd} 10^{10sd} 11^{9sd} 9^{10gs} 12^{10sd} **0-1-5 £415**

Must Be So *J J Bridger* a45
4 b f So Factual (USA) - Ovideo
9^{7sd} 6^{10sd} 11^{8sd} 9^{8sd} **0-0-4**

Mustajed *B R Millman* 90
4 b g Alhaarth (Ire) - Jasarah (Ire)
13^{8g} 14^{7gf} 6^{8gf} 2^{10g} 1^{10gf} 3^{10gs} 2^{10g} 3^{12gs} 11^{11gf} 1^{12gf} **2-4-10 £25,180**

Mustakhlas (USA) *B P J Baugh* 54 a42
4 ch g Diesis - Katiba (USA)
9^{9sd} 7^{8sd} 5^{9sd} 8^{9sd} 6^{11g} 9^{12sd} 12^{9sd} **0-0-7**

Mustang Ali (Ire) *Dr J R J Naylor* 57 a62
4 ch g Ali-Royal (Ire) - Classic Queen (Ire)
4^{12sd} 7^{12sd} 8^{10sd} 8^{12gf} 3^{12sd} 14^{12g} 1^{12f} 9^{12g} 4^{12g} 8^{14g} 4^{12sd} 3^{12sd} **1-3-12 £3,951**

Mustang Lil *M Wigham* a51
4 b f Mark Of Esteem (Ire) - Quivira
8^{5sd} 8^{5sd} **0-0-2**

Mustapha Kip (Ire) *Miss J R Tooth*
3 b g Bold Edge - Arusha (Ire)
8^{10s} 13^{9sd} **0-0-2**

Mustgodowntothesea (Ire) *F J Bowles* 42 a15
3 ch f Raise A Grand (Ire) - Rainery (Ire)
11^{5sh} 14^{7s} 14^{7s} 10^{6g} 9^{8f} 13^{6gf} 9^{10gf} 9^{5sh} 11^{6sd} **0-0-9**

Mutajammel (Fr) *Sir Michael Stoute* 75
3 b g Kingmambo (USA) - Irtifa
15^{7g} 8^{10gf} **0-0-2**

Mutamaasek (USA) *Lady Herries* 63
3 b/br g Swain (Ire) - Tamgeed (USA)
6^{8g} 13^{10s} **0-0-2**

Mutamared (USA) *K A Ryan* 96
5 ch g Nureyev (USA) - Alydariel (USA)
4^{7gs} 6^{8g} 1^{6gf} 13^{6g} 1^{6g} 15^{6s} **2-0-6 £15,190**

Mutamarres *Sir Michael Stoute* 86
2 b c Green Desert (USA) - Injaad
3^{7g} 2^{7gf} 1^{7s} 3^{7g} **1-3-4 £10,185**

Mutarafaa (USA) *D Shaw* a38
6 b g Red Ransom (USA) - Mashaarif (USA)
3^{6sd} 8^{7sd} 6^{6sd} 7^{7sd} **0-1-4 £185**

Mutared (Ire) *N P Littmoden* a57
7 b g Marju (Ire) - Shahaada (USA)
1^{8sd} 4^{8ss} 3^{8sd} **1-1-3 £1,695**

Mutassem (Fr) *E F Vaughan* 64 a62
4 b g Fasliyev (USA) - Fee Eria (Fr)
6^{6sd} 3^{6sd} 4^{8sd} 1^{7sd} 2^{7s} 1^{7sd} 3^{8sd} **2-3-7 £4,592**

Mutawaffer *R A Fahey* 106
4 b g Marju (Ire) - Absaar (USA)
4^{6gs} 22^{7gf} 8^{7gs} 5^{6gf} 17^{6gs} 7^{6gs} 8^{8s} 10^{8g} **0-1-8 £1,174**

Mutawajid (Ire) *R Hannon* 100
2 b c Zafonic (USA) - Zeiting (Ire)
2^{6gf} 2^{6g} 1^{6gs} 6^{6gs} 4^{6g} 7^{6gf} **1-2-6 £19,252**

Mutawaqed (Ire) *M A Magnusson* 85
7 ch g Zafonic (USA) - Waqood (USA)
9^{6gf} 19^{6gs} 15^{7g} 21^{6gs} **0-0-4**

Mutayam *D A Nolan* 55
5 b g Compton Place - Final Shot
15^{6gs} 16^{5gf} 9^{5g} 5^{5gf} 15^{5g} 11^{5g} 6^{5g} 14^{5gf} **0-0-8**

Muy Bien *J R Jenkins* a28
4 ch c Daggers Drawn (USA) - Primula Bairn
11^{6sd} 7^{7sd} **0-0-2**

Muzdaher (Ire) *M Johnston* 89
3 b c Danzig (USA) - Horatia (Ire)
2^{8gf} 2^{8gf} 1^{7gf} 2^{7gf} 5^{7gf} 1^{8gf} 10^{8gs} **2-3-7 £18,266**

Muzdaherha *G A Butler* 76 a40
3 ch f Entrepreneur - Guilty Secret (Ire)
12^{10gs} 6^{9sd} 10^{8g} 2^{10gf} 7^{10gf} 10^{12sd} 5^{8gs} 2^{10gf} 1^{12g} 15^{10s} **1-2-10 £5,880**

Muzher (Ire) *B W Hills* 81
2 ch c Indian Ridge - Almurooj
7^{7gf} 2^{6g} **0-1-2 £1,744**

Muzio Scevola (Ire) *M R Channon* a38
4 ch g Titus Livius (Fr) - Dancing Sunset (Ire)
8^{12sd} **0-0-1**

My *J Noseda* 62
2 b f King's Best (USA) - Maskunah (Ire)
8^{6gf} 6^{6gs} 7^{5g} 11^{6gs} **0-0-4**

My Amalie (Ire) *C E Brittain* 90
2 b f Galileo (Ire) - Princess Amalie (USA)
4^{6gf} 6^{6g} 7^{8gf} **0-0-3 £1,420**

My Boo *T Keddy* 59 a45
3 b f Sri Pekan (USA) - Malwiya (USA)
8^{8gf} 4^{7sd} 9^{7f} 7^{12gf} 11^{10g} 11^{12sd} 8^{9sd} 9^{17sd} 9^{12sd} 1^{12sd} **1-0-10 £1,405**

My Diss Sire *E A L Dunlop* 73 a53
3 b c Vettori (Ire) - Never Diss Miss
3^{8f} 3^{8g} 7^{10gf} 4^{8f} 15^{8gf} 9^{9sd} **0-2-6 £1,610**

My Dream (Ire) *S Kirk* 33 a44
3 b f King's Theatre (Ire) - Dream Chaser
10^{6sd} 10^{8g} 19^{7gf} **0-0-3**

My Gacho (Ire) *T D Barron* 79 a78

3 b g Shinko Forest (Ire) - Floralia
$1^{6sd}\ 4^{6sd}\ 1^{6sd}\ 7^{6g}\ 2^{6gf}\ 2^{6gf}\ 3^{6g}\ 5^{6g}\ 4^{6gf}\ 12^{5gs}$
$6^{6sd}\ 2^{6sd}\ 5^{6sd}$ **2-4-13 £17,602**

My Galliano (Ire) *B G Powell* 71 a49
9 b g Muharib (USA) - Hogan Stand
$9^{10sd}\ 6^{12gf}\ 1^{10g}\ 6^{12g}$ **1-0-4 £4,018**

My Girl Pearl (Ire) *M S Saunders* 57 a52
5 b m Sri Pekan (USA) - Desert Bloom (Fr)
$4^{7sd}\ 10^{7sd}\ 16^{7gs}\ 9^{6f}\ 9^{6gf}\ 8^{5sd}\ 8^{7gf}\ 8^{7g}\ 1^{6gf}$
$2^{6gf}\ 15^{6gs}\ 13^{7sd}\ 1^{7sd}\ 9^{7ss}$ **2-1-14**
£5,966

My Immortal *M C Pipe* 92 a78
3 b c Monsun (Ger) - Dame Kiri (Fr)
$3^{12s}\ 2^{12sd}\ 3^{12gf}\ 1^{14s}\ 1^{16gf}\ 10^{15gs}$ **2-3-6**
£12,691

My Lady Valentine *P Winkworth* 53
2 b f Bahamian Bounty - Laser Light Lady
$9^{5g}\ 7^{5s}\ 1^{5f}\ 7^{6g}\ 7^{5gf}\ 7^{6f}$ **1-0-6 £3,347**

My Last Bean (Ire) *M R Bosley* a22
8 gr g Soviet Lad (USA) - Meanz Beanz
12^{17sd} **0-0-1**

My Legal Eagle (Ire) *E G Bevan* 71 a50
11 b g Law Society (USA) - Majestic Nurse
$6^{14sd}\ 7^{17sd}\ 6^{15gs}\ 3^{16s}\ 2^{14gs}\ 2^{14g}\ 6^{16gf}\ 8^{18g}$
$7^{14g}\ 3^{15gf}\ 5^{13gf}\ 6^{14gf}\ 5^{14gf}\ 12^{14gf}\ 11^{14gs}\ 4^{16gf}$
$7^{16gf}\ 8^{17sf}$ **0-4-18 £3,587**

My Lilli (Ire) *P Mitchell* 19 a55
5 b m Marju (Ire) - Tamburello (Ire)
$6^{8sd}\ 8^{10sd}\ 1^{7sd}\ 8^{8sd}\ 2^{10sd}\ 3^{8sd}\ 11^{8sd}\ 5^{10sd}$
$4^{7sd}\ 15^{8gf}\ 12^{7g}\ 4^{9sf}\ 1^{10sd}$ **2-2-13**
£3,956

My Lovely Lady (Ire) *M L W Bell* 65
2 b f Cape Cross (Ire) - Lace Flower
$13^{8g}\ 4^{8g}$ **0-0-2 £356**

My Maite (Ire) *R Ingram* a48
6 b g Komaite (USA) - Mena
9^{9sd} **0-0-1**

My Michelle *B Palling* 64 a38
4 b f Ali-Royal (Ire) - April Magic
$2^{7gs}\ 1^{7s}\ 6^{7gf}\ 3^{8hy}\ 8^{8sf}$ **1-1-5 £5,769**

My Obsession (Ire) *John Berry* 68
3 b g Spectrum (Ire) - Little Love
$3^{6s}\ 3^{6g}$ **0-2-2 £1,249**

My Only Sunshine *M J Wallace* 74 a66
6 b g First Trump - Fiveofive (Ire)
$11^{6sd}\ 4^{5gs}\ 6^{6gs}\ 2^{6s}\ 7^{5gf}\ 13^{6g}\ 2^{6gs}\ 12^{6g}\ 9^{6g}$
0-2-9 £2,505

My Paris *K A Ryan* 109
4 b g Paris House - My Desire
$20^{8g}\ 5^{7gf}\ 2^{8gs}\ 4^{10s}\ 6^{8gf}\ 16^{7gs}\ 1^{7g}\ 12^{8gf}\ 1^{8s}$
3^{9s} **2-2-10 £56,700**

My Pension (Ire) *P Howling* 50 a76
4 b g Orpen (USA) - Woodenitbenice (USA)
$7^{9sd}\ 1^{10sd}\ 9^{10sd}\ 6^{10sd}\ 18^{10gf}\ 10^{9sd}\ 14^{8g}\ 14^{10g}$
$4^{9sd}\ 6^{8sd}\ 10^{9sd}\ 7^{9sd}$ **1-0-12 £3,653**

My Petra *A King* 73
2 b f Midnight Legend - Lac Marmot (Fr)
$3^{8gs}\ 2^{8s}$ **0-2-2 £1,812**

My Place Or Yours *Miss Gay Kelleway* a32
3 gr f Tagula (Ire) - Absalla (Ire)
10^{7sd} **0-0-1**

My Precious Girl (Ire) *Miss Z C Davison*
3 b f Charnwood Forest (Ire) - Sea Glen (Ire)
$13^{10sd}\ 9^{12gf}$ **0-0-2**

My Princess (Ire) *N A Callaghan* 88
3 b f Danehill Dancer (Ire) - Shanoora (Ire)
$10^{8g}\ 5^{7gf}\ 1^{8f}\ 6^{8gf}\ 3^{8gs}\ 3^{9g}\ 1^{8g}\ 9^{7g}$
2-0-8 £18,554

My Putra (USA) *P F I Cole* 73
3 b/br c Silver Hawk (USA) - Petite Triomphe (USA)
$4^{11gs}\ 2^{12gf}$ **0-1-2 £1,910**

My Rascal (Ire) *J Balding* 61
3 b g Imperial Ballet (Ire) - Derena (Fr)
$11^{8g}\ 6^{6gf}\ 7^{6gf}\ 1^{6g}\ 11^{5s}$ **1-0-5 £3,684**

My Reflection *D Shaw* a22
2 b g Cape Cross (Ire) - There's Two (Ire)
$14^{7s}\ 9^{6hy}\ 8^{6sd}$ **0-0-3**

My Vee Tee (Ire) *Mrs P N Dutfield* 36 a11
3 b g Orpen (USA) - Zabeta
$10^{11g}\ 10^{11gs}\ 11^{8g}\ 12^{7gf}\ 12^{7g}\ 12^{5sd}$
0-0-6

Myannabanana (Ire) *Derek Kane* 54 a11
4 ch g Woodborough (USA) - Raging Storm
$11^{11sd}\ 9^{9sd}\ 7^{12g}$ **0-0-3**

Mycenean Prince (USA) *R C Guest* 49
2 b c Swain (Ire) - Nijinsky's Beauty (USA)
$11^{6gf}\ 7^{6g}\ 12^{7g}$ **0-0-3**

Mykeyta *J G Given* 32
2 b f Key Of Luck (USA) - Mylania
$8^{5f}\ 9^{6g}\ 16^{6gf}$ **0-0-3**

Mynd *R M Whitaker* 67 a66
5 b g Atraf - Prim Lass
$4^{5sd}\ 7^{5sd}\ 9^{5sd}\ 6^{5gs}\ 1^{5hy}\ 4^{6s}\ 7^{5gs}\ 7^{5g}\ 5^{5g}\ 7^{5ft}$
$2^{5s}\ 7^{6sd}\ 5^{5sd}$ **1-1-13 £4,778**

Myrtle Bay (Ire) *K R Burke* 73 a75
2 bl c Pennekamp (USA) - Moneypenny (Ger)
$5^{7gs}\ 3^{7g}\ 2^{8sd}\ 12^{8gf}$ **0-2-4 £1,539**

Mysteriosa *M L W Bell* 46 a54
3 b f Mujahid (USA) - Mrs Gray
$9^{9sd}\ 10^{8sd}\ 2^{7sd}\ 11^{8g}\ 10^{10gf}$ **0-1-5 £826**

Mystery Lot (Ire) *A King* 86
3 b f Revoque (Ire) - Mystery Bid
$1^{10s}\ 4^{10gs}\ 2^{10gf}\ 9^{11gs}\ 4^{10s}\ 8^{10hy}$ **1-1-6**
£7,456

Mystery Pips *N Tinkler* 57 a51
5 b m Bin Ajwaad (Ire) - Le Shuttle
$2^{5sd}\ 3^{5sd}\ 1^{5sd}\ 9^{5sd}\ 13^{5gf}\ 8^{5sd}\ 7^{5gf}\ 2^{5gf}\ 2^{5gf}$
$5^{5f}\ 1^{5gf}\ 2^{5sd}\ 13^{5sd}$ **2-5-13 £7,230**

Mystic Forest *Miss J A Camacho* a27
6 b g Charnwood Forest (Ire) - Mystic Beauty (Ire)
$10^{14ft}\ 12^{17sd}$ **0-0-2**

Mystic Lad *Jamie Poulton* 44 a78
4 gr g Magic Ring (Ire) - Jilly Woo
$3^{7sd}\ 4^{10sd}\ 3^{8sd}\ 1^{8sd}\ 9^{8sd}\ 9^{8g}\ 13^{8gf}\ 11^{8gf}\ 3^{8sd}$
1-3-9 £5,564

Mystic Man (Fr) *K A Ryan* 87 a87
7 b g Cadeaux Genereux - Shawanni
$11^{8gs}\ 8^{7s}\ 4^{7gs}\ 10^{8gf}\ 2^{8gf}\ 10^{8gf}\ 1^{7gf}\ 4^{7g}\ 1^{7gf}$
$5^{8gf}\ 2^{8gf}\ 11^{7g}\ 1^{7sd}\ 3^{7ft}\ 14^{7g}\ 1^{6sd}\ 2^{7sd}$
4-3-17 £23,555

Mystic Mountain *P D Niven*
2 b g Monashee Mountain (USA) - Mystic Memory
15^{7s} **0-0-1**

Mystic Mover *N A Callaghan*
2 b f Danehill Dancer (Ire) - Kaguyahime
11^{6gf} **0-0-1**

Mystic Promise (Ire) *Mrs N Macauley*
4 gr g Among Men (USA) - Ivory's Promise
$14^{12sd}\ 11^{7g}\ 12^{8sd}$ **0-0-3**

Mystic Queen (Ire) *A P Jarvis* 18 a34
2 b f Woodborough (USA) - Speed Queen (Ire)

11^{6gf} 6^{6sd} **0-0-2**

Mystic Roll *B J Meehan* 74 a43
2 br c Medicean - Pain Perdu (Ire)
7^{7f} 3^{8g} 8^{7sd} **0-1-3 £670**

Mystic Storm *Lady Herries* 48 a60
2 b g Medicean - Mrs Nash
10^{7gf} 9^{7sd} **0-0-2**

Mystical Ayr (Ire) *Miss L A Perratt* 69
3 br f Namid - Scanno's Choice (Ire)
4^{6gf} 7^{5g} 6^{5gf} 2^{7g} 1^{8s} 1^{8s} 2^{7hy} **2-2-7 £8,711**

Mystical Land (Ire) *J H M Gosden* 104
3 b c Xaar - Samsung Spirit
1^{5g} 6^{5g} **1-0-2 £5,205**

Mystified (Ire) *R F Fisher* 62 a62
2 b g Raise A Grand (Ire) - Sunrise (Ire)
3^{7gf} 5^{7g} 5^{7gf} 1^{7gf} 8^{8gf} 8^{8g} 3^{7g} 8^{7sf} 8^{9sd} 2^{9sd} **1-3-10 £5,424**

Mytass *J A Pickering* 48 a48
2 b g Averti (Ire) - Emerald Dream (Ire)
8^{5hy} 5^{6f} 5^{7f} 8^{6gf} 3^{7f} 7^{8gf} 6^{7g} 20^{8g} 9^{7gf} 9^{7g} 11^{7g} 5^{7ss} 8^{7sd} 6^{9sd} 8^{9sd} **0-1-15 £421**

Mythical Charm *J J Bridger* 65 a58
6 b m Charnwood Forest (Ire) - Triple Tricks (Ire)
5^{10sd} 6^{10g} 4^{8sd} 6^{7s} 4^{7f} 9^{6g} 7^{9s} 2^{10f} 1^{8gs} 1^{8gf} 6^{8f} 10^{8g} 9^{9gf} 13^{10gf} 7^{7gs} 3^{8gs} 11^{10sd} 1^{10sd} 2^{8sd} 7^{7sd} **3-3-20 £11,216**

Mythical King (Ire) *R Lee* 59
8 b g Fairy King (USA) - Whatcombe (USA)
9^{18g} 3^{18g} 2^{15gf} 8^{16gf} 7^{16gf} **0-2-5 £2,055**

Mythical River *J J Quinn* 44 a30
2 b f Mujahid (USA) - Stygian (USA)
11^{6g} 7^{5gs} 8^{6g} 5^{6sd} **0-0-4**

Myths And Verses *T D Easterby* 62
2 b f Primo Valentino (Ire) - Romantic Myth
2^{5g} 7^{5gf} 6^{5s} 6^{5gf} 3^{5gf} 2^{5gf} 4^{6gf} 7^{6gf} 2^{6gf} 5^{6gf} **0-4-10 £4,430**

Mytori *D Shaw* 37
3 ch f Vettori (Ire) - Markievicz (Ire)
7^{6gf} 9^{6gf} 10^{8g} 12^{7ss} **0-0-4**

Mytton's Bell (Ire) *A Bailey* 64 a61
3 b f Bold Edge - Ionian Secret
9^{9sd} 11^{6sd} 2^{5sd} 3^{5gs} 5^{5s} 2^{5gs} 7^{5g} 7^{6g} 3^{7g} 1^{6sd} 11^{5g} 16^{7gf} 1^{7sd} 18^{6hy} 11^{9sd} 13^{7sd} **2-4-16 £7,843**

Mytton's Dream *R Brotherton* 56 a56
3 br f Diktat - Courtisane
2^{7sd} 5^{7sd} 6^{6sd} 1^{7sd} 2^{7sd} 5^{8g} 5^{8gf} 10^{8g} 14^{8gf} 16^{7gf} 12^{7sd} 10^{7sd} 5^{7sf} **1-2-13 £4,037**

Mytton's Pride *A Bailey* 66 a34
2 b g Tagula (Ire) - Pictina
6^{5gf} 9^{5gs} 1^{5g} 11^{5gf} 5^{5gf} 12^{5g} 12^{5g} 10^{5sd} **1-0-8 £12,064**

Na Bac Leis *R Johnson* a50
5 ch g Bijou D'Inde - Risk The Witch
6^{14sd} 4^{12sd} **0-0-2 £257**

Nabir (Fr) *P D Niven* a74
5 gr g Linamix (Fr) - Nabagha (Fr)
8^{14sf} 6^{11sd} 5^{12sd} **0-0-3**

Nadira (Ire) *E A L Dunlop* 53
3 b f Nashwan (USA) - Doomna (Ire)
11^{8g} 6^{10gf} **0-0-2**

Naemi (Ger) *S L Keightley* a22
3 b f Tannenkonig (Ire) - Noanah (Ger)
8^{9sd} **0-0-1**

Nahaar (Ire) *M P Tregoning* 60
2 b g Royal Applause - Elhida (Ire)
8^{6gf} 6^{6g} **0-0-2**

Naheef (Ire) *Saeed Bin Suroor* 100
6 b g Marju (Ire) - Golden Digger (USA)
10^{10gs} 5^{12g} **0-0-2 £700**

Naivety *G G Margarson* 62 a49
3 ch f Machiavellian (USA) - Innocence
4^{10f} 9^{10gf} 6^{10g} 9^{8gf} 8^{9g} 9^{10g} 7^{10hy} 8^{12ss} 13^{10sd} 10^{10sd} 7^{10sd} 9^{10sd} **0-0-12 £323**

Najaaba (USA) *Miss J Feilden* 85 a90
5 b m Bahhare (USA) - Ashbilya (USA)
8^{9sd} 7^{8sd} 1^{7sd} 6^{10sd} 4^{8gs} 5^{8g} 2^{7g} 6^{8g} 8^{7g} **1-1-9 £10,871**

Najeebon (Fr) *M R Channon* 89
6 ch g Cadeaux Genereux - Jumairah Sun (Ire)
1^{6s} 6^{6g} 5^{6g} 3^{6f} 4^{6gf} 9^{6gf} 7^{6g} 2^{6gf} 11^{6gs} 4^{6g} 2^{6g} 9^{6gs} 12^{7gf} 5^{6g} 16^{6gs} **1-3-15 £13,843**

Nakatani (Ire) *Mrs A V Roberts*
3 b g Raphane (USA) - Cnocma (Ire)
10^{8s} **0-0-1**

Nakheel *M Johnston* 109
2 b c Sadler's Wells (USA) - Matiya (Ire)
1^{8gf} 1^{8gs} **2-0-2 £23,940**

Nakwa (Ire) *E J Alston* 59
7 b g Namaqualand (USA) - Cajo (Ire)
8^{12s} 9^{14g} PU^{14gs} **0-0-3**

Namat (Ire) *W Jarvis* 86
4 b f Daylami (Ire) - Masharik (Ire)
1^{10gs} 1^{12gf} 7^{12gf} 4^{12gf} 15^{12g} **2-0-5 £11,312**

Namathej *E A L Dunlop* 84
3 ch f Halling (USA) - Badaayer (USA)
4^{8gf} 1^{9gs} 2^{11gf} 2^{10gf} 2^{10gf} 4^{10gf} 5^{10gs} **1-3-7 £11,502**

Named At Dinner *Miss Lucinda V Russell* 7
4 ch g Halling (USA) - Salanka (Ire)
13^{11gs} **0-0-1**

Namid Drive (Ire) *J S Wainwright* 32 a15
3 b c Namid - Daniella Drive (USA)
18^{6g} 8^{6s} 7^{7gf} 5^{7gf} 14^{7gf} 5^{6g} 11^{6sd} 14^{7sd} **0-0-8**

Namid Reprobate (Ire) *P F I Cole* 78
2 br c Namid - Morning Surprise
6^{7gf} 5^{5g} 1^{6g} 1^{6s} **2-0-4 £11,032**

Namir (Ire) *Stef Liddiard* 89 a66
3 b g Namid - Danalia (Ire)
2^{6g} 1^{5s} 1^{5gs} 3^{5gf} 7^{5gf} 8^{5gf} 12^{5g} 14^{5g} 18^{5hy} 16^{5s} 4^{6sd} 11^{6sd} 6^{6sd} 12^{5sd} **2-2-14 £18,724**

Namking *C W Thornton* a50
3 b g Namid - Kingdom Queen (Ire)
6^{9sd} 7^{7sd} **0-0-2**

Namoos (USA) *J L Dunlop* 66
2 b/br f Sahm (USA) - Shuhrah (USA)
3^{6g} **0-0-1 £745**

Namroc (Ire) *E F Vaughan* 92
4 b g Indian Ridge - Hesperia
4^{8gf} 6^{8g} 7^{10gf} 4^{10gf} 8^{12gs} 11^{10g} **0-1-6 £1,828**

Namroud (USA) *R A Fahey* 88 a83
6 b g Irish River (Fr) - Top Line (Fr)
6^{6g} 1^{7s} 2^{7gs} 6^{7g} 1^{8g} 6^{8g} 10^{8gf} 6^{8g} 13^{8g} 1^{8hy} 9^{8sd} **3-1-11 £30,419**

Namu *B W Hills* 72
2 b f Mujahid (USA) - Sheraton Heights
7^{6gs} 2^{6gs} 6^{5g} 2^{7gf} 3^{7gf} 2^{6gf} 2^{6hy} **0-5-7**
£5,848

Nan Jan *R Ingram* 57 a81
3 b f Komaite (USA) - Dam Certain (Ire)
7^{10sd} 1^{7sd} 9^{7gf} 8^{7gs} 8^{6gf} 6^{7gf} 2^{7sd} 1^{6ss} 1^{6sd}
5^{7sd} 9^{9sd} **3-1-11 £12,632**

Nan Scurry (Fr) *J Noseda* 64
3 b f Danehill (USA) - Prends Ca (Ire)
13^{7gf} 2^{6g} 3^{6gf} 2^{6gf} 3^{6f} **0-4-5 £3,578**

Nanna (Ire) *R Hollinshead* 44
4 b f Danetime (Ire) - Pre Catelan
6^{6g} 8^{5g} 14^{5gf} **0-0-3**

Nannina *J H M Gosden* 114
2 b f Medicean - Hill Hopper (Ire)
1^{6gf} 5^{6g} 3^{6gf} 1^{7g} 1^{8g} **3-1-5 £136,353**

Nanton (USA) *P F I Cole* 90
3 gr/ro g Spinning World (USA) - Grab The Green (USA)
5^{10gs} 5^{10gf} 2^{10gf} 3^{10gf} 1^{8gf} 1^{8gf} 3^{8gs} 9^{9g} 3^{9gf}
1^{9gf} 10^{9gs} **3-3-11 £18,664**

Nantucket Sound (USA) *P Howling* 59 a74
4 b g Quiet American (USA) - Anna
11^{13sd} 6^{11sd} 7^{12sd} 3^{12sd} 6^{12sd} 7^{10s} 7^{10gf} 6^{10gf}
9^{13gf} 2^{11g} 4^{16g} 8^{11gf} 7^{16gs} 15^{16gf} 10^{14gf} 3^{12sd}
7^{12sd} 6^{10g} **0-3-18 £1,743**

Nantyglo *M L W Bell* 103
2 b f Mark Of Esteem (Ire) - Bright Halo (Ire)
4^{6gs} 1^{6gf} 2^{6g} 3^{7gf} 3^{6gf} 9^{7gs} **1-3-6**
£18,520

Napapijri (Fr) *W G M Turner* 7
3 gr f Highest Honor (Fr) - Les Marettes (Fr)
18^{12gs} 11^{9sd} 12^{7gf} **0-0-3**

Naqi *W J Haggas* 65
2 ch f Cadeaux Genereux - Farha (USA)
5^{5gf} 4^{5gf} 2^{5gs} 4^{5gs} **0-1-4 £1,907**

Narciso (Ger) *M W Easterby* a51
5 ch g Acatenango (Ger) - Notturna
2^{17sd} **0-1-1 £424**

Narvik (Ire) *M A Jarvis* 86
2 ch c Galileo (Ire) - Arctic Hunt (Ire)
1^{7g} **1-0-1 £4,959**

Nashaab (USA) *P D Evans* 97
8 b g Zafonic (USA) - Tajannub (USA)
14^{8gf} 6^{8g} 9^{8gf} 13^{10gs} 3^{7gf} 3^{7gf} 4^{9gf} 11^{7gf}
8^{8gf} 4^{8gf} 9^{10gf} 11^{8gf} 4^{9g} 7^{8g} 15^{8g}
0-3-15 £7,156

Nasheej (USA) *R Hannon* 108
2 b f Swain (Ire) - El Nafis (USA)
1^{7g} 3^{7gf} 1^{7g} 1^{8gf} 3^{8g} **3-1-5 £92,661**

Nassau Street *D J S Ffrench Davis* 22
5 gr g Bahamian Bounty - Milva
5^{8g} 11^{10f} 8^{10gf} **0-0-3**

Nassiria *C E Brittain* 38 a67
4 b f Singspiel (Ire) - Naskhi
8^{8gs} 12^{12sd} **0-0-2**

Nastrelli (Ire) *Sir Michael Stoute* 63
2 b c Mozart (Ire) - Dawnsio (Ire)
8^{7gf} **0-0-1**

Natalie Jane (Ire) *G A Butler* 107 a82
3 ch f Giant's Causeway (USA) - Kirk
4^{10sd} 1^{10gf} 3^{12gf} 2^{12gs} 5^{12gf} 10^{10s} **1-2-6**
£25,520

Nathan Detroit *P J Makin* 39 a42
5 b g Entrepreneur - Mainly Sunset
10^{8sd} 12^{9sd} 4^{7sd} 11^{7gf} 11^{7gf} **0-0-5**

Nation State *G L Moore* a68
4 b c Sadler's Wells (USA) - Native Justice (USA)
5^{13sd} **0-0-1**

National Dress *Sir Mark Prescott* 34 a47
2 b f Singspiel (Ire) - National Treasure
6^{6sd} 8^{6gf} 9^{6sd} 14^{7sd} **0-0-4**

National Trust *Sir Michael Stoute* 97
3 b c Sadler's Wells (USA) - National Treasure
4^{10g} 1^{10gs} 5^{12gf} 11^{12s} 4^{12gf} 11^{15gs} **1-0-6**
£6,671

Native American *M A Jarvis* 73
3 b g Indian Lodge (Ire) - Summer Siren (Fr)
1^{10s} 12^{12gs} 5^{10gf} **1-0-3 £5,655**

Native Tiptoes *Miss Gay Kelleway* 56
2 b f Arkadian Hero (USA) - Waltham Skylark
9^{6s} 13^{6s} **0-0-2**

Native Title *D Nicholls* 94
7 b g Pivotal - Bermuda Lily
2^{5g} 4^{5g} 27^{6gf} 6^{5gs} 10^{6gf} 4^{6g} 4^{5g} 5^{5gf} 11^{5s}
14^{6gs} 13^{6g} **0-3-11 £9,680**

Natural Force (Ire) *Saeed Bin Suroor* 76 a90
2 b c King's Best (USA) - Wolf Cleugh (Ire)
4^{6gs} 3^{7g} 1^{8gf} 1^{8sd} **2-1-4 £8,898**

Naughty By Nature *Sir Michael Stoute* 68
2 b g Machiavellian (USA) - Rumpipumpy
5^{7gf} 6^{8gf} 4^{8g} **0-0-3 £350**

Naughty Girl (Ire) *John A Harris* 54 a40
5 b m Dr Devious (Ire) - Mary Magdalene
7^{7sd} 9^{9sd} 11^{6sd} 11^{7sd} 14^{7g} 1^{8g} **1-0-6**
£1,512

Naughty Nod (Ire) *K R Burke* 67
2 b g Intikhab (USA) - Quelle Celtique (Fr)
3^{6f} 9^{6g} 11^{5g} 10^{7gf} 3^{8g} 4^{10g} 12^{8s} **0-3-7**
£3,025

Nautical *A W Carroll* 79 a76
7 gr g Lion Cavern (USA) - Russian Royal (USA)
8^{8gf} 2^{7g} 2^{6gf} 2^{6gf} 1^{6g} 2^{6gf} 4^{7gf} 12^{6gs} 8^{5g}
7^{6gf} 6^{9sd} **1-5-11 £10,655**

Nautico *Miss L A Perratt* 40
2 ch f Compton Place - Sabre Lady
5^{6g} 7^{6gs} **0-0-2**

Navajo Warrior (Ire) *T D Easterby* 27
2 b c Namid - Nassma (Ire)
11^{7gs} 11^{8gs} **0-0-2**

Naval Attache *P A Blockley* a51
3 b g Slip Anchor - Cayla
11^{14sf} 2^{9sd} 3^{7sd} **0-2-3 £633**

Naval Force *Ian Williams* 44 a71
3 b g Forzando - Barsham
9^{7sd} 4^{10sd} 7^{12g} 1^{8sd} 17^{10g} 7^{12f} **1-0-6**
£3,148

Navigation (Ire) *T J Etherington* 71
3 ch g Bahamian Bounty - Bridge Pool
4^{6f} 2^{5gf} 5^{5gf} 11^{6g} 5^{6g} 1^{6f} 6^{5g} 6^{5g} 4^{5s}
1-1-9 £4,842

Nawaadi *M P Tregoning* 78
2 b g Intikhab (USA) - Elhilmeya (Ire)
4^{6g} 6^{8gs} **0-0-2 £288**

Nawamees (Ire) *G L Moore* 93 a93
7 b g Darshaan - Truly Generous (Ire)
8^{10sd} 15^{12g} 9^{11gf} 2^{12gs} 2^{16sd} **0-2-5**
£6,816

Nawaqees *J L Dunlop* 76
2 b c Danehill (USA) - Elrafa Ah (USA)

7^{6gf} 4^{6g} 6^{6gf} 1^{7hy} 3^{8g} 5^{8s} **1-1-6 £8,614**

Nawayea *M P Tregoning* 66 a70
2 b f Lujain (USA) - Shallat (Ire)
3^{5sd} 4^{6g} **0-1-2 £846**

Nawow *P D Cundell* 72 a79
5 b g Blushing Flame (USA) - Fair Test
1^{13sd} 8^{12sd} 3^{16sd} 4^{12sd} 3^{14gs} 5^{14g} 4^{14gf} **1-2-7 £6,071**

Nayyir *G A Butler* 121
7 ch g Indian Ridge - Pearl Kite (USA)
3^{7g} 4^{8s} 6^{7g} 4^{7g} **0-1-4 £23,750**

Nazaaha (USA) *A G Newcombe* 66 a59
3 gr f Elnadim (USA) - Taatof (Ire)
4^{6gf} 3^{6g} 10^{7g} 2^{7sd} **0-1-4 £1,921**

Ndola *B J Curley* 51 a51
6 b g Emperor Jones (USA) - Lykoa
1^{11sd} 13^{10sd} 1^{10g} **2-0-3 £2,940**

Ne Oublie *J Mackie* 51
3 b c Makbul - Parkside Prospect
11^{6g} 3^{5f} 8^{5gs} UR^{5gs} **0-0-4 £413**

Neardown Beauty (Ire) *I A Wood* 60 a64
2 br f Bahhare (USA) - Habla Me (Ire)
3^{7sd} 8^{8gf} 2^{7g} 3^{8g} 5^{8sd} 5^{7sd} **0-3-6 £2,111**

Neardown Bishop *I A Wood*
3 b g Imperial Ballet (Ire) - Firedancer
12^{12g} **0-0-1**

Neardown Maid *I A Wood* 24 a18
2 b f Bertolini (USA) - Edgeaway
10^{6sd} 9^{7g} **0-0-2**

Nearly A Fool *P Howling* a65
7 b g Komaite (USA) - Greenway Lady
8^{7sd} 7^{9sd} 6^{7sd} 10^{8sd} 3^{8sd} 6^{8sd} **0-1-6 £377**

Nebraska City *D W Thompson* 49 a47
4 b g Piccolo - Scarlet Veil
14^{10sd} 4^{6gf} 8^{8gf} 9^{6f} 7^{5gs} 5^{7g} 3^{7sd} 4^{8sd} **0-2-8 £213**

Neckar Valley (Ire) *Miss J E Foster* 72
6 b g Desert King (Ire) - Solar Attraction (Ire)
5^{12gs} 2^{12s} 8^{13gs} 6^{10gf} 9^{11gf} 9^{12g} 6^{12g} 15^{16g} **0-1-8 £1,233**

Ned Ludd (Ire) *R Hannon* 81
2 b c Montjeu (Ire) - Zanella (Ire)
5^{6f} 2^{7gf} 8^{7gf} 5^{8g} **0-1-4 £1,528**

Nee Lemon Left *A Berry* 35 a21
3 b f Puissance - Via Dolorosa
7^{5sd} 8^{5gs} 8^{7gf} 14^{5sd} 13^{6ft} 14^{8sd} **0-0-6**

Needwood Scot *C N Kellett* 63
4 b g Danzig Connection (USA) - Needwood Nymph
10^{7g} 3^{10g} 6^{10g} 9^{9gf} **0-1-4 £537**

Neferura *E S McMahon* 51 a27
3 b f Mister Baileys - Boadicea's Chariot
6^{8g} 10^{7sd} 15^{8g} 8^{8gf} 16^{5gf} 10^{5gf} 6^{7g} 7^{8s} 6^{12f} 6^{16sd} 9^{9sd} **0-0-11**

Nefski Alexander (USA) *P F I Cole* 64
2 b c Minardi (USA) - Reluctant Guest (USA)
9^{7gf} **0-0-1**

Negas (Ire) *J Howard Johnson* 55
3 b g Titus Livius (Fr) - Alzeam (Ire)
4^{8gf} 11^{8gf} **0-0-2**

Neideen (Ire) *R M Beckett* 67
3 ch f Elnadim (USA) - Mynador (USA)
3^{7gf} 2^{7gf} 4^{7gf} 4^{7g} **0-2-4 £2,254**

Neil's Legacy (Ire) *Miss L A Perratt* 55 a32
3 br f Second Empire (Ire) - Eliade (Ire)
6^{8sd} 6^{11gf} 8^{8gf} 5^{12g} 12^{13s} 1^{10s} 6^{9hy} **1-0-7 £3,406**

Nell Tupp *G Woodward* 55
2 b g Killer Instinct - Eternal Triangle (USA)
14^{6g} 13^{6gf} 3^{6g} **0-0-3 £658**

Nelson (Pol) *P J Hobbs* 17
3 ch g Fourth Of June (USA) - Neustria (Pol)
10^{8g} **0-0-1**

Nelsons Column (Ire) *G M Moore* 76
2 b g Benny The Dip (USA) - Sahara Rose
2^{6g} 2^{6gf} 2^{8gs} 3^{9g} 6^{10g} **0-4-5 £3,875**

Nemetona *Lady Herries* 49
3 b f Zieten (USA) - Golconda (Ire)
10^{8g} **0-0-1**

Nemo Fugat (Ire) *P J Hassett* 64
6 b g Danehill Dancer (Ire) - Do The Right Thing
7^{6gf} 3^{6s} 3^{7g} 5^{7g} 13^{8g} 15^{6gf} 11^{9g} 6^{7s} 3^{7sd} 14^{5g} **0-3-10 £1,194**

Neon Blue *R M Whitaker* 76 a50
4 b/br g Atraf - Desert Lynx (Ire)
8^{7s} 6^{7gs} 11^{7gf} 16^{7g} 9^{7gf} 1^{6gf} 1^{7gf} 3^{7g} 13^{7gf} 9^{7sd} **2-1-10 £10,928**

Nepal (Ire) *M Mullineaux* 63
3 ch f Monashee Mountain (USA) - Zetonic
2^{8s} 8^{8gs} 4^{8gf} 9^{8g} 12^{7gf} **0-1-5 £1,436**

Nephetriti Way (Ire) *P R Chamings* 77 a77
4 b f Docksider (USA) - Velvet Appeal (Ire)
3^{6g} 5^{6gf} 3^{6gf} 3^{6gf} 12^{6gs} 8^{6g} 1^{7sd} 7^{7sd} **1-0-8 £7,457**

Nepro (Ire) *E J Creighton* 61
3 b c Orpen (USA) - My Gray (Fr)
6^{8g} 9^{8g} 3^{8g} 2^{8sd} 2^{8sd} 2^{8sd} 2^{6sd} 7^{5gf} **0-0-8 £16,935**

Neptune *J C Fox* a48
9 b g Dolphin Street (Fr) - Seal Indigo (Ire)
8^{16sd} 8^{12sd} 5^{13sd} 5^{12sd} 8^{16sd} 3^{12sd} 7^{14sd} 2^{12sd} 5^{12sd} 7^{13sd} **0-2-10 £631**

Nero's Return (Ire) *M Johnston* 98
4 b g Mujadil (USA) - Snappy Dresser
1^{8gs} 7^{7s} 4^{8g} 2^{8g} 3^{9g} 5^{9gf} 7^{10f} 4^{8g} 7^{10g} 3^{10gs} 12^{8gs} 10^{11gf} 9^{9g} 1^{9gf} 10^{10gf} 22^{9s} 10^{10g} 3^{8hy} **2-5-18 £39,844**

Nerone (Ger) *P Monteith* 49
4 gr g Sternkoenig (Ire) - Nordwahl (Ger)
9^{16gf} 10^{12gs} 15^{12s} **0-0-3**

Nesno (USA) *J D Bethell* 80
2 ch c Royal Academy (USA) - Cognac Lady (USA)
3^{7s} 4^{7gf} 3^{7g} 14^{8s} **0-2-4 £1,375**

Nessen Dorma (Ire) *J G Given* 95
4 b g Entrepreneur - Goldilocks (Ire)
7^{13gs} 8^{14s} 1^{12s} 4^{16g} 2^{12gf} 4^{14gf} 2^{12gf} 4^{12g} 2^{12gs} 5^{12gs} 8^{12s} 6^{12hy} 13^{12hy} **1-5-13 £16,416**

Nettlebed *G L Moore* a40
2 b f Averti (Ire) - Rash Gift
8^{7sd} **0-0-1**

Networker *K G Reveley* 24
2 ch g Danzig Connection (USA) - Trevorsninepoints
12^{6gf} 15^{6g} **0-0-2**

Neutral Night (Ire) *T G McCourt* 71 a18
5 b m Night Shift (USA) - Neutrality (Ire)
9^{7sd} 11^{8sd} 6^{10g} 5^{8gf} 5^{10f} 6^{8f} 4^{7g} 7^{8gf} 3^{5g} 8^{6sd} **0-1-10 £685**

Neutrino *L M Cumani* 81

3 b g Mtoto - Fair Seas
8^{12g} 1^{10gs} 7^{11gf} 4^{10gf} 2^{12g} 7^{12gs} 7^{12g}
1-2-7 £5,885

Nevada Desert (Ire) *R M Whitaker* 83 a88
5 b g Desert King (Ire) - Kayanga
9^{10sd} 1^{8s} 5^{10gf} 4^{8g} 2^{8gf} 5^{8gf} 6^{8g} 5^{8g} 3^{10gf} 4^{7gf} 4^{10gf} 9^{8gs} 8^{10gf} 3^{9gs} 1^{9sd} 5^{9sd} 8^{9sf}
2-3-17 £19,974

Neven *Miss Lucinda V Russell* 39
6 b g Casteddu - Rose Burton
14^{7gs} 10^{7gf} 6^{8gf} 7^{8gf} 10^{13gf} **0-0-5**

Never Away *N A Callaghan* 44 a54
3 b f Royal Applause - Waypoint
12^{6s} 6^{9sd} 9^{8f} 17^{7f} 3^{10f} 5^{10f} 12^{12g} 3^{8sd}
0-2-8 £635

Never Forget Bowie *R Allan* 48 a41
9 b g Superpower - Heldigvis
9^{9sd} 11^{9sd} 11^{8sd} 12^{12sd} 12^{9gf} 8^{13gf} 4^{8gf} 12^{8gf} 5^{9gf} 3^{8gf} **0-1-10 £440**

Never Promise (Fr) *C Roberts*
7 b m Cadeaux Genereux - Yazeanhaa (USA)
14^{8sd} **0-0-1**

Never Say Deya *M R Channon* 55
2 b f Dansili - Dream On Deya (Ire)
15^{6gf} 4^{7s} 11^{8g} **0-0-3 £262**

Never Without Me *J F Coupland* 67 a8
5 ch g Mark Of Esteem (Ire) - Festival Sister
11^{5hy} 4^{6g} 6^{5f} 16^{5gf} 9^{5gf} 12^{5gf} 10^{5gs} 7^{5gf} 4^{5gf} 6^{5g} 11^{5g} 1^{5gs} 3^{6gf} 4^{5g} 12^{5sd} **1-3-15 £5,917**

Neverletme Go (Ire) *G Wragg* 86
3 b f Green Desert (USA) - Cassandra Go (Ire)
1^{5gf} 2^{5gf} 1^{5gf} 4^{6g} **2-1-4 £16,518**

Nevinstown (Ire) *C Grant* 62 a58
5 b g Lahib (USA) - Moon Tango (Ire)
1^{6sd} 2^{6gf} 10^{6sd} 13^{8sd} 12^{8sd} **1-1-5 £2,301**

Nevsky Bridge *D McCain* 55 a47
3 b f Soviet Star (USA) - Pontressina (USA)
6^{10f} 7^{8g} 9^{9sd} 11^{8s} 3^{8sd} 2^{12sd} **0-2-6 £797**

New Art (USA) *J Noseda* 92
2 br c Gone West (USA) - Sopran Mariduff
6^{5gf} 1^{5f} 1^{6gf} 3^{6g} **2-1-4 £19,560**

New Blood (Ire) *J M Bradley* 21
2 b c Beckett (Ire) - Utmost (Ire)
10^{6gs} 9^{5f} 12^{7gs} 13^{6gf} **0-0-4**

New Day Dawning *C Smith* a22
4 ch f First Trump - Tintinara
6^{7sd} 8^{7sd} **0-0-2**

New England *W M Brisbourne* 59 a55
3 ch g Bachir (Ire) - West Escape
10^{7gs} 7^{7f} 6^{8gf} 8^{8gs} 10^{8gf} 8^{9sd} 5^{7sd} 6^{7sd} 1^{9ss}
1-0-9 £1,481

New Girlfriend (Ire) *Robert Collet* 114
2 b f Diesis - New Story (USA)
1^{5g} 1^{6g} 5^{6s} **2-0-3 £72,277**

New Guinea *M A Jarvis* 59
2 b c Fantastic Light (USA) - Isle Of Spice (USA)
10^{8gf} **0-0-1**

New Journey (Ire) *H J Collingridge* 35
3 b g Cape Cross (Ire) - Desert Skimmer (USA)
12^{7gs} 9^{6g} **0-0-2**

New Morning (Ire) *M A Jarvis* 112
4 b f Sadler's Wells (USA) - Hellenic
1^{10gf} 4^{10gf} 7^{10g} **1-0-3 £34,319**

New Options *Peter Grayson* 55 a63
8 b g Formidable (USA) - No Comebacks
3^{5gf} 3^{5sd} 17^{5gf} 10^{6gf} 5^{5g} 4^{5gs} 5^{6gf} 1^{5sd} 6^{5gf} 5^{5gf} 6^{5gf} 5^{5ft} 8^{5sd} **1-2-13 £3,368**

New Proposal (Ire) *A P Jarvis* 57
3 b g Orpen (USA) - Woodenitbenice (USA)
9^{8gs} 11^{7g} 7^{6gf} **0-0-3**

New Realm (USA) *H J Collingridge* 68 a65
3 b g Red Ransom (USA) - Mystery Rays (USA)
6^{10sd} 3^{10gf} 9^{10g} 7^{12sd} 15^{8f} **0-0-5 £521**

New Seeker *C G Cox* 118
5 b g Green Desert (USA) - Ahbab (Ire)
2^{8g} 6^{8gs} 9^{7g} 1^{8gf} 1^{7gf} 3^{8gf} 1^{7gf} 3^{7g} 9^{7gs}
3-3-9 £196,090

New South Wales *Saeed Bin Suroor* 104
5 b h In The Wings - Temora (Ire)
1^{12g} **1-0-1 £9,430**

New Wave *C F Wall* 69 a76
3 b g Woodman (USA) - Vanishing Point (USA)
4^{7sd} 2^{7sd} 3^{7sd} 8^{8gs} 4^{7g} 10^{8g} **0-2-6 £2,258**

New Wish (Ire) *S B Clark* 56 a55
5 b g Ali-Royal (Ire) - False Spring (Ire)
13^{8s} 4^{7sd} 4^{9sd} 6^{7sd} 5^{9sd} 13^{11g} 3^{6g} 4^{8gf} 12^{7g} 3^{9sd} 5^{8sd} 10^{6g} **0-3-12 £818**

Newcastles Owen (Ire) *R Johnson*
2 b g Elnadim (USA) - Brittas Blues (Ire)
11^{7s} **0-0-1**

Newcorp Lad *Mrs G S Rees* 61 a51
5 b g Komaite (USA) - Gleam Of Gold
11^{8s} 11^{8g} 8^{9f} 11^{9gf} 11^{8gf} 9^{10g} 13^{9gf} 1^{8g} 6^{9g} 11^{9gf} 7^{12sd} **1-0-11 £3,532**

Newkeylets *I Semple* 49
2 b f Diktat - Jay Gee Ell
6^{6s} 5^{5gf} 4^{6gs} 11^{6s} **0-0-4 £285**

Newnham (Ire) *J R Boyle* 76 a77
4 ch g Theatrical - Brief Escapade (Ire)
9^{10g} 3^{10gf} 4^{12sd} 7^{12gf} 6^{12gs} 2^{12sd} 2^{12sd}
0-4-7 £3,161

Newport Boy (Ire) *R Hannon* 19
2 b c Montjeu (Ire) - Dream Chaser
14^{6gf} **0-0-1**

Newsround *D W Chapman* a57
3 ch g Cadeaux Genereux - Ring The Relatives
13^{6sd} 11^{6sd} **0-0-2**

Newtonian (USA) *J Parkes* 24 a75
6 ch g Distant View (USA) - Polly Adler (USA)
2^{12sd} 1^{12sd} 4^{12sd} 17^{12g} 11^{14gs} 5^{12sf} **1-1-6 £4,894**

Newtown Villa *C E Brittain* 47
3 b f Spectrum (Ire) - New Abbey
8^{11gs} 9^{12g} **0-0-2**

Next Flight (Ire) *R E Barr* 57 a36
6 b g Woodborough (USA) - Sans Ceriph (Ire)
9^{16g} 2^{16gs} 5^{14gf} 3^{16sd} 1^{13s} 11^{14gf} **1-1-6 £4,168**

Next Ness (Ire) *R F Fisher* 55
2 b g Indian Lodge (Ire) - Fauna (Ire)
4^{5g} 11^{6sd} 4^{6gf} 9^{6gf} PU^{6sd} 4^{7hy} **0-0-6 £1,324**

Next Time (Ire) *M J Polglase* 14 a49
3 b f Danetime (Ire) - Muckross Park
10^{6sd} 9^{5sd} 8^{5sd} 3^{5sd} 5^{5sd} 9^{5g} **0-0-6 £634**

Ngauruhoe (Ire) *John Berry* 47
3 b f Desert Sun - Snowcap (Ire)
7^{6gf} 5^{6gf} 11^{8gf} 14^{6gf} 6^{8s} 7^{7g} 5^{11g} **0-0-7**

Nice Tune *C E Brittain* 83 a82
3 b f Diktat - Military Tune (Ire)
9^{8gs} 5^{7f} 4^{6gf} 1^{7gf} 11^{8gf} 6^{9s} 5^{7g} 6^{8gf} 5^{8g} 2^{8sd} 4^{10sd} 2^{8sd} **1-2-12 £7,868**

Nicholas Nickelby *M J Polglase* a60
5 gr g Fayruz - Alasib
2^{8sd} 9^{6sd} **0-1-2 £734**

Niciara (Ire) *M C Chapman*
8 b g Soviet Lad (USA) - Verusa (Ire)
18^{16gs} **0-0-1**

Nick's Nikita (Ire) *S Kirk* 73
2 ch f Pivotal - Elaine's Honor (USA)
8^{7g} 3^{7g} 10^{7gf} 5^{8g} **0-1-4 £1,022**

Nico's Girl *M W Easterby* 51 a49
2 ch f Mark Of Esteem (Ire) - Naskhi
2^{5sd} 4^{5gf} 6^{5gf} 2^{5sd} 12^{6g} 10^{6sd} 4^{7gf} 10^{7g} 4^{7gf} 13^{7sd} 6^{9sd} 8^{7sd} 6^{9sd} **0-2-13 £1,850**

Nicozetto (Fr) *N Wilson* 50
5 b g Nicolotte - Arcizette (Fr)
9^{12gs} 9^{8g} 8^{9g} 3^{11g} 14^{10gs} **0-1-5 £399**

Nidhaal (Ire) *E A L Dunlop* 104
2 ch f Observatory (USA) - Jeed (Ire)
1^{6gs} 2^{6gf} 1^{6gf} 5^{6g} **2-1-4 £40,774**

Nietzsche (Ire) *R J Hodges* 65
4 b c Sadler's Wells (USA) - Wannabe
5^{8g} 12^{10s} 7^{10gf} 10^{12gf} 12^{8g} **0-0-5**

Nifty Major *N E Berry* a28
8 b g Be My Chief (USA) - Nifty Fifty (Ire)
7^{5sd} 14^{5ss} 12^{5sd} **0-0-3**

Nifty Roy *I McMath*
5 b g Royal Applause - Nifty Fifty (Ire)
10^{8sd} 15^{17f} **0-0-2**

Nigella *E S McMahon* 85 a75
2 b f Band On The Run - Yabint El Sham
5^{5g} 1^{5sd} 2^{5gf} 6^{5gf} 6^{6gf} 4^{5gf} 2^{5g} **1-2-7 £36,693**

Night Air (Ire) *J J Quinn* 98 a101
4 b g Night Shift (USA) - Pippas Song
1^{7sd} 1^{8sd} 1^{9sd} 16^{8gf} 8^{7gf} 11^{7gf} PU^{9sd} **3-0-7 £42,601**

Night Cap (Ire) *T D McCarthy* a47
6 ch g Night Shift (USA) - Classic Design
4^{7sd} **0-0-1**

Night Club *B Smart* 54
2 b f Mozart (Ire) - Dance By Night
9^{6gf} 5^{7gf} 8^{7gs} **0-0-3**

Night Crescendo (USA) *Mrs A J Perrett* 82 a85
2 b/br c Diesis - Night Fax (USA)
6^{7gf} 3^{7gf} 1^{8sd} **1-1-3 £4,544**

Night Cru *C F Wall* 72
2 b g Night Shift (USA) - Jouet
7^{6gf} 5^{7gs} 3^{7g} 9^{7gs} **0-1-4 £760**

Night Explosion (Ire) *D J S Ffrench Davis* 25 a45
7 ch g Night Shift (USA) - Voodoo Rocket
12^{7sd} 4^{8sd} 9^{9sd} 17^{10g} 14^{8g} 6^{7sd} **0-0-6**

Night Groove (Ire) *N P Littmoden* 63 a64
2 b c Night Shift (USA) - Taysala (Ire)
13^{6gf} 7^{6g} 7^{8s} 5^{7gs} 14^{6g} 7^{9sd} 1^{9sd} 11^{8sd} 10^{9sd} **1-0-9 £2,893**

Night Guest (Ire) *R E Barr*
3 b g Danehill Dancer (Ire) - Meadow Grass (Ire)
11^{7gf} **0-0-1**

Night Hour (Ire) *M P Tregoning* 95
3 b c Entrepreneur - Witching Hour (Ire)
6^{12gs} 4^{10gf} **0-0-2 £1,699**

Night In (Ire) *D R Loder* 75 a72
2 b g Night Shift (USA) - Sherannda (USA)
3^{6sd} 1^{5g} **1-1-2 £4,830**

Night Of Joy (Ire) *M A Jarvis* 79
3 b f King's Best (USA) - Gilah (Ire)
10^{9gf} 8^{8g} 9^{8g} **0-0-3**

Night Out (Fr) *G C Bravery* 49
3 b f Night Shift (USA) - My Lucky Day (Fr)
8^{8g} 15^{10g} 9^{8gf} 13^{10sd} PU^{8gs} 16^{8hy} **0-0-6**

Night Pearl (Ire) *E J Alston* a37
4 b f Night Shift (USA) - Miss Pickpocket (Ire)
9^{5sd} **0-0-1**

Night Prospector *G L Moore* 102 a90
5 b g Night Shift (USA) - Pride Of My Heart
9^{5gf} 3^{5gs} 11^{5gf} 9^{5sd} 6^{5s} 11^{5gf} 11^{5s} 9^{5g} 17^{5gs} 3^{6gs} 10^{6sd} **0-2-11 £4,814**

Night Rainbow (Ire) *A J Lidderdale* 58 a56
2 ch f Night Shift (USA) - Teresita
9^{7g} 5^{7gf} 3^{6sd} 8^{7sd} **0-1-4 £914**

Night Reveller (Ire) *M C Chapman* 33 a5
2 b f Night Shift (USA) - Tir-An-Oir (Ire)
10^{7gf} 8^{5g} 9^{5g} 10^{7gf} 9^{5g} 15^{7g} 7^{5gf} 7^{6gf} 12^{7gf} 13^{6g} 9^{7sd} **0-0-11**

Night Sight (USA) *Mrs S Lamyman* 75 a67
8 b g Eagle Eyed (USA) - El Hamo (USA)
5^{10g} 4^{10gf} 11^{12gf} 2^{10gf} 4^{12g} 6^{12gf} 2^{10g} 2^{16g} 11^{12g} 6^{16gf} 7^{12gf} 3^{17sd} 5^{14ss} 4^{14sd} **0-4-14 £7,652**

Night Spot *R Charlton* 89
4 ch g Night Shift (USA) - Rash Gift
4^{10gs} 10^{10s} 4^{10g} 2^{12g} 19^{12gs} 6^{12gf} 2^{10gf} 5^{10g} 13^{10gf} **0-4-9 £11,593**

Night Storm *S Dow* 67 a69
4 b f Night Shift (USA) - Monte Calvo
11^{7sd} 8^{7sd} 7^{7sd} 9^{8sd} 6^{6sd} 5^{6sd} 1^{6sd} 5^{7sd} 10^{6sd} 8^{6gf} 13^{6gf} 9^{7sd} 8^{6gf} 6^{6gf} 1^{7g} 1^{8hd} 9^{7f} 2^{8g} 3^{8gf} 8^{7sd} 1^{10sd} 4^{9sd} **4-2-22 £13,576**

Night Warrior (Ire) *N P Littmoden* 49 a58
5 b g Alhaarth (Ire) - Miniver (Ire)
12^{10sd} 8^{13sd} 12^{10sd} 6^{10gf} 6^{13gs} 8^{10g} 5^{12f} 3^{12sd} 4^{14sd} 11^{14g} 9^{11sd} 1^{8sd} 1^{12ss} 5^{10sd} 2^{9ss} **2-2-15 £3,485**

Night Wolf (Ire) *Jamie Poulton* 61 a64
5 gr g Indian Ridge - Nicer (Ire)
4^{8sd} 1^{8f} 5^{8gf} 4^{8sd} 17^{8gf} 2^{7f} 9^{8f} 1^{8f} 5^{7sd} **2-1-9 £8,358**

Nightfall (USA) *Saeed Bin Suroor* 47
3 b c Rahy (USA) - Quality Gift
10^{6g} **0-0-1**

Nightwing *Miss Gay Kelleway* 34 a61
3 b g Lujain (USA) - Rasmalai
6^{7sd} 8^{7sd} 6^{9sd} 9^{8hy} 13^{8g} 9^{9sd} 12^{10gf} 10^{10sd} 12^{7sd} **0-0-9**

Nihal (Ire) *M Johnston* 82
2 b f Singspiel (Ire) - Katie McLain (USA)
4^{6gf} 4^{7gs} 1^{7g} 1^{7gf} 8^{8gf} **2-0-5 £21,047**

Nikita Sunrise (Ire) *E J Alston* a2
3 ch f Namid - Shun
9^{7sd} 8^{6sd} **0-0-2**

Nikki Bea (Ire) *Jamie Poulton* a48
2 ch f Titus Livius (Fr) - Strong Feeling (USA)
4^{7sd} **0-0-1 £276**

Nilsatisoptimum (USA) *M Mullineaux* 59 a43
2 ch c Gilded Time (USA) - Fluid Emotion (USA)
8^{7s} 8^{7gf} 5^{7g} 7^{5sd} **0-0-4**

Nimble Star *C W Fairhurst* 31 a34
2 b f Foxhound (USA) - Deerlet
12^{5g} 6^{6gf} 6^{5gf} 7^{5sd} 11^{6gf} **0-0-5**

Nimello (USA) *A G Newcombe* 67 a87
9 b g Kingmambo (USA) - Zakota (Ire)
7^{9sd} 6^{8sd} 1^{9sd} 3^{10gs} 7^{7sd} 1^{9sd} 13^{9gs} 9^{7sd} 11^{9sd}
2^{8sd} 7^{9sd} **2-2-11 £7,527**

Nimrana Fort *J L Dunlop* 65
2 b c Indian Ridge - Ninotchka (USA)
13^{7gf} 11^{7gs} 4^{7s} **0-0-3 £254**

Nina Fontenail (Fr) *B R Millman* 67 a49
4 gr f Kaldounevees (Fr) - Ninon Fontenail (Fr)
2^{10sd} 2^{12g} 1^{12gf} 2^{13gs} 1^{12gf} 2^{12gf} 8^{14gs}
2-4-7 £9,235

Ninah *J M Bradley* 49
4 b f First Trump - Alwal
9^{6g} 4^{10f} 8^{8g} 8^{7gf} 5^{10g} 2^{8hd} 3^{8f} 14^{8f} 4^{7g} 11^{8g}
0-2-10 £1,000

Ninja Storm (Ire) *G L Moore* 46 a49
3 b g Namid - Swan Lake (Ire)
8^{6sd} 8^{5s} 9^{5f} 6^{5gf} 14^{5sd} 9^{6sd} **0-0-6**

Ninth House (USA) *D J Daly* 81 a59
3 b c Chester House (USA) - Ninette (USA)
3^{10gf} 9^{10s} 1^{9sd} **1-1-3 £3,664**

Niobe *B Smart* 68
2 ch f Pivotal - Notturna
1^{5gf} 12^{6gs} **1-0-2 £5,541**

Niobe's Way *P R Chamings* 71 a14
4 b f Singspiel (Ire) - Arietta's Way (Ire)
6^{12gf} 5^{14gf} 11^{14g} 9^{14gs} 2^{14s} 6^{18gf} 13^{14sd}
0-1-7 £963

Nipping (Ire) *Robert Collet* 110
3 b f Night Shift (USA) - Zelda (Ire)
11^{6hy} 5^{5s} 5^{5g} 2^{5g} 2^{6g} 1^{5gs} 10^{5gf} 1^{5g} 15^{5gs}
10^{5gf} **2-2-10 £66,207**

Nisr *Miss Gay Kelleway* 72 a53
8 b g Grand Lodge (USA) - Tharwa (Ire)
3^{6s} 5^{6g} 3^{6gf} 5^{7gf} 5^{6g} 5^{6g} 7^{5sd} 4^{7sf} 11^{7sd}
4^{7sd} 2^{8sd} 4^{10sd} **0-3-12 £1,342**

Nistaki (USA) *T D Easterby* 78
4 ch c Miswaki (USA) - Brandywine Belle (USA)
15^{8s} 11^{8g} 8^{8g} 6^{6gf} 8^{6f} 9^{6gf} 1^{6g} 2^{6g}
1-1-8 £6,063

Niteowl Lad (Ire) *J Balding* 84
3 ch g Tagula (Ire) - Mareha (Ire)
17^{6gf} 10^{5g} 3^{5gf} 6^{5g} 1^{5gf} 6^{5gs} 1^{5gf} 1^{5g}
3-1-8 £17,839

Nivelle *R Hannon* 81
2 b f Imperial Ballet (Ire) - Funny Wave
5^{5gf} 1^{5gf} 5^{6gf} 2^{5g} 10^{5gf} 14^{5gf} 8^{5g} **1-1-7**
£6,258

Nivernais *H Candy* 82
6 b g Forzando - Funny Wave
5^{6s} 10^{6gs} 4^{6g} 14^{5gf} 6^{6gf} 5^{6gs} **0-0-6**
£557

No Commission (Ire) *R F Fisher* 61 a67
3 b g General Monash (USA) - Price Of Passion
5^{7sd} 3^{7sd} 10^{7sd} 4^{7gf} 3^{9sd} 7^{8gf} 8^{9gf} 10^{7sd} 8^{7f}
9^{11gf} 14^{6g} 7^{6gf} 13^{8gf} **0-2-13 £1,562**

No Girls Allowed *D Shaw* 17
5 ch g Cotation - Marcroft
13^{5gf} 12^{7sd} **0-0-2**

No Grouse *E J Alston* 76 a69
5 b g Pursuit Of Love - Lady Joyce (Fr)
1^{7gf} 11^{7gs} 7^{6sd} 1^{6gf} 3^{7gs} 8^{6gs} 8^{7gf} 8^{7g} 6^{7gf}
13^{7g} 5^{7sd} 9^{6sd} 9^{7sd} **2-1-13 £12,158**

No Inkling (Ire) *M J Attwater* 44 a44
2 b f Xaar - No Tippling (Ire)
13^{6g} 10^{7gf} 14^{7g} 9^{6s} 9^{5sd} 5^{5sd} **0-0-6**

No Mercy *M P Muggeridge*
9 ch g Faustus (USA) - Nashville Blues (Ire)
12^{7sd} 9^{8sd} 15^{12sd} **0-0-3**

No Overtime (Ire) *M D I Usher* 51
2 b f Danetime (Ire) - Mulling It Over (Ire)
9^{5g} 10^{5gf} 6^{5gf} 4^{5gf} 2^{5f} 1^{5g} 9^{5gf} 12^{6sf}
1-1-8 £4,128

No Time (Ire) *M J Polglase* 75 a91
5 b h Danetime (Ire) - Muckross Park
8^{6sd} 2^{5sd} 7^{5sd} 4^{6sd} 5^{6sd} 9^{5gf} **0-1-6**
£5,009

Noah Jameel *A G Newcombe* 64
3 ch c Mark Of Esteem (Ire) - Subtle One (Ire)
2^{7gs} **0-1-1 £1,135**

Nobbler *J W Hills* 64 a48
3 br g Classic Cliche (Ire) - Nicely (Ire)
10^{12g} 2^{12gs} 7^{14gf} 8^{12sd} 5^{16gs} 5^{16g} 4^{18gf} 5^{16g}
12^{17gs} **0-1-9 £1,081**

Nobelix (Ire) *J R Fanshawe* 77 a58
3 gr g Linamix (Fr) - Nataliana
4^{8sd} 10^{8gs} 6^{10s} 4^{8gf} 4^{10gf} 2^{10g} 3^{10g} 1^{11s} 3^{12gs}
3^{12g} **1-5-10 £8,190**

Nobelmann (Ger) *A W Carroll* a1
6 ch g Lomitas - Ninova (Ger)
11^{8sd} **0-0-1**

Noble Calling (Fr) *R J Hodges* 40
8 b g Caller I.D. (USA) - Specificity (USA)
9^{12gf} **0-0-1**

Noble Duty (USA) *Saeed Bin Suroor* 48
3 b c Dubai Millennium - Nijinsky's Lover (USA)
14^{10g} **0-0-1**

Noble Edge *P A Blockley* 54 a54
2 ch g Bold Edge - Noble Soul
10^{5g} 7^{5hy} 7^{6gf} 2^{6g} 2^{5gf} 4^{6gf} 4^{5s} 9^{7ss} 6^{7sd}
1^{9sd} **1-2-10 £4,719**

Noble Future *E F Vaughan* 79 a72
3 b g Averti (Ire) - Gold Luck (USA)
4^{7gf} 2^{10sd} 2^{8gs} 4^{12sd} 1^{8g} 6^{10g} **1-2-6**
£6,504

Noble Gent (Ire) *Saeed Bin Suroor* 84
2 b c Danehill (USA) - Blanche Dubois
3^{7gs} 1^{7gf} 4^{8g} **1-1-3 £5,944**

Noble Locks (Ire) *J W Unett*
7 ch g Night Shift (USA) - Imperial Graf (USA)
11^{7sd} **0-0-1**

Noble Mind *P G Murphy* 37 a69
4 b g Mind Games - Lady Annabel
3^{12sd} 2^{12sd} 13^{14sd} 9^{12gf} 15^{12gs} 10^{12sd}
0-2-6 £1,555

Noble Minstrel *S C Williams* 29 a60
2 ch c Fantastic Light (USA) - Sweetness Herself
12^{7gf} 7^{6sd} **0-0-2**

Noble Mount *A B Haynes* 59 a59
4 b g Muhtarram (USA) - Our Poppet (Ire)
4^{6sd} 8^{6sd} 8^{7sd} 4^{6g} 10^{6g} 1^{5gf} 3^{5g} 19^{6gf} 6^{6sd}
9^{7sd} 7^{6sd} 7^{6sd} **1-2-12 £3,968**

Noble Nova *M R Channon* 60
2 br f Fraam - Noble Destiny

5^{6gf} 5^{6f} 3^{5gf} 4^{7gf} 7^{6gf} 7^{6f} 1^{6gs} 4^{7gf} 6^{7gf}
13^{7gs} **1-0-10 £3,541**

Noble Pasao (Ire) *N G Richards* 57
8 b g Alzao (USA) - Belle Passe
9^{12gs} **0-0-1**

Noble Pursuit *R E Barr* 37 a44
8 b g Pursuit Of Love - Noble Peregrine
7^{8sd} 5^{9sd} 6^{9f} 4^{10gf} 4^{10s} 12^{14gf} **0-0-6**

Nocatee (Ire) *P C Haslam* 25 a51
4 b g Vettori (Ire) - Rosy Sunset (Ire)
3^{16sd} 10^{16gs} **0-1-2 £409**

Nod's Star *Mrs L C Jewell* 42
4 ch f Starborough - Barsham
6^{12s} **0-0-1**

Nodina *S C Williams* 62 a59
3 gr g Primo Dominie - Princess Tara
5^{7gf} 5^{7gf} 7^{6gf} 5^{6sd} 12^{7gf} 6^{7gf} **0-0-6**

Nojoom (Ire) *E A L Dunlop* 46
2 b f Alhaarth (Ire) - Elauyun (Ire)
8^{7gs} 7^{7g} **0-0-2**

Nona *Jedd O'Keeffe* 57
2 ch f Halling (USA) - Zarma (Fr)
11^{7gf} 8^{8gs} 8^{7s} **0-0-3**

Nona's Lass *C N Kellett* a23
8 b m Clantime - Festive Lassie
7^{12sd} 11^{10gs} 13^{13sd} **0-0-3**

Noora (Ire) *C G Cox* 81
4 ch f Bahhare (USA) - Esteraad (Ire)
5^{9gf} 9^{10gf} 4^{8gf} 7^{8g} 1^{8gf} 4^{8gf} 1^{10gf} **2-0-7**
£10,770

Noorain *Stef Liddiard* 52 a52
3 ch f Kabool - Abeyr
13^{8g} 15^{6hy} 8^{7gs} 10^{7gf} 15^{7gf} 3^{7f} 7^{7gf} 5^{9sd}
8^{10gf} 2^{9sd} 2^{8sd} 6^{7f} 1^{8sd} 3^{8sd} 10^{7sd}
1-4-15 £2,898

Nopekan (Ire) *Mrs K Waldron* 56
5 b g Sri Pekan (USA) - Giadamar (Ire)
10^{16gf} **0-0-1**

Nopleazinu *Unknown*
5 ch m Sure Blade (USA) - Vado Via
11^{9sd} **0-0-1**

Nor'Wester *J R Fanshawe* 69 a60
3 br g Inchinor - Princess Nawaal (USA)
7^{7sd} 6^{8g} 2^{7gf} **0-1-3 £1,136**

Norcroft *Mrs C A Dunnett* 78 a76
3 b g Fasliyev (USA) - Norcroft Joy
7^{8sd} 18^{6hy} 2^{6sd} 2^{6g} 10^{7gf} 11^{6f} 2^{6sd} 1^{6gf} 2^{8sd}
6^{7gf} 11^{5g} 8^{5g} 2^{6sd} 14^{6g} 1^{6sd} 6^{6sd} **2-5-16**
£14,396

Nordwind (Ire) *W R Swinburn* 96
4 b g Acatenango (Ger) - Narola (Ger)
4^{12f} 6^{14g} 16^{12f} 8^{12g} **0-0-4 £1,454**

Norman Beckett *M R Channon* 69 a64
2 b g Beckett (Ire) - Classic Coral (USA)
3^{6gf} 12^{6gf} 4^{6gf} 1^{7f} 5^{7gs} 3^{6g} 7^{7gs} 10^{8sd}
1-1-8 £5,339

Norman Norman *W S Kittow* a53
3 b g Double Trigger (Ire) - Nour El Sahar (USA)
8^{12sd} 9^{10sd} 10^{12sd} 4^{10sd} 8^{10sd} **0-0-5**

Norse Dancer (Ire) *D R C Elsworth* 125
5 b h Halling (USA) - River Patrol
1^{9gf} 5^{8g} 5^{11gy} 6^{10gf} 2^{12gf} 5^{10g} 8^{10gy} 11^{12gs}
11^{12gf} **1-1-9 £204,543**

North Fleet *J M Bradley*
2 b g Bertolini (USA) - Rhiann
8^{5gf} **0-0-1**

North Light (Ire) *Sir Michael Stoute* 121
4 b c Danehill (USA) - Sought Out (Ire)
2^{10gf} **0-1-1 £11,000**

North Point (Ire) *Derek Kane* 24
7 b g Definite Article - Friendly Song
11^{12sd} 8^{8f} **0-0-2**

North Shore (Ire) *R Hannon* 80
3 b c Soviet Star (USA) - Escape Path
4^{8g} 4^{8gs} 4^{9g} 8^{9gf} 3^{7g} 3^{7gf} 5^{6gf} 5^{9g} 5^{7gf} 3^{7gs}
4^{8f} **0-4-11 £4,521**

North Walk (Ire) *K A Ryan* 83
2 b g Monashee Mountain (USA) - Celtic Link (Ire)
7^{6g} 4^{5gf} 4^{6gf} 1^{7gf} 10^{7g} 1^{6s} 3^{7hy} **2-1-7**
£11,251

Northern Boy (USA) *T D Barron* 75
2 ch c Lure (USA) - Catala (USA)
3^{7gs} 2^{7g} **0-2-2 £2,105**

Northern Chorus (Ire) *A Dickman* 62
2 ch c Distant Music (USA) - Nationalartgallery (Ire)
12^{5gf} 4^{5gf} 5^{5gf} 4^{5gf} **0-0-4 £280**

Northern Desert (Ire) *P W Hiatt* 72 a85
6 b g Desert Style (Ire) - Rosie's Guest (Ire)
4^{7sd} 1^{8sd} 5^{8sd} 3^{7sd} 5^{7sd} 10^{7g} 20^{8g} 9^{7gs} 10^{8g}
5^{7sd} 3^{8sd} 2^{8sd} **1-3-12 £11,036**

Northern Empire (Ire) *B J Meehan* 103
2 ch c Namid - Bumble
2^{5gf} 2^{5g} 1^{5gf} 2^{6gs} **1-3-4 £26,539**

Northern Games *K A Ryan* 31
6 b g Mind Games - Northern Sal
15^{6g} PU^{6gf} **0-0-2**

Northern Nymph *R Hollinshead* 67
6 b g Makbul - Needwood Sprite
5^{16s} 3^{14gs} 3^{12gf} 5^{14gf} 8^{14gf} **0-1-5**
£1,158

Northern Ruler *R E Barr* 19
5 gr g Lugana Beach - Aimee Jane (USA)
10^{7f} 11^{10gf} 9^{12gf} **0-0-3**

Northern Secret *A M Balding* 31
3 b f Sinndar (Ire) - Northern Goddess
14^{8f} **0-0-1**

Northern Svengali (Ire) *D A Nolan* 54
9 b g Distinctly North (USA) - Trilby's Dream (Ire)
6^{5s} UR^{5gf} 10^{6gf} 8^{5g} 9^{6g} **0-0-5**

Northerner (Ire) *J R Norton* 53
2 b c Mark Of Esteem (Ire) - Ensorceleuse (Fr)
9^{6gf} 9^{7s} 9^{9g} **0-0-3**

Northside Lodge (Ire) *W R Swinburn* 74 a77
7 b g Grand Lodge (USA) - Alongside
6^{12sd} 13^{10g} 10^{10gf} 8^{12gf} 2^{10gf} 2^{10gf} 1^{10gf} 3^{10g}
10^{12gf} 11^{9sd} 9^{9sf} 7^{12sd} **1-3-12 £7,049**

Norton (Ire) *T G Mills* 101
8 ch g Barathea (Ire) - Primrose Valley
5^{8gs} 9^{8gs} 1^{8g} 14^{8gf} 11^{8gf} 6^{8gf} 2^{8gf} 5^{9gf}
1-1-8 £19,012

Norton Rose *T J Fitzgerald* 8
3 ch f Dr Fong (USA) - Bonica
14^{8g} 14^{10g} 14^{10g} **0-0-3**

Norwegian *Ian Williams* 53 a57
4 b g Halling (USA) - Chicarica (USA)
5^{9sd} 4^{10g} 9^{8gf} 5^{8gf} 14^{11gf} 5^{10gf} 5^{10g} 20^{8gf}
0-0-8

Nosferatu (Ire) *Mrs A J Perrett* 78
2 b c In The Wings - Gothic Dream (Ire)
3^{8gf} **0-1-1 £888**

Not Allowed *G C Bravery* 56
2 b f Mujadil (USA) - Croeso Cynnes
13^{6g} 5^{6gf} 6^{6gf} 6^{5f} 8^{7g} 7^{8g} **0-0-6**

Not Amused (UAE) *Ian Williams* a66
5 ch g Indian Ridge - Amusing Time (Ire)
11^{12sd} 10^{12sd} 5^{12sd} 6^{12sd} 6^{14sd} **0-0-5**

Not So Dusty *P J Makin* 73 a86
5 b g Primo Dominie - Ann's Pearl (Ire)
2^{5sd} 6^{5sd} 13^{5s} 13^{5g} 11^{5gf} 6^{5g} 9^{5gs} 6^{6sd}
0-1-8 £2,067

Nota Bene *D R C Elsworth* 116
3 b c Zafonic (USA) - Dodo (Ire)
1^{6gf} 1^{6gf} 11^{5gf} **2-0-3 £25,765**

Notability (Ire) *M A Jarvis* 103
3 b c King's Best (USA) - Noble Rose (Ire)
2^{8gs} 1^{8gs} 2^{8g} 9^{8gf} **1-2-4 £40,804**

Notable Guest (USA) *Sir Michael Stoute* 117
4 b c Kingmambo (USA) - Yenda
1^{10gf} 1^{12f} 16^{10g} 1^{11gf} 3^{11gf} **3-0-5**
£84,500

Notable Tiger (USA) *Saeed Bin Suroor* 47
3 br c Tiger Ridge (USA) - Notable Girl (USA)
7^{7g} **0-0-1**

Notjustaprettyface (USA) *H Morrison* 98
3 b/br f Red Ransom (USA) - Maudie May (USA)
10^{5s} 6^{5gf} 3^{6g} 3^{5g} 8^{6g} 5^{5gf} 3^{5gf} 8^{6g} 12^{6s}
0-3-9 £8,840

Notnowcato *Sir Michael Stoute* 107
3 ch c Inchinor - Rambling Rose
3^{7gf} 1^{8gf} 7^{9gf} 13^{7g} 2^{8gs} 1^{8gs} **2-2-6**
£29,819

Notte Italiana (Ire) *J Pearce* 55
3 b f Mtoto - Nordic Way (Ire)
11^{10g} 7^{11g} 8^{12f} 8^{10gf} 2^{14g} 2^{16gf} 2^{14g} 1^{14hy}
1-3-8 £5,118

Noubian (USA) *M P Tregoning* 78 a72
3 ch c Diesis - Beraysim
1^{9sd} 3^{9g} 7^{10s} 6^{8gf} 3^{10gf} **1-2-5 £5,913**

Noul (USA) *J S Moore* 41 a69
6 ch g Miswaki (USA) - Water Course (USA)
8^{6sd} 1^{7sd} 2^{8sd} 5^{9sd} 9^{9sd} 8^{8sd} 8^{9sd} 6^{7gf} 13^{8gf}
9^{8sd} **1-1-10 £3,327**

Nounou *D J Daly* 80 a74
4 b c Starborough - Watheeqah (USA)
1^{13sd} 2^{14gs} 1^{16gf} 6^{16gf} 5^{18gf} **2-1-5**
£9,607

Nouveau Riche (Ire) *H Morrison* 69
4 ch f Entrepreneur - Dime Bag
UR^{8gf} 7^{10gf} 10^{12g} **0-0-3**

Nova Tor (Ire) *Peter Grayson* 62 a71
3 b f Trans Island - Nordic Living (Ire)
5^{6sd} 6^{6sd} 1^{5sd} 10^{6gs} 1^{5sd} 9^{5gs} 8^{5gf} 6^{6gf} 9^{5sd}
8^{7sd} 5^{5sd} 5^{6sd} 5^{5sd} 11^{6sd} 6^{5sd} **2-0-15**
£5,817

Novelina (Ire) *W J Haggas* 55 a61
3 b f Fusaichi Pegasus (USA) - Novelette
3^{7sd} 9^{8g} 4^{7f} **0-1-3 £524**

Now And Again *I W McInnes* 50 a46
6 b g Shaamit (Ire) - Sweet Allegiance
5^{9sd} 8^{9sd} 3^{9sd} 1^{10gs} 9^{10sd} 13^{8g} **1-1-6**
£1,543

Now And Zen *M D Hammond*
3 b g Whittingham (Ire) - Uaeflame (Ire)
16^{6g} **0-0-1**

Now Look Away (Ire) *E S McMahon* 47 a58
4 b g Dushyantor (USA) - Where's Carol
3^{9sd} 9^{7sd} 10^{7sd} 12^{7gs} 9^{7gf} 11^{7g} 4^{7s} 11^{6g}
6^{6sd} 6^{7sd} 3^{8sd} 3^{9sf} PU^{8sd} **0-3-13 £941**

Nowaday (Ger) *T P Tate* 66
3 b g Dashing Blade - Notre Dame (Ger)
3^{10s} 8^{15gs} 9^{12gf} 1^{16g} **1-1-4 £6,216**

Nowell House *M W Easterby* 62
9 ch g Polar Falcon (USA) - Langtry Lady
10^{14s} 13^{16g} 12^{16g} **0-0-3**

Nudrah *J L Dunlop* 74
2 b f Green Desert (USA) - Sayedati Eljamilah (USA)
3^{6gs} 1^{6gf} 11^{6g} **1-1-3 £5,727**

Nufoos *M Johnston* 107
3 b f Zafonic (USA) - Desert Lynx (Ire)
4^{6s} 2^{7g} 2^{6g} 1^{7gf} 2^{7g} 5^{8g} **1-3-6**
£42,437

Nuit Sombre (Ire) *J G M O'Shea* 88
5 b g Night Shift (USA) - Belair Princess (USA)
1^{11gf} 18^{10gs} 8^{12f} 10^{11gs} **1-0-4 £3,733**

Nukhbah (USA) *A G Newcombe* 52
4 b f Bahri (USA) - El Nafis (USA)
5^{10gf} 11^{10f} 8^{17f} **0-0-3**

Numanthia (Ire) *Miss J R Gibney* a59
3 b f Barathea (Ire) - Lafite
6^{8sd} 11^{9sd} 4^{9sd} 10^{9sd} **0-0-4 £255**

Numeric (Ger) *J H M Gosden* 70
2 br c Singspiel (Ire) - Narola (Ger)
6^{8hy} 2^{10hy} **0-1-2 £1,013**

Numero Due *G M Moore* 86
3 b g Sinndar (Ire) - Kindle
6^{8s} 8^{10g} 2^{12gf} 2^{12gf} 1^{14gf} 1^{16gf} 2^{16g} 4^{15s}
2-3-8 £15,929

Nut (Ire) *J W Hills* 65
2 b f Fasliyev (USA) - La Rosetta (Ire)
6^{6gf} 9^{6gf} 3^{6g} 10^{5gf} **0-1-4 £657**

Nutley Queen (Ire) *M Appleby* 17 a45
6 b m Eagle Eyed (USA) - Secret Hideaway (USA)
6^{10sd} 13^{11sd} 5^{9sd} 5^{9sd} 6^{10sd} 4^{12sd} 8^{9sd} 8^{12g}
4^{12sd} **0-0-9**

Nuwara Eliya *G A Butler* 83
3 ch g Grand Lodge (USA) - Delirious Moment (Ire)
4^{7gf} 5^{8gf} 1^{10g} 10^{12s} 6^{12g} **1-0-5 £8,978**

Nuzzle *N G Richards* 37 a40
5 b m Salse (USA) - Lena (USA)
11^{8sd} 5^{9sd} 10^{14sd} 10^{7sd} 7^{9f} 2^{7f} 5^{8f} 7^{10s}
0-1-8 £732

Nyarhini *G Wragg* 76 a69
2 b f Fantastic Light (USA) - Nuryana
6^{6s} 1^{6sd} **1-0-2 £3,873**

O'Tara (Ire) *M H Tompkins* 77
2 b c Danehill (USA) - Utr (USA)
2^{7s} **0-1-1 £1,187**

Oakbridge (Ire) *D J Wintle* 75 a51
3 b c Indian Ridge - Chauncy Lane (Ire)
7^{10gf} 1^{6gf} 5^{7gs} 11^{6g} 15^{7gf} 12^{10g} 16^{10gf} 10^{5sf}
11^{7sd} **1-0-9 £5,557**

Oakley Absolute *R Hannon* 69 a69
3 ch c Bluegrass Prince (Ire) - Susie Oakley Vii
7^{7sd} 5^{8sd} 5^{9sd} 9^{8gs} 3^{10gf} 1^{10g} 4^{11g} 2^{10g} 1^{10gf}
3^{10gf} 2^{10f} 4^{10sd} **2-4-12 £11,410**

Oases *D Shaw* 51 a41
6 ch g Zilzal (USA) - Markievicz (Ire)
6^{7sd} 5^{7gf} 10^{6gs} 5^{6g} 13^{6sd} 6^{6g} 8^{7gs} 4^{6gf} 6^{6gf}
18^{6gf} **0-0-10 £278**

Oasis Star (Ire) *W R Swinburn* 83

4 b f Desert King (Ire) - Sound Tap (Ire)
13^{7gf} 11^{8gs} 9^{7gf} **0-0-3**

Oasis Sun (Ire) *J R Best* 46
2 ch f Desert Sun - Albaiyda (Ire)
8^{6gf} 10^{7g} 11^{6g} **0-0-3**

Oasis Way (Gr) *P R Chamings* 67
3 b f Wadood (USA) - Northern Moon
8^{8gs} 2^{9g} 7^{10f} 7^{9g} 4^{9g} 7^{8g} **0-1-6 £1,929**

Oatcake *G A Butler* 67
3 ch f Selkirk (USA) - Humble Pie
10^{6s} 3^{6g} 3^{8gf} **0-2-3 £1,672**

Obay *M Todhunter* a75
4 ch g Kingmambo (USA) - Parade Queen (USA)
10^{12sd} 9^{17sd} **0-0-2**

Obe Bold (Ire) *A Berry* 63 a55
4 b f Orpen (USA) - Capable Kate (Ire)
10^{6sd} 10^{5sd} 8^{6sd} 5^{6sd} 11^{6sd} 10^{5gf} 5^{6s} 7^{5g} 5^{6gs} 10^{6g} 4^{6gf} 4^{7f} 11^{6gf} 9^{6gf} 6^{5gf} 9^{5gf} 3^{6gf} 9^{5gf} 5^{6f} 6^{6g} 16^{6f} 3^{5sd} 9^{6sd} 7^{5sd} 7^{6sd}
0-2-25 £1,589

Obe Brave *M R Channon* 82
2 b c Agnes World (USA) - Pass The Rose (Ire)
1^{6g} **1-0-1 £5,668**

Obe Gold *M R Channon* 109
3 b g Namaqualand (USA) - Gagajulu
1^{6g} 2^{7gf} 4^{7hy} 7^{6gy} 14^{7gf} 4^{6g} 15^{5g} 10^{6g} 7^{7gf} 16^{6g} 7^{6gf} 2^{6g} 10^{6s} **1-2-13 £21,300**

Obe One *J Howard Johnson* 69
5 b g Puissance - Plum Bold
5^{6s} 11^{6gs} 4^{6gf} 7^{6f} 7^{6gf} 8^{7gf} **0-0-6 £276**

Obergurgl (Ire) *Mrs A Duffield* 29 a62
2 b g Titus Livius (Fr) - Lorella (Ire)
16^{5gf} 8^{5g} 3^{6sd} 6^{5sd} **0-1-4 £562**

Oberon's Prize *D R C Elsworth* 53
3 b g King's Theatre (Ire) - Taj Victory
11^{9gs} 5^{12f} **0-0-2**

Obezyana (USA) *G A Huffer* 79 a90
3 ch g Rahy (USA) - Polish Treaty (USA)
6^{7gf} 7^{11gs} 11^{8s} 9^{10gs} 1^{8g} 1^{8sd} **2-0-6**
£10,639

Oblique (Ire) *Sir Mark Prescott* 103
3 b f Giant's Causeway (USA) - On Call
1^{9g} 1^{10g} 1^{12g} 1^{12g} 4^{14g} 1^{12g} **5-0-6**
£40,231

Oblo (Ire) *B Palling* 47
2 b g Observatory (USA) - Londonnet (Ire)
14^{5s} 12^{5sd} 2^{6f} 5^{6g} 12^{8sd} **0-1-5 £820**

Obrigado (USA) *W J Haggas* 86 a87
5 b g Bahri (USA) - Glorious Diamond (USA)
2^{8gf} 11^{8gs} 3^{8gf} 9^{8gf} 7^{6g} 3^{8gf} 1^{8sd} 4^{9sd}
1-2-8 £10,840

Obscene *M J Polglase* 66
2 b g Key Of Luck (USA) - Scene (Ire)
13^{8s} 7^{8s} 6^{10s} **0-0-3 £352**

Observatory Star (Ire) *T D Easterby* 77
2 br c Observatory (USA) - Pink Sovietstaia (Fr)
5^{6gf} 1^{6gf} 11^{7gs} 5^{6g} 10^{6g} **1-0-5 £4,114**

Obstreperous Way *P R Chamings* 35 a54
3 ch g Dr Fong (USA) - Fleet Key
8^{10sd} 7^{10sd} 15^{12gf} 10^{12sd} 10^{8gf} **0-0-5**

Obvious Charm *R Charlton* 58
3 b f Machiavellian (USA) - Clear Attraction (USA)
9^{10s} 9^{12gf} 5^{10gf} 13^{10gf} **0-0-4**

Ocean Avenue (Ire) *C A Horgan* 80 a29
6 b g Dolphin Street (Fr) - Trinity Hall
6^{10gf} 11^{12gf} 11^{13gf} 5^{12gf} 13^{12sd} **0-0-5**
£245

Ocean Gift *D R C Elsworth* 90
3 b g Cadeaux Genereux - Sea Drift (Fr)
9^{10g} 4^{8g} 2^{7gf} 1^{7gf} 11^{6gf} 9^{7s} 6^{5g} 1^{6g} 5^{6gf} 10^{6g} **2-1-10 £14,600**

Ocean King (USA) *W M Brisbourne* 64 a63
4 ch g Sky Classic (Can) - From Sea To Sea (Can)
9^{9g} 5^{14gf} 9^{7sd} 2^{14sd} 6^{14sd} **0-1-5 £849**

Ocean Of Dreams (Fr) *J D Bethell* 52 a81
2 b c Ocean Of Wisdom (USA) - Tifosa (USA)
3^{5f} 6^{5gs} 1^{6sd} 1^{6sd} 1^{6sd} **3-0-5 £14,026**

Ocean Of Storms (Ire) *N I M Rossiter* 66 a65
10 b/br g Arazi (USA) - Moon Cactus
5^{10ft} 8^{8ft} 13^{9ft} RR^{10ft} 5^{8gf} 10^{8gs} 8^{9gf} 8^{10gs} 8^{8gs} **0-0-9 £178**

Ocean Pride (Ire) *R Hannon* 87 a64
2 b c Lend A Hand - Irish Understudy (Ity)
3^{5gs} 1^{5gs} 3^{6gf} 2^{7sd} 4^{7gs} 1^{7s} 6^{8g} 3^{7gf} 10^{7gs} 3^{7s} **2-2-10 £15,373**

Ocean Rock *C A Horgan* a61
4 b g Perugino (USA) - Polistatic
9^{10sd} 5^{16gs} 12^{13sd} 1^{14sd} 6^{14sd} 5^{17sd} 3^{16sd} 1^{12sd} 4^{16sd} 5^{12sd} **2-1-10 £4,537**

Ocean Sunrise (Ire) *M Johnston* 63
2 b f Danehill (USA) - Wind Silence (USA)
7^{6g} 3^{6gf} 18^{6s} **0-1-3 £672**

Ocean Tide *R Ford* 70
8 b g Deploy - Dancing Tide
5^{18gs} 5^{16g} **0-0-2 £303**

Ocean Valentine *H R A Cecil* 58
2 gr c King Charlemagne (USA) - Dolly Bevan
4^{7gf} **0-0-1 £318**

Oceancookie (Ire) *A M Balding* 72
3 b f Dashing Blade - Sankaty Light (USA)
4^{8g} 1^{7g} 4^{7gf} 7^{7gf} **1-1-4 £4,171**

Oceanico Dot Com (Ire) *A Berry* 74 a65
3 br f Hernando (Fr) - Karen Blixen
6^{5gs} 9^{5gf} 3^{5g} 9^{5gs} 6^{5gf} 7^{6gf} 3^{5s} 13^{5s} 4^{5sd} **0-2-9 £2,450**

Oceans Apart *P F I Cole* 89
2 ch f Desert Prince (Ire) - Ffestiniog (Ire)
2^{5gf} 3^{5s} 1^{5gf} 6^{6gf} 11^{6gf} 1^{6gf} 5^{6gf} **2-2-7**
£20,544

Ochil Hills Dancer (Ire) *A Crook* 35 a28
3 b f Bluebird (USA) - Classic Dilemma
12^{5gf} 8^{5gf} 7^{5gs} 7^{7gf} 14^{6gf} 9^{5gf} 12^{5gf} 7^{5sd} 10^{6gf} **0-0-9**

Ochre Bay *R Hollinshead* 78 a72
2 b c Polar Prince (Ire) - Cloudy Reef
5^{5gf} 1^{5g} 6^{6s} 8^{6sd} 4^{6sd} **1-0-5 £4,835**

Ockums Razor (Ire) *N A Callaghan* 61
2 b c Mozart (Ire) - Merlannah (Ire)
7^{5g} 6^{6gs} 3^{5gf} **0-1-3 £560**

Ocotillo *James Moffatt* a49
5 b g Mark Of Esteem (Ire) - Boojum
5^{9sd} 10^{9sd} 13^{9sd} **0-0-3**

October Ben *M D I Usher* 54
2 b f Killer Instinct - Birmania (Ire)
7^{6gf} **0-0-1**

October Mist (Ire) *K G Reveley* 56
11 gr g Roselier (Fr) - Bonny Joe
8^{10gf} 10^{14g} **0-0-2**

October Sun *Miss D Mountain* 28
2 b c Dansili - Autumn Pride (USA)

10^{8hy} 10^{10hy} **0-0-2**

Odabella (Ire) *John Berry* a45
5 b m Selkirk (USA) - Circe's Isle
5^{9sd} 8^{12sd} **0-0-2**

Oddsmaker (Ire) *M A Barnes* 80 a77
4 b g Barathea (Ire) - Archipova (Ire)
9^{7sd} 19^{8g} 15^{10s} 10^{11s} 10^{8g} 5^{10g} 4^{8gf} 9^{8g} 11^{8gf} 10^{8g} 12^{8gf} 11^{12gs} 12^{8gf} **0-1-13 £536**

Odiham *H Morrison* 98 a101
4 b g Deploy - Hug Me
4^{12gf} 1^{16sd} 5^{16g} 4^{16sd} 8^{14g} 5^{15gs} 19^{18gs} **1-0-7 £18,693**

Oeuf A La Neige *G C H Chung* 61
5 b g Danehill (USA) - Reine De Neige
8^{6gf} 12^{6gs} 7^{5g} **0-0-3**

Ofaraby *M A Jarvis* 105 a105
5 b g Sheikh Albadou - Maristax
8^{10gf} 12^{10gf} 1^{10gs} 2^{10gs} 4^{10g} 2^{10sd} 1^{10g} 8^{10gs} **2-3-8 £38,030**

Off Beat (USA) *J K Price* a38
4 ch g Mister Baileys - Off Off (USA)
7^{7sd} **0-0-1**

Off Colour *Mrs A J Perrett* 79
3 b/br c Rainbow Quest (USA) - Air Of Distinction (Ire)
2^{10g} 2^{12gs} 9^{14g} **0-2-3 £2,165**

Off Hire *C Smith* 43 a43
9 b g Clantime - Lady Pennington
8^{6sd} 6^{5sd} 5^{6sd} 9^{5sd} 7^{6sd} 5^{6g} 8^{5sd} 2^{5ss} 8^{5sd} 5^{5sd} **0-1-10 £422**

Ogee *Sir Michael Stoute* 64 a70
2 ch g Generous (Ire) - Aethra (USA)
9^{8gf} 7^{8hy} 5^{9sd} **0-0-3**

Oggy Oggy Oggy *Peter Grayson* a32
2 ch f Fraam - Princess Poquito
4^{5sd} 10^{7sd} **0-0-2**

Oh Boy (Ire) *J M Bradley* 64 a49
5 b g Tagula (Ire) - Pretty Sally (Ire)
9^{8f} 8^{8g} 10^{8g} 5^{8gf} 10^{8gf} 4^{7gf} 10^{8gf} 9^{7gf} 13^{8g} 7^{8sd} 10^{7gf} **0-1-11 £325**

Oh Danny Boy *Julian Poulton* 67 a75
4 b g Cadeaux Genereux - Final Shot
10^{8s} 3^{10g} 1^{9sd} 10^{8sd} 8^{9sd} **1-1-5 £3,921**

Oh Dara (USA) *M J Attwater* 66 a67
3 b f Aljabr (USA) - Sabaah Elfull
7^{6sd} 8^{6sd} 8^{5sd} 5^{5gs} 6^{6sd} **0-0-5**

Oh Glory Be (USA) *R Hannon* 50 a45
2 b f Dixieland Band (USA) - Long View (USA)
11^{7s} 12^{8sd} **0-0-2**

Oh How Lovely (USA) *A P O'Brien* 101
2 ch f Storm Cat (USA) - Flat Fleet Feet (USA)
11^{7gf} 2^{6f} 1^{7gf} 6^{7g} 4^{7y} 5^{7gs} **1-1-6 £13,720**

Oh So Hardy *M A Allen* 44
4 b/br f Fleetwood (Ire) - Miss Hardy
9^{16g} 14^{16gs} 10^{14s} 6^{15gf} **0-0-4**

Oh So Rosie (Ire) *J S Moore* a61
5 b m Danehill Dancer (Ire) - Shinkoh Rose (Fr)
1^{8sd} **1-0-1 £2,928**

Oh Sunny Boy (Ire) *B G Powell* 45
4 b g Desert Sun - Naivement (Ire)
7^{8f} 18^{8gf} 4^{10g} 4^{12gf} 5^{12gf} **0-0-5**

Ohana *N A Callaghan* 33 a68
2 b c Mark Of Esteem (Ire) - Subya
21^{8gs} 2^{7sd} 7^{7sd} 3^{8sd} 5^{8sd} **0-1-5 £2,007**

Ok Pal *T G Mills* 87 a97
5 b g Primo Dominie - Sheila's Secret (Ire)
5^{5g} 10^{5g} 8^{5g} 4^{5gf} 12^{5g} 3^{5gs} 12^{5hy} 1^{5sd} 1^{5sd} **2-1-9 £14,432**

Okoboji (Ire) *J A Osborne* a32
4 ch c Indian Ridge - Pool Party (USA)
12^{7sd} **0-0-1**

Oktis Morilious (Ire) *A W Carroll* 44 a44
4 b g Octagonal (NZ) - Nottash (Ire)
7^{17sd} 7^{17sd} 15^{12sd} 4^{12gf} PU^{12sd} 6^{10sd} 5^{14sf} 4^{9sd} 11^{10sd} **0-0-9 £272**

Old Bailey (USA) *G L Moore* 24 a76
5 gr g Lit De Justice (USA) - Olden Lek (USA)
1^{6sd} 7^{7sd} 2^{6sd} 5^{6sd} 2^{7sd} 3^{6sd} 7^{6sd} 1^{6sd} 10^{7g} 11^{6sd} 5^{6sd} 11^{6gs} 7^{6sd} 12^{6sd} 18^{7g} 11^{6sd} 14^{7sd} **2-3-17 £8,265**

Old Barns (Ire) *G A Swinbank* 36
5 b g Nucleon (USA) - Surfer Katie (Ire)
11^{9g} 8^{8g} **0-0-2**

Old Harry *E A Wheeler* 42 a13
5 b g Case Law - Supreme Thought
10^{5gf} 6^{6g} 7^{5sd} **0-0-3**

Old Time Dancing *M J Wallace* 57 a49
2 b f Danehill Dancer (Ire) - Rare Old Times (Ire)
6^{6gs} 9^{7sd} 9^{6sd} 10^{5sd} **0-0-4**

Oldenway *R A Fahey* 81 a71
6 b g Most Welcome - Sickle Moon
UR^{11s} 14^{10gs} 10^{10gf} 4^{12gf} 4^{10gf} 1^{10gf} 4^{10gf} 1^{10g} 5^{12gf} 5^{10gf} 6^{12g} 12^{12g} 12^{10g} 2^{9hy} 4^{9sd} 8^{12sd} 2^{12sd} 3^{12sd} **2-3-18 £16,455**

Oligarch (Ire) *N A Callaghan* 93
3 b c Monashee Mountain (USA) - Courtier
2^{7gf} 4^{8gs} 7^{7gs} 11^{7g} 1^{10gf} 3^{10g} 5^{10g} 6^{10g} 5^{10gf} 15^{8g} **1-2-10 £12,976**

Olivair (Ire) *M E Sowersby* 47
2 b f Daggers Drawn (USA) - Exhibit Air (Ire)
5^{5s} 12^{5gs} 11^{6gf} 3^{7gf} 2^{7f} 6^{7g} **0-2-6 £1,470**

Olivia Rose (Ire) *J Pearce* 85
6 b m Mujadil (USA) - Santana Lady (Ire)
5^{8s} 8^{10gs} 12^{11g} 7^{10gf} 1^{10gf} **1-0-5 £6,754**

Olivia Twist *W G M Turner* 30 a40
3 ch f Fraam - Tricata
4^{12s} 5^{12sd} **0-0-2 £258**

Olivino (Ger) *S Dow* a60
4 ch c Second Set (Ire) - Osdemona (Ger)
10^{9} 5^{10} 2^{11g} 5^{10} 1^{10f} 7^{11s} 6^{9g} 1^{10g} 14^{7sd} 8^{10sd} 4^{10sd} **2-0-11 £6,951**

Ollie George (Ire) *A M Balding* 69 a69
2 ch c Fruits Of Love (USA) - The Iron Lady (Ire)
10^{6gf} 3^{7sd} 2^{8s} **0-2-3 £1,467**

Ollijay *Mrs H Dalton* 32 a43
4 b g Wolfhound (USA) - Anthem Flight (USA)
7^{9sd} 9^{9sd} 8^{7sd} 11^{12s} 10^{10g} **0-0-5**

Olympian Odyssey *B W Hills* 89
2 b c Sadler's Wells (USA) - Field Of Hope (Ire)
3^{7gf} 2^{7gf} 1^{7s} **1-2-3 £6,674**

Omaha City (Ire) *B Gubby* 73
11 b g Night Shift (USA) - Be Discreet
11^{8gf} 14^{8gf} 7^{8g} 6^{8gf} 8^{8gf} 2^{7g} **0-1-6 £1,095**

Oman Gulf (USA) *J G Given* 82
4 b g Diesis - Dabaweyaa
2^{11g} 10^{11g} 11^{10g} 4^{8gf} 11^{8g} 5^{8gf} 11^{9gf} 5^{10gf} 6^{12gf} **0-1-9 £1,667**

Omneya *D M Simcock* 39
2 b f Mister Baileys - Silent Miracle (Ire)
$9^{6gs}\ 7^{6gf}\ 8^{5g}$ **0-0-3**

On Air (USA) *M Johnston* 69
2 gr/ro f Cozzene (USA) - Cumulate (USA)
$3^{8gf}\ 9^{8gs}$ **0-1-2 £1,114**

On Angels Wings *G F Bridgwater*
3 b g Polar Prince (Ire) - Crown Angel (USA)
$12^{9sd}\ 11^{7sd}\ 12^{10gf}$ **0-0-3**

On Every Street *R Bastiman* 32
4 b g Singspiel (Ire) - Nekhbet
$14^{8gf}\ 10^{9f}\ 14^{8gf}\ 10^{10s}$ **0-0-4**

On The Bright Side *D Nicholls* 48
3 b f Cyrano De Bergerac - Jade Pet
$5^{6gf}\ 11^{6gf}\ 9^{6gf}\ 4^{7g}\ 12^{8gs}$ **0-0-5 £268**

On The Side *Mrs J R Ramsden* 60 a63
2 b g Shinko Forest (Ire) - Apple Sauce
$7^{5gf}\ 7^{5g}\ 2^{5sd}\ 9^{6g}\ 9^{6f}\ 3^{5sd}\ 4^{6gf}$ **0-2-7 £1,535**

On The Trail *D W Chapman* 48 a56
8 ch g Catrail (USA) - From The Rooftops (Ire)
$11^{6sd}\ 5^{6sd}\ 8^{6sd}\ 5^{6gs}\ 6^{5sd}\ 11^{5sd}\ 9^{5hy}\ 11^{6sd}\ 15^{5gf}\ 5^{6sd}\ 16^{5gf}\ 15^{5g}\ 6^{5g}\ 11^{5gf}\ 13^{5g}\ 5^{5sd}\ 13^{6sd}\ 3^{5sd}\ 1^{5sd}\ 8^{5sd}\ 8^{5sd}\ 12^{6sd}\ 12^{5sd}$ **1-1-23 £1,696**

On The Waterline (Ire) *P D Evans* 66
3 b f Compton Place - Miss Waterline
$10^{6g}\ 6^{6gf}\ 9^{6gf}\ 13^{6gs}\ 11^{7g}\ 12^{7sd}$ **0-0-6**

On The Wing *A P Jarvis* 76
4 b f Pivotal - Come Fly With Me
$9^{10gf}\ 4^{8gf}\ 14^{8gf}$ **0-0-3 £553**

Once In A Bluemoon (Ire) *A Berry*
2 ch f Beckett (Ire) - Ma Bella Luna
$4^{5gf}\ 6^{7gf}\ 12^{6g}$ **0-0-3**

One For Gretta (Ire) *M J Polglase* 5
3 ch f Timeless Times (USA) - Bay Of Bengal (Ire)
$11^{6gf}\ 15^{5gf}$ **0-0-2**

One Great Idea (Ire) *T D Barron* 69
3 b g Night Shift (USA) - Scenaria (Ire)
$5^{6g}\ 5^{5gf}\ 1^{5gf}\ 8^{6gf}\ 11^{6gf}\ 4^{5g}\ 9^{5s}$ **1-0-7 £3,718**

One Last Time *Miss B Sanders* 35 a45
5 b g Primo Dominie - Leap Of Faith (Ire)
$14^{7s}\ 16^{5gs}\ 11^{6g}\ 13^{6gf}\ 5^{8sd}\ 3^{6sd}\ 4^{7sd}\ 5^{7sd}$ **0-1-8 £209**

One More Round (USA) *N P Littmoden* 109 a101
7 b g Ghazi (USA) - Life Of The Party (USA)
$2^{6gf}\ 6^{8gf}\ 6^{7gf}\ 7^{7g}\ 10^{7gy}\ 7^{7sd}$ **0-1-6 £11,458**

One Night In Paris (Ire) *M J Wallace* 63 a63
2 b/br f Danetime (Ire) - Forget Paris (Ire)
$8^{6gf}\ 5^{6sd}\ 5^{6gs}\ 3^{7g}$ **0-1-4 £569**

One Of Each (Ire) *D Carroll* 30 a4
3 ch f Indian Lodge (Ire) - Indian City
$10^{5sd}\ 6^{5f}$ **0-0-2**

One Putra (Ire) *M A Jarvis* 109
3 b c Indian Ridge - Triomphale (USA)
$3^{6s}\ 5^{6gs}\ 7^{5g}\ 1^{5gf}\ 8^{6g}\ 6^{6gs}\ 3^{6gf}\ 12^{5g}\ 2^{6g}\ 3^{6s}$ **1-4-10 £25,746**

One To Win (Ire) *J Noseda* 96 a73
3 b f Cape Cross (Ire) - Safe Exit (Fr)
$3^{10sd}\ 1^{10gf}\ 1^{10g}\ 12^{12s}\ 4^{10g}\ 9^{12g}$ **2-1-6 £13,300**

One Trick Pony *Karen McLintock* 62
2 ch g Timeless Times (USA) - Lavernock Lady
$7^{5s}\ 2^{5g}\ 1^{5s}\ 1^{5g}\ 4^{6g}\ 2^{5g}\ 5^{5g}\ 1^{5g}\ 13^{5gf}\ 13^{5g}$ **3-2-10 £13,945**

One Upmanship *D G Bridgwater* 49 a59
4 ch g Bahamian Bounty - Magnolia
$4^{8sd}\ 3^{10sd}\ 5^{8sd}\ 5^{12sd}\ 2^{12gs}\ 9^{13sd}\ 4^{10g}\ 6^{10f}\ 6^{10f}\ 5^{13gs}\ 5^{12g}\ 8^{10f}\ 10^{12gf}\ 7^{10gf}\ 7^{12sd}$ **0-2-15 £1,116**

One Way Ticket *J M Bradley* 88 a38
5 ch h Pursuit Of Love - Prima Cominna
$2^{5gs}\ 8^{5gs}\ 4^{5gf}\ 2^{5gf}\ 3^{5gs}\ 11^{5g}\ 1^{5gf}\ 1^{5gf}\ 8^{5gf}\ 2^{6gf}\ 1^{5f}\ 10^{5gf}\ 10^{5g}\ 2^{5g}\ 13^{5gf}\ 15^{5g}\ 9^{5sd}$ **3-6-17 £21,898**

Oneiro Way (Ire) *P R Chamings* 67
3 b g King's Best (USA) - Koumiss
5^{7gf} **0-0-1**

Online Investor *C Smith* 49 a70
6 b g Puissance - Anytime Baby
$9^{5sd}\ 3^{5sd}\ 8^{6sd}\ 7^{6sd}\ 8^{5gf}\ 9^{6sd}$ **0-1-6 £417**

Only For Gold *Dr P Pritchard* 49 a29
10 b g Presidium - Calvanne Miss
$8^{6sd}\ 3^{6g}\ 7^{10s}\ 14^{7gf}\ 13^{5g}\ 13^{7gf}\ 11^{8g}\ 15^{8gf}\ 14^{8gf}\ 7^{5gf}$ **0-1-10 £616**

Only If I Laugh *M J Attwater* 53 a62
4 ch g Piccolo - Agony Aunt
$6^{6sd}\ 5^{7sd}\ 5^{7sd}\ 9^{6sd}\ 10^{5sd}\ 9^{5sd}\ 8^{6sd}\ 8^{6gs}\ 4^{6sd}\ 7^{6gf}\ 1^{6gf}\ 7^{6g}\ 8^{6gf}\ 2^{8gf}\ 7^{8gs}\ 12^{8gf}$ **1-1-16 £3,902**

Onlytime Will Tell *D Nicholls* 81
7 ch g Efisio - Prejudice
$12^{6g}\ 6^{7gf}\ 1^{6g}\ 16^{9g}\ 9^{7g}$ **1-0-5 £4,046**

Onyergo (Ire) *J R Weymes* 68
3 b g Polish Precedent (USA) - Trick (Ire)
$5^{8g}\ 3^{7f}\ 3^{9gf}\ 14^{7g}\ 5^{7gf}\ 2^{9f}\ 17^{8gf}\ 3^{9s}\ 2^{10s}\ 3^{12g}\ 4^{12s}$ **0-3-11 £5,213**

Ooh Aah Camara (Ire) *R C Guest* 97
2 b f Danehill Dancer (Ire) - Simla Bibi
$4^{5gs}\ 4^{5g}\ 1^{5s}\ 2^{5gs}\ 1^{5gs}\ 3^{5gs}\ 2^{6g}\ 7^{6gf}\ 7^{5gs}\ 11^{5gf}\ 17^{7gf}$ **2-3-11 £33,959**

Oonagh Maccool (Ire) *M P Tregoning* 81
3 ch f Giant's Causeway (USA) - Alidiva
$1^{8g}\ 1^{8gs}$ **2-0-2 £14,160**

Oops (Ire) *J F Coupland* 44 a34
6 b g In The Wings - Atsuko (Ire)
$15^{14f}\ 10^{14sd}\ 2^{16gs}\ 4^{16gf}$ **0-1-4 £1,326**

Opal Warrior *P W D'Arcy* 50 a61
2 b f Orpen (USA) - Indian Wardance (Ity)
$5^{5gf}\ 2^{7sd}\ 1^{6sd}\ 6^{7sd}$ **1-1-4 £1,844**

Opalite *M A Jarvis* 56
3 ch f Opening Verse (USA) - Gem
$8^{8g}\ 4^{8gf}\ 4^{10gf}\ 7^{10gf}\ 8^{12gf}$ **0-0-5 £830**

Open Mind *R P Elliott* a2
4 b f Mind Games - Primum Tempus
$9^{6sd}\ 13^{5sd}$ **0-0-2**

Open Verse (USA) *M J Wallace* 69 a63
2 b f Black Minnaloushe (USA) - Anytimeatall (USA)
$6^{6gf}\ 5^{8g}\ 2^{7sd}$ **0-1-3 £1,400**

Opening Ceremony (USA) *R A Fahey* 95
6 br m Quest For Fame - Gleam Of Light (Ire)
$2^{11g}\ 6^{9gf}\ 2^{9gf}\ 13^{10g}\ 3^{10gf}\ 3^{10gf}\ 8^{10gs}\ 4^{11gf}\ 1^{10gf}$ **1-2-9 £19,917**

Opera Belle *A P Jarvis* 72 a63
3 b f Dr Fong (USA) - Opera Lover (Ire)
$4^{9gs}\ 9^{8g}\ 3^{11gf}\ 16^{11gs}\ 5^{8s}\ 6^{12g}\ 7^{11g}\ 5^{10sd}\ 8^{12gs}\ 15^{12sd}$ **0-0-10 £803**

Opera Cape *S Kirk* 114
2 b c Barathea (Ire) - Optaria

3^{7gf} 2^{7f} 1^{7gs} 1^{7s} 2^{7gs} 3^{7gs} **2-4-6**
£120,804

Opera Comica *J H M Gosden* 76 a59
2 b f Dr Fong (USA) - Comic (Ire)
7^{7gf} 5^{8g} 2^{8g} 2^{8gs} 6^{10sd} **0-2-5 £2,628**

Opera Knight *A W Carroll* 43 a56
5 ch g In The Wings - Sans Escale (USA)
7^{9sd} 10^{12sd} 7^{9sd} 11^{10g} 13^{9sd} 6^{8g} 11^{10gf} 18^{8gf} 9^{8f} RR^{11g} 6^{10sd} **0-0-11**

Opera Writer (Ire) *T D Easterby* 69
2 b c Rossini (USA) - Miss Flite (Ire)
4^{6gf} 3^{6g} 4^{5g} **0-1-3 £1,419**

Ophistrolie (Ire) *J R Weymes* 46 a39
3 b g Foxhound (USA) - Thoughtful Kate
10^{8gs} 13^{10gs} 4^{10g} 3^{11g} 9^{10g} 4^{11f} 11^{12f} 8^{16s} 4^{12gf} 5^{12gf} 7^{13sd} 11^{12g} 5^{13g} **0-1-13 £428**

Oporto (UAE) *M A Jarvis* 54
2 b f Jade Robbery (USA) - Potentille (Ire)
9^{7g} **0-0-1**

Opportune (Ger) *W M Brisbourne* 54
10 br g Shirley Heights - On The Tiles
7^{12gf} 10^{15gf} 6^{15gf} **0-0-3**

Optical Seclusion (Ire) *T J Etherington* 58 a20
2 b g Second Empire (Ire) - Theda
4^{7gf} 10^{6g} 7^{7g} 4^{6g} 9^{6sd} **0-0-5 £600**

Optimum (Ire) *J T Stimpson* a67
3 br g King's Best (USA) - Colour Dance
8^{10sd} 2^{9sd} 2^{11sd} 3^{12sd} **0-3-4 £2,610**

Oquawka (USA) *E A L Dunlop* 62
2 b/br c Quiet American (USA) - Yazeanhaa (USA)
8^{8gf} **0-0-1**

Orange Dancer (Ire) *H Morrison* 69
2 b f Danehill Dancer (Ire) - Strelitzia (SAF)
6^{6gf} 3^{6gs} 5^{5gs} **0-1-3 £487**

Orange Stravinsky *Sir Michael Stoute* 72
2 b g Stravinsky (USA) - Orange Sunset (Ire)
10^{7g} 5^{8g} 5^{7gf} 16^{8hy} **0-0-4**

Orange Touch (Ger) *Mrs A J Perrett* 102
5 b g Lando (Ger) - Orange Bowl
7^{13f} 7^{12gs} 7^{12hy} **0-0-3**

Oranges And Lemons (Fr) *C E Brittain* 61
2 b f Zafonic (USA) - Tarte Aux Pommes (USA)
5^{5g} 11^{6gs} 7^{5g} **0-0-3**

Orangino *J S Haldane* 42
7 b g Primo Dominie - Sweet Jaffa
10^{6gs} 13^{6f} 7^{7gf} 5^{9f} 4^{8gf} 4^{9gf} 12^{9gf} 5^{12gf}
0-0-8 £523

Oranmore Castle (Ire) *B W Hills* 86
3 b g Giant's Causeway (USA) - Twice The Ease
1^{6gf} 5^{6gf} 20^{6g} 6^{6gf} 7^{5gs} 13^{6gf} 7^{5g} 15^{6g}
1-0-8 £4,696

Oratorio (Ire) *A P O'Brien* 126 a107
3 b c Danehill (USA) - Mahrah (USA)
4^{8gf} 2^{8g} 10^{12g} 3^{8gf} 1^{10gf} 1^{10gy} 4^{10gs} 11^{10ft}
2-2-8 £745,615

Orcadian *J M P Eustace* 109
4 b g Kirkwall - Rosy Outlook (USA)
10^{12s} 6^{12f} 3^{12gf} 6^{10g} 1^{12g} 8^{16s} 3^{12hy}
1-1-7 £23,144

Orchard Supreme *R Hannon* 68 a75
2 ch c Titus Livius (Fr) - Bogus Penny (Ire)
8^{5gf} 10^{6g} 11^{6gf} 6^{8gs} 1^{7s} 9^{8hy} 2^{7sd} 2^{6sd} 2^{6sd} 1^{6sd} **2-3-10 £11,802**

Orchestration (Ire) *M J Attwater* 43 a63
4 ch g Stravinsky (USA) - Mora (Ire)
9^{7sd} 3^{6sd} 8^{7sd} 8^{6sd} 1^{6sd} 3^{5sd} 2^{6sd} 6^{6sd} 7^{7g} 9^{5gf} 6^{6g} 8^{6sd} 1^{5sd} 3^{5sd} 3^{5sd} 1^{5sd} 1^{6sd} 1^{5sd} 5^{6sd} **5-5-19 £8,792**

Ordnance Row *R Hannon* 90
2 b c Mark Of Esteem (Ire) - Language Of Love
7^{7gf} 2^{7gf} 2^{7s} 1^{7s} **1-2-4 £10,051**

Orenay (USA) *M J Wallace* 74 a50
3 ch g Grand Slam (USA) - Moonfire
3^{9s} 3^{7hy} 7^{7f} 7^{7gf} 7^{7sd} 11^{8sd} 11^{7sd} **0-2-7**
£1,510

Oriental Warrior *Saeed Bin Suroor* 5
4 b c Alhaarth (Ire) - Oriental Fashion (Ire)
6^{7hy} **0-0-1 £201**

Oriental Way (Gr) *P R Chamings* a19
3 b f Fascinating Way (Gr) - Light Wind (Gr)
11^{9sd} **0-0-1**

Orientor *J S Goldie* 117
7 b h Inchinor - Orient
8^{6g} 2^{5gs} 8^{6s} 2^{5gf} 12^{5gf} 12^{6f} 4^{5gf} 3^{6gs} 16^{5gf} 12^{6g} 12^{5gs} 6^{5s} **0-2-12 £28,773**

Original Source (Ire) *J Howard Johnson* 75
2 b c Danehill Dancer (Ire) - Kirana
1^{6g} 11^{6gs} 5^{6gf} 13^{8g} 12^{7g} **1-0-5 £4,446**

Orinocovsky (Ire) *N P Littmoden* a65
6 ch g Grand Lodge (USA) - Brillantina (Fr)
3^{14sd} 3^{14sd} 5^{12sd} 12^{16sd} **0-2-4 £904**

Orion Bell *M Johnston* 47 a13
3 b c Robellino (USA) - Fez
12^{8sd} 7^{7g} 6^{10s} 5^{10g} 11^{12f} 12^{10gs} 11^{12gf}
0-0-7

Orion Express *M Hill* 37
4 b g Bahhare (USA) - Kaprisky (Ire)
12^{11sd} 12^{8gf} 13^{14gs} **0-0-3**

Orions Eclipse *M J Gingell* 38 a14
4 b f Magic Ring (Ire) - Belle De Nuit (Ire)
7^{8gs} 9^{10g} 10^{10gs} 6^{7sd} 14^{8g} **0-0-5**

Orlar (Ire) *J A Osborne* 69 a73
3 b f Green Desert (USA) - Soviet Maid (Ire)
16^{10gf} 12^{10gf} 3^{8sd} 3^{9sd} 7^{10gf} 4^{10gf} 9^{10gf}
0-2-7 £1,501

Orpen Quest (Ire) *M J Attwater* 33 a53
3 b g Orpen (USA) - Pursuit Of Truth (USA)
5^{6sd} 8^{5gf} 8^{5gs} 8^{7sf} 3^{8ss} 3^{8sd} 4^{9sd} **0-2-7**
£422

Orpen Wide (Ire) *M C Chapman* 74 a82
3 b g Orpen (USA) - Melba (Ire)
1^{6sd} 1^{6sd} 9^{5sd} 7^{6sd} 6^{5sd} 3^{7sd} 11^{7s} 7^{8g} 10^{12gs} 7^{7g} 6^{7gf} 1^{5gf} 4^{5g} 5^{5g} 3^{6g} 13^{5g} 12^{6g} 6^{5gf} 6^{5gs} 9^{6g} 6^{6g} 1^{8gf} 7^{8s} 17^{7s} 12^{6sd} **4-1-25**
£17,105

Orpen's Astaire (Ire) *Jedd O'Keeffe*
2 b c Orpen (USA) - Rhythm And Style (USA)
14^{7s} **0-0-1**

Orpendonna (Ire) *K A Ryan* 51 a66
3 b f Orpen (USA) - Tetradonna (Ire)
2^{8sd} 5^{7sd} 7^{7g} 9^{8gf} 12^{8gf} 13^{7gf} **0-1-6**
£1,072

Orphan (Ire) *K R Burke* 86
3 b g Orpen (USA) - Ballinlee (Ire)
2^{6s} 1^{6gs} 4^{6s} 3^{6g} 1^{6gf} 6^{6gf} 7^{6gs} 12^{7hy}
2-2-8 £35,638

Orphina (Ire) *J L Dunlop* 64
2 b f Orpen (USA) - Keralba (USA)
9^{6gf} 8^{6gs} 2^{6gf} **0-1-3 £868**

Orpington *D K Weld* 108
4 b g Hernando (Fr) - Oops Pettie

6^{13sh} 2^{14gf} 1^{14gf} 18^{14g} 8^{14gf} **1-1-5**
£33,191

Orpsie Boy (Ire) *N P Littmoden* 81 a86
2 b c Orpen (USA) - Nordicolini (Ire)
8^{6sd} 1^{5gf} 2^{6gf} 5^{6gf} 9^{5gf} 1^{6sd} 3^{6sd} **2-2-7**
£14,041

Orrezzo (Ger) *G E Jones* 51
5 br g Zinaad - Ordessa (Ger)
7^{10g} 16^{10g} **0-0-2**

Orthodox *G L Moore* 55 a62
6 gr g Baryshnikov (Aus) - Sancta
10^{10sd} 12^{12sd} 10^{16sd} 11^{12sd} 9^{15s} 5^{12sd}
0-0-6

Orvietan (Ire) *M Johnston* 49
2 b c Sadler's Wells (USA) - Fiamma (Ire)
9^{8g} 11^{8gs} **0-0-2**

Oscar Snowman *M P Tregoning* 72
2 b c Selkirk (USA) - Chilly Start (Ire)
4^{7gf} **0-0-1 £424**

Oscillator *G A Butler* 71
2 b c Pivotal - Craigmill
4^{8s} **0-0-1 £415**

Osolomio (Ire) *J G Given* 29
2 b g Singspiel (Ire) - Inanna
9^{7g} **0-0-1**

Osorio (Ger) *M Johnston* 46
5 ch h Surumu (Ger) - Ocotal
12^{12s} 8^{10g} **0-0-2**

Ostfanni (Ire) *M Todhunter* 62
5 b m Spectrum (Ire) - Ostwahl (Ire)
6^{14gf} 4^{12gf} 10^{14s} **0-0-3 £279**

Otago (Ire) *J R Best* 76 a73
4 b g Desert Sun - Martino
2^{13sd} 4^{14sd} 3^{10g} 8^{12gf} 8^{10gf} 1^{10gf} 15^{12g} 4^{10g}
PU^{10g} 16^{8gs} 11^{12sd} **1-2-11 £6,518**

Otelcaliforni (USA) *J Noseda* a54
2 b f Gulch (USA) - Ive Gota Bad Liver (USA)
7^{7sd} **0-0-1**

Otis B Driftwood *M Quinn* 60 a63
2 b c Tipsy Creek (USA) - Gi La High
3^{5g} 4^{5gf} 9^{5gf} 9^{5gf} 1^{5sd} 6^{6sd} 14^{5g} 6^{5sd}
1-1-8 £3,569

Oude (USA) *Saeed Bin Suroor* 109
3 b/br c Dubai Millennium - Chosen Lady (USA)
19^{7gf} 2^{8gs} **0-1-2 £7,700**

Ouija Board *E A L Dunlop* 119
4 b f Cape Cross (Ire) - Selection Board
7^{10gf} 1^{12g} 2^{10y} 5^{12f} 1^{12gf} **2-1-5**
£796,888

Oulan Bator (Fr) *R A Fahey* 64
5 b g Astair (Fr) - Scarieuse (Fr)
3^{8sd} 1^{10sd} 1^{10sd} 16^{8s} 15^{10g} 5^{9gf} 1^{9gf} 3^{11gf}
14^{10s} 12^{10g} 3^{9g} **3-1-11 £17,953**

Ouninpohja (Ire) *G A Swinbank* 109
4 b g Imperial Ballet (Ire) - Daziyra (Ire)
16^{10gs} 3^{10gf} 5^{12gf} 1^{12gf} 1^{10g} 1^{12g} 1^{12gf} 1^{12g}
5-1-8 £48,316

Our Choice (Ire) *N P Littmoden* 73 a73
3 b g Indian Danehill (Ire) - Spring Daffodil
2^{9sd} 8^{10s} 5^{12gf} 8^{12sd} 4^{10gf} 3^{12gf} 2^{14gf} 2^{13gf}
1^{12gf} 2^{16gf} 1^{14sd} **2-5-11 £11,826**

Our Claudio *Mrs C A Dunnett*
3 b c Mind Games - Possessive Lady
11^{7sd} 11^{7sd} **0-0-2**

Our Destiny *A W Carroll* a61
7 b g Mujadil (USA) - Superspring
2^{9sd} 4^{10sd} 13^{9sd} **0-1-3 £832**

Our Fugitive (Ire) *A W Carroll* 81
3 gr c Titus Livius (Fr) - Mystical Jumbo
5^{5gs} 9^{5g} 16^{5g} 17^{5hy} 6^{6s} **0-0-5 £154**

Our Glenard *J E Long* 46 a35
6 b g Royal Applause - Loucoum (Fr)
9^{10sd} 3^{12gf} 6^{10g} 6^{12gf} 10^{10f} 12^{10g} **0-1-6**
£425

Our Imperial Bay (USA) *Jennie Candlish* a41
6 b g Smart Strike (Can) - Heat Lightning (USA)
4^{14sd} 3^{14sd} 8^{14sd} 8^{14sd} **0-1-4 £206**

Our Kes (Ire) *P Howling* a82
3 gr f Revoque (Ire) - Gracious Gretclo
1^{7sd} **1-0-1 £3,382**

Our Little Secret (Ire) *A Berry* 63 a41
3 ch f Rossini (USA) - Sports Post Lady (Ire)
6^{5sd} 3^{5g} 2^{5s} 5^{5g} 7^{5g} 12^{5gf} 1^{5g} 2^{5gf} 4^{5g} 5^{5gf}
5^{5s} 4^{5s} **1-3-12 £5,899**

Our Louis *J S Wainwright* 23 a22
3 b f Abou Zouz (USA) - Ninfa Of Cisterna
12^{5f} 9^{5gs} 11^{5sd} **0-0-3**

Our Mary (Ire) *Robert Gray* 55 a60
2 b f Mujadil (USA) - Desert Gem
6^{5g} 13^{7gf} 5^{6gf} 2^{6sf} **0-1-4 £846**

Our Monogram *R M Beckett* 72
9 b g Deploy - Darling Splodge
17^{16gs} 7^{18g} 1^{18g} 3^{16gf} 6^{16gf} 1^{17g} 11^{17g}
2-1-7 £8,795

Our Serendipity *K G Reveley* 55
2 ch f Presidium - Berl's Gift
12^{5g} 7^{6gs} 14^{5gf} **0-0-3**

Our Sheila *B Smart* 69 a48
2 ch f Bahamian Bounty - Shifting Mist
5^{5gf} 2^{5gf} 3^{5gf} 7^{6g} 10^{5gs} 7^{6gf} 8^{6gf} 5^{7sd}
0-1-8 £2,078

Our Sion *Mrs A M Thorpe*
5 b g Dreams End - Millfields Lady
13^{9sd} **0-0-1**

Our Sue *R A Fahey* 48
2 ch f Dr Fong (USA) - Evening Charm (Ire)
7^{7gf} 7^{7g} **0-0-2**

Our Teddy (Ire) *P A Blockley* 82 a83
5 ch g Grand Lodge (USA) - Lady Windley
9^{8sd} 7^{8sd} 6^{10gs} 3^{8gf} 5^{8gf} 8^{12gf} 2^{8gf} 4^{10gf} 8^{10gf}
4^{8gf} 5^{8gf} 8^{12gf} **0-1-12 £3,821**

Our Time (Ire) *H S Howe* 55
2 b f Danetime (Ire) - Tolomena
13^{6gs} 7^{5gf} 9^{7gf} **0-0-3**

Ours (Ire) *J D Bethell* 60
2 b g Mark Of Esteem (Ire) - Ellebanna
12^{6g} 2^{6gf} 5^{6g} 7^{7g} **0-1-4 £2,000**

Out After Dark *C G Cox* 111
4 b g Cadeaux Genereux - Midnight Shift (Ire)
6^{6s} 2^{6gs} 1^{5gf} 4^{6g} 1^{5gf} 1^{5g} 9^{5g} 5^{6gs} 2^{5s} 1^{6gf}
14^{6g} **4-3-11 £74,611**

Out For A Stroll *S C Williams* 78 a73
6 b g Zamindar (USA) - The Jotter
8^{6sd} 10^{7s} 8^{7gf} 9^{7g} 12^{8gf} 5^{7g} 11^{7g} 3^{9gf} 1^{8gf}
1^{8g} 1^{8g} 5^{7s} 1^{8gs} 8^{6gf} 4^{8gf} 3^{7sd} 10^{8sd}
4-3-17 £20,232

Out Of India *B Smart* 71 a65
3 b f Marju (Ire) - Tide Of Fortune
6^{8hy} 2^{7sd} 13^{7g} 2^{8gf} 6^{7gf} 6^{7sd} 10^{7sd} 4^{9sd} 1^{7gf}
1-2-9 £7,086

Out The Ordinary *E S McMahon* 76
2 b c Whittingham (Ire) - Special One
2^{5gs} 3^{5gf} 2^{5g} 2^{5gf} 5^{5gs} 6^{5g} 13^{6gf} **0-4-7 £3,974**

Outer Hebrides *Stef Liddiard* 87 a87
4 b g Efisio - Reuval
7^{7sd} 5^{7sd} 11^{7sd} 4^{7sd} 1^{7sd} 8^{7s} 1^{6g} 2^{6gf} 4^{6gf} 3^{6gf} 6^{6gf} 6^{6g} 1^{7gs} 5^{7g} 3^{7gf} 13^{7g} 4^{7gf} **3-4-17 £25,687**

Outlook *N P Littmoden* 67 a77
2 ch c Observatory (USA) - Area Girl
2^{6sd} 3^{6gs} 1^{7sd} 1^{6sd} 6^{7sd} 1^{6sd} 1^{6gs} 7^{7g} 4^{7sd} 9^{8sd} 2^{8sd} **4-3-11 £19,245**

Outrageous Flirt (Ire) *A Dickman* 57 a57
3 b f Indian Lodge (Ire) - Sofia Aurora (USA)
10^{6s} 7^{7g} 12^{8g} 1^{8gf} 3^{7sd} 6^{8gf} 4^{7f} 3^{8gf} 3^{6gf} 1^{7gs} 6^{8gf} 6^{7s} **2-3-12 £6,318**

Outside Half (Ire) *L Corcoran* 47 a48
3 ch g Raise A Grand (Ire) - Lindas Delight
12^{7sd} 14^{8s} 2^{11f} 13^{16g} 8^{12gf} 5^{14g} 6^{16g} 3^{13sd} **0-2-8 £1,065**

Outward (USA) *R Bastiman* 34 a12
5 b g Gone West (USA) - Seebe (USA)
11^{7sd} 11^{6g} 8^{8g} 4^{7gf} **0-0-4 £256**

Ovation Way (Gr) *P R Chamings* 59 a53
3 ch c Military Fashion - Analampi (Gr)
7^{9sd} 6^{8gf} 5^{8s} **0-0-3**

Over The Limit (Ire) *Mrs A J Perrett* 41
3 b f Diktat - Premiere Cuvee
10^{6s} 12^{8g} **0-0-2**

Over To You Bert *R J Hodges* 44
6 b g Overbury (Ire) - Silvers Era
1^{8s} 19^{7gs} 6^{8g} **1-0-3 £1,500**

Overdrawn (Ire) *Mrs S J Smith* 64 a62
4 b g Daggers Drawn (USA) - In Denial (Ire)
11^{8gf} 6^{8sd} 5^{7gf} 5^{10gs} 12^{9gf} 10^{8g} 5^{7gf} 14^{7f} 10^{7s} **0-0-9**

Overjoy Way *P R Chamings* 62 a50
3 b f Cadeaux Genereux - May Light
2^{7s} 16^{6gf} 9^{7gf} 11^{7sd} **0-1-4 £884**

Overlook *A M Balding* 57
2 b f Generous (Ire) - Spurned (USA)
5^{8gs} 9^{8s} **0-0-2**

Overlord Way (Gr) *P R Chamings* a82
3 br c Tony Galvin (Gr) - Fortunate Way (Gr)
2^{8sd} 2^{10sd} 1^{9sd} 10^{7sd} 10^{9sf} 11^{9sd} **1-2-6 £5,323**

Overstayed (Ire) *P A Blockley* 87
2 ch g Titus Livius (Fr) - Look Nonchalant (Ire)
1^{5hy} 7^{5gs} 2^{5g} 5^{5gf} 5^{6g} 6^{5g} 22^{6gf} **1-1-7 £7,882**

Overstrand (Ire) *Robert Gray* 64
6 b g In The Wings - Vaison La Romaine
8^{16g} 8^{14gf} 6^{14gs} 7^{12g} **0-0-4**

Overtop Way (Gr) *P R Chamings* 62
3 b g Denebola Way (Gr) - Dada (Gr)
9^{10g} 4^{7gs} 11^{8gf} 6^{8gs} 2^{9gf} 2^{8gf} **0-3-6 £2,897**

Overwing (Ire) *R Hannon* 74 a71
2 b f Fasliyev (USA) - Sierva (Ger)
3^{6gf} 2^{5gf} 2^{5gs} 5^{5gs} 3^{5g} 4^{5gf} 7^{5gs} 7^{5sd} 1^{5sd} **1-5-9 £9,776**

Owed *Robert Gray* 24 a71
3 b g Lujain (USA) - Nightingale
2^{6sd} 8^{6sd} 15^{7g} 11^{7sd} 2^{6sd} 3^{7sd} 8^{7sd} 16^{6g} 1^{6sd} 9^{5sd} 7^{9sd} 2^{6sd} 1^{7sd} 1^{7sd} **3-4-14 £9,765**

Owners Biscuits *M Johnston* 48
2 gr f Diktat - Delta Tempo (Ire)
6^{5s} 4^{5gf} 5^{6s} 11^{6gs} 11^{7g} **0-0-5 £257**

Oxford Street Pete (Ire) *A Bailey* 21
3 b g Rossini (USA) - Thabeh
10^{7g} **0-0-1**

Pab Special (Ire) *K R Burke* 65 a65
2 b g City On A Hill (USA) - Tinos Island (Ire)
11^{6gf} 2^{6gf} 5^{7sd} **0-1-3 £1,317**

Pace Shot (Ire) *G L Moore* 80 a77
3 b g Montjeu (Ire) - Pacific Grove
5^{8s} 2^{8g} 3^{11gf} 4^{12sd} 2^{12sd} 16^{9g} **0-2-6 £3,205**

Pacific Breeze (Ire) *J Jay* 42 a32
3 b f Turtle Island (Ire) - C'Est Egal (Ire)
8^{12s} 13^{10g} 11^{10gf} 2^{10gf} 12^{13sd} 14^{8sd} 5^{11sd} **0-1-7 £432**

Pacific Pride *J Howard Johnson* 103
2 b c Compton Place - Only Yours
3^{5g} 2^{6gf} 1^{6gf} 10^{6g} 11^{6gf} 7^{6hy} **1-1-6 £20,830**

Pack Of Lies *Rae Guest* a29
3 b f Lake Coniston (Ire) - Sylvan Dancer (Ire)
7^{6ft} 13^{5sd} 10^{5sd} 3^{5sd} **0-1-4 £208**

Packing Hero (USA) *W J Haggas* 74
2 b/br g Black Minnaloushe (USA) - Splendid (Ire)
3^{6gf} 2^{5g} 1^{6g} **1-2-3 £7,713**

Pactolos Way *P R Chamings* 56
2 b c Docksider (USA) - Arietta's Way (Ire)
7^{8g} 8^{7gs} 5^{7s} **0-0-3**

Paddy Boy (Ire) *J R Boyle* a32
4 br g Overbury (Ire) - Arts Project (Ire)
9^{14sd} **0-0-1**

Paddy Moon *J G Given* 52 a45
2 b g Lujain (USA) - Tara Moon
6^{6sd} 5^{6s} 7^{6hy} **0-0-3**

Paddy's Place (Ire) *M Blanshard* 49
2 b f Compton Place - Lamarita
11^{6gf} 12^{6g} 5^{5g} 13^{5gf} 9^{6sd} **0-0-5**

Paddys Tern *N M Babbage* 53 a57
3 b g Fraam - Great Tern
3^{10sd} 5^{10sd} 7^{11gs} 13^{12s} 10^{10sd} **0-1-5 £642**

Paddywack (Ire) *D W Chapman* 59 a64
8 b g Bigstone (Ire) - Millie's Return (Ire)
9^{6sd} 11^{5sd} 13^{6s} 10^{6g} 9^{6sd} 13^{6g} 6^{5gf} 4^{5sd} 8^{6gf} 5^{5gf} 6^{5g} 10^{6sd} 8^{6sd} 4^{5sd} **0-0-14**

Padre Nostro (Ire) *J R Holt* 60 a62
6 ch g Grand Lodge (USA) - Meglio Che Posso (Ire)
5^{13gf} 5^{12gf} 4^{10g} 13^{11g} 10^{9sd} 4^{11sd} **0-0-6 £297**

Pagan Crest *Mrs A J Perrett* 62
2 ch g Indian Ridge - Maria Theresa
5^{6gf} 6^{7g} 6^{6gf} 4^{7gs} 8^{7g} **0-1-5 £146**

Pagan Dance (Ire) *Mrs A J Perrett* 92
6 b g Revoque (Ire) - Ballade D'Ainhoa (Fr)
8^{12s} 8^{12g} 15^{16g} 8^{14gs} 3^{13gf} 3^{12gf} 7^{12hy} **0-2-7 £2,430**

Pagan Magic (USA) *T G McCourt* 70
4 b g Diesis - Great Lady Slew (USA)
18^{14s} 5^{12gf} 2^{12gs} 6^{14gf} 3^{11g} 7^{12gs} **0-2-6 £2,699**

Pagan Quest *J A R Toller* 59 a62
3 b g Lujain (USA) - Rohita (Ire)
11^{6g} 3^{6f} 2^{5gf} 10^{6g} 2^{6ft} 6^{7sd} **0-2-6**

£2,318

Pagan Sky (Ire) *Miss Venetia Williams* 93 a94
6 ch g Inchinor - Rosy Sunset (Ire)
$2^{10s}\ 19^{12g}\ 12^{12gf}\ 11^{10gf}\ 12^{10gs}\ 1^{10s}\ 3^{10gf}$
$3^{10g}\ 4^{10g}\ 2^{12sd}\ 6^{12sd}$ **1-4-11 £23,598**

Pagan Storm (USA) *Mrs L Stubbs* 36 a48
5 ch g Tabasco Cat (USA) - Melodeon (USA)
$8^{9sd}\ 5^{7sd}\ 2^{7sd}\ 2^{7sd}\ 10^{9sd}\ 2^{6sd}\ 10^{7s}\ 1^{6sd}\ 11^{7gf}$
$9^{7gf}\ 16^{7gs}$ **1-3-11 £2,806**

Pagan Sword *Mrs A J Perrett* 93 a73
3 ch g Selkirk (USA) - Vanessa Bell (Ire)
$3^{7sd}\ 1^{10sd}\ 1^{10gs}\ 6^{11gs}\ 1^{10gf}\ 3^{10gf}\ 10^{11gs}\ 2^{12f}$
1^{10gf} **4-3-9 £27,758**

Paint The Lily (Ire) *F Watson* 47
4 b f Barathea (Ire) - Chocolate Box
$4^{10s}\ 8^{12g}\ 11^{12f}\ 13^{12g}\ 20^{8gf}\ 8^{8gf}\ 6^{9s}$
0-0-7 £268

Pairumani's Girl (Ire) *J L Dunlop* 77
2 b f Pairumani Star (Ire) - Persian Fantasia
$6^{6gf}\ 8^{7f}\ 2^{8g}\ 10^{8g}$ **0-1-4 £1,205**

Palace Episode (USA) *K A Ryan* 114
2 b/br c Machiavellian (USA) - Palace Weekend (USA)
$1^{6f}\ 1^{7g}\ 3^{8g}\ 5^{7gs}\ 1^{8hy}$ **3-1-5 £160,480**

Palace Theatre (Ire) *T D Barron* a75
4 b g Imperial Ballet (Ire) - Luminary
$11^{5sd}\ 4^{6sd}$ **0-0-2 £513**

Palace Walk (Fr) *B G Powell* a51
3 b g Sinndar (Ire) - Page Bleue
$12^{10sd}\ 7^{12sd}$ **0-0-2**

Palais (Ire) *John A Harris*
10 b g Darshaan - Dance Festival
11^{14gf} **0-0-1**

Palais Polaire *J A Geake* 35
3 ch f Polar Falcon (USA) - Palace Street (USA)
9^{6g} **0-0-1**

Palamedes *Robert Gray* 81 a68
6 b g Sadler's Wells (USA) - Kristal Bridge
$10^{12gf}\ 8^{12sd}\ 1^{14gs}\ 17^{14gs}\ 9^{14ss}$ **1-0-5**
£4,213

Palatinate (Fr) *H Candy* 49
3 br g Desert Prince (Ire) - Dead Certain
14^{8gs} **0-0-1**

Palatine Dancer (Ire) *R W Price* 16 a38
3 ch f Namid - Esquiline (USA)
$10^{10gs}\ 5^{10g}\ 5^{6sd}\ 8^{6sd}\ 14^{5sd}\ 5^{5sd}$ **0-0-6**

Palawan *K A Ryan* a61
9 br g Polar Falcon (USA) - Krameria
$8^{5sd}\ 3^{5sd}\ 11^{6sd}$ **0-1-3 £375**

Pallas Royale (Ire) *M Johnston* 46
3 b g Montjeu (Ire) - Russian Rebel
$8^{9gf}\ 9^{10gs}\ 3^{10s}$ **0-0-3 £632**

Pamir (Ire) *L M Cumani* 76 a86
3 b g Namid - Mijouter (Ire)
$3^{6hy}\ 6^{6g}\ 5^{6g}\ 1^{6sd}\ \text{DSQ}^{6sd}\ 3^{7sd}\ 3^{7sd}$ **1-3-7**
£6,921

Panadin (Ire) *V Smith* 53 a36
3 b g Desert King (Ire) - Strident Note
$8^{8g}\ 9^{8g}\ 10^{10sd}\ 14^{16sd}$ **0-0-4**

Pango *H Morrison* 104
6 ch g Bluegrass Prince (Ire) - Riverine
$3^{7gf}\ 5^{8g}\ 2^{8gs}\ 1^{7g}\ 3^{7gf}\ 3^{7g}\ 1^{7gs}\ 18^{7gs}\ 6^{6s}$
2-4-9 £30,378

Panjandrum *R A Harris* 53 a67
7 b g Polar Falcon (USA) - Rengaine (Fr)
$5^{5sd}\ 7^{6sd}\ 4^{5sd}\ 7^{6sd}\ 6^{6sd}\ 5^{6gf}\ 9^{5gf}\ 7^{7gf}\ 8^{6sd}$
$12^{5g}\ 4^{5sd}$ **0-0-11**

Panshir (Fr) *Julian Poulton* 70 a49
4 ch g Unfuwain (USA) - Jalcamin (Ire)
$9^{6gf}\ 15^{6g}\ 13^{7g}\ 17^{7hy}\ 7^{7sd}$ **0-0-5**

Pantomime Prince *R Hannon* 68
2 b g Royal Applause - Floppie (Fr)
$2^{6gf}\ 7^{6gf}$ **0-1-2 £1,496**

Panzer (Ger) *D McCain* 78 a69
4 b g Vettori (Ire) - Prompt
$6^{9sd}\ 8^{9sd}\ 4^{12gf}\ 2^{12gf}\ 1^{12gf}\ 11^{14g}\ 9^{14s}$
1-2-7 £7,517

Papal Bull *Sir Michael Stoute* 82
2 b c Montjeu (Ire) - Mialuna
$4^{7gf}\ 2^{8g}\ 1^{7gf}$ **1-1-3 £7,202**

Papality *W Jarvis* 75
3 b f Giant's Causeway (USA) - Papabile (USA)
$2^{10gf}\ 3^{10g}\ 4^{12gf}\ 5^{10gs}\ 2^{10gf}\ 4^{10g}\ 1^{10gf}$
1-3-7 £8,634

Paparaazi (Ire) *R A Fahey* 78 a70
3 b g Victory Note (USA) - Raazi
$4^{8sd}\ 4^{7sd}\ 2^{8g}\ 5^{8gs}\ 4^{8gf}\ 1^{10g}\ 8^{10s}\ 10^{10g}$
1-1-8 £6,972

Papaspyros (Ire) *J J Quinn* 57 a53
2 ch g Fayruz - Pennant Flame (Ire)
$6^{5g}\ 5^{5g}\ 5^{5sd}\ 13^{5g}\ 6^{5sd}\ 10^{6sd}$ **0-0-6**

Pape Clement (Ire) *D K Ivory* 58 a51
3 ch g Diesis - Prima Voce (Ire)
$12^{10gs}\ 13^{7sd}\ 5^{7gf}\ 8^{6gf}$ **0-0-4**

Papeete (Ger) *Miss B Sanders* 74
4 b f Alzao (USA) - Prairie Vela
$1^{12f}\ 4^{13f}\ 7^{13gf}\ 1^{16gf}\ 4^{14gs}\ 8^{12g}\ 1^{12g}\ 7^{16g}\ 4^{12gs}$
3-0-9 £14,310

Paper Doll *B P J Baugh* a57
3 ch f Mister Baileys - Grand Coronet
$6^{8sd}\ 9^{9sd}\ 2^{8sd}\ 9^{10sd}\ 6^{7sd}\ 4^{8sd}\ 4^{8sd}\ 5^{9sd}\ 10^{7sd}$
$5^{8sd}\ 5^{9sd}$ **0-1-11 £736**

Paper Talk (USA) *B W Hills* 99
3 br c Unbridled's Song (USA) - Journalist (Ire)
$1^{7gf}\ 4^{7gf}\ 1^{8gf}\ 3^{8gf}\ 4^{7g}$ **2-2-5 £24,668**

Papineau *Saeed Bin Suroor* 115
5 ch h Singspiel (Ire) - Early Rising (USA)
$5^{14gs}\ 16^{20gf}$ **0-0-2 £3,500**

Pappas Ruby (USA) *J S Goldie* 32
2 b f Red Ransom (USA) - Pappa Reale
$9^{6g}\ 8^{7g}$ **0-0-2**

Pappy (Ire) *A W Carroll* 38 a21
4 b f Petardia - Impressive Lady
$10^{9sd}\ 9^{7sd}\ 8^{6sd}\ 4^{7g}\ 10^{8gf}\ 9^{10g}\ 11^{7f}$
0-0-7

Par Excellence *W G M Turner* 50 a53
2 gr f Wizard King - Great Intent
$5^{5sd}\ 5^{5gs}\ 5^{5sd}\ 2^{5gs}\ 3^{6gf}\ 4^{6g}\ 1^{5sd}\ 7^{5gf}\ 2^{5gf}$
$6^{5g}\ 5^{5gf}$ **1-3-11 £5,640**

Parade Ground *M A Jarvis*
2 b g Mark Of Esteem (Ire) - Winning Girl
14^{7s} **0-0-1**

Paradise Expected *P W Chapple-Hyam* 49
2 ch f North Briton - Phenomenon
8^{8hy} **0-0-1**

Paradise Flight (Ire) *K A Ryan* 72 a63
4 ch f In The Wings - Aloft (Ire)
$1^{16sd}\ 2^{16g}\ 8^{16gf}\ 4^{20s}\ 4^{16g}\ 1^{17gf}\ 3^{18gf}\ 3^{16gf}$
2-3-8 £12,538

Paradise Isle *C F Wall* 108
4 b f Bahamian Bounty - Merry Rous

$9^{5s}\ 1^{6g}\ 8^{5g}\ 10^{6g}\ 15^{6gf}\ 1^{6g}\ 4^{6s}$ **2-0-7 £19,263**

Paradise Mill (USA) *J H M Gosden* 77
3 b f Horse Chestnut (SAF) - Eaton Place (Ire)
$2^{8g}\ 4^{10gs}\ 1^{10g}$ **1-1-3 £5,309**

Paradise Street (Ire) *J R Fanshawe* 45
2 b f Machiavellian (USA) - Tani (USA)
$13^{7gf}\ 17^{8s}$ **0-0-2**

Paradise Valley *Stef Liddiard* 12 a51
5 b g Groom Dancer (USA) - Rose De Reve (Ire)
$13^{16sd}\ 15^{10gs}\ 5^{17sd}\ 10^{12ss}\ 6^{14sf}\ 10^{16sd}\ 12^{14ss}$ **0-0-7**

Parazone *E J O'Neill* a58
2 b c Superior Premium - Instinction
$10^{8sd}\ 5^{6sd}\ 3^{7sd}$ **0-1-3 £210**

Parc Aux Boules *R Charlton* 56 a58
4 gr g Royal Applause - Aristocratique
$5^{5sd}\ 2^{6sd}\ 2^{7sd}\ 7^{7sd}\ 2^{7sd}\ 9^{8sd}\ 1^{6sd}\ 7^{6gs}$ **1-3-8 £4,012**

Parchment (Ire) *J Howard Johnson* 59
3 ch g Singspiel (Ire) - Hannalou (Fr)
$11^{8s}\ 3^{7gf}\ 6^{11gf}$ **0-1-3 £543**

Paris Bell *T D Easterby* 88
3 gr g Paris House - Warning Bell
$13^{6hy}\ 12^{6s}\ 1^{6s}\ 5^{6gf}\ 5^{6gs}\ 7^{6gf}\ 4^{6gs}\ 6^{6gf}\ 19^{6g}\ 10^{6gs}\ 3^{6hy}\ 10^{7s}$ **1-1-12 £10,748**

Paris Dreamer *R A Fahey* a49
4 b f Paris House - Stoproveritate
$3^{8sd}\ 1^{12sd}\ 2^{14sd}$ **1-2-3 £2,102**

Paris Heights *R M Whitaker* 60
3 gr g Paris House - Petra Nova
$3^{6s}\ 8^{7s}\ 10^{6g}\ 1^{7gf}\ 4^{7gf}\ 2^{7g}\ 5^{8gf}\ 7^{7gf}\ 2^{7gs}\ 4^{8gf}\ 8^{8gf}\ 4^{8s}$ **1-4-12 £4,192**

Paris Power *D Morris* 32 a28
2 b g Superpower - Gables Turner
$8^{5gs}\ 10^{5gf}\ 8^{6gf}\ 8^{8hy}\ 10^{10sd}$ **0-0-5**

Paris St Germain (Ire) *Miss V Haigh* 31
2 b f Definite Article - Key To Paris (Arg)
3^{5g} **0-0-1 £516**

Paris Tapis *P S McEntee* 6 a31
3 gr f Paris House - Time Of Night (USA)
$10^{6s}\ 11^{5sd}\ 15^{5gf}\ 12^{5sd}\ 12^{7f}$ **0-0-5**

Parisette *H R A Cecil* 78
3 b f Dansili - Moulin Rouge
$1^{8g}\ 4^{8s}\ 7^{8gs}\ 6^{7f}\ 11^{7gf}$ **1-0-5 £5,396**

Parisi Princess *D L Williams* 21 a45
4 ch f Shaddad (USA) - Crambella (Ire)
$5^{10sd}\ 4^{7sd}\ 10^{8gf}\ 9^{11gf}\ 15^{10f}$ **0-0-5**

Parisian Playboy *Jedd O'Keeffe* 56
5 gr g Paris House - Exordium
$11^{7s}\ 4^{7s}\ 2^{8g}\ 5^{8s}\ 8^{8gs}\ 6^{7g}\ 7^{8g}\ 5^{6s}\ 11^{6gf}\ 4^{7s}$ **0-2-10 £827**

Parisien Star (Ire) *J R Boyle* 64 a54
9 ch g Paris House - Auction Maid (Ire)
$8^{10sd}\ 12^{12gf}\ 15^{10gf}\ 4^{10gf}\ 6^{10gf}\ 9^{10g}\ 3^{9gf}$ **0-2-7 £1,234**

Park Approach (Ire) *D J Daly* 44 a56
3 gr f Indian Ridge - Abyat (USA)
$12^{6gf}\ 11^{5gf}\ 3^{7gf}\ 13^{6gf}\ 8^{6sd}\ 6^{5sd}\ 11^{5sd}$ **0-0-7 £513**

Park Ave Princess (Ire) *M J Polglase* a24
4 b f Titus Livius (Fr) - Satinette
6^{12sd} **0-0-1**

Park Lane Princess (Ire) *D M Simcock* 58
2 ch f King Of Kings (Ire) - Heated Debate (USA)
$3^{7g}\ 4^{7g}$ **0-1-2 £714**

Park Law (Ire) *J H M Gosden* 79
3 b f Fasliyev (USA) - Blanche Dubois
9^{7gs} **0-0-1**

Park Romance (Ire) *B J Meehan* 86
3 b f Dr Fong (USA) - Park Charger
$7^{8gf}\ 16^{8g}$ **0-0-2**

Park Star *D Shaw* 49 a53
5 b m Gothenberg (Ire) - Miriam
$11^{6sd}\ 4^{6sd}\ 9^{6sd}\ 7^{5sd}\ 8^{6g}\ 16^{8g}\ 14^{7sd}\ 1^{6sd}\ 6^{6sd}\ 5^{6sd}\ 9^{7sd}$ **1-0-11 £1,419**

Parkie Malarkey (Ire) *M Dods*
2 b f Shinko Forest (Ire) - Thornby Park
$15^{6gf}\ 11^{5g}$ **0-0-2**

Parkside Pursuit *J M Bradley* 73
7 b g Pursuit Of Love - Ivory Bride
$10^{5gf}\ 5^{5g}\ 8^{5f}\ 14^{5gf}\ 3^{6g}\ 7^{5gf}\ 10^{5gf}\ 10^{5gf}\ 2^{5gf}\ 1^{5gf}\ 10^{5g}\ 8^{5gs}\ 2^{5f}\ 2^{5g}\ 3^{5gf}\ 3^{6f}\ 3^{5gf}\ 14^{5gs}$ **1-7-18 £9,868**

Parkview Love (USA) *D Shaw* 64 a74
4 b/br g Mister Baileys - Jerre Jo Glanville (USA)
$11^{12sd}\ 7^{12sd}\ 8^{10sd}\ 5^{11g}\ 11^{8g}\ 10^{7gf}\ 3^{7sd}\ 5^{6gs}\ 4^{7sd}\ 7^{6sd}\ 1^{8sd}\ 8^{7g}\ 12^{7sd}\ 2^{8sf}\ 1^{7sd}\ 2^{8sd}\ 5^{7sd}\ 8^{8sd}$ **2-3-18 £8,752**

Parnassian *J A Geake* 80
5 ch g Sabrehill (USA) - Delphic Way
$3^{7gs}\ 9^{8g}\ 8^{10s}\ 5^{11g}\ 13^{8gf}\ 7^{10g}\ 2^{10gs}\ 8^{8g}\ 2^{8g}\ 5^{10g}\ 1^{10hy}$ **1-3-11 £7,553**

Parsley's Return *M Wigham* 54 a48
3 b g Danzero (Aus) - The Frog Queen
$1^{8sd}\ 11^{9sd}\ 5^{9gf}\ 2^{10f}\ 3^{8g}\ 1^{12gf}\ 7^{12sd}\ 6^{13sd}\ 12^{10sd}$ **2-2-9 £4,019**

Participation *J H M Gosden* 83
2 b c Dansili - Andaleeb (USA)
$6^{8gf}\ 7^{8g}\ 1^{7gf}$ **1-0-3 £4,946**

Partners In Jazz (USA) *T D Barron* 105
4 gr g Jambalaya Jazz (USA) - Just About Enough (USA)
$7^{6gs}\ 1^{6s}\ 6^{6g}\ 2^{7g}\ 4^{7gs}\ 3^{7gf}\ 11^{6gs}\ 15^{6g}\ 12^{7g}$ **1-3-9 £34,484**

Party Belle *C E Brittain* 43 a56
2 b f Silver Patriarch (Ire) - Third Party
$5^{5gf}\ 8^{7sd}\ 2^{9sd}\ 3^{7sd}$ **0-1-4 £984**

Party Boss *C E Brittain* 103 a107
3 gr c Silver Patriarch (Ire) - Third Party
$1^{9sd}\ 1^{9sd}\ 1^{7sd}\ 1^{7sd}\ 1^{8sd}\ 12^{8gf}\ 5^{11g}\ 6^{7gs}\ 16^{8gf}\ 11^{7g}\ 7^{8g}\ 5^{7sd}$ **5-0-12 £102,235**

Party Ploy *K R Burke* 65
7 b g Deploy - Party Treat (Ire)
$11^{12s}\ 8^{12gs}\ 11^{12gf}\ 6^{12gf}\ 2^{12f}$ **0-1-5 £838**

Party Princess (Ire) *S Parr* 63 a64
4 b f Orpen (USA) - Summer Queen
$6^{6sd}\ 5^{6g}\ 11^{6gf}\ 12^{6g}\ 11^{7sd}\ 15^{5gf}\ 1^{6g}\ 15^{6gf}\ 11^{6g}\ 17^{6g}\ 12^{7gf}\ 6^{7sf}\ 11^{6sd}$ **1-0-13 £3,519**

Pas De Surprise *P D Evans* a48
7 b g Dancing Spree (USA) - Supreme Rose
$4^{8sd}\ 4^{9sd}\ 8^{9sd}\ 7^{9sd}$ **0-0-4**

Paso Doble *B R Millman* 55 a74
7 b g Dancing Spree (USA) - Delta Tempo (Ire)
$4^{8sd}\ 8^{8sd}\ 10^{6sd}\ 7^{9sd}\ 3^{9sd}\ 3^{7sd}\ 9^{8gf}\ 8^{10s}\ 4^{10gf}\ 10^{10g}\ 9^{11gf}\ 1^{7sd}\ 1^{7sd}\ 7^{8sd}$ **2-2-14 £7,333**

Pass The Port *D Haydn Jones* 81 a84
4 ch g Docksider (USA) - One Of The Family
$6^{7sd}\ 11^{9sd}\ 7^{9sd}\ 6^{12sd}\ 1^{12sd}\ 2^{14gs}\ 2^{13s}\ 5^{14s}\ 3^{14gf}\ 2^{13gs}\ 10^{14g}\ 11^{15s}\ 2^{12sf}\ 1^{12sd}\ 2^{12sd}$

2-5-15 £19,598

Passion Fruit *C W Fairhurst* 81
4 b f Pursuit Of Love - Reine De Thebes (Fr)
1^{6gs} 4^{7gf} 3^{7gf} 1^{7g} 1^{7g} 12^{7g} 2^{7gf} 5^{7gf} 4^{7g} 5^{7hy} **3-3-10 £15,391**

Passion Rules (Ire) *M G Quinlan* a69
2 ch c Carrowkeel (Ire) - Mauras Pride (Ire)
1^{8sd} **1-0-1 £3,783**

Passionately Royal *R A Fahey* 74
3 b g Royal Applause - Passionelle
1^{7g} 1^{8gs} 3^{8gf} 9^{8g} 14^{8gf} 11^{8gf} **2-0-6 £10,872**

Past Tender (Ire) *E J O'Neill* 93 a86
2 br c Indian Danehill (Ire) - Escudo (Ire)
1^{5gf} 6^{5g} 3^{5gf} 3^{5f} 2^{6sd} 2^{6gf} **1-2-6 £11,152**

Pastoral Pursuits *H Morrison* 123
4 b c Bahamian Bounty - Star
7^{8gf} 1^{6gs} **1-0-2 £145,000**

Pat Malone *Lucinda Featherstone*
5 b g Jumbo Hirt (USA) - A Sharp
12^{8sd} **0-0-1**

Patau *C J Down* 56 a56
3 ch c Inchinor - Haste
7^{13sd} 9^{14g} **0-0-2**

Patavellian (Ire) *R Charlton* 113
7 b/br g Machiavellian (USA) - Alessia
6^{6gf} 7^{6s} 2^{6gf} 12^{6g} 3^{7g} 7^{6g} 1^{6g} 5^{5gs} 4^{6gs} **1-2-9 £36,861**

Patavium (Ire) *E J O'Neill* 72
2 b c Titus Livius (Fr) - Arcevia (Ire)
2^{8gf} 10^{8gf} 3^{7g} 11^{8g} **0-2-4 £1,592**

Patavium Prince (Ire) *J R Best* 65
2 ch g Titus Livius (Fr) - Hoyland Common (Ire)
4^{5gf} 7^{5gf} 9^{6gf} **0-0-3 £378**

Patitiri (USA) *E A L Dunlop* a29
2 ch f Rahy (USA) - Dharma (USA)
12^{7sd} **0-0-1**

Patoma (Ire) *Miss E C Lavelle* a62
2 b g Vettori (Ire) - Heresheis
7^{8sd} 8^{10sd} 6^{8sd} **0-0-3**

Patricia Philomena (Ire) *T D Barron* 56
7 br m Prince Of Birds (USA) - Jeewan
12^{12gf} 3^{12f} 2^{12gf} 6^{15g} 3^{13gf} 5^{11gf} **0-3-6 £1,707**

Patrician Dealer *M S Saunders* 10
3 br g Millkom - Double Fault (Ire)
6^{10f} **0-0-1**

Patrixprial *M H Tompkins* 67
4 gr g Linamix (Fr) - Magnificent Star (USA)
10^{17g} **0-0-1**

Patronage *Jonjo O'Neill* 81 a69
3 b g Royal Applause - Passionate Pursuit
5^{10sd} 2^{10gf} 3^{10gf} 2^{12gf} 1^{11gf} 14^{10gs} 9^{11gf} 5^{10gf} **1-3-8 £7,466**

Patternmaker (USA) *W Jarvis* 74 a69
3 b/br g Elnadim (USA) - Attasliyah (Ire)
2^{6s} 2^{6g} 5^{5f} 1^{6gf} 6^{6s} 9^{6gf} 4^{6sd} 11^{6sd} 6^{5sd} **1-2-9 £6,017**

Patxaran (Ire) *P C Haslam* 80
3 b f Revoque (Ire) - Stargard
1^{9gs} 1^{11gf} 2^{10gf} 5^{12gs} 9^{12g} 6^{12g} **2-1-6 £7,852**

Paula Jo *J S Wainwright*
3 b f Factual (USA) - Superstream
12^{7gf} 13^{7gf} 13^{6f} **0-0-3**

Paula Lane *R Curtis* a39
5 b m Factual (USA) - Colfax Classic
13^{13sd} 10^{11sd} **0-0-2**

Paulas Jazz (Ire) *M G Quinlan* 40 a62
2 b c Tagula (Ire) - Sodfahh
3^{8sd} 9^{7g} **0-1-2 £474**

Pauline's Prince *R Hollinshead* 84 a61
3 b c Polar Prince (Ire) - Etma Rose (Ire)
6^{6sd} 5^{6s} 4^{7g} 6^{5s} 7^{7gf} 7^{7gf} 8^{6gf} 5^{7sd} 4^{6g} 7^{7gf} **0-0-10 £863**

Pauls Plain *P W Hiatt*
4 b g Young Buster (Ire) - On The Wagon
17^{8g} **0-0-1**

Pauvic (Ire) *Mrs A Duffield* 46 a56
2 b g Fayruz - Turntable (Ire)
5^{5sd} 4^{5f} 1^{5sd} 13^{6gf} 16^{5hy} 8^{5sd} 4^{5sd} **1-0-7 £1,452**

Pavie (Ire) *Miss J R Gibney* 50 a38
3 ch f Elnadim (USA) - Courtlandt Queen (USA)
8^{7g} 6^{8gs} 5^{8gf} 12^{7sf} 5^{7sd} **0-0-5**

Pavilion *Miss K B Boutflower* 8
3 b f Robellino (USA) - Chiltern Court (USA)
14^{10sd} 8^{11gf} 13^{16g} **0-0-3**

Pawan (Ire) *Miss A Stokell* 80 a91
5 ch g Cadeaux Genereux - Born To Glamour
3^{6sd} 6^{5sd} 5^{5sd} 3^{7sd} 2^{5sd} 2^{6sd} 1^{7sd} 9^{8sd} 5^{6sd} 7^{7gf} 5^{8s} 8^{6s} 2^{7gs} 9^{8g} 7^{8gf} 14^{7f} 9^{6sd} 3^{5g} 5^{6g} 2^{5s} 7^{6sd} 4^{5sd} 4^{5sd} 4^{6sd} **1-7-24 £16,495**

Pawn Broker *Miss J R Tooth* 86
8 ch g Selkirk (USA) - Dime Bag
6^{10gf} 6^{8gs} 14^{8gf} 10^{10gf} 9^{8gf} 7^{10g} **0-0-6 £762**

Pawn In Life (Ire) *M J Polglase* a71
7 b g Midhish - Lady-Mumtaz
2^{8sd} 1^{8sd} 10^{9sd} 1^{8sd} 5^{8sd} 3^{7sd} 8^{7sd} 9^{8sd} 17^{7gf} 12^{12sd} 11^{7sd} 11^{6sd} 12^{8sd} 7^{7sd} 11^{8sd} 12^{8sd} 7^{8sd} 10^{8sd} 3^{8sd} **2-3-19 £8,062**

Pawtucket (Ire) *Saeed Bin Suroor* 38
2 b c Cape Cross (Ire) - Manchaca (Fr)
11^{8gs} **0-0-1**

Pax *D Nicholls* 79
8 ch g Brief Truce (USA) - Child's Play (USA)
3^{5s} 3^{6s} 15^{5gs} 10^{6f} 9^{6gf} 14^{6gs} 3^{6gf} 5^{7gf} 2^{7g} 12^{7gf} **0-3-10 £3,953**

Pax Romana (Ire) *P D Cundell* 81
3 b f Alzao (USA) - Forest Lair
4^{10s} 1^{12s} 6^{15gs} 4^{11g} 8^{11f} 13^{12gf} 13^{10gs} **1-1-7 £6,450**

Pay On (Ire) *W Jarvis* 35
2 ch c Danehill Dancer (Ire) - Richly Deserved (Ire)
13^{6g} 10^{7s} **0-0-2**

Pay The Silver *M F Harris* 64
7 gr g Petong - Marjorie's Memory (Ire)
12^{10g} 4^{10g} 9^{12g} 6^{10s} 10^{12g} **0-0-5 £309**

Pay Time *R E Barr* 55 a44
6 ch m Timeless Times (USA) - Payvashooz
9^{5sd} 7^{7g} 3^{8gf} 6^{7sd} 5^{6f} 10^{6gf} 11^{6f} 3^{7g} 9^{6gf} 8^{6gf} 14^{7g} **0-2-11 £1,303**

Pays D'Amour (Ire) *D A Nolan* 44
8 b g Pursuit Of Love - Lady Of The Land
9^{6gs} 10^{7g} 11^{5gf} 8^{6gf} 12^{6g} 13^{7g} 8^{6gf} 6^{6gf} 13^{6gf} 12^{6g} **0-0-10**

Peace And Love (Ire) *M A Magnusson* 73
2 ch f Fantastic Light (USA) - Muschana

4^{5gf} 1^{5g} 7^{5gs} 8^{6gf} 7^{7gf} 12^{7g} 10^{5g} 9^{5g}
1-0-8 £5,774

Peace Emblem (Ire) *J W Unett* 46 a53
4 b f Bahhare (USA) - Beseeching (Ire)
4^{9sd} 7^{9sd} 7^{9sd} 3^{9sd} 3^{9sd} 1^{9sd} 5^{12sd} 2^{12sd} 5^{10s} 10^{9sd} 3^{9sd} 4^{12sd} 6^{10f} 6^{14sd} 6^{9sf} 4^{11g} 4^{9sf} 14^{10sd} 6^{9ss} **1-4-19 £3,451**

Peace Lily *R F Johnson Houghton* 62
3 b f Dansili - Shall We Run
14^{8g} 3^{6gf} 13^{7gf} 6^{6gf} 5^{6gs} 19^{6g} **0-1-6 £748**

Peace Offering (Ire) *D Nicholls* 104
5 b g Victory Note (USA) - Amnesty Bay
6^{5s} 5^{6hy} 13^{6sh} 4^{5g} 2^{5g} 5^{5gf} 2^{6gs} 3^{5g} 13^{6g}
0-3-9 £23,743

Peace Treaty (Ire) *S R Bowring* a5
4 b f Turtle Island (Ire) - Beautyofthepeace (Ire)
11^{9sd} 11^{12sd} 10^{7sd} **0-0-3**

Peaceful Frontier *C Smith*
3 b f Monashee Mountain (USA) - Edge Of Darkness
12^{6sd} **0-0-1**

Peak Of Perfection (Ire) *M A Jarvis* 92 a64
4 b g Deploy - Nsx
12^{12gf} 6^{12s} 2^{14g} 12^{16sd} 11^{14gs} 13^{15gs} 5^{14g}
0-1-7 £4,630

Peak Park (USA) *P L Gilligan* 60 a77
5 br g Dynaformer (USA) - Play Po (USA)
3^{16sd} 5^{16sd} 1^{16sd} 1^{14sd} 1^{16sd} 18^{20s} 8^{16sd} 9^{16g} 8^{16gf} 1^{16sf} 4^{14ss} 3^{14sd} **4-2-12 £14,756**

Peak Seasons (Ire) *W De Best-Turner* 64
2 ch c Raise A Grand (Ire) - Teresian Girl (Ire)
12^{6gf} 4^{6gf} 2^{6g} 4^{6gf} 7^{6s} 14^{7s} **0-1-6 £3,014**

Pearl Farm *C A Horgan* 57 a53
4 b f Foxhound (USA) - Trinity Hall
2^{6g} 5^{6gf} 3^{6gs} 4^{7gf} 6^{7sd} **0-1-5 £1,749**

Pearl Fisher (Ire) *D Carroll* a48
4 ch f Foxhound (USA) - Naivity (Ire)
9^{7sd} 11^{9sd} 11^{9sd} 12^{9sd} 8^{12sd} 12^{7sd} 6^{7sd}
0-0-7

Pearl Island (USA) *D J Wintle* a32
4 b g Kingmambo (USA) - Mother Of Pearl (Ire)
8^{8sd} 17^{5g} 8^{8sd} **0-0-3**

Pearl King (Ire) *M A Jarvis* 94
3 gr g Daylami (Ire) - Regal Opinion (USA)
5^{8gf} 1^{8g} 6^{10s} 2^{8gf} 4^{8gs} 2^{8g} 2^{10g} 3^{10g}
1-4-8 £20,108

Pearl Of Love (Ire) *M Johnston* 100
4 b c Peintre Celebre (USA) - Aunt Pearl (USA)
10^{12gf} 4^{8gs} 22^{8gf} 8^{12gs} **0-0-4 £1,045**

Pearl's A Singer (Ire) *E McNamara* 71 a68
3 ch f Spectrum (Ire) - Cultured Pearl (Ire)
8^{8s} 4^{9sd} 5^{14g} 2^{12gf} 1^{14g} 1^{12f} SU^{11gf} 5^{12s} 3^{13gf} 7^{12gf} **2-1-10 £8,673**

Pearl's Girl *W J Haggas* 72
2 gr f King's Best (USA) - Karsiyaka (Ire)
3^{7s} **0-1-1 £664**

Pearly King (USA) *Sir Michael Stoute* 46
2 br c Kingmambo (USA) - Mother Of Pearl (Ire)
14^{7g} **0-0-1**

Pearly Poll *R M Beckett* 78 a68
2 ch f Prince Sabo - Bit Of A Tart
2^{6g} 1^{6hy} 11^{7sd} **1-1-3 £4,656**

Pearson Glen (Ire) *James Moffatt* 36 a62
6 ch g Dolphin Street (Fr) - Glendora
2^{9sd} 6^{10sd} 10^{9sd} 14^{8g} 13^{12gf} 9^{14sd} **0-1-6 £833**

Peas 'n Beans (Ire) *M L W Bell* 51 a60
2 ch g Medicean - No Sugar Baby (Fr)
15^{8gf} 6^{8g} 10^{7sd} **0-0-3**

Pedlar Of Dreams (Ire) *Stef Liddiard* 36 a17
3 b f Fayruz - Beautyofthepeace (Ire)
10^{6sd} 6^{5g} 7^{6f} 12^{6gs} **0-0-4**

Pedlar Of Luck *A G Newcombe* a23
2 ch c Zaha (Can) - Victoriet
7^{6sd} **0-0-1**

Pedrillo *Sir Mark Prescott* 107
4 b g Singspiel (Ire) - Patria (USA)
13^{8gs} 9^{8gf} 1^{9g} 23^{9s} **1-0-4 £18,200**

Pedro Jack (Ire) *M A Buckley* 45 a41
8 b g Mujadil (USA) - Festival Of Light
5^{6g} 17^{6gf} 7^{7sd} **0-0-3**

Pee Jay's Dream *M W Easterby* 63 a54
3 ch g Vettori (Ire) - Langtry Lady
12^{11gs} 10^{10gs} 4^{12sd} 4^{14gf} 3^{14gf} 2^{16s} 4^{14g} 2^{13s} 2^{15s} **0-4-9 £3,539**

Peephole *P J Makin* 57 a51
2 ch g Pursuit Of Love - Goodwood Lass (Ire)
10^{8g} 8^{8gf} 9^{8gs} 7^{10sd} 3^{9sd} **0-1-5 £207**

Peeress *Sir Michael Stoute* 117
4 ch f Pivotal - Noble One
1^{7gs} 2^{9g} 1^{8gf} 3^{8g} 1^{8gs} 4^{7gs} **3-0-6 £248,400**

Peewit (Ire) *R F Johnson Houghton* 39
3 b f Namid - Petomi
11^{8gs} 10^{7gf} 15^{7g} **0-0-3**

Peggy Holder *C W Thornton* 16
2 ch f Dancing Spree (USA) - Peggotty
13^{7g} 12^{8gf} 14^{7gf} **0-0-3**

Pekan One *M A Jarvis* 66 a47
3 ch c Grand Lodge (USA) - Ballet
7^{12sd} 5^{10g} 7^{12gs} 8^{10gs} **0-0-4**

Pelham Crescent (Ire) *R Hannon* 76 a75
2 ch c Giant's Causeway (USA) - Sweet Times
9^{7g} 4^{7gf} 2^{7g} 1^{6gs} 6^{8g} 6^{8g} 11^{7hy} 14^{7sd} 2^{8sd} 6^{7sd} **1-2-10 £8,526**

Pella *M Blanshard* 66
4 ch f Hector Protector (USA) - Norpella
11^{8gf} 5^{8gs} 8^{8s} 8^{8g} 6^{8g} 9^{8gf} 1^{10g} 3^{12gs}
1-1-8 £4,472

Penalty Clause (Ire) *Lucinda Featherstone*
5 b g Namaqualand (USA) - Lady Be Lucky (Ire)
12^{12sd} 11^{17sf} **0-0-2**

Penalty Kick (Ire) *N A Callaghan* 74
3 b c Montjeu (Ire) - Dafrah (USA)
11^{9gf} 7^{8gf} 7^{8gs} 3^{11gs} 7^{12gs} 8^{12g} **0-1-6 £550**

Penang Cinta *G A Butler* 40 a48
2 b c Halling (USA) - Penang Pearl (Fr)
19^{7gf} 6^{6sd} 10^{5sd} **0-0-3**

Penang Sapphire *R M Beckett* 59 a27
3 b g Spectrum (Ire) - Penang Pearl (Fr)
7^{6s} 3^{5s} 19^{6gs} 12^{8g} 8^{8gf} 10^{7g} 10^{6sd}
0-0-7 £415

Pending (Ire) *R A Fahey* 66 a63
4 b g Pennekamp (USA) - Dolcezza (Fr)
11^{9sd} 10^{7sd} 2^{8gf} 6^{8gf} 1^{8g} 6^{8gf} 5^{8f} 5^{8gf} 12^{8gf} 9^{8gs} 2^{8sd} 5^{8sd} 2^{8sd} **1-3-13 £5,729**

Penel (Ire) *P T Midgley* 57 a55
4 b g Orpen (USA) - Jayess Elle

3^{6sd} 2^{8g} 10^{6sd} 9^{8gs} 10^{9sd} 4^{10g} 15^{9gf} 6^{10g} 15^{12g} 7^{11sd} 12^{8sd} **0-2-11 £1,823**

Penkenna Princess (Ire) *R M Beckett* 108
3 b f Pivotal - Tiriana
1^{7gs} 16^{8gf} 2^{8gy} 5^{8g} 7^{10gs} 6^{8gs} 4^{8s} **1-1-7 £96,411**

Penmara *M H Tompkins* 59
2 b f Mtoto - Pendulum
9^{6gf} 8^{7gf} 6^{6gf} 3^{10g} **0-1-4 £555**

Penmon Point (Ire) *N Tinkler* 40
2 b g Foxhound (USA) - Brandon Princess
9^{5g} 9^{6gs} 11^{5g} 6^{5gf} **0-0-4**

Pennautier (Ire) *P A Blockley* 50 a50
3 gr f Paris House - Traci's Castle (Ire)
6^{8sd} 7^{9sd} 3^{6gs} 8^{8g} 8^{6gs} 6^{5gf} 12^{6s} 5^{6f} 11^{10f} 11^{7gf} 8^{7gf} 11^{7sf} **0-1-12 £742**

Pennestamp (Ire) *J G M O'Shea* 42
3 b c Pennekamp (USA) - Sopran Marida (Ire)
12^{12f} 6^{12f} 4^{11gs} 18^{7gf} 9^{10g} **0-0-5**

Penny Glitters *J A Glover* 72
2 br f Benny The Dip (USA) - Lucy Glitters (USA)
5^{6gf} 8^{6g} **0-0-2**

Penny Island (Ire) *A King* 52
3 b g Trans Island - Sparklingsovereign
8^{10gf} 11^{8gf} **0-0-2**

Penny Pictures (Ire) *M C Pipe* 84
6 b g Theatrical - Copper Creek
12^{20gf} 10^{16gs} 31^{18gs} **0-0-3**

Penny Stall *Miss E C Lavelle* 52 a56
4 b f Silver Patriarch (Ire) - Madiyla
6^{10gs} 12^{9sd} **0-0-2**

Penny Thoughts *E S McMahon* 56 a29
2 b f Prince Sabo - United Passion
4^{5g} 9^{5sd} 13^{5sf} **0-0-3 £261**

Penny Wedding (Ire) *Miss J Feilden* 75 a54
3 b f Pennekamp (USA) - Eilean Shona
1^{10s} 8^{12g} 4^{10s} 7^{10sd} **1-0-4 £3,564**

Penny Whisper (Ire) *M Dods* 66
2 b f Orpen (USA) - Ionian Secret
1^{5s} 4^{5g} 7^{5gs} 6^{6gf} 1^{7g} 9^{8gs} **2-0-6 £7,899**

Pensata *Miss L A Perratt* 40
2 b f Compton Place - Artistic Merit
10^{5g} 6^{5g} 9^{6g} **0-0-3**

Pension Fund *M W Easterby* 3
11 b g Emperor Fountain - Navarino Bay
15^{11g} 13^{10s} **0-0-2**

Pentecost *A M Balding* 109 a75
6 ch g Tagula (Ire) - Boughtbyphone
1^{8s} 6^{8g} 3^{8gf} 11^{8s} 6^{9g} 5^{8gf} 12^{8sd} 17^{10gs} **1-0-8 £16,312**

Penway *A Sadik* a62
4 b g Groom Dancer (USA) - Imani
6^{8sd} 3^{10sd} 5^{7sd} 5^{7sd} 6^{7sd} 4^{12sd} 13^{9sd} 10^{11sd} 13^{9sd} 10^{9ss} **0-1-10 £790**

Penwell Hill (USA) *M J Attwater* 53 a86
6 b g Distant View (USA) - Avie's Jill (USA)
8^{8sd} 12^{9sd} 5^{11sd} 4^{8sd} 1^{8sd} 12^{8sd} 14^{11g} 5^{7gf} 16^{8gf} 11^{8f} 2^{6sd} 11^{7gf} 11^{9sd} 10^{9sd} **1-1-14 £8,224**

Peopleton Brook *J M Bradley* 86 a72
3 b c Compton Place - Merch Rhyd-Y-Grug
1^{5g} 1^{5gf} 3^{5g} 2^{5gf} 1^{5gf} 2^{5gs} 2^{5gf} 2^{5g} 3^{5g} 16^{5gs} 7^{5g} 3^{5s} 7^{5sd} **3-7-13 £29,895**

Pepper Road *R Bastiman* 56 a41
6 ch g Elmaamul (USA) - Floral Spark
16^{7s} 3^{8g} 10^{8gf} 5^{8gf} 8^{8gf} 5^{7f} 2^{7gf} 4^{8f} 5^{7sd} **0-2-9 £1,500**

Peppermint Tea (Ire) *M L W Bell* 53 a64
3 b f Intikhab (USA) - Karayb (Ire)
2^{6sd} 3^{8gs} 5^{8gf} **0-0-3 £1,790**

Peppertree Lane (Ire) *M Johnston* 80
2 ch c Peintre Celebre (USA) - Salonrolle (Ire)
3^{7g} 3^{7gs} **0-2-2 £2,450**

Pequenita *R C Guest* a30
5 b m Rudimentary (USA) - Sierra Madrona (USA)
8^{12sd} **0-0-1**

Percheron (Ire) *P A Blockley* 43
3 ch g Perugino (USA) - Silvery Halo (USA)
10^{6gf} 11^{6gf} 10^{8gf} 16^{7gf} **0-0-4**

Percussionist (Ire) *J Howard Johnson* 117
4 b g Sadler's Wells (USA) - Magnificient Style (USA)
2^{14gs} 12^{20gf} **0-1-2 £30,800**

Percy Douglas *Miss A Stokell* 62 a51
5 b h Elmaamul (USA) - Qualitair Dream
11^{5sd} 9^{6sd} 4^{5sd} 6^{5sd} 2^{5s} 8^{5sd} 5^{5g} 4^{5sd} 15^{5gf} 11^{5g} 10^{6gf} 13^{8gf} 7^{5g} 9^{6g} 9^{5gf} 11^{5gf} 15^{5gf} 8^{5ss} **0-1-18 £2,068**

Percy's Pearl (USA) *D R C Elsworth* 82
3 ch g Rainbow Quest (USA) - Ridgewood Pearl
1^{8gs} 3^{8gf} 12^{10gf} **1-1-3 £4,622**

Peregrine Hawk (Ire) *Patrick Morris* 19 a51
4 ch g Perugino (USA) - Follow The Wind
5^{7sd} 12^{9sd} 6^{7sd} 2^{8sd} 2^{8sd} 6^{8sd} 10^{7f} 14^{10gf} **0-2-8 £838**

Pererin *N B King* 41 a18
4 b g Whittingham (Ire) - Antithesis (Ire)
9^{7sd} 12^{6sd} 12^{7sd} 3^{10gs} 5^{7s} 7^{10f} 12^{10gf} **0-1-7 £190**

Perez (Ire) *Pat Eddery* a69
3 b g Mujadil (USA) - Kahla
2^{7sd} **0-1-1 £998**

Perfect Balance (Ire) *D W Thompson* 53 a55
4 b/br g Shinko Forest (Ire) - Tumble
2^{12sd} 6^{12sd} 5^{12sd} 14^{12g} 11^{11g} 4^{13gs} 6^{12g} 4^{10g} 3^{13s} 3^{15s} **0-4-10 £1,823**

Perfect Beat (Ire) *Saeed Bin Suroor* 71
2 b f Fasliyev (USA) - Dancing Drop
10^{5gf} 4^{6gf} **0-0-2 £437**

Perfect Blend *B W Hills* 79
3 gr f Linamix (Fr) - Picture Princess
7^{7gs} 3^{7gs} 2^{8gs} 1^{8gf} 4^{8g} **1-3-5 £6,737**

Perfect Choice (Ire) *B J Meehan* 86
3 gr g Daylami (Ire) - Fairy Contessa (Ire)
14^{10gf} 5^{8gf} 15^{8g} 13^{8g} **0-0-4 £473**

Perfect Design *J R Boyle*
3 b f Killer Instinct - Farrh Nouriya (Ire)
9^{12sd} **0-0-1**

Perfect Image *M P Tregoning*
3 b f Makbul - Perfect Timing
11^{10gf} **0-0-1**

Perfect Order (USA) *N A Callaghan* 58 a46
2 b/br f Red Ransom (USA) - Ideal Index (USA)
12^{7f} 5^{6g} 10^{5gf} 11^{6gf} 10^{6sd} 6^{6sd} **0-0-6**

Perfect Punch *K G Reveley* 21
6 b g Reprimand - Aliuska (Ire)
16^{12s} **0-0-1**

Perfect Solution (Ire) *J A R Toller* 64
3 ch f Entrepreneur - Pearl Barley (Ire)
4^{6g} 7^{7gf} 1^{6gs} 14^{6g} **1-0-4 £5,442**

Perfect Story (Ire) *J A R Toller* 80 a84
3 b f Desert Story (Ire) - Shore Lark (USA)
2^{8sd} 2^{8sd} 3^{7sd} 1^{6gf} 2^{6gf} 3^{7gf} 3^{6s} 1^{7sd} 1^{7sd} 5^{6sd} **3-6-10 £21,283**

Perfect Tone (USA) *M A Magnusson* 79 a67
3 ch f Silver Hawk (USA) - Copper Cachet (USA)
3^{10gf} 1^{10sd} 3^{10gf} 8^{12gf} **1-2-4 £5,544**

Perfect Treasure (Ire) *J A R Toller* a65
2 ch f Night Shift (USA) - Pitrizza (Ire)
7^{5sd} 2^{6sd} **0-1-2 £1,237**

Perfectionist *J A R Toller* 50
3 b f In The Wings - Lady Donatella
14^{8gf} 7^{7gf} 11^{8g} 13^{10gf} 7^{8g} **0-0-5**

Perfectperformance (USA) *Saeed Bin Suroor*
3 ch c Rahy (USA) - Balistroika (USA)
5^{11gf} **0-0-1 £1,625**

Perfidious (USA) *J R Boyle* 71 a72
7 b g Lear Fan (USA) - Perfolia (USA)
9^{9sd} 12^{12sd} 11^{10sd} 3^{10sd} 2^{12sd} 11^{10sd} 5^{12g} 5^{12gf} 3^{11s} 1^{12g} 4^{12sd} 3^{12gs} 11^{12sd} 8^{14sd} **1-5-14 £6,642**

Perfumery *J H M Gosden* 62 a45
3 b f Dubai Millennium - Sweet Willa (USA)
9^{8g} 5^{10gs} 9^{13sd} **0-0-3**

Perianth (Ire) *J G M O'Shea* a45
3 ch c Bluebird (USA) - Meandering Rose (USA)
5^{6sd} 5^{7sd} 12^{9ss} **0-0-3**

Perle D'Or (Ire) *W J Haggas* 88
4 b f Entrepreneur - Rose Society
1^{10gs} 8^{10gf} 7^{12g} 1^{10gs} 5^{10g} 4^{11gs} 3^{12hy} 15^{10hy} **2-1-8 £33,373**

Permanex Pride (Ire) *D R C Elsworth* 81
2 ch g Ashkalani (Ire) - Lycia
6^{7gs} 1^{7gf} **1-0-2 £3,198**

Perranporth Lad *Miss Victoria Roberts*
2 b g Mazurek - Valmaranda (USA)
15^{6g} **0-0-1**

Persea (Ire) *D E Cantillon* a62
4 b f Fasliyev (USA) - Final Farewell (USA)
10^{7sd} 2^{6sd} 1^{6sd} 6^{6sd} **1-1-4 £4,633**

Persephone Heights *M Madgwick* a27
5 br m Golden Heights - Jalland
7^{10sd} 7^{16sd} **0-0-2**

Persian Carpet *Unknown* 55
3 b f Desert Style (Ire) - Kuwah (Ire)
4^{6s} 16^{8g} 5^{7g} 2^{8gf} 5^{10g} **0-1-5 £1,140**

Persian Conqueror (Ire) *J L Dunlop* 46
2 b g Sinndar (Ire) - Persian Fantasy
11^{8gf} 6^{8gs} 11^{8g} **0-0-3**

Persian Express (USA) *B W Hills* 71
2 b f Bahri (USA) - Istikbal (USA)
8^{7s} 4^{9g} 1^{7f} 8^{7gs} **1-0-4 £5,099**

Persian Genie (Ire) *Miss J S Davis* 53
4 br f Grand Lodge (USA) - Persia (Ire)
7^{12f} 6^{18g} 2^{17g} 8^{16g} 8^{16gs} **0-1-5 £1,114**

Persian Khanoom (Ire) *B R Millman* 47 a46
3 b f Royal Applause - Kshessinskaya
9^{7sd} 18^{7gs} 14^{7gf} 10^{8gf} 3^{10sd} 4^{10g} 8^{10sd} **0-2-7 £211**

Persian Lightning (Ire) *J L Dunlop* 111
6 b g Sri Pekan (USA) - Persian Fantasy
5^{10gf} 1^{11g} 14^{10gf} **1-0-3 £16,760**

Persian Majesty (Ire) *W R Swinburn* 103
5 b g Grand Lodge (USA) - Spa
4^{11g} 3^{10gf} 4^{12gf} 11^{8gf} 9^{12gs} **0-0-5 £4,501**

Persian Rock (Ire) *B R Millman* 85
3 b g Namid - Cairo Lady (Ire)
7^{6gf} 14^{6gf} 2^{7gs} 5^{6gs} 19^{7gf} 9^{8g} **0-1-6 £2,684**

Persona (Ire) *J Noseda* 65
3 b f Night Shift (USA) - Alonsa (Ire)
4^{8g} 6^{10gf} 7^{8g} SU^{10gf} 4^{9gf} **0-0-5 £618**

Pertemps Green *T D Barron* 62
2 b c Green Desert (USA) - Pure Misk
4^{5g} **0-0-1 £525**

Pertemps Heroine *A D Smith* 49
2 b f Arkadian Hero (USA) - Watheeqah (USA)
4^{5s} 13^{6gf} 6^{7f} **0-0-3 £271**

Pertemps Job *A D Smith* a43
4 b c First Trump - Happy And Blessed (Ire)
5^{9sd} 3^{9sd} 14^{10s} **0-1-3 £216**

Pertemps Magus *A D Smith* 71 a17
5 b m Silver Wizard (USA) - Brilliant Future
1^{6gs} 13^{6gf} 3^{6g} 11^{6gs} 4^{6gs} 12^{7sd} **1-1-6 £5,566**

Peruvian Prince (USA) *J A R Toller* 81 a71
3 b g Silver Hawk (USA) - Inca Dove (USA)
2^{8g} 5^{10g} 8^{8sd} 2^{8f} **0-1-4 £3,542**

Peruvian Style (Ire) *J M Bradley* 60 a79
4 b g Desert Style (Ire) - Lady's Vision (Ire)
9^{7sd} 5^{7sd} 2^{7sd} 9^{7sd} 4^{5sd} 13^{6f} 11^{6gs} 7^{8f} 8^{8g} 8^{6f} **0-1-10 £828**

Pespita (Ire) *P J McBride* 63 a69
4 b f Desert King (Ire) - Platin Lady (Ire)
5^{8sd} 1^{8sd} 8^{10g} 4^{10sd} 9^{12gf} 4^{10g} 7^{10gf} **1-0-7 £2,457**

Petana *Peter Grayson* 51 a53
5 gr m Petong - Duxyana (Ire)
8^{5sd} 1^{5sd} 7^{6sd} 3^{5sd} 8^{5sd} 9^{7sd} 10^{6sd} 10^{5gf} 10^{5gf} 7^{5sd} 15^{5g} 2^{6gf} 5^{6f} 4^{5gf} 4^{5gf} 8^{5gf} 10^{5gf} 4^{5sd} 9^{5sd} 6^{5sd} **1-2-20 £4,536**

Petardias Magic (Ire) *G A Huffer* 88 a74
4 ch g Petardia - Alexander Confranc (Ire)
7^{6sd} 4^{6sd} 9^{6sd} 9^{5gs} 1^{6sd} 3^{6gs} 7^{6g} 7^{6gs} 13^{6gs} 10^{6gf} 9^{7g} 11^{6g} 4^{7sd} **1-1-13 £5,233**

Peter Island (Fr) *J Gallagher* 78 a65
2 b c Dansili - Catania (USA)
8^{7gf} 7^{7sd} 5^{7gf} 1^{7gf} 9^{8gf} 14^{7g} **1-0-6 £4,837**

Peter Paul Rubens (USA) *P F I Cole* 114
4 ch c Belong To Me (USA) - Skybox (USA)
5^{6gf} 3^{6f} 4^{7gf} 10^{7gf} 4^{7gf} **0-2-5 £17,455**

Peter's Imp (Ire) *A Berry* 53
10 b g Imp Society (USA) - Catherine Clare
5^{12gs} 4^{16gf} 1^{11g} 3^{11gf} 7^{13gs} 3^{10gf} 5^{10g} 5^{16gf} 9^{12g} **1-2-9 £4,222**

Peters Delite *R A Fahey* 74 a59
3 b g Makbul - Steadfast Elite (Ire)
2^{7s} 2^{6gs} 3^{7gs} 2^{7s} 2^{7g} 4^{7gf} 8^{7g} 7^{8gf} 9^{7sd} **0-5-9 £8,041**

Peters Ploy *T Keddy* a35
5 ch g Deploy - Alpi Dora
5^{11sd} 5^{9sd} 9^{12sd} **0-0-3**

Petite Colleen (Ire) *D Haydn Jones* a46
4 b f Desert Sun - Nishiki (USA)
8^{12sd} **0-0-1**

Petite Girl *J L Spearing*
3 gr f Daylami (Ire) - Pagoda (Fr)
11^{8sd} 16^{8gs} **0-0-2**

Petite Mac *N Bycroft* 61 a29
5 b m Timeless Times (USA) - Petite Elite
12^{5sd} 4^{5g} 4^{5g} 5^{6gf} 2^{5gf} 8^{5gf} 2^{6g} 1^{6gf} 5^{6gf} 4^{6g} 9^{7g} 11^{6g} 13^{5ss} **1-3-13 £5,889**

Petite Paramour (Ire) *Miss Gay Kelleway* 64 a62
4 b f Malmsey (USA) - Fleet Petite (Ire)
7^{10sd} 9^{12g} 1^{10g} 9^{10sd} 0^{11g} 5^{10g} 8^{11gs} 9^{12gf} 8^{10g} 6^{12sd} 11^{10g} 11^{15gf} 9^{12sd} 3^{14sd} 5^{14sd} **1-1-15 £9,900**

Petite Rouge *Mrs A M Thorpe*
5 ch m Elmaamul (USA) - Elrayahin
8^{12f} **0-0-1**

Petite Spectre *R Hannon* 60 a39
3 ch f Spectrum (Ire) - Petite Epaulette
7^{6gf} 6^{7gf} 11^{7g} 12^{8g} 4^{8g} 12^{10sd} **0-0-6 £359**

Petrichan (Ire) *K A Ryan* 43
2 b g Medicean - Numancia (Ire)
12^{6s} 15^{6gf} 10^{7g} 9^{7gf} **0-0-4**

Petrolero (Arg) *James Moffatt* 36
6 gr g Perfect Parade (USA) - Louise (Arg)
7^{17f} **0-0-1**

Petrula *K A Ryan* 73
6 ch g Tagula (Ire) - Bouffant
5^{12gf} 6^{12gf} **0-0-2**

Petticoat Hill (UAE) *Eoin Doyle* 61
3 b f Timber Country (USA) - Crinolette (Ire)
4^{10gf} PU^{12g} **0-0-2 £352**

Pevensey (Ire) *M A Buckley* 93
3 b g Danehill (USA) - Champaka (Ire)
7^{8hy} 8^{8gf} 2^{8gf} 7^{8g} 4^{12gf} 4^{10gs} 4^{10gf} 1^{10gf} 7^{10g} 5^{10g} 5^{10g} 8^{12g} 3^{10s} **1-2-13 £20,574**

Phantasmagoria *W R Swinburn* 56 a73
3 b f Fraam - Magic Moment
3^{7sd} 4^{7gf} **0-1-2 £1,070**

Phantom Song (Ire) *J A Osborne* 56 a48
3 gr g Shinko Forest (Ire) - Natural Pearl
7^{6sd} 5^{6sd} 18^{6gs} 5^{6gs} 2^{5gf} 1^{5f} 8^{5f} 9^{6gs} 10^{5g} **1-1-9 £3,393**

Phantom Whisper *B R Millman* 85 a79
2 b g Makbul - La Belle Vie
1^{5sd} 1^{5g} 7^{5gf} 7^{5g} 12^{5gf} 9^{6g} 4^{5gs} **2-0-7 £20,159**

Pharaoh Prince *G Prodromou* 42 a61
4 b g Desert Prince (Ire) - Kinlochewe
15^{8s} 15^{10gf} 7^{8sd} 14^{10gf} 2^{10sd} 2^{9sf} 3^{13sd} 1^{12sd} 3^{12sd} 8^{14sd} **1-4-10 £2,976**

Pharia (USA) *J H M Gosden* 37
2 b f Kingmambo (USA) - Harpia (USA)
9^{7gs} 16^{8g} **0-0-2**

Pharoah's Gold (Ire) *D Burchell* a55
7 b g Namaqualand (USA) - Queen Nefertiti (Ire)
5^{6sd} 2^{8sd} 1^{9sd} 7^{9sd} 9^{8sd} 10^{8sd} 10^{7s} 3^{7sd} 6^{7sd} 5^{7sd} 6^{7sd} 10^{9sd} 10^{10sd} **1-2-13 £4,196**

Pheckless *J M Bradley* 53 a58
6 ch g Be My Guest (USA) - Phlirty
7^{6sd} 11^{7sd} 14^{7sd} 1^{8sd} 9^{7sd} 1^{7sd} 7^{6sd} 5^{8sd} 7^{8f} 4^{7gf} 10^{7f} 8^{6sd} 4^{7sd} **2-0-13 £4,519**

Phi Phi (Ire) *Rae Guest* 56 a65
3 b f Fasliyev (USA) - Council Rock
2^{6sd} 8^{6g} 1^{8sd} 8^{8gf} 14^{10gf} 9^{8gf} 3^{8gs} 8^{8gf} 10^{8gf} 13^{7gf} 15^{8s} 1^{8g} 9^{9sd} 7^{8sf} **2-2-14 £5,275**

Philharmonic *R A Fahey* 104
4 b g Victory Note (USA) - Lambast
2^{5g} 1^{5gf} 10^{5gf} 16^{6gs} 17^{6g} **1-1-5 £15,084**

Phills Pearl *D Burchell*
2 gr f Piccolo - Cole Slaw
11^{6sd} **0-0-1**

Philosophic *Mrs L C Jewell*
11 b g Be My Chief (USA) - Metaphysique (Fr)
8^{12sd} **0-0-1**

Phinerine *R A Harris* 60 a63
2 ch g Bahamian Bounty - Golden Panda
11^{6sd} 5^{7sd} 2^{5gf} 5^{5gf} 8^{5gf} 3^{6sd} 7^{6sd} 2^{6sd} 4^{6sd} 2^{6sd} 5^{7sd} **0-4-11 £2,937**

Phlaunt *R F Johnson Houghton* 49 a31
3 b f Faustus (USA) - Phlirty
7^{6g} 6^{8g} 9^{7sd} **0-0-3**

Phluke *R F Johnson Houghton* 81 a78
4 b g Most Welcome - Phlirty
1^{8sd} 5^{9gs} 2^{8sd} 2^{7gf} 5^{8g} 1^{7gf} 3^{7gf} 1^{7f} 2^{7gf} 8^{7sd} 8^{7gf} 16^{7g} **3-4-12 £19,896**

Phoebe Woodstock (Ire) *W R Swinburn* 76
3 ch f Grand Lodge (USA) - Why So Silent
3^{10gf} 2^{10gf} **0-2-2 £2,460**

Phoenix Eye *M Mullineaux* 57 a53
4 b c Tragic Role (USA) - Eye Sight
3^{14sd} 2^{12sd} 7^{12gf} 7^{14sd} 6^{12gs} 5^{12f} 9^{14sd} 6^{16gf} 8^{12g} 4^{12gf} 5^{12gf} 3^{14gf} 9^{16s} 3^{17sf} 1^{9sd} 12^{9sd} **1-4-16 £3,006**

Phoenix Reach (Ire) *A M Balding* 119
5 b h Alhaarth (Ire) - Carroll's Canyon (Ire)
1^{12gf} 5^{10gf} 2^{10s} 10^{12gf} **1-1-4 £846,854**

Phone In *Unknown* 50 a51
2 b g Sinndar (Ire) - Patria (USA)
8^{7s} 11^{7sd} 7^{6hy} **0-0-3**

Phone Tapping *Mrs L B Normile*
4 b g Robellino (USA) - Miss Party Line (USA)
11^{11s} **0-0-1**

Phred *I A Wood*
5 ch g Safawan - Phlirty
11^{16sd} **0-0-1**

Phrenologist *Andrew Reid* a44
5 gr g Mind Games - Leading Princess (Ire)
11^{6sd} 10^{5sd} 8^{6sd} 7^{8sd} **0-0-4**

Physical (Ire) *Mrs A J Perrett* 69 a66
3 b g Efisio - St Clair
14^{8g} 10^{6s} 14^{7gf} 7^{7g} 6^{7sd} 10^{8g} 9^{7sd} **0-0-7**

Piano Man *J C Fox* 66 a64
3 b g Atraf - Pinup
6^{8g} 12^{8g} 6^{10g} 7^{8gf} 7^{10gf} 6^{9sd} 9^{9sd} **0-0-7**

Pianoforte (USA) *E J Alston* 69 a76
3 b g Grand Slam (USA) - Far Too Loud (Can)
6^{8sd} 1^{7sd} 2^{7sd} 10^{7gf} 9^{7g} 16^{7gf} 11^{8g} 16^{8s} **1-1-8 £5,495**

Pic Up Sticks *B G Powell* 95
6 gr g Piccolo - Between The Sticks
5^{6gf} 9^{7gf} 4^{6g} 9^{5g} 18^{6gf} 9^{6gf} 10^{6g} 5^{5gs} 14^{5s} 14^{6gf} 1^{6gf} 4^{6gf} **1-1-12 £18,659**

Picacho (Ire) *J L Dunlop* 32
2 b f Sinndar (Ire) - Gentle Thoughts
16^{7gf} 14^{8s} **0-0-2**

Picador *Sir Mark Prescott* 39 a25
2 b g Pivotal - Candescent
10^{6sd} 9^{5g} 14^{6g} **0-0-3**

Piccelina *D M Simcock* 68
2 ch f Piccolo - Zabelina (USA)
6^{5f} 5^{5g} 2^{5gf} 1^{5gf} 10^{5g} 10^{5g} 16^{5gf} **1-1-7**

£4,502

Piccled *E J Alston* 78 a88
7 b g Piccolo - Creme De Menthe (Ire)
7^{5g} 6^{5gf} 10^{5gs} RR^{5gf} 12^{5gs} 8^{5g} 11^{5g} 12^{5s} 7^{5sf} 2^{5sd} RR^{5sd} **0-1-11 £1,681**

Piccleyes *M J Polglase* 50 a63
4 b g Piccolo - Dark Eyed Lady (Ire)
3^{6sd} 7^{8sd} 9^{7sd} 9^{6sd} 6^{6sd} 8^{6gf} 12^{6gs} 15^{6g} 1^{6sd} 5^{6sd} 7^{6sd} 18^{6g} 9^{6gf} 11^{7gf} 12^{5g} 6^{8hd} 7^{7sf} 7^{5ss} **1-1-18 £3,182**

Piccolo Prince *E J Alston* 68 a61
4 ch g Piccolo - Aegean Flame
9^{6sd} 7^{6gs} 6^{6gf} 10^{5gf} 1^{6s} 13^{6g} 7^{5gf} 11^{6gf} 11^{6gf} 4^{6sd} 10^{7sd} **1-0-11 £5,310**

Piccolomini *M Johnston* 76
3 b g Diktat - La Dama Bonita (USA)
2^{8s} 2^{9gs} 2^{10s} 2^{10gs} 8^{10g} 9^{10gs} 11^{11gs} 11^{11g} 3^{12gf} 7^{12g} **0-4-10 £6,070**

Piccostar *A B Haynes* 64 a69
2 b f Piccolo - Anneliina
2^{5sd} 1^{5sd} 5^{5sd} 2^{5g} 3^{5f} 5^{6sd} 5^{5gs} 6^{6sd} 4^{6gf} 4^{5gf} 9^{6gf} **1-2-11 £6,731**

Pick Of The Crop *J R Jenkins* 45 a41
4 ch g Fraam - Fresh Fruit Daily
10^{8sd} 11^{7sd} 12^{8sd} 4^{10f} 5^{10g} 10^{11gf} **0-0-6**

Pickapeppa *R F Johnson Houghton* 66 a57
3 ch f Piccolo - Cajole (Ire)
7^{6sd} 9^{6g} 11^{7gf} 9^{6gf} **0-0-4**

Pickett *E J O'Neill* 100 a54
2 b c Piccolo - Poly Blue (Ire)
8^{6sd} 1^{5gs} 2^{5gf} 1^{6gf} 2^{5gs} 8^{6gf} 6^{5g} **2-2-7 £33,414**

Picot De Say *C Roberts* 60
3 b g Largesse - Facsimile
12^{8g} 11^{10gf} 5^{10g} 1^{11g} **1-0-4 £2,933**

Pictavia (Ire) *J S Bolger* 111
3 ch f Sinndar (Ire) - Insijaam (USA)
7^{8gf} 3^{12g} 10^{12gf} 8^{12gf} 3^{9gy} 2^{9g} 2^{10gf} **0-4-7 £72,317**

Picture Show (USA) *C E Brittain* 58
2 b f Swain (Ire) - Impetuous Image (USA)
4^{7gf} 9^{7gf} **0-0-2 £312**

Piddies Pride (Ire) *Miss Gay Kelleway* 68 a58
3 b f Indian Lodge (Ire) - Fairybird (Fr)
10^{7sd} 1^{6sd} 4^{6sd} 8^{5sd} 1^{6sd} 11^{7sd} 4^{7sd} 4^{6sd} 13^{9sd} 4^{6sd} 3^{6g} 6^{7gs} 2^{6gf} 10^{7s} 8^{6gf} 9^{7gf} 1^{6g} 13^{7sd} **3-2-18 £9,609**

Pie Corner *M Madgwick* 28
3 ch g Fumo Di Londra (Ire) - Ballystate
11^{7gf} 17^{10g} 10^{6g} **0-0-3**

Pieter Brueghel (USA) *D Nicholls* 99
6 b g Citidancer (USA) - Smart Tally (USA)
4^{6s} 16^{6gs} 8^{6s} 2^{6g} 1^{6gf} 12^{6gf} 7^{6gs} 2^{6gs} 2^{6gf} 21^{6g} **1-3-10 £35,343**

Piety (Ire) *M Johnston* 70
2 b f Danehill (USA) - Quest Of Passion (Fr)
2^{7s} **0-1-1 £969**

Pigeon Island *H Candy* a77
2 gr c Daylami (Ire) - Morina (USA)
2^{10sd} 2^{9sd} **0-2-2 £2,635**

Pike Bishop (Ire) *R Charlton* 99
3 b c Namid - Pink Cashmere (Ire)
7^{5gf} 7^{6g} 2^{5gf} 7^{6gf} 3^{6gs} 9^{6gs} **0-1-6 £6,259**

Pilca (Fr) *R M Stronge* a54
5 ch g Pistolet Bleu (Ire) - Caricoe
5^{9sd} 7^{12sd} 12^{8sd} 7^{9sd} **0-0-4**

Pillars Of Wisdom *J L Dunlop* 83
3 ch c Desert Prince (Ire) - Eurolink Mischief
4^{8gs} 9^{8g} 5^{10g} 2^{10f} 6^{11gf} 1^{8f} 10^{10g} 2^{7g} 1^{7gs} **2-2-9 £11,553**

Pin Spotter *M E Sowersby* 15
2 ch f Bahamian Bounty - Persian Fountain (Ire)
13^{7gf} 10^{8g} 14^{10g} **0-0-3**

Pinafore *H Morrison* 53 a57
3 ch f Fleetwood (Ire) - Shi Shi
13^{7gf} 10^{6gs} 3^{7sd} 5^{7gf} 4^{6gf} 9^{6sd} **0-2-6 £385**

Pinch Of Salt (Ire) *A M Balding* 86
2 b c Hussonet (USA) - Granita (Chi)
5^{7gs} 8^{8gf} 2^{8gf} **0-1-3 £984**

Pinchbeck *M A Jarvis* 83 a89
6 b g Petong - Veuve Hoornaert (Ire)
13^{6s} 11^{6gs} 16^{6s} 1^{6sd} 13^{6g} 3^{6gs} 3^{7sd} 9^{7sd} 1^{6sd} **2-2-9 £16,995**

Pine Bay *B Gubby* 73
4 b f Sure Blade (USA) - Opuntia
6^{6g} 4^{6f} 7^{6g} 8^{6gf} 2^{7g} 3^{7gf} 9^{6g} 7^{6gf} 2^{6g} 3^{6gf} 2^{6gs} 9^{7g} F^{6gf} **0-5-13 £6,666**

Pine Cone (Ire) *A King* 84
3 ch f Dr Fong (USA) - Pine Needle
2^{8gf} 4^{8g} 1^{10g} 2^{10gs} 3^{10gs} 4^{10g} **1-3-6 £8,904**

Pink Bay *W S Kittow* 71 a41
3 b f Forzando - Singer On The Roof
6^{7sd} 2^{6g} 9^{7gf} 13^{7sd} 1^{6gf} 3^{7f} 3^{8f} 12^{8s} **1-3-8 £5,428**

Pink Pyjamas *J A R Toller* a35
2 ch f Compton Place - Pagan Princess
19^{6gf} 9^{6sd} 11^{6sd} **0-0-3**

Pink Shoes (Ire) *L M Cumani* 48
3 b f Sadler's Wells (USA) - Dangerous Diva (Ire)
5^{10gf} 14^{10g} 14^{10gs} **0-0-3**

Pink Tourmaline *Mrs H O Graham* 35
3 br f Diktat - June Brilly (Ire)
9^{7gf} 9^{8gf} 10^{7g} **0-0-3**

Pinpoint (Ire) *W R Swinburn* 101 a79
3 b g Pivotal - Alessia (Ger)
2^{8sd} 4^{8gf} 1^{8g} 2^{8s} 5^{8gs} 1^{8g} **2-2-6 £18,312**

Pins 'n Needles (Ire) *C A Cyzer* a35
4 gr f Mark Of Esteem (Ire) - Khalisiyn
10^{8sd} **0-0-1**

Pinson (Ire) *J-C Rouget* 120
3 gr c Halling (USA) - Tadorne (Fr)
2^{8vs} 1^{8g} 1^{9g} 1^{9g} 1^{10vs} 10^{10gs} **4-1-6 £103,547**

Pintle *J L Spearing* 87
5 b m Pivotal - Boozy
8^{7g} 6^{7g} 11^{7gf} 1^{7gf} 8^{7g} 17^{7gf} **1-0-6 £4,182**

Pip's Baby *S Kirk* 57 a63
2 ch c Groom Dancer (USA) - Captivating (Ire)
16^{6gf} 7^{7gf} 6^{7gf} 2^{7sd} 1^{8sd} **1-1-5 £1,908**

Piper General (Ire) *J Mackie* 36 a79
3 br g General Monash (USA) - Pipewell (Ire)
3^{10sd} 5^{10sd} 3^{10sd} 12^{11g} 1^{12ss} 1^{14sd} 1^{12sd} **3-2-7 £10,674**

Piper Lily *M Blanshard* 61 a49
3 b f Piccolo - Polly Golightly
11^{6s} 6^{5g} 4^{5gf} 13^{5gf} 11^{6gf} 7^{5gf} 6^{6gf} 4^{6g} 8^{6gf}

18^{7g} 5^{6sd} 9^{7sd} **0-0-12 £371**

Piper's Ash (USA) *R Charlton* 49
3 b f Royal Academy (USA) - Merida
9^{6gf} **0-0-1**

Piping Shrike (Ire) *R M Flower* 42 a25
3 b g Princely Heir (Ire) - Sherabi (Ire)
8^{7s} 11^{10s} 8^{9g} 20^{7gf} 11^{8sd} **0-0-5**

Pippa's Dancer (Ire) *W R Muir* 80 a62
3 b f Desert Style (Ire) - Soreze (Ire)
3^{6gs} 7^{6gs} 1^{5f} 12^{5gf} 9^{6gf} 4^{6gf} 12^{7sd} 12^{7g}
1-0-8 £4,407

Pippilongstocking *E G Bevan* 35 a11
3 b f Makbul - Princess Ermyn
12^{9sd} 6^{12g} **0-0-2**

Pippins Corner *M A Allen*
3 b f Piccolo - Newlands Corner
15^{12sd} **0-0-1**

Pips Assertive Way *A W Carroll* 39
4 ch f Nomadic Way (USA) - Return To Brighton
7^{10gs} **0-0-1**

Pips Pearl (Ire) *Mrs P N Dutfield* 44 a21
3 b f Lil's Boy (USA) - Penka (Ire)
10^{8sd} 9^{11g} 11^{10sd} 6^{7gf} 3^{6s} 3^{8gf} 9^{7gf} 3^{8f} 2^{10g}
4^{10f} 7^{12gf} **0-4-11 £2,269**

Piquet *J J Bridger* 47 a58
7 br m Mind Games - Petonellajill
2^{10sd} 2^{10sd} 11^{8sd} 10^{10sd} 13^{10sd} 7^{12sd} 4^{10gf}
2^{10sd} 3^{12sd} 9^{10sd} 7^{10sd} 4^{9gf} 6^{9gf} 6^{10sd} 4^{8gf}
13^{16g} 11^{10sd} 7^{10sd} **0-5-18 £3,877**

Piroetta *J A Osborne* 53 a27
3 b f Averti (Ire) - Bint Albadou (Ire)
5^{7gf} 7^{6g} 12^{8gf} 12^{7sd} 5^{6ss} **0-0-5**

Pirouettes (Ire) *E R Oertel* 48 a48
5 b m Royal Applause - Dance Serenade (Ire)
7^{12sd} 1^{9sd} 8^{9sd} 3^{8sd} 3^{8sd} 3^{8gf} **1-3-6**
£2,444

Pirouetting *B W Hills* 77
2 b f Pivotal - Jitterbug (Ire)
8^{6gs} 4^{6s} **0-0-2 £524**

Pitbull *Mrs G S Rees* 62 a44
2 b c Makbul - Piccolo Cativo
6^{6sd} 5^{5gf} 3^{6gf} 9^{5g} 5^{6g} **0-0-5 £464**

Pitcairn Island *D W P Arbuthnot* 28
3 ch f Indian Ridge - Girl From Ipanema
13^{7gf} 11^{8gf} 15^{11g} **0-0-3**

Pitch Hill *W Jarvis* 4
2 b c Dansili - Break Point
24^{7s} **0-0-1**

Pitch Up (Ire) *T G Mills* 83
3 b g Cape Cross (Ire) - Uhud (Ire)
7^{6gf} 11^{5gf} 3^{6gf} 10^{6gf} 9^{5gs} **0-1-5**
£1,078

Pitsi Kahtoh *P W Hiatt* 43
3 b f Petoski - Plectrum
6^{10gf} 7^{10f} 9^{8gs} 6^{12gf} 11^{14g} 11^{11g} **0-0-6**

Pittsburgh *A M Balding* 57 a66
3 ch g Nashwan (USA) - Oatey
5^{9sd} 13^{10g} 12^{12sd} 8^{9sd} **0-0-4**

Pivotal Era *C F Wall* 27
2 ch g Pivotal - Femme Savante
7^{6gf} **0-0-1**

Pivotal Flame *E S McMahon* 111
3 b c Pivotal - Reddening
4^{7gs} 17^{8gf} 13^{8g} 6^{7gf} 3^{7gs} 11^{7gf} 3^{7g} 3^{7gf} 7^{7gs}
0-3-9 £19,055

Pivotal Point *P J Makin* 97
5 b g Pivotal - True Precision
9^{6g} 19^{6gs} **0-0-2**

Pivotal Role *Sir Mark Prescott* 65 a63
3 ch f Pivotal - Heckle
7^{8gs} 5^{10gs} 5^{9sd} **0-0-3**

Pivotal's Princess (Ire) *E S McMahon* 99
3 ch f Pivotal - Art Princess (Ire)
1^{5gf} 1^{5gf} 1^{5gs} 1^{5gf} 5^{5g} 3^{6s} 3^{5gs} 6^{5g}
4-2-8 £34,879

Pix *S Kirk* 54 a54
2 b f Bertolini (USA) - Fair Kai (Ire)
7^{5gs} 6^{5s} 10^{5sd} 8^{5gf} 4^{7sd} 7^{7gf} 10^{5f} 3^{7f} 3^{8sd}
3^{8sd} 4^{10sd} 9^{9sd} 4^{9sd} **0-3-13 £1,014**

Plain Champagne (Ire) *Dr J R J Naylor* 30 a30
3 b f Victory Note (USA) - Paddys Cocktail (Ire)
13^{8f} 8^{8sd} 11^{10gs} **0-0-3**

Planet (Ire) *M L W Bell* 82
3 b g Soviet Star (USA) - Laurentia (USA)
4^{11gs} 1^{12g} 4^{15gs} 1^{11g} 3^{10g} 9^{12gf} 12^{11gs}
2-1-7 £9,354

Planters Punch (Ire) *G M Moore* 65
4 b g Cape Cross (Ire) - Jamaican Punch (Ire)
14^{12g} 15^{10gf} 13^{10gf} 6^{12s} **0-0-4**

Plateau *D Nicholls* 91
6 b g Zamindar (USA) - Painted Desert
4^{5gs} 17^{5g} 7^{5g} 1^{5gf} 13^{6gf} 4^{5gs} 7^{5s} 2^{5gf} 10^{5gs}
1-1-9 £9,851

Platinum Boy (Ire) *M Wellings* 15 a47
5 b g Goldmark (USA) - Brown Foam
12^{9sd} 8^{9sd} 3^{9sd} 3^{9sd} 11^{9sd} 6^{13sd} 9^{10sd} 10^{12gf}
0-2-8 £426

Platinum Charmer (Ire) *K R Burke* 68 a65
5 b g Kahyasi - Mystic Charm
8^{14sd} 5^{13sd} 6^{12sd} 9^{12sd} 11^{12gs} 1^{11gf} 1^{12gf} 1^{10f}
1^{12f} 3^{12gf} 10^{13gf} 2^{10g} 5^{10gf} 6^{12f} 1^{12g} 7^{14ft}
6^{14gf} 1^{12s} 9^{12sd} 7^{12sd} **6-2-20 £21,984**

Platinum Chief *R Ford* a39
4 b g Puissance - Miss Beverley
6^{12sd} 8^{10sd} **0-0-2**

Platinum Hound (Ire) *H Morrison* 48
2 b f Vettori (Ire) - Dog Rose (SAF)
9^{7g} **0-0-1**

Platinum Pirate *K R Burke* 42 a41
4 b g Merdon Melody - Woodland Steps
8^{9sd} 8^{10sd} 8^{8sd} 7^{10g} 11^{10gs} 5^{9sd} 5^{10s}
0-0-7

Platinum Princess *Saeed Bin Suroor* 68
2 br f Diktat - Nachtigall (Fr)
2^{7s} **0-1-1 £969**

Platnix (Ire) *R J Baker* 33
3 b f Perugino (USA) - Familiar Quest (Ire)
14^{8g} 11^{8g} 8^{7sd} **0-0-3**

Plattocrat *R P Elliott* a30
5 b g Dancing Spree (USA) - No Comebacks
6^{7sd} 11^{7sd} 8^{8sd} 8^{17sd} 11^{17sd} 8^{5sd} **0-0-6**

Plausabelle *A W Carroll* 66 a74
4 b f Royal Applause - Sipsi Fach
1^{9sd} 1^{9sd} 1^{8sd} 2^{9sd} 4^{9sd} 1^{8sd} 5^{10g} 8^{10sd} 15^{10gf}
6^{7s} 9^{6g} **4-1-11 £13,265**

Play Coy *T D Barron* 60
2 b g First Trump - Lady Caroline Lamb (Ire)
4^{5s} 8^{6gf} **0-0-2 £312**

Play Master (Ire) *B Smart* 56 a62
4 b g Second Empire (Ire) - Madam Waajib (Ire)

9^{10gs} 6^{8sd} 6^{8sd} 9^{8sd} **0-0-4**

Play Me *P W Chapple-Hyam* 93
3 b f Nashwan (USA) - Mrs Moonlight
3^{10gs} 3^{10s} 10^{12g} 1^{10g} **1-1-4 £10,871**

Play The Ball (USA) *G A Butler* a80
3 ch g Boundary (USA) - Copper Play (USA)
3^{7sd} 11^{7ft} 10^{9ft} **0-1-3 £1,039**

Play Up Pompey *J J Bridger* 62
3 b g Dansili - Search For Love (Fr)
10^{7g} 5^{10f} 9^{7gs} 10^{8gf} 3^{10g} 5^{10f} 6^{9gs} 3^{10g} 6^{11gf} 6^{12s} 3^{10gf} 6^{10gf} 5^{10g} 4^{8gs} 14^{8s} **0-3-15 £1,675**

Playful *R M Beckett* 96
2 b f Piccolo - Autumn Affair
1^{5g} 6^{5gf} 3^{6g} 4^{5gf} 1^{5gf} 6^{5g} **2-1-6 £16,816**

Playful Act (Ire) *J H M Gosden* 111
3 b f Sadler's Wells (USA) - Magnificient Style (USA)
1^{12gf} 2^{12gf} 10^{12g} 8^{10gs} **1-1-4 £106,951**

Playful Dane (Ire) *W S Cunningham* 96
8 b g Dolphin Street (Fr) - Omicida (Ire)
12^{5gf} 2^{5gf} 6^{5g} 1^{5gf} 2^{5gf} 3^{5gs} 5^{5gs} 1^{5g} 11^{5hy} **2-3-9 £28,302**

Playtime Blue *Mrs H Sweeting* 61
5 b g Komaite (USA) - Miss Calculate
11^{6gf} 2^{5gf} 6^{5gf} 4^{5gf} 9^{5gf} **0-1-5 £1,134**

Playtotheaudience *R A Fahey* 89
2 b g Royal Applause - Flyfisher (USA)
2^{6gf} 1^{6gf} 13^{6g} **1-1-3 £5,659**

Plea Bargain *J H M Gosden* 111
3 b c Machiavellian (USA) - Time Saved
1^{8gs} 2^{10gs} 1^{12gf} 4^{12g} **2-1-4 £122,769**

Pleasant *L G Cottrell* 65
4 b f Topanoora - Devon Peasant
9^{10g} 13^{10gf} 4^{12gf} 4^{12f} 1^{12gs} **1-0-5 £4,134**

Pleasant Home (USA) *C McGaughey III* a124
4 b/br f Seeking The Gold (USA) - Our Country Place (USA)
3^{9g} 1^{8ft} 1^{8g} 4^{9sy} 3^{6ft} 2^{7my} 2^{9ft} 1^{9ft} **3-2-8 £689,854**

Pleasing *J L Dunlop* 20 a64
2 b f Dr Fong (USA) - Trounce
7^{6s} 3^{6sd} 4^{8sd} **0-1-3 £825**

Pleasure Time *C Smith* a44
12 ch g Clantime - First Experience
11^{5sd} 6^{5sd} 9^{5sd} 2^{5sd} 4^{5sd} **0-1-5 £415**

Plectrum (USA) *P W Chapple-Hyam* 93
4 ch g Awesome Again (Can) - Berceau (USA)
3^{7g} 2^{7gf} 3^{9g} 1^{8gs} **1-3-4 £12,401**

Plenty Cried Wolf *R A Fahey* 70
3 b g Wolfhound (USA) - Plentitude (Fr)
4^{11s} 10^{8gf} 13^{10s} 1^{11gf} 2^{10s} 13^{12g} **1-1-6 £5,045**

Plough Maite *D E Cantillon* 37 a39
2 b g Komaite (USA) - Plough Hill
10^{6gf} 5^{7g} 7^{6sd} **0-0-3**

Plum *C A Dwyer* a47
5 br m Pivotal - Rose Chime (Ire)
5^{7sd} 5^{7sd} 11^{9sd} **0-0-3**

Plum Blossom *P J Makin* 43 a30
2 br f Beat All (USA) - Plum Bold
8^{7f} 11^{6g} 7^{5sd} **0-0-3**

Plum Pudding (Ire) *R Hannon* 79
2 b c Elnadim (USA) - Karayb (Ire)
10^{6gf} 3^{7gf} 6^{8gf} 8^{7s} **0-1-4 £942**

Plummet (USA) *D J Daly* 30
4 b f Silver Hawk (USA) - Fairy Heights (Ire)
12^{12g} 12^{10gs} **0-0-2**

Plumpie Mac (Ire) *N Bycroft* 16
4 b f Key Of Luck (USA) - Petrine (Ire)
12^{6g} 7^{12s} **0-0-2**

Plutocrat *L Lungo* 70
9 b g Polar Falcon (USA) - Choire Mhor
4^{16gf} 5^{14g} **0-0-2 £315**

Pocket Too *Jean-Rene Auvray* 12 a59
2 b g Fleetwood (Ire) - Pocket Venus (Ire)
9^{6f} 9^{7sd} 6^{9sd} **0-0-3**

Pocketwood *Jean-Rene Auvray* 83 a70
3 b g Fleetwood (Ire) - Pocket Venus (Ire)
5^{10sd} 5^{10sd} 2^{11gs} 2^{10s} 2^{12gs} 3^{15gs} 7^{14gf} 13^{14s} 1^{12gs} **1-4-9 £10,825**

Poetry 'n Passion *C A Cyzer* 3
4 b f Polish Precedent (USA) - Ghassanah
16^{7g} 11^{12g} **0-0-2**

Point Man (Ire) *J W Payne* a11
5 b g Pivotal - Pursuit Of Truth (USA)
8^{7sd} **0-0-1**

Point Of Dispute *P D Evans* 29 a75
10 b g Cyrano De Bergerac - Opuntia
2^{6sd} 3^{7sd} 3^{6sd} 6^{6sd} 2^{9sd} 7^{7sd} 10^{7sd} 4^{6sd} 7^{9sd} 11^{6gf} **0-4-10 £2,959**

Point Pleasant *E A L Dunlop* a51
2 b g Grand Lodge (USA) - Follow That Dream
7^{8sd} **0-0-1**

Poirot *J Howard Johnson* 55
3 b g Montjeu (Ire) - Opari (Ire)
5^{12gf} 4^{9gs} 9^{8g} **0-0-3 £271**

Poise (Ire) *Sir Michael Stoute* 78
4 b f Rainbow Quest (USA) - Crepe Ginger (Ire)
5^{10s} **0-0-1 £1,250**

Poker Player (Ire) *G C Bravery* 82 a76
3 ch g Raise A Grand (Ire) - Look Nonchalant (Ire)
4^{7sd} 2^{8g} 2^{8gf} 2^{8g} 4^{8gs} 6^{8gf} 1^{6g} **1-3-7 £9,516**

Pokermilliondotcom *A P Jones* 42 a11
2 b g Mujahid (USA) - Addicted To Love
8^{5gs} 2^{5g} 8^{5g} 7^{5sd} 3^{6f} 14^{8gf} **0-1-6 £1,553**

Polar Bear *W J Haggas* 114
5 ch g Polar Falcon (USA) - Aim For The Top (USA)
3^{7gs} 8^{7s} 1^{9gf} 2^{8s} **1-2-4 £30,972**

Polar Ben *J R Fanshawe* 116
6 b g Polar Falcon (USA) - Woodbeck
8^{8g} 4^{7s} 4^{7gf} 2^{8gf} 4^{8g} 3^{8gs} 1^{7hy} 6^{8s} **1-2-8 £22,470**

Polar Blizzard (Ire) *P W D'Arcy* 33
2 ch c Raise A Grand (Ire) - Polar Lady
10^{5gs} 10^{5gf} 12^{6gs} 16^{7g} **0-0-4**

Polar Dancer *H Steinmetz* a65
4 b f Polar Falcon (USA) - Petonica (Ire)
1^{10s} 2^{11g} 4^{9s} 7^{9g} 1^{11g} 3^{11s} 2^{11g} 10^{11s} 6^{11g} 1^{15g} 5^{17sd} **3-0-11 £9,999**

Polar Dawn *B R Millman* 66 a61
3 b f Polar Falcon (USA) - Leave At Dawn
6^{8g} 7^{8gf} 6^{8g} 15^{7gf} 1^{8gf} 6^{10f} 6^{10gs} 5^{8f} 5^{8g} 2^{8hd} 7^{7g} 4^{8gs} 6^{9sd} 7^{10sd} **1-1-14 £6,132**

Polar Force *Mrs C A Dunnett* 80 a69
5 ch g Polar Falcon (USA) - Irish Light (USA)
14^{5sd} 10^{7sd} 1^{6gs} 4^{5gf} 2^{6gf} 9^{6gf} 11^{6gf} 3^{6sd} 9^{6g} 8^{6gs} 1^{5s} 8^{5gs} 1^{5gf} 1^{6g} 17^{5g} 13^{6sd}

4-3-16 £17,127

Polar Haze *J Pearce* 52 a48
8 ch g Polar Falcon (USA) - Sky Music
9^{6sd} 8^{6sd} 6^{6sd} 7^{6sd} 4^{6s} 5^{6sd} 5^{7g} 3^{7g} 6^{6sd} 6^{6gf} 3^{6gf} 2^{6f} 8^{6f} 4^{6g} 8^{6sd} 8^{6sd} 3^{6ss} 9^{6sd} 5^{6sd} **0-4-19 £1,522**

Polar Jem *G G Margarson* 105
5 b m Polar Falcon (USA) - Top Jem
1^{12gf} 4^{10gf} 4^{10g} 5^{12gf} 6^{12g} 1^{12g} **2-0-6 £41,250**

Polar Kingdom *J J Quinn* 53 a78
7 b g Pivotal - Scarlet Lake
6^{6sd} 14^{5gs} 11^{5gf} 14^{6g} 15^{6g} **0-0-5**

Polar Magic *J R Fanshawe* 102
4 ch g Polar Falcon (USA) - Enchant
1^{7g} 2^{7gf} 3^{7gf} 2^{7gs} 13^{7gf} 5^{8s} 3^{8g} **1-3-7 £28,658**

Polar Sun *J R Fanshawe* 71 a82
4 b g Polar Falcon (USA) - Barford Lady
2^{9sd} 6^{9sd} 11^{9sd} 5^{7gs} 14^{7hy} **0-1-5 £1,185**

Polar Tryst *Lady Herries* 59
6 ch m Polar Falcon (USA) - Lovers Tryst
7^{12gf} **0-0-1**

Polar Way *Mrs A J Perrett* 93
6 ch g Polar Falcon (USA) - Fetish
8^{7g} 17^{7gf} **0-0-2**

Polden Milkmaid *J A Geake* 13 a34
4 b f Atraf - Maid Of Mischief
10^{7sd} 12^{7sd} 11^{6gf} **0-0-3**

Pole Dancer *W S Kittow* 40 a52
2 b g Polish Precedent (USA) - Pounelta
15^{7f} 10^{8gf} 6^{8sd} **0-0-3**

Polesworth *C N Kellett* a53
3 b f Wizard King - Nicholas Mistress
8^{9sd} 4^{8sd} 1^{7sd} 1^{7sd} 11^{6sd} 11^{8gf} 5^{7sd} 6^{7sd} 8^{8sd} 6^{7ss} 7^{5sd} 10^{7sd} 3^{6ss} **2-1-13 £3,116**

Poliama *D Burchell* 45
3 b f Polish Precedent (USA) - Amal
7^{8gf} **0-0-1**

Policy Maker (Ire) *E Lellouche* 120
5 b h Sadler's Wells (USA) - Palmeraie (USA)
5^{12g} 2^{12gs} 12^{12gf} 2^{13gs} **0-2-4 £88,113**

Polish Corridor *M Dods* 87
6 b g Danzig Connection (USA) - Possibility
2^{10gs} **0-1-1 £3,294**

Polish Eagle *E A L Dunlop* 73 a63
3 b c Polish Precedent (USA) - Tinashaan (Ire)
3^{9sd} 5^{11gs} 1^{10g} **1-1-3 £4,025**

Polish Effigy *B W Duke* a6
2 b g Bertolini (USA) - Corn Dolly (Ire)
16^{6g} 11^{6sd} **0-0-2**

Polish Emperor (USA) *W R Swinburn* 96 a101
5 ch g Polish Precedent (USA) - Empress Jackie (USA)
5^{5sd} 1^{5sd} 4^{5g} 5^{5gs} 9^{5gs} 20^{5g} 1^{5gf} 7^{5gf} 5^{5gf} 9^{5s} 3^{5gf} 7^{5g} 8^{5g} 12^{6sd} 3^{5sf} 7^{5sd} 8^{6sd} **2-2-17 £24,588**

Polish Flame *K G Reveley* 67
7 b g Blushing Flame (USA) - Lady Emm
12^{12s} 3^{13s} 3^{13gs} 5^{16gf} 2^{16g} **0-3-5 £2,568**

Polish Index *J R Jenkins* 57 a46
3 b g Polish Precedent (USA) - Glossary
10^{7gf} 9^{8gf} 6^{9sd} 9^{10hy} **0-0-4**

Polish Power (Ger) *J S Moore* 66 a66
5 br h Halling (USA) - Polish Queen
4^{13sd} 3^{10g} 15^{10g} 2^{10s} 18^{12g} 7^{12gf} 14^{11g} 11^{16gs} 10^{10g} **0-2-9 £1,955**

Polish Rhapsody (Ire) *J A Supple* a25
4 b f Charnwood Forest (Ire) - Polish Rhythm (Ire)
12^{9sd} 11^{12sd} **0-0-2**

Polish Rose *Miss G Browne* a28
4 ch f Polish Precedent (USA) - Messila Rose
9^{13sd} 11^{9sd} **0-0-2**

Polish Spirit *B R Millman* 68 a53
10 b g Emarati (USA) - Gentle Star
14^{12sd} 12^{11gs} 5^{10s} 1^{10s} 3^{10hy} 3^{10gf} 1^{10g} 2^{10g} 4^{10gf} 8^{12f} 9^{10gf} 11^{11g} 7^{10gs} 9^{10g} 6^{10gs} **2-3-15 £8,160**

Polish Welcome *S C Williams*
2 ch f Polish Precedent (USA) - Three White Sox
16^{6s} **0-0-1**

Political Intrigue *H R A Cecil* 94
3 b c Dansili - Quandary (USA)
10^{12s} 2^{10gf} 1^{12gf} 1^{12gf} 10^{12gf} 7^{12s} **2-1-6 £14,125**

Politkovskaya *T H Caldwell*
2 ch f Medicean - Soluce
16^{6g} 5^{6hy} **0-0-2 £260**

Pollensa Lady *A Crook* 1
5 b m Abzu - Whitegates Lady
7^{12gf} **0-0-1**

Polliwilline (Ire) *R Hannon* 76
2 b f Mull Of Kintyre (USA) - Zelah (Ire)
5^{6g} 1^{6gs} 7^{5g} 9^{6s} **1-0-4 £3,168**

Polygonal (Fr) *E R Oertel* 101
5 b g Octagonal (NZ) - Sectarine (Fr)
21^{8g} 3^{10gf} 8^{12f} 8^{10gf} 13^{10gf} 6^{10f} **0-1-6 £2,332**

Pomfret Lad *J J Quinn* 85
7 b g Cyrano De Bergerac - Lucky Flinders
13^{6s} 2^{6f} 3^{6gf} 11^{5gf} 2^{5s} 2^{6gf} 9^{6gf} 3^{6g} 3^{6gs} 21^{6g} 9^{7s} **0-6-11 £11,846**

Pommes Frites *W R Muir* 79 a81
2 b f Bertolini (USA) - Picolette
2^{6gs} 4^{5g} 4^{5gf} 1^{6gs} 11^{6gs} 7^{6gs} 8^{7s} 1^{7sf} 5^{7sd} 5^{7sd} **2-1-10 £8,775**

Pompadour *J Noseda* 66
3 b f King's Best (USA) - Tanzilla
3^{6gf} **0-0-1 £530**

Pompey Blue *P J McBride* a50
4 b f Abou Zouz (USA) - Habla Me (Ire)
4^{5sd} 7^{6sd} 9^{5sd} 8^{5sd} 8^{5sd} **0-0-5**

Pompey Chimes *J A Geake* a13
5 b g Forzando - Silver Purse
12^{7sd} 10^{8sd} **0-0-2**

Ponente *Mrs H Dalton* 29 a49
3 b f Robellino (USA) - Polmara (Ire)
4^{8sd} 7^{9sd} 7^{8sd} 4^{9sd} 13^{8s} **0-0-5**

Pont Neuf (Ire) *A Crook* 70
5 b m Revoque (Ire) - Petite Maxine
1^{12s} 5^{12s} 4^{12gf} 5^{10s} 10^{13gf} 3^{12g} 4^{12g} 5^{12gs} 5^{12gf} 8^{12g} **1-1-10 £4,664**

Pontefract Glory *M Dods* 52
2 b g Lujain (USA) - Final Glory
8^{7s} 7^{8gf} 8^{7gf} **0-0-3**

Ponty Carlo (Ire) *T D Easterby* 47
2 b c Mujadil (USA) - Distant Shore (Ire)
8^{6gf} **0-0-1**

Pop Play Again *G A Swinbank*

4 ch g Vettori (Ire) - Bellair
9^{11g} **0-0-1**

Pop Princess *P F I Cole* 46
2 ch f Compton Place - Thundercloud
9^{5gs} 6^{7gf} **0-0-2**

Pop Up Again *G A Swinbank* 58
5 ch m Bahamian Bounty - Bellair
6^{7gf} 8^{7g} 6^{8gf} 10^{6gf} 4^{7gf} 2^{7f} 5^{8g} **0-1-7 £1,137**

Poppys Footprint (Ire) *K A Ryan* 85 a71
4 ch f Titus Livius (Fr) - Mica Male (Ity)
11^{7gs} 3^{8gf} 5^{8g} 6^{7gf} 8^{8gf} 7^{8gf} 8^{7sd} 3^{9sd} **0-2-8 £2,136**

Port 'n Starboard *C A Cyzer* 57 a66
4 ch g Polar Falcon (USA) - Sally Slade
6^{8sd} 7^{16sd} 4^{12f} 2^{10sd} 3^{10sd} 4^{12sd} 12^{10sd} **0-2-7 £2,193**

Port D'Argent (Ire) *Mrs H O Graham* 47
3 b f Docksider (USA) - Petite-D-Argent
5^{10g} 3^{12gs} 7^{8gf} 11^{14gf} 4^{10f} 6^{16f} 9^{11gf} **0-1-7 £422**

Port St Charles (Ire) *P R Chamings* a45
8 b/br g Night Shift (USA) - Safe Haven
8^{6sd} **0-0-1**

Portacarron (Ire) *Eamon Tyrrell* 68 a50
3 b f Rossini (USA) - Night Patrol (Ire)
5^{7gf} 9^{8g} 1^{7g} 25^{8gf} 11^{9sd} **1-0-5 £4,900**

Portal *J R Fanshawe* 78
2 b f Hernando (Fr) - White Palace
1^{7gf} **1-0-1 £2,737**

Portcullis *M A Jarvis* 76
2 b c Pivotal - Frond
3^{7g} 4^{8gf} **0-1-2 £1,019**

Porters (USA) *R Hannon* 82 a83
2 b/br c Minardi (USA) - Time For The Show (USA)
5^{7gf} 1^{7gf} 5^{7gf} 7^{8gs} 5^{7gf} 3^{7sd} 2^{7sd} 2^{7sd} 2^{7sd} **1-4-9 £9,451**

Porthcawl *Mrs A J Perrett* 91
4 b f Singspiel (Ire) - Dodo (Ire)
3^{8g} 1^{8gf} 5^{8gf} 9^{7g} **1-1-4 £9,215**

Portland *B W Hills*
2 b c Zafonic (USA) - Bayswater
11^{7s} **0-0-1**

Portmeirion *S C Williams* 70 a41
4 b f Polish Precedent (USA) - India Atlanta
5^{9gs} 7^{8gf} 8^{9sd} 3^{8gf} 1^{6s} 4^{6gs} 1^{6gf} 2^{6g} **2-2-8 £8,147**

Porto Santo (Fr) *P Demercastel* 110
2 b c Kingsalsa (USA) - Exciting Times (Fr)
1^{5hy} 1^{6g} 3^{8s} **2-0-3 £37,642**

Portrayal (USA) *Saeed Bin Suroor* 111
3 b f Saint Ballado (Can) - True Glory (Ire)
1^{10s} **1-0-1 £16,240**

Poseidon Adventure (Ire) *A P O'Brien* 105
2 b c Sadler's Wells (USA) - Fanny Cerrito (USA)
2^{7y} 1^{8gs} 4^{8s} **1-1-3 £17,154**

Positive Profile (Ire) *P C Haslam* 77
7 b g Definite Article - Leyete Gulf (Ire)
5^{14gf} **0-0-1**

Possessed *T D McCarthy* 71 a74
2 b f Desert Prince (Ire) - Obsessive (USA)
2^{7gf} 4^{7f} 1^{9sd} 5^{8sd} 6^{8sd} **1-1-5 £6,034**

Postage Stampe *D M Simcock* 74
2 b f Singspiel (Ire) - Jaljuli
1^{7g} **1-0-1 £3,090**

Postgraduate (Ire) *H Morrison* 97
3 b c Almutawakel - Institutrice (Ire)
1^{7s} 16^{8gf} 7^{7g} 5^{8gs} 2^{8g} **1-1-5 £12,151**

Posthaste *Mrs G S Rees* 7
2 b f High Estate - Post Mistress (Ire)
10^{8gs} **0-0-1**

Postmaster *R Ingram* 72 a40
3 b g Dansili - Post Modern (USA)
5^{8g} 11^{8g} 7^{10g} 9^{12g} 16^{10gs} 14^{10sd} **0-0-6**

Potent Heir (USA) *Saeed Bin Suroor* 82
3 b c Forest Wildcat (USA) - Penniless Heiress (USA)
10^{5gf} 6^{6g} **0-0-2**

Pound Sign *M L W Bell* 78
2 ch c Singspiel (Ire) - Profit Alert (Ire)
4^{7g} 2^{7g} **0-1-2 £1,957**

Pout (Ire) *John Joseph Murphy* 95 a96
3 b f Namid - Symphony (Ire)
1^{6gy} 8^{9g} 9^{5g} 12^{7gf} 3^{6y} 3^{5ys} 4^{6s} 5^{6vs} 5^{8sd} **1-2-9 £21,349**

Poutu (Fr) *A Berry* 27
2 b f Acteur Francais (USA) - Sanctus Lady (Ire)
7^{5gf} 8^{7gf} 10^{7ft} 12^{7g} **0-0-4**

Powder Blue *Saeed Bin Suroor* 62
3 b f Daylami (Ire) - Blue Duster (USA)
4^{7gf} 2^{7g} **0-1-2 £1,498**

Power Assisted *C F Wall* 72
2 ch f Observatory (USA) - Caribbean Star
6^{5gf} 4^{5g} 3^{5gf} 3^{6g} 3^{6gf} **0-3-5 £1,865**

Power Broker *P F I Cole* 74
2 b c Mark Of Esteem (Ire) - Galatrix
9^{6f} 4^{6gs} 4^{6gf} 3^{7gs} **0-1-4 £2,326**

Power Glory *R A Fahey* 52 a34
3 b g Namaqualand (USA) - Belamcanda
12^{8gf} 5^{11gs} 10^{10gf} 4^{14gf} 11^{2g} 13^{14g} 15^{12gs} 4^{11sd} **1-0-8 £3,677**

Power Of Future (Ger) *H R A Cecil* 65
2 ch f Definite Article - Pik Konigin (Ger)
5^{7s} **0-0-1**

Power Politics (USA) *Saeed Bin Suroor* 76
2 b c Seeking The Gold (USA) - Stormy Pick (USA)
2^{5gf} 1^{5gf} **1-0-2 £8,528**

Power Strike (USA) *Mrs L B Normile* 51 a43
4 b g Coronado's Quest (USA) - Galega
3^{12gf} 6^{13g} 4^{12g} 6^{14sd} **0-1-4 £784**

Power To Burn *K Bell* a46
4 b g Superpower - Into The Fire
2^{7sd} 5^{8sd} 3^{7sd} 10^{7sd} **0-2-4 £631**

Powerscourt *A P O'Brien* 124
5 b h Sadler's Wells (USA) - Rainbow Lake
5^{12gf} 4^{12f} 2^{10g} 1^{10y} **1-0-4 £372,750**

Poyle Caitlin (Ire) *Miss B Sanders* 62 a25
3 b f Bachir (Ire) - Poyle Fizz
4^{8gf} 8^{8s} 6^{8f} 13^{10sd} **0-0-4 £327**

Poyle Jenny *Miss B Sanders* a33
6 b m Piccolo - Poyle Amber
11^{7sd} 8^{8sd} **0-0-2**

Pragmatica *R M H Cowell* 57 a60
4 b f Inchinor - Isabella Gonzaga
7^{8sd} 3^{9sd} 5^{8sd} 5^{7sd} 6^{6gf} 7^{6gf} 3^{9sd} 2^{8f} 2^{7g} 2^{7gf} 5^{7g} 12^{9sd} 4^{7sd} 10^{6sd} 8^{6sd} **0-5-15 £4,492**

Prairie Law (Ger) *B N Pollock* 52 a14
5 b g Law Society (USA) - Prairie Charm (Ire)
12^{12sd} 2^{10g} 10^{12sd} 11^{12g} 11^{13gs} 4^{13gf} 3^{12g} 14^{12gf} 1^{11gf} 6^{10g} 17^{11gf} **1-2-11 £4,075**

Prairie Oyster *Andrew Reid* 68
4 b f Emperor Jones (USA) - Soba Up
8^{6gs} 6^{10gf} 8^{10gf} 2^{8gf} 6^{8gf} 4^{8gs} 11^{8g} 7^{8g} PU^{8s} **0-1-9 £1,582**

Prairie Sun (Ger) *Mrs A Duffield* 76
4 b f Law Society (USA) - Prairie Flame (Ire)
1^{16gf} 1^{14f} 1^{16s} 1^{14gf} 3^{17gf} 2^{16gf} 4^{14gf} 7^{16g} 10^{12g} **4-2-9 £18,325**

Prakara (Ire) *L M Cumani* 52
3 ch f Indian Ridge - Prima Volta
7^{8gs} 4^{8gf} 7^{10gf} 11^{8gs} **0-0-4 £448**

Pralin Star (Ire) *Mrs H Sweeting*
3 ch g Daggers Drawn (USA) - Polaregina (Fr)
9^{8sd} **0-0-1**

Pre Eminance (Ire) *C R Egerton* 73 a52
4 b g Peintre Celebre (USA) - Sorb Apple (Ire)
6^{7g} 2^{11g} 8^{12g} 3^{10g} 10^{12sd} 10^{12gs} **0-2-6 £1,721**

Precautionary *Miss J Feilden* 70 a55
2 b f Green Desert (USA) - Well Warned
2^{6gf} 3^{6g} 5^{6gf} 3^{7sd} **0-3-4 £2,816**

Precious Dancer *W R Muir* a46
2 b c Sinndar (Ire) - Crodelle (Ire)
7^{9sd} 9^{8sd} **0-0-2**

Precious Mystery (Ire) *A King* 75 a66
5 ch m Titus Livius (Fr) - Ascoli
3^{13sd} 3^{14sd} 1^{15gs} 4^{15s} 3^{14gs} 13^{20s} 9^{16g} 6^{16g} 2^{14sd} 4^{14sd} 10^{17sd} **1-4-11 £7,720**

Precious Sammi *Julian Poulton* 11
3 b g Mark Of Esteem (Ire) - Night Over Day
11^{7gf} 11^{8gf} **0-0-2**

Pregnant Pause (Ire) *S Kirk* a54
4 b g General Monash (USA) - Dissidentia (Ire)
9^{8sd} 8^{9sd} 3^{7sd} 8^{6sd} 7^{7sd} 3^{8sd} 8^{8sd} **0-2-7 £395**

Prejudicial *M Johnston* 59
2 ch c Efisio - Queenie
2^{5hy} 6^{5g} 10^{5s} **0-1-3 £1,433**

Prelude *W M Brisbourne* 63 a53
4 b f Danzero (Aus) - Dancing Debut
9^{12s} 3^{10s} 9^{9sd} 10^{9gf} 8^{10g} 6^{12g} 2^{10gs} 3^{12gf} 2^{10gs} 2^{10s} 2^{11g} 10^{11gs} 3^{11gs} **0-6-13 £8,316**

Premier Cru *Andrew Turnell* 2 a57
2 b c King's Best (USA) - No Rehearsal (Fr)
13^{8gs} 10^{9sd} 4^{7sd} **0-0-3 £307**

Premier Fantasy *W J Haggas* 63 a70
3 b g Pivotal - Hemaca
11^{6gs} 19^{6gf} 10^{5gs} 6^{5sd} 11^{6sd} **0-0-5**

Premier Grand *R Craggs* 54 a71
5 ch g Case Law - Seamill (Ire)
6^{6f} 10^{6sd} 2^{6sd} 4^{6g} 12^{6gf} **0-2-5 £1,518**

Premier Prospect (USA) *T D Barron* 63
4 b/br f Sahm (USA) - Tadwin
16^{6s} 5^{7gf} 2^{6gf} 7^{6gf} 2^{6gf} 2^{6gf} 12^{6s} 4^{6gf} 1^{6gf} **1-3-9 £6,926**

Premier Rouge *David Marnane* 71 a69
4 b g Croco Rouge (Ire) - Petit Point (Ire)
4^{7sd} 1^{8g} 2^{8f} 4^{10sd} 4^{12gf} 1^{10gf} **1-1-6 £5,225**

Premier Times *M D Hammond* 52
3 ch g Timeless Times (USA) - Lady Magician
15^{8g} 12^{7s} 1^{9g} 6^{10gf} 6^{12gf} 8^{12g} 9^{7gf} 8^{14g} **1-0-8 £2,607**

Prenup (Ire) *L M Cumani* 76
4 ch f Diesis - Mutual Consent (Ire)
5^{12s} 6^{10gf} 6^{12gf} **0-0-3**

Present Oriented (USA) *M C Chapman*
4 ch g Southern Halo (USA) - Shy Beauty (Can)
PU^{10gs} 11^{6gf} 7^{10gf} **0-0-3**

Presenter (Ire) *M Sheppard* 51 a44
5 ch g Cadeaux Genereux - Moviegoer
6^{7sd} 9^{12sd} 13^{9sd} 3^{8s} 4^{7gs} **0-2-5 £465**

Preskani *Mrs N Macauley* 33 a65
3 b g Sri Pekan (USA) - Lamarita
5^{8sd} 3^{7sd} 10^{6sd} 10^{6g} 7^{7sd} 10^{6g} 4^{6sd} 4^{7sd} 5^{8sd} 3^{7ss} 2^{7sd} 1^{7sd} 1^{6ss} 1^{8sd} **3-2-14 £6,168**

Press Express (Ire) *M L W Bell* 81
3 ch g Entrepreneur - Nawaji (USA)
13^{8gf} 15^{7gf} 2^{10g} 1^{9gf} 2^{10gf} 7^{12g} 1^{10gf} **2-2-7 £12,489**

Pressure Putt *W J Haggas* 78 a78
2 ch g Tipsy Creek (USA) - Carnbrea Belle (Ire)
6^{7gf} 1^{7gf} 4^{7s} 3^{7sf} 5^{8sd} **1-2-5 £4,588**

Presto Shinko (Ire) *R Hannon* 110 a95
4 b g Shinko Forest (Ire) - Swift Chorus
1^{6sd} 6^{6g} 1^{6gs} 10^{6s} 2^{6g} 2^{6gf} 3^{6gf} 15^{6gs} 7^{7g} 1^{6gf} 1^{6g} 1^{6g} 1^{6s} **6-3-13 £140,987**

Presumptive (Ire) *R Charlton* 92
5 b g Danehill (USA) - Demure
2^{6gs} 7^{8g} 1^{7gf} 17^{8g} **1-1-4 £14,726**

Prettilini *A W Carroll* 68 a57
2 ch f Bertolini (USA) - Pretiosa (Ire)
3^{5g} 5^{5sd} 2^{6g} 10^{7gs} 9^{5gf} 5^{6g} 5^{6g} 2^{6g} 5^{5gf} 6^{7g} 4^{5sd} 1^{5sd} **1-3-12 £4,785**

Pretty Flamingo (Ire) *Thomas Cooper* a52
5 ch m Lycius (USA) - Scribbling (USA)
4^{13sd} 8^{14sd} **0-0-2**

Pretty Kool *S C Williams* 67
5 b m Inchinor - Carrie Kool
8^{6gf} 1^{5gf} 8^{5gf} 2^{5gs} 2^{5g} 9^{5gf} 9^{5gf} **1-2-7 £6,110**

Pretty Woman (Ire) *S C Williams* 39 a45
3 ch f Night Shift (USA) - Kind Of Cute
5^{7sd} 11^{10g} 6^{10sd} 11^{12gf} 11^{8sd} 6^{8g} **0-0-6**

Pride (Fr) *A De Royer-Dupre* 123
5 b m Peintre Celebre (USA) - Specificity (USA)
6^{11vs} 6^{12g} 1^{10s} 1^{12gs} 7^{12gs} 2^{10gs} 2^{10gf} **2-2-7 £464,173**

Pride Of Joy *D K Ivory* 8
2 ch f Pursuit Of Love - Ivory's Joy
15^{5gf} **0-0-1**

Pride Of Kinloch *K A Ryan* 64 a34
5 ch m Dr Devious (Ire) - Stormswept (USA)
11^{7sd} 9^{6g} 1^{7gs} 12^{7gf} 5^{6gf} 5^{7g} 10^{8hy} 8^{8ss} **1-0-8 £3,601**

Pride Of London (Ire) *P S McEntee* 37 a12
3 b f Danetime (Ire) - Kavana (Ire)
13^{6sd} 5^{6s} 13^{7gf} 5^{8gf} 17^{10g} 4^{8f} 9^{10g} 6^{10f} 4^{10g} 8^{8gf} **0-0-10**

Pride Of Nation (Ire) *L M Cumani* 82
3 b c Danehill Dancer (Ire) - Anita Via (Ire)
2^{8gf} 2^{8g} 1^{8g} **1-2-3 £6,180**

Pride Of Poona (Ire) *D M Simcock* 26 a13
3 b f Indian Ridge - Scandalous
7^{7gf} 10^{9sd} **0-0-2**

Prima Markova *D J Daly* a31
2 b f Mark Of Esteem (Ire) - Ball Gown
9^{9sd} **0-0-1**

Primarily *A Berry* 71 a23
3 b g Mind Games - Prim N Proper

2^{6s} 2^{6s} 3^{7gs} 8^{6gf} 3^{6g} 8^{6sd} 3^{6gf} 2^{6gf} 3^{6g} 6^{6gf} 8^{6hy} **0-7-11 £5,484**

Primary (USA) *W J Haggas* 87
2 b c Giant's Causeway (USA) - Prospective (USA)
1^{7gs} 1^{7gf} 8^{7gs} **2-0-3 £12,837**

Primatech (Ire) *K A Morgan* 12 a44
4 b f Priolo (USA) - Ida Lupino (Ire)
5^{7sd} 8^{6sd} 4^{7sd} 5^{7sd} 9^{6sd} 8^{6sd} 13^{6gs} 2^{6sd} 14^{6g} **0-1-9 £440**

Prime Contender *O Sherwood* 72 a78
3 b g Efisio - Gecko Rouge
11^{8g} 5^{8f} 11^{10gf} 3^{8g} 4^{8gf} 1^{8g} 1^{10sd} **2-1-7 £9,059**

Prime Meridian *J Nicol* 63 a69
2 ch c Observatory (USA) - Marie La Rose (Fr)
14^{8gs} 3^{9sd} 1^{9sf} **1-1-3 £3,018**

Prime Number (Ire) *G A Butler* 97
3 gr g King's Best (USA) - Majinskaya (Fr)
3^{7g} 3^{7gf} 1^{9g} 11^{10s} 1^{8gf} 8^{8g} 1^{8gf} 11^{10g} **3-2-8 £18,938**

Prime Offer *P J McBride* 64
9 b g Primo Dominie - Single Bid
10^{8gf} 5^{8g} 3^{8gf} **0-1-3 £550**

Prime Powered (Ire) *G L Moore* 76 a74
4 b g Barathea (Ire) - Caribbean Quest
11^{10gs} 13^{12gs} 8^{11g} 6^{12gf} 10^{10gs} 6^{10gs} 7^{12gs} 1^{12sd} 12^{12sd} **1-0-9 £3,397**

Prime Recreation *P S Felgate* 72 a16
8 b g Primo Dominie - Night Transaction
5^{5gs} 3^{5s} 11^{5g} 11^{5g} 14^{5gs} 5^{5gs} 12^{5gf} 15^{5gf} 12^{5sd} **0-0-9 £620**

Primed Up (Ire) *G L Moore* 69 a27
3 b g Rainbow Quest (USA) - Cape Mist (USA)
12^{10g} 5^{8gf} 7^{10gf} 9^{9gf} 7^{8gf} 14^{10sd} **0-0-6**

Primeshade Promise *D Burchell* 63 a59
4 ch f Opening Verse (USA) - Bonnie Lassie
10^{7sd} 9^{9sd} 3^{9sd} 1^{8gs} 5^{7s} 4^{7g} 2^{9sd} 2^{9sd} 6^{9sd} 2^{8g} 15^{8gf} **1-4-11 £6,471**

Primo Gold *W R Swinburn* 55 a52
2 b g Primo Valentino (Ire) - Bullion
11^{6g} 9^{6sd} 3^{7sd} **0-1-3 £509**

Primo Way *I Semple* 96
4 b c Primo Dominie - Waypoint
10^{6gs} 1^{7g} 12^{7gf} 2^{8g} 3^{7gf} 9^{8g} 16^{6g} 6^{6g} 15^{7gs} **1-2-9 £12,849**

Primondo (Ire) *J R Fanshawe* 63
3 b g Montjeu (Ire) - Tagiki (Ire)
9^{8gf} 11^{10gs} 3^{12gs} **0-1-3 £850**

Primrose Lane (Jpn) *D R Loder* 70
3 b f Sunday Silence (USA) - Oenothera (Ire)
8^{7gf} 2^{10f} 9^{8gs} **0-1-3 £1,292**

Primus Inter Pares (Ire) *D Nicholls* 96
4 b g Sadler's Wells (USA) - Life At The Top
5^{10hy} 7^{8s} 11^{8gs} 19^{8gf} 8^{6g} 14^{6gs} **0-0-6 £359**

Prince Aaron (Ire) *C N Allen* 111
5 b g Marju (Ire) - Spirito Libro (USA)
1^{6gf} 4^{7gf} 2^{6gf} 8^{7gf} 4^{6gf} 5^{5gf} 7^{6gf} 4^{5gf} **1-1-8 £58,972**

Prince Algarhoud *G L Moore* 28 a48
2 b g Josr Algarhoud (Ire) - Hi Hoh (Ire)
13^{6gf} 5^{6f} 11^{6gf} 12^{7sd} 6^{7sd} **0-0-5**

Prince Ary *B W Hills* 70
2 b g Desert Prince (Ire) - Aryaf (Can)
3^{7g} 4^{7gf} 7^{6gs} 18^{6g} **0-1-4 £1,121**

Prince Charlemagne (Ire) *N P Littmoden* 54
2 br c King Charlemagne (USA) - Ciubanga (Ire)
12^{6gf} 11^{7s} 7^{6gf} 11^{7gs} **0-0-4**

Prince Charming *J H M Gosden* 87
3 b c Royal Applause - Miss Primula
6^{6g} 7^{6g} **0-0-2 £450**

Prince Cyrano *W J Musson* 78 a61
6 b g Cyrano De Bergerac - Odilese
1^{6g} 10^{6gf} 7^{6gf} 11^{5gs} 10^{6gf} 8^{6gs} 8^{6g} 5^{6gs} 1^{6gf} 13^{6g} 8^{6sd} **2-0-11 £9,383**

Prince Darius *P W Chapple-Hyam*
2 br g Efisio - Celt Song (Ire)
11^{8gf} **0-0-1**

Prince Dayjur (USA) *J Pearce* 83 a85
6 b/br g Dayjur (USA) - Distinct Beauty (USA)
1^{7sd} 4^{6sd} 1^{7sd} 8^{7sd} 13^{8g} 2^{7sd} 2^{7gf} 9^{8g} **2-2-8 £9,112**

Prince Du Soleil (Fr) *J R Jenkins*
9 b g Cardoun (Fr) - Revelry (Fr)
15^{6gs} **0-0-1**

Prince Duval (Ire) *E F Vaughan* 55 a49
2 b g Desert Prince (Ire) - Ladylishandra (Ire)
8^{6g} 3^{7gs} 7^{8sd} 6^{8gs} **0-1-4 £432**

Prince Einar *M W Easterby* 5
2 b g Averti (Ire) - Westcourt Pearl
12^{5gf} 12^{5gs} **0-0-2**

Prince Evelith (Ger) *J A Glover* 63
2 b g Dashing Blade - Peace Time (Ger)
2^{7gf} 7^{7gf} 3^{6s} 15^{7s} **0-2-4 £1,110**

Prince Ivor *P R Rodford*
5 b g Polar Falcon (USA) - Mistook (USA)
13^{7sd} **0-0-1**

Prince Kirk (Fr) *E Borromeo* 115
5 b h Selkirk (USA) - Princess Manila (Can)
1^{10hy} 5^{9gf} 9^{8gf} **1-0-3 £38,342**

Prince Minata (Ire) *M Appleby* 14
10 b g Machiavellian (USA) - Aminata
11^{8hd} **0-0-1**

Prince Namid *Mrs A Duffield* 87
3 b g Namid - Fen Princess (Ire)
3^{5gf} 9^{5gf} 2^{6g} 3^{5gf} 4^{5s} 2^{6gf} 7^{6gs} 3^{5gs} 14^{6hy} 6^{5s} **0-5-10 £8,284**

Prince Nureyev (Ire) *B R Millman* 96
5 b g Desert King (Ire) - Annaletta
7^{10s} 13^{10gf} 9^{8gf} 4^{10g} 2^{10gf} 11^{10gf} 6^{10s} 19^{10gf} 4^{10g} 13^{10gs} **0-1-10 £5,010**

Prince Of Blues (Ire) *M Mullineaux* 57 a46
7 b g Prince Of Birds (USA) - Reshift
13^{5gs} 8^{5sd} 13^{5sd} 9^{7sd} 8^{5g} 11^{5sd} 7^{5g} **0-0-7**

Prince Of Gold *R Hollinshead* 68 a69
5 b h Polar Prince (Ire) - Gold Belt (Ire)
9^{6sd} 5^{7sd} 3^{7sd} 6^{7sd} 3^{5sd} 5^{5gs} 8^{6sd} 2^{6s} 10^{6gs} 4^{6g} 2^{6gf} 8^{7g} 6^{6sd} 5^{6gf} 5^{6gf} 5^{6sd} 4^{6sd} 6^{7sd} 6^{9gf} 7^{9sd} 7^{9sd} 6^{9sd} 1^{7ss} **1-4-23 £5,375**

Prince Of Light (Ire) *M Johnston* 102
2 ch c Fantastic Light (USA) - Miss Queen (USA)
3^{6gf} 1^{6gs} 1^{6g} 1^{6gf} 5^{6gs} **3-0-5 £51,300**

Prince Of Love (Ire) *Jedd O'Keeffe* 72
2 b c Fruits Of Love (USA) - Teodora (Ire)
8^{7gf} 5^{7gf} 9^{6g} 1^{8g} 1^{8gs} **2-0-5 £8,385**

Prince Of Medina *J R Best* 53
2 ch g Fraam - Medina De Rioseco
15^{5gf} 7^{5gf} 11^{6gs} **0-0-3**

Prince Of Perles *D Shaw* a30

4 b g Mind Games - Pearls
7^{6sd} 12^{6sd} 11^{5sd} **0-0-3**

Prince Of The May *H Morrison* 57
3 ch g Bluegrass Prince (Ire) - Maytime
8^{8gf} 10^{8g} 3^{8gf} **0-1-3 £552**

Prince Of The Wood (Ire) *A Bailey* a38
5 ch g Woodborough (USA) - Ard Dauphine (Ire)
12^{13sd} **0-0-1**

Prince Of Thebes (Ire) *A M Balding* 99
4 b g Desert Prince (Ire) - Persian Walk (Fr)
2^{7gf} 18^{7g} 4^{7gf} 8^{7s} 7^{7gf} 1^{7gf} 4^{7g} 7^{7gs}
1-1-8 £12,882

Prince Picasso *Sir Mark Prescott* 43
2 b g Lomitas - Auspicious
10^{6gf} 10^{7gf} 13^{5gf} **0-0-3**

Prince Prospect *Mrs L Stubbs* a49
9 b g Lycius (USA) - Princess Dechtra (Ire)
3^{12sd} 10^{12sd} 11^{9sd} **0-1-3 £211**

Prince Pyramus *J J Quinn* 36 a37
7 b g Pyramus (USA) - Rekindled Flame (Ire)
7^{7gf} 5^{7sd} **0-0-2**

Prince Rama *B J Meehan* 65 a64
2 b g Royal Applause - Romoosh
6^{6gf} 8^{5gf} 8^{6gf} 6^{7gf} 7^{7gf} 4^{6g} 10^{6f} 10^{6gs} 2^{7ft}
0-1-9 £1,288

Prince Richard *B Smart* 45
2 b g Diktat - Princess Latifa
17^{7g} 12^{7gf} 13^{8s} **0-0-3**

Prince Samos (Ire) *R Hannon* 94 a74
3 b c Mujadil (USA) - Sabaniya (Fr)
1^{8sd} 1^{8gs} 6^{7gs} 7^{8g} 6^{8g} 5^{10g} 2^{8gf} 5^{8g} 5^{10g} 6^{10g}
10^{8gs} **2-1-11 £20,881**

Prince Slayer *T P McGovern* a43
9 b g Batshoof - Top Sovereign
12^{10sd} **0-0-1**

Prince Tamino *H Morrison* 67 a83
2 b g Mozart (Ire) - Premiere Dance (Ire)
8^{6gf} 3^{7g} 1^{6sd} 2^{6sd} **1-2-4 £6,486**

Prince Tum Tum (USA) *D W Barker* 104 a109
5 b g Capote (USA) - La Grande Epoque (USA)
1^{6sd} 5^{6sd} 7^{8ft} 3^{8gf} 9^{9sd} 2^{7gs} 6^{7sd} 5^{6gf} 17^{6gf}
10^{9g} 6^{7s} 4^{6g} 1^{9gf} 17^{7g} 7^{6sd} 6^{6sf} 2^{6sd}
2-3-17 £28,291

Prince Valentine *G L Moore* 42 a49
4 b g My Best Valentine - Affaire De Coeur
7^{10f} 5^{7f} 15^{7g} 4^{10sd} 9^{8g} 3^{10sd} 4^{8sd} 3^{10sd} 2^{12sd}
0-3-9 £852

Prince Valluga (Ire) *W R Swinburn*
2 ch g Desert Prince (Ire) - Valluga (Ire)
13^{7gf} **0-0-1**

Prince Vector *A King* 88
3 b g Vettori (Ire) - The In-Laws (Ire)
13^{8g} 3^{10gf} 2^{10gf} 2^{12gf} 3^{9gs} 1^{10gf} 4^{11gf} 2^{10g}
1-5-8 £11,577

Prince Vettori *D J Coakley* 51 a67
3 b g Vettori (Ire) - Bombalarina (Ire)
PU^{8gf} 11^{8gf} 11^{11gf} 2^{9sd} 7^{9sd} 11^{10g} 13^{10sd}
1^{8sd} **1-1-8 £2,574**

Prince Woodman (USA) *B J Meehan* 92
2 b c Woodman (USA) - Queen Mama (USA)
1^{6gs} **1-0-1 £6,318**

Prince Zafonic *W Jarvis* 60
2 ch c Zafonic (USA) - Kite Mark
7^{7s} **0-0-1**

Princeable Lady (Ire) *J A Pickering* 52 a54
3 b f Desert Prince (Ire) - Saucy Maid (Ire)
2^{6sd} 6^{7sd} 10^{8sd} 11^{6sd} 7^{7sd} 1^{8gf} 4^{8gf} 10^{9sf}
11^{7sd} 11^{9sd} 4^{6sd} 3^{9sd} **1-2-12 £3,971**

Princelet (Ire) *M A Jarvis* 82
3 b g Desert Prince (Ire) - Soeur Ti (Fr)
3^{10gf} 1^{10g} **1-1-2 £3,978**

Princely Vale (Ire) *W G M Turner* 69 a62
3 b g Princely Heir (Ire) - Lomalou (Ire)
5^{7sd} 11^{7sd} 9^{8sd} 3^{7sd} 8^{6gf} 6^{5gf} 5^{6f} 4^{6g} 2^{6gf}
4^{6gf} 4^{5s} **0-2-11 £2,164**

Princelywallywogan *I A Wood* 79 a67
3 b g Princely Heir (Ire) - Dublivia
3^{7sd} 4^{7sd} 11^{8gs} 8^{7sd} 1^{8gf} 7^{8g} 5^{8gf} 14^{10g} 3^{10sd}
1^{10gs} 11^{8sd} **2-2-11 £11,865**

Princes Theatre *M W Easterby* 38
7 b g Prince Sabo - Frisson
10^{7g} PU^{8gf} **0-0-2**

Princess Arwen *Mrs Barbara Waring* 51 a45
3 b f Magic Ring (Ire) - Absolutelystunning
7^{5gf} 6^{6g} 6^{6sd} 13^{5g} 5^{6sd} 8^{8g} 1^{7sd} 10^{7ss}
1-0-8 £1,473

Princess Bankes *Miss Gay Kelleway* a31
4 b f Vettori (Ire) - Lady Bankes (Ire)
9^{12sd} **0-0-1**

Princess Charlmane (Ire) *C J Teague*
2 b f King Charlemagne (USA) - Bint Alreeys
10^{5gf} **0-0-1**

Princess Cleo *T D Easterby* 78 a73
2 ch f Mark Of Esteem (Ire) - Classy Cleo (Ire)
6^{6g} 2^{5sd} 2^{5gf} 1^{6gs} 9^{6gs} **1-2-5 £29,454**

Princess Cocoa (Ire) *R A Fahey* 46
2 b f Desert Sun - Daily Double (Fr)
9^{7gf} 7^{7g} **0-0-2**

Princess Galadriel *J M P Eustace* 67
4 b f Magic Ring (Ire) - Prim Lass
13^{7g} 4^{8f} 3^{7g} 4^{7gf} 9^{7gf} 17^{7gf} 10^{10gf}
0-1-7 £1,277

Princess Kai (Ire) *R Ingram* a49
4 b f Cayman Kai (Ire) - City Princess
10^{6sd} 10^{5sd} 6^{6sd} 8^{6sd} 11^{5sd} **0-0-5**

Princess Karla (Ire) *J W Unett* a53
3 b f Fayruz - Mystique Air (Ire)
2^{7sd} 10^{9sd} 11^{9sd} 9^{9sd} 10^{9sd} 11^{8sd} **0-1-6**
£1,260

Princess Kiotto *T D Easterby* 78
4 b f Desert King (Ire) - Ferghana Ma
8^{16s} 4^{16gf} 1^{16g} 7^{17gf} 2^{16gf} **1-1-5 £6,562**

Princess Lavinia *G Wragg* 50
2 ch f Fraam - Affaire De Coeur
14^{7s} **0-0-1**

Princess Nada *Saeed Bin Suroor* 74
2 b f Barathea (Ire) - Zomaradah
10^{7gs} 2^{8g} 2^{8s} **0-2-3 £3,113**

Princess Of Aeneas (Ire) *I Semple* 56
2 b f Beckett (Ire) - Romangoddess (Ire)
5^{7gf} 7^{7s} **0-0-2**

Princess Patavium *P C Haslam* 31
2 b f Titus Livius (Fr) - Multi-Sofft
7^{5s} 6^{7f} **0-0-2**

Princess Perfect (Ire) *G M Moore* 52 a40
4 b f Danehill Dancer (Ire) - Resiusa (Ity)
8^{7g} 12^{7s} 10^{7sd} 11^{9sd} 6^{11gf} 12^{12g} 11^{8g} 12^{9sf}
0-0-8

Princess Society (Ire) *E A L Dunlop* 64
2 b f Desert Prince (Ire) - Ballet Society (Fr)

7^{6gf} 6^{7gf} **0-0-2**

Princess Zaha *A G Newcombe* 42
3 b f Zaha (Can) - Otaru (Ire)
11^{8gf} **0-0-1**

Principal Witness (Ire) *T G Dascombe* 77 a65
4 b g Definite Article - Double Eight (Ire)
6^{8s} 12^{7g} 10^{8gf} 11^{10gf} 3^{8g} 5^{8sd} 7^{12s} 2^{14sd} 4^{14sd} **0-2-9 £1,486**

Principessa *B Palling* a44
4 b f Machiavellian (USA) - Party Doll
9^{10sd} 9^{12sd} **0-0-2**

Prinquet (USA) *C E Brittain* 6
2 ch f Marquetry (USA) - Princess Kris
16^{7g} **0-0-1**

Printsmith (Ire) *J R Norton* a53
8 br m Petardia - Black And Blaze
5^{9sd} 13^{9sd} 5^{9sd} 8^{8sd} 2^{8sd} 2^{8sd} 11^{9sd} 8^{8sd} 8^{8sd} 5^{9sd} 13^{8sd} 6^{11ss} 7^{11sd} 9^{9sd} **0-2-14 £833**

Priorina (Ire) *D Haydn Jones* 56 a56
3 b f Priolo (USA) - Strina (Ire)
3^{8sd} 6^{7sd} 13^{7sd} 10^{7sd} 9^{10f} 2^{8f} 5^{7g} 2^{7gf} 10^{7gf} 10^{8sd} 2^{7sf} 2^{8sd} **0-5-12 £3,639**

Priors Hill (Ire) *Saeed Bin Suroor* 97
2 b c Danehill (USA) - Lailati (USA)
1^{8s} 3^{8gf} **1-1-2 £7,070**

Prithee *J H M Gosden* 71
3 b f Barathea (Ire) - Bina Ridge
2^{8g} 3^{10g} 9^{10gs} **0-2-3 £2,046**

Private Benjamin *M R Hoad* a62
5 gr g Ridgewood Ben - Jilly Woo
10^{13sd} 3^{13sd} 12^{12sd} 11^{14gf} **0-1-4 £527**

Private Business (USA) *B W Hills* 103
2 gr/ro c Cozzene (USA) - Privity (USA)
1^{6gs} 5^{7gs} 1^{8gf} 3^{8gf} 4^{7gs} **2-1-5 £17,391**

Private Lives (UAE) *D R C Elsworth* 63
3 b c Timber Country (USA) - Personal Business (USA)
8^{10g} 5^{14g} **0-0-2**

Privy Seal (Ire) *D K Weld* 100
4 b g Cape Cross (Ire) - Lady Joshua (Ire)
7^{10gf} 12^{10gf} 10^{10gf} 8^{10gs} 10^{12gy} 15^{10g} 10^{10g} **0-0-7**

Prize Fighter (Ire) *Jonjo O'Neill* 96
3 b g Desert Sun - Papal
3^{10gs} 3^{9gf} 19^{8gf} 17^{8gs} 8^{8s} **0-1-5 £4,550**

Prizeman (USA) *J A Geake* 54
7 b g Prized (USA) - Shuttle (USA)
20^{10gs} 19^{8gs} 13^{10gf} **0-0-3**

Pro Tempore *David Pinder* 59
3 b f Fraam - Record Time
15^{6gs} 7^{6gf} 6^{6gf} 12^{6gf} 2^{5gf} 3^{5g} 6^{5gf} **0-2-7 £1,304**

Proclamation (Ire) *J Noseda* 128
3 gr c King's Best (USA) - Shamarra (Fr)
6^{10s} 1^{8g} 1^{7gf} 1^{8s} 11^{6g} **3-0-5 £231,275**

Procrastinate (Ire) *R F Fisher* 53 a53
3 ch g Rossini (USA) - May Hinton
3^{7sd} 6^{9sd} 8^{9sd} 4^{9sd} 6^{7gs} 8^{9sd} 5^{7g} 3^{8gs} 4^{10gf} 9^{12g} 11^{8gf} **0-1-11 £1,199**

Procreate (Ire) *Miss L A Perratt* 29
5 b g Among Men (USA) - Woodbury Princess
12^{6gs} 8^{8gf} 14^{7g} 7^{8gf} 8^{7gf} **0-0-5**

Profit's Reality (Ire) *M J Attwater* 99
3 br g Key Of Luck (USA) - Teacher Preacher (Ire)
2^{7g} 1^{8gs} 8^{8g} 1^{10gf} 4^{10gf} 6^{10gs} 8^{10g} 8^{10g} **2-1-8 £21,740**

Profitable *B W Hills* a66
2 b f Daylami (Ire) - Manuetti (Ire)
4^{8sd} **0-0-1 £290**

Prokofiev (USA) *Jonjo O'Neill*
9 br g Nureyev (USA) - Aviara (USA)
16^{14g} **0-0-1**

Promotion *Sir Michael Stoute* 106
5 b g Sadler's Wells (USA) - Tempting Prospect
4^{10gf} 5^{10gf} 5^{12gf} 11^{10gs} **0-0-4 £3,935**

Proper Lady (Ire) *S Kirk* 57
2 b f Danehill Dancer (Ire) - Promising Lady
16^{7g} 7^{7f} 7^{7g} 4^{8hd} 9^{7g} **0-0-5 £267**

Propinquity *W R Swinburn* 95
3 b g Primo Dominie - Lydia Maria
11^{8g} 14^{12gf} **0-0-2**

Proprioception (Ire) *A King* 55
3 ch f Danehill Dancer (Ire) - Pepper And Salt (Ire)
5^{10gf} 7^{10g} 6^{10g} 14^{12gs} **0-0-4**

Prospect Court *J W Unett* 68 a52
3 ch g Pivotal - Scierpan (USA)
12^{7gf} 7^{6g} 12^{6g} 9^{6gf} 9^{6sd} 5^{6sd} 6^{7sd} **0-0-7**

Prospect Hill (Ire) *K A Morgan* a27
7 ch g Nucleon (USA) - Ann Hill (Ire)
11^{6sd} 8^{5sd} 9^{5sd} 11^{6sd} **0-0-4**

Prospect Park *C Laffon-Parias* 116
4 b c Sadler's Wells (USA) - Brooklyn's Dance (Fr)
1^{10g} 6^{12g} 1^{10g} 11^{10gs} **2-0-4 £43,263**

Prospect Point *C A Dwyer* a42
3 ch f Cayman Kai (Ire) - Sassy Lady (Ire)
5^{6sd} 3^{8sd} 8^{8sd} 8^{7sd} 5^{6sd} 8^{5sd} **0-1-6 £206**

Protagonist *B N Pollock* 24 a32
7 b/br g In The Wings - Fatah Flare (USA)
14^{16g} 10^{12sd} 13^{12sd} **0-0-3**

Protecting Heights (Ire) *M E Sowersby*
4 br g Hector Protector (USA) - Height Of Fantasy (Ire)
13^{14gs} 14^{14gs} 12^{12hy} **0-0-3**

Protection Money *L P Grassick* a38
5 ch g Hector Protector (USA) - Three Piece
8^{12sd} 11^{17sd} **0-0-2**

Protective *J G Given*
4 ch g Hector Protector (USA) - You Make Me Real (USA)
21^{12hy} **0-0-1**

Protester *W A O'Gorman* 53 a31
2 b c Agnes World (USA) - Galine
8^{6sd} 10^{6g} **0-0-2**

Proud Killer *J R Jenkins* 52
2 b g Killer Instinct - Thewaari (USA)
12^{7gf} 7^{6s} **0-0-2**

Proud Scholar (USA) *Mrs A J Perrett* 54 a56
3 br f Royal Academy (USA) - Proud Fact (USA)
3^{7f} 12^{8gf} 13^{10sd} **0-1-3 £550**

Proud Western (USA) *B Ellison* 57
7 b/br g Gone West (USA) - Proud Lou (USA)
10^{6gs} 12^{6gs} 1^{5gf} 11^{5gf} 10^{5gf} 12^{5gf} 5^{8gf} 8^{8gf} 11^{6gf} **1-0-9 £2,975**

Prowess (Ire) *B W Hills* 79
2 ch f Peintre Celebre (USA) - Yawl
4^{7gf} 7^{8g} **0-0-2 £572**

Proxenia *R Hannon* 72
2 ch f Pursuit Of Love - Radiant
3^{5gf} 2^{6g} 2^{6gf} 2^{6gf} 2^{6gs} 2^{7gf} 9^{7gf} 11^{6g} **0-6-8 £13,821**

Pseudonym (Ire) *M F Harris* 68 a65

3 ch g Daylami (Ire) - Stage Struck (Ire)
6^{10gf} 7^{10sd} 4^{10g} 14^{12gs} 3^{10sd} **0-1-5 £804**

Psychiatrist *R Hannon* 95 a99
4 ch g Dr Devious (Ire) - Zahwa
2^{7sd} 12^{7g} 4^{7gs} 5^{7gf} 8^{7g} 6^{7g} 7^{7gs} 12^{7sd} 4^{7sd} 2^{8sd} 1^{8sd} **1-2-11 £12,761**

Psychic Star *W R Swinburn* 93
2 b f Diktat - Southern Psychic (USA)
1^{7g} 2^{7g} 5^{7g} 4^{7gf} **1-1-4 £5,446**

Psycho Cat *P A Blockley* 71 a69
2 b g Hunting Lion (Ire) - Canadian Capers
8^{8gf} 5^{7gf} 7^{8gs} 10^{6hy} 7^{7sd} 1^{7ss} 1^{6sd} 2^{9sd} 10^{9sd} **2-1-9 £6,048**

Ptarmigan Ridge *Miss L A Perratt* 88
9 b h Sea Raven (Ire) - Panayr
8^{5g} 7^{5gs} 13^{5s} 14^{5g} 4^{6gs} 5^{5gf} 10^{5g} 9^{5g} 13^{5g} **0-1-9 £2,896**

Ptolemac Cosmology *M L W Bell* 30
2 b g Galileo (Ire) - Crystal Ring (Ire)
11^{8hy} **0-0-1**

Public Eye *L A Dace* 59 a46
4 b g Zafonic (USA) - Stardom
7^{7g} 4^{7f} 7^{8sd} 7^{8gf} 3^{11g} 4^{12gf} 9^{14gf} 12^{10sd} **0-1-8 £1,123**

Public Forum *Sir Michael Stoute* 99
3 b c Rainbow Quest (USA) - Valentine Girl
1^{11gs} **1-0-1 £6,991**

Pugilist *B J Meehan* 89
3 b g Fraam - Travel Mystery
2^{8gf} 2^{10gf} 1^{9gs} 8^{10gf} 4^{10gf} **1-2-5 £7,371**

Pukka (Ire) *L M Cumani* 104
4 b c Sadler's Wells (USA) - Puce
4^{12g} 15^{10gf} 6^{13gf} 4^{12hy} 6^{12s} **0-0-5 £3,381**

Pukka Tique *R Hollinshead* 70
2 b g Groom Dancer (USA) - Surf Bird
9^{7g} 3^{7g} 6^{8g} 30^{6g} 4^{8gs} **0-1-5 £820**

Pulse *Miss J R Tooth* 72 a50
7 b g Salse (USA) - French Gift
4^{5sd} 11^{5sd} 4^{5gs} 1^{5sd} 2^{5gf} 1^{5gs} 4^{5gf} 3^{6f} 4^{5f} 7^{6g} 5^{5gf} 1^{5gf} 2^{5gf} 8^{5gf} 7^{5f} 10^{6gf} 5^{5g} 9^{5g} 7^{5sd} 7^{5sd} **3-4-20 £15,721**

Punctilious *Saeed Bin Suroor* 116
4 b f Danehill (USA) - Robertet (USA)
5^{10gf} 7^{12gf} 1^{12gs} 1^{12g} 4^{15gf} 10^{10y} **2-0-6 £167,490**

Punctuation *C E Brittain* 49 a36
3 b c Groom Dancer (USA) - Shady Point (Ire)
3^{8f} 14^{6gf} 7^{8sd} **0-0-3 £627**

Punjabi *Mrs G S Rees* 52 a55
2 b g Komaite (USA) - Competa
8^{7g} 8^{6gf} 8^{8gs} 12^{8sd} 3^{9sd} **0-1-5 £213**

Punta Galera (Ire) *R Hannon* 93
2 br c Zafonic (USA) - Kobalt Sea (Fr)
5^{7gf} 2^{6gf} 6^{8gs} 1^{8gf} 5^{8gf} **1-1-5 £8,311**

Pure Fiction *R Hannon* 73
2 b f Zilzal (USA) - Once Upon A Time
6^{5g} 1^{7gf} 3^{7gf} **1-0-3 £4,698**

Pure Illusion (Ire) *J H M Gosden* 92
2 b f Danehill (USA) - Saintly Speech (USA)
3^{7gf} 1^{7g} 5^{8gf} **1-1-3 £6,863**

Pure Imagination (Ire) *J M Bradley* 86
4 ch g Royal Academy (USA) - Ivory Bride
4^{6s} 9^{6gf} 5^{6g} 1^{7gf} 7^{6s} 9^{7g} 7^{7gf} 2^{7gf} 5^{7gf} 5^{8gs} 3^{8gf} 8^{8gf} 1^{6g} 8^{7gf} 1^{8g} 2^{7g} **3-3-16 £17,940**

Pure Mischief (Ire) *C R Dore* a67
6 b g Alhaarth (Ire) - Bellissi (Ire)
6^{10sd} 6^{8sd} UR^{9sd} **0-0-3**

Purple Dancer (Fr) *G A Swinbank* 61
3 b g Daylami (Ire) - Stage Manner
6^{7s} 10^{9gf} 4^{7f} 5^{12gf} 6^{8gf} 10^{10gf} 2^{10gs} **0-1-7 £1,408**

Purple Door *R M Beckett* 49 a32
3 b f Daggers Drawn (USA) - Carreamia
9^{7gf} RO^{7g} 3^{7gs} 7^{8g} 3^{7gs} 3^{7gs} 7^{8sd} **0-3-7 £1,723**

Pushy Guest (USA) *G G Margarson* 50
2 ch c Stravinsky (USA) - Saucy Blondy (USA)
14^{6gf} 9^{6gf} 6^{6gf} 7^{6gs} 14^{7gf} **0-0-5**

Puskas (Ire) *M R Channon* 96
2 b g King's Best (USA) - Chiquita Linda (Ire)
6^{5gs} 1^{5gf} 3^{5gf} 6^{6s} 5^{6gf} 6^{6gs} **1-1-6 £7,806**

Puteri Sas (Ire) *P F I Cole* 66
2 b f Fasliyev (USA) - Puteri Wentworth
3^{7g} **0-1-1 £1,081**

Putra Kuantan *M A Jarvis* 97
5 b g Grand Lodge (USA) - Fade
8^{8gs} 13^{8g} 8^{8gf} 5^{9g} 2^{10gf} 4^{10g} **0-1-6 £3,838**

Putra Pekan *M A Jarvis* 110
7 b h Grand Lodge (USA) - Mazarine Blue
3^{8g} 9^{7gs} 15^{8gf} 14^{9g} 8^{8g} **0-0-5 £3,000**

Putra Sas (Ire) *P F I Cole* a96
4 b c Sri Pekan (USA) - Puteri Wentworth
8^{12sd} **0-0-1**

Puya *H Candy* 84
3 b f Kris - Pervenche
1^{7gf} 11^{7gf} **1-0-2 £4,290**

Pyramid *P L Gilligan* a53
3 ch g Pivotal - Mary Cornwallis
12^{6g} 13^{7g} 3^{8sd} **0-1-3 £604**

Pyrrhic *G L Moore* a47
6 b g Salse (USA) - Bint Lariaaf (USA)
8^{12sd} 3^{10sd} 7^{10sd} 9^{8sd} **0-1-4 £210**

Qaadmah (Ire) *D Selvaratnam* 70
3 b f Dubai Millennium - Zahrat Dubai
10^{10gf} 5^{11g} 8^{10gs} 14^{10gf} 10^{6ft} **0-0-5**

Qaasi (USA) *M Johnston* 75
3 ch g Rahy (USA) - Recording (USA)
4^{8gf} 4^{11g} 3^{8g} **0-0-3 £1,969**

Qadar (Ire) *N P Littmoden* 99
3 b g Xaar - Iktidar
4^{6g} 3^{7g} 12^{7gf} **0-1-3 £3,074**

Qik Dip (Ire) *P D Evans* 55
2 b g Desert Style (Ire) - Noble Clare (Ire)
15^{6gf} 14^{6gs} 9^{8g} **0-0-3**

Qobtaan (USA) *M R Bosley* a65
6 b g Capote (USA) - Queen's Gallery (USA)
11^{9sd} 1^{9sd} 12^{9sd} 8^{8sd} 10^{7sd} **1-0-5 £3,540**

Quadrophenia *J G Given* 63
2 b f College Chapel - Truly Madly Deeply
2^{5gf} 1^{5g} 7^{6s} **1-1-3 £4,145**

Quaffle *M Johnston* 40
2 b g Pivotal - Fairy Flight (Ire)
5^{7g} 10^{6gs} 13^{7gf} **0-0-3**

Quaker Boy *M Dods* 59
2 b c Agnes World (USA) - La Brise (Ire)

7^{5g} 3^{5f} 6^{6gf} 4^{5gf} 5^{5gf} **0-0-5 £815**

Qualify *M R Channon* 75 a71
2 b g Mark Of Esteem (Ire) - Raneen Alwatar
8^{7gf} 3^{8gs} 4^{9sd} 3^{10g} 2^{8gf} 1^{8hy} **1-3-6 £6,265**

Qualitair Wings *J Hetherton* 72 a65
6 b g Colonel Collins (USA) - Semperflorens
6^{7g} 10^{8g} 5^{7gs} 1^{8g} 5^{8g} 9^{9s} 4^{8gf} 5^{8g} 4^{8gf} 4^{8g} 7^{8s} 6^{8g} 2^{8gf} 4^{9g} 3^{8gf} 2^{10gs} 1^{9sd} 3^{10sd} **2-4-18 £13,212**

Quality Street *P Butler* 79
3 ch f Fraam - Pusey Street Girl
1^{5gf} 2^{5g} 2^{5gf} 3^{5gf} 8^{5g} **1-3-5 £5,238**

Quantica (Ire) *N Tinkler* 60 a55
6 b g Sri Pekan (USA) - Touche-A-Tout (Ire)
2^{6sd} 3^{6sd} 2^{6gf} 6^{6g} 2^{6gs} 5^{6gs} 11^{6gf} 3^{6s} 1^{7gf} 8^{6gf} 6^{7gf} 2^{7s} 11^{6hy} **1-6-13 £8,213**

Quantum (Ire) *J H M Gosden* 60
2 b f Alhaarth (Ire) - Frappe (Ire)
8^{7g} 4^{8gs} **0-0-2 £256**

Quantum Leap *S Dow* 78 a82
8 b g Efisio - Prejudice
3^{7sd} 2^{6sd} 2^{7sd} 1^{7sd} 3^{7sd} 8^{7sd} 10^{7gs} 11^{7g} 10^{7gf} 1^{7gf} 4^{7gf} 7^{9g} 6^{7gf} 13^{7sd} 12^{7g} 7^{7g} 8^{8sd} 7^{8sd} 5^{8sd} **2-4-19 £14,903**

Quarry Island (Ire) *M Todhunter* 30
4 b f Turtle Island (Ire) - Last Quarry
9^{14gf} **0-0-1**

Quasimodo (Ire) *A W Carroll* 66
3 b c Night Shift (USA) - Daziyra (Ire)
2^{8hy} 3^{8sh} 1^{9hy} 3^{7hy} 6^{10gf} **1-3-5 £7,301**

Quatre Saisons *H R A Cecil* 68
3 ch c Bering - Inseparable
3^{10s} 5^{11g} 7^{10s} **0-0-3 £642**

Quebecois *P D Evans* 25
2 b c Zaha (Can) - Fanciful (Fr)
13^{6s} 16^{6g} 11^{6gf} **0-0-3**

Quedex *R J Price* 78
9 b g Deploy - Alwal
8^{14g} 11^{18gs} **0-0-2**

Queen Charlotte (Ire) *R Ingram* a45
6 ch m Tagula (Ire) - Tisima (Fr)
9^{10sd} **0-0-1**

Queen Cleopatra (Ire) *A P O'Brien* 98
2 b f Kingmambo (USA) - Sequoyah (Ire)
4^{6g} 5^{6s} 9^{7gs} 5^{7gs} **0-0-4 £2,346**

Queen Cobra (Ire) *H Morrison* 79 a65
2 b f Indian Rocket - Miss Sabre
10^{6gf} 1^{5sd} 1^{5hy} **2-0-3 £8,343**

Queen Jean *T D Easterby* 50
2 ch f Pivotal - Composition
8^{6gf} 5^{5g} 6^{6gs} 10^{7gf} **0-0-4**

Queen Lucia (Ire) *J G Given* a10
4 b f Pursuit Of Love - Inquirendo (USA)
13^{7sd} **0-0-1**

Queen Nefitari *M W Easterby* 45 a28
3 b f Celtic Swing - Opalette
9^{7sd} 9^{9s} 12^{12gf} 6^{14g} 10^{11sd} **0-0-5**

Queen Of Diamonds (Ire) *Mrs P N Dutfield* 47
2 b f Fruits Of Love (USA) - Royal Jubilee (Ire)
16^{8gs} 6^{10hy} **0-0-2**

Queen Of Fire *M R Channon* 96
2 b f Dr Fong (USA) - Sonic Sapphire
1^{6gf} 4^{6g} 9^{6gf} 7^{6g} **1-0-4 £10,663**

Queen Of Iceni *J L Dunlop* 79
3 b f Erhaab (USA) - Princess Genista
2^{9gs} 6^{12gs} 6^{12gs} 7^{10gf} 8^{10gf} 2^{15s} 15^{16g} 5^{14s} 1^{14g} 9^{16s} **1-2-10 £7,729**

Queen Of Night *D W Chapman* 75 a72
5 b m Piccolo - Cardinal Press
4^{6sd} 6^{5sd} 3^{5sd} 9^{7sd} RR^{5sd} 4^{5sd} 5^{6sd} 7^{5sd} 11^{6sd} 6^{5gs} 5^{5gf} 12^{5g} 5^{5g} 2^{6sd} 7^{5gf} 3^{5gf} 9^{5gf} 18^{5gf} 3^{5g} 5^{5gf} 10^{5g} 6^{5g} **0-4-22 £3,879**

Queen Tara *G Prodromou* 14
3 b f Kayf Tara - Lucy Tufty
14^{8g} **0-0-1**

Queen Tomyra (Ire) *L M Cumani* 84 a88
3 b f Montjeu (Ire) - Kama Tashoof
2^{10sd} 8^{10gf} 1^{12sd} 4^{12g} **1-1-4 £5,738**

Queen's Best *Sir Michael Stoute* 87
2 b f King's Best (USA) - Cloud Castle
2^{6g} 1^{6s} **1-1-2 £5,549**

Queen's Composer (Ire) *B Smart* 75 a75
2 b c Mozart (Ire) - Queen Leonor (Ire)
2^{7s} 2^{7hy} 2^{8sd} 2^{8ss} **0-4-4 £4,645**

Queen's Dancer *M R Channon* 69 a59
3 b f Groom Dancer (USA) - Special Beat
7^{12g} 8^{12gs} 1^{12gs} 6^{12gf} 1^{12gf} 3^{10f} 6^{12f} 10^{10gf} 5^{10gf} 3^{12g} 3^{10hy} 6^{14ss} **2-3-12 £8,234**

Queen's Echo *M Dods* 72
4 b f Wizard King - Sunday News'N'Echo (USA)
3^{6s} 2^{7g} 6^{7g} 2^{7s} 1^{8s} 6^{9s} 12^{7gf} 14^{8gf} 15^{8gf} **1-3-9 £6,685**

Queen's Lodge (Ire) *J S Wainwright* 91
5 ch m Grand Lodge (USA) - Manilia (Fr)
1^{6gf} 10^{6gf} 6^{6gs} 12^{8gf} 9^{6g} 12^{6g} 11^{6gf} 21^{7s} **1-0-8 £6,802**

Queen's Night (Ire) *M R Channon* 72
2 b f Night Shift (USA) - D D's Jakette (USA)
2^{5gf} 2^{6gf} 4^{5gf} 6^{7gf} 12^{6gf} 10^{7gf} 13^{5gs} **0-2-7 £9,815**

Queen's Pudding (Ire) *J R Fanshawe* 78
2 b f Royal Applause - Gooseberry Pie
1^{6g} **1-0-1 £4,524**

Queens Bounty *Robert Gray* 46 a4
2 b f Bahamian Bounty - Queen Shirley (Ire)
6^{5gs} 7^{5sd} 2^{5gf} 5^{6gf} **0-1-4 £724**

Queens Hand (Ire) *G A Swinbank* 59
3 b f Lend A Hand - Winchester Queen (Ire)
3^{9gs} 4^{8gs} 4^{9s} 1^{7f} **1-1-4 £3,962**

Queens Rhapsody *A Bailey* 78 a81
5 gr g Baryshnikov (Aus) - Digamist Girl (Ire)
10^{7sd} 4^{7gs} 11^{8gf} 10^{7gs} 12^{10g} 14^{8g} 4^{6hy} 6^{7sd} 9^{6sf} 3^{6sd} 3^{7sd} 5^{7sd} **0-3-12 £2,435**

Queenstown (Ire) *B A Pearce* 36 a66
4 b g Desert Style (Ire) - Fanciful (Ire)
8^{10sd} 1^{8sd} 7^{8sd} 12^{7s} 11^{8sd} 7^{7gf} 8^{7sd} 4^{8sd} 14^{6s} 7^{10sd} 15^{12sd} 8^{7sd} 10^{10sd} 8^{11sd} **1-0-14 £2,944**

Quel Fontenailles (Fr) *L A Dace* a66
7 b g Tel Quel (Fr) - Sissi Fontenailles (Fr)
12^{9sd} 4^{12sd} 1^{13sd} 9^{12sd} 5^{12sd} **1-0-5 £2,920**

Querida *J H M Gosden* 52
2 ch f Rainbow Quest (USA) - Qirmazi (USA)
8^{6gs} **0-0-1**

Querido (USA) *Saeed Bin Suroor* 89
3 b c Spectrum (Ire) - Polent
9^{8g} 5^{12gf} 4^{16gf} 11^{16g} 10^{12g} **0-0-5 £829**

Quest On Air *J R Jenkins* 39 a48
6 b g Star Quest - Stormy Heights

2^{14sd} 4^{12sd} 2^{12sd} 4^{11sd} 2^{12sd} 1^{12sd} 4^{11gs} 2^{12sd} 3^{12sd} 5^{11sd} 7^{12sd} **1-5-11 £3,357**

Question Mark *Andrew Reid* 47 a47
3 b g Polar Falcon (USA) - Frankie Fair (Ire)
16^{7g} 14^{7sd} 9^{6gf} 15^{5gf} 10^{6sd} 10^{6sd} 2^{6sd} 9^{5sd} **0-1-8 £422**

Questive *E A L Dunlop* a42
2 b c Rainbow Quest (USA) - Hawait Al Barr
7^{9sd} **0-0-1**

Queue Up *A G Newcombe* 63 a58
3 b g Royal Applause - Faraway Lass
6^{7g} 4^{7gf} 9^{6gf} 9^{7sd} 8^{9sd} 2^{7sd} 2^{7sd} 9^{7sf} 9^{7sd} **0-3-9 £1,141**

Quick *M C Pipe* 46
5 b g Kahyasi - Prompt
10^{18g} **0-0-1**

Quick Move *H R A Cecil* 42
3 b c Selkirk (USA) - Flit (USA)
10^{10g} **0-0-1**

Quickfire *Sir Michael Stoute* 102
3 b f Dubai Millennium - Daring Miss
2^{10s} 5^{8gf} 2^{7gs} 11^{6g} 5^{7g} 3^{8gf} **0-2-6 £27,236**

Quiet Embrace *B W Hills* a54
2 ch f Sunday Silence (USA) - Flying Kiss (Ire)
11^{7sd} **0-0-1**

Quiet Millfit (USA) *R Ingram* a27
9 b g Quiet American (USA) - Millfit (USA)
9^{13sd} **0-0-1**

Quiet Reading (USA) *M R Bosley* a65
8 b g Northern Flagship (USA) - Forlis Key (USA)
5^{8sd} 4^{7sd} 6^{7sd} 9^{9sd} 9^{8sd} 5^{8ss} 4^{8sd} 3^{8sd} 1^{8sd} **1-1-9 £3,424**

Quiet Royal (USA) *Mme C Head-Maarek* 108
2 b f Royal Academy (USA) - Wakigoer (USA)
4^{5g} 1^{7gs} 2^{7vs} 2^{8gs} 1^{7gs} **2-2-5 £93,588**

Quiet Times (Ire) *K A Ryan* a102
6 ch g Dolphin Street (Fr) - Super Times
RR^{5sd} 3^{6sd} 1^{6sd} 7^{5ft} 7^{6ft} 9^{6sd} 11^{7sd} 4^{6sd} 9^{5sf} 11^{6sd} 2^{6sd} **1-2-11 £16,900**

Quiff *Sir Michael Stoute* 102
4 b f Sadler's Wells (USA) - Wince
4^{10g} **0-0-1 £2,500**

Quincannon (USA) *W M Brisbourne* 54 a67
4 b g Kayrawan (USA) - Sulalat
3^{7sd} 4^{7sd} 1^{6sd} 4^{6sd} 7^{6sd} 6^{7sd} 7^{9sd} 5^{7sd} 11^{9sd} 7^{7g} 8^{7f} 5^{7sd} 6^{8gf} 6^{7gf} 2^{7sd} 2^{7sd} 6^{8gf} 2^{7sd} 2^{7gf} 8^{7sd} 2^{7sd} **1-6-21 £6,995**

Quince (Ire) *J Pearce* 83 a78
2 b c Fruits Of Love (USA) - Where's Charlotte
11^{7gf} 8^{7gf} 15^{6gf} 1^{7gf} 1^{7g} 1^{8gf} 9^{8s} 6^{8sd} 7^{8sd} **3-0-9 £16,202**

Quintillion *T J Etherington*
4 gr g Petong - Lady Quinta (Ire)
9^{7sd} 12^{6sd} **0-0-2**

Quintin *T D Easterby* 38
2 ch f Spinning World (USA) - Quadri
13^{8gf} **0-0-1**

Quito (Ire) *D W Chapman* 119 a93
8 b r Machiavellian (USA) - Qirmazi (USA)
9^{6sd} 8^{7sd} 5^{6g} 1^{6gf} 2^{7s} 1^{7s} 4^{6gf} 5^{7g} 9^{6f} 2^{6g} 2^{6gf} 9^{6gs} 8^{8s} 2^{7gf} 1^{6g} 3^{8g} 7^{7gf} 9^{6g} 8^{6gs} **3-5-19 £88,021**

Quizzene (USA) *M Johnston* 90
3 gr g Cozzene (USA) - Company Binness (USA)
2^{12g} 1^{10gs} 1^{12gs} 12^{12gf} 15^{12gs} 10^{15gs} **2-1-6 £20,912**

Quizzical Question (Ire) *L M Cumani* a68
3 ch f Bob Back (USA) - Quality Of Life
1^{10sd} **1-0-1 £3,571**

Quote Unquote *J Parkes* 71 a57
2 ch f Allied Forces (USA) - Quiz Time
2^{5gf} 3^{5sd} 2^{5f} 6^{5g} 4^{5sd} 2^{5sd} 3^{6sd} 6^{6sd} **0-5-8 £3,988**

Qusoor (Ire) *J L Dunlop* 89
2 b f Fasliyev (USA) - Winsa (USA)
5^{6gf} 3^{6gf} 1^{5gf} 1^{6g} 5^{5gf} 3^{5gf} 1^{5g} 8^{6s} **3-2-8 £21,166**

Qutang *W J Haggas* 65
2 ch g Dr Fong (USA) - Ravine
10^{6gs} 4^{6gf} 3^{6gf} 13^{5gf} 5^{7gs} **0-1-5 £966**

Rabbit *Mrs A L M King* a38
4 b f Muhtarram (USA) - Ninia (USA)
11^{7sd} **0-0-1**

Rabitatit (Ire) *J G M O'Shea* 49
4 b f Robellino (USA) - Coupled
8^{8g} 6^{8f} 7^{10g} 4^{8gf} 9^{8gf} **0-0-5 £266**

Raccoon (Ire) *T D Barron* 75
5 b g Raphane (USA) - Kunucu (Ire)
16^{5g} 13^{5g} 7^{5gf} 7^{5g} 13^{5g} 2^{6gf} 2^{6gf} 5^{5g} **0-2-8 £2,296**

Race For The Stars (USA) *A P O'Brien* 101
2 b f Fusaichi Pegasus (USA) - La Lorgnette (Can)
2^{6g} 9^{7g} 1^{7g} 1^{7gs} **2-1-4 £35,232**

Race The Ace *J L Dunlop* 93
4 b g First Trump - Princess Genista
4^{18g} 7^{16gf} 2^{16gs} **0-1-3 £3,874**

Race To The Music (USA) *D R Loder* 87
2 ch c Stravinsky (USA) - Chasethewildwind (USA)
1^{5gf} 1^{6gf} **2-0-2 £9,464**

Racer Forever (USA) *J H M Gosden* 100
2 b c Rahy (USA) - Ras Shaikh (USA)
6^{6s} 2^{6gs} 1^{6gf} 5^{6gf} 5^{5g} **1-1-5 £10,108**

Rack And Ruin (Ire) *R Hannon* 58
2 b f King's Best (USA) - Your Village (Ire)
5^{5s} 5^{5gs} 8^{6gs} 4^{5g} **0-0-4 £259**

Radiant Bride *P A Blockley* 8 a30
5 ch m Groom Dancer (USA) - Radiancy (Ire)
5^{16sd} 12^{10f} **0-0-2**

Radiator Rooney (Ire) *Patrick Morris* 65 a61
2 br g Elnadim (USA) - Queen Of The May (Ire)
11^{7gf} 6^{7g} 4^{6f} 2^{6g} 7^{7f} 8^{5g} 3^{5sd} **0-2-7 £2,513**

Radical Attraction (USA) *R Hannon* a39
2 b/br f Silver Hawk (USA) - Running Flame (Ind)
10^{10sd} **0-0-1**

Radius *H Morrison* 65 a74
2 b g Lujain (USA) - Georgianna (Ire)
7^{6gs} 4^{7g} 2^{6sd} **0-1-3 £1,508**

Radlett Lady *D K Ivory* 51 a52
4 ch f Wolfhound (USA) - Royal Dream
8^{6sd} 1^{5sd} 5^{5sd} 1^{6sd} 6^{6sd} 9^{6sd} 4^{6s} 2^{6gs} 8^{7sf} 3^{6sd} 5^{5sd} 6^{6sd} 4^{6sd} **2-2-13 £4,053**

Radmore Spirit *P D Evans* 43 a36
5 b m Whittingham (Ire) - Ruda (Fr)
6^{7sd} 7^{9sd} 12^{8sd} 8^{7sd} 3^{8g} 11^{10s} **0-1-6 £213**

Raetihi *P S Felgate* a13
4 b f Wizard King - Foreno
10^{6ss} 9^{5sd} 6^{5sd} **0-0-3**

Rafelite *Lady Herries* 64 a56
3 b f Fraam - Megan's Flight
5^{10gs} 8^{10gf} 11^{9sd} 6^{12gs} 13^{12gf} 14^{12sd}
0-0-6

Rafferty (Ire) *T D Barron* 83 a97
6 ch g Lion Cavern (USA) - Badawi (USA)
2^{8sd} 3^{7sd} 6^{7sd} 5^{8sd} 7^{10sd} 5^{8sd} 3^{7gs} 3^{7g} 6^{7gf}
1^{7ft} 16^{6hy} 5^{7s} 9^{7sd} **1-4-13 £13,854**

Raffish *M Scudamore* 68 a64
3 ch g Atraf - Valadon
10^{10g} 8^{12g} 15^{12gs} 10^{12gf} 6^{14f} 8^{14g} 6^{12sd} 1^{10gf}
9^{10gf} **1-0-9 £2,961**

Rafters Music (Ire) *Julian Poulton* 45 a66
10 b g Thatching - Princess Dixieland (USA)
5^{6sd} 3^{7sd} 5^{7sd} 3^{6sd} 11^{6sd} 8^{6sd} 6^{6f} 12^{6hy} 9^{7sf}
0-2-9 £737

Rag Tag (Ire) *A M Balding* 87
2 b g Tagula (Ire) - Lovat Spring (USA)
5^{5gf} 3^{5gf} 1^{5gf} 2^{5f} 14^{5gs} 5^{5gf} **1-0-6**
£5,814

Ragasah *E R Oertel* 41 a51
7 b m Glory Of Dancer - Slight Risk
1^{7sd} 8^{10sd} 7^{7sd} 5^{9sd} 2^{8sd} 8^{10sd} 7^{8sd} 5^{8sd} 2^{7sd}
7^{7g} 12^{7sd} 6^{8gf} 4^{10g} 1^{7sd} 4^{7sd} 3^{8ss} 4^{7sd} 1^{7sd}
3-3-18 £5,569

Raheed (Ire) *Mrs C A Dunnett* 37 a56
4 b g Daggers Drawn (USA) - In Due Course (USA)
7^{7sd} 9^{7sd} 10^{7g} 7^{6sd} 9^{8g} **0-0-5**

Raheel (Ire) *Evan Williams* a61
5 ch g Barathea (Ire) - Tajawuz
12^{12sd} 6^{12sd} 3^{10sd} 8^{10sd} 3^{9sd} 10^{10sd} 16^{12sd}
7^{12gf} **0-2-8 £743**

Rahjel Sultan *E S McMahon* 53 a36
7 b g Puissance - Dalby Dancer
8^{8gs} 6^{8g} 6^{8sd} **0-0-3**

Rahy's Crown (USA) *R Hannon* 59
2 b c Rahy (USA) - Inca Princess (USA)
11^{7gs} 9^{7g} 12^{8gs} **0-0-3**

Rain Holly (Ire) *R A Harris* 59 a20
3 b f Indian Rocket - Holly Bird
6^{7g} 8^{6f} 7^{8f} 3^{7gf} 6^{7gf} 10^{7sf} 15^{12sd} **0-1-7**
£604

Rain Stops Play (Ire) *M R Channon* 84
3 b g Desert Prince (Ire) - Pinta (Ire)
2^{9g} 8^{8hy} 5^{8gf} 4^{7gs} 4^{7gf} 12^{7g} 8^{7gf} 6^{8g} 1^{7g}
17^{7gf} 11^{8g} 6^{7hy} **1-1-12 £10,330**

Rainbow Bay *R A Fahey* 71
2 b c Komaite (USA) - Bollin Victoria
2^{6g} 4^{5gf} 2^{5g} 4^{6gf} **0-2-4 £3,446**

Rainbow Iris *B Smart* 63 a37
3 b/br f Mister Baileys - Kastaway
5^{5gs} 4^{6gs} 8^{6gf} 6^{7f} 4^{7g} 6^{6sd} 10^{6gf} 13^{5gf} 11^{5sd}
10^{6sd} **0-0-10 £876**

Rainbow Rising (Ire) *J Howard Johnson* 93
3 b/br g Desert King (Ire) - Fantastic Bid (USA)
1^{6g} 3^{6gs} 7^{6g} 6^{6g} 13^{5gs} 7^{5hy} **1-1-6**
£7,256

Rainbow River (Ire) *M C Chapman* a37
7 ch g Rainbows For Life (Can) - Shrewd Girl (USA)
11^{11sd} 12^{8sd} 10^{7sd} **0-0-3**

Rainbow Sky *B W Hills* 76 a23
3 b f Rainbow Quest (USA) - Safayn (USA)
7^{10gf} 6^{11gs} 3^{10gf} 1^{11gf} 5^{10gf} 7^{10gs} 14^{12sd}
1-1-7 £5,070

Rainbow Treasure (Ire) *J S Goldie* 32
3 ch f Rainbow Quest (USA) - Gaily Royal (Ire)
7^{8s} 10^{8g} 17^{8s} **0-0-3**

Rainbow's Classic *K A Ryan* 70
2 b c Muhtarram (USA) - Legend Of Aragon
3^{7gf} 3^{7s} 6^{8gf} 7^{8g} **0-2-4 £1,014**

Rainbows Guest (Ire) *A M Balding* 58 a73
2 ch f Indian Lodge (Ire) - Maura's Guest (Ire)
15^{7g} 9^{7s} 2^{7sd} 11^{7s} 1^{7sd} **1-1-5 £4,023**

Rainstorm *T Wall* 29 a36
10 b g Rainbow Quest (USA) - Katsina (USA)
9^{9sd} 8^{10gf} 10^{10f} 12^{10f} **0-0-4**

Raise The Heights (Ire) *C Tinkler* a57
2 b c Orpen (USA) - Blue Heights (Ire)
8^{7sd} 6^{8sd} **0-0-2**

Rajaall *M R Channon* 76 a70
2 b c Royal Applause - Gorgeous Dancer (Ire)
5^{7gf} 7^{9gf} 5^{8s} 5^{10sd} **0-0-4**

Rajam *G A Harker* 47
7 b g Sadler's Wells (USA) - Rafif (USA)
6^{14gf} **0-0-1**

Rajayoga *M H Tompkins* 54 a37
4 ch g Kris - Optimistic
4^{11sd} 7^{14sd} 4^{16gs} **0-0-3 £263**

Rajeem *C E Brittain* 92
2 b f Diktat - Magic Sister
10^{6gf} 8^{8s} 4^{7gf} 1^{8g} 1^{8s} **2-0-5 £18,630**

Rajwa (USA) *Saeed Bin Suroor* 82
3 ch c Dubai Millennium - Zelanda (Ire)
10^{7g} **0-0-1**

Rakata (USA) *P F I Cole* 72 a75
3 b f Quiet American (USA) - Haleakala (Ire)
5^{8gf} 8^{8g} 3^{8s} 2^{9gf} 3^{9sd} 1^{7g} 4^{7hy} **1-4-7**
£8,599

Rakti *M A Jarvis* 129
6 b h Polish Precedent (USA) - Ragera (Ire)
1^{8f} 2^{8gf} 4^{8g} 6^{10gs} 11^{8gf} **1-1-5**
£212,211

Rambling Socks *S R Bowring* 48 a58
2 ch f Rambling Bear - Cledeschamps
12^{6gs} 5^{7s} 6^{6g} 15^{6g} 7^{7sd} 6^{9sd} 2^{6sd} **0-1-7**
£420

Rambo Blue *G J Smith*
5 b g Elmaamul (USA) - Copper Trader
12^{9ss} **0-0-1**

Rampage *W J Haggas* 75 a83
4 ch f Pivotal - Noor El Houdah (Ire)
2^{6g} 1^{6sd} 1^{7sd} **2-1-3 £8,834**

Rampallion *Unknown* 87
2 b c Daylami (Ire) - Minute Waltz
1^{8gs} **1-0-1 £7,176**

Ramsgill (USA) *N P Littmoden* 69 a69
3 b g Prized (USA) - Crazee Mental
9^{7g} 4^{7f} 5^{8gf} 6^{8gf} 1^{10sd} 4^{11g} 2^{10g} 1^{10sd} 4^{9sd}
7^{10sd} **2-2-10 £10,272**

Rancho Cucamonga (Ire) *T D Barron* 80 a85
3 ch f Raphane (USA) - Kunucu (Ire)
2^{6sd} 3^{6sd} 2^{7sd} 1^{6sd} 8^{6s} 13^{6gs} 4^{6gf} 4^{6g} 1^{6sd}
5^{6g} 3^{6gf} 1^{6g} 9^{6gs} 9^{6gs} 19^{5g} 14^{6s} **3-4-16**
£18,258

Randalls Touch *C Smith* 48 a6
3 b g Mind Games - L A Touch
10^{7sd} 6^{5s} 7^{5s} 11^{5f} 11^{5g} **0-0-5**

Random Call (USA) *Sir Michael Stoute* 69
2 b f War Chant (USA) - Lignify (Arg)
1^{7hy} **1-0-1 £4,329**

Random Quest *B J Llewellyn* 79

7 b g Rainbow Quest (USA) - Anne Bonny
11^{14gs} 8^{16gs} 14^{16g} 9^{21s} 7^{16gf} **0-0-5**

Rani Two *W M Brisbourne* 73
6 b m Wolfhound (USA) - Donya
5^{10gf} 10^{11g} 2^{10gf} 9^{10g} 8^{12gs} **0-1-5 £2,135**

Ransacker *C E Brittain* 56
3 b g Bahamian Bounty - Hazy Heights
12^{7g} 10^{10g} **0-0-2**

Raphoola (Ire) *Andre Hermans* a41
4 b f Raphane (USA) - Acicula (Ire)
6^{5sd} 12^{6sd} **0-0-2**

Rapich *J L Spearing* 29
2 b f Josr Algarhoud (Ire) - Vax Rapide
12^{6gf} 17^{7g} **0-0-2**

Rapid Flow *W M Brisbourne* a24
3 b g Fasliyev (USA) - Fleet River (USA)
8^{7sd} **0-0-1**

Rapid River *P D Evans* 72 a62
3 b f Lahib (USA) - Cast A Spell
3^{6sd} 3^{5g} 2^{5gs} 13^{5s} 1^{5sd} 8^{6sd} 14^{5sd} **1-3-7 £3,421**

Rapsgate (Ire) *R Hannon* 79 a69
2 b f Mozart (Ire) - Lady Rushmore (Ire)
3^{5g} 3^{5gf} 2^{5g} 8^{5gf} 8^{6g} 3^{5gf} 28^{6g} 6^{5g} 2^{6sd} 12^{6sd} 1^{5sd} **1-5-11 £9,491**

Rare Breed *Mrs L Stubbs* 75
2 b g Foxhound (USA) - Rare Indigo
3^{5g} 1^{5gs} **1-1-2 £4,180**

Rare Coincidence *R F Fisher* 63 a67
4 ch g Atraf - Green Seed (Ire)
9^{8sd} 6^{9sd} 2^{9sd} 6^{11gs} 1^{9sd} 7^{9sd} 4^{8gs} 5^{8s} 5^{8gf} 8^{8s} 5^{9s} 7^{9sd} 11^{9gs} 1^{12sd} 3^{11gf} 1^{12f} 9^{12g} 2^{12gf} 2^{12gf} 5^{14gf} 7^{12gf} 9^{15s} 8^{12sd} 8^{12sd} **3-4-24 £12,826**

Rare Cross (Ire) *J R Fanshawe* 90
3 b f Cape Cross (Ire) - Hebrides
3^{5gf} 8^{5gf} **0-1-2 £2,348**

Rarefied (Ire) *T D Easterby* 65
4 b g Danehill (USA) - Tenuous
11^{11g} 8^{8gf} 6^{10g} 7^{12g} 4^{10g} 8^{12g} 15^{10g} **0-0-7 £444**

Rashida *M Appleby* 67 a73
3 b f King's Best (USA) - Nimble Lady (Aus)
5^{7gf} 1^{9sd} 9^{10g} 8^{8gf} 16^{8s} **1-0-5 £4,128**

Rasid (USA) *C A Dwyer* 63 a69
7 b g Bahri (USA) - Makadir (USA)
3^{12sd} 8^{12sd} 5^{9sd} 4^{9sd} 4^{12sd} 10^{12s} 3^{12sd} 11^{14g} 5^{11gf} 3^{10sd} 10^{12sd} 11^{10g} 8^{10gf} 13^{10gf} 9^{10g} 12^{10sd} 12^{10sd} 6^{10sd} **0-3-18 £1,762**

Raslan *M Johnston* 41
2 b c Lomitas - Rosia (Ire)
18^{8gs} **0-0-1**

Rasseem (Ire) *Simon Earle* 37 a49
3 b f Fasliyev (USA) - Yorba Linda (Ire)
5^{7sd} 9^{6sd} 1^{6sd} 5^{5sd} 10^{6gf} 12^{6f} 12^{6sd} **1-0-7 £2,583**

Rathmullan *E A Wheeler* 44 a59
6 ch g Bluegrass Prince (Ire) - National Time (USA)
6^{6sd} 6^{7sd} 1^{7g} 6^{9sd} 8^{8g} 13^{7gs} 15^{7gf} 10^{8gf} 15^{8g} 7^{8hd} **1-0-10 £1,305**

Rathor (Ire) *H R A Cecil* 105
3 b/br c Machiavellian (USA) - Raisonnable
2^{10gs} 2^{9gf} 2^{10gf} 1^{10gf} 1^{8gf} 6^{8gf} 5^{8g} **2-3-7 £16,353**

Rathuil (Ire) *Garvan Donnelly* 33 a40
5 b g Barathea (Ire) - Landlady (Fr)
12^{8gf} 10^{10sd} **0-0-2**

Raucous (Ger) *T P Tate* 74
2 b g Zinaad - Roseola (Ger)
4^{8gs} 4^{10g} **0-0-2 £859**

Raul Sahara *P A Blockley* 55 a55
3 b g Makbul - Sheraton Heights
5^{6sd} 6^{9sd} 4^{6sd} 6^{7gf} 7^{7gs} 2^{8gf} 9^{10hd} 4^{9sd} 8^{9sd} 9^{8sd} **0-1-10 £978**

Rave Reviews (Ire) *J L Dunlop* 110
4 b f Sadler's Wells (USA) - Pieds De Plume (Fr)
4^{12s} 5^{12g} 4^{14s} 11^{12g} 2^{10hy} **0-1-5 £54,312**

Ravel (Ire) *M R Bosley* 35 a54
4 b g Fasliyev (USA) - Lili Cup (Fr)
6^{6sd} 3^{5sd} 7^{6sd} 4^{6sd} 4^{7sd} 8^{7sd} 8^{6f} 18^{6f} 4^{7sd} 9^{7sd} 8^{6sd} **0-1-11 £879**

Raven (Ire) *M E Sowersby* 18
3 b f Alzao (USA) - Eman's Joy
9^{7gs} 11^{7gf} 19^{6g} **0-0-3**

Ravenglass (USA) *J G M O'Shea*
6 b h Miswaki (USA) - Urus (USA)
10^{15s} **0-0-1**

Ravish *W J Haggas* 57
2 b f Efisio - Looks Sensational (USA)
4^{7gf} 13^{7gf} **0-0-2 £378**

Rawaabet (Ire) *P W Hiatt* 75 a76
3 b g Bahhare (USA) - Haddeyah (USA)
8^{7sd} 1^{8sd} 6^{9sd} 6^{10sd} 9^{9g} 5^{8g} 2^{8gs} 12^{8gf} 2^{8gf} 8^{8gf} 12^{8g} 13^{8g} **1-2-12 £5,609**

Rawdon (Ire) *M L W Bell* 93 a76
4 b g Singspiel (Ire) - Rebecca Sharp
2^{9sd} 2^{11g} 1^{11gf} 1^{10g} 7^{10gf} 3^{12gs} 5^{10gf} 1^{11gs} 18^{12hy} **3-3-9 £24,847**

Raybers Magic *J R Weymes* a12
4 b f Magic Ring (Ire) - Kirkadian
6^{8sd} **0-0-1**

Raydiation (USA) *B J Meehan* 72 a64
2 br c Dynaformer (USA) - Gemini (Arg)
5^{8gf} 6^{10sd} **0-0-2**

Rayhani (USA) *M P Tregoning* 80
2 b c Theatrical - Bahr Alsalaam (USA)
5^{8gf} 1^{9gf} 10^{8s} **1-0-3 £4,849**

Raymond's Pride *K A Ryan* 89 a73
5 b g Mind Games - Northern Sal
2^{6sd} 3^{7sd} 11^{7sd} 7^{7sd} 12^{6sd} 1^{6s} 9^{6g} 12^{7gf} 27^{6g} 4^{5gs} 1^{6hy} **2-3-11 £15,130**

Raza Cab (Ire) *Miss K M George* 68 a67
3 b g Intikhab (USA) - Laraissa
10^{7gf} 1^{8gf} 11^{7gf} 10^{8gf} 11^{7sd} 5^{9sd} **1-0-6 £4,095**

Raze *Sir Michael Stoute* 74
3 ch f Halling (USA) - Rive (USA)
1^{10gf} 6^{11gf} 6^{12g} **1-0-3 £4,576**

Razed *Unknown* 66
2 b g King's Best (USA) - Key Academy
9^{7gf} 1^{8gf} 19^{7s} **1-0-3 £4,104**

Razkalla (USA) *Saeed Bin Suroor* 118
7 b g Caerleon (USA) - Larrocha (Ire)
2^{12gf} 1^{12gf} 2^{12gf} 3^{11g} 14^{20gf} 4^{12g} 16^{12g} **1-2-7 £294,915**

Reaching Out (Ire) *N J Henderson* 82 a64
3 b g Desert Prince (Ire) - Alwiyda (USA)
6^{7sd} 2^{8gs} 1^{10gf} 2^{10g} 2^{11gf} 6^{8g} 6^{12gf} 2^{10gs} 7^{10g} 9^{10g} **1-4-10 £8,958**

Read Federica *Sir Michael Stoute* 90
3 ch f Fusaichi Pegasus (USA) - Reading Habit (USA)
11^{7gf} 4^{8gs} **0-0-2 £778**

Ready Teddy Go *J Ryan* 16 a42
3 b g Danzig Connection (USA) - Mariette
9^{6g} 10^{10sd} 14^{8hd} 6^{9sd} **0-0-4**

Real Bond *B Smart* 60 a36
3 b g Mind Games - Bond Girl
8^{6sd} 3^{6s} 8^{6g} 5^{5g} 3^{6gs} 6^{6gf} **0-2-6 £1,007**

Real Cool Cat (USA) *M Johnston* 75
3 gr f Storm Cat (USA) - Hail Kris (USA)
8^{7gf} 1^{10gf} 1^{10gf} 2^{12g} 3^{10g} 2^{10g} 2^{10gf} **2-4-7 £15,917**

Real Quality (USA) *I Semple* 104
3 b g Elusive Quality (USA) - Pleasant Prize (USA)
1^{8gs} 14^{8g} 6^{8gf} 6^{10g} 2^{10g} **1-1-5 £16,730**

Realism (Fr) *R A Fahey* 104
5 b g Machiavellian (USA) - Kissing Cousin (Ire)
5^{10gf} 2^{10g} 5^{10gf} 3^{10g} 13^{10gs} 1^{10g} 25^{9s} 1^{10g} **2-2-8 £61,722**

Reality Time (Ire) *J A Osborne* 60 a57
2 b f Daggers Drawn (USA) - Vitality
7^{6g} 6^{6g} 4^{6sd} 8^{6g} **0-0-4**

Really Given (Ire) *M P Tregoning* 63
2 b f Alhaarth (Ire) - Really Gifted (Ire)
13^{6gf} 7^{7gf} 5^{6gs} 13^{7gs} **0-0-4**

Reap *J Pearce* 64 a62
7 b g Emperor Jones (USA) - Corn Futures
4^{9sd} 4^{9sd} 3^{8s} **0-1-3 £1,161**

Reason (Ire) *D W Chapman* 57 a27
7 b g Sadler's Wells (USA) - Marseillaise
7^{11g} 11^{12sd} 7^{12sd} **0-0-3**

Rebel Leader *W R Muir* 75
8 br g Ezzoud (Ire) - Haitienne (Fr)
11^{8gs} **0-0-1**

Rebel Raider (Ire) *B N Pollock* a57
6 b g Mujadil (USA) - Emily's Pride
4^{9sd} 7^{9sd} 9^{8sd} **0-0-3**

Rebel Rebel (Ire) *R J Frankel* 115
3 b c Revoque (Ire) - French Quarter
1^{8gs} 4^{9gf} 2^{8gf} 4^{8g} 3^{10y} **1-1-5 £140,370**

Rebelling (Ire) *R F Johnson Houghton* 64
2 ch c Peintre Celebre (USA) - El Divino (Ire)
12^{7gs} 6^{8g} 6^{8gs} **0-0-3**

Rebellion *Saeed Bin Suroor* 75
2 b c Mozart (Ire) - Last Resort
3^{8gf} 3^{7s} 3^{8hy} **0-3-3 £1,717**

Rebellious Spirit *J G Given* 62 a71
2 b g Mark Of Esteem (Ire) - Robellino Miss (USA)
6^{8gf} 2^{7sd} 2^{6sd} **0-2-3 £2,102**

Rebuttal (USA) *B J Meehan* 101
3 b c Mr Greeley (USA) - Reboot (USA)
5^{8g} **0-0-1 £750**

Recalcitrant *S Dow* 59
2 b c Josr Algarhoud (Ire) - Lady Isabell
9^{7gf} 6^{8g} 14^{8gs} **0-0-3**

Rectangle (Ire) *M D Hammond* 65
5 ch g Fayruz - Moona (USA)
7^{5g} 10^{5f} 2^{5gf} 8^{6f} 4^{5gf} 10^{6g} **0-1-6 £1,682**

Rectangle Blue *M D Hammond* a4
3 b g Atraf - Golden Decoy
8^{11sd} **0-0-1**

Red Acer (Ire) *Mrs N S Sharpe*
4 ch g Shinko Forest (Ire) - Another Baileys
9^{12sd} **0-0-1**

Red Admiral (USA) *Saeed Bin Suroor* 98
3 b g Red Ransom (USA) - Ausherra (USA)
6^{10gf} 12^{12gs} 5^{14gf} 1^{12gs} **1-0-4 £7,264**

Red Affleck (USA) *G G Margarson* 75 a61
3 b g Nicholas (USA) - Lucie Mon Amour (USA)
10^{7gf} 6^{7g} 11^{7gf} 7^{7g} 9^{8sd} 9^{7sd} 2^{7gs} 10^{7gs} 5^{7gs} **0-1-9 £1,099**

Red Apache (Ire) *H J Collingridge* 8
3 b g Namid - Special Dissident
6^{6gf} **0-0-1**

Red Ash (USA) *B W Hills* 91
2 ch c Woodman (USA) - Bermuda Girl (USA)
8^{6gf} 1^{7gf} **1-0-2 £5,733**

Red Birr (Ire) *P R Webber* 64 a69
4 b g Bahhare (USA) - Cappella (Ire)
15^{10gs} 7^{10s} 7^{8gs} 9^{10gs} 6^{10gs} 9^{10gf} 9^{10hy} 1^{10sd} **1-0-8 £2,886**

Red Bloom *Sir Michael Stoute* 115
4 b f Selkirk (USA) - Red Camellia
5^{9gf} 1^{8gf} 2^{10gf} 3^{10gs} 2^{10s} 1^{10gf} 6^{10gs} **2-3-7 £153,585**

Red Bluff (Ire) *H Alexander* 25
5 b g Waky Nao - Reine Rouge (Ger)
19^{10g} 10^{12gs} **0-0-2**

Red Bullet *A G Newcombe*
3 ch c Hatim (USA) - Enchanted Goddess
9^{10gf} **0-0-1**

Red Cape (Fr) *N A Callaghan* a81
2 b c Cape Cross (Ire) - Muirfield (Fr)
6^{6sd} 1^{7sd} 2^{8sd} **1-1-3 £5,124**

Red Chairman *R Johnson* 68 a82
3 br g Red Ransom (USA) - Chine
2^{10sd} 2^{9sd} 3^{9sd} 3^{12sd} 11^{9sd} 3^{7g} 12^{10s} 11^{7g} **0-5-8 £5,024**

Red Clubs (Ire) *B W Hills* 116
2 br c Red Ransom (USA) - Two Clubs
6^{5gf} 1^{5g} 1^{6gf} 1^{6gf} 7^{6gs} 3^{6g} 2^{6g} 2^{6gs} 4^{7gs} **3-2-9 £148,229**

Red Contact (USA) *Julian Poulton* 76 a91
4 b g Sahm (USA) - Basma (USA)
10^{9sd} 2^{7sd} 2^{8sd} 10^{8sd} 13^{7s} 8^{8gf} 4^{8gf} 21^{8gs} 7^{7gf} 17^{9gf} **0-2-10 £6,772**

Red Damson (Ire) *Sir Mark Prescott* 98
4 b g Croco Rouge (Ire) - Damascene (Ire)
6^{14gs} 2^{16g} 1^{14gf} 1^{17ys} **2-1-4 £18,000**

Red Delirium *R Brotherton* a48
9 b g Robellino (USA) - Made Of Pearl (USA)
6^{8sd} 9^{8sd} 6^{11sd} 11^{12sd} 6^{11sd} 6^{12sd} 9^{12sd} **0-0-7**

Red Diadem *W J Haggas* a70
2 b f Pivotal - Red Tiara (USA)
4^{7sd} **0-0-1 £303**

Red Duster (USA) *M L W Bell* 75
2 b/br c Red Ransom (USA) - Logiciel
9^{6gs} 3^{9g} **0-1-2 £748**

Red Emerald *P D Evans* 52 a42
2 b f Makbul - Partenza (USA)
3^{5s} 1^{5s} 6^{5s} 7^{5sd} 8^{6gf} 2^{6f} 5^{6gf} 8^{7sd} 11^{7g} **1-1-9 £4,359**

Red Evie (Ire) *M L W Bell* 52
2 b f Intikhab (USA) - Malafemmena (Ire)
9^{8g} **0-0-1**

Red Finesse *M A Jarvis* 62

3 b f Soviet Star (USA) - Jouet
7^{6g} 3^{6g} **0-1-2 £571**

Red Forest (Ire) *J Mackie* 74 a61
6 b g Charnwood Forest (Ire) - High Atlas
13^{14gf} 3^{14gs} 8^{12g} 9^{14gf} 2^{16g} 5^{16g} 9^{14gf} 7^{14gf} 2^{14gf} 7^{17sd} 7^{14ss} 6^{14sd} **0-3-12 £3,012**

Red Heaven *D R Loder* a56
3 b f Benny The Dip (USA) - Heavenly Ray (USA)
4^{8sd} **0-0-1**

Red Hot Ruby *P T Midgley* a33
4 ch f Komaite (USA) - Gleam Of Gold
10^{5sd} 9^{6sd} 11^{5sd} **0-0-3**

Red Hussar *R J Price* 24 a50
3 ch g Muhtarram (USA) - Miss Bussell
8^{8sd} 10^{10gf} 12^{8g} 8^{9sd} 10^{8gs} 14^{11g} 12^{9sd} **0-0-7**

Red Iris (Ire) *P C Haslam* 21
2 ch f Soviet Star (USA) - Last Rolo
9^{5gf} 15^{6gf} 8^{7gf} **0-0-3**

Red Lancer *R A Fahey* 105 a101
4 ch g Deploy - Miss Bussell
8^{10sd} 7^{12sd} 7^{9sd} 3^{10g} 7^{12s} 7^{10g} 5^{13gs} 2^{11g} 6^{10g} 10^{10gf} 2^{12gf} 8^{10g} 4^{10g} 6^{11gf} 7^{13gf} 7^{12g} 8^{12gs} 8^{12hy} **0-2-18 £34,940**

Red Lantern *M J Attwater* 45 a42
4 ch g Young Ern - Croft Sally
9^{6sd} 12^{5sd} 16^{6gs} 10^{5gf} 9^{7gf} 6^{10g} 4^{8gf} 11^{9sd} 6^{8g} 8^{12sd} 10^{10g} 4^{9sd} 9^{7ss} 9^{9sd} **0-0-14 £275**

Red Light Runner *K A Ryan* 13
3 gr g Mind Games - Sweet Whisper
12^{6sd} 10^{7gf} **0-0-2**

Red Monarch (Ire) *P A Blockley* 51 a65
4 ch g Woodborough (USA) - Sans Ceriph (Ire)
8^{6sd} 8^{5sd} 11^{6s} 2^{6sd} 7^{6s} 10^{6sd} 9^{7g} **0-1-7 £1,040**

Red Mountain *D W Barker* 11 a38
4 b g Unfuwain (USA) - Red Cascade (Ire)
5^{17sd} 4^{14sd} 6^{14sd} 10^{16f} 10^{12gf} **0-0-5**

Red Opera *Sir Mark Prescott* 74
3 ch g Nashwan (USA) - La Papagena
1^{14gf} 4^{14g} 9^{16gf} **1-0-3 £3,806**

Red Peony *Sir Mark Prescott* 105
3 b f Montjeu (Ire) - Red Azalea
6^{8gf} 6^{12gf} 6^{10gf} 2^{10g} 1^{12gf} 2^{12g} 8^{14hy} **1-2-7 £27,138**

Red Pride (Ire) *R Hannon* 55
2 b c Fasliyev (USA) - True Love
15^{6gf} 9^{6g} 5^{5g} 17^{7gs} 13^{6gs} **0-0-5**

Red Racketeer (USA) *E A L Dunlop* 99
3 b c Red Ransom (USA) - Furajet (USA)
1^{10g} 4^{10s} 1^{10g} 2^{12gs} 3^{10g} 1^{10g} 6^{10s} **3-1-7 £28,682**

Red Rackham (Ire) *J Nicol* 28 a46
5 b g Groom Dancer (USA) - Manarah
10^{13sd} 9^{10sd} 12^{12gf} **0-0-3**

Red River Rebel *J R Norton* 59 a51
7 b g Inchinor - Bidweaya (USA)
8^{12sd} 10^{12sd} 5^{14sd} 6^{12g} 1^{12g} 3^{12g} 1^{12g} 5^{12g} 7^{12f} 11^{14g} **2-0-10 £8,327**

Red River Rock (Ire) *T J Fitzgerald* 55
3 b g Spectrum (Ire) - Ann's Annie (Ire)
12^{7g} 13^{8g} 12^{8gf} 4^{10g} **0-0-4 £384**

Red Rocks (Ire) *B J Meehan* 87
2 b c Galileo (Ire) - Pharmacist (Ire)
9^{8gf} 3^{8g} 2^{8gs} **0-2-3 £3,652**

Red Rocky *R Hollinshead* 45
4 b f Danzero (Aus) - Post Mistress (Ire)
11^{7sd} 10^{7g} 10^{11g} **0-0-3**

Red Romeo *G A Swinbank* 89 a91
4 ch g Case Law - Enchanting Eve
21^{6gf} 10^{7gf} 8^{6gf} 5^{8gf} 8^{8g} 7^{7g} 1^{7gf} 16^{7gf} 2^{8sd} 10^{7sd} **1-1-10 £8,157**

Red Rudy *R M Beckett* 69 a62
3 ch g Pivotal - Piroshka
8^{8gf} 6^{9sd} 2^{8g} 4^{8gf} 7^{8g} 4^{9gf} 7^{8gf} 5^{8g} **0-2-8 £3,149**

Red Sail *Dr J D Scargill* 70 a60
4 ch f Dr Fong (USA) - Manhattan Sunset (USA)
5^{10gf} 5^{11f} 6^{12gf} 4^{15gf} 8^{12g} 3^{12sd} 4^{12sd} 9^{12gs} 4^{12sd} **0-1-9 £905**

Red Sam (Ire) *M L W Bell* 31 a46
3 ch g Desert King (Ire) - Mustique Dream
9^{8sd} 7^{10gf} 5^{10gs} **0-0-3**

Red Sans *P Mitchell* a62
3 b c Rainbow Quest (USA) - Sarah Georgina
4^{10sd} 4^{10sd} **0-0-2 £623**

Red Scorpion (USA) *W M Brisbourne* 68
6 ch g Nureyev (USA) - Pricket (USA)
3^{15gf} PU^{15gf} **0-1-2 £638**

Red September *D L Williams*
8 b g Presidium - Tangalooma
13^{10f} **0-0-1**

Red Skelton (Ire) *Ms Deborah J Evans* a63
4 ch g Croco Rouge (Ire) - Newala
3^{9sd} 12^{12sd} 11^{9sd} 9^{9sd} 10^{9gf} 15^{11g} **0-1-6 £519**

Red Sovereign *D G Bridgwater* 80 a69
4 b f Danzig Connection (USA) - Ruby Princess (Ire)
7^{6sd} 2^{5sd} 3^{5sd} 5^{6sd} 15^{5gf} 7^{6gf} 1^{5f} 9^{5gf} 3^{5gf} 8^{5f} 6^{5gf} 11^{6gf} 1^{6gs} 5^{6g} 17^{6gf} 10^{5gs} 3^{5sd} 6^{5sd} 7^{6sd} **2-3-19 £12,606**

Red Spell (Ire) *R Hannon* 95 a108
4 ch g Soviet Star (USA) - A-To-Z (Ire)
21^{8g} 3^{8g} 7^{9g} 1^{8g} 7^{7gf} 5^{8gf} 12^{8g} 3^{9gf} 6^{10sd} 13^{8gs} 2^{7sd} 1^{7sd} 1^{8sd} 6^{7sd} **3-3-14 £41,985**

Red Sun *J Mackie* 68 a48
8 b g Foxhound (USA) - Superetta
9^{16sd} 8^{14gs} 1^{16gs} 5^{16g} 8^{16f} 4^{16gf} 2^{16gf} 5^{16g} 13^{12g} 8^{14gf} **1-1-10 £5,051**

Red Tsarina *V Smith* 13
2 b f Russian Red - Tudor Bay Lady
16^{7gf} 14^{7g} **0-0-2**

Red Vixen (Ire) *C N Allen* a47
2 b f Agnes World (USA) - West Escape
13^{7sd} 8^{7sd} 9^{7sd} **0-0-3**

Red Warning *W R Muir* 33
2 b g Diktat - Red Rosein
13^{7gf} **0-0-1**

Redbank (Ire) *S Dow* 51 a38
4 b g Night Shift (USA) - Bush Rose
6^{6sd} 5^{8f} 7^{6g} 15^{7g} 14^{7gf} **0-0-5**

Redeye Special *D R Loder* 64
3 b f Efisio - Red May (Ire)
1^{6g} **1-0-1 £3,740**

Redi (Ity) *A M Balding* 53
4 b g Danehill Dancer (Ire) - Rossella
7^{12g} 8^{12g} **0-0-2**

Redoubtable (USA) *D W Chapman* 29 a52

14 b h Grey Dawn II - Seattle Rockette (USA)
10^{6sd} 1^{5sd} 11^{6sd} 9^{6sd} 9^{6sd} 7^{6sd} 5^{6sd} 5^{5sd} 4^{5sd} 8^{5gf} 11^{5gf} 10^{6sd} 12^{8g} 7^{6sd} 9^{9sd} **1-0-15 £1,473**

Redspin (Ire) *J S Moore* 65 a38
5 ch g Spectrum (Ire) - Trendy Indian (Ire)
1^{16gs} 6^{22s} 7^{16gf} 13^{17g} 11^{15gf} 6^{16gs} 5^{15gf} 8^{16sd} 12^{16sd} **1-0-9 £3,324**

Redswan *A E Jones* 2
10 ch g Risk Me (Fr) - Bocas Rose
11^{9sd} 17^{7gf} **0-0-2**

Reduit *Mrs A J Perrett* 55
7 ch g Lion Cavern (USA) - Soolaimon (Ire)
9^{10g} **0-0-1**

Redwood Rocks (Ire) *B Smart* 78
4 b g Blush Rambler (USA) - Crisp And Cool (USA)
6^{7gs} 13^{7f} 6^{7g} 1^{7f} 1^{8f} 9^{8gf} 8^{7g} **2-0-7 £6,945**

Redwood Star *P L Gilligan* 75
5 b m Piccolo - Thewaari (USA)
5^{5gf} 5^{5gf} 1^{5f} 10^{6g} 1^{5f} 3^{5gf} 2^{5g} 1^{5f} 3^{5f} 3^{5gf} 12^{5gf} **3-3-11 £18,545**

Reeds Rains *D A Nolan* 18
7 b m Mind Games - Me Spede
11^{5gs} 12^{5gf} 13^{8gf} 14^{8g} 7^{5gf} 8^{5gf} **0-0-6**

Reedsman (Ire) *R C Guest* 32
4 ch g Fayruz - The Way She Moves
6^{7g} 8^{6g} **0-0-2**

Reefscape *A Fabre* 119
4 gr c Linamix (Fr) - Coraline
2^{11vs} 3^{12g} 5^{12gs} 2^{13gs} 2^{15s} 1^{16gs} 1^{20gs} 2^{16s} 6^{12gf} **2-4-9 £270,519**

Reem Three *L M Cumani* a63
2 b f Mark Of Esteem (Ire) - Jumaireyah
7^{7sd} 2^{9sf} **0-1-2 £737**

Refa'Ah (Ire) *Barry Potts*
6 b m Lahib (USA) - Shurooq (USA)
8^{16sd} **0-0-1**

Reflecting (Ire) *J W Hills* a65
2 gr f Daylami (Ire) - Church Light
3^{7sd} **0-1-1 £696**

Reflex Blue *R J Price* a54
8 b g Ezzoud (Ire) - Briggsmaid
1^{17sd} 3^{17sd} 8^{17sd} 9^{17sd} 4^{12sd} 7^{17sd} 3^{14sd} 3^{12ss} **1-3-8 £3,853**

Reformation (Ire) *M F Harris*
2 ch c Spinning World (USA) - Individual (USA)
3^{5f} 8^{6f} **0-0-2 £514**

Regal Aaron *C J Teague*
2 b c Easycall - Regal Academy (Ire)
8^{5gf} **0-0-1**

Regal Attire (USA) *A M Balding* 79
3 ch c Kingmambo (USA) - Style Setter (USA)
2^{10gf} 4^{12g} 6^{12g} **0-1-3 £1,865**

Regal Connection (USA) *M Johnston* 76
2 b f Deputy Commander (USA) - Clever Empress
7^{6g} 2^{8g} 3^{8gf} 2^{9g} 1^{8g} 5^{8gs} **1-3-6 £7,992**

Regal Dream (Ire) *J W Hills* 77 a75
3 b c Namid - Lovely Me (Ire)
1^{5sd} 7^{5sd} 4^{6sd} 4^{6sd} 6^{5gf} 1^{6f} 4^{6g} 6^{7sd} 1^{7gf} 2^{7gf} 6^{7f} 1^{7sd} 5^{7sd} 8^{7g} 11^{7g} **4-1-15 £22,642**

Regal Fantasy (Ire) *P A Blockley* a11
5 b m King's Theatre (Ire) - Threesome (USA)
11^{14sd} 11^{16sd} 8^{11sd} **0-0-3**

Regal Gallery (Ire) *C A Horgan* 49 a68
7 b m Royal Academy (USA) - Polistatic
8^{12sd} 6^{10sd} 7^{10g} **0-0-3**

Regal Lass *J G Given* 45
2 b f Royal Applause - Faraway Lass
5^{5gf} 11^{5g} 9^{5g} **0-0-3**

Regal Magic (Ire) *J H M Gosden* 40 a41
2 b f Sadler's Wells (USA) - Regal Portrait (Ire)
7^{8s} 9^{10sd} **0-0-2**

Regal Performer (Ire) *S Kirk*
4 b g Ali-Royal (Ire) - Khatiynza
6^{14sd} **0-0-1**

Regal Rap *Ian Williams* 56
3 b g Royal Applause - Dust
18^{6s} 13^{6s} 4^{5sh} 23^{6y} 13^{6gy} 11^{8g} 13^{7gf} **0-1-7 £290**

Regal Royale *Sir Michael Stoute* 78
2 b g Medicean - Regal Rose
1^{6gf} 7^{7g} **1-0-2 £7,085**

Regal Setting (Ire) *J Howard Johnson* 83
4 br g King's Theatre (Ire) - Cartier Bijoux
10^{12g} **0-0-1**

Regal Song (Ire) *T J Etherington* a26
9 b g Anita's Prince - Song Beam
12^{6sd} 11^{7sd} 12^{5sd} 13^{6sd} **0-0-4**

Regal Velvet *J H M Gosden* 71
2 b f Halling (USA) - Ruthless Rose (USA)
4^{7g} **0-0-1 £406**

Regency Malaya *M F Harris* a42
4 b f Sri Pekan (USA) - Paola (Fr)
4^{9sd} 9^{10sd} 7^{9sd} **0-0-3**

Regency Red (Ire) *W M Brisbourne* 53 a61
7 ch g Dolphin Street (Fr) - Future Romance
5^{11sd} 2^{12sd} 2^{14sd} 2^{11sd} 1^{12sd} 5^{9sd} 3^{12sd} 4^{12f} 3^{12gf} 7^{11gf} 3^{12sd} 11^{14sd} 9^{12gf} 1^{12gf} 5^{12g} 8^{11g} 8^{12gf} 9^{12sd} 3^{12sd} 4^{12sd} 1^{9ss} **3-7-21 £10,734**

Regent's Secret (USA) *J S Goldie* 87
5 br g Cryptoclearance (USA) - Misty Regent (Can)
12^{10g} 4^{9g} 4^{10gf} 4^{10g} 7^{9gs} 1^{9gf} 1^{9gf} 2^{9gf} 7^{10gf} 2^{9gf} 1^{9gf} 2^{9gf} 2^{8gf} 4^{9gf} 8^{9g} 10^{10s} 5^{9hy} **3-6-17 £24,290**

Reggae Rhythm (Ire) *A J Lidderdale* 62 a69
11 b g Be My Native (USA) - Invery Lady
2^{17sd} 1^{17sd} 5^{16g} 1^{17sf} 3^{16g} 3^{18gs} 2^{17sd} 2^{16sd} 1^{17sd} **3-5-9 £9,802**

Regina *Sir Michael Stoute* 97
3 b f Green Desert (USA) - Dazzle
6^{5gf} 2^{5gf} 16^{5g} 10^{6gs} **0-1-4 £4,697**

Regis Flight *Miss K B Boutflower* 39 a49
3 b g Piccolo - Anthem Flight (USA)
6^{7sd} 16^{6g} 15^{8gf} 9^{5gf} 9^{6g} 12^{5sd} **0-0-6**

Registrar *Mrs A J Perrett* 79
3 ch c Machiavellian (USA) - Confidante (USA)
2^{8g} 2^{9g} 2^{7g} 3^{8gs} 1^{7gs} 7^{7gf} **1-4-6 £9,685**

Regulated (Ire) *P A Blockley* 49 a34
4 b g Alzao (USA) - Royal Hostess (Ire)
8^{10f} 8^{9sd} 5^{12gf} 7^{12g} **0-0-4**

Rehearsal *L Lungo* 98 a98
4 b g Singspiel (Ire) - Daralaka (Ire)
3^{12f} 3^{11gf} 15^{10gf} 3^{12sd} **0-3-4 £16,015**

Rehearsed (Ire) *H Morrison* 66
2 ch f In The Wings - Emilia Romagna (USA)
8^{7g} 7^{7g} 7^{8gs} **0-0-3**

Reinstated (Ire) *B W Hills* 34
2 b f Galileo (Ire) - Miletrian (Ire)
16^{7s} **0-0-1**

Relative Hero (Ire) *Miss S J Wilton* 44 a44
5 ch g Entrepreneur - Aunty (Fr)
12^{14sd} 10^{12sd} 7^{12sd} 4^{12sd} 8^{11sd} 6^{10g} 3^{12gf} 4^{12gf} 6^{14gf} **0-1-9 £848**

Relaxed Gesture (Ire) *Christophe Clement* 123
4 ch c Indian Ridge - Token Gesture (Ire)
1^{9f} 1^{10f} 2^{10f} 2^{11f} 2^{12g} 3^{11f} 1^{12y} **3-3-7 £689,065**

Released (USA) *J H M Gosden* 70
3 b f Red Ransom (USA) - Ispirata (Ire)
5^{8g} **0-0-1**

Reluctant Suitor *Jedd O'Keeffe* 72
3 b g Singspiel (Ire) - Belle Esprit
9^{9gf} 8^{12g} 2^{12gf} 4^{12gf} 7^{14gf} 6^{16gf} **0-1-6 £2,009**

Rem Time (Ire) *John Berry* 49 a52
5 b m Fraam - Any Dream (Ire)
2^{10gf} 4^{10g} 1^{9sd} 4^{10sd} 16^{12g} **1-2-5 £2,365**

Remaal (Ire) *M P Tregoning* 76
3 ch f Unfuwain (USA) - Marah
1^{12gf} 2^{12gf} 5^{10gs} 4^{14g} 6^{12g} **1-1-5 £6,940**

Remarkable Story *J H M Gosden* 32
3 b f Mark Of Esteem (Ire) - Spinning The Yarn
13^{10gs} **0-0-1**

Rembrandt Quality (USA) *Mrs A J Perrett* 69 a71
2 b c Elusive Quality (USA) - My Sister Sarah (USA)
5^{8gs} 3^{7sd} 5^{8sd} **0-1-3 £637**

Remember Ramon (USA) *M J Wallace* 58 a75
2 ch c Diesis - Future Act (USA)
9^{6gf} 3^{10sd} **0-1-2 £762**

Remington (Ire) *B Palling* 69
7 ch g Indian Ridge - Sea Harrier
1^{7g} 13^{7gf} 7^{8g} 7^{10gf} **1-0-4 £3,571**

Reminiscent (Ire) *B P J Baugh* 60 a62
6 b g Kahyasi - Eliza Orzeszkowa (Ire)
1^{12gf} 3^{11gf} 7^{12g} 2^{16gf} 10^{16s} 4^{14ft} 7^{14sd} 6^{16sf} 7^{14sd} **1-2-9 £5,704**

Remus Lupin *F P Murtagh* a48
4 b g Wolfhound (USA) - Incharder (Ire)
3^{13sd} **0-0-1 £414**

Ren's Magic *J R Jenkins*
7 gr g Petong - Bath
8^{10gs} **0-0-1**

Renada *J Howard Johnson* 68
3 b f Sinndar (Ire) - Asterita
3^{9gs} 4^{9gs} 9^{11g} 10^{11g} 4^{14gf} **0-0-5 £1,101**

Renderoc (USA) *J S Moore* 88 a82
2 ch c Mt. Livermore (USA) - Rewarding (USA)
7^{7g} 2^{7gf} 1^{8gf} 2^{7gf} 1^{7sd} 6^{8g} 3^{7g} **2-3-7 £17,755**

Renee Lard (Ire) *A Berry* 31
2 ch f Titus Livius (Fr) - Miss Body (Ire)
9^{7gf} 10^{7g} **0-0-2**

Renegade (Ire) *Mrs L J Mongan* 64 a60
4 b g Fasliyev (USA) - Arcade
5^{5y} 5^{5g} 2^{5g} 5^{5gf} 10^{6f} 6^{5gy} 4^{5ys} 5^{5sd} 6^{6sd} 9^{9sd} 10^{6sd} **0-1-11 £1,391**

Reno's Magic *W G M Turner* a32
4 b f Hello Mister - Mountain Magic
10^{5sd} 10^{5sd} 11^{6sd} **0-0-3**

Repeat (Ire) *J W Unett* a57
5 ch g Night Shift (USA) - Identical (Ire)
1^{6sd} 3^{7sd} 8^{6sd} 3^{7sd} 7^{9sd} 13^{6sd} 10^{7sd} 13^{8sd} 9^{7ss} 6^{9sd} 3^{7sd} 8^{9sd} **1-3-12 £2,432**

Requiem (USA) *D J Daly* 16
3 b f Royal Anthem (USA) - Bonus (USA)
16^{8gf} **0-0-1**

Residential *K A Ryan* 28
4 ch g Zilzal (USA) - House Hunting
8^{11gf} 7^{9gf} 13^{8sd} **0-0-3**

Resistance Heroine *W Jarvis* 70 a20
3 b f Dr Fong (USA) - Odette
6^{7sd} 4^{7g} 7^{7gf} 13^{8gf} 5^{7gf} 2^{8f} 9^{7sd} **0-1-7 £1,609**

Resonate (Ire) *A G Newcombe* 87 a74
7 b h Erin's Isle - Petronelli (USA)
3^{10sd} 6^{9sd} 5^{10sd} 8^{10g} 3^{12gf} 13^{12g} 3^{12f} 4^{12g} 4^{10gf} 5^{12sd} 3^{10sd} **0-4-11 £13,704**

Resplendent Glory (Ire) *T G Mills* 111 a96
3 ch c Namid - Aoife (Ire)
1^{6sd} 1^{6sd} 3^{6gf} 1^{6gs} 1^{6gs} 1^{5gf} 1^{5gf} **6-1-7 £95,130**

Resplendent Nova *T G Mills* 72 a87
3 b g Pivotal - Santiburi Girl
6^{7sd} 2^{8sd} 1^{7sd} 15^{9g} 4^{7gs} 10^{8gf} 2^{9sd} 11^{8gf} 5^{8sd} 7^{7gf} 3^{6sd} 1^{7sd} 14^{7sd} **2-3-13 £13,011**

Resplendent One (Ire) *T G Mills* 102
4 b g Marju (Ire) - Licentious
4^{8g} 3^{8gs} 8^{9g} 11^{8g} 18^{10gf} 8^{8gs} **0-2-6 £10,500**

Resplendent Prince *T G Mills* 58 a72
3 ch g Primo Dominie - Last Result
6^{7sd} 20^{7g} 17^{8g} 7^{6gf} 4^{7sd} 7^{7gf} 7^{8sd} 4^{7sd} **0-0-8 £541**

Ressource (Fr) *G L Moore* a37
6 b g Broadway Flyer (USA) - Rayonne
7^{17sd} 12^{13sd} **0-0-2**

Restart (Ire) *Lucinda Featherstone* 67 a64
4 b g Revoque (Ire) - Stargard
3^{14sd} 4^{14gs} 5^{14g} 2^{20s} 17^{18g} 4^{17g} **0-2-6 £2,978**

Restoration (Fr) *Noel Meade* 83
3 gr g Zafonic (USA) - Restless Mixa (Ire)
1^{8gs} 6^{10gs} 4^{11gs} 10^{12gf} 3^{8gf} 5^{8gs} 4^{8gs} **1-1-7 £7,260**

Retina (Swi) *J G Portman* 36
2 b f Xaar - Razida (Ire)
12^{5gf} 13^{7gf} **0-0-2**

Retirement *R M Stronge* 68 a43
6 b g Zilzal (USA) - Adeptation (USA)
6^{8g} 3^{8s} 8^{10sd} 3^{8gf} 11^{8gf} 8^{9sd} 11^{8sd} **0-2-7 £1,192**

Reunite (Ire) *Saeed Bin Suroor* 75
2 ch f Kingmambo (USA) - Allez Les Trois (USA)
1^{8hy} **1-0-1 £3,312**

Reverence *E J Alston* 108
4 ch g Mark Of Esteem (Ire) - Imperial Bailiwick (Ire)
2^{6g} 1^{5gs} 10^{6g} 1^{5gs} 1^{5gs} 1^{5hy} **4-1-6 £32,974**

Reversionary *M W Easterby* a58
4 b g Poyle George - Harold's Girl (Fr)
3^{8sd} 2^{8sd} 6^{9sd} 11^{9sd} 3^{8sd} 2^{8sd} 7^{7sd} **0-4-7 £1,568**

Reveur *M Mullineaux* 49 a73
2 b f Rossini (USA) - Without Warning (Ire)
10^{5gf} 8^{6gf} 10^{5gf} 9^{6g} 1^{7sd} **1-0-5 £4,061**

Revien (Ire) *Miss J R Tooth* 64 a64
3 b c Rossini (USA) - Kazimiera (Ire)
3^{6sd} 1^{5sd} 6^{5sd} 3^{6sd} 7^{7gs} 15^{6gf} 2^{5gs} 9^{5gf} 9^{6sd} 6^{6sd} 10^{5sd} **1-3-11 £6,274**

Reviewer (Ire) *M Meade* 53
7 b g Sadler's Wells (USA) - Clandestina (USA)
9^{14g} **0-0-1**

Reviving (Ire) *R F Johnson Houghton* 78
2 b g Fasliyev (USA) - Hartstown House (Ire)
3^{5gf} 2^{5gf} 2^{5gf} 13^{6gs} 14^{5g} **0-3-5 £2,869**

Revolve *Mrs L J Mongan* 40 a52
5 b g Pivotal - Alpine Time (Ire)
3^{10g} 8^{10g} 5^{8g} 14^{10sd} 2^{13g} 4^{13sd} 1^{10sd} 13^{10sd} **1-2-8 £2,226**

Revolving World (Ire) *T J Fitzgerald* 25
2 b c Spinning World (USA) - Mannakea (USA)
15^{7g} **0-0-1**

Rezzago (USA) *W R Swinburn* 86 a82
5 b g Night Shift (USA) - Western Friend (USA)
2^{7gf} 4^{7g} 1^{6sd} 1^{6sd} 1^{6gf} 3^{6g} **3-3-6 £16,217**

Rhapsody In Silver (Fr) *J Jay*
3 gr c Medaaly - Concert
7^{14gf} PU^{12gs} **0-0-2**

Rhetorical *P Butler* 20 a35
4 b g Unfuwain (USA) - Miswaki Belle (USA)
12^{10sd} 11^{12sd} 10^{15gf} **0-0-3**

Rhinebird *J R Fanshawe* a67
2 b g Lomitas - Twitcher's Delight
5^{7sd} **0-0-1**

Rhinefield Lass *J S Goldie* 11 a31
5 ch m Bijou D'Inde - Rhinefield Beauty (Ire)
8^{5sd} 14^{5g} 16^{6f} **0-0-3**

Rhodes *M J Wallace* a33
2 ch g Tomba - Princess Zepoli
13^{7sd} **0-0-1**

Rhodesian Winner (Ger) *Frau Marion Rotering* 113
6 ch h Snurge - Rhodesia (Ger)
2^{11g} 1^{14g} 1^{15g} 3^{14gs} 3^{12gf} 7^{16gs} **2-0-6 £57,947**

Rhoslan (Ire) *Mrs P N Dutfield* 33 a41
3 b g Trans Island - Flimmering
12^{6sd} 10^{6sd} 5^{8sd} 9^{9sd} 8^{8sd} 6^{8g} 7^{8gf} 12^{6gf} 10^{6gf} 8^{8gf} 9^{10g} 11^{6f} **0-0-12**

Rhuby River (Ire) *R Dickin* 35
3 b f Bahhare (USA) - Westside Flyer
6^{8s} 13^{7g} 10^{9sd} 12^{9sd} **0-0-4**

Ribald *M L W Bell* 58
2 b f Alhaarth (Ire) - Reactress (USA)
14^{7gf} 4^{7g} 3^{8hd} 10^{8g} **0-1-4 £917**

Ribbons Of Gold *A G Newcombe* 33 a40
3 b f Primo Dominie - In Love Again (Ire)
11^{6g} 11^{7sd} 6^{5sd} 5^{6f} 8^{5f} 11^{6gf} **0-0-6**

Ribh *C E Brittain* 86
2 b f Zafonic (USA) - Torgau (Ire)
4^{5gf} 2^{6gs} **0-1-2 £3,192**

Rice Mother (Ire) *M Johnston* 64
3 b f Indian Ridge - Persian Secret (Fr)
4^{9gs} 7^{8g} 6^{7g} 3^{7f} 6^{8gs} 1^{10g} 5^{10g} **1-1-7 £4,894**

Rich Albi *T D Easterby* 52
3 b g Mind Games - Bollin Sophie
8^{7g} 8^{5g} 11^{6gf} **0-0-3**

Richie Boy *Jennie Candlish* 15
4 b c Dr Fong (USA) - Alathezal (USA)
10^{14sd} 12^{8s} **0-0-2**

Richtee (Ire) *R A Fahey* 76
4 ch f Desert Sun - Santarene (Ire)
8^{14g} 5^{10s} 1^{12gf} 7^{13s} 1^{12gs} 3^{13gf} 4^{12gf} 9^{12gf} **2-0-8 £9,733**

Richterhoffen (Ire) *R Hannon* 77 a78
2 b c Mull Of Kintyre (USA) - Bradwell (Ire)
4^{6gf} 1^{7gf} 8^{6gf} 11^{6g} 11^{6g} 4^{6sd} **1-0-6 £5,681**

Ride Safari *P Winkworth* 11 a43
3 b g Fraam - Vocation (Ire)
9^{6sd} 8^{8sd} 12^{8sd} 16^{7g} **0-0-4**

Ridge Boy (Ire) *R Hannon* 89
4 b c Indian Ridge - Bold Tina (Ire)
4^{8g} 2^{8gf} 2^{9g} 9^{8gf} 3^{8gs} 4^{9g} **0-4-6 £12,713**

Ridgeway Cross (Ire) *E R Oertel* 55 a61
2 gr f Cape Cross (Ire) - Karatisa (Ire)
7^{6gf} 4^{6gf} 4^{6sd} 22^{5gf} 10^{6gs} 10^{6gf} 5^{6gf} 6^{7sd} 11^{6s} 8^{7sd} 7^{7sd} **0-0-11 £936**

Ridicule *J G Portman* 32 a29
6 b g Piccolo - Mockingbird
10^{5sd} 8^{7s} 9^{6g} 13^{6g} **0-0-4**

Rievaulx Rebel *M W Easterby* 48
2 b g Averti (Ire) - Hispaniola (Ire)
5^{5gf} 8^{6gf} 10^{7g} 5^{6gf} 7^{6gf} 6^{7g} **0-0-6**

Right Again *A P Jarvis* 95
2 b c Lujain (USA) - Doliouchka
5^{5g} 5^{6s} 2^{6g} 1^{7gf} 4^{7gs} 7^{7s} 6^{8gf} **1-1-7 £8,437**

Right Answer *T D Easterby* 95
3 b f Lujain (USA) - Quiz Show
8^{5gf} 7^{5g} 9^{5gf} 6^{5g} 9^{5gs} 9^{5gf} 12^{5g} **0-0-7 £420**

Right Key (Ire) *Kevin Prendergast* 108
3 b f Key Of Luck (USA) - Sarifa (Ire)
6^{8s} 5^{10hy} 1^{10g} 1^{12gf} 4^{12gf} RR^{12g} 1^{14gf} 12^{12g} **3-0-8 £120,035**

Right Ted (Ire) *R Hannon* 75
2 b f Mujadil (USA) - Islandagore (Ire)
5^{6g} 3^{7f} 1^{7gf} 6^{7gf} **1-1-4 £4,373**

Right To Roam (Ire) *J A R Toller* 52
3 b g Namid - Lloc
4^{5gf} 4^{5gf} **0-0-2 £598**

Rightful Ruler *B W Hills* 75 a72
3 b g Montjoy (USA) - Lady Of The Realm
4^{8sd} 2^{9sd} 3^{9sd} 3^{10f} 6^{10gf} 10^{10gf} 9^{8gf} 6^{10hd} **0-2-8 £2,512**

Righty Ho *W H Tinning* 38 a33
11 b g Reprimand - Challanging
8^{12sd} 11^{12gf} 5^{14f} **0-0-3**

Riley Boys (Ire) *J G Given* 86
4 ch g Most Welcome - Scarlett Holly
4^{8gs} 6^{7s} 4^{10gs} 3^{8f} 6^{8s} 7^{8g} 2^{8gf} 7^{8gf} 1^{8g} 19^{10gs} 9^{8gf} 16^{9gs} 18^{7s} **1-2-13 £11,832**

Rileys Dream *B J Llewellyn* 44 a30
6 b m Rudimentary (USA) - Dorazine
8^{7gf} 4^{5gf} 6^{6f} 9^{7g} 9^{5hd} 7^{6f} 13^{7sd} **0-0-7 £264**

Rill *J H M Gosden* 65
3 ch f Unfuwain (USA) - River Cara (USA)
1^{12f} **1-0-1 £3,386**

Ring Of Destiny *J Jay* 83 a45
6 b g Magic Ring (Ire) - Canna
5^{12gf} 9^{12gf} 5^{12g} 11^{12gs} 3^{10gf} 8^{10gf} 4^{12gs} 16^{12sd}

0-1-8 £1,009

Ringarooma *C N Allen* 56 a64
3 b f Erhaab (USA) - Tatouma (USA)
8^{7g} 9^{7s} 5^{8sd} 4^{10gs} 16^{10g} 3^{7g} 8^{7sd} 8^{6sd} 9^{6sd} **0-1-9 £551**

Ringmoor Down *D W P Arbuthnot* 106
6 b m Pivotal - Floppie (Fr)
3^{5gf} 3^{6gf} 9^{5gf} 8^{5gf} **0-2-4 £8,800**

Ringsend Lady (Ire) *Barry Potts* 54
4 b f Desert Story (Ire) - Entracte
9^{7gf} 12^{7g} 8^{7g} 8^{9gf} 14^{8g} **0-0-5**

Ringsider (Ire) *G A Butler* 98 a94
4 ch g Docksider (USA) - Red Comes Up (USA)
4^{12gf} 8^{10g} 8^{12gf} 3^{13sd} 3^{12gf} 9^{12f} 7^{10sd} **0-2-7 £6,920**

Rio De Janeiro (Ire) *P R Chamings* 71
4 b g Sadler's Wells (USA) - Alleged Devotion (USA)
17^{10s} 7^{11g} 19^{14s} **0-0-3**

Rio Riva *Miss J A Camacho* 95 a92
3 b c Pivotal - Dixie Favor (USA)
3^{6g} 2^{7gs} 2^{7s} 1^{7gf} 15^{7g} 1^{8g} 4^{9sd} **2-3-7 £23,220**

Riotous Applause *J R Fanshawe* 96
2 b f Royal Applause - Wiener Wald (USA)
6^{6g} 1^{6g} 7^{6g} **1-0-3 £3,939**

Riotous Assembly *B Smart* 53
2 b g Dansili - Pretty Pollyanna
10^{8s} 13^{8s} **0-0-2**

Ripples Maid *J A Geake* 51
2 b f Dansili - Rivers Rhapsody
10^{6g} **0-0-1**

Riquewihr *P Howling* 71 a67
5 ch m Compton Place - Juvenilia (Ire)
5^{6sd} 4^{7sd} 2^{7sd} 1^{7sd} 4^{7sd} 6^{7sd} 11^{6sd} 6^{6sd} 2^{5s} 6^{6g} 1^{6hy} 8^{6sd} 8^{6sd} 7^{6gs} 7^{6gs} 12^{5g} 11^{6sd} **2-2-17 £8,603**

Rise *Andrew Reid* a71
4 b f Polar Falcon (USA) - Splice
10^{6sd} 4^{7sd} 6^{6sd} 8^{6sd} 3^{6sd} 5^{7sd} **0-1-6 £653**

Rising Cross *J R Best* 101
2 bl f Cape Cross (Ire) - Woodrising
5^{5gs} 4^{5s} 5^{5g} 1^{7gf} 1^{7gs} 4^{7gf} 1^{7g} 4^{7g} 4^{7s} 2^{7g} 6^{8gf} **3-1-11 £37,278**

Rising Shadow (Ire) *T D Barron* 98
4 b g Efisio - Jouet
2^{6s} 6^{5gf} 6^{6gs} 1^{6g} 3^{6g} 3^{6g} 2^{6g} 10^{6gs} 11^{6g} 5^{6gs} 3^{6s} 5^{7gs} 8^{6s} **1-5-13 £26,690**

Risk Free *P D Evans* a64
8 ch g Risk Me (Fr) - Princess Lily
2^{9sd} 8^{9sd} 1^{9sd} 2^{9sd} 2^{9sd} 4^{8sd} 3^{8sd} 8^{9sd} **1-4-8 £4,518**

Risk Runner (Ire) *A King* 73
2 b g Mull Of Kintyre (USA) - Fizzygig
4^{8s} 2^{8gf} 5^{8gs} 8^{8g} 1^{8hy} **1-1-5 £5,897**

Riska King *P A Blockley* 73 a55
5 b g Forzando - Artistic Licence
10^{7sd} 3^{7s} 13^{9sd} 9^{8gs} 6^{7f} 9^{7g} 11^{7gf} 13^{8s} 12^{9sd} **0-1-9 £1,056**

Ritsi *Mrs A J Perrett* 66
2 b g Marju (Ire) - Anna Comnena (Ire)
9^{7gs} 4^{7gf} 10^{8g} 12^{8g} **0-0-4 £366**

Rivelli (Ire) *B R Foster*
6 b m Lure (USA) - Kama Tashoof
12^{8s} **0-0-1**

River Alhaarth (Ire) *P W Chapple-Hyam* 86
3 b c Alhaarth (Ire) - Sudden Interest (Fr)
2^{9g} **0-1-1 £2,171**

River Biscuit (USA) *M J Polglase* 54 a66
3 ch g Diesis - Elle Est Revenue (Ire)
7^{7sd} 5^{9sd} 5^{7sd} 10^{8gf} **0-0-4**

River Bravo (Ire) *P W Chapple-Hyam* 83
2 b c Indian Ridge - Sheer Spirit (Ire)
5^{7gs} 1^{6g} **1-0-2 £4,212**

River Card *Michael Hourigan* 55
3 ch f Zaha (Can) - Light Hand
4^{6g} 13^{6f} 8^{7gs} 4^{8g} 16^{8gs} 2^{8g} **0-1-6 £1,230**

River Crossing *T D Easterby* 73
2 b f Zafonic (USA) - Vax Star
1^{5gf} 7^{6gf} 17^{6g} **1-0-3 £3,607**

River Falcon *J S Goldie* 102
5 b g Pivotal - Pearly River
5^{5gs} 1^{5s} 1^{5s} 5^{5g} 5^{6f} 8^{5s} 3^{6gs} 10^{6g} 9^{6s} 8^{5hy} **2-1-10 £31,926**

River Gypsy *D R C Elsworth* 69 a57
4 b g In The Wings - River Erne (USA)
4^{10sd} 9^{10g} 5^{10gs} **0-0-3 £268**

River Iris *Lucinda Featherstone*
4 ch f Riverhead (USA) - Barkston Singer
14^{10gf} **0-0-1**

River Kintyre *B W Hills* 81
2 b c Mull Of Kintyre (USA) - Our Pleasure (Ire)
4^{5g} 1^{5gs} 16^{6g} 19^{6gf} **1-0-4 £9,025**

River Lark (USA) *M Wigham* 37 a8
6 b m Miswaki (USA) - Gold Blossom (USA)
9^{5sd} 9^{5s} 9^{6g} **0-0-3**

River Lena (Ire) *M Johnston* 84
2 b f Spectrum (Ire) - Insijaam (USA)
3^{7g} 2^{7f} 1^{7g} 4^{8gf} **1-2-4 £7,774**

River Line (USA) *C W Fairhurst* 23
4 b g Keos (USA) - Portio (USA)
7^{9gf} 14^{12g} **0-0-2**

River Logic (Ire) *J Howard Johnson* 54
2 b c Fasliyev (USA) - Grey Again
12^{6gf} 4^{6f} 4^{6gf} 8^{7gf} 12^{6gf} **0-0-5 £743**

River Mist Image (USA) *J R Fanshawe* 71 a60
3 ch f Swain (Ire) - Cat's Image (Can)
3^{8gs} 5^{8g} 3^{8gf} 9^{10sd} **0-2-4 £1,497**

River Of Babylon *M L W Bell* 87 a59
4 b f Marju (Ire) - Isle Of Flame
8^{7sd} 6^{7g} 2^{8gs} 1^{7g} 7^{7g} 3^{7g} 4^{8gf} 1^{7gf} 5^{7gf} 2^{7s} 3^{7gs} 6^{7gf} **2-3-12 £23,808**

River Of Diamonds *R A Harris* 56 a46
4 b g Muhtarram (USA) - City Gambler
6^{13sd} 11^{12sd} 1^{10g} 9^{10gf} 15^{10g} 7^{12g} 11^{9sf} 10^{11sd} 6^{8ss} **1-0-9 £2,578**

River Of Fire *C N Kellett* 33 a35
7 ch g Dilum (USA) - Bracey Brook
5^{12sd} 7^{14g} 13^{14gf} **0-0-3**

River Royale *P W Chapple-Hyam* 95
3 b c Royal Applause - Trundley Wood
1^{7gs} 1^{7gf} **2-0-2 £13,268**

River Thames *J A R Toller* 98
2 b c Efisio - Dashing Water
3^{6g} 1^{6gf} 1^{6g} 3^{5hy} 8^{6gf} **2-2-5 £18,156**

Riverhill (Ire) *J Howard Johnson* 25
2 b c Mull Of Kintyre (USA) - Thrill Seeker (Ire)
9^{7gf} **0-0-1**

Riverside Drive (Ire) *J Pearce*

2 b f Priolo (USA) - Alizee (Ire)
13^{7s} **0-0-1**

Rivetting *Sir Mark Prescott* a33
2 b g Vettori (Ire) - Frog
8^{6sd} 7^{6sd} 11^{7sd} **0-0-3**

Riviera Red (Ire) *L Montague Hall* a51
5 b g Rainbow Quest (USA) - Banquise (Ire)
12^{16sd} 12^{10sd} 13^{10sd} 1^{8sd} **1-0-4 £1,423**

Riyadh *T P Tate*
7 ch g Caerleon (USA) - Ausherra (USA)
19^{20s} **0-0-1**

Riyalma (Ire) *Sir Michael Stoute* 75
2 b f Selkirk (USA) - Riyafa (Ire)
2^{8gf} **0-1-1 £1,736**

Ro Eridani *Miss S E Forster*
5 b m Binary Star (USA) - Hat Hill
12^{8gf} **0-0-1**

Road Rage (Ire) *E A L Dunlop*
3 b f Giant's Causeway (USA) - Endorsement
11^{10g} **0-0-1**

Road To Love (Ire) *M Johnston* 85
2 ch g Fruits Of Love (USA) - Alpine Flair (Ire)
7^{6f} 10^{6gf} 1^{8gs} 3^{8s} **1-1-4 £6,630**

Roan Raider (USA) *R C Guest* 28
5 gr/ro g El Prado (Ire) - Flirtacious Wonder (USA)
13^{8gf} 15^{6gf} 14^{5gf} 11^{7sd} **0-0-4**

Roar Blizzard (Ire) *H J Collingridge* 53 a43
7 b h Roar (USA) - Ragtime Rumble (USA)
11^{12sd} 6^{8gf} 8^{9sd} 4^{10gf} 2^{8gf} **0-2-5 £911**

Rob Leach *G L Moore* a59
8 b g Robellino (USA) - Arc Empress Jane (Ire)
5^{12sd} **0-0-1**

Rob Roy (USA) *Sir Michael Stoute* 118
3 b/br c Lear Fan (USA) - Camanoe (USA)
2^{8gf} 19^{8gf} 3^{8gs} 1^{8gs} 14^{10gs} **1-1-5 £41,650**

Robbie Can Can *A W Carroll* 69 a68
6 b g Robellino (USA) - Can Can Lady
4^{9sd} 2^{11g} 11^{10gf} 6^{15gf} 7^{14gs} 7^{11s} 3^{12g} 5^{16g} 4^{10s} 3^{14sd} **0-4-10 £3,122**

Robbie Will *F Jordan* 57
4 b g Robellino (USA) - Life's Too Short (Ire)
3^{10s} 7^{10gs} 10^{12gs} 12^{12gf} 10^{13gf} 11^{12g} **0-1-6 £870**

Robbo *K G Reveley* 59
11 b g Robellino (USA) - Basha (USA)
4^{18gs} **0-0-1 £412**

Robeson *G Haine* 73 a44
3 br g Primo Dominie - Montserrat
5^{8gf} 4^{10gf} 8^{10g} 4^{10gf} 11^{10sd} **0-0-5 £645**

Robin Sharp *J Akehurst* a39
7 ch h First Trump - Mo Stopher
14^{8sd} 11^{8sd} 11^{8sd} 4^{7sd} 7^{8sd} 10^{8ss} 13^{7sd} 8^{8sd} **0-0-8**

Robinzal *T D Easterby* 68
3 b g Zilzal (USA) - Sulitelma (USA)
12^{8s} 5^{6s} 3^{6gs} 5^{6s} 12^{7gf} 1^{7f} 9^{7gf} 1^{8s} **2-1-8 £7,163**

Robmantra *B J Llewellyn* 53 a53
3 b g Prince Sabo - Eliza Jane
3^{5sd} 4^{6sd} 5^{5sd} 6^{6sd} 4^{6s} 9^{5g} 4^{5s} 5^{6gs} 6^{5gf} 8^{5g} 9^{6f} **0-1-11 £676**

Robury *E J Alston* 41 a29
3 b g Robellino (USA) - Youdontsay
4^{6sd} 3^{7gf} 13^{7gs} 18^{6gf} 14^{7sd} **0-1-5 £211**

Robustian *R F Johnson Houghton* 75
2 b g Robellino (USA) - Pontressina (USA)
5^{6gf} 1^{6gf} 8^{6g} 3^{6g} **1-1-4 £5,232**

Robwillcall *A C Whillans* 49
5 b m Timeless Times (USA) - Lavernock Lady
12^{5g} 5^{5s} 2^{6gf} 10^{6gf} 7^{5f} 3^{6f} 2^{8gf} 2^{8gf} **0-4-8 £3,286**

Rocamadour *M R Channon* 115
3 b c Celtic Swing - Watch Me (Ire)
1^{9gf} 1^{10gf} 3^{11g} 4^{8gf} 3^{8g} **2-2-5 £197,752**

Rochdale *M A Jarvis* 75
2 ch g Bertolini (USA) - Owdbetts (Ire)
9^{6gs} 1^{6g} 4^{6gf} **1-0-3 £4,528**

Roches Fleuries (Ire) *Andrew Turnell* 46
5 b m Barathea (Ire) - Princess Caraboo (Ire)
7^{12gf} PU^{12gf} **0-0-2**

Rochesis *Miss K B Boutflower* 72
2 b f Mujahid (USA) - Northern Bird
2^{6gf} 1^{6g} **1-1-2 £2,604**

Rock Chick *J H M Gosden* 74 a65
3 ch f Halling (USA) - Band (USA)
4^{10sd} 5^{10gf} 4^{10gs} 5^{8s} 2^{10s} 3^{10gf} 2^{9sd} 3^{9sd} **0-3-8 £3,977**

Rock Concert *I W McInnes* a63
7 b m Bishop Of Cashel - Summer Pageant
3^{11sd} 8^{12sd} 9^{8sd} 5^{9sd} 10^{9sd} 6^{12sd} 8^{9sd} **0-1-7 £513**

Rock Dove (Ire) *Sir Mark Prescott* 72
3 b f Danehill (USA) - Littlefeather (Ire)
7^{5g} 12^{6s} **0-0-2**

Rock Fever (Ire) *Peter Grayson* 47 a52
3 ch f Desert Sun - Icefern
15^{8gs} 10^{6gs} 4^{6gf} 2^{5sd} 2^{5sd} 9^{5gf} 15^{6gf} 2^{6sd} 10^{6sd} 6^{5sd} 8^{5sd} 7^{6sd} 5^{6sd} 1^{5sd} **1-3-14 £3,414**

Rock Haven (Ire) *W R Swinburn* 68
3 b g Danehill Dancer (Ire) - Mahabba (USA)
5^{8g} 8^{8g} 3^{8g} 8^{10gf} 4^{10gf} 8^{11g} **0-1-6 £687**

Rock Lobster *J G Given* 71
4 b g Desert Sun - Distant Music
5^{8s} 4^{8gf} 2^{9f} 2^{12f} 4^{11gf} 11^{10g} 7^{10g} UR^{12g} **0-3-8 £2,899**

Rock Music *D R Loder* 87 a88
3 ch c Singspiel (Ire) - Stack Rock
5^{6sd} 1^{8sd} 4^{9sd} 11^{7gs} **1-0-4 £5,245**

Rock Of Cloonavery (Ire) *J A Osborne* 66
2 b g Desert Prince (Ire) - Mackla
3^{7s} 8^{8g} 9^{8gs} **0-0-3 £961**

Rock Xaar (Ire) *J Pearce* 40
3 b f Xaar - Miss Golden Sands
8^{8g} **0-0-1**

Rockburst *K R Burke* 75
3 b f Xaar - Topwinder (USA)
6^{6gf} 13^{7gf} 10^{7gf} 8^{7gf} 9^{6g} **0-0-5**

Rockerfella Lad (Ire) *M Todhunter* 60
5 b g Danetime (Ire) - Soucaro
6^{8gs} 6^{9g} 12^{8s} **0-0-3**

Rocket (Ire) *H J Manners* 30
4 ch g Cadeaux Genereux - Prends Ca (Ire)
12^{8sd} 6^{8gf} 15^{6gs} 6^{6gf} 19^{6f} **0-0-5**

Rocket Force (USA) *N Wilson* 78
5 ch g Spinning World (USA) - Pat Us (USA)
18^{8g} 1^{12g} 6^{14gf} 4^{14gf} 8^{12g} 4^{11gs} 9^{10s} **1-1-7 £5,760**

Rockley Bay (Ire) *Mrs L C Jewell* a41
4 b g Mujadil (USA) - Kilkee Bay (Ire)
9^{5sd} 12^{6sd} 8^{7sd} 7^{6sd} **0-0-4**

Rockpiler *J Howard Johnson* 63
3 b g Halling (USA) - Emma Peel
5^{11gf} 3^{12gf} 5^{12gf} **0-0-3 £525**

Rocky Agenda (Ire) *G A Harker*
4 b g Fort Morgan (USA) - Floating Agenda (USA)
8^{14g} **0-0-1**

Rocky Reppin *J Balding* a56
5 b g Rock City - Tino Reppin
1^{7sd} 6^{10sd} 8^{7sd} 1^{7sd} 10^{8sd} 5^{8sd} 3^{7sd} 4^{7sd} 2^{7sd} 8^{7sd} 6^{7sd} 7^{7sd} 11^{7ss} **2-2-13 £4,911**

Rockys Girl *R Flint* 48 a37
3 b f Piccolo - Lady Rockstar
7^{7g} 5^{10f} 9^{10f} 7^{10g} 5^{7g} 11^{9sd} 9^{8sd} 3^{11g} 3^{12sd} 8^{10g} 2^{14hy} 6^{11sd} **0-3-12 £1,142**

Rodeo *B W Hills* 75
2 ch c Pivotal - Flossy
16^{6gs} 4^{7s} **0-0-2 £291**

Rogue *A M Balding* a47
3 b f Royal Applause - Mystique
3^{5sd} **0-1-1 £497**

Rohaani (USA) *Sir Michael Stoute* 104
3 ch c High Yield (USA) - Strawberry's Charm (USA)
1^{10g} 1^{9gf} 1^{8g} 4^{10gf} **3-1-4 £29,642**

Roko *D Shaw* a33
3 b g Komaite (USA) - Robert's Daughter
10^{6sd} 5^{5sd} 7^{6sd} 14^{6sd} 7^{5sd} 11^{5sd} **0-0-6**

Rol'Over Beethoven (Fr) *A P O'Brien* 84
2 b c Mozart (Ire) - Don't Worry Me (Ire)
3^{7gf} 3^{7g} 3^{6gs} **0-2-3 £3,118**

Rolex Free (Arg) *D Flood* a59
7 ch g Friul (Arg) - Karolera (Arg)
6^{13sd} 4^{12sd} 1^{9sd} 8^{9sd} **1-0-4 £2,534**

Roll The Dice (Ire) *R Hannon* 72
2 b c Sinndar (Ire) - Piffle
7^{6s} 4^{7g} 4^{7gs} 5^{7g} F^{8gf} **0-0-5 £823**

Rollerbird *A M Balding* 64
3 b f Sinndar (Ire) - Speedybird (Ire)
5^{7g} 3^{8g} **0-1-2 £1,048**

Roman Army (Ire) *A M Balding* 65
3 b g Trans Island - Contravene (Ire)
12^{8g} 4^{10g} 5^{13g} 3^{13gf} 11^{12g} 9^{17gs} **0-1-6 £580**

Roman Empire *K A Ryan* a62
5 b g Efisio - Gena Ivor (USA)
7^{7sd} 5^{7sd} 12^{7sd} 3^{8sf} 5^{8sd} **0-1-5 £374**

Roman History (Ire) *Robert Gray* 61 a48
2 b g Titus Livius (Fr) - Tetradonna (Ire)
10^{5g} 6^{6gf} 3^{7sd} 2^{7g} 11^{7gf} 9^{7gf} 16^{7gf} 2^{7g} 4^{8gf} 20^{8s} 6^{7gf} 8^{7sd} **0-3-12 £2,973**

Roman Maze *W M Brisbourne* 102 a91
5 ch g Lycius (USA) - Maze Garden (USA)
4^{7sd} 3^{7sd} 2^{6sd} 1^{6sd} 3^{6sd} 8^{6sd} 3^{7gf} 1^{7gf} 2^{6s} 6^{7gf} 1^{8gf} 2^{6g} 14^{7g} 5^{7gs} 7^{6s} 9^{7sd} **3-5-16 £57,667**

Roman Quest *H Morrison* 51
2 b c Lujain (USA) - Roma
13^{8g} 9^{7gf} **0-0-2**

Roman Quintet (Ire) *D W P Arbuthnot* 79 a75
5 ch g Titus Livius (Fr) - Quintellina
11^{10sd} 3^{6sd} 1^{8sd} 2^{7gf} 11^{6g} 2^{6gf} 3^{6gf} 8^{6gf} 1^{6gs} **2-4-9 £12,597**

Roman The Park (Ire) *T D Easterby* 45 a43
4 b f Titus Livius (Fr) - Missfortuna
6^{8sd} 3^{9gf} 9^{8g} 8^{7gs} **0-1-4 £218**

Roman Villa (USA) *R Charlton* 77
3 b c Chester House (USA) - Danzante (USA)
3^{8g} 7^{10gf} 1^{8gf} 7^{10gs} **1-1-4 £5,634**

Romanova (Ire) *D R Loder* a17
3 b f Grand Lodge (USA) - Millitrix
9^{8sd} **0-0-1**

Romantic Evening (Ire) *E S McMahon* 101
2 ch c Dr Fong (USA) - By Candlelight (Ire)
3^{6g} 1^{6g} 3^{7gf} **1-2-3 £10,837**

Romany Nights (Ire) *Miss Gay Kelleway* 87 a69
5 b g Night Shift (USA) - Gipsy Moth
5^{6gf} 8^{5gf} 3^{6gf} 9^{6gf} 1^{6gf} 4^{6s} 1^{6g} 11^{6gf} 7^{7gf} 14^{6gf} 12^{6g} 7^{7s} 6^{5sd} 9^{6sd} 6^{6sd} **2-1-15 £17,283**

Romany Prince *S Gollings* 91
6 b g Robellino (USA) - Vicki Romara
16^{19gs} 6^{18gs} **0-0-2 £233**

Rome (Ire) *G P Enright* 56 a62
6 br g Singspiel (Ire) - Ela Romara
14^{12sd} 6^{14gf} 6^{14gf} 10^{12sd} **0-0-4**

Romil Star (Ger) *K R Burke* 57 a82
8 b g Chief's Crown (USA) - Romelia (USA)
11^{12sd} 1^{12sd} 1^{12sd} 10^{12sd} 2^{11sd} 5^{12sd} 5^{12sd} 8^{12g} 10^{12gf} 4^{12sd} 7^{12gs} 7^{12sd} 12^{12gf} 6^{12gf} 8^{12sd} 4^{14sd} 1^{12sd} 7^{14sd} 2^{14sd} 6^{11sd} **3-2-20 £12,240**

Rondo *T D Barron* 65
2 b g Piccolo - Flourish
4^{5g} **0-0-1 £272**

Ronnie From Donny (Ire) *C J Teague* 44 a55
5 b g Eagle Eyed (USA) - New Rochelle (Ire)
11^{7sd} 4^{6sd} 11^{6gs} 9^{5sd} 6^{6sd} 9^{7f} 18^{7gf} 12^{6gf} 12^{6gf} 8^{6g} **0-0-10**

Ronnies Lad *J R Norton* 52 a56
3 b g Lake Coniston (Ire) - Lycius Touch
8^{8sd} 8^{7sd} 9^{7sd} 4^{6sd} 3^{10sd} 1^{7sd} 8^{9sd} 11^{8gf} 13^{8g} 5^{10gf} 7^{10g} 3^{7gf} 10^{8gf} 12^{7g} 8^{8g} 11^{10g} 10^{10g} **1-1-17 £4,044**

Ronsard (Ire) *Mrs H Dalton* 72 a73
3 b g Spectrum (Ire) - Touche-A-Tout (Ire)
7^{9sd} 2^{9sd} 16^{9g} 11^{9sd} 7^{8gs} 4^{8g} 12^{7gf} 4^{8g} 7^{7sd} 4^{8g} 3^{8g} 6^{8s} 6^{8s} 1^{9sd} **1-3-14 £6,047**

Rood Boy (Ire) *Andrew Turnell* a58
4 b g Great Commotion (USA) - Cnocma (Ire)
5^{8sf} 1^{11sd} **1-0-2 £1,419**

Roodeye *R F Johnson Houghton* 98
3 b f Inchinor - Roo
4^{6g} 6^{6gs} 2^{6gf} 3^{7gf} 4^{7g} 1^{7gf} 4^{7gs} 8^{8f} 6^{7g} 6^{7g} 10^{6s} **1-3-11 £19,717**

Rooftop Protest (Ire) *T Hogan* 87
8 b g Thatching - Seattle Siren (USA)
8^{12sh} 2^{12hy} 8^{20s} 4^{16gf} 4^{13gf} 7^{16gf} 3^{17f} 9^{16gf} 8^{16g} 2^{16g} 3^{16gf} 11^{16g} 1^{16g} **1-4-13 £17,860**

Rooks Bridge (Ire) *G A Ham* a45
3 ch g General Monash (USA) - Lisa's Pride (Ire)
6^{6sd} **0-0-1**

Roonah (Fr) *Karen McLintock* 58 a14
2 b f Xaar - Caer Mecene (Fr)
6^{5g} 3^{5g} 2^{6g} 8^{7s} 12^{7sf} **0-2-5 £1,377**

Rooster Rellik *T D McCarthy* a26
3 ch g Mark Of Esteem (Ire) - Amaretto Flame (Ire)
11^{10sd} 10^{12sd} 18^{10g} **0-0-3**

Rosapenna (Ire) *C F Wall* 79 a71
3 b f Spectrum (Ire) - Blaine (USA)

$2^{6sd}\ 2^{7gs}\ 1^{6f}\ 4^{6gf}\ 3^{6g}\ 1^{6f}\ 4^{6g}\ 2^{6gf}\ 6^{6gf}$
2-4-9 £12,783

Roscommon *E J O'Neill* 65
2 br c Fraam - Gaelic Air
1^{6gf} **1-0-1 £2,982**

Rose Amber *J J Bridger*
4 ch f Double Trigger (Ire) - Sun Follower
11^{10sd} **0-0-1**

Rose Bien *P J McBride* 63 a54
3 b/br f Bien Bien (USA) - Madame Bovary
$5^{7gf}\ 6^{9gf}\ 2^{12sd}\ 3^{11gf}\ 5^{12sd}$ **0-2-5 £1,547**

Rose Muwasim *E A L Dunlop* 57
2 ch f In The Wings - Muwasim (USA)
4^{7gs} **0-0-1 £343**

Rose Of Glenshee (Ire) *Mrs A Duffield* 20
3 ch f Titus Livius (Fr) - Scotia Rose
$6^{12gf}\ 8^{9f}$ **0-0-2**

Rose Of Inchinor *M P Tregoning* 69
2 b f Inchinor - Rosa Canina
$11^{6gf}\ 2^{5gs}\ 3^{6g}\ 3^{5g}$ **0-3-4 £3,016**

Rose Of York (Ire) *Mrs A M Thorpe* a32
5 b m Emarati (USA) - True Ring
$9^{7sd}\ 2^{8sd}\ 9^{7sd}\ 8^{7sd}$ **0-1-4 £438**

Rosebank Lady *M Appleby*
2 b f Tomba - Dona Krista
10^{7s} **0-0-1**

Rosecliff *A M Balding* 79 a67
3 b g Montjeu (Ire) - Dance Clear (Ire)
$4^{8sd}\ 3^{9g}\ 2^{10gs}\ 1^{12gf}\ 7^{12gf}\ 8^{12gs}$ **1-2-6**
£10,358

Rosein *Mrs G S Rees* 71 a62
3 b f Komaite (USA) - Red Rosein
$7^{6sd}\ 7^{6gf}\ 4^{5s}\ 9^{6sd}\ 7^{5g}\ 15^{7g}$ **0-0-6 £576**

Roses In May (USA) *Dale Romans* a127
5 b/br h Devil His Due (USA) - Tell A Secret (USA)
$2^{9ft}\ 1^{10ft}$ **1-1-2 £1,924,479**

Rosie Mac *N Bycroft* 47
4 ch f First Trump - Carol Again
$7^{10gf}\ 6^{10gf}\ 5^{12gf}\ 6^{10gf}\ 8^{12g}\ 9^{10s}\ 3^{10gf}\ 9^{10gf}$
14^{10g} **0-0-9 £475**

Rosie Muir *Mrs A L M King* 35
3 br f Mind Games - Step On Degas
$15^{7g}\ 11^{5g}\ 7^{5f}\ 15^{5g}\ 11^{5g}$ **0-0-5**

Rosie's Result *M Todhunter* 53
5 ch g Case Law - Precious Girl
$7^{5gf}\ 9^{5gf}\ 13^{5g}\ 2^{5gf}\ 5^{5g}\ 12^{5gf}\ 8^{5gf}\ 16^{6gf}$
0-1-8 £876

Rosiella *M Blanshard* 46 a56
3 b f Tagula (Ire) - Queen Of Silk (Ire)
$13^{7sd}\ 10^{6sd}\ 6^{6hy}\ 12^{5gf}\ 12^{7gf}\ 5^{6gf}\ 11^{6g}\ 10^{7gf}$
$10^{6gs}\ 5^{5s}\ 4^{6sd}\ 2^{6sd}\ 7^{7sd}$ **0-1-13 £419**

Rosinka (Ire) *J L Dunlop* 89
2 b f Soviet Star (USA) - Last Drama (Ire)
$2^{6gf}\ 1^{6s}$ **1-1-2 £12,799**

Rosita Mia (Ire) *W G M Turner* 64 a37
2 ch f Dr Fong (USA) - Intercede
$9^{6sd}\ 12^{8sd}\ 2^{6gs}\ 6^{6hy}$ **0-1-4 £1,278**

Roslea Lady (Ire) *J R Fanshawe* 59 a61
2 b f Alhaarth (Ire) - Aguinaga (Ire)
$5^{7sd}\ 4^{8gs}\ 5^{9sd}$ **0-0-3 £380**

Ross Is Boss *C J Teague* 16
3 gr g Paris House - Billie Grey
$14^{7gf}\ 7^{6f}\ 8^{5gf}$ **0-0-3**

Ross Moor *Mrs A J Perrett* 68
3 b c Dansili - Snipe Hall
$4^{6gf}\ 9^{7g}\ 5^{10gf}\ 2^{11g}\ 14^{8gf}$ **0-1-5 £1,702**

Rossall Point *R Allan*
4 b g Fleetwood (Ire) - Loch Clair (Ire)
8^{13gs} **0-0-1**

Rossbeigh (Ire) *D R Loder* 76
3 b c Alhaarth (Ire) - Ring Of Kerry (Ire)
$3^{10g}\ 3^{12gs}$ **0-2-2 £1,481**

Rossin Gold (Ire) *P Monteith* 55
3 b g Rossini (USA) - Sacred Heart (Ire)
$6^{8gf}\ 9^{9gf}\ 4^{12gf}\ 5^{12gf}\ 5^{13s}$ **0-0-5 £267**

Rosthwaite (Ire) *E S McMahon* 71 a44
2 b f Desert Style (Ire) - Thirlmere
$3^{5sd}\ 7^{6g}\ 7^{6g}\ 1^{5gf}\ 5^{5gf}\ 6^{6g}\ 2^{5gf}\ 3^{6g}\ 3^{6g}$
1-4-9 £6,042

Rosti *Miss L A Perratt* a39
5 b g Whittingham (Ire) - Uaeflame (Ire)
$5^{7sd}\ 4^{8sd}\ 6^{7sd}\ 17^{8s}$ **0-0-4**

Rosy Finch (USA) *Sir Mark Prescott* a49
2 ch f Theatrical - Chitka (USA)
6^{7sd} **0-0-1**

Rothesay Dancer *J S Goldie* 71
2 b f Lujain (USA) - Rhinefield Beauty (Ire)
$9^{5g}\ 3^{5s}\ 5^{5gs}\ 3^{5gf}\ 12^{5gf}\ 3^{5gf}\ 2^{5gf}\ 3^{5gf}\ 2^{5gf}$
$7^{5g}\ 2^{5gf}\ 1^{5gf}$ **1-7-12 £11,535**

Rotuma (Ire) *M Dods* 71 a57
6 b g Tagula (Ire) - Cross Question (USA)
$11^{8s}\ 3^{10s}\ 6^{10g}\ 8^{11gf}\ 11^{10g}\ 6^{10gf}\ 4^{10g}\ 11^{10g}$
$5^{11gf}\ 3^{10g}\ 2^{10g}\ 5^{10s}\ 6^{10gf}\ 8^{10gf}\ 4^{10g}\ 2^{10s}\ 1^{9sd}$
3^{10sd} **1-5-18 £5,543**

Rouge Blanc (USA) *G A Harker*
5 b m King Of Kings (Ire) - Style N' Elegance (USA)
$14^{17gf}\ 9^{16f}$ **0-0-2**

Rouge Et Noir *K G Reveley* 56 a42
7 b g Hernando (Fr) - Bayrouge (Ire)
$8^{12g}\ 2^{14f}\ 1^{17f}\ 13^{14gf}\ 4^{15g}\ 3^{16gf}\ 8^{14gf}\ 5^{16gf}$
$3^{16gf}\ 6^{17sf}$ **1-1-10 £5,736**

Rowan Lodge (Ire) *M H Tompkins* 83
3 ch g Indian Lodge (Ire) - Tirol Hope (Ire)
$5^{6hy}\ 3^{6s}\ 8^{6g}\ 3^{7g}\ 5^{7gs}\ 10^{8gf}\ 5^{7s}$ **0-2-7**
£3,288

Rowan Pursuit *J Akehurst* 51 a59
4 b f Pursuit Of Love - Golden Seattle (Ire)
$9^{8sd}\ 5^{7sd}\ 2^{8sd}\ 1^{8sd}\ 4^{8sd}\ 4^{10sd}\ 2^{8sd}\ 3^{8sd}\ 8^{10s}$
$2^{10sd}\ 5^{10f}\ 8^{10sd}\ 11^{10sd}\ 2^{8f}$ **1-5-14**
£6,056

Rowan Warning *J R Boyle* 67 a31
3 b g Diktat - Golden Seattle (Ire)
$2^{7f}\ 4^{8g}\ 4^{9g}\ 3^{8g}\ 3^{9gf}\ 6^{11g}\ 4^{8g}\ 7^{9sd}$ **0-3-8**
£3,752

Rowanberry *R M H Cowell* 53 a36
3 b f Bishop Of Cashel - Raintree Venture
$6^{6sd}\ 4^{6gf}\ 2^{5gf}\ 1^{6gf}\ 3^{6g}\ 9^{5g}$ **1-2-6**
£4,527

Roxanne Mill *K A Ryan* 28 a25
7 b m Cyrano De Bergerac - It Must Be Millie
$12^{6sd}\ 14^{5sd}\ 10^{5gs}$ **0-0-3**

Roy McAvoy (Ire) *M A Barnes* 12
7 b g Danehill (USA) - Decadence
12^{7gf} **0-0-1**

Roya *R Hannon* 67
2 b c Daylami (Ire) - Aegean Dream (Ire)
$12^{7gf}\ 5^{8gf}\ 9^{8g}$ **0-0-3**

Royal Agreement *R Hannon* 55
2 b c Royal Applause - Another Fantasy (Ire)
$11^{6gs}\ 8^{7gf}\ 8^{6gf}\ 9^{6g}\ 6^{8f}$ **0-0-5**

Royal Alchemist *M D I Usher* 107
3 b f Kingsinger (Ire) - Pure Gold
2^{7gs} 5^{7gs} 5^{8gf} 7^{8gf} 6^{8g} 7^{10gs} 2^{10s} 3^{10hy}
0-3-8 £26,776

Royal Amaretto (Ire) *C Smith* 52 a15
11 b g Fairy King (USA) - Melbourne Miss
12^{9sd} 11^{9sd} 6^{10gs} 13^{10s} **0-0-4**

Royal Amnesty *G C H Chung* 53
2 b c Desert Prince (Ire) - Regal Peace
8^{5gf} 9^{5gf} 8^{6gf} **0-0-3**

Royal Atalza (Fr) *G A Huffer* 66 a59
8 gr g Saint Preuil (Fr) - Crystalza (Fr)
10^{16sd} 5^{15gf} 3^{14gf} 10^{16sd} 2^{16g} 5^{14gf} 4^{16gf} 12^{14sd}
0-2-8 £2,105

Royal Auditon *T T Clement* 65 a68
4 ch f First Trump - Loriner's Lass
3^{12sd} 3^{14s} 6^{12gf} 2^{12sd} 14^{16sd} **0-3-5**
£1,856

Royal Awakening (Ire) *R E Barr* 38 a37
4 b g Ali-Royal (Ire) - Morning Surprise
11^{9sd} 10^{8g} 9^{7sd} 8^{6gf} 7^{7g} 9^{11gf} **0-0-6**

Royal Axminster *Mrs P N Dutfield* 47 a56
10 b g Alzao (USA) - Number One Spot
3^{12sd} 7^{14sd} 13^{13sd} 7^{12g} 4^{11gf} 5^{12g} 6^{11gf} 1^{12sd}
1^{12ss} **2-1-9 £3,350**

Royal Cavalier *R Hollinshead* 90
8 b g Prince Of Birds (USA) - Gold Belt (Ire)
7^{12gf} 4^{10gf} 11^{12f} 13^{12gf} 5^{12gf} 7^{12g} 10^{14g}
0-0-7 £1,207

Royal Challenge *M H Tompkins* 85
4 b g Royal Applause - Anotheranniversary
9^{6s} 5^{7gf} 10^{6gf} 6^{7g} 1^{6g} 7^{6g} 9^{7gf} 4^{7g} 13^{7s}
1-0-9 £4,518

Royal Charter *D R Loder* a34
3 b c Royal Applause - Upend
10^{8sd} 14^{10sd} 9^{10sd} **0-0-3**

Royal Citadel (Ire) *C G Cox* 70
2 b f City On A Hill (USA) - Royal Baldini (USA)
4^{5f} 2^{6g} **0-1-2 £1,084**

Royal Composer (Ire) *T D Easterby* 73
2 b c Mozart (Ire) - Susun Kelapa (USA)
3^{6gf} 8^{6gs} **0-0-2 £1,125**

Royal Cozyfire (Ire) *B Palling* 43 a29
3 b g Revoque (Ire) - Mystic Thoughts (Ire)
13^{6gs} 11^{6gs} 9^{6f} 9^{7g} 14^{6f} 8^{6g} 5^{6gf} 6^{6sd} 14^{6gf}
11^{5sd} **0-0-10**

Royal Curtsy *Sir Mark Prescott* 54
2 b f Pivotal - Fen Princess (Ire)
7^{5f} 10^{7g} 7^{6gs} **0-0-3**

Royal Devon (Ire) *Mrs P N Dutfield* 46
2 b g Mujadil (USA) - Cookawara (Ire)
11^{6gs} 7^{7g} 11^{8g} **0-0-3**

Royal Dignitary (USA) *D Nicholls* 82
5 br g Saint Ballado (Can) - Star Actress (USA)
8^{8s} 14^{8gs} 6^{7f} 5^{9g} 7^{8gf} 13^{8gs} 3^{7gf} 3^{9gf} 1^{8gf}
12^{8g} **1-2-10 £9,313**

Royal Distant (USA) *M W Easterby* 58
4 ch f Distant View (USA) - Encorenous (USA)
8^{12g} 6^{12gf} **0-0-2**

Royal Embrace *D Shaw* 50 a53
2 b g Bertolini (USA) - Tight Spin
18^{5g} 6^{5s} 9^{8gf} 4^{6hy} 2^{7sd} 14^{8sd} 8^{8sd} **0-1-7**
£1,161

Royal Engineer *Unknown* 77
2 b g Royal Applause - Iris May
5^{5g} 1^{5gf} 6^{6g} **1-0-3 £4,525**

Royal Envoy (Ire) *B W Hills* 76
2 b c Royal Applause - Seven Notes
8^{6gf} 5^{6gs} **0-0-2**

Royal Fantasy (Ire) *J R Fanshawe* 52
2 b/br f King's Best (USA) - Dreams
13^{7g} **0-0-1**

Royal Fashion (Ire) *I W McInnes* a27
5 b m Ali-Royal (Ire) - Fun Fashion (Ire)
13^{9sd} 10^{6sd} **0-0-2**

Royal Flight *D J Daly* 49
4 b g Royal Applause - Duende
3^{6gf} **0-1-1 £435**

Royal Flynn *M Dods* 75
3 b g Royal Applause - Shamriyna (Ire)
1^{12g} 2^{12g} 7^{12gf} 3^{12g} 7^{12gs} 8^{14gf} 8^{12gf} 5^{10g} 5^{12gf}
4^{11gs} **1-2-10 £5,906**

Royal Game *M L W Bell* 41 a28
3 b g Vettori (Ire) - Ground Game
10^{10g} 12^{9sd} 7^{11f} 10^{16g} 4^{12g} **0-0-5 £268**

Royal Glen (Ire) *W S Coltherd* 49
7 b m Royal Abjar (USA) - Sea Glen (Ire)
5^{10gf} **0-0-1**

Royal Grand *J R Weymes* a21
5 ch h Prince Sabo - Hemline
12^{6sd} **0-0-1**

Royal Island (Ire) *M Johnston* 106
3 b c Trans Island - Royal House (Fr)
7^{8gs} 1^{8hy} 2^{10s} 5^{12g} 4^{8g} 1^{8gf} 2^{8s} 4^{8g}
2-2-8 £31,765

Royal Jelly *J H M Gosden* 76
3 b f King's Best (USA) - Baked Alaska
7^{7f} 6^{8gs} 7^{8g} **0-0-3**

Royal Jet *M R Channon* 91
3 b g Royal Applause - Red Bouquet
11^{10g} 1^{10f} 9^{10gf} 6^{12gf} 4^{10gf} 2^{11gf} 2^{10g} 2^{10g}
1^{12g} 10^{10g} 4^{12gf} 2^{12g} 3^{11gf} 2^{12g} **2-6-14**
£26,792

Royal Lass *Rae Guest* a18
2 b f Fraam - Sabotini
8^{5sd} 10^{7sd} 12^{7sd} **0-0-3**

Royal Logic *M R Channon*
4 b f Royal Applause - Lucie Edward
12^{8sd} **0-0-1**

Royal Lustre *M Todhunter* 23 a53
4 b g Deputy Minister (Can) - Snow Bride (USA)
4^{12sd} 2^{12sd} 3^{12sd} 8^{12sd} 5^{12gf} 8^{9gf} **0-2-6**
£836

Royal Master *P C Haslam* 65 a60
3 b g Royal Applause - High Sevens
3^{6sd} 11^{8gf} 8^{8g} 7^{8gf} 2^{8g} 6^{10gf} 2^{8gf} **0-3-7**
£2,734

Royal Melbourne (Ire) *Miss J A Camacho* 66 a57
5 ch g Among Men (USA) - Calachuchi
3^{12sd} 12^{11sd} 1^{12s} 9^{12gs} 2^{12g} 3^{12sd} 2^{14sd} 11^{14sd}
8^{12gs} 3^{12gf} 4^{12s} 4^{12s} **1-6-12 £7,125**

Royal Millennium (Ire) *M R Channon* 107
7 b g Royal Academy (USA) - Galatrix
4^{6g} 10^{6s} 4^{6f} 15^{6gs} 6^{6g} **0-0-5 £14,900**

Royal Miss *R M Beckett* 59
3 b f Royal Applause - Foreign Mistress
12^{8g} 2^{8s} 6^{10f} 8^{10f} 7^{10g} 7^{10s} 19^{8gf} **0-1-7**
£1,066

Royal Moon (USA) *T D Barron* 50
2 ch g Royal Academy (USA) - Wedding Gift (Fr)

10^{6f} 6^{7gf} 7^{7gf} **0-0-3**

Royal Nite Owl *J Balding* a43
4 b g Royal Applause - Nite-Owl Dancer
6^{5sd} 5^{5sd} 2^{5sd} **0-1-3 £417**

Royal Orissa *D Haydn Jones* 96
3 b g Royal Applause - Ling Lane
1^{6gs} 3^{6s} 5^{6g} 11^{7gf} 16^{7gf} 12^{6gf} 22^{7gs}
1-1-7 £9,889

Royal Pardon *R C Guest* 55
3 b f Royal Applause - Miss Mercy (Ire)
8^{7gs} 7^{6f} 3^{6gf} 3^{7gf} 8^{7f} **0-2-5 £919**

Royal Pavillion (Ire) *W J Musson*
4 b g Cape Cross (Ire) - Regal Scintilla
PU^{6sd} **0-0-1**

Royal Power (Ire) *M R Channon* 96
2 b c Xaar - Magic Touch
3^{5gs} 5^{5s} 2^{5gf} 1^{7g} 3^{7s} 2^{7s} 2^{7gy} **1-4-7**
£40,046

Royal Premier (Ire) *H J Collingridge* 62
2 b c King's Theatre (Ire) - Mystic Shadow (Ire)
6^{7s} 12^{8g} 5^{8s} 17^{8hy} **0-0-4**

Royal Prince *J R Fanshawe* 106
4 gr c Royal Applause - Onefortheditch (USA)
2^{8g} 5^{8g} 4^{8gf} 3^{10gf} 4^{8gf} 5^{7gf} 2^{9gf} 13^{9s}
0-4-8 £18,471

Royal Proposal *L M Cumani* 98
2 b f King's Best (USA) - Mrs Ting (USA)
1^{8g} 2^{7gf} **1-1-2 £7,191**

Royal Punch *T D Easterby* 42
2 b f Royal Applause - Macina (Ire)
9^{6gf} **0-0-1**

Royal Racer (Fr) *J R Best* 15
7 b g Danehill (USA) - Green Rosy (USA)
7^{9gf} **0-0-1**

Royal Rebel *M Johnston* 105
9 b g Robellino (USA) - Greenvera (USA)
8^{16g} 6^{22f} **0-0-2 £525**

Royal Reservation *P W Chapple-Hyam* 64 a73
2 b c Royal Applause - Wig Wam (Ire)
6^{6gf} 6^{7gf} 1^{8sd} **1-0-3 £3,785**

Royal Sailor (Ire) *Julian Poulton* 61 a50
3 b g Bahhare (USA) - Old Tradition (Ire)
6^{12gf} 4^{9gf} 5^{10gf} 16^{10g} 11^{12sd} 11^{12ss} 7^{8sd}
0-0-7 £269

Royal Sapphire (USA) *M Johnston* 51
3 b c Kingmambo (USA) - Amethyst (Ire)
7^{9g} **0-0-1**

Royal Session (Ire) *D Carroll* a12
5 b m Accordion - Mrs Keppel
8^{12sd} 11^{7sd} **0-0-2**

Royal Shakespeare (Fr) *S Gollings* a61
6 b g King's Theatre (Ire) - Persian Walk (Fr)
8^{14sd} **0-0-1**

Royal Song *D Shaw* 32
2 b c Royal Applause - La Caprice (USA)
10^{5gs} 7^{6gf} 10^{5g} **0-0-3**

Royal Storm (Ire) *Mrs A J Perrett* 106
6 b h Royal Applause - Wakayi
7^{7g} 3^{6gf} 12^{6f} 4^{7g} 24^{7gf} 4^{7gs} 9^{7g} 7^{7g} 7^{7gf}
0-0-9 £12,270

Royal Tavira Girl (Ire) *M G Quinlan* 53
2 b f Orpen (USA) - Just Like Annie (Ire)
9^{5f} **0-0-1**

Royal Trigger *Ian Williams* a54
5 b g Double Trigger (Ire) - Jeronime (USA)
13^{12sd} 4^{14sd} 11^{17sd} **0-0-3**

Royal Upstart *M B Shears* 37
4 b g Up And At 'Em - Tycoon Tina
5^{8sd} 10^{12s} 4^{10g} 15^{12gf} **0-0-4**

Royal Wedding *N J Gifford* 69 a74
3 b g King's Best (USA) - Liaison (USA)
1^{8sd} 6^{9sd} 2^{9sd} 15^{10g} 7^{8gs} 4^{10f} 15^{11g}
1-2-7 £5,947

Royal Windmill (Ire) *M D Hammond* 53 a17
6 b g Ali-Royal (Ire) - Salarya (Fr)
10^{6sd} 4^{6gs} 9^{7g} 4^{6g} 2^{7gf} 2^{7gf} 6^{6gf} 12^{7g} 20^{6gf}
15^{6gf} **0-2-10 £1,750**

Royal Wish *J M P Eustace* 39
3 b f Royal Applause - Be My Wish
14^{6gf} 6^{7g} **0-0-2**

Royale Acadou (Fr) *Mrs L J Mongan* 56 a20
7 b/br m Cadoudal (Fr) - Girl Vamp (Fr)
4^{12gf} 9^{12gf} 13^{12sd} 16^{16g} **0-0-4 £362**

Royale Pearl *R Ingram* a47
5 gr m Cloudings (Ire) - Ivy Edith
3^{16sd} 9^{13sd} **0-1-2 £202**

Royalties *M A Allen*
3 b f Mujahid (USA) - Rock Face
9^{10gs} **0-0-1**

Royle Dancer *R Hollinshead* 56 a63
2 b g Makbul - Foxtrot Pie
10^{6sd} 8^{6gf} 7^{7gf} 13^{6g} 2^{7sf} **0-1-5 £1,111**

Rozaria *J Balding*
2 b f Defacto (USA) - Archello (Ire)
14^{6gf} **0-0-1**

Rubber (Ire) *R Hannon* 85
2 b f Namid - Bold Fashion (Fr)
3^{6gs} 3^{6gf} 5^{5gf} **0-2-3 £2,239**

Rubenstar (Ire) *M H Tompkins* 78
2 b g Soviet Star (USA) - Ansariya (USA)
12^{6gf} 6^{6g} 5^{6g} 2^{7gf} 1^{6gf} 14^{6g} 1^{7g} **2-1-7**
£10,031

Rubies *R F Johnson Houghton* 76
3 ch f Inchinor - Fur Will Fly
2^{6gf} 4^{7gf} 5^{6gs} 4^{7g} 4^{6gf} 1^{6g} 7^{5g} **1-1-7**
£6,355

Rubileo *Mrs A J Perrett* 56 a46
2 b f Galileo (Ire) - Ruby Affair (Ire)
5^{7gf} 9^{7sd} 12^{10sd} **0-0-3**

Ruby Brown *C A Cyzer* 67 a69
3 b f Polar Falcon (USA) - Raspberry Sauce
6^{7gf} 6^{8gs} 12^{8gf} 2^{8sd} **0-1-4 £1,112**

Ruby Legend *K G Reveley* 57
7 b g Perpendicular - Singing High
11^{9f} 9^{8gf} 12^{8gf} 4^{11gf} 4^{10g} 14^{11g} 2^{10s} 2^{9gf}
12^{8gf} 5^{10gf} 9^{10gs} 16^{10s} **0-3-12 £2,560**

Ruby Muja *T G McCourt* 52 a48
3 b f Mujahid (USA) - Ruby Julie
4^{5sd} 6^{5sd} 3^{5sd} 7^{5sd} 5^{9gf} 12^{6g} 14^{5g} **0-0-7**
£412

Ruby Murray *B J Meehan* a51
3 b f Zafonic (USA) - Poppadam
6^{9sd} 5^{8sd} 3^{9sd} **0-1-3 £519**

Ruby Rocket (Ire) *H Morrison* 105
4 b f Indian Rocket - Geht Schnell
7^{6gf} 4^{7g} 5^{6g} 1^{6g} 2^{6s} 4^{6gs} **1-1-6**
£27,979

Ruby Rubble *K R Burke* 50
2 b f Distant Music (USA) - Topwinder (USA)
3^{6f} 10^{7g} 7^{5g} **0-0-3 £542**

Ruby Sunrise (Ire) *B P J Baugh* 47 a55
3 ch f Polish Precedent (USA) - Kinlochewe
3^{6sd} 7^{7sd} 8^{7sd} 6^{7gs} 9^{8gf} 5^{7sd} 7^{8gf} 12^{8gf} 2^{7sd} 20^{7gf} 8^{6ft} 9^{7sd} **0-2-12 £1,078**

Ruby Wine *J M P Eustace* 105
3 b f Kayf Tara - Cribella (USA)
4^{10gs} 1^{10gf} 4^{12gf} 5^{12gs} 8^{10g} **1-0-5 £21,991**

Ruby's Dream *J M Bradley* 61
3 b f Tipsy Creek (USA) - Sure Flyer (Ire)
8^{5gs} 9^{6s} 11^{5gf} 10^{6g} 2^{6gf} 4^{6gf} 1^{6g} 6^{6s} 2^{6g} 4^{6g} 4^{6gf} 6^{7g} 15^{6g} 17^{6g} **1-3-14 £8,694**

Rudaki *M E Sowersby* 54 a56
3 ch g Opening Verse (USA) - Persian Fountain (Ire)
14^{10s} 6^{8gf} 5^{9gf} 12^{12gf} 4^{10gs} 1^{9sf} **1-1-6 £1,777**

Rudi's Pet (Ire) *D Nicholls* 80
11 ch g Don't Forget Me - Pink Fondant
8^{6g} 6^{6g} 4^{5g} 2^{6gf} 2^{5gf} 1^{5gf} 1^{5f} 12^{5s} 7^{5gf} 7^{5gf} **2-3-10 £14,887**

Ruffed *M A Jarvis* 47 a52
4 br g First Trump - Maristax
2^{12sd} 11^{10gs} 7^{11gf} 6^{12sd} **0-1-4 £1,036**

Ruffie (Ire) *Miss Gay Kelleway* 52 a65
2 b f Medicean - Darling Lover (USA)
5^{6gf} 6^{7gf} 8^{6g} 6^{7s} 2^{7sd} 1^{9sd} **1-1-6 £4,182**

Ruggtah *P D Niven* 52
4 gr f Daylami (Ire) - Raneen Alwatar
9^{12s} 10^{12g} 9^{12gf} **0-0-3**

Ruin *John A Harris*
7 b g Polish Precedent (USA) - Trojan Desert
16^{12s} **0-0-1**

Rule For Ever *M Johnston* 75
3 br g Diktat - Tous Les Jours (USA)
3^{11s} 9^{12gf} 6^{12gf} 5^{12gf} 1^{14gf} 2^{16gf} 1^{17g} 4^{16gf} 8^{18gs} **2-0-9 £12,390**

Ruler's Gold (USA) *Saeed Bin Suroor* 79
2 b c Rahy (USA) - Crystal Crossing (Ire)
3^{8gs} **0-1-1 £828**

Ruling Reef *M D I Usher* 57 a44
3 b f Diktat - Horseshoe Reef
11^{7sd} 6^{8sd} 5^{10g} 14^{10g} 8^{11f} 1^{8f} 15^{10f} 4^{10f} 9^{8f} 2^{10s} 1^{10gs} 8^{11g} 11^{10g} 10^{9sd} **2-1-14 £8,309**

Rum Destiny (Ire) *J S Wainwright* a7
6 b g Mujadil (USA) - Ruby River
12^{6sd} **0-0-1**

Ruman (Ire) *M J Attwater* 62 a58
3 b g Fayruz - Starway To Heaven (Ity)
6^{6s} 3^{6gs} 1^{6gs} 4^{7gf} 9^{6gs} 8^{8sf} 5^{7sd} **1-2-7 £3,406**

Rumbalara *X Nakkachdji* 81
3 b f Intikhab (USA) - Bint Zamayem (Ire)
2^{10g} 7^{10gf} 0^{10gs} **0-1-3 £2,126**

Rumbling Bridge *Miss J S Davis* 22
4 ch g Air Express (Ire) - Rushing River (USA)
12^{12g} **0-0-1**

Rumplestiltskin (Ire) *A P O'Brien* 112
2 b f Danehill (USA) - Monevassia (USA)
1^{6g} 1^{6g} 3^{6gf} 1^{7g} 1^{7g} 1^{8gs} **5-1-6 £350,807**

Run On *D G Bridgwater* 37 a37
7 b h Runnett - Polar Storm (Ire)
6^{6sd} 7^{7sd} 9^{6f} 13^{5ss} **0-0-4**

Runaway Ruby *B J McMath* 36 a25
11 ch m Respect - Chrislim Vii
14^{7g} 10^{8gf} 7^{7f} 9^{6sd} 11^{6g} **0-0-5**

Rundear (Ire) *M R Channon* 37
2 b f Danehill Dancer (Ire) - Comprehension (USA)
6^{5gs} 8^{5g} **0-0-2**

Running On Empty *Ms Deborah J Evans* 20 a17
2 b g College Chapel - Abstone Queen
9^{7gf} 9^{7sd} 11^{5sd} **0-0-3**

Running Times (USA) *H J Manners* a19
8 b g Brocco (USA) - Concert Peace (USA)
9^{10sd} **0-0-1**

Ruse *J R Fanshawe* a41
2 b f Diktat - Reuval
6^{7sd} **0-0-1**

Russalka *Julian Poulton* 47 a36
4 b f Opening Verse (USA) - Philarmonique (Fr)
8^{8gf} 4^{8g} 8^{9sd} 4^{10g} 14^{13sd} 5^{10g} 5^{8hy} **0-0-7**

Russian Applause *P R Chamings* a52
5 b g Royal Applause - Zeffirella
6^{8sd} 14^{7sd} **0-0-2**

Russian Cafe (Ire) *N Tinkler* 36 a28
4 b f Stravinsky (USA) - Bistro (USA)
9^{6sd} 12^{6s} 18^{8g} 14^{6f} 12^{7gs} 10^{11gf} **0-0-6**

Russian General (Ire) *P F I Cole* 47 a65
3 b c Soviet Star (USA) - Azra (Ire)
6^{8sd} 15^{8gf} 14^{7gs} 6^{8gf} 8^{6f} **0-0-5**

Russian Rio (Ire) *P C Haslam* a40
3 b g Imperial Ballet (Ire) - L'Harmonie (USA)
7^{5sd} **0-0-1**

Russian Rocket (Ire) *Mrs C A Dunnett* 64 a57
3 b g Indian Rocket - Soviet Girl (Ire)
9^{5g} 8^{5gs} 9^{6sd} **0-0-3**

Russian Symphony (USA) *C R Egerton* 95 a98
4 ch g Stravinsky (USA) - Backwoods Teacher (USA)
2^{7sd} 1^{6sd} 2^{6sd} 3^{6sd} 3^{6g} 7^{6g} 4^{6gf} 6^{6gs} 2^{6gf} 16^{6gs} 2^{6sd} 7^{7sd} 11^{6sd} **1-6-13 £22,900**

Rust En Vrede *D Carroll* 33
6 b g Royal Applause - Souveniers
15^{8gf} 7^{10gf} **0-0-2**

Rustler *R Charlton* 82
3 b c Green Desert (USA) - Borgia
8^{8gs} 7^{8g} 2^{8gf} 6^{10gf} 2^{8gs} 2^{9g} 1^{8f} 1^{8gs} **2-3-8 £11,320**

Rutters Rebel (Ire) *N Tinkler* 55
4 b g Entrepreneur - No Quest (Ire)
6^{12gf} 10^{14gf} 8^{12gf} 10^{12g} 14^{10g} 14^{10gf} 18^{12g} **0-0-7**

Ryan's Bliss (Ire) *T D McCarthy* 48 a48
5 b m Danetime (Ire) - Raja Moulana
8^{8sd} 11^{8sd} 8^{10s} 9^{10sd} 4^{10sd} 11^{10sd} 10^{10sd} 7^{12gf} 2^{8sd} 3^{11g} **0-2-10 £536**

Ryan's Future (Ire) *J Akehurst* 87
5 b h Danetime (Ire) - Era
14^{10gf} 7^{10gf} 12^{10s} 4^{12gf} 1^{10g} 5^{10g} 7^{10hy} 12^{12hy} **1-0-8 £6,873**

Ryan's Quest (Ire) *T D McCarthy* a48
6 b m Mukaddamah (USA) - Preponderance (Ire)
9^{5sd} 4^{5sd} 4^{5sd} 8^{5sd} 7^{6sd} 8^{6sd} **0-0-6 £569**

Rydal (USA) *E J Alston* 90 a94
4 ch g Gilded Time (USA) - Tennis Partner (USA)
2^{6sd} 9^{5ft} 2^{6sd} 3^{7sd} 5^{6g} 11^{6gf} 9^{6g} 11^{7gs} 7^{5g} 2^{6sd} 8^{6gf} 2^{5sd} **0-5-12 £18,789**

Ryedale Ovation (Ire) *T D Easterby* 79
2 b g Royal Applause - Passe Passe (USA)

5^{5g} 1^{5g} 3^{5g} 8^{6g} **1-0-4 £9,599**

Ryedane (Ire) *T D Easterby* 84 a81
3 b g Danetime (Ire) - Miss Valediction (Ire)
11^{6g} 1^{5gf} 7^{6gf} 8^{6gf} 13^{5gs} 11^{5gs} 10^{5s} 1^{6sd} **2-0-8 £9,652**

Ryhope Chief (Ire) *M F Harris* 46
2 b g Indian Danehill (Ire) - Rachel Pringle (Ire)
7^{7g} 10^{6g} 9^{6f} 9^{8gf} **0-0-4**

Rymer's Rascal *E J Alston*
13 b g Rymer - City Sound
12^{9sd} **0-0-1**

Saabiq (USA) *C E Brittain* 95
2 br f Grand Slam (USA) - Lucky Lineage (USA)
6^{6gf} 1^{6gf} 7^{7s} 2^{6gf} 7^{7gs} 11^{7gs} **1-1-6 £10,782**

Saadigg (Ire) *M A Jarvis* 92
3 b g Indian Danehill (Ire) - White Cap'S
1^{12g} 3^{11f} 8^{16gf} **1-1-3 £11,196**

Saameq (Ire) *A C Whillans* 22 a59
4 b g Bahhare (USA) - Tajawuz
1^{12sd} 8^{11sd} 9^{17sd} 8^{12sd} 10^{12gs} 15^{12g} 5^{12s} 5^{12sd} 1^{12sd} **2-0-9 £4,468**

Sabana (Ire) *J M Bradley* a47
7 b g Sri Pekan (USA) - Atyaaf (USA)
6^{6sd} 9^{6sd} 8^{6sd} **0-0-3**

Sabbeeh (USA) *Saeed Bin Suroor* 114
4 b c Red Ransom (USA) - Capistrano Day (USA)
7^{7gf} 9^{8gf} 4^{7g} 2^{7g} 3^{8s} 2^{7g} 2^{7hy} **0-5-7 £23,794**

Sabbiosa (Ire) *J L Dunlop* 67 a56
3 b f Desert Prince (Ire) - Alla Marcia (Ire)
1^{8g} 4^{10f} 14^{10gf} 11^{10sd} **1-0-4 £4,033**

Sabo Prince *J M Bradley* 47 a37
3 ch g Atraf - Moving Princess
9^{6sd} 4^{6sd} 5^{6sd} 9^{6g} 5^{6sd} 1^{7gf} 14^{7g} 15^{7gf} 10^{6g} **1-0-9 £3,129**

Sabre D'Argent (USA) *Saeed Bin Suroor* 109
5 br h Kris S (USA) - Sterling Pound (USA)
1^{10gf} **1-0-1 £8,444**

Sabrina Brown *J A Geake* 91 a46
4 br f Polar Falcon (USA) - So True
7^{7g} 1^{6gs} 17^{6gf} 12^{7s} 11^{8sd} 10^{6sd} **1-0-6 £6,805**

Saccharine *M J Polglase* a10
4 b f Whittingham (Ire) - Sweet And Lucky
8^{12sd} 11^{8sd} **0-0-2**

Sachin *J R Boyle* 57 a65
4 b g Bijou D'Inde - Dark Kristal (Ire)
7^{10s} 3^{10sd} 14^{10g} 6^{10gf} 10^{12sd} 6^{10sd} 15^{10gf} 18^{10g} 4^{12sd} 9^{10sd} 6^{12g} 5^{12sd} **0-1-12 £534**

Sachsenwalzer (Ger) *C Grant* 56 a21
7 ch g Top Waltz (Fr) - Stairway To Heaven (Ger)
4^{10s} 4^{8gf} 5^{8gf} 10^{7gf} 8^{8sd} **0-0-5 £257**

Sacranun *L M Cumani* 88
3 ch c Pivotal - Spanish Craft (Ire)
5^{8s} 3^{10gs} 2^{10s} 1^{10gf} **1-2-4 £10,360**

Saddell (Ire) *T D Easterby* 22
2 b f Mull Of Kintyre (USA) - Sharpe's Lady
7^{5s} 8^{5gs} 12^{6gf} **0-0-3**

Saddler's Quest *B P J Baugh* a40
8 b g Saddlers' Hall (Ire) - Seren Quest
5^{12sd} 11^{13sd} **0-0-2**

Saddlers Boy *R Johnson*
7 b g Saddlers' Hall (Ire) - Miss Poll Flinders
12^{10s} **0-0-1**

Sadie *M W Easterby*
2 b f Foxhound (USA) - Prima Sinfonia
9^{5s} **0-0-1**

Sadie's Star (Ire) *M Dods* 39
3 b f Indian Lodge (Ire) - Nishiki (USA)
5^{9gs} 9^{7gf} 8^{10g} 14^{14gf} **0-0-4**

Sadler's Cove (Fr) *Mrs A M Thorpe* 46 a53
7 b g King's Theatre (Ire) - Mine D'Or (Fr)
4^{16sd} 2^{12sd} 2^{16sd} 14^{12sd} 10^{16sd} 8^{13sd} 11^{13sd} 12^{12sd} 4^{12gf} 9^{12sd} **0-2-10 £1,880**

Sadlers Senor (Ire) *J O'Reilly* 35
3 b g Imperial Ballet (Ire) - Mechilie
15^{9gf} 4^{12f} 7^{11gf} UR^{16g} 13^{8sd} **0-0-5 £264**

Safaah *G Prodromou* a38
2 b c Almushtarak (Ire) - Lawn Order
9^{7sd} **0-0-1**

Safari *R J Hodges* 50
2 b f Namaqualand (USA) - Breakfast Creek
11^{5g} 8^{5gf} 9^{7g} 6^{5f} **0-0-4**

Safari Mischief *P Winkworth* 67
2 b g Primo Valentino (Ire) - Night Gypsy
4^{5hy} 3^{5f} 5^{6g} 9^{7gf} 6^{5g} **0-0-5 £915**

Safari Sunset (Ire) *P Winkworth* 95
3 b g Fayruz - Umlani (Ire)
5^{5gs} 19^{5g} 4^{6gf} 6^{7s} 12^{7g} 14^{6g} 6^{6gf} 5^{6g} 11^{6gs} **0-0-9 £2,837**

Safe Harbour *Sir Mark Prescott* a45
3 b f Docksider (USA) - Number One Spot
6^{6sd} 8^{6sd} 5^{6sd} F^{9gf} **0-0-4**

Safe Shot *Mrs J C McGregor* 47
6 b g Salse (USA) - Optaria
6^{9gf} 10^{14gf} 10^{12gf} 5^{12f} 5^{12gf} 7^{12g} **0-0-6**

Safendonseabiscuit *S Kirk* a62
3 b c Danzig Connection (USA) - The Fugative
2^{6sd} **0-1-1 £842**

Saffa Garden (Ire) *C E Brittain* 17 a33
3 b f King's Best (USA) - Allegheny River (USA)
13^{7gf} 7^{6sd} 7^{8sd} 13^{5sd} 9^{8sd} **0-0-5**

Saffron Fox *J G Portman* 70 a76
4 ch f Safawan - Fox Oa (Fr)
4^{10sd} 8^{11gs} 3^{12s} 10^{20s} 3^{18g} 6^{14gf} 4^{16sd} 7^{14gs} 3^{16sd} 11^{17sd} 2^{16sf} 10^{16sd} 7^{16sd} **0-3-13 £3,534**

Saffron River *R Hollinshead* a53
4 b c Polar Prince (Ire) - Cloudy Reef
8^{5sd} 8^{7sd} 6^{6sd} 8^{6sd} 8^{6sd} **0-0-5**

Saffwah (Ire) *Saeed Bin Suroor* 82
2 b f King's Best (USA) - Saafeya (Ire)
2^{6gf} **0-1-1 £1,752**

Safirah *W M Brisbourne* 69 a57
4 b f Singspiel (Ire) - Princess Haifa (USA)
9^{10g} 7^{12g} 9^{12gf} 4^{10gf} 4^{12gf} 4^{12gf} 5^{11gf} 9^{12g} 5^{11gf} 5^{12sd} **0-0-10 £1,129**

Safqa *B W Hills* 70
2 b f Singspiel (Ire) - Shamah
3^{7s} **0-1-1 £882**

Safranine (Ire) *Miss A Stokell* 54 a52
8 b m Dolphin Street (Fr) - Webbiana
2^{5sd} 4^{5sd} 5^{5sd} 2^{6sd} 8^{6sd} 8^{5sd} 11^{6sd} 11^{5gf} 9^{5sd} 20^{6gf} 9^{5g} 9^{5gf} 3^{5gf} 6^{5sd} 6^{5sd} 11^{5sd} 10^{5ss} **0-3-17 £1,917**

Safsoof (USA) *Saeed Bin Suroor* 93 a82
3 b c Gilded Time (USA) - Halcyon Bird (Ire)
6^{9ft} 6^{7gf} 3^{7gf} 6^{7gf} 2^{7g} 1^{7gf} 9^{7gs} **1-2-7 £10,934**

Sahaat *C R Dore* 57 a56
7 b/br g Machiavellian (USA) - Tawaaded (Ire)
10^{16sd} 10^{12sd} 10^{13sd} 12^{10g} 8^{10g} 9^{12gf} 11^{12g} 10^{16gf} **0-0-8**

Sahara Mist (Ire) *D Shaw* a15
3 b f Desert Style (Ire) - Tereed Elhawa
8^{6sd} 8^{7sd} 7^{8sd} 7^{8sd} 9^{6s} **0-0-5**

Sahara Prince (Ire) *K A Morgan* 89 a63
5 b h Desert King (Ire) - Chehana
13^{6hy} 11^{6sh} 1^{7gf} 8^{8gf} 21^{6gf} 3^{7g} 13^{7gf} 12^{8g} 17^{8g} 11^{7sd} 7^{7sd} 5^{7sd} **1-1-12 £8,106**

Sahara Secret (Ire) *D Shaw* a26
2 b f Revoque (Ire) - Buddy And Soda (Ire)
10^{5sd} 14^{6sd} 11^{7sd} **0-0-3**

Sahara Silk (Ire) *D Shaw* 69 a67
4 b f Desert Style (Ire) - Buddy And Soda (Ire)
7^{6sd} 7^{5sd} 13^{5sd} 11^{5sd} 3^{5sd} 13^{5g} 1^{5gf} 1^{5gf} 2^{5gf} 9^{6gf} 5^{6sd} 1^{5gf} 6^{5g} 4^{5g} 5^{5gf} **3-2-15 £17,465**

Sahara Style *R Hollinshead* 44 a54
2 b g Desert Style (Ire) - Scapavia (Fr)
11^{8s} 8^{9sd} 3^{8ss} 13^{8sd} 7^{9sd} **0-1-5 £596**

Sahara Sun (Ire) *W R Muir* 49 a20
2 b f Desert Sun - Perfect Rainbow
9^{8g} 9^{8sd} **0-0-2**

Sahara Sunset (Ire) *D Shaw* 22
3 b f Desert Style (Ire) - Ervedya (Ire)
10^{6gs} 12^{6g} 11^{5sd} 18^{5s} **0-0-4**

Saharan Song (Ire) *Jean-Rene Auvray* a57
4 ch f Singspiel (Ire) - Sahara Baladee (USA)
6^{10sd} 4^{9sd} **0-0-2**

Sahem (Ire) *T J Fitzgerald* 12
8 b g Sadler's Wells (USA) - Sumava (Ire)
11^{12gf} **0-0-1**

Sahf London *G L Moore* 37
2 b g Vettori (Ire) - Lumiere D'Espoir (Fr)
11^{9gf} 5^{9gs} **0-0-2 £387**

Saida Lenasera (Fr) *Mrs P Sly* 71
4 b f Fasliyev (USA) - Lanasara
2^{16gs} 1^{16g} 3^{14g} 2^{16gf} 3^{16s} 8^{15gf} **1-3-6 £6,004**

Saif Sareea *R A Fahey* 69
5 b g Atraf - Slipperose
4^{10gs} 1^{10g} 8^{10gs} 1^{10g} 8^{10g} 4^{8gf} 4^{10s} **2-2-7 £7,296**

Sailing Days *C A Cyzer* 63 a55
3 b f Kris - Uncharted Waters
11^{7gs} 5^{8g} 5^{11gs} 3^{8sd} 11^{10gs} 3^{9g} 5^{12sd} **0-2-7 £2,244**

Sailor A'Hoy *M Mullineaux*
9 b g Handsome Sailor - Eye Sight
13^{12gs} **0-0-1**

Saint Bernadette *J J Quinn* 21
2 b f Bertolini (USA) - Primulette
8^{5g} 11^{5g} **0-0-2**

Saint Etienne (Ire) *A M Balding* 92
4 b f Robellino (USA) - Stop Out
5^{6g} 6^{5gs} 7^{5s} 3^{6gf} 5^{6gf} 1^{6gf} 8^{6gs} 2^{6f} **1-2-8 £24,637**

Saint Lazare (Ire) *J G Given* 39 a29
4 b c Peintre Celebre (USA) - Height Of Passion
13^{14gs} 14^{10gf} 13^{12sd} 9^{13gs} 13^{13gs} **0-0-5**

Saint Liam (USA) *R Dutrow Jr* a129
5 b h Saint Ballado (Can) - Quiet Dance (USA)
1^{9ft} 6^{10ft} 1^{9ft} 2^{9ft} 1^{9ft} 1^{10ft} **4-1-6 £1,900,313**

Saint Nick *J J Bridger*
2 b g Delta Dancer - Queen's Hat
11^{6sd} **0-0-1**

Sainte Just (Ire) *W J Musson* 65 a71
6 b g Polish Precedent (USA) - Charlotte Corday
6^{11sd} 1^{12sd} 3^{13sd} 4^{13sd} 7^{13s} **1-1-5 £4,178**

Saintly Place *C Smith* 45 a55
4 ch g Compton Place - Always On A Sunday
5^{7sd} 7^{6sd} 1^{5sd} 10^{5gf} 13^{6gf} 15^{5gf} 15^{5gf} 18^{8gf} 5^{6sd} 9^{5sd} **1-0-10 £1,442**

Saintly Rachel (Ire) *C F Swan* 101
7 b m Religiously (USA) - Ursha (Ire)
1^{10s} 2^{12ys} 3^{10s} 3^{12gf} 7^{12f} 5^{11g} **1-2-6 £22,620**

Saintly Thoughts (USA) *R J Hodges* 32 a55
10 b/br g St Jovite (USA) - Free Thinker (USA)
4^{17sd} 1^{17sd} 7^{17sd} 1^{16sd} 5^{17sd} 8^{17sd} 12^{16g} 11^{17sd} 6^{16sd} 9^{16g} **2-0-10 £5,478**

Sakabula (USA) *G C Bravery* 66
2 b f King Of Kings (Ire) - Sianema
6^{6gf} 1^{6gs} 9^{6g} 10^{8gf} **1-0-4 £4,241**

Sake (Ire) *N Tinkler* 69
3 b g Shinko Forest (Ire) - Drosera (Ire)
4^{8g} 2^{8g} 7^{8g} 1^{7gf} 3^{8gs} 6^{8g} 2^{8gf} 8^{8g} 5^{8gf} 8^{8gf} 8^{8g} **1-3-11 £9,117**

Salamanca *S Kirk* 101 a92
3 ch f Pivotal - Salanka (Ire)
6^{7gs} 9^{7s} 11^{6gf} 11^{7gf} 2^{7g} 2^{7s} 5^{7g} 3^{6g} 10^{7gf} 1^{8g} 11^{8gs} 9^{8sd} **1-3-12 £40,797**

Salesin *L M Cumani* 69
2 ch c Lomitas - Elisita (Arg)
5^{8s} **0-0-1**

Salford Artist *D R C Elsworth* 74
3 ch g Zafonic (USA) - Highland Rhapsody (Ire)
5^{9gs} 2^{8g} **0-1-2 £1,184**

Salinas (Ger) *M F Harris* 78 a77
6 b g Macanal (USA) - Santa Ana (Ger)
1^{8g} 5^{10g} 7^{10sd} 11^{8sd} **1-0-4 £5,531**

Salinger (USA) *Andrew Turnell* 73 a61
3 b g Lear Fan (USA) - Sharp Flick (USA)
6^{10gs} 1^{6g} 20^{7gf} 6^{8gf} 6^{7gs} 12^{7hy} 3^{10sd} **1-1-7 £3,443**

Salinja (USA) *Mrs A J Perrett* 99
3 b g Boundary (USA) - Lasha (USA)
1^{10gs} 8^{9g} 2^{9gf} 2^{8gf} 7^{10gs} 1^{10g} 10^{9gf} 3^{10s} **2-3-8 £28,968**

Salisbury Plain *N I M Rossiter* a29
4 b c Mark Of Esteem (Ire) - Wild Pavane
12^{8sd} **0-0-1**

Salisbury World (Ire) *D R C Elsworth* 45 a58
2 ch g Spinning World (USA) - Dinka Raja (USA)
10^{6s} 6^{6sd} **0-0-2**

Salon Prive *C A Cyzer* 67 a76
5 b g Green Desert (USA) - Shot At Love (Ire)
1^{5sd} 4^{5sd} 3^{5sd} 3^{6sd} 1^{5sd} 8^{5gs} 2^{5gs} 9^{5g} 5^{5gs} 7^{6sd} 12^{5sd} 8^{5sd} **2-3-12 £10,442**

Salt Man *M P Tregoning* a77
2 b c Mtoto - Romaneh
1^{8sd} **1-0-1 £4,524**

Saltango (Ger) *A M Hales* 71
6 b g Acatenango (Ger) - Salde (Ger)
12^{11gf} **0-0-1**

Saltburn Lad (Ire) *J W Hills* 68 a52

3 b c Sadler's Wells (USA) - Highest Accolade
8^{9sd} 4^{11s} 2^{12g} 11^{14g} 6^{14gf} 13^{14gs} 5^{12g}
0-1-7 £1,339

Saluscraggie *K G Reveley* 49
3 b f Most Welcome - Upper Caen
7^{6g} 9^{10gf} 10^{8g} **0-0-3**

Salut D'Amour (Ire) *J Noseda* 99
2 ch f Danehill Dancer (Ire) - Juno Madonna (Ire)
2^{5s} 1^{5gs} 4^{5gs} 1^{5g} 2^{5gf} 2^{6g} 6^{8g} **2-3-7**
£53,531

Salut Saint Cloud *G L Moore* 55 a35
4 b g Primo Dominie - Tiriana
14^{12sd} 7^{16g} **0-0-2**

Salute (Ire) *P G Murphy* 93 a88
6 b g Muhtarram (USA) - Alasib
4^{12sd} 4^{12sd} 7^{12gf} 2^{12gf} 1^{12g} 7^{16sd} 12^{12gf} 12^{12g}
9^{12sd} 7^{11sd} **1-1-10 £15,336**

Salute Him (Ire) *M R Channon* 87
2 b c Mull Of Kintyre (USA) - Living Legend (Ity)
1^{5s} 3^{5gf} 6^{6gf} 1^{7gs} 2^{8g} 7^{8s} **2-1-6**
£10,369

Salute The General *W R Muir* 71 a79
2 ch c Mark Of Esteem (Ire) - Oiselina (Fr)
9^{7gs} 5^{8gs} 4^{8sd} 2^{8sd} 2^{9sd} 2^{8sd} 1^{8sd} **1-3-7**
£6,901

Salvestro *Mrs A J Perrett* 65 a65
2 b c Medicean - Katy Nowaitee
8^{6gf} 9^{7g} 13^{7g} 4^{7gf} 6^{7gs} 4^{7sd} 10^{7sd} **0-0-7**
£787

Salviati (USA) *J M Bradley* 87
8 b g Lahib (USA) - Mother Courage
20^{5gs} 13^{6gf} 14^{5g} 11^{5gf} 2^{5gf} 7^{5gf} 3^{5gf} 2^{5g}
6^{5gs} 2^{5gf} 5^{5gf} 9^{5g} 9^{5g} 6^{5g} 6^{5gs} 9^{5g} 5^{5g}
0-4-17 £10,868

Sam The Sorcerer *J R Norton* a42
4 b g Wizard King - Awham (USA)
8^{6sd} 5^{8sd} 3^{7sd} 11^{7sd} 10^{7sd} 6^{6sd} 13^{7ss} 5^{7sd}
12^{9sd} **0-1-9 £211**

Sam's Secret *J A Glover* 75
3 b f Josr Algarhoud (Ire) - Twilight Time
9^{7gf} 3^{6gf} 2^{7gf} 12^{7g} 10^{7gs} 2^{7gf} 2^{7g} 1^{7gf} 6^{7gf}
14^{7gf} **1-4-10 £9,084**

Samalan *J Parkes* 19
3 b g Grey Desire - Shalari (Ire)
5^{9gs} 14^{8gf} 15^{10g} **0-0-3**

Samara Sound *A G Newcombe* 11 a32
4 b c Savahra Sound - Hosting
11^{6sd} 8^{7g} **0-0-2**

Samarai *L M Cumani* 54
3 ch g Tagula (Ire) - Gandini
9^{6gf} 6^{7gf} **0-0-2**

Samba Beat *R F Marvin*
6 ch m Efisio - Special Beat
10^{7sd} **0-0-1**

Sambarina (Ire) *C G Cox* 50
3 b f Victory Note (USA) - Brazilia
6^{7gf} 13^{7g} **0-0-2**

Sambertini *T D Easterby* 45
2 b f Bertolini (USA) - Samadilla (Ire)
7^{5s} 7^{5s} 8^{6gf} 8^{7f} **0-0-4**

Samson Quest *N P Littmoden* 56 a62
3 b g Cyrano De Bergerac - Zenita (Ire)
4^{6gs} 2^{5g} 11^{6sd} 10^{6gf} 3^{7gf} 9^{7g} 4^{7gf} 1^{8sd} 7^{7sd}
11^{9sd} 5^{7sd} **1-2-11 £4,873**

Samsouma (Ire) *C E Brittain* 53 a50
2 b f Marju (Ire) - St Bride's Bay
5^{6gf} 13^{6gf} 7^{7sd} 6^{7sd} **0-0-4**

Samuel Charles *C R Dore* 56 a77
7 b g Green Desert (USA) - Hejraan (USA)
3^{7sd} 1^{7sd} 2^{6sd} 9^{7gs} 3^{7gf} 2^{7sd} 11^{7g} 4^{7sd} 7^{8sd}
5^{8sd} 6^{7sd} PU^{7sd} **1-3-12 £7,964**

Samuel John Peploe (Ire) *G L Moore* 14
3 b g Intikhab (USA) - Sadalsud (Ire)
12^{8g} **0-0-1**

Samurai Way *Saeed Bin Suroor* 79
3 b c Darshaan - Truly Special
2^{12f} **0-1-1 £1,060**

San Antonio *Mrs P Sly* 94 a96
5 b g Efisio - Winnebago
15^{10gs} 1^{8s} 1^{8g} 1^{8g} 4^{8s} 2^{7gf} 5^{7gf} 3^{8gf} 5^{7gf}
3^{8gf} 11^{8gs} 2^{6sd} 4^{8sd} **3-4-13 £30,755**

San Deng *W R Muir* 69 a69
3 gr g Averti (Ire) - Miss Mirror
2^{7gf} 1^{8gf} 4^{8gf} 11^{8gf} 5^{10g} 4^{10g} 3^{11g} 2^{12gf} 6^{12sd}
6^{12gf} **1-3-10 £7,435**

San Gimignano (Ire) *W Jarvis* 50
2 ch f City On A Hill (USA) - A La Longue (Ger)
15^{6g} 14^{7g} **0-0-2**

San Hernando *D R C Elsworth* a66
5 b g Hernando (Fr) - Sandrella (Ire)
8^{13sd} 7^{16sd} **0-0-2**

San Michele *Denis P Quinn* 44 a38
3 b f Vettori (Ire) - La Piazza (Ire)
9^{7gf} 10^{8g} 7^{9sd} 6^{10g} 12^{8gf} **0-0-5**

Sanchi (Ire) *Saeed Bin Suroor* 81
3 b c Darshaan - Samara (Ire)
1^{10g} 4^{12hy} **1-0-2 £4,663**

Sancia (Ire) *K J Condon* 71
3 ch f Docksider (USA) - Salabella
2^{7gf} 2^{8gf} 4^{9gy} 7^{7gf} 9^{7g} 9^{9gf} 8^{10g} 9^{8y}
0-2-8 £3,176

Sanctity *J R Fanshawe* 56
2 ch f Pivotal - Blessed Honour
7^{6g} 8^{6g} **0-0-2**

Sand And Stars (Ire) *M H Tompkins* 84
4 ch f Dr Devious (Ire) - Charm The Stars
3^{12gf} 17^{12g} 4^{12gf} 9^{12gf} 4^{14gf} 7^{13gs} 3^{12g}
0-3-7 £4,318

Sand Cat *D M Simcock* 89 a89
2 b c Cadeaux Genereux - Desert Lynx (Ire)
3^{5g} 3^{6gf} 5^{5s} 1^{6sd} 1^{5g} 3^{6sd} 13^{6g} 5^{6gf} 8^{6gs}
7^{6sd} **2-2-10 £12,651**

Sand Fairy (Ire) *M A Jarvis* 78
3 b f Desert King (Ire) - Kinetic Force (USA)
2^{10g} 3^{10g} 9^{10gf} 3^{8gf} 10^{8gf} 3^{8gs} 5^{8g} **0-4-7**
£5,607

Sand Iron (Ire) *S L Keightley* 61 a56
3 b f Desert Style (Ire) - Mettlesome
10^{8s} 9^{9sd} 1^{7s} 8^{8gs} 8^{6sd} **1-0-5 £3,096**

Sand Repeal (Ire) *Miss J Feilden* 69 a69
3 b g Revoque (Ire) - Columbian Sand (Ire)
3^{12s} 3^{12g} 13^{14g} 5^{12sd} 17^{14s} **0-2-5**
£1,371

Sand Sprite (Ire) *Sir Michael Stoute* 45
2 b f Green Desert (USA) - Fleet Amour (USA)
12^{7s} **0-0-1**

Sanders Boy *J R Norton* 39 a8
2 gr c Arkadian Hero (USA) - Rising Of The Moon (Ire)
13^{6g} 7^{5gf} 10^{5gf} 10^{6sd} **0-0-4**

Sandglass *Mrs A J Perrett* 76
2 b f Zafonic (USA) - Clepsydra

2^{8gs} **0-1-1 £2,208**

Sandhill Jack *A G Newcombe* a28
4 b g Muhtarram (USA) - Astern (USA)
9^{13sd} 10^{16sd} **0-0-2**

Sandorra *M Brittain* 58
7 b m Emperor Jones (USA) - Oribi
1^{7gs} 13^{7sd} 7^{7gf} **1-0-3 £2,632**

Sands Crooner (Ire) *D Shaw* 78 a71
2 b c Imperial Ballet (Ire) - Kurfuffle
6^{5gs} 4^{5gs} 5^{5gs} 5^{5gf} 5^{5sd} 6^{5gf} 8^{5g} 6^{5sd} 5^{5sd}
4^{5sf} 7^{5sd} 3^{5ss} 3^{5sd} **0-2-13 £2,843**

Sands Of Barra (Ire) *N A Callaghan* 73 a74
2 gr g Marju (Ire) - Purple Risks (Fr)
6^{7gf} 9^{7gf} 7^{6sd} 4^{8f} 8^{8gf} 1^{7gs} 6^{8hy} 9^{8sd} 6^{8sd}
1^{7sd} **2-0-10 £8,442**

Sandwith *James Moffatt* 69 a58
2 ch g Perryston View - Bodfari Times
8^{6g} 5^{5gf} 2^{5gf} 9^{5g} 8^{5gf} 5^{6sd} 10^{7sd} 9^{6sd}
0-1-8 £858

Sandy Bay (Ire) *W G Harrison* 47 a39
6 b g Spectrum (Ire) - Karinski (USA)
7^{9sd} 8^{8g} 7^{12gf} 9^{16f} 10^{12gf} 9^{8gf} 6^{8gf} 4^{9gf} 7^{9gf}
4^{12gf} **0-0-10 £262**

Sandy's Legend (USA) *Jamie Poulton* 54 a67
3 ch g Tale Of The Cat (USA) - Avasand (USA)
7^{10sd} 10^{12gf} 14^{6g} 16^{8g} 9^{9sd} **0-0-5**

Sangiovese *H Morrison* 83 a60
6 b g Piccolo - Kaprisky (Ire)
8^{8sd} 10^{10s} 3^{11s} 1^{10g} 8^{10s} 3^{10gf} 4^{10gs} 5^{12f} 5^{11gf}
1-2-9 £7,863

Sant Elena *G Wragg* 69
2 ch f Efisio - Argent Du Bois (USA)
4^{6g} 1^{6s} **1-0-2 £2,644**

Santa Fe (Ire) *Sir Michael Stoute* 92
3 b c Green Desert (USA) - Shimna
9^{9gf} 4^{7gs} 16^{8gf} **0-0-3 £1,400**

Santando *C E Brittain* 72 a92
5 b g Hernando (Fr) - Santarem (USA)
6^{10sd} 6^{12sd} 5^{10sd} 6^{12sd} 7^{16gs} 17^{12g} 9^{14gf} 7^{12gf}
10^{12sd} 8^{12gs} 2^{11gf} 8^{10s} 2^{13sd} **0-2-13**
£3,577

Santerno (Ire) *E J O'Neill* 62 a48
2 b f Desert Style (Ire) - Mugello
2^{6sd} 2^{5gf} 4^{5gf} **0-2-3 £3,570**

Santiago Star (Ire) *A M Balding* 85 a55
2 ch c Hussonet (USA) - Normandy (Chi)
7^{6sd} 4^{7gf} 4^{7gs} 1^{7g} 3^{8s} 1^{8f} **2-0-6**
£25,728

Santiburi Lad (Ire) *N Wilson* 60
8 b g Namaqualand (USA) - Suggia
19^{10g} 6^{10gf} 9^{10g} 15^{10gf} 12^{10g} 17^{14s} 13^{14sd}
0-0-7

Saoire *Ms F M Crowley* 109
3 ch f Pivotal - Polish Descent (Ire)
6^{8gf} 1^{8gy} 8^{10gf} 6^{12gf} 5^{8gy} **1-0-5**
£168,541

Sapienza *C E Brittain* 64 a45
2 ch f Singspiel (Ire) - Kameez (Ire)
2^{7g} 2^{8g} 8^{8sd} **0-2-3 £2,309**

Saposcat (Ire) *Dr P Pritchard*
5 b g Groom Dancer (USA) - Dance Of Joy
13^{10gs} 17^{12g} **0-0-2**

Sapphire Dream *A Bailey* 69 a47
3 b f Mind Games - Bombay Sapphire
4^{6gs} 7^{6gf} 12^{5g} 10^{5gf} 6^{6gf} 9^{6g} 7^{6gf} 7^{5s} 8^{7sf}
5^{5sd} 8^{6sd} 8^{5sd} **0-0-12 £807**

Sapphire Sky *D K Ivory* a37
4 b/br f Compton Place - Jewel (Ire)
9^{6sd} 11^{6sd} 6^{5sd} 7^{5sd} **0-0-4**

Sapphire Storm (Ire) *Miss D A McHale* 62 a48
2 b f Elnadim (USA) - Blu Tu Miami (USA)
11^{5gf} 3^{5gf} 2^{6gf} 6^{6f} 2^{6gs} 3^{5gf} 4^{6gf} 3^{7gf} 2^{6gs}
10^{6gf} 3^{5sd} 4^{6gs} 8^{6gf} 8^{6g} 10^{6sf} **0-6-15**
£4,543

Sara Mana Mou *J G Portman* 13
2 b f Medicean - Sarabah (Ire)
12^{7g} 8^{8g} **0-0-2**

Saraba (Fr) *Mrs L J Mongan* 74 a68
4 gr f Soviet Star (USA) - Sarliya (Ire)
2^{9sd} 2^{12sd} 2^{12s} 2^{12s} 12^{11g} 3^{10g} 5^{9g} 6^{10gs}
0-5-8 £4,839

Sarah's Art (Ire) *N A Callaghan* 44 a26
2 gr c City On A Hill (USA) - Treasure Bleue (Ire)
9^{6gf} 13^{6gs} 15^{6g} 9^{5sd} **0-0-4**

Saristar *P F I Cole* 82
4 b f Starborough - Sari
7^{6g} 15^{6s} 6^{6g} 7^{6gf} 11^{6gs} **0-0-5**

Sarn *M Mullineaux* 35
6 b g Atraf - Covent Garden Girl
10^{11gf} 5^{13gs} 9^{16gf} 11^{14gf} **0-0-4**

Saros (Ire) *B Smart* 68 a62
4 b/br g Desert Sun - Fight Right (Fr)
2^{7sd} 3^{8f} RR^{9sd} 5^{8gf} 9^{8gf} 16^{8gf} 9^{8gf} **0-1-7**
£1,794

Sarraaf (Ire) *I Semple* 69 a66
9 ch g Perugino (USA) - Blue Vista (Ire)
4^{7g} 1^{7gf} 2^{7f} 5^{7g} 13^{9gs} 4^{7f} 2^{7g} 3^{7g} 8^{8gf} 3^{8gf}
1^{8gf} 3^{8gf} 10^{8gf} 4^{8gf} 6^{7g} 1^{7sd} 4^{8sf} 3^{9sd}
3-6-18 £14,877

Sarwin (USA) *W J Musson* 51
2 gr/ro c Holy Bull (USA) - Olive The Twist (USA)
12^{7s} 12^{6g} 11^{6g} **0-0-3**

Sasso *Jonjo O'Neill* 81
3 b g Efisio - Sioux
8^{8gf} 9^{8g} 9^{8gf} F^{8gs} 7^{10g} 2^{10gs} 1^{10s} **1-1-7**
£5,836

Sastre (Ire) *A M Hales* 23
3 b f Bluebird (USA) - No Rehearsal (Fr)
14^{8g} 16^{7gs} 12^{8s} **0-0-3**

Satchem (Ire) *Saeed Bin Suroor* 107
3 br c Inchinor - Mohican Princess
9^{8gf} **0-0-1**

Satin Doll *M P Tregoning* a50
2 b f Diktat - Unconditional Love (Ire)
8^{7sd} 9^{6sd} **0-0-2**

Satin Kiss (USA) *Saeed Bin Suroor* 66 a109
3 b f Seeking The Gold (USA) - Satin Flower (USA)
1^{8ft} 1^{9ft} 17^{8gf} 9^{6g} **2-0-4 £169,270**

Satin Rose *K J Burke* 51
3 b f Lujain (USA) - Shamwari (USA)
9^{10gf} 6^{14gf} 4^{12gf} 1^{12gf} 8^{12gf} 15^{16s} 5^{12gf} 10^{10g}
6^{12g} **1-0-9 £3,764**

Satisfaction (Ire) *E J O'Neill* 61
2 b c Dansili - Presentation (Ire)
6^{7g} **0-0-1**

Saturday's Child (Fr) *M S Saunders* a19
3 ch f Hamas (Ire) - Pleasant Whisper (Fr)
9^{6sd} **0-0-1**

Saucepot *Miss J R Tooth* 50 a54
3 ch f Bold Edge - Apple Sauce

7^{5sd} 7^{5sd} 5^{6sd} 17^{6gf} 17^{6gs} 12^{6g} 5^{5gf} 13^{5gf} 7^{5f} 18^{6gf} 8^{8gf} 5^{6gf} 3^{6g} 3^{6sd} 12^{6f} 7^{7sd} 2^{6sd} 9^{5sd} 5^{6sd} 12^{6sd} 11^{6sd} 13^{6sd} 11^{6sd} **0-2-23 £1,255**

Saucy *A W Carroll* 58 a61
4 b f Muhtarram (USA) - So Saucy
6^{10sd} 1^{10sd} 4^{10sd} 1^{10g} 1^{10sd} 5^{10f} 5^{12g} **3-0-7 £4,669**

Sauterelle (Ire) *Thomas Mullins* 64 a68
5 br m Key Of Luck (USA) - Haysong (Ire)
11^{10sd} 7^{16g} 8^{10g} 6^{14g} 6^{11g} 6^{11f} 3^{12gf} 3^{12gf} 10^{12gy} 9^{13gf} **0-2-10 £2,157**

Savannah Pride (Ire) *E R Oertel* 64 a43
2 b f Namid - Milady Lillie (Ire)
6^{5gf} 4^{5gf} 3^{6g} 5^{5gf} 7^{6gf} 9^{7gf} 1^{6gf} 11^{6sd} 11^{6s} 10^{6sd} **1-1-10 £3,878**

Savernake Blue *M R Channon* 81
2 b c Mtoto - Mrs Malaprop
3^{7gf} 4^{7gf} 1^{7g} **1-1-3 £3,842**

Savernake Brave (Ire) *Mrs H Sweeting* 45 a59
4 b g Charnwood Forest (Ire) - Jordinda (Ire)
10^{7sd} 11^{7sd} 11^{7sd} 3^{8sd} 1^{7sd} 13^{7f} 14^{8gf} 11^{7sd} 14^{7g} 3^{8g} 5^{8sd} 12^{9sd} 7^{7sd} 9^{7sd} **1-2-14 £3,199**

Savile's Delight (Ire) *R Brotherton* 83 a75
6 b g Cadeaux Genereux - Across The Ice (USA)
4^{6sd} 12^{7sd} 7^{7sd} 2^{6sd} 1^{5sd} 5^{5sd} 3^{5gs} 12^{6g} 5^{6s} 1^{5gf} 8^{6gf} 8^{6sd} 5^{5g} 5^{5s} 15^{5g} 9^{6sd} 3^{6sd} 13^{6sd} **2-3-18 £13,424**

Saville Road *D J Daly* 96
2 br c Mozart (Ire) - In Full Cry (USA)
1^{6gf} 6^{6g} 2^{7gf} 8^{6g} **1-1-4 £5,857**

Saviours Spirit *T G Mills* 76 a80
4 ch g Komaite (USA) - Greenway Lady
3^{5sd} 8^{5sd} 6^{5gs} 6^{6g} 11^{6gs} 9^{6gs} **0-1-6 £1,026**

Savoie *H R A Cecil* 64
3 ch f Grand Lodge (USA) - Spry
5^{11gf} 10^{9gs} 7^{10gf} **0-0-3**

Savoy Chapel *A W Carroll* 50 a72
3 br c Xaar - Royal Gift
2^{7sd} 2^{8sd} 2^{7sd} 1^{7sd} 7^{8sd} 1^{7sd} 1^{8sd} 2^{8sd} 11^{8g} 8^{10gf} 12^{9sd} 11^{8gf} 10^{8sd} 10^{8sd} 10^{9sd} 12^{9sd} **3-4-16 £13,942**

Sawari *C E Brittain* 53 a38
3 b f Zafonic (USA) - Nefeli
9^{8gf} 5^{8s} 11^{7g} 10^{6sd} 13^{9sd} **0-0-5 £358**

Sawwaah (Ire) *D Nicholls* 89
8 b g Marju (Ire) - Just A Mirage
12^{8gs} 2^{8gf} 5^{7gs} 5^{8gs} 7^{8gf} 9^{8g} 6^{9g} 3^{9gf} 7^{8s} 2^{8gf} 2^{9gf} 2^{9gf} 1^{8gf} 3^{9gf} 1^{9g} 10^{8gf} **2-5-16 £19,498**

Saxon Lil (Ire) *J L Spearing* 80 a45
3 b f Second Empire (Ire) - Salva
5^{7sd} 13^{10sd} 8^{9sd} 3^{7gs} 6^{8gs} 5^{7s} 4^{7s} 1^{7gf} 3^{7f} 4^{8gf} 1^{7gf} 1^{7f} 1^{7g} 1^{7gf} 3^{7gs} 3^{7g} 9^{8g} 6^{8g} **5-4-18 £27,608**

Saxon Saint *M D I Usher* 77 a30
2 b g Josr Algarhoud (Ire) - Antithesis (Ire)
5^{5sd} 6^{5g} 3^{6f} 11^{5g} 2^{5gf} 1^{5gs} 1^{5g} 1^{5gs} 2^{5s} 1^{5gs} 3^{6g} 6^{5gf} 9^{5g} **4-2-13 £24,445**

Saxon Star (Ire) *M D I Usher* 59 a9
2 b g Vettori (Ire) - Thicket
11^{6gf} 8^{6gf} 6^{7gf} 14^{8s} 9^{6gf} 15^{7gf} 8^{7ss} **0-0-7**

Scamperdale *Miss K M George* 46 a58
3 br g Compton Place - Miss Up N Go
6^{8g} 4^{10sd} 7^{9sd} 2^{9sd} **0-1-4 £1,201**

Scandal Keeper (USA) *Saeed Bin Suroor* 84
2 b/br c Danzig (USA) - Canny Miss (Aus)
2^{6g} 1^{6s} **1-1-2 £8,393**

Scarlet Flyer (USA) *G L Moore* 79
2 b c Gilded Time (USA) - Tennis Partner (USA)
3^{6g} 3^{5gf} 2^{7g} 5^{6gf} 1^{6f} 12^{6gs} **1-3-6 £9,298**

Scarlet Invader (Ire) *J L Dunlop* 78
3 b g Indian Ridge - Scarlet Plume
13^{8g} 5^{8g} 1^{7gs} 9^{7gf} 7^{8g} 10^{7s} 13^{7g} 10^{7gf} PU^{7g} **1-0-9 £3,751**

Scarlet Knight *P Mitchell* 87 a85
2 b c Lujain (USA) - Gem
3^{5g} 1^{5hy} 2^{5gf} 4^{6g} 6^{6g} 7^{8gf} 6^{7gs} 4^{9gs} 1^{6sd} 5^{8sd} **2-2-10 £17,310**

Scarlet Mix (Fr) *B G Powell* a43
4 gr g Linamix (Fr) - Scarlet Raider (USA)
7^{16sd} **0-0-1**

Scarlet Pastorale *P C Haslam* 13
2 b f Vettori (Ire) - Show Me Genius (USA)
9^{5g} 8^{6gf} **0-0-2**

Scarlett Rose *Dr J D Scargill* 52 a58
4 b f Royal Applause - Billie Blue
9^{7g} 12^{7gf} 3^{7sd} **0-1-3 £382**

Scarrabus (Ire) *A Crook* 62
4 b g Charnwood Forest (Ire) - Errazuriz (Ire)
10^{13gs} 9^{14g} 9^{12gf} 3^{13f} **0-1-4 £625**

Scarrots *A W Carroll* 21
11 b g Mazilier (USA) - Bath
10^{10gf} **0-0-1**

Scary Night (Ire) *M J Gingell* a54
5 b g Night Shift (USA) - Private Bucks (USA)
7^{5sd} 6^{6sd} 2^{5sd} 7^{5sd} 5^{5sd} 8^{5sd} 14^{10s} 9^{7sd} 13^{6sd} 11^{7gf} 14^{8sd} **0-1-11 £832**

Scattered Empire (Ire) *Peter Grayson* a34
2 b g Second Empire (Ire) - Scatter Brain
9^{7ft} 13^{5sd} 9^{6sd} 8^{5sd} 10^{5ss} **0-0-5**

Scenic Flight *O O'Neill* a16
4 b f Distant View (USA) - Bird Of Time (Ire)
8^{7sd} 12^{9sd} **0-0-2**

Scherzo A La Russe (USA) *A G Newcombe* 57 a36
2 b/br f Stravinsky (USA) - Zadracarta (Can)
6^{5g} 5^{5gf} 5^{5f} 13^{5gf} 12^{5g} 10^{6sd} 5^{7sd} **0-0-7**

Schinken Otto (Ire) *J M Jefferson* 45
4 ch c Shinko Forest (Ire) - Athassel Rose (Ire)
5^{12gs} **0-0-1**

Sciatin (Ire) *L M Cumani* 89
2 b c Alhaarth (Ire) - Robalana (USA)
4^{7g} 1^{7s} 2^{8gf} 4^{8g} **1-1-4 £9,410**

Scissors (Ire) *Miss J Feilden* a21
3 ch f Desert King (Ire) - Clipping
10^{8sd} 8^{9sd} **0-0-2**

Scooby Dude (Ire) *Ms Deborah J Evans* 78 a78
2 b g Tagula (Ire) - Miraculous (Ire)
2^{5gs} 1^{5gf} 2^{5gf} 8^{5f} 3^{5g} 6^{5g} 3^{6sd} 6^{5sd} 4^{5sd} **1-3-9 £12,006**

Scorchio (Ire) *B Smart* a50
4 b g Desert Sun - White-Wash
1^{9sf} 6^{12sd} 9^{9ss} **1-0-3 £1,433**

Scorpio Sally (Ire) *M D Hammond* 47
3 b f Mujadil (USA) - Clear Procedure (USA)
8^{8g} 7^{9s} 7^{12gf} 8^{12gf} 9^{10gf} 8^{16g} 7^{16s} 7^{14g} 4^{12g} **0-0-9**

Scorpion (Ire) *A P O'Brien* 123
3 b c Montjeu (Ire) - Ardmelody
1^{10sh} 2^{10gy} 16^{11g} 2^{12gf} 1^{12g} 1^{15hy} 10^{12gs}
3-2-7 £659,897

Scot Love (Ire) *J Noseda* 71
2 b c Dansili - Fashion
6^{6gs} 5^{6s} **0-0-2**

Scotch House *Robert Gray*
3 ch f Selkirk (USA) - Top Shop
7^{11g} 10^{14g} RR^{12g} **0-0-3**

Scotch Pancake *D R C Elsworth* 81
2 ch f Selkirk (USA) - Galette
2^{8g} **0-1-1 £1,508**

Scotchman (Ire) *R Simpson* 70 a46
2 b c Danehill Dancer (Ire) - Mistress Mac (Ire)
4^{5g} 3^{5g} 4^{6gf} 6^{5gs} 4^{7ft} **0-1-5 £1,449**

Scotland The Brave *J D Bethell* 74
5 ch m Zilzal (USA) - Hunters Of Brora (Ire)
16^{7g} 5^{7s} 3^{7g} 3^{7s} 6^{8g} 5^{8g} 8^{8gf} 7^{8gs} 2^{8s} 1^{7hy}
1-3-10 £6,538

Scots Guard (Ire) *J D Bethell* 39
4 b g Selkirk (USA) - Island Race
10^{8g} 9^{11gf} 8^{10gs} 12^{8gf} **0-0-4**

Scott *J Jay* 66 a69
4 gr g Polar Falcon (USA) - Circled (USA)
10^{12gf} 5^{11g} 3^{16sd} 8^{12gf} 4^{12gs} 3^{12g} 10^{14gs} 2^{12sd}
3^{12sd} 12^{16sd} **0-5-10 £2,657**

Scott's Mill *M Johnston* 37
3 ch g Unfuwain (USA) - Mill On The Floss
5^{12g} 8^{12s} 11^{12s} **0-0-3**

Scottendale *J G Given* 56
3 ch f Zilzal (USA) - Mountain Lodge
7^{8g} 9^{8gf} 12^{11g} **0-0-3**

Scottish Play (Ire) *G A Butler* 71 a52
3 b g Selkirk (USA) - Gold Script (Fr)
12^{8gf} 13^{8gf} 3^{7gf} 11^{7gf} 6^{8f} 11^{12gf} 9^{10sd}
0-1-7 £546

Scottish River (USA) *M D I Usher* 85 a78
6 b g Thunder Gulch (USA) - Overbrook
11^{9sd} 14^{10sd} 1^{12sd} 12^{10sd} 5^{8sd} 15^{11gs} 2^{9sd}
4^{11sd} 6^{10gf} 1^{10gf} 1^{10gf} 11^{10gf} 5^{10g} 5^{10gf} 14^{9gs}
1^{12gf} 10^{12g} 11^{10gs} 6^{12gs} 17^{10g} 4^{9sd} 8^{10sd} 4^{9sd}
5^{10sd} **4-1-24 £15,819**

Scottish Stage (Ire) *Sir Michael Stoute* 100 a70
2 ch f Selkirk (USA) - Drama Class (Ire)
1^{7sd} 2^{7gs} **1-1-2 £9,486**

Scotty Boy (Ire) *G L Moore* 63
2 b c Sadler's Wells (USA) - Goncharova (USA)
8^{8gs} 5^{8s} **0-0-2**

Scotty's Future (Ire) *D Nicholls* 76
7 b g Namaqualand (USA) - Persian Empress (Ire)
3^{8gf} 2^{11gf} 5^{9f} 4^{11g} 7^{8gf} 6^{8gf} 3^{9g} **0-3-7**
£2,882

Screen Test *A P Jarvis* 67 a61
3 b f Danzero (Aus) - Audition
5^{8sd} 4^{9sd} 4^{10sd} 4^{11gf} 12^{10gs} 6^{10g} 13^{8gf}
0-0-7 £806

Screenplay *Miss Sheena West* 73 a69
4 ch g In The Wings - Erudite
5^{10sd} 2^{12sd} 1^{12sd} 4^{14gs} 1^{15s} 3^{14g} 6^{20s} 6^{16gf}
4^{16gf} **2-2-9 £9,250**

Screwdriver *Miss J R Tooth* 84 a81
3 b g Entrepreneur - Lust
5^{7gs} 17^{7gf} 17^{6g} 7^{7gs} 2^{8gf} 4^{7gs} 6^{7gf} 8^{7sd} 8^{7s}
3^{7sd} 10^{8sd} 6^{8sd} 6^{7sd} **0-2-13 £4,428**

Scriptwriter (Ire) *Saeed Bin Suroor* 95
3 b g Sadler's Wells (USA) - Dayanata
1^{10gf} 1^{12gf} **2-0-2 £12,502**

Scroll *P Howling* 63 a67
2 b c Mark Of Esteem (Ire) - Bella Bellisimo (Ire)
7^{5gf} 5^{5f} 5^{8sd} 3^{7g} 8^{7gs} 7^{8g} 7^{7g} 4^{8sd} 6^{9sd} 10^{9sd}
8^{7sd} 3^{7sd} **0-2-12 £1,465**

Scrooby Baby *M J Polglase* 47
3 b f Mind Games - Lunar Music
8^{5gs} 6^{5gf} 14^{6g} 16^{5g} 6^{8g} **0-0-5**

Scrummage *Sir Michael Stoute* 53
2 b c Sinndar (Ire) - Ghariba
7^{7s} **0-0-1**

Scuba (Ire) *H Morrison* 53 a64
3 b c Indian Danehill (Ire) - March Star (Ire)
11^{6sd} 5^{7s} 10^{6gs} 7^{7gs} 10^{7gf} 5^{7sd} 10^{6hy} 2^{7sd}
2^{6sd} 4^{7sd} **0-2-10 £1,610**

Scurra *A C Whillans* 58
6 b g Spectrum (Ire) - Tamnia
7^{12s} 4^{12g} 2^{13s} 7^{13s} 5^{16gf} 8^{16g} 3^{14gf} 8^{12gf} 15^{12gf}
0-3-9 £1,737

Scutch Mill (Ire) *Miss K M George* 71 a69
3 ch c Alhaarth (Ire) - Bumble
4^{6sd} 4^{7sd} 3^{8sd} 4^{10sd} 6^{10sd} 1^{8sd} 8^{10gs} 2^{10g} 5^{10gs}
4^{12f} 7^{10sd} **1-2-11 £5,882**

Scuzme (Ire) *B Ellison* 48
2 br g Xaar - Decatur
11^{6gf} 6^{7gf} 7^{8g} **0-0-3**

Sea Fern *Karen McLintock* 43
4 b g Petong - Duxyana (Ire)
15^{7gs} 9^{6f} 11^{7g} 11^{6gf} **0-0-4**

Sea Frolic (Ire) *Jennie Candlish* 51 a51
4 b f Shinko Forest (Ire) - Centre Travel
1^{8gf} 1^{8gf} 4^{10gf} 14^{8gf} 3^{7g} 6^{7sf} 7^{9sd} 2^{8sd} 1^{8ss}
3-3-9 £7,501

Sea Gift (USA) *Saeed Bin Suroor* 74
3 ch f A.P. Indy (USA) - Ocean Queen (USA)
1^{10f} **1-0-1 £3,737**

Sea Grain (Ire) *J S Wainwright* 63
2 b g Beckett (Ire) - Tara View (Ire)
6^{5g} 2^{5gs} 8^{5g} 10^{7g} **0-1-4 £1,358**

Sea Heir (Ire) *R A Fahey* 57 a54
3 b/br g Princely Heir (Ire) - Isla Bonita
5^{9g} 12^{9gf} 2^{8sd} 8^{9ss} **0-1-4 £424**

Sea Hunter *M R Channon* 100
3 b c Lend A Hand - Ocean Grove (Ire)
UR^{7g} 6^{8gs} 3^{7g} 3^{8gf} 3^{7gf} 1^{7gf} 1^{7g} 1^{7g} 3^{8gf}
7^{7g} **3-3-10 £37,499**

Sea Kestrel (USA) *M Johnston* a59
3 br g Silver Hawk (USA) - By Land By Sea (USA)
4^{8sd} 6^{9sd} PU^{10g} **0-0-3 £268**

Sea Map *D E Cantillon* 54 a62
3 ch g Fraam - Shehana (USA)
6^{10sd} 20^{8g} 11^{10g} 4^{10sd} 13^{10g} 2^{12gf} 1^{12sd} 9^{16g}
7^{12sd} 8^{12gs} 1^{11hy} 1^{12sd} **3-1-12 £8,582**

Sea Of Calm (USA) *E A L Dunlop* 72
2 b f Quiet American (USA) - Ocean Ridge (USA)
8^{8g} **0-0-1**

Sea Of Serenity (Ire) *P A Blockley* 47
2 b f Namid - Serenity
8^{5g} 14^{6gf} **0-0-2**

Sea Salt *T D Barron* 69
2 b g Titus Livius (Fr) - Carati
9^{6g} 5^{6gs} 4^{6gf} **0-0-3 £330**

Sea Storm (Ire) *D R MacLeod* 89 a85

7 b g Dolphin Street (Fr) - Prime Interest (Ire)
8^{7gs} 4^{8gf} 11^{7gs} 14^{10gf} 3^{7f} 3^{7g} 3^{8g} 1^{8gs} 8^{8gf} 11^{7gf} 13^{7g} 14^{9gs} 6^{7g} 6^{8sd} 10^{9sd} **1-3-15**
£11,820

Sea The World (Ire) *D Shaw* a42
5 b g Inzar (USA) - Annie's Travels (Ire)
12^{5sd} 11^{5sd} 10^{5sd} 11^{6sd} **0-0-4**

Sea Wall *R Charlton* 95
3 b g Giant's Causeway (USA) - Spout
3^{11gs} 2^{12gs} 1^{12g} 9^{12gf} 1^{12f} 4^{14gf} **2-2-6**
£14,649

Seabow (USA) *Saeed Bin Suroor* 79
2 b c Rainbow Quest (USA) - Dream Bay (USA)
6^{7gs} **0-0-1**

Seafield Towers *Miss L A Perratt* 69
5 ch g Compton Place - Midnight Spell
6^{5f} 13^{5g} 1^{5g} 3^{6gf} 4^{6gf} **1-1-5 £4,417**

Sealed Bid *M W Easterby* 41
2 b g Zilzal (USA) - Thea (USA)
10^{5gf} 9^{5gs} **0-0-2**

Sealily (Ire) *Mrs A Duffield* 49
4 gr f Docksider (USA) - Hariyana (Ire)
9^{7g} 10^{8s} 4^{7gf} 5^{7f} 5^{7g} 8^{8gf} 5^{8gf} 6^{8gf}
0-0-8

Seallarain *A Berry* 35
2 ch f Perryston View - Bergliot
10^{5g} 7^{5gs} 9^{5gf} 10^{6g} 6^{5s} **0-0-5**

Seasons Estates *B R Millman* 83 a62
3 b f Mark Of Esteem (Ire) - La Fazenda
9^{7sd} 2^{8g} 9^{7f} 1^{8gs} 6^{7gf} 1^{8gf} 5^{8g} 16^{8gs} 15^{10gf}
2-1-9 £8,439

Seasons Parks *B R Millman* 66
3 b f Desert Prince (Ire) - Fantazia
15^{8gf} 8^{10gf} 2^{8gs} **0-1-3 £1,698**

Seattle Robber *P A Blockley* 66 a62
3 b g Robellino (USA) - Seattle Ribbon (USA)
5^{8sd} 5^{9sd} 3^{7sd} 2^{9sd} 7^{9sd} 4^{10sd} 3^{12sd} 3^{12sd} 4^{10g} 3^{10f} 11^{12g} 1^{9gf} 4^{10gf} 2^{8gf} 8^{10hd} 5^{9sd}
1-6-16 £8,136

Seattle Spy (USA) *G A Huffer* 56 a51
2 b/br g Catienus (USA) - Theyrplayinoursong (USA)
6^{6gs} 6^{7g} 11^{7gf} 6^{7gf} 8^{8sd} 6^{7sd} **0-0-6**

Sebaaq (USA) *M P Tregoning* 59
2 ch g Rahy (USA) - Malibu Karen (USA)
15^{6s} 9^{6gs} 8^{6gf} 6^{7g} **0-0-4**

Secam (Pol) *Mrs P Townsley* 42 a65
6 gr g Alywar (USA) - Scytia (Pol)
1^{8sd} 2^{7sd} 1^{7sd} 1^{8sd} 7^{8sd} 7^{8f} 8^{7sd} 9^{8sd}
3-1-8 £6,388

Second Pick (Ire) *R J Hodges*
9 b g Doubletour (USA) - Wurli
11^{12sd} **0-0-1**

Second Reef *E J Alston* 69 a67
3 b g Second Empire (Ire) - Vax Lady
1^{7g} 6^{6gf} 6^{8gf} 13^{6g} 5^{8g} 14^{8s} 3^{7sd} **1-1-7**
£4,404

Second User *J R Jenkins* a7
4 b g Zilzal (USA) - Glossary
8^{7sd} 10^{9sd} 9^{7sd} **0-0-3**

Second Wind *D A Nolan*
10 ch g Kris - Rimosa's Pet
13^{8gf} 13^{6g} **0-0-2**

Secret Affair *A King* 64 a66
3 b g Piccolo - Secret Circle
6^{7gf} 3^{8sd} 11^{10gs} 13^{10gf} 6^{8gf} 6^{8sd} **0-1-6**
£370

Secret Assassin (Ire) *W R Muir* 74 a45
2 b g Daggers Drawn (USA) - Lypharden (Ire)
10^{6gf} 7^{6sd} 5^{5gs} 3^{7gf} 3^{6gf} 3^{6gs} 2^{7gf} 3^{7g} 8^{8g} 3^{7g} **0-6-10 £3,491**

Secret Cavern (USA) *M Appleby* 55 a32
3 b g Lion Cavern (USA) - River Dyna (USA)
4^{7gf} 6^{10s} 16^{10g} 9^{8gf} 13^{8gf} 10^{6sd} **0-0-6**
£287

Secret Dell (Ire) *R Brotherton*
9 b g Doyoun - Summer Silence (USA)
12^{14sd} **0-0-1**

Secret History (USA) *M Johnston* 106
3 b f Bahri (USA) - Ravnina (USA)
1^{8hy} 1^{7s} 2^{8g} 1^{10s} 3^{9g} 5^{12gf} 10^{10gs} 8^{11g}
3-1-8 £68,526

Secret Liaison *Sir Mark Prescott* 73
2 gr g Medicean - Courting
7^{6gf} 3^{6gf} 4^{6gf} **0-1-3 £824**

Secret Night *J A R Toller* 83 a86
2 gr f Dansili - Night Haven
9^{5gf} 3^{5g} 4^{5gf} 2^{5gf} 1^{5g} 10^{5gf} 3^{5g} 5^{6s} 1^{6sd} 7^{6sd} 2^{6sd} **2-4-11 £13,103**

Secret Of Secrets *L R James*
4 b g Timeless Times (USA) - Sophisticated Baby
14^{6s} 10^{6gs} **0-0-2**

Secret Place *E A L Dunlop* 96 a102
4 ch g Compton Place - Secret Circle
2^{8sd} 17^{7g} 4^{7gf} 14^{7g} 12^{7gf} 18^{7g} **0-1-6**
£5,524

Secret Tender (Ire) *J R Weymes* 57 a50
2 ch g Beckett (Ire) - Mystery Bid
6^{6g} 9^{6f} 6^{6gf} 13^{6gf} 2^{7gf} 5^{8sd} 7^{7ss} 3^{10sd} 8^{9sd}
0-2-9 £1,250

Secret Vision (USA) *R M H Cowell* 47 a58
4 ch f Distant View (USA) - Secret Angel
5^{7sd} 1^{6sd} 8^{6sd} 6^{5sd} 8^{6sd} 4^{6f} 11^{6gf} 10^{6f} 8^{7sd} 3^{6sd} 9^{6sd} 14^{6sd} 1^{5sd} 1^{6sd} 9^{5sd} 3^{5ss}
3-2-16 £6,687

Secret's Out *W M Brisbourne* a32
9 b g Polish Precedent (USA) - Secret Obsession (USA)
13^{9sd} **0-0-1**

Secretary General (Ire) *P F I Cole* 92
4 b c Fasliyev (USA) - Katie McLain (USA)
14^{10gs} 7^{12gf} 11^{12gf} 8^{10s} 2^{10gf} 6^{10g} 10^{12gf} 18^{12g} 5^{8gf} 4^{10gs} 3^{8gf} 5^{8g} 10^{10s} **0-2-13**
£4,226

Secretive Dancer (Ire) *S C Williams* 47
3 b f Night Shift (USA) - Lanelle (USA)
13^{8g} 12^{8gf} 8^{8g} **0-0-3**

Sedge (USA) *P T Midgley* 59 a61
5 b g Lure (USA) - First Flyer (USA)
3^{6sd} 1^{7sd} 12^{7sd} 6^{7sd} 5^{8sd} 4^{7f} 5^{8gf} **1-1-7**
£3,137

Seejay *B R Johnson* 49 a49
5 b m Bahamian Bounty - Grand Splendour
8^{12sd} 11^{10sd} 3^{12sd} 2^{8sd} 7^{9sd} 1^{8f} 10^{12sd} 7^{12f} 14^{8f} **1-2-9 £3,138**

Seesawmilu (Ire) *E J Alston* 38
2 b g Almutawakel - Clos De Tart (Ire)
7^{5s} 11^{5s} 7^{5gf} **0-0-3**

Segoria (Ire) *A M Hales* 60 a58
3 b f Shinko Forest (Ire) - Moon Tango (Ire)
4^{6s} 11^{5hy} 11^{6g} 6^{6f} 15^{7g} 10^{5y} 5^{5f} 7^{6sd} 1^{6sd} 3^{7sd} 2^{6sd} 1^{6sd} **2-2-12 £4,028**

Seifi *B Ellison* 61

6 b g Hector Protector (USA) - Garconniere
1^{16gf} 1^{14gf} 2^{16g} 11^{17gf} **2-1-4 £7,397**

Seigneur *C E Brittain* 64
2 b c Diktat - Hazy Heights
14^{7g} 7^{8gf} 9^{8g} 8^{7gf} **0-0-4**

Seldemosa *M S Saunders* a64
4 br f Selkirk (USA) - Baldemosa (Fr)
3^{8sd} 1^{9sd} 2^{8sd} 4^{9sd} 4^{9sd} 4^{8sd} **1-2-6 £5,010**

Selebela *L M Cumani* 91
4 ch f Grand Lodge (USA) - Risarshana (Fr)
4^{10s} 6^{12gf} **0-0-2 £2,920**

Selective *A W Carroll* 92
6 b g Selkirk (USA) - Portelet
8^{6g} 5^{8gs} 5^{7f} 13^{7gf} 3^{8g} 9^{6gf} 23^{7gf} 15^{8gs} **0-1-8 £1,960**

Self Belief *M C Chapman* 50 a45
4 b f Easycall - Princess Of Spain
6^{6sd} 7^{5sd} 2^{7sd} 5^{6sd} 12^{8sd} 6^{7sd} 8^{8sd} 4^{6s} 6^{6sd} 6^{6sd} 16^{6gf} 11^{8gf} 7^{6gf} 16^{6gf} 10^{6sd} **0-1-15 £719**

Self Defense *Miss E C Lavelle* 114
8 b g Warning - Dansara
3^{13g} 6^{12gf} 2^{12g} 7^{12gs} 2^{12gs} **0-2-5 £30,450**

Self Discipline *B W Hills* 51
3 b g Dansili - Cosh (USA)
7^{7gs} 13^{7gf} **0-0-2**

Self Respect (USA) *J Noseda* 89 a73
3 b g Lear Fan (USA) - Cap Of Dignity
1^{9sd} 2^{12gs} 1^{12gs} 5^{14gf} 7^{12gf} 2^{12s} 2^{11gs} **2-3-7 £19,546**

Selika (Ire) *K F Clutterbuck* 68 a61
3 ch g Daggers Drawn (USA) - Hint-Of-Romance (Ire)
2^{10gs} 13^{12gs} 5^{12gs} 3^{10s} 2^{10gf} 5^{8gf} 6^{11gf} 9^{10g} 16^{8g} 7^{12gf} 9^{10gf} 2^{9sd} 9^{14sd} **0-3-13 £3,377**

Selkirk Storm (Ire) *M W Easterby* 42 a33
3 b g Trans Island - Force Divine (Fr)
10^{6s} 14^{6gs} 10^{5sd} 10^{6s} 8^{5gf} 10^{5g} **0-0-6**

Sellasia *J S Moore* 46 a27
2 b f Alhaarth (Ire) - Spry
8^{6g} 8^{6gf} 6^{7sd} 8^{5gf} **0-0-4**

Selma *D R C Elsworth* 61 a70
3 ch f Selkirk (USA) - Mish Mish
3^{8sd} 2^{10sd} 2^{10sd} 1^{8sd} 6^{7sd} 8^{8gs} **1-3-6 £6,392**

Semah's Parc *Mrs A M Naughton* 26
7 b g Pure Melody (USA) - Semah's Dream
16^{12g} 13^{12gf} 5^{13s} **0-0-3**

Semele (Ire) *T D Easterby* 2
2 b f Muhtarram (USA) - Pasithea (Ire)
10^{7s} 11^{8gf} **0-0-2**

Semenovskii *Miss B Sanders* 74 a72
5 b g Fraam - Country Spirit
13^{6g} 3^{6gf} 7^{6g} 9^{5gf} 1^{5gs} 5^{6sd} **1-1-6 £5,396**

Semi Detached (Ire) *J R Boyle* 75
2 b c Distant Music (USA) - Relankina (Ire)
3^{7gs} 2^{8g} 10^{8gs} **0-2-3 £2,148**

Semper Paratus (USA) *V Smith* 38 a49
6 b g Foxhound (USA) - Bletcha Lass (Aus)
5^{7sd} 6^{7sd} 6^{7sd} 12^{7sd} 13^{6s} 8^{7s} 3^{7sd} 7^{6g} 9^{8ss} 3^{8sd} 5^{8sd} **0-2-11 £423**

Sendinpost *S C Williams* 39 a56
2 b f Dansili - Colleville
14^{7s} 6^{6sd} **0-0-2**

Sendintank *S C Williams* 106
5 ch g Halling (USA) - Colleville
7^{16g} 3^{14g} 7^{14g} 1^{15gs} 3^{16g} **1-2-5 £30,350**

Seneschal *A B Haynes* 90 a73
4 b g Polar Falcon (USA) - Broughton Singer (Ire)
9^{8gf} 2^{7gs} 7^{7gf} 7^{7gf} 9^{8gf} 10^{6gs} 13^{8gs} 6^{8g} 11^{10hy} 8^{8sd} 3^{7sd} 6^{7sd} 3^{6sd} **0-3-13 £3,367**

Senior Whim *P R Webber* 41
3 b g Lahib (USA) - Euphorie (Ger)
8^{12s} 11^{12sd} 4^{12gf} 5^{16g} **0-0-4**

Sennen Cove *R Bastiman* 44 a30
6 ch g Bering - Dame Laura (Ire)
6^{7sd} 14^{6sd} 9^{6sd} 7^{6g} 9^{7gf} 6^{8gf} 5^{7g} 11^{6f} 8^{7f} 4^{6g} 8^{8g} **0-0-11**

Senor Benny (USA) *M McDonagh* 108
6 br h Benny The Dip (USA) - Senora Tippy (USA)
4^{5s} 6^{7hy} 2^{5sh} 28^{6gf} 8^{6gy} 7^{5g} 9^{5gf} 14^{5gy} 10^{6gy} 7^{5ys} 6^{6s} 11^{6s} **0-1-12 £8,197**

Senor Bond (USA) *A M Hales* 66 a53
4 ch g Hennessy (USA) - Troppa Freska (USA)
10^{7sd} 4^{7gf} 3^{8g} 4^{7gf} 8^{8g} 10^{9sd} 6^{9f} 1^{8gf} 1^{8gf} 2^{8gf} 12^{8gf} 13^{8gs} 12^{10sd} 3^{8sd} 3^{10sd} **2-4-15 £8,909**

Senor Dali (Ire) *J L Dunlop* 71
2 ch c Peintre Celebre (USA) - Far Fetched (Ire)
5^{8gf} 4^{8gs} **0-0-2 £391**

Senor Eduardo *S Gollings* 51 a55
8 gr g Terimon - Jasmin Path
9^{11sd} 4^{10sd} 2^{10sd} 3^{10sd} 10^{10g} 7^{10gs} 10^{10gf} 12^{10gf} 14^{8sd} 5^{10sd} **0-2-10 £1,274**

Senor Set (Ger) *P A Blockley* 59 a60
4 b g Second Set (Ire) - Shine Share (Ire)
6^{9sd} 3^{12gs} 10^{12sd} 14^{16g} 16^{10g} 11^{14ft} 9^{11sd} 11^{16sf} **0-1-8 £731**

Sensuous *R Hannon* 77
2 b f Royal Applause - Zafaaf
5^{7g} 2^{7gf} 17^{7gf} **0-1-3 £3,270**

Sentiero Rosso (USA) *B Ellison* 86
3 b g Intidab (USA) - Kheyrah (USA)
4^{6s} 3^{6gs} 10^{6g} 4^{6s} 1^{5g} 8^{6gf} 11^{5gs} 6^{5g} 13^{5g} 4^{5s} **1-2-10 £10,691**

Sentinel *P W Chapple-Hyam* 92
6 ch g Hector Protector (USA) - Soolaimon (Ire)
3^{16gs} 5^{12gf} 8^{16g} **0-1-3 £2,040**

Septimus (Ire) *A P O'Brien* 108
2 b c Sadler's Wells (USA) - Caladira (Ire)
1^{7gy} 1^{8g} 3^{8hy} **2-0-3 £92,926**

Seraph *O Brennan*
5 ch g Vettori (Ire) - Dahlawise (Ire)
6^{12gf} **0-0-1**

Serbelloni *M D Hammond* 82 a83
5 b g Spectrum (Ire) - Rose Vibert
1^{14sd} 1^{17sd} 4^{13s} 4^{14g} 5^{16gf} 5^{14gf} 8^{16g} **2-1-7 £11,488**

Serene Pearl (Ire) *G M Moore* 29
3 b f Night Shift (USA) - Shanjah
15^{7s} 16^{6g} 3^{9g} 13^{8gf} **0-1-4 £372**

Serevi (Ire) *J Noseda* 70
2 b c Cape Cross (Ire) - Winter Tern (USA)
9^{6s} 2^{5g} **0-1-2 £1,288**

Sergeant Cecil *B R Millman* 116
6 ch g King's Signet (USA) - Jadidh
12^{12gs} 2^{12f} 3^{12g} 1^{16g} 3^{14gs} 1^{14g} 2^{18g} 1^{18gs} **3-4-8 £344,244**

Sergeant Lewis *R M Flower* 37 a68
3 gr g Mind Games - Silver Blessings
2^{7sd} 2^{7sd} 3^{6sd} 6^{7sd} 1^{6sd} 11^{6gs} 16^{7gs} 6^{6sd} 10^{6sd} 11^{7sd} **1-3-10 £6,341**

Sergeant Slipper *C Smith* 51 a46
8 ch g Never So Bold - Pretty Scarce
6^{6sd} 7^{6sd} 3^{6sd} 13^{5sd} 6^{6sd} 5^{6sd} 9^{6sd} 6^{6sd} 1^{6gs} 5^{5s} 11^{6sd} 5^{6sd} 5^{6sd} 7^{6sd} **1-1-14 £1,553**

Sergeant Small (Ire) *John Berry* 31
3 b g Dr Devious (Ire) - Yavarro
11^{0gs} 12^{12sd} **0-0-2**

Serieux *D Nicholls* 87
6 b g Cadeaux Genereux - Seranda (Ire)
6^{8s} 12^{10gf} 13^{7gf} 1^{7g} 9^{7gf} 6^{7f} 17^{8gs} 5^{7s} 16^{6g} 8^{8g} **1-0-10 £7,442**

Serjeant At Arms (Ire) *P D Evans* 61 a69
6 b g Bluebird (USA) - Curiously
9^{12sd} 7^{14sd} 7^{14sd} 3^{11g} 13^{12g} 9^{15gf} **0-1-6 £538**

Serramanna *Dr J R J Naylor* 63 a64
4 ch f Grand Lodge (USA) - Spry
10^{12s} 9^{10sd} 10^{12gf} 11^{13f} 12^{7gs} 8^{9g} 13^{7gf} 3^{12g} 1^{12g} 2^{10s} 11^{10g} 11^{1gf} 11^{1g} 5^{12sd} 5^{12sd} 6^{12g} 7^{12s} 10^{12sd} **3-2-18 £9,799**

Serre Chevalier (Ire) *W R Swinburn* 112
4 b g Marju (Ire) - Ski Lodge (Ire)
3^{6gs} 6^{6gs} 1^{7gf} 12^{7gf} 1^{7gf} 1^{7g} 1^{7gf} 5^{7g} **4-1-8 £44,664**

Servillia (Ire) *W R Swinburn* a62
2 b f Dansili - Housekeeper (Ire)
3^{8sd} **0-1-1 £503**

Ses Seline *John A Harris*
4 b f Salse (USA) - Absentee
7^{12sd} 10^{8sd} **0-0-2**

Sessile (USA) *J H M Gosden* a55
2 b/br f Forestry (USA) - Madam Lagonza (USA)
5^{7sd} **0-0-1**

Set Alight *Mrs C A Dunnett* 73 a77
4 b f Forzando - Me Spede
2^{7sd} 1^{7sd} 1^{7sd} 1^{7sd} 1^{7sd} 4^{7sd} 3^{7sd} 13^{7s} 3^{6gf} 9^{6gf} 11^{7gf} 12^{7sd} 13^{8sd} 7^{8sd} **4-3-14 £14,812**

Set Barabbas Free *Joseph Quinn* 42
6 b g Bishop Of Cashel - Salanka (Ire)
13^{11s} 5^{7gs} 10^{7y} **0-0-3**

Settle (Ire) *M Flannery* 45 a44
6 b g Ali-Royal (Ire) - Airport
1^{8g} 5^{8g} 8^{16gf} 3^{12s} 12^{10gf} 8^{9ss} **1-1-6 £4,813**

Settlement Craic (Ire) *T G Mills* 91
4 b g Ela-Mana-Mou - Medway (Ire)
6^{10gs} 4^{12g} **0-0-2 £1,276**

Seven Magicians (USA) *Sir Michael Stoute* 104
3 b/br f Silver Hawk (USA) - Mambo Jambo (USA)
2^{11g} 1^{10gf} 6^{12gf} 6^{12gf} **1-1-4 £17,316**

Seven No Trumps *J M Bradley* 83 a69
8 ch g Pips Pride - Classic Ring (Ire)
1^{5gs} 12^{5gs} 2^{5gs} 7^{6sd} 4^{5s} 10^{5gs} 6^{6gf} 8^{5gf} 9^{5gf} 2^{5gf} 1^{5s} 8^{5gs} 3^{5f} 7^{5g} 13^{6gs} 7^{5g} 2^{5gs} 4^{5gf} 5^{5gf} 4^{5gs} 5^{5g} 12^{6g} 6^{5s} **2-4-23 £12,155**

Seven Samurai *J W Hills* 81 a85
2 b c Mark Of Esteem (Ire) - Eishin Eleuthera (Ire)
8^{7sd} 4^{7gf} 1^{7g} 3^{8g} 3^{8g} 1^{7sd} **2-2-6 £11,903**

Seven Shirt *E G Bevan* 32 a30
4 b g Great Dane (Ire) - Bride's Answer
6^{8sd} 8^{9sd} 9^{10g} 10^{8sd} **0-0-4**

Severely (Fr) *B W Hills* 62 a35
3 b f Cape Cross (Ire) - Sevres (USA)
10^{8sd} 8^{11g} 5^{10g} 11^{6g} 5^{14gf} **1-0-5 £2,976**

Sew'N'So Character (Ire) *M Blanshard* 98 a98
4 b g Imperial Ballet (Ire) - Hope And Glory (USA)
3^{8g} 5^{8g} 1^{8gs} 10^{8gf} 10^{8g} 3^{8g} 3^{8sd} 8^{10gs} 3^{8gf} 8^{8gf} 8^{8g} 3^{8gs} 4^{8gs} 13^{8gs} **1-5-14 £24,310**

Sewmore Character *M Blanshard* 42 a57
5 b g Hector Protector (USA) - Kylo Rhoa
7^{9sd} 6^{9sd} 9^{12sd} 5^{8sd} 12^{9sd} 3^{8sd} 13^{10sd} 8^{8f} **0-1-8 £477**

Sewmuch Character *M Blanshard* 62 a69
6 b g Magic Ring (Ire) - Diplomatist
10^{6sd} 4^{6sd} 5^{6s} 11^{6f} 7^{8gf} 14^{6g} 9^{8gf} 3^{7gf} 9^{7gf} 8^{6gs} 14^{6g} **0-0-11 £937**

Seyaadi *E A L Dunlop* 85
3 b g Intikhab (USA) - Sioux Chef
4^{10g} 1^{9gs} **1-0-2 £5,226**

Sforzando *Mrs L Stubbs* 70 a67
4 b f Robellino (USA) - Mory Kante (USA)
5^{7gf} 6^{7g} 2^{7gf} 8^{7gf} 6^{8f} 10^{10gf} 1^{8gs} 10^{9sd} 5^{9sd} 3^{9sd} **1-2-10 £5,354**

Sgt Pepper (Ire) *O Sherwood* 61
4 b g Fasliyev (USA) - Amandine (Ire)
14^{7gs} **0-0-1**

Sgt Schultz (Ire) *J S Moore* 65 a58
2 b g In The Wings - Ann's Annie (Ire)
10^{7gf} 5^{7sd} 13^{7g} 3^{7gf} 5^{8gs} 4^{7g} 14^{7gs} **0-0-7 £882**

Shaaban (Ire) *R J Price* 55 a67
4 b g Woodman (USA) - Ashbilya (USA)
14^{10sd} 3^{8sd} 3^{9sd} 6^{9sd} 7^{10s} 1^{9sd} 2^{12sd} 11^{14sd} 5^{10g} 11^{9sd} 9^{8g} 11^{10gf} **1-3-12 £3,438**

Shaamit's All Over *B A Pearce* a39
6 br m Shaamit (Ire) - First Time Over
4^{8sd} 8^{12sd} 5^{8sd} 7^{12sd} 6^{12sd} 7^{12sd} **0-0-6**

Shaanbar (Ire) *J Hetherton* 52
3 b f Darshaan - Barbara Frietchie (Ire)
4^{12gf} 11^{12s} 8^{10gf} 6^{12g} 8^{16g} **0-0-5 £428**

Shabernak (Ire) *M L W Bell* 113
6 gr g Akarad (Fr) - Salinova (Fr)
4^{14s} 2^{13gs} 6^{12g} 1^{16gf} 10^{16s} **1-1-5 £34,383**

Shade Cozy (USA) *A M Balding* 60 a74
3 gr c Cozzene (USA) - Fire And Shade (USA)
5^{8sd} 4^{8g} 11^{8g} 3^{9sd} 1^{6sd} **1-1-5 £3,778**

Shades Of Beige (UAE) *M Johnston* 74
3 b f Timber Country (USA) - Idrica
3^{10gf} 3^{12gf} 4^{10gf} **0-1-3 £1,915**

Shades Of Green *N A Callaghan* 61 a50
3 b f Loup Sauvage (USA) - Green Light (Fr)
4^{10gf} 1^{11f} 7^{12sd} 3^{10g} 3^{12f} **1-0-5 £4,048**

Shadow Jumper (Ire) *M J Attwater* 50 a67
4 b g Dayjur (USA) - Specifically (USA)
12^{6sd} 9^{8sd} 2^{6sd} 8^{7sd} 8^{6sd} 13^{6gs} 5^{6sd} 3^{6sd} 9^{6sd} 1^{5sd} 2^{6s} 10^{6sd} 7^{5sd} 1^{6sd} 4^{6sd} 6^{7sd} 3^{6sd} 3^{6sd} **2-4-18 £5,647**

Shadowfax *Miss Gay Kelleway* 49
5 b g Anabaa (USA) - Prends Ca (Ire)
12^{8sd} 18^{8gs} 7^{6f} 9^{5gf} 16^{6gf} **0-0-5**

Shady Minstrel (Ire) *M J Attwater* 52
2 ch c Monashee Mountain (USA) - China Silk (Ire)
10^{7gf} 4^{7s} 7^{8gs} 13^{10g} **0-0-4**

Shaheer (Ire) *P Howling* 64 a59
3 b g Shahrastani (USA) - Atmospheric Blues (Ire)
10^{8g} 5^{8gf} 8^{8gf} 4^{8gs} 17^{10gs} 10^{9sd} 10^{8ss} 2^{9sf} 7^{9sd} 3^{10sd} 7^{10sd} **0-2-11 £1,554**

Shahin (USA) *M P Tregoning* 96
2 b c Kingmambo (USA) - String Quartet (Ire)
5^{7g} 2^{8gf} 1^{8gs} **1-1-3 £9,544**

Shahzan House (Ire) *Stef Liddiard* 104 a84
6 b h Sri Pekan (USA) - Nsx
2^{10gs} 2^{10gs} 9^{10s} 4^{10gs} 10^{8gf} 8^{9sd} **0-3-6 £12,526**

Shake The Spear (Ire) *Miss J R Tooth* 41 a52
2 b c Lear Spear (USA) - Milladella (Fr)
8^{7sd} 11^{7gf} **0-0-2**

Shakerattleandroll (Ire) *Mrs L Richards* 71 a71
4 b g Dr Fong (USA) - Speedybird (Ire)
6^{12sd} 1^{11g} 14^{12sd} **1-0-3 £3,477**

Shalati Princess *J C Fox* a43
4 b f Bluegrass Prince (Ire) - Shalati (Fr)
11^{10sd} 9^{13sd} 3^{12sd} **0-1-3 £369**

Sham Ruby *M R Bosley* 28 a28
3 ch f Tagula (Ire) - Bistro (USA)
12^{6g} 11^{7sd} **0-0-2**

Shaman *G L Moore* a17
8 b g Fraam - Magic Maggie
14^{10sd} **0-0-1**

Shamara (Ire) *C F Wall* 58
5 b m Spectrum (Ire) - Hamara (Fr)
8^{9gf} **0-0-1**

Shamardal (USA) *Saeed Bin Suroor* 127 a69
3 b c Giant's Causeway (USA) - Helsinki
9^{9ft} 1^{8s} 1^{11g} 1^{8gf} **3-0-4 £900,471**

Shamdala (Ire) *A De Royer-Dupre* 114
3 b f Grand Lodge (USA) - Shamadara (Ire)
2^{11gs} 1^{12g} 1^{12g} 6^{12g} 1^{15g} 1^{15s} 3^{16s} 4^{12gf} **4-2-8 £176,774**

Shameless *H Alexander* a15
8 ch g Prince Daniel (USA) - Level Edge
7^{8sd} **0-0-1**

Shami *D W Chapman* 57 a52
6 ch h Rainbow Quest (USA) - Bosra Sham (USA)
10^{8gs} 12^{7gs} 20^{9gs} 11^{9sd} 10^{9sd} 8^{8sd} **0-0-6**

Shamila *G A Butler* 79 a72
2 b f Green Desert (USA) - Shamaiel (Ire)
2^{7sd} 2^{6s} **0-2-2 £3,428**

Shamrock Bay *J G Given* 74
3 b f Celtic Swing - Kabayil
1^{10gf} 6^{10g} 6^{10gs} 6^{10gs} **1-0-4 £6,454**

Shamrock City (Ire) *P Howling* a58
8 b g Rock City - Actualite
11^{9sd} 4^{7sd} 7^{8sd} **0-0-3**

Shamrock Tea *M E Sowersby* 9
4 b g Imperial Ballet (Ire) - Yellow Ribbon (Ire)
16^{7s} 14^{6s} 8^{7gs} **0-0-3**

Shamsada (Ire) *R H Macnabb* 59
5 b m Kahyasi - Shamawna (Ire)
6^{14g} 2^{12s} 10^{15s} 11^{14sd} **0-1-4 £913**

Shamsalmaidan (Ire) *C E Brittain* 59
2 ch f Fantastic Light (USA) - Maggi For Margaret
10^{7gf} 3^{7g} 5^{8g} **0-0-3 £692**

Shamwari Fire (Ire) *I W McInnes* 55 a23
5 ch g Idris (Ire) - Bobby's Dream
2^{10g} 11^{8g} 8^{9gf} 5^{10gf} 8^{10gf} 9^{8f} 4^{10gf} 8^{8f} 4^{10gf} 3^{8gs} 5^{8gf} 7^{9sd} 12^{10sd} **0-3-13 £1,029**

Shandrani (Ger) *D G Bridgwater* 37
6 b g Komtur (USA) - Strockida (Ger)
10^{10sd} 6^{10sd} 8^{12sd} 6^{8gf} 13^{7gf} **0-0-5**

Shanghai Lily (Ire) *Sir Michael Stoute* 26
3 b f King's Best (USA) - Marlene-D
19^{8gf} **0-0-1**

Shankly Bond (Ire) *B Smart* 73 a76
3 b g Danehill Dancer (Ire) - Fanellan
2^{10s} 3^{8gf} 3^{9f} 8^{12g} 1^{12gf} 7^{12sd} 3^{10gf} 3^{12gf} 1^{9sd} **2-4-9 £10,371**

Shannkara's Quest (USA) *J R Holt* 30
4 b/br g Coronado's Quest (USA) - Shannkara (Ire)
8^{7gf} 7^{6g} **0-0-2**

Shannon House *M J McGrath* 61 a48
2 ch c Inchinor - Sulitelma (USA)
11^{7gf} 6^{7g} 3^{7g} 11^{8g} 13^{7sd} 14^{8sd} **0-1-6 £510**

Shannon Springs (Ire) *Andrew Turnell* 96
3 b g Darshaan - Our Queen Of Kings
1^{12gf} 5^{12gs} 13^{12gf} DSQ^{12s} 15^{10g} 1^{10g} 4^{10g} 9^{10g} **2-0-8 £18,063**

Shannon's Dream *P W Hiatt*
9 gr m Anshan - Jenny's Call
11^{12sd} **0-0-1**

Shape Up (Ire) *R Craggs* 83 a86
5 b g Octagonal (NZ) - Bint Kaldoun (Ire)
2^{12sd} 3^{12sd} 1^{12sd} 3^{12sd} 5^{14gs} **1-3-5 £9,898**

Shapira (Ger) *Andreas Lowe* 113
4 ch f Kornado - Semplice (Ire)
4^{9gf} 3^{8g} 2^{8gs} 4^{8gs} 6^{8s} **0-2-5 £48,472**

Sharaab (USA) *D E Cantillon* 43 a56
4 b/br g Erhaab (USA) - Ghashtah (USA)
10^{10sd} 6^{10sd} 10^{12sd} 7^{10gf} 9^{8gf} **0-0-5**

Sharaby (Ire) *E A L Dunlop* 73 a72
3 b f Cadeaux Genereux - Shawanni
2^{7g} 2^{6g} 2^{7gs} 1^{7gf} 8^{7gf} 3^{7sd} 7^{7sd} 1^{7gf} 4^{7gf} 3^{8s} 3^{7gf} **2-6-11 £13,232**

Sharadi (Ire) *V Smith* 81
4 b g Desert Sun - Sharadiya (Ire)
14^{13s} 14^{14gf} 11^{16g} 5^{17gf} 1^{18gf} 5^{16gs} 7^{16gf} **1-0-7 £6,698**

Shardakhan (Ire) *G L Moore* a39
3 b g Dr Devious (Ire) - Sharamana (Ire)
8^{12sd} **0-0-1**

Shardda *F Watson*
5 b m Barathea (Ire) - Kronengold (USA)
18^{8s} **0-0-1**

Shardia (Ire) *J Jay* a45
2 b f Marju (Ire) - Shabarana (Fr)
5^{7sd} **0-0-1**

Shareb (USA) *B W Hills* 64
3 b c El Prado (Ire) - My Hansel (USA)
5^{8gs} 12^{8g} **0-0-2**

Shared Dreams *L M Cumani* 96
3 b f Seeking The Gold (USA) - Coretta (Ire)
2^{8gf} 2^{8g} 1^{10gf} 3^{10gf} 3^{10gf} 7^{12g} **1-3-6 £12,486**

Shares (Ire) *P Monteith* 51
5 b g Turtle Island (Ire) - Glendora
11^{12s} **0-0-1**

Shariki (USA) *Saeed Bin Suroor* 81
2 b/br c Spectrum (Ire) - Zahrat Dubai
2^{8g} 1^{8s} **1-1-2 £4,638**

Sharoura *R A Fahey* 60 a32
9 ch m Inchinor - Kinkajoo

1 0^{6sd} 5^{6gs} 13^{7g} 2^{6gf} 14^{6g} 20^{6g} 13^{6sd} 12^{7sd} **0-1-8 £858**

Sharp As A Tack (Ire) *C F Wall* 52
3 b f Zafonic (USA) - Pretty Sharp
14^{6gf} **0-0-1**

Sharp Diversion (USA) *J G Given* 44
3 ch f Diesis - Jamie De Vil (USA)
4^{5s} 17^{6gf} 10^{5s} 9^{6gf} **0-0-4 £324**

Sharp Duo (Ire) *M S Saunders* 59
2 ch g Daggers Drawn (USA) - Fay's Song (Ire)
6^{7s} 2^{7gf} 6^{8s} 5^{7gf} 7^{8gf} **0-1-5 £1,044**

Sharp Hat *D W Chapman* 51 a51
11 b g Shavian - Madam Trilby
6^{6sd} 5^{6sd} 7^{6sd} 2^{6sd} 5^{5sd} 7^{6g} 7^{6gf} 9^{6gf} 16^{6g} **0-1-9 £417**

Sharp N Frosty *W M Brisbourne* 62 a56
3 b g Somayda (Ire) - Wily Miss
1^{10gs} 8^{10s} 10^{10g} 6^{12sd} 9^{11gf} 7^{14gf} **1-0-6 £3,332**

Sharp Reply (USA) *Sir Michael Stoute* 96
3 b g Diesis - Questonia
7^{8hy} 7^{7gs} 13^{8gf} 1^{12gf} 2^{12f} **1-1-5 £5,936**

Sharp Stanley (Ire) *J R Best* 45 a34
2 ch g Daggers Drawn (USA) - Racing Brenda
9^{5gf} 9^{6sd} 13^{5gf} **0-0-3**

Sharp Thrust (Ire) *A P Jarvis* 74 a66
2 b g Daggers Drawn (USA) - Oumaladia (Ire)
3^{6gf} 5^{7sd} 4^{5sd} **0-1-3 £1,114**

Sharp Tune (USA) *J J Sheehan* 51
3 ch g Diesis - Moonflute (USA)
15^{8gs} 12^{8gs} 10^{8g} 16^{7gf} **0-0-4**

Sharpcut (Ire) *A Bailey* 33
6 b g Alhaarth (Ire) - Safiya (USA)
10^{12g} 10^{12g} **0-0-2**

Sharpe Image (Ire) *G M Moore* 38
2 b f Bluebird (USA) - Silvretta (Ire)
5^{7s} **0-0-1**

Sharplaw Autumn (USA) *W J Haggas* 78
2 b f Red Ransom (USA) - Hawzah
2^{7gf} **0-1-1 £1,522**

Sharplaw Star *W J Haggas* 91
3 b f Xaar - Hamsah (Ire)
11^{5gf} 2^{5gf} 14^{5g} 15^{5gf} **0-1-4 £4,533**

Sharpsburg (USA) *Unknown* 79
2 b c Giant's Causeway (USA) - Sofitina (USA)
2^{8gf} **0-1-1 £1,434**

Shashana (Ire) *Sir Michael Stoute* 62
3 ch f King's Best (USA) - Sheshara (Ire)
2^{10gf} 6^{10gf} **0-1-2 £1,532**

Shastye (Ire) *J H M Gosden* 104
4 b f Danehill (USA) - Saganeca (USA)
1^{12g} 2^{12gf} 5^{12gf} 7^{12gf} **1-1-4 £15,587**

Shatin Leader *Miss L A Perratt* 49
3 b f Atraf - Star Dancer
6^{5gs} 5^{5gs} 9^{5s} 15^{6g} 8^{5gf} 1^{6gf} 11^{5gf} 8^{6gf} 12^{5g} **1-0-9 £2,674**

Shawanda (Ire) *A De Royer-Dupre* 123
3 b f Sinndar (Ire) - Shamawna (Ire)
2^{11hy} 1^{10vs} 1^{11s} 1^{12g} 1^{12gf} 1^{12gs} 6^{12gs} **5-1-7 £313,182**

Shaydreambeliever *R A Fahey* 71
2 ch g Daggers Drawn (USA) - Aunt Sadie
3^{5g} 7^{5g} 6^{6g} 9^{6gf} 1^{6gf} 4^{7gf} 4^{7s} 1^{8g} 3^{8gf} **2-2-9 £19,811**

Shaymee's Girl *J Ryan* 37 a25
4 b f Wizard King - Mouchez Le Nez (Ire)
12^{6sd} 9^{5gf} 14^{6gs} 12^{6sd} 15^{5g} 11^{5ss} **0-0-6**

She Whispers (Ire) *G C H Chung* 60 a52
2 b f Royal Applause - Zariyba (Ire)
7^{5gf} 3^{6f} 3^{6gf} 6^{7gs} 11^{7sd} 6^{7gf} 5^{7sd} 1^{6sd} 3^{6sd} **1-3-9 £3,942**

She Who Dares Wins *L R James* 9 a52
5 b m Atraf - Mirani (Ire)
2^{5sd} 2^{5sd} 15^{5gf} 13^{5sd} **0-2-4 £1,244**

She's Dunnett *Mrs C A Dunnett* 43
2 b f Diktat - College Night (Ire)
9^{5g} 10^{6gf} 14^{6gf} 8^{5f} **0-0-4**

She's Enchanted *Miss J R Tooth* 20
5 b m Emarati (USA) - Enchanting Kate
12^{6gf} 11^{7sd} **0-0-2**

She's Expensive (Ire) *I A Wood* 38 a35
3 b f Spectrum (Ire) - Pirouette
18^{8gf} 7^{8s} 8^{10g} 6^{10sd} 13^{8sd} 11^{10g} **0-0-6**

She's My Dream (Ire) *A J Lidderdale* a6
3 ch f General Monash (USA) - She's My Love
13^{7sd} **0-0-1**

She's My Outsider *I A Wood* 83 a58
3 b f Docksider (USA) - Solar Flare (Ire)
13^{7g} 10^{7gf} 3^{8f} 8^{8gf} 3^{8g} 19^{9g} 2^{8g} 6^{8g} 8^{7hy} 12^{7sd} **0-2-10 £4,035**

She's Our Beauty (Ire) *D Nicholls* 66
2 b f Imperial Ballet (Ire) - Eleonora D'Arborea
9^{5s} 1^{5gs} 4^{5g} 5^{5gf} 5^{5gf} **1-0-5 £2,951**

She's Our Lass (Ire) *D Carroll* 77 a66
4 b f Orpen (USA) - Sharadja (Ire)
6^{10gs} 8^{8gf} 8^{9sd} 8^{9gs} 9^{9sd} 8^{9sd} 7^{9sd} **0-0-7**

Shebaan *P S McEntee* a38
4 b f Compton Place - Chairmans Daughter
9^{7sd} 11^{10sd} 12^{7sd} **0-0-3**

Sheboygan (Ire) *J G Given* 93
3 ch f Grand Lodge (USA) - White Satin (Ire)
1^{8s} 14^{8gy} 7^{8gf} 8^{7g} **1-0-4 £8,323**

Shekan Star *K G Reveley* 51 a53
3 b f Sri Pekan (USA) - Celestial Welcome
7^{10gs} 5^{8g} 2^{10s} 6^{8g} 6^{8gf} 9^{11g} 6^{10g} 4^{8g} 2^{9sd} 1^{11g} 2^{12sd} 4^{9sd} 3^{12sd} **1-4-13 £3,078**

Shelhom *M A Jarvis* 83
2 b g Green Desert (USA) - Felawnah (USA)
1^{7s} **1-0-1 £3,305**

Sheliak *B S Rothwell* a26
4 b f Binary Star (USA) - Flo's Choice (Ire)
11^{9s} 5^{12sd} **0-0-2**

Shellatana *J M Bradley* 50
2 b f Mister Baileys - Altizaf
6^{6gf} 4^{6f} 20^{6g} **0-0-3**

Sheltonstopcat *J G Given* 59
2 ch g Mister Baileys - Arminda
13^{6gf} 11^{7s} 10^{8gf} **0-0-3**

Sherbourne *M Madgwick* 2 a44
3 b f Tipsy Creek (USA) - Margarets First
2^{7sd} 6^{8sd} 4^{7sd} 12^{7sd} 3^{6sd} 10^{9sd} 4^{6sd} 12^{5sd} 7^{6gs} 7^{7s} **0-2-10 £619**

Shergael (Ire) *J L Spearing* 53 a53
4 b g Barathea (Ire) - Shergress
8^{9sd} 9^{9sd} 13^{8g} 11^{8gs} 4^{10gf} 9^{10gf} 7^{11g} 8^{10gs} **0-1-8**

Sheriff's Deputy *J W Unett* 65 a67
5 b g Atraf - Forest Fantasy
2^{9sd} 3^{9sd} 4^{9sd} 4^{11g} 4^{8gf} 7^{8gf} 10^{12sd} **0-3-7 £2,515**

Shermeen (Ire) *J A Osborne* 98
2 b f Desert Style (Ire) - Cover Girl (Ire)
3^{5g} 1^{5gf} 9^{5gf} 18^{5gf} 3^{5g} 1^{5s} 1^{6gf} 5^{7gf} 3^{5g}
3-3-9 £27,260

Shes Minnie *J G M O'Shea* 67
2 b f Bertolini (USA) - Wintzig
5^{5g} 2^{6g} 2^{5f} 2^{6gf} 4^{6g} 9^{7gf} **0-3-6 £3,563**

Shesthebiscuit *J Parkes* 65 a11
3 b f Diktat - Selvi
5^{6gf} 2^{7gf} 4^{7gs} 16^{7gf} 7^{8g} 12^{8sd} **0-1-6 £1,801**

Shibumi *J R Best* 11
4 ch f Cigar - Hurricane Rose
16^{11g} 15^{8f} **0-0-2**

Shielaligh *B R Millman* 59 a59
4 ch f Aragon - Sheesha (USA)
2^{7sd} 5^{7sd} 3^{6sd} 2^{6sd} 4^{6sd} 5^{6s} 3^{6hy} 13^{7gf} 5^{6g} 3^{6g} 10^{7gf} 6^{7sd} 5^{8gf} 5^{8gs} 5^{7gf} 5^{7sd} 7^{8sd} 6^{7sd}
0-5-18 £2,985

Shifty *D Carroll* 69 a61
6 b g Night Shift (USA) - Crodelle (Ire)
2^{8sd} 5^{9sd} 1^{8sd} 2^{9sd} 4^{9sd} 4^{8sd} 7^{9sd} 3^{8sd} 1^{8sd} 1^{7sd} 1^{7g} 1^{8s} 14^{8s} **5-3-13 £13,624**

Shifty Night (Ire) *Mrs C A Dunnett* 61 a68
4 b f Night Shift (USA) - Bean Island (USA)
2^{6sd} 6^{6sd} 3^{6sd} 1^{6sd} 7^{6sd} 2^{6sd} 1^{6sd} 1^{6sd} 7^{6sd} 1^{7s} 4^{6gf} 4^{6sd} 12^{6g} 13^{6gs} 7^{6sd} 6^{9sd} 9^{7sd}
4-3-17 £14,124

Shine Bright *R Hannon* 53
2 ch f Fantastic Light (USA) - Beyond Doubt
11^{7gf} 14^{8gs} **0-0-2**

Shingle Street (Ire) *Miss Venetia Williams* 71
3 b g Bahhare (USA) - Sandystones
6^{10s} 2^{12gf} **0-1-2 £1,032**

Shinko (Ire) *Miss J Feilden* 64 a52
2 b f Shinko Forest (Ire) - Sharp Circle (Ire)
11^{5g} 3^{6sd} 9^{6g} 2^{6g} 9^{6gf} 2^{7g} 12^{8g} **0-3-7 £2,460**

Shinko Femme (Ire) *M E Sowersby* 51 a19
4 b f Shinko Forest (Ire) - Kilshanny
14^{7s} 5^{7gf} 7^{7g} 10^{8gf} 5^{7gf} 15^{6g} 2^{7g} 12^{8gf} 11^{7g} 8^{8sd} **0-1-10 £856**

Shiny Thing (USA) *A King* 65
3 br f Lear Fan (USA) - Juliet's Jewel (USA)
7^{10gf} 1^{10f} 3^{10gs} 4^{12g} 6^{12gf} **1-0-5 £3,935**

Shipmaster *A King* 70
2 b g Slip Anchor - Cover Look (SAF)
9^{7g} 7^{8g} 5^{8gs} **0-0-3**

Shire (Ire) *D R C Elsworth* 66
3 br g Trans Island - Trebles (Ire)
10^{8g} 4^{8f} 9^{10gf} 14^{10gf} 6^{10gf} **0-0-5 £478**

Shirley Oaks (Ire) *Miss Z C Davison* 56 a53
7 b m Sri Pekan (USA) - Duly Elected
1^{6sd} 6^{6sd} 6^{7sd} 4^{7sd} 7^{6sd} 5^{6sd} 9^{6sd} 3^{6s} 4^{6s} 12^{7gf} 8^{7s} 8^{7gf} 3^{7gf} 9^{6gf} 8^{5gf} 2^{6gf} 11^{6s} 12^{6gf} 4^{6sd} 12^{6g} 5^{6sd} 7^{6ss} **1-3-22 £3,131**

Shirley Racquet *Mrs A J Bowlby* 41
2 b f Mark Of Esteem (Ire) - Royal Dream
12^{6gf} 7^{6gs} 10^{7gf} **0-0-3**

Shirocco (Ger) *A Fabre* 127
4 b c Monsun (Ger) - So Sedulous (USA)
3^{12gs} 4^{12gs} 1^{12y} **1-0-3 £699,330**

Shogun Prince (Ire) *A King* 80 a78
2 b c Shinko Forest (Ire) - Lady Of Dreams (Ire)
6^{6gs} 3^{6sd} 1^{7sd} 2^{7gs} **1-2-4 £5,049**

Shohrah (Ire) *M P Tregoning* 95
3 ch f Giant's Causeway (USA) - Taqreem (Ire)
5^{7gs} 6^{8f} 7^{10gf} 9^{10s} **0-0-4 £1,250**

Sholto *J O'Reilly* 54 a42
7 b g Tragic Role (USA) - Rose Mill
9^{5sd} 16^{5hy} 7^{6s} 9^{5gs} 14^{6gf} 6^{7gf} 18^{6gf} 5^{6gf} 2^{5g} 7^{6sf} **0-1-10 £431**

Shopfitter *Mrs C A Dunnett* 50
2 b c Sugarfoot - Madam Wurlitzer
11^{6gf} 3^{6gf} 16^{6g} 7^{7gf} 10^{7gf} 11^{6sd} 12^{9sd}
0-0-7 £1,386

Shore Thing (Ire) *M H Tompkins* 58
2 b c Docksider (USA) - Spicebird (Ire)
15^{7s} 8^{7s} **0-0-2**

Short Change (Ire) *A W Carroll* 53
6 b g Revoque (Ire) - Maafi Esm
12^{13gs} 13^{12gf} 3^{10s} 3^{12g} 8^{10gf} 8^{10g} **0-2-6 £776**

Short Chorus *J Balding* 47 a21
4 ch f Inchinor - Strawberry Song
14^{5gs} 6^{5g} 14^{5gf} 13^{6s} 8^{5g} 11^{5g} 9^{5sd}
0-0-7

Short Dance (USA) *B W Hills* 99
2 b f Hennessy (USA) - Clog Dance
3^{6gf} 1^{6gf} 4^{7gs} 1^{7gs} **2-1-4 £21,323**

Short Skirt *Sir Michael Stoute* 94
2 br f Diktat - Much Too Risky
1^{7gs} 7^{7gs} **1-0-2 £4,459**

Shortbread *J L Dunlop* 69
3 ch c Selkirk (USA) - Breadcrumb
3^{12gs} 8^{16gf} 15^{14gf} 17^{10gf} **0-1-4 £548**

Shortest Day *Sir Michael Stoute* 89
2 b f Zafonic (USA) - Winter Solstice
8^{7gf} 2^{7gf} 3^{7gf} 1^{8g} **1-2-4 £8,197**

Shot To Fame (USA) *W R Swinburn* 111
6 b g Quest For Fame - Exocet (USA)
5^{8gf} 4^{8gs} 6^{8g} 8^{10gf} 15^{11gf} 19^{9s} 6^{8gs}
0-0-7 £2,210

Shotley Dancer *N Bycroft* 53 a31
6 ch m Danehill Dancer (Ire) - Hayhurst
5^{14sd} 10^{16g} 6^{8gf} 6^{12g} 4^{16gf} 3^{10gs} 9^{14g} 12^{10g} 6^{10g} 14^{17g} 12^{14s} 5^{12sd} **0-1-12 £921**

Show Me The Lolly (Fr) *P J McBride* 54 a57
5 b m Sri Pekan (USA) - Sugar Lolly (USA)
7^{10g} 2^{8g} 16^{7s} 9^{8gf} 8^{9sd} 7^{10f} 3^{7g} 2^{9sd} 1^{8f} 4^{8gf} 2^{7sd} 3^{9sd} 2^{9sd} 4^{7gf} 3^{7sf} 2^{10sd} 6^{7sd} 2^{9sd}
1-11-18 £8,628

Show Thyme *K A Ryan* 57 a35
2 ch g Compton Place - Souadah (USA)
10^{6g} 8^{6g} 12^{6gf} 10^{7sd} **0-0-4**

Showtime Annie *A Bailey* 59 a58
4 b f Wizard King - Rebel County (Ire)
5^{9sd} 5^{9sd} 2^{9sd} 4^{9sd} 5^{9sd} 4^{8sd} 6^{8s} 10^{9gs} 3^{8s} 13^{8g} 6^{10gs} 6^{9gs} 10^{8gf} 2^{8g} 9^{9g} 8^{7s} 6^{8s} 9^{7hy} 7^{9sf} 5^{11sd} **0-3-20 £2,961**

Showtime Faye *A Bailey* a40
3 b f Overbury (Ire) - Rebel County (Ire)
11^{8sd} 2^{8sd} 12^{9sd} 12^{8sd} **0-1-4 £409**

Shrine Mountain (USA) *J R Holt* 42 a66
3 b g Distorted Humor (USA) - Fancy Ruler (USA)
9^{8s} 5^{6sd} 17^{8gf} 13^{7gf} 10^{9sd} 8^{7sd} **0-0-6**

Shrink *M Dods* 79
4 b f Mind Games - Miss Mercy (Ire)
1^{5g} 1^{5g} 2^{5f} 5^{6gf} **2-1-4 £11,253**

Shropshirelass *P S McEntee* 49 a51

2 b f Beat All (USA) - Emma-Lyne
17^{7gf} 9^{5gf} 4^{5sd} 9^{6gf} 12^{7sd} **0-0-5 £262**

Shugula (Ire) *Ms J S Doyle* 47 a47
3 ch f Tagula (Ire) - Rose Of Shuaib (Ire)
7^{10sd} 11^{10gf} 8^{9sd} 8^{12gf} 14^{10g} 12^{7gf} **0-0-6**

Shunkawakhan (Ire) *G C H Chung* 65 a66
2 b c Indian Danehill (Ire) - Special Park (USA)
2^{5gs} 2^{6sd} 7^{7sd} 17^{5hy} **0-2-4 £2,604**

Shush *C E Brittain* 66 a71
7 b g Shambo - Abuzz
2^{10gf} 1^{12sd} 10^{10sd} 7^{10g} 5^{10gf} 6^{10g} **1-1-6 £3,547**

Shy Glance (USA) *J H M Gosden*
3 b c Red Ransom (USA) - Royal Shyness
16^{10s} **0-0-1**

Siakira *I A Wood* 65 a50
2 ch f Golden Snake (USA) - Minette
5^{7gf} 7^{7gf} 6^{7gs} 11^{7g} 4^{7f} 3^{8gs} 3^{6s} 6^{8sd} **0-1-8 £4,850**

Sian Thomas *David Marnane* 75 a73
4 ch f Magic Ring (Ire) - Midnight Break
2^{12sd} 1^{13sd} 2^{12sd} 12^{14g} 2^{14sd} 2^{14sd} 1^{13gf} 5^{15gf} 8^{13gf} 2^{13gf} 10^{12gy} 9^{12gy} 4^{14y} 23^{10g} **2-4-14 £12,602**

Sicilian (Ire) *B W Hills* 70
2 b g Sadler's Wells (USA) - Hula Angel (USA)
7^{6gs} 5^{7g} 8^{8gf} **0-0-3**

Sidney Charles (Ire) *J A B Old*
3 br g Mister Baileys - Distant Music
15^{10gs} 8^{12gs} **0-0-2**

Sidonius (Pol) *Mrs P Townsley* a31
5 b g Special Power - Solera (Pol)
8^{10sd} **0-0-1**

Siegfrieds Night (Ire) *M C Chapman* 55
4 ch g Night Shift (USA) - Shelbiana (USA)
6^{10hy} 10^{12gf} 15^{10gs} **0-0-3 £215**

Siena Gold *B J Meehan* 95
3 b/br f Key Of Luck (USA) - Corn Futures
10^{7gs} 5^{6s} 2^{6g} 6^{6gf} **0-0-4 £3,230**

Siena Star (Ire) *Robert Gray* 67
7 b g Brief Truce (USA) - Gooseberry Pie
12^{12gf} **0-0-1**

Sienna Storm (Ire) *M H Tompkins* 77
2 b c Peintre Celebre (USA) - Saint Ann (USA)
13^{7g} 1^{8gs} 7^{8gs} **1-0-3 £5,070**

Siera Spirit (Ire) *M G Quinlan* 40 a57
4 b f Desert Sun - Jay And-A (Ire)
6^{7sd} 13^{6sd} 5^{6s} **0-0-3**

Sierra *A W Carroll* 56 a62
4 ch f Dr Fong (USA) - Warning Belle
3^{7sd} 9^{8sd} 9^{9sd} 7^{8hy} 7^{7sd} 4^{7gf} 4^{7gf} 7^{9sd} 15^{8gf} 11^{7sf} **0-1-10 £1,121**

Sierra Vista *D W Barker* 105 a77
5 ch m Atraf - Park Vista
5^{5sd} 3^{6s} 2^{5gs} 16^{5gf} 4^{6gf} 9^{6g} 1^{6g} 1^{5gs} 4^{6gf} 9^{6g} 1^{5s} 5^{6gs} 13^{6g} 8^{5g} 1^{5g} 2^{6s} 18^{6g} 4^{6g} 1^{5s} **5-3-19 £80,304**

Sigismundus (Ire) *J R Boyle* a69
2 b g Mozart (Ire) - Bella Vie (Ire)
12^{6g} 1^{7sd} **1-0-2 £4,138**

Sign Of Luck (Ire) *C E Brittain* 66
3 ch f Daylami (Ire) - Ascot Cyclone (USA)
6^{9gs} 7^{12gf} **0-0-2**

Signal Hill *W J Haggas* 57 a7
2 ch g Observatory (USA) - Rose Des Andes (Ire)
3^{7gf} 8^{7sd} 6^{7s} **0-1-3 £496**

Signatory (USA) *J H M Gosden* 93
3 b c Kris S (USA) - Escrow Agent (USA)
2^{10gf} 1^{10gs} 2^{11g} **1-2-3 £8,909**

Signor Albertini (Ire) *P C Haslam* 21 a31
2 b g Bertolini (USA) - Snow Eagle (Ire)
10^{6g} 11^{6sd} 13^{8gf} **0-0-3**

Signor Peltro *H Candy* 76
2 b g Bertolini (USA) - Pewter Lass
1^{6gs} 15^{6gf} 14^{7gs} **1-0-3 £3,591**

Signor Whippee *A Berry* 41 a47
2 ch g Observatory (USA) - Revoltosa (Ire)
16^{6gf} 9^{5g} 8^{5g} 6^{6gs} 4^{6gf} 7^{5gf} 3^{5sd} 8^{5sd} **0-1-8 £1,180**

Signora Panettiera (Fr) *M R Channon* a18
4 ch f Lord Of Men - Karaferya (USA)
8^{14sd} **0-0-1**

Silberweide (Ger) *M F Harris* a46
6 ch m Motley (USA) - Stairway To Heaven (Ger)
4^{8sd} 12^{9sd} **0-0-2**

Silca's Sister *M R Channon* 114
2 ch f Inchinor - Silca-Cisa
5^{6gs} 1^{6gf} 1^{6s} **2-0-3 £147,427**

Silent Jo (Jpn) *Saeed Bin Suroor* 87
3 b c Sunday Silence (USA) - Jo Knows (USA)
5^{12g} 8^{12gf} 4^{11g} 2^{11gf} 2^{14s} 1^{12f} 4^{12g} **1-2-7 £7,498**

Silent Spring (USA) *B W Hills* 63 a59
3 b f Honour And Glory (USA) - Polar Bird
4^{7gs} 8^{7sd} 5^{6gf} 11^{6gf} 12^{6g} 2^{5sd} 6^{6sf} **0-1-7 £1,594**

Silent Storm *C A Cyzer* 71 a78
5 ch g Zafonic (USA) - Nanda
6^{9sd} 5^{6sd} 8^{7sd} 10^{6sd} 4^{8sd} 8^{7sd} 1^{8sd} 7^{7g} 2^{7sd} 4^{9sd} 5^{7sd} 3^{8gf} 7^{7sd} 7^{12sd} 11^{8sd} 8^{9sd} 5^{9sd} 1^{6sd} **2-2-18 £9,613**

Silent Street *K G Reveley* 53
2 b g Celtic Swing - Smart Spirit (Ire)
8^{5g} 6^{6gf} 12^{6g} 6^{8g} **0-0-4**

Silent Times (Ire) *E J O'Neill* 112
2 b c Danehill Dancer (Ire) - Recoleta (USA)
2^{7gs} 1^{7gs} 2^{7s} 3^{7g} 1^{7gs} **2-2-5 £59,801**

Silent Witness (Aus) *A S Cruz* 128
6 b g El Moxie (USA) - Jade Tiara (Aus)
1^{5g} 1^{5gy} 1^{6gf} 1^{7gf} 2^{8gf} 3^{8f} 1^{6f} **5-2-7 £1,370,696**

Silidan *T P Tate* 90
2 b g Dansili - In Love Again (Ire)
1^{6gf} 4^{6g} 12^{6g} 1^{7gf} 2^{7gf} **2-1-5 £13,501**

Silistra *Mrs L C Jewell*
6 gr g Sadler's Wells (USA) - Dundel (Ire)
8^{10s} **0-0-1**

Silk And Scarlet *A P O'Brien* 106
3 b f Sadler's Wells (USA) - Danilova (USA)
6^{8vs} 4^{8s} 5^{12g} 6^{12gf} 11^{10f} **0-0-5 £27,890**

Silk Fan (Ire) *W R Swinburn* 91
4 b f Unfuwain (USA) - Alikhlas
15^{8gs} 7^{8gs} 6^{7gf} 8^{7gf} **0-0-4 £324**

Silk Merchant (Ire) *J Howard Johnson* 61
2 b c Distant Music (USA) - Space Travel
12^{6g} 6^{5g} **0-0-2**

Silken Act (Can) *Mrs A J Perrett* 76
2 b f Theatrical - Silca Key Service
5^{7gf} 5^{8g} **0-0-2**

Silken Sky *D J Coakley* 79 a71
2 b c Septieme Ciel (USA) - Westwood (Fr)
6^{6f} 9^{7gf} 1^{6sd} 6^{7s} 22^{6g} **1-0-5 £3,090**

Silloth Spirit *Mrs A M Naughton* 19
5 b g Atraf - Gaelic Air
12^{7gf} 16^{7gf} 12^{8g} 16^{17f} **0-0-4**

Silsong (USA) *Miss Gay Kelleway* 61 a51
3 ch f Stephen Got Even (USA) - Silver Trainor (USA)
6^{8g} 15^{7gf} 3^{10g} 2^{10sd} 2^{12ss} 4^{12sd} 6^{12sd}
0-3-7 £2,215

Silvabella (Ire) *D Haydn Jones* a14
2 gr f Monashee Mountain (USA) - Siva (Fr)
8^{7sd} **0-0-1**

Silvaline *T Keddy* 79
6 gr g Linamix (Fr) - Upend
10^{11gs} 9^{10s} 12^{10gf} 11^{12gf} 5^{10g} 9^{10g} 10^{10gf}
7^{9gs} 5^{10g} 6^{10g} 10^{10gf} **0-0-11 £531**

Silver Bangle *S Kirk* 54 a31
2 gr f Robellino (USA) - Silver Charm
6^{6g} 4^{6f} 3^{7g} 11^{7sd} 13^{7gf} **0-1-5 £526**

Silver Bank *M W Easterby* 39
2 b f Silver Patriarch (Ire) - Piggy Bank
9^{5g} 7^{5gf} 10^{5g} **0-0-3**

Silver Bark *E A L Dunlop* a67
3 b f Royal Applause - Argent Du Bois (USA)
4^{7sd} **0-0-1 £260**

Silver Blue (Ire) *R Hannon* 95 a88
2 ch c Indian Lodge (Ire) - Silver Echo
6^{6g} 3^{6gf} 1^{7sd} 3^{7g} 1^{8gf} 4^{8g} 10^{8g} **2-2-7**
£12,583

Silver Chariot *B W Hills* 39 a70
2 gr c Silver Patriarch (Ire) - Asian Love
20^{7gs} 8^{7sd} 1^{7sd} **1-0-3 £3,100**

Silver Court *R J Price* 46
3 b g Silver Patriarch (Ire) - Double Stake (USA)
6^{10g} 8^{10hy} 3^{8gf} 3^{10gs} 12^{7sd} **0-2-5 £720**

Silver Crest *E S McMahon* 89
2 gr c Zilzal (USA) - Red Typhoon
2^{5gs} 3^{5gs} 7^{5g} 4^{5gf} 1^{5gf} 14^{6gf} **1-2-6**
£7,598

Silver Dane (Ire) *Mrs C A Dunnett* 64 a64
3 b g Danetime (Ire) - Silver Prairie (Ire)
7^{6sd} 7^{6sd} 2^{5sd} 6^{5sd} 3^{5sd} 5^{5s} 7^{5f} 6^{6g} 10^{5gf}
6^{6sd} 1^{5gf} 2^{5gf} 5^{5gf} 10^{5gf} 9^{5ft} **1-3-15**
£6,592

Silver Dip *B W Hills* 77
2 gr f Gulch (USA) - Silver Bandana (USA)
7^{7g} 1^{7gf} 12^{7gf} **1-0-3 £10,627**

Silver Dreamer (Ire) *H S Howe* 46 a56
3 b f Brave Act - Heads We Called (Ire)
14^{8gf} 5^{12sd} 7^{12g} 11^{16g} 7^{12sd} **0-0-5**

Silver Fern (Ire) *Eoin Doyle* 49
3 b f Lujain (USA) - Remuria (USA)
21^{6s} 8^{10f} 8^{12gy} 9^{8g} **0-0-4**

Silver Highlight (Can) *A M Balding* 94
3 gr/ro f Silver Charm (USA) - Rare Opportunity (USA)
6^{10gs} 4^{10gf} 1^{10f} **1-0-3 £66,967**

Silver Island *R M H Cowell* 43 a47
4 ch g Silver Patriarch (Ire) - Island Maid
11^{7sd} 2^{7sd} 12^{9sd} 13^{7sd} 10^{6sd} 2^{6g} 12^{6gs} 1^{5sd}
15^{6g} **1-2-9 £2,233**

Silver Jade *C J Teague* 9
4 b f Silver Patriarch (Ire) - Kinraddie
8^{10gf} 9^{14g} **0-0-2**

Silver Mont (Ire) *Mrs A Duffield* 56
2 b c Montjeu (Ire) - Silvernus
11^{9g} 5^{8g} 11^{10g} **0-0-3**

Silver Morgan *A B Haynes* a24
3 gr g Silver Patriarch (Ire) - Liberatrice (Fr)
14^{10sd} 8^{12gf} **0-0-2**

Silver Nun *T D Easterby* 28
2 b f Mind Games - Sapphire Mill
10^{5gs} 14^{5gf} 13^{6gf} **0-0-3**

Silver Palace (Ire) *D Mullarkey* a58
4 b g Night Shift (USA) - French Quartet (Ire)
12^{10sd} 12^{12sd} **0-0-2**

Silver Prophet (Ire) *M R Bosley* 69 a54
6 gr g Idris (Ire) - Silver Heart
13^{12g} 4^{13gs} 5^{12gf} 5^{12sd} 7^{12gs} 5^{12gs} 4^{12gs}
0-0-7 £601

Silver Reign *J A Geake* 50 a39
4 gr g Prince Sabo - Primo Donna Magna
9^{6gs} 16^{7gf} 5^{6s} 9^{6f} 10^{5gf} 10^{6gs} 3^{6sd}
0-1-7 £211

Silver Rhythm *K R Burke*
4 ch f Silver Patriarch (Ire) - Party Treat (Ire)
PU^{12sd} **0-0-1**

Silver Rocket *I A Wood* 46 a42
2 b f Cyrano De Bergerac - Exit
12^{5g} 6^{5gs} 2^{5gf} 4^{5f} 4^{5sd} 6^{5gf} 2^{5gf} 10^{5sd} 6^{5gf}
0-2-9 £1,411

Silver Sail *J S Wainwright* 46
2 gr f Daylami (Ire) - Fiveofive (Ire)
6^{5g} 8^{5g} 5^{6gf} 7^{6g} 10^{7gf} **0-0-5**

Silver Seeker (USA) *A R Dicken* 47
5 gr g Seeking The Gold (USA) - Zelanda (Ire)
5^{16gf} 4^{16gs} 8^{14gf} 5^{16gf} 13^{13s} 3^{12gf} 2^{12f} 8^{12gf}
16^{13s} **0-3-9 £1,277**

Silver Silence (Jpn) *M J Wallace* 67
4 b/br g Sunday Silence (USA) - Island Of Silver (USA)
8^{16gs} 11^{12gf} 16^{9g} 11^{10g} 13^{10gf} 9^{9gf} 8^{10gf}
0-0-7

Silver Song *J L Dunlop* 58
3 gr c Silver Patriarch (Ire) - Singing The Blues
4^{12s} 8^{14g} 12^{14g} 9^{16gs} 5^{18gf} 3^{16g} 9^{16g} 11^{17gs}
0-1-8 £845

Silver Visage (Ire) *Miss J Feilden* 63 a62
3 b g Lujain (USA) - About Face
6^{8gf} 1^{7g} 3^{6f} 13^{7gf} 3^{6gf} 4^{7sd} 9^{8sd} **1-2-7**
£3,903

Silverhay *T D Barron* 76
4 b g Inchinor - Moon Spin
7^{8s} 5^{8f} 4^{8g} 4^{7gf} 5^{10gf} 2^{10gf} 7^{10gs} 10^{10gs} 3^{8g}
11^{11gs} 10^{10s} 1^{10g} 11^{10gf} 4^{10gf} 14^{10s}
1-4-15 £7,754

Silverstein (USA) *J H M Gosden* 79
4 b/br c Seeking The Gold (USA) - Salchow (USA)
3^{8g} **0-1-1 £758**

Silvertown *L Lungo* 81
10 b g Danehill (USA) - Docklands (USA)
1^{14gf} 1^{16gf} **2-0-2 £13,558**

Simlet *E W Tuer* 40
10 b g Forzando - Besito
3^{16f} **0-1-1 £520**

Simon's Seat (USA) *S C Burrough* a63
6 ch g Woodman (USA) - Spire (USA)
2^{16sd} 2^{14sd} 2^{16sd} 4^{17sd} 2^{14sd} 14^{12gf} 5^{17sd}
0-4-7 £3,292

Simonda *Mrs A J Perrett* 97
4 ch f Singspiel (Ire) - Jetbeeah (Ire)

1^{10g} 6^{12g} 13^{12gs} 5^{14s} 9^{14gs} 3^{12g} 5^{14hy}
1-0-7 £11,696

Simple Exchange (Ire) *D K Weld* 111 a106
4 b c Danehill (USA) - Summer Trysting (USA)
3^{7gf} 8^{10gf} 7^{8gf} 6^{10sd} **0-0-4 £5,008**

Simplify *T M Jones* 71 a75
3 b g Fasliyev (USA) - Simplicity
5^{7sd} 4^{8hy} 5^{7g} 9^{7g} 6^{8gs} 2^{8sd} 2^{8sd} 2^{8gf} 1^{8gf}
8^{10gs} 8^{9g} 7^{8f} 12^{8f} 13^{8s} **1-3-14 £6,917**

Simply Sid *W H Tinning* 17
4 b g Presidium - Chadwick's Ginger
9^{11gf} **0-0-1**

Simply St Lucia *J R Weymes* 68 a68
3 b f Charnwood Forest (Ire) - Mubadara (Ire)
4^{7sd} 2^{8g} 6^{9sd} 3^{7f} 6^{8gf} 1^{8s} 9^{8gf} 8^{9ft} 15^{8s}
2^{8sf} 3^{8sd} **1-3-11 £7,602**

Simply Sunshine (Ire) *D W P Arbuthnot* 85
3 b f Desert Sun - Summer Fashion
1^{7gs} 15^{8gf} 4^{7gf} 7^{8gf} 7^{8gf} **1-0-5 £7,272**

Simply The Guest (Ire) *N Tinkler* 27 a71
6 b g Mujadil (USA) - Ned's Contessa (Ire)
6^{6sd} 1^{11sd} 1^{9sd} 1^{12sd} 7^{12sd} 14^{12g} 6^{11sd} 12^{14sd}
8^{11sd} 12^{8sd} 11^{8sd} 11^{8sd} **3-0-12 £9,265**

Simpsons Gamble (Ire) *R M Flower*
2 b g Tagula (Ire) - Kiva
10^{6sd} 13^{7sd} RO^{5g} 15^{6g} **0-0-4**

Simpsons Mount (Ire) *R M Flower* 80 a80
4 ch g Tagula (Ire) - Brunswick
1^{5s} 7^{6g} 1^{5g} 8^{5f} 12^{5gf} 12^{6gf} 6^{5gf} 2^{5g} 2^{6sd}
3^{5gf} 4^{5s} 4^{5gs} 4^{5g} 5^{5s} **2-3-14 £15,917**

Simpsons Ross (Ire) *R M Flower* a47
2 br g Imperial Ballet (Ire) - Brunswick
10^{6sd} 10^{6sd} **0-0-2**

Sin City *Unknown* 76
2 b c Sinndar (Ire) - Turn Of A Century
7^{7gf} 5^{7g} 5^{7gf} 1^{8gf} **1-0-4 £5,187**

Sincerely *B W Hills* 66 a52
3 b f Singspiel (Ire) - Noble Form
7^{7g} 4^{8s} 3^{8gf} 5^{7g} 2^{7g} 2^{7sd} 6^{7sd} **0-3-7**
£3,616

Sindapour (Ire) *M C Pipe* 76
7 b g Priolo (USA) - Sinntara (Ire)
11^{14gf} 11^{20gf} **0-0-2**

Sindirana (Ire) *Sir Michael Stoute* 83
2 br f Kalanisi (Ire) - Sinndiya (Ire)
1^{7g} 4^{8s} **1-0-2 £6,453**

Singalong *D J Daly* 78
3 b f Singspiel (Ire) - No Frills (Ire)
3^{8g} 3^{8g} 2^{8gf} 3^{9gf} **0-4-4 £3,611**

Singhalongtasveer *W Storey* 50
3 b g Namaqualand (USA) - Felinwen
10^{7s} 2^{8gs} 2^{10gf} 13^{10gf} 5^{8gf} 4^{9gf} 10^{9gf} 2^{11gf}
0-3-8 £3,208

Single Track Mind *J R Boyle* 40 a48
7 b g Mind Games - Compact Disc (Ire)
3^{8sd} 12^{7sd} 7^{7gf} 10^{9sd} 8^{8sd} 5^{7sd} 10^{9sf}
0-1-7 £207

Singlet *D J Daly* 71 a61
4 ch g Singspiel (Ire) - Ball Gown
6^{14sd} 7^{12sd} 9^{10gs} 1^{10g} 2^{10gs} 3^{10g} 2^{10s}
1-3-7 £6,911

Singular *J H M Gosden* 75
2 ch f Zafonic (USA) - Tenuous
2^{7g} 4^{8s} **0-1-2 £1,886**

Sinjaree *Mrs S Lamyman* a27
7 b g Mark Of Esteem (Ire) - Forthwith
7^{11sd} 9^{9sd} 10^{8sd} **0-0-3**

Sinnbad *M Johnston* 35
2 b c Sinndar (Ire) - Funny Girl (Ire)
6^{8g} **0-0-1**

Sinner Or Saint (Ire) *T D Easterby* 68
2 ch c Sinndar (Ire) - Hillquest
PU^{7gf} 5^{7gf} 8^{8gf} 2^{7g} 3^{8g} **0-2-5 £2,587**

Sinnomore (Ire) *M A Magnusson* a73
3 ch g Sinndar (Ire) - Demure
2^{10sd} 4^{12sd} **0-1-2 £1,600**

Sion Hill (Ire) *M C Chapman* 61 a59
4 b g Desert Prince (Ire) - Mobilia
10^{7sd} 10^{8sd} 9^{8sd} 11^{11sd} 5^{9sd} 9^{7sd} 3^{6sd} 2^{7g}
2^{7sd} 3^{7g} 4^{8s} 8^{7sd} 3^{8gf} 15^{7f} 7^{8gf} 9^{9sd} 4^{6g}
9^{8gf} 9^{7g} 10^{5sd} 5^{6sd} **0-6-21 £2,040**

Sir Arthur (Ire) *M Johnston* 48
2 ch c Desert Prince (Ire) - Park Express
5^{6gf} **0-0-1**

Sir Bluebird (Ire) *R Hannon* 62
3 ch g Bluebird (USA) - Persian Tapestry
13^{6gf} 3^{6gf} 12^{7g} 8^{7gf} 9^{8gs} 3^{7s} 13^{7g} 7^{10g} 4^{7gf}
0-3-9 £1,100

Sir Bond (Ire) *B Smart* 73 a63
4 ch g Desert Sun - In Tranquility (Ire)
1^{8sd} 2^{8sd} 1^{8sd} 1^{9sd} 2^{7s} 1^{7g} 7^{8g} 4^{9gf} 10^{8gs}
9^{7g} 9^{8g} **4-2-11 £9,261**

Sir Desmond *Rae Guest* 86 a80
7 gr g Petong - I'm Your Lady
5^{6g} 10^{6gf} 7^{6g} 3^{6g} 13^{6gs} 8^{6g} 2^{6gs} 9^{6gs} 5^{5sd}
8^{6sf} 5^{6sd} **0-2-11 £3,760**

Sir Don (Ire) *D Nicholls* 51
6 b g Lake Coniston (Ire) - New Sensitive
19^{6gf} 13^{6f} 17^{7g} 14^{6gf} 12^{6gs} 9^{7f} **0-0-6**

Sir Edward Burrow (Ire) *W Storey*
7 b g Distinctly North (USA) - Alalja (Ire)
14^{14sd} **0-0-1**

Sir Edward Elgar (Ire) *J H M Gosden* 82
3 b c King's Best (USA) - Lady Elgar (Ire)
4^{9g} 3^{10gf} 3^{10g} 1^{10gs} **1-2-4 £5,267**

Sir Edwin Landseer (USA) *Christian Wroe* 89 a85
5 gr/ro h Lit De Justice (USA) - Wildcat Blue (USA)
6^{6ft} 2^{6ft} 7^{6ft} 9^{6g} 1^{6g} 6^{5s} 2^{6gs} 2^{6gs} 6^{6g} 3^{5g}
4^{6ft} 4^{6ft} 10^{7g} 1^{5ft} **2-4-14 £22,998**

Sir Ernest (Ire) *D Shaw* 36 a65
4 b g Daggers Drawn (USA) - Kyra Crown (Ire)
10^{5sd} 8^{5sd} 7^{5sd} 1^{5sd} 7^{5sd} 14^{5sd} 11^{5sd} 12^{5gs}
15^{5gf} 9^{5g} 14^{5g} 12^{5gf} **1-0-12 £2,625**

Sir Francis (Ire) *Mrs L Stubbs* a67
7 b g Common Grounds - Red Note
4^{7sd} 4^{7sd} 11^{7sd} **0-0-3 £264**

Sir Gerard *J R Fanshawe* 69 a80
2 b c Marju (Ire) - Chapeau
4^{7g} 1^{7sd} **1-0-2 £4,333**

Sir Haydn *J R Jenkins* 71 a83
5 ch g Definite Article - Snowscape
2^{10sd} 1^{10sd} 2^{10sd} 1^{10sd} 1^{9sd} 8^{10gf} 6^{10g} 8^{10gf}
6^{10gf} 9^{8sd} 7^{10g} 12^{12sd} 7^{11sd} 5^{9sd} 2^{10sd}
3-3-15 £14,887

Sir Loin *N Tinkler* 68
4 ch g Compton Place - Charnwood Queen
17^{5hy} 1^{5g} 12^{5f} 11^{5gf} 17^{5gf} 3^{5g} 12^{5g} 19^{5gf}
5^{5gf} 8^{5gf} **1-1-10 £3,800**

Sir Mikeale *G Prodromou* a19
2 b c Easycall - Sleep Standing (Ire)

8^{5ss} **0-0-1**

Sir Monty (USA) *Mrs A J Perrett* 77
3 ch g Cat's Career (USA) - Lady Of Meadowlane (USA)
9^{11g} 4^{10gf} 1^{11gf} 6^{12gs} 2^{14gf} 3^{14gf} 2^{16g} 1^{16g} **2-4-8 £10,448**

Sir Night (Ire) *Jedd O'Keeffe* 56
5 b g Night Shift (USA) - Highly Respected (Ire)
7^{12sd} 5^{10g} 1^{10gf} 7^{12f} 5^{12gf} 4^{9gf} 10^{11gf} 6^{11g} **1-0-8 £1,952**

Sir Nod *Miss J A Camacho* 79 a89
3 b g Tagula (Ire) - Nordan Raider
6^{7s} 10^{7g} 12^{7sd} 2^{6g} 1^{6g} 10^{5gs} 2^{6sd} **1-2-7 £10,344**

Sir Northerndancer (Ire) *B Ellison* 56 a31
6 b h Danehill Dancer (Ire) - Lady At War
11^{7gf} 6^{7s} 9^{6sd} 4^{7gs} 5^{6gf} 4^{6gs} 14^{7g} 9^{6sd} 10^{7gf} **0-0-9**

Sir Orpen (Ire) *T D Barron* 79
2 gr g Orpen (USA) - Yalciyna
8^{5gf} 2^{5gf} 2^{6g} 2^{6gs} 16^{6gf} 9^{6g} **0-3-6 £14,252**

Sir Percy *M P Tregoning* 119
2 b c Mark Of Esteem (Ire) - Percy's Lass
1^{6g} 1^{6gf} 1^{7s} 1^{7gs} **4-0-4 £201,632**

Sir Sandrovitch (Ire) *R A Fahey* 64 a69
9 b g Polish Patriot (USA) - Old Downie
1^{5sd} 1^{5sd} 2^{5sd} 3^{5sd} 8^{5sd} 3^{5sd} 12^{5gs} 5^{5gf} 5^{5gf} 10^{5gf} 2^{5gf} 2^{5gf} 7^{5g} 8^{5g} 5^{6f} 1^{5gf} 9^{5g} UR^{5g} 4^{5gf} 6^{5sd} 2^{5sd} 5^{6sd} 3^{5sd} 4^{5sd} **3-7-24 £15,137**

Sir Sidney *J G Given* 76 a59
5 b g Shareef Dancer (USA) - Hattaafeh (Ire)
9^{14gs} 6^{10g} 4^{11gf} 6^{12gf} 10^{8g} DSQ^{9g} 5^{12sd} **0-0-7 £288**

Sir Xaar (Ire) *B Smart* 110
2 b/br c Xaar - Cradle Brief (Ire)
1^{6gf} 1^{6gf} 4^{6gf} 6^{7gs} 5^{7s} 2^{6gf} 5^{6g} 1^{6gf} 2^{6gf} **3-2-9 £55,685**

Siraj *J Ryan* 67 a64
6 b g Piccolo - Masuri Kabisa (USA)
2^{6sd} 1^{6sd} 5^{6sd} 2^{7s} 9^{7gf} 3^{6s} 5^{6g} 12^{7gs} 16^{7hy} 10^{7sd} **1-3-10 £5,357**

Sirbrit *W J Musson* 53
2 b g Cadeaux Genereux - Evening Promise
5^{6gf} 7^{5g} 12^{6s} **0-0-3**

Sirce (Ire) *D J Coakley* 90 a82
3 b f Josr Algarhoud (Ire) - Trading Aces
1^{11gs} 1^{10s} 3^{12gf} 2^{12gf} 2^{12g} 1^{12sd} 2^{12g} 1^{12gs} 14^{12hy} **4-4-9 £30,725**

Sister Eugenie (Ire) *S Kirk* 52 a46
3 b f Indian Lodge (Ire) - Skerray
9^{7gf} 5^{8s} 3^{6gf} 13^{6gf} 12^{8gf} 16^{8f} 4^{8sd} 11^{8sd} **0-1-8 £625**

Sister Gee (Ire) *R Hollinshead* 47 a42
3 b f Desert Story (Ire) - My Gloria (Ire)
9^{6gf} 10^{6gs} 7^{6sd} 4^{5g} 3^{7gs} 8^{7sd} **0-1-6 £537**

Siula Grande (Ire) *W McKeown* 28
2 ch c Raise A Grand (Ire) - Starry Skies (USA)
11^{6g} 7^{7gf} 15^{6gf} **0-0-3**

Sivivatu (USA) *J Noseda* 81
2 b c Stravinsky (USA) - Belle Sultane (USA)
6^{7gf} 1^{6gf} 5^{6g} **1-0-3 £4,394**

Siwa *E A L Dunlop* a62
2 b f Green Desert (USA) - Criquette
4^{6sf} **0-0-1 £313**

Six Of One *R Rowe* 46 a45
7 b g Kahyasi - Ten To Six
10^{16sd} 6^{14gs} 8^{18g} **0-0-3**

Sixtilsix (Ire) *I W McInnes* a34
4 ch g Night Shift (USA) - Assafiyah (Ire)
8^{8sd} **0-0-1**

Skelligs Rock (Ire) *A W Carroll* a51
5 b g Key Of Luck (USA) - Drew (Ire)
9^{12sd} 11^{9sd} **0-0-2**

Skelthwaite *Miss D A McHale* 43 a30
4 b g Desert Story (Ire) - Skip To Somerfield
10^{11sd} 6^{8sd} 7^{10g} 6^{10gf} 5^{8f} 9^{6g} **0-0-6**

Skezahra *T M Jones* 39 a13
2 b f Zaha (Can) - Skedaddle
7^{5gs} 4^{5g} 13^{6gs} 11^{6g} 20^{6s} 13^{10sd} **0-0-6**

Skhilling Spirit *T D Barron* 95
2 b g Most Welcome - Calcavella
5^{6g} 8^{5s} 3^{5gf} 5^{5g} 1^{5gf} 7^{6gf} 3^{6gf} 1^{6gf} 7^{6g} 2^{6gf} 1^{6s} **3-3-11 £38,392**

Ski Jump (USA) *R A Fahey* 90
5 gr g El Prado (Ire) - Skiable (Ire)
2^{14s} 5^{14g} 4^{20gf} 1^{12gs} 3^{14gf} 12^{12g} 5^{12g} 2^{12gf} 5^{13gs} 8^{20s} **1-3-10 £22,954**

Skiddaw Jones *M A Barnes* 33
5 b g Emperor Jones (USA) - Woodrising
3^{14g} 9^{12f} **0-0-2 £423**

Skiddaw Wolf *B Smart* 74 a51
3 ch f Wolfhound (USA) - Stealthy
6^{5gf} 6^{5sd} 1^{6f} 2^{6gf} 2^{6gf} 4^{6gf} 7^{5gf} 7^{6gf} **1-2-8 £8,519**

Skidmark *Miss J R Tooth* 72 a103
4 b g Pennekamp (USA) - Flourishing (Ire)
6^{10sd} 6^{10sd} 6^{10sd} 14^{9gf} 17^{8gs} 10^{12sd} 9^{8sd} 7^{10sd} **0-0-8 £1,077**

Skidrow *M L W Bell* 97
3 b g Bachir (Ire) - Flourishing (Ire)
9^{10gf} 9^{9gf} 5^{8gf} 1^{8g} 5^{8gs} 10^{8g} 2^{8gs} **1-1-7 £11,975**

Skin Sure Thing *A D Smith* 22 a32
2 b f Zaha (Can) - Bay Bianca (Ire)
11^{5f} 9^{7f} 5^{7ft} **0-0-3**

Skip Of Colour *P A Blockley* 20 a61
5 b g Rainbow Quest (USA) - Minskip (USA)
8^{6sd} 9^{6sd} 16^{7g} 9^{9sd} **0-0-4**

Skippit John *Ronald Thompson* 49
3 b g Abou Zouz (USA) - Lady Quinta (Ire)
10^{6sd} 9^{5s} 9^{6g} 7^{7gf} 13^{7gf} **0-0-5**

Skit *R Charlton* 51
2 b g In The Wings - Skew
10^{8g} **0-0-1**

Sky At Night (Ire) *P Mitchell* 50
2 b c Beckett (Ire) - Grade A Star (Ire)
7^{7f} 5^{7gf} 6^{8gf} 2^{8gf} **0-1-4 £856**

Sky Crusader *R Ingram* 97 a94
3 b c Mujahid (USA) - Red Cloud (Ire)
5^{9g} 1^{7g} 4^{8gf} 6^{7gf} 2^{7g} 9^{8gf} 9^{9gf} 3^{7gs} 8^{8g} 5^{7sd} **1-3-10 £30,224**

Sky High Guy (Ire) *S Kirk* a32
2 b c Galileo (Ire) - Well Bought (Ire)
12^{10sd} **0-0-1**

Sky Lodge *M W Easterby* 48
2 ch g Indian Lodge (Ire) - Jumairah Sunset
3^{5s} 8^{5gf} 11^{6gf} 12^{7g} **0-1-4 £521**

Sky Quest (Ire) *W R Swinburn* 89
7 b g Spectrum (Ire) - Rose Vibert

10^{10gf} 7^{9gf} 11^{10g} 12^{10gf} 7^{10gf} 10^{11gf} 5^{12gf}
0-0-7

Skye Boat Song *J Jay* a34
2 b c Inchinor - Nebulae (Ire)
6^{7sd} **0-0-1**

Skye's Folly (USA) *Mrs P Sly* 84
5 b g Kris S (USA) - Bittersweet Hour (USA)
4^{16s} 9^{16gf} 5^{14g} 8^{16gf} 2^{14g} 1^{17g} 3^{16gs} F^{17sd}
1-2-8 £6,939

Skyelady *Miss J A Camacho* 88
2 b f Dansili - Song Of Skye
1^{5s} 6^{5gs} 8^{5g} 2^{6g} 10^{7gf} 6^{7g} 7^{6g} 9^{7hy}
1-1-8 £9,361

Skylarker (USA) *W S Kittow* 86
7 b g Sky Classic (Can) - O My Darling (USA)
5^{10gs} 2^{12gf} 9^{12g} 3^{14gf} 10^{12gs} 8^{12gf} 3^{10s} 10^{10gs}
4^{12gf} **0-2-9 £6,115**

Skylarking (Ire) *J R Fanshawe* a44
2 ch f Docksider (USA) - Surfing
8^{7sd} 9^{6sd} **0-0-2**

Skyscape *Thomas Cooper* 90
3 b f Zafonic (USA) - Aquarelle
7^{10gf} 4^{10gf} 1^{8gf} 15^{8gy} 3^{8gf} 3^{7y} 1^{9gf} 10^{8g} 17^{8sh}
2-2-9 £15,486

Slack Willy Hilly *R Hannon* 45 a46
2 br g Dansili - Fleet Key
7^{5sd} 5^{5sd} 4^{5g} 7^{5gs} 7^{7s} 9^{7gf} 6^{8gf} **0-0-7**

Slate Grey *K R Burke* 46
3 gr g Paris House - Slipperose
7^{5gf} 5^{7gs} 6^{7g} 20^{6gf} **0-0-4**

Slavonic (USA) *K A Ryan* 69 a67
4 ch g Royal Academy (USA) - Cyrillic (USA)
12^{16sd} 9^{9sd} 2^{7sd} 7^{8g} 2^{8s} 5^{8gf} 1^{7g} 4^{7g} 4^{8gf}
4^{8gf} 1^{8gf} 5^{10s} 3^{10g} 7^{12gs} 12^{12sd} **2-3-15**
£10,107

Sleep Tight *B W Duke*
3 b c Dracula (Aus) - Pillowing
9^{12gs} **0-0-1**

Sleeping Indian *J H M Gosden* 121
4 b c Indian Ridge - Las Flores (Ire)
1^{7g} 5^{8s} 1^{7g} 2^{7gf} 5^{8g} 2^{7gs} **2-2-6**
£99,540

Sleeping Storm (Ire) *B J Meehan* 85
2 b f Danehill Dancer (Ire) - Caribbean Escape
6^{7g} 6^{7gf} 1^{6gf} 12^{6gf} **1-0-4 £4,355**

Slew Charm (Fr) *Noel T Chance* 66 a13
3 b g Marathon (USA) - Slew Bay (Fr)
10^{10sd} 2^{10g} 8^{11g} 3^{11s} 4^{11hy} 2^{11g} 4^{12g} 7^{11gs}
11^{9sd} **0-1-9 £6,631**

Sling Back (Ire) *Eamon Tyrrell* 70 a70
4 b f Desert Style (Ire) - Arabian Princess
3^{6sd} 2^{7sd} 12^{8sd} 3^{7sd} 8^{8gf} 2^{7sd} 8^{5g} 1^{7gf} 4^{6gf}
5^{8f} 10^{7gf} 6^{8g} 9^{7g} 16^{8ys} 12^{8gf} 2^{7gf} 3^{9sd} 7^{6sd}
1-6-18 £12,304

Slip Catch (Ire) *W Jarvis* a61
3 b f Intikhab (USA) - Buckle (Ire)
4^{10sd} 5^{9sd} **0-0-2 £262**

Slip Dance (Ire) *Eamon Tyrrell* 101 a88
3 br f Celtic Swing - Hawala (Ire)
5^{8ft} 1^{9s} 4^{7gf} 14^{8gf} 13^{8gy} 2^{6g} 9^{7gf} 6^{6gf} 7^{6gs}
4^{6s} 1^{5gf} 8^{5g} **2-1-12 £45,317**

Slipperfoot *J J Quinn* 51 a27
2 ch f Sugarfoot - She's A Breeze
3^{5g} 3^{5gf} 15^{6s} 8^{5sd} **0-1-4 £1,156**

Small Amount *W Jenks* a35
5 ch m Sir Harry Lewis (USA) - Pretty Scarce
10^{9sd} 15^{11g} 6^{9sd} 9^{9sf} **0-0-4**

Small Time Blues (Ire) *J Parkes* 20 a40
3 b f Danetime (Ire) - Barinia
11^{9sd} 3^{6sd} 14^{5g} 16^{7s} 14^{7sd} 11^{7sd} 7^{11sd} 10^{8sd}
5^{8sd} 8^{7sd} **0-0-10 £627**

Smart Ass (Ire) *J S Moore* 47
2 b f Shinko Forest (Ire) - Jayess Elle
6^{5f} 4^{5gf} 3^{5f} **0-1-3 £636**

Smart Boy Prince (Ire) *C Smith* 40
4 b g Princely Heir (Ire) - Miss Mulaz (Fr)
11^{16gf} 14^{16gf} **0-0-2**

Smart Cassie *Mrs A Duffield* 77
2 ch f Allied Forces (USA) - Katy-Q (Ire)
1^{5f} 3^{5gf} 12^{5gs} 3^{5gf} 3^{5g} 5^{6s} **1-2-6**
£6,621

Smart Danny *J J Quinn* a36
4 gr g Danzero (Aus) - She's Smart
7^{9sd} 6^{6sd} **0-0-2**

Smart Enough *M A Magnusson* 77
2 gr c Cadeaux Genereux - Good Enough (Fr)
7^{8gs} **0-0-1**

Smart Gal (Ire) *J L Dunlop* 71
2 ch f Galileo (Ire) - Spring Easy (Ire)
5^{7gs} 8^{8g} 3^{8gf} 5^{8g} **0-1-4 £868**

Smart Golden Boy (Ire) *Mrs L C Jewell* a52
2 ch g Raise A Grand (Ire) - Stoneware
8^{8sd} 7^{7sd} **0-0-2**

Smart John *Ian Williams* 77
5 b g Bin Ajwaad (Ire) - Katy-Q (Ire)
5^{10s} 6^{13gs} 4^{12gf} 4^{12gf} 1^{13gf} 3^{14gf} 2^{12gf} 5^{12g}
4^{13gf} 2^{12g} 2^{12gs} 6^{12g} **1-4-12 £10,121**

Smart Pick *Mrs L Williamson* 57
2 ch f Piccolo - Nevita
6^{5s} 2^{5f} 6^{5gf} 7^{5g} 4^{7g} **0-1-5 £1,149**

Smart Scot *B P J Baugh* a44
6 ch g Selkirk (USA) - Amazing Bay
7^{7sd} 4^{7sd} 2^{7sd} 6^{7sd} 8^{7sd} **0-1-5 £742**

Smart Starprincess (Ire) *P A Blockley* a49
4 b f Soviet Star (USA) - Takeshi (Ire)
7^{5sd} 7^{5sd} 10^{5sd} **0-0-3**

Smart Tiger (Ger) *N P Littmoden* a74
3 b g Tiger Hill (Ire) - Smoke Signal (Ire)
6^{10g} 4^{11g} 2^{11g} 1^{10g} 1^{10s} 3^{10sd} **2-1-6**
£6,752

Smiddy Hill *R Bastiman* 83
3 b f Factual (USA) - Hello Hobson'S (Ire)
5^{5g} 7^{5f} 6^{5gf} 11^{5g} 13^{5g} 13^{5gf} 6^{5g} 20^{5g} 11^{5s}
0-0-9 £154

Smile For Us *C Drew* 25 a55
2 b g Whittingham (Ire) - Don't Smile
12^{5gf} 6^{7sd} 14^{7gs} 5^{7sd} **0-0-4**

Smirfys Night *E S McMahon* 54 a57
6 b g Tina's Pet - Nightmare Lady
4^{6g} 10^{6gf} 2^{6sd} 11^{5gf} 4^{6g} 11^{6g} 10^{6gf} 2^{5sd}
4^{5gf} 6^{5g} 1^{7sd} 7^{7sd} **1-4-12 £3,272**

Smirfys Party *W M Brisbourne* 55 a53
7 ch g Clantime - Party Scenes
3^{5sd} 5^{5sd} 4^{5sd} 11^{6f} 5^{5sd} 8^{6g} 7^{6gf} 6^{5g} 8^{6g}
3^{6gf} 5^{6sd} 11^{7ss} **0-2-12 £834**

Smith N Allan Oils *C Smith* a65
6 b g Bahamian Bounty - Grand Splendour
2^{7sd} 4^{7sd} 9^{7sd} 7^{7sd} **0-1-4 £736**

Smitten Kitten *B J Meehan* 75 a51
2 b f Green Desert (USA) - Queens Music (USA)
8^{6gf} 4^{7g} 7^{7sd} 6^{8g} 5^{7g} **0-0-5 £325**

Smoke Alarm *N P Littmoden* 43 a50
2 gr c Almutawakel - Allarm Grey (USA)
12^{6sd} 5^{6sd} 9^{5f} 9^{8g} **0-0-4**

Smokey Blue *M J Wallace* a58
2 gr c Tomba - Misty Goddess (Ire)
9^{7sd} **0-0-1**

Smokey Brown *J C Fox* 3 a22
2 b g Inchinor - Holy Smoke
16^{8gs} 9^{9sd} **0-0-2**

Smokey Ridge *H J Collingridge* 28
3 b f Namid - Chimere (Fr)
10^{6g} **0-0-1**

Smokey The Bear *A P Jones* 60
3 ch g Fumo Di Londra (Ire) - Noble Soul
3^{6f} 6^{5gs} 10^{6gf} 11^{6f} 16^{7g} 12^{7gf} 11^{7gf}
0-0-7 £516

Smokin Beau *N P Littmoden* 96 a108
8 b g Cigar - Beau Dada (Ire)
4^{5sd} 9^{6g} 2^{5g} 2^{6s} 9^{5g} 15^{6f} 1^{5sd} 13^{5s} 19^{6gs}
15^{5gf} 18^{6gs} 12^{5s} 17^{6g} 14^{6gf} 3^{6gs} 13^{6s} 11^{6sd}
13^{5sf} **1-3-18 £22,048**

Smokin Grey *L Wells* a29
5 gr m Terimon - Wollow Maid
9^{12sd} 13^{12sd} 11^{12sd} **0-0-3**

Smokin Joe *J R Best* 50 a88
4 b g Cigar - Beau Dada (Ire)
4^{7sd} 4^{8sd} 7^{6sd} 6^{7sd} 15^{6g} 11^{7sd} 11^{8sd}
0-0-7 £1,070

Smokincanon *W G M Turner* 49 a47
3 ch g Fumo Di Londra (Ire) - Secret Miss
8^{6gf} 4^{7sd} **0-0-2**

Smoking Star *C E Brittain* 54 a37
2 b f Observatory (USA) - Gitane (Fr)
7^{7f} 9^{6g} 3^{6g} 7^{7sd} 6^{6sd} **0-1-5 £212**

Smooch *R M H Cowell* 92 a65
2 b f Inchinor - Two Step
5^{5sd} 1^{5sd} 1^{5gs} 2^{5gf} 5^{5g} 9^{6g} 3^{5g} 4^{5gf} 2^{5gs} 7^{5g}
6^{5hy} 5^{5g} 26^{6g} 3^{5sd} **2-2-14 £26,794**

Smooth Jazz *M R Channon* 72
3 b c Zafonic (USA) - Halska
6^{8gf} 2^{9g} 4^{9gs} 5^{11gf} 4^{8gf} 9^{8gf} **0-1-6**
£1,868

Smooth Mover *S C Williams* 31
3 b g Mister Baileys - Dancing Heights (Ire)
16^{10g} 15^{10gs} **0-0-2**

Smoothie (Ire) *Ian Williams* a57
7 gr g Definite Article - Limpopo
5^{12sd} 12^{14sd} **0-0-2**

Smoothly Does It *Mrs A J Bowlby* 71 a66
4 b g Efisio - Exotic Forest
7^{10sd} 4^{10g} 3^{8hy} 2^{8gs} 4^{10g} 7^{8g} **0-2-6**
£2,349

Snails Castle (Ire) *E W Tuer* 36
6 b g Danehill (USA) - Bean Island (USA)
11^{13s} 4^{16f} **0-0-2 £260**

Snake Skin *J Gallagher* 55 a58
2 ch f Golden Snake (USA) - Silken Dalliance
9^{5g} 4^{6f} 12^{5g} 1^{7g} 2^{7f} 8^{7gf} 10^{7gf} 2^{8hy} 3^{7sd}
3^{8sd} 10^{8sd} **1-4-11 £6,721**

Snap *Liam McAteer* 85
4 ch g Dr Fong (USA) - Reactress (USA)
4^{7g} 2^{7gs} 7^{7gf} 10^{8gf} 4^{8g} 7^{7g} 16^{10g} 2^{8hy} 1^{8sh}
1-2-9 £23,425

Snark (Ire) *P J Makin* 54 a76
2 b c Cape Cross (Ire) - Agoer
10^{6g} 1^{7sd} **1-0-2 £4,287**

Sneem's Rock *P R Hedger* 38 a62
4 br c Daylami (Ire) - Urchin (Ire)
7^{10sd} 6^{10sd} 3^{10sd} 3^{10sd} 8^{11gs} 11^{8sd} **0-2-6**
£838

Snookered Again *M W Easterby* 34 a59
3 b g Lujain (USA) - Highest Bid (Fr)
14^{10gf} 8^{8s} 9^{12sd} 10^{10g} 15^{10g} **0-0-5**

Snoqualmie Boy *D R C Elsworth* a77
2 b c Montjeu (Ire) - Seattle Ribbon (USA)
4^{10sd} 4^{8sd} **0-0-2 £661**

Snow Bunting *Jedd O'Keeffe* 69 a58
7 ch g Polar Falcon (USA) - Marl
9^{7gf} 4^{6gf} 4^{6g} 3^{7g} 7^{7gf} 8^{6g} 8^{7g} 7^{8g} 12^{6g} 4^{7sd}
1^{7sd} **1-2-11 £4,224**

Snow Crystal (Ire) *D R Loder* 75
2 ch f Kingmambo (USA) - Crystal Spray
1^{7f} **1-0-1 £4,075**

Snow Symphony (Ire) *D M Simcock* 59
2 b g Distant Music (USA) - Snowspin
6^{8gf} 7^{8gf} 9^{8gf} **0-0-3**

Snow Tempest (USA) *T G Mills* 56 a50
3 b g Theatrical - January's Storm (USA)
9^{10sd} 13^{10sd} 11^{16g} **0-0-3**

Snow Wolf *J M Bradley* 78 a67
4 ch g Wolfhound (USA) - Christmas Rose
6^{5sd} 9^{6sd} 6^{5g} 3^{5f} 19^{6gf} 10^{6f} 7^{6f} 10^{6g} 4^{6gf}
4^{6f} 2^{5s} 8^{5gf} 7^{5g} 13^{6g} 3^{5gs} 5^{5s} 7^{5sd}
0-3-17 £3,672

Snow's Ride *M D Hammond* 59
5 gr g Hernando (Fr) - Crodelle (Ire)
9^{18gs} **0-0-1**

Snowberry Hill (USA) *K A Ryan* 68
2 b c Woodman (USA) - Class Skipper (USA)
7^{6gf} 5^{7g} 5^{7gf} 9^{8gf} **0-0-4**

Snowed Under *J D Bethell* 81
4 gr g Most Welcome - Snowy Mantle
7^{10s} 2^{10gf} 1^{10gf} 1^{10gf} 3^{10gf} 2^{10gs} 1^{10g} 5^{10gf}
15^{10gs} 12^{10g} **3-2-10 £22,150**

So Elegant (Ire) *J Jay* 50 a57
3 b f Bahhare (USA) - Soignee
4^{8sd} 1^{9sd} 8^{10g} 13^{10g} 1^{10g} 17^{12g} 1^{10sd} 7^{12sf}
1^{13sd} 4^{10sd} **4-0-10 £5,904**

So Independent *C R Wilson*
3 b f Tipsy Creek (USA) - So Bold
12^{8s} 17^{7g} 10^{16gf} **0-0-3**

So Sober (Ire) *D Shaw* a39
7 b g Common Grounds - Femme Savante
5^{5sd} 12^{5sd} 3^{5sd} 5^{5sd} **0-1-4 £209**

So Sure (Ire) *J G M O'Shea* a41
5 b g Definite Article - Zorilla
8^{12sd} 11^{12sd} **0-0-2**

Soar *J R Fanshawe* 83
3 b f Danzero (Aus) - Splice
6^{5gf} **0-0-1 £156**

Soba Jones *J Balding* 69 a75
8 b g Emperor Jones (USA) - Soba
2^{6sd} 4^{6sd} 8^{6sd} 5^{6sd} 6^{7sd} 2^{6sd} 3^{6sd} 4^{6g} 8^{6g}
4^{5gf} 12^{6gf} 3^{5gf} 12^{5gf} 10^{5g} 9^{7sd} 4^{5sd}
0-5-16 £4,414

Society Music (Ire) *M Dods* 84
3 b f Almutawakel - Society Fair (Fr)
7^{7g} 2^{8g} 6^{9s} 1^{8gs} 1^{8gf} 2^{8gs} 9^{8g} 7^{8g} 6^{8g}
2-2-9 £14,003

Socks For Glenn *M S Saunders* 76 a49

5 ch g Factual (USA) - Payvashooz
10^{5sd} 12^{5gs} **0-0-2**

Sofelia (Ire) *R Hannon* 61
2 b c Mull Of Kintyre (USA) - Petite Liqueurelle (Ire)
5^{6gf} 2^{7gf} 13^{7gs} 6^{6gs} 13^{8gf} 17^{6gs} 11^{8g}
0-0-7 £1,488

Sofie *W J Haggas* 62
2 ch f Efisio - Krista
5^{6gf} 14^{6g} **0-0-2**

Sofinella (Ire) *A W Carroll* 71
2 gr f Titus Livius (Fr) - Mystical Jumbo
3^{5gf} 1^{5g} 5^{5g} 8^{6s} **1-1-4 £4,409**

Sofisio *Miss S J Wilton* 38 a48
8 ch g Efisio - Legal Embrace (Can)
9^{9sd} 7^{12sd} 3^{12sd} 4^{16gf} 5^{17sf} **0-1-5 £418**

Soft Centre *Mrs A J Perrett* 80
2 ch f Zafonic (USA) - Foodbroker Fancy (Ire)
10^{7gf} 1^{7g} 7^{7gs} **1-0-3 £3,708**

Soft Focus (Ire) *J A Osborne* 56 a56
3 b f Spectrum (Ire) - Creme Caramel (USA)
4^{6sd} 2^{7sd} 1^{7sd} 7^{7sd} 3^{6sd} 17^{7gf} 6^{6f} 5^{7gf}
1-1-8 £4,275

Soft Gold *D M Simcock* 64
2 ch g Zaha (Can) - Soft Touch (Ger)
4^{5g} 7^{6gf} 3^{6gf} 2^{6gf} 4^{6f} 9^{6gf} 4^{6g} 5^{6g} **0-2-8**
£1,782

Soft Pearl (Ire) *A Dickman* 34
2 ch f Titus Livius (Fr) - Tread Softly (Ire)
9^{6gf} 12^{6g} 8^{7g} 8^{7g} **0-0-4**

Sohgol (Ire) *L M Cumani* 81
3 ch f Singspiel (Ire) - Arruhan (Ire)
12^{8g} 15^{8gs} 2^{10gf} 3^{10f} 5^{12gf} 5^{10g} 1^{8gf} 11^{8gf}
1-2-8 £9,188

Soho Square *M Johnston* 72
2 ch c Generous (Ire) - Stardance (USA)
5^{8hd} 3^{8s} **0-1-2 £832**

Sokoke *D A Nolan* 33
4 ch g Compton Place - Sally Green (Ire)
8^{5s} 13^{6g} 10^{5gf} 11^{5gf} **0-0-4**

Sol Rojo *M J Attwater* 42 a61
3 b g Efisio - Shining Cloud
1^{9sd} 7^{10gf} 6^{7gf} 8^{8sd} 4^{9sf} 4^{8sd} 7^{8sd} **1-0-7**
£2,830

Solanich *R Hannon* 67 a57
3 ch g Inchinor - Gussy Marlowe
5^{8gs} 15^{8gf} 3^{7gs} 3^{6gf} 13^{8gf} 6^{7sd} 7^{7gf} 14^{6gf}
12^{6gf} 9^{7sd} **0-2-10 £1,053**

Solar Falcon *A G Newcombe* 54 a33
3 ch f Polar Falcon (USA) - Beryl
8^{8g} 7^{8gf} 10^{10f} 11^{10g} 7^{10sd} **0-0-5**

Solar Power (Ire) *J R Fanshawe* 100 a91
4 b f Marju (Ire) - Next Round (Ire)
5^{5s} 5^{6g} 7^{6sd} 2^{7g} 4^{7gf} 10^{7g} 2^{6g} 13^{6s} 2^{6gs}
0-3-9 £12,256

Solarias Quest *A King* 82
3 b g Pursuit Of Love - Persuasion
1^{12gs} 7^{12gf} 7^{12gf} 1^{12g} 16^{12g} **2-0-5**
£15,063

Soldier's Tale (USA) *J Noseda* 117
4 ch c Stravinsky (USA) - Myrtle
1^{6gs} 1^{6g} 4^{6gs} **2-0-3 £55,118**

Sole Agent (Ire) *G L Moore* 66
3 b g Trans Island - Seattle Siren (USA)
10^{14g} 5^{14s} 6^{17gs} **0-0-3**

Solent (Ire) *R Hannon* 96
3 b c Montjeu (Ire) - Stylish
1^{8g} 16^{8gf} 7^{8g} 5^{10g} 4^{12gf} 6^{12s} 1^{12gf} **2-0-7**
£22,438

Solicitude *D Haydn Jones* 45 a69
2 ch f Bertolini (USA) - Sibilant
13^{6g} 1^{7sd} 3^{7sd} **1-1-3 £4,034**

Solipsist (Ire) *N I M Rossiter* 53
4 ch g Grand Lodge (USA) - Mijouter (Ire)
4^{12gs} 8^{12gf} **0-0-2 £274**

Solo Flight *H Morrison* 95
8 gr g Mtoto - Silver Singer
6^{12gs} 9^{12f} 1^{10gf} 5^{10g} 6^{10gf} 17^{11gf} 11^{10gf} 4^{12gs}
9^{10gs} **1-1-9 £11,271**

Solo Star *Miss J A Camacho* 54
2 ch f Observatory (USA) - Aura Of Grace (USA)
9^{5s} 13^{5g} 7^{6g} 1^{7gf} 3^{7f} 2^{7g} **1-2-6**
£4,227

Solomon's Mine (USA) *M J Polglase* 71 a68
6 b g Rahy (USA) - Shes A Sheba (USA)
10^{9sd} 11^{9sd} 4^{11sd} 9^{16sd} 8^{14sd} 1^{18gs} 6^{16gs} 20^{20s}
1-0-8 £4,588

Solskjaer (Ire) *A P O'Brien* 118
5 b h Danehill (USA) - Lyndonville (Ire)
7^{7hy} 1^{8hy} 2^{10gs} 2^{8sh} 6^{11gy} 8^{8gf} 4^{10gf} 4^{10g} 8^{8gf}
2^{8gf} **1-3-10 £55,367**

Solute (Ger) *M Meade*
2 ch f Zilzal (USA) - See Me Well (Ire)
15^{6gf} **0-0-1**

Solva *B J Meehan* 71
2 b f Singspiel (Ire) - Annapurna (Ire)
4^{7gs} 7^{7gf} 2^{8g} 6^{8g} **0-1-4 £1,767**

Solway Firth *M P Tregoning* a68
3 b c Mark Of Esteem (Ire) - Whitehaven
1^{10sd} 15^{10gf} **1-0-2 £5,148**

Some Diva *W R Swinburn* a59
2 ch f Dr Fong (USA) - Dorothea Brooke (Ire)
5^{6sd} **0-0-1**

Somerby (Ire) *J W Hills* 11 a28
2 b g Sadler's Wells (USA) - Oriental Mystique
15^{8gs} 11^{8sd} **0-0-2**

Somerset West (Ire) *J R Best* 56 a62
5 b g Catrail (USA) - Pizzazz
5^{7sd} 4^{5sd} 2^{5sd} 11^{6sd} 16^{7g} 14^{10gf} 16^{7gf} 5^{5gf}
5^{6gf} 18^{8gf} 11^{6g} 11^{5gf} **0-1-12 £834**

Something (Ire) *T G Mills* 95
3 b c Trans Island - Persian Polly
4^{6gs} 1^{7gf} 20^{7gf} 15^{7gs} **1-0-4 £5,291**

Something Exciting *D R C Elsworth* 113
3 ch f Halling (USA) - Faraway Waters
1^{10gf} 2^{12g} 4^{12gf} 5^{10gs} 3^{10gf} 6^{12gs} **1-2-6**
£121,316

Sometimes Lucky *C Smith* 50 a17
2 br c Key Of Luck (USA) - Quarry (Ire)
7^{5s} 8^{5gs} 8^{5gf} 3^{5g} 4^{6gf} 8^{6gs} 12^{5sd} **0-1-7**
£2,843

Somewhere My Love *P Butler* 11 a61
4 br f Pursuit Of Love - Grand Coronet
6^{7sd} 4^{8sd} 12^{10sd} 9^{7sd} 7^{8sd} 9^{12gf} 11^{10sd} 17^{8gf}
13^{9sd} 10^{10sd} 8^{10sd} **0-0-11**

Somnus *T D Easterby* 115
5 b g Pivotal - Midnight's Reward
4^{6s} 13^{6gs} 10^{7g} 4^{6g} 6^{7s} 5^{7gs} **0-0-6**
£19,150

Somoya *M A Jarvis* 38 a58
2 b f Elnadim (USA) - Seven Wonders (USA)

14^{6gs} 4^{5sd} 6^{5sd} **0-0-3 £234**

Son Altesse *Dr J D Scargill* 39 a53
3 br g Tipsy Creek (USA) - Fabulous Night (Fr)
7^{6sd} 14^{7sd} 12^{7gf} 10^{6sd} 13^{6gf} 9^{6f} **0-0-6**

Son Of Bathwick (Ire) *B R Millman* 57
3 b g Dr Fong (USA) - Bathwick Babe (Ire)
7^{8g} 16^{8gs} 4^{8gf} 12^{8f} **0-0-4 £319**

Son Of Greek Myth (USA) *G L Moore* 7 a67
4 b g Silver Hawk (USA) - Greek Myth (Ire)
6^{12sd} 3^{12sd} 10^{10g} **0-0-3 £534**

Son Of Sophie *C N Kellett* 39 a35
3 b g Band On The Run - Fair Enchantress
6^{6sd} 9^{7sd} 7^{7gf} 7^{7sd} **0-0-4**

Son Of Thunder (Ire) *M Dods* 70
4 ch g Dr Fong (USA) - Sakura Queen (Ire)
5^{8g} 15^{8g} 1^{9f} 5^{8gf} 1^{9gf} 9^{8gf} 4^{9gf} 5^{9gf} 11^{8gf}
6^{8g} 8^{8gf} 8^{9gf} **2-0-12 £7,209**

Sonderborg *J Mackie* 50 a53
4 b f Great Dane (Ire) - Nordico Princess
5^{8sd} 9^{10sd} 13^{10g} 5^{10sd} 13^{10gf} 2^{7g} 3^{7sf} 2^{8sd}
7^{7sd} 2^{8ss} 2^{8sd} 5^{8sd} **0-5-12 £2,371**

Song Huntress *D G Bridgwater* 50 a55
2 b f Foxhound (USA) - Eastern Lyric
8^{6gf} 8^{6g} 5^{6gf} 1^{5gf} 1^{5s} 5^{5g} 8^{5sd} 3^{5f} 3^{6gf} 2^{6gf}
2^{5sd} **2-3-11 £8,332**

Song Koi *Jennie Candlish* a38
4 b f Sri Pekan (USA) - Eastern Lyric
10^{6sd} 8^{6sd} 9^{5sd} **0-0-3**

Song Of Passion (Ire) *R Hannon* 66 a78
2 b f Orpen (USA) - Bint Al Balad (Ire)
4^{6gs} 1^{7sd} **1-0-2 £4,902**

Song Of Silence (USA) *E A L Dunlop* 67 a65
2 b f Unbridled's Song (USA) - State Secret
7^{6gf} 11^{7g} 7^{7sd} 4^{7sd} 4^{7sf} 2^{8sd} 4^{7sd} **0-1-7**
£1,868

Song Of Songs *J R Fanshawe* 102
3 b g Singspiel (Ire) - Thea (USA)
5^{8gs} 4^{10gf} 1^{10gf} 1^{10s} 6^{10gs} **2-0-5**
£18,436

Song Of Vala *R Charlton* 82
4 ch g Peintre Celebre (USA) - Yanka (USA)
6^{8g} 4^{8gf} 6^{8gs} 1^{8gf} 2^{8g} 6^{8gf} **1-2-6**
£22,591

Song Sparrow *G A Butler* 55 a56
3 b f Vettori (Ire) - Fanfare
2^{12sd} 6^{12sd} 4^{11gf} 6^{12sd} 16^{11gf} **0-1-5 £846**

Song Thrush (USA) *P F I Cole* 89
3 gr/ro f Unbridled's Song (USA) - Virgin Michael (USA)
9^{7gs} 2^{8s} 6^{10gf} 8^{7gf} 14^{8gf} 6^{10gf} **0-1-6**
£3,577

Songerie *Sir Mark Prescott* 111
3 b f Hernando (Fr) - Summer Night
4^{10gs} 4^{13g} 3^{15gf} 4^{13s} **0-1-4 £32,914**

Songgaria *J G M O'Shea* a35
3 b f Kingsinger (Ire) - Paula's Joy
10^{7sd} 10^{8sd} **0-0-2**

Songlark *Saeed Bin Suroor* 113
5 br h Singspiel (Ire) - Negligent
1^{12gf} 3^{16g} 6^{12gs} **1-1-3 £31,900**

Sonic Anthem (USA) *D Nicholls* 54 a73
3 b g Royal Anthem (USA) - Whisperifyoudare (USA)
3^{7f} 12^{7g} 2^{7f} 7^{8gf} 6^{7gf} 3^{8gf} **0-3-6**
£1,920

Sonntag Blue (Ire) *Miss J Feilden* 55 a58
3 b g Bluebird (USA) - Laura Margaret
3^{8sd} 4^{8sd} 2^{8sd} 4^{8gf} 3^{12sd} 5^{12sd} 1^{8gf} 5^{9sd} 1^{7sd}
2-0-9 £6,446

Sonny Mac *B J Meehan* 46
2 b c Pivotal - Sea Drift (Fr)
11^{7s} **0-0-1**

Sonny Parkin *G A Huffer* 83 a78
3 b g Spinning World (USA) - No Miss Kris (USA)
5^{7sd} 2^{7sd} 3^{8s} 8^{10g} 1^{8gf} 4^{8gf} 3^{8g} 3^{8gf} 15^{8gf}
12^{10g} 6^{8sd} 3^{8sd} 6^{8sd} **1-5-13 £9,077**

Sonny Santino *R Hannon* 90
2 b c Bertolini (USA) - Irish Impulse (USA)
3^{6s} 2^{6gf} 1^{7gf} 2^{7g} 3^{7g} 2^{8s} 13^{6gf} 11^{8g}
1-3-8 £11,609

Sonoma (Ire) *B S Rothwell* 44 a36
5 ch m Dr Devious (Ire) - Mazarine Blue (USA)
16^{16g} 15^{16gs} 10^{16gf} 4^{16sd} 4^{16gf} 6^{14f} 3^{16gf} 9^{14gf}
0-0-8 £423

Soothsay (Ire) *J W Hills* 65 a74
2 b f Mujadil (USA) - Second Omen
6^{5gs} 1^{6gf} 5^{6sd} 2^{7gs} 1^{7sd} **2-1-5 £8,138**

Sooyou Sir (Ire) *Mrs A Duffield* 55
3 b/br g Orpen (USA) - Naivement (Ire)
4^{12gf} 4^{12gs} 6^{16g} **0-0-3 £260**

Sophie'Jo *H R A Cecil* 69
2 b f Agnes World (USA) - Maureena (Ire)
4^{6gf} 2^{6gf} 13^{7g} 3^{8s} **0-2-4 £2,697**

Sophist (Ire) *J Noseda* 70
2 b c Montjeu (Ire) - Cordon Bleu (USA)
8^{7gs} 5^{8gs} **0-0-2**

Sorbiesharry (Ire) *Mrs N Macauley* 55 a79
6 gr g Sorbie Tower (Ire) - Silver Moon
6^{8sd} 4^{11sd} 6^{9sd} 4^{8sd} 1^{9sd} 1^{9sd} 5^{9sd} 3^{9sd} 2^{12sd}
1^{9sd} 1^{9sd} 2^{8sd} 11^{10gf} 10^{14sd} 8^{8gf} 8^{7sd} 5^{10gf}
8^{9sd} 12^{8gf} 6^{9sd} 5^{9sd} 4^{8sd} 9^{11sd} 7^{9sd} 5^{12sd}
4-3-25 £16,730

Sorceress *J Gallagher* 29 a28
3 b f Wizard King - Aonia
10^{7sd} 8^{7gf} 10^{12sd} **0-0-3**

Sorrel Point *H J Collingridge* a34
2 b c Bertolini (USA) - Lightning Princess
9^{7sd} **0-0-1**

Sotik Star (Ire) *P J Makin* 73
2 b c Elnadim (USA) - Crystal Springs (Ire)
14^{6g} 3^{6gs} 2^{6g} **0-2-3 £1,864**

Soto *M W Easterby* 77 a59
2 b g Averti (Ire) - Belle Of The Blues (Ire)
2^{5g} 1^{5sd} 2^{5s} 5^{5g} 5^{5f} 4^{6gs} 2^{6gf} 5^{7gf} 8^{6gf} 6^{6gs}
5^{6g} 7^{6s} **1-3-12 £8,754**

Sotonian (Hol) *P S Felgate* 7 a34
12 br g Statoblest - Visage
6^{5sd} 16^{6gf} **0-0-2**

Soufah (Ire) *J L Dunlop* 59
3 b g Desert Style (Ire) - Entracte
11^{8g} 8^{8gf} **0-0-2**

Soul Dance *P J Makin* 28 a33
4 b f Imperial Ballet (Ire) - Piccante
5^{5sd} 7^{5f} 13^{5sd} **0-0-3**

Soul Provider (Ire) *G Prodromou* 76 a47
4 ch f Danehill Dancer (Ire) - Wing And A Prayer (Ire)
11^{7g} 1^{6g} 13^{8gf} 8^{6g} 7^{8gf} 4^{8sd} 6^{6g} 3^{8g} 12^{9sd}
1^{5sd} **2-1-10 £3,122**

Soulacroix *Mrs A J Perrett* 97
4 b g Kylian (USA) - California Dreamin
7^{10gs} 7^{12gs} 7^{16g} 6^{15gs} 3^{11gf} 1^{12gs} 2^{12s}
1-2-7 £16,378

Soumillon *Ms Deborah J Evans*
3 gr f Benny The Dip (USA) - Kembla
16^{10g} **0-0-1**

Sound And Vision (Ire) *M Dods* 62 a61
3 b g Fayruz - Lyrical Vision (Ire)
3^{7s} 10^{8g} 2^{8g} 2^{8gf} 12^{10sd} 2^{8s} 5^{10gf} 4^{12gf} 2^{8gf} 3^{8gf} 3^{8g} 5^{11gs} 2^{8ss} 5^{7sd} 7^{8sd} 6^{9ss} **0-7-16 £5,963**

Sound Breeze *M Johnston* 107
3 ch c Giant's Causeway (USA) - Madame Est Sortie (Fr)
1^{8g} 1^{8g} 1^{8gf} 1^{10s} **4-0-4 £34,311**

Sound Of Fleet (USA) *P F I Cole* 62 a57
4 ch g Cozzene (USA) - Tempo (USA)
10^{12gf} 8^{10g} 5^{12gf} 9^{10gf} 19^{12f} 4^{10g} 6^{12sd} PU^{11gf} **0-1-8 £300**

Sound That Alarm *P Mitchell* 73 a38
3 b g Groom Dancer (USA) - Warning Star
5^{6g} 4^{7s} 1^{6hy} 9^{6gf} 7^{8gf} 12^{7sd} 12^{7gf} 6^{8gs} 11^{10sd} 7^{6g} 12^{6sd} **1-0-11 £3,222**

Sounds Simla (Ire) *Rae Guest* 80
2 b f Indian Rocket - Evocative (Ire)
1^{5gs} 7^{5s} 3^{6gf} 3^{5g} 1^{6gf} 6^{6gs} 7^{6gf} 2^{6gf} **2-2-8 £13,011**

South Cape *M R Channon* 96
2 b g Cape Cross (Ire) - Aunt Ruby (USA)
1^{6gf} 3^{6gs} 5^{6hy} **1-1-3 £9,407**

South Hill *M Blanshard* 39 a42
2 b f Marju (Ire) - Briggsmaid
15^{7g} 9^{7sd} 8^{8hd} **0-0-3**

South O'The Border *T G Mills* 82 a79
3 b g Wolfhound (USA) - Abbey's Gal
2^{12g} 6^{13g} 1^{10gf} 3^{10gf} 2^{10gf} 1^{10f} 3^{10gf} 1^{10gs} 2^{10s} 9^{11gf} 9^{10sd} **3-5-11 £20,649**

Southborough Lad *Mrs C A Dunnett* 27
2 ch g Woodborough (USA) - Caribbee Beach (Ire)
8^{5g} 9^{5gf} 11^{6sd} 9^{5g} 7^{8g} 14^{7gf} **0-0-6**

Southburgh (Ire) *Mrs C A Dunnett* 17 a15
4 b g Spectrum (Ire) - College Night (Ire)
12^{7sd} 12^{8s} 12^{12ss} **0-0-3**

Southern Bazaar (USA) *M E Sowersby* 52 a60
4 ch g Southern Halo (USA) - Sunday Bazaar (USA)
9^{7sd} 6^{8sd} 4^{10sd} 16^{10g} 18^{10g} 5^{14sd} 4^{11gf} 9^{14gf} 7^{12gf} 11^{12gf} **0-0-10**

Southern Shore (Ire) *D Burchell* 62
3 ch g Erhaab (USA) - Intisab
8^{7gf} 13^{8gf} 15^{10g} 10^{12gf} 1^{12gf} **1-0-5 £2,555**

Southern Tide (USA) *J J Sheehan* 44 a53
3 b c Southern Halo (USA) - My Own Lovely Lee (USA)
5^{8sd} 6^{6sd} 3^{9sd} 4^{8sd} 1^{9sd} 4^{9sd} 7^{9sd} 8^{10g} 8^{10sd} 7^{9g} 16^{8gf} **1-1-11 £3,150**

Southgate Lady (Ire) *N P Littmoden* 36 a25
2 b f Night Shift (USA) - German Lady
12^{6gf} 15^{5gs} 10^{7sd} 7^{7sd} **0-0-4**

Southport Star (Ire) *J R Fanshawe* 67
2 b g King's Best (USA) - Danzig's Girl (USA)
5^{7gs} 5^{7gf} **0-0-2**

Souvenance *Sir Mark Prescott* 99
2 b f Hernando (Fr) - Summer Night
2^{7gf} 1^{7gf} 9^{8gs} 3^{8gs} **1-2-4 £12,958**

Sovereign Dreamer (USA) *P F I Cole* 64
5 b g Kingmambo (USA) - Spend A Dream (USA)
8^{14gs} 4^{12f} 18^{18g} 2^{12gf} 4^{12f} 2^{12f} **0-2-6 £2,264**

Sovereign Spirit (Ire) *W R Swinburn* 60 a66
3 b g Desert Prince (Ire) - Sheer Spirit (Ire)
5^{10gf} 3^{11gf} 13^{12gf} 6^{12g} 5^{14g} 1^{14sd} 2^{14sd} **1-2-7 £4,306**

Sovereign State (Ire) *D W Thompson* 55 a50
8 b g Soviet Lad (USA) - Portree
3^{13sd} 11^{12sd} 7^{16gs} 2^{14gf} 7^{14f} 4^{14f} 7^{12f} 8^{12f} 2^{13gf} 16^{12gf} 7^{14g} **0-4-11 £1,786**

Sovereignty (Jpn) *I Semple* 72 a74
3 b g King's Best (USA) - Calando (USA)
2^{8sd} 3^{8sd} 4^{8g} 3^{7g} 4^{8gf} 1^{7gf} 8^{7gf} 4^{7gf} 13^{6gf} 6^{7sd} 2^{7gf} **1-3-11 £8,119**

Soviet Joy (Ire) *D Carroll* a28
4 b/br g Russian Revival (USA) - Danny's Joy (Ire)
7^{12sd} **0-0-1**

Soviet Legend (Ire) *T J Etherington* 41 a51
2 b c Soviet Star (USA) - Another Legend (USA)
12^{5gf} 16^{6gf} 9^{5gf} 7^{7gf} 15^{8gf} 7^{6sd} 1^{5sd} 7^{5sd} **1-0-8 £1,463**

Soviet Promise (Ire) *G G Margarson* 38
2 b f Soviet Star (USA) - Akarita (Ire)
7^{7f} 11^{5gf} 11^{7gs} 12^{7gs} **0-0-4**

Soviet Sceptre (Ire) *R T Phillips* 60 a50
4 ch g Soviet Star (USA) - Princess Sceptre
10^{10sd} 15^{12sd} 8^{10sd} 6^{10s} 6^{14g} 7^{13sd} 8^{17g} 1^{12g} **1-0-8 £3,161**

Soviet Song (Ire) *J R Fanshawe* 124
5 b m Marju (Ire) - Kalinka (Ire)
3^{8gf} 1^{8g} 2^{8s} **1-2-3 £196,300**

Soviet Terms *M Johnston* 44
2 b f Soviet Star (USA) - Sharp Terms
7^{6gf} 7^{6f} **0-0-2**

Soviet Threat (Ire) *A G Juckes* a76
4 ch g Soviet Star (USA) - Veiled Threat (Ire)
1^{7sd} 1^{7sd} 7^{8sd} 3^{8sd} 9^{9sd} 7^{7sd} **2-1-6 £5,282**

Soviet Times (Ire) *J R Fanshawe* 42
4 ch f Soviet Star (USA) - Ridge The Times (USA)
6^{6gf} **0-0-1**

Sovietta (Ire) *A G Newcombe* 65 a24
4 b f Soviet Star (USA) - La Riveraine (USA)
9^{12sd} 8^{14sd} 6^{12s} 1^{12hy} 17^{12gf} 9^{12sd} **1-0-6 £3,388**

Sowerby *M Brittain* 38
3 b g Grey Desire - Brief Star (Ire)
13^{6g} **0-0-1**

Soyuz (Ire) *K A Ryan*
5 ch g Cadeaux Genereux - Welsh Mist
PU^{7sd} **0-0-1**

Space Cowboy (Ire) *G L Moore* 61
5 b h Anabaa (USA) - Lady Moranbon (USA)
6^{12gf} **0-0-1**

Space To Run *R P Elliott* a1
3 ch f Dancing Spree (USA) - Approved Quality (Ire)
12^{9sd} 10^{8sd} **0-0-2**

Spaceman *L M Cumani* 49
2 b c In The Wings - Souk (Ire)
16^{8gs} 9^{7s} **0-0-2**

Spanish Ace *A M Balding* 88
4 b g First Trump - Spanish Heart
11^{5gs} 11^{6gf} 17^{6g} 4^{5gf} 7^{5gf} 7^{6g} 10^{6gs} **0-0-7 £540**

Spanish Don *D R C Elsworth* 108
7 b g Zafonic (USA) - Spanish Wells (Ire)
2^{9g} 10^{10g} 18^{8gf} 8^{8gf} 7^{8gf} 4^{9gf} 18^{9s} **0-1-7 £13,971**

Spanish Lace *Miss J A Camacho* a64
2 b f Hernando (Fr) - Kabayil
4^{9sd} 3^{9sd} **0-1-2 £554**

Spanish Law *M Dods* 57
3 b g Zaha (Can) - Misty Moon
9^{7g} 15^{8g} 12^{8gf} 1^{7gf} 2^{8gf} **1-1-5 £2,338**

Spanish Music *R Ingram* 64 a46
3 b f Piccolo - Raffelina (USA)
13^{7g} 3^{5gf} 3^{5gf} 6^{6g} 5^{6g} 7^{6gf} 11^{6g} 9^{6sd} 6^{6sd} 7^{10sd} 12^{8sd} 5^{9sd} **0-0-12 £1,273**

Spanish Rainbow (Ire) *J L Dunlop* 67
2 ch f Rainbow Quest (USA) - Spanish Lady (Ire)
8^{7gf} 7^{8g} **0-0-2**

Spanish Ridge (Ire) *J L Dunlop* 79
3 b g Indian Ridge - Spanish Lady (Ire)
8^{10gs} 8^{10gf} 4^{10gf} 1^{12f} 7^{14s} 2^{16g} 2^{17gs} **1-2-7 £6,267**

Spanish Star *Mrs N Macauley* a45
8 b g Hernando (Fr) - Desert Girl
5^{12sd} 5^{12sd} 8^{9sd} 10^{11sd} 1^{11sd} 7^{11sd} 5^{12ss} **1-0-7 £1,426**

Spanish Story *A M Balding* 44
2 br f Vettori (Ire) - Spanish Heart
13^{8gs} 6^{8hy} **0-0-2**

Spanky's Ladder (Ire) *J Noseda* 85
3 br c Zafonic (USA) - Blasted Heath
3^{7g} 7^{8s} 1^{8gf} **1-1-3 £5,708**

Spark Up *J W Unett* a59
5 b m Lahib (USA) - Catch The Flame (USA)
3^{7sd} 12^{9sd} 12^{9sd} 6^{7sd} 3^{7sd} 1^{7sd} 4^{6sd} 6^{9sd} 2^{7sd} 4^{7sd} 4^{9sd} 2^{7sd} 5^{9sd} 1^{9sd} 7^{7sf} 12^{9sd} **2-4-16 £6,750**

Sparkbridge (Ire) *R F Fisher* 60
2 b g Mull Of Kintyre (USA) - Persian Velvet (Ire)
2^{6gf} 6^{7g} 8^{6gf} 4^{7g} 10^{7sd} **0-1-5 £1,759**

Sparkwell *B W Hills* 77
3 b c Dansili - West Devon (USA)
2^{7gf} 2^{7g} 1^{7gf} 8^{7gf} **1-2-4 £5,874**

Spartan Odyssey *A Bailey* a49
4 b g Overbury (Ire) - Spartan Native
13^{9sd} 6^{12sd} **0-0-2**

Spasiba *Sir Mark Prescott* 48 a52
2 b f Pivotal - Skimra
6^{7f} 7^{6sd} 9^{7f} 11^{7g} 15^{10g} 10^{7sd} **0-0-6**

Speagle (Ire) *Anthony Mullins* a67
3 ch c Desert Sun - Pohutakawa (Fr)
1^{12sd} 8^{12sd} 14^{12g} **1-0-3 £4,108**

Speakerboxxx *P F I Cole* 60 a60
3 ch g Zafonic (USA) - Trounce
11^{7gf} 16^{8g} 5^{6g} 1^{7sd} 5^{8ss} 11^{8sd} **1-0-6 £1,457**

Spear (Ire) *D R Loder* 78 a86
3 b c Almutawakel - Les Hurlants (Ire)
15^{9g} 4^{12gf} 3^{10gf} 4^{14f} 1^{12sd} 2^{12sd} 5^{14g} 5^{12sd} **1-2-8 £6,649**

Spear Thistle *Mrs N Smith* 90
3 ch g Selkirk (USA) - Ardisia (USA)
12^{10gf} 5^{10gs} 4^{10gf} 2^{11gf} 4^{14s} 2^{16g} **0-3-6 £5,605**

Spearit (Ire) *D R C Elsworth* 77 a78
2 ch c Lear Spear (USA) - French Gift
3^{6g} 6^{6g} 4^{6f} 3^{6s} 10^{6s} 1^{5sd} 5^{6sd} **1-2-7 £8,636**

Special Gold *T D Easterby* 74
3 b c Josr Algarhoud (Ire) - Inya Lake
7^{6g} 3^{6s} 4^{5gf} 1^{5gs} 2^{6f} 2^{5g} 7^{5gf} 14^{5gs} **1-3-8 £7,715**

Special Lad *P F I Cole* 89 a85
3 b g Spectrum (Ire) - Oh Hebe (Ire)
11^{11g} 13^{8gs} 10^{10gs} 11^{10gf} 1^{7gf} 1^{6gf} 3^{7gf} 6^{6g} 1^{6gf} 5^{6sd} **3-1-10 £15,855**

Special Moment (Ire) *B W Hills* 68
2 b f Sadler's Wells (USA) - Upper Circle
6^{7gf} 4^{8gs} **0-0-2 £554**

Special Time (SAF) *A M Balding* 42 a30
3 b f Fort Wood (USA) - Popular (SAF)
13^{7g} 9^{7sd} **0-0-2**

Specialise *D W Barker*
3 b f Atraf - Summerhill Special (Ire)
5^{10gf} **0-0-1**

Specialised Lady *S Kirk* 51 a43
2 b f Labeeb - Eurolink Cafe
5^{7sd} 5^{7gf} 7^{8gf} **0-0-3**

Speciosa (Ire) *Mrs P Sly* 108
2 b f Danehill Dancer (Ire) - Specifically (USA)
2^{6gf} 8^{6gf} 3^{7g} 1^{7g} 3^{8gf} 1^{7gs} **2-3-6 £57,255**

Spectacular Dancer (Ire) *Mrs H Dalton* 26 a31
3 b g Fasliyev (USA) - Committal (USA)
16^{7g} 8^{6s} 9^{6sd} 15^{6g} **0-0-4**

Spectacular Show (Ire) *M Quinn* 74
2 ch f Spectrum (Ire) - Stage Presence (Ire)
11^{6gs} 3^{5f} 1^{5s} 6^{6gf} 5^{6g} 5^{5hy} **1-1-6 £5,608**

Spectait *Sir Mark Prescott* 94 a85
3 b g Spectrum (Ire) - Shanghai Girl
1^{7sd} 1^{9sd} 1^{7gs} 4^{8g} **3-0-4 £16,595**

Spectested (Ire) *A W Carroll* 63 a64
4 ch g Spectrum (Ire) - Nisibis
1^{17sd} 4^{12sd} 7^{12sd} 2^{14sd} 2^{15gs} 8^{16g} 3^{20s} 12^{18g} 10^{18g} 11^{14sd} **1-3-10 £6,704**

Spector (Ire) *J J Sheehan* 25
5 gr g Spectrum (Ire) - Safkana (Ire)
13^{12gf} **0-0-1**

Spectral Star *J R Fanshawe* 68 a72
3 b f Unfuwain (USA) - Hyperspectra
5^{8g} 7^{11g} 2^{12sd} **0-1-3 £1,072**

Spectrometer *Ian Williams* 53
8 ch g Rainbow Quest (USA) - Selection Board
9^{14gf} 6^{15s} **0-0-2**

Speed Dial Harry (Ire) *K R Burke* 71 a75
3 b g General Monash (USA) - Jacobina
5^{5sd} 5^{5sd} 12^{6hy} 1^{5s} 5^{6hy} 4^{5gf} 5^{6sd} 5^{6sd} 5^{5gf} 7^{5gs} 6^{6sd} 2^{7sd} **1-1-12 £3,973**

Speed Of Sound *A M Balding* 60
3 ch f Zafonic (USA) - Blue Siren
8^{5gf} 8^{6gf} **0-0-2**

Speed Six *Peter Grayson* 14 a17
3 b g Groom Dancer (USA) - Another Fantasy (Ire)
11^{6sd} 11^{6sd} 12^{5gf} 9^{5g} 10^{8gf} **0-0-5**

Speedfit Free (Ire) *Miss A Stokell* a9
8 b g Night Shift (USA) - Dedicated Lady (Ire)
7^{7sd} 11^{6sd} **0-0-2**

Speedie Rossini (Ire) *S C Williams* a45
3 b g Rossini (USA) - Skatt
2^{6sd} 3^{5sd} 2^{8sd} 11^{6gf} 9^{6f} **0-3-5 £1,650**

Speedy Sam *K R Burke* 77
2 b c Medicean - Warning Star
2^{8g} 2^{8s} **0-2-2 £3,664**

Speedy Spirit *M Salaman* 23 a33

3 ch f Wolfhound (USA) - Ansellady
7^{6sd} 10^{5sd} 13^{6f} 8^{7sd} 14^{7f} 6^{6sd} **0-0-6**

Speightstown *P F I Cole* 71
3 gr c Grand Lodge (USA) - Farfala (Fr)
11^{10g} 6^{12g} 10^{10gs} 5^{13gf} 4^{16gf} 7^{16g} 11^{12gs}
0-0-7 £386

Spell Casting (USA) *M H Tompkins* 75
2 b c Kingmambo (USA) - Copper Play (USA)
7^{8g} 3^{8s} **0-0-2 £896**

Spence Appeal (Ire) *C Roberts* 58 a71
3 b g Nicolotte - It's All Academic (Ire)
1^{8sd} 2^{9sd} 2^{8sd} 2^{10sd} 2^{8sd} 4^{10sd} 3^{9sd} 2^{10g}
1-6-8 £8,055

Spes Bona (USA) *G M Moore* 48
4 b g Rakeen (USA) - Novelette
8^{7gf} 16^{10gf} 9^{11gf} **0-0-3**

Sphinx (Fr) *Jamie Poulton* 41 a72
7 b g Snurge - Egyptale
9^{16gs} 7^{12sd} 4^{12sd} **0-0-3 £260**

Spiccata *R Hannon* 46 a40
2 b f Mozart (Ire) - Sardonic
9^{6gf} 15^{6g} 12^{7sd} **0-0-3**

Spider Power (Ire) *Saeed Bin Suroor* 82
2 b c Royal Applause - America Calling (USA)
9^{6gf} 6^{7g} 2^{6g} 2^{6gf} 3^{6f} 1^{5g} **1-3-6 £9,842**

Spiders Web *G L Moore* 34
5 gr g Linamix (Fr) - Cattermole (USA)
5^{12g} **0-0-1**

Spin King (Ire) *J M Bradley* 66 a43
4 b g Intikhab (USA) - Special Dissident
5^{7f} 11^{7g} 5^{7gf} 6^{7f} 10^{7sd} 9^{8g} 10^{7g} 9^{6gs} 11^{6gf}
10^{8hd} 10^{7sf} **0-0-11**

Spindor (USA) *M A Magnusson* 67 a67
6 ch g Spinning World (USA) - Doree (USA)
6^{7gf} 1^{7sd} 4^{8f} 12^{6gf} 13^{7sd} **1-0-5 £4,123**

Spinetail Rufous (Ire) *B A Pearce* 56 a60
7 b g Prince Of Birds (USA) - Miss Kinabalu
5^{7sd} 9^{6sd} 5^{5sd} 8^{5gf} 5^{6g} 3^{7gs} 8^{6gf} 11^{7gf} 4^{6gf}
10^{6f} 8^{6s} **0-1-11 £698**

Spinnakers Girl *J R Weymes* a14
3 b f Bluegrass Prince (Ire) - Brac Princess (Ire)
11^{9sd} 4^{8sd} **0-0-2 £257**

Spinning Coin *J G Portman* 86
3 b f Mujahid (USA) - Cointosser (Ire)
8^{11gs} 3^{12g} 1^{12g} 1^{12g} 1^{12gf} 2^{12gf} 6^{12s} 2^{12g} 3^{14s}
3-4-9 £18,277

Spinning Dancer (Ire) *N P Littmoden*
2 b f Spinning World (USA) - Fair McLain (Ire)
14^{6gs} **0-0-1**

Spinning Gold *Miss Gay Kelleway* 46
2 ch f Spinning World (USA) - Blue Birds Fly
8^{6gf} 10^{7gs} 11^{7g} **0-0-3**

Spinning Queen *B W Hills* 100
2 ch f Spinning World (USA) - Our Queen Of Kings
1^{6g} 4^{6gf} 3^{6g} 5^{7g} 4^{7g} 8^{8gf} 6^{7gs} **1-1-7**
£18,728

Spinning Ruby *R M Beckett* 76
2 b f Pivotal - Red Rabbit
5^{6gf} 1^{6gs} **1-0-2 £3,168**

Spirit Of Arosa (Ire) *J Akehurst* 68
2 b f Dansili - Vettorina (Ire)
6^{6gf} 5^{6gf} **0-0-2**

Spirit Of Chester (Ire) *M Johnston* 60
3 b f Lend A Hand - It Takes Two (Ire)
9^{7gf} 2^{6f} **0-1-2 £820**

Spirit Of Coniston *M Wellings* 63 a58
2 b c Lake Coniston (Ire) - Kigema (Ire)
9^{5hy} 11^{5gs} 5^{5gf} 7^{5g} 5^{5gf} 4^{5gf} 2^{5gf} 5^{6gf} 2^{5gf}
9^{6gf} 2^{5sd} 9^{5sd} 7^{5sd} **0-3-13 £4,550**

Spirit Of France (Ire) *M Johnston* 98
3 b g Anabaa (USA) - Les Planches
7^{8gs} 4^{6gf} 4^{6gs} 6^{6gf} 4^{6gs} 11^{6g} 2^{7gf} 1^{6gf} 9^{6gf}
3^{7s} 8^{7g} 5^{6gs} 12^{8gf} 1^{8g} 3^{8g} 10^{7gs} **2-3-16**
£50,295

Spiritual Peace (Ire) *K A Ryan* 75
2 b c Cadeaux Genereux - Emerald Peace (Ire)
3^{6gf} 2^{6gf} 7^{7g} **0-2-3 £2,672**

Spitfire Bob (USA) *M E Sowersby* 44 a55
6 b g Mister Baileys - Gulf Cyclone (USA)
12^{10gf} 15^{12gf} 6^{10g} 10^{10gf} 5^{8gf} 9^{14gf} 14^{8gf}
1^{8sd} 9^{8ss} 4^{12sd} **1-0-10 £2,559**

Spitting Image (Ire) *M Johnston* 59 a80
5 ch m Spectrum (Ire) - Decrescendo (Ire)
8^{16g} 7^{16g} 4^{14sd} 6^{16f} 1^{16gf} 7^{16gf} 10^{16g} 2^{16gf}
6^{14gf} 3^{17g} 2^{16g} 3^{17g} 7^{14gf} 1^{17sd} 5^{17sd} 6^{14sd}
1^{16sd} **3-4-17 £13,401**

Spitzensparkes (Ire) *J J Quinn* 49 a27
2 ch f Tagula (Ire) - Danita (Ire)
4^{5gs} 3^{5gf} 4^{5gf} 10^{6gf} 4^{6gf} 12^{6gf} 13^{7gf} 8^{5sd}
8^{6sd} **0-1-9 £501**

Splodger Mac (Ire) *N Bycroft* 52
6 b g Lahib (USA) - Little Love
7^{7gf} 8^{7g} 6^{7gf} 14^{8gf} 9^{8gf} 5^{8gf} 2^{8gs} 16^{8s}
0-1-8 £1,094

Sporting Gesture *M W Easterby* 89
8 ch g Safawan - Polly Packer
9^{14gs} 8^{12gs} 12^{14s} 2^{12f} 1^{12gf} 13^{20gf} 13^{12gf} 5^{12gf}
1^{12gf} 2^{12f} 13^{12g} 1^{12gf} 4^{12gf} 4^{12g} **3-2-14**
£31,323

Spree (Ire) *R Hannon* 83
3 gr f Dansili - Ibiza (Ger)
6^{6gs} 7^{5gf} 4^{6gf} 6^{5gf} 9^{5g} 6^{6gs} 16^{6s} **0-0-7**
£1,150

Spree Vision *P Monteith* 34
9 b g Suave Dancer (USA) - Regent's Folly (Ire)
10^{13s} 5^{10s} **0-0-2**

Spring Breeze *M Dods* 77
4 ch g Dr Fong (USA) - Trading Aces
1^{16g} 3^{16gs} 3^{16gf} 5^{16f} 2^{16gf} 8^{16g} 1^{16gf}
2-3-7 £8,662

Spring Charm (Ire) *K A Morgan* 60
3 ch f Inchinor - Arabis
6^{10f} 7^{10gf} 4^{13gf} 5^{12gf} 6^{10gf} **0-0-5 £290**

Spring Dancer *P T Midgley* 32
4 b f Imperial Ballet (Ire) - Roxy Music (Ire)
11^{7gf} 16^{6gf} 15^{6gf} 12^{7g} **0-0-4**

Spring Dream (Ire) *M R Channon* 61
2 gr f Kalanisi (Ire) - Zest (USA)
6^{7gf} 4^{8g} 5^{8s} **0-0-3 £649**

Spring Goddess (Ire) *A P Jarvis* 87 a90
4 b f Daggers Drawn (USA) - Easter Girl
1^{8sd} 11^{10g} 8^{8gf} 11^{8g} 7^{8gs} 13^{10sd} 2^{7gf}
1-1-7 £9,052

Spring In His Step (USA) *B J Meehan* 56
2 b g Mr Greeley (USA) - Fairy Song (Ire)
8^{7gf} **0-0-1**

Spring Jim *J R Fanshawe* 97
4 b g First Trump - Spring Sixpence
1^{10gs} 6^{10gf} 3^{10g} 2^{12g} 11^{12g} **1-2-5**
£19,927

Spring Pursuit *E G Bevan* 59

9 b g Rudimentary (USA) - Pursuit Of Truth (USA)
6^{13s} 1^{15s} 6^{14s} **1-0-3 £3,501**

Spring Surprise *B R Johnson* a65
4 b f Hector Protector (USA) - Tender Moment (Ire)
11^{12sd} **0-0-1**

Spring Time Girl *B Ellison* 56 a32
3 b f Timeless Times (USA) - Daira
14^{6g} 8^{7sd} 3^{7gs} 3^{8gf} 2^{8gf} 14^{10gf} 4^{7gf} 4^{8f} 1^{8gf}
6^{8g} 6^{10gf} 8^{8s} **1-3-12 £4,258**

Springalong (USA) *R A Harris* 46
5 ch g Gone West (USA) - Seven Springs (USA)
6^{7gf} 7^{8gf} 14^{10sd} **0-0-3**

Springwood Blues (Ire) *J S Wainwright*
2 b f Bluebird (USA) - Fun Board (Fr)
8^{7g} **0-0-1**

Sprouston (Fr) *J Noseda* 64
2 ch g Grand Lodge (USA) - River Fantasy (USA)
12^{6gf} 5^{7gf} 8^{7g} 10^{6gs} **0-0-4**

Spunger *R M Beckett* 67 a48
2 b f Fraam - Complimentary Pass
4^{5gs} 11^{5gf} 6^{5sd} 3^{7sd} 3^{7gf} 1^{8g} 1^{10g} **2-2-7**
£10,443

Spy Glass *J L Dunlop* 83 a80
2 gr c Observatory (USA) - Heather Mix
2^{7gf} 3^{7f} 1^{8s} 3^{9sd} **1-1-4 £5,634**

Spy Gun (USA) *T Wall* 42 a56
5 ch g Mt. Livermore (USA) - Takeover Target (USA)
7^{7sd} 6^{6sd} 2^{6sd} 5^{7sd} 5^{6sd} 13^{7sd} 4^{6s} 5^{9sd} 4^{9sd}
9^{6gf} 8^{9sd} 5^{6sd} 9^{9sd} 10^{8sd} 5^{7sd} 2^{6sd} 1^{7sd} 8^{7ss}
7^{7ss} **1-2-19 £2,294**

Spy Master *J Parkes* a36
7 b g Green Desert (USA) - Obsessive (USA)
8^{5sd} 4^{7sd} 8^{7sd} 6^{6sd} **0-0-4**

Spycatcher (USA) *A C Whillans* 15
5 b g Dixieland Band (USA) - Secret Seeker (USA)
18^{9gs} 8^{16f} **0-0-2**

Squadron Leader (Ire) *R Hannon* 71 a67
2 b g Imperial Ballet (Ire) - Tancholo
10^{6gs} 2^{6g} 4^{7sd} 7^{6g} 3^{6s} 6^{7sf} **0-2-6**
£2,396

Squaw Dance *W J Haggas* 101
3 ch f Indian Ridge - Likely Story (Ire)
11^{8s} 12^{8gf} 3^{8gf} 2^{7gf} 5^{10gf} **0-2-5**
£7,182

Squirtle (Ire) *H Morrison* 62
2 ch f In The Wings - Manilia (Fr)
8^{6gs} 9^{6gf} 3^{6g} 7^{7gs} 8^{6gs} **0-0-5 £716**

Squirtle Turtle *P F I Cole* 36 a50
5 ch g Peintre Celebre (USA) - Hatton Gardens
13^{15gs} 9^{12s} 8^{12gf} 8^{12sd} 5^{10g} **0-0-5**

Sri Diamond *S Kirk* 89 a102
5 b g Sri Pekan (USA) - Hana Marie
1^{8sd} 1^{10sd} 4^{9sd} 1^{8g} 14^{10gs} 1^{12sd} 5^{10sd}
4-0-7 £40,624

Sri Lipis *P F I Cole* 77 a73
3 ch c Cadeaux Genereux - Katrina (Ire)
3^{11g} 6^{12s} 10^{12sd} 6^{12gf} 9^{10sd} 6^{12sd} 1^{12sd}
1-1-7 £4,145

Sriology (Ire) *G Prodromou* 58 a58
4 b g Sri Pekan (USA) - Sinology
3^{9sd} 9^{11sd} 3^{10sd} 6^{10sd} 4^{11s} 10^{12s} 1^{8g} 1^{8s} 7^{10gf}
8^{9sd} 6^{10g} 16^{10g} 8^{8hy} 5^{9sd} 4^{8sf} 7^{8sd} 8^{10sd} 2^{8sd}
2-3-18 £4,533

St Andrews (Ire) *M A Jarvis* 115
5 b h Celtic Swing - Viola Royale (Ire)
2^{10gs} 2^{10hy} 4^{10gs} 6^{8gf} 1^{8gf} 4^{9g} 7^{8s} 5^{8gs} 3^{9gs}
1^{8s} **2-3-10 £60,068**

St Andrews Storm (USA) *R Hannon* 87
3 b c Storm Creek (USA) - L'Amour Toujours (USA)
7^{7gf} 6^{7gf} 6^{7s} 18^{8gf} 7^{6g} 15^{6g} 4^{8gf} 6^{7gs}
0-0-8 £718

St Austell *A M Hales* 43 a63
5 b g Compton Place - Paris Joelle (Ire)
2^{6sd} 5^{6sd} 5^{6sd} 2^{6sd} 3^{5sd} 8^{5sd} 9^{5gf} 6^{6sd} 6^{5sd}
13^{6sd} 7^{5sd} **0-3-11 £2,342**

St Barchan (Ire) *A G Juckes* 13
4 ch g Grand Lodge (USA) - Moon Tango (Ire)
13^{10gf} **0-0-1**

St Ivian *Mrs N Macauley* 50 a65
5 b g Inchinor - Lamarita
5^{6sd} 8^{6sd} 8^{6sd} 4^{6sd} 3^{7sd} 2^{6sd} 4^{6sd} 8^{5sd} 4^{6sd}
7^{7gf} 3^{6sd} 9^{6gf} 1^{7sd} 5^{6sd} 1^{7sd} 10^{7sd} 3^{6sd} 14^{8gf}
3^{6sd} 3^{5g} 2^{5ft} 6^{6g} 5^{7sd} 3^{6sd} 5^{5ss} 3^{5sd} 7^{7sd}
2-9-27 £10,560

St Petersburg *M H Tompkins* 105 a96
5 ch g Polar Falcon (USA) - First Law
19^{8g} 4^{7gs} 5^{7s} 9^{7s} 20^{8gf} 18^{7gs} 1^{7s} 6^{8gs} 11^{9s}
5^{8gs} 2^{8s} 14^{10sd} **1-1-12 £23,743**

St Savarin (Fr) *R A Fahey* 82
4 ch g Highest Honor (Fr) - Sacara (Ger)
1^{11s} 5^{10gs} **1-0-2 £7,223**

Staff Nurse (Ire) *N Wilson* a52
5 b m Night Shift (USA) - Akebia (USA)
2^{12sd} 3^{14sd} 1^{11sd} 3^{12sd} 16^{10gf} 3^{12sd} 11^{11sd} 3^{12sd}
5^{11sd} **1-5-9 £3,320**

Stagbury Hill (USA) *J W Hills* 99
3 ch g Woodman (USA) - Shalabia
6^{7gf} 4^{8gs} 15^{8g} **0-0-3 £898**

Stage Flight *B J Meehan* 98
2 b f In The Wings - Midsummernitedream (Ger)
6^{6gs} 5^{7s} 2^{7s} 1^{7g} 4^{7gs} **1-1-5 £7,648**

Stage Gift (Ire) *Sir Michael Stoute* 70
2 ch g Cadeaux Genereux - Stage Struck (Ire)
7^{7gs} 3^{7g} 2^{7gf} **0-1-3 £2,462**

Stage School (USA) *M Johnston* 72
3 b/br f Sunday Silence (USA) - Danseur Fabuleux (USA)
1^{7s} 9^{8gs} 1^{10gf} **2-0-3 £7,514**

Stage Secret (Ire) *Miss E C Lavelle* 93 a86
4 ch g Zilzal (USA) - Tuxford Hideaway
2^{7sd} 3^{7sd} 7^{6gs} 1^{7gf} 3^{7g} 11^{7gf} 10^{7gf} 2^{6gf} 6^{6g}
2^{7gf} **1-5-10 £19,010**

Stagecoach Emerald *R W Price* 65 a52
3 ch g Spectrum (Ire) - Musician
7^{9sd} 6^{8g} 8^{10gf} **0-0-3**

Stagecoach Ruby *Mrs L C Jewell* 22 a32
4 b f Bijou D'Inde - Forum Girl (USA)
9^{10sd} 5^{12sd} 13^{13sd} 10^{10sd} 10^{12g} 4^{10gs}
0-0-6

Stagnite *K McAuliffe* 64 a63
5 ch g Compton Place - Superspring
5^{5sd} 3^{5sd} 5^{6sd} 2^{5sd} 2^{6gf} 7^{6gf} 4^{6gf} 3^{5f} 1^{5f}
6^{5sd} 4^{6f} 2^{5gf} 5^{5gf} 11^{5g} 11^{6g} 12^{5s} 11^{7sf} 2^{7sd}
1^{6sd} 8^{7sd} 3^{6sd} 5^{7sd} 8^{5sd} **2-7-23 £8,994**

Stainley (Ire) *J D Bethell* 69
2 b g Elnadim (USA) - Fizz Up
10^{6gf} 6^{6gf} 1^{7g} 9^{7gf} 11^{8g} 2^{7s} 17^{7g} 9^{7s}
1-1-8 £8,357

Stallone *N Wilson* 72 a79
8 ch g Brief Truce (USA) - Bering Honneur (USA)
2^{12sd} 6^{14sd} 6^{12gf} 2^{12gf} SU^{11gf} **0-2-5**
£2,123

Stamford Blue *R A Harris* 66 a48
4 b g Bluegrass Prince (Ire) - Fayre Holly (Ire)
11^{6sd} 7^{6sd} 7^{6sd} 7^{6s} UR^{6s} 12^{6f} 1^{6s} 11^{6g} 1^{7gf} 1^{8gf} 5^{8g} 9^{7gf} 7^{7gf} 6^{8hd} 6^{7sf} 2^{7gf} **3-1-16 £11,969**

Stan's Girl *I A Wood* 51 a42
3 b f Fraam - Gigetta (Ire)
6^{6sd} 9^{5sd} 1^{5g} 12^{5f} 8^{6sd} 15^{6gs} 15^{6gf} 6^{5f} **1-0-8 £1,645**

Stanbury (USA) *M R Channon*
3 ch g Zamindar (USA) - Staffin
11^{8gs} **0-0-1**

Stance *G L Moore* a78
6 b g Salse (USA) - De Stael (USA)
6^{16sd} **0-0-1**

Stancomb Wills (Ire) *M H Tompkins* 74 a61
3 b g Trans Island - First Nadia
12^{10gs} 1^{12f} 5^{12g} 3^{14gf} 14^{11gs} 6^{12gs} 11^{12sd} **1-0-7 £4,488**

Stand Ready *L Wells* 33 a27
3 b f Perryston View - Leave It To Lib
13^{10sd} 12^{12sd} 7^{10gf} 11^{8f} **0-0-4**

Stanley Arthur *D Nicholls* 20
3 b g Mind Games - Midnight Orchid (Ire)
9^{7g} 9^{5f} **0-0-2**

Stanley Bay (Ire) *T D Easterby* 53
2 ch f Namid - Joy St Clair (Ire)
8^{5s} 12^{5gs} 5^{6f} 11^{6f} 5^{7g} 8^{5g} **0-0-6**

Stanley Wolfe (Ire) *James Moffatt* 33
2 b g City On A Hill (USA) - Quatredil (Ire)
10^{5g} 9^{6gf} 8^{5gf} 4^{5gf} 9^{5g} **0-0-5 £265**

Star Applause *J S Goldie* 46 a42
5 b m Royal Applause - Cominna
14^{5sd} 5^{5sd} 8^{5gf} 10^{5sd} 7^{5gf} 15^{5g} 10^{5g} **0-0-7**

Star Cluster *H R A Cecil* 88
2 b f Observatory (USA) - Didicoy (USA)
1^{7gf} **1-0-1 £4,270**

Star Crowned (USA) *B J Meehan* a72
2 b c Kingmambo (USA) - Fashion Star (USA)
3^{6sf} **0-1-1 £626**

Star Fern *M J Attwater* 37 a53
4 br g Young Ern - Christening (Ire)
7^{6sd} 13^{7sd} 13^{6s} 6^{5gf} 8^{5gf} 7^{6gf} 2^{8sd} 3^{8sd} 8^{8ss} 5^{7sd} 2^{9sd} 1^{9sd} 5^{9ss} **1-3-13 £2,843**

Star Lad (Ire) *R Brotherton* a41
5 ch g Lake Coniston (Ire) - Simply Special (Ire)
7^{6sd} 7^{6sd} 3^{7sd} 11^{7sd} 4^{5sd} 8^{6sd} 11^{7sd} **0-1-7 £209**

Star Magnitude (USA) *S Dow* 63 a67
4 ch g Distant View (USA) - Stellaria (USA)
1^{7sd} 12^{7gs} **1-0-2 £3,464**

Star Member (Ire) *Ian Williams* 91
6 b g Hernando (Fr) - Constellation (Ire)
14^{16g} 13^{14gs} 15^{14g} **0-0-3**

Star Of Canterbury (Ire) *A P Jarvis* 70
2 ch g Beckett (Ire) - Villa Nova (Ire)
6^{8gf} 13^{8g} **0-0-2**

Star Of Erhaab *E A Wheeler* a3
2 b c Erhaab (USA) - Star Glade
10^{7sd} **0-0-1**

Star Of Kildare (Ire) *N Tinkler* 6
3 b f Raphane (USA) - Lady Fleetsin (Ire)
8^{5g} 14^{5g} **0-0-2**

Star Of Light *B J Meehan* 100 a87
4 b g Mtoto - Star Entry
2^{8sd} 9^{8g} 10^{10gf} 3^{8gf} 1^{8g} 5^{8g} 1^{10gf} 2^{10g} 1^{10gf} 16^{9s} **3-3-10 £90,600**

Star Of Siam (Ire) *Mrs P N Dutfield* 38
2 ch f Elnadim (USA) - Thoroughly (Ire)
13^{5gf} **0-0-1**

Star Of The Stag *Dr J D Scargill* 24
2 b f Observatory (USA) - Jade Vine (Ire)
8^{6gs} 8^{7g} 17^{6g} 11^{8gf} **0-0-4**

Star Ovation (Ire) *T J Fitzgerald* a47
8 ch g Fourstars Allstar (USA) - Standing Ovation
8^{8sd} **0-0-1**

Star Rising *W J Musson* 59
3 ch f Most Welcome - My Greatest Star
10^{8gf} 6^{8gs} 7^{8gf} 7^{10gs} 13^{10g} 9^{10s} **0-0-6**

Star Sensation (Ire) *N Tinkler* 44
5 b/br m Sri Pekan (USA) - Dancing Sensation (USA)
14^{8s} 19^{8g} 11^{10gf} 12^{7gf} 10^{8gf} **0-0-5**

Star Side (Ire) *C Tinkler* 17 a65
3 b c Ashkalani (Ire) - Rachel Pringle (Ire)
5^{10sd} 7^{9sd} 16^{12gs} **0-0-3**

Star Sign *D W Barker* 45
3 b f Robellino (USA) - Amid The Stars
10^{9g} 8^{10f} 7^{10gf} 12^{8g} 5^{9s} 10^{10s} **0-0-6**

Star Welcome *W J Musson* 59 a59
4 ch f Most Welcome - My Greatest Star
4^{9sd} 2^{10sd} 7^{11s} 6^{10s} 6^{10gf} 1^{10gs} 3^{10g} 4^{12g} 9^{12sd} 2^{12sd} 9^{12sd} 6^{12ss} 4^{10sd} **1-3-13 £5,578**

Star Wood (Ire) *R Charlton* 62
3 b f Montjeu (Ire) - Woodwin (Ire)
6^{12gs} 6^{12gf} 11^{10g} 7^{10gs} **0-0-4**

Starboard Light *W G M Turner* 48
2 b f Mark Of Esteem (Ire) - Light Ship
10^{5gf} 7^{6gs} 5^{7gf} **0-0-3**

Starchy *M Johnston* 89
3 b f Cadeaux Genereux - Sahara Star
3^{7g} 9^{7gf} 6^{8gs} 10^{8gs} **0-1-4 £1,484**

Starcraft (NZ) *L M Cumani* 127 a113
5 ch h Soviet Star (USA) - Flying Floozie (NZ)
3^{8gf} 6^{10gf} 1^{8g} 1^{8g} 7^{10ft} **2-1-5 £275,020**

Starcross Maid *J F Coupland* 52 a53
3 ch f Zaha (Can) - Maculatus (USA)
8^{9sd} 6^{7g} 5^{8g} 8^{10gf} 3^{8gf} 4^{8gf} 4^{9sd} 11^{9sd} 3^{8sd} 12^{8s} 2^{8sd} 7^{8ss} 10^{9sd} **0-4-13 £1,156**

Starcross Venture *R A Fahey*
4 b f Orpen (USA) - Maculatus (USA)
11^{8sd} **0-0-1**

Starduster *B R Millman* 71
3 gr f Paris House - To The Stars (Ire)
5^{5s} 3^{5f} 10^{5gf} 2^{5g} 5^{6gf} 4^{5gf} 1^{5gf} 4^{5gs} 4^{5gf} 15^{6g} **1-2-10 £7,047**

Stargazer Jim (Fr) *W J Haggas* 77 a83
3 br g Fly To The Stars - L'Americaine (USA)
5^{7sd} 4^{8gf} 1^{9sd} 2^{10gf} 5^{10g} 3^{10s} 4^{10hy} 1^{10sd} **2-1-8 £10,358**

Stargem *J Pearce* 74 a75
4 b f Compton Place - Holy Smoke
3^{6sd} 1^{6sd} 2^{6sd} 1^{5sd} 12^{5sd} 7^{6g} 9^{6f} 7^{5gf} 2^{5gf} 2^{5f} 3^{5g} 7^{5f} 11^{6g} 4^{5gs} **2-5-14 £13,534**

Starlight Gazer *J A Geake* 74
2 b c Observatory (USA) - Dancing Fire (USA)
3^{6gf} **0-1-1 £1,005**

Starlight River (Ire) *J Parkes* 45 a46
3 b f Spectrum (Ire) - Prosaic Star (Ire)

4^{6sd} 12^{7sd} 12^{6sd} 11^{5sd} 4^{8sd} 9^{6sd} 7^{7gf} 3^{5f} 15^{5gf} 9^{5sd} 10^{5sd} 7^{6ss} **0-1-12 £392**

Starmix *G A Harker* 25
4 br g Linamix (Fr) - Danlu (USA)
15^{7g} 6^{16gf} **0-0-2**

Starship (Ire) *W J Haggas* a75
2 b f Galileo (Ire) - Council Rock
5^{8sd} 2^{7sd} 1^{7sd} **1-1-3 £4,853**

Start Of Authority *J Gallagher* 49
4 ch g Muhtarram (USA) - Heiden's Delight (USA)
13^{8gf} 6^{6gf} 6^{6f} 4^{7g} 4^{7g} 4^{12f} 13^{11g} **0-2-7 £264**

Startengo (Ire) *D R C Elsworth* a58
2 ch c Nashwan (USA) - Virgin Hawk (USA)
7^{8sd} **0-0-1**

Startori *B Smart* 84
2 b f Vettori (Ire) - Celestial Welcome
2^{7g} 3^{7gf} 4^{7g} 1^{7g} 1^{7gs} 3^{8gs} **2-1-6 £32,112**

State Dilemma (Ire) *D Shaw* 72 a79
4 b g Green Desert (USA) - Nuriva (USA)
7^{8sd} 13^{9sd} 17^{8g} 13^{7g} 12^{6gf} 8^{5s} 12^{7sd} 8^{6s} 14^{6gf} 15^{6g} 5^{6sd} **0-0-11**

State Of Balance *K Bell* a56
7 ch m Mizoram (USA) - Equilibrium
5^{10sd} 6^{10sd} 5^{10sd} **0-0-3**

Statophane (Ire) *J S Moore*
5 b g Raphane (USA) - Life On The Street
12^{7sd} **0-0-1**

Staunchly (Ire) *L M Cumani* 42 a37
3 b f Namid - Sidelined (Ire)
9^{6g} 5^{7g} 6^{8sd} **0-0-3**

Stavros (Ire) *J S Wainwright* 34
5 b g General Monash (USA) - Rivers Rainbow
8^{6g} 8^{6f} **0-0-2**

Stay Close *A M Balding* 76 a75
3 b g Belong To Me (USA) - Cymbala (Fr)
1^{7sd} 1^{7sd} 4^{7s} 8^{8g} 8^{7gf} **2-0-5 £7,622**

Steak N Kidney (USA) *M Wigham* 27
2 b/br c Wild Again (USA) - Top Slipper (Fr)
15^{7gf} **0-0-1**

Steal The Thunder *A Berry* 39
3 br g Timeless Times (USA) - Lavernock Lady
8^{7gs} 11^{6gs} 4^{5gf} 5^{5s} 9^{5s} 15^{5f} **0-0-6**

Stedfast McStaunch (Ire) *B J Meehan* a92
3 gr g Desert Style (Ire) - Aneydia (Ire)
3^{9sd} **0-1-1 £2,305**

Steel Blue *R M Whitaker* 94 a58
5 b g Atraf - Something Blue
10^{6g} 12^{5g} 3^{6s} 23^{6gf} 7^{6g} 10^{6gf} 10^{6gf} 4^{6g} 10^{6gf} 12^{6gs} 4^{6g} 20^{6g} 1^{7s} 13^{7gs} 3^{5hy} 9^{6sd} 7^{7s} **1-3-17 £12,367**

Steel City Boy (Ire) *D Carroll*
2 b c Bold Fact (USA) - Balgren (Ire)
9^{6gf} **0-0-1**

Steel Grey *M Brittain*
4 gr g Grey Desire - Call Me Lucky
11^{7gf} 7^{10g} **0-0-2**

Steely Dan *J R Best* 34 a92
6 b g Danzig Connection (USA) - No Comebacks
10^{7sd} 6^{8sd} 1^{7sd} 7^{10sd} 8^{8sd} 9^{12sd} 11^{10gf} 11^{8gf} **1-0-8 £5,999**

Steenberg (Ire) *M H Tompkins* 112
6 ch h Flying Spur (Aus) - Kip's Sister
2^{7hy} 2^{6s} 3^{6g} 3^{6g} 6^{7gs} 11^{7g} 9^{6g} 5^{7sh} 9^{9gs} **0-4-9 £46,786**

Stella Marais (Ire) *C Hennessy* a59
4 b f Second Empire (Ire) - Karakapa (Fr)
1^{7sd} 8^{8g} **1-0-2 £2,928**

Stellar Brilliant (USA) *Sir Michael Stoute* 78
3 b/br f Kris S (USA) - Subeen
2^{10gf} 1^{10gs} **1-1-2 £4,820**

Stellenbosch (USA) *J W Hills* 67
2 b c Cape Town (USA) - New Account (USA)
15^{7g} 4^{8gs} 8^{7f} **0-0-3 £240**

Stellite *J S Goldie* 69 a72
5 ch g Pivotal - Donation
2^{6sd} 3^{7sd} 2^{9sd} 4^{7sd} 4^{9sd} 3^{7gs} 5^{6gf} 13^{6g} 2^{8gf} 1^{7s} 2^{9sd} **1-6-11 £7,260**

Step Perfect (USA) *G M Moore* 37
4 b g Royal Academy (USA) - Gossiping (USA)
12^{11gf} 8^{9gf} **0-0-2**

Stephanie's Mind *M Quinn* 48 a61
3 b f Mind Games - Adorable Cherub (USA)
2^{6sd} 2^{6sd} 1^{5sd} 13^{5sd} 11^{5gf} 8^{5g} 9^{6sd} 10^{6gs} 9^{6gs} 3^{5sd} 10^{6sd} **1-3-11 £6,642**

Stephanies Dream *M J Attwater* 67 a36
2 b f Groom Dancer (USA) - Broughtons Lure (Ire)
3^{5gs} 3^{5g} 5^{5g} 6^{8g} 14^{8gs} 9^{8sd} **0-2-6 £1,976**

Steppe Dancer (Ire) *D J Coakley* a74
2 b c Fasliyev (USA) - Exemina (USA)
5^{7sd} **0-0-1**

Stepping Up (Ire) *Unknown* 106
2 ch c Soviet Star (USA) - Rise And Fall
1^{6gf} 3^{7g} 7^{7gs} **1-1-3 £10,899**

Sterling Magic (Ire) *P W Chapple-Hyam* 57
2 b c Monashee Mountain (USA) - Chardania (Ire)
6^{7g} 4^{7gf} PU^{6sd} **0-0-3 £261**

Sterling Supporter *D W Thompson* 57 a3
3 b f Josr Algarhoud (Ire) - Riyoom (USA)
5^{10gf} 2^{9gf} 12^{8gf} 6^{10gf} 11^{7g} 9^{7sd} **0-0-6 £1,045**

Stetchworth Prince *D R Loder* 108
3 b c Cadeaux Genereux - Elfin Laughter
3^{7gf} 4^{8g} 3^{7gf} 4^{6g} 1^{6gs} 6^{5gf} **1-3-6 £22,114**

Steve Austin *S C Williams* 20 a19
2 b g Zafonic (USA) - Degree
15^{7gf} 12^{6sd} **0-0-2**

Stevedore (Ire) *J R Boyle* 68 a75
4 ch c Docksider (USA) - La Belle Katherine (USA)
5^{8f} 2^{8g} 1^{8gf} 2^{7gf} 8^{7sd} 2^{7f} 10^{7g} 1^{8gf} 12^{8gf} 2^{9sd} 1^{8sf} 3^{8sd} 1^{8sd} **4-5-13 £16,818**

Stevie Wonderboy (USA) *Doug O'Neill* a119
2 ch c Stephen Got Even (USA) - Heat Lightning (USA)
2^{6ft} 3^{6ft} 1^{7ft} 1^{7ft} 1^{9ft} **3-0-5 £511,531**

Stevmarie Star *J A Glover* a28
3 b f Muhtarram (USA) - Cabaret Artiste
8^{7sd} 12^{7sd} 13^{7sd} **0-0-3**

Sticky Mint (Ire) *M Blanshard* 47 a25
2 b f Inchinor - Creme De Menthe (Ire)
5^{5gf} 5^{5gf} 12^{6gf} 9^{6sd} **0-0-4**

Stiletta Star *A M Balding* 72
3 br f Robellino (USA) - Loch Sabre
5^{6gs} 13^{6gf} **0-0-2**

Sting In Her Tail (Ire) *M W Easterby*
2 b f Marju (Ire) - Barbizou (Fr)
14^{5gf} 10^{6sd} 11^{7sd} **0-0-3**

Sting Like A Bee (Ire) *J S Goldie* 58 a46
6 b g Ali-Royal (Ire) - Hidden Agenda (Fr)
8^{8gs} 11^{8g} 3^{10gs} 6^{8gf} 5^{11gf} 2^{10g} 7^{10s} 8^{8gf} 2^{8gf} 11^{9g} 11^{8s} 10^{9sd} **0-3-12 £2,561**

Stoic Leader (Ire) *R F Fisher* 96 a81
5 b g Danehill Dancer (Ire) - Starlust
5^{7sd} 8^{8sd} 5^{9sd} 4^{7sd} 6^{8sd} 1^{8g} 1^{8gf} 1^{7f} 5^{7g} 5^{7gs} 3^{7g} 4^{8gf} 14^{8g} 5^{8gf} 14^{8gf} 3^{7g} 7^{8g} 11^{8gf} 4^{8gf} 5^{8gf} 8^{8gf} 5^{8hy} 6^{8sd} 7^{9sd} 9^{7sd} 8^{9sd} 5^{8sd}
3-2-27 £32,280

Stokesies Luck (Ire) *J L Spearing* 31
2 br c King Charlemagne (USA) - Lesley's Fashion
14^{6g} **0-0-1**

Stokesies Wish *J L Spearing* 69
5 ch m Fumo Di Londra (Ire) - Jess Rebec
15^{6g} 12^{5gf} 3^{6gs} 3^{6gs} 6^{6g} 7^{6gs} 4^{6g} 13^{6g}
0-2-8 £1,824

Stolen *W R Muir* 20 a44
3 b g Groom Dancer (USA) - Jezyah (USA)
10^{10gf} 12^{11g} 10^{12sd} **0-0-3**

Stolen Glance *M W Easterby* a50
2 b f Mujahid (USA) - Stolen Melody
4^{5sd} 12^{7gf} 12^{6sd} 4^{8sd} **0-0-4 £290**

Stolen Hours (USA) *J Akehurst* 87
5 b/br h Silver Deputy (Can) - Fasta (USA)
2^{12gf} 2^{14gf} 4^{12gf} 1^{12gf} **1-2-4 £8,424**

Stolen Song *J Ryan* 57 a60
5 b g Sheikh Albadou - Sparky's Song
13^{16sd} 12^{14gs} 7^{12f} UR^{16g} 12^{16gs} 1^{10gf} 15^{10g} 2^{11gf} 6^{11g} 6^{14sd} 11^{12sd} 3^{14ss} 8^{11sd} **1-2-13 £4,374**

Stoneacre Boy (Ire) *Peter Grayson* 63 a66
2 ch g City On A Hill (USA) - Sans Ceriph (Ire)
9^{6gs} 2^{5sd} 3^{5gf} 4^{5g} 10^{5g} **0-2-5 £1,848**

Stoneacre Fred (Ire) *Peter Grayson* a40
2 br g Lend A Hand - Election Special
10^{7sd} 9^{9sf} 8^{9sd} **0-0-3**

Stoneacre Girl (Ire) *Peter Grayson* 8 a35
2 ch f Rossini (USA) - Ring Of Light
5^{5g} 6^{5sd} 10^{5sd} 7^{6f} 7^{5sd} **0-0-5**

Stoneacre Lad (Ire) *Peter Grayson* 58 a75
2 b c Bluebird (USA) - Jay And-A (Ire)
6^{5sd} 8^{5gf} 10^{5gf} 1^{5sd} 11^{7sd} 1^{5sd} 5^{6sd}
2-0-7 £10,466

Stoneacre Lil (Ire) *Peter Grayson* 25 a49
2 b f Fasliyev (USA) - Lady Ounavarra (Ire)
14^{6gf} 4^{7gf} 11^{8gf} 2^{10sd} **0-1-4 £675**

Stonecrabstomorrow (Ire) *P F I Cole* a76
2 b c Fasliyev (USA) - Tordasia (Ire)
2^{5sd} 2^{6sf} **0-2-2 £2,487**

Stonehaugh (Ire) *J Howard Johnson* 69
2 b c King Charlemagne (USA) - Canary Bird (Ire)
6^{6g} 3^{6gf} 6^{8gf} **0-0-3 £855**

Stonor Lady (USA) *Miss Sheena West* a42
4 b/br f French Deputy (USA) - Blush With Love (USA)
9^{12sd} 8^{9sd} **0-0-2**

Stoop To Conquer *A W Carroll* 85
5 b g Polar Falcon (USA) - Princess Genista
4^{14s} **0-1-1 £861**

Storm Centre *A M Balding* 70
3 ch g Pivotal - Long View
4^{6f} 3^{6g} 5^{8g} **0-1-3 £860**

Storm Chase (USA) *A P Jarvis* 67 a61
3 b/br g Awad (USA) - Night Duja (USA)
10^{6sd} 11^{7sd} 2^{7gs} 3^{7sd} 1^{6gf} 8^{6gf} 2^{7f} 15^{8gf} 2^{7gf} 5^{8gf} 14^{7gf} 14^{7g} **1-4-12 £7,361**

Storm Of Arabia (Ire) *W R Swinburn* 66 a51
2 b g Intikhab (USA) - Mauradell (Ire)
8^{7gf} 9^{7f} 10^{7sd} **0-0-3**

Storm On The Run (Ire) *R Hannon* 77
2 b c Desert Prince (Ire) - Happy Dancer (USA)
2^{5g} 2^{6g} **0-2-2 £2,584**

Storm Prospect *C Tinkler* 57 a62
2 b g Mujahid (USA) - Bajan Blue
8^{8s} 6^{8sd} **0-0-2**

Stormingmichaelori *N Wilson* 49
2 b g Vettori (Ire) - Stormswept (USA)
15^{5gf} 5^{5gf} 6^{7g} 6^{6g} **0-0-4**

Stormville (Ire) *M Brittain* 48 a41
8 b g Catrail (USA) - Haut Volee
9^{9sd} 5^{7gs} 7^{7g} **0-0-3**

Stormy Love (Ire) *M Johnston* 63
3 ch c Giant's Causeway (USA) - Hula Angel (USA)
3^{8gf} 4^{10g} **0-1-2 £1,418**

Stormy Monday *J W Hills* 66
2 b f Cadeaux Genereux - Hasta (USA)
9^{6gf} 4^{6g} 1^{6gs} 11^{7gf} **1-0-4 £3,539**

Stormy Nature (Ire) *W R Swinburn* 74 a78
4 b/br f Mujadil (USA) - Ossana (USA)
7^{7sd} 6^{7sd} 5^{7sd} 4^{8g} 4^{8f} **0-0-5 £569**

Stormy River (Fr) *N Clement* 111
2 gr c Verglas (Ire) - Miss Bio (Fr)
2^{8g} 1^{7s} 2^{8s} **1-2-3 £60,148**

Storyville *Doug Watson* a71
3 br g Lujain (USA) - Slow Jazz (USA)
1^{6sd} 12^{7ft} **1-0-2 £4,075**

Straffan (Ire) *J Hetherton* 64 a61
3 b/br f Shinko Forest (Ire) - Katherine Gorge (USA)
1^{5sd} 1^{6sd} 8^{5sd} 6^{5gs} 1^{6g} 1^{5gs} 15^{6gf} 3^{5s} 17^{5gf} 6^{5gs} 9^{6g} 6^{6gf} 11^{5f} 8^{5gf} 10^{5gf} 8^{7gf} 18^{6gf} 9^{6g} 9^{6gf} 4^{5g} 12^{5sd} 3^{5sd} 8^{7sd} 13^{6sd} 4^{5sd} 2^{6ss}
4-2-26 £12,701

Straight As A Die *R J Hodges* 43 a32
2 b f Pyramus (USA) - Tenderetta
2^{5g} 11^{6g} 7^{6gf} 6^{6g} 8^{6sd} **0-1-5 £836**

Strategic Mount *P F I Cole* 68
2 b c Montjeu (Ire) - Danlu (USA)
5^{8g} 6^{8gs} **0-0-2**

Stratham (Ire) *E J O'Neill* 79 a70
2 b c Mozart (Ire) - Bean Island (USA)
7^{5g} 2^{5gf} 2^{5gf} 3^{6sd} 2^{5gf} 2^{6gf} 1^{6gf} **1-5-7 £12,114**

Strathclyde (Ire) *A M Hales* 45 a51
6 b g Petong - It's Academic
14^{7sd} 9^{5sd} 12^{5gf} 17^{5g} 9^{5f} 6^{5g} 6^{5sd} 6^{5sd} 3^{5sd} 2^{6ss} **0-2-10 £631**

Strathtay *M Appleby* 59
3 ch f Pivotal - Cressida
5^{5gs} 6^{6gf} 11^{6s} 9^{6gs} 6^{8gf} 2^{9s} 7^{8g} 5^{10gf}
0-1-8 £1,261

Stravara *R Hollinshead* 76
2 b g Kayf Tara - Stravsea
8^{10g} 5^{8s} 1^{8hy} **1-0-3 £2,143**

Stravmour *R Hollinshead* a56
9 ch h Seymour Hicks (Fr) - La Stravaganza
6^{12sd} 5^{12sd} 1^{14sd} 7^{17sd} 5^{17sd} 4^{14sd} 2^{12sd} 2^{16sd} 5^{14sd} 2^{12sd} 2^{14sd} **1-4-11 £3,977**

Stravonian *G A Swinbank* 25
5 b g Luso - In The Evening (Ire)
7^{9gf} 7^{12gs} **0-0-2**

Strawberry Dale (Ire) *J D Bethell* 102
3 b f Bering - Manchaca (Fr)
7^{8gs} 9^{8gf} 6^{7gf} 1^{8gf} 7^{8g} 15^{9s} 1^{10hy} **2-0-7**
£23,516

Strawberry Leaf *R Charlton* 86 a77
3 ch f Unfuwain (USA) - Satin Bell
2^{7sd} 3^{8sd} 1^{8gf} 1^{9s} **2-2-4 £14,795**

Strawberry Lolly *Sir Michael Stoute* 67
2 b f Lomitas - Strawberry Morn (Can)
5^{7g} **0-0-1**

Strawberry Patch (Ire) *Miss L A Perratt* 44
6 b g Woodborough (USA) - Okino (USA)
16^{5gf} 13^{5gf} **0-0-2**

Stream Of Gold (Ire) *Sir Michael Stoute* 116
4 b c Rainbow Quest (USA) - River Dancer
1^{8g} 4^{8g} 4^{9g} 4^{10gf} **1-0-4 £68,750**

Stream Of Passion *M R Channon* 31
3 ch f Vettori (Ire) - Between The Sticks
11^{7gf} 9^{8s} **0-0-2**

Street Ballad (Ire) *G M Moore* 45
3 b f Fasliyev (USA) - Nancy Maloney (Ire)
13^{5g} 7^{5gs} 2^{6g} 9^{6g} 10^{7gf} 11^{7gf} **0-1-6**
£760

Street Games *D G Bridgwater* a41
6 b g Mind Games - Pusey Street
12^{12sd} 6^{12sd} 9^{10sd} 6^{9sd} 10^{8g} **0-0-5**

Street Life (Ire) *W J Musson* 74 a74
7 ch g Dolphin Street (Fr) - Wolf Cleugh (Ire)
13^{10sd} 2^{12sd} 12^{10gs} 5^{10s} 9^{11g} 13^{10g} 5^{10hy}
0-1-7 £1,072

Street Warrior (Ire) *C G Cox* 74
2 b g Royal Applause - Anne Bonny
10^{7gs} 2^{7g} 4^{7gf} **0-1-3 £1,807**

Strength 'n Honour *Miss K M George* 91 a84
5 b g Hernando (Fr) - Seasonal Splendour (Ire)
8^{10sd} 7^{13sd} 8^{12g} 12^{16g} 2^{10gs} **0-1-5**
£1,512

Strensall *R E Barr* 78 a46
8 b g Beveled (USA) - Payvashooz
9^{6sd} 5^{5gs} 5^{5g} 10^{5gf} 8^{5gf} 1^{5gf} 7^{5f} 7^{5gf} 3^{5f}
3^{5g} 12^{5g} 6^{5gf} 8^{5s} 3^{5g} 11^{5gf} 6^{5g} **1-3-16**
£8,128

Stretton (Ire) *J D Bethell* 83 a75
7 br g Doyoun - Awayil (USA)
13^{10gf} 15^{10gf} 9^{10gf} 8^{10g} 12^{10gf} 11^{10gs} 7^{11gf}
2^{10gf} 7^{12g} 2^{12g} 1^{12sd} 12^{12sf} **1-2-12**
£6,474

Strictly Speaking (Ire) *R Brotherton*
8 b g Sri Pekan (USA) - Gaijin
13^{9sd} 13^{14sd} **0-0-2**

Strider *P D Evans* 64 a63
4 ch g Pivotal - Sahara Belle (USA)
12^{7sd} 10^{9sd} 9^{8sd} 9^{9sd} 3^{10s} 3^{10g} 16^{12hy} 9^{10g}
3^{10g} 1^{10gf} 7^{13gf} 3^{10gf} 5^{10g} 18^{10g} 12^{10gf}
1-3-15 £5,600

Strife (Ire) *R Hannon* 50
2 b g Stravinsky (USA) - Fife (Ire)
14^{6gf} 10^{6gs} 16^{7g} 10^{8gs} **0-0-4**

Strike Gold *S Kirk* 50 a59
3 b g Mujahid (USA) - Gracious Beauty (USA)
6^{8sd} 15^{8g} 14^{8g} 10^{10gf} 5^{6gf} 12^{7gf} 14^{8f}
0-0-7

Strike Up The Band *D Nicholls* 106
2 b c Cyrano De Bergerac - Green Supreme
1^{5g} 2^{5gs} 1^{5gf} 2^{5gf} 2^{5f} 1^{5gs} **3-3-6**
£75,558

Striking Ambition *R Charlton* 118
5 b h Makbul - Lady Roxanne
1^{5sh} 6^{6s} 13^{5gf} 1^{6g} 13^{7g} 1^{6g} 2^{5gs} **3-1-7**
£122,794

Striking Endeavour *G C Bravery* 36
3 b c Makbul - Nineteenth Of May
17^{7g} **0-0-1**

Striking Sound (USA) *Patrick Morris* a29
7 gr m Rubiano (USA) - Hobe Sound
8^{10sd} **0-0-1**

Strobinia (Ire) *R M Beckett* a41
3 b f Soviet Star (USA) - Robinia (USA)
6^{7sd} **0-0-1**

Stroller (Ire) *J R Fanshawe* 57 a76
4 b f Sadler's Wells (USA) - Gravieres (Fr)
1^{10sd} 4^{10sd} 7^{12s} **1-0-3 £4,057**

Strong Approach (Ire) *T D Barron* 69
2 ch g Fruits Of Love (USA) - Shragraddy Lass (Ire)
6^{5g} 6^{5gf} 2^{6gf} 2^{6gf} 8^{6f} **0-1-5 £2,839**

Strong Hand *M W Easterby* 91
5 b m First Trump - Better Still (Ire)
5^{7gs} 14^{8g} 10^{8s} 3^{8gs} 1^{9gf} 1^{11gf} 1^{11g} 12^{12f}
3^{10gs} 4^{10gf} **3-2-10 £18,621**

Stronghold *J H M Gosden* 109
3 b c Danehill (USA) - Insinuate (USA)
3^{8gs} 2^{8g} 1^{8gf} 3^{10gf} 1^{8gs} 1^{8g} 9^{8s} **3-3-7**
£29,378

Stroppy (Ire) *N P Littmoden* 28
2 b f Xaar - Khalisiyn
18^{6gf} 17^{6g} **0-0-2**

Strudel (Ire) *Sir Mark Prescott* 93 a82
3 b f Spectrum (Ire) - Griddle Cake (Ire)
7^{6sd} 1^{8gs} 7^{9g} 6^{8gs} 5^{11gs} 1^{10s} 7^{12sd} 12^{10hy}
2-0-8 £9,518

Strut *R Charlton* 99
2 ch f Danehill Dancer (Ire) - Boast
11^{6gf} 5^{6gf} 1^{5gf} 1^{5gf} 4^{6gf} 3^{6g} **2-1-6**
£25,620

Stunning Spark *S Dow*
3 b f Fraam - Lady Jo
13^{12sd} **0-0-1**

Sturbury *J W Mullins* 42 a14
3 b f Topanoora - Carry Me (Ire)
11^{12gf} 12^{10sd} 10^{6gf} **0-0-3**

Style Princess (Ire) *D Carroll* 53
2 b f Desert Style (Ire) - Torretta (Ire)
5^{6gf} **0-0-1**

Stylish Dancer *A J Chamberlain* 39 a13
4 b f Muhtarram (USA) - Iltimas (USA)
11^{8g} 8^{12sd} **0-0-2**

Stylish Sunrise (Ire) *I A Wood* 35 a48
4 b g Desert Style (Ire) - Anita At Dawn (Ire)
7^{12sd} 9^{16sd} 4^{16sd} 7^{16gs} 6^{10f} 13^{12g} 8^{16gf}
0-0-7

Stylistic (Ire) *Patrick Morris* 68
4 b f Daggers Drawn (USA) - Treasure (Ire)
27^{7hy} 6^{5g} 10^{5g} 3^{6f} 2^{6gf} 3^{6gf} 8^{7gf} 3^{9f} 14^{10gy}
0-3-9 £3,282

Sualda (Ire) *R A Fahey* 83
6 b g Idris (Ire) - Winning Heart
11^{14gs} 6^{11g} 3^{12g} 8^{12gf} 3^{12gs} 3^{12gf} 2^{12gf} 4^{12g}
3^{12g} 6^{12g} **0-5-10 £12,034**

Subcity (Ire) *K McAuliffe* 47 a51
3 b g Trans Island - Solas Abu (Ire)
11^{8sd} 10^{9sd} 9^{6gs} 5^{5gs} 12^{6gf} 13^{5sd} 17^{10g}

0-0-7

Subpoena *Saeed Bin Suroor* 98
3 b c Diktat - Trefoil
3^{8gf} 9^{10g} 13^{8gf} 3^{8gf} 3^{7gf} 2^{8gs} 2^{8hy} **0-1-7 £8,519**

Subsidise (Ire) *J G Given* a55
2 br g Key Of Luck (USA) - Haysong (Ire)
11^{9sd} 4^{8sd} 7^{8sd} **0-0-3 £301**

Subtle Affair (Ire) *M G Quinlan* 78 a48
3 b f Barathea (Ire) - Uncertain Affair (Ire)
4^{12sd} 5^{12g} 1^{11gs} 8^{10gf} 9^{10gf} 11^{14hy} 4^{17s} 15^{13vs} **1-0-8 £4,725**

Subyan Dreams *P W Chapple-Hyam* 91 a63
3 b f Spectrum (Ire) - Subya
1^{7sd} 10^{7gf} 3^{6g} 9^{7g} **1-0-4 £3,977**

Succeed (Ire) *Mrs H Sweeting* 63 a64
2 b f Elnadim (USA) - Pico
7^{5gf} 4^{5gf} 8^{6sd} 4^{6sd} 2^{5f} 10^{5gf} 7^{5gf} 5^{5sd} 4^{5sd} **0-1-9 £1,349**

Succession *Sir Mark Prescott* 103
3 ch f Groom Dancer (USA) - Pitcroy
9^{8f} 2^{9g} 3^{8g} 1^{8g} **1-2-4 £16,241**

Successor *M D I Usher* 60 a54
5 ch g Entrepreneur - Petralona (USA)
11^{10g} 9^{8sd} 14^{10gf} 15^{10gf} 8^{10gf} 8^{13gf} 11^{13gf} 3^{10sd} 1^{10s} 2^{10gf} 3^{10gf} 11^{10gs} 10^{12gf} 9^{11g} 12^{12sf} 7^{10sd} 5^{9sf} 9^{9sd} 1^{10sd} 7^{10sd} 2^{10sd} **2-4-21 £6,123**

Sudden Edge *H Candy* 66
3 b g Bold Edge - Surprise Surprise
4^{7s} 4^{6gs} 4^{6g} **0-0-3 £859**

Sudden Impulse *A D Brown* 16 a40
4 b f Silver Patriarch (Ire) - Sanshang (Fr)
7^{13sd} 9^{10sd} 12^{8g} 8^{7sd} 12^{7ss} 12^{9ss} **0-0-6**

Suesam *B R Millman* 69
2 b f Piccolo - Barnacla (Ire)
3^{5gs} 6^{5gf} 1^{6gf} 5^{6gf} 6^{6gf} 13^{7gs} 12^{6s} **1-0-7 £7,480**

Suffolk House *K A Ryan* a40
3 b g Paris House - Suffolk Girl
5^{7sd} 13^{8sd} **0-0-2**

Suggestive *W J Haggas* 115 a117
7 b g Reprimand - Pleasuring
3^{7g} 9^{8gf} 3^{7gf} 9^{7gs} 6^{7gf} 1^{7g} 2^{7gf} 1^{7sd} **2-2-8 £43,347**

Sugitani (USA) *N B King* 60 a62
3 b g Kingmambo (USA) - Lady Reiko (Ire)
7^{10gf} 6^{12g} 18^{10gf} 2^{10f} 4^{8ss} 8^{14sd} 3^{12sd} **0-1-7 £1,211**

Suhezy (Ire) *Robert Gray* 52
2 b f Orpen (USA) - Ervedya (Ire)
5^{5g} 4^{5s} 5^{5g} 8^{5gf} 3^{5g} 1^{7g} 6^{7gf} **1-1-7 £4,815**

Suits Me *Julian Poulton* 71
2 ch c Bertolini (USA) - Fancier Bit
1^{7gf} 1^{8gf} **2-0-2 £6,803**

Suivez Moi (Ire) *M F Harris* 72
3 ch c Daggers Drawn (USA) - Pamiers
16^{10gf} 3^{10g} 2^{10gf} 2^{10gf} 3^{9g} 8^{12gs} 5^{10s} **0-4-7 £4,638**

Sukuma (Ire) *A M Balding* a58
3 ch f Highest Honor (Fr) - Selva (Ire)
3^{8sd} 12^{8sd} 13^{7sd} **0-1-3 £414**

Summer Bounty *F Jordan* 80 a49
9 b g Lugana Beach - Tender Moment (Ire)
2^{10gs} 9^{10gf} 10^{9sd} 7^{11gf} 5^{10gs} 8^{10g} 10^{13gf} 4^{8s} 7^{10hy} 5^{12sd} 11^{12sd} 5^{10sd} **0-1-12 £2,380**

Summer Charm *W Jarvis* 76 a77
3 b f Dansili - Regent's Folly (Ire)
2^{7sd} 5^{7sd} 1^{10gf} 3^{13g} 2^{12gf} 2^{12f} 1^{12g} 1^{14g} 1^{12sd} 3^{11gf} 13^{11sd} 8^{12sd} **3-5-12 £14,054**

Summer Flight (Ire) *J H M Gosden* 50
3 b f Danehill (USA) - Summerosa (USA)
9^{10gf} **0-0-1**

Summer Force *C N Kellett* 37 a43
3 ch g Tina's Pet - Hustle An Bustle (USA)
8^{6sd} 8^{6sd} 9^{7gs} 13^{9sd} 13^{8sd} **0-0-5**

Summer Joy *D K Ivory* a3
4 b f Myfontaine - Marycee (Ire)
14^{7sd} 5^{12sd} 12^{10sd} **0-0-3**

Summer Lodge *M H Tompkins* 67
2 b c Indian Lodge (Ire) - Summer Siren (Fr)
12^{6g} 4^{7g} 4^{8g} **0-0-3 £516**

Summer Recluse (USA) *J M Bradley* 74 a74
6 gr g Cozzene (USA) - Summer Retreat (USA)
5^{7sd} 9^{7gs} 13^{7gf} 6^{9gs} 8^{7gs} 9^{7gf} 6^{6f} 8^{5g} 3^{6gf} 5^{6g} 2^{6f} 7^{7gf} 9^{7sd} 3^{6gf} 1^{6f} 8^{6gf} 6^{7g} 1^{6g} 2^{6g} 2^{6g} 10^{6g} 2^{7sd} 4^{6sd} 5^{6sd} **2-6-24 £13,827**

Summer Serenade *L M Cumani*
4 b f Sadler's Wells (USA) - Summer Sonnet
7^{12sd} **0-0-1**

Summer Shades *W M Brisbourne* 71 a65
7 b m Green Desert (USA) - Sally Slade
2^{7sd} 3^{8sd} 7^{7g} 3^{7f} 4^{8f} 7^{8gf} 10^{7gf} 5^{8gf} 4^{8gf} 8^{8g} 8^{8g} 4^{8f} 4^{8g} **0-2-13 £3,351**

Summer Wave (Ire) *Saeed Bin Suroor* 66
2 b f King's Best (USA) - Asfurah (USA)
2^{5g} 5^{5gf} **0-1-2 £1,496**

Summer's Eve *H Candy* 61
2 gr f Singspiel (Ire) - Early Rising (USA)
11^{7g} **0-0-1**

Summerise *Miss J R Gibney* 75 a75
4 b f Atraf - Summerhill Special (Ire)
9^{8sd} 1^{10gf} 1^{10sd} 1^{10sd} 2^{10gf} 3^{12gf} 3^{10sd} 2^{10gs} 4^{12gf} 3^{10gs} 8^{10gs} 11^{10gf} 9^{12sd} **3-4-13 £14,250**

Summertime Parkes *H Candy* a62
2 ch f Silver Patriarch (Ire) - Summerhill Spruce
3^{7sd} **0-1-1 £549**

Summitville *J G Given* 113
5 b m Grand Lodge (USA) - Tina Heights
2^{9gf} 2^{8gf} 3^{10gf} 3^{10gf} 1^{8f} 4^{9g} 2^{8gs} 4^{10hy} 16^{11f} **1-3-9 £104,582**

Sumora (Ire) *G A Butler* 107 a97
3 b f Danehill (USA) - Rain Flower (Ire)
5^{7sd} 2^{5s} 5^{6gf} 6^{5sd} 8^{5gf} 2^{5g} 4^{6gf} 5^{5gf} **0-3-8 £18,373**

Sumptuous *Sir Michael Stoute* 75
2 b f Pivotal - Fabulous
3^{7gf} 6^{7s} **0-0-2 £2,151**

Sun And Showers (Ire) *J H M Gosden* 73
3 b g Rainbow Quest (USA) - Las Flores (Ire)
6^{10gf} 15^{10g} 7^{14gf} 4^{10g} 4^{12gs} **0-0-5 £510**

Sun Bian *A M Balding* a71
3 b c Makbul - Silken Dalliance
5^{5sd} 2^{7sd} 3^{6sd} 9^{7sd} **0-2-4 £1,272**

Sun Bird (Ire) *R Allan* 78
7 ch g Prince Of Birds (USA) - Summer Fashion
8^{12g} 15^{16g} 17^{20gf} **0-0-3**

Sun Catcher (Ire) *R Hannon* 81 a65
2 b g Cape Cross (Ire) - Taalluf (USA)
8^{6gf} 6^{6gs} 9^{7g} 10^{6gs} 1^{6gf} 10^{6sd} 10^{6gs}
1-0-7 £4,804

Sun Hill *C W Fairhurst* 69 a75
5 b g Robellino (USA) - Manhattan Sunset (USA)
9^{12sd} 9^{9sd} 6^{17sd} 11^{16g} 3^{12sd} 8^{16gs} 2^{16g} 8^{16g}
4^{14sd} 3^{16gf} 7^{16gf} 16^{14s} 5^{16sf} 1^{14ss} 6^{14sd} 8^{16sd}
1-1-16 £6,483

Sun King *K G Reveley* 55
8 ch g Zilzal (USA) - Opus One
10^{12gf} 14^{12s} **0-0-2**

Sun Kissed (Jpn) *Saeed Bin Suroor* 93
3 ch c Sunday Silence (USA) - Flying Kiss (Ire)
9^{9gf} 5^{10gf} **0-0-2 £345**

Sunblush (UAE) *M R Channon* 55
3 br f Timber Country (USA) - Tanami
10^{7gs} 10^{8g} **0-0-2**

Sunbolt (Ire) *T D Barron* 60
2 b g Barathea (Ire) - Sunset (Ire)
3^{7gf} 12^{8gf} **0-1-2 £637**

Suncliff *Mrs A Duffield* 27
3 b g Most Welcome - Marjorie's Orchid
7^{7f} 8^{10g} 8^{12gf} **0-0-3**

Sundance (Ire) *H J Collingridge* 80 a80
3 ch g Namid - Titchwell Lass
11^{6gf} 8^{5g} 8^{7sd} 6^{5gs} 13^{6g} **0-0-5**

Sunday City (Jpn) *P Bowen* 73
4 ch g Sunday Silence (USA) - Diamond City (USA)
2^{10g} 4^{12f} 5^{12g} 3^{10gf} **0-3-4 £3,338**

Sunday Smile *M Johnston* 76
2 b f Sunday Silence (USA) - Sensation
5^{6gf} 3^{6gf} 1^{7gf} 13^{7gf} **1-1-4 £5,149**

Sunday Symphony *Saeed Bin Suroor* 105
3 br g Sunday Silence (USA) - Darrery
2^{12gf} 2^{12gs} 3^{14gf} 3^{12gf} **0-4-4 £20,073**

Sunderland Echo (Ire) *B Ellison* 55 a42
2 ch f Tagula (Ire) - La Alla Wa Asa (Ire)
5^{7gf} 8^{7sd} 8^{7s} **0-0-3**

Sundried Tomato *D W Chapman* a76
6 b g Lugana Beach - Little Scarlett
6^{6sd} 9^{6sd} 3^{6sd} 9^{7sd} 9^{7sd} 9^{6sd} 7^{6sd} 9^{5sd} 8^{7sd}
9^{5sd} **0-1-10 £428**

Sundrop (Jpn) *Saeed Bin Suroor* 112
4 b f Sunday Silence (USA) - Oenothera (Ire)
1^{9g} 2^{8gf} 7^{8g} 5^{10y} 5^{10f} 14^{10y} 1^{9f} **2-1-7**
£137,565

Sungio *B P J Baugh* a62
7 b g Halling (USA) - Time Or Never (Fr)
3^{17sd} 2^{16sd} 4^{16sd} 5^{13sd} 2^{16sd} 3^{16sd} 13^{17sd} 13^{17sd}
9^{13sd} 9^{12sd} 6^{14sd} 7^{16sd} **0-4-12 £2,759**

Sunisa (Ire) *J Mackie* 78 a64
4 b f Daggers Drawn (USA) - Winged Victory (Ire)
7^{12gf} 9^{9sd} **0-0-2**

Sunlit Skies *Sir Mark Prescott* 62
3 b f Selkirk (USA) - Shimmering Sea
5^{7gf} 6^{7g} 8^{6gf} **0-0-3**

Sunny Afternoon *Miss E C Lavelle* 62 a59
5 ch m Atraf - Pinup
10^{8gf} 14^{8g} 8^{7gf} 13^{9sd} 4^{6sd} **0-0-5 £225**

Sunny Disposition (Ire) *E F Vaughan* 31 a38
2 b c Desert Sun - Madam Waajib (Ire)
10^{8sd} 10^{8hy} 12^{9sd} **0-0-3**

Sunny Haze *Mrs P N Dutfield* 17
2 ch f Compton Place - Sunrise Girl
12^{5f} 11^{6f} 7^{8gf} **0-0-3**

Sunny Parkes *M Mullineaux* 56
2 ch f Arkadian Hero (USA) - Janette Parkes
5^{6g} 7^{7g} 9^{8gs} 8^{6g} 10^{6g} **0-0-5**

Sunny Times (Ire) *J M P Eustace* 52 a48
3 b f Raise A Grand (Ire) - Dragon Star
2^{7sd} 5^{7gf} 1^{7gs} 5^{8gf} 11^{7sd} 8^{8g} 7^{8sd} **1-1-7**
£3,394

Sunnyside Royale (Ire) *R Bastiman* 35
6 b g Ali-Royal (Ire) - Kuwah (Ire)
11^{14f} **0-0-1**

Sunridge Fairy (Ire) *L R James* 44 a51
6 b m Definite Article - Foxy Fairy (Ire)
10^{8sd} 3^{14sd} 7^{12gs} 2^{11sd} 6^{12sd} 2^{12sd} 3^{12g} 8^{14f}
9^{14gf} **0-4-9 £1,423**

Sunrise Safari (Ire) *P Winkworth* 97
2 b c Mozart (Ire) - Lady Scarlett
3^{5s} 2^{5gf} 3^{5g} 9^{5gf} 3^{5gf} 3^{6f} 6^{6gf} 4^{6g} **0-4-8**
£8,636

Sunset Darling (Ire) *R A Fahey* 20
2 b f Distant Music (USA) - Dissidentia (Ire)
10^{5g} **0-0-1**

Sunset Dreamer (USA) *P Mitchell* 48 a41
4 ch f Boundary (USA) - Quaff (USA)
8^{8sd} 10^{7sd} 2^{8f} 4^{6f} 15^{7g} 11^{8gf} 17^{8gf} 10^{7gf}
4^{6sd} 14^{7sd} **0-1-10 £726**

Sunset King (USA) *R J Hodges* 33
5 b g King Of Kings (Ire) - Sunset River (USA)
13^{6gs} 18^{7gf} 13^{8g} **0-0-3**

Sunset Ridge (Ire) *Rae Guest* 59
2 b f Indian Ridge - Barbara Frietchie (Ire)
8^{6g} 4^{6gf} 4^{6gs} 14^{6gf} **0-0-4 £243**

Sunset Strip *M R Channon* 79 a76
3 b g Josr Algarhoud (Ire) - Shady Street (USA)
3^{7sd} 3^{10g} 1^{9sd} 5^{12gs} 6^{9gf} 3^{10gs} 9^{10g} **1-2-7**
£6,904

Sunshine On Me *C F Wall* 73 a67
4 ch f Kris - Degannwy
4^{12sd} 4^{12sd} 3^{11s} 3^{9sd} 5^{10f} 8^{10f} 1^{10sd} 1^{10g} 1^{10gf}
4^{10g} 3^{10s} 14^{10hy} **3-3-12 £11,775**

Supa Tramp *J R Fanshawe* a42
2 b g Kayf Tara - Shirley Superstar
6^{9sd} **0-0-1**

Supaseus *H Morrison* 91
2 b c Spinning World (USA) - Supamova (USA)
9^{8gf} 2^{8gs} **0-1-2 £1,566**

Super Canyon *J Pearce* a50
7 ch g Gulch (USA) - Marina Park
6^{6sd} 9^{7sd} 12^{6sd} 13^{7sd} 11^{7sd} 14^{6gs} 3^{6sd} 9^{7sd}
9^{6sd} **0-1-9 £208**

Super Dominion *R Hollinshead* 36 a57
8 ch g Superpower - Smartie Lee
1^{9sd} 6^{7sd} 1^{10sd} 3^{10sd} 9^{10sd} 5^{10sd} 5^{10sd} 4^{9sd}
3^{9sd} 8^{12sd} 11^{12hy} 7^{9sd} 7^{11g} 3^{9sd} 9^{10g} 12^{9sd}
1^{9sd} 3^{9sd} **3-4-18 £8,438**

Super Fellow (Ire) *C N Kellett* a46
11 b g Shy Groom (USA) - Killough
5^{17sd} **0-0-1**

Super Frank (Ire) *G A Butler* 48 a48
2 b c Cape Cross (Ire) - Lady Joshua (Ire)
11^{7gf} 6^{7sd} 5^{6hy} **0-0-3**

Super King *A D Brown* 59 a56
4 b g Kingsinger (Ire) - Super Sisters (Aus)
15^{10g} 14^{10g} 6^{9gf} 6^{10g} 5^{8g} 9^{8g} 12^{12gf} 15^{10s}
3^{9sd} 10^{9sf} 10^{7sd} 13^{9sd} 8^{8sd} **0-1-13**

£420

Super Song *P D Evans* a39
5 b g Desert Prince (Ire) - Highland Rhapsody (Ire)
4^{6sd} 8^{7sd} **0-0-2**

Supercast (Ire) *J S Moore* 87
2 b g Alhaarth (Ire) - Al Euro (Fr)
3^{5g} 1^{5gf} 2^{5gf} 4^{5gs} 12^{6g} 8^{5g} 10^{5g} **1-1-7**
£9,820

Superclean *Mrs A L M King* 32
5 ch m Environment Friend - Star Mover
10^{12sd} 9^{12g} 5^{12s} **0-0-3**

Superior Bay *R A Fahey*
2 b f Superior Premium - Star Of Flanders
12^{6sd} **0-0-1**

Superior Hand (Ire) *R A Fahey* 40 a46
3 b c Lend A Hand - Cantata (Ire)
8^{6sd} 8^{6g} **0-0-2**

Superior Star *R A Fahey* 64
2 b g Superior Premium - Lindfield Belle (Ire)
5^{5s} 10^{5gf} 7^{6gf} 5^{6gf} 4^{6gf} **0-0-5 £275**

Supershot (Ire) *O Brennan* 61
7 b g Son Of Sharp Shot (Ire) - One To Two (Ire)
6^{8g} 9^{12gf} 3^{9f} 9^{10gf} **0-0-4 £389**

Superstitious (Ire) *A De Mieulle* 75
3 b g Bluebird (USA) - Stellar Empress (USA)
4^{6gs} 2^{6s} 1^{6g} 1^{6g} 2^{6gf} 0^{8g} **2-3-6**
£14,133

Supreme Charter *M Johnston* 81
2 b g Diktat - Alchi (USA)
7^{5gs} 5^{6g} 4^{6gf} 1^{7gf} 2^{7g} 3^{8g} 2^{8g} 7^{8g} **1-3-8**
£11,388

Supreme Kiss *T Keddy* 65 a65
2 b f Barathea Guest - Kiss Me Again (Ire)
4^{5g} 4^{5sd} 3^{5gf} 3^{5gf} 6^{6sd} 2^{5g} 6^{6gf} 8^{6gf} 8^{5g} 8^{5gf}
0-3-10 £3,101

Supreme Salutation *D K Ivory* 71 a63
9 ch g Most Welcome - Cardinal Press
8^{8sd} 10^{8sd} 13^{8g} 10^{8g} 14^{8gf} 12^{8gs} 5^{10gs} 13^{8g}
2^{8sd} 8^{8g} 16^{12sd} 11^{8gs} 5^{7hy} 8^{7sd} 6^{8hy}
0-1-15 £1,072

Surdoue *P Howling* 51 a59
5 b g Bishop Of Cashel - Chatter's Princess
7^{11sd} 1^{12sd} 3^{11sd} 5^{8sd} 3^{12sd} 1^{8g} 5^{11gs} 12^{9sd}
10^{8sd} 9^{12sd} 3^{12ss} 4^{8sd} 2^{11sd} 3^{11sd} **2-5-14**
£4,633

Surely Truly (Ire) *K R Burke* 79 a81
2 b f Trans Island - Londubh
5^{6s} 2^{5sd} 7^{5g} 4^{5g} 1^{6gs} 1^{6gf} 2^{6g} 4^{6g} 8^{6gs} 3^{6sd}
2-2-10 £16,244

Surf City *R A Harris* 67 a69
2 ch c Distant Music (USA) - Tolyatti
2^{6sd} 9^{6gf} 5^{7g} 10^{7gf} 9^{8g} 12^{7sd} 7^{6sd} 7^{6sd}
0-1-8 £1,188

Surface To Air *Mrs P N Dutfield* 56
4 b g Samraan (USA) - Travelling Lady
4^{15gs} 7^{15s} 8^{12hy} 3^{17g} 10^{16g} **0-1-5 £896**

Surrey Downs Girl *R W Price* 4
3 ch f Lake Coniston (Ire) - Kingston Girl
9^{6f} 18^{7g} 18^{6gf} **0-0-3**

Surwaki (USA) *C G Cox*
3 b c Miswaki (USA) - Quinella
PU^{7gf} **0-0-1**

Susiedil (Ire) *D Nicholls* 40 a46
4 b f Mujadil (USA) - Don't Take Me (Ire)
1^{8sd} 13^{8sd} 9^{8sd} 4^{8gf} 7^{8gf} 4^{12gf} 11^{15g} 5^{9sd}
4^{9sd} 9^{12sf} 6^{8ss} 6^{8sd} **1-0-12 £1,494**

Suspicious Minds *J W Mullins* 47
4 b f Anabaa (USA) - Paloma Bay (Ire)
12^{14gs} 6^{12f} **0-0-2**

Suturia *W R Muir* 55 a52
3 b f Cadeaux Genereux - Cream Tease
3^{6sd} 11^{7sd} 5^{7sd} 9^{9sd} 4^{7gs} 4^{7sd} 5^{7sd} 3^{7gf} 2^{7gf}
11^{8gf} 4^{7g} 8^{7f} **0-3-12 £2,135**

Suzie Fong *H Candy* 9
2 b f Dr Fong (USA) - Limuru
14^{6gf} **0-0-1**

Suzy Bliss *W R Swinburn* 100
2 b f Spinning World (USA) - Poppy Carew (Ire)
5^{7f} 1^{7g} 4^{8gf} 5^{7gs} **1-0-4 £9,235**

Swahili Dancer (USA) *M D Hammond* 52 a31
4 b g Swain (Ire) - Bella Ballerina
6^{12sd} 6^{9s} **0-0-2**

Swains Bridge (USA) *L M Cumani* 68
3 b c Swain (Ire) - Saraa Ree (USA)
6^{8gf} 3^{8g} **0-1-2 £800**

Swainson (USA) *P Mitchell* 76 a46
4 br c Swain (Ire) - Lyphard's Delta (USA)
11^{11g} 13^{10gf} 3^{12gf} 4^{12gf} 5^{11s} 10^{10sd} **0-1-6**
£1,483

Swallow Falls (Ire) *D McCain*
3 b f Lake Coniston (Ire) - Common Cause
13^{8gf} **0-0-1**

Swallow Senora (Ire) *T D Barron* 54 a39
3 b f Entrepreneur - Sangra (USA)
4^{7gf} PU^{7g} 8^{7gf} 10^{6g} 3^{7sd} 6^{7sd} **0-1-6**
£488

Swan Maiden (USA) *J Noseda* 68
2 ch f Swain (Ire) - Robust (USA)
7^{7s} 1^{7g} **1-0-2 £4,979**

Swan Queen *J L Dunlop* 33
2 br f In The Wings - Bronzewing
17^{7s} **0-0-1**

Swanky Star (Ire) *D J S Ffrench Davis* 21 a20
3 b f Orpen (USA) - Haajra (Ire)
14^{6hy} 8^{5gf} 10^{6sd} **0-0-3**

Swayze (Ire) *N P Littmoden* 59 a57
2 b g Marju (Ire) - Dance Of Love (Ire)
7^{6s} 6^{6hy} 6^{7sd} **0-0-3**

Sweeney Todd (Ire) *J G Portman* a36
3 ch g Raise A Grand (Ire) - Optional
10^{10sd} 10^{8sd} **0-0-2**

Sweep The Board (Ire) *M Hill* 46 a21
4 b g Fasliyev (USA) - Fun Board (Fr)
7^{9g} 5^{12gf} 11^{17f} 8^{12g} 19^{5g} 11^{9sf} **0-0-6**

Sweet Afton (Ire) *Eamon Tyrrell* 98
2 b f Mujadil (USA) - Victory Peak
2^{6g} 3^{6f} 1^{5f} 5^{6gf} 2^{5gf} 10^{6gf} 10^{6g} **1-3-7**
£16,290

Sweet Boulangere *R Hannon* 68
2 ch f Grand Lodge (USA) - Cybinka
7^{6gf} 5^{6gf} 3^{6gf} 7^{6g} 16^{7gf} 13^{8g} **0-0-6**
£654

Sweet Cherokee *C N Kellett* 19 a31
2 b f Mind Games - Sioux Lady
9^{5sd} 11^{7sd} 12^{6gf} 9^{5gs} **0-0-4**

Sweet Emily *J R Fanshawe* 73 a67
3 ch f Inchinor - Thamud (Ire)
4^{7g} 4^{7gs} 7^{8sd} 4^{8f} 1^{7g} **1-0-5 £4,181**

Sweet Game (Ire) *J H M Gosden* 47
2 gr f Dixieland Band (USA) - Good Game (USA)

12^{6gf} **0-0-1**

Sweet Indulgence (Ire) *W J Musson* 87 a79
4 ch g Inchinor - Silent Indulgence (USA)
8^{10sd} 14^{10s} 6^{8g} 5^{10gf} 6^{10gf} 4^{10g} 4^{12gs} 3^{12gf} 1^{12gs} 8^{15gs} 3^{14gs} 29^{18gs} **1-3-12 £10,691**

Sweet Jain *E A L Dunlop* 45 a36
2 b f Lujain (USA) - Kingdom Queen (Ire)
8^{7sd} 14^{7gf} 12^{7gs} 4^{7gf} 4^{6g} 5^{6g} **0-0-6 £272**

Sweet Lime (Ire) *B Smart* 76
2 b c Danehill Dancer (Ire) - Lime Hill Honey (Ire)
4^{6g} 2^{7gs} 3^{7g} 10^{7hy} **0-1-4 £3,431**

Sweet Lorraine *T G Mills* 63
3 b f Dashing Blade - Royal Future (Ire)
7^{8g} 8^{7f} 10^{10gf} **0-0-3**

Sweet Namibia (Ire) *J W Hills* 73
3 ch f Namid - Almond Flower (Ire)
1^{5s} 6^{5g} 5^{6gf} 8^{6gf} 14^{6g} **1-0-5 £4,212**

Sweet Pickle *J R Boyle* 62 a65
4 b f Piccolo - Sweet Wilhelmina
2^{7sd} 10^{6sd} 11^{7sd} 1^{7sd} 1^{7sd} 3^{7f} 5^{8f} 4^{7g} 3^{7sd} 7^{7sd} 6^{7gf} 1^{7sf} 9^{6sd} 5^{7sd} **3-3-14 £10,470**

Sweet Potato (Ire) *J Balding* 57 a61
3 b f Monashee Mountain (USA) - Villafranca (Ire)
3^{7sd} 1^{8sd} 5^{12g} 6^{12g} 6^{10g} 5^{8g} 5^{8gf} 8^{8gf} 4^{8s} 7^{10g} 10^{9sd} 9^{7gs} 6^{7gs} 8^{7gf} **1-1-14 £3,500**

Sweet Rosella *G M Moore* a21
2 b f Alhaarth (Ire) - Thamud (Ire)
6^{5sd} **0-0-1**

Sweet Royale *S C Williams* 20
3 b f Royal Applause - Sorara
10^{5gf} **0-0-1**

Sweet Sioux *W R Swinburn* 65 a42
3 ch f Halling (USA) - Mohican Girl
9^{8gf} 5^{10gf} 5^{12gf} 8^{12gf} 4^{10gf} 13^{12sd} 12^{12sd} **0-0-7**

Sweet Stream (Ity) *J E Hammond* 114
5 b m Shantou (USA) - Snug Dinner (Ire)
1^{10g} 1^{15gf} 8^{12gf} **2-0-3 £84,596**

Sweet Talking Girl *J M Bradley* 31
5 b m Bin Ajwaad (Ire) - Arabellajill
9^{5sd} 6^{5f} 10^{7gf} 9^{7s} **0-0-4**

Sweetest Revenge (Ire) *M D I Usher* 73 a67
4 ch f Daggers Drawn (USA) - Joza
5^{6sd} 11^{7sd} 10^{6sd} 9^{6sd} 3^{6sd} 5^{7g} 6^{6gs} 2^{7sd} 4^{7sd} 3^{6g} 3^{6sd} 1^{5g} 12^{5gf} 1^{5sd} 1^{5gs} 3^{5f} 6^{5s} 6^{5g} 7^{6sd} 11^{6sd} **3-5-20 £11,691**

Sweetly Sharp (Ire) *A Berry* 48 a39
2 ch f Daggers Drawn (USA) - Pecan Pie (Ire)
6^{5sd} 1^{5s} 4^{5g} 3^{6gf} 5^{6g} 5^{5g} 9^{7f} 10^{7sd} 7^{7gf} 11^{6gf} **1-1-10 £3,592**

Sweetwater (Ger) *Seamus Lynch* 40 a53
5 b m Goofalik (USA) - Safrane (Ger)
2^{12sd} 3^{14sd} 6^{12sd} 2^{12sd} 1^{17sd} 12^{17sd} 2^{14sd} 12^{17sd} 7^{12sd} 5^{17sd} 7^{12sd} 11^{12gf} 9^{12g} **1-4-13 £3,732**

Swell Lad *S Gollings* 49 a27
3 b g Sadler's Wells (USA) - Lydara (USA)
4^{12s} 16^{10f} 13^{10sd} **0-0-3 £308**

Swift Alchemist *Mrs H Sweeting*
5 b m Fleetwood (Ire) - Pure Gold
14^{10s} **0-0-1**

Swift Dame (Ire) *B J Meehan* 21 a28
3 b f Montjeu (Ire) - Velvet Appeal (Ire)
12^{8sd} 10^{6sd} 9^{10sd} 9^{8s} **0-0-4**

Swift Fury (Ire) *T D Easterby* 9
2 br f Bluebird (USA) - Golden Diamont (Ire)
6^{5g} **0-0-1**

Swift Oscar *J W Hills* 82 a88
3 b g Mark Of Esteem (Ire) - Surf Bird
1^{8sd} 4^{8gf} 10^{8gf} 2^{8sd} 5^{7gf} 2^{7gf} 6^{7sd} 12^{7sd} 5^{7gf} **1-2-9 £12,185**

Swift Sailor *M Johnston* 103 a104
4 gr g Slip Anchor - New Wind (Ger)
1^{14gs} 2^{19gs} 3^{14g} 5^{20gf} 11^{16g} 3^{16sd} 7^{14gs} 19^{14g} 1^{18gs} 20^{18gs} **2-3-10 £51,239**

Swinbrook (USA) *J A R Toller* 87 a76
4 ch g Stravinsky (USA) - Dance Diane (USA)
8^{6gf} 10^{6g} 6^{7sd} 2^{6gf} 3^{7g} 1^{6s} **1-2-6 £6,139**

Swindon (USA) *P F I Cole* 72 a9
3 b f Kingmambo (USA) - Dance Design (Ire)
3^{12gf} 6^{12ss} **0-1-2 £533**

Swing *J Balding* 31 a35
3 b g Dansili - Blues Indigo
12^{6g} 9^{5g} 7^{7sd} 13^{6sd} 18^{7gf} **0-0-5**

Swing The Ring (Ire) *Bruce Hellier* 99
2 b c Rossini (USA) - Sharkiyah (Ire)
4^{6g} 1^{6g} 3^{8g} 3^{6gf} 5^{6g} 6^{7s} **1-1-6 £42,494**

Swinton *M Brittain* 32 a19
4 gr g Grey Desire - Portite Sophie
7^{10s} 11^{8sd} **0-0-2**

Swords *P Howling* 64 a53
3 b g Vettori (Ire) - Pomorie (Ire)
7^{12g} 10^{15gs} 9^{8g} 3^{7sd} 3^{8sd} 3^{12sd} 2^{9ss} **0-4-7 £1,056**

Sworn In (USA) *N I M Rossiter*
4 ch c Kingmambo (USA) - Under Oath (USA)
5^{22f} **0-0-1 £875**

Sydney Symphony *E J O'Neill* 83 a73
3 b c Daylami (Ire) - Hagwah (USA)
6^{10sd} 1^{9sd} 4^{8g} 10^{9gf} 10^{10gf} 10^{10g} 5^{12sd} 8^{10gs} 4^{9sd} 13^{11g} 4^{12sd} **1-0-11 £4,787**

Sydneyroughdiamond *M Mullineaux* 58 a66
3 b g Whittingham (Ire) - November Song
5^{7sd} 2^{6sd} 4^{6sd} 6^{6g} 4^{5s} 10^{8gs} 7^{5s} 13^{10gf} 11^{10g} 9^{6ft} 18^{6hy} 9^{7sd} 7^{8ss} 7^{9sd} 9^{11sd} **0-1-15 £1,558**

Sylva Royal (Ire) *C E Brittain* a54
4 gr f Royal Applause - Trim Star
5^{7sd} 10^{8sd} 15^{8g} **0-0-3**

Symphonia (Ire) *N P Littmoden* 44 a41
2 br f Zafonic (USA) - Simplicity
11^{6gf} 6^{5g} 5^{7g} 3^{8hd} 10^{9sd} 18^{7g} 8^{8sd} **0-0-7 £625**

Synonymy *M Blanshard* 64
2 b c Sinndar (Ire) - Peony
10^{8g} 7^{8g} 16^{8s} **0-0-3**

Taakeed *D Selvaratnam* 87
3 b c Mark Of Esteem (Ire) - Walimu (Ire)
5^{10gs} 1^{8hy} 10^{8gf} 3^{8g} 9^{8gf} 18^{9g} 13^{7ft} **1-1-7 £5,050**

Tabadul (Ire) *E A L Dunlop* 92
4 b g Cadeaux Genereux - Amaniy (USA)
15^{8g} 10^{7gf} 1^{10gf} 6^{10g} 6^{8gs} 4^{8gs} 2^{8g} 5^{8s} **1-2-8 £12,654**

Tabaret *R M Whitaker* 103
2 ch c Bertolini (USA) - Luanshya
2^{5g} 3^{5f} 1^{5g} 10^{5gs} 1^{5g} 3^{5g} **2-3-6 £34,906**

Taboor (Ire) *R M H Cowell* 62 a57
7 b g Mujadil (USA) - Christoph's Girl
8^{5gs} 13^{6gf} 9^{5f} 13^{5gf} 13^{5gf} 1^{5gf} 1^{5gs} 3^{5gs} 6^{5g} 2^{6gs} 10^{5gf} 10^{5gs} 4^{6sd} **2-2-13 £8,946**

Tabulate *P L Gilligan* 31
2 b f Dansili - Let Alone
10^{8hy} **0-0-1**

Tacid *Dr J D Scargill* 50 a47
3 b f Diktat - Defined Feature (Ire)
9^{8g} 10^{7gf} 8^{8gf} 14^{7f} 2^{8s} 2^{8g} 6^{8f} 1^{8g} 9^{8sd} 3^{9sd} 3^{7sd} **1-4-11 £3,302**

Tadlil *E A L Dunlop* 55
3 b c Pivotal - Pretty Poppy
8^{7gf} 5^{6s} 6^{7gf} **0-0-3**

Tafaahum (USA) *B J Llewellyn* 28
4 b g Erhaab (USA) - Makadir (USA)
5^{10s} 8^{12gs} 8^{10g} **0-0-3**

Taffrail *D Burchell* a49
7 b g Slip Anchor - Tizona
8^{12sd} **0-0-1**

Tafilah *P W D'Arcy* 54 a54
2 b f Foxhound (USA) - Petra Nova
2^{5s} 5^{5g} 4^{5sd} 3^{5g} 4^{5gs} 6^{6gf} 8^{7sd} 6^{7sd} 4^{7sd} 2^{9sd} 5^{9sd} 2^{7sd} **0-4-12 £3,041**

Tafiya *G A Butler* 80
2 b f Bahri (USA) - Fickle
2^{7g} **0-1-1 £1,624**

Tag Team (Ire) *John A Harris* 59 a87
4 ch g Tagula (Ire) - Okay Baby (Ire)
6^{5sd} 6^{6sd} 6^{5sd} 1^{5sd} 6^{5gs} 7^{6sd} 3^{6g} 3^{6g} 2^{6sd} 13^{5g} 11^{5gf} 12^{6g} 16^{5gf} 5^{5sd} 2^{5sd} 3^{6sd} 6^{5sd} 4^{5sd} 1^{5sd} **2-5-19 £9,393**

Taggin'Along (Ire) *M D I Usher* 11
2 b g Tagula (Ire) - Sweet Alma
PU^{6f} 10^{6g} 14^{8sd} **0-0-3**

Tagula Bay (Ire) *T D Easterby* 75 a27
3 b f Tagula (Ire) - Nezool Almatar (Ire)
5^{7g} 7^{6s} 3^{6gs} 7^{6g} 3^{5g} 11^{6sd} 3^{6g} 2^{5gs} 2^{5g} 8^{6gs} 13^{6hy} **0-5-11 £5,039**

Tagula Blue (Ire) *J A Glover* 57
5 b g Tagula (Ire) - Palace Blue (Ire)
5^{8gf} 11^{8g} 10^{10gf} **0-0-3**

Tagula Island (Ire) *W G M Turner* a26
3 ch f Tagula (Ire) - Rosy Scintilla (Ire)
11^{6sd} 11^{7sd} **0-0-2**

Tagula Sunrise (Ire) *R A Fahey* 89
3 ch f Tagula (Ire) - Lady From Limerick (Ire)
8^{6hy} 2^{7g} 12^{8g} 4^{7g} 13^{6gf} 1^{7s} 5^{8g} 7^{6gs} 23^{7gs} **1-1-9 £30,129**

Tahirah *Rae Guest* a92
5 b m Green Desert (USA) - Kismah
3^{9sd} **0-1-1 £2,257**

Tahrir (Ire) *B W Hills* 96
3 gr f Linamix (Fr) - Miss Sacha (Ire)
1^{7gf} 3^{8s} 6^{8gf} 3^{7g} 4^{7gf} 1^{7gf} 7^{6s} 2^{6s} **2-2-8 £31,601**

Tahtheeb (Ire) *M P Tregoning* 100 a99
4 b f Muhtarram (USA) - Mihnah (Ire)
3^{10sd} 3^{14gf} 3^{10gf} 6^{12g} **0-3-4 £8,174**

Taili *D A Nolan*
4 b f Taipan (Ire) - Doubtfire
13^{15g} **0-0-1**

Taipan Tommy (Ire) *S Dow* 53 a56
3 ch g Shinko Forest (Ire) - Adieu Cherie (Ire)
5^{5sd} 7^{5sd} 2^{6sd} 3^{5sd} 12^{7gs} 14^{7gs} 10^{7gf} 2^{6f} 7^{5f} 3^{6f} 10^{6f} 4^{6sf} 5^{5sd} 5^{6sd} 8^{6sd} 8^{5sd} **0-3-16 £2,603**

Taiyo *G C Bravery* 51 a52
5 b m Tagula (Ire) - Tharwa (Ire)
9^{7s} 5^{7g} 3^{7gf} 1^{7sd} 14^{8gf} 16^{7g} **1-1-6 £3,098**

Taj India (USA) *N J Hawke*
3 b/br g Gone West (USA) - Circle Of Gold (Ire)
10^{12sd} **0-0-1**

Takafu (USA) *W J Haggas* 86
3 b g Lemon Drop Kid (USA) - Proper Protocol (USA)
5^{8gf} 8^{10g} 1^{10gf} 3^{12g} 11^{14s} **1-1-5 £7,323**

Takanewa (Ire) *J Howard Johnson* 48
2 b f Danetime (Ire) - Lady Ingabelle (Ire)
8^{6gf} **0-0-1**

Take A Bow *P R Chamings* 111
4 b c Royal Applause - Giant Nipper
2^{8gf} 1^{8gs} **1-1-2 £17,722**

Take A Mile (Ire) *B G Powell* 67 a62
3 ch g Inchinor - Bu Hagab (Ire)
9^{8gs} 12^{8gs} 18^{10f} 1^{10s} 2^{10hd} 4^{9ft} 7^{10s} **1-1-7 £4,541**

Take It There *R Hannon* 68
3 ch f Cadeaux Genereux - Feel Free (Ire)
13^{8gf} 6^{9g} 5^{8f} **0-0-3**

Take No Notice (Ire) *K R Burke* 40 a40
2 b f Imperial Ballet (Ire) - North Telstar
9^{7gf} 17^{7gf} 4^{7ft} 10^{9sd} **0-0-4**

Take The Plunge *L G Cottrell* 24 a42
3 br f Benny The Dip (USA) - Pearly River
10^{8sd} 10^{7sd} 7^{9sd} 12^{10g} 9^{12gf} 7^{9sf} 10^{13g} **0-0-7**

Takemetoyourheart *I A Wood* 7 a7
3 ch f Zaha (Can) - Mother Molly (USA)
8^{8g} 11^{6sd} **0-0-2**

Takes Tutu (USA) *K R Burke* 84 a83
6 b g Afternoon Deelites (USA) - Lady Affirmed (USA)
2^{7sd} 2^{7sd} 10^{7sd} 5^{8sd} 2^{8sd} 3^{8gf} 2^{7g} 1^{8gf} 5^{8gf} 13^{8gf} 14^{8g} 7^{8gf} 11^{8gf} 4^{7sd} 5^{8sd} 4^{9sd} 12^{8sd} **1-5-17 £21,397**

Takhleed (USA) *M P Tregoning* 83
3 b g Stravinsky (USA) - Bold Threat (Can)
4^{7gf} 4^{7g} 1^{6gf} 9^{6gf} 3^{6gf} 14^{7gf} **1-0-6 £7,409**

Takhmin (Ire) *A Al Raihe* 92
3 b c Almutawakel - Magdalene (Fr)
1^{10gs} 2^{12s} 7^{11f} 11^{10g} 9^{10ft} **1-0-5 £6,318**

Takitwo *P D Cundell* 48
2 b g Delta Dancer - Tiama (Ire)
8^{6gf} 10^{6g} 15^{6gs} **0-0-3**

Takoda (Ire) *R F Johnson Houghton* 79
2 b g Namid - Madame Claude (Ire)
2^{5s} 1^{5s} 3^{5s} 7^{5gf} 11^{5gf} 5^{5gs} 5^{6gf} 8^{5gf} **1-1-8 £5,664**

Takrit (Ire) *C E Brittain* 51
3 b f Giant's Causeway (USA) - Mockery
5^{14s} 3^{12gf} 9^{12s} **0-0-3 £519**

Talbot Avenue *M Mullineaux* 108
7 b g Puissance - Dancing Daughter
6^{6gf} 5^{7gf} 5^{6gf} 3^{5gs} 3^{5s} 8^{5g} 10^{5gf} 4^{6f} 3^{6gf} 5^{6g} 2^{5gf} 11^{5gf} 4^{5gf} 9^{6g} **0-4-14 £22,220**

Talcen Gwyn (Ire) *M F Harris* 78 a69
3 b g Fayruz - Cheerful Knight (Ire)

11^{5gs} 12^{6gs} 1^{5gf} 5^{6f} 3^{5g} 8^{5gf} 6^{6gf} 5^{5g} 4^{5f} 4^{5gf} 4^{5gs} 2^{6gf} 7^{5gf} 8^{6f} 6^{5s} 5^{5gf} 4^{5gs} 10^{5sd} 8^{6sd} 3^{5sd} **1-4-20 £8,579**

Tally (Ire) *D G Bridgwater* 58 a64
5 ch g Tagula (Ire) - Sally Chase
8^{6sd} 7^{6sd} 9^{6sd} 6^{7sd} 5^{6sd} 2^{5sd} 4^{6sd} 4^{7sd} 5^{6sd} 3^{5gs} 5^{6s} 5^{6gs} 2^{7gs} 5^{7sd} 3^{7gf} 8^{8gf} 12^{6gf} 13^{8gf} 5^{8gs} 3^{7s} **0-5-20 £2,911**

Tallyhobye *J R Weymes* 56
2 b c Foxhound (USA) - Bebe De Cham
7^{5g} 9^{5s} 3^{6s} 4^{7gf} 2^{7gf} 11^{7g} 6^{7gf} 4^{8gf} 6^{8g} **0-1-9 £2,109**

Tamagin (USA) *J W Unett* 70
2 b c Stravinsky (USA) - Luia (USA)
6^{5g} 7^{5f} 5^{6g} 6^{5gs} 9^{7g} 4^{6g} 10^{5g} **0-1-7 £337**

Tamalain (USA) *Mrs A J Perrett* 74
3 b f Royal Academy (USA) - Woodland Orchid (Ire)
2^{8gf} 7^{8g} 2^{8s} 8^{8f} 2^{10gf} 10^{10gs} **0-3-6 £4,872**

Tamarella (Ire) *J A Glover* 37 a34
5 b m Tamarisk (Ire) - Miss Siham (Ire)
18^{5g} 11^{5gf} 4^{5gf} 7^{5sd} **0-0-4**

Tamino (Ire) *H Morrison* 56
2 b c Mozart (Ire) - Stop Out
12^{6gs} 9^{6g} 9^{6g} **0-0-3**

Taminos Love *Sir Michael Stoute* 80
2 b c Lomitas - Tamise (USA)
4^{7s} 2^{8gf} 1^{8gs} **1-1-3 £5,796**

Taminoula (Ire) *P Mitchell* 69 a70
4 b f Tagula (Ire) - Taormina (Ire)
4^{13sd} 4^{12sd} 5^{12sd} 9^{10gf} 6^{10gf} 9^{12sd} 3^{9g} 3^{7g} 1^{7gf} 2^{8gf} 9^{8g} 8^{8gf} 9^{8gf} 4^{9sd} 8^{6sd} **1-3-15 £6,968**

Tamora *A P Jarvis* 47 a51
3 ch f Dr Fong (USA) - Tahara (Ire)
10^{8sd} 7^{10sd} 10^{11gs} 11^{12g} 11^{10sd} 12^{10g} 5^{10gf} 8^{12sd} 6^{8gf} **0-0-9**

Tancred Imp *D W Barker* 25
4 b f Atraf - Tancred Mischief
15^{16g} 7^{12sd} 9^{12gs} **0-0-3**

Tancred Miss *D W Barker* a45
6 b m Presidium - Mischievous Miss
1^{7sd} 10^{7sd} **1-0-2 £1,473**

Tancred Sprite *D W Barker*
3 b f Atraf - Tancred Mischief
13^{8gf} **0-0-1**

Tancred Times *C F Wall* 61
10 ch m Clantime - Mischievous Miss
8^{6g} 8^{5gf} 10^{6g} 14^{6gf} 3^{6gf} 7^{6gf} **0-1-6 £437**

Tanforan *K McAuliffe* 81 a72
3 b g Mujahid (USA) - Florentynna Bay
3^{7sd} 5^{7sd} 5^{8s} 8^{7g} 9^{8g} 2^{7g} 1^{8g} 14^{8g} 3^{7gf} 7^{8g} 1^{7g} 10^{8gf} 1^{8g} 10^{7g} 8^{9sd} **3-3-15 £20,379**

Tangarita *A M Balding* 54 a16
2 b f Tagula (Ire) - Santa Isobel
9^{6sd} 11^{6gs} 4^{6g} 7^{8g} **0-0-4 £369**

Tangible *Liam McAteer* 78
3 b f Hernando (Fr) - Trinity Reef
1^{14gf} 2^{14g} 3^{16gf} 8^{16g} **1-1-4 £8,334**

Tank (Ire) *Miss Sheena West*
4 ch g Woodborough (USA) - Fiddes (Ire)
16^{12sd} **0-0-1**

Tanne Blixen *P S Felgate* 23 a34
4 b f Great Dane (Ire) - Night Transaction
6^{5sd} 10^{5sd} 6^{5sd} 8^{5gs} **0-0-4**

Tannenberg (Ire) *G A Swinbank* 73
4 b g Polish Precedent (USA) - Upper Strata
6^{9g} 11^{7g} 2^{11gf} 3^{12gf} 3^{13gf} 6^{14gf} **0-2-6 £3,182**

Tanning *A W Carroll* 55 a44
3 b f Atraf - Gerundive (USA)
9^{8sd} 9^{7sd} 5^{7sd} 7^{8sd} 6^{7f} 13^{7g} 4^{7f} 4^{8gf} 11^{7gf} 5^{8s} 3^{10gf} 8^{8f} 9^{10gf} 2^{10f} 3^{9sf} 4^{10g} 3^{13g} 2^{11hy} 5^{11sd} 7^{14sf} 7^{12sd} 1^{10sd} **1-5-22 £3,768**

Tantien *John A Harris* 47
3 b f Diktat - Tahilla
12^{8gs} 7^{8g} 4^{6s} 9^{7f} 10^{7gs} 12^{8gf} 12^{7g} **0-0-7**

Tanwir *M G Quinlan* 57
4 b f Unfuwain (USA) - Al Amlah (USA)
7^{14s} 12^{13gs} 10^{12gf} **0-0-3**

Tanzani (USA) *K A Ryan* 51
3 b g Giant's Causeway (USA) - Aunt Pearl (USA)
8^{8gs} 3^{6gf} 4^{7g} 10^{8s} **0-1-4 £783**

Tanzanite (Ire) *D W P Arbuthnot* 92
3 b f Revoque (Ire) - Resume (Ire)
4^{10s} 5^{8g} 3^{10gs} 2^{10gf} 6^{9s} 8^{8gf} 1^{8gs} 4^{8g} 4^{8g} 1^{8gs} 2^{8gs} 1^{11gs} 5^{10s} 12^{10gs} **3-3-14 £30,618**

Tap My Feet (USA) *C E Brittain* 69
2 b/br f Kingmambo (USA) - Ozena (USA)
9^{6gf} 4^{6gf} 6^{6gf} 6^{7g} 8^{5gf} **0-0-5 £539**

Tapa *A M Balding* 71 a66
3 b f Tagula (Ire) - Tweed Mill
1^{6s} 3^{7g} 4^{6g} 14^{6gf} 9^{6gf} 7^{6gf} 4^{6sd} 3^{6g} 15^{5gs} 5^{6ss} 3^{6sd} **1-3-11 £5,496**

Tapau (Ire) *J M Bradley* a40
7 b m Nicolotte - Urtica (Ire)
10^{6sd} 10^{7sd} **0-0-2**

Tappit (Ire) *L R James* 40 a32
6 b g Mujadil (USA) - Green Life
13^{5sd} 5^{6gf} 18^{6g} 10^{11sd} 10^{6sd} 6^{6sd} **0-0-6**

Tara King *A B Haynes* a43
3 b f Deploy - Trinity Hall
5^{12sd} **0-0-1**

Tara Too (Ire) *D W P Arbuthnot* 83
2 b f Danetime (Ire) - Gone With The Wind (Ire)
4^{6gs} 1^{5g} 6^{6gf} 4^{7gs} 21^{6g} 7^{8s} **1-0-6 £6,254**

Tarabut *E A L Dunlop* 83
3 b f Green Desert (USA) - Nabadhaat (USA)
8^{8g} 3^{14gf} 2^{14g} 4^{14gf} 3^{14gf} 1^{14gf} 1^{16g} 5^{15gf} 1^{16gf} 2^{17g} **3-4-10 £17,238**

Taragan *J J Quinn* 53
3 b f Kayf Tara - Morgannwg (Ire)
1^{11gf} 13^{12f} 2^{14g} **1-1-3 £3,931**

Taranai (Ire) *B W Duke* a37
4 ch f Russian Revival (USA) - Miss Flite (Ire)
12^{14sd} 4^{13sd} 11^{14sd} **0-0-3**

Taranaki *Miss E C Lavelle* 79 a74
7 b g Delta Dancer - Miss Ticklepenny
5^{7sd} 7^{7sd} 3^{6sd} 6^{6sd} 7^{7sd} 11^{7gs} 7^{7s} 8^{6gs} 17^{8g} 8^{7gf} 2^{7gf} 2^{7gf} 3^{7gf} 7^{7g} 8^{7gf} 22^{7gf} 6^{7sd} **0-4-17 £3,757**

Tarandot (Ire) *G G Margarson* 97
4 b f Singspiel (Ire) - Rifada
2^{12s} 5^{12gf} 7^{10gf} 3^{12g} 5^{14g} 7^{14s} 8^{12gf} 1^{14hy} 17^{12hy} **1-2-9 £20,430**

Taranis *Unknown* 45 a40

2 b g Lomitas - Woodbeck
7^{6sd} 13^{6g} 14^{6g} **0-0-3**

Taras Leader *J J Quinn* 47
2 b f Bertolini (USA) - Early Call
4^{5gs} 12^{6g} 9^{6g} **0-0-3**

Taras Tornado *J J Quinn* 54 a41
2 b f Distant Music (USA) - Yellow Ribbon (Ire)
5^{5s} 8^{5gs} 6^{5sd} 8^{6gf} 9^{6s} 2^{6hy} 8^{7sd} **0-1-7 £1,299**

Tarfah (USA) *G A Butler* 109
4 b f Kingmambo (USA) - Fickle
1^{8gs} 1^{9gf} 5^{8gf} **2-0-3 £48,490**

Targer Place *T T Clement* a62
2 ch g Compton Place - Floral Spark
4^{5sd} **0-0-1**

Targgis *M A Jarvis* 61 a48
3 b f Mtoto - Fair Shirley (Ire)
6^{12gf} 8^{10g} 8^{12sd} **0-0-3**

Tarkeez (USA) *N P Littmoden* 44 a8
4 b g Lear Fan (USA) - Mt Morna (USA)
7^{8gf} 20^{10gf} 11^{8sd} 14^{10gs} **0-0-4**

Tarraman (USA) *M Johnston* 97
3 b c Fusaichi Pegasus (USA) - Gerri N Jo Go (USA)
1^{8g} 5^{8gf} 13^{8gf} 2^{10g} **1-1-4 £16,655**

Tartan Special *K R Burke* 62 a63
3 b g Fasliyev (USA) - Colchica
4^{6sd} 3^{6g} 14^{6gf} 5^{7s} 10^{6gf} 9^{6sd} 9^{8gf} 7^{9f} 5^{6gf} **0-1-9 £802**

Tartatartufata *D Shaw* 81 a79
3 b f Tagula (Ire) - It's So Easy
3^{5sd} 3^{5sd} 1^{5sd} 2^{5s} 2^{5gs} 1^{5s} 1^{5sd} 1^{5gs} 6^{5gf} 8^{5gs} 5^{5g} 6^{5sd} **4-4-12 £21,736**

Tartiruga (Ire) *B G Powell* 50 a41
4 b g Turtle Island (Ire) - Palio Flyer
8^{9sd} 4^{10s} **0-0-2**

Tartouche *Lady Herries* 106
4 b f Pursuit Of Love - Megan's Flight
1^{12gf} 2^{12g} 3^{11g} 1^{14s} 4^{12g} **2-2-5 £55,447**

Tasalla *M A Jarvis*
2 b c Polish Precedent (USA) - Bahirah
11^{6s} **0-0-1**

Tasdeed *Saeed Bin Suroor* 100
3 ch c Cadeaux Genereux - Miss Universe (Ire)
2^{7gs} 7^{10s} **0-1-2 £3,147**

Tashkandi (Ire) *P Bowen* 102
5 gr h Polish Precedent (USA) - Tashiriya (Ire)
7^{9gf} 6^{8gf} **0-0-2**

Tashyra (Ire) *A M Balding* a36
3 b f Tagula (Ire) - Shiyra
6^{5sd} **0-0-1**

Tasjeel (USA) *Saeed Bin Suroor* 59
2 b f Aljabr (USA) - Siyadah (USA)
7^{8gf} 5^{8g} **0-0-2**

Task Complete *J A Osborne* 49
2 ch f Bahamian Bounty - Taskone
11^{6gf} 7^{6gf} 9^{5gs} **0-0-3**

Tasneef (USA) *T D McCarthy* 24 a42
6 b g Gulch (USA) - Min Alhawa (USA)
10^{10sd} 13^{10g} 13^{10sd} 15^{12sd} **0-0-4**

Tass Heel (Ire) *B J Llewellyn* a56
6 b g Danehill (USA) - Mamouna (USA)
8^{16sd} **0-0-1**

Tata Naka *Mrs C A Dunnett* 67 a54
5 ch m Nashwan (USA) - Overcast (Ire)
6^{10gs} 9^{10s} 13^{12sd} 7^{10g} 11^{10gf} 11^{10gf} 10^{10gf} 8^{10g} 10^{12sd} 12^{12sd} **0-0-10**

Tatstheticket *J Balding* 29 a29
2 b c Diktat - Dekelsmary
15^{6gs} 11^{5g} 13^{7sd} 11^{6sd} 5^{5sd} **0-0-5**

Tatweer (Ire) *D Shaw* 55 a45
5 b g Among Men (USA) - Sandystones
5^{10sd} 8^{10sd} 9^{9sd} 14^{7s} 6^{6sd} 8^{8gf} 3^{8g} 8^{8gf} 18^{9gf} **0-1-9 £580**

Tau Ceti *R M Beckett* 113
6 b h Hernando (Fr) - Napoli
1^{10s} **1-0-1 £16,240**

Tavalu (USA) *Saeed Bin Suroor* 68
3 b g Kingmambo (USA) - Larrocha (Ire)
3^{10gf} 9^{12gf} 4^{14gf} **0-1-3 £837**

Tawaaf *P W Chapple-Hyam* a67
2 b c Medicean - Yasalam (Ire)
6^{6sd} 1^{6sd} **1-0-2 £2,880**

Tawaafud *B W Hills* 78
2 b f Nashwan (USA) - Intimaa (Ire)
2^{7gs} 3^{8g} **0-2-2 £2,126**

Tawaassol (USA) *Sir Michael Stoute* 70
2 b c War Chant (USA) - Montecito (USA)
3^{6s} **0-1-1 £888**

Tawqeet (USA) *J L Dunlop* 113
3 ch c Kingmambo (USA) - Caerless (Ire)
4^{10gf} 1^{12gf} 5^{12gs} 3^{12s} 1^{14gf} 3^{15hy} 3^{14g} **2-1-7 £83,807**

Tax Free (Ire) *D Nicholls* 107
3 b g Tagula (Ire) - Grandel
1^{7gs} 3^{8gf} 1^{7gf} 1^{6g} 1^{6g} **4-1-5 £108,170**

Taxman (Ire) *C E Brittain* 68 a69
3 ch g Singspiel (Ire) - Love Of Silver (USA)
9^{10sd} 3^{14gf} 7^{14g} 5^{14gf} 3^{14gs} 3^{14g} 6^{14gf} 6^{16gf} 2^{14gf} 1^{16gf} 2^{12sd} 3^{12sd} **1-5-12 £7,769**

Tay Bridge (Ire) *M L W Bell* 48
2 ch g Tagula (Ire) - Wild Liffey (USA)
11^{8gs} UR^{7g} 9^{8g} 7^{7gf} **0-0-4**

Tayash *A W Carroll*
5 b g Fleetwood (Ire) - Wassl's Sister
10^{17sd} 13^{14sd} **0-0-2**

Tayif *P A Blockley* a62
9 gr g Taufan (USA) - Rich Lass
4^{6sd} 6^{6sd} 11^{6sd} 3^{6sd} 5^{6sd} **0-1-5 £428**

Taylor Maid *R M H Cowell* 50 a44
3 b f First Trump - Island Maid
11^{7sd} 5^{8sd} 10^{6gf} 10^{5gf} 2^{6gf} 4^{6gf} 5^{6sd} 5^{6f} 13^{5g} 7^{6sd} 10^{7sd} 2^{9sd} 11^{7sd} 7^{9sd} **0-3-14 £1,536**

Tayman (Ire) *G Wragg* 58
3 b/br g Sinndar (Ire) - Sweet Emotion (Ire)
4^{8gs} 9^{10g} **0-0-2 £288**

Tayside Mover *I Semple* 18
3 b g Namaqualand (USA) - Pretty Average
8^{9gf} 6^{11gs} 14^{9g} 9^{8s} **0-0-4**

Tbm Can *W M Brisbourne* 54 a59
6 b g Rock City - Fire Sprite
5^{12sd} 9^{14sd} 7^{12g} 4^{12gf} **0-0-4**

Tcherina (Ire) *T D Easterby* 84
3 b f Danehill Dancer (Ire) - Forget Paris (Ire)
3^{8hy} 4^{10g} 2^{12gs} 10^{12g} 4^{12g} 5^{14gf} 14^{12gs} 1^{12g} 3^{12s} **1-2-9 £13,675**

Te Quiero *Miss Gay Kelleway* a101
7 gr g Bering - Ma Lumiere (Fr)
3^{8sd} 1^{7sd} 7^{9sd} 10^{7sd} 9^{10sd} 5^{7sd} 11^{9sd} 11^{8sd} 9^{9sd} 12^{10sd} **1-1-10 £16,042**

Teach To Preach (USA) *B W Hills* 63
2 ch c Pulpit (USA) - Chateaubaby (USA)
10^{7gs} **0-0-1**

Team-Mate (Ire) *Miss J Feilden* a56
7 b g Nashwan (USA) - Ustka
12^{14gs} 15^{12sd} 11^{12sd} 9^{12sd} **0-0-4**

Tears Of A Clown (Ire) *J A Osborne* a64
2 b c Galileo (Ire) - Mood Swings (Ire)
4^{7sd} **0-0-1 £350**

Teatro (Ire) *M A Jarvis* 45
2 gr c Daylami (Ire) - Star Of The Course (USA)
10^{8gs} **0-0-1**

Tecktal (Fr) *L M Cumani* 61
2 ch f Pivotal - Wenge (USA)
9^{6gs} 7^{6gf} 7^{7g} **0-0-3**

Teddy Monty (Ire) *M Quinn* 55 a51
2 b g Bold Fact (USA) - Mount Soufriere (Ire)
11^{5gf} 8^{5gf} 6^{6gf} 7^{6g} 6^{5f} 5^{6gf} 16^{6gs} 7^{6sd} 6^{7sd} 6^{6sd} **0-0-10**

Tedsdale Mac *N Bycroft* 67
6 ch g Presidium - Stilvella
7^{6s} 1^{6gf} 13^{8g} 13^{7gf} 4^{8gf} 4^{7gf} 5^{8g} 4^{7gs} 4^{6s} 6^{5gf} 11^{8gf} 9^{7g} 14^{8gf} 16^{10s} **1-1-14 £5,636**

Tedstale (USA) *K A Ryan* 90 a84
7 ch g Irish River (Fr) - Carefree Kate (USA)
2^{9sd} 8^{8sd} 9^{9sd} 5^{8sd} 8^{8gf} 7^{10gf} 4^{10s} 1^{12gf} 1^{12g} 10^{12gf} 2^{12gs} 11^{12g} 9^{10gf} 14^{12gs} 1^{14sf} 6^{12sd} 2^{16sd} **3-3-17 £20,894**

Tee El Cee *J D Bethell* 27
3 b f Lujain (USA) - Dona Filipa
8^{6gf} 11^{6f} 12^{7gf} **0-0-3**

Tee Jay Kassidy *Julian Poulton* 60 a62
5 b g Petong - Priceless Fantasy
10^{7sd} 7^{10sd} 5^{8sd} 6^{8f} 16^{10gf} 7^{8gf} **0-0-6**

Teeba (USA) *J L Dunlop* 96
3 ch f Seeking The Gold (USA) - Shadayid (USA)
1^{8gf} 2^{8gf} 3^{8s} **1-1-3 £15,393**

Teenage Rampage *W M Brisbourne* 33
3 b g Prince Sabo - Sorridar
14^{6g} 10^{7gf} 10^{5g} 6^{5gf} 7^{6gf} **0-0-5**

Tees Components *K G Reveley* 93
10 b g Risk Me (Fr) - Lady Warninglid
15^{19gs} 16^{16g} 8^{14gs} 3^{20s} **0-1-4 £1,328**

Teide Lady *Rae Guest* 67
2 ch f Nashwan (USA) - Oshiponga
6^{7s} 2^{8gs} 6^{8g} **0-1-3 £966**

Telegonus *G Wragg* 44
2 b c Fantastic Light (USA) - Circe's Isle
11^{6s} 12^{7s} **0-0-2**

Telegram Sam (Ire) *P A Blockley* 25
3 b g Soviet Star (USA) - She's The Tops
13^{10s} 9^{12f} 5^{12gf} 7^{16sd} **0-0-4**

Telepathic (Ire) *A Berry* 60
5 b g Mind Games - Madrina
13^{6sd} 3^{6gs} 9^{6s} 5^{6gs} 1^{6gs} 3^{5gf} 10^{6gf} 12^{6g} 6^{6f} 6^{6gs} 10^{6gs} 15^{5gf} 19^{6g} 8^{7g} 14^{6gf} **1-2-15 £4,021**

Tell *J L Dunlop* 84
2 b c Green Desert (USA) - Cephalonie (USA)
1^{6g} 2^{7gf} **1-1-2 £6,622**

Tell The Trees *M C Pipe* 42
4 br f Tamure (Ire) - Bluebell Copse
8^{16gf} **0-0-1**

Temper Tantrum *J R Best* 61 a66
7 b g Pursuit Of Love - Queenbird
7^{7sd} 7^{10sd} 3^{8sd} 2^{10sd} 1^{8sd} 14^{10gf} 5^{8f} 2^{8f} 6^{10f} 10^{10g} 7^{7g} 3^{8hd} 14^{8gs} 16^{8gf} 5^{8sd} 4^{7sd} 11^{7sd} 9^{10sd} **1-4-18 £5,535**

Temperance (Ire) *S Kirk* 61
2 b f Orpen (USA) - Alberjas (Ire)
12^{7gf} 7^{8g} **0-0-2**

Tempestuous Sea (Ire) *T D Barron* 56
2 ch f Tagula (Ire) - Mrs Siddons (Ire)
4^{5g} 9^{5gs} 5^{5gf} **0-0-3 £330**

Temple Belle Xpres *S R Bowring* 10 a34
3 b f Overbury (Ire) - Kustom Kit Xpres
10^{7sd} 3^{11sd} 15^{8gf} 8^{7gf} **0-1-4 £207**

Temple Place (Ire) *M L W Bell* 98
4 b c Sadler's Wells (USA) - Puzzled Look (USA)
17^{10gs} 10^{10gs} 1^{8gf} 11^{8g} 3^{8gf} 8^{10gf} 10^{10gy} **1-1-7 £13,205**

Templet (USA) *W G Harrison* 62 a81
5 b g Souvenir Copy (USA) - Two Step Trudy (USA)
3^{9sd} 4^{9sd} 4^{7sd} 10^{7gs} 9^{9gs} 7^{8f} 8^{8g} 10^{10g} 6^{9gf} 6^{8gf} 8^{11g} 4^{9hy} UR^{17sd} 10^{9sd} **0-1-14 £2,346**

Tempsford (USA) *Jonjo O'Neill* 106
5 b g Bering - Nadra (Ire)
1^{12gf} 2^{13gs} 30^{18gs} **1-1-3 £12,613**

Tempsford Flyer (Ire) *J W Hills* 75
2 b c Fasliyev (USA) - Castellane (Fr)
8^{7g} 4^{7f} 5^{8g} **0-0-3 £308**

Ten Carat *Mrs A J Perrett* 97
5 ch g Grand Lodge (USA) - Emerald (USA)
4^{16gs} 2^{21s} 3^{18gs} 25^{18gs} **0-1-4 £11,298**

Ten Commandments (Ire) *J A Osborne* 43
2 br f Key Of Luck (USA) - Zoudie
10^{7g} 6^{7gf} 3^{8gf} **0-1-3 £381**

Ten Downing Street (Ire) *J A Osborne* 78
2 br g Mujadil (USA) - Karen Blixen
4^{5gf} 3^{5gf} 2^{6gf} 3^{5gf} 1^{5gs} **1-3-5 £6,211**

Ten For Fun (Fr) *M J Polglase* a26
2 b g Millkom - Verrokia (Fr)
9^{10sd} 13^{9sd} 12^{7sd} **0-0-3**

Ten Shun *M J Polglase* 50 a54
2 ch g Pivotal - Mint Royale (Ire)
9^{7gf} 9^{7gf} 10^{7g} 3^{7sd} 5^{6sf} 8^{6sd} 6^{8sd} 4^{8sd} **0-1-8 £381**

Ten To The Dozen *J A Osborne* 71
2 b g Royal Applause - Almost Amber (USA)
2^{6gs} **0-1-1 £992**

Ten-Cents *C F Wall* 67 a65
3 b f Dansili - Daylight Dreams
8^{7sd} 6^{8sd} 5^{10gf} 6^{9sd} 3^{8g} 10^{8gs} 8^{7gf} 6^{8sd} 5^{10gf} 4^{7gs} 4^{7g} 3^{7gf} 8^{8sd} 4^{10sd} **0-2-14 £1,809**

Tender Falcon *R J Hodges* 95
5 br g Polar Falcon (USA) - Tendresse (Ire)
1^{12gs} 10^{12g} **1-0-2 £12,391**

Tender The Great (Ire) *V Smith* 33 a55
2 br f Indian Lodge (Ire) - Tender Guest (Ire)
18^{7s} 5^{9sd} **0-0-2**

Tender Trap (Ire) *T G Mills* 45 a88
7 b g Sadler's Wells (USA) - Shamiyda (USA)
5^{14s} 7^{16sd} 11^{16gs} BD^{17sd} **0-0-4 £700**

Tennessee Belle (Ire) *C N Allen* 38 a40
3 b f Lahib (USA) - Spirito Libro (USA)
9^{6g} 8^{7g} 11^{6ft} 8^{6sd} 4^{7sd} 4^{8sd} **0-0-6**

Tennis Star (Ire) *R Charlton* 76
2 b g Montjeu (Ire) - Fabled Lifestyle

4^{8g} 3^{8gs} **0-1-2 £1,098**

Tent (Ire) *J A Osborne* 86 a62
2 b c Distant Music (USA) - Cheeky Weeky
4^{6gf} 1^{6f} 11^{6gf} 4^{7sd} 2^{8gf} 3^{8gf} **1-1-6**
£7,082

Teorban (Pol) *D J S Ffrench Davis* 60
6 b g Don Corleone - Tabaka (Pol)
5^{16gf} 8^{16s} 4^{17f} **0-0-3 £293**

Tequila Rose (Ire) *A Bailey* 50 a18
2 b f Danehill Dancer (Ire) - Enthrone (USA)
11^{5gf} 7^{5gs} 9^{5g} 5^{5gf} 9^{5gs} 6^{6gs} 11^{6sd} **0-0-7**

Tequila Sheila (Ire) *K R Burke* 66 a77
3 ch f Raise A Grand (Ire) - Hever Rosina
4^{7g} 11^{8gs} 9^{7g} 2^{6sd} 7^{6gf} 4^{6sd} 13^{7sd} 3^{7sd} 6^{7sd}
9^{7sd} 7^{6ss} 6^{7sd} 6^{9sd} 7^{9sd} **0-2-14 £3,131**

Terentia *E S McMahon* 68
2 br f Diktat - Agrippina
6^{6gs} 1^{5g} **1-0-2 £4,472**

Terenzium (Ire) *L M Cumani* 63 a61
3 br c Cape Cross (Ire) - Tatanka (Ity)
10^{10sd} 8^{10g} 8^{10gs} 17^{8g} 7^{8g} 14^{8g} 4^{8sd} 8^{8f} 10^{6gf}
0-0-9 £268

Terlan (Ger) *P Monteith* 56
7 b g Medicus (Ger) - Taxodium (Ger)
11^{12s} 14^{12gs} **0-0-2**

Terminate (Ger) *N P Littmoden* 79 a75
3 ch g Acatenango (Ger) - Taghareed (USA)
1^{10sd} 1^{10sd} 2^{10sd} 11^{12gs} 7^{12gf} 2^{10gf} 12^{12gf} 2^{10g}
3^{10g} 11^{11gs} **2-4-10 £13,130**

Terraquin (Ire) *J J Bridger* 53 a40
5 b g Turtle Island (Ire) - Play The Queen (Ire)
10^{8sd} 11^{6gs} 6^{8gs} 12^{7gf} 2^{10gs} 11^{8sd} **0-1-6**
£842

Tesary *E A L Dunlop* 97
3 b f Danehill (USA) - Baldemara (Fr)
1^{6hy} 6^{6s} 2^{6gf} 2^{7gf} 1^{7f} 6^{7gs} 6^{6g} **2-2-7**
£24,776

Tesoro *P A Blockley* a22
2 b g Compton Place - Zenita (Ire)
7^{7sd} 11^{7sd} **0-0-2**

Tetcott (Ire) *A G Newcombe* 48 a58
4 ch f Definite Article - Charlene Lacy (Ire)
7^{8sd} 14^{11gs} 9^{9sd} 4^{8gf} 1^{9sd} 7^{9sd} F^{8g} **1-0-7**
£2,664

Tetra Sing (Ire) *P C Haslam* 41
3 b f Sinndar (Ire) - Tetralogy (USA)
3^{12s} 15^{14gf} 8^{12gf} **0-0-3 £516**

Tetragon (Ire) *A Bailey* 70
5 b g Octagonal (NZ) - Viva Verdi (Ire)
4^{8g} 10^{10s} 3^{9s} 1^{11g} 13^{11g} 12^{9sd} **1-0-6**
£4,536

Teutonic (Ire) *R F Fisher* 29 a43
4 b f Revoque (Ire) - Classic Ring (Ire)
13^{10sd} 8^{14sd} 10^{14sd} 8^{9sd} 6^{14g} 6^{9gf} 11^{10sd}
0-0-7

Tewitfield Lass *A Berry* a27
3 b f Bluegrass Prince (Ire) - Madam Marash (Ire)
7^{9sd} **0-0-1**

Texas Gold *W R Muir* 110 a104
7 ch g Cadeaux Genereux - Star Tulip
9^{5gs} 8^{5gf} 6^{5gs} 13^{6g} 6^{5g} 16^{5gf} 3^{6g} 2^{5g} 2^{5sd}
1^{5gf} 1^{5g} 2^{5gf} 7^{5gf} 8^{6g} 11^{5gs} **2-4-15**
£55,944

Teyaar *M Wellings* a51
9 b g Polar Falcon (USA) - Music In My Life (Ire)
5^{5sd} 10^{6sd} 6^{5sd} 1^{6sd} 6^{5sd} 12^{5sd} **1-0-6**
£1,645

Thaayer *I A Wood* a42
10 b g Wolfhound (USA) - Hamaya (USA)
7^{6sd} 5^{6sd} **0-0-2**

Thakafaat (Ire) *J L Dunlop* 107
3 b f Unfuwain (USA) - Frappe (Ire)
1^{10g} 2^{10gf} 1^{12gf} 7^{12gf} 10^{15gf} **2-1-5**
£99,220

Thalberg *M A Jarvis* 37
2 gr c Highest Honor (Fr) - Stage Manner
14^{7gf} **0-0-1**

Tharua (Ire) *E R Oertel* 55 a59
3 b f Indian Danehill (Ire) - Peig Sayers (Ire)
5^{9sd} 2^{9sd} 8^{9s} 6^{8f} 3^{8gf} 6^{7gs} 3^{8s} 3^{10gf} 6^{10sd}
3^{12sd} 2^{12sd} 1^{16sd} 4^{14ss} 7^{17sd} 6^{16sd} 1^{12sd}
2-5-16 £6,553

That Look *D E Cantillon* a54
2 b g Compton Admiral - Mudflap
6^{9sd} 9^{8sd} 6^{7sd} **0-0-3**

That's Blue Chip *P W D'Arcy* 46 a53
2 b g Namid - Star Cast (Ire)
10^{5gf} 5^{5sd} **0-0-2**

The Abbess *H Candy* 90
3 gr f Bishop Of Cashel - Nisha
5^{7gf} 20^{7g} **0-0-2 £536**

The Bard Song (Ire) *E J O'Neill* 59
2 b c Shinko Forest (Ire) - Minstrelina (USA)
4^{7g} 9^{7gf} 8^{7gf} 15^{8g} **0-0-4 £242**

The Baroness (Ire) *E R Oertel* 11 a51
5 b m Blues Traveller (Ire) - Wicken Wonder (Ire)
8^{5sd} 12^{6sd} 4^{5sd} 7^{5sd} 9^{6sd} 5^{5sd} 4^{5sd} 13^{5f} 4^{5sd}
9^{6sd} 7^{6sd} **0-0-11**

The Bear *I Semple* 93
2 ch g Rambling Bear - Precious Girl
1^{5s} 4^{5s} 4^{5f} 9^{6gs} 1^{6g} **2-0-5 £14,834**

The Beduth Navi *D G Bridgwater* 7 a49
5 b g Forzando - Sweets (Ire)
5^{17sd} 3^{17sd} 4^{14sd} 2^{17sd} 4^{17sd} 2^{13sd} 11^{14gf}
0-3-7 £1,099

The Best Yet *A G Newcombe* a57
7 ch h King's Signet (USA) - Miss Klew
9^{7sd} 11^{6sd} PU^{8sf} **0-0-3**

The Bonus King *J Jay* 73
5 b g Royal Applause - Selvi
2^{8g} 7^{8s} 8^{7gf} 5^{6gf} 11^{7g} 3^{8gf} 8^{8gf} 1^{7gf} 3^{8f}
6^{8gf} 9^{7g} **1-2-11 £5,973**

The Border Cub *Niall Moran* a2
3 b f Lujain (USA) - Full Stop (Ire)
13^{6sd} 11^{6sd} 4^{6sd} **0-0-3 £313**

The Buck (Ire) *M G Quinlan* 61
2 ch c Quws - Erin Anam Cara (Ire)
9^{6gf} 3^{7gf} 7^{7g} 2^{7gf} 10^{8f} **0-2-5 £1,766**

The Cat's Whiskers (NZ) *P W Chapple-Hyam* 79
5 b m Tale Of The Cat (USA) - Good Faith (NZ)
10^{6gf} 16^{6g} 11^{7g} **0-0-3**

The Cayterers *J M Bradley* 54
3 b g Cayman Kai (Ire) - Silky Smooth (Ire)
9^{6g} 4^{8g} **0-0-2 £296**

The Chequered Lady *T D McCarthy* 62 a68
3 b f Benny The Dip (USA) - Hymne D'Amour (USA)
2^{12sd} 7^{10sd} 5^{11g} 7^{12sd} 6^{12g} **0-1-5 £2,510**

The City Kid (Ire) *P D Evans* 75 a75
2 b f Danetime (Ire) - Unfortunate
5^{5g} 11^{6gf} 7^{5gf} 3^{6g} 6^{6gf} 9^{6gs} 2^{6hy} 1^{6sd} 1^{6sd}

6^{8sd} **2-2-10 £8,445**

The Classic Fox *K W Hogg* 29
2 b g Foxhound (USA) - Classic Storm
7^{5gs} 10^{5gf} 9^{7gf} 12^{6gf} 10^{6gf} 8^{8gf} 9^{8gf}
0-0-7

The Clown *W R Muir* 38 a50
4 b g Russian Revival (USA) - Fashion Bride (Ire)
10^{9sd} 9^{10sd} 4^{12sd} 8^{10gs} 11^{8gf} 5^{10sd} **0-0-6**
£259

The Cobbler *V Smith* a42
6 b g Glory Of Dancer - Lady Eccentric (Ire)
7^{7sd} 9^{7sd} 11^{10sd} **0-0-3**

The Coires (Ire) *R Hannon* 91
3 b g Green Desert (USA) - Purple Heather (USA)
11^{8g} 6^{9gf} 2^{10f} 1^{8gf} 2^{9g} 2^{10gf} **1-3-6**
£16,495

The Composer *M Blanshard* 83
3 b g Royal Applause - Superspring
6^{8gs} 5^{8gs} 8^{9gf} 14^{10gf} 13^{9g} 5^{12g} 7^{11gs}
0-0-7 £314

The Connor Fella *F P Murtagh* 49
4 b g Kris - Flower Fairy (Fr)
5^{9gs} 6^{14gf} 6^{8gf} 15^{10g} **0-0-4**

The Cooie (Ire) *J D Bethell* 40
3 b g Sadler's Wells (USA) - Propensity
8^{10g} 12^{12gf} 5^{10gf} 13^{14g} **0-0-4**

The Count (Fr) *F P Murtagh*
6 b g Sillery (USA) - Dear Countess (Fr)
14^{8gf} **0-0-1**

The Crooked Ring *P D Evans* 94
3 b g Magic Ring (Ire) - My Bonus
2^{5s} 4^{6s} 9^{6s} 16^{6gf} 7^{6gf} 17^{6gf} 4^{6g} 5^{6gf} 6^{7gf}
12^{7g} 9^{6gf} 16^{7g} **0-1-12 £5,188**

The Cross Fox *P D Evans* a4
3 gr g Wizard King - Megs Pearl
10^{9sd} **0-0-1**

The Crunch (Ire) *Daniel Mark Loughnane* 35 a28
4 b f College Chapel - Lady Tristram
7^{6s} 11^{6s} 16^{5sh} 10^{5s} 8^{7s} 10^{7g} 8^{6sd} **0-0-7**

The Dunion *Miss L A Perratt* 21
2 br c Beckett (Ire) - Dacian (USA)
18^{6g} 6^{7g} 8^{6gs} **0-0-3**

The Fairy Flag (Ire) *A Bailey* a14
7 ch m Inchinor - Good Reference (Ire)
9^{12sd} **0-0-1**

The Fisio *S Gollings* 74 a69
5 b g Efisio - Misellina (Fr)
6^{5gf} 8^{5gf} 7^{5gs} 1^{5g} 7^{5g} 8^{5sd} 5^{5sf} 3^{5sd}
1-1-8 £6,106

The Flying Peach *W M Brisbourne* 38 a37
2 ch f Observatory (USA) - Taffeta (Ire)
10^{6s} 7^{6gf} 7^{7sd} 12^{7gf} 11^{8gs} 10^{8gf} **0-0-6**

The Footballresult *C N Kellett* a16
4 b f The West (USA) - Bunny Gee
12^{9sd} **0-0-1**

The Fun Merchant *J Pearce* 76 a66
4 b g Mind Games - Sinking
5^{8sd} 6^{8g} 1^{8gs} 16^{8gf} 7^{8g} 9^{7gf} 8^{9sd} 1^{8gf} 12^{8gf}
2-0-9 £7,868

The Gaikwar (Ire) *R A Harris* 81 a73
6 b g Indian Ridge - Broadmara (Ire)
5^{9sd} 1^{9sd} 6^{9sd} 7^{8gs} 5^{8gs} 3^{7gf} 1^{8g} 6^{12gf} 2^{7gf}
4^{8f} 2^{8g} 2^{8gf} 2^{9gf} 4^{8gs} 4^{8gs} 2^{8gf} 2^{8f} 2^{8g} 2^{8g}
4^{8gf} 1^{9gf} 4^{8g} 7^{9sd} 2^{8gs} 9^{9sd} **3-11-25**
£23,838

The Gambler *Ian Emmerson* 37 a44
5 ch g First Trump - Future Options
4^{6sd} 12^{7sd} 7^{7sd} 3^{6sd} 6^{5sd} 15^{6s} 12^{9g} 14^{6gf}
19^{7gf} **0-1-9 £210**

The Geezer *D R C Elsworth* 119
3 ch c Halling (USA) - Polygueza (Fr)
1^{11g} 1^{10gs} 2^{10s} 8^{12g} 3^{12gf} 1^{12gf} 1^{12gs} 2^{12g} 2^{15hy}
4^{15s} **4-3-10 £239,191**

The Great Delaney *Miss D A McHale* 39
2 b c Inchinor - Top
13^{7gf} 12^{6gs} 10^{7sd} **0-0-3**

The Grey One (Ire) *J M Bradley* 58
2 gr c Dansili - Marie Dora (Fr)
6^{6g} 5^{6g} 6^{7g} 15^{6g} **0-0-4**

The History Man (Ire) *M W Easterby* 76
2 b g Titus Livius (Fr) - Handsome Anna (Ire)
2^{5g} 2^{5gf} 3^{5gs} 3^{6f} 1^{5gf} 12^{6gs} 10^{6g} 9^{6s} 1^{6hy}
2-4-9 £15,581

The Jabr (Ire) *A M Balding* 48
2 gr c Aljabr (USA) - Vital Laser (USA)
8^{6gf} **0-0-1**

The Jailer *J G M O'Shea* 41
2 b f Mujahid (USA) - Once Removed
7^{6gf} 6^{7g} 8^{7gf} 14^{7gf} **0-0-4**

The Job *A D Smith* 55 a54
4 ch g Dancing Spree (USA) - Bay Bianca (Ire)
7^{9sd} 5^{9sd} 5^{8sd} 3^{8sd} 9^{8g} 5^{7sd} 3^{7gf} 12^{8f} 4^{8f}
2^{7ss} 1^{7sd} 7^{7ss} **1-3-12 £2,868**

The Jobber (Ire) *M Blanshard* 90 a89
4 b g Foxhound (USA) - Clairification (Ire)
1^{5g} 14^{5s} 1^{5gs} 3^{5gs} 8^{5gs} 17^{5gs} 4^{5gf} 4^{6sd} 9^{5sd}
2-0-9 £18,900

The Keep *R E Barr* 47 a51
3 ch f Shinko Forest (Ire) - Poyle Amber
7^{6sd} 2^{5sd} 5^{5f} 4^{6g} 16^{5gf} 12^{7g} 8^{5gf} 16^{5gf} 10^{7sd}
8^{7sd} **0-1-10 £1,013**

The Kiddykid (Ire) *P D Evans* 114
5 b g Danetime (Ire) - Mezzanine
2^{6g} 3^{6gf} 1^{6s} 6^{6gy} 13^{6f} 14^{6g} 5^{7gf} 7^{7g} 10^{6gs}
1-2-9 £67,780

The King Of Rock *A G Newcombe* a35
4 b g Nicolotte - Lv Girl (Ire)
7^{10sd} **0-0-1**

The Lady Caster *D Morris* 58
2 ch f City On A Hill (USA) - Cinnamon Lady
6^{5gf} 5^{5gf} 12^{6gs} 6^{5f} 3^{5s} 22^{7gf} 12^{5gs} 15^{5gf}
0-0-8 £734

The Lady Mandarin *G Wragg*
2 b f Groom Dancer (USA) - Lonely Shore
11^{6sd} **0-0-1**

The Last Cast *H Morrison* 17
6 ch g Prince Of Birds (USA) - Atan's Gem (USA)
16^{16g} 34^{18gs} **0-0-2**

The Last Drop (Ire) *B W Hills* 75
2 b c Galileo (Ire) - Epping
5^{7gf} **0-0-1**

The Last Sabo *P W D'Arcy*
3 b g Prince Sabo - Classic Fan (USA)
12^{8sd} 12^{9sd} **0-0-2**

The Last Turn *A Berry* 16
3 b f Danzig Connection (USA) - Its My Turn
9^{9gf} 5^{5gs} 7^{8gs} 13^{7gf} **0-0-4 £382**

The Leather Wedge (Ire) *R Johnson* 77 a74
6 b g Hamas (Ire) - Wallflower
UR^{5sd} 2^{5sd} 3^{5sd} 1^{5sd} 5^{5s} 15^{5hy} 1^{5g} 1^{5f} 9^{5gf}

2^{5gs} 10^{5gf} 3^{5gf} 3^{5g} 7^{5gf} 11^{5g} 2^{5g} 10^{5gf} 7^{5g}
2^{5sd} **3-6-19 £17,509**

The London Gang *P D Evans* 72 a62
2 b c Mind Games - Nom Francais
2^{5gs} 6^{5g} 2^{5sd} 4^{6gf} 5^{6gf} 1^{6g} 7^{7gf} 4^{6g} 6^{6gf} 4^{6gs}
5^{6g} 14^{6g} 5^{5hy} **1-2-13 £9,584**

The Loose Screw (Ire) *G M Moore* 46
7 b g Bigstone (Ire) - Princess Of Dance (Ire)
11^{7g} 8^{7g} 5^{8s} 7^{9g} 9^{8g} 5^{10g} 8^{8gf} 13^{8gf}
0-0-8

The Lord *W G M Turner* 97 a89
5 b g Averti (Ire) - Lady Longmead
5^{5sd} 5^{6sd} 7^{6sd} 8^{5sd} 1^{5gs} 1^{5gs} 3^{5g} 5^{5gs} 2^{5gs}
13^{5g} 7^{5gf} 16^{5hy} 8^{6s} 10^{5sf} 5^{5sd} 3^{5sd} 9^{6sd}
2-3-17 £29,066

The Moon And Back (USA) *M P Tregoning* 27
2 ch f Sky Classic (Can) - Fly To The Moon (USA)
7^{6g} **0-0-1**

The Names Bond *N G Richards* a30
7 b g Tragic Role (USA) - Artistic Licence
10^{12sd} **0-0-1**

The Nawab (Ire) *J L Dunlop* 94
3 ch c Almutawakel - Eschasse (USA)
7^{8gf} 5^{10g} 4^{11gf} 4^{12gf} 1^{15gf} 2^{16gf} 1^{16gf} 1^{20s}
PU^{17s} **3-1-9 £22,671**

The Nibbler *G C H Chung*
4 b g General Monash (USA) - Spoilt Again
12^{6gf} 11^{9sd} **0-0-2**

The Number *Miss D A McHale* 68 a65
4 gr g Silver Wizard (USA) - Elite Number (USA)
5^{9sd} 1^{7sd} 10^{9sd} 8^{7sd} 1^{7g} 13^{8gf} 9^{6s} 18^{7gf} 16^{7f}
15^{7gs} 13^{6sd} 9^{8sd} 12^{7sd} 6^{12sd} 13^{7g} 15^{8gf} 13^{7gf}
2-0-17 £6,400

The Old Soldier *A Dickman* 57
7 b g Magic Ring (Ire) - Grecian Belle
5^{5gf} 1^{7gf} 3^{6gs} 1^{7gf} 5^{6gf} 4^{7g} 6^{7gf} 16^{6gf}
2-1-8 £5,080

The Osteopath (Ire) *M Dods* 71
2 ch c Danehill Dancer (Ire) - Miss Margate (Ire)
3^{5gs} 4^{6gf} 6^{6g} 5^{6g} 5^{7g} **0-1-5 £936**

The Pen *P C Haslam* 54
3 ch f Lake Coniston (Ire) - Come To The Point
8^{10gf} 9^{8gf} 7^{8gf} 10^{9gf} 6^{10gf} **0-0-5**

The Plainsman *P W Hiatt* 49 a58
3 b g Atraf - Mylania
8^{7sd} 2^{8sd} 3^{8sd} 6^{12sd} 5^{10sd} 12^{12gf} 8^{12g} 4^{12g}
6^{10g} 12^{13sd} 10^{11sd} **0-2-11 £1,702**

The Player *A M Balding* 72 a70
6 b g Octagonal (NZ) - Patria (USA)
7^{8g} 5^{8sd} 7^{10gf} 3^{12g} 3^{12gf} 6^{11gs} 10^{12g}
0-1-7 £1,358

The Preacher *J G Given* 42
2 b g Namaqualand (USA) - Bustling Around
8^{8hy} **0-0-1**

The Prince *Ian Williams* 86 a60
11 b g Machiavellian (USA) - Mohican Girl
1^{8gf} 1^{8gf} 7^{10gf} 3^{9sf} **2-1-4 £8,093**

The Rebound Kid *G A Huffer* a47
3 b g Royal Applause - Hayhurst
5^{7sd} **0-0-1**

The Rip *R M Stronge* 62
4 ch g Definite Article - Polgwynne
4^{9f} 5^{10gf} 2^{10g} 6^{9gf} 14^{11g} **0-1-5 £1,323**

The Roan Runner *B P J Baugh*
7 gr g Nalchik (USA) - Grey Runner
8^{12sd} **0-0-1**

The Salwick Flyer (Ire) *A Berry* 53
2 b g Tagula (Ire) - Shimla (Ire)
7^{5gf} 5^{6g} 7^{6gs} 8^{7s} **0-0-4**

The Snatcher (Ire) *R Hannon* 88
2 b c Indian Danehill (Ire) - Saninka (Ire)
2^{5hy} 2^{6gs} 1^{5s} 2^{6gf} 1^{6g} 4^{5gf} 9^{7gf} 15^{6gf} 1^{6g}
5^{6g} 2^{6s} **3-4-11 £27,357**

The Spook *Miss L A Perratt* 38 a32
5 b g Bin Ajwaad (Ire) - Rose Mill
8^{12gs} 9^{9sd} 11^{9gs} **0-0-3**

The Spread *M Blanshard* 57
2 ch f Alhaarth (Ire) - Evie Hone (Ire)
9^{7gs} 10^{7f} **0-0-2**

The Struie *P W Chapple-Hyam* 71 a46
2 b f Observatory (USA) - My Way (Ire)
4^{7g} 8^{7gf} 10^{7sd} **0-0-3 £285**

The Tatling (Ire) *J M Bradley* 118
8 br g Perugino (USA) - Aunty Eileen
7^{5s} 5^{5gf} 7^{5gf} 8^{6f} 3^{5gf} 2^{5s} 2^{5gf} 2^{5g} 1^{5gf} 6^{5gs}
5^{6gs} **1-4-11 £107,506**

The Terminator (Ire) *A Berry* 35 a19
3 b g Night Shift (USA) - Surmise (USA)
6^{10gs} 9^{7gf} 10^{8gf} 11^{8gf} 5^{7gf} 7^{8gf} 12^{9sd}
0-0-7

The Terrier *G A Swinbank* 76
2 b f Foxhound (USA) - Branston Gem
4^{5gs} 3^{5gf} 1^{5gf} 1^{5g} 6^{6s} **2-1-5 £8,017**

The Thrifty Bear *C W Fairhurst* 69
2 ch g Rambling Bear - Prudent Pet
4^{6gf} 1^{6gf} 10^{5g} **1-0-3 £6,822**

The Trader (Ire) *M Blanshard* 117
7 ch g Selkirk (USA) - Snowing
3^{6gy} 1^{5g} 16^{6gs} 7^{7g} 14^{5gf} 3^{5g} 6^{5gf} 8^{5gs}
1-1-8 £59,154

The Varlet *D Burchell* a41
5 b g Groom Dancer (USA) - Valagalore
9^{12sd} **0-0-1**

The Violin Player (USA) *H J Collingridge* 89 a92
4 b g King Of Kings (Ire) - Silk Masque (USA)
5^{10sd} 1^{12sd} 1^{12sd} 2^{12sd} 1^{12sd} 10^{12gs} 3^{10gf} 3^{12gf}
3^{11gf} 6^{10gf} 4^{10gf} 10^{10s} 5^{10gf} 11^{10gf} 4^{12sd} 7^{12sd}
3^{12sd} 5^{12sd} **3-4-18 £25,678**

The Visualiser (USA) *Saeed Bin Suroor* 82
2 gr/ro c Giant's Causeway (USA) - Smokey Mirage (USA)
3^{7gf} 8^{7g} 1^{7g} 5^{8g} 5^{10s} **1-1-5 £7,804**

The Way We Were *T G Mills* 70
4 ch g Vettori (Ire) - Pandrop
11^{7s} 4^{10gf} **0-0-2 £280**

The Whistling Teal *G Wragg* 116
9 b g Rudimentary (USA) - Lonely Shore
4^{12gs} 3^{12gf} 2^{14g} 10^{16s} **0-1-4 £47,851**

The Wild Swan (USA) *A P O'Brien* 95
2 b c Storm Cat (USA) - Luna Wells (Ire)
1^{6g} 3^{6hy} **1-1-2 £11,696**

The Wizard Mul *W Storey* 55
5 br g Wizard King - Longden Pride
3^{9g} 7^{8s} 3^{11g} 4^{12gf} 14^{10s} **0-3-5 £1,110**

Theas Dance *M Johnston* 25
3 b f Danzig (USA) - Teggiano (Ire)
16^{8s} 14^{6s} 8^{7gf} 14^{7f} **0-0-4**

Theatre (USA) *Jamie Poulton* 79 a79
6 b g Theatrical - Fasta (USA)
2^{16sd} 5^{13s} 8^{14gs} 7^{20s} 2^{16gs} 10^{14gf} 6^{16gf} 3^{21s}
2^{16gf} **0-4-9 £10,462**

Theatre Belle *Ms Deborah J Evans* 16 a44
4 b f King's Theatre (Ire) - Cumbrian Rhapsody
12^{9sd} 2^{12sd} 8^{14sd} 10^{12sd} 14^{14g} **0-1-5 £411**

Theatre Lady (Ire) *P D Evans* a46
7 b m King's Theatre (Ire) - Littlepace
4^{12sd} **0-0-1**

Theatre Of Dreams *D Nicholls* 74
3 b g Averti (Ire) - Loch Fyne
9^{5s} 11^{5gf} 6^{5f} 8^{5gs} 7^{5gf} 3^{5gf} 9^{5f} 12^{6gf} 13^{5g} **0-1-9 £1,037**

Theatre Royal *A M Balding* 68
2 b f Royal Applause - Rada's Daughter
3^{6gf} 6^{7g} **0-0-2 £748**

Theatre Time (USA) *Ian Williams* 66
5 b g Theatrical - Kyka (USA)
7^{10g} **0-0-1**

Theatre Tinka (Ire) *R Hollinshead* 55 a60
6 b g King's Theatre (Ire) - Orange Grouse (Ire)
5^{12sd} 10^{12sd} 2^{12sd} 7^{12sd} 5^{12gf} 5^{11gf} 11^{12sd} 5^{12sf} **0-1-8 £734**

Thebestisyettocome *T G Mills* 57 a62
3 b c Montjeu (Ire) - French Quartet (Ire)
8^{10sd} 14^{10g} 10^{8gf} 5^{10gf} 4^{10g} 1^{10sd} 4^{10f} **1-1-7 £2,922**

Theflyingscottie *J D Frost* 35
3 gr g Paris House - Miss Flossa (Fr)
13^{7g} 14^{8hd} **0-0-2**

Thegeordieduchess (Ire) *G A Swinbank* a50
4 b f Revoque (Ire) - Tirhala (Ire)
8^{12sd} **0-0-1**

Themesofgreen *M R Channon* 54 a24
4 ch g Botanic (USA) - Harmonia
12^{8sd} 17^{7g} 16^{8gf} 12^{10g} 1^{8g} 8^{8g} **1-0-6 £1,477**

Theosony *H Morrison* 59 a62
3 b f Singspiel (Ire) - New Fortune (Fr)
11^{8gf} 6^{12sd} **0-0-2**

Thewhirlingdervish (Ire) *T D Easterby* 74
7 ch g Definite Article - Nomadic Dancer (Ire)
6^{14g} 9^{14gf} 6^{17gf} **0-0-3**

They All Laughed *T G Mills* 60
2 ch g Zafonic (USA) - Royal Future (Ire)
11^{7gf} 14^{7g} 8^{7gs} 8^{6g} **0-0-4**

Think Lucky *M Johnston* 62
2 br g Zafonic (USA) - Hyde Hall
7^{6g} 4^{8gf} 3^{8gf} 6^{10g} **0-1-4 £519**

Third Empire *C Grant* 71
4 b g Second Empire (Ire) - Tahnee
1^{9s} 9^{8g} 9^{8s} 11^{10g} **1-0-4 £3,464**

This Is My Song *Mrs A J Perrett* 73 a15
3 b f Polish Precedent (USA) - Narva
3^{10s} 9^{9gs} 3^{10gs} 13^{12sd} SU^{10gf} **0-2-5 £1,037**

Thistle *J Howard Johnson* 77
4 ch c Selkirk (USA) - Ardisia (USA)
5^{7g} 4^{8gf} 4^{11gf} 6^{10gf} **0-0-4 £548**

Thomas A Beckett (Ire) *P R Chamings* 62 a50
2 b g Beckett (Ire) - Kenema (Ire)
3^{6g} 14^{7g} 7^{6f} 13^{7sd} **0-0-4 £631**

Thomas Of Bathwick *B R Millman* 64
2 b c Beckett (Ire) - Bathwick Babe (Ire)
2^{5s} 4^{6gf} 8^{6gf} 5^{7s} **0-1-4 £1,657**

Thornaby Green *T D Barron* 67 a51
4 b g Whittingham (Ire) - Dona Filipa
4^{7g} 4^{6gs} 13^{6gf} 13^{6g} 12^{6gs} 5^{7g} 6^{6f} 7^{7gf} 9^{6gf} 8^{7gf} 7^{8gf} 6^{8gf} 6^{7f} 6^{8gf} 4^{8g} 6^{8gf} 4^{8s} 5^{9hy} 1^{8ss} 6^{8sd} **1-2-20 £2,241**

Thornber Court (Ire) *R Hollinshead* 47 a52
3 b f Desert Sun - Goldfinch
10^{5s} 7^{5gs} 5^{5sd} 6^{5f} 7^{5hd} **0-0-5**

Thornfield Clo (Ire) *Unknown* 36
2 gr f Zafonic (USA) - Flounce
11^{6gf} 13^{6gf} 11^{6gf} **0-0-3**

Thornton Princess *B S Rothwell* 65
2 b f Most Welcome - Princess Emily (Ire)
3^{5g} 8^{5gs} 4^{7g} 2^{6gf} 8^{5g} 16^{6g} 5^{6gs} 10^{6gf} 13^{6s} **0-2-9 £2,238**

Thornton Tara *B S Rothwell* 40
3 b f Kayf Tara - Lindrick Lady (Ire)
8^{7g} 4^{10g} 8^{10gs} 9^{14g} **0-0-4 £263**

Thorntoun Piccolo *J S Goldie* 58 a34
3 ch f Groom Dancer (USA) - Massorah (Fr)
4^{8s} 10^{9sd} 4^{7g} 16^{7gf} 2^{6gs} 7^{7gf} 11^{6g} 10^{6gf} **0-1-8 £1,727**

Thorny Mandate *R F Johnson Houghton* 67 a62
3 b g Diktat - Rosa Canina
10^{10g} 3^{10g} 8^{10gf} 5^{12g} 1^{10sd} 2^{10g} 3^{11g} 6^{10gs} **1-3-8 £5,539**

Thorpeness (Ire) *P D Cundell* a47
6 b g Barathea (Ire) - Brisighella (Ire)
5^{12sd} **0-0-1**

Thoughtsofstardom *W M Brisbourne* 64 a67
2 b g Mind Games - Alustar
10^{5gf} 1^{5gf} 4^{5g} UR^{5gf} 7^{5gs} 9^{5g} 1^{5sd} 4^{6sd} 8^{6sd} 5^{5sd} **2-0-10 £6,390**

Three Boars *S Gollings* 61 a52
3 ch g Most Welcome - Precious Poppy
9^{10gs} 11^{10f} 10^{12g} 5^{12sd} 2^{10g} 1^{10f} 6^{10g} 4^{12gf} **1-1-8 £3,789**

Three Counties (Ire) *N I M Rossiter*
4 b c Danehill (USA) - Royal Show (Ire)
8^{13gs} 8^{14gf} **0-0-2**

Three Feathers *M Salaman* 40 a17
2 b c Averti (Ire) - Jane Grey
9^{5gf} 11^{6gs} 9^{7sd} **0-0-3**

Three Graces (Ger) *Saeed Bin Suroor* 112
5 ch g Peintre Celebre (USA) - Trefoil
6^{8gf} 3^{8gf} 4^{7g} 1^{7gf} 8^{7gf} **1-1-5 £22,723**

Three Pennies *V Smith* a47
3 b f Pennekamp (USA) - Triple Zee (USA)
11^{8sd} 9^{7s} 7^{9sd} 7^{9sd} **0-0-4**

Three Secrets (Ire) *G G Margarson* 69
4 b f Danehill (USA) - Castilian Queen (USA)
9^{9gf} 8^{7g} 9^{8g} **0-0-3**

Three Ships *Miss J Feilden* 45 a59
4 ch g Dr Fong (USA) - River Lullaby (USA)
11^{9sd} 4^{8sd} 5^{8sd} 7^{8gf} 1^{9sd} 13^{10sd} **1-0-6 £1,521**

Three Strikes (Ire) *A G Newcombe* 17 a54
3 b f Selkirk (USA) - Special Oasis
4^{7sd} 11^{6sd} 12^{6sd} 11^{5sd} 18^{7gf} 7^{6f} 13^{7gf} **0-0-7**

Three Strings (USA) *P D Niven* 52
2 b c Stravinsky (USA) - Just Cause
11^{6gf} 6^{7gf} 14^{6g} 7^{8g} 19^{8g} **0-0-5**

Three Thieves (UAE) *M Johnston* 77
2 ch c Jade Robbery (USA) - Melisendra (Fr)
6^{6gf} 2^{10g} 1^{9g} **1-1-3 £7,357**

Three Wrens (Ire) *D J Daly* 82 a91

3 b f Second Empire (Ire) - Three Terns (USA)
3^{8g} 1^{8gf} 2^{8g} 1^{8sd} 2^{7sd} 4^{8sd} **2-3-6 £14,266**

Threeball (Ire) *J J Quinn* a31
2 b f Beckett (Ire) - Wicken Wonder (Ire)
7^{5sd} 9^{6sd} **0-0-2**

Threezedzz *P D Evans* 79 a51
7 ch g Emarati (USA) - Exotic Forest
10^{7sd} 11^{6s} 10^{7g} 9^{7g} 3^{8g} **0-1-5 £707**

Through The Rye *E W Tuer* 52
9 ch g Sabrehill (USA) - Baharlilys
5^{16gs} 6^{16g} 2^{16s} **0-1-3 £1,047**

Throw The Dice *K A Ryan* 89
3 b g Lujain (USA) - Euridice (Ire)
6^{6gs} 2^{6gf} 18^{6gf} 20^{8gf} 6^{7gf} 11^{6gf} **0-1-6 £4,240**

Thru The Keyhole *B J Meehan* 53 a56
2 b f Key Of Luck (USA) - Radiancy (Ire)
8^{5gf} 5^{6sd} 7^{6g} 12^{6g} 5^{5sd} **0-0-5**

Thumpers Dream *H R A Cecil* 71
2 b f Cape Cross (Ire) - Perfect Peach
4^{7s} **0-0-1 £332**

Thunder Calling (USA) *P F I Cole* 60
3 b f Thunder Gulch (USA) - Glorious Calling (USA)
6^{10gs} PU^{9sd} **0-0-2**

Thunder Rock (Ire) *Sir Michael Stoute* 91
3 b c King's Best (USA) - Park Express
3^{10gf} 1^{11g} 3^{10g} **1-2-3 £6,467**

Thunderclap *J J Quinn* a38
6 b/br g Royal Applause - Gloriana
10^{8sd} 11^{8sd} **0-0-2**

Thunderwing (Ire) *K R Burke* 91
3 b/br g Indian Danehill (Ire) - Scandisk (Ire)
2^{10gs} 7^{10gs} 7^{9g} 8^{9g} 8^{8g} 7^{8g} 4^{9hy} 2^{7s} **0-2-8 £5,599**

Thurlestone Rock *B J Meehan* 86 a76
5 ch g Sheikh Albadou - Don't Smile
8^{7sd} 11^{6sd} 9^{6sd} 3^{7sd} 4^{6sd} 1^{6gs} 14^{6gs} 14^{6g} 7^{5gf} 6^{6g} 14^{6gs} **1-1-11 £8,090**

Thwaab *F Watson* 28
13 b g Dominion - Velvet Habit
12^{12f} 8^{8gf} **0-0-2**

Thyolo (Ire) *C G Cox* 100
4 ch g Bering - Topline (Ger)
5^{10gf} 6^{10gf} 3^{10gf} 10^{10g} 4^{10gs} 11^{11gf} 13^{9g} 14^{10gf} 6^{10g} **0-1-9 £5,937**

Ti Adora (Ire) *P W D'Arcy* 76 a80
3 b f Montjeu (Ire) - Wavy Up (Ire)
2^{10gf} 1^{11gf} 1^{12gf} 1^{12sd} 6^{12g} 6^{12sf} **3-1-6 £10,677**

Tiamo *M H Tompkins* 81
3 ch c Vettori (Ire) - Speed To Lead (Ire)
13^{12gf} 4^{14gf} 1^{14g} 1^{16g} 3^{15s} 9^{14gf} 7^{16gf} 6^{14s} 8^{14s} **2-0-9 £12,055**

Tiana *J H M Gosden* 97
2 b f Diktat - Hill Welcome
9^{6gf} 1^{6gf} 3^{7gs} **1-1-3 £6,215**

Tiber Tiger (Ire) *N P Littmoden* 81 a45
5 b g Titus Livius (Fr) - Genetta
1^{7g} 4^{8g} 1^{7f} 3^{8gf} 5^{8g} 4^{7f} 7^{8gf} 17^{8g} 7^{7gf} 13^{8s} 10^{7gf} 5^{8g} 10^{7sd} **2-2-13 £8,852**

Tiber Tilly *N P Littmoden* 77 a69
2 b f King Charlemagne (USA) - Clarice Orsini
6^{5gf} 8^{6g} 3^{5gf} 1^{6gs} 6^{6g} 6^{7gf} 11^{7gf} 4^{5g} 11^{6gs} 5^{5sd} 8^{6sd} **1-1-11 £12,068**

Ticero *K A Ryan* 71 a74
4 ch g First Trump - Lucky Flinders
9^{8sd} 1^{10sd} 6^{10sd} 10^{10sd} 3^{9sd} 5^{10g} 3^{12s} 8^{11g} 3^{12gf} 5^{12gf} **1-2-10 £5,284**

Tick The Box (USA) *B J Meehan* 59
2 ch g Mt. Livermore (USA) - Brave New Boundary (USA)
7^{5gs} 9^{5g} 1^{5gs} **1-0-3 £3,435**

Tickers Way *C Drew* 58
4 gr g Cloudings (Ire) - Zany Lady
10^{12gf} 4^{12gf} 6^{14s} **0-0-3 £665**

Ticki Tori (Ire) *Julian Poulton* 76 a62
3 b f Vettori (Ire) - Lamees (USA)
2^{10s} 2^{10g} 4^{8gs} 6^{12sd} **0-2-4 £2,503**

Tictactoe *D J Daly* 40
4 b f Komaite (USA) - White Valley (Ire)
8^{6gs} **0-0-1**

Tides *J A Osborne* a46
4 b f Bahamian Bounty - Petriece
11^{7sd} **0-0-1**

Tidy (Ire) *M D Hammond* 83 a77
5 b g Mujadil (USA) - Neat Shilling (Ire)
4^{7sd} 3^{8s} 3^{7g} 15^{6hy} 10^{7s} 16^{7s} **0-2-6 £1,864**

Tiegs (Ire) *P W Hiatt* 57 a20
3 ch f Desert Prince (Ire) - Helianthus
7^{10g} 3^{14s} 4^{12gs} 8^{12gf} 7^{13g} 9^{12sd} **0-1-6 £908**

Tiffin Brown *P C Haslam* 45 a39
3 br g Erhaab (USA) - Cockatrice
8^{7sd} 11^{9sd} 8^{8sd} 11^{12gf} 5^{12gf} 1^{16g} 11^{16gf} **1-0-7 £3,250**

Tiffin Deano (Ire) *H J Manners* 62 a56
3 b g Mujadil (USA) - Xania
1^{6sd} 10^{6sd} 2^{7s} 3^{5s} 9^{8gf} 10^{6gf} 11^{7s} 6^{10g} 14^{7sd} 8^{7sd} **1-1-10 £4,025**

Tiffin Jo (Ire) *P C Haslam* 25
2 b f Fruits Of Love (USA) - Kick The Habit
17^{6gf} 11^{7gf} 10^{8gf} **0-0-3**

Tiger Bond *B Smart* a13
3 br g Diktat - Blackpool Belle
9^{7sd} **0-0-1**

Tiger Dance (USA) *A P O'Brien* 100
3 b c Storm Cat (USA) - Mariah's Storm (USA)
7^{8gs} 6^{7gs} **0-0-2 £1,350**

Tiger Dawn (Ire) *R A Harris* 42 a41
3 b g Anabaa (USA) - Armorique (Ire)
16^{8gs} 11^{7gf} 9^{6sd} 17^{7gf} 8^{7g} 14^{8f} **0-0-6**

Tiger Frog (USA) *J Mackie* 55
6 b g French Deputy (USA) - Woodyoubelieveit (USA)
7^{12s} 9^{12g} **0-0-2**

Tiger Hunter *P Howling* 45 a57
3 b g Lake Coniston (Ire) - Daynabee
1^{6sd} 4^{7sd} 8^{6sd} 4^{7sd} 9^{6sd} 12^{6gs} 14^{5gf} 9^{7gf} 6^{7f} 12^{6g} 13^{6sd} 11^{6sd} 8^{7sd} 12^{6sd} **1-0-14 £2,940**

Tiger King (Ger) *P Monteith* 64
4 b g Tiger Hill (Ire) - Tennessee Girl (Ger)
11^{10g} 12^{11gs} **0-0-2**

Tiger Tiger (Fr) *Jamie Poulton* 102 a93
4 b c Tiger Hill (Ire) - Adorable Emilie (Fr)
10^{12ft} 10^{10ft} 7^{10gs} 1^{10gs} 3^{10s} 5^{10gs} 4^{12g} 8^{12gs} 4^{12sd} **1-1-9 £18,671**

Tiggers Touch *A W Carroll* 31 a30
3 b f Fraam - Beacon Silver
10^{9sd} 14^{7gf} 11^{8g} 10^{7g} 12^{6ft} 12^{9sf} 12^{7sd}

0-0-7

Tight Squeeze *P W Hiatt* 86 a90
8 br m Petoski - Snowline
10^{9sd} 7^{10sd} 7^{12sd} 4^{12sd} 3^{10sd} 5^{10sd} 1^{12gs} 5^{14g} 10^{12sd} 3^{11g} 3^{12gf} 5^{10gf} 4^{12g} 5^{12g} 7^{10gf} 3^{12gf} 7^{12gf} 3^{12g} 2^{12gs} 2^{14g} 10^{16g} 8^{12gs} 11^{12sd}
1-4-23 £12,510

Tignasse (Fr) *G L Moore* a44
4 b f Double Bed (Fr) - Off Guard (Fr)
9^{10sd} **0-0-1**

Tilen (Ire) *J A Glover* 44
2 ch g Bluebird (USA) - New Sensitive
8^{8gf} 12^{7s} 13^{8hy} **0-0-3**

Tilla *Mrs A J Hamilton-Fairley* 42 a7
5 b m Bin Ajwaad (Ire) - Tosca
9^{12g} SU^{14g} 13^{14sd} **0-0-3**

Tillands (USA) *D R Loder* 42
3 b g Bahri (USA) - Tillandsia (Ire)
10^{8g} **0-0-1**

Tillingborn Dancer (Ire) *M D Hammond* 46
3 b g Imperial Ballet (Ire) - Exhibit Air (Ire)
9^{10g} 14^{8g} 11^{10gf} 12^{8s} 8^{10s} 11^{12g} **0-0-6**

Tillurium (Ire) *M Meade* 46 a36
2 b f Alzao (USA) - Jus'Chillin' (Ire)
10^{5f} 8^{7gf} 10^{5g} 12^{6g} 7^{9sd} **0-0-5**

Tilly Floss *Stef Liddiard*
3 ch f Piccolo - Lv Girl (Ire)
11^{6sd} 10^{10g} **0-0-2**

Tilly's Dream *Julian Poulton* 69 a62
2 ch f Arkadian Hero (USA) - Dunloe (Ire)
9^{7g} 4^{5sd} 5^{6sd} 5^{7sd} 1^{6gf} 6^{6sd} **1-0-6**
£3,371

Tilt *J R Fanshawe* 78 a79
3 b g Daylami (Ire) - Tromond
1^{8s} 5^{10s} 4^{12sd} 3^{14g} 4^{16g} **1-1-5 £5,915**

Tiltili (Ire) *P C Haslam* 38
2 ch f Spectrum (Ire) - Alexander Confranc (Ire)
7^{5g} 6^{7g} **0-0-2**

Timberlake *Miss E C Lavelle* 53 a59
3 b f Bluegrass Prince (Ire) - Ambience Lady
9^{8g} 12^{12gf} 7^{10sd} 14^{12gs} 10^{10gs} **0-0-5**

Time For Life (USA) *H J Collingridge* 85 a80
2 b/br c Woodman (USA) - Marie's Star (USA)
2^{6g} 1^{6sd} 3^{8g} 5^{6sd} 4^{8sd} 3^{8sd} **1-3-6**
£6,595

Time For Mee *J S Wainwright*
3 ch f Timeless Times (USA) - Heemee
12^{6gf} 11^{6g} 15^{8gf} **0-0-3**

Time For You *J M Bradley* 42
3 b f Vettori (Ire) - La Fija (USA)
12^{6s} 7^{6s} 19^{8g} 8^{8f} 9^{8gs} 10^{8gf} 19^{10f} 5^{8hd}
0-0-8

Time Marches On *K G Reveley* 51 a21
7 b g Timeless Times (USA) - Tees Gazette Girl
6^{12sd} 3^{12gf} 6^{12f} 2^{16f} 2^{16gf} **0-3-5 £2,313**

Time N Time Again *Peter Grayson* 64 a88
7 b g Timeless Times (USA) - Primum Tempus
5^{6sd} 6^{5sd} 10^{6sd} 3^{6sd} 6^{6sd} 6^{5hy} 6^{6s} 19^{6g} 8^{6g} 12^{5gf} 7^{5gf} 9^{7sd} 8^{6g} 8^{6sd} 3^{6gf} 7^{6gf} 5^{6gf} 2^{6gf} 7^{6gf} 3^{6g} **0-4-20 £3,184**

Time On *J L Dunlop* 68
2 b f Sadler's Wells (USA) - Time Away (Ire)
18^{7gf} 7^{7gs} 3^{8s} **0-1-3 £708**

Time Out (Ire) *A M Balding* 68
2 b c Alhaarth (Ire) - Waif
3^{8g} 7^{8gs} **0-1-2 £644**

Time To Regret *J S Wainwright* 58
5 b g Presidium - Scoffera
7^{8s} 10^{8gs} 19^{8g} 9^{8gs} 9^{7gf} 4^{8gf} 4^{7gf} 6^{8g} 11^{8gf} 2^{8gf} 4^{8g} 1^{8hy} **1-2-12 £4,397**

Time To Relax (Ire) *J J Quinn* 57 a48
4 b f Orpen (USA) - Lassalia
13^{10g} 5^{8s} 2^{7gs} 1^{9sd} 9^{11gs} **1-1-5 £3,349**

Time To Remember (Ire) *R A Fahey* 35
7 b g Pennekamp (USA) - Bequeath (USA)
11^{7s} 13^{7f} 13^{6gf} **0-0-3**

Times Review (USA) *C A Dwyer* 68 a74
4 b c Crafty Prospector (USA) - Previewed (USA)
8^{7sd} 5^{5sd} 8^{6sd} 8^{6s} 8^{6g} 14^{7g} 4^{7f} 4^{6gf} 8^{6gf} 2^{5g} 8^{6gf} 5^{5g} 2^{5g} 5^{5gf} 15^{5s} 5^{6sd} 5^{5sd}
0-2-17 £4,076

Tin And Lint *G G Margarson* 73
2 ch c Bahamian Bounty - Nopalea
6^{5g} 5^{6gs} 1^{5g} 5^{6g} 2^{5g} 8^{6gf} **1-1-6 £5,383**

Tina's Magic *Mrs G S Rees*
2 ch f Primitive Rising (USA) - Night Transaction
12^{9sd} 12^{9sd} **0-0-2**

Tincture *M L W Bell* 89
3 b f Dr Fong (USA) - Miss D'Ouilly (Fr)
9^{8g} 3^{11gs} 14^{12s} **0-0-3 £5,500**

Tinian *Miss Tracy Waggott* a46
7 b g Mtoto - Housefull
7^{8sd} 4^{8sd} 3^{9sd} 4^{8sd} 5^{9sd} **0-1-5 £211**

Tinker's First *Mrs N Macauley* 3
3 b f First Trump - Tinker Osmaston
12^{6g} 17^{7gf} **0-0-2**

Tinstre (Ire) *P W Hiatt* a20
7 ch g Dolphin Street (Fr) - Satin Poppy
13^{13sd} 14^{12sd} **0-0-2**

Tintac *E J O'Neill* 38 a52
4 b f Intikhab (USA) - Susquehanna Days (USA)
6^{7s} 12^{8g} 10^{9sd} 2^{8sd} 6^{7sd} 10^{7gf} 10^{9sd}
0-1-7 £425

Tintawn Gold (Ire) *S Woodman* 31 a50
5 b m Rudimentary (USA) - Clear Ahead
2^{10sd} 3^{10sd} 9^{10sd} 6^{10sd} 6^{12gf} 4^{13sd} 9^{10g} 11^{10sd} 10^{10sd} **0-2-9 £634**

Tiny Tim (Ire) *A M Balding* 47 a49
7 b g Brief Truce (USA) - Nonnita
2^{6sd} 2^{6sd} 2^{6sd} 4^{7sd} 4^{7sd} 3^{7sd} 3^{7g} 5^{7sd} 8^{7sd} 2^{6s} 6^{6g} 4^{7ss} 10^{6sd} **0-6-13 £2,418**

Tioga Gold (Ire) *L R James* a32
6 b g Goldmark (USA) - Coffee Bean
7^{12sd} 10^{14sd} 8^{12sd} **0-0-3**

Tip Toes (Ire) *Mrs C A Dunnett* 31 a37
3 b f Bianconi (USA) - Tip Tap Toe (USA)
9^{9sd} 7^{11sd} 5^{12sd} 4^{11hy} 13^{12ss} 11^{10sd} **0-0-6**

Tipes *C J Down* 57 a54
3 b c Gleaming (Ire) - Annalena (Ire)
9^{10gs} 11^{13sd} 8^{14g} 10^{12sd} 2^{14sd} 1^{16sd} **1-1-6**
£1,859

Tipo (Ger) *D Flood*
4 ch c Big Shuffle (USA) - Triple Transe (USA)
12^{7g} PU^{7f} **0-0-2**

Tipsy Lad *D J S Ffrench Davis* 49 a61
3 b g Tipsy Creek (USA) - Perfidy (Fr)
9^{8sd} 11^{7sd} 9^{7sd} 7^{8sd} 9^{8sd} 7^{9sd} 11^{10sd} 7^{7sd} 9^{6gf} 19^{8gf} 19^{6gf} 1^{7sd} 6^{8sd} 1^{7sf} 2^{6g} 5^{9sd} 2^{7sd} 2^{7sd} 3^{6sd} **2-4-19 £5,559**

Tipsy Lady *Miss K M George*

4 b f Intikhab (USA) - Creme De Menthe (Ire)
10^{9sd} 12^{7sd} **0-0-2**

Tipsy Lillie *Julian Poulton* 59 a47
3 ch f Tipsy Creek (USA) - Belle De Nuit (Ire)
2^{6s} 12^{6gf} 9^{5gf} 13^{6g} 8^{7g} 10^{7gf} 18^{7gf} 5^{5sd} 6^{6sd} 3^{5sd} 7^{5sd} **0-2-11 £1,288**

Tiptoeing *M H Tompkins* 65 a64
2 b f Tipsy Creek (USA) - Grove Dancer
8^{6g} 5^{6gs} 3^{7sd} 12^{8g} 13^{8sd} **0-1-5 £698**

Tirailleur (Ire) *J R Boyle* 43 a51
5 b m Eagle Eyed (USA) - Tiralle (Ire)
6^{8sd} 8^{8sd} 4^{8sd} 7^{10sd} 12^{6f} 16^{7f} 5^{8f} 4^{8g} 2^{9sd} 4^{7sd} 1^{8ss} 11^{8sd} 3^{8sd} 3^{8ss} **1-2-14 £2,295**

Tirol Livit (Ire) *N Wilson* 25 a52
2 ch g Titus Livius (Fr) - Orange Royale (Ire)
12^{6gf} 11^{7gf} 3^{7ft} **0-1-3 £377**

Titian Saga (Ire) *C N Allen* 79
2 ch f Titus Livius (Fr) - Nordic Living (Ire)
10^{6gf} 1^{6gf} 8^{6gf} **1-0-3 £4,813**

Titian Time (USA) *J H M Gosden* 97
3 b f Red Ransom (USA) - Timely
12^{8gy} 7^{8s} 4^{8gf} 10^{8gf} **0-0-4 £1,400**

Titinius (Ire) *M D Hammond* 79
5 ch g Titus Livius (Fr) - Maiyria (Ire)
14^{8gf} 3^{7f} 14^{6gf} 4^{7gf} 6^{8gf} 17^{7g} **0-1-6 £1,572**

Titus Alone (Ire) *B Smart* 101
2 ch c Titus Livius (Fr) - Swan Sea (USA)
1^{5gf} 1^{5gf} 1^{5f} 8^{5gf} 7^{6g} 9^{5hy} **3-0-6 £30,116**

Titus Lumpus (Ire) *R M Flower* a57
2 b g Titus Livius (Fr) - Carabosse
12^{7sd} 11^{8sd} 7^{7sd} **0-0-3**

Titus Maximus (Ire) *G A Butler* 72 a63
2 ch c Titus Livius (Fr) - Haraabah (USA)
13^{5gs} 1^{5g} 10^{5g} 6^{5sd} **1-0-4 £3,419**

Titus Salt (USA) *M D Hammond* 53 a42
4 ch g Gentlemen (Arg) - Farewell Partner (USA)
6^{8sd} 6^{11sd} 10^{9sd} 12^{8g} 3^{8gf} 2^{8gf} 4^{8gf} 6^{8gf} 5^{10g} 14^{10g} **0-2-10 £1,290**

Titus Wonder (Ire) *P A Blockley* 52 a50
2 ch f Titus Livius (Fr) - Morcote (Ire)
4^{5sd} 8^{5s} 6^{5sd} 4^{6g} 8^{6f} 6^{5gf} **0-0-6**

Tiviski (Ire) *E J Alston* 68 a56
3 b f Desert Style (Ire) - Mummys Best
8^{7g} 9^{8s} 8^{7gs} 3^{6s} 13^{5g} 5^{6gf} 7^{6gf} 7^{5s} 1^{6sd} **1-1-9 £3,610**

Tiyoun (Ire) *Jedd O'Keeffe* 85
7 b g Kahyasi - Taysala (Ire)
4^{16gf} **0-0-1 £1,034**

Tizzy's Law *E F Vaughan* 56 a44
4 b f Case Law - Bo' Babbity
14^{5gf} 10^{6g} 9^{6ss} 9^{7sd} 10^{8sd} **0-0-5**

To Arms *T D Easterby* 63
3 b g Mujahid (USA) - Toffee
5^{10gf} 6^{8gf} 4^{8g} 5^{10g} 9^{11g} **0-0-5 £315**

To Be Fare (Ire) *J Pearce* 28 a39
5 ch g Eagle Eyed (USA) - Petrolea Girl
19^{7gf} 13^{8f} 9^{6sd} 5^{7sd} **0-0-4**

To Sender *J H M Gosden* 93
2 b c King's Best (USA) - Return (USA)
1^{6f} 12^{6gf} **1-0-2 £5,443**

Toberogan (Ire) *W A Murphy* 67
4 b g Docksider (USA) - Beltisaal (Fr)
1^{6s} 7^{6gs} 2^{6y} 5^{6y} 9^{7gf} 2^{6gf} 4^{6g} 8^{6g} 3^{6ys} 15^{6s} **1-4-10 £7,899**

Todman Avenue (USA) *L M Cumani* 92
3 b/br c Lear Fan (USA) - Three Wishes
2^{10hy} 9^{10g} 5^{12gf} 11^{10s} **0-0-4 £4,397**

Toffee Treat *J M P Eustace* 50
2 b f Mujahid (USA) - Toffolux
8^{5gf} 7^{6gf} **0-0-2**

Toffee Vodka (Ire) *J W Hills* 80 a84
3 b f Danehill Dancer (Ire) - Vieux Carre
2^{9sd} 3^{7f} 14^{8gs} 3^{7gf} 3^{7f} 3^{8gs} 1^{8sd} **1-4-7 £9,552**

Tojoneski *I W McInnes* 51 a46
6 b g Emperor Jones (USA) - Sampower Lady
7^{7sd} 6^{8sd} 7^{9sd} 9^{8g} 8^{7g} 7^{8s} 2^{8gf} 4^{10gs} 2^{12f} 1^{13gf} 3^{12gf} 10^{12g} 2^{10f} 4^{12g} 2^{11g} 4^{10sd} 8^{10sd} **1-6-17 £5,626**

Tokewanna *W M Brisbourne* 58 a67
5 b m Danehill (USA) - High Atlas
7^{9sd} 7^{8sd} 1^{9sd} 5^{9sd} 9^{9sd} 3^{8gf} 10^{8gf} 2^{7g} 3^{8f} 4^{8gf} 4^{8gf} 9^{8gf} 7^{7f} 1^{8g} 17^{7g} 6^{8gf} 6^{9sd} 9^{9sd} **2-3-18 £9,417**

Toldo (Ire) *G M Moore* 95
3 gr g Tagula (Ire) - Mystic Belle (Ire)
4^{10g} 3^{12g} 4^{12gs} 1^{12gf} 4^{11gf} 2^{12gf} 4^{12g} 4^{13gs} 1^{15s} 2^{17s} **2-4-10 £24,459**

Tolinis Girl *B Smart* 52
2 b f Bertolini (USA) - Skiddaw Bird
2^{5gf} 6^{6gf} 6^{5gf} 7^{6g} 12^{6gs} 11^{6s} **0-1-6 £472**

Tolpuddle (Ire) *T Stack* 110
5 b g College Chapel - Tabdea (USA)
9^{8s} 4^{10s} 3^{10g} 1^{8sh} 6^{9g} 12^{7sh} **1-1-6 £29,684**

Tom Forest *K A Ryan* 81
3 b g Forest Wildcat (USA) - Silk Masque (USA)
8^{7gf} 1^{7gs} 1^{7g} 3^{7gf} 10^{7gf} 4^{7gf} 12^{6g} 6^{7g} 15^{8g} 3^{7hy} 9^{8s} **2-2-11 £10,869**

Tom From Bounty *W De Best-Turner* a43
5 ch g Opera Ghost - Tempus Fugit
6^{9sd} 9^{7sd} 7^{7sd} 7^{11sd} **0-0-4**

Tom Tun *J Balding* 102
10 b g Bold Arrangement - B Grade
2^{6g} 3^{5s} 1^{6s} 14^{6gs} 6^{6g} 15^{6gs} 14^{6s} 4^{5hy} 6^{6s} **1-2-9 £15,689**

Tomasino *K G Reveley* 80
7 br g Celtic Swing - Bustinetta
4^{13gs} 1^{12s} 8^{11g} 2^{14gs} 1^{12gf} 2^{12gf} 2^{12gf} 3^{12gf} 2^{14gf} 3^{12gf} **2-6-10 £13,534**

Tombalina *C J Teague* 43 a50
2 ch f Tomba - Ashkernazy (Ire)
7^{5gf} 12^{6gf} 2^{5s} 7^{5gf} 5^{5sd} 4^{5g} 2^{5sd} 5^{5sd} 2^{5sd} 11^{5sd} 10^{5sd} 1^{5ss} **1-3-12 £3,226**

Tomina *Miss E C Lavelle* 72 a75
5 b g Deploy - Cavina
8^{16sd} 5^{14g} **0-0-2**

Tommy Smith *P T Midgley* 67 a51
7 ch g Timeless Times (USA) - Superstream
17^{5g} 13^{5gf} 2^{5gf} 12^{5f} 10^{5gf} 5^{5gf} 16^{5gf} 1^{5g} 7^{5gf} 6^{6sd} 17^{5gf} **1-1-11 £5,876**

Tommy Toogood (Ire) *B W Hills* 56
2 b c Danehill (USA) - On The Nile (Ire)
9^{6gf} **0-0-1**

Tommytyler (Ire) *D Carroll* a55
6 b g Goldmark (USA) - John's Ballad (Ire)
2^{7sd} 2^{8sd} 9^{8sd} 3^{8sd} 2^{8sd} 6^{8sd} 5^{8ss} **0-4-7**

£2,312

Tomobel *M H Tompkins* 46
3 b f Josr Algarhoud (Ire) - Eileen's Lady
10^{9gf} **0-0-1**

Tomoohat (USA) *Sir Michael Stoute* 87
3 b f Danzig (USA) - Crystal Downs (USA)
9^{8gs} **0-0-1**

Tomthevic *J M Bradley* 53 a46
7 ch g Emarati (USA) - Madame Bovary
3^{5sd} 5^{5gf} 6^{5f} 4^{6f} 3^{5f} 6^{5f} 13^{5g} 2^{5f} 5^{6f} 6^{5f}
9^{5g} 4^{5g} 11^{5hd} 10^{5f} 11^{5g} 8^{5g} 2^{5sd} **0-5-17**
£1,887

Ton-Chee *F P Murtagh* 29
6 b g Vettori (Ire) - Najariya
6^{17f} 5^{16gf} 5^{14g} **0-0-3**

Toni Alcala *R F Fisher* 70 a67
6 b g Ezzoud (Ire) - Etourdie (USA)
6^{13sd} 3^{16sd} 4^{14sd} 4^{16g} 3^{16gf} 4^{16g} 3^{14g} 5^{16gf}
4^{12gf} 5^{14f} 3^{16f} 3^{14gs} 3^{16gf} 5^{16g} 3^{16gf} 3^{16g} 6^{16g}
10^{14gf} 3^{14g} 2^{17sf} 3^{17sd} **0-9-21 £7,475**

Tonight (Ire) *W M Brisbourne* 50 a21
3 b g Imperial Ballet (Ire) - No Tomorrow (Ire)
13^{10g} 4^{11gf} UR^{11gf} 8^{10g} 10^{12sd} 11^{10s}
0-0-6 £262

Tony James (Ire) *C E Brittain* 110 a52
3 b c Xaar - Sunset Ridge (Fr)
16^{8ft} 13^{9ft} 4^{7gf} 8^{8gf} 11^{8s} 12^{6gs} **0-0-6**
£1,400

Tony The Tap *N A Callaghan* 95 a86
4 b g Most Welcome - Laleston
6^{6gf} 2^{6g} 4^{7f} 5^{6g} 5^{5gf} 2^{5gs} 3^{5gf} 7^{5gs} 2^{6s} 6^{6sd}
0-5-10 £14,373

Tony Tie *J S Goldie* 74 a55
9 b g Ardkinglass - Queen Of The Quorn
9^{8s} 9^{8gf} 12^{9gs} 6^{8g} 3^{10s} 9^{8g} 4^{8gs} 8^{8g} 3^{8gf}
4^{8g} 7^{10gf} 5^{10gf} 16^{9gf} 10^{8g} 3^{10g} 1^{8gf} 8^{10gf}
10^{9sd} **1-3-18 £7,342**

Tootsy *Miss J Feilden* a49
3 b f Dansili - Totom
11^{7sd} 9^{7sd} 5^{7sd} 8^{6sd} 11^{7sd} 10^{7g} **0-0-6**

Top Dirham *M W Easterby* 85
7 ch g Night Shift (USA) - Miller's Melody
4^{8s} 9^{8g} 1^{7gf} 6^{8gf} 11^{7gs} 6^{7gf} 2^{8g} **1-1-7**
£10,688

Top Gear *D R C Elsworth* 87
3 b c Robellino (USA) - Bundle
1^{10gf} **1-0-1 £4,774**

Top Jaro (Fr) *T P Tate* 68
2 b g Marathon (USA) - Shahmy (USA)
1^{8g} 11^{8s} **1-0-2 £4,416**

Top Line Dancer (Ire) *Simon Earle* a4
4 b c Fasliyev (USA) - Twafeaj (USA)
12^{7sd} 15^{8gs} **0-0-2**

Top Man Tee *D J Daly* 79 a76
3 gr c Vettori (Ire) - Etienne Lady (Ire)
7^{8g} 3^{8g} 2^{10g} 1^{10gs} 8^{8sd} **1-2-5 £5,533**

Top Mark *H Morrison* 76 a82
3 b g Mark Of Esteem (Ire) - Red White And Blue
9^{8gf} 6^{8s} 2^{7gf} 2^{7f} 1^{7sd} 9^{7hy} **1-2-6**
£9,626

Top Of The Class (Ire) *P D Evans* 40
8 b m Rudimentary (USA) - School Mum
7^{12gf} 8^{11g} 8^{10f} 14^{10f} 6^{10s} **0-0-5**

Top Place *B A Pearce* a42
4 b f Compton Place - Double Top (Ire)
7^{6sd} 10^{5sd} 6^{6sd} 13^{6sd} 11^{5sd} 3^{10sd} 10^{12sd} 11^{8g}
0-1-8 £207

Top Seed (Ire) *M R Channon* 102 a92
4 b g Cadeaux Genereux - Midnight Heights
6^{12gf} 8^{10gf} 5^{12gf} 6^{13sd} 9^{10gs} 5^{12g} 5^{12gf} 6^{10gf}
6^{10s} 7^{10gf} 12^{12g} 8^{12gf} **0-0-12 £3,275**

Top Son *R Curtis*
6 b g Komaite (USA) - Top Yard
15^{11gf} **0-0-1**

Top Spec (Ire) *J Pearce* 81 a78
4 b g Spectrum (Ire) - Pearl Marine (Ire)
12^{10s} 10^{10gs} 12^{10gf} 2^{10g} 3^{10gf} 6^{10gf} 6^{12gs} 5^{10gf}
3^{10s} 2^{10g} 3^{10gs} 3^{10gf} 5^{10gs} 1^{10gf} 7^{12sd}
1-5-15 £12,524

Top Style (Ire) *G A Harker* 66
7 ch g Topanoora - Kept In Style
1^{13gs} 1^{13gf} 2^{16gf} 8^{14gf} 10^{14g} **2-1-5**
£8,147

Top The Charts *R Hannon* 89
3 b g Singspiel (Ire) - On The Tide
3^{8g} 2^{8g} 5^{10gf} 2^{10gf} 4^{10g} 2^{10g} 8^{12s} 3^{11g} 4^{10gs}
1^{12hd} 1^{12gf} 8^{14s} 2^{12gs} **2-6-13 £17,403**

Top Trees *W S Kittow* 58 a47
7 b g Charnwood Forest (Ire) - Low Line
3^{12g} 4^{15gf} 4^{12f} 4^{14gf} 6^{14g} 13^{16g} 9^{17f} 4^{16g} 5^{17sd}
9^{14sd} 4^{14ss} **0-3-11 £1,906**

Toparudi *M H Tompkins* 78
4 b g Rudimentary (USA) - Topatori (Ire)
11^{10gs} 10^{7g} 4^{10g} 2^{11gs} SU^{11gf} 2^{10hy} 3^{10hy}
0-3-7 £5,220

Topatoo *M H Tompkins* 80
3 ch f Bahamian Bounty - Topatori (Ire)
3^{8g} 2^{7s} 9^{8gf} 7^{7gf} 3^{8g} 1^{8g} 3^{8gf} 8^{8gs} 5^{9gs}
1-4-9 £12,803

Topflight Wildbird *Mrs G S Rees* 27 a43
2 br f Diktat - Jamarj
13^{6g} 10^{6gs} 5^{7sd} **0-0-3**

Topiary Ted *P L Clinton* 73
3 ch g Zafonic (USA) - Lovely Lyca
2^{8gf} 8^{8g} 5^{8g} 10^{8gf} 12^{7gf} 11^{8gf} 6^{8gf} 9^{10g} 8^{8gf}
DSQ^{7gs} 8^{7gf} 3^{6gs} **0-2-12 £1,897**

Topkat (Ire) *M C Pipe* 88
4 b g Simply Great (Fr) - Kitty's Sister
1^{12gf} 7^{14g} 4^{15gf} 2^{12g} 3^{12g} 5^{12gs} **1-2-6**
£16,229

Topple *P W Hiatt* 13
4 b f Master Willie - Top Cover
14^{10g} 12^{12sd} **0-0-2**

Toppling *J M Bradley* 42 a38
7 b g Cadeaux Genereux - Topicality (USA)
7^{5sd} 12^{6sd} 9^{6g} 11^{6gf} 15^{6f} **0-0-5**

Topton (Ire) *P Howling* 70 a62
11 b g Royal Academy (USA) - Circo
7^{8sd} 6^{9sd} 9^{10sd} 7^{8g} 11^{8gs} 4^{8gf} 10^{8g} 3^{8gf} 3^{8gf}
9^{8gf} 9^{8g} 2^{8gf} 3^{8s} 8^{8gf} 7^{8gf} 14^{8gf} 9^{8gf} 10^{9gf}
1^{9sd} 13^{8sf} **1-4-20 £6,101**

Toque *H Morrison* 63
3 ch f King's Best (USA) - Barboukh
10^{10s} 4^{8g} 2^{8g} 7^{8gf} 5^{8gf} 9^{8gf} 6^{8g} 6^{9g} 4^{8hd}
10^{8f} **0-2-10 £1,522**

Tora Petcha (Ire) *R Hollinshead* 82
2 b c Bahhare (USA) - Magdalene (Fr)
6^{6gf} 1^{6gf} 14^{6g} 7^{7s} 7^{6g} 11^{6g} 15^{6g} **1-0-7**
£7,312

Torcello (Ire) *Barry Potts* 68
7 b g Royal Academy (USA) - Vanya

2^{10g} 2^{10f} 2^{13f} 8^{12gf} 12^{16g} **0-3-5 £2,854**

Torgiano (Ire) *P Monteith* 21
4 b g Cadeaux Genereux - Delimara (Ire)
7^{11g} **0-0-1**

Torinmoor (USA) *Mrs A J Perrett* 99
4 ch g Intikhab (USA) - Tochar Ban (USA)
3^{10gs} 2^{10gf} 6^{10gs} 4^{10g} 9^{10gf} 2^{10g} **0-3-6 £9,836**

Torquemada (Ire) *W Jarvis* 69
4 ch g Desert Sun - Gaelic's Fantasy (Ire)
2^{7f} 5^{7gf} 4^{7g} 9^{7gf} 5^{7gs} 12^{6gs} 4^{7gf} 2^{7g} **0-3-8 £3,335**

Torrens (Ire) *R A Fahey* 88
3 b g Royal Anthem (USA) - Azure Lake (USA)
14^{8g} 7^{10gf} 4^{10gf} 1^{12g} 1^{10gf} 3^{11gf} 7^{12s} 1^{10gf} 7^{10g} 5^{10g} 8^{10s} **3-0-11 £23,901**

Torrent *D W Chapman* 61 a57
10 ch g Prince Sabo - Maiden Pool
5^{5sd} 5^{5sd} 4^{5sd} 6^{5sd} 1^{5sd} 10^{5gs} 1^{5sd} 5^{5g} 6^{5gf} 6^{5gf} 7^{5gf} 3^{5f} 10^{5gf} 3^{5g} 9^{5g} 6^{5gf} 12^{5gf} 3^{5gf} 16^{6g} 6^{5gf} 9^{5sd} 6^{5sd} 8^{5ss} 2^{5sd} 8^{6sd} **2-4-25 £4,985**

Torrid Kentavr (USA) *B Ellison* 81
8 b g Trempolino (USA) - Torrid Tango (USA)
1^{8s} 5^{8g} 4^{8g} 2^{10gs} 3^{10g} 4^{12gf} 2^{10gs} 2^{12gs} 10^{12hy} **1-3-9 £16,547**

Tosco (Ger) *D Flood* 34 a49
5 b g Second Set (Ire) - Tosca Rhea
8^{5sd} 8^{7sd} 9^{6sd} 9^{7sd} 11^{8sd} 3^{6sd} 9^{7gs} 11^{7sd} **0-1-8 £209**

Toshi (USA) *I Semple* 86 a77
3 b g Kingmambo (USA) - Majestic Role (Fr)
2^{10g} 2^{10f} 2^{9gs} 1^{9gs} 11^{10gs} 2^{9gf} 9^{10g} 3^{8g} 12^{9sd} 7^{9sf} 6^{9sd} **1-5-11 £11,273**

Toss The Caber (Ire) *K G Reveley* 58
3 ch g Dr Devious (Ire) - Celtic Fling
5^{6s} 9^{10s} 2^{8gf} 1^{8gf} 4^{8gf} 1^{9gf} 6^{9gf} 16^{10g} 16^{10gf} **2-1-9 £7,187**

Total Impact *C A Cyzer* 56 a34
2 ch g Pivotal - Rise 'n Shine
10^{6sd} 5^{6gs} **0-0-2**

Total Turtle (Ire) *T D Easterby* 90 a89
6 b g Turtle Island (Ire) - Chagrin D'Amour (Ire)
17^{16g} 6^{14g} 9^{18gs} 4^{16sd} **0-0-4 £1,168**

Totally Scottish *K G Reveley* 57
9 b g Mtoto - Glenfinlass
2^{22s} 2^{16gs} **0-2-2 £2,126**

Totally Yours (Ire) *W R Muir* 83 a14
4 b f Desert Sun - Total Aloof
9^{6gs} 7^{6gf} 12^{6gf} 18^{7s} 12^{7sd} **0-0-5**

Touch And Weld (Ire) *B W Duke*
4 ch f Weld - Princess Touchee (Ire)
14^{10g} **0-0-1**

Touch Of Ebony (Ire) *C Roberts* a58
6 b g Darshaan - Cormorant Wood
2^{11sd} **0-1-1 £424**

Touch Of Ivory (Ire) *R A Fahey* 55
2 b f Rossini (USA) - Windomen (Ire)
6^{6gf} 3^{6f} 5^{6gf} 4^{7gf} 8^{7gf} 7^{7gf} 5^{7gf} 3^{7gf} 5^{7g} **0-2-9 £1,380**

Touch Of Land (Fr) *H-A Pantall* 121
5 b h Lando (Ger) - Touch Of Class (Ger)
4^{9g} 4^{10gf} 1^{10gs} 5^{10y} 1^{10s} 13^{10gs} 5^{10gf} **2-0-7 £156,545**

Touch Of Silk (Ire) *B W Hills* 55
3 ch f Night Shift (USA) - Blew Her Top (USA)
7^{5s} 17^{6gf} 8^{5g} **0-0-3**

Touch Of Spice *J R Jenkins*
3 ch g Lake Coniston (Ire) - Soft Touch (Ger)
13^{6g} **0-0-1**

Tough Love *T D Easterby* 85
6 ch g Pursuit Of Love - Food Of Love
6^{8gf} 4^{8gf} 2^{7f} 2^{7gf} 8^{8gf} 2^{8gf} 6^{7g} 4^{8gf} 5^{8gf} 8^{8gf} 14^{8gf} **0-3-11 £10,609**

Tough Queen (USA) *N J Hawke*
4 b f Diesis - Here To Eternity (Fr)
15^{10g} **0-0-1**

Tour D'Amour (Ire) *Stef Liddiard* 64 a65
2 b f Fruits Of Love (USA) - Touraneena
9^{5sd} 3^{5sd} 15^{5s} 5^{6gs} 8^{6f} 4^{6gf} 3^{7gf} 1^{7gf} 7^{7g} 7^{7sd} 14^{7gf} 6^{6g} 4^{7g} 6^{7sd} 9^{9sd} 2^{7ss} 9^{6sd} 1^{7sd} **2-3-18 £8,350**

Tournedos (Ire) *J Akehurst* 108
3 b c Rossini (USA) - Don't Care (Ire)
7^{6s} 7^{6g} 10^{5gf} 7^{6g} 1^{5gf} 7^{5s} 5^{5g} 4^{5g} 4^{5g} 12^{5gf} **1-0-10 £24,969**

Tous Les Deux *R F Johnson Houghton* 76
2 b g Efisio - Caerosa
2^{5gs} 1^{5gf} 5^{6gf} 10^{5g} **1-1-4 £5,724**

Tower Hill (Ire) *M A Jarvis* 42 a71
2 b g Grand Lodge (USA) - Champaka (Ire)
14^{7gs} 4^{9sd} 4^{10sd} **0-0-3 £692**

Towerofcharlemagne (Ire) *Miss Gay Kelleway*
2 ch c King Charlemagne (USA) - Nozet
9^{6s} **0-0-1**

Town End Tom *R Craggs* 47 a56
3 b g Entrepreneur - Prima Silk
5^{6sd} 1^{5sd} 7^{6sd} 8^{5sd} 14^{6f} 3^{5f} 14^{5f} 9^{5sd} 12^{5gf} 8^{5g} **1-1-10 £2,970**

Town House *B P J Baugh* 52 a51
3 gr f Paris House - Avondale Girl (Ire)
8^{5sd} 9^{5gf} 10^{5gf} 10^{5gf} 13^{5gf} 4^{5sd} 17^{5gf} **0-0-7**

Townsville (Ire) *D J Daly* 33 a55
3 b g Soviet Star (USA) - Valmarana (USA)
11^{10g} 6^{12sd} 7^{9sd} **0-0-3**

Toy Top (USA) *M Dods* 61 a11
2 gr/ro f Tactical Cat (USA) - I'Ll Flutter By (USA)
6^{6s} 7^{6gf} 9^{6f} 12^{6f} 8^{5gf} 5^{5g} 3^{5gf} 10^{5sd} **0-1-8 £528**

Trace Clip *N I M Rossiter* 68 a56
7 b g Zafonic (USA) - Illusory
8^{5sd} 5^{5g} 6^{6f} 7^{7f} 11^{6gf} 10^{7f} 8^{6gs} 9^{5ss} **0-0-8**

Trackattack *P Howling* 51 a46
3 ch g Atraf - Verbena (Ire)
7^{9sd} 12^{7sd} 10^{7sd} 5^{10gs} 1^{10gf} 5^{12sd} 4^{12sd} 8^{12sd} 5^{10f} 10^{17sd} 4^{7sd} **1-0-11 £3,376**

Trafalgar Bay (Ire) *S Kirk* 90
2 b c Fruits Of Love (USA) - Chatsworth Bay (Ire)
2^{7gf} 1^{7g} 6^{8gf} 4^{7g} 1^{6gs} **2-1-5 £11,820**

Trafalgar Day *L M Cumani* 62
2 b c Mark Of Esteem (Ire) - Rosy Sunset (Ire)
12^{7gs} 11^{7s} 9^{8hy} **0-0-3**

Trafalgar Square *Rae Guest* 83
3 b c King's Best (USA) - Pat Or Else
5^{8hy} 6^{8g} 6^{8gf} 9^{10gf} 3^{8gf} 1^{7gs} 4^{7g} 1^{7gf} 3^{8g} 7^{7hy} **2-1-10 £14,334**

Tragedian (USA) *J H M Gosden* 97 a79
3 ch c Theatrical - Foreign Courier (USA)
1^{10sd} 7^{10gs} 4^{11gf} **1-0-3 £5,598**

Traianos (USA) *P F I Cole* 72 a65
3 b/br c Mt. Livermore (USA) - Shiitake (USA)
6^{8gs} 16^{8g} 8^{7gf} 5^{10sd} 6^{10gf} 12^{7sd} 4^{10gs} **0-1-7**

Trance (Ire) *T D Barron* 88 a83
5 ch g Bahhare (USA) - Lady Of Dreams (Ire)
11^{16g} 7^{14gf} 1^{14gs} 4^{14g} 9^{16g} 10^{12gf} 7^{12gs} 6^{12g} 8^{12g} 6^{13g} 15^{14s} 2^{14sd} 1^{14sd} 4^{12sd} **2-1-14 £13,429**

Tranquilizer *D J Coakley* 56 a70
3 b f Dr Fong (USA) - Tranquillity
3^{10s} 3^{9sd} 12^{10gf} 8^{8gf} 1^{9sd} 3^{9ft} 1^{12sd} **2-3-7 £7,524**

Trans Sonic *A P Jarvis* 86
2 ch g Trans Island - Sankaty Light (USA)
11^{6gf} 2^{6gs} 14^{6gf} 7^{7gf} 9^{6gs} 6^{6g} **0-1-6 £1,502**

Trans Vision (Ire) *A Berry* 51 a21
2 b f Trans Island - Embroidery
7^{5s} 7^{5gf} 5^{5s} 12^{6gf} 3^{5g} 4^{5gf} 6^{5sd} 15^{5gf} 7^{6gf} 15^{5gf} **0-1-10 £696**

Transaction (Ire) *J M P Eustace* 73 a59
3 ch g Trans Island - Meranie Girl (Ire)
10^{6gf} 8^{7gf} 11^{7gf} 8^{6gf} 13^{6g} 15^{5gs} 7^{8f} 12^{8g} 6^{6sd} 12^{7sd} **0-0-10**

Transgress (Ire) *Miss J R Tooth* 26
3 b g Trans Island - Ned's Contessa (Ire)
8^{10g} **0-0-1**

Transit *B Ellison* 41
6 b g Lion Cavern (USA) - Black Fighter (USA)
7^{12gf} **0-0-1**

Transvestite (Ire) *J W Hills* 83
3 b g Trans Island - Christoph's Girl
2^{8g} 4^{8g} 5^{9gf} 4^{8gf} 4^{10gf} 5^{10gf} 1^{8g} 6^{9g} 7^{9gs} 10^{10g} **1-1-10 £10,224**

Transylvania *C J Teague*
10 b m Wolfhound (USA) - Slava (USA)
12^{9sd} **0-0-1**

Trappeto (Ire) *C Smith* 57 a47
3 b c Barathea (Ire) - Campiglia (Ire)
6^{10gf} 8^{8gf} 3^{8gf} 7^{7g} 5^{8gf} 9^{10g} 5^{7sd} **0-1-7 £563**

Traprain (Ire) *M A Jarvis* 86 a57
3 b g Mark Of Esteem (Ire) - Nassma (Ire)
3^{10g} 5^{10g} 3^{8g} 6^{8sd} 1^{9gf} 6^{10g} 7^{10s} 1^{10g} **2-2-8 £11,134**

Travelling Times *Julian Poulton* 49 a47
6 ch g Timeless Times (USA) - Bollin Sophie
4^{6sd} 13^{6g} 3^{5g} 6^{6gf} 6^{5f} 5^{6f} 4^{6gf} 19^{6gf} 8^{6s} 11^{8gf} 4^{6sd} 4^{7ss} 2^{8ss} **0-2-13 £798**

Travolta *C G Cox* 59
2 b g Dansili - Generous Diana
7^{8gs} **0-0-1**

Traytonic *D Nicholls* 111
4 b g Botanic (USA) - Lady Parker (Ire)
5^{6s} 15^{6gs} 1^{6gf} 5^{7gf} 3^{6g} 16^{6g} 19^{6g} 12^{6g} **1-0-8 £17,964**

Treason Trial *Stef Liddiard* 73 a28
4 b g Peintre Celebre (USA) - Pampabella (Ire)
5^{12gf} 2^{14gf} 3^{16g} 3^{14gf} 12^{12sd} 8^{16g} 1^{14s} 7^{15s} **1-2-8 £7,885**

Treasure Cay *P W D'Arcy* 101 a95
4 ch c Bahamian Bounty - Madame Sisu
2^{5sd} 4^{5sd} 1^{5sd} 4^{5sd} 5^{5sd} 3^{5gs} 6^{5gf} 2^{5f} 8^{5g} 3^{5gf} 2^{5g} 6^{6gf} 8^{6g} 2^{6g} 8^{6s} 2^{5g} 1^{5gf} **2-7-17 £40,109**

Treasure House (Ire) *J Jay* 65
4 b g Grand Lodge (USA) - Royal Wolff
15^{6gs} 10^{6g} **0-0-2**

Treasure Trail *Ian Williams* a40
6 b g Millkom - Forever Shineing
8^{12sd} **0-0-1**

Treat Me Wild (Ire) *R Hannon* 56
3 ch f Loup Sauvage (USA) - Goes A Treat (Ire)
6^{6gf} 6^{6g} 6^{7gf} **0-0-3**

Trebello *J R Boyle* 51 a51
4 b g Robellino (USA) - Trempkate (USA)
8^{10gf} 10^{12sd} 8^{12gf} 4^{12sd} 4^{14sd} 7^{12g} 3^{14sd} 5^{13sd} 3^{14hy} **0-2-9 £567**

Treble Seven (USA) *C E Brittain* 56 a55
3 b/br f Fusaichi Pegasus (USA) - Nemea (USA)
6^{10s} 7^{9gf} 9^{6gf} 7^{6sd} 9^{7gf} 5^{10sd} 11^{11gf} 7^{8g} 3^{8f} 4^{8g} 6^{7sd} 11^{7sd} **0-1-12 £1,287**

Tree Roofer *N P Littmoden* a46
6 b g King's Signet (USA) - Armaiti
8^{5sd} 7^{6sd} 6^{5sd} 11^{5sd} 4^{6sd} 4^{5sd} 2^{6sd} 4^{6ss} 13^{5sd} 7^{5sd} **0-1-10 £418**

Treetops Hotel (Ire) *B R Johnson* 59 a61
6 ch g Grand Lodge (USA) - Rousinette
7^{6sd} 5^{7sd} 8^{7sd} 12^{8sd} 18^{7gf} 9^{6s} 1^{8f} 5^{10gf} 3^{9sd} 3^{8f} 1^{10g} 16^{12gs} 6^{10sd} **2-2-13 £5,619**

Tregarron *R Hannon* 75 a61
4 br g Efisio - Language Of Love
7^{6sd} 2^{7gs} 4^{8g} 5^{7gf} 1^{8gf} 8^{7g} 9^{6gs} 9^{8g} 3^{7gs} 4^{8hy} 7^{7sd} 3^{7sd} **1-3-12 £6,083**

Tregenna *R M H Cowell* a44
4 b f Forzando - Nineteenth Of May
6^{8sd} 9^{12sd} 4^{9sd} 1^{9sd} 7^{9sd} 9^{9sd} **1-0-6 £1,473**

Tremane Flyer (Ire) *Mrs A Naughton* 33 a4
5 gr m Lycius (USA) - Burishki
13^{9sd} 11^{12sd} 13^{7ys} 17^{8g} 11^{7gf} 13^{13gf} 7^{7f} 16^{10gf} **0-0-8**

Tremar *T G Mills* 99 a103
3 b c Royal Applause - Sabina
3^{7sd} 8^{7gs} 6^{6gs} 6^{6vs} **0-1-4 £9,000**

Trempjane *R Hannon* 54
3 b f Lujain (USA) - Trempkate (USA)
13^{7g} **0-0-1**

Tresor Secret (Fr) *J Gallagher* 44 a64
5 b g Green Desert (USA) - Tresor (USA)
2^{12sd} 1^{12sd} 12^{14gs} 1^{12sd} **2-1-4 £7,786**

Trevian *J M Bradley* 63 a52
4 ch g Atraf - Ascend (Ire)
8^{14sd} 6^{6g} 9^{8g} 14^{7gf} 8^{6gs} 10^{8gf} 2^{7g} 1^{8g} 7^{7gf} 2^{7gf} 8^{8s} 6^{7sd} 11^{9sd} **1-2-13 £6,233**

Trevira (Ire) *I W McInnes* 49
4 ch g Grand Lodge (USA) - That'Ll Be The Day (Ire)
10^{10gs} 7^{9gs} 13^{8g} 9^{10g} 18^{10gs} 16^{10g} **0-0-6**

Trew Class *M H Tompkins* 99
4 ch f Inchinor - Inimitable
3^{10g} 1^{10gf} 1^{10gf} 5^{10gf} 1^{10gf} 5^{10gf} 3^{10g} 6^{9gf} 16^{10gf} 26^{9s} **3-2-10 £31,685**

Trew Flight (USA) *M H Tompkins* a55
3 b g Rahy (USA) - Magdala (Ire)
9^{9sd} 12^{9sd} **0-0-2**

Trew Style *M H Tompkins* 73 a73
3 ch g Desert King (Ire) - Southern Psychic (USA)
8^{7gf} 3^{10gf} 16^{10gf} 3^{10s} 5^{12s} 3^{12sd} **0-3-6 £1,903**

Trials 'n Tribs *C A Cyzer* 53 a56

3 b f Rainbow Quest (USA) - Seasonal Splendour (Ire)
8^{10sd} 3^{12sd} 7^{10gf} 7^{10f} 4^{10gf} 13^{12gf} 4^{12f} 3^{12sd} 3^{12sd} 2^{12sd} 3^{16sd} **0-5-11 £2,270**

Tribal Chief (Ire) *J A R Toller* 35
3 b c Desert Prince (Ire) - Lehua (Ire)
12^{8g} **0-0-1**

Tribe *Sir Michael Stoute* 73
3 b g Danehill (USA) - Leo Girl (USA)
10^{8gf} 5^{10gs} 3^{8g} **0-1-3 £794**

Tribute (Ire) *Mrs H Dalton* 74
4 b g Green Desert (USA) - Zooming (Ire)
11^{5gf} 11^{5gf} 2^{6g} 10^{6gf} 1^{6f} 4^{6gf} 14^{6gf} 3^{6f} 9^{6gf} 12^{6f} 11^{5g} **1-2-11 £5,339**

Trick Cyclist *M W Easterby* 77 a62
4 b g Mind Games - Sabonis (USA)
8^{5gs} 12^{6s} 20^{6g} 2^{5g} 1^{5gf} 2^{5f} 2^{5g} 5^{5gf} 6^{5g} 5^{5g} 3^{5gf} 13^{6sd} 9^{5sd} **1-4-13 £9,813**

Trick Of Light *Mrs A J Perrett* 78
3 b f Dansili - Stardom
1^{10g} **1-0-1 £2,597**

Trick Or Treat *J G Given* 55 a38
2 b f Lomitas - Trick Of Ace (USA)
8^{6g} 7^{6g} 10^{6sd} **0-0-3**

Trickstep *D McCain* a51
4 b g Imperial Ballet (Ire) - Trick Of Ace (USA)
5^{12sd} 6^{16sd} 9^{10sd} 13^{10sd} **0-0-4**

Tricky Venture *Mrs L C Jewell* 71 a69
5 gr g Linamix (Fr) - Ukraine Venture
1^{10sd} 2^{11sd} 4^{10s} 15^{10g} 12^{10sd} 15^{11g} 11^{10hy} 16^{12sd} 6^{10sd} 5^{10sd} **1-1-10 £4,202**

Triffid *R A Fahey* a48
3 b g Dracula (Aus) - Rockfest (USA)
5^{6sd} 7^{7sd} 8^{6sd} 6^{9sd} 8^{9sd} 9^{7ss} **0-0-6**

Trifti *C A Cyzer* 63 a85
4 b g Vettori (Ire) - Time For Tea (Ire)
6^{7sd} 8^{10sd} 10^{7sd} 1^{7sd} 1^{7sd} 10^{7g} 5^{10gf} 13^{8f} 6^{9sd} 7^{11g} 1^{9sd} 3^{9sd} 8^{8sd} 1^{9sf} **4-1-14 £16,849**

Trigony (Ire) *T D Easterby* 56
3 b g Brave Act - Lulu Island
5^{10s} 7^{10g} 7^{12f} 5^{14gf} **0-0-4**

Trim Image *I W McInnes* 71
3 br f Averti (Ire) - Altizaf
3^{5gs} 8^{5gf} 12^{5gs} **0-1-3 £1,032**

Trimlestown (Ire) *H Candy* a63
2 b c Orpen (USA) - Courtier
9^{7sd} 3^{7sd} **0-1-2 £615**

Trimwaki (USA) *M R Channon* 60
2 b g Miswaki (USA) - My Trim (USA)
11^{7gf} 3^{7gf} 3^{7gf} 5^{7s} 9^{8f} 5^{8f} 12^{10g} 7^{7g} 6^{8g} 5^{7gs} **0-1-10 £1,316**

Trinculo (Ire) *D Nicholls* 93 a87
8 b g Anita's Prince - Fandangerina (USA)
7^{5sd} 4^{6sd} 10^{6g} 1^{5g} 1^{5gf} 1^{5g} 4^{5gf} 1^{5s} 14^{5gs} **4-0-9 £28,028**

Trinity (Ire) *M Brittain* 39
9 b h College Chapel - Kaskazi
10^{7g} **0-0-1**

Trinity Rose *M Johnston* 37
2 ch f Generous (Ire) - Stylish Rose (Ire)
9^{8s} **0-0-1**

Trinivantes (Ire) *R M Beckett*
2 b c Raphane (USA) - Boadicea
13^{7gf} **0-0-1**

Triple Jump *T D Easterby* 69
4 ch g Inchinor - Meteoric
14^{10g} 15^{8g} 6^{10gs} 5^{10gf} 8^{8g} **0-0-5 £255**

Triple Two *E A L Dunlop* 86
3 ch f Pivotal - Tara's Girl (Ire)
9^{7g} 1^{7gf} 6^{7g} 3^{7gf} 7^{7g} **1-0-5 £9,036**

Triple Zero (Ire) *A P Jarvis* 64
3 b f Raise A Grand (Ire) - Locorotondo (Ire)
16^{9g} 6^{7gf} 7^{10gs} 11^{7gf} 1^{8f} 9^{7s} 5^{7gf} 3^{8gf} 1^{6gf} 12^{5gf} **2-1-10 £7,259**

Trishay *J R Boyle*
4 gr f Petong - Marjorie's Memory (Ire)
17^{8g} **0-0-1**

Triskaidekaphobia *K R Burke* 92
2 b c Bertolini (USA) - Seren Teg
5^{5gf} 5^{5g} 1^{5gf} 6^{5gs} 1^{5g} 16^{5gf} 7^{5g} 4^{5gf} 5^{5g} 1^{5g} **3-0-10 £26,160**

Tritonville Lodge (Ire) *Miss E C Lavelle* 84 a77
3 b g Grand Lodge (USA) - Olean
5^{10gf} 3^{12sd} 2^{10gs} 2^{12g} 5^{12gs} **0-3-5 £3,810**

Trivandrun (Ire) *M Johnston* 73
3 b/br f Lend A Hand - Indiaca (Ger)
6^{7gs} 4^{9gf} 1^{8g} 8^{8g} **1-0-4 £5,771**

Trofana Falcon *H J Collingridge* a45
5 b g Polar Falcon (USA) - Silk St James
7^{10sd} 5^{13sd} 10^{10sd} 17^{10g} **0-0-4**

Trojan Flight *Mrs J R Ramsden* 87
4 ch g Hector Protector (USA) - Fairywings
2^{6s} 1^{5gs} 3^{5gf} 3^{6gf} 4^{6s} 1^{6f} 6^{6gf} 3^{6gf} 6^{5g} 6^{5gs} 6^{5gf} 2^{6gf} 9^{6g} 6^{6g} 4^{5gs} 9^{6gs} 7^{6s} 2^{7s} **2-8-18 £27,282**

Trombone Tom *J R Norton* 63 a65
2 b c Superior Premium - Nine To Five
1^{6g} 4^{5gs} 3^{5g} 10^{6s} 4^{6sd} 5^{6sd} 7^{5sd} **1-0-7 £4,009**

Tromp *D J Coakley* 78 a78
4 ch g Zilzal (USA) - Sulitelma (USA)
1^{10sd} 1^{12sd} 1^{11g} 6^{12g} 5^{12sd} 12^{11sd} **3-0-6 £14,080**

Troodos Jet *K W Hogg* 27
4 b g Atraf - Costa Verde
13^{6s} 8^{6gs} 14^{5gf} 14^{6g} 19^{8gf} **0-0-5**

Trophy Pride (USA) *B J Meehan* 69 a77
2 b f Lion Cavern (USA) - Trophy Bride (USA)
5^{6gf} 2^{6g} 12^{6gf} 2^{5g} 2^{5g} 1^{5sd} **1-3-6 £8,935**

Tropical Son *D Shaw* 15 a53
6 b g Distant Relative - Douce Maison (Ire)
10^{12sd} 5^{12sd} 2^{10sd} 3^{9sd} 2^{10sd} 2^{13sd} 3^{14sd} 2^{12sd} 10^{11s} 11^{10s} 9^{9sd} 9^{14sd} 8^{12sf} 6^{9sf} **0-6-14 £2,165**

Trotters Bottom *Andrew Reid* 69 a71
4 b g Mind Games - Fleeting Affair
5^{6g} 14^{5g} 6^{5gf} 11^{5gf} 6^{6sd} 10^{6f} 5^{5gs} 12^{5g} **0-0-8**

Trouble Maker *A M Balding* 60 a55
4 b g Green Desert (USA) - River Abouali
10^{7gf} 4^{6g} 5^{6g} 3^{6gs} 3^{6sd} 9^{6hy} **0-2-6 £1,046**

Trouble Mountain (USA) *M W Easterby* 78
8 br g Mt. Livermore (USA) - Trouble Free (USA)
6^{11s} 12^{10g} 2^{10g} 12^{10gf} 12^{10g} 4^{10gs} 3^{11gf} 12^{10gs} 8^{10s} 13^{10g} 10^{10gf} 7^{10gf} 5^{10hy} **0-2-13 £3,542**

Truckle *C W Fairhurst* 60 a70
3 b g Vettori (Ire) - Proud Titania (Ire)

8^{9sd} 5^{11sd} 8^{12g} 9^{8gf} 11^{9sd} **0-0-5**

True (Ire) *Mrs S Lamyman* 53 a43
4 ch f Barathea (Ire) - Bibliotheque (USA)
6^{7g} 17^{10g} 5^{8gf} 7^{10gf} 11^{8gf} 9^{10gf} 4^{12f} 12^{14gf} 6^{12sd} 9^{10g} **0-1-10**

True Cause (USA) *Saeed Bin Suroor* 100
2 ch c Storm Cat (USA) - Dearly
2^{7gs} 1^{8g} 1^{8gf} 5^{8g} **2-1-4 £23,979**

True Companion *N P Littmoden* 93 a83
6 b g Brief Truce (USA) - Comanche Companion
12^{12sd} 1^{12sd} 4^{12sd} 3^{12sd} 1^{10g} 1^{10s} 2^{10s} 10^{10gs} 5^{12g} 14^{12gs} 16^{10gs} 12^{12gs} 4^{10g} 4^{10hy} 6^{9sf} 2^{12sd} **3-4-16 £17,011**

True Dream *M Meade* 77
2 ch c Mark Of Esteem (Ire) - Crystal Cavern (USA)
2^{7gf} 5^{7g} 1^{8hd} **1-1-3 £4,986**

True Lover (Ger) *J W Mullins* 101
8 b g Winged Love (Ire) - Truneba (Ger)
6^{12g} 13^{18gs} **0-0-2 £600**

True Magic *J D Bethell* 79 a69
4 b f Magic Ring (Ire) - True Precision
6^{5sd} 19^{5hy} 2^{5f} 8^{6gf} 4^{5gf} 10^{5gf} 5^{5g} 14^{6gf} 3^{5gf} 9^{5gf} 13^{5g} **0-2-11 £3,661**

True Night *D Nicholls* 91
8 b g Night Shift (USA) - Dead Certain
12^{7gs} 12^{8gf} 2^{7g} 8^{7gf} 1^{8g} 7^{7gf} 17^{8g} 19^{7gf} 14^{8gs} 7^{8gf} 10^{8gf} 4^{9gf} 5^{9g} 9^{8gf} **1-1-14 £10,298**

True Ruby *S Kirk* a33
2 b f Josr Algarhoud (Ire) - St James's Antigua (Ire)
8^{9sf} **0-0-1**

True To Yourself (USA) *J G Given* a55
4 b g Royal Academy (USA) - Romilly
10^{12sd} 2^{12sd} 3^{14sd} 1^{14sd} 4^{12sd} 5^{12sd} 6^{12sd} 5^{11sd} **1-2-8 £1,972**

True Valentine *A Berry* 45
2 br f Primo Valentino (Ire) - Prim N Proper
9^{5gs} 9^{5f} 4^{5g} 10^{6gf} 4^{5gf} 2^{5g} 8^{6gf} **0-1-7 £838**

Truly Fruitful (Ire) *K R Burke* 66
2 ch g Fruits Of Love (USA) - Truly Flattering
7^{7gs} 1^{7gf} 9^{7g} 4^{7g} **1-0-4 £4,420**

Truman *John A Harris* 64 a49
4 b g Entrepreneur - Sabria (USA)
10^{10gf} 9^{9sd} 7^{7sd} 8^{10gf} 2^{10gf} 6^{10g} **0-1-6 £862**

Trust Rule *M W Easterby* 84
5 b g Selkirk (USA) - Hagwah (USA)
11^{12s} 8^{12f} 10^{14gf} 4^{16gf} 13^{12gf} 4^{12g} 14^{12g} 6^{14gf} 11^{14s} **0-0-9 £1,271**

Trusted Mole (Ire) *W M Brisbourne* 48
7 b g Eagle Eyed (USA) - Orient Air
6^{13gf} 7^{11gf} **0-0-2**

Tryandstopme *J A Osborne* 65 a59
2 b f Fraam - Heavenly Abstone
3^{5sd} 2^{5sd} 3^{5g} 7^{5g} 7^{6gs} 3^{5gf} 5^{5g} 8^{5gf} **0-2-8 £2,672**

Trymore (Ire) *A M Balding* a68
3 ch c Tagula (Ire) - Marimar (Ire)
6^{8sd} 3^{8sd} 11^{10s} **0-1-3 £493**

Trysting Grove (Ire) *E G Bevan* a28
4 b f Cape Cross (Ire) - Elton Grove (Ire)
10^{10sd} 11^{12sd} 13^{12sd} **0-0-3**

Tsaroxy (Ire) *J Howard Johnson* 86
3 b g Xaar - Belsay
1^{8gf} 15^{8gf} 5^{8g} 7^{7g} 8^{6gf} 8^{8gf} 11^{7hy} **1-0-7 £7,014**

Tshukudu *Mrs A L M King* 37
4 ch f Fleetwood (Ire) - Pab's Choice
9^{8g} 4^{12s} 11^{10g} **0-0-3**

Tsini *M P Tregoning* 26
2 b f Alhaarth (Ire) - Susquehanna Days (USA)
13^{6gf} **0-0-1**

Tubber Streams (Ire) *B A Pearce* 23
8 b g Great Marquess - Much Obliged
11^{8gf} **0-0-1**

Tucker *D R C Elsworth* 109
3 b c Inchinor - Tender Moment (Ire)
1^{7gf} 10^{8gf} 1^{8gf} 2^{8g} 6^{8gf} 10^{8s} 7^{8g} 7^{10gf} **2-1-8 £22,710**

Tuckerman *F J Bowles* 49 a46
4 b c Gulch (USA) - Remuria (USA)
12^{9g} 5^{10sd} **0-0-2**

Tuckers Point (Ire) *J A Osborne* 67
2 b f Mujadil (USA) - Romanovna
7^{6gf} 7^{5g} 4^{6gs} 13^{7g} **0-0-4 £249**

Tudor Oak (Ire) *Mark Campion* 51
3 b g Woods Of Windsor (USA) - Tacheo
8^{7gs} 16^{10gf} 8^{10gf} 5^{7gf} 8^{7gs} 12^{8g} **0-0-6**

Tufton *Saeed Bin Suroor* 90
2 b c King's Best (USA) - Mythical Magic
1^{6gf} 2^{7g} **1-1-2 £7,241**

Tulipa (Pol) *T R George* 78
6 ch m Jape (USA) - Truly Best (Pol)
1^{12gf} 4^{13gf} **1-0-2 £2,596**

Tumbleweed Glory (Ire) *B J Meehan* 70
2 b g Marju (Ire) - Tathkara (USA)
9^{7gs} 3^{7gf} 3^{8g} **0-1-3 £1,532**

Tungsten Strike (USA) *Mrs A J Perrett* 110
4 ch g Smart Strike (Can) - Bathilde (Ire)
7^{12g} 2^{16g} 7^{16s} 1^{14gf} 9^{16g} 2^{16gs} **1-2-6 £59,793**

Tuning Fork *J Akehurst* 64 a47
5 b g Alzao (USA) - Tuning
15^{9g} 15^{7g} 16^{10g} 8^{8gf} 10^{9g} 11^{8gf} 10^{7s} 9^{13sd} 12^{16sd} **0-0-9**

Turbo (Ire) *M W Easterby* 91
6 b g Piccolo - By Arrangement (Ire)
7^{10gs} 7^{12gs} 9^{10gf} 18^{12g} 7^{10g} 4^{15s} 7^{12f} 7^{10gs} **0-0-8 £526**

Turf Princess *Ian Emmerson* a50
4 b f Wizard King - Turf Moor (Ire)
5^{6sd} 12^{6sd} 4^{6sd} 11^{6sd} 6^{7sd} **0-0-5**

Turftanzer (Ger) *Don Enrico Incisa* a34
6 b g Lomitas - Tower Bridge (Ger)
5^{12sd} 10^{8sd} **0-0-2**

Turibius *T E Powell* 73 a72
6 b g Puissance - Compact Disc (Ire)
7^{6sd} 10^{5sd} 11^{5gf} 14^{7g} 15^{6f} 7^{5gf} 7^{5gf} 1^{5g} 11^{6gf} 7^{5g} 14^{5gf} 7^{6sd} 5^{5sd} **1-0-13 £2,748**

Turkana Girl *G Wragg* 62
3 ch f Hernando (Fr) - Miss Penton
11^{10gf} 10^{10gf} 3^{7gf} 6^{7gf} **0-1-4 £660**

Turkish Sultan (Ire) *T D Easterby* 76
2 b c Anabaa (USA) - Odalisque (Ire)
2^{7gf} 2^{7g} 9^{8gs} **0-2-3 £2,132**

Turks And Caicos (Ire) *P C Haslam*
4 b/br g Turtle Island (Ire) - Need You Badly
8^{12sd} **0-0-1**

Turks Wood (Ire) *Anthony Mullins* 77
3 b g Charnwood Forest (Ire) - Nairasha (Ire)
3^{8g} 2^{8gf} 2^{7f} 1^{7f} 4^{7gf} 4^{7gf} 8^{12g} 3^{9gf}
1-4-8 £8,300

Turn 'n Burn *C A Cyzer* 79 a79
4 b g Unfuwain (USA) - Seasonal Splendour (Ire)
1^{12sd} 6^{12sd} 13^{17sd} 9^{14g} 4^{12sd} 6^{16sd} 8^{14gf} 4^{14gf} 3^{16g} **1-2-9 £6,289**

Turn Around *P A Blockley* 55 a77
5 b g Pivotal - Bemuse
6^{10s} 2^{9sd} 1^{6sd} 7^{7sd} 2^{6sd} 9^{7gf} **1-2-6 £5,001**

Turn Me On (Ire) *M L W Bell* 74 a60
2 b g Tagula (Ire) - Jacobina
3^{5sd} 3^{5gf} **0-2-2 £1,326**

Turn Of Phrase (Ire) *Robert Gray* 65
6 b g Cadeaux Genereux - Token Gesture (Ire)
3^{12g} 12^{14gf} 6^{14gf} **0-1-3 £609**

Turn On The Style *Peter Grayson* 83
3 ch g Pivotal - Elegant Rose
1^{6s} 4^{6gf} 2^{5gs} 2^{6g} 8^{6gs} **1-1-5 £12,078**

Turnaround (Ger) *Mrs J R Ramsden* 69
3 gr g Highest Honor (Fr) - Tamacana
14^{7g} 8^{5s} UR^{6gs} **0-0-3**

Turner *W M Brisbourne* 67
4 gr g El Prado (Ire) - Gaily Royal (Ire)
15^{10g} 14^{11gf} 3^{12gf} 4^{13gf} 5^{10gf} 1^{16gf} 6^{16gf}
1-1-7 £6,503

Turner's Touch *G L Moore* 67 a68
3 ch g Compton Place - Chairmans Daughter
5^{8sd} 3^{8sd} 6^{8g} 2^{8gf} 5^{10gf} 4^{10g} 10^{10sd} 6^{10f} 10^{8sd} 3^{10sd} 1^{10sd} **1-3-11 £3,896**

Turnkey *M R Channon* 106
3 br g Pivotal - Persian Air
1^{6s} 6^{7gs} 2^{6y} 5^{6gs} 9^{6gs} 3^{7sh} **1-2-6 £19,523**

Turnstile *J Howard Johnson* 99
4 gr g Linamix (Fr) - Kissing Gate (USA)
1^{14g} 16^{14s} 2^{14gf} 8^{16gs} 1^{13gf} 10^{13gf} 11^{15gs}
2-1-7 £14,201

Turnstone *D R Loder* a78
3 b g Pivotal - Adeptation (USA)
1^{8sd} 3^{10sd} **1-0-2 £4,432**

Turtle Bay *B Storey* 64
3 ch f Dr Fong (USA) - My Valentina
6^{9gs} 6^{8g} **0-0-2**

Turtle Bowl (Ire) *F Rohaut* 117
3 b c Dyhim Diamond (Ire) - Clara Bow (Fr)
1^{7gf} 1^{7hy} 4^{8vs} 8^{8s} 1^{8g} 1^{8g} **4-0-6 £218,128**

Turtle Love (Ire) *B D Leavy*
6 b m Turtle Island (Ire) - A Little Loving
9^{14sd} **0-0-1**

Turtle Magic (Ire) *R A Harris* 23
3 b f Turtle Island (Ire) - Theda
8^{6hy} 11^{6sd} 9^{6gf} 15^{6s} 9^{8f} 13^{8gf} **0-0-6**

Turtle Patriarch (Ire) *Mrs A J Perrett* 65
4 b g Turtle Island (Ire) - La Doyenne (Ire)
3^{10s} 5^{13gs} 13^{12gf} 7^{10gf} 11^{10s} **0-1-5 £525**

Turtle Soup (Ire) *T R George* 76
9 b g Turtle Island (Ire) - Lisa's Favourite
4^{16gs} **0-0-1 £539**

Tuscan Dream *A Berry* 22 a38
10 b g Clantime - Excavator Lady
12^{5sd} 10^{5sd} 4^{5sd} 19^{5gf} 10^{5f} **0-0-5**

Tuscan Flyer *R Bastiman* 53 a51
7 b g Clantime - Excavator Lady
15^{6s} 6^{6g} 10^{5gf} 14^{5gf} 10^{5gf} 2^{6f} 3^{6gf} 4^{6sd} 1^{5f} 11^{5gf} 6^{5sd} **1-2-11 £2,786**

Tuscan Treaty *P J McBride* 52 a48
5 b m Brief Truce (USA) - Fiorenz (USA)
11^{7g} 8^{8gf} 6^{8g} 13^{8gf} 13^{7g} 2^{8f} 10^{8g} 2^{9sd} 1^{9sd} 2^{10sd} 5^{7sd} **1-3-11 £3,215**

Tuscany Queen (Ire) *R Hannon* 51
2 b f Titus Livius (Fr) - Queen Molly
4^{5g} 5^{6g} 15^{6gf} **0-0-3**

Tuscany Rose *W R Muir* 44
2 ch f Medicean - Rosewood Belle (USA)
12^{6gs} 12^{8g} 7^{8g} **0-0-3**

Tuscarora (Ire) *A W Carroll* 71 a74
6 b m Revoque (Ire) - Fresh Look (Ire)
3^{7sd} 4^{7sd} 4^{7sd} 4^{7sd} 3^{7gf} 3^{7s} 3^{7gf} 2^{8f} 3^{8f} 4^{8g} 2^{7gf} 2^{7g} 7^{6gf} 6^{7gf} 10^{7gs} 11^{9sd} **0-7-16 £9,788**

Tutu Much (Ire) *M A Magnusson* 53
3 b f Sadler's Wells (USA) - Filia Ardross
1^{12g} **1-0-1 £3,380**

Tuvalu (Ger) *A M Balding* 75 a66
3 ch g Dashing Blade - Tepana (Ger)
2^{10sd} 6^{10sd} 5^{10sd} 3^{11sd} 3^{12g} 3^{12gs} **0-4-6 £2,792**

Twentyfirst Dansar *A D Smith* 56 a57
2 b g Zahran (Ire) - Joker's Luck
6^{5gs} 1^{5g} 13^{6gs} 18^{5gf} 9^{7sd} 3^{9sd} 12^{8sd}
1-1-7 £3,353

Twentytwosilver (Ire) *N J Hawke* 56 a30
5 gr/ro g Emarati (USA) - St Louis Lady
2^{12gf} 17^{12gf} 7^{12gf} 9^{12sd} 11^{8hd} **0-1-5 £1,275**

Twice Nightly *J D Bethell* 28
3 b g Wolfhound (USA) - Dusty's Darling
8^{7f} 6^{6gs} **0-0-2**

Twilight Avenger (Ire) *M J Polglase* 59 a44
2 b g Dr Fong (USA) - Asterita
8^{5gf} 16^{5s} 3^{5f} 12^{7gs} 3^{7f} 4^{7sd} 6^{7g} 10^{7sd} 6^{7gf} 4^{8gf} 11^{8gf} 12^{10g} 8^{7gf} 6^{7sd} 10^{5sd} 5^{6sd}
0-1-16 £1,345

Twill (Ire) *H Morrison* 57 a80
2 ch g Barathea (Ire) - Khafaya
10^{8s} 8^{8sd} 1^{8ss} **1-0-3 £4,012**

Twin Peaks (Ire) *D R Loder* 71 a78
3 b g Monashee Mountain (USA) - Goldenfort Queen (Ire)
1^{7sd} 14^{8gf} 6^{10gs} **1-0-3 £4,104**

Twindego *T D Barron* 66
2 b g Komaite (USA) - On The Wagon
8^{5s} 3^{6gf} 3^{6gf} **0-2-3 £1,418**

Twinkling Star *Mrs A J Perrett* a51
3 b f King Of Kings (Ire) - Miss Twinkletoes (Ire)
14^{12sd} 11^{12sd} 8^{12sd} **0-0-3**

Twinned (Ire) *J S Moore* 64 a65
2 ch g Soviet Star (USA) - Identical (Ire)
3^{5gs} 2^{5f} 3^{5gf} 15^{5gf} 2^{5g} 5^{5gf} 12^{5g} 10^{5gs} 3^{5sd} 9^{5sf} **0-3-10 £4,193**

Twist Bookie (Ire) *J S Moore* 41 a56
5 br g Perugino (USA) - Twist Scarlett (Ger)
9^{9sd} 8^{8sd} 7^{8s} 12^{8g} **0-0-4**

Two Chimneys (USA) *K A Ryan* 50 a54
3 b f Deputy Commander (USA) - Take Heart (USA)
7^{7gf} 13^{7g} 6^{8g} 6^{9sd} 11^{8sd} **0-0-5**

Two Johns *N Wilson*

2 b g Sugarfoot - Hymn Book (Ire)
$10^{8gs}\ 7^{7g}\ 11^{8g}$ **0-0-3**

Two Of A Kind (Ire) *Miss L V Davis*
5 ch g Ashkalani (Ire) - Dulcinea
10^{14sd} **0-0-1**

Twyla Tharp (Ire) *J H M Gosden* 107
3 b f Sadler's Wells (USA) - Sumoto
$1^{9gs}\ 2^{12gf}\ 8^{12gf}\ 6^{13s}\ 3^{14hy}$ **1-2-5 £37,432**

Tybalt *T G McCourt* 73
3 b g Polar Falcon (USA) - Once Removed
$5^{8gf}\ 11^{8g}\ 1^{10gs}\ 6^{10g}\ 9^{10s}\ 8^{10g}\ 4^{12g}$ **1-1-7 £3,858**

Tycheros *S C Williams* 50 a58
3 b g Polar Falcon (USA) - Marie De Flandre (Fr)
$9^{6sd}\ 7^{6s}\ 5^{12g}\ 11^{16g}\ 9^{16s}\ 4^{12sd}\ 2^{11g}\ 1^{12sd}\ 1^{17sd}\ 7^{14sd}$ **2-1-10 £3,401**

Tychy *S C Williams* 90
6 ch m Suave Dancer (USA) - Touch Of White
$17^{6g}\ 7^{5g}\ 15^{5g}$ **0-0-3**

Tyne *T D Barron* 46
4 b g Komaite (USA) - High Typha
$15^{5g}\ 14^{6gf}$ **0-0-2**

Tyneham *W G M Turner* a47
5 b h Robellino (USA) - Diamond Wedding (USA)
$10^{8sd}\ 9^{14sd}$ **0-0-2**

Typhoon Ginger (Ire) *G Woodward* 65
10 ch m Archway (Ire) - Pallas Viking
$10^{8gf}\ 5^{8gf}\ 12^{10gf}\ 5^{10gs}\ 1^{8gf}\ 4^{8g}\ 6^{10g}\ 5^{8gf}\ 15^{10s}$ **1-0-9 £6,817**

Typhoon Tilly *C R Egerton* 72 a73
8 b g Hernando (Fr) - Meavy
$1^{12sd}\ 1^{12sd}\ 4^{12sd}\ 6^{12sd}\ 7^{12sd}\ 5^{15gf}\ 8^{14gf}\ 5^{12gf}\ 1^{14g}\ 4^{12sd}\ 4^{14sf}$ **3-1-11 £10,416**

Tyrone Sam *K A Ryan* 73 a76
3 b g Mind Games - Crystal Sand (Ger)
$2^{7sd}\ 3^{7sd}\ 2^{6sd}\ 14^{6g}\ 2^{6gf}\ 3^{6gf}\ 12^{7gf}$ **0-5-7 £5,623**

Tyson Returns *A J Chamberlain* a42
3 b g Mujahid (USA) - Mabrookah
$9^{8sd}\ 9^{8sd}\ 6^{9sd}\ 14^{8s}\ 16^{8gf}$ **0-0-5**

Tyzack (Ire) *Stef Liddiard* 60
4 b g Fasliyev (USA) - Rabea (USA)
1^{7gf} **1-0-1 £3,803**

Uandi *J Akehurst* 14 a54
2 b f Singspiel (Ire) - Krajina (Fr)
$8^{6hy}\ 5^{9sd}\ 11^{8sd}$ **0-0-3**

Ugly Sister (USA) *G C Bravery* a41
3 gr f Aljabr (USA) - Cinderella Ball (USA)
$4^{8sd}\ 6^{10sd}$ **0-0-2**

Ugo Fire (Ire) *Kevin Prendergast* 106
2 b f Bluebird (USA) - Quiet Mouse (USA)
$7^{5s}\ 4^{5sh}\ 1^{6sh}\ 4^{6g}\ 3^{7gf}\ 4^{6g}\ 3^{6g}\ 2^{7g}\ 1^{7y}$ **2-3-9 £123,628**

Uhoomagoo *K A Ryan* 102 a99
7 b g Namaqualand (USA) - Point Of Law
$10^{8gf}\ 8^{8gf}\ 1^{7sd}\ 7^{7gf}\ 5^{7g}\ 4^{9g}\ 10^{7gf}\ 10^{7gf}\ 12^{8gf}\ 1^{7g}\ 1^{7gf}\ 11^{7gs}\ 4^{7gs}\ 11^{7sd}$ **3-1-14 £68,169**

Uhuru Dawn (Ire) *Andre Hermans* 43 a51
5 b g Fayruz - Come Dancing
$9^{7sd}\ 7^{6sd}\ 8^{6sd}\ 3^{8vs}\ 0^{7g}\ 0^{6g}\ 0^{8s}$ **0-1-7 £1,702**

Uhuru Peak *M W Easterby* 62
4 ch g Bal Harbour - Catherines Well
$11^{7s}\ 20^{8g}\ 1^{6f}\ 1^{8gf}\ 8^{8gf}\ 2^{7gf}\ 10^{8gf}$ **2-1-7 £7,031**

Uig *H S Howe* 78
4 ch f Bien Bien (USA) - Madam Zando
$8^{10g}\ 3^{12s}\ 11^{10gf}\ 5^{10g}\ 4^{10gf}\ 1^{10s}\ 3^{10g}\ 1^{10gf}\ 4^{9s}\ 2^{10gf}\ 4^{10gs}\ 11^{10g}$ **2-2-12 £21,135**

Ullah Pendragon (Ire) *M J Polglase* 53 a38
2 gr g Beckett (Ire) - Marathon Maid
$10^{5g}\ 9^{6gf}\ 4^{7f}\ 6^{7sd}$ **0-0-4 £257**

Ulshaw *J M Bradley* 52 a45
8 ch g Salse (USA) - Kintail
$7^{14sd}\ 6^{14sd}\ 7^{14sd}\ 4^{17sd}\ 5^{14sd}\ 2^{12g}\ 1^{12gf}\ 2^{12hy}\ 8^{13sd}\ 6^{17g}\ 9^{13s}\ 12^{10gf}\ 7^{12g}\ 7^{12g}\ 12^{10gf}\ 6^{10g}\ 7^{10g}\ 5^{12gs}\ 5^{14sd}\ 6^{16sd}$ **1-2-20 £3,964**

Ulysees (Ire) *I Semple* 76 a51
6 b g Turtle Island (Ire) - Tamasriya (Ire)
$1^{6gs}\ 9^{6gs}\ 4^{7s}\ 5^{8gs}\ 5^{8g}\ 4^{7g}\ 6^{8g}\ 11^{6sd}\ 8^{9sd}$ **1-1-9 £4,594**

Umlilo *J H M Gosden* 59
3 b f Mtoto - Ingozi
$3^{8gs}\ 6^{10g}\ 5^{9g}$ **0-1-3 £387**

Umniya (Ire) *M R Channon* 87
3 b f Bluebird (USA) - Sparky's Song
$7^{8gs}\ 13^{7gf}\ 15^{9gf}\ 10^{8g}\ 4^{8gf}\ 7^{8s}$ **0-0-6 £518**

Umthoulah (Ire) *K R Burke* 78
3 br f Unfuwain (USA) - Susquehanna Days (USA)
1^{12gf} **1-0-1 £4,782**

Un Autre Espere *C C Bealby* a16
6 b g Golden Heights - Drummer's Dream (Ire)
$10^{7sd}\ 11^{9sd}\ 6^{8sd}\ 10^{12sd}$ **0-0-4**

Una Momenta *J S Wainwright*
2 ch f Timeless Times (USA) - Lady Magician
14^{6gf} **0-0-1**

Unasuming (Ire) *J Pearce* 40 a53
2 b f Orpen (USA) - Untold
$13^{8g}\ 5^{8sd}\ 13^{10sd}$ **0-0-3**

Unavailable (Ire) *M A Magnusson* 77 a97
4 b f Alzao (USA) - Maid Of Killeen (Ire)
$6^{10sd}\ 10^{12f}\ 7^{12g}\ 4^{13g}$ **0-0-4 £948**

Unbridled's Dream (USA) *C A Cyzer* 65 a57
4 gr/ro g Unbridled's Song (USA) - Diamond Dream (Fr)
$7^{7sd}\ 3^{7f}\ 7^{9g}\ 5^{10gf}\ 7^{11gf}\ 10^{10gf}\ 10^{9sd}\ 12^{16sd}\ 13^{10gs}$ **0-1-9 £530**

Uncle Bernon *J A Geake* 42
6 ch g Pivotal - Magical Veil
13^{6g} **0-0-1**

Uncle Bulgaria (Ire) *G C Bravery* 71
3 b g Alhaarth (Ire) - Istibshar (USA)
$2^{8g}\ 1^{8g}\ 6^{8gf}\ 15^{8g}\ 5^{8gs}\ 4^{8s}\ 15^{8s}\ 10^{10hy}$ **1-2-8 £4,196**

Uncle John *M E Sowersby* 48 a65
4 b g Atraf - Bit O' May
$7^{12sd}\ 8^{12gf}\ 12^{12gs}\ 6^{9gf}\ 1^{12gf}\ 12^{10gf}$ **1-0-6 £2,590**

Under Fire (Ire) *A W Carroll* a55
2 b g Lear Spear (USA) - Kahyasi Moll (Ire)
$8^{7sd}\ 5^{9sf}\ 7^{7sd}$ **0-0-3**

Under My Spell *P D Evans* 76
4 b f Wizard King - Gagajulu
$7^{6gf}\ 4^{6gf}\ 7^{6gf}\ 4^{7gf}\ 6^{7g}\ 3^{8g}\ 4^{7gf}\ 6^{8f}$ **0-1-8 £1,679**

Under My Thumb (Ire) *E J O'Neill* 91
2 b c Desert Style (Ire) - Petite Maxine
$7^{7gf}\ 2^{7f}\ 1^{7g}\ 1^{7f}\ 1^{7gf}\ 4^{8g}\ 4^{10g}$ **3-1-7 £13,386**

Under The Rainbow *P W Chapple-Hyam* 88
2 gr f Fantastic Light (USA) - Farfala (Fr)
17^{8g} 1^{8gf} 1^{10s} **2-0-3 £19,402**

Underscore (USA) *J H M Gosden* 87
3 ch c Spinning World (USA) - Speed Dialer (USA)
2^{8g} 1^{8gs} 6^{10g} 11^{8g} **1-1-4 £6,732**

Undertheinfluence (Ire) *C N Kellett* a26
6 b m Great Commotion (USA) - Katie Craig (Ire)
8^{11sd} 10^{10sd} 7^{7sd} 12^{8sd} **0-0-4**

Underthemistletoe (Ire) *R E Barr* 46 a35
3 b f Lujain (USA) - Christmas Kiss
5^{6sd} 4^{5sd} 4^{6sd} 2^{6gf} 12^{6gf} 6^{7g} 6^{7g} 9^{6gf} 12^{7sd}
0-1-9 £1,081

Undeterred *T D Barron* 84
9 ch g Zafonic (USA) - Mint Crisp (Ire)
6^{6f} 11^{6gf} 8^{6g} 7^{6gf} 4^{6f} 3^{6gf} 4^{6f} 8^{6gf} 1^{6gf}
1^{6gf} 1^{6gf} 4^{6gf} **3-1-12 £13,130**

Unfurled (Ire) *J L Dunlop* 116
3 ch c Unfuwain (USA) - Peony
1^{10g} 1^{11gf} 7^{12g} 2^{12gs} 2^{14g} **2-2-5**
£44,790

Union Jack Jackson (Ire) *J G Given* 63 a59
3 b g Daggers Drawn (USA) - Beechwood Quest (Ire)
5^{10sd} 10^{8gf} 11^{6gf} 9^{8g} 7^{8gf} 14^{8g} 11^{9sd}
0-0-7

Unique Moment *M Johnston* 68
2 ch f Vettori (Ire) - Lonesome
3^{7g} 6^{7gf} 3^{7gf} 1^{7gf} 5^{7gf} 8^{8gs} 5^{8g} **1-1-7**
£5,502

United Nations *N Wilson* 83
4 ch g Halling (USA) - Congress (Ire)
11^{10s} 16^{10gf} 12^{8gs} 12^{8g} 6^{10gf} 10^{9gf}
0-0-6

United Spirit (Ire) *Jedd O'Keeffe* 65 a71
4 b f Fasliyev (USA) - Atlantic Desire (Ire)
8^{9sd} 4^{12sd} 6^{12sd} 3^{9sd} 8^{9sd} 7^{10gf} 7^{8gf} 8^{7gf} 11^{8gf}
9^{10gf} 2^{10gf} 4^{10gf} 7^{10gf} 16^{12g} **0-2-14**
£2,164

Unleaded *J Akehurst* a41
5 ch m Danzig Connection (USA) - Mo Stopher
9^{14sd} 7^{16sd} 13^{14sd} 4^{16sd} **0-0-4**

Unleash (USA) *P J Hobbs* 91
6 ch g Benny The Dip (USA) - Lemhi Go (USA)
14^{19gs} **0-0-1**

Unlimited *Mrs A Duffield* 73
3 b g Bold Edge - Cabcharge Blue
2^{5g} 4^{5g} 6^{5g} 7^{5gf} 1^{5gf} 2^{5g} 8^{5gf} 10^{5g} 4^{5g} 4^{5s}
6^{5s} **1-4-11 £7,631**

Uno Mente *E S McMahon* a41
6 b m Mind Games - One Half Silver (Can)
9^{7sd} 3^{7sd} 4^{8ss} **0-1-3 £215**

Unperturbed *Robert Gray* 23
5 ch m Unfuwain (USA) - Mudflap
8^{16gf} **0-0-1**

Unprecedented (Ire) *T T Clement* a32
4 br g Primo Dominie - Misellina (Fr)
4^{6sd} **0-0-1**

Unreal *B W Hills* 67
3 b f Dansili - Illusory
9^{5f} 12^{6g} **0-0-2**

Unreservedly *P F I Cole* 33 a6
3 b f Cadeaux Genereux - Iberian Dancer (Can)
8^{6sd} 8^{7gs} **0-0-2**

Unrestricted *C F Wall* 58 a55
3 ch f Mark Of Esteem (Ire) - Generous Lady
5^{10gf} 5^{10sd} 6^{10gs} 7^{10g} **0-0-4**

Unscrupulous *J R Fanshawe* 108
6 ch g Machiavellian (USA) - Footlight Fantasy (USA)
1^{7gf} **1-0-1 £9,700**

Unshakable (Ire) *Bob Jones* 98
6 b g Eagle Eyed (USA) - Pepper And Salt (Ire)
10^{10gf} 10^{8g} 2^{8g} 1^{8gs} 4^{8gs} **1-1-5**
£91,890

Unsuited *J E Long* 63
6 b m Revoque (Ire) - Nagnagnag (Ire)
8^{9gf} 8^{10gf} 8^{10g} 5^{10g} **0-0-4**

Untimely *H Morrison* 69
3 ch f Inchinor - All The Time
10^{8gf} 5^{10g} 8^{10gs} 1^{8gf} 3^{10gs} **1-0-5**
£3,071

Up At Dawn *M Blanshard* 44
2 b f Inchinor - Up And About
16^{7f} 10^{8g} 12^{8g} **0-0-3**

Up Dee Creek *Daniel Mark Loughnane* 52 a29
3 ch f Tipsy Creek (USA) - Sandra Dee (Ire)
13^{6sh} 9^{5sh} 5^{7s} 9^{7g} 10^{7g} 13^{8gf} 10^{8g} 14^{7sd}
0-0-8

Up Tempo (Ire) *K A Ryan* 79 a76
7 b g Flying Spur (Aus) - Musical Essence
7^{7sd} 3^{6sd} 6^{8sd} 12^{8g} 2^{6s} 1^{6g} 3^{6gf} 3^{6gf} 11^{6gf}
1-4-9 £6,299

Up The Order *J Pearce*
3 b f Forzando - Art Deco Lady
8^{12sd} 8^{10f} **0-0-2**

Upper Hand *M R Channon* 101
2 ch c Mark Of Esteem (Ire) - Pelagia (Ire)
1^{6gs} 5^{6gs} 2^{6gs} 4^{5hy} 15^{6g} **1-1-5 £23,646**

Upthedowns (Ire) *T D Barron* 63 a51
2 b g Beckett (Ire) - Golden Charm (Ire)
4^{6g} 4^{7g} 3^{7gf} 1^{6g} 2^{6gf} 16^{6s} 7^{7sf} 11^{6sd}
1-2-8 £4,523

Urabande *Julian Poulton*
3 b f Tipsy Creek (USA) - La Belle Mystere
17^{5s} 13^{7sd} **0-0-2**

Urban Calm *J W Unett* 60 a53
4 b f Cadeaux Genereux - Silver Sun
12^{5sd} 3^{7sd} 8^{7sd} 13^{9sd} 9^{6sd} 1^{5sd} 5^{6sd} 1^{6s} 9^{5sd}
10^{5sd} 6^{6sd} 6^{5sd} **2-1-12 £5,348**

Urban Knight *M J Gingell* a21
4 br g Dracula (Aus) - Anhaar
5^{12sd} 13^{12sd} **0-0-2**

Urban Rose *J W Unett* 55 a52
4 b f Piccolo - Blue Lamp (USA)
9^{7sd} 11^{6g} 5^{6gf} 6^{5sd} **0-0-4**

Urban Tiger (Ger) *A King* 80
2 b g Marju (Ire) - Ukraine Venture
3^{6gf} 3^{7gf} 4^{7g} 2^{8gf} 4^{9gf} 13^{7gs} **0-3-6**
£7,532

Ushindi (Ire) *M L W Bell* 66
3 b f Montjeu (Ire) - Fern
13^{7g} 5^{7gf} 17^{10gf} 12^{7gf} 3^{10g} 1^{12gf} 6^{14gf}
1-1-7 £3,404

Usk Poppy *D R C Elsworth* a52
2 b f Mark Of Esteem (Ire) - Wars (Ire)
7^{6sd} **0-0-1**

Ustad (Ire) *P L Gilligan* 69
3 br g Giant's Causeway (USA) - Winsa (USA)
6^{11gs} 9^{15gs} 13^{9sd} PU^{12ss} **0-0-4**

Utterly Heaven (Ire) *D K Weld* 106
3 b f Danehill (USA) - Epicure's Garden (USA)

4^{8s} 1^{7hy} 4^{8gy} 9^{8gf} 7^{8gy} **1-0-5 £19,031**

Vacation (Ire) *V Smith* 64
2 b c King Charlemagne (USA) - Lady Peculiar (Can)
3^{6hy} **0-1-1 £664**

Vadawina (Ire) *A Fabre* 116
3 b f Unfuwain (USA) - Vadaza (Fr)
1^{12vs} 1^{11gs} 1^{10g} 4^{11g} **3-0-4 £151,036**

Vademecum *B Smart* 38 a61
4 br g Shinko Forest (Ire) - Sunshine Coast
7^{6sd} 7^{6sd} 1^{6sd} 10^{7sd} 13^{6sd} 9^{7g} 8^{7g} **1-0-7 £1,456**

Vague (USA) *J Noseda* 99
2 b f Elusive Quality (USA) - April In Kentucky (USA)
5^{6gf} 1^{6gf} 2^{6gf} 2^{7gf} 4^{7g} **1-2-5 £25,192**

Vague Star (Ity) *R Ingram* 74 a68
3 b c Soviet Star (USA) - Simova (USA)
5^{5sd} 10^{5g} 6^{5g} 4^{5f} 1^{5gs} 9^{5gs} 16^{7g} 4^{5sd} 11^{5sf} 10^{5sd} 9^{6sd} **1-0-11 £4,856**

Val D'Isere *B J Meehan* a49
3 ch c Tomba - Dancing Diana
4^{7sd} 14^{7sd} **0-0-2**

Val De Maal (Ire) *Miss J A Camacho* 69 a63
5 ch g Eagle Eyed (USA) - Miss Bojangles
8^{7sd} 15^{6gs} 9^{7sd} 3^{7sd} 3^{7sd} 7^{6sd} 4^{6sd} 2^{6sd} 16^{6g} 3^{6g} 1^{6s} 4^{6sd} 2^{6g} 4^{6g} **1-6-14 £6,579**

Valance (Ire) *C R Egerton* 83
5 br g Bahhare (USA) - Glowlamp (Ire)
9^{14gf} 1^{12gf} 7^{16gf} 6^{13gf} **1-0-4 £16,997**

Vale De Lobo *P F Nicholls* 83
3 b f Loup Sauvage (USA) - Frog
5^{8gs} 2^{10gf} 1^{10g} 7^{10gf} 5^{11gs} 4^{12gs} **1-1-6 £7,129**

Valentin (Ire) *R Hannon* 87
3 ch f King Of Kings (Ire) - Slip Ashore (Ire)
9^{7g} 7^{7gf} 7^{10gf} 8^{10g} 10^{7f} **0-0-5**

Valentine Jak (Ire) *B R Millman* 15
2 b c Imperial Ballet (Ire) - Yahe (Ire)
8^{5gs} 11^{6gf} 9^{6g} **0-0-3**

Valentine's Pet *A W Carroll* 36 a31
5 b m My Best Valentine - Fabulous Pet
9^{10gs} 12^{12g} 10^{9sf} 8^{8sd} 9^{10sd} **0-0-5**

Valentino Swing (Ire) *J L Spearing* 74 a58
2 ch g Titus Livius (Fr) - Farmers Swing (Ire)
10^{6gf} 1^{6f} 1^{6gf} 4^{7sd} 6^{7gs} 1^{6g} **3-0-6 £11,031**

Valentino Taffi *S C Williams* a36
2 b g Primo Valentino (Ire) - Drudwen
8^{7sd} 11^{7sd} **0-0-2**

Valerie *L M Cumani* 55 a57
2 b f Sadler's Wells (USA) - Horatia (Ire)
15^{8gs} 7^{8sd} **0-0-2**

Valet *J G M O'Shea* 15
3 b g Kayf Tara - Val De Fleurie (Ger)
12^{10gs} **0-0-1**

Valeureux *J Hetherton* a49
7 ch g Cadeaux Genereux - La Strada
5^{14sd} **0-0-1**

Valhar *J R Jenkins* 36 a49
2 b f Diktat - Diamond Jayne (Ire)
12^{6s} 8^{6sd} 6^{7sd} **0-0-3**

Valiant Act (Ire) *D M Simcock* a47
3 b f Brave Act - Jungle Story (Ire)
6^{7sd} 6^{8sd} **0-0-2**

Valiant Romeo *R Bastiman* 63
5 b g Primo Dominie - Desert Lynx (Ire)
8^{6s} 1^{5gf} 4^{5gf} 5^{5f} 2^{5g} 2^{5g} 1^{5gf} 6^{5gf} 7^{5gf} 14^{5gf} **2-2-10 £7,506**

Valiant Shadow (Ger) *W Jarvis* 60
3 b g Winged Love (Ire) - Vangelis
10^{8gf} 19^{10g} 12^{10gs} 2^{10g} 5^{12gf} 11^{16gf} **0-1-6 £772**

Validation *P S McEntee* a44
3 b f Lake Coniston (Ire) - Khadino
9^{7sd} 6^{7sd} 9^{7sd} 3^{8sd} 15^{10gf} **0-0-5 £204**

Valixir (Ire) *A Fabre* 126
4 b c Trempolino (USA) - Vadlamixa (Fr)
3^{9gf} 1^{9g} 1^{8gf} 1^{8g} 3^{8gs} 5^{8g} 10^{8y} **3-1-7 £340,360**

Valjarv (Ire) *N P Littmoden* 92
4 b f Bluebird (USA) - Iktidar
7^{6gf} 2^{6gf} 8^{7gf} 10^{6g} 5^{7gf} 6^{6g} 6^{6gf} 5^{7gf} 15^{6gs} **0-1-9 £4,305**

Valley Parader *J R Norton* 25
2 b g Dansili - Glamorous
13^{7s} 8^{8gs} 18^{7g} **0-0-3**

Valuable Gift *J G M O'Shea* a40
8 ch g Cadeaux Genereux - Valbra
6^{7sd} 10^{9sd} 15^{8g} **0-0-3**

Value Plus (Ire) *T J Fitzgerald* 34
3 b f Mujadil (USA) - Brittas Blues (Ire)
8^{6s} 9^{6gf} **0-0-2**

Vamose (Ire) *Miss Gay Kelleway* 65 a64
4 ro g Victory Note (USA) - Narrow Band (Ire)
7^{9sd} 6^{12gf} 4^{9g} 4^{12g} **0-1-4 £1,785**

Vamp *R M Beckett* 83
4 b f Dracula (Aus) - Circe
7^{10gf} 2^{9gf} 3^{10gf} 4^{12gf} 4^{12g} 8^{10gf} 7^{10g} 1^{10gs} 1^{10s} **2-2-9 £7,436**

Vanadium *J G Given* 89
3 b g Dansili - Musianica
1^{6g} 3^{7gf} 1^{7g} 7^{8gf} 5^{8gf} 5^{7gf} 2^{6gs} 15^{6gs} **2-2-8 £14,361**

Vanbrugh (Fr) *Patrick G Kelly* 44 a76
5 ch g Starborough - Renovate
6^{16sd} 1^{16sd} 1^{14sd} 12^{16sd} 1^{16sd} PU^{14sd} 5^{16sd} 1^{11sd} 6^{12g} 12^{12ys} **4-0-10 £11,038**

Vancouver Gold (Ire) *K R Burke* 76 a67
3 b f Monashee Mountain (USA) - Forest Berries (Ire)
1^{7sd} 3^{8s} 16^{8g} **1-1-3 £3,806**

Vandenberghe *J A Osborne* 17
6 b g Millkom - Child Star (Fr)
13^{12g} **0-0-1**

Vanderlin *A M Balding* 114
6 ch g Halling (USA) - Massorah (Fr)
1^{7gs} 2^{7g} 14^{8gf} 2^{7gf} 8^{7gs} 1^{7f} 4^{8y} 2^{8f} 4^{6y} **2-3-9 £169,553**

Vanilla Delight (Ire) *J Howard Johnson* 75
2 b f Orpen (USA) - Fantastic Bid (USA)
5^{7gf} 1^{7gf} **1-0-2 £4,546**

Vanilla Moon *J R Jenkins* 45 a50
5 b m Emperor Jones (USA) - Daarat Alayaam (Ire)
10^{11sd} 4^{13sd} 2^{12gf} 9^{11g} 12^{10gf} **0-1-5 £870**

Vanish (Ire) *D R Loder* 46
3 b f Barathea (Ire) - Silver Hut (USA)
10^{8gf} 6^{10s} **0-0-2**

Vanishing Dancer (Swi) *B Ellison* 33 a60
8 ch g Llandaff (USA) - Vanishing Prairie (USA)
12^{18gs} 1^{12sd} 10^{17sd} 13^{16sf} **1-0-4 £2,528**

Var (USA) *C E Brittain* 113

6 b/br h Forest Wildcat (USA) - Loma Preata (USA)
$8^{5gf}\ 6^{5gf}\ 5^{6f}$ **0-0-3 £8,964**

Varuni (Ire) *P L Clinton* a50
4 b f Ali-Royal (Ire) - Sauvignon (Ire)
$10^{10sd}\ 4^{13sd}\ 8^{13sd}\ 8^{12sd}\ 13^{12gf}\ 14^{11sd}$
0-0-6 £263

Vaudevire *Peter Grayson* a43
4 b g Dancing Spree (USA) - Approved Quality (Ire)
$9^{5sd}\ 12^{5sd}\ 7^{5sd}\ 9^{5sd}\ 7^{6sd}\ 6^{5sd}\ 5^{5sd}\ 9^{5sd}\ 1^{5sd}$
10^{6ss} **1-0-10 £2,898**

Vaughan *H D Daly* 99
4 b g Machiavellian (USA) - Labibeh (USA)
$13^{12s}\ 1^{12gf}\ 5^{12f}\ 9^{12gf}\ 10^{14gs}\ 16^{14g}\ 3^{12g}\ 1^{12gs}$
2-1-8 £20,479

Veba (USA) *B W Hills* 64 a62
2 ch g Black Minnaloushe (USA) - Make Over (USA)
$7^{6gf}\ 4^{7sd}\ 6^{6gf}$ **0-0-3 £240**

Vegas Boys *N A Callaghan* 76
2 b g Royal Applause - Brief Glimpse (Ire)
$9^{7g}\ 5^{6gs}\ 5^{6g}\ 1^{6gf}\ 3^{6gf}\ 9^{6g}$ **1-1-6**
£4,191

Vehari *M Scudamore* 25 a35
2 ch g Tomba - Nannie Annie
$13^{6gf}\ 11^{8sd}\ 10^{7sd}$ **0-0-3**

Veiled Applause *R M Beckett* 63
2 b g Royal Applause - Scarlet Veil
$7^{6gf}\ 7^{5gs}\ 8^{5g}$ **0-0-3**

Velocitas *W M Brisbourne* 49 a56
4 b g Magic Ring (Ire) - Folly Finnesse
$9^{12sd}\ 9^{10s}\ 8^{12gf}\ 6^{14gs}\ 10^{14sd}\ 6^{10gf}\ 7^{8gf}\ 12^{11g}$
$2^{10g}\ 3^{9sd}\ 1^{9ss}$ **1-2-11 £2,064**

Velvet Heights (Ire) *J L Dunlop* 86
3 b c Barathea (Ire) - Height Of Fantasy (Ire)
$6^{10g}\ 5^{12g}\ 6^{14g}\ 3^{14g}\ 3^{16g}\ 2^{15s}$ **0-3-6**
£4,646

Velvet Touch *D M Simcock* 46 a49
4 b f Danzig Connection (USA) - Soft Touch (Ger)
$10^{5sd}\ 4^{5sd}\ 7^{5sd}\ 4^{5sd}\ 9^{5sd}\ 3^{5sd}\ 10^{5sd}\ 2^{5sd}\ 8^{5sd}$
$8^{5sd}\ 5^{5gf}\ 17^{6gf}\ 4^{5f}\ 3^{5f}\ 7^{5sd}\ 6^{5ss}\ 4^{5sd}$
0-3-17 £1,042

Velvet Valley (USA) *Sir Michael Stoute* 64
2 ch c Gone West (USA) - Velvet Morning (USA)
7^{7gf} **0-0-1**

Velvet Waters *R F Johnson Houghton* 77 a68
4 b f Unfuwain (USA) - Gleaming Water
$14^{14g}\ 2^{12gf}\ 3^{12gf}\ 2^{11f}\ 5^{12gf}\ 2^{12g}\ 7^{12sd}\ 4^{12g}$
$5^{14gf}\ 2^{13gf}\ 2^{11g}\ 5^{12gf}\ 8^{12sd}$ **0-6-13**
£8,775

Venables (USA) *D Nicholls* 92 a60
4 ch g Stravinsky (USA) - Hope For A Breeze (Can)
$9^{6gf}\ 29^{6gf}\ 19^{6g}\ 10^{7sd}\ 11^{5s}$ **0-0-5**

Vendors Mistake (Ire) *Andrew Reid* 39 a50
4 b f Danehill (USA) - Sunspangled (Ire)
$8^{7sd}\ 7^{5sd}\ 3^{6sd}\ 5^{6sd}\ 8^{7sd}\ 7^{10g}\ 6^{12gf}$ **0-1-7**
£209

Veneer (Ire) *Miss Gay Kelleway* 76 a61
3 b g Woodborough (USA) - Sweet Lass
$10^{10sd}\ 1^{9gs}\ 11^{9sd}\ 13^{8gf}\ 10^{8sd}\ 18^{7hy}\ 12^{9sd}$
$14^{8sd}\ 6^{8sd}\ 6^{8sd}$ **1-0-10 £4,758**

Venetian King (USA) *J Howard Johnson* 73
3 b g King Of Kings (Ire) - Vena (Ire)
$3^{9gf}\ 4^{7g}\ 1^{10gf}$ **1-1-3 £5,975**

Venetian Lullaby (USA) *T D Barron* 65
3 b/br f Lear Fan (USA) - Wellomond (Fr)
1^{8s} **1-0-1 £3,503**

Venetian Princess (Ire) *P Howling* 49 a49
3 b f Desert Style (Ire) - Dance With Care
$8^{8gf}\ 9^{8g}\ 9^{8gf}\ 11^{8g}\ 6^{7g}\ 6^{8sd}\ 2^{8sd}\ 1^{8sd}\ 6^{8sd}$
1-1-9 £1,884

Venetian Romance (Ire) *D J S Ffrench Davis*
4 ch f Desert Story (Ire) - Cipriani
11^{12ss} **0-0-1**

Veneto (Ire) *M R Channon* 49
2 ch g Spinning World (USA) - Padua (Ire)
$8^{7gf}\ 7^{7gf}\ 10^{7g}$ **0-0-3**

Vengeance Of Rain (NZ) *D Ferraris* 127
4 b g Zabeel (NZ) - Danelagh (Aus)
$1^{8gf}\ 1^{10g}\ 1^{10gy}\ 1^{10gf}\ 1^{12g}\ 8^{7g}\ 5^{8gf}\ 1^{10gf}\ 1^{10gf}$
7-0-9 £2,301,229

Verbier (USA) *N A Callaghan* 53
3 b f Fusaichi Pegasus (USA) - Oh Nellie (USA)
$13^{7gf}\ 10^{8g}\ 7^{7gf}$ **0-0-3**

Verification *J Howard Johnson* 66
2 ch c Medicean - Viewfinder (USA)
$5^{8gf}\ 10^{8s}\ 8^{7s}$ **0-0-3**

Veritable *S Kirk* 31
3 br f So Factual (USA) - Madam Trilby
$9^{6gf}\ 10^{5gs}$ **0-0-2**

Verite *M J Polglase* 68 a57
2 b g Foxhound (USA) - Blushing Victoria
$3^{5g}\ 6^{5gf}\ 5^{5sd}\ 1^{5gf}\ 10^{5gf}\ 8^{5gf}\ 3^{5gf}\ 7^{6g}\ 9^{5gs}$
1-0-9 £6,692

Vermilion Creek *R Hollinshead* 44 a37
6 b m Makbul - Cloudy Reef
$8^{9sd}\ 11^{9sd}\ 8^{8g}\ 7^{8s}\ 7^{8g}\ 9^{8gf}\ 7^{10gf}\ 7^{10f}$
0-0-8

Veronica's Girl *P R Hedger* 30 a66
2 b f Desert Prince (Ire) - Veronica Franco
$12^{8gs}\ 3^{8sd}\ 1^{7sd}$ **1-1-3 £4,309**

Versify *Julian Poulton* 7 a46
3 br f Vettori (Ire) - Tirolina (Ire)
$10^{10sd}\ 5^{9gf}$ **0-0-2**

Verstone (Ire) *R F Fisher* 41
3 b f Brave Act - Golden Charm (Ire)
$11^{7sd}\ 4^{14g}\ 4^{16g}\ 5^{16gf}\ 5^{14g}$ **0-1-5 £513**

Vertigo Blue *C W Thornton* 37 a37
2 b g Averti (Ire) - Soft Colours
$9^{5gf}\ 9^{6g}\ 16^{6g}\ 7^{9sd}\ 9^{9sd}$ **0-0-5**

Very Agreeable *W R Swinburn* a59
2 b f Pursuit Of Love - Oomph
3^{9sf} **0-1-1 £368**

Very Wise *W J Haggas* 92
3 b g Pursuit Of Love - With Care
$6^{8gf}\ 4^{9gf}\ 15^{10gs}\ 4^{10gf}\ 4^{8s}$ **0-0-5 £2,549**

Vesta Flame *Miss L V Davis* a22
4 b f Vettori (Ire) - Ciel De Feu (USA)
$UR^{8sd}\ 6^{12sd}$ **0-0-2**

Vettorious *Mrs P Sly* 51 a47
3 ch g Vettori (Ire) - Sleepless
$8^{9gf}\ 15^{8s}\ 10^{7g}\ 4^{11gf}\ 1^{8g}\ 5^{9sd}\ 10^{8ss}$
1-0-7 £1,750

Veverka *W S Kittow* 40 a35
4 b f King's Theatre (Ire) - Once Smitten (Ire)
$11^{8g}\ 7^{10g}\ 8^{12sd}$ **0-0-3**

Viable *Mrs P Sly* 71
3 b g Vettori (Ire) - Danseuse Davis (Fr)
$3^{10gs}\ 10^{10gf}\ 5^{12gf}\ 2^{10gf}\ 14^{10gf}\ 10^{8gf}\ 8^{10gf}$
0-2-7 £2,593

Vibe *R J Price* 63 a50
4 gr g Danzero (Aus) - Courting
$9^{8s}\ 8^{8hy}\ 2^{8f}\ 8^{10g}\ 11^{8g}\ 9^{8gf}\ 9^{8gf}\ 8^{7g}\ 7^{9sd}$

4^{7sf} 9^{9sd} 5^{9ss} **0-1-12 £1,401**

Vicars Destiny *Mrs S Lamyman* 78
7 b m Sir Harry Lewis (USA) - Church Leap
4^{18gs} 3^{16gs} 1^{22s} 1^{20s} 6^{18gf} 6^{16gf} 5^{16g} 5^{18gs} 7^{17g} 9^{18gs} **2-0-10 £14,128**

Vicat Cole *Mrs L J Mongan* a65
4 ch g Hector Protector (USA) - Dancing Spirit (Ire)
2^{10sd} **0-1-1 £1,072**

Vice Admiral *M W Easterby* 70
2 ch g Vettori (Ire) - Queen Of Scotland (Ire)
9^{8gf} 7^{7s} 6^{7g} 14^{10g} 16^{7g} 21^{7s} **0-0-6**

Vicious Knight *D Nicholls* 93
7 b g Night Shift (USA) - Myth
12^{8gs} 1^{7f} 13^{8g} 10^{7gf} 17^{8gs} 3^{8gf} 7^{7g}
1-1-7 £9,502

Vicious Prince (Ire) *R M Whitaker* 76
6 b g Sadler's Wells (USA) - Sunny Flower (Fr)
14^{14s} DSQ^{16s} 5^{12g} 1^{16g} 3^{16g} 2^{17g} 7^{20s}
1-1-7 £7,237

Vicious Warrior *R M Whitaker* 89 a86
6 b g Elmaamul (USA) - Ling Lane
11^{8gf} 7^{10gf} 4^{8gf} 10^{9gf} 3^{8g} 2^{8g} 16^{8gs} 6^{8gf} 11^{8gf} 16^{8gf} 4^{8g} 12^{8gf} 3^{8sd} 6^{8sd} **0-3-14**
£7,007

Vicky Pollard *A Berry* 57
2 b f King Charlemagne (USA) - Day Star
6^{5gf} 6^{5gf} 5^{5gf} 13^{5sd} **0-0-4**

Victimised (Ire) *A B Haynes* a40
3 b g Victory Note (USA) - Eurolink Virago
5^{5sd} 5^{5sd} 8^{6sd} 10^{6sd} **0-0-4**

Victor Buckwell *B Ellison* 43 a45
3 br g Pivotal - Lonely Shore
7^{9s} 2^{11sd} 7^{12gf} 13^{12gf} 8^{8gf} **0-1-5 £414**

Victor Rossini (Ire) *G C H Chung* a57
3 ch c Rossini (USA) - Right To The Top
6^{7sd} 7^{7sd} 5^{9sd} **0-0-3**

Victoria Peek (Ire) *D Nicholls* 67
3 b f Cape Cross (Ire) - Night Spirit (Ire)
7^{7gs} 9^{6gf} 7^{6s} 4^{5gf} 3^{6f} 1^{6g} 1^{6gf} 4^{6gf} 6^{5gf} 6^{6gf}
2-1-10 £7,769

Victoriana *H J Collingridge* 44 a34
4 b f Wolfhound (USA) - Silk St James
10^{7g} 12^{8gf} 13^{6sd} 13^{7sd} 14^{6g} 13^{9sd} 5^{6sd}
0-0-7

Victory Design (Ire) *J Noseda* 80
3 b c Danehill (USA) - Sun Silk (USA)
3^{8g} 1^{9g} 2^{8gf} 6^{10g} **1-2-4 £7,377**

Victory Hymn (Ire) *M R Channon* 16
3 b f Victory Note (USA) - Nordic Union (Ire)
20^{10g} 16^{7g} **0-0-2**

Victory Quest (Ire) *Mrs S Lamyman* 67 a71
5 b g Victory Note (USA) - Marade (USA)
7^{11sd} 6^{12sd} 12^{17sd} 3^{16sd} 6^{16s} 8^{12sd} **0-1-6**
£517

Vienna's Boy (Ire) *W J Musson* 77 a73
4 b g Victory Note (USA) - Shinkoh Rose (Fr)
8^{6s} 6^{6gs} 8^{6gs} 6^{7gf} 9^{8gf} 7^{8gs} 4^{7sd} 8^{7g} 5^{6sd} 1^{7sd} 6^{7sd} **1-0-11 £3,000**

Viewforth *I Semple* 74 a65
7 b g Emarati (USA) - Miriam
2^{5sd} 10^{6gs} 2^{6gs} 2^{5gf} 1^{5g} 2^{6s} 6^{5gf} 4^{6f} 7^{5g} 4^{6gs} 12^{6sd} 11^{6hy} **1-5-12 £9,433**

Vigorous (Ire) *M Todhunter* 58
5 b m Danetime (Ire) - Merrily
14^{6gf} 4^{5gf} 11^{5gf} 7^{5g} 11^{6gf} 9^{6gf} **0-0-6**
£324

Vijay (Ire) *W G Harrison* 49 a11
6 ch g Eagle Eyed (USA) - Foolish Fun
9^{5sd} 15^{6gf} 4^{5g} 14^{5gf} 14^{6gs} **0-0-5 £312**

Viking Spirit *W R Swinburn* 102
3 b g Mind Games - Dane Dancing (Ire)
2^{6g} 3^{6gf} 3^{6g} 7^{7g} 10^{6g} **0-3-5 £17,916**

Viking Star (Ire) *A D Brown* 38 a38
4 b g Indian Rocket - Nordic Flavour (Ire)
13^{5sh} 11^{8g} 7^{7f} 8^{7gf} 8^{11g} 11^{14sd} 5^{8g} 12^{7sd} 7^{9sd} **0-0-9**

Villa Sonata *J R Fanshawe* a62
2 b f Mozart (Ire) - Villa Carlotta
3^{7sd} **0-1-1 £604**

Villago (Ger) *E W Tuer* 70
5 b g Laroche (Ger) - Village (Ger)
4^{14gs} 2^{16g} 1^{16g} 4^{17g} 3^{16gf} 5^{16g} 4^{17g} 7^{18gs}
1-2-8 £7,871

Villarosi (Ire) *P W Chapple-Hyam* a53
3 b f Rossini (USA) - Trinida
5^{10sd} **0-0-1**

Villarrica (USA) *Sir Michael Stoute* 80
3 ch f Selkirk (USA) - Melikah (Ire)
1^{11gf} 5^{12f} 5^{12gf} 1^{10g} 5^{11gf} **2-0-5 £7,363**

Vinando *C R Egerton* 106
4 ch c Hernando (Fr) - Sirena (Ger)
20^{14g} 2^{12hy} 4^{16g} 4^{18gs} 3^{14gs} 2^{16hy} **0-4-6**
£24,235

Vincent Vegas *Mrs S Lamyman* 7 a17
2 b g Foxhound (USA) - Annie's Song
14^{6g} 11^{5gs} 9^{5sd} 17^{8s} **0-0-4**

Vindication *R M H Cowell* 78
5 ch g Compton Place - Prince's Feather (Ire)
11^{6g} 7^{6gs} 17^{7g} 3^{7f} 9^{6f} 8^{6gf} 2^{7f} 5^{7gf} 6^{7gf} 13^{8gf} 2^{7g} 4^{7g} 7^{7g} **0-4-13 £4,643**

Viniyoga *M H Tompkins* 33 a11
3 b g Cadeaux Genereux - Optimistic
13^{10g} 9^{10gf} 12^{10gf} 8^{12s} 14^{12sd} **0-0-5**

Vinnie Roe (Ire) *D K Weld* 119
7 b/br h Definite Article - Kayu
1^{14gf} 3^{20gf} 3^{12gf} 3^{14g} 8^{16gs} **1-2-5**
£115,534

Vino *B W Hills* a38
2 b f Efisio - Polo
9^{6sd} **0-0-1**

Vino Venus *Miss Sheena West* 22
3 b f Tipsy Creek (USA) - Galaxy Glow
10^{10g} 13^{8f} 8^{11gs} **0-0-3**

Vinska (USA) *J W Hills* 49 a35
2 br f Stravinsky (USA) - Konvincha (USA)
9^{8sd} 8^{8g} 11^{7gf} **0-0-3**

Vintage Times (Ire) *R A Fahey* 37 a44
3 b/br g Namid - Vintage Escape (Ire)
9^{8g} 10^{5sd} 13^{6sf} **0-0-3**

Violent Velocity (Ire) *J J Quinn* 66
2 b c Namid - Lear's Crown (USA)
5^{6g} 4^{7s} **0-0-2**

Violet Avenue *G A Swinbank* 59 a7
4 ch f Muhtarram (USA) - Ivoronica
3^{8s} 15^{8g} 8^{9s} 8^{9gf} 12^{8sd} 8^{10g} **0-1-6**
£539

Violet Ballerina (Ire) *B J Meehan* 72
2 b f Namid - Violet Spring (Ire)
4^{6gf} 1^{7gf} 5^{7hy} 12^{7gs} **1-0-4 £5,171**

Violet Park *B J Meehan* 101 a83

4 b f Pivotal - Petonellajill
1^{8g} 6^{7g} 14^{7gf} 10^{7gf} 4^{7sd} 6^{7g} 2^{7g} 13^{7gf} 2^{8s}
1-2-9 £15,441

Violette *Sir Mark Prescott* 110
2 b f Observatory (USA) - Odette
1^{6g} 2^{5f} 7^{6gf} 2^{6gf} 1^{6gf} 1^{7gf} 1^{6g} 2^{6gf} 2^{7gs} 3^{7gs}
4-3-10 £125,864

Virgin Soldier (Ire) *G A Swinbank* 74
9 ch g Waajib - Never Been Chaste
11^{16g} 4^{16gf} 8^{16gf} **0-0-3 £267**

Virgin's Tears *D E Cantillon*
3 b f Bishop Of Cashel - Lola Mora
6^{6s} 11^{5g} 11^{8gf} **0-0-3**

Virginia Rose (Ire) *J G Given* 54
2 b f Galileo (Ire) - Rispoto
6^{7s} **0-0-1**

Virginia Waters (USA) *A P O'Brien* 115
3 b f Kingmambo (USA) - Legend Maker (Ire)
1^{7ys} 1^{8gf} 8^{8gy} 4^{12g} 6^{8gf} 6^{10gs} 3^{8gy} 10^{8gs}
2-1-8 £278,192

Virtue *C F Swan* 82
3 ch f Vettori (Ire) - Zenith
2^{10gs} 1^{10gf} 1^{12g} 9^{12g} **2-1-4 £11,660**

Viscount Rossini *D Haydn Jones* a43
3 b/br g Rossini (USA) - Spain
7^{9sd} 4^{12sd} 8^{12sd} 5^{12sd} **0-0-4 £316**

Vision Victory (Ger) *T P Tate* a29
3 b g Dashing Blade - Val D'Isere (Ger)
13^{11sd} 10^{9sd} **0-0-2**

Visionist (Ire) *J A Osborne* 98
3 b g Orpen (USA) - Lady Taufan (Ire)
11^{7gf} 2^{6g} 13^{6gf} 9^{6gf} 5^{7g} 17^{7gs} **0-1-6**
£3,240

Vista Bella *M A Jarvis* 108 a77
3 b f Diktat - Cox Orange (USA)
1^{7sd} 1^{8gs} 3^{8gf} **2-1-3 £58,049**

Vittorioso (Ire) *B P J Baugh* a51
4 b g Victory Note (USA) - Miss Anita (Ire)
4^{11sd} 13^{10sd} 7^{10sd} 4^{12sd} 2^{8sd} 2^{7sd} 9^{7sd} 7^{6sd}
13^{7sd} **0-2-9 £833**

Viva Forever (Fr) *A M Hales* 5
6 br m Lando (Ger) - Very Mighty (Fr)
11^{12g} **0-0-1**

Viva Volta *T D Easterby* 68
2 b c Superior Premium - La Volta
3^{5gf} 1^{5gf} 15^{6g} 18^{6g} 19^{6s} **1-1-5 £4,569**

Vivre Sa Vie *Sir Mark Prescott* 30 a49
4 ch f Nashwan (USA) - La Strada
6^{11sd} 9^{12g} **0-0-2**

Vixen Virago *Jane Southcombe* 50 a29
2 ch f Foxhound (USA) - Le Pin
11^{8sd} 9^{6gs} 6^{5sd} 11^{6g} **0-0-4**

Viz (Ire) *Sir Mark Prescott* 102 a81
3 b f Darshaan - For Example (USA)
3^{10g} 2^{12gf} 1^{12sd} 2^{14gf} 7^{12s} 3^{12gs} 1^{12gs}
2-4-7 £35,186

Vizulize *A W Carroll* 30 a64
6 b m Robellino (USA) - Euridice (Ire)
6^{12sd} 2^{10sd} 5^{10sd} 2^{9sd} 1^{9sd} 5^{10sd} 1^{9sd} 4^{9sd} 4^{8sd}
4^{9sd} 1^{9sd} 10^{10g} 14^{11gf} 15^{8gf} 7^{9sd} 6^{10sd} 11^{7sd}
3-2-17 £6,398

Vlasta Weiner *J M Bradley* 33 a66
5 b g Magic Ring (Ire) - Armaiti
1^{7sd} 2^{5sd} 2^{6sd} 4^{7sd} 1^{6sd} 6^{7sd} 5^{6sd} 5^{5sd} 14^{6g}
10^{8g} 1^{6sd} 2^{5sd} 8^{6g} 12^{5ss} 1^{7sd} 1^{6sd} 7^{6sd} 4^{6sd}
5-3-18 £12,310

Vocative (Ger) *P C Haslam* 58 a25
3 gr f Acatenango (Ger) - Vadinaxa (Fr)
8^{11sd} 10^{14gf} 3^{12g} **0-0-3 £642**

Vodkatini *P J Makin* 60 a70
2 b g Bertolini (USA) - Cold Blow
12^{8g} 4^{7s} 5^{7sd} 4^{8sd} **0-0-4 £572**

Voice Mail *A M Balding* 84
6 b g So Factual (USA) - Wizardry
12^{8g} 2^{7g} 8^{8gf} 3^{11gf} 9^{10g} 7^{10gf} 1^{8f} 10^{10gf} 3^{8f}
9^{9gs} 2^{8gf} 7^{10gf} 3^{8g} 6^{10gf} 6^{8f} 14^{8gs}
1-3-16 £15,915

Voile (Ire) *L M Cumani* 102
4 b f Barathea (Ire) - Samriah (Ire)
3^{7g} 7^{8gf} 9^{8gf} **0-1-3 £5,500**

Voir Dire *Mrs P N Dutfield* 61
3 b g Vettori (Ire) - Bobbie Dee
5^{12s} 6^{14g} 8^{16gs} **0-0-3**

Volitio *S Kirk* 44
3 b g Mind Games - Millie's Lady (Ire)
17^{8g} 12^{7gf} 8^{10gf} 16^{12gf} 14^{12gf} **0-0-5**

Voluptuous *T H Caldwell*
5 b m Polish Precedent (USA) - Alzianah
12^{9sd} **0-0-1**

Von Wessex *W G M Turner* 61 a38
3 b g Wizard King - Gay Da Cheen (Ire)
7^{6hy} 3^{5gf} 8^{6sd} 8^{6f} **0-1-4 £368**

Vonadaisy *R A Harris* 32 a53
4 b f Averti (Ire) - Vavona
10^{6sd} 4^{7sd} 8^{9sd} 8^{8sd} 11^{8sd} 15^{6gf} 10^{7f} 9^{7f}
0-0-8

Vondova *R Hannon* 68
3 b f Efisio - Well Proud (Ire)
12^{7gf} 7^{6g} 14^{8g} **0-0-3**

Voom *M R Channon* 16
3 b f Fraam - Natalie Jay
12^{6gf} 11^{8f} 15^{7g} **0-0-3**

Vortex *Miss Gay Kelleway* 115 a117
6 b g Danehill (USA) - Roupala (USA)
2^{9sd} 5^{8g} 1^{7sd} 7^{9g} 1^{7gf} 1^{7g} 3^{8sd} 14^{7gs} 7^{6g}
2^{8sd} 2^{7gf} 10^{7sd} **3-4-12 £78,205**

Votsi (USA) *Saeed Bin Suroor* 52
2 ch f A.P. Indy (USA) - Set In Motion (USA)
5^{7f} 6^{8gf} **0-0-2**

Vracca *M C Pipe* 82
3 ch f Vettori (Ire) - Crystal Cavern (USA)
2^{9g} 10^{9hy} 5^{11gs} 1^{10g} 3^{10g} 9^{12gs} 11^{13gf} 9^{10g}
7^{10g} **1-1-9 £11,254**

Vrisaki (Ire) *M E Sowersby* 32 a51
4 b g Docksider (USA) - Kingdom Queen (Ire)
4^{12sd} 1^{8sd} 4^{11sd} 4^{8sd} 11^{10sd} 12^{10g} 14^{8g} 12^{8g}
10^{12sd} **1-0-9 £1,449**

Vrubel (Ire) *J R Holt* 1 a48
6 ch g Entrepreneur - Renzola
2^{9sd} 12^{10s} 16^{10g} **0-1-3 £375**

Waddon (Ire) *C G Cox* 70
2 b c Green Desert (USA) - Baldemara (Fr)
4^{6gf} 4^{5gs} 4^{6f} **0-0-3 £1,154**

Wadmaan *R J Hodges* 72
6 b g Singspiel (Ire) - Rum Cay (USA)
6^{10gs} 17^{10gs} 6^{16g} **0-0-3**

Wafani *John Berry* 8
6 b g Mtoto - Wafa (Ire)
8^{10f} **0-0-1**

Wages *Evan Williams* a65

5 b g Lake Coniston (Ire) - Green Divot
11[10sd] **0-0-1**

Waggledance (Ire) *J S Wainwright* 59
3 b g Mujadil (USA) - Assertive Lass (USA)
15[6s] 7[6gs] 6[5gf] 6[5g] 4[5gf] 9[6g] 9[6gf] 11[8g]
0-0-8 £263

Wahchi (Ire) *M W Easterby* 64
6 ch g Nashwan (USA) - Nafhaat (USA)
11[9g] 8[8g] 1[10gf] 7[11gf] **1-0-4 £4,134**

Wahoo Sam (USA) *K A Ryan* 83
5 ch g Sandpit (Brz) - Good Reputation (USA)
10[8g] 5[8gf] 7[8g] 10[8gs] 1[8gf] 4[9gf] 1[10gf] 10[9g] 18[9gs]
2-0-9 £11,566

Wainwright (Ire) *P A Blockley* 66 a74
5 b g Victory Note (USA) - Double Opus (Ire)
9[7sd] 3[6sd] 3[6sd] 8[7sd] 1[6sd] 2[6gs] 6[8g] 3[6gs] 1[6gf]
9[6gf] 8[8gf] 7[7gf] 4[7gs] 6[5sd] 2[6sd] 3[7sd] **2-6-16**
£11,727

Wait For The Will (USA) *G L Moore* 83 a78
9 ch g Seeking The Gold (USA) - You'd Be Surprised (USA)
12[12gf] 13[12gf] 20[12g] 2[12g] 6[12g] 2[14gf] 7[13gf] 9[12sd]
6[12sd] 5[13sd] **0-2-10 £4,533**

Waiting For Mary (Ire) *J G M O'Shea* 62
2 b f Tagula (Ire) - Lady Abigail (Ire)
9[6g] 3[6gf] 1[7g] 6[7gf] 6[7g] 5[7gf] **1-0-6**
£3,968

Wake (USA) *M Johnston* 72 a65
5 b g Storm Cat (USA) - Ladies Cruise (USA)
12[8sd] 10[10ft] 10[8g] **0-0-3**

Wake Up Maggie (Ire) *C F Wall* 109 a90
2 b f Xaar - Kalagold (Ire)
1[5gf] 2[5sd] 1[6g] 2[6g] **2-2-4 £149,479**

Waki Naki Noo (USA) *B Smart* 69
2 b c Miswaki (USA) - Dippers (USA)
5[6g] **0-0-1**

Walk In The Park (Ire) *J E Hammond* 121
3 b c Montjeu (Ire) - Classic Park
2[11g] 2[12g] 8[12gf] **0-2-3 £291,107**

Walklikeanegyptian (Ire) *R Hannon* 77
2 b f Danehill (USA) - Ahdaab (USA)
6[5g] 4[5gf] 5[5gf] 4[5gf] 1[5gf] **1-0-5 £4,324**

Walkonthewildside *D R Loder* 103
3 b c Giant's Causeway (USA) - Wannabe Grand (Ire)
1[7g] 1[7gf] **2-0-2 £16,165**

Walnut Grove *T D Barron* 50
2 b f Forzando - Final Rush
6[6gf] 4[5g] 7[5gf] **0-0-3 £263**

Waltzing Wizard *A Berry* a53
6 b g Magic Ring (Ire) - Legendary Dancer
8[7sd] 4[7sd] 11[8sd] 3[9sd] 7[8sd] 2[8sd] PU[7g] **0-2-7**
£631

Wanchai Lad *D Nicholls* 92
4 b g Danzero (Aus) - Frisson
13[5gs] 13[5gf] 1[5gf] 7[5f] 6[5gf] 9[6g] 3[5s] 9[5s] 7[6gs]
2[5gs] 8[5gs] 14[5hy] **1-2-12 £16,643**

Wandering Act (Ire) *A W Carroll* 41 a37
3 b g Brave Act - Cwm Deri (Ire)
9[7sd] 8[7gs] 16[8g] 8[9sd] 6[10g] 10[12f] 10[10g] 5[12f]
8[9sf] 7[8gs] 7[9sd] **0-0-11**

Wanna Shout *R Dickin* 48 a56
7 b m Missed Flight - Lulu
10[8sd] 12[9sd] 10[9sd] 1[9sd] 11[9sd] 6[8gf] 12[9sd] 9[9sd]
2[8sd] **1-1-9 £1,893**

Wannabe Posh (Ire) *J L Dunlop* 58
2 b f Grand Lodge (USA) - Wannabe
9[7g] 12[7g] 10[7g] **0-0-3**

Wansdyke Lass *M R Channon* 63
3 b f Josr Algarhoud (Ire) - Silankka
3[9s] 10[10gs] 12[8g] 1[10gs] 5[9s] 5[10gf] 7[12gf]
1-1-7 £3,060

War At Sea (Ire) *M P Tregoning* 84
3 b g Bering - Naval Affair (Ire)
1[8gf] 12[9gf] 4[10g] 7[11gf] 8[12g] **1-0-5 £8,086**

War Dancer *E A Wheeler* 40
3 b g Wolfhound (USA) - Batchworth Dancer
13[6s] 10[6g] **0-0-2**

War Feather *T D McCarthy* 44 a45
3 b c Selkirk (USA) - Sit Alkul (USA)
14[13sd] 12[10gs] 7[10sd] **0-0-3**

War Owl (USA) *Ian Williams* 74 a77
8 gr g Linamix (Fr) - Ganasheba (USA)
9[11g] 7[10g] 9[11g] 3[10g] 8[10gs] 3[12gf] 3[12sd] 1[14sd] 2[12sd]
1-4-9 £5,592

War Pennant *M R Channon* 69 a69
3 b g Selkirk (USA) - Bunting
12[10sd] 1[12sd] 4[12g] 3[12g] 8[12gf] **1-2-5**
£5,112

War Sword (USA) *G A Butler* 42
2 ch c Diesis - Lamsat Al Hob
11[7gs] **0-0-1**

Warbreck *C R Egerton* a47
4 ch g Selkirk (USA) - Wigging
7[16sd] 4[12sd] 8[12sd] **0-0-3 £260**

Warden Warren *Mrs C A Dunnett* 70 a75
7 b g Petong - Silver Spell
12[7sd] 6[7sd] 10[8sd] 12[8sd] 12[7g] 15[8gf] 9[7g] 11[7gf]
5[7gf] 9[7gf] 1[7gf] 13[8gf] 16[7g] 11[7sd] 7[8sd] 10[8sd]
1-0-16 £4,323

Wares Home (Ire) *K R Burke* a51
4 b g Indian Rocket - Pepilin
3[7sd] 5[7sd] 5[7sd] 13[7sd] **0-1-4 £211**

Warlingham (Ire) *P Howling* 57 a55
7 b g Catrail (USA) - Tadjnama (USA)
5[7sd] 5[7sd] 6[7sd] 3[9sd] 3[9sd] 6[9sd] 10[7sd] 8[8sd] 1[6gf]
2[7g] 1[7f] 9[7gf] 2[6gf] 8[7f] 2[7gf] 17[6gf] 12[6f] 15[6f]
8[7s] **2-5-19 £8,053**

Warren Place *J Hetherton* a47
5 ch g Presidium - Coney Hills
3[7sd] 9[7sd] 8[7sd] 3[6sd] 10[7sd] **0-1-5 £1,049**

Warrsan (Ire) *C E Brittain* 122
7 b h Caerleon (USA) - Lucayan Princess
4[12gf] 4[12g] 5[10gf] 4[12gf] 1[12g] 8[12gs] 13[12f] 12[12gf]
1-0-8 £380,075

Warsaw Pact (Ire) *Sir Mark Prescott* 49 a49
2 b g Polish Precedent (USA) - Always Friendly
5[6gs] 5[7s] 7[9sd] **0-0-3**

Wasalat (USA) *Miss Gay Kelleway* 76
3 b f Bahri (USA) - Saabga (USA)
6[6gs] 8[6gf] 2[7f] 1[10gf] 7[10g] **1-1-5 £4,734**

Washabul *R Hollinshead* 25 a20
2 b f Makbul - Washm (USA)
12[8hy] 11[6sd] 13[9sd] **0-0-3**

Washbrook *M D Hammond* 46
4 b g Royal Applause - Alacrity
8[8g] 13[10gf] 12[10g] 17[10gf] **0-0-4**

Wasseema (USA) *Sir Michael Stoute* 73
2 br f Danzig (USA) - Vantive (USA)
3[6gf] **0-1-1 £872**

Wassfa *C E Brittain* 71
2 b f Mark Of Esteem (Ire) - Mistle Song

3^{7gf} 4^{7gf} **0-0-2 £1,546**

Watch Out Jess *M Madgwick* 52
2 gr f Averti (Ire) - Out Line
7^{6g} 5^{6f} 5^{5gs} 6^{5gf} 9^{5gf} **0-0-5**

Watchmyeyes (Ire) *R W Price* 69 a82
3 ch g Bold Fact (USA) - Shadow Smile (Ire)
7^{7sd} 4^{10gs} 7^{8gf} 9^{7gf} 4^{8sd} 17^{8gf} 7^{7sd} 7^{8g} 7^{10sd} **0-0-9 £1,346**

Watchtower (Ire) *Saeed Bin Suroor* 69
3 ch c Dubai Millennium - Balisada
4^{8g} **0-0-1 £295**

Water Pistol *Mrs A J Perrett* 63
3 b g Double Trigger (Ire) - Water Flower
10^{11g} 6^{14g} 8^{14gf} 6^{14s} 6^{16g} **0-0-5**

Waterfront Dancer *J R Best* 40
3 b g Groom Dancer (USA) - Azula
10^{10g} 10^{10g} 7^{8f} 5^{11gs} 8^{12gf} 18^{8g} 6^{11hy} **0-0-7**

Waterline Lover *P D Evans* 49 a18
3 ch f Efisio - Food Of Love
3^{7s} 3^{6gf} 11^{6g} 10^{6hy} 8^{6sd} **0-2-5 £744**

Waterline Twenty (Ire) *P D Evans* 81 a83
2 b f Indian Danehill (Ire) - Taisho (Ire)
1^{5g} 7^{5gf} 6^{6g} 1^{5f} 3^{5sd} 7^{6gf} 11^{5g} **2-0-7 £7,143**

Waterloo Corner *R Craggs* 71 a67
3 b g Cayman Kai (Ire) - Rasin Luck
4^{9sd} 2^{9sd} 2^{7sd} 3^{7sd} 3^{10g} **0-3-5 £3,109**

Waterside (Ire) *G L Moore* 86 a89
6 ch g Lake Coniston (Ire) - Classic Ring (Ire)
1^{7sd} 9^{7sd} 4^{7sd} 3^{7sd} 5^{7gs} 5^{7g} 3^{8g} 10^{7g} 3^{7gs} 13^{7g} 1^{9gf} 3^{7gf} 4^{8gs} 4^{8gf} 3^{8gf} 5^{8sd} 1^{8sd} 4^{8sd} **3-5-18 £24,728**

Waterways (Ire) *P J Prendergast* 103
2 b f Alhaarth (Ire) - Buckle (Ire)
3^{5s} 1^{5hy} 2^{5hy} 1^{5gy} 2^{6g} 3^{5gs} 2^{5y} 4^{6gy} **2-5-8 £67,480**

Waverley (Ire) *H Morrison* 102
6 b g Catrail (USA) - Marble Halls (Ire)
6^{10gf} 9^{14g} 5^{10s} **0-0-3 £1,170**

Wavertree Dream *J R Best* 28
4 b g Dushyantor (USA) - Dream On Deya (Ire)
17^{8gf} 7^{14gf} **0-0-2**

Wavertree One Off *D R C Elsworth* 55 a62
3 b g Diktat - Miss Clarinet
10^{8gs} 11^{10gf} 13^{10g} 5^{10s} 11^{16sd} 5^{10sd} **0-0-6**

Wavertree Warrior (Ire) *N P Littmoden* 83 a83
3 br g Indian Lodge (Ire) - Karamana
3^{9gs} 1^{8gf} 5^{8gf} 5^{8g} 1^{8sd} 5^{10f} 2^{9gs} 2^{7hy} 9^{8sd} 5^{8sd} **2-3-10 £17,848**

Way To The Stars *A M Balding* 60
2 gr f Dansili - Reason To Dance
12^{7g} **0-0-1**

Wayward Shot (Ire) *M W Easterby* 67
3 b g Desert Prince (Ire) - Style Parade (USA)
1^{8gf} 10^{10s} 11^{8g} 10^{7g} 9^{8g} 4^{8gf} 4^{7gf} 1^{8gf} 9^{8s} **2-0-9 £8,722**

Wazir (USA) *J H M Gosden* 98
3 b/br c Pulpit (USA) - Top Order (USA)
2^{7gf} 9^{7gf} 8^{7g} **0-1-3 £3,113**

Waziri (Ire) *M Sheppard* 65 a49
4 b g Mtoto - Euphorie (Ger)
12^{11g} 8^{10g} 6^{10gf} 10^{12g} 11^{12sd} **0-0-5**

We Are The Chelsea (USA) *M Johnston* 67
3 b c Woodman (USA) - Why Not Willie (Can)
4^{8s} 6^{9g} 4^{8g} 6^{9gf} 15^{8gf} **0-0-5 £848**

We'Re Stonybroke (Ire) *G C H Chung* a62
6 b g College Chapel - Mokaite
1^{6sd} 5^{6sd} 3^{7sd} 9^{7sd} 4^{6sd} 8^{8sd} 13^{6sd} 18^{7hy} 16^{5s} 14^{7sd} **1-1-10 £3,383**

We'll Meet Again *M W Easterby* 60 a61
5 ch g Bin Ajwaad (Ire) - Tantalizing Song (Can)
6^{8sd} 3^{9sd} 4^{10g} 1^{9sd} 2^{9sd} 4^{8gf} 4^{9sd} 7^{9sd} 4^{9sd} 1^{8ss} 5^{9sd} 4^{8sd} 8^{8sd} **2-2-13 £6,925**

Weakest Link *E J Alston* 56 a50
4 b g Mind Games - Sky Music
5^{6sd} 5^{6sd} 7^{5sd} 2^{5s} 8^{6gs} 2^{5gf} 7^{6gf} 11^{5gf} 4^{6gf} 17^{6gf} 6^{5sd} **0-2-11 £2,291**

Web Racer (Ire) *B Storey* 8
3 b f Bold Fact (USA) - Sky Lover
14^{7gf} 12^{8f} 7^{12gf} **0-0-3**

Webbswood Lad (Ire) *Stef Liddiard* 65 a60
4 b g Robellino (USA) - Poleaxe
3^{12g} 12^{10s} 4^{12sd} 3^{12ss} 6^{17sd} **0-1-5 £1,298**

Webster *M Blanshard* 21 a62
3 b g Kingsinger (Ire) - Worsted
4^{7sd} 4^{6sd} 6^{7sd} 7^{6sd} 19^{6gf} 9^{6sd} **0-0-6 £633**

Wedaad *Sir Michael Stoute* 81
2 ch f Fantastic Light (USA) - My First Romance
1^{7f} 8^{8g} 3^{7g} 2^{7gf} **1-2-4 £8,338**

Wedding Party *Mrs A J Perrett* 87
3 ch f Groom Dancer (USA) - Ceanothus (Ire)
16^{8g} 16^{7g} 3^{8g} 12^{8gs} **0-1-4 £1,164**

Wednesdays Boy (Ire) *P D Niven* 47 a58
2 b c Alhaarth (Ire) - Sheen Falls (Ire)
13^{5g} 5^{5gs} 11^{6f} 9^{6gf} 8^{7g} 6^{7s} 4^{6sd} **0-0-7 £281**

Wee Charlie Castle (Ire) *G C H Chung* 70 a55
2 b g Sinndar (Ire) - Seasonal Blossom (Ire)
6^{6gf} 3^{6gf} 8^{6g} 2^{6gf} 4^{7f} 8^{7g} 2^{7gf} 3^{6gf} 2^{7gf} 12^{8gf} 8^{9sd} 11^{7sd} 12^{6sd} 5^{9sd} 2^{9sd} **0-6-15 £7,065**

Wee Dinns (Ire) *M C Pipe* 81
4 b f Marju (Ire) - Tir-An-Oir (Ire)
10^{10g} 9^{10gf} 8^{10gs} 8^{10g} 2^{10g} 3^{10gf} 6^{10s} **0-2-7 £2,129**

Weecandoo (Ire) *C N Allen* 82 a85
7 b m Turtle Island (Ire) - Romantic Air
8^{9sd} 6^{10sd} 9^{12gf} 3^{8gs} 7^{9gf} 9^{10gf} 5^{10s} **0-1-7 £3,551**

Weekend Fever (Ire) *M Johnston* 75
2 b g Indian Danehill (Ire) - Hajal (Ire)
6^{6g} 5^{6gf} 1^{6gf} 6^{7s} 6^{7g} 12^{8hy} **1-0-6 £2,607**

Weet A Head (Ire) *R Hollinshead* 75 a69
4 b g Foxhound (USA) - Morale
7^{10gs} 2^{10s} 8^{12gf} 4^{10g} 1^{11gs} 16^{10s} 7^{10g} 13^{10hy} 6^{9sd} 3^{12sd} 3^{11sd} **1-3-11 £5,989**

Weet An Haul *T Wall* a2
4 b g Danzero (Aus) - Island Ruler
10^{8sd} 14^{12gf} 12^{9sd} **0-0-3**

Weet N Measures *T Wall* a6
3 b g Weet-A-Minute (Ire) - Weet Ees Girl (Ire)
10^{7sd} **0-0-1**

Weet Watchers *T Wall* 48 a31
5 b g Polar Prince (Ire) - Weet Ees Girl (Ire)
10^{6s} 11^{6gf} 7^{5gf} 18^{7gf} 12^{6sd} 20^{5g} 15^{8gs} 13^{9sf} **0-0-8**

Weet Yer Tern (Ire) *P A Blockley* 44 a58
3 b g Brave Act - Maxime (Ire)
14^{8gf} 3^{7sd} 13^{8gs} 17^{7gf} 14^{6gf} 13^{8f} 8^{6g} 5^{9sd} 10^{9sd} 6^{9sd} 7^{7sd} **0-1-11 £368**

Weightless *Mrs A J Perrett* 116
5 ch g In The Wings - Orford Ness
1^{10g} 6^{10g} 5^{10g} 5^{10gf} **1-0-4 £31,420**

Welcome Approach *J R Weymes* 77 a12
2 b c Most Welcome - Lucky Thing
7^{5sd} 1^{5gf} 2^{6g} 3^{5gf} 8^{6gf} 5^{8gf} 3^{6gf} 7^{6f} 11^{6g} 16^{6s} **1-2-10 £8,760**

Welcome Releaf *Julian Poulton* a57
2 ch g Most Welcome - Mint Leaf (Ire)
7^{5sd} 6^{5sd} **0-0-2**

Welcome Spirit *J S Haldane*
2 b g Most Welcome - Valadon
11^{8gf} **0-0-1**

Welcome Stranger *J M P Eustace* 110
5 b g Most Welcome - Just Julia
10^{8g} 4^{7s} 10^{8gf} 2^{8g} 1^{10gf} 3^{11gf} 6^{10g} 5^{11gf} **1-1-8 £33,300**

Well Armed (USA) *C E Brittain* 97 a78
2 b c Tiznow (USA) - Well Dressed (USA)
10^{7gs} 5^{6gf} 8^{7g} 4^{8gf} 2^{7gs} 4^{8g} 11^{7gs} 1^{10sd} **1-1-8 £9,053**

Well Established (Ire) *M A Jarvis* 84
3 b g Sadler's Wells (USA) - Riveryev (USA)
1^{10s} 15^{12gs} 5^{10s} **1-0-3 £4,173**

Well Guarded (Ire) *C R Egerton* a75
2 b c Sadler's Wells (USA) - En Garde (USA)
2^{7sd} **0-1-1 £1,280**

Welling (Ire) *M P Tregoning* 79 a70
3 b/br c Darshaan - Felona
10^{10gf} 7^{10s} 5^{10sd} **0-0-3**

Wellington Hall (Ger) *P W Chapple-Hyam* 85 a85
7 b g Halling (USA) - Wells Whisper (Fr)
2^{10gs} 6^{10gf} 2^{12gf} 3^{12gs} 12^{12gf} 6^{10g} 7^{12hy} 5^{12sd} 6^{12sd} **0-3-9 £4,696**

Wells O'Wearie *I Semple* 16
3 b f Imperial Ballet (Ire) - Sandblaster
10^{8f} **0-0-1**

Welsh Cake *Mrs A J Perrett* 61
2 b f Fantastic Light (USA) - Khubza
11^{6gf} 2^{6gf} 13^{7s} **0-1-3 £1,063**

Welsh Dragon *A M Balding* 49
2 b c Cape Cross (Ire) - Blorenge
5^{5gf} 10^{6gs} 15^{6g} **0-0-3**

Welsh Emperor (Ire) *T P Tate* 114
6 b g Emperor Jones (USA) - Simply Times (USA)
7^{6s} 1^{7s} 3^{6s} 6^{7g} 8^{6g} 1^{6gs} 2^{6gs} **2-2-7 £67,298**

Welsh Touch (Ire) *Miss J Feilden* 63
3 b f Second Empire (Ire) - Touch Of White
6^{8s} 10^{7gf} 1^{6g} 7^{6g} 10^{6gf} 12^{7gf} **1-0-6 £3,851**

Welsh Whisper *S A Brookshaw* 45 a45
6 b m Overbury (Ire) - Grugiar
6^{5sd} 7^{7sd} 12^{6sd} 10^{9sd} 3^{7s} 9^{9sd} 5^{9sd} **0-1-7 £220**

Welsh Wind (Ire) *M Wigham* a64
9 b g Tenby - Bavaria
7^{9sd} 1^{8sd} 2^{8sd} 5^{10sd} 4^{9sd} 4^{9sd} 9^{9sf} **1-1-7 £3,337**

Wembury Point (Ire) *B G Powell* 58 a58
3 gr g Monashee Mountain (USA) - Lady Celina (Fr)
9^{12sd} 11^{7sd} 9^{7sd} 3^{8sd} 3^{10g} 3^{9sd} 5^{10gf} 13^{11g} 8^{12sd} 7^{14sd} **0-3-10 £1,166**

Wendals *Rae Guest* 67
2 br f Xaar - Runelia
5^{7gf} **0-0-1**

Wendy's Girl (Ire) *R P Elliott* a60
4 b f Ashkalani (Ire) - Mrs Evans (Ire)
9^{6sd} 7^{6sd} 1^{6sd} 3^{5sd} 4^{5sd} 6^{7sd} **1-1-6 £3,354**

Wensleydale Star *T D Barron* 59
2 b g Alzao (USA) - Janiceland (Ire)
10^{5g} 7^{7gf} 7^{7gf} 18^{8g} **0-0-4**

Wessex (USA) *P A Blockley* 83 a97
5 ch g Gone West (USA) - Satin Velvet (USA)
1^{8sd} 1^{7sd} 2^{8sd} 3^{8sd} 2^{7sd} 2^{8g} 8^{7gf} 8^{7ft} 7^{6gs} 12^{8sd} 1^{6sd} 4^{7sd} 1^{7sd} **4-4-13 £24,978**

West Beck Lily *I W McInnes*
3 ch f Factual (USA) - Littlebeck
11^{6sd} 13^{5gf} 12^{6sd} **0-0-3**

West End Wonder (Ire) *D Burchell* a44
6 b g Idris (Ire) - Miss Plum
3^{14sd} 5^{14sd} 4^{14sd} 8^{12sd} **0-1-4 £184**

West Hill (Ire) *D McCain* 53
4 b g Gone West (USA) - Altamura (USA)
5^{12gf} 7^{12gs} 16^{11g} 7^{10gf} 15^{11gs} **0-0-5**

West Of Amarillo (USA) *J H M Gosden* 100
2 b c Gone West (USA) - Navarra (USA)
1^{6gf} 7^{7gs} 7^{7g} **1-0-3 £4,832**

West Point *M D Hammond* 48
8 ch g Unfuwain (USA) - Western Reel (USA)
10^{12g} 9^{12gf} **0-0-2**

Westborough (Ire) *N Tinkler* 54 a41
4 ch g Woodborough (USA) - Filey Brigg
11^{6sd} 11^{6gf} 11^{6gf} 10^{6f} 14^{6gf} 4^{6s} 4^{5gf} 10^{6g} 6^{6sd} 9^{6g} 3^{6sd} **0-2-11 £214**

Westbrook Blue *W G M Turner* 91 a73
3 b c Kingsinger (Ire) - Gold And Blue (Ire)
10^{5sd} 7^{6gs} 3^{5gs} 1^{5s} 1^{5gs} 9^{6gf} 7^{5gf} 10^{5gs} 5^{5g} 10^{5gf} 9^{6g} 21^{5hy} **2-1-12 £26,237**

Westcote (USA) *K A Ryan* a66
4 b f Gone West (USA) - Kingscote
7^{9sd} 2^{8sd} 1^{9sd} 4^{7sd} **1-1-4 £4,712**

Westcourt Dream *M W Easterby* 61 a56
5 ch m Bal Harbour - Katie's Kitty
2^{9gf} 14^{10gf} 2^{10gf} 1^{11gf} 3^{9gf} 12^{10g} 11^{10gf} 3^{10g} 11^{10s} 4^{9sd} **1-4-10 £6,170**

Wester Lodge (Ire) *J M P Eustace* 78
3 ch g Fraam - Reamzafonic
13^{10gs} 3^{12gf} 1^{12g} 4^{12f} 8^{14gf} **1-0-5 £5,862**

Western Bluebird (Ire) *Miss Kate Milligan*
7 b g Bluebird (USA) - Arrastra
18^{16g} **0-0-1**

Western Command (Ger) *Mrs N Macauley* a40
9 b g Saddlers' Hall (Ire) - Western Friend (USA)
6^{12sd} 12^{11sd} 6^{9sd} **0-0-3**

Western House (USA) *M Johnston* 80
3 gr g Gulch (USA) - Star Brightly (USA)
6^{8g} 2^{11gf} 5^{11gf} 7^{13g} 10^{16gf} **0-1-5 £1,128**

Western Roots *M Appleby* 63 a76
4 ch g Dr Fong (USA) - Chrysalis
3^{7sd} 2^{9sd} 2^{9sd} 2^{7sd} 2^{10sd} 6^{10sd} 11^{9sd} 3^{7gf} 15^{9gs} 10^{8gf} 5^{9sd} 5^{9gf} 1^{9sd} 1^{9sd} 3^{9sd} **2-7-15 £11,254**

Westerner *E Lellouche* 129
6 b h Danehill (USA) - Walensee
1^{16vs} 1^{16g} 1^{20gf} 3^{12g} 2^{12gs} 5^{12gf} **3-2-6**
£580,789

Westfield Boy *N P Littmoden* 39 a8
3 b g Unfuwain (USA) - Pick Of The Pops
13^{8gs} 13^{10gs} 11^{9sd} **0-0-3**

Westlake Bond (Ire) *B Smart* 38 a40
3 b f Josr Algarhoud (Ire) - Rania
8^{6gf} 10^{5s} 9^{6sf} **0-0-3**

Westland (USA) *Mrs A J Perrett* 87
3 gr g Cozzene (USA) - Cherie Yvonne (USA)
4^{8g} 2^{8gf} **0-1-2 £2,652**

Westmead Etoile *J R Jenkins* a34
5 b m Unfuwain (USA) - Glossary
5^{7sd} 5^{8sd} 8^{7sd} 11^{7sd} **0-0-4**

Westmoreland Road (USA) *Mrs A J Perrett* 24
5 b g Diesis - Tia Gigi (USA)
5^{12gf} **0-0-1 £332**

What Do You Know *G A Butler* a73
2 b g Compton Place - How Do I Know
1^{6sd} 4^{6sd} **1-0-2 £3,784**

What-A-Dancer (Ire) *P D Evans* 77 a89
8 b g Dancing Dissident (USA) - Cool Gales
6^{6sd} 5^{10sd} 7^{10sd} 9^{7sd} 7^{8sd} 7^{7sd} 6^{7sd} 6^{6sd} 6^{7sd}
7^{7sd} 13^{7g} 1^{7f} 1^{7gf} 8^{8g} 4^{7gf} 4^{7gf} 1^{8gf} 7^{8gf}
3^{7f} **3-1-19 £13,344**

Whatatodo *M L W Bell* 57
3 b f Compton Place - Emerald Dream (Ire)
9^{8gf} 6^{6f} 4^{8gf} 16^{7g} 2^{7f} 10^{7gf} 1^{8gf} 5^{8gf}
1-1-8 £4,602

Whatizzit *E A L Dunlop* a69
2 b f Galileo (Ire) - Wosaita
2^{9sd} 1^{9sd} **1-1-2 £4,836**

Whazzat *B W Hills* 100
3 b f Daylami (Ire) - Wosaita
6^{8g} 12^{10gs} 2^{10hy} 8^{13vs} **0-1-4 £6,799**

Whenwillitwin *J S Moore* a50
4 b g Bluegrass Prince (Ire) - Madam Marash (Ire)
4^{10sd} 7^{10sd} 10^{12sd} **0-0-3**

Where's Broughton *W J Musson* 61 a69
2 ch f Cadeaux Genereux - Tuxford Hideaway
8^{6s} 3^{7sd} **0-1-2 £696**

Where's That Tiger (USA) *A P O'Brien* 96
2 ch c Storm Cat (USA) - Blissful (USA)
1^{5sh} 4^{5hy} 4^{5gf} **1-0-3 £11,143**

Which Key (Ire) *Mrs K Walton*
2 b/br f Key Of Luck (USA) - Kudrow (Ire)
9^{6gf} 10^{7f} 18^{7gf} **0-0-3**

Whinhill House *D W Barker* 96 a79
5 ch g Paris House - Darussalam
1^{6sd} 1^{6sd} 9^{6sd} 1^{5sd} 5^{6sd} 13^{7g} 2^{5gs} 1^{5gs} 17^{6g}
1^{5gf} 1^{5f} 2^{5gf} 7^{5gf} 14^{5g} 1^{5gf} 9^{5gf} 8^{6gf} 7^{5gf}
14^{5g} **7-2-19 £37,072**

Whiplash (Ire) *K O Cunningham-Brown* 7 a38
4 b g Orpen (USA) - La Colombari (Ity)
12^{8sd} 11^{7sd} 10^{7gf} **0-0-3**

Whippasnapper *J R Best* 64 a64
5 b g Cayman Kai (Ire) - Give Us A Treat
11^{6sd} 10^{6gs} 11^{6gs} 1^{7gf} 2^{6sd} 2^{7sd} **1-2-6**
£4,158

Whipper (USA) *Robert Collet* 124
4 b c Miesque's Son (USA) - Myth To Reality (Fr)
3^{8gs} 4^{8g} 1^{7g} 2^{8gs} 4^{8g} 4^{8y} **1-2-6**
£261,187

Whipper In *P C Haslam* 61 a49
2 ch f Foxhound (USA) - Come To The Point
5^{5gs} 7^{5gf} 3^{5sd} 4^{5gf} 2^{6s} 4^{5sd} **0-3-6**
£2,265

Whirling *M C Pipe* 56 a42
3 ch f Groom Dancer (USA) - Supersonic
9^{12sd} 11^{12sd} 12^{16g} 1^{12g} **1-0-4 £3,495**

Whirly Bird *Mrs A J Perrett* 98 a81
4 b f Nashwan (USA) - Inchyre
1^{10sd} 1^{10g} 1^{11gf} 3^{12g} **3-0-4 £17,582**

Whisper Inthe Wind (Ire) *Miss J Feilden* 63
2 ch f King Charlemagne (USA) - Persian Mistress (Ire)
7^{6gf} 5^{6g} 6^{5gf} 8^{5f} 4^{7g} 13^{6gf} **0-0-6 £539**

Whispering Death *W J Haggas* 75
3 br g Pivotal - Lucky Arrow
7^{8gs} 5^{12f} 2^{14gf} 1^{14gf} 1^{14gf} 1^{14g} 2^{12s} **3-2-7**
£12,169

Whispering Melody *Mervyn Torrens* 45 a13
4 gr g Royal Applause - La Nureyeva (USA)
SU^{12g} 7^{7s} 10^{5g} 13^{9gf} 9^{7s} 6^{6ss} **0-0-6**

Whistle 'n Flute *M R Channon* 34
3 b c Piccolo - Miletrian Cares (Ire)
12^{6gf} 14^{6s} 12^{7gf} **0-0-3**

Whistle Blowing (Ire) *D McCain* 51 a41
3 b g Forzando - Philgwyn
5^{8g} 2^{10gf} 11^{12sd} **0-1-3 £951**

Whistler *Miss J R Tooth* 98 a71
8 ch g Selkirk (USA) - French Gift
6^{5gs} 9^{5g} 3^{5g} 10^{5gs} 7^{5s} 1^{5gs} 9^{5g} 9^{6f} 13^{5g}
8^{5g} 2^{5gs} 5^{5gf} 15^{5s} 13^{5s} 16^{5gf} 7^{5g} 12^{5gs} 6^{5g}
13^{5hy} 7^{5sd} 9^{7sd} **1-1-21 £16,963**

Whistleupthewind *J M P Eustace* 20 a24
2 b f Piccolo - The Frog Queen
10^{5sd} 11^{6gs} **0-0-2**

Whistling Along *J M Bradley* 43
3 b c Atraf - Forest Song
12^{6gf} 13^{6hy} 7^{5gf} 10^{5f} 6^{7gf} 18^{6gf} 10^{5hd} 15^{7g}
14^{6f} **0-0-9**

Whitbarrow (Ire) *A W Carroll* 90 a82
6 b g Royal Abjar (USA) - Danccini (Ire)
8^{5g} 17^{6gs} 5^{6s} 8^{6g} 9^{5gs} 5^{5g} 7^{5gf} 6^{5gs} 6^{5hy}
3^{5sd} 4^{5sd} **0-1-11 £1,842**

Whitby Echo (Ire) *R Hollinshead* 61 a45
3 b g Entrepreneur - Nom De Plume (USA)
9^{7g} 9^{10gf} 3^{10g} 2^{12g} 18^{12g} 12^{12sd} **0-1-6**
£1,793

Whitcomb (USA) *J Mackie* 38
5 b/br h Skip Away (USA) - Whitebread (USA)
10^{14gs} 14^{14g} 17^{20s} **0-0-3**

White Bear (Fr) *P D Evans* 73 a69
3 ch g Gold Away (Ire) - Danaide (Fr)
3^{8sd} 5^{8sd} 3^{6g} 3^{8gf} 6^{7g} 8^{10gf} 2^{6f} 2^{6g} 3^{6gs} 2^{7g}
6^{5gs} 5^{5gf} 7^{7gs} 4^{7gf} 3^{6gf} 2^{7sd} 3^{6sf} 2^{7sd}
0-11-18 £7,923

White Ladder (Ire) *P F I Cole* 66
2 br c Marju (Ire) - Lady Rachel (Ire)
11^{6s} 5^{6gf} **0-0-2**

White Ledger (Ire) *R E Peacock* a28
6 ch g Ali-Royal (Ire) - Boranwood (Ire)
7^{6sd} **0-0-1**

White Lightening (Ire) *J Howard Johnson* 50
2 ch g Indian Ridge - Mille Miglia (Ire)
9^{6g} **0-0-1**

White O' Morn *J W Unett* a16
6 gr m Petong - I'm Your Lady

11^{5sd} 13^{6sd} **0-0-2**

White Star Magic *K G Wingrove* 26 a51
3 ch g Bluegrass Prince (Ire) - Bless
3^{7sd} 3^{6sd} 4^{7sd} 11^{9sd} 4^{9sd} 3^{8sd} 6^{9gs} 15^{10g} 5^{9sd} 8^{9sd} 8^{9ss} **0-2-11 £940**

Whitethorne *R A Fahey* 73 a48
3 b f Mujadil (USA) - Sharpthorne (USA)
2^{6sd} 8^{6g} 6^{7gs} 7^{6f} 1^{7gs} 1^{7f} 2^{8gf} 1^{7g} 2^{7gf} 13^{7gf} 5^{7gf} 3^{7g} **3-4-12 £14,853**

Whitgift Rock *S Dow* 75 a78
4 b g Piccolo - Fly South
5^{8sd} 2^{8sd} 3^{8sd} 2^{9g} 3^{12g} 7^{10gf} 5^{10gf} 8^{10g} **0-4-8 £3,984**

Whitkirk Star (Ire) *S P Griffiths*
4 b g Alhaarth (Ire) - Three Stars
14^{12sd} **0-0-1**

Whitsbury Common *D R C Elsworth* 61
3 b f Lujain (USA) - Vallauris
7^{8gf} 9^{8gs} 9^{8f} 6^{10f} **0-0-4**

Whitsbury Cross *D R C Elsworth* 89
4 b c Cape Cross (Ire) - Vallauris
1^{8gf} 1^{10gf} 5^{10gf} 11^{10gf} **2-0-4 £16,524**

Who's Winning (Ire) *B G Powell* 91 a91
4 ch g Docksider (USA) - Quintellina
9^{5sd} 2^{6sd} 2^{6sd} 8^{5gs} 1^{6g} 13^{6g} 6^{6gf} 4^{5g} 11^{6gf} 4^{6g} 12^{6gf} 4^{6g} 12^{6gf} 10^{7g} 15^{7gf} **1-4-15 £16,268**

Whole Grain *B R Millman* a43
4 b f Polish Precedent (USA) - Mill Line
3^{12vs} 3^{15vs} 10^{12g} 5^{11sd} **0-0-4 £2,872**

Whoopee (USA) *J G Given* 38
2 b/br f Mozart (Ire) - Time For A Wedding (USA)
8^{6gf} **0-0-1**

Whoopsie *J A Glover* 61
3 b f Unfuwain (USA) - Oops Pettie
1^{12gf} 9^{12gf} 6^{14gf} 1^{16s} 5^{17g} 4^{16s} 3^{16g} 7^{16gf} 6^{15s} **2-1-9 £5,182**

Why Harry *J J Quinn*
3 b g Cyrano De Bergerac - Golden Ciel (USA)
13^{5sd} **0-0-1**

Why Now *K A Ryan* 81 a77
3 b f Dansili - Questionable
3^{6g} 1^{6g} 4^{6g} 3^{5gf} 1^{5gf} 7^{5gs} 7^{7sd} **2-2-7 £12,292**

Why Whisper *B Smart* 42 a42
2 gr c Forzando - Sweet Whisper
8^{5g} 7^{6sd} 10^{7gf} 9^{6sf} 8^{6sd} **0-0-5**

Whyamihere *M G Quinlan* 30
2 gr c Bertolini (USA) - Paris Mist
11^{5s} 10^{6gf} **0-0-2**

Wicked Daze (Ire) *Sir Mark Prescott* 66
2 ch g Generous (Ire) - Thrilling Day
16^{6gf} 2^{7g} 6^{7gf} **0-1-3 £1,154**

Wicked Uncle *S Gollings* 71 a79
6 b g Distant Relative - The Kings Daughter
7^{5sd} 11^{5sd} 12^{5sd} 17^{6s} 9^{5gf} 6^{5f} 12^{5g} 9^{5g} 1^{5sd} 3^{5sd} 3^{5sf} 6^{6sd} **1-2-12 £4,029**

Wig Wam Bam (Ire) *R A Fahey* 50
2 b f Indian Rocket - Almasa
10^{5gf} 3^{5f} 3^{5gs} 6^{5gf} 5^{5gf} **0-2-5 £951**

Wiggy Smith *H Candy* 92 a92
6 ch g Master Willie - Monsoon
11^{10gs} 4^{10s} 4^{10g} 4^{10sd} **0-0-4 £2,449**

Wigwam Willie (Ire) *K A Ryan* 88
3 b g Indian Rocket - Sweet Nature (Ire)
2^{7g} 10^{7g} 2^{8g} 1^{7hy} 15^{7s} **1-2-5 £10,931**

Wild Fell Hall (Ire) *W R Swinburn* 72
2 ch c Grand Lodge (USA) - Genoa
6^{8g} 15^{8s} **0-0-2**

Wild Pitch *P Mitchell* 73 a67
4 ch g Piccolo - Western Horizon (USA)
2^{10sd} 4^{10sd} 3^{10sd} 7^{12sd} 4^{10f} 1^{12sd} 1^{10gf} 11^{12gf} 9^{12gf} 15^{12sd} **2-2-10 £8,817**

Wild Savannah *J H M Gosden* 106 a106
3 b c Singspiel (Ire) - Apache Star
3^{8gf} 5^{10g} 1^{10gf} 2^{12g} 10^{12gf} 1^{10g} 6^{10gf} 2^{12sd} 3^{10sd} **2-4-9 £26,107**

Wild Tide *D W Thompson* 26
6 b m Runnett - Polly Two
14^{7g} 9^{8gf} 13^{10s} **0-0-3**

Wild Wild Wes *R Ingram*
5 ch g The West (USA) - Dam Certain (Ire)
13^{10sd} **0-0-1**

Wild Winner (Ire) *L M Cumani* 40
3 b f Desert King (Ire) - Allons Enfants (USA)
2^{10gs} 1^{10gs} 2^{10gs} 11^{10g} **1-0-4 £12,624**

Wilford Maverick (Ire) *M J Attwater* 54 a53
3 b g Fasliyev (USA) - Lioness
8^{7sd} 10^{6sd} 1^{6sd} 9^{6sd} 10^{6sd} 2^{6s} 7^{6gf} 5^{7sd} 12^{7gf} 9^{6sd} 10^{6g} 2^{7sd} 7^{8sd} **1-2-13 £2,721**

Will He Wish *S Gollings* 94 a94
9 b g Winning Gallery - More To Life
9^{8gs} 11^{8gf} 3^{7gf} 2^{7gf} 5^{7gf} 3^{7gf} 15^{7gf} 1^{7gf} 8^{7g} 14^{7gs} 11^{8sd} 4^{6sf} 1^{6sd} **2-2-13 £20,418**

Will The Till *J M Bradley* 69
3 b g Fraam - Prim Ajwaad
3^{7gf} 7^{8gf} 3^{7g} 9^{8gs} 4^{7gf} 1^{8g} 3^{8gf} 9^{8gf} **1-4-8 £5,117**

Willheconquertoo *I W McInnes* 74 a78
5 ch g Primo Dominie - Sure Care
3^{5sd} 2^{5sd} 9^{5sd} 4^{5sd} 3^{6sd} 3^{6sd} 9^{6sd} 10^{6gf} 6^{5f} 3^{5gf} 5^{7f} 5^{5f} 3^{6g} 9^{6f} 3^{6sd} 1^{6sd} 5^{6sd} 8^{6sd} **1-7-18 £9,962**

Willhego *J R Best* 73 a77
4 ch g Pivotal - Woodrising
2^{10gf} UR^{10g} 17^{12g} 2^{8s} 1^{8g} 7^{8g} 8^{13sd} 7^{12sd} 1^{10sd} **2-2-9 £9,676**

Willhewiz *M S Saunders* 85 a78
5 b g Wizard King - Leave It To Lib
1^{6g} 2^{6gf} 1^{6gf} 6^{5gf} 5^{6gf} 5^{6g} 5^{6g} 13^{6gf} 2^{6sd} **2-2-9 £10,998**

William John *B Ellison* 51 a57
2 b c Foxhound (USA) - Classy Relation
8^{5g} 4^{5s} 9^{6g} 8^{6g} 5^{9sd} 10^{8g} 7^{10g} **0-0-7 £311**

William Tell (Ire) *M D Hammond* 68 a42
3 b g Rossini (USA) - Livry (USA)
4^{10gs} 1^{10g} 11^{8g} 7^{10g} 13^{9sd} 6^{10gf} 5^{10gf} **1-0-7 £3,266**

Willmar (Ire) *W J Haggas* 50 a46
2 b f Zafonic (USA) - Showering
7^{5g} 7^{5sd} 3^{5gf} 12^{5gf} 10^{7g} **0-1-5 £525**

Willofcourse *H Candy* 40
4 b g Aragon - Willyet
13^{6gf} 8^{6g} **0-0-2**

Willows World *Miss D Mountain* 25
2 b f Agnes World (USA) - Branston Jewel (Ire)
12^{6g} 14^{6g} 9^{7hy} **0-0-3**

Wilom (Ger) *M R Hoad* 29 a42
7 ch g Lomitas - Whispering Willows

7^{10sd} 10^{7sd} 4^{8g} 6^{7f} 17^{7gs} **0-0-5**

Wilson Blyth *A Berry* a42
7 b g Puissance - Pearls
10^{5sd} **0-0-1**

Wilson Star (Ire) *J R Boyle* 89 a42
2 b g Tagula (Ire) - Naked Poser (Ire)
7^{5sd} 1^{6g} 3^{6gf} 4^{6g} 6^{7s} **1-1-5 £8,588**

Wiltshire (Ire) *P A Blockley* 54 a65
3 br g Spectrum (Ire) - Mary Magdalene
1^{7sd} UR^{7sd} 1^{8sd} 8^{8sd} 7^{9sd} 13^{8g} 5^{6sd} 4^{8f} 9^{12gf} 5^{9sf} **2-0-10 £6,384**

Win Alot *M C Chapman* 29
7 b g Aragon - Having Fun
12^{12g} **0-0-1**

Wind Chime (Ire) *A G Newcombe* 74 a59
8 ch h Arazi (USA) - Shamisen
2^{10sd} 2^{9sd} 11^{10sd} 5^{9sd} 1^{8g} 4^{8gf} 7^{9sd} 15^{8s} 4^{8gf} 5^{8gf} 4^{8sd} 8^{9sd} **1-2-12 £6,660**

Wind Shuffle (Ger) *T P Tate* 46
2 b g Big Shuffle (USA) - Wiesensturmerin (Ger)
5^{7gf} **0-0-1**

Windermere Island *M L W Bell* 77 a63
3 b f Cadeaux Genereux - Corndavon (USA)
6^{6sd} 8^{6sd} 4^{7sd} 10^{8g} 1^{7f} 10^{7gf} 1^{7gf} 8^{7gf} **2-0-8 £8,690**

Windhover *M Johnston* 80
3 b c King's Best (USA) - Light Fresh Air (USA)
12^{8gs} 3^{8g} 1^{7f} 8^{7g} 13^{8gs} 4^{9gf} **1-1-6 £4,782**

Windmill Lane *J A Geake*
8 b m Saddlers' Hall (Ire) - Alpi Dora
6^{14sd} **0-0-1**

Winds Of Change *M Johnston* 58
2 gr f King's Best (USA) - New Wind (Ger)
11^{7gf} 3^{8g} 6^{8s} **0-1-3 £866**

Winds Of Time (Ire) *Mrs A J Perrett* 91 a79
3 b f Danehill (USA) - Windmill
4^{7gf} 6^{7gf} 8^{9s} 5^{8f} 8^{10gf} 11^{8g} 12^{8sd} **0-0-7 £1,522**

Windsor Knot (Ire) *Saeed Bin Suroor* 101
3 ch c Pivotal - Triple Tie (USA)
3^{10g} **0-0-1 £3,300**

Windwood (Ire) *J W Hills* 45 a51
3 b g Piccolo - Presently
15^{8g} 11^{7gs} 13^{8gf} 6^{7gf} 9^{8sd} 12^{7f} 7^{7gf} **0-0-7**

Windy Prospect *C R Dore* 79 a68
3 ch g Intikhab (USA) - Yellow Ribbon (Ire)
9^{8gs} 7^{6gf} 16^{6gf} 16^{6gs} 9^{7ft} 15^{7s} 8^{6sd} 8^{8sd} 7^{7sd} 3^{8sd} **0-1-10 £861**

Wing Collar *T D Easterby* 89
4 b g In The Wings - Riyoom (USA)
7^{14s} 3^{14gf} 8^{12gf} 2^{14gf} 1^{14gf} 6^{16gf} 1^{14gf} **2-1-7 £18,013**

Wing Commander *R A Fahey* 93 a63
6 b g Royal Applause - Southern Psychic (USA)
11^{9sd} 17^{8g} 1^{8f} 7^{8gf} 5^{8gf} 6^{8gf} 7^{8gf} 17^{8gf} 1^{9gf} **2-0-9 £17,133**

Winged Cupid (Ire) *M Johnston* 111
2 b c In The Wings - Sweet Emotion (Ire)
1^{8gf} 1^{8gf} 2^{8hy} **2-1-3 £64,166**

Winged D'Argent (Ire) *M Johnston* 113
4 b/br g In The Wings - Petite-D-Argent
3^{16gs} 1^{14s} 4^{16s} 3^{16g} 5^{20gf} 8^{14g} 9^{16s} **1-2-7 £35,574**

Wingman (Ire) *J W Hills* 91 a88
3 b g In The Wings - Precedence (Ire)
13^{8gs} 4^{8gf} 5^{9gf} 7^{10g} 5^{12gf} 5^{12gf} 8^{12sd} 5^{11g} 2^{12hy} 4^{12hy} 8^{12sd} **0-2-11 £10,004**

Wings Of Dawn *M P Tregoning* 53
2 b f In The Wings - Petit Point (Ire)
12^{7g} 13^{7gf} 8^{7gf} 14^{8g} **0-0-4**

Wings Of Morning (Ire) *D Carroll* a51
4 ch g Fumo Di Londra (Ire) - Hay Knot
8^{7sd} 10^{9sd} 8^{5sd} 2^{7sd} 11^{7sd} 5^{8sd} 4^{7sd} 4^{7sd} 6^{8sd} **0-1-9 £422**

Wings Of Speed *H Morrison* a35
2 b f Pursuit Of Love - Fleeting Vision (Ire)
9^{7sd} 9^{9sd} 10^{9sd} **0-0-3**

Wingspeed (Ire) *Mrs A J Perrett* 74 a66
3 b g Bluebird (USA) - Aneeda
2^{8gf} 2^{10gf} 2^{8sd} 4^{9g} 10^{10g} 4^{8gf} 2^{10g} 3^{14g} **0-5-8 £5,100**

Winners Delight *A P Jarvis* 80 a88
4 ch g First Trump - Real Popcorn (Ire)
5^{12sd} 3^{12sd} 9^{12sd} 5^{12sd} 6^{11gs} 5^{12gs} 10^{12gf} **0-0-7 £1,018**

Winning Venture *A W Carroll* 69 a42
8 b g Owington - Push A Button
15^{7g} 8^{8gs} 14^{8gf} 7^{8sd} 11^{9sd} **0-0-5**

Winsabonus *P T Midgley*
5 b g Defacto (USA) - Heart Broken
13^{8sd} **0-0-1**

Winslow Boy (USA) *P Monteith* 56
4 b/br g Expelled (USA) - Acusteal (USA)
5^{13gs} 6^{16gf} **0-0-2**

Winter Coral (Fr) *Mrs N S Sharpe* 10
3 ch f Pennekamp (USA) - Winter Water (Fr)
6^{12vs} 13^{10gf} **0-0-2**

Winter Moon *B R Millman* 43
3 b f Mujadil (USA) - Crofters Ceilidh
11^{6gs} 8^{5f} **0-0-2**

Winthorpe (Ire) *J J Quinn* 70 a74
5 b g Tagula (Ire) - Zazu
3^{6sd} 3^{6sd} 2^{7sd} 8^{5sd} 7^{7sd} 10^{6gf} 3^{6g} 7^{5gf} 9^{6gf} 2^{5g} 2^{6gf} 14^{6gf} 8^{5g} 6^{6gf} 8^{5g} 2^{5gf} 6^{5ft} 4^{6hy} **0-8-18 £6,219**

Wise Choice *N P Littmoden* 52
2 b c Green Desert (USA) - Ballykett Lady (USA)
19^{7g} 7^{6g} 12^{8gf} 8^{10g} **0-0-4**

Wise Dennis *A P Jarvis* 108
3 b g Polar Falcon (USA) - Bowden Rose
6^{8gf} 1^{7s} 21^{7gf} 6^{8gs} 8^{7g} 5^{9gf} 8^{7gf} **1-0-7 £17,925**

Wise Kid *P T Midgley* 2
2 b g Cloudings (Ire) - Samana Cay
10^{5g} 11^{7gf} 10^{5sd} 12^{5gs} **0-0-4**

Wise Owl *J Pearce* 76 a84
3 b g Danehill (USA) - Mistle Thrush (USA)
8^{6gf} 7^{10s} 8^{7gf} 5^{9gf} 4^{14gf} 6^{11gf} 5^{12g} 9^{14s} 1^{12sd} **1-0-9 £4,429**

Wise Tale *P D Niven* 55 a18
6 b g Nashwan (USA) - Wilayif (USA)
10^{14gf} 7^{14gf} 5^{14g} 8^{14sd} **0-0-4**

Wise Wager (Ire) *R A Fahey* 75 a52
3 b f Titus Livius (Fr) - Londubh
13^{5s} 10^{5s} 14^{5gf} 4^{5f} 8^{5sd} 4^{5gf} 3^{5gf} 2^{5gf} 4^{5gf} 3^{5gf} 6^{5gf} 2^{5gf} 9^{5gs} **0-5-13 £5,421**

Wishin And Hopin *A G Newcombe* a31
4 b g Danzig Connection (USA) - Trina's Pet

9^{12sd} **0-0-1**

Wistman (UAE) *D Nicholls* 62
4 br g Woodman (USA) - Saik (USA)
16^{7f} 8^{8gf} 13^{8g} **0-0-3**

Witchcraft *D Shaw* 11 a59
4 b g Zilzal (USA) - Witch Of Fife (USA)
10^{10sd} 7^{9sd} 4^{6sd} 3^{8sd} 3^{9sd} 11^{8s} 2^{7sd} 5^{7sd} 2^{9sd} 8^{9sd} 8^{9sd} 5^{9sd} 2^{8sd} 1^{8sd} 6^{8sd} 6^{8sd} **1-5-16 £3,929**

Witchelle *R Craggs* 65 a66
4 br f Wizard King - Tachelle (Ire)
4^{9sd} 1^{8sd} 3^{8sd} 4^{7sd} 2^{7f} 9^{6gf} **1-2-6 £5,802**

Witches Broom *C A Cyzer* a40
4 b f Fraam - Carte Blanche
9^{7sd} 6^{7sd} 8^{5sd} 12^{7sd} **0-0-4**

Witchry *A G Newcombe* 81 a76
3 gr g Green Desert (USA) - Indian Skimmer (USA)
9^{6gs} 10^{5s} 5^{5f} 12^{5gs} 5^{6gf} 4^{6sd} **0-0-6 £225**

Witchy Vibes *M Appleby* 26 a12
3 ch f Tomba - Risk The Witch
7^{6gs} 7^{6s} 10^{5sd} 9^{6sd} 8^{6sd} 7^{7gf} 7^{12gf} **0-0-7**

With Honours *T J Fitzgerald* 27 a27
3 b f Bien Bien (USA) - Fair Test
9^{8gf} 7^{12sd} **0-0-2**

With Interest *A M Balding* 82
2 b c Selkirk (USA) - With Fascination (USA)
1^{7gf} **1-0-1 £4,966**

With Reason (USA) *Saeed Bin Suroor* 116
7 ch g Nashwan (USA) - Just Cause
2^{8g} 6^{7gf} **0-1-2 £9,200**

With Style *E A L Dunlop* 76
2 b f Grand Lodge (USA) - Coyote
9^{7gf} 2^{7gf} **0-1-2 £3,270**

Withering Lady (Ire) *Mrs P N Dutfield* 67 a66
3 b f Tagula (Ire) - Princess Oberon (Ire)
2^{6sd} 3^{5sd} 9^{6sd} 10^{6g} 10^{5gf} 6^{5gf} 14^{6gf} 6^{6g} 8^{5gf} 9^{5gs} 6^{5f} 7^{5s} 8^{5gf} **0-2-13 £2,076**

Without A Paddle *Daniel Mark Loughnane* 71 a44
2 ch g Woodborough (USA) - Sandra Dee (Ire)
14^{6y} 5^{5gf} 7^{5gf} 3^{5f} 3^{5g} 5^{6gf} 9^{7f} 2^{6g} 3^{5g} 13^{6s} 8^{6sd} **0-3-11 £3,873**

Without A Trace (Ire) *E A L Dunlop* 107
3 b f Darshaan - Star Profile (Ire)
6^{8g} 3^{8gf} 6^{8s} 1^{11s} 1^{12g} 1^{12gf} 2^{14s} 3^{13s} 3^{15s} 10^{14hy} 5^{16s} **3-2-11 £43,829**

Witty Girl *M J Polglase* a24
3 b f Whittingham (Ire) - Zando's Charm
9^{7sd} 11^{7sd} **0-0-2**

Witwatersrand (Ire) *B W Hills* 71 a57
3 b f Unfuwain (USA) - Valley Of Gold (Fr)
4^{9gs} 6^{9sd} 1^{8g} 10^{9ft} **1-0-4 £4,460**

Wiz In *T Keddy* 39 a38
3 gr g Wizard King - Great Intent
7^{7sd} 10^{8sd} 5^{12gf} **0-0-3**

Wizard Looking *J S Wainwright* 68 a47
4 b g Wizard King - High Stepping (Ire)
7^{8sd} 2^{10g} 1^{10gf} 1^{11g} 2^{12g} 7^{11gf} 3^{12g} 9^{14gf} **2-3-8 £8,632**

Wizard Of Us *M Mullineaux* 38
5 b g Wizard King - Sian's Girl
18^{10g} 14^{8g} **0-0-2**

Wizard Prince *R A Harris* 50 a45
2 b g Wizard King - Choral Dancer (USA)
6^{5g} 9^{5sd} 3^{6g} 3^{6gf} 10^{6g} 4^{7f} 5^{5f} 7^{5sd} 9^{5g} 8^{5sd} 13^{6sd} **0-1-11 £735**

Wizard Quay *W G M Turner* 49
2 b g Wizard King - Roonah Quay (Ire)
4^{5f} 8^{7gs} 10^{7g} 14^{7gf} 2^{6g} 4^{7gf} 16^{7gs} **0-2-7 £946**

Wizardmicktee (Ire) *A Bailey* 33 a41
3 b g Monashee Mountain (USA) - Epsilon
11^{6f} 12^{6sd} 5^{7gf} 10^{6gf} 16^{6g} 12^{6sd} 9^{9sd} **0-0-7**

Wizards Princess *D W Thompson* 31
5 b m Wizard King - Chalice
10^{9gs} **0-0-1**

Wizby *P D Evans* 55 a28
2 b f Wizard King - Diamond Vanessa (Ire)
1^{5gs} 5^{5s} 3^{5gs} 1^{6g} 5^{7f} 7^{7g} 3^{6gf} 12^{7sd} 6^{6gf} 8^{6gf} 10^{6s} 12^{7sd} **2-1-12 £7,188**

Wodhill Be *D Morris* 45 a49
5 b m Danzig Connection (USA) - Muarij
7^{7sd} 2^{7sd} 5^{7sd} 3^{7sd} 5^{7sd} 7^{7s} 5^{7g} 3^{7sd} 7^{7sd} 5^{7gf} 10^{7g} 10^{8gf} 5^{7gs} 1^{7sd} 4^{7sd} 7^{8g} 6^{8sd} 5^{7ss} 1^{7sd} 10^{7sd} **2-3-20 £3,756**

Wodhill Gold *D Morris* 35 a46
4 ch g Dancing Spree (USA) - Golden Filigree
7^{8sd} 3^{8sd} 10^{10g} 7^{11sd} 3^{8ss} 4^{9sd} 1^{9sd} **1-2-7 £1,866**

Wolds Dancer *T D Easterby* 57
3 b f Fraam - Dancing Em
11^{8g} 12^{8gf} 2^{8g} 3^{9gf} 7^{12g} 7^{10g} 14^{10g} **0-2-7 £1,990**

Wolf Hammer (USA) *J Howard Johnson* 62
3 ch g Diesis - Polly's Link (USA)
7^{6g} 8^{7f} 16^{6g} **0-0-3**

Wolf Pack *C E Brittain*
3 b c Green Desert (USA) - Warning Shadows (Ire)
13^{7g} **0-0-1**

Wolfe Tone (Ire) *A P O'Brien* 113
4 b c Sadler's Wells (USA) - Angelic Song (Can)
3^{10hy} 1^{13f} 4^{16g} 4^{20gf} **1-0-4 £37,734**

Wolfman *D W Barker* a30
3 ch g Wolfhound (USA) - Madam Millie
10^{6gf} 11^{6sf} **0-0-2**

Won Of A Few *M Wigham* a34
5 b g Danzig Connection (USA) - Wonderful Day
6^{6sd} 9^{7sd} 12^{6sd} **0-0-3**

Wonderful Desert *L M Cumani* 57
2 b f Green Desert (USA) - One So Wonderful
7^{6gf} 10^{6gf} 7^{7gf} **0-0-3**

Wonderful Mind *T D Easterby* 72
3 b g Mind Games - Signs And Wonders
3^{5f} 5^{5gf} 3^{5gf} 7^{5gf} 10^{5gs} 12^{5gf} 10^{6gf} 10^{5g} **0-1-8 £2,115**

Wonderful One (Ire) *J H M Gosden* 52
2 ch f Nashwan (USA) - Ring The Relatives
12^{7s} **0-0-1**

Wonky Donkey *S C Williams* a52
4 b g Piccolo - Salinas
6^{5sd} 10^{6sd} 7^{5sd} 11^{5sd} **0-0-4**

Wood Dalling (USA) *W G Harrison* 44
7 b g Woodman (USA) - Cloelia (USA)
17^{7gs} 10^{7gf} 10^{8gf} 12^{8g} 11^{8gf} 11^{8gf} **0-0-6**

Wood Fern (UAE) *W M Brisbourne* 47 a56
5 b g Green Desert (USA) - Woodsia
5^{9sd} 5^{8f} 4^{8g} 9^{9sd} **0-0-4**

Wood Spirit (Ire) *Mrs P N Dutfield* 40
3 b f Woodborough (USA) - Windomen (Ire)
7^{10f} 9^{12gf} 13^{10gf} 12^{8g} **0-0-4**

Wood Sprite *J G Given* 47
3 b f Mister Baileys - Woodbeck
2^{14g} 7^{14s} 13^{12g} **0-1-3 £1,054**

Woodbury *Mrs H Sweeting* 55
6 b m Woodborough (USA) - Jeewan
9^{6g} 8^{6g} 7^{6gf} 8^{6f} 4^{6gf} 5^{6f} 9^{7gf} **0-0-7**
£279

Woodcote (Ire) *C G Cox* 100
3 b g Monashee Mountain (USA) - Tootle
5^{7gf} 8^{6s} 9^{6gf} 2^{6g} 18^{5s} 18^{6g} 19^{6gf} **0-1-7**
£13,457

Woodcote Place *P R Chamings* a70
2 b c Lujain (USA) - Giant Nipper
2^{7sd} 4^{7sd} **0-1-2 £1,512**

Woodcracker *M L W Bell* 105
4 ch g Docksider (USA) - Hen Harrier
2^{10gf} 17^{10g} 16^{11gf} 14^{10g} 28^{9s} **0-1-5**
£4,665

Woodford Consult *M W Easterby* 59 a62
3 b f Benny The Dip (USA) - Chicodove
8^{12f} 5^{12g} 1^{12gf} 2^{14g} 3^{12gf} 6^{12gf} 10^{14g} 4^{12sd}
4^{16sd} **1-2-9 £5,694**

Woodland Lodge (Ire) *M Johnston* 46
3 b f Grand Lodge (USA) - Ultra Finesse (USA)
6^{12gf} 5^{12f} **0-0-2**

Woodlands Belle *B G Powell* 36
2 ch f Woodborough (USA) - Blushing Belle
8^{5sd} 14^{6gs} 16^{8g} 6^{6gf} 15^{8gf} 10^{7f} **0-0-6**

Woodlands Flower *A P Jarvis* 50 a49
2 b f Mujahid (USA) - Glascoed
6^{5gf} 10^{5g} 6^{6sd} 3^{7gf} 4^{7f} 11^{7gs} 8^{7gf} **0-1-7**
£819

Woodnook *J A R Toller* 75
2 b f Cadeaux Genereux - Corndavon (USA)
3^{6gf} 3^{5g} 1^{5g} **1-2-3 £6,963**

Woodsley House (Ire) *Mrs P N Dutfield* 83
3 b c Orpen (USA) - Flame And Shadow (Ire)
7^{8gs} 10^{8gs} 2^{6gs} **0-1-3 £1,680**

Woodudance (USA) *Eamon Tyrrell* a38
3 br f You And I (USA) - Lina Cavalieri
10^{5sd} **0-0-1**

Woodwee *J R Weymes* 57 a61
2 ch g Woodborough (USA) - Evaporate
8^{5g} 2^{5sd} 5^{5sd} 5^{6g} 7^{5g} 1^{5s} 3^{5gf} 6^{6gf} 10^{6gs}
8^{5sd} 8^{7g} 1^{6sf} 4^{6sd} 2^{7sd} 5^{6sd} **2-2-15**
£7,379

Woodwool *H Candy* a34
3 br f Benny The Dip (USA) - Woodcrest
6^{7sd} 5^{9sd} **0-0-2**

Woolacombe Dream *M J Wallace* 63
3 b f Orpen (USA) - Cadeau Elegant
4^{7gf} 5^{6gf} **0-0-2 £262**

Woolett (Fr) *Daniel Mark Loughnane* 61 a14
5 b m Starborough - Voodoo Child (USA)
0^{10g} 4^{9g} 3^{9gf} 14^{9g} 8^{8y} 19^{16s} 10^{8sd} **0-0-7**
£2,305

Woolfall Blue (Ire) *G G Margarson* 87
2 gr c Bluebird (USA) - Diamond Waltz (Ire)
9^{6gs} 6^{6gf} 2^{7g} 2^{7g} 7^{8vs} **0-2-5 £2,441**

Woolfall Joanna *G G Margarson* a38
3 gr f Petong - Real Princess
7^{7sd} 9^{7sd} 8^{6sd} 8^{8sd} **0-0-4**

Woolfall King (Ire) *G G Margarson* 46
2 b g King Charlemagne (USA) - Bazaar Promise
15^{6gf} 10^{7g} 10^{6gs} 6^{7hy} 15^{8hy} **0-0-5**

Woolly Back (Ire) *A C Whillans* 63
4 b g Alzao (USA) - Hopping Higgins (Ire)
4^{12gs} 9^{10s} 10^{12g} 5^{9gs} 10^{10gf} 10^{10g} **0-0-6**

Woolly Bully *G A Huffer* 61
2 b c Robellino (USA) - Belle Ile (USA)
13^{7gs} 6^{6s} 6^{8hy} **0-0-3**

Woolsack (USA) *H Morrison* a72
3 ch c Spinning World (USA) - Rich And Famous (Fr)
1^{6sd} **1-0-1 £4,046**

Woolstone Boy (USA) *J Jay* 18 a63
4 ch g Will's Way (USA) - My Pleasure (USA)
11^{10sd} 15^{10g} 15^{12g} 1^{12sd} 1^{16sd} 1^{12sd} 8^{12sd} 8^{14sd}
3-0-8 £5,943

Wor Kid *A C Whillans*
3 br f Charnwood Forest (Ire) - Patience Please
PU^{8g} **0-0-1**

Word Perfect *M W Easterby* 81
3 b f Diktat - Better Still (Ire)
6^{6s} 6^{6s} 10^{6gf} 11^{6g} 19^{6g} 13^{6gs} 10^{7hy} 3^{7hy}
0-1-8 £908

Working Late *D T Hughes* 58
3 b c Night Shift (USA) - All The Luck (USA)
6^{8gf} 9^{7gf} 9^{7gf} **0-0-3**

Worlaby Dale *Mrs S Lamyman* 37 a40
9 b g Terimon - Restandbethankful
3^{14sd} 4^{17sd} 5^{12sd} 5^{14g} 7^{18gf} 6^{16g} 7^{18gs}
0-1-7 £208

World At My Feet *N Bycroft* 60
3 b f Wolfhound (USA) - Rehaab
16^{5s} 7^{5g} 8^{5f} 8^{6f} 6^{7gf} 13^{6g} 8^{6g} 8^{5gf} 3^{8gf}
6^{8gs} 3^{10g} **0-2-11 £954**

World In Action (Ire) *A P Jarvis* 65
2 b/br g Spinning World (USA) - Pretty Procida (USA)
11^{7gf} 11^{8gf} 3^{7gf} 5^{8g} **0-1-4 £494**

World Series (Ire) *P Mitchell* 79 a74
3 b g Almutawakel - Mezzanine
8^{8gf} 4^{8sd} 1^{7gf} 4^{8gf} 10^{7gf} 5^{7sd} 6^{8gs} **1-0-7**
£3,995

Worldly Pursuit *B Smart* 50 a13
2 ch f Spinning World (USA) - Final Pursuit
14^{6g} 7^{6gf} 10^{7sd} **0-0-3**

Worth A Grand (Ire) *J J Bridger* 58 a52
3 br g Raise A Grand (Ire) - Ballykett Pride (Ire)
11^{8sd} 4^{8sd} 10^{8sd} 9^{10sd} 11^{7sd} 5^{8sd} 1^{7s} 4^{6s}
7^{6sd} 5^{7s} 7^{6gs} 6^{7gf} 15^{10g} 5^{7g} 6^{7s} 6^{6g}
1-0-16 £2,808

Worth Abbey *A W Carroll* 52 a64
3 b g Mujadil (USA) - Housefull
1^{7sd} 9^{6sd} 9^{6sd} 7^{7sd} 11^{6sd} 9^{9sd} 7^{8gf} 13^{7gs} 5^{9sd}
4^{9sd} 11^{8g} 1^{9sd} 4^{9sd} 9^{9sd} 16^{7gs} **2-0-15**
£6,078

Wotavadun (Ire) *K McAuliffe* 18 a25
2 ch g King Of Kings (Ire) - Blush With Love (USA)
10^{6g} 12^{6sd} 13^{6g} **0-0-3**

Wotchalike (Ire) *R J Price* 71 a81
3 ch c Spectrum (Ire) - Juno Madonna (Ire)
2^{10sd} 3^{10sd} 3^{10sd} 3^{9sd} 13^{9g} 9^{10gs} 7^{15gs} 3^{12gs}
9^{16g} 12^{14s} UR^{17sd} 11^{12sd} 7^{9sd} 6^{12sd}
0-2-14 £7,499

Wovoka (Ire) *M R Channon* 98 a63
2 b g Mujadil (USA) - Common Cause
1^{5g} 3^{5s} 6^{5sd} 8^{7gs} 2^{6gf} 5^{6gf} 1^{6gf} 2^{6gf} 2^{6g} 2^{6g}
4^{5gs} 3^{7s} 5^{7g} 1^{7gs} 8^{6gs} 1^{9sh} **4-5-16**
£51,360

Wozani Dancer (Ire) *G A Huffer* 56 a32
3 b g Danehill Dancer (Ire) - Lauretta Blue (Ire)
9^{10g} 8^{8gs} 9^{12sd} 19^{8gf} 17^{8gf} **0-0-5**

Wrenlane *R A Fahey* 65 a52
4 ch g Fraam - Hi Hoh (Ire)
5^{10gf} 12^{8g} 6^{7gf} 6^{8gs} 9^{8sd} **0-0-5**

Wrighty Almighty (Ire) *J Noseda* 85
3 b g Danehill Dancer (Ire) - Persian Empress (Ire)
1^{6gf} 1^{6g} 4^{6gf} 5^{7gf} 10^{6g} **2-0-5 £11,834**

Writ (Ire) *Andrew Reid* 27 a63
3 ch g Indian Lodge (Ire) - Carnelly (Ire)
14^{7g} 12^{10sd} 2^{9sd} 13^{8gf} 8^{8sd} 1^{7sd} 11^{7sd}
1-1-7 £4,089

Wroot Danielle (Ire) *D W Whillans* 61
5 b g Fayruz - Pounding Beat
1^{9gs} 9^{8gs} 12^{8gs} **1-0-3 £3,627**

Wujood *H Morrison* 79 a64
3 b g Alzao (USA) - Rahayeb
3^{11s} 6^{14g} 8^{12gf} 2^{8gf} 1^{8gs} 6^{9gf} 10^{9sd} UR^{8s} 11^{10sd}
1-1-9 £9,083

Wulimaster (USA) *Sir Michael Stoute* 71
2 b/br c Silver Hawk (USA) - Kamaina (USA)
5^{7gf} **0-0-1**

Wunderbra (Ire) *M L W Bell* 84 a77
4 b f Second Empire (Ire) - Supportive (Ire)
3^{5sd} 1^{5g} 16^{5gf} **1-1-3 £7,609**

Wunderwood (USA) *Lady Herries* 111
6 b g Faltaat (USA) - Jasoorah (Ire)
4^{10gs} 1^{12g} 5^{12gf} 8^{12gs} 20^{12hy} **1-0-5**
£20,810

Wyatt Earp (Ire) *R A Fahey* 90 a89
4 b g Piccolo - Tribal Lady
10^{5gf} 2^{5g} 3^{6f} 1^{6gf} 9^{6g} 4^{6g} 12^{5g} 10^{6g} 6^{7g}
6^{6gs} 13^{7g} 1^{7s} 2^{7sd} 5^{8sd} **2-4-14**
£25,927

Wychbury (USA) *Mrs H Dalton* 77 a56
4 ch g Swain (Ire) - Garden Rose (Ire)
9^{9sd} 11^{9sd} 17^{10g} 7^{7g} 4^{8gf} 3^{8gs} 1^{8g} 1^{9gf} 3^{8gf}
6^{8g} 7^{10gf} 15^{9gs} 11^{8sd} **2-3-13 £8,378**

Wyoming *John Allen* 53
4 ch f Inchinor - Shoshone
1^{12s} **1-0-1 £1,494**

Xaar Breeze *Rae Guest* 30
2 b f Xaar - Dicentra
11^{6gf} 11^{6g} 10^{7g} **0-0-3**

Xaara Doon (Ire) *M J Attwater* 15
3 b f Xaar - Hill Of Doon (Ire)
11^{8gs} 12^{12sd} **0-0-2**

Xaarist (Ire) *T P Tate* 59
3 b g Xaar - Can Can Lady
4^{12s} 4^{16g} 14^{16s} **0-1-3 £681**

Xacobeo (Ire) *R Hannon* 62 a4
3 b c Montjeu (Ire) - Afisiak
7^{10gs} 3^{12s} 12^{12sd} **0-1-3 £625**

Xaloc Bay (Ire) *R A Harris* a33
7 br g Charnwood Forest (Ire) - Royal Jade
10^{7sd} 7^{8sd} 7^{8sd} 9^{8sd} 6^{7sd} 12^{7sd} **0-0-6**

Xaluna Bay (Ire) *W R Muir* 64 a73
2 br f Xaar - Lunadine (Fr)
7^{6g} 6^{6g} 1^{5sd} 11^{6sd} **1-0-4 £3,042**

Xanadu *Miss L A Perratt* 40
9 ch g Casteddu - Bellatrix
14^{6gs} 13^{6gs} 12^{5gf} 8^{5gf} 20^{6g} 10^{6gf} 8^{6gf}
0-0-7

Xeight Express (Ire) *A Bailey*
3 b f Ashkalani (Ire) - Believing
13^{8ss} 11^{7ss} **0-0-2**

Xenia *J G Given* 15 a31
2 b f Labeeb - Known Class (USA)
9^{7s} 11^{9sf} 10^{9sd} **0-0-3**

Xenophile *J L Dunlop* 28
2 ch c Elnadim (USA) - Femme Femme (USA)
10^{7gs} **0-0-1**

Xpres Boy (Ire) *S R Bowring* a58
2 b g Tagula (Ire) - Highly Motivated
7^{7sd} 17^{6g} 4^{6sd} 1^{7sd} **1-0-4 £3,316**

Xpres Digital *S R Bowring* 73 a84
4 b g Komaite (USA) - Kustom Kit Xpres
4^{6sd} 5^{6sd} 8^{7sd} 1^{6sd} 3^{6sd} 5^{7sd} 1^{6sd} 3^{6g} 13^{7g}
14^{6g} 13^{6g} **2-2-11 £7,727**

Xsynna *Miss M E Rowland* a4
9 b g Cyrano De Bergerac - Rose Ciel (Ire)
9^{6sd} **0-0-1**

Xtra Torrential (USA) *D M Simcock* 100 a70
3 b c Torrential (USA) - Offering (USA)
11^{8ft} 8^{9ft} 3^{8gs} **0-1-3 £3,080**

Ya Late Maite *E S McMahon* 50
2 ch f Komaite (USA) - Plentitude (Fr)
11^{6gf} 4^{6g} 18^{6g} 9^{7g} **0-0-4 £283**

Yajbill (Ire) *M R Channon* 102
3 b c Royal Applause - Tee Cee
2^{6s} 7^{6gf} 5^{5gf} 8^{6g} 3^{5gf} 15^{6gf} **0-1-6**
£8,779

Yakimov (USA) *D J Wintle* 91
6 ch g Affirmed (USA) - Ballet Troupe (USA)
2^{8gf} 2^{7gf} 2^{8gs} 15^{7gf} 15^{7s} 4^{7s} **0-4-6**
£8,120

Yallingup *T M Jones* 36 a36
2 b f Muhtarram (USA) - Boomerang Blade
12^{6sd} 5^{5f} 6^{6sd} 6^{6gf} **0-0-4**

Yamato Pink *Mrs H Sweeting* 47 a53
4 ch f Bijou D'Inde - Time Or Never (Fr)
4^{6sd} 4^{7sd} 3^{7sd} 2^{6sd} 6^{6gf} 3^{7f} 10^{8gf} 8^{6f} 4^{7g}
6^{7f} 7^{7g} 2^{7sd} 11^{7sd} 12^{6sd} **0-4-14**
£1,945

Yameell *David Marnane* 66
3 b g King's Best (USA) - Maid Of Kashmir (Ire)
10^{8g} 5^{11gf} 2^{9gs} **0-1-3 £1,085**

Yankee George (Ire) *M R Channon* 94
2 b g Cape Cross (Ire) - Yankee Dancer
2^{7gf} 1^{7gf} 1^{7g} 4^{7gf} 8^{7s} 2^{7gf} 7^{7hy} 1^{6gs} 6^{5g} 2^{6g}
2^{6gs} 10^{7hy} **3-4-12 £23,657**

Yankeedoodledandy (Ire) *B G Powell* 81 a74
4 b g Orpen (USA) - Laura Margaret
18^{20gf} 4^{15gf} 4^{16g} 4^{16gf} 6^{12sd} **0-0-5**
£1,560

Yaqoot *M Johnston* 39
3 b f Pivotal - Princess Minnie
8^{6g} **0-0-1**

Yardstick *S Kirk* a45
3 ch c Inchinor - Fair Verona (USA)
6^{9sd} 10^{8sd} **0-0-2**

Yarqus *C E Brittain* 89 a77
2 b c Diktat - Will You Dance
8^{7f} 2^{7gf} 4^{7s} 5^{7g} 2^{9sd} 2^{8gf} 1^{8gs} **1-3-7**
£8,502

Yashin (Ire) *P A Blockley* 64 a62
4 b g Soviet Star (USA) - My Mariam
12^{10sd} 7^{9sd} 6^{10s} 4^{10gf} 14^{6gs} 10^{10gs} 14^{12gf}
4^{10gf} 6^{8gs} 9^{8sf} 11^{8sd} 4^{11sd} **0-1-12 £708**

Yasoodd *M R Channon* 106
2 br c Inchinor - Needwood Epic
5^{5g} 1^{7gs} 3^{7gs} 6^{7s} 2^{7s} 4^{7g} 4^{7g} 6^{7gs} **1-2-8**
£27,293

Yassooma (Ire) *R C Guest* 50
2 b g King Of Kings (Ire) - Statistic (USA)
13^{6gf} 12^{8gs} 10^{8g} **0-0-3**

Yawmi *R A Harris* 67 a104
5 ch h Zafonic (USA) - Reine Wells (Ire)
8^{12sd} 7^{10gf} 3^{8sd} 4^{10gf} 4^{12gf} 6^{12sd} 7^{8sd} 2^{12sd}
3^{10sd} **0-3-9 £2,259**

Yazaar *J H M Gosden* 67
3 ch c Rainbow Quest (USA) - Love And Affection (USA)
9^{8gf} 6^{11s} 3^{11gf} 2^{14gf} 11^{14gf} **0-1-5**
£1,699

Yeats (Ire) *A P O'Brien* 122
4 b c Sadler's Wells (USA) - Lyndonville (Ire)
2^{10hy} 1^{12g} 9^{12gs} 4^{14g} 6^{12y} **1-0-5**
£163,936

Yeldham Lady *A J Chamberlain* a50
3 b f Mujahid (USA) - Future Options
3^{7sd} 2^{8sd} 3^{8sd} 7^{8sd} 1^{9sd} 8^{7sd} 10^{9sd} 9^{10sd}
1-3-8 £3,549

Yellow Card *N A Callaghan* 50 a69
2 ch g Inchinor - Tranquillity
6^{6s} 4^{5sd} 4^{5sd} **0-0-3 £562**

Yenaled *P S McEntee* 65 a76
8 gr g Rambo Dancer (Can) - Fancy Flight (Fr)
5^{8sd} 13^{14g} 7^{9gf} 11^{13g} 7^{12gf} 1^{12g} 8^{14s} 9^{12sf}
5^{12sd} 2^{12sd} 4^{12sd} **1-1-11 £4,319**

Yeoman Lad *M J Gingell* a20
5 b g Groom Dancer (USA) - First Amendment (Ire)
9^{10sd} **0-0-1**

Yeoman's Girl *A M Balding* 43 a39
2 b f Slip Anchor - Rasmalai
9^{9g} 10^{8g} 6^{8gs} 8^{8sd} **0-0-4**

Yes Dear *M R Channon* 62
2 ch f Fantastic Light (USA) - Abeyr
6^{7gf} 13^{8g} **0-0-2**

Yo Pedro (Ire) *J R Fanshawe* 86 a82
3 b g Mark Of Esteem (Ire) - Morina (USA)
6^{7sd} 1^{8sd} 4^{8gs} 7^{7gf} 12^{8gs} **1-0-5 £4,553**

Yomalo (Ire) *Rae Guest* 99 a99
5 ch m Woodborough (USA) - Alkariyh (USA)
2^{5g} 5^{6gf} 1^{6gf} 2^{6gf} 4^{6gf} 3^{6gf} 5^{6gf} 4^{6g} 6^{6g} 2^{5sf}
9^{6sd} **1-5-11 £29,403**

York Cliff *W M Brisbourne* 69 a70
7 b g Marju (Ire) - Azm
2^{9sd} 4^{9sd} 3^{12sd} 7^{12sd} 4^{9s} 9^{9gs} 4^{10g} 2^{10gf} 8^{11gf}
6^{12g} 4^{12sd} 3^{9sd} 3^{12sd} 2^{14sd} 2^{12sd} 3^{12sd} 8^{14sd}
0-8-17 £6,431

Yorke's Folly (USA) *C W Fairhurst* 54 a36
4 b f Stravinsky (USA) - Tommelise (USA)
3^{5g} 6^{5gf} 9^{6gf} 4^{6g} 4^{5g} 2^{5gf} 3^{5gf} 12^{5gf} 8^{5sd}
0-4-9 £2,647

Yorker (USA) *Ms Deborah J Evans* 53 a56
7 b g Boundary (USA) - Shallows (USA)
7^{9sd} 2^{7sd} 7^{9sd} 6^{9sd} 4^{9sd} 4^{9sd} 10^{6gf} 10^{7sd} 5^{8gs}
11^{8sf} 9^{8ss} **0-1-11 £1,093**

Yorkie *J Pearce* 59 a66
6 b g Aragon - Light The Way
9^{6g} 11^{6f} 4^{5g} 4^{5f} 1^{6g} 2^{7sd} 5^{6hy} 3^{7sd} 2^{7sd}
1-3-9 £3,177

Yorkies Boy *Miss J S Davis* 56
10 gr g Clantime - Slipperose
17^{6g} 9^{5gs} 7^{6g} 3^{7g} 4^{7gf} 10^{6s} 11^{6g} 11^{6gf} 6^{6gf}
16^{8gf} 3^{6f} 6^{6gs} 9^{6f} 13^{6f} 13^{7g} **0-3-15**
£943

Yorkshire Blue *J S Goldie* 71 a54
6 b g Atraf - Something Blue
6^{6sd} 4^{8g} 5^{7gf} 1^{7g} 2^{6g} 6^{6g} 1^{6gf} 4^{6gf} 3^{6gf} 13^{6g}
15^{6g} 5^{6gs} 9^{7gf} 9^{6hy} **2-2-14 £10,758**

Yorkshire Lad (Ire) *Miss Gay Kelleway* 77 a68
3 b g Second Empire (Ire) - Villaminta (Ire)
1^{6sd} 6^{7sd} 4^{5sd} 1^{6gf} 8^{6s} 6^{5gf} 10^{5g} 6^{6sd} 12^{6sd}
11^{6sd} 7^{5sd} **2-0-11 £7,520**

Yorkshire Owl *Mrs H Dalton* 56 a29
4 b/br g Marju (Ire) - Rosa Canina
7^{8g} 6^{8gf} 7^{8g} 10^{7sd} 10^{14sd} **0-0-5**

You Call That Art (USA) *R Hannon* 79
2 b f Royal Academy (USA) - Support The Arts (USA)
9^{7s} 5^{7gs} 2^{6g} 2^{6s} 4^{6s} **0-2-5 £4,864**

You Too *M Johnston* 68
3 b f Monsun (Ger) - You Are The One
13^{10gs} 3^{11gs} 1^{14gf} **1-0-3 £4,041**

You're My Son *A B Haynes* 32
3 b g Bold Edge - Sheer Nectar
11^{8g} 10^{8gs} **0-0-2**

Youaremysunshine (Ire) *I A Wood* 63
3 b f Bahhare (USA) - Another Rainbow (Ire)
10^{10g} 8^{8gf} 5^{10f} **0-0-3**

Youmzain (Ire) *M R Channon* 87
2 b c Sinndar (Ire) - Sadima (Ire)
9^{7gs} 3^{8gf} 1^{8g} **1-1-3 £4,153**

Young Bertie *H Morrison* 64
2 ch c Bertolini (USA) - Urania
7^{6g} 5^{6gf} 12^{6g} 10^{5hy} **0-0-4**

Young Boldric *K Bell* 43
3 b g Faustus (USA) - Bold Byzantium
9^{8gs} 8^{8gs} 11^{12gf} 13^{8g} **0-0-4**

Young Dennis (Ire) *Miss M E Rowland*
3 b g Imperial Ballet (Ire) - Giulia Muriel
10^{10g} **0-0-1**

Young Flavio *J M Bradley* 67 a48
2 b g Mark Of Esteem (Ire) - Flavian
5^{5sd} 9^{6gf} 1^{6gf} 7^{6g} 6^{5g} 2^{7g} 1^{7gf} 12^{6gf} 14^{7gs}
6^{5sd} 11^{7sf} **2-1-11 £8,013**

Young Kate *J R Best* 50 a50
4 b f Desert King (Ire) - Stardyn
10^{10gf} 2^{9sf} 2^{8g} 1^{9sd} 2^{8sd} 2^{8sd} 5^{10sd} 10^{10sd}
1-4-8 £3,190

Young Mick *G G Margarson* 57 a59
3 br g King's Theatre (Ire) - Just Warning
4^{12g} 5^{10gf} 7^{10gf} 11^{8g} 14^{8s} 4^{9sd} 3^{9sd} 10^{7sd}
0-1-8 £707

Young Mr Grace (Ire) *T D Easterby* 87
5 b h Danetime (Ire) - Maid Of Mourne
9^{8gs} 2^{7s} 12^{8gs} 5^{8s} 14^{8g} 6^{7gs} 10^{8gf} 8^{8g} 4^{7g}
3^{7gf} 12^{8gs} 10^{8g} 8^{7s} **0-1-13 £5,350**

Young Rooney *M Mullineaux* 71
5 b g Danzig Connection (USA) - Lady Broker
13^{12gs} 4^{8gs} 4^{12gf} 12^{14s} 10^{10hy} **0-1-5**
£715

Young Scotton *J Howard Johnson* 63
5 b g Cadeaux Genereux - Broken Wave
5^{9g} 4^{8g} **0-0-2 £420**

Young Thomas (Ire) *James Moffatt* 38 a11
3 ch g Inchinor - Splicing
9^{7gf} 6^{11gs} 7^{8g} 11^{9s} 11^{7sd} **0-0-5**

Young Valentino *A W Carroll* 59 a32
3 ch g Komaite (USA) - Caprice

1^{6g} 15^{6g} 15^{6gf} 10^{5sd} 12^{7sd} 14^{7sd} **1-0-6**
£3,081

Youngs Forth *A W Carroll* 49 a47
5 b m Most Welcome - Pegs
2^{7sd} 14^{8g} 9^{7gf} 9^{10f} 8^{8g} **0-1-5 £426**

Your Amount (Ire) *A King* 76 a78
2 b g Beckett (Ire) - Sin Lucha (USA)
7^{7sd} 3^{8sd} 4^{7s} 10^{8gf} 1^{7g} 12^{6sd} 6^{7hy} **1-1-7**
£4,844

Youralittlemiller *P G Murphy* 52
2 b f Kalanisi (Ire) - Jam (Ire)
4^{6gf} 3^{7gf} 9^{7gf} **0-1-3 £851**

Yours Sincerely (Ire) *P A Blockley* 52 a44
3 ch g Mark Of Esteem (Ire) - Evrobi (Ire)
7^{10gf} 14^{6f} 17^{5g} 9^{8sd} 4^{7sd} 7^{7sd} 10^{9sd} 8^{6ss}
0-0-8

Yourturnwillcome (Ire) *T G McCourt* 57
3 b f Definite Article - Zani Girl (Ity)
8^{11s} 7^{10y} 9^{10g} 7^{7gf} 17^{10gf} 5^{10s} **0-0-6**

Zaafran *M A Jarvis* 59
2 b f Singspiel (Ire) - Roshani (Ire)
7^{7s} **0-0-1**

Zaal *J A Osborne* 94 a96
2 ch g Alhaarth (Ire) - Balladonia
5^{6gf} 2^{6gf} 1^{6f} 1^{7sd} 5^{7sd} 1^{8s} **3-1-6**
£17,997

Zabadani *Mrs A J Perrett* 19
3 ch f Zafonic (USA) - Bloudan (USA)
13^{10g} **0-0-1**

Zabeel House *E A L Dunlop* 87
2 b g Anabaa (USA) - Divine Quest
2^{6gf} 1^{6gf} 7^{7gs} 3^{6g} 5^{8g} **1-1-5 £7,159**

Zabeel Palace *D R Loder* 93 a81
3 b g Grand Lodge (USA) - Applecross
1^{10sd} 1^{10gf} **2-0-2 £13,620**

Zabeel Tower *M R Channon* 72
2 b c Anabaa (USA) - Bint Kaldoun (Ire)
4^{7g} 15^{7g} 16^{7gf} 4^{8gs} 2^{8g} 3^{7gs} 4^{8g} 18^{8hy}
0-2-8 £2,974

Zac's Spree *Julian Poulton* a21
6 b g Dancing Spree (USA) - Zac's Desire
12^{12sd} **0-0-1**

Zafantage *S Kirk* 69
2 ch f Zafonic (USA) - Up On Points
6^{6gf} 11^{6g} 6^{6gf} 3^{6gf} 1^{7f} 5^{7gs} 3^{7s} 5^{7gf} 8^{7gf}
20^{6g} 9^{7gs} **1-1-11 £11,524**

Zafarilla (Ire) *J Noseda* 42
2 b f Zafonic (USA) - Claustra (Fr)
17^{5s} 5^{5gf} 5^{5f} **0-0-3**

Zafarshah (Ire) *R A Harris* 71 a62
6 b g Danehill (USA) - Zafarana (Fr)
2^{7sd} 5^{8sd} 3^{9sd} 8^{9sd} 6^{7sd} 11^{7sd} 1^{7g} 3^{7gs} 1^{7gs}
5^{7gf} 7^{7g} 2^{7gf} 5^{8gf} 4^{8g} 5^{7gf} 9^{8gf} 9^{8gf} 4^{8g} 7^{8gf}
2^{8sd} 12^{8gs} 10^{9sd} 4^{7sd} 8^{7sd} 6^{7sd} **2-6-25**
£9,198

Zaffeu *N P Littmoden* 53 a59
4 ch g Zafonic (USA) - Leaping Flame (USA)
6^{17sd} 1^{12sd} 4^{12sd} 13^{12sd} 1^{12sd} 3^{17sd} 4^{12sd} 4^{14sd}
4^{11f} 7^{12gf} 5^{11g} 3^{14sd} 16^{12gf} 6^{16sd} 3^{14sd} 4^{14sd}
2-3-16 £7,319

Zagora (Ire) *R A Fahey* a54
3 ch f Docksider (USA) - Cape Clear
6^{9sd} **0-0-1**

Zagreus (Ger) *M W Easterby* 52 a35
3 gr g Fasliyev (USA) - Zephyrine (Ire)
11^{6sd} 13^{6g} 5^{7g} 9^{7gf} 5^{10g} 3^{12g} **0-1-6**
£537

Zahara Joy *D W Thompson* 59
2 ch f Cayman Kai (Ire) - Enjoy (Ire)
7^{6gf} 4^{7gf} 3^{7gf} 6^{7s} 8^{6g} 9^{7gf} **0-1-6 £812**

Zaharath Al Bustan *M R Channon* 74
2 ch f Gulch (USA) - Cayman Sunset (Ire)
2^{6gf} 3^{7gf} 2^{7f} 4^{7gf} 2^{7g} 2^{7gf} **0-4-6**
£7,841

Zaheyah *T Hogan* 64 a47
3 gr f Dansili - Arinaga
10^{7sd} 4^{7g} 11^{7gf} 10^{10g} **0-0-4 £325**

Zahunda (Ire) *M J Gingell* a44
6 b m Spectrum (Ire) - Gift Of Glory (Fr)
3^{7sd} 6^{9sd} 8^{7sd} 4^{7sd} 5^{6sd} 10^{9sd} 14^{7s} **0-1-7**
£210

Zaif (Ire) *D R C Elsworth* 82
2 b c Almutawakel - Colourful (Fr)
11^{7gf} 2^{8gs} **0-1-2 £1,566**

Zak Attack *J Jay* a61
4 ch g Young Ern - Premiere Moon
6^{6sd} 3^{7sd} **0-1-2 £418**

Zalimar (Ire) *L M Cumani* 88
3 b f Montjeu (Ire) - Zanella (Ire)
4^{10gf} 2^{12gf} 5^{11gf} 2^{12gf} 1^{12gf} 1^{14g} 2^{12g} 9^{12g}
2-4-8 £15,269

Zalkani (Ire) *B G Powell* 54 a81
5 ch g Cadeaux Genereux - Zallaka (Ire)
1^{10sd} 8^{10sd} 2^{12sd} 3^{10sd} 2^{10sd} 5^{11gs} 13^{8gf} 7^{10f}
2^{10gf} 4^{8gf} 13^{10g} 2^{10gf} 13^{12sd} 8^{7sd} 3^{8sd} 2^{8sd}
3^{12sd} 6^{8sd} 5^{9sd} 6^{12sd} 8^{8sd} **1-9-21**
£12,187

Zalongo *Sir Michael Stoute* 105
3 ch c Zafonic (USA) - Tamassos
2^{10gf} 3^{10gs} 9^{10gf} 12^{10g} 5^{12g} 5^{12s} **0-2-6**
£11,243

Zalycia *Mrs C A Dunnett*
2 ch f Zilzal (USA) - Double Top (Ire)
16^{5gf} **0-0-1**

Zalzaar (Ire) *C G Cox* 56
3 b g Xaar - Zalamalec (USA)
4^{7g} **0-0-1 £280**

Zamala *J L Dunlop* 72
2 b f King's Best (USA) - Ajayib (USA)
3^{7gs} 3^{7gs} 6^{8gs} **0-1-3 £1,452**

Zamalik (USA) *M A Jarvis* 68
2 b/br c Machiavellian (USA) - Ashbilya (USA)
6^{8g} 6^{8gf} **0-0-2**

Zambach (Ire) *E F Vaughan* 71
2 br f Namid - Marliana (Ire)
5^{6gs} 1^{6gf} 1^{6g} 8^{6g} **2-0-4 £10,491**

Zambezi River *J M Bradley* a36
6 ch g Zamindar (USA) - Double River (USA)
9^{6sd} 10^{7sd} 9^{6sd} 11^{7g} 18^{7gf} 7^{5sd} **0-0-6**

Zamboozle (Ire) *D R C Elsworth* 77
3 ch c Halling (USA) - Blue Sirocco
9^{7g} 4^{10gf} 8^{11gf} 1^{11g} 5^{12f} 4^{12s} **1-0-6**
£4,717

Zandeed (Ire) *A C Whillans* 51 a39
7 b g Inchinor - Persian Song
11^{8gf} 17^{8gf} 12^{9g} 11^{7s} 3^{8s} 3^{9hy} 8^{8sd} 7^{12ss}
0-2-8 £938

Zanderido *B S Rothwell* 51 a13
3 b g Forzando - Triple Concerto
12^{10gf} 2^{7s} 8^{6s} 3^{6f} 18^{6f} 13^{7f} 18^{7gf} 12^{7gs}

7^{7ss} 12^{9sd} **0-2-10 £1,289**

Zando *E G Bevan* 48 a59
3 b g Forzando - Rockin' Rosie
5^{9sd} 7^{10gf} 5^{8gf} 11^{10g} 13^{12f} **0-0-5**

Zanjeer *N Wilson* 75
5 b g Averti (Ire) - Cloudslea (USA)
17^{8g} 13^{8g} 7^{7gf} PU^{7g} 2^{8g} 1^{7gf} 4^{7gf} 1^{7g} 3^{7g}
2-2-9 £10,387

Zantero *W M Brisbourne* a45
3 b g Danzero (Aus) - Cruinn A Bhord
3^{6sd} 7^{5sd} 12^{8sd} 11^{9sd} 12^{9sd} 13^{6ss} **0-1-6**
£412

Zap Attack *J Parkes* a35
5 b g Zafonic (USA) - Rappa Tap Tap (Fr)
7^{7sd} 9^{8sd} **0-0-2**

Zarabad (Ire) *K R Burke* 82 a39
3 b c King's Best (USA) - Zarannda (Ire)
6^{8g} 13^{9sd} **0-0-2 £242**

Zarakash (Ire) *Jonjo O'Neill* 77
5 b g Darshaan - Zarannda (Ire)
7^{14gf} **0-0-1**

Zariano *T D Barron* 41 a65
5 b g Emperor Jones (USA) - Douce Maison (Ire)
1^{8sd} 2^{9sd} 6^{8sd} 3^{7sd} 2^{7sd} 9^{9sd} 11^{7s} 9^{7sd} 14^{7f}
9^{7gf} **1-3-10 £4,820**

Zarin (Ire) *D W Chapman* a41
7 b g Inzar (USA) - Non Dimenticar Me (Ire)
9^{7sd} 8^{7sd} 6^{8sd} 10^{6sd} **0-0-4**

Zarneeta *W De Best-Turner*
4 b f Tragic Role (USA) - Compton Amber
8^{17sd} **0-0-1**

Zarova (Ire) *M W Easterby* 62 a56
3 gr c Zafonic (USA) - Estarova (Fr)
2^{8sd} 14^{8gs} 3^{8f} 8^{9gf} 6^{8gf} 3^{10gf} 1^{10gf} 2^{12gf} 4^{10g}
6^{9sd} **1-5-10 £7,406**

Zarzu *C R Dore* 84 a93
6 b g Magic Ring (Ire) - Rivers Rhapsody
6^{5sd} 4^{5sd} 9^{5sd} 3^{5sd} 2^{5gs} 9^{5gs} 17^{5gs} 13^{5gf} 3^{5g}
16^{5g} 9^{5g} 8^{6gf} **0-3-12 £9,961**

Zastra's Pride *W G M Turner* 31 a17
2 ch f Zaha (Can) - Strath Kitten
9^{5gs} 6^{5sd} 13^{6g} 5^{8gf} **0-0-4**

Zato (Ire) *M R Channon* 104
2 ch c Zafonic (USA) - Top Table
4^{5gs} 1^{5gf} 1^{6gf} 6^{6gf} 2^{6g} 3^{6gf} 1^{7s} 5^{8gs} 3^{8gs}
3-1-9 £46,152

Zaville *M A Jarvis* 72
3 gr f Zafonic (USA) - Colleville
4^{11gs} 2^{14gf} 4^{14g} 4^{16gf} **0-1-4 £1,618**

Zavone (Ire) *R Hannon* 95
2 br c Zafonic (USA) - Irish Teen (USA)
3^{5gf} 1^{5gf} 1^{5g} **2-0-3 £20,034**

Zayn Zen *M A Jarvis* 98 a104
3 ch f Singspiel (Ire) - Roshani (Ire)
1^{8g} 6^{8gf} 3^{7gf} 3^{7gf} 2^{8g} 1^{10gs} 2^{11gf} 5^{10s} 1^{8sd}
4^{10sd} **3-4-10 £37,123**

Zazous *J J Bridger* 56 a54
4 b g Zafonic (USA) - Confidentiality (USA)
7^{8gs} 8^{6f} 2^{7gs} 5^{8gf} 8^{7gf} 3^{5g} 7^{6sd} 3^{7sd} 1^{5sd}
8^{7sd} 7^{7sd} 3^{6sd} 6^{6sd} 3^{6sd} **1-5-14 £3,784**

Zealand *R A Fahey* a60
5 ch g Zamindar (USA) - Risanda
3^{11sd} **0-1-1 £413**

Zed Candy (Fr) *J T Stimpson* 53
2 b g Medicean - Intrum Morshaan (Ire)
7^{8s} **0-0-1**

Zeeba (Ire) *L M Cumani* 77 a76
3 b f Barathea (Ire) - Donya
2^{12sd} 2^{10f} 1^{12gs} **1-2-3 £5,634**

Zeena *C A Horgan* 54 a51
3 b f Unfuwain (USA) - Forest Fire (Swe)
9^{8gf} 5^{10f} 4^{10s} 4^{10sd} 3^{10g} 8^{12sd} 5^{12sd} **0-0-7**
£1,120

Zeitgeist (Ire) *J Howard Johnson* 105
4 b g Singspiel (Ire) - Diamond Quest
6^{12gf} 9^{12s} 1^{12gf} 5^{14g} **1-0-4 £43,500**

Zell (Ire) *E J Alston* 31
2 b f Lend A Hand - Skisette
8^{7gf} **0-0-1**

Zeloso *M F Harris* a53
7 b g Alzao (USA) - Silk Petal
3^{17sd} 4^{14sd} 1^{13sd} 6^{13sd} 1^{14sd} 13^{12sd} 3^{13sd} 2^{14sd}
2^{17sd} 7^{12sd} 3^{13sd} 5^{14sd} **2-5-12 £6,255**

Zendaro *W M Brisbourne* 68
3 b g Danzero (Aus) - Countess Maud
8^{8gf} 2^{7f} 1^{7gf} 3^{7gf} 8^{8gf} 7^{8g} 16^{7gf} **1-2-7**
£5,115

Zennerman (Ire) *W M Brisbourne* 84
2 b g Observatory (USA) - Precocious Miss (USA)
10^{5gs} 1^{5gf} 4^{6gf} 2^{6g} 1^{7s} 10^{7gs} 3^{8gf} 7^{8gf} 5^{8g}
9^{8g} **2-1-10 £10,278**

Zenno Rob Roy (Jpn) *Kazuo Fujisawa* 124
5 b h Sunday Silence (USA) - Roamin Rachel (USA)
3^{11f} 2^{10g} 2^{10f} 3^{12f} 8^{12f} **0-4-5**
£869,257

Zephrina *Jedd O'Keeffe* 27
2 b f Zafonic (USA) - Fairlee Mixa (Fr)
10^{6g} 13^{6gf} **0-0-2**

Zerlina (USA) *J Ryan* 61 a87
4 b f Singspiel (Ire) - Tass
2^{8sd} 5^{8gf} 3^{7sd} 12^{8gf} 4^{7ft} 5^{8sd} 12^{9sf}
0-2-7 £3,502

Zero (Ire) *M A Jarvis* a72
2 b c Halling (USA) - Zonda
5^{8sd} **0-0-1**

Zero Tolerance (Ire) *T D Barron* 109
5 ch g Nashwan (USA) - Place De L'Opera
12^{8gs} 1^{10s} 12^{10g} 19^{10gs} 16^{10g} 5^{9g} 3^{8gs} 1^{8s}
2-1-8 £35,626

Zeydnaa (Ire) *C R Wilson* 54 a40
5 b g Bahhare (USA) - Hadawah (USA)
11^{8gf} 7^{12gf} 3^{11gf} 5^{14gf} 3^{12g} 4^{16g} 6^{14gf} 1^{16gf}
8^{17sd} **1-3-9 £3,941**

Zhitomir *M Dods* 76 a66
7 ch g Lion Cavern (USA) - Treasure Trove (USA)
2^{7s} 2^{7sd} 1^{7gs} 2^{7g} 5^{7gs} 8^{7gf} 2^{7g} 3^{7g} 12^{7g} 2^{7g}
4^{7s} 12^{9sd} **1-7-12 £14,361**

Zhukhov (Ire) *B Smart* 57 a43
2 ch c Allied Forces (USA) - Karameg (Ire)
8^{6g} 4^{6g} 3^{7g} 9^{6g} 6^{7sd} **0-0-5 £477**

Zidane *J R Fanshawe* 71
3 b c Danzero (Aus) - Juliet Bravo
2^{6g} 1^{6gf} **1-1-2 £4,991**

Ziet D'Alsace (Fr) *A W Carroll* a64
5 b m Zieten (USA) - Providenc Mill (Fr)
2^{8sd} 4^{9sd} 1^{7sd} 7^{7sd} 9^{7sd} 1^{7sd} 2^{7sd} **2-2-7**
£7,094

Zietory *P F I Cole* 75 a55
5 b m Zieten (USA) - Fairy Story (Ire)
9^{8sd} 8^{8gf} **0-0-2**

Zietzig (Ire) *D Nicholls* a40
8 b g Zieten (USA) - Missing You
4^{7sd} 7^{7sd} 12^{6sd} **0-0-3**

Ziggy Zen *C J Mann* 70
6 br g Muhtarram (USA) - Springs Welcome
4^{14gs} 11^{15gf} **0-0-2 £274**

Zilcash *A King* 56 a76
2 b g Mujahid (USA) - Empty Purse
7^{6gf} 1^{8sd} **1-0-2 £3,318**

Zilch *M L W Bell* 98
7 ch g Zilzal (USA) - Bunty Boo
9^{6g} 1^{7s} 7^{8gs} 13^{7gf} 10^{7g} 13^{8s} **1-0-6 £13,499**

Zilmy (Ire) *W R Swinburn* 22
4 ch g Zilzal (USA) - My Lewicia (Ire)
8^{7gf} **0-0-1**

Zimbali *J M Bradley* 59 a41
3 ch f Lahib (USA) - Dawn
10^{5sd} 7^{5sd} 9^{5gs} 4^{5gs} 11^{6gs} 6^{5f} 5^{5gf} 4^{6f} 3^{6g} 8^{6gf} 2^{5f} 8^{5f} 7^{5g} 2^{5s} 7^{5gf} 10^{6g} 11^{7sf} 11^{5sd} **0-4-18 £2,997**

Zingbat (Ire) *J G Given* 29
2 b c Rainbow Quest (USA) - Shastri (USA)
14^{8s} **0-0-1**

Zinging *J J Bridger* 44 a52
6 b g Fraam - Hi Hoh (Ire)
1^{7sd} 6^{7sd} 7^{10sd} 8^{7sd} 10^{7sd} 2^{7g} 4^{10sd} 14^{7s} 12^{8sd} 9^{8g} 8^{5sd} 13^{8sd} **1-1-12 £1,853**

Zipadeedoodah *P J Makin* 61 a54
3 b c Bluebird (USA) - River Divine (USA)
4^{5gs} 5^{6g} 5^{6gf} 4^{6sd} **0-0-4 £275**

Zizou (Ire) *P R Hedger* 68 a59
2 b g Fantastic Light (USA) - Search Committee (USA)
12^{6gf} 2^{7g} 9^{7f} 6^{7gf} 13^{8f} 9^{6gs} 2^{8g} 8^{7sd} 10^{10sd} **0-2-9 £2,789**

Zizzle *I A Wood* a55
3 ch c Zaha (Can) - Maria Cappuccini
10^{10sd} 5^{8sd} 10^{7sd} **0-0-3**

Zohar (USA) *B J Meehan* 95
3 b g Aljabr (USA) - Dafnah (USA)
6^{9gf} 8^{10gs} 3^{7gf} **0-1-3 £2,077**

Zolash (Ire) *Mrs L C Jewell* a49
3 b g General Monash (USA) - Zolba (Ire)
5^{8sd} 10^{9sd} 11^{10sd} 7^{11hy} 10^{8sd} 3^{8sd} 9^{8sd} 9^{7sd} **0-1-8 £211**

Zomerlust *J J Quinn* 95
3 b g Josr Algarhoud (Ire) - Passiflora
8^{6s} 2^{6s} 4^{6gf} 1^{6gs} 15^{6g} 10^{6g} 8^{7gf} 4^{6g} 6^{7gs} **1-3-9 £14,934**

Zonergem *Lady Herries* 87 a91
7 ch g Zafonic (USA) - Anasazi (Ire)
8^{10gs} 15^{10gs} 6^{10sd} **0-0-3 £218**

Zonic *R M H Cowell* 34 a36
3 b f Zafonic (USA) - Ferber's Follies (USA)
7^{7f} 14^{7gf} 13^{7gf} 9^{7sd} 8^{9sd} **0-0-5**

Zonic Boom (Fr) *Mrs H Dalton* 67 a51
5 b/br g Zafonic (USA) - Rosi Zambotti (Ire)
7^{10sd} 8^{8gs} 7^{10hy} 1^{8gf} 5^{9f} 1^{9g} 4^{11gf} 11^{11g} 3^{9gf} 5^{11gf} 4^{10g} **2-0-11 £7,483**

Zonnebeke *Mrs C A Dunnett* 26 a43
4 b f Orpen (USA) - Canlubang
9^{7sd} 8^{9sd} 4^{8sd} 13^{7s} 5^{7gf} 7^{8f} **0-0-6**

Zoom Zoom *Mrs L Stubbs* 91 a84
5 b h Abou Zouz (USA) - Iltimas (USA)
1^{6sd} 5^{6sd} 2^{6sd} 1^{6s} 12^{6gs} **2-1-5 £12,318**

Zoripp (Ire) *J G Given* 53 a56
3 b g Spectrum (Ire) - Allspice
9^{7f} 12^{10sd} 10^{10g} 14^{10g} 2^{7gf} 12^{8gf} 7^{7gf} 3^{10g} 5^{12sd} 1^{11sd} 2^{12ss} **1-3-11 £3,317**

Zorn *P Howling* 60 a69
6 br g Dilum (USA) - Very Good
5^{8sd} 3^{7sd} 2^{6sd} 2^{6sd} 7^{7sd} 1^{6sd} 1^{6sd} 4^{6sd} 1^{6sd} 6^{7sd} 12^{6sd} 8^{7sd} 12^{7gf} 7^{7sd} 4^{6gs} 6^{6g} 10^{6gf} 13^{7sd} **3-3-18 £10,791**

Zorooni *M A Jarvis* a60
2 b f Josr Algarhoud (Ire) - Zeyaarah (USA)
3^{7sd} 6^{7sd} **0-1-2 £476**

Zowington *C F Wall* 95 a85
3 gr c Zafonic (USA) - Carmela Owen
11^{6g} 4^{6gf} 1^{6sd} 6^{6gf} 2^{5s} 10^{5gs} 1^{6s} 10^{6sd} **2-1-8 £17,493**

Zozarharry (Ire) *P A Trueman*
7 b g Nicolotte - Miss Butterfield
16^{6gs} 14^{6sd} **0-0-2**

Zuhair *R A Fahey* 67
12 ch g Mujtahid (USA) - Ghzaalh (USA)
5^{5f} **0-0-1**

Zuleta *B D Leavy* 46 a46
4 ch f Vettori (Ire) - Victoria
7^{11sd} 5^{17sd} 7^{12sd} 7^{13sd} 6^{12gf} 15^{12f} **0-0-6**

Zurbaran (Ire) *S L Keightley* 79
2 ch c Alhaarth (Ire) - Broken Romance (Ire)
7^{7gf} 2^{8hy} **0-1-2 £985**